# Getting
# Financial
# Aid

# Getting Financial Aid

**2017**

Eleventh Edition

The College Board, New York

**About the College Board**

The College Board is a mission-driven not-for-profit organization that connects students to college success and opportunity. Founded in 1900, the College Board was created to expand access to higher education. Today, the membership association is made up of over 6,000 of the world's leading educational institutions and is dedicated to promoting excellence and equity in education. Each year, the College Board helps more than seven million students prepare for a successful transition to college through programs and services in college readiness and college success — including the SAT® and the Advanced Placement Program®. The organization also serves the education community through research and advocacy on behalf of students, educators, and schools.

For further information, visit www.collegeboard.org.

Editorial inquiries concerning this book should be directed to Guidance Publications, The College Board, 250 Vesey Street, New York, NY 10281; or telephone 800-323-7155.

Copies of this book are available from your local bookseller or may be ordered from College Board Publications, P.O. Box 7500, London, KY 40742-7500. The book may also be ordered online through the College Board Store at www.collegeboard.org. The price is $23.99.

ISBN: 978-1-4573-0775-1

Printed in the United States of America

Distributed by Macmillan. For information on bulk purchases please contact Macmillan Corporate and Premium Sales Department at (800) 221-7945 x5442.

# Contents

# List of Figures

# List of Tables

# List of Worksheets

# Preface

Financial aid is a great equalizer. In 2015, almost $239 billion in aid was awarded from government and private sources. Coupled with the wide range of lower-cost college options available, financial aid should make a college education affordable for just about everyone.

Yet, according to the American Council on Education, each year *millions* of students who are eligible for this boon don't even apply for it. We assume these students are either unaware of the possibility of aid, or mistakenly believe financial aid is not for them.

And many parents and students who apply for financial aid find the process to be confusing, even intimidating. Like the tax code, the forms and guidelines appear to be full of exceptions, convolutions and incomprehensible terms.

But it doesn't have to be that way. A central aim of this book is to take the confusion and intimidation out of the process by giving clear and direct explanations of what financial aid is all about and simple, step-by-step directions for how to get it. By combining these explanations and directions with costs and financial aid facts for every accredited college that reports this data, we hope this book will achieve our ultimate goal of connecting students to colleges that match both their needs and their means.

## Acknowledgments

We gratefully acknowledge the contributions of the many individuals who originally helped bring the first edition of this book into being. George Ochoa, our writer for Part I of this book, "Financial Aid, Step by Step," transformed a complicated and intricate subject into clear and simple language. Renée Gernand provided leadership and editorial guidance throughout the project. Kathie Little and the late Jack Joyce, our resident experts on financial aid at the time, reviewed the content and kept our course true, as did Sandy Baum, Cindy Bailey, Myra Baas Smith and Linda Peckham.

While we had the advantage of many "in-house" resources, we also relied upon the knowledge and advice of seven financial aid officers who took time from their busy schedules to give us interviews: Vincent Amoroso of Johns Hopkins University, Bonnie Lee Behm of Villanova University, Elizabeth Bickford of the University of Oregon (retired), Joe Paul Case of Amherst College, Mary San Agustin of Palomar College, Mike Scott of Texas Christian University and Forrest Stuart of Rhodes College (now at Furman University). We hope you will find their insight and advice, quoted throughout Part I, as illuminating as we did.

For the current edition, we relied on our resident experts Ami Boshardt, Ted Jamieson and Robin Casanova for help with updating the information in Parts I and II. The descriptions of colleges presented in Part III, "Financial Aid, College by College," were compiled from the College Board's Annual Survey of Colleges in the spring of 2016. The college data were collected, edited and verified by a team of editors led by Chris Hagan, with the assistance of Stan Bernstein. Jenny Xie, Randy Peery, Sara Millones, Kayla Tompkins, David Christ, Karen Villa, Jameeka Watkins, Scott Nicoll and Cedric Crawley compiled, edited and verified the data. Technical support was provided by Doris Chow, Assar Tarazi, John Reynolds, Enrique Lara, Wayne Lau, Priyanka Sabapathy, and Srinivas Bachu. The team of programmers and typesetters at DataStream Content Solutions, Inc., converted the database into readable pages.

We wish to give special acknowledgment to Stan Bernstein, who recently retired. It is with sincere appreciation that we thank him for his many years of yeoman service both to the College Board and to the entire higher education community.

*Tom Vanderberg, Senior Editor*
*Guidance Publications*

# How to Use This Book

## Part I: Financial Aid, Step by Step

The first chapter, "Yes, You Can Afford College," establishes our central point: a college can be found to fit any budget. If you are skeptical about that, please start here — we think we make a strong case.

The chapters that follow (Steps 1 through 11) provide easy-to-follow directions on how to get financial aid, including what you need to know, what you need to do, and when you need to do it.

These steps are presented in a logical sequence. But depending upon your own circumstances — where you are in the college application process, what kinds of colleges you're applying to, and the policies of those colleges — you may need to take the steps in a slightly different order, skip some steps, or do some steps simultaneously. A planning calendar on the inside front cover will help you stay on track.

Financial aid forms often use jargon that can at times seem vague or confusing. Terms like "need" and "cost of attendance" have specific meanings that might not be the same as what you would assume. Throughout Part I, you'll find key terms defined in "Know the Lingo" sidebars (you'll also find a detailed, comprehensive glossary at the end of this book). Other sidebars emphasize or illustrate the main points of each step.

Throughout Part I, you'll find graphs, charts, and tables that summarize information and let you compare different financial aid options. You'll also find checklists and sample worksheets that will help you plan and keep track of your applications.

# Part II: Tables and Worksheets

One of the worksheets that you'll find in Part II will help you compare the financial aid award letters that you'll receive from colleges. To drive home the point that no two award letters are alike, we've included two samples of actual award letters that were sent to the same student by two different universities (the names of which we've changed).

Part II also includes a series of worksheets that you can use to estimate how much the federal government will say you should pay for college out of pocket. These worksheets are designed for dependent students and their parents. If you are an independent student, you can do the same thing with the online tools on collegeboard.org. Finally, in Part II you'll find lists of state aid programs, state-sponsored 529 college savings plans and other useful places to find more information.

# Part III: Financial Aid College by College

This is where we help you get the "financial aid picture" at specific colleges, including the scholarships they offer to entering students, and their required forms and deadlines. To place this picture in context, we give you brief facts about the kind of college it is, and its basic costs. This information can help you compare the colleges you are considering and find colleges that look affordable. But keep in mind that the financial aid figures are mostly based on averages, meaning many students will be above or below these benchmarks.

The college descriptions in Part III are arranged alphabetically by state or territory. Running headers at the top of each page will help you orient yourself and find schools quickly. An alphabetical index of all the colleges in the book appears in Part IV.

Every college described in this book is accredited by an agency recognized by the U.S. Department of Education. Accreditation is a process in which an outside agency ensures that a college meets certain basic standards — it's a stamp of approval on the college's teaching, facilities and administration. For financial aid purposes, accreditation by a federally recognized agency means that federal student aid dollars can be used to attend the institution.

*The College Board College Handbook* also includes full descriptions of the colleges in this book, going beyond the cost and financial aid details presented here to include information about admission requirements, academics, housing, student life, athletics and more.

# Where the College Information Comes From

The information in the college descriptions comes from the College Board's most recent Annual Survey of Colleges, which was conducted in the spring of 2016. Every college reported its own cost and financial aid information to us. Where possible, our staff of editors verified the information by consulting third-party sources, including public university system or district offices, state education departments and the federal government's Integrated Postsecondary Educational Database System. The information presented was current at the time this book went to press in May 2016 — but be warned that it may have changed by the time you're reading this. Once you have narrowed down a list of colleges that you're interested in, you should confirm critical information, such as financial aid application deadlines and requirements, by visiting the colleges' websites or contacting their financial aid offices.

# What's in the College Descriptions

Each college description begins with a shaded box that contains the name of the college, the city or town where it's located, its website address, and its six-digit "federal code" — the code you will need in order to have the information in your FAFSA (Free Application for Federal Student Aid) sent to the college. If a college requires the College Board's CSS/Financial Aid PROFILE®, its four-digit CSS code also appears in this box. (The CSS code is the same code you use to send SAT® and SAT Subject Tests™ scores and AP® Exam scores to a college; the federal code is only used for the FAFSA.)

Below the college name box you'll find a brief summary of what type of college it is — whether it's a four-year private university, a two-year community college or a four-year culinary school run on a for-profit basis. (Definitions of all the different types of schools you might find here are in the glossary.) You'll also find information about the number of students who were enrolled in the 2015–16 school year, and the relative difficulty of obtaining admission to the college.

### BASIC COSTS

"Basic Costs" lists the tuition, fees, room and board charged by the college. The date indicates the school year for which these numbers apply — if the college was unable to report final or projected figures for the upcoming school year, last year's figures are given. If the college combines tuition, fees, and room and board expenses, that single figure is given as a comprehensive fee.

It's important to note that these figures do not include other out-of-pocket costs, such as books, supplies, transportation and personal expenses. These costs can be substantial, depending upon where and how you live, and what you study. But since these costs vary widely from student to student, we felt it would be misleading to display average amounts.

## FINANCIAL AID PICTURE

The core of each college's description is the information about the financial aid it offers. Again, the date indicates the school year for which the college reported numbers — either the current year or the prior year. Depending on the aid programs offered by the college and the figures they reported, you may see one or several of these elements of the financial aid picture:

- **Students with Need.** This shows how financial aid was given to students who could not afford the full cost of attending the college on their own (a full explanation of how "need" is determined is found in Part I, Step 1). The focus is on the entering freshman class but, if a college was unable to provide that breakdown, the numbers are for all undergraduates. Most colleges disclosed the average percentage of need met by financial aid packages, and the relative proportion of aid given as scholarships and grants as opposed to loans or work-study jobs. Use this data to get a sense of how likely a college is to meet your full need, and how much aid will probably come in the form of loans.

- **Students Without Need.** Even though a student does not need financial aid, it's still possible that a college will provide aid based on merit or other criteria, such as alumni affiliation or minority status. That's what is shown here. If a college has a policy of only awarding aid to students who have need, this is also stated here.

- **Scholarships Offered.** This gives details on merit scholarships offered by the college and their criteria for being awarded. Here you can get a sense of whether your GPA or SAT scores put you in the right ballpark for a merit-based grant. You'll also find information about the number of student-athletes who were given a scholarship by the college, and the average award.

- **Cumulative Student Debt.** This tells you how many students borrowed money to pay for college and how much they owed, on average, when they graduated. This is another way for you to measure how much of a college's aid will be loan based. The numbers here only include student loans taken out through the college — not PLUS loans, private education loans or other borrowing done through a third-party lender.

**FINANCIAL AID PROCEDURES**

The financial aid application forms required by the college, and the priority date and/or deadlines that the financial aid office has set, appear here. This section also includes information about notification — that is, when you can expect to hear back from the financial aid office after applying, and by when they will need your final answer about whether you'll be attending. Unless otherwise noted, all dates given in this section are for applicants who intend to enroll in the fall of 2017. If you plan to apply for admission to the spring 2018 term or later, contact the college's financial aid office to find out about their policies and deadlines.

**CONTACT**

The final section of each college description lists the mailing address of the school's financial aid office.

# Part IV: Scholarship Lists

If you want to zero in on colleges that offer scholarships for your particular talents and interests, the lists in Part IV will help you do that. Arranged alphabetically by state, these lists will point you to colleges that offer scholarships for a variety of achievements. Please note that, in many cases, merit is not the only criterion used by the college when awarding aid: It may require recipients to also demonstrate financial need by submitting the FAFSA or another financial aid form.

At some colleges, every applicant is automatically considered for merit scholarships. At others, you have to specifically apply for a given scholarship. And in some cases, a scholarship is only open to you if you've been recommended by your principal, school counselor or teacher.

## What's in the Scholarship Lists

Each list points to colleges that offer aid for a specific talent or area of interest.

**Academics.** This list names colleges that offer merit aid for academic achievement. Typical criteria include the classes you've taken, your GPA and your standardized test scores.

**Art.** This list includes colleges that offer merit aid for artistic ability, as reflected by grades in art classes, teacher recommendations and/or a portfolio you submit to the college.

**Athletics.** If a college offers scholarships for a certain sport, it will be listed here. The letters "M" and "W" indicate whether the scholarship is available to men, women or both. Please note that, at most colleges, only a very few athletes receive significant scholarships. No one should rely on athletic achievements alone to get into college or to pay for it. Instead, make sure your academic record is solid, and be sure to apply for need-based financial aid by submitting the FAFSA and any other required forms.

**Music/Drama.** This list includes colleges and conservatories that offer merit aid for talent in the performing arts, as reflected by grades in music, dance or drama classes; teacher recommendations; and/or an audition or a submitted tape.

**ROTC.** Three lists are included here, one each for the Air Force, Army and Naval Reserve Officers' Training Corps. (Marine Corps ROTC is included in Naval ROTC; the Coast Guard and Merchant Marine do not have ROTC programs.) The schools listed may not necessarily have all their ROTC programs on campus; they may have a sponsorship agreement with a neighboring college or university instead. If you enroll in ROTC, you will need to apply separately for the actual ROTC scholarship from the service branch you've chosen — the money doesn't come automatically. (For information on how much money is awarded and how to apply, consult *The College Board Scholarship Handbook*, or visit your local recruiting station.) Some colleges offer additional institutional scholarships for ROTC candidates from their own funds, beyond what's awarded by the Department of Defense.

# Part I
Financial Aid Step by Step

# Yes, You Can Afford College

Yes, you can afford college. How do we know? Because most colleges are not as expensive as you think. Because if a college wants you as a student, it will try to help you with financial aid. Because most students get financial aid. And because there are ways to reduce the amount you have to pay now, including working part-time and taking out loans.

This is not what everyone will tell you. You may hear discouraging words like, "Most colleges are expensive" and "You won't qualify for financial aid." People may hint that college is not worth all the trouble. The financial aid forms may look complicated and confusing.

We will show you how to get past these doubts. You *can* afford college, and we will show you how. College is worth the expense; you should apply for financial aid. With our step-by-step guide through the process, you'll sidestep confusion and be able to focus on the important decisions in front of you.

## Why You Can Afford College

Despite media hype about pricey colleges and the soaring cost of higher education, most colleges are not as expensive as you might think. In addition, the published prices of many colleges, though high, are not the whole story. If a college wants you as a student, and if you and your parents don't have enough money, the college will usually offer help so you can attend. That help is financial aid — and because of it, **a college's published tuition and fees are not what most people pay.**

Financial aid is a great equalizer, and most students benefit from it. More than two-thirds of all full-time college students receive grants or scholarships to help them foot the bill. Those grants come either from the government, the college or both, and do not have to be paid back. Many students also receive other forms of help, including federal tax credits and deductions that allow their families to keep more of their money at tax time. Thanks to all this assistance, full-time college students pay, on average, much less than the advertised price of their education. In 2015–16, for example, students at four-year private colleges paid an average net price of $14,890 in tuition and fees instead of the average published price of $32,410. Students at four-year public universities received a proportionally similar discount.

Even expensive colleges are less costly than you might think because they offer more financial aid. Since a high-priced college often awards more assistance than a low-priced one, a particular student might end up paying the same out-of-pocket cost at both, or even less at the college with a higher sticker price. **That's why you shouldn't rule out your "dream college" as too expensive until you find out if it wants you and what kind of financial aid package it will give you.**

That said, there are great deals to be found. At a four-year public college — one supported by a state or local government — the average tuition and fees in 2015–16 were $9,410 a year. That's a 70 percent saving over the $32,410 average charged by private colleges. Another way to save money is to spend your first two years at a community college, which is a public college that specializes in two-year education programs. Published tuition and fees at community colleges averaged just over $3,440 a year — a 63 percent saving over the average at a public four-year college.

Here's one last reason you can afford college: you don't have to pay every penny up front. You can borrow money at a low interest rate and pay it back after your studies are over. There are also ways to reduce the amount you have to pay right now. (*See Step 11 for more on these "out-of-pocket" options.*)

**Figure 1:**
Average Tuition, Fees, Room and Board Charges, 2015–16

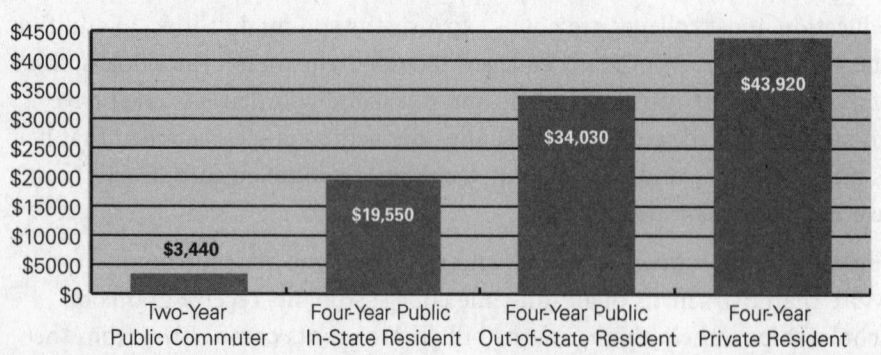

*See Step 3 for more about the components of college costs.*

# Is College Worth It?

Even if you can afford college, is it a good idea? No matter how much financial aid you get, college will still require a sacrifice of money, time, and effort. Kids who go straight to work after high school have more spending money sooner. Does college give enough bang for the buck?

The answer is yes for many reasons including money, job insurance and personal growth.

In terms of money, college clearly pays. The difference in earnings between the typical college graduate and the typical high school graduate has increased sharply over the past three decades: from 25 percent to 69 percent for men, and from 43 percent to 70 percent for women. **College graduates earn almost twice as much over their careers than high school graduates**. Even if you borrow to pay for part of your education, it's still worth it. Provided you borrow intelligently, your increased earnings will help you pay back the loan. (*See Step 11 for more about loans.*)

You might think that the increased earnings from your college education won't make up for the total costs and the years that you won't be in the work force. But Figure 3 on the next page shows otherwise. The grey line shows the cumulative earnings at each age for the average high school graduate

**Figure 2:**
Median Annual Earnings by Education Level

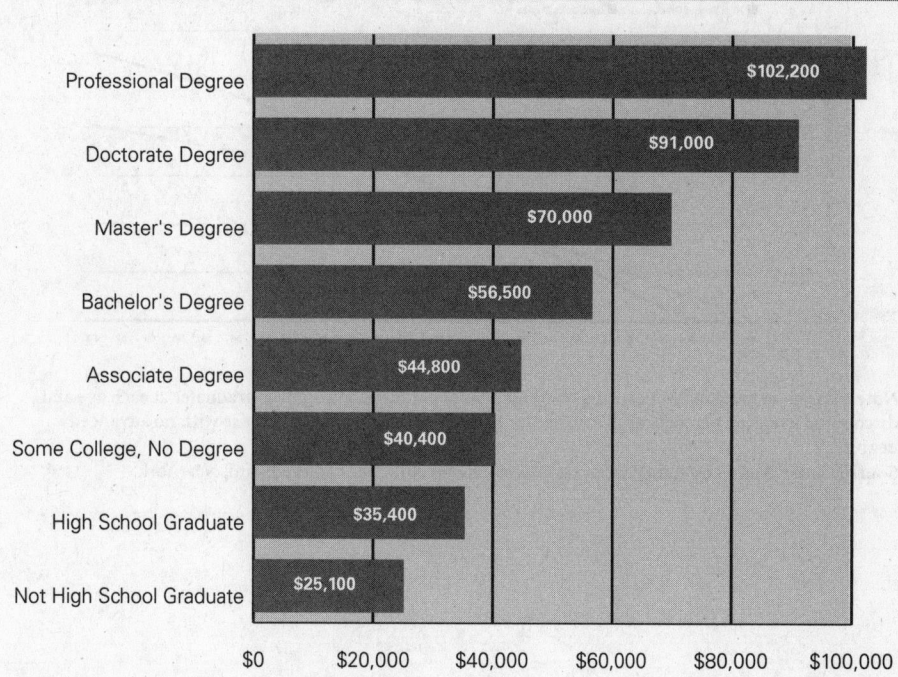

**Note:** Includes full-time, year-round workers age 25 and older.
**Source:** Sandy Baum and Kathleen Payea, *Education Pays 2013*, The College Board, New York.

who enters the workforce full time at the age of 18. The black line shows the cumulative earnings at each age for the average four-year college graduate who enters the workforce at age 22, after subtracting average tuition and fees paid over four years at a public college or university. As you can see, by age 35 the lines intersect. From that point on, the investment in college pays off.

College also provides job insurance in a world whose economy is constantly changing. As new industries develop and many jobs are outsourced to foreign countries, you can compete better with a college degree. A college degree teaches you how to acquire knowledge and put it to use no matter what the circumstances. In fact, some higher-education credential — at least an associate degree — is a minimum to stay employed in the "knowledge economy" of the 21st century. **A mere high school diploma is obsolete; college helps to ensure employment**.

But the value of college can't be reduced to dollars alone. It involves intangibles, things you can't touch directly: how you value yourself, your dreams and your ambitions. If you are an artist, a musician, a writer, a builder, a scientist or a thinker, college will help you cultivate those talents. If you are hoping to find yourself, meet people who are more like you, and meet people who are different and interesting, college can contribute to that search too. College provides rich ground for personal growth.

On every front, as a matter of value for dollars, college is a good buy. You can afford college — and it is worth the price.

**Figure 3:**
Estimated Cumulative Earnings Minus College Costs

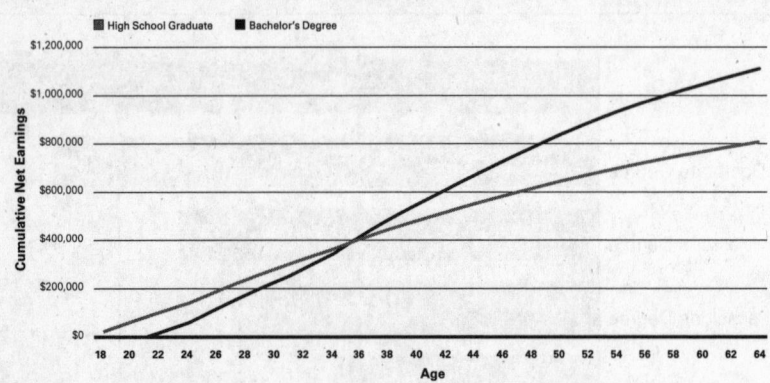

**Notes:** Based on median 2011 earnings for high school graduates and college graduates at each age and discounted using a 3 percent rate. Earnings for B.A. recipients include only those with no advanced degree.
**Source:** Sandy Baum and Kathleen Payea, *Education Pays 2013*, The College Board, New York.

# How This Book Will Help You

Through this book, you will learn how to make college affordable for you. You'll find out exactly what you need to know so you can apply for financial aid, choose an affordable college and control costs while at college. In Part I, we will walk you step-by-step through the process. There are 11 steps in all:

- **Step 1:** You'll find out the key facts about financial aid.
- **Step 2:** You'll get an idea of how much financial aid you can get.
- **Step 3:** You'll see how and why college costs vary.
- **Step 4:** You'll figure out which forms you need to fill out, and when.
- **Step 5:** You'll learn how to fill out the Free Application for Federal Student Aid (FAFSA).
- **Step 6:** You'll find out how to complete the CSS/Financial Aid PROFILE® application (called the PROFILE for short), if your colleges require it.
- **Step 7:** You'll learn how to fill out any other forms a particular college might require.
- **Step 8:** If your family has special circumstances, you'll find out the best way to explain them to colleges.
- **Step 9:** You'll learn about scholarships and other aid you can get from sources outside of a college.
- **Step 10:** You'll learn how to compare award letters from colleges and decide which offer is best for you.
- **Step 11:** You'll learn how to pay your share of the cost of college through work, loans and other means.

In Part II of the book, tables and worksheets will help you make informed decisions and stay in control of the financial aid process. Part III will paint a clear picture of the financial facts about each college you might want to investigate. That includes its costs and its approach to financial aid.

No one will tell you that paying for college is fun. But what you're getting — a college education — is worth it and is within reach. College is a big-ticket purchase that requires careful thought and preparation, like a house or a car. And it shouldn't be done in the dark. This book will guide you into one of the most important purchases you'll ever make — with your eyes wide open.

# Step 1: Let's Go Over the Basics

QUICK
OVERVIEW

The first step to getting financial aid is to understand the basic facts about it. In this step we will explain what financial aid is (money to help you pay for college), what types there are (the kind that comes free and the kind that doesn't), who gets it and where it comes from.

The most important point: almost everyone qualifies for at least one form of financial aid. As long as you apply, the chances are excellent that you will get some.

## Just What Is Financial Aid?

**KNOW THE LINGO**

**Grant** — Money that is given away for free, usually on the basis of who needs it

**Merit scholarship** — Money that is given away for free on the basis of academic qualifications or special talents

**Subsidized loan** — Money that you have to pay back with interest; however, the federal government pays the interest for you while you are in college

**Work-study** — A program in which you take a part-time job to earn money for your education; the federal government pays part of your salary

**Financial aid package** — What a college offers to an accepted student who has applied for aid. Usually a mix of grants, loans and/or work-study.

Financial aid is money given or loaned to you to help you pay for college. Different forms have different rules. The vast majority of aid comes from the federal government, and most of it consists of loans that you must pay back. However, some aid does not require repayment — which makes it the best kind of aid to get.

If you qualify for financial aid, your college will put together an aid "package," usually with different types of aid bundled together. You and your parents will almost certainly still have to pay something, but the aid package will help. Most students qualify for some form of financial aid, so it makes sense to apply for it.

You'll apply for financial aid either at the same time or soon after you apply for admission. You may have to fill out more than one application. At the very least you will fill out the FAFSA, the federal government form. You may also fill out another form, the PROFILE, which many colleges require. And some colleges and state aid agencies require their own financial aid forms, too. The colleges to which you apply will use the forms to figure out what your family can afford to pay and what your "need" is — that is, the difference between what you can pay and what the college actually costs. If the school wants you as a student but sees that you can't handle the whole bill, it will make you a financial aid offer to help you meet your need. If you accept, that financial aid package is your award.

You will need to apply for financial aid every year that you are in college, mainly because your family's financial situation changes yearly. As a result, your financial aid package will probably be somewhat different from year to year.

Financial aid is a helping hand, not a free pass. In the United States, everyone has a right to a free public school education, but not to a free college education. The federal government and most colleges agree that students and their parents are the ones most responsible for paying for college. "The primary responsibility of paying for the student's education lies with the student and his or her parents," says Forrest M. Stuart, the director of financial aid at Furman University in Greenville, S.C. "Financial aid comes in to fill that gap, if you will, between what they can afford and what the college costs." Even so, financial aid can be the deciding factor in whether or not a student attends college.

## Types of Aid

Financial aid may come in many forms. However, all forms can be grouped into two major categories: gift aid and self-help aid.

### GIFT AID

Gift aid is free money, money that you don't have to pay back or work for. Naturally, this is the kind of aid most people want. It can take the form of grants or scholarships.

The terms "grant" and "scholarship" are often used interchangeably to mean free money. But here's the difference. A grant is usually given only on the basis of need, or your family's inability to pay the full cost of college. Scholarships are usually awarded only to those who have "merit," such as proven ability in academics, the arts or athletics. Once you're in college, you may have to maintain a minimum GPA or take certain courses to continue receiving a scholarship.

### SELF-HELP AID

Self-help aid is money that requires a contribution from you. That can mean paying back the money (if the aid is a loan) or working for the money (if the aid is a work-study job).

The most common form of self-help aid is also the most common of any form of financial aid: the loan. A loan is money that you have to pay back with interest. In light of that, you might not consider this aid at all. But it is — a loan means you don't have to pay the full price of college all at once: You can stretch the payments over time, as you would when buying a house or a car. Furthermore, some student loans (such as Perkins loans and Direct Subsidized Stafford loans) are subsidized by the federal government. These loans are interest free while you are in college, and you don't begin to make any payments until six months after you leave college. The federal government subsidizes, or helps to pay, the loan by keeping the interest rate low and by paying that interest while you're enrolled.

Subsidized loans, which are awarded based on need and administered by the college, are the best kind. But you can also take out federal unsubsidized student loans and parent loans, which are also administered by most colleges. However, be careful not to take on more debt than necessary. No matter what kind of loan you take out, you will have to pay it back.

Another form of self-help is work-study. This is financial aid in the form of a job. Since you earn the money through your work, this too may not seem like aid. But it is, because the federal work-study program pays most of your wages. And work-study jobs are usually available right on campus, with limits on your hours so that you won't be unduly distracted from studying.

Aid can also come in the form of tax cuts — income tax deductions and credits for education. But colleges don't award this variety, and you don't apply for it in the same way as you would loans or grants, so we will discuss it separately, in Step 11.

# Who Gets Aid?

Grants and loans are not just for the poorest of the poor, nor are scholarships only for the smartest of the smart. The truth about who gets financial aid is somewhat different from what many people think.

## Those Who Need It

Most financial aid is based on need, not merit. There is money for merit, but most colleges focus their financial aid packages on meeting financial need.

However, there is a lot of confusion about what need means. Many people think it means a state of dire poverty, so that no working-class or middle-class student need apply. "A lot of people think that they either have to be on welfare or Social Security — really poor — to get financial aid, and that's not correct," says Mary San Agustin, director of financial aid and scholarships at Palomar College in San Marcos, Calif. On the other hand, some rich families mistakenly think they are needy because their high living expenses leave them little money for college. "It's this expectation of, I pay my taxes, so my kid should be entitled to some federal financial aid regardless of how much money I make," says Ms. San Agustin.

*Need* simply means that your family can't afford to pay the full cost of a particular college. The *amount* of your need will vary from college to college, because it depends on the cost of attending an individual college. Whether your family has need is determined not by whether you think you are rich or poor, but by the financial aid forms you fill out.

Just fill out the forms. If you do have need, you will be considered for financial aid.

# Those Who Don't

Despite the overall emphasis on need, many colleges do give away money on the basis of merit. They do this to attract the students they want most, and they may award this money even if it is more than the student needs. However, in many cases, the student both needs the money and has earned it on the basis of merit.

**Don't think that only geniuses get merit aid.** At many colleges a "B"-average GPA can put you in the running for merit money. Sometimes a separate application for merit aid is required to put you into consideration; sometimes your application for admission is enough. In either case, don't count yourself out by not applying; apply and let the college decide.

Grants are sometimes awarded based on neither need nor merit. For example, you may get a grant if you are in a certain field of study, are a resident of the state or are a student from the same town as the college. (*See Step 9 for more about grants and scholarships.*)

# Part-Time Students

Some kinds of aid are only available to students enrolled in college full time — usually 12 or more credit hours of courses per semester. But part-time students are eligible for some financial aid. For example, federal programs such as the Stafford loan require only that students be enrolled at least half-time, whereas others, like the Pell Grant, are available to students enrolled less than half-time. Also, some employers offer tuition reimbursement benefits to students who work full time and go to college part time.

# Where the Money Comes From

Financial aid comes from three basic sources: governments (both federal and state), colleges and outside benefactors.

## From the Government

The lion's share of total financial aid awarded in this country comes from the federal government. Almost three-quarters of all student aid is sent from Washington. For undergraduates, the largest chunk of that consists of federal loans, which currently total $62.1 billion a year and represent 34 percent of all student aid. The loans take multiple shapes. Perkins and Stafford loans are for students, while parents may take out a PLUS loan to help pay for their children's educations.

The federal government also funds several grants, including the Pell Grant, the Supplemental Educational Opportunity Grant (SEOG), the Academic Competitiveness Grant and the SMART Grant. The Pell and SEOG are strictly needbased, while the last two are based on both need and academic criteria. The government also funds the federal work-study program.

**KNOW THE LINGO**

**Merit aid** — Aid awarded on the basis of academics, character or talent

**Need-based aid** — Aid awarded on the basis of a family's inability to pay the cost of attending a particular college

**Non-need-based aid** — Aid awarded on some basis other than need or merit, such as grants with eligibility requirements related to field of study or state residence

A much smaller piece of the financial aid pie (5 percent) comes from individual state governments. Most of this aid is for use only at colleges within the state, though a few states offer "portable" aid, which state residents can take with them to a college in another state.

## From the College

A great deal of financial aid comes from individual colleges, using their own "institutional" funds. In fact, colleges award nearly half of all grants. Many, though not all, award merit scholarships as well as need-based grants. They may also offer on-campus job opportunities and loans.

Private colleges give more financial aid than public ones, but their tuition is usually higher as well. Public colleges award less aid, but taxpayer support keeps their tuition lower.

## Outside Grants and Scholarships

Outside grants and scholarships come from sources other than the government or the college. These sources may include corporations like Coca-Cola or community groups like the Elks Club. Some are well known, such as the National Merit Scholarship, but altogether they are a small piece of the financial aid pie: **only 6 percent of all student aid comes from this source.** Pursue them, but don't expect them to outweigh the other aid you will get.

Bear in mind also that your outside scholarship is unlikely to expand the total aid you receive. Most colleges will use an outside scholarship to substitute for some other piece of aid rather than increase the total aid package. Think of your financial aid package as a barrel: when the barrel is full, no more can be added unless something is taken away. The last thing colleges will take away is whatever sum of money your family is expected to contribute. However, at many colleges, the first thing taken away is self-help aid such as loans. Since that could reduce the total amount you will have to

**Figure 4:**
Undergraduate Student Aid (in billions) by Source, 2014–15

pay back later, it is worth applying for outside scholarships. (*See Step 9 for more on these sources of aid.*)

There is a lot of financial aid out there, in many forms. Apply for it — there is a good chance you will get some. These are the main things to know about financial aid:

- It is money to help you pay for college.
- It may come in the form of a gift (grants and scholarships) or in the form of self-help (loans and work-study).
- Most people get it because they need it, though some get it solely because of merit.
- The federal government funds most of it, but states, colleges and outside sources also help.

**QUICK RECAP**

# Step 2: Estimate How Financial Aid Will Work for You

**QUICK OVERVIEW**

Only rarely does a student get a "free ride" scholarship. You and your parents will have to contribute some money to your education — the precise amount will be determined by the college's analysis of financial aid forms you'll fill out. But even before you fill out the forms, you can estimate your share of the cost and begin planning for how to pay it.

## Don't Count Yourself Out

Most college students get some financial aid, but few receive exactly the same financial aid package. Financial aid packages are as individual as the financial circumstances of the students who apply. One family makes $50,000 a year and has two children, a house and a savings account; another makes $50,000 a year but has only one child, a rented apartment and no savings. What financial aid package will each family receive? The answer: It depends on several factors. Families must first submit their applications for consideration by the colleges.

"Probably the question I'm most often asked is, 'Is there a cutoff?'" says Joe Paul Case, the dean and director of financial aid at Amherst College in Amherst, Mass. Financial aid officers agree that there is no single salary cutoff for financial aid — no one income figure that will definitely exclude a student from receiving financial aid. Income is only one criterion for giving out aid: Colleges also consider such factors as family size, number of children in college, and savings. Many students who would be eligible for financial aid fail to apply because they don't realize this.

"I always tell families, don't cut yourself off from the application process," says Bonnie Lee Behm, the director of financial assistance at Villanova University in Villanova, Pa. "Apply and let it work through the system."

Even if you feel absolutely sure that your family doesn't qualify for financial aid, fill out the forms. Your family circumstances might change suddenly — a lost job, health problems, a new child. Then you may need financial aid, and it will help to be in the system already. A college can assist you faster if your financial aid application is on file.

**EXPERT ADVICE**

"We always encourage students to **go ahead and apply** for financial aid even though you may not qualify for anything but a student loan. **At least get the paperwork in**, because if something happens in the middle of the year, we already have the financial aid data we need to make adjustments."

— *Forrest M. Stuart, director of financial aid, Furman University, Greenville, S.C.*

# What "Expected Family Contribution" Means

Even though you probably will qualify for financial aid, it's unlikely that you will get the fabled "full ride." Colleges do sometimes award full tuition — or even full room and board — to a student they greatly want to attract, but that is rare. Almost always, the family is expected to contribute some money. The exact dollar amount will be based on the family's ability to pay. That dollar amount is the expected family contribution, or EFC.

The EFC is carefully calculated to determine what you can afford to pay based on your financial circumstances — no more and no less. The formulas that the federal government and colleges use to calculate EFC are also calibrated to take into account varying costs of living across the country.

In some ways, the concept of EFC works in your favor. No matter what a college costs, so long as it awards you the full financial aid you need you won't have to pay more than your EFC — the amount your family is able to pay. Say your EFC is $8,000. At a college with a total cost of attendance of $11,000, you could get up to $3,000 in financial aid. At a college where the total cost is $25,000, you could get up to $17,000 in aid. **Because of financial aid, any college is at least worth considering; no college should be ruled out in advance as too expensive.**

On the other hand, even though the expected family contribution is based on ability to pay, that does not simply mean how much the family would like to pay. For any purchase, most people would *like* to pay zero dollars. But what they are *able* to pay is how much money they have minus how much they need to keep for other things, such as food, rent, heat and retirement. When colleges award financial aid, they calculate your ability to pay by looking at your income and financial assets as you lay them out in your financial aid application. Using what are called need-analysis formulas, they analyze your data to see how much of the college costs you are able to pay (your EFC) and how much you are unable to pay (your need). How much you would like to pay is not part of the calculation.

# Costs − EFC = Need

Your expected family contribution is your family's share of college costs. Any cost greater than that is your need. Need varies from college to college because it depends on the cost of the individual college. **It's simple arithmetic: College costs minus your EFC equals the amount of aid you need.** At colleges that award enough financial aid to meet your need, the aid package will equal the amount of your need. Costs minus aid equals what you pay.

## Unmet Need (a.k.a. "Gap")

Unfortunately, not all colleges will award enough aid to meet your full need. Some colleges may "gap" your package — that is, not meet your full need. Economics plays a part here. While some colleges may have enough aid dollars available to meet every student's full need, some colleges lack such funds. If your college cannot meet your full need, costs minus aid will still equal what you pay. But what you pay will be more than your EFC. (*See Step 11 for more information on loans* and other ways to help fill such a gap.)

If you do encounter a "gap" in your award, compare the package with the ones you've gotten from other schools, and consider your priorities. Do you want to go to that college, no matter the cost? Or does cost matter more? (*For more on this topic, see Step 10.*)

## It Depends on the College

The amount of aid you get — along with the kind of aid you get, whether gift or self-help — ultimately depends on the college. Formulas and forms are important, but so is the professional judgment of the financial aid officer. And so is the desire of the college to attract you to its campus.

# How Colleges Calculate Your Need

As you saw in Step 1, financial aid comes from two main sources: government money (usually in the form of loans and work-study), and the college's own "institutional" money — usually in the form of grants and scholarships. Your financial aid package will probably contain money from both sources.

Just as there are two main sources of aid, there are two main formulas that colleges use to figure out how much aid you should get. One is called the "Federal Methodology," used for aid coming from government money. Most colleges use it to award their own institutional funds as well. The Federal Methodology is based on the FAFSA, the federal financial aid form.

For aid coming out of their own money, some colleges and scholarship programs use a different formula called the "Institutional Methodology." This is based on the PROFILE (more formally known as the College Board's CSS/Financial Aid PROFILE application) and/or the college's own financial aid application form. (*For more about these forms, see Steps 6 and 7.*) Colleges that use the Institutional Methodology do so because they think it presents a fuller picture of your family's financial situation. "I just think it does a much better job of measuring ability to pay," says Forrest M. Stuart, whose institution, Furman University, requires the PROFILE.

**So what does all this mean to you?** The differences between the two formulas make it possible that your expected family contribution will be lower under one or the other; it all depends on your individual family circumstances, and the individual college(s) you are applying to. You don't have to know how these formulas work or remember what they are called. The thing to remember is that if you apply to several colleges, because of these different formulas you might end up with a different EFC for one college than you do for another.

## Will College Savings Count Against You?

While some families save diligently for their children's college educations, others think this is a mistake. They worry that having a lot of savings will keep colleges from awarding financial aid. **But savings help you more than they hurt you**, and here is why.

When calculating your EFC, colleges subtract what they call an "asset protection allowance" from the amount you have saved. This "allowance" is the amount of money considered reasonable to set aside for educational savings and family emergencies. These "free" savings are not assessed at all. In Federal Methodology, the allowance varies based on the age of the oldest parent, and it can be several tens of thousands of dollars for a married couple in their 40s or 50s. These savings are clearly worth having, since they aren't included when calculating your EFC. (See Table 11 in Part II to get an estimate of what your parents' asset protection allowance may be.)

Even if your family saves more than the asset protection allowance, those savings will be assessed at a maximum rate of only 5.6 percent. So even if 5.6 percent of your excess savings count "against" you when it comes to federal need determination, 94.4 percent count "for" you. You can use them to meet your expected contribution, whatever it turns out to be. That's good news, because your family will be expected to pay much more out of income than out of savings. Most colleges will expect your parents to contribute between 22 and 47 percent of their income toward your EFC.

Essentially, your family will be expected to pay some part of your college costs out of pocket, and if you have savings, you have a pot to draw from. The alternatives are to pay it out of your monthly income or to borrow it — both of which are less appealing choices than using savings. "If I were preparing to send a son or daughter off to school, I would want to have as much savings available to me as I realistically could," says Vincent Amoroso, former director of the Office of Student Financial Services at Johns Hopkins University. "The reason is because, just like in other situations, having money on hand makes it easier for me to make choices that are good for myself and my child."

To be sure, there are other factors your family should consider before saving for college, such as whether they have enough money to save for retirement. But if they can put away any money for college, they should do so without hesitating. (*See Step 11 for information on tax-free college savings plans.*)

**KNOW THE LINGO**

**EFC (Expected Family Contribution)** — How much money a family is expected to pay for college.

**Need** — The difference between your EFC and the cost of attending a particular college you've chosen. Financial aid is designed to meet your need, not your EFC.

**Unmet need** — The difference (if any) between the your need and the financial aid offered by a particular college. Informally, unmet need is also called a **gap**.

**Asset protection allowance** — The amount of money considered reasonable to set aside for educational savings and emergencies, and is therefore not part of your EFC.

# Responsibilities Within the Family

Who should pay for college? Is it entirely the parents' duty, or should the student be responsible? If both, which combination of both? There is no single right answer to questions like these. But families need to discuss the topic, and the sooner the better. Your college will expect someone in the family to make a contribution, and you and your parents should figure out who that is before the bill comes due.

"Families should discuss college costs, family budget, financial aid and financing options at the beginning of the college application process, not at the end," says Carlene Riccelli, a college adviser at Amherst Regional High School in Amherst, Mass. Try to reach decisions that are as specific as possible, so that you each know what's expected of you. Try to make the decisions fair, so that no one feels used. What portion of your summer job income should go toward college? If your family takes out loans, should they be in your name your parents' name or both? Don't forget to discuss ways of keeping costs down, such as living at home and taking community college courses.

If your family is nontraditional, the discussion should include all adults involved in your care. When considering the financial need of students with divorced parents, for example, some colleges that use the Institutional Methodology will assess the income and assets of both natural parents. It will be up to the family to decide how to pay the expected family contribution, but part of that contribution will be based on the income and assets of the parent without custody. (*See Step 8 for more about parental custody and financial aid.*)

While it's important to talk about money, your family also needs to talk about other aspects of choosing a college, such as its academic and social environment. Some of the discussion will have nothing to do with money, but others will have financial aspects: for example, going away to an expensive college versus staying home and commuting to a cheaper one. Step 3 will further explore how to think about these issues. But the important thing is to start having the discussions — financial and otherwise — as early as possible.

# Crunch Some Numbers

If you want a sneak peek at what your expected family contribution will be, crunch some numbers. Part II contains worksheets and tables that you can use to calculate the EFC of a "typical" family under the Federal Methodology. Use the worksheets to add up your income, then subtract deductions and allowances. Total up your assets, too. Apply the formulas in the worksheets to calculate the contribution that is expected from you as a student. Then use the next set of worksheets and tables to calculate your parents' expected contribution. When you're finished, you will have your estimated EFC.

The figure you come up with will only be an estimate. Your actual EFC may be higher or lower, depending on the exact data you ultimately submit and the particular college's financial aid policies. But at least this exercise will give you a ballpark figure for what you can expect to pay.

## Online Calculators

If you'd prefer to estimate your EFC online, there are several websites with special calculators. They include:

- **collegeboard.org** — Our Net Price Calculator lets you "Do the Math" on EFC and to compare your out-of-pocket expenses from one college to another.
- **College and university websites** — These sites also include calculators geared to their individual financial aid policies.

# Your Unique Situation Counts Too

Colleges expect families to contribute some money toward students' education, and the amount they expect is your EFC. But colleges are not just faceless buildings of stone, and your EFC is not fixed in cement. The financial aid officer in charge of distributing a college's financial aid is a human being, and he or she does have some room to adjust how the EFC calculations are made based on your individual circumstances.

Step 8 will go into greater detail on how to notify your college about changes in your family's financial situation, such as a lost job. And Step 10 will discuss how to appeal if you think the college hasn't taken all your circumstances into account. Generally, financial aid officers are sympathetic if you are struggling with problems such as caring for an elderly parent or a lost job. They will be less sympathetic if it seems that you've chosen your financial problems — such as buying a new motorcycle with money that could have gone to pay your college bill. Still, financial aid officers are not heartless, and they will try to help when there is genuine distress.

**QUICK
RECAP**

The American education system expects families to bear as much responsibility for the costs of higher education as they can, but not more. Your family will have to contribute to your college costs, but will also receive help.

- Your family will be required to pay an expected family contribution, or EFC.
- The costs of the college you attend minus the financial aid you receive equals what you pay.
- College savings will not be held against you.

# Step 3: Choosing Colleges, Thinking Costs

**QUICK OVERVIEW**

This step shows you how to think about cost when choosing a college. You'll see why you shouldn't exclude any college from consideration just because of its price. You'll learn what your different college expenses will be, from tuition to pizza money; how costs can vary from college to college; and how to factor in the financial aid package the college is likely to give.

## How to Think About College Costs

When you're thinking about where to apply for college, its "list price" should not be the main consideration. Because financial aid will probably be available to help meet your need, even a college that appears exorbitant may in fact be within reach. A college's published costs are only one part of the equation when it comes to what you'll actually pay. **Until you've applied for and received an offer of financial aid, you won't know the real cost to your family.**

Remember that financial aid works like this: Total cost of attendance *minus* your family's expected family contribution (EFC) *equals* your financial need. As long as the college meets your need, the amount you pay stays the same whatever the price of the college. "I don't think college cost really should be a factor in where students apply for admission," says Vincent Amoroso of Johns Hopkins University. "I say that because your family contribution, in theory, is the same whether you apply to a school that costs $4,000 or to a school that costs $40,000."

In practice, your expected family contribution may actually vary somewhat from college to college. As noted in Step 2, a college using the Federal Methodology to assess your ability to pay might calculate a higher or lower EFC than a college that uses the Institutional Methodology. Even two institutions using the same methodology might calculate slightly different EFCs, depending on how they have treated any special circumstances that may apply to your family. (*See Step 8 for more on special circumstances.*) But

**KNOW THE LINGO**

**Total cost of attendance** — Not just tuition, but also all fees, room and board, transportation, books and supplies, and personal expenses.

**Public college** — A college or university that is subsidized by taxes and other public revenues and governed by a county, state or federal government agency.

**Community college** — A two-year public college subsidized by a local government, such as a county or city.

**Out-of-state tuition** — What public colleges charge students from other states; often more than double the rate for in-state residents.

**Reciprocity agreement** — A deal between neighboring states that allows residents to attend a public college in either state at the in-state tuition rate.

in general, the principle holds that your EFC will be constant from college to college, while your need will vary depending on the price of each college.

**The main thing to consider when applying for college is whether you and that school will be a good fit.** Look for the academic and social aspects that are likely to make you happy and successful there. Are you artistic? Are you mathematical? Do you love to learn for learning's sake? Do you have strong career ambitions in a particular field? Do you long to get away and see the world? Or does it matter more to stay near your family and the place where you grew up? "Students should not just look at a school because it's affordable," says Bonnie Lee Behm of Villanova University. "They should look at a school because it's the right fit for them academically, socially, spiritually and physically. Is cost an important part? Yes. It's a consideration, but only one among many." **And remember — you can find a good fit at more than one college**.

To discover what specific colleges have to offer, research them. You can find a lot of information about majors offered, the composition of the student body, academic policies, and extracurricular and athletic offerings in *The College Board College Handbook*. You can also learn more on the College Search engine on bigfuture.org, and from college guidebooks and websites. If you know people who have gone to the colleges you're considering, talk to them and get their opinions.

So, when deciding which colleges to apply to, don't focus too much on cost. But do be aware of what the costs are; cost may become a factor depending on what financial aid packages you are ultimately offered. Even though your EFC should in principle be the same at all colleges, not all schools always meet full need. And even those that do may meet it with different packages — some with more loans, others with more grants. It makes sense to know what kinds of packages a particular school is likely to give.

By using Part III of this book as a guide, and also by contacting the admissions and financial aid offices of the colleges you're considering, gather as much information as you can about the costs of the school and the type of aid they offer. The rest of Step 3 suggests the kinds of information you should be seeking from each school.

## Choosing Colleges

Both you and your parents should be involved in the discussion about where to apply for college. You will share the responsibility for paying for college, so you should all have a voice. Furthermore, your parents can give you good advice about what colleges to consider based on their life experiences, their knowledge of you, and their understanding of the family finances — even if they themselves have never been to college. The deciding vote, however, should be yours. You are the one who will have to start and finish college, and you are more likely to do so successfully if you have chosen the college yourself. "Only the student knows the fit that he or she will have at a particular institution academically, socially and financially as well," says Forrest Stuart of Furman University.

When you begin choosing where to apply, don't exclude any college. Let every college be on the table, even if it seems too difficult academically or financially. Aim high. Shop around. The best colleges for you may not be the ones that occur to you first.

If a college is a good fit for you, there is probably a way to make it work financially. "Apply to those colleges that you think, okay, maybe we could afford these, but also apply above that level, because some schools may be much more manageable than you expect," says Bonnie Lee Behm of Villanova University.

## Do Consider a "Financial Safety"

Even though all colleges should be on the drawing board, you should also consider applying to a financial "safety" school — one that is a good academic fit and that you feel fairly confident you can afford. Your financial safety school is one you would be happy attending and that has either low published costs or will almost certainly offer enough grant money to make attendance affordable. A public university in your state, a local community college or a private university where you are highly likely to win a merit scholarship might all be financial safeties.

A financial safety is a good idea because your top choices may not give you as much financial aid as you want. "We know students who are really strong academically, but they're not at the top of their class, and they apply to the college of their dreams," says Elizabeth Bickford, director of the Office of Student Financial Aid and Scholarships at the University of Oregon in Eugene. Despite their hopes for a full merit scholarship, such students may find that they can enroll only if they are willing to take out a large amount in unsubsidized loans — something their family may not be willing to do.

In these and other situations, a financial safety is a good backup. For example, if you accept admission to a far-off university, but find that you can't get used to it and want to come back to the financial safety school near home, it will be easier to transfer if you've already applied and been admitted. Still, Elizabeth Bickford says she encourages students to "dream large, because it's your one opportunity. When you go from high school to that first year in college, that's where most of the scholarships are — for entering freshmen. It's your opportunity to make that big step away from home."

**KNOW THE LINGO**

**Need-blind admission** — If a college has a "need-blind admission" policy, this means that it will admit a student solely on the basis of his or her academic merit or other characteristics, regardless of their ability to pay. However, it does not mean the college guarantees to meet full need. You may be admitted, but the college may be unable to offer a financial aid package equal to your need.

**Figure 5:**

Distribution of Full-Time Undergraduates at Four-Year Institutions
by Tuition and Fees, 2015–2016

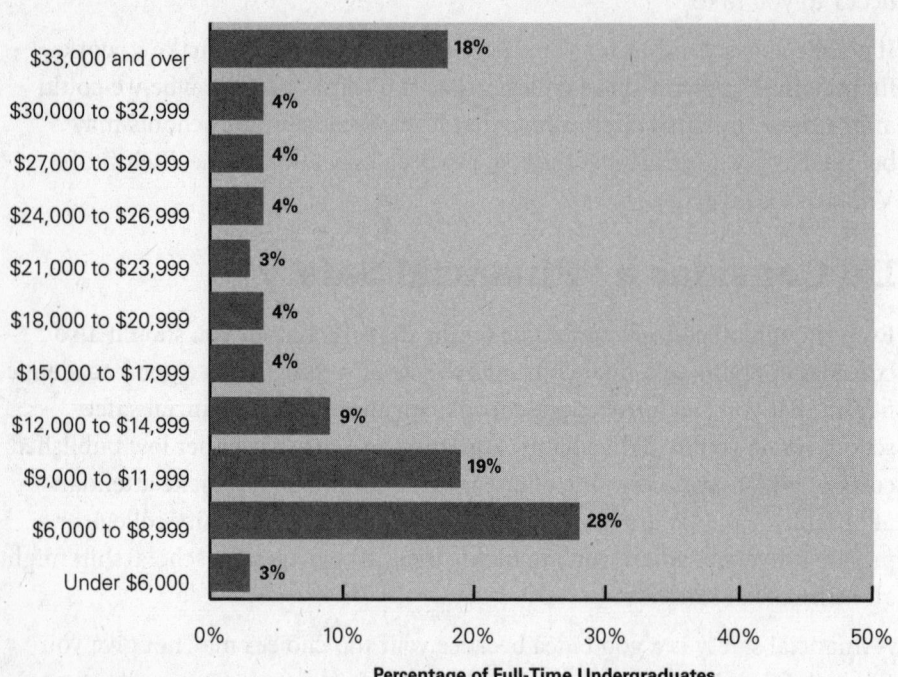

*Sixty percent of full-time undergraduates attend colleges with published
tuition and fee charges of under $15,000. After financial aid, many of those
students pay an even lower "net price" for tuition.*

**Source:** *Annual Survey of Colleges*, The College Board, New York

# Components of College Costs

The price of a college education has several parts. The most obvious is tuition,
the cost of taking courses. Tuition varies depending on how many courses
you take, but full time students pay a flat rate for a full schedule of courses.
If you attend part time, you will likely pay by credit hours, a measure of how
long each class is. Most courses are three credit hours apiece, which usually
translates to three one-hour classes each week. Most full-time students take
an average of four or five courses per semester, for a total of 12 to 15 credit
hours per semester for a full load.

Fees are another component of college costs. Fees are usually billed to all
students as funding for the college's general expenses, such as the library
or student activities. But there may be additional special fees for students
enrolled in certain classes or activities. A chemistry student may pay lab fees,
for example.

Tuition and fees are just one part of what you'll pay for college, and often not
even half. Another large component is room and board. "Room" is the cost
of housing you, and "board" is the cost of food. You may live in a dorm on

campus, or off campus — in an apartment or a house with other students or at home with your parents. You may be on a meal plan where all your meals are prepared for you for one price, or you may fend for yourself, buying groceries and cooking meals. Either way, these basic living expenses are your room and board.

Taken together, tuition, fees, room and board are the largest chunk of college costs. On average, at four-year public colleges across the nation, these elements together make up 80 percent of what students pay for college. Yet there is still another 20 percent of costs to be accounted for. These include:

- Books and supplies — class expenses that are not covered by tuition and will vary depending on the courses you take.

- Transportation expenses — for on-campus students, this is the cost of trips home during holidays; for commuters, this is the cost of either mass transit or a car. Car costs include parking, gas, insurance and maintenance.

- Computer equipment costs — if required by the college. Some colleges may insist that you buy a certain model of computer, or bring your own computer but have special hardware and software installed to make it work on the campus network.

- Personal expenses — everything from snacks outside the meal plan to newspaper subscriptions to haircuts and toothpaste to membership fees for student groups.

# How Costs Can Vary

Each college has different price tags for each of the cost components. For example, books and supplies might cost $1,200 for a typical student at a state university, but $2,500 or more at an art school. Table 1 that follows shows national averages for cost components.

To get specifics for a particular college that you're considering, check its website and look for the school's published estimate of what the average student spends on the different expense categories. The college will use these averages as part of the calculation of your "total cost of attendance," which will partly determine how much aid you're awarded. You can also consult Part III of this book for a school-by-school summary of costs.

However, remember that these average costs are only averages. You are an individual, and you may pay more or less than average, depending on your individual circumstances. For example, if you attend college in California but your family lives in New York, you will pay more for traveling to and from home than if your family is also in California.

Textbook and supply costs can also vary widely depending on your major. If you are an architecture or drafting student, you might have to buy an expensive computer-aided design program that your English major friends won't need. Science students might need to buy a statistical-modeling software package; studio artists a graphic-design suite. At least software like this only has to be bought once and is then used to do work for several classes; furthermore, educational discounts may be available for such purchases. In some programs, students might have to buy supplies that frequently get used up and must be replenished, such as brushes and paints for art students.

Rooming costs will vary a little between different dorm complexes on campus — for example, newer dorms may cost more, and a single room is always more expensive than one shared with a roommate. There will also be differences between various off-campus rooming locations.

Finally, your personal expenses may be higher or lower than average depending on lifestyle factors — but they will almost always be higher than you think. As James Schembari wrote in the *New York Times*, there is always a need for "pizza money" — money to buy pizza, go on a road trip, or hang out at the student union. Books, supplies, travel and everyday expenses "can add $3,000 or more a year, depending on parents' generosity and where their child goes to college," wrote Mr. Schembari.

**Table 1:**
Average Estimated Undergraduate Budgets, 2015–2016

| SECTOR | TUITION AND FEES | BOOKS AND SUPPLIES | ROOM AND BOARD | TRANSPOR- TATION | OTHER EXPENSES | TOTAL EXPENSES* |
|---|---|---|---|---|---|---|
| Public Two-Year | | | | | | |
| Resident | $3,435 | $1,364 | $8,003 | $1,109 | $2,106 | $16,017 |
| Commuter | $3,435 | $1,364 | — | $1,774 | $2,257 | $8,830 |
| Public Four-Year | | | | | | |
| Resident | $9,410 | $1,298 | $10,138 | $1,109 | $2,106 | $24,061 |
| Commuter | $9,410 | $1,298 | — | $1,774 | $2,257 | $14,739 |
| Out-of-State | $23,893 | $1,298 | $10,138 | $1,109 | $2,106 | $38,544 |
| Private Four-Year | | | | | | |
| Resident | $32,410 | $1,249 | $11,516 | $1,033 | $1,628 | $47,831 |
| Commuter | $32,410 | $1,249 | — | $1,774 | $2,257 | $37,690 |

**Note:** Estimates of individual budget items are based on reporting by institutional financial aid offices.
**Source:** *Annual Survey of Colleges*, The College Board, New York, N.Y.

# Ways to Reduce Costs

There are a few time-tested ways of saving money on some of the major cost components of college. To save money on tuition and fees, many students have attended public colleges and community colleges. To save money on room and board, many have commuted rather than roomed on campus. Here are the pros and cons for these money-saving techniques.

## Public vs. Private, In-State vs. Out-of-State

**GOOD TO KNOW**

This section discusses ways to **find inexpensive colleges** during your college search. For tips on how to cut costs once you've enrolled, see Step 11.

Attending a public college in your own state is an excellent way to save money on tuition and fees. Public colleges are subsidized by state taxes, so their tuition and fees for state residents are usually much less than at private colleges — 70 percent less, on average. Depending on the school, the quality of education may be as good or even better than what you would get at a private college.

On the other hand, the true cost picture is more complicated than it looks. Even though private colleges charge more for tuition and fees, most of them also give more scholarships and grants than public colleges do, which helps to even out the costs. "There's an adage that the more expensive the school, the more money they give away," says Mike Scott of Texas Christian University, a private institution.

**Cost isn't everything**. If a particular private school has some valuable characteristic that you want — smaller classes, professors with whom you want to study — it may be worth the extra tuition money. But cost is a factor to consider. If a certain state school can give you all that you want from college, why not go there and save some money?

If you would like to study at a public college or university in another state, be aware that most public schools charge higher tuition to students from out of state than they do to in-state students. Public colleges currently charge an average of $9,410 in tuition and fees to a state resident, but $23,893 to an out-of-state student. The in- and out-of-state rates for specific public colleges and universities are listed in Part III.

### PAYING IN-STATE RATES IN ANOTHER STATE

It is sometimes possible to get the in-state tuition rate, or at least a lowered tuition rate, even if you are an out-of-state student. For example, some state universities have "reciprocity agreements" with neighboring states. South Dakota residents pay tuition rates comparable to state residents at the University of Minnesota and vice versa. There are also discipline-based "consortiums" of public colleges that let you get the in-state tuition rate at another state's public college if your desired major is not available at any public college in your own state.

Your school counselor and state board of education website can give you more information about programs for paying in-state rates in another state.

# Community Colleges

Community colleges are another great way of saving money on tuition and fees. A community college is a two-year school subsidized by a state, county or city. Its cost for tuition and fees is usually much lower than that of a four-year institution — 63 percent lower, on average, than a public four-year college. Community colleges often charge tuition in three tiers — in district, in state and out of state — with the lowest price for those who live in the local district. Though most community colleges do not offer a four-year bachelor's degree (though the number that do are on the rise), they do provide courses whose credits can be transferred toward a bachelor's degree at another college. Because those courses cost much less, this can be a way to save money in your first two years of college — money you can use to help pay for the last two years. Four out of 10 college-bound high school graduates start their college education this way.

There are other reasons to attend a community college besides saving money. If you aren't sure whether you want to go to a four-year college, a community college will give you a sense of what the college experience is like. If you don't know what kind of program you want to pursue — science, art, business or something else — you can explore different subject areas at a community college before committing to a program. And if you need to be able to work, perhaps to support a family, you can work out a more flexible schedule at a community college, where many students work full time and attend classes at night and on weekends.

A community college is also a golden opportunity for students who didn't do well enough in high school to win admission to the college of their choice. Community colleges are open to everyone, and some have agreements with four-year colleges that guarantee admission in the third year for students who have maintained good grades. This is the case in California, according to Mary San Agustin of Palomar College, a community college. If students, she says, "have their heart set in going, let's say, to Stanford or U.C. Berkeley, we have an excellent articulation program that allows them to take the two-year required courses and get guaranteed admissions in their junior year at those schools that they prefer to go to." In this way, **a community college can open the door to a four-year college for you**.

Of course, there are advantages to entering a four-year college as a freshman rather than two years later as a transfer from a community college. Socially and academically, you may enjoy a fuller college experience. "It's all the things that you can't quite name," says Elizabeth Bickford of the University of Oregon. "There is something that you do lose in that transition as an 18- or 19-year-old." But those factors have to be balanced against financial realities, as Ms. Bickford found when she was making her own college decisions. "I'm a community college transfer to a four-year myself. So is my husband. We wouldn't have financially been able to make it if we hadn't done it that way. I think it's a good way to make it if all the support isn't there."

## Living at Home

An obvious way to save money on room and board is to stay home and commute to a college close by. Instead of paying for campus housing and meals — an average cost of $11,516 a year for private colleges — your housing and meal costs remain what they are.

**However, commuting has hidden costs.** You will have transportation expenses that you wouldn't have if you lived on campus. If you can use mass transit, these costs will probably be low enough to make economic sense. But if you have to buy a car and pay for gas and insurance, your transportation costs might end up being close to the costs of on-campus room and board. And if you're thinking of relying on family and friends for rides to and from campus, remember that their schedules may not overlap with yours. Your own schedule may change day to day and semester to semester, depending on your classes and activities. You probably will need your own car if mass transit isn't available.

Also, don't forget that you cost money at home, too. You're still eating and using utilities at home, and you'll inevitably add pick-up meals on campus to those costs. Financial aid packages usually offer help in paying for room and board as well as tuition and fees, so your actual cost for living on campus would probably not be as high as the published price.

We're not saying that commuting isn't a bargain — it usually is. (There are other good reasons to live at home, too.) But if you are thinking of commuting just to save money, don't commit to it until you weigh all the costs and assess the financial aid offers from any "live away" colleges to which you may apply.

## Living Off-Campus

If you don't want to commute but still want to save money on room and board, you might want to consider living off-campus. By residing near campus in an apartment that you share with classmates, you may be able to live more cheaply than you could in the dorms. **But be sure to check the college's policies** — many do not allow freshmen to live off campus if they're under 21 and not living with their parents.

# How to Factor in Financial Aid

Every college publishes an average price for the various cost components, but that published price is probably not the price you will end up paying. Your financial aid package will reduce your actual costs. Yet financial aid packages vary from college to college as much as costs do. In thinking about where you will apply, you need to find out some financial aid basics about each college on your short list. How great a percentage of need does it usually meet? How much aid does it award in grants and how much in loans? Does the college offer any merit scholarships or other forms of aid not based on need?

Part III of this book, "Financial Aid College by College," gives you these financial aid basics, along with a number of other essential facts. These include:

- the school's Web address
- what type of school it is, such as public or private
- how many students are enrolled
- how selective the school is
- basic costs, including tuition, fees, room and board
- financial aid application procedures, including deadlines and required forms
- contact information for the financial aid office

In addition, the "Financial Aid Picture" section of each college's profile tells you how much aid is being distributed to how many students and in what form. This information is useful, but note that it only shows averages. Since few families are "average," the numbers in the financial aid profile shouldn't be considered a guarantee of what you'll get or how much you'll have to pay. For example, in-state students at public colleges usually borrow much less than the average debt per student listed in the profiles, while out-of-state students usually borrow more. You can, however, use the profiles to compare colleges: This college meets a greater percentage of need than most; this college awards a relatively large portion of aid in grants.

# Check with the Financial Aid Office Before You Apply

Before you apply for financial aid, check with the financial aid offices of the colleges to which you're planning to apply for admission — by simply visiting their website, or by talking to them on the phone or in person. Confirm which forms you need to complete and the deadlines. Better to get these details right before you get started than to find out after the fact that you filed too late or didn't file the proper form.

Bear in mind also that each college has its own financial aid policies, such as how outside scholarships are treated and whether or not aid awards can be appealed. When you contact the office, whether long distance or in a campus visit, find out as much as you can about these policies, along with facts about costs and the financial aid process. If possible, schedule an interview with a member of the financial aid staff. They'll give you a lot of information, but don't expect them to offer you aid until they've seen your forms.

**KEEP IN MIND**

The **college profiles in Part III** of this book give the "financial aid picture" for each college, based on averages. Use these profiles to **compare colleges only**; the aid you would get at any college is based on your own individual circumstances, so the amount might be higher or lower than the average for that college.

# Questions to Ask Colleges

Here are some questions worth asking the aid office:

✔ What are your average costs for the first year for:

- tuition and fees
- room and board
- books and supplies
- transportation
- other personal expenses

✔ What is the range of costs for:

- rooms (single, double)
- board (different meal plans)
- tuition rates (flat rate, per credit, etc.)

✔ By how much will total costs increase each year?

✔ How much have tuition and fees and room and board increased over the past three to five years?

✔ Does financial need have an impact on admission decisions?

✔ Does the school offer both need-based and merit-based financial aid?

✔ Do I need to file a separate application for merit-based scholarships?

✔ If the financial aid package isn't enough, under what conditions, if any, will the aid office reconsider the offer?

✔ How will the aid package change from year to year?

✔ What will happen if my family's financial situation changes?

✔ What are the terms and conditions of your aid programs? For example, what are the academic requirements or other conditions for renewing financial aid from year to year?

✔ When can we expect to receive bills from the college? Is there an option to spread the yearly payment over equal monthly installments?

**QUICK RECAP**

When deciding where to apply to college, cost is a factor, but not the most important factor. Don't exclude any college from consideration because of its "sticker price" — what you will actually pay might be much less. Remember:

- Each school has different costs and financial aid policies.

- When choosing colleges to apply to, consider a "financial safety."

- Your costs might vary from the published averages.

- You might be able to save money at a public college or community college or by commuting — but there are pros and cons to all those strategies.

- Research the colleges you're considering and contact their financial aid offices early.

# **Step 4:** Get Ready for the Forms

Depending on where you'll apply, you may need to file up to three kinds of application forms to get financial aid: the FAFSA, the CSS/Financial Aid PROFILE and forms for individual colleges or states. Step 4 gets you ready for those forms. There are two main things to remember. First, file before the deadlines. The early bird — or at least the timely bird — gets the worm. Second, don't be intimidated. The forms are easier to fill out than they look.

## Forms You'll Fill Out

Applying for financial aid is basically a matter of filling out a few financial aid forms on time. The forms may appear complicated, but they are simpler than they look, and millions of people fill them out every year. We will guide you through them so they make sense.

The three steps that follow this one walk you through the application forms you may need to complete: the FAFSA (Step 5), the PROFILE (Step 6) and whatever forms your individual colleges may require (Step 7). This step will help you create a timeline of which colleges require which forms when.

You may not need to fill out all the forms we describe. Most colleges require only one form, the FAFSA. If you do need to fill out more than one form, take heart. Most of the other forms ask for information similar to what the FAFSA requests. Repeating that information may be annoying, but it isn't hard.

### **FAFSA: The Federal Form**

This is the big one. The FAFSA, or Free Application for Federal Student Aid, must be completed by everyone who wants federal government aid. Just about every college financial aid program requires it, even if they also require other forms. Most schools and states use nothing but the FAFSA to determine eligibility for aid.

There is no charge for completing the FAFSA, and it's easy to do. **Don't pay someone to fill it out for you.**

Even though this book presents the financial aid forms in order of FAFSA, PROFILE and institutional forms, **you may need to submit these forms in a different order** depending on the financial aid deadlines of your colleges. In some cases, you may have to file PROFILE a few weeks before FAFSA, or the institutional form on the same day as FAFSA.

### FILING THE FAFSA

**The FAFSA can be filled out and submittted online at www.fafsa.ed.gov** (FAFSA on the Web). The FAFSA website gives lots of help in completing the form. You don't have to stress about making mistakes because the site checks your information as you go along, and it will find any errors for you to correct before submitting. You can also return to your FAFSA online to update or correct information as needed after you have submitted the form.

**The start date for filing the FAFSA has changed.** Are you a high school senior graduating in 2017, planning to start college in the fall of 2017? Then you can access and submit your FAFSA on or after **Oct. 1, 2016**. This is new. Under the old rules, you couldn't file the FAFSA before Jan. 1 of the year for which you're seeking aid. This is a great change, because it eliminates the squeeze many students used to face if they were applying to colleges with early deadlines.

Once it's Oct. 1, however, you should aim to file your FAFSA as soon as possible. Don't be fooled by the federal filing deadline (June 30). **Many college deadlines for financial aid are in February or March**, and they need your FAFSA information by then. So, come October, the earlier that you start working on the FAFSA, the better.

### IF YOU NEED TO USE A PAPER FAFSA

If you are unable to file the FAFSA online, you can request a paper FAFSA by calling 1-800-433-3243. If you are hearing impaired, contact the TTY line at 1-800-730-8913.

On the paper FAFSA you can only list four colleges to receive your information. You can add up to six more later, but you'll have to wait until your FAFSA is processed and you've received your Student Aid Report.

You'll have to allow at least four weeks for mailing and processing before your earliest deadline. Be sure to make a photocopy for your records before mailing.

## PROFILE

In addition to the FAFSA, some colleges and scholarship programs also require that you fill out the CSS/Financial Aid PROFILE to award their own nonfederal funds. They believe this form gives a more complete picture of students' financial circumstances, allowing them to allocate money as fairly as possible. The PROFILE service is administered by the College Board, though the College Board itself does not give out any need-based scholarships.

A few colleges require PROFILE only if you're applying for early decision or early action. Others require it for all applicants. To find out if your colleges require PROFILE, look them up in Part III of this book or refer to the college's websites.

---

**KEEP IN MIND**

**File your FAFSA as early as you can.** When it comes to financial aid, time really is money. Pay attention to college deadlines! **Those who apply late usually get less** than they are entitled to, because there is less money available in the pool.

## KNOW THE LINGO

**FAFSA (Free Application for Federal Student Aid)** — The form that must be completed by everyone applying for federal government aid.

**PROFILE (CSS/Financial Aid PROFILE)** — A Web-based form offered by the College Board and used by some colleges and scholarship programs to award their own financial aid.

**FSA ID (Federal Student Aid ID)** — The username and password used to complete, sign, and submit a FAFSA electronically.

**SAR (Student Aid Report)** — A report generated after you submit your FAFSA that shows your federally calculated EFC. The SAR is sent to you and to the colleges you listed in your FAFSA.

**Priority date** — The date by which applications for financial aid must be received in order to be offered the best possible package. After the priority date, applicants are considered on a first-come, first-served basis until the pool of aid money runs out.

**PROFILE is online only; there are no paper forms.** If you don't have a computer at home, use a computer at your school's guidance office or the library. Once you create a College Board account on collegeboard.org, you can start the PROFILE anytime after October 1st of the year before you intend to start college.

The application will ask about your family and its income and assets. Some colleges also require information from a parent that doesn't live with you, in which case that parent will be asked to complete a separate application.

It's best if you submit the completed PROFILE at least one week before your earliest college financial aid deadline. You can use the same application for multiple colleges, and you'll receive an online acknowledgment confirming the schools to which you're sending the information.

There is a $25 fee to send your PROFILE to one college, plus a fee of $16 for each additional institution. However, depending on the information you submit, you may qualify for a fee waiver. Automatically awarded to low-income, first-time applicants, the fee waiver covers the costs of the PROFILE registration and up to eight school reports.

## College Forms

Some colleges — most of them private — require you to complete their own financial aid form as well as the FAFSA. Usually the forms are not complicated, and filling them out is not a big deal. Mike Scott of Texas Christian University says, "We have a very simple online form, where we just ask a couple of extra questions." Some of the questions are about projected enrollment: "Are they going to be full time or part time? When do they think they're going to graduate?" Others are aimed at matching students to outside sources of aid.

Find out if your colleges require you to file their own form, and if they do, file them on time.

## State Forms

Most states offer need-based financial aid to their residents, and most colleges will require you to apply for it. Ask your school counselor for information on what form you need to complete to apply for state scholarship or grant programs. In many states, the FAFSA alone is enough to establish eligibility for state aid — but some states require their own form. If your state does, find out the deadline and add it to your master timeline for applying for aid. (*A table showing the deadlines for state aid, and which forms each state requires, appears in Step 7.*)

# Know the Deadlines!

Deadlines count. If you're on time, the colleges to which you've applied will have more money to give you; if you're late, they will have less money — or even none. **Late means less money, so be on time!** That means knowing and keeping track of all the financial aid deadlines you have to meet.

This can be tricky, because the deadlines are not all the same. Many schools and states may require you to fill out their own financial aid forms, and those forms may have deadlines that differ from those of the FAFSA or PROFILE. And **keep in mind that a college's due date for financial aid applications is typically different from its due date for admissions applications**.

Many colleges have no firm deadline or closing date for applying for financial aid; rather, they have a "priority" date. Often falling in February or March, the priority date is the date by which the school needs to receive your application to make its most attractive aid offer. After that date, funds may be limited or used up, and you may not get as much aid as you need. "I urge my students to apply for aid by the priority date," says Lauri Benton, a counselor at Columbia High School in Decatur, Ga. "They are more likely to get the aid they need early in the process, when the colleges have ample money to award."

Some colleges accept financial aid applications on a "rolling" basis. This means that applications are reviewed as they come in on a first-come, first-reviewed basis. Applicants are notified — that is, sent a financial aid award letter — a few weeks after they submit their forms. Most colleges that have a priority date will review late applications on a rolling basis. If you're applying to a rolling-applications college that doesn't have any set deadlines or priority dates, you're best off applying by mid-February or early March, when they will probably still have enough money available to meet your need.

Part III of this book, "Financial Aid College by College," lists deadlines and priority dates for colleges, along with their required forms. But it is worth confirming this information with the schools to which you're applying — at least by visiting their websites in November or December. Remember: Time is money. To get the most aid available, apply by the priority date.

## Creating a Timeline for Aid Applications

There are a lot of dates to remember as you apply for financial aid, but they don't have to be overwhelming. You can stay on top of them by making a timeline.

When you've found out the priority dates of the colleges and scholarship programs to which you're applying, as well as those of your state financial aid agency, list them in chronological order. Make that list part of a month-by-month timeline. Don't worry about the past; start the timeline with whatever month you're in now. The chart on the opposite page is an example of the sort of timeline you might construct. (*A blank copy of this chart for you to fill in appears in Part II on page 123.*)

---

**EXPERT ADVICE**

"If you **meet our priority date**, we're going to guarantee you a full package here. You'll get 100 percent of need if you meet that priority deadline. If you don't, then it's what's left over, if we have money left over. And we typically do — but we don't have enough to meet 100 percent of the need of every late applicant."

*— Vincent Amoroso, former director, Student Financial Services, Johns Hopkins University*

**SAMPLE WORKSHEET 1:**
# Meet Your Application Deadlines

|  |  | COLLEGE 1: | COLLEGE 2: | COLLEGE 3: |
|---|---|---|---|---|
|  | College Name | *1st Choice Univ.* | *Private Univ.* | *Financial Safety* |
| FORMS REQUIRED | FAFSA | *Yes* | *Yes* | *Yes* |
|  | PROFILE | *For ED (by 11/1)* | *Yes* | *No* |
|  | State form | *Yes* | *No* | *Yes* |
|  | Institutional form | *No* | *Laptop loaner* | *Yes* |
|  | Tax returns | *Verification only* | *Verification only* | *Yes* |
|  | Other |  |  |  |
| SCHOOL CODES | Federal code | *999999* | *888888* | *777777* |
|  | CSS code | *999Z* | *999X* |  |
| PRIORITY DATE |  | *3/1 (FAFSA, State Form)* | *2/1* | *3/15* |
| CLOSING DATE |  | *None* | *2/15* | *None* |
| AFTER APPLYING | Need to send letter? |  |  |  |
|  | Documentation required? |  |  |  |
| COMPARE AWARDS | Notification date | *12/15* | *4/1* | *2 weeks after applying* |
|  | Reply-by date | *Immediately (if accepted ED)* | *5/1* | *4 weeks after notification* |

*For a blank version of this worksheet that you can photocopy for your own use, see Part II.*

Throughout the period that you're applying for aid, keep your timeline where you can see it, check off what you've done, and remind yourself of what to do next. This will put the deadlines in your control. (*See the inside front cover of this book for a calendar of important dates and reminders.*)

## Do You Get More Money If You Apply Early?

No. If you apply for financial aid Tuesday and another student applies Wednesday, you don't get more money than that student — so long as both of you apply by the deadline (or the priority date). However, when it comes to the college's own funds, and certain "campus-based" federal student aid programs (such as federal work-study), aid is distributed first-come, first-served once that date has passed. If you apply for aid after the college's deadline or priority date, the pool of funds may be used up. So always apply on time.

### WHAT ABOUT EARLY DECISION?

Many schools allow students to apply for admission under early-decision or early-action programs. Whether early acceptance to a school affects the student's financial aid package varies from school to school. Depending on the college, the student accepted early may get more financial aid, less, or the same.

If you are considering early-decision programs, ask each school's financial aid officer: How is financial aid affected if I apply early decision? You may not know exactly what aid you'll get until after you accept. Don't panic: The rules of early decision allow you to turn down the college's acceptance offer if it doesn't offer you enough aid. Just don't put all your eggs into one basket — be sure to apply to a "financial safety school" as well.

## Get Your Stuff Together

For maximum efficiency, gather all the records you need to complete the forms before you sit down to work on them. That will save you a lot of time getting up, hunting around and forgetting where you left off. For both you and your parents, you'll probably need tax returns and related documents (such as W-2 forms), as well as end-of-year pay stubs, bank statements and other financial records. If you're filling out the PROFILE, you will need tax documents from the year that just ended and the previous year. If your parents own their home, you will need current value and mortgage information to fill out the PROFILE.

The FAFSA and PROFILE websites provide preapplication worksheets that you can print out as a way to help you gather your information before filling out the actual application. Use them that way. Add a list of all the records you need to assemble. It should be comprehensive and indicate which records are for all forms and which are for PROFILE only.

**KEEP IN MIND**

When you fill out the FAFSA, both you and one of your parents need a **FSA ID (Federal Student Aid ID)**. This is important: the FSA ID will allow you to sign your FAFSA electronically, which will cut down your processing time. **You and one of your parents must each obtain a FSA ID** at **the FAFSA website**. You should register for your FSA IDs **before you fill out the FAFSA**. Although you will be prompted to get one if you didn't, it might delay processing time, so it's better to get your FSA ID ahead of time.

**EXPERT ADVICE**

If, like many students, you've never filed a tax return, you'll probably find it helpful to **get a blank copy of IRS Form 1040EZ** and the instructions that come with it. This is the simplest tax return form there is, and most high school and college students use it to report their summer and after-school job earnings. If your parents have filed for you in past years, **ask them to walk you through your return** for the last year.

## Establish Eligibility

To be eligible for federal financial aid, among other requirements, you'll have to:

- be a U.S. citizen or eligible noncitizen
- have a valid Social Security number
- not have been convicted of sale or possession of drugs
- if male and at least 18 years old, be registered with the Selective Service (in most cases)

Most of these requirements will not require extra work for most students. But two of them may. If you don't have a Social Security number, get one as soon as possible (go to www.ssa.gov to learn how), and certainly before you file your FAFSA. And if you are male, you can register for the Selective Service through the FAFSA application if you haven't already. If you do have a drug conviction, you may still be able to establish eligibility by completing a treatment program.

## Income Tax Returns

PROFILE asks you for two years of tax information. For example, if you are seeking aid for the 2017–18 academic year you must report income information for both 2015 and 2016. It also asks for estimated income for the next year, which you can base on the prior year's information.

The FAFSA asks you to provide tax information for only one year, the "prior-prior" year. For example, if you are seeking aid for the 2017–18 academic year you only have to provide information from 2015 tax returns. This is another good change because it makes it easier to complete the FAFSA with information imported directly from the IRS, using the IRS Data Retrieval Tool (DRT), rather than with income estimates that may need correcting.

## IRS Data Retrieval Tool

Accessible right from your FAFSA online, this tool allows you or your parents to access the IRS tax return information needed to complete the FAFSA and to transfer the data directly onto your FAFSA form. However, it takes a fair amount of time for your tax return information to become available for transfer from the IRS; up to three weeks if you filed your returns electronically and up to eight weeks if you filed by mail. So keep that in mind if you need to file a late tax return for the year you have to provide information.

**For many colleges, the IRS Data Retrieval process is the preferred means of completing your FAFSA.** If you cannot use this process at the time you initially complete your FAFSA, check with your college(s) to determine how best to update your FAFSA information once your tax returns have been filed.

You'll have to file some forms to get financial aid, but they aren't as difficult as they might look. The main forms are FAFSA and PROFILE, plus whatever other forms your colleges or state may require.

- File on time — filing late can cost you money.

- File your FAFSA online. Get a FSA-ID for yourself and for one of your parents early.

- Make a timeline to keep track of your deadlines, including college priority dates.

- As early as possible, check with your colleges to be sure you know what forms they each require and how they want you to provide tax information.

- Gather together the records you need to fill out the forms.

- If you don't have one already, get a Social Security number.

**QUICK RECAP**

# Step 5: Fill Out the FAFSA

**QUICK OVERVIEW**

The FAFSA may look intimidating, but it's actually pretty easy to fill out. The questions mainly concern your income and assets and those of your parents, but they also touch on other matters, such as your citizenship status and the schools to which you want the FAFSA to be sent. We'll walk you through it, and give you tips about how to avoid delays. Above all: File on time!

## General Advice

Nobody likes to fill out forms. And no one enjoys having to share information about family finances. But the potential result — money to help you pay for college — is well worth it. And you will see in this step that the FAFSA is really pretty simple. While the form has six sections, only one requires financial information, and another is, essentially, "sign here." The online FAFSA also has "skip logic" so you don't have to see questions that don't pertain to you.

Again, remember that you don't have to do the steps in this book in exactly the order presented. If the colleges require you to submit the PROFILE before the FAFSA, then do the PROFILE first, even though we present the FAFSA first. Since the PROFILE requires much of the same information needed to fill out the FAFSA, doing the PROFILE first will make this step much easier.

**Help is available by phone and online** if you have questions about FAFSA. And don't be afraid to call the financial aid offices of the colleges to which you're applying. If you're confused about this or any other aspect of the financial aid process, these offices can help. "People look at the FAFSA and they find it a bit overwhelming initially," says Vincent Amoroso of Johns Hopkins University. "They come to us seeking guidance and reassurance on how to get through the application process. We show them that it's not as complicated as it looks."

**EXPERT ADVICE**

"Our job is to get students through this maze. You'd call a mechanic if your car is broken. Well, why not call us if you have a question about financial aid applications? That's our job — to get you through the process."

— *Bonnie Lee Behm, director of financial assistance, Villanova University*

## Apply on Time

You can file your FAFSA anytime after Oct. 1 of the year before you'll start college. Most college deadlines for financial aid are in March, and some fall as early as February, so don't let time slip by. You have to leave time for your FAFSA to be processed. Be sure to file your online form at least one week before the earliest deadline. Remember: missing your college's deadline or priority date can cost you money.

## Read Instructions Carefully; Fill Out the Form Accurately

With the FAFSA as with all financial aid forms, accuracy is vital. Read the directions. Understand the terms that are being used. Many terms, such as "date of birth," are straightforward, but others, such as "investments," require you to read the instructions carefully so you know what they mean in this context. Even the term "parent," as discussed below, has a special meaning on the FAFSA.

Be as complete and accurate as you can about your financial circumstances. If you submit incorrect data, you might create delays that could endanger your aid. By avoiding errors, you will increase your chances of getting all the aid for which you are eligible.

## Keep Track of Your "Save Key" and FSA ID

You don't have to complete the FAFSA on the Web in one sitting. At the start, you'll create a "Save Key" password that will allow you to leave the application before completing it and to return later.

Get FSA IDs ahead of time for both yourself and for one of your parents so you can sign the form electronically. The FSA IDs can be obtained at StudentAid.gov/fsaid.

## Give Yourself Time

Even though the FAFSA has been made easier, it is still an important form and requires concentration. Take it seriously; don't try to do it on your phone or while multi-tasking. Use a PC or laptop in a quiet place where you won't be distracted, and give yourself a good hour or so to do it right.

**KNOW THE LINGO**

**If you've never filed an income tax return before** — or if your parents file for you — you may not be familiar with these IRS forms:

**1040** — The main form of your tax return, this is a summary of all the taxable income you or your parents made last year, possible deductions from that income, the tax owed on that income, and credits that give some of that tax back.

**W-2** — A tax form prepared by the employer stating how much taxable income they paid you last year, as well as untaxed benefits you or your parents received from them. Information on this form is used on both the 1040 and the FAFSA.

**1099** — A form similar to the W-2 that shows income you received from anyone other than an employer. For example, if one of your parents is an independent contractor, he or she may receive a 1099-MISC showing the nonemployee compensation a client paid them.

**1098** — A tax form showing payments for which you can take a deduction or credit. For example, if you take out a student loan, once you begin repaying it you will receive a 1098-E from your lender every year showing how much interest you paid on the loan.

**Figure 6:**
FAFSA on the Web

# Let's Walk Through It

The FAFSA has five sections that ask questions, each with a common theme.
The exact order or wording of these questions may change from year to year, but
the substance remains more or less the same. And the purpose never changes:
to provide information about yourself and your family that colleges will use to
figure out how much federal student aid you qualify for.

There are a few general tips to keep in mind while filling out the FAFSA:

- The word "you" always means you, the student.

- The word "college" means a college, university, community college or any
  other school beyond high school.

- The phrase "net worth" means the current value of an asset (such as a
  business) minus the amount of debt owed on it.

- Questions about income are for the previous year; questions about assets
  ask for their value as of the day you fill out the form.

- When entering dollar figures, round to the nearest dollar and don't use
  commas or decimal points.

- If you have special financial circumstances that you need to explain, you
  can't do it on the FAFSA. Instead, write to your colleges directly. (*See Step
  8 of this book, "Make Your Special Circumstances Known."*)

Here is a step-by-step walk–through of the key questions on the FAFSA. Since
the online form is interactive, it will automatically skip over some questions or
sections depending on how you answer. For example, if you say that you're not
married, you won't be asked questions about your spouse. For that reason, you
might not see all the questions described here.

# Step One: Questions About Yourself

These questions (labeled "Student Demographics") gather basic information used to identify you and determine which federal and state programs you may qualify for. For example, the question about your citizenship is there because only U.S. citizens (or eligible noncitizens) can get federal student aid.

Here's the main information this section will ask for:

**Your name.** Enter your name exactly as it appears on your Social Security card. If the two don't match, you will be asked a few days later to fix it, slowing down the whole process.

**Your Social Security number (SSN).** As noted in Step 4 of this book, you need to have an SSN to apply for federal aid (you can't even open the online FAFSA without one). If you make an error entering this number on the login page, you can't change it and you have to start over. More delay.

**Whether you're male or female.** This question is only used to determine if you need to register with the Selective Service System. If you are male between the ages of 18 and 25, you must be registered with the Selective Service (the draft) in order to be eligible for federal aid. This requirement applies to any person assigned the sex of male at birth. If you're not registered, you can do it now on the FAFSA.

**Where you live.** Use a permanent home mailing address here, not a school or office address.

**The state in which you legally reside.** You will be asked this question if you have lived in your state for less than five years. Your answer will determine whether you're eligible for scholarships and grants from your state. In some cases, your state of legal residence might be different from the state where you're actually living at the time you fill out the FAFSA. This might be the case if you've recently moved or one of your parents is in the military.

You don't need to request that your information be sent to a state agency; the government will automatically send your processed information to the agency of your state government that administers financial aid programs for state

residents, whether scholarships, grants or loans. Do be aware, however, that some states require an additional financial aid form, as discussed in Step 7 of this book.

**Your permanent telephone number.** Use a permanent home or cell phone number, not a school or office number.

**Your e-mail address.** This is optional, but if you provide it, the government can send your Student Aid Report (SAR) by e-mail instead of snail mail, so it will reach you faster. Supply an e-mail address you check regularly.

**Your marital status as of today.** That means the day you submit your FAFSA. If your marital status changes later, you cannot update it on your FAFSA. In that instance, contact the financial aid office at the colleges you want to attend.

**Whether you are a citizen or an eligible noncitizen.** You are a citizen if you were born in this country or became a citizen through the naturalization process. An eligible noncitizen is someone such as a U.S. permanent resident holding a green card (Permanent Resident Card), or someone who has refugee status who is allowed to live permanently in the United States. It is not someone visiting on a student visa. If you're an eligible noncitizen, you'll have to fill in your Alien Registration Number. If you're neither a citizen nor an eligible noncitizen, you can't get federal aid, but you may be eligible for state or college aid — so you should still fill out the FAFSA, unless you don't have a Social Security number. In that case, call your colleges.

**Whether you've ever been convicted of possessing or selling illegal drugs.** Say "yes" only if the offense occurred while you were receiving federal student aid (unlikely if this is your first FAFSA, in which case you won't even see this question online), it's still on your record, and you were tried as an adult.

**Your high school completion status next year.** Before you can get federal financial aid, you must have completed high school or its equivalent. Select "High school diploma" if you will graduate from a public or private high school this year; "General Educational Development (GED) if you have the GED diploma or expect to pass the GED exam; or "Home schooled" if you will satisfy your state's requirements for successfully completing home schooling at the high school level. If you must select "None of the above," contact the financial aid office at the colleges you want to attend.

**Name, city and state of your high school:** This info will enable your high school to be notified of the status of your application. You don't have to enter the exact full name of your school (in fact you can even leave it blank). When you hit "confirm" you'll get a list of schools in your area, and then you can select the right one.

**What year of college you'll be in next year.** Your answer determines the aid programs for which you qualify.

**What degree will you be working on in the next school year.** Some aid programs are not available for graduate study, a second bachelor's degree or nondegree study. If you are undecided about what type of degree you will be pursuing (for example, if you're applying to both two-year and four-year colleges), check "undecided," but be sure to follow up with each college you're applying to after you've submitted the FAFSA.

**The highest level of education completed by your father and mother.** This won't affect your federal aid, but some states use this information to award scholarships to students who are the first in their family to attend college.

**Whether you're interested in work-study:** The best answer is "yes." Preserve your options. You're not committing to anything, and your answer won't affect the amount of grant money you might get.

## Step Two: School Selection

This is where you indicate which colleges should receive your FAFSA information. You list the colleges, and the government will send the processed information to them for free.

You can list up to 10 colleges online; but if you are using the paper FAFSA, you can only list four. In either case you can add additional schools later, when you get your Student Aid Report (SAR).

**Identify each college by its name or federal school code.** You can find the federal school code in Part III of this book (see Figure 7 below). You can also search for it on the FAFSA Web page. The online FAFSA form also has a good search tool for finding a college by city and state.

**Housing Plans.** For each college, you have to say whether you plan to live on campus, off campus or with your parents. Your answer will affect the housing costs that the school will estimate for you, and therefore your financial need. If you haven't made a decision yet, assume you'll live on campus.

**Figure 7:**

Finding a College's Federal Code

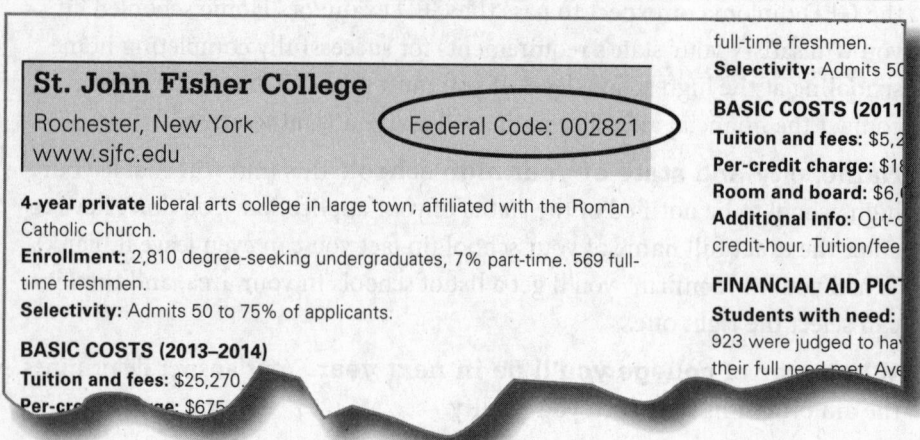

*The Federal Code for each college in Part III of this book can be found in its college description.*

## Step Three: Are You Independent?

The questions in this step determine whether or not you're an independent student. To be considered independent for the purpose of federal student aid eligibility, it doesn't matter if you feel independent, have a job or even live on your own. It also has nothing to do with whether your parents claim you as a dependent on their tax return. But if you can truthfully answer "yes" to at least one of the questions in this step, you will be considered independent.

The things that would classify you as independent are:

• You turn age 24 or older in the year you start college.

- You'll be enrolled in a graduate degree program in the year for which you're seeking aid.

- You're married.

- You have children who get more than half of their support from you.

- You have dependents other than your children or spouse who live with you and get more than half their support from you.

- You're an orphan, or you've been a ward/dependent of the court.

- You're currently serving in, or are a veteran of, the active-duty U.S. armed forces. (If you served only as a reservist and were never activated for reasons other than training, answer "no.")

- You are a homeless, unaccompanied youth (or at risk of being such).

If you are independent, then you can skip the section about your parents' income and assets. But there are certain cases where a college financial aid office will want to know about your parents' finances even if you are an independent. If you do meet one of the criteria on the list above, it's a good idea to ask the colleges to which you're applying whether they'll consider you fully independent for the purpose of awarding their own institutional funds. If one or more of them won't, you should fill out the parent section. The online application will ask you whether you want to fill it out or skip it.

**Are you unable to obtain information about your parents?** Even if it is determined that you are a dependent, you might be able to show special circumstances that will allow you to submit your FAFSA without parental information. Follow the instructions on the FAFSA carefully, and then follow up immediately with the financial aid office at each college you want to attend.

## Step Four: Questions About Your Parents

If you're a dependent student, you have to answer these questions (labeled "Parent Demographics") even if you don't live with your parents. When you're ready to submit the application, you will also need one of your parents to sign it, either on the paper form or by using a PIN on the electronic version.

Modern family life can make the definition of "parent" complicated. But the FAFSA definitions are fairly clear:

- If both your parents are living and married to each other, answer the questions about both of them.

- If only one of your parents is living, answer the questions about him or her.

- If your widowed parent remarried, answer the questions about your stepparent too.

- If you were raised by a single parent, answer the questions about him or her.

- If your parents are divorced or separated, answer the questions about the parent you lived with the most during the past 12 months.

- If that parent remarried, answer the questions about your stepparent, too.

- Don't provide information about grandparents, legal guardians or foster parents. FAFSA doesn't consider them your parents unless they have legally adopted you.

Here's a run-down of the important questions:

**Marital status:** Indicate the status as it is at the time you submit the form.

**Their Social Security numbers:** Unlike you, your parents are not required to have Social Security numbers in order for you to file the FAFSA (but in that case you have to enter zeroes). But if they do have Social Security numbers, they must provide them.

**Their names:** Again, if they have social security cards, their names must exactly match.

**The number of people in your parents' household:** These include you and your parents. The number who will be in college during the next year is also asked for: that also includes you (but not your parents). These questions affect how much money your parents will be expected to contribute to your education.

## Step Five: Your Parents' Financial Information

OK, this is usually the most complicated part of the FAFSA. But this section has been greatly simplified. For the most part, it asks for the same information that your parents must provide on their federal income tax form, and even points out exactly where they can find that information. The main questions are:

**If either of your parents is a "dislocated worker."** Answer "yes" if one (or both) of your parents has been laid off or has lost their business and is still unemployed. "Dislocated worker" also includes a stay-at-home mom or dad who no longer receives support from a spouse and can't find a job. If you answer "yes" to this question, you should also contact the financial aid office at each college you are applying to. *(See Step 8, "Make Your Special Circumstances Known.")*

**Whether anyone in the household received certain federal benefits.** A "yes" answer to any of the listed programs, such as free or reduced-price lunch or supplemental nutrition assistance (food stamps), will likely result in a determination that your family should not be expected to contribute any money toward your education.

**Whether they're eligible to file the 1040A or 1040EZ tax form.** It's to your advantage if they can answer yes, they're eligible to file this form. If they would normally file the 1040A but filed the full 1040 only to take advantage of an education tax benefit relating to a child already in college, they can still check this box.

---

**EXPERT ADVICE**

"**Some people overthink the FAFSA** questions. They'll get to what we would see as straightforward questions: 'How many are in your household?' And then 'How many in your household go to college?' Well, some families will list every person who's ever lived in the household and then every member who has ever attended college. And actually **what we want to know** is, how many are living in your household now, and how many of them are in college now."

— *Elizabeth Bickford, director, Office of Student Financial Aid and Scholarships, University of Oregon, Eugene*

### GOOD TO KNOW

The FAFSA asks both you and your parents to report the amount of income tax that was paid for the year before last. **The amount they want here is only the federal income tax amount** — don't include Social Security, Medicare, or any of the taxes that are reported in the "other taxes" section of Form 1040. If you or one of your parents was self-employed or had to self-report tip income from a restaurant job, you should keep that in mind.

**Their income tax information:** The IRS Data Retrieval Process is the preferred means of completing the FAFSA (see description that follows). Check with your college(s) to determine how best to update your FAFSA information if no tax returns have been filed.

**What their untaxed income and benefits were.** These include items like earned income credits, welfare benefits, Social Security benefits, child support and other money that didn't get taxed. It also includes any contributions your parents made for the previous tax year to deductible Individual Retirement Accounts (IRAs) or employer-sponsored retirement plans such as 401(k)s or 403(b)s. Add this up on worksheets and fill in the totals on the FAFSA. If you're filling out the worksheets online, the information will appear on the confirmation page you'll see after submitting, which you should print out and keep on file in case a financial aid administrator asks about them later.

**What their assets are.** These include cash, savings and the value of investments, such as stocks and bonds. The amounts to put down are "as of" the day you fill out the FAFSA. Often that is just a best guess, using the most recent bank statements. (Keep in mind that the amount of aid you are entitled to is based much more on family income than on assets.) They do *not* include the home where your parents primarily live (a summer cottage would be included), a family-owned business of less than 100 employees, or a family farm that they live on and operate. However, if your parents own more than one home — a summer cottage, for example, or an investment property — they also should report their equity in that home on the "investments" line. If they own a farm that they don't live on, they also should report the value of that farm as a business. Another thing your parents do not need to include here is any money they have in tax-advantaged retirement accounts, such as IRAs, 401(k)s, 403(b)s and the like.

# The IRS Data Retrieval Tool

The IRS Data Retrieval Tool allows students and parents to access the IRS tax return information needed to complete the FAFSA, and transfer the data directly into their FAFSA from the IRS website.

You can use the IRS retrieval tool to transfer your tax return information if:

- You have filed your tax returns
- You have not filed an amended tax return
- Your marital status has not changed since you filed your tax returns
- You are not filing your tax returns as married, filing separately
- You did not file a Puerto Rican or foreign tax return

You might not be able to use the IRS retrieval tool to transfer your tax return information if you **very recently** filed your tax return.

- If you filed your taxes electronically, allow three weeks for the tool to be available.
- If you filed your taxes by mail, allow eight weeks for the tool to be available.

**The IRS Retrieval Tool is the preferred means of completing your FAFSA.** If you cannot use this process at the time you initially complete your FAFSA, check with your college(s) to determine how best to update your FAFSA information once your tax returns have been filed.

Follow the online instructions to have the IRS data fill in your income data. **Do not change any data once it is transferred to your FAFSA.** Changing any piece of tax data may require follow-up and verification by your college's financial aid office.

# Step Six: Your Own Financial Information

These questions ask about *your* income and assets — whether or not you are independent. Income is how much money you made last year; assets are what you own and the savings you have. If you are married, they also want to know about your spouse's income and assets.

These are the main things that this section asks for:

**Whether you've completed a tax return for the past year.** This means the return that you filed a year ago. If you have, they will ask what form you used, for example, the 1040 or 1040A. If you didn't file any tax return, they will still ask how much you (and, if you have one, your spouse) earned from working.

**Whether you're eligible to file the 1040A or 1040EZ tax form.** The instructions on the FAFSA explain who can file these forms. Most students can. If you can, say yes.

**GOOD TO KNOW**

Most students are eligible to file IRS Form 1040EZ or 1040A as their tax return. Some parents can, too. (The rules determining whether you can are explained in the FAFSA instructions.) **If both you and your parents are eligible to file the 1040A or 1040EZ**, it may turn out that only your income (not your assets) will be assessed when calculating your expected family contribution.

**What income and tax information you and your spouse reported on your tax returns.** Again, these questions are easy to answer if you've already completed your tax return, and if the IRS Data Retrieval tool is available to you. If not, check with your colleges to determine how best to update your FAFSA information.

**The number of people in your household:** This question refers to the number of people in *your* household, if you have one — not your parents'.

**What your untaxed income and benefits were.** Once again, these include items like earned income credits, welfare benefits, Social Security benefits, child support and other money that came to you without being taxed. You will be asked about these in a series of questions on screen. (If you are filling out the paper FAFSA, you should use the worksheets that come with the form to add them all up, then fill in the totals on your FAFSA. Don't submit the worksheets, but keep copies of them on file. A financial aid office may want those details later.)

**What your assets are.** This question is meant to provide a snapshot of your assets, the money or property you currently own. Using current banking statements and investment records, say how much cash and savings you have, as well the total value of any stocks, other investments or investment properties that you might own. If you're still in high school, chances are that you only have a small savings or checking account, which you should report on the line asking for "cash, savings accounts and checking accounts." You may also have some government savings bonds, certificates of deposit (CDs) or a few shares of stock; those should be reported on the line asking about "investments."

Don't include any college savings accounts in this step unless you are independent (you answered "yes" to any question in FAFSA Step Three) and they are owned by you in your own name.

## Step Seven: Review Your Answers, Then Sign and Submit

This is easy, but it's still an important step. Take the time to carefully review all your answers for accuracy and spelling — even your name. Be sure to print out your FAFSA if you're filling it out online.

**Preparer's information.** If you or your family paid a fee to someone to fill out your FAFSA, or to advise you on how to fill it out, that person must provide his or her Social Security number or Employment Identification Number (EIN), and must also sign and date the form. This requirement does not apply to school counselors, financial aid administrators, friends or mentors who helped but did not charge a fee.

Pay heed to this warning from the FAFSA website: "Be wary of organizations that charge a fee to submit your application, or to find you money for school. Some are legitimate and some are scams. Generally, **any help that you pay for can be received free** from your school or Federal Student Aid."

**Terms to read before signing.** You'll see a list of terms you must agree to by signing. There is nothing onerous here, but there is a scary-sounding penalty for giving "false or misleading information." This does *not* mean honest mistakes or estimates that turn out to be way off; they're talking about intentional fraud.

If your parents provided financial information, one of them also needs to sign. Use your PINs to sign electronically — don't use the "print signature page and mail" option. It just wastes time.

Be sure to keep clicking on "next" until you get to the confirmation page! Your FAFSA is not truly submitted until then.

## FAFSA Step Eight: Confirmation

You're done! Be sure to print the confirmation page, and save it to your hard drive as well. If you don't have a printer, write down the confirmation number, date and time. This is your proof that your FAFSA was received.

If you file using the paper form, make a photocopy of it before mailing it, and keep that photocopy together with the worksheets you filled out and all the records you used.

# Check Your Student Aid Report!

After you submit your FAFSA, you'll receive your Student Aid Report, or SAR. How long it will take for you to receive it, and in what form, will depend on how you filed the FAFSA. If you filed FAFSA on the Web and signed it with your PIN, you should recieve it immediately, or at most within one to three days. If you filed a paper FAFSA and did not provide an e-mail address, you'll receive a paper SAR within about four weeks.

In whatever form the SAR reaches you, check it over carefully. It will include a summary detailing the information you supplied on the FAFSA. Make sure this information is correct. If not, then you must make corrections. It's easy to do — just go back to www.fafsa.ed.gov, log in and click on "Make FAFSA Corrections." You can also add or remove colleges this way.

Make corrections only if the data on the SAR doesn't accurately represent your family's financial situation at the time the FAFSA was originally filed. For example, if you mistyped a number, or if the federal data-entry clerk misread your handwriting, correct that. But **don't make changes that reflect changes to your income or assets since you filed the FAFSA.** If important changes of that sort have happened — such as a lost job — inform your colleges individually rather than through the FAFSA. (*See Step 8, "Make Your Special Circumstances Known."*)

**KEEP IN MIND**

**You have to leave time for your FAFSA to be processed.** If you're filing on paper, allow at least four weeks before your earliest college or state deadline. If you're filing online, leave at least one week before the earliest deadline.

**KEEP IN MIND**

Eligibility for **federal student aid does not automatically continue** from one year to the next. You have to reapply every year that you're in college. Do that by filling out a **Renewal FAFSA**. This is a partially preformatted version of the FAFSA that you can use so long as you applied for federal aid the previous year.

At the top of the SAR, you should also see an estimate of your EFC: the amount of money your family is expected to contribute toward college costs. You might not see an EFC if there is incorrect or missing information that made it impossible to process your data. If that happens to you, submit the necessary corrections and you'll get your EFC estimate. **The actual EFC calculated by a given college may be different than what you'll see here**, especially if that college uses a different formula, or if its financial aid office has adjusted your EFC based on special circumstances that you brought to the college's attention.

The colleges you requested to receive your FAFSA information will automatically get your SAR. At the corrections stage, you'll have an opportunity to add more colleges to receive your FAFSA information. You can also give a school permission to add itself to the list. Just provide the college with the Data Release Number (DRN) that will be provided on your SAR. The school will use your DRN to access your application record.

The SAR gives you an estimate of how much money your family is expected to pay for college, but not how much financial aid you'll receive. You'll find that out when your individual colleges send you their award letters. Even so, by filing your FAFSA, you've taken a big step toward getting those letters.

If the expected family contribution (EFC) indicated on the SAR looks too high for your family to afford, you should talk to your parents and discuss other financing options with them. (*See Step 11, "Consider Your Out-of-Pocket Options."*) It could also mean that you need to explain some special financial circumstances to the colleges to which you've applied (see Step 8).

**QUICK RECAP**

The FAFSA is easier than it looks. Most of it is about your income and assets, and that of your parents. Remember:

- File on time. Submit your FAFSA as soon as possible, especially if your colleges have early financial aid deadlines or priority dates.
- Use the IRS data retrieval tool to transfer your tax return information.
- Read instructions.
- Be accurate.
- Reapply every year.

# Step 6: Fill Out the PROFILE (If Required)

Whether you have to fill out the CSS/Financial Aid PROFILE depends on the colleges to which you're applying. If you do, you'll find it mainly asks for "more of the same" — information about your family's income, expenses and assets — rather than something completely new. The online form is customized to your situation, so you won't be presented with too many questions that don't apply to you. However, the application does take time to fill out, so leave yourself plenty of time to submit it before your colleges' deadlines.

## General Advice

Step 6 is to fill out the CSS/Financial Aid PROFILE® — but only if you need to. If the schools to which you're applying don't require this financial aid form, you don't have to complete it. Find out if they require it by checking Part III of this book or the colleges' websites.

The PROFILE is administered by the College Board, a not-for-profit association of schools and colleges (and the publisher of this book). It is available online only: You can't file on paper. The upside of this is that PROFILE is available 24 hours a day, seven days a week. Furthermore, its system of online edits alerts you to missing or incorrect information before you submit the application, eliminating a potential source of delays. Firewall protection and data encryption protect the information you submit about your family and their finances. The downside is that if you don't have a computer with Internet access at home, you will have to use one at your school, a library or a parent's workplace.

The PROFILE doesn't replace the FAFSA: You still need to complete that, too, because that's the form required for federal student aid, which any college will expect you to seek before they give away their own institutional funds. The schools that require the PROFILE do so because they believe it gives a more complete account of your financial situation to guide them in awarding their own funds. The College Board provides the colleges with your PROFILE information, and the colleges use it to calculate your expected family contribution and your need.

Since it's designed to give a more complete picture of your finances, it is not surprising that the PROFILE is longer than the FAFSA. It's the same general concept, but you'll need to gather more records to answer all the questions, and it will take more time to fill out.

## Create Your Account and File Early

Because the PROFILE form is more involved, and because colleges may ask for additional information even after the form is filed, it's important to begin the process well before your colleges' deadlines and leave yourself lots of time to fill out the application. The College Board usually processes your PROFILE information overnight, but it can take longer when application submissions peak closer to school deadlines. Also, don't assume it can all be completed in one session; you may need to return to the form if a college asks for supplemental information. Fortunately, you can go back and forth to your application online, rather than having to finish it in one sitting.

It's best to submit the PROFILE at least one week before your earliest financial aid priority date. Remember, colleges use PROFILE information to determine who gets their limited grant dollars. If you file late, you will have to make do with whatever funds, if any, are left over.

## Preparing for the PROFILE

Get ready for the PROFILE by collecting important financial documents like tax forms, business and farm statements, and information about other income and assets. Having a PDF copy of your family's tax forms will help speed things along. You can also download and print out the *PROFILE Student Guide and Application Instructions* from the PROFILE site.

The FAFSA and the PROFILE will both ask you to provide family income information from two years prior to the year you plan to enter college. However, you'll need to gather more records to fill out the PROFILE than you will for the FAFSA.

For example, expect to answer a few questions about your parents' income for the most recent year or the year just before you enter college and about the anticipated year to come. There are also questions about your projected summer and school-year earnings during your first year in college. The purpose of this is to give financial aid officers a better idea of your family's financial circumstances over time.

**EXPERT ADVICE**

Most schools that require the PROFILE use it when they're investing a lot of their own institutional dollars into need-based programs. We use it because **the PROFILE gives us an added, more in-depth look** at a family's financial strength. Our ultimate goal is to give the right dollars to the right students at the right time, and this PROFILE application helps us do that."

— *Vincent Amoroso, former director, Office of Student Financial Services, Johns Hopkins University*

**GOOD TO KNOW**

**Help is available** to get you through the PROFILE application. If you're not sure about how to answer any question, **check the online Help Desk** that's built into the online application. If you can't find an answer to your question there, contact the PROFILE help line, either by e-mail (**help@cssprofile.org**) or by phone (**305-829-9793**).

You can also contact the financial aid office at the college to which you're applying. In addition, your high school counselor may be able to answer your questions.

## Documents You'll Need Before You Fill Out Your PROFILE

It's a good idea to gather the necessary records before you start and have them handy as you work on the PROFILE. You'll need records for both yourself and your parents.

✔ Federal income tax return from 2 years prior to the year you start college

✔ Federal income tax return for the year before you start college, if completed, or pay stubs and other income-related records

✔ W-2 forms and other records of money earned for those two years

✔ Records of untaxed income for those two years

✔ Current bank statements and mortgage information

✔ Records of stocks, bonds, trusts and other investments

Because the FAFSA and the PROFILE use the same tax year information to answer a majority of their questions, it may be helpful to complete the PROFILE soon after you complete the FAFSA while the information is still top of mind. The financial aid deadline dates provided by your colleges are important considerations when making this decision.

# Starting the PROFILE Application

Just like registering ahead of time for a FSA ID, **it's best to begin the PROFILE well before the first college's deadline.** You can gain access to the PROFILE application through your College Board account. Creating the username and password for the account is free; you may have done this already if you previously accessed bigfuture.org to search for colleges or register for the SAT. If you don't have Internet access at home, ask your school counselor or librarian if you can use one of the school's computers.

It's important to start collecting documents for the PROFILE as soon as you're sure about where you'll be applying for aid, but in any case at least one week before the earliest financial aid filing date you need to meet. Accounts can be created at any time and the PROFILE application can be started beginning Oct. 1 of the year before you intend to start college. Once you begin, you can either complete your application then and there or return to it at a later time. Your PROFILE application will be customized to your circumstances based on the information you give as you complete the application.

Most families will have to pay a fee of $25 to have their PROFILE sent to one college, plus $16 for each additional college. The fee can be paid with most major credit cards or bank debit cards. Low-income families applying for the first time may qualify for a fee waiver (see sidebar).

## Let's Walk Through It

Your PROFILE application may contain up to 16 sections; depending on your family's situation, a number of sub-sections may or may not be included. The application includes questions about you and your finances and questions about your parents and their finances. There is a place for you to explain in your own words any special financial circumstances and a place for any supplemental questions that may be required by one or more of the schools to which you're applying. In addition, if your parents are divorced or separated, your noncustodial parent might need to complete an online Noncustodial PROFILE (be mindful of your college deadlines and allow sufficient time for this.)

To help you fill out the PROFILE, there are instructions online that you can follow, along with other avenues for help. A few general points to keep in mind:

- If a financial question (such as one about income or assets) doesn't apply to you, enter a zero (0).

- If a nonfinancial question (such as a year or a name) doesn't apply to you, leave it blank. If the field is required, just enter N/A.

**GOOD TO KNOW**

If you come from a low-income family, and you are applying for financial aid for the first time, **you may be eligible for a fee waiver** covering registration costs and up to eight school reports. Information that you provide on the PROFILE form determines if you are eligible. **You will automatically get the fee waiver if you qualify —** you don't have to apply for it separately.

- Round all money amounts to the nearest dollar. Don't enter commas or cents.

When you fill out the application, don't be surprised if you don't see all the questions or sections that are mentioned here. The PROFILE is customized to your situation. That means that when you complete the form, any sections that are known not to apply to you won't even be presented and individual questions that aren't relevant will be greyed out. For example, if your parents are married, you won't be shown any questions that assume you have a noncustodial parent.

## Your Basic Information

The PROFILE begins by asking for some basic information about you, such as your date of birth, where you live, whether you are a U.S. citizen, a veteran, married, etc. These questions usually won't involve looking up documents; just answer them straightforwardly. Some of them (such as the questions about date of birth and being a veteran) are intended to clarify whether you're a dependent or an independent student.

## College Information

This section focuses on where you are in school now, and lets you select which colleges should receive your PROFILE application. When selecting the colleges or scholarship programs where you would like to have your PROFILE report sent, you will also answer if you are a new college student and where you expect to live for each school. You can add more colleges or programs to this list after you register, or even after filing your application.

**Figure 8:**
Finding a College's CSS code

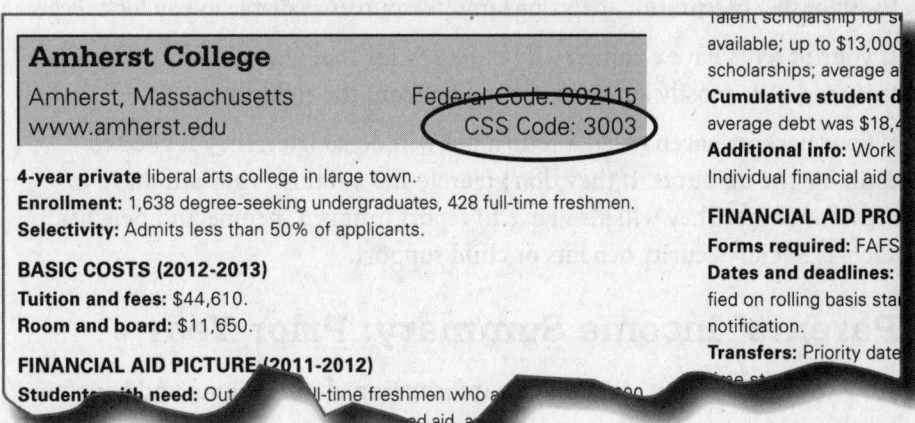

*CSS Code for each college in Part III of this book can be found in its college description.*

# Your Parents' Information

This section asks for some basic information from your parents. The term "parents" as PROFILE understands it might need some defining. It basically means your custodial parents, the people with whom you live. If both your parents are living, married to each other and have custody of you, answer the questions about both of them. But if that isn't the case, follow these rules:

- If your birth or adoptive parents are divorced, separated or were never married, then you only need to provide information about the parent with whom you live. If you lived with both equally in the past 12 months, answer the questions about the parent who provided most of your financial support.

- If you have a widowed or single parent or a legal guardian, answer the questions only about that person.

- If your parent (as defined above) has married or remarried, include information about your stepparent too.

Your parents should use this section to provide information about themselves, including name, date of birth, employment status, and whether they themselves are in college or graduate school. Some of these questions have to do with clarifying financial strength — for example, the question about what kind of retirement plans your parents have. Some are just matters of housekeeping, such as their preferred daytime telephone number in case they need to be contacted.

# Parents' Income and Benefits for the "Prior-Prior" Year

In this section, your parents report their income and benefits from two years before the year you intend to start college. That should be the same tax information you used to complete your FAFSA. Information in this section is used to establish a baseline for analyzing family resources available to pay for college.

If your parents have a completed tax return for that year on hand, filling in this section is mostly a matter of copying from the right lines.

If your parents haven't filed a return but will do so later, they'll need to estimate the amounts. If they don't plan to file a return, they still have to report income. They will also have to report untaxed income and benefits, such as Social Security benefits or child support.

# Parents' Income Summary: Prior Year

Here your parents are asked to give information about income and benefits for the year before the year you intend to start college. This is part of a three year set of data that is meant to give the PROFILE colleges a long-term view of your family's finances. This section asks for that year's earnings from work, other taxable income, and untaxed income. Worksheets are provided to assist you calculate any untaxed income and benefits.

# Parents' Income Summary: Anticipated Income

Here your parents have to estimate how much they expect to receive in income and benefits during the year in which you start college. Again, the idea is to establish as clear a picture as possible about your family's finances in the long term, and to show whether the years before you started college was typical or not. Your parents will have to estimate work income, other taxable income, and untaxed income and benefits. In this section they will also be able to, explain any unusual increases or decreases in income and benefits (10 percent or more) from last year.

# Parent Income not Reported on Taxes

Some forms of income don't show up on tax forms. This section asks if there are other sources of income that your family is receiving.

# Parent Address Information

In this section your parents are asked for some additional information about your family's residence(s) and housing.

# Parents' Assets

This section asks about your parents' assets because these are resources that can help them finance college. There are questions about cash and savings and checking accounts (with their value as of the day you fill out the form). If they own their home, there are questions to determine home equity, the difference between the current market value of their home and the outstanding mortgage debt.

There are also questions about the current market value of any other assets they own, including investments and other real estate. They also need to include educational savings accounts, such as 529 prepaid tuition or college savings plans or Coverdell savings accounts that they've opened for you or your siblings.

# Business Assets and Farm Assets

These sections will only appear if your parents indicated ownership in a business or farm. There will be questions about value, debt, number of employees, tax form filed and if you live on the farm.

# Parents' Expenses

This section asks about certain special expenses your parents might have. These are not just any expenses, such as grocery bills or vacation airfare, but specific costs that might legitimately affect their ability to pay for college. Included here are child support payments, certain educational costs, and medical and dental expenses not covered by insurance.

# Information About a Noncustodial Parent

If your parents are divorced or separated, this section asks for information about the parent who doesn't have custody of you. But it should be filled out by your custodial parent. If for any reason you can't get sufficient information about the noncustodial parent, there is an opportunity to explain why. Many colleges want this information because they believe it is the responsibility of both your biological or adoptive parents to pay for your college costs, even if they no longer live together, and even if the parent who does have custody of you has remarried. That's why, after you've filled out this section and submitted your PROFILE, they may request that your noncustodial parent fill out a supplemental form, the Noncustodial PROFILE. The section you're filling out here is not that supplemental form; your noncustodial parent will fill out that form if it's required.

# Your Own Income and Benefits

This section asks about your own income and benefits, if any, from two years before the year you intend to start college.

If you have a completed tax return for that year, this section is mostly a matter of copying the amounts from the correct lines, such as the adjusted gross income and income tax paid. If you didn't file a return but you did make some money that year, you'll have to report it. Untaxed income also goes in this section. A worksheet is available for you to tally it up.

# Your Expected Summer/School-Year Resources for the Coming School Year

Here you're asked to state your expected resources for this coming summer and this coming school year. You're also asked about scholarships you expect to get from sources other than the colleges to which you're applying and how much money your parents think they'll be able to pay for your college expenses.

This may seem like a strange series of questions, especially if you don't know yet where you'll be going to college next year, or where (even if) you'll be working. But colleges that use the PROFILE want to have as clear a picture as possible of your future resources, not just your past ones. For example, if you currently have an after-school job but will leave that job when you graduate, the financial aid offices need to know that the income from that job won't be available to you anymore once you've started college.

Do the best you can to estimate these figures. If you're not sure how to answer in your particular case, check the PROFILE help online or contact the financial aid office at the college to which you're applying.

## Your Own Assets

This section asks about your assets — the money or property you, the student, currently own. These too affect your ability to pay for college. You need to list any cash you have and any checking or savings accounts in your name. Give their value as of the day you're filling out the application. You should also include any investments, such as certificates of deposit, savings bonds, stocks or real estate that you own. If you have any Individual Retirement Accounts (IRAs) or other tax-advantaged retirement accounts, you should also list them here.

If you're an independent student, then any money you have in 529 prepaid tuition or college savings plans or Coverdell savings accounts should be included here. If you're a dependent, those will be considered your parents' assets, and the information about them should go in the Parent Assets.

This section will also ask you to answer questions about any trust accounts your parents or other relatives may have established for you. A trust account is money that is held for you by somebody else until you reach a certain age, at which point it becomes yours. Colleges want to know about this because if you have a trust, that money will eventually reach your hands, lowering your ultimate financial need. If you have any trust accounts, list their value here and answer the questions about them. But don't include money in Section 529 plans; those aren't the same as trusts.

## Your Expenses for the Previous Year

You'll only see these questions if you're an independent student. If you are, you'll be asked about any child support you or your spouse paid to a former spouse and any medical and dental expenses you had last year that weren't covered by insurance. Most colleges will consider these expenses in determining your financial need.

## Household Summary

This section asks questions about other dependent members of your household. If you are a dependent student, you will be shown the Parents' Household version. If you are an independent student, you will be asked questions about your household in the Student's Household version, and if required by your school, your parents' household in the Parents' Household section.

The questions in this section ask for more information about these household members: their names, how they're related to you, their ages, and to what extent you or your parents are required to pay for their school or college education last year and next year. The reason for these questions is that if household members other than you are enrolled in college, and your family is paying heavily to fund those educations, the colleges may take this into account when they determine the expected family contribution (EFC) to your own education. If there are younger children in the family, the colleges will assume that a certain portion of the household's income and assets need to be saved for their college educations, which will also affect your EFC.

# Explanations/Special Circumstances

This section gives you a chance to explain anything unusual in your application or any special circumstances that affect your family's ability to pay for college. Categories are provided to give examples of when an additional explanation will be helpful to the colleges reviewing your application. You can mention, for example, reasons for unusually high medical or dental expenses, steep rises or falls in income from year to year, or loss of employment. You should also give information about any outside scholarships you've been awarded. This allows the PROFILE colleges to better understand your financial picture.

In addition to telling the colleges about anything you think it's important that they know about, you should also use this section to expand on your answers to certain questions in previous sections, if there wasn't an explanation box provided per the instructions that you'll find on the PROFILE website. For example, you can provide details about tuition benefits, gifts from relatives, etc.

You're limited to 2,000 characters (about 300 words) in this section. If you need more space, send the information directly to your colleges, including your name and Social Security number on all correspondence. (**See Step 8 for tips on how to let your college know about your special circumstances**.)

# Supplemental Information

You will only see this section if one or more of the colleges to which you're applying requires more information. In that case, you'll see additional questions here. Your answers to these questions will be used only by the colleges that ask for them. Some of the questions colleges ask here are used to determine your eligibility for purely need-based financial aid; others are used to determine if you're eligible for scholarships that have non-need-based criteria.

Here are some examples of the types of questions you might see:

- What is the year, make and model of the family's primary car?

- Do you or either of your parents receive free food or housing as a job benefit?

- What is your family's religious denomination? (This information will be used to determine scholarship eligibility.)

- In what field of study do you plan to major?

# After Submitting Your PROFILE

**GOOD TO KNOW**

**If only one of your birth parents has custody of you**, your college may still require information from both parents. If that happens, the main PROFILE application collects information from one parent, and the **Noncustodial PROFILE** collects information from the other. After the information is processed, the college will complete the EFC calculation. How to divide up payment of the EFC among you and your parents is a family decision.

After you complete your PROFILE, you'll receive an online PROFILE acknowledgment that confirms the colleges to which you're sending the information and gives you the opportunity to review any data you submitted. You should print the acknowledgment, which includes the list of colleges and the data you entered on the form. Once you submit your PROFILE, you can't revise your information online for the colleges you selected. Use the printed acknowledgment to make changes, if necessary, to the PROFILE information, and send those corrections directly to your colleges. It is best if the PROFILE is only sent to colleges only once, so try to have it as complete as possible when you submit. If you do need to make changes, you can re-enter the application to make updates. Some colleges may prefer to receive updates by paper, so check with your colleges for their preference.

The College Board analyzes your data and reports it to the colleges to which you're applying. The schools then apply their own institutional policies to figure out your expected family contribution (EFC). From this analysis, they determine how great your need is and how much institutional financial aid to give you.

## SENDING YOUR PROFILE TO ADDITIONAL COLLEGES

You can delete colleges from your list of schools only before you submit the application. After that, all the listed colleges will get your information. But you can add colleges whenever you want, even after you submit the application. Just go to the PROFILE website and click on "Add Colleges to Submitted Application." The fee is $16 for each additional college or program to which you want your information sent.

When you add additional colleges, you will also be given the opportunity to update or correct any of the information on your original application. Please note, however, that this new information will only be sent to the colleges you're adding. You should directly contact the colleges to which you submitted your original application to update your information with them.

## SUPPLEMENTAL PROFILE FORMS

Some colleges require supplemental information that's not on the PROFILE application. For example, a college may require a Noncustodial PROFILE if you don't live with both of your birth parents. When you register for the PROFILE and indicate that your biological or adoptive parents are not married, you will receive an e-mail with instructions, a temporary password and a link to an application that you should forward to your noncustodial parent to complete. This form can be completed only by the noncustodial parent.

Be aware that these follow-ups take additional time. All the more reason to leave yourself plenty of time to file the PROFILE before your college financial aid deadlines.

Since the PROFILE form is customized, the application may not necessarily be the same length as the FAFSA. In some cases the PROFILE will contain more questions than the FAFSA and in some cases it will contain fewer. The main difference is that it tries to get a more complete picture of your family's finances. A few points to keep in mind:

- File early.
- The PROFILE is online only, so you have to submit it on a computer.
- There are fees, but students from low-income families may qualify for a fee waiver.
- After you submit your PROFILE, you'll get an online acknowledgment confirming that you submitted it. You can make corrections, but you should check with your colleges first.
- Depending on your circumstances, you or one of your parents may have to submit supplemental information to one or more of your colleges.

**QUICK RECAP**

# Step 7: Fill Out Any Other Required Forms

**QUICK OVERVIEW**

The FAFSA and PROFILE are the big ones, but don't forget to file any other forms that may be required by your state or by the colleges to which you're applying. You don't want to have your application for financial aid marked "incomplete" because you didn't file a one-page form. These forms can vary widely from college to college, and from state to state.

## Some Colleges Have Their Own Financial Aid Application

Some colleges have their own forms that you have to submit in addition to the FAFSA and the PROFILE. A purpose of the form may be to get more information about your finances, or to find out if you're a member of a particular group that is eligible for a special scholarship or grant. If a college requires such a form from all first-time applicants, its description in Part III of the book will say "institutional form required" under the "application procedures" section. Contact the financial aid office at your colleges to find out more.

The good news is that these forms are generally not long or complicated — they are usually just a page or two in length. They manage to stay short because they are intended not to duplicate the FAFSA or PROFILE forms but to supplement them and help the financial aid office keep track of applications. Such a "one pager" might, for example, ask for basic identifying information, some demographic facts and whether you are interested in loans and work-study. This kind of form is typical at community colleges and most four-year public colleges. "It's almost like an update form," Mary San Agustin says of the institutional form currently in use at her institution, Palomar College. "It's basically just a supplemental form in case any changes occurred since the time the student applied for admission or completed the FAFSA."

Sometimes a college might require a longer form that asks questions about your finances that are about as broad and deep as the FAFSA or PROFILE. Usually this only happens with colleges that use their own formulas to calculate need, but choose not to use the PROFILE to help them with it.

Another reason a college might require its own financial aid form is if it requires every student to have a computer on campus. Such schools sometimes have a supplemental form that qualifies needy applicants for a stipend to buy a computer, or places them in a "loaner" program so they can borrow one. The University of Virginia has two forms that deal with computers. One form is for its "laptop loaner" program, and a different form is for a "one-time computer expense" that allows students who want to buy a laptop to add the purchase price to their cost of attendance; that way their aid package may cover the cost.

Still another kind of institutional form is one for early decision applicants. Such a form works as a sort of "pre-read" meant to help students get an early estimate of their expected family contribution and the financial aid package they will receive if they accept an early-decision offer. (The rules of early decision require them to accept the offer if the college offers enough financial aid for them to attend.) Some schools offer a similar pre-read form for student athletes who are being recruited by a coach.

## Scholarship and Grant Forms

Some colleges require a separate form for students applying for merit scholarships. This isn't always the case: At many schools, every student who applies for admission is automatically considered for merit scholarships. But at some schools, you must file a separate application for merit scholarships. The rules may even differ from department to department, depending on your major. For example, if you want to major in theater or music performance, you might have to audition. Contact the financial aid office at your colleges for more details, and check with the department in which you're interested in majoring.

Some institutional forms ask questions to find out if you qualify for financial aid funds set aside for students with particular characteristics. For example, the college might offer grants that are only available to children of alumni or descendants of the town's founding families. At most colleges, these grants are part of the need-based aid program, so you have to demonstrate need through the FAFSA along with proving you have the right qualifications for the grant.

## Verification of Your Tax Return

Some colleges require you to provide your family's federal or state tax returns for verification. **"Verification" doesn't mean that you did something wrong**. It's not like an IRS audit, where only suspicious tax returns are selected for special scrutiny. Since colleges disburse federal money — in the form of grants, work-study and loans — they are required by law to check the information that a certain percentage of financial aid applicants have submitted.

Not all colleges ask for this information the same way. Some will require you to use the IRS Data Retrieval process; some might require official tax transcripts; others might just want photocopies of the returns. Check directly with the college to verify how you should submit the returns, and if they also require any attached schedules or the W-2s or 1099s you received from employers and banks. Usually you'll also have to fill out a form that allows colleges to confirm details, like how many of your siblings are enrolled in college. The college may ask you to send your documents directly to the financial aid office, or it might ask you to send them to the College Board's Institutional Documentation (IDOC) service.

Some colleges will request verification if the data you submitted on the FAFSA looks unusual. As an extreme example, people who reported that they had no income may be asked how they supported themselves.

# State Forms

Most states rely on the FAFSA to award their need-based grants and loans to students. But a few states have their own financial aid forms. For example, New York State has an application for its Tuition Assistance Program (TAP) that is sent to eligible students who submit a FAFSA.

Even though the thought of filling out yet another form may seem burdensome, and you feel sure that you won't qualify for the state aid program, fill it out. If you don't, your application might be marked "incomplete" at your colleges. These state forms are usually short and don't take long to fill out, especially once you do the prep work of filling out the FAFSA. **When you file the FAFSA online, you'll be automatically directed to your state's form.** (If you file the FAFSA paper form, you'll usually have to send away for a paper copy of your state form.)

**Table 2:**
State Aid Deadlines

| STATE | FORM(S) REQUIRED | DEADLINE | NOTES |
|---|---|---|---|
| Alaska | FAFSA | 6/30<br>1/1 | Performance Scholarship<br>Priority date for Alaska Education Grant |
| Arkansas | FAFSA | 6/1 | Higher Education Opportunity Grant<br>Academic Challenge awards |
| California | FAFSA, state form | 3/2<br>9/2 | Initial awards<br>Additional community college awards |
| Connecticut | FAFSA, state form | 2/15 | Priority date |
| Delaware | FAFSA | 4/15 | |
| District of Columbia | FAFSA, DC form | 5/1<br>6/30 | FAFSA<br>DC form |
| Florida | FAFSA | 5/15 | |
| Idaho | FAFSA, state form | 3/1 | |
| Illinois | FAFSA | 1/1 | Priority date |
| Indiana | FAFSA | 3/10 | |
| Iowa | FAFSA | 7/1 | |
| Kansas | FAFSA, state form | 4/1 | Priority date |
| Kentucky | FAFSA | 1/1 | Priority date |
| Louisiana | FAFSA | 7/1 | |
| Maine | FAFSA | 5/1 | |
| Maryland | FAFSA | 3/1 | |
| Massachusetts | FAFSA | 5/1 | Priority date |
| Michigan | FAFSA | 3/1 | |
| Minnesota | FAFSA | 30 days after start of term | |
| Missouri | FAFSA | 4/1 | |
| Montana | FAFSA | 3/1 | Priority date |
| Mississippi | FAFSA | 3/31<br>9/15 | HELP Scholarship<br>MTAG and MESG Grants |
| Nevada | | 1/1 | Priority date |
| New Jersey | FAFSA | 6/1<br>10/1<br>3/1 | Tuition Aid Grant applicants<br>All other applicants<br>Spring-term applicants only |
| New York | FAFSA, state form | 6/30 | |
| North Carolina | | 1/1 | Priority date |
| North Dakota | FAFSA | 4/15 | Priority date |
| Ohio | FAFSA | 10/1 | |
| Oklahoma | FAFSA | 3/1 | Priority date |
| Oregon | FAFSA | 3/1 | Opportunity Grant; asap after 1/1 for OSAC Private Scholarships |
| Pennsylvania | FAFSA, state form | 5/1<br>8/1 | 4-year degree candidates<br>Other applicants |
| Rhode Island | FAFSA | 3/1 | Priority date |

| STATE | FORM(S) REQUIRED | DEADLINE | NOTES |
|---|---|---|---|
| South Carolina | FAFSA | 1/1 | Priority date for SC Commission on Higher Education Grants |
| | | 6/30 | Tuition Grants |
| Tennessee | FAFSA | 2/15 | Tennessee Promise |
| | | 3/1 | State Grant |
| Texas | | 3/15 | |
| Vermont | | 1/1 | Priority date |
| Washington | FAFSA | 1/1 | Priority date |
| West Virginia | FAFSA, state form | 3/1 | Promise Scholarship |
| | | 4/15 | Higher Education Grant |

*Residents of states not listed in this table should contact their state aid office directly. See "Contact Information for State Aid Programs" in Part II.*

**QUICK RECAP**

In addition to the FAFSA and PROFILE, some states and colleges have financial aid forms of their own. Here's what to know about them:

- They're usually short.
- Their questions vary from school to school and from state to state.
- They may determine if you're eligible for special grants.
- They may help verify your financial information, perhaps through questions about your tax returns.
- If state aid is available, apply for it, or your colleges might consider your financial aid application incomplete.
- If one of your colleges requires an institutional application, fill it out, or you'll disqualify yourself from financial aid.

# **Step 8:** Make Your Special Circumstances Known

**QUICK OVERVIEW**

If something in your family's financial life can't be explained on the financial aid forms, make sure your colleges know about it. These "special circumstances" may include a lost job, high medical expenses or supporting an extended family. Colleges are willing to listen and, if you make your case, may be able to improve your financial aid package by taking those circumstances into account. This step is about how to prepare your case.

## Be a Person, Not Just a Form

Sometimes the financial aid forms you fill out don't tell the whole story. They may not show that your family sends money every month to support relatives in another country. Since the forms are based on the previous year's tax forms, they may not reveal this year's events: how one of your parents just lost a job, or will be shifting from full-time to half-time work. When the forms don't adequately report a special circumstance that affects your family's ability to pay for college, let your college know — it may change how much financial aid you get!

**Even if you're not sure your circumstance qualifies as special, speak up**. The financial aid office will let you know whether it qualifies. Don't think you're limited to communicating with your college only through the financial aid forms. If there's any doubt in your mind about whether those forms give a true picture of your family's situation, feel free to go beyond the form and contact the financial aid office. **Be a person, not just a form**. There are two reasons to do this: It guarantees that the college knows how much you are able to pay, and it shows that you're interested in the college — which may affect the lengths to which they'll go to help you.

### Using the Financial Aid Forms

In some cases, you can inform your colleges of special circumstances through the financial aid forms themselves — the FAFSA, PROFILE and institutional forms (Steps 5, 6 and 7, respectively, of this book). If you're supporting children, if you've been in the military, or if your parents are divorced, your FAFSA will make that clear. For colleges requiring PROFILE, you can use that form to describe special financial circumstances, list special family expenses, such as your family's medical and dental expenses, or any private school tuition that your parents might pay for your younger siblings.

While forms may serve well enough, it may still be a good idea to write a letter or schedule a visit. If there's any doubt in your mind about whether forms convey your situation, definitely contact the college.

## Going Beyond the Forms

You may have special circumstances that aren't covered by the forms. Or financially significant events may happen after you submit the forms — events that may be too complicated to explain in a simple correction. If that happens, communicate with the aid office as soon as possible after any financial hardships arise. The sooner you act, the sooner the college can adjust your award — and the more likely they will still have funds available to do so.

**Even after you start college, if a financial emergency occurs, let the school know**. The financial aid director can often help needy students with unusual expenses, such as medical costs, emergency trips home or funding to allow them to take an unpaid internship in the summer instead of working for money.

# How to Contact the College

A letter to the financial aid office explaining your circumstances is often the best way to state your case. Some schools have a form specifically for explaining special circumstances; it's worth asking your colleges what they prefer. The more closely you follow their procedures, the more likely you are to be heard.

No matter how you communicate with your college, be polite, clear and specific. **Remember, you're trying to put a face to the form, so make it a friendly one**. You'll get further by calmly presenting your situation and giving as many relevant specifics as possible. For example, if your parent got laid off, the school might want to know what the prospects for reemployment might be, whether your parent has filed for unemployment benefits and, if so, the amount of the benefit payments awarded. Don't be surprised or offended if the college responds to you with a request for documentation, such as a copy of your most recent tax return or pay stub.

## The Special Circumstances Form

Some colleges have a form through which you can let them know about special circumstances. "The purpose of the form is not to make everybody jump through a hoop," says Forrest Stuart, the director of financial aid at Furman. "It's to help the parents and the student put on paper all the information we need to help them out."

## Communicating by Letter

With many schools, the best way to contact the aid office is in a letter. Often, it can strengthen your case to enclose photocopies of supporting documentation with the letter — for example, a paper showing your parent was laid off. The aid officer may also ask you for specific documentation.

After sending your letter, follow up with the financial aid office a week or two later to make sure they received it and to see if they have any questions. You can do this by e-mail or telephone. If you live close by, or have scheduled a campus visit, you should also visit the aid office, but call first to make an appointment.

## E-Mail

Some colleges prefer to have you contact them by e-mail. At the University of Oregon, applicants can communicate their special financial circumstances through the school's website, where they can find an e-mail address for the financial aid office. "That way, they can do it whenever they think about it," says Elizabeth Bickford, the financial aid director.

# Examples of Special Situations

Many circumstances can affect your family's ability to pay for college. They may include a change in your financial situation from what was reported in the financial aid forms, such as a lost job, emergency expenses, health problems or even a windfall that misrepresents your usual level of income.

Family ties can also have financial implications, such as supporting an extended family or going through a divorce. And if you've served in the military, there are some special instructions you need to follow on the financial aid forms.

## Change in Financial Situation

Financial aid officers want to know not only that your financial aid situation changed, but why it changed. Certain types of changes are more likely than others to persuade them to give you more financial aid. Generally, aid officers will look more kindly on circumstances that are beyond your control, rather than the result of poor planning. For example, if your father gets laid off because his company has fallen on hard times, that is more likely to get attention than if he retires early to spend more time golfing. And the college is more likely to turn a sympathetic eye to necessary roof repairs than a loan to install a backyard Jacuzzi.

---

**EXPERT ADVICE**

"**We must have documentation**, and what we really like too is a nice **letter explaining the situation**. But on top of that, we also like to have a phone call or, if the student's already on campus, to have them come in and talk to us. That way, we can have a **dialogue about the situation** and give them some direction on what to provide to us and how to provide it."

— *Vincent Amoroso, former director, Office of Student Financial Services, Johns Hopkins University*

---

**GOOD TO KNOW**

If you're explaining your special financial circumstances by letter, it's best to send it to the financial aid office via mail or fax, so that it can be **easily incorporated into your file**. Write and format it as a standard business letter. **Put your name and Social Security Number** in the first paragraph, so the financial aid office won't have trouble matching the letter to your file.

## LOST JOB OR LOST INCOME

If you or your parents had a job when you filled out the FAFSA, and now don't, that will clearly affect your ability to pay. Even if you receive a severance package or collect unemployment benefits, your long-term ability to pay will still be reduced. This is information your financial aid office needs to know. For Palomar College, you would fill out a form that allows the financial aid office to override the FAFSA data with the new data. "You have to still report the previous year's income," according to Palomar's Mary San Agustin, "but we override it with the current-year income."

The FAFSA form asks if you or a parent is a "dislocated worker." But don't think answering "yes" to that question is sufficient to alert colleges to the problem. They will want to know more, and the more information you give them, the more likely they can help you. And given the large number of job losses caused by the current recession, you should try to give them this information as soon as possible. Remember, there is a limit to the amount of financial aid funds available.

Equally important are unusual changes in other sources of income besides wages and salaries. For example, suppose a student's mother became disabled and had to stop working, and her employer's disability insurance plan gave her a large percentage of her salary in the year for which her income was reported on the FAFSA, but a much lower percentage afterward. The FAFSA will show a larger income than she will be receiving once the student arrives in college. This change in disability benefits, like a lost job, needs to be explained to the college.

## EMERGENCY SAVINGS DRAWDOWN

An emergency may force your family to spend some of the savings that you reported on the financial aid forms. For example, suppose your house is damaged by a fire the day after you submit the FAFSA. Your family needs to spend a large amount of money to pay for the repairs. Depending on where the money comes from — regular savings, a retirement account, borrowing through a home-equity loan — this will have different effects on your need calculation. But no matter what the emergency or the source of the money you wind up spending is, you should tell the aid office.

Sometimes one crisis will have several different effects. A hurricane might not only destroy an applicant's home, but also put the family breadwinners temporarily out of work. In such a case, make sure the aid office knows about all the different effects on your financial situation.

## HEALTH PROBLEMS

A serious health problem in your family can involve both an emergency savings drawdown to pay for medical expenses, and loss of income if the patient is too sick to work. If someone in your family has recently become disabled, developed a chronic illness or had major surgery, this has a clear impact on your family's ability to pay for college. Your college's financial aid office should be able to help.

A letter, or the school's own "special circumstances" form (if they have one), is a good way to let a college know about your family's medical problem. But the financial aid forms provide some paths as well. The PROFILE form allows you to list medical expenses that weren't covered by insurance last year, and estimate the same for this year. You can also explain high medical expenses in the "Explanations/Special Circumstances" section. The FAFSA, on the other hand, doesn't ask specifically about medical expenses. If your college only uses the FAFSA, and you have unusually high medical expenses, a letter to the college makes sense.

### WINDFALL

In financial terms, a windfall is a sum of money you didn't expect to get, which is normally a good thing — but even a windfall can have its downside. On your financial aid forms, if you received a windfall last year, that makes your annual income look higher than it normally is, which will tend to raise your expected family contribution (EFC).

Some windfalls are better than others. A windfall is usually understood as a genuine, one-time boost to your finances. It might be an inheritance from an aunt you never knew or an unusually high year-end bonus from your job. If you get such a windfall, inform the aid office that your reported income was higher than usual, and that they shouldn't expect a repeat performance.

But some windfalls not only make your annual income look bigger than it is, but represent an overall loss to your financial position. Examples include a severance package on losing your job, or an early withdrawal from a retirement plan, such as an IRA, to cover an emergency. In both situations, your records for that year show a boost in income, but that apparent good news conceals bad financial news — that you lost your job in one case, and suffered a massive hit to your retirement savings in the other. If you experience this kind of windfall, explain the reality to your aid office.

## Family Ties

Not every family has two parents married to each other. And some families have stronger ties to grandparents, uncles, aunts and cousins than others. Different families live in different ways. The way your family lives may have financial implications that your financial aid office should recognize.

### SUPPORTING EXTENDED FAMILY

The financial aid forms tell the colleges about how many people live in your household, including you, your parents and your siblings. But many families give financial support to an extended family of relatives who live outside the household. Immigrant families, for example, often send money regularly to grandparents, aunts or uncles in another country. Since that decreases the amount you have available to pay for college, make sure the financial aid office knows about it.

### DIVORCED OR SEPARATED PARENTS

If your parents have divorced or separated, make sure the colleges know how that has affected your ability to pay. To do this, follow the rules on the financial aid forms. For the FAFSA, provide only the information about the parent you lived with more during the past 12 months (your custodial parent) — and, if that parent has remarried, your stepparent. For the PROFILE, provide not only that data but also information on your other parent, the one who does not have custody of you — your noncustodial parent.

Some colleges that use PROFILE will also want your noncustodial parent to submit information separately on the Noncustodial PROFILE. That information will be confidential; you and your custodial parent won't be able to see the data the other parent provides, nor will that parent see yours. However, the information submitted by your noncustodial parent will affect the college's calculation of your total expected family contribution (EFC). If you don't think it will be possible to get your noncustodial parent to fill out the form, let the college know. However, the school isn't likely to waive its requirement for the form for anything less than a significant reason.

In the parent-income section of either the FAFSA or PROFILE, a custodial parent who is receiving alimony or child support payments should report only what he or she received, not what he or she was supposed to receive. In certain circumstances, documented evidence that your noncustodial parent is behind in payments could help support your case if you appeal your award.

## Military Service

If you're currently serving in the active-duty military or the reserves, or if you are a veteran, don't assume that your military benefits alone will meet your full financial need. At most institutions, they no longer will. Benefits or not, you should apply for financial aid by submitting the FAFSA and any other required forms.

When filling out these forms, there are a few points to remember. Read the instructions carefully to make sure you qualify as a veteran for purposes of federal student aid. You should report housing allowances, subsistence allowances and untaxed combat pay as income. But don't include veterans' education benefits or ROTC scholarships when answering the questions about your untaxed income. The colleges consider them outside resources to be reported separately. (*See Step 9 for more information on outside resources.*)

Veterans are as liable as anyone to the special situations discussed earlier, from lost jobs to medical crises. That includes windfalls. For example, if you received a lot of combat pay last year but have now been discharged and won't receive it again, you should explain that to the colleges.

**QUICK
RECAP**

If there are special circumstances that affect your ability to pay for college, let your college know.

- Tell the college financial aid office as soon as you know about your special circumstances — either before you get your award or afterward.
- If you have to go beyond the forms, write a letter, e-mail, call or visit.
- Explain your situation clearly, documenting it where appropriate.
- The situations that may affect your ability to pay range from a lost job or high medical bills to status as a veteran or an undocumented immigrant.

# **Step 9:** Look for Scholarships

**QUICK OVERVIEW**

It's worth it to look for financial aid beyond what you'll get from colleges and federal student aid programs. This "outside money" probably won't amount to a "full ride," but it can help. Begin your search for outside scholarships around the time you start looking for a college because many scholarships have early deadlines.

## Scholarships Colleges Give You vs. Scholarships You Get on Your Own

**KNOW THE LINGO**

**Outside money** — Grants and scholarships that come from sources other than colleges or the federal government, such as states and private organizations.

**Portable money** — Grants and scholarships that you can take with you to whichever college you attend.

**College-offered money** — Grants and scholarships that colleges award from their own funds.

Financial aid doesn't come only from the government and colleges. It also comes in the form of scholarships from outside sources, including states and private donors. This money doesn't come looking for you: You have to find the programs that fit you and apply. You will have to qualify for the scholarship in some way, whether through academic merit, artistic talent or fitting some set of criteria, like being a person of Japanese descent living in New Jersey. **Very few outside scholarships offer anything close to full tuition, fees, room and board**. But they're worth the search because every little bit helps.

The scholarships you can get from outside sources are not exactly like the scholarships you might get from your college. These are the basic facts to know about each type.

### **College-Offered Scholarships**

In most cases, you don't have to apply separately for the scholarships that colleges award. You're automatically considered for them when you apply to the school. If you qualify, the college will include the scholarship in your financial aid package as they see fit. However, some colleges have merit-based scholarships for which you must apply separately.

To find out what the rules are for scholarship aid at your colleges, contact the schools or look at their websites, which usually describe the process for applying for scholarships under "admission" and then under "financial aid." Be sure to do this research *before* you submit your application for admission. At some colleges, you have to indicate on your admissions application that you are applying for a special scholarship; for example, this is true of Boston University's Trustee Scholar Program. At others, you don't have to apply for special scholarships until after you've submitted your application for admission.

Many college merit scholarships have to be renewed from year to year. To make sure yours is renewed, know the school's criteria for keeping it — for example, maintaining a certain GPA. Different scholarships will have different criteria at each college.

## Outside Scholarships: State Sources

Almost every state offers scholarships to their residents. These scholarships are usually available only for state residents attending colleges within the state, though a few states offer "portable" aid that a state resident can take to a college in another state.

Take the time to research scholarships and grants in your state. Almost every state has a department of education website that describes state scholarships and how to apply for them. These are usually separate from the state-sponsored, need-based financial aid programs for which you apply through the FAFSA or the state's own financial aid form, such as the Tuition Assistance Program (TAP) in New York State. An example of a state-sponsored, merit-based scholarship program with a separate application process is Florida's Merit Scholars Award, for which applicants must show high academic achievement.

## Outside Scholarships: Private Sources

Private scholarships are offered by many sources, including foundations, corporations, civic groups, religious organizations, veterans' associations and the military. The Society of Women Engineers offers the Bechtel Corporation Scholarship to high-achieving female students of engineering. United Methodist Scholarships are available to students who belong to that Christian denomination. The Senator George J. Mitchell Scholarship Research Institute offers awards to Maine residents studying in state.

Don't assume you have to be a genius to get a private scholarship. Although many scholarship programs consider academic merit, a range of conditions may qualify you for a scholarship, including interests, ethnic background and community work. The Los Padres Foundation grants scholarships to low-income Latino students. California students pursuing a career in agriculture are eligible for a California Farm Bureau Scholarship.

Most scholarships come with limits. Though a few programs will pay full tuition, the amount of most awards is much smaller, as little as $500 or $1,000.

## MYTH/FACT

**Myth:** "Untold millions" of scholarship dollars are available for use every year.

**Fact:** Private scholarships are only a small segment of the overall money available for college — **just 6 percent** of all aid to undergraduates. True, that share currently amounts to over 11 billion a year, but that's dwarfed by the $172.6 billion paid out by other sources. Grants from federal, college and state funds, in that order, are likely to be much more important in your overall financial aid package. It's worth looking for private scholarships, but don't count on them as your sole source of funding.

Many awards are limited to the freshman year of study. Fortunately, other scholarships are only for later years. The Bechtel Corporation Scholarship, for example, is just for women in their sophomore, junior or senior year of study. And once you've declared a major you may find yourself eligible for a scholarship that is aimed only at students in your academic discipline.

# Searching for Scholarships

Searching for private scholarships takes effort. But there are a number of Web-based scholarship search engines, like the ones on bigfuture.org and fastweb. com, that can help you zero in on scholarships for which you may qualify. If you like using this book, you might prefer to search for scholarships using the *College Board Scholarship Handbook*. It describes more than 2,400 outside scholarships, internships and loan programs, and is indexed by eligibility requirements — such as minority status, religious affiliation and state of residence — to help you match yourself to the programs.

**Beware of commercial scholarship search companies** that offer to help you find scholarships for a fee. Some do a responsible job, but many charge exorbitant fees and make fraudulent claims. For example, if they "guarantee" you a scholarship or promise to "do all the work for you," they are probably lying. Getting a scholarship is never guaranteed and, no matter what, you are going to have to do some work to apply.

Your school counselor may be of more help. Many private scholarships send application forms directly to school counselors. Tell your counselor in your junior year or early in your senior year that you are interested in applying for private scholarships.

**Searching for scholarships takes time, so start early.** You'll need time to find them, request information, gather materials, and complete your application. So look for scholarships as soon as you can — in the summer before your senior year, or by October or November of that year.

## Look Locally

When looking for scholarships, it pays to look locally. The fact is, you are more likely to obtain a scholarship from a local organization than from a state or national one.

On the local level, you will be competing with a smaller pool of applicants and are more likely to have characteristics that interest the donors. Again, your school counselor can help. The counseling office will have a file of local scholarships — from banks, the Kiwanis, the local garden club and other groups. Let your counselor know you are looking for scholarships; stop by the counseling office regularly to read the scholarship files or check the scholarship bulletin board. The office may also use Internet announcements, e-mail postings or newsletters to spread the word about scholarship programs to interested students.

Local businesses can also be a source of scholarship money. If you have a part-time job after school or a summer job, check to see if the company that employs you has a scholarship program or offers tuition assistance. For example, Chick-fil-A has a well-known scholarship program for its restaurant employees. Some companies provide their employees with a dependent tuition-assistance benefit. That means one of your parents might be able to get his or her employer to pay some of your tuition.

## Military Scholarships and Education Benefits

In return for military service, the armed forces offer a variety of college scholarships and education-assistance plans. For example, in the Reserve Officer Training Corps (ROTC) program offered by the Army, Navy and Air Force, you get scholarship assistance for college while being trained as a military officer. When you graduate, you are commissioned as an officer in the reserves and begin your term of military service.

Educational assistance for veterans is available in most states. If you're a veteran, contact your state veterans' administration for complete information and application forms.

# Applying for Scholarships

Once you find the programs for which you qualify, you have to apply. This may mean not only another form to fill out, but compiling supporting documents, such as transcripts, recommendations and an essay. Depending on the program, you may have to provide evidence of leadership, patriotism, depth of character, desire to serve or financial need. Get to know the requirements of each scholarship as early as possible, so you can do any necessary extra work on time.

A few pointers to remember:

**Apply early!** Apply as early as possible to scholarship programs. If you can, do it in the fall of your senior year, even if the deadlines aren't until February or March. Very often, scholarship programs will have awarded all their funds for the year on a first-come, first-served basis before their stated deadline.

**Follow directions.** Read instructions carefully and do what they say. Scholarship programs receive hundreds and even thousands of applications. Don't lose out because of failure to submit a school transcript or to provide appropriate recommendations. If you have a question about your eligibility for a particular scholarship or how to complete the application, contact the scholarship sponsors.

**Be organized.** It's a good idea to create a separate file for each scholarship and sort them by their due dates. Track application deadlines and requirements using Worksheet 2 (**a blank copy of this worksheet appears in Part II**). In one place, store the different supporting documents you may need, such as transcripts, standardized test scores and letters of recommendation.

**Check your work.** Proofread your applications for spelling or grammatical errors, fill in all blanks, and make sure your handwriting is legible.

**Keep copies of everything.** If application materials get lost, having copies on file will make it easier to resend the application quickly.

**Reapply.** Some programs only offer money for the first year of college, but others can be renewed each subsequent year. If your program is one of them, it pays to reapply once you're in college.

SAMPLE WORKSHEET 2:
# Scholarship Application Planner

|  | PROGRAM 1 | PROGRAM 2 | PROGRAM 3 |
|---|---|---|---|
| PROGRAM/SPONSOR | Wyzant College Scholarship | Young Naturalist Awards | Town Bank |
| ELIGIBILITY REQUIREMENTS | Competition/talent | Competition/talent | Need, local residency |
| TYPE OF AWARD | Scholarship | Scholarship | Internship |
| AMOUNT OF AWARD | $10,000, $3,000, $2,000 | $50 to $2,500 | $2,500 |
| CAN BE USED FOR | Tuition/fees | Any expense | Any expense |
| CAN BE USED AT | Any college | Any college | In-state colleges |
| DEADLINE | May 1 | Mar. 1 | April 1 |
| FORMS REQUIRED | Application and essay | Web form | Application (includes need analysis) |
| TEST SCORES REQUIRED | None | None | SAT |
| ESSAY OR ACADEMIC SAMPLE | Essay | Essay, research project | None required |
| RECOMMENDATIONS | None | None | One teacher (Mr. Filmer), Local branch manager |
| NOTIFICATION BEGINS | Not sure | Not sure | May 15 |
| REQUIREMENTS TO KEEP AFTER FRESHMAN YEAR | One-time payment only | One-time payment only | Based on performance during internship |

*For a blank version of this worksheet that you can photocopy for your own use, see Part II.*

# How a Scholarship Can Affect Your Financial Aid Package

**SCHOLARSHIP PROFILE**

The **Coca-Cola Scholars Program** is one example of the many sources of private scholarship aid. Run by the Coca-Cola Scholars Foundation, this annual program issues 150 national awards of $20,000 each. To be eligible, you must be a high school senior with a minimum 3.00 GPA at the end of junior year, and demonstrate high academic achievement, leadership and service orientation. Finalists attend an interview.

If a college to which you're applying hasn't met your full need — that is, if there's a "gap" in your financial aid award — outside scholarships can be used to fill that gap. That will make the college much more affordable and give you more choices when it comes time to decide which college you want to attend.

If, on the other hand, a college is already meeting your full need, it works a little differently. It would be nice if your outside scholarship were added on top of all your other financial aid to make your total aid package even bigger. But it probably won't be. Following federal policy, your college will most likely count any outside scholarship or tuition assistance you receive as an "outside resource" that decreases your aid package dollar for dollar. So the total amount of your financial aid package will be exactly the same.

You might think this is unfair: This is money you found and, in the case of employer tuition assistance and veteran's benefits, money you earned. On the other hand, it is money that's available to pay for your education without your having to dip into your income and assets. The philosophy behind financial aid is that everyone should pay what they can out of income and assets (your expected family contribution, or EFC), and then financial aid, including any outside resources, makes up the difference. The only way you can pay less than your EFC is if you get so many outside scholarships that they exceed your financial need. This is highly unlikely.

However, **it is still worth getting outside scholarships**. For one thing, it increases your freedom to choose a college regardless of cost. "If I'm a student, the more money that I can bring to the table for myself, the better position I'm going to be in to exercise choices that I might want to make," says Vincent Amoroso of Johns Hopkins University. For another thing, many colleges will use your outside scholarship money to reduce the self-help part of your aid package first — loans and work-study. This can significantly reduce the amount of money you'll owe after college or the time you'll need to spend working during college.

At some colleges, your outside scholarships will not be used to reduce your gift aid (grants and scholarships) unless the amount exceeds your self-help aid. Colleges that don't meet your full financial need may first apply outside scholarships toward filling the gap. Most colleges decide these issues on a case-by-case basis, but a few have stated policies that they publish on their financial aid Web page or will share with you if asked.

In making admission decisions, admission offices are likely to look on outside scholarships favorably. Students who have searched for and found outside scholarships on their own will probably be seen as students with initiative and a sense of responsibility. That makes the student a stronger candidate for admission.

If you win a scholarship after you've already submitted your FAFSA and/ or PROFILE, tell the colleges to which you've applied. Many schools have a special form specifically designed for you to submit this information. If you don't tell the colleges about a scholarship, it could jeopardize your eligibility for federal aid.

# Tax Effects

Your outside scholarship may be taxed as income — this depends on the use for which it's designated by the program that awards the scholarship. Generally, scholarship dollars used for costs that are purely educational, such as tuition and fees, will be tax free. But money used for living expenses, transportation or books will be taxed as unearned income. The scholarship program will let you know how much (if any) of your award is taxable, and will send you a copy of the IRS's Form 1098 at the end of each tax year.

If your employer gives you tuition assistance, it's tax free up to $5,250 a year. After that amount, it's taxable. If you get tuition assistance from your parent's employer, that will be included in your parents' taxable income, but they probably will be able to offset some or most of that with an education tax break (see Table 6 in Step 11 for more info.)

It takes work to hunt down and apply for outside scholarships, but it's worth it. Just remember:

- Outside scholarships will probably provide only a small part of the money you need for college, but every little bit helps.
- There are national and statewide scholarships programs, but look locally too.
- Websites, books and your school counselor can help you match outside scholarships to your qualifications.
- Search and apply early, and follow instructions.
- Your outside scholarship may affect the financial aid package awarded by your college, and it may be taxable as income.

**QUICK RECAP**

# Step 10: Weigh the Offers

**QUICK OVERVIEW**

After you've submitted all the financial aid forms, you'll receive offers of financial aid from the colleges that have accepted you. This step will help you weigh these award letters and make an informed decision based on an "apples to apples" comparison of the packages. If an award leaves you with a larger out-of-pocket share than you think your family can handle, you can appeal.

## Comparing Award Letters from Colleges

Soon after a college accepts you for admission, it will send you a financial aid award letter. The letter will detail what you'll get — the financial aid package the college is offering you. It will contain an outline of the expected costs you will incur during a year at the college, your expected family contribution (EFC) toward those costs, and the types and amounts of financial aid the college is offering to make up the difference.

The letter will also contain instructions on how to accept the aid package and how to contact the aid office if you have any questions or want to appeal the award.

It's best to wait until you have the award letters from all the different colleges that have accepted you before deciding which one to accept. If you have questions, wait until you've gotten answers from all the financial aid offices involved before you decide.

The offers in your award letters will differ. The amount and type of aid given will vary, and the letters may also differ in format, especially in how they itemize costs. Since most offers will only describe aid for your first year, an important question to ask is what you should expect to receive after that. Offers that look very similar for year one can be very different for subsequent years.

**KNOW THE LINGO**

**Aid package** — The total amount of all financial aid being offered to a student by a college.

**Award letter** — A document that a college sends to a student detailing the financial aid package. It indicates the type and amount of each scholarship, grant, loan or work-study opportunity being offered.

**Appeal** — A request that a college reconsider its financial aid package.

## SAMPLE WORKSHEET 3:
# Compare Your Awards

| | COLLEGE 1 | COLLEGE 2 | COLLEGE 3 |
|---|---|---|---|
| **Step 1.** For each college, list its name, award deadline, and the total cost of attendance (this figure should be in your award letter; if not, refer to the college website or contact the financial aid office). | | | |
| Name of college | Private Univ. | Small College | Regional State |
| Award deadline date | 5/1 | 5/1 | 4 weeks |
| Total cost of attendance | $31,825 | $33,410 | $15,566 |
| **Step 2.** List the financial aid awards each school is offering. Don't forget that grants, scholarships and work-study do not have to be repaid, while all loans must be repaid. | | | |
| Grants and scholarships | | | |
| • Pell Grant (federal) | | | |
| • SEOG (federal) | | | |
| • State | can't use | $2,000 | $2,000 |
| • College | $12,700 | $13,785 | $941 |
| • Other | | | |
| Total grants/scholarships | $12,700 | $15,785 | $2,941 |
| Percentage of package that is grant/scholarship | 60% | 74% | 53% |
| Work-study opportunities | $2,000 | $1,000 | |
| Subsidized Stafford loan | | | |
| Unsubsidized Stafford loan | $2,625 | $2,625 | $2,625 |
| Perkins loan | $4,000 | $2,000 | |
| Other loan(s) | | | |
| Total loans | $6,625 | $4,625 | $2,625 |
| Percentage of package that is work or loans | 40% | 26% | 47% |
| Total financial aid award | $21,325 | $21,410 | $5,566 |
| **Step 3.** In the rows below, calculate what it will actually cost you to attend each college by subtracting the total financial aid award (row b) from the total cost of attendance (row a) to see the net cost (row c). | | | |
| a) Total cost of attendance | $31,825 | $33,410 | $15,566 |
| b) Total financial aid award | $21,325 | $21,410 | $5,566 |
| c) Net cost to attend (a minus b) | $10,500 | $12,000 | $10,000 |

*For a blank version of this worksheet that you can photocopy for your own use, see Part II.*

## EXPERT ADVICE

"It's **not simply the dollar amount of the grant or scholarship** that families should focus on. They need to **lay out, side by side, the full picture**. What's the cost of attendance, including out-of-pocket expenses? What's the family contribution? What are the elements of aid? What's going to happen with loans, with work?"

*— Joe Paul Case, dean and director of financial aid, Amherst College, Amherst, Mass.*

In weighing the offers, the important thing is to compare apples to apples and not apples to oranges. For example, just because School A offers $10,000 in financial aid while School B only offers $8,000 doesn't necessarily mean School A has the better deal. If School A's aid package has $3,000 in grants and $7,000 in loans, but School B has $6,000 in grants and $2,000 in loans, School B is offering you more free money (grants) than School A.

There is another reason why a financial aid package may not be as big as it seems: higher costs. If one school's costs are higher than another's, you may be left with a higher out-of-pocket expense even after subtracting a "bigger" aid package. **Don't be dazzled by a large award. Instead, look for the bottom line: your net cost to attend the school.**

Here's a true story to illustrate this further. **Two sample award letters appear in Part II.** These were taken from actual letters received by a student. Only the names of the colleges involved have been changed, to "Blue University" and "Green University." The student's first-choice college was Blue U, which cost about $2,000 more than Green U. When she first compared the letters, she was very upset because it looked like Green U was giving her a much bigger scholarship, and much more total aid.

But her school counselor showed her that Blue U was actually offering the better deal. First of all, the grants and scholarship from Green U only looked bigger because they were presented as a total. Secondly, the student loans offered by Blue U (Stafford and Perkins) were subsidized, while the Stafford loan offered by Green U was not. That meant at Green U she would have to pay interest on the loan while she was in college. And third, the $14,810 Green U was "offering" as a parent PLUS loan wasn't really aid at all, but just an option for how her family could pay for their contribution. Bottom line, the true cost to her would be about the same at both colleges, even though Blue U is more expensive.

The College Board has an online "Compare Your Aid Awards" tool on bigfuture.org that lets you do this kind of side-by-side comparison of your awards. You can also use Worksheet 3 in this book to break out the different components of costs and aid packages and compare them side by side (a blank copy of this worksheet appears in Part II). When doing this analysis, keep an eye out for both quantity and quality. On the quantity side, for example, the "Family Share of Costs" figure tells you the amount of money your family will be expected to contribute. Your family will need to decide whether this amount is affordable. Look especially for evidence of "gapping," the practice of leaving a gap between the cost of attendance and the money accounted for by aid and EFC. You will be expected to fill that gap — in effect increasing your EFC.

On the quality side, consider the figures for "% of Award That Is Gift Aid" and "% of Award That Is Loan." The higher the proportion of gift aid (grant or scholarships) to loans, the better the award.

## Loans vs. Grants

All other things being equal, it's better to receive a grant or scholarship than a loan. For that reason, a financial aid package with a high percentage of gift aid is more attractive, on the face of it, than one with a high percentage of loans. But you might want to take the award that offers more loans and less gift aid, if that college is a better fit for you overall.

In any event, don't be surprised if your award includes loans. Most aid packages contain them. Loans are optional; you don't have to take them out. But if offered as part of a need-based aid package, they can be an excellent way to help finance your education. The alternative — taking only grant aid and trying to pay the costs that the loans would cover out of pocket — could put your family under much more financial stress than the loan would.

It's usually in your best interest to accept subsidized Stafford and Perkins loans that are part of the aid package. The repayment terms are good and the government pays the interest while you're in school. Unsubsidized loans — such as unsubsidized Stafford, PLUS loan and private loans from a bank — should be studied more carefully to make sure the terms are acceptable. You should understand the specific terms of each loan, including its interest rate, the origination fee, the term of the loan and the grace period before repayment begins. You should also realize that unsubsidized loans are not need based and are typically used to help your families pay their EFC. If a college offers them as part of your aid package, consider them as an option, but don't weigh them equally with subsidized loans in the package.

Work-study jobs are also optional, but if you're offered one and you can manage the time, take it. Having a job on campus brings in income, expands your social networks, allows you to make contacts with professors and administrators, and gives you experience that can improve your résumé.

# Appealing Your Award

Even though your award letters are printed in black and white, they aren't necessarily the last word. It is possible to appeal the awards to ask the colleges to reconsider their aid packages. There is no guarantee that they will grant your request, but there are circumstances where it's worth trying.

One reason you might appeal a package is if it has a lot of unsubsidized loans. However, bear in the mind that the college probably offered those loans because there wasn't enough gift aid to go around. Another reason to appeal is if you don't think you can afford the expected family contribution. You will need to have evidence to make that case. The college based its calculation of your EFC on the financial information you submitted. If you think this calculation was wrong, ask the financial aid office how it was made and see if you can find out if a mistake occurred. It will help if you have special circumstances that weren't communicated in your financial aid forms, such as a recent layoff; situations like this will clearly demonstrate why your

**KEEP IN MIND**

> **Just because you're awarded a loan** to pay part of your college costs **doesn't mean you have to accept it**. If your family has funds available in savings or current income, you can use these funds if you prefer. The downside is that you'll have less money available now, which could put your family under financial stress. The upside is that you won't have to pay the money back later with interest.

**KNOW THE LINGO**

There are three types of federal loans for educational expenses:

**Stafford** — Loan to students. May be subsidized (if student demonstrates need) or unsubsidized. If subsidized, the government pays the interest on the loan while the student is in college.

**PLUS** — A federal loan for parents to cover college costs not met by financial aid. Not subsidized.

**Perkins** — Subsidized loan to students with exceptional need. Perkins-loan debt may be forgiven if the borrower enters a career in the public service.

# Questions to Ask About Your Award

These are some questions to ask your college financial aid office if you're awarded gift aid:

✔ What do I have to do to keep my scholarship — do I have to do anything more than maintain satisfactory academic progress?

✔ Is there a minimum GPA or other condition?

✔ Is the scholarship renewable in subsequent years?

✔ If I win an outside scholarship, what happens to my aid?

Questions to ask if you're awarded a loan:

✔ What are the terms of my loan?

✔ What is the interest rate, and when do I start repayment?

✔ How much will I owe by the time I graduate?

✔ What will my monthly repayment be?

✔ By how much will my loan increase after my first year?

Questions to ask if you're awarded work-study:

✔ Do I have a "guaranteed" job, or will I have to find one?

✔ How are jobs assigned?

✔ How many hours per week will I be expected to work?

✔ What is the hourly wage?

✔ How often will I be paid?

✔ Will I be paid directly, or will my student account get credited?

family would have difficulty paying its EFC. (*See Step 8, "Make Your Special Circumstances Known."*)

"I've changed financial aid packages on appeal if somebody can demonstrate why they can't afford it," says Forrest Stuart of Furman University. "It may be the need analysis just didn't take some things into account. If they can show me where there's a real problem, even to the point where they show me their monthly budget, I might say, 'Man, you are right. You've got these medical expenses or you've got this and that. Let me see if I can help you.' I am not perfect, and the need analysis is not perfect, and we'll sometimes overlook something."

Still another reason for appealing an award is if you have better offers from other colleges, and would like to see if this college can match them. Some aid offices will consider matching a better offer from another college. But most will only hear an appeal that's based on your family's financial circumstances. "We don't bargain," says Mike Scott of Texas Christian University. "We just don't want to play that game of, 'Well, we'll give you more money simply because another school gave you more money.'"

You might see the entire appeal process as essentially negotiation or bargaining — trying to get as much as possible from the school you'd like to attend. However, most financial aid officers loathe the term "negotiate." Your appeal will have a better chance of success if it appears not a matter of haggling but of providing information not previously available to the financial aid office.

It will also help your cause if you are obviously doing your part to fund your education. A student who accepts the self-help components of a school's financial aid package will be more likely to get extra help than one who declined them. "If the student is not willing to somehow contribute, either by working or taking out a student loan, then we are very unlikely to give them any extra money," says Mike Scott.

A phone call is a good way to start the appeal process, even though most colleges will want you to put your reasons for an appeal in writing. Some have a specific form for appeals; others would like for you to state your case in a letter. Find out the college's preferred procedure by calling or checking their website. No matter how you file your appeal, your case will be stronger if you can provide data to back it up. A few days after filing your appeal, follow up with a phone call or, if possible, by visiting the aid office. Within a short time, the college will let you know its decision.

If you receive a revised award, take the new award letter and compare it to your other aid packages. **It's best not to decide where to enroll until you've received the final offer from each college.** But keep in mind the deadline set by each college for acceptance of its award. If you miss the deadline, you could lose the package. If you do need more time, try asking the college for an extension.

# Follow Up: Accepting an Award

Once you've compared all the awards and any appeals have been ruled upon, you and your family will have to decide on a college. Many factors, including costs and financial aid, will be in play. If your first-choice college has accepted you but not given as much aid as you'd hoped, the choice may be difficult. Do you go to your first-choice college even though it's a financial risk for your family, or to a second-choice college your family can safely afford?

In the end, your own preferences should have the greatest weight. Most of the loan debt, payable after graduation, will be on your shoulders. And your personal happiness at the school will have a major influence on whether you graduate successfully. If your family can put together a sensible financial plan to pay the costs, the best choice is the one that fits you best academically and personally.

Follow whatever instructions came in the award packet. If you're being asked for more information, send it. Complete any forms that came with the award letter. Sign the letter and return it by the due date.

**EXPERT ADVICE**

"I tell families **not to use the word 'negotiate.'** If an aid package is much lower than what's being offered by similar institutions, families should call and ask if there is additional information that may make a difference."

— *Carlene Riccelli, college adviser, Amherst Regional High School, Amherst, Mass.*

**QUICK
RECAP**

When you receive your award letters from colleges, you'll have to decide which offer to accept.

- Compare apples to apples, analyzing the awards to see what the real costs and financial aid elements are.
- Just because loans are offered, you don't have to accept them. But they're worth considering, especially if they're subsidized loans.
- If you appeal an award, you'll be on stronger ground if you can demonstrate circumstances that weren't previously made clear to the school.
- Your decision about which offer to accept should be based not just on cost but on how well the college fits you academically, socially and personally.

# Step 11: Consider Your Out-of-Pocket Options

**QUICK OVERVIEW**

Financial aid is intended to cover the difference between your expected family contribution (EFC) and the total cost of college. However, you still have to pay your EFC and whatever gap there might be between the aid you received and your financial need. This step is about ways to meet those out-of-pocket costs.

## Making Up the Difference

For almost every family, college is going to cost money. Even a generous financial aid package will usually leave you with some bills to pay. Some packages will meet less than your full need and leave you spending more than your EFC.

But you can afford to make up this difference between the total cost of attendance and the aid you're receiving if you take advantage of the various resources available to you. There are a number of programs and strategies that can help you save, pay or borrow for college.

**KNOW THE LINGO**

**EFC (Expected Family Contribution)** — How much money a family is expected to pay for college out of pocket, based on the family's ability to pay.

**Need** — The difference between your EFC and the cost of attending a particular college you've chosen. Financial aid is designed to meet your need, not your EFC.

**Unmet need** — The difference (if any) between your need and the financial aid offered by a particular college. Informally, unmet need is also called a **gap**.

## Save for It

You shouldn't spend your entire family savings on college: You need to leave some for other uses, such as retirement and emergency medical costs. But it makes sense to use some of your savings for college.

Don't worry if your family doesn't already have a huge sum of money saved for college. **Every little bit helps, and it's never too late to start saving.** Even while you're applying to college, your family can start saving. Try to save as much as you can from summer and after-school jobs, and encourage your parents to set aside some money from every paycheck. Talk with your parents about how much money you and they already have saved for your college costs, and discuss how your family can afford the rest of the bill.

Don't believe anyone who says you shouldn't save for college because it will reduce your chances of getting financial aid. As noted in Step 2, savings are worth having so you can pay out-of-pocket costs without having to borrow. Very little, if any, of your parents' savings are counted against you when your financial need is determined. "Parents should not avoid saving because, frankly, a family that has saved has a resource to draw on, whereas a family that hasn't is totally dependent on current income and loans," says Joe Paul Case, dean and director of financial aid at Amherst College in Amherst, Mass.

There are a number of places families can put their savings. The most traditional is a regular bank savings account, which pays a little interest and offers freedom to withdraw and deposit money at any time. A certificate of deposit (CD) has stricter rules about when you can withdraw money, but it usually pays higher interest than a savings account. Both of these options are good for short-term, flexible savings. But neither has any tax incentives — tax breaks that make them especially attractive for college savings.

The following savings vehicles do come with tax breaks:

**529 college savings plan.** Also known as the QTP (Qualified Tuition Program), these are tax-advantaged accounts sponsored by the various states. Interest earned in these plans is not taxed as income, and some states also offer a state income-tax deduction for contributions their residents make to the state's plan. There are no income restrictions, and contribution limits are high. Grandparents, uncles and aunts are also allowed to contribute to the plan, even if they don't live in the same state as you and your parents — in fact, you don't have to be a resident of a state to contribute to its plan, and you can withdraw funds from a state's plan to pay for expenses at a college in another state. Most plans offer a few different investment types, such as a fund that invests in stocks or one that invests in bonds.

**Coverdell Education Savings Account.** These tax-free trust or custodial accounts are similar to 529s, but they're sponsored by banks and brokerage houses instead of states, and therefore offer a greater range of investment choices. They can be used to pay private elementary and high school costs as well as college costs, unlike 529s, which can only be used for college costs. Total contributions for the student can't be more than $2,000 in a given year, and your family income has to be less than $110,000 (for single filers) or $220,000 (for joint filers). You can contribute to both a 529 and a Coverdell in the same year for the same student.

**529 prepaid tuition plan.** Like the 529 college savings plans, these are sponsored by the states, but they work differently. A 529 prepaid tuition plan lets a family make advance tuition payments years before their children will enter college. That allows them to "lock in" today's tuition rates instead of paying the higher rates likely to prevail years from now. Provided the student is admitted, the plans are guaranteed to be honored by public universities and some private colleges in the state that sponsors the plan. However, these plans have drawbacks. They can only be used for tuition and fees, not for room, board or other supplemental costs. When that's combined with the fact that the tuition rates are only locked in for in-state colleges, most parents prefer the more flexible 529 savings plans.

**Independent 529 prepaid tuition plan.** This is a special 529 prepaid tuition plan sponsored by a group of private colleges and universities and administered by TIAA-CREF. For more information, visit www.independent529plan.org.

**U.S. savings bonds.** If your parents pay for some of your college costs by cashing in U.S. government savings bonds, the interest that has accumulated on the bond may be tax exempt. That means the interest won't be taxed as income and your tax bill will be smaller. The bond must be issued after 1989 and your parent must have been age 24 or older when the bond was issued. This deduction can't overlap with any other education tax break, and you can't use two different tax breaks to pay for the same expense.

**Individual Retirement Account (IRA).** Generally, it's not a good idea to raid the family retirement funds, such as IRAs, to pay for college. "We tell parents all the time, you can borrow money to pay for your kid's education. You cannot borrow money to retire with," says Mike Scott of Texas Christian University. It's usually better to take out a PLUS loan than to diminish retirement assets. Still, if your family does need to go into an IRA to pay college expenses, the government doesn't charge the 10 percent additional tax you would ordinarily have to pay for breaking open an IRA before age 59½.

# Table 3:
## Comparison of Education Savings Options

| | COVERDELL EDUCATION SAVINGS ACCOUNT | 529 COLLEGE SAVINGS PLAN (QUALIFIED TUITION PROGRAM) | 529 PREPAID TUITION PLAN | U.S. GOVERNMENT SAVINGS BONDS | UNIFORM GIFTS TO MINORS ACT ACCOUNT | INDIVIDUAL RETIREMENT ACCOUNT |
|---|---|---|---|---|---|---|
| **Tax advantages** | Earnings in account not taxed as income | Earnings in account not taxed as income<br><br>Some states allow residents to deduct contributions for state income tax purposes | Earnings in account not taxed as income<br><br>Some states allow residents to deduct contributions for state income tax purposes | Interest earned is not taxed if used for qualified expenses | Interest earned is taxed at child's rate | Exception to the 10% early withdrawal penalty rule |
| **Expenses that qualify** | • Tuition & fees<br>• Books & supplies<br>• Room & board (if at least half-time)<br>• Expenses for special needs services<br>• K-12 education expenses | • Tuition & fees<br>• Books & supplies<br>• Room & board (if at least half-time)<br>• Computer<br>• Special needs services | Tuition & fees | • Tuition & fees<br>• Contributions to a Coverdell or 529 | Any expense (not limited to education) | • Tuition & fees<br>• Books & supplies<br>• Room & board (if at least half-time)<br>• Special needs services |
| **Contribution limits** | $2,000 per year | None | None | None | None | $5,500 per year ($6,500 if over 50) |
| **Income phaseout for benefits** | $95,000–$110,000 (single filers)<br><br>$190,000–$220,000 (joint filers) | None | None | Varies by income and filing status | None | Varies by type of account |
| **Other limitations** | Assets must be distributed by age 30<br><br>Must pay 10% penalty if distributions not used for qualified expenses | Must pay 10% penalty if distributions not used for qualified expenses | Benefits may only be used at colleges that participate in the plan<br><br>Must pay 10% penalty if distributions not used for qualified expenses | Applies only to Series EE or Series I bonds issued after 1989 and purchased after owner turned 24 | Counted as student asset for financial aid purposes | Interest earned will still be taxed at your regular rate |

# Work for It

Besides a summer job, you might also want to consider working during the school year to help meet expenses. There are two basic approaches. You can go to college full time while working part time, or you can hold a full-time job while attending college part time.

## Full-Time Student, Part-Time Job

If you're offered a work-study job as part of your financial aid package, the earnings from that job will go toward your college costs. Even if you're not offered work-study, you may still be able to find a part-time job on or near campus. You can also work during the summer to make money to put toward college.

Work has benefits beyond the extra income it generates. Studies have shown that students who work part time get better grades and are more likely to finish college than those who don't work at all. If the job is on campus, it can enhance your college experience by giving you a chance to meet people beyond your circle of friends and classmates.

On the other hand, don't work so many hours that you jeopardize your ability to get through college. **If you're going to college full time, the recommended workload is about 10 to 15 hours a week**. If you work more than 20 hours a week, you're likely to get overloaded and put yourself at risk of dropping out. If you take fewer courses to make time for work, you may drop below full-time status, which could make you ineligible for many grants and scholarships. If your financial situation makes you feel that you have to work more hours, it might be better to borrow more money so you don't have to work so much.

## Part-Time Student, Full-Time Job

A different (and much more difficult) way of approaching work is to be a full-time worker who goes to college part time. This is possible as long as you don't take too many credits in one semester. If you try for more than six to eight credits (two courses) while working full time, you'll probably have trouble getting everything done. On the other hand, if you take fewer than six credits a semester, you won't be eligible for need-based subsidized Stafford or Perkins loans or a Pell Grant.

Working full time while going to school part time is an especially attractive way to pay for an associate degree or a vocational certificate. Most community colleges cater to working students and offer classes at night to meet their needs. If you take six credits per semester, you can probably earn an associate degree in four or five years.

If you're planning on earning a bachelor's degree, however, you should strongly consider attending college full time and borrowing money to replace the income that you won't be earning through a job. Why? If you take only six credits a semester, it will take 10 years to earn a bachelor's! You will probably

---

**EXPERT ADVICE**

"**Work gives students structure.** First, they have to be somewhere. They have to be doing something at certain times of the week, which helps them manage their time. Second, if the job is on campus, they get involved with an office or a department or a faculty member, and that helps to **strengthen that student's connection with that school**, which always enhances the academic experience."

— *Vincent Amoroso, former director, Office of Student Financial Services, Johns Hopkins University* earn more money in the long run if you get that bachelor's in the usual four or five years, and concentrate on your career after you've earned that degree.

Some employers offer tuition assistance or scholarship money to employees who are attending college. Check to see if your employer is one of them. For a typical educational assistance program, up to $5,250 of those benefits will be tax free each year.

## Co-op and Internship Programs

Many colleges sponsor internships or "co-op" (cooperative) programs with local employers. Some interns and almost all co-op participants receive payment from their employers along with academic credit. In co-op programs, you may be able to alternate periods of full-time work and full-time study. Often the business at which you intern hires you after graduation, or at least recommends you to others. Internship and co-op programs can help you make money, get academic credit, gain job experience and make contacts with potential employers. If you are fairly certain about what career you want to pursue, a co-op program in that career can be the best way to earn your degree.

## Promising to Work Later

Holding a job during college is not the only way of using work to pay your college costs. There are several programs that allow you to commit to work in public service after graduation in exchange for either a non-need-based scholarship while in college or a stipend that can be used to repay student loans after college. The ROTC program is an example of the former, and AmeriCorps is an example of the latter.

### ROTC

In return for military service, the armed forces offer career training and a number of educational benefits to help pay for college, including full college scholarships and education assistance plans. If that deal sounds good to you, check with the Reserve Officers' Training Corps (ROTC) office at your high school or on your college campus. Each branch of the military offers ROTC training. Part IV of this book contains lists of colleges that offer ROTC programs for each service branch.

### OTHER SERVICE PROGRAMS

AmeriCorps is a network of national service programs for which you can work as a volunteer, full or part time, for up to a year. After completing a term of service with AmeriCorps, you're eligible for an education award, which can be used either to repay student loans or to pay for college tuition. The amount of the award depends on how long you worked for the program, and for how many hours each week. For more information, go to www.americorps.org.

Another type of program is one that hinges on your financial aid package and the profession you choose after college. If you received a Perkins loan as part of your package, the loan may be forgiven if you enter certain professions serving the public, such as teaching, nursing or law enforcement.

**KEEP IN MIND**

As noted in Step 2, you will be **expected to contribute** a larger percentage of your **work income to college costs** than your parents will. In general, you will be expected to pay about 50 percent of your earnings toward college.

# Borrow It

To borrow money is to spend today what you'll earn in the future. You will have to pay the loan back, with interest, when you start earning money after college. A loan can be intimidating because it assumes you'll have the money for repayment, and you may not feel sure of that.

There are many forms of "bad debt" in our society, such as credit card debt, where you borrow money on unfavorable terms to buy consumer goods that will have little or no value in a year. But an education loan is a "good debt." That's because you are borrowing money on favorable terms to achieve an outcome — higher lifetime earnings — that will more than pay back the loan.

Loans are available that your family can use to borrow money to meet your EFC. The most common types are the unsubsidized Stafford and the PLUS loan, both of which are guaranteed by the federal government, but there are also state and private sources.

## How Much Should You Borrow?

If your family decides to borrow money to pay for college, they should consider the total debt that you will carry after graduation. That total debt includes any subsidized, need-meeting loans that you accept as part of the college's aid package as well as any non-need-based loans your family takes out to meet the EFC. When you pay back that debt, you'll do so in the form of monthly payments, and those payments should be affordable based on the income you're likely to have. The total monthly payment will usually be similar to a car payment — $200 to $300 a month. But the amount will vary with the amount borrowed and interest rate offered.

Table 4 that follows will help you determine what your monthly payment will be. It shows monthly repayment over 10 years for a loan of $10,000 at various interest rates. To calculate a monthly payment for a loan amount not listed on the table, multiply the amount borrowed by the repayment factor for your interest rate. For example, if you borrowed $12,500 at 7.5 percent, your monthly payment would be $148.46 ($12,500 × .0118770).

There are some ways to make your repayment burden lighter after college. Many lenders will offer to cut your interest rate a bit if you make your first 12 monthly payments on time. If you borrow from multiple federal loan programs, such as the Perkins, subsidized Stafford and unsubsidized Stafford, you can consolidate these loans after graduation, which will simplify things by allowing you to make only one payment a month. Consolidation also gives you the option of "re-amortizing" your loans — that means stretching your payments over a longer period of time than you would normally have left to repay the debt. If you re-amortize when you consolidate, you will usually have a lower monthly payment, but will pay more interest over the total life of all the loans.

**KNOW THE LINGO**

**Principal** — The portion of debt that is left over from the amount you originally borrowed.

**Interest** — The portion of debt that has been charged to you by the lender as a fee for loaning you the principal.

**Table 4:**

Calculating Your Monthly Loan Payment

| AMOUNT OF LOAN | INTEREST RATE | REPAYMENT FACTOR | MONTHLY PAYMENT |
|---|---|---|---|
| $10,000 | 4.00% | .010125 | $101.25 |
| | 4.50% | .010364 | $103.64 |
| | 5.00% | .010607 | $106.07 |
| | 5.50% | .010853 | $108.53 |
| | 6.00% | .011102 | $111.02 |
| | 6.50% | .011355 | $113.55 |
| | 7.00% | .011611 | $116.11 |
| | 7.50% | .011870 | $118.70 |
| | 8.00% | .012133 | $121.33 |
| | 8.50% | .012399 | $123.99 |
| | 9.00% | .012668 | $126.68 |

**GOOD TO KNOW**

When you start paying back your educational loan, remember that the **interest may be tax deductible**. To a maximum of $2,500 per year, you can deduct the interest you pay from your income, which will lower your tax bite. In effect, the government will be subsidizing your loan. This is true for every kind of education loan, including PLUS loans.

# Types of Non-Need-Based Loans

There are three basic types of loans you can use to pay your out-of-pocket costs: federal, state and private.

## FEDERAL LOANS

Federal loans have relatively low interest rates and are guaranteed by the federal government. This means that if you don't pay your loan back to the lender (though, of course, you should), the federal government will. That encourages lenders to lend you money even if you're a student with no credit history and little employment record.

Two basic kinds of federal loans are used for paying an EFC, one for students, one for parents:

**Student Loans (Direct Unsubsidized Stafford).** While **subsidized** Stafford loans are need-based, meaning they are only awarded to students that demonstrate financial need for aid, an **unsubsidized** Stafford loan is available to anyone who submits the FAFSA, no matter what their financial situation. You don't even have to apply for it.

With a Direct Unsubsidized Stafford loan, you borrow money directly from the federal government, but the loan is provided through your college. You'll be charged only the interest while you're in school, and you can choose to either make monthly interest payments while you're in school, or let the interest accrue (accumulate) until you begin repaying the loan after school. If you let the interest accrue, you won't have to make any monthly payments while you're in college; but the interest will be "capitalized" (added) into the principal of the loan, so your monthly payments after college will be somewhat larger than they would have been if you had paid the interest during college.

Whether or not you let interest accrue, six months after leaving school (your grace period), you have to begin paying back both the principal and the interest. For loans disbursed after July 1, 2015, the interest rate is the same as for subsidized Stafford loans: 4.29 percent. It's possible that Congress might change the interest rate for new loans disbursed in future years; you can check the current rate on Student Aid on the Web at www.studentaid.ed.gov.

**Direct PLUS Loans for parents.** With a PLUS loan, your parents borrow money to pay for your education directly from the federal government (but through your college). They can borrow any amount up to your total cost of attendance minus the financial aid you receive. To get a PLUS loan, you must have submitted the FAFSA, and your parents will probably have to fill out an application from the college's financial aid office and pass a credit review.

Your parents will have to start making payments on the entire debt — both the principal and the interest — as soon as the loan money is disbursed to the school; but they can request that payments be deferred until after you leave school, in which case the interest charged while you are in school will be accrued and added to the principal.

The interest rate for Direct PLUS loans is a fixed rate of 6.84% for loans disbursed on or after July 1, 2015. Again, Congress might change the rate for new loans disbursed in future years, so check for the current rate on Student Aid on the Web at www.studentaid.ed.gov.

**What if I have trouble repaying the loan?** Under certain circumstances, such as economic hardship, you can postpone repayment of a federal student loan by applying for a deferment (during which no interest accumulates) or forbearance (during which it does). Under exceptional circumstances, such as total disability or teaching in a designated low-income school, some borrowers get a loan discharge, or cancellation of the debt. These rules apply to all federal student loans, and may also apply to parent PLUS loans in certain situations.

### STATE LOANS

Some states sponsor loan programs for students and parents in their state. These loans are usually neither subsidized nor based on need. Check with your state financial aid agency to find out more.

### PRIVATE LOANS

Federal student loans are not available from private lenders. Under the Direct Loan Program, Stafford student loans and PLUS parent loans come directly from the U.S. Department of Education, and loan funds are provided through the college. You or your parents can always take out a loan from a private lender, the same as a car loan for example. But that route is generally the worst way to finance a college education.

### HOME-EQUITY LOANS

Many parents consider taking out a loan against their home equity to pay for their children's higher education. While this may be an attractive option for your family, you should keep in mind that, unlike PLUS loans and other education loans, home-equity loans do come with the condition that if you can't pay back the loan, the bank can foreclose on your house.

## Table 5:
Comparison of Education Loan Options

| | DIRECT SUBSIDIZED STAFFORD | PERKINS | DIRECT UNSUBSIDIZED STAFFORD | DIRECT PLUS | PRIVATE/ ALTERNATIVE EDUCATION LOAN | HOME EQUITY LOAN OR LINE OF CREDIT |
|---|---|---|---|---|---|---|
| BORROWING LIMIT | $3,500 first year $4,500 second year $5,500 third and fourth years Higher limits if parents were denied a PLUS loan | $5,500/year $27,500 undergraduate maximum | $5,500 first year $6,500 second year $7,500 third and fourth years Higher limits if parents were denied a PLUS loan | Maximum is difference between total cost of attendance and financial aid awarded | Depends on lender and credit check | Depends on credit check and home equity |
| INTEREST RATES | In school: 0% In repayment: 4.29% (fixed) as of July 1, 2015 | In school: 0% In repayment: 5% (fixed) | In school: 4.66% (fixed) In repayment: 4.29% (fixed) as of July 1, 2015 | 6.84% (fixed) as of July 1, 2015 | Depends on lender and credit check; may be fixed or variable | Depends on lender and credit check; may be fixed or variable |
| PROS | Interest that accumulates while you're in college paid by federal government | No fees Interest that accumulates while you're in college paid by federal government Debt may be forgiven if you enter a career in the public service | Option of not making pay-ments during college and "capitalizing" accrued interest into the loan upon graduation Same deferment and forbearance rules as subsidized loans | No collateral required | | Can use money for noneducational purposes Repayment term may be longer than for federal loans |
| CONS | Only available to students with financial need 1% loan fee | Only available to students with financial need Amount of loan you're offered subject to col-lege financial aid office's discretion | 1% loan fee | Parents must pass credit check to take out loan Parents must begin paying interest immediately 4.3% origina-tion fee | Borrower must pass credit check Parents may have to cosign May have high origination fees | Home used as collateral for loan Can take several months to secure loan; may need to have house appraised |

# Cut It

You can cut what you will have to spend on college by reducing the amount of time you have to spend in college. This is an especially smart move if it looks like college won't be affordable even after you contribute all you can from savings, current income and loans. But cutting college time in order to cut college costs is an idea worth considering for other reasons as well.

## Getting a Jump on College Credits

Tuition, the cost of taking classes, is usually based on the number of credit-hours required for a degree. But you can cut the cost of tuition by earning some of those credits ahead of time at your own high school or a community college. By doing this, you may also be able to reduce the number of semesters you have to spend in college, which will cut not only your tuition costs but all other costs, such as room and board. Some colleges offer accelerated programs that will help you do that.

### AP®/CLEP®

The Advanced Placement Program® (AP®) and the College-Level Examination Program® (CLEP®), which are sponsored by the College Board, help you earn college credit. The programs differ in various ways. For example, students take AP courses as part of their high school curriculum, but they can prepare to take the CLEP examinations by any number of means — in school, on the job or by just reading books in their spare time. These programs are similar, however, in that you earn credit by taking an examination and receiving a score that your college accepts.

Colleges differ as to which programs, courses and scores they accept and how much credit they grant. But every credit you receive means a credit you don't have to pay for in college. Depending on your exam scores and your college's policies, you may be able to graduate a semester or even a year early if you've taken enough CLEP or AP Exams.

To learn more about AP go to apstudent.collegeboard.org

To find out if a college you're interested in grants credit for CLEP, use the CLEP College Search tool at clep.collegeboard.org.

### TAKE COMMUNITY COLLEGE CLASSES OVER THE SUMMER

Courses at a community college usually cost much less than at a four-year college. Find out if there are courses you can take at a local community college in the summers and transfer to your four-year college. For example, if you don't have the knowledge of a certain subject that you need to pass a CLEP exam, you may still be able to take that course at a community college over the summer and transfer the credit to your four-year college.

**OTHER ACCELERATED PROGRAMS**

Some colleges offer an "accelerated program" designed for students who want to graduate in three years. These programs require a lot of work and dedication, but they will cut your college costs substantially by eliminating an entire year of expenses. It's possible to get through these programs if you're determined.

## Cutting Other Expenses

Tuition is not the only college cost you can cut. Room, board, books, supplies, transportation — all of these add substantially to your total college bill. (Most people are shocked at what college textbooks cost these days.) Here are some suggestions to reduce these expenses:

**BOOKS**

- ✔ Buy used textbooks instead of new ones.
- ✔ Comparison shop for textbooks online.
- ✔ Sell your textbooks at the end of the semester.

**ROOM AND BOARD**

- ✔ Live off campus in a house or apartment that you share with classmates. That can be cheaper than a college dorm. (But check the policy at the college you want to attend — many require freshmen to live on campus.)
- ✔ If you plan to live in a dorm in your sophomore year and beyond, try to get a position as a resident adviser and the free room and board that comes with it.

**TRANSPORTATION**

- ✔ If you're commuting to school, carpool with a classmate from your area.

# Education Tax Breaks

Federal student aid isn't the only way that Uncle Sam can help you pay for college. There are also tax breaks available for higher-education costs. By reducing the amount your family has to pay the government at tax time, these programs amount to federal subsidies for out-of-pocket costs. Some of them take the form of tax credits, which cut your taxes dollar for dollar: That is, a $1 tax credit would make your tax bill $1 smaller. Others take the form of tax deductions, which lower the amount of your income that is subject to tax, indirectly lowering your tax bill.

There are two federal income tax credits for college expenses: the **American Opportunity credit** and the **Lifetime Learning credit**. These tax credits let your family reduce the taxes they pay dollar-for dollar, but each credit is for a different amount and has different requirements. And for any one student, a family can only elect to use only one of these credits on the same tax return.

The American Opportunity credit is worth up to $2,500 per year for each eligible student in the family. Unlike most tax credits, if the amount of the credit is more than the amount of tax owed, all or a portion of the excess may be received as a refund. This credit is available for the *first four years* of college. To be eligible, a student must be enrolled at least half-time; and the credit can only be claimed for four tax years for each student in the family. If a family has more than one student in college, it can claim the American Opportunity credit for one student and the Lifetime Learning credit for another student in the same year.

The Lifetime Learning credit is worth up to $2,000 per tax return for educational expenses paid on behalf of all eligible students in the family. You don't get a refund if you can't use all of the credit, but there is *no limit on the number of years* this credit can be claimed for a student. If a family has more than one student in college, it can claim the American Opportunity credit for one student, and the Lifetime Learning credit for another student in the same year.

For each of these tax credits, the amount of the credit depends on your family's income. The American Opportunity credit is gradually reduced if your family's adjusted gross income is more than $180,000 if you have two parents filing a joint return and $90,000 for a parent filing singly. The Lifetime Learning credit phases out after $130,000 for joint returns and $65,000 for single returns.

If your family's income is too high to qualify for either of these tax credits, there's also a tax deduction that may help. With the tuition and fees deduction, you can deduct up to $4,000 of college tuition and fees if your family income isn't more than $65,000 (for single filers) or $130,000 (for joint filers); the deduction is up to $2,000 if your family income isn't more than $80,000 (for single filers) or $160,000 (for joint filers). If you claim this deduction, you can't claim the American Opportunity or Lifetime Learning credits for the same student that year.

Interest paid on student loans is tax deductible up to a maximum of $2,500 per year. This benefit applies to all loans used to pay for college, including PLUS loans. To be eligible for this deduction, your family's income has to be less than $80,000 (for single filers) or $160,000 (for joint filers). The tax break is only for the amount of interest you paid, not the amount you borrowed.

Some states also allow you to take tax credits or deductions from your state income taxes. Find out about yours from your state government.

## Table 6:
### Federal Income Tax Benefits for Higher Education

| | AMERICAN OPPORTUNITY CREDIT | LIFETIME LEARNING CREDIT | TUITION AND FEES DEDUCTION | STUDENT LOAN INTEREST DEDUCTION |
|---|---|---|---|---|
| **AVAILABLE FOR** | Tuition, fees, books, supplies and equipment<br><br>1st four years of undergraduate study only<br><br>Associate and bachelor's degree programs only | Tuition and fees only<br><br>All years of study<br><br>Any degree program, also nondegree courses to acquire job skills | Tuition and fees only<br><br>All years of study<br><br>Attendance at any postsecondary institution participating in a federal student aid program | Any higher education cost<br><br>All years of study<br><br>Any degree program |
| **MAXIMUM VALUE** | $2,500 credit per student | $2,000 credit per family | Up to $4,000 deduction taken as an adjustment to gross income | $2,500 deduction from taxable income |
| **MAXIMUM INCOME FOR ELIGIBILITY** | $80,000–$90,000 (single filers)<br><br>$160,000–$180,000 (joint filers) | $55,000–$65,000 (single filers)<br><br>$110,000–$130,000 (joint filers) | $65,000 (single filers)<br><br>$130,000 (joint filers) | $65,000–$80,000 (single filers)<br><br>$130,000–$160,000 (joint filers) |
| **CONDITIONS** | Student must be enrolled at least half-time<br><br>Cannot claim the Lifetime Learning credit for the same student in the same year | Cannot claim the American Opportunity credit for the same student in the same year | Cannot claim either the American Opportunity credit or the Lifetime Learning credit for the same student in the same year | Student must have been enrolled at least half-time |

**QUICK RECAP**

To deal with out-of-pocket college costs, you have several options. You can draw on savings or current income to pay, or you can borrow some portion of the total bill. And you can cut the costs.

- Several savings options, including U.S. savings bonds, 529s and Coverdell accounts, have tax benefits that can also help.
- You can work during college or promise to work later through programs like ROTC or AmeriCorps.
- You can borrow through student or parent loans.
- You can reduce your costs by such means as taking college-level courses for credit before you enter college.
- Tax breaks can help you meet college costs.

# Once You're in College

**QUICK OVERVIEW**

Once you're in college, you shouldn't be preoccupied with paying for it. Academics, extracurricular activities and making friends are more important. But there are some things you need to do to stay on target financially. This chapter will tell you what they are.

## Reapply for Aid Each Year!

Don't forget to reapply to renew your aid package every year! Check at your financial aid office to make sure you have the right forms and know what the deadlines are. Most colleges have a renewal deadline for financial aid that's a week or two later than the deadline for new applicants.

When you renew, don't expect your aid package to stay exactly the same. It may become more loan heavy each year, with more money in subsidized loans. The borrowing limits on the subsidized Stafford loan are higher for sophomores than for freshmen, and even higher for juniors and seniors. Also, keep in mind that some scholarships and grants are for freshmen only.

While you're reapplying for the financial aid you already have, keep an eye out for new opportunities. As you move on to higher grades and declare a major, you may become eligible for outside scholarships that weren't open to you in the past. Follow the guidelines in Step 9 to look for outside sources of money.

**EXPERT ADVICE**

"There are students who tell me that the reason they didn't pass their class was they're **too busy working**, because they need the money to support themselves. And I tell them, you need to determine your priorities. There's a limit of how much financial aid I can give you to help offset that."

— *Mary San Agustin, director of financial aid and scholarships, Palomar College, San Marcos, Calif.*

## Stay on Track

The next thing to keep in mind is that you have to maintain eligibility for financial aid. For federal student aid, stay in school at least half-time, and avoid illegal drugs. A drug-related conviction can lead to suspension or revocation of your federal-aid eligibility.

You don't have to maintain a particular GPA to maintain federal eligibility (though you do have to meet your individual school's standards for "satisfactory academic progress"). But the financial aid your college gives you, such as scholarships, may have specific academic requirements. Do your best in all your classes and stay on track academically, not only because it will help you get the most out of college but because it will help you keep your financial aid. To maintain or establish eligibility for academic scholarships, an on-campus job such as a teaching or research assistant, or a "co-op" program between your department and a local employer, you'll need to be in good academic standing.

## Maintain Grades

To keep up your grades, you'll have to make decisions about how to spend your time. It's important to build social relationships, pursue extracurricular activities, and earn money through work, but balance those against the need to maintain a good academic record. If you have a job, don't work so hard at it that you jeopardize your aid eligibility.

## Don't Stay Too Long

Did you know that only about one-third of all students who enter a four-year college graduate in four years? Most take six or more years to earn a bachelor's degree. Obviously, the longer you stay in college, the more it's going to cost you — not only in tuition, fees, room, board and other expenses, but also in lost earnings from a delayed career.

**Make it a goal to graduate on time**. Make sure you are on track to complete your college's core requirements, as well as the core requirements for your major.

Speaking of majors, don't feel that you need to rush into choosing one. Except for some very specialized career and technical institutes, most colleges and universities allow you to take time during your first two years to take classes in different fields and make sure you know enough to choose a major that fits your interests and abilities. On the other hand, don't wait so long that you neglect to take the courses that are requirements for a major. You don't want to have to pay for an extra semester to get your biology degree because you didn't take that required organic chemistry course your sophomore year.

## Transferring from a Community College

If you're going to a community college, and plan to transfer to a four-year college, **make sure you know all the transfer requirements** — including whatever courses are needed for the major you intend to declare. It helps if your community college has an articulation agreement with the four-year college specifying exactly what courses are required for transfer. Almost all community colleges have a transfer adviser on staff who can help you make sure you're on track. Get to know your adviser and check in with him or her regularly.

### MYTH/FACT

**Myth:** Only certain majors will lead to high earnings after graduation.

**Fact:** Don't be fooled. If you're not drawn to the major, you probably won't like the work and will leave that field before you ever reach the high earnings. Instead, **choose a major based on your interests and talents**, not on someone else's predictions of industrial trends. And remember that many of today's highest paying fields — such as marketing and software engineering — require critical thinking skills that you will acquire in courses like anthropology and philosophy. To learn more about specific academic fields and what it's like to major in them, read the College Board's *Book of Majors*.

# Watch Your Personal Expenses

The purpose of financial aid is to give you the money you need to pay for college costs. But that aid can quickly become too little if you spend too much. To avoid overspending, live within your means and don't run up frivolous debt. That means sticking to a budget and avoiding credit cards.

## Student Budgeting

To live within your means, all you have to do is not spend more than you receive in income. The best way to do that is to create a budget at the beginning of each semester and stick to it. Your budget should list the funds you will receive (such as money from parents, savings, work, grants and loans), subtract how much money you plan to spend on given items (such as tuition, fees, room, board, books, clothes and recreation) and calculate the difference — the bottom line. If the bottom line is a negative number — that is, if your expenses exceed your income — you're overspending. Once you have a budget where your income is equal to or greater than your expenses, follow it, and you'll be living within your means.

To create a budget, first examine what you have actually been spending, then **set priorities if you're spending too much**. That alone can help you to spend less, as you realize you can make do with one latte a day instead of two. "You start making conscious decisions about what it is that you want to do," says Elizabeth Bickford of the University of Oregon at Eugene. "You're actually just taking control over your financial spending."

By all means have fun, but don't spend too much money on nonessential items like DVDs, high-end clothes or trips to the beach. Some of your friends at college may have more money than you, but don't let social pressure push you into trying to spend like they do. Learn to suggest ordering pizza from the local hangout instead of driving to an expensive restaurant.

Save money wherever you can — for example, limit your cell phone use to free times. Comparison shop for groceries and supplies. And don't visit the ATM too often: It's too easy to withdraw money and overspend. See collegeboard.org for more advice on budgeting and financial planning.

## Credit Card Debt

Be especially careful with your credit cards. They can be convenient for paying for big-ticket items like textbooks and airplane tickets, if you use them sparingly and pay off the entire amount when you get the bill. But if you abuse them, they can land you in a world of trouble.

**A credit card is essentially a high-interest loan.** Pulling it out at a cash register to make an impulse purchase may give you a feeling of freedom, but you won't feel free once you get the bill — especially when you're still paying interest on that impulse purchase months or years later. If you let the debt accumulate, it may swell so much that you won't be able to pay down the debt. This can affect your future academic career. If you miss payments on your credit cards, or if your credit card debt is high, you can hurt your credit rating. A bad credit rating can harm your chances of getting student loans to pay for graduate school, or a car loan when you start working. It can even prevent you from getting a job with certain security-conscious employers, such as banks or government agencies.

Use credit cards only when you know you can repay the debt promptly. Save them for emergencies. (A spring-break vacation is not an emergency.) Think through each credit card purchase before you spend. If you do get in over your head with credit card use, cut your expenses and talk to your family and financial aid administrator for more guidance.

## Saving for Future Needs

While you're trying to live within your means, it's also wise to save for the future. Savings will give you greater freedom to cope with college and personal costs to come. If at all possible, make sure your budget includes money set aside for future needs. Your parents, of course, should do the same.

Try to save what you can from the jobs you have during the school year and in the summer. Think about the following as goals for your savings:

Students should think about …

- ✔ Next year's college expenses
- ✔ Application fees and tuition for graduate school
- ✔ A vacation with friends after you graduate
- ✔ Moving to another city after you graduate
- ✔ The unexpected (such as traveling to a friend's wedding or a family funeral)

Parents should think about …

- ✔ Next year's college expenses
- ✔ College expenses for younger children (if any)
- ✔ Retirement
- ✔ The unexpected (such as making it through a layoff or paying for a child's wedding)

# Final Thoughts

Once you're in college, you may sometimes wonder if it's worth it. Can your family afford the expense? Will you be able to repay your student loans? If you've made reasonable choices along the way, the answer is yes. If you ever have doubts, visit your school's career center and do some research into the fields of work you might enter. Find out how much money you're likely to be earning when you first graduate, and how much five years later. A light might go on for you, as Elizabeth Bickford has often observed with other students. "When they see that relationship, many students say, 'Oh, wait a second, I can do that.'"

You will be able to pay back your student loans. College is a sound investment. You can afford college!

**QUICK RECAP**

Once you're in college, make sure you stay on track financially.

- Reapply for aid every year.
- Maintain your federal eligibility by staying in school the right number of hours and avoiding illegal drugs.
- Keep up your grades. Don't let them get derailed by too much time spent on work or other nonacademic activities.
- Declare a major at a suitable time.
- Make a budget and stick to it.
- Be wary of credit cards.
- Save for future expenses.
- Keep an eye out for new sources of outside scholarships.
- Remember that college is worth it!

# Part II

## WORKSHEET 1:
# Meet Your Application Deadlines

| | | COLLEGE 1: | COLLEGE 2: | COLLEGE 3: |
|---|---|---|---|---|
| | College Name | *1st Choice Univ.* | *Private Univ.* | *Financial Safety* |
| FORMS REQUIRED | FAFSA | | | |
| | PROFILE | | | |
| | State form | | | |
| | Institutional form | | | |
| | Tax returns | | | |
| | Other | | | |
| SCHOOL CODES | Federal code | | | |
| | CSS code | | | |
| PRIORITY DATE | | | | |
| CLOSING DATE | | | | |
| AFTER APPLYING | Need to send letter? | | | |
| | Documentation required? | | | |
| COMPARE AWARDS | Notification date | | | |
| | Reply-by date | | | |

## WORKSHEET 2:
# Scholarship Application Planner

|  | PROGRAM 1 | PROGRAM 2 | PROGRAM 3 |
|---|---|---|---|
| PROGRAM/SPONSOR |  |  |  |
| ELIGIBILITY REQUIREMENTS |  |  |  |
| TYPE OF AWARD |  |  |  |
| AMOUNT OF AWARD |  |  |  |
| CAN BE USED FOR |  |  |  |
| CAN BE USED AT |  |  |  |
| DEADLINE |  |  |  |
| FORMS REQUIRED |  |  |  |
| TEST SCORES REQUIRED |  |  |  |
| ESSAY OR ACADEMIC SAMPLE |  |  |  |
| RECOMMENDATIONS |  |  |  |
| NOTIFICATION BEGINS |  |  |  |
| REQUIREMENTS TO KEEP AFTER FRESHMAN YEAR |  |  |  |

## WORKSHEET 3:
# Compare Your Awards

| | COLLEGE 1 | COLLEGE 2 | COLLEGE 3 |
|---|---|---|---|
| **Step 1.** For each college, list its name, award deadline and total cost of attendance (this figure should be in your award letter; if not, refer to the college website or contact the financial aid office). | | | |
| Name of college | | | |
| Award deadline date | | | |
| Total cost of attendance | | | |
| **Step 2.** List the financial aid awards each school is offering. Don't forget that grants, scholarships and work-study do not have to be repaid, while all loans must be repaid. | | | |
| Grants and scholarships | | | |
| • Pell Grant (federal) | | | |
| • SEOG (federal) | | | |
| • State | | | |
| • College | | | |
| • Other | | | |
| Total grants/scholarships | | | |
| Percentage of package that is grant/scholarship | | | |
| Work-study opportunities | | | |
| Subsidized Stafford loan | | | |
| Unsubsidized Stafford loan | | | |
| Perkins loan | | | |
| Other loan(s) | | | |
| Total loans | | | |
| Percentage of package that is work or loans | | | |
| Total financial aid award | | | |
| **Step 3.** In the rows below, calculate what it will actually cost you to attend each college by subtracting the total financial aid award (row b) from the total cost of attendance (row a) to see the net cost (row c). | | | |
| a) Total cost of attendance | | | |
| b) Total financial aid award | | | |
| c) Net cost to attend (a minus b) | | | |

**Figure 9:**
Sample Financial Aid Award Letter 1

---

**Blue University**      Cost of Attendance: $ 28,706.00

CLASS: 2021

March 22, 2017

TENTATIVE
FINANCIAL AWARD NOTIFICATION FOR 2017–2018

Based on the information that you submitted on your FAFSA and to our office,
**Blue University** can offer you the following TENTATIVE awards.

This package is based on an award period from 09/10/17 to 06/06/18.

| AID AWARD | ACCEPT AWARD | | OFFERED AMOUNT |
|---|---|---|---|
| | Yes | NO | |
| FEDERAL PERKINS LOAN | _____ | _____ | $1,143 |
| STATE WORK-STUDY | _____ | _____ | $2,400 |
| BLUE EDUCATIONAL GRANT | _____ | _____ | $3,538 |
| UNIVERSITY SCHOLARSHIP | _____ | _____ | $2,000 |
| RESIDENCE HALL GRANT | _____ | _____ | $2,000 |
| FEDERAL STAFFORD LOAN – SUB. | _____ | _____ | $2,625 |

Finalize your financial aid award as soon as possible by forwarding to our office the forms listed on the Missing Documents Form included with this letter.

Please read the important information pamphlet! Indicate your intent by checking whether or not you accept each aid award, then sign and return this letter in order to reserve your award(s).

Please refer to the Cost Worksheet to help determine your expenses for the academic year.

If direct loan amounts desired are less than above, please indicate below:

    Requested Federal Stafford Loan (Sub.)    $ _____
    Requested Federal Perkins Loan         $ _____

I acknowledge that I have read and will comply with all the supporting information in the Important Information Pamphlet. Furthermore, if I receive any financial assistance not included in this award letter, including tuition waivers or employer reimbursement, I will notify your office immediately.

Signature _____    Date _____1

**Figure 10:**
Sample Financial Aid Award Letter 2

**Green University** | Office of Student Financial Planning

Cost of Attendance: $ 26,005.00

March 1, 2017

**Step 1. Circle A for Accept or D for Decline for each individual award where indicated below:**

|  | Fall 2017 | Spring 2018 | Total | A / D |
|---|---|---|---|---|
| Presidential Freshman Scholarship | $3,250 | $3,250 | $6,500 | A / D |
| **Green University Grant** | $705 | $705 | $1,410 | A / D |
| **Total Grants and Scholarships** |  |  | **$7,910** |  |
| Federal Unsubsidized Stafford Loan | $1,313 | $1,312 | $2,625 | A / D |
| **Total Student Loans** |  |  | **$2,625** |  |
| Federal College Work-Study | $330 | $330 | $660 | A / D |
| Federal PLUS Loan and/or Green Partnership Loan | $7,405 | $7,405 | $14,810 |  |

**Step 2. Please note the following:**

Your awards are based on full-time enrollment for the fall and spring terms and residence hall occupancy for the fall and spring terms (for financial aid purposes, full-time is defined as 12 credits or more per term).

You have been offered loan(s) that require separate loan materials.

The amount of your Green University Grant was based upon residence hall occupancy for the fall and spring terms. A change in housing status may result in a reduction of this award.

**Step 3. Please list other financial assistance, scholarships, or loans you will receive not indicated above. List the scholarship/donor name and the expected amount (example: Elks Club $100).**

| Name | Amount |
|---|---|
|  |  |
|  |  |

**Step 4. Attention: Your awards are not final until you complete the items on the ACTION REQUESTED page.**

# Estimate Your EFC Under Federal Methodology

## WORKSHEET 4A:
### Estimate a Dependent Student's Expected Contribution

| STUDENT'S INCOME | |
|---|---|
| 1. Taxable income ("adjusted gross income" from IRS Form 1040) | $ |
| 2. Untaxed income/benefits | + |
| 3. Taxable student aid | - |
| 4. Total student's income (sum of lines 1 and 2, minus line 3) | = |
| **Allowances** | |
| 5. U.S. income tax paid (from IRS Form 1040) | |
| 6. State and other taxes paid (% from Table 7 x line 4) | + |
| 7. F.I.C.A. (Table 8) | + |
| 8. Income protection allowance | $6,000 |
| 9. Parents' negative available income offset (line 20 of parents' worksheet, if negative) | + |
| 10. Total allowances (sum of lines 5-9) | = |
| 11. Available income (line 4 minus line 10) | = |
| 12. Available income assessment rate | x 0.50 |
| 13. Contribution from income (line 11 x line 12; if negative, enter $0) | = |
| **Student's Assets*** | |
| 14. Cash, savings and checking accounts | |
| 15. Other real estate/investment equity | + |
| 16. Business/nonfamily farm equity | + |
| 17. Net worth (sum of lines 14-16) | = |
| 18. Asset assessment rate | x 0.20 |
| 19. Contribution from assets (line 17 x line 18; if simple needs test or negative, enter $0) | = |
| **Contribution**** | |
| 20. Total Student Contribution (sum of lines 13 and 19) | = |

* If you are eligible to file an IRS 1040A or 1040EZ form, or you are not required to file a tax return, and your parents' taxable income is less than $50,000, no assets are included in the methodology.

** If your parents' adjusted gross income is $24,000 or less, and they file or are eligible to file an IRS 1040A or 1040EZ form, no contribution is expected.

## WORKSHEET 4B:
# Estimate the Parents' Expected Contribution

| Parents' Income | |
|---|---|
| 1.    Taxable income ("adjusted gross income" from IRS Form 1040) | $ |
| 2.    Untaxed income/benefits | + |
| 3.    Income exclusions (child support paid + education tax credits + taxable combat pay) | - |
| 4.    Total parents' income (sum of lines 1 and 2, minus line 3) | = |
| **Allowances** | |
| 5.    U.S. income tax paid (from IRS Form 1040) | |
| 6.    State and other taxes paid (% from Table 7 x line 4) | + |
| 7.    F.I.C.A. paid (Table 8) | + |
| 8.    Employment allowance (Table 8) | + |
| 9.    Income protection allowance (Table 9) | + |
| 10.   Total allowances (sum of lines 5-9) | = |
| 11.   Available income (line 4 minus line 10; may be negative) | = |
| **Parents' Assets*** | |
| 12.   Cash, savings and checking accounts | |
| 13.   Other real estate/investment equity | + |
| 14.   Adjusted business/nonfamily farm equity (Table 10) | + |
| 15.   Net worth (sum of lines 12-14) | = |
| 16.   Education Savings and Asset protection allowance (Table 11) | - |
| 17.   Discretionary net worth (line 15 minus line 16) | = |
| 18.   Conversion percentage | x 12% |
| 19.   Contribution from assets (line 17 x line 18; if simple needs test or negative, enter $0) | = |
| 20.   Adjusted available income (sum of line 11 and line 19; may be negative) | = |
| **Contribution**** | |
| 21.   Total contribution (calculate using line 20 and Table 12) | = |
| 22.   Number of dependent children in college at least half time | ÷ |
| 23.   Parents' contribution for student (line 21 divided by line 22; if negative, enter $0) | = |

* If your parents are eligible to file an IRS 1040A or 1040EZ form, or are not required to file a tax return and their taxable income is less than $50,000, no assets are included in the methodology.

** If your parents' adjusted gross income is $24,000 or less, and they are eligible to file an IRS 1040A or 1040EZ form, or are not required to file a tax return, no contribution is expected.

**TABLE 7:** 2016–2017 Federal EFC Allowances for State Taxes

| | Parents TOTAL INCOME | | Student TOTAL INCOME |
|---|---|---|---|
| | $ 0-14,999 | $15,000 or more | Any amount |
| Alabama (AL) | 3% | 2% | 2% |
| Alaska (AK) | 2 | 1 | 0 |
| American Samoa (AS) | 2 | 1 | 1 |
| Arizona (AZ) | 4 | 3 | 2 |
| Arkansas (AR) | 4 | 3 | 3 |
| California (CA) | 7 | 6 | 5 |
| Canada (CN) | 2 | 1 | 1 |
| Colorado (CO) | 4 | 3 | 3 |
| Connecticut (CT) | 8 | 7 | 5 |
| Delaware (DE) | 5 | 4 | 3 |
| District of Columbia (DC) | 7 | 6 | 5 |
| Federated States of Micronesia (FM) | 2 | 1 | 1 |
| Florida (FL) | 3 | 2 | 1 |
| Georgia (GA) | 5 | 4 | 3 |
| Guam (GU) | 2 | 1 | 1 |
| Hawaii (HI) | 5 | 4 | 4 |
| Idaho (ID) | 5 | 4 | 3 |
| Illinois (IL) | 6 | 5 | 3 |
| Indiana (IN) | 4 | 3 | 3 |
| Iowa (IA) | 5 | 4 | 3 |
| Kansas (KS) | 5 | 4 | 3 |
| Kentucky (KY) | 5 | 4 | 4 |
| Louisiana (LA) | 3 | 2 | 2 |
| Maine (ME) | 6 | 5 | 4 |
| Marshall Islands (MH) | 2 | 1 | 1 |
| Maryland (MD) | 8 | 7 | 5 |
| Massachusetts (MA) | 6 | 5 | 4 |
| Mexico (MX) | 2 | 1 | 1 |
| Michigan (MI) | 4 | 3 | 3 |
| Minnesota (MN) | 6 | 5 | 4 |
| Mississippi | 3 | 2 | 2 |
| Missouri (MO) | 4 | 3 | 3 |
| Montana (MT) | 4 | 3 | 3 |
| Nebraska (NE) | 5 | 4 | 3 |
| Nevada (NV) | 2 | 1 | 1 |
| New Hampshire (NH) | 5 | 4 | 1 |
| New Jersey (NJ) | 9 | 8 | 4 |
| New Mexico (NM) | 3 | 2 | 2 |
| New York (NY) | 9 | 8 | 6 |
| North Carolina (NC) | 5 | 4 | 4 |
| North Dakota (ND) | 2% | 1% | 1% |
| Northern Mariana Islands (MP) | 2 | 1 | 1 |
| Ohio (OH) | 5 | 4 | 3 |
| Oklahoma (OK) | 3 | 2 | 2 |
| Oregon (OR) | 7 | 6 | 5 |
| Palau (PW) | 2 | 1 | 1 |
| Pennsylvania (PA) | 5 | 4 | 3 |
| Puerto Rico (PR) | 2 | 1 | 1 |
| Rhode Island (RI) | 7 | 6 | 3 |
| South Carolina (SC) | 4 | 3 | 3 |
| South Dakota (SD) | 2 | 1 | 1 |
| Tennessee (TN) | 2 | 1 | 1 |
| Texas (TX) | 3 | 2 | 1 |
| Utah (UT) | 5 | 4 | 3 |
| Vermont (VT) | 6 | 5 | 3 |
| Virgin Islands (VI) | 2 | 1 | 1 |
| Virginia (VA) | 6 | 5 | 4 |
| Washington (WA) | 3 | 2 | 1 |
| West Virginia (WV) | 3 | 2 | 2 |
| Wisconsin (WI) | 7 | 6 | 4 |
| Wyoming (WY) | 1 | 0 | 1 |
| Not Reported (NR) | 2 | 1 | 1 |

**TABLE 8:** Federal EFC Allowances for FICA and Employment

FICA: WAGES

| | |
|---|---|
| $1 to $118,500 | 7.65% of income earned by each wage earner (maximum $9,065.25 per person) |
| $118,501 or more | $9,065.25 + 1.45% of income earned above $118,500 by each wage earner |

| | |
|---|---|
| EMPLOYMENT ALLOWANCE | 35% of lesser earned income to a maximum $4,000 (single parent: 35% of earned income to a maximum of $4,000) |

**TABLE 9:** Federal EFC Income Protection Allowance for Parents

| Family Size (including student) | Number in College | | | | |
|---|---|---|---|---|---|
| | 1 | 2 | 3 | 4 | 5 |
| 2 | $ 17,840 | $ 14,790 | | | |
| 3 | 22,220 | 19,180 | $ 16,130 | | |
| 4 | 27,440 | 24,390 | 21,350 | $ 18,300 | |
| 5 | 32,380 | 29,320 | 26,290 | 23,240 | $ 20,200 |
| 6 | 37,870 | 34,820 | 31,780 | 28,730 | 25,690 |

For each additional family member, add $4,270.
For each additional college student, subtract $3,040.

**TABLE 10:** Federal EFC Adjusted Net Worth of a Business or Farm

| NET WORTH | ADJUSTED NET WORTH | | |
|---|---|---|---|
| Less than $1 | $ | 0 | |
| $1 to 125,000 | $ | 0 | + 40% of net worth |
| $125,001 to 380,000 | $ | 50,000 | + 50% of net worth over $125,000 |
| $380,001 to 635,000 | $ | 177,500 | + 60% of net worth over $380,000 |
| $635,001 or more | $ | 330,500 | + 100% of net worth over $635,000 |

**TABLE 11:** Federal EFC Education Savings and Asset Protection Allowance for Parents

| AGE OF OLDER PARENT OR STUDENT | COUPLE/ MARRIED | UNMARRIED/ SINGLE |
|---|---|---|
| 25 or under | $ 0 | $ 0 |
| 26 | 1,000 | 500 |
| 27 | 2,100 | 1,100 |
| 28 | 3,100 | 1,600 |
| 29 | 4,100 | 2,100 |
| 30 | 5,200 | 2,600 |
| 31 | 6,200 | 3,200 |
| 32 | 7,200 | 3,700 |
| 33 | 8,300 | 4,200 |
| 34 | 9,300 | 4,700 |
| 35 | 10,300 | 5,300 |
| 36 | 11,400 | 5,800 |
| 37 | 12,400 | 6,300 |
| 38 | 13,400 | 6,800 |
| 39 | 14,500 | 7,400 |
| 40 | 15,500 | 7,900 |
| 41 | 15,900 | 8,100 |
| 42 | 16,300 | 8,300 |
| 43 | 16,600 | 8,500 |
| 44 | 17,000 | 8,600 |
| 45 | 17,400 | 8,800 |
| 46 | 17,800 | 9,000 |
| 47 | 18,300 | 9,200 |
| 48 | 18,700 | 9,400 |
| 49 | 19,200 | 9,700 |
| 50 | 19,700 | 9,900 |
| 51 | 20,200 | 10,100 |
| 52 | 20,700 | 10,400 |
| 53 | 21,300 | 10,600 |
| 54 | 21,800 | 10,900 |
| 55 | 22,400 | 11,100 |
| 56 | 23,000 | 11,400 |
| 57 | 23,700 | 11,700 |
| 58 | 24,300 | 12,000 |
| 59 | 25,000 | 12,300 |
| 60 | 25,700 | 12,600 |
| 61 | 26,400 | 12,900 |
| 62 | 27,200 | 13,200 |
| 63 | 27,900 | 13,600 |
| 64 | 28,800 | 13,900 |
| 65 or over | 29,600 | 14,300 |

**TABLE 12:** Federal EFC Parents' Contribution from Adjusted Available Income (AAI)

| ADJUSTED AVAILABLE INCOME (AAI) | TOTAL CONTRIBUTIONS FROM INCOME | |
|---|---|---|
| Less than $ -3,409 (3,409) | $ | -750 |
| $(3,409) to 15,900 | | 22% of AI |
| $ 15,901 to 20,000 | $ 3,498 | + 25% of AAI over $ 15,900 |
| $ 20,001 to 24,100 | $ 4,523 | + 29% of AAI over $ 20,000 |
| $ 24,101 to 28,200 | $ 5,712 | + 34% of AAI over $ 24,100 |
| $ 28,201 to 32,200 | $ 7,106 | + 40% of AAI over $ 28,200 |
| $ 32,201 or more | $ 8,706 | + 47% of AAI over $ 32,200 |

# Contact Information for State Aid Programs

**ALABAMA**
Alabama Commission on
Higher Education
P.O. Box 302000
Montgomery, AL 36130-2000
334-242-1998
www.ache.state.al.us

**ALASKA**
Alaska Commission on Postsecondary Education
P.O. Box 110505
Juneau, AK 99811-0505
800-441-2962
www.acpe.alaska.gov/

**ARIZONA**
Arizona Department of Education
1535 West Jefferson Street
Phoenix, AZ 85007
800-352-4558
www.azed.gov/

**ARKANSAS**
Arkansas Department of Higher Education
423 Main Street, Suite 400
Little Rock, AR 72201
501-371-2000
www.adhe.edu

**CALIFORNIA**
California Student Aid Commission
P.O. Box 419026
Rancho Cordova, CA 95741-9026
888-224-7268
www.csac.ca.gov

**COLORADO**
Colorado Department of Education
201 East Colfax Avenue
Denver, CO 80203
303-866-6600
www.cde.state.co.us

**CONNECTICUT**
Connecticut Office of Higher Education
61 Woodland Street
Hartford, CT 06105-2326
860-947-1800
www.ctohe.org

**DELAWARE**
Delaware Higher Education Office
John G. Townsend Building
401 Federal Street, Suite 2
Dover, DE 19901
302-735-4000
www.doe.k12.de.us/dheo

**DISTRICT OF COLUMBIA**
Office of the State Superintendent
of Education
810 First Street, NE, 9th Floor
Washington, DC 20002
202-727-6436
www.seo.dc.gov

**FLORIDA**
Florida Department of Education
Office of Student Financial Assistance
325 W. Gaines Street, Suite 1314
Tallahassee, FL 32399-0400
888-827-2004
www.floridastudentfinancialaid.org

**GEORGIA**
Georgia Student Finance Commission
2082 East Exchange Place
Tucker, GA 30084
800-505-4732
www.gsfc.org

**GUAM**
University of Guam
Student Financial Aid Office
UOG Station
Mangilao, GU 96923
671-735-2288
www.uog.edu

**HAWAII**
Hawaii State Department
of Education
1390 Miller Street
Honolulu, HI 96813
808-586-3230
www.hawaiipublicschools.org

**IDAHO**
Idaho State Department of Education
650 West State Street
P.O. Box 83720
Boise, ID 83720-0027
800-432-4601
www.sde.idaho.gov

**ILLINOIS**
Illinois Student Assistance Commission
1755 Lake Cook Road
Deerfield, IL 60015-5209
800-899-4722
www.isac.org

**INDIANA**
State Student Assistance Commission of Indiana
101 West Ohio Street, Suite 300
Indianapolis, IN 46204
888-528-4719
www.in.gov/ssaci

**IOWA**
Iowa College Student
Aid Commission
430 East Grand Avenue, FL 3
Des Moines, IA 50309
877-272-4456
www.iowacollegeaid.gov

**KANSAS**
Kansas Board of Regents
1000 SW Jackson Street, Suite 520
Topeka, KS 66612-1368
785-296-3421
www.kansasregents.org

**KENTUCKY**
KHEAA Student Aid Branch
100 Airport Road
Frankfort, KY 40602
800-928-8926
www.kheaa.com

**LOUISIANA**
Louisiana Office of Student
Financial Assistance
P.O. Box 91202
Baton Rouge, LA 70821-9202
800-259-5626
www.osfa.la.gov

**MAINE**
Finance Authority of Maine
Education Assistance Division
P.O. Box 949
5 Community Drive
Augusta, ME 04332-0949
800-228-3734
www.famemaine.com

**MARYLAND**
Maryland Higher Education Commission
Office of Student Financial Assistance
6 N. Liberty St.
Baltimore, MD 21201
800-974-0203
www.mhec.state.md.us

**MASSACHUSETTS**
Massachusetts Department of Higher Education
Office of Student Financial Assistance
454 Broadway, Suite 200
Revere, MA 02151
617-391-6070
www.osfa.mass.edu

**MICHIGAN**
Michigan Higher Education Assistance Authority
Office of Scholarships and Grants
P.O. Box 30462
Lansing, MI 48909-7962
888-447-2687
www.michigan.gov/mistudentaid

**MINNESOTA**
Minnesota Office of Higher Education
1450 Energy Park Drive, Suite 350
St. Paul, MN 55108-5227
800-657-3866
www.ohe.state.mn.us

**MISSISSIPPI**
Mississippi Office of Student Financial Aid
3825 Ridgewood Road
Jackson, MS 39211-6453
800-327-2980
www.mississippi.edu/riseupms/

**MISSOURI**
Missouri Department of
Higher Education
205 Jefferson Street
P.O. Box 1469
Jefferson City, MO 65102-1469
800-473-6757
www.dhe.mo.gov

**MONTANA**
Montana Board of Regents
P.O. Box 203201
2500 Broadway Street
Helena, MT 59620-3201
406-444-6570
http://mus.edu/board/

**NEBRASKA**
Coordinating Commission for Postsecondary Education
P.O. Box 95005
Lincoln, NE 68509-5005
402-471-2847
www.ccpe.nebraska.gov

**NEVADA**
Nevada Department of Education
700 East Fifth Street
Carson City, NV 89701
775-687-9220
www.doe.nv.gov

**NEW HAMPSHIRE**
New Hampshire Postsecondary Education Commission
101 Pleasant Street
Concord, NH 03301-3860
603-271-3494
www.education.nh.gov/highered/

**NEW JERSEY**
HESAA Grants & Scholarships
P.O. Box 540
Trenton, NJ 08625-0540
800-792-8670
www.hesaa.org

**NEW MEXICO**
New Mexico Higher Education Department
2044 Galisteo Street
Santa Fe, NM 87505
505-476-8400
www.hed.state.nm.us

**NEW YORK**
New York State Higher Education Services Corporation
99 Washington Avenue
Albany, NY 12255
888-697-4372
www.hesc.ny.gov

**NORTH CAROLINA**
North Carolina State Education Assistance Authority
P.O. Box 14103
Research Triangle Park, NC 27709
919-549-8614
www.ncseaa.edu

**NORTH DAKOTA**
North Dakota University System
10th Floor, State Capitol
600 East Boulevard Ave, Dept. 215
Bismarck, ND 58505-0230
701-328-2960
www.ndus.edu

**OHIO**
Ohio Board of Regents
25 South Front Street
Columbus, OH 43215
614-466-6000
www.ohiohighered.org/

**OKLAHOMA**
Oklahoma State Regents for
Higher Education
Tuition Aid Grant Program
655 Research Parkway, Suite 200
Oklahoma City, OK 73104
405-225-9100
www.okhighered.org

**OREGON**
Oregon Student Assistance Commission
1500 Valley River Drive, Suite 100
Eugene, OR 97401
800-452-8807
www.oregonstudentaid.gov

**PENNSYLVANIA**
Pennsylvania Higher Education Assistance Agency
P.O. Box 8157
Harrisburg, PA 17105-8157
800-692-7392
www.pheaa.org

**PUERTO RICO**
Departmento de Educacion
P.O. Box 190759
San Juan, PR 00919-0759
787-759-2000
www.de.gobierno.pr

**RHODE ISLAND**
Rhode Island Higher Education Assistance Authority
560 Jefferson Boulevard, Suite 100
Warwick, RI 02886-1304
800-922-9855
www.riheaa.org

**SOUTH CAROLINA**
South Carolina Commission on Higher Education
1122 Lady Street, Suite 300
Columbia, SC 29201
803-737-2260
www.che.sc.gov

**SOUTH DAKOTA**
South Dakota Department
of Education
Office of Finance and Management
800 Governors Drive
Pierre, SD 57501
605-773-3134
www.doe.sd.gov/

**TENNESSEE**
Tennessee Student Assistance Corporation
404 James Robertson Parkway,
Suite 1510, Parkway Towers
Nashville, TN 37243-0820
800-342-1663
www.tn.gov.collegepays

**TEXAS**
Texas Higher Education Coordinating Board
Student Loan Programs
P.O. Box 12788-2788
Austin, TX 78711
800-242-3062
www.hhloans.com

**UTAH**
Utah Higher Education
Assistance Authority
P.O. Box 145110
Salt Lake City, UT 84114-5110
877-336-7378
www.uheaa.org

**VERMONT**
Vermont Student Assistance Corporation
P.O. Box 2000
Winooski, VT 05404
800-642-3177
www.vsac.org

**VIRGIN ISLANDS**
Financial Aid Office, Virgin Islands Board of Education
P.O. Box 11900
St. Thomas, VI 00801
340-774-4546
www.myviboe.com

**VIRGINIA**
State Council of Higher Education
for Virginia
James Monroe Building
101 North 14th Street, 10th Fl.
Richmond, VA 23219
804-225-2600
www.schev.edu

**WASHINGTON**
Washington Student Achievement Council
917 Lakeridge Way SW
Olympia, WA 98502
(360) 753-7800
www.wsac.wa.gov

**WEST VIRGINIA**
West Virginia Higher Education Policy Commission
1018 Kanawha Boulevard East, Suite 700
Charleston, WV 25301
304-558-2101
www.wvhepc.com

**WISCONSIN**
Wisconsin Higher Educational
Aids Board
P. O. Box 7885
Madison, WI 53707-7885
608-267-2206
www.heab.state.wi.us

**WYOMING**
Wyoming Department of Education
2300 Capitol Avenue
Hathaway Building, Second Floor
Cheyenne, WY 82002-2060
307-777-7675
www.k12.wy.us

# Part III

Financial Aid College
by College

# Alabama

## Alabama Agricultural and Mechanical University

Huntsville, Alabama
www.aamu.edu                    Federal Code: 001002

**4-year public** university and agricultural college in large city.
**Enrollment:** 4,055 undergrads.

**BASIC COSTS (2015-2016)**
**Tuition and fees:** $9,214; out-of-state residents $16,984.
**Per-credit charge:** $259; out-of-state residents $518.
**Room and board:** $6,340.
**Additional info:** Health Insurance for domestic students: $152; Health Insurance for international students: $1,632. Tuition/fee waivers available for minority students.

**FINANCIAL AID PICTURE**
**Students with need:** Need-based aid available for full-time and part-time students. Work study available weekends and for part-time students.
**Students without need:** No-need awards available for athletics, minority status.
**Scholarships offered:** Presidential Scholarship: full tuition, course fees, room and board, $1,000 for books and supplies per semester; for students with 3.5 GPA or higher. Provost Scholarship: full tuition, course fees, room and board, $800 for books and supplies per semester; for students with 3.4 GPA or higher. Dean's Scholarship: full tuition, course fees, room and board, $500 for books and supplies per semester; for students with 3.3 GPA or higher.

**FINANCIAL AID PROCEDURES**
**Forms required:** FAFSA, institutional form.
**Dates and Deadlines:** Closing date 3/1. Applicants notified on a rolling basis starting 4/15; must reply within 2 week(s) of notification.

**CONTACT**
Darryl Jackson, Director of Student Financial Aid
Box 908, Normal, AL 35762
(256) 372-5400

## Alabama State University

Montgomery, Alabama
www.alasu.edu                    Federal Code: 001005

**4-year public** university in small city.
**Enrollment:** 4,740 undergrads, 8% part-time. 1,006 full-time freshmen.
**Selectivity:** Admits less than 50% of applicants.

**BASIC COSTS (2015-2016)**
**Tuition and fees:** $8,720; out-of-state residents $15,656.
**Per-credit charge:** $289; out-of-state residents $578.
**Room and board:** $5,422.

**FINANCIAL AID PICTURE (2015-2016)**
**Students with need:** Out of 797 full-time freshmen who applied for aid, 796 were judged to have need. Of these, 753 received aid, and 239 had their full need met. Average financial aid package met 77% of need; average scholarship/grant was $5,621; average loan was $3,482. For part-time students, average financial aid package was $10,067.
**Students without need:** 16 full-time freshmen who did not demonstrate need for aid received scholarships/grants; average award was $6,320. No-need awards available for academics, alumni affiliation, art, athletics, job skills, leadership, minority status, music/drama, religious affiliation, ROTC.

**Scholarships offered:** 35 full-time freshmen received athletic scholarships; average amount $11,295.

**FINANCIAL AID PROCEDURES**
**Forms required:** FAFSA.
**Dates and Deadlines:** Priority date 4/1; no closing date. Applicants notified on a rolling basis starting 5/1.
**Transfers:** Applicants notified on a rolling basis starting 5/1.

**CONTACT**
Marcus Byrd, Director of Financial Aid
PO Box 271, Montgomery, AL 36101-0271
(334) 229-4323

## Amridge University

Montgomery, Alabama
www.amridgeuniversity.edu        Federal Code: 016885

**4-year private** virtual university in small city, affiliated with Church of Christ.
**Enrollment:** 308 undergrads, 46% part-time. 4 full-time freshmen.
**Selectivity:** Open admission; but selective for some programs.

**BASIC COSTS (2015-2016)**
**Tuition and fees:** $6,900.
**Per-credit charge:** $250.

**FINANCIAL AID PICTURE (2015-2016)**
**Students with need:** Out of 4 full-time freshmen who applied for aid, 3 were judged to have need. Of these, 3 received aid, and 3 had their full need met. Average financial aid package met 100% of need; average scholarship/grant was $4,120; average loan was $3,120. For part-time students, average financial aid package was $4,350.
**Students without need:** No-need awards available for academics, leadership, religious affiliation.

**FINANCIAL AID PROCEDURES**
**Forms required:** FAFSA, institutional form.
**Dates and Deadlines:** Applicants notified on a rolling basis.
**Transfers:** No deadline. Applicants notified on a rolling basis.

**CONTACT**
Starr Fain, Financial Aid Director
1200 Taylor Road, Montgomery, AL 36117-3553
(800) 351-4040 ext. 7523

## Athens State University

Athens, Alabama
www.athens.edu                   Federal Code: 001008

**Upper-division public** liberal arts and teachers college in large town.
**Enrollment:** 2,904 undergrads, 58% part-time.

**BASIC COSTS (2015-2016)**
**Tuition and fees:** $6,270; out-of-state residents $11,790.

**FINANCIAL AID PICTURE (2014-2015)**
**Students with need:** Average financial aid package for all full-time undergraduates was $10,057; for part-time $8,293. 45% awarded as scholarships/grants, 55% awarded as loans/jobs. Work study available nights, weekends, and for part-time students.
**Students without need:** No-need awards available for academics, alumni affiliation, art, athletics, leadership, minority status.

**FINANCIAL AID PROCEDURES**
**Forms required:** FAFSA.
**Dates and Deadlines:** Applicants notified on a rolling basis starting 6/1; must reply within 3 week(s) of notification.

**CONTACT**
Mary Chambliss, Director, Student Financial Services
300 North Beaty Street, Athens, AL 35611
(256) 233-8170

## Auburn University
Auburn, Alabama
www.auburn.edu                    Federal Code: 001009

**4-year public** university in small city.
**Enrollment:** 21,551 undergrads, 9% part-time. 4,592 full-time freshmen.
**Selectivity:** Admits over 75% of applicants.

**BASIC COSTS (2015-2016)**
**Tuition and fees:** $10,424; out-of-state residents $28,040.
**Per-credit charge:** $367; out-of-state residents $1,101.
**Room and board:** $12,584.

**FINANCIAL AID PICTURE (2014-2015)**
**Students with need:** Out of 2,887 full-time freshmen who applied for aid, 1,790 were judged to have need. Of these, 1,790 received aid, and 334 had their full need met. Average financial aid package met 50% of need; average scholarship/grant was $8,635; average loan was $3,863. For part-time students, average financial aid package was $5,778.
**Students without need:** 1,253 full-time freshmen who did not demonstrate need for aid received scholarships/grants; average award was $7,358.
**Scholarships offered: Merit:** Freshmen and General Scholarships; up to full-tuition; require 28 ACT/1240 SAT and 3.25 GPA. National Merit and National Achievement Finalists; full-tuition plus additional benefits. **Athletic:** 85 full-time freshmen received athletic scholarships; average amount $30,561.
**Additional info:** State of Alabama has pre-paid college tuition plan for residents.

**FINANCIAL AID PROCEDURES**
**Forms required:** FAFSA.
**Dates and Deadlines:** Priority date 3/1; no closing date. Applicants notified on a rolling basis starting 10/2.
**Transfers:** No deadline. Applicants notified on a rolling basis; must reply within 2 week(s) of notification.

**CONTACT**
Mike Reynolds, Director, Student Financial Services
Quad Center, Auburn, AL 36849-5111
(334) 844-4080

## Auburn University at Montgomery
Montgomery, Alabama
www.aum.edu                      Federal Code: 008310

**4-year public** university in small city.
**Enrollment:** 4,142 undergrads, 26% part-time. 568 full-time freshmen.
**Selectivity:** Admits over 75% of applicants. GED not accepted.

**BASIC COSTS (2015-2016)**
**Tuition and fees:** $9,350; out-of-state residents $20,210.
**Per-credit charge:** $290; out-of-state residents $652.
**Room and board:** $5,520.

**FINANCIAL AID PICTURE (2015-2016)**
**Students with need:** Out of 450 full-time freshmen who applied for aid, 395 were judged to have need. Of these, 395 received aid, and 48 had their full need met. For part-time students, average financial aid package was $5,875.
**Students without need:** 59 full-time freshmen who did not demonstrate need for aid received scholarships/grants; average award was $4,626.

**Scholarships offered:** Achievement Scholarship, AUM Freshman Leadership Scholarship, Deichelmann Memorial Scholarship, Freshman Housing Scholarship, Recognition Scholarship, Warhawk Scholarship.

**FINANCIAL AID PROCEDURES**
**Forms required:** FAFSA.
**Dates and Deadlines:** Priority date 3/1; no closing date. Applicants notified on a rolling basis starting 4/15.

**CONTACT**
Anthony Richey, Director of Financial Aid
PO Box 244023, Montgomery, AL 36124-4023
(334) 244-3571

## Bevill State Community College
Jasper, Alabama
www.bscc.edu                     Federal Code: 005733

**2-year public** community college in small town.
**Enrollment:** 3,210 undergrads, 43% part-time. 760 full-time freshmen.
**Selectivity:** Open admission; but selective for some programs.

**BASIC COSTS (2015-2016)**
**Tuition and fees:** $4,678; out-of-state residents $8,358.
**Per-credit charge:** $115; out-of-state residents $230.
**Room and board:** $1,850.
**Additional info:** Tuition/fee waivers available for unemployed or children of unemployed.

**FINANCIAL AID PICTURE**
**Students with need:** Need-based aid available for full-time and part-time students.
**Students without need:** No-need awards available for academics, leadership, music/drama.

**FINANCIAL AID PROCEDURES**
**Forms required:** FAFSA.
**Dates and Deadlines:** Priority date 5/1; no closing date. Applicants notified on a rolling basis starting 7/1.

**CONTACT**
Melissa Stowe, Assistan Dean for Admissions, Financial Aid, & Student Records
1411 Indiana Avenue, Jasper, AL 35501
(205) 387-0511 ext. 5814

## Birmingham-Southern College
Birmingham, Alabama
www.bsc.edu                      Federal Code: 001012

**4-year private** liberal arts college in very large city, affiliated with United Methodist Church.
**Enrollment:** 1,346 undergrads, 1% part-time. 441 full-time freshmen.
**Selectivity:** Admits 50 to 75% of applicants.

**BASIC COSTS (2015-2016)**
**Tuition and fees:** $33,128.
**Room and board:** $11,440.

**FINANCIAL AID PICTURE (2015-2016)**
**Students with need:** Out of 347 full-time freshmen who applied for aid, 288 were judged to have need. Of these, 288 received aid, and 107 had their full need met. Average financial aid package met 74% of need; average scholarship/grant was $5,538; average loan was $4,348. Need-based aid available for part-time students.

**Students without need:** 153 full-time freshmen who did not demonstrate need for aid received scholarships/grants; average award was $21,955. No-need awards available for academics, alumni affiliation, art, leadership, music/drama, religious affiliation, ROTC, state/district residency.

**Scholarships offered:** Neal and Anne Berte Scholarship: full tuition; based on academic achievement; 1 awarded. Blount-Monaghan/Vulcan Materials Company Scholarship: full tuition; based on academic achievement; 1 awarded. William Jones and Elizabeth Perry Rushton Scholarship: full tuition, room and board, fees, books, $2,000 travel stipend; based on academic achievement; 1 awarded. Phi Beta Kappa: full tuition; based on academic achievement. United Methodist Scholarship: $1,000-$2,500; awarded to United Methodist with recommendation from senior United Methodist Minister.

**Additional info:** Auditions required for music, theatre, dance applicants seeking scholarships. Portfolios required for art applicants seeking scholarships, and essays recommended for all applicants seeking scholarships.

**FINANCIAL AID PROCEDURES**
**Forms required:** FAFSA, state aid form.
**Dates and Deadlines:** Priority date 3/1; no closing date. Applicants notified on a rolling basis starting 3/1; must reply by 5/1.
**Transfers:** No deadline. Applicants notified on a rolling basis starting 3/1; must reply within 2 week(s) of notification.

**CONTACT**
Brian Quisenberry, Director of Financial Aid Services
900 Arkadelphia Road, Birmingham, AL 35254
(205) 226-4688

# Central Alabama Community College
Alexander City, Alabama
www.cacc.edu          Federal Code: 001007

**2-year public** community college in large town.
**Enrollment:** 1,594 undergrads, 40% part-time. 391 full-time freshmen.
**Selectivity:** Open admission; but selective for some programs.

**BASIC COSTS (2015-2016)**
**Tuition and fees:** $4,320; out-of-state residents $7,770.
**Per-credit charge:** $115; out-of-state residents $230.

**FINANCIAL AID PICTURE (2014-2015)**
**Students with need:** 70% of average financial aid package awarded as scholarships/grants, 30% awarded as loans/jobs. Need-based aid available for part-time students. Work study available nights.
**Students without need:** No-need awards available for academics, athletics, music/drama, state/district residency.

**FINANCIAL AID PROCEDURES**
**Forms required:** FAFSA.
**Dates and Deadlines:** Priority date 7/15; no closing date. Applicants notified on a rolling basis.

**CONTACT**
Cindy Entrekin, Director of Financial Aid
1675 Cherokee Road, Alexander City, AL 35010
(256) 215-4251

# Chattahoochee Valley Community College
Phenix City, Alabama
www.cv.edu          Federal Code: 012182

**2-year public** community college in small city.
**Enrollment:** 1,806 undergrads.

**Selectivity:** Open admission; but selective for some programs.

**BASIC COSTS (2015-2016)**
**Tuition and fees:** $4,380; out-of-state residents $7,830.
**Per-credit charge:** $115; out-of-state residents $230.

**FINANCIAL AID PICTURE**
**Students with need:** Need-based aid available for full-time and part-time students. Work study available nights, weekends, and for part-time students.
**Students without need:** No-need awards available for academics, art, athletics, leadership, music/drama.

**FINANCIAL AID PROCEDURES**
**Forms required:** FAFSA.
**Dates and Deadlines:** Priority date 7/1; no closing date. Applicants notified on a rolling basis; must reply within 1 week(s) of notification.

**CONTACT**
Joan Waters, Director of Financial Aid
2602 College Drive, Phenix City, AL 36869
(334) 291-4915

# Columbia Southern University
Orange Beach, Alabama
www.columbiasouthern.edu          Federal Code: 041215

**4-year for-profit** virtual university in small town.
**Enrollment:** 24,282 undergrads, 49% part-time. 797 full-time freshmen.
**Selectivity:** Open admission.

**BASIC COSTS (2016-2017)**
**Tuition and fees:** $6,335.
**Per-credit charge:** $210.

**FINANCIAL AID PICTURE**
**Students with need:** Need-based aid available for full-time and part-time students.

**FINANCIAL AID PROCEDURES**
**Forms required:** FAFSA, institutional form.
**Dates and Deadlines:** Applicants notified on a rolling basis.
**Transfers:** No deadline. Applicants notified on a rolling basis.

**CONTACT**
Pat Troup, VP Business Affairs
21982 University Lane, Orange Beach, AL 36561
(251) 981-3771 ext. 1226

# Concordia College
Selma, Alabama
www.ccal.edu          Federal Code: 010554

**4-year private** liberal arts college in large town, affiliated with Lutheran Church - Missouri Synod.
**Enrollment:** 610 undergrads.
**Selectivity:** Open admission.

**BASIC COSTS (2015-2016)**
**Tuition and fees:** $10,120.
**Room and board:** $5,600.
**Additional info:** Tuition/fee waivers available for adults.

**FINANCIAL AID PICTURE**
**Students with need:** Need-based aid available for full-time and part-time students.
**Students without need:** This college awards aid only to students with need.

**FINANCIAL AID PROCEDURES**

**Forms required:** FAFSA, state aid form, institutional form.

**Dates and Deadlines:** Priority date 4/1; closing date 4/15. Applicants notified on a rolling basis starting 6/15; must reply within 2 week(s) of notification.

**CONTACT**

Tharsteen Bridges, Financial Aid Administrator

1712 Broad Street, Selma, AL 36701

(334) 847-5700 ext. 160

## Enterprise State Community College
Enterprise, Alabama
www.escc.edu                    Federal Code: 001015

**2-year public** community college in large town.

**Enrollment:** 1,529 undergrads, 41% part-time. 293 full-time freshmen.

**Selectivity:** Open admission.

**BASIC COSTS (2015-2016)**

**Tuition and fees:** $4,320; out-of-state residents $7,770.

**Per-credit charge:** $115; out-of-state residents $230.

**FINANCIAL AID PICTURE (2014-2015)**

**Students with need:** 77% of average financial aid package awarded as scholarships/grants, 23% awarded as loans/jobs.

**Students without need:** No-need awards available for academics, art, athletics, leadership, music/drama, state/district residency.

**FINANCIAL AID PROCEDURES**

**Forms required:** FAFSA.

**Dates and Deadlines:** Priority date 6/15; no closing date. Applicants notified on a rolling basis starting 6/1; must reply within 2 week(s) of notification.

**Transfers:** Applicants notified on a rolling basis starting 6/1; must reply within 2 week(s) of notification.

**CONTACT**

Henry Quisenberry, Director of Financial Aid

Box 1300, Enterprise, AL 36331

(334) 347-2623 ext. 2214

## Faulkner State Community College
Bay Minette, Alabama
www.faulknerstate.edu           Federal Code: 001060

**2-year public** community college in large town.

**Enrollment:** 4,372 undergrads, 41% part-time. 1,078 full-time freshmen.

**Selectivity:** Open admission; but selective for some programs.

**BASIC COSTS (2015-2016)**

**Tuition and fees:** $4,320; out-of-state residents $7,770.

**Per-credit charge:** $115; out-of-state residents $230.

**Room and board:** $5,800.

**FINANCIAL AID PICTURE (2014-2015)**

**Students with need:** 53% of average financial aid package awarded as scholarships/grants, 47% awarded as loans/jobs. Work study available nights.

**Students without need:** No-need awards available for academics, art, athletics, leadership, music/drama.

**FINANCIAL AID PROCEDURES**

**Forms required:** FAFSA, institutional form.

**Dates and Deadlines:** Priority date 7/1; no closing date. Applicants notified on a rolling basis starting 7/1; must reply within 2 week(s) of notification.

**CONTACT**

James Theeuwes, Director of Financial Aid

1900 Highway 31 South, Bay Minette, AL 36507

(251) 580-2151

## Faulkner University
Montgomery, Alabama
www.faulkner.edu                Federal Code: 001003

**4-year private** university and liberal arts college in large city, affiliated with Church of Christ.

**Enrollment:** 2,282 undergrads, 22% part-time. 381 full-time freshmen.

**Selectivity:** Admits 50 to 75% of applicants.

**BASIC COSTS (2015-2016)**

**Tuition and fees:** $19,280.

**Per-credit charge:** $590.

**Room and board:** $7,130.

**Additional info:** Required fee includes additional cost per semester for iPad and required software. After 4 semesters and bachelor degree completion, students own the iPad. Tuition/fee waivers available for adults, minority students, unemployed or children of unemployed.

**FINANCIAL AID PICTURE (2014-2015)**

**Students with need:** Out of 348 full-time freshmen who applied for aid, 331 were judged to have need. Of these, 331 received aid, and 25 had their full need met. Average financial aid package met 61% of need; average scholarship/grant was $11,419; average loan was $3,002. For part-time students, average financial aid package was $6,582.

**Students without need:** 21 full-time freshmen who did not demonstrate need for aid received scholarships/grants; average award was $5,339. No-need awards available for academics, alumni affiliation, athletics, music/drama, religious affiliation, state/district residency.

**Scholarships offered:** 37 full-time freshmen received athletic scholarships; average amount $5,454.

**FINANCIAL AID PROCEDURES**

**Forms required:** FAFSA, state aid form, institutional form.

**Dates and Deadlines:** Priority date 3/15; closing date 8/1. Applicants notified on a rolling basis starting 5/1; must reply within 3 week(s) of notification.

**Transfers:** No deadline. Applicants notified on a rolling basis; must reply within 3 week(s) of notification.

**CONTACT**

William Jackson, Director of Financial Aid

5345 Atlanta Highway, Montgomery, AL 36109-3398

(334) 386-7195

## Gadsden State Community College
Gadsden, Alabama
www.gadsdenstate.edu            Federal Code: 001017

**2-year public** community and technical college in small city.

**Enrollment:** 4,613 undergrads.

**Selectivity:** Open admission; but selective for some programs.

**BASIC COSTS (2015-2016)**

**Tuition and fees:** $4,020; out-of-state residents $7,470.

**Per-credit charge:** $115; out-of-state residents $230.

**Room and board:** $3,600.

**Additional info:** Tuition/fee waivers available for minority students, unemployed or children of unemployed.

**FINANCIAL AID PICTURE**

**Students with need:** Need-based aid available for full-time and part-time students.

**Students without need:** No-need awards available for academics, alumni affiliation, art, athletics, job skills, leadership, minority status, music/drama, state/district residency.

**FINANCIAL AID PROCEDURES**

**Forms required:** FAFSA, institutional form.

**Dates and Deadlines:** Priority date 4/15; no closing date. Applicants notified on a rolling basis starting 6/10.

**CONTACT**
Jacqueline Clark, Director of Financial Services
1001 George Wallace Drive, Gadsden, AL 35902-0227
(256) 549-8267

## George C. Wallace Community College at Dothan
Dothan, Alabama
www.wallace.edu                    Federal Code: 001018

**2-year public** community college in small city.
**Enrollment:** 4,173 undergrads, 49% part-time. 747 full-time freshmen.
**Selectivity:** Admits over 75% of applicants.

**BASIC COSTS (2015-2016)**
**Tuition and fees:** $4,260; out-of-state residents $7,710.
**Per-credit charge:** $115; out-of-state residents $230.

**FINANCIAL AID PICTURE (2014-2015)**
**Students with need:** 99% of average financial aid package awarded as scholarships/grants, 1% awarded as loans/jobs.
**Students without need:** No-need awards available for academics, athletics, leadership.

**FINANCIAL AID PROCEDURES**
**Forms required:** FAFSA.
**Dates and Deadlines:** Priority date 5/1; no closing date. Applicants notified on a rolling basis.

**CONTACT**
Erma Perry, Director of Financial Aid
1141 Wallace Drive, Dothan, AL 36303-0943
(334) 687-3543 ext. 4285

## George C. Wallace State Community College at Selma
Selma, Alabama
www.wccs.edu                    Federal Code: 005699

**2-year public** community and technical college in large town.
**Enrollment:** 1,498 undergrads.
**Selectivity:** Open admission; but selective for some programs.

**BASIC COSTS (2015-2016)**
**Tuition and fees:** $4,020; out-of-state residents $8,040.
**Per-credit charge:** $134; out-of-state residents $268.

**FINANCIAL AID PICTURE (2014-2015)**
**Students with need:** Average financial aid package for all full-time undergraduates was $2,320. 98% awarded as scholarships/grants, 2% awarded as loans/jobs. Need-based aid available for part-time students. Work study available nights.
**Students without need:** This college awards aid only to students with need.

**FINANCIAL AID PROCEDURES**
**Forms required:** FAFSA.
**Dates and Deadlines:** Priority date 8/1; no closing date. Applicants notified on a rolling basis starting 6/15; must reply within 2 week(s) of notification.
**Transfers:** No deadline. Applicants notified on a rolling basis; must reply within 2 week(s) of notification.

**CONTACT**
Anessa Kidd, Director of Financial Aid
PO Box 2530, Selma, AL 36702-2530
(334) 876-9286

## Heritage Christian University
Florence, Alabama
www.hcu.edu                    Federal Code: 015370

**4-year private** virtual Bible college in large town, affiliated with Church of Christ.
**Enrollment:** 60 undergrads.

**BASIC COSTS (2015-2016)**
**Tuition and fees:** $12,030.
**Per-credit charge:** $373.
**Room and board:** $3,840.

**FINANCIAL AID PICTURE**
**Students with need:** Need-based aid available for full-time and part-time students.

**FINANCIAL AID PROCEDURES**
**Forms required:** FAFSA.
**Dates and Deadlines:** Priority date 6/1; no closing date. Applicants notified on a rolling basis starting 6/1; must reply by 7/28 or within 2 week(s) of notification.
**Transfers:** No deadline. Applicants notified on a rolling basis; must reply by 7/28 or within 3 week(s) of notification.

**CONTACT**
Mechelle Thompson, Financial Aid Director
3625 Helton Drive, Florence, AL 35630
(256) 766-6610 ext. 224

## Herzing University: Birmingham
Birmingham, Alabama
www.herzing.edu                    Federal Code: 010193

**4-year for-profit** business and technical college in very large city.
**Enrollment:** 305 undergrads.

**BASIC COSTS (2015-2016)**
**Additional info:** Certificate programs: $13,670 to $26,820. Associate programs: $26,180 to $53,640. Bachelor's programs: $61,515 to $88,065.

**FINANCIAL AID PICTURE**
**Students with need:** Need-based aid available for full-time students.
**Students without need:** This college awards aid only to students with need.

**FINANCIAL AID PROCEDURES**
**Forms required:** FAFSA.

**CONTACT**
Kentray Sims, Director of Financial Services
280 West Valley Avenue, Birmingham, AL 35209
(205) 916-2800

## Huntingdon College
Montgomery, Alabama
www.huntingdon.edu                    Federal Code: 001019

**4-year private** liberal arts college in small city, affiliated with United Methodist Church.

**Enrollment:** 1,160 undergrads, 23% part-time. 252 full-time freshmen.
**Selectivity:** Admits 50 to 75% of applicants.

## BASIC COSTS (2015-2016)
**Tuition and fees:** $25,050.
**Per-credit charge:** $1,000.
**Room and board:** $8,850.
**Additional info:** Tuition at time of enrollment locked for 4 years.

## FINANCIAL AID PICTURE (2015-2016)
**Students with need:** Out of 242 full-time freshmen who applied for aid, 209 were judged to have need. Of these, 209 received aid, and 28 had their full need met. Average financial aid package met 62% of need; average scholarship/grant was $15,320; average loan was $3,264. For part-time students, average financial aid package was $6,654.
**Students without need:** 43 full-time freshmen who did not demonstrate need for aid received scholarships/grants; average award was $10,420. No-need awards available for academics, alumni affiliation, leadership, music/drama, religious affiliation, ROTC, state/district residency.

## FINANCIAL AID PROCEDURES
**Forms required:** FAFSA.
**Dates and Deadlines:** Priority date 3/1; no closing date. Applicants notified on a rolling basis starting 3/1; must reply by 5/1 or within 2 week(s) of notification.
**Transfers:** No deadline. Applicants notified on a rolling basis starting 3/1; must reply by 5/1 or within 2 week(s) of notification. Transfer student should be in good academic standing at previous institution and cannot be in default on any previous student loans. While Academic Transfer scholarships are merit-based according to GPA, need-based aid (i.e. FAFSA) contingent upon eligibility and good-standing within Title IV.

## CONTACT
Belinda Duett, Director of Student Financial Aid
1500 East Fairview Avenue, Montgomery, AL 36106-2148
(334) 833-4428

# Huntsville Bible College
Huntsville, Alabama
www.hbc1.edu                    Federal Code: 038943

**4-year private** Bible college in small city.
**Enrollment:** 74 undergrads.
**Selectivity:** Open admission.

## BASIC COSTS (2015-2016)
**Tuition and fees:** $5,320.
**Per-credit charge:** $175.

## FINANCIAL AID PICTURE
**Students with need:** Need-based aid available for full-time students.
**Students without need:** This college awards aid only to students with need.

## FINANCIAL AID PROCEDURES
**Forms required:** FAFSA.
**Dates and Deadlines:** Priority date 4/1; closing date 6/30. Applicants notified by 8/15; must reply by 9/1.
**Transfers:** Priority date 8/1; closing date 8/15.

## CONTACT
Jacqueline Robinson, Financial Officer
904 Oakwood Avenue, Huntsville, AL 35811-1632
(256) 536-7235

# Jacksonville State University
Jacksonville, Alabama
www.jsu.edu                    Federal Code: 001020

**4-year public** university in small town.
**Enrollment:** 6,625 undergrads, 19% part-time. 1,169 full-time freshmen.
**Selectivity:** Admits 50 to 75% of applicants.

## BASIC COSTS (2015-2016)
**Tuition and fees:** $9,000; out-of-state residents $18,000.
**Per-credit charge:** $300; out-of-state residents $600.
**Room and board:** $7,128.

## FINANCIAL AID PICTURE (2014-2015)
**Students with need:** Out of 1,108 full-time freshmen who applied for aid, 1,083 were judged to have need. Of these, 1,083 received aid. For part-time students, average financial aid package was $7,008.
**Students without need:** No-need awards available for academics, alumni affiliation, art, athletics, leadership, music/drama, ROTC, state/district residency.
**Scholarships offered:** Four-year tuition scholarship: for entering freshmen from Alabama; 28 ACT or 1230 SAT.

## FINANCIAL AID PROCEDURES
**Forms required:** FAFSA, institutional form.
**Dates and Deadlines:** Priority date 3/15; no closing date. Applicants notified on a rolling basis starting 4/16; must reply within 2 week(s) of notification.

## CONTACT
Vickie Adams, Director of Financial Aid
700 Pelham Road North, Jacksonville, AL 36265-1602
(256) 782-5006

# Jefferson Davis Community College
Brewton, Alabama
www.jdcc.edu                    Federal Code: 001021

**2-year public** nursing and community college in small town.
**Enrollment:** 1,033 undergrads, 44% part-time. 258 full-time freshmen.
**Selectivity:** Open admission; but selective for some programs.

## BASIC COSTS (2015-2016)
**Tuition and fees:** $4,020; out-of-state residents $7,470.
**Per-credit charge:** $115; out-of-state residents $230.
**Room only:** $3,000.

## FINANCIAL AID PICTURE
**Students with need:** Need-based aid available for full-time and part-time students. Work study available nights.
**Students without need:** No-need awards available for academics, athletics, leadership.

## FINANCIAL AID PROCEDURES
**Forms required:** FAFSA.
**Dates and Deadlines:** Applicants notified on a rolling basis; must reply within 2 week(s) of notification.
**Transfers:** Must reply within 2 week(s) of notification.

## CONTACT
Vanessa Kyles, Director of Financial Aid
PO Box 958, Brewton, AL 36427
(251) 809-1516

## Jefferson State Community College
Birmingham, Alabama
www.jeffstateonline.com                Federal Code: 001022

**2-year public** community college in large city.
**Enrollment:** 7,381 undergrads.
**Selectivity:** Open admission; but selective for some programs.

**BASIC COSTS (2015-2016)**
**Tuition and fees:** $4,380; out-of-state residents $7,830.
**Per-credit charge:** $115; out-of-state residents $230.

**FINANCIAL AID PICTURE**
**Students with need:** Need-based aid available for full-time and part-time students. Work study available nights.
**Students without need:** No-need awards available for academics, art, leadership, music/drama.
**Additional info:** Any Alabama resident over age 60 may attend classes tuition free, on a space available basis.

**FINANCIAL AID PROCEDURES**
**Forms required:** FAFSA, institutional form.
**Dates and Deadlines:** Closing date 5/1. Applicants notified on a rolling basis starting 6/1.
**Transfers:** Transfer students not eligible for academic scholarships until 12 hours have been completed on campus.

**CONTACT**
Theresa Mays, Financial Aid Director
2601 Carson Road, Birmingham, AL 35215-3098
(205) 856-8509

## Judson College
Marion, Alabama
www.judson.edu                Federal Code: 001023

**4-year private** liberal arts college for women in small town, affiliated with Baptist faith.
**Enrollment:** 373 undergrads.
**Selectivity:** Admits 50 to 75% of applicants.

**BASIC COSTS (2015-2016)**
**Tuition and fees:** $16,850.
**Per-credit charge:** $534.
**Room and board:** $9,686.

**FINANCIAL AID PICTURE**
**Students with need:** Need-based aid available for full-time and part-time students. Work study available nights, weekends, and for part-time students.
**Students without need:** No-need awards available for academics, art, athletics, music/drama, religious affiliation, ROTC, state/district residency.
**Scholarships offered:** Full Tuition Scholarship: given to National Merit Finalists or students with 29 ACT and 3.5 GPA; up to 5 awarded. Honor Scholarships: 1 for full-tuition, 2 for $2,500, 3 for $2,000; awarded based on exam scores. Music scholarships: variable amounts awarded based on audition.

**FINANCIAL AID PROCEDURES**
**Forms required:** FAFSA, state aid form.
**Dates and Deadlines:** Priority date 3/1; no closing date. Applicants notified on a rolling basis starting 3/1; must reply within 2 week(s) of notification.
**Transfers:** No deadline. Applicants notified on a rolling basis starting 3/1; must reply within 2 week(s) of notification.

**CONTACT**
Anita Smith, Interim Director of Financial Aid
302 Bibb Street, Marion, AL 36756
(334) 683-5157

## Lawson State Community College
Birmingham, Alabama
www.lawsonstate.edu                Federal Code: 001059

**2-year public** community college in small city.
**Enrollment:** 3,090 undergrads.
**Selectivity:** Open admission; but selective for some programs.

**BASIC COSTS (2015-2016)**
**Tuition and fees:** $4,320; out-of-state residents $7,800.
**Per-credit charge:** $116; out-of-state residents $232.
**Room and board:** $4,760.

**FINANCIAL AID PICTURE**
**Students with need:** Need-based aid available for full-time and part-time students. Work study available nights.
**Students without need:** This college awards aid only to students with need.

**FINANCIAL AID PROCEDURES**
**Forms required:** FAFSA.
**Dates and Deadlines:** Closing date 6/1. Applicants notified on a rolling basis starting 8/1; must reply within 2 week(s) of notification.

**CONTACT**
Cassandra Byrd, Director of Student Financial Services
3060 Wilson Road SW, Birmingham, AL 35221-1717
(205) 929-6380

## Lurleen B. Wallace Community College
Andalusia, Alabama
www.lbwcc.edu                Federal Code: 008988

**2-year public** community college in small town.
**Enrollment:** 1,412 undergrads, 27% part-time. 447 full-time freshmen.
**Selectivity:** Open admission.

**BASIC COSTS (2015-2016)**
**Tuition and fees:** $4,320; out-of-state residents $7,770.
**Per-credit charge:** $115; out-of-state residents $230.

**FINANCIAL AID PICTURE (2014-2015)**
**Students with need:** Need-based aid available for full-time and part-time students.
**Students without need:** No-need awards available for academics, art, athletics, leadership, music/drama.

**FINANCIAL AID PROCEDURES**
**Forms required:** FAFSA.
**Dates and Deadlines:** Closing date 8/1. Applicants notified on a rolling basis.

**CONTACT**
Donna Bass, Director of Financial Aid, Andalusia Campus
Box 1418, Andalusia, AL 36420
(334) 881-2272

## Miles College
Birmingham, Alabama
www.miles.edu                Federal Code: 001028

**4-year private** liberal arts college in very large city, affiliated with Christian Methodist Episcopal Church.
**Enrollment:** 1,690 undergrads.
**Selectivity:** Open admission; but selective for some programs.

**BASIC COSTS (2015-2016)**
**Tuition and fees:** $11,604.
**Per-credit charge:** $448.
**Room and board:** $7,042.
**Additional info:** Room and Board cost range between $5,882 and $7,042; depending upon the dormitory to which the individual is assigned.

**FINANCIAL AID PICTURE**
**Students with need:** Need-based aid available for full-time and part-time students.
**Students without need:** This college awards aid only to students with need.

**FINANCIAL AID PROCEDURES**
**Forms required:** FAFSA, state aid form.
**Dates and Deadlines:** Priority date 4/15; no closing date. Applicants notified on a rolling basis starting 7/15; must reply within 2 week(s) of notification.

**CONTACT**
P Lanier, Financial Aid Administrator
5500 Myron Massey Boulevard, Fairfield, AL 35064
(205) 929-1665

## Northeast Alabama Community College
Rainsville, Alabama
www.nacc.edu                    Federal Code: 001031

**2-year public** community college in rural community.
**Enrollment:** 2,051 undergrads, 43% part-time. 485 full-time freshmen.
**Selectivity:** Open admission.

**BASIC COSTS (2015-2016)**
**Tuition and fees:** $4,320; out-of-state residents $7,770.
**Per-credit charge:** $115; out-of-state residents $230.

**FINANCIAL AID PICTURE**
**Students with need:** Need-based aid available for full-time and part-time students.
**Students without need:** No-need awards available for academics, art, leadership, minority status, music/drama.

**FINANCIAL AID PROCEDURES**
**Forms required:** FAFSA.
**Dates and Deadlines:** Applicants notified on a rolling basis.

**CONTACT**
Nixon Willmon, Director of Financial Aid
Admissions Office, NACC, Rainsville, AL 35986-0159
(256) 228-6001 ext. 2327

## Northwest-Shoals Community College
Muscle Shoals, Alabama
www.nwscc.edu                    Federal Code: 005697

**2-year public** community and technical college in large town.
**Enrollment:** 3,022 undergrads, 46% part-time. 592 full-time freshmen.
**Selectivity:** Open admission; but selective for some programs.

**BASIC COSTS (2015-2016)**
**Tuition and fees:** $4,291; out-of-state residents $7,741.
**Per-credit charge:** $115; out-of-state residents $230.
**Additional info:** Tuition/fee waivers available for minority students, unemployed or children of unemployed.

**FINANCIAL AID PICTURE (2014-2015)**
**Students with need:** 59% of average financial aid package awarded as scholarships/grants, 41% awarded as loans/jobs. Need-based aid available for part-time students. Work study available nights.

**Students without need:** No-need awards available for academics, art, leadership, minority status, music/drama.

**FINANCIAL AID PROCEDURES**
**Forms required:** FAFSA.
**Dates and Deadlines:** Priority date 4/1; closing date 8/1. Applicants notified on a rolling basis starting 6/1; must reply within 2 week(s) of notification.
**Transfers:** No deadline. Applicants notified on a rolling basis starting 6/1; must reply within 2 week(s) of notification. Students without 1-year Alabama residency before fall term ineligible for state grant.

**CONTACT**
Lindsey Peck, Director of Student Financial Aid Services Temporary
PO Box 2545, Muscle Shoals, AL 35662-2545
(256) 331-6232

## Oakwood University
Huntsville, Alabama
www.oakwood.edu                    Federal Code: 001033

**4-year private** liberal arts college in small city, affiliated with Seventh-day Adventists.
**Enrollment:** 1,687 undergrads.
**Selectivity:** Admits less than 50% of applicants.

**BASIC COSTS (2015-2016)**
**Tuition and fees:** $16,720.
**Room and board:** $9,312.

**FINANCIAL AID PICTURE**
**Students with need:** Need-based aid available for full-time students.
**Students without need:** No-need awards available for academics, leadership, religious affiliation, state/district residency.

**FINANCIAL AID PROCEDURES**
**Forms required:** FAFSA, state aid form.
**Dates and Deadlines:** Closing date 4/15. Applicants notified on a rolling basis starting 4/1.

**CONTACT**
Joylin Trotman, Director of Financial Aid
7000 Adventist Boulevard, NW, Huntsville, AL 35896
(256) 726-7208

## Remington College: Mobile
Mobile, Alabama
http://mobile.remingtoncollege.edu   Federal Code: 026055

**2-year private** career college in large city.
**Enrollment:** 881 undergrads.
**Selectivity:** Open admission.

**BASIC COSTS (2015-2016)**
**Additional info:** Tuition for associate degree programs, $33,900; tuition for diploma programs vary and range from $15,995 to $20,995.

**FINANCIAL AID PICTURE**
**Students with need:** Need-based aid available for full-time students. Work study available nights.
**Students without need:** This college awards aid only to students with need.

**FINANCIAL AID PROCEDURES**
**Forms required:** FAFSA.

**CONTACT**
James Dunn, National Director of Financial Aid
828 Downtowner Loop West, Mobile, AL 36609-5404
(251) 343-8200

## Samford University
Birmingham, Alabama
www.samford.edu                    Federal Code: 001036

**4-year private** university in small city, affiliated with Baptist faith.
**Enrollment:** 3,145 undergrads, 3% part-time. 728 full-time freshmen.
**Selectivity:** Admits over 75% of applicants.

### BASIC COSTS (2015-2016)
**Tuition and fees:** $28,370.
**Per-credit charge:** $920.
**Room and board:** $10,234.

### FINANCIAL AID PICTURE (2014-2015)
**Students with need:** Out of 576 full-time freshmen who applied for aid, 350 were judged to have need. Of these, 350 received aid, and 87 had their full need met. Average financial aid package met 69% of need; average scholarship/grant was $14,744; average loan was $3,196. For part-time students, average financial aid package was $7,397.
**Students without need:** 336 full-time freshmen who did not demonstrate need for aid received scholarships/grants; average award was $10,036. No-need awards available for academics, alumni affiliation, art, athletics, leadership, minority status, music/drama, religious affiliation, ROTC, state/district residency.
**Scholarships offered:** 20 full-time freshmen received athletic scholarships; average amount $28,306.

### FINANCIAL AID PROCEDURES
**Forms required:** FAFSA, state aid form.
**Dates and Deadlines:** Priority date 3/1; no closing date. Applicants notified on a rolling basis starting 3/1; must reply by 5/1.
**Transfers:** Applicants notified on a rolling basis. Student must be fully admitted and all transcripts must be received by admissions office.

### CONTACT
Lane Smith, Director of Student Financial Services
800 Lakeshore Drive, Birmingham, AL 35229
(205) 726-2905

## Selma University
Selma, Alabama
www.selmauniversity.org            Federal Code: 040673

**4-year private** university in large town, affiliated with Baptist faith.
**Enrollment:** 399 undergrads.
**Selectivity:** Open admission.

### BASIC COSTS (2015-2016)
**Tuition and fees:** $6,605.
**Room and board:** $5,000.
**Additional info:** Tuition/fee waivers available for minority students.

### FINANCIAL AID PICTURE
**Students with need:** Need-based aid available for full-time and part-time students. Work study available weekends and for part-time students.
**Students without need:** This college awards aid only to students with need.

### FINANCIAL AID PROCEDURES
**Forms required:** FAFSA, institutional form.
**Dates and Deadlines:** Priority date 5/1; closing date 6/30. Applicants notified on a rolling basis starting 8/23; must reply within 2 week(s) of notification.
**Transfers:** Closing date 5/1. Applicants notified on a rolling basis; must reply within 2 week(s) of notification.

### CONTACT
Nerieko Stephens, Director of Financial Aid
1501 Lapsley Street, Selma, AL 36701

## Shelton State Community College
Tuscaloosa, Alabama
www.sheltonstate.edu               Federal Code: 005691

**2-year public** community and technical college in small city.
**Enrollment:** 4,477 undergrads, 51% part-time. 707 full-time freshmen.
**Selectivity:** Open admission.

### BASIC COSTS (2015-2016)
**Tuition and fees:** $4,020; out-of-state residents $7,470.
**Per-credit charge:** $115; out-of-state residents $230.

### FINANCIAL AID PICTURE
**Students with need:** Need-based aid available for full-time and part-time students. Work study available nights.
**Students without need:** This college awards aid only to students with need.

### FINANCIAL AID PROCEDURES
**Forms required:** FAFSA.
**Dates and Deadlines:** Priority date 6/30; no closing date. Applicants notified on a rolling basis starting 7/30.

### CONTACT
Rhonda Smith, Director of Fiancial Aid
9500 Old Greensboro Road, Tuscaloosa, AL 35405-8522
(205) 391-2376

## Snead State Community College
Boaz, Alabama
www.snead.edu                      Federal Code: 001038

**2-year public** community college in small town.
**Enrollment:** 2,179 undergrads.
**Selectivity:** Open admission.

### BASIC COSTS (2015-2016)
**Tuition and fees:** $4,380; out-of-state residents $7,830.
**Per-credit charge:** $115; out-of-state residents $230.
**Room and board:** $3,110.

### FINANCIAL AID PICTURE (2014-2015)
**Students with need:** 80% of average financial aid package awarded as scholarships/grants, 20% awarded as loans/jobs. Need-based aid available for part-time students. Work study available nights.
**Students without need:** No-need awards available for academics, alumni affiliation, art, athletics, leadership, music/drama.

### FINANCIAL AID PROCEDURES
**Forms required:** FAFSA.
**Dates and Deadlines:** Applicants notified on a rolling basis starting 4/15.

### CONTACT
Amanda Childress, Financial Aid Coordinator
PO Box 734, Boaz, AL 35957-0734
(256) 840-4127

## Southeastern Bible College
Birmingham, Alabama
www.sebc.edu                       Federal Code: 013857

**4-year private** Bible college in very large city, affiliated with nondenominational tradition.
**Enrollment:** 151 undergrads.
**Selectivity:** Admits over 75% of applicants.

**BASIC COSTS (2015-2016)**
Tuition and fees: $12,600.
Per-credit charge: $405.
Room and board: $4,975.

**FINANCIAL AID PICTURE**
Students with need: Need-based aid available for full-time and part-time students.
Students without need: No-need awards available for academics, leadership.

**FINANCIAL AID PROCEDURES**
Forms required: FAFSA, institutional form.
Dates and Deadlines: Priority date 4/1; no closing date.

**CONTACT**
Joanne Belin, Director of Financial Aid
2545 Valleydale Road, Birmingham, AL 35244-2083
(205) 970-9215

## Southern Union State Community College

Wadley, Alabama
www.suscc.edu          Federal Code: 001040

2-year public community and technical college in small city.
Enrollment: 4,734 undergrads.
Selectivity: Open admission; but selective for some programs.

**BASIC COSTS (2015-2016)**
Tuition and fees: $4,020; out-of-state residents $7,470.
Per-credit charge: $115; out-of-state residents $230.
Room and board: $3,200.

**FINANCIAL AID PICTURE**
Students with need: Need-based aid available for full-time and part-time students.
Students without need: No-need awards available for alumni affiliation, art, athletics.

**FINANCIAL AID PROCEDURES**
Forms required: FAFSA.
Dates and Deadlines: Priority date 4/1; no closing date. Applicants notified on a rolling basis.

**CONTACT**
Pam Jones, Director of Financial Aid
750 Roberts Street, Wadley, AL 36276
(256) 395-2215

## Spring Hill College

Mobile, Alabama
www.shc.edu          Federal Code: 001041

4-year private liberal arts college in large city, affiliated with Roman Catholic Church.
Enrollment: 1,365 undergrads, 2% part-time. 429 full-time freshmen.
Selectivity: Admits less than 50% of applicants.

**BASIC COSTS (2015-2016)**
Tuition and fees: $34,091.
Per-credit charge: $975.
Room and board: $12,090.

**FINANCIAL AID PICTURE (2015-2016)**
Students with need: Out of 371 full-time freshmen who applied for aid, 321 were judged to have need. Of these, 321 received aid, and 81 had their

full need met. Average financial aid package met 78% of need; average scholarship/grant was $25,257; average loan was $3,410. For part-time students, average financial aid package was $4,525.
Students without need: 90 full-time freshmen who did not demonstrate need for aid received scholarships/grants; average award was $22,122. No-need awards available for academics, alumni affiliation, art, athletics, job skills, leadership, minority status, ROTC, state/district residency.
Scholarships offered: 33 full-time freshmen received athletic scholarships; average amount $6,729.

**FINANCIAL AID PROCEDURES**
Forms required: FAFSA, state aid form.
Dates and Deadlines: Priority date 3/1; no closing date. Applicants notified on a rolling basis starting 2/15; must reply by 5/1 or within 2 week(s) of notification.
Transfers: No deadline. Applicants notified on a rolling basis starting 3/1; must reply within 2 week(s) of notification.

**CONTACT**
Ellen Foster, Director of Financial Aid
4000 Dauphin Street, Mobile, AL 36608-1791
(800) 548-7886

## Stillman College

Tuscaloosa, Alabama
www.stillman.edu          Federal Code: 001044

4-year private liberal arts college in small city, affiliated with Presbyterian Church (USA).
Enrollment: 1,000 undergrads. 280 full-time freshmen.

**BASIC COSTS (2015-2016)**
Tuition and fees: $15,938.
Per-credit charge: $539.
Room and board: $5,952.

**FINANCIAL AID PICTURE (2015-2016)**
Students with need: Out of 230 full-time freshmen who applied for aid, 230 were judged to have need. Of these, 230 received aid, and 198 had their full need met. Average financial aid package met 75% of need; average scholarship/grant was $2,791; average loan was $2,406. For part-time students, average financial aid package was $5,953.
Students without need: 4 full-time freshmen who did not demonstrate need for aid received scholarships/grants; average award was $8,467. No-need awards available for academics, alumni affiliation, athletics, state/district residency.
Scholarships offered: 10 full-time freshmen received athletic scholarships; average amount $2,090.

**FINANCIAL AID PROCEDURES**
Forms required: FAFSA, state aid form.
Dates and Deadlines: Priority date 4/15; closing date 8/15. Applicants notified on a rolling basis starting 3/1; must reply by 7/31 or within 4 week(s) of notification.
Transfers: Priority date 3/15; no deadline. Applicants notified on a rolling basis starting 10/15; must reply by 3/15 or within 4 week(s) of notification.

**CONTACT**
Jacqueline Morris, Director of Financial Aid
3601 Stillman Boulevard, Tuscaloosa, AL 35403
(205) 366-8844

## Talladega College

Talladega, Alabama
www.talladega.edu          Federal Code: 001046

4-year private liberal arts college in large town, affiliated with United Church of Christ.

**Enrollment:** 1,016 undergrads.

**Selectivity:** Open admission; but selective for some programs.

## BASIC COSTS (2015-2016)

**Tuition and fees:** $13,828.

**Per-credit charge:** $466.33.

**Room and board:** $6,704.

**Additional info:** Less than 12 or more than 18 credit hours; $466.33 per credit hour.

## FINANCIAL AID PICTURE

**Students with need:** Need-based aid available for full-time and part-time students.

**Students without need:** This college awards aid only to students with need.

## FINANCIAL AID PROCEDURES

**Forms required:** FAFSA, state aid form, institutional form.

**Dates and Deadlines:** Closing date 3/1. Applicants notified on a rolling basis starting 2/1; must reply within 2 week(s) of notification.

**Transfers:** Priority date 3/1; no deadline. Applicants notified on a rolling basis; must reply within 2 week(s) of notification.

## CONTACT

627 West Battle Street, Talladega, AL 35160

(256) 761-6256

## Troy University

Troy, Alabama

www.troy.edu          Federal Code: 001047

**4-year public** university in large town.

**Enrollment:** 13,989 undergrads, 36% part-time. 1,697 full-time freshmen.

**Selectivity:** Admits over 75% of applicants.

## BASIC COSTS (2015-2016)

**Tuition and fees:** $9,646; out-of-state residents $18,256.

**Per-credit charge:** $287; out-of-state residents $574.

**Room and board:** $6,525.

## FINANCIAL AID PICTURE (2015-2016)

**Students with need:** For part-time students, average financial aid package was $4,903.

**Students without need:** No-need awards available for academics, alumni affiliation, art, athletics, leadership, minority status, music/drama, ROTC.

## FINANCIAL AID PROCEDURES

**Forms required:** FAFSA, institutional form.

**Dates and Deadlines:** Closing date 5/1. Applicants notified on a rolling basis starting 5/1; must reply within 2 week(s) of notification.

## CONTACT

Carol Ballard, Vice Chancellor, Financial Aid

University Avenue, Adams Administration 111, Troy, AL 36082

(334) 670-3186

## Tuskegee University

Tuskegee, Alabama

www.tuskegee.edu          Federal Code: 001050

**4-year private** university in small town.

**Enrollment:** 2,485 undergrads, 2% part-time. 645 full-time freshmen.

**Selectivity:** Admits 50 to 75% of applicants.

## BASIC COSTS (2015-2016)

**Tuition and fees:** $21,535.

**Room and board:** $9,104.

## FINANCIAL AID PICTURE (2014-2015)

**Students with need:** Out of 645 full-time freshmen who applied for aid, 628 were judged to have need. Of these, 628 received aid. Average financial aid package met 70% of need; average scholarship/grant was $1,500; average loan was $7,500. Need-based aid available for part-time students.

**Students without need:** 175 full-time freshmen who did not demonstrate need for aid received scholarships/grants; average award was $12,750. No-need awards available for academics, athletics, ROTC, state/district residency.

**Scholarships offered:** 47 full-time freshmen received athletic scholarships; average amount $18,250.

## FINANCIAL AID PROCEDURES

**Forms required:** FAFSA, institutional form.

**Dates and Deadlines:** Closing date 3/31. Applicants notified on a rolling basis starting 5/15; must reply within 2 week(s) of notification.

**Transfers:** Priority date 3/31. Applicants notified on a rolling basis.

## CONTACT

Advergus James, Director of Financial Aid Services

Margaret Murray Washington Hall, Tuskegee, AL 36088

(334) 724-4733

## University of Alabama

Tuscaloosa, Alabama

www.ua.edu          Federal Code: 001051

**4-year public** university in small city.

**Enrollment:** 31,005 undergrads, 8% part-time. 6,794 full-time freshmen.

**Selectivity:** Admits 50 to 75% of applicants.

## BASIC COSTS (2015-2016)

**Tuition and fees:** $10,170; out-of-state residents $25,950.

**Room and board:** $9,030.

## FINANCIAL AID PICTURE (2014-2015)

**Students with need:** Out of 4,504 full-time freshmen who applied for aid, 3,224 were judged to have need. Of these, 3,120 received aid, and 861 had their full need met. Average financial aid package met 58% of need; average scholarship/grant was $13,123; average loan was $3,494. For part-time students, average financial aid package was $6,053.

**Students without need:** 1,849 full-time freshmen who did not demonstrate need for aid received scholarships/grants; average award was $14,135. No-need awards available for academics, alumni affiliation, art, athletics, leadership, minority status, music/drama, ROTC, state/district residency.

**Scholarships offered:** 92 full-time freshmen received athletic scholarships; average amount $24,153.

## FINANCIAL AID PROCEDURES

**Forms required:** FAFSA.

**Dates and Deadlines:** Priority date 3/1; no closing date. Applicants notified on a rolling basis starting 4/1; must reply within 3 week(s) of notification.

**Transfers:** No deadline. Applicants notified on a rolling basis. Scholarship opportunities for transfer students.

## CONTACT

Helen Allen, Director, Student Financial Aid

Box 870132, Tuscaloosa, AL 35487-0132

(205) 348-6756

## University of Alabama at Birmingham

Birmingham, Alabama

www.uab.edu          Federal Code: 001052

**4-year public** university in very large city.

**Enrollment:** 11,383 undergrads, 26% part-time. 1,719 full-time freshmen.

## BASIC COSTS (2015-2016)

**Tuition and fees:** $9,596; out-of-state residents $21,956.
**Per-credit charge:** $305; out-of-state residents $717.
**Room and board:** $9,850.

## FINANCIAL AID PICTURE

**Students with need:** Need-based aid available for full-time and part-time students.

**Students without need:** No-need awards available for academics, alumni affiliation, art, athletics, leadership, minority status, music/drama, ROTC.

**Scholarships offered:** Presidential Recognition, Presidential, and Endowed Scholarships: full tuition and required fees for 4 years (up to 15 credit hours per semester for fall and spring only); for in-state students with 33-36 ACT and 3.5 GPA (supplemental application required). Golden Excellence Scholarship: $7,500 per year; for in-state students with 30-32 ACT and 3.5 GPA. Collegiate Honors Scholarship: $5,500 per year; for in-state students with 27-29 ACT and 3.5 GPA or 30-36 ACT and 3.0-3.49 GPA. Breakthrough Scholarship: $3,000 per year; for in-state students with 24-26 ACT and 3.5 GPA. Academic Achievement Scholarship: $2,000 per year; for in-state students with 20-23 ACT and 3.5 GPA or 24-29 ACT and 3.0-3.49 GPA. Blazer Elite Scholarship: $15,000 per year; for out-of-state students with 30-36 ACT and 3.5 GPA. Blazer Gold Scholarship: $12,000 per year; for out-of-state students with 26-29 ACT and 3.5 GPA. Blazer Pride Scholarship: $10,000 per year; for out-of-state students with 24-25 ACT and 3.5 GPA or 26-36 ACT and 3.0-3.49 GPA. Blazer Distinction Scholarship: $7,500 per year, for out-of-state students with 20-23 ACT and 3.5 GPA or 24-25 ACT and 3.0-3.49 GPA. National Merit Finalist/National Achievement Finalist/National Hispanic Recognition Program Scholar Awards: full tuition and required fees for 4 years (up to 15 credit hours per semester for fall and spring only), annual on-campus housing allotment, and a one-time $2,500 stipend to be used for experiential learning (study away, internships, co-ops, etc.); National Merit Finalists must name UAB as first choice with NMSC. National Achievement Finalists and National Hispanic Recognition Program Scholars must send a copy of their Finalist letter and certificate to the UAB Undergraduate Admissions Office.

## FINANCIAL AID PROCEDURES

**Forms required:** FAFSA.

**Dates and Deadlines:** Priority date 3/1; no closing date. Applicants notified on a rolling basis starting 3/15; must reply within 4 week(s) of notification.

**Transfers:** Applicants notified on a rolling basis; must reply within 4 week(s) of notification.

## CONTACT

Helen McIntyre, Director of Financial Aid
1720 2nd Avenue South, Birmingham, AL 35294-4600
(205) 934-8223

# University of Alabama in Huntsville

Huntsville, Alabama
www.uah.edu                    Federal Code: 001055

**4-year public** university in small city.
**Enrollment:** 5,829 undergrads, 19% part-time. 1,027 full-time freshmen.
**Selectivity:** Admits over 75% of applicants.

## BASIC COSTS (2015-2016)

**Tuition and fees:** $9,128; out-of-state residents $20,622.
**Room and board:** $9,205.
**Additional info:** Each college has required course fees which vary by college.

## FINANCIAL AID PICTURE (2015-2016)

**Students with need:** Out of 1,026 full-time freshmen who applied for aid, 555 were judged to have need. Of these, 548 received aid, and 149 had their full need met. Average financial aid package met 74% of need; average scholarship/grant was $10,630; average loan was $5,511. For part-time students, average financial aid package was $5,155.

**Students without need:** 365 full-time freshmen who did not demonstrate need for aid received scholarships/grants; average award was $10,063. No-need awards available for academics, art, athletics, leadership, minority status, music/drama, ROTC.

**Scholarships offered:** 65 full-time freshmen received athletic scholarships; average amount $7,042.

**Additional info:** Application deadline for institutional scholarships is December 1.

## FINANCIAL AID PROCEDURES

**Forms required:** FAFSA.

**Dates and Deadlines:** Priority date 4/1; closing date 7/31. Applicants notified on a rolling basis starting 4/1; must reply within 2 week(s) of notification.

**Transfers:** First-time regularly admitted transfer students who have earned a minimum of 24 transfer credits from an accredited institution of higher learning considered for one-time transfer scholarship award. Super Scholar Transfer Scholarship requires 3.50 college GPA and is currently valued at $3,000 renewable for an additional year. UAH Transfer Merit Scholarship requires 3.00 college GPA and is currently valued at $1,500 renewable for an additional year. Students must be admitted to UAH to be eligible for these awards. Priority consideration is given to students who are admitted to UAH by June 1. Students admitted after the priority deadline may be eligible for awards as funding is available.

## CONTACT

Andy Weaver, Director of Student Financial Services
UAH Office of Undergraduate Admissions, Huntsville, AL 35899
(256) 824-6241

# University of Mobile

Mobile, Alabama
www.umobile.edu                    Federal Code: 001029

**4-year private** university and liberal arts college in small city, affiliated with Baptist faith.
**Enrollment:** 1,437 undergrads, 11% part-time. 280 full-time freshmen.
**Selectivity:** Admits 50 to 75% of applicants.

## BASIC COSTS (2015-2016)

**Tuition and fees:** $19,970.
**Per-credit charge:** $695.
**Room and board:** $9,670.

## FINANCIAL AID PICTURE (2015-2016)

**Students with need:** Out of 242 full-time freshmen who applied for aid, 214 were judged to have need. Of these, 214 received aid, and 214 had their full need met. Average financial aid package met 69% of need; average scholarship/grant was $5,177; average loan was $3,679. For part-time students, average financial aid package was $9,430.

**Students without need:** 26 full-time freshmen who did not demonstrate need for aid received scholarships/grants; average award was $7,648. No-need awards available for academics, alumni affiliation, athletics, music/drama, religious affiliation.

**Scholarships offered:** 8 full-time freshmen received athletic scholarships; average amount $20,386.

## FINANCIAL AID PROCEDURES

**Forms required:** FAFSA, state aid form, institutional form.
**Dates and Deadlines:** Applicants notified on a rolling basis starting 2/1.

## CONTACT

Marie Batson, Associate Vice President for Enrollment Management
5735 College Parkway, Mobile, AL 36613-2842
(251) 442-2252

## University of Montevallo
Montevallo, Alabama
www.montevallo.edu                    Federal Code: 001004

**4-year public** university and liberal arts college in small town.
**Enrollment:** 2,553 undergrads.
**Selectivity:** Admits 50 to 75% of applicants.

**BASIC COSTS (2015-2016)**
**Tuition and fees:** $11,410; out-of-state residents $22,780.
**Per-credit charge:** $358; out-of-state residents $737.
**Room and board:** $6,900.

**FINANCIAL AID PICTURE (2015-2016)**
**Students with need:** Average financial aid package met 58% of need; average scholarship/grant was $9,087; average loan was $3,377. For part-time students, average financial aid package was $7,025.
**Students without need:** No-need awards available for academics, art, athletics, leadership, minority status, music/drama, religious affiliation, ROTC.

**FINANCIAL AID PROCEDURES**
**Forms required:** FAFSA.
**Dates and Deadlines:** Priority date 4/1; no closing date. Applicants notified on a rolling basis starting 4/20; must reply within 2 week(s) of notification.

**CONTACT**
Bob Walker, Director of Financial Aid
Palmer Hall, Station 6030, Montevallo, AL 35115-6000
(205) 665-6050

## University of North Alabama
Florence, Alabama
www.una.edu                    Federal Code: 001016

**4-year public** university in large town.
**Enrollment:** 5,723 undergrads, 13% part-time. 931 full-time freshmen.
**Selectivity:** Admits 50 to 75% of applicants.

**BASIC COSTS (2015-2016)**
**Tuition and fees:** $9,508; out-of-state residents $17,128.
**Per-credit charge:** $254; out-of-state residents $508.
**Room and board:** $6,516.

**FINANCIAL AID PICTURE (2014-2015)**
**Students with need:** Out of 666 full-time freshmen who applied for aid, 579 were judged to have need. Of these, 567 received aid, and 58 had their full need met. Average financial aid package met 56% of need; average scholarship/grant was $4,139; average loan was $2,889. For part-time students, average financial aid package was $5,245.
**Students without need:** 145 full-time freshmen who did not demonstrate need for aid received scholarships/grants; average award was $3,900. No-need awards available for academics, alumni affiliation, art, athletics, job skills, leadership, minority status, music/drama, religious affiliation, ROTC, state/district residency.
**Scholarships offered:** 44 full-time freshmen received athletic scholarships; average amount $7,844.

**FINANCIAL AID PROCEDURES**
**Forms required:** FAFSA.
**Dates and Deadlines:** Priority date 6/1; no closing date. Applicants notified on a rolling basis starting 3/30.

**CONTACT**
Shauna James, Director, Student Financial Services
One Harrison Plaza, UNA Box 5011, Florence, AL 35632-0001
(256) 765-4278

## University of South Alabama
Mobile, Alabama
www.southalabama.edu                    Federal Code: 001057

**4-year public** university in small city.
**Enrollment:** 11,457 undergrads, 18% part-time. 2,030 full-time freshmen.
**Selectivity:** Admits over 75% of applicants.

**BASIC COSTS (2015-2016)**
**Tuition and fees:** $8,790; out-of-state residents $17,580.
**Per-credit charge:** $293; out-of-state residents $586.
**Room and board:** $7,250.
**Additional info:** Tuition/fee waivers available for minority students.

**FINANCIAL AID PICTURE (2014-2015)**
**Students with need:** Out of 1,795 full-time freshmen who applied for aid, 1,351 were judged to have need. Of these, 1,351 received aid, and 168 had their full need met. Average financial aid package met 57% of need; average scholarship/grant was $7,057; average loan was $3,454. For part-time students, average financial aid package was $7,693.
**Students without need:** 408 full-time freshmen who did not demonstrate need for aid received scholarships/grants; average award was $5,257. No-need awards available for academics, alumni affiliation, art, athletics, job skills, leadership, minority status, music/drama, ROTC, state/district residency.
**Scholarships offered:** 58 full-time freshmen received athletic scholarships; average amount $18,648.

**FINANCIAL AID PROCEDURES**
**Forms required:** FAFSA, institutional form.

**CONTACT**
Marla Sklopan, Director, Financial Aid
Meisler Hall, Suite 2500, Mobile, AL 36688-0002
(800) 305-6828

## University of West Alabama
Livingston, Alabama
www.uwa.edu                    Federal Code: 001024

**4-year public** university in small town.
**Enrollment:** 1,913 undergrads, 11% part-time. 350 full-time freshmen.
**Selectivity:** Admits 50 to 75% of applicants.

**BASIC COSTS (2015-2016)**
**Tuition and fees:** $9,062; out-of-state residents $16,206.
**Per-credit charge:** $292; out-of-state residents $584.
**Room and board:** $7,480.

**FINANCIAL AID PICTURE (2014-2015)**
**Students with need:** Out of 312 full-time freshmen who applied for aid, 268 were judged to have need. Of these, 266 received aid, and 8 had their full need met. Average financial aid package met 24% of need; average scholarship/grant was $5,170. For part-time students, average financial aid package was $7,123.
**Students without need:** 35 full-time freshmen who did not demonstrate need for aid received scholarships/grants; average award was $4,760. No-need awards available for academics, alumni affiliation, art, athletics, leadership, music/drama, state/district residency.
**Scholarships offered:** *Merit:* Trustee Scholarships: available for students who have qualifying ACT scores; amounts vary depending on the student's composite ACT score. *Athletic:* 45 full-time freshmen received athletic scholarships; average amount $5,440.

**FINANCIAL AID PROCEDURES**
**Forms required:** FAFSA.
**Dates and Deadlines:** Priority date 3/1; no closing date. Applicants notified on a rolling basis starting 4/15; must reply within 2 week(s) of notification.

**Transfers:** Priority date 2/12; no deadline. Applicants notified on a rolling basis; must reply within 2 week(s) of notification.

### CONTACT

Don Rainer, Director of Financial Aid
Station 4, Livingston, AL 35470
(205) 652-3576

## Virginia College in Huntsville

Huntsville, Alabama
www.vc.edu                    Federal Code: 030106

**4-year for-profit** business and technical college in small city.
**Enrollment:** 597 undergrads.
**Selectivity:** Open admission.

### BASIC COSTS (2015-2016)

**Additional info:** Diploma programs; $13,392-$23,220. Associate degree programs; $37,152-$40,700. Bachelor degree programs; $69,660-$75,702. Cost of books and supplies included in program tuition. All costs are subject to change.

### FINANCIAL AID PICTURE

**Students with need:** Need-based aid available for full-time and part-time students. Work study available nights, weekends, and for part-time students.

### FINANCIAL AID PROCEDURES

**Forms required:** FAFSA, institutional form.
**Dates and Deadlines:** Applicants notified on a rolling basis.

### CONTACT

Samantha Williams, Director of Financial Aid
2800 Bob Wallace Avenue, Huntsville, AL 35805
(256) 533-7387

## Wallace State Community College at Hanceville

Hanceville, Alabama
www.wallacestate.edu              Federal Code: 007871

**2-year public** health science and community college in small town.
**Enrollment:** 4,822 undergrads, 46% part-time. 875 full-time freshmen.
**Selectivity:** Open admission; but selective for some programs.

### BASIC COSTS (2015-2016)

**Tuition and fees:** $4,320; out-of-state residents $7,770.
**Per-credit charge:** $115; out-of-state residents $230.
**Room only:** $1,800.

### FINANCIAL AID PICTURE

**Students with need:** Need-based aid available for full-time and part-time students. Work study available nights.
**Students without need:** This college awards aid only to students with need.

### FINANCIAL AID PROCEDURES

**Forms required:** FAFSA.
**Dates and Deadlines:** Priority date 5/1; no closing date. Applicants notified on a rolling basis starting 7/15; must reply within 2 week(s) of notification.
**Transfers:** No deadline.

### CONTACT

Becky Graves, Director of Student Financial Aid
801 Main Street NW/PO Box 2000, Hanceville, AL 35077-2000
(256) 352-8182

# Alaska

## Alaska Bible College

Palmer, Alaska
www.akbible.edu               Federal Code: 014325

**4-year private** Bible college in small town, affiliated with nondenominational tradition.
**Enrollment:** 29 undergrads.
**Selectivity:** Open admission; but selective for some programs.

### BASIC COSTS (2015-2016)

**Tuition and fees:** $9,300.
**Room and board:** $5,400.

### FINANCIAL AID PICTURE

**Students with need:** Need-based aid available for full-time and part-time students. Work study available nights, weekends, and for part-time students.
**Students without need:** No-need awards available for academics.

### FINANCIAL AID PROCEDURES

**Forms required:** FAFSA, institutional form.
**Dates and Deadlines:** Priority date 5/30; no closing date. Must reply within 2 week(s) of notification.
**Transfers:** Closing date 7/31. Applicants notified by 8/31; must reply within 2 week(s) of notification.

### CONTACT

Sandy Anderson, Financial Aid
248 East Elmwood Avenue, Palmer, AK 99645
(907) 745-3201

## Alaska Pacific University

Anchorage, Alaska
www.alaskapacific.edu            Federal Code: 001061

**4-year private** university and liberal arts college in large city, affiliated with United Methodist Church.
**Enrollment:** 291 undergrads.
**Selectivity:** Admits less than 50% of applicants.

### BASIC COSTS (2015-2016)

**Tuition and fees:** $19,680.
**Room and board:** $7,000.

### FINANCIAL AID PICTURE

**Students with need:** Need-based aid available for full-time and part-time students. Work study available nights, weekends, and for part-time students.
**Students without need:** No-need awards available for academics, alumni affiliation, art, leadership, music/drama, religious affiliation, state/district residency.

### FINANCIAL AID PROCEDURES

**Forms required:** FAFSA.
**Dates and Deadlines:** Priority date 4/15; no closing date. Applicants notified on a rolling basis starting 2/1; must reply within 4 week(s) of notification.
**Transfers:** Priority date 6/1; no deadline. Applicants notified on a rolling basis starting 2/1; must reply within 2 week(s) of notification.

### CONTACT

Phong Moua, Director, Student Financial Services
4101 University Drive, Anchorage, AK 99508-3051
(907) 564-8341

## Charter College
Anchorage, Alaska
www.chartercollege.edu          Federal Code: 017377

**4-year for-profit** junior and technical college in large city.
**Enrollment:** 3,256 undergrads.
**Selectivity:** Open admission.

### BASIC COSTS (2015-2016)
**Additional info:** Tuition and fees vary depending on program. Examples of Bachelor Degree Programs: Business Management Accounting; $78,800; Criminal Justice; $41,400. Associate Programs: Business Management Practice; $41,370; Paralegal Studies; $41,376. All costs are subject to change.

### FINANCIAL AID PICTURE
**Students with need:** Need-based aid available for full-time and part-time students.

### FINANCIAL AID PROCEDURES
**Forms required:** FAFSA.
**Dates and Deadlines:** Applicants notified on a rolling basis; must reply within 5 week(s) of notification.

### CONTACT
2221 East Northern Lights Boulevard, Suite 120, Anchorage, AK 99508
(907) 777-1314

## Ilisagvik College
Barrow, Alaska
www.ilisagvik.edu          Federal Code: 034613

**2-year public** community college in rural community.
**Enrollment:** 77 undergrads, 62% part-time. 20 full-time freshmen.
**Selectivity:** Open admission.

### BASIC COSTS (2015-2016)
**Tuition and fees:** $3,340; out-of-state residents $3,340.
**Per-credit charge:** $125; out-of-state residents $125.
**Room and board:** $15,000.

### FINANCIAL AID PICTURE (2014-2015)
**Students with need:** 88% of average financial aid package awarded as scholarships/grants, 12% awarded as loans/jobs. Need-based aid available for part-time students. Work study available nights, weekends, and for part-time students.
**Students without need:** This college awards aid only to students with need.

### FINANCIAL AID PROCEDURES
**Forms required:** FAFSA.
**Dates and Deadlines:** Closing date 4/15. Applicants notified by 4/15.

### CONTACT
Eta-Starr Edwardsen, Financial Aid Manager
100 Stevenson Road, Barrow, AK 99723
(907) 852-1708

## University of Alaska Anchorage
Anchorage, Alaska
www.uaa.alaska.edu          Federal Code: 011462

**4-year public** university in large city.
**Enrollment:** 12,352 undergrads, 45% part-time. 1,339 full-time freshmen.
**Selectivity:** Open admission; but selective for some programs.

### BASIC COSTS (2015-2016)
**Tuition and fees:** $6,414; out-of-state residents $20,394.

**Per-credit charge:** $183; out-of-state residents $649.
**Room and board:** $10,254.

### FINANCIAL AID PICTURE (2015-2016)
**Students with need:** Out of 1,160 full-time freshmen who applied for aid, 784 were judged to have need. Of these, 714 received aid, and 106 had their full need met. Average financial aid package met 59% of need; average scholarship/grant was $3,476; average loan was $3,202. For part-time students, average financial aid package was $5,988.
**Students without need:** 95 full-time freshmen who did not demonstrate need for aid received scholarships/grants; average award was $3,362. No-need awards available for academics, art, athletics, leadership, minority status, music/drama, ROTC.
**Scholarships offered:** 14 full-time freshmen received athletic scholarships; average amount $2,517.

### FINANCIAL AID PROCEDURES
**Forms required:** FAFSA.
**Dates and Deadlines:** Priority date 4/1; no closing date. Applicants notified on a rolling basis starting 2/1; must reply within 4 week(s) of notification.
**Transfers:** Closing date 4/15.

### CONTACT
Sonya Stein, Director, Student Financial Assistance
PO Box 141629, Anchorage, AK 99514-1629
(907) 786-1480

## University of Alaska Fairbanks
Fairbanks, Alaska
www.uaf.edu          Federal Code: 001063

**4-year public** university in small city.
**Enrollment:** 5,445 undergrads, 39% part-time. 739 full-time freshmen.
**Selectivity:** Open admission; but selective for some programs. GED not accepted.

### BASIC COSTS (2015-2016)
**Tuition and fees:** $6,804; out-of-state residents $20,784.
**Per-credit charge:** $183; out-of-state residents $649.
**Room and board:** $8,380.

### FINANCIAL AID PICTURE (2014-2015)
**Students with need:** Out of 682 full-time freshmen who applied for aid, 390 were judged to have need. Of these, 378 received aid, and 77 had their full need met. Average financial aid package met 60% of need; average scholarship/grant was $7,188; average loan was $2,784. For part-time students, average financial aid package was $4,416.
**Students without need:** 131 full-time freshmen who did not demonstrate need for aid received scholarships/grants; average award was $3,643. No-need awards available for academics, art, athletics, music/drama, state/district residency.
**Scholarships offered:** 16 full-time freshmen received athletic scholarships; average amount $9,848.

### FINANCIAL AID PROCEDURES
**Forms required:** FAFSA, institutional form.
**Dates and Deadlines:** Priority date 2/15; closing date 7/1. Applicants notified on a rolling basis starting 3/1; must reply within 2 week(s) of notification.
**Transfers:** Must reply within 2 week(s) of notification.

### CONTACT
Deanna Dieringer, Director of Financial Aid
PO Box 757480, Fairbanks, AK 99775-7480
(888) 474-7256

## University of Alaska Southeast

Juneau, Alaska
www.uas.alaska.edu                    Federal Code: 001065

**4-year public** university and liberal arts college in large town.
**Enrollment:** 1,591 undergrads.

### BASIC COSTS (2015-2016)

**Tuition and fees:** $6,990; out-of-state residents $20,970.
**Per-credit charge:** $183; out-of-state residents $649.
**Room and board:** $8,400.

### FINANCIAL AID PICTURE

**Students with need:** Need-based aid available for full-time and part-time students. Work study available nights, weekends, and for part-time students.
**Students without need:** No-need awards available for academics, job skills, leadership, music/drama, state/district residency.
**Additional info:** Transfer, continuing, and freshman scholarship deadline March 1.

### FINANCIAL AID PROCEDURES

**Forms required:** FAFSA.
**Dates and Deadlines:** Priority date 4/15; no closing date. Applicants notified on a rolling basis starting 3/1; must reply within 3 week(s) of notification.

### CONTACT

Corinne Soltis, Assistant Director/VA Certifying Official
11120 Glacier Highway, Juneau, AK 99801-8681
(907) 796-6255

# Arizona

## Arizona Christian University

Phoenix, Arizona
www.arizonachristian.edu              Federal Code: 007113

**4-year private** Bible and liberal arts college in very large city, affiliated with nondenominational tradition.
**Enrollment:** 644 undergrads, 3% part-time. 154 full-time freshmen.
**Selectivity:** Admits 50 to 75% of applicants.

### BASIC COSTS (2016-2017)

**Tuition and fees:** $23,896.
**Per-credit charge:** $958.
**Room and board:** $9,548.

### FINANCIAL AID PICTURE (2014-2015)

**Students with need:** Out of 144 full-time freshmen who applied for aid, 123 were judged to have need. Of these, 123 received aid, and 18 had their full need met. Average financial aid package met 62% of need; average scholarship/grant was $3,905; average loan was $2,931. For part-time students, average financial aid package was $9,715.
**Students without need:** 53 full-time freshmen who did not demonstrate need for aid received scholarships/grants; average award was $4,159. No-need awards available for academics, athletics, leadership, music/drama.
**Scholarships offered:** 10 full-time freshmen received athletic scholarships; average amount $5,400.

### FINANCIAL AID PROCEDURES

**Forms required:** FAFSA.
**Dates and Deadlines:** Applicants notified on a rolling basis.
**Transfers:** No deadline. Applicants notified on a rolling basis.

### CONTACT

Steven Young, Director of Financial Aid
2625 East Cactus Road, Phoenix, AZ 85032-7042
(602) 386-4106

## Arizona State University

Tempe, Arizona
www.asu.edu                           Federal Code: 001081

**4-year public** university in small city.
**Enrollment:** 41,222 undergrads, 8% part-time. 7,594 full-time freshmen.
**Selectivity:** Admits over 75% of applicants.

### BASIC COSTS (2015-2016)

**Tuition and fees:** $10,156; out-of-state residents $25,456.
**Per-credit charge:** $677; out-of-state residents $1,033.
**Room and board:** $11,061.

### FINANCIAL AID PICTURE (2014-2015)

**Students with need:** Out of 6,039 full-time freshmen who applied for aid, 4,409 were judged to have need. Of these, 4,409 received aid, and 1,021 had their full need met. Average financial aid package met 71% of need; average scholarship/grant was $12,181; average loan was $3,097. For part-time students, average financial aid package was $7,704.
**Students without need:** 2,070 full-time freshmen who did not demonstrate need for aid received scholarships/grants; average award was $8,332. No-need awards available for academics, art, athletics, leadership, music/drama, state/district residency.
**Scholarships offered:** 34 full-time freshmen received athletic scholarships; average amount $15,825.

### FINANCIAL AID PROCEDURES

**Forms required:** FAFSA.
**Dates and Deadlines:** Priority date 3/1; no closing date. Applicants notified on a rolling basis starting 3/1.

### CONTACT

Melissa Pizzo, Dean, Admissions and Financial Aid Services
PO Box 870112, Tempe, AZ 85287-0112
(855) 278-5080

## Arizona Western College

Yuma, Arizona
www.azwestern.edu                     Federal Code: 001071

**2-year public** community college in small city.
**Enrollment:** 6,120 undergrads, 62% part-time. 774 full-time freshmen.
**Selectivity:** Open admission; but selective for some programs.

### BASIC COSTS (2016-2017)

**Tuition and fees:** $2,655; out-of-state residents $8,650.
**Per-credit charge:** $80; out-of-state residents $278.
**Room and board:** $6,559.

### FINANCIAL AID PICTURE (2014-2015)

**Students with need:** 92% of average financial aid package awarded as scholarships/grants, 8% awarded as loans/jobs. Need-based aid available for part-time students. Work study available nights, weekends, and for part-time students.
**Students without need:** No-need awards available for academics, art, athletics, leadership, minority status, music/drama.

### FINANCIAL AID PROCEDURES

**Forms required:** FAFSA, institutional form.
**Dates and Deadlines:** Priority date 4/1; no closing date. Applicants notified on a rolling basis starting 5/1.

### CONTACT

Lisa Seale, Director of Financial Aid
PO Box 929, Yuma, AZ 85366-0929
(928) 344-7634

## Art Institute of Phoenix

Phoenix, Arizona
www.artinstitutes.edu/phoenix          Federal Code: 040513

**3-year for-profit** culinary school and visual arts college in very large city.
**Enrollment:** 1,009 undergrads.

### BASIC COSTS (2015-2016)
**Additional info:** Diploma programs range from $23,088-$26,455; Associates programs: $43,290; Bachelors programs: $86,580. Books, supplies, fees range depending on program level and course of study. All costs are subject to change.

### FINANCIAL AID PICTURE
**Students with need:** Need-based aid available for full-time and part-time students.

### FINANCIAL AID PROCEDURES
**Forms required:** FAFSA.

### CONTACT
Abigail Garcia, Director of Administrative and Financial Services
2233 West Dunlap Avenue, Phoenix, AZ 85021-2859

## Brookline College: Phoenix

Phoenix, Arizona
www.brooklinecollege.edu          Federal Code: 022188

**2-year for-profit** nursing and career college in very large city.
**Enrollment:** 1,429 undergrads.
**Selectivity:** Open admission.

### BASIC COSTS (2015-2016)
**Additional info:** Diploma programs: $15,225-$20,000; Associate degree programs: $30,000-$31,800; Bachelor's degree programs: $15,500-$85,000. Fees vary by course and program. All fees are subject to change.

### FINANCIAL AID PICTURE
**Students with need:** Need-based aid available for full-time students.
**Students without need:** This college awards aid only to students with need.

### FINANCIAL AID PROCEDURES
**Forms required:** FAFSA, institutional form.

### CONTACT
Genna Gillary, Corporate Manager of Financial Aid
2445 West Dunlap Avenue, Suite 100, Phoenix, AZ 85021-5820
(602) 644-7110

## Brookline College: Tempe

Tempe, Arizona
www.brooklinecollege.edu          Federal Code: 022188

**2-year for-profit** branch campus and career college in very large city.
**Enrollment:** 418 undergrads.
**Selectivity:** Open admission; but selective for some programs.

### BASIC COSTS (2015-2016)
**Additional info:** Diploma programs: $15,225-$28,500; Associate degree programs: $30,000. Fees vary by course and program. All fees are subject to change.

### FINANCIAL AID PICTURE
**Students with need:** Need-based aid available for full-time students.
**Students without need:** This college awards aid only to students with need.

### FINANCIAL AID PROCEDURES
**Forms required:** FAFSA, institutional form.

### CONTACT
Genna Gillary, Corporate Manager of Financial Aid
1140-1150 South Priest Drive, Tempe, AZ 85281-5240
(480) 545-8755

## Brookline College: Tucson

Tucson, Arizona
www.brooklinecollege.edu          Federal Code: 022188

**2-year for-profit** branch campus and career college in very large city.
**Enrollment:** 507 undergrads.
**Selectivity:** Open admission.

### BASIC COSTS (2015-2016)
**Additional info:** Diploma programs: $12,750-$15,225; Associate degree programs: $30,000; Bachelor's degree programs: Criminal Justice: $60,00. Fees vary by course and program. All fees are subject to change.

### FINANCIAL AID PICTURE
**Students with need:** Need-based aid available for full-time and part-time students.
**Students without need:** This college awards aid only to students with need.

### FINANCIAL AID PROCEDURES
**Forms required:** FAFSA, institutional form.

### CONTACT
Genna Gillary, Corporate Manager of Financial Aid
5441 East 22nd Street, Suite 125, Tucson, AZ 85711-5444
(602) 644-7090

## Central Arizona College

Coolidge, Arizona
www.centralaz.edu          Federal Code: 007283

**2-year public** community college in small city.
**Enrollment:** 5,462 undergrads.
**Selectivity:** Open admission; but selective for some programs.

### BASIC COSTS (2015-2016)
**Tuition and fees:** $2,460; out-of-state residents $10,740.
**Per-credit charge:** $82; out-of-state residents $164.
**Room and board:** $6,800.

### FINANCIAL AID PICTURE
**Students with need:** Need-based aid available for full-time and part-time students. Work study available nights, weekends, and for part-time students.

### FINANCIAL AID PROCEDURES
**Forms required:** FAFSA.
**Dates and Deadlines:** Priority date 5/1; closing date 7/15. Must reply within 3 week(s) of notification.

### CONTACT
Elisa Juarez, Director of Financial Aid
Admissions Office, Coolidge, AZ 85128-9030
(520) 494-5425

## Chandler-Gilbert Community College

Chandler, Arizona
www.cgc.maricopa.edu          Federal Code: 030722

**2-year public** community college in small city.
**Enrollment:** 9,234 undergrads, 61% part-time. 680 full-time freshmen.

**Selectivity:** Open admission; but selective for some programs.

## BASIC COSTS (2015-2016)
**Tuition and fees:** $2,550; out-of-state residents $9,780.
**Per-credit charge:** $84; out-of-state residents $325.

## FINANCIAL AID PICTURE
**Students with need:** Work study available nights, weekends, and for part-time students.

## CONTACT
Timothy Wolsey, Director of Financial Aid
2626 East Pecos Road, Chandler, AZ 85225-2499
(855) 622-2332

## Cochise College
Douglas, Arizona
www.cochise.edu                Federal Code: 001072

**2-year public** community college in large town.
**Enrollment:** 3,949 undergrads, 57% part-time. 553 full-time freshmen.
**Selectivity:** Open admission; but selective for some programs.

## BASIC COSTS (2016-2017)
**Tuition and fees:** $2,370; out-of-state residents $7,500.
**Per-credit charge:** $79; out-of-state residents $250.
**Room and board:** $6,564.

## FINANCIAL AID PICTURE (2014-2015)
**Students with need:** Out of 466 full-time freshmen who applied for aid, 386 were judged to have need. Of these, 379 received aid. For part-time students, average financial aid package was $3,442.
**Students without need:** 15 full-time freshmen who did not demonstrate need for aid received scholarships/grants; average award was $1,615.
**Scholarships offered:** 46 full-time freshmen received athletic scholarships; average amount $3,875.

## FINANCIAL AID PROCEDURES
**Forms required:** FAFSA.
**Dates and Deadlines:** Priority date 5/1; closing date 6/15. Applicants notified on a rolling basis starting 6/1.
**Transfers:** Applicants notified on a rolling basis starting 6/1. Official college or university transcripts for all institutions previously attended required.

## CONTACT
Karen Emmer, Director of Financial Aid
901 North Colombo Avenue, Sierra Vista, AZ 85635-2317
(520) 515-5417

## DeVry University: Phoenix
Phoenix, Arizona
www.devry.edu                Federal Code: 008322

**4-year for-profit** university in large city.
**Enrollment:** 730 undergrads.

## BASIC COSTS (2015-2016)
**Tuition and fees:** $17,132.
**Per-credit charge:** $609.

## FINANCIAL AID PICTURE
**Students with need:** Need-based aid available for full-time and part-time students.
**Students without need:** This college awards aid only to students with need.

## FINANCIAL AID PROCEDURES
**Forms required:** FAFSA.

**Dates and Deadlines:** Applicants notified on a rolling basis.

## CONTACT
2149 West Dunlap Avenue, Phoenix, AZ 85021-2995
(602) 870-9229

## Dine College
Tsaile, Arizona
www.dinecollege.edu                Federal Code: 008246

**2-year public** community college in rural community.
**Enrollment:** 1,369 undergrads.
**Selectivity:** Open admission.

## BASIC COSTS (2015-2016)
**Tuition and fees:** $1,730; out-of-state residents $1,730.

## FINANCIAL AID PICTURE (2014-2015)
**Students with need:** 99% of average financial aid package awarded as scholarships/grants, 1% awarded as loans/jobs. Need-based aid available for part-time students.
**Students without need:** This college awards aid only to students with need.

## FINANCIAL AID PROCEDURES
**Forms required:** FAFSA, institutional form.
**Dates and Deadlines:** Priority date 4/15; closing date 10/31. Applicants notified on a rolling basis starting 3/1; must reply within 4 week(s) of notification.
**Transfers:** Priority date 3/17; no deadline. Applicants notified on a rolling basis starting 3/17; must reply within 8 week(s) of notification.

## CONTACT
Formon Thompson, Financial Aid Director
PO Box C 04, Tsaile, AZ 86556
(928) 724-6857

## Eastern Arizona College
Thatcher, Arizona
www.eac.edu                Federal Code: 001073

**2-year public** community college in large town.
**Enrollment:** 4,524 undergrads, 61% part-time. 692 full-time freshmen.
**Selectivity:** Open admission; but selective for some programs.

## BASIC COSTS (2015-2016)
**Tuition and fees:** $2,080; out-of-state residents $9,580.
**Per-credit charge:** $100; out-of-state residents $235.
**Room and board:** $5,980.

## FINANCIAL AID PICTURE (2014-2015)
**Students with need:** Out of 665 full-time freshmen who applied for aid, 562 were judged to have need. Of these, 314 received aid, and 31 had their full need met. Average financial aid package met 27% of need; average scholarship/grant was $6,560. For part-time students, average financial aid package was $3,298.
**Students without need:** 35 full-time freshmen who did not demonstrate need for aid received scholarships/grants; average award was $3,237. No-need awards available for academics, art, athletics, leadership, music/drama, state/district residency.
**Scholarships offered:** *Merit:* Departmental Scholarships; in-state tuition; based on 2.5 GPA. Academic Scholarships; in-state tuition; based on 3.0 GPA. Performing Arts Scholarships; amounts vary; based on 2.5 GPA and audition. *Athletic:* 13 full-time freshmen received athletic scholarships; average amount $3,326.

**Additional info:** Limited number of tuition waivers for New Mexico residents. Unlimited number of waivers for those meeting WUE requirements.

**FINANCIAL AID PROCEDURES**
**Forms required:** FAFSA, institutional form.
**Dates and Deadlines:** Priority date 3/1; no closing date. Applicants notified on a rolling basis starting 3/15.
**Transfers:** No deadline. Applicants notified on a rolling basis starting 3/15.

**CONTACT**
Bill Osborn, Director of Financial Aid
615 North Stadium Avenue, Thatcher, AZ 85552-0769
(928) 428-8287

## Embry-Riddle Aeronautical University: Prescott Campus
Prescott, Arizona
www.embryriddle.edu          Federal Code: 001479

**4-year private** university in large town.
**Enrollment:** 2,193 undergrads, 5% part-time. 579 full-time freshmen.
**Selectivity:** Admits over 75% of applicants.

**BASIC COSTS (2015-2016)**
**Tuition and fees:** $33,144.
**Per-credit charge:** $1,331.
**Room and board:** $9,990.

**FINANCIAL AID PICTURE**
**Students with need:** Need-based aid available for full-time and part-time students.

**FINANCIAL AID PROCEDURES**
**Forms required:** FAFSA.
**Dates and Deadlines:** Priority date 3/1; no closing date. Applicants notified on a rolling basis; must reply within 4 week(s) of notification.

**CONTACT**
Debra Hintz, Director, Financial Aid-Prescott Campus
3700 Willow Creek Road, Prescott, AZ 86301-3720
(928) 777-3765

## Estrella Mountain Community College
Avondale, Arizona
www.estrellamountain.edu          Federal Code: 031563

**2-year public** community college in small city.
**Enrollment:** 7,735 undergrads, 63% part-time. 865 full-time freshmen.
**Selectivity:** Open admission.

**BASIC COSTS (2015-2016)**
**Tuition and fees:** $2,550; out-of-state residents $9,780.

**FINANCIAL AID PICTURE**
**Students with need:** Need-based aid available for full-time and part-time students. Work study available nights.
**Students without need:** No-need awards available for leadership.

**FINANCIAL AID PROCEDURES**
**Dates and Deadlines:** Priority date 4/1; no closing date. Applicants notified on a rolling basis starting 4/15.

**CONTACT**
Rosanna Short, Director, Financial Aid
3000 North Dysart Road, Avondale, AZ 85392
(623) 935-8930

## GateWay Community College
Phoenix, Arizona
www.gatewaycc.edu          Federal Code: 008303

**2-year public** community and technical college in very large city.
**Enrollment:** 5,653 undergrads.
**Selectivity:** Open admission; but selective for some programs.

**BASIC COSTS (2015-2016)**
**Tuition and fees:** $2,550; out-of-state residents $9,780.

**FINANCIAL AID PICTURE**
**Students with need:** Need-based aid available for full-time and part-time students. Work study available nights, weekends, and for part-time students.
**Students without need:** No-need awards available for athletics.

**FINANCIAL AID PROCEDURES**
**Forms required:** FAFSA, institutional form.
**Dates and Deadlines:** Closing date 4/15. Applicants notified on a rolling basis; must reply within 4 week(s) of notification.

**CONTACT**
Suzanne Ringle, Director of Financial Aid
108 North 40th Street, Phoenix, AZ 85034
(602) 286-8115

## Grand Canyon University
Phoenix, Arizona
www.gcu.edu          Federal Code: 001074

**4-year for-profit** university in very large city.
**Enrollment:** 39,400 undergrads.

**BASIC COSTS (2015-2016)**
**Tuition and fees:** $17,150.
**Per-credit charge:** $688.
**Room and board:** $7,900.

**FINANCIAL AID PICTURE**
**Students with need:** Need-based aid available for full-time and part-time students. Work study available nights, weekends, and for part-time students.
**Students without need:** No-need awards available for academics, alumni affiliation, art, athletics, leadership, minority status, music/drama, religious affiliation, ROTC, state/district residency.

**FINANCIAL AID PROCEDURES**
**Forms required:** FAFSA.
**Dates and Deadlines:** Applicants notified on a rolling basis.
**Transfers:** No deadline. Applicants notified on a rolling basis.

**CONTACT**
Chris Linderson, Vice President of Financial Aid
3300 West Camelback Road, Phoenix, AZ 85017-8562
(800) 800-9776

## Mesa Community College
Mesa, Arizona
www.mesacc.edu          Federal Code: 001077

**2-year public** community college in very large city.
**Enrollment:** 21,491 undergrads.
**Selectivity:** Open admission; but selective for some programs.

**BASIC COSTS (2015-2016)**
**Tuition and fees:** $2,535; out-of-state residents $9,765.
**Per-credit charge:** $84; out-of-state residents $325.

## FINANCIAL AID PICTURE

**Students with need:** Need-based aid available for full-time and part-time students.

**Students without need:** No-need awards available for academics, athletics.

**Additional info:** Awards available for Maricopa County residents.

## FINANCIAL AID PROCEDURES

**Forms required:** FAFSA, institutional form.

**Dates and Deadlines:** Priority date 5/1; no closing date. Applicants notified on a rolling basis starting 7/1.

**Transfers:** Priority date 7/13. Applicants notified on a rolling basis.

## CONTACT

Patricia Peppin, Financial Aid

1833 West Southern Avenue, Mesa, AZ 85202

(480) 471-7400

## Mohave Community College
Kingman, Arizona

www.mohave.edu                    Federal Code: 011864

**2-year public** community college in small city.

**Enrollment:** 3,199 undergrads.

**Selectivity:** Open admission; but selective for some programs.

## BASIC COSTS (2015-2016)

**Tuition and fees:** $2,640; out-of-state residents $8,715.

**Per-credit charge:** $81; out-of-state residents $284.

## FINANCIAL AID PICTURE

**Students with need:** Need-based aid available for full-time and part-time students. Work study available nights.

**Students without need:** This college awards aid only to students with need.

## FINANCIAL AID PROCEDURES

**Forms required:** FAFSA, institutional form.

**Dates and Deadlines:** Priority date 4/15; closing date 7/15. Applicants notified on a rolling basis starting 5/1; must reply within 2 week(s) of notification.

## CONTACT

Shannon Sheaff, Director of Financial Aid

1971 Jagerson Avenue, Kingman, AZ 86409

(866) 664-2832

## Northcentral University
Prescott Valley, Arizona

www.ncu.edu                    Federal Code: 038133

**Upper-division for-profit** virtual university in large town.

**Enrollment:** 181 undergrads.

## BASIC COSTS (2015-2016)

**Additional info:** Bachelor degree programs: range from $10,526-$13,310; Associates programs: $1,296 per credit hour. Books, supplies, fees range depending on program level and course of study. All costs are subject to change.

## FINANCIAL AID PICTURE

**Students with need:** Need-based aid available for full-time and part-time students.

## FINANCIAL AID PROCEDURES

**Dates and Deadlines:** Applicants notified on a rolling basis; must reply within 4 week(s) of notification.

**Transfers:** No deadline. Applicants notified on a rolling basis.

## CONTACT

Ian Cooper, Director Learner Financial Services

8667 East Hartford Drive, Scottsdale, AZ 85255

(888) 327-2877 ext. 8080

## Northern Arizona University
Flagstaff, Arizona

www.nau.edu                    Federal Code: 001082

**4-year public** university in small city.

**Enrollment:** 24,992 undergrads, 19% part-time. 4,418 full-time freshmen.

**Selectivity:** Admits over 75% of applicants.

## BASIC COSTS (2015-2016)

**Tuition and fees:** $10,358; out-of-state residents $23,348.

**Room and board:** $9,132.

**Additional info:** Tuition at time of enrollment locked for 4 years.

## FINANCIAL AID PICTURE (2014-2015)

**Students with need:** Out of 3,903 full-time freshmen who applied for aid, 3,011 were judged to have need. Of these, 2,908 received aid, and 413 had their full need met. Average financial aid package met 62% of need; average scholarship/grant was $6,838; average loan was $3,343. For part-time students, average financial aid package was $6,709.

**Students without need:** 602 full-time freshmen who did not demonstrate need for aid received scholarships/grants; average award was $7,081. No-need awards available for academics, alumni affiliation, art, athletics, leadership, minority status, music/drama, ROTC, state/district residency.

**Scholarships offered:** 58 full-time freshmen received athletic scholarships; average amount $16,776.

**Additional info:** Guaranteed fixed tuition for 4 years and guaranteed gift aid for 4 years.

## FINANCIAL AID PROCEDURES

**Forms required:** FAFSA.

**Dates and Deadlines:** Priority date 2/1; no closing date. Applicants notified on a rolling basis starting 2/1.

**Transfers:** No deadline. Applicants notified on a rolling basis.

## CONTACT

Nydia Nittmann, Director of Financial Aid

PO Box 4084, Flagstaff, AZ 86011-4084

(928) 523-4951

## Northland Pioneer College
Holbrook, Arizona

www.npc.edu                    Federal Code: 011862

**2-year public** community and technical college in small town.

**Enrollment:** 3,233 undergrads.

**Selectivity:** Open admission; but selective for some programs.

## BASIC COSTS (2015-2016)

**Tuition and fees:** $2,110; out-of-state residents $10,270.

**Per-credit charge:** $68; out-of-state residents $325.

## FINANCIAL AID PICTURE

**Students with need:** Need-based aid available for full-time and part-time students. Work study available nights, weekends, and for part-time students.

**Students without need:** No-need awards available for academics, art, job skills, leadership, minority status, music/drama, state/district residency.

## FINANCIAL AID PROCEDURES

**Forms required:** FAFSA, institutional form.

**Dates and Deadlines:** Priority date 6/1; no closing date. Applicants notified on a rolling basis starting 5/15; must reply within 2 week(s) of notification.

**Transfers:** No deadline. Applicants notified on a rolling basis.

**CONTACT**
Beaulah Bob-Pennypacker, Financial Aid Coordinator
PO Box 610, Holbrook, AZ 86025-0610
(928) 524-7626

## Paradise Valley Community College
Phoenix, Arizona
www.pvc.maricopa.edu            Federal Code: 026236

**2-year public** community college in very large city.
**Enrollment:** 2,867 full-time undergrads.
**Selectivity:** Open admission.

**BASIC COSTS (2015-2016)**
**Tuition and fees:** $2,550; out-of-state residents $9,780.

**FINANCIAL AID PICTURE**
**Students with need:** Need-based aid available for full-time and part-time students.

**FINANCIAL AID PROCEDURES**
**Forms required:** FAFSA.
**Dates and Deadlines:** Applicants notified on a rolling basis starting 6/1.

**CONTACT**
Ken Clarke, Director of Financial Aid
18401 North 32nd Street, Phoenix, AZ 85032
(602) 787-7100

## Phoenix College
Phoenix, Arizona
www.phoenixcollege.edu            Federal Code: 001078

**2-year public** community college in very large city.
**Enrollment:** 9,921 undergrads, 69% part-time. 742 full-time freshmen.
**Selectivity:** Open admission; but selective for some programs.

**BASIC COSTS (2016-2017)**
**Tuition and fees:** $2,550; out-of-state residents $9,780.

**FINANCIAL AID PICTURE (2015-2016)**
**Students with need:** 65% of average financial aid package awarded as scholarships/grants, 35% awarded as loans/jobs. Work study available weekends and for part-time students.

**FINANCIAL AID PROCEDURES**
**Forms required:** FAFSA.
**Dates and Deadlines:** Priority date 6/30; no closing date. Applicants notified on a rolling basis.

**CONTACT**
Cindy Ramos, Director
1202 West Thomas Road, Phoenix, AZ 85013
(602) 285-7425

## Pima Community College
Tucson, Arizona
www.pima.edu            Federal Code: 007266

**2-year public** community and technical college in very large city.
**Enrollment:** 33,082 undergrads.
**Selectivity:** Open admission; but selective for some programs.

**BASIC COSTS (2015-2016)**
**Tuition and fees:** $2,450; out-of-state residents $10,745.
**Per-credit charge:** $76; out-of-state residents $352.

**FINANCIAL AID PICTURE**
**Students with need:** Need-based aid available for full-time and part-time students.
**Students without need:** No-need awards available for academics, alumni affiliation, art, athletics, minority status, music/drama.

**FINANCIAL AID PROCEDURES**
**Forms required:** FAFSA.
**Dates and Deadlines:** Priority date 4/4; no closing date. Applicants notified on a rolling basis starting 5/1; must reply within 2 week(s) of notification.

**CONTACT**
Anna Reese, Executive Director of Financial Aid
4905B East Broadway, Tucson, AZ 85709-1120
(520) 206-4950

## Prescott College
Prescott, Arizona
www.prescott.edu            Federal Code: 013659

**4-year private** liberal arts college in small city.
**Enrollment:** 395 undergrads, 24% part-time. 35 full-time freshmen.
**Selectivity:** Admits 50 to 75% of applicants.

**BASIC COSTS (2015-2016)**
**Tuition and fees:** $27,503.
**Room and board:** $7,200.

**FINANCIAL AID PICTURE (2015-2016)**
**Students with need:** Out of 28 full-time freshmen who applied for aid, 27 were judged to have need. Of these, 27 received aid, and 3 had their full need met. Average financial aid package met 75% of need; average scholarship/grant was $18,461; average loan was $3,840. For part-time students, average financial aid package was $10,222.
**Students without need:** 8 full-time freshmen who did not demonstrate need for aid received scholarships/grants; average award was $4,750. No-need awards available for academics, leadership.

**FINANCIAL AID PROCEDURES**
**Forms required:** FAFSA.
**Dates and Deadlines:** Priority date 3/1; no closing date. Applicants notified on a rolling basis starting 3/15.
**Transfers:** No deadline. Applicants notified on a rolling basis starting 3/15; must reply within 4 week(s) of notification. Dean's 21st Century Global Leader Scholarship: $10,000 per year; 2200 SAT/33 ACT or 3.25 college GPA, proof of volunteering, superior application rating. Merit Scholarship: $8,000 per year; 1550 SAT/23 ACT or 3.0 GPA, proof of volunteering, superior application rating. Phi Theta Kappa Scholarship: $2,000 per year.

**CONTACT**
Mary Frances Causey, Director of Financial Aid
220 Grove Avenue, Prescott, AZ 86301
(928) 350-1111

## Refrigeration School
Phoenix, Arizona
www.refrigerationschool.com            Federal Code: 014127

**2-year for-profit** technical college in very large city.
**Enrollment:** 1,185 undergrads.
**Selectivity:** Open admission; but selective for some programs.

**BASIC COSTS (2015-2016)**
**Tuition and fees:** $20,325.

**FINANCIAL AID PICTURE (2014-2015)**
**Students with need:** 44% of average financial aid package awarded as scholarships/grants, 56% awarded as loans/jobs.

## CONTACT

Melanie Zuverink, Financial Aid Director
4210 East Washington Street, Phoenix, AZ 85034-1816
(602) 275-7133

## Rio Salado College

Tempe, Arizona
www.riosalado.edu                      Federal Code: 014483

**2-year public** community college in very large city.
**Enrollment:** 58,980 undergrads.
**Selectivity:** Open admission; but selective for some programs.

### BASIC COSTS (2015-2016)

**Tuition and fees:** $2,560; out-of-state residents $9,790.
**Per-credit charge:** $84; out-of-state residents $325.

### FINANCIAL AID PICTURE

**Students with need:** Need-based aid available for full-time and part-time students.
**Students without need:** This college awards aid only to students with need.

### FINANCIAL AID PROCEDURES

**Forms required:** FAFSA, institutional form.
**Dates and Deadlines:** Priority date 6/30; no closing date. Applicants notified on a rolling basis starting 6/30.

### CONTACT

Nanci Regehr, Director of Financial Aid
2323 West 14th Street, Tempe, AZ 85281
(480) 517-8310

## Scottsdale Community College

Scottsdale, Arizona
www.scottsdalecc.edu                   Federal Code: 008304

**2-year public** community college in small city.
**Enrollment:** 3,445 undergrads.
**Selectivity:** Open admission.

### BASIC COSTS (2015-2016)

**Tuition and fees:** $2,550; out-of-state residents $9,780.
**Per-credit charge:** $84; out-of-state residents $325.

### FINANCIAL AID PICTURE

**Students with need:** Need-based aid available for full-time and part-time students.
**Students without need:** No-need awards available for academics, athletics.

### FINANCIAL AID PROCEDURES

**Forms required:** FAFSA.
**Dates and Deadlines:** Priority date 6/1; no closing date. Applicants notified on a rolling basis starting 7/1; must reply by 7/15 or within 3 week(s) of notification.
**Transfers:** Priority date 7/1; no deadline. Applicants notified on a rolling basis starting 7/1.

### CONTACT

Stacie Beck, Director of Financial Aid
9000 East Chaparral Road, Scottsdale, AZ 85256-2626
(480) 423-6549

## South Mountain Community College

Phoenix, Arizona
www.southmountaincc.edu                Federal Code: 015001

**2-year public** community college in very large city.
**Enrollment:** 1,340 undergrads.
**Selectivity:** Open admission.

### BASIC COSTS (2016-2017)

**Tuition and fees:** $2,550; out-of-state residents $9,780.
**Per-credit charge:** $84; out-of-state residents $325.

### FINANCIAL AID PICTURE

**Students with need:** Need-based aid available for full-time and part-time students. Work study available nights, weekends, and for part-time students.
**Students without need:** No-need awards available for academics, athletics, minority status, music/drama.

### FINANCIAL AID PROCEDURES

**Forms required:** FAFSA.
**Dates and Deadlines:** Priority date 5/1; no closing date. Applicants notified on a rolling basis starting 5/15; must reply within 3 week(s) of notification.

### CONTACT

Inez Moreno-Weinert, Director of Financial Aid and Placement
7050 South 24th Street, Phoenix, AZ 85042
(602) 243-8300

## Southwest University of Visual Arts

Tucson, Arizona
www.suva.edu                           Federal Code: 024915

**4-year for-profit** visual arts college in very large city.
**Enrollment:** 161 undergrads.

### BASIC COSTS (2015-2016)

**Tuition and fees:** $22,944.
**Additional info:** Estimated total costs for books and supplies for each program: $3,900-$4,750.

### FINANCIAL AID PICTURE

**Students with need:** Need-based aid available for full-time and part-time students. Work study available nights, weekends, and for part-time students.
**Students without need:** This college awards aid only to students with need.
**Scholarships offered:** Board of Trustees Scholarship: Transfer Student Scholarship; Scholarship for Continuing Students.

### FINANCIAL AID PROCEDURES

**Forms required:** FAFSA.
**Transfers:** No deadline. Applicants notified on a rolling basis.

### CONTACT

Julie Mairs
2525 North Country Club Road, Tucson, AZ 85716
(520) 325-0123

## Tohono O'odham Community College

Sells, Arizona
www.tocc.edu                           Federal Code: 037844

**2-year public** community college in rural community.
**Enrollment:** 192 undergrads, 58% part-time. 14 full-time freshmen.
**Selectivity:** Open admission.

### BASIC COSTS (2015-2016)

**Tuition and fees:** $2,055; out-of-state residents $4,620.

**Room only:** $2,400.

## FINANCIAL AID PICTURE (2014-2015)

**Students with need:** 99% of average financial aid package awarded as scholarships/grants, 1% awarded as loans/jobs. Need-based aid available for part-time students.

**Students without need:** This college awards aid only to students with need.

## FINANCIAL AID PROCEDURES

**Forms required:** FAFSA, institutional form.

**Dates and Deadlines:** Applicants notified on a rolling basis.

## CONTACT

Alvaro Rivera, Financial Aid Director
PO Box 3129, Sells, AZ 85634-3129
(520) 383-8401 ext. 41

## University of Arizona

Tucson, Arizona
www.arizona.edu
Federal Code: 001083

**4-year public** university in very large city.

**Enrollment:** 33,364 undergrads, 11% part-time. 6,974 full-time freshmen.

**Selectivity:** Admits over 75% of applicants.

## BASIC COSTS (2015-2016)

**Tuition and fees:** $11,400; out-of-state residents $32,600.

**Room and board:** $9,840.

**Additional info:** Tuition/fee waivers available for minority students.

## FINANCIAL AID PICTURE (2014-2015)

**Students with need:** Out of 5,183 full-time freshmen who applied for aid, 3,837 were judged to have need. Of these, 3,691 received aid, and 501 had their full need met. Average financial aid package met 59% of need; average scholarship/grant was $10,134; average loan was $3,299. For part-time students, average financial aid package was $8,871.

**Students without need:** 1,888 full-time freshmen who did not demonstrate need for aid received scholarships/grants; average award was $8,164. No-need awards available for academics, art, athletics, music/drama.

**Scholarships offered:** *Merit:* Various merit scholarships available. National Merit scholarship: $6,000-$10,000 a year. *Athletic:* 36 full-time freshmen received athletic scholarships; average amount $20,317.

**Additional info:** Arizona Assurance Program; provides housing, books, and tuition for all new, incoming resident freshmen; must be Pell-eligible with combined family income less than $42,500; funding provided as grants, scholarships, and federal work-study.

## FINANCIAL AID PROCEDURES

**Forms required:** FAFSA. CSS PROFILE required for some; subset of applicants asked to comply based on FAFSA information.

**Dates and Deadlines:** Priority date 3/1; no closing date. Applicants notified on a rolling basis starting 2/1.

**Transfers:** Priority date 3/1. Awards based on academic factors for both residents and non-residents and vary in amount each year.

## CONTACT

Elizabeth Acree
1428 East University Boulevard, Tucson, AZ 85721-0040
(520) 621-1858

## Western International University

Tempe, Arizona
www.west.edu
Federal Code: 014970

**4-year for-profit** university and business college in very large city.

**Enrollment:** 1,157 undergrads. 216 full-time freshmen.

**Selectivity:** Open admission.

## BASIC COSTS (2015-2016)

**Per-credit charge:** $250.

**Additional info:** $250 per-credit-hour for online undergraduate course; includes books and supplies.

## FINANCIAL AID PICTURE

**Students with need:** Need-based aid available for full-time students.

**Students without need:** This college awards aid only to students with need.

## FINANCIAL AID PROCEDURES

**Forms required:** FAFSA, institutional form.

**Dates and Deadlines:** Applicants notified on a rolling basis.

**Transfers:** No deadline. Applicants notified on a rolling basis.

## CONTACT

Beth Carlisle, Director of Finance
1601 West Fountainhead Parkway, Tempe, AZ 85282
(602) 943-2311

## Yavapai College

Prescott, Arizona
www.yc.edu
Federal Code: 001079

**2-year public** community college in large town.

**Enrollment:** 8,273 undergrads.

**Selectivity:** Open admission; but selective for some programs.

## BASIC COSTS (2015-2016)

**Tuition and fees:** $2,250; out-of-state residents $10,560.

**Per-credit charge:** $75; out-of-state residents $353.

**Room and board:** $8,858.

## FINANCIAL AID PICTURE

**Students with need:** Need-based aid available for full-time and part-time students.

**Students without need:** No-need awards available for academics, athletics.

## FINANCIAL AID PROCEDURES

**Forms required:** FAFSA.

**Dates and Deadlines:** Priority date 4/1; no closing date. Applicants notified on a rolling basis.

## CONTACT

Terri Eckel, Financial Aid Operations
1100 East Sheldon Street, Prescott, AZ 86301
(928) 776-2152

# Arkansas

## Arkansas Baptist College

Little Rock, Arkansas
www.arkansasbaptist.edu
Federal Code: 001087

**4-year private** liberal arts college in small city, affiliated with American Baptist Churches in the USA.

**Enrollment:** 989 undergrads.

**Selectivity:** Open admission.

## BASIC COSTS (2015-2016)

**Tuition and fees:** $8,760.

**Per-credit charge:** $335.

**Room and board:** $7,826.

## FINANCIAL AID PICTURE

**Students with need:** Need-based aid available for full-time and part-time students.

**Students without need:** This college awards aid only to students with need.

## FINANCIAL AID PROCEDURES

**Forms required:** FAFSA.

**Dates and Deadlines:** Closing date 4/1. Applicants notified on a rolling basis starting 6/15.

## CONTACT

Phillip Rodgers, Director of Financial Aid
1621 Dr. Martin Luther King Drive, Little Rock, AR 72202
(501) 420-1226

# Arkansas Northeastern College

Blytheville, Arkansas
www.anc.edu                                    Federal Code: 012860

**2-year public** community college in large town.

**Enrollment:** 1,361 undergrads.

**Selectivity:** Open admission; but selective for some programs.

## BASIC COSTS (2015-2016)

**Tuition and fees:** $2,180; out-of-district residents $2,480; out-of-state residents $3,980.

**Per-credit charge:** $65; out-of-district residents $75; out-of-state residents $125.

## FINANCIAL AID PICTURE (2014-2015)

**Students with need:** 97% of average financial aid package awarded as scholarships/grants, 3% awarded as loans/jobs. Need-based aid available for part-time students.

**Students without need:** No-need awards available for academics, art, minority status, music/drama, state/district residency.

## FINANCIAL AID PROCEDURES

**Forms required:** FAFSA, institutional form.

**Dates and Deadlines:** Priority date 4/15; no closing date. Applicants notified on a rolling basis starting 3/1; must reply within 2 week(s) of notification.

## CONTACT

Mindy Walker, Director of Financial Aid
PO Box 1109, Blytheville, AR 72316-1109
(870) 762-1020 ext. 1160

# Arkansas State University

State University, Arkansas
www.astate.edu                                 Federal Code: 001090

**4-year public** university in small city.

**Enrollment:** 8,909 undergrads, 19% part-time. 1,542 full-time freshmen.

**Selectivity:** Admits 50 to 75% of applicants.

## BASIC COSTS (2015-2016)

**Tuition and fees:** $8,050; out-of-state residents $14,050.

**Per-credit charge:** $200; out-of-state residents $400.

**Room and board:** $8,140.

**Additional info:** There is a College Support Assessment Fee, $22 per-credit hour for undergraduate students and $52 per-credit hour for graduate students, for the Colleges of Business, Engineering, Nursing & Health Professions, and Sciences & Mathematics.

## FINANCIAL AID PICTURE (2015-2016)

**Students with need:** Out of 1,478 full-time freshmen who applied for aid, 1,426 were judged to have need. Of these, 1,411 received aid, and 577 had

their full need met. Average financial aid package met 62% of need; average scholarship/grant was $10,000; average loan was $6,200. Need-based aid available for part-time students.

**Students without need:** 225 full-time freshmen who did not demonstrate need for aid received scholarships/grants; average award was $5,000. No-need awards available for academics, alumni affiliation, art, athletics, leadership, minority status, music/drama, ROTC, state/district residency.

**Scholarships offered:** 75 full-time freshmen received athletic scholarships; average amount $13,200.

## FINANCIAL AID PROCEDURES

**Forms required:** FAFSA, institutional form.

**Dates and Deadlines:** Priority date 2/15; closing date 7/1. Applicants notified on a rolling basis starting 6/1; must reply within 2 week(s) of notification.

**Transfers:** Applicants notified on a rolling basis starting 6/1; must reply within 2 week(s) of notification.

## CONTACT

Terry Finney, Director of Financial Aid and Scholarships
PO Box 1570, State University, AR 72467-1570
(870) 972-2310

# Arkansas State University Mid-South

West Memphis, Arkansas
www.asumidsouth.edu                            Federal Code: 015862

**2-year public** community and junior college in large town.

**Enrollment:** 1,896 undergrads. 187 full-time freshmen.

**Selectivity:** Open admission.

## BASIC COSTS (2015-2016)

**Tuition and fees:** $3,190; out-of-district residents $3,790; out-of-state residents $4,990.

**Per-credit charge:** $90; out-of-district residents $110; out-of-state residents $150.

## FINANCIAL AID PICTURE (2014-2015)

**Students with need:** Out of 174 full-time freshmen who applied for aid, 173 were judged to have need. Of these, 173 received aid. Average financial aid package met 29% of need. Need-based aid available for part-time students.

**Students without need:** 1 full-time freshmen who did not demonstrate need for aid received scholarships/grants; average award was $1,350. No-need awards available for academics, state/district residency.

## FINANCIAL AID PROCEDURES

**Forms required:** FAFSA, institutional form.

**Dates and Deadlines:** Priority date 4/30; no closing date. Applicants notified on a rolling basis starting 6/1; must reply within 2 week(s) of notification.

## CONTACT

Carol McHann, Director of Financial Aid
2000 West Broadway, West Memphis, AR 72301
(870) 733-6741

# Arkansas State University: Beebe

Beebe, Arkansas
www.asub.edu                                   Federal Code: 001090

**2-year public** community college in small town.

**Enrollment:** 2,889 undergrads, 30% part-time. 689 full-time freshmen.

**Selectivity:** Open admission; but selective for some programs.

## BASIC COSTS (2015-2016)

**Tuition and fees:** $3,330; out-of-state residents $5,430.

**Per-credit charge:** $96; out-of-state residents $166.

**Room and board:** $4,842.

### FINANCIAL AID PICTURE

**Students with need:** Need-based aid available for full-time and part-time students. Work study available nights, weekends, and for part-time students.
**Students without need:** No-need awards available for academics, leadership, music/drama.

### FINANCIAL AID PROCEDURES

**Forms required:** FAFSA, institutional form.
**Dates and Deadlines:** Priority date 6/1; no closing date. Applicants notified on a rolling basis starting 6/1; must reply within 2 week(s) of notification.
**Transfers:** No deadline. Applicants notified on a rolling basis.

### CONTACT

Louise Driver, Director of Financial Aid
PO Box 1000, Beebe, AR 72012-1000
(501) 882-8245

## Arkansas State University: Mountain Home

Mountain Home, Arkansas
www.asumh.edu                Federal Code: 901090

**2-year public** community and technical college in large town.
**Enrollment:** 1,224 undergrads.
**Selectivity:** Open admission; but selective for some programs.

### BASIC COSTS (2015-2016)

**Tuition and fees:** $3,420; out-of-state residents $5,400.
**Per-credit charge:** $92; out-of-state residents $158.

### FINANCIAL AID PICTURE

**Students with need:** Need-based aid available for full-time and part-time students.
**Students without need:** No-need awards available for academics, alumni affiliation, leadership, state/district residency.
**Scholarships offered:** Academic Distinction Scholarship: full tuition; for qualified Arkansas residents.
**Additional info:** Satisfactory academic progress policy for Title IV aid.

### FINANCIAL AID PROCEDURES

**Forms required:** FAFSA, institutional form.
**Dates and Deadlines:** Priority date 6/1; no closing date. Applicants notified on a rolling basis starting 5/1; must reply within 2 week(s) of notification.
**Transfers:** No deadline. Applicants notified on a rolling basis starting 7/1; must reply within 2 week(s) of notification. All final academic transcripts required prior to awarding Title IV aid.

### CONTACT

Clay Berry, Director of Financial Aid
1600 South College Street, Mountain Home, AR 72653
(870) 508-6100 ext. 195

## Arkansas Tech University

Russellville, Arkansas
www.atu.edu                Federal Code: 001089

**4-year public** university and liberal arts college in large town.
**Enrollment:** 8,799 undergrads, 20% part-time. 1,863 full-time freshmen.
**Selectivity:** Admits over 75% of applicants.

### BASIC COSTS (2015-2016)

**Tuition and fees:** $7,740; out-of-state residents $14,190.
**Per-credit charge:** $215; out-of-state residents $430.
**Room and board:** $6,918.

### FINANCIAL AID PICTURE (2014-2015)

**Students with need:** Out of 1,786 full-time freshmen who applied for aid, 1,275 were judged to have need. Of these, 1,262 received aid, and 81 had their full need met. Average financial aid package met 62% of need; average scholarship/grant was $4,552; average loan was $3,003. For part-time students, average financial aid package was $5,662.
**Students without need:** 477 full-time freshmen who did not demonstrate need for aid received scholarships/grants; average award was $5,748. No-need awards available for academics, athletics, leadership, music/drama, ROTC, state/district residency.
**Scholarships offered:** 67 full-time freshmen received athletic scholarships; average amount $5,254.

### FINANCIAL AID PROCEDURES

**Forms required:** FAFSA, institutional form.
**Dates and Deadlines:** Priority date 3/15; no closing date. Applicants notified on a rolling basis starting 3/15; must reply within 4 week(s) of notification.
**Transfers:** No deadline. Applicants notified on a rolling basis starting 5/1; must reply within 2 week(s) of notification.

### CONTACT

Shirley Goines, Director of Student Financial Aid
1605 Coliseum Drive, Suite 141, Russellville, AR 72801-2222
(479) 968-0399

## Black River Technical College

Pocahontas, Arkansas
www.blackrivertech.edu                Federal Code: 011948

**2-year public** technical college in small town.
**Enrollment:** 1,745 undergrads.
**Selectivity:** Open admission; but selective for some programs.

### BASIC COSTS (2015-2016)

**Tuition and fees:** $3,240; out-of-state residents $6,330.
**Per-credit charge:** $86; out-of-state residents $189.

### FINANCIAL AID PICTURE

**Students with need:** Need-based aid available for full-time and part-time students.
**Students without need:** No-need awards available for academics, leadership, minority status, music/drama, state/district residency.

### FINANCIAL AID PROCEDURES

**Forms required:** FAFSA, institutional form.
**Dates and Deadlines:** Priority date 4/1; closing date 6/30. Applicants notified on a rolling basis starting 4/1.
**Transfers:** No deadline.

### CONTACT

Brandi Chester, Financial Aid Director
Highway 304 East, Pocahontas, AR 72455
(870) 248-4000 ext. 4020

## Central Baptist College

Conway, Arkansas
www.cbc.edu                Federal Code: 001093

**4-year private** Bible college in large town, affiliated with Baptist faith.
**Enrollment:** 769 undergrads, 19% part-time. 108 full-time freshmen.

### BASIC COSTS (2015-2016)

**Tuition and fees:** $14,400.
**Per-credit charge:** $430.
**Room and board:** $7,500.

**FINANCIAL AID PICTURE**

**Students with need:** Need-based aid available for full-time and part-time students. Work study available nights, weekends, and for part-time students.
**Students without need:** No-need awards available for academics, alumni affiliation, athletics, leadership, music/drama, religious affiliation.

**FINANCIAL AID PROCEDURES**

**Forms required:** FAFSA, institutional form.
**Dates and Deadlines:** Priority date 7/1; closing date 8/1. Applicants notified on a rolling basis starting 4/1.
**Transfers:** No deadline. Applicants notified on a rolling basis.

**CONTACT**

Tonya Hammontree, Director of Financial Aid
1501 College Avenue, Conway, AR 72034
(501) 205-8809

## College of the Ouachitas
Malvern, Arkansas
www.coto.edu                    Federal Code: 009976

**2-year public** community and technical college in small town.
**Enrollment:** 764 undergrads, 35% part-time. 118 full-time freshmen.
**Selectivity:** Open admission; but selective for some programs.

**BASIC COSTS (2015-2016)**
**Tuition and fees:** $3,620; out-of-state residents $6,410.
**Per-credit charge:** $93; out-of-state residents $186.

**FINANCIAL AID PICTURE (2014-2015)**
**Students with need:** Need-based aid available for full-time and part-time students. Work study available nights.
**Students without need:** No-need awards available for academics.

**FINANCIAL AID PROCEDURES**
**Forms required:** FAFSA.
**Dates and Deadlines:** Applicants notified on a rolling basis starting 7/1; must reply within 6 week(s) of notification.
**Transfers:** No deadline. Applicants notified on a rolling basis; must reply within 6 week(s) of notification.

**CONTACT**
Vickie Young, Director of Financial Aid
One College Circle, Malvern, AR 72104
(501) 337-5000 ext. 1122

## Cossatot Community College of the University of Arkansas
De Queen, Arkansas
www.cccua.edu                    Federal Code: 012432

**2-year public** community college in small town.
**Enrollment:** 969 undergrads.
**Selectivity:** Open admission; but selective for some programs.

**BASIC COSTS (2015-2016)**
**Tuition and fees:** $2,670; out-of-district residents $3,030; out-of-state residents $5,820.
**Per-credit charge:** $65; out-of-district residents $77; out-of-state residents $170.

**FINANCIAL AID PICTURE**
**Students with need:** Need-based aid available for full-time and part-time students. Work study available nights.
**Additional info:** Active or honorably discharged military and their dependents receive tuition discounts.

**FINANCIAL AID PROCEDURES**

**Forms required:** FAFSA, institutional form.
**Dates and Deadlines:** Priority date 5/1; no closing date. Applicants notified on a rolling basis starting 3/1.
**Transfers:** Applicants notified on a rolling basis starting 3/1.

**CONTACT**

Denise Hammond, Director of Financial Aid
183 College Drive, De Queen, AR 71832
(870) 584-4471

## Crowley's Ridge College
Paragould, Arkansas
www.crc.edu                    Federal Code: 001095

**2-year private** liberal arts college in large town, affiliated with Church of Christ.
**Enrollment:** 176 undergrads.
**Selectivity:** Open admission.

**BASIC COSTS (2015-2016)**
**Tuition and fees:** $11,300.
**Room and board:** $6,100.

**FINANCIAL AID PICTURE**
**Students with need:** Work study available nights, weekends, and for part-time students.
**Students without need:** No-need awards available for academics, athletics, leadership, music/drama.

**FINANCIAL AID PROCEDURES**
**Forms required:** FAFSA.
**Dates and Deadlines:** Applicants notified on a rolling basis starting 5/30.
**Transfers:** No deadline. Applicants notified on a rolling basis.

**CONTACT**
David Goff, Director of Financial Aid
100 College Drive, Paragould, AR 72450
(870) 236-6901 ext. 119

## East Arkansas Community College
Forrest City, Arkansas
www.eacc.edu                    Federal Code: 012260

**2-year public** community college in large town.
**Enrollment:** 1,268 undergrads.
**Selectivity:** Open admission; but selective for some programs.

**BASIC COSTS (2015-2016)**
**Tuition and fees:** $2,790; out-of-district residents $3,090; out-of-state residents $3,600.
**Per-credit charge:** $82; out-of-district residents $92; out-of-state residents $109.

**FINANCIAL AID PICTURE**
**Students with need:** Need-based aid available for full-time and part-time students.
**Students without need:** This college awards aid only to students with need.

**FINANCIAL AID PROCEDURES**
**Forms required:** FAFSA.
**Dates and Deadlines:** Priority date 3/1; closing date 7/1. Applicants notified on a rolling basis starting 5/15; must reply within 2 week(s) of notification.

**CONTACT**
Alvin Coleman, Director of Financial Aid
1700 Newcastle Road, Forrest City, AR 72335-2204
(870) 633-4480 ext. 225

## Ecclesia College
Springdale, Arkansas
www.ecollege.edu                    Federal Code: 038553

**4-year private** Bible and liberal arts college in large town, affiliated with interdenominational tradition.
**Enrollment:** 193 undergrads, 12% part-time. 68 full-time freshmen.
**Selectivity:** Admits 50 to 75% of applicants.

**BASIC COSTS (2016-2017)**
**Tuition and fees:** $16,090.
**Per-credit charge:** $475.
**Room and board:** $5,010.
**Additional info:** Tuition/fee waivers available for adults.

**FINANCIAL AID PICTURE**
**Students with need:** Need-based aid available for full-time and part-time students. Work study available nights, weekends, and for part-time students.
**Students without need:** No-need awards available for academics, athletics, job skills, leadership, music/drama.

**FINANCIAL AID PROCEDURES**
**Forms required:** FAFSA.
**Dates and Deadlines:** Applicants notified on a rolling basis starting 7/1.
**Transfers:** No deadline. Applicants notified on a rolling basis starting 2/1; must reply within 4 week(s) of notification.

**CONTACT**
Linda Sutherland, Director of Financial Aid
9653 Nations Drive, Springdale, AR 72762
(479) 248-7236

## Harding University
Searcy, Arkansas
www.harding.edu                    Federal Code: 001097

**4-year private** university in large town, affiliated with Church of Christ.
**Enrollment:** 4,442 undergrads, 8% part-time. 1,065 full-time freshmen.
**Selectivity:** Admits over 75% of applicants.

**BASIC COSTS (2015-2016)**
**Tuition and fees:** $17,670.
**Per-credit charge:** $570.
**Room and board:** $6,668.

**FINANCIAL AID PICTURE (2014-2015)**
**Students with need:** Out of 926 full-time freshmen who applied for aid, 693 were judged to have need. Of these, 689 received aid, and 239 had their full need met. Average financial aid package met 81% of need; average scholarship/grant was $10,070; average loan was $6,799. For part-time students, average financial aid package was $9,006.
**Students without need:** 220 full-time freshmen who did not demonstrate need for aid received scholarships/grants; average award was $6,742. No-need awards available for academics, alumni affiliation, art, athletics, leadership, music/drama, religious affiliation, ROTC, state/district residency.
**Scholarships offered:** 50 full-time freshmen received athletic scholarships; average amount $6,451.

**FINANCIAL AID PROCEDURES**
**Forms required:** FAFSA.
**Dates and Deadlines:** Priority date 4/15; no closing date. Applicants notified on a rolling basis starting 2/15; must reply within 2 week(s) of notification.
**Transfers:** No deadline.

**CONTACT**
Jonathan Roberts, Director of Student Financial Services
915 East Market Avenue, Searcy, AR 72149-2255
(501) 279-4257

## Henderson State University
Arkadelphia, Arkansas
www.hsu.edu                    Federal Code: 001098

**4-year public** university and liberal arts college in large town.
**Enrollment:** 3,096 undergrads, 11% part-time. 698 full-time freshmen.
**Selectivity:** Admits 50 to 75% of applicants.

**BASIC COSTS (2015-2016)**
**Tuition and fees:** $7,809; out-of-state residents $14,409.
**Per-credit charge:** $207; out-of-state residents $427.
**Room and board:** $6,500.
**Additional info:** Miscellaneous expenses range from $1800 to $2600/year and transportation ranges from $2000 to $3000/year.

**FINANCIAL AID PICTURE (2014-2015)**
**Students with need:** Out of 679 full-time freshmen who applied for aid, 641 were judged to have need. Of these, 609 received aid, and 216 had their full need met. Average financial aid package met 91% of need; average scholarship/grant was $4,641; average loan was $3,069. For part-time students, average financial aid package was $5,399.
**Students without need:** 52 full-time freshmen who did not demonstrate need for aid received scholarships/grants; average award was $5,565. No-need awards available for academics, alumni affiliation, art, athletics, job skills, leadership, minority status, music/drama, ROTC, state/district residency.
**Scholarships offered:** 59 full-time freshmen received athletic scholarships; average amount $4,573.

**FINANCIAL AID PROCEDURES**
**Dates and Deadlines:** Priority date 4/15; no closing date. Applicants notified on a rolling basis starting 3/1; must reply within 2 week(s) of notification.
**Transfers:** No deadline. Applicants notified on a rolling basis starting 3/1; must reply within 2 week(s) of notification.

**CONTACT**
Vicki Taylor, Director of Financial Aid
1100 Henderson Street, Arkadelphia, AR 71999-0001
(870) 230-5094

## Hendrix College
Conway, Arkansas
www.hendrix.edu                    Federal Code: 001099

**4-year private** liberal arts college in small city, affiliated with United Methodist Church.
**Enrollment:** 1,303 undergrads. 397 full-time freshmen.
**Selectivity:** Admits over 75% of applicants.

**BASIC COSTS (2015-2016)**
**Tuition and fees:** $40,870.
**Per-credit charge:** $1,267.
**Room and board:** $11,244.

**FINANCIAL AID PICTURE (2015-2016)**
**Students with need:** Out of 375 full-time freshmen who applied for aid, 295 were judged to have need. Of these, 295 received aid, and 111 had their full need met. Average financial aid package met 89% of need; average scholarship/grant was $32,929; average loan was $3,245. For part-time students, average financial aid package was $2,694.
**Students without need:** 100 full-time freshmen who did not demonstrate need for aid received scholarships/grants; average award was $25,216. No-need awards available for academics, art, leadership, music/drama.

**FINANCIAL AID PROCEDURES**
**Forms required:** FAFSA.

**Dates and Deadlines:** Priority date 3/1; no closing date. Applicants notified on a rolling basis starting 3/1; must reply by 5/1 or within 4 week(s) of notification.

**Transfers:** Applicants notified on a rolling basis starting 3/1; must reply by 5/1.

**CONTACT**
Kristina Burford, Director of Financial Aid
1600 Washington Avenue, Conway, AR 72032-3080
(501) 450-1368

## John Brown University
Siloam Springs, Arkansas
www.jbu.edu                          Federal Code: 001100

**4-year private** university and liberal arts college in large town, affiliated with interdenominational tradition.
**Enrollment:** 1,685 undergrads, 9% part-time. 318 full-time freshmen.
**Selectivity:** Admits 50 to 75% of applicants.

**BASIC COSTS (2015-2016)**
**Tuition and fees:** $24,468.
**Per-credit charge:** $780.
**Room and board:** $8,664.
**Additional info:** Tuition/fee waivers available for adults.

**FINANCIAL AID PICTURE (2014-2015)**
**Students with need:** Out of 279 full-time freshmen who applied for aid, 229 were judged to have need. Of these, 229 received aid, and 44 had their full need met. Average financial aid package met 77% of need; average scholarship/grant was $16,475; average loan was $2,874. For part-time students, average financial aid package was $2,053.
**Students without need:** 87 full-time freshmen who did not demonstrate need for aid received scholarships/grants; average award was $14,384. No-need awards available for academics, alumni affiliation, art, athletics, leadership, music/drama, ROTC.
**Scholarships offered:** 13 full-time freshmen received athletic scholarships; average amount $9,902.

**FINANCIAL AID PROCEDURES**
**Forms required:** FAFSA, state aid form.
**Dates and Deadlines:** Priority date 3/1; no closing date. Applicants notified on a rolling basis starting 3/1; must reply by 5/1 or within 4 week(s) of notification.
**Transfers:** No deadline. Applicants notified on a rolling basis starting 3/1; must reply by 5/1 or within 4 week(s) of notification.

**CONTACT**
Kim Eldridge, Director of Financial Aid
2000 West University Street, Siloam Springs, AR 72761-2121
(877) 528-4636

## Lyon College
Batesville, Arkansas
www.lyon.edu                          Federal Code: 001088

**4-year private** liberal arts college in large town, affiliated with Presbyterian Church (USA).
**Enrollment:** 676 undergrads. 211 full-time freshmen.
**Selectivity:** Admits 50 to 75% of applicants.

**BASIC COSTS (2015-2016)**
**Tuition and fees:** $25,280.
**Room and board:** $8,110.

**FINANCIAL AID PICTURE (2015-2016)**
**Students with need:** Average financial aid package met 73% of need; average scholarship/grant was $18,124; average loan was $3,400. For part-time students, average financial aid package was $500.
**Students without need:** No-need awards available for academics, art, athletics, leadership, music/drama, religious affiliation, state/district residency.
**Scholarships offered:** Brown Scholarship: tuition, room, board, and mandatory fees; based on high school record, standardized test scores; 3 awarded. Anderson Scholarship; tuition and mandatory fees; based on high school record, test scores; 4 awarded.

**FINANCIAL AID PROCEDURES**
**Forms required:** FAFSA, state aid form.
**Dates and Deadlines:** Priority date 3/15; no closing date. Applicants notified on a rolling basis starting 3/1; must reply by 8/15.
**Transfers:** No deadline. Applicants notified on a rolling basis starting 3/1; must reply within 2 week(s) of notification.

**CONTACT**
Tommy Tucker, Director of Student Financial Assistance
PO Box 2317, Batesville, AR 72501-2317
(870) 307-7257

## National Park College
Hot Springs, Arkansas
www.npcc.edu                          Federal Code: 012105

**2-year public** liberal arts and technical college in large town.
**Enrollment:** 3,244 undergrads.
**Selectivity:** Open admission; but selective for some programs.

**BASIC COSTS (2015-2016)**
**Tuition and fees:** $3,160; out-of-district residents $3,460; out-of-state residents $4,540.
**Per-credit charge:** $88; out-of-district residents $98; out-of-state residents $134.

**FINANCIAL AID PICTURE**
**Students with need:** Need-based aid available for full-time and part-time students. Work study available nights, weekends, and for part-time students.
**Students without need:** No-need awards available for academics, minority status, music/drama, state/district residency.

**FINANCIAL AID PROCEDURES**
**Forms required:** FAFSA, institutional form.
**Dates and Deadlines:** Priority date 7/1; no closing date. Applicants notified on a rolling basis.
**Transfers:** Transfer applicants must furnish evidence of good standing at previous institution to qualify for financial aid.

**CONTACT**
101 College Drive, Hot Springs, AR 71913
(501) 760-4235

## North Arkansas College
Harrison, Arkansas
www.northark.edu                      Federal Code: 012261

**2-year public** community and technical college in large town.
**Enrollment:** 2,157 undergrads.
**Selectivity:** Open admission; but selective for some programs.

**BASIC COSTS (2015-2016)**
**Tuition and fees:** $2,550; out-of-district residents $3,270; out-of-state residents $5,400.

## FINANCIAL AID PICTURE

**Students with need:** Need-based aid available for full-time and part-time students. Work study available nights.

**Students without need:** No-need awards available for academics, athletics, state/district residency.

## FINANCIAL AID PROCEDURES

**Forms required:** FAFSA, institutional form.

**Dates and Deadlines:** Priority date 5/1; no closing date. Applicants notified on a rolling basis starting 5/1.

**Transfers:** No deadline. Applicants notified on a rolling basis starting 5/1.

## CONTACT

Jennifer Haddock, Director of Financial Aid

1515 Pioneer Drive, Harrison, AR 72601

(870) 391-3266

# Northwest Arkansas Community College

Bentonville, Arkansas

www.nwacc.edu                     Federal Code: 030633

**2-year public** community college in small city.

**Enrollment:** 5,205 undergrads.

**Selectivity:** Open admission; but selective for some programs.

## BASIC COSTS (2015-2016)

**Tuition and fees:** $3,208; out-of-district residents $4,633; out-of-state residents $4,708.

**Per-credit charge:** $75; out-of-district residents $123; out-of-state residents $125.

## FINANCIAL AID PICTURE

**Students with need:** Need-based aid available for full-time and part-time students. Work study available nights, weekends, and for part-time students.

**Students without need:** No-need awards available for academics, leadership, music/drama, state/district residency.

## FINANCIAL AID PROCEDURES

**Forms required:** FAFSA, institutional form.

**Dates and Deadlines:** Priority date 4/1; no closing date. Applicants notified on a rolling basis starting 4/1; must reply within 2 week(s) of notification.

## CONTACT

Michelle Cordell, Director of Financial Aid

One College Drive, Bentonville, AR 72712

(479) 619-4329

# Ouachita Baptist University

Arkadelphia, Arkansas

www.obu.edu                       Federal Code: 001102

**4-year private** liberal arts college in large town, affiliated with Baptist faith.

**Enrollment:** 1,471 undergrads, 2% part-time. 412 full-time freshmen.

**Selectivity:** Admits 50 to 75% of applicants.

## BASIC COSTS (2016-2017)

**Tuition and fees:** $24,940.

**Per-credit charge:** $675.

**Room and board:** $7,380.

## FINANCIAL AID PICTURE (2015-2016)

**Students with need:** Out of 376 full-time freshmen who applied for aid, 290 were judged to have need. Of these, 290 received aid, and 91 had their full need met. Average financial aid package met 83% of need; average scholarship/grant was $14,052; average loan was $2,545. For part-time students, average financial aid package was $11,238.

**Students without need:** 117 full-time freshmen who did not demonstrate need for aid received scholarships/grants; average award was $9,875. No-need awards available for academics, alumni affiliation, art, athletics, job skills, leadership, minority status, music/drama, religious affiliation, ROTC, state/district residency.

**Scholarships offered:** 31 full-time freshmen received athletic scholarships; average amount $5,342.

## FINANCIAL AID PROCEDURES

**Forms required:** FAFSA, state aid form.

**Dates and Deadlines:** Priority date 1/15; closing date 6/1. Applicants notified on a rolling basis starting 11/1.

## CONTACT

Susan Hurst, Director of Student Financial Services

OBU Box 3776, Arkadelphia, AR 71998-0001

(870) 245-5570

# Ozarka College

Melbourne, Arkansas

www.ozarka.edu                    Federal Code: 013217

**2-year public** community and technical college in rural community.

**Enrollment:** 1,326 undergrads.

**Selectivity:** Open admission; but selective for some programs.

## BASIC COSTS (2015-2016)

**Tuition and fees:** $3,445; out-of-state residents $6,385.

**Per-credit charge:** $88; out-of-state residents $186.

## FINANCIAL AID PICTURE

**Students with need:** Need-based aid available for full-time and part-time students.

## FINANCIAL AID PROCEDURES

**Forms required:** FAFSA.

**Dates and Deadlines:** Applicants notified on a rolling basis; must reply within 2 week(s) of notification.

## CONTACT

Laura Lawrence, Financial Aid Director

218 College Drive, Melbourne, AR 72556-0010

(870) 368-7371 ext. 2010

# Philander Smith College

Little Rock, Arkansas

www.philander.edu                 Federal Code: 001103

**4-year private** liberal arts college in small city, affiliated with United Methodist Church.

**Enrollment:** 584 undergrads, 6% part-time. 112 full-time freshmen.

## BASIC COSTS (2015-2016)

**Tuition and fees:** $12,414.

**Per-credit charge:** $495.

**Room and board:** $8,250.

## FINANCIAL AID PICTURE (2014-2015)

**Students with need:** Out of 106 full-time freshmen who applied for aid, 106 were judged to have need. Of these, 106 received aid, and 3 had their full need met. Average financial aid package met 59% of need; average scholarship/grant was $12,026; average loan was $3,075. For part-time students, average financial aid package was $7,393.

**Students without need:** 4 full-time freshmen who did not demonstrate need for aid received scholarships/grants; average award was $13,744. No-need awards available for academics, athletics, music/drama, religious affiliation.

**Scholarships offered:** 1 full-time freshmen received athletic scholarships; average amount $3,528.

**FINANCIAL AID PROCEDURES**

**Forms required:** FAFSA.

**Dates and Deadlines:** Priority date 3/1; no closing date. Applicants notified on a rolling basis starting 3/1; must reply within 2 week(s) of notification.

**Transfers:** Must reply within 2 week(s) of notification.

**CONTACT**

Kisa Hinton, Director of Financial Aid
900 Daisy Bates Drive, Little Rock, AR 72202-3718
(501) 370-5350

## Phillips Community College of the University of Arkansas

Helena, Arkansas
www.pccua.edu                    Federal Code: 001104

**2-year public** community college in large town.

**Enrollment:** 708 undergrads.

**Selectivity:** Open admission; but selective for some programs.

**BASIC COSTS (2015-2016)**

**Tuition and fees:** $2,593; out-of-district residents $2,968; out-of-state residents $4,325.

**Per-credit charge:** $67; out-of-district residents $80; out-of-state residents $125.

**FINANCIAL AID PICTURE**

**Students with need:** Need-based aid available for full-time and part-time students. Work study available nights.

**Students without need:** This college awards aid only to students with need.

**Additional info:** Tuition waivers given to firefighters and law enforcement officers.

**FINANCIAL AID PROCEDURES**

**Forms required:** FAFSA.

**Dates and Deadlines:** Priority date 4/12; closing date 6/12. Applicants notified on a rolling basis starting 4/12; must reply within 2 week(s) of notification.

**CONTACT**

Barbra Stevenson, Director of Financial Aid
1000 Campus Drive, Helena, AR 72342
(870) 338-6474 ext. 1160

## Pulaski Technical College

North Little Rock, Arkansas
www.pulaskitech.edu               Federal Code: 014167

**2-year public** community and technical college in small city.

**Enrollment:** 6,844 undergrads.

**Selectivity:** Open admission; but selective for some programs.

**BASIC COSTS (2015-2016)**

**Tuition and fees:** $4,590; out-of-state residents $6,330.

**Per-credit charge:** $110; out-of-state residents $168.

**FINANCIAL AID PICTURE**

**Students with need:** Need-based aid available for full-time and part-time students.

**FINANCIAL AID PROCEDURES**

**Forms required:** FAFSA, institutional form.

**Dates and Deadlines:** Closing date 5/15. Applicants notified on a rolling basis starting 5/1; must reply within 2 week(s) of notification.

**CONTACT**

Lavonne Juhl, Director Financial Aid
3000 West Scenic Drive, North Little Rock, AR 72118-3347
(501) 812-2289

## Rich Mountain Community College

Mena, Arkansas
www.rmcc.edu                     Federal Code: 012435

**2-year public** community college in small town.

**Enrollment:** 500 undergrads, 33% part-time. 128 full-time freshmen.

**Selectivity:** Open admission; but selective for some programs.

**BASIC COSTS (2015-2016)**

**Tuition and fees:** $3,060; out-of-district residents $3,480; out-of-state residents $6,750.

**Per-credit charge:** $72; out-of-district residents $86; out-of-state residents $195.

**FINANCIAL AID PICTURE (2014-2015)**

**Students with need:** 99% of average financial aid package awarded as scholarships/grants, 1% awarded as loans/jobs. Need-based aid available for part-time students.

**Students without need:** No-need awards available for academics.

**FINANCIAL AID PROCEDURES**

**Forms required:** FAFSA, institutional form.

**Dates and Deadlines:** Priority date 7/1; no closing date. Applicants notified on a rolling basis starting 6/1; must reply within 2 week(s) of notification.

**CONTACT**

Mary Standerfer, Director of Financial Aid
1100 College Drive, Mena, AR 71953
(479) 394-7622 ext. 1420

## South Arkansas Community College

El Dorado, Arkansas
www.southark.edu                 Federal Code: 013858

**2-year public** community and junior college in large town.

**Enrollment:** 1,183 undergrads, 49% part-time. 175 full-time freshmen.

**Selectivity:** Open admission; but selective for some programs.

**BASIC COSTS (2015-2016)**

**Tuition and fees:** $2,990; out-of-district residents $3,380; out-of-state residents $5,660.

**Per-credit charge:** $83; out-of-district residents $96; out-of-state residents $172.

**FINANCIAL AID PICTURE**

**Students with need:** Need-based aid available for full-time and part-time students.

**FINANCIAL AID PROCEDURES**

**Forms required:** FAFSA, institutional form.

**Dates and Deadlines:** Closing date 7/1. Applicants notified on a rolling basis starting 7/1; must reply within 2 week(s) of notification.

**CONTACT**

Veronda Tatum, Director of Financial Aid
Box 7010, El Dorado, AR 71731-7010
(870) 864-7133

## Southeast Arkansas College
Pine Bluff, Arkansas
www.seark.edu                     Federal Code: 005707

**2-year public** community college in small city.
**Enrollment:** 1,291 undergrads.
**Selectivity:** Open admission; but selective for some programs.

**BASIC COSTS (2015-2016)**
**Tuition and fees:** $3,070; out-of-state residents $5,590.

**FINANCIAL AID PICTURE**
**Students with need:** Need-based aid available for full-time and part-time students. Work study available nights.
**Students without need:** No-need awards available for academics, leadership, state/district residency.

**FINANCIAL AID PROCEDURES**
**Forms required:** FAFSA.
**Dates and Deadlines:** Priority date 6/1; no closing date. Applicants notified on a rolling basis starting 5/1; must reply within 2 week(s) of notification.

**CONTACT**
Donna Cox, Director of Financial Aid
1900 Hazel Street, Pine Bluff, AR 71603
(870) 543-5909

## Southern Arkansas University
Magnolia, Arkansas
www.saumag.edu                    Federal Code: 001107

**4-year public** university in large town.
**Enrollment:** 2,859 undergrads, 7% part-time. 699 full-time freshmen.
**Selectivity:** Admits 50 to 75% of applicants.

**BASIC COSTS (2015-2016)**
**Tuition and fees:** $7,881; out-of-state residents $11,451.
**Per-credit charge:** $217; out-of-state residents $336.
**Room and board:** $5,704.

**FINANCIAL AID PICTURE (2014-2015)**
**Students with need:** Out of 669 full-time freshmen who applied for aid, 583 were judged to have need. Of these, 579 received aid, and 207 had their full need met. Average financial aid package met 81% of need; average scholarship/grant was $4,732; average loan was $2,984. For part-time students, average financial aid package was $6,165.
**Students without need:** 82 full-time freshmen who did not demonstrate need for aid received scholarships/grants; average award was $5,249. No-need awards available for academics, alumni affiliation, art, athletics, leadership, minority status, music/drama, state/district residency.
**Scholarships offered:** 25 full-time freshmen received athletic scholarships; average amount $3,063.

**FINANCIAL AID PROCEDURES**
**Forms required:** FAFSA.
**Dates and Deadlines:** Priority date 7/1; no closing date. Applicants notified on a rolling basis starting 4/15; must reply within 2 week(s) of notification.

**CONTACT**
Marcela McRae-Brunson, Director of Financial Aid
Box 9382, Magnolia, AR 71754-9382
(870) 235-4025

## Southern Arkansas University Tech
Camden, Arkansas
www.sautech.edu                   Federal Code: 007738

**2-year public** community and technical college in large town.
**Enrollment:** 697 undergrads, 29% part-time. 160 full-time freshmen.
**Selectivity:** Open admission; but selective for some programs.

**BASIC COSTS (2015-2016)**
**Tuition and fees:** $3,240; out-of-state residents $4,680.
**Room only:** $1,300.

**FINANCIAL AID PICTURE**
**Students with need:** Need-based aid available for full-time and part-time students. Work study available nights, weekends, and for part-time students.
**Students without need:** No-need awards available for academics, state/district residency.

**FINANCIAL AID PROCEDURES**
**Forms required:** FAFSA.
**Dates and Deadlines:** Priority date 6/1; no closing date. Applicants notified on a rolling basis starting 5/1.
**Transfers:** Priority date 4/15; closing date 6/1. Applicants notified on a rolling basis starting 5/1.

**CONTACT**
Jennifer Williams, Director of Financial Aid
PO Box 3499, Camden, AR 71711-1599
(870) 574-4511

## University of Arkansas
Fayetteville, Arkansas
www.uark.edu                      Federal Code: 001108

**4-year public** university in small city.
**Enrollment:** 21,806 undergrads, 11% part-time. 4,871 full-time freshmen.
**Selectivity:** Admits 50 to 75% of applicants.

**BASIC COSTS (2015-2016)**
**Tuition and fees:** $8,522; out-of-state residents $21,826.
**Per-credit charge:** $234.26; out-of-state residents $677.73.
**Room and board:** $9,880.

**FINANCIAL AID PICTURE (2015-2016)**
**Students with need:** Need-based aid available for full-time and part-time students.

**FINANCIAL AID PROCEDURES**
**Forms required:** FAFSA.

**CONTACT**
Wendy Stouffer, Executive Director of Scholarship/Financial Aid
232 Silas H. Hunt Hall, Fayetteville, AR 72701
(479) 575-3806

## University of Arkansas at Fort Smith
Fort Smith, Arkansas
www.uafs.edu                      Federal Code: 001110

**4-year public** university in small city.
**Enrollment:** 5,989 undergrads.
**Selectivity:** Open admission; but selective for some programs.

**BASIC COSTS (2015-2016)**
**Tuition and fees:** $6,322; out-of-state residents $14,122.
**Per-credit charge:** $150; out-of-state residents $410.
**Room and board:** $8,068.

**FINANCIAL AID PICTURE**

**Students with need:** Need-based aid available for full-time and part-time students. Work study available nights, weekends, and for part-time students.
**Students without need:** No-need awards available for academics, athletics, job skills, leadership, music/drama.

**FINANCIAL AID PROCEDURES**

**Forms required:** FAFSA.
**Dates and Deadlines:** Priority date 6/15; no closing date. Applicants notified on a rolling basis starting 3/1; must reply within 4 week(s) of notification.
**Transfers:** No deadline. Applicants notified on a rolling basis starting 3/1; must reply within 4 week(s) of notification.

**CONTACT**

David Seward, Director of Financial Aid
PO Box 3649, Fort Smith, AR 72913-3649
(479) 788-7090

## University of Arkansas at Little Rock
Little Rock, Arkansas
www.ualr.edu                    Federal Code: 001161

**4-year public** university in small city.
**Enrollment:** 7,888 undergrads.

**BASIC COSTS (2015-2016)**
**Tuition and fees:** $8,108; out-of-state residents $19,178.
**Room and board:** $7,228.

**FINANCIAL AID PICTURE**
**Students with need:** Need-based aid available for full-time and part-time students. Work study available weekends and for part-time students.
**Students without need:** No-need awards available for academics, art, athletics, leadership, music/drama.

**FINANCIAL AID PROCEDURES**
**Forms required:** FAFSA, state aid form.
**Dates and Deadlines:** Priority date 3/1; no closing date. Applicants notified on a rolling basis starting 5/1.

**CONTACT**
Carlia Smith, Director of Financial Aid
2801 South University Avenue, Little Rock, AR 72204-1099
(501) 569-3035

## University of Arkansas at Monticello
Monticello, Arkansas
www.uamont.edu                  Federal Code: 001085

**4-year public** university and technical college in large town.
**Enrollment:** 3,733 undergrads.
**Selectivity:** Open admission; but selective for some programs.

**BASIC COSTS (2015-2016)**
**Tuition and fees:** $6,447; out-of-state residents $12,297.
**Per-credit charge:** $150; out-of-state residents $345.
**Room and board:** $6,189.

**FINANCIAL AID PICTURE**
**Students with need:** Need-based aid available for full-time and part-time students. Work study available nights, weekends, and for part-time students.
**Students without need:** No-need awards available for academics, athletics, job skills, leadership, music/drama, ROTC, state/district residency.

**FINANCIAL AID PROCEDURES**
**Forms required:** FAFSA.
**Dates and Deadlines:** Priority date 5/1; no closing date. Applicants notified on a rolling basis starting 5/1; must reply within 2 week(s) of notification.

**CONTACT**
Susan Brewer, Director of Financial Aid
Box 3600, Monticello, AR 71656
(870) 460-1050

## University of Arkansas at Pine Bluff
Pine Bluff, Arkansas
www.uapb.edu                    Federal Code: 001086

**4-year public** university in small city.
**Enrollment:** 2,526 undergrads, 9% part-time. 671 full-time freshmen.
**Selectivity:** Admits less than 50% of applicants.

**BASIC COSTS (2015-2016)**
**Tuition and fees:** $6,308; out-of-state residents $11,978.
**Per-credit charge:** $151; out-of-state residents $340.
**Room and board:** $7,270.
**Additional info:** Tuition/fee waivers available for minority students.

**FINANCIAL AID PICTURE**
**Students with need:** Need-based aid available for full-time and part-time students. Work study available weekends and for part-time students.
**Students without need:** No-need awards available for academics, alumni affiliation, art, athletics, leadership, minority status, music/drama, religious affiliation, ROTC, state/district residency.

**FINANCIAL AID PROCEDURES**
**Forms required:** FAFSA.
**Dates and Deadlines:** Priority date 4/15; no closing date. Applicants notified on a rolling basis starting 3/1.
**Transfers:** Must supply financial aid transcript from prior college or university.

**CONTACT**
Janice Kearney, Director, Student Financial Aid
1200 North University Drive, Mail Slot 4981, Pine Bluff, AR 71601-2799
(870) 575-8302

## University of Arkansas for Medical Sciences
Little Rock, Arkansas
www.uams.edu                    Federal Code: 001109

**4-year public** university and health science college in large city.
**Enrollment:** 761 undergrads.

**BASIC COSTS (2015-2016)**
**Tuition and fees:** $7,785; out-of-state residents $17,895.
**Per-credit charge:** $260; out-of-state residents $597.
**Additional info:** Tuition/fee waivers available for minority students.

**FINANCIAL AID PICTURE**
**Students with need:** Need-based aid available for full-time and part-time students.
**Students without need:** No-need awards available for academics, state/district residency.

**FINANCIAL AID PROCEDURES**
**Forms required:** FAFSA, institutional form.
**Dates and Deadlines:** Applicants notified on a rolling basis starting 5/1; must reply within 4 week(s) of notification.
**Transfers:** Priority date 5/15; no deadline. Applicants notified by 1/15.

**CONTACT**
Gloria Kemp, Director of Student Financial Services
4301 West Markham Street, Little Rock, AR 72205
(501) 686-6128

## University of Arkansas: Community College at Batesville

Batesville, Arkansas
www.uaccb.edu                    Federal Code: 014042

**2-year public** community college in small town.
**Enrollment:** 1,090 undergrads.
**Selectivity:** Open admission; but selective for some programs.

### BASIC COSTS (2015-2016)

**Tuition and fees:** $2,850; out-of-district residents $3,240; out-of-state residents $5,220.
**Per-credit charge:** $70; out-of-district residents $83; out-of-state residents $149.

### FINANCIAL AID PICTURE

**Students with need:** Need-based aid available for full-time students. Work study available nights, weekends, and for part-time students.
**Students without need:** This college awards aid only to students with need.

### FINANCIAL AID PROCEDURES

**Forms required:** FAFSA.
**Dates and Deadlines:** Applicants notified on a rolling basis starting 3/1; must reply within 2 week(s) of notification.

### CONTACT

Kristen Cross, Director of Financial Aid
Box 3350, Batesville, AR 72503
(870) 612-2036

## University of Arkansas: Community College at Hope

Hope, Arkansas
www.uacch.edu                    Federal Code: 005732

**2-year public** community and technical college in small town.
**Enrollment:** 1,045 undergrads, 37% part-time. 190 full-time freshmen.
**Selectivity:** Open admission; but selective for some programs.

### BASIC COSTS (2015-2016)

**Tuition and fees:** $2,480; out-of-district residents $2,660; out-of-state residents $4,790.
**Per-credit charge:** $63; out-of-district residents $69; out-of-state residents $140.

### FINANCIAL AID PICTURE (2014-2015)

**Students with need:** 97% of average financial aid package awarded as scholarships/grants, 3% awarded as loans/jobs. Need-based aid available for part-time students. Work study available nights.
**Students without need:** No-need awards available for academics.

### FINANCIAL AID PROCEDURES

**Forms required:** FAFSA, institutional form.
**Dates and Deadlines:** Closing date 7/6. Applicants notified on a rolling basis starting 1/1; must reply within 4 week(s) of notification.
**Transfers:** No deadline. Applicants notified on a rolling basis.

### CONTACT

Becky Wilson, Director of Financial Aid
2500 South Main, Hope, AR 71802-0140
(870) 722-8264

## University of Arkansas: Community College at Morrilton

Morrilton, Arkansas
www.uaccm.edu                    Federal Code: 005245

**2-year public** community college in small town.
**Enrollment:** 1,970 undergrads, 31% part-time. 498 full-time freshmen.
**Selectivity:** Admits 50 to 75% of applicants.

### BASIC COSTS (2015-2016)

**Tuition and fees:** $3,575; out-of-district residents $3,785; out-of-state residents $4,880.
**Per-credit charge:** $85; out-of-district residents $92; out-of-state residents $128.

### FINANCIAL AID PICTURE (2015-2016)

**Students with need:** Out of 469 full-time freshmen who applied for aid, 395 were judged to have need. Of these, 374 received aid, and 20 had their full need met. Average financial aid package met 49% of need; average scholarship/grant was $2,710; average loan was $1,571. For part-time students, average financial aid package was $5,408.
**Students without need:** 42 full-time freshmen who did not demonstrate need for aid received scholarships/grants; average award was $915. No-need awards available for academics, leadership, state/district residency.

### FINANCIAL AID PROCEDURES

**Forms required:** FAFSA, institutional form.
**Dates and Deadlines:** Priority date 7/1; no closing date.
**Transfers:** Applicants notified on a rolling basis starting 5/1.

### CONTACT

Teresa Cash, Director of Financial Aid
1537 University Boulevard, Morrilton, AR 72110
(501) 977-2055

## University of Central Arkansas

Conway, Arkansas
www.uca.edu                      Federal Code: 001092

**4-year public** university in small city.
**Enrollment:** 9,340 undergrads, 12% part-time. 1,986 full-time freshmen.
**Selectivity:** Admits over 75% of applicants.

### BASIC COSTS (2015-2016)

**Tuition and fees:** $7,889; out-of-state residents $13,806.
**Per-credit charge:** $198; out-of-state residents $395.
**Room and board:** $5,982.

### FINANCIAL AID PICTURE

**Students with need:** Need-based aid available for full-time students. Work study available nights, weekends, and for part-time students.
**Students without need:** No-need awards available for academics, art, athletics, leadership, minority status, music/drama, ROTC, state/district residency.
**Additional info:** Room and board may be paid monthly.

### FINANCIAL AID PROCEDURES

**Forms required:** FAFSA.
**Dates and Deadlines:** Priority date 4/15; closing date 7/1. Applicants notified on a rolling basis starting 5/4.

### CONTACT

Cheryl Lyons, Director of Student Financial Aid
201 Donaghey Avenue, Conway, AR 72035
(501) 450-3140

## University of the Ozarks
Clarksville, Arkansas
www.ozarks.edu                    Federal Code: 001094

**4-year private** university and liberal arts college in small town, affiliated with Presbyterian Church (USA).
**Enrollment:** 640 undergrads, 1% part-time. 210 full-time freshmen.
**Selectivity:** Admits over 75% of applicants.

**BASIC COSTS (2015-2016)**
**Tuition and fees:** $24,350.
**Room and board:** $7,190.
**Additional info:** Tuition/fee waivers available for minority students.

**FINANCIAL AID PICTURE**
**Students with need:** Need-based aid available for full-time and part-time students. Work study available nights, weekends, and for part-time students.
**Students without need:** No-need awards available for academics, alumni affiliation, art, leadership, minority status, music/drama, religious affiliation, state/district residency.
**Additional info:** Walton International Scholarship Program provides full scholarships to selected Central American and Mexican residents.

**FINANCIAL AID PROCEDURES**
**Forms required:** FAFSA.
**Dates and Deadlines:** Priority date 2/15; no closing date. Applicants notified on a rolling basis starting 3/1; must reply within 2 week(s) of notification.

**CONTACT**
Jana Hart, Dean of Admission and Financial Aid
415 North College Avenue, Clarksville, AR 72830-2880
(479) 979-1221

## Williams Baptist College
Walnut Ridge, Arkansas
www.wbcoll.edu                    Federal Code: 001106

**4-year private** liberal arts college in small town, affiliated with Southern Baptist Convention.
**Enrollment:** 491 undergrads, 2% part-time. 162 full-time freshmen.
**Selectivity:** Admits 50 to 75% of applicants.

**BASIC COSTS (2015-2016)**
**Tuition and fees:** $16,430.
**Per-credit charge:** $640.
**Room and board:** $7,000.

**FINANCIAL AID PICTURE (2014-2015)**
**Students with need:** Out of 127 full-time freshmen who applied for aid, 100 were judged to have need. Of these, 100 received aid. For part-time students, average financial aid package was $8,631.
**Students without need:** No-need awards available for academics, art, athletics, leadership, minority status, music/drama, religious affiliation, state/district residency.
**Scholarships offered:** *Merit:* Trustee's Scholarship: up to full tuition, room and board; based on 30 ACT and 3.5 GPA; 1 awarded; renewable for 4 years with 3.25 GPA with at least 15 credit hours per semester. *Athletic:* 111 full-time freshmen received athletic scholarships; average amount $4,452.
**Additional info:** Art scholarship applicants must submit portfolio.

**FINANCIAL AID PROCEDURES**
**Forms required:** FAFSA.
**Dates and Deadlines:** Priority date 5/1; no closing date. Applicants notified on a rolling basis starting 4/1; must reply within 2 week(s) of notification.
**Transfers:** Priority date 4/1; no deadline. Applicants notified on a rolling basis starting 4/1; must reply within 2 week(s) of notification.

**CONTACT**
Barbara Turner, Director of Financial Aid
PO Box 3665, Walnut Ridge, AR 72476
(870) 759-4112

# California

## Academy of Art University
San Francisco, California
www.academyart.edu                Federal Code: 007531

**4-year for-profit** university and visual arts college in very large city.
**Enrollment:** 8,969 undergrads, 41% part-time. 704 full-time freshmen.
**Selectivity:** Open admission.

**BASIC COSTS (2016-2017)**
**Tuition and fees:** $26,490.
**Per-credit charge:** $873.
**Room and board:** $15,250.

**FINANCIAL AID PICTURE (2014-2015)**
**Students with need:** Out of 366 full-time freshmen who applied for aid, 322 were judged to have need. Of these, 300 received aid, and 10 had their full need met. Average financial aid package met 29% of need; average scholarship/grant was $9,290; average loan was $3,121. For part-time students, average financial aid package was $5,637.
**Students without need:** 15 full-time freshmen who did not demonstrate need for aid received scholarships/grants; average award was $5,584. No-need awards available for academics, art, athletics.
**Scholarships offered:** 30 full-time freshmen received athletic scholarships; average amount $19,866.
**Additional info:** Numerous summer grant programs available.

**FINANCIAL AID PROCEDURES**
**Forms required:** FAFSA, institutional form.
**Dates and Deadlines:** Priority date 3/1; no closing date. Applicants notified on a rolling basis starting 3/15; must reply within 2 week(s) of notification.
**Transfers:** No deadline. Applicants notified on a rolling basis.

**CONTACT**
Joe Vollaro, Executive Vice President for Financial Aid/Compliance
79 New Montgomery Street, San Francisco, CA 94105-3410
(415) 618-6273

## Academy of Couture Art
Beverly Hills, California
www.academyofcoutureart.edu       Federal Code: 041855

**4-year private** institute of couture fashion design in very large city.
**Enrollment:** 17 undergrads.
**Selectivity:** Open admission; but selective for some programs.

**BASIC COSTS (2015-2016)**
**Tuition and fees:** $22,338.
**Per-credit charge:** $556.
**Additional info:** Tuition at time of enrollment locked for 4 years.

**FINANCIAL AID PICTURE (2014-2015)**
**Students with need:** 33% of average financial aid package awarded as scholarships/grants, 67% awarded as loans/jobs. Need-based aid available for part-time students.
**Students without need:** This college awards aid only to students with need.

## FINANCIAL AID PROCEDURES

**Forms required:** FAFSA, state aid form.

**Dates and Deadlines:** Priority date 3/2; no closing date. Applicants notified on a rolling basis starting 3/2.

**Transfers:** No deadline. Applicants notified on a rolling basis. Maximum college transfer credits cannot exceed 45% of the entire quarter credits hours needed for graduation.

## CONTACT

Robert Rice, Director of Financial Aid

8484 Wilshire Boulevard Suite 730, Beverly Hills, CA 90211

(310) 360-8888 ext. 110

## Allan Hancock College

Santa Maria, California

www.hancockcollege.edu          Federal Code: 001111

**2-year public** community college in small city.

**Enrollment:** 8,716 undergrads.

**Selectivity:** Open admission; but selective for some programs.

### BASIC COSTS (2015-2016)

**Tuition and fees:** $1,418; out-of-state residents $6,968.

**Per-credit charge:** $46; out-of-state residents $231.

### FINANCIAL AID PICTURE

**Students with need:** Need-based aid available for full-time and part-time students.

**Students without need:** This college awards aid only to students with need.

### FINANCIAL AID PROCEDURES

**Forms required:** FAFSA.

**Dates and Deadlines:** Priority date 5/1; no closing date. Applicants notified on a rolling basis starting 6/1.

### CONTACT

Robert Parisi, Dean, Student Services

800 South College Drive, Santa Maria, CA 93454-6399

(805) 922-6966 ext. 3200

## Alliant International University

San Diego, California

www.alliant.edu          Federal Code: 011117

**4-year private** university in very large city.

**Enrollment:** 675 undergrads.

**Selectivity:** Open admission; but selective for some programs.

### BASIC COSTS (2015-2016)

**Tuition and fees:** $20,740.

**Per-credit charge:** $680.

**Room and board:** $7,790.

**Additional info:** Tuition/fee waivers available for minority students.

### FINANCIAL AID PICTURE

**Students with need:** Need-based aid available for full-time and part-time students. Work study available nights, weekends, and for part-time students.

**Students without need:** No-need awards available for academics, alumni affiliation, athletics, leadership.

**Scholarships offered:** Grants and scholarships available based on GPA and SAT/ACT scores.

### FINANCIAL AID PROCEDURES

**Forms required:** FAFSA.

**Dates and Deadlines:** Closing date 3/2. Applicants notified on a rolling basis starting 2/1; must reply within 3 week(s) of notification.

## CONTACT

Deborah Spindler, Director of Financial Aid

10455 Pomerado Road, San Diego, CA 92131-1799

(858) 635-4559

## American Academy of Dramatic Arts: West

Los Angeles, California

www.aada.edu          Federal Code: 014801

**2-year private** performing arts college in very large city.

**Enrollment:** 275 undergrads.

### BASIC COSTS (2015-2016)

**Tuition and fees:** $30,650.

### FINANCIAL AID PICTURE

**Students with need:** Need-based aid available for full-time students. Work study available nights, weekends, and for part-time students.

**Students without need:** This college awards aid only to students with need.

**Additional info:** The Academy participates in various federal and state financial aid programs and offers a choice of payment plans. The Academy offers a variety of scholarships and assistance opportunities and a choice of payment plans for International Students. The Academy also participates with foreign government aid programs, if available.

### FINANCIAL AID PROCEDURES

**Forms required:** institutional form.

**Dates and Deadlines:** Priority date 7/1; no closing date. Applicants notified on a rolling basis starting 6/1; must reply within 3 week(s) of notification.

### CONTACT

John Bloch, President

1336 N. La Brea Avenue, Los Angeles, CA 90028

(323) 464-2777 ext. 105

## American Jewish University

Bel-Air, California

www.college.aju.edu          Federal Code: 002741

**4-year private** university and liberal arts college in very large city, affiliated with Jewish faith.

**Enrollment:** 150 undergrads.

### BASIC COSTS (2015-2016)

**Tuition and fees:** $29,608.

**Per-credit charge:** $1,184.

**Room and board:** $15,170.

### FINANCIAL AID PICTURE

**Students with need:** Need-based aid available for full-time and part-time students. Work study available weekends and for part-time students.

**Students without need:** No-need awards available for leadership, minority status, music/drama, state/district residency.

### FINANCIAL AID PROCEDURES

**Forms required:** FAFSA, institutional form.

**Dates and Deadlines:** Priority date 3/2; no closing date. Applicants notified on a rolling basis starting 1/1; must reply by 6/30.

**Transfers:** Priority date 7/1; no deadline. Applicants notified on a rolling basis; must reply within 3 week(s) of notification.

### CONTACT

Larisa Zadoyen, Director of Financial Aid

Office of Undergraduate Admissions, Bel-Air, CA 90077

(310) 476-9777 ext. 222

## American River College
Sacramento, California
www.arc.losrios.edu          Federal Code: 001232

**2-year public** community college in large city.
**Enrollment:** 19,923 undergrads.
**Selectivity:** Open admission; but selective for some programs.

**BASIC COSTS (2015-2016)**
**Tuition and fees:** $1,416; out-of-state residents $7,956.
**Per-credit charge:** $46; out-of-state residents $264.
**Additional info:** Tuition/fee waivers available for minority students.

**FINANCIAL AID PICTURE**
**Students with need:** Need-based aid available for full-time and part-time students.
**Students without need:** This college awards aid only to students with need.

**FINANCIAL AID PROCEDURES**
**Forms required:** FAFSA.
**Dates and Deadlines:** Priority date 3/2; closing date 6/30. Applicants notified on a rolling basis starting 7/1; must reply within 2 week(s) of notification.

**CONTACT**
Chad Funk, Financial Aid Supervisor
4700 College Oak Drive, Sacramento, CA 95841
(916) 484-8437

## Antelope Valley College
Lancaster, California
www.avc.edu          Federal Code: 001113

**2-year public** liberal arts and technical college in large city.
**Enrollment:** 10,056 undergrads.
**Selectivity:** Open admission; but selective for some programs.

**BASIC COSTS (2015-2016)**
**Tuition and fees:** $1,420; out-of-state residents $7,420.
**Per-credit charge:** $46; out-of-state residents $246.

**FINANCIAL AID PICTURE (2014-2015)**
**Students with need:** 83% of average financial aid package awarded as scholarships/grants, 17% awarded as loans/jobs. Need-based aid available for part-time students.

**FINANCIAL AID PROCEDURES**
**Forms required:** FAFSA, state aid form.
**Dates and Deadlines:** Applicants notified on a rolling basis starting 7/15; must reply within 2 week(s) of notification.
**Transfers:** Priority date 3/2; no deadline. Applicants notified on a rolling basis.

**CONTACT**
Nichelle Williams, Director of Financial Aid
3041 West Avenue K, Lancaster, CA 93536-5426
(661) 722-6337

## Antioch University Santa Barbara
Santa Barbara, California
www.antiochsb.edu          Federal Code: 003010

**Upper-division private** university and liberal arts college in small city.
**Enrollment:** 117 undergrads, 30% part-time.

**BASIC COSTS (2015-2016)**
**Tuition and fees:** $18,120.

**FINANCIAL AID PICTURE (2014-2015)**
**Students with need:** 40% of average financial aid package awarded as scholarships/grants, 60% awarded as loans/jobs. Need-based aid available for part-time students. Work study available nights, weekends, and for part-time students.

**FINANCIAL AID PROCEDURES**
**Forms required:** FAFSA.
**Dates and Deadlines:** Priority date 4/15; no closing date. Applicants notified on a rolling basis; must reply within 4 week(s) of notification.
**Transfers:** Priority date 4/1; no deadline.

**CONTACT**
Heather Hartwell, Financial Aid Counselor
602 Anacapa Street, Santa Barbara, CA 93101
(805) 962-8179 ext. 5108

## Art Center College of Design
Pasadena, California
www.artcenter.edu          Federal Code: 001116

**4-year private** visual arts college in small city.
**Enrollment:** 1,890 undergrads, 16% part-time. 181 full-time freshmen.
**Selectivity:** Admits over 75% of applicants.

**BASIC COSTS (2016-2017)**
**Tuition and fees:** $40,596.
**Per-credit charge:** $1,669.

**FINANCIAL AID PICTURE**
**Students with need:** Need-based aid available for full-time and part-time students.

**CONTACT**
Victoria Amezcua, Director of Financial Aid
1700 Lida Street, Pasadena, CA 91103
(626) 396-2215

## Art Institute of California: Hollywood
North Hollywood, California
www.artinstitutes.edu/hollywood          Federal Code: 031254

**4-year for-profit** culinary school and visual arts college in very large city.
**Enrollment:** 1,602 undergrads.

**BASIC COSTS (2015-2016)**
**Additional info:** Diploma programs range from $25,014-$30,005, books and supplies range from $600-$800, room and board ranges from $14,920-$18,650. Associates programs range from $46,770-$49,438, books and supplies range from $1,050-$1,400, room and board $29,840. Bachelors programs range from from $93,390-$95,070, books and supplies range from $2,450-$2,800, room and board $55,950.

**FINANCIAL AID PICTURE**
**Students with need:** Need-based aid available for full-time and part-time students.

**CONTACT**
Adis Ceballos, Director of Student Financial Services
5250 Lankershim Boulevard, North Hollywood, CA 91601
(818) 299-5151

## Art Institute of California: Los Angeles
Santa Monica, California
www.artinstitutes.edu/losangeles    Federal Code: 007470

**2-year for-profit** visual arts and career college in large city.
**Enrollment:** 1,436 undergrads.

### BASIC COSTS (2015-2016)
**Additional info:** Diploma programs range from $24,496-$30,789, books and supplies range from $600-$800, room and board ranges from $15,576-$19,470. Associates programs range from $47,055-$49,444, books and supplies range from $1,050-$1,400, room and board range from $23,382-31,176. Bachelors programs range from from $93,678-$95,854, books and supplies range from $2,450-$2,800, room and board $58,410.

### FINANCIAL AID PICTURE
**Students with need:** Need-based aid available for full-time and part-time students. Work study available nights, weekends, and for part-time students.
**Students without need:** No-need awards available for academics.

### FINANCIAL AID PROCEDURES
**Forms required:** FAFSA.
**Dates and Deadlines:** Applicants notified on a rolling basis.

### CONTACT
Cynthia Galarza, Director of Student Financial Services
2900 31st Street, Santa Monica, CA 90405-3035
(310) 752-4700

## Art Institute of California: Orange County
Santa Ana, California
www.artinstitutes.edu/orangecounty
Federal Code: 007236

**3-year for-profit** culinary school and visual arts college in very large city.
**Enrollment:** 1,417 undergrads.

### BASIC COSTS (2015-2016)
**Additional info:** Diploma programs range from $24,496-$30,778, books and supplies range from $600-$800, room and board ranges from $15,588-$19,485. Associates programs range from $47,055-$49,433, books and supplies range from $1,050-$1,400, room and board range from $23,382-31,176. Bachelors programs range from from $93,6785-$95,843, books and supplies range from $2,450-$2,800, room and board $58,455.

### FINANCIAL AID PICTURE
**Students with need:** Need-based aid available for full-time and part-time students. Work study available nights, weekends, and for part-time students.
**Students without need:** No-need awards available for academics, art, minority status.

### FINANCIAL AID PROCEDURES
**Forms required:** FAFSA, state aid form.
**Dates and Deadlines:** Applicants notified on a rolling basis; must reply within 2 week(s) of notification.

### CONTACT
Silvia Dimas, Director of Student Financial Services
3601 West Sunflower Avenue, Santa Ana, CA 92704-7931
(714) 830-0202

## Art Institute of California: San Diego
San Diego, California
www.artinstitutes.edu/sandiego    Federal Code: 016471

**3-year for-profit** visual arts college in very large city.
**Enrollment:** 1,634 undergrads.

### BASIC COSTS (2015-2016)
**Additional info:** Diploma programs range from $24,496-$30,778, books and supplies range from $600-$800, room and board ranges from $15,176-$18970. Associates programs range from $47,076-$49,433, books and supplies range from $1,050-$1,400, room and board $30,352. Bachelors programs range from from $93,696-$95,843, books and supplies range from $2,450-$2,800, room and board $56,910.

### FINANCIAL AID PICTURE
**Students with need:** Need-based aid available for full-time students.

### FINANCIAL AID PROCEDURES
**Forms required:** FAFSA.

### CONTACT
Laverne Arberry-Lamb, Director of Student Financial Services
7650 Mission Valley Road, San Diego, CA 92108-4423

## Ashford University
San Diego, California
www.ashford.edu    Federal Code: 001881

**4-year for-profit** university in very large city.
**Enrollment:** 36,405 undergrads. 636 full-time freshmen.
**Selectivity:** Open admission.

### BASIC COSTS (2015-2016)
**Tuition and fees:** $10,480.
**Per-credit charge:** $420.
**Room and board:** $6,300.

### FINANCIAL AID PICTURE
**Students with need:** Need-based aid available for full-time and part-time students. Work study available nights, weekends, and for part-time students.

### FINANCIAL AID PROCEDURES
**Forms required:** FAFSA, institutional form.
**Dates and Deadlines:** Priority date 3/1; no closing date. Applicants notified on a rolling basis starting 2/15; must reply within 2 week(s) of notification.
**Transfers:** Students with 3.50 GPA eligible for President's Scholarship, 3.25-3.49 eligible for Provost's Scholarship and 3.00-3.24 eligible for Dean's Scholarship.

### CONTACT
Bridget McGuire, Senior Vice President, Financial Aid and Services
8620 Spectrum Center Boulevard, San Diego, CA 92123
(866) 711-1700

## Azusa Pacific University
Azusa, California
www.apu.edu    Federal Code: 001117

**4-year private** university in small city, affiliated with interdenominational tradition.
**Enrollment:** 5,862 undergrads, 9% part-time. 1,039 full-time freshmen.
**Selectivity:** Admits over 75% of applicants.

### BASIC COSTS (2015-2016)
**Tuition and fees:** $34,754.
**Per-credit charge:** $1,424.
**Room and board:** $9,218.
**Additional info:** Tuition/fee waivers available for minority students.

### FINANCIAL AID PICTURE (2014-2015)
**Students with need:** Out of 942 full-time freshmen who applied for aid, 845 were judged to have need. Of these, 844 received aid, and 96 had their full need met. Average financial aid package met 35% of need; average

scholarship/grant was $10,581; average loan was $3,712. For part-time students, average financial aid package was $8,990.

**Students without need:** 139 full-time freshmen who did not demonstrate need for aid received scholarships/grants; average award was $9,432. No-need awards available for academics, athletics, leadership, minority status, music/drama, religious affiliation, ROTC.

**Scholarships offered:** 36 full-time freshmen received athletic scholarships; average amount $20,225.

### FINANCIAL AID PROCEDURES
**Forms required:** FAFSA, institutional form.
**Dates and Deadlines:** Priority date 3/2; closing date 7/1. Applicants notified on a rolling basis starting 3/1; must reply within 3 week(s) of notification.
**Transfers:** Cal Grants not available to first time applicants who are seniors.

### CONTACT
Todd Ross, Director of Student Financial Services
901 East Alosta Avenue, Azusa, CA 91702-7000
(626) 812-3009

## Barstow Community College
Barstow, California
www.barstow.edu          Federal Code: 001119

**2-year public** community college in large town.
**Enrollment:** 1,178 undergrads.
**Selectivity:** Open admission.

### BASIC COSTS (2015-2016)
**Tuition and fees:** $1,388; out-of-state residents $7,388.
**Per-credit charge:** $46; out-of-state residents $246.

### FINANCIAL AID PICTURE
**Students with need:** Need-based aid available for full-time and part-time students.
**Students without need:** This college awards aid only to students with need.

### FINANCIAL AID PROCEDURES
**Forms required:** FAFSA.
**Dates and Deadlines:** Closing date 6/17. Applicants notified on a rolling basis starting 7/1.

### CONTACT
Danielle Cordova, Financial Aid Officer
2700 Barstow Road, Barstow, CA 92311-9984
(760) 252-2411 ext. 7205

## Berkeley City College
Berkeley, California
www.berkeleycitycollege.edu     Federal Code: 014311

**2-year public** community college in small city.
**Enrollment:** 3,840 undergrads.
**Selectivity:** Open admission.

### BASIC COSTS (2015-2016)
**Tuition and fees:** $1,420; out-of-state residents $7,810.
**Per-credit charge:** $46; out-of-state residents $259.
**Additional info:** Tuition/fee waivers available for adults, minority students, unemployed or children of unemployed.

### FINANCIAL AID PICTURE
**Students with need:** Need-based aid available for full-time and part-time students.
**Students without need:** This college awards aid only to students with need.

### FINANCIAL AID PROCEDURES
**Dates and Deadlines:** Applicants notified on a rolling basis.

### CONTACT
Loan Nguyen, Financial Aid Supervisor
2050 Center Street, Berkeley, CA 94704
(510) 981-2878

## Bethesda University of California
Anaheim, California
www.buc.edu          Federal Code: 032663

**4-year private** university in large city, affiliated with Christian Church.
**Enrollment:** 256 undergrads.
**Selectivity:** GED not accepted.

### BASIC COSTS (2015-2016)
**Tuition and fees:** $7,930.
**Per-credit charge:** $251.

### FINANCIAL AID PICTURE
**Students with need:** Need-based aid available for full-time and part-time students.
**Students without need:** This college awards aid only to students with need.

### FINANCIAL AID PROCEDURES
**Forms required:** FAFSA, institutional form.
**Dates and Deadlines:** Applicants notified on a rolling basis starting 6/30.
**Transfers:** No deadline.

### CONTACT
William Lee, Director of Financial Aid
730 North Euclid Street, Anaheim, CA 92801
(714) 683-1413

## Biola University
La Mirada, California
www.biola.edu          Federal Code: 001122

**4-year private** university and Bible college in large town, affiliated with interdenominational tradition.
**Enrollment:** 4,219 undergrads, 3% part-time. 827 full-time freshmen.
**Selectivity:** Admits 50 to 75% of applicants.

### BASIC COSTS (2015-2016)
**Tuition and fees:** $34,498.
**Per-credit charge:** $1,438.
**Room and board:** $9,791.
**Additional info:** Tuition/fee waivers available for minority students.

### FINANCIAL AID PICTURE (2014-2015)
**Students with need:** Average financial aid package met 51% of need; average scholarship/grant was $15,270; average loan was $3,123. For part-time students, average financial aid package was $12,559.
**Students without need:** No-need awards available for academics, alumni affiliation, art, athletics, leadership, minority status, music/drama.
**Scholarships offered:** Scholarships for Underrepresented Groups of Ethnicity: up to $6,500; based on GPA and ethnicity. Community Service Scholarship: $2,700; based on demonstration of outstanding spiritual leadership. Alumni Dependent Scholarship: $500; given to students whose parents completed 30 units of coursework at Biola University.

### FINANCIAL AID PROCEDURES
**Forms required:** FAFSA.
**Dates and Deadlines:** Priority date 3/1; no closing date. Applicants notified on a rolling basis starting 1/1.

**Transfers:** No deadline. Applicants notified on a rolling basis starting 3/1.

**CONTACT**
Jonathan Choy, Director of Financial Aid
13800 Biola Avenue, La Mirada, CA 90639-0001
(562) 903-4742

## Brandman University
Irvine, California
www.brandman.edu          Federal Code: 041618

**4-year private** virtual university in large city.
**Enrollment:** 3,595 undergrads, 67% part-time. 12 full-time freshmen.
**Selectivity:** Admits 50 to 75% of applicants.

**FINANCIAL AID PICTURE**
**Students with need:** Need-based aid available for full-time and part-time students.
**Students without need:** No-need awards available for academics.

**FINANCIAL AID PROCEDURES**
**Forms required:** FAFSA.
**Dates and Deadlines:** Applicants notified on a rolling basis starting 6/1.
**Transfers:** No deadline. Applicants notified on a rolling basis starting 6/1.

**CONTACT**
Greg Ball, Assistant Vice Chancellor, Financial Aid
16355 Laguna Canyon Road, Irvine, CA 92618

## Brooks Institute
Ventura, California
www.brooks.edu          Federal Code: 001123

**3-year for-profit** visual arts college in small city.
**Enrollment:** 415 undergrads.

**BASIC COSTS (2015-2016)**
**Tuition and fees:** $20,320.

**FINANCIAL AID PICTURE**
**Students with need:** Need-based aid available for full-time and part-time students. Work study available nights, weekends, and for part-time students.

**FINANCIAL AID PROCEDURES**
**Forms required:** FAFSA, institutional form.
**Dates and Deadlines:** Priority date 3/2; no closing date. Applicants notified on a rolling basis starting 5/1.
**Transfers:** No deadline. Applicants notified on a rolling basis.

**CONTACT**
Steve Hamaker, Director of Finance & Operations
5301 North Ventura Avenue, Ventura, CA 93001
(866) 394-1726

## Butte College
Oroville, California
www.butte.edu          Federal Code: 006972

**2-year public** community college in small city.
**Enrollment:** 11,164 undergrads, 49% part-time. 1,290 full-time freshmen.
**Selectivity:** Open admission; but selective for some programs.

**BASIC COSTS (2015-2016)**
**Tuition and fees:** $1,496; out-of-state residents $7,796.
**Per-credit charge:** $46; out-of-state residents $256.

**FINANCIAL AID PICTURE (2014-2015)**
**Students with need:** 76% of average financial aid package awarded as scholarships/grants, 24% awarded as loans/jobs. Need-based aid available for part-time students.
**Students without need:** This college awards aid only to students with need.

**FINANCIAL AID PROCEDURES**
**Forms required:** FAFSA.
**Dates and Deadlines:** Priority date 5/1; no closing date. Applicants notified on a rolling basis starting 7/9.

**CONTACT**
Tammera Shinar, Director, Financial Aid & Veteran Services
3536 Butte Campus Drive, Oroville, CA 95965
(530) 895-2311

## Cabrillo College
Aptos, California
www.cabrillo.edu          Federal Code: 001124

**2-year public** community college in large town.
**Enrollment:** 7,785 undergrads.
**Selectivity:** Open admission; but selective for some programs.

**BASIC COSTS (2015-2016)**
**Tuition and fees:** $1,411; out-of-state residents $7,411.
**Per-credit charge:** $46; out-of-state residents $246.

**FINANCIAL AID PICTURE**
**Students with need:** Need-based aid available for full-time and part-time students.

**FINANCIAL AID PROCEDURES**
**Forms required:** FAFSA, institutional form.
**Dates and Deadlines:** Applicants notified on a rolling basis starting 7/31; must reply within 3 week(s) of notification.
**Transfers:** Academic transcript required.

**CONTACT**
Tama Bolton, Director of Enrollment Services
6500 Soquel Drive, Aptos, CA 95003
(831) 479-6415

## California Baptist University
Riverside, California
www.calbaptist.edu          Federal Code: 001125

**4-year private** university in large city, affiliated with Southern Baptist Convention.
**Enrollment:** 6,630 undergrads, 14% part-time. 1,094 full-time freshmen.
**Selectivity:** Admits 50 to 75% of applicants.

**BASIC COSTS (2015-2016)**
**Tuition and fees:** $30,384.
**Per-credit charge:** $1,099.
**Room and board:** $9,540.

**FINANCIAL AID PICTURE (2015-2016)**
**Students with need:** Out of 994 full-time freshmen who applied for aid, 898 were judged to have need. Of these, 882 received aid, and 85 had their full need met. Average financial aid package met 60% of need; average scholarship/grant was $16,838; average loan was $3,828. For part-time students, average financial aid package was $7,847.
**Students without need:** 76 full-time freshmen who did not demonstrate need for aid received scholarships/grants; average award was $7,668. No-need awards available for academics, art, athletics, music/drama, religious affiliation, ROTC.

**Scholarships offered: Merit:** Matching room and board scholarship for recipients of the ROTC scholarships. Yellow Ribbon Scholarship for qualified veterans. **Athletic:** 70 full-time freshmen received athletic scholarships; average amount $14,132.

**FINANCIAL AID PROCEDURES**

**Forms required:** FAFSA, state aid form.

**Dates and Deadlines:** Priority date 3/2; no closing date. Applicants notified on a rolling basis starting 3/2; must reply by 6/1.

**Transfers:** No deadline. Applicants notified on a rolling basis starting 12/15; must reply by 6/1.

**CONTACT**

Rebecca Sanchez, Director of Financial Aid

8432 Magnolia Avenue, Riverside, CA 92504-3297

(951) 343-4236

## California Christian College

Fresno, California

www.calchristiancollege.edu          Federal Code: 014128

**4-year private** Bible college in large city, affiliated with Free Will Baptists.

**Enrollment:** 18 undergrads, 39% part-time. 1 full-time freshmen.

**Selectivity:** Open admission.

**BASIC COSTS (2016-2017)**

**Tuition and fees:** $8,990.

**Per-credit charge:** $350.

**Room only:** $4,800.

**FINANCIAL AID PICTURE (2015-2016)**

**Students with need:** Out of 1 full-time freshmen who applied for aid, 1 were judged to have need. Of these, 1 received aid. Average financial aid package met 34% of need; average scholarship/grant was $6,275. For part-time students, average financial aid package was $4,960.

**Students without need:** This college awards aid only to students with need.

**FINANCIAL AID PROCEDURES**

**Forms required:** FAFSA, institutional form.

**Dates and Deadlines:** Priority date 3/2; no closing date. Applicants notified on a rolling basis starting 5/1.

**CONTACT**

Melinda Scroggins, Financial Aid Coordinator

5364 E. Belmont, Fresno, CA 93727

(559) 251-4215 ext. 1006

## California College of the Arts

San Francisco, California

www.cca.edu          Federal Code: 001127

**4-year private** visual arts college in very large city.

**Enrollment:** 1,504 undergrads, 5% part-time. 272 full-time freshmen.

**Selectivity:** Admits over 75% of applicants.

**BASIC COSTS (2016-2017)**

**Tuition and fees:** $45,466.

**Room only:** $9,320.

**FINANCIAL AID PICTURE (2014-2015)**

**Students with need:** Out of 158 full-time freshmen who applied for aid, 146 were judged to have need. Of these, 146 received aid, and 7 had their full need met. Average financial aid package met 63% of need; average scholarship/grant was $25,417; average loan was $3,540. For part-time students, average financial aid package was $12,199.

**Students without need:** 86 full-time freshmen who did not demonstrate need for aid received scholarships/grants; average award was $10,859. No-need awards available for academics, art.

**Scholarships offered:** Creative Achievement Scholarship: up to $20,000 annually; renewable; based on academic achievement and strength of admissions portfolios.

**Additional info:** Application deadline for merit scholarships February 1.

**FINANCIAL AID PROCEDURES**

**Forms required:** FAFSA, state aid form.

**Dates and Deadlines:** Priority date 2/1; no closing date. Applicants notified by 4/1.

**Transfers:** No deadline. Applicants notified on a rolling basis starting 3/1. Scholarships available for community college transfer students.

**CONTACT**

Dewayne Barnes, Director of Financial Aid

1111 Eighth Street, San Francisco, CA 94107-2247

(415) 703-9528

## California College San Diego

San Diego, California

www.cc-sd.edu

**4-year private** business and health science college in very large city.

**Enrollment:** 1,075 undergrads.

**Selectivity:** Open admission.

**BASIC COSTS (2015-2016)**

**Additional info:** 20-month Associate programs: Business Management & Accounting $42,389, Computer Programming $42,273, Computer Technology & Networking $42,408, Graphic Arts $42,387, Medical Specialties $42,411, Respiratory Therapy $49,504. 36-month Bachelor programs: Accounting $74,753, Business Administration $74,620, Computer Science $74,700, Health Information Management $74,700, Healthcare Administration $74,778, Respiratory Therapy $81,719. All fees & books included.

**FINANCIAL AID PICTURE**

**Students with need:** Need-based aid available for full-time and part-time students.

**FINANCIAL AID PROCEDURES**

**Forms required:** FAFSA, state aid form, institutional form.

**CONTACT**

Tony Roman, Lean Financial Planner

6602 Convoy Court, Suite 100, San Diego, CA 92111

(619) 680-4430

## California Institute of Integral Studies

San Francisco, California

www.ciis.edu          Federal Code: 012154

**Upper-division private** university in very large city.

**Enrollment:** 102 undergrads, 15% part-time.

**BASIC COSTS (2015-2016)**

**Tuition and fees:** $18,315.

**Per-credit charge:** $748.

**Additional info:** Above tuition and fees are for fall and spring semesters. Most students also attend in the summer, which would add $8970 in tuition and $215 in fees.

**FINANCIAL AID PICTURE (2014-2015)**

**Students with need:** Average financial aid package for all full-time undergraduates was $20,269; for part-time $15,331. 39% awarded as scholarships/grants, 61% awarded as loans/jobs. Work study available nights, weekends, and for part-time students.

**Students without need:** No-need awards available for academics, alumni affiliation, art, job skills, leadership, minority status, music/drama, ROTC, state/district residency.

## FINANCIAL AID PROCEDURES
**Dates and Deadlines:** Closing date 4/15.
**Transfers:** No deadline.

## CONTACT
Michael Szkotak, Financial Aid Director
1453 Mission Street, San Francisco, CA 94103
(415) 575-6156

## California Institute of Technology
Pasadena, California       Federal Code: 001131
www.caltech.edu       CSS Code: 4034

**4-year private** university in small city.
**Enrollment:** 1,001 undergrads. 241 full-time freshmen.
**Selectivity:** Admits less than 50% of applicants.

### BASIC COSTS (2016-2017)
**Tuition and fees:** $47,577.
**Room and board:** $14,100.

### FINANCIAL AID PICTURE (2015-2016)
**Students with need:** Out of 181 full-time freshmen who applied for aid, 140 were judged to have need. Of these, 140 received aid, and 140 had their full need met. Average financial aid package met 100% of need; average scholarship/grant was $37,873; average loan was $3,349.
**Students without need:** 2 full-time freshmen who did not demonstrate need for aid received scholarships/grants; average award was $5,000.

### FINANCIAL AID PROCEDURES
**Forms required:** FAFSA, CSS PROFILE, state aid form, institutional form.
**Dates and Deadlines:** Priority date 3/2; no closing date. Applicants notified by 4/15; must reply by 5/1 or within 2 week(s) of notification.
**Transfers:** Priority date 3/1; no deadline.

### CONTACT
Don Crewell, Director of Financial Aid
383 South Hill Avenue, Mail Code 10-90, Pasadena, CA 91125
(626) 395-6280

## California Institute of the Arts
Valencia, California       Federal Code: 001132
www.calarts.edu       CSS Code: 4049

**4-year private** visual arts and performing arts college in small city.
**Enrollment:** 942 undergrads, 1% part-time. 193 full-time freshmen.
**Selectivity:** Admits less than 50% of applicants.

### BASIC COSTS (2015-2016)
**Tuition and fees:** $43,876.
**Room and board:** $11,165.

### FINANCIAL AID PICTURE (2015-2016)
**Students with need:** Out of 150 full-time freshmen who applied for aid, 147 were judged to have need. Of these, 140 received aid, and 38 had their full need met. For part-time students, average financial aid package was $32,032.
**Students without need:** No-need awards available for academics, art, minority status, music/drama.

### FINANCIAL AID PROCEDURES
**Forms required:** FAFSA, CSS PROFILE.

**Dates and Deadlines:** Priority date 2/15; no closing date. Applicants notified on a rolling basis starting 4/1; must reply by 5/1 or within 3 week(s) of notification.
**Transfers:** Applicants notified by 4/1; must reply by 5/1 or within 3 week(s) of notification.

## CONTACT
Robin Bailey-Chen, Director of Financial Aid
24700 McBean Parkway, Valencia, CA 91355
(661) 253-7869

## California Lutheran University
Thousand Oaks, California
www.callutheran.edu       Federal Code: 001133

**4-year private** university and liberal arts college in small city, affiliated with Evangelical Lutheran Church in America.
**Enrollment:** 2,802 undergrads, 5% part-time. 595 full-time freshmen.
**Selectivity:** Admits 50 to 75% of applicants.

### BASIC COSTS (2016-2017)
**Tuition and fees:** $39,760.
**Per-credit charge:** $1,265.
**Room and board:** $13,060.

### FINANCIAL AID PICTURE (2015-2016)
**Students with need:** Out of 584 full-time freshmen who applied for aid, 445 were judged to have need. Of these, 445 received aid, and 89 had their full need met. Average financial aid package met 73% of need; average scholarship/grant was $24,073; average loan was $3,450. For part-time students, average financial aid package was $18,101.
**Students without need:** 131 full-time freshmen who did not demonstrate need for aid received scholarships/grants; average award was $18,850. No-need awards available for academics, alumni affiliation, art, leadership, minority status, music/drama, religious affiliation, state/district residency.
**Scholarships offered:** Academic Scholarships: range from $3,000 up to $15,000 per year; based on GPA, test scores, and class rank at time of Admission. Presidential Scholarship Program: $17,000 up to full tuition; additional application required. Visual and Performing Arts Scholarships: $1,000-$6,000; application deadline of February 1 and audition with department deadline of February 22.

### FINANCIAL AID PROCEDURES
**Forms required:** FAFSA, state aid form.
**Dates and Deadlines:** Priority date 3/1; closing date 7/1. Applicants notified on a rolling basis starting 3/15; must reply within 2 week(s) of notification.
**Transfers:** No deadline. Applicants notified on a rolling basis starting 3/15; must reply within 2 week(s) of notification.

### CONTACT
Jerry McKeen, Director of Financial Aid
60 West Olsen Road #1350, Thousand Oaks, CA 91360-2787
(805) 493-3115

## California Maritime Academy
Vallejo, California
www.csum.edu       Federal Code: 001134

**4-year public** university and maritime college in small city.
**Enrollment:** 1,072 undergrads, 3% part-time. 220 full-time freshmen.
**Selectivity:** Admits over 75% of applicants.

### BASIC COSTS (2015-2016)
**Tuition and fees:** $6,536; out-of-state residents $17,696.
**Room and board:** $11,756.

## FINANCIAL AID PICTURE (2015-2016)

**Students with need:** Out of 122 full-time freshmen who applied for aid, 122 were judged to have need. Of these, 122 received aid, and 35 had their full need met. Need-based aid available for part-time students.

**Students without need:** This college awards aid only to students with need.

**Additional info:** US Maritime Administration provides annual incentive payment of $3,000 per student, with certain conditions. Tuition waiver for children of deceased or disabled California veterans.

## FINANCIAL AID PROCEDURES

**Forms required:** FAFSA.

**Dates and Deadlines:** Priority date 3/2; no closing date. Applicants notified on a rolling basis starting 4/1.

## CONTACT

Craig Yamamoto, Director of Financial Aid
200 Maritime Academy Drive, Vallejo, CA 94590
(707) 654-1287

# California Polytechnic State University: San Luis Obispo

San Luis Obispo, California
www.calpoly.edu                                    Federal Code: 001143

**4-year public** university in large town.
**Enrollment:** 19,971 undergrads, 4% part-time. 4,648 full-time freshmen.
**Selectivity:** Admits less than 50% of applicants.

## BASIC COSTS (2015-2016)

**Tuition and fees:** $9,000; out-of-state residents $20,160.
**Room and board:** $12,009.
**Additional info:** International Student Fee of $300 per quarter.

## FINANCIAL AID PICTURE (2014-2015)

**Students with need:** Out of 3,619 full-time freshmen who applied for aid, 1,954 were judged to have need. Of these, 1,885 received aid, and 184 had their full need met. Average financial aid package met 56% of need; average scholarship/grant was $3,177; average loan was $3,276. For part-time students, average financial aid package was $5,578.

**Students without need:** 649 full-time freshmen who did not demonstrate need for aid received scholarships/grants; average award was $2,072. No-need awards available for academics, alumni affiliation, art, athletics, job skills, leadership, music/drama, ROTC, state/district residency.

**Scholarships offered:** 104 full-time freshmen received athletic scholarships; average amount $3,411.

**Additional info:** College-administered financial aid is not available for undergraduate international students.

## FINANCIAL AID PROCEDURES

**Forms required:** FAFSA.

**Dates and Deadlines:** Priority date 3/2; no closing date. Applicants notified on a rolling basis starting 4/1.

## CONTACT

Lois Kelly, Director, Financial Aid
Admissions Office, Cal Poly, San Luis Obispo, CA 93407-0031
(805) 756-2927

# California State Polytechnic University: Pomona

Pomona, California
www.cpp.edu                                        Federal Code: 001144

**4-year public** university in small city.
**Enrollment:** 22,034 undergrads, 11% part-time. 2,656 full-time freshmen.

**Selectivity:** Admits less than 50% of applicants.

## BASIC COSTS (2015-2016)

**Tuition and fees:** $6,976; out-of-state residents $18,136.
**Room and board:** $15,238.
**Additional info:** Published fees may increase when public funding in inadequate. All CSU fees should be regarded as estimates, subject to change upon approval by The Board of Trustees.

## FINANCIAL AID PICTURE (2015-2016)

**Students with need:** Out of 2,265 full-time freshmen who applied for aid, 1,795 were judged to have need. Of these, 1,680 received aid, and 32 had their full need met. Average financial aid package met 58% of need; average scholarship/grant was $10,396; average loan was $3,443. For part-time students, average financial aid package was $8,386.

**Students without need:** 2 full-time freshmen who did not demonstrate need for aid received scholarships/grants; average award was $2,000. No-need awards available for academics, alumni affiliation, athletics, leadership, state/district residency.

**Scholarships offered:** 5 full-time freshmen received athletic scholarships; average amount $1,400.

## FINANCIAL AID PROCEDURES

**Forms required:** FAFSA.

**Dates and Deadlines:** Priority date 3/2; no closing date. Applicants notified on a rolling basis starting 4/1; must reply within 2 week(s) of notification.

## CONTACT

Diana Minor, Director of Financial Aid
3801 West Temple Avenue, Pomona, CA 91768-4019
(909) 869-3700

# California State University: Bakersfield

Bakersfield, California
www.csub.edu                                       Federal Code: 007993

**4-year public** university and liberal arts college in small city.
**Enrollment:** 7,985 undergrads, 17% part-time. 1,397 full-time freshmen.
**Selectivity:** Admits over 75% of applicants. GED not accepted.

## BASIC COSTS (2015-2016)

**Tuition and fees:** $6,811; out-of-state residents $17,971.
**Room and board:** $12,561.

## FINANCIAL AID PICTURE (2014-2015)

**Students with need:** Average financial aid package met 21% of need; average scholarship/grant was $4,128; average loan was $1,100. For part-time students, average financial aid package was $3,747.

**Students without need:** This college awards aid only to students with need.

**Scholarships offered:** 162 full-time freshmen received athletic scholarships; average amount $755.

## FINANCIAL AID PROCEDURES

**Forms required:** FAFSA, state aid form.

**Dates and Deadlines:** Priority date 3/2; no closing date. Applicants notified on a rolling basis starting 4/15; must reply within 3 week(s) of notification.

## CONTACT

Ron Radney, Director of Financial Aid & Scholarships
9001 Stockdale Highway, Bakersfield, CA 93311-1099
(661) 664-2011

## California State University: Channel Islands

Camarillo, California
www.csuci.edu                    Federal Code: 039803

**4-year public** university in small city.
**Enrollment:** 5,625 undergrads.

### BASIC COSTS (2015-2016)
**Tuition and fees:** $6,532; out-of-state residents $17,692.
**Room and board:** $14,858.

### FINANCIAL AID PICTURE
**Students with need:** Need-based aid available for full-time and part-time students. Work study available nights, weekends, and for part-time students.
**Students without need:** No-need awards available for academics, leadership, state/district residency.

### FINANCIAL AID PROCEDURES
**Forms required:** FAFSA.
**Dates and Deadlines:** Priority date 3/2; no closing date. Applicants notified by 4/7.

### CONTACT
Sunshine Garcia, Director of Financial Aid
One University Drive, Camarillo, CA 93012
(805) 437-8530

## California State University: Chico

Chico, California
www.csuchico.edu                 Federal Code: 001146

**4-year public** university and liberal arts college in small city.
**Enrollment:** 16,127 undergrads, 10% part-time. 2,757 full-time freshmen.
**Selectivity:** Admits 50 to 75% of applicants.

### BASIC COSTS (2015-2016)
**Tuition and fees:** $7,026; out-of-state residents $18,182.
**Room and board:** $12,234.

### FINANCIAL AID PICTURE (2014-2015)
**Students with need:** Out of 2,493 full-time freshmen who applied for aid, 1,982 were judged to have need. Of these, 1,945 received aid, and 371 had their full need met. Average financial aid package met 68% of need; average scholarship/grant was $10,486; average loan was $3,431. For part-time students, average financial aid package was $13,985.
**Students without need:** No-need awards available for academics, art, athletics, leadership, minority status, music/drama, religious affiliation.
**Scholarships offered:** President's Scholar Award: 10 awards at $12,000 each; 12 awards at $1,000 each.

### FINANCIAL AID PROCEDURES
**Forms required:** FAFSA.
**Dates and Deadlines:** Priority date 3/2; no closing date. Applicants notified on a rolling basis starting 3/2.

### CONTACT
Dan Reed, Director of Financial Aid
400 West First Street, Chico, CA 95929-0722
(530) 898-6451

## California State University: Dominguez Hills

Carson, California
www.csudh.edu                    Federal Code: 001141

**4-year public** university in small city.
**Enrollment:** 12,526 undergrads, 27% part-time. 1,286 full-time freshmen.

**Selectivity:** Admits 50 to 75% of applicants.

### BASIC COSTS (2015-2016)
**Tuition and fees:** $6,278; out-of-state residents $17,438.
**Room and board:** $12,790.
**Additional info:** Tuition/fee waivers available for adults.

### FINANCIAL AID PICTURE (2014-2015)
**Students with need:** Out of 1,248 full-time freshmen who applied for aid, 1,156 were judged to have need. Of these, 1,142 received aid, and 19 had their full need met. Average financial aid package met 36% of need; average scholarship/grant was $5,320; average loan was $1,551. For part-time students, average financial aid package was $4,712.
**Students without need:** 63 full-time freshmen who did not demonstrate need for aid received scholarships/grants; average award was $3,792. No-need awards available for academics, alumni affiliation, art, athletics, leadership, music/drama.
**Scholarships offered:** 1 full-time freshmen received athletic scholarships; average amount $1,500.

### FINANCIAL AID PROCEDURES
**Forms required:** FAFSA.
**Dates and Deadlines:** Priority date 3/2; no closing date. Applicants notified on a rolling basis starting 2/28.
**Transfers:** Applicants notified on a rolling basis starting 4/1; must reply within 3 week(s) of notification.

### CONTACT
Delores Lee, Director of Financial Aid
1000 East Victoria Street, Carson, CA 90747
(310) 243-3696

## California State University: East Bay

Hayward, California
www.csueastbay.edu               Federal Code: 001138

**4-year public** university in small city.
**Enrollment:** 12,924 undergrads, 14% part-time. 1,730 full-time freshmen.
**Selectivity:** Admits 50 to 75% of applicants.

### BASIC COSTS (2015-2016)
**Tuition and fees:** $6,564; out-of-state residents $17,724.
**Room and board:** $12,849.

### FINANCIAL AID PICTURE (2015-2016)
**Students with need:** Out of 1,031 full-time freshmen who applied for aid, 998 were judged to have need. Of these, 983 received aid, and 21 had their full need met. Average financial aid package met 63% of need; average scholarship/grant was $9,540; average loan was $5,054. For part-time students, average financial aid package was $7,486.
**Students without need:** No-need awards available for academics, athletics, music/drama.

### FINANCIAL AID PROCEDURES
**Forms required:** FAFSA.
**Dates and Deadlines:** Priority date 3/2; no closing date. Applicants notified on a rolling basis starting 3/30; must reply within 3 week(s) of notification.

### CONTACT
Rhonda Johnson, Director of Financial Aid
25800 Carlos Bee Boulevard, Hayward, CA 94542-3095
(510) 885-3018

## California State University: Fresno

Fresno, California
www.csufresno.edu                Federal Code: 001147

**4-year public** university in very large city.
**Enrollment:** 21,076 undergrads, 16% part-time. 2,599 full-time freshmen.

**Selectivity:** Admits 50 to 75% of applicants.

### BASIC COSTS (2015-2016)
**Tuition and fees:** $6,298; out-of-state residents $17,458.
**Room and board:** $10,604.
**Additional info:** Tuition/fee waivers available for adults, minority students, unemployed or children of unemployed.

### FINANCIAL AID PICTURE (2015-2016)
**Students with need:** Average financial aid package met 70% of need; average scholarship/grant was $9,984; average loan was $3,115. For part-time students, average financial aid package was $9,321.
**Students without need:** No-need awards available for academics, art, athletics, leadership, music/drama, ROTC, state/district residency.

### FINANCIAL AID PROCEDURES
**Forms required:** FAFSA.
**Dates and Deadlines:** Priority date 3/2; no closing date. Applicants notified on a rolling basis starting 4/1; must reply within 3 week(s) of notification.
**Transfers:** No deadline. Applicants notified on a rolling basis starting 4/1; must reply within 3 week(s) of notification.

### CONTACT
Denise Tardell, Associate Director of Financial Aid
5150 North Maple Avenue, M/S JA 57, Fresno, CA 93740-8026
(559) 278-2182

## California State University: Fullerton
Fullerton, California
www.fullerton.edu                    Federal Code: 001137

**4-year public** university in small city.
**Enrollment:** 33,009 undergrads, 18% part-time. 4,287 full-time freshmen.
**Selectivity:** Admits less than 50% of applicants.

### BASIC COSTS (2015-2016)
**Tuition and fees:** $6,436; out-of-state residents $17,596.
**Room and board:** $14,574.

### FINANCIAL AID PICTURE
**Students with need:** Need-based aid available for full-time and part-time students. Work study available nights, weekends, and for part-time students.
**Students without need:** No-need awards available for academics, art, athletics, leadership, music/drama.
**Additional info:** Fee waiver for children of veterans killed in action or with service-connected disability whose annual income is $5,000 or less.

### FINANCIAL AID PROCEDURES
**Forms required:** FAFSA.
**Dates and Deadlines:** Priority date 3/2; closing date 6/6. Applicants notified on a rolling basis; must reply within 4 week(s) of notification.
**Transfers:** No deadline. Applicants notified on a rolling basis; must reply within 4 week(s) of notification.

### CONTACT
Cecilia Schouwe, Director of Financial Aid
P.O. Box 6900, Fullerton, CA 92834-6900
(657) 278-3125

## California State University: Long Beach
Long Beach, California
www.csulb.edu                    Federal Code: 001139

**4-year public** university in large city.
**Enrollment:** 32,079 undergrads, 17% part-time. 3,505 full-time freshmen.
**Selectivity:** Admits less than 50% of applicants.

### BASIC COSTS (2015-2016)
**Tuition and fees:** $6,452; out-of-state residents $17,612.
**Room and board:** $11,880.

### FINANCIAL AID PICTURE (2015-2016)
**Students with need:** Average financial aid package met 81% of need; average scholarship/grant was $7,786; average loan was $3,366. For part-time students, average financial aid package was $10,621.
**Students without need:** No-need awards available for academics, art, athletics, job skills, leadership, music/drama, state/district residency.
**Scholarships offered:** President's Scholar Award: full tuition and fees, campus housing, books.

### FINANCIAL AID PROCEDURES
**Forms required:** FAFSA.
**Dates and Deadlines:** Priority date 3/2; no closing date. Applicants notified on a rolling basis starting 3/25; must reply within 3 week(s) of notification.
**Transfers:** Community college EOP students may be eligible for grant.

### CONTACT
Nicholas Valdivia, Director of Financial Aid
1250 Bellflower Boulevard, Long Beach, CA 90840-0106
(562) 985-4641

## California State University: Los Angeles
Los Angeles, California
www.calstatela.edu                    Federal Code: 001140

**4-year public** university in very large city.
**Enrollment:** 23,405 undergrads, 13% part-time. 3,688 full-time freshmen.
**Selectivity:** Admits 50 to 75% of applicants.

### BASIC COSTS (2015-2016)
**Tuition and fees:** $6,344; out-of-state residents $15,272.
**Room and board:** $12,834.

### FINANCIAL AID PICTURE (2015-2016)
**Students with need:** Out of 2,383 full-time freshmen who applied for aid, 2,210 were judged to have need. Of these, 2,142 received aid, and 266 had their full need met. Average financial aid package met 69% of need; average scholarship/grant was $9,713; average loan was $3,193. For part-time students, average financial aid package was $10,066.
**Students without need:** 54 full-time freshmen who did not demonstrate need for aid received scholarships/grants; average award was $1,646.
**Scholarships offered:** 4 full-time freshmen received athletic scholarships; average amount $4,287.

### FINANCIAL AID PROCEDURES
**Forms required:** FAFSA.
**Dates and Deadlines:** Priority date 3/2; no closing date. Applicants notified on a rolling basis starting 4/1; must reply within 3 week(s) of notification.

### CONTACT
Tamie Nguyen, Director of Center for Student Financial Aid
5151 State University Drive SA101, Los Angeles, CA 90032
(323) 343-6260

## California State University: Monterey Bay
Seaside, California
www.csumb.edu                    Federal Code: 032603

**4-year public** liberal arts and teachers college in large town.
**Enrollment:** 6,657 undergrads, 7% part-time. 1,049 full-time freshmen.
**Selectivity:** Admits less than 50% of applicants.

## BASIC COSTS (2015-2016)
**Tuition and fees:** $6,119; out-of-state residents $17,279.
**Room and board:** $10,542.

## FINANCIAL AID PICTURE (2015-2016)
**Students with need:** Out of 932 full-time freshmen who applied for aid, 738 were judged to have need. Of these, 666 received aid, and 99 had their full need met. Average financial aid package met 65% of need; average scholarship/grant was $10,558; average loan was $3,327. For part-time students, average financial aid package was $6,670.
**Students without need:** No-need awards available for academics, athletics, leadership, state/district residency.
**Scholarships offered:** 37 full-time freshmen received athletic scholarships; average amount $2,841.

## FINANCIAL AID PROCEDURES
**Forms required:** FAFSA, state aid form.
**Dates and Deadlines:** Priority date 3/2; closing date 5/20. Applicants notified on a rolling basis starting 4/1.

## CONTACT
Angeles Fuentes, Director of Financial Aid Services
100 Campus Center, Student Services Building, Seaside, CA 93955-8001
(831) 582-5100

## California State University: Northridge
Northridge, California
www.csun.edu
Federal Code: 001153

**4-year public** university in very large city.
**Enrollment:** 36,917 undergrads, 18% part-time. 5,450 full-time freshmen.
**Selectivity:** Admits less than 50% of applicants.

## BASIC COSTS (2015-2016)
**Tuition and fees:** $6,549; out-of-state residents $17,709.
**Room and board:** $10,981.

## FINANCIAL AID PICTURE (2014-2015)
**Students with need:** Out of 4,814 full-time freshmen who applied for aid, 4,629 were judged to have need. Of these, 4,629 received aid. For part-time students, average financial aid package was $12,473.
**Students without need:** 788 full-time freshmen who did not demonstrate need for aid received scholarships/grants; average award was $1,173. No-need awards available for academics, athletics, state/district residency.
**Scholarships offered:** 56 full-time freshmen received athletic scholarships; average amount $11,450.

## FINANCIAL AID PROCEDURES
**Forms required:** FAFSA.
**Dates and Deadlines:** Priority date 3/2; no closing date. Applicants notified on a rolling basis starting 4/1.

## CONTACT
Lili Vidal, Director of Financial Aid
18111 Nordhoff Street, Northridge, CA 91330-8207
(818) 677-4085

## California State University: Sacramento
Sacramento, California
www.csus.edu
Federal Code: 001233

**4-year public** university in very large city.
**Enrollment:** 27,244 undergrads, 19% part-time. 3,473 full-time freshmen.
**Selectivity:** Admits 50 to 75% of applicants.

## BASIC COSTS (2015-2016)
**Tuition and fees:** $6,872; out-of-state residents $18,032.

**Room and board:** $13,460.

## FINANCIAL AID PICTURE (2014-2015)
**Students with need:** Out of 3,128 full-time freshmen who applied for aid, 2,649 were judged to have need. Of these, 2,582 received aid, and 329 had their full need met. Average financial aid package met 63% of need; average scholarship/grant was $8,522; average loan was $3,119. For part-time students, average financial aid package was $7,250.
**Students without need:** 8 full-time freshmen who did not demonstrate need for aid received scholarships/grants; average award was $1,000.

## FINANCIAL AID PROCEDURES
**Forms required:** FAFSA.
**Dates and Deadlines:** Applicants notified on a rolling basis starting 4/23; must reply within 4 week(s) of notification.

## CONTACT
Craig Yamamoto, Financial Aid Director
6000 J Street, Sacramento, CA 95819-6048
(916) 278-6554

## California State University: San Bernardino
San Bernardino, California
www.csusb.edu
Federal Code: 001142

**4-year public** university and liberal arts college in small city.
**Enrollment:** 17,721 undergrads, 11% part-time. 2,906 full-time freshmen.
**Selectivity:** Admits 50 to 75% of applicants.

## BASIC COSTS (2015-2016)
**Tuition and fees:** $6,579; out-of-state residents $17,739.
**Room and board:** $10,023.

## FINANCIAL AID PICTURE (2015-2016)
**Students with need:** Out of 2,757 full-time freshmen who applied for aid, 2,527 were judged to have need. Of these, 2,466 received aid, and 290 had their full need met. Average financial aid package met 65% of need; average scholarship/grant was $8,696; average loan was $3,260. For part-time students, average financial aid package was $5,350.
**Students without need:** 6 full-time freshmen who did not demonstrate need for aid received scholarships/grants; average award was $6,333.
**Scholarships offered:** 4 full-time freshmen received athletic scholarships; average amount $2,825.

## FINANCIAL AID PROCEDURES
**Forms required:** FAFSA, state aid form.
**Dates and Deadlines:** Priority date 3/2; no closing date. Applicants notified on a rolling basis starting 4/1.

## CONTACT
Roseanna Ruiz, Director of Financial Aid
5500 University Parkway, San Bernardino, CA 92407-2397
(909) 537-7800

## California State University: Stanislaus
Turlock, California
www.csustan.edu
Federal Code: 001157

**4-year public** business and liberal arts college in small city.
**Enrollment:** 8,093 undergrads, 16% part-time. 1,220 full-time freshmen.
**Selectivity:** Admits 50 to 75% of applicants.

## BASIC COSTS (2015-2016)
**Tuition and fees:** $6,700; out-of-state residents $17,860.
**Room and board:** $10,090.
**Additional info:** Tuition/fee waivers available for adults.

## FINANCIAL AID PICTURE

**Students with need:** Need-based aid available for full-time and part-time students. Work study available nights, weekends, and for part-time students.
**Students without need:** No-need awards available for academics, alumni affiliation, art, athletics, leadership, minority status, music/drama, state/district residency.

## FINANCIAL AID PROCEDURES

**Forms required:** FAFSA, state aid form.
**Dates and Deadlines:** Priority date 3/2; no closing date. Applicants notified on a rolling basis starting 3/15; must reply within 3 week(s) of notification.
**Transfers:** No deadline. Applicants notified on a rolling basis starting 3/15; must reply within 3 week(s) of notification.

## CONTACT

Noelia Gonzales, Director of Financial Aid and Scholarships
One University Circle, Turlock, CA 95382-0256
(209) 667-3336

# California University of Management and Sciences

Anaheim, California
www.calums.edu                    Federal Code: 041331

**4-year private** university and business college in very large city.
**Enrollment:** 39 undergrads. 10 full-time freshmen.

## BASIC COSTS (2015-2016)

**Tuition and fees:** $9,570.

## FINANCIAL AID PICTURE (2014-2015)

**Students with need:** Average financial aid package for all full-time undergraduates was $20,000. 34% awarded as scholarships/grants, 66% awarded as loans/jobs.
**Students without need:** This college awards aid only to students with need.

## FINANCIAL AID PROCEDURES

**Forms required:** FAFSA, institutional form.
**Dates and Deadlines:** Priority date 9/1; closing date 9/15. Applicants notified on a rolling basis; must reply within 2 week(s) of notification.
**Transfers:** No deadline. Applicants notified on a rolling basis; must reply within 2 week(s) of notification.

## CONTACT

Jeffrey Beasca, Chief Compliance Officer
721 North Euclid Streeet, Anaheim, CA 92801-4116
(714) 533-3946

# Canada College

Redwood City, California
www.canadacollege.edu              Federal Code: 006973

**2-year public** community college in small city.
**Enrollment:** 3,844 undergrads, 90% part-time. 111 full-time freshmen.
**Selectivity:** Open admission; but selective for some programs.

## BASIC COSTS (2015-2016)

**Tuition and fees:** $1,436; out-of-state residents $8,006.
**Per-credit charge:** $46; out-of-state residents $265.

## FINANCIAL AID PICTURE (2014-2015)

**Students with need:** 92% of average financial aid package awarded as scholarships/grants, 8% awarded as loans/jobs. Need-based aid available for part-time students.

## FINANCIAL AID PROCEDURES

**Forms required:** FAFSA.

**Dates and Deadlines:** Priority date 3/2; no closing date. Applicants notified on a rolling basis starting 5/1; must reply within 2 week(s) of notification.

## CONTACT

Margie Carrington, Financial Aid Director
4200 Farm Hill Boulevard, Redwood City, CA 94061
(650) 306-3116

# Cerro Coso Community College

Ridgecrest, California
www.cerrocoso.edu                  Federal Code: 010111

**2-year public** community college in large town.
**Enrollment:** 2,580 undergrads.
**Selectivity:** Open admission.

## BASIC COSTS (2015-2016)

**Tuition and fees:** $1,382; out-of-state residents $8,642.
**Per-credit charge:** $46; out-of-state residents $288.

## FINANCIAL AID PICTURE

**Students with need:** Need-based aid available for full-time and part-time students. Work study available nights.

## FINANCIAL AID PROCEDURES

**Forms required:** FAFSA.
**Dates and Deadlines:** Priority date 5/15; no closing date. Applicants notified on a rolling basis starting 6/1; must reply within 2 week(s) of notification.

## CONTACT

JoAnn Spiller, Director of Financial Aid and Scholarships
3000 College Heights Boulevard, Ridgecrest, CA 93555-7777
(760) 384-6221

# Chabot College

Hayward, California
www.chabotcollege.edu              Federal Code: 001162

**2-year public** community college in large city.
**Enrollment:** 8,998 undergrads.
**Selectivity:** Open admission; but selective for some programs.

## BASIC COSTS (2015-2016)

**Tuition and fees:** $1,414; out-of-state residents $8,704.
**Per-credit charge:** $46; out-of-state residents $289.

## FINANCIAL AID PICTURE

**Students with need:** Work study available nights, weekends, and for part-time students.
**Additional info:** Tuition and/or fee waivers for low-income students.

## FINANCIAL AID PROCEDURES

**Forms required:** FAFSA, institutional form.
**Dates and Deadlines:** Priority date 8/1; no closing date. Applicants notified on a rolling basis.

## CONTACT

Kathryn Linzmeyer, Director of Financial Aid
25555 Hesperian Boulevard, Hayward, CA 94545
(510) 723-6746

# Chaffey College

Rancho Cucamonga, California
www.chaffey.edu                    Federal Code: 001163

**2-year public** community college in small city.
**Enrollment:** 14,699 undergrads.

**Selectivity:** Open admission.

**BASIC COSTS (2015-2016)**
**Tuition and fees:** $1,414; out-of-state residents $7,744.
**Per-credit charge:** $46; out-of-state residents $257.
**Additional info:** Tuition/fee waivers available for adults.

**FINANCIAL AID PICTURE**
**Students with need:** Need-based aid available for full-time and part-time students.
**Students without need:** No-need awards available for academics.
**Additional info:** State of California Board of Governors fee waivers to qualified state residents. Criteria for eligibility: households which receive public assistance, meet state's low income guidelines, and demonstrate need as defined by Title IV programs.

**FINANCIAL AID PROCEDURES**
**Forms required:** FAFSA.
**Dates and Deadlines:** Applicants notified on a rolling basis starting 7/15; must reply within 2 week(s) of notification.

**CONTACT**
Karen Sanders, Financial Aid Supervisor
5885 Haven Avenue, Rancho Cucamonga, CA 91737-3002
(909) 652-6006

## Chapman University
Orange, California
www.chapman.edu          Federal Code: 001164

**4-year private** university and liberal arts college in very large city, affiliated with Christian Church (Disciples of Christ).
**Enrollment:** 6,281 undergrads, 4% part-time. 1,419 full-time freshmen.
**Selectivity:** Admits less than 50% of applicants.

**BASIC COSTS (2016-2017)**
**Tuition and fees:** $48,710.
**Per-credit charge:** $1,500.
**Room and board:** $14,368.

**FINANCIAL AID PICTURE (2014-2015)**
**Students with need:** Out of 1,080 full-time freshmen who applied for aid, 870 were judged to have need. Of these, 870 received aid, and 155 had their full need met. Average financial aid package met 77% of need; average scholarship/grant was $16,998; average loan was $3,851. For part-time students, average financial aid package was $14,825.
**Students without need:** 338 full-time freshmen who did not demonstrate need for aid received scholarships/grants; average award was $16,020. No-need awards available for academics, alumni affiliation, art, music/drama, religious affiliation.

**FINANCIAL AID PROCEDURES**
**Forms required:** FAFSA.
**Dates and Deadlines:** Priority date 3/2; no closing date. Applicants notified on a rolling basis starting 3/15; must reply within 3 week(s) of notification.
**Transfers:** No deadline. Applicants notified on a rolling basis starting 3/15; must reply within 3 week(s) of notification.

**CONTACT**
Jim Whitaker, Associate Vice Chancellor of Enrollment Management and Chief Financial Aid Officer
Admission Office, Orange, CA 92866
(714) 997-6741

## Charles Drew University of Medicine and Science
Los Angeles, California
www.cdrewu.edu          Federal Code: 013653

**4-year private** university and health science college in very large city.
**Enrollment:** 85 undergrads, 38% part-time.

**BASIC COSTS (2015-2016)**
**Tuition and fees:** $16,150.
**Per-credit charge:** $535.

**FINANCIAL AID PICTURE (2014-2015)**
**Students with need:** Average financial aid package for all full-time undergraduates was $10,376; for part-time $5,745. 28% awarded as scholarships/grants, 72% awarded as loans/jobs. Work study available nights, weekends, and for part-time students.
**Students without need:** No-need awards available for academics, leadership.

**FINANCIAL AID PROCEDURES**
**Forms required:** FAFSA.
**Dates and Deadlines:** Applicants notified on a rolling basis.
**Transfers:** No deadline. Applicants notified on a rolling basis.

**CONTACT**
LaNae Herrera, Director of Financial Aid
1731 East 120th Street, Los Angeles, CA 90059
(323) 563-4824

## Citrus College
Glendora, California
www.citruscollege.edu          Federal Code: 001166

**2-year public** community college in small city.
**Enrollment:** 9,475 undergrads.
**Selectivity:** Open admission.

**BASIC COSTS (2015-2016)**
**Tuition and fees:** $1,450; out-of-state residents $8,170.
**Per-credit charge:** $46; out-of-state residents $270.

**FINANCIAL AID PICTURE (2014-2015)**
**Students with need:** 90% of average financial aid package awarded as scholarships/grants, 10% awarded as loans/jobs. Need-based aid available for part-time students. Work study available nights, weekends, and for part-time students.

**FINANCIAL AID PROCEDURES**
**Forms required:** FAFSA.
**Dates and Deadlines:** Closing date 3/1. Applicants notified on a rolling basis; must reply within 2 week(s) of notification.

**CONTACT**
Carol Thomas, Director of Financial Aid
1000 West Foothill Boulevard, Glendora, CA 91741-1899
(626) 914-8592

## City College of San Francisco
San Francisco, California
www.ccsf.edu          Federal Code: 012874

**2-year public** community college in very large city.
**Enrollment:** 13,638 undergrads.
**Selectivity:** Open admission; but selective for some programs.

**BASIC COSTS (2015-2016)**
**Tuition and fees:** $1,414; out-of-state residents $7,954.
**Per-credit charge:** $46; out-of-state residents $264.
**Additional info:** Tuition/fee waivers available for unemployed or children of unemployed.

**FINANCIAL AID PICTURE**
**Students with need:** Work study available nights, weekends, and for part-time students.
**Additional info:** Board of Governor fee waiver for low income students.

**FINANCIAL AID PROCEDURES**
**Forms required:** FAFSA.
**Dates and Deadlines:** Priority date 3/1; no closing date. Applicants notified on a rolling basis starting 7/1.

**CONTACT**
Jorge Bell, Dean, Financial Aid
Office of Admissions and Records E-107, San Francisco, CA 94112
(415) 239-3576

## Claremont McKenna College
Claremont, California                    Federal Code: 001170
www.cmc.edu                              CSS Code: 4054

**4-year private** liberal arts college in large town.
**Enrollment:** 1,325 undergrads. 343 full-time freshmen.
**Selectivity:** Admits less than 50% of applicants.

**BASIC COSTS (2015-2016)**
**Tuition and fees:** $49,045.
**Room and board:** $15,280.

**FINANCIAL AID PICTURE (2015-2016)**
**Students with need:** Out of 190 full-time freshmen who applied for aid, 141 were judged to have need. Of these, 141 received aid, and 141 had their full need met. Average financial aid package met 100% of need; average scholarship/grant was $39,775; average loan was $3,987. Need-based aid available for part-time students.
**Students without need:** 16 full-time freshmen who did not demonstrate need for aid received scholarships/grants; average award was $15,713. No-need awards available for academics, leadership, ROTC.
**Scholarships offered:** McKenna Achievement Award: $10,000 for 4 years; based on strong academic record and outstanding leadership and involvement. Seaver Leadership Scholarship: full tuition for 4 years; awarded to students who demonstrate exceptional promise to become leaders intent on making a positive impact in the world. Interdisciplinary Science Scholarship: full tuition for 4 years; awarded to students who want to major in a science and a non-science and have financial need.

**FINANCIAL AID PROCEDURES**
**Forms required:** FAFSA, CSS PROFILE, state aid form.
**Dates and Deadlines:** Priority date 1/1; closing date 2/1. Applicants notified by 4/1; must reply by 5/1.
**Transfers:** Closing date 4/1. Applicants notified by 5/15; must reply by 6/1.

**CONTACT**
Clint Gasaway, Director of Financial Aid
888 Columbia Avenue, Claremont, CA 91711
(909) 621-8356

## Coastline Community College
Fountain Valley, California
www.coastline.edu                        Federal Code: 013536

**2-year public** community college in small city.
**Enrollment:** 7,361 undergrads.

**Selectivity:** Open admission.
**BASIC COSTS (2015-2016)**
**Tuition and fees:** $1,400; out-of-state residents $8,330.
**Per-credit charge:** $46; out-of-state residents $277.
**Additional info:** Tuition/fee waivers available for unemployed or children of unemployed.

**FINANCIAL AID PICTURE**
**Students with need:** Need-based aid available for full-time and part-time students.
**Students without need:** This college awards aid only to students with need.
**Additional info:** Board of Governor's Grant: statewide fee waiver program for students or dependents receiving HFOL/TANF, SSI, General Relief, or whose income meets set standards or who are considered eligible through Federal needs analysis.

**FINANCIAL AID PROCEDURES**
**Forms required:** FAFSA, institutional form.
**Dates and Deadlines:** Priority date 3/2; no closing date. Applicants notified on a rolling basis starting 8/1; must reply within 2 week(s) of notification.

**CONTACT**
Steve Woodyard, Director of Financial Aid
11460 Warner Avenue, Fountain Valley, CA 92708
(714) 241-6239

## Cogswell Polytechnical College
San Jose, California
www.cogswell.edu                         Federal Code: 001177

**4-year for-profit** business and engineering college in small city.
**Enrollment:** 630 undergrads, 16% part-time. 106 full-time freshmen.
**Selectivity:** Admits 50 to 75% of applicants.

**BASIC COSTS (2015-2016)**
**Tuition and fees:** $16,640.
**Room only:** $8,000.

**FINANCIAL AID PICTURE (2015-2016)**
**Students with need:** 50% of average financial aid package awarded as scholarships/grants, 50% awarded as loans/jobs. Need-based aid available for part-time students.
**Students without need:** No-need awards available for academics.

**FINANCIAL AID PROCEDURES**
**Forms required:** FAFSA.
**Dates and Deadlines:** Priority date 3/1; no closing date. Applicants notified on a rolling basis starting 4/30; must reply within 4 week(s) of notification.
**Transfers:** No deadline. Applicants notified by 4/1; must reply within 4 week(s) of notification.

**CONTACT**
Yariela Perez, Financial Aid Manager
191 Baypointe Parkway, San Jose, CA 95134
(800) 264-7955

## Coleman University
San Diego, California
www.coleman.edu                          Federal Code: 009273

**4-year private** university and technical college in very large city.
**Enrollment:** 364 undergrads, 16% part-time. 35 full-time freshmen.
**Selectivity:** Open admission; but selective for some programs.

**BASIC COSTS (2016-2017)**
**Tuition and fees:** $20,725.

**Per-credit charge:** $345.

## FINANCIAL AID PICTURE

**Students with need:** Need-based aid available for full-time and part-time students. Work study available nights.

**Students without need:** This college awards aid only to students with need.

## FINANCIAL AID PROCEDURES

**Forms required:** FAFSA, institutional form.

**Dates and Deadlines:** Applicants notified on a rolling basis starting 1/4; must reply within 1 week(s) of notification.

**Transfers:** No deadline. Applicants notified on a rolling basis starting 1/4; must reply within 1 week(s) of notification.

## CONTACT

Axel Hernandez, Director of Financial Aid
8888 Balboa Avenue, San Diego, CA 92123
(858) 499-0202

## College of Marin

Kentfield, California
www.marin.edu
Federal Code: 001178

**2-year public** community college in small town.

**Enrollment:** 2,672 undergrads.

**Selectivity:** Open admission; but selective for some programs.

## BASIC COSTS (2015-2016)

**Tuition and fees:** $1,418; out-of-state residents $8,888.

**Per-credit charge:** $46; out-of-state residents $295.

## FINANCIAL AID PICTURE

**Students with need:** Need-based aid available for full-time and part-time students.

**Students without need:** This college awards aid only to students with need.

## FINANCIAL AID PROCEDURES

**Forms required:** FAFSA.

**Dates and Deadlines:** Priority date 3/2; no closing date. Applicants notified on a rolling basis starting 5/15.

## CONTACT

David Cook, Director of Financial Aid
835 College Avenue, Kentfield, CA 94904
(415) 457-8811 ext. 7405

## College of San Mateo

San Mateo, California
www.collegeofsanmateo.edu
Federal Code: 001181

**2-year public** community college in small city.

**Enrollment:** 5,263 undergrads.

**Selectivity:** Open admission; but selective for some programs.

## BASIC COSTS (2015-2016)

**Tuition and fees:** $1,418; out-of-state residents $8,288.

**Per-credit charge:** $46; out-of-state residents $275.

## FINANCIAL AID PICTURE

**Students with need:** Need-based aid available for full-time and part-time students.

**Students without need:** This college awards aid only to students with need.

## FINANCIAL AID PROCEDURES

**Forms required:** FAFSA.

**Dates and Deadlines:** Applicants notified on a rolling basis starting 6/15.

**Transfers:** No deadline. Applicants notified on a rolling basis.

## CONTACT

Claudia Menjivar, Director of Financial Aid
1700 West Hillsdale Boulevard, San Mateo, CA 94402-3784
(650) 574-6147

## College of the Canyons

Santa Clarita, California
www.canyons.edu
Federal Code: 008903

**2-year public** community college in large city.

**Enrollment:** 14,279 undergrads, 57% part-time. 1,352 full-time freshmen.

**Selectivity:** Open admission; but selective for some programs.

## FINANCIAL AID PICTURE (2015-2016)

**Students with need:** 80% of average financial aid package awarded as scholarships/grants, 20% awarded as loans/jobs. Need-based aid available for part-time students. Work study available nights, weekends, and for part-time students.

**Students without need:** No-need awards available for academics, alumni affiliation, art, athletics, job skills, leadership, minority status, music/drama, religious affiliation, ROTC, state/district residency.

## FINANCIAL AID PROCEDURES

**Forms required:** FAFSA, state aid form, institutional form.

**Dates and Deadlines:** Closing date 3/2. Applicants notified on a rolling basis starting 6/1; must reply within 4 week(s) of notification.

**Transfers:** No deadline.

## CONTACT

Thomas Bilbruck, Director, Financial Aid and Scholarships
26455 Rockwell Canyon Road, Santa Clarita, CA 91355
(661) 362-3242

## College of the Desert

Palm Desert, California
www.collegeofthedesert.edu
Federal Code: 001182

**2-year public** community college in small city.

**Enrollment:** 7,179 undergrads.

**Selectivity:** Open admission; but selective for some programs.

## BASIC COSTS (2015-2016)

**Tuition and fees:** $1,380; out-of-state residents $7,380.

**Per-credit charge:** $46; out-of-district residents $246.

**Additional info:** Tuition/fee waivers available for adults, minority students, unemployed or children of unemployed.

## FINANCIAL AID PICTURE

**Students with need:** Need-based aid available for full-time and part-time students. Work study available nights, weekends, and for part-time students.

**Students without need:** No-need awards available for academics, art, minority status, music/drama.

## FINANCIAL AID PROCEDURES

**Forms required:** FAFSA.

**Dates and Deadlines:** Priority date 3/2; no closing date. Applicants notified on a rolling basis starting 7/1.

**Transfers:** No deadline. Applicants notified on a rolling basis starting 7/1.

## CONTACT

Ken Lira, Director of Financial Aid
43500 Monterey Avenue, Palm Desert, CA 92260
(760) 773-2532

## College of the Redwoods
Eureka, California
www.redwoods.edu                     Federal Code: 001185

**2-year public** community college in large town.
**Enrollment:** 2,635 undergrads.
**Selectivity:** Open admission; but selective for some programs.

**BASIC COSTS (2015-2016)**
**Tuition and fees:** $1,418; out-of-state residents $7,598.
**Per-credit charge:** $46; out-of-state residents $252.
**Room and board:** $7,560.
**Additional info:** Optional $10 student fee and $10 technology fee.

**FINANCIAL AID PICTURE**
**Students with need:** Need-based aid available for full-time and part-time students.

**FINANCIAL AID PROCEDURES**
**Forms required:** FAFSA, institutional form.
**Dates and Deadlines:** Priority date 4/15; no closing date. Applicants notified on a rolling basis starting 5/1; must reply within 6 week(s) of notification.

**CONTACT**
Lynn Thiesen, Director of Financial Aid
7351 Tompkins Hill Road, Eureka, CA 95501-9300
(707) 476-4182

## College of the Siskiyous
Weed, California
www.siskiyous.edu                    Federal Code: 001187

**2-year public** community and junior college in small town.
**Enrollment:** 788 undergrads. 276 full-time freshmen.
**Selectivity:** Open admission; but selective for some programs.

**BASIC COSTS (2015-2016)**
**Tuition and fees:** $1,430; out-of-state residents $8,060.
**Per-credit charge:** $46; out-of-state residents $267.
**Room and board:** $8,925.

**FINANCIAL AID PICTURE (2014-2015)**
**Students with need:** 63% of average financial aid package awarded as scholarships/grants, 37% awarded as loans/jobs. Need-based aid available for part-time students. Work study available nights, weekends, and for part-time students.
**Students without need:** This college awards aid only to students with need.

**FINANCIAL AID PROCEDURES**
**Forms required:** FAFSA.
**Dates and Deadlines:** Priority date 4/30; no closing date. Applicants notified on a rolling basis starting 6/1; must reply within 2 week(s) of notification.
**Transfers:** No deadline. Applicants notified on a rolling basis. Academic transcripts required.

**CONTACT**
Janette Harris, Director of Financial Aid
800 College Avenue, Weed, CA 96094-2899
(530) 938-5500

## Columbia College
Sonora, California
www.gocolumbia.edu                   Federal Code: 007707

**2-year public** community college in small town.
**Enrollment:** 1,595 undergrads.

**Selectivity:** Open admission.

**BASIC COSTS (2015-2016)**
**Tuition and fees:** $1,418; out-of-state residents $7,988.
**Per-credit charge:** $46; out-of-state residents $265.

**FINANCIAL AID PICTURE**
**Students with need:** Need-based aid available for full-time and part-time students.
**Students without need:** No-need awards available for academics.

**FINANCIAL AID PROCEDURES**
**Forms required:** FAFSA, state aid form, institutional form.
**Dates and Deadlines:** Priority date 3/2; closing date 6/1. Applicants notified on a rolling basis starting 6/15; must reply within 2 week(s) of notification.

**CONTACT**
Marnie Shively, Director of Student Financial Services
11600 Columbia College Drive, Sonora, CA 95370
(209) 588-5105

## Columbia College Hollywood
Tarzana, California
www.columbiacollege.edu

**4-year private** visual arts college in very large city.
**Enrollment:** 330 undergrads.
**Selectivity:** Open admission; but selective for some programs.

**BASIC COSTS (2015-2016)**
**Tuition and fees:** $21,200.
**Room and board:** $11,970.

**FINANCIAL AID PICTURE**
**Students with need:** Need-based aid available for full-time and part-time students. Work study available nights, weekends, and for part-time students.
**Students without need:** This college awards aid only to students with need.

**FINANCIAL AID PROCEDURES**
**Forms required:** FAFSA, state aid form.
**Dates and Deadlines:** Priority date 3/2; closing date 5/30. Applicants notified on a rolling basis starting 3/30; must reply within 2 week(s) of notification.
**Transfers:** No deadline. Applicants notified on a rolling basis starting 3/30; must reply within 2 week(s) of notification.

**CONTACT**
Jan Hastings, Fianancial Aid Manager
18618 Oxnard Street, Tarzana, CA 91356
(818) 345-8414

## Concordia University Irvine
Irvine, California
www.cui.edu                          Federal Code: 013885

**4-year private** university and liberal arts college in small city, affiliated with Lutheran Church - Missouri Synod.
**Enrollment:** 1,853 undergrads, 7% part-time. 334 full-time freshmen.
**Selectivity:** Admits 50 to 75% of applicants.

**BASIC COSTS (2015-2016)**
**Tuition and fees:** $31,690.
**Per-credit charge:** $925.
**Room and board:** $9,890.
**Additional info:** Tuition/fee waivers available for adults.

**FINANCIAL AID PICTURE (2015-2016)**
**Students with need:** Out of 296 full-time freshmen who applied for aid, 258 were judged to have need. Of these, 258 received aid, and 48 had their

full need met. Average financial aid package met 72% of need; average scholarship/grant was $20,127; average loan was $3,421. For part-time students, average financial aid package was $6,234.

**Students without need:** 56 full-time freshmen who did not demonstrate need for aid received scholarships/grants; average award was $9,834. No-need awards available for academics, athletics, music/drama, religious affiliation.

**Scholarships offered: *Merit:*** Presidential Honors: up to full tuition; based on 3.9-4.0 GPA and 1300 SAT or 29 ACT. Regent: up to $12,500; based on 3.8-4.0 GPA. Provost: up to $10,000; based on 3.4 -3.79 GPA. Dean's: up to $7,500; based on 3.0-3.39 GPA. Phi Theta Kappa: up to $6,000; based on 2.50-4.00 GPA. ***Athletic:*** 18 full-time freshmen received athletic scholarships.

**FINANCIAL AID PROCEDURES**
**Forms required:** FAFSA, state aid form.
**Dates and Deadlines:** Closing date 3/2. Applicants notified on a rolling basis starting 3/15; must reply within 4 week(s) of notification.
**Transfers:** Priority date 3/2. Applicants notified on a rolling basis starting 3/15; must reply within 4 week(s) of notification.

**CONTACT**
Lori McDonald, Director of Financial Aid
1530 Concordia West, Irvine, CA 92612-3203
(949) 214-3066

## Copper Mountain College
Joshua Tree, California
www.cmccd.edu                Federal Code: 035424

**2-year public** community college in small town.
**Enrollment:** 1,375 undergrads.
**Selectivity:** Open admission; but selective for some programs.

**BASIC COSTS (2015-2016)**
**Tuition and fees:** $1,380; out-of-state residents $7,110.
**Per-credit charge:** $46; out-of-state residents $237.

**FINANCIAL AID PICTURE**
**Students with need:** Need-based aid available for full-time and part-time students.

**FINANCIAL AID PROCEDURES**
**Forms required:** FAFSA.
**Dates and Deadlines:** Priority date 3/2; no closing date.

**CONTACT**
Brian Heinemann, Director of Financial Aid
6162 Rotary Way, Joshua Tree, CA 92252
(866) 366-3791 ext. 4235

## Crafton Hills College
Yucaipa, California
www.craftonhills.edu          Federal Code: 009272

**2-year public** community college in small city.
**Enrollment:** 3,422 undergrads.
**Selectivity:** Open admission.

**BASIC COSTS (2015-2016)**
**Tuition and fees:** $1,425; out-of-state residents $7,425.
**Per-credit charge:** $46; out-of-state residents $246.
**Additional info:** Tuition/fee waivers available for adults, minority students, unemployed or children of unemployed.

**FINANCIAL AID PICTURE**
**Students with need:** Need-based aid available for full-time and part-time students. Work study available nights.

**Students without need:** This college awards aid only to students with need.

**FINANCIAL AID PROCEDURES**
**Forms required:** FAFSA, institutional form.
**Dates and Deadlines:** Priority date 4/15; closing date 6/2. Applicants notified on a rolling basis starting 7/31; must reply within 2 week(s) of notification.
**Transfers:** Priority date 1/2; closing date 3/2.

**CONTACT**
John Muskavitch, Director of Financial Aid
11711 Sand Canyon Road, Yucaipa, CA 92399-1799
(909) 794-2161 ext. 3242

## Cuyamaca College
El Cajon, California
www.cuyamaca.edu             Federal Code: 014435

**2-year public** community college in small city.
**Enrollment:** 5,814 undergrads.
**Selectivity:** Open admission.

**BASIC COSTS (2015-2016)**
**Tuition and fees:** $1,428; out-of-state residents $7,428.
**Per-credit charge:** $46; out-of-state residents $246.

**FINANCIAL AID PICTURE**
**Students with need:** Work study available nights, weekends, and for part-time students.

**FINANCIAL AID PROCEDURES**
**Forms required:** FAFSA.
**Dates and Deadlines:** Priority date 3/2; no closing date. Applicants notified on a rolling basis; must reply within 2 week(s) of notification.

**CONTACT**
Ray Reyes, Financial Aid Director
900 Rancho San Diego Parkway, El Cajon, CA 92019-4304
(619) 660-4201

## Cypress College
Cypress, California
www.cypresscollege.edu        Federal Code: 001193

**2-year public** community college in small city.
**Enrollment:** 9,348 undergrads, 65% part-time. 665 full-time freshmen.
**Selectivity:** Open admission.

**BASIC COSTS (2015-2016)**
**Tuition and fees:** $1,414; out-of-state residents $7,684.
**Per-credit charge:** $46; out-of-state residents $255.

**FINANCIAL AID PICTURE**
**Students with need:** Need-based aid available for full-time and part-time students.

**FINANCIAL AID PROCEDURES**
**Forms required:** FAFSA.

**CONTACT**
Chinh Pham, Director of Financial Aid
9200 Valley View Street, Cypress, CA 90630
(714) 484-7114

## De Anza College

Cupertino, California
www.deanza.edu
Federal Code: 004480

**2-year public** community college in large town.
**Enrollment:** 22,620 undergrads.
**Selectivity:** Open admission; but selective for some programs.

**BASIC COSTS (2015-2016)**
**Tuition and fees:** $1,427; out-of-state residents $8,267.
**Per-credit charge:** $31; out-of-state residents $183.

**FINANCIAL AID PICTURE**
**Students with need:** Need-based aid available for full-time and part-time students.
**Students without need:** This college awards aid only to students with need.

**FINANCIAL AID PROCEDURES**
**Forms required:** FAFSA.
**Dates and Deadlines:** Applicants notified on a rolling basis starting 5/15; must reply within 2 week(s) of notification.

**CONTACT**
Lisa Mandy, Director of Financial Aid
21250 Stevens Creek Boulevard, Cupertino, CA 95014
(408) 864-8718

## Deep Springs College

Dyer, Nevada
www.deepsprings.edu
Federal Code: 015483

**2-year private** liberal arts college for men in rural community.
**Enrollment:** 28 undergrads. 15 full-time freshmen.

**BASIC COSTS (2015-2016)**
**Additional info:** All students receive a full scholarship covering tuition, room and board. Students buy their own books and necessary supplies.

**FINANCIAL AID PICTURE (2014-2015)**
**Students with need:** Need-based aid available for full-time students.
**Students without need:** 15 full-time freshmen who did not demonstrate need for aid received scholarships/grants. No-need awards available for academics, job skills, leadership.
**Additional info:** Every admitted student is awarded a scholarship for the full cost of tuition and room and board. For students in need, additional funds are available for books, travel, and incidental expenses.

**FINANCIAL AID PROCEDURES**
**Forms required:** institutional form.
**Dates and Deadlines:** Applicants notified by 4/15.
**Transfers:** Transfer students are also eligible for admission and, like all other students, receive a full scholarship for tuition and room and board.

**CONTACT**
David Neidorf, President
Applications Committee, Dyer, NV 89010-9803
(760) 872-2000 ext. 45

## Design Institute of San Diego

San Diego, California
www.disd.edu
Federal Code: 016233

**4-year for-profit** career college in very large city.
**Enrollment:** 148 undergrads, 44% part-time. 7 full-time freshmen.

**BASIC COSTS (2015-2016)**
**Tuition and fees:** $18,664.
**Room and board:** $11,268.

**FINANCIAL AID PICTURE**
**Students with need:** Work study available nights, weekends, and for part-time students.
**Scholarships offered:** Building the Legacy Scholarship offered.
**Additional info:** Financial aid is available for those who qualify. A free Preliminary Financial Aid Profile will be done for anyone who has applied to the college. This profile is an estimate of financial aid eligibility for grants and loans.

**FINANCIAL AID PROCEDURES**
**Dates and Deadlines:** Applicants notified on a rolling basis.

**CONTACT**
Jackie Gloria, Financial Aid Direcotr
8555 Commerce Avenue, San Diego, CA 92121
(858) 566-1200 ext. 1023

## DeVry University: Pomona

Pomona, California
www.devry.edu
Federal Code: 023329

**4-year for-profit** university in small city.
**Enrollment:** 1,501 undergrads.

**BASIC COSTS (2015-2016)**
**Tuition and fees:** $17,132.
**Per-credit charge:** $609.

**FINANCIAL AID PICTURE**
**Students with need:** Need-based aid available for full-time and part-time students.
**Students without need:** This college awards aid only to students with need.

**FINANCIAL AID PROCEDURES**
**Forms required:** FAFSA.
**Dates and Deadlines:** Applicants notified on a rolling basis.

**CONTACT**
901 Corporate Center Drive, Pomona, CA 91768-2642

## Diablo Valley College

Pleasant Hill, California
www.dvc.edu
Federal Code: 001191

**2-year public** community college in large town.
**Enrollment:** 9,588 undergrads.
**Selectivity:** Open admission.

**BASIC COSTS (2015-2016)**
**Tuition and fees:** $1,390; out-of-state residents $8,080.
**Per-credit charge:** $46; out-of-state residents $269.

**FINANCIAL AID PICTURE**
**Students with need:** Need-based aid available for full-time and part-time students.

**FINANCIAL AID PROCEDURES**
**Forms required:** FAFSA, state aid form, institutional form.
**Dates and Deadlines:** Priority date 3/2; closing date 5/1. Applicants notified on a rolling basis starting 6/1; must reply within 2 week(s) of notification.

**CONTACT**
Emily Stone, Dean, CalWORKS, EOPS/CARE, Financial Aid and Scholarship
321 Golf Club Road, Pleasant Hill, CA 94523-1529
(925) 696-2009

## Dominican University of California

San Rafael, California
www.dominican.edu          Federal Code: 001196

**4-year private** university in small city.
**Enrollment:** 1,358 undergrads, 14% part-time. 261 full-time freshmen.
**Selectivity:** Admits over 75% of applicants.

### BASIC COSTS (2015-2016)
**Tuition and fees:** $42,550.
**Per-credit charge:** $1,760.
**Room and board:** $13,940.

### FINANCIAL AID PICTURE (2014-2015)
**Students with need:** Out of 237 full-time freshmen who applied for aid, 213 were judged to have need. Of these, 213 received aid, and 31 had their full need met. Average financial aid package met 71% of need; average scholarship/grant was $24,442; average loan was $3,362. For part-time students, average financial aid package was $9,781.
**Students without need:** 24 full-time freshmen who did not demonstrate need for aid received scholarships/grants; average award was $15,973. No-need awards available for academics, alumni affiliation, athletics, leadership, minority status, music/drama.
**Scholarships offered:** 4 full-time freshmen received athletic scholarships; average amount $5,673.
**Additional info:** 4-year guarantee program.

### FINANCIAL AID PROCEDURES
**Forms required:** FAFSA, institutional form.
**Dates and Deadlines:** Priority date 3/2; no closing date. Applicants notified on a rolling basis starting 3/15; must reply within 2 week(s) of notification.
**Transfers:** Must reply within 2 week(s) of notification.

### CONTACT
Shanon Little, Director of Financial Aid
50 Acacia Avenue, San Rafael, CA 94901-2298
(415) 257-1350

## East Los Angeles College

Monterey Park, California
www.elac.edu          Federal Code: 001222

**2-year public** community college in very large city.
**Enrollment:** 17,536 undergrads.
**Selectivity:** Open admission; but selective for some programs.

### BASIC COSTS (2015-2016)
**Tuition and fees:** $1,402; out-of-state residents $7,312.
**Per-credit charge:** $46; out-of-state residents $243.
**Additional info:** Tuition/fee waivers available for unemployed or children of unemployed.

### FINANCIAL AID PICTURE
**Students with need:** Need-based aid available for full-time and part-time students. Work study available nights, weekends, and for part-time students.
**Students without need:** This college awards aid only to students with need.
**Additional info:** Need-based enrollment fee waivers available through a state aid program.

### FINANCIAL AID PROCEDURES
**Forms required:** FAFSA, institutional form.
**Dates and Deadlines:** Priority date 4/30; no closing date. Applicants notified on a rolling basis; must reply within 4 week(s) of notification.
**Transfers:** No deadline.

### CONTACT
Lindy Fong, Financial Aid Manager
1301 Avenida Cesar Chavez, Monterey Park, CA 91754-6099
(323) 265-8738

## El Camino College

Torrance, California
www.elcamino.edu          Federal Code: 001197

**2-year public** community and junior college in very large city.
**Enrollment:** 32,699 full-time undergrads. 32,696 full-time freshmen.
**Selectivity:** Open admission; but selective for some programs.

### BASIC COSTS (2015-2016)
**Tuition and fees:** $1,419; out-of-state residents $8,469.
**Per-credit charge:** $46; out-of-state residents $281.
**Additional info:** Tuition/fee waivers available for adults.

### FINANCIAL AID PICTURE
**Students with need:** Need-based aid available for full-time and part-time students.
**Students without need:** No-need awards available for academics, art, athletics, leadership, music/drama.
**Additional info:** Students may apply for Pell grants until June 30.

### FINANCIAL AID PROCEDURES
**Forms required:** FAFSA, institutional form.
**Dates and Deadlines:** Priority date 3/2; closing date 6/30. Applicants notified on a rolling basis starting 7/15.
**Transfers:** Outside scholarships must be reported to financial aid office.

### CONTACT
Melissa Guess, Director of Financial Aid
16007 Crenshaw Boulevard, Torrance, CA 90506
(310) 660-3593 ext. 3493

## Empire College

Santa Rosa, California
www.empcol.edu          Federal Code: 009032

**2-year for-profit** business college in large city.
**Enrollment:** 377 undergrads, 14% part-time. 251 full-time freshmen.
**Selectivity:** Open admission; but selective for some programs.

### BASIC COSTS (2015-2016)
**Additional info:** Associates degree programs range from $25,585-$27,680, Books range from $4,000-$5,400. Undergraduate Certificates Health Administration - range from $9,905-$19,350, Books and supplies range from $1,600-$4,600.

### FINANCIAL AID PICTURE (2014-2015)
**Students with need:** Out of 226 full-time freshmen who applied for aid, 226 were judged to have need. Of these, 226 received aid.
**Students without need:** This college awards aid only to students with need.
**Scholarships offered:** Dean's Scholarship for high school seniors: 10 awarded; $250-$1,500. Dean's Scholarships for Empire College students: 7 awarded; $250-$1,000. Based on academic achievement, letter of intent, extracurricular activities and letter of recommendation.

### FINANCIAL AID PROCEDURES
**Forms required:** FAFSA.
**Dates and Deadlines:** Applicants notified on a rolling basis.

### CONTACT
Mary O'Brien, Financial Aid Officer
3035 Cleveland Avenue, Santa Rosa, CA 95403-2100
(707) 546-4000

## Feather River College

Quincy, California
www.frc.edu
Federal Code: 008597

**2-year public** community and liberal arts college in small town.
**Enrollment:** 1,646 undergrads, 54% part-time. 355 full-time freshmen.
**Selectivity:** Open admission.

**BASIC COSTS (2015-2016)**
**Tuition and fees:** $1,461; out-of-state residents $7,491.
**Per-credit charge:** $46; out-of-state residents $247.
**Room only:** $5,350.
**Additional info:** Tuition/fee waivers available for adults, unemployed or children of unemployed.

**FINANCIAL AID PICTURE (2014-2015)**
**Students with need:** 72% of average financial aid package awarded as scholarships/grants, 28% awarded as loans/jobs. Need-based aid available for part-time students. Work study available nights, weekends, and for part-time students.
**Students without need:** This college awards aid only to students with need.

**FINANCIAL AID PROCEDURES**
**Forms required:** FAFSA.
**Dates and Deadlines:** Priority date 3/2; no closing date. Applicants notified on a rolling basis starting 4/1; must reply within 3 week(s) of notification.

**CONTACT**
Andre Vandervelden, Financial Aid Director
570 Golden Eagle Avenue, Quincy, CA 95971
(530) 283-0202 ext. 283

## Foothill College

Los Altos Hills, California
www.foothill.edu
Federal Code: 001199

**2-year public** community college in large town.
**Enrollment:** 6,740 undergrads.
**Selectivity:** Open admission; but selective for some programs.

**BASIC COSTS (2015-2016)**
**Tuition and fees:** $1,503; out-of-state residents $8,343.
**Per-credit charge:** $31; out-of-state residents $183.

**FINANCIAL AID PICTURE (2015-2016)**
**Students with need:** Need-based aid available for full-time and part-time students. Work study available nights, weekends, and for part-time students.
**Scholarships offered:** Chancellor's Scholarship: for first-time freshmen who graduate with a 3.5 GPA from Santa Clara or San Mateo County as Chancellor's Scholar; $2,000.

**FINANCIAL AID PROCEDURES**
**Forms required:** FAFSA, institutional form.
**Dates and Deadlines:** Priority date 3/30; no closing date. Applicants notified on a rolling basis starting 5/1; must reply within 3 week(s) of notification.

**CONTACT**
Kevin Harral, Director, Financial Aid
12345 El Monte Road, Los Altos Hills, CA 94022
(650) 949-7245

## Fremont College

Cerritos, California
www.fremont.edu
Federal Code: 030399

**2-year for-profit** branch campus and career college in very large city.
**Enrollment:** 276 undergrads.

**Selectivity:** Open admission; but selective for some programs and for out-of-state students.

**BASIC COSTS (2015-2016)**
**Additional info:** Bachelor's in Business Leadership, Healthcare Mgmt - $35,495, Associate's in Healthcare Information Technology - $35,685, Sports & Rehabilitation Therapy - $34,085, Multimedia Design, Digital Marketing, Paralegal - $35,495, Undergraduate Certificates Health Administration - $17,435, Massage Therapy - $22,885, Web & Mobile Marketing - $17,840. Books and supplies included in tuition cost. Tuition/fee waivers available for unemployed or children of unemployed.

**FINANCIAL AID PICTURE**
**Students with need:** Need-based aid available for full-time students.
**Students without need:** This college awards aid only to students with need.

**FINANCIAL AID PROCEDURES**
**Forms required:** FAFSA, institutional form.

**CONTACT**
Lori Prince, Director of Finance
18000 Studebaker Road, Cerritos, CA 90703
(562) 809-5100

## Fresno City College

Fresno, California
www.fresnocitycollege.edu
Federal Code: 001307

**2-year public** community and liberal arts college in very large city.
**Enrollment:** 16,384 undergrads.
**Selectivity:** Open admission; but selective for some programs.

**BASIC COSTS (2015-2016)**
**Tuition and fees:** $1,420; out-of-state residents $8,470.
**Per-credit charge:** $46; out-of-state residents $281.
**Additional info:** Tuition/fee waivers available for adults, minority students, unemployed or children of unemployed.

**FINANCIAL AID PICTURE**
**Students with need:** Need-based aid available for full-time and part-time students.
**Students without need:** This college awards aid only to students with need.
**Additional info:** Board of Governors Grant Program to offset enrollment fees based on untaxed income, low income, or calculated need. Students qualifying for program also automatically exempt from health fees. March 2 application deadline for California grants.

**FINANCIAL AID PROCEDURES**
**Forms required:** FAFSA, state aid form.
**Dates and Deadlines:** Priority date 4/15; closing date 6/30. Applicants notified on a rolling basis starting 4/1.

**CONTACT**
Frank Ramon, Financial Aid Director
1101 East University Avenue, Fresno, CA 93741
(559) 442-8279

## Fresno Pacific University

Fresno, California
www.fresno.edu
Federal Code: 001253

**4-year private** university and liberal arts college in large city, affiliated with Mennonite Brethren Church.
**Enrollment:** 2,570 undergrads.

## BASIC COSTS (2015-2016)

**Tuition and fees:** $27,854.
**Room and board:** $7,690.

## FINANCIAL AID PICTURE

**Students with need:** Need-based aid available for full-time and part-time students. Work study available nights, weekends, and for part-time students.
**Students without need:** No-need awards available for academics, athletics, leadership, music/drama, religious affiliation.

## FINANCIAL AID PROCEDURES

**Forms required:** FAFSA.
**Dates and Deadlines:** Closing date 3/2. Applicants notified on a rolling basis starting 3/2; must reply by 7/30 or within 3 week(s) of notification.
**Transfers:** No deadline.

## CONTACT

Gary Nicholes, Director of Student Financial Services
1717 South Chestnut Avenue, Fresno, CA 93702-4709
(559) 453-2041

## Fullerton College

Fullerton, California
www.fullcoll.edu                    Federal Code: 001201

**2-year public** community and technical college in small city.
**Enrollment:** 13,268 undergrads, 57% part-time. 1,154 full-time freshmen.
**Selectivity:** Open admission.

## BASIC COSTS (2015-2016)

**Tuition and fees:** $1,443; out-of-state residents $7,713.
**Per-credit charge:** $46; out-of-state residents $255.
**Additional info:** Tuition/fee waivers available for adults, minority students, unemployed or children of unemployed.

## FINANCIAL AID PICTURE (2015-2016)

**Students with need:** 93% of average financial aid package awarded as scholarships/grants, 7% awarded as loans/jobs. Need-based aid available for part-time students.

## FINANCIAL AID PROCEDURES

**Forms required:** FAFSA.
**Dates and Deadlines:** Applicants notified on a rolling basis.

## CONTACT

Greg Ryan, Director of Financial Aid & Veterans Services
321 East Chapman Avenue, Fullerton, CA 92832-2095
(714) 992-7050

## Glendale Community College

Glendale, California
www.glendale.edu                    Federal Code: 001203

**2-year public** community college in small city.
**Enrollment:** 8,156 undergrads.
**Selectivity:** Open admission; but selective for some programs.

## BASIC COSTS (2015-2016)

**Tuition and fees:** $1,416; out-of-state residents $7,566.
**Per-credit charge:** $46; out-of-state residents $251.

## FINANCIAL AID PICTURE

**Students with need:** Need-based aid available for full-time and part-time students. Work study available nights, weekends, and for part-time students.
**Students without need:** This college awards aid only to students with need.

## FINANCIAL AID PROCEDURES

**Forms required:** FAFSA, institutional form.

**Dates and Deadlines:** Priority date 4/15; no closing date. Applicants notified on a rolling basis starting 6/15; must reply within 2 week(s) of notification.
**Transfers:** No deadline.

## CONTACT

Patricia Hurley, Director of Financial Aid
1500 North Verdugo Road, Glendale, CA 91208-2809
(818) 240-1000 ext. 5916

## Golden Gate University

San Francisco, California
www.ggu.edu                    Federal Code: 001205

**4-year private** university in very large city.
**Enrollment:** 435 undergrads.

## BASIC COSTS (2015-2016)

**Tuition and fees:** $18,300.
**Per-credit charge:** $610.

## FINANCIAL AID PICTURE

**Students with need:** Need-based aid available for full-time and part-time students. Work study available nights.
**Students without need:** This college awards aid only to students with need.

## FINANCIAL AID PROCEDURES

**Forms required:** FAFSA, institutional form.
**Dates and Deadlines:** Priority date 1/2; no closing date. Applicants notified on a rolling basis; must reply within 3 week(s) of notification.
**Transfers:** Priority date 6/14; no deadline. Applicants notified on a rolling basis starting 1/2; must reply within 3 week(s) of notification.

## CONTACT

Louis Riccardi
536 Mission Street, San Francisco, CA 94105-2968
(415) 442-7270

## Grossmont College

El Cajon, California
www.grossmont.edu                    Federal Code: 001208

**2-year public** nursing and community college in small city.
**Enrollment:** 13,253 undergrads.
**Selectivity:** Open admission; but selective for some programs.

## BASIC COSTS (2015-2016)

**Tuition and fees:** $1,418; out-of-state residents $7,418.
**Per-credit charge:** $46; out-of-state residents $246.

## FINANCIAL AID PICTURE

**Students with need:** Need-based aid available for full-time and part-time students. Work study available nights, weekends, and for part-time students.
**Students without need:** This college awards aid only to students with need.

## FINANCIAL AID PROCEDURES

**Forms required:** FAFSA.
**Dates and Deadlines:** Priority date 3/2; closing date 6/30. Applicants notified on a rolling basis starting 7/15; must reply within 2 week(s) of notification.

## CONTACT

Michael Copenhaver, Director of Financial Aid
8800 Grossmont College Drive, El Cajon, CA 92020
(619) 644-7129

## Hartnell College
Salinas, California
www.hartnell.edu                    Federal Code: 001209

2-year public community college in small city.
**Enrollment:** 10,226 undergrads, 74% part-time. 732 full-time freshmen.
**Selectivity:** Open admission; but selective for some programs.

**BASIC COSTS (2015-2016)**
**Tuition and fees:** $1,400; out-of-state residents $7,040.
**Per-credit charge:** $46; out-of-state residents $234.

**FINANCIAL AID PICTURE (2014-2015)**
**Students with need:** 98% of average financial aid package awarded as scholarships/grants, 2% awarded as loans/jobs.

**FINANCIAL AID PROCEDURES**
**Forms required:** FAFSA.
**Dates and Deadlines:** Priority date 8/1; no closing date. Applicants notified on a rolling basis.

**CONTACT**
Mary Dominguez, Dean Student Affairs
411 Central Avenue, Salinas, CA 93901
(831) 755-6806

## Harvey Mudd College
Claremont, California
https://www.hmc.edu/admission/      Federal Code: 001171
                                     CSS Code: 4341

4-year private engineering and liberal arts college in small city.
**Enrollment:** 812 undergrads. 194 full-time freshmen.
**Selectivity:** Admits less than 50% of applicants.

**BASIC COSTS (2016-2017)**
**Tuition and fees:** $50,749.
**Per-credit charge:** $1,574.
**Room and board:** $16,506.

**FINANCIAL AID PICTURE (2014-2015)**
**Students with need:** Out of 134 full-time freshmen who applied for aid, 103 were judged to have need. Of these, 103 received aid, and 103 had their full need met. Average financial aid package met 100% of need; average scholarship/grant was $41,635; average loan was $3,742. Need-based aid available for part-time students.
**Students without need:** 41 full-time freshmen who did not demonstrate need for aid received scholarships/grants; average award was $11,310. No-need awards available for academics.
**Scholarships offered:** Harvey S. Mudd Merit Award: for first-time first-year students in science and technology programs; $10,000 annually for 4 years; must maintain minimum 2.75 GPA. Harvey Mudd College-sponsored National Merit Scholarships: from $1,000 to $2,000; based on need.
**Additional info:** Students can use 100% of their outside awards toward first reducing the need-based portion of their student loans and/or Federal Work Study award. Once need-based student loans and/or Federal Work Study award have been completely eliminated, any additional outside scholarships may reduce need-based Harvey Mudd Scholarship only. However, to maximize financial aid eligibility, students may retain need-based student loans and/or Federal Work Study award up to their federal need.

**FINANCIAL AID PROCEDURES**
**Forms required:** FAFSA, CSS PROFILE, state aid form.
**Dates and Deadlines:** Priority date 2/1; closing date 2/1. Applicants notified by 4/1; must reply by 5/1 or within 2 week(s) of notification.
**Transfers:** Closing date 3/2. Applicants notified by 5/15; must reply by 6/10 or within 2 week(s) of notification.

**CONTACT**
Gilma Lopez, Director of Financial Aid
301 Platt Boulevard, Claremont, CA 91711-5901
(909) 621-8055

## Holy Names University
Oakland, California
www.hnu.edu                         Federal Code: 001183

4-year private university in large city, affiliated with Roman Catholic Church.
**Enrollment:** 624 undergrads, 17% part-time. 81 full-time freshmen.
**Selectivity:** Admits less than 50% of applicants.

**BASIC COSTS (2015-2016)**
**Tuition and fees:** $35,666.
**Per-credit charge:** $1,206.
**Room and board:** $12,072.

**FINANCIAL AID PICTURE (2014-2015)**
**Students with need:** Out of 78 full-time freshmen who applied for aid, 70 were judged to have need. Of these, 70 received aid, and 7 had their full need met. Average financial aid package met 70% of need; average scholarship/grant was $26,831; average loan was $3,749. For part-time students, average financial aid package was $12,309.
**Students without need:** 11 full-time freshmen who did not demonstrate need for aid received scholarships/grants; average award was $13,810. No-need awards available for academics, athletics, leadership, music/drama, religious affiliation, state/district residency.
**Scholarships offered:** *Merit:* Aspiring Leadership Grant: $5,500 annually; based on 2.70-2.99 GPA. Honors Scholarship: $8,500 annually; based on 3.00-3.29 GPA. Dean's Scholarship: $9,500 annually; based on 3.30-3.49 GPA. President's Scholarship: $11,000 annually; based on 3.50-3.74 GPA. Regent's Scholarship: $12,000 annually; based on 3.75+ GPA. Durocher Scholarship: full tuition; campus residency required; based on evidence of leadership, contributions to school and/or community and academic achievement, minimum GPA 3.75, minimum SAT 1100 (exclusive of Writing); 1 awarded per year. *Athletic:* 9 full-time freshmen received athletic scholarships; average amount $13,103.

**FINANCIAL AID PROCEDURES**
**Forms required:** FAFSA.
**Dates and Deadlines:** Priority date 3/2; no closing date. Applicants notified on a rolling basis starting 9/1; must reply by 8/26 or within 2 week(s) of notification.
**Transfers:** No deadline. Applicants notified on a rolling basis starting 9/1; must reply by 5/1 or within 2 week(s) of notification.

**CONTACT**
Tam Lee-Operario, Director of Financial Aid
3500 Mountain Boulevard, Oakland, CA 94619-1699
(510) 436-1327

## Hope International University
Fullerton, California
www.hiu.edu                         Federal Code: 001252

4-year private university and liberal arts college in small city, affiliated with Christian Church.
**Enrollment:** 843 undergrads, 25% part-time. 84 full-time freshmen.
**Selectivity:** Admits less than 50% of applicants.

**BASIC COSTS (2015-2016)**
**Tuition and fees:** $28,550.
**Per-credit charge:** $1,230.
**Room and board:** $9,050.

## FINANCIAL AID PICTURE (2014-2015)
**Students with need:** Out of 78 full-time freshmen who applied for aid, 72 were judged to have need. Of these, 72 received aid, and 15 had their full need met. Average financial aid package met 42% of need; average scholarship/grant was $15,468; average loan was $3,372. For part-time students, average financial aid package was $10,751.
**Students without need:** No-need awards available for academics, athletics, leadership, music/drama.
**Scholarships offered:** 38 full-time freshmen received athletic scholarships; average amount $12,300.

## FINANCIAL AID PROCEDURES
**Forms required:** FAFSA, institutional form.
**Dates and Deadlines:** Priority date 3/2; no closing date. Applicants notified on a rolling basis starting 2/15; must reply within 2 week(s) of notification.
**Transfers:** No deadline. Applicants notified on a rolling basis starting 2/15; must reply within 2 week(s) of notification.

## CONTACT
Shannon O'Shields, Director of Student Financial Services
2500 East Nutwood Avenue, Fullerton, CA 92831-3199
(714) 879-3901 ext. 2232

# Humboldt State University
Arcata, California
www.humboldt.edu                    Federal Code: 001149

**4-year public** university and liberal arts college in large town.
**Enrollment:** 8,210 undergrads, 6% part-time. 1,364 full-time freshmen.
**Selectivity:** Admits over 75% of applicants.

## BASIC COSTS (2015-2016)
**Tuition and fees:** $7,196; out-of-state residents $18,356.
**Room and board:** $12,380.

## FINANCIAL AID PICTURE (2014-2015)
**Students with need:** Out of 1,248 full-time freshmen who applied for aid, 1,038 were judged to have need. Of these, 1,004 received aid, and 90 had their full need met. Average financial aid package met 71% of need; average scholarship/grant was $9,236; average loan was $5,580. For part-time students, average financial aid package was $8,914.
**Students without need:** 38 full-time freshmen who did not demonstrate need for aid received scholarships/grants; average award was $442. No-need awards available for academics, alumni affiliation, athletics, minority status, state/district residency.
**Scholarships offered:** 21 full-time freshmen received athletic scholarships; average amount $4,001.

## FINANCIAL AID PROCEDURES
**Forms required:** FAFSA.
**Dates and Deadlines:** Priority date 3/1; no closing date. Applicants notified on a rolling basis starting 4/1; must reply within 4 week(s) of notification.
**Transfers:** Need is most salient factor for some programs.

## CONTACT
Peggy Metzger, Director of Financial Aid
One Harpst Street, Arcata, CA 95521-8299
(707) 826-4321

# Humphreys College
Stockton, California
www.humphreys.edu              Federal Code: 001212

**4-year private** business, liberal arts and teachers college in large city.
**Enrollment:** 617 undergrads.

## BASIC COSTS (2015-2016)
**Tuition and fees:** $13,212.
**Per-credit charge:** $367.

## FINANCIAL AID PICTURE
**Students with need:** Need-based aid available for full-time and part-time students. Work study available nights, weekends, and for part-time students.
**Students without need:** No-need awards available for academics.

## FINANCIAL AID PROCEDURES
**Forms required:** FAFSA.
**Dates and Deadlines:** Applicants notified on a rolling basis starting 8/15; must reply within 2 week(s) of notification.

## CONTACT
Rita Franco, Financial Aid Director
6650 Inglewood Avenue, Stockton, CA 95207-3896
(209) 478-0800 ext. 3903

# Imperial Valley College
Imperial, California
www.imperial.edu              Federal Code: 001214

**2-year public** nursing and community college in large town.
**Enrollment:** 8,043 undergrads.
**Selectivity:** Open admission; but selective for some programs.

## BASIC COSTS (2015-2016)
**Tuition and fees:** $1,414; out-of-state residents $8,014.
**Per-credit charge:** $46; out-of-state residents $266.
**Additional info:** Tuition/fee waivers available for adults.

## FINANCIAL AID PICTURE
**Students with need:** Need-based aid available for full-time and part-time students. Work study available nights, weekends, and for part-time students.
**Students without need:** This college awards aid only to students with need.

## FINANCIAL AID PROCEDURES
**Forms required:** FAFSA.
**Dates and Deadlines:** Priority date 3/2; closing date 6/30. Applicants notified on a rolling basis starting 5/1.
**Transfers:** No deadline. Applicants notified on a rolling basis.

## CONTACT
Lisa Seals, Director of Financial Aid
Box 158, Imperial, CA 92251-0158
(760) 355-6266

# Irvine Valley College
Irvine, California
www.ivc.edu              Federal Code: 025395

**2-year public** community college in small city.
**Enrollment:** 9,957 undergrads.
**Selectivity:** Open admission.

## BASIC COSTS (2015-2016)
**Tuition and fees:** $1,418; out-of-state residents $8,048.
**Per-credit charge:** $46; out-of-state residents $267.
**Additional info:** Tuition/fee waivers available for minority students.

## FINANCIAL AID PICTURE
**Students with need:** Need-based aid available for full-time and part-time students. Work study available nights.
**Students without need:** This college awards aid only to students with need.

**FINANCIAL AID PROCEDURES**

**Forms required:** FAFSA, state aid form, institutional form.

**Dates and Deadlines:** Applicants notified on a rolling basis starting 4/30.

**CONTACT**

Darryl Cox, Director of Financial Aid

5500 Irvine Center Drive, Irvine, CA 92618-4399

(949) 451-5287

## John F. Kennedy University

Pleasant Hill, California

www.jfku.edu                    Federal Code: 004484

**Upper-division private** university in large town.

**Enrollment:** 251 undergrads.

**Selectivity:** Open admission; but selective for some programs.

**BASIC COSTS (2015-2016)**

**Tuition and fees:** $17,469.

**Per-credit charge:** $478.

**FINANCIAL AID PICTURE**

**Students with need:** Need-based aid available for full-time and part-time students.

**Students without need:** This college awards aid only to students with need.

**FINANCIAL AID PROCEDURES**

**Forms required:** FAFSA, institutional form.

**Dates and Deadlines:** Priority date 3/2; no closing date. Applicants notified on a rolling basis; must reply within 4 week(s) of notification.

**Transfers:** Priority date 4/1.

**CONTACT**

Mindy Bergeron, Director of Financial Aid

100 Ellinwood Way, Pleasant Hill, CA 94523-4817

(925) 969-3385

## John Paul the Great Catholic University

Escondido, California

www.jpcatholic.com              Federal Code: 041937

**4-year private** university in small city, affiliated with Roman Catholic Church.

**Enrollment:** 206 undergrads, 6% part-time. 56 full-time freshmen.

**Selectivity:** Admits over 75% of applicants.

**BASIC COSTS (2015-2016)**

**Tuition and fees:** $24,900.

**Per-credit charge:** $667.

**Room only:** $8,100.

**Additional info:** Tuition at time of enrollment locked for 4 years.

**FINANCIAL AID PICTURE (2014-2015)**

**Students with need:** Out of 46 full-time freshmen who applied for aid, 46 were judged to have need. Of these, 46 received aid, and 2 had their full need met. Average financial aid package met 45% of need; average scholarship/grant was $9,391; average loan was $3,111. For part-time students, average financial aid package was $12,355.

**Students without need:** 1 full-time freshmen who did not demonstrate need for aid received scholarships/grants; average award was $6,000. No-need awards available for academics, leadership.

**FINANCIAL AID PROCEDURES**

**Forms required:** FAFSA, institutional form.

**Dates and Deadlines:** Closing date 4/15. Applicants notified on a rolling basis starting 12/1; must reply by 5/1 or within 2 week(s) of notification.

**CONTACT**

Lisa Williams, Director of Financial Aid

220 West Grand Avenue, Escondido, CA 92025

(858) 653-6740 ext. 1303

## Kaplan College: Riverside

Riverside, California

www.riverside.kaplancollege.com    Federal Code: 030445

**2-year for-profit** junior and technical college in very large city.

**Enrollment:** 167 undergrads.

**Selectivity:** Open admission.

**BASIC COSTS (2015-2016)**

**Additional info:** Associate programs: Criminal Justice; $29,292. Diploma programs: Dental Assistant; $17,120; Massage Therapy; Medical Assistant, Medical Billing and Coding Specialist $15,304.

**FINANCIAL AID PICTURE**

**Students with need:** Need-based aid available for full-time students. Work study available nights.

**Students without need:** This college awards aid only to students with need.

**FINANCIAL AID PROCEDURES**

**Forms required:** FAFSA, institutional form.

**Transfers:** No deadline.

**CONTACT**

Cynthia Arevalo

4040 Vine Street, Riverside, CA 92507

(818) 672-3000

## Kaplan College: Sacramento

Sacramento, California

https://www.kaplancollege.com/sacramento-ca

                                Federal Code: 016720

**2-year for-profit** technical college in large city.

**Enrollment:** 429 undergrads.

**Selectivity:** Open admission; but selective for some programs.

**BASIC COSTS (2015-2016)**

**Additional info:** Associate degree program: Criminal Justice; $29,292. Diploma programs: Vocational Nursing; $31,685; Dental Assistant; $17,122; Medical Assistant, Medical Office Specialist $15,727.

**FINANCIAL AID PICTURE**

**Students with need:** Need-based aid available for full-time students.

**Students without need:** This college awards aid only to students with need.

**CONTACT**

Ryan Smith, Director of Finance

4330 Watt Avenue, Suite 400, Sacramento, CA 95821

(916) 649-8168

## La Sierra University

Riverside, California

www.lasierra.edu                Federal Code: 001215

**4-year private** university, Bible and liberal arts college in large city, affiliated with Seventh-day Adventists.

**Enrollment:** 2,020 undergrads, 9% part-time. 428 full-time freshmen.

**Selectivity:** Admits less than 50% of applicants.

**BASIC COSTS (2015-2016)**
Tuition and fees: $30,471.
Per-credit charge: $815.
Room and board: $7,800.

**FINANCIAL AID PICTURE**
Students with need: Need-based aid available for full-time and part-time students. Work study available nights, weekends, and for part-time students.
Students without need: No-need awards available for academics, art, athletics, leadership, music/drama, religious affiliation.
Scholarships offered: Sports and Honors Scholarship available for qualified students.

**FINANCIAL AID PROCEDURES**
Forms required: FAFSA, state aid form.
Dates and Deadlines: Priority date 3/2; closing date 8/15. Applicants notified on a rolling basis starting 4/15; must reply by 8/5 or within 2 week(s) of notification.
Transfers: Closing date 7/1. Applicants notified by 8/15; must reply by 9/1 or within 2 week(s) of notification. Every student whose balance is not completely covered by financial aid must make a payment of at least one-third of the balance due by the published deadline before each quarter. There will continue to be three standard payment options available. Year-in-Advance: Pay the full year's charges minus confirmed aid by the published deadline for Fall and receive a 7% discount. Quarter-in-Advance: Pay each quarter's charges minus confirmed aid by the published deadline for that quarter and receive a 2% discount. Monthly Payment: Pay in three monthly installments for each quarter, with the first payment due by that quarter's published deadline. A $30 fee applies for each quarter that this option is chosen.

**CONTACT**
Elina Bascom, Director of Student Financial Services
4500 Riverwalk Parkway, Riverside, CA 92515-8247
(951) 785-2175

## Laguna College of Art and Design
Laguna Beach, California
www.lcad.edu                    Federal Code: 016517

**4-year private** visual arts college in small city.
Enrollment: 567 undergrads, 10% part-time. 66 full-time freshmen.
Selectivity: Admits less than 50% of applicants.

**BASIC COSTS (2016-2017)**
Tuition and fees: $28,950.
Per-credit charge: $1,206.
Room only: $9,400.

**FINANCIAL AID PICTURE (2014-2015)**
Students with need: Out of 47 full-time freshmen who applied for aid, 47 were judged to have need. Of these, 47 received aid. Need-based aid available for part-time students.
Students without need: No-need awards available for art.
Additional info: Need and merit-based scholarship deadline June 1st.

**FINANCIAL AID PROCEDURES**
Forms required: FAFSA, institutional form.
Dates and Deadlines: Applicants notified on a rolling basis; must reply within 2 week(s) of notification.
Transfers: No deadline. Applicants notified on a rolling basis.

**CONTACT**
Christopher Brown, Director of Admission and Financial Aid
2222 Laguna Canyon Road, Laguna Beach, CA 92651-1136
(949) 376-6000 ext. 223

## Lake Tahoe Community College
South Lake Tahoe, California
www.ltcc.edu                    Federal Code: 012907

**2-year public** community college in large town.
Enrollment: 1,457 undergrads.
Selectivity: Open admission.

**BASIC COSTS (2015-2016)**
Tuition and fees: $1,415; out-of-state residents $7,670.
Per-credit charge: $31; out-of-state residents $170.

**FINANCIAL AID PICTURE**
Students with need: Need-based aid available for full-time and part-time students. Work study available nights.

**FINANCIAL AID PROCEDURES**
Forms required: FAFSA.
Dates and Deadlines: Closing date 6/30. Applicants notified on a rolling basis starting 7/1; must reply within 2 week(s) of notification.

**CONTACT**
Julie Cathie, Director of Financial Aid
One College Drive, South Lake Tahoe, CA 96150-4524
(530) 541-4660 ext. 236

## Las Positas College
Livermore, California
www.laspositascollege.edu           Federal Code: 030357

**2-year public** community college in small city.
Enrollment: 6,162 undergrads.
Selectivity: Open admission.

**BASIC COSTS (2015-2016)**
Tuition and fees: $1,436; out-of-state residents $8,726.
Per-credit charge: $46; out-of-district residents $289; out-of-state residents $289.
Additional info: Tuition/fee waivers available for unemployed or children of unemployed.

**FINANCIAL AID PICTURE**
Students with need: Need-based aid available for full-time students.

**FINANCIAL AID PROCEDURES**
Forms required: institutional form.
Dates and Deadlines: Priority date 5/1; no closing date. Applicants notified on a rolling basis starting 7/1; must reply within 2 week(s) of notification.

**CONTACT**
Andi Schreibman, Financial Aid Officer
3033 Collier Canyon Road, Livermore, CA 94551
(925) 424-1580

## Lassen Community College
Susanville, California
www.lassencollege.edu               Federal Code: 001217

**2-year public** community college in large town.
Enrollment: 2,183 undergrads, 69% part-time. 151 full-time freshmen.
Selectivity: Open admission; but selective for some programs.

**BASIC COSTS (2015-2016)**
Tuition and fees: $1,407; out-of-state residents $7,392.
Per-credit charge: $46; out-of-state residents $249.
Room only: $2,800.

**FINANCIAL AID PICTURE (2014-2015)**

**Students with need:** 79% of average financial aid package awarded as scholarships/grants, 21% awarded as loans/jobs.

**Students without need:** This college awards aid only to students with need.

**Additional info:** Board of Governors Grant: low-income California residents can have registration fees waived.

**FINANCIAL AID PROCEDURES**

**Forms required:** FAFSA.

**Dates and Deadlines:** Priority date 7/1; no closing date. Applicants notified on a rolling basis starting 7/1; must reply within 2 week(s) of notification.

**Transfers:** No deadline.

**CONTACT**

Matt Levine, Director of Financial Aid

PO Box 3000, Susanville, CA 96130

(530) 251-8849

## Le Cordon Bleu College of Culinary Arts: Los Angeles

Pasadena, California

www.chefs.edu/los-angeles          Federal Code: 032103

**2-year for-profit** culinary school in very large city.

**Enrollment:** 1,350 undergrads.

**Selectivity:** Open admission.

**BASIC COSTS (2015-2016)**

**Additional info:** Certificate programs: $19,500. Associate programs: $40,000. Books and supplies are included.

**FINANCIAL AID PICTURE**

**Students with need:** Need-based aid available for full-time and part-time students. Work study available nights, weekends, and for part-time students.

**FINANCIAL AID PROCEDURES**

**Forms required:** FAFSA.

**Dates and Deadlines:** Applicants notified on a rolling basis.

**Transfers:** No deadline.

**CONTACT**

Gabriela Arzate, Director of Student Finance

530 East Colorado Boulevard, Pasadena, CA 91101

(626) 229-1300

## Le Cordon Bleu College of Culinary Arts: San Francisco

San Francisco, California

www.chefs.edu/San-Francisco          Federal Code: 015698

**2-year for-profit** culinary school and career college in very large city.

**Enrollment:** 442 undergrads.

**BASIC COSTS (2015-2016)**

**Additional info:** Certificate programs: $19,500. Associate programs: $40,000. Books and supplies are included.

**FINANCIAL AID PICTURE**

**Students with need:** Need-based aid available for full-time students.

**FINANCIAL AID PROCEDURES**

**Forms required:** FAFSA, state aid form.

**Dates and Deadlines:** Applicants notified on a rolling basis; must reply within 1 week(s) of notification.

**CONTACT**

Director of Financial Aid

350 Rhode Island Street, San Francisco, CA 94103

(415) 771-3500

## Life Pacific College

San Dimas, California

www.lifepacific.edu          Federal Code: 016029

**4-year private** Bible college in large town, affiliated with Christian Church.

**Enrollment:** 520 undergrads.

**BASIC COSTS (2015-2016)**

**Tuition and fees:** $13,320.

**Per-credit charge:** $530.

**Room and board:** $7,246.

**FINANCIAL AID PICTURE**

**Students with need:** Need-based aid available for full-time and part-time students.

**Students without need:** No-need awards available for academics.

**FINANCIAL AID PROCEDURES**

**Forms required:** FAFSA.

**Dates and Deadlines:** Applicants notified on a rolling basis starting 6/1.

**CONTACT**

Becky Huyck, Director of Financial Aid

Attn: Admissions, San Dimas, CA 91773

(909) 599-5433 ext. 325

## Lincoln University

Oakland, California

www.lincolnuca.edu          Federal Code: 006975

**4-year private** university and business college in very large city.

**Enrollment:** 162 undergrads.

**BASIC COSTS (2015-2016)**

**Tuition and fees:** $10,200.

**Per-credit charge:** $410.

**FINANCIAL AID PICTURE**

**Students with need:** Need-based aid available for full-time and part-time students.

**Students without need:** This college awards aid only to students with need.

**FINANCIAL AID PROCEDURES**

**Forms required:** FAFSA.

**Dates and Deadlines:** Priority date 3/22; closing date 8/22. Applicants notified by 12/1; must reply by 1/2.

**Transfers:** Applicants notified by 12/1; must reply by 1/1.

**CONTACT**

James Peterson, Chief Financial Aid Director

401 15th Street, Oakland, CA 94612

(510) 628-8023

## Loma Linda University

Loma Linda, California

www.llu.edu          Federal Code: 001218

**3-year private** university and health science college in large town, affiliated with Seventh-day Adventists.

**Enrollment:** 1,071 undergrads.

**BASIC COSTS (2015-2016)**
**Tuition and fees:** $32,572.
**Room only:** $2,910.

**FINANCIAL AID PICTURE**
**Students with need:** Need-based aid available for full-time and part-time students.

**FINANCIAL AID PROCEDURES**
**Forms required:** FAFSA.
**Transfers:** Priority date 3/2; no deadline. Applicants notified on a rolling basis starting 4/1; must reply within 4 week(s) of notification.

**CONTACT**
Verdell Schaefer, Director of Financial Aid
Admissions Processing, Loma Linda, CA 92350
(909) 558-4509

## Long Beach City College
Long Beach, California
www.lbcc.edu                    Federal Code: 001219

**2-year public** community college in large city.
**Enrollment:** 16,317 undergrads.
**Selectivity:** Open admission.

**BASIC COSTS (2015-2016)**
**Tuition and fees:** $1,418; out-of-state residents $9,188.
**Per-credit charge:** $46; out-of-state residents $305.

**FINANCIAL AID PICTURE**
**Students with need:** Need-based aid available for full-time and part-time students.
**Students without need:** This college awards aid only to students with need.

**FINANCIAL AID PROCEDURES**
**Forms required:** FAFSA, institutional form.
**Dates and Deadlines:** Priority date 5/29; no closing date. Applicants notified on a rolling basis starting 7/6; must reply within 2 week(s) of notification.

**CONTACT**
Lillian Justice, Director of Financial Aid and Veterans Affairs
4901 East Carson Street, Long Beach, CA 90808
(562) 938-4257

## Los Angeles City College
Los Angeles, California
www.lacitycollege.edu           Federal Code: 001223

**2-year public** community college in very large city.
**Enrollment:** 9,959 undergrads.
**Selectivity:** Open admission.

**BASIC COSTS (2015-2016)**
**Tuition and fees:** $1,402; out-of-state residents $8,062.
**Per-credit charge:** $46; out-of-state residents $268.

**FINANCIAL AID PICTURE**
**Students with need:** Need-based aid available for full-time and part-time students.
**Students without need:** This college awards aid only to students with need.
**Additional info:** Fee waivers available for public assistance and Social Security insurance recipients; fee credits available for low income families.

**FINANCIAL AID PROCEDURES**
**Forms required:** FAFSA.
**Dates and Deadlines:** Priority date 3/2; no closing date. Applicants notified on a rolling basis starting 7/6; must reply within 2 week(s) of notification.
**Transfers:** No deadline. Applicants notified by 7/1.

**CONTACT**
Jeremy Villar, Dean of Student Services
855 North Vermont Avenue, Los Angeles, CA 90029-3589
(323) 953-4000 ext. 2025

## Los Angeles Harbor College
Wilmington, California
www.lahc.edu                    Federal Code: 001224

**2-year public** community college in small city.
**Enrollment:** 6,636 undergrads.
**Selectivity:** Open admission.

**BASIC COSTS (2015-2016)**
**Tuition and fees:** $1,404; out-of-state residents $7,194.
**Per-credit charge:** $46; out-of-state residents $239.

**FINANCIAL AID PICTURE**
**Students with need:** Need-based aid available for full-time and part-time students. Work study available nights, weekends, and for part-time students.
**Students without need:** This college awards aid only to students with need.

**FINANCIAL AID PROCEDURES**
**Forms required:** FAFSA, institutional form.
**Dates and Deadlines:** Priority date 3/2; no closing date. Applicants notified on a rolling basis; must reply within 2 week(s) of notification.
**Transfers:** Closing date 5/15.

**CONTACT**
Sheila Millman, Financial Aid Manager
1111 Figueroa Place, Wilmington, CA 90744-2397
(310) 233-4320

## Los Angeles Mission College
Sylmar, California
www.lamission.edu               Federal Code: 012550

**2-year public** community college in large town.
**Enrollment:** 7,295 undergrads.
**Selectivity:** Open admission.

**BASIC COSTS (2015-2016)**
**Tuition and fees:** $1,404; out-of-state residents $7,854.
**Per-credit charge:** $46; out-of-state residents $261.

**FINANCIAL AID PICTURE (2014-2015)**
**Students with need:** 94% of average financial aid package awarded as scholarships/grants, 6% awarded as loans/jobs. Need-based aid available for part-time students.
**Additional info:** Board of Governors Fee Waiver available to those in receipt of TANF (CalWORKS), Social Security Insurance, or General Relief. Students may also qualify based on family income.

**FINANCIAL AID PROCEDURES**
**Forms required:** FAFSA.
**Dates and Deadlines:** Priority date 5/1; no closing date. Applicants notified on a rolling basis starting 5/1.

**CONTACT**
Dennis Schroeder, Financial Aid Director
13356 Eldridge Avenue, Sylmar, CA 91342-3245
(818) 364-7648

## Los Angeles Pierce College
Woodland Hills, California
www.piercecollege.edu                    Federal Code: 001226

**2-year public** community college in very large city.
**Enrollment:** 14,714 undergrads.
**Selectivity:** Open admission; but selective for some programs.

**BASIC COSTS (2015-2016)**
**Tuition and fees:** $1,404; out-of-state residents $7,854.
**Per-credit charge:** $46; out-of-state residents $261.

**FINANCIAL AID PICTURE**
**Students with need:** Need-based aid available for full-time and part-time students. Work study available nights, weekends, and for part-time students.
**Students without need:** This college awards aid only to students with need.

**FINANCIAL AID PROCEDURES**
**Forms required:** FAFSA, institutional form.
**Dates and Deadlines:** Priority date 3/2; no closing date. Applicants notified on a rolling basis starting 8/1.

**CONTACT**
Anafe Robinson, Director of Financial Aid, Scholarships & Veterans
6201 Winnetka Avenue, Woodland Hills, CA 91371
(818) 719-6428

## Los Angeles Southwest College
Los Angeles, California
www.lasc.edu                             Federal Code: 007047

**2-year public** community college in very large city.
**Enrollment:** 4,578 undergrads.
**Selectivity:** Open admission; but selective for some programs.

**BASIC COSTS (2015-2016)**
**Tuition and fees:** $1,402; out-of-state residents $8,062.
**Per-credit charge:** $46; out-of-state residents $268.

**FINANCIAL AID PICTURE**
**Students with need:** Need-based aid available for full-time and part-time students.
**Additional info:** Board of Governors Enrollment Fee Waiver available to students receiving AFDC, SSI/SSP, or General Assistance. May also qualify on basis of income.

**FINANCIAL AID PROCEDURES**
**Forms required:** FAFSA.
**Dates and Deadlines:** Applicants notified on a rolling basis; must reply within 2 week(s) of notification.

**CONTACT**
Kathaleen Stiger, Financial Aid Director
1600 West Imperial Highway, Los Angeles, CA 90047-4899
(323) 241-5328

## Los Angeles Trade and Technical College
Los Angeles, California
www.lattc.edu                            Federal Code: 001227

**2-year public** community and technical college in very large city.
**Enrollment:** 8,610 undergrads.
**Selectivity:** Open admission; but selective for some programs.

**BASIC COSTS (2015-2016)**
**Tuition and fees:** $1,418; out-of-state residents $7,868.

**Per-credit charge:** $46; out-of-state residents $261.

**FINANCIAL AID PICTURE**
**Students with need:** Need-based aid available for full-time and part-time students. Work study available nights, weekends, and for part-time students.
**Students without need:** This college awards aid only to students with need.

**FINANCIAL AID PROCEDURES**
**Forms required:** FAFSA.
**Dates and Deadlines:** Priority date 5/1; closing date 6/30. Applicants notified on a rolling basis.
**Transfers:** No deadline.

**CONTACT**
Cecilia Kwan, Financial Aid Manager
400 West Washington Boulevard, Los Angeles, CA 90015-4181
(213) 744-9016

## Los Angeles Valley College
Valley Glen, California
www.lavc.edu                             Federal Code: 001228

**2-year public** community college in very large city.
**Enrollment:** 11,870 undergrads.
**Selectivity:** Open admission; but selective for some programs.

**BASIC COSTS (2015-2016)**
**Tuition and fees:** $1,404; out-of-state residents $7,854.
**Per-credit charge:** $46; out-of-state residents $261.

**FINANCIAL AID PICTURE**
**Students with need:** Need-based aid available for full-time and part-time students.
**Students without need:** This college awards aid only to students with need.

**FINANCIAL AID PROCEDURES**
**Forms required:** FAFSA.
**Dates and Deadlines:** Priority date 5/1; no closing date. Applicants notified on a rolling basis.

**CONTACT**
Vernon Bridges, Financial Aid Manager
5800 Fulton Avenue, Valley Glen, CA 91401-4096
(818) 947-2412

## Los Medanos College
Pittsburg, California
www.losmedanos.edu                       Federal Code: 010340

**2-year public** community college in small city.
**Enrollment:** 3,924 undergrads.
**Selectivity:** Open admission.

**BASIC COSTS (2015-2016)**
**Tuition and fees:** $1,390; out-of-state residents $7,540.
**Per-credit charge:** $46; out-of-state residents $251.

**FINANCIAL AID PICTURE**
**Students with need:** Need-based aid available for full-time and part-time students.
**Students without need:** This college awards aid only to students with need.

**FINANCIAL AID PROCEDURES**
**Forms required:** FAFSA, state aid form.

**Dates and Deadlines:** Priority date 3/2; no closing date. Applicants notified on a rolling basis starting 6/1; must reply within 2 week(s) of notification.
**Transfers:** No deadline. Applicants notified by 6/1.

**CONTACT**
Loretta Canto-Williams, Director of Financial Aid
2700 East Leland Road, Pittsburg, CA 94565
(925) 439-2181 ext. 3139

## Loyola Marymount University
Los Angeles, California
www.lmu.edu                    Federal Code: 001234

**4-year private** university in very large city, affiliated with Roman Catholic Church.
**Enrollment:** 6,162 undergrads, 2% part-time. 1,348 full-time freshmen.
**Selectivity:** Admits 50 to 75% of applicants.

**BASIC COSTS (2015-2016)**
**Tuition and fees:** $42,794.
**Per-credit charge:** $1,747.
**Room and board:** $13,630.

**FINANCIAL AID PICTURE (2014-2015)**
**Students with need:** Out of 1,067 full-time freshmen who applied for aid, 757 were judged to have need. Of these, 757 received aid, and 174 had their full need met. Average financial aid package met 68% of need; average scholarship/grant was $20,271; average loan was $5,220. For part-time students, average financial aid package was $10,321.
**Students without need:** 438 full-time freshmen who did not demonstrate need for aid received scholarships/grants; average award was $9,662. No-need awards available for academics, alumni affiliation, art, music/drama, religious affiliation, ROTC.
**Scholarships offered: Merit:** Range from $1,000 to $15,000. Trustee Scholarship: Full tuition, fees, room and board, selection based on academic accomplishments and interview process; typically 10 each year. Presidential Scholarship: $25,000 and up, based on academic accomplishments and interview process; typically 20 each year. Arrupe Scholarships: Range from $12,500 to full tuition, based on academic accomplishments. LMU Achievement Awards: Range from $1,000 and up, based on academic accomplishments. **Athletic:** 39 full-time freshmen received athletic scholarships; average amount $24,803.

**FINANCIAL AID PROCEDURES**
**Forms required:** FAFSA.
**Dates and Deadlines:** Priority date 2/1; closing date 5/30. Must reply by 5/1 or within 4 week(s) of notification.
**Transfers:** Priority date 3/2; no deadline. Applicants notified on a rolling basis starting 6/1; must reply within 3 week(s) of notification.

**CONTACT**
Maureen Weatherall, Vice Provost, Enrollment Management
1 LMU Drive, Los Angeles, CA 90045-2659
(310) 338-2753

## Marymount California University
Rancho Palos Verdes, California
www.marymountcalifornia.edu      Federal Code: 010474

**4-year private** liberal arts college in large town, affiliated with Roman Catholic Church.
**Enrollment:** 1,059 undergrads, 4% part-time. 228 full-time freshmen.
**Selectivity:** Admits 50 to 75% of applicants.

**BASIC COSTS (2015-2016)**
**Tuition and fees:** $34,130.

**Per-credit charge:** $1,430.
**Room and board:** $13,780.

**FINANCIAL AID PICTURE (2014-2015)**
**Students with need:** Out of 146 full-time freshmen who applied for aid, 144 were judged to have need. Of these, 144 received aid, and 38 had their full need met. Average financial aid package met 86% of need; average scholarship/grant was $25,010; average loan was $3,500. For part-time students, average financial aid package was $15,974.
**Students without need:** 23 full-time freshmen who did not demonstrate need for aid received scholarships/grants; average award was $10,087. No-need awards available for art, athletics, music/drama.
**Scholarships offered: Merit:** President's Scholarship: $8,000; Academic GPA: 3.30 and above; SAT 1530 or ACT 22. Dean's Scholarship: $6,000; Academic GPA 3.00-3.29; SAT 1410 or ACT 20. Achievement Scholarship: $4,500; Academic GPA 2.80-2.99; SAT 1210 or ACT 17. Deadline May 1. All admitted students considered. Renewable for one additional consecutive year. **Athletic:** 35 full-time freshmen received athletic scholarships; average amount $10,136.

**FINANCIAL AID PROCEDURES**
**Forms required:** FAFSA.
**Dates and Deadlines:** Priority date 3/2; no closing date. Applicants notified by 3/1.

**CONTACT**
Barbara Grimm, Director of Financial Aid
30800 Palos Verdes Drive East, Rancho Palos Verdes, CA 90275-6299
(310) 303-7217

## The Master's College
Santa Clarita, California
www.masters.edu                Federal Code: 001220

**4-year private** liberal arts and seminary college in small city, affiliated with nondenominational tradition.
**Enrollment:** 1,133 undergrads, 14% part-time. 194 full-time freshmen.
**Selectivity:** Admits over 75% of applicants.

**BASIC COSTS (2016-2017)**
**Tuition and fees:** $31,970.
**Per-credit charge:** $1,325.
**Room and board:** $10,300.

**FINANCIAL AID PICTURE (2014-2015)**
**Students with need:** Out of 184 full-time freshmen who applied for aid, 166 were judged to have need. Of these, 166 received aid, and 28 had their full need met. Average financial aid package met 71% of need; average scholarship/grant was $19,919; average loan was $3,214. For part-time students, average financial aid package was $5,877.
**Students without need:** 28 full-time freshmen who did not demonstrate need for aid received scholarships/grants; average award was $12,400. No-need awards available for academics, alumni affiliation, art, athletics, leadership, music/drama.
**Scholarships offered:** 10 full-time freshmen received athletic scholarships; average amount $16,334.

**FINANCIAL AID PROCEDURES**
**Forms required:** FAFSA, state aid form, institutional form.
**Dates and Deadlines:** Priority date 3/2; no closing date. Applicants notified on a rolling basis starting 2/18; must reply by 5/1 or within 2 week(s) of notification.
**Transfers:** No deadline. Applicants notified on a rolling basis starting 2/18; must reply by 5/1 or within 2 week(s) of notification.

**CONTACT**
Gary Edwards, Director of Financial Aid
Office of Admissions, Santa Clarita, CA 91321-1200
(661) 259-3540 ext. 2290

# Mendocino College
Ukiah, California
www.mendocino.edu                    Federal Code: 011672

**2-year public** community college in large town.
**Enrollment:** 1,439 undergrads.
**Selectivity:** Open admission.

## BASIC COSTS (2015-2016)
**Tuition and fees:** $1,420; out-of-state residents $7,420.
**Per-credit charge:** $46; out-of-state residents $246.
**Additional info:** Tuition/fee waivers available for unemployed or children of unemployed.

## FINANCIAL AID PICTURE
**Students with need:** Need-based aid available for full-time and part-time students. Work study available nights.
**Students without need:** No-need awards available for academics, leadership, music/drama, state/district residency.

## FINANCIAL AID PROCEDURES
**Forms required:** FAFSA.
**Dates and Deadlines:** Priority date 5/31; no closing date. Applicants notified on a rolling basis starting 7/1; must reply within 2 week(s) of notification.
**Transfers:** No deadline. Applicants notified on a rolling basis.

## CONTACT
Ulises Velasco, Director of Financial Aid
1000 Hensley Creek/Box 3000, Ukiah, CA 95482
(707) 468-3110

# Menlo College
Atherton, California
www.menlo.edu                        Federal Code: 001236

**4-year private** business and liberal arts college in small city.
**Enrollment:** 765 undergrads, 3% part-time. 150 full-time freshmen.
**Selectivity:** Admits less than 50% of applicants.

## BASIC COSTS (2016-2017)
**Tuition and fees:** $39,950.
**Per-credit charge:** $1,636.
**Room and board:** $13,150.

## FINANCIAL AID PICTURE (2015-2016)
**Students with need:** Out of 140 full-time freshmen who applied for aid, 131 were judged to have need. Of these, 131 received aid, and 18 had their full need met. Average financial aid package met 70% of need; average scholarship/grant was $28,530; average loan was $3,159. For part-time students, average financial aid package was $16,832.
**Students without need:** 75 full-time freshmen who did not demonstrate need for aid received scholarships/grants; average award was $15,488. No-need awards available for academics, athletics.
**Scholarships offered:** 40 full-time freshmen received athletic scholarships; average amount $17,478.

## FINANCIAL AID PROCEDURES
**Forms required:** FAFSA.
**Dates and Deadlines:** Priority date 3/2; closing date 8/1. Applicants notified on a rolling basis starting 12/15; must reply by 5/1 or within 2 week(s) of notification.
**Transfers:** Closing date 12/15. Applicants notified on a rolling basis starting 12/1; must reply by 5/1 or within 2 week(s) of notification.

## CONTACT
Jessica Ayres, Director, Office of Financial Aid
1000 El Camino Real, Atherton, CA 94027
(650) 543-3880

# Merritt College
Oakland, California
www.merritt.edu                      Federal Code: 001267

**2-year public** community college in large city.
**Enrollment:** 3,155 undergrads.
**Selectivity:** Open admission.

## BASIC COSTS (2015-2016)
**Tuition and fees:** $1,420; out-of-state residents $8,020.
**Per-credit charge:** $46; out-of-state residents $266.
**Additional info:** Tuition/fee waivers available for unemployed or children of unemployed.

## FINANCIAL AID PICTURE
**Students with need:** Need-based aid available for full-time and part-time students.

## FINANCIAL AID PROCEDURES
**Forms required:** FAFSA, institutional form.
**Dates and Deadlines:** Priority date 4/1; closing date 6/30. Applicants notified on a rolling basis starting 6/1.

## CONTACT
Alice Freeman, Financial Aid Coordinator
12500 Campus Drive, Oakland, CA 94619
(510) 436-2465

# Mills College
Oakland, California
www.mills.edu                        Federal Code: 001238

**4-year private** liberal arts college for women in large city.
**Enrollment:** 852 undergrads, 5% part-time. 139 full-time freshmen.
**Selectivity:** Admits over 75% of applicants.

## BASIC COSTS (2015-2016)
**Tuition and fees:** $44,258.
**Room and board:** $12,390.

## FINANCIAL AID PICTURE (2015-2016)
**Students with need:** Out of 133 full-time freshmen who applied for aid, 113 were judged to have need. Of these, 110 received aid, and 26 had their full need met. Average financial aid package met 94% of need; average scholarship/grant was $36,050; average loan was $4,815. For part-time students, average financial aid package was $28,828.
**Students without need:** 34 full-time freshmen who did not demonstrate need for aid received scholarships/grants; average award was $24,149. No-need awards available for academics, leadership, music/drama.

## FINANCIAL AID PROCEDURES
**Forms required:** FAFSA, state aid form.
**Dates and Deadlines:** Priority date 2/1; closing date 2/15. Applicants notified on a rolling basis starting 3/1; must reply by 5/1 or within 2 week(s) of notification.
**Transfers:** Priority date 3/2; closing date 7/15. Applicants notified on a rolling basis starting 4/15; must reply by 5/1 or within 2 week(s) of notification.

## CONTACT
Jeff Hardie, Assistant Vice President for Student Financial Services
5000 MacArthur Boulevard, Oakland, CA 94613
(510) 430-2000

## MiraCosta College
Oceanside, California
www.miracosta.edu                  Federal Code: 001239

**2-year public** community and junior college in large city.
**Enrollment:** 12,320 undergrads, 69% part-time. 1,256 full-time freshmen.
**Selectivity:** Open admission; but selective for some programs.

### BASIC COSTS (2015-2016)
**Tuition and fees:** $1,428; out-of-state residents $7,428.
**Per-credit charge:** $46; out-of-state residents $246.

### FINANCIAL AID PICTURE
**Students with need:** Need-based aid available for full-time and part-time students. Work study available nights.
**Additional info:** Waiver of in-state fees for eligible low-income students.

### FINANCIAL AID PROCEDURES
**Forms required:** FAFSA, state aid form, institutional form.
**Dates and Deadlines:** Priority date 4/12; no closing date. Applicants notified on a rolling basis; must reply within 1 week(s) of notification.
**Transfers:** Priority date 4/4; no deadline.

### CONTACT
Michael Dear, Director, Financial Aid and Scholarships
One Barnard Drive, Oceanside, CA 92056-3899
(760) 795-6711

## Modesto Junior College
Modesto, California
www.mjc.edu                  Federal Code: 001240

**2-year public** community and junior college in large city.
**Enrollment:** 16,253 undergrads, 62% part-time. 1,483 full-time freshmen.
**Selectivity:** Open admission; but selective for some programs.

### BASIC COSTS (2015-2016)
**Tuition and fees:** $1,416; out-of-state residents $7,926.
**Per-credit charge:** $46; out-of-state residents $263.

### FINANCIAL AID PICTURE
**Students with need:** Need-based aid available for full-time and part-time students. Work study available nights, weekends, and for part-time students.
**Students without need:** This college awards aid only to students with need.
**Additional info:** Modesto Junior College scholarship priority deadline 12/15.

### FINANCIAL AID PROCEDURES
**Forms required:** FAFSA, state aid form, institutional form.
**Dates and Deadlines:** Priority date 3/2; no closing date. Applicants notified on a rolling basis starting 5/1; must reply within 2 week(s) of notification.

### CONTACT
Peggy Fikse, Director, Student Financial Services
435 College Avenue, Modesto, CA 95350-5800

## Monterey Peninsula College
Monterey, California
www.mpc.edu                  Federal Code: 001242

**2-year public** community college in large town.
**Enrollment:** 4,256 undergrads.
**Selectivity:** Open admission; but selective for some programs.

### BASIC COSTS (2015-2016)
**Tuition and fees:** $1,450; out-of-state residents $7,450.
**Per-credit charge:** $46; out-of-state residents $246.

**Additional info:** Tuition/fee waivers available for adults, minority students, unemployed or children of unemployed.

### FINANCIAL AID PICTURE
**Students with need:** Need-based aid available for full-time and part-time students.

### FINANCIAL AID PROCEDURES
**Forms required:** FAFSA, institutional form.
**Dates and Deadlines:** Closing date 6/30. Applicants notified on a rolling basis starting 6/1.

### CONTACT
Francisco Tostado, Director of Student Financial Services
980 Fremont Street, Monterey, CA 93940-4799
(831) 646-4000

## Moorpark College
Moorpark, California
www.moorparkcollege.edu                  Federal Code: 007115

**2-year public** community college in small city.
**Enrollment:** 10,232 undergrads.
**Selectivity:** Open admission; but selective for some programs.

### BASIC COSTS (2015-2016)
**Tuition and fees:** $1,448; out-of-state residents $8,348.
**Per-credit charge:** $46; out-of-state residents $276.

### FINANCIAL AID PICTURE
**Students with need:** Need-based aid available for full-time and part-time students.
**Students without need:** This college awards aid only to students with need.

### FINANCIAL AID PROCEDURES
**Forms required:** FAFSA, state aid form.
**Dates and Deadlines:** Priority date 5/14; no closing date. Applicants notified on a rolling basis starting 6/15.
**Transfers:** Priority date 5/16. Applicants notified by 6/16.

### CONTACT
Kimberly Korinke, Financial Aid Officer
7075 Campus Road, Moorpark, CA 93021
(805) 378-1463

## Mount Saint Mary's University
Los Angeles, California
www.msmu.edu                  Federal Code: 001243

**4-year private** university and liberal arts college for women in very large city, affiliated with Roman Catholic Church.
**Enrollment:** 2,779 undergrads, 23% part-time. 532 full-time freshmen.
**Selectivity:** Admits over 75% of applicants.

### BASIC COSTS (2015-2016)
**Tuition and fees:** $35,944.
**Per-credit charge:** $1,456.
**Room and board:** $11,117.

### FINANCIAL AID PICTURE (2015-2016)
**Students with need:** Out of 513 full-time freshmen who applied for aid, 503 were judged to have need. Of these, 502 received aid, and 27 had their full need met. Average financial aid package met 73% of need; average scholarship/grant was $20,134; average loan was $3,656. Need-based aid available for part-time students.

**Students without need:** 28 full-time freshmen who did not demonstrate need for aid received scholarships/grants; average award was $16,710. No-need awards available for academics, alumni affiliation, music/drama.

**FINANCIAL AID PROCEDURES**
**Forms required:** FAFSA.
**Dates and Deadlines:** Priority date 3/1; no closing date. Applicants notified on a rolling basis starting 3/1; must reply by 5/1.
**Transfers:** No deadline. Applicants notified on a rolling basis starting 3/1; must reply by 5/1 or within 3 week(s) of notification.

**CONTACT**
La Royce Housely, Director of Student Financing
12001 Chalon Road, Los Angeles, CA 90049
(310) 954-4195

## Mount San Antonio College
Walnut, California
www.mtsac.edu                                 Federal Code: 001245

**2-year public** community college in small city.
**Enrollment:** 26,431 undergrads, 62% part-time. 2,577 full-time freshmen.
**Selectivity:** Open admission.

**BASIC COSTS (2015-2016)**
**Tuition and fees:** $1,418; out-of-state residents $8,228.
**Per-credit charge:** $46; out-of-state residents $273.

**FINANCIAL AID PICTURE**
**Students with need:** Need-based aid available for full-time and part-time students.
**Students without need:** This college awards aid only to students with need.

**FINANCIAL AID PROCEDURES**
**Forms required:** FAFSA.
**Dates and Deadlines:** Priority date 3/2; no closing date. Applicants notified on a rolling basis starting 7/1.

**CONTACT**
Chau Dao, Director Financial Aid
1100 North Grand Avenue, Walnut, CA 91789
(909) 274-4450

## Mount San Jacinto College
San Jacinto, California
www.msjc.edu                                  Federal Code: 001246

**2-year public** community college in small city.
**Enrollment:** 8,336 undergrads.
**Selectivity:** Open admission; but selective for some programs.

**BASIC COSTS (2015-2016)**
**Tuition and fees:** $1,394; out-of-state residents $7,724.
**Per-credit charge:** $46; out-of-state residents $257.

**FINANCIAL AID PICTURE**
**Students with need:** Need-based aid available for full-time and part-time students. Work study available nights.
**Students without need:** No-need awards available for academics, music/drama.
**Additional info:** Board of Governors Grant Program for state residents to defray cost of enrollment fees.

**FINANCIAL AID PROCEDURES**
**Forms required:** FAFSA, institutional form.
**Dates and Deadlines:** Priority date 3/2; no closing date. Applicants notified on a rolling basis starting 5/1; must reply within 3 week(s) of notification.

**Transfers:** No deadline.

**CONTACT**
Leisa Navarro, Financial Aid Supervisor
1499 North State Street, San Jacinto, CA 92583
(951) 487-3245

## Mt. Sierra College
Monrovia, California
www.mtsierra.edu                              Federal Code: 031287

**3-year for-profit** visual arts and business college in large city.
**Enrollment:** 530 undergrads.

**BASIC COSTS (2015-2016)**
**Tuition and fees:** $15,588.
**Per-credit charge:** $395.
**Additional info:** Mandatory California State STRF fee, currently $0, laptop expense $500-$1,600, depending on program.

**FINANCIAL AID PICTURE**
**Students with need:** Need-based aid available for full-time and part-time students.

**FINANCIAL AID PROCEDURES**
**Forms required:** FAFSA.
**Transfers:** No deadline. Applicants notified on a rolling basis.

**CONTACT**
Lida Castillo, Financial Aid Director
101 East Huntington Drive, Monrovia, CA 91016
(626) 873-2100

## MTI College
Sacramento, California
www.mticollege.edu                            Federal Code: 012912

**2-year for-profit** business and technical college in large city.
**Enrollment:** 1,020 undergrads.

**BASIC COSTS (2015-2016)**
**Additional info:** Diploma programs range from $12,050-$17,185, books and supplies range from $1,444-$2,773, Associates programs range from $12,325-$14,439, books and supplies range from $1,033-$2,098.

**FINANCIAL AID PICTURE**
**Students with need:** Need-based aid available for full-time students. Work study available nights.

**CONTACT**
Paula Perez, Director of Financial Aid
5221 Madison Avenue, Sacramento, CA 95841
(916) 339-1500

## National University
La Jolla, California
www.nu.edu                                    Federal Code: 011460

**4-year private** university in very large city.
**Enrollment:** 8,555 undergrads, 62% part-time. 7 full-time freshmen.
**Selectivity:** Open admission; but selective for some programs.

**BASIC COSTS (2015-2016)**
**Tuition and fees:** $12,744.
**Per-credit charge:** $354.

## FINANCIAL AID PICTURE (2015-2016)

**Students with need:** 26% of average financial aid package awarded as scholarships/grants, 74% awarded as loans/jobs. Need-based aid available for part-time students.

## FINANCIAL AID PROCEDURES

**Forms required:** FAFSA, state aid form, institutional form.
**Dates and Deadlines:** Applicants notified on a rolling basis.
**Transfers:** No deadline.

## CONTACT

Valerie Ryan, Director of Financial Aid
11255 North Torrey Pines Road, La Jolla, CA 92037-1011
(858) 642-8500

## NewSchool of Architecture & Design

San Diego, California
www.newschoolarch.edu          Federal Code: 030439

**5-year for-profit** visual arts and liberal arts college in very large city.
**Enrollment:** 403 undergrads, 10% part-time. 55 full-time freshmen.

## BASIC COSTS (2016-2017)

**Tuition and fees:** $26,463.
**Per-credit charge:** $751.

## FINANCIAL AID PICTURE (2015-2016)

**Students with need:** Average financial aid package met 31% of need; average scholarship/grant was $11,013; average loan was $4,161. For part-time students, average financial aid package was $8,597.

## CONTACT

Diondrae Collier, Director of Financial Aid
1249 F Street, San Diego, CA 92101
(619) 681-8818

## Notre Dame de Namur University

Belmont, California
www.ndnu.edu          Federal Code: 001179

**4-year private** university and liberal arts college in large town, affiliated with Roman Catholic Church.
**Enrollment:** 1,097 undergrads.

## BASIC COSTS (2015-2016)

**Tuition and fees:** $32,608.
**Per-credit charge:** $1,039.
**Room and board:** $13,006.

## FINANCIAL AID PICTURE

**Students with need:** Need-based aid available for full-time and part-time students. Work study available nights, weekends, and for part-time students.
**Students without need:** No-need awards available for academics, art, athletics, leadership, music/drama, religious affiliation, ROTC.
**Scholarships offered:** Presidential Scholarships: up to $26,000 per year; based on academic merit and leadership. Emerging Artist Scholarship: up to $9,500 annually; based on demonstrated talent in the performing and fine arts. Belmont Scholarships: up to $9,000 annually; based on merit. Bay Area Catholic High School: up to $7,500 per year to one student from each of Bay Area Catholic high schools.

## FINANCIAL AID PROCEDURES

**Forms required:** FAFSA. CSS PROFILE accepted but not required.
**Dates and Deadlines:** Priority date 3/2; no closing date. Applicants notified on a rolling basis starting 2/15; must reply by 5/1 or within 2 week(s) of notification.

## CONTACT

Wilbert Lleses, Director of Financial Aid
1500 Ralston Avenue, Belmont, CA 94002-1908
(650) 508-3600

## Occidental College

Los Angeles, California          Federal Code: 001249
www.oxy.edu          CSS Code: 4581

**4-year private** liberal arts college in very large city, affiliated with nondenominational tradition.
**Enrollment:** 2,088 undergrads, 1% part-time. 545 full-time freshmen.
**Selectivity:** Admits less than 50% of applicants.

## BASIC COSTS (2015-2016)

**Tuition and fees:** $49,248.
**Room and board:** $13,946.

## FINANCIAL AID PICTURE (2014-2015)

**Students with need:** Out of 374 full-time freshmen who applied for aid, 311 were judged to have need. Of these, 310 received aid, and 310 had their full need met. Average financial aid package met 100% of need; average scholarship/grant was $37,998; average loan was $4,635. For part-time students, average financial aid package was $25,185.
**Students without need:** 64 full-time freshmen who did not demonstrate need for aid received scholarships/grants; average award was $11,236. No-need awards available for academics, leadership, music/drama, state/district residency.
**Scholarships offered:** Margaret Bundy Scott Scholarship: $25,000. President's Scholarship: $17,500; awarded to top 10-15% of incoming class based on academic achievement, leadership, and citizenship.
**Additional info:** Work-study programs are available during the day when students are not in class.

## FINANCIAL AID PROCEDURES

**Forms required:** FAFSA, CSS PROFILE, state aid form.
**Dates and Deadlines:** Priority date 2/1; closing date 2/1. Applicants notified by 4/1; must reply by 5/1.
**Transfers:** Closing date 3/2. Applicants notified by 6/15; must reply within 2 week(s) of notification. California residents must apply for Cal Grant by completing FAFSA and CSAC's GPA verification form by March 2. For all applicants, FAFSA is due March 2; Profile is due April 1,.

## CONTACT

Maureen Goldberg, Director of Financial Aid
1600 Campus Road, Los Angeles, CA 90041
(323) 259-2548

## Ohlone College

Fremont, California
www.ohlone.edu          Federal Code: 004481

**2-year public** community college in large city.
**Enrollment:** 7,105 undergrads, 59% part-time. 608 full-time freshmen.
**Selectivity:** Open admission; but selective for some programs.

## BASIC COSTS (2015-2016)

**Tuition and fees:** $1,418; out-of-state residents $8,378.
**Per-credit charge:** $46; out-of-state residents $278.
**Additional info:** Tuition/fee waivers available for adults, minority students, unemployed or children of unemployed.

## FINANCIAL AID PICTURE (2014-2015)

**Students with need:** 93% of average financial aid package awarded as scholarships/grants, 7% awarded as loans/jobs. Need-based aid available for part-time students.

**FINANCIAL AID PROCEDURES**
**Forms required:** FAFSA.
**Dates and Deadlines:** Must reply within 2 week(s) of notification.

**CONTACT**
Deborah Griffin, Director, Financial Aid
43600 Mission Boulevard, Fremont, CA 94539-0390
(510) 659-6150

## Orange Coast College
Costa Mesa, California
www.orangecoastcollege.edu        Federal Code: 001250

**2-year public** community college in small city.
**Enrollment:** 16,150 undergrads, 57% part-time. 1,515 full-time freshmen.
**Selectivity:** Open admission.

**BASIC COSTS (2015-2016)**
**Tuition and fees:** $1,418; out-of-state residents $8,348.
**Per-credit charge:** $46; out-of-state residents $277.
**Additional info:** Tuition/fee waivers available for adults, minority students, unemployed or children of unemployed.

**FINANCIAL AID PICTURE**
**Students with need:** Need-based aid available for full-time and part-time students.

**FINANCIAL AID PROCEDURES**
**Forms required:** FAFSA, state aid form.
**Dates and Deadlines:** Priority date 3/2; no closing date. Applicants notified on a rolling basis; must reply within 2 week(s) of notification.

**CONTACT**
Financial Aid Director
2701 Fairview Road, Costa Mesa, CA 92628-5005
(714) 432-5508

## Otis College of Art and Design
Los Angeles, California
www.otis.edu        Federal Code: 001251

**4-year private** visual arts college in very large city.
**Enrollment:** 1,088 undergrads.

**BASIC COSTS (2015-2016)**
**Tuition and fees:** $40,504.
**Per-credit charge:** $1,280.

**FINANCIAL AID PICTURE**
**Students with need:** Need-based aid available for full-time and part-time students. Work study available nights, weekends, and for part-time students.
**Students without need:** No-need awards available for academics, art.

**FINANCIAL AID PROCEDURES**
**Forms required:** FAFSA, state aid form.
**Dates and Deadlines:** Priority date 2/15; no closing date. Applicants notified on a rolling basis starting 3/1; must reply within 2 week(s) of notification.

**CONTACT**
Jessika Vasquez-Huerta, Director of Financial Aid
9045 Lincoln Boulevard, Los Angeles, CA 90045-9785
(310) 665-6880

## Pacific Oaks College
Pasadena, California
www.pacificoaks.edu        Federal Code: 001255

**Upper-division private** teachers college in small city.
**Enrollment:** 543 undergrads.

**BASIC COSTS (2015-2016)**
**Tuition and fees:** $22,740.
**Per-credit charge:** $758.

**FINANCIAL AID PICTURE**
**Students with need:** Need-based aid available for full-time and part-time students. Work study available nights, weekends, and for part-time students.
**Students without need:** This college awards aid only to students with need.

**FINANCIAL AID PROCEDURES**
**Dates and Deadlines:** Priority date 4/15; no closing date. Applicants notified on a rolling basis starting 5/1; must reply by 5/15 or within 4 week(s) of notification.

**CONTACT**
Seph Rodriguez, Director of Financial Aid
55 Eureka Street, Pasadena, CA 91103
(626) 397-1350

## Pacific States University
Los Angeles, California
www.psuca.edu        Federal Code: 031633

**4-year private** university in very large city.
**Enrollment:** 14 undergrads.
**Selectivity:** Open admission; but selective for some programs.

**BASIC COSTS (2015-2016)**
**Tuition and fees:** $16,005.
**Per-credit charge:** $345.
**Additional info:** Tuition at time of enrollment locked for 4 years.

**FINANCIAL AID PICTURE**
**Students with need:** Need-based aid available for full-time students.
**Students without need:** No-need awards available for academics.

**FINANCIAL AID PROCEDURES**
**Forms required:** FAFSA, institutional form.

**CONTACT**
James Cummings, Director of Financial Aid
3424 Wilshire Boulevard 12th floor, Los Angeles, CA 90010
(323) 731-2383 ext. 211

## Pacific Union College
Angwin, California
www.puc.edu        Federal Code: 001258

**4-year private** liberal arts college in small town, affiliated with Seventh-day Adventists.
**Enrollment:** 1,507 undergrads, 10% part-time. 250 full-time freshmen.
**Selectivity:** Admits less than 50% of applicants.

**BASIC COSTS (2016-2017)**
**Tuition and fees:** $28,329.
**Per-credit charge:** $810.
**Room and board:** $7,920.
**Additional info:** Student Health Plan $750/year.

**FINANCIAL AID PICTURE (2015-2016)**

**Students with need:** Out of 250 full-time freshmen who applied for aid, 201 were judged to have need. Of these, 201 received aid, and 2 had their full need met. Average financial aid package met 60% of need; average scholarship/grant was $18,417; average loan was $2,828. Need-based aid available for part-time students.

**Students without need:** 49 full-time freshmen who did not demonstrate need for aid received scholarships/grants; average award was $2,772. No-need awards available for academics, alumni affiliation, art, athletics, leadership, music/drama, religious affiliation.

**Scholarships offered:** 10 full-time freshmen received athletic scholarships; average amount $2,700.

**FINANCIAL AID PROCEDURES**

**Forms required:** FAFSA, institutional form.

**Dates and Deadlines:** Priority date 3/2; no closing date. Applicants notified on a rolling basis starting 4/1; must reply within 3 week(s) of notification.

**Transfers:** No deadline. Applicants notified on a rolling basis starting 4/1; must reply within 3 week(s) of notification.

**CONTACT**

Laurie Wheeler, Director of Student Financial Services
One Angwin Avenue, Angwin, CA 94508-9707
(707) 965-7200

## Palo Verde College

Blythe, California
www.paloverde.edu                    Federal Code: 001259

**2-year public** community college in large town.

**Enrollment:** 450 undergrads.

**Selectivity:** Open admission; but selective for some programs.

**BASIC COSTS (2015-2016)**

**Tuition and fees:** $1,380; out-of-state residents $7,890.

**Per-credit charge:** $46; out-of-state residents $263.

**FINANCIAL AID PICTURE**

**Students with need:** Need-based aid available for full-time and part-time students. Work study available nights.

**Students without need:** This college awards aid only to students with need.

**FINANCIAL AID PROCEDURES**

**Forms required:** FAFSA, state aid form, institutional form.

**Dates and Deadlines:** Applicants notified on a rolling basis starting 7/1; must reply within 4 week(s) of notification.

**CONTACT**

Diana Mendez, Financial Aid Officer
One College Drive, Blythe, CA 92225
(760) 921-5536

## Palomar College

San Marcos, California
www.palomar.edu                    Federal Code: 001260

**2-year public** community college in small city.

**Enrollment:** 12,286 undergrads.

**Selectivity:** Open admission; but selective for some programs.

**BASIC COSTS (2015-2016)**

**Tuition and fees:** $1,428; out-of-state residents $7,428.

**Per-credit charge:** $46; out-of-state residents $246.

**FINANCIAL AID PICTURE**

**Students with need:** Need-based aid available for full-time and part-time students. Work study available nights.

**Students without need:** This college awards aid only to students with need.

**FINANCIAL AID PROCEDURES**

**Forms required:** FAFSA, institutional form.

**Dates and Deadlines:** Priority date 4/1; no closing date. Applicants notified on a rolling basis starting 6/1.

**Transfers:** No deadline.

**CONTACT**

Mary San Agustin, Director of Financial Aid, Scholarships & Veterans Services
1140 West Mission Road, San Marcos, CA 92069-1487
(760) 891-7510

## Patten University

Oakland, California
www.patten.edu                    Federal Code: 004490

**4-year private** university and liberal arts college in large city, affiliated with interdenominational tradition.

**Enrollment:** 1,492 undergrads.

**Selectivity:** Open admission; but selective for some programs.

**BASIC COSTS (2015-2016)**

**Tuition and fees:** $3,432.

**FINANCIAL AID PICTURE**

**Students with need:** Need-based aid available for full-time and part-time students.

**FINANCIAL AID PROCEDURES**

**Forms required:** institutional form.

**CONTACT**

Denis Clark, Financial Aid Director
2433 Coolidge Avenue, Oakland, CA 94601-2699
(510) 261-8500 ext. 7747

## Pepperdine University

Malibu, California
www.pepperdine.edu                    Federal Code: 001264

**4-year private** university and liberal arts college in small city, affiliated with Church of Christ.

**Enrollment:** 3,514 undergrads, 8% part-time. 743 full-time freshmen.

**Selectivity:** Admits less than 50% of applicants.

**BASIC COSTS (2016-2017)**

**Tuition and fees:** $50,022.

**Per-credit charge:** $1,565.

**Room and board:** $14,330.

**FINANCIAL AID PICTURE (2015-2016)**

**Students with need:** Out of 736 full-time freshmen who applied for aid, 405 were judged to have need. Of these, 401 received aid, and 64 had their full need met. Average financial aid package met 73% of need; average scholarship/grant was $32,440; average loan was $5,774. For part-time students, average financial aid package was $28,836.

**Students without need:** 185 full-time freshmen who did not demonstrate need for aid received scholarships/grants; average award was $13,491. No-need awards available for academics, art, athletics, leadership, music/drama, religious affiliation.

**Scholarships offered:** 33 full-time freshmen received athletic scholarships; average amount $39,743.

**FINANCIAL AID PROCEDURES**

**Forms required:** FAFSA.

**Dates and Deadlines:** Closing date 2/15. Applicants notified by 4/15; must reply by 5/1.

**CONTACT**
Janet Lockhart, Director of Financial Assistance
24255 Pacific Coast Highway, Malibu, CA 90263-4392
(310) 506-4301

## Pitzer College
Claremont, California     Federal Code: 001172
www.pitzer.edu     CSS Code: 4619

**4-year private** liberal arts college in large town.
**Enrollment:** 1,067 undergrads, 3% part-time. 267 full-time freshmen.
**Selectivity:** Admits less than 50% of applicants.

**BASIC COSTS (2015-2016)**
**Tuition and fees:** $48,670.
**Room and board:** $15,210.

**FINANCIAL AID PICTURE (2015-2016)**
**Students with need:** Out of 149 full-time freshmen who applied for aid, 109 were judged to have need. Of these, 109 received aid, and 109 had their full need met. Average financial aid package met 100% of need; average scholarship/grant was $42,479; average loan was $2,631. For part-time students, average financial aid package was $25,570.
**Students without need:** 3 full-time freshmen who did not demonstrate need for aid received scholarships/grants; average award was $5,000. No-need awards available for academics, leadership, ROTC.
**Scholarships offered:** Trustee Community Scholar Award: $5,000 per year; based on extraordinary academic achievement, outstanding leadership or exceptional community service.

**FINANCIAL AID PROCEDURES**
**Forms required:** FAFSA, CSS PROFILE, state aid form.
**Dates and Deadlines:** Closing date 2/1. Applicants notified by 4/1; must reply by 5/1.
**Transfers:** Closing date 3/1. Applicants notified by 5/15; must reply by 6/15.

**CONTACT**
Robin Thompson, Director of Financial Aid
1050 North Mills Avenue, Claremont, CA 91711-6101
(909) 621-8208

## Platt College: Los Angeles
Alhambra, California
www.plattcollege.edu     Federal Code: 030627

**2-year for-profit** visual arts and technical college in very large city.
**Enrollment:** 661 undergrads.

**BASIC COSTS (2015-2016)**
**Additional info:** Medical Sciences: certificate $1,795-$31,941; associate $26,913.50-$45,798; bachelor's $24,867.50-$66,858.50. Legal Studies: certificate/diploma $26,981-$31,515.50; associate $31,816-$37,919; Bachelor's $72,936.50-$78,939.50.

**FINANCIAL AID PICTURE**
**Students with need:** Need-based aid available for full-time and part-time students. Work study available nights.

**FINANCIAL AID PROCEDURES**
**Forms required:** FAFSA, institutional form.
**Dates and Deadlines:** Priority date 3/2; no closing date. Applicants notified on a rolling basis starting 1/1.

**CONTACT**
Nina Martinez, Financial Aid Director
1000 South Fremont Avenue A9W, Alhambra, CA 91803
(626) 300-5444 ext. 230

## Platt College: Ontario
Ontario, California
www.plattcollege.edu     Federal Code: 030627

**4-year for-profit** branch campus and technical college in small city.
**Enrollment:** 431 undergrads.

**BASIC COSTS (2015-2016)**
**Additional info:** Medical Sciences: certificate $1,795-$31,941; associate $26,913.50-$45,798; bachelor's $24,867.50-$66,858.50. Legal Studies: certificate/diploma $26,981-$31,515.50; associate $31,816-$37,919; Bachelor's $72,936.50-$78,939.50.

**FINANCIAL AID PICTURE**
**Students with need:** Need-based aid available for full-time and part-time students. Work study available nights.
**Scholarships offered:** Presidential Scholarship, CAPPS Scholarship, Imagine America Scholarship: $1,000 each; based on application and essay; approximately 100 plus available per calendar year.

**FINANCIAL AID PROCEDURES**
**Forms required:** FAFSA, institutional form.
**Dates and Deadlines:** Priority date 3/2; no closing date. Applicants notified on a rolling basis starting 1/1.
**Transfers:** No deadline.

**CONTACT**
Rosemarie Young, Regional Director of Compliance and Civil Rights
3700 Inland Empire Boulevard, Ontario, CA 91764
(909) 941-9410

## Platt College: San Diego
San Diego, California
www.platt.edu     Federal Code: 023043

**4-year for-profit** visual arts and technical college in very large city.
**Enrollment:** 369 undergrads. 72 full-time freshmen.
**Selectivity:** Open admission; but selective for some programs and for out-of-state students.

**BASIC COSTS (2015-2016)**
**Additional info:** Medical Sciences: certificate $1,795-$31,941; associate $26,913.50-$45,798; bachelor's $24,867.50-$66,858.50. Legal Studies: certificate/diploma $26,981-$31,515.50; associate $31,816-$37,919; Bachelor's $72,936.50-$78,939.50.

**FINANCIAL AID PICTURE**
**Students with need:** Need-based aid available for full-time and part-time students.

**FINANCIAL AID PROCEDURES**
**Forms required:** FAFSA, state aid form, institutional form.
**Dates and Deadlines:** Closing date 3/2. Applicants notified on a rolling basis; must reply within 1 week(s) of notification.

**CONTACT**
Opel Oliver, Director of Financial Aid
6250 El Cajon Boulevard, San Diego, CA 92115
(619) 265-0107

## Point Loma Nazarene University
San Diego, California
www.pointloma.edu                    Federal Code: 001262

**4-year private** university and liberal arts college in very large city, affiliated with Church of the Nazarene.
**Enrollment:** 2,760 undergrads, 6% part-time. 587 full-time freshmen.
**Selectivity:** Admits 50 to 75% of applicants.

**BASIC COSTS (2015-2016)**
**Tuition and fees:** $32,400.
**Per-credit charge:** $1,325.
**Room and board:** $9,800.

**FINANCIAL AID PICTURE (2014-2015)**
**Students with need:** Out of 515 full-time freshmen who applied for aid, 421 were judged to have need. Of these, 421 received aid, and 77 had their full need met. Average financial aid package met 64% of need; average scholarship/grant was $16,970; average loan was $3,611. For part-time students, average financial aid package was $10,528.
**Students without need:** 104 full-time freshmen who did not demonstrate need for aid received scholarships/grants; average award was $11,553. No-need awards available for academics, art, athletics, music/drama, religious affiliation, ROTC.
**Scholarships offered:** 13 full-time freshmen received athletic scholarships; average amount $11,919.

**FINANCIAL AID PROCEDURES**
**Forms required:** FAFSA.
**Dates and Deadlines:** Priority date 3/2; no closing date. Applicants notified on a rolling basis starting 12/15; must reply by 5/15.

**CONTACT**
Pam Macias, Director of Financial Aid
3900 Lomaland Drive, San Diego, CA 92106-2899
(619) 849-2068

## Pomona College
Claremont, California              Federal Code: 001173
www.pomona.edu                          CSS Code: 4607

**4-year private** liberal arts college in large town.
**Enrollment:** 1,640 undergrads.

**BASIC COSTS (2015-2016)**
**Tuition and fees:** $47,620.
**Room and board:** $15,150.

**FINANCIAL AID PICTURE**
**Students with need:** Need-based aid available for full-time and part-time students.
**Students without need:** This college awards aid only to students with need.
**Additional info:** Financial aid awards loan-free for all eligible students.

**FINANCIAL AID PROCEDURES**
**Forms required:** FAFSA, CSS PROFILE, state aid form.
**Dates and Deadlines:** Priority date 3/1; closing date 3/1. Applicants notified by 4/1; must reply by 5/1.
**Transfers:** Closing date 3/1. Must reply by 6/1. Candidates required to submit financial aid transcript from previous institution directly to the college.

**CONTACT**
Mary Booker, Director of Financial Aid
333 North College Way, Claremont, CA 91711-6312
(909) 621-8205

## Professional Golfers Career College
Temecula, California
www.golfcollege.edu                  Federal Code: 033673

**2-year for-profit** golf academy in small city.
**Enrollment:** 311 undergrads.

**BASIC COSTS (2015-2016)**
**Tuition and fees:** $15,000.

**FINANCIAL AID PICTURE**
**Students with need:** Need-based aid available for full-time students.

**FINANCIAL AID PROCEDURES**
**Transfers:** No deadline.

**CONTACT**
Ann Martin, Financial Aid Director
26109 Ynez Road, Temecula, CA 92591
(800) 877-4380

## Providence Christian College
Pasadena, California
www.providencecc.edu

**4-year private** liberal arts college in large city, affiliated with nondenominational tradition.
**Enrollment:** 145 undergrads. 70 full-time freshmen.

**BASIC COSTS (2015-2016)**
**Tuition and fees:** $27,173.
**Per-credit charge:** $1,037.
**Room and board:** $8,213.

**FINANCIAL AID PICTURE (2015-2016)**
**Students with need:** Out of 68 full-time freshmen who applied for aid, 65 were judged to have need. Of these, 65 received aid. Average financial aid package met 60% of need; average scholarship/grant was $8,000; average loan was $5,500. For part-time students, average financial aid package was $5,000.
**Students without need:** 2 full-time freshmen who did not demonstrate need for aid received scholarships/grants; average award was $10,250. No-need awards available for academics, athletics, leadership, music/drama, religious affiliation.
**Scholarships offered:** 1 full-time freshmen received athletic scholarships; average amount $12,000.

**FINANCIAL AID PROCEDURES**
**Forms required:** FAFSA, institutional form.
**Dates and Deadlines:** Priority date 3/1; closing date 5/1. Applicants notified on a rolling basis starting 3/1; must reply by 5/1 or within 3 week(s) of notification.
**Transfers:** No deadline. Applicants notified on a rolling basis; must reply by 5/1 or within 3 week(s) of notification.

**CONTACT**
Tina Bos, Director of Financial Aid
1539 East Howard Street, Pasadena, CA 91104

## Reedley College
Reedley, California
www.reedleycollege.edu               Federal Code: 001308

**2-year public** community college in large town.
**Enrollment:** 11,184 undergrads.
**Selectivity:** Open admission.

## BASIC COSTS (2015-2016)
**Tuition and fees:** $1,420; out-of-state residents $8,470.
**Per-credit charge:** $46; out-of-state residents $281.
**Room and board:** $6,668.
**Additional info:** Tuition/fee waivers available for adults, minority students, unemployed or children of unemployed.

## FINANCIAL AID PICTURE
**Students with need:** Need-based aid available for full-time and part-time students.
**Students without need:** This college awards aid only to students with need.
**Additional info:** Board of Governors fee waiver available for low-income students. Book voucher available for EOPS students.

## FINANCIAL AID PROCEDURES
**Forms required:** FAFSA, state aid form.
**Dates and Deadlines:** Priority date 3/2; no closing date. Applicants notified on a rolling basis starting 3/2; must reply within 3 week(s) of notification.
**Transfers:** Priority date 4/15. March 2 deadline for California grants.

## CONTACT
Chris Cortes, Director of Financial Aid
995 North Reed Avenue, Reedley, CA 93654
(559) 638-3641

# Rio Hondo College
Whittier, California
www.riohondo.edu          Federal Code: 001269

**2-year public** community college in small city.
**Enrollment:** 9,113 undergrads.
**Selectivity:** Open admission; but selective for some programs.

## BASIC COSTS (2015-2016)
**Tuition and fees:** $1,452; out-of-state residents $7,452.
**Per-credit charge:** $46; out-of-state residents $246.

## FINANCIAL AID PICTURE (2014-2015)
**Students with need:** 98% of average financial aid package awarded as scholarships/grants, 2% awarded as loans/jobs. Need-based aid available for part-time students.

## FINANCIAL AID PROCEDURES
**Forms required:** FAFSA.
**Dates and Deadlines:** Priority date 7/15; no closing date. Applicants notified on a rolling basis.

## CONTACT
Yvonne Gutierrez-Sandoval, Director Financial Aid
3600 Workman Mill Road, Whittier, CA 90601-1699
(562) 908-3411

# Riverside City College
Riverside, California
www.rcc.edu          Federal Code: 001270

**2-year public** community college in large city.
**Enrollment:** 13,294 undergrads.
**Selectivity:** Open admission; but selective for some programs.

## BASIC COSTS (2015-2016)
**Tuition and fees:** $1,416; out-of-state residents $7,416.
**Per-credit charge:** $46; out-of-state residents $246.
**Additional info:** Tuition/fee waivers available for adults, unemployed or children of unemployed.

## FINANCIAL AID PICTURE
**Students with need:** Need-based aid available for full-time and part-time students. Work study available nights, weekends, and for part-time students.
**Students without need:** No-need awards available for academics, alumni affiliation, art, leadership, minority status, music/drama, state/district residency.

## FINANCIAL AID PROCEDURES
**Forms required:** FAFSA, institutional form.
**Dates and Deadlines:** Priority date 3/1; no closing date. Applicants notified on a rolling basis starting 7/1.
**Transfers:** Students who received financial aid at another institution and earned less than 2.0 GPA ineligible for aid during first semester. Students must complete 6 units and earn 2.0 GPA to be eligible.

## CONTACT
Elizabeth Hilton, Director of Student Financial Services
4800 Magnolia Avenue, Riverside, CA 92506
(951) 222-8710

# Sacramento City College
Sacramento, California
www.scc.losrios.edu          Federal Code: 001233

**2-year public** community college in large city.
**Enrollment:** 15,932 undergrads.
**Selectivity:** Open admission.

## BASIC COSTS (2015-2016)
**Tuition and fees:** $1,416; out-of-state residents $7,956.
**Per-credit charge:** $46; out-of-state residents $264.

## FINANCIAL AID PICTURE
**Students with need:** Need-based aid available for full-time and part-time students. Work study available nights, weekends, and for part-time students.

## FINANCIAL AID PROCEDURES
**Forms required:** FAFSA, state aid form.
**Dates and Deadlines:** Priority date 3/2; no closing date. Applicants notified on a rolling basis starting 7/1; must reply within 2 week(s) of notification.
**Transfers:** Priority date 5/30.

## CONTACT
Rukiya Bates, Financial Aid Supervisor
3835 Freeport Boulevard, Sacramento, CA 95822
(916) 558-2546

# Saddleback College
Mission Viejo, California
www.saddleback.edu          Federal Code: 008918

**2-year public** community college in small city.
**Enrollment:** 10,309 undergrads, 56% part-time. 1,057 full-time freshmen.
**Selectivity:** Open admission; but selective for some programs.

## BASIC COSTS (2015-2016)
**Tuition and fees:** $1,418; out-of-state residents $8,678.
**Per-credit charge:** $46; out-of-state residents $288.

## FINANCIAL AID PICTURE (2014-2015)
**Students with need:** 84% of average financial aid package awarded as scholarships/grants, 16% awarded as loans/jobs. Need-based aid available for part-time students.
**Students without need:** This college awards aid only to students with need.

## FINANCIAL AID PROCEDURES
**Forms required:** FAFSA.

**Dates and Deadlines:** Closing date 6/30. Applicants notified on a rolling basis starting 4/1.

**CONTACT**
Ruth Higgins, Interim Director, Financial Aid and Scholarships
28000 Marguerite Parkway, Mission Viejo, CA 92692
(949) 582-4860

## St. Mary's College of California
Moraga, California
www.stmarys-ca.edu                    Federal Code: 001302

**4-year private** liberal arts college in large town, affiliated with Roman Catholic Church.
**Enrollment:** 2,916 undergrads, 9% part-time. 652 full-time freshmen.
**Selectivity:** Admits over 75% of applicants.

**BASIC COSTS (2016-2017)**
**Tuition and fees:** $44,360.
**Per-credit charge:** $1,583.
**Room and board:** $14,880.

**FINANCIAL AID PICTURE (2015-2016)**
**Students with need:** Out of 547 full-time freshmen who applied for aid, 470 were judged to have need. Of these, 469 received aid, and 65 had their full need met. Average financial aid package met 72% of need; average scholarship/grant was $28,521; average loan was $3,769. For part-time students, average financial aid package was $6,000.
**Students without need:** 156 full-time freshmen who did not demonstrate need for aid received scholarships/grants; average award was $18,578. No-need awards available for academics, athletics, leadership, music/drama, religious affiliation.
**Scholarships offered:** *Merit:* Honors at Entrance Scholarship: $13,000 annually based on 3.7 GPA and 1200 SAT/27 ACT (SAT score exclusive of Writing). Presidential Scholars Scholarships: $11,000 annually based on 3.8 GPA and 1350 SAT (exclusive of writing) recipients also receive Honors at Entrance Scholarship for total of $24,000 annually. Lasallian Scholarship: $11,000 annually based on attendance at a U.S. Lasallian high school. Gael Scholarships: $11,000 annually based on students noteworthy extracurricular involvement and demanding college preparatory schedules that include rigorous senior schedules with a GPA above 3.26. All scholarships are for fall term applicants admitted by March 1. *Athletic:* 19 full-time freshmen received athletic scholarships; average amount $40,585.

**FINANCIAL AID PROCEDURES**
**Forms required:** FAFSA.
**Dates and Deadlines:** Priority date 2/15; no closing date. Applicants notified on a rolling basis starting 2/1; must reply by 5/1.
**Transfers:** Closing date 2/15. Applicants notified on a rolling basis starting 3/20; must reply by 5/1. To receive consideration for all types of financial aid, transfer students must be admitted by March 1 prior to fall term. Honors at Entrance Scholarship; $13,000 annually; based on 3.5 GPA with 30 transferable credits.

**CONTACT**
Priscilla Muha, Director of Financial Aid
Box 4800, Moraga, CA 94575-4800
(925) 631-4370

## Samuel Merritt University
Oakland, California
www.samuelmerritt.edu                Federal Code: 007012

**Upper-division private** health science and nursing college in large city.
**Enrollment:** 584 undergrads.

**Selectivity:** GED not accepted.

**BASIC COSTS (2015-2016)**
**Tuition and fees:** $44,166.
**Per-credit charge:** $1,861.

**FINANCIAL AID PICTURE**
**Students with need:** Need-based aid available for full-time and part-time students. Work study available nights, weekends, and for part-time students.
**Students without need:** No-need awards available for academics, leadership, minority status.
**Additional info:** Ongoing private scholarships available. Students eligible to work in Medical Center (associated with college).

**FINANCIAL AID PROCEDURES**
**Transfers:** Priority date 3/2; no deadline. Applicants notified on a rolling basis; must reply within 3 week(s) of notification.

**CONTACT**
Mary Robinson, Director of Financial Aid
370 Hawthorne Avenue, Oakland, CA 94609-9954
(510) 869-1550

## San Diego Christian College
Santee, California
www.sdcc.edu                          Federal Code: 012031

**4-year private** liberal arts college in small city, affiliated with nondenominational tradition.
**Enrollment:** 878 undergrads, 19% part-time. 106 full-time freshmen.
**Selectivity:** Admits 50 to 75% of applicants.

**BASIC COSTS (2016-2017)**
**Tuition and fees:** $29,550.
**Per-credit charge:** $1,210.
**Room and board:** $10,974.

**FINANCIAL AID PICTURE (2014-2015)**
**Students with need:** 96% of average financial aid package awarded as scholarships/grants, 4% awarded as loans/jobs. Need-based aid available for part-time students. Work study available nights, weekends, and for part-time students.
**Students without need:** No-need awards available for academics, alumni affiliation, athletics, leadership, music/drama, state/district residency.
**Scholarships offered:** Early Acceptance Award: $1000: available to applicants who have turned in all admission materials by January 15th.

**FINANCIAL AID PROCEDURES**
**Forms required:** FAFSA, state aid form, institutional form.
**Dates and Deadlines:** Priority date 3/2; closing date 7/15. Applicants notified on a rolling basis starting 4/1; must reply by 5/1 or within 4 week(s) of notification.
**Transfers:** Applicants notified on a rolling basis starting 4/1; must reply by 5/1 or within 4 week(s) of notification. Transfer students with at least 30 units earned at one institution fall under a different Academic Scholarship awarding grid than first time freshman.

**CONTACT**
Daniel Reed, Director of Financial Aid
200 Riverview Parkway, Santee, CA 92071-5822
(619) 201-8730

## San Diego City College
San Diego, California
www.sdcity.edu                        Federal Code: 001273

**2-year public** community and junior college in very large city.
**Enrollment:** 9,977 undergrads.

**Selectivity:** Open admission.

**BASIC COSTS (2015-2016)**
**Tuition and fees:** $1,418; out-of-state residents $7,208.
**Per-credit charge:** $46; out-of-state residents $239.
**Additional info:** Tuition/fee waivers available for unemployed or children of unemployed.

**FINANCIAL AID PICTURE (2014-2015)**
**Students with need:** 90% of average financial aid package awarded as scholarships/grants, 10% awarded as loans/jobs. Need-based aid available for part-time students.
**Students without need:** This college awards aid only to students with need.

**FINANCIAL AID PROCEDURES**
**Forms required:** FAFSA.
**Dates and Deadlines:** Priority date 4/15; no closing date. Applicants notified on a rolling basis starting 7/1; must reply within 4 week(s) of notification.
**Transfers:** No deadline. Applicants notified on a rolling basis starting 7/1. Aid is limited to remaining eligibility based on receipt of aid from previous college.

**CONTACT**
Greg Sanchez, Financial Aid Manager
1313 Park Boulevard, San Diego, CA 92101-4787
(619) 388-3501

## San Diego Mesa College
San Diego, California
www.sdmesa.edu                    Federal Code: 001275

**2-year public** community college in very large city.
**Enrollment:** 15,343 undergrads.
**Selectivity:** Open admission.

**BASIC COSTS (2015-2016)**
**Tuition and fees:** $1,418; out-of-state residents $7,208.
**Per-credit charge:** $46; out-of-state residents $239.

**FINANCIAL AID PICTURE (2014-2015)**
**Students with need:** Need-based aid available for full-time and part-time students.
**Students without need:** This college awards aid only to students with need.

**FINANCIAL AID PROCEDURES**
**Forms required:** FAFSA.
**Dates and Deadlines:** Priority date 3/2; no closing date. Applicants notified on a rolling basis starting 6/15; must reply within 3 week(s) of notification.
**Transfers:** No deadline.

**CONTACT**
Gilda Maldonado, Financial Aid Officer
7250 Mesa College Drive, San Diego, CA 92111
(619) 388-2817

## San Diego Miramar College
San Diego, California
www.sdmiramar.edu                    Federal Code: 014172

**2-year public** community college in very large city.
**Enrollment:** 11,710 undergrads.
**Selectivity:** Open admission.

**BASIC COSTS (2015-2016)**
**Tuition and fees:** $1,437; out-of-state residents $7,227.
**Per-credit charge:** $46; out-of-state residents $239.

**Additional info:** Tuition/fee waivers available for unemployed or children of unemployed.

**FINANCIAL AID PICTURE**
**Students with need:** Need-based aid available for full-time and part-time students.
**Additional info:** Private scholarships available.

**FINANCIAL AID PROCEDURES**
**Forms required:** FAFSA.
**Dates and Deadlines:** Priority date 3/2; closing date 6/30. Applicants notified on a rolling basis; must reply within 3 week(s) of notification.
**Transfers:** No deadline. Transfers advised to apply early.

**CONTACT**
Adela Jacobson, Financial Aid Officer
10440 Black Mountain Road, San Diego, CA 92126-2999
(619) 388-7864

## San Diego State University
San Diego, California
www.sdsu.edu                    Federal Code: 001151

**4-year public** university in very large city.
**Enrollment:** 29,234 undergrads, 11% part-time. 4,955 full-time freshmen.
**Selectivity:** Admits less than 50% of applicants.

**BASIC COSTS (2015-2016)**
**Tuition and fees:** $6,976; out-of-state residents $18,136.
**Room and board:** $15,826.

**FINANCIAL AID PICTURE (2015-2016)**
**Students with need:** Out of 3,700 full-time freshmen who applied for aid, 2,600 were judged to have need. Of these, 2,500 received aid, and 260 had their full need met. Average financial aid package met 66% of need; average scholarship/grant was $10,000; average loan was $3,200. For part-time students, average financial aid package was $7,900.
**Students without need:** 100 full-time freshmen who did not demonstrate need for aid received scholarships/grants; average award was $4,900. No-need awards available for academics, alumni affiliation, art, athletics, leadership, music/drama, ROTC, state/district residency.
**Scholarships offered:** 100 full-time freshmen received athletic scholarships; average amount $16,000.

**FINANCIAL AID PROCEDURES**
**Forms required:** FAFSA, state aid form.
**Dates and Deadlines:** Priority date 4/1; closing date 3/2. Applicants notified on a rolling basis starting 3/15.
**Transfers:** Applicants notified on a rolling basis starting 3/15.

**CONTACT**
Rose Pasenelli, Director of Financial Aid
5500 Campanile Drive, San Diego, CA 92182-7455
(619) 594-6323

## San Francisco Art Institute
San Francisco, California
www.sfai.edu                    Federal Code: 003948

**4-year private** visual arts college in very large city.
**Enrollment:** 404 undergrads, 6% part-time. 85 full-time freshmen.
**Selectivity:** Admits 50 to 75% of applicants.

**BASIC COSTS (2015-2016)**
**Tuition and fees:** $41,272.
**Per-credit charge:** $1,770.
**Room and board:** $15,666.

## FINANCIAL AID PICTURE (2015-2016)

**Students with need:** Out of 57 full-time freshmen who applied for aid, 50 were judged to have need. Of these, 50 received aid. Average financial aid package met 50% of need; average scholarship/grant was $5,060; average loan was $1,730. For part-time students, average financial aid package was $9,346.

**Students without need:** 28 full-time freshmen who did not demonstrate need for aid received scholarships/grants; average award was $6,547. No-need awards available for academics, alumni affiliation, art.

**Scholarships offered:** Several awards based on portfolio reviews during application for admissions process.

## FINANCIAL AID PROCEDURES

**Forms required:** FAFSA.

**Dates and Deadlines:** Priority date 3/1; no closing date. Applicants notified on a rolling basis starting 3/1; must reply within 2 week(s) of notification.

**Transfers:** Priority date 3/2; no deadline. Applicants notified on a rolling basis starting 4/1; must reply within 3 week(s) of notification.

## CONTACT

Annita Alldredge, Director of Financial Aid

SFAI - Admissions Office, San Francisco, CA 94133

(415) 749-4520

# San Francisco Conservatory of Music

San Francisco, California        Federal Code: 001278

www.sfcm.edu                     CSS Code: 4744

**4-year private** music college in very large city.

**Enrollment:** 157 undergrads, 1% part-time. 33 full-time freshmen.

**Selectivity:** Admits less than 50% of applicants.

## BASIC COSTS (2015-2016)

**Tuition and fees:** $42,210.

**Per-credit charge:** $1,816.

**Room only:** $11,900.

**Additional info:** Municipal Transportation Fee is now included within the Comprehensive fee, included within the Required Fees.

## FINANCIAL AID PICTURE (2015-2016)

**Students with need:** Out of 32 full-time freshmen who applied for aid, 31 were judged to have need. Of these, 31 received aid, and 9 had their full need met. Average financial aid package met 47% of need; average scholarship/grant was $21,500; average loan was $5,508. For part-time students, average financial aid package was $11,413.

**Students without need:** 6 full-time freshmen who did not demonstrate need for aid received scholarships/grants; average award was $14,000. No-need awards available for music/drama.

## FINANCIAL AID PROCEDURES

**Forms required:** FAFSA. CSS/Financial Aid PROFILE required of international applicants for any need-based scholarship funding. The school code for this is: 4744.

**Dates and Deadlines:** Priority date 2/15; closing date 3/1. Applicants notified on a rolling basis starting 4/1; must reply within 2 week(s) of notification.

**Transfers:** Applicants notified on a rolling basis starting 4/1; must reply within 2 week(s) of notification.

## CONTACT

Doris Howard, Director of Financial Aid

50 Oak Street, San Francisco, CA 94102

(415) 503-6235

# San Francisco State University

San Francisco, California

www.sfsu.edu                     Federal Code: 001154

**4-year public** university in very large city.

**Enrollment:** 25,867 undergrads, 15% part-time. 3,932 full-time freshmen.

**Selectivity:** Admits 50 to 75% of applicants.

## BASIC COSTS (2015-2016)

**Tuition and fees:** $6,476; out-of-state residents $17,636.

**Room and board:** $13,434.

**Additional info:** Excluded from the required fees is an optional fee of $2.00 (Student Involvement and Representation Fee). For 2015-2016: Room Only (on campus): $8,090; Board Only (On campus meal plan): $4,144 for all undergraduates, including first-time freshmen.

## FINANCIAL AID PICTURE (2015-2016)

**Students with need:** Out of 3,478 full-time freshmen who applied for aid, 2,897 were judged to have need. Of these, 2,742 received aid, and 823 had their full need met. Average financial aid package met 76% of need; average scholarship/grant was $9,203; average loan was $3,331. For part-time students, average financial aid package was $11,198.

**Students without need:** This college awards aid only to students with need.

**Scholarships offered:** *Merit:* Presidential Scholarship: 3.8 GPA and California residency required. *Athletic:* 26 full-time freshmen received athletic scholarships; average amount $7,001.

## FINANCIAL AID PROCEDURES

**Forms required:** FAFSA.

**Dates and Deadlines:** Priority date 3/2; no closing date. Applicants notified on a rolling basis starting 4/15; must reply by 4/15 or within 2 week(s) of notification.

## CONTACT

Barbara Hubler, Director of Financial Aid

1600 Holloway Avenue, San Francisco, CA 94132

(415) 338-7000

# San Joaquin Delta College

Stockton, California

www.deltacollege.edu             Federal Code: 001280

**2-year public** community college in large city.

**Enrollment:** 14,373 undergrads, 58% part-time. 8,067 full-time freshmen.

**Selectivity:** Open admission; but selective for some programs.

## BASIC COSTS (2015-2016)

**Tuition and fees:** $1,380; out-of-state residents $7,950.

**Per-credit charge:** $46; out-of-state residents $265.

## FINANCIAL AID PICTURE (2014-2015)

**Students with need:** Out of 8,067 full-time freshmen who applied for aid, 6,516 were judged to have need. Of these, 5,290 received aid, and 7 had their full need met. Average financial aid package met 31% of need; average scholarship/grant was $5,180; average loan was $2,633. For part-time students, average financial aid package was $4,704.

**Students without need:** No-need awards available for academics, athletics.

**Additional info:** Enrollment fee waivers available for low-income California residents.

## FINANCIAL AID PROCEDURES

**Forms required:** FAFSA, institutional form.

**Dates and Deadlines:** Closing date 6/30. Applicants notified on a rolling basis starting 4/1; must reply within 3 week(s) of notification.

**Transfers:** No deadline.

## CONTACT

Tina Lent, Director of Financial Aid, Scholarships & Veterans Services
5151 Pacific Avenue, Stockton, CA 95207-6370
(209) 954-5115

# San Joaquin Valley College

Visalia, California
www.sjvc.edu                          Federal Code: 021207

**2-year for-profit** junior college in small city.
**Enrollment:** 1,892 undergrads.
**Selectivity:** Open admission; but selective for some programs.

## BASIC COSTS (2015-2016)

**Additional info:** Certificate programs range from $14,415-$40,500, Associates programs range from $28,830-$58,970, books and supplies included in tuition.

## FINANCIAL AID PICTURE

**Students with need:** Need-based aid available for full-time students.

## FINANCIAL AID PROCEDURES

**Forms required:** FAFSA, state aid form, institutional form.

## CONTACT

Kevin Robinson, Vice President of Student Financial Services
8400 West Mineral King Avenue, Visalia, CA 93291-9283
(559) 651-2500

# San Jose City College

San Jose, California
www.sjcc.edu                          Federal Code: 001282

**2-year public** community college in very large city.
**Enrollment:** 4,833 undergrads.
**Selectivity:** Open admission.

## BASIC COSTS (2015-2016)

**Tuition and fees:** $1,418; out-of-state residents $7,538.
**Per-credit charge:** $46; out-of-state residents $250.

## FINANCIAL AID PICTURE

**Students with need:** Need-based aid available for full-time and part-time students.
**Students without need:** This college awards aid only to students with need.
**Additional info:** Board of Governors Grant (fee waivers) available to all qualified applicants.

## FINANCIAL AID PROCEDURES

**Forms required:** FAFSA.
**Dates and Deadlines:** Applicants notified on a rolling basis; must reply within 4 week(s) of notification.

## CONTACT

Takeo Kubo, Dean of Enrollment Services
2100 Moorpark Avenue, San Jose, CA 95128-2798
(408) 288-3741

# San Jose State University

San Jose, California
www.sjsu.edu                          Federal Code: 001155

**4-year public** university and liberal arts college in very large city.
**Enrollment:** 26,822 undergrads, 19% part-time. 3,620 full-time freshmen.

**Selectivity:** Admits 50 to 75% of applicants.

## BASIC COSTS (2015-2016)

**Tuition and fees:** $7,378; out-of-state residents $18,538.
**Room and board:** $14,217.

## FINANCIAL AID PICTURE (2014-2015)

**Students with need:** Out of 2,757 full-time freshmen who applied for aid, 2,347 were judged to have need. Of these, 2,255 received aid, and 1,419 had their full need met. Average financial aid package met 88% of need; average scholarship/grant was $9,354; average loan was $7,595. For part-time students, average financial aid package was $16,363.
**Students without need:** This college awards aid only to students with need.
**Scholarships offered:** 10 full-time freshmen received athletic scholarships; average amount $16,096.

## FINANCIAL AID PROCEDURES

**Forms required:** FAFSA.
**Dates and Deadlines:** Priority date 3/2; closing date 6/15.

## CONTACT

Coleetta Mcelroy, Director of Financial Aid & Scholarships
One Washington Square, San Jose, CA 95192-0016
(408) 283-7500

# Santa Barbara City College

Santa Barbara, California
www.sbcc.edu                          Federal Code: 001285

**2-year public** community college in small city.
**Enrollment:** 13,699 undergrads.
**Selectivity:** Open admission; but selective for some programs.

## BASIC COSTS (2015-2016)

**Tuition and fees:** $1,478; out-of-state residents $9,458.
**Per-credit charge:** $46; out-of-state residents $312.
**Additional info:** Tuition/fee waivers available for unemployed or children of unemployed.

## FINANCIAL AID PICTURE

**Students with need:** Need-based aid available for full-time and part-time students.
**Additional info:** California residents may qualify for Board of Governor's Financial Assistance Program, which will allow institutions to waive enrollment fee.

## FINANCIAL AID PROCEDURES

**Forms required:** FAFSA.
**Dates and Deadlines:** Applicants notified on a rolling basis starting 5/1; must reply within 2 week(s) of notification.

## CONTACT

Brad Hardison, Director of Financial Aid
721 Cliff Drive, Santa Barbara, CA 93109-2394
(805) 965-0581 ext. 2716

# Santa Clara University

Santa Clara, California                Federal Code: 001326
www.scu.edu                            CSS Code: 4851

**4-year private** university in small city, affiliated with Roman Catholic Church.
**Enrollment:** 5,344 undergrads, 1% part-time. 1,261 full-time freshmen.
**Selectivity:** Admits less than 50% of applicants.

## BASIC COSTS (2015-2016)

**Tuition and fees:** $45,300.
**Room and board:** $13,425.

## FINANCIAL AID PICTURE (2015-2016)
**Students with need:** Out of 761 full-time freshmen who applied for aid, 515 were judged to have need. Of these, 494 received aid, and 216 had their full need met. Average financial aid package met 81% of need; average scholarship/grant was $26,964; average loan was $3,394. Need-based aid available for part-time students.
**Students without need:** 304 full-time freshmen who did not demonstrate need for aid received scholarships/grants; average award was $14,523. No-need awards available for academics, athletics, music/drama, ROTC.
**Scholarships offered:** 62 full-time freshmen received athletic scholarships; average amount $32,101.

## FINANCIAL AID PROCEDURES
**Forms required:** FAFSA, CSS PROFILE.
**Dates and Deadlines:** Priority date 2/1; no closing date. Applicants notified by 4/1; must reply by 5/1 or within 2 week(s) of notification.
**Transfers:** No deadline. Applicants notified on a rolling basis starting 4/1; must reply by 5/1 or within 2 week(s) of notification.

## CONTACT
Dean of Financial Services
500 El Camino Real, Santa Clara, CA 95053
(408) 554-4505

# Santa Monica College
Santa Monica, California
www.smc.edu                    Federal Code: 001286

**2-year public** community college in small city.
**Enrollment:** 24,770 undergrads.
**Selectivity:** Open admission; but selective for some programs.

## BASIC COSTS (2015-2016)
**Tuition and fees:** $1,444; out-of-state residents $10,114.
**Per-credit charge:** $46; out-of-state residents $335.

## FINANCIAL AID PICTURE
**Students with need:** Need-based aid available for full-time and part-time students.

## FINANCIAL AID PROCEDURES
**Forms required:** FAFSA, institutional form.
**Dates and Deadlines:** Applicants notified on a rolling basis starting 7/1; must reply within 2 week(s) of notification.
**Transfers:** No deadline.

## CONTACT
Steve Myrow, Director of Financial Aid
1900 Pico Boulevard, Santa Monica, CA 90405-1628
(310) 434-4343

# Santa Rosa Junior College
Santa Rosa, California
www.santarosa.edu              Federal Code: 001287

**2-year public** community college in small city.
**Enrollment:** 12,640 undergrads.
**Selectivity:** Open admission; but selective for some programs.

## BASIC COSTS (2015-2016)
**Tuition and fees:** $1,420; out-of-state residents $7,330.
**Per-credit charge:** $46; out-of-state residents $243.

## FINANCIAL AID PICTURE
**Students with need:** Need-based aid available for full-time and part-time students. Work study available nights.

**Students without need:** No-need awards available for academics, art, leadership, music/drama, state/district residency.
**Additional info:** California's Board of Governors Program provides fee waivers for applicants with need.

## FINANCIAL AID PROCEDURES
**Forms required:** FAFSA.
**Dates and Deadlines:** Priority date 3/1; no closing date. Applicants notified on a rolling basis starting 4/15.

## CONTACT
Jana Cox, Director of Financial Services
1501 Mendocino Avenue, Santa Rosa, CA 95401-4395
(707) 521-7948

# Santiago Canyon College
Orange, California
www.sccollege.edu

**2-year public** community college in small city.
**Enrollment:** 4,662 undergrads.
**Selectivity:** Open admission.

## BASIC COSTS (2015-2016)
**Tuition and fees:** $1,418; out-of-state residents $8,018.
**Per-credit charge:** $46; out-of-state residents $266.
**Additional info:** Tuition/fee waivers available for adults, minority students, unemployed or children of unemployed.

## FINANCIAL AID PICTURE
**Students with need:** Need-based aid available for full-time and part-time students.
**Students without need:** This college awards aid only to students with need.

## FINANCIAL AID PROCEDURES
**Forms required:** FAFSA, state aid form, institutional form.
**Dates and Deadlines:** Priority date 7/1; no closing date. Applicants notified on a rolling basis starting 6/1.
**Transfers:** No deadline. Applicants notified by 6/1.

## CONTACT
Syed Rizvi, Associate Dean of Student Support Services
8045 East Chapman Avenue, Orange, CA 92869
(714) 628-4876

# Scripps College
Claremont, California            Federal Code: 001174
www.scrippscollege.edu           CSS Code: 4693

**4-year private** liberal arts college for women in large town.
**Enrollment:** 968 undergrads. 249 full-time freshmen.
**Selectivity:** Admits less than 50% of applicants.

## BASIC COSTS (2015-2016)
**Tuition and fees:** $49,152.
**Room and board:** $15,108.

## FINANCIAL AID PICTURE (2014-2015)
**Students with need:** Out of 141 full-time freshmen who applied for aid, 88 were judged to have need. Of these, 88 received aid, and 88 had their full need met. Average financial aid package met 100% of need; average scholarship/grant was $37,042; average loan was $3,060. For part-time students, average financial aid package was $24,082.
**Students without need:** 53 full-time freshmen who did not demonstrate need for aid received scholarships/grants; average award was $15,576. No-need awards available for academics, leadership.

**Scholarships offered:** James E. Scripps Scholarship: variable amount up to half-tuition; renewable; for distinguished young women whose intellectual and personal promise can be developed with a Scripps education.

### FINANCIAL AID PROCEDURES
**Forms required:** FAFSA, CSS PROFILE, state aid form.
**Dates and Deadlines:** Closing date 2/1. Applicants notified by 4/1; must reply by 5/1.
**Transfers:** Priority date 4/1. Applicants notified by 5/1; must reply by 6/1. Students applying for admission as a transfer student should be aware that financial aid may be limited or unavailable.

### CONTACT
Patrick Moore, Director of Financial Aid
1030 Columbia Avenue, Claremont, CA 91711-3905
(909) 621-8275

## Shasta Bible College and Graduate School
Redding, California
www.shasta.edu                    Federal Code: 016802

**4-year private** Bible and seminary college in small city, affiliated with Baptist faith.
**Enrollment:** 51 undergrads.

### BASIC COSTS (2015-2016)
**Tuition and fees:** $11,260.
**Per-credit charge:** $350.
**Room only:** $2,800.

### FINANCIAL AID PICTURE
**Students with need:** Need-based aid available for full-time and part-time students.
**Students without need:** No-need awards available for music/drama.

### FINANCIAL AID PROCEDURES
**Forms required:** FAFSA.
**Dates and Deadlines:** Closing date 8/1. Applicants notified on a rolling basis.

### CONTACT
Linda Iles, Financial Aid Director
2951 Goodwater Avenue, Redding, CA 96002
(530) 221-4275 ext. 32

## Shasta College
Redding, California
www.shastacollege.edu                Federal Code: 001289

**2-year public** community and junior college in small city.
**Enrollment:** 6,056 undergrads.
**Selectivity:** Open admission; but selective for some programs.

### BASIC COSTS (2015-2016)
**Tuition and fees:** $1,418; out-of-state residents $7,718.
**Per-credit charge:** $46; out-of-state residents $256.

### FINANCIAL AID PICTURE
**Students with need:** Need-based aid available for full-time and part-time students.
**Students without need:** This college awards aid only to students with need.

### FINANCIAL AID PROCEDURES
**Forms required:** FAFSA, institutional form.

**Dates and Deadlines:** Priority date 3/2; no closing date. Applicants notified on a rolling basis starting 7/1.

### CONTACT
Benna Starrett, Director of Financial Aid
Box 496006, Redding, CA 96049-6006
(530) 225-4735

## Sierra College
Rocklin, California
www.sierracollege.edu                Federal Code: 001290

**2-year public** community college in small city.
**Enrollment:** 13,800 undergrads.
**Selectivity:** Open admission; but selective for some programs.

### BASIC COSTS (2015-2016)
**Tuition and fees:** $1,428; out-of-state residents $7,428.
**Per-credit charge:** $46; out-of-state residents $245.
**Room and board:** $7,400.

### FINANCIAL AID PICTURE
**Students with need:** Need-based aid available for full-time and part-time students. Work study available nights, weekends, and for part-time students.

### FINANCIAL AID PROCEDURES
**Forms required:** FAFSA.
**Dates and Deadlines:** Priority date 3/2; no closing date. Applicants notified on a rolling basis starting 5/15.
**Transfers:** No deadline.

### CONTACT
Linda Williams, Financial Aid Program Manager
5000 Rocklin Road, Rocklin, CA 95677-3397
(916) 660-7310

## Simpson University
Redding, California
www.simpsonu.edu                    Federal Code: 001291

**4-year private** university in small city, affiliated with Christian and Missionary Alliance.
**Enrollment:** 959 undergrads, 3% part-time. 88 full-time freshmen.
**Selectivity:** Admits 50 to 75% of applicants.

### BASIC COSTS (2015-2016)
**Tuition and fees:** $25,200.
**Per-credit charge:** $1,050.
**Room and board:** $8,050.
**Additional info:** Tuition/fee waivers available for minority students.

### FINANCIAL AID PICTURE (2015-2016)
**Students with need:** Out of 88 full-time freshmen who applied for aid, 77 were judged to have need. Of these, 77 received aid, and 7 had their full need met. Average financial aid package met 73% of need; average scholarship/grant was $17,794; average loan was $3,392. For part-time students, average financial aid package was $8,022.
**Students without need:** 8 full-time freshmen who did not demonstrate need for aid received scholarships/grants; average award was $11,447. No-need awards available for academics, alumni affiliation, athletics, leadership, minority status, music/drama, religious affiliation, state/district residency.
**Scholarships offered:** 3 full-time freshmen received athletic scholarships; average amount $15,500.
**Additional info:** Work-study programs available.

### FINANCIAL AID PROCEDURES
**Forms required:** FAFSA, state aid form.

**Dates and Deadlines:** Priority date 3/2; no closing date. Applicants notified on a rolling basis starting 3/2.

**CONTACT**
Melissa Hudson, Director of Financial Aid
2211 College View Drive, Redding, CA 96003-8606
(530) 226-4111

## Skyline College
San Bruno, California
www.skylinecollege.edu          Federal Code: 007713

**2-year public** community college in small city.
**Enrollment:** 4,911 undergrads, 68% part-time. 353 full-time freshmen.
**Selectivity:** Open admission; but selective for some programs.

**BASIC COSTS (2015-2016)**
**Tuition and fees:** $1,446; out-of-state residents $8,076.
**Per-credit charge:** $46; out-of-state residents $267.

**FINANCIAL AID PICTURE (2014-2015)**
**Students with need:** For part-time students, average financial aid package was $1,457.

**FINANCIAL AID PROCEDURES**
**Forms required:** FAFSA, institutional form.
**Dates and Deadlines:** Priority date 5/2; no closing date. Applicants notified on a rolling basis starting 5/1; must reply within 2 week(s) of notification.

**CONTACT**
Regina Morrison, Director of Financial Aid
3300 College Drive, San Bruno, CA 94066-1662
(650) 738-4236

## Soka University of America
Aliso Viejo, California
www.soka.edu          Federal Code: 038144

**4-year private** university and liberal arts college in large town.
**Enrollment:** 433 undergrads. 127 full-time freshmen.
**Selectivity:** Admits less than 50% of applicants.

**BASIC COSTS (2016-2017)**
**Tuition and fees:** $29,372.
**Per-credit charge:** $1,224.
**Room and board:** $11,812.

**FINANCIAL AID PICTURE (2015-2016)**
**Students with need:** Out of 127 full-time freshmen who applied for aid, 112 were judged to have need. Of these, 112 received aid, and 112 had their full need met. Average financial aid package met 100% of need; average scholarship/grant was $24,750; average loan was $5,369. For part-time students, average financial aid package was $10,830.
**Students without need:** 9 full-time freshmen who did not demonstrate need for aid received scholarships/grants; average award was $12,333. No-need awards available for academics, athletics, leadership, minority status.
**Scholarships offered:** *Merit:* Global Merit Scholarship: Full Ride (up to cost of attendance); annually; renewable up to 8 semesters. Soka Merit Scholarship: renewable up to 8 semesters. Makiguchi Scholarship: Full Ride (up to cost of attendance); annually; renewable up to 8 semesters; to one international applicant who has graduated from high school in an African nation.
*Athletic:* 5 full-time freshmen received athletic scholarships; average amount $6,399.
**Additional info:** All admitted students whose annual family income is $60,000 or less qualify for Soka Opportunity Scholarship, which covers full

tuition. All admitted students to the BA in Liberal Arts program will be considered for additional scholarship opportunities for higher income levels. 100% of continuing students who were eligible for need-based financial assistance received a need-based scholarship or grant.

**FINANCIAL AID PROCEDURES**
**Forms required:** FAFSA, state aid form.
**Dates and Deadlines:** Priority date 2/15; closing date 3/2. Applicants notified on a rolling basis starting 3/15; must reply by 5/1 or within 4 week(s) of notification.
**Transfers:** Must reply by 5/1 or within 4 week(s) of notification.

**CONTACT**
Stacey Choi, Manager of Financial Aid
One University Drive, Aliso Viejo, CA 92656-8081
(949) 480-4342

## Sonoma State University
Rohnert Park, California
www.sonoma.edu          Federal Code: 001156

**4-year public** university and liberal arts college in large town.
**Enrollment:** 8,550 undergrads, 14% part-time. 1,461 full-time freshmen.

**BASIC COSTS (2015-2016)**
**Tuition and fees:** $7,324; out-of-state residents $18,484.
**Room and board:** $12,814.

**FINANCIAL AID PICTURE**
**Students with need:** Need-based aid available for full-time and part-time students.
**Students without need:** No-need awards available for academics, alumni affiliation, art, athletics, leadership, minority status, music/drama.
**Additional info:** Pell Grant recipients see no increase in their fees, students with family incomes of $75,000 or less will pay no fees at all.

**FINANCIAL AID PROCEDURES**
**Forms required:** FAFSA.
**Dates and Deadlines:** Priority date 1/31; no closing date. Applicants notified on a rolling basis starting 3/25; must reply within 2 week(s) of notification.

**CONTACT**
Susan Gutierrez, Director, Financial Aid
1801 East Cotati Avenue, Rohnert Park, CA 94928-3609
(707) 664-2389

## Southern California Institute of Architecture
Los Angeles, California
www.sciarc.edu          Federal Code: 014073

**5-year private** visual arts college in very large city.
**Enrollment:** 255 undergrads. 34 full-time freshmen.
**Selectivity:** Admits 50 to 75% of applicants.

**BASIC COSTS (2015-2016)**
**Tuition and fees:** $42,220.

**FINANCIAL AID PICTURE (2014-2015)**
**Students with need:** Out of 8 full-time freshmen who applied for aid, 8 were judged to have need. Of these, 8 received aid, and 2 had their full need met. Average financial aid package met 5% of need; average scholarship/grant was $13,294. Need-based aid available for part-time students.
**Students without need:** 3 full-time freshmen who did not demonstrate need for aid received scholarships/grants; average award was $15,000. No-need awards available for academics, state/district residency.

**FINANCIAL AID PROCEDURES**
**Forms required:** FAFSA, institutional form.
**Dates and Deadlines:** Closing date 3/2. Applicants notified on a rolling basis starting 3/15; must reply within 3 week(s) of notification.
**Transfers:** Applicants notified on a rolling basis starting 3/15; must reply within 3 week(s) of notification.

**CONTACT**
Christopher Banks, Finance Director
960 E 3rd Street, Los Angeles, CA 90013
(213) 356-5376

## Southwestern College
Chula Vista, California
www.swccd.edu          Federal Code: 001294

**2-year public** community college in small city.
**Enrollment:** 11,472 undergrads.
**Selectivity:** Open admission; but selective for some programs.

**BASIC COSTS (2015-2016)**
**Tuition and fees:** $1,428; out-of-state residents $7,218.
**Per-credit charge:** $46; out-of-state residents $239.

**FINANCIAL AID PICTURE**
**Students with need:** Need-based aid available for full-time and part-time students. Work study available nights, weekends, and for part-time students.

**FINANCIAL AID PROCEDURES**
**Forms required:** FAFSA.
**Dates and Deadlines:** Applicants notified on a rolling basis starting 7/1.

**CONTACT**
Patti Larkin, Director of Financial Aid
900 Otay Lakes Road, Chula Vista, CA 91910-7297
(619) 482-6357

## Stanbridge College
Irvine, California
www.stanbridge.edu

**4-year for-profit** health science and technical college in large city.
**Enrollment:** 926 undergrads.
**Selectivity:** Open admission; but selective for some programs.

**BASIC COSTS (2015-2016)**
**Comprehensive fee:** $34,995.
**Additional info:** Tuition at time of enrollment locked for 4 years.

**FINANCIAL AID PICTURE**
**Students with need:** Need-based aid available for full-time and part-time students.
**Students without need:** This college awards aid only to students with need.

**FINANCIAL AID PROCEDURES**
**Forms required:** FAFSA, state aid form, institutional form.
**Dates and Deadlines:** Closing date 3/2. Applicants notified on a rolling basis starting 1/1; must reply by 2/15 or within 6 week(s) of notification.
**Transfers:** Priority date 1/1. Applicants notified on a rolling basis starting 1/1; must reply by 2/15 or within 6 week(s) of notification.

**CONTACT**
Brian Silvano, Director of HR & Financial Services
2041 Business Center Drive, Suite 107, Irvine, CA 92612

## Stanford University
Stanford, California          Federal Code: 001305
www.stanford.edu             CSS Code: 4704

**4-year private** university and liberal arts college in small city.
**Enrollment:** 6,994 undergrads. 1,678 full-time freshmen.
**Selectivity:** Admits less than 50% of applicants.

**BASIC COSTS (2015-2016)**
**Tuition and fees:** $46,320.
**Room and board:** $14,107.

**FINANCIAL AID PICTURE (2014-2015)**
**Students with need:** Out of 997 full-time freshmen who applied for aid, 811 were judged to have need. Of these, 790 received aid, and 738 had their full need met. Average financial aid package met 100% of need; average scholarship/grant was $43,291; average loan was $2,580. Need-based aid available for part-time students.
**Students without need:** No-need awards available for athletics.
**Scholarships offered:** *Merit:* SoFi Parent Loan program provides a non-federal education loan option for parents of undergraduate students. *Athletic:* 116 full-time freshmen received athletic scholarships; average amount $30,902.
**Additional info:** For parents with total annual income below $65,000 and typical assets for this income range, parent contribution toward educational costs not expected. Students will still be expected to contribute from their income and savings. For parents with total annual income below $125,000 and typical assets for this income range, the expected parent contribution will be low enough to ensure that all tuition charges are covered with need-based scholarship, federal and state grants, and/or outside scholarship funds. Families with incomes at higher levels (typically up to $200,000) may also qualify for assistance, especially if more than one family member is enrolled in college.

**FINANCIAL AID PROCEDURES**
**Forms required:** FAFSA, CSS PROFILE.
**Dates and Deadlines:** Priority date 2/15; no closing date. Applicants notified on a rolling basis starting 4/1; must reply by 5/1.
**Transfers:** Priority date 3/15.

**CONTACT**
Karen Cooper, Director, Financial Aid
Montag Hall, Stanford, CA 94305-6106
(650) 723-3058

## SUM Bible College & Theological Seminary
Oakland, California
www.sum.edu          Federal Code: 037524

**4-year private** Bible and seminary college in very large city, affiliated with Assemblies of God.
**Enrollment:** 446 undergrads, 15% part-time. 7 full-time freshmen.
**Selectivity:** Open admission; but selective for some programs.

**BASIC COSTS (2015-2016)**
**Tuition and fees:** $8,400.
**Per-credit charge:** $260.
**Room only:** $2,400.
**Additional info:** Additional $520 charge for those required to attend the Mardi Gras practicum. Board plan not available.

**FINANCIAL AID PICTURE**
**Students with need:** Need-based aid available for full-time and part-time students.
**Students without need:** No-need awards available for academics, leadership, religious affiliation.

## FINANCIAL AID PROCEDURES
**Forms required:** FAFSA.
**Transfers:** No deadline. Applicants notified on a rolling basis.

## CONTACT
Kathryn Mangan, Financial Aid Director
735 105th Avenue, Oakland, CA 94603
(510) 567-6174

## Taft College
Taft, California
www.taftcollege.edu                    Federal Code: 001309

**2-year public** community college in small town.
**Enrollment:** 2,284 undergrads.
**Selectivity:** Open admission.

## BASIC COSTS (2015-2016)
**Tuition and fees:** $1,380; out-of-state residents $7,380.
**Per-credit charge:** $46; out-of-state residents $246.
**Room and board:** $4,707.

## FINANCIAL AID PICTURE
**Students with need:** Need-based aid available for full-time and part-time students. Work study available nights.
**Students without need:** No-need awards available for academics.
**Scholarships offered:** Taft College Merit Awards: $250; for students from local high schools; available for 2 years; based on GPA of 3.0 or higher. Taft College High School Merit Award: $600; for students from local high schools. Taft College Nonresident Awards: $4,230; applied to nonresident tuition; available for 1 year; based on GPA of 3.0 or higher.

## FINANCIAL AID PROCEDURES
**Forms required:** FAFSA, institutional form.
**Dates and Deadlines:** Applicants notified on a rolling basis; must reply within 4 week(s) of notification.
**Transfers:** No deadline.

## CONTACT
Barbara Amerio, Director of Financial Aid
29 Cougar Court, Taft, CA 93268
(661) 763-7762

## Thomas Aquinas College
Santa Paula, California
www.thomasaquinas.edu                  Federal Code: 023580

**4-year private** liberal arts college in rural community, affiliated with Roman Catholic Church.
**Enrollment:** 377 undergrads. 79 full-time freshmen.
**Selectivity:** Admits over 75% of applicants.

## BASIC COSTS (2016-2017)
**Tuition and fees:** $24,500.
**Per-credit charge:** $681.
**Room and board:** $7,950.

## FINANCIAL AID PICTURE (2015-2016)
**Students with need:** Out of 67 full-time freshmen who applied for aid, 62 were judged to have need. Of these, 62 received aid, and 62 had their full need met. Average financial aid package met 100% of need; average scholarship/grant was $14,711; average loan was $3,233.
**Students without need:** This college awards aid only to students with need.

## FINANCIAL AID PROCEDURES
**Forms required:** FAFSA, state aid form, institutional form.

**Dates and Deadlines:** Closing date 3/2. Applicants notified on a rolling basis starting 2/1; must reply by 5/1 or within 2 week(s) of notification.

## CONTACT
Gregory Becher, Director of Financial Aid
10000 Ojai Road, Santa Paula, CA 93060-9621
(800) 634-9797

## Trident University International
Cypress, California
www.trident.edu                         Federal Code: 041279

**4-year for-profit** virtual university in very large city.
**Enrollment:** 4,760 undergrads.
**Selectivity:** Open admission.

## BASIC COSTS (2015-2016)
**Per-credit charge:** $375.
**Additional info:** The tuition cost for the Bachelors program (100-400 level courses) is $375 per semester credit hour or $1,500 per course (All Trident courses are 4 semester credit hours). The tuition cost for Retired Military or Veterans of the military or Partnerships in the Bachelors program (100-400 level courses) is $300 per semester credit hour or $1,200 per course. The tuition cost for military students using Military Tuition Assistance; military spouses or Partnerships in the Bachelors program (100-400 level courses) is $250 per semester credit hour or $1,000 per course.

## FINANCIAL AID PICTURE
**Students with need:** Need-based aid available for full-time and part-time students.

## FINANCIAL AID PROCEDURES
**Forms required:** FAFSA, institutional form.
**Transfers:** No deadline.

## CONTACT
Taisha Wright, Director of Financial Aid
Attn: Office of the Registrar, Cypress, CA 90630
(714) 816-0366 ext. 1061

## University of California: Berkeley
Berkeley, California
www.berkeley.edu                        Federal Code: 001312

**4-year public** university in small city.
**Enrollment:** 27,496 undergrads, 3% part-time. 5,510 full-time freshmen.
**Selectivity:** Admits less than 50% of applicants.

## BASIC COSTS (2015-2016)
**Tuition and fees:** $13,431; out-of-state residents $38,139.
**Room and board:** $15,562.

## FINANCIAL AID PICTURE (2015-2016)
**Students with need:** Out of 3,044 full-time freshmen who applied for aid, 2,494 were judged to have need. Of these, 2,494 received aid, and 479 had their full need met. Average financial aid package met 78% of need; average scholarship/grant was $20,864; average loan was $6,686. For part-time students, average financial aid package was $22,142.
**Students without need:** 351 full-time freshmen who did not demonstrate need for aid received scholarships/grants; average award was $6,737. No-need awards available for academics, athletics, leadership.
**Scholarships offered:** *Merit:* University Scholarship, President's Undergraduate Fellowships, Regents and Chancellor's Scholarships, Alumni Scholarships. *Athletic:* 81 full-time freshmen received athletic scholarships; average amount $26,155.

**Additional info:** For resident families whose gross income ranges from $80,000 to $150,000 annually and who have typical assets, parents' contribution capped at maximum of 15% of total income. Tuition and registration fee for low-income California residents covered under the Blue and Gold Opportunity Plan.

### FINANCIAL AID PROCEDURES

**Forms required:** FAFSA, state aid form.
**Dates and Deadlines:** Closing date 3/2. Applicants notified by 3/31; must reply by 5/1.
**Transfers:** Applicants notified by 4/15.

### CONTACT

Rachelle Feldman, Director of Financial Aid
110 Sproul Hall, #5800, Berkeley, CA 94720-5800
(510) 642-6000

## University of California: Davis

Davis, California
www.ucdavis.edu                          Federal Code: 001313

**4-year public** university in small city.
**Enrollment:** 28,239 undergrads, 1% part-time. 5,383 full-time freshmen.
**Selectivity:** Admits less than 50% of applicants.

### BASIC COSTS (2015-2016)

**Tuition and fees:** $13,951; out-of-state residents $38,659.
**Room and board:** $14,517.

### FINANCIAL AID PICTURE

**Students with need:** Need-based aid available for full-time and part-time students. Work study available nights, weekends, and for part-time students.
**Students without need:** This college awards aid only to students with need.

### FINANCIAL AID PROCEDURES

**Forms required:** FAFSA, state aid form.
**Dates and Deadlines:** Priority date 3/2; no closing date. Applicants notified on a rolling basis starting 3/16.

### CONTACT

Deborah Agee, Director of Financial Aid
178 Mrak Hall, One Shields Ave, Davis, CA 95616
(530) 752-2390

## University of California: Irvine

Irvine, California
www.uci.edu                              Federal Code: 001314

**4-year public** university in small city.
**Enrollment:** 25,256 undergrads, 2% part-time. 5,426 full-time freshmen.
**Selectivity:** Admits less than 50% of applicants.

### BASIC COSTS (2015-2016)

**Tuition and fees:** $14,750; out-of-state residents $39,458.
**Room and board:** $12,947.
**Additional info:** Required fees include $1,497 for our student health insurance plan. Although this is a mandatory fee, if a student is covered through private insurance, he or she can waive out.

### FINANCIAL AID PICTURE (2014-2015)

**Students with need:** Out of 4,320 full-time freshmen who applied for aid, 3,646 were judged to have need. Of these, 3,575 received aid, and 914 had their full need met. Average financial aid package met 85% of need; average scholarship/grant was $18,619; average loan was $6,384. For part-time students, average financial aid package was $15,366.

**Students without need:** 55 full-time freshmen who did not demonstrate need for aid received scholarships/grants; average award was $9,593.
**Scholarships offered:** 26 full-time freshmen received athletic scholarships; average amount $18,360.
**Additional info:** UC Blue & Gold Opportunity Plan guarantees that needy in-state students from families earning less than $80,000/yr have system-wide tuition and fees paid through scholarships and grants.

### FINANCIAL AID PROCEDURES

**Forms required:** FAFSA, state aid form.
**Dates and Deadlines:** Priority date 3/3; closing date 6/20. Applicants notified on a rolling basis starting 4/1.

### CONTACT

Brice Kikuchi, Interim Director, Financial Aid & Scholarships
260 Aldrich Hall, Irvine, CA 92697-1075
(949) 824-8262

## University of California: Los Angeles

Los Angeles, California
www.ucla.edu                             Federal Code: 001315

**4-year public** university in very large city.
**Enrollment:** 29,575 undergrads, 2% part-time. 5,753 full-time freshmen.
**Selectivity:** Admits less than 50% of applicants.

### BASIC COSTS (2015-2016)

**Tuition and fees:** $12,753; out-of-state residents $35,631.
**Room and board:** $13,452.

### FINANCIAL AID PICTURE (2014-2015)

**Students with need:** Average financial aid package met 83% of need; average scholarship/grant was $20,255; average loan was $7,168. For part-time students, average financial aid package was $15,747.
**Students without need:** 117 full-time freshmen who did not demonstrate need for aid received scholarships/grants; average award was $4,494. No-need awards available for academics, art, job skills, ROTC.
**Scholarships offered:** 60 full-time freshmen received athletic scholarships; average amount $26,146.

### FINANCIAL AID PROCEDURES

**Forms required:** FAFSA.
**Dates and Deadlines:** Priority date 3/2; no closing date. Applicants notified on a rolling basis starting 3/15.

### CONTACT

Ronald Johnson, Director, Financial Aid Office
1147 Murphy Hall, Los Angeles, CA 90095-1436
(310) 206-0400

## University of California: Merced

Merced, California
www.ucmerced.edu                         Federal Code: 041271

**4-year public** university in small city.
**Enrollment:** 6,237 undergrads, 1% part-time. 1,548 full-time freshmen.
**Selectivity:** Admits 50 to 75% of applicants.

### BASIC COSTS (2015-2016)

**Tuition and fees:** $13,208; out-of-state residents $37,913.
**Room and board:** $15,646.

### FINANCIAL AID PICTURE (2014-2015)

**Students with need:** Out of 1,496 full-time freshmen who applied for aid, 1,389 were judged to have need. Of these, 1,381 received aid, and 477 had their full need met. Average financial aid package met 88% of need; average

scholarship/grant was $21,477; average loan was $4,771. For part-time students, average financial aid package was $12,792.

**Students without need:** 7 full-time freshmen who did not demonstrate need for aid received scholarships/grants; average award was $10,521. No-need awards available for academics, leadership.

**Scholarships offered:** *Merit:* Regents' Scholarships: based on strength and breadth of academic program, grades, personal statement, extracurricular activities, community activities, first-generation status, other indicators of academic excellence and promise. *Athletic:* 2 full-time freshmen received athletic scholarships; average amount $750.

**FINANCIAL AID PROCEDURES**

**Forms required:** FAFSA.

**Dates and Deadlines:** Closing date 3/2. Applicants notified on a rolling basis starting 4/1; must reply by 6/1.

**Transfers:** Applicants notified on a rolling basis starting 3/2.

**CONTACT**

Ron Radney, Director, Financial Aid & Scholarships
5200 North Lake Road, Merced, CA 95343-5603
(209) 228-7178

# University of California: Riverside
Riverside, California
www.ucr.edu                    Federal Code: 001316

**4-year public** university in large city.
**Enrollment:** 18,598 undergrads. 4,023 full-time freshmen.
**Selectivity:** Admits 50 to 75% of applicants.

**BASIC COSTS (2015-2016)**
**Tuition and fees:** $13,527; out-of-state residents $38,235.
**Room and board:** $15,700.

**FINANCIAL AID PICTURE (2014-2015)**
**Students with need:** Out of 3,667 full-time freshmen who applied for aid, 3,167 were judged to have need. Of these, 3,117 received aid, and 760 had their full need met. Average financial aid package met 85% of need; average scholarship/grant was $20,872; average loan was $6,116. For part-time students, average financial aid package was $15,545.

**Students without need:** 78 full-time freshmen who did not demonstrate need for aid received scholarships/grants; average award was $5,155. No-need awards available for academics, alumni affiliation, art, athletics, leadership, music/drama, state/district residency.

**Scholarships offered:** 16 full-time freshmen received athletic scholarships; average amount $20,086.

**FINANCIAL AID PROCEDURES**

**Forms required:** FAFSA, state aid form.
**Dates and Deadlines:** Priority date 3/2; closing date 6/15. Applicants notified on a rolling basis starting 3/1; must reply by 5/1 or within 3 week(s) of notification.
**Transfers:** Closing date 6/1. Applicants notified on a rolling basis starting 3/1; must reply by 6/1 or within 3 week(s) of notification.

**CONTACT**

Jose Aguilar, Director of Financial Aid
Undergraduate Admissions, Riverside, CA 92521
(951) 827-3878

# University of California: San Diego
La Jolla, California
www.ucsd.edu                    Federal Code: 001317

**4-year public** university in large town.
**Enrollment:** 23,850 undergrads. 5,286 full-time freshmen.

**BASIC COSTS (2015-2016)**
**Tuition and fees:** $13,557; out-of-state residents $38,265.
**Room and board:** $12,071.

**FINANCIAL AID PICTURE (2015-2016)**
**Students with need:** Out of 3,599 full-time freshmen who applied for aid, 2,711 were judged to have need. Of these, 2,552 received aid, and 873 had their full need met. Average financial aid package met 86% of need; average scholarship/grant was $18,362; average loan was $5,434. For part-time students, average financial aid package was $15,453.

**Students without need:** 90 full-time freshmen who did not demonstrate need for aid received scholarships/grants; average award was $10,814. No-need awards available for academics, art, athletics, leadership, minority status, music/drama.

**Scholarships offered:** 17 full-time freshmen received athletic scholarships; average amount $2,206.

**FINANCIAL AID PROCEDURES**

**Forms required:** FAFSA, state aid form.
**Dates and Deadlines:** Priority date 3/2; closing date 6/1. Applicants notified on a rolling basis starting 3/15; must reply within 3 week(s) of notification.
**Transfers:** Applicants notified on a rolling basis; must reply within 3 week(s) of notification.

**CONTACT**

Ann Klein, Director of Financial Aid
9500 Gilman Drive, 0021, La Jolla, CA 92093-0021
(858) 534-4480

# University of California: Santa Barbara
Santa Barbara, California
www.ucsb.edu                    Federal Code: 001320

**4-year public** university in small city.
**Enrollment:** 20,606 undergrads, 2% part-time. 4,725 full-time freshmen.
**Selectivity:** Admits less than 50% of applicants.

**BASIC COSTS (2015-2016)**
**Tuition and fees:** $13,865; out-of-state residents $38,573.
**Room and board:** $14,192.

**FINANCIAL AID PICTURE (2014-2015)**
**Students with need:** Out of 3,872 full-time freshmen who applied for aid, 3,053 were judged to have need. Of these, 2,959 received aid, and 855 had their full need met. Average financial aid package met 83% of need; average scholarship/grant was $20,515; average loan was $6,130. For part-time students, average financial aid package was $17,645.

**Students without need:** 71 full-time freshmen who did not demonstrate need for aid received scholarships/grants; average award was $12,062. No-need awards available for academics, alumni affiliation, athletics, ROTC.

**Scholarships offered:** 38 full-time freshmen received athletic scholarships; average amount $10,592.

**FINANCIAL AID PROCEDURES**

**Forms required:** FAFSA.
**Dates and Deadlines:** Priority date 3/2; closing date 5/31. Must reply within 2 week(s) of notification.
**Transfers:** California residents must apply for a CAL grant from the California Student Aid Commission; must complete and submit FAFSA by March 2.

**CONTACT**

Mike Miller, Director of Financial Aid
1210 Cheadle Hall, Santa Barbara, CA 93106-2014
(805) 893-2432

# University of California: Santa Cruz
Santa Cruz, California
www.ucsc.edu                                    Federal Code: 001321

**4-year public** university in small city.
**Enrollment:** 16,231 undergrads, 3% part-time. 4,019 full-time freshmen.
**Selectivity:** Admits 50 to 75% of applicants.

## BASIC COSTS (2015-2016)
**Tuition and fees:** $13,446; out-of-state residents $36,582.
**Room and board:** $14,730.
**Additional info:** Tuition/fee waivers available for unemployed or children of unemployed.

## FINANCIAL AID PICTURE (2014-2015)
**Students with need:** Out of 3,368 full-time freshmen who applied for aid, 2,772 were judged to have need. Of these, 2,685 received aid, and 489 had their full need met. Average financial aid package met 81% of need; average scholarship/grant was $19,339; average loan was $6,477. For part-time students, average financial aid package was $15,431.
**Students without need:** 345 full-time freshmen who did not demonstrate need for aid received scholarships/grants; average award was $4,860. No-need awards available for academics, alumni affiliation, art, leadership, music/drama.
**Scholarships offered:** Regents Scholarships; $4,000-$6,000 per year for 4 years; for outstanding academic achievement.
**Additional info:** Blue and Gold Opportunity Plan covers the educational and student services fees for CA residents whose family earns less than $80,000 a year. Blue and Gold students with sufficient financial need can qualify for more grant aid to reduce the cost of attendance.

## FINANCIAL AID PROCEDURES
**Forms required:** FAFSA, state aid form.
**Dates and Deadlines:** Closing date 3/2. Applicants notified on a rolling basis starting 4/1; must reply within 4 week(s) of notification.
**Transfers:** The Karl S. Pister Leadership Opportunity Awards Program established by a former chancellor increases opportunities for talented community college students who want to transfer to UCSC. Candidates, nominated by the regional community college presidents, must have overcome adverse socioeconomic circumstances, have a demonstrated commitment to assisting and improving the lives of others and have financial aid eligibility. One recipient is named from each of 13 regional community colleges. Awards are $10,000 per year for 2 years.

## CONTACT
Michelle Whittingham, Associate Vice Chancellor, Enrollment Management
Cook House, 1156 High Street, Santa Cruz, CA 95064
(831) 459-2963

# University of La Verne
La Verne, California
www.laverne.edu                                 Federal Code: 001216

**4-year private** university in large town.
**Enrollment:** 2,859 undergrads, 3% part-time. 720 full-time freshmen.
**Selectivity:** Admits less than 50% of applicants.

## BASIC COSTS (2016-2017)
**Tuition and fees:** $40,063.
**Per-credit charge:** $1,083.
**Room and board:** $12,710.

## FINANCIAL AID PICTURE (2015-2016)
**Students with need:** Out of 665 full-time freshmen who applied for aid, 624 were judged to have need. Of these, 624 received aid, and 66 had their full need met. Average financial aid package met 31% of need; average

scholarship/grant was $11,116; average loan was $3,749. For part-time students, average financial aid package was $19,436.
**Students without need:** 92 full-time freshmen who did not demonstrate need for aid received scholarships/grants; average award was $20,998. No-need awards available for academics, alumni affiliation, art, leadership, minority status, music/drama, religious affiliation.

## FINANCIAL AID PROCEDURES
**Forms required:** FAFSA, state aid form.
**Dates and Deadlines:** Priority date 3/2; no closing date. Applicants notified on a rolling basis starting 3/1; must reply within 2 week(s) of notification.

## CONTACT
Diane Anchundia, Director, Financial Aid Office
1950 Third Street, La Verne, CA 91750
(800) 649-0160

# University of Redlands
Redlands, California
www.redlands.edu                                Federal Code: 001322

**4-year private** university and liberal arts college in small city.
**Enrollment:** 3,452 undergrads, 22% part-time. 525 full-time freshmen.
**Selectivity:** Admits 50 to 75% of applicants.

## BASIC COSTS (2015-2016)
**Tuition and fees:** $44,900.
**Room and board:** $13,090.

## FINANCIAL AID PICTURE
**Students with need:** Need-based aid available for full-time and part-time students.
**Students without need:** No-need awards available for academics, art, music/drama.

## FINANCIAL AID PROCEDURES
**Forms required:** FAFSA, state aid form.
**Dates and Deadlines:** Closing date 3/2. Applicants notified on a rolling basis starting 2/28; must reply by 6/1.
**Transfers:** No deadline.

## CONTACT
Alisha Aguilar, Director of Financial Aid
1200 East Colton Avenue, Redlands, CA 92373-0999
(909) 748-8047

# University of San Diego
San Diego, California
www.sandiego.edu                                Federal Code: 010395

**4-year private** university in very large city, affiliated with Roman Catholic Church.
**Enrollment:** 5,551 undergrads, 3% part-time. 1,129 full-time freshmen.
**Selectivity:** Admits 50 to 75% of applicants.

## BASIC COSTS (2015-2016)
**Tuition and fees:** $44,586.
**Per-credit charge:** $1,515.
**Room and board:** $12,042.

## FINANCIAL AID PICTURE (2014-2015)
**Students with need:** Out of 826 full-time freshmen who applied for aid, 642 were judged to have need. Of these, 634 received aid, and 98 had their full need met. Average financial aid package met 73% of need; average scholarship/grant was $25,383; average loan was $5,937. For part-time students, average financial aid package was $18,261.

**Students without need:** 271 full-time freshmen who did not demonstrate need for aid received scholarships/grants; average award was $14,656. No-need awards available for academics, athletics, leadership, music/drama, religious affiliation, ROTC.
**Scholarships offered:** 29 full-time freshmen received athletic scholarships; average amount $40,710.

## FINANCIAL AID PROCEDURES

**Forms required:** FAFSA.
**Dates and Deadlines:** Priority date 3/2; no closing date. Applicants notified on a rolling basis starting 3/1; must reply by 5/1 or within 3 week(s) of notification.
**Transfers:** Entering transfer students are not eligible for institutional merit-based scholarships.

## CONTACT

Judith Lewis Logue, Director of Financial Aid Services
5998 Alcala Park, San Diego, CA 92110-2492
(619) 260-4720

## University of San Francisco

San Francisco, California          Federal Code: 001325
www.usfca.edu                      CSS Code: 4850

**4-year private** university in very large city, affiliated with Roman Catholic Church.
**Enrollment:** 6,682 undergrads, 4% part-time. 1,265 full-time freshmen.
**Selectivity:** Admits 50 to 75% of applicants.

### BASIC COSTS (2016-2017)
**Tuition and fees:** $44,494.
**Per-credit charge:** $1,565.
**Room and board:** $13,990.

### FINANCIAL AID PICTURE (2015-2016)
**Students with need:** Out of 866 full-time freshmen who applied for aid, 715 were judged to have need. Of these, 706 received aid, and 54 had their full need met. For part-time students, average financial aid package was $9,998.
**Students without need:** 802 full-time freshmen who did not demonstrate need for aid received scholarships/grants; average award was $13,409. No-need awards available for academics, athletics, ROTC.
**Scholarships offered:** *Merit:* University Scholars Program: up to $20,000 per year for 8 UG Semesters; must have 3.8 weighted GPA as calculated by USF admissions and combined SAT of 1320 on Critical Reading and Math sections or minimum ACT composite test score of 30. Applicants must apply for admission no later than November 15 under the Early Action Plan for the following year. Renewal automatic as long as 3.25 GPA achieved each semester. *Athletic:* 38 full-time freshmen received athletic scholarships; average amount $43,605.
**Additional info:** Most aid to international students is for athletics.

### FINANCIAL AID PROCEDURES
**Forms required:** FAFSA, CSS PROFILE.
**Dates and Deadlines:** Priority date 1/15; no closing date. Applicants notified on a rolling basis starting 4/1; must reply within 4 week(s) of notification.
**Transfers:** Must reply within 4 week(s) of notification.

### CONTACT
Susan Murphy, Senior Associate Dean, Director, Enrollment and Financial Services
2130 Fulton Street, San Francisco, CA 94117-1080
(415) 422-2620

## University of Southern California

Los Angeles, California          Federal Code: 001328
www.usc.edu                      CSS Code: 4852

**4-year private** university in very large city.
**Enrollment:** 18,518 undergrads, 3% part-time. 3,093 full-time freshmen.
**Selectivity:** Admits less than 50% of applicants. GED not accepted.

### BASIC COSTS (2016-2017)
**Tuition and fees:** $52,283.
**Per-credit charge:** $1,733.
**Room and board:** $14,348.

### FINANCIAL AID PICTURE (2014-2015)
**Students with need:** Out of 1,786 full-time freshmen who applied for aid, 1,031 were judged to have need. Of these, 1,030 received aid, and 1,015 had their full need met. Average financial aid package met 100% of need; average scholarship/grant was $34,948; average loan was $5,195. For part-time students, average financial aid package was $21,716.
**Students without need:** 678 full-time freshmen who did not demonstrate need for aid received scholarships/grants; average award was $21,275. No-need awards available for academics, alumni affiliation, art, athletics, leadership, music/drama, ROTC.
**Scholarships offered:** *Merit:* Trustee Scholarship: full tuition; approximately 100 awards annually; finalists invited to mandatory interview. Presidential Scholarship: one-half tuition; approximately 200 awarded annually; finalists invited to a mandatory interview. National Merit Presidential Scholarship: one-half tuition; number of awards varies; admitted Freshmen who are National Merit Finalists and who designate USC as their first-choice college. Deans Scholarship: one-quarter tuition; approximately 50 awards annually; Mork Family Scholarship: full tuition plus $5,000 living stipend; 10 awards annually; Stamps Leadership Scholarship: full tuition plus $5,000 enrichment fund (research, overseas study, etc.); 5 awards annually. *Athletic:* 87 full-time freshmen received athletic scholarships; average amount $56,533.

### FINANCIAL AID PROCEDURES
**Forms required:** FAFSA, CSS PROFILE.
**Dates and Deadlines:** Priority date 2/16; no closing date. Applicants notified by 4/1; must reply by 5/1.
**Transfers:** Applicants notified by 5/1.

### CONTACT
Thomas McWhorter, Dean of Financial Aid
Office of Admission, Los Angeles, CA 90089-0911
(213) 740-4444

## University of the Pacific

Stockton, California
www.pacific.edu                  Federal Code: 001329

**4-year private** university in large city.
**Enrollment:** 3,720 undergrads, 2% part-time. 934 full-time freshmen.
**Selectivity:** Admits 50 to 75% of applicants.

### BASIC COSTS (2015-2016)
**Tuition and fees:** $42,934.
**Per-credit charge:** $1,463.
**Room and board:** $12,858.

### FINANCIAL AID PICTURE (2015-2016)
**Students with need:** Out of 762 full-time freshmen who applied for aid, 667 were judged to have need. Of these, 667 received aid, and 87 had their full need met. For part-time students, average financial aid package was $17,521.
**Students without need:** 193 full-time freshmen who did not demonstrate need for aid received scholarships/grants; average award was $13,173. No-need awards available for academics, athletics, leadership, music/drama, religious affiliation.

**Scholarships offered:** 24 full-time freshmen received athletic scholarships; average amount $41,423.

## FINANCIAL AID PROCEDURES
**Forms required:** FAFSA.
**Dates and Deadlines:** Priority date 2/15; no closing date. Applicants notified on a rolling basis starting 3/1.

## CONTACT
Lynn Fox, Director of Financial Aid
3601 Pacific Avenue, Stockton, CA 95211-0197
(209) 946-2011

# University of the West
Rosemead, California
www.uwest.edu                    Federal Code: 036963

**4-year private** business and liberal arts college in small city, affiliated with Buddhist faith.
**Enrollment:** 99 undergrads.

## BASIC COSTS (2015-2016)
**Tuition and fees:** $13,110.
**Per-credit charge:** $409.
**Room and board:** $6,920.

## FINANCIAL AID PICTURE
**Students with need:** Need-based aid available for full-time and part-time students. Work study available nights, weekends, and for part-time students.
**Students without need:** No-need awards available for academics, leadership.
**Scholarships offered:** Lotus Scholarship: up to $10,000 per year depending on academic merits and financial need. President's Fellowship: full-tuition award. Dean's Fellowship: half-tuition award. Campus Life Leadership Fellowship: full tuition and room and board award plus $1,000 scholarship. Campus Life Assistance Fellowship: full room and board award plus $1,000 scholarship. UWest Scholarship: $1,000 to $2,000 per academic year. Drs. Allen and Lily Huang Student Leadership Award: $2,000, one award each year. Lotus Scholarships: $10,000 or $5,000 per year.

## FINANCIAL AID PROCEDURES
**Forms required:** FAFSA, institutional form.
**Transfers:** No deadline.

## CONTACT
Lezli Fang, Financial Aid Officer
1409 North Walnut Grove Avenue, Rosemead, CA 91770
(626) 571-8811 ext. 138

# Vanguard University of Southern California
Costa Mesa, California
www.vanguard.edu                 Federal Code: 001293

**4-year private** university and liberal arts college in small city, affiliated with Assemblies of God.
**Enrollment:** 1,941 undergrads.

## BASIC COSTS (2015-2016)
**Tuition and fees:** $30,050.
**Room and board:** $9,150.

## FINANCIAL AID PICTURE
**Students with need:** Need-based aid available for full-time students.
**Students without need:** No-need awards available for academics, athletics, music/drama, religious affiliation.

## FINANCIAL AID PROCEDURES
**Forms required:** FAFSA, state aid form.
**Dates and Deadlines:** Closing date 3/2. Applicants notified on a rolling basis starting 4/1; must reply within 3 week(s) of notification.
**Transfers:** Applicants notified on a rolling basis.

## CONTACT
Christina Padilla, Director of Financial Aid
55 Fair Drive, Costa Mesa, CA 92626-9601
(714) 955-5490

# Ventura College
Ventura, California
www.venturacollege.edu           Federal Code: 001334

**2-year public** community college in small city.
**Enrollment:** 8,951 undergrads.
**Selectivity:** Open admission; but selective for some programs.

## BASIC COSTS (2015-2016)
**Tuition and fees:** $1,418; out-of-state residents $8,738.
**Per-credit charge:** $46; out-of-state residents $290.

## FINANCIAL AID PICTURE
**Students with need:** Need-based aid available for full-time and part-time students.

## FINANCIAL AID PROCEDURES
**Forms required:** FAFSA, state aid form.
**Dates and Deadlines:** Priority date 3/2; no closing date. Applicants notified on a rolling basis.

## CONTACT
Alma Rodriguez, Director, Financial Aid
4667 Telegraph Road, Ventura, CA 93003
(805) 654-6369

# Victor Valley College
Victorville, California
www.vvc.edu                      Federal Code: 001335

**2-year public** community college in small city.
**Enrollment:** 7,283 undergrads, 62% part-time. 638 full-time freshmen.
**Selectivity:** Open admission.

## BASIC COSTS (2015-2016)
**Tuition and fees:** $1,390; out-of-state residents $7,180.
**Per-credit charge:** $46; out-of-state residents $239.

## FINANCIAL AID PICTURE
**Students with need:** Need-based aid available for full-time and part-time students.
**Additional info:** Board of Governors grant pays enrollment fee in full for low-income students.

## FINANCIAL AID PROCEDURES
**Forms required:** FAFSA, state aid form, institutional form.
**Dates and Deadlines:** Priority date 3/2; no closing date. Applicants notified on a rolling basis starting 8/1; must reply within 4 week(s) of notification.

## CONTACT
Jason Judkins, Director, Financial Aid
18422 Bear Valley Road, Victorville, CA 92392-5850
(760) 245-4271 ext. 2917

## West Coast University: Los Angeles

North Hollywood, California
www.westcoastuniversity.edu        Federal Code: 036983

**4-year for-profit** health science and nursing college in very large city.
**Enrollment:** 1,435 undergrads.

**BASIC COSTS (2015-2016)**
**Tuition and fees:** $33,731.
**Per-credit charge:** $1,836.

**FINANCIAL AID PICTURE**
**Students with need:** Need-based aid available for full-time and part-time students. Work study available nights, weekends, and for part-time students.
**Students without need:** No-need awards available for academics.

**FINANCIAL AID PROCEDURES**
**Forms required:** FAFSA, state aid form, institutional form.
**Dates and Deadlines:** Closing date 6/30. Applicants notified on a rolling basis.

**CONTACT**
Tracy Cabuco, Director of Financial Aid
12215 Victory Boulevard, North Hollywood, CA 91606
(818) 299-5500

## West Coast University: Ontario

Ontario, California
www.westcoastuniversity.edu        Federal Code: 036983

**4-year for-profit** branch campus and nursing college in small city.
**Enrollment:** 1,061 undergrads.
**Selectivity:** Open admission; but selective for some programs.

**BASIC COSTS (2015-2016)**
**Tuition and fees:** $33,731.
**Per-credit charge:** $1,836.

**FINANCIAL AID PICTURE**
**Students with need:** Need-based aid available for full-time and part-time students. Work study available nights, weekends, and for part-time students.
**Students without need:** No-need awards available for academics.

**FINANCIAL AID PROCEDURES**
**Forms required:** FAFSA, state aid form, institutional form.
**Dates and Deadlines:** Closing date 6/30. Applicants notified on a rolling basis.

**CONTACT**
Raylena Figueroa, Director of Financial Aid
2855 East Guasti Road, Ontario, CA 91761
(909) 467-6100

## West Coast University: Orange County

Anaheim, California
www.westcoastuniversity.edu        Federal Code: 036983

**4-year for-profit** branch campus and nursing college in large city.
**Enrollment:** 1,477 undergrads.
**Selectivity:** Open admission; but selective for some programs.

**BASIC COSTS (2015-2016)**
**Tuition and fees:** $33,175.
**Per-credit charge:** $1,836.

**FINANCIAL AID PICTURE**
**Students with need:** Need-based aid available for full-time and part-time students. Work study available nights, weekends, and for part-time students.

**Students without need:** No-need awards available for academics.

**FINANCIAL AID PROCEDURES**
**Forms required:** FAFSA, state aid form, institutional form.
**Dates and Deadlines:** Closing date 6/30. Applicants notified on a rolling basis.

**CONTACT**
Teresa Salcedo, Director of Financial Aid
1477 South Manchester Avenue, Anaheim, CA 92802
(714) 782-1700

## West Hills College: Coalinga

Coalinga, California
www.westhillscollege.com        Federal Code: 001176

**2-year public** community college in small town.
**Enrollment:** 1,985 undergrads.
**Selectivity:** Open admission.

**BASIC COSTS (2015-2016)**
**Tuition and fees:** $1,380; out-of-state residents $8,430.
**Per-credit charge:** $46; out-of-state residents $281.
**Room and board:** $7,977.
**Additional info:** Tuition/fee waivers available for unemployed or children of unemployed.

**FINANCIAL AID PICTURE**
**Students with need:** Need-based aid available for full-time and part-time students.

**FINANCIAL AID PROCEDURES**
**Forms required:** FAFSA.
**Dates and Deadlines:** Priority date 3/2; no closing date. Applicants notified on a rolling basis starting 6/1.

**CONTACT**
Mary Mello, Director of Financial Aid
300 Cherry Lane, Coalinga, CA 93210
(559) 934-2310

## West Los Angeles College

Culver City, California
www.wlac.edu        Federal Code: 008596

**2-year public** community college in large town.
**Enrollment:** 6,134 undergrads.
**Selectivity:** Open admission.

**BASIC COSTS (2015-2016)**
**Tuition and fees:** $1,404; out-of-state residents $7,854.
**Per-credit charge:** $46; out-of-state residents $261.
**Additional info:** Tuition/fee waivers available for unemployed or children of unemployed.

**FINANCIAL AID PICTURE**
**Students with need:** Need-based aid available for full-time and part-time students.
**Students without need:** This college awards aid only to students with need.
**Additional info:** California residents may qualify for Board of Governors Grant Program.

**FINANCIAL AID PROCEDURES**
**Forms required:** FAFSA.
**Dates and Deadlines:** Applicants notified on a rolling basis; must reply within 4 week(s) of notification.
**Transfers:** No deadline.

**CONTACT**
Glenn Schenk, Financial Aid Director
9000 Overland Avenue, Culver City, CA 90230
(310) 287-4533

## Westmont College
Santa Barbara, California
www.westmont.edu                    Federal Code: 001341

**4-year private** liberal arts college in small city, affiliated with
nondenominational tradition.
**Enrollment:** 1,284 undergrads. 337 full-time freshmen.
**Selectivity:** Admits over 75% of applicants.

### BASIC COSTS (2015-2016)
**Tuition and fees:** $41,360.
**Per-credit charge:** $1,850.
**Room and board:** $13,040.

### FINANCIAL AID PICTURE (2015-2016)
**Students with need:** Out of 287 full-time freshmen who applied for aid,
230 were judged to have need. Of these, 230 received aid, and 48 had their
full need met. Average financial aid package met 81% of need; average
scholarship/grant was $25,289; average loan was $4,510.
**Students without need:** 82 full-time freshmen who did not demonstrate
need for aid received scholarships/grants; average award was $14,411. No-
need awards available for academics, art, athletics, leadership, minority status, music/drama.
**Scholarships offered: _Merit:_** Scholarships automatically awarded to entering
students based on GPA and SAT or ACT scores (first-year students) or college academic GPA (transfers): renewable annually; unlimited number
awarded until class is full. First-year scholarships: Presidential, $14,000, must
maintain 3.25 GPA; Provost, $12,000, must maintain 3.0 GPA; Dean's,
$10,000, must maintain 2.75 GPA. **_Athletic:_** 5 full-time freshmen received
athletic scholarships; average amount $5,500.

### FINANCIAL AID PROCEDURES
**Forms required:** FAFSA, institutional form. PROFILE accepted but not
required.
**Dates and Deadlines:** Priority date 3/1; no closing date. Applicants notified
on a rolling basis starting 2/1; must reply by 5/1 or within 2 week(s) of notification.
**Transfers:** No deadline. Applicants notified on a rolling basis starting 4/1;
must reply by 5/1 or within 2 week(s) of notification. Transfer students may
qualify for academic merit scholarships.

### CONTACT
Sean Smith, Director of Financial Aid
955 La Paz Road, Santa Barbara, CA 93108-1089
(888) 963-4624

## Westwood College: Inland Empire
Upland, California
www.westwood.edu/locations/california/inland-empire-
campus                    Federal Code: 007548

**3-year for-profit** career college in small city.
**Enrollment:** 1,644 undergrads.

### BASIC COSTS (2015-2016)
**Additional info:** Electronics Technology: AOS $34,825. Information Technol-
ogy: AOS $34,825. Business Administration: AAS $36,428. Computer Aided
Design/Architectural Drafting: AAS $38,367. Construction Management: AAS
$36,428. Criminal Justice: AAS $38,717. Graphic Design: AAS $40,278.

Health Information Technology: AAS $40,296. Healthcare Office Administra-
tion: AAS $35,259. Medical Assisting: AAS $27,251. Medical Insurance Coding & Billing: AAS $35,259. Paralegal: AAS $33,250. Business Administration:
Major in Healthcare Management: BS $72,856. Business Administration:
Major in Management: BS $72,856. Business Administration: Major in Mar-
keting Mangagement: BS $72,856. Construction Management: BS $72,856.
Criminal Justice: Major in Administration: BS $77,434. Graphic Design: Major
in Visual Communications: BS $76,720. Information & Network Technologies:
Major in Network Management: BS $69,650. Medical Assisting: DP $19,465.
Additional costs and fees such as books, tool kits, lab fee and online fees
may apply.

### FINANCIAL AID PICTURE
**Students with need:** Need-based aid available for full-time and part-time students.

### FINANCIAL AID PROCEDURES
**Forms required:** FAFSA, institutional form.
**Dates and Deadlines:** Must reply within 1 week(s) of notification.
**Transfers:** No deadline.

### CONTACT
Audri Williams, Director of Student Finance
20 West Seventh Street, Upland, CA 91786
(909) 931-7599

## Whittier College
Whittier, California
www.whittier.edu                    Federal Code: 001342

**4-year private** liberal arts college in small city.
**Enrollment:** 1,645 undergrads, 2% part-time. 445 full-time freshmen.
**Selectivity:** Admits 50 to 75% of applicants.

### BASIC COSTS (2015-2016)
**Tuition and fees:** $43,080.
**Room and board:** $12,672.

### FINANCIAL AID PICTURE (2015-2016)
**Students with need:** Out of 402 full-time freshmen who applied for aid,
358 were judged to have need. Of these, 358 received aid, and 79 had their
full need met. Average financial aid package met 79% of need; average
scholarship/grant was $33,748; average loan was $4,772. For part-time students, average financial aid package was $23,576.
**Students without need:** 63 full-time freshmen who did not demonstrate
need for aid received scholarships/grants; average award was $24,341. No-
need awards available for academics, alumni affiliation, art, minority status,
music/drama.
**Additional info:** Auditions required for talent scholarship applicants in art,
music, and theater.

### FINANCIAL AID PROCEDURES
**Forms required:** FAFSA.
**Dates and Deadlines:** Priority date 3/1; closing date 6/30. Applicants notified
on a rolling basis starting 2/15; must reply within 2 week(s) of notification.
**Transfers:** Priority date 2/1. Applicants notified on a rolling basis starting 3/1;
must reply by 6/1 or within 2 week(s) of notification.

### CONTACT
Julie Aldama, Director of Financial Aid
13406 East Philadelphia Street, Whittier, CA 90608-0634
(562) 907-4285

## William Jessup University
Rocklin, California
www.jessup.edu                    Federal Code: 001281

**4-year private** university, Bible and liberal arts college in small city, affiliated with nondenominational tradition.
**Enrollment:** 1,093 undergrads, 17% part-time. 146 full-time freshmen.
**Selectivity:** Admits over 75% of applicants.

**BASIC COSTS (2015-2016)**
**Tuition and fees:** $26,480.
**Per-credit charge:** $670.
**Room and board:** $10,278.

**FINANCIAL AID PICTURE (2015-2016)**
**Students with need:** Out of 140 full-time freshmen who applied for aid, 126 were judged to have need. Of these, 126 received aid, and 25 had their full need met. Average financial aid package met 71% of need; average scholarship/grant was $19,174; average loan was $3,424. For part-time students, average financial aid package was $9,547.
**Students without need:** 13 full-time freshmen who did not demonstrate need for aid received scholarships/grants; average award was $7,923. No-need awards available for academics, art, athletics, leadership, minority status, music/drama, religious affiliation, state/district residency.
**Scholarships offered:** 6 full-time freshmen received athletic scholarships; average amount $10,207.

**FINANCIAL AID PROCEDURES**
**Forms required:** FAFSA.
**Dates and Deadlines:** Priority date 3/2; no closing date. Applicants notified on a rolling basis starting 3/2; must reply within 3 week(s) of notification.

**CONTACT**
John Swan, Director of Financial Aid
2121 University Ave, Rocklin, CA 95765
(916) 577-2233

## Woodbury University
Burbank, California             Federal Code: 001343
www.woodbury.edu                     CSS Code: 4955

**4-year private** university in very large city.
**Enrollment:** 1,245 undergrads, 13% part-time. 136 full-time freshmen.
**Selectivity:** Admits 50 to 75% of applicants.

**BASIC COSTS (2015-2016)**
**Tuition and fees:** $36,408.
**Per-credit charge:** $1,166.
**Room and board:** $10,668.

**FINANCIAL AID PICTURE (2015-2016)**
**Students with need:** Out of 115 full-time freshmen who applied for aid, 106 were judged to have need. Of these, 105 received aid, and 6 had their full need met. Average financial aid package met 53% of need; average scholarship/grant was $19,891; average loan was $3,605. For part-time students, average financial aid package was $10,343.
**Students without need:** 27 full-time freshmen who did not demonstrate need for aid received scholarships/grants; average award was $12,089. No-need awards available for academics.

**FINANCIAL AID PROCEDURES**
**Forms required:** FAFSA, CSS PROFILE, institutional form.
**Dates and Deadlines:** Priority date 11/15; closing date 2/1. Applicants notified on a rolling basis starting 11/30.
**Transfers:** No deadline. Applicants notified on a rolling basis starting 4/1; must reply by 5/1 or within 2 week(s) of notification.

**CONTACT**
Celeastia Williams, Director
7500 Glenoaks Boulevard, Burbank, CA 91504-1052
(818) 767-0888 ext. 273

## Yeshiva Ohr Elchonon Chabad/West Coast Talmudical Seminary
Los Angeles, California
yoec@yoec.edu                   Federal Code: 015975

**4-year private** rabbinical and seminary college for men in very large city, affiliated with Jewish faith.
**Enrollment:** 160 undergrads. 59 full-time freshmen.
**Selectivity:** Admits 50 to 75% of applicants.

**BASIC COSTS (2015-2016)**
**Tuition and fees:** $13,900.
**Room and board:** $7,350.
**Additional info:** Tuition/fee waivers available for minority students.

**FINANCIAL AID PICTURE**
**Students with need:** Need-based aid available for full-time students.
**Students without need:** This college awards aid only to students with need.

**FINANCIAL AID PROCEDURES**
**Forms required:** FAFSA, state aid form, institutional form.
**Dates and Deadlines:** Priority date 1/15; closing date 6/30. Applicants notified by 5/1; must reply by 7/1.

**CONTACT**
Hendy Tauber, Financial Aid Administrator
7215 Waring Avenue, Los Angeles, CA 90046
(323) 937-3763 ext. 112

## Yuba College
Marysville, California
http://yc.yccd.edu              Federal Code: 001344

**2-year public** community college in small city.
**Enrollment:** 6,461 undergrads, 58% part-time. 763 full-time freshmen.
**Selectivity:** Open admission; but selective for some programs.

**BASIC COSTS (2015-2016)**
**Tuition and fees:** $1,400; out-of-state residents $8,000.
**Per-credit charge:** $46; out-of-state residents $266.
**Additional info:** Tuition/fee waivers available for adults.

**FINANCIAL AID PICTURE**
**Students with need:** Need-based aid available for full-time and part-time students.
**Students without need:** No-need awards available for academics, athletics, job skills, minority status, music/drama.
**Additional info:** Tuition fee waiver based on Board of Governors Grant.

**FINANCIAL AID PROCEDURES**
**Forms required:** FAFSA.
**Dates and Deadlines:** Priority date 8/7; closing date 3/1. Applicants notified on a rolling basis starting 4/1.

**CONTACT**
Martin Gutierrez, Dean for EOP&S and Financial Aid
2088 North Beale Road, Marysville, CA 95901
(530) 741-6939

# Colorado

## Adams State University
Alamosa, Colorado
www.adams.edu                    Federal Code: 001345

**4-year public** liberal arts college in small town.
**Enrollment:** 2,169 undergrads, 20% part-time. 430 full-time freshmen.

**BASIC COSTS (2015-2016)**
**Tuition and fees:** $8,574; out-of-state residents $19,086.
**Per-credit charge:** $227; out-of-state residents $665.
**Room and board:** $7,900.

**FINANCIAL AID PICTURE (2015-2016)**
**Students with need:** Out of 411 full-time freshmen who applied for aid, 331 were judged to have need. Of these, 330 received aid, and 2 had their full need met. Average financial aid package met 56% of need; average scholarship/grant was $7,876; average loan was $3,149. For part-time students, average financial aid package was $7,363.
**Students without need:** No-need awards available for academics, alumni affiliation, art, athletics, leadership, minority status, music/drama, state/district residency.

**FINANCIAL AID PROCEDURES**
**Forms required:** FAFSA.
**Dates and Deadlines:** Applicants notified on a rolling basis starting 4/30.
**Transfers:** No deadline. Applicants notified on a rolling basis starting 4/30; must reply within 4 week(s) of notification.

**CONTACT**
Philip Schroeder, Director of Financial Aid
208 Edgemont Boulevard, Alamosa, CO 81101
(719) 587-7306

## Aims Community College
Greeley, Colorado
www.aims.edu                    Federal Code: 007582

**2-year public** community college in small city.
**Enrollment:** 3,586 undergrads, 52% part-time. 459 full-time freshmen.
**Selectivity:** Open admission; but selective for some programs.

**BASIC COSTS (2015-2016)**
**Tuition and fees:** $2,281; out-of-district residents $3,432; out-of-state residents $13,018.
**Per-credit charge:** $67; out-of-district residents $106; out-of-state residents $425.

**FINANCIAL AID PICTURE**
**Students with need:** Need-based aid available for full-time and part-time students. Work study available nights, weekends, and for part-time students.

**FINANCIAL AID PROCEDURES**
**Forms required:** FAFSA.
**Dates and Deadlines:** Priority date 3/15; no closing date. Applicants notified on a rolling basis starting 6/1.

**CONTACT**
Nancy Gray, Director of Student Financial Assistance
4911 West 20th Street, Greeley, CO 80634
(970) 339-6548

## Arapahoe Community College
Littleton, Colorado
www.arapahoe.edu

**2-year public** community college in large town.
**Enrollment:** 7,673 undergrads, 76% part-time. 361 full-time freshmen.
**Selectivity:** Open admission; but selective for some programs.

**BASIC COSTS (2015-2016)**
**Tuition and fees:** $4,117; out-of-state residents $16,264.
**Per-credit charge:** $131; out-of-state residents $535.
**Additional info:** In-state tuition based upon assumption of Colorado Opportunity Fund waiver of $75 per-credit hour.

**FINANCIAL AID PICTURE (2014-2015)**
**Students with need:** Need-based aid available for full-time and part-time students. Work study available nights, weekends, and for part-time students.
**Students without need:** No-need awards available for academics, alumni affiliation, art, leadership, minority status, music/drama, state/district residency.
**Scholarships offered:** President's Scholarship: based on 3.0 GPA, references. College Bound Scholarship: based on high GED score. All awards $750 for full-time students, $375 for half-time, $563 for three-quarters time.

**FINANCIAL AID PROCEDURES**
**Forms required:** FAFSA.
**Dates and Deadlines:** Priority date 4/1; no closing date. Applicants notified on a rolling basis starting 4/15; must reply by 11/1.

**CONTACT**
PO Box 9002, Littleton, CO 80160-9002

## Bel-Rea Institute of Animal Technology
Denver, Colorado
www.bel-rea.com                    Federal Code: 012670

**2-year for-profit** technical college in very large city.
**Enrollment:** 489 undergrads.

**FINANCIAL AID PICTURE**
**Students with need:** Need-based aid available for full-time students.
**Students without need:** This college awards aid only to students with need.

**FINANCIAL AID PROCEDURES**
**Forms required:** FAFSA.
**Dates and Deadlines:** Priority date 8/31; no closing date. Applicants notified on a rolling basis starting 8/15.
**Transfers:** No deadline.

**CONTACT**
Stasi Botinelli, Financial Aid Director
1681 South Dayton Street, Denver, CO 80247
(303) 751-8700

## CollegeAmerica: Colorado Springs
Colorado Springs, Colorado
www.collegeamerica.edu

**4-year private** career college in large city.
**Enrollment:** 430 undergrads.
**Selectivity:** Open admission.

**BASIC COSTS (2015-2016)**
**Additional info:** Tuition varies by program. Associate's programs range from $34,390 to $48,251 for the complete program. Bachelor's programs range from $55,800 to $74,753 for the complete program.

**FINANCIAL AID PICTURE**

**Students with need:** Need-based aid available for full-time and part-time students.

**FINANCIAL AID PROCEDURES**

**Forms required:** FAFSA, institutional form.

**CONTACT**

Sonia Martinez, Director of Financial Aid
3645 Citadel Drive South, Colorado Springs, CO 80909

## CollegeAmerica: Denver

Denver, Colorado
www.collegeamerica.edu            Federal Code: 025943

**2-year private** nursing and technical college in very large city.
**Enrollment:** 204 undergrads.
**Selectivity:** Open admission.

**BASIC COSTS (2015-2016)**

**Additional info:** Tuition varies by program. Associate's programs range from $34,390 to $48,251 for the complete program. Bachelor's programs range from $55,800 to $74,753 for the complete program.

**FINANCIAL AID PICTURE**

**Students with need:** Need-based aid available for full-time students.
**Students without need:** This college awards aid only to students with need.
**Scholarships offered:** High School Academic Scholarship: based on outcome of OLSAT exam. Number awarded has no limit. A limited number of Associate Degree and Bachelor Degree Scholarships are available at the Denver campus. Basis for selection: 500 word essay. Reviewed by scholarship committee. Number of awards vary per quarter.

**FINANCIAL AID PROCEDURES**

**Forms required:** FAFSA, institutional form.
**Dates and Deadlines:** Applicants notified on a rolling basis; must reply within 4 week(s) of notification.
**Transfers:** No deadline. Applicants notified on a rolling basis.

**CONTACT**

Sonia Martinez, Regional Director of Central Financial Aid
1385 South Colorado Boulevard, 5th Floor, Denver, CO 80222-1912
(303) 300-8740

## Colorado Christian University

Lakewood, Colorado
www.ccu.edu            Federal Code: 009401

**4-year private** university and liberal arts college in large city, affiliated with nondenominational tradition.
**Enrollment:** 3,862 undergrads.

**BASIC COSTS (2015-2016)**

**Tuition and fees:** $27,986.
**Room and board:** $10,580.

**FINANCIAL AID PICTURE**

**Students with need:** Need-based aid available for full-time and part-time students. Work study available nights, weekends, and for part-time students.
**Students without need:** No-need awards available for academics, athletics, leadership, music/drama.

**FINANCIAL AID PROCEDURES**

**Forms required:** FAFSA.
**Dates and Deadlines:** Priority date 3/15; no closing date. Applicants notified on a rolling basis starting 4/1; must reply by 5/1 or within 4 week(s) of notification.

**Transfers:** Priority date 3/1; no deadline. Applicants notified by 3/10; must reply within 4 week(s) of notification.

**CONTACT**

Steve Woodburn, Director of Student Financial Aid
8787 West Alameda Avenue, Lakewood, CO 80226
(303) 963-3230

## Colorado College

Colorado Springs, Colorado       Federal Code: 001347
www.coloradocollege.edu          CSS Code: 4072

**4-year private** liberal arts college in large city.
**Enrollment:** 2,096 undergrads. 583 full-time freshmen.
**Selectivity:** Admits less than 50% of applicants.

**BASIC COSTS (2015-2016)**

**Tuition and fees:** $48,996.
**Room and board:** $11,215.

**FINANCIAL AID PICTURE (2015-2016)**

**Students with need:** Out of 290 full-time freshmen who applied for aid, 226 were judged to have need. Of these, 226 received aid, and 225 had their full need met. Average financial aid package met 100% of need; average scholarship/grant was $45,232; average loan was $2,563. Need-based aid available for part-time students.
**Students without need:** 43 full-time freshmen who did not demonstrate need for aid received scholarships/grants; average award was $9,490. No-need awards available for academics, athletics, leadership.
**Scholarships offered:** 15 full-time freshmen received athletic scholarships; average amount $44,790.

**FINANCIAL AID PROCEDURES**

**Forms required:** FAFSA, CSS PROFILE.
**Dates and Deadlines:** Closing date 2/15. Applicants notified by 3/15; must reply by 5/1.
**Transfers:** Closing date 3/1. Applicants notified by 4/15; must reply by 5/15.

**CONTACT**

James Swanson, Director of Financial Aid
14 East Cache La Poudre Street, Colorado Springs, CO 80903-9854
(800) 260-6458

## Colorado Heights University

Denver, Colorado
www.chu.edu            Federal Code: 032893

**4-year private** business and liberal arts college in very large city.
**Enrollment:** 107 undergrads.

**BASIC COSTS (2015-2016)**

**Tuition and fees:** $8,796.
**Per-credit charge:** $275.
**Room only:** $1,750.

**FINANCIAL AID PICTURE**

**Students with need:** Need-based aid available for full-time and part-time students.
**Students without need:** This college awards aid only to students with need.

**FINANCIAL AID PROCEDURES**

**Forms required:** FAFSA.
**Dates and Deadlines:** Applicants notified on a rolling basis.
**Transfers:** No deadline. Applicants notified on a rolling basis.

**CONTACT**
Beba Predic, Director of Finance
3001 South Federal Boulevard, Denver, CO 80236
(303) 937-4202

## Colorado Mesa University
Grand Junction, Colorado
www.coloradomesa.edu          Federal Code: 001358

**4-year public** community and liberal arts college in small city.
**Enrollment:** 8,628 undergrads, 17% part-time. 2,030 full-time freshmen.
**Selectivity:** Admits over 75% of applicants.

**BASIC COSTS (2015-2016)**
**Tuition and fees:** $8,008; out-of-state residents $19,363.
**Per-credit charge:** $240; out-of-state residents $618.
**Room and board:** $10,526.

**FINANCIAL AID PICTURE**
**Students with need:** Need-based aid available for full-time and part-time students. Work study available nights, weekends, and for part-time students.
**Students without need:** No-need awards available for academics, alumni affiliation, art, athletics, leadership, music/drama.

**FINANCIAL AID PROCEDURES**
**Forms required:** FAFSA.
**Dates and Deadlines:** Applicants notified on a rolling basis starting 4/1; must reply within 2 week(s) of notification.
**Transfers:** No deadline. Applicants notified on a rolling basis starting 4/1.

**CONTACT**
Curt Martin, Director of Financial Aid
1100 North Avenue, Grand Junction, CO 81501-3122
(970) 248-1396

## Colorado Mountain College
Glenwood Springs, Colorado
www.coloradomtn.edu          Federal Code: 004506

**2-year public** community and liberal arts college in small town.
**Enrollment:** 4,023 undergrads, 89% part-time. 87 full-time freshmen.
**Selectivity:** Open admission; but selective for some programs.

**BASIC COSTS (2015-2016)**
**Tuition and fees:** $2,010; out-of-district residents $3,510; out-of-state residents $11,490.
**Per-credit charge:** $57; out-of-district residents $107; out-of-state residents $373.
**Room and board:** $9,000.

**FINANCIAL AID PICTURE**
**Students with need:** Need-based aid available for full-time and part-time students. Work study available nights, weekends, and for part-time students.
**Students without need:** This college awards aid only to students with need.

**FINANCIAL AID PROCEDURES**
**Forms required:** FAFSA.
**Dates and Deadlines:** Priority date 3/31; no closing date. Applicants notified on a rolling basis; must reply within 4 week(s) of notification.
**Transfers:** Transfer scholarships available for Colorado residents with 3.0 GPA and minimum 20 credit hours from previous schools.

**CONTACT**
Tom Valles, Director of Student Financial Aid
802 Grand Avenue, Glenwood Springs, CO 81601
(970) 947-8277

## Colorado Northwestern Community College
Rangely, Colorado
www.cncc.edu          Federal Code: 001359

**2-year public** community college in rural community.
**Enrollment:** 649 undergrads.
**Selectivity:** Open admission; but selective for some programs.

**BASIC COSTS (2015-2016)**
**Tuition and fees:** $4,210; out-of-state residents $6,999.
**Per-credit charge:** $131; out-of-state residents $223.
**Room and board:** $6,654.
**Additional info:** In-state tuition based upon assumption of Colorado Opportunity Fund waiver of $75 per-credit hour.

**FINANCIAL AID PICTURE (2014-2015)**
**Students with need:** 56% of average financial aid package awarded as scholarships/grants, 44% awarded as loans/jobs. Need-based aid available for part-time students. Work study available nights, weekends, and for part-time students.
**Students without need:** No-need awards available for academics, athletics, leadership.
**Scholarships offered:** Academic Scholarships: $200-$1,000; for Colorado residents based on grades, specific talent, area of study; requires application, essay, informal interview, 2.5 GPA.

**FINANCIAL AID PROCEDURES**
**Forms required:** FAFSA, institutional form.
**Dates and Deadlines:** Priority date 5/1; no closing date. Applicants notified on a rolling basis starting 5/15; must reply within 4 week(s) of notification.
**Transfers:** No deadline.

**CONTACT**
Tresa England, Director, Financial Aid
500 Kennedy Drive, Rangely, CO 81648
(970) 675-3204

## Colorado School of Healing Arts
Lakewood, Colorado
www.csha.net          Federal Code: 035844

**2-year for-profit** career college in small city.
**Enrollment:** 176 undergrads.
**Selectivity:** Open admission.

**FINANCIAL AID PICTURE**
**Students with need:** Need-based aid available for full-time and part-time students.
**Students without need:** This college awards aid only to students with need.

**FINANCIAL AID PROCEDURES**
**Forms required:** FAFSA.

**CONTACT**
Andrea Niece, Financial Aid Administrator
7655 West Mississippi Avenue, Suite 100, Lakewood, CO 80226
(303) 986-2320 ext. 26

## Colorado School of Mines
Golden, Colorado
www.mines.edu          Federal Code: 001348

**4-year public** university and engineering college in large town.
**Enrollment:** 4,533 undergrads, 4% part-time. 998 full-time freshmen.

**Selectivity:** Admits less than 50% of applicants.

### BASIC COSTS (2015-2016)
**Tuition and fees:** $17,353; out-of-state residents $34,828.
**Per-credit charge:** $508; out-of-state residents $1,090.
**Room and board:** $11,008.

### FINANCIAL AID PICTURE (2014-2015)
**Students with need:** Out of 829 full-time freshmen who applied for aid, 522 were judged to have need. Of these, 522 received aid, and 133 had their full need met. Average financial aid package met 62% of need; average scholarship/grant was $4,347; average loan was $3,599. For part-time students, average financial aid package was $6,749.
**Students without need:** 318 full-time freshmen who did not demonstrate need for aid received scholarships/grants; average award was $7,911. No-need awards available for academics, alumni affiliation, athletics, music/drama, ROTC.
**Scholarships offered:** 45 full-time freshmen received athletic scholarships; average amount $7,628.

### FINANCIAL AID PROCEDURES
**Forms required:** FAFSA.
**Dates and Deadlines:** Priority date 3/1; closing date 10/1. Applicants notified on a rolling basis starting 3/1; must reply by 5/1.
**Transfers:** Applicants notified on a rolling basis starting 3/15; must reply by 5/1. Federal aid only (Pell grant and Stafford loan). No aid available for second undergraduate degree candidates.

### CONTACT
Jill Robertson, Director of Financial Aid
Undergraduate Admissions Office, Golden, CO 80401-6114
(303) 273-3301

## Colorado School of Trades
Lakewood, Colorado
www.schooloftrades.edu              Federal Code: 013513

**2-year for-profit** technical college in small city.
**Enrollment:** 153 undergrads.
**Selectivity:** Open admission.

### FINANCIAL AID PICTURE
**Students with need:** Need-based aid available for full-time students.

### FINANCIAL AID PROCEDURES
**Forms required:** FAFSA, institutional form.

### CONTACT
Robert Martin, President
1575 Hoyt Street, Lakewood, CO 80215-2945
(303) 233-4697 ext. 44

## Colorado State University
Fort Collins, Colorado              Federal Code: 001350
www.colostate.edu              CSS Code: 4075

**4-year public** university in small city.
**Enrollment:** 23,009 undergrads, 7% part-time. 4,064 full-time freshmen.
**Selectivity:** Admits over 75% of applicants.

### BASIC COSTS (2015-2016)
**Tuition and fees:** $10,558; out-of-state residents $27,267.
**Per-credit charge:** $377; out-of-state residents $1,251.
**Room and board:** $10,794.

### FINANCIAL AID PICTURE (2014-2015)
**Students with need:** Out of 3,520 full-time freshmen who applied for aid, 2,181 were judged to have need. Of these, 1,990 received aid, and 692 had

their full need met. Average financial aid package met 64% of need; average scholarship/grant was $7,274; average loan was $5,099. For part-time students, average financial aid package was $6,501.
**Students without need:** 688 full-time freshmen who did not demonstrate need for aid received scholarships/grants; average award was $4,179. No-need awards available for academics, alumni affiliation, art, athletics, leadership, music/drama, state/district residency.
**Scholarships offered:** 28 full-time freshmen received athletic scholarships; average amount $18,582.
**Additional info:** Colorado students who have a family Adjusted Gross Income (AGI) on their federal income tax return(s) of $57,000 or less (and who meet other eligibility requirements) given grants to cover at least one-half the cost of tuition. Students who are eligible for a federal Pell Grant receive 100% of base tuition and standard fees.

### FINANCIAL AID PROCEDURES
**Forms required:** FAFSA. CSS PROFILE required for first-time domestic applicants.
**Dates and Deadlines:** Priority date 3/1; no closing date. Applicants notified on a rolling basis starting 3/1.

### CONTACT
Tom Biedscheid, Director of Student Financial Aid
Office of Admissions/Colorado State University, Fort Collins, CO 80523-1062
(970) 491-6321

## Colorado State University: Pueblo
Pueblo, Colorado
www.csupueblo.edu              Federal Code: 001365

**4-year public** university in small city.
**Enrollment:** 4,227 undergrads, 15% part-time. 877 full-time freshmen.

### BASIC COSTS (2015-2016)
**Tuition and fees:** $8,281; out-of-state residents $19,851.
**Per-credit charge:** $228.58; out-of-state residents $687.14.
**Room and board:** $9,636.

### FINANCIAL AID PICTURE
**Students with need:** Need-based aid available for full-time and part-time students. Work study available nights, weekends, and for part-time students.
**Students without need:** No-need awards available for academics, alumni affiliation, art, athletics, job skills, leadership, minority status, music/drama, ROTC, state/district residency.
**Scholarships offered:** Merit scholarships of $2,000 or more are awarded to admitted students with a cumulative weighted GPA of 3.5 or higher and either an ACT composite score of 25 or higher or SAT composite (math and verbal) of 1120 or higher. Admitted entering first-year students who have either a 3.8 GPA or 26 ACT Composite or 1200 SAT Composite will be invited to apply for the 25 places available each year in the Honors Program; other interested students may also apply. Tuition awards will be available to students who are accepted to the program.

### FINANCIAL AID PROCEDURES
**Forms required:** FAFSA.
**Dates and Deadlines:** Closing date 3/1. Applicants notified on a rolling basis starting 3/15; must reply within 3 week(s) of notification.

### CONTACT
Sean McGivney, Director of Financial Aid
2200 Bonforte Boulevard, Pueblo, CO 81001-4901
(719) 549-2753

## Colorado Technical University
Colorado Springs, Colorado
www.coloradotech.edu                 Federal Code: 010148

**4-year for-profit** university and technical college in large city.
**Enrollment:** 1,144 undergrads.
**Selectivity:** Open admission; but selective for some programs.

**BASIC COSTS (2015-2016)**
**Per-credit charge:** $325.
**Additional info:** Associate programs: $30,225-$30,387.50. Bachelor's programs: $58,500-$60,450. Technology fee: $125 per term.

**FINANCIAL AID PICTURE**
**Students with need:** Need-based aid available for full-time and part-time students. Work study available nights, weekends, and for part-time students.
**Students without need:** No-need awards available for academics, ROTC.

**FINANCIAL AID PROCEDURES**
**Forms required:** FAFSA.
**Dates and Deadlines:** Applicants notified on a rolling basis starting 6/30.
**Transfers:** No deadline.

**CONTACT**
Cindy Rubek, Director of Student Financial Services
4435 North Chestnut Street, Colorado Springs, CO 80907
(719) 598-0200

## Community College of Aurora
Aurora, Colorado
www.ccaurora.edu                 Federal Code: 016058

**2-year public** community college in large city.
**Enrollment:** 5,405 undergrads, 79% part-time. 216 full-time freshmen.
**Selectivity:** Open admission.

**BASIC COSTS (2015-2016)**
**Tuition and fees:** $4,163; out-of-state residents $16,310.
**Per-credit charge:** $131; out-of-state residents $535.

**FINANCIAL AID PICTURE**
**Students with need:** Need-based aid available for full-time and part-time students.
**Students without need:** No-need awards available for academics, minority status, music/drama, state/district residency.

**FINANCIAL AID PROCEDURES**
**Forms required:** FAFSA.
**Dates and Deadlines:** Priority date 6/1; no closing date. Applicants notified on a rolling basis starting 7/15.

**CONTACT**
John Young, Executive Director, Financial Aid
16000 East CentreTech Parkway, Aurora, CO 80011-9036
(303) 360-4709

## Community College of Denver
Denver, Colorado
www.ccd.edu                 Federal Code: 009542

**2-year public** community college in very large city.
**Enrollment:** 8,003 undergrads.
**Selectivity:** Open admission; but selective for some programs.

**BASIC COSTS (2015-2016)**
**Tuition and fees:** $4,916; out-of-state residents $17,063.
**Per-credit charge:** $131; out-of-state residents $535.

**Additional info:** In-state tuition based upon assumption of Colorado Opportunity Fund waiver of $75 per-credit hour.

**FINANCIAL AID PICTURE**
**Students with need:** Need-based aid available for full-time and part-time students.
**Students without need:** No-need awards available for academics, leadership, state/district residency.

**FINANCIAL AID PROCEDURES**
**Forms required:** FAFSA, institutional form.
**Dates and Deadlines:** Priority date 4/15; no closing date. Applicants notified on a rolling basis.

**CONTACT**
Thad Spaulding, Director of Financial Aid
Campus Box 201, PO Box 173363, Denver, CO 80217-3363
(303) 556-5503

## Denver School of Nursing
Denver, Colorado
www.denverschoolofnursing.edu

**4-year for-profit** nursing college in very large city.
**Enrollment:** 653 full-time undergrads.

**BASIC COSTS (2015-2016)**
**Additional info:** Total tuition and fees for Bachelor of Science in Nursing Completion program, $54,923. Total Tuition and fees for the Associate Degree in Nursing Completion Program is $43,837.

**FINANCIAL AID PICTURE**
**Students with need:** Need-based aid available for full-time and part-time students.
**Students without need:** This college awards aid only to students with need.

**FINANCIAL AID PROCEDURES**
**Forms required:** FAFSA.

**CONTACT**
Geri Reichmuth, Director of Financial Aid
1401 19th Street, Denver, CO 80202

## DeVry University: Westminster
Westminster, Colorado
www.devry.edu                 Federal Code: 014831

**4-year for-profit** university in very large city.
**Enrollment:** 409 undergrads.

**BASIC COSTS (2015-2016)**
**Tuition and fees:** $17,132.
**Per-credit charge:** $609.

**FINANCIAL AID PICTURE**
**Students with need:** Need-based aid available for full-time and part-time students.
**Students without need:** This college awards aid only to students with need.

**FINANCIAL AID PROCEDURES**
**Forms required:** FAFSA.
**Dates and Deadlines:** Applicants notified on a rolling basis.

**CONTACT**
1870 West 122nd Avenue, Westminster, CO 80234-2010
(303) 329-3340

## Fort Lewis College

Durango, Colorado
www.fortlewis.edu                    Federal Code: 001353

**4-year public** business and liberal arts college in large town.
**Enrollment:** 3,570 undergrads, 6% part-time. 758 full-time freshmen.
**Selectivity:** Admits over 75% of applicants.

### BASIC COSTS (2015-2016)
**Tuition and fees:** $7,601; out-of-state residents $17,817.
**Per-credit charge:** $244; out-of-state residents $670.
**Room and board:** $9,130.
**Additional info:** Tuition/fee waivers available for minority students.

### FINANCIAL AID PICTURE (2014-2015)
**Students with need:** Out of 656 full-time freshmen who applied for aid, 523 were judged to have need. Of these, 522 received aid, and 81 had their full need met. Average financial aid package met 90% of need; average scholarship/grant was $4,902; average loan was $3,325. For part-time students, average financial aid package was $4,629.
**Students without need:** 157 full-time freshmen who did not demonstrate need for aid received scholarships/grants; average award was $3,362. No-need awards available for academics, alumni affiliation, art, athletics, leadership, music/drama, state/district residency.
**Scholarships offered:** *Merit:* Presidential Scholarship: $8,000 out-of-state, $2,000 in-state; 121 admission index required. Provost Scholarship: $7,000 out-of-state, $1,500 in-state; 110-120 admission index required. Dean's Scholarship: $6,000 out-of-state, $1,000 in-state; 101-109 admission index required. Academic Promise Scholarship: $4,000 out-of-state, $750 in-state; 92-100 admission index required. New Mexico Reciprocal Scholarship: New Mexico residents are given in-state tuition rates; based on 3.5 GPA; number of awards limited. *Athletic:* 71 full-time freshmen received athletic scholarships; average amount $5,562.
**Additional info:** Tuition waived for Native Americans of federally recognized tribes; census number and Certificate of Indian Blood must accompany application.

### FINANCIAL AID PROCEDURES
**Forms required:** FAFSA.
**Dates and Deadlines:** Priority date 2/15; no closing date. Applicants notified by 3/1; must reply by 9/16.
**Transfers:** No deadline. Applicants notified on a rolling basis.

### CONTACT
Tracey Piccoli, Director of Financial Aid
1000 Rim Drive, Durango, CO 81301-3999
(970) 247-7073

## Front Range Community College

Westminster, Colorado
www.frontrange.edu                    Federal Code: 007933

**2-year public** community college in large city.
**Enrollment:** 15,551 undergrads, 67% part-time. 1,029 full-time freshmen.
**Selectivity:** Open admission.

### BASIC COSTS (2015-2016)
**Tuition and fees:** $4,310; out-of-state residents $16,457.
**Per-credit charge:** $131; out-of-state residents $535.
**Additional info:** In-state tuition based upon assumption of Colorado Opportunity Fund waiver of $75 per-credit hour.

### FINANCIAL AID PICTURE (2014-2015)
**Students with need:** 59% of average financial aid package awarded as scholarships/grants, 41% awarded as loans/jobs. Need-based aid available for part-time students. Work study available nights, weekends, and for part-time students.

**Students without need:** No-need awards available for academics, job skills, leadership, state/district residency.

### FINANCIAL AID PROCEDURES
**Forms required:** FAFSA, institutional form.
**Dates and Deadlines:** Priority date 5/1; no closing date. Applicants notified on a rolling basis starting 4/15; must reply within 3 week(s) of notification.

### CONTACT
Carolee Goldsmith, Director of Financial Aid
3645 West 112th Avenue, Westminster, CO 80031
(303) 439-9454

## IntelliTec College

Colorado Springs, Colorado
http://intelliteccollege.com          Federal Code: 008635

**2-year for-profit** technical college in large city.
**Enrollment:** 828 undergrads.
**Selectivity:** Open admission.

### FINANCIAL AID PICTURE
**Students with need:** Need-based aid available for full-time and part-time students. Work study available nights.
**Students without need:** This college awards aid only to students with need.

### FINANCIAL AID PROCEDURES
**Forms required:** FAFSA, state aid form, institutional form.
**Dates and Deadlines:** Applicants notified on a rolling basis.
**Transfers:** No deadline.

### CONTACT
Kristy Sanchez, Lead Financial Services Representative
2315 East Pikes Peak Avenue, Colorado Springs, CO 80909
(719) 632-7626

## IntelliTec College: Grand Junction

Grand Junction, Colorado
http://intelliteccollege.com          Federal Code: 030669

**2-year for-profit** technical college in small city.
**Enrollment:** 145 undergrads.
**Selectivity:** Open admission.

### FINANCIAL AID PICTURE
**Students with need:** Need-based aid available for full-time students.
**Students without need:** This college awards aid only to students with need.

### FINANCIAL AID PROCEDURES
**Forms required:** FAFSA.
**Dates and Deadlines:** Applicants notified on a rolling basis.
**Transfers:** No deadline.

### CONTACT
Mike Grove, Chief Financial Aid Officer
772 Horizon Drive, Grand Junction, CO 81506
(970) 245-8101

## Johnson & Wales University: Denver

Denver, Colorado
www.jwu.edu                    Federal Code: 003404

**4-year private** college in large city.
**Enrollment:** 1,356 undergrads, 10% part-time. 341 full-time freshmen.

**Selectivity:** Admits over 75% of applicants.

**BASIC COSTS (2015-2016)**
**Tuition and fees:** $30,681.
**Room and board:** $11,499.

**FINANCIAL AID PICTURE (2015-2016)**
**Students with need:** Out of 325 full-time freshmen who applied for aid, 281 were judged to have need. Of these, 281 received aid, and 48 had their full need met. Average financial aid package met 74% of need; average scholarship/grant was $9,346; average loan was $3,390. For part-time students, average financial aid package was $13,681.
**Students without need:** 39 full-time freshmen who did not demonstrate need for aid received scholarships/grants; average award was $11,224. No-need awards available for academics, alumni affiliation, job skills, leadership, state/district residency.

**FINANCIAL AID PROCEDURES**
**Forms required:** FAFSA.
**Dates and Deadlines:** Applicants notified on a rolling basis starting 3/1; must reply within 2 week(s) of notification.

**CONTACT**
Lynn Robinson, Chief Financial Aid Officer
7150 Montview Boulevard, Denver, CO 80220
(800) 342-5598 ext. 4648

## Lamar Community College
Lamar, Colorado
www.lamarcc.edu                  Federal Code: 001355

**2-year public** community college in small town.
**Enrollment:** 476 undergrads, 28% part-time. 115 full-time freshmen.
**Selectivity:** Open admission; but selective for some programs.

**BASIC COSTS (2015-2016)**
**Tuition and fees:** $4,329; out-of-state residents $7,118.
**Per-credit charge:** $131; out-of-state residents $223.
**Room and board:** $6,070.
**Additional info:** In-state tuition based upon assumption of Colorado Opportunity Fund waiver of $75 per-credit hour.

**FINANCIAL AID PICTURE (2014-2015)**
**Students with need:** 58% of average financial aid package awarded as scholarships/grants, 42% awarded as loans/jobs. Need-based aid available for part-time students.
**Students without need:** No-need awards available for academics, athletics, minority status, state/district residency.

**FINANCIAL AID PROCEDURES**
**Forms required:** FAFSA.
**Dates and Deadlines:** Priority date 4/1; no closing date. Applicants notified on a rolling basis starting 4/15.
**Transfers:** No deadline.

**CONTACT**
Teale Hemphill, Director of Financial Aid
2401 South Main Street, Lamar, CO 81052-3999

## Metropolitan State University of Denver
Denver, Colorado
www.msudenver.edu                  Federal Code: 001360

**4-year public** liberal arts college in very large city.
**Enrollment:** 20,584 undergrads.

**BASIC COSTS (2015-2016)**
**Tuition and fees:** $6,420; out-of-state residents $19,257.

**Per-credit charge:** $292; out-of-state residents $785.

**FINANCIAL AID PICTURE**
**Students with need:** Need-based aid available for full-time and part-time students.

**FINANCIAL AID PROCEDURES**
**Forms required:** FAFSA.
**Dates and Deadlines:** Applicants notified on a rolling basis starting 3/15.
**Transfers:** No deadline.

**CONTACT**
Cindy Hejl, Director of Financial Aid
Campus Box 16, Denver, CO 80217

## Morgan Community College
Fort Morgan, Colorado
www.morgancc.edu                  Federal Code: 009981

**2-year public** community college in large town.
**Enrollment:** 1,172 undergrads.
**Selectivity:** Open admission; but selective for some programs.

**BASIC COSTS (2015-2016)**
**Tuition and fees:** $4,097; out-of-state residents $16,244.
**Per-credit charge:** $131; out-of-state residents $535.

**FINANCIAL AID PICTURE**
**Students with need:** Need-based aid available for full-time and part-time students. Work study available nights, weekends, and for part-time students.

**FINANCIAL AID PROCEDURES**
**Forms required:** FAFSA.
**Dates and Deadlines:** Closing date 4/2. Applicants notified on a rolling basis.

**CONTACT**
Sally Nestor, Director of Financial Aid
920 Barlow Road, Fort Morgan, CO 80701
(970) 542-3100

## Naropa University
Boulder, Colorado
www.naropa.edu                  Federal Code: 014652

**4-year private** university and liberal arts college in small city.
**Enrollment:** 396 undergrads, 7% part-time. 43 full-time freshmen.
**Selectivity:** Admits over 75% of applicants.

**BASIC COSTS (2015-2016)**
**Tuition and fees:** $30,750.
**Per-credit charge:** $995.
**Room and board:** $9,604.

**FINANCIAL AID PICTURE (2015-2016)**
**Students with need:** Out of 40 full-time freshmen who applied for aid, 36 were judged to have need. Of these, 36 received aid. Average financial aid package met 68% of need; average scholarship/grant was $18,092; average loan was $5,620. For part-time students, average financial aid package was $32,293.
**Students without need:** This college awards aid only to students with need.

**FINANCIAL AID PROCEDURES**
**Forms required:** FAFSA, state aid form.
**Dates and Deadlines:** Priority date 3/1; no closing date. Applicants notified on a rolling basis starting 3/1; must reply within 4 week(s) of notification.

**CONTACT**
Nancy Morrell, Director of Student Financial Aid
2130 Arapahoe Avenue, Boulder, CO 80302-6697
(303) 546-3534

## Nazarene Bible College
Colorado Springs, Colorado
www.nbc.edu                    Federal Code: 013007

**4-year private** Bible college in very large city, affiliated with Church of the Nazarene.
**Enrollment:** 760 undergrads, 85% part-time. 1 full-time freshmen.
**Selectivity:** Open admission.

**BASIC COSTS (2015-2016)**
**Tuition and fees:** $14,250.
**Per-credit charge:** $450.

**FINANCIAL AID PICTURE**
**Students with need:** Need-based aid available for full-time and part-time students. Work study available nights, weekends, and for part-time students.
**Students without need:** No-need awards available for academics, minority status, religious affiliation.

**FINANCIAL AID PROCEDURES**
**Forms required:** FAFSA.
**Dates and Deadlines:** Applicants notified on a rolling basis starting 8/1.
**Transfers:** No deadline. Applicants notified on a rolling basis.

**CONTACT**
Jenny Madsen, Director of Financial Aid
1111 Academy Park Loop, Colorado Springs, CO 80910-3704
(719) 884-5050

## Northeastern Junior College
Sterling, Colorado
www.njc.edu                    Federal Code: 001361

**2-year public** community and junior college in large town.
**Enrollment:** 1,063 undergrads, 19% part-time. 312 full-time freshmen.
**Selectivity:** Open admission; but selective for some programs.

**BASIC COSTS (2015-2016)**
**Tuition and fees:** $4,515; out-of-state residents $7,304.
**Per-credit charge:** $125; out-of-state residents $223.
**Room and board:** $7,504.
**Additional info:** In-state tuition based upon assumption of Colorado Opportunity Fund waiver of $75 per-credit hour. Tuition/fee waivers available for adults, minority students.

**FINANCIAL AID PICTURE (2014-2015)**
**Students with need:** 53% of average financial aid package awarded as scholarships/grants, 47% awarded as loans/jobs. Need-based aid available for part-time students. Work study available nights, weekends, and for part-time students.
**Students without need:** No-need awards available for academics, alumni affiliation, art, athletics, job skills, leadership, music/drama, state/district residency.
**Additional info:** Need-based financial aid available to part-time students taking 6 credits or more per semester.

**FINANCIAL AID PROCEDURES**
**Forms required:** FAFSA, institutional form.
**Dates and Deadlines:** Priority date 3/1; no closing date. Applicants notified on a rolling basis starting 4/15; must reply within 3 week(s) of notification.
**Transfers:** No deadline. Applicants notified on a rolling basis starting 4/15; must reply within 3 week(s) of notification.

**CONTACT**
Alice Weingardt, Financial Aid Director
100 College Avenue, Sterling, CO 80751-2399
(970) 521-6751

## Otero Junior College
La Junta, Colorado
https://www.ojc.edu            Federal Code: 001362

**2-year public** community and junior college in small town.
**Enrollment:** 1,410 undergrads.
**Selectivity:** Open admission; but selective for some programs.

**BASIC COSTS (2015-2016)**
**Tuition and fees:** $4,209; out-of-state residents $6,998.
**Per-credit charge:** $131; out-of-state residents $223.
**Room and board:** $6,306.

**FINANCIAL AID PICTURE (2014-2015)**
**Students with need:** 73% of average financial aid package awarded as scholarships/grants, 27% awarded as loans/jobs. Need-based aid available for part-time students. Work study available nights, weekends, and for part-time students.
**Students without need:** No-need awards available for academics, athletics, state/district residency.

**FINANCIAL AID PROCEDURES**
**Forms required:** FAFSA.
**Dates and Deadlines:** Priority date 4/1; no closing date. Applicants notified on a rolling basis starting 4/1; must reply within 2 week(s) of notification.
**Transfers:** No deadline. Applicants notified on a rolling basis starting 4/1; must reply within 2 week(s) of notification.

**CONTACT**
Angela Moore, Financial Aid Director
1802 Colorado Avenue, La Junta, CO 81050
(719) 384-6834

## Pikes Peak Community College
Colorado Springs, Colorado
www.ppcc.edu                   Federal Code: 008896

**2-year public** community college in large city.
**Enrollment:** 12,448 undergrads, 60% part-time. 1,212 full-time freshmen.
**Selectivity:** Open admission.

**BASIC COSTS (2015-2016)**
**Tuition and fees:** $4,218; out-of-state residents $16,365.
**Per-credit charge:** $131; out-of-state residents $536.
**Additional info:** In-state tuition based upon assumption of Colorado Opportunity Fund waiver of $75 per-credit hour.

**FINANCIAL AID PICTURE (2014-2015)**
**Students with need:** Average financial aid package met 40% of need; average scholarship/grant was $4,200; average loan was $3,000. For part-time students, average financial aid package was $7,500.
**Students without need:** 25 full-time freshmen who did not demonstrate need for aid received scholarships/grants; average award was $500.

**FINANCIAL AID PROCEDURES**
**Forms required:** FAFSA.
**Dates and Deadlines:** Priority date 3/31; closing date 7/1. Applicants notified on a rolling basis; must reply within 2 week(s) of notification.

**CONTACT**
Ron Swartwood, Director of Financial Aid
5675 South Academy Boulevard, Colorado Springs, CO 80906-5498
(719) 502-3000

## Platt College: Aurora

Aurora, Colorado
www.plattcolorado.edu            Federal Code: 030149

**4-year for-profit** nursing college in very large city.
**Enrollment:** 198 undergrads.
**Selectivity:** Open admission; but selective for some programs.

**BASIC COSTS (2015-2016)**
**Tuition and fees:** $19,786.
**Additional info:** Additiona fees may apply.

**FINANCIAL AID PICTURE**
**Students with need:** Need-based aid available for full-time students.
**Students without need:** This college awards aid only to students with need.

**FINANCIAL AID PROCEDURES**
**Forms required:** FAFSA, institutional form.
**Dates and Deadlines:** Applicants notified on a rolling basis.

**CONTACT**
Margie Rose, Director of Financial Aid
3100 South Parker Road, Aurora, CO 80014-3141
(303) 369-5151

## Pueblo Community College

Pueblo, Colorado
www.pueblocc.edu            Federal Code: 014829

**2-year public** community college in small city.
**Enrollment:** 4,893 undergrads, 61% part-time. 277 full-time freshmen.
**Selectivity:** Open admission; but selective for some programs.

**BASIC COSTS (2015-2016)**
**Tuition and fees:** $4,479; out-of-state residents $16,626.
**Per-credit charge:** $131; out-of-state residents $535.
**Additional info:** In-state tuition based upon assumption of Colorado Opportunity Fund waiver of $75 per-credit hour.

**FINANCIAL AID PICTURE**
**Students with need:** Need-based aid available for full-time and part-time students. Work study available nights.
**Students without need:** No-need awards available for academics, art, job skills, leadership, music/drama.

**FINANCIAL AID PROCEDURES**
**Forms required:** FAFSA.
**Dates and Deadlines:** Priority date 3/15; no closing date. Applicants notified on a rolling basis starting 4/1.
**Transfers:** No deadline. Applicants notified on a rolling basis starting 4/1.

**CONTACT**
Monica Hardwick, Director of Financial Aid
900 West Orman Avenue, Pueblo, CO 81004-1499
(719) 549-3020

## Red Rocks Community College

Lakewood, Colorado
www.rrcc.edu            Federal Code: 009543

**2-year public** community and career college in small city.
**Enrollment:** 7,789 undergrads.
**Selectivity:** Open admission.

**BASIC COSTS (2015-2016)**
**Tuition and fees:** $4,353; out-of-state residents $16,499.

**Per-credit charge:** $131; out-of-state residents $536.

**FINANCIAL AID PICTURE**
**Students with need:** Need-based aid available for full-time and part-time students.
**Students without need:** No-need awards available for academics, leadership, minority status, state/district residency.

**FINANCIAL AID PROCEDURES**
**Forms required:** FAFSA.
**Dates and Deadlines:** Priority date 4/1; no closing date. Applicants notified on a rolling basis starting 5/1.

**CONTACT**
Linda Crook, Director of Financial Aid
13300 West Sixth Avenue, Lakewood, CO 80228-1255
(303) 914-6256

## Redstone College

Broomfield, Colorado
www.redstone.edu            Federal Code: 007297

**2-year for-profit** technical college in small city.
**Enrollment:** 552 undergrads.
**Selectivity:** Open admission.

**BASIC COSTS (2015-2016)**
**Additional info:** Tuition and fees for entire Associate degree program $33,455 to $40,219 depending on program.

**FINANCIAL AID PICTURE**
**Students with need:** Need-based aid available for full-time students.
**Students without need:** This college awards aid only to students with need.

**FINANCIAL AID PROCEDURES**
**Forms required:** FAFSA, state aid form.
**Dates and Deadlines:** Applicants notified on a rolling basis; must reply within 2 week(s) of notification.

**CONTACT**
Alicia Harbin, Financial Aid Director
10851 West 120th Avenue, Broomfield, CO 80021-3401

## Regis University

Denver, Colorado
www.regis.edu            Federal Code: 001363

**4-year private** university and liberal arts college in very large city, affiliated with Roman Catholic Church.
**Enrollment:** 4,414 undergrads, 45% part-time. 481 full-time freshmen.
**Selectivity:** Admits 50 to 75% of applicants.

**BASIC COSTS (2016-2017)**
**Tuition and fees:** $33,935.
**Per-credit charge:** $1,035.
**Room and board:** $10,040.

**FINANCIAL AID PICTURE (2014-2015)**
**Students with need:** Out of 384 full-time freshmen who applied for aid, 334 were judged to have need. Of these, 334 received aid, and 53 had their full need met. Average financial aid package met 83% of need; average scholarship/grant was $21,173; average loan was $3,634. For part-time students, average financial aid package was $9,939.
**Students without need:** 131 full-time freshmen who did not demonstrate need for aid received scholarships/grants; average award was $14,007. No-need awards available for academics, athletics, leadership, music/drama, religious affiliation, ROTC, state/district residency.

**Scholarships offered:** 34 full-time freshmen received athletic scholarships; average amount $13,954.

## FINANCIAL AID PROCEDURES
**Forms required:** FAFSA.
**Dates and Deadlines:** Priority date 5/31; no closing date. Applicants notified on a rolling basis starting 3/15.
**Transfers:** Applicants notified by 4/1.

## CONTACT
Ellie Miller, Director of Financial Aid
3333 Regis Boulevard, Mail Code A12, Denver, CO 80221-1099
(800) 388-2366 ext. 4126

## Rocky Mountain College of Art & Design
Denver, Colorado
www.rmcad.edu                    Federal Code: 013991

**4-year for-profit** visual arts college in very large city.
**Enrollment:** 1,074 undergrads, 36% part-time. 76 full-time freshmen.
**Selectivity:** Open admission.

## BASIC COSTS (2016-2017)
**Tuition and fees:** $15,870.
**Per-credit charge:** $594.

## FINANCIAL AID PICTURE (2014-2015)
**Students with need:** 37% of average financial aid package awarded as scholarships/grants, 63% awarded as loans/jobs. Need-based aid available for part-time students. Work study available nights, weekends, and for part-time students.
**Students without need:** No-need awards available for academics, art, state/district residency.

## FINANCIAL AID PROCEDURES
**Forms required:** FAFSA.
**Dates and Deadlines:** Priority date 3/15; no closing date. Applicants notified on a rolling basis starting 4/1; must reply within 2 week(s) of notification.
**Transfers:** Must reply within 2 week(s) of notification.

## CONTACT
Michael Dulay, Senior Financial Aid Program Manager
1600 Pierce Street, Denver, CO 80214
(303) 505-6675

## Trinidad State Junior College
Trinidad, Colorado
www.trinidadstate.edu              Federal Code: 001368

**2-year public** community college in small town.
**Enrollment:** 1,216 undergrads.
**Selectivity:** Open admission; but selective for some programs.

## BASIC COSTS (2015-2016)
**Tuition and fees:** $4,353; out-of-state residents $7,142.
**Per-credit charge:** $130; out-of-state residents $223.
**Room and board:** $6,274.
**Additional info:** In-state tuition based upon assumption of Colorado Opportunity Fund waiver of $75 per-credit hour.

## FINANCIAL AID PICTURE
**Students with need:** Need-based aid available for full-time and part-time students. Work study available nights.
**Students without need:** No-need awards available for academics, athletics, state/district residency.

## FINANCIAL AID PROCEDURES
**Forms required:** FAFSA.

**Dates and Deadlines:** Priority date 5/1; no closing date. Applicants notified on a rolling basis starting 6/15.

## CONTACT
Wilma Atencio, Financial Aid Director
600 Prospect Street, Trinidad, CO 81082
(719) 846-5553

## United States Air Force Academy
USAF Academy, Colorado
www.academyadmissions.com          Federal Code: 001369

**4-year public** liberal arts and military college in large city.
**Enrollment:** 4,111 undergrads. 1,162 full-time freshmen.
**Selectivity:** Admits less than 50% of applicants.

## BASIC COSTS (2016-2017)
**Additional info:** All cadet expenses, including tuition, room and board and supplies are paid for by the federal government.

## CONTACT
HQ USAFA/RR 2304 Cadet Drive, Suite 2400, USAF Academy, CO 80840-5025

## University of Colorado Boulder
Boulder, Colorado
www.colorado.edu                   Federal Code: 001370

**4-year public** university in small city.
**Enrollment:** 26,491 undergrads, 6% part-time. 6,170 full-time freshmen.
**Selectivity:** Admits over 75% of applicants.

## BASIC COSTS (2015-2016)
**Tuition and fees:** $11,091; out-of-state residents $34,125.
**Room and board:** $13,194.

## FINANCIAL AID PICTURE (2015-2016)
**Students with need:** Out of 4,134 full-time freshmen who applied for aid, 2,616 were judged to have need. Of these, 2,526 received aid, and 1,109 had their full need met. Average financial aid package met 81% of need; average scholarship/grant was $10,283; average loan was $5,354. For part-time students, average financial aid package was $12,872.
**Students without need:** 1,953 full-time freshmen who did not demonstrate need for aid received scholarships/grants; average award was $8,628. No-need awards available for academics, alumni affiliation, art, athletics, leadership, music/drama, ROTC, state/district residency.
**Scholarships offered:** *Merit:* Presidential Scholars Program; $15,000 per year during freshman and sophomore years, $12,500 per year during junior and senior years; for out-of-state freshmen in top 1-3% of admitted out-of-state freshman class, based on GPA, class rank, and test scores; renewable based on minimum GPA. Chancellor's Achievement Scholarship; $25,000 over four years; for top 25% of out-of-state admitted new freshmen, based on GPA, class rank, and test scores; renewable based on minimum GPA. Norlin Scholars Program; $5,000; based on excellent academic or creative ability; 20-30 annual awards; renewable contingent upon academic progress. President Joseph A. Sewall Award; $5,000 per year; for Colorado residents; based on GPA and SAT/ACT. President Horace M. Hale Award; $3,500 per year; for Colorado residents; based on GPA and SAT/ACT. President James H. Baker Award; $2,500 per year; for Colorado residents; based on GPA and SAT/ACT. *Athletic:* 57 full-time freshmen received athletic scholarships; average amount $28,476.

## FINANCIAL AID PROCEDURES
**Forms required:** FAFSA. PROFILE accepted but not required.
**Dates and Deadlines:** Priority date 3/1; no closing date. Applicants notified on a rolling basis starting 3/15; must reply within 3 week(s) of notification.

**Transfers:** Some financial aid programs available exclusively to transfer students.

**CONTACT**
Gwen Pomper, Director of Financial Aid
Regent Administrative Center 125, Boulder, CO 80309-0552
(303) 492-5091

## University of Colorado Colorado Springs
Colorado Springs, Colorado
www.uccs.edu                    Federal Code: 004509

**4-year public** university in large city.
**Enrollment:** 9,480 undergrads, 22% part-time. 1,661 full-time freshmen.
**Selectivity:** Admits over 75% of applicants.

**BASIC COSTS (2015-2016)**
**Tuition and fees:** $9,428; out-of-state residents $22,298.
**Room and board:** $9,500.
**Additional info:** Students in the Western Undergraduate Exchange program pay 150% of in-state tuition rather than the full out-of-state tuition. Also, most students affiliated with the military are eligible for in-state tuition rates.

**FINANCIAL AID PICTURE (2014-2015)**
**Students with need:** Out of 1,494 full-time freshmen who applied for aid, 1,090 were judged to have need. Of these, 979 received aid, and 29 had their full need met. Average financial aid package met 52% of need; average scholarship/grant was $5,657; average loan was $3,289. For part-time students, average financial aid package was $6,250.
**Students without need:** 189 full-time freshmen who did not demonstrate need for aid received scholarships/grants; average award was $1,396. No-need awards available for academics, alumni affiliation, athletics, leadership, ROTC, state/district residency.
**Scholarships offered:** 65 full-time freshmen received athletic scholarships; average amount $4,508.

**FINANCIAL AID PROCEDURES**
**Forms required:** FAFSA.
**Dates and Deadlines:** Priority date 3/1; no closing date. Applicants notified on a rolling basis starting 4/15.

**CONTACT**
Jevita Rogers, Director of Financial Aid
1420 Austin Bluffs Parkway, Colorado Springs, CO 80918
(719) 255-3460

## University of Colorado Denver
Denver, Colorado
www.ucdenver.edu                Federal Code: 006740

**4-year public** university in very large city.
**Enrollment:** 10,786 undergrads, 26% part-time. 1,248 full-time freshmen.
**Selectivity:** Admits 50 to 75% of applicants.

**BASIC COSTS (2015-2016)**
**Tuition and fees:** $10,389; out-of-state residents $29,319.
**Room and board:** $9,603.

**FINANCIAL AID PICTURE (2014-2015)**
**Students with need:** Out of 1,080 full-time freshmen who applied for aid, 867 were judged to have need. Of these, 792 received aid, and 39 had their full need met. Average financial aid package met 45% of need; average scholarship/grant was $6,559; average loan was $2,840. For part-time students, average financial aid package was $6,062.

**Students without need:** 44 full-time freshmen who did not demonstrate need for aid received scholarships/grants; average award was $3,708. No-need awards available for academics, art, leadership, music/drama, state/district residency.
**Additional info:** Pell eligible, full-time students receive a financial aid package that includes a combination of grants, scholarships, and a work-study award sufficient to fund the student's share of tuition, fees, and estimated book expenses. An eligible student may remain in the program for up to 10 semesters or completion of a bachelor's degree.

**FINANCIAL AID PROCEDURES**
**Forms required:** FAFSA.
**Dates and Deadlines:** Applicants notified on a rolling basis starting 3/24.
**Transfers:** No deadline. Applicants notified on a rolling basis.

**CONTACT**
Justin Jaramillo, Director of Financial Aid - Interim
Box 173364, Campus Box 167, Denver, CO 80217-3364
(303) 556-2886

## University of Denver
Denver, Colorado              Federal Code: 001371
www.du.edu                    CSS Code: 4842

**4-year private** university in very large city.
**Enrollment:** 5,739 undergrads, 5% part-time. 1,415 full-time freshmen.
**Selectivity:** Admits 50 to 75% of applicants.

**BASIC COSTS (2016-2017)**
**Tuition and fees:** $46,422.
**Per-credit charge:** $1,258.
**Room and board:** $12,021.

**FINANCIAL AID PICTURE (2015-2016)**
**Students with need:** Out of 935 full-time freshmen who applied for aid, 657 were judged to have need. Of these, 657 received aid, and 191 had their full need met. Average financial aid package met 82% of need; average scholarship/grant was $30,860; average loan was $3,357. For part-time students, average financial aid package was $29,219.
**Students without need:** 501 full-time freshmen who did not demonstrate need for aid received scholarships/grants; average award was $18,550. No-need awards available for academics, art, athletics, leadership, music/drama.
**Scholarships offered:** 47 full-time freshmen received athletic scholarships; average amount $33,529.

**FINANCIAL AID PROCEDURES**
**Forms required:** FAFSA, CSS PROFILE.
**Dates and Deadlines:** Priority date 2/15; no closing date. Applicants notified by 3/22; must reply by 5/1.

**CONTACT**
Tom Willoughby, Vice Chancellor, Enrollment
2197 South University Boulevard, Denver, CO 80208
(303) 871-4020

## University of Northern Colorado
Greeley, Colorado
www.unco.edu                    Federal Code: 001349

**4-year public** university in small city.
**Enrollment:** 9,108 undergrads.

**BASIC COSTS (2015-2016)**
**Tuition and fees:** $8,166; out-of-state residents $19,752.
**Per-credit charge:** $253; out-of-state residents $713.25.
**Room and board:** $10,360.

**Additional info:** Costs reflect student share of tuition after the Colorado College Opportunity Fund.

## FINANCIAL AID PICTURE

**Students with need:** Need-based aid available for full-time and part-time students. Work study available nights, weekends, and for part-time students.
**Students without need:** No-need awards available for academics, athletics, music/drama.

## FINANCIAL AID PROCEDURES

**Forms required:** FAFSA.
**Dates and Deadlines:** Priority date 3/1; no closing date. Applicants notified on a rolling basis starting 3/1; must reply within 4 week(s) of notification.

## CONTACT

Marty Somero, Director of Financial Aid
501 20th Street, Campus Box 10, Greeley, CO 80639
(970) 351-2502

## Western State Colorado University

Gunnison, Colorado
www.western.edu
Federal Code: 001372

**4-year public** university and liberal arts college in small town.
**Enrollment:** 1,951 undergrads, 6% part-time. 464 full-time freshmen.
**Selectivity:** Admits over 75% of applicants.

### BASIC COSTS (2015-2016)

**Tuition and fees:** $8,451; out-of-state residents $19,455.
**Per-credit charge:** $243; out-of-state residents $702.
**Room and board:** $9,307.
**Additional info:** Tuition/fee waivers available for unemployed or children of unemployed.

### FINANCIAL AID PICTURE (2015-2016)

**Students with need:** Out of 433 full-time freshmen who applied for aid, 263 were judged to have need. Of these, 263 received aid, and 22 had their full need met. Average financial aid package met 58% of need; average scholarship/grant was $7,409; average loan was $3,112. For part-time students, average financial aid package was $3,937.
**Students without need:** 138 full-time freshmen who did not demonstrate need for aid received scholarships/grants; average award was $4,405. No-need awards available for academics, alumni affiliation, art, athletics, leadership, music/drama.
**Scholarships offered:** *Merit:* Academic Excellence Award; $1,000; based on 3.5 GPA and 22 ACT/1010 SAT. Non-resident Leadership Award; $2,500; based on 3.2 GPA, 990 SAT, leadership activities. SAT scores exclusive of Writing. *Athletic:* 34 full-time freshmen received athletic scholarships; average amount $4,869.

### FINANCIAL AID PROCEDURES

**Forms required:** FAFSA.
**Dates and Deadlines:** Priority date 4/1; no closing date. Applicants notified on a rolling basis starting 4/1; must reply by 5/1 or within 4 week(s) of notification.

### CONTACT

Carrie Esquibel, Director of Financial Aid
600 North Adams Street, Gunnison, CO 81231
(970) 943-3085

## Westwood College: Aurora

Aurora, Colorado
www.westwood.edu/locations/colorado/denver-south-campus
Federal Code: 007548

**4-year for-profit** career college in very large city.
**Enrollment:** 276 undergrads.

### BASIC COSTS (2015-2016)

**Additional info:** Business Administration: AAS $35,686. Computer Aided Design/Architectural Drafting: AAS $38,367. Construction Management: AAS $35,686. Criminal Justice: AAS $38,717. Graphic Design: AAS $40,278. Healthcare Office Administration: AAS $33.586. Medical Assisting: AAS $33,586. Information Technology: AOS $34,825. Business Administration: Major in Management: BS $71,372. Construction Management: BS $71,372. Criminal Justice: Major in Administration: BS $77,434. Medical Assisting: DP $23,990. Additional costs and fees such as books, tool kits, lab fee and online fees may apply.

### FINANCIAL AID PICTURE

**Students with need:** Need-based aid available for full-time and part-time students.

### FINANCIAL AID PROCEDURES

**Forms required:** FAFSA, state aid form, institutional form.
**Dates and Deadlines:** Applicants notified on a rolling basis; must reply within 2 week(s) of notification.

### CONTACT

Abigail Barnes, Director of Student Finance
350 Blackhawk Street, Aurora, CO 80011
(303) 975-5029

## Westwood College: Denver North

Denver, Colorado
www.westwood.edu/locations/colorado/denver-north-campus
Federal Code: 007548

**4-year for-profit** career college in very large city.
**Enrollment:** 863 undergrads.

### BASIC COSTS (2015-2016)

**Additional info:** Business Administration: AAS $35,686. Computer Aided Design/Architectural Drafting: AAS $38,367. Construction Management: AAS $35,686. Criminal Justice: AAS $38,717. Dental Assisting: AAS $29,897. Graphic Design: AAS $40,278. Health Information Technology: AAS $38,384. Healthcare Office Administration: AAS $33,586. Medical Assisting: AAS $33,586. Paralegal: AAS $33,250. Automotive Technology: AOS $36,533. Information Technology: AOS $34,825. Business Administration: Major in Management: BS $71,372. Construction Management: BS $71,372. Criminal Justice: Major in Administration: BS $77,434. Information & Network Technologies: Major in CISCO Network Systems: BS $69,650. Medical Assisting: DP $23,990. Additional costs and fees such as books, tool kits, lab fee and online fees may apply.

### FINANCIAL AID PICTURE

**Students with need:** Need-based aid available for full-time and part-time students.
**Students without need:** No-need awards available for academics, state/district residency.

### FINANCIAL AID PROCEDURES

**Forms required:** FAFSA, state aid form, institutional form.
**Dates and Deadlines:** Applicants notified on a rolling basis starting 1/1; must reply within 2 week(s) of notification.
**Transfers:** No deadline.

### CONTACT

Armando Guardiola, Director, Financial Aid
7350 North Broadway, Denver, CO 80221
(720) 542-5631

# Connecticut

## Albertus Magnus College
New Haven, Connecticut
www.albertus.edu                    Federal Code: 001374

**4-year private** liberal arts college in small city, affiliated with Roman Catholic Church.
**Enrollment:** 1,188 undergrads, 14% part-time. 142 full-time freshmen.
**Selectivity:** Admits over 75% of applicants.

### BASIC COSTS (2015-2016)
**Tuition and fees:** $29,650.
**Per-credit charge:** $1,215.
**Room and board:** $13,608.

### FINANCIAL AID PICTURE (2014-2015)
**Students with need:** 71% of average financial aid package awarded as scholarships/grants, 29% awarded as loans/jobs. Need-based aid available for part-time students. Work study available nights, weekends, and for part-time students.
**Students without need:** No-need awards available for academics, state/district residency.

### FINANCIAL AID PROCEDURES
**Forms required:** FAFSA.
**Dates and Deadlines:** Priority date 3/15; no closing date. Applicants notified on a rolling basis starting 4/15; must reply within 2 week(s) of notification.
**Transfers:** No deadline. Must reply within 2 week(s) of notification.

### CONTACT
Michele Cochran, Director of Financial Aid
700 Prospect Street, New Haven, CT 06511-1189
(203) 773-8508

## Asnuntuck Community College
Enfield, Connecticut
www.asnuntuck.edu                    Federal Code: 011150

**2-year public** community and technical college in large town.
**Enrollment:** 1,295 undergrads, 52% part-time. 227 full-time freshmen.
**Selectivity:** Open admission.

### BASIC COSTS (2015-2016)
**Tuition and fees:** $4,052; out-of-state residents $12,116.
**Per-credit charge:** $150; out-of-state residents $450.

### FINANCIAL AID PICTURE
**Students with need:** Need-based aid available for full-time and part-time students. Work study available nights, weekends, and for part-time students.

### FINANCIAL AID PROCEDURES
**Forms required:** FAFSA, institutional form.
**Dates and Deadlines:** Closing date 6/1. Applicants notified on a rolling basis starting 7/1; must reply within 2 week(s) of notification.
**Transfers:** Financial aid transcript required.

### CONTACT
Donna Jones-Searle, Director of Financial Aid
170 Elm Street, Enfield, CT 06082
(860) 253-3000 ext. 3030

## Capital Community College
Hartford, Connecticut
www.ccc.commnet.edu                    Federal Code: 007635

**2-year public** community and technical college in small city.
**Enrollment:** 3,110 undergrads, 74% part-time. 260 full-time freshmen.
**Selectivity:** Open admission; but selective for some programs.

### BASIC COSTS (2015-2016)
**Tuition and fees:** $4,052; out-of-state residents $12,116.
**Per-credit charge:** $150; out-of-state residents $450.
**Additional info:** Tuition/fee waivers available for minority students.

### FINANCIAL AID PICTURE
**Students with need:** Need-based aid available for full-time and part-time students. Work study available nights, weekends, and for part-time students.
**Students without need:** This college awards aid only to students with need.

### FINANCIAL AID PROCEDURES
**Forms required:** FAFSA.
**Dates and Deadlines:** Closing date 7/15. Applicants notified on a rolling basis starting 7/15; must reply within 2 week(s) of notification.
**Transfers:** Closing date 7/1.

### CONTACT
Margaret Malaspina, Director of Financial Aid
950 Main Street, Hartford, CT 06103-1207
(860) 906-5127

## Central Connecticut State University
New Britain, Connecticut
www.ccsu.edu                    Federal Code: 001378

**4-year public** university in small city.
**Enrollment:** 9,693 undergrads, 20% part-time. 1,351 full-time freshmen.
**Selectivity:** Admits 50 to 75% of applicants.

### BASIC COSTS (2015-2016)
**Tuition and fees:** $10,460; out-of-state residents $21,570.
**Per-credit charge:** $207; out-of-state residents $212.
**Room and board:** $11,134.

### FINANCIAL AID PICTURE (2015-2016)
**Students with need:** 55% of average financial aid package awarded as scholarships/grants, 45% awarded as loans/jobs. Need-based aid available for part-time students. Work study available nights, weekends, and for part-time students.
**Students without need:** No-need awards available for academics, athletics, minority status.

### FINANCIAL AID PROCEDURES
**Forms required:** FAFSA.
**Dates and Deadlines:** Priority date 3/1; closing date 9/15. Applicants notified on a rolling basis starting 4/1; must reply within 2 week(s) of notification.
**Transfers:** Priority date 4/15. Applicants notified on a rolling basis.

### CONTACT
Richard Bishop, Director of Financial Aid
1615 Stanley Street, New Britain, CT 06050
(860) 832-2200

## Charter Oak State College
New Britain, Connecticut
www.charteroak.edu                    Federal Code: 032343

**4-year public** virtual career college in small city.
**Enrollment:** 1,634 undergrads, 80% part-time.

## BASIC COSTS (2015-2016)
**Tuition and fees:** $9,009; out-of-state residents $11,619.
**Per-credit charge:** $276; out-of-state residents $363.

## FINANCIAL AID PICTURE (2014-2015)
**Students with need:** Average financial aid package for all full-time undergraduates was $7,983; for part-time $4,812. 37% awarded as scholarships/grants, 63% awarded as loans/jobs.

## FINANCIAL AID PROCEDURES
**Forms required:** FAFSA.
**Dates and Deadlines:** Priority date 4/15; no closing date. Applicants notified on a rolling basis.
**Transfers:** No deadline. Applicants notified on a rolling basis.

## CONTACT
Deborah Flinn, Director of Financial Aid
55 Paul Manafort Drive, New Britain, CT 06053
(860) 515-3703

## Connecticut College
New London, Connecticut          Federal Code: 001379
www.conncoll.edu                 CSS Code: 3284

**4-year private** liberal arts college in large town.
**Enrollment:** 1,854 undergrads. 483 full-time freshmen.
**Selectivity:** Admits less than 50% of applicants.

## BASIC COSTS (2015-2016)
**Tuition and fees:** $49,350.
**Per-credit charge:** $1,460.
**Room and board:** $13,615.

## FINANCIAL AID PICTURE (2015-2016)
**Students with need:** Out of 309 full-time freshmen who applied for aid, 284 were judged to have need. Of these, 284 received aid, and 284 had their full need met. Average financial aid package met 100% of need; average scholarship/grant was $37,224; average loan was $3,314. Need-based aid available for part-time students.
**Students without need:** This college awards aid only to students with need.

## FINANCIAL AID PROCEDURES
**Forms required:** FAFSA, CSS PROFILE.
**Dates and Deadlines:** Priority date 2/1; no closing date. Applicants notified by 4/1; must reply by 5/1.

## CONTACT
Sean Martin, Director of Financial Aid Services
270 Mohegan Avenue, New London, CT 06320
(860) 439-2058

## Eastern Connecticut State University
Willimantic, Connecticut
www.easternct.edu                Federal Code: 001425

**4-year public** university and liberal arts college in large town.
**Enrollment:** 4,767 undergrads, 10% part-time. 871 full-time freshmen.
**Selectivity:** Admits 50 to 75% of applicants.

## BASIC COSTS (2015-2016)
**Tuition and fees:** $10,016; out-of-state residents $22,286.
**Per-credit charge:** $467; out-of-state residents $472.
**Room and board:** $12,108.

## FINANCIAL AID PICTURE (2014-2015)
**Students with need:** Out of 790 full-time freshmen who applied for aid, 577 were judged to have need. Of these, 550 received aid. Need-based aid available for part-time students.

## FINANCIAL AID PROCEDURES
**Forms required:** FAFSA.
**Dates and Deadlines:** Priority date 3/1; no closing date. Applicants notified on a rolling basis starting 3/1; must reply by 5/1.

## CONTACT
83 Windham Street, Willimantic, CT 06226-2295
(860) 465-5286

## Fairfield University
Fairfield, Connecticut           Federal Code: 001385
www.fairfield.edu                CSS Code: 3390

**4-year private** university in small city, affiliated with Roman Catholic Church.
**Enrollment:** 3,863 undergrads, 4% part-time. 965 full-time freshmen.
**Selectivity:** Admits 50 to 75% of applicants.

## BASIC COSTS (2016-2017)
**Tuition and fees:** $46,000.
**Per-credit charge:** $725.
**Room and board:** $13,860.
**Additional info:** Tuition/fee waivers available for minority students.

## FINANCIAL AID PICTURE (2015-2016)
**Students with need:** Out of 718 full-time freshmen who applied for aid, 483 were judged to have need. Of these, 483 received aid, and 129 had their full need met. Average financial aid package met 80% of need; average scholarship/grant was $25,764; average loan was $3,773. For part-time students, average financial aid package was $7,947.
**Students without need:** 365 full-time freshmen who did not demonstrate need for aid received scholarships/grants; average award was $13,543. No-need awards available for academics, alumni affiliation, art, athletics, leadership, music/drama.
**Scholarships offered:** *Merit:* Academic scholarship: $7,000-$25,000; based on high school academic achievement and leadership; renewable for four years; 90% of students received financial aid. *Athletic:* 72 full-time freshmen received athletic scholarships; average amount $23,059.
**Additional info:** Veteran's Pride Program provides tuition discounts for children of qualified veterans. Bridgeport Tuition Program provides free tuition to qualified students from City of Bridgeport with family income under $50,000.

## FINANCIAL AID PROCEDURES
**Forms required:** FAFSA, CSS PROFILE.
**Dates and Deadlines:** Closing date 2/15. Applicants notified by 4/1; must reply by 5/1.
**Transfers:** Closing date 5/1. Applicants notified on a rolling basis starting 4/1; must reply within 3 week(s) of notification.

## CONTACT
Diana Draper, Director of Financial Aid
1073 North Benson Road, Fairfield, CT 06824
(203) 254-4125

## Gateway Community College
New Haven, Connecticut
www.gatewayct.edu                Federal Code: 008303

**2-year public** community college in small city.
**Enrollment:** 6,542 undergrads.
**Selectivity:** Open admission; but selective for some programs.

## BASIC COSTS (2015-2016)
**Tuition and fees:** $4,052; out-of-state residents $12,116.
**Per-credit charge:** $150; out-of-state residents $450.

**FINANCIAL AID PICTURE**

**Students with need:** Need-based aid available for full-time and part-time students. Work study available nights, weekends, and for part-time students.
**Students without need:** This college awards aid only to students with need.

**FINANCIAL AID PROCEDURES**

**Forms required:** FAFSA, institutional form.
**Dates and Deadlines:** Applicants notified on a rolling basis; must reply within 2 week(s) of notification.

**CONTACT**

Raymond Zeek, Director of Financial Aid
20 Church Street, New Haven, CT 06510
(203) 285-2013

## Goodwin College

East Hartford, Connecticut
www.goodwin.edu                    Federal Code: 015833

**2-year private** health science and career college in small city.
**Enrollment:** 3,287 undergrads, 82% part-time. 176 full-time freshmen.
**Selectivity:** Open admission; but selective for some programs.

**FINANCIAL AID PICTURE**

**Students with need:** Need-based aid available for full-time and part-time students. Work study available nights.
**Students without need:** This college awards aid only to students with need.

**FINANCIAL AID PROCEDURES**

**Forms required:** FAFSA, institutional form.
**Dates and Deadlines:** Applicants notified on a rolling basis starting 7/1.
**Transfers:** No deadline. Applicants notified on a rolling basis starting 8/1.

**CONTACT**

Mark Malboeuf, Director of Financial Aid
One Riverside Drive, East Hartford, CT 06118-9980
(860) 727-6723

## Holy Apostles College and Seminary

Cromwell, Connecticut
www.holyapostles.edu                Federal Code: 001389

**4-year private** liberal arts and seminary college in large town, affiliated with Roman Catholic Church.
**Enrollment:** 95 undergrads, 33% part-time. 8 full-time freshmen.
**Selectivity:** Admits over 75% of applicants.

**BASIC COSTS (2015-2016)**
**Tuition and fees:** $9,670.
**Per-credit charge:** $320.
**Additional info:** All courses, all degree programs, now $320 per credit hour.

**FINANCIAL AID PICTURE (2014-2015)**

**Students with need:** Average financial aid package for all full-time undergraduates was $10,500; for part-time $8,500. 32% awarded as scholarships/grants, 68% awarded as loans/jobs.
**Students without need:** This college awards aid only to students with need.

**FINANCIAL AID PROCEDURES**

**Forms required:** FAFSA.
**Dates and Deadlines:** Closing date 6/30. Applicants notified on a rolling basis starting 8/25; must reply within 2 week(s) of notification.
**Transfers:** No deadline. Applicants notified on a rolling basis; must reply within 2 week(s) of notification.

**CONTACT**

Debora Johnston, Financial Aid Director
33 Prospect Hill Road, Cromwell, CT 06416-2005
(860) 632-3020

## Housatonic Community College

Bridgeport, Connecticut
www.hcc.commnet.edu                 Federal Code: 004513

**2-year public** community college in small city.
**Enrollment:** 4,808 undergrads.
**Selectivity:** Open admission; but selective for some programs.

**BASIC COSTS (2015-2016)**
**Tuition and fees:** $4,042; out-of-state residents $12,106.
**Per-credit charge:** $150; out-of-state residents $450.

**FINANCIAL AID PICTURE**

**Students with need:** Need-based aid available for full-time and part-time students.
**Students without need:** This college awards aid only to students with need.

**FINANCIAL AID PROCEDURES**

**Forms required:** FAFSA.
**Dates and Deadlines:** Priority date 11/1; closing date 5/1. Applicants notified on a rolling basis starting 6/1.

**CONTACT**

Barbara Surowiec, Director of Financial Aid
900 Lafayette Boulevard, Bridgeport, CT 06604-4704
(203) 332-5047

## Lincoln College of New England

Southington, Connecticut
www.lincolncollegene.edu

**2-year for-profit** culinary school and business college in small town.
**Enrollment:** 715 undergrads.
**Selectivity:** Open admission.

**BASIC COSTS (2015-2016)**
**Tuition and fees:** $19,940.
**Room and board:** $9,200.

**FINANCIAL AID PICTURE**

**Students with need:** Need-based aid available for full-time and part-time students. Work study available nights, weekends, and for part-time students.
**Students without need:** No-need awards available for academics.

**FINANCIAL AID PROCEDURES**

**Dates and Deadlines:** Applicants notified on a rolling basis starting 1/1.

**CONTACT**

Rachel Bourjolly, Regional Director of Financial Aid
2279 Mount Vernon Road, Southington, CT 06489-1057
(860) 668-3515

## Lyme Academy College of Fine Arts

Old Lyme, Connecticut
www.lymeacademy.edu                 Federal Code: 030794

**4-year private** visual arts college in small town.
**Enrollment:** 78 undergrads.

PART III: FINANCIAL AID COLLEGE BY COLLEGE

## BASIC COSTS (2015-2016)
**Tuition and fees:** $31,360.
**Per-credit charge:** $1,235.
**Room only:** $7,000.

## FINANCIAL AID PICTURE
**Students with need:** Need-based aid available for full-time and part-time students. Work study available nights, weekends, and for part-time students.
**Students without need:** No-need awards available for academics, art, leadership.

## FINANCIAL AID PROCEDURES
**Forms required:** FAFSA.
**Dates and Deadlines:** Priority date 2/15; closing date 4/15. Applicants notified on a rolling basis starting 3/1; must reply by 5/1 or within 2 week(s) of notification.
**Transfers:** Closing date 7/31. Applicants notified on a rolling basis starting 2/15; must reply by 5/1 or within 2 week(s) of notification.

## CONTACT
Jim Falconer, Director of Financial Aid
84 Lyme Street, Old Lyme, CT 06371
(860) 434-3571 ext. 114

# Manchester Community College
Manchester, Connecticut
www.mcc.commnet.edu    Federal Code: 001392

**2-year public** community college in small city.
**Enrollment:** 5,952 undergrads, 62% part-time. 659 full-time freshmen.
**Selectivity:** Open admission; but selective for some programs.

## BASIC COSTS (2015-2016)
**Tuition and fees:** $4,042; out-of-state residents $12,106.
**Per-credit charge:** $150; out-of-state residents $450.

## FINANCIAL AID PICTURE (2014-2015)
**Students with need:** 96% of average financial aid package awarded as scholarships/grants, 4% awarded as loans/jobs. Need-based aid available for part-time students.

## FINANCIAL AID PROCEDURES
**Forms required:** FAFSA.
**Dates and Deadlines:** Priority date 5/15; closing date 8/13. Applicants notified on a rolling basis starting 5/1; must reply within 2 week(s) of notification.

## CONTACT
Ivette Rivera-Dreyer, Director of Financial Aid
PO Box 1046, MS#12, Manchester, CT 06045-1046
(860) 512-3380

# Middlesex Community College
Middletown, Connecticut
www.mxcc.edu    Federal Code: 008038

**2-year public** community college in large town.
**Enrollment:** 2,534 undergrads.
**Selectivity:** Open admission; but selective for some programs.

## BASIC COSTS (2015-2016)
**Tuition and fees:** $4,052; out-of-state residents $12,116.
**Per-credit charge:** $150; out-of-state residents $450.

## FINANCIAL AID PICTURE
**Students with need:** Need-based aid available for full-time and part-time students.

**Students without need:** This college awards aid only to students with need.
**Additional info:** Tuition and/or fee waiver for veterans.

## FINANCIAL AID PROCEDURES
**Forms required:** FAFSA, institutional form.
**Dates and Deadlines:** Priority date 6/1; no closing date. Applicants notified on a rolling basis starting 7/1; must reply within 2 week(s) of notification.
**Transfers:** Closing date 9/1.

## CONTACT
Irene Martin, Director of Financial Aid
100 Training Hill Road, Middletown, CT 06457-4889
(860) 343-5741

# Mitchell College
New London, Connecticut    Federal Code: 001393
www.mitchell.edu    CSS Code: 3528

**4-year private** liberal arts college in small city.
**Enrollment:** 659 undergrads.

## BASIC COSTS (2015-2016)
**Tuition and fees:** $31,000.
**Room and board:** $12,500.

## FINANCIAL AID PICTURE
**Students with need:** Need-based aid available for full-time and part-time students. Work study available nights, weekends, and for part-time students.
**Students without need:** No-need awards available for academics, alumni affiliation, art, leadership.

## FINANCIAL AID PROCEDURES
**Forms required:** FAFSA, CSS PROFILE.
**Dates and Deadlines:** Priority date 3/1; no closing date. Applicants notified on a rolling basis starting 2/15; must reply within 3 week(s) of notification.

## CONTACT
Jacklyn Stoltz, Director of Financial Aid
437 Pequot Avenue, New London, CT 06320-4498
(860) 701-5040

# Naugatuck Valley Community College
Waterbury, Connecticut
www.nv.edu    Federal Code: 006982

**2-year public** community and technical college in small city.
**Enrollment:** 6,302 undergrads, 63% part-time. 834 full-time freshmen.
**Selectivity:** Open admission; but selective for some programs.

## BASIC COSTS (2015-2016)
**Tuition and fees:** $4,052; out-of-state residents $12,116.
**Per-credit charge:** $150; out-of-state residents $450.

## FINANCIAL AID PICTURE
**Students with need:** Need-based aid available for full-time and part-time students.
**Students without need:** This college awards aid only to students with need.

## FINANCIAL AID PROCEDURES
**Forms required:** FAFSA.
**Dates and Deadlines:** Priority date 4/1; no closing date. Applicants notified on a rolling basis starting 6/1.
**Transfers:** Financial aid transcripts required from all previous schools attended.

**CONTACT**
Catherine Hardy, Director of Financial Aid Services
750 Chase Parkway, Waterbury, CT 06708-3089
(203) 575-8006

## Norwalk Community College
Norwalk, Connecticut
http://norwalk.edu/default.asp          Federal Code: 001399

**2-year public** community college in small city.
**Enrollment:** 4,714 undergrads, 58% part-time. 626 full-time freshmen.
**Selectivity:** Open admission; but selective for some programs.

**BASIC COSTS (2015-2016)**
**Tuition and fees:** $4,042; out-of-state residents $12,106.
**Per-credit charge:** $150; out-of-state residents $450.

**FINANCIAL AID PICTURE**
**Students with need:** Need-based aid available for full-time and part-time students.
**Students without need:** No-need awards available for academics, alumni affiliation.

**FINANCIAL AID PROCEDURES**
**Forms required:** FAFSA.
**Dates and Deadlines:** Priority date 7/7; no closing date. Applicants notified on a rolling basis starting 7/1; must reply within 2 week(s) of notification.

**CONTACT**
Norma McNerney, Director of Financial Aid
188 Richards Avenue, Norwalk, CT 06854-1655
(203) 857-7023

## Paier College of Art
Hamden, Connecticut
www.paiercollegeofart.edu          Federal Code: 007459

**4-year for-profit** visual arts college in small city.
**Enrollment:** 112 undergrads, 23% part-time. 10 full-time freshmen.
**Selectivity:** Admits over 75% of applicants.

**BASIC COSTS (2015-2016)**
**Tuition and fees:** $15,445.

**FINANCIAL AID PICTURE (2014-2015)**
**Students with need:** Out of 9 full-time freshmen who applied for aid, 6 were judged to have need. Of these, 6 received aid. Average financial aid package met 83% of need; average scholarship/grant was $7,880; average loan was $3,374. For part-time students, average financial aid package was $5,477.

**FINANCIAL AID PROCEDURES**
**Forms required:** FAFSA.
**Dates and Deadlines:** Priority date 4/16; closing date 8/1. Applicants notified on a rolling basis starting 6/1; must reply within 3 week(s) of notification.
**Transfers:** Applicants notified on a rolling basis starting 6/1; must reply within 3 week(s) of notification.

**CONTACT**
John DeRose, Director of Financial Aid
20 Gorham Avenue, Hamden, CT 06514-3902
(203) 287-3034

## Post University
Waterbury, Connecticut
www.post.edu          Federal Code: 001401

**4-year for-profit** university and business college in small city.
**Enrollment:** 720 undergrads, 2% part-time. 201 full-time freshmen.
**Selectivity:** Admits less than 50% of applicants.

**BASIC COSTS (2015-2016)**
**Tuition and fees:** $27,350.
**Per-credit charge:** $875.
**Room and board:** $10,500.

**FINANCIAL AID PICTURE (2014-2015)**
**Students with need:** Out of 178 full-time freshmen who applied for aid, 172 were judged to have need. Of these, 172 received aid, and 27 had their full need met. Average financial aid package met 55% of need; average scholarship/grant was $16,655; average loan was $364. For part-time students, average financial aid package was $7,812.
**Students without need:** 5 full-time freshmen who did not demonstrate need for aid received scholarships/grants; average award was $9,000.
**Scholarships offered: Merit:** Post University annually awards two full-tuition scholarships to outstanding incoming students pursuing a degree at the Malcolm Baldrige School of Business. The University also offers a full tuition scholarship to one outstanding student from Naugatuck Valley Community College. Eligibility criteria are available on the University website. Academic merit scholarships available based on GPA and test scores; renewable contingent upon maintaining specific GPA. **Athletic:** 38 full-time freshmen received athletic scholarships; average amount $14,078.

**FINANCIAL AID PROCEDURES**
**Forms required:** FAFSA.
**Dates and Deadlines:** Priority date 3/15; no closing date. Applicants notified on a rolling basis starting 4/15; must reply by 5/1 or within 3 week(s) of notification.
**Transfers:** No deadline. Applicants notified on a rolling basis starting 4/15; must reply within 1 week(s) of notification.

**CONTACT**
Michelle Gambacini, Director of Office of Student Finance
800 Country Club Road, Waterbury, CT 06723-2540
(203) 596-4571

## Quinebaug Valley Community College
Danielson, Connecticut
www.qvcc.commnet.edu          Federal Code: 010530

**2-year public** community and technical college in large town.
**Enrollment:** 1,530 undergrads.
**Selectivity:** Open admission.

**BASIC COSTS (2015-2016)**
**Tuition and fees:** $4,047; out-of-state residents $12,111.
**Per-credit charge:** $150; out-of-state residents $450.

**FINANCIAL AID PICTURE**
**Students with need:** Need-based aid available for full-time and part-time students. Work study available nights.
**Students without need:** This college awards aid only to students with need.

**FINANCIAL AID PROCEDURES**
**Forms required:** FAFSA.
**Dates and Deadlines:** Closing date 8/1. Applicants notified on a rolling basis starting 5/1.

**CONTACT**
Kimberly Rich, Financial Aid Director
742 Upper Maple Street, Danielson, CT 06239-1440
(860) 412-7208

## Quinnipiac University

| Hamden, Connecticut | Federal Code: 001402 |
| www.quinnipiac.edu | CSS Code: 3712 |

**4-year private** university in small city.
**Enrollment:** 6,931 undergrads, 3% part-time. 1,901 full-time freshmen.
**Selectivity:** Admits 50 to 75% of applicants.

**BASIC COSTS (2016-2017)**
**Tuition and fees:** $43,940.
**Per-credit charge:** $995.
**Room and board:** $15,170.

**FINANCIAL AID PICTURE (2015-2016)**
**Students with need:** Out of 1,548 full-time freshmen who applied for aid, 1,222 were judged to have need. Of these, 1,215 received aid, and 226 had their full need met. Average financial aid package met 67% of need; average scholarship/grant was $21,166; average loan was $3,550. For part-time students, average financial aid package was $9,278.
**Students without need:** 533 full-time freshmen who did not demonstrate need for aid received scholarships/grants; average award was $16,944. No-need awards available for academics, athletics.
**Scholarships offered:** *Merit:* Academic scholarships; $9,000-$24,000 per year; based on class rank and SAT/ACT scores; renewable with full-time status and 3.0 GPA. *Athletic:* 74 full-time freshmen received athletic scholarships; average amount $34,658.

**FINANCIAL AID PROCEDURES**
**Forms required:** FAFSA, CSS PROFILE.
**Dates and Deadlines:** Priority date 3/1; no closing date. Applicants notified on a rolling basis starting 2/15; must reply by 5/1 or within 2 week(s) of notification.
**Transfers:** No deadline. Applicants notified on a rolling basis starting 3/1; must reply by 5/1 or within 2 week(s) of notification. Students transferring with 2 years of full-time college work and 3.5 GPA may be eligible for transfer scholarship.

**CONTACT**
Dominic Yoia, Associate Vice President and University Director of Financial Aid
275 Mount Carmel Avenue, Hamden, CT 06518-1908
(203) 582-8750

## Sacred Heart University

| Fairfield, Connecticut | Federal Code: 001403 |
| www.sacredheart.edu | CSS Code: 3780 |

**4-year private** university in large town, affiliated with Roman Catholic Church.
**Enrollment:** 5,109 undergrads, 13% part-time. 1,290 full-time freshmen.
**Selectivity:** Admits 50 to 75% of applicants.

**BASIC COSTS (2015-2016)**
**Tuition and fees:** $37,170.
**Per-credit charge:** $600.
**Room and board:** $14,140.
**Additional info:** Tuition/fee waivers available for adults, minority students.

**FINANCIAL AID PICTURE (2015-2016)**
**Students with need:** Out of 1,152 full-time freshmen who applied for aid, 908 were judged to have need. Of these, 908 received aid, and 158 had

their full need met. Average financial aid package met 57% of need; average scholarship/grant was $15,547; average loan was $4,065. For part-time students, average financial aid package was $6,008.
**Students without need:** 365 full-time freshmen who did not demonstrate need for aid received scholarships/grants; average award was $12,316. No-need awards available for academics, alumni affiliation, art, athletics, leadership, music/drama, religious affiliation, state/district residency.
**Scholarships offered:** 58 full-time freshmen received athletic scholarships; average amount $17,951.

**FINANCIAL AID PROCEDURES**
**Forms required:** FAFSA, CSS PROFILE.
**Dates and Deadlines:** Priority date 2/15; no closing date. Applicants notified on a rolling basis starting 3/1; must reply within 2 week(s) of notification.
**Transfers:** Closing date 2/15. Applicants notified on a rolling basis; must reply within 2 week(s) of notification.

**CONTACT**
Julie Savino, Executive Director, University Financial Assistance
5151 Park Avenue, Fairfield, CT 06825
(203) 371-7980

## St. Vincent's College

| Bridgeport, Connecticut | |
| www.stvincentscollege.edu | Federal Code: 006191 |

**2-year private** health science college in small city, affiliated with Roman Catholic Church.
**Enrollment:** 669 undergrads, 93% part-time. 5 full-time freshmen.
**Selectivity:** Admits 50 to 75% of applicants.

**BASIC COSTS (2015-2016)**
**Tuition and fees:** $17,850.
**Per-credit charge:** $595.

**FINANCIAL AID PICTURE (2014-2015)**
**Students with need:** Out of 4 full-time freshmen who applied for aid, 4 were judged to have need. Of these, 4 received aid, and 2 had their full need met. Average financial aid package met 47% of need; average scholarship/grant was $5,410; average loan was $3,500. For part-time students, average financial aid package was $5,052.
**Students without need:** 2 full-time freshmen who did not demonstrate need for aid received scholarships/grants; average award was $5,700. No-need awards available for academics.

**FINANCIAL AID PROCEDURES**
**Forms required:** FAFSA.
**Dates and Deadlines:** Priority date 3/15; no closing date. Applicants notified on a rolling basis; must reply within 4 week(s) of notification.

**CONTACT**
Dorothy Martin-Hatcher, Director of Financial Aid
2800 Main Street, Bridgeport, CT 06606
(203) 576-5513

## Southern Connecticut State University

| New Haven, Connecticut | |
| www.southernct.edu | Federal Code: 001406 |

**4-year public** university in small city.
**Enrollment:** 8,106 undergrads, 15% part-time. 1,394 full-time freshmen.
**Selectivity:** Admits 50 to 75% of applicants.

**BASIC COSTS (2015-2016)**
**Tuition and fees:** $9,600; out-of-state residents $21,870.
**Per-credit charge:** $494; out-of-state residents $509.

Room and board: $11,614.

**FINANCIAL AID PICTURE (2015-2016)**

**Students with need:** Out of 1,146 full-time freshmen who applied for aid, 968 were judged to have need. Of these, 968 received aid, and 257 had their full need met. Average financial aid package met 67% of need; average scholarship/grant was $5,583; average loan was $3,676. For part-time students, average financial aid package was $10,574.

**Students without need:** 46 full-time freshmen who did not demonstrate need for aid received scholarships/grants; average award was $4,145. No-need awards available for academics, alumni affiliation, athletics, job skills, ROTC, state/district residency.

**Scholarships offered:** *Merit:* General Academic Achievement Awards; 90 awarded. Presidential Scholarships, Trustees Scholarships available. *Athletic:* 15 full-time freshmen received athletic scholarships; average amount $11,583.

**FINANCIAL AID PROCEDURES**

**Forms required:** FAFSA.

**Dates and Deadlines:** Priority date 3/5; closing date 3/9. Applicants notified on a rolling basis starting 4/11; must reply within 2 week(s) of notification.

**Transfers:** Applicants notified on a rolling basis starting 6/15; must reply within 2 week(s) of notification.

**CONTACT**

Gloria Lee, Director of Financial Aid & Scholarships
131 Farnham Avenue, New Haven, CT 06515-1202
(203) 392-5222

## Three Rivers Community College
Norwich, Connecticut
www.threerivers.edu                    Federal Code: 009765

**2-year public** community and technical college in large town.
**Enrollment:** 3,949 undergrads.
**Selectivity:** Open admission; but selective for some programs.

**BASIC COSTS (2015-2016)**

**Tuition and fees:** $4,052; out-of-state residents $12,116.
**Per-credit charge:** $150; out-of-state residents $450.

**FINANCIAL AID PICTURE**

**Students with need:** Need-based aid available for full-time and part-time students. Work study available nights, weekends, and for part-time students.
**Students without need:** This college awards aid only to students with need.
**Scholarships offered:** Various scholarships; $75 to $500.

**FINANCIAL AID PROCEDURES**

**Forms required:** FAFSA.

**Dates and Deadlines:** Priority date 5/1; no closing date. Applicants notified on a rolling basis; must reply within 2 week(s) of notification.

**Transfers:** No deadline.

**CONTACT**

Hong-Yu Kovic, Financial Aid Counselor
Admissions Office, Norwich, CT 06360-6598
(860) 215-9040

## Trinity College
Hartford, Connecticut                    Federal Code: 001414
www.trincoll.edu                         CSS Code: 3899

**4-year private** liberal arts college in large city.
**Enrollment:** 2,251 undergrads.
**Selectivity:** Admits less than 50% of applicants.

**BASIC COSTS (2015-2016)**

**Tuition and fees:** $50,776.
**Per-credit charge:** $1,615.
**Room and board:** $13,144.
**Additional info:** Tuition/fee waivers available for adults.

**FINANCIAL AID PICTURE**

**Students with need:** Need-based aid available for full-time and part-time students. Work study available nights, weekends, and for part-time students.
**Students without need:** No-need awards available for academics, leadership.

**FINANCIAL AID PROCEDURES**

**Forms required:** FAFSA, CSS PROFILE.

**Dates and Deadlines:** Priority date 2/1; closing date 3/1. Applicants notified by 4/1; must reply by 5/1 or within 2 week(s) of notification.

**Transfers:** Closing date 4/1. Applicants notified on a rolling basis starting 5/15; must reply within 2 week(s) of notification.

**CONTACT**

Kelly O'Brien, Director of Financial Aid
300 Summit Street, Hartford, CT 06106
(860) 297-2046

## Tunxis Community College
Farmington, Connecticut
www.tunxis.edu                    Federal Code: 009764

**2-year public** community college in large town.
**Enrollment:** 3,517 undergrads, 55% part-time. 560 full-time freshmen.
**Selectivity:** Open admission; but selective for some programs.

**BASIC COSTS (2015-2016)**

**Tuition and fees:** $4,052; out-of-state residents $12,116.
**Per-credit charge:** $150; out-of-state residents $450.

**FINANCIAL AID PICTURE**

**Students with need:** Need-based aid available for full-time and part-time students. Work study available nights, weekends, and for part-time students.
**Students without need:** No-need awards available for academics.
**Additional info:** Financial aid available to all students showing need. Part-time students encouraged to apply.

**FINANCIAL AID PROCEDURES**

**Forms required:** FAFSA.

**Dates and Deadlines:** Priority date 6/1; no closing date. Applicants notified on a rolling basis starting 3/1.

**CONTACT**

David Welsh, Director of Financial Aid
271 Scott Swamp Road, Farmington, CT 06032-3187
(860) 606-9501

## United States Coast Guard Academy
New London, Connecticut
www.uscga.edu                    Federal Code: 001415

**4-year public** engineering and military college in small city.
**Enrollment:** 898 undergrads. 291 full-time freshmen.
**Selectivity:** Admits less than 50% of applicants.

**BASIC COSTS (2016-2017)**

**Tuition and fees:** $978.
**Additional info:** For US Citizens, room, tuition, and board at the Coast Guard Academy are paid for by the government. In addition, all US Cadets

receive pay totaling $12,324.00 per year. Cadet pay is furnished by the government for uniforms, equipment, textbooks, and other expenses incidental to training.

**CONTACT**
Cadet Finance Manager
31 Mohegan Avenue, New London, CT 06320

## University of Bridgeport
Bridgeport, Connecticut
www.bridgeport.edu                    Federal Code: 001416

**4-year private** university in small city.
**Enrollment:** 2,897 undergrads, 27% part-time. 408 full-time freshmen.
**Selectivity:** Admits 50 to 75% of applicants.

**BASIC COSTS (2015-2016)**
**Tuition and fees:** $30,850.
**Per-credit charge:** $960.
**Room and board:** $12,990.

**FINANCIAL AID PICTURE**
**Students with need:** Need-based aid available for full-time and part-time students. Work study available nights, weekends, and for part-time students.
**Students without need:** No-need awards available for academics, art, athletics, leadership, music/drama.
**Scholarships offered:** Academic Excellence and Leadership Scholarship; up to full tuition, room, and board; for students ranking in the top quarter of high school class with 1200 SAT. Academic Scholarship; up to full tuition; for students in the top quarter of class and 1100 SAT. Academic Grant; up to half-tuition; for students in top half of class and 1100 SAT. Challenge Grant; $3,000; for students in the top half of class and 1000 SAT. All SAT scores exclusive of Writing.

**FINANCIAL AID PROCEDURES**
**Forms required:** FAFSA.
**Dates and Deadlines:** Priority date 3/1; no closing date. Applicants notified on a rolling basis starting 4/1; must reply within 4 week(s) of notification.
**Transfers:** No deadline. Applicants notified on a rolling basis starting 4/1; must reply by 5/1 or within 2 week(s) of notification.

**CONTACT**
Christine Falzerano, Director of Student Financial Services
126 Park Avenue, Bridgeport, CT 06604
(203) 576-4568

## University of Connecticut
Storrs, Connecticut
www.uconn.edu                    Federal Code: 007997

**4-year public** university in large town.
**Enrollment:** 18,451 undergrads, 3% part-time. 3,766 full-time freshmen.
**Selectivity:** Admits 50 to 75% of applicants.

**BASIC COSTS (2016-2017)**
**Tuition and fees:** $13,366; out-of-state residents $34,908.
**Per-credit charge:** $439; out-of-state residents $1,337.
**Room and board:** $12,436.

**FINANCIAL AID PICTURE (2015-2016)**
**Students with need:** Out of 2,986 full-time freshmen who applied for aid, 2,028 were judged to have need. Of these, 1,984 received aid, and 350 had their full need met. Average financial aid package met 58% of need; average scholarship/grant was $13,096; average loan was $3,420. For part-time students, average financial aid package was $7,609.

**Students without need:** 511 full-time freshmen who did not demonstrate need for aid received scholarships/grants; average award was $7,689. No-need awards available for academics, art, athletics, leadership, minority status, music/drama.
**Scholarships offered:** 100 full-time freshmen received athletic scholarships; average amount $31,377.
**Additional info:** Institution offers variety of need-based financial aid programs. Financial assistance packages may include grants, loans and work-study awards.

**FINANCIAL AID PROCEDURES**
**Forms required:** FAFSA.
**Dates and Deadlines:** Priority date 3/1; no closing date. Applicants notified on a rolling basis starting 3/1; must reply within 4 week(s) of notification.

**CONTACT**
Mona Lucas, Director of Student Financial Aid Services
2131 Hillside Road, Unit 3088, Storrs, CT 06269-3088
(860) 486-2819

## University of Hartford
West Hartford, Connecticut
www.hartford.edu                    Federal Code: 001422

**4-year private** university in small city.
**Enrollment:** 5,028 undergrads, 10% part-time. 1,419 full-time freshmen.
**Selectivity:** Admits 50 to 75% of applicants.

**BASIC COSTS (2016-2017)**
**Tuition and fees:** $37,790.
**Per-credit charge:** $520.
**Room and board:** $11,986.
**Additional info:** Tuition/fee waivers available for minority students.

**FINANCIAL AID PICTURE (2015-2016)**
**Students with need:** Out of 1,269 full-time freshmen who applied for aid, 1,115 were judged to have need. Of these, 1,112 received aid, and 154 had their full need met. Average financial aid package met 68% of need; average scholarship/grant was $21,295; average loan was $3,528. For part-time students, average financial aid package was $6,146.
**Students without need:** 255 full-time freshmen who did not demonstrate need for aid received scholarships/grants; average award was $15,845. No-need awards available for academics, alumni affiliation, art, athletics, job skills, leadership, minority status, music/drama.
**Scholarships offered:** 14 full-time freshmen received athletic scholarships; average amount $34,782.

**FINANCIAL AID PROCEDURES**
**Forms required:** FAFSA.
**Dates and Deadlines:** Priority date 2/1; no closing date. Applicants notified on a rolling basis starting 3/1; must reply by 5/1 or within 2 week(s) of notification.

**CONTACT**
Victoria Hampton, Director of Student Financial Assistance
Bates House, West Hartford, CT 06117-1599
(860) 768-4296

## University of New Haven
West Haven, Connecticut
www.newhaven.edu                    Federal Code: 001397

**4-year private** university in small city.
**Enrollment:** 4,942 undergrads, 7% part-time. 1,237 full-time freshmen.
**Selectivity:** Admits over 75% of applicants.

PART III: FINANCIAL AID COLLEGE BY COLLEGE

## BASIC COSTS (2015-2016)
**Tuition and fees:** $35,650.
**Per-credit charge:** $1,145.
**Room and board:** $14,720.

## FINANCIAL AID PICTURE (2015-2016)
**Students with need:** Out of 1,073 full-time freshmen who applied for aid, 973 were judged to have need. Of these, 973 received aid, and 146 had their full need met. Average financial aid package met 61% of need; average scholarship/grant was $19,888; average loan was $3,467. For part-time students, average financial aid package was $5,727.
**Students without need:** 155 full-time freshmen who did not demonstrate need for aid received scholarships/grants; average award was $15,364. No-need awards available for academics, art, athletics.
**Scholarships offered:** 3 full-time freshmen received athletic scholarships; average amount $10,666.

## FINANCIAL AID PROCEDURES
**Forms required:** FAFSA.
**Dates and Deadlines:** Closing date 3/1. Applicants notified on a rolling basis starting 3/1; must reply within 2 week(s) of notification.

## CONTACT
Karen Flynn, Director of Financial Aid
300 Boston Post Road, West Haven, CT 06516-1916
(203) 932-7315

## University of Saint Joseph
West Hartford, Connecticut
www.usj.edu                          Federal Code: 001409

**4-year private** liberal arts college for women in small city, affiliated with Roman Catholic Church.
**Enrollment:** 904 undergrads, 15% part-time. 211 full-time freshmen.
**Selectivity:** Admits over 75% of applicants.

## BASIC COSTS (2015-2016)
**Tuition and fees:** $36,140.
**Per-credit charge:** $780.
**Room and board:** $14,850.

## FINANCIAL AID PICTURE
**Students with need:** Need-based aid available for full-time students.
**Students without need:** No-need awards available for academics, leadership, minority status.

## FINANCIAL AID PROCEDURES
**Forms required:** FAFSA.
**Dates and Deadlines:** Applicants notified on a rolling basis starting 2/15.
**Transfers:** No deadline. Applicants notified on a rolling basis starting 2/15.

## CONTACT
Ashley Dutton, Director of Financial Aid
1678 Asylum Avenue, West Hartford, CT 06117
(866) 442-8752

## Wesleyan University
Middletown, Connecticut          Federal Code: 001424
www.wesleyan.edu                      CSS Code: 3959

**4-year private** university and liberal arts college in large town.
**Enrollment:** 2,819 undergrads. 757 full-time freshmen.
**Selectivity:** Admits less than 50% of applicants.

## BASIC COSTS (2016-2017)
**Tuition and fees:** $50,912.
**Room and board:** $13,950.

**Additional info:** Comprehensive residential fee for juniors & seniors is $15,858.

## FINANCIAL AID PICTURE (2015-2016)
**Students with need:** Out of 390 full-time freshmen who applied for aid, 372 were judged to have need. Of these, 372 received aid, and 372 had their full need met. Average financial aid package met 100% of need; average scholarship/grant was $43,059; average loan was $3,068.
**Students without need:** This college awards aid only to students with need.
**Scholarships offered:** Freeman Asian Scholars: for international first-year applicants from select East and Southeast Asian countries; 22 awarded.
**Additional info:** Most families whose income is below $60,000 will not be packaged with loans; grant aid will replace the standard loan in the package. Other students demonstrating significant need will graduate with 4-year packaged loan debt of $10,000 or $14,000 depending on need level. All other students will have their 4-year packaged loan debt reduced by about 30%.

## FINANCIAL AID PROCEDURES
**Forms required:** FAFSA, CSS PROFILE.
**Dates and Deadlines:** Closing date 2/15. Applicants notified by 4/1; must reply by 5/1.
**Transfers:** Priority date 4/1; closing date 4/1. Applicants notified by 5/15; must reply by 6/1 or within 2 week(s) of notification. No financial aid available for international transfer candidates.

## CONTACT
Robert Coughlin, Director of Financial Aid
70 Wyllys Avenue, Middletown, CT 06459-0260
(860) 685-2800

## Western Connecticut State University
Danbury, Connecticut
www.wcsu.edu                          Federal Code: 001380

**4-year public** university in small city.
**Enrollment:** 5,081 undergrads, 16% part-time. 774 full-time freshmen.
**Selectivity:** Admits 50 to 75% of applicants.

## BASIC COSTS (2015-2016)
**Tuition and fees:** $9,516; out-of-state residents $21,786.
**Per-credit charge:** $207; out-of-state residents $212.
**Room and board:** $11,738.

## FINANCIAL AID PICTURE (2014-2015)
**Students with need:** Out of 659 full-time freshmen who applied for aid, 543 were judged to have need. Of these, 536 received aid, and 46 had their full need met. Average financial aid package met 50% of need; average scholarship/grant was $6,050; average loan was $3,550. For part-time students, average financial aid package was $5,925.
**Students without need:** 8 full-time freshmen who did not demonstrate need for aid received scholarships/grants; average award was $8,515. No-need awards available for academics, art, minority status, music/drama.

## FINANCIAL AID PROCEDURES
**Forms required:** FAFSA, institutional form.
**Dates and Deadlines:** Priority date 3/15; no closing date. Applicants notified on a rolling basis starting 4/15; must reply by 5/1 or within 2 week(s) of notification.

## CONTACT
Melissa Stephens, Director of Student Financial Assistance
181 White Street, Danbury, CT 06810-6826
(203) 837-8581

## Yale University

New Haven, Connecticut        Federal Code: 001426
www.yale.edu                          CSS Code: 3987

**4-year private** university in small city.
**Enrollment:** 5,528 undergrads. 1,364 full-time freshmen.
**Selectivity:** Admits less than 50% of applicants.

### BASIC COSTS (2015-2016)
**Tuition and fees:** $47,600.
**Room and board:** $14,600.

### FINANCIAL AID PICTURE (2015-2016)
**Students with need:** Out of 843 full-time freshmen who applied for aid, 694 were judged to have need. Of these, 694 received aid, and 694 had their full need met. Average financial aid package met 100% of need; average scholarship/grant was $50,359; average loan was $2,266. Need-based aid available for part-time students.
**Students without need:** This college awards aid only to students with need.
**Additional info:** All scholarships based on demonstrated need.

### FINANCIAL AID PROCEDURES
**Forms required:** FAFSA, CSS PROFILE, institutional form.
**Dates and Deadlines:** Priority date 3/1; closing date 3/1. Applicants notified by 4/1; must reply by 5/1.

### CONTACT
Caesar Storlazzi, Director of University Financial Aid
Yale Undergraduate Admissions, New Haven, CT 06520-8234
(203) 432-2700

# Delaware

## Delaware College of Art and Design

Wilmington, Delaware
www.dcad.edu                     Federal Code: 041398

**2-year private** visual arts college in large city.
**Enrollment:** 155 undergrads, 9% part-time. 65 full-time freshmen.
**Selectivity:** Admits 50 to 75% of applicants.

### BASIC COSTS (2015-2016)
**Tuition and fees:** $23,945.
**Per-credit charge:** $975.
**Room and board:** $11,850.

### FINANCIAL AID PICTURE
**Students with need:** Need-based aid available for full-time and part-time students. Work study available nights, weekends, and for part-time students.
**Students without need:** No-need awards available for academics, art.

### FINANCIAL AID PROCEDURES
**Forms required:** FAFSA.
**Dates and Deadlines:** Priority date 4/1; no closing date. Applicants notified on a rolling basis; must reply within 2 week(s) of notification.
**Transfers:** No deadline. Applicants notified on a rolling basis; must reply within 2 week(s) of notification.

### CONTACT
Nicole Little, Director of Financial Aid
600 North Market Street, Wilmington, DE 19801
(302) 622-8000 ext. 105

## Delaware State University

Dover, Delaware
www.desu.edu                     Federal Code: 001428

**4-year public** university in large town.
**Enrollment:** 3,654 undergrads.

### BASIC COSTS (2015-2016)
**Tuition and fees:** $7,532; out-of-state residents $16,138.
**Per-credit charge:** $280; out-of-state residents $638.
**Room and board:** $10,820.

### FINANCIAL AID PICTURE
**Students with need:** Need-based aid available for full-time and part-time students.
**Students without need:** This college awards aid only to students with need.
**Additional info:** Students must file FAFSA by 3/15 every year.

### FINANCIAL AID PROCEDURES
**Forms required:** FAFSA.
**Dates and Deadlines:** Priority date 3/15; closing date 7/1. Applicants notified on a rolling basis starting 4/1; must reply by 7/10.
**Transfers:** Closing date 2/15.

### CONTACT
Stephen Ampersand, Assistant Vice President of Student Financial Services
1200 North DuPont Highway, Dover, DE 19901
(302) 857-6250

## Delaware Technical Community College: Jack F. Owens Campus

Georgetown, Delaware
https://www.dtcc.edu/our-campuses/georgetown
                                 Federal Code: 007053

**2-year public** community and technical college in small town.
**Enrollment:** 3,852 undergrads.
**Selectivity:** Open admission; but selective for some programs.

### BASIC COSTS (2015-2016)
**Tuition and fees:** $3,568; out-of-state residents $8,458.
**Per-credit charge:** $136; out-of-state residents $340.

### FINANCIAL AID PICTURE
**Students with need:** Need-based aid available for full-time and part-time students.
**Students without need:** This college awards aid only to students with need.

### FINANCIAL AID PROCEDURES
**Forms required:** FAFSA.
**Dates and Deadlines:** Priority date 6/1; no closing date. Applicants notified on a rolling basis starting 5/1; must reply within 2 week(s) of notification.

### CONTACT
Veronica Oney, Financial Aid Officer
21179 College Drive, Georgetown, DE 19947
(302) 855-5692

## Delaware Technical Community College: Stanton/Wilmington Campus
Newark, Delaware
https://www.dtcc.edu/our-campuses/stanton
Federal Code: 021449

**2-year public** community and technical college in small city.
**Enrollment:** 6,076 undergrads.
**Selectivity:** Open admission; but selective for some programs.

**BASIC COSTS (2015-2016)**
**Tuition and fees:** $3,568; out-of-state residents $8,458.
**Per-credit charge:** $136; out-of-state residents $340.

**FINANCIAL AID PICTURE**
**Students with need:** Need-based aid available for full-time and part-time students.
**Students without need:** This college awards aid only to students with need.

**FINANCIAL AID PROCEDURES**
**Forms required:** FAFSA.
**Dates and Deadlines:** Priority date 6/1; no closing date. Applicants notified on a rolling basis starting 5/1; must reply within 2 week(s) of notification.

**CONTACT**
Debra Troxler, Student Financial Aid Officer
400 Stanton-Christiana Road, Newark, DE 19713
(302) 571-5380

## Delaware Technical Community College: Terry Campus
Dover, Delaware
https://www.dtcc.edu/our-campuses/dover
Federal Code: 011727

**2-year public** community and technical college in large town.
**Enrollment:** 2,732 undergrads.
**Selectivity:** Open admission; but selective for some programs.

**BASIC COSTS (2015-2016)**
**Tuition and fees:** $3,568; out-of-state residents $8,458.
**Per-credit charge:** $136; out-of-state residents $340.

**FINANCIAL AID PICTURE**
**Students with need:** Need-based aid available for full-time and part-time students.
**Students without need:** This college awards aid only to students with need.

**FINANCIAL AID PROCEDURES**
**Forms required:** FAFSA.
**Dates and Deadlines:** Priority date 6/1; no closing date. Applicants notified on a rolling basis starting 5/1; must reply within 2 week(s) of notification.

**CONTACT**
Jennifer Grunden, Financial Aid Director
100 Campus Drive, Dover, DE 19901
(302) 857-1040

## Goldey-Beacom College
Wilmington, Delaware
www.gbc.edu
Federal Code: 001429

**4-year private** business college in small city.
**Enrollment:** 620 undergrads.

**BASIC COSTS (2015-2016)**
**Tuition and fees:** $22,950.
**Per-credit charge:** $765.
**Room only:** $5,800.

**FINANCIAL AID PICTURE**
**Students with need:** Need-based aid available for full-time and part-time students. Work study available nights, weekends, and for part-time students.
**Students without need:** No-need awards available for academics, athletics.

**FINANCIAL AID PROCEDURES**
**Forms required:** FAFSA.
**Dates and Deadlines:** Priority date 4/15; closing date 7/15. Applicants notified on a rolling basis starting 3/1; must reply within 2 week(s) of notification.
**Transfers:** Applicants notified on a rolling basis starting 3/1; must reply within 2 week(s) of notification.

**CONTACT**
Jane Lysle, Dean of Enrollment Management
4701 Limestone Road, Wilmington, DE 19808
(302) 225-6265

## University of Delaware
Newark, Delaware
www.udel.edu
Federal Code: 001431

**4-year public** university in large town.
**Enrollment:** 17,575 undergrads, 4% part-time. 4,169 full-time freshmen.
**Selectivity:** Admits 50 to 75% of applicants.

**BASIC COSTS (2015-2016)**
**Tuition and fees:** $12,520; out-of-state residents $31,420.
**Per-credit charge:** $468; out-of-state residents $1,255.
**Room and board:** $12,146.

**FINANCIAL AID PICTURE (2015-2016)**
**Students with need:** Out of 3,694 full-time freshmen who applied for aid, 2,348 were judged to have need. Of these, 2,234 received aid, and 1,134 had their full need met. Average financial aid package met 76% of need; average scholarship/grant was $9,756; average loan was $6,605. For part-time students, average financial aid package was $12,424.
**Students without need:** This college awards aid only to students with need.
**Scholarships offered:** *Merit:* Scholarships ranging from $1,000 to full cost of education. *Athletic:* 123 full-time freshmen received athletic scholarships; average amount $11,107.
**Additional info:** 12/15 application deadline to receive scholarship consideration. Sibling/parent tuition credit plan. Senior citizen tuition credit for state residents over 60.

**FINANCIAL AID PROCEDURES**
**Forms required:** FAFSA.
**Dates and Deadlines:** Priority date 2/1; closing date 3/15. Applicants notified on a rolling basis starting 3/15; must reply by 5/1 or within 3 week(s) of notification.
**Transfers:** No deadline. Aid usually limited to federal and state programs.

**CONTACT**
Melissa Stone, Director of Student Financial Services
210 South College Avenue, Newark, DE 19716
(302) 831-2126

## Wesley College
Dover, Delaware
www.wesley.edu                    Federal Code: 001433

**4-year private** liberal arts college in large town, affiliated with United Methodist Church.
**Enrollment:** 1,457 full-time undergrads.

### BASIC COSTS (2015-2016)
**Tuition and fees:** $25,020.
**Room and board:** $10,970.

### FINANCIAL AID PICTURE
**Students with need:** Need-based aid available for full-time and part-time students. Work study available nights, weekends, and for part-time students.
**Students without need:** This college awards aid only to students with need.

### FINANCIAL AID PROCEDURES
**Forms required:** FAFSA, institutional form.
**Dates and Deadlines:** Priority date 2/1; no closing date. Applicants notified on a rolling basis starting 1/1; must reply within 2 week(s) of notification.
**Transfers:** No deadline. Applicants notified on a rolling basis; must reply within 2 week(s) of notification.

### CONTACT
Michael Hall, Director of Student Financial Planning
120 North State Street, Dover, DE 19901-3875
(302) 736-2494

## Wilmington University
New Castle, Delaware
www.wilmu.edu                     Federal Code: 007948

**4-year private** liberal arts college in large town.
**Enrollment:** 9,238 undergrads, 57% part-time. 345 full-time freshmen.
**Selectivity:** Open admission.

### BASIC COSTS (2015-2016)
**Tuition and fees:** $10,430.
**Per-credit charge:** $346.

### FINANCIAL AID PICTURE
**Students with need:** Need-based aid available for full-time and part-time students. Work study available nights, weekends, and for part-time students.
**Students without need:** No-need awards available for academics, athletics.

### FINANCIAL AID PROCEDURES
**Forms required:** FAFSA.
**Dates and Deadlines:** Priority date 4/30; no closing date. Applicants notified on a rolling basis starting 8/5; must reply within 2 week(s) of notification.

### CONTACT
Nicole McDaniel-Smith, Director of Financial Aid
320 N Dupont Highway, New Castle, DE 19720
(302) 328-9401 ext. 107

# District of Columbia

## American University
Washington, District of Columbia     Federal Code: 001434
www.american.edu                      CSS Code: 5007

**4-year private** university in very large city, affiliated with United Methodist Church.
**Enrollment:** 7,300 undergrads, 4% part-time. 1,779 full-time freshmen.
**Selectivity:** Admits less than 50% of applicants.

### BASIC COSTS (2016-2017)
**Tuition and fees:** $44,593.
**Per-credit charge:** $1,467.
**Room and board:** $14,526.

### FINANCIAL AID PICTURE (2015-2016)
**Students with need:** Average financial aid package met 91% of need; average scholarship/grant was $27,104; average loan was $3,684. For part-time students, average financial aid package was $8,318.
**Students without need:** This college awards aid only to students with need.
**Scholarships offered:** United Methodist scholarship; supplemental application required.
**Additional info:** Early decision applicants must submit estimated AU institutional financial aid application by 11/15 and a FASFA as soon as possible after Jan 1.

### FINANCIAL AID PROCEDURES
**Forms required:** FAFSA. CSS Profile and FAFSA must be completed by freshmen who are seeking need-based aid.
**Dates and Deadlines:** Closing date 2/15. Applicants notified by 4/1; must reply by 5/1 or within 4 week(s) of notification.
**Transfers:** Priority date 3/1. Phi Theta Kappa scholarship available.

### CONTACT
Brian Lee Sang, Assistant Vice Provost, Financial Aid
4400 Massachusetts Avenue NW, Washington, DC 20016-8001
(202) 885-6500

## Catholic University of America
Washington, District of Columbia     Federal Code: 001437
www.cua.edu                           CSS Code: 5104

**4-year private** university in very large city, affiliated with Roman Catholic Church.
**Enrollment:** 3,462 undergrads, 4% part-time. 904 full-time freshmen.
**Selectivity:** Admits over 75% of applicants.

### BASIC COSTS (2015-2016)
**Tuition and fees:** $40,932.
**Per-credit charge:** $1,600.
**Room and board:** $13,356.

### FINANCIAL AID PICTURE (2015-2016)
**Students with need:** Average financial aid package met 79% of need; average scholarship/grant was $24,379; average loan was $4,161. For part-time students, average financial aid package was $8,961.
**Students without need:** No-need awards available for academics, alumni affiliation, music/drama, religious affiliation.

## FINANCIAL AID PROCEDURES

**Forms required:** FAFSA, CSS PROFILE.

**Dates and Deadlines:** Priority date 2/1; closing date 4/10. Applicants notified on a rolling basis starting 3/20; must reply by 5/1 or within 2 week(s) of notification.

**Transfers:** Priority date 2/1; no deadline. Applicants notified on a rolling basis starting 4/1; must reply by 5/1 or within 2 week(s) of notification.

## CONTACT

Joe Dobrota, Director of Financial Aid

102 Father O'Connell Hall, Washington, DC 20064

(202) 319-5307

# Gallaudet University

Washington, District of Columbia

www.gallaudet.edu                    Federal Code: 001443

**4-year private** university and liberal arts college in very large city.

**Enrollment:** 989 undergrads, 3% part-time. 170 full-time freshmen.

**Selectivity:** Admits 50 to 75% of applicants.

## BASIC COSTS (2015-2016)

**Tuition and fees:** $15,604.

**Per-credit charge:** $628.

**Room and board:** $12,630.

## FINANCIAL AID PICTURE (2014-2015)

**Students with need:** Out of 151 full-time freshmen who applied for aid, 142 were judged to have need. Of these, 141 received aid, and 18 had their full need met. Average financial aid package met 70% of need; average scholarship/grant was $19,278; average loan was $3,072. Need-based aid available for part-time students.

**Students without need:** 7 full-time freshmen who did not demonstrate need for aid received scholarships/grants; average award was $5,286. No-need awards available for leadership.

**Additional info:** Institution receives substantial aid from state vocational rehabilitation agencies, supplemented by institutional grants when needed.

## FINANCIAL AID PROCEDURES

**Forms required:** FAFSA.

**Dates and Deadlines:** Applicants notified on a rolling basis starting 3/1.

## CONTACT

Shondra Dickson Mitchell, Interim Director of Financial Aid

800 Florida Avenue, NE, Washington, DC 20002

(202) 651-5290

# George Washington University

Washington, District of Columbia    Federal Code: 001444

www.gwu.edu/explore                  CSS Code: 5246

**4-year private** university in very large city.

**Enrollment:** 10,901 undergrads, 8% part-time. 2,410 full-time freshmen.

**Selectivity:** Admits less than 50% of applicants.

## BASIC COSTS (2015-2016)

**Tuition and fees:** $50,435.

**Room and board:** $12,050.

**Additional info:** Tuition at time of enrollment locked for 4 years.

## FINANCIAL AID PICTURE (2014-2015)

**Students with need:** Out of 1,530 full-time freshmen who applied for aid, 1,116 were judged to have need. Of these, 1,105 received aid, and 530 had their full need met. Average financial aid package met 89% of need; average scholarship/grant was $27,843; average loan was $5,006. For part-time students, average financial aid package was $9,241.

**Students without need:** 740 full-time freshmen who did not demonstrate need for aid received scholarships/grants; average award was $18,993. No-need awards available for academics, art, athletics, music/drama, ROTC.

**Scholarships offered:** 50 full-time freshmen received athletic scholarships; average amount $46,243.

**Additional info:** Auditions required for performing arts scholarships.

## FINANCIAL AID PROCEDURES

**Forms required:** FAFSA, CSS PROFILE.

**Dates and Deadlines:** Closing date 2/1. Applicants notified on a rolling basis starting 3/24; must reply by 5/1.

**Transfers:** Closing date 5/1.

## CONTACT

Daniel Small, Director of Student Financial Assistance

2121 I Street NW, Suite 201, Washington, DC 20052

(202) 994-6620

# Georgetown University

Washington, District of Columbia    Federal Code: 001445

www.georgetown.edu                   CSS Code: 5244

**4-year private** university in very large city, affiliated with Roman Catholic Church.

**Enrollment:** 7,168 undergrads, 3% part-time. 1,567 full-time freshmen.

**Selectivity:** Admits less than 50% of applicants.

## BASIC COSTS (2015-2016)

**Tuition and fees:** $48,611.

**Per-credit charge:** $2,002.

**Room and board:** $15,160.

## FINANCIAL AID PICTURE (2015-2016)

**Students with need:** Out of 1,031 full-time freshmen who applied for aid, 632 were judged to have need. Of these, 632 received aid, and 632 had their full need met. Average financial aid package met 100% of need; average scholarship/grant was $42,794; average loan was $2,845. Need-based aid available for part-time students.

**Students without need:** No-need awards available for athletics.

**Scholarships offered:** 92 full-time freshmen received athletic scholarships; average amount $19,342.

## FINANCIAL AID PROCEDURES

**Forms required:** FAFSA, CSS PROFILE.

**Dates and Deadlines:** Priority date 2/1; no closing date. Applicants notified by 4/1; must reply by 5/1 or within 2 week(s) of notification.

**Transfers:** Priority date 3/1. Applicants notified by 5/15; must reply by 5/30 or within 2 week(s) of notification.

## CONTACT

Patricia McWade, Dean of Student Financial Services

Room 103 White Gravenor Hall, Washington, DC 20057

(202) 687-4547

# Howard University

Washington, District of Columbia

www.howard.edu                       Federal Code: 001448

**4-year private** university in very large city.

**Enrollment:** 6,796 undergrads, 6% part-time. 1,615 full-time freshmen.

**Selectivity:** Admits less than 50% of applicants.

## BASIC COSTS (2015-2016)

**Tuition and fees:** $23,970.

**Per-credit charge:** $980.

**Room and board:** $10,740.

**FINANCIAL AID PICTURE (2014-2015)**

**Students with need:** Out of 1,433 full-time freshmen who applied for aid, 1,334 were judged to have need. Of these, 1,313 received aid, and 306 had their full need met. Average financial aid package met 75% of need; average scholarship/grant was $6,623; average loan was $4,076. Need-based aid available for part-time students.

**Students without need:** 181 full-time freshmen who did not demonstrate need for aid received scholarships/grants; average award was $27,031. No-need awards available for academics, alumni affiliation, art, athletics, leadership, music/drama, religious affiliation, ROTC.

**Scholarships offered:** 65 full-time freshmen received athletic scholarships; average amount $22,279.

**FINANCIAL AID PROCEDURES**

**Forms required:** FAFSA.

**Dates and Deadlines:** Priority date 2/1; closing date 5/1. Applicants notified on a rolling basis starting 2/16; must reply by 2/16 or within 3 week(s) of notification.

**Transfers:** Priority date 2/1; closing date 5/1. Applicants notified by 6/1; must reply within 3 week(s) of notification.

**CONTACT**

Brian Johnson, Associate Director - Financial Aid
2400 Sixth Street NW, Washington, DC 20059
(202) 806-2820

## Trinity Washington University
Washington, District of Columbia
www.trinitydc.edu          Federal Code: 001460

**4-year private** liberal arts college in very large city, affiliated with Roman Catholic Church.

**Enrollment:** 2,129 undergrads.

**BASIC COSTS (2015-2016)**

**Tuition and fees:** $22,780.

**Room and board:** $10,080.

**FINANCIAL AID PICTURE**

**Students with need:** Need-based aid available for full-time and part-time students.

**Students without need:** No-need awards available for academics, alumni affiliation, leadership.

**FINANCIAL AID PROCEDURES**

**Forms required:** FAFSA.

**Dates and Deadlines:** Priority date 3/1; closing date 4/1. Applicants notified on a rolling basis starting 2/1; must reply within 2 week(s) of notification.

**CONTACT**

Meghan Howard, Director of Financial Aid
125 Michigan Avenue, NE, Washington, DC 20017
(202) 884-9530

## University of the District of Columbia
Washington, District of Columbia
www.udc.edu          Federal Code: 007015

**4-year public** university and liberal arts college in very large city.

**Enrollment:** 4,463 undergrads.

**Selectivity:** Admits less than 50% of applicants.

**BASIC COSTS (2015-2016)**

**Tuition and fees:** $7,421.

**Room and board:** $13,200.

**FINANCIAL AID PICTURE**

**Students with need:** Need-based aid available for full-time and part-time students. Work study available nights, weekends, and for part-time students.

**Students without need:** This college awards aid only to students with need.

**FINANCIAL AID PROCEDURES**

**Forms required:** FAFSA.

**Dates and Deadlines:** Applicants notified on a rolling basis starting 6/1; must reply by 8/28 or within 2 week(s) of notification.

**Transfers:** No deadline. Applicants notified on a rolling basis starting 6/1; must reply by 8/28 or within 2 week(s) of notification.

**CONTACT**

Steve Schissler, AVP Financial Aid and Enrollment Services
4200 Connecticut Avenue NW, Washington, DC 20008
(419) 530-8700

## University of the Potomac
Washington, District of Columbia
www.potomac.edu          Federal Code: 032183

**3-year for-profit** business college in very large city.

**Enrollment:** 341 undergrads.

**Selectivity:** Open admission.

**BASIC COSTS (2015-2016)**

**Additional info:** Bacholer degree program: $541; Associate degree programs: $541; certificates: $250. Books and supplies range depending on program level and course of study. All costs are subject to change.

**FINANCIAL AID PICTURE**

**Students with need:** Need-based aid available for full-time and part-time students.

**FINANCIAL AID PROCEDURES**

**Forms required:** FAFSA, institutional form.

**Dates and Deadlines:** Applicants notified on a rolling basis; must reply within 4 week(s) of notification.

**CONTACT**

David Rivers, Director of Financial Aid
4000 Chesapeake Street NW, Washington, DC 20016
(602) 734-4372

# Florida

## Adventist University of Health Sciences
Orlando, Florida
www.adu.edu          Federal Code: 031155

**4-year private** university and health science college in large city, affiliated with Seventh-day Adventists.

**Enrollment:** 1,704 undergrads, 63% part-time. 88 full-time freshmen.

**Selectivity:** Admits 50 to 75% of applicants.

**BASIC COSTS (2016-2017)**

**Tuition and fees:** $13,480.

**Per-credit charge:** $430.

**Room and board:** $4,200.

**FINANCIAL AID PICTURE (2014-2015)**

**Students with need:** Out of 83 full-time freshmen who applied for aid, 76 were judged to have need. Of these, 71 received aid, and 4 had their full need met. Average financial aid package met 26% of need; average scholarship/grant was $5,846; average loan was $2,871. For part-time students, average financial aid package was $5,105.

**Students without need:** 6 full-time freshmen who did not demonstrate need for aid received scholarships/grants; average award was $4,268. No-need awards available for state/district residency.

### FINANCIAL AID PROCEDURES

**Forms required:** FAFSA, institutional form.

**Dates and Deadlines:** Priority date 4/10; no closing date. Applicants notified on a rolling basis starting 3/1.

### CONTACT

Rebecca Valencia, Director of Financial Aid
671 Winyah Drive, Orlando, FL 32803
(407) 303-9203

## Art Institute of Fort Lauderdale
Fort Lauderdale, Florida
www.aifl.edu                          Federal Code: 010195

**4-year for-profit** visual arts and technical college in large city.
**Enrollment:** 1,514 undergrads.

### BASIC COSTS (2015-2016)
**Tuition and fees:** $22,105.
**Per-credit charge:** $489.
**Room only:** $6,345.

### FINANCIAL AID PICTURE
**Students with need:** Need-based aid available for full-time and part-time students. Work study available nights, weekends, and for part-time students.
**Students without need:** No-need awards available for academics.
**Scholarships offered:** Art Institute Merit Awards; $200-300 per quarter; based on GPA.
**Additional info:** Internal scholarships available. Financial planning program allows personalized service to budget and meet college costs through individualized payment plans.

### FINANCIAL AID PROCEDURES
**Forms required:** FAFSA.

### CONTACT
Joy Cummings, Director of Student Financial Service
1799 SE 17th Street, Fort Lauderdale, FL 33316
(954) 308-2165

## Ave Maria University
Ave Maria, Florida
www.avemaria.edu                      Federal Code: 039413

**4-year private** university and liberal arts college in small town, affiliated with Roman Catholic Church.
**Enrollment:** 1,061 undergrads, 1% part-time. 303 full-time freshmen.
**Selectivity:** Admits less than 50% of applicants.

### BASIC COSTS (2015-2016)
**Tuition and fees:** $19,430.
**Room and board:** $10,233.

### FINANCIAL AID PICTURE
**Students with need:** Need-based aid available for full-time and part-time students. Work study available nights, weekends, and for part-time students.
**Students without need:** No-need awards available for academics, athletics, leadership, music/drama, religious affiliation, state/district residency.

### FINANCIAL AID PROCEDURES
**Forms required:** FAFSA, state aid form.

**Dates and Deadlines:** Priority date 4/1; no closing date. Applicants notified on a rolling basis starting 10/1.

### CONTACT
Anne Hart, Director of Financial Aid
5050 Ave Maria Boulevard, Ave Maria, FL 34142-9505

## Baptist College of Florida
Graceville, Florida
www.baptistcollege.edu                Federal Code: 013001

**4-year private** Bible and teachers college in small town, affiliated with Southern Baptist Convention.
**Enrollment:** 460 undergrads, 28% part-time. 39 full-time freshmen.
**Selectivity:** Admits 50 to 75% of applicants.

### BASIC COSTS (2016-2017)
**Tuition and fees:** $10,000.
**Per-credit charge:** $320.
**Room and board:** $4,888.

### FINANCIAL AID PICTURE (2015-2016)
**Students with need:** Average financial aid package met 30% of need; average scholarship/grant was $5,687; average loan was $3,131. For part-time students, average financial aid package was $3,865.
**Students without need:** No-need awards available for academics, minority status, music/drama, religious affiliation.

### FINANCIAL AID PROCEDURES
**Forms required:** FAFSA, state aid form, institutional form.
**Dates and Deadlines:** Priority date 4/1; closing date 4/15. Applicants notified on a rolling basis starting 6/15; must reply within 4 week(s) of notification.
**Transfers:** No deadline.

### CONTACT
Stephanie Powell, Director of Financial Aid
5400 College Drive, Graceville, FL 32440-3306
(850) 263-3261 ext. 461

## Barry University
Miami Shores, Florida
www.barry.edu                         Federal Code: 001466

**4-year private** university in large town, affiliated with Roman Catholic Church.
**Enrollment:** 3,703 undergrads, 15% part-time. 430 full-time freshmen.
**Selectivity:** Admits 50 to 75% of applicants.

### BASIC COSTS (2015-2016)
**Tuition and fees:** $28,800.
**Per-credit charge:** $865.
**Room and board:** $10,600.

### FINANCIAL AID PICTURE (2015-2016)
**Students with need:** Out of 372 full-time freshmen who applied for aid, 355 were judged to have need. Of these, 354 received aid, and 22 had their full need met. Average financial aid package met 66% of need; average scholarship/grant was $11,272; average loan was $3,210. For part-time students, average financial aid package was $5,858.
**Students without need:** 42 full-time freshmen who did not demonstrate need for aid received scholarships/grants; average award was $10,956. No-need awards available for academics, art, athletics, music/drama.
**Scholarships offered:** 20 full-time freshmen received athletic scholarships; average amount $18,140.

### FINANCIAL AID PROCEDURES
**Forms required:** FAFSA.

**Dates and Deadlines:** Applicants notified on a rolling basis starting 1/25.

**CONTACT**

H. Dart Humeston, Director of Financial Aid

11300 NE Second Avenue, Miami Shores, FL 33161-6695

(305) 899-3673

## Beacon College

Leesburg, Florida

www.beaconcollege.edu          Federal Code: 033733

**4-year private** liberal arts college in large town.

**Enrollment:** 274 undergrads, 3% part-time. 52 full-time freshmen.

**Selectivity:** Admits 50 to 75% of applicants.

**BASIC COSTS (2015-2016)**

**Tuition and fees:** $34,680.

**Per-credit charge:** $830.

**Room and board:** $10,250.

**FINANCIAL AID PICTURE (2014-2015)**

**Students with need:** Out of 36 full-time freshmen who applied for aid, 12 were judged to have need. Of these, 12 received aid. Average financial aid package met 75% of need; average scholarship/grant was $7,000; average loan was $5,500. Need-based aid available for part-time students.

**Students without need:** 13 full-time freshmen who did not demonstrate need for aid received scholarships/grants; average award was $7,000. No-need awards available for academics, leadership, state/district residency.

**Additional info:** Work-study programs offered based on financial need.

**FINANCIAL AID PROCEDURES**

**Forms required:** FAFSA, state aid form.

**Dates and Deadlines:** Priority date 4/1; no closing date. Applicants notified on a rolling basis starting 5/1; must reply within 2 week(s) of notification.

**Transfers:** No deadline. Applicants notified on a rolling basis starting 5/1; must reply within 2 week(s) of notification.

**CONTACT**

Shawna Wells-Booth, Financial Aid Director

105 East Main Street, Leesburg, FL 34748

(352) 638-9733

## Bethune-Cookman University

Daytona Beach, Florida

www.cookman.edu          Federal Code: 001467

**4-year private** liberal arts college in small city, affiliated with United Methodist Church.

**Enrollment:** 3,666 undergrads, 5% part-time. 927 full-time freshmen.

**Selectivity:** Admits 50 to 75% of applicants.

**BASIC COSTS (2015-2016)**

**Tuition and fees:** $14,410.

**Per-credit charge:** $560.

**Room and board:** $8,710.

**Additional info:** Tuition at time of enrollment locked for 4 years.

**FINANCIAL AID PICTURE (2014-2015)**

**Students with need:** Out of 927 full-time freshmen who applied for aid, 902 were judged to have need. Of these, 902 received aid, and 40 had their full need met. Average financial aid package met 52% of need; average scholarship/grant was $10,571; average loan was $3,633. Need-based aid available for part-time students.

**Students without need:** This college awards aid only to students with need.

**FINANCIAL AID PROCEDURES**

**Forms required:** FAFSA.

**Dates and Deadlines:** Priority date 4/1; no closing date. Applicants notified on a rolling basis starting 4/1; must reply within 3 week(s) of notification.

**CONTACT**

Joseph Coleman, Director of Financial Aid

640 Dr. Mary McLeod Bethune Boulevard, Daytona Beach, FL 32114-3099

(800) 553-9369

## Broward College

Fort Lauderdale, Florida

www.broward.edu          Federal Code: 001500

**2-year public** community college in small city.

**Enrollment:** 38,127 undergrads, 68% part-time. 3,616 full-time freshmen.

**Selectivity:** Open admission; but selective for some programs.

**BASIC COSTS (2015-2016)**

**Tuition and fees:** $3,405; out-of-state residents $11,058.

**Per-credit charge:** $113; out-of-state residents $368.

**Additional info:** Bachelor programs charged at higher tuition rates. Tuition/fee waivers available for adults, minority students.

**FINANCIAL AID PICTURE (2015-2016)**

**Students with need:** 80% of average financial aid package awarded as scholarships/grants, 20% awarded as loans/jobs. Need-based aid available for part-time students. Work study available nights, weekends, and for part-time students.

**Students without need:** No-need awards available for academics, athletics, leadership, state/district residency.

**FINANCIAL AID PROCEDURES**

**Forms required:** FAFSA, institutional form.

**Dates and Deadlines:** Priority date 4/15; no closing date. Applicants notified on a rolling basis starting 6/1.

**Transfers:** No deadline.

**CONTACT**

Marielena DeSanctis, Vice President of Student Affairs

225 East Las Olas Boulevard, Fort Lauderdale, FL 33301

## Brown Mackie College: Miami

Miami, Florida

www.brownmackie.edu          Federal Code: 005127

**2-year for-profit** business and career college in very large city.

**Enrollment:** 919 undergrads.

**Selectivity:** Open admission.

**BASIC COSTS (2015-2016)**

**Tuition and fees:** $19,145.

**Per-credit charge:** $391.

**FINANCIAL AID PICTURE**

**Students with need:** Work study available nights.

**Students without need:** No-need awards available for academics, state/district residency.

**CONTACT**

Ingrid Ayala, Director of Financial Aid

One Herald Plaza, Miami, FL 33132

(305) 341-6600

## Carlos Albizu University
Miami, Florida
www.albizu.edu                    Federal Code: 010724

**4-year private** university in very large city.
**Enrollment:** 262 undergrads, 51% part-time. 6 full-time freshmen.

### BASIC COSTS (2015-2016)
**Tuition and fees:** $10,194.
**Per-credit charge:** $323.

### FINANCIAL AID PICTURE
**Students with need:** Need-based aid available for full-time and part-time students. Work study available nights.
**Students without need:** This college awards aid only to students with need.

### FINANCIAL AID PROCEDURES
**Forms required:** FAFSA, institutional form.
**Dates and Deadlines:** Priority date 6/1; no closing date. Applicants notified on a rolling basis starting 2/1.
**Transfers:** No deadline. Applicants notified on a rolling basis.

### CONTACT
Ramona Morales, Financial Aid Director
2173 NW 99th Avenue, Miami, FL 33172
(305) 593-1223 ext. 153

## Chipola College
Marianna, Florida
www.chipola.edu                   Federal Code: 001472

**2-year public** community college in small town.
**Enrollment:** 1,425 undergrads, 47% part-time. 153 full-time freshmen.
**Selectivity:** Open admission; but selective for some programs.

### BASIC COSTS (2015-2016)
**Tuition and fees:** $3,060; out-of-state residents $8,891.

### FINANCIAL AID PICTURE
**Students with need:** Need-based aid available for full-time and part-time students. Work study available nights.
**Students without need:** No-need awards available for academics, alumni affiliation, art, athletics, job skills, leadership, minority status, music/drama.

### FINANCIAL AID PROCEDURES
**Forms required:** FAFSA, institutional form.
**Dates and Deadlines:** Priority date 5/1; no closing date. Applicants notified on a rolling basis starting 1/2; must reply within 2 week(s) of notification.

### CONTACT
Beverly Hambright, Director of Financial Aid
3094 Indian Circle, Marianna, FL 32446
(850) 718-2223

## City College: Miami
Miami, Florida
www.citycollege.edu               Federal Code: 025154

**2-year private** career college in large city.
**Enrollment:** 228 undergrads.

### BASIC COSTS (2015-2016)
**Tuition and fees:** $14,550.
**Per-credit charge:** $320.
**Additional info:** Additional program fees are charged per credit hour or per course.

### FINANCIAL AID PICTURE
**Students with need:** Need-based aid available for full-time and part-time students.
**Students without need:** This college awards aid only to students with need.

### FINANCIAL AID PROCEDURES
**Forms required:** FAFSA, institutional form.
**Dates and Deadlines:** Applicants notified on a rolling basis.

### CONTACT
Armando Rios, President
9300 South Dadeland Boulevard, Miami, FL 33156
(305) 666-9242

## College of Business and Technology: Cutler Bay
Cutler Bay, Florida
www.cbt.edu                       Federal Code: 030716

**2-year for-profit** technical and career college in very large city.
**Enrollment:** 78 undergrads. 17 full-time freshmen.
**Selectivity:** Open admission.

### BASIC COSTS (2015-2016)
**Additional info:** Tuition per semester credit $498; enrollment fee $150; student services fee $120; additional fees vary by program.

### FINANCIAL AID PICTURE (2014-2015)
**Students with need:** 37% of average financial aid package awarded as scholarships/grants, 63% awarded as loans/jobs. Need-based aid available for part-time students. Work study available nights.
**Students without need:** This college awards aid only to students with need.

### FINANCIAL AID PROCEDURES
**Forms required:** FAFSA.
**Transfers:** No deadline.

### CONTACT
Yazmin Palma, Director of Financial Aid
19151 South Dixie Highway, #203, Cutler Bay, FL 33157

## College of Business and Technology: Flagler
Miami, Florida
www.cbt.edu                       Federal Code: 030716

**2-year for-profit** technical and career college in very large city.
**Enrollment:** 288 undergrads. 82 full-time freshmen.
**Selectivity:** Open admission.

### BASIC COSTS (2015-2016)
**Additional info:** Tuition per semester credit $498; enrollment fee $150; student services fee $120; additional fees vary by program.

### FINANCIAL AID PICTURE (2014-2015)
**Students with need:** 40% of average financial aid package awarded as scholarships/grants, 60% awarded as loans/jobs. Need-based aid available for part-time students. Work study available nights.
**Students without need:** This college awards aid only to students with need.

### FINANCIAL AID PROCEDURES
**Forms required:** FAFSA.
**Transfers:** No deadline.

**CONTACT**
Yazmin Palma, Financial Aid Director
8230 West Flagler Street, Miami, FL 33144

## College of Business and Technology: Hialeah

Hialeah, Florida
www.cbt.edu                    Federal Code: 030716

**2-year for-profit** technical and career college in large city.
**Enrollment:** 200 undergrads. 85 full-time freshmen.
**Selectivity:** Open admission.

**BASIC COSTS (2015-2016)**
**Additional info:** Tuition per semester credit $498; enrollment fee $150; student services fee $120; additional fees vary by program.

**FINANCIAL AID PICTURE (2014-2015)**
**Students with need:** 43% of average financial aid package awarded as scholarships/grants, 57% awarded as loans/jobs. Need-based aid available for part-time students. Work study available nights.
**Students without need:** This college awards aid only to students with need.

**FINANCIAL AID PROCEDURES**
**Forms required:** FAFSA.
**Transfers:** No deadline.

**CONTACT**
Yazmin Palma, Financial Aid Director
935 West 49th Street Suite 203, Hialeah, FL 33012-3436

## College of Business and Technology: Kendall

Miami, Florida
www.cbt.edu                    Federal Code: 030716

**2-year for-profit** technical and career college in very large city.
**Enrollment:** 10 undergrads. 1 full-time freshmen.
**Selectivity:** Open admission.

**BASIC COSTS (2015-2016)**
**Additional info:** Tuition per semester credit $498; enrollment fee $150; student services fee $120; additional fees vary by program.

**FINANCIAL AID PICTURE (2014-2015)**
**Students with need:** 67% of average financial aid package awarded as scholarships/grants, 33% awarded as loans/jobs. Need-based aid available for part-time students. Work study available nights.
**Students without need:** This college awards aid only to students with need.

**FINANCIAL AID PROCEDURES**
**Forms required:** FAFSA.

**CONTACT**
Yazmin Palma, Financial Aid Director
8700 W Flagler Street, Miami, FL 33174

## College of Business and Technology: Miami Gardens

Miami Gardens, Florida
www.cbt.edu                    Federal Code: 030716

**2-year for-profit** technical and career college in small city.
**Enrollment:** 72 undergrads. 12 full-time freshmen.

**Selectivity:** Open admission.

**FINANCIAL AID PICTURE (2014-2015)**
**Students with need:** 58% of average financial aid package awarded as scholarships/grants, 42% awarded as loans/jobs. Need-based aid available for part-time students. Work study available nights.
**Students without need:** This college awards aid only to students with need.

**FINANCIAL AID PROCEDURES**
**Forms required:** FAFSA.
**Transfers:** No deadline.

**CONTACT**
Yazmin Palma, Director of Financial Aid
5190 NW 167th Street, Miami Gardens, FL 33014-6338

## College of Central Florida

Ocala, Florida
www.cf.edu                    Federal Code: 001471

**2-year public** community college in small city.
**Enrollment:** 6,937 undergrads, 60% part-time. 900 full-time freshmen.
**Selectivity:** Open admission; but selective for some programs.

**BASIC COSTS (2015-2016)**
**Tuition and fees:** $3,213; out-of-state residents $12,656.
**Per-credit charge:** $107; out-of-state residents $422.
**Additional info:** Bachelor programs charged at higher tuition rates. Tuition/fee waivers available for minority students.

**FINANCIAL AID PICTURE**
**Students with need:** Need-based aid available for full-time and part-time students.
**Students without need:** No-need awards available for academics, athletics, minority status, music/drama, state/district residency.

**FINANCIAL AID PROCEDURES**
**Forms required:** FAFSA.

**CONTACT**
Maureen Anderson, Director, Financial Aid
3001 SW College Road, Ocala, FL 34474-4415
(352) 873-5803 ext. 1340

## Daytona State College

Daytona Beach, Florida
www.daytonastate.edu                    Federal Code: 001475

**2-year public** community and technical college in large city.
**Enrollment:** 10,856 undergrads, 58% part-time. 847 full-time freshmen.
**Selectivity:** Open admission; but selective for some programs.

**BASIC COSTS (2015-2016)**
**Tuition and fees:** $3,134; out-of-state residents $12,204.
**Additional info:** Bachelor programs charged at higher tuition rates.

**FINANCIAL AID PICTURE (2014-2015)**
**Students with need:** Out of 737 full-time freshmen who applied for aid, 602 were judged to have need. Of these, 580 received aid. Need-based aid available for part-time students.
**Students without need:** No-need awards available for academics, athletics, leadership, music/drama, state/district residency.
**Scholarships offered:** 23 full-time freshmen received athletic scholarships; average amount $6,175.

**FINANCIAL AID PROCEDURES**
**Forms required:** FAFSA.

**Dates and Deadlines:** Priority date 5/15; no closing date. Applicants notified on a rolling basis starting 3/15.

**CONTACT**
Kevin McCrary, Director of Financial Aid
Admissions Office Daytona State College, Daytona Beach, FL 32114
(386) 506-3000 ext. 3015

## DeVry University: Miramar
Miramar, Florida
www.devry.edu

**4-year for-profit** university in large town.
**Enrollment:** 503 undergrads.

**BASIC COSTS (2015-2016)**
**Tuition and fees:** $17,132.
**Per-credit charge:** $609.

**FINANCIAL AID PICTURE**
**Students with need:** Need-based aid available for full-time and part-time students.
**Students without need:** This college awards aid only to students with need.

**FINANCIAL AID PROCEDURES**
**Forms required:** FAFSA.
**Dates and Deadlines:** Applicants notified on a rolling basis.

**CONTACT**
Assistant Director of Student Finance
2300 SW 145th Avenue, Miramar, FL 33027
(954) 499-9700

## DeVry University: Orlando
Orlando, Florida
www.devry.edu                    Federal Code: 022966

**4-year for-profit** university in very large city.
**Enrollment:** 914 undergrads.

**BASIC COSTS (2015-2016)**
**Tuition and fees:** $17,132.
**Per-credit charge:** $609.

**FINANCIAL AID PICTURE**
**Students with need:** Need-based aid available for full-time and part-time students.
**Students without need:** This college awards aid only to students with need.

**FINANCIAL AID PROCEDURES**
**Forms required:** FAFSA.
**Dates and Deadlines:** Applicants notified on a rolling basis.

**CONTACT**
Director of Student Finance
4000 Millennia Boulevard, Orlando, FL 32839-2426
(407) 345-2800

## Digital Media Arts College
Boca Raton, Florida
www.dmac.edu                    Federal Code: 041274

**3-year for-profit** visual arts college in large city.
**Enrollment:** 300 undergrads.

**Selectivity:** Open admission.

**BASIC COSTS (2015-2016)**
**Tuition and fees:** $17,610.
**Per-credit charge:** $582.

**FINANCIAL AID PICTURE**
**Students with need:** Need-based aid available for full-time and part-time students.
**Students without need:** No-need awards available for art.

**FINANCIAL AID PROCEDURES**
**Forms required:** FAFSA.
**Dates and Deadlines:** Applicants notified on a rolling basis starting 1/1; must reply within 4 week(s) of notification.
**Transfers:** No deadline. Applicants notified on a rolling basis starting 1/1.

**CONTACT**
Sharon Scheible, Director of Financial Aid
5400 Broken Sound Boulevard, Boca Raton, FL 33487

## Eastern Florida State College
Cocoa, Florida
www.easternflorida.edu           Federal Code: 001470

**2-year public** community college in very large city.
**Enrollment:** 12,736 undergrads.
**Selectivity:** Open admission; but selective for some programs.

**BASIC COSTS (2015-2016)**
**Tuition and fees:** $3,130; out-of-state residents $12,183.
**Per-credit charge:** $104; out-of-state residents $406.

**FINANCIAL AID PICTURE**
**Students with need:** Need-based aid available for full-time and part-time students.
**Students without need:** No-need awards available for academics, athletics.

**FINANCIAL AID PROCEDURES**
**Forms required:** FAFSA.
**Dates and Deadlines:** Priority date 4/15; closing date 6/30. Applicants notified on a rolling basis starting 6/1; must reply within 2 week(s) of notification.
**Transfers:** Transfer students must complete at least 15 credit hours with 3.5 GPA to be considered for merit scholarship.

**CONTACT**
Indira Dzadovsky, Director of Financial Aid/ Veteran Affairs
1519 Clearlake Road, Cocoa, FL 32922-9987
(321) 433-5530

## Eckerd College
St. Petersburg, Florida
www.eckerd.edu                   Federal Code: 001487

**4-year private** liberal arts college in large city, affiliated with Presbyterian Church (USA).
**Enrollment:** 1,779 undergrads, 2% part-time. 448 full-time freshmen.
**Selectivity:** Admits 50 to 75% of applicants.

**BASIC COSTS (2016-2017)**
**Tuition and fees:** $41,538.
**Per-credit charge:** $1,412.
**Room and board:** $11,336.

**FINANCIAL AID PICTURE (2014-2015)**
**Students with need:** Out of 448 full-time freshmen who applied for aid, 368 were judged to have need. Of these, 368 received aid, and 79 had their

full need met. Average financial aid package met 88% of need; average scholarship/grant was $22,273; average loan was $3,328. For part-time students, average financial aid package was $31,439.

**Students without need:** 175 full-time freshmen who did not demonstrate need for aid received scholarships/grants; average award was $16,280. No-need awards available for academics, art, athletics, music/drama, state/district residency.

**Scholarships offered: *Merit:*** Academic scholarships: $10,000 to $16,000 per year; available to entering freshmen with strong scholastic records regardless of financial need. Transfer scholarships: $6,000-11,000. Artistic Achievement Awards: music, theater, visual arts and creative writing; limited number available through separate application process. Freshman Research Associateships also available. ***Athletic:*** 10 full-time freshmen received athletic scholarships; average amount $24,564.

### FINANCIAL AID PROCEDURES

**Forms required:** FAFSA.

**Dates and Deadlines:** Priority date 3/1; no closing date. Applicants notified on a rolling basis starting 2/20.

### CONTACT

Patricia Watkins, Director of Financial Aid
4200 54th Avenue South, St. Petersburg, FL 33711
(727) 864-8334

## Edward Waters College

Jacksonville, Florida
www.ewc.edu
Federal Code: 001478

**4-year private** liberal arts college in very large city, affiliated with African Methodist Episcopal Church.

**Enrollment:** 933 undergrads.

### BASIC COSTS (2015-2016)

**Tuition and fees:** $12,525.

**Per-credit charge:** $472.

**Room and board:** $7,282.

### FINANCIAL AID PICTURE

**Students with need:** Need-based aid available for full-time and part-time students. Work study available nights, weekends, and for part-time students.

### FINANCIAL AID PROCEDURES

**Forms required:** FAFSA.

**Dates and Deadlines:** Closing date 4/15. Applicants notified on a rolling basis starting 5/1; must reply within 2 week(s) of notification.

### CONTACT

Janice Nowak, Director of Financial Aid
1658 Kings Road, Jacksonville, FL 32209
(904) 470-8190

## Embry-Riddle Aeronautical University

Daytona Beach, Florida
www.embryriddle.edu
Federal Code: 001479

**4-year private** university in small city.

**Enrollment:** 5,247 undergrads, 7% part-time. 1,270 full-time freshmen.

**Selectivity:** Admits 50 to 75% of applicants.

### BASIC COSTS (2015-2016)

**Tuition and fees:** $33,218.

**Per-credit charge:** $1,331.

**Room and board:** $10,382.

### FINANCIAL AID PICTURE

**Students with need:** Need-based aid available for full-time and part-time students.

### FINANCIAL AID PROCEDURES

**Forms required:** FAFSA.

**Dates and Deadlines:** Priority date 3/1; no closing date. Applicants notified on a rolling basis starting 3/1; must reply within 4 week(s) of notification.

### CONTACT

Barbara Dryden, Director of Financial Aid
600 South Clyde Morris Boulevard, Daytona Beach, FL 32114-3900
(386) 226-6300

## Embry-Riddle Aeronautical University: Worldwide Campus

Daytona Beach, Florida
www.embryriddle.edu
Federal Code: 001479

**4-year private** virtual university in small city.

**Enrollment:** 10,478 undergrads, 71% part-time. 77 full-time freshmen.

**Selectivity:** Admits 50 to 75% of applicants.

### BASIC COSTS (2015-2016)

**Tuition and fees:** $8,520.

**Per-credit charge:** $355.

**Additional info:** Undergraduate tuition is $355 per credit hour. Discounted Tuition rates are available for Active Duty Military Personnel. Embry-Riddle Worldwide does not offer housing.

### FINANCIAL AID PICTURE

**Students with need:** Need-based aid available for full-time and part-time students.

### FINANCIAL AID PROCEDURES

**Forms required:** FAFSA.

**Dates and Deadlines:** Priority date 4/15; no closing date. Applicants notified on a rolling basis starting 3/1; must reply within 4 week(s) of notification.

### CONTACT

Dagmar Bowen, Director of Financial Aid, Worldwide Campus
Attn: Worldwide Imaging, Daytona Beach, FL 32114-3900
(866) 567-7202

## Everglades University: Boca Raton

Boca Raton, Florida
www.evergladesuniversity.edu
Federal Code: 031085

**4-year private** university in small city.

**Enrollment:** 192 undergrads. 27 full-time freshmen.

**Selectivity:** Admits over 75% of applicants.

### BASIC COSTS (2016-2017)

**Tuition and fees:** $15,993.

**Per-credit charge:** $627.

**Additional info:** Tuition for each undergraduate semester of 12 credits is $7,524. Education fees are $400 per semester for on-campus students. First-time students pay a one-time $145 registration fee upon initial enrollment. Online students pay $800 per semester in education fees.

### FINANCIAL AID PICTURE (2015-2016)

**Students with need:** 57% of average financial aid package awarded as scholarships/grants, 43% awarded as loans/jobs. Work study available nights, weekends, and for part-time students.

### FINANCIAL AID PROCEDURES

**Forms required:** FAFSA, institutional form.

**Dates and Deadlines:** Applicants notified on a rolling basis.

**Transfers:** No deadline.

**CONTACT**
Seeta Singh-Moonilall, Director of Financial Aid
5002 T-REX Avenue, Suite 100, Boca Raton, FL 33431
(561) 912-1211

## Everglades University: Orlando
Maitland, Florida
www.evergladesuniversity.edu　　　Federal Code: 031085

**4-year private** university and branch campus college in large city.
**Enrollment:** 135 undergrads. 19 full-time freshmen.
**Selectivity:** Admits over 75% of applicants.

### BASIC COSTS (2016-2017)
**Tuition and fees:** $15,993.
**Per-credit charge:** $627.
**Additional info:** Tuition for each undergraduate semester of 12 credits is $7,524. Education fees are $400 per semester for on-campus students. First-time students pay a one-time $145 registration fee upon initial enrollment. Online students pay $800 per semester in education fees.

### FINANCIAL AID PICTURE (2015-2016)
**Students with need:** 64% of average financial aid package awarded as scholarships/grants, 36% awarded as loans/jobs. Work study available nights, weekends, and for part-time students.

### FINANCIAL AID PROCEDURES
**Forms required:** FAFSA, institutional form.
**Transfers:** No deadline.

### CONTACT
Seeta Singh-Moonilall, Regional Director of Financial Aid
850 Trafalgar Court Suite 100, Maitland, FL 32751
(866) 289-1078

## Flagler College
Saint Augustine, Florida
www.flagler.edu　　　Federal Code: 007893

**4-year private** liberal arts college in large town.
**Enrollment:** 2,702 undergrads, 4% part-time. 622 full-time freshmen.
**Selectivity:** Admits 50 to 75% of applicants.

### BASIC COSTS (2015-2016)
**Tuition and fees:** $16,900.
**Per-credit charge:** $560.
**Room and board:** $9,350.

### FINANCIAL AID PICTURE (2015-2016)
**Students with need:** Out of 531 full-time freshmen who applied for aid, 399 were judged to have need. Of these, 399 received aid, and 58 had their full need met. Average financial aid package met 58% of need; average scholarship/grant was $9,324; average loan was $3,153. For part-time students, average financial aid package was $4,689.
**Students without need:** 138 full-time freshmen who did not demonstrate need for aid received scholarships/grants; average award was $2,157. No-need awards available for academics, art, athletics, job skills, leadership, minority status, music/drama, religious affiliation, state/district residency.
**Scholarships offered:** 24 full-time freshmen received athletic scholarships; average amount $10,584.

### FINANCIAL AID PROCEDURES
**Forms required:** FAFSA, state aid form.
**Dates and Deadlines:** Priority date 3/1; no closing date. Applicants notified on a rolling basis starting 3/1; must reply within 2 week(s) of notification.
**Transfers:** No deadline. Applicants notified on a rolling basis starting 3/1; must reply within 2 week(s) of notification. Transfer students receiving

Florida-sponsored aid must notify Florida Office of Student Financial Assistance of their transfer.

**CONTACT**
Sheia Pleasant-Doine, Director of Financial Aid
74 King Street, St. Augustine, FL 32084
(800) 304-4208

## Florida Agricultural and Mechanical University
Tallahassee, Florida
www.famu.edu　　　Federal Code: 001480

**4-year public** university in small city.
**Enrollment:** 7,705 undergrads, 10% part-time. 1,388 full-time freshmen.
**Selectivity:** Admits 50 to 75% of applicants.

### BASIC COSTS (2015-2016)
**Tuition and fees:** $5,785; out-of-state residents $17,725.
**Per-credit charge:** $188; out-of-state residents $586.
**Room and board:** $10,100.

### FINANCIAL AID PICTURE (2014-2015)
**Students with need:** Out of 1,369 full-time freshmen who applied for aid, 1,226 were judged to have need. Of these, 1,225 received aid, and 233 had their full need met. Average financial aid package met 77% of need; average scholarship/grant was $7,619; average loan was $3,466. For part-time students, average financial aid package was $8,986.
**Students without need:** 19 full-time freshmen who did not demonstrate need for aid received scholarships/grants; average award was $8,491. No-need awards available for academics, art, athletics, leadership, music/drama, ROTC.
**Scholarships offered:** 50 full-time freshmen received athletic scholarships; average amount $13,014.

### FINANCIAL AID PROCEDURES
**Forms required:** FAFSA.
**Dates and Deadlines:** Priority date 3/1; no closing date. Applicants notified on a rolling basis starting 4/15.
**Transfers:** No deadline. Applicants notified on a rolling basis starting 4/15.

### CONTACT
Lisa Stewart, Director of Financial Aid
444 Gamble Street Lucy Moten, Room 204, Tallahassee, FL 32307-3200
(850) 599-3730

## Florida Atlantic University
Boca Raton, Florida
www.fau.edu　　　Federal Code: 001481

**4-year public** university in small city.
**Enrollment:** 24,228 undergrads, 35% part-time. 3,296 full-time freshmen.
**Selectivity:** Admits 50 to 75% of applicants.

### BASIC COSTS (2015-2016)
**Tuition and fees:** $6,039; out-of-state residents $21,595.
**Per-credit charge:** $201; out-of-state residents $720.
**Room and board:** $11,748.

### FINANCIAL AID PICTURE (2015-2016)
**Students with need:** Out of 2,770 full-time freshmen who applied for aid, 2,099 were judged to have need. Of these, 2,066 received aid, and 181 had their full need met. Average financial aid package met 54% of need; average scholarship/grant was $7,321; average loan was $5,998. For part-time students, average financial aid package was $12,180.

**Students without need:** 95 full-time freshmen who did not demonstrate need for aid received scholarships/grants; average award was $3,896. No-need awards available for academics, athletics, leadership, music/drama, state/district residency.

**Scholarships offered:** 47 full-time freshmen received athletic scholarships; average amount $9,594.

## FINANCIAL AID PROCEDURES
**Forms required:** FAFSA.

**Dates and Deadlines:** Priority date 3/1; closing date 6/30. Applicants notified on a rolling basis starting 3/15; must reply by 8/23.

**Transfers:** Applicants notified on a rolling basis starting 3/15; must reply by 8/23.

## CONTACT
Tracy Boulukos, Assistant Provost for Enrollment Management
777 Glades Road, Boca Raton, FL 33431
(561) 297-2738

## Florida College
Temple Terrace, Florida
www.floridacollege.edu          Federal Code: 001482

**4-year private** liberal arts college in large town.
**Enrollment:** 550 undergrads, 2% part-time. 226 full-time freshmen.
**Selectivity:** Admits over 75% of applicants.

### BASIC COSTS (2015-2016)
**Tuition and fees:** $16,074.
**Per-credit charge:** $600.
**Room and board:** $8,090.

### FINANCIAL AID PICTURE (2014-2015)
**Students with need:** Out of 195 full-time freshmen who applied for aid, 169 were judged to have need. Of these, 169 received aid, and 11 had their full need met. Average financial aid package met 58% of need; average scholarship/grant was $6,008; average loan was $3,161. For part-time students, average financial aid package was $3,783.

**Students without need:** 37 full-time freshmen who did not demonstrate need for aid received scholarships/grants; average award was $3,112. No-need awards available for academics, athletics, music/drama, state/district residency.

**Scholarships offered:** 27 full-time freshmen received athletic scholarships; average amount $3,096.

### FINANCIAL AID PROCEDURES
**Forms required:** FAFSA, state aid form.
**Dates and Deadlines:** Closing date 9/30. Applicants notified on a rolling basis starting 3/30; must reply within 2 week(s) of notification.
**Transfers:** No deadline. Applicants notified on a rolling basis starting 3/30; must reply within 2 week(s) of notification.

### CONTACT
Stephen Blaylock, Financial Aid Director
119 North Glen Arven Avenue, Temple Terrace, FL 33617
(813) 988-5131 ext. 131

## Florida College of Natural Health: Bradenton
Bradenton, Florida
www.fcnh.com

**2-year for-profit** health science and career college in small city.
**Enrollment:** 143 undergrads.
**Selectivity:** Open admission; but selective for some programs.

### BASIC COSTS (2015-2016)
**Additional info:** Therapeutic Massage; $12,529, books & supplies; $870. Advanced Therapeutic Massage; $16,644, books & supplies $1,040. Advanced Paramedical Skin Care; $17,761, books & supplies; $1,934. A.S. Advanced Therapeutic Massage; $22,189, books & supplies; $1,629. A.S. Therapeutic Massage and Skin Care; $23,414, books & supplies; $2,502. A.S. Advanced Paramedical Skin Care; $23,307, books & supplies; $2,523.

### FINANCIAL AID PICTURE
**Students with need:** Need-based aid available for full-time students.
**Students without need:** This college awards aid only to students with need.

### FINANCIAL AID PROCEDURES
**Forms required:** FAFSA.
**Dates and Deadlines:** Applicants notified on a rolling basis.

### CONTACT
Lora Miller, Financial Aid Officer
616 67th Street Circle East, Bradenton, FL 34208

## Florida College of Natural Health: Maitland
Maitland, Florida
www.fcnh.com          Federal Code: 030086

**2-year for-profit** health science and junior college in large town.
**Enrollment:** 418 undergrads.

### BASIC COSTS (2015-2016)
**Additional info:** Therapeutic Massage $12,529, books & supplies $870. Advanced Therapeutic Massage $16,644, books & supplies $1,040. Skin Care and Electrology $10,379, books & supplies $1,755. Advanced Paramedical Skin Care $17,761, books & supplies $1,934. A.S. Advanced Therapeutic Massage $22,189, books & supplies $1,629. A.S. Therapeutic Massage and Skin Care $23,414, books & supplies $2,502. A.S. Advanced Paramedical Skin Care $23,307, books & supplies $2,523.

### FINANCIAL AID PICTURE
**Students with need:** Need-based aid available for full-time students.
**Students without need:** This college awards aid only to students with need.

### FINANCIAL AID PROCEDURES
**Forms required:** FAFSA.
**Dates and Deadlines:** Applicants notified on a rolling basis.

### CONTACT
Lavern Walden, Director of Financial Aid
2600 Lake Lucien Drive; Suite 240, Maitland, FL 32751
(954) 975-6400

## Florida College of Natural Health: Miami
Miami, Florida
www.fcnh.com          Federal Code: 030086

**2-year for-profit** branch campus and community college in very large city.
**Enrollment:** 202 undergrads.
**Selectivity:** Open admission; but selective for some programs.

### BASIC COSTS (2015-2016)
**Additional info:** Therapeutic Massage $12,533, books & supplies $870. Advanced Therapeutic Massage $16,649, books & supplies $1,040. Skin Care and Electrology $10,387, books & supplies $1,755. Advanced Paramedical Skin Care $17,771, books & supplies $1,934. A.S. Advanced Therapeutic Massage $22,198, books & supplies $1,629. A.S. Therapeutic Massage and

Skin Care $23,427, books & supplies $2,502. A.S. Advanced Paramedical Skin Care $23,319, books & supplies $2,523.

**FINANCIAL AID PICTURE**

**Students with need:** Need-based aid available for full-time students.

**Students without need:** This college awards aid only to students with need.

**FINANCIAL AID PROCEDURES**

**Forms required:** FAFSA.

**Dates and Deadlines:** Applicants notified on a rolling basis.

**CONTACT**

Jorge Villasante, Director of Financial Aid

7925 Northwest 12th Street, Suite 201, Miami, FL 33126

(954) 975-6400

## Florida College of Natural Health: Pompano Beach

Pompano Beach, Florida

www.fcnh.com                          Federal Code: 030086

**2-year for-profit** junior college in very large city.

**Enrollment:** 203 undergrads.

**Selectivity:** Open admission; but selective for some programs.

**BASIC COSTS (2015-2016)**

**Additional info:** Therapeutic Massage $12,525, books & supplies $870. Advanced Therapeutic Massage $16,639, books & supplies $1,040. Skin Care and Electrology $10,370, books & supplies $1,755. Advanced Paramedical Skin Care $17,752, books & supplies $1,934. A.S. Advanced Therapeutic Massage $22,181, books & supplies $1,629. A.S. Therapeutic Massage and Skin Care $23,402, books & supplies $2,502. A.S. Advanced Paramedical Skin Care $23,294, books & supplies $2,523.

**FINANCIAL AID PICTURE**

**Students with need:** Need-based aid available for full-time students.

**Students without need:** This college awards aid only to students with need.

**FINANCIAL AID PROCEDURES**

**Forms required:** FAFSA.

**Dates and Deadlines:** Applicants notified on a rolling basis.

**CONTACT**

Helen Wilson, Director of Financial Aid

2001 West Sample Road, Suite 100, Pompano Beach, FL 33064

(954) 975-6400

## Florida Gateway College

Lake City, Florida

www.fgc.edu                           Federal Code: 001501

**2-year public** community college in large town.

**Enrollment:** 1,996 undergrads, 65% part-time. 167 full-time freshmen.

**Selectivity:** Open admission; but selective for some programs.

**BASIC COSTS (2015-2016)**

**Tuition and fees:** $3,100; out-of-state residents $11,747.

**Additional info:** Bachelor programs charged at higher tuition rates. Tuition/fee waivers available for minority students.

**FINANCIAL AID PICTURE**

**Students with need:** Need-based aid available for full-time and part-time students.

**Students without need:** No-need awards available for academics, leadership, minority status, music/drama, state/district residency.

**Scholarships offered:** Top 20% Scholarship: $1,000/year; top 20% of graduating class; must complete 70% of all attempted classes and maintain 2.0 GPA. Florida Bright Futures Scholarship: must submit completed (error-free) Florida Financial Aid Application during last year of high school (after 12/1 and prior to graduation).

**FINANCIAL AID PROCEDURES**

**Forms required:** FAFSA, institutional form.

**Dates and Deadlines:** Priority date 6/1; no closing date. Applicants notified on a rolling basis starting 6/1; must reply within 2 week(s) of notification.

**CONTACT**

Anita Westberry, Director of Financial Aid

149 SE College Place, Lake City, FL 32025-2007

(386) 754-4282

## Florida Gulf Coast University

Fort Myers, Florida

www.fgcu.edu                          Federal Code: 032553

**4-year public** university in small city.

**Enrollment:** 13,430 undergrads, 20% part-time. 2,734 full-time freshmen.

**Selectivity:** Admits 50 to 75% of applicants.

**BASIC COSTS (2015-2016)**

**Tuition and fees:** $6,118; out-of-state residents $25,161.

**Room and board:** $8,820.

**FINANCIAL AID PICTURE (2014-2015)**

**Students with need:** Out of 1,944 full-time freshmen who applied for aid, 1,271 were judged to have need. Of these, 1,271 received aid, and 126 had their full need met. Average financial aid package met 51% of need; average scholarship/grant was $5,070; average loan was $6,799. For part-time students, average financial aid package was $6,964.

**Students without need:** 125 full-time freshmen who did not demonstrate need for aid received scholarships/grants; average award was $2,272. No-need awards available for academics, alumni affiliation, athletics, leadership, minority status, music/drama, religious affiliation, state/district residency.

**Scholarships offered:** 24 full-time freshmen received athletic scholarships; average amount $5,816.

**FINANCIAL AID PROCEDURES**

**Forms required:** FAFSA, state aid form, institutional form.

**Dates and Deadlines:** Priority date 3/1; closing date 6/30. Applicants notified on a rolling basis starting 2/15.

**Transfers:** Applicants notified on a rolling basis.

**CONTACT**

Jorge Lopez-Rosado, Director of Student Financial Services

10501 FGCU Boulevard South, Fort Myers, FL 33965-6565

(239) 590-7920

## Florida Institute of Technology

Melbourne, Florida                    Federal Code: 001469

www.fit.edu                           CSS Code: 5080

**4-year private** university in small city.

**Enrollment:** 3,320 undergrads, 4% part-time. 644 full-time freshmen.

**Selectivity:** Admits 50 to 75% of applicants.

**BASIC COSTS (2015-2016)**

**Tuition and fees:** $39,290.

**Per-credit charge:** $1,115.

**Room and board:** $13,500.

**FINANCIAL AID PICTURE (2015-2016)**

**Students with need:** Out of 439 full-time freshmen who applied for aid, 383 were judged to have need. Of these, 383 received aid, and 153 had

their full need met. Average financial aid package met 87% of need; average scholarship/grant was $27,045; average loan was $3,436. For part-time students, average financial aid package was $13,176.

**Students without need:** 210 full-time freshmen who did not demonstrate need for aid received scholarships/grants; average award was $16,191. No-need awards available for academics, alumni affiliation, athletics, music/drama, ROTC, state/district residency.

**Scholarships offered:** 29 full-time freshmen received athletic scholarships; average amount $23,249.

### FINANCIAL AID PROCEDURES
**Forms required:** FAFSA, CSS PROFILE.
**Dates and Deadlines:** Priority date 3/1; no closing date. Applicants notified on a rolling basis starting 2/15; must reply by 5/1 or within 4 week(s) of notification.
**Transfers:** No deadline. Applicants notified on a rolling basis starting 2/15; must reply by 5/1 or within 4 week(s) of notification.

### CONTACT
Jay Lally, Director of Financial Aid
150 West University Boulevard, Melbourne, FL 32901-6975
(321) 674-8070

## Florida International University
Miami, Florida
www.fiu.edu                    Federal Code: 009635

**4-year public** university in very large city.
**Enrollment:** 40,225 undergrads, 37% part-time. 4,209 full-time freshmen.
**Selectivity:** Admits less than 50% of applicants.

### BASIC COSTS (2015-2016)
**Tuition and fees:** $6,556; out-of-state residents $18,955.
**Per-credit charge:** $206; out-of-state residents $619.
**Room and board:** $10,870.

### FINANCIAL AID PICTURE (2014-2015)
**Students with need:** Out of 2,817 full-time freshmen who applied for aid, 2,790 were judged to have need. Of these, 2,563 received aid, and 356 had their full need met. Average financial aid package met 27% of need; average scholarship/grant was $6,311; average loan was $2,065. For part-time students, average financial aid package was $5,832.
**Students without need:** 666 full-time freshmen who did not demonstrate need for aid received scholarships/grants; average award was $4,346. No-need awards available for academics, art, athletics, minority status, music/drama, state/district residency.
**Scholarships offered:** 90 full-time freshmen received athletic scholarships; average amount $14,781.

### FINANCIAL AID PROCEDURES
**Forms required:** FAFSA.
**Dates and Deadlines:** Priority date 3/1; closing date 5/15. Applicants notified on a rolling basis; must reply by 5/1.
**Transfers:** Applicants notified on a rolling basis; must reply by 5/1.

### CONTACT
Francisco Valines, Director of Financial Aid
Modesto Maidique Campus, PC 140, Miami, FL 33199
(305) 348-7000

## Florida Keys Community College
Key West, Florida
www.fkcc.edu                    Federal Code: 001485

**2-year public** community college in large town.
**Enrollment:** 819 undergrads.

**Selectivity:** Open admission; but selective for some programs.

### BASIC COSTS (2015-2016)
**Tuition and fees:** $3,277; out-of-state residents $13,162.
**Per-credit charge:** $82.78; out-of-state residents $331.11.
**Room only:** $8,131.

### FINANCIAL AID PICTURE
**Students with need:** Need-based aid available for full-time and part-time students.
**Students without need:** No-need awards available for academics, art, leadership, minority status.

### FINANCIAL AID PROCEDURES
**Forms required:** FAFSA, institutional form.
**Dates and Deadlines:** Priority date 5/1; no closing date. Applicants notified on a rolling basis starting 6/15; must reply within 2 week(s) of notification.
**Transfers:** Closing date 5/1. Florida Student Assistance Grant available to students paying Florida resident tuition.

### CONTACT
Joyce Lubeck-Sonenberg, Director of Financial Aid
5901 College Road, Key West, FL 33040
(305) 809-3523

## Florida Memorial University
Miami Gardens, Florida
www.fmuniv.edu                    Federal Code: 001486

**4-year private** liberal arts college in very large city, affiliated with American Baptist Churches in the USA.
**Enrollment:** 1,399 undergrads.

### BASIC COSTS (2015-2016)
**Tuition and fees:** $15,280.
**Room and board:** $5,040.

### FINANCIAL AID PICTURE
**Students with need:** Need-based aid available for full-time and part-time students.
**Additional info:** Need-based financial aid available to part-time students taking 6 credits or more per semester.

### FINANCIAL AID PROCEDURES
**Dates and Deadlines:** Applicants notified on a rolling basis; must reply within 2 week(s) of notification.
**Transfers:** Priority date 3/15; closing date 4/15.

### CONTACT
Calvin Davis, Director of Financial Aid
15800 NW 42nd Avenue, Miami Gardens, FL 33054
(305) 430-1168

## Florida National University
Hialeah, Florida
www.fnu.edu                    Federal Code: 017069

**2-year for-profit** junior college in very large city.
**Enrollment:** 2,389 undergrads, 10% part-time. 372 full-time freshmen.
**Selectivity:** Open admission; but selective for some programs.

### BASIC COSTS (2015-2016)
**Tuition and fees:** $13,090.
**Per-credit charge:** $525.
**Additional info:** Tuition at time of enrollment locked for 2 years.

**FINANCIAL AID PICTURE (2014-2015)**
**Students with need:** 40% of average financial aid package awarded as scholarships/grants, 60% awarded as loans/jobs. Need-based aid available for part-time students.
**Students without need:** This college awards aid only to students with need.

**FINANCIAL AID PROCEDURES**
**Forms required:** FAFSA, institutional form.
**Dates and Deadlines:** Applicants notified on a rolling basis.

**CONTACT**
Omar Sanchez, Vice President of Assessment and Reasearch/Director of Financial Aid
4425 West Jose Regueiro (20th) Avenue, Hialeah, FL 33012
(305) 821-3333 ext. 1003

## Florida Southern College
Lakeland, Florida
www.flsouthern.edu
Federal Code: 001488

**4-year private** liberal arts college in small city, affiliated with United Methodist Church.
**Enrollment:** 2,306 undergrads, 2% part-time. 692 full-time freshmen.
**Selectivity:** Admits less than 50% of applicants.

**BASIC COSTS (2015-2016)**
**Tuition and fees:** $31,460.
**Per-credit charge:** $900.
**Room and board:** $10,210.

**FINANCIAL AID PICTURE (2015-2016)**
**Students with need:** Out of 633 full-time freshmen who applied for aid, 505 were judged to have need. Of these, 505 received aid, and 145 had their full need met. Average financial aid package met 75% of need; average scholarship/grant was $20,621; average loan was $5,366. For part-time students, average financial aid package was $15,675.
**Students without need:** 187 full-time freshmen who did not demonstrate need for aid received scholarships/grants; average award was $19,014. No-need awards available for academics, alumni affiliation, art, athletics, job skills, leadership, minority status, music/drama, religious affiliation, ROTC, state/district residency.
**Scholarships offered:** *Merit:* McClug Scholarship; based on 1290 SAT (exclusive of Writing) or 29 ACT, rank in top 5% of class, and 3.5 GPA; 3 awarded. Hollingsworth Scholarship; based on 1290 SAT (exclusive of Writing) or 29 ACT and 3.5 GPA. *Athletic:* 31 full-time freshmen received athletic scholarships; average amount $14,679.

**FINANCIAL AID PROCEDURES**
**Forms required:** FAFSA, institutional form.
**Dates and Deadlines:** Priority date 3/1; closing date 7/1. Applicants notified on a rolling basis starting 3/1; must reply within 3 week(s) of notification.
**Transfers:** No deadline. Applicants notified on a rolling basis; must reply within 2 week(s) of notification.

**CONTACT**
William Healy, Director of Financial Aid
111 Lake Hollingsworth Drive, Lakeland, FL 33801-5698
(863) 680-4140

## Florida SouthWestern State College
Fort Myers, Florida
www.fsw.edu
Federal Code: 001477

**2-year public** liberal arts college in small city.
**Enrollment:** 14,885 undergrads, 64% part-time. 1,884 full-time freshmen.

**Selectivity:** Open admission; but selective for some programs.

**BASIC COSTS (2015-2016)**
**Tuition and fees:** $3,341; out-of-state residents $13,039.
**Additional info:** Bachelor programs charged at higher tuition rates.

**FINANCIAL AID PICTURE (2014-2015)**
**Students with need:** Out of 1,570 full-time freshmen who applied for aid, 1,318 were judged to have need. Of these, 1,248 received aid, and 40 had their full need met. Average financial aid package met 48% of need; average scholarship/grant was $5,307; average loan was $3,011. For part-time students, average financial aid package was $4,241.
**Students without need:** 85 full-time freshmen who did not demonstrate need for aid received scholarships/grants; average award was $3,190. No-need awards available for academics, art, athletics, leadership, music/drama.

**FINANCIAL AID PROCEDURES**
**Forms required:** FAFSA, institutional form.
**Dates and Deadlines:** Priority date 5/1; closing date 9/16. Applicants notified on a rolling basis starting 6/30.

**CONTACT**
8099 College Parkway, Fort Myers, FL 33919
(239) 489-9346

## Florida State College at Jacksonville
Jacksonville, Florida
www.fscj.edu
Federal Code: 001484

**2-year public** community and junior college in very large city.
**Enrollment:** 21,565 undergrads, 69% part-time. 1,517 full-time freshmen.
**Selectivity:** Open admission; but selective for some programs.

**BASIC COSTS (2015-2016)**
**Tuition and fees:** $3,146; out-of-state residents $12,038.
**Additional info:** Bachelor programs charged at higher tuition rates.

**FINANCIAL AID PICTURE**
**Students with need:** Need-based aid available for full-time and part-time students. Work study available nights, weekends, and for part-time students.
**Students without need:** No-need awards available for academics, alumni affiliation, art, athletics, job skills, leadership, minority status, music/drama.

**FINANCIAL AID PROCEDURES**
**Forms required:** FAFSA, institutional form.
**Dates and Deadlines:** Priority date 8/1; no closing date.

**CONTACT**
Angie Nickel, Associate Director of Financial Aid
501 West State Street, Jacksonville, FL 32202
(904) 632-3154

## Florida State University
Tallahassee, Florida
www.fsu.edu
Federal Code: 001489

**4-year public** university in small city.
**Enrollment:** 32,290 undergrads, 10% part-time. 5,994 full-time freshmen.
**Selectivity:** Admits 50 to 75% of applicants.

**BASIC COSTS (2015-2016)**
**Tuition and fees:** $6,507; out-of-state residents $21,673.
**Per-credit charge:** $215; out-of-state residents $721.
**Room and board:** $10,264.

**FINANCIAL AID PICTURE (2014-2015)**
**Students with need:** Out of 4,952 full-time freshmen who applied for aid, 2,999 were judged to have need. Of these, 2,966 received aid, and 419 had

their full need met. Average financial aid package met 62% of need; average scholarship/grant was $8,203; average loan was $3,581. For part-time students, average financial aid package was $7,714.

**Students without need:** 588 full-time freshmen who did not demonstrate need for aid received scholarships/grants; average award was $3,355. No-need awards available for academics, art, athletics, leadership, music/drama, ROTC, state/district residency.

**Scholarships offered:** 84 full-time freshmen received athletic scholarships; average amount $17,057.

**FINANCIAL AID PROCEDURES**

**Forms required:** FAFSA, state aid form.

**Dates and Deadlines:** Applicants notified on a rolling basis starting 4/5.

**CONTACT**

Darryl Marshall, Director of Financial Aid
PO Box 3062400, Tallahassee, FL 32306-2400
(850) 644-0539

## Florida Technical College: Orlando
Orlando, Florida
www.ftccollege.edu          Federal Code: 015670

**2-year for-profit** junior and technical college in large city.

**Enrollment:** 2,977 undergrads.

**Selectivity:** Open admission.

**BASIC COSTS (2015-2016)**

**Additional info:** Diploma programs $995-$22,635. Associate degree programs $31,555-$34,259. Bachelor's degree programs $58,985-$59,335. Other fees vary by program.

**FINANCIAL AID PICTURE**

**Students with need:** Need-based aid available for full-time and part-time students.

**Students without need:** This college awards aid only to students with need.

**FINANCIAL AID PROCEDURES**

**Forms required:** FAFSA.

**Dates and Deadlines:** Applicants notified on a rolling basis.

**CONTACT**

Jennie Gomeztagle, Financial Services
12900 Challenger Parkway, Orlando, FL 32826-2707
(407) 447-7300

## Fortis College: Winter Park
Winter Park, Florida
www.fortis.edu          Federal Code: 022455

**2-year for-profit** technical college in very large city.

**Enrollment:** 14 undergrads.

**Selectivity:** Open admission.

**BASIC COSTS (2015-2016)**

**Additional info:** Diploma programs: Dental Assisting $18,500; Medical Assisting $14,995; Medical Assisting with Basic X-Ray Operation $18,500; Medical Billing and Coding $18,025; Medical Office Basic X-Ray Technician $18,500; Sterile Processing Technology $15,836. Associate degree programs: Criminal Justice $27,912; Healthcare Management $15,991; Surgical Technology $35,000; Nursing $47,332. All program costs include tuition, books, supplies, exams, and immunizations (where required).

**FINANCIAL AID PICTURE**

**Students with need:** Need-based aid available for full-time students.

**Students without need:** This college awards aid only to students with need.

**FINANCIAL AID PROCEDURES**

**Forms required:** FAFSA.

**CONTACT**

Cathy Lane, Corporate Finance Director
1573 West Fairbanks Avenue, Suite 100, Winter Park, FL 32789
(407) 843-3984

## Full Sail University
Winter Park, Florida
www.fullsail.edu          Federal Code: 016812

**4-year for-profit** visual arts and music college in very large city.

**Enrollment:** 17,318 undergrads.

**Selectivity:** Open admission; but selective for some programs.

**BASIC COSTS (2015-2016)**

**Additional info:** Tuition ranges from $31,000-$77,500 for the entire degree program, including books, lab fees, and other educational charges. Does not include Project LaunchBox - an Apple computer and software package.

**FINANCIAL AID PICTURE**

**Students with need:** Need-based aid available for full-time students. Work study available nights, weekends, and for part-time students.

**FINANCIAL AID PROCEDURES**

**Forms required:** FAFSA.

**Dates and Deadlines:** Applicants notified on a rolling basis; must reply within 2 week(s) of notification.

**CONTACT**

3300 University Boulevard, Winter Park, FL 32792-7429
(407) 679-0100 ext. 2300

## Gulf Coast State College
Panama City, Florida
www.gulfcoast.edu          Federal Code: 001490

**2-year public** community college in small city.

**Enrollment:** 4,258 undergrads, 56% part-time. 144 full-time freshmen.

**Selectivity:** Open admission; but selective for some programs.

**BASIC COSTS (2015-2016)**

**Tuition and fees:** $2,963; out-of-state residents $10,791.

**Additional info:** Bachelor programs charged at higher tuition rates.

**FINANCIAL AID PICTURE (2014-2015)**

**Students with need:** 73% of average financial aid package awarded as scholarships/grants, 27% awarded as loans/jobs. Need-based aid available for part-time students. Work study available nights, weekends, and for part-time students.

**Students without need:** No-need awards available for academics, athletics, job skills, leadership, minority status, music/drama, state/district residency.

**FINANCIAL AID PROCEDURES**

**Forms required:** FAFSA.

**Dates and Deadlines:** Priority date 5/15; closing date 7/1. Applicants notified on a rolling basis starting 7/1.

**Transfers:** Priority date 11/1; no deadline.

**CONTACT**

Chris Westlake, Executive Director, Financial Aid
5230 West US Highway 98, Panama City, FL 32401-1041
(850) 872-3845

## Hillsborough Community College
Tampa, Florida
www.hccfl.edu                          Federal Code: 007870

**2-year public** community college in large city.
**Enrollment:** 23,138 undergrads, 55% part-time. 3,042 full-time freshmen.
**Selectivity:** Open admission; but selective for some programs.

**BASIC COSTS (2015-2016)**
**Tuition and fees:** $3,132; out-of-state residents $11,388.

**FINANCIAL AID PICTURE (2014-2015)**
**Students with need:** 55% of average financial aid package awarded as scholarships/grants, 45% awarded as loans/jobs. Need-based aid available for part-time students. Work study available nights, weekends, and for part-time students.
**Students without need:** No-need awards available for academics, art, athletics, minority status, music/drama.

**FINANCIAL AID PROCEDURES**
**Forms required:** FAFSA, institutional form.
**Dates and Deadlines:** Applicants notified on a rolling basis.

**CONTACT**
Tierra Smith, Director of Financial Aid
Box 31127, Tampa, FL 33631-3127
(877) 736-2575

## Hobe Sound Bible College
Hobe Sound, Florida
www.hsbc.edu                           Federal Code: 015463

**4-year private** Bible college in small town, affiliated with interdenominational tradition.
**Enrollment:** 59 undergrads.

**BASIC COSTS (2015-2016)**
**Tuition and fees:** $6,090.
**Per-credit charge:** $275.
**Room and board:** $5,840.

**FINANCIAL AID PICTURE**
**Students with need:** Need-based aid available for full-time and part-time students.
**Students without need:** No-need awards available for academics, leadership.

**FINANCIAL AID PROCEDURES**
**Forms required:** FAFSA.
**Dates and Deadlines:** Closing date 8/1.

**CONTACT**
Joanna Wetherald, Director of Financial Aid
PO Box 1065, Hobe Sound, FL 33475
(772) 546-5534 ext. 1003

## Hodges University
Naples, Florida
www.hodges.edu                         Federal Code: 030375

**4-year private** university in small city.
**Enrollment:** 1,476 undergrads, 33% part-time. 122 full-time freshmen.

**BASIC COSTS (2015-2016)**
**Tuition and fees:** $16,400.
**Per-credit charge:** $530.

**FINANCIAL AID PICTURE (2015-2016)**
**Students with need:** Out of 112 full-time freshmen who applied for aid, 101 were judged to have need. Of these, 101 received aid, and 28 had their full need met. Average financial aid package met 70% of need; average scholarship/grant was $3,100; average loan was $3,050. For part-time students, average financial aid package was $7,675.
**Students without need:** 6 full-time freshmen who did not demonstrate need for aid received scholarships/grants; average award was $300. No-need awards available for academics.

**FINANCIAL AID PROCEDURES**
**Forms required:** FAFSA.
**Dates and Deadlines:** Priority date 8/15; no closing date. Applicants notified on a rolling basis starting 7/7.
**Transfers:** No deadline. Applicants notified on a rolling basis.

**CONTACT**
Joe Gilchrist, Vice President of Student Financial Assistance
2655 Northbrooke Drive, Naples, FL 34119
(239) 513-1122

## Indian River State College
Fort Pierce, Florida
www.irsc.edu                           Federal Code: 001493

**2-year public** community college in small city.
**Enrollment:** 14,044 undergrads, 64% part-time. 1,079 full-time freshmen.
**Selectivity:** Open admission; but selective for some programs.

**BASIC COSTS (2015-2016)**
**Tuition and fees:** $3,115; out-of-state residents $11,715.
**Additional info:** Bachelor programs charged at higher tuition rates.

**FINANCIAL AID PICTURE**
**Students with need:** Need-based aid available for full-time and part-time students.
**Students without need:** No-need awards available for academics, athletics, minority status, music/drama, state/district residency.

**FINANCIAL AID PROCEDURES**
**Forms required:** FAFSA, institutional form.
**Dates and Deadlines:** Priority date 7/18; no closing date. Applicants notified on a rolling basis starting 5/15.

**CONTACT**
Mary Lewis, Director of Financial Aid
3209 Virginia Avenue, Fort Pierce, FL 34981-5596
(772) 462-7450

## International Academy of Design and Technology: Tampa
Tampa, Florida
www.academy.edu                        Federal Code: 030314

**4-year for-profit** visual arts and technical college in very large city.
**Enrollment:** 600 undergrads.
**Selectivity:** Open admission.

**BASIC COSTS (2015-2016)**
**Additional info:** Associate programs: $32,800. Bachelor's programs: $64,800.

**FINANCIAL AID PICTURE**
**Students with need:** Need-based aid available for full-time and part-time students. Work study available nights, weekends, and for part-time students.
**Students without need:** No-need awards available for academics.

**FINANCIAL AID PROCEDURES**
Forms required: FAFSA.

**CONTACT**
Tim Coppola, Vice President of Finance
5104 Eisenhower Boulevard, Tampa, FL 33634
(813) 880-8056

## Jacksonville University
Jacksonville, Florida
www.ju.edu                                   Federal Code: 001495

**4-year private** university and liberal arts college in very large city.
**Enrollment:** 2,964 undergrads, 31% part-time. 486 full-time freshmen.
**Selectivity:** Admits 50 to 75% of applicants.

**BASIC COSTS (2016-2017)**
Tuition and fees: $33,930.
Per-credit charge: $1,130.
Room and board: $13,550.

**FINANCIAL AID PICTURE (2015-2016)**
**Students with need:** Out of 476 full-time freshmen who applied for aid, 421 were judged to have need. Of these, 421 received aid, and 101 had their full need met. Average financial aid package met 88% of need; average scholarship/grant was $19,055; average loan was $2,506. For part-time students, average financial aid package was $8,360.
**Students without need:** 40 full-time freshmen who did not demonstrate need for aid received scholarships/grants; average award was $15,860. No-need awards available for academics, art, athletics, leadership, music/drama, ROTC.
**Scholarships offered:** 76 full-time freshmen received athletic scholarships; average amount $18,814.

**FINANCIAL AID PROCEDURES**
Forms required: FAFSA, institutional form.
Dates and Deadlines: Priority date 3/31; no closing date. Applicants notified on a rolling basis starting 2/20.
Transfers: No deadline. Applicants notified on a rolling basis.

**CONTACT**
Karen Laverdiere, Financial Aid Director
2800 University Boulevard North, Jacksonville, FL 32211-3394
(904) 256-7060

## Johnson & Wales University: North Miami
North Miami, Florida
www.jwu.edu                                   Federal Code: 003404

**4-year private** university in large city.
**Enrollment:** 1,752 undergrads, 10% part-time. 317 full-time freshmen.
**Selectivity:** Admits over 75% of applicants.

**BASIC COSTS (2015-2016)**
Tuition and fees: $29,226.
Room and board: $11,100.

**FINANCIAL AID PICTURE (2015-2016)**
**Students with need:** Out of 298 full-time freshmen who applied for aid, 263 were judged to have need. Of these, 263 received aid, and 25 had their full need met. Average financial aid package met 69% of need; average scholarship/grant was $10,213; average loan was $3,371. For part-time students, average financial aid package was $21,722.

**Students without need:** 25 full-time freshmen who did not demonstrate need for aid received scholarships/grants; average award was $9,280. No-need awards available for academics, alumni affiliation, leadership, state/district residency.

**FINANCIAL AID PROCEDURES**
Forms required: FAFSA.
Dates and Deadlines: Applicants notified on a rolling basis starting 3/1; must reply within 2 week(s) of notification.

**CONTACT**
Lynn Robinson, Director, Financial Aid
1701 Northeast 127th Street, North Miami, FL 33181
(800) 342-5598

## Johnson University: Florida
Kissimmee, Florida
www.fcc.edu                                   Federal Code: 015192

**4-year private** Bible and teachers college in small city, affiliated with Christian Church.
**Enrollment:** 201 undergrads.

**BASIC COSTS (2015-2016)**
Tuition and fees: $14,270.
Per-credit charge: $440.
Room only: $3,200.

**FINANCIAL AID PICTURE**
**Students with need:** Need-based aid available for full-time and part-time students. Work study available nights, weekends, and for part-time students.
**Students without need:** No-need awards available for academics, alumni affiliation, leadership, music/drama, religious affiliation, state/district residency.

**FINANCIAL AID PROCEDURES**
Forms required: FAFSA, institutional form.
Dates and Deadlines: Priority date 5/1; closing date 7/15. Applicants notified on a rolling basis starting 3/1.
Transfers: Available only if funding remains.

**CONTACT**
1011 Bill Beck Boulevard, Kissimmee, FL 34744-4402
(407) 569-1368

## Jones College
Jacksonville, Florida
www.jones.edu                                 Federal Code: 001497

**4-year private** business college in very large city.
**Enrollment:** 445 undergrads.
**Selectivity:** Open admission.

**BASIC COSTS (2015-2016)**
Tuition and fees: $9,240.
Per-credit charge: $305.

**FINANCIAL AID PICTURE**
**Students with need:** Need-based aid available for full-time and part-time students. Work study available nights.
**Students without need:** This college awards aid only to students with need.
**Additional info:** All new students offered Annie Harper Jones Scholarship during their first semester if enrolled in at least 6 hours.

**FINANCIAL AID PROCEDURES**
Forms required: FAFSA.

**Dates and Deadlines:** Priority date 8/1; no closing date. Applicants notified on a rolling basis starting 7/1.

**Transfers:** No deadline. Applicants notified on a rolling basis starting 7/1.

**CONTACT**

Becky Davis, Financial Assistant Director

5353 Arlington Expressway, Jacksonville, FL 32211

(904) 743-1122 ext. 100

## Jose Maria Vargas University

Pembroke Pines, Florida

www.jmvu.edu                      Federal Code: 041620

**4-year for-profit** university in small city.

**Enrollment:** 154 undergrads.

**Selectivity:** Open admission.

**FINANCIAL AID PICTURE**

**Students with need:** Need-based aid available for full-time and part-time students.

**Students without need:** No-need awards available for academics.

**FINANCIAL AID PROCEDURES**

**Forms required:** FAFSA, state aid form, institutional form.

**Dates and Deadlines:** Applicants notified on a rolling basis; must reply within 2 week(s) of notification.

**Transfers:** No deadline. Applicants notified on a rolling basis; must reply within 2 week(s) of notification.

**CONTACT**

Edith Paredes, Director of Financial Aid

10131 Pines Boulevard, Pembroke Pines, FL 33026

(954) 322-4460

## Keiser University

West Palm Beach, Florida

www.keiseruniversity.edu          Federal Code: 015159

**4-year private** health science and career college in large city.

**Enrollment:** 15,939 undergrads, 46% part-time. 1,258 full-time freshmen.

**Selectivity:** Admits 50 to 75% of applicants.

**BASIC COSTS (2015-2016)**

**Tuition and fees:** $9,162.

**FINANCIAL AID PICTURE (2014-2015)**

**Students with need:** 43% of average financial aid package awarded as scholarships/grants, 57% awarded as loans/jobs. Need-based aid available for part-time students.

**Students without need:** No-need awards available for academics, alumni affiliation, job skills, leadership.

**FINANCIAL AID PROCEDURES**

**Forms required:** FAFSA.

**CONTACT**

Frederick Pfeffer, Associate Vice Chancellor-Student Financial Services

2600 North Military Trail, West Palm Beach, FL 33409

(954) 776-4476

## Key College

Dania Beach, Florida

www.keycollege.edu                Federal Code: 015191

**2-year for-profit** business and technical college in very large city.

**Enrollment:** 59 undergrads.

**BASIC COSTS (2015-2016)**

**Additional info:** Total program costs: certificates $14,780-$25,865, books and supplies $1,839-$2,100; associates $22,170-$33,255, books and supplies; $2,000-$3,170. Tuition at time of enrollment locked for 2 years.

**FINANCIAL AID PICTURE**

**Students with need:** Need-based aid available for full-time and part-time students.

**Students without need:** This college awards aid only to students with need.

**Scholarships offered:** Key College Scholarships and Employers Scholarships: merit based; approximately 10 scholarships of $1,000 each, awarded during the academic year.

**Additional info:** Federal Supplemental Educational Opportunities Grant (FSEOG), PELL grant, ACG, FFEL (federal loan program) available; direct loans offered.

**FINANCIAL AID PROCEDURES**

**Forms required:** FAFSA, institutional form.

**CONTACT**

Amber Young, Director of Financial Services

225 East Dania Beach Boulevard, Dania Beach, FL 33004-3046

(954) 923-4440

## Lake-Sumter State College

Leesburg, Florida

www.lssc.edu                      Federal Code: 001502

**2-year public** community and junior college in small city.

**Enrollment:** 1,786 full-time undergrads.

**Selectivity:** Open admission; but selective for some programs.

**BASIC COSTS (2015-2016)**

**Tuition and fees:** $3,172; out-of-state residents $13,276.

**Additional info:** Bachelor programs charged at higher tuition rates.

**FINANCIAL AID PICTURE**

**Students with need:** Need-based aid available for full-time and part-time students. Work study available nights.

**Students without need:** No-need awards available for academics, art, athletics, leadership, minority status, state/district residency.

**FINANCIAL AID PROCEDURES**

**Forms required:** FAFSA, institutional form.

**Dates and Deadlines:** Priority date 5/29; no closing date. Applicants notified on a rolling basis.

**Transfers:** No deadline. Applicants notified on a rolling basis.

**CONTACT**

Audrey Williams, Financial Aid Director

9501 US Highway 441, Leesburg, FL 34788-8751

(352) 365-3567

## Lincoln College of Technology: West Palm Beach

West Palm Beach, Florida

www.lincolnedu.com                Federal Code: 016095

**2-year for-profit** technical college in small city.

**Enrollment:** 713 undergrads.

**Selectivity:** Open admission.

**BASIC COSTS (2015-2016)**

**Additional info:** Diploma programs: $16,281-$28,351. Associate programs: $18,994-$42,053. Bachelor programs: $55,681-$65,674. Costs include total tuition, materials, tool fees, and registration fee.

## FINANCIAL AID PICTURE

**Students with need:** Need-based aid available for full-time students. Work study available nights, weekends, and for part-time students.

## FINANCIAL AID PROCEDURES

**Forms required:** FAFSA, institutional form.
**Dates and Deadlines:** Applicants notified on a rolling basis.

## CONTACT

Elizabeth Layton, Director of Student Financial Services
2410 Metrocentre Boulevard, West Palm Beach, FL 33407
(561) 842-8324

## Lynn University
Boca Raton, Florida
www.lynn.edu                    Federal Code: 001505

**4-year private** university in small city.
**Enrollment:** 1,957 undergrads, 5% part-time. 514 full-time freshmen.
**Selectivity:** Admits over 75% of applicants.

### BASIC COSTS (2016-2017)
**Tuition and fees:** $36,150.
**Room and board:** $11,640.

### FINANCIAL AID PICTURE (2015-2016)
**Students with need:** Out of 461 full-time freshmen who applied for aid, 276 were judged to have need. Of these, 276 received aid, and 276 had their full need met. Average financial aid package met 55% of need; average scholarship/grant was $10,427; average loan was $3,931. For part-time students, average financial aid package was $5,921.
**Students without need:** 159 full-time freshmen who did not demonstrate need for aid received scholarships/grants; average award was $11,682. No-need awards available for academics, alumni affiliation, athletics, leadership, music/drama.
**Scholarships offered:** *Merit:* Based on HS GPA and/or test scores: National Merit Scholarship for full tuition up to 16 credits each semester (10 available award per academic year). Presidential Scholarship for Full tuition and room and board up to 16 credits each semester (2 available award per academic year); Dean's Scholarship for $12,000 per academic year (159 recipients in 2014-15); Merit Scholarship for $10,000 per academic year (96 recipients in 2014-15); Academic Grant for $6,000 per academic year (50 recipients in 2014-15). *Athletic:* 112 full-time freshmen received athletic scholarships; average amount $10,914.

### FINANCIAL AID PROCEDURES
**Forms required:** FAFSA.
**Dates and Deadlines:** Priority date 3/1; no closing date. Applicants notified on a rolling basis starting 2/1; must reply within 2 week(s) of notification.
**Transfers:** No deadline. Applicants notified on a rolling basis; must reply within 2 week(s) of notification. Up to $10,000 of need met to include federal, state and institutional aid.

### CONTACT
John Chambers, Director of Student Financial Assistance
3601 North Military Trail, Boca Raton, FL 33431-5598
(561) 237-7185

## Miami Dade College
Miami, Florida
www.mdc.edu/main               Federal Code: 001506

**2-year public** community college in very large city.
**Enrollment:** 57,884 undergrads, 58% part-time. 8,410 full-time freshmen.
**Selectivity:** Open admission; but selective for some programs.

### BASIC COSTS (2015-2016)
**Tuition and fees:** $3,547; out-of-state residents $12,075.
**Per-credit charge:** $118; out-of-state residents $403.
**Additional info:** Bachelor programs charged at higher tuition rates.

### FINANCIAL AID PICTURE (2014-2015)
**Students with need:** Out of 6,866 full-time freshmen who applied for aid, 6,865 were judged to have need. Of these, 6,864 received aid, and 4,873 had their full need met. Average financial aid package met 64% of need; average scholarship/grant was $5,370; average loan was $2,244. For part-time students, average financial aid package was $3,674.
**Students without need:** 184 full-time freshmen who did not demonstrate need for aid received scholarships/grants; average award was $1,124. No-need awards available for academics, art, athletics, music/drama, state/district residency.
**Scholarships offered:** 24 full-time freshmen received athletic scholarships; average amount $3,045.

### FINANCIAL AID PROCEDURES
**Forms required:** FAFSA.
**Dates and Deadlines:** Priority date 3/15; closing date 6/30. Applicants notified on a rolling basis starting 5/15.
**Transfers:** No deadline. Applicants notified on a rolling basis.

### CONTACT
Mercedes Amaya, Associate V.P. - Student Financial Services
11011 SW 104th Street, Miami, FL 33176-3393
(305) 237-0382

## New College of Florida
Sarasota, Florida
www.ncf.edu                    Federal Code: 039574

**4-year public** liberal arts college in small city.
**Enrollment:** 852 undergrads. 261 full-time freshmen.
**Selectivity:** Admits 50 to 75% of applicants.

### BASIC COSTS (2015-2016)
**Tuition and fees:** $6,916; out-of-state residents $29,944.
**Per-credit charge:** $192; out-of-state residents $832.
**Room and board:** $8,932.

### FINANCIAL AID PICTURE (2015-2016)
**Students with need:** Out of 238 full-time freshmen who applied for aid, 145 were judged to have need. Of these, 145 received aid, and 69 had their full need met. Average financial aid package met 89% of need; average scholarship/grant was $9,832; average loan was $2,649.
**Students without need:** 93 full-time freshmen who did not demonstrate need for aid received scholarships/grants; average award was $2,717. No-need awards available for academics, state/district residency.

### FINANCIAL AID PROCEDURES
**Forms required:** FAFSA.
**Dates and Deadlines:** Priority date 2/15; no closing date. Applicants notified on a rolling basis starting 3/15; must reply by 5/1 or within 2 week(s) of notification.
**Transfers:** No deadline. Applicants notified on a rolling basis starting 3/15; must reply by 5/1 or within 2 week(s) of notification.

### CONTACT
Tara Karas, Director of Financial Aid
5800 Bay Shore Road, Sarasota, FL 34243-2109
(941) 487-5000

## North Florida Community College
Madison, Florida
www.nfcc.edu                          Federal Code: 001508

**2-year public** community college in rural community.
**Enrollment:** 1,167 undergrads.
**Selectivity:** Open admission; but selective for some programs.

**BASIC COSTS (2015-2016)**
**Tuition and fees:** $3,084; out-of-state residents $12,018.

**FINANCIAL AID PICTURE**
**Students with need:** Need-based aid available for full-time and part-time students. Work study available nights, weekends, and for part-time students.
**Students without need:** This college awards aid only to students with need.

**FINANCIAL AID PROCEDURES**
**Forms required:** FAFSA.
**Dates and Deadlines:** Priority date 5/15; no closing date. Applicants notified on a rolling basis starting 6/20; must reply within 2 week(s) of notification.

**CONTACT**
Amelia Mulkey, Director of Financial Aid
325 NW Turner Davis Drive, Madison, FL 32340
(850) 973-1621

## Northwest Florida State College
Niceville, Florida
www.nwfsc.edu                         Federal Code: 001510

**2-year public** technical college in large town.
**Enrollment:** 4,604 undergrads.
**Selectivity:** Open admission.

**BASIC COSTS (2015-2016)**
**Tuition and fees:** $3,120; out-of-state residents $11,941.
**Additional info:** Bachelor programs charged at higher tuition rate. Certificates and ATD diplomas charted at a lower tuition rate. Tuition/fee waivers available for minority students.

**FINANCIAL AID PICTURE**
**Students with need:** Need-based aid available for full-time and part-time students.
**Students without need:** No-need awards available for academics, leadership, minority status, ROTC, state/district residency.

**FINANCIAL AID PROCEDURES**
**Forms required:** FAFSA, institutional form.
**Dates and Deadlines:** Priority date 4/1; no closing date. Applicants notified on a rolling basis starting 2/1; must reply within 2 week(s) of notification.
**Transfers:** Academic transcript evaluated to determine student eligibility for financial aid.

**CONTACT**
Patricia Bennett, Director of Financial Aid/Veterans Affairs
100 College Boulevard, Niceville, FL 32578-1347
(850) 729-5370

## Nova Southeastern University
Fort Lauderdale, Florida
www.nova.edu                          Federal Code: 001509

**4-year private** university in small city.
**Enrollment:** 4,565 undergrads, 30% part-time. 633 full-time freshmen.
**Selectivity:** Admits 50 to 75% of applicants.

**BASIC COSTS (2015-2016)**
**Tuition and fees:** $27,660.
**Per-credit charge:** $897.
**Room and board:** $10,874.

**FINANCIAL AID PICTURE (2015-2016)**
**Students with need:** Out of 566 full-time freshmen who applied for aid, 473 were judged to have need. Of these, 458 received aid, and 73 had their full need met. Average financial aid package met 81% of need; average scholarship/grant was $18,946; average loan was $2,344. For part-time students, average financial aid package was $21,561.
**Students without need:** This college awards aid only to students with need.
**Scholarships offered: *Merit:*** President's Scholarship; up to full tuition; based on GPA and SAT/ACT; over 100 awarded. Dean's Scholarship; $1,000-$9,500; based on GPA and SAT/ACT; 825 awarded. Razor's Edge Scholarship; $10,000; based on leadership qualities and academics; 20 awarded. ***Athletic:*** 27 full-time freshmen received athletic scholarships; average amount $20,082.

**FINANCIAL AID PROCEDURES**
**Forms required:** FAFSA, state aid form.
**Dates and Deadlines:** Applicants notified on a rolling basis.

**CONTACT**
Stephanie Brown, Vice President, Enrollment and Student Services
3301 College Avenue, Fort Lauderdale, FL 33314
(954) 262-3380

## Palm Beach Atlantic University
West Palm Beach, Florida
www.pba.edu                           Federal Code: 008849

**4-year private** university and liberal arts college in small city, affiliated with interdenominational tradition.
**Enrollment:** 2,587 undergrads, 7% part-time. 547 full-time freshmen.
**Selectivity:** Admits over 75% of applicants.

**BASIC COSTS (2015-2016)**
**Tuition and fees:** $27,050.
**Per-credit charge:** $645.
**Room and board:** $8,932.

**FINANCIAL AID PICTURE (2015-2016)**
**Students with need:** Out of 476 full-time freshmen who applied for aid, 401 were judged to have need. Of these, 401 received aid, and 90 had their full need met. Average financial aid package met 67% of need; average scholarship/grant was $17,554; average loan was $3,339. For part-time students, average financial aid package was $6,293.
**Students without need:** 146 full-time freshmen who did not demonstrate need for aid received scholarships/grants; average award was $12,546. No-need awards available for academics, alumni affiliation, art, athletics, leadership, music/drama, ROTC, state/district residency.
**Scholarships offered:** 25 full-time freshmen received athletic scholarships; average amount $8,656.

**FINANCIAL AID PROCEDURES**
**Forms required:** FAFSA, state aid form.
**Dates and Deadlines:** Priority date 5/1; no closing date. Applicants notified on a rolling basis starting 3/1; must reply by 5/1.
**Transfers:** No deadline. Applicants notified on a rolling basis starting 3/1; must reply by 5/1. Florida residential undergraduate students eligible for grant from state if enrolled full-time.

**CONTACT**
Joseph Bryan, Director of Financial Aid
901 South Flagler Drive, West Palm Beach, FL 33416-4708
(561) 803-2126

## Palm Beach State College
Lake Worth, Florida
www.palmbeachstate.edu          Federal Code: 001512

**2-year public** community college in large town.
**Enrollment:** 26,351 undergrads, 69% part-time. 1,794 full-time freshmen.
**Selectivity:** Open admission; but selective for some programs.

**BASIC COSTS (2015-2016)**
**Tuition and fees:** $3,030; out-of-state residents $10,890.
**Per-credit charge:** $101; out-of-state residents $363.

**FINANCIAL AID PICTURE**
**Students with need:** Work study available nights, weekends, and for part-time students.
**Students without need:** No-need awards available for academics, alumni affiliation, athletics, leadership, state/district residency.

**FINANCIAL AID PROCEDURES**
**Forms required:** FAFSA, institutional form.
**Dates and Deadlines:** Priority date 7/1; no closing date. Applicants notified on a rolling basis; must reply within 2 week(s) of notification.

**CONTACT**
Chuck Zettler, Director of Student Financial Aid
4200 Congress Avenue, Lake Worth, FL 33461
(561) 868-3330

## Pasco-Hernando State College
New Port Richey, Florida
www.phsc.edu          Federal Code: 010652

**2-year public** community college in large town.
**Enrollment:** 11,207 undergrads, 60% part-time. 1,133 full-time freshmen.
**Selectivity:** Open admission; but selective for some programs.

**BASIC COSTS (2015-2016)**
**Tuition and fees:** $3,155; out-of-state residents $12,032.
**Additional info:** Bachelor programs charged at higher tuition rates.

**FINANCIAL AID PICTURE (2014-2015)**
**Students with need:** 72% of average financial aid package awarded as scholarships/grants, 28% awarded as loans/jobs. Need-based aid available for part-time students. Work study available nights, weekends, and for part-time students.
**Students without need:** No-need awards available for academics, athletics, minority status.
**Additional info:** Childcare assistance grants available to eligible students.

**FINANCIAL AID PROCEDURES**
**Forms required:** FAFSA.
**Dates and Deadlines:** Applicants notified on a rolling basis.

**CONTACT**
Rebecca Shanafelt, Director of Financial Aid/Veterans Services
10230 Ridge Road, New Port Richey, FL 34654-5199
(727) 816-3463

## Pensacola State College
Pensacola, Florida
www.pensacolastate.edu          Federal Code: 001513

**2-year public** community college in small city.
**Enrollment:** 7,836 undergrads, 58% part-time. 949 full-time freshmen.
**Selectivity:** Open admission; but selective for some programs.

**BASIC COSTS (2015-2016)**
**Tuition and fees:** $3,137; out-of-state residents $12,593.
**Additional info:** Bachelor programs charged at higher tuition rates.

**FINANCIAL AID PICTURE**
**Students with need:** Need-based aid available for full-time and part-time students.
**Students without need:** No-need awards available for academics, athletics, leadership, music/drama, state/district residency.

**FINANCIAL AID PROCEDURES**
**Forms required:** FAFSA.
**Dates and Deadlines:** Priority date 5/1; no closing date. Applicants notified on a rolling basis starting 3/1; must reply within 2 week(s) of notification.
**Transfers:** All transfers must submit prior college transcripts for evaluation before Federal and State Aid eligibility is determined.

**CONTACT**
Karen Kessler, Director of Financial Aid
1000 College Boulevard, Pensacola, FL 32504-8998
(850) 484-1680

## Polk State College
Winter Haven, Florida
www.polk.edu          Federal Code: 001514

**2-year public** community college in large town.
**Enrollment:** 8,436 undergrads, 66% part-time. 594 full-time freshmen.
**Selectivity:** Open admission; but selective for some programs.

**BASIC COSTS (2015-2016)**
**Tuition and fees:** $3,367; out-of-state residents $12,272.
**Additional info:** Bachelor programs charged at higher tuition rates.

**FINANCIAL AID PICTURE (2014-2015)**
**Students with need:** Out of 536 full-time freshmen who applied for aid, 488 were judged to have need. Of these, 487 received aid, and 54 had their full need met. Average financial aid package met 39% of need; average scholarship/grant was $4,540; average loan was $2,760. For part-time students, average financial aid package was $3,508.
**Students without need:** 18 full-time freshmen who did not demonstrate need for aid received scholarships/grants; average award was $1,178. No-need awards available for academics, athletics, leadership, state/district residency.
**Scholarships offered:** 34 full-time freshmen received athletic scholarships; average amount $2,309.

**FINANCIAL AID PROCEDURES**
**Forms required:** FAFSA.
**Dates and Deadlines:** Priority date 5/15; no closing date. Applicants notified on a rolling basis.

**CONTACT**
Marcia Conliffe, Director of Student Financial Services
999 Avenue H NE, Winter Haven, FL 33881-4299
(863) 298-6850

## Rasmussen College: Fort Myers
Fort Myers, Florida
www.rasmussen.edu

**4-year for-profit** career college in small city.
**Enrollment:** 642 undergrads.
**Selectivity:** Open admission; but selective for some programs.

**BASIC COSTS (2016-2017)**
**Tuition and fees:** $13,455.

**Per-credit charge:** $299.
**Additional info:** Full-time tuition varies according to program of study. Required course materials fee of $150 per course.

**FINANCIAL AID PICTURE**
**Students with need:** Need-based aid available for full-time and part-time students.

**FINANCIAL AID PROCEDURES**
**Forms required:** FAFSA, institutional form.
**Dates and Deadlines:** Applicants notified on a rolling basis.

**CONTACT**
Debora Murray, Director of Financial Aid
9160 Forum Corporate Parkway, Suite 100, Fort Myers, FL 33905-7805

## Rasmussen College: New Port Richey
New Port Richey, Florida
www.rasmussen.edu          Federal Code: 008501

**4-year for-profit** career college in small city.
**Enrollment:** 637 undergrads.
**Selectivity:** Open admission; but selective for some programs.

**BASIC COSTS (2016-2017)**
**Tuition and fees:** $13,455.
**Per-credit charge:** $299.

**FINANCIAL AID PICTURE**
**Students with need:** Need-based aid available for full-time and part-time students.

**FINANCIAL AID PROCEDURES**
**Forms required:** FAFSA, institutional form.
**Dates and Deadlines:** Applicants notified on a rolling basis.

**CONTACT**
Debora Murray, Director of Student Financial Services
8661 Citizens Drive, New Port Richey, FL 34654
(727) 942-0069

## Rasmussen College: Ocala
Ocala, Florida
www.rasmussen.edu          Federal Code: 008501

**4-year for-profit** career college in small city.
**Enrollment:** 1,305 undergrads.
**Selectivity:** Open admission; but selective for some programs.

**BASIC COSTS (2016-2017)**
**Tuition and fees:** $13,455.
**Per-credit charge:** $299.

**FINANCIAL AID PICTURE**
**Students with need:** Need-based aid available for full-time and part-time students.

**FINANCIAL AID PROCEDURES**
**Forms required:** FAFSA, institutional form.
**Dates and Deadlines:** Applicants notified on a rolling basis.

**CONTACT**
Debora Murray, Director of Financial Aid
2221 Southwest 46th Court, Ocala, FL 34474
(352) 629-1941 ext. 130

## Rasmussen College: Tampa/Brandon
Tampa, Florida
www.rasmussen.edu

**4-year for-profit** branch campus and career college in large city.
**Enrollment:** 583 undergrads.
**Selectivity:** Open admission; but selective for some programs.

**BASIC COSTS (2016-2017)**
**Tuition and fees:** $13,455.
**Per-credit charge:** $299.
**Additional info:** Full-time tuition varies according to program of study. Required course materials fee of $150 per course.

**FINANCIAL AID PICTURE**
**Students with need:** Need-based aid available for full-time and part-time students.

**FINANCIAL AID PROCEDURES**
**Forms required:** FAFSA, institutional form.
**Dates and Deadlines:** Applicants notified on a rolling basis.

**CONTACT**
Debora Murray, Financial Aid Director
4042 Park Oak Boulevard, Tampa, FL 33610

## Remington College: Tampa
Tampa, Florida
www.tampa.remingtoncollege.edu   Federal Code: 007586

**4-year private** technical college in very large city.
**Enrollment:** 350 undergrads.

**BASIC COSTS (2015-2016)**
**Additional info:** Diploma programs: $15,995-$19,990. Associate programs, $33,900. Bachelor's program: $24,700.

**FINANCIAL AID PICTURE**
**Students with need:** Need-based aid available for full-time students.
**Students without need:** This college awards aid only to students with need.

**FINANCIAL AID PROCEDURES**
**Forms required:** FAFSA, institutional form.

**CONTACT**
Shavonne Roberts, Director of Student Financial Services
6302 East Dr. Martin Luther King Jr. Boulevard, Tampa, FL 33619
(813) 935-5700 ext. 217

## Ringling College of Art and Design
Sarasota, Florida
www.ringling.edu          Federal Code: 012574

**4-year private** visual arts college in small city.
**Enrollment:** 1,258 undergrads, 6% part-time. 305 full-time freshmen.
**Selectivity:** Admits over 75% of applicants.

**BASIC COSTS (2015-2016)**
**Tuition and fees:** $41,480.
**Per-credit charge:** $1,780.
**Room and board:** $13,850.

**FINANCIAL AID PICTURE (2015-2016)**
**Students with need:** Average financial aid package met 50% of need; average scholarship/grant was $17,652; average loan was $6,969. For part-time students, average financial aid package was $20,115.
**Students without need:** No-need awards available for academics, art.

## FINANCIAL AID PROCEDURES

**Forms required:** FAFSA.

**Dates and Deadlines:** Priority date 3/1; no closing date. Applicants notified on a rolling basis starting 4/1.

**Transfers:** No deadline. Applicants notified on a rolling basis starting 3/1.

## CONTACT

Lee Harrell, Director of Financial Aid

2700 North Tamiami Trail, Sarasota, FL 34234-5895

(941) 359-7534

## Rollins College

Winter Park, Florida

www.rollins.edu                    Federal Code: 001515

**4-year private** liberal arts college in large town.

**Enrollment:** 1,948 undergrads. 493 full-time freshmen.

**Selectivity:** Admits 50 to 75% of applicants.

### BASIC COSTS (2015-2016)

**Tuition and fees:** $44,760.

**Room and board:** $13,910.

### FINANCIAL AID PICTURE (2015-2016)

**Students with need:** Out of 325 full-time freshmen who applied for aid, 272 were judged to have need. Of these, 271 received aid, and 49 had their full need met. Average financial aid package met 71% of need; average scholarship/grant was $30,035; average loan was $3,720. Need-based aid available for part-time students.

**Students without need:** 159 full-time freshmen who did not demonstrate need for aid received scholarships/grants; average award was $18,836. No-need awards available for academics, art, athletics, leadership, music/drama, state/district residency.

**Scholarships offered:** *Merit:* Presidential, Alonzo Rollins; $4,000-$15,000 per year; based on academic record; 130 available per year. Donald Cram; $3,000-$5,000 per year; based on academic record, science major; 10 available per year. *Athletic:* 15 full-time freshmen received athletic scholarships; average amount $22,125.

**Additional info:** Audition required for theater arts and music scholarship applicants. Portfolio required for art scholarships.

### FINANCIAL AID PROCEDURES

**Forms required:** FAFSA.

**Dates and Deadlines:** Priority date 3/1; no closing date. Applicants notified on a rolling basis starting 3/1.

**Transfers:** Priority date 4/15; no deadline.

### CONTACT

Steve Booker, Director of Financial Aid

1000 Holt Avenue, Campus Box 2720, Winter Park, FL 32789

(407) 646-2395

## Saint Johns River State College

Palatka, Florida

www.sjrstate.edu                    Federal Code: 001523

**2-year public** community college in large town.

**Enrollment:** 4,962 undergrads, 64% part-time. 604 full-time freshmen.

**Selectivity:** Open admission; but selective for some programs.

### BASIC COSTS (2015-2016)

**Tuition and fees:** $3,180; out-of-state residents $11,608.

**Additional info:** Bachelor programs charged at higher tuition rates. Tuition and fees combined as fees are also variable based on in-state / out-of-state residency.

## FINANCIAL AID PICTURE

**Students with need:** Need-based aid available for full-time and part-time students.

## FINANCIAL AID PROCEDURES

**Forms required:** FAFSA.

**Dates and Deadlines:** Priority date 7/1; no closing date. Applicants notified on a rolling basis.

## CONTACT

Daniel Barkowitz, Dean of Enrollment Management

5001 St. Johns Avenue, Palatka, FL 32177-3897

(386) 312-4040

## Saint Leo University

Saint Leo, Florida

www.saintleo.edu                    Federal Code: 001526

**4-year private** university in rural community, affiliated with Roman Catholic Church.

**Enrollment:** 2,367 undergrads, 4% part-time. 656 full-time freshmen.

**Selectivity:** Admits 50 to 75% of applicants.

### BASIC COSTS (2015-2016)

**Tuition and fees:** $20,830.

**Room and board:** $9,870.

### FINANCIAL AID PICTURE (2015-2016)

**Students with need:** Out of 579 full-time freshmen who applied for aid, 505 were judged to have need. Of these, 504 received aid, and 66 had their full need met. Average financial aid package met 68% of need; average scholarship/grant was $14,862; average loan was $3,428. For part-time students, average financial aid package was $12,446.

**Students without need:** 148 full-time freshmen who did not demonstrate need for aid received scholarships/grants; average award was $6,248. No-need awards available for academics, alumni affiliation, athletics, leadership, minority status, religious affiliation, state/district residency.

**Scholarships offered:** 25 full-time freshmen received athletic scholarships; average amount $12,127.

### FINANCIAL AID PROCEDURES

**Forms required:** FAFSA, state aid form.

**Dates and Deadlines:** Priority date 3/1; no closing date. Applicants notified on a rolling basis starting 1/1.

### CONTACT

Melinda Clark, Assistant Vice President of Financial Aid

Box 6665 MC2008, Saint Leo, FL 33574-6665

(800) 240-7658

## St. Petersburg College

Saint Petersburg, Florida

www.spcollege.edu                    Federal Code: 001528

**2-year public** community college in large city.

**Enrollment:** 27,354 undergrads.

**Selectivity:** Open admission; but selective for some programs.

### BASIC COSTS (2015-2016)

**Tuition and fees:** $3,353; out-of-state residents $11,607.

**Additional info:** Bachelor programs charged at higher tuition rates.

### FINANCIAL AID PICTURE

**Students with need:** Need-based aid available for full-time and part-time students. Work study available nights, weekends, and for part-time students.

**Students without need:** No-need awards available for academics, art, athletics, minority status, music/drama.

## FINANCIAL AID PROCEDURES

**Forms required:** FAFSA, state aid form.

**Dates and Deadlines:** Priority date 4/15; no closing date. Applicants notified on a rolling basis starting 5/15; must reply within 2 week(s) of notification.

### CONTACT

Michael Bennett, Associate Vice-President Financial Aid Services
Box 13489, St. Petersburg, FL 33733-3489
(727) 791-2485

## Saint Thomas University
Miami Gardens, Florida
www.stu.edu                           Federal Code: 001468

**4-year private** university in very large city, affiliated with Roman Catholic Church.

**Enrollment:** 882 undergrads, 7% part-time. 194 full-time freshmen.

**Selectivity:** Admits less than 50% of applicants.

### BASIC COSTS (2015-2016)

**Tuition and fees:** $27,780.

**Per-credit charge:** $932.

**Room and board:** $7,720.

### FINANCIAL AID PICTURE (2014-2015)

**Students with need:** 46% of average financial aid package awarded as scholarships/grants, 54% awarded as loans/jobs.

**Students without need:** No-need awards available for academics, athletics, leadership.

### FINANCIAL AID PROCEDURES

**Forms required:** FAFSA.

**Dates and Deadlines:** Priority date 4/1; no closing date. Applicants notified on a rolling basis starting 3/1.

**Transfers:** Priority date 4/15.

### CONTACT

Yadani Rivero, Associate Director of Financial Aid
16401 Northwest 37th Avenue, Miami Gardens, FL 33054-6459
(305) 628-6547

## Santa Fe College
Gainesville, Florida
www.sfcollege.edu                     Federal Code: 001519

**2-year public** community college in small city.

**Enrollment:** 14,998 undergrads.

**Selectivity:** Open admission; but selective for some programs.

### BASIC COSTS (2015-2016)

**Tuition and fees:** $3,203; out-of-state residents $11,487.

**Additional info:** Bachelor programs charged at higher tuition rates. Tuition/fee waivers available for minority students.

### FINANCIAL AID PICTURE

**Students with need:** Need-based aid available for full-time and part-time students.

**Students without need:** No-need awards available for academics, art, athletics, leadership, minority status, music/drama, state/district residency.

### FINANCIAL AID PROCEDURES

**Forms required:** FAFSA.

**Dates and Deadlines:** Priority date 3/15; closing date 6/30. Applicants notified by 8/1.

**Transfers:** Must have minimum 2.0 GPA to be eligible for financial aid.

### CONTACT

Kamia Mwango, Acting Director of Financial Aid
3000 NW 83rd Street, R-112, Gainesville, FL 32606-6210
(352) 395-5480

## Schiller International University
Largo, Florida
www.schiller.edu                      Federal Code: 023141

**4-year for-profit** university in small city.

**Enrollment:** 145 undergrads.

**Selectivity:** Open admission.

### BASIC COSTS (2015-2016)

**Additional info:** Total program costs: associates $35,400-$47,190; bachelor's $35,400-$70,800.

### FINANCIAL AID PICTURE

**Students with need:** Need-based aid available for full-time and part-time students. Work study available nights.

**Students without need:** No-need awards available for academics, alumni affiliation, leadership, minority status, state/district residency.

**Scholarships offered:** One-fourth tuition awards; available to students possessing an outstanding academic record and potential; 50 available for one or two semesters. Knowledge Tuition Awards; one-fourth tuition; available to students with good academic records and financial need; 20 available for one or two semesters.

**Additional info:** Special scholarship program for US students studying abroad at European campuses of Schiller. Work-study available to students taking 2 or more courses.

### FINANCIAL AID PROCEDURES

**Forms required:** FAFSA, state aid form, institutional form.

**Dates and Deadlines:** Closing date 4/1. Applicants notified on a rolling basis starting 5/1; must reply within 3 week(s) of notification.

**Transfers:** No deadline. Applicants notified on a rolling basis.

### CONTACT

Andre Sergeyev, Financial Aid Advisor
8560 Ulmerton Road, Largo, FL 33771
(727) 736-5082 ext. 253

## Seminole State College of Florida
Sanford, Florida
www.seminolestate.edu                 Federal Code: 001520

**2-year public** community college in large town.

**Enrollment:** 15,792 undergrads, 62% part-time. 1,631 full-time freshmen.

**Selectivity:** Open admission; but selective for some programs.

### BASIC COSTS (2015-2016)

**Tuition and fees:** $3,074; out-of-state residents $11,399.

**Additional info:** Bachelor programs charged at higher tuition rates.

### FINANCIAL AID PICTURE

**Students with need:** Need-based aid available for full-time and part-time students.

**Students without need:** No-need awards available for academics, art, athletics, leadership, minority status, music/drama, state/district residency.

### FINANCIAL AID PROCEDURES

**Forms required:** FAFSA.

**Dates and Deadlines:** Priority date 7/1; no closing date. Applicants notified on a rolling basis starting 4/1.

**Transfers:** Priority date 5/31; no deadline. Applicants notified on a rolling basis starting 4/1.

PART III: FINANCIAL AID COLLEGE BY COLLEGE

**CONTACT**
Roseann Amato, Director of Financial Aid
100 Weldon Boulevard, Sanford, FL 32773-6199
(407) 708-4722 ext. 3422

## South Florida State College
Avon Park, Florida
www.southflorida.edu          Federal Code: 001522

**2-year public** community and technical college in small town.
**Enrollment:** 2,049 undergrads, 60% part-time. 184 full-time freshmen.
**Selectivity:** Open admission; but selective for some programs.

**BASIC COSTS (2015-2016)**
**Tuition and fees:** $3,136; out-of-state residents $11,829.
**Additional info:** Bachelor programs charged at higher tuition rates. Tuition/fee waivers available for minority students.

**FINANCIAL AID PICTURE (2014-2015)**
**Students with need:** 91% of average financial aid package awarded as scholarships/grants, 9% awarded as loans/jobs. Need-based aid available for part-time students.
**Students without need:** No-need awards available for academics, athletics, leadership, minority status, music/drama, state/district residency.

**FINANCIAL AID PROCEDURES**
**Forms required:** FAFSA.
**Dates and Deadlines:** Priority date 4/15; no closing date. Applicants notified on a rolling basis starting 4/1.
**Transfers:** Students must maintain satisfactory academic progress.

**CONTACT**
Jerry Donna, Director of Financial Aid
600 West College Drive, Avon Park, FL 33825
(863) 453-6661 ext. 7254

## Southeastern University
Lakeland, Florida
www.seu.edu          Federal Code: 001521

**4-year private** liberal arts and teachers college in small city, affiliated with Assemblies of God.
**Enrollment:** 3,412 undergrads, 8% part-time. 801 full-time freshmen.
**Selectivity:** Admits less than 50% of applicants.

**BASIC COSTS (2015-2016)**
**Tuition and fees:** $22,840.
**Per-credit charge:** $910.
**Room and board:** $9,148.

**FINANCIAL AID PICTURE (2014-2015)**
**Students with need:** Out of 739 full-time freshmen who applied for aid, 641 were judged to have need. Of these, 638 received aid, and 73 had their full need met. Average financial aid package met 65% of need; average scholarship/grant was $13,603; average loan was $3,265. For part-time students, average financial aid package was $5,897.
**Students without need:** 104 full-time freshmen who did not demonstrate need for aid received scholarships/grants; average award was $6,556. No-need awards available for academics, alumni affiliation, athletics, job skills, leadership, minority status, music/drama, religious affiliation, state/district residency.
**Scholarships offered:** 22 full-time freshmen received athletic scholarships; average amount $7,491.

**FINANCIAL AID PROCEDURES**
**Forms required:** FAFSA.

**Dates and Deadlines:** Priority date 2/15; no closing date. Applicants notified on a rolling basis starting 3/15; must reply within 6 week(s) of notification.
**Transfers:** Must reply within 6 week(s) of notification.

**CONTACT**
Rebekah Burdick, Director of Student Financial Services
1000 Longfellow Boulevard, Lakeland, FL 33801-6034
(863) 667-5024

## Southern Technical College
Fort Myers, Florida
www.southerntech.edu          Federal Code: 016068

**2-year private** career college in large city.
**Enrollment:** 15,389 undergrads.
**Selectivity:** Open admission; but selective for some programs.

**BASIC COSTS (2015-2016)**
**Additional info:** Full program costs: diplomas $11,346-$19,150, books and supplies $184; associates $33,570-$47,654, books and supplies up to $825; bachelor's $69,350-$74,975, books and supplies up to $825.

**FINANCIAL AID PICTURE**
**Students with need:** Need-based aid available for full-time and part-time students. Work study available nights, weekends, and for part-time students.

**FINANCIAL AID PROCEDURES**
**Forms required:** FAFSA.
**Dates and Deadlines:** Applicants notified on a rolling basis.
**Transfers:** No deadline. Applicants notified on a rolling basis.

**CONTACT**
Laura Selvey, Director of Financial Aid
1685 Medical Lane, Ft. Myers, FL 33907-1108
(813) 630-4401

## State College of Florida, Manatee-Sarasota
Bradenton, Florida
www.scf.edu          Federal Code: 001504

**2-year public** nursing and community college in small city.
**Enrollment:** 9,848 undergrads, 60% part-time. 947 full-time freshmen.
**Selectivity:** Open admission; but selective for some programs.

**BASIC COSTS (2015-2016)**
**Tuition and fees:** $3,074; out-of-state residents $11,596.
**Additional info:** Bachelor programs charged at higher tuition rates.

**FINANCIAL AID PICTURE (2015-2016)**
**Students with need:** 59% of average financial aid package awarded as scholarships/grants, 41% awarded as loans/jobs. Need-based aid available for part-time students. Work study available nights, weekends, and for part-time students.
**Students without need:** No-need awards available for academics, art, athletics, music/drama, state/district residency.

**FINANCIAL AID PROCEDURES**
**Forms required:** FAFSA.
**Dates and Deadlines:** Priority date 6/1; closing date 7/28. Applicants notified on a rolling basis starting 3/15.

**CONTACT**
Director of Financial Aid
Box 1849, Bradenton, FL 34206-1849

## Stetson University
DeLand, Florida
www.stetson.edu       Federal Code: 001531

**4-year private** university in large town.
**Enrollment:** 3,042 undergrads, 2% part-time. 982 full-time freshmen.
**Selectivity:** Admits 50 to 75% of applicants.

### BASIC COSTS (2016-2017)
**Tuition and fees:** $43,240.
**Per-credit charge:** $1,111.
**Room and board:** $12,326.

### FINANCIAL AID PICTURE (2015-2016)
**Students with need:** Out of 871 full-time freshmen who applied for aid, 760 were judged to have need. Of these, 760 received aid, and 178 had their full need met. Average financial aid package met 78% of need; average scholarship/grant was $28,926; average loan was $3,674. For part-time students, average financial aid package was $10,567.
**Students without need:** 183 full-time freshmen who did not demonstrate need for aid received scholarships/grants; average award was $24,048. No-need awards available for academics, alumni affiliation, art, athletics, leadership, minority status, music/drama, religious affiliation, ROTC, state/district residency.
**Scholarships offered:** 31 full-time freshmen received athletic scholarships; average amount $24,036.

### FINANCIAL AID PROCEDURES
**Forms required:** FAFSA.
**Dates and Deadlines:** Priority date 3/15; no closing date. Applicants notified on a rolling basis starting 3/1; must reply within 2 week(s) of notification.

### CONTACT
Susan Merchant, Director of Financial Aid
Campus Box 8378, DeLand, FL 32723
(386) 822-7120

## Tallahassee Community College
Tallahassee, Florida
www.tcc.fl.edu       Federal Code: 001533

**2-year public** community college in small city.
**Enrollment:** 11,357 undergrads, 51% part-time. 2,056 full-time freshmen.
**Selectivity:** Open admission; but selective for some programs.

### BASIC COSTS (2015-2016)
**Tuition and fees:** $3,025; out-of-state residents $11,288.

### FINANCIAL AID PICTURE (2014-2015)
**Students with need:** Out of 1,561 full-time freshmen who applied for aid, 1,079 were judged to have need. Of these, 1,050 received aid. Need-based aid available for part-time students.
**Students without need:** No-need awards available for academics, art, athletics, leadership, music/drama, state/district residency.

### FINANCIAL AID PROCEDURES
**Forms required:** FAFSA, institutional form.
**Dates and Deadlines:** Priority date 6/1; no closing date. Applicants notified on a rolling basis starting 6/1; must reply within 2 week(s) of notification.

### CONTACT
William Spiers, Director of Financial Aid
444 Appleyard Drive, Tallahassee, FL 32304
(850) 201-8399

## Talmudic University
Miami Beach, Florida
www.talmudicu.edu       Federal Code: 013814

**4-year private** rabbinical college for men in very large city, affiliated with Jewish faith.
**Enrollment:** 29 undergrads.

### BASIC COSTS (2015-2016)
**Tuition and fees:** $13,000.
**Room and board:** $8,000.

### FINANCIAL AID PICTURE
**Students with need:** Need-based aid available for full-time and part-time students. Work study available nights, weekends, and for part-time students.
**Students without need:** This college awards aid only to students with need.

### FINANCIAL AID PROCEDURES
**Forms required:** FAFSA, institutional form.
**Dates and Deadlines:** Applicants notified on a rolling basis.

### CONTACT
Peggy Loewy Wellisch, Chief Financial Aid Officer
4000 Alton Road, Miami Beach, FL 33140
(305) 534-050

## Trinity Baptist College
Jacksonville, Florida
www.tbc.edu

**4-year private** Bible and teachers college in very large city.
**Enrollment:** 280 undergrads. 113 full-time freshmen.

### BASIC COSTS (2015-2016)
**Tuition and fees:** $11,040.
**Room and board:** $6,270.

### FINANCIAL AID PICTURE (2014-2015)
**Students with need:** Out of 106 full-time freshmen who applied for aid, 100 were judged to have need. Of these, 100 received aid. Need-based aid available for part-time students.
**Students without need:** No-need awards available for academics, leadership, state/district residency.
**Scholarships offered:** Dollar-for-dollar matching scholarship for all students who are awarded the Florida Academic Bright Futures Scholarship or the Florida Medallion Bright Futures Scholarship. Students must be admitted for enrollment at Trinity Baptist College to be eligible for a matching scholarship.

### FINANCIAL AID PROCEDURES
**Dates and Deadlines:** Applicants notified on a rolling basis starting 1/1; must reply within 2 week(s) of notification.
**Transfers:** Applicants notified on a rolling basis starting 1/1; must reply within 2 week(s) of notification. Transfer must provide copies of official transcripts from all previous schools before financial aid at Trinity Baptist College is packaged and offered.

### CONTACT
Mark Elkins, Financial Aid
800 Hammond Boulevard, Jacksonville, FL 32221

## Trinity College of Florida
Trinity, Florida
www.trinitycollege.edu       Federal Code: 030282

**4-year private** Bible college in small city, affiliated with interdenominational tradition.

**Enrollment:** 202 undergrads, 18% part-time. 32 full-time freshmen.
**Selectivity:** Admits over 75% of applicants.

**BASIC COSTS (2015-2016)**
**Tuition and fees:** $15,690.
**Per-credit charge:** $495.
**Room and board:** $6,450.

**FINANCIAL AID PICTURE (2015-2016)**
**Students with need:** Out of 28 full-time freshmen who applied for aid, 25 were judged to have need. Of these, 25 received aid. Average financial aid package met 48% of need; average scholarship/grant was $7,445; average loan was $6,567. For part-time students, average financial aid package was $9,029.
**Students without need:** 5 full-time freshmen who did not demonstrate need for aid received scholarships/grants; average award was $1,560. No-need awards available for academics.

**FINANCIAL AID PROCEDURES**
**Forms required:** FAFSA, institutional form.
**Dates and Deadlines:** Priority date 3/15; closing date 9/15. Applicants notified on a rolling basis starting 1/5; must reply within 2 week(s) of notification.
**Transfers:** No deadline. Applicants notified on a rolling basis starting 1/5; must reply within 2 week(s) of notification.

**CONTACT**
Sue Wayne, Financial Aid Director
2430 Welbilt Boulevard, Trinity, FL 34655-4401
(727) 376-6911 ext. 310

# University of Central Florida
Orlando, Florida
www.ucf.edu                     Federal Code: 003954

**4-year public** university in very large city.
**Enrollment:** 54,120 undergrads, 31% part-time. 6,200 full-time freshmen.
**Selectivity:** Admits less than 50% of applicants.

**BASIC COSTS (2015-2016)**
**Tuition and fees:** $6,368; out-of-state residents $22,467.
**Per-credit charge:** $212; out-of-state residents $749.
**Room and board:** $9,554.

**FINANCIAL AID PICTURE (2014-2015)**
**Students with need:** Out of 5,552 full-time freshmen who applied for aid, 3,860 were judged to have need. Of these, 3,713 received aid, and 320 had their full need met. Average financial aid package met 55% of need; average scholarship/grant was $5,382; average loan was $3,630. For part-time students, average financial aid package was $5,765.
**Students without need:** 510 full-time freshmen who did not demonstrate need for aid received scholarships/grants; average award was $3,382. No-need awards available for academics, alumni affiliation, athletics, leadership, ROTC, state/district residency.
**Scholarships offered:** *Merit:* Academic scholarships: $2,000-$24,000 over 4-year period, freshmen automatically considered. *Athletic:* 58 full-time freshmen received athletic scholarships; average amount $13,213.

**FINANCIAL AID PROCEDURES**
**Forms required:** FAFSA.
**Dates and Deadlines:** Priority date 3/1; closing date 6/30. Applicants notified on a rolling basis starting 3/15; must reply within 3 week(s) of notification.

**CONTACT**
Alicia Keaton, Director of Financial Aid
Box 160111, Orlando, FL 32816-0111
(407) 823-2827

# University of Florida
Gainesville, Florida
www.ufl.edu                     Federal Code: 001535

**4-year public** university in small city.
**Enrollment:** 33,972 undergrads, 10% part-time. 7,094 full-time freshmen.
**Selectivity:** Admits less than 50% of applicants.

**BASIC COSTS (2015-2016)**
**Tuition and fees:** $6,381; out-of-state residents $28,658.
**Per-credit charge:** $149; out-of-state residents $856.
**Room and board:** $9,650.

**FINANCIAL AID PICTURE (2014-2015)**
**Students with need:** Out of 5,467 full-time freshmen who applied for aid, 3,344 were judged to have need. Of these, 3,296 received aid, and 902 had their full need met. Average financial aid package met 99% of need; average scholarship/grant was $7,874; average loan was $3,990. Need-based aid available for part-time students.
**Students without need:** 321 full-time freshmen who did not demonstrate need for aid received scholarships/grants; average award was $2,131. No-need awards available for academics, alumni affiliation, art, athletics, leadership, minority status, music/drama, state/district residency.
**Scholarships offered:** 86 full-time freshmen received athletic scholarships; average amount $16,666.

**FINANCIAL AID PROCEDURES**
**Forms required:** FAFSA.
**Dates and Deadlines:** Priority date 3/15; no closing date. Applicants notified on a rolling basis starting 4/15.
**Transfers:** Closing date 3/15. Applicants notified on a rolling basis starting 4/15.

**CONTACT**
Richard Wilder, Director of Student Financial Aid
201 Criser Hall-PO Box 114000, Gainesville, FL 32611-4000
(352) 392-1275

# University of Miami
Coral Gables, Florida              Federal Code: 001536
www.miami.edu                      CSS Code: 5815

**4-year private** university in small city.
**Enrollment:** 10,768 undergrads, 4% part-time. 2,057 full-time freshmen.
**Selectivity:** Admits less than 50% of applicants.

**BASIC COSTS (2015-2016)**
**Tuition and fees:** $45,724.
**Per-credit charge:** $1,850.
**Room and board:** $13,066.

**FINANCIAL AID PICTURE (2015-2016)**
**Students with need:** Out of 2,056 full-time freshmen who applied for aid, 1,564 were judged to have need. Of these, 1,259 received aid, and 1,256 had their full need met. Average financial aid package met 99% of need; average scholarship/grant was $11,456; average loan was $3,874. For part-time students, average financial aid package was $12,699.
**Students without need:** 442 full-time freshmen who did not demonstrate need for aid received scholarships/grants; average award was $8,973. No-need awards available for academics, athletics, music/drama, ROTC, state/district residency.
**Scholarships offered:** *Merit:* About 45% of incoming freshman receive a merit-based scholarship based on academic performance in high school and standardized test scores. Scholarships range from $8,000 annually to full cost of attendance plus an enrichment stipend. *Athletic:* 60 full-time freshmen received athletic scholarships; average amount $50,277.

## FINANCIAL AID PROCEDURES

**Forms required:** FAFSA, CSS PROFILE.

**Dates and Deadlines:** Priority date 1/1; closing date 4/15. Applicants notified on a rolling basis starting 1/20; must reply by 5/1.

**Transfers:** Priority date 3/1. Applicants notified by 3/25; must reply by 5/1.

## CONTACT

Raymond Nault-Hix, Executive Director of Financial Assistance Services
PO Box 248025, Coral Gables, FL 33124-4616
(305) 284-5212

# University of North Florida
Jacksonville, Florida
www.unf.edu
Federal Code: 009841

**4-year public** university in very large city.

**Enrollment:** 13,562 undergrads, 30% part-time. 1,513 full-time freshmen.

**Selectivity:** Admits 50 to 75% of applicants.

## BASIC COSTS (2015-2016)

**Tuition and fees:** $6,394; out-of-state residents $20,112.

**Per-credit charge:** $143; out-of-state residents $600.

**Room and board:** $9,487.

## FINANCIAL AID PICTURE (2015-2016)

**Students with need:** Out of 1,282 full-time freshmen who applied for aid, 857 were judged to have need. Of these, 807 received aid, and 179 had their full need met. Average financial aid package met 90% of need; average scholarship/grant was $7,680; average loan was $3,220. For part-time students, average financial aid package was $6,699.

**Students without need:** 131 full-time freshmen who did not demonstrate need for aid received scholarships/grants; average award was $3,071. No-need awards available for academics, athletics, leadership, minority status, music/drama, state/district residency.

**Scholarships offered:** 40 full-time freshmen received athletic scholarships; average amount $8,583.

## FINANCIAL AID PROCEDURES

**Forms required:** FAFSA.

**Dates and Deadlines:** Closing date 4/1. Applicants notified on a rolling basis starting 3/15.

**Transfers:** Priority date 4/1; no deadline. Applicants notified on a rolling basis; must reply within 2 week(s) of notification. Students must submit financial aid transcripts from previous institutions attended.

## CONTACT

Anissa Agne, Director of Financial Aid
1 UNF Drive, Jacksonville, FL 32224-7699
(904) 620-5555

# University of South Florida
Tampa, Florida
www.usf.edu
Federal Code: 001537

**4-year public** university in very large city.

**Enrollment:** 30,314 undergrads, 22% part-time. 4,124 full-time freshmen.

**Selectivity:** Admits less than 50% of applicants.

## BASIC COSTS (2015-2016)

**Tuition and fees:** $6,410; out-of-state residents $17,324.

**Per-credit charge:** $211; out-of-district residents $211; out-of-state residents $575.

**Room and board:** $9,400.

**Additional info:** Tuition/fee waivers available for unemployed or children of unemployed.

## FINANCIAL AID PICTURE (2014-2015)

**Students with need:** Out of 3,537 full-time freshmen who applied for aid, 2,680 were judged to have need. Of these, 2,568 received aid, and 398 had their full need met. Average financial aid package met 62% of need; average scholarship/grant was $9,173; average loan was $4,949. For part-time students, average financial aid package was $8,106.

**Students without need:** 761 full-time freshmen who did not demonstrate need for aid received scholarships/grants; average award was $2,657. No-need awards available for academics, art, athletics, leadership, music/drama, state/district residency.

**Scholarships offered:** 61 full-time freshmen received athletic scholarships; average amount $9,610.

**Additional info:** Deferred tuition payment plan available for late financial aid recipients.

## FINANCIAL AID PROCEDURES

**Forms required:** FAFSA.

**Dates and Deadlines:** Priority date 3/1; no closing date. Applicants notified on a rolling basis starting 3/15.

## CONTACT

Billie Hamilton, Director of Financial Aid
4202 East Fowler Avenue, SVC 1036, Tampa, FL 33620-9951
(813) 974-4700

# University of South Florida: Sarasota-Manatee
Sarasota, Florida
www.usfsm.edu
Federal Code: 001537

**4-year public** university in small city.

**Enrollment:** 1,762 undergrads, 45% part-time. 91 full-time freshmen.

**Selectivity:** Admits less than 50% of applicants.

## BASIC COSTS (2015-2016)

**Tuition and fees:** $5,587; out-of-state residents $16,502.

**Per-credit charge:** $140; out-of-state residents $504.

## FINANCIAL AID PICTURE (2014-2015)

**Students with need:** Out of 79 full-time freshmen who applied for aid, 61 were judged to have need. Of these, 55 received aid, and 7 had their full need met. Average financial aid package met 54% of need; average scholarship/grant was $7,798; average loan was $3,999. For part-time students, average financial aid package was $7,550.

**Students without need:** 6 full-time freshmen who did not demonstrate need for aid received scholarships/grants; average award was $1,625. No-need awards available for academics, alumni affiliation, art, athletics, job skills, leadership, minority status, music/drama, religious affiliation, state/district residency.

## FINANCIAL AID PROCEDURES

**Forms required:** FAFSA.

**Dates and Deadlines:** Priority date 3/1; no closing date. Applicants notified on a rolling basis starting 3/15.

## CONTACT

Gabriela Vega, Director of Financial Aid
8350 North Tamiami Trail, Sarasota, FL 34243
(941) 359-4330

# University of Tampa
Tampa, Florida
www.ut.edu
Federal Code: 001538

**4-year private** university and liberal arts college in large city.

**Enrollment:** 7,061 undergrads, 3% part-time. 1,752 full-time freshmen.

**Selectivity:** Admits 50 to 75% of applicants.

**BASIC COSTS (2016-2017)**
**Tuition and fees:** $27,740.
**Per-credit charge:** $550.
**Room and board:** $10,196.

**FINANCIAL AID PICTURE (2014-2015)**
**Students with need:** Out of 1,417 full-time freshmen who applied for aid, 1,113 were judged to have need. Of these, 1,112 received aid, and 1,111 had their full need met. Average financial aid package met 62% of need; average scholarship/grant was $13,276; average loan was $3,318. For part-time students, average financial aid package was $5,057.
**Students without need:** 466 full-time freshmen who did not demonstrate need for aid received scholarships/grants; average award was $7,750. No-need awards available for academics, art, athletics, leadership, music/drama, ROTC.
**Scholarships offered: Merit:** Presidential Scholarships: up to $9,000; 3.5 GPA. Dean's Scholarships: up to $8,000; 3.2 GPA. Departmental scholarships also awarded. Merit scholarships awarded at time of admission for new freshmen up to $14,000, for new transfers up to $7,000, for international freshmen and transfers up to $8,000. **Athletic:** 70 full-time freshmen received athletic scholarships; average amount $6,547.

**FINANCIAL AID PROCEDURES**
**Forms required:** FAFSA.
**Dates and Deadlines:** Priority date 1/1; no closing date. Applicants notified on a rolling basis starting 3/1; must reply by 5/1 or within 3 week(s) of notification.
**Transfers:** No deadline. Applicants notified on a rolling basis starting 3/1; must reply within 3 week(s) of notification. Transfer scholarships available; Phi Theta Kappa Scholarships.

**CONTACT**
Jacqueline LaTorella, Director of Financial Aid
401 West Kennedy Boulevard, Tampa, FL 33606-1490
(813) 253-6239

## University of West Florida
Pensacola, Florida
www.uwf.edu                    Federal Code: 003955

**4-year public** university in small city.
**Enrollment:** 9,786 undergrads, 28% part-time. 1,196 full-time freshmen.
**Selectivity:** Admits less than 50% of applicants.

**BASIC COSTS (2015-2016)**
**Tuition and fees:** $6,569; out-of-state residents $19,451.
**Per-credit charge:** $219; out-of-state residents $648.
**Room and board:** $9,912.

**FINANCIAL AID PICTURE (2014-2015)**
**Students with need:** Out of 1,032 full-time freshmen who applied for aid, 809 were judged to have need. Of these, 785 received aid, and 118 had their full need met. Average financial aid package met 53% of need; average scholarship/grant was $6,752; average loan was $3,438. For part-time students, average financial aid package was $4,927.
**Students without need:** 144 full-time freshmen who did not demonstrate need for aid received scholarships/grants; average award was $1,972. No-need awards available for academics, alumni affiliation, art, athletics, minority status, music/drama, ROTC.
**Scholarships offered:** 20 full-time freshmen received athletic scholarships; average amount $9,780.

**FINANCIAL AID PROCEDURES**
**Forms required:** FAFSA.
**Dates and Deadlines:** Priority date 3/15; no closing date. Applicants notified on a rolling basis starting 3/1.

**Transfers:** Applicants notified on a rolling basis.

**CONTACT**
Janice Bass, Director of Financial Aid
11000 University Parkway, Pensacola, FL 32514-5750
(850) 474-2400

## Valencia College
Orlando, Florida
www.valenciacollege.edu          Federal Code: 006750

**2-year public** community college in very large city.
**Enrollment:** 36,537 undergrads.
**Selectivity:** Open admission; but selective for some programs.

**BASIC COSTS (2015-2016)**
**Tuition and fees:** $3,092; out-of-state residents $11,729.
**Additional info:** Bachelor programs charged at higher tuition rates.

**FINANCIAL AID PICTURE**
**Students with need:** Need-based aid available for full-time and part-time students. Work study available nights.

**FINANCIAL AID PROCEDURES**
**Forms required:** FAFSA.
**Dates and Deadlines:** Closing date 3/15. Applicants notified on a rolling basis starting 4/2; must reply within 2 week(s) of notification.
**Transfers:** No deadline.

**CONTACT**
Christen Christensen, Director, Financial Aid
PO Box 3028, Orlando, FL 32802-3028
(407) 299-5000

## Warner University
Lake Wales, Florida
www.warner.edu                   Federal Code: 008848

**4-year private** liberal arts college in large town, affiliated with Church of God.
**Enrollment:** 1,027 undergrads.

**BASIC COSTS (2015-2016)**
**Tuition and fees:** $19,754.
**Room and board:** $7,924.

**FINANCIAL AID PICTURE**
**Students with need:** Need-based aid available for full-time and part-time students.
**Students without need:** No-need awards available for academics, alumni affiliation, art, athletics, leadership, music/drama, religious affiliation, state/district residency.

**FINANCIAL AID PROCEDURES**
**Forms required:** FAFSA, state aid form.
**Dates and Deadlines:** Priority date 5/1; no closing date. Applicants notified on a rolling basis starting 3/15; must reply within 2 week(s) of notification.
**Transfers:** Priority date 10/1; closing date 5/15. Applicants notified on a rolling basis; must reply within 2 week(s) of notification.

**CONTACT**
Lorrie Steedley, Financial Aid Director
13895 Highway 27, Lake Wales, FL 33859
(863) 638-7202

## Webber International University

Babson Park, Florida
www.webber.edu                    Federal Code: 001540

**4-year private** university and business college in rural community.
**Enrollment:** 688 undergrads.

**BASIC COSTS (2015-2016)**
**Tuition and fees:** $22,326.
**Per-credit charge:** $316.
**Room and board:** $8,712.
**Additional info:** Tuition/fee waivers available for adults.

**FINANCIAL AID PICTURE**
**Students with need:** Need-based aid available for full-time and part-time students. Work study available nights, weekends, and for part-time students.
**Students without need:** No-need awards available for academics, athletics, leadership.

**FINANCIAL AID PROCEDURES**
**Forms required:** FAFSA, institutional form.
**Dates and Deadlines:** Priority date 5/1; closing date 8/1. Applicants notified on a rolling basis starting 4/1; must reply within 4 week(s) of notification.
**Transfers:** Eligibility for academic scholarships predicated on 12 hours of transferable credit.

**CONTACT**
Kathleen Wilson, Registrar
1201 North Scenic Highway, Babson Park, FL 33827-0096
(863) 638-2930

# Georgia

## Agnes Scott College

Decatur, Georgia
www.agnesscott.edu                 Federal Code: 001542

**4-year private** liberal arts college for women in very large city, affiliated with Presbyterian Church (USA).
**Enrollment:** 846 undergrads, 1% part-time. 271 full-time freshmen.
**Selectivity:** Admits 50 to 75% of applicants.

**BASIC COSTS (2016-2017)**
**Tuition and fees:** $38,472.
**Per-credit charge:** $1,593.
**Room and board:** $11,520.

**FINANCIAL AID PICTURE (2015-2016)**
**Students with need:** Out of 249 full-time freshmen who applied for aid, 220 were judged to have need. Of these, 220 received aid, and 60 had their full need met. Average financial aid package met 84% of need; average scholarship/grant was $27,535; average loan was $3,391. For part-time students, average financial aid package was $7,025.
**Students without need:** 51 full-time freshmen who did not demonstrate need for aid received scholarships/grants; average award was $27,090. No-need awards available for academics, leadership, minority status, music/drama, religious affiliation.

**FINANCIAL AID PROCEDURES**
**Forms required:** FAFSA. PROFILE required for early decision/early action applicants.
**Dates and Deadlines:** Priority date 2/15; closing date 5/1. Applicants notified on a rolling basis starting 3/1; must reply by 5/1 or within 3 week(s) of notification.
**Transfers:** Merit scholarships available.

**CONTACT**
Patrick Bonones, Director of Financial Aid
141 East College Avenue, Decatur, GA 30030-3797
(404) 471-6395

## Albany State University

Albany, Georgia
www.asurams.edu                   Federal Code: 001544

**4-year public** university in small city.
**Enrollment:** 2,988 undergrads, 15% part-time. 473 full-time freshmen.
**Selectivity:** Admits 50 to 75% of applicants.

**BASIC COSTS (2015-2016)**
**Tuition and fees:** $6,460; out-of-state residents $19,280.
**Per-credit charge:** $162; out-of-state residents $590.
**Room and board:** $7,698.

**FINANCIAL AID PICTURE**
**Students with need:** Need-based aid available for full-time and part-time students. Work study available nights, weekends, and for part-time students.
**Students without need:** No-need awards available for academics, alumni affiliation, athletics, music/drama, ROTC, state/district residency.

**FINANCIAL AID PROCEDURES**
**Forms required:** FAFSA.
**Dates and Deadlines:** Priority date 4/15; closing date 6/30. Applicants notified on a rolling basis starting 1/7; must reply within 2 week(s) of notification.
**Transfers:** Must reply within 2 week(s) of notification.

**CONTACT**
Thomas Harris, Director of Financial Aid
504 College Drive, Albany, GA 31705-2796
(229) 430-4650

## Albany Technical College

Albany, Georgia
www.albanytech.edu                Federal Code: 005601

**2-year public** technical college in small city.
**Enrollment:** 3,894 undergrads.
**Selectivity:** Open admission; but selective for some programs.

**BASIC COSTS (2015-2016)**
**Tuition and fees:** $3,182; out-of-state residents $5,852.
**Per-credit charge:** $89; out-of-state residents $178.

**FINANCIAL AID PICTURE**
**Students with need:** Need-based aid available for full-time and part-time students. Work study available nights.
**Students without need:** No-need awards available for academics, state/district residency.

**FINANCIAL AID PROCEDURES**
**Forms required:** FAFSA, state aid form.
**Dates and Deadlines:** Applicants notified on a rolling basis starting 5/1.

**CONTACT**
Helen Catt, Financial Aid Director
1704 South Slappy Boulevard, Albany, GA 31701-3514
(229) 430-3506

## Andrew College
Cuthbert, Georgia
www.andrewcollege.edu          Federal Code: 001545

**2-year private** junior and liberal arts college in small town, affiliated with United Methodist Church.
**Enrollment:** 307 undergrads, 2% part-time. 149 full-time freshmen.
**Selectivity:** Admits 50 to 75% of applicants.

**BASIC COSTS (2015-2016)**
**Tuition and fees:** $14,924.
**Room and board:** $9,182.

**FINANCIAL AID PICTURE (2014-2015)**
**Students with need:** Out of 130 full-time freshmen who applied for aid, 113 were judged to have need. Of these, 113 received aid. Need-based aid available for part-time students.
**Students without need:** No-need awards available for academics, alumni affiliation, art, athletics, leadership, music/drama, religious affiliation, state/district residency.

**FINANCIAL AID PROCEDURES**
**Forms required:** FAFSA, state aid form, institutional form.
**Dates and Deadlines:** Priority date 4/1; closing date 8/1. Applicants notified on a rolling basis starting 4/15.

**CONTACT**
Daiquiri Tyson, Director of Financial Aid
501 College Street, Cuthbert, GA 39840-1395
(229) 732-5958

## Armstrong State University
Savannah, Georgia
www.armstrong.edu          Federal Code: 001546

**4-year public** university in small city.
**Enrollment:** 6,331 undergrads, 27% part-time. 635 full-time freshmen.
**Selectivity:** Admits 50 to 75% of applicants.

**BASIC COSTS (2015-2016)**
**Tuition and fees:** $6,332; out-of-state residents $19,152.
**Per-credit charge:** $161.93; out-of-state residents $589.27.
**Room and board:** $10,498.

**FINANCIAL AID PICTURE (2014-2015)**
**Students with need:** Out of 576 full-time freshmen who applied for aid, 402 were judged to have need. Of these, 402 received aid. Average financial aid package met 49% of need; average scholarship/grant was $1,500; average loan was $4,500. For part-time students, average financial aid package was $12,900.
**Students without need:** 295 full-time freshmen who did not demonstrate need for aid received scholarships/grants. No-need awards available for academics, alumni affiliation, art, athletics, job skills, leadership, minority status, music/drama, ROTC, state/district residency.
**Scholarships offered:** 23 full-time freshmen received athletic scholarships; average amount $2,909.
**Additional info:** Armstrong Commitment Fund provided to students in sophomore, junior or senior year. Students must demonstrate need, complete financial literacy training, and participate in community service activities.

**FINANCIAL AID PROCEDURES**
**Forms required:** FAFSA.
**Dates and Deadlines:** Priority date 3/15; closing date 4/20. Must reply within 2 week(s) of notification.

**CONTACT**
Kaye O'Neal, Financial Aid Director
11935 Abercorn Street, Savannah, GA 31419-1997
(912) 344-3266

## Art Institute of Atlanta
Atlanta, Georgia
www.artinstitutes.edu/atlanta          Federal Code: 009270

**4-year for-profit** culinary school and visual arts college in very large city.
**Enrollment:** 2,623 undergrads.

**BASIC COSTS (2015-2016)**
**Additional info:** Diploma programs: $20,381-$30,412, books and supplies $450-$600, room and board $15,024-$18,780. Associate programs: $44,354-$47,791, books and supplies $1,100-$1,450, room and board $30,048. Bachelor's programs: $88,047-$92,101, books and supplies $1,100-$2,250, room and board $56,340.

**FINANCIAL AID PICTURE**
**Students with need:** Need-based aid available for full-time and part-time students. Work study available nights, weekends, and for part-time students.
**Students without need:** No-need awards available for academics, art, state/district residency.
**Scholarships offered:** Art Institutes Scholarship Competition awards $2,000-$56,064 depending on program to winning high school seniors selected on merits of written essay, original artwork, resume, letter(s) of recommendation, and high school academic achievement; up to 1 full-tuition, 2 half-tuition, and 24 partial-tuition scholarships available. Art Institutes Culinary Scholarship Competition awards $2,000-$32,704 to winning high school seniors selected through three-part elimination-style competition to prove academic ability, culinary expertise, and commitment to succeed; up to 1 full-tuition or 2 partial-tuition scholarships available. Various other scholarships and awards available.

**FINANCIAL AID PROCEDURES**
**Forms required:** FAFSA, state aid form.
**Dates and Deadlines:** Applicants notified on a rolling basis starting 3/15.

**CONTACT**
Chris Schwarzer, Director of Administrative and Financial Services
6600 Peachtree Dunwoody Road, NE, Atlanta, GA 30328
(770) 394-8300

## Athens Technical College
Athens, Georgia
www.athenstech.edu          Federal Code: 005600

**2-year public** community and technical college in small city.
**Enrollment:** 4,563 undergrads.
**Selectivity:** Open admission; but selective for some programs.

**BASIC COSTS (2015-2016)**
**Tuition and fees:** $3,218; out-of-state residents $5,888.
**Per-credit charge:** $89; out-of-state residents $178.

**FINANCIAL AID PICTURE**
**Students with need:** Need-based aid available for full-time and part-time students.
**Students without need:** No-need awards available for academics, leadership.

**FINANCIAL AID PROCEDURES**
**Forms required:** FAFSA.
**Dates and Deadlines:** Applicants notified on a rolling basis starting 6/15; must reply within 2 week(s) of notification.

**CONTACT**
Wanda Hicks, Director of Financial Aid
800 US Highway 29 North, Athens, GA 30601-1500
(706) 355-5009

## Atlanta Metropolitan College
Atlanta, Georgia
www.atlm.edu                          Federal Code: 012165

**2-year public** junior college in very large city.
**Enrollment:** 2,700 undergrads.

**BASIC COSTS (2015-2016)**
**Tuition and fees:** $3,830; out-of-state residents $11,752.
**Per-credit charge:** $97; out-of-state residents $361.

**FINANCIAL AID PICTURE**
**Students with need:** Need-based aid available for full-time and part-time students. Work study available nights, weekends, and for part-time students.
**Students without need:** This college awards aid only to students with need.

**FINANCIAL AID PROCEDURES**
**Forms required:** FAFSA, state aid form.
**Dates and Deadlines:** Closing date 6/1. Applicants notified on a rolling basis; must reply by 6/30.
**Transfers:** Priority date 6/1; closing date 6/30. Applicants notified on a rolling basis; must reply by 6/30.

**CONTACT**
Alicia Scott, Director
1630 Metropolitan Parkway, SW, Atlanta, GA 30310-4498
(404) 756-4002

## Atlanta Technical College
Atlanta, Georgia
www.atlantatech.edu                   Federal Code: 008543

**2-year public** community and technical college in very large city.
**Enrollment:** 3,558 undergrads, 62% part-time. 4,282 full-time freshmen.
**Selectivity:** Open admission; but selective for some programs.

**BASIC COSTS (2015-2016)**
**Tuition and fees:** $3,274; out-of-state residents $5,944.
**Per-credit charge:** $89; out-of-state residents $178.

**FINANCIAL AID PICTURE (2014-2015)**
**Students with need:** Need-based aid available for part-time students.

**FINANCIAL AID PROCEDURES**
**Forms required:** state aid form.
**Dates and Deadlines:** Priority date 3/1; no closing date. Applicants notified on a rolling basis starting 4/15.

**CONTACT**
Melody Hodge, Interim Director of Financial Aid
1560 Metropolitan Parkway, SW, Atlanta, GA 30310-4446
(404) 225-4400

## Augusta University
Augusta, Georgia
www.augusta.edu                        Federal Code: 001579

**4-year public** university in small city.
**Enrollment:** 4,776 undergrads.
**Selectivity:** Admits 50 to 75% of applicants. GED not accepted.

**BASIC COSTS (2015-2016)**
**Tuition and fees:** $10,418; out-of-state residents $29,084.
**Per-credit charge:** $283; out-of-state residents $905.
**Room only:** $4,600.

**FINANCIAL AID PICTURE (2015-2016)**
**Students with need:** 49% of average financial aid package awarded as scholarships/grants, 51% awarded as loans/jobs. Need-based aid available for part-time students.
**Students without need:** No-need awards available for academics, alumni affiliation, art, athletics, job skills, leadership, minority status, music/drama, religious affiliation, ROTC, state/district residency.

**FINANCIAL AID PROCEDURES**
**Forms required:** FAFSA.
**Dates and Deadlines:** Closing date 3/1. Applicants notified on a rolling basis starting 3/1; must reply within 2 week(s) of notification.

**CONTACT**
Brenda Burney, Director of Financial Aid
Benet House, 1120 15th Street, Augusta, GA 30912
(706) 737-1524

## Bainbridge State College
Bainbridge, Georgia
www.bainbridge.edu                     Federal Code: 011074

**2-year public** agricultural, community and technical college in large town.
**Enrollment:** 2,401 undergrads, 66% part-time. 182 full-time freshmen.

**BASIC COSTS (2015-2016)**
**Tuition and fees:** $3,772; out-of-state residents $11,366.
**Per-credit charge:** $91; out-of-state residents $344.

**FINANCIAL AID PICTURE**
**Students with need:** Need-based aid available for full-time and part-time students.
**Students without need:** This college awards aid only to students with need.

**FINANCIAL AID PROCEDURES**
**Forms required:** FAFSA, institutional form.
**Dates and Deadlines:** Priority date 6/1; closing date 8/1. Applicants notified on a rolling basis starting 6/1; must reply within 2 week(s) of notification.
**Transfers:** Priority date 6/11.

**CONTACT**
Sybil Smith, Director of Financial Aid
2500 East Shotwell Street, Bainbridge, GA 39818-0990
(229) 243-6920

## Bauder College
Atlanta, Georgia
www.bauder.edu                         Federal Code: 011574

**4-year for-profit** career college in very large city.
**Enrollment:** 751 undergrads.
**Selectivity:** Open admission; but selective for some programs.

**BASIC COSTS (2015-2016)**
**Additional info:** Bachelor's programs: Business Administration $70,125; Business Administration - Accounting $70,452; Business Administration - Fashion Merchandising $72,772; Criminal Justice $73,139. Associate programs: $34,275-$46,723. Certificate program: Medical Assisting $15,568. Diploma program: Practical Nursing $23,395.

**FINANCIAL AID PICTURE**
**Students with need:** Need-based aid available for full-time and part-time students. Work study available nights, weekends, and for part-time students.
**Students without need:** This college awards aid only to students with need.

## FINANCIAL AID PROCEDURES

**Forms required:** FAFSA, institutional form.

**Dates and Deadlines:** Applicants notified on a rolling basis starting 7/15.

## CONTACT

Rhonda King, Director of Financial Aid

384 Northyards Boulevard NW, Ste 190, Atlanta, GA 30313

(404) 237-7573

## Berry College

Mount Berry, Georgia

www.berry.edu

Federal Code: 001554

CSS Code: 5059

**4-year private** liberal arts college in large town.

**Enrollment:** 2,089 undergrads, 1% part-time. 575 full-time freshmen.

**Selectivity:** Admits 50 to 75% of applicants.

## BASIC COSTS (2015-2016)

**Tuition and fees:** $31,996.

**Per-credit charge:** $1,059.

**Room and board:** $11,190.

## FINANCIAL AID PICTURE (2015-2016)

**Students with need:** Out of 523 full-time freshmen who applied for aid, 410 were judged to have need. Of these, 410 received aid, and 120 had their full need met. Average financial aid package met 84% of need; average scholarship/grant was $22,244; average loan was $4,092. For part-time students, average financial aid package was $8,339.

**Students without need:** 165 full-time freshmen who did not demonstrate need for aid received scholarships/grants; average award was $13,562. No-need awards available for academics, art, leadership, minority status, music/drama, religious affiliation.

**Scholarships offered:** Georgia Tuition Equalization Grant; $700; for Georgia residents who attend in-state private institutions. HOPE Scholarship; $3,600 annually; for Georgia residents from eligible high schools with at least B average in college prep coursework.

**Additional info:** All students encouraged to work on-campus up to 16 hours per week.

## FINANCIAL AID PROCEDURES

**Forms required:** FAFSA, state aid form. Not require for domestic applicants.

**Dates and Deadlines:** Priority date 3/1; no closing date. Applicants notified on a rolling basis starting 2/15; must reply by 5/1.

**Transfers:** No deadline. Applicants notified on a rolling basis starting 11/15.

## CONTACT

Donna Childres, Director of Financial Aid

PO Box 490159, Mount Berry, GA 30149-0159

(706) 236-1714

## Beulah Heights University

Atlanta, Georgia

www.beulah.edu

Federal Code: 030763

**5-year private** university, Bible, business and seminary college in very large city, affiliated with nondenominational tradition.

**Enrollment:** 400 undergrads.

**Selectivity:** Open admission.

## BASIC COSTS (2015-2016)

**Tuition and fees:** $9,390.

**Per-credit charge:** $303.

**Room only:** $5,000.

**Additional info:** An additional fee of $100 is incurred for each on-line course in which a student is registered.

## FINANCIAL AID PICTURE

**Students with need:** Need-based aid available for full-time and part-time students. Work study available nights, weekends, and for part-time students.

## FINANCIAL AID PROCEDURES

**Forms required:** FAFSA.

**Dates and Deadlines:** Priority date 2/1; closing date 6/30. Applicants notified on a rolling basis.

**Transfers:** No deadline. Applicants notified on a rolling basis; must reply within 1 week(s) of notification.

## CONTACT

Robin Harrell, Director of Financial Aid

892 Berne Street SE, Atlanta, GA 30316

(404) 627-2681 ext. 124

## Brenau University

Gainesville, Georgia

www.brenau.edu

Federal Code: 001556

**4-year private** university and liberal arts college for women in large town.

**Enrollment:** 1,556 undergrads, 37% part-time. 191 full-time freshmen.

**Selectivity:** Admits 50 to 75% of applicants.

## BASIC COSTS (2015-2016)

**Tuition and fees:** $25,878.

**Per-credit charge:** $849.

**Room and board:** $11,998.

## FINANCIAL AID PICTURE

**Students with need:** Need-based aid available for full-time and part-time students. Work study available nights, weekends, and for part-time students.

**Students without need:** No-need awards available for academics, art, athletics, leadership, music/drama.

## FINANCIAL AID PROCEDURES

**Forms required:** FAFSA, state aid form.

**Dates and Deadlines:** Priority date 4/1; no closing date. Applicants notified on a rolling basis starting 3/1.

## CONTACT

Pam Barrett, Director of Financial Aid

500 Washington Street SE, Gainesville, GA 30501

(770) 534-6152

## Brewton-Parker College

Mount Vernon, Georgia

www.bpc.edu

Federal Code: 001557

**4-year private** liberal arts college in small town, affiliated with Southern Baptist Convention.

**Enrollment:** 432 undergrads.

## BASIC COSTS (2015-2016)

**Tuition and fees:** $16,180.

**Room and board:** $7,930.

## FINANCIAL AID PICTURE

**Students with need:** Need-based aid available for full-time and part-time students. Work study available nights, weekends, and for part-time students.

**Students without need:** No-need awards available for academics, athletics, leadership, religious affiliation, state/district residency.

**Scholarships offered:** Scholarships available for academic achievement and SAT scores for incoming freshman transfer students, ranging from $1,500-$3,000 per academic year, available for four years.

## FINANCIAL AID PROCEDURES

**Forms required:** FAFSA, state aid form.

**Dates and Deadlines:** Priority date 3/15; closing date 7/1. Applicants notified on a rolling basis starting 3/15; must reply within 2 week(s) of notification.

**CONTACT**

Chris Dooley, Director of Financial Aid

Brewton-Parker College # 2011, Mount Vernon, GA 30445

(912) 583-3215

## Carver College

Atlanta, Georgia

www.carver.edu                    Federal Code: 036353

**4-year private** Bible and liberal arts college in very large city.

**Enrollment:** 115 undergrads.

**BASIC COSTS (2015-2016)**

**Tuition and fees:** $9,860.

**Per-credit charge:** $390.

**Room and board:** $6,600.

**FINANCIAL AID PICTURE**

**Students with need:** Need-based aid available for full-time students.

**Students without need:** This college awards aid only to students with need.

**FINANCIAL AID PROCEDURES**

**Forms required:** FAFSA, institutional form.

**CONTACT**

Sheri Jefferson, Financial Aid Director

3870 Cascade Road, SW, Atlanta, GA 30331

(404) 527-4520 ext. 205

## Central Georgia Technical College

Warner Robins, Georgia

www.centralgatech.edu            Federal Code: 005763

**2-year public** community and technical college in small city.

**Enrollment:** 7,833 undergrads, 66% part-time.

**Selectivity:** Open admission; but selective for some programs.

**BASIC COSTS (2015-2016)**

**Tuition and fees:** $3,208; out-of-state residents $5,878.

**Per-credit charge:** $89; out-of-state residents $178.

**FINANCIAL AID PICTURE**

**Students with need:** Need-based aid available for full-time and part-time students.

**Students without need:** No-need awards available for academics, athletics, state/district residency.

**FINANCIAL AID PROCEDURES**

**Forms required:** FAFSA, state aid form, institutional form.

**Dates and Deadlines:** Closing date 7/15.

**CONTACT**

Jackie White, Director, Financial Aid

80 Cohen Walker Drive, Warner Robins, GA 31088

(478) 757-3422

## Chattahoochee Technical College

Marietta, Georgia

www.chattahoocheetech.edu        Federal Code: 005620

**2-year public** community and technical college in large city.

**Enrollment:** 9,819 undergrads.

**Selectivity:** Open admission; but selective for some programs.

**BASIC COSTS (2015-2016)**

**Tuition and fees:** $3,216; out-of-state residents $5,886.

**Per-credit charge:** $89; out-of-state residents $178.

**FINANCIAL AID PICTURE**

**Students with need:** Need-based aid available for full-time and part-time students. Work study available nights, weekends, and for part-time students.

**FINANCIAL AID PROCEDURES**

**Forms required:** FAFSA.

**Dates and Deadlines:** Applicants notified on a rolling basis.

**CONTACT**

Kristie Teasley, Director of Financial Aid

980 South Cobb Drive, SE, Marietta, GA 30060-3300

(770) 528-4531

## Clark Atlanta University

Atlanta, Georgia

www.cau.edu                        Federal Code: 001559

**4-year private** university in very large city, affiliated with United Methodist Church.

**Enrollment:** 2,741 undergrads, 4% part-time. 828 full-time freshmen.

**Selectivity:** Admits 50 to 75% of applicants.

**BASIC COSTS (2016-2017)**

**Tuition and fees:** $21,945.

**Per-credit charge:** $828.

**Room and board:** $10,478.

**FINANCIAL AID PICTURE (2015-2016)**

**Students with need:** Out of 788 full-time freshmen who applied for aid, 761 were judged to have need. Of these, 759 received aid, and 338 had their full need met. Average financial aid package met 39% of need; average scholarship/grant was $4,870; average loan was $2,072. For part-time students, average financial aid package was $4,179.

**Students without need:** 1 full-time freshmen who did not demonstrate need for aid received scholarships/grants; average award was $9,940. No-need awards available for academics, art, athletics, leadership, minority status, music/drama, religious affiliation, ROTC, state/district residency.

**Scholarships offered:** 1 full-time freshmen received athletic scholarships; average amount $10,005.

**FINANCIAL AID PROCEDURES**

**Forms required:** FAFSA, state aid form.

**Dates and Deadlines:** Priority date 3/1; no closing date. Applicants notified on a rolling basis starting 4/1.

**CONTACT**

James Stotts, Director of Financial Aid

223 James P. Brawley Drive, SW, Atlanta, GA 30314-4391

(404) 880-6018

## Clayton State University

Morrow, Georgia

www.clayton.edu                    Federal Code: 008976

**4-year public** university in small city.

**Enrollment:** 5,878 undergrads, 41% part-time. 434 full-time freshmen.

**Selectivity:** Admits less than 50% of applicants.

**BASIC COSTS (2015-2016)**

**Tuition and fees:** $6,312; out-of-state residents $19,132.

**Per-credit charge:** $161; out-of-state residents $589.27.

**Room and board:** $9,484.

## FINANCIAL AID PICTURE (2014-2015)

**Students with need:** Out of 412 full-time freshmen who applied for aid, 375 were judged to have need. Of these, 375 received aid, and 17 had their full need met. Average financial aid package met 52% of need; average scholarship/grant was $6,535; average loan was $3,402. For part-time students, average financial aid package was $8,177.

**Students without need:** 3 full-time freshmen who did not demonstrate need for aid received scholarships/grants; average award was $2,041. No-need awards available for academics, athletics, music/drama.

**Scholarships offered:** 26 full-time freshmen received athletic scholarships; average amount $3,750.

## FINANCIAL AID PROCEDURES

**Forms required:** FAFSA, state aid form.

**Dates and Deadlines:** Priority date 7/15; no closing date. Applicants notified on a rolling basis.

**Transfers:** No deadline. Applicants notified on a rolling basis.

## CONTACT

Patricia Barton, Director of Financial Aid
2000 Clayton State Boulevard, Morrow, GA 30260-0285
(678) 466-4185

## College of Coastal Georgia
Brunswick, Georgia
www.ccga.edu
Federal Code: 001558

**4-year public** liberal arts college in large town.
**Enrollment:** 3,039 undergrads, 36% part-time. 620 full-time freshmen.
**Selectivity:** Admits 50 to 75% of applicants.

### BASIC COSTS (2015-2016)
**Tuition and fees:** $4,434; out-of-state residents $12,692.
**Per-credit charge:** $103; out-of-state residents $378.
**Room and board:** $9,416.

### FINANCIAL AID PICTURE
**Students with need:** Need-based aid available for full-time and part-time students. Work study available nights.
**Students without need:** No-need awards available for academics, alumni affiliation, athletics.

### FINANCIAL AID PROCEDURES
**Forms required:** FAFSA, state aid form.
**Dates and Deadlines:** Priority date 6/1; no closing date. Applicants notified on a rolling basis starting 4/1.
**Transfers:** No deadline. Applicants notified on a rolling basis.

### CONTACT
Terral Harris, Director of Financial Aid
One College Drive, Brunswick, GA 31520
(912) 279-5722

## Columbus State University
Columbus, Georgia
www.columbusstate.edu
Federal Code: 001561

**4-year public** university and liberal arts college in small city.
**Enrollment:** 6,711 undergrads, 27% part-time. 939 full-time freshmen.
**Selectivity:** Admits 50 to 75% of applicants. GED not accepted.

### BASIC COSTS (2015-2016)
**Tuition and fees:** $7,056; out-of-state residents $20,274.
**Per-credit charge:** $174; out-of-state residents $615.
**Room and board:** $9,374.

## FINANCIAL AID PICTURE (2015-2016)

**Students with need:** Out of 861 full-time freshmen who applied for aid, 691 were judged to have need. Of these, 687 received aid, and 122 had their full need met. Average financial aid package met 70% of need; average scholarship/grant was $4,994; average loan was $3,483. For part-time students, average financial aid package was $7,275.

**Students without need:** 42 full-time freshmen who did not demonstrate need for aid received scholarships/grants; average award was $1,776. No-need awards available for academics, alumni affiliation, art, athletics, job skills, leadership, minority status, music/drama, ROTC.

**Scholarships offered:** 43 full-time freshmen received athletic scholarships; average amount $5,178.

## FINANCIAL AID PROCEDURES

**Forms required:** FAFSA.

**Dates and Deadlines:** Priority date 5/1; no closing date. Applicants notified on a rolling basis starting 5/15; must reply within 4 week(s) of notification.

## CONTACT

Russ Romandini, Director of Financial Aid
4225 University Avenue, Columbus, GA 31907-5645
(706) 507-8807

## Columbus Technical College
Columbus, Georgia
www.columbustech.edu
Federal Code: 005624

**2-year public** technical college in small city.
**Enrollment:** 3,739 undergrads.
**Selectivity:** Open admission; but selective for some programs.

### BASIC COSTS (2015-2016)
**Tuition and fees:** $3,228; out-of-state residents $5,898.
**Per-credit charge:** $89; out-of-state residents $178.

### FINANCIAL AID PICTURE
**Students with need:** Need-based aid available for full-time and part-time students.

### FINANCIAL AID PROCEDURES
**Forms required:** FAFSA.
**Dates and Deadlines:** Applicants notified on a rolling basis.

### CONTACT
Debbie Henshaw, Director of Financial Aid
928 Manchester Expressway, Columbus, GA 31904-6572
(706) 649-1859

## Covenant College
Lookout Mountain, Georgia
www.covenant.edu
Federal Code: 003484

**4-year private** liberal arts college in small city, affiliated with Presbyterian Church in America (PCA).
**Enrollment:** 1,007 undergrads, 1% part-time. 265 full-time freshmen.
**Selectivity:** Admits over 75% of applicants.

### BASIC COSTS (2015-2016)
**Tuition and fees:** $31,320.
**Room and board:** $9,170.

### FINANCIAL AID PICTURE (2014-2015)
**Students with need:** Out of 215 full-time freshmen who applied for aid, 172 were judged to have need. Of these, 172 received aid, and 53 had their full need met. Average financial aid package met 80% of need; average scholarship/grant was $18,152; average loan was $5,915. For part-time students, average financial aid package was $10,487.

**Students without need:** 76 full-time freshmen who did not demonstrate need for aid received scholarships/grants; average award was $12,064. No-need awards available for academics, alumni affiliation, art, job skills, leadership, minority status, music/drama, religious affiliation, state/district residency.

**Scholarships offered:** Maclellan Scholars Program; minimum SAT 1200 (exclusive of Writing) or ACT 27, high school GPA 3.3. Presidential Scholarship; based on GPA, leadership, Christian commitment, extracurricular activities, work experience, references.

### FINANCIAL AID PROCEDURES
**Forms required:** FAFSA, state aid form.
**Dates and Deadlines:** Applicants notified on a rolling basis starting 2/1; must reply within 3 week(s) of notification.
**Transfers:** Some scholarships may be depleted for mid-semester transfers, such as athletic, diversity or music.

### CONTACT
Brenda Rapier, Director of Financial Aid
14049 Scenic Highway, Lookout Mountain, GA 30750
(706) 419-1126

## Dalton State College
Dalton, Georgia
www.daltonstate.edu    Federal Code: 003956

**4-year public** liberal arts and teachers college in large town.
**Enrollment:** 4,671 undergrads. 928 full-time freshmen.

### BASIC COSTS (2015-2016)
**Tuition and fees:** $4,056; out-of-state residents $12,314.
**Per-credit charge:** $103; out-of-state residents $378.
**Room only:** $4,500.

### FINANCIAL AID PICTURE (2014-2015)
**Students with need:** Out of 770 full-time freshmen who applied for aid, 669 were judged to have need. Of these, 582 received aid, and 349 had their full need met. Average financial aid package met 90% of need; average scholarship/grant was $3,500; average loan was $2,550. Need-based aid available for part-time students.
**Students without need:** No-need awards available for academics, leadership, minority status, state/district residency.

### FINANCIAL AID PROCEDURES
**Forms required:** FAFSA.
**Dates and Deadlines:** Applicants notified on a rolling basis starting 4/1.
**Transfers:** No deadline. Applicants notified on a rolling basis.

### CONTACT
Carol Jones, Director of Student Financial Aid
650 College Drive, Dalton, GA 30720
(706) 272-4545

## Darton College
Albany, Georgia
www.darton.edu    Federal Code: 001543

**2-year public** community college in small city.
**Enrollment:** 5,990 undergrads.
**Selectivity:** Open admission; but selective for some programs.

### BASIC COSTS (2015-2016)
**Tuition and fees:** $3,940; out-of-state residents $11,534.
**Per-credit charge:** $91; out-of-state residents $344.
**Room and board:** $9,770.

### FINANCIAL AID PICTURE
**Students with need:** Need-based aid available for full-time and part-time students. Work study available nights, weekends, and for part-time students.
**Students without need:** No-need awards available for academics, alumni affiliation, art, athletics, music/drama, state/district residency.
**Additional info:** Auditions, portfolios, essays, extracurricular activities impact scholarship decisions.

### FINANCIAL AID PROCEDURES
**Forms required:** FAFSA, state aid form, institutional form.
**Dates and Deadlines:** Applicants notified on a rolling basis; must reply within 3 week(s) of notification.

### CONTACT
Haley Hooks, Director of Financial Aid
2400 Gillionville Road, Albany, GA 31707-3098
(229) 317-6746

## DeVry University: Decatur
Decatur, Georgia
www.devry.edu    Federal Code: 009224

**4-year for-profit** university in large town.
**Enrollment:** 1,684 undergrads.

### BASIC COSTS (2015-2016)
**Tuition and fees:** $17,132.
**Per-credit charge:** $609.

### FINANCIAL AID PICTURE
**Students with need:** Need-based aid available for full-time and part-time students.
**Students without need:** This college awards aid only to students with need.

### FINANCIAL AID PROCEDURES
**Forms required:** FAFSA.
**Dates and Deadlines:** Applicants notified on a rolling basis.

### CONTACT
One West Court Square, Suite 100, Decatur, GA 30030-2556
(404) 292-7900

## East Georgia State College
Swainsboro, Georgia
www.ega.edu    Federal Code: 010997

**2-year public** community and junior college in small town.
**Enrollment:** 3,001 undergrads.
**Selectivity:** Admits less than 50% of applicants.

### BASIC COSTS (2015-2016)
**Tuition and fees:** $3,612; out-of-state residents $12,092.
**Per-credit charge:** $89; out-of-state residents $344.
**Room and board:** $7,542.

### FINANCIAL AID PICTURE
**Students with need:** Need-based aid available for full-time and part-time students.
**Students without need:** No-need awards available for academics, leadership, state/district residency.

### FINANCIAL AID PROCEDURES
**Forms required:** FAFSA, state aid form, institutional form.
**Dates and Deadlines:** Priority date 6/1; no closing date. Applicants notified on a rolling basis starting 6/1; must reply within 2 week(s) of notification.
**Transfers:** Students must provide EGSC with final official transcripts from all institutions previously attended prior to aid being awarded.

## CONTACT

Karen Jones, Associate VP of Enrollment Management
131 College Circle, Swainsboro, GA 30401-2699
(478) 289-2012

## Emmanuel College

Franklin Springs, Georgia
www.ec.edu                    Federal Code: 001563

**4-year private** liberal arts and teachers college in rural community, affiliated with Pentecostal Holiness Church.
**Enrollment:** 762 undergrads, 3% part-time. 232 full-time freshmen.
**Selectivity:** Admits less than 50% of applicants.

### BASIC COSTS (2015-2016)
**Tuition and fees:** $18,870.
**Per-credit charge:** $775.
**Room and board:** $7,200.

### FINANCIAL AID PICTURE (2015-2016)
**Students with need:** 59% of average financial aid package awarded as scholarships/grants, 41% awarded as loans/jobs. Need-based aid available for part-time students. Work study available nights, weekends, and for part-time students.
**Students without need:** No-need awards available for academics, art, athletics, job skills, leadership, music/drama, religious affiliation, state/district residency.

### FINANCIAL AID PROCEDURES
**Forms required:** FAFSA, state aid form, institutional form.
**Dates and Deadlines:** Priority date 5/1; closing date 6/15. Applicants notified on a rolling basis starting 3/1; must reply within 2 week(s) of notification.
**Transfers:** Applicants notified on a rolling basis starting 3/1; must reply within 2 week(s) of notification.

### CONTACT
Niki Stinson, Director of Financial Aid
181 Spring Street, Franklin Springs, GA 30639-0129
(706) 245-2843

## Emory University

Atlanta, Georgia                Federal Code: 001564
www.emory.edu                   CSS Code: 5187

**4-year private** university in very large city, affiliated with United Methodist Church.
**Enrollment:** 6,770 undergrads, 1% part-time. 1,357 full-time freshmen.
**Selectivity:** Admits less than 50% of applicants. GED not accepted.

### BASIC COSTS (2016-2017)
**Tuition and fees:** $47,954.
**Per-credit charge:** $1,971.
**Room and board:** $13,486.

### FINANCIAL AID PICTURE
**Students with need:** Need-based aid available for full-time and part-time students. Work study available nights, weekends, and for part-time students.
**Students without need:** No-need awards available for academics, art, leadership, music/drama, religious affiliation, state/district residency.
**Scholarships offered:** Emory and Goizueta Scholars programs: two-thirds tuition to full cost; based on academic merit of incoming first-year students, requires nomination by appropriate high school official by November 1 of senior year; renewable for four years of undergraduate study.
**Additional info:** Loan replacement grant and loan cap program available to students from families with total annual incomes of $100,000 or less who demonstrate need for financial aid.

### FINANCIAL AID PROCEDURES
**Forms required:** FAFSA, CSS PROFILE.
**Dates and Deadlines:** Priority date 2/15; closing date 3/1. Applicants notified by 4/1; must reply by 5/1.
**Transfers:** No deadline. Applicants notified on a rolling basis starting 5/1. Limitations on aid available to transfer students. Financial aid filing deadline for transfers is 30 days following transfer student admission date.

### CONTACT
John Leach, Director of Financial Aid
1390 Oxford Road NE, 3rd Floor, Atlanta, GA 30322
(800) 727-6039

## Fort Valley State University

Fort Valley, Georgia
www.fvsu.edu                    Federal Code: 001566

**4-year public** liberal arts and teachers college in small town.
**Enrollment:** 3,250 undergrads.

### BASIC COSTS (2015-2016)
**Tuition and fees:** $6,566; out-of-state residents $19,386.
**Per-credit charge:** $162; out-of-state residents $590.
**Room and board:** $7,778.

### FINANCIAL AID PICTURE
**Students with need:** Need-based aid available for full-time and part-time students.
**Students without need:** No-need awards available for academics, athletics, music/drama.
**Additional info:** Financial aid transcripts must be received from former institutions before application for aid will be considered complete and reviewed for awards.

### FINANCIAL AID PROCEDURES
**Forms required:** FAFSA.
**Dates and Deadlines:** Priority date 3/1; no closing date. Applicants notified on a rolling basis starting 3/15; must reply within 1 week(s) of notification.

### CONTACT
Eula Solomon, Director of Financial Aid
1005 State University Drive, Fort Valley, GA 31030-4313
(478) 825-6351

## Georgia College and State University

Milledgeville, Georgia          Federal Code: 001602
www.gcsu.edu                    CSS Code: 5252

**4-year public** university and liberal arts college in large town.
**Enrollment:** 5,935 undergrads, 7% part-time. 1,463 full-time freshmen.
**Selectivity:** Admits over 75% of applicants.

### BASIC COSTS (2015-2016)
**Tuition and fees:** $9,170; out-of-state residents $27,518.
**Room and board:** $11,612.

### FINANCIAL AID PICTURE (2014-2015)
**Students with need:** Out of 1,266 full-time freshmen who applied for aid, 767 were judged to have need. Of these, 761 received aid. Average financial aid package met 25% of need; average scholarship/grant was $4,544; average loan was $3,302. For part-time students, average financial aid package was $6,181.
**Students without need:** 25 full-time freshmen who did not demonstrate need for aid received scholarships/grants; average award was $1,683. No-need awards available for academics, alumni affiliation, art, athletics, leadership, music/drama, state/district residency.

**Scholarships offered: *Merit:*** Trustee Scholarships: $6,000 per year for four years. Presidential Scholarships: $4,000 per year for four years. Vincent Scholarship: $3,000 per year. Scholarships based on superior academic accomplishments, include stipends to be used toward study abroad programs. ***Athletic:*** 26 full-time freshmen received athletic scholarships; average amount $4,002.

**FINANCIAL AID PROCEDURES**
**Forms required:** FAFSA, CSS PROFILE.
**Dates and Deadlines:** Priority date 3/1; no closing date. Applicants notified on a rolling basis starting 3/1.
**Transfers:** Filing priority date of March 1 for programs with limited funding . Priority date of July 31 in order to have aid funds available to meet payment deadline.

**CONTACT**
Cathy Crawley, Director of Financial Aid
Campus Box 23, Milledgeville, GA 31061-0490
(478) 445-5149

## Georgia Gwinnett College
Lawrenceville, Georgia
www.ggc.edu

**4-year public** liberal arts college in large town.
**Enrollment:** 10,998 undergrads, 30% part-time. 2,077 full-time freshmen.
**Selectivity:** Admits over 75% of applicants.

**BASIC COSTS (2015-2016)**
**Tuition and fees:** $5,648; out-of-state residents $16,152.
**Per-credit charge:** $118; out-of-state residents $441.
**Room and board:** $12,300.

**FINANCIAL AID PICTURE (2015-2016)**
**Students with need:** Out of 1,904 full-time freshmen who applied for aid, 1,646 were judged to have need. Of these, 1,603 received aid, and 413 had their full need met. Average financial aid package met 35% of need; average scholarship/grant was $4,983; average loan was $3,350. For part-time students, average financial aid package was $6,488.
**Students without need:** No-need awards available for academics, athletics.
**Scholarships offered:** 15 full-time freshmen received athletic scholarships; average amount $6,372.

**FINANCIAL AID PROCEDURES**
**Forms required:** FAFSA.
**Dates and Deadlines:** Priority date 7/1; no closing date. Applicants notified on a rolling basis starting 5/15.
**Transfers:** No deadline. Applicants notified on a rolling basis.

**CONTACT**
Kimberly Jordan, Director of Financial Aid
1000 University Center Lane, Lawrenceville, GA 30043
(678) 407-5701

## Georgia Highlands College
Rome, Georgia
www.highlands.edu          Federal Code: 009507

**2-year public** community and liberal arts college in large town.
**Enrollment:** 5,748 undergrads, 53% part-time. 950 full-time freshmen.

**BASIC COSTS (2015-2016)**
**Tuition and fees:** $3,660; out-of-state residents $12,188.
**Per-credit charge:** $90.87; out-of-state residents $344.

**FINANCIAL AID PICTURE (2014-2015)**
**Students with need:** 84% of average financial aid package awarded as scholarships/grants, 16% awarded as loans/jobs. Need-based aid available for part-time students. Work study available nights.
**Students without need:** No-need awards available for academics, art.
**Additional info:** All Federal Work Study students must be Pell eligible and taking a minimum of 6 credit hours.

**FINANCIAL AID PROCEDURES**
**Forms required:** FAFSA, state aid form.
**Dates and Deadlines:** Priority date 7/1; closing date 4/1. Applicants notified on a rolling basis starting 4/1; must reply within 2 week(s) of notification.
**Transfers:** No deadline. Applicants notified on a rolling basis starting 5/1; must reply within 2 week(s) of notification. Transfer students are only eligible for aid not used at previous institution in the same aid year and/or the maximum eligibility allowed for a given term. Transfer students cannot receive Federal Aid at two institutions during the same term.

**CONTACT**
Megan Simpson, Director of Financial Aid
3175 Cedartown Highway, Rome, GA 30161
(706) 295-6311

## Georgia Institute of Technology
Atlanta, Georgia          Federal Code: 001569
www.gatech.edu          CSS Code: 5248

**4-year public** university in large city.
**Enrollment:** 14,460 undergrads, 6% part-time. 2,805 full-time freshmen.
**Selectivity:** Admits less than 50% of applicants. GED not accepted.

**BASIC COSTS (2015-2016)**
**Tuition and fees:** $12,204; out-of-state residents $32,396.
**Room and board:** $10,716.

**FINANCIAL AID PICTURE (2014-2015)**
**Students with need:** Out of 1,634 full-time freshmen who applied for aid, 806 were judged to have need. Of these, 783 received aid, and 286 had their full need met. Average financial aid package met 84% of need; average scholarship/grant was $7,953; average loan was $3,788. For part-time students, average financial aid package was $7,313.
**Students without need:** 570 full-time freshmen who did not demonstrate need for aid received scholarships/grants; average award was $6,694. No-need awards available for academics, athletics, leadership, music/drama, ROTC, state/district residency.
**Scholarships offered: *Merit:*** Prospective students may apply for a President's Scholarship covering all tuition and fees, including meals and standard room. For in-state students, part of this is expected to be the Zell Miller/HOPE Scholarship provided by the State of Georgia. For out-of-state students, this includes a tuition waiver, which reduces the cost of tuition to the same as that of an in-state student. When added to the other awards the student has received (HOPE/Zell Miller Scholarship, National Merit award, etc.) this will be equal to the official total cost of attendance, as determined by the Office of Scholarships and Financial Aid. ***Athletic:*** 38 full-time freshmen received athletic scholarships; average amount $16,340.

**FINANCIAL AID PROCEDURES**
**Forms required:** FAFSA, institutional form. CSS PROFILE required for domestic, first-time applicants.
**Dates and Deadlines:** Priority date 2/15; closing date 2/15. Applicants notified by 4/15; must reply by 5/1.
**Transfers:** Priority date 5/1; closing date 5/1. Applicants notified by 6/15. Student must be officially admitted, all final transcripts must be received, and transcripts must be articulated.

**CONTACT**
Marie Mons, Director of Student Financial Planning and Services
Office of Undergraduate Admissions, Atlanta, GA 30332-0320
(404) 894-4160

## Georgia Military College
Milledgeville, Georgia
www.gmc.edu                    Federal Code: 001571

**2-year public** community and military college in large town.
**Enrollment:** 6,840 undergrads.
**Selectivity:** Open admission; but selective for some programs.

### BASIC COSTS (2015-2016)
**Tuition and fees:** $5,453; out-of-state residents $5,453.
**Per-credit charge:** $122.

### FINANCIAL AID PICTURE
**Students with need:** Need-based aid available for full-time and part-time students. Work study available nights.
**Students without need:** No-need awards available for athletics, leadership, ROTC, state/district residency.
**Additional info:** Institutional aid offered to those enrolled in Cadet Corps who reside on campus.

### FINANCIAL AID PROCEDURES
**Forms required:** FAFSA, state aid form.
**Dates and Deadlines:** Applicants notified on a rolling basis.
**Transfers:** No deadline. Applicants notified on a rolling basis. Transfer students must submit financial aid transcript from any prior post-secondary institutions.

### CONTACT
Alisa Stephens, Director of Financial Aid
201 East Greene Street, Milledgeville, GA 31061
(478) 387-4842

## Georgia Perimeter College
Clarkston, Georgia
www.gpc.edu                    Federal Code: 001562

**2-year public** junior and liberal arts college in very large city.
**Enrollment:** 18,678 undergrads, 62% part-time. 2,090 full-time freshmen.
**Selectivity:** Admits 50 to 75% of applicants.

### BASIC COSTS (2015-2016)
**Tuition and fees:** $3,758; out-of-state residents $11,352.
**Per-credit charge:** $91; out-of-state residents $344.

### FINANCIAL AID PICTURE (2014-2015)
**Students with need:** Out of 1,686 full-time freshmen who applied for aid, 1,543 were judged to have need. Of these, 1,543 received aid, and 35 had their full need met. Average financial aid package met 52% of need; average scholarship/grant was $4,587; average loan was $2,996. For part-time students, average financial aid package was $4,763.
**Students without need:** 60 full-time freshmen who did not demonstrate need for aid received scholarships/grants; average award was $1,364. No-need awards available for academics, alumni affiliation, art, athletics, job skills, leadership, minority status, music/drama, religious affiliation, ROTC, state/district residency.
**Scholarships offered:** 44 full-time freshmen received athletic scholarships; average amount $5,680.

### FINANCIAL AID PROCEDURES
**Forms required:** FAFSA.
**Dates and Deadlines:** Closing date 6/1. Applicants notified on a rolling basis; must reply within 3 week(s) of notification.
**Transfers:** Priority date 6/1; no deadline.

### CONTACT
Ron Stark, Executive Vice President for Administrative and Financial Affairs
555 North Indian Creek Drive, Clarkston, GA 30021-2361
(678) 891-3535

## Georgia Piedmont Technical College
Clarkston, Georgia
www.gptc.edu                   Federal Code: 016582

**2-year public** technical college in large city.
**Enrollment:** 4,050 undergrads.
**Selectivity:** Open admission; but selective for some programs.

### BASIC COSTS (2015-2016)
**Tuition and fees:** $3,374; out-of-state residents $6,044.
**Per-credit charge:** $89; out-of-state residents $178.

### FINANCIAL AID PICTURE
**Students with need:** Need-based aid available for full-time and part-time students. Work study available nights, weekends, and for part-time students.
**Students without need:** No-need awards available for academics, minority status.

### FINANCIAL AID PROCEDURES
**Forms required:** FAFSA.
**Dates and Deadlines:** Closing date 8/20. Applicants notified on a rolling basis.
**Transfers:** No deadline.

### CONTACT
Lakisha Sanders, Assistant Vice President of Financial Aid
495 North Indian Creek Drive, Clarkston, GA 30021-2397
(404) 297-9522 ext. 1160

## Georgia Southern University
Statesboro, Georgia
www.georgiasouthern.edu        Federal Code: 001572

**4-year public** university in large town.
**Enrollment:** 17,173 undergrads, 8% part-time. 3,476 full-time freshmen.
**Selectivity:** Admits 50 to 75% of applicants. GED not accepted.

### BASIC COSTS (2015-2016)
**Tuition and fees:** $7,318; out-of-state residents $20,536.
**Per-credit charge:** $174; out-of-state residents $615.
**Room and board:** $9,800.

### FINANCIAL AID PICTURE (2014-2015)
**Students with need:** Out of 3,270 full-time freshmen who applied for aid, 2,306 were judged to have need. Of these, 2,255 received aid, and 290 had their full need met. Average financial aid package met 55% of need; average scholarship/grant was $7,098; average loan was $4,183. For part-time students, average financial aid package was $6,541.
**Students without need:** 109 full-time freshmen who did not demonstrate need for aid received scholarships/grants; average award was $1,831. No-need awards available for academics, alumni affiliation, art, athletics, leadership, minority status, music/drama, ROTC, state/district residency.
**Scholarships offered:** *Merit:* 1906 Scholars; tuition for 4 years; 10 awards annually. UHP Scholarships; $1,500 for 4 years; 10 awards annually. Foundation Scholars; $1,500 for 4 years; 10 awards annually. Miscellaneous renewable and non-renewable awards; ranging from $500-$5,000. *Athletic:* 33 full-time freshmen received athletic scholarships; average amount $12,773.
**Additional info:** Majority of available scholarships are need-blind.

### FINANCIAL AID PROCEDURES
**Forms required:** FAFSA.
**Dates and Deadlines:** Priority date 4/20; no closing date. Applicants notified on a rolling basis starting 4/20.
**Transfers:** No deadline. Applicants notified on a rolling basis starting 4/20.

### CONTACT
Connie Murphey, Director of Financial Aid
PO Box 8024, Statesboro, GA 30458
(912) 478-5413

PART III: FINANCIAL AID COLLEGE BY COLLEGE

## Georgia Southwestern State University
Americus, Georgia
www.gsw.edu                    Federal Code: 001573

**4-year public** university and liberal arts college in large town.
**Enrollment:** 2,305 undergrads, 29% part-time. 374 full-time freshmen.
**Selectivity:** Admits 50 to 75% of applicants.

### BASIC COSTS (2015-2016)
**Tuition and fees:** $6,234; out-of-state residents $19,054.
**Per-credit charge:** $162; out-of-state residents $589.
**Room and board:** $7,390.

### FINANCIAL AID PICTURE (2015-2016)
**Students with need:** Out of 350 full-time freshmen who applied for aid, 272 were judged to have need. Of these, 270 received aid, and 36 had their full need met. Average financial aid package met 58% of need; average scholarship/grant was $4,941; average loan was $3,435. For part-time students, average financial aid package was $7,375.
**Students without need:** 38 full-time freshmen who did not demonstrate need for aid received scholarships/grants; average award was $2,253. No-need awards available for academics, alumni affiliation, art, athletics, leadership, music/drama, state/district residency.
**Scholarships offered:** 9 full-time freshmen received athletic scholarships; average amount $2,234.

### FINANCIAL AID PROCEDURES
**Forms required:** FAFSA.
**Dates and Deadlines:** Priority date 4/15; closing date 6/15. Applicants notified on a rolling basis starting 5/1; must reply within 8 week(s) of notification.

### CONTACT
Angela Bryant, Director of Financial Aid
800 Georgia Southwestern State University Drive, Americus, GA 31709-9957
(229) 928-1378

## Georgia State University
Atlanta, Georgia
www.gsu.edu                    Federal Code: 001574

**4-year public** university in very large city.
**Enrollment:** 24,452 undergrads, 23% part-time. 3,641 full-time freshmen.
**Selectivity:** Admits 50 to 75% of applicants. GED not accepted.

### BASIC COSTS (2015-2016)
**Tuition and fees:** $10,686; out-of-state residents $28,896.
**Per-credit charge:** $286; out-of-state residents $893.
**Room and board:** $10,728.

### FINANCIAL AID PICTURE (2014-2015)
**Students with need:** Out of 3,494 full-time freshmen who applied for aid, 2,985 were judged to have need. Of these, 2,937 received aid, and 259 had their full need met. Average financial aid package met 62% of need; average scholarship/grant was $5,089. For part-time students, average financial aid package was $7,597.
**Students without need:** No-need awards available for academics, alumni affiliation, art, athletics, job skills, leadership, minority status, music/drama, religious affiliation, ROTC, state/district residency.

### FINANCIAL AID PROCEDURES
**Forms required:** FAFSA.
**Dates and Deadlines:** Closing date 4/1. Applicants notified on a rolling basis starting 3/1.
**Transfers:** Applicants notified on a rolling basis starting 3/1; must reply by 11/1.

### CONTACT
Louis Scott, Director of Student Financial Aid
Box 4009, Atlanta, GA 30302-4009
(404) 413-2400

## Gordon State College
Barnesville, Georgia
www.gordonstate.edu                    Federal Code: 001575

**2-year public** liberal arts college in small town.
**Enrollment:** 4,084 undergrads.
**Selectivity:** Admits 50 to 75% of applicants.

### BASIC COSTS (2015-2016)
**Tuition and fees:** $4,164; out-of-state residents $12,422.
**Per-credit charge:** $103; out-of-state residents $378.
**Room and board:** $6,210.

### FINANCIAL AID PICTURE (2014-2015)
**Students with need:** Need-based aid available for part-time students. Work study available nights, weekends, and for part-time students.
**Students without need:** No-need awards available for academics, athletics, music/drama, state/district residency.

### FINANCIAL AID PROCEDURES
**Forms required:** FAFSA, state aid form.
**Dates and Deadlines:** Priority date 5/1; closing date 6/1. Applicants notified on a rolling basis starting 4/1.

### CONTACT
Jody DeFore, Director of Financial Aid
419 College Drive, Barnesville, GA 30204
(678) 359-5990

## Gupton Jones College of Funeral Service
Decatur, Georgia
www.gupton-jones.edu                    Federal Code: 010771

**2-year private** technical college in very large city.
**Enrollment:** 212 undergrads.
**Selectivity:** Open admission.

### BASIC COSTS (2015-2016)
**Tuition and fees:** $11,100.
**Per-credit charge:** $250.
**Additional info:** Books are included in tuition.

### FINANCIAL AID PICTURE
**Students with need:** Need-based aid available for full-time and part-time students.
**Students without need:** This college awards aid only to students with need.

### FINANCIAL AID PROCEDURES
**Forms required:** FAFSA.
**Dates and Deadlines:** Applicants notified on a rolling basis.

### CONTACT
James Hinz, Dean
5141 Snapfinger Woods Drive, Decatur, GA 30035
(770) 593-2257

## Gwinnett College

Lilburn, Georgia
www.gwinnettcollege.edu     Federal Code: 025830

**2-year for-profit** junior and career college in large city.
**Enrollment:** 352 undergrads.
**Selectivity:** Open admission; but selective for some programs.

### BASIC COSTS (2015-2016)
**Tuition and fees:** $9,850.

### FINANCIAL AID PICTURE
**Students with need:** Need-based aid available for full-time and part-time students.

### FINANCIAL AID PROCEDURES
**Forms required:** FAFSA.
**Dates and Deadlines:** Applicants notified on a rolling basis.

### CONTACT
James Davidson, Director of Financial Aid
4230 Highway 29, Lilburn, GA 30047
(770) 381-7200

## Gwinnett Technical College

Lawrenceville, Georgia
www.gwinnetttech.edu

**2-year public** technical college in large town.
**Enrollment:** 7,234 undergrads.
**Selectivity:** Open admission; but selective for some programs.

### BASIC COSTS (2015-2016)
**Tuition and fees:** $3,238; out-of-state residents $5,908.
**Per-credit charge:** $89; out-of-state residents $178.

### FINANCIAL AID PICTURE
**Students with need:** Need-based aid available for full-time and part-time students.

### FINANCIAL AID PROCEDURES
**Forms required:** FAFSA.
**Dates and Deadlines:** Closing date 7/8.

### CONTACT
Karen Laverdiere
5150 Sugarloaf Parkway, Lawrenceville, GA 30043-5702

## Herzing University: Atlanta

Atlanta, Georgia
www.herzing.edu     Federal Code: 014030

**3-year for-profit** business and technical college in very large city.
**Enrollment:** 393 undergrads.

### BASIC COSTS (2015-2016)
**Additional info:** Tuition for diploma programs: $6,450-$8,555 per semester. Associate programs: $12,900 per year; Bachelor's programs: $12,900-$19,320 per year.

### FINANCIAL AID PICTURE
**Students with need:** Need-based aid available for full-time and part-time students. Work study available nights.
**Students without need:** No-need awards available for academics.

### FINANCIAL AID PROCEDURES
**Forms required:** FAFSA, institutional form.
**Dates and Deadlines:** Applicants notified on a rolling basis.

### CONTACT
Stephanie Gunby, Director of Financial Aid
3393 Peachtree Road NE, Suite 1003, Atlanta, GA 30326
(404) 816-4533

## Kennesaw State University

Kennesaw, Georgia
www.kennesaw.edu     Federal Code: 001577

**4-year public** university in large town.
**Enrollment:** 29,842 undergrads, 24% part-time. 4,741 full-time freshmen.
**Selectivity:** Admits 50 to 75% of applicants. GED not accepted.

### BASIC COSTS (2015-2016)
**Tuition and fees:** $7,326; out-of-state residents $20,782.
**Per-credit charge:** $178; out-of-state residents $626.
**Room and board:** $10,210.

### FINANCIAL AID PICTURE
**Students with need:** Need-based aid available for full-time and part-time students. Work study available nights.
**Students without need:** No-need awards available for academics, alumni affiliation, art, athletics, job skills, leadership, minority status, music/drama, ROTC, state/district residency.

### FINANCIAL AID PROCEDURES
**Forms required:** FAFSA.
**Dates and Deadlines:** Priority date 4/1; no closing date. Applicants notified on a rolling basis starting 4/1.
**Transfers:** No deadline. Applicants notified on a rolling basis starting 4/1.

### CONTACT
Ron Day, Director of Financial Aid
3391 Town Point Drive, Kennesaw, GA 30144
(770) 423-6074

## LaGrange College

LaGrange, Georgia
www.lagrange.edu     Federal Code: 001578

**4-year private** liberal arts college in large town, affiliated with United Methodist Church.
**Enrollment:** 905 undergrads, 5% part-time. 233 full-time freshmen.
**Selectivity:** Admits 50 to 75% of applicants.

### BASIC COSTS (2015-2016)
**Tuition and fees:** $27,510.
**Per-credit charge:** $1,120.
**Room and board:** $11,240.

### FINANCIAL AID PICTURE (2014-2015)
**Students with need:** Out of 225 full-time freshmen who applied for aid, 213 were judged to have need. Of these, 213 received aid, and 70 had their full need met. Average financial aid package met 75% of need; average scholarship/grant was $15,282; average loan was $3,274. For part-time students, average financial aid package was $7,626.
**Students without need:** 12 full-time freshmen who did not demonstrate need for aid received scholarships/grants; average award was $10,067. No-need awards available for academics, art, leadership, music/drama, religious affiliation, state/district residency.
**Scholarships offered:** Presidential: tuition, room and board; competitive. Fellows: $12,500 per year; competitive. Founders: $10,000 per year; competitive. Hilltop: $7,500 per year. Gateway: $5,500 per year.

### FINANCIAL AID PROCEDURES
**Forms required:** FAFSA, state aid form.

**Dates and Deadlines:** Priority date 3/1; no closing date. Applicants notified on a rolling basis starting 3/15; must reply within 4 week(s) of notification.
**Transfers:** No deadline. Applicants notified on a rolling basis starting 3/1; must reply within 3 week(s) of notification.

**CONTACT**
Michelle Reeves, Director of Financial Aid
601 Broad Street, LaGrange, GA 30240-2999
(706) 880-8241

## Life University
Marietta, Georgia
www.life.edu                          Federal Code: 014170

**4-year private** university in very large city.
**Enrollment:** 718 undergrads, 27% part-time. 93 full-time freshmen.
**Selectivity:** Admits 50 to 75% of applicants.

**BASIC COSTS (2015-2016)**
**Tuition and fees:** $10,860.

**FINANCIAL AID PICTURE (2015-2016)**
**Students with need:** Out of 82 full-time freshmen who applied for aid, 74 were judged to have need. Of these, 74 received aid. Average financial aid package met 24% of need; average scholarship/grant was $5,000; average loan was $3,500. For part-time students, average financial aid package was $6,700.
**Students without need:** No-need awards available for academics, alumni affiliation, athletics, leadership, minority status, state/district residency.
**Scholarships offered:** 1 full-time freshmen received athletic scholarships; average amount $11,000.

**FINANCIAL AID PROCEDURES**
**Forms required:** FAFSA.
**Dates and Deadlines:** Priority date 3/15; no closing date. Applicants notified on a rolling basis starting 3/1.
**Transfers:** Priority date 3/15; no deadline. Applicants notified on a rolling basis.

**CONTACT**
Melissa Waters, Director of Financial Aid
1269 Barclay Circle, Marietta, GA 30060
(770) 426-2944

## Luther Rice University
Lithonia, Georgia
www.LutherRice.edu                    Federal Code: 031009

**4-year private** university, Bible and seminary college in very large city, affiliated with Baptist faith.
**Enrollment:** 408 undergrads. 3 full-time freshmen.
**Selectivity:** Open admission.

**BASIC COSTS (2015-2016)**
**Tuition and fees:** $7,920.
**Per-credit charge:** $244.

**FINANCIAL AID PICTURE (2014-2015)**
**Students with need:** Out of 3 full-time freshmen who applied for aid, 1 were judged to have need. Of these, 1 received aid. For part-time students, average financial aid package was $8,776.
**Students without need:** 2 full-time freshmen who did not demonstrate need for aid received scholarships/grants; average award was $589. No-need awards available for academics.

**FINANCIAL AID PROCEDURES**
**Forms required:** FAFSA.

**Dates and Deadlines:** Applicants notified on a rolling basis.
**Transfers:** No deadline. Applicants notified on a rolling basis.

**CONTACT**
Casey Kuffrey, Director of Financial Aid
3038 Evans Mill Road, Lithonia, GA 30038

## Mercer University
Macon, Georgia
www.mercer.edu                        Federal Code: 001580

**4-year private** university in small city.
**Enrollment:** 2,851 undergrads, 2% part-time. 827 full-time freshmen.
**Selectivity:** Admits 50 to 75% of applicants.

**BASIC COSTS (2015-2016)**
**Tuition and fees:** $34,450.
**Per-credit charge:** $1,138.
**Room and board:** $10,898.

**FINANCIAL AID PICTURE (2015-2016)**
**Students with need:** Out of 827 full-time freshmen who applied for aid, 609 were judged to have need. Of these, 609 received aid, and 289 had their full need met. Average financial aid package met 89% of need; average scholarship/grant was $25,648; average loan was $8,776. For part-time students, average financial aid package was $10,301.
**Students without need:** 201 full-time freshmen who did not demonstrate need for aid received scholarships/grants; average award was $20,226. No-need awards available for academics, art, athletics, job skills, leadership, music/drama, religious affiliation, ROTC, state/district residency.
**Scholarships offered:** *Merit:* Various scholarships; primarily based on GPA, SAT/ACT, and personal interview; early applications given highest consideration. National Merit finalists and semi-finalists guaranteed full-tuition scholarships. *Athletic:* 38 full-time freshmen received athletic scholarships; average amount $20,114.

**FINANCIAL AID PROCEDURES**
**Forms required:** FAFSA, state aid form, institutional form.
**Dates and Deadlines:** Priority date 4/1; no closing date. Applicants notified on a rolling basis starting 3/15; must reply within 2 week(s) of notification.
**Transfers:** No deadline. Applicants notified on a rolling basis starting 3/15; must reply within 2 week(s) of notification.

**CONTACT**
Maria Hammett, Associate Vice President, Student Financial Planning
1501 Mercer University Drive, Macon, GA 31207-0001
(478) 301-2670

## Middle Georgia State College
Macon, Georgia
www.mga.edu                           Federal Code: 001581

**4-year public** liberal arts college in small city.
**Enrollment:** 7,164 undergrads.

**BASIC COSTS (2015-2016)**
**Tuition and fees:** $4,522; out-of-state residents $13,308.
**Per-credit charge:** $109; out-of-state residents $402.
**Room and board:** $8,210.

**FINANCIAL AID PICTURE**
**Students with need:** Need-based aid available for full-time and part-time students. Work study available nights, weekends, and for part-time students.
**Students without need:** No-need awards available for academics, alumni affiliation, art, athletics, job skills, leadership, minority status, music/drama, state/district residency.

## FINANCIAL AID PROCEDURES

**Forms required:** FAFSA.

**Dates and Deadlines:** Closing date 7/16. Applicants notified on a rolling basis starting 5/1.

## CONTACT

Lee Ann Kirkland, Director of Financial Aid
100 College Station Drive, Macon, GA 31206
(478) 471-2800

## Morehouse College

Atlanta, Georgia
www.morehouse.edu                    Federal Code: 001582

**4-year private** liberal arts college for men in very large city.

**Enrollment:** 2,163 undergrads, 4% part-time. 598 full-time freshmen.

**Selectivity:** Admits over 75% of applicants.

### BASIC COSTS (2016-2017)

**Tuition and fees:** $26,742.

**Room and board:** $13,322.

### FINANCIAL AID PICTURE (2015-2016)

**Students with need:** Out of 590 full-time freshmen who applied for aid, 522 were judged to have need. Of these, 514 received aid, and 57 had their full need met. Average financial aid package met 50% of need; average scholarship/grant was $15,904; average loan was $3,611. For part-time students, average financial aid package was $9,799.

**Students without need:** No-need awards available for academics, alumni affiliation, art, athletics, job skills, leadership, music/drama, ROTC, state/district residency.

**Scholarships offered:** 27 full-time freshmen received athletic scholarships; average amount $19,747.

### FINANCIAL AID PROCEDURES

**Forms required:** FAFSA, state aid form.

**Dates and Deadlines:** Priority date 2/15; closing date 4/1. Applicants notified on a rolling basis; must reply within 2 week(s) of notification.

**Transfers:** Priority date 2/15; no deadline. Applicants notified on a rolling basis; must reply within 2 week(s) of notification.

### CONTACT

Sheryl Spivey, Director of Financial Aid
830 Westview Drive SW, Atlanta, GA 30314
(404) 653-7750

## North Georgia Technical College

Clarkesville, Georgia
www.northgatech.edu                    Federal Code: 005619

**2-year public** community and technical college in small town.

**Enrollment:** 2,414 undergrads, 61% part-time. 326 full-time freshmen.

**Selectivity:** Open admission; but selective for some programs.

### BASIC COSTS (2015-2016)

**Tuition and fees:** $3,218; out-of-state residents $5,888.

**Per-credit charge:** $89; out-of-state residents $178.

**Room and board:** $4,000.

### FINANCIAL AID PICTURE (2014-2015)

**Students with need:** 64% of average financial aid package awarded as scholarships/grants, 36% awarded as loans/jobs. Need-based aid available for part-time students. Work study available nights, weekends, and for part-time students.

### FINANCIAL AID PROCEDURES

**Forms required:** FAFSA.

**Dates and Deadlines:** Applicants notified on a rolling basis.

## CONTACT

Audra Jimenez, Director of Financial Aid
1500 Highway 197 North, Clarkesville, GA 30523
(706) 754-7726

## Oglethorpe University

Atlanta, Georgia
www.oglethorpe.edu                    Federal Code: 001586

**4-year private** liberal arts college in very large city.

**Enrollment:** 1,125 undergrads, 6% part-time. 319 full-time freshmen.

**Selectivity:** Admits over 75% of applicants.

### BASIC COSTS (2016-2017)

**Tuition and fees:** $35,425.

**Per-credit charge:** $1,467.

**Room and board:** $12,710.

### FINANCIAL AID PICTURE (2015-2016)

**Students with need:** Out of 282 full-time freshmen who applied for aid, 259 were judged to have need. Of these, 259 received aid, and 47 had their full need met. Average financial aid package met 78% of need; average scholarship/grant was $27,004; average loan was $3,325. For part-time students, average financial aid package was $7,335.

**Students without need:** 60 full-time freshmen who did not demonstrate need for aid received scholarships/grants; average award was $17,939. No-need awards available for academics, art, leadership, music/drama, religious affiliation, state/district residency.

### FINANCIAL AID PROCEDURES

**Forms required:** FAFSA, state aid form.

**Dates and Deadlines:** Priority date 2/15; no closing date. Applicants notified on a rolling basis starting 3/1; must reply by 5/1 or within 2 week(s) of notification.

**Transfers:** No deadline.

### CONTACT

Chris Summers, Director of Financial Aid
4484 Peachtree Road NE, Atlanta, GA 30319-2797
(404) 364-8356

## Oxford College of Emory University

Oxford, Georgia                    Federal Code: 001565
www.oxford.emory.edu                    CSS Code: 5186

**2-year private** branch campus and liberal arts college in large town, affiliated with United Methodist Church.

**Enrollment:** 935 undergrads. 485 full-time freshmen.

**Selectivity:** Admits less than 50% of applicants. GED not accepted.

### BASIC COSTS (2016-2017)

**Tuition and fees:** $43,254.

**Per-credit charge:** $1,775.

**Room and board:** $12,006.

### FINANCIAL AID PICTURE

**Students with need:** Need-based aid available for full-time and part-time students. Work study available nights, weekends, and for part-time students.

**Students without need:** No-need awards available for academics, leadership, religious affiliation, state/district residency.

**Scholarships offered:** Woodruff Scholarships; full tuition, room and board for 4 years. Dean's Scholarship; full tuition for 4 years. Faculty Scholarships; half tuition for 4 years. 2-year scholarships; range from $8,000-$10,000 a year.

**Additional info:** Loan reduction program for families with annual assessed incomes of $100,000 or less who demonstrate need.

**FINANCIAL AID PROCEDURES**
**Forms required:** FAFSA, CSS PROFILE, state aid form.
**Dates and Deadlines:** Priority date 2/15; closing date 3/1. Applicants notified on a rolling basis starting 4/1; must reply by 5/1.

**CONTACT**
Jennifer Patil, Associate Dean for Financial Aid and Enrollment
122 Few Circle, Oxford, GA 30054-1418
(770) 784-8303

## Paine College
Augusta, Georgia
www.paine.edu                     Federal Code: 001587

**4-year private** liberal arts college in large city, affiliated with Christian Methodist Episcopal Church.
**Enrollment:** 551 undergrads, 8% part-time. 125 full-time freshmen.
**Selectivity:** Admits less than 50% of applicants.

**BASIC COSTS (2015-2016)**
**Tuition and fees:** $12,912.
**Per-credit charge:** $481.
**Room and board:** $6,094.

**FINANCIAL AID PICTURE**
**Students with need:** Need-based aid available for full-time and part-time students. Work study available nights, weekends, and for part-time students.
**Students without need:** No-need awards available for academics, alumni affiliation, athletics, music/drama, religious affiliation, ROTC.

**FINANCIAL AID PROCEDURES**
**Forms required:** FAFSA, state aid form.
**Dates and Deadlines:** Priority date 3/1; no closing date. Applicants notified on a rolling basis starting 5/1; must reply within 2 week(s) of notification.

**CONTACT**
Consuelo Quinn, Interim Director of Financial Aid
1235 15th Street, Augusta, GA 30901-3182
(706) 821-8262

## Piedmont College
Demorest, Georgia
www.piedmont.edu                  Federal Code: 001588

**4-year private** liberal arts and teachers college in rural community, affiliated with Christian Church.
**Enrollment:** 1,259 undergrads, 10% part-time. 275 full-time freshmen.
**Selectivity:** Admits 50 to 75% of applicants.

**BASIC COSTS (2015-2016)**
**Tuition and fees:** $21,990.
**Per-credit charge:** $917.
**Room and board:** $9,050.
**Additional info:** Tuition/fee waivers available for adults.

**FINANCIAL AID PICTURE (2015-2016)**
**Students with need:** Out of 252 full-time freshmen who applied for aid, 227 were judged to have need. Of these, 227 received aid, and 49 had their full need met. Average financial aid package met 75% of need; average scholarship/grant was $17,050; average loan was $3,337. For part-time students, average financial aid package was $4,557.
**Students without need:** 47 full-time freshmen who did not demonstrate need for aid received scholarships/grants; average award was $12,085. No-need awards available for academics, alumni affiliation, art, leadership, music/drama, religious affiliation, state/district residency.

**Scholarships offered:** Academic scholarships; based on superior academics, leadership, and extracurricular activities.

**FINANCIAL AID PROCEDURES**
**Forms required:** FAFSA, state aid form, institutional form.
**Dates and Deadlines:** Priority date 5/1; no closing date. Applicants notified on a rolling basis; must reply within 2 week(s) of notification.
**Transfers:** No deadline. Applicants notified on a rolling basis; must reply within 2 week(s) of notification.

**CONTACT**
David McMillion, Director of Financial Aid
1021 Central Avenue, Demorest, GA 30535-0010
(706) 776-0114

## Point University
West Point, Georgia
www.point.edu                     Federal Code: 001547

**4-year private** Bible and liberal arts college in small town, affiliated with Christian Church.
**Enrollment:** 1,337 undergrads, 12% part-time. 264 full-time freshmen.
**Selectivity:** Admits less than 50% of applicants.

**BASIC COSTS (2015-2016)**
**Tuition and fees:** $18,500.
**Room and board:** $6,600.

**FINANCIAL AID PICTURE (2014-2015)**
**Students with need:** 44% of average financial aid package awarded as scholarships/grants, 56% awarded as loans/jobs. Need-based aid available for part-time students. Work study available nights.
**Students without need:** No-need awards available for academics, athletics, leadership.

**FINANCIAL AID PROCEDURES**
**Forms required:** FAFSA, state aid form.
**Dates and Deadlines:** Priority date 6/1; closing date 8/1. Applicants notified on a rolling basis starting 3/1; must reply within 3 week(s) of notification.
**Transfers:** Priority date 3/25; no deadline. Applicants notified on a rolling basis starting 3/1.

**CONTACT**
Janifer Morgan, Director of Financial Aid
507 West 10th Street, West Point, GA 31833
(404) 385-1018

## Reinhardt University
Waleska, Georgia
www.reinhardt.edu                 Federal Code: 001589

**4-year private** liberal arts and teachers college in rural community, affiliated with United Methodist Church.
**Enrollment:** 1,237 undergrads, 9% part-time. 310 full-time freshmen.
**Selectivity:** Admits over 75% of applicants.

**BASIC COSTS (2015-2016)**
**Tuition and fees:** $20,266.
**Per-credit charge:** $665.
**Room and board:** $7,568.

**FINANCIAL AID PICTURE (2014-2015)**
**Students with need:** Out of 298 full-time freshmen who applied for aid, 252 were judged to have need. Of these, 250 received aid, and 29 had their full need met. Average financial aid package met 57% of need; average scholarship/grant was $11,105; average loan was $3,191. For part-time students, average financial aid package was $5,280.

**Students without need:** 75 full-time freshmen who did not demonstrate need for aid received scholarships/grants; average award was $6,412. No-need awards available for academics, art, athletics, music/drama, religious affiliation, state/district residency.

**Scholarships offered:** 42 full-time freshmen received athletic scholarships; average amount $7,184.

### FINANCIAL AID PROCEDURES

**Forms required:** FAFSA, state aid form.

**Dates and Deadlines:** Priority date 7/1; no closing date. Applicants notified on a rolling basis starting 3/1; must reply within 2 week(s) of notification.

**Transfers:** No deadline.

### CONTACT

Angela Harlow, Director of Financial Aid
7300 Reinhardt Circle, Waleska, GA 30183-2981
(770) 720-5667

## Savannah College of Art and Design
Savannah, Georgia
www.scad.edu                    Federal Code: 015022

**4-year private** visual arts and performing arts college in small city.

**Enrollment:** 9,939 undergrads, 17% part-time. 2,004 full-time freshmen.

**Selectivity:** Admits 50 to 75% of applicants.

### BASIC COSTS (2015-2016)

**Tuition and fees:** $34,470.

**Per-credit charge:** $766.

**Room and board:** $13,677.

### FINANCIAL AID PICTURE (2015-2016)

**Students with need:** Out of 1,437 full-time freshmen who applied for aid, 1,172 were judged to have need. Of these, 1,172 received aid, and 131 had their full need met. Average financial aid package met 16% of need; average scholarship/grant was $5,363; average loan was $3,005. For part-time students, average financial aid package was $15,090.

**Students without need:** 779 full-time freshmen who did not demonstrate need for aid received scholarships/grants; average award was $10,351. No-need awards available for academics, alumni affiliation, art, athletics, job skills, leadership, minority status, music/drama, ROTC.

**Scholarships offered:** 21 full-time freshmen received athletic scholarships; average amount $31,171.

**Additional info:** Degree-seeking students can be awarded maximum of one scholarship from the college, but may receive additional scholarships from other sources, as well as additional forms of financial aid. Scholarships based on academic achievement are awarded through the admission office.

### FINANCIAL AID PROCEDURES

**Forms required:** FAFSA, state aid form.

**Dates and Deadlines:** Applicants notified on a rolling basis starting 3/1; must reply within 4 week(s) of notification.

**Transfers:** No deadline. Applicants notified on a rolling basis. Transfer students are eligible to apply for academic and portfolio scholarships.

### CONTACT

Kim Beveridge, Director of Financial Aid
PO Box 2072, Savannah, GA 31402-2072
(912) 525-5100

## Savannah Technical College
Savannah, Georgia
www.savannahtech.edu            Federal Code: 005618

**2-year public** technical college in large city.

**Enrollment:** 4,784 undergrads.

**Selectivity:** Open admission; but selective for some programs.

### BASIC COSTS (2015-2016)

**Tuition and fees:** $3,188; out-of-state residents $5,858.

**Per-credit charge:** $89; out-of-state residents $178.

### FINANCIAL AID PICTURE

**Students with need:** Need-based aid available for full-time and part-time students.

**Students without need:** No-need awards available for academics, leadership, minority status, state/district residency.

### FINANCIAL AID PROCEDURES

**Forms required:** FAFSA.

**Dates and Deadlines:** Applicants notified on a rolling basis.

### CONTACT

Faith Anderson, Financial Aid Director
5717 White Bluff Road, Savannah, GA 31401-5521
(912) 443-5776

## Shorter University
Rome, Georgia
www.shorter.edu                 Federal Code: 001591

**4-year private** liberal arts college in large town, affiliated with Southern Baptist Convention.

**Enrollment:** 1,300 full-time undergrads.

### BASIC COSTS (2015-2016)

**Tuition and fees:** $20,976.

**Per-credit charge:** $400.

**Room and board:** $9,500.

### FINANCIAL AID PICTURE

**Students with need:** Need-based aid available for full-time and part-time students. Work study available nights.

**Students without need:** No-need awards available for academics, art, athletics, music/drama, religious affiliation, state/district residency.

**Additional info:** Cost is reduced for all in-state students by state tuition equalization grant program. College matches for out-of-state full-time students.

### FINANCIAL AID PROCEDURES

**Forms required:** FAFSA, state aid form, institutional form.

**Dates and Deadlines:** Priority date 4/1; no closing date. Applicants notified on a rolling basis starting 3/1; must reply within 2 week(s) of notification.

**Transfers:** Priority date 4/15; no deadline. Applicants notified on a rolling basis starting 3/31; must reply within 2 week(s) of notification.

### CONTACT

Colleen Lassiter, Financial Aid Director
315 Shorter Avenue, Rome, GA 30165
(706) 233-7227

## South Georgia State College
Douglas, Georgia
www.sgsc.edu                    Federal Code: 001592

**4-year public** liberal arts college in large town.

**Enrollment:** 2,635 undergrads, 31% part-time. 933 full-time freshmen.

**Selectivity:** Admits 50 to 75% of applicants.

### BASIC COSTS (2015-2016)

**Tuition and fees:** $3,756; out-of-state residents $11,350.

**Per-credit charge:** $90; out-of-state residents $344.

**Room and board:** $8,250.

**FINANCIAL AID PICTURE**

**Students with need:** Need-based aid available for full-time and part-time students.

**Students without need:** No-need awards available for academics.

**FINANCIAL AID PROCEDURES**

**Forms required:** FAFSA, institutional form.

**Dates and Deadlines:** Priority date 6/1; no closing date. Applicants notified on a rolling basis starting 7/6; must reply within 2 week(s) of notification.

**Transfers:** No deadline.

**CONTACT**

Latoya Curtis, Director of Financial Aid

100 West College Park Drive, Douglas, GA 31533-5098

(912) 260-4282

## South University: Savannah

Savannah, Georgia

www.southuniversity.edu          Federal Code: 013039

**4-year for-profit** university in small city.

**Enrollment:** 777 undergrads.

**BASIC COSTS (2015-2016)**

**Additional info:** Associate programs: $44,615-$50,250, books and supplies $3,200-$3,600. Bachelor's programs: $44,665-$83,500, books and supplies $3,200-$6,000.

**FINANCIAL AID PICTURE**

**Students with need:** Need-based aid available for full-time students.

**FINANCIAL AID PROCEDURES**

**Forms required:** FAFSA, state aid form.

**Dates and Deadlines:** Applicants notified on a rolling basis starting 9/1.

**CONTACT**

Tressa Brush, Director of Financial Aid

709 Mall Boulevard, Savannah, GA 31406

(912) 201-8000

## Southeastern Technical College

Vidalia, Georgia

www.southeasterntech.edu          Federal Code: 030665

**2-year public** technical college in large town.

**Enrollment:** 1,665 undergrads.

**Selectivity:** Open admission; but selective for some programs.

**BASIC COSTS (2015-2016)**

**Tuition and fees:** $3,308; out-of-state residents $5,978.

**Per-credit charge:** $89; out-of-state residents $178.

**FINANCIAL AID PICTURE**

**Students with need:** Need-based aid available for full-time and part-time students. Work study available nights.

**Students without need:** No-need awards available for state/district residency.

**FINANCIAL AID PROCEDURES**

**Forms required:** FAFSA, state aid form.

**Dates and Deadlines:** Applicants notified on a rolling basis starting 4/6.

**CONTACT**

Mitchell Fagler, Executive Director of Student Affairs/Financial Aid

3001 East First Street, Vidalia, GA 30474

(478) 289-2268

## Southern Regional Technical College

Thomasville, Georgia

www.southernregional.edu          Federal Code: 005615

**2-year public** technical college in large town.

**Enrollment:** 2,277 undergrads.

**Selectivity:** Open admission; but selective for some programs.

**BASIC COSTS (2015-2016)**

**Tuition and fees:** $3,148; out-of-state residents $5,818.

**Per-credit charge:** $89; out-of-state residents $178.

**FINANCIAL AID PICTURE**

**Students with need:** Need-based aid available for full-time and part-time students. Work study available nights.

**Students without need:** No-need awards available for state/district residency.

**FINANCIAL AID PROCEDURES**

**Forms required:** FAFSA.

**Dates and Deadlines:** Applicants notified on a rolling basis starting 7/1.

**CONTACT**

Judi Lowworn, Director of Financial Aid

15689 US Highway 19 North, Thomasville, GA 31792-9960

(229) 225-5036

## Spelman College

Atlanta, Georgia

www.spelman.edu          Federal Code: 001594

**4-year private** liberal arts college for women in very large city.

**Enrollment:** 2,142 undergrads, 2% part-time. 564 full-time freshmen.

**Selectivity:** Admits less than 50% of applicants. GED not accepted.

**BASIC COSTS (2015-2016)**

**Tuition and fees:** $26,388.

**Room and board:** $12,363.

**FINANCIAL AID PICTURE (2015-2016)**

**Students with need:** Out of 544 full-time freshmen who applied for aid, 495 were judged to have need. Of these, 494 received aid, and 40 had their full need met. Average financial aid package met 35% of need; average scholarship/grant was $11,056; average loan was $3,722. For part-time students, average financial aid package was $9,155.

**Students without need:** No-need awards available for academics, alumni affiliation, music/drama, state/district residency.

**FINANCIAL AID PROCEDURES**

**Forms required:** FAFSA, institutional form.

**Dates and Deadlines:** Priority date 2/1; no closing date. Applicants notified on a rolling basis starting 2/15; must reply within 2 week(s) of notification.

**Transfers:** Priority date 2/1; no deadline. Applicants notified on a rolling basis starting 2/15; must reply within 2 week(s) of notification. No special aid for transfer students for the first year.

**CONTACT**

Lenora Jackson, Associate Vice President, Enrollment Management

350 Spelman Lane SW, Campus Box 277, Atlanta, GA 30314-4399

(404) 681-3643 ext. 5212

## Thomas University

Thomasville, Georgia

www.thomasu.edu          Federal Code: 001555

**4-year private** university and liberal arts college in large town.

**Enrollment:** 745 undergrads.

**Selectivity:** Open admission; but selective for some programs.

**BASIC COSTS (2015-2016)**
**Tuition and fees:** $16,400.
**Per-credit charge:** $610.
**Room only:** $4,650.

**FINANCIAL AID PICTURE**
**Students with need:** Need-based aid available for full-time and part-time students.
**Students without need:** No-need awards available for academics, athletics, leadership, state/district residency.

**FINANCIAL AID PROCEDURES**
**Forms required:** FAFSA, state aid form.
**Dates and Deadlines:** Priority date 5/1; no closing date. Applicants notified on a rolling basis.
**Transfers:** Student must submit official academic transcripts from all colleges attended. Financial aid received during current academic year from previous school will be verified through the National Student Loan Data System (NSLDS).

**CONTACT**
Chrissy Gass, Director of Financial Aid
1501 Millpond Road, Thomasville, GA 31792-7499
(229) 226-1621 ext. 1002

## Toccoa Falls College
Toccoa Falls, Georgia
www.tfc.edu                Federal Code: 001596

**4-year private** Bible and liberal arts college in large town, affiliated with Christian and Missionary Alliance.
**Enrollment:** 773 undergrads, 9% part-time. 148 full-time freshmen.
**Selectivity:** Admits less than 50% of applicants.

**BASIC COSTS (2016-2017)**
**Tuition and fees:** $22,910.
**Per-credit charge:** $863.
**Room and board:** $7,635.

**FINANCIAL AID PICTURE (2014-2015)**
**Students with need:** Out of 135 full-time freshmen who applied for aid, 119 were judged to have need. Of these, 119 received aid, and 19 had their full need met. Average financial aid package met 64% of need; average scholarship/grant was $13,981; average loan was $3,271. For part-time students, average financial aid package was $5,066.
**Students without need:** 24 full-time freshmen who did not demonstrate need for aid received scholarships/grants; average award was $9,434. No-need awards available for academics.

**FINANCIAL AID PROCEDURES**
**Forms required:** FAFSA, institutional form.
**Dates and Deadlines:** Priority date 5/1; closing date 8/1. Applicants notified on a rolling basis starting 3/1; must reply within 2 week(s) of notification.
**Transfers:** No deadline. Applicants notified on a rolling basis starting 3/1; must reply within 2 week(s) of notification.

**CONTACT**
Stuart Spires, Director of Student Financial Services
PO Box 800899, Toccoa Falls, GA 30598
(706) 886-7299 ext. 5435

## Truett-McConnell College
Cleveland, Georgia
www.truett.edu              Federal Code: 001597

**4-year private** liberal arts college in small town, affiliated with Southern Baptist Convention.

**Enrollment:** 752 undergrads, 9% part-time. 207 full-time freshmen.
**Selectivity:** Admits over 75% of applicants.

**BASIC COSTS (2015-2016)**
**Tuition and fees:** $17,900.
**Per-credit charge:** $575.
**Room and board:** $7,220.

**FINANCIAL AID PICTURE (2015-2016)**
**Students with need:** Out of 199 full-time freshmen who applied for aid, 178 were judged to have need. Of these, 178 received aid, and 29 had their full need met. Average financial aid package met 64% of need; average scholarship/grant was $11,579; average loan was $3,697. For part-time students, average financial aid package was $5,558.
**Students without need:** 29 full-time freshmen who did not demonstrate need for aid received scholarships/grants; average award was $6,643. No-need awards available for academics, alumni affiliation, athletics, leadership, minority status, music/drama, religious affiliation, state/district residency.
**Scholarships offered:** 22 full-time freshmen received athletic scholarships; average amount $3,800.

**FINANCIAL AID PROCEDURES**
**Forms required:** FAFSA, state aid form, institutional form.
**Dates and Deadlines:** Priority date 4/1; no closing date. Applicants notified on a rolling basis starting 3/15; must reply within 2 week(s) of notification.
**Transfers:** No deadline. Applicants notified on a rolling basis starting 3/1; must reply within 2 week(s) of notification.

**CONTACT**
Truitt Franklin, Director of Financial Aid
100 Alumni Drive, Cleveland, GA 30528
(800) 226-8621

## University of Georgia
Athens, Georgia
www.uga.edu                Federal Code: 001598

**4-year public** university in small city.
**Enrollment:** 27,328 undergrads, 6% part-time. 5,274 full-time freshmen.
**Selectivity:** Admits 50 to 75% of applicants.

**BASIC COSTS (2015-2016)**
**Tuition and fees:** $11,622; out-of-state residents $29,832.
**Room and board:** $9,436.

**FINANCIAL AID PICTURE (2015-2016)**
**Students with need:** Out of 4,429 full-time freshmen who applied for aid, 2,328 were judged to have need. Of these, 2,304 received aid, and 683 had their full need met. Average financial aid package met 78% of need; average scholarship/grant was $10,210; average loan was $3,260. For part-time students, average financial aid package was $6,869.
**Students without need:** 181 full-time freshmen who did not demonstrate need for aid received scholarships/grants; average award was $3,118. No-need awards available for academics, athletics, ROTC, state/district residency.
**Scholarships offered:** 95 full-time freshmen received athletic scholarships; average amount $18,346.

**FINANCIAL AID PROCEDURES**
**Forms required:** FAFSA.
**Dates and Deadlines:** Priority date 3/1; no closing date. Applicants notified on a rolling basis starting 5/1; must reply within 2 week(s) of notification.

**CONTACT**
Bonnie Joerschke, Director of Student Financial Aid
Terrell Hall, Athens, GA 30602-1633
(706) 542-6147

## University of North Georgia
Dahlonega, Georgia
www.ung.edu                    Federal Code: 001585

**4-year public** university and liberal arts college in large town.
**Enrollment:** 16,048 undergrads, 28% part-time. 2,904 full-time freshmen.
**Selectivity:** Admits 50 to 75% of applicants.

**BASIC COSTS (2015-2016)**
**Tuition and fees:** $7,178; out-of-state residents $20,720.
**Per-credit charge:** $179; out-of-state residents $630.
**Room and board:** $7,642.

**FINANCIAL AID PICTURE (2014-2015)**
**Students with need:** Out of 2,672 full-time freshmen who applied for aid, 1,790 were judged to have need. Of these, 1,701 received aid, and 1,058 had their full need met. Average financial aid package met 68% of need; average scholarship/grant was $5,945; average loan was $3,775. For part-time students, average financial aid package was $6,252.
**Students without need:** 260 full-time freshmen who did not demonstrate need for aid received scholarships/grants; average award was $1,100. No-need awards available for academics, alumni affiliation, art, athletics, leadership, minority status, music/drama, ROTC, state/district residency.
**Scholarships offered:** 62 full-time freshmen received athletic scholarships; average amount $4,502.

**FINANCIAL AID PROCEDURES**
**Forms required:** FAFSA.
**Dates and Deadlines:** Applicants notified on a rolling basis starting 4/1; must reply within 2 week(s) of notification.

**CONTACT**
Jill Rayner, Director of Financial Aid
82 College Circle, Dahlonega, GA 30597
(706) 864-1412

## University of West Georgia
Carrollton, Georgia
www.westga.edu                 Federal Code: 001601

**4-year public** university in large town.
**Enrollment:** 10,753 undergrads, 18% part-time. 2,343 full-time freshmen.
**Selectivity:** Admits 50 to 75% of applicants.

**BASIC COSTS (2015-2016)**
**Tuition and fees:** $7,188; out-of-state residents $20,406.
**Per-credit charge:** $175; out-of-state residents $615.
**Room and board:** $9,698.
**Additional info:** Tuition/fee waivers available for adults, minority students.

**FINANCIAL AID PICTURE (2015-2016)**
**Students with need:** Out of 2,253 full-time freshmen who applied for aid, 1,879 were judged to have need. Of these, 1,851 received aid, and 1,099 had their full need met. Average financial aid package met 46% of need; average scholarship/grant was $4,961; average loan was $3,400. For part-time students, average financial aid package was $7,483.
**Students without need:** 133 full-time freshmen who did not demonstrate need for aid received scholarships/grants; average award was $2,102. No-need awards available for academics, alumni affiliation, art, athletics, job skills, leadership, minority status, music/drama, religious affiliation.
**Scholarships offered:** 51 full-time freshmen received athletic scholarships; average amount $4,881.

**FINANCIAL AID PROCEDURES**
**Forms required:** FAFSA.
**Dates and Deadlines:** Priority date 4/1; closing date 7/1. Applicants notified on a rolling basis starting 5/1.

**CONTACT**
Philip Hawkins, Director of Financial Aid
1601 Maple Street, Carrollton, GA 30118
(678) 839-6421

## Valdosta State University
Valdosta, Georgia
www.valdosta.edu               Federal Code: 001599

**4-year public** university in small city.
**Enrollment:** 8,744 undergrads, 17% part-time. 1,524 full-time freshmen.
**Selectivity:** Admits 50 to 75% of applicants.

**BASIC COSTS (2015-2016)**
**Tuition and fees:** $7,342; out-of-state residents $20,560.
**Per-credit charge:** $175; out-of-state residents $615.
**Room and board:** $7,912.

**FINANCIAL AID PICTURE (2014-2015)**
**Students with need:** Out of 1,427 full-time freshmen who applied for aid, 1,168 were judged to have need. Of these, 1,168 received aid, and 250 had their full need met. Average financial aid package met 98% of need; average scholarship/grant was $6,943; average loan was $3,389. For part-time students, average financial aid package was $14,641.
**Students without need:** 20 full-time freshmen who did not demonstrate need for aid received scholarships/grants; average award was $2,662. No-need awards available for academics, art, athletics, minority status, music/drama, ROTC, state/district residency.
**Scholarships offered:** 20 full-time freshmen received athletic scholarships; average amount $5,264.

**FINANCIAL AID PROCEDURES**
**Forms required:** FAFSA.
**Dates and Deadlines:** Priority date 4/1; closing date 3/1. Applicants notified on a rolling basis starting 3/15.
**Transfers:** Priority date 4/1; closing date 3/1. Applicants notified on a rolling basis starting 4/15.

**CONTACT**
Doug Tanner, Director of Financial Aid
1500 North Patterson Street, Valdosta, GA 31698-0170
(229) 333-5935

## Wesleyan College
Macon, Georgia
www.wesleyancollege.edu        Federal Code: 001600

**4-year private** nursing and liberal arts college for women in small city, affiliated with United Methodist Church.
**Enrollment:** 660 undergrads, 22% part-time. 106 full-time freshmen.
**Selectivity:** Admits less than 50% of applicants.

**BASIC COSTS (2015-2016)**
**Tuition and fees:** $20,290.
**Per-credit charge:** $480.
**Room and board:** $9,020.
**Additional info:** Tuition/fee waivers available for adults.

**FINANCIAL AID PICTURE (2014-2015)**
**Students with need:** Out of 83 full-time freshmen who applied for aid, 81 were judged to have need. Of these, 81 received aid, and 15 had their full need met. Average financial aid package met 77% of need; average scholarship/grant was $16,450; average loan was $4,895. For part-time students, average financial aid package was $7,337.

**Students without need:** 23 full-time freshmen who did not demonstrate need for aid received scholarships/grants; average award was $11,496. No-need awards available for academics, alumni affiliation, art, job skills, leadership, minority status, music/drama, religious affiliation, state/district residency.

**Scholarships offered:** Academic Scholarships; $1,000 up to tuition and standard room/board; based on minimum 1100 SAT (exclusive of Writing) or 25 ACT and 3.75 GPA, or 1200 SAT (exclusive of Writing) or 27 ACT and 3.5 GPA. Leadership Awards and scholarships for music, art, and theater; range from $1,000-$18,500.

**FINANCIAL AID PROCEDURES**
**Forms required:** FAFSA, state aid form, institutional form.
**Dates and Deadlines:** Closing date 4/15. Applicants notified on a rolling basis starting 3/1; must reply by 5/1 or within 3 week(s) of notification.
**Transfers:** Priority date 7/15; no deadline. Applicants notified on a rolling basis starting 3/15; must reply within 3 week(s) of notification. Scholarships available based on number of hours and GPA transferred in, with minimum 30 semester or 45 quarter hours and 3.0 GPA required.

**CONTACT**
Danielle Lodge, Financial Aid Director
4760 Forsyth Road, Macon, GA 31210-4462
(478) 757-3902

## West Georgia Technical College
Waco, Georgia
www.westgatech.edu                    Federal Code: 005614

**2-year public** technical college in small city.
**Enrollment:** 6,431 undergrads.
**Selectivity:** Open admission; but selective for some programs.

**BASIC COSTS (2015-2016)**
**Tuition and fees:** $3,288; out-of-state residents $5,958.
**Per-credit charge:** $89; out-of-state residents $178.

**FINANCIAL AID PICTURE**
**Students with need:** Need-based aid available for full-time and part-time students. Work study available nights.
**Students without need:** No-need awards available for state/district residency.

**FINANCIAL AID PROCEDURES**
**Forms required:** FAFSA, state aid form, institutional form.
**Dates and Deadlines:** Applicants notified on a rolling basis; must reply within 1 week(s) of notification.
**Transfers:** Aid must be in order or cash paid at registration for classes.

**CONTACT**
Anna English, Executive Director of Financial Aid
176 Murphy Campus Boulevard, Waco, GA 30182
(706) 845-4323

## Wiregrass Georgia Technical College
Valdosta, Georgia
www.wiregrass.edu                    Federal Code: 005256

**2-year public** technical college in small city.
**Enrollment:** 499 undergrads.
**Selectivity:** Open admission; but selective for some programs.

**BASIC COSTS (2015-2016)**
**Tuition and fees:** $3,268; out-of-state residents $5,938.
**Per-credit charge:** $89; out-of-state residents $178.

**FINANCIAL AID PICTURE**
**Students with need:** Need-based aid available for full-time and part-time students. Work study available nights.
**Students without need:** No-need awards available for academics, job skills, state/district residency.

**FINANCIAL AID PROCEDURES**
**Forms required:** FAFSA, state aid form, institutional form.
**Dates and Deadlines:** Applicants notified on a rolling basis starting 6/1.

**CONTACT**
Shelia Thomas, Financial Aid Director
4089 Val Tech Road, Valdosta, GA 31602
(229) 333-2107

## Young Harris College
Young Harris, Georgia
www.yhc.edu                    Federal Code: 001604

**4-year private** liberal arts college in rural community, affiliated with United Methodist Church.
**Enrollment:** 1,166 undergrads. 1,157 full-time freshmen.

**BASIC COSTS (2015-2016)**
**Tuition and fees:** $28,197.
**Per-credit charge:** $900.
**Room and board:** $9,876.

**FINANCIAL AID PICTURE (2014-2015)**
**Students with need:** Out of 929 full-time freshmen who applied for aid, 836 were judged to have need. Of these, 836 received aid, and 160 had their full need met. Average financial aid package met 78% of need; average scholarship/grant was $19,671; average loan was $3,679. For part-time students, average financial aid package was $10,876.
**Students without need:** 321 full-time freshmen who did not demonstrate need for aid received scholarships/grants; average award was $18,646. No-need awards available for academics, art, athletics, job skills, leadership, music/drama, state/district residency.
**Scholarships offered:** Academic Scholarships; $11,000-$14,000; based on index including GPA and SAT/ACT. Additional awards to a percentage of recipients range from $1,000 to full tuition, room and board.

**FINANCIAL AID PROCEDURES**
**Forms required:** FAFSA, state aid form.
**Dates and Deadlines:** Priority date 5/1; no closing date. Applicants notified on a rolling basis starting 2/15; must reply within 2 week(s) of notification.

**CONTACT**
Linda Adams, Financial Aid Director
PO Box 116, Young Harris, GA 30582-0116
(706) 379-3111

# Hawaii

## Brigham Young University-Hawaii
Laie, Hawaii
www.byuh.edu                    Federal Code: 001606

**4-year private** university and liberal arts college in small town, affiliated with Church of Jesus Christ of Latter-day Saints.
**Enrollment:** 2,681 undergrads.
**Selectivity:** GED not accepted.

## BASIC COSTS (2015-2016)
**Tuition and fees:** $5,100.
**Room and board:** $5,802.
**Additional info:** 100% higher tuition and per-credit-hour charges for students who are not members of The Church of Jesus Christ of Latter-day Saints.

## FINANCIAL AID PICTURE
**Students with need:** Need-based aid available for full-time and part-time students.
**Students without need:** No-need awards available for academics, art, athletics, leadership, music/drama, state/district residency.

## FINANCIAL AID PROCEDURES
**Forms required:** FAFSA.
**Dates and Deadlines:** Closing date 3/15. Applicants notified by 5/1; must reply by 8/31.

## CONTACT
Michael Tejada, Financial Aid and Student Accounts Manager
55-220 Kulanui Street, #1973, Laie, HI 96762-1294
(808) 675-3539

## Chaminade University of Honolulu
Honolulu, Hawaii
www.chaminade.edu                    Federal Code: 001605

**4-year private** university in large city, affiliated with Roman Catholic Church.
**Enrollment:** 1,217 undergrads, 2% part-time. 239 full-time freshmen.
**Selectivity:** Admits over 75% of applicants.

## BASIC COSTS (2015-2016)
**Tuition and fees:** $21,924.
**Per-credit charge:** $722.
**Room and board:** $12,290.
**Additional info:** Nursing tuition $26,930.

## FINANCIAL AID PICTURE (2014-2015)
**Students with need:** Out of 215 full-time freshmen who applied for aid, 180 were judged to have need. Of these, 180 received aid, and 40 had their full need met. Average financial aid package met 74% of need; average scholarship/grant was $4,858; average loan was $3,264. For part-time students, average financial aid package was $16,360.
**Students without need:** 58 full-time freshmen who did not demonstrate need for aid received scholarships/grants; average award was $8,016. No-need awards available for academics, athletics, minority status, religious affiliation, ROTC, state/district residency.
**Scholarships offered:** 6 full-time freshmen received athletic scholarships; average amount $3,792.

## FINANCIAL AID PROCEDURES
**Forms required:** FAFSA.
**Dates and Deadlines:** Priority date 2/15; no closing date. Must reply within 4 week(s) of notification.
**Transfers:** No deadline. Applicants notified on a rolling basis.

## CONTACT
Amy Takiguchi, Director of Financial Aid
3140 Waialae Avenue, Honolulu, HI 96816
(808) 735-4780

## Hawaii Pacific University
Honolulu, Hawaii
www.hpu.edu                          Federal Code: 007279

**4-year private** university and liberal arts college in large city.
**Enrollment:** 3,940 undergrads, 28% part-time. 473 full-time freshmen.

**Selectivity:** Admits over 75% of applicants.

## BASIC COSTS (2016-2017)
**Tuition and fees:** $23,460.
**Per-credit charge:** $740.
**Room and board:** $13,899.

## FINANCIAL AID PICTURE
**Students with need:** Need-based aid available for full-time and part-time students. Work study available nights, weekends, and for part-time students.
**Students without need:** No-need awards available for academics, alumni affiliation, athletics, leadership, music/drama, ROTC.

## FINANCIAL AID PROCEDURES
**Forms required:** FAFSA.
**Dates and Deadlines:** Priority date 3/1; no closing date. Applicants notified on a rolling basis starting 4/1; must reply within 3 week(s) of notification.
**Transfers:** No deadline. Must reply within 3 week(s) of notification.

## CONTACT
James Oshiro, Executive Director of Financial Aid
1 Aloha Tower Drive, Honolulu, HI 96813
(808) 544-0253

## University of Hawaii at Hilo
Hilo, Hawaii
www.hilo.hawaii.edu                  Federal Code: 001611

**4-year public** university and liberal arts college in large town.
**Enrollment:** 3,124 undergrads, 19% part-time. 371 full-time freshmen.
**Selectivity:** Admits 50 to 75% of applicants.

## BASIC COSTS (2015-2016)
**Tuition and fees:** $7,332; out-of-state residents $19,788.
**Per-credit charge:** $288; out-of-state residents $807.
**Room and board:** $8,414.

## FINANCIAL AID PICTURE
**Students with need:** Need-based aid available for full-time and part-time students.
**Students without need:** No-need awards available for academics, art, leadership, music/drama, state/district residency.
**Additional info:** Hawaii student incentive grants and tuition waivers (merit and need-based) available to Hawaii residents at participating institutions.

## FINANCIAL AID PROCEDURES
**Forms required:** FAFSA.
**Dates and Deadlines:** Priority date 3/1; no closing date. Applicants notified on a rolling basis starting 3/1; must reply within 3 week(s) of notification.

## CONTACT
Lynette Egusa, Director of Financial Aid
200 West Kawili Street, Hilo, HI 96720-4091
(808) 932-7449

## University of Hawaii at Manoa
Honolulu, Hawaii
www.manoa.hawaii.edu                 Federal Code: 001610

**4-year public** university in very large city.
**Enrollment:** 13,320 undergrads, 16% part-time. 1,638 full-time freshmen.
**Selectivity:** Admits over 75% of applicants.

## BASIC COSTS (2015-2016)
**Tuition and fees:** $11,164; out-of-state residents $31,516.
**Per-credit charge:** $431; out-of-state residents $1,279.
**Room and board:** $10,980.
**Additional info:** Tuition/fee waivers available for minority students.

## FINANCIAL AID PICTURE (2014-2015)

**Students with need:** Out of 1,412 full-time freshmen who applied for aid, 940 were judged to have need. Of these, 934 received aid, and 326 had their full need met. Average financial aid package met 76% of need; average scholarship/grant was $9,904; average loan was $3,907. For part-time students, average financial aid package was $10,237.

**Students without need:** 331 full-time freshmen who did not demonstrate need for aid received scholarships/grants; average award was $11,092. No-need awards available for academics, alumni affiliation, art, athletics, leadership, music/drama, ROTC, state/district residency.

**Scholarships offered:** 38 full-time freshmen received athletic scholarships; average amount $21,189.

**Additional info:** Hawaii student incentive grants and tuition waivers (merit and need-based) available to Hawaii residents at participating institutions.

## FINANCIAL AID PROCEDURES

**Forms required:** FAFSA.

**Dates and Deadlines:** Priority date 3/1; no closing date. Applicants notified on a rolling basis starting 4/1; must reply by 5/1 or within 4 week(s) of notification.

**Transfers:** No deadline. Applicants notified on a rolling basis starting 3/15; must reply within 4 week(s) of notification.

## CONTACT

Jodie Kuba, Director of Financial Aid
2600 Campus Road, QLCSS 001, Honolulu, HI 96822
(808) 956-7251

# University of Hawaii: Hawaii Community College

Hilo, Hawaii
www.hawaii.hawaii.edu          Federal Code: 005258

**2-year public** community college in small city.
**Enrollment:** 2,354 undergrads.
**Selectivity:** Open admission.

## BASIC COSTS (2015-2016)

**Tuition and fees:** $3,660; out-of-state residents $9,900.
**Per-credit charge:** $120; out-of-state residents $328.

## FINANCIAL AID PICTURE

**Students with need:** Need-based aid available for full-time and part-time students.

**Students without need:** This college awards aid only to students with need.

**Additional info:** Hawaii student incentive grants and tuition waivers (merit and need-based) available to Hawaii residents.

## FINANCIAL AID PROCEDURES

**Forms required:** FAFSA.

**Dates and Deadlines:** Priority date 4/1; no closing date. Applicants notified on a rolling basis starting 2/1; must reply within 2 week(s) of notification.

**Transfers:** Applicants notified by 2/1; must reply within 2 week(s) of notification. Residents of Guam, Federated States of Micronesia, Palau, Marianas Islands and certain other island nations considered residents for tuition purpose.

## CONTACT

Jason Cifra, VCSA
200 West Kawili Street, Hilo, HI 96720-4091

# University of Hawaii: Honolulu Community College

Honolulu, Hawaii
www2.honolulu.hawaii.edu          Federal Code: 001612

**2-year public** community and technical college in very large city.
**Enrollment:** 3,261 undergrads.
**Selectivity:** Open admission; but selective for out-of-state students.

## BASIC COSTS (2015-2016)

**Tuition and fees:** $3,630; out-of-state residents $9,870.
**Per-credit charge:** $120; out-of-state residents $328.

## FINANCIAL AID PICTURE

**Students with need:** Need-based aid available for full-time and part-time students.

**Students without need:** No-need awards available for academics, state/district residency.

**Additional info:** Hawaii student incentive grants and tuition waivers (merit and need-based) available to Hawaii residents at participating institutions.

## FINANCIAL AID PROCEDURES

**Forms required:** FAFSA.

**Dates and Deadlines:** Priority date 4/1; no closing date. Applicants notified on a rolling basis starting 7/1; must reply within 3 week(s) of notification.

## CONTACT

Jannine Oyama, Financial Aid Officer
874 Dillingham Boulevard, Honolulu, HI 96817
(808) 845-9116

# University of Hawaii: Kapiolani Community College

Honolulu, Hawaii
www.kcc.hawaii.edu          Federal Code: 001613

**2-year public** community college in very large city.
**Enrollment:** 7,994 undergrads.
**Selectivity:** Open admission; but selective for some programs.

## BASIC COSTS (2015-2016)

**Tuition and fees:** $3,660; out-of-state residents $9,900.
**Per-credit charge:** $120; out-of-state residents $328.

## FINANCIAL AID PICTURE

**Students with need:** Need-based aid available for full-time and part-time students.

**Students without need:** This college awards aid only to students with need.

## FINANCIAL AID PROCEDURES

**Forms required:** FAFSA.

**Dates and Deadlines:** Priority date 4/1; no closing date. Applicants notified on a rolling basis starting 4/1; must reply within 2 week(s) of notification.

**Transfers:** No deadline. Applicants notified on a rolling basis.

## CONTACT

Jennifer Bradley, Financial Aid Manager
4303 Diamond Head Road, Honolulu, HI 96816-4421
(808) 734-9555

# University of Hawaii: Kauai Community College

Lihue, Hawaii
www.kauai.hawaii.edu                    Federal Code: 001614

**2-year public** community college in small city.
**Enrollment:** 1,098 undergrads.
**Selectivity:** Open admission; but selective for out-of-state students.

## BASIC COSTS (2015-2016)
**Tuition and fees:** $3,708; out-of-state residents $9,948.
**Per-credit charge:** $120; out-of-state residents $328.

## FINANCIAL AID PICTURE
**Students with need:** Work study available nights.
**Additional info:** Hawaii student incentive grants and tuition waivers (merit and need-based) available to Hawaii residents.

## FINANCIAL AID PROCEDURES
**Forms required:** FAFSA, institutional form.
**Dates and Deadlines:** Priority date 3/1; closing date 5/1. Applicants notified on a rolling basis starting 5/1.
**Transfers:** Academic transcript evaluation by end of first semester is required.

## CONTACT
Rebecca Thompson, Financial Aid Officer
3-1901 Kaumualii Highway, Lihue, HI 96766-9500
(808) 245-8360

# University of Hawaii: Leeward Community College

Pearl City, Hawaii
www.lcc.hawaii.edu                    Federal Code: 004549

**2-year public** community college in large town.
**Enrollment:** 5,789 undergrads.
**Selectivity:** Open admission.

## BASIC COSTS (2015-2016)
**Tuition and fees:** $3,655; out-of-state residents $9,895.
**Per-credit charge:** $120; out-of-state residents $328.

## FINANCIAL AID PICTURE
**Students with need:** Need-based aid available for full-time and part-time students.
**Additional info:** Leveraging Educational Assistance Partnership (LEAP) funds or tuition waivers available to students with financial need.

## FINANCIAL AID PROCEDURES
**Forms required:** FAFSA.
**Dates and Deadlines:** Priority date 4/15; no closing date. Applicants notified on a rolling basis starting 6/1; must reply within 2 week(s) of notification.

## CONTACT
Aileen Lum-Akana, Financial Aid Director
96-045 Ala Ike, Pearl City, HI 96782
(808) 455-0606

# University of Hawaii: Maui College

Kahului, Hawaii
www.maui.hawaii.edu

**2-year public** community college in small city.
**Enrollment:** 3,149 undergrads, 61% part-time. 352 full-time freshmen.
**Selectivity:** Open admission; but selective for some programs.

## BASIC COSTS (2015-2016)
**Tuition and fees:** $3,726; out-of-state residents $9,966.
**Per-credit charge:** $120; out-of-state residents $328.
**Additional info:** Tuition/fee waivers available for minority students.

## FINANCIAL AID PICTURE
**Students with need:** Need-based aid available for full-time and part-time students. Work study available nights.

## FINANCIAL AID PROCEDURES
**Forms required:** FAFSA, institutional form.
**Dates and Deadlines:** Closing date 4/1. Applicants notified on a rolling basis starting 6/1; must reply within 4 week(s) of notification.

## CONTACT
Kilohana Miller, Interim Financial Aid Director
310 West Kaahumanu Avenue, Kahului, HI 96732-1617
(808) 984-3277

# University of Hawaii: West Oahu

Kapolei, Hawaii
www.uhwo.hawaii.edu                    Federal Code: 014315

**4-year public** liberal arts and teachers college in large town.
**Enrollment:** 2,517 undergrads, 43% part-time. 126 full-time freshmen.
**Selectivity:** Admits 50 to 75% of applicants.

## BASIC COSTS (2015-2016)
**Tuition and fees:** $7,152; out-of-state residents $19,608.
**Per-credit charge:** $288; out-of-state residents $807.

## FINANCIAL AID PICTURE (2014-2015)
**Students with need:** Out of 126 full-time freshmen who applied for aid, 126 were judged to have need. Of these, 126 received aid. Average financial aid package met 50% of need; average scholarship/grant was $727; average loan was $592. For part-time students, average financial aid package was $4,686.
**Students without need:** No-need awards available for academics.

## FINANCIAL AID PROCEDURES
**Forms required:** FAFSA.
**Dates and Deadlines:** Priority date 4/1; no closing date. Applicants notified on a rolling basis starting 4/1; must reply within 2 week(s) of notification.
**Transfers:** No deadline. Applicants notified by 7/1.

## CONTACT
Lester Ishimoto, Financial Aid Officer
91-1001 Farrington Highway, Kapolei, HI 96707
(808) 454-4700

# University of Hawaii: Windward Community College

Kaneohe, Hawaii
www.wcc.hawaii.edu                    Federal Code: 010390

**2-year public** community college in small city.
**Enrollment:** 2,460 undergrads.
**Selectivity:** Open admission.

## BASIC COSTS (2015-2016)
**Tuition and fees:** $3,640; out-of-state residents $9,880.
**Per-credit charge:** $120; out-of-state residents $328.
**Additional info:** Tuition/fee waivers available for minority students.

## FINANCIAL AID PICTURE
**Students with need:** Need-based aid available for full-time and part-time students.

**Students without need:** No-need awards available for academics.

**Additional info:** Hawaii student incentive grants and tuition waivers (merit and need-based) available to Hawaii residents.

### FINANCIAL AID PROCEDURES
**Forms required:** FAFSA.

**Dates and Deadlines:** Priority date 4/1; no closing date. Applicants notified on a rolling basis starting 3/15; must reply within 2 week(s) of notification.

### CONTACT
Steven Chigawa, Financial Aid Officer
45-720 Kea'ahala Road, Kaneohe, HI 96744
(808) 235-7449

# Idaho

## Boise Bible College
Boise, Idaho
www.boisebible.edu          Federal Code: 015783

**4-year private** Bible college in small city, affiliated with nondenominational tradition.

**Enrollment:** 144 undergrads.

### BASIC COSTS (2015-2016)
**Tuition and fees:** $11,670.
**Per-credit charge:** $375.
**Room and board:** $3,150.

### FINANCIAL AID PICTURE
**Students with need:** Need-based aid available for full-time and part-time students.

**Students without need:** No-need awards available for academics, leadership, music/drama, religious affiliation.

### FINANCIAL AID PROCEDURES
**Forms required:** FAFSA, institutional form.

**Dates and Deadlines:** Priority date 5/1; no closing date. Applicants notified on a rolling basis starting 5/2; must reply by 8/1 or within 2 week(s) of notification.

**Transfers:** Financial aid and academic transcripts must be on file before federal aid is awarded.

### CONTACT
Joyce Anderson, Financial Aid Officer
8695 West Marigold Street, Boise, ID 83714-1220
(208) 376-7731

## Boise State University
Boise, Idaho
www.boisestate.edu          Federal Code: 001616

**4-year public** university in small city.

**Enrollment:** 15,964 undergrads, 25% part-time. 2,155 full-time freshmen.

**Selectivity:** Admits over 75% of applicants.

### BASIC COSTS (2015-2016)
**Tuition and fees:** $6,876; out-of-state residents $20,926.
**Per-credit charge:** $273; out-of-state residents $523.
**Room and board:** $6,938.

### FINANCIAL AID PICTURE (2014-2015)
**Students with need:** Out of 1,421 full-time freshmen who applied for aid, 1,348 were judged to have need. Of these, 1,312 received aid, and 250 had

their full need met. Average financial aid package met 62% of need; average scholarship/grant was $5,245; average loan was $3,191. For part-time students, average financial aid package was $5,381.

**Students without need:** 256 full-time freshmen who did not demonstrate need for aid received scholarships/grants; average award was $1,268. No-need awards available for academics, alumni affiliation, art, athletics, music/drama.

**Scholarships offered:** 28 full-time freshmen received athletic scholarships; average amount $2,893.

### FINANCIAL AID PROCEDURES
**Forms required:** FAFSA.

**Dates and Deadlines:** Priority date 2/15; no closing date. Applicants notified on a rolling basis starting 3/15; must reply by 4/12 or within 4 week(s) of notification.

**Transfers:** No deadline. Applicants notified on a rolling basis; must reply within 2 week(s) of notification. Financial aid transcripts required from all postsecondary schools attended whether or not financial aid was received.

### CONTACT
Diana Fairchild, Director of Financial Aid
1910 University Drive, Boise, ID 83725-1320
(208) 426-1664

## Brigham Young University-Idaho
Rexburg, Idaho
www.byui.edu          Federal Code: 001625

**4-year private** university in large town, affiliated with Church of Jesus Christ of Latter-day Saints.

**Enrollment:** 20,390 undergrads.

### BASIC COSTS (2015-2016)
**Tuition and fees:** $3,830.
**Per-credit charge:** $160.
**Room and board:** $4,000.

### FINANCIAL AID PICTURE
**Students with need:** Need-based aid available for full-time and part-time students.

**Students without need:** No-need awards available for academics, alumni affiliation, art, leadership, music/drama.

**Additional info:** Application deadline for merit scholarships 3/1.

### FINANCIAL AID PROCEDURES
**Forms required:** FAFSA.

**Dates and Deadlines:** Priority date 5/1; no closing date. Applicants notified on a rolling basis starting 2/1.

### CONTACT
Aaron Sanns, Financial Aid and Scholarship Director
120 Kimball Building, Rexburg, ID 83460-1615
(208) 496-1600

## Broadview University: Boise
Meridian, Idaho
www.broadviewuniversity.edu          Federal Code: 011166

**2-year for-profit** career college in large town.

**Enrollment:** 142 undergrads.

**Selectivity:** Open admission.

### BASIC COSTS (2015-2016)
**Tuition and fees:** $18,027.
**Per-credit charge:** $372.

**FINANCIAL AID PICTURE**

**Students with need:** Need-based aid available for full-time and part-time students.

**FINANCIAL AID PROCEDURES**

**Forms required:** FAFSA, institutional form.

**Dates and Deadlines:** Applicants notified on a rolling basis starting 7/1; must reply within 2 week(s) of notification.

**CONTACT**

Cynthianna Hamrick, Director of Financial Aid

2750 East Gala Court, Meridian, ID 83642

(208) 577-2900

## College of Idaho

Caldwell, Idaho

www.collegeofidaho.edu                    Federal Code: 001617

**4-year private** liberal arts college in large town.

**Enrollment:** 1,034 undergrads, 3% part-time. 201 full-time freshmen.

**Selectivity:** Admits over 75% of applicants.

**BASIC COSTS (2016-2017)**

**Tuition and fees:** $27,425.

**Per-credit charge:** $1,060.

**Room and board:** $8,990.

**Additional info:** Tuition/fee waivers available for adults.

**FINANCIAL AID PICTURE (2015-2016)**

**Students with need:** Out of 177 full-time freshmen who applied for aid, 156 were judged to have need. Of these, 156 received aid, and 39 had their full need met. Average financial aid package met 87% of need; average scholarship/grant was $3,831; average loan was $3,391. For part-time students, average financial aid package was $13,508.

**Students without need:** 30 full-time freshmen who did not demonstrate need for aid received scholarships/grants; average award was $16,455. No-need awards available for academics, alumni affiliation, athletics, job skills, ROTC.

**Scholarships offered:** 27 full-time freshmen received athletic scholarships; average amount $3,741.

**FINANCIAL AID PROCEDURES**

**Forms required:** FAFSA, institutional form.

**Dates and Deadlines:** Priority date 2/1; no closing date. Applicants notified on a rolling basis starting 3/15; must reply within 3 week(s) of notification.

**Transfers:** No deadline. Applicants notified on a rolling basis starting 1/31; must reply within 3 week(s) of notification.

**CONTACT**

Jennifer Worden, Director of Student Financial Aid Services

2112 Cleveland Boulevard, Caldwell, ID 83605-4432

(208) 459-5307

## College of Southern Idaho

Twin Falls, Idaho

www.csi.edu                    Federal Code: 001619

**2-year public** community and junior college in large town.

**Enrollment:** 9,300 undergrads.

**Selectivity:** Open admission; but selective for some programs.

**BASIC COSTS (2015-2016)**

**Tuition and fees:** $3,600; out-of-district residents $5,100; out-of-state residents $8,400.

**Per-credit charge:** $120; out-of-district residents $170; out-of-state residents $280.

**Room and board:** $5,540.

**FINANCIAL AID PICTURE**

**Students with need:** Need-based aid available for full-time and part-time students.

**Additional info:** Out-of-state tuition waivers based on GPA and activities.

**FINANCIAL AID PROCEDURES**

**Forms required:** FAFSA.

**Dates and Deadlines:** Priority date 3/1; no closing date. Applicants notified on a rolling basis starting 4/30; must reply within 3 week(s) of notification.

**CONTACT**

Jennifer Zimmers, Director of Student Financial Aid

Box 1238, Twin Falls, ID 83303-1238

(208) 732-6273

## College of Western Idaho

Nampa, Idaho

www.cwidaho.cc                    Federal Code: 042118

**2-year public** community and technical college in large city.

**Enrollment:** 8,376 undergrads.

**Selectivity:** Open admission; but selective for some programs.

**BASIC COSTS (2015-2016)**

**Tuition and fees:** $4,080; out-of-district residents $5,080; out-of-state residents $9,000.

**Per-credit charge:** $136; out-of-district residents $186; out-of-state residents $300.

**FINANCIAL AID PICTURE**

**Students with need:** Need-based aid available for full-time and part-time students. Work study available nights, weekends, and for part-time students.

**Students without need:** No-need awards available for academics, leadership, minority status.

**FINANCIAL AID PROCEDURES**

**Forms required:** FAFSA.

**Dates and Deadlines:** Priority date 7/15; no closing date. Applicants notified on a rolling basis starting 3/1; must reply within 4 week(s) of notification.

**Transfers:** No deadline. Applicants notified on a rolling basis starting 3/1; must reply within 4 week(s) of notification.

**CONTACT**

Nicole McMillin, Director of Financial Aid

MS 3000, Nampa, ID 83653

(208) 562-3000

## Eastern Idaho Technical College

Idaho Falls, Idaho

www.eitc.edu                    Federal Code: 011133

**2-year public** technical college in small city.

**Enrollment:** 553 undergrads.

**Selectivity:** Open admission; but selective for some programs.

**BASIC COSTS (2015-2016)**

**Tuition and fees:** $2,334; out-of-state residents $8,550.

**Per-credit charge:** $103; out-of-state residents $205.

**FINANCIAL AID PICTURE**

**Students with need:** Need-based aid available for full-time and part-time students.

**Students without need:** No-need awards available for academics, job skills, state/district residency.

**FINANCIAL AID PROCEDURES**

**Forms required:** FAFSA, institutional form.

**Dates and Deadlines:** Priority date 6/1; no closing date. Applicants notified on a rolling basis starting 6/6.

### CONTACT
Shayna Sharp, Director of Financial Aid
1600 South 25th East, Idaho Falls, ID 83404-5788
(208) 524-3000 ext. 3389

## Idaho State University
Pocatello, Idaho
www.isu.edu                                    Federal Code: 001620

**4-year public** university in small city.
**Enrollment:** 8,977 undergrads, 23% part-time. 1,571 full-time freshmen.
**Selectivity:** Admits over 75% of applicants.

### BASIC COSTS (2015-2016)
**Tuition and fees:** $6,784; out-of-state residents $20,182.
**Per-credit charge:** $339; out-of-state residents $556.
**Room and board:** $6,338.

### FINANCIAL AID PICTURE (2014-2015)
**Students with need:** Out of 1,100 full-time freshmen who applied for aid, 910 were judged to have need. Of these, 894 received aid, and 66 had their full need met. Average financial aid package met 48% of need; average scholarship/grant was $4,992; average loan was $3,051. For part-time students, average financial aid package was $5,088.
**Students without need:** 158 full-time freshmen who did not demonstrate need for aid received scholarships/grants; average award was $1,934. No-need awards available for academics, alumni affiliation, art, athletics, leadership, minority status, music/drama, ROTC, state/district residency.
**Scholarships offered:** 41 full-time freshmen received athletic scholarships; average amount $9,601.

### FINANCIAL AID PROCEDURES
**Forms required:** FAFSA.
**Dates and Deadlines:** Priority date 3/1; no closing date. Applicants notified on a rolling basis starting 4/1.
**Transfers:** Closing date 3/1. Applicants notified on a rolling basis starting 3/1.

### CONTACT
James Martin, Director of Financial Aid
921 South 8th Stop 8270, Pocatello, ID 83209-8270
(208) 282-2756

## Lewis-Clark State College
Lewiston, Idaho
www.lcsc.edu                                   Federal Code: 001621

**4-year public** liberal arts and technical college in large town.
**Enrollment:** 3,035 undergrads, 26% part-time. 491 full-time freshmen.
**Selectivity:** Admits over 75% of applicants.

### BASIC COSTS (2015-2016)
**Tuition and fees:** $6,000; out-of-state residents $17,000.
**Per-credit charge:** $307.
**Room and board:** $6,360.

### FINANCIAL AID PICTURE (2014-2015)
**Students with need:** Out of 463 full-time freshmen who applied for aid, 378 were judged to have need. Of these, 378 received aid, and 36 had their full need met. Average financial aid package met 57% of need; average scholarship/grant was $5,185; average loan was $2,906. For part-time students, average financial aid package was $5,492.

**Students without need:** 65 full-time freshmen who did not demonstrate need for aid received scholarships/grants; average award was $2,251. No-need awards available for academics, alumni affiliation, art, athletics, job skills, leadership, minority status, music/drama, religious affiliation.
**Scholarships offered:** 6 full-time freshmen received athletic scholarships; average amount $7,764.

### FINANCIAL AID PROCEDURES
**Forms required:** FAFSA, institutional form.
**Dates and Deadlines:** Closing date 3/1. Applicants notified on a rolling basis starting 4/15; must reply within 2 week(s) of notification.

### CONTACT
Laura Hughes, Director of Financial Aid
500 Eighth Avenue, Lewiston, ID 83501-2698
(208) 792-2224

## North Idaho College
Coeur d'Alene, Idaho
www.nic.edu                                    Federal Code: 001623

**2-year public** community college in large town.
**Enrollment:** 5,779 undergrads.

### BASIC COSTS (2015-2016)
**Tuition and fees:** $4,012; out-of-district residents $5,282; out-of-state residents $9,952.
**Room and board:** $7,450.
**Additional info:** Tuition/fee waivers available for minority students.

### FINANCIAL AID PICTURE
**Students with need:** Need-based aid available for full-time and part-time students. Work study available weekends and for part-time students.
**Students without need:** No-need awards available for academics, art, athletics, leadership, minority status, music/drama, state/district residency.

### FINANCIAL AID PROCEDURES
**Forms required:** FAFSA.
**Dates and Deadlines:** Priority date 3/15; no closing date. Applicants notified on a rolling basis starting 4/1; must reply within 2 week(s) of notification.

### CONTACT
Joe Bekken, Director of Financial Aid
1000 West Garden Avenue, Coeur d'Alene, ID 83814-2199
(208) 769-3368

## Northwest Nazarene University
Nampa, Idaho
www.nnu.edu                                    Federal Code: 001624

**4-year private** university in small city, affiliated with Church of the Nazarene.
**Enrollment:** 1,290 undergrads, 10% part-time. 263 full-time freshmen.
**Selectivity:** Admits 50 to 75% of applicants.

### BASIC COSTS (2016-2017)
**Tuition and fees:** $28,150.
**Per-credit charge:** $1,199.
**Room and board:** $7,000.

### FINANCIAL AID PICTURE (2015-2016)
**Students with need:** Average financial aid package met 77% of need; average scholarship/grant was $16,946; average loan was $7,511. Need-based aid available for part-time students.
**Students without need:** No-need awards available for academics, athletics, leadership, music/drama, religious affiliation, ROTC.

### FINANCIAL AID PROCEDURES
**Forms required:** FAFSA.

**Dates and Deadlines:** Priority date 3/1; no closing date. Applicants notified on a rolling basis starting 2/15; must reply within 3 week(s) of notification.

**CONTACT**
Ann Crabb, Director of Financial Aid
623 South University Boulevard, Nampa, ID 83686-5897
(208) 467-8422

## Stevens-Henager College: Boise
Boise, Idaho
www.stevenshenager.edu                    Federal Code: 003674

**2-year for-profit** technical and career college in small city.
**Enrollment:** 350 undergrads.
**Selectivity:** Open admission; but selective for some programs.

**BASIC COSTS (2015-2016)**
**Additional info:** Associate programs: $42,387-$58,692. Bachelor's programs: $31,620-$74,778. Amounts are for the entire program and include books and supplies.

**FINANCIAL AID PICTURE**
**Students with need:** Need-based aid available for full-time students.
**Students without need:** This college awards aid only to students with need.

**FINANCIAL AID PROCEDURES**
**Forms required:** FAFSA.

**CONTACT**
Ali Earle, Business Officer
1444 S Entertainment Avenue, Boise, ID 83709
(208) 383-4540 ext. 1804

## University of Idaho
Moscow, Idaho
www.uidaho.edu                    Federal Code: 001626

**4-year public** university in large town.
**Enrollment:** 7,826 undergrads, 7% part-time. 1,554 full-time freshmen.
**Selectivity:** Admits 50 to 75% of applicants.

**BASIC COSTS (2015-2016)**
**Tuition and fees:** $7,020; out-of-state residents $21,024.
**Per-credit charge:** $351; out-of-state residents $1,051.
**Room and board:** $8,328.
**Additional info:** Tuition/fee waivers available for minority students.

**FINANCIAL AID PICTURE (2014-2015)**
**Students with need:** Out of 1,446 full-time freshmen who applied for aid, 1,099 were judged to have need. Of these, 1,079 received aid, and 396 had their full need met. Average financial aid package met 80% of need; average scholarship/grant was $4,660; average loan was $5,474. For part-time students, average financial aid package was $7,704.
**Students without need:** 364 full-time freshmen who did not demonstrate need for aid received scholarships/grants; average award was $5,337. No-need awards available for academics, alumni affiliation, art, athletics, leadership, minority status, music/drama, ROTC, state/district residency.
**Scholarships offered:** 43 full-time freshmen received athletic scholarships; average amount $18,967.

**FINANCIAL AID PROCEDURES**
**Forms required:** FAFSA.
**Dates and Deadlines:** Priority date 2/15; no closing date. Applicants notified on a rolling basis starting 3/30; must reply within 4 week(s) of notification.
**Transfers:** No deadline. Applicants notified on a rolling basis starting 3/30; must reply within 4 week(s) of notification.

**CONTACT**
Daniel Davenport, Director Student Financial Aid
875 Perimeter Drive MS 4264, Moscow, ID 83844-4264
(208) 885-6312

# Illinois

## American Academy of Art
Chicago, Illinois
www.aaart.edu                    Federal Code: 001628

**4-year private** visual arts college in very large city.
**Enrollment:** 317 undergrads, 29% part-time. 59 full-time freshmen.
**Selectivity:** Open admission.

**BASIC COSTS (2015-2016)**
**Tuition and fees:** $31,050.

**FINANCIAL AID PICTURE**
**Students with need:** Work study available nights.
**Students without need:** No-need awards available for art.

**FINANCIAL AID PROCEDURES**
**Forms required:** FAFSA, institutional form.
**Dates and Deadlines:** Applicants notified on a rolling basis.
**Transfers:** Financial aid transcript from previously attended college required.

**CONTACT**
Ione Fitzgerald, Financial Aid Director
332 South Michigan Avenue, Suite 300, Chicago, IL 60604-4302
(312) 461-0600

## Augustana College
Rock Island, Illinois
www.augustana.edu                    Federal Code: 001633

**4-year private** liberal arts college in large city, affiliated with Evangelical Lutheran Church in America.
**Enrollment:** 2,454 undergrads. 726 full-time freshmen.
**Selectivity:** Admits less than 50% of applicants. GED not accepted.

**BASIC COSTS (2016-2017)**
**Tuition and fees:** $39,621.
**Per-credit charge:** $1,700.
**Room and board:** $10,037.

**FINANCIAL AID PICTURE (2014-2015)**
**Students with need:** Out of 663 full-time freshmen who applied for aid, 578 were judged to have need. Of these, 576 received aid, and 140 had their full need met. Average financial aid package met 87% of need; average scholarship/grant was $24,025; average loan was $3,721.
**Students without need:** 147 full-time freshmen who did not demonstrate need for aid received scholarships/grants; average award was $21,008. No-need awards available for academics, alumni affiliation, art, music/drama, religious affiliation.
**Scholarships offered:** Presidential Scholarship: $24,000; 30 ACT or 1260 SAT and rank in the top ten percent of high school class. Dean's Scholarship: $19,000; 25 ACT or 1140 SAT and rank in the top 20 percent of high school class. Founders Scholarship: $17,000; must plan to enroll full-time. Transfer Scholarship: $8,000-$18,000; demonstrated outstanding academic performance in previous college studies.

**FINANCIAL AID PROCEDURES**
**Forms required:** FAFSA, institutional form.

**Dates and Deadlines:** Priority date 2/1; no closing date. Applicants notified on a rolling basis starting 3/1; must reply by 5/1.

**Transfers:** Priority date 5/1; no deadline. Applicants notified on a rolling basis.

### CONTACT

Sue Standley, Director of Financial Assistance
639 38th Street, Rock Island, IL 61201-2296
(309) 794-7207

## Aurora University

Aurora, Illinois
www.aurora.edu                   Federal Code: 001634

**4-year private** university in large city.

**Enrollment:** 3,567 undergrads, 12% part-time. 630 full-time freshmen.

**Selectivity:** Admits over 75% of applicants.

### BASIC COSTS (2016-2017)

**Tuition and fees:** $22,830.

**Room and board:** $10,000.

**Additional info:** Tuition/fee waivers available for adults.

### FINANCIAL AID PICTURE (2015-2016)

**Students with need:** Out of 586 full-time freshmen who applied for aid, 534 were judged to have need. Of these, 534 received aid, and 65 had their full need met. Average financial aid package met 78% of need; average scholarship/grant was $15,972; average loan was $3,234. For part-time students, average financial aid package was $6,741.

**Students without need:** 93 full-time freshmen who did not demonstrate need for aid received scholarships/grants; average award was $11,428. No-need awards available for academics, alumni affiliation, art, music/drama, religious affiliation, ROTC, state/district residency.

**Scholarships offered:** Board of Trustees scholarships: $13,000. James E. Crimi Presidential Scholarships: $12,000. Dean's Scholarships: $11,000. Aurora University Opportunity Grants: $9,000. AU Promise Grant: $3,000.

**Additional info:** Undocumented students may be considered for limited institutional financial aid based on an internal financial aid document.

### FINANCIAL AID PROCEDURES

**Forms required:** FAFSA.

**Dates and Deadlines:** Priority date 1/1; no closing date. Applicants notified on a rolling basis starting 3/1.

**Transfers:** No deadline. Applicants notified on a rolling basis; must reply by 5/1 or within 3 week(s) of notification.

### CONTACT

Heather Granart, Dean of Student Financial Services
347 South Gladstone Avenue, Aurora, IL 60506-4892
(630) 844-6190

## Benedictine University

Lisle, Illinois
www.ben.edu                    Federal Code: 001767

**4-year private** university and liberal arts college in large town, affiliated with Roman Catholic Church.

**Enrollment:** 3,749 undergrads.

### BASIC COSTS (2015-2016)

**Tuition and fees:** $29,620.

**Per-credit charge:** $905.

**Room and board:** $8,630.

**Additional info:** Tuition/fee waivers available for adults.

### FINANCIAL AID PICTURE

**Students with need:** Need-based aid available for full-time and part-time students. Work study available nights, weekends, and for part-time students.

**Students without need:** No-need awards available for academics, alumni affiliation, athletics, leadership, music/drama, ROTC, state/district residency.

### FINANCIAL AID PROCEDURES

**Forms required:** FAFSA.

**Dates and Deadlines:** Priority date 3/1; no closing date. Applicants notified on a rolling basis starting 2/1; must reply within 2 week(s) of notification.

**Transfers:** No deadline. Applicants notified on a rolling basis starting 3/15; must reply within 2 week(s) of notification.

### CONTACT

Diane Battistella, Senior Associate Dean
5700 College Road, Lisle, IL 60532
(630) 829-6100

## Benedictine University at Springfield

Springfield, Illinois
www.ben.edu/springfield            Federal Code: 001761

**2-year private** branch campus college in small city, affiliated with Roman Catholic Church.

**Enrollment:** 771 undergrads.

### FINANCIAL AID PICTURE

**Students with need:** Need-based aid available for full-time and part-time students. Work study available nights, weekends, and for part-time students.

**Students without need:** No-need awards available for academics, art, athletics, leadership, religious affiliation.

### FINANCIAL AID PROCEDURES

**Forms required:** FAFSA.

**Dates and Deadlines:** Priority date 4/15; no closing date. Applicants notified on a rolling basis starting 4/15; must reply within 2 week(s) of notification.

### CONTACT

1500 North Fifth Street, Springfield, IL 62702-2694
(217) 525-1420

## Black Hawk College

Moline, Illinois
www.bhc.edu                    Federal Code: 001638

**2-year public** community college in large town.

**Enrollment:** 3,441 undergrads, 47% part-time. 481 full-time freshmen.

**Selectivity:** Open admission; but selective for some programs.

### BASIC COSTS (2015-2016)

**Tuition and fees:** $4,050; out-of-district residents $7,500; out-of-state residents $7,650.

**Per-credit charge:** $135; out-of-district residents $250; out-of-state residents $255.

**Additional info:** Tuition for five contiguous counties is $180 per credit hour. Online courses are $150 per credit hour in-state;$175 per credit hour out-of-state.

### FINANCIAL AID PICTURE (2014-2015)

**Students with need:** Out of 480 full-time freshmen who applied for aid, 320 were judged to have need. Of these, 292 received aid, and 46 had their full need met. Average financial aid package met 72% of need; average scholarship/grant was $2,306; average loan was $1,614. For part-time students, average financial aid package was $1,780.

**Students without need:** 43 full-time freshmen who did not demonstrate need for aid received scholarships/grants; average award was $1,856. No-need awards available for academics, art, athletics, leadership, music/drama, state/district residency.

**Scholarships offered: Merit:** Scholarship program; based on need and/or merit. Tuition awards; awarded to students who graduate in the top 10% of their class. **Athletic:** 52 full-time freshmen received athletic scholarships; average amount $2,356.

**Additional info:** 5/15 deadline for scholarships.

**FINANCIAL AID PROCEDURES**

**Forms required:** FAFSA.

**Dates and Deadlines:** Priority date 5/15; no closing date. Applicants notified on a rolling basis starting 5/1.

**Transfers:** No deadline. Applicants notified on a rolling basis.

**CONTACT**

Joanna Dye, Director, Financial Aid
6600-34th Avenue, Moline, IL 61265-5899
(309) 796-5400

## Blackburn College
Carlinville, Illinois
www.blackburn.edu
Federal Code: 001639

**4-year private** liberal arts college in small town, affiliated with Presbyterian Church (USA).

**Enrollment:** 579 undergrads, 3% part-time. 167 full-time freshmen.

**Selectivity:** Admits 50 to 75% of applicants.

**BASIC COSTS (2016-2017)**

**Tuition and fees:** $21,162.

**Per-credit charge:** $680.

**Room and board:** $7,364.

**FINANCIAL AID PICTURE (2014-2015)**

**Students with need:** Out of 156 full-time freshmen who applied for aid, 136 were judged to have need. Of these, 136 received aid, and 30 had their full need met. Average financial aid package met 76% of need; average scholarship/grant was $13,988; average loan was $2,948. For part-time students, average financial aid package was $6,805.

**Students without need:** 33 full-time freshmen who did not demonstrate need for aid received scholarships/grants; average award was $4,515. No-need awards available for academics, state/district residency.

**Additional info:** Each resident student works 160 hours per semester.

**FINANCIAL AID PROCEDURES**

**Forms required:** FAFSA.

**Dates and Deadlines:** Priority date 3/1; no closing date. Applicants notified on a rolling basis starting 3/1; must reply within 4 week(s) of notification.

**Transfers:** No deadline. Applicants notified on a rolling basis; must reply within 4 week(s) of notification.

**CONTACT**

Jane Kelsey, Director of Financial Aid
700 College Avenue, Carlinville, IL 62626
(217) 854-5774

## Blessing-Rieman College of Nursing
Quincy, Illinois
www.brcn.edu
Federal Code: 006214

**4-year private** health science and nursing college in large town.

**Enrollment:** 233 undergrads, 18% part-time.

**Selectivity:** Admits 50 to 75% of applicants.

**BASIC COSTS (2016-2017)**

**Tuition and fees:** $22,900.

**Per-credit charge:** $763.

**FINANCIAL AID PICTURE (2014-2015)**

**Students with need:** Average financial aid package for all full-time undergraduates was $5,260; for part-time $5,260. 39% awarded as scholarships/grants, 61% awarded as loans/jobs.

**Students without need:** No-need awards available for academics, alumni affiliation, leadership, state/district residency.

**Additional info:** Financial aid for freshmen and sophomores administered by Culver-Stockton College and Quincy University. Institution does not have first time, full-time students, only junior and senior students.

**FINANCIAL AID PROCEDURES**

**Forms required:** FAFSA.

**Dates and Deadlines:** Priority date 3/1; closing date 4/1.

**Transfers:** Applicants notified on a rolling basis starting 12/15.

**CONTACT**

Kevin Turnbull, Financial Aid Coordinator
PO Box 7005, Quincy, IL 62305
(217) 228-5520 ext. 6993

## Bradley University
Peoria, Illinois
www.bradley.edu
Federal Code: 001641

**4-year private** university in large city.

**Enrollment:** 4,436 undergrads, 5% part-time. 948 full-time freshmen.

**Selectivity:** Admits 50 to 75% of applicants.

**BASIC COSTS (2015-2016)**

**Tuition and fees:** $31,480.

**Per-credit charge:** $830.

**Room and board:** $9,700.

**FINANCIAL AID PICTURE (2014-2015)**

**Students with need:** Out of 837 full-time freshmen who applied for aid, 647 were judged to have need. Of these, 646 received aid, and 128 had their full need met. Average financial aid package met 72% of need; average scholarship/grant was $15,901; average loan was $4,704. Need-based aid available for part-time students.

**Students without need:** 111 full-time freshmen who did not demonstrate need for aid received scholarships/grants; average award was $9,871. No-need awards available for academics, alumni affiliation, art, athletics, leadership, minority status, music/drama.

**Scholarships offered:** 41 full-time freshmen received athletic scholarships; average amount $20,259.

**FINANCIAL AID PROCEDURES**

**Forms required:** FAFSA.

**Dates and Deadlines:** Priority date 3/1; no closing date. Applicants notified on a rolling basis starting 3/1; must reply by 5/1 or within 2 week(s) of notification.

**Transfers:** No deadline. Applicants notified by 3/1; must reply by 5/1 or within 2 week(s) of notification.

**CONTACT**

Dave Pardieck, Financial Assistance Director
1501 W. Bradley Avenue, Peoria, IL 61625
(309) 677-3089

## Carl Sandburg College

Galesburg, Illinois
www.sandburg.edu                    Federal Code: 007265

**2-year public** community college in large town.
**Enrollment:** 1,516 undergrads.
**Selectivity:** Open admission; but selective for some programs.

**BASIC COSTS (2015-2016)**
**Tuition and fees:** $4,650; out-of-district residents $6,540; out-of-state residents $7,680.
**Per-credit charge:** $150; out-of-district residents $213; out-of-state residents $251.

**FINANCIAL AID PICTURE**
**Students with need:** Need-based aid available for full-time students.
**Students without need:** No-need awards available for academics, art, athletics, music/drama.

**FINANCIAL AID PROCEDURES**
**Forms required:** FAFSA, institutional form.
**Dates and Deadlines:** Priority date 5/1; no closing date. Applicants notified on a rolling basis starting 5/1; must reply by 8/25 or within 2 week(s) of notification.
**Transfers:** Must reply by 8/25. Tuition guarantee provides no increase in tuition up to three years as long as enrolled full-time.

**CONTACT**
Lisa Hanson, Director of Financial Aid
2400 Tom L. Wilson Boulevard, Galesburg, IL 61401
(309) 341-5283

## City Colleges of Chicago: Harold Washington College

Chicago, Illinois
www.ccc.edu

**2-year public** community college in very large city.
**Enrollment:** 7,943 undergrads.
**Selectivity:** Open admission; but selective for some programs.

**BASIC COSTS (2015-2016)**
**Tuition and fees:** $3,506; out-of-district residents $9,206; out-of-state residents $11,906.

**FINANCIAL AID PICTURE**
**Students with need:** Need-based aid available for full-time and part-time students. Work study available nights.
**Students without need:** This college awards aid only to students with need.

**FINANCIAL AID PROCEDURES**
**Forms required:** FAFSA.
**Dates and Deadlines:** Applicants notified on a rolling basis.

**CONTACT**
Elina Fonseca, Financial Aid Director
30 East Lake Street, Chicago, IL 60601
(312) 553-6041

## City Colleges of Chicago: Harry S. Truman College

Chicago, Illinois
www.ccc.edu

**2-year public** community college in very large city.
**Enrollment:** 4,135 undergrads.

**Selectivity:** Open admission; but selective for some programs.

**BASIC COSTS (2015-2016)**
**Tuition and fees:** $3,506; out-of-district residents $9,206; out-of-state residents $11,906.

**FINANCIAL AID PICTURE**
**Students with need:** Need-based aid available for full-time and part-time students. Work study available nights, weekends, and for part-time students.
**Students without need:** This college awards aid only to students with need.

**FINANCIAL AID PROCEDURES**
**Forms required:** FAFSA.
**Dates and Deadlines:** Applicants notified on a rolling basis.

**CONTACT**
Robert Evans, Financial Aid Director
1145 West Wilson Avenue, Chicago, IL 60640
(773) 907-4810

## City Colleges of Chicago: Kennedy-King College

Chicago, Illinois
www.ccc.edu

**2-year public** community college in very large city.
**Enrollment:** 2,821 undergrads.
**Selectivity:** Open admission.

**BASIC COSTS (2015-2016)**
**Tuition and fees:** $3,506; out-of-district residents $9,206; out-of-state residents $11,906.

**FINANCIAL AID PICTURE**
**Students with need:** Need-based aid available for full-time and part-time students.
**Students without need:** This college awards aid only to students with need.

**FINANCIAL AID PROCEDURES**
**Forms required:** FAFSA.
**Dates and Deadlines:** Applicants notified on a rolling basis; must reply within 2 week(s) of notification.

**CONTACT**
Tabitha O'Neil, Financial Aid Director
6301 South Halsted Street, Chicago, IL 60621
(773) 602-5133

## City Colleges of Chicago: Malcolm X College

Chicago, Illinois
www.ccc.edu

**2-year public** community college in very large city.
**Enrollment:** 4,027 undergrads.
**Selectivity:** Open admission; but selective for some programs.

**BASIC COSTS (2015-2016)**
**Tuition and fees:** $3,506; out-of-district residents $9,206; out-of-state residents $11,906.

**FINANCIAL AID PICTURE**
**Students with need:** Need-based aid available for full-time and part-time students.
**Students without need:** This college awards aid only to students with need.

**FINANCIAL AID PROCEDURES**

**Forms required:** FAFSA, institutional form.

**Dates and Deadlines:** Applicants notified on a rolling basis; must reply within 2 week(s) of notification.

**CONTACT**

Tamika Davenport, Financial Aid Director

1900 West Van Buren Street, Chicago, IL 60612

## City Colleges of Chicago: Olive-Harvey College

Chicago, Illinois

www.ccc.edu

**2-year public** community college in very large city.

**Enrollment:** 2,149 undergrads.

**Selectivity:** Open admission; but selective for some programs.

**BASIC COSTS (2015-2016)**

**Tuition and fees:** $3,506; out-of-district residents $9,206; out-of-state residents $11,906.

**FINANCIAL AID PICTURE**

**Students with need:** Need-based aid available for full-time and part-time students.

**FINANCIAL AID PROCEDURES**

**Forms required:** FAFSA.

**Dates and Deadlines:** Applicants notified on a rolling basis.

**CONTACT**

Jolander Jeffries, Financial Aid Director

10001 South Woodlawn Avenue, Chicago, IL 60628

(773) 291-6391

## City Colleges of Chicago: Richard J. Daley College

Chicago, Illinois

www.ccc.edu

**2-year public** community college in very large city.

**Enrollment:** 3,953 undergrads.

**Selectivity:** Open admission; but selective for some programs.

**BASIC COSTS (2015-2016)**

**Tuition and fees:** $3,506; out-of-district residents $9,206; out-of-state residents $11,906.

**FINANCIAL AID PICTURE**

**Students with need:** Need-based aid available for full-time students.

**FINANCIAL AID PROCEDURES**

**Forms required:** FAFSA.

**Dates and Deadlines:** Applicants notified on a rolling basis.

**Transfers:** College work study jobs and Federal Supplemental Educational Opportunity Grant (SEOG) may not be available to transfers.

**CONTACT**

Loucynda White, Financial Aid Director

7500 South Pulaski Road, Chicago, IL 60652

(773) 838-7581

## City Colleges of Chicago: Wilbur Wright College

Chicago, Illinois

www.ccc.edu

**2-year public** community college in very large city.

**Enrollment:** 7,691 undergrads.

**Selectivity:** Open admission.

**BASIC COSTS (2015-2016)**

**Tuition and fees:** $3,506; out-of-district residents $9,206; out-of-state residents $11,906.

**FINANCIAL AID PICTURE**

**Students with need:** Need-based aid available for full-time and part-time students.

**FINANCIAL AID PROCEDURES**

**Forms required:** FAFSA, institutional form.

**Dates and Deadlines:** Applicants notified on a rolling basis.

**CONTACT**

Inesha Kelly, Financial Aid Director

4300 North Narragansett Avenue, Chicago, IL 60634-4276

(773) 481-8100

## College of DuPage

Glen Ellyn, Illinois

www.cod.edu                    Federal Code: 006656

**2-year public** community college in large town.

**Enrollment:** 16,535 undergrads, 56% part-time. 2,574 full-time freshmen.

**Selectivity:** Open admission; but selective for some programs.

**BASIC COSTS (2015-2016)**

**Tuition and fees:** $4,320; out-of-district residents $9,930; out-of-state residents $12,030.

**Per-credit charge:** $144; out-of-district residents $331; out-of-state residents $401.

**FINANCIAL AID PICTURE (2014-2015)**

**Students with need:** Out of 1,964 full-time freshmen who applied for aid, 1,124 were judged to have need. Of these, 1,043 received aid. For part-time students, average financial aid package was $3,993.

**Students without need:** 105 full-time freshmen who did not demonstrate need for aid received scholarships/grants; average award was $3,639. No-need awards available for academics, art, leadership, minority status, music/drama, state/district residency.

**FINANCIAL AID PROCEDURES**

**Forms required:** FAFSA.

**Dates and Deadlines:** Priority date 4/30; no closing date. Applicants notified on a rolling basis starting 6/1; must reply within 2 week(s) of notification.

**Transfers:** No deadline. Applicants notified on a rolling basis; must reply within 2 week(s) of notification. Must have financial aid application on file indicating previous institutions attended.

**CONTACT**

Earl Dowling, Associate Vice President Enrollment Management

425 Fawell Boulevard, Glen Ellyn, IL 60137-6599

(630) 942-2380

## College of Lake County

Grayslake, Illinois

www.clcillinois.edu            Federal Code: 007694

**2-year public** community college in large town.

**Enrollment:** 11,466 undergrads.

**Selectivity:** Open admission; but selective for some programs.

**BASIC COSTS (2015-2016)**
**Tuition and fees:** $3,870; out-of-district residents $8,955; out-of-state residents $11,855.
**Per-credit charge:** $99; out-of-district residents $256; out-of-state residents $345.
**Additional info:** Tuition/fee waivers available for minority students.

**FINANCIAL AID PICTURE**
**Students with need:** Need-based aid available for full-time and part-time students. Work study available nights.
**Students without need:** No-need awards available for academics, alumni affiliation, art, athletics, leadership, minority status, music/drama.
**Scholarships offered:** Academic Achievement Scholarship: based on GPA and student essay; tuition and fees.

**FINANCIAL AID PROCEDURES**
**Forms required:** FAFSA.
**Dates and Deadlines:** Priority date 6/3; no closing date. Applicants notified on a rolling basis starting 6/15; must reply within 2 week(s) of notification.

**CONTACT**
Erin Fowles, Director, Financial Aid
19351 West Washington Street, Grayslake, IL 60030-1198
(847) 543-2062

## Columbia College Chicago
Chicago, Illinois
www.colum.edu                    Federal Code: 001665

**4-year private** visual arts and liberal arts college in very large city.
**Enrollment:** 8,519 undergrads.

**BASIC COSTS (2015-2016)**
**Tuition and fees:** $24,344.
**Per-credit charge:** $816.
**Room and board:** $13,482.

**FINANCIAL AID PICTURE**
**Students with need:** Need-based aid available for full-time and part-time students.
**Students without need:** No-need awards available for academics, art, leadership, music/drama, state/district residency.

**FINANCIAL AID PROCEDURES**
**Forms required:** FAFSA, institutional form. Accepted but not required for domestic applicants.
**Dates and Deadlines:** Priority date 5/1; no closing date. Applicants notified on a rolling basis.

**CONTACT**
Cynthia Grunden, Assistant VP of Student Financial Services
600 South Michigan Avenue, Chicago, IL 60605-1996
(866) 705-0200

## Concordia University Chicago
River Forest, Illinois
www.cuchicago.edu                Federal Code: 001666

**4-year private** university and liberal arts college in large town, affiliated with Lutheran Church - Missouri Synod.
**Enrollment:** 1,441 undergrads. 300 full-time freshmen.

**BASIC COSTS (2015-2016)**
**Tuition and fees:** $29,520.
**Per-credit charge:** $895.
**Room and board:** $8,992.

**FINANCIAL AID PICTURE (2014-2015)**
**Students with need:** Out of 290 full-time freshmen who applied for aid, 271 were judged to have need. Of these, 271 received aid, and 36 had their full need met. Average financial aid package met 76% of need; average scholarship/grant was $19,060; average loan was $3,206. For part-time students, average financial aid package was $6,489.
**Students without need:** 29 full-time freshmen who did not demonstrate need for aid received scholarships/grants; average award was $15,062. No-need awards available for academics, alumni affiliation, music/drama, religious affiliation.
**Scholarships offered:** Presidential Honors: full tuition; selection by essay; 5 per year. Presidential Scholarships: up to $12,000; selection by ACT and GPA. Community Awards: up to $7,000; selection by ACT and GPA. Transfer Honors: up to $10,000; selection by GPA. Music Scholarships: amount varies; selection by audition.

**FINANCIAL AID PROCEDURES**
**Forms required:** FAFSA.
**Dates and Deadlines:** Priority date 2/1; closing date 6/1. Applicants notified on a rolling basis starting 1/24.
**Transfers:** No deadline. Applicants notified on a rolling basis; must reply within 4 week(s) of notification.

**CONTACT**
Aida Asencio-Pinto, Director of Financial Aid
7400 Augusta Street, River Forest, IL 60305-1499
(708) 209-3113

## Danville Area Community College
Danville, Illinois
www.dacc.edu                     Federal Code: 001669

**2-year public** community college in large town.
**Enrollment:** 1,885 undergrads, 47% part-time. 301 full-time freshmen.
**Selectivity:** Open admission.

**BASIC COSTS (2015-2016)**
**Tuition and fees:** $3,900; out-of-district residents $6,150; out-of-state residents $6,150.
**Per-credit charge:** $115; out-of-district residents $190; out-of-state residents $190.

**FINANCIAL AID PICTURE (2014-2015)**
**Students with need:** 86% of average financial aid package awarded as scholarships/grants, 14% awarded as loans/jobs. Need-based aid available for part-time students. Work study available nights, weekends, and for part-time students.
**Students without need:** No-need awards available for academics, art, athletics, leadership, minority status, music/drama, state/district residency.

**FINANCIAL AID PROCEDURES**
**Forms required:** FAFSA, institutional form.
**Dates and Deadlines:** Priority date 7/1; no closing date. Applicants notified on a rolling basis starting 4/1.
**Transfers:** NSLDS reviewed before aid disbursed.

**CONTACT**
Janet Ingargiola, Director of Financial Aid
2000 East Main Street, Danville, IL 61832
(217) 443-8891

## DePaul University
Chicago, Illinois
www.depaul.edu                   Federal Code: 001671

**4-year private** university in very large city, affiliated with Roman Catholic Church.

**Enrollment:** 15,683 undergrads, 13% part-time. 2,551 full-time freshmen.
**Selectivity:** Admits 50 to 75% of applicants.

## BASIC COSTS (2015-2016)
**Tuition and fees:** $36,361.
**Per-credit charge:** $585.
**Room and board:** $12,873.

## FINANCIAL AID PICTURE (2014-2015)
**Students with need:** Out of 2,180 full-time freshmen who applied for aid, 1,806 were judged to have need. Of these, 1,803 received aid, and 196 had their full need met. Average financial aid package met 65% of need; average scholarship/grant was $1,969; average loan was $3,601. For part-time students, average financial aid package was $9,426.
**Students without need:** 626 full-time freshmen who did not demonstrate need for aid received scholarships/grants; average award was $13,940. No-need awards available for academics, art, athletics, leadership, music/drama, ROTC, state/district residency.
**Scholarships offered:** 59 full-time freshmen received athletic scholarships; average amount $21,577.

## FINANCIAL AID PROCEDURES
**Forms required:** FAFSA.
**Dates and Deadlines:** Priority date 3/1; no closing date. Applicants notified on a rolling basis starting 3/15.
**Transfers:** Priority date 2/28; no deadline. Applicants notified on a rolling basis starting 5/1; must reply by 8/1.

## CONTACT
Paula Luff, Director of Financial Aid
1 East Jackson Boulevard Suite 9000, Chicago, IL 60604-2287
(312) 362-8610

## DeVry University: Chicago
Chicago, Illinois
www.devry.edu                    Federal Code: 010727

**4-year for-profit** university in very large city.
**Enrollment:** 1,149 undergrads.

## BASIC COSTS (2015-2016)
**Tuition and fees:** $17,132.
**Per-credit charge:** $609.
**Additional info:** Annual tuition: $10,810-$21,163; fees $50-$90.

## FINANCIAL AID PICTURE
**Students with need:** Need-based aid available for full-time and part-time students.
**Students without need:** This college awards aid only to students with need.

## FINANCIAL AID PROCEDURES
**Forms required:** FAFSA.
**Dates and Deadlines:** Applicants notified on a rolling basis.

## CONTACT
Milena Dobrina, Director of Financial Aid
3300 North Campbell Avenue, Chicago, IL 60618-5994
(773) 929-8509

## Dominican University
River Forest, Illinois
www.dom.edu                    Federal Code: 001750

**4-year private** university and liberal arts college in large town, affiliated with Roman Catholic Church.
**Enrollment:** 2,241 undergrads, 8% part-time. 483 full-time freshmen.

**Selectivity:** Admits 50 to 75% of applicants.

## BASIC COSTS (2015-2016)
**Tuition and fees:** $30,670.
**Per-credit charge:** $1,010.
**Room and board:** $9,380.

## FINANCIAL AID PICTURE (2015-2016)
**Students with need:** Out of 458 full-time freshmen who applied for aid, 435 were judged to have need. Of these, 435 received aid, and 28 had their full need met. Average financial aid package met 76% of need; average scholarship/grant was $21,975; average loan was $3,333. For part-time students, average financial aid package was $9,661.
**Students without need:** 40 full-time freshmen who did not demonstrate need for aid received scholarships/grants; average award was $9,697. No-need awards available for academics, alumni affiliation, art, minority status, religious affiliation.
**Scholarships offered:** Presidential Scholarships; $16,000. Dean's Scholarships; $13,500. University Honor Scholarships; $11,500. Achievement Scholarships; $7,000-$9,900. Merit Scholarships; $7,500-$15,000. All based on ACT/SAT and GPA. Ida Brechtel Scholarships; $7,500; for students majoring in chemistry or biology/chemistry. Alice Welsh Skilling Scholarship; $7,500; for students majoring in visual arts. Residence Life Award; $3,000.

## FINANCIAL AID PROCEDURES
**Forms required:** FAFSA.
**Dates and Deadlines:** Priority date 2/15; no closing date. Applicants notified on a rolling basis starting 3/15; must reply within 2 week(s) of notification.
**Transfers:** No deadline. Applicants notified on a rolling basis starting 3/15; must reply within 3 week(s) of notification.

## CONTACT
Victoria Lamick, Director of Financial Aid
7900 West Division Street, River Forest, IL 60305-1099
(708) 524-6809

## East-West University
Chicago, Illinois
www.eastwest.edu                    Federal Code: 015310

**4-year private** university in very large city.
**Enrollment:** 512 undergrads.
**Selectivity:** Open admission; but selective for some programs.

## BASIC COSTS (2015-2016)
**Tuition and fees:** $20,145.
**Room and board:** $8,811.

## FINANCIAL AID PICTURE
**Students with need:** Need-based aid available for full-time and part-time students.
**Students without need:** No-need awards available for academics.
**Additional info:** Foreign students eligible for institutional scholarship.

## FINANCIAL AID PROCEDURES
**Forms required:** FAFSA.
**Dates and Deadlines:** Closing date 3/31. Applicants notified on a rolling basis starting 1/4; must reply within 4 week(s) of notification.
**Transfers:** Closing date 4/1.

## CONTACT
Cesar Campos, Director of Financial Aid
816 South Michigan Avenue, Chicago, IL 60605-2185
(312) 939-0111

## Eastern Illinois University
Charleston, Illinois
www.eiu.edu                                Federal Code: 001674

**4-year public** university in large town.
**Enrollment:** 7,063 undergrads, 12% part-time. 1,136 full-time freshmen.
**Selectivity:** Admits 50 to 75% of applicants.

**BASIC COSTS (2015-2016)**
**Tuition and fees:** $11,312; out-of-state residents $13,442.
**Per-credit charge:** $285; out-of-state residents $356.
**Room and board:** $9,546.
**Additional info:** Tuition at time of enrollment locked for 4 years.

**FINANCIAL AID PICTURE (2015-2016)**
**Students with need:** Out of 1,053 full-time freshmen who applied for aid, 794 were judged to have need. Of these, 786 received aid, and 60 had their full need met. Average financial aid package met 64% of need; average scholarship/grant was $3,629; average loan was $3,165. For part-time students, average financial aid package was $6,134.
**Students without need:** 160 full-time freshmen who did not demonstrate need for aid received scholarships/grants; average award was $3,560. No-need awards available for academics, art, athletics, leadership, music/drama, ROTC.
**Scholarships offered:** *Merit:* Commitment to Excellence Scholarship; for entering freshmen who demonstrated high academic achievement based on GPA and ACT; renewable, based on maintaining basic requirements. *Athletic:* 36 full-time freshmen received athletic scholarships; average amount $8,090.

**FINANCIAL AID PROCEDURES**
**Forms required:** FAFSA.
**Dates and Deadlines:** Priority date 3/1; no closing date. Applicants notified on a rolling basis starting 3/1; must reply within 2 week(s) of notification.

**CONTACT**
Mandi Starwalt, Interim Senior Associate Director of Financial Aid and Scholarships
600 Lincoln Avenue, Charleston, IL 61920
(217) 581-3713

## Elgin Community College
Elgin, Illinois
www.elgin.edu                              Federal Code: 001675

**2-year public** community college in small city.
**Enrollment:** 8,167 undergrads, 61% part-time. 900 full-time freshmen.
**Selectivity:** Open admission; but selective for some programs.

**BASIC COSTS (2015-2016)**
**Tuition and fees:** $3,580; out-of-district residents $13,030; out-of-state residents $14,950.
**Per-credit charge:** $119; out-of-district residents $434; out-of-state residents $498.

**FINANCIAL AID PICTURE**
**Students with need:** Need-based aid available for full-time and part-time students. Work study available nights, weekends, and for part-time students.
**Students without need:** No-need awards available for academics, alumni affiliation, art, athletics, job skills, leadership, minority status, music/drama, religious affiliation, ROTC, state/district residency.

**FINANCIAL AID PROCEDURES**
**Forms required:** FAFSA, institutional form.
**Dates and Deadlines:** Priority date 6/1; no closing date. Applicants notified on a rolling basis starting 4/6; must reply within 3 week(s) of notification.

**CONTACT**
Amy Perrin, Director of Financial Aid & Scholarships
1700 Spartan Drive, Elgin, IL 60123-7193
(847) 214-7520

## Elmhurst College
Elmhurst, Illinois
www.elmhurst.edu                           Federal Code: 001676

**4-year private** liberal arts college in large town, affiliated with United Church of Christ.
**Enrollment:** 2,752 undergrads, 4% part-time. 478 full-time freshmen.
**Selectivity:** Admits 50 to 75% of applicants.

**BASIC COSTS (2015-2016)**
**Tuition and fees:** $34,450.
**Per-credit charge:** $973.
**Room and board:** $9,816.

**FINANCIAL AID PICTURE (2015-2016)**
**Students with need:** Out of 468 full-time freshmen who applied for aid, 408 were judged to have need. Of these, 408 received aid, and 123 had their full need met. Average financial aid package met 80% of need; average scholarship/grant was $24,766; average loan was $3,467. For part-time students, average financial aid package was $9,745.
**Students without need:** 66 full-time freshmen who did not demonstrate need for aid received scholarships/grants; average award was $18,802. No-need awards available for academics, alumni affiliation, art, minority status, music/drama, religious affiliation, ROTC, state/district residency.
**Scholarships offered:** Presidential Scholarship: up to $18,000. Dean's Scholarship: up to $16,000. Founder's Scholarship: up to $12,000. Trustee Scholarship: up to $10,000 Combination test scores and GPA considered.

**FINANCIAL AID PROCEDURES**
**Forms required:** FAFSA.
**Dates and Deadlines:** Priority date 2/1; no closing date. Applicants notified on a rolling basis starting 2/16; must reply within 3 week(s) of notification.
**Transfers:** No deadline. Applicants notified on a rolling basis; must reply within 3 week(s) of notification.

**CONTACT**
Ruth Pusich, Director of Student Financial Services
190 South Prospect Avenue, Elmhurst, IL 60126-3296
(630) 617-3075

## Eureka College
Eureka, Illinois
www.eureka.edu                             Federal Code: 001678

**4-year private** liberal arts college in small town, affiliated with Christian Church (Disciples of Christ).
**Enrollment:** 654 undergrads.

**BASIC COSTS (2015-2016)**
**Tuition and fees:** $20,510.
**Per-credit charge:** $575.
**Room and board:** $8,635.

**FINANCIAL AID PICTURE**
**Students with need:** Need-based aid available for full-time and part-time students. Work study available nights, weekends, and for part-time students.
**Students without need:** No-need awards available for academics, alumni affiliation, art, leadership, music/drama, religious affiliation.
**Scholarships offered:** Reagan Fellows Program: full tuition; 5 awarded. Sandifer Mentorships: fully paid mentorship anywhere in the world at end of

sophomore year; all freshmen eligible. Eureka College Ministry Fellowship: full tuition scholarships; 2 available each year.

## FINANCIAL AID PROCEDURES

**Forms required:** FAFSA.

**Dates and Deadlines:** Priority date 4/15; no closing date. Applicants notified on a rolling basis starting 2/1; must reply by 5/1 or within 3 week(s) of notification.

**Transfers:** No deadline. Applicants notified on a rolling basis; must reply within 2 week(s) of notification.

## CONTACT

Ellen Rigsby, Director of Financial Aid
300 East College Avenue, Eureka, IL 61530-1500
(309) 467-6311

# Governors State University

University Park, Illinois
www.govst.edu                   Federal Code: 009145

**4-year public** university in large town.
**Enrollment:** 3,526 undergrads, 47% part-time. 203 full-time freshmen.
**Selectivity:** Open admission; but selective for some programs.

## BASIC COSTS (2015-2016)

**Tuition and fees:** $10,246; out-of-state residents $18,406.
**Per-credit charge:** $272; out-of-state residents $544.
**Room only:** $5,238.
**Additional info:** Board plans are declining balance, so lower and higher balances are available and can be changed at any time. Tuition/fee waivers available for minority students.

## FINANCIAL AID PICTURE (2014-2015)

**Students with need:** 41% of average financial aid package awarded as scholarships/grants, 59% awarded as loans/jobs. Need-based aid available for part-time students. Work study available nights, weekends, and for part-time students.
**Students without need:** No-need awards available for academics.

## FINANCIAL AID PROCEDURES

**Forms required:** FAFSA.

**Dates and Deadlines:** Priority date 5/1; closing date 10/1. Applicants notified on a rolling basis starting 3/1; must reply within 2 week(s) of notification.

**Transfers:** Must reply within 2 week(s) of notification.

## CONTACT

John Perry, Financial Aid Director
One University Parkway, University Park, IL 60484
(708) 534-4480

# Greenville College

Greenville, Illinois
www.greenville.edu               Federal Code: 001684

**4-year private** liberal arts college in small town, affiliated with Free Methodist Church of North America.
**Enrollment:** 1,042 undergrads, 2% part-time. 259 full-time freshmen.
**Selectivity:** Admits 50 to 75% of applicants.

## BASIC COSTS (2015-2016)

**Tuition and fees:** $25,088.
**Room and board:** $8,288.

## FINANCIAL AID PICTURE (2014-2015)

**Students with need:** Out of 245 full-time freshmen who applied for aid, 225 were judged to have need. Of these, 225 received aid, and 29 had their full need met. Average financial aid package met 77% of need; average

scholarship/grant was $16,806; average loan was $3,518. For part-time students, average financial aid package was $6,940.

**Students without need:** 33 full-time freshmen who did not demonstrate need for aid received scholarships/grants; average award was $8,477. No-need awards available for academics, alumni affiliation, art, minority status, religious affiliation.

**Scholarships offered:** McAllaster Honors Scholarship; $12,000; 3.5 GPA and 27 ACT/1210 SAT. President's Scholarships; $9,000; 3.0 GPA, 27 ACT/1210 SAT, and leadership qualities. Dean's Scholarship; $8,000; 3.0 GPA, 22 ACT/1020 SAT and leadership qualities. Character & Service Scholarship; $500-$5,000, 2.5 GPA.

## FINANCIAL AID PROCEDURES

**Forms required:** FAFSA.

**Dates and Deadlines:** Priority date 2/1; no closing date. Applicants notified on a rolling basis starting 3/1.

**Transfers:** No deadline. Applicants notified on a rolling basis; must reply within 3 week(s) of notification.

## CONTACT

Marilae Latham, Director of Financial Aid
315 East College Avenue, Greenville, IL 62246
(618) 664-7111

# Harper College

Palatine, Illinois
www.harpercollege.edu             Federal Code: 003961

**2-year public** community college in small city.
**Enrollment:** 11,636 undergrads. 1,392 full-time freshmen.
**Selectivity:** Open admission; but selective for some programs.

## BASIC COSTS (2015-2016)

**Tuition and fees:** $4,007; out-of-district residents $11,717; out-of-state residents $13,982.
**Per-credit charge:** $113.75; out-of-district residents $370.75; out-of-state residents $446.25.

## FINANCIAL AID PICTURE (2014-2015)

**Students with need:** Out of 931 full-time freshmen who applied for aid, 738 were judged to have need. Of these, 599 received aid, and 19 had their full need met. Average financial aid package met 47% of need; average scholarship/grant was $4,991; average loan was $2,874. For part-time students, average financial aid package was $3,348.

**Students without need:** 78 full-time freshmen who did not demonstrate need for aid received scholarships/grants; average award was $1,797. No-need awards available for academics, art, leadership, minority status, music/drama, state/district residency.

**Scholarships offered:** Distinguished Scholar Award; full tuition and fees, renewable for second year; based on 27 ACT with 23 math, 20 reading, and 19 English OR 3.5/4.0 or 4.5/5.0 GPA. Trustee Scholarship; based on 2.5/4.0 or 3.5/4.0 GPA and high school's recommendation.

## FINANCIAL AID PROCEDURES

**Forms required:** FAFSA.

**Dates and Deadlines:** Closing date 3/1. Applicants notified on a rolling basis starting 3/1; must reply within 2 week(s) of notification.

**Transfers:** No deadline. Applicants notified on a rolling basis starting 3/1; must reply within 2 week(s) of notification.

## CONTACT

Laura McGee, Director, Scholarships and Financial Assistance
1200 West Algonquin Road, Palatine, IL 60067-7398
(847) 925-6248

## Heartland Community College

Normal, Illinois
www.heartland.edu                    Federal Code: 030838

**2-year public** community college in small city.
**Enrollment:** 3,354 undergrads, 46% part-time. 379 full-time freshmen.
**Selectivity:** Open admission; but selective for some programs.

### BASIC COSTS (2015-2016)
**Tuition and fees:** $4,260; out-of-district residents $8,520; out-of-state residents $12,780.
**Per-credit charge:** $142; out-of-district residents $284; out-of-state residents $426.

### FINANCIAL AID PICTURE
**Students with need:** Need-based aid available for full-time and part-time students. Work study available nights, weekends, and for part-time students.
**Students without need:** No-need awards available for academics, alumni affiliation, athletics, job skills, leadership, minority status, state/district residency.

### FINANCIAL AID PROCEDURES
**Forms required:** FAFSA, institutional form.
**Dates and Deadlines:** Priority date 4/1; no closing date. Applicants notified on a rolling basis starting 5/15; must reply within 2 week(s) of notification.

### CONTACT
Todd Burns, Director of Financial Aid
1500 West Raab Road, Normal, IL 61761
(309) 268-8020

## Highland Community College

Freeport, Illinois
www.highland.edu                     Federal Code: 001681

**2-year public** community college in large town.
**Enrollment:** 1,511 undergrads, 40% part-time. 324 full-time freshmen.
**Selectivity:** Open admission; but selective for some programs.

### BASIC COSTS (2015-2016)
**Tuition and fees:** $4,290; out-of-district residents $6,510; out-of-state residents $6,780.
**Per-credit charge:** $123; out-of-district residents $197; out-of-state residents $206.

### FINANCIAL AID PICTURE (2014-2015)
**Students with need:** Out of 285 full-time freshmen who applied for aid, 236 were judged to have need. Of these, 222 received aid. Average financial aid package met 34% of need; average scholarship/grant was $5,038; average loan was $2,686. For part-time students, average financial aid package was $2,737.
**Students without need:** 15 full-time freshmen who did not demonstrate need for aid received scholarships/grants; average award was $4,421. No-need awards available for academics, athletics.
**Scholarships offered:** 2 full-time freshmen received athletic scholarships; average amount $220.

### FINANCIAL AID PROCEDURES
**Forms required:** FAFSA, institutional form.
**Dates and Deadlines:** Applicants notified on a rolling basis starting 8/1; must reply within 2 week(s) of notification.
**Transfers:** No deadline. Applicants notified on a rolling basis starting 4/1.

### CONTACT
Kathy Bangasser, Director of Financial Aid
2998 West Pearl City Road, Freeport, IL 61032-9341
(815) 599-3559

## Illinois Central College

East Peoria, Illinois
www.icc.edu                          Federal Code: 006753

**2-year public** community college in large town.
**Enrollment:** 7,425 undergrads, 55% part-time. 701 full-time freshmen.
**Selectivity:** Open admission; but selective for some programs.

### BASIC COSTS (2015-2016)
**Tuition and fees:** $4,050; out-of-state residents $10,050.
**Per-credit charge:** $135; out-of-state residents $290.

### FINANCIAL AID PICTURE
**Students with need:** Need-based aid available for full-time and part-time students.
**Students without need:** No-need awards available for academics, athletics, minority status, music/drama, state/district residency.

### FINANCIAL AID PROCEDURES
**Forms required:** FAFSA.
**Dates and Deadlines:** Priority date 6/1; no closing date. Applicants notified on a rolling basis starting 5/1; must reply within 2 week(s) of notification.

### CONTACT
Beth McClain, Dean of Enrollment Management
1 College Drive, East Peoria, IL 61635-0001
(309) 694-5311

## Illinois College

Jacksonville, Illinois
www.ic.edu                           Federal Code: 001688

**4-year private** liberal arts college in large town, affiliated with Presbyterian Church (USA).
**Enrollment:** 942 undergrads. 254 full-time freshmen.
**Selectivity:** Admits 50 to 75% of applicants.

### BASIC COSTS (2015-2016)
**Tuition and fees:** $31,660.
**Per-credit charge:** $970.
**Room and board:** $9,190.

### FINANCIAL AID PICTURE (2014-2015)
**Students with need:** Out of 240 full-time freshmen who applied for aid, 222 were judged to have need. Of these, 222 received aid, and 47 had their full need met. Average financial aid package met 87% of need; average scholarship/grant was $22,274; average loan was $4,416. For part-time students, average financial aid package was $4,217.
**Students without need:** 32 full-time freshmen who did not demonstrate need for aid received scholarships/grants; average award was $16,268. No-need awards available for academics, art, music/drama.
**Scholarships offered:** College transfer scholarship; available with 12 transferable credit hours and minimum 3.0 GPA.

### FINANCIAL AID PROCEDURES
**Forms required:** FAFSA.
**Dates and Deadlines:** Priority date 1/31; no closing date. Applicants notified on a rolling basis starting 2/15; must reply within 2 week(s) of notification.
**Transfers:** No deadline. Applicants notified on a rolling basis starting 6/1; must reply within 2 week(s) of notification.

### CONTACT
Katherine Taylor, Director of Financial Aid
1101 West College Avenue, Jacksonville, IL 62650
(217) 245-3035

## Illinois Eastern Community Colleges: Frontier Community College

Fairfield, Illinois
www.iecc.edu/fcc                    Federal Code: 014090

**2-year public** community college in small town.
**Enrollment:** 341 undergrads, 48% part-time. 80 full-time freshmen.
**Selectivity:** Open admission; but selective for some programs.

**BASIC COSTS (2015-2016)**
**Tuition and fees:** $2,950; out-of-district residents $8,512; out-of-state residents $10,378.
**Per-credit charge:** $83; out-of-district residents $268; out-of-state residents $330.

**FINANCIAL AID PICTURE**
**Students with need:** Need-based aid available for full-time and part-time students.
**Students without need:** No-need awards available for academics, athletics, state/district residency.

**FINANCIAL AID PROCEDURES**
**Forms required:** FAFSA, institutional form.
**Dates and Deadlines:** Applicants notified on a rolling basis starting 8/1; must reply within 2 week(s) of notification.

**CONTACT**
Lori Noe, Financial Aid Coordinator
Two Frontier Drive, Fairfield, IL 62837-9801
(618) 842-3711

## Illinois Eastern Community Colleges: Lincoln Trail College

Robinson, Illinois
www.iecc.edu/ltc                    Federal Code: 009786

**2-year public** community college in small town.
**Enrollment:** 546 undergrads, 26% part-time. 154 full-time freshmen.
**Selectivity:** Open admission; but selective for some programs.

**BASIC COSTS (2015-2016)**
**Tuition and fees:** $2,950; out-of-district residents $8,512; out-of-state residents $10,378.
**Per-credit charge:** $83; out-of-district residents $268; out-of-state residents $330.

**FINANCIAL AID PICTURE**
**Students with need:** Need-based aid available for full-time and part-time students.
**Students without need:** No-need awards available for academics, athletics, state/district residency.

**FINANCIAL AID PROCEDURES**
**Forms required:** FAFSA, institutional form.
**Dates and Deadlines:** Applicants notified on a rolling basis starting 8/1; must reply within 2 week(s) of notification.

**CONTACT**
Aaron White, Coordinator of Financial Aid
11220 State Highway 1, Robinson, IL 62454-5707
(618) 544-8657

## Illinois Eastern Community Colleges: Olney Central College

Olney, Illinois
www.iecc.edu/occ                    Federal Code: 001742

**2-year public** community college in small town.
**Enrollment:** 805 undergrads, 26% part-time. 180 full-time freshmen.
**Selectivity:** Open admission; but selective for some programs.

**BASIC COSTS (2015-2016)**
**Tuition and fees:** $2,950; out-of-district residents $8,512; out-of-state residents $10,378.
**Per-credit charge:** $83; out-of-district residents $268; out-of-state residents $330.

**FINANCIAL AID PICTURE**
**Students with need:** Need-based aid available for full-time and part-time students.
**Students without need:** No-need awards available for academics, athletics, state/district residency.

**FINANCIAL AID PROCEDURES**
**Forms required:** FAFSA, institutional form.
**Dates and Deadlines:** Applicants notified on a rolling basis starting 8/1; must reply within 2 week(s) of notification.

**CONTACT**
Veralee Harris, Financial Aid Coordinator
305 North West Street, Olney, IL 62450
(618) 395-7777

## Illinois Eastern Community Colleges: Wabash Valley College

Mount Carmel, Illinois
www.iecc.edu/wvc                    Federal Code: 001779

**2-year public** community college in small town.
**Enrollment:** 702 undergrads, 30% part-time. 224 full-time freshmen.
**Selectivity:** Open admission; but selective for some programs.

**BASIC COSTS (2015-2016)**
**Tuition and fees:** $2,950; out-of-district residents $8,512; out-of-state residents $10,378.
**Per-credit charge:** $83; out-of-district residents $268; out-of-state residents $330.

**FINANCIAL AID PICTURE**
**Students with need:** Need-based aid available for full-time and part-time students.
**Students without need:** No-need awards available for academics, athletics, state/district residency.

**FINANCIAL AID PROCEDURES**
**Forms required:** FAFSA, institutional form.
**Dates and Deadlines:** Applicants notified on a rolling basis starting 8/1; must reply within 2 week(s) of notification.

**CONTACT**
Mary Johnson, Financial Aid Coordinator
2200 College Drive, Mount Carmel, IL 62863-2657
(618) 262-8641

## Illinois Institute of Art: Chicago

Chicago, Illinois
www.ilic.artinstitutes.edu          Federal Code: 012584

**4-year for-profit** visual arts college in very large city.
**Enrollment:** 1,807 undergrads.

## BASIC COSTS (2015-2016)

**Additional info:** Diploma programs: $23,334-$27,665, books and supplies $800-$950. Associate programs: $44,019-$46,802, books and supplies $1,500. Bachelor's programs: $87,489-$92,372, books and supplies $3,000.

## FINANCIAL AID PICTURE

**Students with need:** Need-based aid available for full-time and part-time students.

## FINANCIAL AID PROCEDURES

**Forms required:** FAFSA.

**Dates and Deadlines:** Priority date 5/1; no closing date. Applicants notified on a rolling basis.

## CONTACT

350 North Orleans Street, Chicago, IL 60654

# Illinois Institute of Art: Schaumburg

Schaumburg, Illinois
www.artinstitutes.edu/schaumburg  Federal Code: 012584

**3-year for-profit** visual arts and career college in small city.
**Enrollment:** 902 undergrads.
**Selectivity:** Open admission.

## BASIC COSTS (2015-2016)

**Additional info:** Associate programs: $43,620-$44,019, books and supplies $1,500. Bachelor's programs: $87,090-$88,584, books and supplies $3,000.

## FINANCIAL AID PICTURE

**Students with need:** Need-based aid available for full-time and part-time students. Work study available nights, weekends, and for part-time students.
**Students without need:** No-need awards available for academics, art.
**Scholarships offered:** Scholarships based on GPA and talent-based scholarships available.

## FINANCIAL AID PROCEDURES

**Forms required:** FAFSA.
**Dates and Deadlines:** Priority date 3/1; no closing date.
**Transfers:** No deadline. Applicants notified on a rolling basis.

## CONTACT

Joe Payne, Director of Student Financial Services
1000 North Plaza Drive, Schaumburg, IL 60173
(800) 314-3450

# Illinois Institute of Technology

Chicago, Illinois
www.iit.edu  Federal Code: 001691

**4-year private** university and engineering college in very large city.
**Enrollment:** 2,923 undergrads, 5% part-time. 440 full-time freshmen.
**Selectivity:** Admits 50 to 75% of applicants.

## BASIC COSTS (2015-2016)

**Tuition and fees:** $43,680.
**Room and board:** $11,300.

## FINANCIAL AID PICTURE (2014-2015)

**Students with need:** Out of 309 full-time freshmen who applied for aid, 283 were judged to have need. Of these, 283 received aid, and 61 had their full need met. Average financial aid package met 83% of need; average scholarship/grant was $32,136; average loan was $3,657. For part-time students, average financial aid package was $13,681.
**Students without need:** 152 full-time freshmen who did not demonstrate need for aid received scholarships/grants; average award was $24,656. No-need awards available for academics, alumni affiliation, leadership, ROTC.

**Scholarships offered:** Heald Academic Scholarships; $12,000-$25,000. Camras Scholar Program; full tuition and advanced access to research and leadership development; top 5% of applicant pool. Crown Scholarship; full tuition for five years; first-year full-time architecture student; one offered.

## FINANCIAL AID PROCEDURES

**Forms required:** FAFSA.
**Dates and Deadlines:** Priority date 2/1; no closing date. Applicants notified on a rolling basis starting 3/1.
**Transfers:** No deadline. Applicants notified on a rolling basis starting 3/15.

## CONTACT

Abigail McGrath, Director of Financial Aid
10 West 33rd Street, Chicago, IL 60616-3793
(312) 567-7219

# Illinois State University

Normal, Illinois
www.ilstu.edu  Federal Code: 001692

**4-year public** university in small city.
**Enrollment:** 18,343 undergrads, 7% part-time. 3,618 full-time freshmen.
**Selectivity:** Admits over 75% of applicants.

## BASIC COSTS (2016-2017)

**Tuition and fees:** $13,666; out-of-state residents $21,482.
**Per-credit charge:** $359.47; out-of-state residents $620.
**Room and board:** $9,850.
**Additional info:** Tuition at time of enrollment locked for 4 years; tuition/fee waivers available for adults.

## FINANCIAL AID PICTURE

**Students with need:** Need-based aid available for full-time and part-time students. Work study available nights, weekends, and for part-time students.
**Students without need:** No-need awards available for academics, alumni affiliation, art, athletics, leadership, music/drama, ROTC.
**Scholarships offered:** Various non-need based merit scholarships available, including Presidential Scholars' Program, Provost's Scholarship, and Dean's Scholarship.

## FINANCIAL AID PROCEDURES

**Forms required:** FAFSA.
**Dates and Deadlines:** Priority date 3/1; no closing date. Applicants notified on a rolling basis starting 4/1; must reply within 2 week(s) of notification.

## CONTACT

Jana Albrecht, Director of Financial Aid
Campus Box 2200, Normal, IL 61790-2200
(309) 438-2231

# Illinois Valley Community College

Oglesby, Illinois
www.ivcc.edu  Federal Code: 001705

**2-year public** community college in small town.
**Enrollment:** 2,572 undergrads.
**Selectivity:** Open admission; but selective for some programs.

## BASIC COSTS (2015-2016)

**Tuition and fees:** $3,580; out-of-district residents $9,944; out-of-state residents $10,752.
**Per-credit charge:** $112; out-of-district residents $324; out-of-state residents $351.

## FINANCIAL AID PICTURE

**Students with need:** Need-based aid available for full-time and part-time students. Work study available nights.

**Students without need:** No-need awards available for academics, art, athletics, leadership, music/drama.

**Scholarships offered:** Foundation scholarships available.

### FINANCIAL AID PROCEDURES

**Forms required:** FAFSA.

**Dates and Deadlines:** Priority date 3/1; no closing date. Applicants notified on a rolling basis starting 3/1.

### CONTACT

Patty Williamson, Director, Financial Aid

815 North Orlando Smith Avenue, Oglesby, IL 61348-9693

(815) 224-0438

## Illinois Wesleyan University

Bloomington, Illinois

www.iwu.edu　　　　　　　　　Federal Code: 001696

**4-year private** university and liberal arts college in small city.

**Enrollment:** 1,834 undergrads, 1% part-time. 450 full-time freshmen.

**Selectivity:** Admits 50 to 75% of applicants.

### BASIC COSTS (2015-2016)

**Tuition and fees:** $42,490.

**Per-credit charge:** $1,322.

**Room and board:** $9,796.

### FINANCIAL AID PICTURE (2015-2016)

**Students with need:** Out of 389 full-time freshmen who applied for aid, 300 were judged to have need. Of these, 300 received aid, and 135 had their full need met. Average financial aid package met 87% of need; average scholarship/grant was $26,251; average loan was $4,318.

**Students without need:** 147 full-time freshmen who did not demonstrate need for aid received scholarships/grants; average award was $19,615. No-need awards available for academics, art, music/drama.

**Scholarships offered:** Academic scholarships based on high school academic performance, recommendations, testing. Talent awards available in music, art, theater, and musical theater. Limited number of full-tuition awards in music.

### FINANCIAL AID PROCEDURES

**Forms required:** FAFSA, institutional form.

**Dates and Deadlines:** Priority date 3/1; no closing date. Applicants notified on a rolling basis starting 3/1; must reply by 5/1.

**Transfers:** No deadline. Applicants notified on a rolling basis; must reply by 5/1 or within 3 week(s) of notification.

### CONTACT

Scott Seibring, Director of Financial Aid

PO Box 2900, Bloomington, IL 61702-2900

(309) 556-3096

## International Academy of Design and Technology: Chicago

Chicago, Illinois

www.iadtchicago.edu　　　　　Federal Code: 021603

**4-year for-profit** visual arts and technical college in very large city.

**Enrollment:** 229 undergrads.

**Selectivity:** Open admission.

### BASIC COSTS (2015-2016)

**Additional info:** Associate degree program tuition $38,400. Bachelor's degree program tuition $72,000. Books included in tuition. Application fee $50.

### FINANCIAL AID PICTURE

**Students with need:** Need-based aid available for full-time and part-time students.

**Students without need:** This college awards aid only to students with need.

**Additional info:** College work study programs available to day and evening students.

### FINANCIAL AID PROCEDURES

**Forms required:** FAFSA.

**Dates and Deadlines:** Applicants notified on a rolling basis.

**Transfers:** No deadline. Applicants notified on a rolling basis; must reply within 2 week(s) of notification.

### CONTACT

Andrea Watkins, Associate Director of Financial Aid

One North State Street, Suite 500, Chicago, IL 60602

(312) 980-9200 ext. 9251

## John A. Logan College

Carterville, Illinois

www.jalc.edu　　　　　　　　　Federal Code: 008076

**2-year public** community college in small town.

**Enrollment:** 2,600 undergrads.

**Selectivity:** Open admission; but selective for some programs.

### FINANCIAL AID PICTURE

**Students with need:** Need-based aid available for full-time and part-time students.

**Students without need:** This college awards aid only to students with need.

### FINANCIAL AID PROCEDURES

**Forms required:** FAFSA, institutional form.

**Dates and Deadlines:** Priority date 5/1; no closing date. Applicants notified on a rolling basis starting 5/1.

### CONTACT

Sherry Summary, Director for Student Financial Assistance

700 Logan College Road, Carterville, IL 62918

(618) 985-3741 ext. 8308

## John Wood Community College

Quincy, Illinois

www.jwcc.edu　　　　　　　　　Federal Code: 012813

**2-year public** community college in large town.

**Enrollment:** 1,612 undergrads.

**Selectivity:** Open admission; but selective for some programs.

### BASIC COSTS (2015-2016)

**Tuition and fees:** $4,614; out-of-state residents $7,914.

**Per-credit charge:** $147; out-of-state residents $257.

### FINANCIAL AID PICTURE

**Students with need:** Need-based aid available for full-time and part-time students. Work study available nights, weekends, and for part-time students.

**Scholarships offered:** Non-need based scholarships and awards are available. Interested students must apply and be selected. Area organizations also have scholarships and awards available.

### FINANCIAL AID PROCEDURES

**Forms required:** FAFSA.

**Dates and Deadlines:** Applicants notified on a rolling basis starting 3/1.

## CONTACT
Melanie Lechtenberg, Director of Financial Aid
1301 South 48th Street, Quincy, IL 62305-8736
(217) 641-4336

## Joliet Junior College
Joliet, Illinois
www.jjc.edu                  Federal Code: 001699

**2-year public** community and junior college in small city.
**Enrollment:** 11,945 undergrads.
**Selectivity:** Open admission; but selective for some programs and for out-of-state students.

### BASIC COSTS (2015-2016)
**Tuition and fees:** $3,450; out-of-district residents $10,530; out-of-state residents $11,190.
**Per-credit charge:** $115; out-of-district residents $320; out-of-state residents $342.

### FINANCIAL AID PICTURE
**Students with need:** Need-based aid available for full-time and part-time students. Work study available nights, weekends, and for part-time students.
**Students without need:** No-need awards available for academics.

### FINANCIAL AID PROCEDURES
**Forms required:** FAFSA, institutional form.
**Dates and Deadlines:** Closing date 6/12. Applicants notified on a rolling basis starting 5/15.

### CONTACT
David Seward, Director of Financial Aid
1215 Houbolt Road, Joliet, IL 60431-8938
(815) 729-9020 ext. 2701

## Judson University
Elgin, Illinois
www.judsonu.edu              Federal Code: 001700

**4-year private** university and liberal arts college in small city, affiliated with American Baptist Churches in the USA.
**Enrollment:** 1,077 undergrads, 32% part-time. 145 full-time freshmen.
**Selectivity:** Open admission; but selective for some programs.

### BASIC COSTS (2016-2017)
**Tuition and fees:** $28,700.
**Per-credit charge:** $1,165.
**Room and board:** $9,650.

### FINANCIAL AID PICTURE (2015-2016)
**Students with need:** Out of 171 full-time freshmen who applied for aid, 160 were judged to have need. Of these, 160 received aid, and 30 had their full need met. Average financial aid package met 68% of need; average scholarship/grant was $10,414; average loan was $4,317. For part-time students, average financial aid package was $10,412.
**Students without need:** 17 full-time freshmen who did not demonstrate need for aid received scholarships/grants; average award was $8,558. No-need awards available for academics, alumni affiliation, art, athletics, leadership, music/drama, religious affiliation.
**Scholarships offered:** *Merit:* Trustees' Scholarship: $16,000; based on ACT/SAT and GPA. President's Scholarship: $14,000; based on ACT/SAT and GPA. Dean's Scholarship: $12,000; based on ACT/SAT and GPA. Faculty Scholarship: $10,000; based on ACT/SAT and GPA. University Scholarship: $8,000; based on ACT/SAT and GPA. *Athletic:* 73 full-time freshmen received athletic scholarships; average amount $4,817.

### FINANCIAL AID PROCEDURES
**Forms required:** FAFSA.
**Dates and Deadlines:** Priority date 2/15; closing date 5/1. Applicants notified on a rolling basis starting 3/1; must reply by 5/1 or within 4 week(s) of notification.
**Transfers:** No deadline. Applicants notified on a rolling basis starting 3/1; must reply by 5/1 or within 4 week(s) of notification.

### CONTACT
Diana Winton, Interim Director of Financial Aid
1151 North State Street, Elgin, IL 60123-1404
(847) 628-2530

## Kankakee Community College
Kankakee, Illinois
www.kcc.edu                  Federal Code: 007690

**2-year public** community college in large town.
**Enrollment:** 2,539 undergrads, 64% part-time. 233 full-time freshmen.
**Selectivity:** Open admission; but selective for some programs.

### BASIC COSTS (2015-2016)
**Tuition and fees:** $4,080; out-of-district residents $9,120; out-of-state residents $17,760.
**Per-credit charge:** $122; out-of-district residents $290; out-of-state residents $578.

### FINANCIAL AID PICTURE
**Students with need:** Need-based aid available for full-time and part-time students. Work study available nights.
**Students without need:** No-need awards available for athletics.

### FINANCIAL AID PROCEDURES
**Forms required:** FAFSA.
**Dates and Deadlines:** Closing date 7/13. Applicants notified on a rolling basis; must reply within 4 week(s) of notification.
**Transfers:** Applicants notified on a rolling basis; must reply within 4 week(s) of notification.

### CONTACT
Deanna Thompson, Director of Financial Aid
100 College Drive, Kankakee, IL 60901-6505
(815) 802-8550

## Kaskaskia College
Centralia, Illinois
www.kaskaskia.edu            Federal Code: 001701

**2-year public** community college in large town.
**Enrollment:** 2,370 undergrads, 43% part-time. 155 full-time freshmen.
**Selectivity:** Open admission; but selective for some programs.

### BASIC COSTS (2015-2016)
**Tuition and fees:** $3,930; out-of-district residents $6,990; out-of-state residents $12,330.
**Per-credit charge:** $115; out-of-district residents $217; out-of-state residents $395.

### FINANCIAL AID PICTURE (2015-2016)
**Students with need:** Out of 118 full-time freshmen who applied for aid, 118 were judged to have need. Of these, 102 received aid. Average financial aid package met 65% of need; average scholarship/grant was $1,308. For part-time students, average financial aid package was $1,797.
**Students without need:** No-need awards available for academics, athletics, state/district residency.

**FINANCIAL AID PROCEDURES**

**Forms required:** FAFSA.

**Dates and Deadlines:** Priority date 5/15; no closing date. Applicants notified on a rolling basis starting 4/1; must reply within 2 week(s) of notification.

**Transfers:** No deadline. Applicants notified on a rolling basis.

**CONTACT**

Jill Klosterman, Director of Financial Aid

27210 College Road, Centralia, IL 62801

(618) 545-3080

## Kendall College

Chicago, Illinois

www.kendall.edu

Federal Code: 001703

**4-year for-profit** culinary school and teachers college in very large city.

**Enrollment:** 1,516 undergrads.

**BASIC COSTS (2015-2016)**

**Tuition and fees:** $25,248.

**Per-credit charge:** $655.

**Room only:** $10,350.

**Additional info:** Tuition and fees quoted are for School of Culinary Arts.

**FINANCIAL AID PICTURE**

**Students with need:** Need-based aid available for full-time and part-time students. Work study available nights, weekends, and for part-time students.

**Students without need:** No-need awards available for academics, alumni affiliation, job skills.

**FINANCIAL AID PROCEDURES**

**Forms required:** FAFSA.

**Dates and Deadlines:** Priority date 4/15; no closing date. Applicants notified on a rolling basis starting 1/1; must reply within 2 week(s) of notification.

**Transfers:** No deadline. Applicants notified on a rolling basis; must reply within 2 week(s) of notification.

**CONTACT**

Frank Arce, Director of Financial Aid

900 N. North Branch Street, Chicago, IL 60642-4278

(312) 752-2070

## Kishwaukee College

Malta, Illinois

www.kishwaukeecollege.edu

Federal Code: 007684

**2-year public** community college in rural community.

**Enrollment:** 4,900 undergrads.

**Selectivity:** Open admission; but selective for some programs.

**BASIC COSTS (2015-2016)**

**Tuition and fees:** $3,930; out-of-district residents $9,690; out-of-state residents $15,390.

**Per-credit charge:** $119; out-of-district residents $311; out-of-state residents $501.

**FINANCIAL AID PICTURE**

**Students with need:** Need-based aid available for full-time and part-time students. Work study available nights, weekends, and for part-time students.

**Students without need:** No-need awards available for academics, athletics, leadership, music/drama, state/district residency.

**FINANCIAL AID PROCEDURES**

**Forms required:** FAFSA, institutional form.

**Dates and Deadlines:** Priority date 5/1; no closing date. Applicants notified on a rolling basis starting 5/1; must reply within 2 week(s) of notification.

**Transfers:** Must reply within 2 week(s) of notification. Some state programs not available to sophomore status students.

**CONTACT**

Pamela Wagener, Director, Financial Aid/Veterans Affairs

21193 Malta Road, Malta, IL 60150-9699

(815) 825-2086 ext. 2240

## Knox College

Galesburg, Illinois

www.knox.edu

Federal Code: 001704

**4-year private** liberal arts college in large town.

**Enrollment:** 1,374 undergrads, 1% part-time. 386 full-time freshmen.

**Selectivity:** Admits 50 to 75% of applicants.

**BASIC COSTS (2016-2017)**

**Tuition and fees:** $43,285.

**Room and board:** $9,330.

**FINANCIAL AID PICTURE (2015-2016)**

**Students with need:** Out of 347 full-time freshmen who applied for aid, 316 were judged to have need. Of these, 316 received aid, and 73 had their full need met. Average financial aid package met 91% of need; average scholarship/grant was $32,565; average loan was $4,892. Need-based aid available for part-time students.

**Students without need:** 68 full-time freshmen who did not demonstrate need for aid received scholarships/grants; average award was $20,514. No-need awards available for academics, art, leadership, music/drama.

**Scholarships offered:** Scholarships awarded based on academic achievement, visual and performing arts, writing, service and leadership, and math.

**FINANCIAL AID PROCEDURES**

**Forms required:** FAFSA, institutional form.

**Dates and Deadlines:** Priority date 2/1; no closing date. Applicants notified on a rolling basis starting 2/15; must reply by 5/1.

**Transfers:** Priority date 2/1. Applicants notified on a rolling basis starting 2/15; must reply by 6/1.

**CONTACT**

Ann Brill, Director of Financial Aid

2 East South Street, Galesburg, IL 61401

(309) 341-7149

## Lake Forest College

Lake Forest, Illinois

www.lakeforest.edu

Federal Code: 001706

**4-year private** liberal arts college in large town.

**Enrollment:** 1,559 undergrads, 1% part-time. 356 full-time freshmen.

**Selectivity:** Admits 50 to 75% of applicants.

**BASIC COSTS (2015-2016)**

**Tuition and fees:** $42,644.

**Room and board:** $9,570.

**FINANCIAL AID PICTURE**

**Students with need:** Need-based aid available for full-time students.

**Students without need:** No-need awards available for academics, alumni affiliation, art, leadership, music/drama.

**FINANCIAL AID PROCEDURES**

**Forms required:** FAFSA.

**Dates and Deadlines:** Priority date 2/15; closing date 5/1. Applicants notified on a rolling basis starting 3/1; must reply by 5/1 or within 2 week(s) of notification.

**Transfers:** Applicants notified on a rolling basis starting 3/15; must reply by 5/1.

**CONTACT**
Gerard Cebrzynski, Financial Aid Director
555 North Sheridan Road, Lake Forest, IL 60045-2338
(847) 735-5015

## Lake Land College
Mattoon, Illinois
www.lakelandcollege.edu          Federal Code: 007644

**2-year public** community college in large town.
**Enrollment:** 3,387 undergrads. 895 full-time freshmen.
**Selectivity:** Open admission; but selective for some programs.

**BASIC COSTS (2015-2016)**
**Tuition and fees:** $3,507; out-of-district residents $7,328; out-of-state residents $13,130.

**FINANCIAL AID PICTURE**
**Students with need:** Need-based aid available for full-time and part-time students. Work study available nights, weekends, and for part-time students.
**Students without need:** No-need awards available for academics, athletics.

**FINANCIAL AID PROCEDURES**
**Forms required:** FAFSA.
**Dates and Deadlines:** Priority date 5/1; no closing date. Applicants notified on a rolling basis starting 6/1.
**Transfers:** No deadline.

**CONTACT**
Paula Carpenter, Director of Financial Aid and Veteran Services
5001 Lake Land Boulevard, Mattoon, IL 61938-9366
(217) 234-5231

## Lakeview College of Nursing
Danville, Illinois
www.lakeviewcol.edu          Federal Code: 010501

**Upper-division private** nursing college in large town.
**Enrollment:** 324 undergrads, 18% part-time.

**BASIC COSTS (2015-2016)**
**Tuition and fees:** $14,400.
**Per-credit charge:** $480.

**FINANCIAL AID PICTURE**
**Students with need:** Need-based aid available for full-time and part-time students.
**Students without need:** This college awards aid only to students with need.

**FINANCIAL AID PROCEDURES**
**Forms required:** FAFSA, institutional form.
**Transfers:** Priority date 4/15; no deadline.

**CONTACT**
Janet Ingargiola, Director of Financial Aid
903 North Logan Avenue, Danville, IL 61832
(217) 554-6887

## Le Cordon Bleu College of Culinary Arts: Chicago
Chicago, Illinois
www.chefs.edu/Chicago          Federal Code: 016758

**2-year for-profit** culinary school in very large city.
**Enrollment:** 958 undergrads.
**Selectivity:** Open admission.

**BASIC COSTS (2015-2016)**
**Additional info:** Certificate programs: $19,500. Associate programs: $40,000. Books and supplies are included.

**FINANCIAL AID PICTURE**
**Students with need:** Need-based aid available for full-time and part-time students. Work study available nights.

**FINANCIAL AID PROCEDURES**
**Forms required:** FAFSA, institutional form.
**Dates and Deadlines:** Applicants notified on a rolling basis.
**Transfers:** No deadline. Applicants notified on a rolling basis.

**CONTACT**
Nathan Nimrick, Director of Student Finance
361 West Chestnut, Chicago, IL 60610-3050
(312) 944-0882

## Lewis and Clark Community College
Godfrey, Illinois
www.lc.edu          Federal Code: 010020

**2-year public** community college in large town.
**Enrollment:** 3,599 undergrads.
**Selectivity:** Open admission; but selective for some programs.

**BASIC COSTS (2015-2016)**
**Tuition and fees:** $4,440; out-of-district residents $10,920; out-of-state residents $14,160.
**Per-credit charge:** $108; out-of-district residents $324; out-of-state residents $432.

**FINANCIAL AID PICTURE**
**Students with need:** Need-based aid available for full-time and part-time students.

**FINANCIAL AID PROCEDURES**
**Forms required:** FAFSA.
**Dates and Deadlines:** Priority date 6/1; no closing date. Applicants notified on a rolling basis starting 8/1; must reply within 3 week(s) of notification.
**Transfers:** No deadline. Applicants notified on a rolling basis.

**CONTACT**
Angela Weaver, Director, Financial Aid
5800 Godfrey Road, Godfrey, IL 62035-2466
(618) 468-2223

## Lewis University
Romeoville, Illinois
www.lewisu.edu          Federal Code: 001707

**4-year private** university in large town, affiliated with Roman Catholic Church.
**Enrollment:** 4,529 undergrads, 16% part-time. 700 full-time freshmen.
**Selectivity:** Admits 50 to 75% of applicants.

**BASIC COSTS (2016-2017)**
**Tuition and fees:** $30,050.

**Per-credit charge:** $880.

**Room and board:** $10,320.

**Additional info:** Tuition/fee waivers available for adults.

### FINANCIAL AID PICTURE (2015-2016)

**Students with need:** Out of 668 full-time freshmen who applied for aid, 604 were judged to have need. Of these, 604 received aid, and 145 had their full need met. Average financial aid package met 81% of need; average scholarship/grant was $16,992; average loan was $3,366. For part-time students, average financial aid package was $8,500.

**Students without need:** 89 full-time freshmen who did not demonstrate need for aid received scholarships/grants; average award was $12,077. No-need awards available for academics, alumni affiliation, art, athletics, music/drama, religious affiliation, ROTC.

**Scholarships offered:** 12 full-time freshmen received athletic scholarships; average amount $13,773.

### FINANCIAL AID PROCEDURES

**Forms required:** FAFSA.

**Dates and Deadlines:** Priority date 2/1; closing date 5/1. Applicants notified on a rolling basis starting 2/1; must reply by 5/1 or within 2 week(s) of notification.

**Transfers:** Applicants notified on a rolling basis starting 2/1; must reply by 5/1 or within 2 week(s) of notification.

### CONTACT

Janeen Decharinte, Director of Financial Aid Services

Unit #297, Romeoville, IL 60446-2200

(815) 836-5263

## Lincoln Christian University

Lincoln, Illinois

www.lincolnchristian.edu          Federal Code: 001708

**4-year private** university and Bible college in large town, affiliated with Church of Christ.

**Enrollment:** 514 undergrads, 21% part-time. 70 full-time freshmen.

**Selectivity:** Admits 50 to 75% of applicants.

### BASIC COSTS (2015-2016)

**Tuition and fees:** $17,400.

**Per-credit charge:** $430.

**Room and board:** $7,430.

### FINANCIAL AID PICTURE (2014-2015)

**Students with need:** Out of 66 full-time freshmen who applied for aid, 56 were judged to have need. Of these, 56 received aid, and 3 had their full need met. Average financial aid package met 51% of need; average scholarship/grant was $8,297; average loan was $3,188. Need-based aid available for part-time students.

**Students without need:** 10 full-time freshmen who did not demonstrate need for aid received scholarships/grants; average award was $3,823. No-need awards available for academics.

**Scholarships offered:** 4 full-time freshmen received athletic scholarships; average amount $6,025.

### FINANCIAL AID PROCEDURES

**Forms required:** FAFSA.

**Dates and Deadlines:** Priority date 3/1; no closing date. Applicants notified on a rolling basis starting 3/1; must reply within 4 week(s) of notification.

### CONTACT

Nancy Siddens, Director of Student Financial Aid

100 Campus View Drive, Lincoln, IL 62656-2111

(217) 732-3168 ext. 2304

## Lincoln College

Lincoln, Illinois

www.lincolncollege.edu          Federal Code: 001709

**2-year private** junior and liberal arts college in large town.

**Enrollment:** 1,200 undergrads. 599 full-time freshmen.

### BASIC COSTS (2015-2016)

**Tuition and fees:** $17,900.

**Room and board:** $7,100.

**Additional info:** Tuition at time of enrollment locked for 2 years.

### FINANCIAL AID PICTURE (2014-2015)

**Students with need:** Out of 581 full-time freshmen who applied for aid, 559 were judged to have need. Of these, 542 received aid, and 15 had their full need met. Average financial aid package met 46% of need; average scholarship/grant was $125. For part-time students, average financial aid package was $6,197.

**Students without need:** No-need awards available for academics, alumni affiliation, art, athletics, leadership, music/drama.

**Scholarships offered:** 19 full-time freshmen received athletic scholarships; average amount $7,859.

**Additional info:** Auditions recommended for music, speech, theater, broadcasting, and dance scholarship candidates, portfolios recommended for art and technical theater scholarship candidates.

### FINANCIAL AID PROCEDURES

**Forms required:** FAFSA.

**Dates and Deadlines:** Priority date 4/1; no closing date. Applicants notified on a rolling basis starting 6/1; must reply within 3 week(s) of notification.

**Transfers:** No deadline. Applicants notified on a rolling basis.

### CONTACT

Chris Steckmann, Director of Financial Aid

300 Keokuk Street, Lincoln, IL 62656

(217) 732-3155 ext. 231

## Lincoln Land Community College

Springfield, Illinois

www.llcc.edu          Federal Code: 007170

**2-year public** community and junior college in small city.

**Enrollment:** 3,831 undergrads.

**Selectivity:** Open admission; but selective for some programs.

### BASIC COSTS (2015-2016)

**Tuition and fees:** $3,630; out-of-district residents $6,930; out-of-state residents $10,230.

**Per-credit charge:** $110; out-of-district residents $220; out-of-state residents $330.

**Additional info:** Tuition/fee waivers available for minority students.

### FINANCIAL AID PICTURE

**Students with need:** Need-based aid available for full-time and part-time students. Work study available nights.

**Students without need:** No-need awards available for academics, athletics, minority status, state/district residency.

### FINANCIAL AID PROCEDURES

**Forms required:** FAFSA, institutional form.

**Dates and Deadlines:** Closing date 6/30. Applicants notified on a rolling basis starting 4/15; must reply within 2 week(s) of notification.

### CONTACT

Lisa Collier, Associate Vice President, Financial Aid

5250 Shepherd Road, Springfield, IL 62794-9256

(217) 786-2237

# Loyola University Chicago
Chicago, Illinois
www.luc.edu                          Federal Code: 001710

**4-year private** university in very large city, affiliated with Roman Catholic Church.
**Enrollment:** 10,276 undergrads, 7% part-time. 2,190 full-time freshmen.
**Selectivity:** Admits 50 to 75% of applicants.

**BASIC COSTS (2016-2017)**
**Tuition and fees:** $42,032.
**Per-credit charge:** $751.
**Room and board:** $13,770.

**FINANCIAL AID PICTURE (2015-2016)**
**Students with need:** Out of 1,823 full-time freshmen who applied for aid, 1,504 were judged to have need. Of these, 1,499 received aid, and 216 had their full need met. Average financial aid package met 80% of need; average scholarship/grant was $20,960; average loan was $3,947. For part-time students, average financial aid package was $13,834.
**Students without need:** 595 full-time freshmen who did not demonstrate need for aid received scholarships/grants; average award was $15,511. No-need awards available for academics, art, athletics, leadership, music/drama, religious affiliation, ROTC.
**Scholarships offered:** 16 full-time freshmen received athletic scholarships; average amount $27,342.

**FINANCIAL AID PROCEDURES**
**Forms required:** FAFSA.
**Dates and Deadlines:** Priority date 3/1; no closing date. Applicants notified on a rolling basis starting 2/15; must reply within 3 week(s) of notification.
**Transfers:** FAFSA must be filed by 3/1 to receive Illinois map grant.

**CONTACT**
Nancy Merz, Dir., Financial Aid
1032 West Sheridan Road., Chicago, IL 60660
(312) 915-7803

# MacCormac College
Chicago, Illinois
www.maccormac.edu                    Federal Code: 001716

**2-year private** community and junior college in very large city.
**Enrollment:** 198 undergrads.

**BASIC COSTS (2015-2016)**
**Tuition and fees:** $12,820.

**FINANCIAL AID PICTURE**
**Students with need:** Need-based aid available for full-time and part-time students.
**Students without need:** No-need awards available for academics, leadership.
**Scholarships offered:** The MAC Honor is based on ACT and high school class rank. The High School Business Club Scholarship, which awards $1,800, requires an ACT of at least 20, a GPA of at least 3.0, and membership in a high school business club. The Founders Scholarship, which awards $1,200, requires an ACT of at least 20, a GPA of at least 3.0, and participation in school, community, charity organizations or church.

**FINANCIAL AID PROCEDURES**
**Forms required:** FAFSA.
**Dates and Deadlines:** Closing date 8/15. Must reply within 2 week(s) of notification.

**CONTACT**
Rathenia Hunter, Director of Financial Aid
29 East Madison Street, Chicago, IL 60602
(312) 922-1884 ext. 209

# MacMurray College
Jacksonville, Illinois
www.mac.edu                          Federal Code: 001717

**4-year private** liberal arts college in large town, affiliated with United Methodist Church.
**Enrollment:** 571 undergrads.
**Selectivity:** Admits 50 to 75% of applicants.

**BASIC COSTS (2015-2016)**
**Tuition and fees:** $24,172.
**Per-credit charge:** $750.
**Room and board:** $8,112.
**Additional info:** Two year frozen tuition plan in place. Students receive one tuition increase across 4 years. Students residing on campus all 4 years receive 8th semester of room and board free. Tuition at time of enrollment locked for 4 years; tuition/fee waivers available for adults.

**FINANCIAL AID PICTURE**
**Students with need:** Need-based aid available for full-time and part-time students. Work study available nights, weekends, and for part-time students.
**Students without need:** No-need awards available for academics, alumni affiliation, leadership, religious affiliation, state/district residency.
**Scholarships offered:** Academic scholarships: $6,000-$15,000 per year; based on merit; 3 freshman selected for full-tuition scholarships. Transfer scholarships: up to $10,000; based on academic merit. Leadership scholarship: $5,000; based on committee selection; awarded to one incoming female freshman annually. Alumni referral scholarships: up to $1,000 per year. Children of alumni scholarships: $1,000 per year. Church-matching scholarships: up to $1,500 per year.
**Additional info:** Merit scholarships for accepted, enrolled freshman and transfer students based on academic record and notified upon admission. Frozen tuition offered for full-time degree seeking new students for their first two years. Students residing on campus for four years will get the 8th semester of room and board waived.

**FINANCIAL AID PROCEDURES**
**Forms required:** FAFSA.
**Dates and Deadlines:** Priority date 2/1; no closing date. Applicants notified on a rolling basis starting 3/1; must reply within 2 week(s) of notification.
**Transfers:** No deadline. Applicants notified on a rolling basis starting 3/1; must reply within 2 week(s) of notification. Phi Theta Kappa members receive $2,500 per year.

**CONTACT**
Laci Engelbrecht, Director of Financial Aid
447 East College Avenue, Jacksonville, IL 62650-2590
(217) 479-7041

# McHenry County College
Crystal Lake, Illinois
www.mchenry.edu                      Federal Code: 007691

**2-year public** community college in large town.
**Enrollment:** 4,486 undergrads, 55% part-time. 630 full-time freshmen.
**Selectivity:** Open admission; but selective for some programs.

**BASIC COSTS (2016-2017)**
**Tuition and fees:** $3,314; out-of-district residents $10,666; out-of-state residents $13,497.
**Per-credit charge:** $101; out-of-district residents $346; out-of-state residents $440.

**FINANCIAL AID PICTURE**
**Students with need:** Need-based aid available for full-time and part-time students. Work study available nights, weekends, and for part-time students.

**Students without need:** No-need awards available for academics, athletics, leadership, music/drama, state/district residency.

**Scholarships offered:** President's Scholarship; full tuition for 2 years; based on talent in academic areas; students must complete portfolio and have 3.0 GPA. Founding Faculty Scholarship; full tuition for 2 years; based on GPA and essay.

**Additional info:** Students can apply throughout the award year for federal and state aid. Students with physical handicaps or learning disabilities may apply for special needs scholarship.

### FINANCIAL AID PROCEDURES

**Forms required:** FAFSA, institutional form.

**Dates and Deadlines:** Priority date 6/1; no closing date. Applicants notified on a rolling basis starting 5/1.

### CONTACT

Leana Davis, Director of Financial Aid
8900 US Highway 14, Crystal Lake, IL 60012-2738
(815) 455-8761

## McKendree University

Lebanon, Illinois
www.mckendree.edu                    Federal Code: 001722

**4-year private** university and liberal arts college in small town, affiliated with United Methodist Church.

**Enrollment:** 2,292 undergrads, 21% part-time. 400 full-time freshmen.

**Selectivity:** Admits 50 to 75% of applicants.

### BASIC COSTS (2016-2017)

**Tuition and fees:** $28,740.

**Per-credit charge:** $910.

**Room and board:** $9,200.

### FINANCIAL AID PICTURE (2015-2016)

**Students with need:** Average financial aid package met 75% of need; average scholarship/grant was $20,705; average loan was $3,887. For part-time students, average financial aid package was $5,181.

**Students without need:** No-need awards available for academics, alumni affiliation, art, athletics, leadership, music/drama, religious affiliation.

**Scholarships offered:** Dean's Scholarships; $10,000 annually; based on 3.0 GPA or 22 ACT. Presidential Scholarships; $10,000 annually; based on 3.0 GPA and 22 ACT. Honor's Scholarships; $13,000 annually; based on 3.6 GPA and 27 ACT. Leadership Scholarship; up to $5,000 annually; available to students that have been awarded McKendree University Presidential or Honor's Scholarship and attend Leadership Scholarship Event, during which they complete two personal interviews and submit an essay. Community Service Scholarship; highly competitive; up to $4,000 annually; must be enrolled full-time; have a 2.5 GPA; and a record of volunteering in high school.

### FINANCIAL AID PROCEDURES

**Forms required:** FAFSA.

**Dates and Deadlines:** Applicants notified by 3/1.

**Transfers:** No deadline. Applicants notified by 3/1; must reply within 4 week(s) of notification.

### CONTACT

Elizabeth Juehne, Director of Financial Aid
701 College Road, Lebanon, IL 62254-1299
(618) 537-6828

## Midstate College

Peoria, Illinois
www.midstate.edu                    Federal Code: 004568

**4-year for-profit** business college in small city.

**Enrollment:** 521 undergrads, 70% part-time. 3 full-time freshmen.

**Selectivity:** Open admission; but selective for some programs and for out-of-state students.

### BASIC COSTS (2015-2016)

**Tuition and fees:** $16,230.

**Per-credit charge:** $381.

### FINANCIAL AID PICTURE

**Students with need:** Need-based aid available for full-time and part-time students. Work study available nights, weekends, and for part-time students.

**Students without need:** No-need awards available for academics.

### FINANCIAL AID PROCEDURES

**Forms required:** FAFSA, institutional form.

**Dates and Deadlines:** Applicants notified on a rolling basis; must reply within 4 week(s) of notification.

### CONTACT

Irene Bimrose, Director of Financial Assistance
411 West Northmoor Road, Peoria, IL 61614-3558
(309) 692-4092 ext. 1210

## Millikin University

Decatur, Illinois
www.millikin.edu                    Federal Code: 001724

**4-year private** university in small city, affiliated with Presbyterian Church (USA).

**Enrollment:** 2,013 undergrads, 2% part-time. 476 full-time freshmen.

**Selectivity:** Admits 50 to 75% of applicants.

### BASIC COSTS (2016-2017)

**Tuition and fees:** $31,924.

**Per-credit charge:** $449.

**Room and board:** $11,190.

### FINANCIAL AID PICTURE (2014-2015)

**Students with need:** Out of 461 full-time freshmen who applied for aid, 418 were judged to have need. Of these, 418 received aid, and 107 had their full need met. Average financial aid package met 85% of need; average scholarship/grant was $9,192; average loan was $4,348. For part-time students, average financial aid package was $6,173.

**Students without need:** 42 full-time freshmen who did not demonstrate need for aid received scholarships/grants; average award was $13,705. No-need awards available for academics, alumni affiliation, art, leadership, minority status, music/drama.

**Scholarships offered:** Scholarships for students who demonstrate significant potential for contributing to campus life; renewable for 4 years of attendance.

### FINANCIAL AID PROCEDURES

**Forms required:** FAFSA.

**Dates and Deadlines:** Priority date 1/31; no closing date. Applicants notified on a rolling basis starting 3/1; must reply by 5/1 or within 4 week(s) of notification.

**Transfers:** Priority date 1/31; no deadline. Applicants notified on a rolling basis starting 3/1.

### CONTACT

Cheryl Howerton, Director of Financial Aid
1184 West Main Street, Decatur, IL 62522-2084
(217) 424-6317

## Monmouth College

Monmouth, Illinois
www.monmouthcollege.edu                    Federal Code: 001725

**4-year private** liberal arts college in small town, affiliated with Presbyterian Church (USA).

**Enrollment:** 1,174 undergrads, 1% part-time. 273 full-time freshmen.
**Selectivity:** Admits 50 to 75% of applicants.

## BASIC COSTS (2015-2016)
**Tuition and fees:** $34,200.
**Room and board:** $8,060.

## FINANCIAL AID PICTURE (2015-2016)
**Students with need:** Out of 257 full-time freshmen who applied for aid, 237 were judged to have need. Of these, 237 received aid, and 50 had their full need met. Average financial aid package met 88% of need; average scholarship/grant was $26,884; average loan was $3,573. For part-time students, average financial aid package was $14,817.
**Students without need:** 36 full-time freshmen who did not demonstrate need for aid received scholarships/grants; average award was $21,613. No-need awards available for academics, art, leadership, music/drama, religious affiliation.

## FINANCIAL AID PROCEDURES
**Forms required:** FAFSA.
**Dates and Deadlines:** Priority date 1/1; no closing date. Applicants notified on a rolling basis starting 2/15; must reply by 5/1 or within 2 week(s) of notification.
**Transfers:** Priority date 2/1; no deadline. Applicants notified on a rolling basis; must reply by 8/15.

## CONTACT
Jayne Schreck, Assoc. VP of Financial Aid
700 East Broadway, Monmouth, IL 61462-1998
(309) 457-2129

# Moody Bible Institute
Chicago, Illinois
www.moody.edu              Federal Code: 001727

**4-year private** Bible and seminary college in very large city, affiliated with interdenominational tradition.
**Enrollment:** 2,976 undergrads.

## BASIC COSTS (2015-2016)
**Tuition and fees:** $12,290.
**Per-credit charge:** $310.
**Room and board:** $11,870.

## FINANCIAL AID PICTURE
**Students with need:** Need-based aid available for full-time and part-time students.
**Students without need:** This college awards aid only to students with need.
**Additional info:** Aid available to upperclassmen is based on private and not federal/state sources.

## FINANCIAL AID PROCEDURES
**Forms required:** institutional form.
**Dates and Deadlines:** Applicants notified on a rolling basis; must reply by 7/1.
**Transfers:** No deadline. Applicants notified on a rolling basis; must reply by 7/1.

## CONTACT
Heather Shalley, Director of Financial Aid
820 N LaSalle Boulevard, Chicago, IL 60610
(312) 329-4178

# Moraine Valley Community College
Palos Hills, Illinois
www.morainevalley.edu       Federal Code: 007692

**2-year public** community and junior college in large town.
**Enrollment:** 11,235 undergrads, 47% part-time. 1,761 full-time freshmen.
**Selectivity:** Open admission; but selective for some programs.

## BASIC COSTS (2015-2016)
**Tuition and fees:** $3,996; out-of-district residents $8,916; out-of-state residents $10,326.
**Per-credit charge:** $116; out-of-district residents $280; out-of-state residents $327.

## FINANCIAL AID PICTURE (2014-2015)
**Students with need:** 88% of average financial aid package awarded as scholarships/grants, 12% awarded as loans/jobs. Need-based aid available for part-time students. Work study available nights.
**Students without need:** No-need awards available for academics, alumni affiliation, athletics, leadership, state/district residency.

## FINANCIAL AID PROCEDURES
**Forms required:** FAFSA, institutional form.
**Dates and Deadlines:** Priority date 5/1; no closing date. Applicants notified on a rolling basis starting 6/15; must reply within 2 week(s) of notification.

## CONTACT
Carissa Davis, Director of Financial Aid
9000 West College Parkway, Palos Hills, IL 60465-2478
(708) 974-5726

# Morrison Institute of Technology
Morrison, Illinois
www.morrisontech.edu        Federal Code: 008880

**2-year private** technical college in small town.
**Enrollment:** 91 undergrads. 55 full-time freshmen.
**Selectivity:** Open admission.

## BASIC COSTS (2015-2016)
**Tuition and fees:** $15,590.
**Room only:** $3,900.

## FINANCIAL AID PICTURE
**Students with need:** Need-based aid available for full-time and part-time students. Work study available nights, weekends, and for part-time students.
**Students without need:** No-need awards available for academics.

## FINANCIAL AID PROCEDURES
**Forms required:** FAFSA, institutional form.
**Dates and Deadlines:** Applicants notified on a rolling basis; must reply within 2 week(s) of notification.

## CONTACT
Julie Damhoff, Financial Aid Director
701 Portland Avenue, Morrison, IL 61270-2959
(815) 772-7218 ext. 203

# Morton College
Cicero, Illinois
www.morton.edu             Federal Code: 001728

**2-year public** community college in small city.
**Enrollment:** 3,008 undergrads, 58% part-time. 433 full-time freshmen.
**Selectivity:** Open admission; but selective for some programs and for out-of-state students.

**BASIC COSTS (2015-2016)**
**Tuition and fees:** $3,440; out-of-district residents $7,280; out-of-state residents $9,200.
**Per-credit charge:** $88; out-of-district residents $216; out-of-state residents $280.

**FINANCIAL AID PICTURE**
**Students with need:** Need-based aid available for full-time and part-time students. Work study available nights, weekends, and for part-time students.

**FINANCIAL AID PROCEDURES**
**Forms required:** FAFSA, institutional form.
**Dates and Deadlines:** Priority date 6/1; no closing date. Applicants notified on a rolling basis starting 8/3.

**CONTACT**
Yolanda Freemon, Director of Financial Aid
3801 South Central Avenue, Cicero, IL 60804-4398
(708) 656-8000 ext. 2426

## National University of Health Sciences
Lombard, Illinois
www.nuhs.edu                    Federal Code: 001732

**4-year private** university and health science college in large town.
**Enrollment:** 130 undergrads.

**BASIC COSTS (2015-2016)**
**Tuition and fees:** $11,368.
**Per-credit charge:** $350.
**Additional info:** Tuition and fees quoted are for Bachelor's program: Biomedical Science. Associate program: Massage Therapy $12,702, books and supplies $400.

**FINANCIAL AID PICTURE**
**Students with need:** Need-based aid available for full-time and part-time students.

**FINANCIAL AID PROCEDURES**
**Transfers:** No deadline.

**CONTACT**
Robert Dame, Director of Financial Aid
200 East Roosevelt Road, Lombard, IL 60148-4583
(630) 889-6700

## North Central College
Naperville, Illinois
www.northcentralcollege.edu        Federal Code: 001734

**4-year private** liberal arts college in small city, affiliated with United Methodist Church.
**Enrollment:** 2,633 undergrads, 2% part-time. 599 full-time freshmen.
**Selectivity:** Admits 50 to 75% of applicants.

**BASIC COSTS (2015-2016)**
**Tuition and fees:** $35,421.
**Per-credit charge:** $979.
**Room and board:** $10,545.

**FINANCIAL AID PICTURE (2015-2016)**
**Students with need:** Out of 558 full-time freshmen who applied for aid, 484 were judged to have need. Of these, 484 received aid, and 70 had their full need met. Average financial aid package met 81% of need; average scholarship/grant was $23,861; average loan was $3,429. For part-time students, average financial aid package was $14,035.

**Students without need:** 115 full-time freshmen who did not demonstrate need for aid received scholarships/grants; average award was $17,230. No-need awards available for academics, art, leadership, minority status, music/drama, religious affiliation, ROTC, state/district residency.
**Scholarships offered:** Numerous merit and talent scholarship opportunities available.

**FINANCIAL AID PROCEDURES**
**Forms required:** FAFSA.
**Dates and Deadlines:** Applicants notified on a rolling basis starting 3/1; must reply within 4 week(s) of notification.
**Transfers:** No deadline. Applicants notified on a rolling basis starting 3/1; must reply within 4 week(s) of notification.

**CONTACT**
Martin Reba, Director of Financial Aid
30 North Brainard Street, Naperville, IL 60566-7063
(630) 637-5600

## North Park University
Chicago, Illinois
www.northpark.edu                Federal Code: 001735

**4-year private** university and liberal arts college in very large city, affiliated with Evangelical Covenant Church of America.
**Enrollment:** 2,140 undergrads.
**Selectivity:** Admits less than 50% of applicants.

**BASIC COSTS (2015-2016)**
**Tuition and fees:** $25,740.
**Per-credit charge:** $858.
**Room and board:** $8,580.

**FINANCIAL AID PICTURE**
**Students with need:** Need-based aid available for full-time students. Work study available nights.
**Students without need:** No-need awards available for academics, art, music/drama, religious affiliation.

**FINANCIAL AID PROCEDURES**
**Forms required:** FAFSA.
**Dates and Deadlines:** Priority date 5/1; closing date 8/1. Applicants notified on a rolling basis starting 10/1; must reply by 5/1 or within 3 week(s) of notification.
**Transfers:** Priority date 6/1. Applicants notified on a rolling basis starting 10/1; must reply within 3 week(s) of notification.

**CONTACT**
Lucy Shaker, Director of Financial Aid
3225 West Foster Avenue Box 19, Chicago, IL 60625-4895
(773) 244-5506

## Northeastern Illinois University
Chicago, Illinois
www.neiu.edu                    Federal Code: 001693

**4-year public** university in very large city.
**Enrollment:** 7,979 undergrads, 44% part-time. 708 full-time freshmen.
**Selectivity:** Admits 50 to 75% of applicants.

**BASIC COSTS (2016-2017)**
**Tuition and fees:** $11,698; out-of-state residents $20,098.
**Per-credit charge:** $349; out-of-state residents $699.
**Additional info:** Tuition at time of enrollment locked for 4 years.

**FINANCIAL AID PICTURE (2015-2016)**
**Students with need:** Out of 622 full-time freshmen who applied for aid, 498 were judged to have need. Of these, 419 received aid, and 1 had their

full need met. Average financial aid package met 18% of need; average scholarship/grant was $7,550; average loan was $3,057. For part-time students, average financial aid package was $5,556.

**Students without need:** 11 full-time freshmen who did not demonstrate need for aid received scholarships/grants; average award was $2,160. No-need awards available for academics, art, leadership, music/drama, ROTC.

## FINANCIAL AID PROCEDURES

**Forms required:** FAFSA.

**Dates and Deadlines:** Priority date 2/28; no closing date. Applicants notified on a rolling basis starting 3/15; must reply within 2 week(s) of notification.

## CONTACT

Maureen Amos, Director of Financial Aid
5500 North St. Louis Avenue, Chicago, IL 60625
(773) 442-5010

## Northern Illinois University

DeKalb, Illinois
www.niu.edu                    Federal Code: 001737

**4-year public** university in large town.
**Enrollment:** 14,952 undergrads, 12% part-time. 2,546 full-time freshmen.
**Selectivity:** Admits 50 to 75% of applicants.

## BASIC COSTS (2015-2016)

**Tuition and fees:** $12,202; out-of-district residents $15,988; out-of-state residents $21,242.
**Per-credit charge:** $315.52; out-of-district residents $441.73; out-of-state residents $617.
**Room and board:** $9,670.
**Additional info:** Tuition at time of enrollment locked for 4 years.

## FINANCIAL AID PICTURE (2014-2015)

**Students with need:** Out of 2,361 full-time freshmen who applied for aid, 2,025 were judged to have need. Of these, 2,020 received aid, and 142 had their full need met. Average financial aid package met 63% of need; average scholarship/grant was $9,083; average loan was $3,443. For part-time students, average financial aid package was $6,406.

**Students without need:** 356 full-time freshmen who did not demonstrate need for aid received scholarships/grants; average award was $4,710. No-need awards available for academics, alumni affiliation, art, athletics, leadership, music/drama, ROTC.

**Scholarships offered:** *Merit:* University Scholars; full tuition, fees, on-campus room and board; 33 ACT and either top 5% HS class or 3.75 GPA. NIU Scholars; $7,000; 27 ACT and either top 5% or 3.75 GPA. Northern Academic Scholarship; $4,000; 25-26 ACT and either top 10% or 3.0 GPA or 27 ACT and above; 6-10% of class or 3.0-3.74 GPA. Centennial Scholarship; $3,000; 22-24 ACT and either top 10% or 3.0 GPA. Red & Black Award; $3,000; 19-21 ACT and either top 10% or 3.0 GPA; or 22 ACT and above; 11-25% of class. Out-of-State Huskie Scholarship; $9,466; resident of Iowa, Indiana, Missouri, or Wisconsin; 19 ACT and either top 50% or 2.75 GPA. DeKalb County Scholarship; $4,000; DeKalb County public high school graduate with variable criteria (cannot be combined with other scholarships). Pre-Law Scholarship; $2,000; for pre-law majors with 28 ACT and 3.5 GPA. Huskie Legacy Award; $1,000; incoming child of alumnus/alumna. *Athletic:* 44 full-time freshmen received athletic scholarships; average amount $21,372.

## FINANCIAL AID PROCEDURES

**Forms required:** FAFSA.

**Dates and Deadlines:** Priority date 3/1; no closing date. Applicants notified on a rolling basis starting 3/15.

**Transfers:** No deadline. Applicants notified on a rolling basis starting 3/15. Two year, $2,000/yr. transfer scholarship available with 3.5 cumulative transfer GPA and 30 transferable hours completed at time of admission.

## CONTACT

Rebecca Babel, Director of Student Financial Aid
1425 West Lincoln Highway, DeKalb, IL 60115-2854
(815) 753-1395

## Northwestern College

Chicago, Illinois
www.nc.edu                    Federal Code: 012362

**2-year for-profit** technical and career college in very large city.
**Enrollment:** 973 undergrads, 66% part-time. 54 full-time freshmen.
**Selectivity:** Open admission; but selective for some programs.

## BASIC COSTS (2015-2016)

**Tuition and fees:** $21,195.
**Per-credit charge:** $465.

## FINANCIAL AID PICTURE

**Students with need:** Need-based aid available for full-time and part-time students. Work study available nights.

**Students without need:** No-need awards available for academics, alumni affiliation.

**Scholarships offered:** Academic Scholarship: $600 per quarter up to six quarters. Board of Directors: $800 per quarter up to six quarters. Centennial: amount varies. Educational Achievement Scholarship: $600 per quarter up to six quarters. Community Scholarship: $800 per quarter up to six quarters. Early Acceptance Scholarship: amount varies. Scholastic Scholarship: $667 per quarter up to six quarters. Presidential Scholarship: $800 per quarter up to six quarters. Excellence Scholarship: $1,200 per quarter up to six quarters. Transfer Student Scholarship: $400 per quarter up to four quarters. Student Success Scholarship: Summer quarter only up to $1,000. American Hero Tuition and First Responders Tuition Discount: 15%. Legacy Tuition Discount: 10%.

**Additional info:** State grant programs for Illinois residents and alternative loans offered.

## FINANCIAL AID PROCEDURES

**Forms required:** FAFSA, institutional form.

**Dates and Deadlines:** Priority date 2/15; closing date 6/30. Applicants notified on a rolling basis starting 1/2; must reply within 4 week(s) of notification.

## CONTACT

Patricia Kilian, Director of Financial Aid
4811 N. Milwaukee Avenue, STE 203, Chicago, IL 60630
(847) 233-7700 ext. 2103

## Northwestern University

Evanston, Illinois                    Federal Code: 001739
www.northwestern.edu                    CSS Code: 1565

**4-year private** university in small city.
**Enrollment:** 8,819 undergrads, 6% part-time. 2,017 full-time freshmen.
**Selectivity:** Admits less than 50% of applicants.

## BASIC COSTS (2015-2016)

**Tuition and fees:** $49,047.
**Room and board:** $14,936.

## FINANCIAL AID PICTURE (2015-2016)

**Students with need:** Out of 1,188 full-time freshmen who applied for aid, 982 were judged to have need. Of these, 982 received aid, and 950 had their full need met. Average financial aid package met 100% of need; average scholarship/grant was $42,088; average loan was $3,961.

**Students without need:** 88 full-time freshmen who did not demonstrate need for aid received scholarships/grants; average award was $3,189. No-need awards available for athletics, music/drama.

**Scholarships offered:** 105 full-time freshmen received athletic scholarships; average amount $39,796.

### FINANCIAL AID PROCEDURES

**Forms required:** FAFSA, CSS PROFILE.

**Dates and Deadlines:** Priority date 3/5; closing date 3/5. Applicants notified by 4/15; must reply by 5/1 or within 2 week(s) of notification.

**Transfers:** Closing date 6/1. Transfer student aid limited for first year.

### CONTACT

Carolyn Lindley, University Director of Financial Aid

1801 Hinman Avenue, Evanston, IL 60208-3060

(847) 491-7400

## Oakton Community College
Des Plaines, Illinois
www.oakton.edu                          Federal Code: 009896

**2-year public** community college in small city.

**Enrollment:** 2,788 full-time undergrads.

**Selectivity:** Open admission; but selective for some programs.

### BASIC COSTS (2015-2016)

**Tuition and fees:** $3,518; out-of-district residents $9,510; out-of-state residents $11,640.

**Per-credit charge:** $111; out-of-district residents $311; out-of-state residents $382.

### FINANCIAL AID PICTURE (2014-2015)

**Students with need:** 95% of average financial aid package awarded as scholarships/grants, 5% awarded as loans/jobs. Need-based aid available for part-time students. Work study available nights, weekends, and for part-time students.

**Students without need:** No-need awards available for academics, art, athletics, leadership, minority status, music/drama, state/district residency.

**Scholarships offered:** Oakton Merit Scholarship Program; tuition and related fees; first-time, in-district, freshmen in top 10% of high school class.

### FINANCIAL AID PROCEDURES

**Forms required:** FAFSA, institutional form.

**Dates and Deadlines:** Priority date 3/1; no closing date. Applicants notified on a rolling basis starting 3/1; must reply within 2 week(s) of notification.

**Transfers:** Applicants notified on a rolling basis starting 5/1.

### CONTACT

Jamie Petersen, Director of Financial Aid

Enrollment Center, Des Plaines, IL 60016

(847) 635-1708

## Olivet Nazarene University
Bourbonnais, Illinois
www.olivet.edu                          Federal Code: 001741

**4-year private** university and liberal arts college in small city, affiliated with Church of the Nazarene.

**Enrollment:** 3,389 undergrads, 10% part-time. 733 full-time freshmen.

**Selectivity:** Admits over 75% of applicants.

### BASIC COSTS (2016-2017)

**Tuition and fees:** $33,940.

**Per-credit charge:** $1,373.

**Room and board:** $7,900.

### FINANCIAL AID PICTURE (2015-2016)

**Students with need:** Out of 700 full-time freshmen who applied for aid, 631 were judged to have need. Of these, 631 received aid, and 167 had their full need met. Average financial aid package met 80% of need; average scholarship/grant was $21,424; average loan was $2,465. Need-based aid available for part-time students.

**Students without need:** 102 full-time freshmen who did not demonstrate need for aid received scholarships/grants; average award was $15,790. No-need awards available for academics, alumni affiliation, art, athletics, leadership, music/drama, religious affiliation, ROTC, state/district residency.

**Scholarships offered:** 27 full-time freshmen received athletic scholarships; average amount $9,820.

### FINANCIAL AID PROCEDURES

**Dates and Deadlines:** Priority date 3/1; no closing date. Applicants notified on a rolling basis starting 1/15; must reply within 2 week(s) of notification.

**Transfers:** No deadline. Applicants notified on a rolling basis starting 1/15; must reply within 2 week(s) of notification.

### CONTACT

Greg Bruner, Director of Financial Aid

One University Avenue, Bourbonnais, IL 60914

(815) 939-5249

## Parkland College
Champaign, Illinois
www.parkland.edu                          Federal Code: 007118

**2-year public** community college in small city.

**Enrollment:** 7,958 undergrads.

**Selectivity:** Open admission; but selective for some programs.

### BASIC COSTS (2015-2016)

**Tuition and fees:** $4,215; out-of-district residents $10,095; out-of-state residents $14,985.

**Per-credit charge:** $125; out-of-district residents $321; out-of-state residents $484.

### FINANCIAL AID PICTURE

**Students with need:** Need-based aid available for full-time students. Work study available nights.

**Students without need:** No-need awards available for academics, art, athletics, leadership, minority status, music/drama, state/district residency.

### FINANCIAL AID PROCEDURES

**Forms required:** FAFSA, institutional form.

**Dates and Deadlines:** Closing date 3/1. Applicants notified on a rolling basis starting 6/1; must reply within 2 week(s) of notification.

### CONTACT

Tim Wendt, Director of Enrollment Services

2400 West Bradley Avenue, Champaign, IL 61821-1899

(217) 351-2222

## Prairie State College
Chicago Heights, Illinois
www.prairiestate.edu                          Federal Code: 001640

**2-year public** community college in large town.

**Enrollment:** 4,571 undergrads.

**Selectivity:** Open admission; but selective for some programs.

### BASIC COSTS (2015-2016)

**Tuition and fees:** $4,290; out-of-district residents $9,750; out-of-state residents $11,550.

**Per-credit charge:** $121; out-of-district residents $303; out-of-state residents $363.

## FINANCIAL AID PICTURE

**Students with need:** Need-based aid available for full-time and part-time students. Work study available nights, weekends, and for part-time students.

## FINANCIAL AID PROCEDURES

**Forms required:** FAFSA, institutional form.

**Dates and Deadlines:** Closing date 7/1. Applicants notified on a rolling basis; must reply within 2 week(s) of notification.

## CONTACT

Alice Garcia, Director of Financial Aid

202 South Halsted Street, Chicago Heights, IL 60411

(708) 709-3523

## Principia College

Elsah, Illinois

www.principiacollege.edu

Federal Code: 001744

CSS Code: 1630

**4-year private** liberal arts college in rural community, affiliated with First Church of Christ, Scientist (Christian Science).

**Enrollment:** 449 undergrads, 2% part-time. 79 full-time freshmen.

**Selectivity:** Admits over 75% of applicants.

## BASIC COSTS (2016-2017)

**Tuition and fees:** $27,980.

**Per-credit charge:** $916.

**Room and board:** $11,030.

## FINANCIAL AID PICTURE (2015-2016)

**Students with need:** Out of 59 full-time freshmen who applied for aid, 51 were judged to have need. Of these, 51 received aid, and 22 had their full need met. Average financial aid package met 99% of need; average scholarship/grant was $26,094; average loan was $5,727. Need-based aid available for part-time students.

**Students without need:** 41 full-time freshmen who did not demonstrate need for aid received scholarships/grants; average award was $24,300. No-need awards available for academics, alumni affiliation, leadership.

**Scholarships offered:** Trustee Scholarship; full-tuition; based on GPA and SAT/ACT. Chairman's Scholarship; 3/4 tuition; based on GPA and SAT/ACT. President's Scholarship; 1/2 tuition; based on GPA and SAT/ACT. Dean's Scholarship; 1/4 tuition; based on GPA and SAT/ACT. Arthur Schulz, Jr. Alumni Scholarship; $4,500; based on GPA and SAT/ACT. Children and grandchildren of alumni scholarships; based on GPA. Founders' Scholarships; 1/4 to full-tuition; awarded to students who demonstrate deep commitment to Christian Science, character, and citizenship as evidenced by active participation in these areas.

## FINANCIAL AID PROCEDURES

**Forms required:** CSS PROFILE, institutional form.

**Dates and Deadlines:** Closing date 3/1. Applicants notified by 4/1.

**Transfers:** Priority date 3/1.

## CONTACT

Tamara Gavaletz, Director of Admissions and Financial Aid

One Maybeck Place, Elsah, IL 62028-9799

(800) 277-4648 ext. 2813

## Quincy University

Quincy, Illinois

www.quincy.edu

Federal Code: 001745

**4-year private** university and liberal arts college in large town, affiliated with Roman Catholic Church.

**Enrollment:** 1,065 undergrads, 4% part-time. 278 full-time freshmen.

**Selectivity:** Admits 50 to 75% of applicants.

## BASIC COSTS (2015-2016)

**Tuition and fees:** $26,998.

**Per-credit charge:** $700.

**Room and board:** $10,000.

## FINANCIAL AID PICTURE (2015-2016)

**Students with need:** Out of 266 full-time freshmen who applied for aid, 240 were judged to have need. Of these, 239 received aid, and 64 had their full need met. Average financial aid package met 87% of need; average scholarship/grant was $19,246; average loan was $5,131. For part-time students, average financial aid package was $6,514.

**Students without need:** 33 full-time freshmen who did not demonstrate need for aid received scholarships/grants; average award was $11,761. No-need awards available for academics, alumni affiliation, art, athletics, leadership, music/drama.

**Scholarships offered:** *Merit:* Academic scholarships: $8,000-$15,000 per year; based on ACT and high school GPA; unlimited number awarded. *Athletic:* 21 full-time freshmen received athletic scholarships; average amount $6,440.

## FINANCIAL AID PROCEDURES

**Forms required:** FAFSA.

**Dates and Deadlines:** Priority date 3/21; no closing date. Applicants notified on a rolling basis starting 3/1; must reply by 5/1 or within 2 week(s) of notification.

## CONTACT

Lisa Flack, Director of Financial Aid

1800 College Avenue, Quincy, IL 62301-2699

(217) 228-5260

## Rasmussen College: Aurora

Aurora, Illinois

www.rasmussen.edu

**2-year for-profit** branch campus and career college in small city.

**Enrollment:** 369 undergrads.

**Selectivity:** Open admission; but selective for some programs.

## BASIC COSTS (2016-2017)

**Tuition and fees:** $13,455.

**Per-credit charge:** $299.

## FINANCIAL AID PICTURE

**Students with need:** Need-based aid available for full-time and part-time students.

## FINANCIAL AID PROCEDURES

**Forms required:** FAFSA, institutional form.

**Dates and Deadlines:** Applicants notified on a rolling basis.

## CONTACT

Debora Murray, Director of Financial Services

2363 Sequoia Drive, Suite 131, Aurora, IL 60506

## Rasmussen College: Mokena/Tinley Park

Mokena, Illinois

www.rasmussen.edu

**4-year for-profit** career college in large town.

**Enrollment:** 234 undergrads.

**Selectivity:** Admits over 75% of applicants.

## BASIC COSTS (2016-2017)

**Tuition and fees:** $13,455.

**Per-credit charge:** $299.

**FINANCIAL AID PICTURE**

**Students with need:** Need-based aid available for full-time and part-time students.

**FINANCIAL AID PROCEDURES**

**Forms required:** FAFSA, institutional form.

**Dates and Deadlines:** Applicants notified on a rolling basis.

**CONTACT**

Debora Murray, Director of Financial Services
8650 West Spring Lake Road, Mokena, IL 60448

## Rasmussen College: Rockford

Rockford, Illinois
www.rasmussen.edu

**2-year for-profit** career college in small city.

**Enrollment:** 587 undergrads.

**Selectivity:** Open admission; but selective for some programs.

**BASIC COSTS (2016-2017)**

**Tuition and fees:** $13,455.

**Per-credit charge:** $299.

**FINANCIAL AID PICTURE**

**Students with need:** Need-based aid available for full-time and part-time students.

**FINANCIAL AID PROCEDURES**

**Forms required:** FAFSA, institutional form.

**Dates and Deadlines:** Applicants notified on a rolling basis.

**CONTACT**

Debora Murray, Director of Financial Services
6000 East State Street, Fourth Floor, Rockford, IL 61108-2513

## Rasmussen College: Romeoville/Joliet

Romeoville, Illinois
www.rasmussen.edu

**2-year for-profit** career college in large town.

**Enrollment:** 532 undergrads.

**Selectivity:** Open admission; but selective for some programs.

**BASIC COSTS (2016-2017)**

**Tuition and fees:** $13,455.

**Per-credit charge:** $299.

**FINANCIAL AID PICTURE**

**Students with need:** Need-based aid available for full-time and part-time students.

**FINANCIAL AID PROCEDURES**

**Forms required:** FAFSA, institutional form.

**Dates and Deadlines:** Applicants notified on a rolling basis.

**CONTACT**

Debora Murray, Director of Financial Services
400 West Normantown Road, Romeoville, IL 60446

## Rend Lake College

Ina, Illinois
www.rlc.edu                                    Federal Code: 007119

**2-year public** community college in rural community.

**Enrollment:** 1,632 undergrads, 29% part-time. 518 full-time freshmen.

**Selectivity:** Open admission; but selective for some programs.

**BASIC COSTS (2015-2016)**

**Tuition and fees:** $3,300; out-of-district residents $4,905; out-of-state residents $4,950.

**Per-credit charge:** $95; out-of-district residents $148; out-of-state residents $150.

**FINANCIAL AID PICTURE (2014-2015)**

**Students with need:** Out of 478 full-time freshmen who applied for aid, 451 were judged to have need. Of these, 448 received aid, and 147 had their full need met. Average financial aid package met 59% of need; average scholarship/grant was $1,285. For part-time students, average financial aid package was $1,130.

**FINANCIAL AID PROCEDURES**

**Forms required:** FAFSA.

**Dates and Deadlines:** Applicants notified on a rolling basis starting 3/15; must reply within 4 week(s) of notification.

**Transfers:** No deadline. Applicants notified on a rolling basis starting 3/15; must reply within 4 week(s) of notification.

**CONTACT**

Cheri Rushing, Director of Financial Aid
468 North Ken Gray Parkway, Ina, IL 62846
(618) 437-5321 ext. 1385

## Resurrection University

Chicago, Illinois
www.resu.edu                                   Federal Code: 022141

**Upper-division private** health science and nursing college in very large city, affiliated with Roman Catholic Church.

**Enrollment:** 391 undergrads.

**BASIC COSTS (2015-2016)**

**Tuition and fees:** $25,142.

**Per-credit charge:** $808.

**FINANCIAL AID PICTURE**

**Students with need:** Need-based aid available for full-time and part-time students. Work study available nights, weekends, and for part-time students.

**Students without need:** No-need awards available for academics, alumni affiliation.

**FINANCIAL AID PROCEDURES**

**Forms required:** FAFSA.

**Transfers:** Priority date 4/1; no deadline. Applicants notified on a rolling basis starting 4/1; must reply within 3 week(s) of notification.

**CONTACT**

Shirley Howell, Financial Aid Officer
1431 North Claremont Avenue, Chicago, IL 60622
(773) 252-6446

## Richland Community College

Decatur, Illinois
www.richland.edu                               Federal Code: 010879

**2-year public** community college in small city.

**Enrollment:** 2,855 undergrads.

**Selectivity:** Open admission; but selective for some programs.

**BASIC COSTS (2015-2016)**

**Tuition and fees:** $3,732; out-of-district residents $5,757; out-of-state residents $13,662.

**Per-credit charge:** $114; out-of-district residents $182; out-of-state residents $445.

## FINANCIAL AID PICTURE
**Students with need:** Need-based aid available for full-time and part-time students. Work study available nights.
**Students without need:** No-need awards available for academics, art, leadership, music/drama.

## FINANCIAL AID PROCEDURES
**Forms required:** FAFSA.
**Dates and Deadlines:** Priority date 7/25; no closing date. Applicants notified on a rolling basis starting 3/20.
**Transfers:** No deadline. Applicants notified on a rolling basis.

## CONTACT
Carmin Ross, Director of Financial Aid
One College Park, Decatur, IL 62521
(217) 875-7200 ext. 271

## Robert Morris University: Chicago
Chicago, Illinois
www.robertmorris.edu                    Federal Code: 001746

**4-year private** university in very large city.
**Enrollment:** 2,681 undergrads, 5% part-time. 871 full-time freshmen.
**Selectivity:** Admits less than 50% of applicants.

## BASIC COSTS (2016-2017)
**Tuition and fees:** $25,950.
**Per-credit charge:** $717.
**Room and board:** $12,600.

## FINANCIAL AID PICTURE (2014-2015)
**Students with need:** Out of 835 full-time freshmen who applied for aid, 809 were judged to have need. Of these, 780 received aid, and 37 had their full need met. Average financial aid package met 51% of need; average scholarship/grant was $12,301; average loan was $3,855. For part-time students, average financial aid package was $8,574.
**Students without need:** 41 full-time freshmen who did not demonstrate need for aid received scholarships/grants; average award was $10,909. No-need awards available for academics, art, athletics, leadership, music/drama, ROTC, state/district residency.
**Scholarships offered:** 576 full-time freshmen received athletic scholarships; average amount $8,818.

## FINANCIAL AID PROCEDURES
**Forms required:** FAFSA.
**Dates and Deadlines:** Applicants notified on a rolling basis.
**Transfers:** No deadline. Applicants notified on a rolling basis.

## CONTACT
Leigh Brinson, Vice President of Financial Services
401 South State Street, Chicago, IL 60605
(312) 935-4077

## Rock Valley College
Rockford, Illinois
www.rockvalleycollege.edu               Federal Code: 1747

**2-year public** community college in small city.
**Enrollment:** 6,796 undergrads, 56% part-time. 736 full-time freshmen.
**Selectivity:** Open admission; but selective for some programs.

## BASIC COSTS (2015-2016)
**Tuition and fees:** $3,044; out-of-district residents $8,264; out-of-state residents $15,374.
**Per-credit charge:** $91; out-of-district residents $265; out-of-state residents $502.

## FINANCIAL AID PICTURE (2014-2015)
**Students with need:** Need-based aid available for part-time students. Work study available nights.

## FINANCIAL AID PROCEDURES
**Forms required:** FAFSA, institutional form.
**Dates and Deadlines:** Priority date 5/1; no closing date. Applicants notified on a rolling basis; must reply within 4 week(s) of notification.

## CONTACT
James Heller, Director of Financial Aid
3301 North Mulford Road, Rockford, IL 61114-5699
(815) 921-4150

## Rockford Career College
Rockford, Illinois
www.rockfordcareercollege.edu          Federal Code: 008545

**2-year for-profit** career college in small city.
**Enrollment:** 484 undergrads.
**Selectivity:** Open admission.

## FINANCIAL AID PICTURE
**Students with need:** Need-based aid available for full-time and part-time students. Work study available nights.
**Students without need:** This college awards aid only to students with need.

## FINANCIAL AID PROCEDURES
**Forms required:** FAFSA.
**Dates and Deadlines:** Applicants notified on a rolling basis.

## CONTACT
Lisa Ruch, Director of Financial Aid
1130 South Alpine Road, Rockford, IL 61108
(815) 967-7314

## Rockford University
Rockford, Illinois
www.rockford.edu                        Federal Code: 001748

**4-year private** liberal arts college in small city.
**Enrollment:** 1,033 undergrads, 11% part-time. 147 full-time freshmen.

## BASIC COSTS (2015-2016)
**Tuition and fees:** $28,330.
**Per-credit charge:** $745.
**Room and board:** $7,940.

## FINANCIAL AID PICTURE (2014-2015)
**Students with need:** Out of 142 full-time freshmen who applied for aid, 134 were judged to have need. Of these, 134 received aid, and 17 had their full need met. Average financial aid package met 71% of need; average scholarship/grant was $16,491; average loan was $3,907. For part-time students, average financial aid package was $7,949.
**Students without need:** 13 full-time freshmen who did not demonstrate need for aid received scholarships/grants; average award was $12,710. No-need awards available for academics, alumni affiliation, leadership, minority status, music/drama, state/district residency.

## FINANCIAL AID PROCEDURES
**Forms required:** FAFSA.
**Dates and Deadlines:** Priority date 3/1; no closing date. Applicants notified on a rolling basis starting 3/1; must reply within 4 week(s) of notification.

## CONTACT

Todd Fischer-Free, Assistant Vice President of Student Administrative Services

5050 East State Street, Rockford, IL 61108-2311

(815) 226-3383

# Roosevelt University

Chicago, Illinois

www.roosevelt.edu

Federal Code: 001749

**4-year private** university in very large city.

**Enrollment:** 3,727 undergrads.

## BASIC COSTS (2015-2016)

**Tuition and fees:** $27,300.

**Per-credit charge:** $737.

**Room and board:** $12,980.

## FINANCIAL AID PICTURE

**Students with need:** Need-based aid available for full-time and part-time students. Work study available nights, weekends, and for part-time students.

**Students without need:** No-need awards available for academics, alumni affiliation, art, job skills, minority status.

## FINANCIAL AID PROCEDURES

**Forms required:** FAFSA, institutional form.

**Dates and Deadlines:** Priority date 3/1; no closing date. Applicants notified on a rolling basis starting 2/1; must reply within 2 week(s) of notification.

**Transfers:** Applicants notified on a rolling basis starting 3/1; must reply within 2 week(s) of notification.

## CONTACT

Jeanne Locarnini, Assistant Provost, Financial Aid

430 S Michigan Ave, Chicago, IL 60605-1394

(866) 421-0935

# Rush University

Chicago, Illinois

www.rushu.rush.edu

Federal Code: 009800

**Upper-division private** health science and nursing college in very large city.

**Enrollment:** 134 undergrads, 26% part-time.

## BASIC COSTS (2015-2016)

**Tuition and fees:** $33,857.

**Per-credit charge:** $555.

**Additional info:** Tuition/fee waivers available for minority students.

## FINANCIAL AID PICTURE

**Students with need:** Need-based aid available for full-time and part-time students.

**Students without need:** No-need awards available for academics, minority status.

## FINANCIAL AID PROCEDURES

**Transfers:** Priority date 3/1.

## CONTACT

Michael Frechette, Director of Student Financial Aid

College Admissions, Chicago, IL 60612

(312) 942-6256

# Saint Anthony College of Nursing

Rockford, Illinois

www.sacn.edu

Federal Code: 009987

**Upper-division private** nursing college in small city, affiliated with Roman Catholic Church.

**Enrollment:** 233 undergrads.

## BASIC COSTS (2015-2016)

**Tuition and fees:** $23,566.

**Per-credit charge:** $713.

## FINANCIAL AID PICTURE

**Students with need:** Need-based aid available for full-time and part-time students.

**Students without need:** No-need awards available for academics, leadership.

## FINANCIAL AID PROCEDURES

**Transfers:** Closing date 6/30. Applicants notified on a rolling basis starting 4/15.

## CONTACT

Serrita Woods, Financial Aid Officer

5658 East State Street, Rockford, IL 61108-2468

(815) 395-5089

# St. Francis Medical Center College of Nursing

Peoria, Illinois

www.sfmccon.edu

Federal Code: 006240

**Upper-division private** nursing college in small city, affiliated with Roman Catholic Church.

**Enrollment:** 402 undergrads, 29% part-time.

## BASIC COSTS (2016-2017)

**Tuition and fees:** $19,980.

**Per-credit charge:** $580.

**Room only:** $3,500.

## FINANCIAL AID PICTURE (2014-2015)

**Students with need:** Average financial aid package for all full-time undergraduates was $12,306; for part-time $8,477. 36% awarded as scholarships/grants, 64% awarded as loans/jobs.

**Students without need:** No-need awards available for academics, alumni affiliation.

**Additional info:** OSF Saint Francis Medical Center Education student loan available to full-time students on a limited basis. Tuition waiver program for hospital employees available.

## FINANCIAL AID PROCEDURES

**Forms required:** FAFSA, institutional form.

**Dates and Deadlines:** Priority date 6/1; no closing date. Must reply within 4 week(s) of notification.

**Transfers:** No deadline. Applicants notified on a rolling basis starting 5/15; must reply within 4 week(s) of notification.

## CONTACT

Nancy Perryman, Coordinator of Student Finance, Financial Assistance

511 NE Greenleaf Street, Peoria, IL 61603-3783

(309) 655-4119

## St. John's College
Springfield, Illinois
www.stjohnscollegespringfield.edu   Federal Code: 030980

**Upper-division private** nursing college in small city, affiliated with Roman Catholic Church.
**Enrollment:** 121 undergrads, 12% part-time.
**Selectivity:** Open admission; but selective for some programs.

### BASIC COSTS (2015-2016)
**Tuition and fees:** $19,237.
**Per-credit charge:** $753.
**Additional info:** Tuition at time of enrollment locked for 2 years.

### FINANCIAL AID PICTURE (2014-2015)
**Students with need:** Average financial aid package for all full-time undergraduates was $9,000; for part-time $1,000. 35% awarded as scholarships/grants, 65% awarded as loans/jobs. Work study available nights, weekends, and for part-time students.
**Students without need:** No-need awards available for alumni affiliation, minority status.

### FINANCIAL AID PROCEDURES
**Transfers:** Priority date 2/15; no deadline. Applicants notified on a rolling basis starting 4/1; must reply within 12 week(s) of notification.

### CONTACT
Timothy Marten, Financial Aid Officer
729 East Carpenter Street, Springfield, IL 62702-5321
(217) 544-6464 ext. 44705

## Saint Xavier University
Chicago, Illinois
www.sxu.edu                           Federal Code: 001768

**4-year private** university in very large city, affiliated with Roman Catholic Church.
**Enrollment:** 2,940 undergrads.

### BASIC COSTS (2015-2016)
**Tuition and fees:** $30,920.
**Per-credit charge:** $650.
**Room and board:** $10,620.

### FINANCIAL AID PICTURE
**Students with need:** Need-based aid available for full-time and part-time students.
**Students without need:** No-need awards available for academics, athletics, music/drama.

### FINANCIAL AID PROCEDURES
**Forms required:** FAFSA.
**Dates and Deadlines:** Priority date 2/15; no closing date. Applicants notified on a rolling basis starting 2/1; must reply by 5/1 or within 2 week(s) of notification.
**Transfers:** Applicants notified on a rolling basis starting 2/15; must reply by 5/1 or within 2 week(s) of notification.

### CONTACT
Susan Swisher, Director of Financial aid
3700 West 103rd Street, Chicago, IL 60655
(773) 298-3073

## Sauk Valley Community College
Dixon, Illinois
www.svcc.edu                          Federal Code: 001752

**2-year public** community college in large town.
**Enrollment:** 1,532 undergrads, 46% part-time. 317 full-time freshmen.
**Selectivity:** Open admission; but selective for some programs.

### BASIC COSTS (2016-2017)
**Tuition and fees:** $3,258; out-of-district residents $9,110; out-of-state residents $9,716.

### FINANCIAL AID PICTURE (2014-2015)
**Students with need:** Out of 145 full-time freshmen who applied for aid, 113 were judged to have need. Of these, 103 received aid. Average financial aid package met 23% of need; average scholarship/grant was $4,814; average loan was $2,117. For part-time students, average financial aid package was $3,079.
**Students without need:** 20 full-time freshmen who did not demonstrate need for aid received scholarships/grants; average award was $2,795. No-need awards available for academics, athletics, minority status, state/district residency.
**Scholarships offered:** 14 full-time freshmen received athletic scholarships; average amount $2,684.

### FINANCIAL AID PROCEDURES
**Forms required:** FAFSA, institutional form.
**Dates and Deadlines:** Priority date 8/5; no closing date. Applicants notified on a rolling basis starting 3/20; must reply within 4 week(s) of notification.
**Transfers:** No deadline. Applicants notified on a rolling basis starting 3/20; must reply within 4 week(s) of notification.

### CONTACT
Jennifer Schultz, Coordinator of Financial Aid
173 Illinois Route 2, Dixon, IL 61021-9112
(815) 288-5511 ext. 339

## School of the Art Institute of Chicago
Chicago, Illinois
www.saic.edu                          Federal Code: 001753

**4-year private** visual arts college in very large city.
**Enrollment:** 2,843 undergrads, 8% part-time. 573 full-time freshmen.
**Selectivity:** Admits 50 to 75% of applicants.

### BASIC COSTS (2015-2016)
**Tuition and fees:** $43,960.
**Per-credit charge:** $1,438.
**Room and board:** $12,850.

### FINANCIAL AID PICTURE (2014-2015)
**Students with need:** Need-based aid available for full-time and part-time students. Work study available nights, weekends, and for part-time students.
**Students without need:** No-need awards available for academics, art.
**Scholarships offered:** Merit scholarships; $2,000 to full tuition; renewable.

### FINANCIAL AID PROCEDURES
**Forms required:** FAFSA.
**Dates and Deadlines:** Priority date 3/15; no closing date. Applicants notified on a rolling basis starting 3/1.
**Transfers:** No deadline. Applicants notified on a rolling basis.

### CONTACT
Patrick James, Director of Financial Aid
36 South Wabash Avenue, Chicago, IL 60603
(312) 629-6600

## Shawnee Community College
Ullin, Illinois
www.shawneecc.edu                    Federal Code: 007693

**2-year public** community college in rural community.
**Enrollment:** 1,819 undergrads.
**Selectivity:** Open admission; but selective for some programs.

### BASIC COSTS (2016-2017)
**Tuition and fees:** $2,970; out-of-district residents $4,920; out-of-state residents $4,980.
**Per-credit charge:** $99; out-of-district residents $164; out-of-state residents $166.

### FINANCIAL AID PICTURE
**Students with need:** Need-based aid available for full-time and part-time students.
**Students without need:** This college awards aid only to students with need.

### FINANCIAL AID PROCEDURES
**Forms required:** FAFSA.
**Dates and Deadlines:** Priority date 9/1; no closing date. Applicants notified on a rolling basis; must reply within 2 week(s) of notification.

### CONTACT
Tammy Capps, Director of Financial Aid
8364 Shawnee College Road, Ullin, IL 62992
(618) 634-3280 ext. 3280

## Shimer College
Chicago, Illinois
www.shimer.edu                       Federal Code: 001756

**4-year private** liberal arts college in very large city.
**Enrollment:** 76 undergrads, 21% part-time. 11 full-time freshmen.

### BASIC COSTS (2015-2016)
**Tuition and fees:** $34,004.
**Room and board:** $11,516.
**Additional info:** Tuition/fee waivers available for adults.

### FINANCIAL AID PICTURE
**Students with need:** Need-based aid available for full-time and part-time students. Work study available nights, weekends, and for part-time students.
**Students without need:** No-need awards available for academics, alumni affiliation.
**Scholarships offered:** Michel de Montaigne Scholarship: half or full tuition; awarded to new students on the basis of merit in writing and discussion; 2 full and 2 half tuition scholarships awarded each year.

### FINANCIAL AID PROCEDURES
**Forms required:** FAFSA.
**Dates and Deadlines:** Applicants notified on a rolling basis starting 3/15; must reply by 5/1.
**Transfers:** Closing date 8/1. Applicants notified on a rolling basis; must reply by 5/1 or within 3 week(s) of notification.

### CONTACT
Janet Henthorn, Financial Aid Officer
3424 South State Street, Chicago, IL 60616
(312) 235-3507

## South Suburban College of Cook County
South Holland, Illinois
www.ssc.edu                          Federal Code: 001769

**2-year public** community college in large town.
**Enrollment:** 4,401 undergrads. 671 full-time freshmen.
**Selectivity:** Open admission; but selective for some programs.

### BASIC COSTS (2016-2017)
**Tuition and fees:** $4,583; out-of-district residents $10,523; out-of-state residents $12,173.
**Per-credit charge:** $135; out-of-district residents $333; out-of-state residents $358.
**Additional info:** Tuition/fee waivers available for adults.

### FINANCIAL AID PICTURE (2014-2015)
**Students with need:** Out of 671 full-time freshmen who applied for aid, 629 were judged to have need. Of these, 629 received aid. Average financial aid package met 65% of need; average scholarship/grant was $4,740. Need-based aid available for part-time students.
**Students without need:** 44 full-time freshmen who did not demonstrate need for aid received scholarships/grants; average award was $181. No-need awards available for academics, art, athletics, music/drama, state/district residency.
**Scholarships offered:** 181 full-time freshmen received athletic scholarships; average amount $1,260.

### FINANCIAL AID PROCEDURES
**Forms required:** FAFSA.
**Dates and Deadlines:** Priority date 6/30; no closing date. Applicants notified on a rolling basis starting 5/1.
**Transfers:** No deadline. Applicants notified on a rolling basis starting 5/11; must reply by 7/15 or within 2 week(s) of notification.

### CONTACT
John Semple, Director
15800 South State Street, South Holland, IL 60473
(708) 596-2000 ext. 2438

## Southeastern Illinois College
Harrisburg, Illinois
www.sic.edu                          Federal Code: 001757

**2-year public** community college in small town.
**Enrollment:** 1,004 undergrads, 30% part-time. 142 full-time freshmen.
**Selectivity:** Open admission; but selective for some programs.

### BASIC COSTS (2015-2016)
**Tuition and fees:** $3,120; out-of-district residents $4,800; out-of-state residents $5,040.

### FINANCIAL AID PICTURE (2014-2015)
**Students with need:** Out of 138 full-time freshmen who applied for aid, 125 were judged to have need. Of these, 125 received aid, and 4 had their full need met. Average financial aid package met 35% of need; average scholarship/grant was $4,677. For part-time students, average financial aid package was $2,871.
**Students without need:** 16 full-time freshmen who did not demonstrate need for aid received scholarships/grants; average award was $1,858. No-need awards available for academics, alumni affiliation, art, athletics, music/drama.
**Scholarships offered:** 6 full-time freshmen received athletic scholarships; average amount $3,657.

### FINANCIAL AID PROCEDURES
**Forms required:** FAFSA.
**Dates and Deadlines:** Priority date 2/15; no closing date. Applicants notified on a rolling basis starting 3/1; must reply within 2 week(s) of notification.

**Transfers:** Priority date 2/28; no deadline. Applicants notified on a rolling basis starting 4/1; must reply within 2 week(s) of notification.

**CONTACT**
Emily Henson, Director of Financial Aid
3575 College Road, Harrisburg, IL 62946
(618) 252-5400 ext. 2450

## Southern Illinois University Carbondale
Carbondale, Illinois
www.siu.edu                              Federal Code: 001758

**4-year public** university in large town.
**Enrollment:** 12,858 undergrads, 12% part-time. 2,151 full-time freshmen.
**Selectivity:** Admits over 75% of applicants.

### BASIC COSTS (2015-2016)
**Tuition and fees:** $13,137; out-of-state residents $26,390.
**Per-credit charge:** $295; out-of-state residents $736.
**Room and board:** $9,996.
**Additional info:** Tuition at time of enrollment locked for 4 years.

### FINANCIAL AID PICTURE (2015-2016)
**Students with need:** Out of 2,027 full-time freshmen who applied for aid, 1,719 were judged to have need. Of these, 1,703 received aid, and 130 had their full need met. Average financial aid package met 62% of need; average scholarship/grant was $8,675; average loan was $3,403. For part-time students, average financial aid package was $9,867.
**Students without need:** 152 full-time freshmen who did not demonstrate need for aid received scholarships/grants; average award was $6,804. No-need awards available for academics, alumni affiliation, art, athletics, leadership, minority status, music/drama, ROTC, state/district residency.
**Scholarships offered:** 48 full-time freshmen received athletic scholarships; average amount $19,342.
**Additional info:** Need-based financial aid available to part-time students enrolled in minimum of 6 semester hours.

### FINANCIAL AID PROCEDURES
**Forms required:** FAFSA.
**Dates and Deadlines:** Priority date 3/1; no closing date. Applicants notified on a rolling basis starting 3/15.
**Transfers:** Must reply within 4 week(s) of notification.

**CONTACT**
Terri Harfst, Director
Undergraduate Admissions, Mailcode 4710, Carbondale, IL 62901
(618) 453-4334

## Southern Illinois University Edwardsville
Edwardsville, Illinois
www.siue.edu                             Federal Code: 001759

**4-year public** university in large town.
**Enrollment:** 11,717 undergrads, 15% part-time. 2,074 full-time freshmen.
**Selectivity:** Admits over 75% of applicants.

### BASIC COSTS (2015-2016)
**Tuition and fees:** $10,247; out-of-state residents $21,740.
**Per-credit charge:** $255; out-of-state residents $639.
**Room and board:** $9,570.
**Additional info:** Tuition at time of enrollment locked for 4 years.

### FINANCIAL AID PICTURE (2015-2016)
**Students with need:** Out of 1,870 full-time freshmen who applied for aid, 1,373 were judged to have need. Of these, 1,340 received aid, and 621 had

their full need met. Average financial aid package met 66% of need; average scholarship/grant was $8,069; average loan was $3,533. For part-time students, average financial aid package was $8,182.
**Students without need:** This college awards aid only to students with need.
**Scholarships offered:** 22 full-time freshmen received athletic scholarships; average amount $16,427.

### FINANCIAL AID PROCEDURES
**Forms required:** FAFSA.
**Dates and Deadlines:** Priority date 3/1; closing date 6/1. Applicants notified on a rolling basis starting 3/15; must reply within 4 week(s) of notification.

**CONTACT**
Sally Mullen, Director of Student Financial Aid
Rendleman Hall, Rm 2120, Edwardsville, IL 62026-1600
(618) 650-3880

## Southwestern Illinois College
Belleville, Illinois
www.swic.edu                             Federal Code: 001636

**2-year public** community college in small city.
**Enrollment:** 9,028 undergrads, 55% part-time. 1,039 full-time freshmen.
**Selectivity:** Open admission; but selective for some programs.

### BASIC COSTS (2015-2016)
**Tuition and fees:** $3,420; out-of-district residents $12,120; out-of-state residents $15,750.
**Per-credit charge:** $109; out-of-district residents $399; out-of-state residents $520.
**Additional info:** Tuition/fee waivers available for adults.

### FINANCIAL AID PICTURE (2014-2015)
**Students with need:** 61% of average financial aid package awarded as scholarships/grants, 39% awarded as loans/jobs. Need-based aid available for part-time students. Work study available nights.
**Students without need:** No-need awards available for academics, art, athletics, leadership, minority status, music/drama, ROTC.

### FINANCIAL AID PROCEDURES
**Forms required:** FAFSA, institutional form.
**Dates and Deadlines:** Priority date 8/1; closing date 5/31. Applicants notified on a rolling basis starting 4/1; must reply within 2 week(s) of notification.

**CONTACT**
Robert Tebbe, Director of Financial Aid
2500 Carlyle Avenue, Belleville, IL 62221-5899
(618) 235-2700 ext. 5288

## Spoon River College
Canton, Illinois
www.src.edu                              Federal Code: 001643

**2-year public** community college in large town.
**Enrollment:** 1,161 undergrads, 37% part-time. 300 full-time freshmen.
**Selectivity:** Open admission; but selective for some programs.

### BASIC COSTS (2015-2016)
**Tuition and fees:** $4,200; out-of-district residents $9,240; out-of-state residents $10,020.
**Per-credit charge:** $120; out-of-district residents $288; out-of-state residents $314.

### FINANCIAL AID PICTURE (2014-2015)
**Students with need:** 68% of average financial aid package awarded as scholarships/grants, 32% awarded as loans/jobs. Need-based aid available for part-time students. Work study available nights.

**Students without need:** No-need awards available for academics, art, athletics, music/drama, state/district residency.

**Scholarships offered:** SRC's Foundation offers many scholarships. The application deadline is March 15. Students are required to complete an application and a FAFSA for the upcoming year.

**Additional info:** Students who have submitted all required forms by the processing deadline are guaranteed to have aid eligibility established by the tuition deadline. All forms submitted after the processing deadline are processed in the order received on a continuing basis.

### FINANCIAL AID PROCEDURES
**Forms required:** FAFSA.

**Dates and Deadlines:** Priority date 6/21; closing date 7/1. Applicants notified on a rolling basis starting 5/15.

### CONTACT
Jo Branson, Director of Financial Aid
23235 North County Road 22, Canton, IL 61520
(309) 649-7030

## Taylor Business Institute
Chicago, Illinois
www.tbiil.edu                     Federal Code: 011810

**2-year for-profit** business college in very large city.
**Enrollment:** 257 undergrads.

### FINANCIAL AID PICTURE
**Students with need:** Need-based aid available for full-time students. Work study available nights.

### FINANCIAL AID PROCEDURES
**Forms required:** FAFSA, state aid form, institutional form.

### CONTACT
Florence Davis, Financial Aid Director
318 West Adams Street, 5th Floor, Chicago, IL 60606
(312) 658-5100

## Trinity Christian College
Palos Heights, Illinois
www.trnty.edu                     Federal Code: 001771

**4-year private** liberal arts college in very large city.
**Enrollment:** 1,152 undergrads, 15% part-time. 190 full-time freshmen.

### BASIC COSTS (2015-2016)
**Tuition and fees:** $26,440.
**Room and board:** $9,390.

### FINANCIAL AID PICTURE (2015-2016)
**Students with need:** Out of 175 full-time freshmen who applied for aid, 151 were judged to have need. Of these, 151 received aid, and 76 had their full need met. For part-time students, average financial aid package was $5,470.

**Students without need:** 21 full-time freshmen who did not demonstrate need for aid received scholarships/grants; average award was $9,455. No-need awards available for academics, alumni affiliation, art, athletics, leadership, minority status, music/drama, religious affiliation.

**Scholarships offered:** 10 full-time freshmen received athletic scholarships; average amount $9,830.

**Additional info:** High school transcripts and ACT/SAT required for merit scholarships.

### FINANCIAL AID PROCEDURES
**Forms required:** FAFSA.

**Dates and Deadlines:** Priority date 2/15; no closing date. Applicants notified on a rolling basis starting 3/1; must reply by 5/1 or within 2 week(s) of notification.

**Transfers:** Applicants notified on a rolling basis starting 3/1; must reply by 5/1 or within 2 week(s) of notification.

### CONTACT
Ryan Zantingh, Director of Financial Aid
6601 West College Drive, Palos Heights, IL 60463
(708) 239-4706

## Trinity College of Nursing & Health Sciences
Rock Island, Illinois
www.trinitycollegeqc.edu          Federal Code: 006225

**4-year private** health science and nursing college in large city.
**Enrollment:** 219 undergrads, 37% part-time. 1 full-time freshmen.
**Selectivity:** Admits 50 to 75% of applicants.

### BASIC COSTS (2016-2017)
**Tuition and fees:** $23,404.
**Per-credit charge:** $687.

### FINANCIAL AID PICTURE (2015-2016)
**Students with need:** Average financial aid package for all full-time undergraduates was $3,011; for part-time $2,665. 47% awarded as scholarships/grants, 53% awarded as loans/jobs.

**Students without need:** This college awards aid only to students with need.

### FINANCIAL AID PROCEDURES
**Forms required:** FAFSA, institutional form.
**Dates and Deadlines:** Applicants notified on a rolling basis starting 1/1.
**Transfers:** No deadline.

### CONTACT
Christine Christopherson, Financial Aid Specialist
2122 25th Avenue, Rock Island, IL 61201-5317
(309) 779-7740

## Trinity International University
Deerfield, Illinois
www.tiu.edu                       Federal Code: 001772

**4-year private** university and liberal arts college in large town, affiliated with Evangelical Free Church of America.
**Enrollment:** 1,010 undergrads. 162 full-time freshmen.

### BASIC COSTS (2015-2016)
**Tuition and fees:** $28,700.
**Per-credit charge:** $1,180.
**Room and board:** $8,830.
**Additional info:** Tuition/fee waivers available for minority students.

### FINANCIAL AID PICTURE (2014-2015)
**Students with need:** Out of 149 full-time freshmen who applied for aid, 133 were judged to have need. Of these, 133 received aid, and 14 had their full need met. Average financial aid package met 71% of need; average scholarship/grant was $6,990; average loan was $4,001. For part-time students, average financial aid package was $6,184.

**Students without need:** 8 full-time freshmen who did not demonstrate need for aid received scholarships/grants; average award was $13,080. No-need awards available for academics, alumni affiliation, athletics, minority status, music/drama, religious affiliation.

**Scholarships offered:** 8 full-time freshmen received athletic scholarships; average amount $7,472.

**FINANCIAL AID PROCEDURES**

**Forms required:** FAFSA.

**Dates and Deadlines:** Priority date 4/1; no closing date. Applicants notified on a rolling basis starting 2/15; must reply within 4 week(s) of notification.

**Transfers:** No deadline. Applicants notified on a rolling basis; must reply within 4 week(s) of notification.

**CONTACT**

Rachael Russiaky, Executive Director for Student Services
2065 Half Day Road, Deerfield, IL 60015
(847) 317-8060

## Triton College
River Grove, Illinois
www.triton.edu          Federal Code: 001773

**2-year public** community and junior college in large town.

**Enrollment:** 8,561 undergrads, 64% part-time. 833 full-time freshmen.

**Selectivity:** Open admission; but selective for some programs.

**BASIC COSTS (2015-2016)**

**Tuition and fees:** $3,870; out-of-district residents $9,370; out-of-state residents $11,629.

**Per-credit charge:** $113; out-of-district residents $296; out-of-state residents $371.

**FINANCIAL AID PICTURE (2014-2015)**

**Students with need:** Out of 550 full-time freshmen who applied for aid, 510 were judged to have need. Of these, 503 received aid. For part-time students, average financial aid package was $6,798.

**Students without need:** 48 full-time freshmen who did not demonstrate need for aid received scholarships/grants; average award was $3,171. No-need awards available for academics, athletics.

**Scholarships offered:** Board of Trustees Honor Scholarship: covers tuition and fees; for in-district high school students in top 10% of graduating class.

**FINANCIAL AID PROCEDURES**

**Forms required:** FAFSA, institutional form.

**Dates and Deadlines:** Priority date 4/15; no closing date. Applicants notified on a rolling basis starting 4/1; must reply within 2 week(s) of notification.

**CONTACT**

Patricia Zinga, Director of Financial Aid
2000 North Fifth Avenue, River Grove, IL 60171
(708) 456-0300 ext. 3441

## University of Chicago
Chicago, Illinois
www.uchicago.edu          Federal Code: 001774

**4-year private** university and liberal arts college in very large city.

**Enrollment:** 5,830 undergrads, 1% part-time. 1,537 full-time freshmen.

**Selectivity:** Admits less than 50% of applicants.

**BASIC COSTS (2015-2016)**

**Tuition and fees:** $50,193.

**Room and board:** $14,772.

**FINANCIAL AID PICTURE (2015-2016)**

**Students with need:** Out of 937 full-time freshmen who applied for aid, 724 were judged to have need. Of these, 724 received aid, and 724 had their full need met. Average financial aid package met 100% of need; average scholarship/grant was $46,854.

**Students without need:** No-need awards available for academics, leadership.

**Additional info:** No Barriers program replaces student loans with grants in all need-based financial aid packages. Grants offered instead of loans in all need based financial aid packages. Families who apply for financial aid do not have to pay a college application fee. Funding available for summer and school-year internships, research positions, study abroad, and career exploration treks for all majors and interests.

**FINANCIAL AID PROCEDURES**

**Forms required:** FAFSA, institutional form.

**Dates and Deadlines:** Closing date 2/15. Applicants notified by 4/1; must reply by 5/1.

**Transfers:** Priority date 4/1; closing date 4/1. Applicants notified on a rolling basis starting 5/1; must reply by 6/1.

**CONTACT**

Amanda Fijal, Executive Director, University Financial Aid & ESA Technologies
1101 East 58th Street, Chicago, IL 60637
(773) 702-8666

## University of Illinois at Chicago
Chicago, Illinois
www.uic.edu          Federal Code: 001776

**4-year public** university in very large city.

**Enrollment:** 17,368 undergrads, 8% part-time. 2,995 full-time freshmen.

**Selectivity:** Admits over 75% of applicants.

**BASIC COSTS (2015-2016)**

**Tuition and fees:** $13,762; out-of-state residents $26,618.

**Room and board:** $10,728.

**Additional info:** Tuition at time of enrollment locked for 4 years; tuition/fee waivers available for minority students.

**FINANCIAL AID PICTURE (2014-2015)**

**Students with need:** Out of 2,737 full-time freshmen who applied for aid, 2,377 were judged to have need. Of these, 2,258 received aid, and 225 had their full need met. Average financial aid package met 62% of need; average scholarship/grant was $13,834; average loan was $3,608. For part-time students, average financial aid package was $10,079.

**Students without need:** 120 full-time freshmen who did not demonstrate need for aid received scholarships/grants; average award was $5,482. No-need awards available for academics, art, athletics, ROTC.

**Scholarships offered:** 20 full-time freshmen received athletic scholarships; average amount $20,102.

**FINANCIAL AID PROCEDURES**

**Forms required:** FAFSA.

**Dates and Deadlines:** Priority date 2/1; no closing date. Applicants notified on a rolling basis starting 3/15; must reply by 5/1.

**CONTACT**

Timothy Opgenorth, Director of the Office of Student Financial Aid
Office of Admissions and Records, UIC, PO Box 5220, Chicago, IL 60607-5220
(312) 996-3126

## University of Illinois at Urbana-Champaign
Champaign, Illinois
http://illinois.edu          Federal Code: 001775

**4-year public** university in small city.

**Enrollment:** 32,170 undergrads, 2% part-time. 6,926 full-time freshmen.

**Selectivity:** Admits 50 to 75% of applicants.

## BASIC COSTS (2015-2016)
**Tuition and fees:** $15,626; out-of-state residents $30,786.
**Room and board:** $11,010.
**Additional info:** Tuition at time of enrollment locked for 4 years.

## FINANCIAL AID PICTURE (2014-2015)
**Students with need:** Out of 5,882 full-time freshmen who applied for aid, 3,346 were judged to have need. Of these, 3,133 received aid, and 436 had their full need met. Average financial aid package met 68% of need; average scholarship/grant was $14,644; average loan was $4,455. For part-time students, average financial aid package was $7,850.
**Students without need:** 848 full-time freshmen who did not demonstrate need for aid received scholarships/grants; average award was $5,525. No-need awards available for academics, alumni affiliation, art, athletics, leadership, minority status, music/drama, ROTC, state/district residency.
**Scholarships offered:** *Merit:* President's Award Program: $1,000-$4,000 for 4 years; for members of historically underrepresented group, with ACT score of 22-23 and in the top quarter of their class, or who have an ACT score of 24 or higher and are in the top half of their class. University Achievement Scholarship: $8,000; criteria set by each college, renewable with 3.0 GPA; 50 available. Matthews Scholars: $2,000 per year, renewable for 4 years if GPA of 3.3 is maintained; criteria includes academic achievement, leadership skills, commitment to campus and community efforts, good sponsor relations, diversity of college gender and ethnicity; approximately 150 available. FMC Award of Excellence: $1,000 a year, non-renewable; criteria set by individual colleges; 20 available. Provost Scholarship: full tuition, renewable with 3.0 GPA; National Achievement, National Hispanic Scholar finalists, or National Merit finalists who have indicated the University of Illinois at Urbana-Champaign as their top choice. Campus Merit: $3,000; students in historically underrepresented groups who are in the top 10 percent of their graduating class. National Merit: $500; National Merit finalists who indicated the University of Illinois as their top choice, renewable with 3.0 GPA. James Hunter Anthony and Gerald Blackshear Scholarship: 1 year of tuition and fees, renewable with 3.0 GPA; incoming freshmen who are graduates of an Illinois high school, with superior academic and leadership qualities; need may be considered. *Athletic:* 36 full-time freshmen received athletic scholarships; average amount $31,373.

## FINANCIAL AID PROCEDURES
**Forms required:** FAFSA.
**Dates and Deadlines:** Priority date 3/15; no closing date. Applicants notified on a rolling basis starting 3/1; must reply by 5/1 or within 3 week(s) of notification.

## CONTACT
Daniel Mann, Director of Student Financial Aid
901 West Illinois, Urbana, IL 61801-3028
(217) 333-0100

# University of Illinois: Springfield
Springfield, Illinois
www.uis.edu                          Federal Code: 009333

**4-year public** university and liberal arts college in small city.
**Enrollment:** 2,857 undergrads, 35% part-time. 302 full-time freshmen.
**Selectivity:** Admits 50 to 75% of applicants.

## BASIC COSTS (2015-2016)
**Tuition and fees:** $11,413; out-of-state residents $20,938.
**Per-credit charge:** $314; out-of-state residents $631.
**Room and board:** $11,550.
**Additional info:** Tuition at time of enrollment locked for 4 years.

## FINANCIAL AID PICTURE (2014-2015)
**Students with need:** Out of 281 full-time freshmen who applied for aid, 233 were judged to have need. Of these, 229 received aid, and 58 had their

full need met. Average financial aid package met 80% of need; average scholarship/grant was $13,210; average loan was $3,237. For part-time students, average financial aid package was $7,130.
**Students without need:** 56 full-time freshmen who did not demonstrate need for aid received scholarships/grants; average award was $8,930. No-need awards available for academics, alumni affiliation, art, athletics, job skills, leadership, minority status, music/drama, state/district residency.
**Scholarships offered:** 12 full-time freshmen received athletic scholarships; average amount $6,844.

## FINANCIAL AID PROCEDURES
**Forms required:** FAFSA.
**Dates and Deadlines:** Priority date 3/1; closing date 11/15. Applicants notified on a rolling basis starting 1/1; must reply within 3 week(s) of notification.
**Transfers:** No deadline. Applicants notified on a rolling basis.

## CONTACT
Carolyn Schloemann, Acting Director, Financial Assistance
One University Plaza, MS UHB 1080, Springfield, IL 62703
(217) 206-6724

# University of St. Francis
Joliet, Illinois
www.stfrancis.edu                    Federal Code: 001664

**4-year private** university and liberal arts college in small city, affiliated with Roman Catholic Church.
**Enrollment:** 1,325 undergrads, 4% part-time. 181 full-time freshmen.
**Selectivity:** Admits 50 to 75% of applicants.

## BASIC COSTS (2016-2017)
**Tuition and fees:** $30,840.
**Per-credit charge:** $825.
**Room and board:** $9,084.

## FINANCIAL AID PICTURE (2015-2016)
**Students with need:** Out of 173 full-time freshmen who applied for aid, 158 were judged to have need. Of these, 158 received aid, and 94 had their full need met. Average financial aid package met 79% of need; average scholarship/grant was $8,815; average loan was $3,637. For part-time students, average financial aid package was $9,446.
**Students without need:** 23 full-time freshmen who did not demonstrate need for aid received scholarships/grants; average award was $10,951. No-need awards available for academics, alumni affiliation, art, athletics, leadership, minority status, music/drama, religious affiliation, state/district residency.
**Scholarships offered:** 16 full-time freshmen received athletic scholarships; average amount $10,431.

## FINANCIAL AID PROCEDURES
**Forms required:** FAFSA, institutional form.
**Dates and Deadlines:** Priority date 2/15; no closing date. Applicants notified on a rolling basis starting 2/15.

## CONTACT
Bruce Foote, Assistant Director for Institutional Research
500 Wilcox Street, Joliet, IL 60435
(866) 890-8331

# VanderCook College of Music
Chicago, Illinois
www.vandercook.edu                   Federal Code: 177800

**4-year private** music and teachers college in very large city.
**Enrollment:** 104 undergrads, 8% part-time. 28 full-time freshmen.

**Selectivity:** Admits over 75% of applicants.

**BASIC COSTS (2015-2016)**
**Tuition and fees:** $26,300.
**Per-credit charge:** $1,020.
**Room and board:** $11,516.

**FINANCIAL AID PICTURE (2014-2015)**
**Students with need:** Out of 27 full-time freshmen who applied for aid, 19 were judged to have need. Of these, 19 received aid. For part-time students, average financial aid package was $4,278.
**Students without need:** 6 full-time freshmen who did not demonstrate need for aid received scholarships/grants; average award was $9,142. No-need awards available for academics, music/drama.
**Additional info:** Musical talent considered for partial tuition waiver.

**FINANCIAL AID PROCEDURES**
**Forms required:** FAFSA.
**Dates and Deadlines:** Priority date 3/1; no closing date. Applicants notified on a rolling basis starting 5/1; must reply within 2 week(s) of notification.
**Transfers:** Priority date 4/1. Must reply by 5/1.

**CONTACT**
Sirena Covington, Director of Financial Aid
3140 South Federal Street, Chicago, IL 60616-3731
(312) 225-6288 ext. 253

## Waubonsee Community College
Sugar Grove, Illinois
www.waubonsee.edu        Federal Code: 006931

**2-year public** community and junior college in small town.
**Enrollment:** 8,055 undergrads.
**Selectivity:** Open admission; but selective for some programs.

**BASIC COSTS (2015-2016)**
**Tuition and fees:** $3,540; out-of-district residents $8,753; out-of-state residents $9,483.

**FINANCIAL AID PICTURE**
**Students with need:** Need-based aid available for full-time and part-time students. Work study available nights.
**Students without need:** No-need awards available for academics, art, athletics, leadership, minority status, music/drama, state/district residency.
**Scholarships offered:** Gustafson Scholarship; provides tuition for 64 semester hours; selected graduates from each in-district school.

**FINANCIAL AID PROCEDURES**
**Forms required:** FAFSA.
**Dates and Deadlines:** Priority date 3/1; no closing date. Applicants notified on a rolling basis starting 4/1.
**Transfers:** Priority date 3/13; no deadline. Applicants notified on a rolling basis starting 4/13.

**CONTACT**
Charles Boudreau, Director of Student Financial Aid Services
Route 47 at Waubonsee Drive, Sugar Grove, IL 60554-9454
(630) 466-7900 ext. 5774

## Western Illinois University
Macomb, Illinois
www.wiu.edu        Federal Code: 001780

**4-year public** university in large town.
**Enrollment:** 9,141 undergrads, 11% part-time. 1,508 full-time freshmen.
**Selectivity:** Admits 50 to 75% of applicants.

**BASIC COSTS (2015-2016)**
**Tuition and fees:** $11,508; out-of-state residents $15,910.
**Per-credit charge:** $293; out-of-state residents $440.
**Room and board:** $9,580.
**Additional info:** Student Insurance $690/semester or $1380 for full academic year. Tuition at time of enrollment locked for 4 years.

**FINANCIAL AID PICTURE (2015-2016)**
**Students with need:** Out of 1,387 full-time freshmen who applied for aid, 1,210 were judged to have need. Of these, 1,178 received aid, and 315 had their full need met. Average financial aid package met 61% of need; average scholarship/grant was $9,935; average loan was $3,481. For part-time students, average financial aid package was $6,838.
**Students without need:** 34 full-time freshmen who did not demonstrate need for aid received scholarships/grants; average award was $1,904. No-need awards available for academics, alumni affiliation, art, athletics, leadership, minority status, music/drama, ROTC.
**Scholarships offered:** *Merit:* Western Commitment Scholarships-Merit: based on high school GPA and ACT/SAT score; 4-year scholarships towards the cost of attendance; award levels of $1,000, $2,000, $3,000, and $10,000 for highest ability; renewable for up to 4 years if maintain eligibility. New freshmen who submit all application materials by May 15 are automatically considered. *Athletic:* 44 full-time freshmen received athletic scholarships; average amount $8,379.
**Additional info:** University funded need-based grant and work program continued for student's undergraduate career with emphasis on graduating in 4 years and maintaining an average of 15 hours/semester and satisfactory academic performance.

**FINANCIAL AID PROCEDURES**
**Forms required:** FAFSA.
**Dates and Deadlines:** Applicants notified on a rolling basis starting 1/15.
**Transfers:** No deadline. Applicants notified on a rolling basis starting 1/15. Transfer students with confirmed Associates degree receive transfer scholarship or book award based on GPA. If they do not qualify for a scholarship, they receive a book award.

**CONTACT**
Mary Lawson, Director of Financial Aid
1 University Circle, Macomb, IL 61455-1390
(309) 298-2446

## Westwood College: O'Hare Airport
Chicago, Illinois
www.westwood.edu/locations/illinois/ohare-airport-campus        Federal Code: 023139

**4-year for-profit** career college in very large city.
**Enrollment:** 784 undergrads.

**BASIC COSTS (2015-2016)**
**Additional info:** Computer-Aided Design/Architectural Drafting: AAS $39,067. Graphic Design: AAS $40,978; BAS $78,120. Information and Network Technologies: AAS $35,525; BAS $71,050. Software Development: BAS $71,050. Business Administration: BAS $74,256. Construction Management: AAS $37,128; BAS $74,256. Criminal Justice: BAS $78,834. Medical Assisting: Diploma $25,685. Additional costs and fees such as books, tool kits, lab fee and online fees may apply.

**FINANCIAL AID PICTURE**
**Students with need:** Need-based aid available for full-time and part-time students.

**FINANCIAL AID PROCEDURES**
**Forms required:** FAFSA, institutional form.
**Dates and Deadlines:** Priority date 3/1; closing date 6/30.

## CONTACT

Tracy Walker, Director of Student Finance

8501 West Higgins Road, Chicago, IL 60631

(773) 380-6852

## Wheaton College

Wheaton, Illinois

www.wheaton.edu　　　　Federal Code: 001781

**4-year private** liberal arts college in small city, affiliated with nondenominational tradition.

**Enrollment:** 2,447 undergrads, 2% part-time. 605 full-time freshmen.

**Selectivity:** Admits 50 to 75% of applicants.

### BASIC COSTS (2015-2016)

**Tuition and fees:** $32,950.

**Per-credit charge:** $1,373.

**Room and board:** $9,200.

### FINANCIAL AID PICTURE (2015-2016)

**Students with need:** Out of 455 full-time freshmen who applied for aid, 353 were judged to have need. Of these, 352 received aid, and 92 had their full need met. Average financial aid package met 88% of need; average scholarship/grant was $22,035; average loan was $4,923. For part-time students, average financial aid package was $17,650.

**Students without need:** 136 full-time freshmen who did not demonstrate need for aid received scholarships/grants; average award was $5,593. No-need awards available for academics, alumni affiliation, art, minority status, music/drama.

**Scholarships offered:** Charles Blanchard President's Award: $5,000 per year for up to 4 years; U.S. citizens with 3.7 GPA on 4.0 scale, plus 1400 SAT/32 ACT; unlimited number available; also available to transfer students. Arthur Holmes Award: $2,500 per year for up to 4 years; U.S. citizens not qualifying for Blanchard Award with 3.6 GPA on 4.0 scale, plus 1330 SAT/30 ACT; unlimited number available; also available to transfer students.

### FINANCIAL AID PROCEDURES

**Forms required:** FAFSA, institutional form.

**Dates and Deadlines:** Priority date 2/15; no closing date. Applicants notified on a rolling basis starting 3/1.

**Transfers:** Priority date 2/15; no deadline. Applicants notified on a rolling basis starting 3/1; must reply by 5/1.

### CONTACT

Karen Belling, Director of Financial Aid

501 College Avenue, Wheaton, IL 60187-5593

(630) 752-5021

# Indiana

## Ancilla College

Donaldson, Indiana

www.ancilla.edu　　　　Federal Code: 001784

**2-year private** junior and liberal arts college in rural community, affiliated with Roman Catholic Church.

**Enrollment:** 468 undergrads, 19% part-time. 155 full-time freshmen.

**Selectivity:** Open admission; but selective for some programs.

### BASIC COSTS (2015-2016)

**Tuition and fees:** $14,330.

**Per-credit charge:** $470.

**Room and board:** $8,500.

### FINANCIAL AID PICTURE (2014-2015)

**Students with need:** Out of 151 full-time freshmen who applied for aid, 149 were judged to have need. Of these, 149 received aid. Need-based aid available for part-time students.

**Students without need:** No-need awards available for academics, athletics, job skills, leadership.

### FINANCIAL AID PROCEDURES

**Forms required:** FAFSA.

**Dates and Deadlines:** Closing date 3/10. Applicants notified on a rolling basis starting 3/10; must reply within 2 week(s) of notification.

**Transfers:** No deadline. Applicants notified on a rolling basis; must reply by 8/1.

### CONTACT

Marcella Hopple, Director of Financial Aid

9601 Union Road, Donaldson, IN 46513

(574) 936-8898 ext. 307

## Anderson University

Anderson, Indiana

www.anderson.edu　　　　Federal Code: 001785

**4-year private** liberal arts college in small city, affiliated with Church of God.

**Enrollment:** 1,760 undergrads, 9% part-time. 421 full-time freshmen.

**Selectivity:** Admits 50 to 75% of applicants.

### BASIC COSTS (2015-2016)

**Tuition and fees:** $27,600.

**Per-credit charge:** $1,147.

**Room and board:** $9,380.

**Additional info:** Tuition/fee waivers available for adults.

### FINANCIAL AID PICTURE

**Students with need:** Need-based aid available for full-time and part-time students. Work study available nights, weekends, and for part-time students.

**Students without need:** No-need awards available for academics, alumni affiliation, art, leadership, minority status, music/drama, religious affiliation.

### FINANCIAL AID PROCEDURES

**Forms required:** FAFSA.

**Dates and Deadlines:** Priority date 3/1; no closing date. Applicants notified on a rolling basis starting 3/1.

**Transfers:** No deadline. Applicants notified on a rolling basis.

### CONTACT

Kenneth Nieman, Director of Student Financial Services

1100 East Fifth Street, Anderson, IN 46012-3495

(765) 641-4182

## Ball State University

Muncie, Indiana

www.bsu.edu　　　　Federal Code: 001786

**4-year public** university in small city.

**Enrollment:** 15,689 undergrads, 7% part-time. 3,492 full-time freshmen.

**Selectivity:** Admits 50 to 75% of applicants.

### BASIC COSTS (2015-2016)

**Tuition and fees:** $9,498; out-of-state residents $25,016.

**Room and board:** $9,656.

### FINANCIAL AID PICTURE (2015-2016)

**Students with need:** Out of 3,287 full-time freshmen who applied for aid, 2,506 were judged to have need. Of these, 2,506 received aid, and 1,117 had their full need met. Average financial aid package met 67% of need;

average scholarship/grant was $5,490; average loan was $3,534. For part-time students, average financial aid package was $7,683.

**Students without need:** 498 full-time freshmen who did not demonstrate need for aid received scholarships/grants; average award was $7,157. No-need awards available for academics, athletics, leadership, minority status, music/drama, ROTC, state/district residency.

**Scholarships offered:** 76 full-time freshmen received athletic scholarships; average amount $21,347.

**FINANCIAL AID PROCEDURES**

**Forms required:** FAFSA.

**Dates and Deadlines:** Priority date 3/15; no closing date. Applicants notified on a rolling basis starting 4/1.

**Transfers:** No deadline. Applicants notified on a rolling basis starting 6/1.

**CONTACT**

John McPherson, Assistant Vice President of Enrollment Services
Office of Admissions, Ball State University, Muncie, IN 47306-0855
(765) 285-5600

## Bethel College

Mishawaka, Indiana
www.bethelcollege.edu                    Federal Code: 001787

**4-year private** liberal arts college in small city, affiliated with Missionary Church.

**Enrollment:** 1,432 undergrads, 18% part-time. 280 full-time freshmen.

**Selectivity:** Admits 50 to 75% of applicants.

**BASIC COSTS (2016-2017)**

**Tuition and fees:** $27,380.

**Room and board:** $8,470.

**Additional info:** Tuition/fee waivers available for adults, minority students.

**FINANCIAL AID PICTURE (2015-2016)**

**Students with need:** Need-based aid available for full-time and part-time students. Work study available nights, weekends, and for part-time students.

**Students without need:** 22 full-time freshmen who did not demonstrate need for aid received scholarships/grants; average award was $14,344. No-need awards available for academics, alumni affiliation, art, athletics, job skills, leadership, minority status, music/drama, religious affiliation, ROTC.

**Scholarships offered:** 11 full-time freshmen received athletic scholarships; average amount $9,644.

**FINANCIAL AID PROCEDURES**

**Forms required:** FAFSA, institutional form.

**Dates and Deadlines:** Priority date 3/1; closing date 3/10. Applicants notified on a rolling basis starting 3/1.

**Transfers:** No deadline. Applicants notified on a rolling basis starting 4/1.

**CONTACT**

Jody Walker, Director of Financial Aid
1001 Bethel Circle, Mishawaka, IN 46545-5591
(574) 807-7277

## Brown Mackie College: South Bend

South Bend, Indiana
www.brownmackie.edu                    Federal Code: 004583

**2-year for-profit** community and technical college in small city.

**Enrollment:** 340 undergrads.

**Selectivity:** Open admission.

**BASIC COSTS (2015-2016)**

**Tuition and fees:** $16,490.

**Per-credit charge:** $327.

**FINANCIAL AID PICTURE**

**Students with need:** Need-based aid available for full-time and part-time students.

**Students without need:** This college awards aid only to students with need.

**FINANCIAL AID PROCEDURES**

**Forms required:** FAFSA.

**Dates and Deadlines:** Applicants notified on a rolling basis; must reply within 1 week(s) of notification.

**CONTACT**

Sue Kempt, Senior Financial Aid Officer
3454 Douglas Road, South Bend, IN 46635

## Butler University

Indianapolis, Indiana
www.butler.edu                    Federal Code: 001788

**4-year private** university in very large city.

**Enrollment:** 4,001 undergrads, 1% part-time. 1,024 full-time freshmen.

**Selectivity:** Admits 50 to 75% of applicants.

**BASIC COSTS (2015-2016)**

**Tuition and fees:** $37,010.

**Per-credit charge:** $1,502.

**Room and board:** $12,055.

**FINANCIAL AID PICTURE (2015-2016)**

**Students with need:** Out of 985 full-time freshmen who applied for aid, 641 were judged to have need. Of these, 641 received aid, and 78 had their full need met. Average financial aid package met 73% of need; average scholarship/grant was $22,533; average loan was $3,982. For part-time students, average financial aid package was $9,814.

**Students without need:** 337 full-time freshmen who did not demonstrate need for aid received scholarships/grants; average award was $14,857. No-need awards available for academics, alumni affiliation, athletics, leadership, music/drama.

**Scholarships offered:** 27 full-time freshmen received athletic scholarships; average amount $30,869.

**FINANCIAL AID PROCEDURES**

**Forms required:** FAFSA.

**Dates and Deadlines:** Priority date 3/1; no closing date. Applicants notified on a rolling basis starting 3/15; must reply within 3 week(s) of notification.

**Transfers:** Priority date 3/15.

**CONTACT**

Melissa Smurdon, Director of Financial Aid
4600 Sunset Avenue, Indianapolis, IN 46208
(317) 940-8200

## Calumet College of St. Joseph

Whiting, Indiana
www.ccsj.edu                    Federal Code: 001834

**4-year private** liberal arts college in small city, affiliated with Roman Catholic Church.

**Enrollment:** 881 undergrads. 115 full-time freshmen.

**Selectivity:** Admits less than 50% of applicants.

**BASIC COSTS (2015-2016)**

**Tuition and fees:** $17,000.

**Per-credit charge:** $530.

**Additional info:** Tuition at time of enrollment locked for 4 years.

## FINANCIAL AID PICTURE (2014-2015)

**Students with need:** Out of 100 full-time freshmen who applied for aid, 92 were judged to have need. Of these, 87 received aid, and 11 had their full need met. Average financial aid package met 66% of need; average scholarship/grant was $6,429; average loan was $3,073. For part-time students, average financial aid package was $5,707.

**Students without need:** 3 full-time freshmen who did not demonstrate need for aid received scholarships/grants; average award was $6,000. No-need awards available for academics, alumni affiliation, art, athletics, leadership, music/drama.

**Scholarships offered:** 73 full-time freshmen received athletic scholarships; average amount $6,741.

**Additional info:** Immediate computerized estimate of financial aid eligibility available to students applying in person. Students with a zero EFC who are state aid and Pell Grant recipients receive institutional aid to cover tuition.

## FINANCIAL AID PROCEDURES

**Forms required:** FAFSA.

**Dates and Deadlines:** Priority date 3/10; no closing date. Applicants notified on a rolling basis starting 4/30; must reply within 2 week(s) of notification.

**Transfers:** No deadline. Applicants notified on a rolling basis. Academic Scholarship for transfer students.

## CONTACT

Lynn Miskus, Vice-President of Business & Finance
2400 New York Avenue, Whiting, IN 46394-2195
(219) 473-4296

# Crossroads Bible College
Indianapolis, Indiana
www.crossroads.edu          Federal Code: 034567

**4-year private** Bible college in very large city.
**Enrollment:** 249 undergrads. 9 full-time freshmen.

## BASIC COSTS (2015-2016)
**Tuition and fees:** $12,400.
**Per-credit charge:** $395.

## FINANCIAL AID PICTURE (2014-2015)
**Students with need:** Out of 9 full-time freshmen who applied for aid, 9 were judged to have need. Of these, 9 received aid, and 9 had their full need met. Average financial aid package met 100% of need; average scholarship/grant was $5,500; average loan was $4,500. For part-time students, average financial aid package was $6,200.
**Students without need:** This college awards aid only to students with need.

## FINANCIAL AID PROCEDURES
**Forms required:** FAFSA, institutional form.
**Dates and Deadlines:** Priority date 3/1; closing date 3/10. Applicants notified on a rolling basis; must reply within 2 week(s) of notification.
**Transfers:** No deadline. Applicants notified on a rolling basis; must reply within 2 week(s) of notification.

## CONTACT
Phyllis Dodson, Senior Director of Financial Aid
601 North Shortridge Road, Indianapolis, IN 46219

# DePauw University
Greencastle, Indiana          Federal Code: 001792
www.depauw.edu          CSS Code: 1166

**4-year private** music and liberal arts college in small town, affiliated with United Methodist Church.
**Enrollment:** 2,223 undergrads. 596 full-time freshmen.

**Selectivity:** Admits 50 to 75% of applicants.

## BASIC COSTS (2015-2016)
**Tuition and fees:** $44,678.
**Per-credit charge:** $1,373.
**Room and board:** $11,700.

## FINANCIAL AID PICTURE
**Students with need:** Need-based aid available for full-time and part-time students. Work study available nights, weekends, and for part-time students.
**Students without need:** No-need awards available for academics, alumni affiliation, leadership, music/drama.
**Scholarships offered:** Holton Scholarships; $1,000 to full tuition; based on exceptional leadership and/or service; 50 awarded.

## FINANCIAL AID PROCEDURES
**Forms required:** FAFSA, CSS PROFILE.
**Dates and Deadlines:** Priority date 2/15; closing date 3/1. Applicants notified on a rolling basis starting 3/15; must reply by 5/1.
**Transfers:** Applicants notified by 3/27; must reply by 5/1.

## CONTACT
Craig Slaughter, Director of Financial Aid
101 East Seminary Street, Greencastle, IN 46135-1611
(765) 658-4030

# Earlham College
Richmond, Indiana
www.earlham.edu          Federal Code: 001793

**4-year private** liberal arts and seminary college in large town, affiliated with Society of Friends (Quaker).
**Enrollment:** 935 undergrads, 1% part-time. 270 full-time freshmen.
**Selectivity:** Admits 50 to 75% of applicants.

## BASIC COSTS (2015-2016)
**Tuition and fees:** $44,390.
**Per-credit charge:** $1,450.
**Room and board:** $9,120.

## FINANCIAL AID PICTURE (2014-2015)
**Students with need:** Out of 254 full-time freshmen who applied for aid, 240 were judged to have need. Of these, 240 received aid, and 44 had their full need met. Average financial aid package met 93% of need; average scholarship/grant was $31,777; average loan was $4,318. Need-based aid available for part-time students.
**Students without need:** 27 full-time freshmen who did not demonstrate need for aid received scholarships/grants; average award was $19,056. No-need awards available for academics, leadership, minority status, religious affiliation.

## FINANCIAL AID PROCEDURES
**Forms required:** FAFSA.
**Dates and Deadlines:** Closing date 3/1. Applicants notified on a rolling basis starting 3/15; must reply by 5/1.
**Transfers:** Priority date 3/1; no deadline. Applicants notified on a rolling basis starting 3/1; must reply by 5/1 or within 3 week(s) of notification. Deadline for State of Indiana Grants, 3/1 (FAFSA date).

## CONTACT
Kathy Gottschalk, Director of Financial Aid
801 National Road West, Richmond, IN 47374-4095
(765) 983-1217

## Franklin College
Franklin, Indiana
www.franklincollege.edu                Federal Code: 001798

**4-year private** liberal arts college in large town, affiliated with American Baptist Churches in the USA.
**Enrollment:** 1,012 undergrads. 327 full-time freshmen.
**Selectivity:** Admits 50 to 75% of applicants.

### BASIC COSTS (2015-2016)
**Tuition and fees:** $29,025.
**Room and board:** $9,040.

### FINANCIAL AID PICTURE (2014-2015)
**Students with need:** Out of 320 full-time freshmen who applied for aid, 281 were judged to have need. Of these, 281 received aid, and 37 had their full need met. Average financial aid package met 71% of need; average scholarship/grant was $17,782; average loan was $3,454. For part-time students, average financial aid package was $7,019.
**Students without need:** 46 full-time freshmen who did not demonstrate need for aid received scholarships/grants; average award was $14,397. No-need awards available for academics, alumni affiliation, art, minority status, music/drama, religious affiliation, state/district residency.

### FINANCIAL AID PROCEDURES
**Forms required:** FAFSA, institutional form.
**Dates and Deadlines:** Priority date 3/1; closing date 3/10. Applicants notified on a rolling basis starting 3/1; must reply by 5/1 or within 4 week(s) of notification.
**Transfers:** Must reply by 5/1 or within 2 week(s) of notification.

### CONTACT
Elizabeth Sappenfield, Director of Financial Aid
101 Branigin Boulevard, Franklin, IN 46131-2623
(317) 738-8075

## Goshen College
Goshen, Indiana
www.goshen.edu                Federal Code: 001799

**4-year private** liberal arts college in large town, affiliated with Mennonite Church.
**Enrollment:** 756 undergrads, 6% part-time. 176 full-time freshmen.
**Selectivity:** Admits 50 to 75% of applicants.

### BASIC COSTS (2016-2017)
**Tuition and fees:** $32,200.
**Per-credit charge:** $1,340.
**Room and board:** $10,300.

### FINANCIAL AID PICTURE (2015-2016)
**Students with need:** Out of 152 full-time freshmen who applied for aid, 134 were judged to have need. Of these, 134 received aid, and 27 had their full need met. Average financial aid package met 88% of need; average scholarship/grant was $25,103; average loan was $3,933. For part-time students, average financial aid package was $9,328.
**Students without need:** 142 full-time freshmen who did not demonstrate need for aid received scholarships/grants; average award was $14,874. No-need awards available for academics, art, athletics, job skills, leadership, minority status, music/drama.
**Scholarships offered:** *Merit:* President's Leadership Award: $19,000; must meet two of the following criteria and submit separate application: 3.8 GPA, 1290 SAT (exclusive of Writing) or 29 ACT, top 5% of class. National Merit semifinalist: 10 awards offered each year; renews annually with 3.2 GPA. CIIE scholarship for first-generation students of color: must have 3.0 GPA and 860 SAT or 18 ACT and complete separate application; 20 awards offered each year. Merit scholarship: levels of $14,000, $12,000, $10,000,

$8,000, $6,000 awarded based on combination of ACT or SAT score and high school GPA available to all applicants who qualify. *Athletic:* 16 full-time freshmen received athletic scholarships; average amount $7,960.

### FINANCIAL AID PROCEDURES
**Forms required:** FAFSA.
**Dates and Deadlines:** Priority date 3/1; no closing date. Applicants notified on a rolling basis starting 2/1; must reply by 5/1 or within 2 week(s) of notification.
**Transfers:** No deadline. Applicants notified on a rolling basis starting 3/1; must reply by 5/1 or within 2 week(s) of notification.

### CONTACT
Joel Short, Director of Financial Aid
1700 South Main Street, Goshen, IN 46526-4724
(574) 535-7525

## Grace College
Winona Lake, Indiana
www.grace.edu                Federal Code: 001800

**4-year private** liberal arts college in small town, affiliated with Brethren Church.
**Enrollment:** 1,604 undergrads, 8% part-time. 355 full-time freshmen.
**Selectivity:** Admits over 75% of applicants.

### BASIC COSTS (2015-2016)
**Tuition and fees:** $22,450.
**Per-credit charge:** $800.
**Room and board:** $8,160.
**Additional info:** Tuition/fee waivers available for minority students.

### FINANCIAL AID PICTURE
**Students with need:** Need-based aid available for full-time and part-time students. Work study available nights, weekends, and for part-time students.
**Students without need:** No-need awards available for academics, art, athletics, leadership, minority status, music/drama, religious affiliation, state/district residency.

### FINANCIAL AID PROCEDURES
**Forms required:** FAFSA.
**Dates and Deadlines:** Closing date 3/1. Applicants notified on a rolling basis starting 3/1; must reply by 5/1.
**Transfers:** Applicants notified by 3/15; must reply by 5/1. Applicants who miss dates for admission and financial aid are notified on rolling basis until class is full.

### CONTACT
Charlette Sauders, Director of Financial Aid Services
200 Seminary Drive, Winona Lake, IN 46590
(574) 372-5100 ext. 6162

## Hanover College
Hanover, Indiana
www.hanover.edu                Federal Code: 001801

**4-year private** liberal arts college in rural community, affiliated with Presbyterian Church (USA).
**Enrollment:** 1,127 undergrads. 304 full-time freshmen.
**Selectivity:** Admits 50 to 75% of applicants. GED not accepted.

### BASIC COSTS (2015-2016)
**Tuition and fees:** $34,514.
**Per-credit charge:** $938.
**Room and board:** $10,452.

## FINANCIAL AID PICTURE (2014-2015)

**Students with need:** 79% of average financial aid package awarded as scholarships/grants, 21% awarded as loans/jobs. Need-based aid available for part-time students. Work study available nights, weekends, and for part-time students.

**Students without need:** No-need awards available for academics, alumni affiliation, art, leadership, minority status, music/drama, religious affiliation, state/district residency.

## FINANCIAL AID PROCEDURES

**Forms required:** FAFSA.

**Dates and Deadlines:** Priority date 3/1; no closing date. Applicants notified by 3/1.

**Transfers:** No deadline. Applicants notified on a rolling basis starting 3/1; must reply by 5/1 or within 2 week(s) of notification.

## CONTACT

Richard Nash, Director of Financial Aid
PO Box 108, Hanover, IN 47243-0108
(812) 866-7029

## Holy Cross College
Notre Dame, Indiana
www.hcc-nd.edu                    Federal Code: 007263

**4-year private** liberal arts college in small city, affiliated with Roman Catholic Church.

**Enrollment:** 546 undergrads, 1% part-time. 122 full-time freshmen.
**Selectivity:** Admits over 75% of applicants.

## BASIC COSTS (2015-2016)

**Tuition and fees:** $27,950.
**Room and board:** $9,975.
**Additional info:** Tuition at time of enrollment locked for 4 years.

## FINANCIAL AID PICTURE (2014-2015)

**Students with need:** Out of 93 full-time freshmen who applied for aid, 72 were judged to have need. Of these, 72 received aid, and 14 had their full need met. Average financial aid package met 61% of need; average scholarship/grant was $15,400; average loan was $3,700. For part-time students, average financial aid package was $3,000.

**Students without need:** 46 full-time freshmen who did not demonstrate need for aid received scholarships/grants; average award was $1,900. No-need awards available for academics, athletics, state/district residency.

**Scholarships offered:** 19 full-time freshmen received athletic scholarships; average amount $7,800.

## FINANCIAL AID PROCEDURES

**Forms required:** FAFSA.

**Dates and Deadlines:** Priority date 3/1; no closing date. Applicants notified on a rolling basis starting 5/1; must reply within 2 week(s) of notification.

**Transfers:** No deadline. Applicants notified on a rolling basis starting 9/1; must reply within 3 week(s) of notification. Merit-based transfer scholarships and need-based assistance grants available.

## CONTACT

Michael Schmaltz, Director of Financial Aid
54515 State Road 933 North, Notre Dame, IN 46556-0308
(574) 239-8400

## Huntington University
Huntington, Indiana
www.huntington.edu             Federal Code: 001803

**4-year private** liberal arts college in large town, affiliated with United Brethren in Christ.

**Enrollment:** 947 undergrads, 6% part-time. 213 full-time freshmen.
**Selectivity:** Admits over 75% of applicants.

## BASIC COSTS (2016-2017)

**Tuition and fees:** $25,400.
**Room and board:** $8,456.
**Additional info:** Tuition/fee waivers available for minority students.

## FINANCIAL AID PICTURE (2015-2016)

**Students with need:** Out of 207 full-time freshmen who applied for aid, 188 were judged to have need. Of these, 159 received aid, and 14 had their full need met. Average financial aid package met 82% of need; average scholarship/grant was $15,542; average loan was $2,770. For part-time students, average financial aid package was $6,818.

**Students without need:** 43 full-time freshmen who did not demonstrate need for aid received scholarships/grants; average award was $9,314. No-need awards available for academics, alumni affiliation, art, athletics, leadership, minority status, music/drama, religious affiliation.

**Scholarships offered:** *Merit:* Horizon Leader Scholarship: covers all fees associated with tuition and housing costs for up to 10 semesters. *Athletic:* 19 full-time freshmen received athletic scholarships; average amount $8,627.

**Additional info:** Loan repayment program offered to qualifying students. This program helps students payback their loans after graduation based on their income.

## FINANCIAL AID PROCEDURES

**Forms required:** FAFSA.

**Dates and Deadlines:** Priority date 3/10; no closing date. Applicants notified on a rolling basis starting 2/15; must reply by 5/1.

**Transfers:** No deadline. Applicants notified on a rolling basis; must reply by 5/1.

## CONTACT

Jerry Davis, Director of Financial Aid
2303 College Avenue, Huntington, IN 46750-1237
(260) 359-4015

## Indiana State University
Terre Haute, Indiana
www.indstate.edu               Federal Code: 001807

**4-year public** university in small city.
**Enrollment:** 10,737 undergrads, 10% part-time. 2,735 full-time freshmen.
**Selectivity:** Admits 50 to 75% of applicants.

## BASIC COSTS (2015-2016)

**Tuition and fees:** $8,580; out-of-state residents $18,708.
**Per-credit charge:** $304; out-of-state residents $656.
**Room and board:** $9,000.

## FINANCIAL AID PICTURE (2014-2015)

**Students with need:** Out of 2,581 full-time freshmen who applied for aid, 2,158 were judged to have need. Of these, 2,083 received aid, and 317 had their full need met. Average financial aid package met 81% of need; average scholarship/grant was $5,589; average loan was $3,079. For part-time students, average financial aid package was $5,260.

**Students without need:** This college awards aid only to students with need.

**Scholarships offered:** 67 full-time freshmen received athletic scholarships; average amount $13,891.

**Additional info:** Financial aid application deadline March 1 for Indiana residents applying for state grant.

## FINANCIAL AID PROCEDURES

**Forms required:** FAFSA.

**Dates and Deadlines:** Priority date 3/1; closing date 7/1. Applicants notified on a rolling basis starting 3/15.

## CONTACT
Crystal Baker, Director of Student Financial Aid
Office of Admissions, John W. Moore Welcome Center, Terre Haute, IN 47809-9989
(800) 841-4744

# Indiana University Bloomington
Bloomington, Indiana
www.iub.edu                    Federal Code: 001809

**4-year public** university in small city.
**Enrollment:** 32,694 undergrads, 3% part-time. 7,697 full-time freshmen.
**Selectivity:** Admits over 75% of applicants.

## BASIC COSTS (2015-2016)
**Tuition and fees:** $10,388; out-of-state residents $33,741.
**Per-credit charge:** $284; out-of-state residents $1,014.
**Room and board:** $9,795.

## FINANCIAL AID PICTURE (2014-2015)
**Students with need:** Out of 5,442 full-time freshmen who applied for aid, 3,479 were judged to have need. Of these, 3,277 received aid, and 901 had their full need met. Average financial aid package met 66% of need; average scholarship/grant was $11,891; average loan was $3,077. For part-time students, average financial aid package was $5,875.
**Students without need:** 1,570 full-time freshmen who did not demonstrate need for aid received scholarships/grants; average award was $6,442. No-need awards available for academics, art, athletics, leadership, minority status, music/drama, religious affiliation, ROTC.
**Scholarships offered:** *Merit:* Honors College Scholarship; $1,000-$6,000. Hudson & Holland; $6,000; 1100 SAT (23 ACT), top 20% class rank, 3.2 GPA, strong consideration given to students from underrepresented minority backgrounds and those who demonstrate commitment to working with underrepresented/disadvantaged populations. Cox Research Scholarship; Indiana residents; awarded to incoming freshmen of exemplary achievement who are interested in working under the direction of a faculty mentor on research and scholarly activities; total value of more than $63,000 over four years, provides funds for tuition, fees, room and board; includes stipend for research work; 1360 SAT (31 ACT), rank in the top 5% of class. Kelley Scholars Program; tuition and fees, room and board, books (overseas study funding, if requested); business major, 1350 SAT (32 ACT), 3.8 GPA, recipients must display excellence in academics, leadership, and extracurricular involvement. School of Music Dean's Award; amounts vary; exceptional talent displayed in audition. 21st Century Scholars Award; in-state instructional fees; Indiana residence, fulfilled terms pledged in eighth grade, filed FAFSA before 3/1 of senior year. Army and Air Force ROTC Scholarships; tuition, fees, books, monthly stipend. All SAT scores listed exclusive of writing. *Athletic:* 69 full-time freshmen received athletic scholarships; average amount $21,291.
**Additional info:** Majority of institutional gift aid merit-based. Some need-based grants go to merit winners with financial need.

## FINANCIAL AID PROCEDURES
**Forms required:** FAFSA.
**Dates and Deadlines:** Priority date 3/10; no closing date. Applicants notified on a rolling basis starting 4/1.

## CONTACT
300 North Jordan Avenue, Bloomington, IN 47405-1106
(812) 855-6500

# Indiana University East
Richmond, Indiana
www.iue.edu                    Federal Code: 001811

**4-year public** university in large town.
**Enrollment:** 3,173 undergrads, 39% part-time. 392 full-time freshmen.
**Selectivity:** Admits 50 to 75% of applicants.

## BASIC COSTS (2015-2016)
**Tuition and fees:** $6,930; out-of-state residents $18,379.
**Per-credit charge:** $211; out-of-state residents $593.

## FINANCIAL AID PICTURE (2014-2015)
**Students with need:** Out of 385 full-time freshmen who applied for aid, 319 were judged to have need. Of these, 314 received aid, and 60 had their full need met. Average financial aid package met 66% of need; average scholarship/grant was $7,210; average loan was $2,761. For part-time students, average financial aid package was $5,062.
**Students without need:** 29 full-time freshmen who did not demonstrate need for aid received scholarships/grants; average award was $1,872. No-need awards available for academics, alumni affiliation, leadership.
**Scholarships offered:** *Merit:* IU East Distinguished Scholars; $24,000 ($6,000 annually for 4 years); rank in top 10% of HS class; exceptional SAT or ACT scores; scholars are also expected to apply and remain eligible for the Honors Program; must attend full time and maintain at least a 3.0 GPA. IU East Valedictorian and Salutatorian Scholarships; $16,000 ($4,000 annually for 4 years); rank 1st or 2nd in HS class; must attend full time and maintain at least a 3.0 GPA. Lingle Scholars; $8,000 ($2,000 annually for 4 years); Wayne County students who apply for and are accepted to the IUE Honors Program are eligible. *Athletic:* 15 full-time freshmen received athletic scholarships; average amount $3,879.

## FINANCIAL AID PROCEDURES
**Forms required:** FAFSA, institutional form.
**Dates and Deadlines:** Priority date 3/10; no closing date. Applicants notified on a rolling basis starting 5/1; must reply within 2 week(s) of notification.

## CONTACT
Sarah Soper, Director, Financial Aid & Scholarships
2325 Chester Boulevard, Richmond, IN 47374-1289
(765) 973-8206

# Indiana University Kokomo
Kokomo, Indiana
www.iuk.edu                    Federal Code: 001814

**4-year public** university in large town.
**Enrollment:** 2,778 undergrads, 23% part-time. 493 full-time freshmen.
**Selectivity:** Admits 50 to 75% of applicants.

## BASIC COSTS (2015-2016)
**Tuition and fees:** $6,941; out-of-state residents $18,379.
**Per-credit charge:** $212; out-of-state residents $593.

## FINANCIAL AID PICTURE (2014-2015)
**Students with need:** Out of 469 full-time freshmen who applied for aid, 365 were judged to have need. Of these, 342 received aid, and 51 had their full need met. Average financial aid package met 65% of need; average scholarship/grant was $7,641; average loan was $2,774. For part-time students, average financial aid package was $5,412.
**Students without need:** 36 full-time freshmen who did not demonstrate need for aid received scholarships/grants; average award was $1,888. No-need awards available for academics, athletics, leadership.
**Scholarships offered:** *Merit:* Herbert Scholarship; incoming freshman with SAT score of 1300 and is in the top 10% of their graduating class, renewable for additional 3 years where cumulative 3.3 GPA is maintained. IU Kokomo Pre-Professional Scholarship Program; $2,500, laptop computer, $1,000 stipend for international travel, faculty mentor, undergraduate research opportunity, tutoring assistance, GRE prep, textbook credit, free software. ESP and STAR Scholarships; any more available. *Athletic:* 7 full-time freshmen received athletic scholarships; average amount $2,286.

## FINANCIAL AID PROCEDURES
**Forms required:** FAFSA.

PART III: FINANCIAL AID COLLEGE BY COLLEGE

**Dates and Deadlines:** Priority date 3/10; no closing date. Applicants notified on a rolling basis starting 3/25; must reply within 4 week(s) of notification.

**CONTACT**
Karen Shaw, Director of Office of Scholarships and Financial Aid
Kelley Student Center, Room 230, Kokomo, IN 46902-9003
(765) 455-9216

## Indiana University Northwest
Gary, Indiana
www.iun.edu                    Federal Code: 001815

**4-year public** university in small city.
**Enrollment:** 4,117 undergrads, 29% part-time. 652 full-time freshmen.
**Selectivity:** Admits over 75% of applicants.

**BASIC COSTS (2015-2016)**
**Tuition and fees:** $6,963; out-of-state residents $18,379.
**Per-credit charge:** $212; out-of-state residents $593.

**FINANCIAL AID PICTURE (2014-2015)**
**Students with need:** Out of 590 full-time freshmen who applied for aid, 431 were judged to have need. Of these, 398 received aid, and 60 had their full need met. Average financial aid package met 68% of need; average scholarship/grant was $7,243; average loan was $2,776. For part-time students, average financial aid package was $5,122.
**Students without need:** 42 full-time freshmen who did not demonstrate need for aid received scholarships/grants; average award was $3,561. No-need awards available for academics, athletics.
**Scholarships offered: Merit:** Valedictorian Scholarship; incoming freshmen ranked first in their high school graduating class. Special Academic Scholarship Tier One; $5,000; incoming full-time freshman who has a 3.5 GPA and a minimum SAT score of 1100 (ACT 24); renewable for 4 years with 3.5 cumulative GPA. Special Academic Scholarship Tier Two; incoming full-time freshman with minimum 3.5 cumulative GPA and a minimum SAT score of 1150 (ACT 25); full tuition waiver for a maximum of 126 credit hours; renewable with a 3.5 cumulative GPA. **Athletic:** 5 full-time freshmen received athletic scholarships; average amount $1,800.

**FINANCIAL AID PROCEDURES**
**Forms required:** FAFSA.
**Dates and Deadlines:** Priority date 3/10; no closing date. Applicants notified on a rolling basis starting 4/15; must reply by 6/30.

**CONTACT**
Harold Burtley, Director, Scholarships and Financial Aid
3400 Broadway, Gary, IN 46408
(219) 980-6778

## Indiana University South Bend
South Bend, Indiana
www.iusb.edu                    Federal Code: 001816

**4-year public** university in small city.
**Enrollment:** 5,165 undergrads, 26% part-time. 866 full-time freshmen.
**Selectivity:** Admits over 75% of applicants.

**BASIC COSTS (2015-2016)**
**Tuition and fees:** $6,986; out-of-state residents $18,379.
**Per-credit charge:** $213; out-of-state residents $593.
**Room only:** $7,150.

**FINANCIAL AID PICTURE (2014-2015)**
**Students with need:** Out of 804 full-time freshmen who applied for aid, 680 were judged to have need. Of these, 658 received aid, and 76 had their full need met. Average financial aid package met 63% of need; average

scholarship/grant was $7,169; average loan was $2,882. For part-time students, average financial aid package was $5,016.
**Students without need:** 62 full-time freshmen who did not demonstrate need for aid received scholarships/grants; average award was $1,598. No-need awards available for academics, athletics.
**Scholarships offered: Merit:** Central Indiana Chapter of the Indiana University Alumni Association: $1,000, four scholarships, student be a resident of Hamilton, Hancock, Hendricks or Marion County, and attending any campus of Indiana University full time in the fall. Pilot Club: $1,000, medical scholarship offered to a current junior who will return to IU South Bend for their senior year; money is for tuition, fees, and/or books. Distinguished Alumni Service Award: $1,000, minimum GPA of 3.5, resident of Indiana, two scholarships for graduating seniors that have a proven record of excellence both in and out of the classroom as demonstrated by both GPA and leadership and service work. **Athletic:** 36 full-time freshmen received athletic scholarships; average amount $877.

**FINANCIAL AID PROCEDURES**
**Forms required:** FAFSA, institutional form.
**Dates and Deadlines:** Priority date 3/10; no closing date. Applicants notified on a rolling basis starting 5/1.

**CONTACT**
Cathy Buckman, Assistant Vice Chancellor for Enrollment Services and Interim Director of Financial Aid
1700 Mishawaka Avenue, South Bend, IN 46634-7111
(574) 520-4357

## Indiana University Southeast
New Albany, Indiana
www.ius.edu                    Federal Code: 001817

**4-year public** university in large town.
**Enrollment:** 5,228 undergrads, 34% part-time. 894 full-time freshmen.
**Selectivity:** Admits over 75% of applicants.

**BASIC COSTS (2015-2016)**
**Tuition and fees:** $6,949; out-of-state residents $18,379.
**Per-credit charge:** $212; out-of-state residents $593.
**Room only:** $6,410.

**FINANCIAL AID PICTURE (2014-2015)**
**Students with need:** Out of 822 full-time freshmen who applied for aid, 646 were judged to have need. Of these, 622 received aid, and 66 had their full need met. Average financial aid package met 60% of need; average scholarship/grant was $6,628; average loan was $3,077. For part-time students, average financial aid package was $4,670.
**Students without need:** 64 full-time freshmen who did not demonstrate need for aid received scholarships/grants; average award was $847. No-need awards available for academics, art, athletics, leadership, minority status, music/drama.
**Scholarships offered: Merit:** Presidential Scholars Award; up to $12,000/year; $6,000 renewable scholarship also provides an additional $6,000 for students living on campus; $1,500 towards a study abroad program, and a laptop; must be an entering first-year student, GPA 3.5+, SAT 1150+ (ACT 25), resident of Indiana. Balfour Scholarship; up to $2,000; for incoming freshman with 1300+ SAT or equivalent ACT, rank in upper 10% of class; renewable for four years with 3.5 GPA. Dr. Sharon Waggoner Scholarship; up to $1,000; for outstanding foreign language student who has completed 2 semesters of foreign language study at IUS. **Athletic:** 10 full-time freshmen received athletic scholarships; average amount $1,594.

**FINANCIAL AID PROCEDURES**
**Forms required:** FAFSA.
**Dates and Deadlines:** Closing date 3/10. Applicants notified on a rolling basis starting 5/1; must reply within 3 week(s) of notification.

## CONTACT

Traci Armes, Director of Financial Aid
4201 Grant Line Road, New Albany, IN 47150-6405
(812) 941-2246

## Indiana University-Purdue University Fort Wayne

Fort Wayne, Indiana
www.ipfw.edu                   Federal Code: 001828

**4-year public** university and branch campus college in large city.
**Enrollment:** 8,746 undergrads. 1,469 full-time freshmen.

### BASIC COSTS (2015-2016)

**Tuition and fees:** $8,080; out-of-state residents $19,408.
**Per-credit charge:** $235; out-of-state residents $613.
**Room only:** $5,980.

### FINANCIAL AID PICTURE (2014-2015)

**Students with need:** Out of 1,354 full-time freshmen who applied for aid, 1,099 were judged to have need. Of these, 1,003 received aid, and 25 had their full need met. Average financial aid package met 47% of need; average scholarship/grant was $4,566; average loan was $2,936. For part-time students, average financial aid package was $5,424.
**Students without need:** 9 full-time freshmen who did not demonstrate need for aid received scholarships/grants; average award was $1,528. No-need awards available for academics, alumni affiliation, art, athletics, leadership, minority status, music/drama, ROTC, state/district residency.
**Scholarships offered:** 15 full-time freshmen received athletic scholarships; average amount $13,304.

### FINANCIAL AID PROCEDURES

**Forms required:** FAFSA.
**Dates and Deadlines:** Priority date 3/10; no closing date. Applicants notified on a rolling basis starting 4/1; must reply within 3 week(s) of notification.

### CONTACT

David Peterson, Director of Financial Aid
2101 East Coliseum Boulevard, Fort Wayne, IN 46805-1499
(260) 481-6820

## Indiana University-Purdue University Indianapolis

Indianapolis, Indiana
www.iupui.edu                   Federal Code: 001813

**4-year public** university in very large city.
**Enrollment:** 21,217 undergrads, 20% part-time. 3,772 full-time freshmen.
**Selectivity:** Admits 50 to 75% of applicants.

### BASIC COSTS (2015-2016)

**Tuition and fees:** $9,056; out-of-state residents $29,774.
**Per-credit charge:** $267; out-of-state residents $958.
**Room and board:** $8,154.

### FINANCIAL AID PICTURE (2014-2015)

**Students with need:** Out of 3,431 full-time freshmen who applied for aid, 2,644 were judged to have need. Of these, 2,552 received aid, and 493 had their full need met. Average financial aid package met 68% of need; average scholarship/grant was $9,403; average loan was $3,306. For part-time students, average financial aid package was $5,250.
**Students without need:** 345 full-time freshmen who did not demonstrate need for aid received scholarships/grants; average award was $5,811. No-need awards available for academics, ROTC.

**Scholarships offered:** *Merit:* Dean's Recognition Scholarship; $11,000 annually for 4 years; minimum HS GPA of 3.5 and score 1200+ SAT (26 ACT); students must attend full time and maintain a 3.0 GPA. IUPUI Service Award; $7,000 annually for 4 years; minimum HS GPA; students must attend full time and maintain a 3.0 GPA and must volunteer for 20 hours of service at IUPUI events annually. IUPUI Undergraduate Research Opportunities Program; offers research project and travel grants and conference travel funds; formal research credits may be earned toward graduation. IUPUI Chancellor's Scholarship; $12,000 annually for 4 years; minimum HS GPA of 3.75 with a minimum 1250 SAT (28 ACT); automatically admitted to the IUPUI Honors College to be considered for renewal, students must attend full time, be an active participant in the Honors College and maintain a 3.3 GPA. *Athletic:* 29 full-time freshmen received athletic scholarships; average amount $13,420.

### FINANCIAL AID PROCEDURES

**Forms required:** FAFSA.
**Dates and Deadlines:** Priority date 3/10; no closing date. Applicants notified on a rolling basis starting 4/1.

### CONTACT

Marvin Smith, Director of Student Financial Services
420 University Boulevard, CE 255, Indianapolis, IN 46202-5143
(317) 274-4162

## Indiana Wesleyan University

Marion, Indiana
www.indwes.edu                   Federal Code: 001822

**4-year private** university and liberal arts college in large town, affiliated with Wesleyan Church.
**Enrollment:** 2,752 undergrads, 2% part-time. 655 full-time freshmen.
**Selectivity:** Admits over 75% of applicants.

### BASIC COSTS (2015-2016)

**Tuition and fees:** $24,728.
**Room and board:** $7,988.

### FINANCIAL AID PICTURE (2014-2015)

**Students with need:** Out of 626 full-time freshmen who applied for aid, 538 were judged to have need. Of these, 538 received aid, and 294 had their full need met. Average financial aid package met 93% of need; average scholarship/grant was $8,673; average loan was $3,772. For part-time students, average financial aid package was $18,937.
**Students without need:** 87 full-time freshmen who did not demonstrate need for aid received scholarships/grants; average award was $7,623. No-need awards available for academics, alumni affiliation, art, athletics, music/drama, ROTC.
**Scholarships offered:** *Merit:* Academic Scholarships; $750-$6,000; 3.2 GPA and 1050 SAT (exclusive of Writing) or 23 ACT required. *Athletic:* 35 full-time freshmen received athletic scholarships; average amount $7,760.

### FINANCIAL AID PROCEDURES

**Forms required:** FAFSA, institutional form.
**Dates and Deadlines:** Closing date 3/10. Applicants notified on a rolling basis starting 3/10.
**Transfers:** Applicants notified on a rolling basis.

### CONTACT

Lisa Montany, Director of Financial Aid
4201 South Washington Street, Marion, IN 46953-4999
(765) 677-2116

**PART III: FINANCIAL AID COLLEGE BY COLLEGE**

## Ivy Tech Community College: Bloomington

Bloomington, Indiana
www.ivytech.edu                    Federal Code: 035213

**2-year public** community college in small city.
**Enrollment:** 4,023 undergrads.
**Selectivity:** Open admission; but selective for some programs.

**BASIC COSTS (2015-2016)**
**Tuition and fees:** $4,115; out-of-state residents $7,992.
**Per-credit charge:** $133.15; out-of-state residents $262.

**FINANCIAL AID PICTURE**
**Students with need:** Need-based aid available for full-time and part-time students. Work study available nights.

**FINANCIAL AID PROCEDURES**
**Forms required:** FAFSA.
**Dates and Deadlines:** Closing date 3/1. Applicants notified on a rolling basis starting 7/1.
**Transfers:** Closing date 3/1.

**CONTACT**
Patt McCafferty, Director of Financial Aid
200 Daniels Way, Bloomington, IN 47404-1511
(812) 332-1559

## Ivy Tech Community College: Central Indiana

Indianapolis, Indiana
www.ivytech.edu                    Federal Code: 009917

**2-year public** community college in very large city.
**Enrollment:** 16,828 undergrads.
**Selectivity:** Open admission; but selective for some programs.

**BASIC COSTS (2015-2016)**
**Tuition and fees:** $4,115; out-of-state residents $7,992.
**Per-credit charge:** $133.15; out-of-state residents $262.

**FINANCIAL AID PICTURE**
**Students with need:** Need-based aid available for full-time and part-time students. Work study available nights.

**FINANCIAL AID PROCEDURES**
**Forms required:** FAFSA.
**Dates and Deadlines:** Closing date 3/1. Applicants notified on a rolling basis starting 7/1.

**CONTACT**
Director of Financial Aid
50 West Fall Creek Parkway North Drive, Indianapolis, IN 46208-5752
(317) 921-4882

## Ivy Tech Community College: Columbus

Columbus, Indiana
www.ivytech.edu                    Federal Code: 010038

**2-year public** community college in large town.
**Enrollment:** 2,248 undergrads.
**Selectivity:** Open admission; but selective for some programs.

**BASIC COSTS (2015-2016)**
**Tuition and fees:** $4,115; out-of-state residents $7,992.
**Per-credit charge:** $133.15; out-of-state residents $262.

**FINANCIAL AID PICTURE**
**Students with need:** Need-based aid available for full-time and part-time students. Work study available nights.

**FINANCIAL AID PROCEDURES**
**Forms required:** FAFSA.
**Dates and Deadlines:** Closing date 3/1. Applicants notified on a rolling basis starting 7/1.

**CONTACT**
Paul Johnston, Director of Financial Aid
4475 Central Avenue, Columbus, IN 47203-1868
(812) 372-9925

## Ivy Tech Community College: East Central

Muncie, Indiana
www.ivytech.edu/eastcentral        Federal Code: 009924

**2-year public** community college in small city.
**Enrollment:** 5,295 undergrads.
**Selectivity:** Open admission; but selective for some programs.

**BASIC COSTS (2015-2016)**
**Tuition and fees:** $4,115; out-of-state residents $7,992.
**Per-credit charge:** $133.15; out-of-state residents $262.

**FINANCIAL AID PICTURE**
**Students with need:** Need-based aid available for full-time and part-time students. Work study available nights.
**Additional info:** Higher Education Aid (HEA), Child of Disabled/Deceased Veterans (CDV), Ivy Tech Scholarships (IVTC) and grants, vocational rehabilitation and veteran's assistance available. None require repayment.

**FINANCIAL AID PROCEDURES**
**Forms required:** FAFSA.
**Dates and Deadlines:** Closing date 3/1. Applicants notified on a rolling basis starting 7/1.

**CONTACT**
Tammy Tomfohrde, Director of Financial Aid
4301 South Cowan Road, Muncie, IN 47302-9448
(765) 289-2291 ext. 1222

## Ivy Tech Community College: Kokomo

Kokomo, Indiana
www.ivytech.edu                    Federal Code: 010041

**2-year public** community college in large town.
**Enrollment:** 2,557 undergrads.
**Selectivity:** Open admission; but selective for some programs.

**BASIC COSTS (2015-2016)**
**Tuition and fees:** $4,115; out-of-state residents $7,992.
**Per-credit charge:** $133.15; out-of-state residents $262.

**FINANCIAL AID PICTURE**
**Students with need:** Need-based aid available for full-time and part-time students. Work study available nights.

**FINANCIAL AID PROCEDURES**
**Forms required:** FAFSA.
**Dates and Deadlines:** Closing date 3/1. Applicants notified on a rolling basis starting 7/1.
**Transfers:** Applicants notified on a rolling basis starting 7/1.

**CONTACT**

Anjanetta Polk, Director of Financial Aid

1815 East Morgan Street, Kokomo, IN 46903-1373

(765) 459-0561

## Ivy Tech Community College: Lafayette

Lafayette, Indiana

www.ivytech.edu                    Federal Code: 010039

**2-year public** community college in large town.

**Enrollment:** 4,106 undergrads.

**Selectivity:** Open admission; but selective for some programs.

**BASIC COSTS (2015-2016)**

**Tuition and fees:** $4,115; out-of-state residents $7,992.

**Per-credit charge:** $133.15; out-of-state residents $262.

**FINANCIAL AID PICTURE**

**Students with need:** Need-based aid available for full-time and part-time students. Work study available nights.

**FINANCIAL AID PROCEDURES**

**Forms required:** FAFSA.

**Dates and Deadlines:** Closing date 3/1. Applicants notified on a rolling basis starting 7/1.

**CONTACT**

Beverly Cooper, Director of Financial Aid

3101 South Creasy Lane, Lafayette, IN 47905-6299

(765) 772-9100

## Ivy Tech Community College: North Central

South Bend, Indiana

www.ivytech.edu                    Federal Code: 008423

**2-year public** community college in small city.

**Enrollment:** 4,911 undergrads.

**Selectivity:** Open admission; but selective for some programs.

**BASIC COSTS (2015-2016)**

**Tuition and fees:** $4,115; out-of-state residents $7,992.

**Per-credit charge:** $133.15; out-of-state residents $262.

**FINANCIAL AID PICTURE**

**Students with need:** Need-based aid available for full-time and part-time students. Work study available nights.

**FINANCIAL AID PROCEDURES**

**Forms required:** FAFSA.

**Dates and Deadlines:** Closing date 3/1. Applicants notified on a rolling basis starting 7/1.

**CONTACT**

Barb Jerzyk, Director of Financial Aid

220 Dean Johnson Boulevard, South Bend, IN 46601-3415

(219) 289-7001

## Ivy Tech Community College: Northeast

Fort Wayne, Indiana

www.ivytech.edu                    Federal Code: 009926

**2-year public** community college in small city.

**Enrollment:** 7,128 undergrads.

**Selectivity:** Open admission; but selective for some programs.

**BASIC COSTS (2015-2016)**

**Tuition and fees:** $4,115; out-of-state residents $7,992.

**Per-credit charge:** $133.15; out-of-state residents $262.

**FINANCIAL AID PICTURE**

**Students with need:** Need-based aid available for full-time and part-time students. Work study available nights.

**FINANCIAL AID PROCEDURES**

**Forms required:** FAFSA.

**Dates and Deadlines:** Closing date 3/1. Applicants notified on a rolling basis starting 7/1.

**CONTACT**

Norman Newman, Director of Financial Aid

3800 North Anthony Boulevard, Fort Wayne, IN 46805-1489

(260) 482-9171

## Ivy Tech Community College: Northwest

Gary, Indiana

www.ivytech.edu                    Federal Code: 010040

**2-year public** community college in small city.

**Enrollment:** 7,551 undergrads, 65% part-time. 609 full-time freshmen.

**Selectivity:** Open admission; but selective for some programs.

**BASIC COSTS (2015-2016)**

**Tuition and fees:** $4,115; out-of-state residents $7,992.

**Per-credit charge:** $133.15; out-of-state residents $262.

**FINANCIAL AID PICTURE**

**Students with need:** Need-based aid available for full-time and part-time students. Work study available nights.

**FINANCIAL AID PROCEDURES**

**Forms required:** FAFSA.

**Dates and Deadlines:** Closing date 3/1. Applicants notified on a rolling basis starting 7/1.

**CONTACT**

Barb Jerzyk, Director of Financial Aid

1440 East 35th Avenue, Gary, IN 46409-1499

(219) 981-1111

## Ivy Tech Community College: Richmond

Richmond, Indiana

www.ivytech.edu                    Federal Code: 010037

**2-year public** community college in large town.

**Enrollment:** 1,980 undergrads.

**Selectivity:** Open admission; but selective for some programs.

**BASIC COSTS (2015-2016)**

**Tuition and fees:** $4,115; out-of-state residents $7,992.

**Per-credit charge:** $133.15; out-of-state residents $262.

**FINANCIAL AID PICTURE**

**Students with need:** Need-based aid available for full-time and part-time students. Work study available nights.

**FINANCIAL AID PROCEDURES**

**Forms required:** FAFSA.

**Dates and Deadlines:** Closing date 3/1. Applicants notified on a rolling basis starting 7/1.

**CONTACT**

Ann Franzen-Roha, Director of Financial Aid

2357 Chester Boulevard, Richmond, IN 47374-1298

(765) 966-2656

## Ivy Tech Community College: South Central

Sellersburg, Indiana
www.ivytech.edu                      Federal Code: 010109

**2-year public** community college in small town.
**Enrollment:** 4,090 undergrads.
**Selectivity:** Open admission; but selective for some programs.

### BASIC COSTS (2015-2016)
**Tuition and fees:** $4,115; out-of-state residents $7,992.
**Per-credit charge:** $133.15; out-of-state residents $262.

### FINANCIAL AID PICTURE
**Students with need:** Need-based aid available for full-time and part-time students. Work study available nights.

### FINANCIAL AID PROCEDURES
**Forms required:** FAFSA.
**Dates and Deadlines:** Closing date 3/1. Applicants notified on a rolling basis starting 7/1.

### CONTACT
Gary Cottrill, Director of Financial Aid
8204 Highway 311, Sellersburg, IN 47172-1897
(812) 246-3301

## Ivy Tech Community College: Southeast

Madison, Indiana
www.ivytech.edu                      Federal Code: 009923

**2-year public** community college in large town.
**Enrollment:** 1,849 undergrads.
**Selectivity:** Open admission; but selective for some programs.

### BASIC COSTS (2015-2016)
**Tuition and fees:** $4,115; out-of-state residents $7,992.
**Per-credit charge:** $133.15; out-of-state residents $262.

### FINANCIAL AID PICTURE
**Students with need:** Need-based aid available for full-time and part-time students. Work study available nights.

### FINANCIAL AID PROCEDURES
**Forms required:** FAFSA.
**Dates and Deadlines:** Closing date 3/1. Applicants notified on a rolling basis starting 7/1.

### CONTACT
Richard Hill, Director of Financial Aid
590 Ivy Tech Drive, Madison, IN 47250-1881
(812) 265-2580 ext. 4148

## Ivy Tech Community College: Southwest

Evansville, Indiana
www.ivytech.edu                      Federal Code: 009925

**2-year public** community college in small city.
**Enrollment:** 4,260 undergrads.
**Selectivity:** Open admission; but selective for some programs.

### BASIC COSTS (2015-2016)
**Tuition and fees:** $4,115; out-of-state residents $7,992.
**Per-credit charge:** $133.15; out-of-state residents $262.

### FINANCIAL AID PICTURE
**Students with need:** Need-based aid available for full-time and part-time students. Work study available nights.

### FINANCIAL AID PROCEDURES
**Forms required:** FAFSA.
**Dates and Deadlines:** Closing date 3/1. Applicants notified on a rolling basis starting 7/1.

### CONTACT
Casey Trela, Director of Financial Aid
3501 First Avenue, Evansville, IN 47710-3398
(812) 426-2865

## Ivy Tech Community College: Wabash Valley

Terre Haute, Indiana
www.ivytech.edu                      Federal Code: 008547

**2-year public** community college in small city.
**Enrollment:** 3,247 undergrads.
**Selectivity:** Open admission; but selective for some programs.

### BASIC COSTS (2015-2016)
**Tuition and fees:** $4,115; out-of-state residents $7,992.
**Per-credit charge:** $133.15; out-of-state residents $262.

### FINANCIAL AID PICTURE
**Students with need:** Need-based aid available for full-time and part-time students. Work study available nights.

### FINANCIAL AID PROCEDURES
**Forms required:** FAFSA.
**Dates and Deadlines:** Closing date 3/1. Applicants notified on a rolling basis starting 7/1.
**Transfers:** Applicants notified on a rolling basis starting 7/1.

### CONTACT
Julie Wonderlin, Director of Financial Aid
8000 South Education Drive, Terre Haute, IN 47802-4898
(812) 299-1121

## Kaplan College: Indianapolis

Indianapolis, Indiana
www.kaplancollege.com                Federal Code: 009777

**2-year for-profit** health science and nursing college in very large city.
**Enrollment:** 501 undergrads.
**Selectivity:** Open admission; but selective for some programs.

### BASIC COSTS (2015-2016)
**Additional info:** Criminal Justice: $31,365. Dental Assistant: $16,450. Electrical Technician: $21,904. Medical Assistant: $16,465. Medical Office Specialist: $16,735. Practical Nursing: $23,340. Spanish for Healthcare Workers: $510.

### FINANCIAL AID PICTURE
**Students with need:** Need-based aid available for full-time students.
**Students without need:** This college awards aid only to students with need.

### CONTACT
Vincent O'Neal, Financial Aid Director
7302 Woodland Drive, Indianapolis, IN 46278-1736
(317) 293-6503

## Manchester University
North Manchester, Indiana
www.manchester.edu                    Federal Code: 001820

**4-year private** pharmacy and liberal arts college in small town, affiliated with Church of the Brethren.
**Enrollment:** 1,239 undergrads, 1% part-time. 396 full-time freshmen.
**Selectivity:** Admits 50 to 75% of applicants.

### BASIC COSTS (2016-2017)
**Tuition and fees:** $30,802.
**Per-credit charge:** $700.
**Room and board:** $9,620.

### FINANCIAL AID PICTURE (2015-2016)
**Students with need:** Average financial aid package met 85% of need; average scholarship/grant was $22,106; average loan was $3,337. Need-based aid available for part-time students.
**Students without need:** No-need awards available for academics, alumni affiliation, leadership, minority status, music/drama, religious affiliation.
**Scholarships offered:** Honors Fellowship; full tuition; based on academics; 2 awarded. Presidential Leadership Award; $2,500 travel grant; 3 awarded. Trustee Scholarships; $12,000; based on merit; 40 awarded to each incoming class. Presidential Scholarships; $9,000; based on merit. Arts, service, modern language scholarships; $9,000; based on merit/ability.
**Additional info:** Students automatically considered for all scholarship programs.

### FINANCIAL AID PROCEDURES
**Forms required:** FAFSA.
**Dates and Deadlines:** Priority date 3/1; no closing date. Applicants notified on a rolling basis starting 3/20.
**Transfers:** Aid eligibility remaining determined by reviewing total credit hours transferred and financial aid transcripts.

### CONTACT
Sherri Shockey, Director of Student Financial Services
604 East College Avenue, North Manchester, IN 46962-0365
(260) 982-5066

## Marian University
Indianapolis, Indiana
www.marian.edu                    Federal Code: 001821

**4-year private** university and liberal arts college in very large city, affiliated with Roman Catholic Church.
**Enrollment:** 1,969 undergrads, 14% part-time. 286 full-time freshmen.
**Selectivity:** Admits 50 to 75% of applicants.

### BASIC COSTS (2015-2016)
**Tuition and fees:** $30,500.
**Per-credit charge:** $1,350.
**Room and board:** $9,436.

### FINANCIAL AID PICTURE
**Students with need:** Need-based aid available for full-time and part-time students. Work study available nights, weekends, and for part-time students.
**Students without need:** No-need awards available for academics, alumni affiliation, art, athletics, leadership, music/drama, religious affiliation.

### FINANCIAL AID PROCEDURES
**Forms required:** FAFSA, institutional form.
**Dates and Deadlines:** Closing date 3/15. Applicants notified on a rolling basis starting 3/15; must reply within 2 week(s) of notification.
**Transfers:** No deadline. Applicants notified on a rolling basis starting 3/15; must reply within 2 week(s) of notification.

### CONTACT
Chad Bir, Director of Financial Aid
3200 Cold Spring Road, Indianapolis, IN 46222-1997
(317) 955-6040

## Oakland City University
Oakland City, Indiana
www.oak.edu                    Federal Code: 001824

**4-year private** university and liberal arts college in small town, affiliated with Baptist General Conference.
**Enrollment:** 539 undergrads, 42% part-time. 76 full-time freshmen.
**Selectivity:** Admits 50 to 75% of applicants.

### BASIC COSTS (2015-2016)
**Tuition and fees:** $22,800.
**Per-credit charge:** $760.
**Room and board:** $9,030.
**Additional info:** Tuition/fee waivers available for minority students, unemployed or children of unemployed.

### FINANCIAL AID PICTURE (2014-2015)
**Students with need:** Out of 74 full-time freshmen who applied for aid, 74 were judged to have need. Of these, 74 received aid. Average financial aid package met 70% of need; average scholarship/grant was $4,726; average loan was $10,907. Need-based aid available for part-time students.
**Students without need:** No-need awards available for academics, athletics, minority status, religious affiliation.

### FINANCIAL AID PROCEDURES
**Forms required:** FAFSA.
**Dates and Deadlines:** Priority date 3/10; no closing date. Applicants notified on a rolling basis starting 5/1.

### CONTACT
Cassie Scraper, Director of Financial Aid
138 North Lucretia Street, Oakland City, IN 47660
(812) 749-1224

## Purdue University
West Lafayette, Indiana
www.purdue.edu                    Federal Code: 001825

**4-year public** university in small city.
**Enrollment:** 29,325 undergrads, 4% part-time. 6,874 full-time freshmen.
**Selectivity:** Admits 50 to 75% of applicants.

### BASIC COSTS (2015-2016)
**Tuition and fees:** $10,002; out-of-state residents $28,804.
**Per-credit charge:** $329; out-of-state residents $930.
**Room and board:** $10,030.
**Additional info:** Differential general service fees: Engineering and new beginning Computer Science undergraduate students pay an additional $2,050 per academic year. Management undergraduate students pay an additional $1,436 per academic year. School of Technology undergraduate students pay an additional $572 per academic year.

### FINANCIAL AID PICTURE (2015-2016)
**Students with need:** Out of 4,898 full-time freshmen who applied for aid, 3,318 were judged to have need. Of these, 3,318 received aid, and 1,580 had their full need met. Average financial aid package met 83% of need; average scholarship/grant was $13,865; average loan was $3,759. For part-time students, average financial aid package was $7,916.
**Students without need:** 747 full-time freshmen who did not demonstrate need for aid received scholarships/grants; average award was $6,534. No-need awards available for academics, athletics, leadership, music/drama, ROTC, state/district residency.

**Scholarships offered:** *Merit:* Trustees Scholarship; $12,000-$16,000 per year to non-Indiana residents; $10,000 per year to Indiana residents; renewable for up to 4 years of continuous full-time enrollment; for exceptional academic achievement, leadership and service. Presidential Scholarship; $5,000-$10,000 per year to non-Indiana residents; $2,000-$8,000 per year to Indiana residents; renewable for up to four years of continuous full-time enrollment; exceptional academic achievement in leadership and service. *Athletic:* 55 full-time freshmen received athletic scholarships; average amount $23,928. **Additional info:** Cooperative work for credit available in many programs. Purdue Promise replaces need based loans with institutional funds after and in conjunction with federal and state eligibility for high-need students; maximum allowable family income is $50,000.

### FINANCIAL AID PROCEDURES
**Forms required:** FAFSA.
**Dates and Deadlines:** Priority date 3/1; no closing date. Applicants notified by 4/15.

### CONTACT
Theodore Malone, Executive Director of Financial Aid
475 Stadium Mall Drive, West Lafayette, IN 47907-2050
(765) 494-0998

## Purdue University Calumet
Hammond, Indiana
www.purduecal.edu                    Federal Code: 001827

**4-year public** university and branch campus college in small city.
**Enrollment:** 8,408 undergrads, 42% part-time. 947 full-time freshmen.
**Selectivity:** Admits 50 to 75% of applicants.

### BASIC COSTS (2015-2016)
**Tuition and fees:** $7,360; out-of-state residents $16,625.
**Per-credit charge:** $221; out-of-state residents $530.
**Room and board:** $7,368.

### FINANCIAL AID PICTURE (2014-2015)
**Students with need:** Out of 836 full-time freshmen who applied for aid, 657 were judged to have need. Of these, 616 received aid, and 41 had their full need met. Average financial aid package met 12% of need; average scholarship/grant was $5,060; average loan was $2,303. For part-time students, average financial aid package was $3,771.
**Students without need:** 68 full-time freshmen who did not demonstrate need for aid received scholarships/grants; average award was $1,557. No-need awards available for academics, athletics, state/district residency.
**Scholarships offered:** 26 full-time freshmen received athletic scholarships; average amount $1,919.

### FINANCIAL AID PROCEDURES
**Forms required:** FAFSA.
**Dates and Deadlines:** Priority date 3/10; closing date 6/30. Applicants notified on a rolling basis starting 4/15; must reply within 2 week(s) of notification.

### CONTACT
Kevin Popa, Financial Aid and Student Accounts
2200 169th Street, Hammond, IN 46323-2094
(219) 989-2301

## Purdue University North Central
Westville, Indiana
www.pnc.edu                    Federal Code: 001826

**4-year public** university in rural community.
**Enrollment:** 3,514 undergrads.

### BASIC COSTS (2015-2016)
**Tuition and fees:** $7,358; out-of-state residents $17,516.
**Per-credit charge:** $221; out-of-state residents $559.

### FINANCIAL AID PICTURE
**Students with need:** Need-based aid available for full-time and part-time students.
**Students without need:** No-need awards available for academics, athletics, leadership.

### FINANCIAL AID PROCEDURES
**Forms required:** FAFSA.
**Dates and Deadlines:** Priority date 3/10; closing date 6/30. Applicants notified on a rolling basis starting 4/1; must reply by 8/1 or within 2 week(s) of notification.
**Transfers:** Priority date 3/1; no deadline.

### CONTACT
Brad Remmenga, Director, Financial Aid and Compliance
1401 South US Highway 421, Westville, IN 46391-9542
(219) 785-5460

## Rose-Hulman Institute of Technology
Terre Haute, Indiana
www.rose-hulman.edu                    Federal Code: 001830

**4-year private** engineering college in small city.
**Enrollment:** 2,233 undergrads, 1% part-time. 545 full-time freshmen.
**Selectivity:** Admits 50 to 75% of applicants. GED not accepted.

### BASIC COSTS (2016-2017)
**Tuition and fees:** $46,210.
**Per-credit charge:** $1,259.
**Room and board:** $13,293.
**Additional info:** Required fees includes student laptop.

### FINANCIAL AID PICTURE (2015-2016)
**Students with need:** Out of 429 full-time freshmen who applied for aid, 340 were judged to have need. Of these, 340 received aid, and 84 had their full need met. Average financial aid package met 77% of need; average scholarship/grant was $25,954; average loan was $3,367. For part-time students, average financial aid package was $35,394.
**Students without need:** 201 full-time freshmen who did not demonstrate need for aid received scholarships/grants; average award was $11,613. No-need awards available for academics, minority status, ROTC.

### FINANCIAL AID PROCEDURES
**Forms required:** FAFSA.
**Dates and Deadlines:** Priority date 3/1; no closing date. Applicants notified on a rolling basis starting 3/10; must reply by 5/1.
**Transfers:** No deadline. Applicants notified on a rolling basis; must reply by 6/1.

### CONTACT
Melinda Middleton, Director of Financial Aid
Office of Admissions, Terre Haute, IN 47803-3999
(800) 248-7448

## Saint Joseph's College
Rensselaer, Indiana
www.saintjoe.edu                    Federal Code: 001833

**4-year private** liberal arts college in small town, affiliated with Roman Catholic Church.
**Enrollment:** 1,009 undergrads, 6% part-time. 249 full-time freshmen.
**Selectivity:** Admits 50 to 75% of applicants.

## BASIC COSTS (2015-2016)

**Tuition and fees:** $28,690.
**Per-credit charge:** $950.
**Room and board:** $8,900.

## FINANCIAL AID PICTURE (2014-2015)

**Students with need:** Out of 221 full-time freshmen who applied for aid, 200 were judged to have need. Of these, 200 received aid, and 52 had their full need met. Average financial aid package met 80% of need; average scholarship/grant was $19,894; average loan was $4,101. For part-time students, average financial aid package was $4,917.

**Students without need:** 21 full-time freshmen who did not demonstrate need for aid received scholarships/grants; average award was $16,449. No-need awards available for academics, alumni affiliation, athletics, music/drama, religious affiliation.

**Scholarships offered:** 7 full-time freshmen received athletic scholarships; average amount $7,830.

## FINANCIAL AID PROCEDURES

**Forms required:** FAFSA.

**Dates and Deadlines:** Priority date 3/1; no closing date. Applicants notified on a rolling basis starting 3/1; must reply by 5/1 or within 2 week(s) of notification.

**Transfers:** No deadline. Applicants notified on a rolling basis starting 9/1; must reply by 5/1 or within 2 week(s) of notification.

## CONTACT

Debra Sizemore, Director of Student Financial Services
Box 890, Rensselaer, IN 47978-0890
(219) 866-6163

# St. Mary-of-the-Woods College

Saint Mary of the Woods, Indiana
www.smwc.edu                    Federal Code: 001835

**4-year private** liberal arts college in rural community, affiliated with Roman Catholic Church.

**Enrollment:** 592 undergrads, 34% part-time. 86 full-time freshmen.
**Selectivity:** Admits 50 to 75% of applicants.

## BASIC COSTS (2015-2016)

**Tuition and fees:** $28,932.
**Per-credit charge:** $496.
**Room and board:** $10,500.
**Additional info:** Tuition at time of enrollment locked for 4 years; tuition/fee waivers available for minority students.

## FINANCIAL AID PICTURE (2014-2015)

**Students with need:** Out of 83 full-time freshmen who applied for aid, 83 were judged to have need. Of these, 83 received aid. For part-time students, average financial aid package was $5,463.

**Students without need:** 3 full-time freshmen who did not demonstrate need for aid received scholarships/grants; average award was $16,403. No-need awards available for academics, alumni affiliation, art, athletics, job skills, leadership, minority status, music/drama, religious affiliation, state/district residency.

**Scholarships offered:** *Merit:* Saint Mother Theodore Guerin Scholarships; 2 per year at $20,000 a year for 4 years, 8 per year at $13,000 a year for 4 years; based on academics, service and leadership. Top Ten on 10 Scholarships; 2 per year at $20,000 a year for 4 years, 8 per year at $13,000 a year for four years; for local students based on academics, service and leadership. Trustees Scholarships; up to $11,000 a year for 4 years; based on academics. Presidential Scholarships; up to $9,000 a year for 4 years; based on academics. Dean's Scholarships; up to $6,000 a year for 4 years; based on academics. Woods Scholarships; up to $4,000 per year for 4 years; based on academics. *Athletic:* 20 full-time freshmen received athletic scholarships; average amount $8,159.

**Additional info:** Portfolio or audition required of applicants who wish to be considered for Creative Arts Scholarship.

## FINANCIAL AID PROCEDURES

**Forms required:** FAFSA.

**Dates and Deadlines:** Closing date 3/10. Applicants notified on a rolling basis starting 12/1; must reply within 6 week(s) of notification.

**Transfers:** Priority date 7/1; no deadline. Applicants notified on a rolling basis starting 12/1; must reply within 8 week(s) of notification. Transfer grants available for students graduating or transferring from Ivy Tech Community College.

## CONTACT

Darla Hopper, Director of Financial Aid
1 St Mary of Woods Coll, Saint Mary of the Woods, IN 47876-1099
(812) 535-5100

# Saint Mary's College

Notre Dame, Indiana
www.saintmarys.edu              Federal Code: 001836

**4-year private** liberal arts college for women in small city, affiliated with Roman Catholic Church.

**Enrollment:** 1,559 undergrads, 1% part-time. 412 full-time freshmen.
**Selectivity:** Admits over 75% of applicants.

## BASIC COSTS (2015-2016)

**Tuition and fees:** $37,400.
**Per-credit charge:** $1,440.
**Room and board:** $11,320.

## FINANCIAL AID PICTURE (2015-2016)

**Students with need:** Out of 363 full-time freshmen who applied for aid, 299 were judged to have need. Of these, 299 received aid, and 76 had their full need met. Average financial aid package met 88% of need; average scholarship/grant was $16,542; average loan was $3,348. For part-time students, average financial aid package was $7,498.

**Students without need:** 104 full-time freshmen who did not demonstrate need for aid received scholarships/grants; average award was $14,688. No-need awards available for academics, art, music/drama.

**Scholarships offered:** Credentials of all admitted candidates automatically reviewed for merit scholarship consideration. Amounts vary depending on academic qualifications, renewable provided minimum GPA requirements are maintained. Grant for the cost of a double room on-campus awarded to any admitted student with a full tuition ROTC scholarship.

**Additional info:** Saint Mary's also accepts veteran benefits and participates in the Yellow Ribbon Program, through which 100% of a student's tuition and fees can be paid.

## FINANCIAL AID PROCEDURES

**Forms required:** FAFSA.

**Dates and Deadlines:** Closing date 3/1. Applicants notified on a rolling basis starting 12/15.

**Transfers:** Priority date 5/15; no deadline. Applicants notified on a rolling basis; must reply by 4/15. To meet Indiana grant deadlines, Indiana residents must submit FAFSA by March 1.

## CONTACT

Kathleen Brown, Director of Financial Aid
122 Le Mans Hall, Notre Dame, IN 46556-5001
(574) 284-4557

# Taylor University

Upland, Indiana
www.taylor.edu                  Federal Code: 001838

**4-year private** university and liberal arts college in small town, affiliated with interdenominational tradition.

**Enrollment:** 1,888 undergrads, 3% part-time. 519 full-time freshmen.
**Selectivity:** Admits over 75% of applicants.

**BASIC COSTS (2015-2016)**
**Tuition and fees:** $30,270.
**Per-credit charge:** $1,058.
**Room and board:** $8,497.
**Additional info:** Per-credit hour charge for 1 to 6 hours: $841; for 7 to 11 hours: $1,058.

**FINANCIAL AID PICTURE (2015-2016)**
**Students with need:** Out of 445 full-time freshmen who applied for aid, 345 were judged to have need. Of these, 345 received aid, and 93 had their full need met. Average financial aid package met 76% of need; average scholarship/grant was $17,653; average loan was $4,429. For part-time students, average financial aid package was $12,799.
**Students without need:** 142 full-time freshmen who did not demonstrate need for aid received scholarships/grants; average award was $12,968. No-need awards available for academics, alumni affiliation, art, athletics, leadership, minority status, music/drama, religious affiliation, state/district residency.
**Scholarships offered:** 27 full-time freshmen received athletic scholarships; average amount $5,306.

**FINANCIAL AID PROCEDURES**
**Forms required:** FAFSA.
**Dates and Deadlines:** Closing date 3/10. Applicants notified on a rolling basis starting 3/1; must reply by 5/1.
**Transfers:** Applicants notified on a rolling basis starting 3/1; must reply by 5/1.

**CONTACT**
Tim Nace, Associate Dean, Enrollment Management and Director of Financial Aid
236 West Reade Avenue, Upland, IN 46989-1001
(765) 998-5358

## Trine University
Angola, Indiana
www.trine.edu                 Federal Code: 001839

**4-year private** university and engineering college in small town.
**Enrollment:** 1,738 undergrads, 2% part-time. 524 full-time freshmen.
**Selectivity:** Admits over 75% of applicants.

**BASIC COSTS (2015-2016)**
**Tuition and fees:** $30,350.
**Per-credit charge:** $935.
**Room and board:** $10,200.
**Additional info:** Tuition for engineering students: $32,300.

**FINANCIAL AID PICTURE (2014-2015)**
**Students with need:** Out of 485 full-time freshmen who applied for aid, 442 were judged to have need. Of these, 442 received aid, and 50 had their full need met. Average financial aid package met 80% of need; average scholarship/grant was $5,796; average loan was $4,533.
**Students without need:** 73 full-time freshmen who did not demonstrate need for aid received scholarships/grants; average award was $11,230. No-need awards available for academics, alumni affiliation, minority status, music/drama.

**FINANCIAL AID PROCEDURES**
**Forms required:** FAFSA.
**Dates and Deadlines:** Priority date 3/1; no closing date. Applicants notified on a rolling basis starting 3/10; must reply by 5/1 or within 2 week(s) of notification.
**Transfers:** Applicants notified on a rolling basis starting 3/1; must reply by 5/1 or within 2 week(s) of notification.

**CONTACT**
Kim Bennett, Executive Director of Admission and Financial Aid
One University Avenue, Angola, IN 46703
(260) 665-4158

## University of Evansville
Evansville, Indiana
www.evansville.edu             Federal Code: 001795

**4-year private** university and liberal arts college in small city, affiliated with United Methodist Church.
**Enrollment:** 2,161 undergrads, 4% part-time. 515 full-time freshmen.
**Selectivity:** Admits 50 to 75% of applicants.

**BASIC COSTS (2015-2016)**
**Tuition and fees:** $32,946.
**Per-credit charge:** $890.
**Room and board:** $11,240.

**FINANCIAL AID PICTURE (2015-2016)**
**Students with need:** Average financial aid package met 86% of need; average scholarship/grant was $24,275; average loan was $3,459. For part-time students, average financial aid package was $8,314.
**Students without need:** 119 full-time freshmen who did not demonstrate need for aid received scholarships/grants; average award was $23,758. No-need awards available for academics, alumni affiliation, art, athletics, music/drama, religious affiliation.
**Scholarships offered:** 35 full-time freshmen received athletic scholarships; average amount $18,943.

**FINANCIAL AID PROCEDURES**
**Forms required:** FAFSA.
**Dates and Deadlines:** Priority date 3/1; no closing date. Applicants notified on a rolling basis starting 3/1; must reply by 8/1.
**Transfers:** Priority date 3/1. Applicants notified on a rolling basis starting 4/1; must reply by 8/1 or within 3 week(s) of notification. Indiana state aid is available for a total of 8 semesters at all schools attended.

**CONTACT**
Cathleen Wright, Director of Financial Aid
1800 Lincoln Avenue, Evansville, IN 47722
(812) 488-2364

## University of Indianapolis
Indianapolis, Indiana
www.uindy.edu                  Federal Code: 001804

**4-year private** university and liberal arts college in very large city, affiliated with United Methodist Church.
**Enrollment:** 4,139 undergrads, 16% part-time. 963 full-time freshmen.
**Selectivity:** Admits 50 to 75% of applicants.

**BASIC COSTS (2015-2016)**
**Tuition and fees:** $26,150.
**Per-credit charge:** $1,080.
**Room and board:** $9,930.

**FINANCIAL AID PICTURE (2014-2015)**
**Students with need:** Out of 878 full-time freshmen who applied for aid, 775 were judged to have need. Of these, 775 received aid, and 97 had their full need met. Average financial aid package met 67% of need; average scholarship/grant was $8,338; average loan was $3,728. For part-time students, average financial aid package was $4,025.
**Students without need:** 125 full-time freshmen who did not demonstrate need for aid received scholarships/grants; average award was $11,327. No-need awards available for academics, alumni affiliation, art, athletics, music/drama, religious affiliation, state/district residency.

**Scholarships offered: *Merit:*** Presidential Scholarship; full tuition; upper 5% of class, 1270 SAT/29 ACT, strong college prep required. Dean's Scholarship; 50% tuition; upper 7% of class, 1270 SAT/29 ACT, demonstrated leadership, strong college prep required. Alumni Scholarship; 30% tuition; upper 15% of class, 1100 SAT/24 ACT, alumnus connection to school required. Service Award; $2,500; based on demonstrated commitment to community volunteerism. United Methodist Award; $2,500; based on demonstrated commitment to church, activities. SAT scores listed are exclusive of writing portion. ***Athletic:*** 87 full-time freshmen received athletic scholarships; average amount $14,098.

**FINANCIAL AID PROCEDURES**

**Forms required:** FAFSA, institutional form.

**Dates and Deadlines:** Closing date 3/10. Applicants notified on a rolling basis starting 3/1; must reply within 3 week(s) of notification.

**Transfers:** No deadline. Applicants notified on a rolling basis starting 3/1.

**CONTACT**

Linda Handy, Director of Financial Aid
1400 East Hanna Avenue, Indianapolis, IN 46227-3697
(317) 788-3217

## University of Notre Dame

Notre Dame, Indiana
www.nd.edu

Federal Code: 001840
CSS Code: 1841

**4-year private** university in small city, affiliated with Roman Catholic Church.
**Enrollment:** 8,425 undergrads. 2,011 full-time freshmen.
**Selectivity:** Admits less than 50% of applicants. GED not accepted.

**BASIC COSTS (2016-2017)**
**Tuition and fees:** $49,685.
**Per-credit charge:** $2,049.
**Room and board:** $14,358.

**FINANCIAL AID PICTURE (2014-2015)**
**Students with need:** Out of 1,346 full-time freshmen who applied for aid, 886 were judged to have need. Of these, 886 received aid, and 881 had their full need met. Average financial aid package met 100% of need; average scholarship/grant was $35,998; average loan was $3,622. Need-based aid available for part-time students.
**Students without need:** 107 full-time freshmen who did not demonstrate need for aid received scholarships/grants; average award was $21,979. No-need awards available for academics, athletics, ROTC.
**Scholarships offered:** 111 full-time freshmen received athletic scholarships; average amount $40,822.

**FINANCIAL AID PROCEDURES**

**Forms required:** FAFSA, CSS PROFILE.

**Dates and Deadlines:** Priority date 2/15; no closing date. Applicants notified on a rolling basis starting 3/28; must reply by 5/1.

**Transfers:** Closing date 3/31. Applicants notified on a rolling basis; must reply within 2 week(s) of notification. Require signed and completed federal tax returns, including all schedules and W-2 forms from both the applicant and the parents of the applicant.

**CONTACT**

Thomas Bear, Executive Director of Student Financial Strategies
220 Main Building, Notre Dame, IN 46556
(574) 631-6436

## University of Saint Francis

Fort Wayne, Indiana
www.sf.edu

Federal Code: 001832

**4-year private** university and liberal arts college in large city, affiliated with Roman Catholic Church.

**Enrollment:** 1,745 undergrads, 14% part-time. 282 full-time freshmen.
**Selectivity:** Admits over 75% of applicants.

**BASIC COSTS (2015-2016)**
**Tuition and fees:** $27,220.
**Per-credit charge:** $830.
**Room and board:** $8,830.

**FINANCIAL AID PICTURE (2014-2015)**
**Students with need:** Out of 274 full-time freshmen who applied for aid, 254 were judged to have need. Of these, 254 received aid, and 49 had their full need met. Average financial aid package met 73% of need; average scholarship/grant was $16,670; average loan was $2,890. For part-time students, average financial aid package was $12,142.
**Students without need:** 27 full-time freshmen who did not demonstrate need for aid received scholarships/grants; average award was $8,624. No-need awards available for academics, art, athletics, music/drama, state/district residency.
**Scholarships offered:** 26 full-time freshmen received athletic scholarships; average amount $6,243.

**FINANCIAL AID PROCEDURES**

**Forms required:** FAFSA.

**Dates and Deadlines:** Priority date 3/10; no closing date. Applicants notified on a rolling basis starting 3/1; must reply by 8/1.

**Transfers:** Priority date 3/10; no deadline. Applicants notified on a rolling basis starting 3/1; must reply by 8/1. USF offers academic scholarships to transfer students based on their cumulative college GPA.

**CONTACT**

Michelle Nisun, Director of Financial Aid
2701 Spring Street, Fort Wayne, IN 46808
(260) 399-8003

## University of Southern Indiana

Evansville, Indiana
www.usi.edu

Federal Code: 001808

**4-year public** university and liberal arts college in small city.
**Enrollment:** 8,058 undergrads, 15% part-time. 1,658 full-time freshmen.
**Selectivity:** Admits 50 to 75% of applicants.

**BASIC COSTS (2015-2016)**
**Tuition and fees:** $7,397; out-of-state residents $17,179.
**Room and board:** $8,276.

**FINANCIAL AID PICTURE (2015-2016)**
**Students with need:** Out of 1,539 full-time freshmen who applied for aid, 1,081 were judged to have need. Of these, 1,081 received aid, and 108 had their full need met. Average financial aid package met 80% of need; average scholarship/grant was $8,137; average loan was $3,288. For part-time students, average financial aid package was $6,185.
**Students without need:** 330 full-time freshmen who did not demonstrate need for aid received scholarships/grants; average award was $2,912. No-need awards available for academics, art, athletics, leadership, music/drama, state/district residency.
**Scholarships offered:** 32 full-time freshmen received athletic scholarships; average amount $3,464.

**FINANCIAL AID PROCEDURES**

**Forms required:** FAFSA.

**Dates and Deadlines:** Priority date 3/1; no closing date. Applicants notified on a rolling basis starting 4/1; must reply by 4/1.

**CONTACT**

Mary Harper, Director of Student Financial Assistance
8600 University Boulevard, Evansville, IN 47712
(812) 464-1767

## Valparaiso University
Valparaiso, Indiana
www.valpo.edu                    Federal Code: 001842

**4-year private** university in large town, affiliated with Lutheran Church.
**Enrollment:** 3,141 undergrads, 2% part-time. 714 full-time freshmen.
**Selectivity:** Admits over 75% of applicants.

### BASIC COSTS (2015-2016)
**Tuition and fees:** $36,160.
**Per-credit charge:** $1,565.
**Room and board:** $10,520.
**Additional info:** Engineering students pay an additional $740 fee.

### FINANCIAL AID PICTURE (2014-2015)
**Students with need:** Out of 650 full-time freshmen who applied for aid,
570 were judged to have need. Of these, 568 received aid, and 392 had
their full need met. Average financial aid package met 94% of need; average
scholarship/grant was $24,489; average loan was $4,852. For part-time students, average financial aid package was $11,673.
**Students without need:** 110 full-time freshmen who did not demonstrate
need for aid received scholarships/grants; average award was $15,590. No-
need awards available for academics, alumni affiliation, art, athletics, leadership, music/drama, religious affiliation, ROTC, state/district residency.
**Scholarships offered: Merit:** Academic Scholarships; $15,000-full tuition.
Departmental and Lutheran Scholarships; amounts vary. **Athletic:** 20 full-
time freshmen received athletic scholarships; average amount $29,485.
**Additional info:** Financial assistance based on need, academic record, talent
available through university.

### FINANCIAL AID PROCEDURES
**Forms required:** FAFSA.
**Dates and Deadlines:** Priority date 3/1; no closing date. Applicants notified
on a rolling basis starting 3/1.
**Transfers:** Transfer students eligible for scholarships based on previous college work. Scholarship amounts vary depending on the GPA at previous institutions.

### CONTACT
Karen Klimczyk, Director of Financial Aid
Kretzmann Hall, 1700 Chapel Drive, Valparaiso, IN 46383-6493
(219) 464-5015

## Vincennes University
Vincennes, Indiana
www.vinu.edu                    Federal Code: 001843

**2-year public** junior college in large town.
**Enrollment:** 7,940 undergrads, 35% part-time. 3,089 full-time freshmen.
**Selectivity:** Open admission; but selective for some programs.

### BASIC COSTS (2015-2016)
**Tuition and fees:** $5,374; out-of-state residents $12,710.
**Per-credit charge:** $171.14; out-of-state residents $415.62.
**Room and board:** $8,732.
**Additional info:** Students from Illinois are charged the in-state tuition rate.

### FINANCIAL AID PICTURE (2014-2015)
**Students with need:** Out of 2,389 full-time freshmen who applied for aid,
2,234 were judged to have need. Of these, 2,234 received aid. Need-based
aid available for part-time students.
**Students without need:** No-need awards available for academics, art, athletics, job skills, leadership, music/drama, state/district residency.
**Scholarships offered:** Presidential Scholarship: $2,500 per year for 4 semes-
ters; SAT score and rank in upper 10% of class; limited in number. Blue &
Gold Scholarship: $1,750 per year for 4 semesters; SAT score and rank in
upper 50% of class; limited number of awards. Indiana Academic Honors/

Technical Honors Diploma: $1,250 per year for 4 semesters. Walters Scholar-
ship: tuition, room and board; for candidates in good standing. Education
Scholarship: for education majors, based on SAT scores and rank in upper
10% of class; 1 awarded. Valedictorian/Salutatorian scholarship: tuition and
housing or tuition and a stipend for commuters.

### FINANCIAL AID PROCEDURES
**Forms required:** FAFSA.
**Dates and Deadlines:** Priority date 3/1; no closing date. Applicants notified
on a rolling basis starting 5/1; must reply by 8/24.
**Transfers:** No deadline. Applicants notified on a rolling basis starting 4/1.
Transfer students must notify the State Student Assistance Commission
within 30 days of start of term.

### CONTACT
Stanley Werne, Director of Financial Aid
1002 North First Street, Vincennes, IN 47591
(812) 888-4361

## Wabash College
Crawfordsville, Indiana
www.wabash.edu                    Federal Code: 001844

**4-year private** liberal arts college for men in large town.
**Enrollment:** 867 undergrads. 238 full-time freshmen.
**Selectivity:** Admits 50 to 75% of applicants.

### BASIC COSTS (2015-2016)
**Tuition and fees:** $39,980.
**Per-credit charge:** $1,639.
**Room and board:** $9,360.

### FINANCIAL AID PICTURE (2015-2016)
**Students with need:** Out of 228 full-time freshmen who applied for aid,
184 were judged to have need. Of these, 183 received aid, and 132 had
their full need met. Average financial aid package met 93% of need; average
scholarship/grant was $28,590; average loan was $3,326. Need-based aid
available for part-time students.
**Students without need:** 15 full-time freshmen who did not demonstrate
need for aid received scholarships/grants; average award was $11,751. No-
need awards available for academics, art, leadership, music/drama.
**Scholarships offered:** Lilly Awards Program: full tuition, room, board, fees;
recognizes outstanding personal achievement and potential for leadership.
Fine Arts Scholarship: up to $15,000; based on creativity/ability; approxi-
mately 16 awarded. Honor Scholarships: up to full tuition; based on competitive exams; approximately 40 awarded. President's Scholarships, Dean's
Scholarships, and Alumni Awards: based on class rank, SAT scores; unlimited number awarded. Awards range from $7,500 to $25,000 per year.

### FINANCIAL AID PROCEDURES
**Forms required:** FAFSA.
**Dates and Deadlines:** Closing date 2/15. Applicants notified by 3/31; must
reply by 5/1 or within 2 week(s) of notification.
**Transfers:** Closing date 2/15. Applicants notified by 3/31; must reply by 5/1
or within 2 week(s) of notification.

### CONTACT
Heidi Carl, Director of Financial Aid
PO Box 352, Crawfordsville, IN 47933
(800) 718-9746

# Iowa

## Allen College
Waterloo, Iowa
www.allencollege.edu          Federal Code: 030691

**4-year private** health science and nursing college in small city.
**Enrollment:** 370 undergrads. 1 full-time freshmen.
**Selectivity:** Admits less than 50% of applicants.

**BASIC COSTS (2015-2016)**
**Tuition and fees:** $19,530.
**Per-credit charge:** $574.
**Room and board:** $7,281.

**FINANCIAL AID PICTURE (2014-2015)**
**Students with need:** Out of 1 full-time freshmen who applied for aid, 1 were judged to have need. Of these, 1 received aid. Average financial aid package met 58% of need; average scholarship/grant was $18,130; average loan was $4,500. For part-time students, average financial aid package was $8,309.
**Students without need:** No-need awards available for academics, leadership, minority status, ROTC.

**FINANCIAL AID PROCEDURES**
**Forms required:** FAFSA, institutional form.
**Dates and Deadlines:** Priority date 5/1; no closing date. Applicants notified on a rolling basis starting 5/1; must reply within 2 week(s) of notification.
**Transfers:** No deadline. Applicants notified on a rolling basis starting 4/1; must reply within 2 week(s) of notification.

**CONTACT**
Kathie Aswegan, Financial Aid Coordinator
1825 Logan Avenue, Waterloo, IA 50703
(319) 226-2003

## Briar Cliff University
Sioux City, Iowa
www.briarcliff.edu          Federal Code: 001846

**4-year private** university and liberal arts college in small city, affiliated with Roman Catholic Church.
**Enrollment:** 942 undergrads, 17% part-time. 206 full-time freshmen.
**Selectivity:** Admits 50 to 75% of applicants.

**BASIC COSTS (2015-2016)**
**Tuition and fees:** $27,910.
**Per-credit charge:** $890.
**Room and board:** $8,124.

**FINANCIAL AID PICTURE (2014-2015)**
**Students with need:** Out of 206 full-time freshmen who applied for aid, 173 were judged to have need. Of these, 173 received aid, and 57 had their full need met. Average financial aid package met 34% of need; average scholarship/grant was $15,058; average loan was $3,865. For part-time students, average financial aid package was $5,072.
**Students without need:** 44 full-time freshmen who did not demonstrate need for aid received scholarships/grants; average award was $1,574. No-need awards available for academics, alumni affiliation, art, athletics, music/drama, religious affiliation.
**Scholarships offered:** *Merit:* Presidential Scholarships; awarded each year for achievement and demonstrated leadership, based on application and on-campus interview; 2-5 awarded. *Athletic:* 159 full-time freshmen received athletic scholarships; average amount $8,145.

**FINANCIAL AID PROCEDURES**
**Forms required:** FAFSA.
**Dates and Deadlines:** Priority date 3/15; no closing date. Applicants notified on a rolling basis starting 3/15; must reply by 5/1 or within 4 week(s) of notification.
**Transfers:** Closing date 3/15.

**CONTACT**
Brian Eben, Assistant Vice President for Enrollment Management
3303 Rebecca Street, Sioux City, IA 51104-2324
(712) 279-5200

## Buena Vista University
Storm Lake, Iowa
www.bvu.edu          Federal Code: 001847

**4-year private** liberal arts college in large town, affiliated with Presbyterian Church (USA).
**Enrollment:** 864 undergrads, 1% part-time. 223 full-time freshmen.
**Selectivity:** Admits 50 to 75% of applicants.

**BASIC COSTS (2015-2016)**
**Tuition and fees:** $31,318.
**Per-credit charge:** $1,053.
**Room and board:** $9,046.

**FINANCIAL AID PICTURE (2015-2016)**
**Students with need:** Out of 201 full-time freshmen who applied for aid, 178 were judged to have need. Of these, 177 received aid, and 36 had their full need met. Average financial aid package met 86% of need; average scholarship/grant was $24,691; average loan was $5,002. For part-time students, average financial aid package was $11,407.
**Students without need:** 45 full-time freshmen who did not demonstrate need for aid received scholarships/grants; average award was $18,956. No-need awards available for academics, art, minority status, music/drama.
**Additional info:** Portfolio required of art scholarship applicants, audition required of music and drama scholarship applicants.

**FINANCIAL AID PROCEDURES**
**Forms required:** FAFSA.
**Dates and Deadlines:** Priority date 6/1; no closing date. Applicants notified on a rolling basis starting 2/15.

**CONTACT**
Leanne Valentine, Director of Financial Assistance
610 West Fourth Street, Storm Lake, IA 50588
(714) 749-2164

## Central College
Pella, Iowa
www.central.edu          Federal Code: 001850

**4-year private** liberal arts college in large town, affiliated with Reformed Church in America.
**Enrollment:** 1,225 undergrads, 1% part-time. 317 full-time freshmen.
**Selectivity:** Admits 50 to 75% of applicants.

**BASIC COSTS (2015-2016)**
**Tuition and fees:** $33,345.
**Per-credit charge:** $1,338.
**Room and board:** $9,980.

**FINANCIAL AID PICTURE (2015-2016)**
**Students with need:** Out of 307 full-time freshmen who applied for aid, 270 were judged to have need. Of these, 270 received aid, and 49 had their full need met. Average financial aid package met 83% of need; average

scholarship/grant was $25,326; average loan was $2,811. For part-time students, average financial aid package was $18,716.

**Students without need:** 85 full-time freshmen who did not demonstrate need for aid received scholarships/grants; average award was $13,177. No-need awards available for academics, alumni affiliation, art, minority status, music/drama, religious affiliation, state/district residency.

**Scholarships offered:** Students may qualify for academic scholarships up to and including three full-tuition scholarships. Funds are also awarded to students who demonstrate skills and talents in a variety of academic areas.

**Additional info:** Funds are awarded to students who qualify as National Merit Finalists.

### FINANCIAL AID PROCEDURES

**Forms required:** FAFSA.

**Dates and Deadlines:** Priority date 3/1; no closing date. Applicants notified on a rolling basis starting 3/1; must reply by 5/1 or within 2 week(s) of notification.

**Transfers:** No deadline. Applicants notified on a rolling basis starting 3/15; must reply by 5/1 or within 2 week(s) of notification. Transfers only eligible for total of 4 years of state funds.

### CONTACT

Wayne Dille, Director of Financial Aid
812 University Street, Pella, IA 50219-1999
(641) 628-5336

## Clarke University
Dubuque, Iowa
www.clarke.edu                    Federal Code: 001852

**4-year private** university and liberal arts college in small city, affiliated with Roman Catholic Church.

**Enrollment:** 861 undergrads, 8% part-time. 174 full-time freshmen.

**Selectivity:** Admits 50 to 75% of applicants.

### BASIC COSTS (2015-2016)

**Tuition and fees:** $29,940.

**Per-credit charge:** $690.

**Room and board:** $9,000.

### FINANCIAL AID PICTURE (2015-2016)

**Students with need:** Out of 168 full-time freshmen who applied for aid, 151 were judged to have need. Of these, 151 received aid, and 45 had their full need met. Average financial aid package met 84% of need; average scholarship/grant was $22,043; average loan was $3,299. For part-time students, average financial aid package was $9,219.

**Students without need:** 23 full-time freshmen who did not demonstrate need for aid received scholarships/grants; average award was $21,863. No-need awards available for academics, alumni affiliation, art, athletics, leadership, music/drama.

**Scholarships offered:** 106 full-time freshmen received athletic scholarships; average amount $5,025.

**Additional info:** Reduced tuition for family members of BVMs.

### FINANCIAL AID PROCEDURES

**Forms required:** FAFSA.

**Dates and Deadlines:** Priority date 4/15; no closing date. Applicants notified on a rolling basis starting 3/15; must reply by 5/1 or within 2 week(s) of notification.

**Transfers:** Applicants notified on a rolling basis starting 3/15; must reply within 2 week(s) of notification.

### CONTACT

Amy Norton, Director of Financial Aid
1550 Clarke Drive, Dubuque, IA 52001-3198
(563) 588-6327

## Clinton Community College
Clinton, Iowa
www.eicc.edu                    Federal Code: 001853

**2-year public** community college in large town.

**Enrollment:** 1,909 undergrads.

**Selectivity:** Open admission; but selective for some programs.

### BASIC COSTS (2015-2016)

**Tuition and fees:** $4,200; out-of-state residents $6,210.

**Per-credit charge:** $140; out-of-state residents $207.

**Additional info:** Online course tuition is $162 per credit hour. Tuition for nearby Illinois counties is $162 per credit hour.

### FINANCIAL AID PICTURE

**Students with need:** Work study available nights.

### FINANCIAL AID PROCEDURES

**Forms required:** FAFSA, institutional form.

**Dates and Deadlines:** Priority date 4/1; no closing date. Applicants notified on a rolling basis starting 5/15; must reply within 2 week(s) of notification.

### CONTACT

Teresa Thiede, Financial Aid Officer
1000 Lincoln Boulevard, Clinton, IA 52732
(563) 244-7070

## Coe College
Cedar Rapids, Iowa
www.coe.edu                    Federal Code: 001854

**4-year private** nursing and liberal arts college in small city, affiliated with Presbyterian Church (USA).

**Enrollment:** 1,338 undergrads, 1% part-time. 377 full-time freshmen.

**Selectivity:** Admits 50 to 75% of applicants.

### BASIC COSTS (2015-2016)

**Tuition and fees:** $39,080.

**Room and board:** $8,510.

**Additional info:** Tuition/fee waivers available for adults.

### FINANCIAL AID PICTURE (2015-2016)

**Students with need:** Out of 353 full-time freshmen who applied for aid, 317 were judged to have need. Of these, 317 received aid, and 63 had their full need met. Average financial aid package met 85% of need; average scholarship/grant was $29,510; average loan was $4,487. For part-time students, average financial aid package was $12,362.

**Students without need:** 57 full-time freshmen who did not demonstrate need for aid received scholarships/grants; average award was $23,438. No-need awards available for academics, alumni affiliation, art, music/drama, ROTC, state/district residency.

**Scholarships offered:** Scholarships for business/economics, music, art, theater, writing, foreign language, science: based on portfolio or audition; available for non-majors except in science and business/economics. Academic Awards: $6,000-$19,000; based on high school achievement.

### FINANCIAL AID PROCEDURES

**Forms required:** FAFSA.

**Dates and Deadlines:** Priority date 3/1; no closing date. Applicants notified on a rolling basis starting 3/15; must reply by 5/1 or within 2 week(s) of notification.

### CONTACT

Barb Hoffman, Director of Financial Aid
1220 First Avenue NE, Cedar Rapids, IA 52402
(319) 399-8540

## Cornell College
Mount Vernon, Iowa
www.cornellcollege.edu          Federal Code: 001856

**4-year private** liberal arts college in small town, affiliated with United Methodist Church.
**Enrollment:** 1,031 undergrads. 276 full-time freshmen.
**Selectivity:** Admits 50 to 75% of applicants.

**BASIC COSTS (2016-2017)**
**Tuition and fees:** $38,925.
**Room and board:** $8,700.

**FINANCIAL AID PICTURE (2015-2016)**
**Students with need:** Out of 239 full-time freshmen who applied for aid, 210 were judged to have need. Of these, 210 received aid, and 49 had their full need met. Average financial aid package met 80% of need; average scholarship/grant was $25,076; average loan was $3,450. For part-time students, average financial aid package was $3,055.
**Students without need:** 65 full-time freshmen who did not demonstrate need for aid received scholarships/grants; average award was $19,675. No-need awards available for academics, alumni affiliation, art, leadership, minority status, music/drama, religious affiliation.

**FINANCIAL AID PROCEDURES**
**Forms required:** FAFSA.
**Dates and Deadlines:** Priority date 3/1; no closing date. Applicants notified on a rolling basis starting 3/1; must reply by 5/1 or within 2 week(s) of notification.
**Transfers:** No deadline. Applicants notified on a rolling basis starting 3/1; must reply by 5/1 or within 2 week(s) of notification.

**CONTACT**
Shannon Amundson, Director of Financial Assistance
600 First Street SW, Mount Vernon, IA 52314-1098
(319) 895-4216

## Des Moines Area Community College
Ankeny, Iowa
www.dmacc.edu          Federal Code: 004589

**2-year public** community college in large town.
**Enrollment:** 12,798 undergrads, 50% part-time. 583 full-time freshmen.
**Selectivity:** Open admission; but selective for some programs.

**BASIC COSTS (2015-2016)**
**Tuition and fees:** $4,290; out-of-state residents $8,580.
**Per-credit charge:** $139; out-of-state residents $278.

**FINANCIAL AID PICTURE**
**Students with need:** Need-based aid available for full-time and part-time students. Work study available nights, weekends, and for part-time students.
**Students without need:** No-need awards available for academics, athletics, state/district residency.
**Scholarships offered:** Foundation Freshmen Scholar Award; full tuition, fees and books for maximum of 15 credit hours per semester based on available funds; open to all high school seniors in top 10% of graduating class.

**FINANCIAL AID PROCEDURES**
**Forms required:** FAFSA.
**Dates and Deadlines:** Priority date 4/1; no closing date. Applicants notified on a rolling basis starting 4/1; must reply within 2 week(s) of notification.

**CONTACT**
DeLores Hawkins, Director of Financial Aid
2006 South Ankeny Boulevard, Ankeny, IA 50023-3993
(515) 964-6282

## Dordt College
Sioux Center, Iowa
www.dordt.edu          Federal Code: 001859

**4-year private** liberal arts college in small town, affiliated with Christian Reformed Church.
**Enrollment:** 1,351 undergrads.
**Selectivity:** Admits 50 to 75% of applicants.

**BASIC COSTS (2015-2016)**
**Tuition and fees:** $28,280.
**Per-credit charge:** $1,160.
**Room and board:** $8,350.
**Additional info:** Tuition/fee waivers available for adults.

**FINANCIAL AID PICTURE (2015-2016)**
**Students with need:** 62% of average financial aid package awarded as scholarships/grants, 38% awarded as loans/jobs. Need-based aid available for part-time students. Work study available nights, weekends, and for part-time students.
**Students without need:** No-need awards available for academics, alumni affiliation, art, athletics, leadership, music/drama, religious affiliation.

**FINANCIAL AID PROCEDURES**
**Forms required:** FAFSA, institutional form.
**Dates and Deadlines:** Priority date 4/1; no closing date. Applicants notified on a rolling basis starting 3/1; must reply within 3 week(s) of notification.
**Transfers:** Closing date 6/1. Applicants notified on a rolling basis starting 10/1.

**CONTACT**
Michael Epema, Director of Financial Aid
498 Fourth Avenue, NE, Sioux Center, IA 51250
(712) 722-6087

## Drake University
Des Moines, Iowa
www.drake.edu          Federal Code: 001860

**4-year private** university in large city.
**Enrollment:** 3,269 undergrads, 3% part-time. 801 full-time freshmen.
**Selectivity:** Admits 50 to 75% of applicants.

**BASIC COSTS (2015-2016)**
**Tuition and fees:** $33,696.
**Room and board:** $9,596.

**FINANCIAL AID PICTURE (2015-2016)**
**Students with need:** Out of 687 full-time freshmen who applied for aid, 546 were judged to have need. Of these, 546 received aid, and 151 had their full need met. Average financial aid package met 76% of need; average scholarship/grant was $19,158; average loan was $3,109. For part-time students, average financial aid package was $10,803.
**Students without need:** 214 full-time freshmen who did not demonstrate need for aid received scholarships/grants; average award was $14,553. No-need awards available for academics, alumni affiliation, art, athletics, minority status, music/drama, ROTC, state/district residency.
**Scholarships offered: Merit:** Drake University Presidential Scholarship; $7,000-$12,000; based on academic merit and awards; unlimited available. National Alumni Scholarship Competition; 6 full-time tuition with room and board and 10 full-time tuition; available to top students. **Athletic:** 27 full-time freshmen received athletic scholarships; average amount $27,188.

**FINANCIAL AID PROCEDURES**
**Forms required:** FAFSA.
**Dates and Deadlines:** Applicants notified on a rolling basis starting 3/1; must reply by 5/1 or within 3 week(s) of notification.

**Transfers:** No deadline. Applicants notified on a rolling basis starting 3/1; must reply by 5/1 or within 2 week(s) of notification. FAFSA must be filed by 7/1 for Iowa Tuition Grant deadline.

**CONTACT**
Christina Marchard, Institutional Research and Academic Compliance Assistant
2507 University Avenue, Des Moines, IA 50311-4505
(515) 271-1865

## Ellsworth Community College
Iowa Falls, Iowa
www.iavalley.cc.ia.us/ecc          Federal Code: 001862

**2-year public** community college in small town.
**Enrollment:** 709 full-time undergrads.
**Selectivity:** Open admission; but selective for some programs.

**BASIC COSTS (2015-2016)**
**Tuition and fees:** $5,520; out-of-state residents $6,480.
**Per-credit charge:** $158; out-of-state residents $190.
**Room and board:** $6,464.
**Additional info:** Tuition/fee waivers available for adults.

**FINANCIAL AID PICTURE**
**Students with need:** Need-based aid available for full-time and part-time students. Work study available nights, weekends, and for part-time students.
**Students without need:** No-need awards available for academics, art, athletics, leadership, minority status, music/drama.
**Scholarships offered:** Academic scholarships; $500-$1,800; based on ACT and GPA; unlimited number offered. Directors Scholarship; $2,300; for those who are 1st or 2nd in class; unlimited number offered.

**FINANCIAL AID PROCEDURES**
**Forms required:** FAFSA, institutional form.
**Dates and Deadlines:** Closing date 4/1. Applicants notified on a rolling basis starting 2/15; must reply within 4 week(s) of notification.
**Transfers:** Priority date 4/15.

**CONTACT**
Tara Miller, Financial Aid Administrator
1100 College Avenue, Iowa Falls, IA 50126
(641) 648-4611 ext. 432

## Emmaus Bible College
Dubuque, Iowa
www.emmaus.edu          Federal Code: 016487

**4-year private** Bible college in small city, affiliated with Brethren Church.
**Enrollment:** 232 undergrads, 4% part-time. 59 full-time freshmen.
**Selectivity:** Admits less than 50% of applicants.

**BASIC COSTS (2016-2017)**
**Tuition and fees:** $16,580.
**Per-credit charge:** $660.
**Room and board:** $7,100.

**FINANCIAL AID PICTURE**
**Students with need:** Need-based aid available for full-time and part-time students.
**Students without need:** No-need awards available for academics, leadership, minority status, music/drama, religious affiliation.

**FINANCIAL AID PROCEDURES**
**Forms required:** FAFSA.
**Dates and Deadlines:** Applicants notified on a rolling basis starting 3/1; must reply within 2 week(s) of notification.

**CONTACT**
Steve Seeman, Financial Aid Director
2570 Asbury Road, Dubuque, IA 52001
(563) 588-8000 ext. 1309

## Faith Baptist Bible College and Theological Seminary
Ankeny, Iowa
www.faith.edu          Federal Code: 007121

**4-year private** Bible and seminary college in large town, affiliated with General Association of Regular Baptist Churches.
**Enrollment:** 227 undergrads.
**Selectivity:** Admits 50 to 75% of applicants.

**BASIC COSTS (2015-2016)**
**Tuition and fees:** $16,600.
**Per-credit charge:** $570.
**Room and board:** $6,732.

**FINANCIAL AID PICTURE**
**Students with need:** Need-based aid available for full-time and part-time students.
**Students without need:** No-need awards available for academics, leadership, music/drama.

**FINANCIAL AID PROCEDURES**
**Forms required:** FAFSA.
**Dates and Deadlines:** Priority date 4/1; no closing date. Applicants notified on a rolling basis starting 3/15.

**CONTACT**
Breck Appell, Financial Assistance Director
1900 NW Fourth Street, Ankeny, IA 50023
(515) 964-0601 ext. 216

## Graceland University
Lamoni, Iowa
www.graceland.edu          Federal Code: 001866

**4-year private** university and liberal arts college in rural community, affiliated with Community of Christ.
**Enrollment:** 1,375 undergrads, 10% part-time. 291 full-time freshmen.
**Selectivity:** Admits less than 50% of applicants.

**BASIC COSTS (2016-2017)**
**Tuition and fees:** $27,010.
**Per-credit charge:** $725.
**Room and board:** $8,280.

**FINANCIAL AID PICTURE (2015-2016)**
**Students with need:** Out of 266 full-time freshmen who applied for aid, 249 were judged to have need. Of these, 248 received aid, and 45 had their full need met. Average financial aid package met 80% of need; average scholarship/grant was $21,114; average loan was $3,694. For part-time students, average financial aid package was $6,540.
**Students without need:** 31 full-time freshmen who did not demonstrate need for aid received scholarships/grants; average award was $15,063. No-need awards available for academics, alumni affiliation, art, athletics, job skills, leadership, music/drama, religious affiliation.
**Scholarships offered:** *Merit:* Study and Faith Scholarship; 50% tuition; for Community of Christ members. Congregational Matching Grants; up to $500 for other faiths. Merit scholarships; up to $14,000; for incoming freshmen based on GPA and ACT/SAT. Fine Arts, Athletic and Computer Science scholarships available. *Athletic:* 40 full-time freshmen received athletic scholarships; average amount $4,953.

**Additional info:** Founders Scholarship will supplement other gift aid until percentage of calculated need has been met.

**FINANCIAL AID PROCEDURES**
**Forms required:** FAFSA.
**Dates and Deadlines:** Applicants notified on a rolling basis starting 2/1; must reply within 2 week(s) of notification.
**Transfers:** No deadline. Applicants notified on a rolling basis; must reply within 2 week(s) of notification.

**CONTACT**
Talia Brown, Director of Enrollment Operations
1 University Place, Lamoni, IA 50140
(866) 472-2352 ext. 2

## Grand View University
Des Moines, Iowa
www.admissions.grandview.edu     Federal Code: 001867

**4-year private** university and liberal arts college in large city, affiliated with Evangelical Lutheran Church in America.
**Enrollment:** 1,889 undergrads, 14% part-time. 267 full-time freshmen.
**Selectivity:** Admits over 75% of applicants.

**BASIC COSTS (2016-2017)**
**Tuition and fees:** $25,474.
**Per-credit charge:** $616.
**Room and board:** $8,172.

**FINANCIAL AID PICTURE (2015-2016)**
**Students with need:** Out of 253 full-time freshmen who applied for aid, 220 were judged to have need. Of these, 220 received aid, and 68 had their full need met. Average financial aid package met 84% of need; average scholarship/grant was $19,812; average loan was $3,955. For part-time students, average financial aid package was $7,398.
**Students without need:** 48 full-time freshmen who did not demonstrate need for aid received scholarships/grants; average award was $9,706. No-need awards available for academics, alumni affiliation, art, athletics, music/drama, religious affiliation, ROTC.
**Scholarships offered:** *Merit:* Presidential Scholarship: $10,000 to full tuition. Dean's Scholarship: $9,000 - $14,000. Director's Award: $8,000 - $12,000. *Athletic:* 169 full-time freshmen received athletic scholarships; average amount $4,923.

**FINANCIAL AID PROCEDURES**
**Dates and Deadlines:** Priority date 3/1; no closing date. Applicants notified on a rolling basis starting 3/1; must reply by 5/1 or within 3 week(s) of notification.
**Transfers:** Priority date 3/1; no deadline. Applicants notified on a rolling basis starting 3/1; must reply by 5/1 or within 3 week(s) of notification.

**CONTACT**
Michele Dunne, Director of Financial Aid
1200 Grandview Avenue, Des Moines, IA 50316-1599
(515) 263-2963

## Grinnell College
Grinnell, Iowa     Federal Code: 001868
www.grinnell.edu     CSS Code: 6252

**4-year private** liberal arts college in small town.
**Enrollment:** 1,667 undergrads. 442 full-time freshmen.
**Selectivity:** Admits less than 50% of applicants.

**BASIC COSTS (2016-2017)**
**Tuition and fees:** $48,758.

**Per-credit charge:** $1,510.
**Room and board:** $11,980.

**FINANCIAL AID PICTURE (2015-2016)**
**Students with need:** Out of 362 full-time freshmen who applied for aid, 306 were judged to have need. Of these, 306 received aid, and 306 had their full need met. Average financial aid package met 100% of need; average scholarship/grant was $37,426; average loan was $3,979. For part-time students, average financial aid package was $7,239.
**Students without need:** 81 full-time freshmen who did not demonstrate need for aid received scholarships/grants; average award was $16,475. No-need awards available for academics, state/district residency.
**Additional info:** Need-blind admission policy, 100% of demonstrated institutional need met for all domestic students, with loan cap programs. Students may apply financial aid to off-campus study programs.

**FINANCIAL AID PROCEDURES**
**Forms required:** FAFSA, CSS PROFILE.
**Dates and Deadlines:** Closing date 2/1. Applicants notified by 4/1; must reply by 5/1.
**Transfers:** Closing date 4/1. Applicants notified by 5/20; must reply by 6/1.

**CONTACT**
Brad Lindberg, Director of Student Financial Aid
1103 Park Street, 2nd Floor, Grinnell, IA 50112-1690
(641) 269-3250

## Hawkeye Community College
Waterloo, Iowa
www.hawkeyecollege.edu     Federal Code: 004595

**2-year public** community and technical college in small city.
**Enrollment:** 3,903 undergrads, 33% part-time. 805 full-time freshmen.
**Selectivity:** Open admission; but selective for some programs.

**BASIC COSTS (2015-2016)**
**Tuition and fees:** $4,785; out-of-state residents $5,535.
**Per-credit charge:** $152; out-of-state residents $177.

**FINANCIAL AID PICTURE**
**Students with need:** Need-based aid available for full-time students. Work study available nights, weekends, and for part-time students.
**Students without need:** No-need awards available for academics, state/district residency.

**FINANCIAL AID PROCEDURES**
**Forms required:** FAFSA.
**Dates and Deadlines:** Priority date 7/1; no closing date. Applicants notified on a rolling basis starting 5/1; must reply within 2 week(s) of notification.

**CONTACT**
Gisella Baker, Director of Financial Aid
Box 8015, Waterloo, IA 50704-8015
(319) 296-4020

## Iowa Central Community College
Fort Dodge, Iowa
www.iowacentral.edu     Federal Code: 004597

**2-year public** community college in large town.
**Enrollment:** 3,454 undergrads, 20% part-time. 1,092 full-time freshmen.
**Selectivity:** Open admission; but selective for some programs.

**BASIC COSTS (2015-2016)**
**Tuition and fees:** $5,130; out-of-state residents $7,275.
**Per-credit charge:** $157; out-of-state residents $229.
**Room and board:** $6,150.

## FINANCIAL AID PICTURE (2015-2016)
**Students with need:** Average financial aid package met 76% of need; average scholarship/grant was $1,167; average loan was $1,610. For part-time students, average financial aid package was $1,390.
**Students without need:** No-need awards available for academics, art, athletics, leadership, music/drama.

## FINANCIAL AID PROCEDURES
**Forms required:** FAFSA.
**Dates and Deadlines:** Priority date 3/15; no closing date. Applicants notified on a rolling basis starting 4/15.

## CONTACT
Darci Bangert, Director of Financial Aid
One Triton Circle, Fort Dodge, IA 50501

# Iowa Lakes Community College
Estherville, Iowa
www.iowalakes.edu                    Federal Code: 001864

**2-year public** community college in small town.
**Enrollment:** 1,307 undergrads, 20% part-time. 530 full-time freshmen.
**Selectivity:** Open admission; but selective for some programs.

## BASIC COSTS (2015-2016)
**Tuition and fees:** $5,322; out-of-state residents $5,652.
**Room and board:** $5,850.

## FINANCIAL AID PICTURE (2014-2015)
**Students with need:** Out of 452 full-time freshmen who applied for aid, 362 were judged to have need. Of these, 360 received aid. Need-based aid available for part-time students.
**Students without need:** This college awards aid only to students with need.
**Scholarships offered:** 95 full-time freshmen received athletic scholarships; average amount $1,856.

## FINANCIAL AID PROCEDURES
**Forms required:** FAFSA, institutional form.
**Dates and Deadlines:** Priority date 4/22; no closing date. Applicants notified on a rolling basis starting 4/15.

## CONTACT
Steve Pelzer, Director of Financial Aid
300 South 18th Street, Estherville, IA 51334-2725
(712) 362-7917

# Iowa State University
Ames, Iowa
www.iastate.edu                    Federal Code: 001869

**4-year public** university in small city.
**Enrollment:** 29,520 undergrads, 5% part-time. 6,013 full-time freshmen.
**Selectivity:** Admits over 75% of applicants.

## BASIC COSTS (2015-2016)
**Tuition and fees:** $7,736; out-of-state residents $20,856.
**Per-credit charge:** $277; out-of-state residents $824.
**Room and board:** $8,070.

## FINANCIAL AID PICTURE (2014-2015)
**Students with need:** Out of 5,091 full-time freshmen who applied for aid, 3,103 were judged to have need. Of these, 3,062 received aid, and 1,075 had their full need met. Average financial aid package met 82% of need; average scholarship/grant was $8,389; average loan was $3,308. For part-time students, average financial aid package was $8,247.

**Students without need:** 2,242 full-time freshmen who did not demonstrate need for aid received scholarships/grants; average award was $3,624. No-need awards available for academics, alumni affiliation, art, athletics, leadership, minority status, music/drama, ROTC, state/district residency.
**Scholarships offered:** 74 full-time freshmen received athletic scholarships; average amount $21,886.
**Additional info:** Short-term loan program available to meet unplanned needs. Financial counseling clinic provides budget and credit education assistance.

## FINANCIAL AID PROCEDURES
**Forms required:** FAFSA.
**Dates and Deadlines:** Priority date 3/1; no closing date. Applicants notified on a rolling basis starting 4/1; must reply by 5/1.
**Transfers:** Priority date 2/15.

## CONTACT
Roberta Johnson, Director of Student Financial Aid
100 Enrollment Services Center, Ames, IA 50011-2011
(515) 294-0066

# Iowa Wesleyan College
Mount Pleasant, Iowa
www.iwc.edu                    Federal Code: 001871

**4-year private** liberal arts college in small town, affiliated with United Methodist Church.
**Enrollment:** 578 undergrads.

## BASIC COSTS (2015-2016)
**Tuition and fees:** $27,286.
**Per-credit charge:** $675.
**Room and board:** $9,576.

## FINANCIAL AID PICTURE
**Students with need:** Need-based aid available for full-time students. Work study available nights, weekends, and for part-time students.
**Students without need:** No-need awards available for academics, alumni affiliation, art, music/drama.
**Scholarships offered:** Unlimited merit based scholarships; based on ACT/SAT and GPA.

## FINANCIAL AID PROCEDURES
**Forms required:** FAFSA.
**Dates and Deadlines:** Priority date 4/1; no closing date. Applicants notified on a rolling basis starting 1/1; must reply within 2 week(s) of notification.
**Transfers:** Applicants notified on a rolling basis.

## CONTACT
Phyllis Whitney, Chief Financial Officer
601 North Main Street, Mount Pleasant, IA 52641-1398
(319) 385-6242

# Iowa Western Community College
Council Bluffs, Iowa
www.iwcc.edu                    Federal Code: 004598

**2-year public** community and technical college in small city.
**Enrollment:** 4,645 undergrads, 29% part-time. 1,586 full-time freshmen.
**Selectivity:** Open admission; but selective for some programs.

## BASIC COSTS (2015-2016)
**Tuition and fees:** $4,888; out-of-state residents $5,038.
**Per-credit charge:** $149; out-of-state residents $154.
**Room and board:** $6,040.

**FINANCIAL AID PICTURE**

**Students with need:** Need-based aid available for full-time and part-time students.

**Students without need:** No-need awards available for athletics, music/drama.

**FINANCIAL AID PROCEDURES**

**Forms required:** FAFSA.

**Dates and Deadlines:** Applicants notified on a rolling basis starting 3/1; must reply within 3 week(s) of notification.

**CONTACT**

Keri Zimmer, Dean of Advising and Academic Success

2700 College Road, Council Bluffs, IA 51502-3004

(800) 432-5852 ext. 3277

## Kaplan University: Cedar Falls
Cedar Falls, Iowa
www.kaplanuniversity.edu/cedar-falls-iowa.aspx
Federal Code: 004586

**4-year for-profit** university and branch campus college in small city.

**Enrollment:** 386 undergrads.

**Selectivity:** Open admission; but selective for some programs.

**BASIC COSTS (2015-2016)**

**Additional info:** Diploma programs: $11,501-$23,410. Associate programs: $30,654-$35,763. Bachelor's programs: $35,763-$66,417.

**FINANCIAL AID PICTURE**

**Students with need:** Need-based aid available for full-time and part-time students. Work study available nights, weekends, and for part-time students.

**Students without need:** This college awards aid only to students with need.

**FINANCIAL AID PROCEDURES**

**Forms required:** FAFSA, institutional form.

**Dates and Deadlines:** Applicants notified on a rolling basis.

**Transfers:** No deadline. Applicants notified on a rolling basis.

**CONTACT**

Amy Kramer, Director of Financial Aid

7009 Nordic Drive, Cedar Falls, IA 50613

## Kaplan University: Cedar Rapids
Cedar Rapids, Iowa
www.kaplanuniversity.edu/cedar-rapids-iowa.aspx
Federal Code: 004220

**2-year for-profit** liberal arts college in small city.

**Enrollment:** 483 undergrads.

**Selectivity:** Open admission; but selective for some programs.

**BASIC COSTS (2015-2016)**

**Additional info:** Diploma programs: $11,501-$23,410. Associate programs: $30,654-$35,763. Bachelor's programs: $35,763-$66,417.

**FINANCIAL AID PICTURE**

**Students with need:** Need-based aid available for full-time and part-time students. Work study available nights, weekends, and for part-time students.

**Students without need:** No-need awards available for academics.

**FINANCIAL AID PROCEDURES**

**Forms required:** FAFSA, institutional form.

**Dates and Deadlines:** Priority date 6/30; no closing date. Applicants notified on a rolling basis.

**Transfers:** Priority date of 07/08 for filing Iowa Tuition Grant application.

**CONTACT**

Robert Brooks, Director of Financial Aid Operations

3165 Edgewood Parkway, SW, Cedar Rapids, IA 52404

## Kaplan University: Davenport
Davenport, Iowa
www.kaplanuniversity.edu/davenport-iowa.aspx
Federal Code: 004586

**4-year for-profit** university in large city.

**Enrollment:** 40,349 undergrads.

**Selectivity:** Open admission; but selective for some programs.

**BASIC COSTS (2015-2016)**

**Additional info:** Diploma programs: $11,501-$23,410. Associate programs: $30,654-$35,763. Bachelor's programs: $35,763-$66,417.

**FINANCIAL AID PICTURE**

**Students with need:** Need-based aid available for full-time and part-time students. Work study available nights.

**Students without need:** No-need awards available for academics.

**FINANCIAL AID PROCEDURES**

**Forms required:** FAFSA, institutional form.

**Dates and Deadlines:** Applicants notified on a rolling basis starting 3/4; must reply by 6/15 or within 2 week(s) of notification.

**CONTACT**

Chris Christopherson, Director of Financial Aid

1801 East Kimberly Road, Suite 1, Davenport, IA 52807-2095

## Kaplan University: Des Moines
Urbandale, Iowa
www.kaplanuniversity.edu/des-moines-iowa.aspx
Federal Code: 004220

**4-year for-profit** university in large city.

**Enrollment:** 780 undergrads.

**Selectivity:** Open admission; but selective for some programs.

**BASIC COSTS (2015-2016)**

**Additional info:** Diploma programs: $11,501-$23,410. Associate programs: $30,654-$35,763. Bachelor's programs: $35,763-$66,417.

**FINANCIAL AID PICTURE**

**Students with need:** Need-based aid available for full-time and part-time students. Work study available nights, weekends, and for part-time students.

**Students without need:** This college awards aid only to students with need.

**FINANCIAL AID PROCEDURES**

**Forms required:** FAFSA, institutional form.

**Dates and Deadlines:** Priority date 6/30; no closing date.

**CONTACT**

Summer Vaselaar, Director of Financial Aid

4655 121st Street, Urbandale, IA 50323

(515) 727-2100

## Kirkwood Community College
Cedar Rapids, Iowa
www.kirkwood.edu
Federal Code: 004076

**2-year public** community college in small city.

**Enrollment:** 9,453 undergrads.

**Selectivity:** Open admission; but selective for some programs.

**BASIC COSTS (2015-2016)**
**Tuition and fees:** $4,490; out-of-state residents $5,390.
**Per-credit charge:** $148; out-of-state residents $178.

**FINANCIAL AID PICTURE**
**Students with need:** Need-based aid available for full-time and part-time students. Work study available nights, weekends, and for part-time students.
**Students without need:** No-need awards available for art, athletics, leadership, music/drama.

**FINANCIAL AID PROCEDURES**
**Forms required:** FAFSA.
**Dates and Deadlines:** Closing date 6/30. Applicants notified on a rolling basis starting 4/1.

**CONTACT**
Jennifer Hughes, Compliance Reporting Manager
6301 Kirkwood Boulevard SW, Cedar Rapids, IA 52404-2068
(319) 398-1274

# Loras College
Dubuque, Iowa
www.loras.edu                    Federal Code: 001873

**4-year private** liberal arts college in small city, affiliated with Roman Catholic Church.
**Enrollment:** 1,444 undergrads, 2% part-time. 389 full-time freshmen.
**Selectivity:** Admits over 75% of applicants.

**BASIC COSTS (2016-2017)**
**Tuition and fees:** $31,525.
**Per-credit charge:** $610.
**Room and board:** $7,697.
**Additional info:** Tuition/fee waivers available for minority students.

**FINANCIAL AID PICTURE (2015-2016)**
**Students with need:** Out of 363 full-time freshmen who applied for aid, 313 were judged to have need. Of these, 313 received aid, and 147 had their full need met. Average financial aid package met 85% of need; average scholarship/grant was $17,682; average loan was $3,855. For part-time students, average financial aid package was $5,422.
**Students without need:** 76 full-time freshmen who did not demonstrate need for aid received scholarships/grants; average award was $19,106. No-need awards available for academics, art.
**Scholarships offered:** Presidential Scholarship: awards up to full tuition for 5 qualified candidates. Breitbach Catholic Thinkers and Leaders Program: selected applicants receive awards of up to $17,000 per year. Loras Merit Award. Pope John Paul II Merit Scholarship. Music Scholarship open to all majors.
**Additional info:** Audition or portfolio recommended for music and art financial aid applicants.

**FINANCIAL AID PROCEDURES**
**Forms required:** FAFSA.
**Dates and Deadlines:** Priority date 4/15; no closing date. Applicants notified on a rolling basis starting 3/1; must reply within 3 week(s) of notification.
**Transfers:** Priority date 3/1; no deadline. Applicants notified on a rolling basis starting 3/1; must reply within 3 week(s) of notification.

**CONTACT**
Julie Dunn, Director of Financial Planning
1450 Alta Vista Street, Dubuque, IA 52001-0178
(563) 588-7136

# Luther College
Decorah, Iowa
www.luther.edu                    Federal Code: 001874

**4-year private** liberal arts college in small town, affiliated with Evangelical Lutheran Church in America.
**Enrollment:** 2,286 undergrads. 623 full-time freshmen.
**Selectivity:** Admits 50 to 75% of applicants.

**BASIC COSTS (2015-2016)**
**Tuition and fees:** $39,190.
**Per-credit charge:** $1,392.
**Room and board:** $7,920.

**FINANCIAL AID PICTURE (2015-2016)**
**Students with need:** Out of 534 full-time freshmen who applied for aid, 456 were judged to have need. Of these, 456 received aid, and 169 had their full need met. Average financial aid package met 89% of need; average scholarship/grant was $24,313; average loan was $4,796. For part-time students, average financial aid package was $24,009.
**Students without need:** 76 full-time freshmen who did not demonstrate need for aid received scholarships/grants; average award was $19,841. No-need awards available for academics, alumni affiliation, art, minority status, music/drama.
**Scholarships offered:** Academic scholarship; $15,000-$19,000; based on class rank and SAT/ACT. National Merit Scholarship; $1,000-$2,000. Diversity Enrichment Scholarship; $2,500-$5,000; awarded to students with broadly diverse and distinctive backgrounds. Church Matching Scholarship; up to $750; for students from member churches. Music scholarship; $2,000-$6,000; plus one scholarship that covers one credit hour of lessons. Legacy Award; $1,000; for children of Luther College alumni. Competitive Nursing scholarship; $1,000; determined by nursing faculty and strength of admission file. Art scholarship; $150-$500; determined by evaluation of portfolio.

**FINANCIAL AID PROCEDURES**
**Forms required:** FAFSA, institutional form.
**Dates and Deadlines:** Priority date 3/1; no closing date. Applicants notified on a rolling basis starting 3/15; must reply by 5/1 or within 4 week(s) of notification.

**CONTACT**
Janice Cordell, Director of Student Financial Planning
700 College Drive, Decorah, IA 52101-1042
(563) 387-1018

# Maharishi University of Management
Fairfield, Iowa
www.mum.edu                    Federal Code: 011113

**4-year private** university and liberal arts college in small town.
**Enrollment:** 344 undergrads, 35% part-time. 21 full-time freshmen.
**Selectivity:** Admits less than 50% of applicants.

**BASIC COSTS (2015-2016)**
**Tuition and fees:** $26,530.
**Room and board:** $7,400.

**FINANCIAL AID PICTURE**
**Students with need:** Need-based aid available for full-time and part-time students. Work study available nights, weekends, and for part-time students.
**Scholarships offered:** Shelley Hoffman Scholarship; $500-$900; applicant must have cerebral palsy, with preference given to students majoring in creative writing; 7 awarded. National Merit Scholarship; full tuition; for NMS finalists; 4 awarded. Ray Prat Scholarship; $500-$1,750; for musically-talented undergraduates; 4 awarded. Girl Scout Gold Award Scholarship; $1,500 renewable; for GS Gold Award recipients; 5 awarded. DeRoy D. Thomas Scholarship; $3,000 each; open to outstanding African American; 1 awarded.

**Additional info:** Students may earn scholarships through volunteer staff program.

### FINANCIAL AID PROCEDURES

**Forms required:** FAFSA.

**Dates and Deadlines:** Priority date 7/15; closing date 7/30. Applicants notified on a rolling basis starting 3/1; must reply within 4 week(s) of notification.

**Transfers:** No deadline. Applicants notified on a rolling basis starting 3/15; must reply within 4 week(s) of notification.

### CONTACT

Dan Wasielewski, Director of Financial Aid
Office of Admissions, Fairfield, IA 52557
(641) 472-1156

## Mercy College of Health Sciences
Des Moines, Iowa
www.mchs.edu                              Federal Code: 006273

**4-year private** health science college in large city, affiliated with Roman Catholic Church.

**Enrollment:** 789 undergrads, 44% part-time. 39 full-time freshmen.

### BASIC COSTS (2015-2016)

**Tuition and fees:** $16,268.
**Per-credit charge:** $563.

### FINANCIAL AID PICTURE

**Students with need:** Need-based aid available for full-time and part-time students. Work study available nights, weekends, and for part-time students.

**Students without need:** No-need awards available for academics, minority status.

### FINANCIAL AID PROCEDURES

**Forms required:** FAFSA.

**Dates and Deadlines:** Priority date 4/15; closing date 7/1. Applicants notified on a rolling basis starting 3/1; must reply within 3 week(s) of notification.

**Transfers:** Priority date 4/15; closing date 7/1. Applicants notified on a rolling basis starting 3/1; must reply within 3 week(s) of notification.

### CONTACT

Joe Brookover, Financial Aid Director
921 Sixth Avenue, Des Moines, IA 50309-1200
(515) 643-6611

## Morningside College
Sioux City, Iowa
www.morningside.edu                       Federal Code: 001879

**4-year private** liberal arts college in small city, affiliated with United Methodist Church.

**Enrollment:** 1,268 undergrads, 2% part-time. 339 full-time freshmen.

**Selectivity:** Admits 50 to 75% of applicants.

### BASIC COSTS (2015-2016)

**Tuition and fees:** $28,155.
**Per-credit charge:** $850.
**Room and board:** $8,710.
**Additional info:** Tuition/fee waivers available for adults.

### FINANCIAL AID PICTURE (2015-2016)

**Students with need:** Need-based aid available for part-time students.

**Students without need:** No-need awards available for academics, alumni affiliation, art, athletics, music/drama, religious affiliation.

**Scholarships offered:** President's Scholarship: $7,500-$12,500; based on 27 ACT and top 10% of class or 3.9 high school GPA. Dean's Scholarship:

$3,000-$7,500; based on 23 ACT or top 20% of class. Mustang Co-Curricular Award: up to $3,000; based on leadership and involvement. National Merit: full tuition. Talent Awards: up to $4,000; based on talents in the areas of art, creative writing, computer technology, mass communications, mock trial, music, and/or theater.

### FINANCIAL AID PROCEDURES

**Forms required:** FAFSA.

**Dates and Deadlines:** Priority date 3/1; no closing date. Applicants notified on a rolling basis starting 3/15.

**Transfers:** No deadline. Applicants notified by 3/1.

### CONTACT

Karen Gagnon, Director Student Financial Planning
1501 Morningside Avenue, Sioux City, IA 51106
(712) 274-5159

## Mount Mercy University
Cedar Rapids, Iowa
www.mtmercy.edu                           Federal Code: 001880

**4-year private** liberal arts college in small city, affiliated with Roman Catholic Church.

**Enrollment:** 1,535 undergrads, 38% part-time. 243 full-time freshmen.

**Selectivity:** Admits 50 to 75% of applicants.

### BASIC COSTS (2015-2016)

**Tuition and fees:** $28,226.
**Per-credit charge:** $768.
**Room and board:** $8,600.

### FINANCIAL AID PICTURE (2015-2016)

**Students with need:** Out of 221 full-time freshmen who applied for aid, 192 were judged to have need. Of these, 191 received aid, and 50 had their full need met. Average financial aid package met 85% of need; average scholarship/grant was $22,373; average loan was $3,460. For part-time students, average financial aid package was $9,687.

**Students without need:** 45 full-time freshmen who did not demonstrate need for aid received scholarships/grants; average award was $16,306. No-need awards available for academics, alumni affiliation, art, athletics, leadership, music/drama, religious affiliation.

**Scholarships offered:** 46 full-time freshmen received athletic scholarships; average amount $4,459.

### FINANCIAL AID PROCEDURES

**Forms required:** FAFSA.

**Dates and Deadlines:** Priority date 3/1; no closing date. Applicants notified on a rolling basis starting 3/15; must reply by 5/1 or within 3 week(s) of notification.

**Transfers:** No deadline. Applicants notified on a rolling basis starting 3/1; must reply within 3 week(s) of notification.

### CONTACT

Bethany Rinderknecht, Director of Financial Aid
1330 Elmhurst Drive NE, Cedar Rapids, IA 52402-4797
(319) 368-6467

## Muscatine Community College
Muscatine, Iowa
www.eicc.edu                              Federal Code: 001882

**2-year public** community college in large town.

**Enrollment:** 1,600 undergrads.

**Selectivity:** Open admission; but selective for some programs.

## BASIC COSTS (2015-2016)

**Tuition and fees:** $4,200; out-of-state residents $6,210.

**Per-credit charge:** $140; out-of-state residents $207.

**Room only:** $4,570.

**Additional info:** Online course tuition is $162 per credit hour.

## FINANCIAL AID PICTURE

**Students with need:** Work study available nights.

## FINANCIAL AID PROCEDURES

**Forms required:** FAFSA.

**Dates and Deadlines:** Priority date 4/20; no closing date. Applicants notified on a rolling basis starting 5/15; must reply within 2 week(s) of notification.

## CONTACT

Robin Jennings, Financial Aid Officer

152 Colorado Street, Muscatine, IA 52761-5396

(563) 288-6060

# North Iowa Area Community College
Mason City, Iowa

www.niacc.edu                    Federal Code: 001877

**2-year public** community college in large town.

**Enrollment:** 1,930 undergrads. 540 full-time freshmen.

**Selectivity:** Open admission; but selective for some programs.

## BASIC COSTS (2015-2016)

**Tuition and fees:** $4,792; out-of-state residents $6,798.

**Room and board:** $6,518.

## FINANCIAL AID PICTURE (2014-2015)

**Students with need:** Out of 490 full-time freshmen who applied for aid, 380 were judged to have need. Of these, 380 received aid, and 95 had their full need met. Average financial aid package met 25% of need; average scholarship/grant was $4,415; average loan was $2,499. For part-time students, average financial aid package was $5,673.

**Students without need:** No-need awards available for academics, art, athletics, leadership.

## FINANCIAL AID PROCEDURES

**Forms required:** FAFSA, institutional form.

**Dates and Deadlines:** Priority date 3/1; no closing date. Applicants notified on a rolling basis starting 4/1; must reply within 2 week(s) of notification.

## CONTACT

Mary Bloomingdale, Director of Financial Aid

500 College Drive, Mason City, IA 50401

(641) 422-4351

# Northeast Iowa Community College
Calmar, Iowa

www.nicc.edu                    Federal Code: 004587

**2-year public** community college in rural community.

**Enrollment:** 2,431 undergrads, 43% part-time. 494 full-time freshmen.

**Selectivity:** Open admission; but selective for some programs.

## BASIC COSTS (2015-2016)

**Tuition and fees:** $5,010; out-of-state residents $5,010.

**Per-credit charge:** $154.

## FINANCIAL AID PICTURE

**Students with need:** Need-based aid available for full-time and part-time students. Work study available nights, weekends, and for part-time students.

**Students without need:** No-need awards available for academics, leadership, state/district residency.

## FINANCIAL AID PROCEDURES

**Forms required:** FAFSA.

**Dates and Deadlines:** Priority date 7/1; no closing date. Applicants notified on a rolling basis starting 5/1.

**Transfers:** No deadline. Applicants notified on a rolling basis; must reply within 2 week(s) of notification.

## CONTACT

Jeff Murphy, Director of Financial Aid

PO Box 400, Calmar, IA 52132

(563) 526-3263 ext. 447

# Northwest Iowa Community College
Sheldon, Iowa

www.nwicc.edu                    Federal Code: 004600

**2-year public** community college in small town.

**Enrollment:** 775 undergrads.

**Selectivity:** Open admission; but selective for some programs.

## BASIC COSTS (2015-2016)

**Tuition and fees:** $5,550; out-of-state residents $5,850.

**Per-credit charge:** $150; out-of-state residents $160.

**Room and board:** $4,942.

## FINANCIAL AID PICTURE

**Students with need:** Need-based aid available for full-time and part-time students.

## FINANCIAL AID PROCEDURES

**Forms required:** FAFSA, institutional form.

**Dates and Deadlines:** Priority date 4/1; no closing date. Applicants notified on a rolling basis starting 5/1.

## CONTACT

Karna Hofmeyer, Financial Aid Director

603 West Park Street, Sheldon, IA 51201

(712) 324-5061 ext. 138

# Northwestern College
Orange City, Iowa

www.nwciowa.edu                    Federal Code: 001883

**4-year private** liberal arts college in small town, affiliated with Reformed Church in America.

**Enrollment:** 1,084 undergrads, 3% part-time. 260 full-time freshmen.

**Selectivity:** Admits 50 to 75% of applicants.

## BASIC COSTS (2015-2016)

**Tuition and fees:** $28,950.

**Room and board:** $8,750.

**Additional info:** Tuition/fee waivers available for adults.

## FINANCIAL AID PICTURE (2015-2016)

**Students with need:** Out of 231 full-time freshmen who applied for aid, 181 were judged to have need. Of these, 181 received aid, and 117 had their full need met. Average financial aid package met 94% of need; average scholarship/grant was $6,370; average loan was $4,322. For part-time students, average financial aid package was $8,416.

**Students without need:** 77 full-time freshmen who did not demonstrate need for aid received scholarships/grants; average award was $12,771. No-need awards available for academics, alumni affiliation, art, athletics, music/drama, religious affiliation, state/district residency.

**Scholarships offered:** 53 full-time freshmen received athletic scholarships; average amount $5,141.

## FINANCIAL AID PROCEDURES

**Forms required:** FAFSA.

**Dates and Deadlines:** Priority date 4/1; closing date 6/30. Applicants notified on a rolling basis starting 3/15; must reply within 3 week(s) of notification.

**Transfers:** No deadline. Applicants notified on a rolling basis starting 3/1. Financial aid transcript required for aid.

## CONTACT

Eric Anderson, Director of Financial Aid
101 Seventh Street SW, Orange City, IA 51041
(712) 707-7131

# St. Ambrose University
Davenport, Iowa
www.sau.edu                          Federal Code: 001889

**4-year private** university and business college in small city, affiliated with Roman Catholic Church.

**Enrollment:** 2,499 undergrads, 10% part-time. 445 full-time freshmen.

**Selectivity:** Admits 50 to 75% of applicants.

## BASIC COSTS (2015-2016)

**Tuition and fees:** $28,380.

**Per-credit charge:** $866.

**Room and board:** $9,582.

**Additional info:** Tuition/fee waivers available for adults.

## FINANCIAL AID PICTURE (2015-2016)

**Students with need:** Average financial aid package met 71% of need; average scholarship/grant was $17,687; average loan was $3,352. For part-time students, average financial aid package was $7,663.

**Students without need:** 75 full-time freshmen who did not demonstrate need for aid received scholarships/grants; average award was $13,492. No-need awards available for academics, alumni affiliation, art, athletics, minority status, music/drama, religious affiliation.

**Scholarships offered: *Merit:*** Ambrose Scholarship; 4.0 GPA and 30 ACT or 1320 SAT required. Presidential Scholarship; 3.8 GPA and ACT 26-29 or SAT 1170-1319 required. SAT scores listed are exclusive of Writing. ***Athletic:*** 42 full-time freshmen received athletic scholarships; average amount $3,915.

**Additional info:** Iowa applicants must apply for financial aid by July 1. Audition required for music, drama scholarship applicants.

## FINANCIAL AID PROCEDURES

**Forms required:** FAFSA.

**Dates and Deadlines:** Priority date 3/16; no closing date. Applicants notified on a rolling basis starting 2/1; must reply within 2 week(s) of notification.

**Transfers:** No deadline. Must reply within 2 week(s) of notification.

## CONTACT

Julie Haack, Director of Financial Aid
518 West Locust Street, Davenport, IA 52803-2898
(563) 333-6000

# St. Luke's College
Sioux City, Iowa
www.stlukescollege.edu               Federal Code: 007291

**2-year private** health science and nursing college in small city.

**Enrollment:** 245 undergrads, 46% part-time. 5 full-time freshmen.

**Selectivity:** Admits over 75% of applicants.

## BASIC COSTS (2016-2017)

**Tuition and fees:** $20,460.

**Per-credit charge:** $525.

## FINANCIAL AID PICTURE (2015-2016)

**Students with need:** Average financial aid package met 75% of need; average scholarship/grant was $3,096; average loan was $4,250. For part-time students, average financial aid package was $15,862.

**Students without need:** No-need awards available for academics, job skills, leadership.

## FINANCIAL AID PROCEDURES

**Forms required:** FAFSA.

**Dates and Deadlines:** Priority date 3/1; no closing date. Applicants notified on a rolling basis starting 4/15; must reply within 2 week(s) of notification.

## CONTACT

Danelle Johannsen, Department Chair, Student and Administrative Services
2800 Pierce Street Suite 410, Sioux City, IA 51104
(712) 279-3377

# Simpson College
Indianola, Iowa
www.simpson.edu                      Federal Code: 001887

**4-year private** liberal arts college in large town, affiliated with United Methodist Church.

**Enrollment:** 1,602 undergrads, 11% part-time. 322 full-time freshmen.

**Selectivity:** Admits over 75% of applicants.

## BASIC COSTS (2015-2016)

**Tuition and fees:** $34,175.

**Per-credit charge:** $380.

**Room and board:** $7,963.

**Additional info:** Tuition/fee waivers available for adults, minority students.

## FINANCIAL AID PICTURE (2015-2016)

**Students with need:** Out of 322 full-time freshmen who applied for aid, 267 were judged to have need. Of these, 267 received aid, and 62 had their full need met. Average financial aid package met 83% of need; average scholarship/grant was $23,831; average loan was $4,842. For part-time students, average financial aid package was $5,628.

**Students without need:** 53 full-time freshmen who did not demonstrate need for aid received scholarships/grants; average award was $20,406. No-need awards available for academics, alumni affiliation, art, leadership, minority status, music/drama, religious affiliation.

**Scholarships offered:** Wesley Service Scholarship; $500 per year; students commit to serve 80 hours of community service a year, keep service journal, read assigned readings, and attend monthly service reflection meetings; number of awards varies. George Washington Carver Scholarship; $15,000 to three-quarters tuition per year; for outstanding freshmen from distinctive and broadly diverse backgrounds who bring in a multicultural perspective; number of awards varies. George Washington Carver Fellowship; 3/4 to full tuition; awarded to outstanding freshmen from distinctive and broadly diverse backgrounds who exhibit potential for leadership and service. John C. Culver Fellowship; range from $16,000 - $20,000 per year, awarded to students who show interest in politics, history, or public service; number of awards varies. Iowa History Center Distinguished Scholarship; range from $16,000 - $20,000 per year, awarded to students who have an interest in Iowa history and the work needed to preserve and promote the history of both the Midwest and the state of Iowa; up to five awarded annually.

**Additional info:** Music and theater scholarships based on audition. Art scholarships based on portfolio.

## FINANCIAL AID PROCEDURES

**Forms required:** FAFSA.

**Dates and Deadlines:** Priority date 4/1; no closing date. Applicants notified on a rolling basis starting 3/15; must reply by 5/1 or within 3 week(s) of notification.

**Transfers:** No deadline. Applicants notified on a rolling basis.

**CONTACT**
Tracie Pavon, Assistant Vice President for Enrollment and Financial Assistance
701 North C Street, Indianola, IA 50125
(515) 961-1630

## Southeastern Community College
West Burlington, Iowa
www.scciowa.edu                    Federal Code: 004603

**2-year public** community and junior college in large town.
**Enrollment:** 1,732 undergrads, 29% part-time. 361 full-time freshmen.
**Selectivity:** Open admission; but selective for some programs.

**BASIC COSTS (2015-2016)**
**Tuition and fees:** $5,000; out-of-state residents $5,150.
**Per-credit charge:** $165; out-of-state residents $170.
**Room and board:** $6,216.

**FINANCIAL AID PICTURE (2015-2016)**
**Students with need:** Out of 316 full-time freshmen who applied for aid, 297 were judged to have need. Of these, 293 received aid. Need-based aid available for part-time students.
**Students without need:** 7 full-time freshmen who did not demonstrate need for aid received scholarships/grants; average award was $2,250. No-need awards available for academics, art, athletics, minority status.
**Scholarships offered:** 6 full-time freshmen received athletic scholarships; average amount $4,194.

**FINANCIAL AID PROCEDURES**
**Forms required:** FAFSA.
**Dates and Deadlines:** Applicants notified on a rolling basis starting 3/1; must reply within 4 week(s) of notification.

**CONTACT**
Gwen Scholer, Financial Aid Director
1500 West Agency Road, West Burlington, IA 52655-0605
(319) 752-2731 ext. 5014

## Southwestern Community College
Creston, Iowa
www.swcciowa.edu                    Federal Code: 001857

**2-year public** community college in small town.
**Enrollment:** 935 undergrads.
**Selectivity:** Open admission; but selective for some programs.

**BASIC COSTS (2015-2016)**
**Tuition and fees:** $4,920; out-of-state residents $5,130.
**Per-credit charge:** $152; out-of-state residents $159.
**Room and board:** $6,450.

**FINANCIAL AID PICTURE (2014-2015)**
**Students with need:** 58% of average financial aid package awarded as scholarships/grants, 42% awarded as loans/jobs. Need-based aid available for part-time students. Work study available nights, weekends, and for part-time students.
**Students without need:** No-need awards available for academics, athletics, leadership, music/drama, state/district residency.

**FINANCIAL AID PROCEDURES**
**Forms required:** FAFSA.
**Dates and Deadlines:** Closing date 7/1. Applicants notified on a rolling basis starting 6/1; must reply within 2 week(s) of notification.
**Transfers:** Applicants notified on a rolling basis starting 6/1; must reply within 2 week(s) of notification.

**CONTACT**
Rebecca Slick, Financial Aid Officer
1501 West Townline Street, Creston, IA 50801
(641) 782-1333

## University of Dubuque
Dubuque, Iowa
www.dbq.edu                    Federal Code: 001891

**4-year private** university and seminary college in small city, affiliated with Presbyterian Church (USA).
**Enrollment:** 1,834 undergrads, 11% part-time. 440 full-time freshmen.
**Selectivity:** Admits over 75% of applicants.

**BASIC COSTS (2015-2016)**
**Tuition and fees:** $27,895.
**Room and board:** $9,070.

**FINANCIAL AID PICTURE (2015-2016)**
**Students with need:** Average financial aid package met 74% of need; average scholarship/grant was $17,272; average loan was $7,446. For part-time students, average financial aid package was $9,201.
**Students without need:** No-need awards available for academics, alumni affiliation, leadership, music/drama, religious affiliation, ROTC.

**FINANCIAL AID PROCEDURES**
**Forms required:** FAFSA.
**Dates and Deadlines:** Priority date 4/1; no closing date. Applicants notified on a rolling basis starting 3/1; must reply within 3 week(s) of notification.
**Transfers:** No deadline. Applicants notified on a rolling basis starting 3/1; must reply within 3 week(s) of notification. Iowa Tuition Grant available to Iowa residents.

**CONTACT**
Timothy Kremer, Dean of Student Financial Planning and Scholarships
2000 University Avenue, Dubuque, IA 52001-5099
(563) 589-3396

## University of Iowa
Iowa City, Iowa
www.uiowa.edu                    Federal Code: 001892

**4-year public** university in small city.
**Enrollment:** 21,927 undergrads, 10% part-time. 4,343 full-time freshmen.
**Selectivity:** Admits over 75% of applicants.

**BASIC COSTS (2015-2016)**
**Tuition and fees:** $8,104; out-of-state residents $27,890.
**Per-credit charge:** $279; out-of-state residents $1,103.
**Room and board:** $9,728.

**FINANCIAL AID PICTURE (2014-2015)**
**Students with need:** Out of 3,333 full-time freshmen who applied for aid, 2,214 were judged to have need. Of these, 2,214 received aid, and 774 had their full need met. Average financial aid package met 70% of need; average scholarship/grant was $8,695; average loan was $4,310. For part-time students, average financial aid package was $8,608.
**Students without need:** 727 full-time freshmen who did not demonstrate need for aid received scholarships/grants; average award was $4,714. No-need awards available for academics, alumni affiliation, art, athletics, leadership, music/drama, ROTC, state/district residency.
**Scholarships offered:** *Merit:* Presidential Scholarship; $13,000 per year for 4 years; based on ACT/SAT, GPA, essay; 20 awarded each year. Old Gold Scholarship; $3,000 per year for 4 years; 30 ACT/1330 SAT and 3.8 GPA

required. National Scholars Award; $4,490 per year for 4 years; for nonresidents who are U.S residents or permanent residents with a Regent Admission Index score of 290. Iowa Scholars Award; $1,000 one-time award; for first-year Iowa residents with 27 ACT/1210 SAT and 3.8 GPA or 30 ACT/1330 SAT and 3.7 GPA. Iowa Heritage Award; $1,500 per year for up to four years; for nonresident students who have a parent, step-parent, legal guardian, or grandparent who graduated from UI. Advantage Iowa Award; from $2,000 to full resident tuition; for first-year students who are U.S. citizens or permanent residents whose enrollment will contribute to a diverse learning environment; eligibility criteria vary, but may include race/ethnicity, socioeconomic factors, first-generation college student, participation in federal Upward Bound program. *Athletic:* 181 full-time freshmen received athletic scholarships; average amount $14,745.

**FINANCIAL AID PROCEDURES**
**Forms required:** FAFSA, institutional form.
**Dates and Deadlines:** Priority date 3/1; no closing date. Applicants notified on a rolling basis starting 3/1; must reply by 5/1 or within 2 week(s) of notification.
**Transfers:** No deadline. Applicants notified on a rolling basis starting 3/15; must reply by 5/1 or within 2 week(s) of notification.

**CONTACT**
Mark Warner, Director of Student Financial Aid
107 Calvin Hall, Iowa City, IA 52242-1396
(319) 335-1450

# University of Northern Iowa
Cedar Falls, Iowa
www.uni.edu                           Federal Code: 001890

**4-year public** university in small city.
**Enrollment:** 9,934 undergrads, 9% part-time. 1,762 full-time freshmen.
**Selectivity:** Admits over 75% of applicants.

**BASIC COSTS (2015-2016)**
**Tuition and fees:** $7,817; out-of-state residents $18,005.
**Per-credit charge:** $277; out-of-state residents $702.
**Room and board:** $8,320.

**FINANCIAL AID PICTURE (2014-2015)**
**Students with need:** Out of 1,520 full-time freshmen who applied for aid, 1,036 were judged to have need. Of these, 1,010 received aid, and 196 had their full need met. Average financial aid package met 68% of need; average scholarship/grant was $4,866; average loan was $3,225. For part-time students, average financial aid package was $6,913.
**Students without need:** 368 full-time freshmen who did not demonstrate need for aid received scholarships/grants; average award was $3,165. No-need awards available for academics, alumni affiliation, art, athletics, leadership, minority status, music/drama, ROTC, state/district residency.
**Scholarships offered:** *Merit:* Presidential Scholarship Award; $8,000/year for up to 4 years; must be in upper 10% of high school class with 29 ACT or Regent Admission Index of 335 and involved in leadership and service activities; 20 available. Distinguished Scholar Award for Iowans; $1,000-$2,500/year, renewable for a 2nd year; for Iowa residents with 28 ACT or Regent Admission Index of 300. *Athletic:* 38 full-time freshmen received athletic scholarships; average amount $6,522.

**FINANCIAL AID PROCEDURES**
**Forms required:** FAFSA.
**Dates and Deadlines:** Applicants notified on a rolling basis starting 3/15.

**CONTACT**
Joyce Morrow, Director Financial Aid and Student Employment
1227 West 27th Street, Cedar Falls, IA 50614-0018
(319) 273-2700

# Upper Iowa University
Fayette, Iowa
www.uiu.edu                           Federal Code: 001893

**4-year private** university and liberal arts college in rural community.
**Enrollment:** 4,022 undergrads, 39% part-time. 433 full-time freshmen.
**Selectivity:** Admits 50 to 75% of applicants.

**BASIC COSTS (2015-2016)**
**Tuition and fees:** $28,138.
**Per-credit charge:** $421.
**Room and board:** $8,058.

**FINANCIAL AID PICTURE (2014-2015)**
**Students with need:** Out of 232 full-time freshmen who applied for aid, 222 were judged to have need. Of these, 221 received aid, and 37 had their full need met. Average financial aid package met 65% of need; average scholarship/grant was $16,563; average loan was $2,610. For part-time students, average financial aid package was $7,186.
**Students without need:** 207 full-time freshmen who did not demonstrate need for aid received scholarships/grants; average award was $13,017. No-need awards available for academics, alumni affiliation, athletics.

**FINANCIAL AID PROCEDURES**
**Forms required:** FAFSA.
**Dates and Deadlines:** Priority date 3/1; no closing date. Applicants notified on a rolling basis starting 3/1; must reply within 9 week(s) of notification.
**Transfers:** No deadline. Applicants notified on a rolling basis starting 7/1; must reply within 8 week(s) of notification.

**CONTACT**
Linda Gebel, Controller
Parker Fox Hall, Fayette, IA 52142
(800) 553-4150 ext. 3

# Vatterott College: Des Moines
Des Moines, Iowa
www.vatterott-college.edu            Federal Code: 026092

**2-year for-profit** health science and technical college in large city.
**Enrollment:** 239 undergrads.
**Selectivity:** Open admission.

**BASIC COSTS (2015-2016)**
**Additional info:** Certificate program: (5 weeks) $4,250. Diploma programs: (40 weeks) $20,384-$21,500; (50 weeks) $24,440. Associate programs: (70 weeks) $31,260-$39,090; (80 weeks) $38,280. Costs include fees, books and supplies.

**FINANCIAL AID PICTURE**
**Students with need:** Need-based aid available for full-time students.
**Students without need:** This college awards aid only to students with need.
**Scholarships offered:** Make the Grade Scholarship; up to $1,000; based on final semester grades; available for 1 year after high school graduation.

**FINANCIAL AID PROCEDURES**
**Forms required:** FAFSA.
**Dates and Deadlines:** Applicants notified on a rolling basis.

**CONTACT**
Afton Erdmann, Financial Aid Administrator
7000 Fleur Drive, Des Moines, IA 50321
(515) 309-9000

## Waldorf University

Forest City, Iowa
www.waldorf.edu
Federal Code: 001895

**4-year private** liberal arts college in small town, affiliated with Evangelical Lutheran Church in America.
**Enrollment:** 1,764 undergrads, 21% part-time. 202 full-time freshmen.
**Selectivity:** Admits 50 to 75% of applicants.

### BASIC COSTS (2015-2016)
**Tuition and fees:** $20,884.
**Per-credit charge:** $550.
**Room and board:** $6,994.

### FINANCIAL AID PICTURE (2015-2016)
**Students with need:** Average financial aid package met 70% of need; average scholarship/grant was $15,383; average loan was $4,218. For part-time students, average financial aid package was $5,566.
**Students without need:** No-need awards available for academics, alumni affiliation, athletics, job skills, leadership, music/drama, religious affiliation, state/district residency.

### FINANCIAL AID PROCEDURES
**Forms required:** FAFSA, institutional form.
**Dates and Deadlines:** Priority date 3/1; no closing date. Applicants notified on a rolling basis starting 3/1; must reply within 2 week(s) of notification.
**Transfers:** Applicants notified on a rolling basis starting 3/1; must reply within 2 week(s) of notification.

### CONTACT
Duane Polsdofer, Director of Student Financial Aid
106 South Sixth Street, Forest City, IA 50436-1713
(641) 585-8120

## Wartburg College

Waverly, Iowa
www.wartburg.edu
Federal Code: 001896

**4-year private** liberal arts college in small town, affiliated with Evangelical Lutheran Church in America.
**Enrollment:** 1,537 undergrads, 4% part-time. 461 full-time freshmen.
**Selectivity:** Admits 50 to 75% of applicants.

### BASIC COSTS (2015-2016)
**Tuition and fees:** $37,190.
**Room and board:** $9,010.

### FINANCIAL AID PICTURE (2014-2015)
**Students with need:** Out of 409 full-time freshmen who applied for aid, 357 were judged to have need. Of these, 357 received aid, and 72 had their full need met. Average financial aid package met 84% of need; average scholarship/grant was $23,885; average loan was $4,658. For part-time students, average financial aid package was $8,352.
**Students without need:** 99 full-time freshmen who did not demonstrate need for aid received scholarships/grants; average award was $19,774. No-need awards available for academics, alumni affiliation, leadership, music/drama, religious affiliation.
**Scholarships offered:** Regents scholarship; up to full tuition, fees, room and board; based on 28 ACT (1240 SAT, exclusive of Writing) or rank in top 10% of class; renewable for 4 years with 3.0 GPA. Presidential Scholarship; up to $6,000 per year; based on 25 ACT (1140 SAT, exclusive of Writing) or rank in top 20% of class or 3.5 GPA; renewable for 4 years with 2.7 GPA. Students who participate in Regents Scholarship competition not eligible for Presidential Scholarship.

### FINANCIAL AID PROCEDURES
**Forms required:** FAFSA.

**Dates and Deadlines:** Priority date 3/1; no closing date. Applicants notified on a rolling basis starting 3/1; must reply within 2 week(s) of notification.

### CONTACT
Jennifer Sassman, Director of Financial Aid
100 Wartburg Boulevard, PO Box 1003, Waverly, IA 50677-0903
(319) 352-8262

## Western Iowa Tech Community College

Sioux City, Iowa
www.witcc.edu
Federal Code: 004590

**2-year public** community college in small city.
**Enrollment:** 3,288 undergrads.
**Selectivity:** Open admission; but selective for some programs.

### BASIC COSTS (2015-2016)
**Tuition and fees:** $5,130; out-of-state residents $5,160.
**Per-credit charge:** $139; out-of-state residents $140.
**Room and board:** $4,800.

### FINANCIAL AID PICTURE
**Students with need:** Need-based aid available for full-time and part-time students. Work study available nights, weekends, and for part-time students.
**Students without need:** No-need awards available for academics, art, leadership, minority status, music/drama.

### FINANCIAL AID PROCEDURES
**Forms required:** FAFSA.
**Dates and Deadlines:** Applicants notified on a rolling basis starting 4/1.

### CONTACT
Le Ann Hoffman, Director of Financial Aid
Box 5199, Sioux City, IA 51102-5199
(712) 274-6402

## William Penn University

Oskaloosa, Iowa
www.wmpenn.edu
Federal Code: 001900

**4-year private** university and liberal arts college in large town, affiliated with Society of Friends (Quaker).
**Enrollment:** 1,464 undergrads, 7% part-time. 221 full-time freshmen.
**Selectivity:** Admits 50 to 75% of applicants.

### BASIC COSTS (2015-2016)
**Tuition and fees:** $23,930.
**Per-credit charge:** $450.
**Room and board:** $6,544.

### FINANCIAL AID PICTURE (2014-2015)
**Students with need:** Out of 197 full-time freshmen who applied for aid, 164 were judged to have need. Of these, 164 received aid. Need-based aid available for part-time students.
**Students without need:** No-need awards available for academics, alumni affiliation, athletics, leadership, music/drama, religious affiliation.
**Scholarships offered:** Participation awards for music, drama, media, cheerleading, dance, religious leadership. Academic scholarships; based on high school GPA and ACT/SAT.

### FINANCIAL AID PROCEDURES
**Forms required:** FAFSA.
**Dates and Deadlines:** Priority date 7/1; no closing date. Applicants notified on a rolling basis starting 1/1; must reply within 3 week(s) of notification.
**Transfers:** No deadline. Applicants notified on a rolling basis starting 1/1.

## CONTACT

Cyndi Peiffer, Director of Financial Aid
201 Trueblood Avenue, Oskaloosa, IA 52577
(641) 673-1060

# Kansas

## Allen County Community College

Iola, Kansas
www.allencc.edu                    Federal Code: 001901

**2-year public** community college in small town.
**Enrollment:** 2,854 undergrads.
**Selectivity:** Open admission.

### BASIC COSTS (2015-2016)

**Tuition and fees:** $2,250; out-of-district residents $2,250; out-of-state residents $2,250.
**Per-credit charge:** $57; out-of-district residents $57; out-of-state residents $57.
**Room and board:** $4,550.

### FINANCIAL AID PICTURE

**Students with need:** Need-based aid available for full-time and part-time students. Work study available nights, weekends, and for part-time students.
**Students without need:** No-need awards available for academics, art, athletics, music/drama, state/district residency.
**Additional info:** Scholarships for livestock judging, cheerleading, choir, dance, drama, art, academic challenge, and student ambassadors.

### FINANCIAL AID PROCEDURES

**Forms required:** FAFSA.
**Dates and Deadlines:** Closing date 6/1. Applicants notified on a rolling basis starting 6/1; must reply within 2 week(s) of notification.
**Transfers:** Priority date 4/1. Applicants notified on a rolling basis starting 3/1.

### CONTACT

Vicki Curry, Director of Financial Aid
1801 North Cottonwood, Iola, KS 66749
(620) 365-5116 ext. 221

## Baker University

Baldwin City, Kansas
www.bakeru.edu                    Federal Code: 001903

**4-year private** liberal arts and teachers college in small town, affiliated with United Methodist Church.
**Enrollment:** 793 undergrads, 1% part-time. 182 full-time freshmen.
**Selectivity:** Admits over 75% of applicants.

### BASIC COSTS (2015-2016)

**Tuition and fees:** $30,080.
**Per-credit charge:** $810.
**Room and board:** $8,270.
**Additional info:** Tuition/fee waivers available for minority students.

### FINANCIAL AID PICTURE (2015-2016)

**Students with need:** Need-based aid available for part-time students.
**Students without need:** No-need awards available for academics, alumni affiliation, art, athletics, music/drama, religious affiliation.

### FINANCIAL AID PROCEDURES

**Forms required:** FAFSA.

---

**Dates and Deadlines:** Priority date 3/1; no closing date. Applicants notified on a rolling basis starting 3/1; must reply within 6 week(s) of notification.
**Transfers:** No deadline. Applicants notified on a rolling basis starting 3/1; must reply within 6 week(s) of notification.

### CONTACT

Jeanne Mott, Senior Director of Financial Aid
618 Eighth Street, Baldwin City, KS 66006-0065
(785) 594-4595

## Barclay College

Haviland, Kansas
www.barclaycollege.edu                    Federal Code: 001917

**4-year private** Bible college in rural community, affiliated with Society of Friends (Quaker).
**Enrollment:** 233 undergrads, 19% part-time. 37 full-time freshmen.
**Selectivity:** Admits 50 to 75% of applicants.

### BASIC COSTS (2015-2016)

**Tuition and fees:** $14,990.
**Per-credit charge:** $295.
**Room and board:** $8,000.

### FINANCIAL AID PICTURE

**Students with need:** Need-based aid available for full-time and part-time students. Work study available nights, weekends, and for part-time students.
**Students without need:** No-need awards available for academics, alumni affiliation, leadership, music/drama, state/district residency.

### FINANCIAL AID PROCEDURES

**Forms required:** FAFSA, institutional form.
**Dates and Deadlines:** Priority date 5/31; closing date 7/15. Applicants notified on a rolling basis starting 1/1; must reply within 4 week(s) of notification.

### CONTACT

Ryan Haase, Director of Student Financial Services
607 North Kingman, Haviland, KS 67059
(620) 862-5252 ext. 41

## Barton County Community College

Great Bend, Kansas
www.bartonccc.edu                    Federal Code: 004608

**2-year public** community college in large town.
**Enrollment:** 2,646 undergrads.
**Selectivity:** Open admission; but selective for some programs.

### BASIC COSTS (2015-2016)

**Tuition and fees:** $2,910; out-of-state residents $3,840.
**Per-credit charge:** $65; out-of-district residents $65; out-of-state residents $65.
**Room and board:** $5,379.

### FINANCIAL AID PICTURE

**Students with need:** Need-based aid available for full-time and part-time students.
**Students without need:** No-need awards available for academics, athletics.

### FINANCIAL AID PROCEDURES

**Forms required:** FAFSA, state aid form.
**Dates and Deadlines:** Priority date 3/1; no closing date. Applicants notified on a rolling basis starting 6/1; must reply within 4 week(s) of notification.

**CONTACT**

Myrna Perkins, Assistant Dean of Student Services/Director of Financial Aid

245 North East 30th Road, Great Bend, KS 67530-9283

(620) 792-2701

## Benedictine College

Atchison, Kansas

www.benedictine.edu                    Federal Code: 010256

**4-year private** liberal arts college in large town, affiliated with Roman Catholic Church.

**Enrollment:** 1,868 undergrads, 1% part-time. 508 full-time freshmen.

**Selectivity:** Admits over 75% of applicants.

**BASIC COSTS (2015-2016)**

**Tuition and fees:** $26,250.

**Per-credit charge:** $695.

**Room and board:** $9,165.

**FINANCIAL AID PICTURE (2015-2016)**

**Students with need:** Out of 439 full-time freshmen who applied for aid, 369 were judged to have need. Of these, 369 received aid, and 96 had their full need met. Average financial aid package met 76% of need; average scholarship/grant was $17,135; average loan was $3,940. For part-time students, average financial aid package was $12,360.

**Students without need:** 95 full-time freshmen who did not demonstrate need for aid received scholarships/grants; average award was $12,435. No-need awards available for academics, alumni affiliation, art, athletics, job skills, leadership, minority status, music/drama, religious affiliation, state/district residency.

**Scholarships offered:** *Merit:* Presidential Scholarship: full tuition; maintain 3.5 GPA; 5 awarded. Dean's Scholarship: partial tuition; maintain 3.5 GPA; 5 awarded. *Athletic:* 42 full-time freshmen received athletic scholarships; average amount $18,254.

**FINANCIAL AID PROCEDURES**

**Forms required:** FAFSA.

**Dates and Deadlines:** Priority date 4/1; no closing date. Applicants notified on a rolling basis starting 2/1; must reply within 2 week(s) of notification.

**Transfers:** No deadline. Applicants notified on a rolling basis. Scholarship available for students transferring 2.0 cumulative GPA.

**CONTACT**

Tony Tanking, Director Financial Aid

1020 North Second Street, Atchison, KS 66002-1499

(913) 360-7484

## Bethany College

Lindsborg, Kansas

www.bethanylb.edu                    Federal Code: 001904

**4-year private** liberal arts college in small town, affiliated with Evangelical Lutheran Church in America.

**Enrollment:** 629 undergrads, 2% part-time. 161 full-time freshmen.

**Selectivity:** Admits over 75% of applicants.

**BASIC COSTS (2015-2016)**

**Tuition and fees:** $26,550.

**Room and board:** $8,100.

**FINANCIAL AID PICTURE**

**Students with need:** Need-based aid available for full-time and part-time students. Work study available nights, weekends, and for part-time students.

**Students without need:** No-need awards available for academics, alumni affiliation, art, athletics, job skills, leadership, minority status, music/drama, religious affiliation, ROTC, state/district residency.

**Additional info:** State financial aid deadline March 15.

**FINANCIAL AID PROCEDURES**

**Forms required:** FAFSA.

**Dates and Deadlines:** Priority date 3/1; no closing date. Applicants notified on a rolling basis; must reply by 8/22.

**CONTACT**

Amy Hoss, Director of Financial Aid

335 East Swensson, Lindsborg, KS 67456-1897

(785) 227-3311 ext. 8248

## Bethel College

North Newton, Kansas

www.bethelks.edu                    Federal Code: 001905

**4-year private** liberal arts college in large town, affiliated with Mennonite Church.

**Enrollment:** 525 undergrads, 3% part-time. 130 full-time freshmen.

**Selectivity:** Admits 50 to 75% of applicants.

**BASIC COSTS (2015-2016)**

**Tuition and fees:** $25,410.

**Per-credit charge:** $910.

**Room and board:** $8,110.

**FINANCIAL AID PICTURE (2015-2016)**

**Students with need:** Average financial aid package met 80% of need; average scholarship/grant was $5,489; average loan was $5,639. For part-time students, average financial aid package was $8,144.

**Students without need:** No-need awards available for academics, alumni affiliation, art, athletics, minority status, music/drama, religious affiliation, state/district residency.

**Scholarships offered:** Scholarships for academically talented students, ranging from 16% to 50% of tuition.

**FINANCIAL AID PROCEDURES**

**Forms required:** FAFSA, institutional form.

**Dates and Deadlines:** Priority date 4/1; no closing date. Applicants notified on a rolling basis starting 2/1; must reply within 2 week(s) of notification.

**Transfers:** No deadline. Applicants notified on a rolling basis starting 2/1; must reply within 2 week(s) of notification.

**CONTACT**

Tony Graber, Director of Financial Aid

300 E 27th Street, North Newton, KS 67117-8061

(800) 522-1887 ext. 232

## Butler Community College

El Dorado, Kansas

www.butlercc.edu                    Federal Code: 001906

**2-year public** community college in large town.

**Enrollment:** 9,363 undergrads.

**Selectivity:** Open admission; but selective for some programs.

**BASIC COSTS (2015-2016)**

**Tuition and fees:** $2,640; out-of-district residents $2,970; out-of-state residents $4,770.

**Per-credit charge:** $69; out-of-district residents $80; out-of-state residents $140.

**Room and board:** $5,650.

**Additional info:** Tuition/fee waivers available for unemployed or children of unemployed.

**FINANCIAL AID PICTURE**

**Students with need:** Need-based aid available for full-time and part-time students. Work study available nights, weekends, and for part-time students.

**Students without need:** No-need awards available for academics, art, athletics, music/drama.

## FINANCIAL AID PROCEDURES

**Forms required:** FAFSA, institutional form.
**Dates and Deadlines:** Priority date 4/1; no closing date. Applicants notified on a rolling basis starting 5/1; must reply within 2 week(s) of notification.
**Transfers:** Students with 90 hours or more must have classes validated by degree-granting 4-year institution.

## CONTACT

Susie Edwards, Director of Financial Aid
901 South Haverhill Road, El Dorado, KS 67042-3280
(316) 322-3121

## Central Christian College of Kansas

McPherson, Kansas
www.centralchristian.edu          Federal Code: 001908

**4-year private** liberal arts college in large town, affiliated with Free Methodist Church of North America.
**Enrollment:** 1,043 undergrads, 2% part-time. 339 full-time freshmen.
**Selectivity:** Admits 50 to 75% of applicants.

## BASIC COSTS (2016-2017)

**Tuition and fees:** $24,690.
**Per-credit charge:** $650.
**Room and board:** $7,950.

## FINANCIAL AID PICTURE

**Students with need:** Need-based aid available for full-time and part-time students. Work study available nights, weekends, and for part-time students.
**Students without need:** No-need awards available for academics, alumni affiliation, athletics, leadership, music/drama, religious affiliation.

## FINANCIAL AID PROCEDURES

**Forms required:** FAFSA.
**Dates and Deadlines:** Priority date 3/1; no closing date. Applicants notified on a rolling basis starting 3/1; must reply within 4 week(s) of notification.
**Transfers:** No deadline. Applicants notified on a rolling basis; must reply within 4 week(s) of notification.

## CONTACT

Nichole Carver, Interim Director of Financial Aid
1200 South Main, McPherson, KS 67460-5740
(620) 241-0723 ext. 389

## Cloud County Community College

Concordia, Kansas
www.cloud.edu          Federal Code: 001909

**2-year public** community college in small town.
**Enrollment:** 1,196 undergrads, 40% part-time. 355 full-time freshmen.
**Selectivity:** Open admission.

## BASIC COSTS (2015-2016)

**Tuition and fees:** $2,820; out-of-district residents $2,970; out-of-state residents $3,120.
**Per-credit charge:** $72; out-of-district residents $79; out-of-state residents $133.
**Room and board:** $5,750.

## FINANCIAL AID PICTURE (2014-2015)

**Students with need:** 59% of average financial aid package awarded as scholarships/grants, 41% awarded as loans/jobs. Need-based aid available for part-time students. Work study available nights, weekends, and for part-time students.

## FINANCIAL AID PROCEDURES

**Forms required:** FAFSA.
**Dates and Deadlines:** Priority date 4/1; no closing date. Applicants notified on a rolling basis starting 5/1; must reply within 4 week(s) of notification.

## CONTACT

Suzi Knoettgen, Director of Student Financial Aid
2221 Campus Drive, Concordia, KS 66901-1002
(785) 243-1435 ext. 280

## Coffeyville Community College

Coffeyville, Kansas
www.coffeyville.edu          Federal Code: 001910

**2-year public** community and technical college in large town.
**Enrollment:** 1,067 undergrads, 10% part-time. 469 full-time freshmen.
**Selectivity:** Open admission.

## BASIC COSTS (2015-2016)

**Tuition and fees:** $2,160; out-of-state residents $3,630.
**Per-credit charge:** $35; out-of-state residents $84.
**Room and board:** $5,551.

## FINANCIAL AID PICTURE

**Students with need:** Need-based aid available for full-time and part-time students. Work study available nights, weekends, and for part-time students.
**Students without need:** No-need awards available for academics, alumni affiliation, art, athletics, leadership, music/drama, state/district residency.

## FINANCIAL AID PROCEDURES

**Forms required:** FAFSA.
**Dates and Deadlines:** Priority date 7/1; no closing date. Applicants notified on a rolling basis starting 6/20.

## CONTACT

Pam Feerer, Director of Financial Aid
400 West 11th Street, Coffeyville, KS 67337-5064
(620) 252-7357

## Colby Community College

Colby, Kansas
www.colbycc.edu          Federal Code: 001911

**2-year public** community college in small town.
**Enrollment:** 1,311 undergrads.
**Selectivity:** Open admission; but selective for some programs.

## BASIC COSTS (2015-2016)

**Tuition and fees:** $3,150; out-of-state residents $4,920.
**Per-credit charge:** $65; out-of-state residents $124.
**Room and board:** $4,460.

## FINANCIAL AID PICTURE

**Students with need:** Need-based aid available for full-time and part-time students. Work study available nights, weekends, and for part-time students.
**Students without need:** No-need awards available for academics, athletics, leadership, music/drama.

## FINANCIAL AID PROCEDURES

**Forms required:** FAFSA, state aid form.
**Dates and Deadlines:** Priority date 6/1; no closing date. Applicants notified on a rolling basis starting 5/1.

## CONTACT

Paula Halvorson, Director of Financial Aid
1255 South Range Avenue, Colby, KS 67701
(785) 460-4695

## Cowley County Community College
Arkansas City, Kansas
www.cowley.edu                        Federal Code: 001902

**2-year public** community and technical college in large town.
**Enrollment:** 3,569 undergrads.
**Selectivity:** Open admission; but selective for some programs.

### BASIC COSTS (2015-2016)
**Tuition and fees:** $2,520; out-of-district residents $2,820; out-of-state residents $4,230.
**Per-credit charge:** $55; out-of-district residents $65; out-of-state residents $112.
**Room and board:** $4,625.
**Additional info:** Oklahoma residents $75 per credit hour for tuition, $29 per credit hour for fees.

### FINANCIAL AID PICTURE
**Students with need:** Need-based aid available for full-time and part-time students.
**Students without need:** No-need awards available for academics, alumni affiliation, art, athletics, leadership, music/drama, state/district residency.

### FINANCIAL AID PROCEDURES
**Forms required:** FAFSA.
**Dates and Deadlines:** Priority date 4/15; no closing date. Applicants notified on a rolling basis starting 1/15; must reply within 2 week(s) of notification.

### CONTACT
Sally Palmer, Director of Financial Aid
PO Box 1147, Arkansas City, KS 67005-1147
(620) 442-0430

## Dodge City Community College
Dodge City, Kansas
www.dc3.edu                           Federal Code: 001913

**2-year public** community and technical college in large town.
**Enrollment:** 1,105 undergrads.
**Selectivity:** Open admission; but selective for some programs.

### BASIC COSTS (2015-2016)
**Tuition and fees:** $2,620; out-of-district residents $2,770; out-of-state residents $3,070.
**Per-credit charge:** $35; out-of-district residents $40; out-of-state residents $50.
**Room and board:** $5,720.

### FINANCIAL AID PICTURE
**Students with need:** Need-based aid available for full-time and part-time students. Work study available nights, weekends, and for part-time students.
**Students without need:** No-need awards available for academics, athletics, music/drama, state/district residency.

### FINANCIAL AID PROCEDURES
**Forms required:** FAFSA, institutional form.
**Dates and Deadlines:** Priority date 3/15; no closing date. Applicants notified on a rolling basis; must reply within 2 week(s) of notification.

### CONTACT
Russ McBee, Director of Financial Aid
2501 North 14th Avenue, Dodge City, KS 67801-2399
(620) 227-9336

## Donnelly College
Kansas City, Kansas
www.donnelly.edu                      Federal Code: 001914

**2-year private** junior and liberal arts college in small city, affiliated with Roman Catholic Church.
**Enrollment:** 262 undergrads, 25% part-time. 62 full-time freshmen.
**Selectivity:** Open admission.

### BASIC COSTS (2015-2016)
**Tuition and fees:** $8,340.
**Per-credit charge:** $275.
**Room and board:** $7,020.

### FINANCIAL AID PICTURE (2015-2016)
**Students with need:** Out of 61 full-time freshmen who applied for aid, 57 were judged to have need. Of these, 57 received aid, and 15 had their full need met. Average financial aid package met 97% of need; average scholarship/grant was $2,526; average loan was $3,286. Need-based aid available for part-time students.
**Students without need:** 52 full-time freshmen who did not demonstrate need for aid received scholarships/grants. No-need awards available for academics, religious affiliation.

### FINANCIAL AID PROCEDURES
**Forms required:** FAFSA, institutional form.
**Dates and Deadlines:** Closing date 4/1. Applicants notified on a rolling basis starting 7/1.
**Transfers:** Priority date 4/1; no deadline. Applicants notified on a rolling basis starting 4/1; must reply within 2 week(s) of notification.

### CONTACT
Erin Anderson, Director of Financial Aid
608 North 18th Street, Kansas City, KS 66102-4210
(913) 621-8740

## Emporia State University
Emporia, Kansas
www.emporia.edu                       Federal Code: 001927

**4-year public** university in large town.
**Enrollment:** 3,730 undergrads, 6% part-time. 732 full-time freshmen.
**Selectivity:** Admits over 75% of applicants.

### BASIC COSTS (2015-2016)
**Tuition and fees:** $5,936; out-of-state residents $18,524.
**Per-credit charge:** $155; out-of-state residents $575.
**Room and board:** $7,967.

### FINANCIAL AID PICTURE (2015-2016)
**Students with need:** Out of 662 full-time freshmen who applied for aid, 529 were judged to have need. Of these, 527 received aid, and 86 had their full need met. Average financial aid package met 64% of need; average scholarship/grant was $5,937; average loan was $5,106. For part-time students, average financial aid package was $5,282.
**Students without need:** 143 full-time freshmen who did not demonstrate need for aid received scholarships/grants; average award was $1,947. No-need awards available for academics, alumni affiliation, art, athletics, job skills, leadership, minority status, music/drama, religious affiliation, state/district residency.
**Scholarships offered:** *Merit:* Hornet Scholars: Based on High School GPA and ACT ($1,000 to $1,800). Foundation Scholars: Based on High School GPA and ACT ($1,900 to $2,700). Presidential Scholars: Based on High School GPA and ACT ($2,500 to $3,600). Valedictorian/Salutatorian Scholarships for students ranked 1 ($500) or 2 ($250) in their class. *Athletic:* 36 full-time freshmen received athletic scholarships; average amount $2,431.
**Additional info:** Institution's own payment plan is available.

## FINANCIAL AID PROCEDURES

**Forms required:** FAFSA, state aid form.

**Dates and Deadlines:** Priority date 3/15; no closing date. Applicants notified on a rolling basis starting 2/2; must reply within 2 week(s) of notification.

**Transfers:** No deadline. Applicants notified on a rolling basis; must reply within 2 week(s) of notification.

## CONTACT

Elaine Henrie, Director of Financial Aid

One Kellogg Circle, Campus Box 4034, Emporia, KS 66801-5415

(620) 341-5457

# Fort Hays State University

Hays, Kansas

www.fhsu.edu                                 Federal Code: 001915

**4-year public** university in large town.

**Enrollment:** 11,503 undergrads, 51% part-time. 857 full-time freshmen.

**Selectivity:** Admits over 75% of applicants.

## BASIC COSTS (2015-2016)

**Tuition and fees:** $4,654; out-of-state residents $13,657.

**Per-credit charge:** $119; out-of-state residents $419.

**Room and board:** $7,477.

## FINANCIAL AID PICTURE (2014-2015)

**Students with need:** Out of 516 full-time freshmen who applied for aid, 429 were judged to have need. Of these, 414 received aid, and 30 had their full need met. Average financial aid package met 47% of need; average scholarship/grant was $4,879; average loan was $2,847. For part-time students, average financial aid package was $4,924.

**Students without need:** 125 full-time freshmen who did not demonstrate need for aid received scholarships/grants; average award was $1,074. No-need awards available for academics, alumni affiliation, art, job skills, leadership, minority status, music/drama, state/district residency.

**Scholarships offered:** 31 full-time freshmen received athletic scholarships; average amount $4,580.

## FINANCIAL AID PROCEDURES

**Forms required:** FAFSA, institutional form.

**Dates and Deadlines:** Priority date 3/1; no closing date. Applicants notified on a rolling basis starting 3/15; must reply within 2 week(s) of notification.

**Transfers:** No deadline. Applicants notified on a rolling basis starting 3/15; must reply within 3 week(s) of notification.

## CONTACT

Craig Karlin, Director of Student Financial Aid

600 Park Street, Hays, KS 67601

(785) 628-4494

# Fort Scott Community College

Fort Scott, Kansas

www.fortscott.edu                            Federal Code: 001916

**2-year public** community college in small town.

**Enrollment:** 1,702 undergrads.

**Selectivity:** Open admission.

## BASIC COSTS (2015-2016)

**Tuition and fees:** $2,825; out-of-district residents $2,915; out-of-state residents $4,595.

**Per-credit charge:** $50; out-of-district residents $53; out-of-state residents $109.

**Room and board:** $5,580.

## FINANCIAL AID PICTURE (2014-2015)

**Students with need:** 51% of average financial aid package awarded as scholarships/grants, 49% awarded as loans/jobs. Need-based aid available for part-time students.

## FINANCIAL AID PROCEDURES

**Forms required:** FAFSA.

**Dates and Deadlines:** Priority date 7/1; no closing date. Applicants notified on a rolling basis starting 10/1.

## CONTACT

Lillie Grubb, Financial Aid Director

2108 S Horton St, Fort Scott, KS 66701

(620) 223-2700 ext. 3522

# Friends University

Wichita, Kansas

www.friends.edu                              Federal Code: 001918

**4-year private** university and liberal arts college in large city, affiliated with nondenominational tradition.

**Enrollment:** 1,417 undergrads. 187 full-time freshmen.

## BASIC COSTS (2015-2016)

**Tuition and fees:** $25,830.

**Per-credit charge:** $855.

**Room and board:** $7,320.

## FINANCIAL AID PICTURE (2014-2015)

**Students with need:** Out of 167 full-time freshmen who applied for aid, 149 were judged to have need. Of these, 149 received aid, and 49 had their full need met. Average financial aid package met 81% of need; average scholarship/grant was $7,423; average loan was $3,188. For part-time students, average financial aid package was $5,522.

**Students without need:** 18 full-time freshmen who did not demonstrate need for aid received scholarships/grants; average award was $12,798. No-need awards available for academics, alumni affiliation, art, athletics, leadership, music/drama, religious affiliation.

**Scholarships offered:** 87 full-time freshmen received athletic scholarships; average amount $4,323.

## FINANCIAL AID PROCEDURES

**Forms required:** FAFSA.

**Dates and Deadlines:** Priority date 3/15; no closing date. Applicants notified on a rolling basis starting 3/1; must reply within 3 week(s) of notification.

**Transfers:** No deadline. Applicants notified on a rolling basis starting 3/1; must reply within 3 week(s) of notification.

## CONTACT

Tony Lubbers, Director of Financial Aid

2100 West University Avenue, Wichita, KS 67213

(800) 794-6945

# Garden City Community College

Garden City, Kansas

www.gcccks.edu                               Federal Code: 001919

**2-year public** community college in large town.

**Enrollment:** 1,953 undergrads.

**Selectivity:** Open admission; but selective for some programs.

## BASIC COSTS (2015-2016)

**Tuition and fees:** $2,816; out-of-state residents $3,424.

**Per-credit charge:** $57; out-of-state residents $76.

**Room and board:** $5,250.

**Additional info:** Border State Tuition Rate extended to residents of the following states: CO, MO, NE, NM, OK, TX.

## FINANCIAL AID PICTURE

**Students with need:** Need-based aid available for full-time and part-time students. Work study available nights, weekends, and for part-time students.

**Students without need:** No-need awards available for academics, art, athletics, job skills, leadership, minority status, music/drama, state/district residency.

## FINANCIAL AID PROCEDURES

**Forms required:** FAFSA, institutional form.

**Dates and Deadlines:** Priority date 3/1; no closing date. Applicants notified on a rolling basis starting 4/15; must reply within 2 week(s) of notification.

## CONTACT

Melinda Harrington, Director of Financial Aid
801 Campus Drive, Garden City, KS 67846-6333
(620) 276-9519

# Grantham University

Lenexa, Kansas
www.grantham.edu                    Federal Code: 041223

**4-year for-profit** virtual university in large city.

**Enrollment:** 11,092 undergrads.

**Selectivity:** Open admission; but selective for some programs.

## BASIC COSTS (2015-2016)

**Tuition and fees:** $16,108.

**Room and board:** $13,568.

## FINANCIAL AID PICTURE

**Students with need:** Need-based aid available for full-time and part-time students.

## FINANCIAL AID PROCEDURES

**Forms required:** FAFSA.

**Transfers:** No deadline. Applicants notified on a rolling basis.

## CONTACT

Lindsay Bridgeman, Director Financial Aid
16025 W 113th Street, Lenexa, KS 66219
(866) 850-2980

# Haskell Indian Nations University

Lawrence, Kansas
www.haskell.edu                    Federal Code: 010438

**4-year public** university in small city.

**Enrollment:** 803 undergrads, 4% part-time. 172 full-time freshmen.

**Selectivity:** Admits 50 to 75% of applicants.

## BASIC COSTS (2015-2016)

**Tuition and fees:** $1,610.

**Room and board:** $248.

## FINANCIAL AID PICTURE

**Students with need:** Need-based aid available for full-time and part-time students. Work study available nights, weekends, and for part-time students.

**Additional info:** Some personal expenses may be offset by Bureau of Indian Affairs grants. Most students qualify for only minimum Pell grant.

## FINANCIAL AID PROCEDURES

**Forms required:** FAFSA.

**Dates and Deadlines:** Priority date 5/15; no closing date. Applicants notified on a rolling basis starting 3/15; must reply within 9 week(s) of notification.

**Transfers:** Priority date 11/8; closing date 4/15.

## CONTACT

Carlene Morris, Financial Aid Officer
155 Indian Avenue #5031, Lawrence, KS 66046-4800
(785) 830-2702

# Hesston College

Hesston, Kansas
www.hesston.edu                    Federal Code: 001920

**2-year private** junior and liberal arts college in small town, affiliated with Mennonite Church.

**Enrollment:** 408 undergrads, 13% part-time. 156 full-time freshmen.

**Selectivity:** Open admission; but selective for some programs.

## BASIC COSTS (2015-2016)

**Tuition and fees:** $25,234.

**Room and board:** $8,144.

## FINANCIAL AID PICTURE (2015-2016)

**Students with need:** Out of 123 full-time freshmen who applied for aid, 111 were judged to have need. Of these, 111 received aid. Need-based aid available for part-time students.

**Students without need:** 3 full-time freshmen who did not demonstrate need for aid received scholarships/grants; average award was $6,667. No-need awards available for academics, alumni affiliation, art, athletics, job skills, music/drama.

**Scholarships offered:** 2 full-time freshmen received athletic scholarships; average amount $5,250.

## FINANCIAL AID PROCEDURES

**Forms required:** FAFSA.

**Dates and Deadlines:** Closing date 4/1. Applicants notified on a rolling basis starting 2/1; must reply within 4 week(s) of notification.

**Transfers:** No deadline. Applicants notified on a rolling basis starting 2/1.

## CONTACT

Marcia Mendez, Financial Aid Director
Box 3000, Hesston, KS 67062-2093
(800) 995-2757

# Highland Community College

Highland, Kansas
www.highlandcc.edu                    Federal Code: 001921

**2-year public** community college in rural community.

**Enrollment:** 1,876 undergrads, 40% part-time. 483 full-time freshmen.

**Selectivity:** Open admission; but selective for out-of-state students.

## BASIC COSTS (2015-2016)

**Tuition and fees:** $2,910; out-of-district residents $3,300; out-of-state residents $3,300.

**Per-credit charge:** $55; out-of-district residents $68; out-of-state residents $68.

**Room and board:** $5,506.

## FINANCIAL AID PICTURE

**Students with need:** Need-based aid available for full-time and part-time students. Work study available nights, weekends, and for part-time students.

**Students without need:** No-need awards available for academics, alumni affiliation, art, athletics, job skills, leadership, music/drama.

**Additional info:** Auditions and portfolios important for certain scholarship candidates.

## FINANCIAL AID PROCEDURES

**Forms required:** FAFSA.

**Dates and Deadlines:** Priority date 4/1; no closing date. Applicants notified on a rolling basis starting 4/15; must reply within 4 week(s) of notification.

**Transfers:** No deadline. Applicants notified on a rolling basis starting 4/1; must reply within 4 week(s) of notification.

**CONTACT**
Amy Lackey, Director of Student Financial Aid
606 West Main Street, Highland, KS 66035
(785) 442-6023

## Hutchinson Community College
Hutchinson, Kansas
www.hutchcc.edu                    Federal Code: 001923

**2-year public** community college in large town.
**Enrollment:** 5,172 undergrads, 59% part-time. 867 full-time freshmen.
**Selectivity:** Open admission; but selective for some programs.

**BASIC COSTS (2015-2016)**
**Tuition and fees:** $2,670; out-of-district residents $2,970; out-of-state residents $3,900.
**Per-credit charge:** $70; out-of-district residents $80; out-of-state residents $111.
**Room and board:** $5,430.
**Additional info:** Residence Hall students pay a $50 social fee.

**FINANCIAL AID PICTURE (2014-2015)**
**Students with need:** Out of 695 full-time freshmen who applied for aid, 504 were judged to have need. Of these, 490 received aid, and 122 had their full need met. Average financial aid package met 41% of need; average scholarship/grant was $3,774; average loan was $2,447. For part-time students, average financial aid package was $4,903.
**Students without need:** 255 full-time freshmen who did not demonstrate need for aid received scholarships/grants; average award was $2,521. No-need awards available for academics, art, athletics, leadership, minority status, music/drama, state/district residency.
**Scholarships offered:** 193 full-time freshmen received athletic scholarships; average amount $3,144.

**FINANCIAL AID PROCEDURES**
**Forms required:** FAFSA, institutional form.
**Dates and Deadlines:** Priority date 2/1; no closing date. Applicants notified on a rolling basis starting 4/1; must reply within 2 week(s) of notification.

**CONTACT**
Nathan Buche, Financial Aid Director
1300 North Plum, Hutchinson, KS 67501
(620) 665-3568

## Independence Community College
Independence, Kansas
www.indycc.edu                    Federal Code: 001924

**2-year public** community college in large town.
**Enrollment:** 642 undergrads, 12% part-time. 275 full-time freshmen.
**Selectivity:** Open admission.

**BASIC COSTS (2015-2016)**
**Tuition and fees:** $3,045; out-of-district residents $3,225; out-of-state residents $4,425.
**Per-credit charge:** $54; out-of-district residents $60; out-of-state residents $100.
**Room and board:** $4,950.

**FINANCIAL AID PICTURE**
**Students with need:** Need-based aid available for full-time and part-time students. Work study available nights, weekends, and for part-time students.

**Students without need:** No-need awards available for academics, art, athletics, music/drama, state/district residency.
**Additional info:** Student labor grants awarded to students not eligible for Federal Work-Study. Students may apply by completing Student Employment Application. Student Support Services (SSS) grants available to eligible participants of the SSS program. Tuition waiver to all persons residing in college's taxing district.

**FINANCIAL AID PROCEDURES**
**Forms required:** FAFSA.
**Dates and Deadlines:** Priority date 4/1; no closing date. Applicants notified on a rolling basis.

**CONTACT**
Wendy Isle, Chief Fiscal Officer
1057 West College Avenue, Independence, KS 67301
(620) 332-5412

## Johnson County Community College
Overland Park, Kansas
www.jccc.edu                    Federal Code: 008244

**2-year public** community college in very large city.
**Enrollment:** 11,608 undergrads.
**Selectivity:** Open admission; but selective for some programs.

**BASIC COSTS (2015-2016)**
**Tuition and fees:** $2,730; out-of-district residents $3,180; out-of-state residents $6,420.
**Per-credit charge:** $75; out-of-district residents $90; out-of-state residents $198.

**FINANCIAL AID PICTURE**
**Students with need:** Need-based aid available for full-time and part-time students.
**Students without need:** No-need awards available for academics.

**FINANCIAL AID PROCEDURES**
**Forms required:** FAFSA, state aid form.
**Dates and Deadlines:** Priority date 4/1; no closing date. Applicants notified on a rolling basis starting 4/15; must reply within 2 week(s) of notification.

**CONTACT**
Christal Williams, Program Director for Student Financial Aid
12345 College Boulevard, Overland Park, KS 66210-1299
(913) 469-3840

## Kansas City Kansas Community College
Kansas City, Kansas
www.kckcc.edu                    Federal Code: 001925

**2-year public** community and career college in very large city.
**Enrollment:** 4,768 undergrads, 61% part-time. 527 full-time freshmen.
**Selectivity:** Open admission; but selective for some programs.

**BASIC COSTS (2015-2016)**
**Tuition and fees:** $2,640; out-of-state residents $6,660.
**Per-credit charge:** $73; out-of-state residents $207.
**Room and board:** $4,800.

**FINANCIAL AID PICTURE (2014-2015)**
**Students with need:** 73% of average financial aid package awarded as scholarships/grants, 27% awarded as loans/jobs. Need-based aid available for part-time students. Work study available nights, weekends, and for part-time students.
**Students without need:** No-need awards available for academics, art, athletics, music/drama.

## FINANCIAL AID PROCEDURES

**Forms required:** FAFSA.

**Dates and Deadlines:** Applicants notified on a rolling basis starting 5/1; must reply within 4 week(s) of notification.

## CONTACT

Mary Dorr, Director of Financial Aid

7250 State Avenue, Kansas City, KS 66112

(913) 288-7697

# Kansas State University
Manhattan, Kansas

www.k-state.edu                    Federal Code: 001928

**4-year public** university in small city.

**Enrollment:** 19,443 undergrads, 9% part-time. 3,691 full-time freshmen.

**Selectivity:** Admits over 75% of applicants.

## BASIC COSTS (2015-2016)

**Tuition and fees:** $9,350; out-of-state residents $23,429.

**Per-credit charge:** $284; out-of-state residents $753.

**Room and board:** $8,380.

## FINANCIAL AID PICTURE (2014-2015)

**Students with need:** Out of 2,853 full-time freshmen who applied for aid, 1,955 were judged to have need. Of these, 1,916 received aid, and 439 had their full need met. Average financial aid package met 78% of need; average scholarship/grant was $4,578; average loan was $3,669. For part-time students, average financial aid package was $8,998.

**Students without need:** 638 full-time freshmen who did not demonstrate need for aid received scholarships/grants; average award was $4,255. No-need awards available for academics, alumni affiliation, art, athletics, leadership, music/drama, ROTC, state/district residency.

**Scholarships offered:** 94 full-time freshmen received athletic scholarships; average amount $10,711.

## FINANCIAL AID PROCEDURES

**Forms required:** FAFSA.

**Dates and Deadlines:** Priority date 3/1; no closing date. Applicants notified on a rolling basis starting 4/1; must reply within 2 week(s) of notification.

## CONTACT

Larry Moeder, Assistant Vice President for Student Financial Assistance and Admissions

119 Anderson Hall, Manhattan, KS 66506

(785) 532-6420

# Kansas Wesleyan University
Salina, Kansas

www.kwu.edu                    Federal Code: 001929

**4-year private** university and liberal arts college in large town, affiliated with United Methodist Church.

**Enrollment:** 665 undergrads, 7% part-time. 142 full-time freshmen.

**Selectivity:** Admits 50 to 75% of applicants.

## BASIC COSTS (2016-2017)

**Tuition and fees:** $28,000.

**Per-credit charge:** $280.

**Room and board:** $8,600.

## FINANCIAL AID PICTURE (2014-2015)

**Students with need:** Out of 141 full-time freshmen who applied for aid, 127 were judged to have need. Of these, 127 received aid, and 28 had their full need met. Average financial aid package met 74% of need; average scholarship/grant was $9,003; average loan was $3,851. For part-time students, average financial aid package was $657.

**Students without need:** 13 full-time freshmen who did not demonstrate need for aid received scholarships/grants; average award was $11,808. No-need awards available for academics, alumni affiliation, art, athletics, job skills, music/drama, religious affiliation.

**Scholarships offered:** 48 full-time freshmen received athletic scholarships; average amount $2,827.

**Additional info:** Awards available for residence hall students: minimum $7,000 for 3.0 GPA plus ACT score of 22 or SAT of 950 (exclusive of Writing); minimum $8,000 for 3.5 GPA plus ACT score of 22 or SAT score of 1030 (exclusive of Writing); minimum $9,000 for 3.75 GPA plus ACT score of 25 or SAT score of 1140 (exclusive of Writing). Application deadline March 15.

## FINANCIAL AID PROCEDURES

**Forms required:** FAFSA.

**Dates and Deadlines:** Closing date 3/15. Applicants notified on a rolling basis starting 2/1; must reply by 8/1 or within 3 week(s) of notification.

**Transfers:** No deadline. Applicants notified on a rolling basis starting 8/1. Academic scholarships based upon cumulative GPA of transferring credit hours.

## CONTACT

Lois Madsen, Director of Student Financial Planning

100 East Claflin Avenue, Salina, KS 67401-6196

(785) 833-4319

# Labette Community College
Parsons, Kansas

www.labette.edu                    Federal Code: 001930

**2-year public** community college in large town.

**Enrollment:** 1,574 undergrads.

**Selectivity:** Open admission; but selective for some programs.

## BASIC COSTS (2015-2016)

**Tuition and fees:** $2,700; out-of-state residents $3,450.

**Per-credit charge:** $48; out-of-state residents $73.

**Additional info:** Tuition/fee waivers available for adults, minority students, unemployed or children of unemployed.

## FINANCIAL AID PICTURE

**Students with need:** Need-based aid available for full-time and part-time students. Work study available nights.

**Students without need:** No-need awards available for academics, leadership.

## FINANCIAL AID PROCEDURES

**Forms required:** FAFSA.

**Dates and Deadlines:** Applicants notified on a rolling basis starting 4/4; must reply within 2 week(s) of notification.

## CONTACT

Kathy Johnston, Director of Financial Aid

200 South 14th Street, Parsons, KS 67357

(620) 820-1219

# Manhattan Area Technical College
Manhattan, Kansas

www.manhattantech.edu                    Federal Code: 005500

**2-year public** technical college in large town.

**Enrollment:** 446 undergrads, 22% part-time. 88 full-time freshmen.

**Selectivity:** Open admission; but selective for some programs.

## BASIC COSTS (2015-2016)

**Tuition and fees:** $3,897; out-of-state residents $3,897.

Per-credit charge: $100.

## FINANCIAL AID PICTURE (2014-2015)
**Students with need:** Out of 80 full-time freshmen who applied for aid, 65 were judged to have need. Of these, 63 received aid, and 2 had their full need met. Average financial aid package met 38% of need; average scholarship/grant was $5,026; average loan was $2,867. For part-time students, average financial aid package was $4,263.
**Students without need:** No-need awards available for academics, leadership.

## FINANCIAL AID PROCEDURES
**Forms required:** FAFSA, institutional form.
**Dates and Deadlines:** Priority date 7/1; no closing date. Applicants notified on a rolling basis.
**Transfers:** Priority date 7/1. Applicants notified on a rolling basis.

## CONTACT
Laura Weiss-Cook, Director of Financial Aid
3136 Dickens Avenue, Manhattan, KS 66503-2499
(785) 320-4541

## Manhattan Christian College
Manhattan, Kansas
www.mccks.edu                  Federal Code: 001931

**4-year private** Bible college in small city, affiliated with Christian Church.
**Enrollment:** 294 undergrads, 22% part-time. 45 full-time freshmen.

### BASIC COSTS (2015-2016)
**Tuition and fees:** $14,290.
**Per-credit charge:** $575.
**Room and board:** $8,254.

### FINANCIAL AID PICTURE
**Students with need:** Need-based aid available for full-time and part-time students.
**Students without need:** No-need awards available for academics, leadership, music/drama.

### FINANCIAL AID PROCEDURES
**Forms required:** FAFSA, state aid form.
**Dates and Deadlines:** Priority date 4/1; no closing date. Applicants notified on a rolling basis starting 4/1; must reply within 2 week(s) of notification.
**Transfers:** Priority date 4/1; no deadline. Applicants notified on a rolling basis; must reply within 2 week(s) of notification.

### CONTACT
Brandon Winter, Financial Aid Counselor
1415 Anderson Avenue, Manhattan, KS 66502

## McPherson College
McPherson, Kansas
www.mcpherson.edu              Federal Code: 001933

**4-year private** liberal arts college in large town, affiliated with Church of the Brethren.
**Enrollment:** 643 undergrads, 4% part-time. 194 full-time freshmen.
**Selectivity:** Admits less than 50% of applicants.

### BASIC COSTS (2015-2016)
**Tuition and fees:** $25,977.
**Per-credit charge:** $250.
**Room and board:** $8,450.

### FINANCIAL AID PICTURE (2014-2015)
**Students with need:** Out of 167 full-time freshmen who applied for aid, 152 were judged to have need. Of these, 152 received aid, and 68 had their

full need met. Average financial aid package met 100% of need; average scholarship/grant was $5,653; average loan was $10,879. For part-time students, average financial aid package was $10,617.
**Students without need:** 37 full-time freshmen who did not demonstrate need for aid received scholarships/grants; average award was $16,142. No-need awards available for academics, alumni affiliation, art, athletics, music/drama, religious affiliation, state/district residency.
**Scholarships offered: Merit:** Presidential Scholarship; $10,000 each year of attendance for four years; competition in fall and spring; 10 awards given per year. **Athletic:** 117 full-time freshmen received athletic scholarships; average amount $4,733.

### FINANCIAL AID PROCEDURES
**Forms required:** FAFSA.
**Dates and Deadlines:** Priority date 3/1; no closing date. Applicants notified on a rolling basis starting 3/1; must reply within 3 week(s) of notification.
**Transfers:** No deadline. Applicants notified on a rolling basis; must reply within 3 week(s) of notification.

### CONTACT
Sara Brubaker, Director of Financial Aid & Admissions Operations
1600 East Euclid Street, McPherson, KS 67460-1402
(620) 242-0400

## MidAmerica Nazarene University
Olathe, Kansas
www.mnu.edu                    Federal Code: 007032

**4-year private** university and liberal arts college in small city, affiliated with Church of the Nazarene.
**Enrollment:** 1,329 undergrads, 20% part-time. 190 full-time freshmen.

### BASIC COSTS (2016-2017)
**Tuition and fees:** $27,650.
**Per-credit charge:** $800.
**Room and board:** $7,900.

### FINANCIAL AID PICTURE
**Students with need:** Need-based aid available for full-time and part-time students.
**Students without need:** No-need awards available for academics, athletics, music/drama, religious affiliation, ROTC.

### FINANCIAL AID PROCEDURES
**Forms required:** FAFSA.
**Dates and Deadlines:** Priority date 3/1; no closing date. Applicants notified on a rolling basis starting 1/30; must reply within 2 week(s) of notification.

### CONTACT
Director of Student Financial Services
2030 East College Way, Olathe, KS 66062-1899
(913) 917-3298

## Neosho County Community College
Chanute, Kansas
www.neosho.edu                 Federal Code: 001936

**2-year public** community college in small town.
**Enrollment:** 2,259 undergrads.
**Selectivity:** Open admission; but selective for some programs.

### BASIC COSTS (2015-2016)
**Tuition and fees:** $2,850; out-of-district residents $2,850; out-of-state residents $2,850.
**Per-credit charge:** $64; out-of-district residents $64; out-of-state residents $64.

**Room and board:** $5,900.

## FINANCIAL AID PICTURE

**Students with need:** Need-based aid available for full-time and part-time students. Work study available nights, weekends, and for part-time students.

**Students without need:** No-need awards available for academics, art, athletics, job skills, leadership, music/drama, state/district residency.

**Scholarships offered:** Visual and performing arts, Academic Challenge stipends, industrial engineering and business scholarship.

## FINANCIAL AID PROCEDURES

**Forms required:** FAFSA.

**Dates and Deadlines:** Priority date 4/1; no closing date. Applicants notified on a rolling basis; must reply within 6 week(s) of notification.

**Transfers:** All academic transcripts and financial aid transcripts must be on file before aid will be awarded.

## CONTACT

Kara Hale, Director of Financial Aid
800 West 14th Street, Chanute, KS 66720
(620) 431-2820 ext. 278

## Newman University

Wichita, Kansas
www.newmanu.edu                    Federal Code: 001939

**4-year private** university and liberal arts college in large city, affiliated with Roman Catholic Church.

**Enrollment:** 1,126 undergrads, 12% part-time. 162 full-time freshmen.

**Selectivity:** Admits 50 to 75% of applicants.

## BASIC COSTS (2015-2016)

**Tuition and fees:** $25,720.

**Per-credit charge:** $831.

**Room and board:** $7,340.

**Additional info:** Tuition/fee waivers available for adults, unemployed or children of unemployed.

## FINANCIAL AID PICTURE

**Students with need:** Need-based aid available for full-time and part-time students. Work study available nights, weekends, and for part-time students.

**Students without need:** No-need awards available for academics, art, athletics, leadership, music/drama.

## FINANCIAL AID PROCEDURES

**Forms required:** FAFSA.

**Dates and Deadlines:** Closing date 3/1. Applicants notified on a rolling basis starting 2/1.

## CONTACT

Charly Smith, Director of Financial Aid
3100 McCormick, Wichita, KS 67213-2097
(316) 942-4291 ext. 2103

## North Central Kansas Technical College

Beloit, Kansas
www.ncktc.edu                    Federal Code: 005265

**2-year public** technical college in small town.

**Enrollment:** 785 undergrads.

**Selectivity:** Open admission.

## BASIC COSTS (2015-2016)

**Tuition and fees:** $3,488; out-of-state residents $3,488.

**Per-credit charge:** $109.

**Room and board:** $5,094.

## FINANCIAL AID PICTURE (2015-2016)

**Students with need:** 35% of average financial aid package awarded as scholarships/grants, 65% awarded as loans/jobs. Need-based aid available for part-time students. Work study available nights.

**Students without need:** No-need awards available for academics, state/district residency.

## FINANCIAL AID PROCEDURES

**Forms required:** FAFSA, state aid form.

## CONTACT

Gary Odle, Financial Aid Director
PO Box 507, Beloit, KS 67420
(785) 738-9028

## Northwest Kansas Technical College

Goodland, Kansas
www.nwktc.edu

**2-year public** technical college in small town.

**Enrollment:** 626 undergrads.

**Selectivity:** Open admission; but selective for some programs.

## BASIC COSTS (2015-2016)

**Tuition and fees:** $8,200; out-of-state residents $8,200.

## FINANCIAL AID PICTURE

**Students with need:** Need-based aid available for full-time and part-time students.

**Students without need:** This college awards aid only to students with need.

## FINANCIAL AID PROCEDURES

**Dates and Deadlines:** Closing date 8/1.

## CONTACT

Penny Nemechek, Financial Aid Coordinator
1209 Harrison, Goodland, KS 67735

## Ottawa University

Ottawa, Kansas
www.ottawa.edu                    Federal Code: 001937

**4-year private** university and liberal arts college in large town, affiliated with American Baptist Churches in the USA.

**Enrollment:** 533 undergrads.

## BASIC COSTS (2015-2016)

**Tuition and fees:** $26,204.

**Per-credit charge:** $1,056.

**Room and board:** $9,194.

## FINANCIAL AID PICTURE

**Students with need:** Need-based aid available for full-time and part-time students. Work study available nights, weekends, and for part-time students.

**Students without need:** No-need awards available for academics, alumni affiliation, athletics, music/drama, religious affiliation.

## FINANCIAL AID PROCEDURES

**Forms required:** FAFSA.

**Dates and Deadlines:** Priority date 3/15; no closing date. Applicants notified on a rolling basis starting 2/1; must reply within 4 week(s) of notification.

**Transfers:** No deadline. Applicants notified on a rolling basis starting 2/1; must reply within 4 week(s) of notification.

## CONTACT

Howard Fischer, Financial Aid Director
1001 South Cedar Street, #17, Ottawa, KS 66067-3399
(785) 242-5200 ext. 5571

## Pittsburg State University

Pittsburg, Kansas
www.pittstate.edu                  Federal Code: 001926

**4-year public** university in large town.
**Enrollment:** 5,700 undergrads, 6% part-time. 1,018 full-time freshmen.
**Selectivity:** Admits over 75% of applicants.

**BASIC COSTS (2015-2016)**
**Tuition and fees:** $6,508; out-of-state residents $16,978.
**Per-credit charge:** $171; out-of-state residents $519.
**Room and board:** $7,372.

**FINANCIAL AID PICTURE (2014-2015)**
**Students with need:** For part-time students, average financial aid package was $4,497.
**Students without need:** No-need awards available for academics, alumni affiliation, art, athletics, leadership, minority status, music/drama, ROTC.

**FINANCIAL AID PROCEDURES**
**Forms required:** FAFSA, state aid form.
**Dates and Deadlines:** Priority date 3/1; no closing date. Applicants notified on a rolling basis starting 3/1; must reply within 2 week(s) of notification.
**Transfers:** No deadline. Applicants notified on a rolling basis. Transfer student scholarships available.

**CONTACT**
Tammy Higgins, Director of Student Financial Assistance
1701 South Broadway, Pittsburg, KS 66762
(620) 235-4240

## Pratt Community College

Pratt, Kansas
www.prattcc.edu                  Federal Code: 001938

**2-year public** community and technical college in small town.
**Enrollment:** 673 full-time undergrads.
**Selectivity:** Open admission; but selective for some programs.

**BASIC COSTS (2015-2016)**
**Tuition and fees:** $2,970; out-of-state residents $3,210.
**Per-credit charge:** $58; out-of-state residents $66.
**Room and board:** $5,422.

**FINANCIAL AID PICTURE**
**Students with need:** Need-based aid available for full-time and part-time students.
**Students without need:** No-need awards available for academics, art, athletics, leadership, minority status, music/drama, state/district residency.

**FINANCIAL AID PROCEDURES**
**Forms required:** FAFSA, institutional form.
**Dates and Deadlines:** Priority date 5/1; closing date 8/1. Applicants notified on a rolling basis starting 2/1; must reply within 2 week(s) of notification.

**CONTACT**
Nikki Powell, Director of Financial Aid
348 Northeast State Route 61, Pratt, KS 67124-8317
(620) 450-2248

## Seward County Community College

Liberal, Kansas
www.sccc.edu                  Federal Code: 008228

**2-year public** community and technical college in large town.
**Enrollment:** 1,629 undergrads. 354 full-time freshmen.

**Selectivity:** Open admission.

**BASIC COSTS (2015-2016)**
**Tuition and fees:** $2,520; out-of-district residents $2,640; out-of-state residents $3,660.
**Per-credit charge:** $51; out-of-district residents $55; out-of-state residents $89.
**Room and board:** $4,680.

**FINANCIAL AID PICTURE**
**Students with need:** Need-based aid available for full-time and part-time students.
**Students without need:** No-need awards available for academics, athletics.

**FINANCIAL AID PROCEDURES**
**Forms required:** FAFSA, institutional form.
**Dates and Deadlines:** Priority date 4/1; no closing date. Applicants notified on a rolling basis starting 6/15; must reply within 4 week(s) of notification.

**CONTACT**
Donna Fisher, Financial Aid Director
1801 North Kansas Avenue, Liberal, KS 67905-1137
(620) 417-1110

## Southwestern College

Winfield, Kansas
www.sckans.edu                  Federal Code: 001940

**4-year private** liberal arts college in large town, affiliated with United Methodist Church.
**Enrollment:** 1,147 undergrads, 59% part-time. 123 full-time freshmen.
**Selectivity:** Admits over 75% of applicants.

**BASIC COSTS (2015-2016)**
**Tuition and fees:** $25,946.
**Per-credit charge:** $1,075.
**Room and board:** $7,080.

**FINANCIAL AID PICTURE (2014-2015)**
**Students with need:** Out of 94 full-time freshmen who applied for aid, 88 were judged to have need. Of these, 88 received aid, and 9 had their full need met. Average financial aid package met 68% of need; average scholarship/grant was $15,738; average loan was $4,724. For part-time students, average financial aid package was $4,791.
**Students without need:** 28 full-time freshmen who did not demonstrate need for aid received scholarships/grants; average award was $7,338. No-need awards available for academics, athletics, leadership, music/drama.
**Scholarships offered:** *Merit:* Presidential Scholarship; based on GPA, SAT/ACT, essay, resume, leadership, community service. Scholarships for major; based on GPA, SAT, essay, interview; 3 awarded. *Athletic:* 17 full-time freshmen received athletic scholarships; average amount $3,649.

**FINANCIAL AID PROCEDURES**
**Forms required:** FAFSA, institutional form.
**Dates and Deadlines:** Priority date 4/1; no closing date. Applicants notified on a rolling basis starting 2/1; must reply within 2 week(s) of notification.
**Transfers:** Priority date 4/1. Applicants notified on a rolling basis starting 2/1; must reply within 2 week(s) of notification. Activity grants and scholarships, except for presidential scholarship and premier scholarships, available to transfer students. Phi Theta Kappa scholarship available for transfer students who are members.

**CONTACT**
Brenda Hicks, Director of Financial Aid
100 College Street, Winfield, KS 67156
(620) 229-6215

## Sterling College
Sterling, Kansas
www.sterling.edu                    Federal Code: 001945

**4-year private** liberal arts college in small town.
**Enrollment:** 659 undergrads, 6% part-time. 143 full-time freshmen.
**Selectivity:** Admits less than 50% of applicants.

### BASIC COSTS (2015-2016)
**Tuition and fees:** $23,350.
**Room and board:** $8,110.

### FINANCIAL AID PICTURE (2015-2016)
**Students with need:** Average financial aid package met 88% of need; average scholarship/grant was $12,180; average loan was $5,008. For part-time students, average financial aid package was $11,838.
**Students without need:** No-need awards available for academics, alumni affiliation, art, athletics, leadership, music/drama.

### FINANCIAL AID PROCEDURES
**Forms required:** FAFSA.
**Dates and Deadlines:** Priority date 3/15; no closing date. Applicants notified on a rolling basis starting 2/1; must reply within 2 week(s) of notification.
**Transfers:** No deadline. Applicants notified on a rolling basis starting 2/1; must reply within 2 week(s) of notification.

### CONTACT
Mitzi Suhler, Financial Aid Director
125 West Cooper, Sterling, KS 67579
(620) 278-4407

## Tabor College
Hillsboro, Kansas
www.tabor.edu                       Federal Code: 001946

**4-year private** liberal arts college in small town, affiliated with Mennonite Brethren Church.
**Enrollment:** 669 undergrads, 18% part-time. 149 full-time freshmen.
**Selectivity:** Admits 50 to 75% of applicants.

### BASIC COSTS (2015-2016)
**Tuition and fees:** $25,320.
**Per-credit charge:** $510.
**Room and board:** $8,880.
**Additional info:** Tuition/fee waivers available for adults.

### FINANCIAL AID PICTURE (2014-2015)
**Students with need:** Out of 147 full-time freshmen who applied for aid, 119 were judged to have need. Of these, 119 received aid, and 15 had their full need met. Average financial aid package met 73% of need; average scholarship/grant was $5,535; average loan was $4,209. For part-time students, average financial aid package was $10,306.
**Students without need:** 62 full-time freshmen who did not demonstrate need for aid received scholarships/grants; average award was $11,419. No-need awards available for academics, alumni affiliation, art, athletics, leadership, music/drama, religious affiliation.
**Scholarships offered:** 110 full-time freshmen received athletic scholarships; average amount $6,078.

### FINANCIAL AID PROCEDURES
**Forms required:** FAFSA.
**Dates and Deadlines:** Priority date 3/1; no closing date. Applicants notified on a rolling basis starting 3/1; must reply within 5 week(s) of notification.
**Transfers:** Priority date 3/1; no deadline. Applicants notified on a rolling basis starting 2/20; must reply within 5 week(s) of notification. Transfer students with over 20 transferable credit hours are not eligible for Presidential, National Merit or Dean's scholarships.

### CONTACT
Sommer Smith, Director of Financial Aid
400 South Jefferson, Hillsboro, KS 67063-7135
(620) 947-3121 ext. 1726

## University of Kansas
Lawrence, Kansas
www.ku.edu                          Federal Code: 001948

**4-year public** university in small city.
**Enrollment:** 18,278 undergrads, 9% part-time. 3,977 full-time freshmen.
**Selectivity:** Admits over 75% of applicants.

### BASIC COSTS (2015-2016)
**Tuition and fees:** $10,802; out-of-state residents $26,640.
**Per-credit charge:** $330; out-of-state residents $858.
**Room and board:** $10,076.
**Additional info:** Tuition at time of enrollment locked for 4 years.

### FINANCIAL AID PICTURE (2014-2015)
**Students with need:** Out of 3,127 full-time freshmen who applied for aid, 2,067 were judged to have need. Of these, 2,008 received aid, and 748 had their full need met. Average financial aid package met 73% of need; average scholarship/grant was $7,001; average loan was $3,409. For part-time students, average financial aid package was $9,045.
**Students without need:** 989 full-time freshmen who did not demonstrate need for aid received scholarships/grants; average award was $5,602. No-need awards available for academics, alumni affiliation, art, athletics, leadership, minority status, music/drama, ROTC, state/district residency.
**Scholarships offered:** 74 full-time freshmen received athletic scholarships; average amount $19,151.

### FINANCIAL AID PROCEDURES
**Forms required:** FAFSA.
**Dates and Deadlines:** Priority date 3/1; no closing date. Applicants notified on a rolling basis starting 4/1; must reply within 4 week(s) of notification.

### CONTACT
Brenda Maigaard, Director
1502 Iowa Street, Lawrence, KS 66045-7576
(785) 864-4700

## University of Kansas Medical Center
Kansas City, Kansas
www.kumc.edu                        Federal Code: 001948

**Upper-division public** university and health science college in very large city.
**Enrollment:** 504 undergrads, 28% part-time.

### BASIC COSTS (2015-2016)
**Tuition and fees:** $9,903; out-of-state residents $24,549.
**Per-credit charge:** $304; out-of-state residents $792.
**Additional info:** Tuition at time of enrollment locked for 2 years.

### FINANCIAL AID PICTURE (2014-2015)
**Students with need:** Average financial aid package for all full-time undergraduates was $16,051; for part-time $9,664. 32% awarded as scholarships/grants, 68% awarded as loans/jobs. Work study available nights, weekends, and for part-time students.
**Students without need:** No-need awards available for academics, leadership, state/district residency.

### CONTACT
Sara Honeck, Director of Student Financial Aid
KUMC Office of Admissions, Mail Stop 4005, Kansas City, KS 66160
(913) 588-5170

## University of St. Mary
Leavenworth, Kansas
www.stmary.edu                    Federal Code: 001943

**4-year private** university in large town, affiliated with Roman Catholic Church.
**Enrollment:** 793 undergrads, 22% part-time. 111 full-time freshmen.
**Selectivity:** Admits less than 50% of applicants.

### BASIC COSTS (2015-2016)
**Tuition and fees:** $25,620.
**Per-credit charge:** $805.
**Room and board:** $7,750.

### FINANCIAL AID PICTURE (2014-2015)
**Students with need:** Out of 91 full-time freshmen who applied for aid, 81 were judged to have need. Of these, 81 received aid. Average financial aid package met 88% of need; average scholarship/grant was $6,658; average loan was $3,476. For part-time students, average financial aid package was $10,456.
**Students without need:** 18 full-time freshmen who did not demonstrate need for aid received scholarships/grants; average award was $13,100. No-need awards available for academics, art, athletics, leadership, music/drama, religious affiliation.
**Scholarships offered: *Merit:*** Essays may be required for scholarship applicants. Auditions recommended for music and drama scholarship applicants. Portfolio reviews for art award applicants. ***Athletic:*** 82 full-time freshmen received athletic scholarships; average amount $1,250.

### FINANCIAL AID PROCEDURES
**Forms required:** FAFSA, state aid form.
**Dates and Deadlines:** Priority date 4/1; no closing date. Applicants notified on a rolling basis starting 2/15; must reply within 2 week(s) of notification.
**Transfers:** No deadline. Applicants notified on a rolling basis starting 2/1; must reply within 2 week(s) of notification.

### CONTACT
Annissa Epperson, Director of Financial Aid
4100 South Fourth Street Trafficway, Leavenworth, KS 66048
(913) 758-6172

## Washburn University
Topeka, Kansas
www.washburn.edu                  Federal Code: 001949

**4-year public** university in small city.
**Enrollment:** 4,900 undergrads, 25% part-time. 757 full-time freshmen.
**Selectivity:** Open admission; but selective for some programs.

### BASIC COSTS (2015-2016)
**Tuition and fees:** $7,910; out-of-state residents $17,750.
**Per-credit charge:** $260; out-of-state residents $588.
**Room and board:** $6,830.

### FINANCIAL AID PICTURE (2015-2016)
**Students with need:** Out of 699 full-time freshmen who applied for aid, 456 were judged to have need. Of these, 456 received aid, and 78 had their full need met. Average financial aid package met 39% of need; average scholarship/grant was $4,850; average loan was $3,438. For part-time students, average financial aid package was $7,755.
**Students without need:** 151 full-time freshmen who did not demonstrate need for aid received scholarships/grants; average award was $3,611. No-need awards available for academics, alumni affiliation, art, athletics, job skills, leadership, minority status, music/drama, religious affiliation, ROTC, state/district residency.
**Scholarships offered:** 39 full-time freshmen received athletic scholarships; average amount $5,670.

### FINANCIAL AID PROCEDURES
**Forms required:** FAFSA.
**Dates and Deadlines:** Priority date 2/15; no closing date. Applicants notified on a rolling basis starting 4/1; must reply within 4 week(s) of notification.
**Transfers:** No deadline. Applicants notified on a rolling basis starting 4/1; must reply within 4 week(s) of notification.

### CONTACT
Kandace Mars, Associate Director of Financial Aid
1700 SW College Avenue, Morgan 100, Topeka, KS 66621
(785) 670-1151

## Wichita Area Technical College
Wichita, Kansas
www.watc.edu                      Federal Code: 005498

**2-year public** technical college in large city.
**Enrollment:** 1,482 undergrads.
**Selectivity:** Open admission; but selective for some programs.

### BASIC COSTS (2015-2016)
**Tuition and fees:** $2,940; out-of-state residents $3,360.
**Per-credit charge:** $67; out-of-state residents $81.
**Additional info:** Tuition for general education courses is $67 per credit hour and fees are $31 per credit hour. Tuition costs vary by program.

### FINANCIAL AID PICTURE
**Students with need:** Need-based aid available for full-time and part-time students. Work study available nights.
**Students without need:** This college awards aid only to students with need.

### FINANCIAL AID PROCEDURES
**Forms required:** FAFSA, CSS PROFILE, institutional form.
**Dates and Deadlines:** Applicants notified on a rolling basis starting 1/1.
**Transfers:** No deadline. Applicants notified on a rolling basis starting 1/1.

### CONTACT
Lacey Ledwich, Director of Financial Aid
4004 North Webb Road, Suite 100, Wichita, KS 67226
(316) 677-9400

## Wichita State University
Wichita, Kansas
www.wichita.edu                   Federal Code: 001950

**4-year public** university in large city.
**Enrollment:** 11,060 undergrads, 23% part-time. 1,366 full-time freshmen.
**Selectivity:** Admits over 75% of applicants.

### BASIC COSTS (2015-2016)
**Tuition and fees:** $7,528; out-of-state residents $15,852.
**Per-credit charge:** $203; out-of-state residents $480.

### FINANCIAL AID PICTURE (2014-2015)
**Students with need:** Out of 1,346 full-time freshmen who applied for aid, 745 were judged to have need. Of these, 736 received aid, and 478 had their full need met. Average financial aid package met 72% of need; average scholarship/grant was $4,486; average loan was $3,728. For part-time students, average financial aid package was $5,269.
**Students without need:** 431 full-time freshmen who did not demonstrate need for aid received scholarships/grants; average award was $1,234. No-need awards available for academics, alumni affiliation, art, athletics.

### FINANCIAL AID PROCEDURES
**Forms required:** FAFSA.

**Dates and Deadlines:** Priority date 3/1; no closing date. Applicants notified on a rolling basis starting 10/15; must reply by 5/1 or within 2 week(s) of notification.

**Transfers:** No deadline. Applicants notified on a rolling basis.

**CONTACT**
Sheelu Surender, Director of Financial Aid
1845 Fairmount, Box 124, Wichita, KS 67260-0124
(316) 978-5337

# Kentucky

## Alice Lloyd College
Pippa Passes, Kentucky
www.alc.edu                    Federal Code: 001951

**4-year private** liberal arts college in rural community.
**Enrollment:** 214 undergrads. 214 full-time freshmen.
**Selectivity:** Admits less than 50% of applicants.

**BASIC COSTS (2015-2016)**
**Tuition and fees:** $11,460.
**Per-credit charge:** $212.
**Room and board:** $5,940.
**Additional info:** Tuition/fee waivers available for minority students.

**FINANCIAL AID PICTURE**
**Students with need:** Need-based aid available for full-time and part-time students. Work study available nights, weekends, and for part-time students.
**Students without need:** No-need awards available for academics, athletics, minority status, state/district residency.
**Scholarships offered:** Alice Lloyd Scholars Program; tuition, room, board, fees, and books; awarded to up to 3 freshmen a year.
**Additional info:** All students receive financial aid through student work program. No student denied admission because of inability to pay. All full-time students required to work minimum of 10 hours per week.

**FINANCIAL AID PROCEDURES**
**Forms required:** FAFSA.
**Dates and Deadlines:** Closing date 2/1. Applicants notified on a rolling basis starting 5/1; must reply by 8/1 or within 4 week(s) of notification.
**Transfers:** Applicants notified on a rolling basis starting 5/1; must reply by 8/1 or within 4 week(s) of notification. Tuition guarantee only for total of 10 semesters of course work from all schools attended.

**CONTACT**
Jacqueline Stewart, Director of Financial Aid
100 Purpose Road, Pippa Passes, KY 41844
(606) 368-6058

## Asbury University
Wilmore, Kentucky
www.asbury.edu                    Federal Code: 001952

**4-year private** university and liberal arts college in small town, affiliated with interdenominational tradition.
**Enrollment:** 1,526 undergrads, 12% part-time. 309 full-time freshmen.
**Selectivity:** Admits 50 to 75% of applicants.

**BASIC COSTS (2016-2017)**
**Tuition and fees:** $28,829.
**Per-credit charge:** $1,093.
**Room and board:** $6,748.

**FINANCIAL AID PICTURE**
**Students with need:** Need-based aid available for full-time and part-time students. Work study available nights, weekends, and for part-time students.
**Students without need:** No-need awards available for academics, alumni affiliation, art, athletics, leadership, minority status, music/drama, religious affiliation, ROTC, state/district residency.

**FINANCIAL AID PROCEDURES**
**Forms required:** FAFSA.
**Dates and Deadlines:** Priority date 3/1; no closing date. Applicants notified on a rolling basis starting 1/31; must reply within 4 week(s) of notification.

**CONTACT**
Ronald Anderson, Director of Financial Aid
One Macklem Drive, Wilmore, KY 40390-1198
(859) 858-3511 ext. 2195

## Beckfield College
Florence, Kentucky
www.beckfield.edu                    Federal Code: 016726

**4-year for-profit** nursing and career college in large town.
**Enrollment:** 808 undergrads.
**Selectivity:** Open admission; but selective for some programs.

**BASIC COSTS (2015-2016)**
**Tuition and fees:** $18,350.

**FINANCIAL AID PICTURE**
**Students with need:** Need-based aid available for full-time and part-time students.
**Students without need:** This college awards aid only to students with need.
**Scholarships offered:** High School scholarship; tuition for one course per quarter for maximum of 8 quarters; must achieve and maintain 3.0 GPA, be enrolled full-time, and enter college in July or October following graduation from high school. Merit scholarship; $100 per quarter; must maintain 4.0 GPA, perfect attendance, and carry at least 8 quarter credit hours.
**Additional info:** Deadline for filing of financial aid forms is end of first week of classes.

**FINANCIAL AID PROCEDURES**
**Forms required:** FAFSA.
**Dates and Deadlines:** Applicants notified on a rolling basis.

**CONTACT**
Kim Villaverde, Corporate Director of Student Financial
16 Spiral Drive, Florence, KY 41042
(859) 371-9393 ext. 1134

## Bellarmine University
Louisville, Kentucky
www.bellarmine.edu                    Federal Code: 001954

**4-year private** university and liberal arts college in very large city, affiliated with Roman Catholic Church.
**Enrollment:** 2,584 undergrads, 5% part-time. 707 full-time freshmen.
**Selectivity:** Admits over 75% of applicants.

**BASIC COSTS (2015-2016)**
**Tuition and fees:** $37,650.
**Per-credit charge:** $850.
**Room and board:** $11,360.

**FINANCIAL AID PICTURE (2015-2016)**
**Students with need:** Out of 678 full-time freshmen who applied for aid, 584 were judged to have need. Of these, 584 received aid, and 137 had

their full need met. Average financial aid package met 77% of need; average scholarship/grant was $23,542; average loan was $3,316. For part-time students, average financial aid package was $9,340.

**Students without need:** 119 full-time freshmen who did not demonstrate need for aid received scholarships/grants; average award was $23,504. No-need awards available for academics, alumni affiliation, art, athletics, leadership, minority status, music/drama, religious affiliation, ROTC, state/district residency.

**Scholarships offered:** *Merit:* Academic awards range from $7,000 to full tuition. *Athletic:* 33 full-time freshmen received athletic scholarships; average amount $8,632.

### FINANCIAL AID PROCEDURES

**Forms required:** FAFSA.

**Dates and Deadlines:** Priority date 2/1; no closing date. Applicants notified on a rolling basis starting 3/15; must reply by 5/1.

**Transfers:** Applicants notified on a rolling basis starting 4/15; must reply within 3 week(s) of notification.

### CONTACT

Heather Boutell, Director of Financial Aid
2001 Newburg Road, Louisville, KY 40205
(502) 272-8124

## Berea College
Berea, Kentucky
www.berea.edu
Federal Code: 001955

**4-year private** liberal arts college in small town.
**Enrollment:** 1,593 undergrads. 432 full-time freshmen.
**Selectivity:** Admits less than 50% of applicants.

### BASIC COSTS (2016-2017)
**Tuition and fees:** $25,470.
**Room and board:** $6,472.

### FINANCIAL AID PICTURE (2015-2016)
**Students with need:** Out of 432 full-time freshmen who applied for aid, 432 were judged to have need. Of these, 432 received aid. Average financial aid package met 96% of need; average scholarship/grant was $32,957; average loan was $908. For part-time students, average financial aid package was $31,267.
**Students without need:** This college awards aid only to students with need.

### FINANCIAL AID PROCEDURES
**Forms required:** FAFSA.
**Dates and Deadlines:** Priority date 2/1; no closing date. Applicants notified on a rolling basis starting 11/1; must reply by 5/1.
**Transfers:** Financial aid transcript from previous school(s) must be received before awarding aid.

### CONTACT
Theresa Lowder, Director of Student Financial Aid Services
CPO 2220, Berea, KY 40404
(859) 985-3310

## Big Sandy Community and Technical College
Prestonsburg, Kentucky
www.bigsandy.kctcs.edu
Federal Code: 001996

**2-year public** community and technical college in small town.
**Enrollment:** 3,250 undergrads.
**Selectivity:** Open admission; but selective for some programs.

### BASIC COSTS (2015-2016)
**Tuition and fees:** $4,650; out-of-state residents $15,690.
**Per-credit charge:** $147; out-of-state residents $515.
**Additional info:** Nonresident students living in contiguous counties are charged a discounted non-resident rate of $294 per credit hour.

### FINANCIAL AID PICTURE
**Students with need:** Need-based aid available for full-time and part-time students.
**Students without need:** No-need awards available for academics.

### FINANCIAL AID PROCEDURES
**Forms required:** FAFSA.
**Dates and Deadlines:** Priority date 4/1; no closing date. Applicants notified on a rolling basis; must reply within 2 week(s) of notification.
**Transfers:** Kentucky State Grant must be transferred by August 1 for fall semester, December 1 for spring semester.

### CONTACT
Denise Trusty, Director of Financial Aid
One Bert T. Combs Drive, Prestonsburg, KY 41653
(606) 886-3863 ext. 67255

## Bluegrass Community and Technical College
Lexington, Kentucky
www.bluegrass.kctcs.edu
Federal Code: 009707

**2-year public** community and technical college in large city.
**Enrollment:** 10,392 undergrads.
**Selectivity:** Open admission; but selective for some programs.

### BASIC COSTS (2015-2016)
**Tuition and fees:** $4,650; out-of-state residents $15,690.
**Per-credit charge:** $147; out-of-state residents $515.
**Additional info:** Nonresident students living in contiguous counties are charged a discounted non-resident rate of $294 per credit hour.

### FINANCIAL AID PICTURE
**Students with need:** Need-based aid available for full-time and part-time students. Work study available nights, weekends, and for part-time students.
**Students without need:** No-need awards available for academics, minority status, state/district residency.

### FINANCIAL AID PROCEDURES
**Forms required:** FAFSA, institutional form.
**Dates and Deadlines:** Priority date 4/15; no closing date. Applicants notified on a rolling basis starting 6/5; must reply within 3 week(s) of notification.
**Transfers:** No deadline. Applicants notified on a rolling basis.

### CONTACT
Runan Pendergrast, Director of Financial Aid
200 Oswald Building, Cooper Drive, Lexington, KY 40506-0235
(859) 246-6216

## Brescia University
Owensboro, Kentucky
www.brescia.edu
Federal Code: 001958

**4-year private** university and liberal arts college in small city, affiliated with Roman Catholic Church.
**Enrollment:** 1,024 undergrads, 25% part-time. 147 full-time freshmen.
**Selectivity:** Admits less than 50% of applicants.

### BASIC COSTS (2015-2016)
**Tuition and fees:** $20,840.
**Per-credit charge:** $570.

**Room and board:** $8,750.

## FINANCIAL AID PICTURE (2014-2015)

**Students with need:** 51% of average financial aid package awarded as scholarships/grants, 49% awarded as loans/jobs. Need-based aid available for part-time students. Work study available nights, weekends, and for part-time students.

**Students without need:** No-need awards available for academics, alumni affiliation, art, athletics, minority status, music/drama, religious affiliation, state/district residency.

## FINANCIAL AID PROCEDURES

**Forms required:** FAFSA.

**Dates and Deadlines:** Priority date 8/1; closing date 8/23. Applicants notified on a rolling basis starting 3/1; must reply within 3 week(s) of notification.

## CONTACT

Kristi Eidson, Director of Financial Aid
717 Frederica Street, Owensboro, KY 42301-3023
(270) 685-3131 ext. 4216

## Brown Mackie College: Hopkinsville

Hopkinsville, Kentucky
www.brownmackie.edu                  Federal Code: 014493

**2-year for-profit** business and junior college in large town.
**Enrollment:** 222 undergrads.
**Selectivity:** Open admission.

## BASIC COSTS (2015-2016)

**Tuition and fees:** $16,490.
**Per-credit charge:** $327.

## FINANCIAL AID PICTURE

**Students with need:** Need-based aid available for full-time students.

## FINANCIAL AID PROCEDURES

**Forms required:** FAFSA.

**Dates and Deadlines:** Applicants notified on a rolling basis.

## CONTACT

Lamisha Sers, Director of Financial Aid
4001 Fort Campbell Boulevard, Hopkinsville, KY 42240
(800) 359-4753

## Campbellsville University

Campbellsville, Kentucky
www.campbellsville.edu            Federal Code: 001959

**4-year private** university in large town, affiliated with Baptist faith.
**Enrollment:** 2,098 undergrads, 11% part-time. 710 full-time freshmen.
**Selectivity:** Admits over 75% of applicants.

## BASIC COSTS (2016-2017)

**Tuition and fees:** $24,596.
**Per-credit charge:** $972.
**Room and board:** $7,896.
**Additional info:** Tuition/fee waivers available for adults, minority students, unemployed or children of unemployed.

## FINANCIAL AID PICTURE (2014-2015)

**Students with need:** Out of 685 full-time freshmen who applied for aid, 644 were judged to have need. Of these, 637 received aid, and 92 had their full need met. Average financial aid package met 73% of need; average scholarship/grant was $15,817; average loan was $3,052. For part-time students, average financial aid package was $5,606.

**Students without need:** 49 full-time freshmen who did not demonstrate need for aid received scholarships/grants; average award was $9,209. No-need awards available for academics, art, athletics, leadership, minority status, music/drama, religious affiliation, state/district residency.

**Scholarships offered:** 43 full-time freshmen received athletic scholarships; average amount $10,558.

**Additional info:** Matching scholarships available for students whose church contributes $200 annually. Performance grants available to members of marching band.

## FINANCIAL AID PROCEDURES

**Forms required:** FAFSA.

**Dates and Deadlines:** Priority date 1/31; no closing date. Applicants notified on a rolling basis starting 3/15; must reply by 5/1 or within 2 week(s) of notification.

**Transfers:** No deadline. Applicants notified on a rolling basis.

## CONTACT

Chris Mapes, Director of Financial Aid
1 University Drive, Campbellsville, KY 42718-2799
(270) 789-5013

## Centre College

Danville, Kentucky
www.centre.edu                    Federal Code: 001961

**4-year private** liberal arts college in large town, affiliated with Presbyterian Church (USA).
**Enrollment:** 1,355 undergrads. 375 full-time freshmen.
**Selectivity:** Admits 50 to 75% of applicants.

## BASIC COSTS (2015-2016)

**Tuition and fees:** $38,200.
**Room and board:** $9,620.

## FINANCIAL AID PICTURE (2015-2016)

**Students with need:** Out of 299 full-time freshmen who applied for aid, 226 were judged to have need. Of these, 226 received aid, and 83 had their full need met. Average financial aid package met 87% of need; average scholarship/grant was $29,311; average loan was $3,718.

**Students without need:** 141 full-time freshmen who did not demonstrate need for aid received scholarships/grants; average award was $20,495. No-need awards available for academics, alumni affiliation, art, leadership, music/drama, ROTC.

**Scholarships offered:** Institutional Merit Award: $9,500 to full tuition; applications must be on file by February 1; renewable. Music and Drama Scholarships: up to $7,500. Guaranteed minimum award available to admitted Centre Fellows and Kentucky Governor's Scholars.

## FINANCIAL AID PROCEDURES

**Forms required:** FAFSA, institutional form.

**Dates and Deadlines:** Priority date 1/31; closing date 1/31. Applicants notified on a rolling basis starting 3/19; must reply by 5/1.

**Transfers:** No deadline. Applicants notified on a rolling basis starting 3/1; must reply within 2 week(s) of notification. Financial aid transcript required.

## CONTACT

John Cuny, VP for Finance and Treasurer
600 West Walnut Street, Danville, KY 40422-1394
(859) 238-5367

## Clear Creek Baptist Bible College

Pineville, Kentucky
www.ccbbc.edu                     Federal Code: 017044

**4-year private** Bible college in small town, affiliated with Southern Baptist Convention.

**Enrollment:** 135 undergrads. 11 full-time freshmen.
**Selectivity:** Open admission; but selective for some programs.

**BASIC COSTS (2015-2016)**
**Tuition and fees:** $8,310.
**Per-credit charge:** $253.
**Room and board:** $3,570.

**FINANCIAL AID PICTURE (2015-2016)**
**Students with need:** Out of 10 full-time freshmen who applied for aid, 10 were judged to have need. Of these, 10 received aid. Average financial aid package met 50% of need; average scholarship/grant was $6,365. For part-time students, average financial aid package was $2,372.
**Students without need:** 1 full-time freshmen who did not demonstrate need for aid received scholarships/grants; average award was $800. No-need awards available for academics, alumni affiliation, religious affiliation.

**FINANCIAL AID PROCEDURES**
**Forms required:** FAFSA, institutional form.
**Dates and Deadlines:** Priority date 6/30; no closing date. Applicants notified on a rolling basis starting 6/1; must reply by 8/1.
**Transfers:** Priority date 5/5; no deadline. Applicants notified on a rolling basis starting 5/5; must reply by 8/1.

**CONTACT**
Sam Risner, Director of Financial Aid
300 Clear Creek Road, Pineville, KY 40977-9754
(606) 337-3196 ext. 142

## Daymar College: Bowling Green
Bowling Green, Kentucky
www.daymarcollege.edu　　Federal Code: 004934

**2-year for-profit** branch campus and career college in small city.
**Enrollment:** 225 undergrads.
**Selectivity:** Open admission.

**BASIC COSTS (2015-2016)**
**Additional info:** Diploma programs: $22,000-$26,500. Associate programs: $33,000. Tuition/fee waivers available for adults.

**FINANCIAL AID PICTURE**
**Students with need:** Need-based aid available for full-time and part-time students. Work study available nights.
**Students without need:** This college awards aid only to students with need.

**FINANCIAL AID PROCEDURES**
**Forms required:** FAFSA.

**CONTACT**
Janice Cutliff, Director of Financial Services
2421 Fitzgerald Industrial Drive, Bowling Green, KY 42101
(270) 843-6750

## Daymar College: Owensboro
Owensboro, Kentucky
www.daymarcollege.edu　　Federal Code: 009313

**2-year for-profit** business and junior college in small city.
**Enrollment:** 94 undergrads.
**Selectivity:** Open admission.

**BASIC COSTS (2015-2016)**
**Additional info:** Diploma programs: $22,000-$26,500. Associate programs: $33,000-$48,000.

**FINANCIAL AID PICTURE**
**Students with need:** Need-based aid available for full-time and part-time students.
**Students without need:** This college awards aid only to students with need.

**FINANCIAL AID PROCEDURES**
**Forms required:** FAFSA.
**Dates and Deadlines:** Applicants notified on a rolling basis.

**CONTACT**
Denise Jernigan, Director of Financial Services
3361 Buckland Square, Owensboro, KY 42301
(270) 926-4040

## Daymar College: Paducah
Paducah, Kentucky　　Federal Code: 013661
www.daymarcollege.edu　　CSS Code: 0669

**2-year for-profit** technical college in small city.
**Enrollment:** 47 undergrads.
**Selectivity:** Open admission.

**BASIC COSTS (2015-2016)**
**Additional info:** Diploma programs: $22,000-$26,500. Associate programs: $33,000.

**FINANCIAL AID PICTURE**
**Students with need:** Need-based aid available for full-time students.

**FINANCIAL AID PROCEDURES**
**Forms required:** FAFSA, CSS PROFILE.
**Dates and Deadlines:** Applicants notified on a rolling basis; must reply within 3 week(s) of notification.

**CONTACT**
JoAnn Price, Financial Aid Officer
509 South 30th Street, Paducah, KY 42001

## Eastern Kentucky University
Richmond, Kentucky
www.eku.edu　　Federal Code: 001963

**4-year public** university in large town.
**Enrollment:** 13,493 undergrads, 16% part-time. 2,729 full-time freshmen.
**Selectivity:** Admits 50 to 75% of applicants.

**BASIC COSTS (2015-2016)**
**Tuition and fees:** $8,600; out-of-state residents $18,090.
**Per-credit charge:** $340; out-of-state residents $735.
**Room and board:** $8,360.

**FINANCIAL AID PICTURE**
**Students with need:** Need-based aid available for full-time and part-time students. Work study available nights, weekends, and for part-time students.
**Students without need:** No-need awards available for academics, alumni affiliation, art, athletics, job skills, leadership, minority status, music/drama, ROTC, state/district residency.

**FINANCIAL AID PROCEDURES**
**Forms required:** FAFSA.
**Dates and Deadlines:** Applicants notified on a rolling basis starting 4/1.

**CONTACT**
Shelley Park, Director of Student Financial Assistance, Scholarship and Veteran Affairs
SSB CPO 54, 521 Lancaster Avenue, Richmond, KY 40475-3102

## Elizabethtown Community and Technical College

Elizabethtown, Kentucky
www.elizabethtown.kctcs.edu   Federal Code: 001991

**2-year public** community and technical college in large town.
**Enrollment:** 4,800 undergrads.
**Selectivity:** Open admission; but selective for some programs.

### BASIC COSTS (2015-2016)
**Tuition and fees:** $4,770; out-of-state residents $15,810.
**Per-credit charge:** $147; out-of-state residents $515.

### FINANCIAL AID PICTURE (2014-2015)
**Students with need:** 61% of average financial aid package awarded as scholarships/grants, 39% awarded as loans/jobs. Need-based aid available for part-time students. Work study available nights, weekends, and for part-time students.
**Students without need:** This college awards aid only to students with need.

### FINANCIAL AID PROCEDURES
**Forms required:** FAFSA.
**Dates and Deadlines:** Priority date 8/1; no closing date. Applicants notified on a rolling basis starting 6/1; must reply within 2 week(s) of notification.
**Transfers:** Priority date 7/11; no deadline. Applicants notified on a rolling basis; must reply within 2 week(s) of notification.

### CONTACT
Michael Barlow, Director of Financial Aid
600 College Street Road, Elizabethtown, KY 42701
(270) 769-2371 ext. 68614

## Georgetown College

Georgetown, Kentucky
www.georgetowncollege.edu   Federal Code: 001964

**4-year private** liberal arts college in large town, affiliated with Baptist faith.
**Enrollment:** 978 undergrads, 7% part-time. 271 full-time freshmen.
**Selectivity:** Admits 50 to 75% of applicants.

### BASIC COSTS (2016-2017)
**Tuition and fees:** $35,850.
**Per-credit charge:** $1,470.
**Room and board:** $9,050.
**Additional info:** Continuing students fee is $50 per semester. The Carte Blanche meal plan provides flexible continuous dining not limited to a fixed number of meals per week.

### FINANCIAL AID PICTURE (2014-2015)
**Students with need:** Out of 263 full-time freshmen who applied for aid, 244 were judged to have need. Of these, 244 received aid, and 12 had their full need met. Average financial aid package met 88% of need; average scholarship/grant was $15,317; average loan was $2,575. Need-based aid available for part-time students.
**Students without need:** 19 full-time freshmen who did not demonstrate need for aid received scholarships/grants; average award was $5,458. No-need awards available for academics, alumni affiliation, art, athletics, leadership, music/drama, religious affiliation, ROTC, state/district residency.
**Scholarships offered:** 9 full-time freshmen received athletic scholarships; average amount $4,278.

### FINANCIAL AID PROCEDURES
**Forms required:** FAFSA.
**Dates and Deadlines:** Priority date 2/1; no closing date. Applicants notified on a rolling basis starting 3/1; must reply by 5/1.

### CONTACT
Bob Fultz, Director of Student Financial Planning
400 East College Street, Georgetown, KY 40324-1696
(502) 863-8027

## Hazard Community and Technical College

Hazard, Kentucky
www.hazard.kctcs.edu   Federal Code: 006962

**2-year public** community and technical college in small town.
**Enrollment:** 1,803 undergrads.
**Selectivity:** Open admission; but selective for some programs and for out-of-state students.

### BASIC COSTS (2015-2016)
**Tuition and fees:** $4,650; out-of-district residents $9,060; out-of-state residents $15,690.
**Per-credit charge:** $147; out-of-district residents $294; out-of-state residents $515.

### FINANCIAL AID PICTURE
**Students with need:** Need-based aid available for full-time and part-time students.
**Students without need:** This college awards aid only to students with need.

### FINANCIAL AID PROCEDURES
**Forms required:** FAFSA.
**Dates and Deadlines:** Priority date 4/1; no closing date. Applicants notified on a rolling basis starting 6/15; must reply within 2 week(s) of notification.

### CONTACT
Chuck Anderson, Financial Aid Director
One Community College Drive, Hazard, KY 41701
(606) 487-3061

## Hopkinsville Community College

Hopkinsville, Kentucky
www.hopkinsville.kctcs.edu   Federal Code: 001994

**2-year public** community college in small city.
**Enrollment:** 3,165 undergrads.
**Selectivity:** Open admission; but selective for some programs.

### BASIC COSTS (2015-2016)
**Tuition and fees:** $4,650; out-of-district residents $9,060; out-of-state residents $15,690.
**Per-credit charge:** $147; out-of-district residents $297; out-of-state residents $515.

### FINANCIAL AID PICTURE
**Students with need:** Need-based aid available for full-time and part-time students. Work study available nights.
**Students without need:** No-need awards available for academics, leadership, minority status, state/district residency.
**Scholarships offered:** The Rotary Scholars Program: two years of full-time study; any graduate of a Christian County high school (beginning with the Class of 2012); 2.5 high school GPA and 95% attendance required.
**Additional info:** ACT required for academic scholarships.

### FINANCIAL AID PROCEDURES
**Forms required:** FAFSA.
**Dates and Deadlines:** Priority date 7/15; no closing date. Applicants notified on a rolling basis starting 7/1.
**Transfers:** No deadline. Applicants notified on a rolling basis.

## CONTACT
Jeff Horton, Chief Financial Officer
PO Box 2100, Hopkinsville, KY 42241-2100
(270) 707-3830

## Jefferson Community and Technical College
Louisville, Kentucky
www.jefferson.kctcs.edu          Federal Code: 006961

**2-year public** community and technical college in large city.
**Enrollment:** 11,588 undergrads.
**Selectivity:** Open admission; but selective for some programs.

### BASIC COSTS (2015-2016)
**Tuition and fees:** $4,650; out-of-state residents $15,690.
**Per-credit charge:** $147; out-of-state residents $515.

### FINANCIAL AID PICTURE
**Students with need:** Need-based aid available for full-time and part-time students.
**Students without need:** No-need awards available for academics, art, minority status.

### FINANCIAL AID PROCEDURES
**Forms required:** FAFSA, institutional form.
**Dates and Deadlines:** Priority date 3/15; no closing date. Applicants notified on a rolling basis starting 6/15; must reply within 3 week(s) of notification.

### CONTACT
Lisa Schrenger, Financial Aid Officer
109 East Broadway, Louisville, KY 40202
(502) 213-2137

## Kentucky Christian University
Grayson, Kentucky
www.kcu.edu          Federal Code: 001965

**4-year private** university and Bible college in small town.
**Enrollment:** 564 undergrads, 12% part-time. 170 full-time freshmen.

### BASIC COSTS (2015-2016)
**Tuition and fees:** $17,810.
**Per-credit charge:** $580.
**Room and board:** $7,800.

### FINANCIAL AID PICTURE
**Students with need:** Need-based aid available for full-time and part-time students. Work study available nights, weekends, and for part-time students.
**Students without need:** No-need awards available for academics, alumni affiliation, leadership, minority status, music/drama, religious affiliation.

### FINANCIAL AID PROCEDURES
**Forms required:** FAFSA.
**Dates and Deadlines:** Priority date 3/1; no closing date. Applicants notified on a rolling basis starting 3/15; must reply within 2 week(s) of notification.

### CONTACT
Jennie Bender, Director of Financial Aid
100 Academic Parkway, Grayson, KY 41143-2205
(606) 474-3226

## Kentucky Mountain Bible College
Jackson, Kentucky
www.kmbc.edu          Federal Code: 030021

**4-year private** Bible college in rural community, affiliated with Kentucky Mountain Holiness Association.
**Enrollment:** 67 undergrads, 18% part-time. 15 full-time freshmen.
**Selectivity:** Admits 50 to 75% of applicants.

### BASIC COSTS (2015-2016)
**Tuition and fees:** $7,460.
**Per-credit charge:** $225.
**Room and board:** $4,750.

### FINANCIAL AID PICTURE (2015-2016)
**Students with need:** Out of 14 full-time freshmen who applied for aid, 14 were judged to have need. Of these, 14 received aid, and 4 had their full need met. Average financial aid package met 65% of need; average scholarship/grant was $5,393; average loan was $6,625. For part-time students, average financial aid package was $5,816.
**Students without need:** No-need awards available for academics, job skills, leadership, music/drama.

### FINANCIAL AID PROCEDURES
**Forms required:** FAFSA, institutional form.
**Dates and Deadlines:** Priority date 5/1; no closing date. Applicants notified on a rolling basis starting 3/15.
**Transfers:** No deadline. Applicants notified on a rolling basis starting 8/30; must reply within 6 week(s) of notification.

### CONTACT
Rosita Marshall, Director of Financial Aid
855 Highway 541, Jackson, KY 41339
(606) 693-5000 ext. 175

## Kentucky State University
Frankfort, Kentucky
www.kysu.edu          Federal Code: 001968

**4-year public** university and liberal arts college in large town.
**Enrollment:** 1,286 undergrads, 15% part-time. 210 full-time freshmen.
**Selectivity:** Admits less than 50% of applicants.

### BASIC COSTS (2015-2016)
**Tuition and fees:** $7,754; out-of-state residents $18,056.
**Per-credit charge:** $307; out-of-state residents $736.
**Room and board:** $6,690.

### FINANCIAL AID PICTURE (2015-2016)
**Students with need:** Out of 192 full-time freshmen who applied for aid, 182 were judged to have need. Of these, 182 received aid, and 45 had their full need met. Average financial aid package met 87% of need; average scholarship/grant was $9,987; average loan was $3,733. For part-time students, average financial aid package was $10,310.
**Students without need:** 16 full-time freshmen who did not demonstrate need for aid received scholarships/grants; average award was $10,810. No-need awards available for academics, alumni affiliation, art, athletics, leadership, music/drama.
**Scholarships offered:** 21 full-time freshmen received athletic scholarships; average amount $10,844.

### FINANCIAL AID PROCEDURES
**Forms required:** FAFSA.
**Dates and Deadlines:** Priority date 4/15; no closing date. Applicants notified on a rolling basis starting 3/15; must reply within 4 week(s) of notification.
**Transfers:** Priority date 4/15. Applicants notified on a rolling basis; must reply within 4 week(s) of notification.

## CONTACT
Victoria Owens, Director of Financial Aid
400 East Main Street, ASB 312, Frankfort, KY 40601
(502) 597-5960

# Kentucky Wesleyan College
Owensboro, Kentucky
www.kwc.edu                    Federal Code: 001969

**4-year private** liberal arts college in small city, affiliated with United Methodist Church.
**Enrollment:** 691 undergrads, 4% part-time. 229 full-time freshmen.

### BASIC COSTS (2015-2016)
**Tuition and fees:** $23,250.
**Per-credit charge:** $640.
**Room and board:** $8,150.

### FINANCIAL AID PICTURE (2014-2015)
**Students with need:** Out of 222 full-time freshmen who applied for aid, 207 were judged to have need. Of these, 206 received aid, and 40 had their full need met. Average financial aid package met 74% of need; average scholarship/grant was $15,663; average loan was $3,153. For part-time students, average financial aid package was $5,828.
**Students without need:** 22 full-time freshmen who did not demonstrate need for aid received scholarships/grants; average award was $11,000. No-need awards available for academics, alumni affiliation, art, athletics, leadership, music/drama, religious affiliation, state/district residency.
**Scholarships offered:** Scholarships range from $1,000 to full tuition. Students compete in on-campus scholarship competitions.

### FINANCIAL AID PROCEDURES
**Forms required:** FAFSA.
**Dates and Deadlines:** Priority date 1/1; no closing date. Applicants notified on a rolling basis starting 2/15; must reply within 2 week(s) of notification.
**Transfers:** No deadline. Applicants notified on a rolling basis starting 11/15; must reply within 2 week(s) of notification.

### CONTACT
Samantha Hays, Director of Financial Aid
3000 Frederica Street, Owensboro, KY 42301
(270) 852-3130

# Lincoln College of Technology: Florence
Florence, Kentucky
www.swcollege.net              Federal Code: 012128

**2-year for-profit** health science and career college in small city.
**Enrollment:** 222 undergrads.
**Selectivity:** Open admission.

### BASIC COSTS (2015-2016)
**Additional info:** Certificate programs: $10,255. Diploma programs: $15,320 to $30,045. Associate programs: $30,515 to $33,048. Costs include total tuition, materials, tool fees, and registration fee.

### FINANCIAL AID PICTURE
**Students with need:** Need-based aid available for full-time and part-time students.
**Students without need:** This college awards aid only to students with need.

### FINANCIAL AID PROCEDURES
**Forms required:** FAFSA.
**Dates and Deadlines:** Applicants notified on a rolling basis.
**Transfers:** No deadline. Applicants notified on a rolling basis.

## CONTACT
Victoria Hubbard, Director of Financial Aid
8095 Connector Drive, Florence, KY 41042
(859) 282-9999

# Lindsey Wilson College
Columbia, Kentucky
www.lindsey.edu                Federal Code: 001972

**4-year private** liberal arts college in small town, affiliated with United Methodist Church.
**Enrollment:** 2,100 undergrads, 2% part-time. 514 full-time freshmen.
**Selectivity:** Open admission; but selective for some programs.

### BASIC COSTS (2015-2016)
**Tuition and fees:** $23,162.
**Per-credit charge:** $955.
**Room and board:** $8,900.

### FINANCIAL AID PICTURE (2015-2016)
**Students with need:** Out of 514 full-time freshmen who applied for aid, 484 were judged to have need. Of these, 484 received aid, and 102 had their full need met. Need-based aid available for part-time students.
**Students without need:** This college awards aid only to students with need.

### FINANCIAL AID PROCEDURES
**Forms required:** FAFSA, institutional form.
**Dates and Deadlines:** Priority date 3/1; no closing date. Applicants notified on a rolling basis starting 5/1; must reply within 2 week(s) of notification.
**Transfers:** Applicants notified on a rolling basis.

### CONTACT
Marilyn Radford, Director of Financial Aid
210 Lindsey Wilson Street, Columbia, KY 42728
(270) 384-8022

# Madisonville Community College
Madisonville, Kentucky
www.madisonville.kctcs.edu     Federal Code: 009010

**2-year public** community college in large town.
**Enrollment:** 2,265 undergrads.
**Selectivity:** Open admission; but selective for some programs.

### BASIC COSTS (2015-2016)
**Tuition and fees:** $4,650; out-of-district residents $9,060; out-of-state residents $15,690.
**Per-credit charge:** $147; out-of-district residents $294; out-of-state residents $515.
**Additional info:** Tuition/fee waivers available for minority students, unemployed or children of unemployed.

### FINANCIAL AID PICTURE
**Students with need:** Need-based aid available for full-time and part-time students. Work study available nights, weekends, and for part-time students.
**Students without need:** No-need awards available for minority status.

### FINANCIAL AID PROCEDURES
**Forms required:** FAFSA, institutional form.
**Dates and Deadlines:** Priority date 7/1; no closing date. Applicants notified on a rolling basis; must reply within 3 week(s) of notification.

### CONTACT
Martha Phelps, Director of Financial Aid
2000 College Drive, Madisonville, KY 42431
(270) 824-8693

## Maysville Community and Technical College
Maysville, Kentucky
www.maysville.kctcs.edu        Federal Code: 006960

**2-year public** community and technical college in small town.
**Enrollment:** 3,184 undergrads.
**Selectivity:** Open admission; but selective for some programs.

**BASIC COSTS (2015-2016)**
**Tuition and fees:** $4,650; out-of-state residents $15,690.
**Per-credit charge:** $147; out-of-state residents $515.
**Additional info:** Nonresident students living in contiguous counties are charged a discounted non-resident rate of $294 per credit hour.

**FINANCIAL AID PICTURE**
**Students with need:** Need-based aid available for full-time and part-time students. Work study available nights.
**Students without need:** No-need awards available for academics.

**FINANCIAL AID PROCEDURES**
**Forms required:** FAFSA, institutional form.
**Dates and Deadlines:** Priority date 4/1; no closing date. Applicants notified on a rolling basis starting 3/1; must reply within 3 week(s) of notification.

**CONTACT**
Sandy Power, Financial Aid Director
1755 US HIghway 68, Maysville, KY 41056
(606) 759-7141 ext. 66404

## Midway College
Midway, Kentucky
www.midway.edu        Federal Code: 001975

**4-year private** liberal arts college for women in small town, affiliated with Christian Church (Disciples of Christ).
**Enrollment:** 916 undergrads.

**BASIC COSTS (2016-2017)**
**Tuition and fees:** $23,250.
**Per-credit charge:** $860.
**Room and board:** $8,400.

**FINANCIAL AID PICTURE**
**Students with need:** Need-based aid available for full-time and part-time students. Work study available nights, weekends, and for part-time students.
**Students without need:** No-need awards available for academics, alumni affiliation, art, athletics, leadership, minority status, religious affiliation.
**Additional info:** Audition required of applicants for music scholarships.

**FINANCIAL AID PROCEDURES**
**Forms required:** FAFSA, institutional form.
**Dates and Deadlines:** Applicants notified on a rolling basis; must reply within 4 week(s) of notification.

**CONTACT**
Kate Ware, Director of Financial Aid
512 East Stephens Street, Midway, KY 40347-1120
(859) 846-5410

## Morehead State University
Morehead, Kentucky
www.moreheadstate.edu        Federal Code: 001976

**4-year public** university in large town.
**Enrollment:** 7,038 undergrads, 13% part-time. 1,452 full-time freshmen.

**Selectivity:** Admits over 75% of applicants.

**BASIC COSTS (2015-2016)**
**Tuition and fees:** $7,966; out-of-state residents $20,114.
**Room and board:** $8,300.
**Additional info:** Tuition/fee waivers available for minority students.

**FINANCIAL AID PICTURE**
**Students with need:** Need-based aid available for full-time and part-time students. Work study available nights, weekends, and for part-time students.
**Students without need:** No-need awards available for academics, alumni affiliation, art, athletics, leadership, minority status, music/drama, ROTC, state/district residency.

**FINANCIAL AID PROCEDURES**
**Forms required:** FAFSA.
**Dates and Deadlines:** Priority date 3/15; no closing date. Applicants notified on a rolling basis.
**Transfers:** No deadline. Applicants notified on a rolling basis. Transfer scholarships available.

**CONTACT**
Donna King, Director of Financial Aid
100 Admissions Center, Morehead, KY 40351
(606) 783-2000

## Murray State University
Murray, Kentucky
www.murraystate.edu        Federal Code: 001977

**4-year public** university in large town.
**Enrollment:** 7,891 undergrads, 11% part-time. 1,490 full-time freshmen.
**Selectivity:** Admits over 75% of applicants.

**BASIC COSTS (2015-2016)**
**Tuition and fees:** $7,608; out-of-state residents $20,712.
**Per-credit charge:** $273; out-of-state residents $819.
**Room and board:** $8,206.
**Additional info:** Murray State has multiple regional tuition rates for residents of states in our region. Regional rates are substantially lower than the out-of-state tuition rate. Tuition/fee waivers available for minority students.

**FINANCIAL AID PICTURE (2014-2015)**
**Students with need:** Out of 1,302 full-time freshmen who applied for aid, 1,028 were judged to have need. Of these, 1,027 received aid, and 248 had their full need met. Average financial aid package met 34% of need; average scholarship/grant was $6,496; average loan was $5,071. For part-time students, average financial aid package was $6,675.
**Students without need:** 166 full-time freshmen who did not demonstrate need for aid received scholarships/grants; average award was $4,911. No-need awards available for academics, alumni affiliation, art, athletics, job skills, leadership, minority status, music/drama, ROTC, state/district residency.
**Scholarships offered:** *Merit:* Excellence Award provides additional $1,000 in scholarship and $500 in housing to one Valedictorian and one Salutatorian at each public high school in our 18 county service region. *Athletic:* 42 full-time freshmen received athletic scholarships; average amount $10,807.
**Additional info:** Racer Promise grant, for first-time freshman from our 18-county service region who demonstrate financial need, covers up to 8 semesters of mandatory tuition and fees.

**FINANCIAL AID PROCEDURES**
**Forms required:** FAFSA, institutional form.
**Dates and Deadlines:** Priority date 2/1; no closing date. Applicants notified on a rolling basis starting 3/15; must reply by 5/1.
**Transfers:** Priority date 2/1; no deadline. Applicants notified on a rolling basis starting 3/15; must reply by 5/1. Transfer Scholarship; students eligible to

apply before entering when transferring 36 or more credit hours with 3.25 GPA.

**CONTACT**
Janet Balok, Director of Financial Aid
102 Curris Center, Murray, KY 42071
(270) 809-2546

## National College: Danville
Danville, Kentucky
www.national-college.edu          Federal Code: 010489

**2-year for-profit** business college in large town.
**Enrollment:** 81 undergrads.
**Selectivity:** Open admission.

**BASIC COSTS (2016-2017)**
**Tuition and fees:** $14,460.
**Per-credit charge:** $317.

**FINANCIAL AID PICTURE**
**Students with need:** Need-based aid available for full-time and part-time students.
**Students without need:** This college awards aid only to students with need.

**FINANCIAL AID PROCEDURES**
**Forms required:** FAFSA.
**Dates and Deadlines:** Applicants notified on a rolling basis.

**CONTACT**
Pam Cotton, Director of Financial Aid and Auditing
115 East Lexington Avenue, Danville, KY 40422
(540) 986-1800

## National College: Florence
Florence, Kentucky
www.national-college.edu          Federal Code: 010489

**2-year for-profit** business college in large town.
**Enrollment:** 40 undergrads.
**Selectivity:** Open admission.

**BASIC COSTS (2016-2017)**
**Tuition and fees:** $14,460.
**Per-credit charge:** $317.

**FINANCIAL AID PICTURE**
**Students with need:** Need-based aid available for full-time and part-time students.
**Students without need:** This college awards aid only to students with need.

**FINANCIAL AID PROCEDURES**
**Forms required:** FAFSA.
**Dates and Deadlines:** Applicants notified on a rolling basis.

**CONTACT**
Pam Cotton, Director of Financial Aid and Auditing
8095 Connector Drive, Florence, KY 41042
(540) 986-1800

## National College: Lexington
Lexington, Kentucky
www.national-college.edu          Federal Code: 010489

**2-year for-profit** business and junior college in small city.
**Enrollment:** 98 undergrads.

**Selectivity:** Open admission; but selective for some programs.

**BASIC COSTS (2016-2017)**
**Tuition and fees:** $14,460.
**Per-credit charge:** $317.

**FINANCIAL AID PICTURE**
**Students with need:** Need-based aid available for full-time and part-time students.
**Students without need:** This college awards aid only to students with need.

**FINANCIAL AID PROCEDURES**
**Forms required:** FAFSA.
**Dates and Deadlines:** Applicants notified on a rolling basis.

**CONTACT**
Pam Cotton, Director of Financial Aid and Auditing
2376 Sir Barton Way, Lexington, KY 40509
(859) 255-0621

## National College: Louisville
Louisville, Kentucky
www.national-college.edu          Federal Code: 010489

**2-year for-profit** business college in large city.
**Enrollment:** 158 undergrads.
**Selectivity:** Open admission; but selective for some programs.

**BASIC COSTS (2016-2017)**
**Tuition and fees:** $14,460.
**Per-credit charge:** $317.

**FINANCIAL AID PICTURE**
**Students with need:** Need-based aid available for full-time and part-time students.
**Students without need:** This college awards aid only to students with need.

**FINANCIAL AID PROCEDURES**
**Forms required:** FAFSA.
**Dates and Deadlines:** Applicants notified on a rolling basis.

**CONTACT**
Pamela Cotton, Director of Financial Aid and Compliance Officer
4205 Dixie Highway, Louisville, KY 40216
(540) 986-1800

## National College: Pikeville
Pikeville, Kentucky
www.national-college.edu          Federal Code: 010489

**2-year for-profit** business college in large town.
**Enrollment:** 137 undergrads.
**Selectivity:** Open admission; but selective for some programs.

**BASIC COSTS (2016-2017)**
**Tuition and fees:** $14,460.
**Per-credit charge:** $317.

**FINANCIAL AID PICTURE**
**Students with need:** Need-based aid available for full-time and part-time students.
**Students without need:** This college awards aid only to students with need.

**FINANCIAL AID PROCEDURES**
**Forms required:** FAFSA.

## CONTACT

Pam Cotton, Director of Financial Aid and Auditing

50 National Collge Boulevard, Pikeville, KY 41501

(540) 986-1800

## National College: Richmond

Richmond, Kentucky

www.national-college.edu            Federal Code: 010489

**2-year for-profit** business college in large town.

**Enrollment:** 61 undergrads.

**Selectivity:** Open admission.

### BASIC COSTS (2016-2017)

**Tuition and fees:** $14,460.

**Per-credit charge:** $317.

### FINANCIAL AID PICTURE

**Students with need:** Need-based aid available for full-time and part-time students.

**Students without need:** This college awards aid only to students with need.

### FINANCIAL AID PROCEDURES

**Forms required:** FAFSA.

**Dates and Deadlines:** Applicants notified on a rolling basis.

### CONTACT

Pam Cotton, Director of Financial Aid and Auditing

125 South Killarney Lane, Richmond, KY 40475

(540) 986-1800

## Northern Kentucky University

Highland Heights, Kentucky

www.nku.edu            Federal Code: 009275

**4-year public** university in small town.

**Enrollment:** 11,302 undergrads, 18% part-time. 2,103 full-time freshmen.

**Selectivity:** Admits over 75% of applicants.

### BASIC COSTS (2015-2016)

**Tuition and fees:** $9,120; out-of-district residents $13,584; out-of-state residents $17,856.

**Per-credit charge:** $364; out-of-district residents $550; out-of-state residents $728.

**Room and board:** $9,078.

### FINANCIAL AID PICTURE (2014-2015)

**Students with need:** Out of 1,858 full-time freshmen who applied for aid, 1,468 were judged to have need. Of these, 1,465 received aid, and 298 had their full need met. Average financial aid package met 68% of need; average scholarship/grant was $5,994; average loan was $3,476. For part-time students, average financial aid package was $7,968.

**Students without need:** 306 full-time freshmen who did not demonstrate need for aid received scholarships/grants; average award was $5,899. No-need awards available for academics, alumni affiliation, art, athletics, leadership, music/drama, ROTC, state/district residency.

**Scholarships offered:** 58 full-time freshmen received athletic scholarships; average amount $12,922.

### FINANCIAL AID PROCEDURES

**Forms required:** FAFSA.

**Dates and Deadlines:** Priority date 2/1; no closing date. Applicants notified on a rolling basis starting 3/15.

**Transfers:** No deadline. Applicants notified on a rolling basis starting 3/1.

## CONTACT

Leah Stewart, Director of Financial Assistance

Administrative Center 400, Northern Kentucky University, Highland Heights, KY 41099

(859) 572-5143

## Owensboro Community and Technical College

Owensboro, Kentucky

www.owensboro.kctcs.edu            Federal Code: 030345

**2-year public** community and technical college in small city.

**Enrollment:** 2,615 undergrads, 46% part-time. 471 full-time freshmen.

**Selectivity:** Open admission; but selective for some programs.

### BASIC COSTS (2015-2016)

**Tuition and fees:** $4,650; out-of-state residents $15,690.

**Per-credit charge:** $147; out-of-state residents $515.

### FINANCIAL AID PICTURE (2014-2015)

**Students with need:** 67% of average financial aid package awarded as scholarships/grants, 33% awarded as loans/jobs. Need-based aid available for part-time students.

**Students without need:** No-need awards available for academics, art, minority status, music/drama, state/district residency.

### FINANCIAL AID PROCEDURES

**Forms required:** FAFSA.

**Dates and Deadlines:** Priority date 4/1; no closing date. Must reply within 2 week(s) of notification.

**Transfers:** Financial aid transcripts from previous institutions may be required.

### CONTACT

Bernice Ayer, Financial Aid Officer

4800 New Hartford Road, Owensboro, KY 42303-1899

(270) 686-4521

## St. Catharine College

St. Catharine, Kentucky

www.sccky.edu            Federal Code: 001983

**4-year private** health science and liberal arts college in small town, affiliated with Roman Catholic Church.

**Enrollment:** 539 undergrads, 5% part-time. 137 full-time freshmen.

**Selectivity:** Open admission; but selective for some programs.

### BASIC COSTS (2015-2016)

**Tuition and fees:** $19,832.

**Per-credit charge:** $660.

**Room and board:** $9,412.

### FINANCIAL AID PICTURE

**Students with need:** Need-based aid available for full-time and part-time students.

**Students without need:** This college awards aid only to students with need.

### FINANCIAL AID PROCEDURES

**Forms required:** FAFSA, institutional form.

**Dates and Deadlines:** Priority date 3/15; no closing date. Applicants notified on a rolling basis.

**Transfers:** Priority date 2/1; no deadline. Applicants notified on a rolling basis.

**CONTACT**

Jeremy Pittman, Director of Financial Aid

2735 Bardstown Road, St. Catharine, KY 40061

(859) 336-5082 ext. 1214

## Somerset Community College

Somerset, Kentucky

www.somerset.kctcs.edu          Federal Code: 001997

**2-year public** community and technical college in large town.

**Enrollment:** 6,995 undergrads.

**Selectivity:** Open admission; but selective for some programs.

**BASIC COSTS (2015-2016)**

**Tuition and fees:** $4,650; out-of-state residents $15,690.

**Per-credit charge:** $147; out-of-state residents $515.

**Additional info:** Nonresident students living in contiguous counties are charged a discounted non-resident rate of $294 per credit hour.

**FINANCIAL AID PICTURE**

**Students with need:** Need-based aid available for full-time and part-time students.

**Students without need:** This college awards aid only to students with need.

**FINANCIAL AID PROCEDURES**

**Forms required:** FAFSA.

**Dates and Deadlines:** Priority date 3/1; no closing date. Applicants notified on a rolling basis starting 5/1; must reply within 2 week(s) of notification.

**Transfers:** Priority date 3/15; closing date 8/15. Applicants notified on a rolling basis starting 5/1; must reply within 2 week(s) of notification.

**CONTACT**

Daniel Patterson, Director of Financial Aid

808 Monticello Street, Somerset, KY 42501

(606) 679-8501 ext. 16640

## Southeast Kentucky Community and Technical College

Cumberland, Kentucky

www.southeast.kctcs.edu          Federal Code: 001998

**2-year public** community and technical college in small town.

**Enrollment:** 2,376 undergrads, 28% part-time. 250 full-time freshmen.

**Selectivity:** Open admission; but selective for some programs.

**BASIC COSTS (2015-2016)**

**Tuition and fees:** $4,650; out-of-state residents $15,690.

**Per-credit charge:** $147; out-of-state residents $515.

**Additional info:** Nonresident students living in contiguous counties are charged a discounted non-resident rate of $294 per credit hour.

**FINANCIAL AID PICTURE**

**Students with need:** Need-based aid available for full-time and part-time students.

**Students without need:** This college awards aid only to students with need.

**Additional info:** March 15 deadline for state financial aid.

**FINANCIAL AID PROCEDURES**

**Forms required:** FAFSA.

**Dates and Deadlines:** Priority date 3/15; no closing date. Must reply within 2 week(s) of notification.

**CONTACT**

Rebecca Parrott, Vice President for Student Affairs

700 College Road, Cumberland, KY 40823

(606) 589-2145

## Spalding University

Louisville, Kentucky

www.spalding.edu          Federal Code: 001960

**4-year private** university in very large city, affiliated with Roman Catholic Church.

**Enrollment:** 1,122 undergrads, 18% part-time. 179 full-time freshmen.

**Selectivity:** Admits 50 to 75% of applicants.

**BASIC COSTS (2015-2016)**

**Tuition and fees:** $23,887.

**Per-credit charge:** $796.25.

**Room and board:** $8,400.

**FINANCIAL AID PICTURE**

**Students with need:** Need-based aid available for full-time and part-time students.

**Students without need:** No-need awards available for academics, alumni affiliation, art, leadership.

**Scholarships offered:** Egan Service Learning Program: covers the cost of a double room on campus; awarded to students who demonstrate leadership in campus activities and agree to complete service hours within the community. Catherine Spalding Grant: a need based award with a maximum dollar amount of $6,500, opportunity for renewal for eight semesters; requires a minimum GPA of 2.0 and completion of FAFSA.

**FINANCIAL AID PROCEDURES**

**Forms required:** FAFSA.

**Dates and Deadlines:** Priority date 1/1; no closing date. Applicants notified on a rolling basis starting 3/31.

**Transfers:** No deadline. Applicants notified on a rolling basis; must reply within 2 week(s) of notification.

**CONTACT**

Michelle Standridge, Interim Director of Financial Aid

845 S Third Street, Louisville, KY 40203

(502) 873-4329

## Spencerian College

Louisville, Kentucky

www.spencerian.edu          Federal Code: 004618

**2-year for-profit** career college in large city.

**Enrollment:** 466 undergrads, 39% part-time. 71 full-time freshmen.

**Selectivity:** Open admission; but selective for some programs.

**BASIC COSTS (2015-2016)**

**Additional info:** Certificate programs range from $13,225-$38,905, books and supplies range from $900-$3,300, room and board ranges from $5,950-$17,850. Associates programs range from $32,485-$52,625, books and supplies range from $2,400-$4,000, room and board ranges from $14,875-$23,800.

**FINANCIAL AID PICTURE (2014-2015)**

**Students with need:** 54% of average financial aid package awarded as scholarships/grants, 46% awarded as loans/jobs. Need-based aid available for part-time students.

**Students without need:** No-need awards available for academics.

**FINANCIAL AID PROCEDURES**

**Forms required:** FAFSA, institutional form.

**CONTACT**

Jill Schuler, Director of Financial Aid

4627 Dixie Highway, Louisville, KY 40216

## Spencerian College: Lexington

Lexington, Kentucky
www.spencerian.edu                     Federal Code: 004618

**2-year for-profit** branch campus college in small city.
**Enrollment:** 76 undergrads.
**Selectivity:** Open admission; but selective for some programs.

### BASIC COSTS (2015-2016)
**Tuition and fees:** $19,260.
**Per-credit charge:** $299.
**Room only:** $5,940.

### FINANCIAL AID PICTURE (2014-2015)
**Students with need:** Need-based aid available for full-time and part-time students.
**Students without need:** This college awards aid only to students with need.

### FINANCIAL AID PROCEDURES
**Forms required:** FAFSA, state aid form, institutional form.
**Dates and Deadlines:** Applicants notified on a rolling basis starting 1/1.
**Transfers:** No deadline. Applicants notified on a rolling basis.

### CONTACT
Brian Highley, Director of Financial Aid/Compliance Officer
2355 Harrodsburg Rd, Lexington, KY 40504
(859) 223-9608 ext. 5441

## Sullivan College of Technology and Design

Louisville, Kentucky
www.sctd.edu                          Federal Code: 012088

**2-year for-profit** visual arts, technical and career college in very large city.
**Enrollment:** 395 undergrads.

### BASIC COSTS (2015-2016)
**Additional info:** Full-program tuition cost ranges from $38,160-$44,520 depending on the program of study. The per-credit-hour tuition rate ranges from $450-$525 also depending on the program of study. The approximate cost of books and supplies per academic year varies by program of study. Required fees are a $200 general fee per quarter plus a fee of $240 for online courses. Rent for a semi-private room is $660 per month or $5,940 for the academic year (9 months/3 quarters). The required meal plan for all housing students includes three meals a day Mon-Fri and brunch and dinner on Sat-Sun (19 meals) and costs $2,985 per academic year. Total room and board for an academic year is $8,925. Tuition at time of enrollment locked for 2 years; tuition/fee waivers available for unemployed or children of unemployed.

### FINANCIAL AID PICTURE (2014-2015)
**Students with need:** 67% of average financial aid package awarded as scholarships/grants, 33% awarded as loans/jobs. Need-based aid available for part-time students.
**Students without need:** No-need awards available for academics, art, job skills.
**Scholarships offered:** Academic Scholarships; up to $3,000; based on class rank, GPA, essay. Scholarship Day Competition; up to $1,500 based upon testing scores. Scholarship Fair Competition; up to $3,000; based upon open competition in electronics, drafting, interior design, computer networking and art skills. Kentucky Skills USA Scholarships; up to $1,500; based upon state championship competitions in such fields as drafting, electronics, etc.

### FINANCIAL AID PROCEDURES
**Forms required:** FAFSA.
**Dates and Deadlines:** Applicants notified on a rolling basis; must reply within 2 week(s) of notification.

**Transfers:** No deadline. Applicants notified on a rolling basis.

### CONTACT
Michelle Smith, Financial Planning Director
3901 Atkinson Square Drive, Louisville, KY 40218-4524
(502) 456-6509 ext. 8240

## Sullivan University

Louisville, Kentucky
www.sullivan.edu                      Federal Code: 004619

**4-year for-profit** university in large city.
**Enrollment:** 2,498 undergrads, 38% part-time. 241 full-time freshmen.

### BASIC COSTS (2015-2016)
**Additional info:** Program and housing costs vary by program.

### FINANCIAL AID PICTURE
**Students with need:** Need-based aid available for full-time and part-time students. Work study available nights.
**Students without need:** This college awards aid only to students with need.

### FINANCIAL AID PROCEDURES
**Forms required:** FAFSA.
**Dates and Deadlines:** Applicants notified on a rolling basis starting 1/2.

### CONTACT
Angela Miller, Director of Financial Planning
3101 Bardstown Road, Louisville, KY 40205
(502) 456-6771

## Thomas More College

Crestview Hills, Kentucky
www.thomasmore.edu                    Federal Code: 002001

**4-year private** liberal arts college in small town, affiliated with Roman Catholic Church.
**Enrollment:** 1,308 undergrads, 3% part-time. 276 full-time freshmen.
**Selectivity:** Admits over 75% of applicants.

### BASIC COSTS (2016-2017)
**Tuition and fees:** $29,450.
**Per-credit charge:** $620.
**Room and board:** $7,304.

### FINANCIAL AID PICTURE (2014-2015)
**Students with need:** Out of 267 full-time freshmen who applied for aid, 248 were judged to have need. Of these, 248 received aid, and 38 had their full need met. Average financial aid package met 74% of need; average scholarship/grant was $17,415; average loan was $3,637. For part-time students, average financial aid package was $4,675.
**Students without need:** 27 full-time freshmen who did not demonstrate need for aid received scholarships/grants; average award was $15,141. No-need awards available for academics, alumni affiliation, art, leadership, minority status, music/drama, religious affiliation, ROTC, state/district residency.

### FINANCIAL AID PROCEDURES
**Forms required:** FAFSA.
**Dates and Deadlines:** Closing date 3/15. Applicants notified on a rolling basis starting 3/1; must reply by 5/1.
**Transfers:** No deadline. Applicants notified on a rolling basis; must reply by 5/1.

### CONTACT
Dyane Foltz, Director of Financial Aid
333 Thomas More Parkway, Crestview Hills, KY 41017-3495
(859) 344-4043

# Transylvania University

Lexington, Kentucky
www.transy.edu                          Federal Code: 001987

**4-year private** liberal arts college in large city, affiliated with Christian
Church (Disciples of Christ).
**Enrollment:** 1,055 undergrads, 1% part-time. 311 full-time freshmen.
**Selectivity:** Admits over 75% of applicants.

## BASIC COSTS (2016-2017)
**Tuition and fees:** $35,830.
**Room and board:** $9,860.

## FINANCIAL AID PICTURE (2015-2016)
**Students with need:** Out of 281 full-time freshmen who applied for aid,
228 were judged to have need. Of these, 228 received aid, and 74 had their
full need met. Average financial aid package met 84% of need; average
scholarship/grant was $23,656; average loan was $3,135. For part-time students, average financial aid package was $10,531.
**Students without need:** 83 full-time freshmen who did not demonstrate
need for aid received scholarships/grants; average award was $16,976. No-
need awards available for academics, art, leadership, minority status, music/
drama, religious affiliation, state/district residency.
**Scholarships offered:** William T. Young Merit Scholarships: 20 awarded; tuition and fees.
**Additional info:** Auditions and portfolios required for music and art scholarships respectively. Essays required for other scholarship programs. Applications for William T. Young scholarships must be received by December 1.

## FINANCIAL AID PROCEDURES
**Forms required:** FAFSA.
**Dates and Deadlines:** Priority date 1/1; no closing date. Applicants notified
on a rolling basis starting 3/15; must reply by 5/1 or within 2 week(s) of notification.
**Transfers:** No deadline. Applicants notified on a rolling basis starting 3/15;
must reply by 8/6.

## CONTACT
David Cecil, Director of Financial Aid
300 North Broadway, Lexington, KY 40508-1797
(859) 233-8239

# Union College

Barbourville, Kentucky
www.unionky.edu                         Federal Code: 001988

**4-year private** liberal arts and teachers college in small town, affiliated with
United Methodist Church.
**Enrollment:** 794 undergrads, 6% part-time. 212 full-time freshmen.
**Selectivity:** Admits 50 to 75% of applicants.

## BASIC COSTS (2015-2016)
**Tuition and fees:** $24,075.
**Per-credit charge:** $340.
**Room and board:** $7,000.

## FINANCIAL AID PICTURE (2015-2016)
**Students with need:** Average financial aid package met 68% of need; average scholarship/grant was $18,504; average loan was $3,667. Need-based
aid available for part-time students.
**Students without need:** No-need awards available for academics, alumni
affiliation, athletics, leadership, music/drama, religious affiliation.

## FINANCIAL AID PROCEDURES
**Forms required:** FAFSA.
**Dates and Deadlines:** Priority date 2/1; no closing date. Applicants notified
on a rolling basis starting 2/15; must reply within 2 week(s) of notification.

**Transfers:** No deadline. Applicants notified on a rolling basis starting 2/15;
must reply within 2 week(s) of notification.

## CONTACT
Andra Butler, Director of Financial Aid
310 College Street, Box 005, Barbourville, KY 40906
(606) 546-1618

# University of Kentucky

Lexington, Kentucky
www.uky.edu                             Federal Code: 001989

**4-year public** university in large city.
**Enrollment:** 22,247 undergrads.

## BASIC COSTS (2015-2016)
**Tuition and fees:** $10,936; out-of-state residents $24,268.
**Per-credit charge:** $404; out-of-state residents $960.
**Room and board:** $9,086.
**Additional info:** Tuition/fee waivers available for adults, minority students.

## FINANCIAL AID PICTURE
**Students with need:** Need-based aid available for full-time and part-time stu-
dents. Work study available weekends and for part-time students.
**Students without need:** No-need awards available for academics, alumni
affiliation, art, athletics, job skills, leadership, minority status, music/drama,
ROTC, state/district residency.

## FINANCIAL AID PROCEDURES
**Forms required:** FAFSA.
**Dates and Deadlines:** Closing date 2/15. Applicants notified on a rolling
basis starting 4/1; must reply within 3 week(s) of notification.
**Transfers:** Priority date 4/1.

## CONTACT
Nimmi Wiggins, Director of Student Financial Aid
100 Funkhouser Building, Lexington, KY 40506-0054
(859) 257-3172

# University of Louisville

Louisville, Kentucky
www.louisville.edu                      Federal Code: 001999

**4-year public** university in very large city.
**Enrollment:** 14,844 undergrads, 18% part-time. 2,726 full-time freshmen.
**Selectivity:** Admits 50 to 75% of applicants.

## BASIC COSTS (2015-2016)
**Tuition and fees:** $10,744; out-of-state residents $24,632.
**Per-credit charge:** $440; out-of-state residents $1,036.
**Room and board:** $8,120.

## FINANCIAL AID PICTURE (2015-2016)
**Students with need:** Out of 2,377 full-time freshmen who applied for aid,
1,802 were judged to have need. Of these, 1,784 received aid, and 472 had
their full need met. Average financial aid package met 64% of need; average
scholarship/grant was $9,568; average loan was $3,153. For part-time students, average financial aid package was $6,527.
**Students without need:** 462 full-time freshmen who did not demonstrate
need for aid received scholarships/grants; average award was $7,884. No-
need awards available for academics, art, athletics, leadership, minority status, music/drama, ROTC, state/district residency.
**Scholarships offered:** 107 full-time freshmen received athletic scholarships;
average amount $22,661.

## FINANCIAL AID PROCEDURES
**Forms required:** FAFSA.

**Dates and Deadlines:** Priority date 2/15; no closing date. Applicants notified on a rolling basis starting 4/1.
**Transfers:** Priority date 3/1.

**CONTACT**
Sandy Neel, Director of Student Financial Aid
2211 South Brook Street, Louisville, KY 40292
(502) 852-5511

## University of Pikeville
Pikeville, Kentucky
www.upike.edu                    Federal Code: 001980

**4-year private** university and liberal arts college in small town, affiliated with Presbyterian Church (USA).
**Enrollment:** 1,244 undergrads, 2% part-time. 175 full-time freshmen.
**Selectivity:** Open admission; but selective for some programs.

**BASIC COSTS (2016-2017)**
**Tuition and fees:** $19,600.
**Per-credit charge:** $817.
**Room and board:** $8,376.

**FINANCIAL AID PICTURE (2015-2016)**
**Students with need:** Average financial aid package met 82% of need; average scholarship/grant was $18,100; average loan was $3,442. For part-time students, average financial aid package was $10,010.
**Students without need:** This college awards aid only to students with need.
**Scholarships offered:** University of Pikeville Promise: full-tuition, four-year scholarship that places emphasis on academics and financial need; applicants must submit ACT and HSGPA, file FAFSA by February 15 of senior year in high school, be a Kentucky resident, display full eligibility for Pell Grant and receive CAP and KTG state grants.

**FINANCIAL AID PROCEDURES**
**Forms required:** FAFSA.
**Dates and Deadlines:** Priority date 2/15; no closing date. Applicants notified on a rolling basis starting 2/1; must reply by 5/1.
**Transfers:** No deadline. Must reply by 5/1 or within 2 week(s) of notification.

**CONTACT**
Judy Bradley, Financial Aid Director
147 Sycamore Street, Pikeville, KY 41501-1194
(606) 218-5251

## University of the Cumberlands
Williamsburg, Kentucky
www.ucumberlands.edu              Federal Code: 001962

**4-year private** university and liberal arts college in small town, affiliated with Baptist faith.
**Enrollment:** 1,817 undergrads, 9% part-time. 433 full-time freshmen.
**Selectivity:** Admits 50 to 75% of applicants.

**BASIC COSTS (2015-2016)**
**Tuition and fees:** $22,000.
**Per-credit charge:** $690.
**Room and board:** $8,500.

**FINANCIAL AID PICTURE (2015-2016)**
**Students with need:** Out of 414 full-time freshmen who applied for aid, 388 were judged to have need. Of these, 388 received aid, and 67 had their full need met. Average financial aid package met 80% of need; average scholarship/grant was $18,932; average loan was $3,438. For part-time students, average financial aid package was $4,336.

**Students without need:** 43 full-time freshmen who did not demonstrate need for aid received scholarships/grants; average award was $9,691. No-need awards available for academics, athletics, job skills, leadership, music/drama, religious affiliation, state/district residency.
**Scholarships offered:** *Merit:* Presidential: up to $22,000; based on outstanding academic credentials; no limit. Dean's: up to $15,000; based on ACT/SAT score and high school GPA; no limit. Kentucky Rogers Scholar: up to full-tuition. Rogers Scholar Graduate: based on ACT/SAT score and GPA; up to 3 per year. Kentucky Governor's Scholar: up to $15,000; GSP graduate; no limit. Christian Leadership: $1,000-$5,000; based on involvement/leadership in church or other religious organizations; no limit. Trustee Scholarship: based upon outstanding academic credentials, letters of recommendations, essays and interview process; full tuition, room and board: up to 5 awarded. Lewis Appalachian Scholarship: based on academic performance and community involvement; available to students from select regions of KY; $1,000; 1 awarded each year. *Athletic:* 61 full-time freshmen received athletic scholarships; average amount $6,064.

**FINANCIAL AID PROCEDURES**
**Forms required:** FAFSA.
**Dates and Deadlines:** Priority date 2/1; no closing date. Applicants notified on a rolling basis starting 3/1; must reply within 2 week(s) of notification.
**Transfers:** Applicants notified on a rolling basis starting 3/1; must reply within 2 week(s) of notification.

**CONTACT**
Steve Allen, Director of Financial Planning
6178 College Station Drive, Williamsburg, KY 40769
(800) 343-1609

## West Kentucky Community and Technical College
Paducah, Kentucky
www.westkentucky.kctcs.edu        Federal Code: 001979

**2-year public** community and technical college in large town.
**Enrollment:** 4,668 undergrads.
**Selectivity:** Open admission; but selective for some programs.

**BASIC COSTS (2015-2016)**
**Tuition and fees:** $4,650; out-of-state residents $15,690.
**Per-credit charge:** $147; out-of-state residents $515.
**Additional info:** Nonresident students living in contiguous counties are charged a discounted non-resident rate of $294 per credit hour.

**FINANCIAL AID PICTURE**
**Students with need:** Need-based aid available for full-time and part-time students.

**FINANCIAL AID PROCEDURES**
**Forms required:** FAFSA.
**Dates and Deadlines:** Priority date 4/1; closing date 7/15. Applicants notified on a rolling basis starting 7/15; must reply within 4 week(s) of notification.

**CONTACT**
Nate Slaton, Director of Financial Aid
4810 Alben Barkley Drive, Paducah, KY 42002-7380
(270) 534-3248

## Western Kentucky University
Bowling Green, Kentucky
www.wku.edu                       Federal Code: 002002

**4-year public** university in small city.
**Enrollment:** 15,119 undergrads, 14% part-time. 3,079 full-time freshmen.

**Selectivity:** Admits over 75% of applicants.

**BASIC COSTS (2015-2016)**
**Tuition and fees:** $9,482; out-of-state residents $24,132.
**Per-credit charge:** $395; out-of-state residents $1,006.
**Room and board:** $7,368.

**FINANCIAL AID PICTURE (2014-2015)**
**Students with need:** Out of 2,697 full-time freshmen who applied for aid, 2,053 were judged to have need. Of these, 2,028 received aid, and 820 had their full need met. Average financial aid package met 40% of need; average scholarship/grant was $5,222; average loan was $3,000. For part-time students, average financial aid package was $9,691.
**Students without need:** 434 full-time freshmen who did not demonstrate need for aid received scholarships/grants; average award was $6,915. No-need awards available for academics, alumni affiliation, art, athletics, job skills, leadership, minority status, music/drama, religious affiliation, ROTC, state/district residency.
**Scholarships offered: *Merit:*** Academic scholarships; $200 to full tuition; number awarded varies. ***Athletic:*** 97 full-time freshmen received athletic scholarships; average amount $12,922.

**FINANCIAL AID PROCEDURES**
**Forms required:** FAFSA.
**Dates and Deadlines:** Priority date 2/15; no closing date. Applicants notified on a rolling basis starting 3/1.
**Transfers:** Transfer students receiving CAP Grant must notify the state agency by December 1 of each year.

**CONTACT**
Cynthia Burnette, Director of Financial Assistance
1906 College Heights Boulevard #11020, Bowling Green, KY 42101
(270) 745-2755

# Louisiana

## Baton Rouge Community College
Baton Rouge, Louisiana
www.mybrcc.edu                    Federal Code: 037303

**2-year public** community college in large city.
**Enrollment:** 7,843 undergrads, 42% part-time. 1,582 full-time freshmen.
**Selectivity:** Open admission.

**BASIC COSTS (2015-2016)**
**Tuition and fees:** $4,054; out-of-state residents $8,132.

**FINANCIAL AID PICTURE**
**Students with need:** Need-based aid available for full-time and part-time students. Work study available weekends and for part-time students.
**Students without need:** No-need awards available for academics, athletics, leadership, minority status, state/district residency.

**FINANCIAL AID PROCEDURES**
**Forms required:** FAFSA, institutional form.
**Dates and Deadlines:** Priority date 4/15; closing date 6/30. Applicants notified on a rolling basis.
**Transfers:** No deadline. Applicants notified on a rolling basis.

**CONTACT**
Rosey Toney, Director of Financial Aid
201 Community College Drive, Baton Rouge, LA 70806
(225) 216-8640

## Bossier Parish Community College
Bossier City, Louisiana
www.bpcc.edu/index.html                    Federal Code: 012033

**2-year public** community college in small city.
**Enrollment:** 5,393 undergrads, 35% part-time. 1,116 full-time freshmen.
**Selectivity:** Open admission.

**BASIC COSTS (2015-2016)**
**Tuition and fees:** $3,971; out-of-state residents $8,648.

**FINANCIAL AID PICTURE (2014-2015)**
**Students with need:** Out of 1,106 full-time freshmen who applied for aid, 1,011 were judged to have need. Of these, 978 received aid, and 18 had their full need met. Average financial aid package met 31% of need; average scholarship/grant was $2,038; average loan was $2,072. For part-time students, average financial aid package was $9,762.
**Students without need:** 3 full-time freshmen who did not demonstrate need for aid received scholarships/grants; average award was $500. No-need awards available for academics, athletics, leadership, minority status, music/drama.
**Scholarships offered:** 18 full-time freshmen received athletic scholarships; average amount $1,681.

**FINANCIAL AID PROCEDURES**
**Forms required:** FAFSA.
**Dates and Deadlines:** Priority date 6/1; no closing date. Applicants notified on a rolling basis starting 4/1; must reply within 3 week(s) of notification.
**Transfers:** No deadline.

**CONTACT**
Vickie Temple, Financial Aid Director
6220 East Texas Street, Bossier City, LA 71111-6922
(318) 678-6026

## Centenary College of Louisiana
Shreveport, Louisiana
www.centenary.edu                    Federal Code: 002003

**4-year private** liberal arts college in large city, affiliated with United Methodist Church.
**Enrollment:** 518 undergrads, 2% part-time. 155 full-time freshmen.
**Selectivity:** Admits 50 to 75% of applicants.

**BASIC COSTS (2015-2016)**
**Tuition and fees:** $33,900.
**Room and board:** $12,350.

**FINANCIAL AID PICTURE (2015-2016)**
**Students with need:** Out of 146 full-time freshmen who applied for aid, 131 were judged to have need. Of these, 131 received aid, and 31 had their full need met. Average financial aid package met 68% of need; average scholarship/grant was $22,356; average loan was $3,297. For part-time students, average financial aid package was $8,736.
**Students without need:** 24 full-time freshmen who did not demonstrate need for aid received scholarships/grants; average award was $20,612. No-need awards available for academics, alumni affiliation, art, music/drama, religious affiliation, state/district residency.

**FINANCIAL AID PROCEDURES**
**Forms required:** FAFSA.
**Dates and Deadlines:** Priority date 2/15; no closing date. Applicants notified on a rolling basis starting 3/15; must reply by 5/1.
**Transfers:** No deadline. Applicants notified on a rolling basis starting 2/15; must reply within 4 week(s) of notification.

**CONTACT**
Lynette Viskozki, Director of Financial Aid
Office of Admission, Shreveport, LA 71104
(318) 869-5137

## Delgado Community College
New Orleans, Louisiana
www.dcc.edu                          Federal Code: 004625

**2-year public** community college in large city.
**Enrollment:** 15,538 undergrads, 57% part-time. 1,414 full-time freshmen.
**Selectivity:** Open admission; but selective for some programs.

**BASIC COSTS (2015-2016)**
**Tuition and fees:** $3,911; out-of-state residents $8,200.

**FINANCIAL AID PICTURE (2014-2015)**
**Students with need:** 42% of average financial aid package awarded as scholarships/grants, 58% awarded as loans/jobs. Need-based aid available for part-time students. Work study available nights.
**Students without need:** No-need awards available for academics, athletics, leadership, music/drama, state/district residency.

**FINANCIAL AID PROCEDURES**
**Forms required:** FAFSA, institutional form.
**Dates and Deadlines:** Priority date 5/1; closing date 7/15. Applicants notified on a rolling basis starting 4/1; must reply within 2 week(s) of notification.

**CONTACT**
Rhonda King, Director of Financial Aid
615 City Park Avenue, New Orleans, LA 70119
(855) 215-8247

## Dillard University
New Orleans, Louisiana
www.dillard.edu                        Federal Code: 002004

**4-year private** university and liberal arts college in large city, affiliated with United Church of Christ.
**Enrollment:** 1,200 undergrads.

**BASIC COSTS (2015-2016)**
**Tuition and fees:** $16,252.
**Room and board:** $9,766.

**FINANCIAL AID PICTURE**
**Students with need:** Need-based aid available for full-time and part-time students. Work study available nights, weekends, and for part-time students.
**Students without need:** This college awards aid only to students with need.

**FINANCIAL AID PROCEDURES**
**Forms required:** FAFSA, institutional form.
**Dates and Deadlines:** Priority date 12/1; closing date 3/1. Applicants notified on a rolling basis starting 3/1; must reply by 5/1 or within 2 week(s) of notification.

**CONTACT**
Theodis Wright, Director of Financial Aid
2601 Gentilly Boulevard, New Orleans, LA 70122-3097
(800) 216-8094

## Grambling State University
Grambling, Louisiana
www.gram.edu                          Federal Code: 002006

**4-year public** university in small town.
**Enrollment:** 4,153 undergrads.

**BASIC COSTS (2015-2016)**
**Tuition and fees:** $7,063; out-of-state residents $16,086.
**Per-credit charge:** $220; out-of-state residents $376.
**Room and board:** $6,478.

**FINANCIAL AID PICTURE**
**Students with need:** Need-based aid available for full-time and part-time students. Work study available nights, weekends, and for part-time students.
**Students without need:** No-need awards available for academics, alumni affiliation, art, athletics, job skills, leadership, minority status, music/drama, religious affiliation, ROTC, state/district residency.

**FINANCIAL AID PROCEDURES**
**Forms required:** FAFSA.
**Dates and Deadlines:** Priority date 4/1; closing date 6/1. Applicants notified on a rolling basis starting 3/1; must reply within 2 week(s) of notification.
**Transfers:** Applicants notified on a rolling basis starting 3/1; must reply within 2 week(s) of notification.

**CONTACT**
Albert Tezno, Director of Student Financial Aid
403 Main Street, GSU Box 4200, Grambling, LA 71245
(318) 274-6190

## Herzing University: Kenner
Kenner, Louisiana
www.herzing.edu                        Federal Code: 020897

**4-year for-profit** branch campus and technical college in very large city.
**Enrollment:** 305 undergrads.

**BASIC COSTS (2015-2016)**
**Additional info:** Certificate programs: $13,670 to $26,820. Associate programs: $26,180 to $53,640. Bachelor's programs: $61,515 to $88,065.

**FINANCIAL AID PICTURE**
**Students with need:** Work study available nights, weekends, and for part-time students.

**CONTACT**
Ava Gomez, Financial Aid Director
2500 Williams Boulevard, Kenner, LA 70062

## ITI Technical College
Baton Rouge, Louisiana
www.iticollege.edu                     Federal Code: 015270

**2-year for-profit** technical and career college in large city.
**Enrollment:** 536 undergrads.
**Selectivity:** Open admission; but selective for some programs.

**BASIC COSTS (2015-2016)**
**Additional info:** Full-time tuition varies by program from $10,550-$27,950. Registration fee $150. Estimated average total books and supplies from $1,875-$3,925.

**FINANCIAL AID PICTURE**
**Students with need:** Need-based aid available for full-time students.
**Students without need:** This college awards aid only to students with need.

## FINANCIAL AID PROCEDURES
**Forms required:** FAFSA.

### CONTACT
Connie Roubique, Financial Aid Director
13944 Airline Highway, Baton Rouge, LA 70817
(225) 752-4233

## Louisiana College
Pineville, Louisiana
www.lacollege.edu                    Federal Code: 002007

**4-year private** liberal arts college in small city, affiliated with Southern Baptist Convention.
**Enrollment:** 881 undergrads, 3% part-time. 211 full-time freshmen.
**Selectivity:** Admits 50 to 75% of applicants.

### BASIC COSTS (2015-2016)
**Tuition and fees:** $15,070.
**Per-credit charge:** $440.
**Room and board:** $5,186.

### FINANCIAL AID PICTURE
**Students with need:** Need-based aid available for full-time and part-time students. Work study available nights, weekends, and for part-time students.
**Students without need:** No-need awards available for academics, art, leadership, music/drama, ROTC.

### FINANCIAL AID PROCEDURES
**Forms required:** FAFSA, institutional form.
**Dates and Deadlines:** Priority date 3/31; no closing date. Applicants notified on a rolling basis starting 3/1; must reply by 5/1 or within 2 week(s) of notification.
**Transfers:** No deadline. Applicants notified on a rolling basis; must reply within 4 week(s) of notification. Scholarships available.

### CONTACT
David Barnard, Director of Financial Aid
LC Box 566, Pineville, LA 71359
(318) 487-7386

## Louisiana State University and Agricultural and Mechanical College
Baton Rouge, Louisiana
www.lsu.edu                    Federal Code: 002010

**4-year public** university and agricultural college in small city.
**Enrollment:** 24,904 undergrads, 6% part-time. 5,619 full-time freshmen.
**Selectivity:** Admits over 75% of applicants.

### BASIC COSTS (2015-2016)
**Tuition and fees:** $8,827; out-of-state residents $26,236.
**Room and board:** $11,200.

### FINANCIAL AID PICTURE
**Students with need:** Need-based aid available for full-time and part-time students. Work study available nights, weekends, and for part-time students.
**Students without need:** No-need awards available for academics, athletics, music/drama, ROTC.

### FINANCIAL AID PROCEDURES
**Forms required:** FAFSA, institutional form.
**Dates and Deadlines:** Priority date 4/1; no closing date. Applicants notified on a rolling basis starting 12/15; must reply by 5/1.
**Transfers:** No deadline. Applicants notified on a rolling basis starting 10/1; must reply by 5/1 or within 3 week(s) of notification.

### CONTACT
Amy Marix
1146 Pleasant Hall, Baton Rouge, LA 70803-2750
(225) 578-3103

## Louisiana State University at Alexandria
Alexandria, Louisiana
www.lsua.edu                    Federal Code: 002011

**4-year public** university in small city.
**Enrollment:** 3,104 undergrads. 426 full-time freshmen.
**Selectivity:** GED not accepted.

### BASIC COSTS (2015-2016)
**Tuition and fees:** $6,158; out-of-state residents $13,150.

### FINANCIAL AID PICTURE (2014-2015)
**Students with need:** Out of 238 full-time freshmen who applied for aid, 238 were judged to have need. Of these, 238 received aid, and 233 had their full need met. Average financial aid package met 98% of need; average scholarship/grant was $4,517; average loan was $2,601. For part-time students, average financial aid package was $6,392.
**Students without need:** 35 full-time freshmen who did not demonstrate need for aid received scholarships/grants; average award was $1,444. No-need awards available for academics, athletics, ROTC.
**Scholarships offered:** 6 full-time freshmen received athletic scholarships; average amount $2,687.

### FINANCIAL AID PROCEDURES
**Forms required:** FAFSA.
**Dates and Deadlines:** Applicants notified on a rolling basis starting 3/1; must reply within 3 week(s) of notification.
**Transfers:** No deadline. Applicants notified on a rolling basis starting 3/1; must reply within 3 week(s) of notification.

### CONTACT
Deron Thaxton, Director of Financial Aid & Scholarships
8100 Highway 71 South, Alexandria, LA 71302-9121
(318) 473-6423

## Louisiana State University at Eunice
Eunice, Louisiana
www.lsue.edu                    Federal Code: 002012

**2-year public** nursing and junior college in large town.
**Enrollment:** 2,673 undergrads.
**Selectivity:** Open admission; but selective for some programs.

### BASIC COSTS (2015-2016)
**Tuition and fees:** $3,828; out-of-state residents $9,192.

### FINANCIAL AID PICTURE
**Students with need:** Need-based aid available for full-time and part-time students.

### FINANCIAL AID PROCEDURES
**Forms required:** FAFSA, institutional form.
**Dates and Deadlines:** Priority date 6/1; no closing date. Applicants notified on a rolling basis starting 4/1; must reply within 2 week(s) of notification.

### CONTACT
Jacqueline LaChapelle, Director of Financial Aid
Box 1129, Eunice, LA 70535
(337) 550-1282

## Louisiana State University Health Sciences Center

New Orleans, Louisiana
www.lsuhsc.edu                    Federal Code: 002014

**Upper-division public** health science and nursing college in large city.
**Enrollment:** 877 undergrads, 33% part-time.

### BASIC COSTS (2015-2016)
**Tuition and fees:** $6,093; out-of-state residents $11,717.
**Per-credit charge:** $325; out-of-state residents $677.
**Room only:** $4,797.

### FINANCIAL AID PICTURE
**Students with need:** Need-based aid available for full-time and part-time students. Work study available nights, weekends, and for part-time students.
**Students without need:** No-need awards available for academics.

### FINANCIAL AID PROCEDURES
**Forms required:** FAFSA, institutional form.
**Dates and Deadlines:** Priority date 4/15; no closing date. Applicants notified on a rolling basis starting 7/1.

### CONTACT
Patrick Gorman, Director of Financial Aid
433 Bolivar Street, New Orleans, LA 70112-2223
(504) 568-4820

## Louisiana State University in Shreveport

Shreveport, Louisiana
www.lsus.edu                      Federal Code: 002013

**4-year public** university and teachers college in large city.
**Enrollment:** 2,444 undergrads, 25% part-time. 347 full-time freshmen.
**Selectivity:** Admits over 75% of applicants.

### BASIC COSTS (2015-2016)
**Tuition and fees:** $6,903; out-of-state residents $20,057.

### FINANCIAL AID PICTURE
**Students with need:** Need-based aid available for full-time and part-time students. Work study available nights, weekends, and for part-time students.
**Students without need:** No-need awards available for academics, athletics.

### FINANCIAL AID PROCEDURES
**Dates and Deadlines:** Applicants notified on a rolling basis.

### CONTACT
Betty McCrary, Director of Student Financial Aid
One University Place, Shreveport, LA 71115-2399
(318) 797-5363

## Louisiana Tech University

Ruston, Louisiana
www.latech.edu                    Federal Code: 002008

**4-year public** university in large town.
**Enrollment:** 7,629 undergrads.
**Selectivity:** GED not accepted.

### BASIC COSTS (2015-2016)
**Tuition and fees:** $8,463; out-of-state residents $25,980.
**Room and board:** $5,670.

### FINANCIAL AID PICTURE
**Students with need:** Need-based aid available for full-time and part-time students.

**Students without need:** No-need awards available for academics, alumni affiliation, art, athletics, job skills, leadership, music/drama, ROTC, state/district residency.

### FINANCIAL AID PROCEDURES
**Forms required:** FAFSA, institutional form.
**Dates and Deadlines:** Priority date 4/15; no closing date. Applicants notified on a rolling basis starting 4/1; must reply within 3 week(s) of notification.
**Transfers:** Priority date 8/1; no deadline. Applicants notified on a rolling basis starting 8/20; must reply within 2 week(s) of notification.

### CONTACT
Aimee Baxter, Director of Student Financial Aid
Box 3178, Ruston, LA 71272
(318) 257-2641

## Loyola University New Orleans

New Orleans, Louisiana
www.loyno.edu                     Federal Code: 002016

**4-year private** university and liberal arts college in large city, affiliated with Roman Catholic Church.
**Enrollment:** 2,583 undergrads, 6% part-time. 644 full-time freshmen.
**Selectivity:** Admits over 75% of applicants.

### BASIC COSTS (2016-2017)
**Tuition and fees:** $38,504.
**Per-credit charge:** $1,052.
**Room and board:** $12,808.

### FINANCIAL AID PICTURE (2015-2016)
**Students with need:** Out of 591 full-time freshmen who applied for aid, 514 were judged to have need. Of these, 513 received aid, and 65 had their full need met. Average financial aid package met 80% of need; average scholarship/grant was $29,994; average loan was $3,672. For part-time students, average financial aid package was $11,930.
**Students without need:** 121 full-time freshmen who did not demonstrate need for aid received scholarships/grants; average award was $16,778. No-need awards available for academics, alumni affiliation, art, athletics, music/drama, ROTC.
**Scholarships offered:** 19 full-time freshmen received athletic scholarships; average amount $12,760.

### FINANCIAL AID PROCEDURES
**Forms required:** FAFSA.
**Dates and Deadlines:** Priority date 3/1; no closing date. Applicants notified by 3/30; must reply within 2 week(s) of notification.
**Transfers:** Priority date 3/1; no deadline. Applicants notified on a rolling basis starting 3/1; must reply within 2 week(s) of notification. Transfer scholarship deadline June 1.

### CONTACT
Carrie Glass, Director of Scholarships and Financial Aid
6363 St. Charles Avenue, New Orleans, LA 70118-6195
(504) 865-3231

## McNeese State University

Lake Charles, Louisiana
www.mcneese.edu                   Federal Code: 002017

**4-year public** university in small city.
**Enrollment:** 6,598 undergrads, 14% part-time. 1,241 full-time freshmen.
**Selectivity:** Admits over 75% of applicants.

### BASIC COSTS (2015-2016)
**Tuition and fees:** $6,658; out-of-state residents $12,000.

PART III: FINANCIAL AID COLLEGE BY COLLEGE

**Room and board:** $5,664.

**FINANCIAL AID PICTURE (2014-2015)**

**Students with need:** Out of 1,133 full-time freshmen who applied for aid, 808 were judged to have need. Of these, 798 received aid. Need-based aid available for part-time students.

**Students without need:** No-need awards available for academics, alumni affiliation, art, athletics, leadership, minority status, music/drama, state/district residency.

**Additional info:** Books may be charged and paid in 2 installments during semester.

**FINANCIAL AID PROCEDURES**

**Forms required:** FAFSA, institutional form.

**Dates and Deadlines:** Priority date 5/1; no closing date. Applicants notified on a rolling basis.

**Transfers:** Transfer students must exhibit satisfactory academic progress at school most recently attended to be eligible for financial aid.

**CONTACT**

Taina Savoit, Director of Financial Aid

MSU Box 91740, Lake Charles, LA 70609-1740

(337) 475-5065

## Nicholls State University

Thibodaux, Louisiana

www.nicholls.edu                    Federal Code: 002005

**4-year public** university in large town.

**Enrollment:** 5,256 undergrads, 13% part-time. 1,183 full-time freshmen.

**Selectivity:** Admits over 75% of applicants.

**BASIC COSTS (2015-2016)**

**Tuition and fees:** $7,378; out-of-state residents $18,310.

**Room and board:** $9,290.

**FINANCIAL AID PICTURE (2014-2015)**

**Students with need:** Out of 1,113 full-time freshmen who applied for aid, 768 were judged to have need. Of these, 760 received aid, and 154 had their full need met. Average financial aid package met 64% of need; average scholarship/grant was $8,207; average loan was $2,551. For part-time students, average financial aid package was $4,490.

**Students without need:** 133 full-time freshmen who did not demonstrate need for aid received scholarships/grants; average award was $3,346. No-need awards available for academics, athletics, leadership, minority status, music/drama, state/district residency.

**Scholarships offered:** 19 full-time freshmen received athletic scholarships; average amount $7,488.

**FINANCIAL AID PROCEDURES**

**Forms required:** FAFSA, institutional form.

**Dates and Deadlines:** Priority date 4/15; closing date 6/30. Applicants notified on a rolling basis.

**Transfers:** Priority date 5/1; no deadline. Applicants notified on a rolling basis.

**CONTACT**

Casie Triche, Director of Financial Aid

PO Box 2004-NSU, Thibodaux, LA 70310

(985) 448-4048

## Northwestern State University

Natchitoches, Louisiana

www.nsula.edu                    Federal Code: 002021

**4-year public** university in large town.

**Enrollment:** 6,836 undergrads, 27% part-time. 1,137 full-time freshmen.

**Selectivity:** Admits 50 to 75% of applicants.

**BASIC COSTS (2015-2016)**

**Tuition and fees:** $7,006; out-of-state residents $17,794.

**Per-credit charge:** $354; out-of-district residents $354.

**Room and board:** $8,584.

**FINANCIAL AID PICTURE (2014-2015)**

**Students with need:** Out of 1,082 full-time freshmen who applied for aid, 857 were judged to have need. Of these, 850 received aid, and 185 had their full need met. For part-time students, average financial aid package was $10,609.

**Students without need:** 150 full-time freshmen who did not demonstrate need for aid received scholarships/grants; average award was $3,648. No-need awards available for academics, alumni affiliation, art, athletics, job skills, leadership, minority status, music/drama, religious affiliation, ROTC, state/district residency.

**Scholarships offered:** 19 full-time freshmen received athletic scholarships; average amount $6,697.

**FINANCIAL AID PROCEDURES**

**Forms required:** FAFSA, institutional form.

**Dates and Deadlines:** Priority date 5/1; no closing date. Applicants notified on a rolling basis starting 5/1; must reply within 4 week(s) of notification.

**Transfers:** No deadline. Applicants notified on a rolling basis starting 5/1; must reply within 4 week(s) of notification.

**CONTACT**

Lauren Jackson, Director of Financial Aid

175 Sam Sibley Drive, Student Services Center, Suite 235, Natchitoches, LA 71497

(800) 823-3008

## Nunez Community College

Chalmette, Louisiana

www.nunez.edu                    Federal Code: 015130

**2-year public** community and technical college in large town.

**Enrollment:** 1,551 undergrads, 48% part-time. 160 full-time freshmen.

**Selectivity:** Open admission; but selective for some programs.

**BASIC COSTS (2015-2016)**

**Tuition and fees:** $3,946; out-of-state residents $7,444.

**Additional info:** Tuition/fee waivers available for minority students.

**FINANCIAL AID PICTURE (2014-2015)**

**Students with need:** 62% of average financial aid package awarded as scholarships/grants, 38% awarded as loans/jobs. Need-based aid available for part-time students. Work study available nights.

**Additional info:** Pell Grants, Stafford Loans, campus work-study, and tuition waiver scholarships available. Louisiana National Guard tuition exemption, teacher tuition exemption, dependents of injured fire-police tuition waivers available.

**FINANCIAL AID PROCEDURES**

**Forms required:** FAFSA.

**Dates and Deadlines:** Priority date 6/1; closing date 8/1.

**Transfers:** Applicant must supply academic transcripts from every post-secondary school attended before aid is awarded.

**CONTACT**

John Whisnant, Financial Aid Officer

3710 Paris Road, Chalmette, LA 70043

(504) 278-6478

## Our Lady of the Lake College

Baton Rouge, Louisiana
www.ololcollege.edu                    Federal Code: 031062

**4-year private** health science and nursing college in large city, affiliated with Roman Catholic Church.
**Enrollment:** 1,485 undergrads.

**BASIC COSTS (2015-2016)**
**Tuition and fees:** $14,816.

**FINANCIAL AID PICTURE (2014-2015)**
**Students with need:** 97% of average financial aid package awarded as scholarships/grants, 3% awarded as loans/jobs.

**FINANCIAL AID PROCEDURES**
**Forms required:** FAFSA, institutional form.
**Dates and Deadlines:** Priority date 3/1; no closing date.

**CONTACT**
Barrye Bailey, Director of Financial Aid
5414 Brittany Drive, Baton Rouge, LA 70808
(225) 768-1714

## Remington College: Baton Rouge

Baton Rouge, Louisiana
http://baton-rouge.remingtoncollege.edu
                                        Federal Code: E00907

**2-year private** technical college in large city.
**Enrollment:** 547 undergrads.
**Selectivity:** Open admission; but selective for some programs.

**BASIC COSTS (2015-2016)**
**Additional info:** Total program tuition: diplomas $15,995-$21,700; associates $33,900.

**FINANCIAL AID PICTURE**
**Students with need:** Need-based aid available for full-time students. Work study available nights.
**Students without need:** This college awards aid only to students with need.

**FINANCIAL AID PROCEDURES**
**Forms required:** FAFSA.
**Dates and Deadlines:** Applicants notified on a rolling basis; must reply within 1 week(s) of notification.

**CONTACT**
James Dunn, National Director of Financial Aid
10551 Coursey Boulevard, Baton Rouge, LA 70816
(225) 236-3200

## Remington College: Lafayette

Lafayette, Louisiana
http://lafayette.remingtoncollege.edu
                                        Federal Code: 005203

**2-year private** junior college in small city.
**Enrollment:** 585 undergrads.
**Selectivity:** Open admission; but selective for some programs.

**BASIC COSTS (2015-2016)**
**Additional info:** Total program tuition: diplomas $15,995-$21,700; associates $33,900.

**FINANCIAL AID PICTURE**
**Students with need:** Need-based aid available for full-time students. Work study available nights.
**Students without need:** This college awards aid only to students with need.

**FINANCIAL AID PROCEDURES**
**Forms required:** FAFSA, institutional form.

**CONTACT**
James Dunn, National Director of Financial Aid
303 Rue Louis XIV, Lafayette, LA 70508

## St. Joseph Seminary College

St. Benedict, Louisiana
www.sjasc.edu                          Federal Code: 002027

**4-year private** liberal arts and seminary college for men in rural community, affiliated with Roman Catholic Church.
**Enrollment:** 137 undergrads. 15 full-time freshmen.

**BASIC COSTS (2015-2016)**
**Tuition and fees:** $16,410.
**Per-credit charge:** $260.
**Room and board:** $14,120.

**FINANCIAL AID PICTURE**
**Students with need:** Need-based aid available for full-time and part-time students.
**Students without need:** No-need awards available for academics, leadership.

**FINANCIAL AID PROCEDURES**
**Forms required:** FAFSA.
**Dates and Deadlines:** Priority date 3/15; no closing date. Applicants notified on a rolling basis starting 7/1; must reply within 4 week(s) of notification.
**Transfers:** Closing date 5/1. Applicants notified on a rolling basis starting 7/1; must reply within 4 week(s) of notification.

**CONTACT**
Katie Plude, Director of Student Financial Aid
75376 River Road, St. Benedict, LA 70457-9990
(985) 867-2248

## South Louisiana Community College

Lafayette, Louisiana
www.solacc.edu                         Federal Code: 039563

**2-year public** community college in small city.
**Enrollment:** 5,640 undergrads.
**Selectivity:** Open admission; but selective for some programs.

**BASIC COSTS (2015-2016)**
**Tuition and fees:** $4,037; out-of-state residents $7,642.

**FINANCIAL AID PICTURE**
**Students with need:** Need-based aid available for full-time and part-time students.
**Students without need:** No-need awards available for academics, leadership, state/district residency.

**FINANCIAL AID PROCEDURES**
**Forms required:** FAFSA, institutional form.
**Dates and Deadlines:** Priority date 5/15; no closing date.

**CONTACT**
Director of Financial Aid
1101 Bertrand Dr., Lafayette, LA 70506-4124
(337) 521-8910

## Southeastern Louisiana University

Hammond, Louisiana
www.southeastern.edu                    Federal Code: 002024

**4-year public** university in large town.
**Enrollment:** 11,028 undergrads, 13% part-time. 2,339 full-time freshmen.
**Selectivity:** Admits over 75% of applicants.

### BASIC COSTS (2015-2016)
**Tuition and fees:** $7,280; out-of-state residents $19,758.
**Per-credit charge:** $303; out-of-state residents $823.
**Room and board:** $7,370.

### FINANCIAL AID PICTURE (2014-2015)
**Students with need:** Out of 2,235 full-time freshmen who applied for aid, 1,654 were judged to have need. Of these, 1,629 received aid, and 181 had their full need met. For part-time students, average financial aid package was $5,383.
**Students without need:** 292 full-time freshmen who did not demonstrate need for aid received scholarships/grants; average award was $2,047. No-need awards available for academics, athletics, job skills, leadership, music/drama, state/district residency.
**Scholarships offered:** *Merit:* Various scholarships: $1,000-$3,500; any student admitted with 24 ACT and 3.0 GPA on a seven-semester transcript qualifies for scholarship. On-campus housing scholarships: range from half-room award to full-room award; based on ACT and GPA. Presidential Honors Scholarship: $2,500-$3,500 plus on-campus housing and meals; based on 30 ACT, 3.0 GPA. *Athletic:* 45 full-time freshmen received athletic scholarships; average amount $7,790.

### FINANCIAL AID PROCEDURES
**Forms required:** FAFSA, institutional form.
**Dates and Deadlines:** Priority date 5/1; no closing date. Applicants notified on a rolling basis starting 4/1; must reply within 2 week(s) of notification.
**Transfers:** Applicants notified on a rolling basis starting 3/1; must reply within 2 week(s) of notification. Financial aid is available for transfer students, including those admitted on probation.

### CONTACT
Charles Cambre, Director of Financial Aid
SLU 10752, Hammond, LA 70402
(985) 549-2244

## Southern University and Agricultural and Mechanical College

Baton Rouge, Louisiana
www.subr.edu                    Federal Code: 002025

**4-year public** university in large city.
**Enrollment:** 5,285 undergrads, 13% part-time. 1,176 full-time freshmen.

### BASIC COSTS (2015-2016)
**Tuition and fees:** $6,766; out-of-state residents $16,116.
**Room and board:** $6,232.

### FINANCIAL AID PICTURE (2015-2016)
**Students with need:** Out of 1,147 full-time freshmen who applied for aid, 1,073 were judged to have need. Of these, 1,054 received aid.
**Students without need:** No-need awards available for academics, athletics, ROTC, state/district residency.
**Scholarships offered:** College of Education, Arts and Humanities Scholarship: full-tuition; based on 22 ACT (or comparable SAT), 3.2 GPA, evidence of community involvement/extracurricular activities; two letters of recommendation. College of Education, Arts and Humanities Scholarship: tuition only; based on 20 ACT (or comparable SAT), 3.0 GPA, evidence of community involvement/extracurricular activities; two letters of recommendation.

### FINANCIAL AID PROCEDURES
**Forms required:** FAFSA.
**Dates and Deadlines:** Priority date 1/31; closing date 3/30. Applicants notified on a rolling basis starting 5/1; must reply within 3 week(s) of notification.
**Transfers:** Closing date 5/31. Applicants notified on a rolling basis starting 5/31; must reply within 3 week(s) of notification.

### CONTACT
Raymond Clarke, Associate Vice Chancellor for Student Success
T.H. Harris Hall, Baton Rouge, LA 70813
(225) 771-2790 ext. 2790

## Southern University at New Orleans

New Orleans, Louisiana
www.suno.edu                    Federal Code: 002026

**4-year public** university in large city.
**Enrollment:** 2,390 undergrads.

### BASIC COSTS (2015-2016)
**Tuition and fees:** $5,781; out-of-state residents $14,682.
**Room and board:** $8,620.

### FINANCIAL AID PICTURE
**Students with need:** Need-based aid available for full-time and part-time students.
**Students without need:** This college awards aid only to students with need.

### FINANCIAL AID PROCEDURES
**Forms required:** FAFSA.
**Dates and Deadlines:** Closing date 4/15. Applicants notified by 5/15; must reply within 1 week(s) of notification.

### CONTACT
Leatrice Latimore, Director of Financial Aid
6801 Press Drive, New Orleans, LA 70126
(504) 286-5263

## Tulane University

New Orleans, Louisiana            Federal Code: 002029
www.tulane.edu                    CSS Code: 6832

**4-year private** university in very large city.
**Enrollment:** 8,262 undergrads, 18% part-time. 1,647 full-time freshmen.
**Selectivity:** Admits less than 50% of applicants.

### BASIC COSTS (2016-2017)
**Tuition and fees:** $51,010.
**Per-credit charge:** $1,964.
**Room and board:** $14,446.

### FINANCIAL AID PICTURE (2014-2015)
**Students with need:** Out of 1,017 full-time freshmen who applied for aid, 645 were judged to have need. Of these, 645 received aid, and 368 had their full need met. Average financial aid package met 96% of need; average scholarship/grant was $30,318; average loan was $6,224. For part-time students, average financial aid package was $11,127.
**Students without need:** 530 full-time freshmen who did not demonstrate need for aid received scholarships/grants; average award was $24,610. No-need awards available for academics, athletics, leadership, music/drama, ROTC, state/district residency.
**Scholarships offered:** *Merit:* Dean's Honor Scholarship: full-tuition. Distinguished Scholars Award: partial tuition. Founders Scholarship: partial tuition. Urban Scholars Award: full-tuition. *Athletic:* 41 full-time freshmen received athletic scholarships; average amount $32,663.

## FINANCIAL AID PROCEDURES

**Forms required:** FAFSA, CSS PROFILE.
**Dates and Deadlines:** Priority date 2/15; no closing date. Applicants notified on a rolling basis starting 3/15.
**Transfers:** Applicants notified on a rolling basis starting 2/1; must reply by 5/1 or within 2 week(s) of notification.

## CONTACT

Michael Goodman, Associate Vice President for Financial Aid
6823 St. Charles Avenue, New Orleans, LA 70118-5680
(504) 865-5723

# University of Holy Cross
New Orleans, Louisiana
www.olhcc.edu                    Federal Code: 002023

**4-year private** liberal arts college in very large city, affiliated with Roman Catholic Church.
**Enrollment:** 940 undergrads.

## BASIC COSTS (2015-2016)

**Tuition and fees:** $13,360.
**Per-credit charge:** $408.

## FINANCIAL AID PICTURE

**Students with need:** Need-based aid available for full-time and part-time students. Work study available nights, weekends, and for part-time students.
**Students without need:** No-need awards available for academics, state/district residency.

## FINANCIAL AID PROCEDURES

**Forms required:** FAFSA.
**Dates and Deadlines:** Priority date 7/1; no closing date. Applicants notified on a rolling basis starting 5/15; must reply within 4 week(s) of notification.
**Transfers:** Must reply within 2 week(s) of notification.

## CONTACT

Anna Vaughan, Financial Aid Coordinator
4123 Woodland Drive, New Orleans, LA 70131-7399
(504) 394-7744

# University of Louisiana at Lafayette
Lafayette, Louisiana
www.louisiana.edu                Federal Code: 002031

**4-year public** university in small city.
**Enrollment:** 15,091 undergrads, 15% part-time. 2,906 full-time freshmen.
**Selectivity:** Admits 50 to 75% of applicants.

## BASIC COSTS (2015-2016)

**Tuition and fees:** $8,552; out-of-state residents $22,280.
**Room and board:** $8,566.

## FINANCIAL AID PICTURE (2014-2015)

**Students with need:** Out of 2,740 full-time freshmen who applied for aid, 1,843 were judged to have need. Of these, 1,825 received aid, and 270 had their full need met. Average financial aid package met 61% of need; average scholarship/grant was $7,695; average loan was $3,133. For part-time students, average financial aid package was $4,896.
**Students without need:** This college awards aid only to students with need.
**Scholarships offered:** 79 full-time freshmen received athletic scholarships; average amount $10,187.

## FINANCIAL AID PROCEDURES

**Forms required:** FAFSA.

**Dates and Deadlines:** Priority date 5/1; no closing date. Applicants notified on a rolling basis starting 4/1; must reply within 2 week(s) of notification.
**Transfers:** Applicants notified on a rolling basis starting 5/1; must reply within 2 week(s) of notification.

## CONTACT

Cindy Perez, Director, Student Financial Aid
Box 41210, Lafayette, LA 70504-1210
(337) 482-6506

# University of Louisiana at Monroe
Monroe, Louisiana
www.ulm.edu                      Federal Code: 002020

**4-year public** university in small city.
**Enrollment:** 5,981 undergrads, 17% part-time. 1,376 full-time freshmen.
**Selectivity:** Admits over 75% of applicants.

## BASIC COSTS (2015-2016)

**Tuition and fees:** $7,658; out-of-state residents $19,758.
**Room and board:** $7,048.

## FINANCIAL AID PICTURE (2015-2016)

**Students with need:** 92% of average financial aid package awarded as scholarships/grants, 8% awarded as loans/jobs. Need-based aid available for part-time students.
**Students without need:** No-need awards available for academics, alumni affiliation, art, athletics, job skills, leadership, minority status, music/drama, religious affiliation, ROTC, state/district residency.

## FINANCIAL AID PROCEDURES

**Forms required:** FAFSA.
**Dates and Deadlines:** Closing date 6/30. Applicants notified on a rolling basis starting 6/1; must reply within 2 week(s) of notification.

## CONTACT

Frankie Everett, Director of Financial Aid
700 University Avenue, Monroe, LA 71209-1160
(318) 342-5320

# University of New Orleans
New Orleans, Louisiana
www.uno.edu                      Federal Code: 002015

**4-year public** university in very large city.
**Enrollment:** 6,185 undergrads, 23% part-time. 905 full-time freshmen.
**Selectivity:** Admits 50 to 75% of applicants.

## BASIC COSTS (2015-2016)

**Tuition and fees:** $8,094; out-of-state residents $21,911.
**Per-credit charge:** $203; out-of-state residents $663.
**Room and board:** $9,515.

## FINANCIAL AID PICTURE (2015-2016)

**Students with need:** Out of 856 full-time freshmen who applied for aid, 728 were judged to have need. Of these, 691 received aid, and 60 had their full need met. Average financial aid package met 66% of need; average scholarship/grant was $5,873; average loan was $3,286. For part-time students, average financial aid package was $4,765.
**Students without need:** 38 full-time freshmen who did not demonstrate need for aid received scholarships/grants; average award was $3,737. No-need awards available for academics, athletics, music/drama.
**Scholarships offered:** 19 full-time freshmen received athletic scholarships; average amount $5,538.
**Additional info:** Students in good academic and financial standing eligible to participate in Extended Payment Plan option.

## FINANCIAL AID PROCEDURES

**Forms required:** FAFSA.

**Dates and Deadlines:** Priority date 1/15; no closing date. Applicants notified on a rolling basis starting 3/15.

**Transfers:** Mid-year transfers must submit financial aid transcript from all post-secondary schools attended. Others submit NSLDS.

## CONTACT

Ann Lockridge, Director Financial Aid and Scholarships

University of New Orleans, 105 Earl K. Long Library, New Orleans, LA 70148

(504) 280-6603

## Xavier University of Louisiana
New Orleans, Louisiana

www.xula.edu                          Federal Code: 002032

**4-year private** university in very large city, affiliated with Roman Catholic Church.

**Enrollment:** 2,344 undergrads, 4% part-time. 684 full-time freshmen.

**Selectivity:** Admits 50 to 75% of applicants.

## BASIC COSTS (2015-2016)

**Tuition and fees:** $22,349.

**Per-credit charge:** $825.

**Room and board:** $8,200.

## FINANCIAL AID PICTURE

**Students with need:** Need-based aid available for full-time and part-time students. Work study available nights, weekends, and for part-time students.

**Students without need:** No-need awards available for academics, art, athletics, music/drama.

## FINANCIAL AID PROCEDURES

**Forms required:** FAFSA.

**Dates and Deadlines:** Priority date 1/1; no closing date. Applicants notified on a rolling basis starting 4/1; must reply within 2 week(s) of notification.

## CONTACT

Mildred Higgins, Director of Financial Aid

One Drexel Drive, New Orleans, LA 70125-1098

(504) 520-7517

# Maine

## Bates College
Lewiston, Maine                        Federal Code: 002036

www.bates.edu                          CSS Code: 3076

**4-year private** liberal arts college in small city.

**Enrollment:** 1,792 undergrads. 516 full-time freshmen.

**Selectivity:** Admits less than 50% of applicants. GED not accepted.

## BASIC COSTS (2015-2016)

**Tuition and fees:** $48,735.

**Room and board:** $14,105.

## FINANCIAL AID PICTURE (2015-2016)

**Students with need:** Out of 254 full-time freshmen who applied for aid, 215 were judged to have need. Of these, 215 received aid, and 215 had their full need met. Average financial aid package met 100% of need; average scholarship/grant was $41,230; average loan was $2,197.

**Students without need:** This college awards aid only to students with need.

**Additional info:** Priority date for filing required financial aid forms for early decision students is 11/15.

## FINANCIAL AID PROCEDURES

**Forms required:** FAFSA, CSS PROFILE.

**Dates and Deadlines:** Closing date 2/15. Applicants notified by 4/1; must reply by 5/1.

**Transfers:** Closing date 1/1. Applicants notified by 6/1; must reply by 6/15.

## CONTACT

Wendy Glass, Director of Student Financial Services

23 Campus Avenue, Lindholm House, Lewiston, ME 04240

(207) 786-6096

## Bowdoin College
Brunswick, Maine                       Federal Code: 002038

www.bowdoin.edu                        CSS Code: 3089

**4-year private** liberal arts college in large town.

**Enrollment:** 1,794 undergrads. 500 full-time freshmen.

**Selectivity:** Admits less than 50% of applicants. GED not accepted.

## BASIC COSTS (2015-2016)

**Tuition and fees:** $48,212.

**Per-credit charge:** $933.

**Room and board:** $13,142.

## FINANCIAL AID PICTURE (2015-2016)

**Students with need:** Out of 280 full-time freshmen who applied for aid, 225 were judged to have need. Of these, 225 received aid, and 225 had their full need met. Average financial aid package met 100% of need; average scholarship/grant was $42,165.

**Students without need:** 20 full-time freshmen who did not demonstrate need for aid received scholarships/grants; average award was $1,000. No-need awards available for academics, leadership.

**Additional info:** Regardless of financial circumstances, students admitted will receive the money they need to attend. International students for regular admission must submit their financial aid applications by January 1st.

## FINANCIAL AID PROCEDURES

**Forms required:** FAFSA, CSS PROFILE.

**Dates and Deadlines:** Closing date 2/15. Applicants notified by 4/5; must reply by 5/1 or within 1 week(s) of notification.

**Transfers:** Closing date 3/1. Applicants notified by 5/1; must reply by 6/1 or within 1 week(s) of notification. Financial aid usually not available for transfer students. Early Decision applicants must submit financial aid applications by November 15 (ED I) and January 1 (ED II).

## CONTACT

Michael Bartini, Director of Student Aid

5000 College Station, Brunswick, ME 04011-8441

(207) 725-3273

## Central Maine Community College
Auburn, Maine

www.cmcc.edu                           Federal Code: 005276

**2-year public** community and technical college in small city.

**Enrollment:** 2,354 undergrads, 47% part-time. 478 full-time freshmen.

**Selectivity:** Open admission; but selective for some programs.

## BASIC COSTS (2015-2016)

**Tuition and fees:** $3,480; out-of-state residents $6,180.

**Per-credit charge:** $90; out-of-state residents $180.

**Room and board:** $7,978.

## FINANCIAL AID PICTURE (2015-2016)

**Students with need:** Average financial aid package met 67% of need; average scholarship/grant was $5,175; average loan was $5,613. For part-time students, average financial aid package was $5,403.

**Additional info:** Tuition and/or fee waivers may be available to orphans, Native Americans, fire fighters, police, disabled veterans, dependents or survivors of veterans killed in line of duty.

## FINANCIAL AID PROCEDURES

**Forms required:** FAFSA.

**Dates and Deadlines:** Priority date 5/1; no closing date. Applicants notified on a rolling basis starting 2/15.

**Transfers:** No deadline. Applicants notified on a rolling basis starting 2/15.

## CONTACT

John Bowie, Director of Financial Aid

1250 Turner Street, Auburn, ME 04210-6498

(207) 755-5273

## Colby College

Waterville, Maine
www.colby.edu

Federal Code: 002039
CSS Code: 3280

**4-year private** liberal arts college in large town.

**Enrollment:** 1,857 undergrads. 508 full-time freshmen.

**Selectivity:** Admits less than 50% of applicants.

## BASIC COSTS (2015-2016)

**Tuition and fees:** $49,120.

**Per-credit charge:** $1,810.

**Room and board:** $12,610.

## FINANCIAL AID PICTURE (2015-2016)

**Students with need:** Out of 253 full-time freshmen who applied for aid, 211 were judged to have need. Of these, 211 received aid, and 211 had their full need met. Average financial aid package met 100% of need; average scholarship/grant was $43,762; average loan was $2,925.

**Additional info:** Packaged loans have been replaced with institutional grants.

## FINANCIAL AID PROCEDURES

**Forms required:** FAFSA. Required if they want to be eligible for any aid beyond federal aid.

**Dates and Deadlines:** Closing date 2/1. Applicants notified by 4/1; must reply by 5/1.

**Transfers:** Closing date 3/1. Applicants notified by 5/30; must reply within 2 week(s) of notification. Students admitted as other than first semester freshmen are eligible for Colby aid for the number of semesters required for graduation as determined by the College at the time of entry.

## CONTACT

Elreo Campbell, Director of Financial Aid and Associate Dean of Admissions and Financial Aid

4800 Mayflower Hill, Waterville, ME 04901-8848

(800) 723-3032

## College of the Atlantic

Bar Harbor, Maine
www.coa.edu

Federal Code: 011385

**4-year private** liberal arts college in small town.

**Enrollment:** 333 undergrads, 2% part-time. 81 full-time freshmen.

**Selectivity:** Admits over 75% of applicants.

## BASIC COSTS (2015-2016)

**Tuition and fees:** $42,084.

**Per-credit charge:** $1,385.

**Room and board:** $9,432.

## FINANCIAL AID PICTURE

**Students with need:** Need-based aid available for full-time and part-time students. Work study available nights, weekends, and for part-time students.

**Students without need:** No-need awards available for academics, leadership.

**Scholarships offered:** Students from selected secondary schools, special programs such as robotics, selected summer programs, may receive $10,000 a year in scholarships; graduates of community colleges with a 3.0 average may be eligible for $15,000 per year scholarship.

**Additional info:** Low-cost classes available for local residents; some business courses covered by grant to the college.

## FINANCIAL AID PROCEDURES

**Forms required:** FAFSA, institutional form.

**Dates and Deadlines:** Closing date 2/15. Applicants notified by 4/1; must reply by 5/1.

**Transfers:** Priority date 2/15. Applicants notified by 4/1; must reply by 5/1. FAFSA must be filed by 5/1 for Maine residents to be eligible for Maine state grant.

## CONTACT

Bruce Hazam, Director of Financial Aid

105 Eden Street, Bar Harbor, ME 04609

(207) 288-5015

## Eastern Maine Community College

Bangor, Maine
www.emcc.edu

Federal Code: 005277

**2-year public** community and technical college in large town.

**Enrollment:** 1,988 undergrads.

**Selectivity:** Open admission; but selective for some programs.

## BASIC COSTS (2015-2016)

**Tuition and fees:** $3,675; out-of-state residents $6,375.

**Per-credit charge:** $90; out-of-state residents $180.

**Room and board:** $8,134.

## FINANCIAL AID PICTURE

**Students with need:** Need-based aid available for full-time and part-time students. Work study available nights, weekends, and for part-time students.

**Students without need:** This college awards aid only to students with need.

## FINANCIAL AID PROCEDURES

**Forms required:** FAFSA.

**Dates and Deadlines:** Priority date 5/1; no closing date. Applicants notified on a rolling basis starting 5/1; must reply within 3 week(s) of notification.

## CONTACT

Candace Ward, Registrar/Financial Aid Director

354 Hogan Road, Bangor, ME 04401

(207) 974-4625

## Husson University

Bangor, Maine
www.husson.edu

Federal Code: 002043

**4-year private** business and health science college in large town.

**Enrollment:** 2,595 undergrads, 15% part-time. 526 full-time freshmen.

**Selectivity:** Admits over 75% of applicants.

## BASIC COSTS (2015-2016)

**Tuition and fees:** $16,582.

**Per-credit charge:** $522.

**Room and board:** $8,922.
**Additional info:** Some programs have additional lab fees, $800 per year for programs within the New England School of Communications.

## FINANCIAL AID PICTURE (2015-2016)

**Students with need:** Out of 492 full-time freshmen who applied for aid, 437 were judged to have need. Of these, 437 received aid, and 88 had their full need met. Average financial aid package met 78% of need; average scholarship/grant was $9,205; average loan was $3,278. For part-time students, average financial aid package was $5,635.
**Students without need:** 41 full-time freshmen who did not demonstrate need for aid received scholarships/grants; average award was $2,010. No-need awards available for academics, leadership.
**Scholarships offered:** President's Academic Scholarship: $16,000 over 4 years; min SAT score of 1500 or 22 on the ACT; A average; ranked at the top of class. Provost's Leadership Scholarship: $8,000-$12,000 over 4 years; min SAT score of 1500 or 22 on the ACT; B average or better; ranked near the top of class; nonathletic activities. Dean's Leadership Scholarship: $4,000-$6,000 over 4 years; min SAT score of 1500 or 22 on the ACT; B average or better; history of strong academic performance; nonathletic activities. Future Educator Scholarship: $8,000 over 4 years; for students accepted in the Teacher Education Pine Tree Scholarship; $8,000 over 4 years; out-of-state recognition scholarship based on SAT scores, class rank, and GPA; awarded to first-year entering students only. Scholarships with an Admissions Application Deadline of April 1, 2015 or Open-Ended (applications must be complete to be considered). Legacy Scholarship: $4,000 over 4 years; student must have had a parent, grandparent, or great grandparent, who graduated from Husson to receive this scholarship. President's Global Scholarship: $4,000-$20,000 over 4 years; based on merit; the student must provide proof of financial responsibility and be eligible for an I-20 student visa for consideration. Transfer Scholarship: $1,000 for a 2.5 GPA per year; $2,000 for a 3.0 GPA per year. Business CEO Scholarship: $2,000 over 4 years; for select business and criminal justice students; based on SAT scores, class rank, and GPA; completed admissions applications must be received no later than April 1, 2015. AHEAD Scholarship (Affirming Husson's Educational Access and Diversity): $8,000 over 4 years; eligible students must come from a multicultural background to be considered for this limited award; completed admissions applications must be received no later than April 1, 2015.

## FINANCIAL AID PROCEDURES

**Forms required:** FAFSA.
**Dates and Deadlines:** Priority date 4/15; no closing date. Applicants notified on a rolling basis starting 4/1; must reply by 5/1 or within 2 week(s) of notification.
**Transfers:** No deadline. Applicants notified on a rolling basis starting 2/20; must reply within 2 week(s) of notification.

## CONTACT

Anne Tabor, Director of Financial Aid
1 College Circle, Bangor, ME 04401-2999
(207) 941-7156

# Kennebec Valley Community College
Fairfield, Maine
www.kvcc.me.edu                 Federal Code: 009826

**2-year public** community, liberal arts and technical college in small town.
**Enrollment:** 1,600 undergrads.
**Selectivity:** Open admission; but selective for some programs.

## BASIC COSTS (2015-2016)
**Tuition and fees:** $3,355; out-of-state residents $6,055.
**Per-credit charge:** $90; out-of-state residents $180.
**Additional info:** Additional lab and technology fees apply to specific programs and courses.

## FINANCIAL AID PICTURE
**Students with need:** Need-based aid available for full-time and part-time students.
**Students without need:** This college awards aid only to students with need.

## FINANCIAL AID PROCEDURES
**Forms required:** FAFSA, institutional form.
**Dates and Deadlines:** Priority date 4/1; no closing date. Applicants notified on a rolling basis starting 5/1.
**Transfers:** No deadline. Applicants notified on a rolling basis.

## CONTACT
Anne Connors, Director of Financial Aid
92 Western Avenue, Fairfield, ME 04937-1367
(207) 453-5121

# Landing School of Boatbuilding and Design
Arundel, Maine
www.landingschool.edu          Federal Code: 016778

**2-year private** career college in small town.
**Enrollment:** 73 undergrads. 14 full-time freshmen.
**Selectivity:** Open admission; but selective for some programs.

## BASIC COSTS (2016-2017)
**Tuition and fees:** $22,296.
**Additional info:** Program fees vary by program.

## FINANCIAL AID PICTURE (2014-2015)
**Students with need:** Out of 11 full-time freshmen who applied for aid, 11 were judged to have need. Of these, 11 received aid.
**Students without need:** This college awards aid only to students with need.

## FINANCIAL AID PROCEDURES
**Forms required:** FAFSA.
**Dates and Deadlines:** Priority date 4/1; no closing date. Applicants notified on a rolling basis starting 3/1; must reply within 3 week(s) of notification.
**Transfers:** No deadline. Applicants notified on a rolling basis; must reply within 3 week(s) of notification.

## CONTACT
Kristy Lank, Director of Admin & Finance
286 River Road, Arundel, ME 04046
(207) 985-7976 ext. 428

# Maine College of Art
Portland, Maine
www.meca.edu                   Federal Code: 011673

**4-year private** visual arts college in small city.
**Enrollment:** 430 undergrads, 4% part-time. 111 full-time freshmen.
**Selectivity:** Admits over 75% of applicants.

## BASIC COSTS (2015-2016)
**Tuition and fees:** $32,290.
**Per-credit charge:** $1,315.
**Room and board:** $10,872.

## FINANCIAL AID PICTURE
**Students with need:** Need-based aid available for full-time and part-time students. Work study available nights, weekends, and for part-time students.
**Students without need:** No-need awards available for academics, art.

## FINANCIAL AID PROCEDURES
**Forms required:** FAFSA.

**Dates and Deadlines:** Priority date 3/1; no closing date. Applicants notified on a rolling basis starting 2/15; must reply within 2 week(s) of notification. **Transfers:** Closing date 4/15. Applicants notified on a rolling basis starting 2/15; must reply within 2 week(s) of notification.

**CONTACT**
Carri Frechette, Director of Financial Aid
522 Congress Street, Portland, ME 04101
(207) 699-5073

## Maine College of Health Professions
Lewiston, Maine
www.mchp.edu                    Federal Code: 006305

**2-year private** health science and nursing college in large town.
**Enrollment:** 184 undergrads, 68% part-time. 3 full-time freshmen.

**BASIC COSTS (2015-2016)**
**Tuition and fees:** $10,900.
**Per-credit charge:** $266.
**Room only:** $1,900.

**FINANCIAL AID PICTURE (2015-2016)**
**Students with need:** For part-time students, average financial aid package was $8,211.
**Students without need:** This college awards aid only to students with need.

**FINANCIAL AID PROCEDURES**
**Forms required:** FAFSA.
**Dates and Deadlines:** Applicants notified on a rolling basis starting 4/1; must reply within 2 week(s) of notification.
**Transfers:** No deadline. Applicants notified on a rolling basis; must reply within 2 week(s) of notification.

**CONTACT**
Nicole DeBlois, Financial Aid Specialist
70 Middle Street, Lewiston, ME 04240
(207) 795-2270

## Maine Maritime Academy
Castine, Maine
www.mainemaritime.edu              Federal Code: 002044

**4-year public** maritime college in rural community.
**Enrollment:** 1,037 undergrads, 1% part-time. 234 full-time freshmen.

**BASIC COSTS (2015-2016)**
**Tuition and fees:** $12,788; out-of-district residents $17,668; out-of-state residents $25,372.
**Room and board:** $9,830.
**Additional info:** USCG mandated Training Cruise/Co-ops have additional fees.

**FINANCIAL AID PICTURE**
**Students with need:** Need-based aid available for full-time and part-time students. Work study available nights, weekends, and for part-time students.
**Students without need:** No-need awards available for academics, leadership, religious affiliation, state/district residency.

**FINANCIAL AID PROCEDURES**
**Forms required:** FAFSA.
**Dates and Deadlines:** Closing date 4/15. Applicants notified on a rolling basis starting 4/1; must reply within 4 week(s) of notification.

**CONTACT**
Kathy Heath, Director of Financial Aid
Pleasant Street, Castine, ME 04420
(207) 326-2339

## Northern Maine Community College
Presque Isle, Maine
www.nmcc.edu                    Federal Code: 005760

**2-year public** community and technical college in small town.
**Enrollment:** 626 undergrads, 36% part-time. 102 full-time freshmen.

**BASIC COSTS (2015-2016)**
**Tuition and fees:** $3,398; out-of-state residents $6,098.
**Per-credit charge:** $90; out-of-state residents $180.
**Room and board:** $7,106.
**Additional info:** Additional lab and technology fees may apply to specific programs and courses. Tuition/fee waivers available for minority students.

**FINANCIAL AID PICTURE (2015-2016)**
**Students with need:** Out of 98 full-time freshmen who applied for aid, 90 were judged to have need. Of these, 90 received aid, and 3 had their full need met. Average financial aid package met 50% of need; average scholarship/grant was $6,270; average loan was $3,006. For part-time students, average financial aid package was $5,067.
**Students without need:** 4 full-time freshmen who did not demonstrate need for aid received scholarships/grants; average award was $1,250.

**FINANCIAL AID PROCEDURES**
**Forms required:** FAFSA, institutional form.
**Dates and Deadlines:** Priority date 5/1; no closing date. Applicants notified on a rolling basis starting 4/15; must reply within 2 week(s) of notification.
**Transfers:** No deadline. Applicants notified on a rolling basis.

**CONTACT**
Norma Smith, Financial Aid Coordinator
33 Edgemont Drive, Presque Isle, ME 04769
(207) 768-2790

## Saint Joseph's College of Maine
Standish, Maine
www.sjcme.edu                    Federal Code: 002051

**4-year private** liberal arts college in small town, affiliated with Roman Catholic Church.
**Enrollment:** 960 undergrads.

**BASIC COSTS (2015-2016)**
**Tuition and fees:** $33,820.
**Per-credit charge:** $1,000.
**Room and board:** $12,510.

**FINANCIAL AID PICTURE**
**Students with need:** Need-based aid available for full-time and part-time students. Work study available nights, weekends, and for part-time students.
**Students without need:** No-need awards available for academics, alumni affiliation, leadership.

**FINANCIAL AID PROCEDURES**
**Forms required:** FAFSA, institutional form.
**Dates and Deadlines:** Priority date 3/1; no closing date. Applicants notified on a rolling basis starting 3/1; must reply within 3 week(s) of notification.

**CONTACT**
Jill Golike, Financial Aid Director
278 Whites Bridge Road, Standish, ME 04084-5236
(800) 752-1266

## Southern Maine Community College
South Portland, Maine
www.smccme.edu                    Federal Code: 005525

**2-year public** community and technical college in large town.
**Enrollment:** 5,233 undergrads, 50% part-time. 915 full-time freshmen.
**Selectivity:** Open admission; but selective for some programs.

### BASIC COSTS (2015-2016)
**Tuition and fees:** $3,485; out-of-state residents $6,185.
**Per-credit charge:** $90; out-of-state residents $180.
**Room and board:** $8,688.

### FINANCIAL AID PICTURE (2014-2015)
**Students with need:** 44% of average financial aid package awarded as scholarships/grants, 56% awarded as loans/jobs. Need-based aid available for part-time students. Work study available nights, weekends, and for part-time students.
**Students without need:** This college awards aid only to students with need.

### FINANCIAL AID PROCEDURES
**Forms required:** FAFSA.
**Dates and Deadlines:** Priority date 5/1; no closing date. Applicants notified on a rolling basis.

### CONTACT
Shaun Gray, Director of Financial Services
2 Fort Road, South Portland, ME 04106
(207) 741-5518

## Thomas College
Waterville, Maine
www.thomas.edu                    Federal Code: 002052

**4-year private** business, liberal arts and teachers college in large town.
**Enrollment:** 855 undergrads, 6% part-time. 256 full-time freshmen.
**Selectivity:** Admits over 75% of applicants.

### BASIC COSTS (2015-2016)
**Tuition and fees:** $24,300.
**Per-credit charge:** $985.
**Room and board:** $10,430.

### FINANCIAL AID PICTURE (2015-2016)
**Students with need:** Average financial aid package met 85% of need; average scholarship/grant was $16,101; average loan was $4,026. For part-time students, average financial aid package was $9,830.
**Students without need:** No-need awards available for academics, alumni affiliation, leadership, state/district residency.

### FINANCIAL AID PROCEDURES
**Forms required:** FAFSA.
**Dates and Deadlines:** Priority date 2/15; no closing date. Applicants notified on a rolling basis starting 3/15; must reply within 2 week(s) of notification.

### CONTACT
Jeannine Bosse, Director of Student Financial Services
180 West River Road, Waterville, ME 04901
(207) 859-1105

## Unity College
Unity, Maine
www.unity.edu                    Federal Code: 006858

**4-year private** liberal arts college in rural community.
**Enrollment:** 643 undergrads, 1% part-time. 198 full-time freshmen.

**Selectivity:** Admits over 75% of applicants.

### BASIC COSTS (2015-2016)
**Tuition and fees:** $26,800.
**Per-credit charge:** $925.
**Room and board:** $9,800.
**Additional info:** Tuition/fee waivers available for minority students.

### FINANCIAL AID PICTURE (2015-2016)
**Students with need:** Out of 157 full-time freshmen who applied for aid, 140 were judged to have need. Of these, 140 received aid, and 18 had their full need met. Average financial aid package met 72% of need; average scholarship/grant was $13,825; average loan was $6,432. For part-time students, average financial aid package was $3,005.
**Students without need:** 24 full-time freshmen who did not demonstrate need for aid received scholarships/grants; average award was $9,500. No-need awards available for academics, leadership, minority status.

### FINANCIAL AID PROCEDURES
**Forms required:** FAFSA.
**Dates and Deadlines:** Priority date 3/1; no closing date. Applicants notified on a rolling basis starting 3/10; must reply within 2 week(s) of notification.
**Transfers:** Priority date 3/10. Applicants notified on a rolling basis starting 3/10; must reply within 2 week(s) of notification.

### CONTACT
Rand Newell, Director of Financial Aid
P.O. 532, Unity, ME 04988-0532
(207) 509-7235

## University of Maine
Orono, Maine
www.umaine.edu                    Federal Code: 002053

**4-year public** university in large town.
**Enrollment:** 8,677 undergrads, 8% part-time. 2,017 full-time freshmen.
**Selectivity:** Admits over 75% of applicants.

### BASIC COSTS (2015-2016)
**Tuition and fees:** $10,610; out-of-state residents $28,880.
**Per-credit charge:** $279; out-of-state residents $888.
**Room and board:** $9,576.
**Additional info:** New England Regional Student Program tuition is $12,570.

### FINANCIAL AID PICTURE (2015-2016)
**Students with need:** Out of 1,873 full-time freshmen who applied for aid, 1,489 were judged to have need. Of these, 1,469 received aid, and 268 had their full need met. Average financial aid package met 82% of need; average scholarship/grant was $10,561; average loan was $3,762. For part-time students, average financial aid package was $11,921.
**Students without need:** 306 full-time freshmen who did not demonstrate need for aid received scholarships/grants; average award was $5,515. No-need awards available for academics, alumni affiliation, art, athletics, job skills, leadership, minority status, music/drama, religious affiliation, ROTC, state/district residency.
**Scholarships offered: *Merit:*** Academic merit scholarships: range in value from $1,000 to $15,000; most awards are renewable for up to eight (8) consecutive semesters; based upon academic performance and full-time enrollment. ***Athletic:*** 9 full-time freshmen received athletic scholarships; average amount $12,350.
**Additional info:** Financial aid is available for students entering in the spring.

### FINANCIAL AID PROCEDURES
**Forms required:** FAFSA.
**Dates and Deadlines:** Priority date 3/1; closing date 5/15. Applicants notified on a rolling basis starting 3/15.
**Transfers:** Priority date 3/1; closing date 5/15.

## CONTACT

Sarah Doheny, Director of Student Financial Aid
5713 Chadbourne Hall, Orono, ME 04469-5713
(207) 581-1324

# University of Maine at Augusta

Augusta, Maine
www.uma.edu                    Federal Code: 006760

**4-year public** university in large town.
**Enrollment:** 3,964 undergrads, 61% part-time. 237 full-time freshmen.
**Selectivity:** Open admission; but selective for some programs.

## BASIC COSTS (2015-2016)

**Tuition and fees:** $7,448; out-of-state residents $16,688.
**Per-credit charge:** $217; out-of-state residents $525.
**Additional info:** New England Regional Student Program tuition is $9,750.

## FINANCIAL AID PICTURE (2015-2016)

**Students with need:** 42% of average financial aid package awarded as scholarships/grants, 58% awarded as loans/jobs. Need-based aid available for part-time students. Work study available nights, weekends, and for part-time students.
**Students without need:** No-need awards available for academics, athletics, leadership, music/drama, state/district residency.

## FINANCIAL AID PROCEDURES

**Forms required:** FAFSA.
**Dates and Deadlines:** Priority date 3/1; no closing date. Applicants notified on a rolling basis starting 3/15; must reply within 2 week(s) of notification.

## CONTACT

Sherry McCollett, Director of Financial Aid
46 University Drive, Augusta, ME 04330
(207) 621-3455

# University of Maine at Farmington

Farmington, Maine
www.umf.maine.edu              Federal Code: 002040

**4-year public** liberal arts and teachers college in small town.
**Enrollment:** 1,766 undergrads, 5% part-time. 410 full-time freshmen.
**Selectivity:** Admits over 75% of applicants.

## BASIC COSTS (2015-2016)

**Tuition and fees:** $9,217; out-of-state residents $18,305.
**Per-credit charge:** $261; out-of-state residents $545.
**Room and board:** $8,970.
**Additional info:** New England Regional Student Program tuition is $12,544. Tuition/fee waivers available for minority students.

## FINANCIAL AID PICTURE (2014-2015)

**Students with need:** Out of 405 full-time freshmen who applied for aid, 351 were judged to have need. Of these, 351 received aid, and 159 had their full need met. Average financial aid package met 86% of need; average scholarship/grant was $8,538; average loan was $5,304. For part-time students, average financial aid package was $8,231.
**Students without need:** 33 full-time freshmen who did not demonstrate need for aid received scholarships/grants; average award was $3,061. No-need awards available for academics, leadership, minority status, music/drama, state/district residency.
**Scholarships offered:** Academic Excellence Scholarship: for students ranking in the top 10% of their graduating class. Distinction Scholarship: for students ranking in the top 20% of their graduating class. Academic Achievement Scholarship: for students ranking in the top 30% of their graduating class. Students from schools that do not report rank will be considered for

these scholarships based on their high school academic courses and grades. The amount awarded varies depending on the scholarship awarded and the residency of the applicant.
**Additional info:** Freshman students from Franklin County, Maine, offered free on-campus housing for their first year at UMF. Federal processor must receive FAFSA by 3/1 in order for applicant to receive priority consideration from campus.

## FINANCIAL AID PROCEDURES

**Forms required:** FAFSA.
**Dates and Deadlines:** Priority date 3/1; no closing date. Applicants notified on a rolling basis starting 3/15.
**Transfers:** Applicants notified on a rolling basis starting 3/15.

## CONTACT

Ronald Milliken, Director of Financial Aid
246 Main Street, Farmington, ME 04938
(207) 778-7100

# University of Maine at Fort Kent

Fort Kent, Maine            Federal Code: 002041
www.umfk.maine.edu              CSS Code: 3393

**4-year public** university and branch campus college in small town.
**Enrollment:** 990 undergrads, 41% part-time. 127 full-time freshmen.
**Selectivity:** Admits over 75% of applicants.

## BASIC COSTS (2015-2016)

**Tuition and fees:** $7,575; out-of-state residents $10,875.
**Per-credit charge:** $220; out-of-state residents $330.
**Room and board:** $7,910.

## FINANCIAL AID PICTURE (2014-2015)

**Students with need:** Out of 109 full-time freshmen who applied for aid, 93 were judged to have need. Of these, 93 received aid, and 58 had their full need met. Average financial aid package met 85% of need; average scholarship/grant was $6,133; average loan was $5,436. For part-time students, average financial aid package was $6,505.
**Students without need:** 6 full-time freshmen who did not demonstrate need for aid received scholarships/grants; average award was $917. No-need awards available for academics, leadership.

## FINANCIAL AID PROCEDURES

**Forms required:** FAFSA, CSS PROFILE, state aid form, institutional form.
**Dates and Deadlines:** Priority date 3/1; no closing date. Applicants notified on a rolling basis starting 3/15.

## CONTACT

Lisa Lipe, Assoc. Director of Financial Aid
23 University Drive, Fort Kent, ME 04743
(207) 834-7607

# University of Maine at Machias

Machias, Maine
www.umm.maine.edu              Federal Code: 002055

**4-year public** university and liberal arts college in rural community.
**Enrollment:** 574 undergrads, 25% part-time. 111 full-time freshmen.

## BASIC COSTS (2015-2016)

**Tuition and fees:** $7,480; out-of-state residents $19,300.
**Per-credit charge:** $222; out-of-state residents $616.
**Room and board:** $8,486.
**Additional info:** New England Regional Student Program tuition is $9,990.

## FINANCIAL AID PICTURE

**Students with need:** Need-based aid available for full-time and part-time students.

**Students without need:** No-need awards available for academics, athletics.

## FINANCIAL AID PROCEDURES

**Forms required:** FAFSA.

**Dates and Deadlines:** Priority date 3/1; no closing date. Applicants notified on a rolling basis starting 3/1.

**Transfers:** Applicants notified on a rolling basis starting 3/1.

## CONTACT

Stephanie Larrabee, Director of Financial Aid

116 O'Brien Avenue, Machias, ME 04654-1397

(207) 255-1203

# University of Maine at Presque Isle

Presque Isle, Maine

www.umpi.edu                              Federal Code: 002033

**4-year public** university in small town.

**Enrollment:** 833 undergrads, 21% part-time. 184 full-time freshmen.

**Selectivity:** Admits over 75% of applicants.

## BASIC COSTS (2015-2016)

**Tuition and fees:** $7,436; out-of-state residents $10,736.

**Per-credit charge:** $220; out-of-state residents $330.

**Room and board:** $8,044.

**Additional info:** New England Regional Student Program tuition is $9,900. Tuition/fee waivers available for minority students.

## FINANCIAL AID PICTURE (2015-2016)

**Students with need:** Out of 166 full-time freshmen who applied for aid, 141 were judged to have need. Of these, 141 received aid, and 84 had their full need met. Average financial aid package met 87% of need; average scholarship/grant was $8,150; average loan was $4,223. For part-time students, average financial aid package was $8,489.

**Students without need:** 13 full-time freshmen who did not demonstrate need for aid received scholarships/grants; average award was $2,063. No-need awards available for academics.

## FINANCIAL AID PROCEDURES

**Forms required:** FAFSA.

**Dates and Deadlines:** Priority date 4/1; no closing date. Applicants notified on a rolling basis starting 3/1; must reply within 2 week(s) of notification.

## CONTACT

Christopher Bell, Director of Student Financial Services

181 Main Street, Presque Isle, ME 04769

(207) 768-9510

# University of New England

Biddeford, Maine

www.une.edu                               Federal Code: 002050

**4-year private** university in small city.

**Enrollment:** 2,271 undergrads, 1% part-time. 624 full-time freshmen.

**Selectivity:** Admits over 75% of applicants.

## BASIC COSTS (2015-2016)

**Tuition and fees:** $34,660.

**Per-credit charge:** $1,180.

**Room and board:** $12,920.

## FINANCIAL AID PICTURE

**Students with need:** Need-based aid available for full-time and part-time students. Work study available nights, weekends, and for part-time students.

**Students without need:** No-need awards available for academics.

**Scholarships offered:** UNE Scholarships and UNE Departmental Award: non-need; based on academic qualifications as determined from GPA and

SAT/ACT scores; must be a full-time undergraduate student and maintain a 2.5 GPA.

## FINANCIAL AID PROCEDURES

**Forms required:** FAFSA.

**Dates and Deadlines:** Priority date 5/1; no closing date. Applicants notified on a rolling basis starting 2/1.

## CONTACT

Paul Henderson, Assistant Vice President of Student Financial Services

11 Hills Beach Road, Biddeford, ME 04005

(207) 602-2404

# University of Southern Maine

Portland, Maine

www.usm.maine.edu                         Federal Code: 009762

**4-year public** university in small city.

**Enrollment:** 5,359 undergrads, 31% part-time. 701 full-time freshmen.

**Selectivity:** Admits over 75% of applicants.

## BASIC COSTS (2015-2016)

**Tuition and fees:** $8,540; out-of-state residents $20,900.

**Per-credit charge:** $253; out-of-state residents $665.

**Room and board:** $9,400.

**Additional info:** New England Regional Student Program tuition is $11,400.

## FINANCIAL AID PICTURE (2014-2015)

**Students with need:** Out of 654 full-time freshmen who applied for aid, 523 were judged to have need. Of these, 522 received aid, and 225 had their full need met. Average financial aid package met 73% of need; average scholarship/grant was $7,212; average loan was $5,845. For part-time students, average financial aid package was $8,701.

**Students without need:** 62 full-time freshmen who did not demonstrate need for aid received scholarships/grants; average award was $4,242. No-need awards available for academics, music/drama, state/district residency.

## FINANCIAL AID PROCEDURES

**Forms required:** FAFSA.

**Dates and Deadlines:** Priority date 2/15; no closing date. Applicants notified on a rolling basis starting 3/15; must reply by 5/1 or within 2 week(s) of notification.

**Transfers:** Applicants notified on a rolling basis; must reply by 5/1 or within 2 week(s) of notification.

## CONTACT

Keith Dubois, Director of Financial Aid Office

PO Box 9300, Portland, ME 04104

(207) 780-5250

# Washington County Community College

Calais, Maine

www.wccc.me.edu                           Federal Code: 009231

**2-year public** community and technical college in small town.

**Enrollment:** 332 undergrads.

**Selectivity:** Open admission; but selective for some programs.

## BASIC COSTS (2015-2016)

**Tuition and fees:** $3,380; out-of-state residents $6,080.

**Per-credit charge:** $90; out-of-state residents $180.

**Room and board:** $5,340.

## FINANCIAL AID PICTURE

**Students with need:** Need-based aid available for full-time and part-time students. Work study available nights.

**Students without need:** No-need awards available for academics.

## FINANCIAL AID PROCEDURES
**Forms required:** FAFSA, institutional form.
**Dates and Deadlines:** Priority date 4/1; closing date 5/1. Applicants notified on a rolling basis starting 5/1; must reply within 2 week(s) of notification.
**Transfers:** Priority date 8/1; no deadline. Applicants notified on a rolling basis; must reply within 2 week(s) of notification.

## CONTACT
William O'Shea, Financial Aid Director
One College Drive, Calais, ME 04619
(207) 454-1033

## York County Community College
Wells, Maine
www.yccc.edu                    Federal Code: 031229

**2-year public** community and technical college in small town.
**Enrollment:** 1,391 undergrads, 67% part-time. 82 full-time freshmen.
**Selectivity:** Open admission.

## BASIC COSTS (2015-2016)
**Tuition and fees:** $3,330; out-of-state residents $6,030.
**Per-credit charge:** $90; out-of-state residents $180.
**Additional info:** Additional lab and technology fees may apply to specific programs and courses. Tuition/fee waivers available for minority students.

## FINANCIAL AID PICTURE (2014-2015)
**Students with need:** Out of 78 full-time freshmen who applied for aid, 61 were judged to have need. Of these, 58 received aid. Average financial aid package met 44% of need; average scholarship/grant was $5,129; average loan was $2,590. For part-time students, average financial aid package was $3,769.
**Students without need:** 9 full-time freshmen who did not demonstrate need for aid received scholarships/grants; average award was $907. No-need awards available for academics, alumni affiliation, art, job skills, leadership, state/district residency.

## FINANCIAL AID PROCEDURES
**Forms required:** FAFSA.
**Dates and Deadlines:** Priority date 5/1; no closing date. Must reply within 2 week(s) of notification.

## CONTACT
David Daigle, Director of Financial Aid
112 College Drive, Wells, ME 04090
(207) 216-4410

# Maryland

## Allegany College of Maryland
Cumberland, Maryland
www.allegany.edu                    Federal Code: 002057

**2-year public** community college in large town.
**Enrollment:** 2,461 undergrads.
**Selectivity:** Open admission; but selective for some programs.

## BASIC COSTS (2015-2016)
**Tuition and fees:** $3,665; out-of-district residents $6,665; out-of-state residents $7,955.
**Per-credit charge:** $114; out-of-district residents $214; out-of-state residents $257.

## FINANCIAL AID PICTURE
**Students with need:** Need-based aid available for full-time and part-time students. Work study available nights.
**Students without need:** No-need awards available for academics, athletics, leadership, state/district residency.

## FINANCIAL AID PROCEDURES
**Forms required:** FAFSA, institutional form.
**Dates and Deadlines:** Priority date 3/1; no closing date. Applicants notified on a rolling basis starting 4/15; must reply within 2 week(s) of notification.

## CONTACT
Vicki Smith, Director of Financial Aid
12401 Willowbrook Road, SE, Cumberland, MD 21502
(301) 784-5213

## Anne Arundel Community College
Arnold, Maryland
www.aacc.edu                    Federal Code: 002058

**2-year public** community college in large town.
**Enrollment:** 12,601 undergrads, 66% part-time. 1,404 full-time freshmen.
**Selectivity:** Open admission; but selective for some programs.

## BASIC COSTS (2015-2016)
**Tuition and fees:** $3,920; out-of-district residents $6,830; out-of-state residents $11,480.
**Per-credit charge:** $105; out-of-district residents $202; out-of-state residents $357.

## FINANCIAL AID PICTURE (2014-2015)
**Students with need:** 71% of average financial aid package awarded as scholarships/grants, 29% awarded as loans/jobs. Need-based aid available for part-time students. Work study available nights, weekends, and for part-time students.

## FINANCIAL AID PROCEDURES
**Forms required:** FAFSA, institutional form.
**Dates and Deadlines:** Priority date 5/15; no closing date. Applicants notified on a rolling basis starting 7/1; must reply within 2 week(s) of notification.

## CONTACT
Richard Heath, Director of Student Financial Services
101 College Parkway, Arnold, MD 21012-1895
(410) 777-2203

## Baltimore City Community College
Baltimore, Maryland
www.bccc.edu                    Federal Code: 002061

**2-year public** community college in very large city.
**Enrollment:** 4,857 undergrads.
**Selectivity:** Open admission; but selective for some programs.

## BASIC COSTS (2015-2016)
**Tuition and fees:** $3,062; out-of-state residents $7,172.
**Per-credit charge:** $88; out-of-state residents $225.

## FINANCIAL AID PICTURE
**Students with need:** Need-based aid available for full-time and part-time students. Work study available nights, weekends, and for part-time students.
**Students without need:** This college awards aid only to students with need.

## FINANCIAL AID PROCEDURES
**Forms required:** FAFSA, state aid form, institutional form.
**Dates and Deadlines:** Priority date 6/1; no closing date. Applicants notified on a rolling basis starting 7/1; must reply within 2 week(s) of notification.

**CONTACT**
Vera Brooks, Director of Financial Aid
2901 Liberty Heights Avenue, Baltimore, MD 21215-7893
(410) 462-8348

## Bowie State University
Bowie, Maryland
www.bowiestate.edu                     Federal Code: 002062

**4-year public** university in small city.
**Enrollment:** 4,298 undergrads, 18% part-time. 550 full-time freshmen.
**Selectivity:** Admits 50 to 75% of applicants.

**BASIC COSTS (2015-2016)**
**Tuition and fees:** $7,657; out-of-state residents $18,140.
**Per-credit charge:** $230; out-of-state residents $660.
**Room and board:** $10,850.

**FINANCIAL AID PICTURE (2014-2015)**
**Students with need:** Out of 461 full-time freshmen who applied for aid, 460 were judged to have need. Of these, 460 received aid, and 216 had their full need met. Average financial aid package met 48% of need; average scholarship/grant was $7,856; average loan was $3,368. For part-time students, average financial aid package was $5,555.
**Students without need:** 20 full-time freshmen who did not demonstrate need for aid received scholarships/grants; average award was $196. No-need awards available for academics, alumni affiliation, art, athletics, music/drama, state/district residency.
**Scholarships offered:** 23 full-time freshmen received athletic scholarships; average amount $3,213.

**FINANCIAL AID PROCEDURES**
**Forms required:** FAFSA.
**Dates and Deadlines:** Closing date 3/1. Applicants notified on a rolling basis starting 4/1; must reply within 2 week(s) of notification.
**Transfers:** Applicants notified on a rolling basis starting 4/1; must reply within 2 week(s) of notification.

**CONTACT**
Linda Gayton, Director of Financial Aid
14000 Jericho Park Road, Bowie, MD 20715
(301) 860-3540

## Capitol Technology University
Laurel, Maryland
www.capitol-college.edu                 Federal Code: 001436

**4-year private** business and engineering college in large town.
**Enrollment:** 441 undergrads.

**BASIC COSTS (2015-2016)**
**Tuition and fees:** $23,508.
**Per-credit charge:** $750.
**Room only:** $5,180.
**Additional info:** On-campus room charge is for triple occupancy room. Tuition at time of enrollment locked for 4 years.

**FINANCIAL AID PICTURE**
**Students with need:** Need-based aid available for full-time and part-time students. Work study available nights, weekends, and for part-time students.
**Students without need:** No-need awards available for academics, alumni affiliation, leadership, minority status.

**FINANCIAL AID PROCEDURES**
**Forms required:** FAFSA, institutional form.

**Dates and Deadlines:** Priority date 3/1; no closing date. Applicants notified on a rolling basis starting 4/1; must reply by 5/1 or within 3 week(s) of notification.

**CONTACT**
Sue Thompson, Director of Financial Aid
11301 Springfield Road, Laurel, MD 20708
(301) 369-2800 ext. 3039

## Carroll Community College
Westminster, Maryland
www.carrollcc.edu                        Federal Code: 031007

**2-year public** community college in large town.
**Enrollment:** 3,154 undergrads, 60% part-time. 538 full-time freshmen.
**Selectivity:** Open admission; but selective for some programs.

**BASIC COSTS (2015-2016)**
**Tuition and fees:** $4,596; out-of-district residents $6,684; out-of-state residents $9,312.
**Per-credit charge:** $153; out-of-district residents $223; out-of-state residents $310.

**FINANCIAL AID PICTURE (2014-2015)**
**Students with need:** 57% of average financial aid package awarded as scholarships/grants, 43% awarded as loans/jobs. Need-based aid available for part-time students. Work study available nights, weekends, and for part-time students.
**Students without need:** No-need awards available for academics, art, job skills, leadership, state/district residency.

**FINANCIAL AID PROCEDURES**
**Forms required:** FAFSA.
**Dates and Deadlines:** Priority date 3/1; no closing date. Must reply within 2 week(s) of notification.

**CONTACT**
John Gay, Director of Financial Aid
1601 Washington Road, Westminster, MD 21157
(410) 386-8437

## Cecil College
North East, Maryland
www.my.cecil.edu                         Federal Code: 008308

**2-year public** community college in large town.
**Enrollment:** 2,402 undergrads.
**Selectivity:** Open admission; but selective for some programs.

**BASIC COSTS (2015-2016)**
**Tuition and fees:** $3,630; out-of-district residents $6,330; out-of-state residents $7,680.
**Per-credit charge:** $100; out-of-district residents $190; out-of-state residents $235.
**Additional info:** Tuition at time of enrollment locked for 2 years.

**FINANCIAL AID PICTURE**
**Students with need:** Need-based aid available for full-time students. Work study available nights, weekends, and for part-time students.
**Students without need:** No-need awards available for academics, alumni affiliation, athletics, job skills, state/district residency.

**FINANCIAL AID PROCEDURES**
**Forms required:** FAFSA.
**Dates and Deadlines:** Priority date 8/1; no closing date. Applicants notified on a rolling basis; must reply within 2 week(s) of notification.

## CONTACT

Amanda Solecki, Director of Financial Aid
One Seahawk Drive, North East, MD 21901
(443) 674-1891

## Chesapeake College

Wye Mills, Maryland
www.chesapeake.edu              Federal Code: 004650

**2-year public** community college in rural community.
**Enrollment:** 1,975 undergrads, 65% part-time. 277 full-time freshmen.
**Selectivity:** Open admission; but selective for some programs.

### BASIC COSTS (2015-2016)

**Tuition and fees:** $4,520; out-of-district residents $6,560; out-of-state residents $8,870.
**Per-credit charge:** $115; out-of-district residents $183; out-of-state residents $260.

### FINANCIAL AID PICTURE (2014-2015)

**Students with need:** 97% of average financial aid package awarded as scholarships/grants, 3% awarded as loans/jobs. Need-based aid available for part-time students.
**Students without need:** No-need awards available for academics, art, athletics, state/district residency.

### FINANCIAL AID PROCEDURES

**Forms required:** FAFSA, institutional form.
**Dates and Deadlines:** Priority date 5/1; no closing date. Applicants notified on a rolling basis starting 5/5; must reply within 2 week(s) of notification.

### CONTACT

Mindy Schaffer, Director of Financial Aid
Box 8, Wye Mills, MD 21679-0008
(410) 827-5803

## College of Southern Maryland

La Plata, Maryland
www.csmd.edu               Federal Code: 002064

**2-year public** community college in large town.
**Enrollment:** 8,358 undergrads.
**Selectivity:** Open admission; but selective for some programs.

### BASIC COSTS (2015-2016)

**Tuition and fees:** $4,428; out-of-district residents $7,638; out-of-state residents $9,889.
**Per-credit charge:** $120; out-of-district residents $207; out-of-state residents $268.

### FINANCIAL AID PICTURE

**Students with need:** Need-based aid available for full-time and part-time students. Work study available nights, weekends, and for part-time students.
**Students without need:** No-need awards available for academics, athletics, leadership.

### FINANCIAL AID PROCEDURES

**Forms required:** FAFSA.
**Dates and Deadlines:** Priority date 3/1; no closing date. Applicants notified on a rolling basis starting 6/15.

### CONTACT

Christian Zimmermann, Director of Financial Assistance
College of Southern Maryland-AOD, La Plata, MD 20646-0910
(301) 934-7531

## Community College of Baltimore County

Baltimore, Maryland
www.ccbcmd.edu               Federal Code: 002063

**2-year public** community college in very large city.
**Enrollment:** 20,630 undergrads, 70% part-time. 1,985 full-time freshmen.
**Selectivity:** Open admission; but selective for some programs.

### BASIC COSTS (2015-2016)

**Tuition and fees:** $4,252; out-of-district residents $7,342; out-of-state residents $10,582.
**Per-credit charge:** $113; out-of-district residents $216; out-of-state residents $324.
**Additional info:** In-State, Out-of-District tuition and fees are $7,342.

### FINANCIAL AID PICTURE

**Students with need:** Need-based aid available for full-time and part-time students. Work study available nights, weekends, and for part-time students.
**Students without need:** No-need awards available for academics, athletics, state/district residency.
**Additional info:** On-campus employment typically available.

### FINANCIAL AID PROCEDURES

**Forms required:** FAFSA.
**Dates and Deadlines:** Priority date 1/9; no closing date. Applicants notified on a rolling basis starting 2/27; must reply within 2 week(s) of notification.

### CONTACT

Virginia Zawodny, Director of Financial Aid
800 South Rolling Road, Baltimore, MD 21228-5317
(443) 840-2222

## Coppin State University

Baltimore, Maryland
www.coppin.edu               Federal Code: 002068

**4-year public** liberal arts college in very large city.
**Enrollment:** 2,885 undergrads.

### BASIC COSTS (2015-2016)

**Tuition and fees:** $6,362; out-of-state residents $11,886.
**Per-credit charge:** $184; out-of-state residents $547.
**Room and board:** $9,359.

### FINANCIAL AID PICTURE

**Students with need:** Need-based aid available for full-time and part-time students.
**Students without need:** No-need awards available for academics, alumni affiliation, athletics, ROTC, state/district residency.
**Scholarships offered:** Gold Freshman Merit Award: $2,000 per year; awarded to freshmen with 950 SAT and 2.5 GPA. Gold Transfer Merit Award: $1,500 per year; awarded to Maryland Community College transfer students with 2.8 GPA and successful completion of 56 credits. Blue Freshman Merit Award: $1,000 per year; awarded to freshman with 900 SAT and 2.5 GPA. Blue Transfer Merit Award: $800 per year; awarded to Maryland Community College transfer students with 2.5 GPA and successful completion of 25 credits. SAT scores exclusive of Writing.
**Additional info:** Funds allocated by State of Maryland for minority students enrolled for at least 6 credits who are Maryland residents and US citizens (Minority Grant).

### FINANCIAL AID PROCEDURES

**Forms required:** FAFSA.
**Dates and Deadlines:** Priority date 3/1; no closing date. Applicants notified on a rolling basis starting 4/15; must reply within 2 week(s) of notification.

**CONTACT**
Mose Cartier, Director of Financial Aid
2500 West North Avenue, Baltimore, MD 21216
(410) 951-3636

## Frederick Community College
Frederick, Maryland
www.frederick.edu                    Federal Code: 002071

**2-year public** community college in small city.
**Enrollment:** 5,043 undergrads.
**Selectivity:** Open admission; but selective for some programs.

**BASIC COSTS (2015-2016)**
**Tuition and fees:** $4,165; out-of-district residents $8,245; out-of-state residents $10,945.
**Per-credit charge:** $116; out-of-district residents $252; out-of-state residents $342.

**FINANCIAL AID PICTURE (2014-2015)**
**Students with need:** 77% of average financial aid package awarded as scholarships/grants, 23% awarded as loans/jobs. Need-based aid available for part-time students.
**Students without need:** No-need awards available for academics, athletics, state/district residency.
**Scholarships offered:** Scholarships available for Frederick County Public Schools students with high GPA who will participate in student ambassador program. Other general scholarships available.

**FINANCIAL AID PROCEDURES**
**Forms required:** FAFSA, institutional form.
**Dates and Deadlines:** Priority date 6/1; no closing date. Applicants notified on a rolling basis starting 5/15; must reply within 2 week(s) of notification.
**Transfers:** Applicants notified on a rolling basis starting 6/1. Financial aid transcripts from prior institutions must be submitted before awards are made.

**CONTACT**
Brenda Dayhoff, Executive Director, Financial Aid
7932 Opossumtown Pike, Frederick, MD 21702
(301) 846-2480

## Frostburg State University
Frostburg, Maryland
www.frostburg.edu                    Federal Code: 002072

**4-year public** university and teachers college in small town.
**Enrollment:** 4,850 undergrads, 15% part-time. 981 full-time freshmen.
**Selectivity:** Admits 50 to 75% of applicants.

**BASIC COSTS (2015-2016)**
**Tuition and fees:** $8,488; out-of-state residents $20,588.
**Per-credit charge:** $257; out-of-state residents $514.
**Room and board:** $8,672.

**FINANCIAL AID PICTURE (2014-2015)**
**Students with need:** Out of 854 full-time freshmen who applied for aid, 631 were judged to have need. Of these, 630 received aid, and 104 had their full need met. Average financial aid package met 60% of need; average scholarship/grant was $7,515; average loan was $3,217. For part-time students, average financial aid package was $4,437.
**Students without need:** 170 full-time freshmen who did not demonstrate need for aid received scholarships/grants; average award was $2,465. No-need awards available for academics, leadership, minority status.

**FINANCIAL AID PROCEDURES**
**Forms required:** FAFSA.

**Dates and Deadlines:** Priority date 3/1; no closing date. Applicants notified on a rolling basis starting 3/15; must reply within 3 week(s) of notification.

**CONTACT**
Angela Hovatter, Director of Financial Aid
101 Braddock Road, Frostburg, MD 21532-1099
(301) 687-4201

## Garrett College
McHenry, Maryland
www.garrettcollege.edu               Federal Code: 010014

**2-year public** community college in rural community.
**Enrollment:** 548 undergrads.
**Selectivity:** Open admission.

**BASIC COSTS (2015-2016)**
**Tuition and fees:** $3,890; out-of-district residents $7,550; out-of-state residents $8,750.
**Per-credit charge:** $98; out-of-district residents $220; out-of-state residents $260.
**Room and board:** $5,910.
**Additional info:** Room and board is for Garrett Hall. Laker Hall charged at a higher rate.

**FINANCIAL AID PICTURE**
**Students with need:** Need-based aid available for full-time and part-time students. Work study available nights, weekends, and for part-time students.
**Students without need:** No-need awards available for academics, athletics, leadership.
**Additional info:** Many merit and need-based local scholarships available.

**FINANCIAL AID PROCEDURES**
**Forms required:** FAFSA.
**Dates and Deadlines:** Priority date 3/1; no closing date. Applicants notified on a rolling basis starting 6/1; must reply within 2 week(s) of notification.

**CONTACT**
Cissy Vansickle, Director of Financial Aid
687 Mosser Road, McHenry, MD 21541
(301) 387-3012

## Goucher College
Baltimore, Maryland                  Federal Code: 002073
www.goucher.edu                      CSS Code: 5257

**4-year private** liberal arts college in small city.
**Enrollment:** 1,466 undergrads, 1% part-time. 389 full-time freshmen.
**Selectivity:** Admits over 75% of applicants.

**BASIC COSTS (2015-2016)**
**Tuition and fees:** $42,180.
**Room and board:** $12,460.

**FINANCIAL AID PICTURE (2015-2016)**
**Students with need:** Out of 312 full-time freshmen who applied for aid, 265 were judged to have need. Of these, 265 received aid, and 58 had their full need met. Average financial aid package met 80% of need; average scholarship/grant was $29,973; average loan was $2,995. For part-time students, average financial aid package was $7,948.
**Students without need:** 123 full-time freshmen who did not demonstrate need for aid received scholarships/grants; average award was $15,799. No-need awards available for academics, art, music/drama.

**FINANCIAL AID PROCEDURES**
**Forms required:** FAFSA, CSS PROFILE.

**Dates and Deadlines:** Priority date 2/1; closing date 4/1. Applicants notified on a rolling basis starting 3/1; must reply by 5/1 or within 2 week(s) of notification.
**Transfers:** Priority date 4/15; no deadline. Applicants notified on a rolling basis starting 4/15; must reply within 2 week(s) of notification.

**CONTACT**
Stephanie Bender, Director of Financial Aid
1021 Dulaney Valley Road, Baltimore, MD 21204-2753
(410) 337-6141

## Hagerstown Community College
Hagerstown, Maryland
www.hagerstowncc.edu          Federal Code: 002074

**2-year public** community college in small city.
**Enrollment:** 3,396 undergrads. 313 full-time freshmen.
**Selectivity:** Open admission; but selective for some programs.

**BASIC COSTS (2015-2016)**
**Tuition and fees:** $3,930; out-of-district residents $5,910; out-of-state residents $7,650.
**Per-credit charge:** $117; out-of-district residents $183; out-of-state residents $241.

**FINANCIAL AID PICTURE (2014-2015)**
**Students with need:** Out of 257 full-time freshmen who applied for aid, 207 were judged to have need. Of these, 194 received aid, and 12 had their full need met. Average financial aid package met 45% of need; average scholarship/grant was $4,247; average loan was $2,702. Need-based aid available for part-time students.
**Students without need:** This college awards aid only to students with need.

**FINANCIAL AID PROCEDURES**
**Forms required:** FAFSA.
**Dates and Deadlines:** Priority date 5/30; no closing date. Applicants notified on a rolling basis starting 4/15.
**Transfers:** No deadline.

**CONTACT**
Carolyn Cox, Director of Financial Aid
11400 Robinwood Drive, Hagerstown, MD 21742-6514
(240) 500-2473

## Harford Community College
Bel Air, Maryland
www.harford.edu          Federal Code: 002075

**2-year public** community college in small city.
**Enrollment:** 5,546 undergrads, 59% part-time. 941 full-time freshmen.
**Selectivity:** Open admission; but selective for some programs.

**BASIC COSTS (2015-2016)**
**Tuition and fees:** $4,176; out-of-district residents $6,786; out-of-state residents $9,396.
**Per-credit charge:** $116; out-of-district residents $203; out-of-state residents $290.

**FINANCIAL AID PICTURE (2014-2015)**
**Students with need:** Out of 659 full-time freshmen who applied for aid, 437 were judged to have need. Of these, 402 received aid. Need-based aid available for part-time students.
**Scholarships offered:** Alfred C. O'Connell Homes Scholarship; full tuition and fees for 2 years; based on 3.25 GPA; 25 awards.

**FINANCIAL AID PROCEDURES**
**Forms required:** FAFSA, institutional form.
**Dates and Deadlines:** Priority date 3/15; no closing date. Applicants notified on a rolling basis starting 4/1; must reply within 2 week(s) of notification.

**CONTACT**
Lynn Lee, Director of Financial Aid
401 Thomas Run Road, Bel Air, MD 21015
(443) 443-2257

## Hood College
Frederick, Maryland
www.hood.edu          Federal Code: 002076

**4-year private** liberal arts college in small city.
**Enrollment:** 1,246 undergrads, 6% part-time. 257 full-time freshmen.
**Selectivity:** Admits over 75% of applicants.

**BASIC COSTS (2015-2016)**
**Tuition and fees:** $35,150.
**Per-credit charge:** $1,005.
**Room and board:** $11,840.

**FINANCIAL AID PICTURE (2015-2016)**
**Students with need:** Out of 233 full-time freshmen who applied for aid, 197 were judged to have need. Of these, 197 received aid, and 43 had their full need met. Average financial aid package met 78% of need; average scholarship/grant was $25,594; average loan was $3,728. For part-time students, average financial aid package was $8,933.
**Students without need:** 54 full-time freshmen who did not demonstrate need for aid received scholarships/grants; average award was $18,077. No-need awards available for academics, alumni affiliation, leadership, minority status, music/drama, ROTC, state/district residency.

**FINANCIAL AID PROCEDURES**
**Forms required:** FAFSA, institutional form.
**Dates and Deadlines:** Priority date 2/15; no closing date. Applicants notified on a rolling basis starting 3/1; must reply by 5/1 or within 4 week(s) of notification.

**CONTACT**
Brenda DiSorbo, Director of Financial Aid
401 Rosemont Avenue, Frederick, MD 21701-8575
(301) 696-3411

## Howard Community College
Columbia, Maryland
www.howardcc.edu          Federal Code: 008175

**2-year public** community college in small city.
**Enrollment:** 9,333 undergrads, 61% part-time. 1,161 full-time freshmen.
**Selectivity:** Open admission; but selective for some programs.

**BASIC COSTS (2015-2016)**
**Tuition and fees:** $4,623; out-of-district residents $7,113; out-of-state residents $8,463.
**Per-credit charge:** $132; out-of-district residents $215; out-of-state residents $260.

**FINANCIAL AID PICTURE (2014-2015)**
**Students with need:** 81% of average financial aid package awarded as scholarships/grants, 19% awarded as loans/jobs. Need-based aid available for part-time students. Work study available nights, weekends, and for part-time students.

**FINANCIAL AID PROCEDURES**
**Forms required:** FAFSA.

**Dates and Deadlines:** Priority date 3/1; no closing date. Applicants notified on a rolling basis starting 5/1.

**CONTACT**
Dawn Lowe, Director of Financial Aid Services
10901 Little Patuxent Parkway, Columbia, MD 21044-3197
(443) 518-1260

## Johns Hopkins University

Baltimore, Maryland       Federal Code: 002077
www.jhu.edu       CSS Code: 5332

**4-year private** university in very large city.
**Enrollment:** 5,334 undergrads. 1,414 full-time freshmen.
**Selectivity:** Admits less than 50% of applicants.

**BASIC COSTS (2015-2016)**
**Tuition and fees:** $49,210.
**Per-credit charge:** $1,624.
**Room and board:** $14,540.

**FINANCIAL AID PICTURE (2014-2015)**
**Students with need:** Out of 914 full-time freshmen who applied for aid, 717 were judged to have need. Of these, 717 received aid, and 702 had their full need met. Average financial aid package met 99% of need; average scholarship/grant was $35,792; average loan was $3,301.
**Students without need:** 11 full-time freshmen who did not demonstrate need for aid received scholarships/grants; average award was $30,263. No-need awards available for academics, athletics, leadership, ROTC, state/district residency.
**Scholarships offered: _Merit:_** Hodson Trust Scholarship: $34,000; annually for 4 years; 20 awards. Westgate Scholarship for engineering freshmen: tuition plus $1,000 for 4 years; academic excellence, leadership, demonstrated research experience required; 2 offered per year per class. Wilson Research grants: $10,000. Baltimore Scholars Program: full tuition scholarship for US citizens or permanent residents who have attended a Baltimore City public school for at least 10th, 11th, and 12th grades and meet a residency requirement. _Athletic:_ 12 full-time freshmen received athletic scholarships; average amount $28,026.
**Additional info:** Selected students receive aid packages without loan expectation, including grants to full need. Private merit aid does not reduce Hopkins grant.

**FINANCIAL AID PROCEDURES**
**Forms required:** FAFSA, CSS PROFILE.
**Dates and Deadlines:** Closing date 3/1. Applicants notified by 4/1; must reply by 5/1.
**Transfers:** Closing date 3/15. Must reply within 2 week(s) of notification. Aid on funds-available basis.

**CONTACT**
Tom McDermott, Director of Student Financial Services
3400 North Charles Street, Mason Hall, Baltimore, MD 21218-2683
(410) 516-8028

## Johns Hopkins University: Peabody Conservatory of Music

Baltimore, Maryland
www.peabody.jhu.edu       Federal Code: E00233

**4-year private** music college in very large city.
**Enrollment:** 265 undergrads.
**Selectivity:** Admits less than 50% of applicants.

**BASIC COSTS (2015-2016)**
**Tuition and fees:** $44,050.

**Per-credit charge:** $1,215.
**Room and board:** $14,200.

**FINANCIAL AID PICTURE**
**Students with need:** Need-based aid available for full-time and part-time students. Work study available nights, weekends, and for part-time students.
**Students without need:** No-need awards available for academics, music/drama.

**FINANCIAL AID PROCEDURES**
**Forms required:** FAFSA, institutional form.
**Dates and Deadlines:** Closing date 2/1. Applicants notified by 4/1; must reply by 5/1.
**Transfers:** Applicants notified by 4/1; must reply by 5/1.

**CONTACT**
Rebecca Polgar, Director Financial Aid
One East Mount Vernon Place, Baltimore, MD 21202
(410) 234-4900

## Kaplan University: Hagerstown

Hagerstown, Maryland
www.hagerstown.kaplanuniversity.edu
      Federal Code: 007946

**2-year for-profit** business and junior college in large town.
**Enrollment:** 854 undergrads.
**Selectivity:** Open admission; but selective for some programs.

**BASIC COSTS (2015-2016)**
**Additional info:** Diploma programs: $11,501-$21,147. Associate programs: $33,390-$35,987. Bachelor's programs: $28,350-$66,780.

**FINANCIAL AID PICTURE**
**Students with need:** Need-based aid available for full-time and part-time students.

**FINANCIAL AID PROCEDURES**
**Forms required:** FAFSA, institutional form.
**Dates and Deadlines:** Applicants notified on a rolling basis starting 6/1; must reply within 2 week(s) of notification.

**CONTACT**
Kristen Brezler, Director of Financial Aid
18618 Crestwood Drive, Hagerstown, MD 21742
(301) 739-2670

## Loyola University Maryland

Baltimore, Maryland       Federal Code: 002078
www.loyola.edu       CSS Code: 5370

**4-year private** university in very large city, affiliated with Roman Catholic Church.
**Enrollment:** 4,031 undergrads, 1% part-time. 1,134 full-time freshmen.
**Selectivity:** Admits 50 to 75% of applicants.

**BASIC COSTS (2015-2016)**
**Tuition and fees:** $45,200.
**Room and board:** $13,310.

**FINANCIAL AID PICTURE (2014-2015)**
**Students with need:** Out of 858 full-time freshmen who applied for aid, 662 were judged to have need. Of these, 662 received aid, and 612 had their full need met. Average financial aid package met 93% of need; average scholarship/grant was $21,995; average loan was $4,190. For part-time students, average financial aid package was $5,500.

**Students without need:** 218 full-time freshmen who did not demonstrate need for aid received scholarships/grants; average award was $17,165. No-need awards available for academics, athletics, ROTC.

**Scholarships offered:** 29 full-time freshmen received athletic scholarships; average amount $29,045.

### FINANCIAL AID PROCEDURES

**Forms required:** FAFSA, CSS PROFILE.

**Dates and Deadlines:** Closing date 2/15. Applicants notified by 3/15; must reply by 5/1.

**Transfers:** No deadline. Applicants notified on a rolling basis starting 5/1; must reply by 7/1.

### CONTACT

Mark Lindenmeyer, Director of Financial Aid / Assistant Vice President for Enrollment

4501 North Charles Street, Baltimore, MD 21210-2699

(410) 617-2576

## Maryland Institute College of Art
Baltimore, Maryland
www.mica.edu                          Federal Code: 002080

**4-year private** visual arts college in very large city.

**Enrollment:** 1,761 undergrads, 1% part-time. 411 full-time freshmen.

**Selectivity:** Admits less than 50% of applicants.

### BASIC COSTS (2016-2017)

**Tuition and fees:** $45,400.

**Per-credit charge:** $1,820.

**Room and board:** $12,450.

### FINANCIAL AID PICTURE

**Students with need:** Need-based aid available for full-time and part-time students. Work study available nights, weekends, and for part-time students.

**Students without need:** No-need awards available for academics, art.

### FINANCIAL AID PROCEDURES

**Forms required:** FAFSA, institutional form.

**Dates and Deadlines:** Closing date 2/15. Applicants notified by 4/6; must reply by 5/1.

**Transfers:** Closing date 3/1. Applicants notified by 4/25; must reply by 5/20.

### CONTACT

Diane Prengaman, Associate Vice President for Financial Aid

1300 Mount Royal Avenue, Baltimore, MD 21217-4134

(410) 225-2285

## McDaniel College
Westminster, Maryland
www.mcdaniel.edu                       Federal Code: 002109

**4-year private** liberal arts college in large town.

**Enrollment:** 1,621 undergrads, 1% part-time. 431 full-time freshmen.

**Selectivity:** Admits over 75% of applicants.

### BASIC COSTS (2015-2016)

**Tuition and fees:** $39,500.

**Per-credit charge:** $1,234.

**Room and board:** $10,300.

### FINANCIAL AID PICTURE (2015-2016)

**Students with need:** Out of 398 full-time freshmen who applied for aid, 352 were judged to have need. Of these, 352 received aid, and 90 had their full need met. Average financial aid package met 84% of need; average scholarship/grant was $31,233; average loan was $3,365. For part-time students, average financial aid package was $11,642.

**Students without need:** 77 full-time freshmen who did not demonstrate need for aid received scholarships/grants; average award was $20,052. No-need awards available for academics, ROTC, state/district residency.

**Scholarships offered:** Academic scholarships: $5,000-$21,000; based on academic credentials. Honors Scholarship Program: $23,000-full tuition; separate competitive process with application due 1/2; interview required. Dorsey Scholars Program: full tuition, room and board; based on 1400 SAT, 3.8 GPA in rigorous curriculum, discussion-based sessions, interviews, essay.

### FINANCIAL AID PROCEDURES

**Forms required:** FAFSA.

**Dates and Deadlines:** Priority date 3/1; no closing date. Applicants notified on a rolling basis starting 3/1; must reply by 5/1 or within 2 week(s) of notification.

**Transfers:** No deadline. Applicants notified on a rolling basis starting 2/15; must reply by 8/1 or within 2 week(s) of notification.

### CONTACT

Zhanna Goltser, Director of Financial Aid

2 College Hill, Westminster, MD 21157-4390

(410) 857-2233

## Montgomery College
Rockville, Maryland
www.montgomerycollege.edu              Federal Code: 006911

**2-year public** community college in very large city.

**Enrollment:** 19,096 undergrads.

**Selectivity:** Open admission; but selective for some programs.

### BASIC COSTS (2015-2016)

**Tuition and fees:** $4,728; out-of-district residents $9,156; out-of-state residents $12,432.

**Per-credit charge:** $118; out-of-district residents $241; out-of-state residents $332.

### FINANCIAL AID PICTURE

**Students with need:** Need-based aid available for full-time and part-time students. Work study available nights, weekends, and for part-time students.

**Students without need:** No-need awards available for academics, alumni affiliation, art, athletics, leadership, minority status, music/drama, state/district residency.

**Scholarships offered:** Board of Trustees Academic Potential Scholarship: first year of tuition; based on GPA and high school nominations; 125 awards available.

### FINANCIAL AID PROCEDURES

**Forms required:** FAFSA, institutional form.

**Dates and Deadlines:** Priority date 5/15; no closing date. Applicants notified on a rolling basis starting 5/30.

**Transfers:** No deadline. Applicants notified on a rolling basis starting 1/1; must reply within 4 week(s) of notification.

### CONTACT

Melissa Gregory, Director of Financial Aid

51 Mannakee Street, Rockville, MD 20850

(240) 567-5100

## Morgan State University
Baltimore, Maryland
www.morgan.edu                         Federal Code: 002083

**4-year public** university in large city.

**Enrollment:** 6,294 undergrads, 11% part-time. 1,159 full-time freshmen.

**Selectivity:** Admits 50 to 75% of applicants.

**BASIC COSTS (2015-2016)**
**Tuition and fees:** $7,508; out-of-state residents $17,182.
**Room and board:** $10,246.
**Additional info:** Tuition/fee waivers available for minority students.

**FINANCIAL AID PICTURE**
**Students with need:** Need-based aid available for full-time and part-time students.

**FINANCIAL AID PROCEDURES**
**Forms required:** FAFSA.
**Dates and Deadlines:** Priority date 4/1; no closing date. Applicants notified on a rolling basis starting 6/1; must reply within 2 week(s) of notification.

**CONTACT**
Tanya Wilkerson, Director of Financial Aid
1700 East Cold Spring Lane, Baltimore, MD 21251
(443) 885-3170

## Mount St. Mary's University
Emmitsburg, Maryland
www.msmary.edu                    Federal Code: 002086

**4-year private** university and liberal arts college in rural community, affiliated with Roman Catholic Church.
**Enrollment:** 1,786 undergrads, 5% part-time. 506 full-time freshmen.
**Selectivity:** Admits 50 to 75% of applicants.

**BASIC COSTS (2016-2017)**
**Tuition and fees:** $39,000.
**Per-credit charge:** $1,250.
**Room and board:** $12,610.
**Additional info:** Tuition/fee waivers available for minority students.

**FINANCIAL AID PICTURE (2015-2016)**
**Students with need:** Out of 455 full-time freshmen who applied for aid, 379 were judged to have need. Of these, 379 received aid, and 87 had their full need met. Average financial aid package met 72% of need; average scholarship/grant was $22,784; average loan was $4,269. For part-time students, average financial aid package was $6,270.
**Students without need:** 124 full-time freshmen who did not demonstrate need for aid received scholarships/grants; average award was $17,270. No-need awards available for academics, art, athletics, leadership, ROTC.
**Scholarships offered: Merit:** Founder's Scholarship: full-tuition scholarship based on on-campus written examination, 3.5 GPA, and SAT scores of 1150 or higher (exclusive of writing) or ACT score of 25 or higher; 2 awards. **Athletic:** 35 full-time freshmen received athletic scholarships; average amount $13,346.

**FINANCIAL AID PROCEDURES**
**Forms required:** FAFSA.
**Dates and Deadlines:** Closing date 3/1. Applicants notified on a rolling basis starting 2/14; must reply by 5/1.
**Transfers:** Scholarships available based on GPA at previous institution.

**CONTACT**
David Reeder, Director of Financial Aid
16300 Old Emmitsburg Road, Emmitsburg, MD 21727
(800) 448-4347

## Notre Dame of Maryland University
Baltimore, Maryland
www.ndm.edu                    Federal Code: 002065

**4-year private** liberal arts college for women in very large city, affiliated with Roman Catholic Church.
**Enrollment:** 1,001 undergrads, 48% part-time. 93 full-time freshmen.

**BASIC COSTS (2015-2016)**
**Tuition and fees:** $33,670.
**Room and board:** $10,930.

**FINANCIAL AID PICTURE (2014-2015)**
**Students with need:** 55% of average financial aid package awarded as scholarships/grants, 45% awarded as loans/jobs. Need-based aid available for part-time students.
**Students without need:** No-need awards available for academics, alumni affiliation, art, leadership, music/drama, ROTC.
**Scholarships offered:** Academic/achievement awards: $6,000 to full tuition. Endowed scholarships: $1,000 to $8,000; variable criteria; usually 20-35 awards.
**Additional info:** Maximum consideration for financial aid if application received by February 15. Auditions and portfolios in areas of art, music and writing considered for scholarships.

**FINANCIAL AID PROCEDURES**
**Forms required:** FAFSA.
**Dates and Deadlines:** Priority date 2/15; no closing date. Applicants notified on a rolling basis starting 3/15; must reply by 5/1 or within 2 week(s) of notification.
**Transfers:** Applicants notified by 3/15; must reply by 5/1 or within 2 week(s) of notification. Specific non-need based merit scholarships available for transfer students. Transfer scholarships: range from $7000 to full tuition.

**CONTACT**
Audrey Brooks, Director of Financial Aid
4701 North Charles Street, Baltimore, MD 21210
(410) 532-5369

## Prince George's Community College
Largo, Maryland
www.pgcc.edu                    Federal Code: 002089

**2-year public** community college in very large city.
**Enrollment:** 12,617 undergrads.
**Selectivity:** Open admission; but selective for some programs.

**BASIC COSTS (2015-2016)**
**Tuition and fees:** $4,550; out-of-district residents $7,190; out-of-state residents $10,100.
**Per-credit charge:** $105; out-of-district residents $193; out-of-state residents $290.

**FINANCIAL AID PICTURE**
**Students with need:** Need-based aid available for full-time and part-time students.
**Students without need:** This college awards aid only to students with need.

**FINANCIAL AID PROCEDURES**
**Forms required:** FAFSA, institutional form.
**Dates and Deadlines:** Priority date 6/1; no closing date. Applicants notified on a rolling basis starting 6/1; must reply within 2 week(s) of notification.

**CONTACT**
Sharon Hasson, Director of Financial Aid
301 Largo Road, Largo, MD 20774
(301) 322-0866

## St. John's College
Annapolis, Maryland
www.sjc.edu                    Federal Code: 002092

**4-year private** liberal arts college in large town.
**Enrollment:** 406 undergrads. 105 full-time freshmen.

**Selectivity:** Admits over 75% of applicants.

### BASIC COSTS (2016-2017)
**Tuition and fees:** $50,228.
**Room and board:** $11,888.

### FINANCIAL AID PICTURE (2015-2016)
**Students with need:** Out of 85 full-time freshmen who applied for aid, 72 were judged to have need. Of these, 72 received aid, and 23 had their full need met. Average financial aid package met 85% of need; average scholarship/grant was $31,235; average loan was $3,715. Need-based aid available for part-time students.
**Students without need:** 32 full-time freshmen who did not demonstrate need for aid received scholarships/grants; average award was $19,401. No-need awards available for academics.
**Scholarships offered:** Academic scholarships range up to $23,000 for the 2016-2017 academic year; students encouraged to apply under Early Action I or II.
**Additional info:** All applicants automatically considered for merit scholarships, and all students completing the FAFSA are considered for need-based financial aid.

### FINANCIAL AID PROCEDURES
**Forms required:** FAFSA, state aid form. International students must complete CSS PROFILE.
**Dates and Deadlines:** Priority date 2/15; no closing date. Applicants notified on a rolling basis starting 12/15; must reply by 5/1 or within 2 week(s) of notification.
**Transfers:** Must reply by 5/1 or within 2 week(s) of notification.

### CONTACT
Dana Kennedy, Director of Financial Aid
60 College Avenue, Annapolis, MD 21401
(410) 626-2502

## St. Mary's College of Maryland
St. Mary's City, Maryland
www.smcm.edu                    Federal Code: 002095

**4-year public** liberal arts college in small town.
**Enrollment:** 1,725 undergrads, 3% part-time. 394 full-time freshmen.
**Selectivity:** Admits over 75% of applicants.

### BASIC COSTS (2015-2016)
**Tuition and fees:** $13,895; out-of-state residents $28,745.
**Room and board:** $12,290.

### FINANCIAL AID PICTURE (2015-2016)
**Students with need:** Out of 320 full-time freshmen who applied for aid, 210 were judged to have need. Of these, 207 received aid, and 18 had their full need met. Average financial aid package met 73% of need; average scholarship/grant was $10,337; average loan was $3,327. For part-time students, average financial aid package was $5,065.
**Students without need:** 122 full-time freshmen who did not demonstrate need for aid received scholarships/grants; average award was $3,856. No-need awards available for academics, alumni affiliation.

### FINANCIAL AID PROCEDURES
**Forms required:** FAFSA.
**Dates and Deadlines:** Priority date 2/28; no closing date. Applicants notified by 4/1; must reply by 5/1.
**Transfers:** Applicants notified by 4/15; must reply within 2 week(s) of notification. All financial aid recipients must have GED or high school diploma. Financial aid transcript required from previous colleges attended.

### CONTACT
Nadine Hutton, Director of Financial Aid
18952 East Fisher Road, St. Mary's City, MD 20686-3001
(240) 895-3000

## Salisbury University
Salisbury, Maryland
www.salisbury.edu               Federal Code: 002091

**4-year public** university and liberal arts college in large town.
**Enrollment:** 7,612 undergrads, 6% part-time. 1,144 full-time freshmen.
**Selectivity:** Admits 50 to 75% of applicants.

### BASIC COSTS (2015-2016)
**Tuition and fees:** $9,086; out-of-state residents $17,432.
**Per-credit charge:** $276; out-of-state residents $623.
**Room and board:** $11,010.

### FINANCIAL AID PICTURE (2014-2015)
**Students with need:** Out of 985 full-time freshmen who applied for aid, 593 were judged to have need. Of these, 572 received aid, and 93 had their full need met. Average financial aid package met 51% of need; average scholarship/grant was $6,323; average loan was $3,128. For part-time students, average financial aid package was $5,177.
**Students without need:** 281 full-time freshmen who did not demonstrate need for aid received scholarships/grants; average award was $2,486. No-need awards available for academics, alumni affiliation, art, leadership, music/drama, ROTC, state/district residency.

### FINANCIAL AID PROCEDURES
**Forms required:** FAFSA.
**Dates and Deadlines:** Priority date 3/1; closing date 12/31. Applicants notified by 3/15; must reply by 5/1.
**Transfers:** No deadline.

### CONTACT
Elizabeth Zimmerman, Director of Financial Aid
1101 Camden Avenue, Salisbury, MD 21801
(410) 543-6165

## Stevenson University
Stevenson, Maryland
www.stevenson.edu               Federal Code: 002107

**4-year private** university in very large city.
**Enrollment:** 3,665 undergrads, 15% part-time. 685 full-time freshmen.
**Selectivity:** Admits 50 to 75% of applicants.

### BASIC COSTS (2015-2016)
**Tuition and fees:** $30,998.
**Room and board:** $12,720.

### FINANCIAL AID PICTURE (2014-2015)
**Students with need:** Out of 655 full-time freshmen who applied for aid, 579 were judged to have need. Of these, 579 received aid, and 56 had their full need met. Average financial aid package met 61% of need; average scholarship/grant was $17,771; average loan was $3,298. For part-time students, average financial aid package was $4,581.
**Students without need:** 95 full-time freshmen who did not demonstrate need for aid received scholarships/grants; average award was $10,805. No-need awards available for academics, art.
**Additional info:** Cooperative Education Program allows students to work in their field of study with area corporations.

### FINANCIAL AID PROCEDURES
**Forms required:** FAFSA.
**Dates and Deadlines:** Priority date 2/15; no closing date. Applicants notified on a rolling basis starting 3/15; must reply by 5/1 or within 2 week(s) of notification.
**Transfers:** Closing date 3/1. Applicants notified on a rolling basis starting 3/1.

### CONTACT

Barbara Miller, Director of Financial Aid

1525 Greenspring Valley Road, Stevenson, MD 21153-0641

(443) 334-3500

## Towson University

Towson, Maryland

www.towson.edu                    Federal Code: 002099

**4-year public** university in small city.

**Enrollment:** 18,806 undergrads, 11% part-time. 2,708 full-time freshmen.

**Selectivity:** Admits 50 to 75% of applicants.

### BASIC COSTS (2015-2016)

**Tuition and fees:** $9,182; out-of-state residents $20,788.

**Per-credit charge:** $278; out-of-state residents $756.

**Room and board:** $11,638.

### FINANCIAL AID PICTURE (2015-2016)

**Students with need:** Out of 2,353 full-time freshmen who applied for aid, 1,599 were judged to have need. Of these, 1,491 received aid, and 203 had their full need met. Average financial aid package met 57% of need; average scholarship/grant was $8,290; average loan was $3,194. For part-time students, average financial aid package was $5,616.

**Students without need:** 298 full-time freshmen who did not demonstrate need for aid received scholarships/grants; average award was $5,206. No-need awards available for academics, alumni affiliation, art, athletics, leadership, music/drama, ROTC, state/district residency.

**Scholarships offered:** *Merit:* Wide variety of merit-based scholarships including several scholarships for students in specific majors. *Athletic:* 82 full-time freshmen received athletic scholarships; average amount $8,800.

### FINANCIAL AID PROCEDURES

**Forms required:** FAFSA, state aid form.

**Dates and Deadlines:** Priority date 2/15; no closing date. Applicants notified on a rolling basis starting 3/21; must reply within 2 week(s) of notification.

**Transfers:** Must reply by 5/15 or within 2 week(s) of notification.

### CONTACT

David Horne, Director of Financial Aid

8000 York Road, Towson, MD 21252-0001

(410) 704-4236

## United States Naval Academy

Annapolis, Maryland

www.usna.edu

**4-year public** military college in large town.

**Enrollment:** 4,525 undergrads. 1,134 full-time freshmen.

**Selectivity:** Admits less than 50% of applicants.

### BASIC COSTS (2016-2017)

**Additional info:** The Naval Academy does not charge tuition, room, board, or any other fees. Medical and dental care is provided by the United States Government. Each midshipman receives a monthly salary to cover costs of books, supplies, uniform, laundry, and equipment including a computer and a printer.

### CONTACT

52 King George Street, Annapolis, MD 21402-1318

## University of Baltimore

Baltimore, Maryland

www.ubalt.edu                    Federal Code: 002102

**4-year public** university and liberal arts college in very large city.

**Enrollment:** 3,307 undergrads, 38% part-time. 137 full-time freshmen.

**Selectivity:** Admits 50 to 75% of applicants.

### BASIC COSTS (2015-2016)

**Tuition and fees:** $8,326; out-of-state residents $19,744.

**Per-credit charge:** $296; out-of-state residents $935.

### FINANCIAL AID PICTURE

**Students with need:** Need-based aid available for full-time and part-time students.

### FINANCIAL AID PROCEDURES

**Forms required:** FAFSA, institutional form.

**Dates and Deadlines:** Applicants notified on a rolling basis.

**Transfers:** Closing date 5/1. Applicants notified on a rolling basis; must reply within 2 week(s) of notification. Scholarship application deadline 3/1.

### CONTACT

Joseph Blevins, Director, Financial Aid

1420 North Charles Street, Baltimore, MD 21201-5779

(410) 837-4763

## University of Maryland: Baltimore

Baltimore, Maryland

www.umaryland.edu                    Federal Code: 002104

**Upper-division public** university and health science college in very large city.

**Enrollment:** 860 undergrads, 28% part-time.

### BASIC COSTS (2015-2016)

**Tuition and fees:** $10,143; out-of-state residents $32,779.

**Per-credit charge:** $365; out-of-state residents $806.

**Additional info:** Tuition and fees vary by program.

### FINANCIAL AID PICTURE

**Students with need:** Need-based aid available for full-time and part-time students. Work study available nights, weekends, and for part-time students.

**Additional info:** Maryland state deadline 3/1.

### FINANCIAL AID PROCEDURES

**Forms required:** FAFSA, state aid form.

**Dates and Deadlines:** Priority date 3/15; no closing date. Applicants notified on a rolling basis starting 4/15; must reply within 2 week(s) of notification.

### CONTACT

Patricia Scott, Associate Director of Financial Aid

220 Arch Street, Baltimore, MD 21201

(410) 706-7347

## University of Maryland: Baltimore County

Baltimore, Maryland

www.umbc.edu                    Federal Code: 002105

**4-year public** university in large city.

**Enrollment:** 11,144 undergrads, 14% part-time. 1,616 full-time freshmen.

**Selectivity:** Admits 50 to 75% of applicants.

### BASIC COSTS (2015-2016)

**Tuition and fees:** $11,006; out-of-state residents $23,770.

**Per-credit charge:** $335; out-of-state residents $864.

**Room and board:** $10,868.

## FINANCIAL AID PICTURE (2014-2015)

**Students with need:** Out of 1,252 full-time freshmen who applied for aid, 820 were judged to have need. Of these, 748 received aid, and 161 had their full need met. Average financial aid package met 61% of need; average scholarship/grant was $8,994; average loan was $3,389. For part-time students, average financial aid package was $5,721.

**Students without need:** 339 full-time freshmen who did not demonstrate need for aid received scholarships/grants; average award was $8,950. No-need awards available for academics, alumni affiliation, art, athletics, music/drama.

**Scholarships offered:** *Merit:* UMBC General Merit Awards: $500-$22,000 per year. Scholars Programs Awards: $5,000-$22,000 per year; includes Center for Women and Information Technology Scholars Program, Humanities Scholars Program, Linehan Artist Scholars Program, Meyerhoff Scholars Program (Sciences and Engineering), and Sondheim Public Affairs Scholars Program, tuition, fees, room and board. *Athletic:* 43 full-time freshmen received athletic scholarships; average amount $10,051.

## FINANCIAL AID PROCEDURES

**Forms required:** FAFSA.

**Dates and Deadlines:** Priority date 2/14; no closing date. Applicants notified on a rolling basis starting 3/25; must reply within 2 week(s) of notification.

**Transfers:** 2-year merit scholarships available for transfer students from community colleges.

## CONTACT

Jane Hickey, Director of Financial Aid & Scholarships
1000 Hilltop Circle, Baltimore, MD 21250
(410) 455-2387

# University of Maryland: College Park

College Park, Maryland
www.maryland.edu          Federal Code: 002103

**4-year public** university in large town.
**Enrollment:** 26,889 undergrads, 6% part-time. 4,128 full-time freshmen.
**Selectivity:** Admits less than 50% of applicants.

## BASIC COSTS (2015-2016)

**Tuition and fees:** $9,996; out-of-state residents $31,144.
**Per-credit charge:** $340; out-of-state residents $1,221.
**Room and board:** $10,972.
**Additional info:** For the upcoming academic year, the tuition figure for junior and senior undergraduate students in business, engineering, and computer science majors is $700 higher, regardless of residency.

## FINANCIAL AID PICTURE (2014-2015)

**Students with need:** Out of 3,174 full-time freshmen who applied for aid, 1,695 were judged to have need. Of these, 1,681 received aid, and 627 had their full need met. Average financial aid package met 78% of need; average scholarship/grant was $11,040; average loan was $4,663. For part-time students, average financial aid package was $9,856.

**Students without need:** 861 full-time freshmen who did not demonstrate need for aid received scholarships/grants; average award was $6,577. No-need awards available for academics, art, athletics, leadership, music/drama, ROTC, state/district residency.

**Scholarships offered:** 27 full-time freshmen received athletic scholarships; average amount $20,282.

**Additional info:** Prepaid tuition plans available through state.

## FINANCIAL AID PROCEDURES

**Forms required:** FAFSA.

**Dates and Deadlines:** Priority date 2/15; no closing date. Applicants notified on a rolling basis starting 4/1; must reply by 5/1.

## CONTACT

Monique Boyd, Director of Financial Aid
Mitchell Building, College Park, MD 20742-5235
(301) 314-9000

# University of Maryland: Eastern Shore

Princess Anne, Maryland
www.umes.edu          Federal Code: 002106

**4-year public** university in rural community.
**Enrollment:** 3,573 undergrads, 8% part-time. 756 full-time freshmen.
**Selectivity:** Admits less than 50% of applicants.

## BASIC COSTS (2015-2016)

**Tuition and fees:** $7,625; out-of-state residents $16,687.
**Per-credit charge:** $208; out-of-state residents $518.
**Room and board:** $9,114.

## FINANCIAL AID PICTURE (2014-2015)

**Students with need:** Out of 739 full-time freshmen who applied for aid, 661 were judged to have need. Of these, 637 received aid, and 1 had their full need met. Average financial aid package met 24% of need. For part-time students, average financial aid package was $3,012.

**Students without need:** 10 full-time freshmen who did not demonstrate need for aid received scholarships/grants; average award was $4,664. No-need awards available for academics, alumni affiliation, art, athletics, leadership, music/drama, ROTC, state/district residency.

**Scholarships offered:** 6 full-time freshmen received athletic scholarships; average amount $17,189.

## FINANCIAL AID PROCEDURES

**Forms required:** FAFSA.

**Dates and Deadlines:** Priority date 3/1; closing date 4/1. Applicants notified on a rolling basis starting 4/15.

**Transfers:** No deadline. Applicants notified on a rolling basis starting 6/15.

## CONTACT

Vera Miles-Heath, Interim Director of Financial Aid
Student Development Center, Suite 1140, Princess Anne, MD 21853
(410) 651-6172

# University of Maryland: University College

Adelphi, Maryland
www.umuc.edu          Federal Code: 011644

**4-year public** virtual university in large town.
**Enrollment:** 36,118 undergrads, 76% part-time. 227 full-time freshmen.
**Selectivity:** Open admission.

## BASIC COSTS (2015-2016)

**Tuition and fees:** $7,146; out-of-state residents $12,426.
**Per-credit charge:** $279; out-of-state residents $499.

## FINANCIAL AID PICTURE (2014-2015)

**Students with need:** Out of 162 full-time freshmen who applied for aid, 156 were judged to have need. Of these, 79 received aid. Average financial aid package met 23% of need; average scholarship/grant was $3,012; average loan was $2,480. For part-time students, average financial aid package was $4,736.

**Students without need:** No-need awards available for academics, leadership.

## FINANCIAL AID PROCEDURES

**Forms required:** FAFSA.

**Dates and Deadlines:** Priority date 6/1; no closing date. Applicants notified on a rolling basis starting 5/1; must reply within 2 week(s) of notification.

**CONTACT**
Eugene Lockett, Vice President and Chief Financial Officer
1616 McCormick Drive, Largo, MD 20774
(301) 985-7510

## Washington Adventist University
Takoma Park, Maryland
www.wau.edu      Federal Code: 002067

**4-year private** liberal arts college in large town, affiliated with Seventh-day Adventists.
**Enrollment:** 765 undergrads.

**BASIC COSTS (2015-2016)**
**Tuition and fees:** $22,790.
**Room and board:** $8,650.

**FINANCIAL AID PICTURE**
**Students with need:** Need-based aid available for full-time and part-time students.
**Students without need:** No-need awards available for academics, alumni affiliation, athletics, religious affiliation.

**FINANCIAL AID PROCEDURES**
**Forms required:** FAFSA.
**Dates and Deadlines:** Priority date 3/1; closing date 3/31. Applicants notified on a rolling basis starting 5/31; must reply within 4 week(s) of notification.

**CONTACT**
Sharon Conway, Director of Financial Aid
7600 Flower Avenue, Takoma Park, MD 20912
(301) 891-4005

## Washington College
Chestertown, Maryland
www.washcoll.edu      Federal Code: 002108

**4-year private** liberal arts college in small town.
**Enrollment:** 1,386 undergrads. 391 full-time freshmen.
**Selectivity:** Admits 50 to 75% of applicants.

**BASIC COSTS (2015-2016)**
**Tuition and fees:** $43,850.
**Room and board:** $10,612.

**FINANCIAL AID PICTURE (2015-2016)**
**Students with need:** Out of 308 full-time freshmen who applied for aid, 266 were judged to have need. Of these, 266 received aid, and 74 had their full need met. Average financial aid package met 91% of need; average scholarship/grant was $29,630; average loan was $3,429. Need-based aid available for part-time students.
**Students without need:** 106 full-time freshmen who did not demonstrate need for aid received scholarships/grants; average award was $17,710. No-need awards available for academics, art, music/drama.
**Scholarships offered:** National Honor Society Scholarship: $50,000 over 4 years; applicant must be member of National Honor Society, National Society of High School Scholars, or Cum Laude Society.

**FINANCIAL AID PROCEDURES**
**Forms required:** FAFSA.
**Dates and Deadlines:** Priority date 3/1; no closing date. Applicants notified on a rolling basis starting 1/5; must reply by 5/1 or within 2 week(s) of notification.

**CONTACT**
Jean Narcum, Director of Financial Aid
300 Washington Avenue, Chestertown, MD 21620-1197
(410) 778-7214

## Wor-Wic Community College
Salisbury, Maryland
www.worwic.edu      Federal Code: 013842

**2-year public** community college in large town.
**Enrollment:** 2,775 undergrads, 69% part-time. 339 full-time freshmen.
**Selectivity:** Open admission; but selective for some programs.

**BASIC COSTS (2015-2016)**
**Tuition and fees:** $3,600; out-of-district residents $7,440; out-of-state residents $9,030.
**Per-credit charge:** $103; out-of-district residents $231; out-of-state residents $284.

**FINANCIAL AID PICTURE**
**Students with need:** Need-based aid available for full-time and part-time students. Work study available nights, weekends, and for part-time students.
**Students without need:** No-need awards available for academics, state/district residency.

**FINANCIAL AID PROCEDURES**
**Forms required:** FAFSA, institutional form.
**Dates and Deadlines:** Priority date 6/1; no closing date. Applicants notified on a rolling basis starting 4/1.

**CONTACT**
Deborah Jenkins, Director of Financial Aid
32000 Campus Drive, Salisbury, MD 21804
(410) 334-2905

# Massachusetts

## American International College
Springfield, Massachusetts
www.aic.edu      Federal Code: 002114

**4-year private** health science and liberal arts college in small city.
**Enrollment:** 1,478 undergrads, 6% part-time. 313 full-time freshmen.
**Selectivity:** Admits 50 to 75% of applicants.

**BASIC COSTS (2015-2016)**
**Tuition and fees:** $31,870.
**Per-credit charge:** $660.
**Room and board:** $12,900.

**FINANCIAL AID PICTURE (2014-2015)**
**Students with need:** Out of 297 full-time freshmen who applied for aid, 288 were judged to have need. Of these, 288 received aid, and 31 had their full need met. Average financial aid package met 67% of need; average scholarship/grant was $22,092; average loan was $3,293. For part-time students, average financial aid package was $8,552.
**Students without need:** 24 full-time freshmen who did not demonstrate need for aid received scholarships/grants; average award was $13,281. No-need awards available for academics, athletics.
**Scholarships offered:** *Merit:* Presidential, Provost, Opportunity Scholarships: $5,000 to $11,000; based on class rank, SAT, GPA. *Athletic:* 23 full-time freshmen received athletic scholarships; average amount $12,505.

## FINANCIAL AID PROCEDURES

**Forms required:** FAFSA.

**Dates and Deadlines:** Priority date 5/1; no closing date. Applicants notified on a rolling basis starting 2/15; must reply within 2 week(s) of notification.

## CONTACT

Sage Stachowiak, Director of Financial Aid
1000 State Street, Springfield, MA 01109
(413) 205-3259

## Amherst College
Amherst, Massachusetts      Federal Code: 002115
www.amherst.edu      CSS Code: 3003

**4-year private** liberal arts college in large town.

**Enrollment:** 1,795 undergrads. 477 full-time freshmen.

**Selectivity:** Admits less than 50% of applicants.

## BASIC COSTS (2015-2016)

**Tuition and fees:** $50,562.

**Room and board:** $13,210.

## FINANCIAL AID PICTURE (2015-2016)

**Students with need:** Out of 322 full-time freshmen who applied for aid, 259 were judged to have need. Of these, 259 received aid, and 259 had their full need met. Average financial aid package met 100% of need; average scholarship/grant was $49,514; average loan was $404.

**Students without need:** This college awards aid only to students with need.

## FINANCIAL AID PROCEDURES

**Forms required:** FAFSA, CSS PROFILE.

**Dates and Deadlines:** Priority date 2/15; no closing date. Applicants notified by 4/1; must reply by 5/1.

## CONTACT

Gail Holt, Dean of Financial Aid
PO Box 5000, Amherst, MA 01002-5000
(413) 542-2296

## Anna Maria College
Paxton, Massachusetts
www.annamaria.edu      Federal Code: 002117

**4-year private** liberal arts college in small town, affiliated with Roman Catholic Church.

**Enrollment:** 1,123 undergrads, 28% part-time. 232 full-time freshmen.

**Selectivity:** Admits over 75% of applicants.

## BASIC COSTS (2015-2016)

**Tuition and fees:** $35,074.

**Room and board:** $13,112.

## FINANCIAL AID PICTURE (2014-2015)

**Students with need:** Need-based aid available for full-time and part-time students. Work study available nights, weekends, and for part-time students.

**Students without need:** No-need awards available for academics, music/drama.

## FINANCIAL AID PROCEDURES

**Forms required:** FAFSA.

**Dates and Deadlines:** Priority date 3/1; no closing date. Applicants notified on a rolling basis starting 4/1.

**Transfers:** No deadline. Applicants notified on a rolling basis starting 4/1; must reply within 4 week(s) of notification. Deadline May 1 for state aid.

## CONTACT

Sandra Pereira, Director of Financial Aid
50 Sunset Lane, Box O, Paxton, MA 01612-1198
(508) 849-3363

## Assumption College
Worcester, Massachusetts
www.assumption.edu      Federal Code: 002118

**4-year private** liberal arts college in small city, affiliated with Roman Catholic Church.

**Enrollment:** 1,979 undergrads. 570 full-time freshmen.

**Selectivity:** Admits over 75% of applicants.

## BASIC COSTS (2015-2016)

**Tuition and fees:** $36,160.

**Per-credit charge:** $1,184.

**Room and board:** $11,264.

**Additional info:** Tuition at time of enrollment locked for 4 years.

## FINANCIAL AID PICTURE (2015-2016)

**Students with need:** Out of 506 full-time freshmen who applied for aid, 430 were judged to have need. Of these, 430 received aid, and 113 had their full need met. Average financial aid package met 72% of need; average scholarship/grant was $20,067; average loan was $3,687. Need-based aid available for part-time students.

**Students without need:** 123 full-time freshmen who did not demonstrate need for aid received scholarships/grants; average award was $14,802. No-need awards available for academics, athletics, music/drama.

**Scholarships offered:** *Merit:* Academic scholarships: $2,500-$22,000 per year; based on academic achievement and leadership talents. *Athletic:* 24 full-time freshmen received athletic scholarships; average amount $5,661.

## FINANCIAL AID PROCEDURES

**Forms required:** FAFSA.

**Dates and Deadlines:** Closing date 2/15. Applicants notified on a rolling basis starting 2/16; must reply by 5/1.

**Transfers:** Closing date 3/31. Applicants notified on a rolling basis starting 3/15.

## CONTACT

William Smith, Director of Financial Aid
500 Salisbury Street, Worcester, MA 01609-1296
(508) 767-7158

## Babson College
Babson Park, Massachusetts      Federal Code: 002121
www.babson.edu      CSS Code: 3075

**4-year private** business college in large town.

**Enrollment:** 2,141 undergrads. 528 full-time freshmen.

**Selectivity:** Admits less than 50% of applicants.

## BASIC COSTS (2016-2017)

**Tuition and fees:** $48,288.

**Room and board:** $15,376.

## FINANCIAL AID PICTURE (2015-2016)

**Students with need:** Average financial aid package met 98% of need; average scholarship/grant was $38,761; average loan was $3,840.

**Students without need:** This college awards aid only to students with need.

**Scholarships offered:** Presidential Scholarship: half tuition; based on high school record, co-curricular achievements, demonstrated leadership, writing skills, standardized test scores; approximately 40 awarded each year. Woman's Leadership Award: one quarter tuition; based on demonstrated leadership experience, future leadership potential, and academic achievement. Diversity Leadership Award: either full or half tuition; awarded to students with the greatest potential for leadership in creating a diverse Babson community. Weissmann Scholarship: full tuition. Global Scholars, full tuition for international students with financial need.

**FINANCIAL AID PROCEDURES**
**Forms required:** FAFSA, CSS PROFILE.
**Dates and Deadlines:** Closing date 2/15. Applicants notified by 4/1; must reply by 5/1.
**Transfers:** Closing date 4/15. Applicants notified by 5/1; must reply by 6/1.

**CONTACT**
Melissa Shaak, Director, Student Financial Services
231 Forest Street, Babson Park, MA 02457-0310
(781) 239-4219

## Bard College at Simon's Rock
Great Barrington, Massachusetts    Federal Code: 009645
www.simons-rock.edu    CSS Code: 3795

**4-year private** liberal arts college in small town.
**Enrollment:** 325 undergrads, 1% part-time. 116 full-time freshmen.
**Selectivity:** Admits over 75% of applicants.

**BASIC COSTS (2015-2016)**
**Tuition and fees:** $50,859.
**Room and board:** $13,660.
**Additional info:** Tuition/fee waivers available for minority students.

**FINANCIAL AID PICTURE**
**Students with need:** Need-based aid available for full-time students. Work study available nights, weekends, and for part-time students.
**Students without need:** No-need awards available for academics, alumni affiliation, minority status, state/district residency.
**Scholarships offered:** Acceleration to Excellence Program: up to full-tuition; for outstanding students who apply during 10th or 11th grade; based on academic excellence, extracurricular distinction, personal motivation, and character.

**FINANCIAL AID PROCEDURES**
**Forms required:** FAFSA, CSS PROFILE, state aid form.
**Dates and Deadlines:** Priority date 2/15; no closing date. Applicants notified on a rolling basis starting 3/15; must reply within 2 week(s) of notification.
**Transfers:** Priority date 2/1; closing date 5/1.

**CONTACT**
Denise Ackerman, Director of Financial Aid
Office of Admission, Great Barrington, MA 01230-1990
(413) 528-7297

## Bay Path University
Longmeadow, Massachusetts
www.baypath.edu    Federal Code: 002122

**4-year private** liberal arts college for women in large town.
**Enrollment:** 1,849 undergrads, 20% part-time. 173 full-time freshmen.
**Selectivity:** Admits over 75% of applicants.

**BASIC COSTS (2015-2016)**
**Tuition and fees:** $31,785.
**Per-credit charge:** $500.
**Room and board:** $13,045.

**FINANCIAL AID PICTURE (2015-2016)**
**Students with need:** Out of 166 full-time freshmen who applied for aid, 160 were judged to have need. Of these, 160 received aid, and 10 had their full need met. Average financial aid package met 76% of need; average scholarship/grant was $24,193; average loan was $4,051. For part-time students, average financial aid package was $7,071.
**Students without need:** 12 full-time freshmen who did not demonstrate need for aid received scholarships/grants; average award was $15,475. No-need awards available for academics.
**Scholarships offered:** 1897 Founders Scholarship: $17,000/year for residents, $12,000/year for commuters. Provost's Scholarship: $15,000/year for residents, $11,000/year for commuters. Dean's Scholarship: $14,000/year for residents, $10,000/year for commuters. Seize the Day Award: $8,000/year for residents, $7,000/year for commuters. Pathways Award: $5,000/year for residents, $5,000/year for commuters.

**FINANCIAL AID PROCEDURES**
**Forms required:** FAFSA.
**Dates and Deadlines:** Priority date 3/1; no closing date. Applicants notified on a rolling basis starting 3/1; must reply within 2 week(s) of notification.
**Transfers:** No deadline. Applicants notified on a rolling basis starting 3/1; must reply within 2 week(s) of notification.

**CONTACT**
Stephanie King, Director of Student Financial Services
588 Longmeadow Street, Longmeadow, MA 01106
(413) 565-1000 ext. 1345

## Bay State College
Boston, Massachusetts
www.baystate.edu    Federal Code: 003965

**2-year for-profit** nursing and career college in very large city.
**Enrollment:** 1,070 undergrads, 38% part-time. 121 full-time freshmen.
**Selectivity:** Admits over 75% of applicants.

**BASIC COSTS (2015-2016)**
**Tuition and fees:** $26,780.
**Per-credit charge:** $876.
**Room and board:** $13,000.
**Additional info:** Tuition is based 30 credits per academic year. Bay State College charges by the credit to offer personalized flexibility on course loads. Online and Evening programs are offered at a considerably reduced rate.

**FINANCIAL AID PICTURE (2014-2015)**
**Students with need:** 37% of average financial aid package awarded as scholarships/grants, 63% awarded as loans/jobs. Need-based aid available for part-time students. Work study available nights, weekends, and for part-time students.
**Students without need:** No-need awards available for academics, alumni affiliation, job skills, leadership.

**FINANCIAL AID PROCEDURES**
**Forms required:** FAFSA.
**Dates and Deadlines:** Priority date 3/15; closing date 6/30. Applicants notified on a rolling basis starting 2/1.

**CONTACT**
Jeanne Stella-Devani, Director of Student Financial Services
122 Commonwealth Avenue, Boston, MA 02116
(617) 217-9066

## Becker College
Worcester, Massachusetts
www.becker.edu    Federal Code: 002123

**4-year private** liberal arts college in small city.
**Enrollment:** 2,036 undergrads, 22% part-time. 407 full-time freshmen.

**Selectivity:** Admits 50 to 75% of applicants.

## BASIC COSTS (2015-2016)
**Tuition and fees:** $34,080.
**Per-credit charge:** $1,355.
**Room and board:** $12,400.

## FINANCIAL AID PICTURE (2015-2016)
**Students with need:** Out of 380 full-time freshmen who applied for aid, 353 were judged to have need. Of these, 353 received aid, and 35 had their full need met. Average financial aid package met 64% of need; average scholarship/grant was $9,038; average loan was $3,449. For part-time students, average financial aid package was $9,647.
**Students without need:** 53 full-time freshmen who did not demonstrate need for aid received scholarships/grants; average award was $13,320. No-need awards available for academics, state/district residency.

## FINANCIAL AID PROCEDURES
**Forms required:** FAFSA.
**Dates and Deadlines:** Priority date 3/15; no closing date. Applicants notified on a rolling basis starting 3/15.

## CONTACT
Heather Ruland, Director of Finacial Aid
Office of Admissions, Worcester, MA 01609
(508) 373-9433

## Benjamin Franklin Institute of Technology
Boston, Massachusetts
www.bfit.edu                    Federal Code: 002151

**2-year private** technical college in very large city.
**Enrollment:** 485 undergrads, 12% part-time. 207 full-time freshmen.

## BASIC COSTS (2015-2016)
**Tuition and fees:** $16,950.
**Per-credit charge:** $707.
**Room and board:** $13,900.

## FINANCIAL AID PICTURE
**Students with need:** Need-based aid available for full-time and part-time students.
**Students without need:** No-need awards available for academics, leadership, state/district residency.

## FINANCIAL AID PROCEDURES
**Forms required:** FAFSA.
**Dates and Deadlines:** Priority date 3/1; no closing date. Applicants notified on a rolling basis starting 3/1; must reply within 3 week(s) of notification.

## CONTACT
Ozie Ratcliff, Director of Student Financial Services
41 Berkeley Street, Boston, MA 02116
(617) 588-1358

## Bentley University
Waltham, Massachusetts          Federal Code: 002124
www.bentley.edu                 CSS Code: 3096

**4-year private** university and business college in small city.
**Enrollment:** 4,137 undergrads, 1% part-time. 978 full-time freshmen.
**Selectivity:** Admits less than 50% of applicants.

## BASIC COSTS (2015-2016)
**Tuition and fees:** $44,085.
**Room and board:** $14,520.

## FINANCIAL AID PICTURE (2014-2015)
**Students with need:** Out of 707 full-time freshmen who applied for aid, 492 were judged to have need. Of these, 491 received aid, and 212 had their full need met. Average financial aid package met 94% of need; average scholarship/grant was $30,356; average loan was $3,882. For part-time students, average financial aid package was $14,532.
**Students without need:** 207 full-time freshmen who did not demonstrate need for aid received scholarships/grants; average award was $17,311. No-need awards available for academics, athletics, leadership, minority status.
**Scholarships offered:** *Merit:* Awards are made through the admission process with no separate application required. Award amounts range from full-tuition (limited number) to one-third tuition. *Athletic:* 14 full-time freshmen received athletic scholarships; average amount $24,617.

## FINANCIAL AID PROCEDURES
**Forms required:** FAFSA. CSS PROFILE is required of students who want to be considered for institutional need-based grants. Deadlines for receipt of CSS Profile: Early Decision 12/1; Regular Decision, 2/1.
**Dates and Deadlines:** Closing date 2/1. Applicants notified by 3/31.
**Transfers:** Closing date 4/15. Applicants notified on a rolling basis starting 4/15. Transfer students are eligible for need-based institutional grants but not academic scholarships.

## CONTACT
Donna Kendall, Executive Director of Financial Assistance and Enrollment Management
175 Forest Street, Waltham, MA 02452-4705
(781) 891-3441

## Berklee College of Music
Boston, Massachusetts           Federal Code: 002126
www.berklee.edu                 CSS Code: 3107

**4-year private** music college in very large city.
**Enrollment:** 5,112 undergrads, 16% part-time. 879 full-time freshmen.
**Selectivity:** Admits less than 50% of applicants.

## BASIC COSTS (2015-2016)
**Tuition and fees:** $40,082.
**Per-credit charge:** $1,378.
**Room and board:** $17,546.

## FINANCIAL AID PICTURE (2015-2016)
**Students with need:** Out of 412 full-time freshmen who applied for aid, 352 were judged to have need. Of these, 338 received aid, and 33 had their full need met. Average financial aid package met 33% of need; average scholarship/grant was $12,674; average loan was $3,694. For part-time students, average financial aid package was $12,738.
**Students without need:** 199 full-time freshmen who did not demonstrate need for aid received scholarships/grants; average award was $16,621. No-need awards available for academics, music/drama.

## FINANCIAL AID PROCEDURES
**Forms required:** FAFSA, CSS PROFILE.
**Dates and Deadlines:** Priority date 3/1; closing date 4/15. Applicants notified on a rolling basis starting 1/31; must reply within 2 week(s) of notification.

## CONTACT
Frank Mullen, Director of Financial Aid
1140 Boylston Street, Boston, MA 02215
(800) 538-3844

## Berkshire Community College
Pittsfield, Massachusetts
www.berkshirecc.edu             Federal Code: 002167

**2-year public** community college in large town.
**Enrollment:** 1,781 undergrads, 60% part-time. 269 full-time freshmen.

**Selectivity:** Open admission; but selective for some programs.

## BASIC COSTS (2015-2016)
**Tuition and fees:** $6,060; out-of-state residents $13,080.
**Per-credit charge:** $26; out-of-state residents $260.

## FINANCIAL AID PICTURE
**Students with need:** Need-based aid available for full-time and part-time students. Work study available nights, weekends, and for part-time students.
**Students without need:** No-need awards available for academics, job skills, leadership, minority status, state/district residency.

## FINANCIAL AID PROCEDURES
**Forms required:** FAFSA.
**Dates and Deadlines:** Applicants notified on a rolling basis starting 6/1.
**Transfers:** No deadline. Applicants notified on a rolling basis.

## CONTACT
Anne Moore, Director of Financial Aid
1350 West Street, Pittsfield, MA 01201-5786
(413) 236-1644

## Boston Architectural College
Boston, Massachusetts
www.the-bac.edu                    Federal Code: 003966

**6-year private** architecture and design college in very large city.
**Enrollment:** 329 undergrads, 2% part-time. 38 full-time freshmen.
**Selectivity:** Open admission; but selective for some programs.

## BASIC COSTS (2015-2016)
**Tuition and fees:** $20,666.
**Per-credit charge:** $1,668.

## FINANCIAL AID PICTURE
**Students with need:** Need-based aid available for full-time and part-time students. Work study available nights, weekends, and for part-time students.
**Students without need:** No-need awards available for academics, art, leadership.

## FINANCIAL AID PROCEDURES
**Forms required:** FAFSA.
**Dates and Deadlines:** Priority date 4/15; no closing date. Applicants notified on a rolling basis starting 3/30; must reply within 2 week(s) of notification.
**Transfers:** No deadline. Applicants notified on a rolling basis starting 3/1; must reply within 2 week(s) of notification.

## CONTACT
Janice Wilkos Greenberg, Director of Financial Aid
320 Newbury Street, Boston, MA 02115-2795
(617) 585-0125

## Boston Baptist College
Boston, Massachusetts
www.boston.edu

**4-year private** Bible college in very large city, affiliated with Baptist faith.
**Enrollment:** 89 undergrads.

## BASIC COSTS (2015-2016)
**Tuition and fees:** $15,040.
**Room and board:** $8,102.

## FINANCIAL AID PICTURE
**Students with need:** Need-based aid available for full-time and part-time students. Work study available nights, weekends, and for part-time students.
**Students without need:** No-need awards available for academics, alumni affiliation, job skills, leadership, religious affiliation.

## FINANCIAL AID PROCEDURES
**Forms required:** FAFSA, state aid form, institutional form.

## CONTACT
Jessica Shannon, Director of Financial Aid
950 Metropolitan Avenue, Boston, MA 02136
(888) 235-2014 ext. 231

## Boston College
Chestnut Hill, Massachusetts        Federal Code: 002128
www.bc.edu                          CSS Code: 3083

**4-year private** university in small city, affiliated with Roman Catholic Church.
**Enrollment:** 9,192 undergrads. 2,288 full-time freshmen.
**Selectivity:** Admits less than 50% of applicants.

## BASIC COSTS (2015-2016)
**Tuition and fees:** $49,324.
**Room and board:** $13,496.

## FINANCIAL AID PICTURE (2014-2015)
**Students with need:** Out of 1,171 full-time freshmen who applied for aid, 926 were judged to have need. Of these, 926 received aid, and 926 had their full need met. Average financial aid package met 100% of need; average scholarship/grant was $34,324; average loan was $3,502. Need-based aid available for part-time students.
**Students without need:** 38 full-time freshmen who did not demonstrate need for aid received scholarships/grants; average award was $20,238. No-need awards available for academics, athletics, leadership, ROTC.
**Scholarships offered:** 61 full-time freshmen received athletic scholarships; average amount $47,468.

## FINANCIAL AID PROCEDURES
**Forms required:** FAFSA, CSS PROFILE.
**Dates and Deadlines:** Priority date 2/1; no closing date. Applicants notified on a rolling basis starting 4/1.
**Transfers:** Priority date 3/15. Must reply within 2 week(s) of notification.

## CONTACT
Mary McGranahan, Director of Financial Aid
140 Commonwealth Avenue, Devlin Hall 208, Chestnut Hill, MA 02467-3809
(617) 552-3300

## Boston Conservatory
Boston, Massachusetts
www.bostonconservatory.edu          Federal Code: 002129

**4-year private** music and performing arts college in very large city.
**Enrollment:** 565 undergrads, 1% part-time. 117 full-time freshmen.
**Selectivity:** Admits less than 50% of applicants.

## BASIC COSTS (2015-2016)
**Tuition and fees:** $43,800.
**Per-credit charge:** $1,670.
**Room and board:** $17,242.

## FINANCIAL AID PICTURE (2014-2015)
**Students with need:** Out of 102 full-time freshmen who applied for aid, 84 were judged to have need. Of these, 84 received aid, and 9 had their full need met. Average financial aid package met 42% of need; average scholarship/grant was $19,012; average loan was $3,215. For part-time students, average financial aid package was $12,055.
**Students without need:** 28 full-time freshmen who did not demonstrate need for aid received scholarships/grants; average award was $12,375. No-need awards available for music/drama.

## FINANCIAL AID PROCEDURES

**Forms required:** FAFSA.

**Dates and Deadlines:** Priority date 3/1; no closing date. Applicants notified by 4/1; must reply by 5/1.

**Transfers:** Applicants notified on a rolling basis starting 4/1; must reply within 4 week(s) of notification.

## CONTACT

Nicole Brennan, Director of Financial Aid

8 The Fenway, Boston, MA 02215

(617) 912-9147

## Boston University

Boston, Massachusetts
www.bu.edu

Federal Code: 002130
CSS Code: 3087

**4-year private** university in very large city.

**Enrollment:** 16,456 undergrads, 2% part-time. 3,628 full-time freshmen.

**Selectivity:** Admits less than 50% of applicants.

### BASIC COSTS (2015-2016)

**Tuition and fees:** $48,436.

**Per-credit charge:** $1,482.

**Room and board:** $14,520.

### FINANCIAL AID PICTURE (2015-2016)

**Students with need:** Out of 1,401 full-time freshmen who applied for aid, 1,320 were judged to have need. Of these, 1,320 received aid, and 525 had their full need met. Average financial aid package met 93% of need; average scholarship/grant was $35,715; average loan was $5,640. For part-time students, average financial aid package was $13,983.

**Students without need:** 203 full-time freshmen who did not demonstrate need for aid received scholarships/grants; average award was $20,990. No-need awards available for academics, alumni affiliation, art, athletics, leadership, music/drama, religious affiliation, ROTC, state/district residency.

**Scholarships offered:** *Merit:* Trustee Scholar Program: full-tuition and fees (renewable); candidates nominated by high school principals, headmasters, or counselors. Presidential Scholarship: $20,000 (renewable); based on exceptionally strong high school academic record. *Athletic:* 74 full-time freshmen received athletic scholarships; average amount $39,897.

**Additional info:** Financial aid deadline for early decision applicants: 11/1; Financial Aid deadline for early decision 2 applicants: 1/3. Graduates of Boston's public high schools who complete financial aid application and demonstrate need will be awarded financial aid packages that contain no loans and meet full demonstrated need.

### FINANCIAL AID PROCEDURES

**Forms required:** FAFSA, CSS PROFILE.

**Dates and Deadlines:** Closing date 2/1. Applicants notified on a rolling basis starting 4/1; must reply by 5/1 or within 2 week(s) of notification.

**Transfers:** Closing date 3/1. Applicants notified on a rolling basis; must reply by 6/1. Transfer students cannot receive duplicate disbursements simultaneously from different institutions.

### CONTACT

Christine McGuire, Associate Vice President & Executive Director of Financial Assistance

233 Bay State Road, Boston, MA 02215

(617) 353-2965

## Brandeis University

Waltham, Massachusetts
www.brandeis.edu

Federal Code: 002133
CSS Code: 3092

**4-year private** university in small city.

**Enrollment:** 3,610 undergrads. 859 full-time freshmen.

**Selectivity:** Admits less than 50% of applicants.

### BASIC COSTS (2015-2016)

**Tuition and fees:** $49,598.

**Per-credit charge:** $1,490.

**Room and board:** $13,706.

### FINANCIAL AID PICTURE (2014-2015)

**Students with need:** Out of 501 full-time freshmen who applied for aid, 413 were judged to have need. Of these, 411 received aid, and 345 had their full need met. Average financial aid package met 97% of need; average scholarship/grant was $38,299; average loan was $3,256. For part-time students, average financial aid package was $29,865.

**Students without need:** 105 full-time freshmen who did not demonstrate need for aid received scholarships/grants; average award was $15,077. No-need awards available for academics.

**Scholarships offered:** Justice Brandeis Scholarships; full tuition. Martin Luther King scholarships; tuition and room and board. Presidential scholarships; $25,000. Dean's Awards; $15,000. Waltham High School scholarships; full tuition.

### FINANCIAL AID PROCEDURES

**Forms required:** FAFSA, CSS PROFILE.

**Dates and Deadlines:** Priority date 2/1; no closing date. Applicants notified by 4/1; must reply by 5/1.

**Transfers:** Priority date 4/1. International transfer students seeking scholarship or need-based financial assistance must apply by 2/1.

### CONTACT

Sherri Avery, Executive Director of Student Financial Services

415 South Street, MS003, Waltham, MA 02453

(781) 736-3700

## Bridgewater State University

Bridgewater, Massachusetts
www.bridgew.edu

Federal Code: 002183

**4-year public** university in large town.

**Enrollment:** 9,497 undergrads, 17% part-time. 1,493 full-time freshmen.

**Selectivity:** Admits over 75% of applicants.

### BASIC COSTS (2015-2016)

**Tuition and fees:** $8,474; out-of-state residents $14,614.

**Per-credit charge:** $38; out-of-state residents $294.

**Room and board:** $11,700.

**Additional info:** Tuition/fee waivers available for minority students, unemployed or children of unemployed.

### FINANCIAL AID PICTURE (2014-2015)

**Students with need:** Out of 1,448 full-time freshmen who applied for aid, 1,117 were judged to have need. Of these, 1,093 received aid, and 92 had their full need met. For part-time students, average financial aid package was $6,690.

**Students without need:** 10 full-time freshmen who did not demonstrate need for aid received scholarships/grants; average award was $1,012. No-need awards available for academics, alumni affiliation, minority status, ROTC, state/district residency.

**Additional info:** Tuition and/or fee waivers for Native Americans. Work-study programs available to half-time and full-time students.

### FINANCIAL AID PROCEDURES

**Forms required:** FAFSA.

**Dates and Deadlines:** Priority date 3/1; no closing date. Applicants notified on a rolling basis starting 4/1.

### CONTACT

Janet Gumbris, Director of Financial Aid

Office of Admission-Welcome Center, Bridgewater, MA 02325

(508) 531-1341

## Bristol Community College
Fall River, Massachusetts
www.bristolcc.edu                    Federal Code: 002176

**2-year public** community college in small city.
**Enrollment:** 8,046 undergrads.
**Selectivity:** Open admission; but selective for some programs.

**BASIC COSTS (2015-2016)**
**Tuition and fees:** $5,505; out-of-state residents $11,685.
**Per-credit charge:** $24; out-of-state residents $230.
**Additional info:** Tuition/fee waivers available for unemployed or children of unemployed.

**FINANCIAL AID PICTURE**
**Students with need:** Need-based aid available for full-time and part-time students. Work study available nights, weekends, and for part-time students.
**Students without need:** No-need awards available for academics, art, leadership, minority status, music/drama.

**FINANCIAL AID PROCEDURES**
**Forms required:** FAFSA, institutional form.
**Dates and Deadlines:** Priority date 5/1; no closing date. Applicants notified on a rolling basis starting 5/1; must reply within 2 week(s) of notification.
**Transfers:** No deadline. Applicants notified on a rolling basis starting 3/1.

**CONTACT**
David Allen, Director of Financial Aid
777 Elsbree Street, Fall River, MA 02720-7395
(508) 678-2811 ext. 2515

## Bunker Hill Community College
Boston, Massachusetts
www.bhcc.edu                    Federal Code: 011210

**2-year public** community college in very large city.
**Enrollment:** 13,187 undergrads, 69% part-time. 825 full-time freshmen.
**Selectivity:** Open admission; but selective for some programs.

**BASIC COSTS (2015-2016)**
**Tuition and fees:** $4,470; out-of-state residents $10,650.
**Per-credit charge:** $24; out-of-state residents $230.
**Additional info:** Tuition/fee waivers available for minority students.

**FINANCIAL AID PICTURE**
**Students with need:** Need-based aid available for full-time and part-time students.
**Students without need:** No-need awards available for academics.

**FINANCIAL AID PROCEDURES**
**Forms required:** FAFSA.
**Dates and Deadlines:** Priority date 5/1; no closing date. Applicants notified on a rolling basis starting 6/1; must reply within 2 week(s) of notification.
**Transfers:** No deadline. Applicants notified on a rolling basis; must reply within 2 week(s) of notification.

**CONTACT**
Melissa Holster, Director of Financial Aid
250 New Rutherford Avenue, Boston, MA 02129-2925
(617) 228-2275

## Cambridge College
Cambridge, Massachusetts
www.cambridgecollege.edu                    Federal Code: 021829

**4-year private** liberal arts and teachers college in small city.
**Enrollment:** 997 undergrads, 76% part-time. 8 full-time freshmen.

**Selectivity:** Open admission.

**BASIC COSTS (2015-2016)**
**Tuition and fees:** $13,400.

**FINANCIAL AID PICTURE (2015-2016)**
**Students with need:** Average financial aid package met 35% of need; average scholarship/grant was $5,707; average loan was $3,500. For part-time students, average financial aid package was $5,976.
**Students without need:** This college awards aid only to students with need.

**FINANCIAL AID PROCEDURES**
**Forms required:** FAFSA.
**Dates and Deadlines:** Priority date 7/15; closing date 10/1. Applicants notified on a rolling basis starting 7/1.

**CONTACT**
Francis Lauder, Director of Financial Aid
1000 Massachusetts Avenue, Cambridge, MA 02138-5304
(800) 877-4723 ext. 1440

## Cape Cod Community College
West Barnstable, Massachusetts
www.capecod.edu                    Federal Code: 002168

**2-year public** community college in small town.
**Enrollment:** 3,057 undergrads.
**Selectivity:** Open admission; but selective for some programs.

**BASIC COSTS (2015-2016)**
**Tuition and fees:** $7,620; out-of-state residents $11,250.
**Per-credit charge:** $24; out-of-state residents $230.
**Additional info:** Tuition/fee waivers available for minority students.

**FINANCIAL AID PICTURE**
**Students with need:** Need-based aid available for full-time and part-time students.
**Students without need:** No-need awards available for academics, art, job skills, leadership, music/drama, state/district residency.

**FINANCIAL AID PROCEDURES**
**Forms required:** FAFSA.
**Dates and Deadlines:** Priority date 5/1; no closing date. Applicants notified on a rolling basis starting 5/1.
**Transfers:** No deadline. Applicants notified on a rolling basis starting 6/1.

**CONTACT**
Sherry Andersen, Director of Financial Aid
2240 Iyannough Road, West Barnstable, MA 02668-1599
(508) 362-2131 ext. 4393

## Clark University
Worcester, Massachusetts          Federal Code: 002139
www.clarku.edu                    CSS Code: 3279

**4-year private** university and liberal arts college in small city.
**Enrollment:** 2,331 undergrads, 1% part-time. 669 full-time freshmen.
**Selectivity:** Admits 50 to 75% of applicants.

**BASIC COSTS (2015-2016)**
**Tuition and fees:** $41,940.
**Room and board:** $8,200.

**FINANCIAL AID PICTURE (2015-2016)**
**Students with need:** Out of 476 full-time freshmen who applied for aid, 379 were judged to have need. Of these, 374 received aid, and 225 had their full need met. Average financial aid package met 93% of need; average

scholarship/grant was $27,747; average loan was $4,671. Need-based aid available for part-time students.

**Students without need:** 225 full-time freshmen who did not demonstrate need for aid received scholarships/grants; average award was $18,798. No-need awards available for academics, leadership.

**Scholarships offered:** Scholarships: $12,000-$18,000 per year; for academic excellence or community service. Presidential LEEP scholarship: full tuition, room and board for four years; awarded to 5 outstanding first year students.

### FINANCIAL AID PROCEDURES

**Forms required:** FAFSA, CSS PROFILE.

**Dates and Deadlines:** Closing date 2/1. Applicants notified by 3/31; must reply by 5/1 or within 2 week(s) of notification.

**Transfers:** Closing date 4/1. Applicants notified on a rolling basis starting 6/1; must reply by 7/1 or within 2 week(s) of notification. Financial aid transcript from previous institution(s) attended required.

### CONTACT

Mary Ellen Severance, Director of Financial Aid and Student Employment
950 Main Street, Worcester, MA 01610-1477
(508) 793-7478

## College of the Holy Cross

Worcester, Massachusetts      Federal Code: 002141
www.holycross.edu      CSS Code: 3282

**4-year private** liberal arts college in small city, affiliated with Roman Catholic Church.

**Enrollment:** 2,885 undergrads. 738 full-time freshmen.

**Selectivity:** Admits less than 50% of applicants.

### BASIC COSTS (2015-2016)

**Tuition and fees:** $47,176.

**Room and board:** $12,748.

### FINANCIAL AID PICTURE (2015-2016)

**Students with need:** Out of 469 full-time freshmen who applied for aid, 404 were judged to have need. Of these, 404 received aid, and 404 had their full need met. Average financial aid package met 100% of need; average scholarship/grant was $34,015; average loan was $4,937.

**Students without need:** 9 full-time freshmen who did not demonstrate need for aid received scholarships/grants; average award was $48,882. No-need awards available for academics, athletics, music/drama, state/district residency.

**Scholarships offered:** 37 full-time freshmen received athletic scholarships; average amount $27,024.

**Additional info:** Cost of tuition above amount of Pell Grant waived for Worcester residents whose families earn less than $50,000.

### FINANCIAL AID PROCEDURES

**Forms required:** FAFSA. CSS PROFILE required of all students applying for institutional aid.

**Dates and Deadlines:** Closing date 2/1. Applicants notified by 4/1; must reply by 5/1.

**Transfers:** Closing date 4/15. Applicants notified by 6/30. Financial aid is limited for transfer students.

### CONTACT

Lynne Myers, Director of Financial Aid
One College Street, Worcester, MA 01610-2395
(508) 793-2265

## Curry College

Milton, Massachusetts
www.curry.edu      Federal Code: 002143

**4-year private** liberal arts college in large town.

**Enrollment:** 2,691 undergrads, 25% part-time. 600 full-time freshmen.

**Selectivity:** Admits over 75% of applicants.

### BASIC COSTS (2015-2016)

**Tuition and fees:** $36,445.

**Room and board:** $13,900.

### FINANCIAL AID PICTURE (2015-2016)

**Students with need:** Out of 487 full-time freshmen who applied for aid, 487 were judged to have need. Of these, 487 received aid, and 46 had their full need met. Average financial aid package met 69% of need; average scholarship/grant was $24,802; average loan was $3,595. For part-time students, average financial aid package was $5,579.

**Students without need:** 107 full-time freshmen who did not demonstrate need for aid received scholarships/grants; average award was $14,173. No-need awards available for academics, alumni affiliation, leadership.

**Scholarships offered:** Trustees Scholarship, Academic Achievement Scholarships, Excellence in Education and Curry Success Scholarships: varying amounts ranging from $3,000-$16,000; based on past academic achievement, promising academic ability, demonstrated leadership skills, character and citizenship, community service and talent.

### FINANCIAL AID PROCEDURES

**Forms required:** FAFSA.

**Dates and Deadlines:** Priority date 3/1; no closing date. Applicants notified on a rolling basis starting 3/1; must reply by 5/1 or within 2 week(s) of notification.

**Transfers:** No deadline. Applicants notified on a rolling basis starting 3/1; must reply by 5/1 or within 2 week(s) of notification.

### CONTACT

Stephanny Elias, Director, Student Financial Services
1071 Blue Hill Avenue, Milton, MA 02186-9984
(617) 333-2354

## Dean College

Franklin, Massachusetts
www.dean.edu      Federal Code: 002144

**2-year private** liberal arts and performing arts college in large town.

**Enrollment:** 1,113 undergrads. 473 full-time freshmen.

**Selectivity:** Admits 50 to 75% of applicants.

### BASIC COSTS (2015-2016)

**Tuition and fees:** $35,720.

**Room and board:** $15,200.

### FINANCIAL AID PICTURE (2015-2016)

**Students with need:** Out of 394 full-time freshmen who applied for aid, 372 were judged to have need. Of these, 372 received aid, and 58 had their full need met. Average financial aid package met 70% of need; average scholarship/grant was $25,206; average loan was $3,112. For part-time students, average financial aid package was $5,074.

**Students without need:** 59 full-time freshmen who did not demonstrate need for aid received scholarships/grants; average award was $19,313. No-need awards available for academics, alumni affiliation, art, athletics, leadership, music/drama.

**Scholarships offered:** *Merit:* Trustee's Scholarship: $10,000-$12,000 per year; based on outstanding academic accomplishments or potential. President's Leadership Scholarship: $8,000-$12,000 per year; given to students with leadership positions during their high school careers. Performing Arts Scholarship: $5,000-$11,000 per year; based on achievement in dance or theater. *Athletic:* 150 full-time freshmen received athletic scholarships; average amount $4,593.

### FINANCIAL AID PROCEDURES

**Forms required:** FAFSA.

**Dates and Deadlines:** Priority date 3/15; no closing date. Applicants notified on a rolling basis starting 2/25; must reply by 5/1 or within 2 week(s) of notification.

**Transfers:** No deadline. Applicants notified on a rolling basis starting 3/1.

**CONTACT**
Frank Mullen, Dean of Student Financial Planning and Services
99 Main Street, Franklin, MA 02038-1994
(508) 541-1518

## Eastern Nazarene College
Quincy, Massachusetts
www.enc.edu                             Federal Code: 002145

**4-year private** liberal arts college in small city, affiliated with Church of the Nazarene.
**Enrollment:** 911 undergrads, 1% part-time. 120 full-time freshmen.
**Selectivity:** Admits 50 to 75% of applicants.

### BASIC COSTS (2016-2017)
**Tuition and fees:** $30,815.
**Room and board:** $9,140.
**Additional info:** Tuition/fee waivers available for minority students.

### FINANCIAL AID PICTURE
**Students with need:** Need-based aid available for full-time and part-time students. Work study available nights, weekends, and for part-time students.
**Students without need:** No-need awards available for academics, alumni affiliation, leadership, religious affiliation, ROTC.
**Scholarships offered:** Academic scholarships: amounts vary based on test scores; minimum 1500 SAT or 21 ACT. Honors Scholar: based on 1800 SAT or 27 ACT. Dean's Scholar: based on 2100 SAT or 32 ACT. Munro Scholar: full-tuition; based on interview and 2100 SAT or 32 ACT. President's Scholar: full-tuition plus room and board; based on interview and 2250 SAT or 34 ACT.
**Additional info:** Participant in Massachusetts University pre-payment plan.

### FINANCIAL AID PROCEDURES
**Forms required:** FAFSA, institutional form.
**Dates and Deadlines:** Priority date 3/1; closing date 8/1. Applicants notified on a rolling basis starting 3/14; must reply by 8/1 or within 2 week(s) of notification.

**CONTACT**
Delinda Hall, Intirim Director of Financial Aid
23 East Elm Avenue, Quincy, MA 02170
(617) 745-3712

## Elms College
Chicopee, Massachusetts
www.elms.edu                            Federal Code: 002140

**4-year private** liberal arts college in small city, affiliated with Roman Catholic Church.
**Enrollment:** 1,268 undergrads, 24% part-time. 182 full-time freshmen.
**Selectivity:** Admits 50 to 75% of applicants.

### BASIC COSTS (2015-2016)
**Tuition and fees:** $32,335.
**Room and board:** $11,708.

### FINANCIAL AID PICTURE (2015-2016)
**Students with need:** Out of 176 full-time freshmen who applied for aid, 169 were judged to have need. Of these, 169 received aid, and 22 had their full need met. Average financial aid package met 72% of need; average scholarship/grant was $22,523; average loan was $3,416. For part-time students, average financial aid package was $7,434.

**Students without need:** 13 full-time freshmen who did not demonstrate need for aid received scholarships/grants; average award was $13,875. No-need awards available for academics, alumni affiliation, leadership, religious affiliation, state/district residency.

### FINANCIAL AID PROCEDURES
**Forms required:** FAFSA.
**Dates and Deadlines:** Priority date 3/1; no closing date. Applicants notified on a rolling basis starting 3/15; must reply by 5/1 or within 2 week(s) of notification.
**Transfers:** No deadline. Applicants notified on a rolling basis starting 3/15.

**CONTACT**
Kristin Hmieleski, Director of Financial Aid
291 Springfield Street, Chicopee, MA 01013-2839
(413) 265-2249

## Emerson College
Boston, Massachusetts                   Federal Code: 002146
www.emerson.edu                         CSS Code: 3367

**4-year private** college of communication and the arts in very large city.
**Enrollment:** 3,784 undergrads, 1% part-time. 915 full-time freshmen.
**Selectivity:** Admits less than 50% of applicants.

### BASIC COSTS (2015-2016)
**Tuition and fees:** $41,052.
**Per-credit charge:** $1,260.
**Room and board:** $15,700.

### FINANCIAL AID PICTURE (2015-2016)
**Students with need:** Out of 692 full-time freshmen who applied for aid, 472 were judged to have need. Of these, 472 received aid, and 55 had their full need met. Average financial aid package met 62% of need; average scholarship/grant was $20,145; average loan was $3,989. For part-time students, average financial aid package was $8,621.
**Students without need:** 115 full-time freshmen who did not demonstrate need for aid received scholarships/grants; average award was $15,280. No-need awards available for academics, leadership, music/drama, state/district residency.
**Scholarships offered:** Trustees Scholarships: half-tuition; honors program students may apply. Dean's Scholarships: $14,000. Emerson Stage Scholarships: amounts vary; based on performing arts audition and academic merit.
**Additional info:** Massachusetts Loan Plan available for parents of dependent undergraduates.

### FINANCIAL AID PROCEDURES
**Forms required:** FAFSA, CSS PROFILE.
**Dates and Deadlines:** Closing date 3/1. Applicants notified by 4/1; must reply by 5/1 or within 3 week(s) of notification.
**Transfers:** Priority date 4/1.

**CONTACT**
Ruthanne Madsen, Vice President for Enrollment, Student Financial Services
120 Boylston Street, Boston, MA 02116-4624
(617) 824-8655

## Emmanuel College
Boston, Massachusetts
www.emmanuel.edu                        Federal Code: 002147

**4-year private** liberal arts college in very large city, affiliated with Roman Catholic Church.
**Enrollment:** 1,865 undergrads, 5% part-time. 555 full-time freshmen.
**Selectivity:** Admits 50 to 75% of applicants.

## BASIC COSTS (2015-2016)

**Tuition and fees:** $36,504.
**Per-credit charge:** $1,134.
**Room and board:** $13,920.

## FINANCIAL AID PICTURE (2015-2016)

**Students with need:** Out of 500 full-time freshmen who applied for aid, 454 were judged to have need. Of these, 454 received aid, and 204 had their full need met. Average financial aid package met 76% of need; average scholarship/grant was $23,170; average loan was $3,660. For part-time students, average financial aid package was $10,780.

**Students without need:** 100 full-time freshmen who did not demonstrate need for aid received scholarships/grants; average award was $14,720. No-need awards available for academics, alumni affiliation, leadership.

## FINANCIAL AID PROCEDURES

**Forms required:** FAFSA.

**Dates and Deadlines:** Priority date 2/15; no closing date. Applicants notified on a rolling basis starting 3/1.

**Transfers:** Priority date 4/1; no deadline. Applicants notified on a rolling basis.

## CONTACT

Jennifer Porter, Associate Vice President for Student Financial Services
400 The Fenway, Boston, MA 02115
(617) 735-9938

## Endicott College

Beverly, Massachusetts
www.endicott.edu                    Federal Code: 002148

**4-year private** liberal arts college in large town.
**Enrollment:** 2,979 undergrads, 10% part-time. 780 full-time freshmen.
**Selectivity:** Admits 50 to 75% of applicants.

## BASIC COSTS (2015-2016)

**Tuition and fees:** $30,292.
**Per-credit charge:** $914.
**Room and board:** $14,112.

## FINANCIAL AID PICTURE (2015-2016)

**Students with need:** Out of 757 full-time freshmen who applied for aid, 557 were judged to have need. Of these, 556 received aid, and 72 had their full need met. Average financial aid package met 60% of need; average scholarship/grant was $9,714; average loan was $3,585. For part-time students, average financial aid package was $6,753.

**Students without need:** 170 full-time freshmen who did not demonstrate need for aid received scholarships/grants; average award was $8,670. No-need awards available for academics, alumni affiliation, art, job skills, leadership, music/drama, religious affiliation, ROTC, state/district residency.

## FINANCIAL AID PROCEDURES

**Forms required:** FAFSA, institutional form.

**Dates and Deadlines:** Priority date 3/15; no closing date. Applicants notified on a rolling basis starting 3/15; must reply within 2 week(s) of notification.

## CONTACT

Marcia Toomey, Director of Financial Aid
376 Hale Street, Beverly, MA 01915-9985
(978) 232-2060

## Fisher College

Boston, Massachusetts
www.fisher.edu                    Federal Code: 002150

**4-year private** business and liberal arts college in very large city.
**Enrollment:** 1,608 undergrads, 28% part-time. 400 full-time freshmen.

**Selectivity:** Admits 50 to 75% of applicants.

## BASIC COSTS (2015-2016)

**Tuition and fees:** $28,942.
**Room and board:** $15,082.

## FINANCIAL AID PICTURE (2014-2015)

**Students with need:** Out of 246 full-time freshmen who applied for aid, 207 were judged to have need. Of these, 205 received aid. For part-time students, average financial aid package was $3,626.

**Students without need:** 52 full-time freshmen who did not demonstrate need for aid received scholarships/grants; average award was $8,370. No-need awards available for academics.

**Scholarships offered:** *Merit:* Fisher Honor Scholarship: $5,000; based on outstanding academic and personal achievement, contribution to school and community; renewable with 3.0 GPA. Presidential Scholarship: $8,000. Achievement Scholarship: $6,000. Opportunity Award: $5,000. Charles River Award: $3,000. *Athletic:* 5 full-time freshmen received athletic scholarships; average amount $12,400.

## FINANCIAL AID PROCEDURES

**Forms required:** FAFSA.

**Dates and Deadlines:** Priority date 3/15; no closing date. Applicants notified on a rolling basis starting 3/1.

**Transfers:** Transfer Student Scholarship; $2,500.

## CONTACT

Pam Walker, Director of Financial Aid
Office of Admissions, Boston, MA 02116
(617) 236-8821

## Fitchburg State University

Fitchburg, Massachusetts
www.fitchburgstate.edu                    Federal Code: 002184

**4-year public** liberal arts and teachers college in small city.
**Enrollment:** 4,048 undergrads, 15% part-time. 724 full-time freshmen.
**Selectivity:** Admits 50 to 75% of applicants.

## BASIC COSTS (2015-2016)

**Tuition and fees:** $9,935; out-of-state residents $16,015.
**Per-credit charge:** $40; out-of-state residents $294.
**Room and board:** $9,210.

## FINANCIAL AID PICTURE (2014-2015)

**Students with need:** Out of 707 full-time freshmen who applied for aid, 510 were judged to have need. Of these, 494 received aid, and 494 had their full need met. Average financial aid package met 76% of need; average scholarship/grant was $6,068; average loan was $3,239. Need-based aid available for part-time students.

**Students without need:** 41 full-time freshmen who did not demonstrate need for aid received scholarships/grants; average award was $1,369. No-need awards available for academics, alumni affiliation, leadership, ROTC, state/district residency.

## FINANCIAL AID PROCEDURES

**Forms required:** FAFSA.

**Dates and Deadlines:** Priority date 3/1; no closing date. Applicants notified on a rolling basis starting 3/15; must reply within 2 week(s) of notification.

## CONTACT

Brindle Denise, Director, Financial Aid
160 Pearl Street, Fitchburg, MA 01420-2697
(978) 665-3156

## Framingham State University
Framingham, Massachusetts
www.framingham.edu                    Federal Code: 002185

**4-year public** university in small city.
**Enrollment:** 4,288 undergrads, 11% part-time. 806 full-time freshmen.
**Selectivity:** Admits 50 to 75% of applicants.

### BASIC COSTS (2015-2016)
**Tuition and fees:** $8,700; out-of-state residents $14,780.
**Per-credit charge:** $41; out-of-state residents $294.
**Room and board:** $10,834.

### FINANCIAL AID PICTURE (2014-2015)
**Students with need:** Out of 754 full-time freshmen who applied for aid, 576 were judged to have need. Of these, 576 received aid, and 130 had their full need met. Average financial aid package met 60% of need; average scholarship/grant was $5,200; average loan was $4,550. For part-time students, average financial aid package was $4,800.
**Students without need:** 67 full-time freshmen who did not demonstrate need for aid received scholarships/grants; average award was $2,325. No-need awards available for academics.
**Scholarships offered:** Senator Paul E. Tsongas Scholarship: full-tuition and fees; available to Massachusetts residents based on 3.75 GPA and test scores; 5 awarded. Merit scholarships: available to students majoring in education, natural or physical sciences based on GPA and test scores.

### FINANCIAL AID PROCEDURES
**Forms required:** FAFSA.
**Dates and Deadlines:** Priority date 3/1; no closing date. Applicants notified on a rolling basis starting 3/15; must reply by 5/1 or within 2 week(s) of notification.
**Transfers:** Priority date 11/1; no deadline. Applicants notified on a rolling basis starting 11/1; must reply within 2 week(s) of notification.

### CONTACT
Deborah Altsher, Director of Financial Aid
PO Box 9101, Framingham, MA 01701-9101
(508) 626-4534

## Franklin W. Olin College of Engineering
Needham, Massachusetts
www.olin.edu                    Federal Code: 039463

**4-year private** engineering college in large town.
**Enrollment:** 333 undergrads. 76 full-time freshmen.
**Selectivity:** Admits less than 50% of applicants.

### BASIC COSTS (2015-2016)
**Tuition and fees:** $48,181.
**Per-credit charge:** $1,500.
**Room and board:** $15,600.
**Additional info:** Required fees include a laptop fee charged to all first year students. Health insurance is also available for those who do not have it for an additional fee.

### FINANCIAL AID PICTURE (2015-2016)
**Students with need:** Out of 50 full-time freshmen who applied for aid, 36 were judged to have need. Of these, 36 received aid, and 35 had their full need met. Average financial aid package met 100% of need; average scholarship/grant was $42,883; average loan was $2,949.
**Students without need:** 40 full-time freshmen who did not demonstrate need for aid received scholarships/grants; average award was $23,458. No-need awards available for academics, leadership.
**Scholarships offered:** The Olin Tuition Scholarship: 50% of tuition for up to 8 semesters; awarded to all matriculated students.

**Additional info:** Financial aid forms not needed for the Olin Tuition Scholarship, which all students receive. FAFSA is required to apply for need-based aid.

### FINANCIAL AID PROCEDURES
**Forms required:** FAFSA.
**Dates and Deadlines:** Closing date 2/15. Applicants notified by 3/21; must reply by 5/1 or within 2 week(s) of notification.
**Transfers:** Closing date 2/15. Applicants notified by 3/21; must reply by 5/1 or within 2 week(s) of notification.

### CONTACT
Jean Ricker, Director of Financial Aid
1000 Olin Way, Needham, MA 02492
(781) 292-2343

## Gordon College
Wenham, Massachusetts
www.gordon.edu                    Federal Code: 002153

**4-year private** liberal arts college in small town, affiliated with nondenominational tradition.
**Enrollment:** 1,664 undergrads, 2% part-time. 440 full-time freshmen.
**Selectivity:** Admits over 75% of applicants.

### BASIC COSTS (2015-2016)
**Tuition and fees:** $35,386.
**Per-credit charge:** $847.
**Room and board:** $10,218.

### FINANCIAL AID PICTURE (2015-2016)
**Students with need:** Out of 378 full-time freshmen who applied for aid, 314 were judged to have need. Of these, 314 received aid, and 49 had their full need met. Average financial aid package met 76% of need; average scholarship/grant was $22,519; average loan was $3,752. For part-time students, average financial aid package was $17,038.
**Students without need:** 123 full-time freshmen who did not demonstrate need for aid received scholarships/grants; average award was $14,337. No-need awards available for academics, alumni affiliation, art, leadership, minority status, music/drama, ROTC, state/district residency.
**Scholarships offered:** Founder's Scholarship; $16,000-$15,000; based on academic achievement. Harold John Ockenga Scholarship; $12,000 to $13,000; based on academic record. T. Leonard Lewis Scholarship; $9,000 to $11,000; based on academic record. Isabel Warwick Wood Scholarship; $7,000 to $8,000; based on academic record. Choral Scholars Program; $5,000; for students with excellent ability/academic performance seeking career in vocal music field. National Merit Finalists and National Achievement Finalist Scholars; 75% of tuition. All scholarships renewable annually.

### FINANCIAL AID PROCEDURES
**Forms required:** FAFSA.
**Dates and Deadlines:** Priority date 3/1; no closing date. Applicants notified on a rolling basis starting 2/15; must reply by 5/1.
**Transfers:** Applicants notified on a rolling basis starting 2/15; must reply by 5/1 or within 2 week(s) of notification.

### CONTACT
Daniel O'Connell, Senior Director of Student Financial Services
255 Grapevine Road, Wenham, MA 01984-1899
(800) 343-1379

## Greenfield Community College
Greenfield, Massachusetts
www.gcc.mass.edu                    Federal Code: 002169

**2-year public** community college in large town.
**Enrollment:** 1,850 undergrads.

**Selectivity:** Open admission; but selective for some programs.

## BASIC COSTS (2015-2016)

**Tuition and fees:** $6,482; out-of-state residents $14,132.
**Per-credit charge:** $26; out-of-state residents $281.
**Additional info:** Tuition/fee waivers available for adults.

## FINANCIAL AID PICTURE

**Students with need:** Need-based aid available for full-time and part-time students. Work study available nights, weekends, and for part-time students.
**Students without need:** This college awards aid only to students with need.

## FINANCIAL AID PROCEDURES

**Forms required:** FAFSA, institutional form.
**Dates and Deadlines:** Priority date 4/15; no closing date. Applicants notified on a rolling basis starting 5/1; must reply within 2 week(s) of notification.

## CONTACT

Linda Dejardins, Director of Financial Aid
One College Drive, Greenfield, MA 01301
(413) 775-1109

## Hampshire College

Amherst, Massachusetts
www.hampshire.edu
Federal Code: 004661
CSS Code: 3447

**4-year private** liberal arts college in large town.
**Enrollment:** 1,396 undergrads. 370 full-time freshmen.
**Selectivity:** Admits 50 to 75% of applicants.

## BASIC COSTS (2016-2017)

**Tuition and fees:** $50,550.
**Room and board:** $13,274.

## FINANCIAL AID PICTURE (2015-2016)

**Students with need:** 81% of average financial aid package awarded as scholarships/grants, 19% awarded as loans/jobs. Work study available nights, weekends, and for part-time students.
**Students without need:** No-need awards available for academics, art, leadership, music/drama.

## FINANCIAL AID PROCEDURES

**Forms required:** FAFSA, CSS PROFILE.
**Dates and Deadlines:** Closing date 2/1. Applicants notified by 4/1; must reply by 5/1 or within 2 week(s) of notification.
**Transfers:** Applicants notified by 4/1; must reply by 5/1. Phi Theta Kappa Scholarship offered in amounts up to $15,000 per year. STEM Scholarship is able to offer a limited number of scholarships, sponsored by the National Science Foundation, to transfer students who wish to study STEM (science, technology, engineering, and mathematics) disciplines. The value of the STEM Scholarship is $10,000 per year.

## CONTACT

Jennifer Lawton, Director of Financial Aid
893 West Street, Amherst, MA 01002-9988
(413) 559-5484

## Harvard College

Cambridge, Massachusetts
www.college.harvard.edu
Federal Code: 002155
CSS Code: 3434

**4-year private** university and liberal arts college in small city.
**Enrollment:** 6,638 undergrads. 1,661 full-time freshmen.
**Selectivity:** Admits less than 50% of applicants.

## BASIC COSTS (2015-2016)

**Tuition and fees:** $45,278.

**Room and board:** $15,381.

## FINANCIAL AID PICTURE (2014-2015)

**Students with need:** Out of 1,030 full-time freshmen who applied for aid, 868 were judged to have need. Of these, 868 received aid, and 868 had their full need met. Average financial aid package met 100% of need; average scholarship/grant was $48,671; average loan was $3,544. Need-based aid available for part-time students.
**Students without need:** This college awards aid only to students with need.

## FINANCIAL AID PROCEDURES

**Forms required:** FAFSA, CSS PROFILE.
**Dates and Deadlines:** Closing date 2/1. Applicants notified by 4/1; must reply by 5/1 or within 2 week(s) of notification.
**Transfers:** Closing date 2/15. Applicants notified by 5/30; must reply within 2 week(s) of notification.

## CONTACT

Sally Donahue, Director of Financial Aid
86 Brattle Street, Cambridge, MA 02138
(617) 495-1581

## Hellenic College/Holy Cross

Brookline, Massachusetts
www.hchc.edu
Federal Code: 002154

**4-year private** liberal arts and seminary college in large town, affiliated with Eastern Orthodox Church.
**Enrollment:** 91 undergrads.

## BASIC COSTS (2015-2016)

**Tuition and fees:** $22,490.
**Per-credit charge:** $950.
**Room and board:** $16,192.
**Additional info:** Parking 425 Health Insurance 2007.

## FINANCIAL AID PICTURE

**Students with need:** Need-based aid available for full-time students. Work study available nights, weekends, and for part-time students.
**Students without need:** This college awards aid only to students with need.

## FINANCIAL AID PROCEDURES

**Forms required:** FAFSA, institutional form.
**Dates and Deadlines:** Closing date 4/1. Applicants notified by 4/1; must reply within 2 week(s) of notification.
**Transfers:** No deadline. Applicants notified on a rolling basis; must reply within 2 week(s) of notification.

## CONTACT

Kevin Derrivan, CFO
50 Goddard Avenue, Brookline, MA 02445
(617) 850-1239

## Holyoke Community College

Holyoke, Massachusetts
www.hcc.edu.
Federal Code: 002170

**2-year public** community college in large town.
**Enrollment:** 5,851 undergrads, 51% part-time. 988 full-time freshmen.
**Selectivity:** Open admission; but selective for some programs.

## BASIC COSTS (2015-2016)

**Tuition and fees:** $5,270; out-of-state residents $11,450.
**Per-credit charge:** $24; out-of-state residents $230.

## FINANCIAL AID PICTURE (2014-2015)

**Students with need:** 77% of average financial aid package awarded as scholarships/grants, 23% awarded as loans/jobs. Need-based aid available for part-time students. Work study available nights.

**Students without need:** No-need awards available for academics, art, leadership, music/drama.

### FINANCIAL AID PROCEDURES

**Forms required:** FAFSA.

**Dates and Deadlines:** Priority date 5/1; no closing date. Applicants notified on a rolling basis starting 5/1; must reply within 2 week(s) of notification.

### CONTACT

Karen Derouin, Director of Financial Aid
303 Homestead Avenue, Holyoke, MA 01040
(413) 552-2150

# Laboure College
Milton, Massachusetts
www.laboure.edu　　　　Federal Code: 006324

**2-year private** health science and nursing college in large town, affiliated with Roman Catholic Church.

**Enrollment:** 808 undergrads, 93% part-time. 3 full-time freshmen.

**Selectivity:** Admits 50 to 75% of applicants.

## BASIC COSTS (2015-2016)

**Tuition and fees:** $34,405.

**Per-credit charge:** $930.

## FINANCIAL AID PICTURE (2014-2015)

**Students with need:** Out of 3 full-time freshmen who applied for aid, 3 were judged to have need. Of these, 3 received aid. Average financial aid package met 80% of need; average scholarship/grant was $5,000; average loan was $3,500. For part-time students, average financial aid package was $5,000.

**Students without need:** No-need awards available for academics, alumni affiliation, leadership, religious affiliation.

### FINANCIAL AID PROCEDURES

**Forms required:** FAFSA.

**Dates and Deadlines:** Priority date 5/1; no closing date. Applicants notified on a rolling basis starting 1/15; must reply within 2 week(s) of notification.

**Transfers:** Priority date 12/1. Applicants notified on a rolling basis starting 12/1; must reply within 2 week(s) of notification.

### CONTACT

Erin Hanlon, Director of Financial Aid
303 Adams Street, Milton, MA 02186
(617) 322-3531

# Lasell College
Newton, Massachusetts
www.lasell.edu　　　　Federal Code: 002158

**4-year private** business and liberal arts college in small city.

**Enrollment:** 1,810 undergrads, 1% part-time. 501 full-time freshmen.

**Selectivity:** Admits over 75% of applicants.

## BASIC COSTS (2016-2017)

**Tuition and fees:** $33,600.

**Room and board:** $13,900.

## FINANCIAL AID PICTURE (2014-2015)

**Students with need:** Out of 450 full-time freshmen who applied for aid, 401 were judged to have need. Of these, 400 received aid, and 76 had their full need met. Average financial aid package met 73% of need; average

scholarship/grant was $22,400; average loan was $2,500. For part-time students, average financial aid package was $16,700.

**Students without need:** 77 full-time freshmen who did not demonstrate need for aid received scholarships/grants; average award was $10,300. No-need awards available for academics, alumni affiliation, leadership.

### FINANCIAL AID PROCEDURES

**Forms required:** FAFSA.

**Dates and Deadlines:** Priority date 2/15; no closing date. Applicants notified on a rolling basis starting 2/15; must reply by 5/1 or within 2 week(s) of notification.

**Transfers:** No deadline. Applicants notified on a rolling basis starting 2/15.

### CONTACT

Michele Kosboth, Director of Student Financial Planning
1844 Commonwealth Avenue, Newton, MA 02466-2709
(617) 243-2227

# Lesley University
Cambridge, Massachusetts
www.lesley.edu　　　　Federal Code: 002160

**4-year private** liberal arts and teachers college in very large city.

**Enrollment:** 1,418 undergrads.

## BASIC COSTS (2015-2016)

**Tuition and fees:** $25,200.

**Per-credit charge:** $555.

**Room and board:** $14,830.

## FINANCIAL AID PICTURE (2015-2016)

**Students with need:** Average financial aid package met 80% of need; average scholarship/grant was $8,614; average loan was $3,805. For part-time students, average financial aid package was $12,709.

**Students without need:** No-need awards available for academics, art, leadership, minority status, state/district residency.

**Scholarships offered:** Freshmen scholarships: $5,000-full tuition; for students with strong academic backgrounds who have shown a commitment to community service and making a difference in the lives of others.

### FINANCIAL AID PROCEDURES

**Forms required:** FAFSA.

**Dates and Deadlines:** Priority date 2/15; no closing date. Applicants notified on a rolling basis starting 2/1.

**Transfers:** Priority date 3/15.

### CONTACT

Scott Jewell, Director of Financial Aid
29 Everett Street, Cambridge, MA 02140-2790
(617) 349-8667

# Massachusetts Bay Community College
Wellesley Hills, Massachusetts
www.massbay.edu　　　　Federal Code: 002171

**2-year public** community college in large town.

**Enrollment:** 3,859 undergrads.

**Selectivity:** Open admission; but selective for some programs.

## BASIC COSTS (2015-2016)

**Tuition and fees:** $5,220; out-of-state residents $11,400.

**Per-credit charge:** $24; out-of-state residents $230.

**Additional info:** Tuition/fee waivers available for unemployed or children of unemployed.

## FINANCIAL AID PICTURE

**Students with need:** Need-based aid available for full-time and part-time students.

## FINANCIAL AID PROCEDURES

**Forms required:** FAFSA.

**Dates and Deadlines:** Priority date 5/1; no closing date. Applicants notified on a rolling basis starting 4/1.

**Transfers:** No deadline. Applicants notified on a rolling basis.

## CONTACT

Elizabeth Enos, Director of Financial Aid
50 Oakland Street, Wellesley Hills, MA 02481
(781) 239-2600

# Massachusetts College of Art and Design
Boston, Massachusetts
www.massart.edu          Federal Code: 002180

**4-year public** visual arts college in very large city.

**Enrollment:** 1,736 undergrads, 11% part-time. 292 full-time freshmen.

**Selectivity:** Admits 50 to 75% of applicants.

## BASIC COSTS (2015-2016)

**Tuition and fees:** $11,725; out-of-state residents $31,225.

**Room and board:** $13,175.

**Additional info:** Tuition/fee waivers available for unemployed or children of unemployed.

## FINANCIAL AID PICTURE (2014-2015)

**Students with need:** Out of 254 full-time freshmen who applied for aid, 198 were judged to have need. Of these, 198 received aid. For part-time students, average financial aid package was $10,792.

**Students without need:** 39 full-time freshmen who did not demonstrate need for aid received scholarships/grants; average award was $8,066. No-need awards available for academics, art, leadership, state/district residency.

**Additional info:** Tuition waiver available to Vietnam veterans.

## FINANCIAL AID PROCEDURES

**Forms required:** FAFSA.

**Dates and Deadlines:** Priority date 3/1; no closing date. Applicants notified on a rolling basis starting 3/15; must reply within 3 week(s) of notification.

**Transfers:** Financial aid transcripts required.

## CONTACT

Aurelio Ramirez, Director of Financial Aid
621 Huntington Avenue, Boston, MA 02115-5882
(617) 879-7850

# Massachusetts College of Liberal Arts
North Adams, Massachusetts
www.mcla.edu          Federal Code: 002187

**4-year public** liberal arts college in large town.

**Enrollment:** 1,423 undergrads, 11% part-time. 270 full-time freshmen.

**Selectivity:** Admits 50 to 75% of applicants.

## BASIC COSTS (2015-2016)

**Tuition and fees:** $9,650; out-of-state residents $18,595.

**Per-credit charge:** $43; out-of-state residents $416.

**Room and board:** $9,828.

**Additional info:** Tuition/fee waivers available for unemployed or children of unemployed.

## FINANCIAL AID PICTURE (2015-2016)

**Students with need:** Out of 264 full-time freshmen who applied for aid, 203 were judged to have need. Of these, 203 received aid, and 145 had their full need met. Average financial aid package met 81% of need; average scholarship/grant was $7,614; average loan was $3,273. For part-time students, average financial aid package was $10,195.

**Students without need:** 31 full-time freshmen who did not demonstrate need for aid received scholarships/grants; average award was $1,986. No-need awards available for academics, art, leadership, minority status, music/drama.

## FINANCIAL AID PROCEDURES

**Forms required:** FAFSA.

**Dates and Deadlines:** Priority date 3/1; no closing date. Applicants notified on a rolling basis starting 3/1; must reply by 5/1 or within 2 week(s) of notification.

## CONTACT

Elizabeth Petri, Director of Financial Aid
375 Church Street, North Adams, MA 01247
(413) 662-5219

# Massachusetts Institute of Technology
Cambridge, Massachusetts          Federal Code: 002178
web.mit.edu          CSS Code: 3514

**4-year private** university in small city.

**Enrollment:** 4,474 undergrads, 1% part-time. 1,050 full-time freshmen.

**Selectivity:** Admits less than 50% of applicants.

## BASIC COSTS (2015-2016)

**Tuition and fees:** $46,704.

**Room and board:** $13,730.

## FINANCIAL AID PICTURE (2014-2015)

**Students with need:** Out of 832 full-time freshmen who applied for aid, 641 were judged to have need. Of these, 641 received aid, and 641 had their full need met. Average financial aid package met 100% of need; average scholarship/grant was $39,882; average loan was $2,869. For part-time students, average financial aid package was $33,825.

**Students without need:** This college awards aid only to students with need.

**Additional info:** Filing deadline 2/15 for CSS PROFILE.

## FINANCIAL AID PROCEDURES

**Forms required:** FAFSA, CSS PROFILE.

**Dates and Deadlines:** Priority date 2/15; closing date 2/15. Applicants notified by 3/14; must reply by 5/1.

**Transfers:** No deadline. Applicants notified by 5/15. Access to MIT funds may be limited to fewer than 8 terms.

## CONTACT

Stuart Schmill, Interim Executive Director of Student Financial Services
77 Massachusetts Avenue, Room 3-108, Cambridge, MA 02139-4307
(617) 258-8600

# Massachusetts Maritime Academy
Buzzards Bay, Massachusetts
www.maritime.edu          Federal Code: 002181

**4-year public** engineering and maritime college in small town.

**Enrollment:** 1,537 undergrads, 2% part-time. 385 full-time freshmen.

**Selectivity:** Admits 50 to 75% of applicants.

## BASIC COSTS (2015-2016)

**Tuition and fees:** $7,256; out-of-state residents $22,310.

**Room and board:** $11,120.

## FINANCIAL AID PICTURE (2015-2016)

**Students with need:** Out of 361 full-time freshmen who applied for aid, 257 were judged to have need. Of these, 257 received aid, and 59 had their full need met. Average financial aid package met 77% of need; average

scholarship/grant was $9,304; average loan was $3,245. Need-based aid available for part-time students.

**Students without need:** 34 full-time freshmen who did not demonstrate need for aid received scholarships/grants; average award was $4,038. No-need awards available for academics, alumni affiliation, leadership.

### FINANCIAL AID PROCEDURES
**Forms required:** FAFSA, institutional form.
**Dates and Deadlines:** Priority date 5/1; no closing date. Applicants notified on a rolling basis starting 3/20.

### CONTACT
Catherine Kedski, Financial Aid Director
101 Academy Drive, Buzzards Bay, MA 02532
(508) 830-5086

## Massasoit Community College
Brockton, Massachusetts
www.massasoit.mass.edu          Federal Code: 002177

**2-year public** community college in small city.
**Enrollment:** 6,738 undergrads, 51% part-time. 1,171 full-time freshmen.
**Selectivity:** Open admission; but selective for some programs.

### BASIC COSTS (2015-2016)
**Tuition and fees:** $5,610; out-of-state residents $11,790.
**Per-credit charge:** $24; out-of-state residents $230.
**Additional info:** Tuition/fee waivers available for unemployed or children of unemployed.

### FINANCIAL AID PICTURE
**Students with need:** Need-based aid available for full-time and part-time students.
**Students without need:** This college awards aid only to students with need.

### FINANCIAL AID PROCEDURES
**Forms required:** FAFSA.
**Dates and Deadlines:** Priority date 4/15; no closing date. Applicants notified on a rolling basis starting 6/1.

### CONTACT
Todd Hughes, Director of Financial Aid
One Massasoit Boulevard, Brockton, MA 02302-3996
(508) 588-9100 ext. 1479

## MCPHS University
Boston, Massachusetts
www.mcphs.edu          Federal Code: 002165

**4-year private** health science and pharmacy college in very large city.
**Enrollment:** 3,877 undergrads, 5% part-time. 751 full-time freshmen.
**Selectivity:** Admits over 75% of applicants.

### BASIC COSTS (2015-2016)
**Tuition and fees:** $30,530.
**Per-credit charge:** $1,090.
**Room and board:** $15,174.

### FINANCIAL AID PICTURE (2015-2016)
**Students with need:** Out of 617 full-time freshmen who applied for aid, 545 were judged to have need. Of these, 545 received aid, and 265 had their full need met. Average financial aid package met 40% of need; average scholarship/grant was $11,523; average loan was $4,664. For part-time students, average financial aid package was $10,240.

**Students without need:** 206 full-time freshmen who did not demonstrate need for aid received scholarships/grants; average award was $11,780. No-need awards available for academics.

### FINANCIAL AID PROCEDURES
**Forms required:** FAFSA.
**Dates and Deadlines:** Priority date 3/15; no closing date. Applicants notified on a rolling basis starting 3/15.
**Transfers:** Massachusetts State Grant deadline May 1.

### CONTACT
Elizabeth Goreham, Executive Director of Enrollment Services
179 Longwood Avenue, Boston, MA 02115-5896
(617) 732-2864

## Merrimack College
North Andover, Massachusetts
www.merrimack.edu          Federal Code: 002120

**4-year private** business and liberal arts college in large town, affiliated with Roman Catholic Church.
**Enrollment:** 3,161 undergrads, 3% part-time. 828 full-time freshmen.
**Selectivity:** Admits over 75% of applicants.

### BASIC COSTS (2015-2016)
**Tuition and fees:** $37,270.
**Per-credit charge:** $1,270.
**Room and board:** $13,875.

### FINANCIAL AID PICTURE (2015-2016)
**Students with need:** Out of 696 full-time freshmen who applied for aid, 604 were judged to have need. Of these, 603 received aid, and 90 had their full need met. Average financial aid package met 62% of need; average scholarship/grant was $19,404; average loan was $3,378. For part-time students, average financial aid package was $6,548.
**Students without need:** 177 full-time freshmen who did not demonstrate need for aid received scholarships/grants; average award was $11,787. No-need awards available for academics, alumni affiliation, athletics, leadership, music/drama, religious affiliation.
**Scholarships offered:** 67 full-time freshmen received athletic scholarships; average amount $24,832.

### FINANCIAL AID PROCEDURES
**Forms required:** FAFSA.
**Dates and Deadlines:** Priority date 2/15; no closing date. Applicants notified by 3/15.
**Transfers:** Priority date 3/15; closing date 7/15. Applicants notified on a rolling basis; must reply within 2 week(s) of notification.

### CONTACT
Adrienne Montgomery, Director of Financial Aid
510 Turnpike Street, Suite 201, North Andover, MA 01845
(978) 837-5186

## Middlesex Community College
Bedford, Massachusetts
www.middlesex.mass.edu          Federal Code: 009936

**2-year public** community college in small city.
**Enrollment:** 8,353 undergrads, 60% part-time. 1,106 full-time freshmen.
**Selectivity:** Open admission; but selective for some programs.

### BASIC COSTS (2015-2016)
**Tuition and fees:** $5,580; out-of-state residents $11,760.
**Per-credit charge:** $181; out-of-state residents $387.
**Additional info:** Tuition/fee waivers available for adults.

## FINANCIAL AID PICTURE

**Students with need:** Need-based aid available for full-time and part-time students.

**Students without need:** This college awards aid only to students with need.

**Additional info:** Application priority date 5/1 for Massachusetts state funds.

## FINANCIAL AID PROCEDURES

**Forms required:** FAFSA, institutional form.

**Dates and Deadlines:** Priority date 5/1; no closing date. Applicants notified on a rolling basis starting 6/1; must reply within 2 week(s) of notification.

## CONTACT

Robert Baumel, Financial Aid Director
33 Kearney Square, Lowell, MA 01852-1987
(978) 656-3242

## Montserrat College of Art

Beverly, Massachusetts
www.montserrat.edu                    Federal Code: 013774

**4-year private** visual arts college in large town.
**Enrollment:** 378 undergrads.

## BASIC COSTS (2015-2016)

**Tuition and fees:** $29,550.
**Room only:** $8,600.

## FINANCIAL AID PICTURE

**Students with need:** Need-based aid available for full-time and part-time students. Work study available nights, weekends, and for part-time students.

**Students without need:** No-need awards available for academics, art.

**Scholarships offered:** Talent Awards: $5,000-$10,000; based on artistic and academic ability.

## FINANCIAL AID PROCEDURES

**Forms required:** FAFSA, institutional form.

**Dates and Deadlines:** Priority date 3/1; no closing date. Applicants notified on a rolling basis starting 3/1; must reply by 5/1 or within 2 week(s) of notification.

**Transfers:** No deadline. Applicants notified on a rolling basis starting 12/20; must reply within 2 week(s) of notification.

## CONTACT

Anne McDermott, Director of Financial Aid
23 Essex Street, Beverly, MA 01915
(978) 921-4242 ext. 1155

## Mount Holyoke College

South Hadley, Massachusetts     Federal Code: 002192
www.mtholyoke.edu                CSS Code: 3529

**4-year private** liberal arts college for women in large town.
**Enrollment:** 2,099 undergrads, 1% part-time. 512 full-time freshmen.
**Selectivity:** Admits 50 to 75% of applicants.

## BASIC COSTS (2015-2016)

**Tuition and fees:** $43,886.
**Per-credit charge:** $1,370.
**Room and board:** $12,860.

## FINANCIAL AID PICTURE (2015-2016)

**Students with need:** Out of 400 full-time freshmen who applied for aid, 336 were judged to have need. Of these, 336 received aid, and 336 had their full need met. Average financial aid package met 100% of need; average scholarship/grant was $32,332; average loan was $3,468. For part-time students, average financial aid package was $25,841.

---

**Students without need:** 66 full-time freshmen who did not demonstrate need for aid received scholarships/grants; average award was $19,312. No-need awards available for academics, leadership.

**Scholarships offered:** Scholarships are awarded competitively to first-year candidates and are renewable for up to eight (8) semesters with full-time status and good academic standing. Amounts range from $10,000 to full tuition. Scholarships are not transferrable to other institutions. Number awarded each year varies; approximately 25% of entering first year students are awarded merit-based awards.

## FINANCIAL AID PROCEDURES

**Forms required:** FAFSA, CSS PROFILE.

**Dates and Deadlines:** Priority date 2/15; closing date 3/1. Applicants notified by 4/1; must reply by 5/1.

**Transfers:** Closing date 5/15. Applicants notified on a rolling basis; must reply within 4 week(s) of notification.

## CONTACT

Kathy Blaisdell, Director of Student Financial Services
Newhall Center, South Hadley, MA 01075-1488
(413) 538-2291

## Mount Ida College

Newton, Massachusetts
www.mountida.edu                 Federal Code: 002193

**4-year private** business and liberal arts college in small city.
**Enrollment:** 1,290 undergrads.

## BASIC COSTS (2015-2016)

**Tuition and fees:** $32,300.
**Per-credit charge:** $875.
**Room and board:** $13,000.

## FINANCIAL AID PICTURE

**Students with need:** Need-based aid available for full-time and part-time students. Work study available nights.

## FINANCIAL AID PROCEDURES

**Forms required:** FAFSA, institutional form.

**Dates and Deadlines:** Priority date 4/15; no closing date. Applicants notified on a rolling basis starting 3/1; must reply within 3 week(s) of notification.

## CONTACT

Dyan Teehan, Director of Financial Aid
777 Dedham Street, Newton, MA 02459
(617) 928-4785

## Mount Wachusett Community College

Gardner, Massachusetts
www.mwcc.edu                     Federal Code: 002172

**2-year public** community college in large town.
**Enrollment:** 3,648 undergrads, 60% part-time. 503 full-time freshmen.
**Selectivity:** Open admission; but selective for some programs.

## BASIC COSTS (2015-2016)

**Tuition and fees:** $6,400; out-of-state residents $12,550.

## FINANCIAL AID PICTURE (2014-2015)

**Students with need:** Out of 482 full-time freshmen who applied for aid, 398 were judged to have need. Of these, 395 received aid, and 22 had their full need met. Average financial aid package met 96% of need; average scholarship/grant was $5,071; average loan was $1,787. For part-time students, average financial aid package was $4,052.

**Students without need:** This college awards aid only to students with need.

## FINANCIAL AID PROCEDURES

**Forms required:** FAFSA.

**Dates and Deadlines:** Priority date 5/1; no closing date. Applicants notified on a rolling basis starting 3/15; must reply within 2 week(s) of notification.

### CONTACT

Kelly Morrissey, Director, FInancial Aid
444 Green Street, Gardner, MA 01440-1000
(978) 632-6600 ext. 169

## New England Conservatory of Music
Boston, Massachusetts
www.necmusic.edu                    Federal Code: 002194

**4-year private** music college in very large city.

**Enrollment:** 381 undergrads, 4% part-time. 89 full-time freshmen.

**Selectivity:** Admits less than 50% of applicants.

### BASIC COSTS (2015-2016)

**Tuition and fees:** $43,055.

**Per-credit charge:** $1,365.

**Room and board:** $13,240.

### FINANCIAL AID PICTURE (2014-2015)

**Students with need:** Out of 55 full-time freshmen who applied for aid, 40 were judged to have need. Of these, 40 received aid, and 5 had their full need met. Average financial aid package met 56% of need; average scholarship/grant was $19,742; average loan was $4,366. For part-time students, average financial aid package was $12,129.

**Students without need:** 47 full-time freshmen who did not demonstrate need for aid received scholarships/grants; average award was $13,892. No-need awards available for academics, music/drama.

### FINANCIAL AID PROCEDURES

**Forms required:** FAFSA, institutional form.

**Dates and Deadlines:** Closing date 12/1. Applicants notified by 4/1; must reply by 5/1 or within 2 week(s) of notification.

### CONTACT

Lauren Urbanek, Director of Financial Aid
290 Huntington Avenue, Boston, MA 02115-5018
(617) 585-1110

## Newbury College
Brookline, Massachusetts
www.newbury.edu                    Federal Code: 007484

**4-year private** business and liberal arts college in large city.

**Enrollment:** 867 undergrads.

**Selectivity:** Admits over 75% of applicants.

### BASIC COSTS (2015-2016)

**Tuition and fees:** $31,408.

**Room and board:** $13,740.

### FINANCIAL AID PICTURE

**Students with need:** Need-based aid available for full-time and part-time students.

**Students without need:** This college awards aid only to students with need.

### FINANCIAL AID PROCEDURES

**Forms required:** FAFSA.

**Dates and Deadlines:** Priority date 3/1; closing date 5/1. Applicants notified on a rolling basis starting 3/1; must reply by 5/1 or within 2 week(s) of notification.

**Transfers:** No deadline. Applicants notified on a rolling basis starting 3/1; must reply by 5/1 or within 2 week(s) of notification.

### CONTACT

Jenny Aguiar, Director of Financial Aid
129 Fisher Avenue, Brookline, MA 02445
(617) 730-7100

## Nichols College
Dudley, Massachusetts
www.nichols.edu                    Federal Code: 002197

**4-year private** business and liberal arts college in rural community.

**Enrollment:** 1,256 undergrads, 8% part-time. 401 full-time freshmen.

**Selectivity:** Admits over 75% of applicants.

### BASIC COSTS (2015-2016)

**Tuition and fees:** $33,300.

**Room and board:** $12,600.

### FINANCIAL AID PICTURE (2014-2015)

**Students with need:** Out of 383 full-time freshmen who applied for aid, 337 were judged to have need. Of these, 337 received aid, and 63 had their full need met. Average financial aid package met 73% of need; average scholarship/grant was $17,842; average loan was $2,529. Need-based aid available for part-time students.

**Students without need:** 43 full-time freshmen who did not demonstrate need for aid received scholarships/grants; average award was $13,860. No-need awards available for academics, alumni affiliation, leadership, ROTC.

### FINANCIAL AID PROCEDURES

**Forms required:** FAFSA.

**Dates and Deadlines:** Priority date 3/1; closing date 6/1. Applicants notified on a rolling basis starting 2/26; must reply within 4 week(s) of notification.

**Transfers:** Applicants notified by 3/1; must reply within 4 week(s) of notification.

### CONTACT

Jennifer Bianco, Director of Financial Aid
PO Box 5000, Dudley, MA 01571-5000
(508) 213-2372

## North Shore Community College
Danvers, Massachusetts
www.northshore.edu                    Federal Code: 002173

**2-year public** community college in small city.

**Enrollment:** 6,197 undergrads, 61% part-time. 714 full-time freshmen.

**Selectivity:** Open admission; but selective for some programs.

### BASIC COSTS (2015-2016)

**Tuition and fees:** $6,420; out-of-state residents $13,380.

**Per-credit charge:** $25; out-of-state residents $257.

**Additional info:** Health Professions Programs have a 150.00 fee per semester. Culinary Arts programs have a 100.00 fee per semester.

### FINANCIAL AID PICTURE

**Students with need:** Need-based aid available for full-time and part-time students.

**Students without need:** This college awards aid only to students with need.

### FINANCIAL AID PROCEDURES

**Forms required:** FAFSA.

**Dates and Deadlines:** Priority date 4/15; no closing date. Applicants notified on a rolling basis starting 4/1; must reply within 2 week(s) of notification.

## CONTACT
Susan Sullivan, Director of Student Financial Services
One Ferncroft Road, Danvers, MA 01923-0840
(978) 762-4000

## Northeastern University
Boston, Massachusetts    Federal Code: 002199
www.northeastern.edu    CSS Code: 3667

**4-year private** university in very large city.
**Enrollment:** 17,913 undergrads. 2,797 full-time freshmen.
**Selectivity:** Admits less than 50% of applicants.

### BASIC COSTS (2015-2016)
**Tuition and fees:** $45,530.
**Room and board:** $15,000.

### FINANCIAL AID PICTURE (2015-2016)
**Students with need:** Out of 1,888 full-time freshmen who applied for aid, 1,243 were judged to have need. Of these, 1,243 received aid, and 1,243 had their full need met. Average financial aid package met 100% of need; average scholarship/grant was $32,339; average loan was $4,608.
**Students without need:** 660 full-time freshmen who did not demonstrate need for aid received scholarships/grants; average award was $20,411. No-need awards available for academics, athletics, leadership, ROTC.
**Scholarships offered:** 59 full-time freshmen received athletic scholarships; average amount $33,439.

### FINANCIAL AID PROCEDURES
**Forms required:** FAFSA, CSS PROFILE.
**Dates and Deadlines:** Priority date 2/15; no closing date. Applicants notified by 4/1; must reply by 5/1.
**Transfers:** Priority date 5/1; no deadline. Applicants notified on a rolling basis.

### CONTACT
Anthony Erwin, Dean of Student Financial Services
200 Kerr Hall, Boston, MA 02115
(617) 373-3190

## Northern Essex Community College
Haverhill, Massachusetts
www.necc.mass.edu    Federal Code: 002174

**2-year public** community and junior college in small city.
**Enrollment:** 6,010 undergrads, 63% part-time. 753 full-time freshmen.
**Selectivity:** Open admission; but selective for some programs.

### BASIC COSTS (2015-2016)
**Tuition and fees:** $5,700; out-of-state residents $12,930.
**Per-credit charge:** $25; out-of-state residents $266.

### FINANCIAL AID PICTURE
**Students with need:** Need-based aid available for full-time and part-time students.
**Students without need:** No-need awards available for academics.

### FINANCIAL AID PROCEDURES
**Forms required:** FAFSA, institutional form.
**Dates and Deadlines:** Priority date 5/1; no closing date. Must reply within 2 week(s) of notification.

### CONTACT
Alexis Fishbone, Director of Financial Aid
100 Elliott Street, Haverhill, MA 01830-2399
(978) 556-3600

## Northpoint Bible College
Haverhill, Massachusetts
www.northpoint.edu    Federal Code: 035705

**4-year private** Bible college in small city, affiliated with Assemblies of God.
**Enrollment:** 234 undergrads, 15% part-time. 39 full-time freshmen.

### BASIC COSTS (2015-2016)
**Tuition and fees:** $11,150.
**Per-credit charge:** $335.
**Room and board:** $8,350.

### FINANCIAL AID PICTURE (2015-2016)
**Students with need:** 37% of average financial aid package awarded as scholarships/grants, 63% awarded as loans/jobs. Need-based aid available for part-time students.
**Students without need:** No-need awards available for academics, leadership, minority status, music/drama, state/district residency.

### FINANCIAL AID PROCEDURES
**Forms required:** FAFSA.
**Dates and Deadlines:** Priority date 6/1; no closing date. Applicants notified on a rolling basis; must reply within 4 week(s) of notification.

### CONTACT
Patricia Stauffer, Financial Aid Director
320 South Main Street, Haverhill, MA 01835
(978) 478-3470

## Pine Manor College
Chestnut Hill, Massachusetts
www.pmc.edu    Federal Code: 002201

**4-year private** liberal arts college in very large city.
**Enrollment:** 354 undergrads, 3% part-time. 96 full-time freshmen.
**Selectivity:** Admits 50 to 75% of applicants.

### BASIC COSTS (2015-2016)
**Tuition and fees:** $27,105.
**Room and board:** $12,890.

### FINANCIAL AID PICTURE
**Students with need:** Need-based aid available for full-time and part-time students. Work study available nights, weekends, and for part-time students.
**Students without need:** No-need awards available for academics, alumni affiliation, leadership.

### FINANCIAL AID PROCEDURES
**Forms required:** FAFSA.
**Dates and Deadlines:** Priority date 5/1; no closing date. Applicants notified on a rolling basis starting 4/1; must reply by 5/1 or within 2 week(s) of notification.
**Transfers:** No deadline. Applicants notified on a rolling basis starting 3/1; must reply by 5/1 or within 2 week(s) of notification.

### CONTACT
Elizabeth Gorra
400 Heath Street, Chestnut Hill, MA 02467
(617) 731-7000

## Quinsigamond Community College
Worcester, Massachusetts
www.qcc.edu    Federal Code: 002175

**2-year public** community college in small city.
**Enrollment:** 7,224 undergrads, 60% part-time. 931 full-time freshmen.

Selectivity: Open admission; but selective for some programs.

## BASIC COSTS (2015-2016)

Tuition and fees: $6,540; out-of-state residents $12,720.
Per-credit charge: $24; out-of-state residents $230.

## FINANCIAL AID PICTURE (2014-2015)

Students with need: 65% of average financial aid package awarded as scholarships/grants, 35% awarded as loans/jobs. Need-based aid available for part-time students. Work study available nights, weekends, and for part-time students.

Students without need: No-need awards available for academics, leadership, minority status.

Additional info: All Pell Grant eligible students applying by May 1 will receive enough grant aid to cover tuition, fees and books.

## FINANCIAL AID PROCEDURES

Forms required: FAFSA.

Dates and Deadlines: Priority date 4/1; no closing date. Applicants notified on a rolling basis starting 4/1.

## CONTACT

Karen Grant, Director of Financial Aid
670 West Boylston Street, Worcester, MA 01606
(508) 854-4261

## Regis College

Weston, Massachusetts
www.regiscollege.edu              Federal Code: 002206

4-year private health science and liberal arts college in large town, affiliated with Roman Catholic Church.

Enrollment: 1,235 undergrads, 22% part-time. 269 full-time freshmen.
Selectivity: Admits over 75% of applicants.

## BASIC COSTS (2015-2016)

Tuition and fees: $37,540.
Per-credit charge: $1,251.
Room and board: $14,380.

## FINANCIAL AID PICTURE (2015-2016)

Students with need: Out of 257 full-time freshmen who applied for aid, 240 were judged to have need. Of these, 240 received aid, and 43 had their full need met. Average financial aid package met 60% of need; average scholarship/grant was $21,525; average loan was $3,361. For part-time students, average financial aid package was $6,454.

Students without need: 26 full-time freshmen who did not demonstrate need for aid received scholarships/grants; average award was $11,367. No-need awards available for academics, alumni affiliation.

Additional info: Family tuition discount scholarship offered during any semester in which 2 or more unmarried, dependent siblings attend as full-time undergraduates.

## FINANCIAL AID PROCEDURES

Forms required: FAFSA.
Dates and Deadlines: Priority date 2/15; no closing date. Applicants notified on a rolling basis starting 3/15.
Transfers: No deadline. Applicants notified on a rolling basis.

## CONTACT

Bonnie Quinn, Director of Financial Aid
235 Wellesley Street, Weston, MA 02493-1571
(781) 768-7180

## Roxbury Community College

Roxbury Crossing, Massachusetts
www.rcc.mass.edu              Federal Code: 011930

2-year public community college in very large city.
Enrollment: 2,216 undergrads.
Selectivity: Open admission; but selective for some programs.

## BASIC COSTS (2015-2016)

Tuition and fees: $4,980; out-of-state residents $11,610.
Per-credit charge: $26; out-of-state residents $387.

## FINANCIAL AID PICTURE

Students with need: Need-based aid available for full-time and part-time students.
Students without need: This college awards aid only to students with need.

## FINANCIAL AID PROCEDURES

Forms required: FAFSA, institutional form.
Dates and Deadlines: Closing date 5/1. Applicants notified on a rolling basis starting 6/15; must reply within 2 week(s) of notification.

## CONTACT

Ray O'Rourke, Director of Financial Aid
1234 Columbus Avenue, Roxbury Crossing, MA 02120-3400
(617) 541-5322

## Salem State University

Salem, Massachusetts
www.salemstate.edu              Federal Code: 002188

4-year public university in large town.
Enrollment: 7,134 undergrads.

## BASIC COSTS (2015-2016)

Tuition and fees: $9,246; out-of-state residents $15,386.
Per-credit charge: $38; out-of-state residents $294.
Room and board: $12,464.

## FINANCIAL AID PICTURE

Students with need: Need-based aid available for full-time and part-time students. Work study available nights, weekends, and for part-time students.
Students without need: No-need awards available for academics.

## FINANCIAL AID PROCEDURES

Forms required: FAFSA.
Dates and Deadlines: Priority date 3/1; closing date 9/1. Applicants notified on a rolling basis starting 3/15; must reply within 2 week(s) of notification.

## CONTACT

Judy Cramer, Director of Financial Aid
352 Lafayette Street, Salem, MA 01970-5353
(978) 542-6112

## School of the Museum of Fine Arts

Boston, Massachusetts
www.smfa.edu              Federal Code: 004667

4-year private visual arts college in very large city.
Enrollment: 278 undergrads, 11% part-time. 34 full-time freshmen.
Selectivity: Admits over 75% of applicants.

## BASIC COSTS (2015-2016)

Tuition and fees: $41,228.
Room only: $10,950.

## FINANCIAL AID PICTURE (2015-2016)
**Students with need:** Average financial aid package met 46% of need; average scholarship/grant was $5,591; average loan was $4,452. For part-time students, average financial aid package was $17,647.
**Students without need:** No-need awards available for academics, art.

## FINANCIAL AID PROCEDURES
**Forms required:** FAFSA.
**Dates and Deadlines:** Closing date 3/15. Applicants notified on a rolling basis starting 4/1; must reply by 5/1 or within 2 week(s) of notification.

## CONTACT
Shaun Thomas, Director of Financial Aid
230 The Fenway, Boston, MA 02115
(800) 776-0135

## Simmons College
Boston, Massachusetts
www.simmons.edu                    Federal Code: 002208

**4-year private** health science and liberal arts college for women in very large city.
**Enrollment:** 1,706 undergrads, 6% part-time. 471 full-time freshmen.
**Selectivity:** Admits 50 to 75% of applicants.

## BASIC COSTS (2015-2016)
**Tuition and fees:** $37,380.
**Room and board:** $14,040.

## FINANCIAL AID PICTURE (2015-2016)
**Students with need:** Out of 411 full-time freshmen who applied for aid, 368 were judged to have need. Of these, 368 received aid, and 54 had their full need met. Average financial aid package met 77% of need; average scholarship/grant was $27,573; average loan was $3,105. For part-time students, average financial aid package was $17,193.
**Students without need:** 95 full-time freshmen who did not demonstrate need for aid received scholarships/grants; average award was $16,292. No-need awards available for academics, alumni affiliation.

## FINANCIAL AID PROCEDURES
**Forms required:** FAFSA, institutional form.
**Dates and Deadlines:** Priority date 3/1; no closing date. Applicants notified on a rolling basis starting 3/15.
**Transfers:** No deadline. Applicants notified on a rolling basis starting 3/15.

## CONTACT
Heather Patenaude, Director of Student Financial Services
300 The Fenway, Boston, MA 02115-5898
(617) 521-2001

## Smith College
Northampton, Massachusetts          Federal Code: 002209
www.smith.edu                       CSS Code: 3762

**4-year private** liberal arts college for women in large town.
**Enrollment:** 2,473 undergrads, 1% part-time. 609 full-time freshmen.
**Selectivity:** Admits less than 50% of applicants.

## BASIC COSTS (2015-2016)
**Tuition and fees:** $46,288.
**Per-credit charge:** $1,440.
**Room and board:** $15,470.

## FINANCIAL AID PICTURE (2015-2016)
**Students with need:** Average financial aid package met 100% of need; average scholarship/grant was $41,802; average loan was $3,289. For part-time students, average financial aid package was $29,388.

**Students without need:** No-need awards available for academics, state/district residency.
**Scholarships offered:** Zollman Scholarships: $20,000; for academic excellence; about 15 awarded. STRIDE scholarship: $15,000; about 50 awarded. Springfield/Holyoke Partnership: full-tuition; for academic excellence in Springfield or Holyoke public high schools; up to 4 awarded.
**Additional info:** Financial aid policy guarantees to meet full financial need, as calculated by college, of all admitted students who have met application deadlines.

## FINANCIAL AID PROCEDURES
**Forms required:** FAFSA, CSS PROFILE, institutional form.
**Dates and Deadlines:** Closing date 2/15. Applicants notified by 4/1; must reply by 5/1.
**Transfers:** Priority date 2/15; closing date 4/1. Applicants notified by 4/1; must reply by 5/1. Applicants who apply after admission decision is made cannot receive college aid until they complete at least 32 credits at Smith.

## CONTACT
David Belanger, Director of Student Financial Services
7 College Lane, Northampton, MA 01063
(413) 585-2530

## Springfield College
Springfield, Massachusetts
www.springfieldcollege.edu          Federal Code: 002211

**4-year private** health science and liberal arts college in small city.
**Enrollment:** 2,138 undergrads. 546 full-time freshmen.

## BASIC COSTS (2015-2016)
**Tuition and fees:** $34,455.
**Room and board:** $13,410.

## FINANCIAL AID PICTURE (2015-2016)
**Students with need:** Out of 512 full-time freshmen who applied for aid, 450 were judged to have need. Of these, 450 received aid, and 39 had their full need met. Average financial aid package met 78% of need; average scholarship/grant was $22,834; average loan was $3,166. For part-time students, average financial aid package was $21,084.
**Students without need:** 76 full-time freshmen who did not demonstrate need for aid received scholarships/grants; average award was $10,462. No-need awards available for academics, alumni affiliation, art, leadership, minority status, music/drama, state/district residency.

## FINANCIAL AID PROCEDURES
**Forms required:** FAFSA, institutional form.
**Dates and Deadlines:** Priority date 3/15; no closing date. Applicants notified on a rolling basis starting 2/7; must reply within 2 week(s) of notification.
**Transfers:** Priority date 5/1. Applicants notified on a rolling basis starting 5/1; must reply by 6/1 or within 2 week(s) of notification.

## CONTACT
Edward Ciosek, Director of Financial Aid
263 Alden Street, Springfield, MA 01109
(413) 748-3108

## Springfield Technical Community College
Springfield, Massachusetts
www.stcc.edu                        Federal Code: 005549

**2-year public** community and technical college in small city.
**Enrollment:** 5,658 undergrads, 53% part-time. 925 full-time freshmen.
**Selectivity:** Open admission; but selective for some programs.

PART III: FINANCIAL AID COLLEGE BY COLLEGE

**BASIC COSTS (2015-2016)**
**Tuition and fees:** $5,436; out-of-state residents $11,946.
**Per-credit charge:** $25; out-of-state residents $242.
**Additional info:** New England reciprocal annual tuition and fees $5811.

**FINANCIAL AID PICTURE (2014-2015)**
**Students with need:** 77% of average financial aid package awarded as scholarships/grants, 23% awarded as loans/jobs. Need-based aid available for part-time students.

**FINANCIAL AID PROCEDURES**
**Forms required:** FAFSA.
**Dates and Deadlines:** Priority date 5/1; no closing date. Applicants notified on a rolling basis starting 4/1.

**CONTACT**
Jeremy Greenhouse, Director of Financial Aid
One Armory Square, Springfield, MA 01102-9000
(413) 755-4214

## Stonehill College
Easton, Massachusetts
www.stonehill.edu
Federal Code: 002217
CSS Code: 3770

**4-year private** liberal arts college in large town, affiliated with Roman Catholic Church.
**Enrollment:** 2,481 undergrads. 656 full-time freshmen.
**Selectivity:** Admits over 75% of applicants.

**BASIC COSTS (2015-2016)**
**Tuition and fees:** $38,550.
**Per-credit charge:** $1,285.
**Room and board:** $14,720.
**Additional info:** Tuition/fee waivers available for minority students, unemployed or children of unemployed.

**FINANCIAL AID PICTURE (2015-2016)**
**Students with need:** Out of 556 full-time freshmen who applied for aid, 429 were judged to have need. Of these, 429 received aid, and 215 had their full need met. Average financial aid package met 92% of need; average scholarship/grant was $25,498; average loan was $3,679. For part-time students, average financial aid package was $11,229.
**Students without need:** 207 full-time freshmen who did not demonstrate need for aid received scholarships/grants; average award was $17,439. No-need awards available for academics, athletics, leadership, ROTC.
**Scholarships offered:** *Merit:* Moreau Honors Scholarship: $25,000. Shields Merit Scholars Program: $8,000-$10,000. Novak/Sakmar/Templeton Scholarship: $2,500-$10,000. Presidential Scholarship: $16,000-$20,000. Dean's Scholarship: $12,000-$14,000. Stonehill Scholarship: $5,000-$10,000. *Athletic:* 13 full-time freshmen received athletic scholarships; average amount $13,471.

**FINANCIAL AID PROCEDURES**
**Forms required:** FAFSA, CSS PROFILE.
**Dates and Deadlines:** Priority date 12/1; closing date 2/1. Applicants notified by 4/1; must reply by 5/1.
**Transfers:** Closing date 4/1. Applicants notified by 5/25. For transfer students who qualify, merit scholarships and need based aid are provided as aid availability allows.

**CONTACT**
Eileen O'Leary, Assistant Vice President for Finance/Director of Student Aid and Finance
320 Washington Street, Easton, MA 02357-0100
(508) 565-1088

## Suffolk University
Boston, Massachusetts
www.suffolk.edu
Federal Code: 002218

**4-year private** university in very large city.
**Enrollment:** 5,454 undergrads, 5% part-time. 1,371 full-time freshmen.
**Selectivity:** Admits over 75% of applicants.

**BASIC COSTS (2015-2016)**
**Tuition and fees:** $33,934.
**Per-credit charge:** $829.
**Room and board:** $14,648.

**FINANCIAL AID PICTURE (2015-2016)**
**Students with need:** Out of 971 full-time freshmen who applied for aid, 876 were judged to have need. Of these, 876 received aid, and 104 had their full need met. Average financial aid package met 69% of need; average scholarship/grant was $9,604; average loan was $3,463. For part-time students, average financial aid package was $14,890.
**Students without need:** 391 full-time freshmen who did not demonstrate need for aid received scholarships/grants; average award was $14,307. No-need awards available for academics, alumni affiliation.
**Scholarships offered:** Various scholarships; amounts vary; based on academic achievement, talent, and contribution to applicant's school and community.
**Additional info:** Foreign students may apply for institutional employment awards.

**FINANCIAL AID PROCEDURES**
**Forms required:** FAFSA.
**Dates and Deadlines:** Closing date 3/1. Applicants notified on a rolling basis starting 2/5; must reply by 5/1 or within 2 week(s) of notification.

**CONTACT**
Christine Perry, Director of Financial Aid
8 Ashburton Place, Boston, MA 02108
(617) 573-8470

## Tufts University
Medford, Massachusetts
www.tufts.edu
Federal Code: 002219
CSS Code: 3901

**4-year private** university in small city.
**Enrollment:** 5,236 undergrads, 1% part-time. 1,360 full-time freshmen.
**Selectivity:** Admits less than 50% of applicants.

**BASIC COSTS (2015-2016)**
**Tuition and fees:** $50,604.
**Room and board:** $13,094.

**FINANCIAL AID PICTURE (2015-2016)**
**Students with need:** Out of 665 full-time freshmen who applied for aid, 513 were judged to have need. Of these, 496 received aid, and 496 had their full need met. Average financial aid package met 100% of need; average scholarship/grant was $40,048; average loan was $2,459. For part-time students, average financial aid package was $35,664.
**Students without need:** This college awards aid only to students with need.
**Scholarships offered:** National Merit Scholarships: $500 for non-need; $2,000 for need.
**Additional info:** Students from families with incomes less than $60,000 receive aid awards in which student loans are replaced by grants.

**FINANCIAL AID PROCEDURES**
**Forms required:** FAFSA, CSS PROFILE.
**Dates and Deadlines:** Closing date 2/15. Applicants notified by 4/1; must reply by 5/1.

**Transfers:** Closing date 3/15. Applicants notified by 6/1; must reply within 2 week(s) of notification.

**CONTACT**

Patricia Reilly, Director of Financial Aid

Bendetson Hall, Medford, MA 02155

(617) 627-2000

# University of Massachusetts Amherst

Amherst, Massachusetts

www.umass.edu                                    Federal Code: 002221

**4-year public** university in large town.

**Enrollment:** 22,405 undergrads, 6% part-time. 4,691 full-time freshmen.

**Selectivity:** Admits 50 to 75% of applicants.

**BASIC COSTS (2015-2016)**

**Tuition and fees:** $14,356; out-of-state residents $30,689.

**Per-credit charge:** $72; out-of-state residents $414.

**Room and board:** $12,028.

**FINANCIAL AID PICTURE (2014-2015)**

**Students with need:** Out of 4,143 full-time freshmen who applied for aid, 2,718 were judged to have need. Of these, 2,661 received aid, and 376 had their full need met. Average financial aid package met 81% of need; average scholarship/grant was $10,480; average loan was $3,685. For part-time students, average financial aid package was $9,622.

**Students without need:** 749 full-time freshmen who did not demonstrate need for aid received scholarships/grants; average award was $5,904. No-need awards available for academics, art, athletics, music/drama, state/district residency.

**Scholarships offered:** *Merit:* Merit scholarships: all applicants automatically considered. *Athletic:* 52 full-time freshmen received athletic scholarships; average amount $22,625.

**FINANCIAL AID PROCEDURES**

**Forms required:** FAFSA.

**Dates and Deadlines:** Priority date 3/1; no closing date. Applicants notified on a rolling basis starting 4/1; must reply by 5/1 or within 2 week(s) of notification.

**CONTACT**

Suzanne Peters, Director of Financial Aid

University Admissions Center, Amherst, MA 01003-9291

(413) 545-0801

# University of Massachusetts Boston

Boston, Massachusetts

www.umb.edu                                    Federal Code: 002222

**4-year public** university in very large city.

**Enrollment:** 12,397 undergrads, 25% part-time. 1,438 full-time freshmen.

**Selectivity:** Admits 50 to 75% of applicants.

**BASIC COSTS (2015-2016)**

**Tuition and fees:** $12,682; out-of-state residents $29,920.

**Per-credit charge:** $72; out-of-state residents $407.

**FINANCIAL AID PICTURE (2014-2015)**

**Students with need:** Out of 1,060 full-time freshmen who applied for aid, 929 were judged to have need. Of these, 929 received aid, and 514 had their full need met. Average financial aid package met 90% of need; average scholarship/grant was $9,909; average loan was $3,077. For part-time students, average financial aid package was $11,222.

**Students without need:** 82 full-time freshmen who did not demonstrate need for aid received scholarships/grants; average award was $6,756. No-need awards available for academics, leadership, state/district residency.

**Additional info:** Some Massachusetts state employees and Massachusetts Vietnam veterans eligible for tuition waiver. Some waivers available based on talent and academic excellence.

**FINANCIAL AID PROCEDURES**

**Forms required:** FAFSA.

**Dates and Deadlines:** Priority date 3/1; no closing date. Applicants notified on a rolling basis starting 3/6.

**CONTACT**

Judy Keyes, Director of Financial Aid Services

100 Morrissey Boulevard, Boston, MA 02125-3393

(617) 287-6300

# University of Massachusetts Dartmouth

Dartmouth, Massachusetts

www.umassd.edu                                    Federal Code: 002210

**4-year public** university in large town.

**Enrollment:** 7,054 undergrads, 12% part-time. 1,416 full-time freshmen.

**Selectivity:** Admits over 75% of applicants.

**BASIC COSTS (2015-2016)**

**Tuition and fees:** $12,588; out-of-state residents $26,173.

**Per-credit charge:** $59; out-of-state residents $337.

**Room and board:** $11,622.

**FINANCIAL AID PICTURE (2015-2016)**

**Students with need:** Out of 1,278 full-time freshmen who applied for aid, 1,071 were judged to have need. Of these, 1,071 received aid, and 436 had their full need met. Average financial aid package met 87% of need; average scholarship/grant was $9,351; average loan was $3,264. For part-time students, average financial aid package was $10,775.

**Students without need:** 131 full-time freshmen who did not demonstrate need for aid received scholarships/grants; average award was $3,948. No-need awards available for academics, minority status, ROTC, state/district residency.

**Scholarships offered:** Chancellor's Merit Scholarship: approximately $2,000; for Massachusetts high school seniors with 1200 SAT (exclusive of Writing) and minimum 3.30 High School GPA; 50 awarded. Solveig E.J. Balestracci Scholarship: $1,000; for academic achievement in marine-related area for residents of New Bedford, Dartmouth, Acushnet, Westport, Mattapoisett, Marion, Rochester or Lakeville; 1 awarded. Boivon Scholarship: $1,000; based on academic involvement in French language and culture. A.J. Carvalho Memorial Scholarship: approximately $5,000; for New Bedford graduates of Portuguese descent with 3.0 GPA. Cranston Foundation Scholarship: $500; for students in the Bioengineering Department.

**FINANCIAL AID PROCEDURES**

**Forms required:** FAFSA.

**Dates and Deadlines:** Priority date 3/1; no closing date.

**CONTACT**

Audra Callahan, Director of Financial Aid

285 Old Westport Road, Dartmouth, MA 02747-2300

(508) 999-8643

# University of Massachusetts Lowell

Lowell, Massachusetts

www.uml.edu                                    Federal Code: 002161

**4-year public** university in small city.

**Enrollment:** 12,494 undergrads, 23% part-time. 1,633 full-time freshmen.

**Selectivity:** Admits 50 to 75% of applicants.

**BASIC COSTS (2015-2016)**
**Tuition and fees:** $13,427; out-of-state residents $20,540.
**Per-credit charge:** $61; out-of-state residents $357.
**Room and board:** $11,670.
**Additional info:** The required fees above or In-State students are $11973. The required fees for Out of State students are $20,558.

**FINANCIAL AID PICTURE (2014-2015)**
**Students with need:** Out of 1,412 full-time freshmen who applied for aid, 1,019 were judged to have need. Of these, 1,019 received aid, and 504 had their full need met. Average financial aid package met 90% of need; average scholarship/grant was $9,343; average loan was $3,438. For part-time students, average financial aid package was $9,720.
**Students without need:** 290 full-time freshmen who did not demonstrate need for aid received scholarships/grants; average award was $4,501. No-need awards available for academics, alumni affiliation, art, athletics, leadership, minority status, music/drama, ROTC, state/district residency.
**Scholarships offered:** 63 full-time freshmen received athletic scholarships; average amount $11,266.

**FINANCIAL AID PROCEDURES**
**Forms required:** FAFSA.
**Dates and Deadlines:** Priority date 3/1; no closing date. Applicants notified on a rolling basis starting 3/21.
**Transfers:** Applicants notified on a rolling basis starting 3/20.

**CONTACT**
Joyce McLaughlin, Director of Financial Aid
University Crossing, Suite 420, 220 Pawtucket Street, Lowell, MA 01854-2874
(978) 934-4220

## Urban College of Boston
Boston, Massachusetts
www.urbancollege.edu            Federal Code: 031305

**2-year private** community college in very large city.
**Enrollment:** 405 undergrads.
**Selectivity:** Open admission.

**BASIC COSTS (2015-2016)**
**Tuition and fees:** $8,900.

**FINANCIAL AID PICTURE**
**Students with need:** Need-based aid available for full-time and part-time students.
**Students without need:** This college awards aid only to students with need.

**FINANCIAL AID PROCEDURES**
**Forms required:** FAFSA.
**Dates and Deadlines:** Priority date 12/10; no closing date. Applicants notified on a rolling basis starting 4/15.

**CONTACT**
Mia Taylor, Director of Financial Aid
178 Tremont Street, Seventh Floor, Boston, MA 02111
(617) 348-6220

## Wellesley College
Wellesley, Massachusetts            Federal Code: 002224
www.wellesley.edu            CSS Code: 3957

**4-year private** liberal arts college for women in large town.
**Enrollment:** 2,188 undergrads. 593 full-time freshmen.
**Selectivity:** Admits less than 50% of applicants.

**BASIC COSTS (2015-2016)**
**Tuition and fees:** $46,836.
**Room and board:** $14,504.

**FINANCIAL AID PICTURE (2015-2016)**
**Students with need:** Average financial aid package met 100% of need; average scholarship/grant was $46,277; average loan was $2,678. Need-based aid available for part-time students.
**Students without need:** This college awards aid only to students with need.
**Additional info:** No student will graduate with more than $12,825 in packaged student loans. Students from families with a calculated income between $60,000 and $100,000 will graduate with no more than $8,600 in packaged student loans. Students from families with the greatest need ($60,000 income or less) will graduate with $0 in packaged student loans; their packages will consist of scholarship and work-study money.

**FINANCIAL AID PROCEDURES**
**Forms required:** FAFSA, CSS PROFILE.
**Dates and Deadlines:** Priority date 2/15; no closing date. Applicants notified by 4/1; must reply by 5/1.
**Transfers:** Closing date 3/1.

**CONTACT**
Scott Juedes, Director of Student Financial Services
106 Central Street, Wellesley, MA 02481-8203
(781) 283-2360

## Wentworth Institute of Technology
Boston, Massachusetts
www.wit.edu            Federal Code: 002225

**4-year private** engineering and technical college in very large city.
**Enrollment:** 4,288 undergrads, 9% part-time. 961 full-time freshmen.
**Selectivity:** Admits 50 to 75% of applicants.

**BASIC COSTS (2015-2016)**
**Tuition and fees:** $30,760.
**Per-credit charge:** $960.
**Room and board:** $13,390.

**FINANCIAL AID PICTURE (2015-2016)**
**Students with need:** Out of 875 full-time freshmen who applied for aid, 776 were judged to have need. Of these, 776 received aid, and 62 had their full need met. For part-time students, average financial aid package was $8,278.
**Students without need:** 243 full-time freshmen who did not demonstrate need for aid received scholarships/grants; average award was $8,751. No-need awards available for academics, leadership, ROTC, state/district residency.
**Scholarships offered:** Applicants for admission automatically considered for merit scholarships.

**FINANCIAL AID PROCEDURES**
**Forms required:** FAFSA.
**Dates and Deadlines:** Priority date 3/1; no closing date. Applicants notified on a rolling basis starting 3/15; must reply within 2 week(s) of notification.
**Transfers:** Review of NSLDS history within 30 days of beginning of enrollment required.

**CONTACT**
Anne-Marie Caruso, Director of Financial Aid
550 Huntington Avenue, Boston, MA 02115
(617) 989-4020

## Western New England University

Springfield, Massachusetts
www.wne.edu                          Federal Code: 002226

4-year private university in small city.
**Enrollment:** 2,726 undergrads, 5% part-time. 719 full-time freshmen.
**Selectivity:** Admits over 75% of applicants.

### BASIC COSTS (2015-2016)
**Tuition and fees:** $34,030.
**Per-credit charge:** $598.
**Room and board:** $12,896.

### FINANCIAL AID PICTURE (2015-2016)
**Students with need:** Out of 662 full-time freshmen who applied for aid, 600 were judged to have need. Of these, 600 received aid, and 69 had their full need met. Average financial aid package met 74% of need; average scholarship/grant was $20,850; average loan was $3,778. For part-time students, average financial aid package was $6,920.
**Students without need:** 89 full-time freshmen who did not demonstrate need for aid received scholarships/grants; average award was $13,671. No-need awards available for academics, music/drama, ROTC.

### FINANCIAL AID PROCEDURES
**Forms required:** FAFSA.
**Dates and Deadlines:** Priority date 4/15; no closing date. Applicants notified on a rolling basis starting 3/1; must reply by 5/1 or within 2 week(s) of notification.
**Transfers:** No deadline. Applicants notified on a rolling basis starting 3/1; must reply by 5/1 or within 2 week(s) of notification.

### CONTACT
Kathy Chambers
1215 Wilbraham Road, Springfield, MA 01119-2684
(800) 325-1122 ext. 2080

## Westfield State University

Westfield, Massachusetts
www.westfield.ma.edu                 Federal Code: 002189

4-year public university in large town.
**Enrollment:** 5,459 undergrads, 10% part-time. 1,220 full-time freshmen.
**Selectivity:** Admits over 75% of applicants.

### BASIC COSTS (2015-2016)
**Tuition and fees:** $8,815; out-of-state residents $14,895.
**Per-credit charge:** $280.
**Room and board:** $10,691.
**Additional info:** Tuition for New England Regional Program: $1,455.

### FINANCIAL AID PICTURE (2014-2015)
**Students with need:** Out of 1,157 full-time freshmen who applied for aid, 819 were judged to have need. Of these, 805 received aid, and 76 had their full need met. Average financial aid package met 60% of need; average scholarship/grant was $5,770; average loan was $3,162. Need-based aid available for part-time students.
**Students without need:** 10 full-time freshmen who did not demonstrate need for aid received scholarships/grants; average award was $4,021. No-need awards available for academics.

### FINANCIAL AID PROCEDURES
**Forms required:** FAFSA.
**Dates and Deadlines:** Priority date 3/1; no closing date. Applicants notified on a rolling basis starting 4/1; must reply within 2 week(s) of notification.
**Transfers:** Priority date 3/1; no deadline. Applicants notified on a rolling basis starting 4/1.

### CONTACT
Catherine Ryan, Director of Financial Aid
577 Western Avenue, Westfield, MA 01086-1630
(413) 572-5218

## Wheaton College

Norton, Massachusetts                Federal Code: 002227
www.wheatoncollege.edu               CSS Code: 3963

4-year private liberal arts college in large town.
**Enrollment:** 1,565 undergrads. 417 full-time freshmen.
**Selectivity:** Admits 50 to 75% of applicants.

### BASIC COSTS (2015-2016)
**Tuition and fees:** $47,700.
**Room and board:** $12,165.

### FINANCIAL AID PICTURE (2015-2016)
**Students with need:** Out of 332 full-time freshmen who applied for aid, 282 were judged to have need. Of these, 282 received aid, and 127 had their full need met. Average financial aid package met 93% of need; average scholarship/grant was $33,905; average loan was $3,953. Need-based aid available for part-time students.
**Students without need:** 98 full-time freshmen who did not demonstrate need for aid received scholarships/grants; average award was $12,906. No-need awards available for academics.
**Scholarships offered:** Balfour Scholarship, Trustee Scholarship, and Community and Regional Scholarship: award amounts vary (up to $20,000) and are renewable annually throughout a student's academic career; available to applicants selected from the top 30% of the applicant pool in recognition of high academic achievement, regardless of financial need.

### FINANCIAL AID PROCEDURES
**Forms required:** FAFSA, CSS PROFILE.
**Dates and Deadlines:** Closing date 2/1. Applicants notified by 4/1; must reply by 5/1.
**Transfers:** Closing date 4/1. Applicants notified on a rolling basis; must reply by 6/1. Financial aid for admitted (transfer) students is determined based on a combined assessment of financial eligibility and the overall academic strength of the candidate.

### CONTACT
Robin Randall, Assistant Vice President for Enrollment and Student Financial Services
26 East Main Street, Norton, MA 02766
(508) 286-8232

## Wheelock College

Boston, Massachusetts
www.wheelock.edu                     Federal Code: 002228

4-year private liberal arts and teachers college in very large city.
**Enrollment:** 809 undergrads, 1% part-time. 216 full-time freshmen.
**Selectivity:** Admits over 75% of applicants.

### BASIC COSTS (2015-2016)
**Tuition and fees:** $33,835.
**Per-credit charge:** $1,020.
**Room and board:** $14,000.

### FINANCIAL AID PICTURE (2015-2016)
**Students with need:** Out of 197 full-time freshmen who applied for aid, 185 were judged to have need. Of these, 185 received aid, and 24 had their full need met. Average financial aid package met 67% of need; average scholarship/grant was $23,325; average loan was $3,373. For part-time students, average financial aid package was $8,994.

**Students without need:** 28 full-time freshmen who did not demonstrate need for aid received scholarships/grants; average award was $13,428. No-need awards available for academics, leadership, state/district residency.
**Scholarships offered:** Dean's and Merit Scholarships: $13,000-$17,000; granted to all first-year students based on GPA and SAT/ACT scores.

**FINANCIAL AID PROCEDURES**
**Forms required:** FAFSA.
**Dates and Deadlines:** Priority date 2/15; no closing date. Applicants notified on a rolling basis starting 3/1; must reply by 5/1.
**Transfers:** Priority date 4/15. Applicants notified on a rolling basis starting 4/1.

**CONTACT**
Roxanne Dumas, Director of Financial Aid
200 The Riverway, Boston, MA 02215-4104
(617) 879-2443

## Williams College
Williamstown, Massachusetts — Federal Code: 002229
www.williams.edu — CSS Code: 3965

**4-year private** liberal arts college in small town.
**Enrollment:** 2,065 undergrads. 551 full-time freshmen.
**Selectivity:** Admits less than 50% of applicants.

**BASIC COSTS (2015-2016)**
**Tuition and fees:** $50,070.
**Room and board:** $13,220.

**FINANCIAL AID PICTURE (2015-2016)**
**Students with need:** Out of 348 full-time freshmen who applied for aid, 276 were judged to have need. Of these, 276 received aid, and 276 had their full need met. Average financial aid package met 100% of need; average scholarship/grant was $48,376; average loan was $2,728.

**FINANCIAL AID PROCEDURES**
**Forms required:** FAFSA, CSS PROFILE.
**Dates and Deadlines:** Priority date 2/1; no closing date. Applicants notified by 4/1; must reply by 5/1.
**Transfers:** Closing date 4/1. Applicants notified by 5/15; must reply within 2 week(s) of notification.

**CONTACT**
Paul Boyer, Director of Financial Aid
PO BOX 487, Williamstown, MA 01267
(413) 597-3131

## Worcester Polytechnic Institute
Worcester, Massachusetts — Federal Code: 002233
www.wpi.edu — CSS Code: 3969

**4-year private** university in small city.
**Enrollment:** 4,177 undergrads, 2% part-time. 1,054 full-time freshmen.
**Selectivity:** Admits less than 50% of applicants.

**BASIC COSTS (2015-2016)**
**Tuition and fees:** $45,590.
**Per-credit charge:** $1,249.
**Room and board:** $13,410.

**FINANCIAL AID PICTURE (2014-2015)**
**Students with need:** Out of 875 full-time freshmen who applied for aid, 709 were judged to have need. Of these, 708 received aid, and 393 had their full need met. Average financial aid package met 79% of need; average scholarship/grant was $23,869; average loan was $2,838. For part-time students, average financial aid package was $11,434.

**Students without need:** 303 full-time freshmen who did not demonstrate need for aid received scholarships/grants; average award was $13,207. No-need awards available for academics, leadership, minority status, ROTC.
**Scholarships offered:** Merit scholarships: typically $10,000-$25,000; renewable for 4 years.

**FINANCIAL AID PROCEDURES**
**Forms required:** FAFSA, CSS PROFILE.
**Dates and Deadlines:** Priority date 2/1; no closing date. Applicants notified on a rolling basis starting 4/1; must reply by 5/1 or within 2 week(s) of notification.
**Transfers:** Closing date 3/1. Applicants notified by 4/15; must reply by 5/1.

**CONTACT**
Monica Blondin, Director, Student Aid and Financial Literacy
100 Institute Road, Worcester, MA 01609-2280
(508) 831-5469

## Worcester State University
Worcester, Massachusetts
www.worcester.edu — Federal Code: 002190

**4-year public** liberal arts and teachers college in small city.
**Enrollment:** 5,049 undergrads, 19% part-time. 785 full-time freshmen.
**Selectivity:** Admits 50 to 75% of applicants.

**BASIC COSTS (2015-2016)**
**Tuition and fees:** $8,857; out-of-state residents $14,937.
**Per-credit charge:** $40; out-of-state residents $294.
**Room and board:** $11,560.

**FINANCIAL AID PICTURE (2014-2015)**
**Students with need:** Out of 743 full-time freshmen who applied for aid, 561 were judged to have need. Of these, 548 received aid, and 196 had their full need met. Average financial aid package met 77% of need; average scholarship/grant was $4,811; average loan was $2,756. For part-time students, average financial aid package was $6,673.
**Students without need:** 23 full-time freshmen who did not demonstrate need for aid received scholarships/grants; average award was $4,414. No-need awards available for academics, ROTC.
**Scholarships offered:** Presidential Scholarship: full in-state tuition and fees; 3.75 GPA and 1200 SAT required; 15 awarded. Tsongas Scholarship: full in-state tuition and fees to Massachusetts residents; 3.75 GPA and 1200 SAT required; 5 awarded. Access Scholarship: $1,000 per year; for under-served groups with 2.5 GPA and 920 SAT; 15 awarded.
**Additional info:** Veterans, Native Americans and those certified by Massachusetts Rehabilitation Commission and Massachusetts Commission for the Blind considered for tuition waivers while funds available. Tuition also waived for needy Massachusetts residents and in-state National Guard members.

**FINANCIAL AID PROCEDURES**
**Forms required:** FAFSA, institutional form.
**Dates and Deadlines:** Priority date 3/1; closing date 5/1. Applicants notified on a rolling basis starting 3/1; must reply within 3 week(s) of notification.

**CONTACT**
Jayne McGinn, Director of Financial Aid
Office of Undergraduate Admission, Worcester, MA 01602-2597
(508) 929-8056

# Michigan

## Adrian College
Adrian, Michigan
www.adrian.edu                    Federal Code: 002234

**4-year private** liberal arts college in large town, affiliated with United Methodist Church.
**Enrollment:** 1,655 full-time undergrads. 480 full-time freshmen.
**Selectivity:** Admits 50 to 75% of applicants.

### BASIC COSTS (2016-2017)
**Tuition and fees:** $34,500.
**Per-credit charge:** $890.
**Room and board:** $11,000.

### FINANCIAL AID PICTURE (2014-2015)
**Students with need:** Out of 452 full-time freshmen who applied for aid, 423 were judged to have need. Of these, 423 received aid, and 51 had their full need met. Average financial aid package met 75% of need; average scholarship/grant was $22,052; average loan was $3,581. For part-time students, average financial aid package was $10,825.
**Students without need:** 55 full-time freshmen who did not demonstrate need for aid received scholarships/grants; average award was $14,894. No-need awards available for academics, alumni affiliation, art, leadership, music/drama, religious affiliation, ROTC, state/district residency.
**Scholarships offered:** Academic scholarships: based on 20 ACT and 3.0 GPA.

### FINANCIAL AID PROCEDURES
**Forms required:** FAFSA.
**Dates and Deadlines:** Priority date 3/1; no closing date. Applicants notified on a rolling basis starting 3/15; must reply by 5/1 or within 2 week(s) of notification.
**Transfers:** No deadline. Applicants notified on a rolling basis starting 3/15; must reply by 5/1 or within 2 week(s) of notification.

### CONTACT
Matthew Rheinecker, Director of Financial Aid
110 South Madison Street, Adrian, MI 49221-2575
(888) 876-0194

## Albion College
Albion, Michigan
www.albion.edu                    Federal Code: 002235

**4-year private** liberal arts college in small town, affiliated with United Methodist Church.
**Enrollment:** 1,360 undergrads. 455 full-time freshmen.
**Selectivity:** Admits over 75% of applicants.

### BASIC COSTS (2015-2016)
**Tuition and fees:** $39,088.
**Per-credit charge:** $1,640.
**Room and board:** $11,060.

### FINANCIAL AID PICTURE (2015-2016)
**Students with need:** Out of 411 full-time freshmen who applied for aid, 362 were judged to have need. Of these, 362 received aid, and 87 had their full need met. Average financial aid package met 91% of need; average scholarship/grant was $32,079; average loan was $4,268.
**Students without need:** 92 full-time freshmen who did not demonstrate need for aid received scholarships/grants; average award was $24,220. No-need awards available for academics, alumni affiliation, art, leadership, music/drama.

**Scholarships offered:** Academic scholarships: $15,000-$23,500 per year; renewable; subject to satisfactory progress; awarded to students with outstanding academic records or unique skills, talents, or abilities.

### FINANCIAL AID PROCEDURES
**Forms required:** FAFSA.
**Dates and Deadlines:** Priority date 2/15; no closing date. Applicants notified on a rolling basis starting 3/15.
**Transfers:** No deadline. Applicants notified on a rolling basis starting 3/15.

### CONTACT
Ann Whitmer, Director of Financial Aid
611 East Porter Street, Albion, MI 49224-1831
(517) 629-0440

## Alma College
Alma, Michigan
www.alma.edu                    Federal Code: 002236

**4-year private** liberal arts college in large town, affiliated with Presbyterian Church (USA).
**Enrollment:** 1,345 undergrads, 1% part-time. 336 full-time freshmen.
**Selectivity:** Admits 50 to 75% of applicants.

### BASIC COSTS (2015-2016)
**Tuition and fees:** $35,806.
**Per-credit charge:** $1,100.
**Room and board:** $9,822.

### FINANCIAL AID PICTURE (2015-2016)
**Students with need:** Out of 318 full-time freshmen who applied for aid, 289 were judged to have need. Of these, 289 received aid, and 57 had their full need met. Average financial aid package met 81% of need; average scholarship/grant was $27,491; average loan was $3,825. For part-time students, average financial aid package was $17,831.
**Students without need:** 46 full-time freshmen who did not demonstrate need for aid received scholarships/grants; average award was $21,206. No-need awards available for academics, alumni affiliation, art, minority status, music/drama, religious affiliation.
**Scholarships offered:** Freshman merit awards of up to $21,000 annually are based on high school GPA and ACT/SAT scores. Transfer student merit awards of up to $19,000 annually are based on college GPA. Top scholars are invited to interview for additional scholarship funds. National Achievement and National Hispanic scholars also are invited to interview for additional scholarship funds that range up to full tuition.
**Additional info:** Auditions required for music, drama, dance scholarship candidates. Portfolios required for art scholarship candidates.

### FINANCIAL AID PROCEDURES
**Forms required:** FAFSA.
**Dates and Deadlines:** Priority date 3/1; no closing date. Applicants notified on a rolling basis starting 3/1; must reply within 3 week(s) of notification.
**Transfers:** No deadline. Applicants notified on a rolling basis starting 3/1; must reply within 3 week(s) of notification.

### CONTACT
Michelle McNier, Director of Financial Aid
614 West Superior Street, Alma, MI 48801-1599
(989) 463-7347

## Alpena Community College
Alpena, Michigan
www.alpenacc.edu                    Federal Code: 002237

**2-year public** community college in large town.
**Enrollment:** 2,000 undergrads.

**Selectivity:** Open admission; but selective for some programs.

## BASIC COSTS (2015-2016)

**Tuition and fees:** $4,170; out-of-district residents $6,210; out-of-state residents $6,210.

**Per-credit charge:** $121; out-of-district residents $189; out-of-state residents $189.

## FINANCIAL AID PICTURE

**Students with need:** Need-based aid available for full-time and part-time students.

**Students without need:** No-need awards available for academics, art, athletics, job skills, leadership, music/drama.

## FINANCIAL AID PROCEDURES

**Forms required:** FAFSA.

**Dates and Deadlines:** Priority date 8/1; no closing date. Applicants notified on a rolling basis starting 5/15; must reply within 3 week(s) of notification.

## CONTACT

Rob Roose, Dean of Students
665 Johnson Street, Alpena, MI 49707
(989) 358-7205

---

# Andrews University

Berrien Springs, Michigan
www.andrews.edu

Federal Code: 002238
CSS Code: 1030

**4-year private** university in small town, affiliated with Seventh-day Adventists.

**Enrollment:** 1,504 undergrads, 8% part-time. 273 full-time freshmen.

**Selectivity:** Admits less than 50% of applicants.

## BASIC COSTS (2015-2016)

**Tuition and fees:** $27,000.

**Per-credit charge:** $1,089.

**Room and board:** $8,532.

## FINANCIAL AID PICTURE (2015-2016)

**Students with need:** Out of 209 full-time freshmen who applied for aid, 182 were judged to have need. Of these, 182 received aid, and 40 had their full need met. Average financial aid package met 86% of need; average scholarship/grant was $6,386; average loan was $3,437. For part-time students, average financial aid package was $16,777.

**Students without need:** 87 full-time freshmen who did not demonstrate need for aid received scholarships/grants; average award was $12,376. No-need awards available for academics, job skills, leadership, music/drama.

## FINANCIAL AID PROCEDURES

**Forms required:** FAFSA, CSS PROFILE, institutional form.

**Dates and Deadlines:** Priority date 3/31; no closing date. Applicants notified on a rolling basis starting 3/15.

## CONTACT

Elynda Bedney, Director of Student Financial Services
100 US Highway 31, Berrien Springs, MI 49104

---

# Aquinas College

Grand Rapids, Michigan
www.aquinas.edu

Federal Code: 002239

**4-year private** liberal arts college in small city, affiliated with Roman Catholic Church.

**Enrollment:** 1,692 undergrads, 9% part-time. 370 full-time freshmen.

**Selectivity:** Admits 50 to 75% of applicants. GED not accepted.

## BASIC COSTS (2016-2017)

**Tuition and fees:** $30,062.

---

**Per-credit charge:** $498.

**Room and board:** $8,814.

**Additional info:** Tuition/fee waivers available for adults.

## FINANCIAL AID PICTURE (2015-2016)

**Students with need:** Out of 337 full-time freshmen who applied for aid, 309 were judged to have need. Of these, 309 received aid, and 57 had their full need met. Average financial aid package met 81% of need; average scholarship/grant was $21,588; average loan was $1,984. For part-time students, average financial aid package was $4,288.

**Students without need:** 46 full-time freshmen who did not demonstrate need for aid received scholarships/grants; average award was $16,026. No-need awards available for academics, alumni affiliation, art, athletics, leadership, minority status, music/drama.

**Scholarships offered: Merit:** Spectrum Scholarship: $3,000, full tuition; awarded to students who have excelled in academics, leadership or community service; renewable. **Athletic:** 16 full-time freshmen received athletic scholarships; average amount $2,906.

## FINANCIAL AID PROCEDURES

**Forms required:** FAFSA.

**Dates and Deadlines:** Priority date 3/1; no closing date. Applicants notified on a rolling basis starting 3/1; must reply within 2 week(s) of notification.

**Transfers:** Priority date 4/15; closing date 7/1. Must reply within 2 week(s) of notification.

## CONTACT

David Steffee, Director of Financial Aid
1607 Robinson Road Southeast, Grand Rapids, MI 49506-1799
(616) 632-2893

---

# Baker College of Auburn Hills

Auburn Hills, Michigan
www.baker.edu

Federal Code: E00466

**4-year private** business and technical college in small city.

**Enrollment:** 3,400 undergrads.

**Selectivity:** Open admission; but selective for some programs.

## BASIC COSTS (2015-2016)

**Tuition and fees:** $10,800.

**Per-credit charge:** $240.

## FINANCIAL AID PICTURE

**Students with need:** Work study available nights, weekends, and for part-time students.

**Students without need:** No-need awards available for academics, alumni affiliation.

## FINANCIAL AID PROCEDURES

**Forms required:** FAFSA, institutional form.

**Dates and Deadlines:** Priority date 2/21; closing date 9/1. Applicants notified on a rolling basis starting 4/1.

**Transfers:** Must have been deemed financial aid-eligible at previous school.

## CONTACT

Greg Little, Financial Aid Director
1500 University Drive, Auburn Hills, MI 48326
(248) 340-0600

---

# Baker College of Cadillac

Cadillac, Michigan
www.baker.edu

Federal Code: E00461

**4-year private** business and health science college in large town.

**Enrollment:** 1,800 undergrads.

**Selectivity:** Open admission.

## BASIC COSTS (2015-2016)
**Tuition and fees:** $10,800.
**Per-credit charge:** $240.
**Room only:** $3,000.

## FINANCIAL AID PICTURE
**Students with need:** Need-based aid available for full-time and part-time students. Work study available nights, weekends, and for part-time students.
**Students without need:** No-need awards available for academics.
**Scholarships offered:** Baker College Career Scholarships: $400 per term for 4 years; based on 2.5 GPA after junior year of high school. Board of Regents Scholarships: half tuition for 4 years; based on 3.5 GPA through grade 11.

## FINANCIAL AID PROCEDURES
**Forms required:** FAFSA, institutional form.
**Dates and Deadlines:** Priority date 2/21; no closing date. Applicants notified on a rolling basis starting 5/1.
**Transfers:** Priority date 3/20; closing date 9/1.

## CONTACT
Kristin Bonney, Financial Aid Officer
9600 East 13th Street, Cadillac, MI 49601
(231) 876-3118

# Baker College of Clinton Township
Clinton Township, Michigan
www.baker.edu                    Federal Code: E00462

**4-year private** business and technical college in very large city.
**Enrollment:** 3,618 undergrads.
**Selectivity:** Open admission; but selective for some programs.

## BASIC COSTS (2015-2016)
**Tuition and fees:** $10,800.
**Per-credit charge:** $240.

## FINANCIAL AID PICTURE
**Students with need:** Need-based aid available for full-time and part-time students. Work study available nights, weekends, and for part-time students.
**Students without need:** No-need awards available for academics, minority status.

## FINANCIAL AID PROCEDURES
**Forms required:** FAFSA, institutional form.
**Dates and Deadlines:** Priority date 2/21; closing date 9/1. Applicants notified on a rolling basis starting 4/1.

## CONTACT
Lisa Harvener, Vice President of Student Services
34950 Little Mack Avenue, Clinton Township, MI 48035
(586) 790-9589

# Baker College of Muskegon
Muskegon, Michigan
www.baker.edu                    Federal Code: E00463

**4-year private** business and technical college in small city.
**Enrollment:** 4,500 undergrads.
**Selectivity:** Open admission; but selective for some programs.

## BASIC COSTS (2015-2016)
**Tuition and fees:** $10,800.
**Per-credit charge:** $240.
**Room only:** $3,000.

## FINANCIAL AID PICTURE
**Students with need:** Need-based aid available for full-time and part-time students. Work study available nights, weekends, and for part-time students.
**Students without need:** No-need awards available for academics, minority status.
**Scholarships offered:** Career Scholarship: $4,800 over 4 years; based on GPA over 3.0. Board Regents Scholarship: one-half tuition for 4 years; based on GPA over 3.5. Alternative Scholarship: one-half tuition for 2 years; based on academic success in alternative high school education program.

## FINANCIAL AID PROCEDURES
**Forms required:** FAFSA, institutional form.
**Dates and Deadlines:** Priority date 2/21; no closing date. Applicants notified on a rolling basis starting 4/1.
**Transfers:** Priority date 3/21.

## CONTACT
Jody Zerlant, Director of Financial Aid
1903 Marquette Avenue, Muskegon, MI 49442
(231) 777-5231

# Baker College of Owosso
Owosso, Michigan
www.baker.edu                    Federal Code: E00464

**4-year private** business and technical college in large town.
**Enrollment:** 3,000 undergrads.
**Selectivity:** Open admission; but selective for some programs.

## BASIC COSTS (2015-2016)
**Tuition and fees:** $10,800.
**Per-credit charge:** $240.
**Room only:** $3,000.

## FINANCIAL AID PICTURE
**Students with need:** Need-based aid available for full-time and part-time students. Work study available nights, weekends, and for part-time students.
**Students without need:** No-need awards available for academics, minority status.

## FINANCIAL AID PROCEDURES
**Forms required:** FAFSA, institutional form.
**Dates and Deadlines:** Priority date 2/21; closing date 9/1. Applicants notified on a rolling basis starting 4/1.
**Transfers:** Priority date 3/21.

## CONTACT
Nicole Patterson, Financial Aid Director
1020 South Washington Street, Owosso, MI 48867
(989) 720-3430

# Baker College of Port Huron
Port Huron, Michigan
www.baker.edu                    Federal Code: E00465

**4-year private** business and technical college in large town.
**Enrollment:** 1,200 undergrads.
**Selectivity:** Open admission; but selective for some programs.

## BASIC COSTS (2015-2016)
**Tuition and fees:** $10,800.
**Per-credit charge:** $240.
**Room only:** $3,000.

## FINANCIAL AID PICTURE
**Students with need:** Need-based aid available for full-time and part-time students. Work study available nights.

**Students without need:** This college awards aid only to students with need.

**FINANCIAL AID PROCEDURES**
**Forms required:** FAFSA, institutional form.
**Dates and Deadlines:** Priority date 2/21; no closing date. Applicants notified on a rolling basis starting 4/1.
**Transfers:** Priority date 3/21; closing date 9/1.

**CONTACT**
Barbara Fosgard, Financial Aid Director
3403 Lapeer Road, Port Huron, MI 48060-2597
(810) 985-7000

## Bay College
Escanaba, Michigan
www.baycollege.edu          Federal Code: 002240

**2-year public** community college in large town.
**Enrollment:** 1,497 undergrads, 53% part-time. 252 full-time freshmen.
**Selectivity:** Open admission; but selective for some programs.

**BASIC COSTS (2015-2016)**
**Tuition and fees:** $4,290; out-of-district residents $6,720; out-of-state residents $10,980.
**Room only:** $3,000.

**FINANCIAL AID PICTURE**
**Students with need:** Need-based aid available for full-time and part-time students. Work study available nights, weekends, and for part-time students.
**Students without need:** No-need awards available for academics.

**FINANCIAL AID PROCEDURES**
**Forms required:** FAFSA.
**Dates and Deadlines:** Priority date 4/1; no closing date. Applicants notified on a rolling basis starting 2/1; must reply within 2 week(s) of notification.

**CONTACT**
Laurie Spangenberg, Financial Aid Director
2001 North Lincoln Road, Escanaba, MI 49829-2511
(906) 217-4032

## Bay Mills Community College
Brimley, Michigan
www.bmcc.edu          Federal Code: 030666

**2-year public** community college in rural community.
**Enrollment:** 461 undergrads.
**Selectivity:** Open admission.

**BASIC COSTS (2015-2016)**
**Tuition and fees:** $3,250; out-of-state residents $3,250.
**Per-credit charge:** $95.

**FINANCIAL AID PICTURE**
**Students with need:** Work study available nights.

**FINANCIAL AID PROCEDURES**
**Forms required:** FAFSA.
**Dates and Deadlines:** Priority date 6/30; no closing date.

**CONTACT**
Tina Miller, Financial Aid Director
12214 West Lakeshore Drive, Brimley, MI 49715
(906) 248-3354 ext. 8437

## Calvin College
Grand Rapids, Michigan
www.calvin.edu          Federal Code: 002241

**4-year private** liberal arts college in large city, affiliated with Christian Reformed Church.
**Enrollment:** 3,788 undergrads, 2% part-time. 941 full-time freshmen.
**Selectivity:** Admits 50 to 75% of applicants.

**BASIC COSTS (2015-2016)**
**Tuition and fees:** $30,660.
**Per-credit charge:** $730.
**Room and board:** $9,690.

**FINANCIAL AID PICTURE (2015-2016)**
**Students with need:** Out of 853 full-time freshmen who applied for aid, 652 were judged to have need. Of these, 652 received aid, and 125 had their full need met. Average financial aid package met 78% of need; average scholarship/grant was $19,240; average loan was $4,059. For part-time students, average financial aid package was $11,078.
**Students without need:** 277 full-time freshmen who did not demonstrate need for aid received scholarships/grants; average award was $10,663. No-need awards available for academics, alumni affiliation, art, leadership, minority status, music/drama, religious affiliation, state/district residency.
**Scholarships offered:** Honors Fellows award: for high-achieving and service-oriented students. Perkins Fellows leadership awards: for high-achieving and service-oriented students. Legacy awards for alumni children. Denominational awards. First generation awards. Various departmental scholarships.

**FINANCIAL AID PROCEDURES**
**Forms required:** FAFSA.
**Dates and Deadlines:** Priority date 2/15; no closing date. Applicants notified on a rolling basis starting 3/15.
**Transfers:** Priority date 3/15; closing date 8/15. Applicants notified on a rolling basis starting 3/15; must reply by 6/1.

**CONTACT**
Paul Witte, Director of Financial Aid
3201 Burton Street Southeast, Grand Rapids, MI 49546
(616) 526-6134

## Central Michigan University
Mount Pleasant, Michigan
www.cmich.edu          Federal Code: 002243

**4-year public** university in large town.
**Enrollment:** 19,954 undergrads, 12% part-time. 3,448 full-time freshmen.
**Selectivity:** Admits 50 to 75% of applicants.

**BASIC COSTS (2015-2016)**
**Tuition and fees:** $11,850; out-of-state residents $23,670.
**Per-credit charge:** $395; out-of-state residents $789.
**Room and board:** $9,088.

**FINANCIAL AID PICTURE (2014-2015)**
**Students with need:** Out of 3,402 full-time freshmen who applied for aid, 2,478 were judged to have need. Of these, 2,402 received aid, and 1,292 had their full need met. Average financial aid package met 83% of need; average scholarship/grant was $8,017; average loan was $6,075. For part-time students, average financial aid package was $9,538.
**Students without need:** 801 full-time freshmen who did not demonstrate need for aid received scholarships/grants; average award was $5,157. No-need awards available for academics, alumni affiliation, art, athletics, leadership, minority status, music/drama, ROTC, state/district residency.
**Scholarships offered:** 42 full-time freshmen received athletic scholarships; average amount $15,056.

**Additional info:** Tuition waiver for Native American students qualifying under state program criteria.

## FINANCIAL AID PROCEDURES

**Forms required:** FAFSA.

**Dates and Deadlines:** Priority date 3/1; no closing date. Applicants notified on a rolling basis starting 4/1.

## CONTACT

Kirk Yats, Director, Scholarships and Financial Aid

Admissions Office, Mount Pleasant, MI 48859

(989) 774-3674

## Cleary University
Howell, Michigan
www.cleary.edu          Federal Code: 002246

**4-year private** university and business college in small city.

**Enrollment:** 206 full-time undergrads.

**Selectivity:** Open admission; but selective for some programs.

## BASIC COSTS (2015-2016)

**Tuition and fees:** $18,750.

**Additional info:** Tuition at time of enrollment locked for 4 years.

## FINANCIAL AID PICTURE

**Students with need:** Need-based aid available for full-time and part-time students. Work study available nights.

**Students without need:** This college awards aid only to students with need.

**Scholarships offered:** Oren Beutler Endowed Scholarship: $750; new or continuing full-time student maintaining 3.0 GPA, demonstrated leadership and service to community; one awarded annually; renewable for 4 years. Scholarship for veteran/military students (honorable discharge only).

**Additional info:** Filing electronically preferred; paper applications available. Tuition guarantee based on continuous enrollment. Essay and recommendations required for scholarship consideration.

## FINANCIAL AID PROCEDURES

**Forms required:** FAFSA.

**Dates and Deadlines:** Priority date 3/1; no closing date. Applicants notified on a rolling basis starting 3/1; must reply within 2 week(s) of notification.

**Transfers:** No deadline. Applicants notified on a rolling basis starting 4/1; must reply within 2 week(s) of notification. Aid eligibility for transfer students is determined using aid already received from the other school.

## CONTACT

Vesta Smith-Campbell, Director of Financial Aid

3750 Cleary Drive, Howell, MI 48843

(517) 338-3015

## College for Creative Studies
Detroit, Michigan
www.collegeforcreativestudies.edu  Federal Code: 006771

**4-year private** visual arts college in very large city.

**Enrollment:** 1,376 undergrads.

## BASIC COSTS (2015-2016)

**Tuition and fees:** $38,950.

**Per-credit charge:** $1,252.

**Room and board:** $8,450.

## FINANCIAL AID PICTURE

**Students with need:** Need-based aid available for full-time and part-time students. Work study available nights, weekends, and for part-time students.

**Students without need:** No-need awards available for academics, art.

## FINANCIAL AID PROCEDURES

**Forms required:** FAFSA.

**Dates and Deadlines:** Priority date 7/1; no closing date. Applicants notified on a rolling basis starting 2/15; must reply within 3 week(s) of notification.

**Transfers:** Priority date 3/21.

## CONTACT

Kristin Moskovitz, Director of Financial Aid

201 East Kirby, Detroit, MI 48202-4034

(313) 664-7495

## Concordia University
Ann Arbor, Michigan
www.cuaa.edu          Federal Code: 002247

**4-year private** liberal arts and teachers college in small city, affiliated with Lutheran Church - Missouri Synod.

**Enrollment:** 562 full-time undergrads. 171 full-time freshmen.

## BASIC COSTS (2015-2016)

**Tuition and fees:** $26,895.

**Per-credit charge:** $1,080.

**Room and board:** $9,300.

## FINANCIAL AID PICTURE (2015-2016)

**Students with need:** Out of 167 full-time freshmen who applied for aid, 156 were judged to have need. Of these, 156 received aid, and 29 had their full need met. Average financial aid package met 70% of need; average scholarship/grant was $16,876; average loan was $4,899. For part-time students, average financial aid package was $8,992.

**Students without need:** 3 full-time freshmen who did not demonstrate need for aid received scholarships/grants; average award was $13,982. No-need awards available for academics, alumni affiliation, art, athletics, leadership, music/drama, religious affiliation.

**Scholarships offered:** 19 full-time freshmen received athletic scholarships.

## FINANCIAL AID PROCEDURES

**Forms required:** FAFSA.

**Dates and Deadlines:** Closing date 3/1. Applicants notified on a rolling basis starting 3/1; must reply within 3 week(s) of notification.

**Transfers:** Priority date 5/1. Applicants notified on a rolling basis; must reply within 3 week(s) of notification.

## CONTACT

Steven Taylor, Director of Financial Aid

4090 Geddes Road, Ann Arbor, MI 48105

(734) 995-7408

## Cornerstone University
Grand Rapids, Michigan
www.cornerstone.edu          Federal Code: 002266

**4-year private** university and liberal arts college in small city, affiliated with interdenominational tradition.

**Enrollment:** 1,912 undergrads, 22% part-time. 325 full-time freshmen.

## BASIC COSTS (2015-2016)

**Tuition and fees:** $26,100.

**Per-credit charge:** $980.

**Room and board:** $8,560.

**Additional info:** Tuition/fee waivers available for minority students.

## FINANCIAL AID PICTURE (2015-2016)

**Students with need:** Out of 298 full-time freshmen who applied for aid, 261 were judged to have need. Of these, 261 received aid, and 30 had their full need met. Average financial aid package met 70% of need; average

scholarship/grant was $17,747; average loan was $3,606. For part-time students, average financial aid package was $4,940.

**Students without need:** 55 full-time freshmen who did not demonstrate need for aid received scholarships/grants; average award was $10,538. No-need awards available for academics, athletics, music/drama.

**Scholarships offered:** *Merit:* Academic scholarships: based on high school GPA and ACT. *Athletic:* 29 full-time freshmen received athletic scholarships; average amount $5,489.

**Additional info:** Audition required for music scholarship applicants.

### FINANCIAL AID PROCEDURES

**Forms required:** FAFSA.

**Dates and Deadlines:** Priority date 3/1; no closing date. Applicants notified on a rolling basis starting 3/1.

**Transfers:** No deadline. Applicants notified by 3/15.

### CONTACT

Carol Carpenter, Student Financial Services
1001 East Beltline NE, Grand Rapids, MI 49525-5897
(616) 222-1424

## Davenport University
Grand Rapids, Michigan
www.davenport.edu                    Federal Code: 015260

**4-year private** university and business college in small city.
**Enrollment:** 5,864 undergrads.
**Selectivity:** Admits over 75% of applicants.

**BASIC COSTS (2015-2016)**
**Tuition and fees:** $19,750.
**Per-credit charge:** $633.
**Room and board:** $10,078.

**FINANCIAL AID PICTURE**
**Students with need:** Need-based aid available for full-time and part-time students. Work study available nights, weekends, and for part-time students.
**Students without need:** No-need awards available for academics, alumni affiliation, athletics, leadership.

**FINANCIAL AID PROCEDURES**
**Forms required:** FAFSA.
**Dates and Deadlines:** Priority date 3/1; no closing date. Applicants notified on a rolling basis starting 3/1; must reply within 2 week(s) of notification.
**Transfers:** No deadline. Applicants notified on a rolling basis.

**CONTACT**
David De Boer, Executive Director of Financial Aid
6191 Kraft Avenue SE, Grand Rapids, MI 49512-9396
(866) 925-3884

## Delta College
University Center, Michigan
www.delta.edu                    Federal Code: 002251

**2-year public** community college in small city.
**Enrollment:** 9,291 undergrads.
**Selectivity:** Open admission.

**BASIC COSTS (2015-2016)**
**Tuition and fees:** $3,495; out-of-district residents $5,370; out-of-state residents $9,870.
**Per-credit charge:** $97; out-of-district residents $159; out-of-state residents $309.

**FINANCIAL AID PICTURE**
**Students with need:** Need-based aid available for full-time and part-time students. Work study available nights.

**Students without need:** No-need awards available for academics, athletics.

### FINANCIAL AID PROCEDURES

**Forms required:** FAFSA.

**Dates and Deadlines:** Applicants notified on a rolling basis; must reply within 2 week(s) of notification.

**Transfers:** No deadline. Applicants notified on a rolling basis.

### CONTACT

Lisa Martens, Interim Financial Aid Director
1961 Delta Road D101, University Center, MI 48710
(989) 686-9080

## Eastern Michigan University
Ypsilanti, Michigan
www.emich.edu                    Federal Code: 002259

**4-year public** university in small city.
**Enrollment:** 17,284 undergrads, 25% part-time. 2,588 full-time freshmen.
**Selectivity:** Admits 50 to 75% of applicants.

**BASIC COSTS (2015-2016)**
**Tuition and fees:** $10,417; out-of-state residents $27,712.
**Per-credit charge:** $296; out-of-state residents $873.
**Room and board:** $9,344.
**Additional info:** Higher course levels charged at higher rates.

**FINANCIAL AID PICTURE (2014-2015)**
**Students with need:** Out of 2,369 full-time freshmen who applied for aid, 1,879 were judged to have need. Of these, 1,862 received aid, and 102 had their full need met. Average financial aid package met 46% of need; average scholarship/grant was $6,255; average loan was $3,257. For part-time students, average financial aid package was $5,277.
**Students without need:** 622 full-time freshmen who did not demonstrate need for aid received scholarships/grants; average award was $4,766. No-need awards available for academics, alumni affiliation, art, athletics, leadership, minority status, music/drama, ROTC, state/district residency.
**Scholarships offered:** 90 full-time freshmen received athletic scholarships; average amount $15,991.

**FINANCIAL AID PROCEDURES**
**Forms required:** FAFSA.
**Dates and Deadlines:** Applicants notified on a rolling basis starting 3/1.
**Transfers:** No deadline. Applicants notified on a rolling basis starting 3/1.

**CONTACT**
Donna Holubik, Director
400 Pierce Hall, Ypsilanti, MI 48197
(734) 487-0455

## Ferris State University
Big Rapids, Michigan
www.ferris.edu                    Federal Code: 002260

**4-year public** university in large town.
**Enrollment:** 12,550 undergrads, 28% part-time. 1,921 full-time freshmen.
**Selectivity:** Admits over 75% of applicants.

**BASIC COSTS (2015-2016)**
**Tuition and fees:** $11,460; out-of-state residents $17,190.
**Per-credit charge:** $382; out-of-state residents $573.
**Room and board:** $9,434.

**FINANCIAL AID PICTURE (2015-2016)**
**Students with need:** Out of 1,796 full-time freshmen who applied for aid, 1,476 were judged to have need. Of these, 1,473 received aid, and 270 had their full need met. Average financial aid package met 71% of need; average

scholarship/grant was $4,560; average loan was $3,640. For part-time students, average financial aid package was $6,650.

**Students without need:** 271 full-time freshmen who did not demonstrate need for aid received scholarships/grants; average award was $4,760. No-need awards available for academics, alumni affiliation, art, athletics, job skills, leadership, minority status, music/drama, ROTC, state/district residency.

**Scholarships offered:** 65 full-time freshmen received athletic scholarships; average amount $7,750.

### FINANCIAL AID PROCEDURES

**Forms required:** FAFSA.

**Dates and Deadlines:** Priority date 2/1; no closing date. Applicants notified on a rolling basis starting 3/15; must reply within 3 week(s) of notification.

**Transfers:** Applicants notified on a rolling basis; must reply within 3 week(s) of notification.

### CONTACT

Sara Dew, Director of Financial Aid

1201 South State Street, CSS 201, Big Rapids, MI 49307-2714

(231) 591-2110

## Finlandia University
Hancock, Michigan
www.finlandia.edu                    Federal Code: 002322

**4-year private** university and liberal arts college in small town, affiliated with Evangelical Lutheran Church in America.

**Enrollment:** 570 undergrads.

**Selectivity:** Open admission; but selective for some programs.

### BASIC COSTS (2015-2016)

**Tuition and fees:** $22,110.

**Room and board:** $7,648.

### FINANCIAL AID PICTURE

**Students with need:** Need-based aid available for full-time and part-time students. Work study available nights, weekends, and for part-time students.

**Students without need:** No-need awards available for academics, leadership, religious affiliation, state/district residency.

**Additional info:** Work/study program; up to $2,800 per year.

### FINANCIAL AID PROCEDURES

**Forms required:** FAFSA, institutional form.

**Dates and Deadlines:** Priority date 3/1; no closing date. Applicants notified on a rolling basis starting 3/1; must reply within 2 week(s) of notification.

**Transfers:** Priority date 3/10; no deadline. Applicants notified on a rolling basis starting 2/1; must reply within 2 week(s) of notification.

### CONTACT

Sandra Turnquist, Director of Financial Aid

601 Quincy Street, Hancock, MI 49930-1882

(906) 487-7261

## Glen Oaks Community College
Centreville, Michigan
www.glenoaks.edu                    Federal Code: 002263

**2-year public** community college in rural community.

**Enrollment:** 680 undergrads.

**Selectivity:** Open admission; but selective for some programs.

### BASIC COSTS (2015-2016)

**Tuition and fees:** $3,960; out-of-district residents $5,610; out-of-state residents $6,870.

### FINANCIAL AID PICTURE

**Students with need:** Need-based aid available for full-time and part-time students. Work study available nights.

**Students without need:** No-need awards available for academics, art, athletics, leadership.

### FINANCIAL AID PROCEDURES

**Forms required:** FAFSA, institutional form.

**Dates and Deadlines:** Applicants notified on a rolling basis.

### CONTACT

Jean Zimmerman, Director of Financial Aid and Scholarship

62249 Shimmel Road, Centreville, MI 49032-9719

(269) 467-9945 ext. 260

## Gogebic Community College
Ironwood, Michigan
www.gogebic.edu                    Federal Code: 002264

**2-year public** community college in small town.

**Enrollment:** 771 undergrads, 33% part-time. 190 full-time freshmen.

**Selectivity:** Open admission; but selective for some programs.

### BASIC COSTS (2015-2016)

**Tuition and fees:** $4,344; out-of-district residents $5,708; out-of-state residents $6,607.

**Per-credit charge:** $106; out-of-district residents $150; out-of-state residents $179.

**Room and board:** $5,804.

### FINANCIAL AID PICTURE

**Students with need:** Need-based aid available for full-time and part-time students. Work study available nights, weekends, and for part-time students.

**Students without need:** No-need awards available for academics, art, athletics, job skills, leadership, music/drama, state/district residency.

### FINANCIAL AID PROCEDURES

**Forms required:** FAFSA.

**Dates and Deadlines:** Priority date 5/1; no closing date. Applicants notified on a rolling basis starting 3/15; must reply within 2 week(s) of notification.

### CONTACT

Sue Forbes, Director of Financial Aid

E4946 Jackson Road, Ironwood, MI 49938

(906) 932-4231 ext. 206

## Grace Bible College
Grand Rapids, Michigan
www.gbcol.edu                    Federal Code: 002265

**4-year private** Bible and liberal arts college in small city, affiliated with Christian Church.

**Enrollment:** 303 undergrads, 5% part-time. 72 full-time freshmen.

**Selectivity:** Admits 50 to 75% of applicants.

### BASIC COSTS (2015-2016)

**Tuition and fees:** $17,850.

**Per-credit charge:** $595.

**Room and board:** $7,400.

### FINANCIAL AID PICTURE (2014-2015)

**Students with need:** Out of 68 full-time freshmen who applied for aid, 60 were judged to have need. Of these, 60 received aid. Average financial aid package met 53% of need; average scholarship/grant was $11,870; average loan was $3,231. For part-time students, average financial aid package was $7,306.

**Students without need:** 12 full-time freshmen who did not demonstrate need for aid received scholarships/grants; average award was $5,088. No-need awards available for academics, music/drama, religious affiliation.

**FINANCIAL AID PROCEDURES**
**Forms required:** FAFSA.
**Dates and Deadlines:** Priority date 3/1; no closing date. Applicants notified on a rolling basis starting 5/15; must reply within 2 week(s) of notification.
**Transfers:** No deadline. Applicants notified on a rolling basis starting 5/15; must reply within 2 week(s) of notification.

**CONTACT**
Kurt Postma, Director of Financial Aid
1011 Aldon Street SW, PO Box 910, Grand Rapids, MI 49509
(616) 261-8557

## Grand Rapids Community College
Grand Rapids, Michigan
www.grcc.edu
Federal Code: 002267

**2-year public** community college in small city.
**Enrollment:** 13,840 undergrads, 68% part-time. 1,661 full-time freshmen.
**Selectivity:** Open admission; but selective for some programs.

**BASIC COSTS (2015-2016)**
**Tuition and fees:** $3,699; out-of-district residents $7,419; out-of-state residents $10,779.
**Per-credit charge:** $108; out-of-district residents $232; out-of-state residents $344.

**FINANCIAL AID PICTURE (2014-2015)**
**Students with need:** 54% of average financial aid package awarded as scholarships/grants, 46% awarded as loans/jobs. Need-based aid available for part-time students. Work study available nights, weekends, and for part-time students.
**Students without need:** No-need awards available for academics.
**Scholarships offered:** Michigan Merit Award: $2,500; based on Michigan Educational Assessment Program scores.
**Additional info:** Tuition reimbursement and/or child-care services for single parents and displaced homemakers who meet Perkins guidelines.

**FINANCIAL AID PROCEDURES**
**Forms required:** FAFSA.
**Dates and Deadlines:** Priority date 4/1; no closing date. Applicants notified on a rolling basis starting 5/1; must reply within 3 week(s) of notification.

**CONTACT**
Ann Isaacson, Director of Financial Aid
143 Bostwick Avenue NE, Grand Rapids, MI 49503-3295
(616) 234-4030

## Grand Valley State University
Allendale, Michigan
www.gvsu.edu

**4-year public** university in large town.
**Enrollment:** 21,889 undergrads, 11% part-time. 4,092 full-time freshmen.
**Selectivity:** Admits over 75% of applicants.

**BASIC COSTS (2015-2016)**
**Tuition and fees:** $11,078; out-of-state residents $15,744.
**Per-credit charge:** $462; out-of-state residents $656.
**Room and board:** $8,360.

**FINANCIAL AID PICTURE (2015-2016)**
**Students with need:** Out of 3,653 full-time freshmen who applied for aid, 2,462 were judged to have need. Of these, 2,439 received aid, and 338 had

their full need met. Average financial aid package met 69% of need; average scholarship/grant was $7,599; average loan was $3,715. For part-time students, average financial aid package was $6,229.
**Students without need:** 742 full-time freshmen who did not demonstrate need for aid received scholarships/grants; average award was $2,712. No-need awards available for academics, alumni affiliation, art, athletics, music/drama, state/district residency.
**Scholarships offered:** 53 full-time freshmen received athletic scholarships; average amount $7,003.

**FINANCIAL AID PROCEDURES**
**Forms required:** FAFSA.
**Dates and Deadlines:** Priority date 3/1; no closing date. Applicants notified on a rolling basis starting 3/3; must reply by 5/1 or within 4 week(s) of notification.
**Transfers:** No deadline. Applicants notified on a rolling basis starting 3/20; must reply within 4 week(s) of notification.

**CONTACT**
1 Campus Drive, Allendale, MI 49401-9403

## Great Lakes Christian College
Lansing, Michigan
www.glcc.edu
Federal Code: 002269

**4-year private** Bible college in small city, affiliated with Christian Church.
**Enrollment:** 174 undergrads.

**BASIC COSTS (2015-2016)**
**Tuition and fees:** $14,540.
**Per-credit charge:** $455.
**Room and board:** $8,500.

**FINANCIAL AID PICTURE (2015-2016)**
**Students with need:** 65% of average financial aid package awarded as scholarships/grants, 35% awarded as loans/jobs. Need-based aid available for part-time students. Work study available nights, weekends, and for part-time students.
**Students without need:** No-need awards available for academics, alumni affiliation, music/drama.

**FINANCIAL AID PROCEDURES**
**Forms required:** FAFSA, state aid form, institutional form.
**Dates and Deadlines:** Closing date 8/1. Applicants notified on a rolling basis starting 5/1; must reply within 3 week(s) of notification.
**Transfers:** Priority date 3/31; closing date 8/31. Applicants notified on a rolling basis; must reply within 3 week(s) of notification. FAFSA due 6/30.

**CONTACT**
Ryan Apple, Financial Aid Director
6211 West Willow Highway, Lansing, MI 48917-1231
(517) 321-0242 ext. 227

## Henry Ford Community College
Dearborn, Michigan
www.hfcc.edu

**2-year public** community college in small city.
**Enrollment:** 11,129 undergrads, 61% part-time. 1,640 full-time freshmen.
**Selectivity:** Open admission; but selective for some programs.

**BASIC COSTS (2015-2016)**
**Tuition and fees:** $3,360; out-of-district residents $5,340; out-of-state residents $7,350.
**Per-credit charge:** $92; out-of-district residents $158; out-of-state residents $225.

## FINANCIAL AID PICTURE (2014-2015)

**Students with need:** 67% of average financial aid package awarded as scholarships/grants, 33% awarded as loans/jobs. Work study available nights, weekends, and for part-time students.

**Students without need:** No-need awards available for academics, athletics.

## FINANCIAL AID PROCEDURES

**Forms required:** FAFSA.

**Dates and Deadlines:** Priority date 6/5; no closing date. Applicants notified on a rolling basis starting 5/15.

## CONTACT

Kevin Culler, Director, Financial Aid
5101 Evergreen Road, Dearborn, MI 48128
(313) 845-9616

## Hillsdale College

Hillsdale, Michigan
www.hillsdale.edu

Federal Code: 002272
CSS Code: 1295

**4-year private** liberal arts college in small town, affiliated with Christian Church.

**Enrollment:** 1,485 undergrads, 2% part-time. 383 full-time freshmen.

**Selectivity:** Admits 50 to 75% of applicants.

## BASIC COSTS (2015-2016)

**Tuition and fees:** $24,592.

**Per-credit charge:** $950.

**Room and board:** $9,760.

## FINANCIAL AID PICTURE (2014-2015)

**Students with need:** Out of 245 full-time freshmen who applied for aid, 187 were judged to have need. Of these, 179 received aid, and 68 had their full need met. Average financial aid package met 60% of need; average scholarship/grant was $7,554; average loan was $6,130. For part-time students, average financial aid package was $4,224.

**Students without need:** 180 full-time freshmen who did not demonstrate need for aid received scholarships/grants; average award was $4,887. No-need awards available for academics, alumni affiliation, art, athletics, leadership, music/drama.

**Scholarships offered:** *Merit:* Distinct Honor Scholarship: full tuition; 5 awarded. Presidential Scholarship: half tuition; 30 awarded. Trustee Scholarship: up to $10,000; 35 awarded. *Athletic:* 57 full-time freshmen received athletic scholarships; average amount $13,269.

**Additional info:** Campus employment available to all students.

## FINANCIAL AID PROCEDURES

**Forms required:** institutional form. CSS PROFILE required for returning students only.

**Dates and Deadlines:** Priority date 5/1; no closing date. Applicants notified on a rolling basis starting 12/1; must reply by 5/1 or within 4 week(s) of notification.

**Transfers:** Applicants notified on a rolling basis starting 2/1; must reply by 5/1 or within 4 week(s) of notification.

## CONTACT

Richard Moeggenberg, Director of Financial Aid
33 East College Street, Hillsdale, MI 49242
(517) 607-2350

## Hope College

Holland, Michigan
www.hope.edu

**4-year private** liberal arts college in small city, affiliated with Reformed Church in America.

**Enrollment:** 3,238 undergrads, 2% part-time. 777 full-time freshmen.

**Selectivity:** Admits 50 to 75% of applicants.

## BASIC COSTS (2015-2016)

**Tuition and fees:** $30,550.

**Room and board:** $9,390.

**Additional info:** Tuition/fee waivers available for minority students.

## FINANCIAL AID PICTURE (2015-2016)

**Students with need:** Average financial aid package met 80% of need; average scholarship/grant was $19,996; average loan was $4,039. For part-time students, average financial aid package was $4,252.

**Students without need:** 216 full-time freshmen who did not demonstrate need for aid received scholarships/grants; average award was $8,159. No-need awards available for academics, art, minority status, music/drama, religious affiliation.

## FINANCIAL AID PROCEDURES

**Forms required:** FAFSA, institutional form.

**Dates and Deadlines:** Priority date 3/1; no closing date. Applicants notified on a rolling basis starting 3/15.

**Transfers:** No deadline. Applicants notified on a rolling basis starting 3/25.

## CONTACT

Thomas Bylsma, Chief Financial Officer
69 East 10th Street, Holland, MI 49422-9000
(616) 395-7765

## Jackson College

Jackson, Michigan
www.jccmi.edu

Federal Code: 002274

**2-year public** community college in small city.

**Enrollment:** 5,180 undergrads.

**Selectivity:** Open admission; but selective for some programs.

## BASIC COSTS (2015-2016)

**Tuition and fees:** $4,890; out-of-district residents $6,300; out-of-state residents $8,640.

**Per-credit charge:** $125; out-of-district residents $172; out-of-state residents $250.

## FINANCIAL AID PICTURE

**Students with need:** Need-based aid available for full-time and part-time students. Work study available nights, weekends, and for part-time students.

**Students without need:** No-need awards available for academics, art, athletics, leadership.

## FINANCIAL AID PROCEDURES

**Forms required:** FAFSA, institutional form.

**Dates and Deadlines:** Priority date 6/15; no closing date. Applicants notified on a rolling basis starting 3/1.

## CONTACT

Kim Cvitkovic, Director of Financial Aid
2111 Emmons Road, Jackson, MI 49201-8399
(517) 796-8410

## Kalamazoo College

Kalamazoo, Michigan
www.kzoo.edu

Federal Code: 002275

**4-year private** liberal arts college in small city.

**Enrollment:** 1,415 undergrads, 1% part-time. 364 full-time freshmen.

**Selectivity:** Admits 50 to 75% of applicants.

## BASIC COSTS (2015-2016)

**Tuition and fees:** $42,946.

**Room and board:** $8,886.

**Additional info:** $1,104 for health insurance if the student has no health insurance.

### FINANCIAL AID PICTURE (2015-2016)

**Students with need:** Out of 304 full-time freshmen who applied for aid, 240 were judged to have need. Of these, 240 received aid, and 139 had their full need met. Average financial aid package met 94% of need; average scholarship/grant was $29,445; average loan was $4,956.

**Students without need:** 117 full-time freshmen who did not demonstrate need for aid received scholarships/grants; average award was $20,273. No-need awards available for academics, alumni affiliation, art, leadership, music/drama.

**Scholarships offered:** Honors Scholarship: $10,000-24,000 annually; based on academic and co-curricular record and accomplishments; varied number awarded. Enlightened Leadership Awards: $5,000; based on written application and/or creative expression portfolio.

**Additional info:** Paid career development internship and senior project experiences available on campus.

### FINANCIAL AID PROCEDURES

**Forms required:** FAFSA.

**Dates and Deadlines:** Priority date 2/15; no closing date. Applicants notified by 3/23; must reply by 5/1.

**Transfers:** Closing date 3/1. Must reply by 5/1.

### CONTACT

Marian Stowers, Director of Financial Aid
1200 Academy Street, Kalamazoo, MI 49006
(269) 337-7192

## Kalamazoo Valley Community College

Kalamazoo, Michigan
www.kvcc.edu                    Federal Code: 006949

**2-year public** community college in small city.

**Enrollment:** 7,479 undergrads, 61% part-time. 868 full-time freshmen.

**Selectivity:** Open admission.

### BASIC COSTS (2015-2016)

**Tuition and fees:** $3,060; out-of-district residents $5,100; out-of-state residents $6,810.

**Per-credit charge:** $95; out-of-district residents $163; out-of-state residents $220.

### FINANCIAL AID PICTURE

**Students with need:** Need-based aid available for full-time and part-time students. Work study available nights, weekends, and for part-time students.

**Students without need:** No-need awards available for academics, athletics.

### FINANCIAL AID PROCEDURES

**Forms required:** FAFSA, institutional form.

**Dates and Deadlines:** Priority date 6/1; no closing date. Applicants notified on a rolling basis starting 5/1; must reply within 2 week(s) of notification.

### CONTACT

Roger Miller, Director of Financial Aid
6767 West O Avenue, Kalamazoo, MI 49003-4070
(269) 488-4340

## Kellogg Community College

Battle Creek, Michigan
www.kellogg.edu                    Federal Code: 002276

**2-year public** community college in small city.

**Enrollment:** 3,943 undergrads, 69% part-time. 238 full-time freshmen.

**Selectivity:** Open admission; but selective for some programs.

### BASIC COSTS (2015-2016)

**Tuition and fees:** $3,375; out-of-district residents $5,228; out-of-state residents $7,313.

**Per-credit charge:** $100; out-of-district residents $161; out-of-state residents $231.

**Additional info:** Current Military Service members pay in-district rates regardless of residency status. Health programs charged at higher rates.

### FINANCIAL AID PICTURE (2014-2015)

**Students with need:** Need-based aid available for full-time and part-time students. Work study available nights.

**Students without need:** No-need awards available for academics, art, athletics, music/drama, state/district residency.

### FINANCIAL AID PROCEDURES

**Forms required:** FAFSA, institutional form.

**Dates and Deadlines:** Priority date 4/1; no closing date. Applicants notified on a rolling basis starting 3/13.

**Transfers:** No deadline. Applicants notified on a rolling basis.

### CONTACT

Nikki Jewell, Director, Financial Aid
450 North Avenue, Battle Creek, MI 49017-3397
(269) 965-4123

## Kettering University

Flint, Michigan
www.kettering.edu                    Federal Code: 002262

**4-year private** university and engineering college in small city.

**Enrollment:** 1,802 undergrads, 3% part-time. 434 full-time freshmen.

**Selectivity:** Admits 50 to 75% of applicants.

### BASIC COSTS (2015-2016)

**Tuition and fees:** $38,430.

**Per-credit charge:** $1,281.

**Room and board:** $7,510.

### FINANCIAL AID PICTURE (2015-2016)

**Students with need:** Out of 421 full-time freshmen who applied for aid, 339 were judged to have need. Of these, 339 received aid, and 38 had their full need met. Average financial aid package met 62% of need; average scholarship/grant was $18,296; average loan was $3,387. Need-based aid available for part-time students.

**Students without need:** 93 full-time freshmen who did not demonstrate need for aid received scholarships/grants; average award was $14,323. No-need awards available for academics.

**Scholarships offered:** Various scholarships: $20,000-$40,000 for 4 years; based on merit. Renewable scholarships: $250-$5,000 per year.

### FINANCIAL AID PROCEDURES

**Forms required:** FAFSA.

**Dates and Deadlines:** Applicants notified on a rolling basis starting 3/1.

**Transfers:** No deadline. Applicants notified on a rolling basis starting 1/31.

### CONTACT

Diane Bice, Director of Financial Aid
1700 University Avenue, Flint, MI 48504-6214
(810) 762-7859

## Kirtland Community College

Roscommon, Michigan
www.kirtland.edu                    Federal Code: 007171

**2-year public** community college in rural community.

**Enrollment:** 1,220 undergrads, 58% part-time. 127 full-time freshmen.

**Selectivity:** Open admission; but selective for some programs.

## BASIC COSTS (2015-2016)

**Tuition and fees:** $3,725; out-of-district residents $4,955; out-of-state residents $7,625.

**Per-credit charge:** $105; out-of-district residents $146; out-of-state residents $235.

**Additional info:** Tuition/fee waivers available for minority students.

## FINANCIAL AID PICTURE (2014-2015)

**Students with need:** Out of 115 full-time freshmen who applied for aid, 108 were judged to have need. Of these, 108 received aid, and 4 had their full need met. Average financial aid package met 47% of need; average scholarship/grant was $5,354; average loan was $1,783. For part-time students, average financial aid package was $4,114.

**Students without need:** 2 full-time freshmen who did not demonstrate need for aid received scholarships/grants; average award was $3,960. No-need awards available for academics, athletics, minority status.

**Scholarships offered:** 4 full-time freshmen received athletic scholarships; average amount $1,471.

**Additional info:** Federal and institutional work-study programs available.

## FINANCIAL AID PROCEDURES

**Forms required:** FAFSA.

**Dates and Deadlines:** Priority date 5/1; no closing date. Applicants notified on a rolling basis.

**Transfers:** No deadline.

## CONTACT

Christin Bates, Director of Financial Aid

10775 North Saint Helen Road, Roscommon, MI 48653

(989) 275-5000 ext. 310

# Kuyper College

Grand Rapids, Michigan

www.kuyper.edu          Federal Code: 002311

**4-year private** Bible and liberal arts college in large city, affiliated with Christian Reformed Church.

**Enrollment:** 252 undergrads, 13% part-time. 46 full-time freshmen.

**Selectivity:** Admits 50 to 75% of applicants.

## BASIC COSTS (2015-2016)

**Tuition and fees:** $19,484.

**Room and board:** $7,260.

## FINANCIAL AID PICTURE (2014-2015)

**Students with need:** Out of 45 full-time freshmen who applied for aid, 38 were judged to have need. Of these, 38 received aid, and 5 had their full need met. Average financial aid package met 78% of need; average scholarship/grant was $14,013; average loan was $3,989. For part-time students, average financial aid package was $10,441.

**Students without need:** 8 full-time freshmen who did not demonstrate need for aid received scholarships/grants; average award was $5,163. No-need awards available for academics, alumni affiliation, leadership, minority status, music/drama.

**Scholarships offered:** Achievement Awards: $1,000-$8,000; based on GPA and ACT. Christian Leadership Scholarship: $2,000; renewable annually; based on Christian service activities; 3.2 GPA. Christian Ministry Scholarship: up to $2,000; renewable annually; based on family's primary source of income. Multicultural Scholarships: $500-$5,000; based on 2.5 GPA, academic record, leadership involvement, essays, cross-cultural experiences, and student's ethnic, cultural and socioeconomic background.

## FINANCIAL AID PROCEDURES

**Forms required:** FAFSA.

**Dates and Deadlines:** Priority date 3/1; no closing date. Applicants notified on a rolling basis starting 3/15; must reply within 2 week(s) of notification.

**Transfers:** No deadline. Applicants notified on a rolling basis starting 3/15; must reply within 2 week(s) of notification.

## CONTACT

Agnes Russell, Director of Financial Aid

3333 East Beltline Avenue NE, Grand Rapids, MI 49525-9781

(616) 988-3656

# Lake Michigan College

Benton Harbor, Michigan

www.lakemichigancollege.edu          Federal Code: 002277

**2-year public** community college in large town.

**Enrollment:** 2,812 undergrads, 60% part-time. 440 full-time freshmen.

**Selectivity:** Open admission; but selective for some programs.

## BASIC COSTS (2015-2016)

**Tuition and fees:** $4,140; out-of-district residents $5,685; out-of-state residents $5,685.

**Per-credit charge:** $94; out-of-district residents $145; out-of-state residents $145.

**Room only:** $7,000.

**Additional info:** Tuition/fee waivers available for adults.

## FINANCIAL AID PICTURE

**Students with need:** Need-based aid available for full-time and part-time students.

**Scholarships offered:** Presidential Scholarship: full tuition and fees; at least 10 scholarships available to new high school graduates each year.

## FINANCIAL AID PROCEDURES

**Forms required:** FAFSA.

**Dates and Deadlines:** Priority date 3/1; no closing date. Applicants notified on a rolling basis starting 4/1; must reply within 2 week(s) of notification.

**Transfers:** No deadline. Must reply within 2 week(s) of notification.

## CONTACT

Susan Fintze, Assistant Director, Financial Aid

2755 East Napier Avenue, Benton Harbor, MI 49022-1899

(269) 927-8112

# Lake Superior State University

Sault Ste. Marie, Michigan

www.lssu.edu          Federal Code: 002293

**4-year public** university and engineering college in large town.

**Enrollment:** 2,212 undergrads, 13% part-time. 393 full-time freshmen.

**Selectivity:** Admits over 75% of applicants.

## BASIC COSTS (2015-2016)

**Tuition and fees:** $10,577; out-of-state residents $10,577.

**Per-credit charge:** $433.

**Room and board:** $9,290.

## FINANCIAL AID PICTURE

**Students with need:** Need-based aid available for full-time and part-time students. Work study available nights, weekends, and for part-time students.

**Students without need:** No-need awards available for academics, athletics, state/district residency.

## FINANCIAL AID PROCEDURES

**Forms required:** FAFSA.

**Dates and Deadlines:** Priority date 3/1; no closing date. Applicants notified on a rolling basis starting 10/1; must reply by 5/1 or within 3 week(s) of notification.

**Transfers:** Closing date 3/1. Applicants notified on a rolling basis starting 3/1.

## CONTACT
Deborah Faust, Director of Financial Aid
650 West Easterday Avenue, Sault Sainte Marie, MI 49783-1699
(906) 635-2678

## Lansing Community College
Lansing, Michigan
www.lcc.edu                           Federal Code: 002278

**2-year public** community college in small city.
**Enrollment:** 12,528 undergrads, 61% part-time. 1,629 full-time freshmen.
**Selectivity:** Open admission; but selective for some programs.

### BASIC COSTS (2015-2016)
**Tuition and fees:** $3,020; out-of-district residents $5,660; out-of-state residents $8,300.
**Per-credit charge:** $88; out-of-district residents $176; out-of-state residents $264.

### FINANCIAL AID PICTURE (2014-2015)
**Students with need:** Need-based aid available for full-time and part-time students. Work study available nights, weekends, and for part-time students.
**Students without need:** No-need awards available for academics, athletics.

### FINANCIAL AID PROCEDURES
**Forms required:** FAFSA.
**Dates and Deadlines:** Closing date 7/19. Applicants notified on a rolling basis starting 2/11.
**Transfers:** Closing date 7/1. Applicants notified on a rolling basis starting 4/3.

### CONTACT
Stephanie Bogard Trapp, Director of Financial Aid
1121 Enrollment Services, Lansing, MI 48901-7210
(517) 483-1200

## Lawrence Technological University
Southfield, Michigan
www.ltu.edu                           Federal Code: 002279

**4-year private** university in small city.
**Enrollment:** 1,967 undergrads, 18% part-time. 329 full-time freshmen.
**Selectivity:** Admits 50 to 75% of applicants.

### BASIC COSTS (2015-2016)
**Tuition and fees:** $30,300.
**Per-credit charge:** $986.
**Room and board:** $9,470.
**Additional info:** Tuition/fee waivers available for unemployed or children of unemployed.

### FINANCIAL AID PICTURE (2014-2015)
**Students with need:** Out of 315 full-time freshmen who applied for aid, 247 were judged to have need. Of these, 246 received aid, and 44 had their full need met. Average financial aid package met 69% of need; average scholarship/grant was $16,867; average loan was $6,440. For part-time students, average financial aid package was $14,325.
**Students without need:** 63 full-time freshmen who did not demonstrate need for aid received scholarships/grants; average award was $16,980. No-need awards available for academics, alumni affiliation, minority status, ROTC, state/district residency.
**Scholarships offered:** 57 full-time freshmen received athletic scholarships; average amount $11,458.
**Additional info:** March 1 state deadline for Michigan Competitive Scholarship and Michigan Tuition Grant.

### FINANCIAL AID PROCEDURES
**Forms required:** FAFSA.
**Dates and Deadlines:** Priority date 4/1; no closing date. Applicants notified on a rolling basis starting 4/1; must reply within 2 week(s) of notification.
**Transfers:** Applicants notified on a rolling basis starting 4/1; must reply within 2 week(s) of notification.

### CONTACT
Dee King, Director of Student Financial Aid
21000 West Ten Mile Road, Southfield, MI 48075-1058
(248) 204-2121

## Macomb Community College
Warren, Michigan
www.macomb.edu                        Federal Code: 008906

**2-year public** community college in small city.
**Enrollment:** 15,955 undergrads, 68% part-time. 1,506 full-time freshmen.
**Selectivity:** Open admission; but selective for some programs.

### BASIC COSTS (2015-2016)
**Tuition and fees:** $3,070; out-of-district residents $5,050; out-of-state residents $6,430.
**Per-credit charge:** $94; out-of-district residents $160; out-of-state residents $206.

### FINANCIAL AID PICTURE
**Students with need:** Need-based aid available for full-time and part-time students. Work study available nights, weekends, and for part-time students.
**Students without need:** No-need awards available for academics, athletics, leadership, music/drama, state/district residency.

### FINANCIAL AID PROCEDURES
**Forms required:** FAFSA, institutional form.
**Dates and Deadlines:** Priority date 4/15; no closing date. Applicants notified on a rolling basis starting 5/15; must reply within 2 week(s) of notification.
**Transfers:** Must submit financial aid transcripts from all institutions attended.

### CONTACT
Doug Levy, Director of Financial Aid
14500 East Twelve Mile Road, Warren, MI 48088-3896
(586) 445-7228

## Madonna University
Livonia, Michigan
www.madonna.edu                       Federal Code: 002282

**4-year private** university and liberal arts college in small city, affiliated with Roman Catholic Church.
**Enrollment:** 2,674 undergrads, 47% part-time. 168 full-time freshmen.
**Selectivity:** Admits 50 to 75% of applicants.

### BASIC COSTS (2015-2016)
**Tuition and fees:** $18,740.
**Per-credit charge:** $620.
**Room and board:** $9,230.

### FINANCIAL AID PICTURE (2014-2015)
**Students with need:** Out of 132 full-time freshmen who applied for aid, 110 were judged to have need. Of these, 110 received aid, and 29 had their full need met. Average financial aid package met 66% of need; average scholarship/grant was $10,894; average loan was $2,994. For part-time students, average financial aid package was $6,512.

**Students without need:** 43 full-time freshmen who did not demonstrate need for aid received scholarships/grants; average award was $7,631. No-need awards available for academics, alumni affiliation, art, athletics, leadership, minority status, music/drama, religious affiliation, state/district residency.
**Scholarships offered:** 26 full-time freshmen received athletic scholarships; average amount $8,950.

**FINANCIAL AID PROCEDURES**
**Forms required:** FAFSA.
**Dates and Deadlines:** Priority date 2/1; no closing date. Applicants notified on a rolling basis starting 3/15; must reply by 9/1 or within 2 week(s) of notification.
**Transfers:** Priority date 2/1; no deadline. Applicants notified on a rolling basis starting 4/15; must reply by 9/1 or within 2 week(s) of notification. Deadline for state aid is March 1.

**CONTACT**
Chris Ziegler, Director of Financial Aid
36600 Schoolcraft Road, Livonia, MI 48150-1176
(734) 432-5664

## Marygrove College
Detroit, Michigan
www.marygrove.edu                    Federal Code: 002284

**4-year private** liberal arts college in very large city, affiliated with Roman Catholic Church.
**Enrollment:** 676 undergrads.
**Selectivity:** Admits 50 to 75% of applicants.

**BASIC COSTS (2015-2016)**
**Tuition and fees:** $20,930.
**Per-credit charge:** $590.
**Room and board:** $7,125.

**FINANCIAL AID PICTURE**
**Students with need:** Need-based aid available for full-time and part-time students.
**Students without need:** This college awards aid only to students with need.

**FINANCIAL AID PROCEDURES**
**Forms required:** FAFSA, institutional form.
**Dates and Deadlines:** Priority date 3/15; no closing date. Applicants notified on a rolling basis starting 5/15; must reply within 2 week(s) of notification.

**CONTACT**
Kimberly Gooden, Director, Enrollment Center
8425 West McNichols Road, Detroit, MI 48221
(313) 927-1692

## Michigan Jewish Institute
West Bloomfield, Michigan
www.mji.edu                    Federal Code: 032843

**4-year private** liberal arts college in very large city, affiliated with Jewish faith.
**Enrollment:** 2,204 undergrads.
**Selectivity:** Open admission; but selective for some programs.

**BASIC COSTS (2015-2016)**
**Tuition and fees:** $10,600.
**Per-credit charge:** $350.

**FINANCIAL AID PICTURE (2014-2015)**
**Students with need:** Need-based aid available for full-time and part-time students. Work study available nights, weekends, and for part-time students.

**Students without need:** This college awards aid only to students with need.

**FINANCIAL AID PROCEDURES**
**Forms required:** FAFSA.
**Dates and Deadlines:** Applicants notified on a rolling basis starting 1/1.
**Transfers:** Priority date 1/1; no deadline. Applicants notified on a rolling basis starting 1/1.

**CONTACT**
Sandra Kittle, Financial Aid Administrator
6888 West Maple Road, West Bloomfield, MI 48322
(248) 414-6900 ext. 2104

## Michigan State University
East Lansing, Michigan
www.msu.edu                    Federal Code: 002290

**4-year public** university in small city.
**Enrollment:** 38,853 undergrads, 9% part-time. 7,991 full-time freshmen.
**Selectivity:** Admits 50 to 75% of applicants.

**BASIC COSTS (2015-2016)**
**Tuition and fees:** $13,560; out-of-state residents $36,360.
**Per-credit charge:** $452; out-of-state residents $1,212.
**Room and board:** $9,474.

**FINANCIAL AID PICTURE (2015-2016)**
**Students with need:** Out of 5,660 full-time freshmen who applied for aid, 3,990 were judged to have need. Of these, 3,819 received aid, and 663 had their full need met. Average financial aid package met 64% of need; average scholarship/grant was $10,723; average loan was $3,375. For part-time students, average financial aid package was $8,501.
**Students without need:** 742 full-time freshmen who did not demonstrate need for aid received scholarships/grants; average award was $9,367. No-need awards available for academics, alumni affiliation, art, athletics, leadership, music/drama, ROTC, state/district residency.
**Scholarships offered:** 50 full-time freshmen received athletic scholarships; average amount $25,583.

**FINANCIAL AID PROCEDURES**
**Forms required:** FAFSA.
**Dates and Deadlines:** Applicants notified on a rolling basis starting 3/15; must reply within 4 week(s) of notification.

**CONTACT**
Richard Shipman, Director of Financial Aid
250 Administration Building, East Lansing, MI 48824
(517) 353-5940

## Michigan Technological University
Houghton, Michigan
www.mtu.edu                    Federal Code: 002292

**4-year public** university in small town.
**Enrollment:** 5,645 undergrads, 5% part-time. 1,276 full-time freshmen.
**Selectivity:** Admits over 75% of applicants.

**BASIC COSTS (2015-2016)**
**Tuition and fees:** $14,286; out-of-state residents $30,250.
**Per-credit charge:** $529; out-of-state residents $1,109.
**Room and board:** $9,857.

**FINANCIAL AID PICTURE (2015-2016)**
**Students with need:** Out of 1,151 full-time freshmen who applied for aid, 857 were judged to have need. Of these, 857 received aid, and 192 had their full need met. Average financial aid package met 81% of need; average

scholarship/grant was $9,417; average loan was $3,218. For part-time students, average financial aid package was $7,687.

**Students without need:** 340 full-time freshmen who did not demonstrate need for aid received scholarships/grants; average award was $4,969. No-need awards available for academics, alumni affiliation, athletics, job skills, leadership, ROTC, state/district residency.

**Scholarships offered:** 54 full-time freshmen received athletic scholarships; average amount $10,815.

### FINANCIAL AID PROCEDURES

**Forms required:** FAFSA.

**Dates and Deadlines:** Priority date 3/1; no closing date. Applicants notified on a rolling basis starting 3/15; must reply by 5/1.

### CONTACT

William Roberts, Director of Financial Aid
1400 Townsend Drive, Houghton, MI 49931-1295
(906) 487-2622

## Mid Michigan Community College

Harrison, Michigan
www.midmich.edu               Federal Code: 006768

**2-year public** community college in small town.

**Enrollment:** 2,942 undergrads.

**Selectivity:** Open admission; but selective for some programs.

### BASIC COSTS (2015-2016)

**Tuition and fees:** $3,580; out-of-district residents $6,400; out-of-state residents $6,400.

**Per-credit charge:** $104; out-of-district residents $188; out-of-state residents $188.

**Additional info:** Tuition/fee waivers available for adults.

### FINANCIAL AID PICTURE

**Students with need:** Need-based aid available for full-time and part-time students. Work study available nights.

**Students without need:** No-need awards available for academics, art.

### FINANCIAL AID PROCEDURES

**Forms required:** FAFSA, institutional form.

**Dates and Deadlines:** Priority date 5/1; no closing date. Applicants notified on a rolling basis starting 4/1; must reply within 2 week(s) of notification.

### CONTACT

Gale Crandell, Financial Aid Director
1375 South Clare Avenue, Harrison, MI 48625-9442
(989) 386-6622

## Monroe County Community College

Monroe, Michigan
www.monroeccc.edu               Federal Code: 002294

**2-year public** community college in large town.

**Enrollment:** 1,500 full-time undergrads.

**Selectivity:** Open admission; but selective for some programs.

### BASIC COSTS (2015-2016)

**Tuition and fees:** $3,730; out-of-district residents $5,980; out-of-state residents $6,580.

**Per-credit charge:** $122; out-of-district residents $197; out-of-state residents $217.

**Additional info:** Tuition/fee waivers available for minority students.

### FINANCIAL AID PICTURE

**Students with need:** Need-based aid available for full-time and part-time students. Work study available nights, weekends, and for part-time students.

**Students without need:** No-need awards available for academics, alumni affiliation, art, leadership, music/drama, state/district residency.

### FINANCIAL AID PROCEDURES

**Forms required:** FAFSA, institutional form.

**Dates and Deadlines:** Priority date 4/1; no closing date. Applicants notified on a rolling basis starting 4/1; must reply within 2 week(s) of notification.

### CONTACT

Valerie Culler, Director of Financial Aid/Placement
1555 South Raisinville Road, Monroe, MI 48161-9746
(734) 384-4135

## Montcalm Community College

Sidney, Michigan
www.montcalm.edu               Federal Code: 002295

**2-year public** community and liberal arts college in rural community.

**Enrollment:** 1,496 undergrads.

**Selectivity:** Open admission; but selective for some programs.

### BASIC COSTS (2015-2016)

**Tuition and fees:** $3,540; out-of-district residents $6,150; out-of-state residents $8,880.

**Per-credit charge:** $100; out-of-district residents $187; out-of-state residents $278.

### FINANCIAL AID PICTURE

**Students with need:** Need-based aid available for full-time and part-time students.

**Students without need:** No-need awards available for academics, state/district residency.

### FINANCIAL AID PROCEDURES

**Forms required:** FAFSA, institutional form.

**Dates and Deadlines:** Priority date 2/15; no closing date. Applicants notified on a rolling basis starting 4/15; must reply within 2 week(s) of notification.

**Transfers:** Priority date 3/1; no deadline. Applicants notified on a rolling basis starting 4/15.

### CONTACT

Traci Nichols, Director of Financial Aid
2800 College Drive, Sidney, MI 48885
(989) 328-1285

## Mott Community College

Flint, Michigan
www.mcc.edu               Federal Code: 002261

**2-year public** community college in small city.

**Enrollment:** 7,556 undergrads, 71% part-time. 612 full-time freshmen.

**Selectivity:** Open admission; but selective for some programs.

### BASIC COSTS (2016-2017)

**Tuition and fees:** $4,666; out-of-district residents $6,260; out-of-state residents $8,598.

**Per-credit charge:** $130; out-of-district residents $183; out-of-state residents $261.

### FINANCIAL AID PICTURE (2014-2015)

**Students with need:** Need-based aid available for full-time and part-time students. Work study available nights.

**Students without need:** No-need awards available for academics, alumni affiliation, art, athletics, leadership, minority status, music/drama, state/district residency.

### FINANCIAL AID PROCEDURES

**Forms required:** FAFSA.

**Dates and Deadlines:** Priority date 6/1; no closing date. Applicants notified on a rolling basis starting 5/1.
**Transfers:** Pell Grants adjusted for amount used at another institution.

**CONTACT**
Emily Varney, Director - Student Financial Services
1401 East Court Street, Flint, MI 48503-2089
(810) 762-0144

## Muskegon Community College
Muskegon, Michigan
www.muskegoncc.edu          Federal Code: 002297

2-year public community college in small city.
**Enrollment:** 3,587 undergrads, 62% part-time. 503 full-time freshmen.
**Selectivity:** Open admission; but selective for some programs.

**BASIC COSTS (2015-2016)**
**Tuition and fees:** $3,790; out-of-district residents $6,340; out-of-state residents $8,500.
**Per-credit charge:** $99; out-of-district residents $184; out-of-state residents $256.

**FINANCIAL AID PICTURE (2014-2015)**
**Students with need:** 76% of average financial aid package awarded as scholarships/grants, 24% awarded as loans/jobs. Need-based aid available for part-time students. Work study available nights, weekends, and for part-time students.

**FINANCIAL AID PROCEDURES**
**Forms required:** FAFSA.
**Dates and Deadlines:** Priority date 5/1; no closing date. Applicants notified on a rolling basis starting 6/1; must reply within 2 week(s) of notification.

**CONTACT**
Bruce Wierda, Director of Financial Aid
221 South Quarterline Road, Muskegon, MI 49442
(231) 777-0221

## North Central Michigan College
Petoskey, Michigan
www.ncmich.edu          Federal Code: 002299

2-year public community college in small town.
**Enrollment:** 2,581 undergrads.
**Selectivity:** Open admission; but selective for some programs.

**BASIC COSTS (2015-2016)**
**Tuition and fees:** $3,708; out-of-district residents $5,725; out-of-state residents $7,195.
**Per-credit charge:** $103; out-of-district residents $170; out-of-state residents $219.
**Room and board:** $6,250.

**FINANCIAL AID PICTURE**
**Students with need:** Need-based aid available for full-time and part-time students. Work study available nights, weekends, and for part-time students.

**FINANCIAL AID PROCEDURES**
**Forms required:** FAFSA, institutional form.
**Dates and Deadlines:** Applicants notified on a rolling basis starting 4/30.

**CONTACT**
Virginia Panoff, Director of Financial Aid
1515 Howard Street, Petoskey, MI 49770
(231) 348-6627

## Northern Michigan University
Marquette, Michigan
www.nmu.edu          Federal Code: 002301

4-year public university in large town.
**Enrollment:** 7,989 undergrads.

**BASIC COSTS (2015-2016)**
**Tuition and fees:** $9,860; out-of-state residents $15,260.
**Per-credit charge:** $373; out-of-state residents $598.
**Room and board:** $9,286.
**Additional info:** Tuition/fee waivers available for minority students.

**FINANCIAL AID PICTURE**
**Students with need:** Need-based aid available for full-time and part-time students. Work study available nights, weekends, and for part-time students.
**Students without need:** No-need awards available for academics, art, athletics, leadership, music/drama, ROTC, state/district residency.
**Scholarships offered:** Talent recognition awards: available in art and design, music, theater. Freshman Fellowship: $1,000 in student employment; 3.5 GPA and 24 ACT. Dr. Edgar L. Harden Scholarship: full scholarship; 3.5 GPA and 24 ACT. National Academic Award: $3,500; minimum 3.0 GPA and 19 ACT; awarded to non-Michigan residents. Merit Excellence Award: $2,750-$3,500; based on 3.0 GPA and 33 ACT. Merit Award: $2,250-$3,000; 3.0 GPA and 30-32 ACT. Scholars Award: $1,250-$2,000; 3.0 GPA and 27-29 ACT. Outstanding Achievement: $750-$1,500; 3.0 GPA and 25-26 ACT.
**Additional info:** Audition or portfolio required for music, drama, and art scholarship applicants. Alumni Dependent Tuition Program gives resident tuition rates to nonresident dependents of NMU alumni who received master's, baccalaureate, or associate degree; renewable.

**FINANCIAL AID PROCEDURES**
**Forms required:** FAFSA.
**Dates and Deadlines:** Priority date 3/1; no closing date. Applicants notified on a rolling basis starting 4/1; must reply within 2 week(s) of notification.
**Transfers:** No deadline. Applicants notified on a rolling basis starting 4/1; must reply within 2 week(s) of notification. Merit-based transfer scholarships available.

**CONTACT**
Michael Rotundo, Director of Financial Aid
1401 Presque Isle Avenue, Marquette, MI 49855
(906) 227-2327

## Northwestern Michigan College
Traverse City, Michigan
www.nmc.edu          Federal Code: 002302

2-year public community and maritime college in large town.
**Enrollment:** 3,938 undergrads.
**Selectivity:** Open admission; but selective for some programs.

**BASIC COSTS (2015-2016)**
**Tuition and fees:** $3,950; out-of-district residents $6,783; out-of-state residents $8,522.
**Per-credit charge:** $96; out-of-district residents $191; out-of-state residents $249.
**Room and board:** $9,850.

**FINANCIAL AID PICTURE**
**Students with need:** Need-based aid available for full-time and part-time students. Work study available nights, weekends, and for part-time students.
**Students without need:** No-need awards available for academics, art, job skills, leadership, minority status, music/drama, ROTC, state/district residency.

**FINANCIAL AID PROCEDURES**
**Forms required:** FAFSA.

**Dates and Deadlines:** Priority date 4/1; no closing date. Applicants notified on a rolling basis starting 5/1; must reply within 2 week(s) of notification.

**CONTACT**
Pam Palermo, Director for Financial Aid
1701 East Front Street, Traverse City, MI 49686
(231) 995-1035

## Northwood University: Michigan
Midland, Michigan
www.northwood.edu                    Federal Code: 004072

**4-year private** university and business college in large town.
**Enrollment:** 1,459 undergrads, 3% part-time. 334 full-time freshmen.
**Selectivity:** Admits 50 to 75% of applicants.

**BASIC COSTS (2015-2016)**
**Tuition and fees:** $24,170.
**Per-credit charge:** $883.
**Room and board:** $9,590.

**FINANCIAL AID PICTURE (2015-2016)**
**Students with need:** Out of 291 full-time freshmen who applied for aid, 232 were judged to have need. Of these, 232 received aid, and 43 had their full need met. Average financial aid package met 67% of need; average scholarship/grant was $5,657; average loan was $3,379. For part-time students, average financial aid package was $9,792.
**Students without need:** 47 full-time freshmen who did not demonstrate need for aid received scholarships/grants; average award was $11,042. No-need awards available for academics, alumni affiliation, athletics, leadership, minority status.
**Scholarships offered: Merit:** Academic scholarships based on test scores and GPA; unlimited number awarded. **Athletic:** 39 full-time freshmen received athletic scholarships; average amount $11,352.

**FINANCIAL AID PROCEDURES**
**Forms required:** FAFSA.
**Dates and Deadlines:** Priority date 3/1; no closing date. Applicants notified on a rolling basis starting 3/1.
**Transfers:** No deadline. Applicants notified on a rolling basis.

**CONTACT**
Mark Martin, Financial Aid Director
4000 Whiting Drive, Midland, MI 48640
(989) 837-4230

## Oakland Community College
Bloomfield Hills, Michigan
www.oaklandcc.edu                    Federal Code: 002303

**2-year public** community college in very large city.
**Enrollment:** 12,202 undergrads.
**Selectivity:** Open admission.

**BASIC COSTS (2015-2016)**
**Tuition and fees:** $2,710; out-of-district residents $5,200; out-of-state residents $7,270.
**Per-credit charge:** $88; out-of-district residents $171; out-of-state residents $240.

**FINANCIAL AID PICTURE**
**Students with need:** Need-based aid available for full-time and part-time students.
**Students without need:** No-need awards available for academics, athletics, job skills.

**FINANCIAL AID PROCEDURES**
**Forms required:** FAFSA.
**Dates and Deadlines:** Priority date 4/15; no closing date. Applicants notified on a rolling basis starting 4/15.
**Transfers:** Closing date 6/30. Applicants notified on a rolling basis starting 6/30. Michigan residency required for aid to transfer students.

**CONTACT**
Wilma Porter, Director of Financial Assistance and Scholarships
2480 Opdyke Road, Bloomfield Hills, MI 48304-2266
(248) 341-2000

## Oakland University
Rochester, Michigan
www.oakland.edu                    Federal Code: 002307

**4-year public** university in small city.
**Enrollment:** 16,733 undergrads, 23% part-time. 2,410 full-time freshmen.
**Selectivity:** Admits 50 to 75% of applicants.

**BASIC COSTS (2015-2016)**
**Tuition and fees:** $11,513; out-of-state residents $23,873.
**Per-credit charge:** $384; out-of-state residents $796.
**Room and board:** $9,250.

**FINANCIAL AID PICTURE (2014-2015)**
**Students with need:** Out of 2,024 full-time freshmen who applied for aid, 1,549 were judged to have need. Of these, 1,482 received aid, and 163 had their full need met. Average financial aid package met 80% of need; average scholarship/grant was $6,897; average loan was $2,956. For part-time students, average financial aid package was $8,868.
**Students without need:** 399 full-time freshmen who did not demonstrate need for aid received scholarships/grants; average award was $5,081. No-need awards available for academics, alumni affiliation, art, athletics, leadership, music/drama.
**Scholarships offered: Merit:** Wide range of scholarships; awarded on basis of accomplishment. **Athletic:** 53 full-time freshmen received athletic scholarships; average amount $14,788.

**FINANCIAL AID PROCEDURES**
**Forms required:** FAFSA.
**Dates and Deadlines:** Priority date 2/15; no closing date. Applicants notified on a rolling basis starting 3/8.

**CONTACT**
Cindy Hermsen, Director of Financial Aid
101 North Foundation Hall, Rochester, MI 48309-4401
(248) 370-2550

## Olivet College
Olivet, Michigan
www.olivetcollege.edu                    Federal Code: 002308

**4-year private** liberal arts college in rural community, affiliated with United Church of Christ.
**Enrollment:** 912 undergrads. 232 full-time freshmen.
**Selectivity:** Admits 50 to 75% of applicants. GED not accepted.

**BASIC COSTS (2015-2016)**
**Tuition and fees:** $24,816.
**Room and board:** $8,400.

**FINANCIAL AID PICTURE (2014-2015)**
**Students with need:** Out of 212 full-time freshmen who applied for aid, 205 were judged to have need. Of these, 205 received aid, and 113 had their full need met. Average financial aid package met 68% of need; average

scholarship/grant was $11,500; average loan was $3,410. For part-time students, average financial aid package was $8,902.

**Students without need:** This college awards aid only to students with need.

**Scholarships offered:** Scholarships: up to $2,000; for students who demonstrate history of community service and civic responsibility during high school or college. Academic merit scholarships: up to full tuition. All scholarships renewable for 4 years.

### FINANCIAL AID PROCEDURES

**Forms required:** FAFSA.

**Dates and Deadlines:** Applicants notified on a rolling basis starting 2/1; must reply within 3 week(s) of notification.

### CONTACT

Libby Jean, Director of Student Services
320 South Main Street, Olivet, MI 49076
(269) 749-7645

## Robert B. Miller College
Battle Creek, Michigan
www.millercollege.edu          Federal Code: 040943

**4-year private** liberal arts college in small city.
**Enrollment:** 327 undergrads.

### BASIC COSTS (2015-2016)
**Tuition and fees:** $11,970.

### FINANCIAL AID PICTURE
**Students with need:** Need-based aid available for full-time and part-time students.
**Students without need:** No-need awards available for academics, leadership.

### FINANCIAL AID PROCEDURES
**Transfers:** No deadline. Applicants notified on a rolling basis starting 4/1.

### CONTACT
Kim Cvitkovic, Director of Financial Aid
450 North Avenue, Battle Creek, MI 49017
(269) 660-8021 ext. 2720

## Rochester College
Rochester Hills, Michigan
www.rc.edu          Federal Code: 002288

**4-year private** liberal arts college in small city, affiliated with Church of Christ.
**Enrollment:** 960 undergrads.

### BASIC COSTS (2015-2016)
**Tuition and fees:** $21,884.
**Per-credit charge:** $649.
**Room and board:** $6,750.
**Additional info:** Tuition/fee waivers available for minority students.

### FINANCIAL AID PICTURE
**Students with need:** Need-based aid available for full-time and part-time students. Work study available nights, weekends, and for part-time students.
**Students without need:** No-need awards available for academics, alumni affiliation, athletics, leadership, music/drama, religious affiliation, state/district residency.

### FINANCIAL AID PROCEDURES
**Forms required:** FAFSA.
**Dates and Deadlines:** Priority date 8/1; no closing date. Applicants notified on a rolling basis starting 1/1; must reply within 2 week(s) of notification.

### CONTACT
Jessica Bristow, Director of Financial Aid
800 West Avon Road, Rochester Hills, MI 48307
(248) 218-2029

## Sacred Heart Major Seminary
Detroit, Michigan
www.shms.edu          Federal Code: 002313

**4-year private** seminary college in very large city, affiliated with Roman Catholic Church.
**Enrollment:** 260 undergrads.

### BASIC COSTS (2015-2016)
**Tuition and fees:** $18,029.
**Per-credit charge:** $421.
**Room and board:** $9,769.
**Additional info:** Theology students pay additional tuition charges. Tuition/fee waivers available for adults.

### FINANCIAL AID PICTURE
**Students with need:** Work study available nights, weekends, and for part-time students.
**Students without need:** No-need awards available for academics, religious affiliation.

### FINANCIAL AID PROCEDURES
**Forms required:** FAFSA, institutional form.
**Dates and Deadlines:** Applicants notified on a rolling basis; must reply within 2 week(s) of notification.
**Transfers:** No deadline. Applicants notified on a rolling basis. Must submit certified high school transcript, copy of high school diploma, copy of GED certificate showing passing score, or college transcript showing associate degree as certification of eligibility; must submit financial aid transcripts from all previous post-secondary institutions attended.

### CONTACT
Kathy Liberski, Director of Financial Aid
2701 Chicago Boulevard, Detroit, MI 48206-1799

## Saginaw Valley State University
University Center, Michigan
www.svsu.edu          Federal Code: 002314

**4-year public** university in small city.
**Enrollment:** 8,434 undergrads, 15% part-time. 1,555 full-time freshmen.
**Selectivity:** Admits over 75% of applicants.

### BASIC COSTS (2015-2016)
**Tuition and fees:** $8,969; out-of-state residents $21,062.
**Per-credit charge:** $284.
**Room and board:** $8,600.

### FINANCIAL AID PICTURE (2015-2016)
**Students with need:** Out of 1,535 full-time freshmen who applied for aid, 1,193 were judged to have need. Of these, 1,193 received aid. Need-based aid available for part-time students.
**Students without need:** No-need awards available for academics, art, athletics, leadership, minority status, music/drama.
**Scholarships offered:** Presidential Scholarships: tuition and selective fees up to 136 credit hours; granted to students who are first or second in high school class with 24 ACT or 3.7 GPA and 28 ACT. Dean's Scholarship: $3,000 per year for four years; 3.0 GPA and 24 ACT. University Foundation Scholarship: tuition and selective fees for four courses and $1,000 to apply toward study abroad or a research project; 3.5 GPA and 24 ACT. University

Scholarship: $1,000 per year for four years; 3.5 GPA. Various private scholarships also available.

## FINANCIAL AID PROCEDURES
**Forms required:** FAFSA.
**Dates and Deadlines:** Priority date 1/1; no closing date. Applicants notified on a rolling basis starting 3/1.
**Transfers:** No deadline. Applicants notified on a rolling basis; must reply within 10 week(s) of notification. Community college scholarship, private scholarships, and Transfer Dean's scholarships available.

## CONTACT
Robert Lemuel, Director of Scholarships and Financial Aid
7400 Bay Road, University Center, MI 48710
(989) 964-4900

# St. Clair County Community College
Port Huron, Michigan
www.sc4.edu                    Federal Code: 002310

**2-year public** community college in large town.
**Enrollment:** 2,694 undergrads.
**Selectivity:** Open admission; but selective for some programs.

## BASIC COSTS (2015-2016)
**Tuition and fees:** $3,600; out-of-district residents $6,480; out-of-state residents $9,240.
**Per-credit charge:** $102; out-of-district residents $198; out-of-state residents $290.

## FINANCIAL AID PICTURE (2015-2016)
**Students with need:** Work study available nights.

## FINANCIAL AID PROCEDURES
**Forms required:** FAFSA.
**Dates and Deadlines:** Priority date 6/1; no closing date. Applicants notified on a rolling basis starting 5/15; must reply within 2 week(s) of notification.
**Transfers:** No deadline. Applicants notified on a rolling basis.

## CONTACT
Josephine Cassar, Executive Director, Financial Assistance
323 Erie Street, Port Huron, MI 48061-5015
(810) 989-5530

# Schoolcraft College
Livonia, Michigan
www.schoolcraft.edu            Federal Code: 002315

**2-year public** culinary school and community college in small city.
**Enrollment:** 10,474 undergrads, 71% part-time. 911 full-time freshmen.
**Selectivity:** Open admission; but selective for some programs.

## BASIC COSTS (2015-2016)
**Tuition and fees:** $3,564; out-of-district residents $4,854; out-of-state residents $6,834.
**Per-credit charge:** $96; out-of-district residents $139; out-of-state residents $205.

## FINANCIAL AID PICTURE (2014-2015)
**Students with need:** Need-based aid available for full-time and part-time students. Work study available nights, weekends, and for part-time students.
**Students without need:** No-need awards available for academics, athletics, leadership, music/drama, state/district residency.
**Scholarships offered:** Trustee Scholarships: $750 per semester (fall and winter); renewable for 2nd year; based on essay, GPA, ACT score trustee application, graduation from local high school;.

## FINANCIAL AID PROCEDURES
**Forms required:** FAFSA.
**Dates and Deadlines:** Applicants notified on a rolling basis starting 6/1.
**Transfers:** No deadline.

## CONTACT
Regina Mosley, Executive Director of Student Financial Services
18600 Haggerty Road, Livonia, MI 48152-2696
(734) 462-4433

# Siena Heights University
Adrian, Michigan
www.sienaheights.edu           Federal Code: 002316

**4-year private** university and liberal arts college in large town, affiliated with Roman Catholic Church.
**Enrollment:** 2,266 undergrads.

## BASIC COSTS (2015-2016)
**Tuition and fees:** $23,750.
**Per-credit charge:** $480.
**Room and board:** $9,710.

## FINANCIAL AID PICTURE
**Students with need:** Need-based aid available for full-time students. Work study available nights, weekends, and for part-time students.

## FINANCIAL AID PROCEDURES
**Dates and Deadlines:** Priority date 3/15; closing date 8/15.
**Transfers:** Priority date 3/1; no deadline.

## CONTACT
Lori Kosarue, Director of Financial Aid
1247 East Siena Heights Drive, Adrian, MI 49221-1796
(517) 264-7110

# Southwestern Michigan College
Dowagiac, Michigan
www.swmich.edu                 Federal Code: 002317

**2-year public** community college in small town.
**Enrollment:** 1,951 undergrads, 43% part-time. 517 full-time freshmen.
**Selectivity:** Open admission; but selective for some programs.

## BASIC COSTS (2015-2016)
**Tuition and fees:** $4,763; out-of-district residents $5,776; out-of-state residents $6,166.
**Per-credit charge:** $113; out-of-district residents $147; out-of-state residents $160.
**Room only:** $5,980.

## FINANCIAL AID PICTURE
**Students with need:** Need-based aid available for full-time and part-time students. Work study available nights, weekends, and for part-time students.
**Students without need:** No-need awards available for academics, art, leadership, music/drama.

## FINANCIAL AID PROCEDURES
**Forms required:** FAFSA, institutional form.
**Dates and Deadlines:** Priority date 7/1; no closing date. Applicants notified on a rolling basis starting 4/1; must reply within 2 week(s) of notification.

## CONTACT
Christine Passer, Director of Financial Aid
58900 Cherry Grove Road, Dowagiac, MI 49047-9793
(800) 456-8675 ext. 2143

## Spring Arbor University
Spring Arbor, Michigan
www.arbor.edu        Federal Code: 002318

**4-year private** university and liberal arts college in rural community, affiliated with Free Methodist Church of North America.
**Enrollment:** 2,307 undergrads, 26% part-time. 290 full-time freshmen.
**Selectivity:** Admits 50 to 75% of applicants.

### BASIC COSTS (2015-2016)
**Tuition and fees:** $25,510.
**Per-credit charge:** $605.
**Room and board:** $8,870.

### FINANCIAL AID PICTURE
**Students with need:** Need-based aid available for full-time and part-time students. Work study available nights, weekends, and for part-time students.
**Students without need:** No-need awards available for academics, art, athletics, minority status, music/drama, religious affiliation.
**Scholarships offered:** Trustee Scholarship: $12,000. President Scholarship: $10,000. Provost Scholarship: $7,500. Faculty Scholarship: $4,000. Partnership Scholarship: $1,000. All based on GPA, class rank, and ACT. National Merit Finalist/Semifinalist: 60% tuition.

### FINANCIAL AID PROCEDURES
**Forms required:** FAFSA.
**Dates and Deadlines:** Priority date 3/1; no closing date. Applicants notified on a rolling basis starting 3/1; must reply within 2 week(s) of notification.
**Transfers:** No deadline. Applicants notified on a rolling basis starting 5/1; must reply within 2 week(s) of notification. Financial aid transcript required from each college previously attended.

### CONTACT
Herbert Rotich, Director of Financial Aid
106 East Main Street, Spring Arbor, MI 49283-9799
(517) 750-6468

## University of Detroit Mercy
Detroit, Michigan
www.udmercy.edu        Federal Code: 002323

**4-year private** university in very large city, affiliated with Roman Catholic Church.
**Enrollment:** 2,586 undergrads, 20% part-time. 503 full-time freshmen.
**Selectivity:** Admits 50 to 75% of applicants.

### BASIC COSTS (2015-2016)
**Tuition and fees:** $38,626.
**Per-credit charge:** $984.
**Room and board:** $8,870.

### FINANCIAL AID PICTURE (2015-2016)
**Students with need:** Out of 455 full-time freshmen who applied for aid, 365 were judged to have need. Of these, 365 received aid, and 62 had their full need met. Average financial aid package met 78% of need; average scholarship/grant was $27,115; average loan was $3,764. For part-time students, average financial aid package was $7,825.
**Students without need:** 134 full-time freshmen who did not demonstrate need for aid received scholarships/grants; average award was $21,817. No-need awards available for academics, alumni affiliation, athletics, religious affiliation, state/district residency.
**Scholarships offered:** *Merit:* Scholarships: $10,000-$21,000 per year; awarded to every full-time freshman student that attends directly out of high school. *Athletic:* 19 full-time freshmen received athletic scholarships; average amount $18,902.

### FINANCIAL AID PROCEDURES
**Forms required:** FAFSA.

**Dates and Deadlines:** Priority date 4/1; no closing date. Applicants notified on a rolling basis starting 3/1.
**Transfers:** No deadline. Applicants notified on a rolling basis starting 3/1.

### CONTACT
Jenny McAlonan, Director of Scholarship and Financial Aid
4001 West McNichols Road, Detroit, MI 48221-3038
(313) 993-3350

## University of Michigan
Ann Arbor, Michigan        Federal Code: 002325
www.umich.edu        CSS Code: 1839

**4-year public** university in small city.
**Enrollment:** 28,120 undergrads, 3% part-time. 6,475 full-time freshmen.
**Selectivity:** Admits less than 50% of applicants.

### BASIC COSTS (2015-2016)
**Tuition and fees:** $13,856; out-of-state residents $43,476.
**Per-credit charge:** $534; out-of-state residents $1,768.
**Room and board:** $10,554.

### FINANCIAL AID PICTURE (2014-2015)
**Students with need:** Out of 3,415 full-time freshmen who applied for aid, 2,539 were judged to have need. Of these, 2,359 received aid, and 1,813 had their full need met. Average financial aid package met 86% of need; average scholarship/grant was $15,006; average loan was $4,254. For part-time students, average financial aid package was $11,847.
**Students without need:** 1,221 full-time freshmen who did not demonstrate need for aid received scholarships/grants; average award was $5,720. No-need awards available for academics, alumni affiliation, art, athletics, leadership, music/drama, religious affiliation, ROTC, state/district residency.
**Scholarships offered:** 156 full-time freshmen received athletic scholarships; average amount $30,285.

### FINANCIAL AID PROCEDURES
**Forms required:** FAFSA, CSS PROFILE.
**Dates and Deadlines:** Closing date 4/30. Applicants notified on a rolling basis starting 3/15.

### CONTACT
Pamela Fowler, Executive Director, Office of Financial Aid
1220 Student Activities Building, Ann Arbor, MI 48109-1316
(734) 763-6600

## University of Michigan: Dearborn
Dearborn, Michigan
www.umd.umich.edu        Federal Code: 002326

**4-year public** university in small city.
**Enrollment:** 6,843 undergrads, 29% part-time. 959 full-time freshmen.
**Selectivity:** Admits 50 to 75% of applicants.

### BASIC COSTS (2015-2016)
**Tuition and fees:** $11,304; out-of-state residents $23,520.
**Per-credit charge:** $430; out-of-state residents $919.

### FINANCIAL AID PICTURE (2015-2016)
**Students with need:** Average financial aid package met 67% of need; average scholarship/grant was $6,909; average loan was $2,868. For part-time students, average financial aid package was $6,729.
**Students without need:** No-need awards available for academics, alumni affiliation, art, athletics, job skills, leadership, minority status, music/drama, ROTC, state/district residency.

### FINANCIAL AID PROCEDURES
**Forms required:** FAFSA.

**Dates and Deadlines:** Priority date 3/1; no closing date. Applicants notified on a rolling basis starting 3/5; must reply within 3 week(s) of notification.
**Transfers:** Priority date 3/1; no deadline. Applicants notified on a rolling basis starting 4/1; must reply within 3 week(s) of notification.

### CONTACT
Katherine Allen, Director of Financial Aid
4901 Evergreen Road, 1145 UC, Dearborn, MI 48128-1491
(313) 593-5000

## University of Michigan: Flint
Flint, Michigan
www.umflint.edu                      Federal Code: 002327

**4-year public** university and branch campus college in small city.
**Enrollment:** 6,255 undergrads, 36% part-time. 595 full-time freshmen.
**Selectivity:** Admits 50 to 75% of applicants.

### BASIC COSTS (2015-2016)
**Tuition and fees:** $10,458; out-of-state residents $19,980.
**Per-credit charge:** $396; out-of-state residents $790.
**Room and board:** $8,178.

### FINANCIAL AID PICTURE (2014-2015)
**Students with need:** Out of 536 full-time freshmen who applied for aid, 451 were judged to have need. Of these, 430 received aid, and 20 had their full need met. Average financial aid package met 70% of need; average scholarship/grant was $6,526; average loan was $3,275. For part-time students, average financial aid package was $9,482.
**Students without need:** 23 full-time freshmen who did not demonstrate need for aid received scholarships/grants; average award was $4,136. No-need awards available for academics, art, leadership, music/drama.
**Scholarships offered:** High school students applying as first-time freshmen have access to more scholarship funds to help pay for their respected UM-Flint education.

### FINANCIAL AID PROCEDURES
**Forms required:** FAFSA, institutional form.
**Dates and Deadlines:** Priority date 3/1; no closing date. Applicants notified on a rolling basis starting 3/15.
**Transfers:** Priority date 2/14; no deadline. Applicants notified on a rolling basis starting 3/1. Self-help aid must be accepted on the student's on-line account before it can be paid.

### CONTACT
Lori Vedder, Financial Aid Director
303 East Kearsley Street, Flint, MI 48502-1950
(810) 762-3444

## Walsh College of Accountancy and Business Administration
Troy, Michigan
www.walshcollege.edu                  Federal Code: 004071

**Upper-division private** business college in large city.
**Enrollment:** 939 undergrads.

### BASIC COSTS (2015-2016)
**Tuition and fees:** $12,820.
**Per-credit charge:** $419.

### FINANCIAL AID PICTURE (2014-2015)
**Students with need:** 26% of average financial aid package awarded as scholarships/grants, 74% awarded as loans/jobs. Need-based aid available for part-time students.
**Students without need:** No-need awards available for academics.

### FINANCIAL AID PROCEDURES
**Transfers:** Priority date 3/1; no deadline. Applicants notified on a rolling basis.

### CONTACT
Catherine Berrahou, Director, Financial Aid
PO Box 7006, Troy, MI 48007-7006
(248) 823-1285

## Wayne County Community College
Detroit, Michigan
www.wcccd.edu                        Federal Code: 009230

**2-year public** community college in very large city.
**Enrollment:** 11,937 undergrads, 75% part-time. 939 full-time freshmen.
**Selectivity:** Open admission; but selective for some programs.

### BASIC COSTS (2016-2017)
**Tuition and fees:** $3,460; out-of-district residents $3,790; out-of-state residents $4,690.
**Per-credit charge:** $105; out-of-district residents $116; out-of-state residents $146.

### FINANCIAL AID PICTURE
**Students with need:** Need-based aid available for full-time and part-time students.

### FINANCIAL AID PROCEDURES
**Forms required:** FAFSA.
**Dates and Deadlines:** Priority date 5/1; no closing date. Applicants notified on a rolling basis starting 5/1.

### CONTACT
Myra Hawkins, District Associate Vice Chancellor of Student Services
801 West Fort Street, Detroit, MI 48226
(313) 496-2865

## Wayne State University
Detroit, Michigan
www.wayne.edu                        Federal Code: 002329

**4-year public** university in very large city.
**Enrollment:** 16,728 undergrads, 31% part-time. 2,101 full-time freshmen.
**Selectivity:** Admits over 75% of applicants.

### BASIC COSTS (2015-2016)
**Tuition and fees:** $11,814; out-of-state residents $25,254.
**Per-credit charge:** $348; out-of-state residents $796.
**Room and board:** $10,061.

### FINANCIAL AID PICTURE (2014-2015)
**Students with need:** Out of 1,828 full-time freshmen who applied for aid, 1,571 were judged to have need. Of these, 1,555 received aid, and 134 had their full need met. Average financial aid package met 57% of need; average scholarship/grant was $7,142; average loan was $3,187. For part-time students, average financial aid package was $6,293.
**Students without need:** 362 full-time freshmen who did not demonstrate need for aid received scholarships/grants; average award was $5,732. No-need awards available for academics, art, athletics, leadership, music/drama.
**Scholarships offered:** 32 full-time freshmen received athletic scholarships; average amount $10,633.
**Additional info:** Need-based institutional grants cover tuition and fees with grants and EFC (no loans).

### FINANCIAL AID PROCEDURES
**Forms required:** FAFSA.

**Dates and Deadlines:** Priority date 3/31; no closing date. Applicants notified on a rolling basis starting 3/31.

**Transfers:** Priority date 3/31; no deadline. Applicants notified on a rolling basis starting 3/31; must reply within 2 week(s) of notification.

### CONTACT

Gabriela Garfield, Senior Director, Financial Aid

PO Box 02759, Detroit, MI 48202-0759

(313) 577-2100

## West Shore Community College

Scottville, Michigan

www.westshore.edu                    Federal Code: 007950

**2-year public** community college in rural community.

**Enrollment:** 815 undergrads.

**Selectivity:** Open admission; but selective for some programs.

### BASIC COSTS (2015-2016)

**Tuition and fees:** $3,052; out-of-district residents $5,122; out-of-state residents $6,772.

### FINANCIAL AID PICTURE

**Students with need:** Need-based aid available for full-time and part-time students. Work study available nights, weekends, and for part-time students.

### FINANCIAL AID PROCEDURES

**Forms required:** FAFSA, institutional form.

**Dates and Deadlines:** Priority date 6/1; no closing date. Applicants notified on a rolling basis starting 5/15; must reply within 2 week(s) of notification.

### CONTACT

Rebekah Schaub, Director of Financial Aid

3000 North Stiles Road, Scottville, MI 49454-0277

(231) 845-5518

## Western Michigan University

Kalamazoo, Michigan

www.wmich.edu                    Federal Code: 002330

**4-year public** university in small city.

**Enrollment:** 18,179 undergrads, 16% part-time. 3,089 full-time freshmen.

**Selectivity:** Admits over 75% of applicants.

### BASIC COSTS (2015-2016)

**Tuition and fees:** $11,029; out-of-state residents $25,713.

**Per-credit charge:** $349; out-of-state residents $857.

**Room and board:** $9,238.

### FINANCIAL AID PICTURE (2015-2016)

**Students with need:** Out of 2,614 full-time freshmen who applied for aid, 2,064 were judged to have need. Of these, 2,064 received aid, and 565 had their full need met. Average financial aid package met 75% of need; average scholarship/grant was $5,075; average loan was $3,170. Need-based aid available for part-time students.

**Students without need:** 321 full-time freshmen who did not demonstrate need for aid received scholarships/grants; average award was $4,900. No-need awards available for academics, alumni affiliation, art, athletics, minority status, music/drama, ROTC, state/district residency.

**Scholarships offered: _Merit:_** Medallion Scholarship: $50,000; based on 3.7 GPA, 26 ACT/1170 SAT; may be renewed for up to 8 consecutive semesters; minimum of 20 available. Dean's Scholarship: $6,000 over 2 years. Residence Hall Award: $4,000; awarded to students living in residence halls for a third year; minimum of 20 available. _**Athletic:**_ 64 full-time freshmen received athletic scholarships; average amount $20,779.

### FINANCIAL AID PROCEDURES

**Forms required:** FAFSA.

**Dates and Deadlines:** Priority date 3/1; no closing date. Applicants notified on a rolling basis starting 3/15.

**Transfers:** No deadline. Applicants notified on a rolling basis starting 3/15.

### CONTACT

Terrell Hodge, Director of Financial Aid

1903 West Michigan Avenue, Kalamazoo, MI 49008-5211

(269) 387-6000

# Minnesota

## Academy College

Bloomington, Minnesota

www.academycollege.edu                    Federal Code: 013505

**2-year for-profit** technical and career college in large city.

**Enrollment:** 116 undergrads, 70% part-time. 3 full-time freshmen.

**Selectivity:** Open admission.

### BASIC COSTS (2015-2016)

**Additional info:** Per-credit-hour charge starts at $355, may vary depending on program level and course of study. There is a one-time student activity fee of $280; annual technology fee $120; estimated books and supplies vary by program and range from $750 to $1,500. All costs are subject to change.

### FINANCIAL AID PICTURE (2014-2015)

**Students with need:** 33% of average financial aid package awarded as scholarships/grants, 67% awarded as loans/jobs. Need-based aid available for part-time students. Work study available nights, weekends, and for part-time students.

### FINANCIAL AID PROCEDURES

**Forms required:** FAFSA, institutional form.

**Dates and Deadlines:** Applicants notified on a rolling basis.

### CONTACT

Kellye MacLeod, Director of Financial Aid

1600 W 82nd St, Bloomington, MN 55431

(952) 851-0066

## Alexandria Technical and Community College

Alexandria, Minnesota

www.alextech.edu                    Federal Code: 005544

**2-year public** community and technical college in large town.

**Enrollment:** 1,628 undergrads.

**Selectivity:** Open admission; but selective for some programs.

### BASIC COSTS (2015-2016)

**Tuition and fees:** $5,402; out-of-state residents $5,402.

### FINANCIAL AID PICTURE (2014-2015)

**Students with need:** 40% of average financial aid package awarded as scholarships/grants, 60% awarded as loans/jobs. Need-based aid available for part-time students.

**Students without need:** This college awards aid only to students with need.

### FINANCIAL AID PROCEDURES

**Forms required:** FAFSA.

**Dates and Deadlines:** Priority date 5/1; no closing date. Applicants notified on a rolling basis starting 6/30; must reply within 2 week(s) of notification.

**Transfers:** No deadline. Applicants notified on a rolling basis; must reply within 2 week(s) of notification.

**CONTACT**

Steve Richards, Dean of Technology & Student Financial Services

1601 Jefferson Street, Alexandria, MN 56308-3799

(320) 762-4540

## Anoka Technical College

Anoka, Minnesota

www.anokatech.edu                    Federal Code: 007350

**2-year public** technical college in large town.

**Enrollment:** 2,095 undergrads.

**Selectivity:** Open admission; but selective for some programs.

**BASIC COSTS (2015-2016)**

**Tuition and fees:** $5,585; out-of-state residents $5,585.

**Per-credit charge:** $167.

**FINANCIAL AID PICTURE**

**Students with need:** Need-based aid available for full-time and part-time students. Work study available nights.

**Students without need:** This college awards aid only to students with need.

**FINANCIAL AID PROCEDURES**

**Forms required:** FAFSA.

**Dates and Deadlines:** Applicants notified on a rolling basis starting 7/1.

**CONTACT**

Sean Johns, Director of Financial Aid

1355 West Highway 10, Anoka, MN 55303

(763) 433-1500

## Anoka-Ramsey Community College

Coon Rapids, Minnesota

www.anokaramsey.edu                    Federal Code: 002332

**2-year public** community college in small city.

**Enrollment:** 8,972 undergrads.

**Selectivity:** Open admission; but selective for some programs.

**BASIC COSTS (2015-2016)**

**Tuition and fees:** $5,014; out-of-state residents $5,014.

**Per-credit charge:** $144.96.

**FINANCIAL AID PICTURE**

**Students with need:** Need-based aid available for full-time and part-time students. Work study available nights, weekends, and for part-time students.

**Students without need:** This college awards aid only to students with need.

**FINANCIAL AID PROCEDURES**

**Forms required:** FAFSA, institutional form.

**Dates and Deadlines:** Priority date 4/1; no closing date. Applicants notified on a rolling basis; must reply within 2 week(s) of notification.

**CONTACT**

Sean Johns, Financial Aid Officer

11200 Mississippi Boulevard NW, Coon Rapids, MN 55433

(763) 433-1500

## Art Institutes International Minnesota

Minneapolis, Minnesota

www.artinstitutes.edu/minneapolis   Federal Code: 010248

**4-year for-profit** culinary school and visual arts college in large city.

**Enrollment:** 820 undergrads.

**Selectivity:** Open admission.

**BASIC COSTS (2015-2016)**

**Tuition and fees:** $23,088.

**Per-credit charge:** $481.

**Room only:** $7,065.

**FINANCIAL AID PICTURE**

**Students with need:** Need-based aid available for full-time and part-time students.

**Students without need:** No-need awards available for academics.

**FINANCIAL AID PROCEDURES**

**Forms required:** FAFSA.

**CONTACT**

Greg Woodard, Director of Administrative and Financial Services

15 South Ninth Street, Minneapolis, MN 55402

(800) 777-3643

## Augsburg College

Minneapolis, Minnesota

www.augsburg.edu                    Federal Code: 002334

**4-year private** liberal arts college in large city, affiliated with Evangelical Lutheran Church in America.

**Enrollment:** 2,492 undergrads, 19% part-time. 391 full-time freshmen.

**Selectivity:** Admits 50 to 75% of applicants.

**BASIC COSTS (2015-2016)**

**Tuition and fees:** $35,465.

**Room and board:** $9,380.

**FINANCIAL AID PICTURE (2014-2015)**

**Students with need:** Out of 358 full-time freshmen who applied for aid, 329 were judged to have need. Of these, 328 received aid, and 31 had their full need met. Average financial aid package met 73% of need; average scholarship/grant was $22,567; average loan was $3,894. For part-time students, average financial aid package was $5,428.

**Students without need:** 57 full-time freshmen who did not demonstrate need for aid received scholarships/grants; average award was $13,949. No-need awards available for academics, alumni affiliation, art, leadership, music/drama, religious affiliation.

**Scholarships offered:** President's Scholarships: up to full tuition annually; 3.7 GPA and ACT/SAT score 27 or higher; number awarded determined annually. Regents Scholarships: $4,000-$10,000; top 30% of class rank or test scores. Must apply before 5/1 for both scholarships.

**FINANCIAL AID PROCEDURES**

**Forms required:** FAFSA.

**Dates and Deadlines:** Priority date 3/15; closing date 8/1. Applicants notified on a rolling basis starting 3/1; must reply within 3 week(s) of notification.

**Transfers:** Priority date 7/1; closing date 8/15. Applicants notified on a rolling basis starting 3/1; must reply by 9/1.

**CONTACT**

Paul Terrio, Director of Enrollment Services

2211 Riverside Avenue, Minneapolis, MN 55454

(612) 330-1046

## Bemidji State University
Bemidji, Minnesota
www.bemidjistate.edu          Federal Code: 002336

**4-year public** university in large town.
**Enrollment:** 4,393 undergrads, 23% part-time. 559 full-time freshmen.
**Selectivity:** Admits over 75% of applicants.

### BASIC COSTS (2015-2016)
**Tuition and fees:** $8,366; out-of-state residents $8,366.
**Per-credit charge:** $257.35; out-of-state residents $257.35.
**Room and board:** $7,690.
**Additional info:** Tuition/fee waivers available for minority students.

### FINANCIAL AID PICTURE (2014-2015)
**Students with need:** Out of 487 full-time freshmen who applied for aid, 344 were judged to have need. Of these, 339 received aid, and 26 had their full need met. Average financial aid package met 68% of need; average scholarship/grant was $5,475; average loan was $3,483. For part-time students, average financial aid package was $5,255.
**Students without need:** 130 full-time freshmen who did not demonstrate need for aid received scholarships/grants; average award was $10,127. No-need awards available for academics, alumni affiliation, art, athletics, job skills, leadership, minority status, music/drama, ROTC.
**Scholarships offered:** 35 full-time freshmen received athletic scholarships; average amount $4,765.

### FINANCIAL AID PROCEDURES
**Forms required:** FAFSA, institutional form.
**Dates and Deadlines:** Closing date 3/31. Applicants notified on a rolling basis starting 3/15.

### CONTACT
Lesa Lawrence, Director of Financial Aid
102 Deputy Hall #13, Bemidji, MN 56601-2699
(218) 755-2034

## Bethany Lutheran College
Mankato, Minnesota
www.blc.edu          Federal Code: 002337

**4-year private** liberal arts college in small city, affiliated with Evangelical Lutheran Synod.
**Enrollment:** 493 undergrads, 3% part-time. 141 full-time freshmen.
**Selectivity:** Admits over 75% of applicants.

### BASIC COSTS (2015-2016)
**Tuition and fees:** $25,300.
**Per-credit charge:** $1,050.
**Room and board:** $7,910.

### FINANCIAL AID PICTURE (2014-2015)
**Students with need:** Out of 132 full-time freshmen who applied for aid, 118 were judged to have need. Of these, 118 received aid, and 16 had their full need met. Average financial aid package met 83% of need; average scholarship/grant was $18,158; average loan was $4,436. For part-time students, average financial aid package was $12,308.
**Students without need:** 17 full-time freshmen who did not demonstrate need for aid received scholarships/grants; average award was $9,111. No-need awards available for academics, alumni affiliation, art, music/drama, ROTC.

### FINANCIAL AID PROCEDURES
**Forms required:** FAFSA, institutional form.
**Dates and Deadlines:** Priority date 4/15; no closing date. Applicants notified on a rolling basis starting 3/1; must reply within 4 week(s) of notification.
**Transfers:** No deadline. Applicants notified on a rolling basis starting 3/1; must reply within 4 week(s) of notification.

### CONTACT
Jeffrey Younge, Director of Financial Aid
700 Luther Drive, Mankato, MN 56001-4490
(507) 344-7328

## Bethel University
St. Paul, Minnesota
www.bethel.edu          Federal Code: 002338

**4-year private** university and liberal arts college in large city, affiliated with Baptist General Conference.
**Enrollment:** 2,875 undergrads, 17% part-time. 614 full-time freshmen.
**Selectivity:** Admits over 75% of applicants.

### BASIC COSTS (2015-2016)
**Tuition and fees:** $34,140.
**Per-credit charge:** $1,417.
**Room and board:** $9,770.

### FINANCIAL AID PICTURE (2015-2016)
**Students with need:** Out of 565 full-time freshmen who applied for aid, 451 were judged to have need. Of these, 451 received aid, and 83 had their full need met. Average financial aid package met 83% of need; average scholarship/grant was $22,123; average loan was $3,988. For part-time students, average financial aid package was $14,797.
**Students without need:** 163 full-time freshmen who did not demonstrate need for aid received scholarships/grants; average award was $13,358. No-need awards available for academics, alumni affiliation, art, leadership, music/drama, state/district residency.

### FINANCIAL AID PROCEDURES
**Forms required:** FAFSA.
**Dates and Deadlines:** Priority date 4/15; no closing date. Applicants notified on a rolling basis starting 3/1.

### CONTACT
Jeffrey Olson, Director of Financial Aid
3900 Bethel Drive, St. Paul, MN 55112-6999
(651) 638-6241

## Capella University
Minneapolis, Minnesota
www.capella.edu          Federal Code: 032673

**4-year for-profit** virtual university in very large city.
**Enrollment:** 8,750 undergrads.
**Selectivity:** Open admission; but selective for some programs.

### BASIC COSTS (2015-2016)
**Additional info:** Tuition varies by program and level. Per-credit-hour for Certificate programs: $387-$787; per-credit-hour for Bachelor's degrees: $315-$371. All costs are subject to change.

### FINANCIAL AID PICTURE
**Students with need:** Need-based aid available for full-time and part-time students.

### CONTACT
Tonia Teasley, VP Learner Services and Operations
225 South Sixth Street, Minneapolis, MN 55402
(888) 227-3552

# Carleton College

Northfield, Minnesota
www.carleton.edu

Federal Code: 002340
CSS Code: 6081

**4-year private** liberal arts college in large town.
**Enrollment:** 1,995 undergrads. 491 full-time freshmen.
**Selectivity:** Admits less than 50% of applicants.

## BASIC COSTS (2015-2016)
**Tuition and fees:** $49,263.
**Room and board:** $12,783.

## FINANCIAL AID PICTURE (2014-2015)
**Students with need:** Out of 377 full-time freshmen who applied for aid, 267 were judged to have need. Of these, 267 received aid, and 267 had their full need met. Average financial aid package met 100% of need; average scholarship/grant was $39,854; average loan was $4,285.
**Students without need:** This college awards aid only to students with need.
**Scholarships offered:** National Merit, National Achievement, National Hispanic Scholars Awards: $2,000 per year; based on outstanding academic achievement and promise.
**Additional info:** Full financial need of all admitted applicants met through combination of work, loans, grants.

## FINANCIAL AID PROCEDURES
**Forms required:** FAFSA, CSS PROFILE.
**Dates and Deadlines:** Closing date 2/15. Applicants notified by 3/31; must reply by 5/1 or within 2 week(s) of notification.
**Transfers:** Closing date 3/15. Applicants notified by 5/15; must reply by 6/1 or within 2 week(s) of notification.

## CONTACT
Rodney Oto, Director of Student Financial Services
100 South College Street, Northfield, MN 55057
(507) 222-4138

# Central Lakes College

Brainerd, Minnesota
www.clcmn.edu

Federal Code: 002339

**2-year public** community and technical college in large town.
**Enrollment:** 2,806 undergrads.
**Selectivity:** Open admission; but selective for some programs.

## BASIC COSTS (2015-2016)
**Tuition and fees:** $5,384; out-of-state residents $5,384.

## FINANCIAL AID PICTURE
**Students with need:** Need-based aid available for full-time and part-time students.

## FINANCIAL AID PROCEDURES
**Forms required:** FAFSA.
**Dates and Deadlines:** Priority date 6/1; no closing date. Applicants notified on a rolling basis starting 6/10; must reply within 2 week(s) of notification.

## CONTACT
Mike Barnaby, Director of Financial Aid
501 West College Drive, Brainerd, MN 56401
(218) 855-8039

# Century College

White Bear Lake, Minnesota
www.century.edu

Federal Code: 010546

**2-year public** community and technical college in large town.
**Enrollment:** 8,202 undergrads, 58% part-time. 790 full-time freshmen.

**Selectivity:** Open admission; but selective for some programs.

## BASIC COSTS (2015-2016)
**Tuition and fees:** $5,391; out-of-state residents $5,391.
**Per-credit charge:** $161.

## FINANCIAL AID PICTURE
**Students with need:** Need-based aid available for full-time and part-time students.
**Students without need:** This college awards aid only to students with need.

## FINANCIAL AID PROCEDURES
**Forms required:** FAFSA.
**Dates and Deadlines:** Priority date 5/1; no closing date. Applicants notified on a rolling basis starting 5/15.
**Transfers:** Priority date 7/1; no deadline. Applicants notified on a rolling basis starting 5/15.

## CONTACT
Pam Engebretson, Financial Aid Director
3300 Century Avenue North, White Bear Lake, MN 55110
(651) 779-3305

# College of St. Benedict

St. Joseph, Minnesota
www.csbsju.edu

Federal Code: 002341

**4-year private** liberal arts college in small town, affiliated with Roman Catholic Church.
**Enrollment:** 1,943 undergrads, 1% part-time. 476 full-time freshmen.
**Selectivity:** Admits 50 to 75% of applicants.

## BASIC COSTS (2015-2016)
**Tuition and fees:** $40,846.
**Per-credit charge:** $1,660.
**Room and board:** $10,231.
**Additional info:** Meal plan is flexible meal plan.

## FINANCIAL AID PICTURE (2015-2016)
**Students with need:** Out of 419 full-time freshmen who applied for aid, 363 were judged to have need. Of these, 363 received aid, and 126 had their full need met. Average financial aid package met 91% of need; average scholarship/grant was $29,368; average loan was $4,515. For part-time students, average financial aid package was $22,467.
**Students without need:** 93 full-time freshmen who did not demonstrate need for aid received scholarships/grants; average award was $17,950. No-need awards available for academics, alumni affiliation, art, leadership, music/drama, ROTC.
**Scholarships offered:** Trustees' Scholarships: $20,000-$22,000 renewable; based on 3.6 GPA, 30 ACT or equivalent SAT, demonstrated leadership and service, faculty interview. President's Scholarships: $15,500-$19,000 renewable; based on GPA, high school rank, ACT/SAT, leadership and service. Dean's Scholarships: $7,000-$15,000 renewable; based on GPA, high school rank, ACT/SAT, leadership and service. Art, music and theater scholarships: up to $4,000 renewable. Intercultural LEAD fellowship: up to $10,000 renewable; based on GPA, leadership, financial need, first generation college students, commitment to intercultural issues and action, from diverse urban high schools; on campus interview required. Army ROTC and ROTC Nursing Scholarships: based on demonstrated leadership potential, GPA, class standing, ACT/SAT, high achievement with broad interests and willingness to take on challenges. Catholic High School Scholarship: $4,000 renewable; for students attending Catholic high schools outside Minnesota. Saints Scholarship: $2,000-$4,000 renewable; for students attending public high schools outside Minnesota. FoCuS Scholarship: $22,000 renewable; for students majoring in chemistry. Bonner Leader Scholarship: $2,500 renewable; for students with strong interest in doing service at CSB/SJU, preference for students with financial need. Legacy Scholarship: $1,000 renewable; mother, father or

grandparent obtained degree from Saint John's or St. Ben's. Benedictine Scholarship: $5,000 renewable; for students from low income families who have completed a college access program such as Upward Bound.
**Additional info:** Scholarship letters will be mailed on a rolling basis approximately two weeks from the time the admission acceptance letter is sent.

## FINANCIAL AID PROCEDURES
**Forms required:** FAFSA, institutional form.
**Dates and Deadlines:** Priority date 3/15; no closing date. Applicants notified on a rolling basis starting 3/15; must reply by 5/1.
**Transfers:** No deadline. Applicants notified on a rolling basis starting 3/15; must reply by 5/1. Phi Theta Kappa Scholarship: $1,500 renewable; for members of Phi Theta Kappa. Idelia Loso Scholarship: $750 for community college transfer students with AA degree majoring in nursing or education.

## CONTACT
Stuart Perry, Executive Director of Financial Aid
College of Saint Benedict/Saint John's University, Collegeville, MN 56321-7155
(320) 363-5388

# College of St. Scholastica
Duluth, Minnesota
www.css.edu                     Federal Code: 002343

**4-year private** liberal arts college in small city, affiliated with Roman Catholic Church.
**Enrollment:** 2,782 undergrads, 18% part-time. 439 full-time freshmen.
**Selectivity:** Admits 50 to 75% of applicants.

## BASIC COSTS (2015-2016)
**Tuition and fees:** $33,994.
**Per-credit charge:** $1,056.
**Room and board:** $8,932.
**Additional info:** Tuition/fee waivers available for minority students.

## FINANCIAL AID PICTURE (2015-2016)
**Students with need:** Out of 402 full-time freshmen who applied for aid, 360 were judged to have need. Of these, 360 received aid, and 95 had their full need met. Average financial aid package met 80% of need; average scholarship/grant was $7,795; average loan was $3,589. For part-time students, average financial aid package was $7,002.
**Students without need:** 42 full-time freshmen who did not demonstrate need for aid received scholarships/grants; average award was $17,529. No-need awards available for academics, alumni affiliation, music/drama, religious affiliation, ROTC, state/district residency.
**Scholarships offered:** Benedictine Scholarship: $5,000-$15,000 per year for up to 4 years. Access Scholarship: $8,500. Both based on GPA, SAT/ACT score; unlimited number awarded. Summit Scholarship: an additional $1,500 for those who qualify for the Benedictine Scholarship and who graduate at the top of their high school class or ACT score greater than 30. Divisional Merit Awards: $4,000; available to transfer students; based on major; unlimited number awarded.

## FINANCIAL AID PROCEDURES
**Forms required:** FAFSA.
**Dates and Deadlines:** Priority date 3/1; no closing date. Applicants notified on a rolling basis starting 3/1; must reply by 5/1 or within 2 week(s) of notification.

## CONTACT
Jon Erickson, Director of Financial Aid
1200 Kenwood Avenue, Duluth, MN 55811-4199
(218) 723-6570

# Concordia College: Moorhead
Moorhead, Minnesota
www.concordiacollege.edu          Federal Code: 002346

**4-year private** liberal arts college in large town, affiliated with Evangelical Lutheran Church in America.
**Enrollment:** 2,104 undergrads, 1% part-time. 540 full-time freshmen.
**Selectivity:** Admits over 75% of applicants.

## BASIC COSTS (2015-2016)
**Tuition and fees:** $35,464.
**Per-credit charge:** $1,380.
**Room and board:** $7,600.

## FINANCIAL AID PICTURE (2014-2015)
**Students with need:** Out of 503 full-time freshmen who applied for aid, 416 were judged to have need. Of these, 416 received aid, and 93 had their full need met. Average financial aid package met 91% of need; average scholarship/grant was $22,242; average loan was $4,637. For part-time students, average financial aid package was $13,215.
**Students without need:** 119 full-time freshmen who did not demonstrate need for aid received scholarships/grants; average award was $14,551. No-need awards available for academics, art, leadership, minority status, music/drama.
**Scholarships offered:** Concordia College Regents Scholarship: tuition for 4 years; based on 4.13 GPA and 33 ACT. Presidential Distinction Scholarships: $17,000 per year up to 4 years; eligibility based on 4.04 GPA and 30 ACT/1770 SAT; approximately 80 awarded. Faculty Scholarships: $16,000 per year up to 4 years; eligibility based on 3.9 GPA and 27 ACT/1770 SAT; approximately 160 awarded. National Merit Scholars; finalists who name Concordia as their first choice receive minimum of $17,000 per year. Excellence Scholarships: $13,000 to $15,000 per year; based on academic achievement. Concordia College Scholarships: $7,000 to $11,000 per year; for students who show strong potential for success and contribution to the Concordia community. Performance Scholarships: $2,500 per year for up to 4 years; for excellence in music performance, theater performance, speech and debate, and visual arts.

## FINANCIAL AID PROCEDURES
**Forms required:** FAFSA.
**Dates and Deadlines:** Priority date 3/1; no closing date. Applicants notified on a rolling basis starting 3/15.
**Transfers:** No deadline. Applicants notified on a rolling basis starting 4/1. Eligible transfer students are offered merit aid limited to the number of semesters needed to complete their degree as determined through the transfer credit evaluation.

## CONTACT
Eric Addington, Director of Financial Aid
901 Eighth Street South, Moorhead, MN 56562
(218) 299-3010

# Concordia University St. Paul
Saint Paul, Minnesota
www.csp.edu                     Federal Code: 002347

**4-year private** university in large city, affiliated with Lutheran Church - Missouri Synod.
**Enrollment:** 2,281 undergrads, 43% part-time. 229 full-time freshmen.
**Selectivity:** Admits 50 to 75% of applicants.

## BASIC COSTS (2016-2017)
**Tuition and fees:** $21,250.
**Room and board:** $8,500.

## FINANCIAL AID PICTURE (2015-2016)
**Students with need:** Out of 212 full-time freshmen who applied for aid, 173 were judged to have need. Of these, 170 received aid, and 21 had their

full need met. Average financial aid package met 66% of need; average scholarship/grant was $12,383; average loan was $3,443. For part-time students, average financial aid package was $7,295.

**Students without need:** 24 full-time freshmen who did not demonstrate need for aid received scholarships/grants; average award was $4,243. No-need awards available for academics, art, athletics, minority status, music/drama, religious affiliation.

**Scholarships offered:** 28 full-time freshmen received athletic scholarships.

**Additional info:** Church districts and local congregations are major sources of aid for church-vocation students.

## FINANCIAL AID PROCEDURES
**Forms required:** FAFSA, state aid form.

**Dates and Deadlines:** Priority date 5/1; no closing date. Applicants notified on a rolling basis starting 3/1.

**Transfers:** No deadline. Applicants notified on a rolling basis. Adult learners in degree completion programs are typically not eligible for most types of institutional scholarships/grants because of discounted tuition rates.

## CONTACT
Jeanie Peck, Director of Financial Aid
1282 Concordia Avenue, Saint Paul, MN 55104-5494
(651) 603-6300

# Crossroads College
Rochester, Minnesota
www.crossroadscollege.edu              Federal Code: 002366

**4-year private** Bible college in small city, affiliated with Christian Church.
**Enrollment:** 96 undergrads.

## BASIC COSTS (2015-2016)
**Tuition and fees:** $16,040.
**Per-credit charge:** $450.
**Room only:** $4,150.

## FINANCIAL AID PICTURE
**Students with need:** Need-based aid available for full-time and part-time students. Work study available nights.

**Students without need:** No-need awards available for academics, leadership, music/drama, religious affiliation.

**Scholarships offered:** Home-Educated Grant: $500 per semester if home-schooled for two years during high school. Travel Grant: $500 per semester for student who resides in states other than Minnesota, Iowa, Wisconsin. Crossroads Matching Grant: church funds matched up to $500 per semester; awarded to first year students.

## FINANCIAL AID PROCEDURES
**Forms required:** FAFSA, institutional form.

**Dates and Deadlines:** Priority date 4/1; closing date 4/15. Applicants notified on a rolling basis starting 2/1; must reply within 4 week(s) of notification.

**Transfers:** Mid-year transfer students will have financial aid calculated with the prior school term award in mind.

## CONTACT
Jason Vagt, Director of Financial Aid
920 Mayowood Road SW, Rochester, MN 55902
(507) 288-4563

# Crown College
Saint Bonifacius, Minnesota
www.crown.edu                        Federal Code: 002383

**4-year private** liberal arts college in small town, affiliated with Christian and Missionary Alliance.
**Enrollment:** 885 full-time undergrads.

## BASIC COSTS (2015-2016)
**Tuition and fees:** $23,740.
**Room and board:** $7,940.
**Additional info:** Tuition/fee waivers available for minority students.

## FINANCIAL AID PICTURE
**Students with need:** Need-based aid available for full-time and part-time students. Work study available nights, weekends, and for part-time students.

**Students without need:** No-need awards available for academics, alumni affiliation, leadership, minority status, music/drama, religious affiliation.

## FINANCIAL AID PROCEDURES
**Forms required:** FAFSA.

**Dates and Deadlines:** Priority date 4/1; no closing date. Applicants notified on a rolling basis starting 4/1; must reply within 3 week(s) of notification.

**Transfers:** No deadline. Applicants notified on a rolling basis; must reply within 3 week(s) of notification. Cannot have attended more than 4 years of college to receive state grant.

## CONTACT
Shannon Schaaf, Director of Financial Aid
8700 College View Drive, Saint Bonifacius, MN 55375-9001
(952) 446-4177

# Dakota County Technical College
Rosemount, Minnesota
www.dctc.edu                          Federal Code: 010402

**2-year public** technical college in large town.
**Enrollment:** 2,359 undergrads, 44% part-time. 563 full-time freshmen.
**Selectivity:** Open admission; but selective for some programs.

## BASIC COSTS (2015-2016)
**Tuition and fees:** $5,713; out-of-state residents $5,713.
**Per-credit charge:** $169.

## FINANCIAL AID PICTURE
**Students with need:** Need-based aid available for full-time and part-time students. Work study available nights.

**Students without need:** No-need awards available for academics, athletics, leadership.

## FINANCIAL AID PROCEDURES
**Forms required:** FAFSA.

**Dates and Deadlines:** Applicants notified on a rolling basis starting 3/15.

**Transfers:** No deadline. FAFSA must be processed within 14 days of the first day of the semester to be considered for Minnesota State Grant for the semester.

## CONTACT
Scott Roelke, Director of Scholarships and Financial Aid
1300 145th Street East, Rosemount, MN 55068
(651) 423-8299

# Dunwoody College of Technology
Minneapolis, Minnesota
www.dunwoody.edu                      Federal Code: 004641

**2-year private** technical college in very large city.
**Enrollment:** 1,043 undergrads, 18% part-time. 170 full-time freshmen.
**Selectivity:** Admits over 75% of applicants.

## BASIC COSTS (2015-2016)
**Tuition and fees:** $24,230.

## FINANCIAL AID PICTURE (2014-2015)
**Students with need:** Out of 164 full-time freshmen who applied for aid, 146 were judged to have need. Of these, 146 received aid, and 8 had their

full need met. Average financial aid package met 31% of need; average scholarship/grant was $5,494; average loan was $3,379. For part-time students, average financial aid package was $5,445.

**Students without need:** 9 full-time freshmen who did not demonstrate need for aid received scholarships/grants; average award was $1,042.

### FINANCIAL AID PROCEDURES

**Forms required:** FAFSA, state aid form.

**Dates and Deadlines:** Priority date 6/1; no closing date. Applicants notified on a rolling basis starting 3/1.

**Transfers:** No deadline. Applicants notified on a rolling basis starting 7/1; must reply within 4 week(s) of notification.

### CONTACT

Barbara Charboneau, Director of Financial Aid

818 Dunwoody Boulevard, Minneapolis, MN 55403-1192

(612) 374-5800

## Fond du Lac Tribal and Community College

Cloquet, Minnesota

www.fdltcc.edu                    Federal Code: E00482

**2-year public** community college in small town.

**Enrollment:** 895 undergrads, 40% part-time. 227 full-time freshmen.

**Selectivity:** Open admission.

### BASIC COSTS (2015-2016)

**Tuition and fees:** $5,258; out-of-state residents $5,258.

**Per-credit charge:** $159.

**Room only:** $3,508.

### FINANCIAL AID PICTURE (2014-2015)

**Students with need:** 65% of average financial aid package awarded as scholarships/grants, 35% awarded as loans/jobs. Need-based aid available for part-time students.

**Students without need:** No-need awards available for academics.

### FINANCIAL AID PROCEDURES

**Forms required:** FAFSA.

**Dates and Deadlines:** Priority date 3/16; no closing date. Applicants notified on a rolling basis starting 4/16.

**Transfers:** Applicants notified on a rolling basis.

### CONTACT

David Sutherland, Director of Financial Aid

2101 14th Street, Cloquet, MN 55720

(218) 879-0816

## Globe University: Minneapolis

Minneapolis, Minnesota

www.globeuniversity.edu            Federal Code: 004642

**4-year for-profit** university and career college in large city.

**Enrollment:** 164 undergrads.

**Selectivity:** Open admission; but selective for some programs.

### BASIC COSTS (2015-2016)

**Tuition and fees:** $18,702.

**Per-credit charge:** $390.

**Additional info:** Per-credit hour charge for 1 to 11 hours, $460; for 12 to 16 hours, $390. Course fees: $10 to $400 per course.

### FINANCIAL AID PICTURE

**Students with need:** Need-based aid available for full-time and part-time students.

### FINANCIAL AID PROCEDURES

**Forms required:** FAFSA, state aid form, institutional form.

**Dates and Deadlines:** Applicants notified on a rolling basis starting 7/1; must reply within 2 week(s) of notification.

### CONTACT

Katie Bergstrom, Financial Aid Manager

80 South 8th Street, Minneapolis, MN 55402

(612) 455-3000

## Globe University: Moorhead

Moorhead, Minnesota

www.globeuniversity.edu            Federal Code: 017145

**4-year for-profit** university and career college in large town.

**Enrollment:** 220 undergrads.

**Selectivity:** Open admission.

### BASIC COSTS (2015-2016)

**Tuition and fees:** $18,702.

**Per-credit charge:** $390.

**Additional info:** Per-credit hour charge for 1 to 11 hours, $460; for 12 to 16 hours, $390. Course fees: $10 to $400 per course.

### FINANCIAL AID PICTURE

**Students with need:** Need-based aid available for full-time and part-time students.

### FINANCIAL AID PROCEDURES

**Forms required:** FAFSA, state aid form, institutional form.

**Dates and Deadlines:** Applicants notified on a rolling basis starting 7/1; must reply within 2 week(s) of notification.

### CONTACT

Trevor Pearson, Financial Aid Manager

2777 34th Street South, Moorhead, MN 56560

(218) 422-1000

## Globe University: Woodbury

Woodbury, Minnesota

www.globeuniversity.edu            Federal Code: 004642

**4-year for-profit** health science and career college in small city.

**Enrollment:** 717 undergrads.

**Selectivity:** Open admission; but selective for some programs.

### BASIC COSTS (2015-2016)

**Tuition and fees:** $18,702.

**Per-credit charge:** $390.

**Additional info:** Per-credit hour charge for 1 to 11 hours, $460; for 12 to 16 hours, $390. Course fees: $10 to $400 per course.

### FINANCIAL AID PICTURE

**Students with need:** Need-based aid available for full-time and part-time students.

### FINANCIAL AID PROCEDURES

**Forms required:** FAFSA, state aid form, institutional form.

**Dates and Deadlines:** Applicants notified on a rolling basis starting 7/1; must reply within 2 week(s) of notification.

### CONTACT

Jill Garcia, Director of Financial Aid

8089 Globe Drive, Woodbury, MN 55125

(651) 730-5100

## Gustavus Adolphus College
St. Peter, Minnesota
www.gustavus.edu                    Federal Code: 002353

**4-year private** liberal arts college in large town, affiliated with Evangelical Lutheran Church in America.
**Enrollment:** 2,376 undergrads, 1% part-time. 619 full-time freshmen.
**Selectivity:** Admits 50 to 75% of applicants.

### BASIC COSTS (2015-2016)
**Tuition and fees:** $41,812.
**Room and board:** $9,176.

### FINANCIAL AID PICTURE (2014-2015)
**Students with need:** Out of 524 full-time freshmen who applied for aid, 464 were judged to have need. Of these, 464 received aid, and 184 had their full need met. Average financial aid package met 93% of need; average scholarship/grant was $28,974; average loan was $3,267.
**Students without need:** 141 full-time freshmen who did not demonstrate need for aid received scholarships/grants; average award was $21,409. No-need awards available for academics, alumni affiliation, art, minority status, music/drama, religious affiliation, state/district residency.
**Scholarships offered:** Presidential Scholarship: $10,000-$14,000. National Merit finalist: $7,500; academic. Legacy Scholarship: $2,500; academic for children or siblings of alumni. Jussi Bjorling Scholarship: $1,000-$4,000; for music; 40 awarded. Anderson Theatre and Dance Scholarship: $2,000; 15 awarded. Dean's Scholarship: $1,000-$10,000; Forensic $500-$2,000.

### FINANCIAL AID PROCEDURES
**Forms required:** FAFSA. CSS PROFILE required of students applying for need-based assistance.
**Dates and Deadlines:** Priority date 3/15; closing date 5/1. Applicants notified on a rolling basis starting 3/15; must reply by 5/1 or within 2 week(s) of notification.
**Transfers:** Applicants notified on a rolling basis starting 12/20; must reply by 5/1 or within 2 week(s) of notification.

### CONTACT
Doug Minter, Director of Student Financial Assistance
800 West College Avenue, St. Peter, MN 56082
(507) 933-7527

## Hamline University
St. Paul, Minnesota
www.hamline.edu                    Federal Code: 002354

**4-year private** university and liberal arts college in very large city, affiliated with United Methodist Church.
**Enrollment:** 2,141 undergrads, 2% part-time. 521 full-time freshmen.
**Selectivity:** Admits 50 to 75% of applicants.

### BASIC COSTS (2015-2016)
**Tuition and fees:** $37,896.
**Per-credit charge:** $1,153.
**Room and board:** $9,736.
**Additional info:** Per credit hour charge is for part time (less than 12 credits).

### FINANCIAL AID PICTURE (2014-2015)
**Students with need:** Out of 484 full-time freshmen who applied for aid, 437 were judged to have need. Of these, 437 received aid, and 90 had their full need met. Average financial aid package met 85% of need; average scholarship/grant was $24,164; average loan was $4,013. For part-time students, average financial aid package was $11,306.
**Students without need:** 73 full-time freshmen who did not demonstrate need for aid received scholarships/grants; average award was $15,889. No-need awards available for academics, alumni affiliation, art, leadership, minority status, music/drama, religious affiliation.

**Scholarships offered:** Academic scholarships: ranging from $10,000 to $23,000. Departmental scholarships: $3,000-$5,000 depending on department. National Merit Finalist Scholarship: $24,000. Bishop Hamline Scholarship-Participation in College Preparedness Program: $3,000. Hamline Heritage Award (legacy scholarship): $2,000. Hamline Firsts Award: $2,500 for first-generation students.

### FINANCIAL AID PROCEDURES
**Forms required:** FAFSA.
**Dates and Deadlines:** Priority date 3/15; no closing date. Applicants notified on a rolling basis starting 3/15; must reply by 5/1 or within 2 week(s) of notification.
**Transfers:** Priority date 4/1; no deadline. Applicants notified on a rolling basis starting 4/1; must reply within 2 week(s) of notification.

### CONTACT
Lynette Wahl, Director of Financial Aid
1536 Hewitt Avenue, St. Paul, MN 55104-1284
(651) 523-3000

## Hennepin Technical College
Brooklyn Park, Minnesota
www.hennepintech.edu                Federal Code: 010491

**2-year public** technical college in small city.
**Enrollment:** 5,052 undergrads, 62% part-time. 321 full-time freshmen.
**Selectivity:** Open admission; but selective for some programs.

### BASIC COSTS (2015-2016)
**Tuition and fees:** $5,159; out-of-state residents $5,159.
**Per-credit charge:** $157.

### FINANCIAL AID PICTURE
**Students with need:** Need-based aid available for full-time and part-time students. Work study available nights, weekends, and for part-time students.
**Students without need:** This college awards aid only to students with need.

### FINANCIAL AID PROCEDURES
**Forms required:** FAFSA, state aid form, institutional form.
**Dates and Deadlines:** Applicants notified on a rolling basis starting 3/1.
**Transfers:** No deadline. Applicants notified on a rolling basis.

### CONTACT
Tim Jacobson, Director
9000 Brooklyn Boulevard, Brooklyn Park, MN 55445
(952) 995-1418

## Institute of Production and Recording
Minneapolis, Minnesota
www.ipr.edu                    Federal Code: 041302

**2-year for-profit** career college in large city.
**Enrollment:** 243 undergrads.
**Selectivity:** Open admission.

### BASIC COSTS (2015-2016)
**Tuition and fees:** $20,450.
**Per-credit charge:** $390.
**Additional info:** Per-credit hour charge for 1 to 13 hours, $460; for 14 to 16 hours, $390. Course fees: $10 to $400 per course.

### FINANCIAL AID PICTURE
**Students with need:** Need-based aid available for full-time and part-time students.

### FINANCIAL AID PROCEDURES
**Forms required:** FAFSA, state aid form, institutional form.

**Dates and Deadlines:** Applicants notified on a rolling basis starting 7/1; must reply within 2 week(s) of notification.

**CONTACT**
JR Hunte, Financial Aid Manager
300 North 1st Avenue, Suite 500, Minneapolis, MN 55401
(612) 244-2800

## Inver Hills Community College
Inver Grove Heights, Minnesota
www.inverhills.edu                    Federal Code: 006935

**2-year public** community college in large town.
**Enrollment:** 4,112 undergrads, 58% part-time. 424 full-time freshmen.
**Selectivity:** Open admission; but selective for some programs.

**BASIC COSTS (2015-2016)**
**Tuition and fees:** $5,288; out-of-state residents $5,288.
**Per-credit charge:** $159.

**FINANCIAL AID PICTURE (2014-2015)**
**Students with need:** 56% of average financial aid package awarded as scholarships/grants, 44% awarded as loans/jobs. Need-based aid available for part-time students. Work study available nights, weekends, and for part-time students.
**Students without need:** This college awards aid only to students with need.

**FINANCIAL AID PROCEDURES**
**Forms required:** FAFSA.
**Dates and Deadlines:** Applicants notified on a rolling basis starting 4/1.
**Transfers:** Priority date 4/1; no deadline. Applicants notified on a rolling basis.

**CONTACT**
Emily Dowdle, Director of Financial Aid
2500 80th Street East, Inver Grove Heights, MN 55076-3224
(651) 450-3495

## Itasca Community College
Grand Rapids, Minnesota
www.itascacc.edu                    Federal Code: 002356

**2-year public** community college in large town.
**Enrollment:** 1,008 undergrads, 25% part-time. 198 full-time freshmen.
**Selectivity:** Open admission; but selective for some programs.

**BASIC COSTS (2015-2016)**
**Tuition and fees:** $5,325; out-of-state residents $6,507.
**Room and board:** $5,340.

**FINANCIAL AID PICTURE (2014-2015)**
**Students with need:** 66% of average financial aid package awarded as scholarships/grants, 34% awarded as loans/jobs. Need-based aid available for part-time students. Work study available nights, weekends, and for part-time students.
**Students without need:** No-need awards available for academics, leadership, state/district residency.

**FINANCIAL AID PROCEDURES**
**Forms required:** FAFSA.
**Dates and Deadlines:** Priority date 5/1; no closing date. Applicants notified on a rolling basis starting 4/20.
**Transfers:** No deadline. Applicants notified on a rolling basis starting 4/20.

**CONTACT**
Nathan Wright, Financial Aid Director
1851 Highway 169 East, Grand Rapids, MN 55744
(218) 322-2320

## Lake Superior College
Duluth, Minnesota
www.lsc.edu                    Federal Code: 005757

**2-year public** community and technical college in small city.
**Enrollment:** 3,349 undergrads, 47% part-time. 345 full-time freshmen.
**Selectivity:** Open admission; but selective for some programs.

**BASIC COSTS (2015-2016)**
**Tuition and fees:** $5,126; out-of-state residents $9,543.

**FINANCIAL AID PICTURE**
**Students with need:** Need-based aid available for full-time and part-time students. Work study available nights, weekends, and for part-time students.
**Students without need:** No-need awards available for academics.

**FINANCIAL AID PROCEDURES**
**Forms required:** FAFSA.
**Dates and Deadlines:** Applicants notified on a rolling basis.
**Transfers:** No deadline.

**CONTACT**
LaNita Robinson, Director of Financial Aid
2101 Trinity Road, Duluth, MN 55811
(218) 733-7616

## Leech Lake Tribal College
Cass Lake, Minnesota
www.lltc.edu                    Federal Code: 030964

**2-year public** community college in small town.
**Enrollment:** 328 undergrads.
**Selectivity:** Open admission.

**BASIC COSTS (2015-2016)**
**Tuition and fees:** $4,920; out-of-state residents $4,920.
**Per-credit charge:** $154.

**FINANCIAL AID PICTURE**
**Students with need:** Need-based aid available for full-time and part-time students.

**FINANCIAL AID PROCEDURES**
**Forms required:** FAFSA, state aid form, institutional form.
**Dates and Deadlines:** Applicants notified on a rolling basis; must reply within 4 week(s) of notification.
**Transfers:** No deadline. Applicants notified on a rolling basis; must reply within 4 week(s) of notification.

**CONTACT**
Heather Broda, Director of Financial Aid
6945 Little Wolf Road NW, Cass Lake, MN 56633
(218) 335-4270

## Macalester College
St. Paul, Minnesota                    Federal Code: 002358
www.macalester.edu                    CSS Code: 6390

**4-year private** liberal arts college in very large city, affiliated with Presbyterian Church (USA).

**Enrollment:** 2,149 undergrads, 1% part-time. 582 full-time freshmen.
**Selectivity:** Admits less than 50% of applicants.

## BASIC COSTS (2015-2016)
**Tuition and fees:** $48,887.
**Per-credit charge:** $1,521.
**Room and board:** $10,874.

## FINANCIAL AID PICTURE (2015-2016)
**Students with need:** Out of 455 full-time freshmen who applied for aid, 399 were judged to have need. Of these, 399 received aid, and 399 had their full need met. Average financial aid package met 100% of need; average scholarship/grant was $37,273; average loan was $3,849. Need-based aid available for part-time students.
**Students without need:** 61 full-time freshmen who did not demonstrate need for aid received scholarships/grants; average award was $14,600. No-need awards available for academics, minority status.
**Scholarships offered:** Merit scholarship: $1,000-$18,000; renewable for four years; based on admission application; over 40% of first-year students were awarded merit-based scholarship in 2015-16.
**Additional info:** College constructs a financial aid package that meets full demonstrated need for all admitted students.

## FINANCIAL AID PROCEDURES
**Forms required:** FAFSA, CSS PROFILE.
**Dates and Deadlines:** Priority date 2/8; closing date 3/1. Applicants notified by 4/1; must reply by 5/1.
**Transfers:** Priority date 4/15. Applicants notified by 5/15; must reply within 2 week(s) of notification.

## CONTACT
David Wheaton, Vice President for Administration & Finance
1600 Grand Avenue, St. Paul, MN 55105-1899
(651) 696-6214

# Martin Luther College
New Ulm, Minnesota
www.mlc-wels.edu                     Federal Code: 002361

**4-year private** college of theology and education in large town, affiliated with Wisconsin Evangelical Lutheran Synod.
**Enrollment:** 747 undergrads, 6% part-time. 198 full-time freshmen.
**Selectivity:** Admits over 75% of applicants.

## BASIC COSTS (2016-2017)
**Tuition and fees:** $13,980.
**Room and board:** $5,510.

## FINANCIAL AID PICTURE (2014-2015)
**Students with need:** Out of 157 full-time freshmen who applied for aid, 128 were judged to have need. Of these, 126 received aid, and 15 had their full need met. Average financial aid package met 66% of need; average scholarship/grant was $7,667; average loan was $3,641. For part-time students, average financial aid package was $7,949.
**Students without need:** 22 full-time freshmen who did not demonstrate need for aid received scholarships/grants; average award was $2,304. No-need awards available for academics, leadership, music/drama, religious affiliation.
**Scholarships offered:** Academic Scholarship: $500; 3.75 GPA after 6 semesters of high school or 27 ACT. Presidential Scholarship: $1,000; to student selected as high school valedictorian or ranked first in class after 7 semesters.

## FINANCIAL AID PROCEDURES
**Forms required:** FAFSA, institutional form.
**Dates and Deadlines:** Priority date 4/15; closing date 4/15. Applicants notified on a rolling basis starting 4/15; must reply by 9/1.

## CONTACT
Mark Bauer, Director of Financial Aid
1995 Luther Court, New Ulm, MN 56073-3965
(507) 354-8221

# McNally Smith College of Music
St. Paul, Minnesota
www.mcnallysmith.edu                 Federal Code: 030012

**4-year private** music and performing arts college in large city.
**Enrollment:** 420 undergrads, 13% part-time. 70 full-time freshmen.
**Selectivity:** Admits less than 50% of applicants.

## BASIC COSTS (2016-2017)
**Tuition and fees:** $27,940.
**Per-credit charge:** $1,040.
**Room and board:** $5,100.
**Additional info:** Tuition at time of enrollment locked for 4 years.

## FINANCIAL AID PICTURE (2014-2015)
**Students with need:** Out of 53 full-time freshmen who applied for aid, 46 were judged to have need. Of these, 46 received aid. Average financial aid package met 27% of need; average scholarship/grant was $5,726; average loan was $1,653. For part-time students, average financial aid package was $3,809.
**Students without need:** 7 full-time freshmen who did not demonstrate need for aid received scholarships/grants; average award was $5,100. No-need awards available for academics, music/drama.
**Scholarships offered:** Merit-based Premier Scholarships are awarded to incoming and returning students who show outstanding promise in their chosen area of study. The merit-based Conclave Music Business Scholarship is presented to an outstanding McNally Smith College of Music Business student each academic year, and includes tuition and a stipend to attend the Conclave Learning Conference in July. Academic Achievement Scholarships are given in recognition of outstanding academic performance. These scholarships are only available to returning students who are not already receiving a Premier Scholarship. Academic Achievement Scholarships do not require an application, and awards for the upcoming fall semester are determined after previous spring semester grades are posted. Students are issued awards automatically based on GPA.

## FINANCIAL AID PROCEDURES
**Forms required:** FAFSA.
**Dates and Deadlines:** Priority date 5/1; closing date 8/1. Applicants notified on a rolling basis starting 3/1; must reply within 3 week(s) of notification.
**Transfers:** Priority date 5/1; closing date 8/1. Applicants notified on a rolling basis starting 3/1; must reply within 3 week(s) of notification.

## CONTACT
Jeffrey Aalbers, Senior Director of Administrative Services
19 Exchange Street East, St. Paul, MN 55101
(800) 594-9500

# Mesabi Range College
Virginia, Minnesota
www.mesabirange.edu                  Federal Code: 004009

**2-year public** community and technical college in large town.
**Enrollment:** 1,373 undergrads.
**Selectivity:** Open admission.

## BASIC COSTS (2015-2016)
**Tuition and fees:** $5,311; out-of-state residents $6,493.
**Per-credit charge:** $177.03; out-of-state residents $197.02.
**Room only:** $4,036.

**FINANCIAL AID PICTURE**

**Students with need:** Need-based aid available for full-time and part-time students. Work study available nights, weekends, and for part-time students.
**Students without need:** No-need awards available for state/district residency.

**FINANCIAL AID PROCEDURES**

**Forms required:** FAFSA, institutional form.
**Dates and Deadlines:** Priority date 4/22; no closing date. Applicants notified on a rolling basis starting 5/1; must reply within 2 week(s) of notification.
**Transfers:** No deadline.

**CONTACT**

Jodi Pontinen, Director of Financial Aid
1001 Chestnut Street West, Virginia, MN 55792-3448
(218) 749-7753

## Metropolitan State University

St. Paul, Minnesota
www.metrostate.edu                    Federal Code: 010374

**4-year public** university in very large city.
**Enrollment:** 7,244 undergrads, 63% part-time. 73 full-time freshmen.

**BASIC COSTS (2015-2016)**

**Tuition and fees:** $7,492; out-of-state residents $14,320.
**Per-credit charge:** $219; out-of-state residents $446.

**FINANCIAL AID PICTURE (2014-2015)**

**Students with need:** 33% of average financial aid package awarded as scholarships/grants, 67% awarded as loans/jobs. Need-based aid available for part-time students. Work study available nights, weekends, and for part-time students.
**Students without need:** No-need awards available for academics, leadership, minority status, state/district residency.

**FINANCIAL AID PROCEDURES**

**Forms required:** FAFSA.
**Dates and Deadlines:** Priority date 3/1; no closing date. Applicants notified on a rolling basis starting 5/1; must reply within 2 week(s) of notification.

**CONTACT**

Lois Larson, Director of Financial Aid
700 East Seventh Street, St. Paul, MN 55106-5000
(651) 793-1414

## Minneapolis Business College

Roseville, Minnesota
www.minneapolisbusinesscollege.edu
                                       Federal Code: 004645

**2-year for-profit** business and technical college in very large city.
**Enrollment:** 235 undergrads.
**Selectivity:** Open admission.

**BASIC COSTS (2015-2016)**

**Tuition and fees:** $14,720.
**Room only:** $6,960.

**FINANCIAL AID PICTURE**

**Students with need:** Need-based aid available for full-time students.
**Students without need:** This college awards aid only to students with need.
**Additional info:** Individual financial planning available for all students to meet the cost of education.

**FINANCIAL AID PROCEDURES**

**Forms required:** FAFSA.

**Dates and Deadlines:** Applicants notified on a rolling basis.

**CONTACT**

Marie Martin, Director of Student Services
1711 West County Road B, Roseville, MN 55113
(651) 636-7406

## Minneapolis College of Art and Design

Minneapolis, Minnesota
www.mcad.edu                          Federal Code: 002365

**4-year private** visual arts college in very large city.
**Enrollment:** 668 undergrads, 2% part-time. 123 full-time freshmen.
**Selectivity:** Admits 50 to 75% of applicants.

**BASIC COSTS (2015-2016)**

**Tuition and fees:** $35,326.
**Per-credit charge:** $1,453.
**Room only:** $5,110.
**Additional info:** Estimated expenses: food $2,130, books/supplies $2,870, personal $900, transportation $432, loan fees $72. Required laptop purchase of $1,500 may be waived if student has a laptop with appropriate specs.

**FINANCIAL AID PICTURE (2014-2015)**

**Students with need:** Out of 118 full-time freshmen who applied for aid, 103 were judged to have need. Of these, 103 received aid, and 16 had their full need met. Average financial aid package met 68% of need; average scholarship/grant was $19,639; average loan was $4,506. For part-time students, average financial aid package was $7,760.
**Students without need:** 19 full-time freshmen who did not demonstrate need for aid received scholarships/grants; average award was $12,736. No-need awards available for academics, alumni affiliation, art.
**Scholarships offered:** Admissions Merit Scholarships: $6,000-$15,000; based on admissions file. Students admitted to the college automatically entered into scholarship competition.

**FINANCIAL AID PROCEDURES**

**Forms required:** FAFSA.
**Dates and Deadlines:** Priority date 3/1; closing date 6/1. Applicants notified on a rolling basis starting 3/1; must reply by 5/1 or within 2 week(s) of notification.
**Transfers:** Priority date 4/1; closing date 7/1. Applicants notified on a rolling basis starting 3/1; must reply by 5/1 or within 2 week(s) of notification. Transfer students may apply for admission by the priority deadline of Feb. 15. Only students accepted will receive an award letter. Complete the FAFSA by March 1. Be sure to include MCAD on the list of schools to receive your FAFSA analysis.

**CONTACT**

Laura Link, Director of Financial Aid
2501 Stevens Avenue, Minneapolis, MN 55404
(612) 874-8782

## Minneapolis Community and Technical College

Minneapolis, Minnesota
www.minneapolis.edu                   Federal Code: 002362

**2-year public** community and technical college in large city.
**Enrollment:** 8,187 undergrads.
**Selectivity:** Open admission; but selective for some programs.

**BASIC COSTS (2015-2016)**

**Tuition and fees:** $5,366; out-of-state residents $5,366.

## FINANCIAL AID PICTURE

**Students with need:** Need-based aid available for full-time and part-time students. Work study available nights, weekends, and for part-time students.
**Students without need:** This college awards aid only to students with need.

## FINANCIAL AID PROCEDURES

**Forms required:** FAFSA.
**Dates and Deadlines:** Priority date 7/12; no closing date. Applicants notified on a rolling basis starting 7/1.
**Transfers:** Priority date 7/22; no deadline. Applicants notified on a rolling basis starting 7/1.

## CONTACT

Angela Christensen, Director of Financial Aid
1501 Hennepin Avenue, Minneapolis, MN 55403-1710
(612) 659-6240

# Minnesota School of Business: Blaine
Blaine, Minnesota
www.msbcollege.edu                    Federal Code: 017145

**4-year for-profit** career college in small city.
**Enrollment:** 239 undergrads.
**Selectivity:** Open admission.

## BASIC COSTS (2015-2016)

**Tuition and fees:** $18,702.
**Per-credit charge:** $390.
**Additional info:** Per-credit hour charge for 1 to 11 hours, $460; for 12 to 16 hours, $390. Course fees: $10 to $400 per course.

## FINANCIAL AID PICTURE

**Students with need:** Need-based aid available for full-time and part-time students.

## FINANCIAL AID PROCEDURES

**Forms required:** FAFSA, institutional form.
**Dates and Deadlines:** Applicants notified on a rolling basis starting 7/1; must reply within 2 week(s) of notification.

## CONTACT

Paul Huber, Financial Aid Manager
3680 Pheasant Ridge Dr. NE, Blaine, MN 55449
(763) 225-8000

# Minnesota School of Business: Brooklyn Center
Brooklyn Center, Minnesota
www.msbcollege.edu                    Federal Code: 017145

**2-year for-profit** career college in large town.
**Enrollment:** 109 undergrads.
**Selectivity:** Open admission.

## BASIC COSTS (2015-2016)

**Tuition and fees:** $18,702.
**Per-credit charge:** $390.
**Additional info:** Per-credit hour charge for 1 to 11 hours, $460; for 12 to 16 hours, $390. Course fees: $10 to $400 per course.

## FINANCIAL AID PICTURE

**Students with need:** Need-based aid available for full-time and part-time students.

## FINANCIAL AID PROCEDURES

**Forms required:** FAFSA, state aid form, institutional form.

**Dates and Deadlines:** Applicants notified on a rolling basis starting 7/1; must reply within 2 week(s) of notification.

## CONTACT

Tyuon Harris, Financial Aid Manager
5910 Shingle Creek Parkway, Brooklyn Center, MN 55430
(763) 566-7777

# Minnesota School of Business: Elk River
Elk River, Minnesota
www.msbcollege.edu                    Federal Code: 017145

**4-year for-profit** university and career college in large town.
**Enrollment:** 236 undergrads.
**Selectivity:** Open admission.

## BASIC COSTS (2015-2016)

**Tuition and fees:** $18,702.
**Per-credit charge:** $390.
**Additional info:** Per-credit hour charge for 1 to 11 hours, $460; for 12 to 16 hours, $390. Course fees: $10 to $400 per course.

## FINANCIAL AID PICTURE

**Students with need:** Need-based aid available for full-time and part-time students.

## FINANCIAL AID PROCEDURES

**Forms required:** FAFSA, state aid form, institutional form.
**Dates and Deadlines:** Applicants notified on a rolling basis starting 7/1; must reply within 2 week(s) of notification.

## CONTACT

Breanna Persons, Financial Aid Manager
11500 193rd Avenue NW, Elk River, MN 55330
(763) 367-7000

# Minnesota School of Business: Lakeville
Lakeville, Minnesota
www.msbcollege.edu                    Federal Code: 017145

**4-year for-profit** university and career college in small city.
**Enrollment:** 195 undergrads.
**Selectivity:** Open admission.

## BASIC COSTS (2015-2016)

**Tuition and fees:** $18,702.
**Per-credit charge:** $390.
**Additional info:** Per-credit hour charge for 1 to 11 hours, $460; for 12 to 16 hours, $390. Course fees: $10 to $400 per course.

## FINANCIAL AID PICTURE

**Students with need:** Need-based aid available for full-time and part-time students.

## FINANCIAL AID PROCEDURES

**Forms required:** FAFSA, state aid form, institutional form.
**Dates and Deadlines:** Applicants notified on a rolling basis starting 7/1; must reply within 2 week(s) of notification.

## CONTACT

Jaclyn Oscarson, Financial Aid Manager
17685 Juniper Path, Lakeville, MN 55044
(952) 892-9000

## Minnesota School of Business: Plymouth
Plymouth, Minnesota
www.msbcollege.edu                Federal Code: 017145

**4-year for-profit** university and career college in small city.
**Enrollment:** 130 undergrads.
**Selectivity:** Open admission.

**BASIC COSTS (2015-2016)**
**Tuition and fees:** $18,702.
**Per-credit charge:** $390.
**Additional info:** Per-credit hour charge for 1 to 11 hours, $460; for 12 to 16 hours, $390. Course fees: $10 to $400 per course.

**FINANCIAL AID PICTURE**
**Students with need:** Need-based aid available for full-time and part-time students.

**FINANCIAL AID PROCEDURES**
**Forms required:** FAFSA, state aid form, institutional form.
**Dates and Deadlines:** Applicants notified on a rolling basis starting 7/1; must reply within 2 week(s) of notification.

**CONTACT**
Holly Weberg, Financial Aid Manager
1455 County Road 101 North, Plymouth, MN 55447
(763) 476-2000

## Minnesota School of Business: Richfield
Richfield, Minnesota
www.msbcollege.edu                Federal Code: 017145

**4-year for-profit** university and career college in large town.
**Enrollment:** 693 undergrads.
**Selectivity:** Open admission; but selective for some programs.

**BASIC COSTS (2015-2016)**
**Tuition and fees:** $18,702.
**Per-credit charge:** $390.
**Additional info:** Per-credit hour charge for 1 to 11 hours, $460; for 12 to 16 hours, $390. Course fees: $10 to $400 per course.

**FINANCIAL AID PICTURE**
**Students with need:** Need-based aid available for full-time and part-time students.

**FINANCIAL AID PROCEDURES**
**Forms required:** FAFSA, state aid form, institutional form.
**Dates and Deadlines:** Applicants notified on a rolling basis starting 7/1; must reply within 2 week(s) of notification.

**CONTACT**
Andrea Howie, Financial Aid Manager
1401 West 76 Street, Suite 500, Richfield, MN 55423
(612) 861-2000

## Minnesota School of Business: Rochester
Rochester, Minnesota
www.msbcollege.edu                Federal Code: 017145

**4-year for-profit** university and career college in small city.
**Enrollment:** 183 undergrads.
**Selectivity:** Open admission.

**BASIC COSTS (2015-2016)**
**Tuition and fees:** $18,702.
**Per-credit charge:** $390.

**Additional info:** Per-credit hour charge for 1 to 11 hours, $460; for 12 to 16 hours, $390. Course fees: $10 to $400 per course.

**FINANCIAL AID PICTURE**
**Students with need:** Need-based aid available for full-time and part-time students.

**FINANCIAL AID PROCEDURES**
**Forms required:** FAFSA, state aid form, institutional form.
**Dates and Deadlines:** Applicants notified on a rolling basis starting 7/1; must reply within 2 week(s) of notification.

**CONTACT**
Chris Cook, Financial Aid Manager
2521 Pennington Drive NW, Rochester, MN 55901
(507) 536-9500

## Minnesota School of Business: St. Cloud
Waite Park, Minnesota
www.msbcollege.edu                Federal Code: 017145

**4-year for-profit** university and career college in small city.
**Enrollment:** 218 undergrads.
**Selectivity:** Open admission.

**BASIC COSTS (2015-2016)**
**Tuition and fees:** $18,702.
**Per-credit charge:** $390.
**Additional info:** Per-credit hour charge for 1 to 11 hours, $460; for 12 to 16 hours, $390. Course fees: $10 to $400 per course.

**FINANCIAL AID PICTURE**
**Students with need:** Need-based aid available for full-time and part-time students.

**FINANCIAL AID PROCEDURES**
**Forms required:** FAFSA, state aid form, institutional form.
**Dates and Deadlines:** Applicants notified on a rolling basis starting 7/1; must reply within 2 week(s) of notification.

**CONTACT**
Eric Hanson, Financial Aid Manager
1201 Second Street South, Waite Park, MN 56387
(866) 403-3333

## Minnesota School of Business: Shakopee
Shakopee, Minnesota
www.msbcollege.edu                Federal Code: 017145

**4-year for-profit** university and career college in large town.
**Enrollment:** 210 undergrads.
**Selectivity:** Open admission.

**BASIC COSTS (2015-2016)**
**Tuition and fees:** $18,702.
**Per-credit charge:** $390.
**Additional info:** Per-credit hour charge for 1 to 11 hours, $460; for 12 to 16 hours, $390. Course fees: $10 to $400 per course.

**FINANCIAL AID PICTURE**
**Students with need:** Need-based aid available for full-time and part-time students.

**FINANCIAL AID PROCEDURES**
**Forms required:** FAFSA, state aid form, institutional form.
**Dates and Deadlines:** Applicants notified on a rolling basis starting 7/1; must reply within 2 week(s) of notification.

**CONTACT**
Laurie Dresow, Financial Aid Manager
1200 Shakopee Town Square, Shakopee, MN 55379
(952) 345-1200

## Minnesota State College - Southeast Technical

Winona, Minnesota
www.southeastmn.edu                    Federal Code: 002393

**2-year public** technical college in large town.
**Enrollment:** 1,538 undergrads, 45% part-time. 149 full-time freshmen.
**Selectivity:** Open admission; but selective for some programs.

**BASIC COSTS (2015-2016)**
**Tuition and fees:** $5,615; out-of-state residents $5,615.

**FINANCIAL AID PICTURE (2014-2015)**
**Students with need:** Out of 128 full-time freshmen who applied for aid, 113 were judged to have need. Of these, 111 received aid, and 3 had their full need met. Average financial aid package met 36% of need; average scholarship/grant was $4,585; average loan was $3,178. For part-time students, average financial aid package was $5,165.
**Students without need:** 8 full-time freshmen who did not demonstrate need for aid received scholarships/grants; average award was $1,763. No-need awards available for academics, leadership.
**Scholarships offered:** 11 full-time freshmen received athletic scholarships; average amount $1,718.

**FINANCIAL AID PROCEDURES**
**Forms required:** FAFSA, state aid form, institutional form.
**Dates and Deadlines:** Applicants notified on a rolling basis; must reply within 3 week(s) of notification.
**Transfers:** Applicants notified on a rolling basis; must reply within 3 week(s) of notification. Mid-year transfer application forms must be accompanied by financial aid transcript.

**CONTACT**
Tammy Vondrasek, Director of Financial Aid
1250 Homer Road, Winona, MN 55987-0409
(507) 453-2639

## Minnesota State Community and Technical College

Fergus Falls, Minnesota
www.minnesota.edu                    Federal Code: 005541

**2-year public** community and technical college in large town.
**Enrollment:** 4,491 undergrads, 44% part-time. 786 full-time freshmen.
**Selectivity:** Open admission.

**BASIC COSTS (2015-2016)**
**Tuition and fees:** $5,361; out-of-state residents $5,361.
**Per-credit charge:** $161; out-of-state residents $161.
**Room only:** $3,000.
**Additional info:** Students can buy a meal card with a starting balance of $900 per semester ($1,800) per academic year.

**FINANCIAL AID PICTURE**
**Students with need:** Need-based aid available for full-time and part-time students. Work study available nights, weekends, and for part-time students.
**Students without need:** No-need awards available for academics, art, leadership, minority status, music/drama, state/district residency.
**Scholarships offered:** Academic and leadership scholarships: $400-$1,000 each; available to 1st and 2nd year students; over 150 awarded annually.

**FINANCIAL AID PROCEDURES**
**Forms required:** FAFSA.
**Dates and Deadlines:** Priority date 6/1; no closing date. Applicants notified on a rolling basis starting 7/1.
**Transfers:** Priority date 7/1; no deadline. Applicants notified on a rolling basis.

**CONTACT**
Wendy Olds, Director of Financial Aid
405 Colfax Avenue SW, Wadena, MN 56482-1447
(218) 846-3810

## Minnesota State University Mankato

Mankato, Minnesota
www.mnsu.edu                    Federal Code: 002360

**4-year public** university in small city.
**Enrollment:** 12,292 undergrads.

**BASIC COSTS (2015-2016)**
**Tuition and fees:** $7,966; out-of-state residents $16,110.
**Per-credit charge:** $310; out-of-state residents $622.
**Room and board:** $8,430.

**FINANCIAL AID PICTURE (2015-2016)**
**Students with need:** Average financial aid package met 70% of need; average scholarship/grant was $5,658; average loan was $3,810. For part-time students, average financial aid package was $6,267.
**Students without need:** No-need awards available for academics, art, athletics, leadership, minority status, music/drama.

**FINANCIAL AID PROCEDURES**
**Forms required:** FAFSA.
**Dates and Deadlines:** Priority date 3/15; no closing date. Applicants notified on a rolling basis starting 3/30; must reply within 2 week(s) of notification.

**CONTACT**
Sandra Loerts, Director of Financial Aid
122 Taylor Center, Mankato, MN 56001
(507) 389-1185

## Minnesota State University Moorhead

Moorhead, Minnesota
www.mnstate.edu                    Federal Code: 002367

**4-year public** university in small city.
**Enrollment:** 5,037 undergrads, 15% part-time. 887 full-time freshmen.
**Selectivity:** Admits over 75% of applicants.

**BASIC COSTS (2015-2016)**
**Tuition and fees:** $8,092; out-of-state residents $15,228.
**Per-credit charge:** $230.25; out-of-state residents $461.
**Room and board:** $7,798.
**Additional info:** Tuition/fee waivers available for minority students.

**FINANCIAL AID PICTURE (2014-2015)**
**Students with need:** Out of 758 full-time freshmen who applied for aid, 512 were judged to have need. Of these, 505 received aid. Need-based aid available for part-time students.
**Students without need:** No-need awards available for academics, alumni affiliation, art, athletics, leadership, minority status, music/drama, state/district residency.
**Additional info:** The financial aid application process consists of several steps. At each step institution may ask for information or additional documentation. The entire process can take 6-12 weeks.

## FINANCIAL AID PROCEDURES

**Forms required:** FAFSA.

**Dates and Deadlines:** Priority date 2/15; no closing date.

**Transfers:** Closing date 6/30.

### CONTACT

Carolyn Zehren, Director of Financial Aid and Scholarships

1104 Seventh Avenue South, Moorhead, MN 56563

(218) 236-2251

## Minnesota West Community and Technical College

Pipestone, Minnesota

www.mnwest.edu                Federal Code: 005263

**2-year public** community and technical college in large town.

**Enrollment:** 1,753 undergrads.

**Selectivity:** Open admission; but selective for some programs.

### BASIC COSTS (2015-2016)

**Tuition and fees:** $5,677; out-of-state residents $5,677.

**Per-credit charge:** $172.

### FINANCIAL AID PICTURE (2014-2015)

**Students with need:** 62% of average financial aid package awarded as scholarships/grants, 38% awarded as loans/jobs. Need-based aid available for part-time students. Work study available nights, weekends, and for part-time students.

### FINANCIAL AID PROCEDURES

**Forms required:** FAFSA.

**Dates and Deadlines:** Priority date 6/9; no closing date. Applicants notified on a rolling basis starting 4/9; must reply within 2 week(s) of notification.

### CONTACT

Jodi Landgaard, Financial Aid Director

1314 North Hiawatha Avenue, Pipestone, MN 56164

(507) 372-3403

## National American University: Bloomington

Bloomington, Minnesota

www.national.edu               Federal Code: E00640

**4-year for-profit** business and nursing college in very large city.

**Enrollment:** 422 undergrads.

**Selectivity:** Open admission.

### BASIC COSTS (2015-2016)

**Tuition and fees:** $16,470.

**Per-credit charge:** $346.

**Additional info:** Additional fees may apply.

### FINANCIAL AID PICTURE

**Students with need:** Need-based aid available for full-time and part-time students. Work study available nights, weekends, and for part-time students.

**Students without need:** No-need awards available for academics.

### FINANCIAL AID PROCEDURES

**Forms required:** FAFSA.

**Dates and Deadlines:** Priority date 8/21; no closing date. Applicants notified on a rolling basis.

### CONTACT

Lindsey Regel, Lead Financial Services Representative

7801 Metro Parkway Suite 200, Bloomington, MN 55425

## Normandale Community College

Bloomington, Minnesota

www.normandale.edu             Federal Code: 007954

**2-year public** community college in very large city.

**Enrollment:** 8,516 undergrads.

**Selectivity:** Open admission; but selective for some programs.

### BASIC COSTS (2015-2016)

**Tuition and fees:** $5,736; out-of-state residents $5,736.

**Per-credit charge:** $162; out-of-state residents $162.

### FINANCIAL AID PICTURE (2014-2015)

**Students with need:** 43% of average financial aid package awarded as scholarships/grants, 57% awarded as loans/jobs. Need-based aid available for part-time students. Work study available nights, weekends, and for part-time students.

**Students without need:** No-need awards available for academics, art, leadership, music/drama, state/district residency.

### FINANCIAL AID PROCEDURES

**Forms required:** FAFSA, state aid form.

**Dates and Deadlines:** Priority date 4/1; no closing date. Applicants notified on a rolling basis starting 4/15.

### CONTACT

Susan Ant, Director, Financial Aid and Scholarships

9700 France Avenue South, Bloomington, MN 55431

(952) 358-8250

## North Central University

Minneapolis, Minnesota

www.northcentral.edu           Federal Code: 002369

**4-year private** university in large city, affiliated with Assemblies of God.

**Enrollment:** 1,301 undergrads.

### BASIC COSTS (2015-2016)

**Tuition and fees:** $21,586.

**Room and board:** $6,584.

### FINANCIAL AID PICTURE

**Students with need:** Need-based aid available for full-time and part-time students. Work study available nights, weekends, and for part-time students.

**Students without need:** No-need awards available for academics, leadership, music/drama.

**Scholarships offered:** President's Scholarship: $2,500 per year; renewable; based on academic performance. Dean's Scholarship: $1,500 per year; renewable; based on academic performance. First Choice Scholarship awarded to those who submit their application early and meet academic criteria.

### FINANCIAL AID PROCEDURES

**Forms required:** FAFSA.

**Dates and Deadlines:** Applicants notified on a rolling basis starting 3/1; must reply within 2 week(s) of notification.

**Transfers:** Priority date 4/15; no deadline. Applicants notified on a rolling basis starting 3/1.

### CONTACT

Donna Jager, Director of Financial Aid

910 Elliot Avenue, Minneapolis, MN 55404

(800) 289-4488 ext. 289

## North Hennepin Community College

Brooklyn Park, Minnesota
www.nhcc.edu                         Federal Code: 002370

**2-year public** community college in small city.
**Enrollment:** 6,173 undergrads, 68% part-time. 507 full-time freshmen.
**Selectivity:** Open admission; but selective for some programs.

### BASIC COSTS (2015-2016)
**Tuition and fees:** $5,383; out-of-state residents $5,383.
**Per-credit charge:** $165.

### FINANCIAL AID PICTURE (2014-2015)
**Students with need:** 56% of average financial aid package awarded as scholarships/grants, 44% awarded as loans/jobs. Need-based aid available for part-time students. Work study available nights, weekends, and for part-time students.
**Students without need:** No-need awards available for academics, art, leadership.
**Additional info:** Computerized financial aid application.

### FINANCIAL AID PROCEDURES
**Forms required:** FAFSA.
**Dates and Deadlines:** Priority date 4/15; no closing date. Applicants notified on a rolling basis starting 6/1.
**Transfers:** No deadline. Applicants notified on a rolling basis.

### CONTACT
Steve Yang, Director of Financial Aid and Scholarships
7411 85th Avenue North, Brooklyn Park, MN 55445
(763) 424-0728

## Northland Community & Technical College

Thief River Falls, Minnesota
www.northlandcollege.edu         Federal Code: 002385

**2-year public** community and technical college in small town.
**Enrollment:** 2,310 undergrads, 46% part-time. 333 full-time freshmen.
**Selectivity:** Open admission; but selective for some programs.

### BASIC COSTS (2015-2016)
**Tuition and fees:** $5,534; out-of-state residents $5,534.
**Per-credit charge:** $165; out-of-state residents $165.

### FINANCIAL AID PICTURE (2014-2015)
**Students with need:** 36% of average financial aid package awarded as scholarships/grants, 64% awarded as loans/jobs. Need-based aid available for part-time students. Work study available nights, weekends, and for part-time students.
**Students without need:** This college awards aid only to students with need.

### FINANCIAL AID PROCEDURES
**Forms required:** FAFSA.
**Dates and Deadlines:** Priority date 5/1; no closing date. Applicants notified on a rolling basis starting 5/15.
**Transfers:** No deadline. Applicants notified on a rolling basis starting 5/1; must reply within 2 week(s) of notification.

### CONTACT
Gerald Schulte, Director of Financial Aid
2022 Central Avenue NE, East Grand Forks, MN 56721
(218) 683-8557

## Northwest Technical College

Bemidji, Minnesota
www.ntcmn.edu                        Federal Code: 005759

**2-year public** technical college in large town.
**Enrollment:** 712 undergrads, 54% part-time. 75 full-time freshmen.
**Selectivity:** Open admission; but selective for some programs.

### BASIC COSTS (2015-2016)
**Tuition and fees:** $5,480; out-of-state residents $5,480.
**Per-credit charge:** $173; out-of-state residents $173.
**Room and board:** $7,690.

### FINANCIAL AID PICTURE (2014-2015)
**Students with need:** 62% of average financial aid package awarded as scholarships/grants, 38% awarded as loans/jobs. Need-based aid available for part-time students. Work study available nights.
**Students without need:** This college awards aid only to students with need.

### FINANCIAL AID PROCEDURES
**Forms required:** FAFSA.
**Dates and Deadlines:** Priority date 6/1; no closing date. Applicants notified on a rolling basis starting 3/1.

### CONTACT
Lesa Lawrence, Director of Financial Aid
905 Grant Avenue Southeast, Bemidji, MN 56601-4907
(218) 333-6600

## Northwestern Health Sciences University

Bloomington, Minnesota
www.nwhealth.edu                     Federal Code: 012328

**Upper-division private** university and health science college in very large city.
**Enrollment:** 163 undergrads, 55% part-time. 3 full-time freshmen.
**Selectivity:** Open admission; but selective for some programs.

### BASIC COSTS (2015-2016)
**Tuition and fees:** $12,267.
**Per-credit charge:** $392.

### FINANCIAL AID PICTURE (2014-2015)
**Students with need:** Need-based aid available for part-time students.
**Students without need:** This college awards aid only to students with need.

### FINANCIAL AID PROCEDURES
**Forms required:** FAFSA.
**Dates and Deadlines:** Priority date 6/1; no closing date. Applicants notified on a rolling basis.

### CONTACT
Susan Neppl, Director of Financial Aid
2501 West 84th Street, Bloomington, MN 55431

## Oak Hills Christian College

Bemidji, Minnesota
www.oakhills.edu                     Federal Code: 016116

**4-year private** Bible college in large town, affiliated with interdenominational tradition.
**Enrollment:** 114 undergrads.

### BASIC COSTS (2015-2016)
**Tuition and fees:** $16,165.

**Room and board:** $5,816.

## FINANCIAL AID PICTURE
**Students with need:** Need-based aid available for full-time and part-time students. Work study available nights, weekends, and for part-time students.
**Students without need:** No-need awards available for academics, alumni affiliation.

## FINANCIAL AID PROCEDURES
**Forms required:** FAFSA, institutional form.
**Dates and Deadlines:** Applicants notified on a rolling basis starting 3/1.
**Transfers:** No deadline. Applicants notified on a rolling basis starting 3/1.

## CONTACT
Matt Myrick, Director of Financial Aid
1600 Oak Hills Road SW, Bemidji, MN 56601-8826
(218) 751-8670 ext. 1284

# Pine Technical & Community College
Pine City, Minnesota
www.pine.edu          Federal Code: 005535

**2-year public** technical college in small town.
**Enrollment:** 1,083 undergrads.
**Selectivity:** Open admission; but selective for some programs.

## BASIC COSTS (2015-2016)
**Tuition and fees:** $5,081; out-of-state residents $9,676.

## FINANCIAL AID PICTURE
**Students with need:** Need-based aid available for full-time and part-time students.
**Students without need:** No-need awards available for academics, state/district residency.

## FINANCIAL AID PROCEDURES
**Forms required:** FAFSA.
**Dates and Deadlines:** Priority date 5/5; no closing date. Applicants notified on a rolling basis starting 6/5.

## CONTACT
Shawn Reynolds, Financial Aid Director
900 Fourth Street SE, Pine City, MN 55063
(320) 629-5100 ext. 161

# Rainy River Community College
International Falls, Minnesota
www.rainyriver.edu          Federal Code: 006775

**2-year public** community and technical college in small town.
**Enrollment:** 278 undergrads, 18% part-time.
**Selectivity:** Open admission.

## BASIC COSTS (2015-2016)
**Tuition and fees:** $5,325; out-of-state residents $6,507.
**Room and board:** $3,840.
**Additional info:** Tuition/fee waivers available for unemployed or children of unemployed.

## FINANCIAL AID PICTURE (2015-2016)
**Students with need:** 54% of average financial aid package awarded as scholarships/grants, 46% awarded as loans/jobs. Need-based aid available for part-time students. Work study available nights, weekends, and for part-time students.
**Students without need:** No-need awards available for academics, alumni affiliation, leadership, minority status, state/district residency.
**Additional info:** Many scholarship and employment opportunities for applicants showing little or no need.

## FINANCIAL AID PROCEDURES
**Forms required:** FAFSA, institutional form.
**Dates and Deadlines:** Priority date 6/1; no closing date. Applicants notified on a rolling basis starting 5/1; must reply within 3 week(s) of notification.

## CONTACT
Scott Riley, Director of Financial Aid
1501 Highway 71, International Falls, MN 56649
(218) 285-7722

# Rasmussen College: Blaine
Blaine, Minnesota
www.rasmussen.edu

**4-year for-profit** branch campus and career college in small city.
**Enrollment:** 770 undergrads.
**Selectivity:** Open admission; but selective for some programs.

## BASIC COSTS (2016-2017)
**Tuition and fees:** $13,455.
**Per-credit charge:** $299.

## FINANCIAL AID PICTURE
**Students with need:** Need-based aid available for full-time and part-time students.

## FINANCIAL AID PROCEDURES
**Forms required:** FAFSA, institutional form.
**Dates and Deadlines:** Applicants notified on a rolling basis.

## CONTACT
Debora Murray, Director of Financial Services
3629 95th Avenue NE, Blaine, MN 55014

# Rasmussen College: Bloomington
Bloomington, Minnesota
www.rasmussen.edu          Federal Code: 011686

**2-year for-profit** branch campus and career college in small city.
**Enrollment:** 809 undergrads.
**Selectivity:** Open admission; but selective for some programs.

## BASIC COSTS (2016-2017)
**Tuition and fees:** $13,455.
**Per-credit charge:** $299.

## FINANCIAL AID PICTURE
**Students with need:** Need-based aid available for full-time and part-time students.

## FINANCIAL AID PROCEDURES
**Forms required:** FAFSA, institutional form.
**Dates and Deadlines:** Applicants notified on a rolling basis.

## CONTACT
Debora Murray, Director of Financial Services
4400 West 78th Street, Bloomington, MN 55435
(952) 545-2000

# Rasmussen College: Brooklyn Park
Brooklyn Park, Minnesota
www.rasmussen.edu

**2-year for-profit** branch campus and career college in small city.
**Enrollment:** 654 undergrads.
**Selectivity:** Open admission; but selective for some programs.

**BASIC COSTS (2016-2017)**
**Tuition and fees:** $13,455.
**Per-credit charge:** $299.

**FINANCIAL AID PICTURE**

**Students with need:** Need-based aid available for full-time and part-time students.

**FINANCIAL AID PROCEDURES**

**Forms required:** FAFSA, institutional form.
**Dates and Deadlines:** Applicants notified on a rolling basis.

**CONTACT**

Debora Murray, Director of Financial Services
8301 93rd Avenue North, Brooklyn Park, MN 55445

## Rasmussen College: Eagan

Eagan, Minnesota
www.rasmussen.edu                    Federal Code: 004648

**2-year for-profit** career college in small city.
**Enrollment:** 629 undergrads.
**Selectivity:** Open admission; but selective for some programs.

**BASIC COSTS (2016-2017)**
**Tuition and fees:** $13,455.
**Per-credit charge:** $299.

**FINANCIAL AID PICTURE**

**Students with need:** Need-based aid available for full-time and part-time students.

**FINANCIAL AID PROCEDURES**

**Forms required:** FAFSA, institutional form.
**Dates and Deadlines:** Applicants notified on a rolling basis.

**CONTACT**

Debora Murray, Director of Financial Services
3500 Federal Drive, Eagan, MN 55122
(651) 687-9000

## Rasmussen College: Lake Elmo/ Woodbury

Lake Elmo, Minnesota
www.rasmussen.edu

**4-year for-profit** career college in small city.
**Enrollment:** 586 undergrads.
**Selectivity:** Open admission; but selective for some programs.

**BASIC COSTS (2016-2017)**
**Tuition and fees:** $13,455.
**Per-credit charge:** $299.

**FINANCIAL AID PICTURE**

**Students with need:** Need-based aid available for full-time and part-time students.

**FINANCIAL AID PROCEDURES**

**Forms required:** FAFSA, institutional form.
**Dates and Deadlines:** Applicants notified on a rolling basis.

**CONTACT**

Debora Murray, Director of Financial Services
8565 Eagle Point Circle, Lake Elmo, MN 55042-8637

## Rasmussen College: Mankato

Mankato, Minnesota
www.rasmussen.edu                    Federal Code: 016845

**2-year for-profit** career college in large town.
**Enrollment:** 672 undergrads.
**Selectivity:** Open admission; but selective for some programs.

**BASIC COSTS (2016-2017)**
**Tuition and fees:** $13,455.
**Per-credit charge:** $299.

**FINANCIAL AID PICTURE**

**Students with need:** Need-based aid available for full-time and part-time students.

**FINANCIAL AID PROCEDURES**

**Forms required:** FAFSA, institutional form.
**Dates and Deadlines:** Applicants notified on a rolling basis.

**CONTACT**

Debora Murray, Director of Financial Services
130 Saint Andrews Drive, Mankato, MN 56001
(507) 625-6556

## Rasmussen College: Moorhead

Moorhead, Minnesota
www.rasmussen.edu

**4-year for-profit** career college in small city.
**Enrollment:** 371 undergrads.
**Selectivity:** Open admission; but selective for some programs.

**BASIC COSTS (2016-2017)**
**Tuition and fees:** $13,455.
**Per-credit charge:** $299.

**FINANCIAL AID PICTURE**

**Students with need:** Need-based aid available for full-time and part-time students.

**FINANCIAL AID PROCEDURES**

**Forms required:** FAFSA, institutional form.
**Dates and Deadlines:** Applicants notified on a rolling basis.

**CONTACT**

Debora Murray, Director of Financial Services
1250 29th Avenue South, Moorhead, MN 56560

## Rasmussen College: St. Cloud

St. Cloud, Minnesota
www.rasmussen.edu                    Federal Code: 008694

**2-year for-profit** career college in small city.
**Enrollment:** 834 undergrads.
**Selectivity:** Open admission; but selective for some programs.

**BASIC COSTS (2016-2017)**
**Tuition and fees:** $13,455.
**Per-credit charge:** $299.

**FINANCIAL AID PICTURE**

**Students with need:** Need-based aid available for full-time and part-time students.

**FINANCIAL AID PROCEDURES**

**Forms required:** FAFSA, institutional form.
**Dates and Deadlines:** Applicants notified on a rolling basis.

**CONTACT**

Debora Murray, Director of Financial Services

226 Park Avenue South, St. Cloud, MN 56301-3713

(320) 251-5600

## Ridgewater College

Willmar, Minnesota

www.ridgewater.edu                    Federal Code: 005252

**2-year public** community and technical college in large town.

**Enrollment:** 3,438 undergrads.

**Selectivity:** Open admission; but selective for some programs.

**BASIC COSTS (2015-2016)**

**Tuition and fees:** $5,402; out-of-state residents $5,402.

**Additional info:** Tuition/fee waivers available for adults.

**FINANCIAL AID PICTURE**

**Students with need:** Need-based aid available for full-time and part-time students. Work study available nights, weekends, and for part-time students.

**Additional info:** Special funds are available for adult transfer students returning or continuing education after a 7-year absence from academic training. ALLISS grants provide reimbursement for one class, up to five credits for one semester.

**FINANCIAL AID PROCEDURES**

**Forms required:** FAFSA, institutional form.

**Dates and Deadlines:** Applicants notified on a rolling basis.

**CONTACT**

Jim Rice, Director of Financial Aid

2101 15th Avenue Northwest, Willmar, MN 56201

(320) 222-7474

## Riverland Community College

Austin, Minnesota

www.riverland.edu                    Federal Code: 002335

**2-year public** community and technical college in large town.

**Enrollment:** 2,173 undergrads.

**Selectivity:** Open admission; but selective for some programs.

**BASIC COSTS (2015-2016)**

**Tuition and fees:** $5,539; out-of-state residents $5,539.

**Per-credit charge:** $165.

**Room only:** $3,000.

**FINANCIAL AID PICTURE (2014-2015)**

**Students with need:** 44% of average financial aid package awarded as scholarships/grants, 56% awarded as loans/jobs. Need-based aid available for part-time students. Work study available nights, weekends, and for part-time students.

**Additional info:** One class tuition-free for Minnesota residents over 25 who have not attended college for at least 7 years.

**FINANCIAL AID PROCEDURES**

**Forms required:** FAFSA.

**Dates and Deadlines:** Priority date 5/15; no closing date. Applicants notified on a rolling basis; must reply within 5 week(s) of notification.

**Transfers:** No deadline. Applicants notified on a rolling basis.

**CONTACT**

Gary Schindler, Financial Aid Director

1900 Eighth Avenue, NW, Austin, MN 55912-1407

(507) 433-0511

## Rochester Community and Technical College

Rochester, Minnesota

www.rctc.edu                    Federal Code: 002373

**2-year public** community and technical college in small city.

**Enrollment:** 6,062 undergrads.

**Selectivity:** Open admission; but selective for some programs.

**BASIC COSTS (2015-2016)**

**Tuition and fees:** $5,637; out-of-state residents $5,637.

**Per-credit charge:** $164.

**FINANCIAL AID PICTURE**

**Students with need:** Need-based aid available for full-time and part-time students. Work study available nights, weekends, and for part-time students.

**FINANCIAL AID PROCEDURES**

**Forms required:** FAFSA.

**Dates and Deadlines:** Priority date 4/15; no closing date. Applicants notified on a rolling basis.

**CONTACT**

Beth Diekmann, Director of Financial Aid

851 30th Avenue SE, Rochester, MN 55904-4999

(507) 285-7271

## St. Catherine University

Saint Paul, Minnesota

www.stkate.edu                    Federal Code: 002342

**4-year private** health science and liberal arts college for women in large city, affiliated with Roman Catholic Church.

**Enrollment:** 3,243 undergrads, 34% part-time. 395 full-time freshmen.

**Selectivity:** Admits 50 to 75% of applicants.

**BASIC COSTS (2015-2016)**

**Tuition and fees:** $35,629.

**Per-credit charge:** $1,164.

**Room and board:** $8,750.

**Additional info:** Evening, weekend, and online baccalaureate students are $548 per credit; associate degree students are $664 per credit.

**FINANCIAL AID PICTURE (2015-2016)**

**Students with need:** Out of 395 full-time freshmen who applied for aid, 347 were judged to have need. Of these, 347 received aid, and 91 had their full need met. Average financial aid package met 92% of need; average scholarship/grant was $9,800; average loan was $3,900. For part-time students, average financial aid package was $17,800.

**Students without need:** 48 full-time freshmen who did not demonstrate need for aid received scholarships/grants; average award was $17,500. No-need awards available for academics, alumni affiliation, leadership, state/district residency.

**Scholarships offered:** St. Catherine of Alexandria Merit Scholarships: $2,000-$6,000; high school seniors in top 15% of class, evidence of academic preparation, outstanding leadership abilities, involvement in extracurricular activities and community service; renewable for 3 years.

**Additional info:** Audition required for music scholarships.

**FINANCIAL AID PROCEDURES**

**Forms required:** FAFSA, institutional form.

**Dates and Deadlines:** Priority date 4/15; no closing date. Applicants notified on a rolling basis starting 3/30; must reply within 2 week(s) of notification.

**Transfers:** Applicants notified on a rolling basis; must reply within 2 week(s) of notification.

**CONTACT**
Elizabeth Stevens, Director of Financial Aid
2004 Randolph Avenue #F-02, St. Paul, MN 55105
(651) 690-6540

## Saint Cloud State University
St. Cloud, Minnesota
www.stcloudstate.edu                    Federal Code: 002377

**4-year public** university in small city.
**Enrollment:** 10,620 undergrads, 17% part-time. 1,793 full-time freshmen.
**Selectivity:** Admits over 75% of applicants.

**BASIC COSTS (2015-2016)**
**Tuition and fees:** $7,814; out-of-state residents $15,732.
**Per-credit charge:** $227; out-of-state residents $491.
**Room and board:** $7,930.

**FINANCIAL AID PICTURE (2015-2016)**
**Students with need:** Out of 1,501 full-time freshmen who applied for aid, 1,104 were judged to have need. Of these, 1,103 received aid, and 132 had their full need met. Average financial aid package met 60% of need; average scholarship/grant was $5,982; average loan was $3,543. For part-time students, average financial aid package was $7,895.
**Students without need:** 396 full-time freshmen who did not demonstrate need for aid received scholarships/grants; average award was $10,338. No-need awards available for academics, art, athletics, minority status, music/drama, ROTC.
**Scholarships offered:** 93 full-time freshmen received athletic scholarships; average amount $5,219.

**FINANCIAL AID PROCEDURES**
**Forms required:** FAFSA.
**Dates and Deadlines:** Priority date 4/15; no closing date. Applicants notified on a rolling basis starting 6/15.
**Transfers:** No deadline. Applicants notified on a rolling basis starting 6/15.

**CONTACT**
Michael Uran, Director of Financial Aid
720 Fourth Avenue South, AS 115, St. Cloud, MN 56301
(320) 308-2047

## St. Cloud Technical and Community College
St Cloud, Minnesota
www.sctcc.edu                    Federal Code: 005534

**2-year public** community and technical college in small city.
**Enrollment:** 4,010 undergrads.
**Selectivity:** Open admission; but selective for some programs.

**BASIC COSTS (2015-2016)**
**Tuition and fees:** $5,325; out-of-state residents $5,325.
**Per-credit charge:** $159.

**FINANCIAL AID PICTURE (2014-2015)**
**Students with need:** 64% of average financial aid package awarded as scholarships/grants, 36% awarded as loans/jobs. Need-based aid available for part-time students. Work study available nights, weekends, and for part-time students.
**Students without need:** No-need awards available for academics, leadership, state/district residency.

**FINANCIAL AID PROCEDURES**
**Forms required:** FAFSA.
**Dates and Deadlines:** Applicants notified on a rolling basis starting 6/1.

**CONTACT**
Anita Baugh, Director of Financial Aid
1540 Northway Drive, St. Cloud, MN 56303
(320) 308-5961

## St. John's University
Collegeville, Minnesota
www.csbsju.edu                    Federal Code: 002379

**4-year private** university and liberal arts college in rural community, affiliated with Roman Catholic Church.
**Enrollment:** 1,742 undergrads, 2% part-time. 451 full-time freshmen.
**Selectivity:** Admits 50 to 75% of applicants.

**BASIC COSTS (2015-2016)**
**Tuition and fees:** $40,226.
**Per-credit charge:** $1,647.
**Room and board:** $9,604.

**FINANCIAL AID PICTURE (2015-2016)**
**Students with need:** Out of 388 full-time freshmen who applied for aid, 340 were judged to have need. Of these, 340 received aid, and 142 had their full need met. Average financial aid package met 93% of need; average scholarship/grant was $28,696; average loan was $2,530. For part-time students, average financial aid package was $4,299.
**Students without need:** 92 full-time freshmen who did not demonstrate need for aid received scholarships/grants; average award was $16,890. No-need awards available for academics, alumni affiliation, art, leadership, music/drama, ROTC, state/district residency.
**Scholarships offered:** Trustees' Scholarships: $20,000-$22,000 renewable; based on 3.6 GPA, 30 ACT/equivalent SAT, demonstrated leadership and service, faculty interview. President's Scholarships: $15,500-$19,000 renewable; based on GPA, high school rank, ACT/SAT, leadership and service. Dean's Scholarships: $7,000-$15,000 renewable; based on GPA, high school rank, ACT/SAT, leadership and service. Art, music and theater scholarships: up to $4,000 renewable. Intercultural LEAD fellowship: up to $10,000 renewable; based on GPA, leadership, financial need, first generation college students, commitment to intercultural issues and action, from diverse urban high schools; on campus interview required. Army ROTC and ROTC Nursing Scholarships: based on demonstrated leadership potential, GPA, class standing, ACT/SAT, high achievement with broad interests and willingness to take on challenges. Catholic High School Scholarship: $4,000 renewable; for students attending Catholic high schools outside Minnesota. Saints Scholarship: $2,000-$4,000 renewable; for students attending public high schools outside Minnesota. FoCuS Scholarship: $22,000 renewable; for students majoring in chemistry. Bonner Leader Scholarship: $2,500 renewable; for students with strong interest in doing service at CSB/SJU, preference for students with financial need. Legacy Scholarship: $1,000 renewable; mother, father or grandparent obtained degree from Saint John's or St. Ben's. Benedictine Scholarship: $5,000 renewable; for students from low income families who have completed a college access program such as Upward Bound.
**Additional info:** Scholarship letters will be mailed on rolling basis approximately 2 weeks from the time admission acceptance letter is sent.

**FINANCIAL AID PROCEDURES**
**Forms required:** FAFSA, institutional form.
**Dates and Deadlines:** Priority date 3/15; no closing date. Applicants notified on a rolling basis starting 3/15; must reply by 5/1.
**Transfers:** Applicants notified on a rolling basis starting 3/15; must reply by 5/1. Phi Theta Kappa Scholarship: $1,500 renewable; for members of Phi Theta Kappa.

**CONTACT**
Robert Piechota, Director of Financial Aid
College of St Benedict/St John's University, Collegeville, MN 56321-7155
(320) 363-3664

## St. Mary's University of Minnesota
Winona, Minnesota
www.smumn.edu                    Federal Code: 002380

**4-year private** university in large town, affiliated with Roman Catholic Church.
**Enrollment:** 1,718 undergrads, 29% part-time. 277 full-time freshmen.
**Selectivity:** Admits over 75% of applicants.

### BASIC COSTS (2016-2017)
**Tuition and fees:** $32,575.
**Per-credit charge:** $1,070.
**Room and board:** $8,635.

### FINANCIAL AID PICTURE (2015-2016)
**Students with need:** Out of 243 full-time freshmen who applied for aid, 214 were judged to have need. Of these, 214 received aid, and 65 had their full need met. Average financial aid package met 81% of need; average scholarship/grant was $23,138; average loan was $2,216. Need-based aid available for part-time students.
**Students without need:** 61 full-time freshmen who did not demonstrate need for aid received scholarships/grants; average award was $16,547. No-need awards available for academics, alumni affiliation, art, leadership, minority status, music/drama.

### FINANCIAL AID PROCEDURES
**Forms required:** FAFSA.
**Dates and Deadlines:** Priority date 3/15; no closing date. Applicants notified on a rolling basis starting 2/1; must reply within 3 week(s) of notification.
**Transfers:** No deadline. Applicants notified on a rolling basis starting 2/1.

### CONTACT
Jayne Wobig, Director of Financial Aid
700 Terrace Heights #2, Winona, MN 55987-1399
(507) 457-1437

## St. Olaf College
Northfield, Minnesota             Federal Code: 002382
www.stolaf.edu                    CSS Code: 6638

**4-year private** liberal arts college in large town, affiliated with Evangelical Lutheran Church in America.
**Enrollment:** 3,005 undergrads. 763 full-time freshmen.
**Selectivity:** Admits less than 50% of applicants.

### BASIC COSTS (2015-2016)
**Tuition and fees:** $42,940.
**Per-credit charge:** $1,343.
**Room and board:** $9,790.

### FINANCIAL AID PICTURE (2015-2016)
**Students with need:** Out of 633 full-time freshmen who applied for aid, 515 were judged to have need. Of these, 515 received aid, and 471 had their full need met. Average financial aid package met 99% of need; average scholarship/grant was $32,224; average loan was $3,674. For part-time students, average financial aid package was $7,376.
**Students without need:** 184 full-time freshmen who did not demonstrate need for aid received scholarships/grants; average award was $16,256. No-need awards available for academics, art, leadership, music/drama.
**Scholarships offered:** Buntrock Scholarship: $24,000. Presidential Scholarship: $18,000. Dean's Scholarship: $15,000. Faculty Scholarship: $12,000. Academic Scholarship: $10,000. National Hispanic Scholar/National Achievement: $7,500. National Merit Scholarship: $7,500. Fine Arts scholarships: $2,000-$11,500. Faculty scholarship: $7,500. All are 4-year renewable; number awarded varies yearly.
**Additional info:** Limited number of music lesson fee waivers available for music majors, awarded on audition basis only.

### FINANCIAL AID PROCEDURES
**Forms required:** FAFSA. CSS PROFILE due February 1.
**Dates and Deadlines:** Priority date 2/1; closing date 3/1. Applicants notified by 4/1; must reply by 5/1.
**Transfers:** No deadline. Applicants notified on a rolling basis; must reply within 2 week(s) of notification.

### CONTACT
Sandy Sundstrom, Director of Student Financial Aid
1520 St. Olaf Avenue, Northfield, MN 55057
(507) 786-3019

## St. Paul College
Saint Paul, Minnesota
www.saintpaul.edu                 Federal Code: 005533

**2-year public** community and technical college in large city.
**Enrollment:** 5,674 undergrads.
**Selectivity:** Open admission; but selective for some programs.

### BASIC COSTS (2015-2016)
**Tuition and fees:** $5,479; out-of-state residents $5,479.

### FINANCIAL AID PICTURE
**Students with need:** Need-based aid available for full-time and part-time students. Work study available nights.
**Students without need:** No-need awards available for leadership.

### FINANCIAL AID PROCEDURES
**Forms required:** FAFSA.
**Dates and Deadlines:** Applicants notified on a rolling basis starting 6/1.
**Transfers:** Priority date 5/1; no deadline. Applicants notified on a rolling basis starting 6/1.

### CONTACT
Adam Johnson, Financial Aid Director
235 Marshall Avenue, Saint Paul, MN 55102-1800
(651) 846-1386

## South Central College
North Mankato, Minnesota
www.southcentral.edu              Federal Code: 005537

**2-year public** community and technical college in large town.
**Enrollment:** 2,907 undergrads.
**Selectivity:** Open admission.

### BASIC COSTS (2015-2016)
**Tuition and fees:** $5,015; out-of-state residents $5,015.

### FINANCIAL AID PICTURE
**Students with need:** Need-based aid available for full-time and part-time students. Work study available nights.

### FINANCIAL AID PROCEDURES
**Forms required:** FAFSA.
**Dates and Deadlines:** Priority date 5/1; no closing date. Applicants notified on a rolling basis starting 6/1.
**Transfers:** No deadline. Applicants notified on a rolling basis starting 6/1.

### CONTACT
Jayne Dinse, Financial Aid Director
1920 Lee Boulevard, North Mankato, MN 56003
(507) 389-7220

## Southwest Minnesota State University
Marshall, Minnesota
www.smsu.edu
Federal Code: 002375

**4-year public** university and liberal arts college in large town.
**Enrollment:** 2,291 undergrads, 20% part-time. 446 full-time freshmen.
**Selectivity:** Admits 50 to 75% of applicants.

### BASIC COSTS (2015-2016)
**Tuition and fees:** $8,337; out-of-state residents $8,337.
**Per-credit charge:** $234.
**Room and board:** $7,572.

### FINANCIAL AID PICTURE (2015-2016)
**Students with need:** Out of 384 full-time freshmen who applied for aid, 277 were judged to have need. Of these, 277 received aid, and 39 had their full need met. Average financial aid package met 51% of need; average scholarship/grant was $5,713; average loan was $3,441. For part-time students, average financial aid package was $5,035.
**Students without need:** 97 full-time freshmen who did not demonstrate need for aid received scholarships/grants; average award was $2,223. No-need awards available for academics, alumni affiliation, art, athletics, leadership, minority status, music/drama, state/district residency.
**Scholarships offered:** 81 full-time freshmen received athletic scholarships; average amount $2,246.

### FINANCIAL AID PROCEDURES
**Forms required:** FAFSA, institutional form.
**Dates and Deadlines:** Priority date 3/1; no closing date. Applicants notified on a rolling basis starting 5/1.

### CONTACT
David Vikander, Director of Financial Aid
1501 State Street, Marshall, MN 56258-1598
(507) 537-6281

## University of Minnesota: Crookston
Crookston, Minnesota
www.crk.umn.edu
Federal Code: 004069

**4-year public** branch campus college in small town.
**Enrollment:** 1,874 undergrads, 37% part-time. 226 full-time freshmen.
**Selectivity:** Admits over 75% of applicants.

### BASIC COSTS (2015-2016)
**Tuition and fees:** $11,646; out-of-state residents $11,646.
**Per-credit charge:** $392; out-of-state residents $392.
**Room and board:** $7,506.

### FINANCIAL AID PICTURE (2015-2016)
**Students with need:** Out of 196 full-time freshmen who applied for aid, 151 were judged to have need. Of these, 150 received aid, and 35 had their full need met. Average financial aid package met 76% of need; average scholarship/grant was $9,760; average loan was $3,300. For part-time students, average financial aid package was $5,772.
**Students without need:** 32 full-time freshmen who did not demonstrate need for aid received scholarships/grants; average award was $2,055. No-need awards available for academics, alumni affiliation, athletics, leadership, minority status, music/drama, ROTC, state/district residency.
**Scholarships offered:** *Merit:* Merit Scholarship: based on a minimum GPA of 3.25 and a minimum ACT score of 21. Presidential Scholarship: $20,000 total ($5,000 annually for four years); based on ACT score of 30 and GPA of 3.25. Chancellor Scholarship: $8,000 total ($4,000 annually for two years); based on ACT score of 27-29 and GPA of 3.25. Distinguished Scholarship: $6,000 total ($3,000 annually for two years); based on ACT score of 25-26 and 3.25 GPA. Merriam Legacy Scholarship: $4,000 total ($2,000 annually for two years); based on ACT score of 23-24 and a 3.25 GPA. Achievement

Scholarship: $2,000; based on ACT score of 21-22 and 3.25 GPA. Students must have earned a cumulative GPA of 3.3 at the end of Spring Semester in order to renew for the following year. *Athletic:* 21 full-time freshmen received athletic scholarships; average amount $3,723.
**Additional info:** Under the University of Minnesota Promise Scholarship (U Promise), eligible new Minnesota resident undergraduates with a family income of up to $100,000 will be guaranteed a U Promise Scholarship. Eligible new freshman and transfer students enrolling for the first time will receive a guaranteed, multi-year, U Promise Scholarship. Eligible new freshmen will receive a guaranteed need-based scholarship, ranging from $500 to $3,500 each year, for four years. Eligible new transfer students will receive a guaranteed, need-based scholarship, ranging from $500 to $1,500 each year, for two years.

### FINANCIAL AID PROCEDURES
**Forms required:** FAFSA.
**Dates and Deadlines:** Priority date 3/1; no closing date. Applicants notified on a rolling basis starting 3/1; must reply within 8 week(s) of notification.
**Transfers:** No deadline. Applicants notified on a rolling basis starting 3/1; must reply within 8 week(s) of notification.

### CONTACT
Melissa Dingmann, Director of Financial Aid
2900 University Avenue, Crookston, MN 56716-5001
(218) 281-8563

## University of Minnesota: Duluth
Duluth, Minnesota
www.d.umn.edu
Federal Code: 002388

**4-year public** university in small city.
**Enrollment:** 8,929 undergrads, 5% part-time. 2,187 full-time freshmen.
**Selectivity:** Admits over 75% of applicants.

### BASIC COSTS (2015-2016)
**Tuition and fees:** $13,082; out-of-state residents $17,032.
**Per-credit charge:** $458; out-of-state residents $609.
**Room and board:** $7,210.

### FINANCIAL AID PICTURE (2014-2015)
**Students with need:** Out of 1,958 full-time freshmen who applied for aid, 1,307 were judged to have need. Of these, 1,272 received aid, and 257 had their full need met. Average financial aid package met 68% of need; average scholarship/grant was $8,276; average loan was $3,933. For part-time students, average financial aid package was $6,312.
**Students without need:** 312 full-time freshmen who did not demonstrate need for aid received scholarships/grants; average award was $2,197. No-need awards available for academics, alumni affiliation, art, athletics, music/drama, ROTC, state/district residency.
**Scholarships offered:** 32 full-time freshmen received athletic scholarships; average amount $7,284.

### FINANCIAL AID PROCEDURES
**Forms required:** FAFSA.
**Dates and Deadlines:** Priority date 3/1. Applicants notified on a rolling basis starting 3/1.
**Transfers:** No deadline. Applicants notified on a rolling basis starting 4/1.

### CONTACT
Brenda Herzig, Director of Financial Aid
Solon Campus Center 25, Duluth, MN 55812-3000
(218) 726-8000

## University of Minnesota: Morris

Morris, Minnesota
www.morris.umn.edu                    Federal Code: 002389

**4-year public** university and liberal arts college in small town.
**Enrollment:** 1,741 undergrads, 4% part-time. 415 full-time freshmen.
**Selectivity:** Admits 50 to 75% of applicants.

### BASIC COSTS (2015-2016)
**Tuition and fees:** $12,846; out-of-state residents $12,846.
**Per-credit charge:** $458; out-of-state residents $458.
**Room and board:** $7,804.

### FINANCIAL AID PICTURE (2015-2016)
**Students with need:** Out of 374 full-time freshmen who applied for aid, 279 were judged to have need. Of these, 278 received aid, and 76 had their full need met. Average financial aid package met 81% of need; average scholarship/grant was $10,921; average loan was $3,168. For part-time students, average financial aid package was $9,790.
**Students without need:** 78 full-time freshmen who did not demonstrate need for aid received scholarships/grants; average award was $3,850. No-need awards available for academics.
**Scholarships offered:** Chancellor's Scholarship: $3,500/year for 4 years; top 5%. Dean's Scholarship: $2,500/year for 4 years; top 10%. Founder's Scholarship: $1,000/year for 4 years; top 20%. National Merit Scholarship: full tuition scholarship for 4 years. Prairie Scholars Award: full tuition/year for 4 years; Morris Scholars Award: $5,000/year for 4 years plus one-time $2,500 research or creative project stipend. President's Distinguished Scholar Award: $1,000 to $3,000/year for four years.
**Additional info:** Land-grant program waiving tuition for Native Americans.

### FINANCIAL AID PROCEDURES
**Forms required:** FAFSA.
**Dates and Deadlines:** Applicants notified on a rolling basis starting 4/1.
**Transfers:** No deadline. Applicants notified on a rolling basis starting 4/1.

### CONTACT
Jill Beauregard, Director of Financial Aid
600 E. 4th St., Morris, MN 56267
(800) 992-8863

## University of Minnesota: Rochester

Rochester, Minnesota
http://r.umn.edu

**4-year public** university and health science college in small city.
**Enrollment:** 402 undergrads, 3% part-time. 88 full-time freshmen.
**Selectivity:** Admits less than 50% of applicants.

### BASIC COSTS (2015-2016)
**Tuition and fees:** $13,232; out-of-state residents $13,232.
**Per-credit charge:** $458; out-of-state residents $458.
**Room and board:** $9,440.

### FINANCIAL AID PICTURE (2015-2016)
**Students with need:** Out of 86 full-time freshmen who applied for aid, 64 were judged to have need. Of these, 64 received aid, and 15 had their full need met. Average financial aid package met 82% of need; average scholarship/grant was $10,270; average loan was $3,332. For part-time students, average financial aid package was $7,577.
**Students without need:** 9 full-time freshmen who did not demonstrate need for aid received scholarships/grants; average award was $1,083. No-need awards available for academics.

### FINANCIAL AID PROCEDURES
**Forms required:** FAFSA.
**Dates and Deadlines:** Priority date 3/1; no closing date. Applicants notified on a rolling basis starting 3/15.

**Transfers:** Applicants notified by 7/1.
### CONTACT
111 South Broadway, Suite 300, Rochester, MN 55904
(507) 258-8457

## University of Minnesota: Twin Cities

Minneapolis, Minnesota
www.umn.edu                    Federal Code: 003969

**4-year public** university in very large city.
**Enrollment:** 30,511 undergrads, 8% part-time. 5,756 full-time freshmen.
**Selectivity:** Admits less than 50% of applicants.

### BASIC COSTS (2015-2016)
**Tuition and fees:** $13,790; out-of-state residents $22,210.
**Per-credit charge:** $471; out-of-state residents $795.
**Room and board:** $9,314.

### FINANCIAL AID PICTURE (2015-2016)
**Students with need:** Out of 4,631 full-time freshmen who applied for aid, 2,881 were judged to have need. Of these, 2,840 received aid, and 844 had their full need met. Average financial aid package met 78% of need; average scholarship/grant was $10,320; average loan was $3,687. For part-time students, average financial aid package was $7,181.
**Students without need:** This college awards aid only to students with need.
**Scholarships offered:** 29 full-time freshmen received athletic scholarships; average amount $5,578.

### FINANCIAL AID PROCEDURES
**Forms required:** FAFSA, institutional form.
**Dates and Deadlines:** Priority date 3/1; no closing date. Applicants notified on a rolling basis starting 2/15.

### CONTACT
240 Williamson Hall, Minneapolis, MN 55455-0213
(612) 624-1111

## University of Northwestern - St. Paul

Saint Paul, Minnesota
www.unwsp.edu                    Federal Code: 002371

**4-year private** university and liberal arts college in very large city, affiliated with nondenominational tradition.
**Enrollment:** 1,945 undergrads.

### BASIC COSTS (2015-2016)
**Tuition and fees:** $28,730.
**Room and board:** $8,954.
**Additional info:** Technology fee for commuting students is $150. Tuition/fee waivers available for minority students.

### FINANCIAL AID PICTURE
**Students with need:** Need-based aid available for full-time and part-time students. Work study available nights, weekends, and for part-time students.
**Students without need:** No-need awards available for academics, alumni affiliation, leadership, music/drama.
**Scholarships offered:** Eagle Scholars Program: $12,000-$15,000 per year; ACT score of 30 or SAT score of 1320; up to 15 awarded yearly to incoming freshmen; renewable annually with successful involvement in program, including a cumulative GPA of 3.65 or higher.
**Additional info:** Students enrolled at least half-time in the FOCUS or Distance Education degree programs may apply for financial aid from the same Federal and state sources as traditional undergraduates. However, their expense budgets and aid are less due to lower tuition.

## FINANCIAL AID PROCEDURES
**Forms required:** FAFSA, institutional form.
**Dates and Deadlines:** Priority date 3/1; closing date 8/1. Applicants notified on a rolling basis starting 3/1; must reply within 2 week(s) of notification.

### CONTACT
Richard Blatchley, Director of Financial Aid
3003 Snelling Avenue North, Saint Paul, MN 55113-1598
(651) 631-5212

## University of St. Thomas
Saint Paul, Minnesota
www.stthomas.edu        Federal Code: 002345

**4-year private** university in very large city, affiliated with Roman Catholic Church.
**Enrollment:** 6,126 undergrads, 3% part-time. 1,420 full-time freshmen.
**Selectivity:** Admits over 75% of applicants.

### BASIC COSTS (2015-2016)
**Tuition and fees:** $38,105.
**Per-credit charge:** $1,165.
**Room and board:** $9,750.

### FINANCIAL AID PICTURE (2015-2016)
**Students with need:** Out of 1,155 full-time freshmen who applied for aid, 874 were judged to have need. Of these, 874 received aid, and 205 had their full need met. Average financial aid package met 88% of need; average scholarship/grant was $20,889; average loan was $7,604. For part-time students, average financial aid package was $10,403.
**Students without need:** 262 full-time freshmen who did not demonstrate need for aid received scholarships/grants; average award was $17,956. No-need awards available for academics, music/drama, ROTC.

### FINANCIAL AID PROCEDURES
**Forms required:** FAFSA.
**Dates and Deadlines:** Priority date 4/1; no closing date. Applicants notified on a rolling basis starting 3/1; must reply within 3 week(s) of notification.

### CONTACT
2115 Summit Avenue, Mail 5017, Saint Paul, MN 55105

## Vermilion Community College
Ely, Minnesota
www.vcc.edu        Federal Code: 002350

**2-year public** community and technical college in small town.
**Enrollment:** 696 undergrads.
**Selectivity:** Open admission.

### BASIC COSTS (2015-2016)
**Tuition and fees:** $5,325; out-of-state residents $6,507.
**Room and board:** $5,660.

### FINANCIAL AID PICTURE
**Students with need:** Need-based aid available for full-time and part-time students. Work study available nights, weekends, and for part-time students.

### FINANCIAL AID PROCEDURES
**Forms required:** FAFSA, institutional form.
**Dates and Deadlines:** Priority date 4/15; no closing date. Applicants notified on a rolling basis starting 4/1.

### CONTACT
1900 East Camp Street, Ely, MN 55731-9989
(218) 235-2153

## Walden University
Minneapolis, Minnesota
www.waldenu.edu        Federal Code: 025402

**4-year for-profit** virtual university in large city.
**Enrollment:** 7,815 undergrads, 90% part-time.
**Selectivity:** Open admission; but selective for some programs.

### BASIC COSTS (2015-2016)
**Tuition and fees:** $14,970.
**Per-credit charge:** $322.

### FINANCIAL AID PICTURE (2014-2015)
**Students with need:** 22% of average financial aid package awarded as scholarships/grants, 78% awarded as loans/jobs. Need-based aid available for part-time students.
**Students without need:** This college awards aid only to students with need.

### FINANCIAL AID PROCEDURES
**Forms required:** FAFSA.
**Dates and Deadlines:** Applicants notified on a rolling basis.
**Transfers:** No deadline. Applicants notified on a rolling basis.

### CONTACT
Teresa Drzewiecki, Exec Director of Financial Aid
100 Washington Ave South, Suite 900, Minneapolis, MN 55401
(410) 843-8506

## Winona State University
Winona, Minnesota
www.winona.edu        Federal Code: 002394

**4-year public** university in large town.
**Enrollment:** 7,816 undergrads, 11% part-time. 1,644 full-time freshmen.
**Selectivity:** Admits 50 to 75% of applicants.

### BASIC COSTS (2015-2016)
**Tuition and fees:** $9,047; out-of-state residents $14,744.
**Per-credit charge:** $235; out-of-state residents $426.
**Room and board:** $8,120.
**Additional info:** Fees include mandatory laptop and tablet lease ($970 / year) for full-time students.

### FINANCIAL AID PICTURE (2014-2015)
**Students with need:** Out of 1,458 full-time freshmen who applied for aid, 1,021 were judged to have need. Of these, 999 received aid, and 90 had their full need met. Average financial aid package met 50% of need; average scholarship/grant was $5,133; average loan was $3,466. For part-time students, average financial aid package was $5,026.
**Students without need:** 312 full-time freshmen who did not demonstrate need for aid received scholarships/grants; average award was $2,017. No-need awards available for academics, alumni affiliation, art, athletics, leadership, minority status, music/drama, ROTC, state/district residency.
**Scholarships offered:** *Merit:* Outstanding Academics Honors Award: $2,500, renewable, top 5% of class, ACT 32 or above. WSU Foundation Board Scholarship: $2,000 renewable, top 15% of class, ACT 28-31, essay/interview. Presidential Honor Scholarships: $1,500 renewable; top 15% of class, ACT 28-31; $1,000, renewable, top 10% of class, ACT 27; $750, renewable, top 15% of class, ACT 26. Resident Tuition Scholarships: $3,400, renewable, to out-of-state students, top 15% of class or ACT 25. *Athletic:* 475 full-time freshmen received athletic scholarships; average amount $2,160.

### FINANCIAL AID PROCEDURES
**Forms required:** FAFSA.
**Dates and Deadlines:** Priority date 5/1; no closing date. Applicants notified on a rolling basis starting 5/1; must reply within 3 week(s) of notification.

**CONTACT**
Mari Livingston, Associate Director of Financial Aid
Office of Admissions, Winona, MN 55987
(800) 342-5978

# Mississippi

## Alcorn State University
Lorman, Mississippi
www.alcorn.edu  Federal Code: 002396

**4-year public** university and agricultural college in rural community.
**Enrollment:** 2,911 undergrads, 12% part-time. 601 full-time freshmen.
**Selectivity:** Admits over 75% of applicants.

**BASIC COSTS (2015-2016)**
**Tuition and fees:** $6,384; out-of-state residents $15,433.
**Room and board:** $8,996.

**FINANCIAL AID PICTURE (2015-2016)**
**Students with need:** Out of 601 full-time freshmen who applied for aid, 594 were judged to have need. Of these, 581 received aid, and 59 had their full need met. Average financial aid package met 91% of need; average scholarship/grant was $6,139; average loan was $3,373. For part-time students, average financial aid package was $11,134.
**Students without need:** 125 full-time freshmen who did not demonstrate need for aid received scholarships/grants; average award was $7,691. No-need awards available for academics, athletics, leadership, ROTC.
**Scholarships offered:** 34 full-time freshmen received athletic scholarships; average amount $12,184.

**FINANCIAL AID PROCEDURES**
**Forms required:** FAFSA, institutional form.
**Dates and Deadlines:** Priority date 3/15; no closing date. Applicants notified on a rolling basis starting 4/1; must reply within 4 week(s) of notification.

**CONTACT**
Juanita Edwards, Director of Financial Aid
1000 ASU Drive #300, Lorman, MS 39096-7500
(601) 877-6190

## Belhaven University
Jackson, Mississippi
www.belhaven.edu  Federal Code: 002397

**4-year private** university and liberal arts college in large city, affiliated with Presbyterian Church (USA).
**Enrollment:** 2,715 undergrads, 47% part-time. 284 full-time freshmen.
**Selectivity:** Admits 50 to 75% of applicants.

**BASIC COSTS (2015-2016)**
**Tuition and fees:** $21,816.
**Per-credit charge:** $425.
**Room and board:** $8,000.

**FINANCIAL AID PICTURE (2014-2015)**
**Students with need:** Out of 265 full-time freshmen who applied for aid, 246 were judged to have need. Of these, 246 received aid, and 87 had their full need met. Average financial aid package met 80% of need; average scholarship/grant was $16,000; average loan was $3,400. For part-time students, average financial aid package was $12,000.

**Students without need:** 38 full-time freshmen who did not demonstrate need for aid received scholarships/grants; average award was $9,500. No-need awards available for academics, alumni affiliation, art, athletics, job skills, leadership, music/drama.
**Scholarships offered:** 2 full-time freshmen received athletic scholarships; average amount $12,750.

**FINANCIAL AID PROCEDURES**
**Forms required:** FAFSA.
**Dates and Deadlines:** Priority date 1/31; no closing date. Applicants notified on a rolling basis starting 2/1.
**Transfers:** No deadline. Applicants notified on a rolling basis.

**CONTACT**
Debbi Braswell, Director of Financial Aid
1500 Peachtree Street, Jackson, MS 39202
(601) 968-5933

## Blue Cliff College: Gulfport
Gulfport, Mississippi
www.bluecliffcollege.edu  Federal Code: 035253

**2-year for-profit** career college in small city.
**Enrollment:** 274 undergrads.

**BASIC COSTS (2015-2016)**
**Additional info:** Diploma programs: Cosmetology $18,080. Massage therapy $13,144; books and supplies $1,250. Dialysis technician $17,450; books and supplies $1,850. Midical/clinical assistant $12,985; books and supplies $1,850. Associate program: Massage therapy $13,144; books and supplies $1,250.

**FINANCIAL AID PICTURE**
**Students with need:** Need-based aid available for full-time and part-time students.
**Students without need:** This college awards aid only to students with need.

**FINANCIAL AID PROCEDURES**
**Forms required:** FAFSA.

**CONTACT**
Judy May, Financial Planner
12251 Bernard Parkway, Gulfport, MS 39503

## Blue Mountain College
Blue Mountain, Mississippi
www.bmc.edu  Federal Code: 002398

**4-year private** liberal arts college in rural community, affiliated with Southern Baptist Convention.
**Enrollment:** 436 undergrads, 9% part-time. 55 full-time freshmen.
**Selectivity:** Admits less than 50% of applicants.

**BASIC COSTS (2015-2016)**
**Tuition and fees:** $10,968.
**Per-credit charge:** $317.
**Room and board:** $5,424.

**FINANCIAL AID PICTURE (2015-2016)**
**Students with need:** Out of 53 full-time freshmen who applied for aid, 44 were judged to have need. Of these, 44 received aid, and 15 had their full need met. Average financial aid package met 63% of need; average scholarship/grant was $6,788; average loan was $3,140. For part-time students, average financial aid package was $6,613.

**Students without need:** 4 full-time freshmen who did not demonstrate need for aid received scholarships/grants; average award was $6,169. No-need awards available for academics, alumni affiliation, art, athletics, leadership, music/drama, religious affiliation, state/district residency.
**Scholarships offered:** *Merit:* ACT/SAT Scholarships: varies from $1,000 to $7,000 per year; based on ACT/SAT score; number varies depending on number of applicants. Valedictorian/Salutatorian Scholarships: $1,000 to $5,000 first year; based on rank in class; unlimited number available. Child of Alumnae/Alumni: $500 first year; must be dependent of graduate; unlimited number available. *Athletic:* 7 full-time freshmen received athletic scholarships; average amount $74,718.

**FINANCIAL AID PROCEDURES**
**Forms required:** FAFSA.
**Dates and Deadlines:** Priority date 3/1; closing date 7/31. Applicants notified on a rolling basis starting 4/1; must reply within 4 week(s) of notification.
**Transfers:** No deadline.

**CONTACT**
Janice Prather, Director of Financial Aid
PO Box 160, Blue Mountain, MS 38610-0160
(662) 685-4771 ext. 145

## Coahoma Community College
Clarksdale, Mississippi
www.coahomacc.edu          Federal Code: 002401

**2-year public** community college in large town.
**Enrollment:** 1,957 undergrads.
**Selectivity:** Open admission; but selective for some programs.

**BASIC COSTS (2015-2016)**
**Tuition and fees:** $2,440; out-of-state residents $3,240.
**Room and board:** $4,220.

**FINANCIAL AID PICTURE**
**Students with need:** Need-based aid available for full-time and part-time students.
**Students without need:** This college awards aid only to students with need.

**FINANCIAL AID PROCEDURES**
**Forms required:** FAFSA, institutional form.
**Dates and Deadlines:** Priority date 4/1; no closing date. Applicants notified on a rolling basis starting 7/1.
**Transfers:** Priority date 3/1.

**CONTACT**
Patricia Brooks, Director of Financial Aid
3240 Friars Point Road, Clarksdale, MS 38614-9799
(662) 627-2571

## Copiah-Lincoln Community College
Wesson, Mississippi
www.colin.edu          Federal Code: 002402

**2-year public** community college in small town.
**Enrollment:** 2,662 undergrads, 12% part-time. 763 full-time freshmen.
**Selectivity:** Open admission; but selective for some programs.

**BASIC COSTS (2015-2016)**
**Tuition and fees:** $2,730; out-of-state residents $4,730.
**Room and board:** $3,400.

**FINANCIAL AID PICTURE**
**Students with need:** Need-based aid available for full-time and part-time students. Work study available nights, weekends, and for part-time students.

**Students without need:** No-need awards available for academics, art, athletics, job skills, leadership, music/drama, state/district residency.

**FINANCIAL AID PROCEDURES**
**Forms required:** FAFSA.
**Dates and Deadlines:** Closing date 4/1. Applicants notified on a rolling basis starting 4/1; must reply within 2 week(s) of notification.

**CONTACT**
Leslie Smith, Director of Financial Aid
PO Box 649, Wesson, MS 39191
(601) 643-8340

## Delta State University
Cleveland, Mississippi
www.deltastate.edu          Federal Code: 002403

**4-year public** university in large town.
**Enrollment:** 2,440 undergrads, 8% part-time. 322 full-time freshmen.

**BASIC COSTS (2015-2016)**
**Tuition and fees:** $6,112.
**Room and board:** $7,592.

**FINANCIAL AID PICTURE (2014-2015)**
**Students with need:** Need-based aid available for full-time and part-time students. Work study available nights, weekends, and for part-time students.
**Students without need:** No-need awards available for academics, alumni affiliation, art, athletics, leadership, music/drama, state/district residency.

**FINANCIAL AID PROCEDURES**
**Forms required:** FAFSA, institutional form.
**Dates and Deadlines:** Priority date 3/1; no closing date. Applicants notified on a rolling basis starting 5/1.
**Transfers:** Closing date 3/1. Applicants notified on a rolling basis starting 5/1.

**CONTACT**
Christie Rocconi, Director of Student Financial Assistance
117 Kent Wyatt Hall, Cleveland, MS 38733
(662) 846-4670

## East Central Community College
Decatur, Mississippi
www.eccc.edu          Federal Code: 002404

**2-year public** community college in rural community.
**Enrollment:** 2,172 undergrads.
**Selectivity:** Open admission; but selective for some programs.

**BASIC COSTS (2015-2016)**
**Tuition and fees:** $2,190; out-of-state residents $4,290.
**Room and board:** $3,340.

**FINANCIAL AID PICTURE**
**Students with need:** Need-based aid available for full-time and part-time students. Work study available nights.
**Students without need:** No-need awards available for academics, art, athletics, leadership, music/drama, state/district residency.

**FINANCIAL AID PROCEDURES**
**Forms required:** FAFSA, state aid form.
**Dates and Deadlines:** Priority date 4/1; no closing date. Applicants notified on a rolling basis starting 7/31; must reply within 2 week(s) of notification.

**CONTACT**
Brenda Carson, Director of Financial Aid
Box 129, Decatur, MS 39327
(601) 635-2111 ext. 378

## East Mississippi Community College
Scooba, Mississippi
www.eastms.edu                           Federal Code: 002405

**2-year public** community college in rural community.
**Enrollment:** 4,296 undergrads, 30% part-time. 915 full-time freshmen.
**Selectivity:** Open admission; but selective for some programs.

**BASIC COSTS (2015-2016)**
**Tuition and fees:** $2,840; out-of-state residents $5,240.
**Room and board:** $4,400.
**Additional info:** Tuition at time of enrollment locked for 2 years; tuition/fee waivers available for adults, minority students.

**FINANCIAL AID PICTURE (2015-2016)**
**Students with need:** 52% of average financial aid package awarded as scholarships/grants, 48% awarded as loans/jobs. Need-based aid available for part-time students.
**Students without need:** No-need awards available for academics, alumni affiliation, art, athletics, leadership, music/drama, state/district residency.

**FINANCIAL AID PROCEDURES**
**Forms required:** FAFSA, state aid form, institutional form.
**Dates and Deadlines:** Priority date 4/1; no closing date. Applicants notified on a rolling basis starting 4/1; must reply within 2 week(s) of notification.
**Transfers:** Applicants notified on a rolling basis starting 4/1.

**CONTACT**
James Gibson, Vice President Enrollment Management
Admissions Office, Scooba, MS 39358
(662) 476-5079

## Hinds Community College
Raymond, Mississippi
www.hindscc.edu                           Federal Code: 002407

**2-year public** branch campus and community college in small town.
**Enrollment:** 10,198 undergrads, 29% part-time. 2,417 full-time freshmen.
**Selectivity:** Open admission; but selective for some programs.

**BASIC COSTS (2015-2016)**
**Tuition and fees:** $2,500; out-of-state residents $5,100.
**Per-credit charge:** $100; out-of-state residents $200.
**Room and board:** $3,960.

**FINANCIAL AID PICTURE (2014-2015)**
**Students with need:** 68% of average financial aid package awarded as scholarships/grants, 32% awarded as loans/jobs. Need-based aid available for part-time students. Work study available nights, weekends, and for part-time students.
**Students without need:** No-need awards available for academics, art, athletics, job skills, leadership, minority status, music/drama, state/district residency.

**FINANCIAL AID PROCEDURES**
**Forms required:** FAFSA.
**Dates and Deadlines:** Priority date 3/15; no closing date. Applicants notified on a rolling basis.
**Transfers:** Financial aid transcripts from all previous colleges must be on file prior to award letter being released.

**CONTACT**
Louanne Langston, District Director of Financial Aid & Student Success
HCC Office of Admissions and Records, Raymond, MS 39154-1100
(601) 857-3223

## Holmes Community College
Goodman, Mississippi
www.holmescc.edu                          Federal Code: 002408

**2-year public** community college in rural community.
**Enrollment:** 6,186 undergrads.
**Selectivity:** Open admission; but selective for some programs.

**BASIC COSTS (2015-2016)**
**Tuition and fees:** $2,450; out-of-state residents $5,030.
**Room and board:** $2,950.

**FINANCIAL AID PICTURE (2014-2015)**
**Students with need:** 76% of average financial aid package awarded as scholarships/grants, 24% awarded as loans/jobs.
**Students without need:** No-need awards available for academics, athletics.
**Scholarships offered:** President's Scholarship: for full-time students; full tuition; requires ACT of 20 or higher. Board of Trustees Scholarship: for full-time students; tuition, room and board; requires ACT of 28 or higher.

**FINANCIAL AID PROCEDURES**
**Forms required:** FAFSA, state aid form, institutional form.
**Dates and Deadlines:** Priority date 6/1; no closing date. Applicants notified on a rolling basis.

**CONTACT**
Gail Muse, Director of Financial Aid
Box 398, Goodman, MS 39079
(662) 472-9027

## Itawamba Community College
Fulton, Mississippi
www.iccms.edu                             Federal Code: 002409

**2-year public** community and technical college in small town.
**Enrollment:** 5,037 undergrads, 25% part-time. 1,213 full-time freshmen.
**Selectivity:** Open admission; but selective for some programs.

**BASIC COSTS (2015-2016)**
**Tuition and fees:** $2,420; out-of-state residents $4,620.
**Room and board:** $3,150.

**FINANCIAL AID PICTURE**
**Students with need:** Need-based aid available for full-time and part-time students.
**Students without need:** No-need awards available for academics, art, athletics, leadership, music/drama, state/district residency.

**FINANCIAL AID PROCEDURES**
**Forms required:** FAFSA, institutional form.
**Dates and Deadlines:** Applicants notified on a rolling basis starting 4/15.

**CONTACT**
Terry Bland, Director of Financial Aid
602 West Hill Street, Fulton, MS 38843-1099
(662) 862-8220

## Jackson State University
Jackson, Mississippi
www.jsums.edu                             Federal Code: 002410

**4-year public** university in small city.
**Enrollment:** 7,422 undergrads, 10% part-time. 1,120 full-time freshmen.
**Selectivity:** Admits 50 to 75% of applicants.

**BASIC COSTS (2015-2016)**
**Tuition and fees:** $6,866; out-of-state residents $16,821.

**Per-credit charge:** $286; out-of-state residents $415.
**Room and board:** $8,226.
**Additional info:** Tuition/fee waivers available for minority students.

### FINANCIAL AID PICTURE (2014-2015)
**Students with need:** Out of 1,120 full-time freshmen who applied for aid, 1,038 were judged to have need. Of these, 1,033 received aid, and 11 had their full need met. Average financial aid package met 36% of need; average scholarship/grant was $5,245; average loan was $3,350. For part-time students, average financial aid package was $5,534.
**Students without need:** 31 full-time freshmen who did not demonstrate need for aid received scholarships/grants; average award was $9,367. No-need awards available for academics, alumni affiliation, athletics, leadership, minority status, music/drama, ROTC.
**Scholarships offered:** 55 full-time freshmen received athletic scholarships; average amount $15,663.16.

### FINANCIAL AID PROCEDURES
**Forms required:** FAFSA.
**Dates and Deadlines:** Priority date 4/15; no closing date. Applicants notified on a rolling basis starting 3/1.
**Transfers:** Priority date 4/15. Applicants notified by 3/1.

### CONTACT
Betty Moncure, Director, Financial Aid
1400 John R. Lynch Street, Jackson, MS 39217
(601) 979-2227

## Jones County Junior College
Ellisville, Mississippi
www.jcjc.edu                     Federal Code: 002411

**2-year public** community and junior college in small town.
**Enrollment:** 4,066 undergrads.
**Selectivity:** Open admission; but selective for some programs.

### BASIC COSTS (2015-2016)
**Tuition and fees:** $2,722; out-of-state residents $4,722.
**Room and board:** $3,600.

### FINANCIAL AID PICTURE
**Students with need:** Need-based aid available for full-time and part-time students. Work study available nights, weekends, and for part-time students.
**Students without need:** No-need awards available for academics, athletics, state/district residency.

### FINANCIAL AID PROCEDURES
**Forms required:** FAFSA, state aid form, institutional form.
**Dates and Deadlines:** Priority date 4/1; no closing date. Applicants notified on a rolling basis starting 6/1; must reply within 2 week(s) of notification.

### CONTACT
Jennifer Suber, Director of Student Financial Aid
900 South Court Street, Ellisville, MS 39437
(601) 477-4040

## Meridian Community College
Meridian, Mississippi
www.meridiancc.edu              Federal Code: 002413

**2-year public** community college in large town.
**Enrollment:** 3,188 undergrads, 23% part-time.
**Selectivity:** Open admission; but selective for some programs.

### BASIC COSTS (2015-2016)
**Tuition and fees:** $2,350; out-of-state residents $3,630.
**Per-credit charge:** $100; out-of-state residents $157.

**Room and board:** $3,450.

### FINANCIAL AID PICTURE
**Students with need:** Need-based aid available for full-time and part-time students.
**Students without need:** No-need awards available for academics, art, athletics, leadership, music/drama, state/district residency.
**Scholarships offered:** Incoming freshmen graduating from a school in Lauderdale County can attend tuition-free.

### FINANCIAL AID PROCEDURES
**Forms required:** FAFSA, institutional form.
**Dates and Deadlines:** Priority date 6/1; no closing date. Applicants notified on a rolling basis starting 5/15; must reply within 2 week(s) of notification.

### CONTACT
Nedra Bradley, Director of Financial Aid
910 Highway 19 North, Meridian, MS 39307-5890
(601) 484-8628

## Millsaps College
Jackson, Mississippi
www.millsaps.edu                Federal Code: 002414

**4-year private** business and liberal arts college in large city, affiliated with United Methodist Church.
**Enrollment:** 756 undergrads, 1% part-time. 223 full-time freshmen.
**Selectivity:** Admits 50 to 75% of applicants.

### BASIC COSTS (2015-2016)
**Tuition and fees:** $35,510.
**Per-credit charge:** $1,026.
**Room and board:** $12,412.

### FINANCIAL AID PICTURE (2015-2016)
**Students with need:** Out of 198 full-time freshmen who applied for aid, 159 were judged to have need. Of these, 159 received aid, and 45 had their full need met. Average financial aid package met 81% of need; average scholarship/grant was $27,019; average loan was $3,553. For part-time students, average financial aid package was $5,660.
**Students without need:** 62 full-time freshmen who did not demonstrate need for aid received scholarships/grants; average award was $24,023. No-need awards available for academics, art, leadership, music/drama, religious affiliation.

### FINANCIAL AID PROCEDURES
**Forms required:** FAFSA.
**Dates and Deadlines:** Priority date 3/1; no closing date. Applicants notified on a rolling basis starting 3/15; must reply by 5/1 or within 2 week(s) of notification.
**Transfers:** No deadline. Applicants notified on a rolling basis; must reply within 2 week(s) of notification.

### CONTACT
Patrick James, Director of Financial Aid
1701 North State Street, Jackson, MS 39210-0001
(601) 974-1220

## Mississippi College
Clinton, Mississippi
www.mc.edu                      Federal Code: 002415

**4-year private** university in large town, affiliated with Southern Baptist Convention.
**Enrollment:** 2,898 undergrads, 8% part-time. 593 full-time freshmen.

**BASIC COSTS (2015-2016)**
**Tuition and fees:** $16,114.
**Per-credit charge:** $477.
**Room and board:** $8,744.

**FINANCIAL AID PICTURE (2015-2016)**
**Students with need:** Out of 513 full-time freshmen who applied for aid, 312 were judged to have need. Of these, 312 received aid, and 34 had their full need met. Average financial aid package met 74% of need; average scholarship/grant was $12,550; average loan was $5,149. For part-time students, average financial aid package was $5,064.
**Students without need:** 229 full-time freshmen who did not demonstrate need for aid received scholarships/grants; average award was $8,089. No-need awards available for academics, alumni affiliation, art, athletics, leadership, music/drama, religious affiliation, ROTC.
**Scholarships offered: *Merit:*** Scholarships up to $1,500 based on various criteria including leadership, academics, church and community involvement; extensive number awarded. ***Athletic:*** 74 full-time freshmen received athletic scholarships; average amount $9,934.
**Additional info:** Student reply date for institutional scholarships: May 1.

**FINANCIAL AID PROCEDURES**
**Forms required:** FAFSA, state aid form.
**Dates and Deadlines:** Priority date 3/1; no closing date. Applicants notified on a rolling basis starting 3/1; must reply by 5/1.
**Transfers:** No deadline. Applicants notified on a rolling basis starting 3/1; must reply by 5/1.

**CONTACT**
Cassandra Sessoms, Coordinator of Institutional Research
Box 4026, Clinton, MS 39058-0001
(601) 925-3464

## Mississippi Delta Community College
Moorhead, Mississippi
www.msdelta.edu                    Federal Code: 002416

**2-year public** community college in rural community.
**Enrollment:** 2,479 undergrads.
**Selectivity:** Open admission; but selective for some programs.

**BASIC COSTS (2015-2016)**
**Tuition and fees:** $2,490; out-of-state residents $4,098.
**Per-credit charge:** $125.
**Room and board:** $2,740.

**FINANCIAL AID PICTURE**
**Students with need:** Need-based aid available for full-time students.
**Students without need:** No-need awards available for academics, athletics, state/district residency.

**FINANCIAL AID PROCEDURES**
**Forms required:** FAFSA, institutional form.
**Dates and Deadlines:** Closing date 8/1. Applicants notified on a rolling basis; must reply within 2 week(s) of notification.

**CONTACT**
Mary Rodgers, Director of Financial Aid
Box 668, Moorhead, MS 38761
(662) 246-6263

## Mississippi Gulf Coast Community College
Perkinston, Mississippi
www.mgccc.edu                    Federal Code: 002419

**2-year public** community college in large city.
**Enrollment:** 8,975 undergrads.

**Selectivity:** Open admission; but selective for some programs.

**BASIC COSTS (2015-2016)**
**Tuition and fees:** $2,800; out-of-state residents $4,646.
**Room and board:** $4,100.

**FINANCIAL AID PICTURE**
**Students with need:** Need-based aid available for full-time students.
**Students without need:** This college awards aid only to students with need.

**FINANCIAL AID PROCEDURES**
**Forms required:** FAFSA, institutional form.
**Dates and Deadlines:** Priority date 6/1; no closing date. Applicants notified on a rolling basis starting 7/1.

**CONTACT**
LaShanda Chamberlain, Director of Financial Aid
PO Box 548, Perkinston, MS 39573
(228) 497-7687

## Mississippi State University
Mississippi State, Mississippi
www.msstate.edu                    Federal Code: 002423

**4-year public** university and agricultural college in large town.
**Enrollment:** 16,712 undergrads, 7% part-time. 2,974 full-time freshmen.
**Selectivity:** Admits 50 to 75% of applicants.

**BASIC COSTS (2015-2016)**
**Tuition and fees:** $7,502; out-of-state residents $20,142.
**Room and board:** $9,068.
**Additional info:** Tuition/fee waivers available for minority students.

**FINANCIAL AID PICTURE (2014-2015)**
**Students with need:** Out of 2,442 full-time freshmen who applied for aid, 2,016 were judged to have need. Of these, 2,007 received aid, and 625 had their full need met. Average financial aid package met 63% of need; average scholarship/grant was $6,244; average loan was $3,375. For part-time students, average financial aid package was $9,026.
**Students without need:** 763 full-time freshmen who did not demonstrate need for aid received scholarships/grants; average award was $5,076. No-need awards available for academics, alumni affiliation, art, athletics, job skills, leadership, minority status, music/drama, ROTC, state/district residency.
**Scholarships offered:** 107 full-time freshmen received athletic scholarships; average amount $13,598.

**FINANCIAL AID PROCEDURES**
**Forms required:** FAFSA, state aid form.
**Dates and Deadlines:** Priority date 3/1; no closing date. Applicants notified on a rolling basis starting 12/1; must reply by 5/1.
**Transfers:** No deadline. Applicants notified on a rolling basis.

**CONTACT**
Paul McKinney, Director
Box 6334, Mississippi State, MS 39762
(662) 325-2450

## Mississippi University for Women
Columbus, Mississippi
www.muw.edu                    Federal Code: 002422

**4-year public** university and liberal arts college in large town.
**Enrollment:** 2,192 undergrads.
**Selectivity:** Admits over 75% of applicants.

**BASIC COSTS (2015-2016)**
**Tuition and fees:** $5,781; out-of-state residents $15,847.
**Per-credit charge:** $241; out-of-state residents $661.
**Room and board:** $6,591.
**Additional info:** Tuition/fee waivers available for adults, minority students.

**FINANCIAL AID PICTURE**
**Students with need:** Need-based aid available for full-time and part-time students. Work study available nights, weekends, and for part-time students.
**Students without need:** No-need awards available for academics, alumni affiliation, leadership, minority status, music/drama, ROTC, state/district residency.

**FINANCIAL AID PROCEDURES**
**Forms required:** FAFSA, state aid form.
**Dates and Deadlines:** Priority date 3/1; no closing date. Applicants notified on a rolling basis starting 3/15; must reply within 2 week(s) of notification.
**Transfers:** Closing date 4/1.

**CONTACT**
Nicole Patrick, Director of Financial Aid
1100 College St. MUW-1613, Columbus, MS 39701
(662) 329-7114

## Northeast Mississippi Community College
Booneville, Mississippi
www.nemcc.edu                    Federal Code: 002426

**2-year public** community college in small town.
**Enrollment:** 3,568 undergrads.
**Selectivity:** Open admission; but selective for some programs.

**BASIC COSTS (2015-2016)**
**Tuition and fees:** $2,452; out-of-state residents $4,702.
**Room and board:** $3,650.

**FINANCIAL AID PICTURE (2014-2015)**
**Students with need:** 73% of average financial aid package awarded as scholarships/grants, 27% awarded as loans/jobs. Need-based aid available for part-time students.
**Students without need:** No-need awards available for academics, alumni affiliation, athletics, leadership, music/drama.

**FINANCIAL AID PROCEDURES**
**Forms required:** FAFSA, institutional form.
**Dates and Deadlines:** Priority date 4/1; no closing date. Applicants notified on a rolling basis.
**Transfers:** No deadline.

**CONTACT**
Greg Windham, Director of Financial Aid
101 Cunningham Boulevard, Booneville, MS 38829

## Northwest Mississippi Community College
Senatobia, Mississippi
www.northwestms.edu              Federal Code: 002427

**2-year public** community college in small town.
**Enrollment:** 8,220 undergrads.
**Selectivity:** Open admission; but selective for some programs.

**BASIC COSTS (2015-2016)**
**Tuition and fees:** $2,550; out-of-state residents $4,950.
**Per-credit charge:** $110; out-of-state residents $210.
**Room and board:** $3,400.

**FINANCIAL AID PICTURE**
**Students with need:** Need-based aid available for full-time students.

**FINANCIAL AID PROCEDURES**
**Forms required:** FAFSA.
**Dates and Deadlines:** Priority date 4/1; no closing date. Applicants notified by 8/16.

**CONTACT**
Director of Financial Aid
4975 Highway 51 North, Senatobia, MS 38668
(662) 562-3271

## Pearl River Community College
Poplarville, Mississippi
www.prcc.edu                     Federal Code: 002430

**2-year public** community college in small town.
**Enrollment:** 4,900 undergrads.
**Selectivity:** Open admission; but selective for some programs.

**BASIC COSTS (2015-2016)**
**Tuition and fees:** $2,900; out-of-state residents $5,298.
**Room and board:** $4,500.

**FINANCIAL AID PICTURE**
**Students with need:** Need-based aid available for full-time and part-time students.
**Students without need:** No-need awards available for academics, alumni affiliation, athletics, leadership, music/drama, state/district residency.

**FINANCIAL AID PROCEDURES**
**Forms required:** FAFSA, institutional form.
**Dates and Deadlines:** Priority date 4/17; no closing date. Applicants notified on a rolling basis.

**CONTACT**
Valerie Horne, Director of Financial Aid
101 Highway 11 North, Poplarville, MS 39470
(601) 403-1212

## Rust College
Holly Springs, Mississippi
www.rustcollege.edu              Federal Code: 002433

**4-year private** liberal arts and teachers college in small town, affiliated with United Methodist Church.
**Enrollment:** 856 undergrads.

**BASIC COSTS (2015-2016)**
**Tuition and fees:** $9,500.
**Per-credit charge:** $396.
**Room and board:** $4,100.
**Additional info:** Tuition at time of enrollment locked for 4 years.

**FINANCIAL AID PICTURE**
**Students with need:** Need-based aid available for full-time and part-time students.
**Students without need:** No-need awards available for academics, leadership, music/drama, religious affiliation, state/district residency.
**Scholarships offered:** Honor Track Scholarship: $11,800; minimum GPA 3.5, ACT 22, SAT 1530. Presidential Scholarship: $3,000; minimum GPA 3.25, ACT 19, SAT 1350. Academic Dean's Scholarship: $2500; minimum GPA 3.0, ACT 17, SAT 1230.

**FINANCIAL AID PROCEDURES**
**Forms required:** FAFSA, institutional form.

**Dates and Deadlines:** Priority date 3/15; closing date 6/30. Applicants notified on a rolling basis starting 4/1; must reply within 2 week(s) of notification.

**Transfers:** No deadline. Applicants notified on a rolling basis starting 4/1; must reply within 2 week(s) of notification.

**CONTACT**
Helen Street, Director of Financial Aid
150 Rust Avenue, Holly Springs, MS 38635-2328
(662) 252-8000 ext. 4062

## Southwest Mississippi Community College
Summit, Mississippi
www.smcc.edu                    Federal Code: 002436

**2-year public** community college in rural community.
**Enrollment:** 1,771 undergrads.
**Selectivity:** Open admission; but selective for some programs.

**BASIC COSTS (2015-2016)**
**Tuition and fees:** $2,720; out-of-state residents $5,420.
**Per-credit charge:** $115; out-of-state residents $120.
**Room and board:** $3,600.

**FINANCIAL AID PICTURE**
**Students with need:** Need-based aid available for full-time and part-time students.

**FINANCIAL AID PROCEDURES**
**Forms required:** FAFSA.
**Dates and Deadlines:** Applicants notified on a rolling basis.

**CONTACT**
Joni Wilkinson, Director of Financial Aid
1156 College Drive, Summit, MS 39666
(601) 276-3708

## Tougaloo College
Tougaloo, Mississippi
www.tougaloo.edu                Federal Code: 002439

**4-year private** liberal arts college in large city, affiliated with United Church of Christ.
**Enrollment:** 857 undergrads, 5% part-time. 154 full-time freshmen.
**Selectivity:** Admits less than 50% of applicants.

**BASIC COSTS (2015-2016)**
**Tuition and fees:** $10,607.
**Per-credit charge:** $423.
**Room and board:** $6,400.
**Additional info:** Tuition/fee waivers available for adults.

**FINANCIAL AID PICTURE**
**Students with need:** Need-based aid available for full-time and part-time students.
**Students without need:** No-need awards available for academics, art, athletics, leadership, music/drama.

**FINANCIAL AID PROCEDURES**
**Forms required:** FAFSA, state aid form, institutional form.
**Dates and Deadlines:** Priority date 4/15; no closing date. Applicants notified on a rolling basis starting 5/1; must reply within 2 week(s) of notification.
**Transfers:** No deadline. Applicants notified on a rolling basis starting 2/1; must reply within 2 week(s) of notification.

**CONTACT**
Maria Thomas, Director of Financial Aid
500 West County Line Road, Tougaloo, MS 39174
(601) 977-7766

## University of Mississippi
University, Mississippi
www.olemiss.edu                 Federal Code: 002440

**4-year public** university in large town.
**Enrollment:** 18,472 undergrads, 7% part-time. 3,762 full-time freshmen.
**Selectivity:** Admits over 75% of applicants.

**BASIC COSTS (2015-2016)**
**Tuition and fees:** $7,444; out-of-state residents $20,674.
**Per-credit charge:** $306; out-of-state residents $857.25.

**FINANCIAL AID PICTURE (2014-2015)**
**Students with need:** Out of 2,779 full-time freshmen who applied for aid, 1,842 were judged to have need. Of these, 1,793 received aid, and 290 had their full need met. Average financial aid package met 75% of need; average scholarship/grant was $8,532; average loan was $3,192. For part-time students, average financial aid package was $1,762.
**Students without need:** 1,325 full-time freshmen who did not demonstrate need for aid received scholarships/grants; average award was $7,231. No-need awards available for academics, alumni affiliation, art, athletics, leadership, music/drama, ROTC, state/district residency.
**Scholarships offered:** 48 full-time freshmen received athletic scholarships; average amount $13,231.

**FINANCIAL AID PROCEDURES**
**Forms required:** FAFSA.
**Dates and Deadlines:** Priority date 3/1; no closing date. Applicants notified on a rolling basis starting 4/1; must reply within 4 week(s) of notification.
**Transfers:** No deadline. Applicants notified on a rolling basis starting 4/1; must reply within 4 week(s) of notification.

**CONTACT**
Laura Diven-Brown, Director of Financial Aid
145 Martindale, University, MS 38677-1848
(800) 891-4596

## University of Mississippi Medical Center
Jackson, Mississippi
www.umc.edu                     Federal Code: 004688

**Upper-division public** health science college in large city.
**Enrollment:** 701 undergrads.
**Selectivity:** Open admission; but selective for some programs. GED not accepted.

**BASIC COSTS (2015-2016)**
**Tuition and fees:** $7,344; out-of-state residents $20,574.
**Per-credit charge:** $306; out-of-state residents $857.

**FINANCIAL AID PICTURE**
**Students with need:** Need-based aid available for full-time and part-time students.
**Students without need:** This college awards aid only to students with need.

**FINANCIAL AID PROCEDURES**
**Forms required:** FAFSA, state aid form, institutional form.
**Dates and Deadlines:** Closing date 4/1. Applicants notified by 7/15; must reply within 2 week(s) of notification.

**CONTACT**
Stacey Mathews, Director of Student Financial Aid
2500 North State Street, Jackson, MS 39216
(601) 984-1117

## University of Southern Mississippi
Hattiesburg, Mississippi
www.usm.edu                              Federal Code: 002441

**4-year public** university in small city.
**Enrollment:** 11,736 undergrads, 13% part-time. 1,585 full-time freshmen.
**Selectivity:** Admits 50 to 75% of applicants.

**BASIC COSTS (2015-2016)**
**Tuition and fees:** $7,224; out-of-state residents $16,094.
**Per-credit charge:** $301; out-of-state residents $671.
**Room and board:** $7,550.

**FINANCIAL AID PICTURE (2014-2015)**
**Students with need:** Out of 1,493 full-time freshmen who applied for aid, 1,247 were judged to have need. Of these, 1,244 received aid, and 346 had their full need met. Average financial aid package met 74% of need; average scholarship/grant was $4,794; average loan was $4,304. For part-time students, average financial aid package was $5,827.
**Students without need:** 199 full-time freshmen who did not demonstrate need for aid received scholarships/grants; average award was $5,627. No-need awards available for academics, alumni affiliation, art, athletics, leadership, music/drama, ROTC, state/district residency.
**Scholarships offered:** 81 full-time freshmen received athletic scholarships; average amount $9,982.

**FINANCIAL AID PROCEDURES**
**Forms required:** FAFSA.
**Dates and Deadlines:** Priority date 3/15; no closing date. Applicants notified on a rolling basis starting 3/15.
**Transfers:** Merit scholarships available to community college transfer students based on college GPA.

**CONTACT**
David Williamson, Director of Financial Aid
118 College Drive #5166, Hattiesburg, MS 39406-0001
(601) 266-4774

## William Carey University
Hattiesburg, Mississippi
www.wmcarey.edu                          Federal Code: 002447

**4-year private** university and liberal arts college in small city, affiliated with Baptist faith.
**Enrollment:** 2,047 undergrads.
**Selectivity:** Open admission; but selective for some programs.

**BASIC COSTS (2015-2016)**
**Tuition and fees:** $11,700.
**Per-credit charge:** $360.
**Room and board:** $5,220.

**FINANCIAL AID PICTURE**
**Students with need:** Need-based aid available for full-time and part-time students. Work study available nights, weekends, and for part-time students.
**Students without need:** No-need awards available for academics, alumni affiliation, art, athletics, music/drama, religious affiliation.

**FINANCIAL AID PROCEDURES**
**Forms required:** FAFSA.
**Dates and Deadlines:** Priority date 4/1; closing date 9/1. Applicants notified on a rolling basis starting 6/1; must reply within 2 week(s) of notification.

**CONTACT**
William Curry, Dean of Enrollment Management & Records
498 Tuscan Avenue, Hattiesburg, MS 39401
(601) 318-6153

# Missouri

## Avila University
Kansas City, Missouri
www.avila.edu                            Federal Code: 002449

**4-year private** university and liberal arts college in very large city, affiliated with Roman Catholic Church.
**Enrollment:** 1,368 undergrads, 16% part-time. 743 full-time freshmen.
**Selectivity:** Admits 50 to 75% of applicants.

**BASIC COSTS (2015-2016)**
**Tuition and fees:** $26,500.
**Per-credit charge:** $650.
**Room and board:** $7,500.
**Additional info:** Tuition/fee waivers available for adults.

**FINANCIAL AID PICTURE (2014-2015)**
**Students with need:** Out of 482 full-time freshmen who applied for aid, 441 were judged to have need. Of these, 441 received aid, and 66 had their full need met. Average financial aid package met 70% of need; average scholarship/grant was $16,486; average loan was $3,443. For part-time students, average financial aid package was $5,527.
**Students without need:** 254 full-time freshmen who did not demonstrate need for aid received scholarships/grants; average award was $9,803. No-need awards available for academics, alumni affiliation, art, athletics, music/drama, religious affiliation.
**Scholarships offered:** 89 full-time freshmen received athletic scholarships; average amount $4,216.
**Additional info:** Financial aid adjusted based on need for increases in tuition.

**FINANCIAL AID PROCEDURES**
**Forms required:** FAFSA, institutional form.
**Dates and Deadlines:** Closing date 4/1. Applicants notified on a rolling basis starting 2/1; must reply within 2 week(s) of notification.
**Transfers:** No deadline. Applicants notified on a rolling basis starting 2/1; must reply within 2 week(s) of notification. Non-need-based academic scholarship available for transfer students.

**CONTACT**
Crystal Bruntz, Director of Financial Aid
11901 Wornall Road, Kansas City, MO 64145-1007
(816) 501-3600

## Baptist Bible College
Springfield, Missouri
www.gobbc.edu                            Federal Code: 013208

**4-year private** Bible and seminary college in small city, affiliated with Baptist faith.
**Enrollment:** 321 undergrads.
**Selectivity:** Open admission.

**BASIC COSTS (2015-2016)**
**Tuition and fees:** $12,850.
**Per-credit charge:** $405.
**Room and board:** $6,550.

## FINANCIAL AID PICTURE

**Students with need:** Need-based aid available for full-time and part-time students.

## FINANCIAL AID PROCEDURES

**Forms required:** FAFSA, institutional form.

**Dates and Deadlines:** Closing date 5/1. Applicants notified on a rolling basis; must reply within 2 week(s) of notification.

## CONTACT

Bob Kotulski, Financial Aid Director
628 East Kearney Street, Springfield, MO 65803
(417) 268-6036

## Bolivar Technical College

Bolivar, Missouri
www.bolivarcollege.org          Federal Code: 035793

**2-year private** branch campus and technical college in small town.
**Enrollment:** 86 undergrads. 16 full-time freshmen.
**Selectivity:** Open admission; but selective for some programs.

## BASIC COSTS (2015-2016)

**Tuition and fees:** $12,982.
**Additional info:** Tuition/fee waivers available for adults.

## FINANCIAL AID PICTURE (2014-2015)

**Students with need:** Out of 16 full-time freshmen who applied for aid, 16 were judged to have need. Of these, 16 received aid, and 16 had their full need met. For part-time students, average financial aid package was $1,444.
**Students without need:** This college awards aid only to students with need.

## FINANCIAL AID PROCEDURES

**Forms required:** FAFSA, institutional form.
**Dates and Deadlines:** Priority date 4/1; no closing date.
**Transfers:** Priority date 4/1; no deadline. Applicants notified on a rolling basis.

## CONTACT

Wendy McGowin, Financial Aid
PO Box 592, Bolivar, MO 65613
(417) 777-5062

## Calvary Bible College and Theological Seminary

Kansas City, Missouri
www.calvary.edu          Federal Code: 002450

**4-year private** Bible and seminary college in large city, affiliated with nondenominational tradition.
**Enrollment:** 226 undergrads, 28% part-time. 36 full-time freshmen.
**Selectivity:** Admits over 75% of applicants.

## BASIC COSTS (2015-2016)

**Tuition and fees:** $11,640.
**Per-credit charge:** $360.
**Room and board:** $5,200.
**Additional info:** Visit web site for detailed information regarding tuition and expenses at Calvary Bible College. Tuition/fee waivers available for minority students.

## FINANCIAL AID PICTURE (2014-2015)

**Students with need:** Out of 30 full-time freshmen who applied for aid, 27 were judged to have need. Of these, 27 received aid, and 6 had their full

need met. Average financial aid package met 74% of need; average scholarship/grant was $6,014; average loan was $3,472. For part-time students, average financial aid package was $10,675.
**Students without need:** 1 full-time freshmen who did not demonstrate need for aid received scholarships/grants; average award was $500. No-need awards available for academics, alumni affiliation, music/drama, religious affiliation, ROTC.

## FINANCIAL AID PROCEDURES

**Forms required:** FAFSA.
**Dates and Deadlines:** Closing date 4/1. Applicants notified on a rolling basis starting 5/1; must reply within 2 week(s) of notification.
**Transfers:** No deadline. Applicants notified on a rolling basis starting 6/1; must reply within 2 week(s) of notification.

## CONTACT

Bob Crank, Financial Aid Director
15800 Calvary Road, Kansas City, MO 64147-1341
(816) 425-6136

## Central Christian College of the Bible

Moberly, Missouri
www.cccb.edu          Federal Code: 014619

**4-year private** Bible college in large town, affiliated with Christian Church.
**Enrollment:** 272 undergrads, 17% part-time. 55 full-time freshmen.

## FINANCIAL AID PICTURE

**Students with need:** Need-based aid available for full-time and part-time students.
**Scholarships offered:** Each semester, 100 open Full-Tuition Scholarships are made available to new or transferring students who have been admitted into a degree or certificate program and attend classes on Moberly campus.

## FINANCIAL AID PROCEDURES

**Dates and Deadlines:** Priority date 4/1; no closing date. Applicants notified on a rolling basis starting 3/1; must reply within 4 week(s) of notification.
**Transfers:** No deadline.

## CONTACT

Rhonda Dunham, Financial Aid Director
911 East Urbandale Drive, Moberly, MO 65270-1997
(888) 263-3900

## Central Methodist University

Fayette, Missouri
www.centralmethodist.edu          Federal Code: E00605

**4-year private** university and liberal arts college in small town, affiliated with United Methodist Church.
**Enrollment:** 1,091 undergrads, 2% part-time. 281 full-time freshmen.
**Selectivity:** Admits 50 to 75% of applicants.

## BASIC COSTS (2016-2017)

**Tuition and fees:** $23,010.
**Per-credit charge:** $210.
**Room and board:** $7,550.

## FINANCIAL AID PICTURE (2015-2016)

**Students with need:** Out of 262 full-time freshmen who applied for aid, 237 were judged to have need. Of these, 237 received aid, and 41 had their full need met. Average financial aid package met 69% of need; average scholarship/grant was $5,086; average loan was $3,471. For part-time students, average financial aid package was $5,899.

**Students without need:** 44 full-time freshmen who did not demonstrate need for aid received scholarships/grants; average award was $14,528. No-need awards available for academics, alumni affiliation, athletics, leadership, music/drama, religious affiliation, ROTC.
**Scholarships offered:** 174 full-time freshmen received athletic scholarships; average amount $6,392.

### FINANCIAL AID PROCEDURES
**Forms required:** FAFSA.
**Dates and Deadlines:** Priority date 3/15; no closing date. Applicants notified on a rolling basis starting 1/1; must reply by 8/5 or within 2 week(s) of notification.
**Transfers:** No deadline. Applicants notified on a rolling basis. Merit based institutional financial aid is determined by college transfer GPA.

### CONTACT
Kristen Gibbs, Director of Financial Assistance
411 Central Methodist Square, Fayette, MO 65248-1198
(660) 248-6245

## Chamberlain College of Nursing: St. Louis
St Louis, Missouri
www.chamberlain.edu          Federal Code: 006385

**4-year for-profit** nursing college in very large city.
**Enrollment:** 510 undergrads.

### BASIC COSTS (2015-2016)
**Tuition and fees:** $18,160.
**Per-credit charge:** $665.
**Additional info:** Tuition quoted is for Nursing courses at $590 per credit. Tuition and fees vary by program.

### FINANCIAL AID PICTURE
**Students with need:** Need-based aid available for full-time and part-time students.
**Students without need:** No-need awards available for academics.
**Scholarships offered:** Tenet Nurse Citizen Award: full tuition; based on application, essay, interview, renewable with 3.25 GPA, 1 awarded. Chancellor's Award: half tuition; for students with 24 ACT, 3.5 GPA; number awarded subject to fund availability. Merit Scholarships: up to $3,000; based on academic achievement; number awarded subject to fund availability.

### FINANCIAL AID PROCEDURES
**Forms required:** FAFSA, institutional form.
**Dates and Deadlines:** Applicants notified on a rolling basis starting 4/1; must reply within 2 week(s) of notification.
**Transfers:** No deadline.

### CONTACT
Michelle Mohn, Financial Counselor
11830 Westline Industrial Drive, Suite 106, St. Louis, MO 63146
(314) 768-5604

## College of the Ozarks
Point Lookout, Missouri
www.cofo.edu          Federal Code: 002500

**4-year private** liberal arts college in small town, affiliated with interdenominational tradition.
**Enrollment:** 1,442 undergrads, 1% part-time. 301 full-time freshmen.
**Selectivity:** Admits less than 50% of applicants.

### BASIC COSTS (2015-2016)
**Tuition and fees:** $18,730.

**Per-credit charge:** $310.
**Room and board:** $6,500.

### FINANCIAL AID PICTURE (2014-2015)
**Students with need:** Out of 246 full-time freshmen who applied for aid, 236 were judged to have need. Of these, 236 received aid, and 53 had their full need met. Average financial aid package met 86% of need; average scholarship/grant was $14,336. For part-time students, average financial aid package was $4,905.
**Students without need:** 64 full-time freshmen who did not demonstrate need for aid received scholarships/grants; average award was $13,595. No-need awards available for academics, art, athletics, leadership, music/drama, ROTC, state/district residency.
**Scholarships offered:** 10 full-time freshmen received athletic scholarships; average amount $3,650.
**Additional info:** The College guarantees to meet 100% of total cost for each full-time student without loans of any kind. All full-time students work on campus in exchange for full financial assistance for tuition.

### FINANCIAL AID PROCEDURES
**Forms required:** FAFSA.
**Dates and Deadlines:** Priority date 2/15; no closing date. Applicants notified on a rolling basis starting 7/1.
**Transfers:** Applicants notified by 7/1.

### CONTACT
Jeff Ford, Financial Aid Director
PO Box 17, Point Lookout, MO 65726-0017
(417) 690-3290

## Columbia College
Columbia, Missouri
www.ccis.edu          Federal Code: 002456

**4-year private** liberal arts college in small city, affiliated with Christian Church (Disciples of Christ).
**Enrollment:** 805 undergrads, 15% part-time. 112 full-time freshmen.
**Selectivity:** Admits 50 to 75% of applicants.

### BASIC COSTS (2015-2016)
**Tuition and fees:** $20,963.
**Room and board:** $8,221.
**Additional info:** Entering students will pay a fixed rate that is good for five consecutive years. Lab fees may apply to some classes, all other fees are covered by cost of tuition. Tuition at time of enrollment locked for 4 years.

### FINANCIAL AID PICTURE (2014-2015)
**Students with need:** Out of 92 full-time freshmen who applied for aid, 77 were judged to have need. Of these, 77 received aid, and 15 had their full need met. Average financial aid package met 64% of need; average scholarship/grant was $4,473; average loan was $2,932. For part-time students, average financial aid package was $7,145.
**Students without need:** 16 full-time freshmen who did not demonstrate need for aid received scholarships/grants; average award was $10,758. No-need awards available for academics, alumni affiliation, art, athletics, leadership, minority status, music/drama, religious affiliation, ROTC, state/district residency.
**Scholarships offered:** *Merit:* Columbia College Scholarship: full tuition, room/board; requires 3.5 GPA, 26 ACT/SAT equivalent, campus visit, interview, essay, 2 letters of recommendation, resume; renewable with 30 semester hours and 3.6 GPA. Presidential Scholarship: full tuition; requires 3.5 GPA, 26 ACT/SAT equivalent, campus visit, interview, essay, 2 letters of recommendation, resume; renewable with 30 semester hours and 3.6 GPA. Capstone scholarship: 60% of tuition; requires 28 ACT/SAT equivalent and 3.6 GPA; renewable with 3.6 GPA and 27 credits earned annually. Keystone Scholarship: 3.4 GPA or GED equivalent; 26 ACT/SAT equivalent; renewable

with 27 credits per year and 3.4 GPA for up to 3 years. *Athletic:* 23 full-time freshmen received athletic scholarships; average amount $13,713.

**FINANCIAL AID PROCEDURES**

**Forms required:** FAFSA.

**Dates and Deadlines:** Priority date 3/1; no closing date. Applicants notified on a rolling basis starting 5/1.

**Transfers:** No deadline. Applicants notified by 5/1.

**CONTACT**

Sharon Abernathy, Director of Financial Aid

1001 Rogers Street, Columbia, MO 65216

(573) 875-7390

## Conception Seminary College
Conception, Missouri

www.conception.edu                    Federal Code: 002467

**4-year private** seminary college for men in rural community, affiliated with Roman Catholic Church.

**Enrollment:** 106 undergrads. 19 full-time freshmen.

**Selectivity:** Admits over 75% of applicants.

**BASIC COSTS (2016-2017)**

**Tuition and fees:** $20,706.

**Room and board:** $12,316.

**FINANCIAL AID PICTURE**

**Students with need:** Need-based aid available for full-time and part-time students. Work study available nights, weekends, and for part-time students.

**Students without need:** No-need awards available for academics.

**FINANCIAL AID PROCEDURES**

**Forms required:** FAFSA.

**Dates and Deadlines:** Applicants notified on a rolling basis starting 8/1; must reply by 8/20.

**CONTACT**

Justin Hernandez, Financial Aid Officer

Box 502, Conception, MO 64433-0502

(660) 944-2851

## Cottey College
Nevada, Missouri

www.cottey.edu                    Federal Code: 002458

**2-year private** liberal arts college for women in small town.

**Enrollment:** 317 undergrads. 145 full-time freshmen.

**BASIC COSTS (2015-2016)**

**Tuition and fees:** $19,300.

**Room and board:** $7,000.

**FINANCIAL AID PICTURE (2014-2015)**

**Students with need:** Out of 123 full-time freshmen who applied for aid, 110 were judged to have need. Of these, 110 received aid, and 44 had their full need met. Average financial aid package met 85.75% of need; average scholarship/grant was $16,894; average loan was $2,827. For part-time students, average financial aid package was $6,191.

**Students without need:** 34 full-time freshmen who did not demonstrate need for aid received scholarships/grants; average award was $11,723. No-need awards available for academics, alumni affiliation, art, athletics, leadership, music/drama.

**Scholarships offered:** 7 full-time freshmen received athletic scholarships; average amount $4,326.

**FINANCIAL AID PROCEDURES**

**Forms required:** FAFSA.

**Dates and Deadlines:** Priority date 3/1; no closing date. Applicants notified on a rolling basis starting 4/1; must reply within 2 week(s) of notification.

**Transfers:** Applicants notified on a rolling basis starting 4/1; must reply within 2 week(s) of notification.

**CONTACT**

Sherry Pennington, Coordinator of Financial Aid

1000 West Austin Boulevard, Nevada, MO 64772

(417) 667-8181 ext. 2190

## Crowder College
Neosho, Missouri

www.crowder.edu                    Federal Code: 002459

**2-year public** community and liberal arts college in small town.

**Enrollment:** 3,923 undergrads, 40% part-time. 898 full-time freshmen.

**Selectivity:** Open admission; but selective for some programs.

**BASIC COSTS (2016-2017)**

**Tuition and fees:** $2,940; out-of-district residents $4,140; out-of-state residents $4,140.

**Per-credit charge:** $82; out-of-district residents $122; out-of-state residents $122.

**Room and board:** $5,002.

**FINANCIAL AID PICTURE (2014-2015)**

**Students with need:** 77% of average financial aid package awarded as scholarships/grants, 23% awarded as loans/jobs. Need-based aid available for part-time students. Work study available nights, weekends, and for part-time students.

**Students without need:** No-need awards available for academics, art, athletics, leadership, minority status, music/drama, state/district residency.

**FINANCIAL AID PROCEDURES**

**Forms required:** FAFSA, institutional form.

**Dates and Deadlines:** Priority date 7/1; no closing date. Applicants notified on a rolling basis starting 5/15; must reply within 4 week(s) of notification.

**CONTACT**

Stephanie Ferguson, Director of Financial Aid

601 Laclede Avenue, Neosho, MO 64850

(417) 451-3223 ext. 5434

## Culver-Stockton College
Canton, Missouri

www.culver.edu                    Federal Code: 002460

**4-year private** liberal arts college in small town, affiliated with Christian Church (Disciples of Christ).

**Enrollment:** 973 undergrads, 5% part-time. 260 full-time freshmen.

**Selectivity:** Admits 50 to 75% of applicants.

**BASIC COSTS (2015-2016)**

**Tuition and fees:** $24,900.

**Per-credit charge:** $570.

**Room and board:** $7,950.

**FINANCIAL AID PICTURE (2015-2016)**

**Students with need:** Out of 234 full-time freshmen who applied for aid, 214 were judged to have need. Of these, 214 received aid, and 30 had their full need met. Average financial aid package met 70% of need; average scholarship/grant was $16,809; average loan was $3,339. For part-time students, average financial aid package was $5,840.

**Students without need:** 27 full-time freshmen who did not demonstrate need for aid received scholarships/grants; average award was $9,531. No-need awards available for academics, alumni affiliation, art, athletics, leadership, music/drama, religious affiliation.

**Scholarships offered:** 32 full-time freshmen received athletic scholarships; average amount $5,488.

## FINANCIAL AID PROCEDURES

**Forms required:** FAFSA.

**Dates and Deadlines:** Priority date 3/1; closing date 6/1. Applicants notified on a rolling basis starting 2/15; must reply within 2 week(s) of notification.

**Transfers:** Must reply within 2 week(s) of notification.

## CONTACT

Tina Wiseman, Director of Financial Aid

One College Hill, Canton, MO 63435-1299

(573) 288-6307

# DeVry University: Kansas City

Kansas City, Missouri

www.devry.edu

**4-year for-profit** university in large city.

**Enrollment:** 423 undergrads.

## BASIC COSTS (2015-2016)

**Tuition and fees:** $17,132.

**Per-credit charge:** $609.

## FINANCIAL AID PICTURE

**Students with need:** Need-based aid available for full-time and part-time students.

**Students without need:** This college awards aid only to students with need.

## FINANCIAL AID PROCEDURES

**Forms required:** FAFSA.

**Dates and Deadlines:** Applicants notified on a rolling basis.

## CONTACT

11224 Holmes Street, Kansas City, MO 64131

(816) 941-0439

# Drury University

Springfield, Missouri

www.drury.edu        Federal Code: 002461

**4-year private** university and liberal arts college in large city, affiliated with United Church of Christ.

**Enrollment:** 1,313 undergrads, 2% part-time. 282 full-time freshmen.

**Selectivity:** Admits 50 to 75% of applicants.

## BASIC COSTS (2016-2017)

**Tuition and fees:** $25,905.

**Room and board:** $8,256.

## FINANCIAL AID PICTURE (2014-2015)

**Students with need:** Out of 234 full-time freshmen who applied for aid, 187 were judged to have need. Of these, 187 received aid, and 42 had their full need met. Average financial aid package met 70% of need; average scholarship/grant was $15,667; average loan was $3,988. For part-time students, average financial aid package was $10,368.

**Students without need:** 99 full-time freshmen who did not demonstrate need for aid received scholarships/grants; average award was $8,464. No-need awards available for academics, alumni affiliation, art, athletics, job skills, leadership, minority status, music/drama, religious affiliation.

**Scholarships offered:** *Merit:* Phi Theta Kappa Scholarship: $1,000. *Athletic:* 31 full-time freshmen received athletic scholarships; average amount $12,500.

## FINANCIAL AID PROCEDURES

**Forms required:** FAFSA, institutional form.

**Dates and Deadlines:** Priority date 2/15; closing date 3/1. Applicants notified on a rolling basis starting 3/1; must reply within 2 week(s) of notification.

**Transfers:** No deadline.

## CONTACT

Becky Ahrens, Director of Financial Aid

900 North Benton Avenue, Springfield, MO 65802-3712

(417) 873-7523

# East Central College

Union, Missouri

www.eastcentral.edu        Federal Code: 008862

**2-year public** community college in large town.

**Enrollment:** 2,543 undergrads, 42% part-time. 550 full-time freshmen.

**Selectivity:** Open admission; but selective for some programs.

## BASIC COSTS (2016-2017)

**Tuition and fees:** $2,850; out-of-district residents $3,900; out-of-state residents $5,610.

**Per-credit charge:** $76; out-of-district residents $111; out-of-state residents $168.

## FINANCIAL AID PICTURE

**Students with need:** Need-based aid available for full-time and part-time students.

**Students without need:** No-need awards available for academics, alumni affiliation, art, athletics, music/drama, state/district residency.

## FINANCIAL AID PROCEDURES

**Forms required:** FAFSA.

**Dates and Deadlines:** Priority date 3/15; no closing date. Applicants notified on a rolling basis starting 4/1.

**Transfers:** No deadline. Applicants notified on a rolling basis starting 4/1.

## CONTACT

Karen Griffin, Director of Financial Aid

1964 Prairie Dell Road, Union, MO 63084-0529

(636) 584-6588

# Evangel University

Springfield, Missouri

www.evangel.edu        Federal Code: 002463

**4-year private** liberal arts college in small city, affiliated with Assemblies of God.

**Enrollment:** 1,723 undergrads, 10% part-time. 329 full-time freshmen.

**Selectivity:** Admits 50 to 75% of applicants.

## BASIC COSTS (2015-2016)

**Tuition and fees:** $21,416.

**Room and board:** $7,582.

## FINANCIAL AID PICTURE (2014-2015)

**Students with need:** Out of 322 full-time freshmen who applied for aid, 283 were judged to have need. Of these, 283 received aid, and 30 had their full need met. Average financial aid package met 67% of need; average scholarship/grant was $12,568; average loan was $3,584. For part-time students, average financial aid package was $7,830.

**Students without need:** This college awards aid only to students with need.

**Scholarships offered:** 21 full-time freshmen received athletic scholarships; average amount $8,923.

## FINANCIAL AID PROCEDURES

**Forms required:** FAFSA.

**Dates and Deadlines:** Priority date 3/1; closing date 7/1. Applicants notified on a rolling basis starting 3/1; must reply within 3 week(s) of notification.

**CONTACT**
Dorynda Carpenter, Director of Student Financial Services
1111 North Glenstone, Springfield, MO 65802
(417) 865-2811 ext. 7300

## Fontbonne University
St. Louis, Missouri
www.fontbonne.edu                Federal Code: 002464

**4-year private** university and liberal arts college in large city, affiliated with Roman Catholic Church.
**Enrollment:** 1,086 undergrads, 18% part-time. 178 full-time freshmen.
**Selectivity:** Admits over 75% of applicants.

**BASIC COSTS (2016-2017)**
**Tuition and fees:** $24,610.
**Per-credit charge:** $648.
**Room and board:** $9,107.

**FINANCIAL AID PICTURE (2015-2016)**
**Students with need:** 46% of average financial aid package awarded as scholarships/grants, 54% awarded as loans/jobs. Need-based aid available for part-time students. Work study available nights, weekends, and for part-time students.
**Students without need:** No-need awards available for academics, alumni affiliation, art, leadership, minority status, music/drama, religious affiliation, state/district residency.
**Scholarships offered:** Presidential Scholarship: up to $19,000 per academic year. Dean's Scholarship: up to $13,000 per academic year. Founder's Scholarship: up to $11,500 per academic year. Alumni Scholarship: up to $8,500 per academic year. Freshman College Scholarship: up to $6,500 per academic year. Griffin Award: up to $4,000 per academic year. Dean's Scholarship: $6,000-$8,000. Alumni Scholarship: $1,000-$6,000. Campus Service Scholarship: $500-$3,000. Art, theater, English, writing and computer science scholarships also available.

**FINANCIAL AID PROCEDURES**
**Forms required:** FAFSA, institutional form.
**Dates and Deadlines:** Priority date 3/15; no closing date. Applicants notified on a rolling basis starting 2/1; must reply within 2 week(s) of notification.
**Transfers:** Priority date 2/1; closing date 4/1. Applicants notified on a rolling basis starting 3/1; must reply within 2 week(s) of notification.

**CONTACT**
Matthew Kearney, Director of Financial Aid
6800 Wydown Boulevard, Saint Louis, MO 63105-3098
(314) 889-1414

## Goldfarb School of Nursing at Barnes-Jewish College
St. Louis, Missouri
www.barnesjewishcollege.edu        Federal Code: 003689

**Upper-division private** nursing college in very large city.
**Enrollment:** 637 undergrads, 11% part-time.

**BASIC COSTS (2016-2017)**
**Tuition and fees:** $19,423.
**Per-credit charge:** $698.

**FINANCIAL AID PICTURE (2014-2015)**
**Students with need:** Average financial aid package for all full-time undergraduates was $2,915; for part-time $3,113. 13% awarded as scholarships/grants, 87% awarded as loans/jobs.

**Students without need:** No-need awards available for academics, leadership, minority status.

**FINANCIAL AID PROCEDURES**
**Forms required:** FAFSA.
**Dates and Deadlines:** Priority date 4/1; no closing date. Applicants notified on a rolling basis.
**Transfers:** No deadline. Applicants notified on a rolling basis.

**CONTACT**
Jason Crowe, Enrollment Manager
4483 Duncan Avenue, St. Louis, MO 63110-1091
(314) 362-9250

## Hannibal-LaGrange University
Hannibal, Missouri
www.hlg.edu                Federal Code: 009089

**4-year private** university and liberal arts college in large town, affiliated with Southern Baptist Convention.
**Enrollment:** 881 full-time undergrads.
**Selectivity:** Admits 50 to 75% of applicants.

**BASIC COSTS (2015-2016)**
**Tuition and fees:** $20,560.
**Room and board:** $3,804.

**FINANCIAL AID PICTURE**
**Students with need:** Need-based aid available for full-time and part-time students.
**Students without need:** No-need awards available for academics, art, athletics, music/drama, religious affiliation.
**Additional info:** Work-study opportunities vary according to on-and off-campus needs.

**FINANCIAL AID PROCEDURES**
**Forms required:** FAFSA, institutional form.
**Dates and Deadlines:** Applicants notified on a rolling basis; must reply by 8/31.
**Transfers:** No deadline.

**CONTACT**
Brice Baumgardner, Financial Aid Director
2800 Palmyra Road, Hannibal, MO 63401
(573) 629-3267

## Harris-Stowe State University
St. Louis, Missouri
www.hssu.edu                Federal Code: 002466

**4-year public** university in large city.
**Enrollment:** 1,363 undergrads, 24% part-time. 265 full-time freshmen.
**Selectivity:** Open admission.

**BASIC COSTS (2015-2016)**
**Tuition and fees:** $5,220; out-of-state residents $9,853.
**Per-credit charge:** $199; out-of-state residents $392.
**Room and board:** $9,140.

**FINANCIAL AID PICTURE (2014-2015)**
**Students with need:** 55% of average financial aid package awarded as scholarships/grants, 45% awarded as loans/jobs. Need-based aid available for part-time students. Work study available nights, weekends, and for part-time students.
**Students without need:** No-need awards available for academics, alumni affiliation, art, athletics, leadership, music/drama, state/district residency.

## FINANCIAL AID PROCEDURES

**Forms required:** FAFSA, institutional form.

**Dates and Deadlines:** Closing date 4/1. Applicants notified on a rolling basis starting 4/1; must reply within 3 week(s) of notification.

**Transfers:** Priority date 4/1. Applicants notified on a rolling basis starting 4/1; must reply within 3 week(s) of notification.

### CONTACT

James Green, Director of Financial Assistance

3026 Laclede Avenue, St. Louis, MO 63103-2199

(314) 340-3500 ext. 3502

## Hickey College

St. Louis, Missouri

www.hickeycollege.edu                    Federal Code: 014209

**4-year for-profit** business and technical college in very large city.

**Enrollment:** 372 undergrads.

**Selectivity:** Open admission; but selective for some programs.

### BASIC COSTS (2015-2016)

**Additional info:** Diploma programs: $13,890-$21,620, books and supplies $1,810-$2,574, room and board $5,920-$8,880. Associate programs: $27,730-$31,710, books and supplies $2,434-$3,328, room and board $11,840-$13,320. Bachelor's program: $21,380, books and supplies $2,413, room and board $17,760.

### FINANCIAL AID PICTURE

**Students with need:** Need-based aid available for full-time students.

### FINANCIAL AID PROCEDURES

**Forms required:** FAFSA.

**Dates and Deadlines:** Applicants notified on a rolling basis.

### CONTACT

Deana Pecoroni, Director, Student Services

940 West Port Plaza, St. Louis, MO 63146

(314) 434-2212 ext. 128

## Jefferson College

Hillsboro, Missouri

www.jeffco.edu                    Federal Code: 002468

**2-year public** community and technical college in rural community.

**Enrollment:** 4,563 undergrads, 50% part-time. 944 full-time freshmen.

**Selectivity:** Open admission; but selective for some programs.

### BASIC COSTS (2015-2016)

**Tuition and fees:** $3,090; out-of-district residents $4,560; out-of-state residents $6,000.

**Room and board:** $5,644.

### FINANCIAL AID PICTURE (2014-2015)

**Students with need:** Out of 886 full-time freshmen who applied for aid, 667 were judged to have need. Of these, 640 received aid, and 19 had their full need met. Average financial aid package met 52% of need; average scholarship/grant was $2,452; average loan was $2,746. For part-time students, average financial aid package was $3,421.

**Students without need:** 1 full-time freshmen who did not demonstrate need for aid received scholarships/grants; average award was $1,482. No-need awards available for academics, art, athletics, leadership, music/drama, state/district residency.

**Scholarships offered:** 49 full-time freshmen received athletic scholarships; average amount $6,117.

### FINANCIAL AID PROCEDURES

**Forms required:** FAFSA.

**Dates and Deadlines:** Priority date 4/1; no closing date. Applicants notified on a rolling basis starting 4/15.

### CONTACT

Sarah Bright, Director of Student Financial Services

1000 Viking Drive, Hillsboro, MO 63050-2441

(636) 481-3212

## Kansas City Art Institute

Kansas City, Missouri

www.kcai.edu                    Federal Code: 002473

**4-year private** visual arts college in large city.

**Enrollment:** 636 undergrads, 1% part-time. 146 full-time freshmen.

**Selectivity:** Admits 50 to 75% of applicants.

### BASIC COSTS (2015-2016)

**Tuition and fees:** $35,270.

**Per-credit charge:** $1,430.

**Room and board:** $10,240.

### FINANCIAL AID PICTURE (2015-2016)

**Students with need:** 74% of average financial aid package awarded as scholarships/grants, 26% awarded as loans/jobs. Need-based aid available for part-time students. Work study available nights, weekends, and for part-time students.

**Students without need:** No-need awards available for academics, art.

**Scholarships offered:** Merit scholarships: priority application dates 2/1 and 3/1; deadline 8/1.

### FINANCIAL AID PROCEDURES

**Forms required:** FAFSA.

**Dates and Deadlines:** Priority date 3/15; closing date 4/1. Applicants notified on a rolling basis starting 4/1; must reply within 2 week(s) of notification.

**Transfers:** No deadline. Applicants notified on a rolling basis starting 4/1; must reply within 2 week(s) of notification.

### CONTACT

Darci Webster, Director of Financial Aid

4415 Warwick Boulevard, Kansas City, MO 64111

(816) 802-3337

## Lincoln University

Jefferson City, Missouri

www.lincolnu.edu                    Federal Code: 002479

**4-year public** university and liberal arts college in large town.

**Enrollment:** 2,247 undergrads, 15% part-time. 585 full-time freshmen.

**Selectivity:** Open admission; but selective for some programs and for out-of-state students.

### BASIC COSTS (2015-2016)

**Tuition and fees:** $7,042; out-of-state residents $13,432.

**Per-credit charge:** $205; out-of-state residents $418.

**Room and board:** $6,070.

### FINANCIAL AID PICTURE (2015-2016)

**Students with need:** Out of 566 full-time freshmen who applied for aid, 530 were judged to have need. Of these, 530 received aid, and 15 had their full need met. Average financial aid package met 62% of need; average scholarship/grant was $6,483; average loan was $6,418. For part-time students, average financial aid package was $6,340.

**Students without need:** No-need awards available for academics, art, athletics, job skills, leadership, minority status, music/drama, ROTC, state/district residency.

**Scholarships offered:** 43 full-time freshmen received athletic scholarships; average amount $4,044.

### FINANCIAL AID PROCEDURES
**Forms required:** FAFSA, institutional form.
**Dates and Deadlines:** Priority date 3/1; no closing date. Applicants notified on a rolling basis starting 3/15; must reply within 2 week(s) of notification.
**Transfers:** No deadline. Applicants notified on a rolling basis starting 3/15; must reply within 2 week(s) of notification.

### CONTACT
Alfred Robinson, Director of Financial Aid and Student Employment
820 Chestnut Street, B7 Young Hall, Jefferson City, MO 65101
(573) 681-6156

## Lindenwood University
St. Charles, Missouri
www.lindenwood.edu          Federal Code: 002480

**4-year private** university and liberal arts college in small city, affiliated with Presbyterian Church (USA).
**Enrollment:** 7,787 undergrads, 7% part-time. 1,217 full-time freshmen.
**Selectivity:** Admits 50 to 75% of applicants.

### BASIC COSTS (2016-2017)
**Tuition and fees:** $16,332.
**Per-credit charge:** $453.
**Room and board:** $8,800.

### FINANCIAL AID PICTURE (2015-2016)
**Students with need:** Out of 827 full-time freshmen who applied for aid, 629 were judged to have need. Of these, 629 received aid, and 200 had their full need met. Average financial aid package met 73% of need; average scholarship/grant was $7,274; average loan was $3,286. For part-time students, average financial aid package was $4,914.
**Students without need:** 467 full-time freshmen who did not demonstrate need for aid received scholarships/grants; average award was $5,701. No-need awards available for academics, art, athletics, leadership, minority status, music/drama, religious affiliation, state/district residency.
**Scholarships offered:** 73 full-time freshmen received athletic scholarships; average amount $7,700.

### FINANCIAL AID PROCEDURES
**Forms required:** FAFSA.
**Dates and Deadlines:** Priority date 4/1; no closing date. Applicants notified on a rolling basis.

### CONTACT
Lori Bode, Director of Financial Aid
209 South Kingshighway, St. Charles, MO 63301
(636) 949-4923

## Logan University
Chesterfield, Missouri
www.logan.edu          Federal Code: 004703

**3-year private** university in very large city.
**Enrollment:** 52 undergrads, 35% part-time.

### BASIC COSTS (2015-2016)
**Tuition and fees:** $8,390.
**Per-credit charge:** $275.

### FINANCIAL AID PICTURE (2014-2015)
**Students with need:** Average financial aid package for all full-time undergraduates was $7,919; for part-time $4,770. 28% awarded as scholarships/grants, 72% awarded as loans/jobs.

### FINANCIAL AID PROCEDURES
**Transfers:** No deadline. Applicants notified on a rolling basis starting 7/16; must reply by 9/16.

### CONTACT
Kerry Hallahan, Director of Financial Aid
1851 Schoettler Road, Chesterfield, MO 63017
(800) 782-3344

## Maryville University of Saint Louis
St. Louis, Missouri
www.maryville.edu          Federal Code: 002482

**4-year private** university in very large city.
**Enrollment:** 2,703 undergrads, 29% part-time. 381 full-time freshmen.
**Selectivity:** Admits 50 to 75% of applicants.

### BASIC COSTS (2015-2016)
**Tuition and fees:** $26,958.
**Per-credit charge:** $766.
**Room and board:** $10,240.

### FINANCIAL AID PICTURE (2015-2016)
**Students with need:** Out of 343 full-time freshmen who applied for aid, 304 were judged to have need. Of these, 304 received aid, and 91 had their full need met. Average financial aid package met 71% of need; average scholarship/grant was $17,196; average loan was $3,311. For part-time students, average financial aid package was $9,131.
**Students without need:** 31 full-time freshmen who did not demonstrate need for aid received scholarships/grants; average award was $13,805. No-need awards available for academics, art, athletics, job skills, leadership, minority status, music/drama, ROTC, state/district residency.
**Scholarships offered:** *Merit:* University Scholars Program: awarded to full-time freshmen with 28 ACT or 1170 SAT (exclusive of Writing), high school GPA 3.5-4.0; interview required. M-PACT Award: awarded to full-time freshmen based on campus activity and impact on student life. *Athletic:* 21 full-time freshmen received athletic scholarships; average amount $16,174.

### FINANCIAL AID PROCEDURES
**Forms required:** FAFSA.
**Dates and Deadlines:** Priority date 3/1; no closing date. Applicants notified on a rolling basis starting 3/1; must reply by 5/1 or within 2 week(s) of notification.
**Transfers:** No deadline. Applicants notified on a rolling basis starting 2/1; must reply by 5/1 or within 2 week(s) of notification. Scholarships available for transfer students.

### CONTACT
Martha Harbaugh, Director of Financial Aid
650 Maryville University Drive, St. Louis, MO 63141-7299
(314) 529-9361

## Metro Business College: Jefferson City
Jefferson City, Missouri
www.metrobusinesscollege.edu          Federal Code: 014710

**2-year for-profit** health science and career college in large town.
**Enrollment:** 80 undergrads, 15% part-time. 9 full-time freshmen.
**Selectivity:** Open admission; but selective for some programs.

### BASIC COSTS (2016-2017)
**Tuition and fees:** $11,375.
**Per-credit charge:** $230.
**Additional info:** Tuition at time of enrollment locked for 2 years.

## FINANCIAL AID PICTURE

**Students with need:** Need-based aid available for full-time and part-time students.

## FINANCIAL AID PROCEDURES

**Forms required:** FAFSA, institutional form.
**Dates and Deadlines:** Applicants notified on a rolling basis.

## CONTACT

Debbie Jenkins, Financial Aid Coordinator
210 El Mercado Plaza, Jefferson City, MO 65109
(573) 635-6600

# Metropolitan Community College - Kansas City
Kansas City, Missouri
www.mcckc.edu                Federal Code: 002484

**2-year public** community college in large city.
**Enrollment:** 15,547 undergrads.
**Selectivity:** Open admission; but selective for some programs.

## BASIC COSTS (2015-2016)

**Tuition and fees:** $2,870; out-of-district residents $5,270; out-of-state residents $6,890.

## FINANCIAL AID PICTURE

**Students with need:** Need-based aid available for full-time students. Work study available nights.
**Students without need:** No-need awards available for academics, athletics, leadership.

## FINANCIAL AID PROCEDURES

**Forms required:** FAFSA, institutional form.
**Dates and Deadlines:** Priority date 5/30; closing date 6/30. Applicants notified on a rolling basis starting 4/8.

## CONTACT

Dena Norris, Director of Student Financial Aid Services
3200 Broadway, Kansas City, MO 64111
(816) 604-1527

# Mineral Area College
Park Hills, Missouri
www.mineralarea.edu           Federal Code: 002486

**2-year public** community college in small town.
**Enrollment:** 2,157 undergrads, 26% part-time. 462 full-time freshmen.
**Selectivity:** Open admission; but selective for some programs.

## BASIC COSTS (2016-2017)

**Tuition and fees:** $3,220; out-of-district residents $4,240; out-of-state residents $5,620.
**Room and board:** $6,994.

## FINANCIAL AID PICTURE (2014-2015)

**Students with need:** 74% of average financial aid package awarded as scholarships/grants, 26% awarded as loans/jobs. Need-based aid available for part-time students.
**Students without need:** No-need awards available for academics, alumni affiliation, art, athletics, leadership, music/drama, state/district residency.

## FINANCIAL AID PROCEDURES

**Forms required:** FAFSA.
**Dates and Deadlines:** Closing date 4/1. Applicants notified on a rolling basis starting 2/15; must reply within 4 week(s) of notification.

## CONTACT

Denise Sebastian, Financial Aid Director
PO Box 1000, Park Hills, MO 63601-1000
(573) 518-2133

# Missouri Baptist University
St. Louis, Missouri
www.mobap.edu                Federal Code: 007540

**4-year private** university and liberal arts college in very large city, affiliated with Baptist faith.
**Enrollment:** 1,719 undergrads, 23% part-time. 254 full-time freshmen.
**Selectivity:** Admits 50 to 75% of applicants.

## BASIC COSTS (2015-2016)

**Tuition and fees:** $23,750.
**Per-credit charge:** $782.
**Room and board:** $9,510.

## FINANCIAL AID PICTURE (2014-2015)

**Students with need:** 46% of average financial aid package awarded as scholarships/grants, 54% awarded as loans/jobs. Need-based aid available for part-time students. Work study available nights, weekends, and for part-time students.
**Students without need:** No-need awards available for academics, alumni affiliation, athletics, leadership, music/drama, religious affiliation.

## FINANCIAL AID PROCEDURES

**Forms required:** FAFSA, institutional form.
**Dates and Deadlines:** Priority date 4/1; no closing date. Applicants notified on a rolling basis starting 4/16; must reply within 2 week(s) of notification.
**Transfers:** Institutional academic scholarships available.

## CONTACT

John Brandt, Director of Student Financial Services
One College Park Drive, St. Louis, MO 63141-8660
(314) 392-2366

# Missouri College
Brentwood, Missouri
www.missouricollege.com       Federal Code: 009795

**2-year for-profit** technical college in large city.
**Enrollment:** 553 undergrads.
**Selectivity:** Open admission; but selective for some programs.

## BASIC COSTS (2015-2016)

**Additional info:** Diploma programs: $10,250-$15,050. Associate programs: $2,200-$35,501. Bachelor's programs: $37,270.

## FINANCIAL AID PICTURE

**Students with need:** Need-based aid available for full-time and part-time students. Work study available nights.

## FINANCIAL AID PROCEDURES

**Forms required:** FAFSA.

## CONTACT

Jennifer Malotte, Director of Student Finance
1405 South Hanley Road, Brentwood, MO 63144
(314) 821-7700

## Missouri Southern State University

Joplin, Missouri
www.mssu.edu                    Federal Code: 002488

**4-year public** university and liberal arts college in small city.
**Enrollment:** 5,202 undergrads, 21% part-time. 792 full-time freshmen.
**Selectivity:** Admits over 75% of applicants.

### BASIC COSTS (2015-2016)

**Tuition and fees:** $5,876; out-of-state residents $11,186.
**Per-credit charge:** $177; out-of-state residents $354.
**Room and board:** $6,622.
**Additional info:** Transportation and miscellaneous expenses $3303.

### FINANCIAL AID PICTURE (2014-2015)

**Students with need:** Out of 683 full-time freshmen who applied for aid, 402 were judged to have need. Of these, 400 received aid, and 100 had their full need met. Average financial aid package met 69% of need; average scholarship/grant was $4,822; average loan was $4,735. For part-time students, average financial aid package was $7,313.
**Students without need:** 101 full-time freshmen who did not demonstrate need for aid received scholarships/grants; average award was $2,481. No-need awards available for academics, alumni affiliation, art, athletics, job skills, leadership, minority status, music/drama, religious affiliation, state/district residency.
**Scholarships offered:** 77 full-time freshmen received athletic scholarships; average amount $2,855.

### FINANCIAL AID PROCEDURES

**Forms required:** FAFSA.
**Dates and Deadlines:** Applicants notified on a rolling basis starting 3/15; must reply by 5/1.

### CONTACT

Rebecca Diskin, Director of Student Financial Aid
3950 East Newman Road, Joplin, MO 64801-1595
(417) 625-9325

## Missouri State University

Springfield, Missouri
www.missouristate.edu           Federal Code: 002503

**4-year public** university in small city.
**Enrollment:** 16,617 undergrads, 13% part-time. 3,203 full-time freshmen.
**Selectivity:** Admits over 75% of applicants.

### BASIC COSTS (2015-2016)

**Tuition and fees:** $7,060; out-of-state residents $13,930.
**Per-credit charge:** $205; out-of-state residents $434.
**Room and board:** $7,868.

### FINANCIAL AID PICTURE (2015-2016)

**Students with need:** Out of 2,817 full-time freshmen who applied for aid, 2,011 were judged to have need. Of these, 1,984 received aid, and 359 had their full need met. Average financial aid package met 64% of need; average scholarship/grant was $6,329; average loan was $3,357. For part-time students, average financial aid package was $6,034.
**Students without need:** 543 full-time freshmen who did not demonstrate need for aid received scholarships/grants; average award was $3,149. No-need awards available for academics, alumni affiliation, art, athletics, job skills, leadership, minority status, music/drama, ROTC, state/district residency.
**Scholarships offered:** *Merit:* Presidential Scholarship: $12,500 per year plus a full waiver of non-resident fees for non-Missouri residents; based on 30 ACT and either top 10% class rank or 3.90 GPA; 30 awarded. Board of Governors Scholarship: $5,000 per year plus a full waiver of non-resident fees;

based on 28 ACT and either top 10% class rank or 3.90 GPA; unlimited number of awards. Provost Scholarship: $2,500 per year plus a full waiver of non-resident fees; based on 26 ACT and either top 20% class rank or 3.70 GPA; unlimited number of awards. Multicultural Leadership Scholarship: $6,250 per year for students in top half of class or 3.00 GPA and who have demonstrated leadership in multicultural school or community activities; 50 awarded. Dean's Scholarship: $1,500 per year plus a full waiver of non-resident fees; based on 24 ACT and either top 10% class rank or 3.90 GPA; unlimited number of awards. *Athletic:* 40 full-time freshmen received athletic scholarships; average amount $13,058.
**Additional info:** Extensive scholarship program offered to freshmen and transfer students. Out-of-state fee stipends available. Student employment service available to assist students in securing employment on campus and in community.

### FINANCIAL AID PROCEDURES

**Forms required:** FAFSA.
**Dates and Deadlines:** Priority date 3/31; no closing date. Applicants notified on a rolling basis starting 3/31; must reply within 4 week(s) of notification.
**Transfers:** No deadline. Applicants notified on a rolling basis.

### CONTACT

Vicki Mattocks, Director of Financial Aid
901 South National Avenue, Springfield, MO 65897
(417) 836-5262

## Missouri State University: West Plains

West Plains, Missouri
www.wp.missouristate.edu        Federal Code: 031060

**2-year public** branch campus and liberal arts college in large town.
**Enrollment:** 1,554 undergrads.
**Selectivity:** Open admission; but selective for some programs.

### BASIC COSTS (2015-2016)

**Tuition and fees:** $3,880; out-of-state residents $7,450.
**Per-credit charge:** $119; out-of-state residents $238.
**Room and board:** $5,590.

### FINANCIAL AID PICTURE

**Students with need:** Need-based aid available for full-time and part-time students. Work study available nights, weekends, and for part-time students.
**Students without need:** No-need awards available for academics, athletics, state/district residency.

### FINANCIAL AID PROCEDURES

**Forms required:** FAFSA, institutional form.
**Dates and Deadlines:** Priority date 3/31; no closing date. Applicants notified on a rolling basis; must reply by 4/15.

### CONTACT

Donna Bassham, Coordinator of Financial Aid
128 Garfield Avenue, West Plains, MO 65775-2715
(417) 255-7243

## Missouri Tech

St. Charles, Missouri
www.motech.edu                  Federal Code: 016272

**4-year for-profit** engineering and technical college in very large city.
**Enrollment:** 108 undergrads.

### BASIC COSTS (2015-2016)

**Additional info:** Certificate program: $11,337, books and supplies $825. Diploma programs: $28,092-$32,350, books and supplies $2,075-$2,400.

Associate programs: $42,882-$47,140, books and supplies $3,175-$3,500. Bachelor's programs: $82,995-$89,545, books and supplies $6,150-$6,650.

### FINANCIAL AID PICTURE

**Students with need:** Need-based aid available for full-time and part-time students.

**Students without need:** This college awards aid only to students with need.

### FINANCIAL AID PROCEDURES

**Forms required:** FAFSA, institutional form.

**Dates and Deadlines:** Applicants notified on a rolling basis.

### CONTACT

Cindy Ann Sinnott, Financial Aid Director
1690 Country Club Plaza Drive, St. Charles, MO 63303
(314) 569-3600 ext. 316

## Missouri University of Science and Technology
Rolla, Missouri
www.mst.edu                    Federal Code: 002517

**4-year public** university in large town.
**Enrollment:** 6,749 undergrads, 10% part-time. 1,273 full-time freshmen.
**Selectivity:** Admits over 75% of applicants.

### BASIC COSTS (2015-2016)

**Tuition and fees:** $9,784; out-of-state residents $26,308.
**Per-credit charge:** $277; out-of-state residents $827.
**Room and board:** $9,464.
**Additional info:** Tuition/fee waivers available for minority students.

### FINANCIAL AID PICTURE (2014-2015)

**Students with need:** Out of 715 full-time freshmen who applied for aid, 677 were judged to have need. Of these, 677 received aid, and 121 had their full need met. Average financial aid package met 33% of need; average scholarship/grant was $9,955; average loan was $6,606. For part-time students, average financial aid package was $7,313.

**Students without need:** 258 full-time freshmen who did not demonstrate need for aid received scholarships/grants; average award was $6,151. No-need awards available for academics, alumni affiliation, athletics, job skills, leadership, minority status, music/drama, religious affiliation, ROTC, state/district residency.

**Scholarships offered:** 56 full-time freshmen received athletic scholarships; average amount $9,402.

### FINANCIAL AID PROCEDURES

**Forms required:** FAFSA.

**Dates and Deadlines:** Priority date 3/1; no closing date. Applicants notified on a rolling basis starting 4/1; must reply within 3 week(s) of notification.

**Transfers:** Special scholarships available to transfer students.

### CONTACT

Bridgette Betz, Director of Financial Assistance
106 Parker Hall, Rolla, MO 65409-1060
(573) 341-4282

## Missouri Valley College
Marshall, Missouri
www.moval.edu                    Federal Code: 002489

**4-year private** liberal arts college in large town, affiliated with Presbyterian Church (USA).
**Enrollment:** 1,380 undergrads, 2% part-time. 434 full-time freshmen.
**Selectivity:** Admits less than 50% of applicants.

### BASIC COSTS (2015-2016)

**Tuition and fees:** $19,750.
**Room and board:** $8,400.
**Additional info:** Fees include all required books.

### FINANCIAL AID PICTURE

**Students with need:** Need-based aid available for full-time and part-time students. Work study available nights, weekends, and for part-time students.

**Students without need:** No-need awards available for academics, state/district residency.

**Scholarships offered:** Talent scholarships: $1,000 to $13,000; for general achievement, 100 awarded.

### FINANCIAL AID PROCEDURES

**Forms required:** FAFSA.

**Dates and Deadlines:** Priority date 3/15; no closing date. Applicants notified on a rolling basis starting 2/1; must reply within 6 week(s) of notification.

**Transfers:** No deadline. Applicants notified on a rolling basis starting 3/14; must reply within 3 week(s) of notification.

### CONTACT

Rachel Robinson, Director of Financial Aid
500 East College Street, Marshall, MO 65340
(660) 831-4176

## Missouri Western State University
St Joseph, Missouri
www.missouriwestern.edu          Federal Code: 002490

**4-year public** university and liberal arts college in small city.
**Enrollment:** 4,420 undergrads, 18% part-time. 803 full-time freshmen.
**Selectivity:** Open admission; but selective for some programs.

### BASIC COSTS (2015-2016)

**Tuition and fees:** $6,652; out-of-state residents $12,810.
**Per-credit charge:** $198; out-of-state residents $403.
**Room and board:** $8,565.

### FINANCIAL AID PICTURE

**Students with need:** Need-based aid available for full-time and part-time students.

**Students without need:** No-need awards available for academics, alumni affiliation, art, athletics, job skills, leadership, minority status, music/drama, state/district residency.

**Scholarships offered:** Golden Griffon Scholarship: up to $10,000 per year for 4 years; 27 ACT, top 10% of class or 3.5 GPA; evidence of involvement in extracurricular activities and community service; 2 essays and personal interview required; application deadline 2/1. President's Academic Scholarship: up to $4,000 per year; 25 ACT and either rank in the top 15% of class or 3.25 GPA required; application deadline 3/1.

### FINANCIAL AID PROCEDURES

**Forms required:** FAFSA, institutional form.

**Dates and Deadlines:** Priority date 3/1; no closing date. Applicants notified on a rolling basis starting 4/5; must reply within 3 week(s) of notification.

**Transfers:** No deadline. Applicants notified on a rolling basis starting 4/15; must reply within 2 week(s) of notification.

### CONTACT

Marilyn Baker, Director of Financial Aid
4525 Downs Drive, Saint Joseph, MO 64507
(816) 271-4361

## Moberly Area Community College
Moberly, Missouri
www.macc.edu     Federal Code: 002491

**2-year public** community college in large town.
**Enrollment:** 5,800 undergrads.
**Selectivity:** Open admission; but selective for some programs.

### BASIC COSTS (2015-2016)
**Tuition and fees:** $3,060; out-of-district residents $4,590; out-of-state residents $6,120.
**Per-credit charge:** $86; out-of-district residents $137; out-of-state residents $188.
**Room and board:** $4,600.

### FINANCIAL AID PICTURE
**Students with need:** Need-based aid available for full-time and part-time students. Work study available nights, weekends, and for part-time students.
**Students without need:** No-need awards available for academics, alumni affiliation, art, athletics, leadership, music/drama.

### FINANCIAL AID PROCEDURES
**Forms required:** FAFSA.
**Dates and Deadlines:** Priority date 4/1; no closing date. Applicants notified on a rolling basis starting 4/1; must reply by 7/15 or within 2 week(s) of notification.

### CONTACT
Amy Hager, Director of Financial Aid
101 College Avenue, Moberly, MO 65270-1304
(660) 263-4110 ext. 301

## National American University: Kansas City
Independence, Missouri
www.national.edu

**4-year for-profit** university in large city.
**Enrollment:** 646 undergrads.
**Selectivity:** Open admission.

### BASIC COSTS (2015-2016)
**Tuition and fees:** $15,885.
**Per-credit charge:** $333.
**Additional info:** Additional fees may apply.

### FINANCIAL AID PICTURE
**Students with need:** Need-based aid available for full-time and part-time students. Work study available nights, weekends, and for part-time students.
**Students without need:** This college awards aid only to students with need.

### FINANCIAL AID PROCEDURES
**Forms required:** FAFSA, institutional form.
**Dates and Deadlines:** Applicants notified on a rolling basis starting 6/4.

### CONTACT
Katie Williams, Financial Services Advisor
3620 Arrowhead Avenue, Independence, MO 64057
(816) 412-7736

## North Central Missouri College
Trenton, Missouri
www.ncmissouri.edu     Federal Code: 002514

**2-year public** community college in small town.
**Enrollment:** 1,085 undergrads.

**Selectivity:** Open admission; but selective for some programs.

### BASIC COSTS (2015-2016)
**Tuition and fees:** $3,180; out-of-district residents $4,170; out-of-state residents $5,340.
**Per-credit charge:** $76; out-of-district residents $109; out-of-state residents $148.
**Room and board:** $5,734.

### FINANCIAL AID PICTURE
**Students with need:** Need-based aid available for full-time and part-time students.
**Students without need:** No-need awards available for academics, athletics, leadership.

### FINANCIAL AID PROCEDURES
**Forms required:** FAFSA, institutional form.
**Dates and Deadlines:** Priority date 7/1; no closing date. Applicants notified on a rolling basis starting 3/15.
**Transfers:** No deadline. Applicants notified on a rolling basis starting 4/1. Transfer students may not receive same awards after transferring since some funds campus-based.

### CONTACT
Megan DeWitt, Financial Aid Director
1301 Main Street, Trenton, MO 64683
(660) 359-3948 ext. 1402

## Northwest Missouri State University
Maryville, Missouri
www.nwmissouri.edu     Federal Code: 002496

**4-year public** university in large town.
**Enrollment:** 5,288 undergrads, 7% part-time. 1,407 full-time freshmen.
**Selectivity:** Admits 50 to 75% of applicants.

### BASIC COSTS (2015-2016)
**Tuition and fees:** $8,459; out-of-state residents $14,779.
**Per-credit charge:** $282; out-of-state residents $492.
**Room and board:** $9,538.
**Additional info:** Tuition/fee waivers available for minority students.

### FINANCIAL AID PICTURE (2014-2015)
**Students with need:** Out of 1,210 full-time freshmen who applied for aid, 903 were judged to have need. Of these, 903 received aid, and 618 had their full need met. Average financial aid package met 77% of need; average scholarship/grant was $7,444; average loan was $3,282. For part-time students, average financial aid package was $4,818.
**Students without need:** 167 full-time freshmen who did not demonstrate need for aid received scholarships/grants; average award was $3,530. No-need awards available for academics, alumni affiliation, art, athletics, job skills, leadership, minority status, music/drama, ROTC, state/district residency.
**Scholarships offered:** 33 full-time freshmen received athletic scholarships; average amount $5,881.

### FINANCIAL AID PROCEDURES
**Forms required:** FAFSA.
**Dates and Deadlines:** Priority date 4/1; no closing date. Applicants notified on a rolling basis starting 3/15.
**Transfers:** No deadline. Applicants notified on a rolling basis starting 5/10; must reply within 4 week(s) of notification. Transfer scholarship based on academic record.

### CONTACT
Del Morley, Director of Financial Assistance
800 University Drive, Maryville, MO 64468-6001
(660) 562-1363

## Ozark Christian College

Joplin, Missouri
www.occ.edu                    Federal Code: 015569

**4-year private** Bible college in small city, affiliated with nondenominational tradition.
**Enrollment:** 742 undergrads.
**Selectivity:** Open admission.

### BASIC COSTS (2015-2016)
**Tuition and fees:** $11,110.
**Per-credit charge:** $345.
**Room and board:** $4,820.

### FINANCIAL AID PICTURE
**Students with need:** Need-based aid available for full-time and part-time students.
**Students without need:** No-need awards available for academics, leadership.

### FINANCIAL AID PROCEDURES
**Forms required:** FAFSA.
**Dates and Deadlines:** Priority date 4/1; no closing date. Applicants notified on a rolling basis starting 4/15; must reply within 3 week(s) of notification.
**Transfers:** Academic transcripts required. ACT scores may qualify student for grants or scholarships.

### CONTACT
Kim Balentine, Director of Financial Aid
1111 North Main Street, Joplin, MO 64801
(417) 624-2518

## Ozarks Technical Community College

Springfield, Missouri
www.otc.edu                    Federal Code: 030830

**2-year public** community and technical college in small city.
**Enrollment:** 13,614 undergrads.
**Selectivity:** Open admission; but selective for some programs.

### BASIC COSTS (2015-2016)
**Tuition and fees:** $3,600; out-of-district residents $5,070; out-of-state residents $6,540.
**Per-credit charge:** $98; out-of-district residents $147; out-of-state residents $196.

### FINANCIAL AID PICTURE (2014-2015)
**Students with need:** 63% of average financial aid package awarded as scholarships/grants, 37% awarded as loans/jobs. Need-based aid available for part-time students.
**Students without need:** This college awards aid only to students with need.

### FINANCIAL AID PROCEDURES
**Forms required:** FAFSA, institutional form.
**Dates and Deadlines:** Closing date 3/31. Applicants notified on a rolling basis starting 5/16.

### CONTACT
Jeff Ford, College Director of Financial Aid
1001 East Chestnut Expressway, Springfield, MO 65802
(417) 447-6930

## Park University

Parkville, Missouri
www.park.edu                    Federal Code: 002498

**4-year private** university in small town.
**Enrollment:** 8,502 undergrads.
**Selectivity:** Admits less than 50% of applicants.

### BASIC COSTS (2015-2016)
**Tuition and fees:** $11,470.
**Per-credit charge:** $369.
**Room and board:** $7,672.
**Additional info:** Active-Duty Military and their dependents; $250 per-credit-hour. Veterans and their dependents; $310 per-credit-hour.

### FINANCIAL AID PICTURE (2014-2015)
**Students with need:** Need-based aid available for full-time and part-time students. Work study available nights, weekends, and for part-time students.
**Students without need:** No-need awards available for academics, alumni affiliation, art, athletics, music/drama.

### FINANCIAL AID PROCEDURES
**Forms required:** FAFSA, institutional form.
**Dates and Deadlines:** Priority date 4/1; closing date 8/1. Applicants notified on a rolling basis starting 4/1; must reply by 8/1 or within 4 week(s) of notification.
**Transfers:** Priority date 4/1; closing date 8/1. Applicants notified on a rolling basis starting 8/1; must reply within 4 week(s) of notification.

### CONTACT
Cathy Colapietro, Executive Director of Student Financial Services
8700 NW River Park Drive, Parkville, MO 64152
(816) 584-6290

## Ranken Technical College

St. Louis, Missouri
www.ranken.edu                    Federal Code: 012500

**2-year private** technical college in very large city.
**Enrollment:** 1,929 undergrads.
**Selectivity:** Open admission.

### FINANCIAL AID PICTURE
**Students with need:** Need-based aid available for full-time and part-time students. Work study available nights.

### FINANCIAL AID PROCEDURES
**Forms required:** FAFSA, institutional form.
**Dates and Deadlines:** Priority date 4/1; no closing date. Applicants notified on a rolling basis starting 4/1.

### CONTACT
Michelle Williams, Financial Aid Director
4431 Finney Avenue, St. Louis, MO 63113
(314) 286-4863

## Research College of Nursing

Kansas City, Missouri
www.researchcollege.edu                    Federal Code: 006392

**4-year for-profit** nursing college in very large city.
**Enrollment:** 293 undergrads, 2% part-time. 57 full-time freshmen.
**Selectivity:** Admits over 75% of applicants.

### BASIC COSTS (2015-2016)
**Tuition and fees:** $34,790.

**Room and board:** $9,055.

**FINANCIAL AID PICTURE**

**Students with need:** Need-based aid available for full-time students.

**Students without need:** No-need awards available for academics, leadership.

**Additional info:** Financial aid handled by Rockhurst University for freshmen and sophomores.

**FINANCIAL AID PROCEDURES**

**Forms required:** FAFSA, institutional form.

**Dates and Deadlines:** Priority date 3/15; no closing date. Applicants notified on a rolling basis starting 3/15.

**Transfers:** Priority date 4/1; no deadline. Applicants notified by 5/1.

**CONTACT**

Maureen McKinnon, Interim Director of Financial Aid

2525 East Meyer Boulevard, Kansas City, MO 64132-1199

(816) 995-2814

## Rockhurst University
Kansas City, Missouri
ww2.rockhurst.edu          Federal Code: 002499

**4-year private** business and liberal arts college in very large city, affiliated with Roman Catholic Church.

**Enrollment:** 1,542 undergrads, 7% part-time. 398 full-time freshmen.

**Selectivity:** Admits 50 to 75% of applicants.

**BASIC COSTS (2016-2017)**

**Tuition and fees:** $34,790.

**Per-credit charge:** $1,134.

**Room and board:** $9,056.

**FINANCIAL AID PICTURE (2014-2015)**

**Students with need:** Out of 361 full-time freshmen who applied for aid, 272 were judged to have need. Of these, 272 received aid, and 49 had their full need met. Average financial aid package met 82% of need; average scholarship/grant was $2,688; average loan was $5,838. For part-time students, average financial aid package was $9,358.

**Students without need:** 70 full-time freshmen who did not demonstrate need for aid received scholarships/grants; average award was $22,957. No-need awards available for academics, alumni affiliation, athletics, leadership, music/drama.

**Scholarships offered:** 57 full-time freshmen received athletic scholarships; average amount $14,637.

**Additional info:** Auditions, portfolios required for some scholarships.

**FINANCIAL AID PROCEDURES**

**Forms required:** FAFSA.

**Dates and Deadlines:** Priority date 3/1; no closing date. Applicants notified on a rolling basis starting 3/1; must reply within 4 week(s) of notification.

**Transfers:** No deadline. Applicants notified on a rolling basis starting 1/30; must reply within 4 week(s) of notification. Scholarships awarded to qualified first-time transfers.

**CONTACT**

Maureen McKinnon, Director of Financial Aid

1100 Rockhurst Road, Kansas City, MO 64110-2561

(816) 501-4600

## St. Charles Community College
Cottleville, Missouri
www.stchas.edu          Federal Code: 017027

**2-year public** community college in small city.

**Enrollment:** 6,301 undergrads, 47% part-time. 1,148 full-time freshmen.

**Selectivity:** Open admission; but selective for some programs.

**BASIC COSTS (2016-2017)**

**Tuition and fees:** $3,090; out-of-district residents $4,560; out-of-state residents $6,600.

**Per-credit charge:** $98; out-of-district residents $147; out-of-state residents $215.

**FINANCIAL AID PICTURE (2014-2015)**

**Students with need:** 79% of average financial aid package awarded as scholarships/grants, 21% awarded as loans/jobs. Need-based aid available for part-time students.

**Students without need:** No-need awards available for academics, art, athletics, leadership, music/drama.

**FINANCIAL AID PROCEDURES**

**Forms required:** FAFSA, institutional form.

**Dates and Deadlines:** Priority date 6/1; no closing date. Applicants notified on a rolling basis starting 4/1; must reply by 8/1.

**Transfers:** Applicants notified on a rolling basis starting 4/1; must reply by 8/1.

**CONTACT**

Kathy Brockgreitens-Gober, Dean of Enrollment Services

4601 Mid Rivers Mall Drive, Cottleville, MO 63376

(636) 922-8270

## St. Louis Christian College
Florissant, Missouri
www.stlchristian.edu          Federal Code: 012580

**4-year private** Bible college in small city, affiliated with Christian Church.

**Enrollment:** 153 undergrads, 18% part-time. 14 full-time freshmen.

**Selectivity:** Admits less than 50% of applicants.

**BASIC COSTS (2015-2016)**

**Tuition and fees:** $9,750.

**Per-credit charge:** $325.

**Room and board:** $4,600.

**FINANCIAL AID PICTURE (2015-2016)**

**Students with need:** Out of 13 full-time freshmen who applied for aid, 12 were judged to have need. Of these, 12 received aid. Average financial aid package met 51% of need; average scholarship/grant was $4,883; average loan was $3,500. For part-time students, average financial aid package was $4,820.

**FINANCIAL AID PROCEDURES**

**Forms required:** FAFSA.

**Dates and Deadlines:** Closing date 8/1. Applicants notified on a rolling basis starting 7/20; must reply within 2 week(s) of notification.

**CONTACT**

Pam Ralls, Financial Aid Director

1360 Grandview Drive, Florissant, MO 63033

(314) 837-6777 ext. 1101

## St. Louis Community College
Saint Louis, Missouri
www.stlcc.edu          Federal Code: 002469

**2-year public** community and junior college in large city.

**Enrollment:** 8,820 undergrads.

**Selectivity:** Open admission.

**BASIC COSTS (2015-2016)**

**Tuition and fees:** $3,090; out-of-district residents $4,470; out-of-state residents $6,150.

**Per-credit charge:** $103; out-of-district residents $149; out-of-state residents $205.

**FINANCIAL AID PICTURE**

**Students with need:** Need-based aid available for full-time and part-time students.

**Students without need:** No-need awards available for academics, art, athletics, leadership, music/drama.

**FINANCIAL AID PROCEDURES**

**Forms required:** FAFSA.

**Dates and Deadlines:** Priority date 4/15; no closing date. Applicants notified on a rolling basis starting 4/1.

**CONTACT**

Paulette Johnson, Manager of Student Financial Aid
300 South Broadway, St. Louis, MO 63102-2800
(314) 644-9117

## Saint Louis University
Saint Louis, Missouri
www.slu.edu          Federal Code: 002506

**4-year private** university in very large city, affiliated with Roman Catholic Church.

**Enrollment:** 7,973 undergrads, 9% part-time. 1,605 full-time freshmen.

**Selectivity:** Admits 50 to 75% of applicants.

**BASIC COSTS (2015-2016)**

**Tuition and fees:** $39,226.

**Per-credit charge:** $1,350.

**Room and board:** $10,640.

**Additional info:** Tuition/fee waivers available for unemployed or children of unemployed.

**FINANCIAL AID PICTURE (2014-2015)**

**Students with need:** Out of 1,329 full-time freshmen who applied for aid, 1,055 were judged to have need. Of these, 1,055 received aid, and 271 had their full need met. Average financial aid package met 76% of need; average scholarship/grant was $23,362; average loan was $3,691. For part-time students, average financial aid package was $7,620.

**Students without need:** 468 full-time freshmen who did not demonstrate need for aid received scholarships/grants; average award was $16,024. No-need awards available for academics, art, athletics, leadership, music/drama, religious affiliation, ROTC.

**Scholarships offered:** *Merit:* Scholarships available for $3,000-$16,000; based on academic achievement, test scores, leadership, and community service. *Athletic:* 48 full-time freshmen received athletic scholarships; average amount $19,118.

**Additional info:** Presidential Scholarship applications due 12/1. Martin Luther King Jr. Scholarship applications have priority date of 2/1. Emergency Scholarship Fund available to assist students and families with special circumstances. Loan program available to assist some students without other financing options. Will match, dollar for dollar, all qualified scholarship gifts of $100 and more.

**FINANCIAL AID PROCEDURES**

**Forms required:** FAFSA.

**Dates and Deadlines:** Priority date 3/1; no closing date. Applicants notified on a rolling basis starting 3/15; must reply by 5/1 or within 4 week(s) of notification.

**Transfers:** No deadline. Applicants notified on a rolling basis starting 3/15; must reply by 5/1 or within 4 week(s) of notification. Students should file FAFSA by 4/1 for Missouri State Funds.

**CONTACT**

Cari Wickliffe, Asst. V.P. and Director of Student Financial Services
One North Grand Boulevard, St. Louis, MO 63103
(314) 977-2350

## St. Luke's College
Kansas City, Missouri
www.saintlukescollege.edu          Federal Code: 009782

**Upper-division private** nursing college in large city, affiliated with Episcopal Church.

**Enrollment:** 434 undergrads.

**BASIC COSTS (2015-2016)**

**Tuition and fees:** $15,164.

**Per-credit charge:** $452.

**FINANCIAL AID PICTURE**

**Students with need:** Need-based aid available for full-time and part-time students.

**FINANCIAL AID PROCEDURES**

**Transfers:** Priority date 4/1; no deadline. Applicants notified on a rolling basis; must reply within 3 week(s) of notification.

**CONTACT**

Jennifer Wright, Director of Financial Aid
624 Westport Road, Kansas City, MO 64111
(816) 932-6742

## Southeast Missouri State University
Cape Girardeau, Missouri
www.semo.edu          Federal Code: 002501

**4-year public** university in large town.

**Enrollment:** 9,098 undergrads, 15% part-time. 1,718 full-time freshmen.

**Selectivity:** Admits over 75% of applicants.

**BASIC COSTS (2016-2017)**

**Tuition and fees:** $6,990; out-of-state residents $12,375.

**Per-credit charge:** $199.3; out-of-state residents $378.8.

**Room and board:** $8,285.

**FINANCIAL AID PICTURE (2014-2015)**

**Students with need:** Out of 1,503 full-time freshmen who applied for aid, 1,101 were judged to have need. Of these, 1,086 received aid, and 148 had their full need met. Average financial aid package met 58% of need; average scholarship/grant was $6,522; average loan was $3,255. For part-time students, average financial aid package was $5,505.

**Students without need:** 409 full-time freshmen who did not demonstrate need for aid received scholarships/grants; average award was $4,430. No-need awards available for academics, alumni affiliation, art, athletics, job skills, leadership, minority status, music/drama, ROTC, state/district residency.

**Scholarships offered:** 38 full-time freshmen received athletic scholarships; average amount $13,475.

**FINANCIAL AID PROCEDURES**

**Forms required:** FAFSA.

**Dates and Deadlines:** Priority date 3/1; no closing date. Applicants notified on a rolling basis starting 4/1; must reply within 3 week(s) of notification.

**Transfers:** Must reply by 8/20 or within 3 week(s) of notification.

**CONTACT**

Karen Walker, Director of Financial Aid Services
One University Plaza MS 3550, Cape Girardeau, MO 63701
(573) 651-2253

## Southwest Baptist University
Bolivar, Missouri
www.sbuniv.edu                    Federal Code: 002502

**4-year private** university in large town, affiliated with Southern Baptist Convention.
**Enrollment:** 2,394 undergrads, 21% part-time. 390 full-time freshmen.

### BASIC COSTS (2015-2016)
**Tuition and fees:** $21,840.
**Room and board:** $7,160.

### FINANCIAL AID PICTURE
**Students with need:** Need-based aid available for full-time and part-time students. Work study available nights, weekends, and for part-time students.
**Students without need:** No-need awards available for academics, alumni affiliation, art, athletics, minority status, music/drama, religious affiliation.

### FINANCIAL AID PROCEDURES
**Forms required:** FAFSA.
**Dates and Deadlines:** Priority date 3/15; no closing date. Applicants notified on a rolling basis starting 3/1; must reply within 2 week(s) of notification.

### CONTACT
Brad Gamble, Director of Financial Aid
1600 University Avenue, Bolivar, MO 65613-2597
(417) 328-1822

## State Fair Community College
Sedalia, Missouri
www.sfccmo.edu                    Federal Code: 007628

**2-year public** community college in large town.
**Enrollment:** 4,050 undergrads.
**Selectivity:** Open admission; but selective for some programs.

### BASIC COSTS (2015-2016)
**Tuition and fees:** $3,000; out-of-district residents $4,200; out-of-state residents $6,000.
**Per-credit charge:** $100; out-of-district residents $140; out-of-state residents $200.
**Room and board:** $5,100.

### FINANCIAL AID PICTURE
**Students with need:** Need-based aid available for full-time and part-time students. Work study available nights, weekends, and for part-time students.
**Students without need:** No-need awards available for academics, art, athletics, music/drama, state/district residency.

### FINANCIAL AID PROCEDURES
**Forms required:** FAFSA.
**Dates and Deadlines:** Priority date 7/1; no closing date. Applicants notified on a rolling basis starting 7/15; must reply within 3 week(s) of notification.
**Transfers:** No deadline. Applicants notified on a rolling basis starting 7/15; must reply within 3 week(s) of notification.

### CONTACT
Lana DeJaynes, Director of Financial Aid
3201 West 16th Street, Sedalia, MO 65301-2199
(660) 596-7295

## State Technical College of Missouri
Linn, Missouri
www.statetechmo.edu                    Federal Code: 004711

**2-year public** technical college in rural community.
**Enrollment:** 1,171 undergrads, 9% part-time. 503 full-time freshmen.

**Selectivity:** Open admission; but selective for some programs.

### BASIC COSTS (2016-2017)
**Tuition and fees:** $5,873; out-of-state residents $10,665.
**Per-credit charge:** $159.75; out-of-state residents $319.5.
**Room and board:** $5,300.

### FINANCIAL AID PICTURE (2014-2015)
**Students with need:** Out of 464 full-time freshmen who applied for aid, 371 were judged to have need. Of these, 371 received aid, and 77 had their full need met. Average financial aid package met 9% of need; average scholarship/grant was $4,809; average loan was $2,913. Need-based aid available for part-time students.
**Students without need:** 11 full-time freshmen who did not demonstrate need for aid received scholarships/grants; average award was $733. No-need awards available for academics, alumni affiliation, state/district residency.
**Scholarships offered:** 24 full-time freshmen received athletic scholarships; average amount $888.

### FINANCIAL AID PROCEDURES
**Forms required:** FAFSA.
**Dates and Deadlines:** Priority date 4/1; no closing date. Applicants notified on a rolling basis starting 4/1; must reply within 3 week(s) of notification.

### CONTACT
Becky Whithaus, Director of Financial Aid
One Technology Drive, Linn, MO 65051
(573) 897-5143

## Stephens College
Columbia, Missouri
www.stephens.edu                    Federal Code: 002512

**4-year private** liberal arts and career college for women in small city.
**Enrollment:** 706 undergrads, 16% part-time. 190 full-time freshmen.
**Selectivity:** Admits 50 to 75% of applicants.

### BASIC COSTS (2015-2016)
**Tuition and fees:** $29,176.
**Room and board:** $9,818.

### FINANCIAL AID PICTURE (2014-2015)
**Students with need:** 49% of average financial aid package awarded as scholarships/grants, 51% awarded as loans/jobs. Need-based aid available for part-time students. Work study available nights, weekends, and for part-time students.
**Students without need:** No-need awards available for academics, alumni affiliation, athletics, leadership, music/drama, state/district residency.
**Scholarships offered:** Stephens Scholars: 75% to 100% tuition for 4 years; competitive for accepted students with 25 ACT/1700 SAT and 3.5 GPA through essays and on-campus interviews; 6 available.

### FINANCIAL AID PROCEDURES
**Forms required:** FAFSA.
**Dates and Deadlines:** Priority date 3/15; no closing date. Applicants notified on a rolling basis starting 3/1.
**Transfers:** Phi Theta Kappa students transferring from 2-year institutions eligible for scholarship.

### CONTACT
Kim Stonecipher-Fisher, Director of Financial Aid
1200 East Broadway, Columbia, MO 65215
(800) 876-7106

## Stevens Institute of Business & Arts

St. Louis, Missouri
www.siba.edu                    Federal Code: 008552

**2-year for-profit** business and liberal arts college in very large city.
**Enrollment:** 61 undergrads. 46 full-time freshmen.
**Selectivity:** Open admission; but selective for some programs.

### FINANCIAL AID PICTURE
**Students with need:** Need-based aid available for full-time and part-time students.
**Students without need:** This college awards aid only to students with need.

### FINANCIAL AID PROCEDURES
**Forms required:** FAFSA.
**Dates and Deadlines:** Applicants notified on a rolling basis.

### CONTACT
Chrissa Siampos, Financial Aid Director
1521 Washington Avenue, St. Louis, MO 63103
(314) 421-0949 ext. 1405

## Texas County Technical College

Houston, Missouri
www.texascountytech.edu         Federal Code: 035793

**2-year private** nursing and technical college in small town.
**Enrollment:** 17 undergrads.
**Selectivity:** Open admission.

### BASIC COSTS (2015-2016)
**Tuition and fees:** $13,348.
**Per-credit charge:** $428.
**Additional info:** Annual fees cost range by the program from $450-$2,794.

### FINANCIAL AID PICTURE (2014-2015)
**Students with need:** Need-based aid available for full-time and part-time students.
**Students without need:** This college awards aid only to students with need.

### FINANCIAL AID PROCEDURES
**Forms required:** FAFSA, state aid form, institutional form.
**Transfers:** No deadline. Applicants notified on a rolling basis.

### CONTACT
Clarice Casebeer, Director of Financial Aid
6915 South Highway 63, Houston, MO 65483
(417) 967-5466

## Three Rivers Community College

Poplar Bluff, Missouri
www.trcc.edu                    Federal Code: 004713

**2-year public** community college in large town.
**Enrollment:** 3,087 undergrads.
**Selectivity:** Open admission; but selective for some programs.

### BASIC COSTS (2015-2016)
**Tuition and fees:** $3,420; out-of-district residents $4,890; out-of-state residents $5,970.
**Per-credit charge:** $85; out-of-district residents $134; out-of-state residents $170.
**Room only:** $3,440.

### FINANCIAL AID PICTURE
**Students with need:** Need-based aid available for full-time and part-time students.
**Students without need:** No-need awards available for academics, athletics, state/district residency.

### FINANCIAL AID PROCEDURES
**Forms required:** FAFSA, institutional form.
**Dates and Deadlines:** Priority date 4/1; no closing date. Applicants notified on a rolling basis starting 6/1; must reply within 2 week(s) of notification.

### CONTACT
Laura Milligan
2080 Three Rivers Boulevard, Poplar Bluff, MO 63901-1308
(573) 840-9607

## Truman State University

Kirksville, Missouri
www.truman.edu                  Federal Code: 002495

**4-year public** university and liberal arts college in large town.
**Enrollment:** 5,290 undergrads, 3% part-time. 1,317 full-time freshmen.
**Selectivity:** Admits over 75% of applicants.

### BASIC COSTS (2015-2016)
**Tuition and fees:** $7,430; out-of-state residents $13,654.
**Per-credit charge:** $298; out-of-state residents $557.
**Room and board:** $8,480.

### FINANCIAL AID PICTURE (2014-2015)
**Students with need:** Out of 1,141 full-time freshmen who applied for aid, 739 were judged to have need. Of these, 739 received aid, and 317 had their full need met. Average financial aid package met 88% of need; average scholarship/grant was $8,180; average loan was $3,663. For part-time students, average financial aid package was $7,588.
**Students without need:** 549 full-time freshmen who did not demonstrate need for aid received scholarships/grants; average award was $5,589. No-need awards available for academics, alumni affiliation, art, athletics, leadership, minority status, music/drama, ROTC, state/district residency.
**Scholarships offered:** *Merit:* Pershing Scholarship: up to full-tuition, average room and board price, up to $4,000 for study-abroad; awarded to outstanding scholars and leaders; 12 awarded. Truman Leadership Award: up to full-tuition, average room and board price; awarded to Missouri residents for demonstrated leadership and academic achievement. Non-Resident Tuition Scholarship: $2,000-$5,000; Available to non-Missouri resident freshmen who meet specified academic parameters to assist with the non-resident portion of tuition; unlimited number available. President's Combined Ability: $2,000-$3,000; specified academic parameters based on GPA & standardized test scores; unlimited number available. *Athletic:* 92 full-time freshmen received athletic scholarships; average amount $4,379.

### FINANCIAL AID PROCEDURES
**Forms required:** FAFSA.
**Dates and Deadlines:** Priority date 4/1; no closing date. Applicants notified on a rolling basis starting 3/1.
**Transfers:** Applicants notified on a rolling basis starting 3/1. Limited number of automatic and competitive awards offered to transfer students.

### CONTACT
Kathy Elsea, Financial Aid Director
100 East Normal Avenue, Kirksville, MO 63501
(660) 785-4130

# University of Central Missouri
Warrensburg, Missouri
www.ucmo.edu                    Federal Code: 02454

**4-year public** university in large town.
**Enrollment:** 9,017 undergrads, 11% part-time. 1,687 full-time freshmen.
**Selectivity:** Admits over 75% of applicants.

## BASIC COSTS (2015-2016)
**Tuition and fees:** $7,321; out-of-state residents $13,767.
**Per-credit charge:** $214; out-of-state residents $429.
**Room and board:** $8,102.

## FINANCIAL AID PICTURE (2014-2015)
**Students with need:** Out of 1,554 full-time freshmen who applied for aid, 1,141 were judged to have need. Of these, 1,141 received aid, and 172 had their full need met. Average financial aid package met 68% of need; average scholarship/grant was $4,242. For part-time students, average financial aid package was $5,656.
**Students without need:** 344 full-time freshmen who did not demonstrate need for aid received scholarships/grants; average award was $2,436. No-need awards available for academics, alumni affiliation, art, athletics, leadership, minority status, music/drama, religious affiliation, ROTC, state/district residency.
**Scholarships offered:** 64 full-time freshmen received athletic scholarships; average amount $5,682.

## FINANCIAL AID PROCEDURES
**Forms required:** FAFSA, institutional form.
**Dates and Deadlines:** Priority date 3/1; no closing date. Applicants notified on a rolling basis starting 3/1; must reply within 2 week(s) of notification.
**Transfers:** No deadline. Must reply within 2 week(s) of notification.

## CONTACT
Angela Karlin, Director of Student Financial Assistance
WDE 1400, Warrensburg, MO 64093
(660) 543-8080

# University of Missouri: Columbia
Columbia, Missouri
www.missouri.edu                Federal Code: 002516

**4-year public** university in small city.
**Enrollment:** 27,393 undergrads, 5% part-time. 6,035 full-time freshmen.
**Selectivity:** Admits over 75% of applicants.

## FINANCIAL AID PICTURE
**Students with need:** Need-based aid available for full-time and part-time students. Work study available nights, weekends, and for part-time students.
**Students without need:** No-need awards available for academics, alumni affiliation, art, athletics, leadership, minority status, music/drama, ROTC, state/district residency.
**Additional info:** Scholarship available for international students based on success during 1st semester.

## FINANCIAL AID PROCEDURES
**Forms required:** FAFSA.
**Dates and Deadlines:** Priority date 3/1; no closing date. Applicants notified on a rolling basis starting 4/1; must reply within 4 week(s) of notification.
**Transfers:** No deadline. Applicants notified on a rolling basis starting 4/1; must reply within 4 week(s) of notification.

## CONTACT
Nicholas Prewett, Director of Student Financial Aid
230 Jesse Hall, Columbia, MO 65211
(573) 882-7506

# University of Missouri: Kansas City
Kansas City, Missouri
www.umkc.edu                    Federal Code: 002518

**4-year public** university in large city.
**Enrollment:** 7,977 undergrads, 19% part-time. 1,021 full-time freshmen.
**Selectivity:** Admits 50 to 75% of applicants.

## BASIC COSTS (2015-2016)
**Tuition and fees:** $9,559; out-of-state residents $22,714.
**Per-credit charge:** $272; out-of-state residents $711.
**Room and board:** $9,772.

## FINANCIAL AID PICTURE (2015-2016)
**Students with need:** Out of 887 full-time freshmen who applied for aid, 692 were judged to have need. Of these, 675 received aid, and 88 had their full need met. Average financial aid package met 62% of need; average scholarship/grant was $8,510; average loan was $5,937. For part-time students, average financial aid package was $6,200.
**Students without need:** 196 full-time freshmen who did not demonstrate need for aid received scholarships/grants; average award was $5,971. No-need awards available for academics, alumni affiliation, art, athletics, leadership, minority status, music/drama, state/district residency.
**Scholarships offered:** *Merit:* Trustees Scholarship available that covers most educational expenses. *Athletic:* 24 full-time freshmen received athletic scholarships; average amount $16,562.
**Additional info:** Many automatic scholarships and non-resident fee waivers available for students who apply for admission by 2/1. Automatic awards range from $1,000 to a complete non-resident fee differential.

## FINANCIAL AID PROCEDURES
**Forms required:** FAFSA.
**Dates and Deadlines:** Priority date 3/1; no closing date. Applicants notified on a rolling basis starting 4/15; must reply within 2 week(s) of notification.
**Transfers:** Applicants notified on a rolling basis; must reply within 2 week(s) of notification.

## CONTACT
Scott Young, Director of Student Financial Aid
5100 Rockhill Road, AC120, Kansas City, MO 64110-2499
(816) 235-1154

# University of Missouri: St. Louis
St. Louis, Missouri
www.umsl.edu                    Federal Code: 002519

**4-year public** university in very large city.
**Enrollment:** 8,276 undergrads, 33% part-time. 501 full-time freshmen.
**Selectivity:** Admits over 75% of applicants.

## BASIC COSTS (2015-2016)
**Tuition and fees:** $10,065; out-of-state residents $25,512.
**Per-credit charge:** $335; out-of-state residents $850.
**Room and board:** $9,052.

## FINANCIAL AID PICTURE (2015-2016)
**Students with need:** Out of 429 full-time freshmen who applied for aid, 366 were judged to have need. Of these, 363 received aid, and 114 had their full need met. Average financial aid package met 79% of need; average scholarship/grant was $11,204; average loan was $3,285. For part-time students, average financial aid package was $6,853.
**Students without need:** 64 full-time freshmen who did not demonstrate need for aid received scholarships/grants; average award was $6,752. No-need awards available for academics, alumni affiliation, art, athletics, music/drama, ROTC, state/district residency.
**Scholarships offered:** *Merit:* Curators' Scholarship: $7,000; 28 ACT, top 5% of high school class, Missouri resident. Chancellor's Scholarship: $5,000; 26

ACT, top 10% of high school class. **Athletic:** 11 full-time freshmen received athletic scholarships; average amount $17,060.

## FINANCIAL AID PROCEDURES

**Forms required:** FAFSA.

**Dates and Deadlines:** Priority date 3/1; no closing date. Applicants notified on a rolling basis starting 4/1; must reply within 2 week(s) of notification.

**Transfers:** Transfer scholarships awarded to new students entering in fall or spring semesters. Must transfer at least 45 credit hours. Students transferring from Missouri 2-year institution must have minimum cumulative GPA of 3.25 for consideration. Students transferring from non-Missouri 2-year institution or any 4-year institution must have minimum cumulative GPA of 3.5 for consideration. Students starting in fall must be admitted by March 15; spring students must be admitted by October 15.

## CONTACT

Anthony Georges, Director of Student Financial Aid
One University Boulevard, St. Louis, MO 63121-4400
(314) 516-5526

## Vatterott College: St. Joseph
Saint Joseph, Missouri
www.vatterott-college.edu           Federal Code: 026092

**2-year for-profit** branch campus and technical college in small city.
**Enrollment:** 231 undergrads.
**Selectivity:** Open admission.

## BASIC COSTS (2015-2016)

**Additional info:** Diploma programs: (30 weeks) $13,350; (40 weeks) $19,800; (50 weeks) $20,800; (60 weeks) $21,050. Associate programs: (70 weeks) $30,559-$34,900. Costs include fees, books and supplies.

## FINANCIAL AID PICTURE

**Students with need:** Need-based aid available for full-time and part-time students.

**Scholarships offered:** Make the Grade Scholarship: up to $1,000; based on high school grades.

## FINANCIAL AID PROCEDURES

**Forms required:** FAFSA.

## CONTACT

Marcia Hurley, Financial Aid Administrator
3131 Frederick Avenue, St. Joseph, MO 64506
(816) 364-5399

## Washington University in St. Louis
St. Louis, Missouri              Federal Code: 002520
www.wustl.edu                    CSS Code: 6929

**4-year private** university in large city.
**Enrollment:** 7,032 undergrads, 4% part-time. 1,721 full-time freshmen.
**Selectivity:** Admits less than 50% of applicants.

## BASIC COSTS (2016-2017)

**Tuition and fees:** $49,770.
**Room and board:** $15,596.

## FINANCIAL AID PICTURE (2015-2016)

**Students with need:** Out of 865 full-time freshmen who applied for aid, 685 were judged to have need. Of these, 678 received aid, and 678 had their full need met. Average financial aid package met 100% of need; average scholarship/grant was $40,752; average loan was $4,926. Need-based aid available for part-time students.

**Students without need:** 189 full-time freshmen who did not demonstrate need for aid received scholarships/grants; average award was $14,355. No-need awards available for academics, art, leadership, ROTC.

**Scholarships offered:** Scholarships up to full tuition plus stipend; renewable for 4 years; based upon academic merit.

**Additional info:** Scholarship funds increased and a program offered to eliminate need-based loans to families of students with incomes of $75,000 or less.

## FINANCIAL AID PROCEDURES

**Forms required:** FAFSA, CSS PROFILE, institutional form.

**Dates and Deadlines:** Closing date 2/1. Applicants notified by 4/1; must reply by 5/1.

## CONTACT

Michael Runiewicz, Director of Student Financial Services
Campus Box 1089, One Brookings Drive, St. Louis, MO 63130-4899
(314) 935-5900

## Webster University
St. Louis, Missouri
www.webster.edu                  Federal Code: 002521

**4-year private** university in very large city.
**Enrollment:** 2,721 undergrads, 15% part-time. 412 full-time freshmen.
**Selectivity:** Admits 50 to 75% of applicants.

## BASIC COSTS (2015-2016)

**Tuition and fees:** $25,500.
**Per-credit charge:** $650.
**Room and board:** $10,860.

## FINANCIAL AID PICTURE (2015-2016)

**Students with need:** Out of 375 full-time freshmen who applied for aid, 298 were judged to have need. Of these, 295 received aid, and 16 had their full need met. Average financial aid package met 69% of need; average scholarship/grant was $10,586; average loan was $3,564. For part-time students, average financial aid package was $7,472.

**Students without need:** 39 full-time freshmen who did not demonstrate need for aid received scholarships/grants; average award was $12,116. No-need awards available for academics, art, leadership, music/drama, state/district residency.

**Scholarships offered:** Presidential Scholarships: full tuition; 3.75 GPA, top 20% class rank, 27 ACT and interview; 5 awarded. Webster Academic Scholarships: $6,500-$15,000; 3.0 GPA and 21 ACT; no limit. Leadership Scholarships: $2,000; 3.3 GPA and 24 ACT, resume of activities; 12 awarded.

## FINANCIAL AID PROCEDURES

**Forms required:** FAFSA, institutional form.

**Dates and Deadlines:** Priority date 4/1; no closing date. Applicants notified on a rolling basis starting 2/1; must reply within 2 week(s) of notification.

**Transfers:** Closing date 4/1. Applicants notified on a rolling basis starting 2/1; must reply within 2 week(s) of notification.

## CONTACT

James Myers, Associate Vice President Undergraduate Admission & Financial Aid
470 East Lockwood Avenue, St. Louis, MO 63119-3194
(314) 968-6992

## Westminster College
Fulton, Missouri
www.westminster-mo.edu           Federal Code: 002523

**4-year private** liberal arts college in large town, affiliated with Presbyterian Church (USA).

**Enrollment:** 930 undergrads, 1% part-time. 239 full-time freshmen.
**Selectivity:** Admits 50 to 75% of applicants.

**BASIC COSTS (2015-2016)**
**Tuition and fees:** $23,480.
**Per-credit charge:** $800.
**Room and board:** $9,340.
**Additional info:** Tuition/fee waivers available for minority students.

**FINANCIAL AID PICTURE (2015-2016)**
**Students with need:** Out of 184 full-time freshmen who applied for aid, 157 were judged to have need. Of these, 157 received aid, and 71 had their full need met. Average financial aid package met 92% of need; average scholarship/grant was $18,524; average loan was $3,087. Need-based aid available for part-time students.
**Students without need:** 80 full-time freshmen who did not demonstrate need for aid received scholarships/grants; average award was $14,636. No-need awards available for academics, alumni affiliation, leadership, minority status, music/drama.

**FINANCIAL AID PROCEDURES**
**Forms required:** FAFSA.
**Dates and Deadlines:** Priority date 2/15; no closing date. Applicants notified on a rolling basis starting 3/15.
**Transfers:** Applicants notified on a rolling basis starting 3/1; must reply within 3 week(s) of notification.

**CONTACT**
Aimee Bristow, Director of Financial Aid
501 Westminster Avenue, Fulton, MO 65251-1299
(573) 592-5365

## William Jewell College
Liberty, Missouri
www.jewell.edu                Federal Code: 002524

**4-year private** liberal arts college in large town.
**Enrollment:** 1,053 undergrads, 3% part-time. 245 full-time freshmen.
**Selectivity:** Admits 50 to 75% of applicants.

**BASIC COSTS (2016-2017)**
**Tuition and fees:** $32,930.
**Per-credit charge:** $945.
**Room and board:** $9,280.

**FINANCIAL AID PICTURE (2015-2016)**
**Students with need:** Out of 217 full-time freshmen who applied for aid, 181 were judged to have need. Of these, 181 received aid, and 101 had their full need met. Average financial aid package met 80% of need; average scholarship/grant was $22,452; average loan was $4,166. Need-based aid available for part-time students.
**Students without need:** 30 full-time freshmen who did not demonstrate need for aid received scholarships/grants; average award was $19,191. No-need awards available for academics, alumni affiliation, athletics, music/drama.
**Scholarships offered: Merit:** Academic scholarships: $10,000-$24,000 awarded at time of admittance; competitive. National Merit Semifinalists: automatically qualify for academic scholarship of $24,000. All academic scholarships available for 8 consecutive semesters with 2.5 GPA. **Athletic:** 26 full-time freshmen received athletic scholarships; average amount $9,370.

**FINANCIAL AID PROCEDURES**
**Forms required:** FAFSA.
**Dates and Deadlines:** Priority date 3/1; no closing date. Applicants notified on a rolling basis starting 3/1; must reply within 2 week(s) of notification.
**Transfers:** Closing date 9/15. Applicants notified on a rolling basis starting 3/15; must reply within 2 week(s) of notification. Transfer students evaluated

individually by financial aid staff to determine number of semesters of aid available.

**CONTACT**
Daniel Holt, Director, Financial Aid and Scholarship Services
500 College Hill, Liberty, MO 64068
(816) 415-5974

## William Woods University
Fulton, Missouri
www.williamwoods.edu          Federal Code: 002525

**4-year private** university and teachers college in large town, affiliated with Christian Church (Disciples of Christ).
**Enrollment:** 962 undergrads, 13% part-time. 200 full-time freshmen.
**Selectivity:** Admits over 75% of applicants.

**BASIC COSTS (2015-2016)**
**Tuition and fees:** $22,160.
**Room and board:** $8,960.

**FINANCIAL AID PICTURE (2014-2015)**
**Students with need:** Out of 127 full-time freshmen who applied for aid, 104 were judged to have need. Of these, 104 received aid, and 23 had their full need met. Average financial aid package met 70% of need; average scholarship/grant was $14,008; average loan was $4,205. For part-time students, average financial aid package was $7,980.
**Students without need:** 48 full-time freshmen who did not demonstrate need for aid received scholarships/grants; average award was $11,114. No-need awards available for academics, alumni affiliation, art, athletics, leadership, music/drama, religious affiliation.
**Scholarships offered: Merit:** LEAD (Leading, Educating, Achieving and Developing) Award: $5,000 for campus residents, $2,500 for commuters; based on commitment to campus and community involvement; renewable each year if commitment has been met in previous year. **Athletic:** 6 full-time freshmen received athletic scholarships; average amount $7,119.

**FINANCIAL AID PROCEDURES**
**Forms required:** FAFSA.
**Dates and Deadlines:** Priority date 3/1; no closing date. Applicants notified on a rolling basis starting 3/15; must reply within 2 week(s) of notification.
**Transfers:** No deadline. Applicants notified on a rolling basis; must reply within 2 week(s) of notification. Transfer students eligible for scholarships based on incoming GPA.

**CONTACT**
Deana Ready, Director of Financial Aid
One University Avenue, Fulton, MO 65251-2388
(573) 592-1793

# Montana

## Blackfeet Community College
Browning, Montana
www.bfcc.edu                  Federal Code: 014902

**2-year public** tribal community college in small town.
**Enrollment:** 462 undergrads, 27% part-time. 111 full-time freshmen.
**Selectivity:** Open admission.

**BASIC COSTS (2015-2016)**
**Tuition and fees:** $2,810; out-of-state residents $2,810.
**Per-credit charge:** $95.

**Additional info:** Tuition at time of enrollment locked for 2 years; tuition/fee waivers available for adults, minority students, unemployed or children of unemployed.

**FINANCIAL AID PICTURE (2015-2016)**

**Students with need:** Out of 92 full-time freshmen who applied for aid, 92 were judged to have need. Of these, 92 received aid. Average financial aid package met 53% of need; average scholarship/grant was $1,530. Need-based aid available for part-time students.

**Students without need:** 19 full-time freshmen who did not demonstrate need for aid received scholarships/grants. No-need awards available for academics, minority status, state/district residency.

**Scholarships offered:** 111 full-time freshmen received athletic scholarships; average amount $53.

**FINANCIAL AID PROCEDURES**

**Forms required:** FAFSA, institutional form.

**Dates and Deadlines:** Applicants notified on a rolling basis starting 8/1; must reply by 3/1.

**Transfers:** No deadline. Applicants notified on a rolling basis starting 8/1.

**CONTACT**

Gaylene DuCharme, Director of Financial Aid

504 SE Boundary, Browning, MT 59417

(406) 338-5421 ext. 2245

# Carroll College

Helena, Montana

www.carroll.edu

Federal Code: 002526

**4-year private** liberal arts college in large town, affiliated with Roman Catholic Church.

**Enrollment:** 1,428 undergrads, 2% part-time. 315 full-time freshmen.

**Selectivity:** Admits 50 to 75% of applicants.

**BASIC COSTS (2015-2016)**

**Tuition and fees:** $30,754.

**Per-credit charge:** $1,254.

**Room and board:** $9,218.

**FINANCIAL AID PICTURE (2014-2015)**

**Students with need:** Out of 271 full-time freshmen who applied for aid, 218 were judged to have need. Of these, 218 received aid, and 57 had their full need met. Average financial aid package met 79% of need; average scholarship/grant was $16,371; average loan was $3,237. For part-time students, average financial aid package was $7,693.

**Students without need:** 94 full-time freshmen who did not demonstrate need for aid received scholarships/grants; average award was $12,976. No-need awards available for academics, art, athletics, leadership, minority status, music/drama, religious affiliation, ROTC.

**Scholarships offered:** 53 full-time freshmen received athletic scholarships; average amount $9,115.

**FINANCIAL AID PROCEDURES**

**Forms required:** FAFSA.

**Dates and Deadlines:** Priority date 3/1; no closing date. Applicants notified on a rolling basis starting 3/1; must reply by 5/1 or within 2 week(s) of notification.

**CONTACT**

Janet Riis, Director of Financial Aid

1601 North Benton Avenue, Helena, MT 59625

(406) 447-5425

# Chief Dull Knife College

Lame Deer, Montana

www.cdkc.edu

Federal Code: 014878

**2-year public** junior college in rural community.

**Enrollment:** 26 undergrads.

**Selectivity:** Open admission.

**BASIC COSTS (2015-2016)**

**Tuition and fees:** $2,260; out-of-state residents $2,260.

**Per-credit charge:** $70.

**FINANCIAL AID PICTURE**

**Students with need:** Need-based aid available for full-time and part-time students. Work study available nights.

**Students without need:** No-need awards available for academics.

**FINANCIAL AID PROCEDURES**

**Forms required:** FAFSA, institutional form.

**Dates and Deadlines:** Priority date 3/1; no closing date. Applicants notified on a rolling basis; must reply within 2 week(s) of notification.

**Transfers:** No deadline. Applicants notified on a rolling basis; must reply within 2 week(s) of notification.

**CONTACT**

Devin Wertman, Director of Financial Aid

Box 98, Lame Deer, MT 59043

(406) 477-6215

# Dawson Community College

Glendive, Montana

www.dawson.edu

Federal Code: 002529

**2-year public** community college in small town.

**Enrollment:** 216 undergrads, 26% part-time. 72 full-time freshmen.

**Selectivity:** Open admission.

**BASIC COSTS (2015-2016)**

**Tuition and fees:** $3,570; out-of-district residents $5,005; out-of-state residents $10,815.

**Per-credit charge:** $65; out-of-district residents $112; out-of-state residents $307.

**Room and board:** $5,575.

**FINANCIAL AID PICTURE**

**Students with need:** Work study available nights, weekends, and for part-time students.

**Students without need:** No-need awards available for academics, art, athletics, music/drama.

**FINANCIAL AID PROCEDURES**

**Forms required:** FAFSA.

**Dates and Deadlines:** Priority date 3/1; no closing date. Applicants notified on a rolling basis starting 5/15; must reply within 2 week(s) of notification.

**CONTACT**

Rory Seeger, Director of Financial Aid

300 College Drive, Glendive, MT 59330

(406) 377-9410

# Flathead Valley Community College

Kalispell, Montana

www.fvcc.edu

Federal Code: 006777

**2-year public** community college in large town.

**Enrollment:** 2,206 undergrads.

**Selectivity:** Open admission; but selective for some programs.

**BASIC COSTS (2015-2016)**
**Tuition and fees:** $3,965; out-of-district residents $5,337; out-of-state residents $11,105.

**FINANCIAL AID PICTURE**
**Students with need:** Need-based aid available for full-time and part-time students.
**Students without need:** No-need awards available for academics, athletics.

**FINANCIAL AID PROCEDURES**
**Forms required:** FAFSA.
**Dates and Deadlines:** Priority date 3/1; no closing date. Applicants notified on a rolling basis starting 4/15; must reply within 2 week(s) of notification.

**CONTACT**
Cynthia Kiefer, Director of Financial Aid
777 Grandview Drive, Kalispell, MT 59901
(406) 756-3849

## Fort Peck Community College
Poplar, Montana
www.fpcc.edu                    Federal Code: 016616

**2-year public** community college in rural community.
**Enrollment:** 323 undergrads.
**Selectivity:** Open admission.

**BASIC COSTS (2015-2016)**
**Tuition and fees:** $2,250; out-of-state residents $2,250.
**Per-credit charge:** $70.
**Room only:** $1,350.
**Additional info:** Tuition/fee waivers available for adults, minority students, unemployed or children of unemployed.

**FINANCIAL AID PICTURE**
**Students with need:** Need-based aid available for full-time and part-time students.
**Students without need:** No-need awards available for academics, minority status, state/district residency.

**FINANCIAL AID PROCEDURES**
**Forms required:** FAFSA, institutional form.
**Dates and Deadlines:** Applicants notified on a rolling basis starting 5/1; must reply within 3 week(s) of notification.
**Transfers:** No deadline. Applicants notified on a rolling basis starting 5/1; must reply within 3 week(s) of notification.

**CONTACT**
Lanette Clark, Financial Aid Director
Box 398, 605 Indian, Poplar, MT 59255-0398
(406) 768-6327

## Great Falls College Montana State University
Great Falls, Montana
www.gfcmsu.edu                    Federal Code: 009314

**2-year public** community college in small city.
**Enrollment:** 1,398 undergrads.
**Selectivity:** Open admission; but selective for some programs.

**BASIC COSTS (2015-2016)**
**Tuition and fees:** $3,130; out-of-state residents $9,382.
**Per-credit charge:** $104; out-of-state residents $364.
**Additional info:** Tuition/fee waivers available for minority students.

**FINANCIAL AID PICTURE**
**Students with need:** Need-based aid available for full-time and part-time students. Work study available nights, weekends, and for part-time students.
**Students without need:** No-need awards available for academics, leadership.

**FINANCIAL AID PROCEDURES**
**Forms required:** FAFSA, institutional form.
**Dates and Deadlines:** Priority date 3/1; no closing date. Applicants notified on a rolling basis starting 4/15.
**Transfers:** No deadline. Applicants notified on a rolling basis; must reply within 3 week(s) of notification.

**CONTACT**
Leah Habel, Director of Financial Aid
2100 16th Avenue South, Great Falls, MT 59405
(800) 446-2698 ext. 4334

## Helena College University of Montana
Helena, Montana
www.umhelena.edu                    Federal Code: 007570

**2-year public** community and technical college in large town.
**Enrollment:** 1,063 undergrads.
**Selectivity:** Open admission.

**BASIC COSTS (2015-2016)**
**Tuition and fees:** $3,062; out-of-state residents $8,358.
**Per-credit charge:** $79; out-of-state residents $255.
**Additional info:** Tuition/fee waivers available for minority students.

**FINANCIAL AID PICTURE**
**Students with need:** Need-based aid available for full-time and part-time students.

**FINANCIAL AID PROCEDURES**
**Forms required:** FAFSA, institutional form.
**Dates and Deadlines:** Priority date 3/1; no closing date. Applicants notified on a rolling basis starting 5/1.
**Transfers:** Applicants notified on a rolling basis starting 5/1.

**CONTACT**
Valerie Curtin, Director of Financial Aid
1115 North Roberts Street, Helena, MT 59601-3098
(406) 447-6916

## Little Big Horn College
Crow Agency, Montana
www.lbhc.edu                    Federal Code: 016135

**2-year private** community college in rural community.
**Enrollment:** 236 undergrads.
**Selectivity:** Open admission.

**BASIC COSTS (2015-2016)**
**Tuition and fees:** $2,860.
**Per-credit charge:** $85.

**FINANCIAL AID PICTURE (2014-2015)**
**Students with need:** 99% of average financial aid package awarded as scholarships/grants, 1% awarded as loans/jobs. Need-based aid available for part-time students.
**Students without need:** This college awards aid only to students with need.

**FINANCIAL AID PROCEDURES**
**Forms required:** FAFSA, institutional form.
**Dates and Deadlines:** Applicants notified on a rolling basis.

**Transfers:** No deadline. Applicants notified on a rolling basis.

**CONTACT**

Beverly Snell, Financial Aid Director
Box 370, Crow Agency, MT 59022
(406) 638-3140

## Miles Community College

Miles City, Montana
www.milescc.edu        Federal Code: 002528

**2-year public** community college in small town.
**Enrollment:** 367 undergrads, 26% part-time. 109 full-time freshmen.
**Selectivity:** Open admission; but selective for some programs.

**BASIC COSTS (2015-2016)**

**Tuition and fees:** $3,945; out-of-district residents $5,085; out-of-state residents $8,085.
**Room and board:** $5,880.

**FINANCIAL AID PICTURE**

**Students with need:** Need-based aid available for full-time and part-time students. Work study available nights, weekends, and for part-time students.
**Students without need:** No-need awards available for academics, athletics, leadership.

**FINANCIAL AID PROCEDURES**

**Forms required:** FAFSA.
**Dates and Deadlines:** Priority date 3/1; no closing date. Applicants notified on a rolling basis starting 4/15; must reply within 4 week(s) of notification.

**CONTACT**

Loren Lancaster, Financial Aid Officer
2715 Dickinson Street, Miles City, MT 59301
(406) 874-6208

## Montana State University

Bozeman, Montana
www.montana.edu        Federal Code: 002532

**4-year public** university in large town.
**Enrollment:** 13,527 undergrads, 15% part-time. 2,173 full-time freshmen.
**Selectivity:** Admits over 75% of applicants.

**BASIC COSTS (2015-2016)**

**Tuition and fees:** $6,968; out-of-state residents $21,961.
**Per-credit charge:** $222; out-of-state residents $847.
**Room and board:** $8,650.
**Additional info:** Tuition/fee waivers available for minority students.

**FINANCIAL AID PICTURE (2014-2015)**

**Students with need:** Out of 1,732 full-time freshmen who applied for aid, 1,192 were judged to have need. Of these, 1,155 received aid, and 106 had their full need met. Average financial aid package met 91% of need; average scholarship/grant was $5,192; average loan was $3,829. For part-time students, average financial aid package was $10,206.
**Students without need:** 32 full-time freshmen who did not demonstrate need for aid received scholarships/grants; average award was $1,381. No-need awards available for academics, alumni affiliation, art, athletics, job skills, leadership, minority status, music/drama, ROTC, state/district residency.
**Scholarships offered:** 9 full-time freshmen received athletic scholarships; average amount $4,864.
**Additional info:** Tuition waiver for honorably discharged veterans, children of members of the United States armed forces who, at the time of entry into service, had legal residence in Montana and who were killed in action or who died as a result of injury, disease, or other disability incurred while in the service.

**FINANCIAL AID PROCEDURES**

**Forms required:** FAFSA.
**Dates and Deadlines:** Priority date 3/1; no closing date. Applicants notified on a rolling basis starting 4/1; must reply within 3 week(s) of notification.
**Transfers:** Priority date 7/1; no deadline.

**CONTACT**

Brandi Payne, Director of Financial Aid Services
PO Box 172190, Bozeman, MT 59717-2190
(406) 994-2845

## Montana State University: Billings

Billings, Montana
www.msubillings.edu        Federal Code: 002530

**4-year public** university and technical college in small city.
**Enrollment:** 3,744 undergrads, 29% part-time. 682 full-time freshmen.
**Selectivity:** Admits over 75% of applicants.

**BASIC COSTS (2015-2016)**

**Tuition and fees:** $5,802; out-of-state residents $17,712.
**Per-credit charge:** $183; out-of-state residents $679.
**Room and board:** $7,214.

**FINANCIAL AID PICTURE (2014-2015)**

**Students with need:** Out of 567 full-time freshmen who applied for aid, 446 were judged to have need. Of these, 443 received aid, and 106 had their full need met. Average financial aid package met 68% of need; average scholarship/grant was $4,599; average loan was $4,997. For part-time students, average financial aid package was $7,625.
**Students without need:** 84 full-time freshmen who did not demonstrate need for aid received scholarships/grants; average award was $1,765. No-need awards available for academics, alumni affiliation, art, athletics, job skills, leadership, minority status, music/drama, ROTC, state/district residency.
**Scholarships offered:** 27 full-time freshmen received athletic scholarships; average amount $2,774.
**Additional info:** Veterans and honors fee waivers offered.

**FINANCIAL AID PROCEDURES**

**Forms required:** FAFSA.
**Dates and Deadlines:** Priority date 3/1; no closing date. Applicants notified on a rolling basis starting 3/1; must reply within 3 week(s) of notification.
**Transfers:** Applicants notified on a rolling basis.

**CONTACT**

Emily Williamson, Director of Financial Aid and Scholarships
1500 University Drive, Billings, MT 59101-0298
(406) 657-2188

## Montana State University: Northern

Havre, Montana
www.msun.edu        Federal Code: 002533

**4-year public** university in large town.
**Enrollment:** 1,218 undergrads.

**BASIC COSTS (2015-2016)**

**Tuition and fees:** $4,871; out-of-state residents $16,841.
**Per-credit charge:** $117; out-of-state residents $516.
**Room and board:** $6,525.
**Additional info:** Out-of-state students pay an additional $106 in fees. Tuition/fee waivers available for minority students.

## FINANCIAL AID PICTURE

**Students with need:** Need-based aid available for full-time and part-time students. Work study available nights, weekends, and for part-time students.
**Students without need:** No-need awards available for academics, athletics.

## FINANCIAL AID PROCEDURES

**Forms required:** FAFSA, institutional form.
**Dates and Deadlines:** Priority date 4/15; no closing date. Applicants notified on a rolling basis starting 5/1; must reply within 4 week(s) of notification.

## CONTACT

Cindy Small, Director of Financial Aid
Box 7751, Havre, MT 59501-7751
(406) 265-3787

## Montana Tech of the University of Montana

Butte, Montana
www.mtech.edu                    Federal Code: 002531

**4-year public** engineering and technical college in large town.
**Enrollment:** 2,447 undergrads, 9% part-time. 440 full-time freshmen.
**Selectivity:** Admits over 75% of applicants.

## BASIC COSTS (2015-2016)

**Tuition and fees:** $6,539; out-of-state residents $19,571.
**Per-credit charge:** $205; out-of-state residents $745.
**Room and board:** $8,562.

## FINANCIAL AID PICTURE (2014-2015)

**Students with need:** Out of 369 full-time freshmen who applied for aid, 260 were judged to have need. Of these, 260 received aid, and 57 had their full need met. Average financial aid package met 66% of need; average scholarship/grant was $5,575; average loan was $3,017. For part-time students, average financial aid package was $7,658.
**Students without need:** 77 full-time freshmen who did not demonstrate need for aid received scholarships/grants; average award was $4,054. No-need awards available for academics, alumni affiliation, athletics, leadership, minority status, music/drama, religious affiliation, state/district residency.
**Scholarships offered:** 10 full-time freshmen received athletic scholarships; average amount $4,026.

## FINANCIAL AID PROCEDURES

**Forms required:** FAFSA.
**Dates and Deadlines:** Priority date 3/1; no closing date. Applicants notified on a rolling basis starting 3/15; must reply within 2 week(s) of notification.
**Transfers:** No deadline. Applicants notified on a rolling basis; must reply within 2 week(s) of notification.

## CONTACT

Mike Richardson, Director of Financial Aid
1300 West Park Street, Butte, MT 59701-8997
(406) 496-4256

## Rocky Mountain College

Billings, Montana
www.rocky.edu                    Federal Code: 002534

**4-year private** liberal arts college in small city, affiliated with United Church of Christ.
**Enrollment:** 906 undergrads, 2% part-time. 240 full-time freshmen.
**Selectivity:** Admits 50 to 75% of applicants.

## BASIC COSTS (2016-2017)

**Tuition and fees:** $26,665.
**Room and board:** $8,133.

## FINANCIAL AID PICTURE (2015-2016)

**Students with need:** Out of 219 full-time freshmen who applied for aid, 194 were judged to have need. Of these, 194 received aid, and 43 had their full need met. Average financial aid package met 77% of need; average scholarship/grant was $18,407; average loan was $3,272. For part-time students, average financial aid package was $10,565.
**Students without need:** 14 full-time freshmen who did not demonstrate need for aid received scholarships/grants; average award was $11,929. No-need awards available for academics, athletics.
**Scholarships offered:** 26 full-time freshmen received athletic scholarships; average amount $4,642.

## FINANCIAL AID PROCEDURES

**Forms required:** FAFSA.
**Dates and Deadlines:** Priority date 3/1; no closing date. Applicants notified on a rolling basis starting 2/15; must reply within 4 week(s) of notification.
**Transfers:** No deadline. Applicants notified on a rolling basis starting 2/15; must reply within 4 week(s) of notification.

## CONTACT

Jessica Francischetti, Director of Financial Assistance
1511 Poly Drive, Billings, MT 59102-1796
(406) 657-1031

## Salish Kootenai College

Pablo, Montana
www.skc.edu                    Federal Code: 015023

**4-year private** liberal arts college in rural community.
**Enrollment:** 818 undergrads.
**Selectivity:** Open admission; but selective for some programs.

## BASIC COSTS (2015-2016)

**Tuition and fees:** $6,279; out-of-state residents $11,463.
**Per-credit charge:** $141.
**Additional info:** Tuition/fee waivers available for minority students.

## FINANCIAL AID PICTURE

**Students with need:** Need-based aid available for full-time and part-time students. Work study available nights, weekends, and for part-time students.

## FINANCIAL AID PROCEDURES

**Forms required:** FAFSA.
**Dates and Deadlines:** Priority date 3/31; no closing date. Applicants notified on a rolling basis starting 7/15; must reply within 6 week(s) of notification.

## CONTACT

Jackie Swain, Financial Aid Director
PO Box 70, Pablo, MT 59855
(406) 275-4855

## Stone Child College

Box Elder, Montana
www.stonechild.edu                    Federal Code: 026109

**2-year public** community and junior college in rural community.
**Enrollment:** 289 undergrads, 45% part-time. 38 full-time freshmen.
**Selectivity:** Open admission.

## BASIC COSTS (2015-2016)

**Tuition and fees:** $2,645; out-of-state residents $2,645.

## FINANCIAL AID PICTURE (2015-2016)

**Students with need:** 36% of average financial aid package awarded as scholarships/grants, 64% awarded as loans/jobs. Need-based aid available for part-time students.

**Additional info:** Scholarships available to high school and GED graduates who apply for college admission during the first term after graduation.

### FINANCIAL AID PROCEDURES
**Forms required:** FAFSA.
**Dates and Deadlines:** Priority date 3/1; no closing date. Applicants notified on a rolling basis.

### CONTACT
Tiffany Galbavy, Financial Aid Director
8294 Upper Box Elder Road, Box Elder, MT 59521
(406) 395-4313 ext. 267

## University of Great Falls
Great Falls, Montana
www.ugf.edu                    Federal Code: 002527

**4-year private** university and liberal arts college in small city, affiliated with Roman Catholic Church.
**Enrollment:** 1,052 undergrads. 163 full-time freshmen.
**Selectivity:** Admits over 75% of applicants.

### BASIC COSTS (2015-2016)
**Tuition and fees:** $22,170.
**Per-credit charge:** $666.
**Room and board:** $7,920.

### FINANCIAL AID PICTURE (2015-2016)
**Students with need:** Out of 144 full-time freshmen who applied for aid, 125 were judged to have need. Of these, 125 received aid, and 1 had their full need met. Average financial aid package met 75% of need; average scholarship/grant was $11,047; average loan was $3,343. For part-time students, average financial aid package was $9,885.
**Students without need:** 19 full-time freshmen who did not demonstrate need for aid received scholarships/grants; average award was $9,739. No-need awards available for academics, alumni affiliation, art, athletics, music/drama, religious affiliation, state/district residency.
**Scholarships offered:** *Merit:* Freshmen scholarships: $1,000-$6,000; based on high school GPA; renewable. *Athletic:* 30 full-time freshmen received athletic scholarships; average amount $11,772.

### FINANCIAL AID PROCEDURES
**Forms required:** FAFSA.
**Dates and Deadlines:** Priority date 3/1; no closing date. Applicants notified on a rolling basis starting 3/1; must reply within 3 week(s) of notification.
**Transfers:** Transfer student scholarships; $2,500-$4,000; based on college GPA; renewable.

### CONTACT
Kelli Engelhardt, Director of Financial Aid
1301 20th Street South, Great Falls, MT 59405
(406) 791-5235

## University of Montana
Missoula, Montana
www.umt.edu                    Federal Code: 002536

**4-year public** university and liberal arts college in small city.
**Enrollment:** 10,632 undergrads, 19% part-time. 1,627 full-time freshmen.
**Selectivity:** Admits over 75% of applicants.

### BASIC COSTS (2015-2016)
**Tuition and fees:** $6,158; out-of-state residents $23,048.
**Per-credit charge:** $182; out-of-state residents $886.
**Room and board:** $8,406.
**Additional info:** Tuition/fee waivers available for minority students.

### FINANCIAL AID PICTURE
**Students with need:** Need-based aid available for full-time and part-time students. Work study available nights, weekends, and for part-time students.
**Students without need:** No-need awards available for academics, athletics, leadership, music/drama, ROTC, state/district residency.
**Additional info:** Fee waivers for minority students available to American Indians with blood quantum eligibility for, or enrolled membership in, a Montana tribe.

### FINANCIAL AID PROCEDURES
**Forms required:** FAFSA.
**Dates and Deadlines:** Priority date 2/15; no closing date. Applicants notified on a rolling basis starting 4/1; must reply within 4 week(s) of notification.
**Transfers:** Applicants notified on a rolling basis starting 4/1.

### CONTACT
Kent McGowan, Director of Financial Aid
Lommasson Center 103, Missoula, MT 59812
(406) 243-5373

## University of Montana: Western
Dillon, Montana
www.umwestern.edu              Federal Code: 002537

**4-year public** liberal arts and teachers college in small town.
**Enrollment:** 1,410 undergrads, 17% part-time. 242 full-time freshmen.
**Selectivity:** Open admission; but selective for some programs.

### BASIC COSTS (2015-2016)
**Tuition and fees:** $4,226; out-of-state residents $15,711.
**Per-credit charge:** $129; out-of-state residents $607.
**Room and board:** $6,994.
**Additional info:** Tuition/fee waivers available for minority students.

### FINANCIAL AID PICTURE (2014-2015)
**Students with need:** Average financial aid package met 16% of need; average scholarship/grant was $2,981; average loan was $3,868. For part-time students, average financial aid package was $3,641.
**Students without need:** 1 full-time freshmen who did not demonstrate need for aid received scholarships/grants; average award was $1,207. No-need awards available for academics, alumni affiliation, art, athletics, leadership, state/district residency.
**Scholarships offered:** *Merit:* Chancellor's Leadership Waiver Scholarship, departmental waiver scholarship, Western Undergraduate Exchange. *Athletic:* 25 full-time freshmen received athletic scholarships; average amount $1,736.
**Additional info:** Tuition waivers available for veterans, war orphans, Native Americans, senior citizens, and dependents of Montana University System employees.

### FINANCIAL AID PROCEDURES
**Forms required:** FAFSA.
**Dates and Deadlines:** Priority date 3/1; no closing date. Applicants notified on a rolling basis starting 4/1; must reply within 4 week(s) of notification.
**Transfers:** No deadline. Applicants notified on a rolling basis starting 4/1; must reply within 4 week(s) of notification. Transfer students must have 2.0 GPA to enter in with good academic standing. Students with transfer GPA below 1.8 must appeal to receive financial aid. Students with transfer GPA between 1.8 and 1.99 enter on financial aid warning.

### CONTACT
Erica Jones, Director of Financial Aid
710 South Atlantic Street, Dillon, MT 59725
(406) 683-7511

# Nebraska

## Bellevue University
Bellevue, Nebraska
www.bellevue.edu                   Federal Code: 002538

**4-year private** university and business college in large city.
**Enrollment:** 6,224 undergrads, 40% part-time. 41 full-time freshmen.
**Selectivity:** Open admission; but selective for some programs.

**BASIC COSTS (2015-2016)**
**Tuition and fees:** $8,700.
**Per-credit charge:** $275.
**Room and board:** $7,285.
**Additional info:** First year we are offering room and board on campus.

**FINANCIAL AID PICTURE**
**Students with need:** Need-based aid available for full-time and part-time students. Work study available nights, weekends, and for part-time students.
**Students without need:** No-need awards available for academics, athletics, leadership.

**FINANCIAL AID PROCEDURES**
**Forms required:** FAFSA, institutional form.
**Dates and Deadlines:** Applicants notified on a rolling basis starting 4/15; must reply within 2 week(s) of notification.
**Transfers:** No deadline. Applicants notified on a rolling basis starting 4/15; must reply within 2 week(s) of notification.

**CONTACT**
Janet Yale, Director, Financial Aid
1000 Galvin Road South, Bellevue, NE 68005-3098
(402) 557-7095

## BryanLGH College of Health Sciences
Lincoln, Nebraska
www.bryanhealthcollege.edu          Federal Code: 006399

**4-year private** health science college in large city, affiliated with United Methodist Church.
**Enrollment:** 590 undergrads.

**BASIC COSTS (2015-2016)**
**Tuition and fees:** $16,350.
**Per-credit charge:** $515.

**FINANCIAL AID PICTURE**
**Students with need:** Need-based aid available for full-time and part-time students.
**Students without need:** No-need awards available for academics, leadership.

**FINANCIAL AID PROCEDURES**
**Forms required:** FAFSA, institutional form.
**Dates and Deadlines:** Closing date 5/1. Applicants notified on a rolling basis starting 5/1; must reply within 3 week(s) of notification.

**CONTACT**
Deborah Wilke, Financial Aid Director
5035 Everett Street, Lincoln, NE 68506
(402) 481-8984

## Central Community College
Grand Island, Nebraska
www.cccneb.edu                      Federal Code: 014468

**2-year public** community and technical college in large town.
**Enrollment:** 3,965 undergrads, 49% part-time. 611 full-time freshmen.
**Selectivity:** Open admission.

**BASIC COSTS (2015-2016)**
**Tuition and fees:** $2,820; out-of-state residents $4,050.
**Per-credit charge:** $82; out-of-state residents $123.
**Room and board:** $6,878.

**FINANCIAL AID PICTURE (2014-2015)**
**Students with need:** Out of 531 full-time freshmen who applied for aid, 429 were judged to have need. Of these, 410 received aid, and 126 had their full need met. Average financial aid package met 78% of need; average scholarship/grant was $2,426; average loan was $1,431. For part-time students, average financial aid package was $2,972.
**Students without need:** 29 full-time freshmen who did not demonstrate need for aid received scholarships/grants; average award was $509. No-need awards available for academics, art, athletics, job skills, leadership, music/drama.
**Scholarships offered:** 21 full-time freshmen received athletic scholarships; average amount $818.
**Additional info:** All students are eligible to apply for a Pell Grant. Students enrolled for at least six semester hours (half-time) are eligible to apply for grants, loans, work study, and scholarships. To be considered for full-time benefits, students must be enrolled for at least 12 credit hours during the semester.

**FINANCIAL AID PROCEDURES**
**Forms required:** FAFSA, institutional form.
**Dates and Deadlines:** Priority date 3/1; no closing date. Applicants notified on a rolling basis starting 2/1; must reply within 2 week(s) of notification.

**CONTACT**
Hylee Asche, Financial Aid Director
3134 West Highway 34, P.O.Box 4903, Grand Island, NE 68802-4903
(308) 398-7424

## Chadron State College
Chadron, Nebraska
www.csc.edu                         Federal Code: 002539

**4-year public** business and liberal arts college in small town.
**Enrollment:** 2,099 undergrads, 18% part-time. 413 full-time freshmen.
**Selectivity:** Open admission; but selective for some programs.

**BASIC COSTS (2015-2016)**
**Tuition and fees:** $6,204; out-of-state residents $6,234.
**Room and board:** $6,506.

**FINANCIAL AID PICTURE**
**Students with need:** Need-based aid available for full-time and part-time students. Work study available nights, weekends, and for part-time students.
**Students without need:** No-need awards available for academics, alumni affiliation, art, athletics, leadership, minority status, music/drama, state/district residency.

**FINANCIAL AID PROCEDURES**
**Forms required:** FAFSA, institutional form.
**Dates and Deadlines:** Priority date 6/1; no closing date. Applicants notified on a rolling basis starting 4/1; must reply within 2 week(s) of notification.

**CONTACT**
Sherry Douglas, Director of Financial Aid
1000 Main Street, Chadron, NE 69337
(308) 432-6230

## Clarkson College
Omaha, Nebraska
www.clarksoncollege.edu                    Federal Code: 009862

**4-year private** health science college in large city, affiliated with Episcopal Church.
**Enrollment:** 765 undergrads.
**Selectivity:** Open admission; but selective for some programs.

### BASIC COSTS (2015-2016)
**Tuition and fees:** $15,210.
**Per-credit charge:** $480.
**Room only:** $4,840.

### FINANCIAL AID PICTURE
**Students with need:** Need-based aid available for full-time and part-time students. Work study available nights, weekends, and for part-time students.
**Students without need:** No-need awards available for academics, alumni affiliation, minority status, religious affiliation.

### FINANCIAL AID PROCEDURES
**Forms required:** FAFSA, institutional form.
**Dates and Deadlines:** Priority date 4/1; no closing date. Applicants notified on a rolling basis starting 4/13; must reply within 3 week(s) of notification.
**Transfers:** Priority date 3/1; no deadline. Applicants notified on a rolling basis starting 3/30.

### CONTACT
Margie Harris, Director of Student Financial Services
101 South 42nd Street, Omaha, NE 68131-2739
(402) 552-2749

## College of Saint Mary
Omaha, Nebraska
www.csm.edu                    Federal Code: 002540

**4-year private** university and liberal arts college for women in large city, affiliated with Roman Catholic Church.
**Enrollment:** 705 undergrads, 4% part-time. 99 full-time freshmen.
**Selectivity:** Admits 50 to 75% of applicants.

### BASIC COSTS (2015-2016)
**Tuition and fees:** $28,964.
**Per-credit charge:** $950.
**Room and board:** $7,400.

### FINANCIAL AID PICTURE (2015-2016)
**Students with need:** Average financial aid package met 75% of need; average scholarship/grant was $19,031; average loan was $2,785. For part-time students, average financial aid package was $5,532.
**Students without need:** No-need awards available for academics, athletics, music/drama.

### FINANCIAL AID PROCEDURES
**Forms required:** FAFSA.
**Dates and Deadlines:** Priority date 3/15; no closing date. Applicants notified on a rolling basis starting 3/15; must reply within 2 week(s) of notification.
**Transfers:** No deadline. Applicants notified on a rolling basis starting 3/15; must reply within 2 week(s) of notification. Scholarships and need based grants available for full-time transfer students.

### CONTACT
Beth Sisk, Director of Financial Aid
7000 Mercy Road, Omaha, NE 68106
(402) 399-2362

## Concordia University
Seward, Nebraska
www.cune.edu                    Federal Code: 002541

**4-year private** university in small town, affiliated with Lutheran Church - Missouri Synod.
**Enrollment:** 1,255 undergrads, 3% part-time. 347 full-time freshmen.
**Selectivity:** Admits over 75% of applicants.

### BASIC COSTS (2016-2017)
**Tuition and fees:** $28,480.
**Per-credit charge:** $860.
**Room and board:** $7,800.

### FINANCIAL AID PICTURE (2015-2016)
**Students with need:** Out of 324 full-time freshmen who applied for aid, 280 were judged to have need. Of these, 280 received aid, and 76 had their full need met. Average financial aid package met 81% of need; average scholarship/grant was $18,413; average loan was $3,450. For part-time students, average financial aid package was $10,318.
**Students without need:** 24 full-time freshmen who did not demonstrate need for aid received scholarships/grants; average award was $16,457. No-need awards available for academics, alumni affiliation, art, athletics, leadership, music/drama, religious affiliation.
**Scholarships offered:** *Merit:* President's scholarship: $18,000 per year; based on GPA and SAT/ACT. Regent's scholarship: $14,000-$15,000 per year; based on GPA and SAT/ACT. Dean's Scholarship: $12,000-$13,000 per year; based on GPA and SAT/ACT. Achievement Award: $8,000-$10,000 per year; based on GPA and SAT/ACT. *Athletic:* 47 full-time freshmen received athletic scholarships; average amount $5,622.

### FINANCIAL AID PROCEDURES
**Forms required:** FAFSA.
**Dates and Deadlines:** Priority date 3/1; no closing date. Applicants notified on a rolling basis starting 3/1; must reply within 4 week(s) of notification.
**Transfers:** Applicants notified on a rolling basis starting 3/1; must reply within 4 week(s) of notification.

### CONTACT
Donna Stehlik, Director of SFS & Financial Aid Compliance
800 North Columbia Avenue, Seward, NE 68434-1556
(800) 535-5494 ext. 7270

## Creative Center
Omaha, Nebraska
www.creativecenter.edu                    Federal Code: 031643

**4-year for-profit** visual arts and career college in large city.
**Enrollment:** 64 undergrads, 6% part-time.
**Selectivity:** Admits over 75% of applicants.

### BASIC COSTS (2016-2017)
**Tuition and fees:** $27,700.

### FINANCIAL AID PICTURE
**Students with need:** Need-based aid available for full-time and part-time students.
**Students without need:** No-need awards available for academics, art.
**Scholarships offered:** President's Award: $1,000. Founder's Award: $2,000. Both awards based on portfolio and high school academics. Andy Arrants Memorial Scholarship: supply kit (approx. $500); based on submitted artwork and essay.

### FINANCIAL AID PROCEDURES
**Forms required:** FAFSA.
**Dates and Deadlines:** Closing date 7/15. Applicants notified on a rolling basis starting 2/1.
**Transfers:** No deadline. Applicants notified on a rolling basis starting 2/1.

## CONTACT

Sandy LaRocca, Director of Financial Aid
10850 Emmet Street, Omaha, NE 68164-2911
(402) 898-1000 ext. 203

# Creighton University
Omaha, Nebraska
www.creighton.edu                    Federal Code: 002542

**4-year private** university in very large city, affiliated with Roman Catholic Church.
**Enrollment:** 4,080 undergrads, 4% part-time. 1,065 full-time freshmen.
**Selectivity:** Admits 50 to 75% of applicants.

## BASIC COSTS (2015-2016)

**Tuition and fees:** $36,422.
**Per-credit charge:** $1,090.
**Room and board:** $10,294.
**Additional info:** Tuition/fee waivers available for adults, minority students.

## FINANCIAL AID PICTURE (2015-2016)

**Students with need:** Out of 853 full-time freshmen who applied for aid, 645 were judged to have need. Of these, 645 received aid, and 179 had their full need met. Average financial aid package met 85% of need; average scholarship/grant was $21,566; average loan was $5,120. Need-based aid available for part-time students.
**Students without need:** 383 full-time freshmen who did not demonstrate need for aid received scholarships/grants; average award was $14,488. No-need awards available for academics, alumni affiliation, art, athletics, leadership, minority status, music/drama, ROTC.
**Scholarships offered:** *Merit:* Diversity Scholarship & Native American Merit Scholarship: $30,000; awarded to students who show commitment to diversity; 3.3 GPA or higher on a 4.0 scale required; applicants evaluated on academic merit, community service, school activities, leadership, and financial need. First-generation college bound students are encouraged to apply. Excellence in the Arts: $4,000; awarded to students who intend to major in music, art, dance, theater, and musical theater. Christina M. Hixson Scholarship in Business Administration: $4,500; awarded to freshman business students from high schools in CO, IA, IL, KA, MN, MO, NE, ND, SD, WI or WY with a minimum of 3.0 GPA. Heider College of Business Administration Ethics and Social Responsibility Scholarship: $2,500; awarded to students with exceptional service accomplishments and leadership potential. Presidential Scholarship: $28,000; awarded to selected applicants in the top 10% of applicant pool, based upon academics. Scott Scholarship: full tuition scholarship in the Heider College of Business Administration; awarded to selected students in the top 10% of applicant pool; based on academics. G. Robert Muchemore Foundation Undergraduate Scholarship: $26,000; awarded to graduates of Nebraska high schools entering as freshmen; based upon academics. *Athletic:* 37 full-time freshmen received athletic scholarships; average amount $16,925.

## FINANCIAL AID PROCEDURES

**Forms required:** FAFSA, institutional form.
**Dates and Deadlines:** Priority date 3/1; no closing date. Applicants notified on a rolling basis starting 3/15; must reply by 3/15 or within 4 week(s) of notification.
**Transfers:** No deadline. Applicants notified on a rolling basis starting 3/10; must reply by 5/1 or within 2 week(s) of notification.

## CONTACT

Paula Kohles, Director of Financial Aid
2500 California Plaza, Omaha, NE 68178-0001
(402) 280-2731

# Doane College
Crete, Nebraska
www.doane.edu                    Federal Code: 002544

**4-year private** liberal arts college in small town, affiliated with United Church of Christ.
**Enrollment:** 1,053 undergrads, 1% part-time. 330 full-time freshmen.
**Selectivity:** Admits over 75% of applicants.

## BASIC COSTS (2015-2016)

**Tuition and fees:** $28,790.
**Per-credit charge:** $940.
**Room and board:** $8,350.

## FINANCIAL AID PICTURE (2015-2016)

**Students with need:** Out of 309 full-time freshmen who applied for aid, 268 were judged to have need. Of these, 268 received aid, and 105 had their full need met. Average financial aid package met 93% of need; average scholarship/grant was $20,993; average loan was $3,568. Need-based aid available for part-time students.
**Students without need:** 20 full-time freshmen who did not demonstrate need for aid received scholarships/grants; average award was $13,464. No-need awards available for academics, alumni affiliation, art, athletics, music/drama, religious affiliation.
**Scholarships offered:** 41 full-time freshmen received athletic scholarships; average amount $5,024.

## FINANCIAL AID PROCEDURES

**Forms required:** FAFSA.
**Dates and Deadlines:** Priority date 2/25; no closing date. Applicants notified on a rolling basis starting 3/15; must reply within 4 week(s) of notification.

## CONTACT

Peggy Tvrdy, Director of Financial Aid
1014 Boswell Avenue, Crete, NE 68333
(402) 826-8260

# Grace University
Omaha, Nebraska
www.graceuniversity.edu                    Federal Code: 002547

**4-year private** university and Bible college in large city, affiliated with interdenominational tradition.
**Enrollment:** 345 undergrads.

## BASIC COSTS (2015-2016)

**Tuition and fees:** $20,548.
**Per-credit charge:** $555.
**Room and board:** $7,228.
**Additional info:** Tuition/fee waivers available for minority students.

## FINANCIAL AID PICTURE

**Students with need:** Need-based aid available for full-time and part-time students.
**Students without need:** No-need awards available for academics, alumni affiliation, athletics, leadership, minority status, music/drama.

## FINANCIAL AID PROCEDURES

**Forms required:** FAFSA.
**Dates and Deadlines:** Priority date 3/1; closing date 4/1. Applicants notified on a rolling basis starting 3/1; must reply within 3 week(s) of notification.
**Transfers:** No deadline. Applicants notified on a rolling basis starting 3/1; must reply within 3 week(s) of notification.

## CONTACT

Ray Miller, Director of Financial Aid
1311 South Ninth Street, Omaha, NE 68108-3629
(402) 449-2810

## Hastings College
Hastings, Nebraska
www.hastings.edu                    Federal Code: 002548

**4-year private** liberal arts college in large town, affiliated with Presbyterian Church (USA).
**Enrollment:** 1,103 undergrads, 1% part-time. 293 full-time freshmen.

### BASIC COSTS (2015-2016)
**Tuition and fees:** $27,300.
**Per-credit charge:** $1,070.
**Room and board:** $8,080.
**Additional info:** Tuition/fee waivers available for adults.

### FINANCIAL AID PICTURE
**Students with need:** Need-based aid available for full-time and part-time students. Work study available nights, weekends, and for part-time students.
**Students without need:** No-need awards available for academics, alumni affiliation, art, athletics, leadership, music/drama.
**Scholarships offered:** Walter Scott Scholarship Competition: full-tuition, for freshman; 3 awarded. Trustees Scholarships: $14,000 per year. President's Scholarships: $13,000 per year. Dean Scholarships: $12,000 per year. Ambassador Scholarships: $10,000 per year. Ringland Scholarships: $8,000 per year. Pro Rege Scholarships: $7,000 per year. Kessler Scholarship: full tuition, for Christian Ministry students; 3 awarded. Christian Ministry scholarships: $5,000 per year; 3 awarded.

### FINANCIAL AID PROCEDURES
**Forms required:** FAFSA, institutional form.
**Dates and Deadlines:** Closing date 5/1. Applicants notified on a rolling basis starting 2/15; must reply within 2 week(s) of notification.
**Transfers:** No deadline. Stafford loans based on number of transferable credits.

### CONTACT
Traci Boeve, Financial Aid Director
710 North Turner Avenue, Hastings, NE 68901-7621
(402) 461-7789

## Kaplan University: Lincoln
Lincoln, Nebraska
www.lincoln.kaplanuniversity.edu     Federal Code: 004721

**2-year for-profit** branch campus college in small city.
**Enrollment:** 548 undergrads.
**Selectivity:** Open admission; but selective for some programs.

### BASIC COSTS (2015-2016)
**Additional info:** Bachelor's degree programs - $66,417, Associate's degree programs range from $30,654-$35,763, Certificate programs range from $11,501-$22,368. Some programs have additional associated fees that are not included in the price of tuition.

### FINANCIAL AID PICTURE
**Students with need:** Need-based aid available for full-time and part-time students. Work study available nights, weekends, and for part-time students.
**Students without need:** This college awards aid only to students with need.

### FINANCIAL AID PROCEDURES
**Forms required:** FAFSA, institutional form.
**Dates and Deadlines:** Applicants notified on a rolling basis starting 2/1.
**Transfers:** No deadline.

### CONTACT
Corinne Combs, Director of Financial Aid
1821 K Street, Lincoln, NE 68508
(402) 474-5315

## Kaplan University: Omaha
Omaha, Nebraska
www.omaha.kaplanuniversity.edu      Federal Code: 008491

**2-year for-profit** career college in large city.
**Enrollment:** 549 undergrads.
**Selectivity:** Open admission; but selective for some programs.

### BASIC COSTS (2015-2016)
**Additional info:** Bachelor's degree programs - $66,417, Associate's degree programs range from $30,654-$35,763, Certificate programs range from $11,501-$22,368. Some programs have additional associated fees that are not included in the price of tuition.

### FINANCIAL AID PICTURE
**Students with need:** Need-based aid available for full-time and part-time students. Work study available nights, weekends, and for part-time students.
**Students without need:** This college awards aid only to students with need.

### FINANCIAL AID PROCEDURES
**Forms required:** FAFSA, institutional form.
**Dates and Deadlines:** Applicants notified on a rolling basis.

### CONTACT
Crystal Faxon, Director Of Financial Aid
5425 North 103rd Street, Omaha, NE 68134
(402) 431-6100

## Little Priest Tribal College
Winnebago, Nebraska
www.littlepriest.edu                 Federal Code: 033233

**2-year private** community college in rural community.
**Enrollment:** 104 undergrads, 35% part-time. 17 full-time freshmen.
**Selectivity:** Open admission.

### FINANCIAL AID PICTURE
**Students with need:** Need-based aid available for full-time and part-time students.

### FINANCIAL AID PROCEDURES
**Forms required:** FAFSA, institutional form.

### CONTACT
Sabariyatty Mohhammad, Director of Financial Aid
PO Box 270, Winnebago, NE 68071
(402) 878-3325

## Metropolitan Community College
Omaha, Nebraska
www.mccneb.edu                       Federal Code: 004432

**2-year public** community and technical college in large city.
**Enrollment:** 12,662 undergrads.
**Selectivity:** Open admission; but selective for some programs.

### BASIC COSTS (2015-2016)
**Tuition and fees:** $2,775; out-of-state residents $4,035.
**Per-credit charge:** $56; out-of-state residents $84.
**Room and board:** $6,255.

### FINANCIAL AID PICTURE
**Students with need:** Need-based aid available for full-time and part-time students.
**Students without need:** No-need awards available for academics.

## FINANCIAL AID PROCEDURES

**Forms required:** FAFSA, institutional form.

**Dates and Deadlines:** Priority date 3/15; no closing date. Applicants notified on a rolling basis starting 4/15.

## CONTACT

Wilma Hjelum, Director of Financial Aid & Veteran Services

Box 3777, Omaha, NE 68103-0777

(402) 457-2330

## Mid-Plains Community College

North Platte, Nebraska

www.mpcc.edu                    Federal Code: 002557

**2-year public** community and technical college in large town.

**Enrollment:** 1,209 undergrads, 37% part-time. 353 full-time freshmen.

**Selectivity:** Open admission; but selective for some programs.

### BASIC COSTS (2015-2016)

**Tuition and fees:** $2,880; out-of-state residents $3,600.

**Per-credit charge:** $81; out-of-state residents $105.

**Room and board:** $5,896.

### FINANCIAL AID PICTURE (2014-2015)

**Students with need:** Out of 292 full-time freshmen who applied for aid, 219 were judged to have need. Of these, 218 received aid, and 82 had their full need met. Average financial aid package met 84% of need; average scholarship/grant was $4,591; average loan was $2,064. For part-time students, average financial aid package was $4,130.

**Students without need:** 69 full-time freshmen who did not demonstrate need for aid received scholarships/grants; average award was $1,452. No-need awards available for academics, art, athletics, music/drama.

**Scholarships offered:** 51 full-time freshmen received athletic scholarships; average amount $4,014.

### FINANCIAL AID PROCEDURES

**Forms required:** FAFSA, institutional form.

**Dates and Deadlines:** Priority date 5/1; no closing date. Applicants notified on a rolling basis starting 5/1; must reply within 3 week(s) of notification.

**Transfers:** Priority date 3/1. Applicants notified on a rolling basis starting 3/5; must reply within 2 week(s) of notification.

### CONTACT

Erinn Brauer, Director of Financial Aid

1101 Halligan Drive, North Platte, NE 69101

(800) 658-4348

## Midland University

Fremont, Nebraska

www.midlandu.edu                    Federal Code: 002553

**4-year private** university and liberal arts college in large town, affiliated with Evangelical Lutheran Church in America.

**Enrollment:** 1,224 undergrads.

### BASIC COSTS (2015-2016)

**Tuition and fees:** $29,400.

**Room and board:** $7,484.

**Additional info:** Tuition/fee waivers available for minority students.

### FINANCIAL AID PICTURE

**Students with need:** Need-based aid available for full-time and part-time students. Work study available nights, weekends, and for part-time students.

**Students without need:** No-need awards available for academics, alumni affiliation, art, athletics, leadership, minority status, music/drama, religious affiliation.

## FINANCIAL AID PROCEDURES

**Forms required:** FAFSA, institutional form.

**Dates and Deadlines:** Priority date 4/15; no closing date. Applicants notified on a rolling basis starting 3/1; must reply within 2 week(s) of notification.

**Transfers:** Priority date 4/1. Applicants notified on a rolling basis starting 4/1; must reply within 2 week(s) of notification.

## CONTACT

Doug Watson, Director of Financial Aid

900 North Clarkson, Fremont, NE 68025

(402) 721-5480

## Nebraska Christian College

Papillion, Nebraska

www.nechristian.edu                    Federal Code: 012976

**4-year private** Bible college in large town, affiliated with Christian Church.

**Enrollment:** 130 undergrads.

### BASIC COSTS (2015-2016)

**Tuition and fees:** $600.

**Per-credit charge:** $625.

**Comprehensive fee:** $22,900.

### FINANCIAL AID PICTURE

**Students with need:** Need-based aid available for full-time and part-time students. Work study available nights, weekends, and for part-time students.

**Students without need:** No-need awards available for academics, leadership, religious affiliation.

### FINANCIAL AID PROCEDURES

**Forms required:** FAFSA, institutional form.

**Dates and Deadlines:** Priority date 6/1; no closing date. Applicants notified on a rolling basis starting 5/5.

### CONTACT

Sarah Nigro, Financial Aid Officer

12550 South 114th Street, Papillion, NE 68046

## Nebraska College of Technical Agriculture

Curtis, Nebraska

www.ncta.unl.edu                    Federal Code: 007358

**2-year public** agricultural college in rural community.

**Enrollment:** 253 undergrads, 6% part-time. 91 full-time freshmen.

**Selectivity:** Open admission.

### BASIC COSTS (2015-2016)

**Tuition and fees:** $4,679; out-of-state residents $9,175.

**Per-credit charge:** $118; out-of-state residents $250.25.

**Room and board:** $6,956.

### FINANCIAL AID PICTURE (2014-2015)

**Students with need:** Average financial aid package met 69% of need; average scholarship/grant was $6,385; average loan was $3,147. Need-based aid available for part-time students.

**Students without need:** No-need awards available for academics, leadership, state/district residency.

### FINANCIAL AID PROCEDURES

**Forms required:** FAFSA.

**Dates and Deadlines:** Priority date 4/1; no closing date. Applicants notified on a rolling basis starting 5/1; must reply within 2 week(s) of notification.

**Transfers:** No deadline. Applicants notified on a rolling basis; must reply within 2 week(s) of notification.

CONTACT

Brenda Kahny, Financial Aid Specialist

404 East 7th Street, Curtis, NE 69025-0069

(308) 367-5207

## Nebraska Indian Community College

Macy, Nebraska

www.thenicc.edu                 Federal Code: 015339

**2-year public** community college in rural community.

**Enrollment:** 132 undergrads. 19 full-time freshmen.

**Selectivity:** Open admission.

### BASIC COSTS (2016-2017)

**Tuition and fees:** $5,150.

**Per-credit charge:** $170.

**Additional info:** Tuition/fee waivers available for minority students.

### FINANCIAL AID PICTURE (2014-2015)

**Students with need:** Out of 18 full-time freshmen who applied for aid, 18 were judged to have need. Of these, 18 received aid. Need-based aid available for part-time students.

**Students without need:** This college awards aid only to students with need.

### FINANCIAL AID PROCEDURES

**Forms required:** FAFSA.

**Dates and Deadlines:** Priority date 9/1; no closing date.

**Transfers:** No deadline. Must reply within 2 week(s) of notification.

### CONTACT

Cecilei Pappan, Financial Aid Director

PO Box 428, Macy, NE 68039-0428

(402) 241-5930

## Nebraska Methodist College of Nursing and Allied Health

Omaha, Nebraska

www.methodistcollege.edu        Federal Code: 009937

**4-year private** health science and nursing college in large city, affiliated with United Methodist Church.

**Enrollment:** 766 undergrads, 38% part-time. 33 full-time freshmen.

### BASIC COSTS (2015-2016)

**Tuition and fees:** $18,109.

**Per-credit charge:** $552.

**Room only:** $6,460.

### FINANCIAL AID PICTURE (2015-2016)

**Students with need:** Out of 28 full-time freshmen who applied for aid, 24 were judged to have need. Of these, 24 received aid. Average financial aid package met 51% of need; average scholarship/grant was $7,872; average loan was $3,520. For part-time students, average financial aid package was $8,233.

**Students without need:** 5 full-time freshmen who did not demonstrate need for aid received scholarships/grants; average award was $5,200. No-need awards available for academics, alumni affiliation, leadership, religious affiliation.

### FINANCIAL AID PROCEDURES

**Forms required:** FAFSA, institutional form.

**Dates and Deadlines:** Priority date 3/1; no closing date. Applicants notified on a rolling basis starting 3/15; must reply within 3 week(s) of notification.

CONTACT

Penny James, Director of Financial Aid

720 North 87th Street, Omaha, NE 68114-2852

(402) 354-7225

## Nebraska Wesleyan University

Lincoln, Nebraska

www.nebrwesleyan.edu            Federal Code: 002555

**4-year private** liberal arts college in small city, affiliated with United Methodist Church.

**Enrollment:** 1,788 undergrads, 17% part-time. 368 full-time freshmen.

**Selectivity:** Admits over 75% of applicants.

### BASIC COSTS (2015-2016)

**Tuition and fees:** $29,800.

**Per-credit charge:** $1,075.

**Room and board:** $8,340.

**Additional info:** Tuition/fee waivers available for adults, minority students.

### FINANCIAL AID PICTURE (2014-2015)

**Students with need:** Out of 332 full-time freshmen who applied for aid, 294 were judged to have need. Of these, 293 received aid, and 71 had their full need met. Average financial aid package met 81% of need; average scholarship/grant was $17,683; average loan was $4,956. For part-time students, average financial aid package was $7,334.

**Students without need:** 67 full-time freshmen who did not demonstrate need for aid received scholarships/grants; average award was $13,701. No-need awards available for academics, alumni affiliation, art, leadership, music/drama.

**Scholarships offered:** Huge-NWU Scholarship: tuition, books, fees, and room and board up to $27,000; competitive; 2 awards per year.

### FINANCIAL AID PROCEDURES

**Forms required:** FAFSA.

**Dates and Deadlines:** Applicants notified on a rolling basis starting 2/1; must reply by 5/1 or within 2 week(s) of notification.

**Transfers:** No deadline. Applicants notified on a rolling basis starting 2/1; must reply within 3 week(s) of notification.

### CONTACT

Thomas Ochsner, Director of Scholarships and Financial Aid

5000 St. Paul Avenue, Lincoln, NE 68504

(402) 465-2212

## Northeast Community College

Norfolk, Nebraska

www.northeast.edu               Federal Code: 002556

**2-year public** community college in large town.

**Enrollment:** 2,726 undergrads.

**Selectivity:** Open admission; but selective for some programs.

### BASIC COSTS (2015-2016)

**Tuition and fees:** $3,165; out-of-state residents $4,215.

**Per-credit charge:** $86; out-of-state residents $121.

**Room and board:** $7,200.

### FINANCIAL AID PICTURE

**Students with need:** Need-based aid available for full-time and part-time students. Work study available nights, weekends, and for part-time students.

**Students without need:** No-need awards available for academics, athletics, music/drama.

### FINANCIAL AID PROCEDURES

**Forms required:** FAFSA, institutional form.

**Dates and Deadlines:** Applicants notified on a rolling basis; must reply within 2 week(s) of notification.

**CONTACT**
Stacy Dieckman, Director of Financial Aid
801 East Benjamin Avenue, Norfolk, NE 68702-0469
(402) 844-7285

## Peru State College
Peru, Nebraska
www.peru.edu                    Federal Code: 002559

**4-year public** liberal arts and teachers college in rural community.
**Enrollment:** 1,472 undergrads, 22% part-time. 250 full-time freshmen.
**Selectivity:** Open admission.

**BASIC COSTS (2015-2016)**
**Tuition and fees:** $6,397; out-of-state residents $6,397.
**Room and board:** $7,018.

**FINANCIAL AID PICTURE**
**Students with need:** Need-based aid available for full-time and part-time students. Work study available nights, weekends, and for part-time students.
**Students without need:** No-need awards available for academics, art, athletics, leadership, music/drama, state/district residency.

**FINANCIAL AID PROCEDURES**
**Forms required:** FAFSA.
**Dates and Deadlines:** Priority date 3/1; no closing date. Applicants notified on a rolling basis starting 3/1; must reply within 2 week(s) of notification.
**Transfers:** Must have financial aid transcripts from all previous schools sent to college.

**CONTACT**
P.O. Box 10, Peru, NE 68421-0010
(402) 872-2228

## Southeast Community College
Lincoln, Nebraska
www.southeast.edu               Federal Code: 007591

**2-year public** community college in small city.
**Enrollment:** 6,537 undergrads.
**Selectivity:** Open admission.

**BASIC COSTS (2015-2016)**
**Tuition and fees:** $2,779; out-of-state residents $3,409.
**Per-credit charge:** $61; out-of-state residents $75.
**Room and board:** $4,647.

**FINANCIAL AID PICTURE**
**Students with need:** Need-based aid available for full-time and part-time students. Work study available nights, weekends, and for part-time students.
**Students without need:** No-need awards available for academics, leadership, minority status, state/district residency.

**FINANCIAL AID PROCEDURES**
**Forms required:** FAFSA, institutional form.
**Dates and Deadlines:** Applicants notified on a rolling basis; must reply within 2 week(s) of notification.

**CONTACT**
Melissa Troyer, Administrative Director of Financial Aid
8800 O Street, Lincoln, NE 68520
(402) 437-2610

## Union College
Lincoln, Nebraska
www.ucollege.edu                Federal Code: 002563

**4-year private** liberal arts college in large city, affiliated with Seventh-day Adventists.
**Enrollment:** 762 undergrads, 5% part-time. 156 full-time freshmen.
**Selectivity:** Admits 50 to 75% of applicants.

**BASIC COSTS (2016-2017)**
**Tuition and fees:** $22,538.
**Per-credit charge:** $894.
**Room and board:** $6,766.

**FINANCIAL AID PICTURE (2014-2015)**
**Students with need:** Out of 128 full-time freshmen who applied for aid, 110 were judged to have need. Of these, 110 received aid, and 28 had their full need met. Average financial aid package met 76% of need; average scholarship/grant was $15,017; average loan was $4,164. For part-time students, average financial aid package was $8,193.
**Students without need:** 43 full-time freshmen who did not demonstrate need for aid received scholarships/grants; average award was $8,719. No-need awards available for academics, state/district residency.
**Additional info:** Special institutional grants offered to all freshmen and sophomores demonstrating exceptional financial need.

**FINANCIAL AID PROCEDURES**
**Forms required:** FAFSA, institutional form.
**Dates and Deadlines:** Applicants notified on a rolling basis starting 12/1; must reply by 9/1.

**CONTACT**
Taryn Rouse, Director of Student Financial Services
3800 South 48th Street, Lincoln, NE 68506-4300
(402) 486-2505

## University of Nebraska - Kearney
Kearney, Nebraska
www.unk.edu                     Federal Code: 002551

**4-year public** university in large town.
**Enrollment:** 4,820 undergrads, 10% part-time. 985 full-time freshmen.
**Selectivity:** Admits over 75% of applicants.

**BASIC COSTS (2015-2016)**
**Tuition and fees:** $6,724; out-of-state residents $12,994.
**Per-credit charge:** $175; out-of-state residents $380.
**Room and board:** $9,230.

**FINANCIAL AID PICTURE (2014-2015)**
**Students with need:** Out of 852 full-time freshmen who applied for aid, 695 were judged to have need. Of these, 689 received aid, and 227 had their full need met. Average financial aid package met 74% of need; average scholarship/grant was $8,200; average loan was $3,386. For part-time students, average financial aid package was $5,932.
**Students without need:** 155 full-time freshmen who did not demonstrate need for aid received scholarships/grants; average award was $4,919. No-need awards available for academics, alumni affiliation, art, athletics, leadership, minority status, music/drama, ROTC, state/district residency.
**Scholarships offered:** 33 full-time freshmen received athletic scholarships; average amount $4,124.

**FINANCIAL AID PROCEDURES**
**Forms required:** FAFSA, institutional form.
**Dates and Deadlines:** Priority date 4/1; no closing date. Applicants notified on a rolling basis starting 3/15; must reply within 2 week(s) of notification.
**Transfers:** No deadline. Applicants notified on a rolling basis starting 3/15.

**CONTACT**
Mary Sommers, Director of Financial Aid
905 West 25th, Kearney, NE 68849
(308) 865-8520

## University of Nebraska - Lincoln
Lincoln, Nebraska
www.unl.edu                              Federal Code: 002565

**4-year public** university in large city.
**Enrollment:** 20,182 undergrads, 7% part-time. 4,628 full-time freshmen.
**Selectivity:** Admits over 75% of applicants.

**BASIC COSTS (2015-2016)**
**Tuition and fees:** $8,279; out-of-state residents $22,446.
**Room and board:** $10,310.

**FINANCIAL AID PICTURE (2014-2015)**
**Students with need:** Out of 3,546 full-time freshmen who applied for aid, 2,544 were judged to have need. Of these, 2,492 received aid, and 572 had their full need met. Average financial aid package met 82% of need; average scholarship/grant was $7,871; average loan was $3,893. For part-time students, average financial aid package was $10,657.
**Students without need:** 571 full-time freshmen who did not demonstrate need for aid received scholarships/grants; average award was $6,485. No-need awards available for academics, alumni affiliation, art, athletics, leadership, music/drama, state/district residency.
**Scholarships offered:** 149 full-time freshmen received athletic scholarships; average amount $11,915.

**FINANCIAL AID PROCEDURES**
**Forms required:** FAFSA.
**Dates and Deadlines:** Priority date 4/1; no closing date. Applicants notified on a rolling basis starting 4/1.
**Transfers:** No deadline. Applicants notified on a rolling basis starting 4/1.

**CONTACT**
Justin Brown, Director of Scholarships and Financial Aid
1410 Q Street, Lincoln, NE 68588-0417
(402) 472-2030

## University of Nebraska - Omaha
Omaha, Nebraska
www.unomaha.edu                          Federal Code: 002554

**4-year public** university in large city.
**Enrollment:** 12,287 undergrads, 22% part-time. 2,060 full-time freshmen.
**Selectivity:** Admits over 75% of applicants.

**BASIC COSTS (2015-2016)**
**Tuition and fees:** $7,573; out-of-state residents $20,368.
**Room and board:** $8,848.

**FINANCIAL AID PICTURE (2014-2015)**
**Students with need:** Out of 1,509 full-time freshmen who applied for aid, 1,203 were judged to have need. Of these, 1,182 received aid, and 307 had their full need met. Average financial aid package met 65% of need; average scholarship/grant was $6,298; average loan was $3,091. For part-time students, average financial aid package was $6,000.
**Students without need:** 139 full-time freshmen who did not demonstrate need for aid received scholarships/grants; average award was $1,880. No-need awards available for academics, alumni affiliation, art, athletics, leadership, minority status, music/drama, ROTC, state/district residency.
**Scholarships offered:** 55 full-time freshmen received athletic scholarships; average amount $6,922.

**FINANCIAL AID PROCEDURES**
**Forms required:** FAFSA.
**Dates and Deadlines:** Priority date 4/1; no closing date. Applicants notified on a rolling basis starting 4/15; must reply within 2 week(s) of notification.

**CONTACT**
Marty Habrock, Director of Financial Aid
6001 Dodge Street, Omaha, NE 68182-0005
(402) 554-2327

## University of Nebraska Medical Center
Omaha, Nebraska
www.unmc.edu                             Federal Code: 006895

**Upper-division public** health science college in very large city.
**Enrollment:** 739 undergrads.

**BASIC COSTS (2015-2016)**
**Additional info:** College of Medicine: resident $28,000; nonresident $69,640; Books/Equipment $1,720. College of Dentistry: resident $28,700; nonresident $70,405; Books/Equipment $8,040. College of Pharmacy: resident $18,330; nonresident $37,770; Books/Equipment $1,130. Tuition is assessed on per semester not credit hour basis. Tuition/fee waivers available for minority students.

**FINANCIAL AID PICTURE**
**Students with need:** Need-based aid available for full-time and part-time students. Work study available nights, weekends, and for part-time students.

**FINANCIAL AID PROCEDURES**
**Forms required:** FAFSA, institutional form.
**Dates and Deadlines:** Closing date 4/1. Applicants notified by 7/1; must reply by 7/30 or within 2 week(s) of notification.
**Transfers:** No deadline. Applicants notified on a rolling basis starting 5/1; must reply within 2 week(s) of notification.

**CONTACT**
Judith Walker, Director of Financial Aid
984230 Nebraska Medical Center, Omaha, NE 68198-4230
(402) 559-4199

## Wayne State College
Wayne, Nebraska
www.wsc.edu                              Federal Code: 002566

**4-year public** liberal arts and teachers college in small town.
**Enrollment:** 2,783 undergrads, 6% part-time. 630 full-time freshmen.
**Selectivity:** Open admission.

**BASIC COSTS (2015-2016)**
**Tuition and fees:** $6,042; out-of-state residents $10,632.
**Per-credit charge:** $153; out-of-state residents $306.
**Room and board:** $6,760.
**Additional info:** Additional Special Rates apply for residents of qualifying states.

**FINANCIAL AID PICTURE (2015-2016)**
**Students with need:** Out of 573 full-time freshmen who applied for aid, 418 were judged to have need. Of these, 407 received aid, and 173 had their full need met. Average financial aid package met 54% of need; average scholarship/grant was $4,323; average loan was $3,242. For part-time students, average financial aid package was $6,938.
**Students without need:** 76 full-time freshmen who did not demonstrate need for aid received scholarships/grants; average award was $2,284. No-need awards available for academics, art, athletics, leadership, minority status, music/drama, religious affiliation, ROTC, state/district residency.

**Scholarships offered:** 50 full-time freshmen received athletic scholarships; average amount $3,281.

## FINANCIAL AID PROCEDURES

**Forms required:** FAFSA.

**Dates and Deadlines:** Priority date 4/1; no closing date. Applicants notified on a rolling basis starting 4/1; must reply within 4 week(s) of notification.

## CONTACT

Annette Kaus, Director of Financial Aid

1111 Main Street, Wayne, NE 68787

(402) 375-7230

## Western Nebraska Community College

Scottsbluff, Nebraska

www.wncc.edu                    Federal Code: 002560

**2-year public** community college in large town.

**Enrollment:** 1,232 undergrads, 37% part-time. 317 full-time freshmen.

**Selectivity:** Open admission; but selective for some programs.

### BASIC COSTS (2016-2017)

**Tuition and fees:** $3,270; out-of-state residents $3,660.

**Per-credit charge:** $91.5; out-of-state residents $104.5.

**Room and board:** $7,010.

**Additional info:** Border state students from Colorado, Wyoming, and South Dakota pay in-state tuition rates.

### FINANCIAL AID PICTURE (2015-2016)

**Students with need:** Out of 237 full-time freshmen who applied for aid, 178 were judged to have need. Of these, 173 received aid. Average financial aid package met 92% of need; average scholarship/grant was $4,859; average loan was $3,194. For part-time students, average financial aid package was $9,305.

**Students without need:** 74 full-time freshmen who did not demonstrate need for aid received scholarships/grants; average award was $1,703. No-need awards available for academics, art, athletics, leadership, music/drama, state/district residency.

**Scholarships offered:** 68 full-time freshmen received athletic scholarships; average amount $6,088.

### FINANCIAL AID PROCEDURES

**Forms required:** FAFSA.

**Dates and Deadlines:** Priority date 3/1; no closing date. Applicants notified on a rolling basis starting 4/1.

**Transfers:** State of Nebraska limits the amount of Nebraska State Grant funds a student receives in any one year.

### CONTACT

Sheila Johns, Director of Financial Aid

1601 East 27th Street, Scottsbluff, NE 69361

(308) 635-6011

## York College

York, Nebraska

www.york.edu                    Federal Code: 002567

**4-year private** liberal arts and teachers college in small town, affiliated with Church of Christ.

**Enrollment:** 392 undergrads. 109 full-time freshmen.

**Selectivity:** Admits 50 to 75% of applicants.

### BASIC COSTS (2016-2017)

**Tuition and fees:** $17,700.

**Per-credit charge:** $600.

**Room and board:** $6,600.

## FINANCIAL AID PICTURE

**Students with need:** Need-based aid available for full-time and part-time students. Work study available nights, weekends, and for part-time students.

**Students without need:** No-need awards available for academics, alumni affiliation, athletics, leadership, music/drama.

## FINANCIAL AID PROCEDURES

**Forms required:** FAFSA.

**Dates and Deadlines:** Priority date 4/1; no closing date. Applicants notified on a rolling basis starting 3/1; must reply within 4 week(s) of notification.

**Transfers:** No deadline. Applicants notified on a rolling basis starting 3/1; must reply within 4 week(s) of notification.

## CONTACT

Brien Alley, Director of Financial Aid

1125 East 8th Street, York, NE 68467

(402) 363-5624

# Nevada

## Art Institute of Las Vegas

Henderson, Nevada

www.artinstitutes.edu/lasvegas          Federal Code: 030846

**3-year for-profit** culinary school and visual arts college in very large city.

**Enrollment:** 952 undergrads.

**Selectivity:** Open admission; but selective for some programs.

### BASIC COSTS (2015-2016)

**Tuition and fees:** $22,645.

**Per-credit charge:** $481.

**Room only:** $5,850.

### FINANCIAL AID PICTURE

**Students with need:** Need-based aid available for full-time and part-time students. Work study available nights, weekends, and for part-time students.

**Students without need:** No-need awards available for academics, state/district residency.

**Scholarships offered:** Academic Competitiveness Grant: up to $750 the first year and up to $1,300 the second year; available to students who are receiving a Pell Grant, are full time in their first or second year of college in a degree program, who graduated from high school in 2005 or later, and who took a program of study in high school that was considered to be rigorous; each eligible student may receive 2 years of ACG; must have a 3.0 GPA at the end of the first year to receive a second year grant. C-CAP Careers Through Culinary Arts Program: approximately $36,000-$72,000; available to students who are enrolled in a C-CAP program. CKYBER National Kitchen and Bath Association VNU Scholarship: provided for students enrolled in a NKBA (National Kitchen and Bath Association) endorsed program; GPA of 2.7 or higher; must be attending full time for the full academic year; Interior Design program students are eligible to apply. Evelyn Keedy Memorial Scholarship: $30,000 tuition; available to high school seniors who show dedication to their education and a desire for a creative career. National Art Honor Society Scholarship: first Place $20,000, second place $10,000, third place $5,000, fourth place $3,000, fifth place $2,000; high school seniors who also belong to the National Art Honor Society may apply; senior class members of the National Art Honor Society are eligible to compete.

### FINANCIAL AID PROCEDURES

**Dates and Deadlines:** Applicants notified on a rolling basis.

**Transfers:** No deadline. Applicants notified on a rolling basis.

### CONTACT

Dana Sirolli, Director of Student Financial Services

2350 Corporate Circle, Henderson, NV 89074-7737

(702) 369-9944

## Career College of Northern Nevada
Sparks, Nevada
www.ccnn.edu                    Federal Code: 026215

**2-year for-profit** career college in large city.
**Enrollment:** 581 undergrads.
**Selectivity:** Open admission.

### FINANCIAL AID PICTURE
**Students with need:** Need-based aid available for full-time students.
**Students without need:** This college awards aid only to students with need.

### FINANCIAL AID PROCEDURES
**Forms required:** FAFSA.
**Dates and Deadlines:** Applicants notified on a rolling basis.

### CONTACT
Patricia Shannon, Director of Financial Aid
1421 Pullman Drive, Sparks, NV 89434
(775) 856-2266

## College of Southern Nevada
Las Vegas, Nevada
www.csn.edu                    Federal Code: 010362

**2-year public** community college in very large city.
**Enrollment:** 28,685 undergrads, 70% part-time. 1,694 full-time freshmen.
**Selectivity:** Open admission; but selective for some programs.

### BASIC COSTS (2015-2016)
**Tuition and fees:** $2,805; out-of-state residents $9,450.
**Per-credit charge:** $88.

### FINANCIAL AID PICTURE
**Students with need:** Work study available nights, weekends, and for part-time students.
**Students without need:** No-need awards available for state/district residency.

### FINANCIAL AID PROCEDURES
**Forms required:** FAFSA.
**Dates and Deadlines:** Priority date 5/1; closing date 6/30. Applicants notified on a rolling basis starting 7/15; must reply within 2 week(s) of notification.

### CONTACT
Director, Student Financial Services
6375 West Charleston Boulevard, Las Vegas, NV 89146-1164
(702) 651-4047

## Great Basin College
Elko, Nevada
www.gbcnv.edu                    Federal Code: 006977

**4-year public** community and teachers college in large town.
**Enrollment:** 1,926 undergrads.
**Selectivity:** Open admission; but selective for some programs.

### BASIC COSTS (2015-2016)
**Tuition and fees:** $2,805; out-of-state residents $9,450.
**Per-credit charge:** $88.
**Room only:** $3,325.

### FINANCIAL AID PICTURE
**Students with need:** Need-based aid available for full-time and part-time students. Work study available nights, weekends, and for part-time students.

### FINANCIAL AID PROCEDURES
**Forms required:** FAFSA.
**Dates and Deadlines:** Priority date 6/1; no closing date. Applicants notified on a rolling basis starting 7/1.
**Transfers:** Priority date 4/1.

### CONTACT
Scott Neilsen, Director of Financial Aid
1500 College Parkway, Elko, NV 89801
(775) 753-2267

## Kaplan College: Las Vegas
Las Vegas, Nevada
www.kaplancollege.com                    Federal Code: 030432

**2-year for-profit** career college in very large city.
**Enrollment:** 944 undergrads.
**Selectivity:** Open admission; but selective for some programs.

### BASIC COSTS (2015-2016)
**Additional info:** Criminal Justice: $292.22 quarter unit credit (95 Credit Hours), total $30,805. Health Information Technology: $293.89 quarter unit credit (94 Credit Hours), total $30,805. Medical Assistant: $297.03 quarter unit credit (51 Credit Hours), total $15,663. Medical Assistant X-Ray Technician: $291.51 quarter unit credit (70 Credit Hours), total $22,045. Medical Billing and Coding Specialist: $289.09 quarter unit credit (51 Credit Hours), total $15,663. Pharmacy Technician: $258.31 quarter unit credit (57 Credit Hours), total $15,663. Phlebotomy Technician: total $995. Practical Nursing: $313.39 quarter unit credit (89 Credit Hours), total $29,731.

### FINANCIAL AID PICTURE
**Students with need:** Need-based aid available for full-time and part-time students. Work study available nights.

### FINANCIAL AID PROCEDURES
**Forms required:** FAFSA, institutional form.
**Transfers:** No deadline. Applicants notified on a rolling basis.

### CONTACT
Carmen Torres, Director of Finance
3535 West Sahara Avenue, Las Vegas, NV 89102
(702) 368-2338

## Nevada State College
Henderson, Nevada
www.nsc.edu                    Federal Code: 041143

**4-year public** nursing, liberal arts and teachers college in large city.
**Enrollment:** 3,429 undergrads, 61% part-time. 215 full-time freshmen.
**Selectivity:** Admits 50 to 75% of applicants.

### BASIC COSTS (2015-2016)
**Tuition and fees:** $5,033; out-of-state residents $15,299.
**Per-credit charge:** $142.

### FINANCIAL AID PICTURE (2015-2016)
**Students with need:** 100% of average financial aid package awarded as scholarships/grants, 0% awarded as loans/jobs. Need-based aid available for part-time students.

### FINANCIAL AID PROCEDURES
**Forms required:** FAFSA, institutional form.
**Dates and Deadlines:** Priority date 3/1; no closing date. Applicants notified on a rolling basis starting 5/1.
**Transfers:** Applicants notified on a rolling basis starting 5/1.

**CONTACT**
Anthony Morrone, Associate Director
1125 Nevada State Drive, Henderson, NV 89002
(702) 992-2150

## Roseman University of Health Sciences
Henderson, Nevada
www.roseman.edu                    Federal Code: 040653

**Upper-division private** university in very large city.
**Enrollment:** 312 undergrads.

**BASIC COSTS (2016-2017)**
**Tuition and fees:** $40,607.
**Per-credit charge:** $644.

**FINANCIAL AID PICTURE (2014-2015)**
**Students with need:** Average financial aid package for all full-time undergraduates was $9,810. 8% awarded as scholarships/grants, 92% awarded as loans/jobs. Need-based aid available for part-time students. Work study available nights, weekends, and for part-time students.
**Students without need:** No-need awards available for academics, leadership.

**FINANCIAL AID PROCEDURES**
**Forms required:** FAFSA.
**Dates and Deadlines:** Applicants notified on a rolling basis starting 5/2; must reply within 4 week(s) of notification.
**Transfers:** No deadline. Applicants notified on a rolling basis starting 1/1; must reply within 4 week(s) of notification.

**CONTACT**
Sally Mickelson, Director of Financial Aid
11 Sunset Way, Henderson, NV 89014-2333
(702) 968-1635

## Sierra Nevada College
Incline Village, Nevada
www.sierranevada.edu                Federal Code: 009192

**4-year private** liberal arts college in small town.
**Enrollment:** 498 undergrads, 2% part-time. 93 full-time freshmen.

**BASIC COSTS (2015-2016)**
**Tuition and fees:** $29,994.
**Per-credit charge:** $1,234.
**Room and board:** $12,066.

**FINANCIAL AID PICTURE (2015-2016)**
**Students with need:** Out of 77 full-time freshmen who applied for aid, 66 were judged to have need. Of these, 66 received aid, and 21 had their full need met. Average financial aid package met 53% of need; average scholarship/grant was $26,237; average loan was $3,299. For part-time students, average financial aid package was $13,494.
**Students without need:** 26 full-time freshmen who did not demonstrate need for aid received scholarships/grants; average award was $15,639. No-need awards available for academics, alumni affiliation, art, athletics, state/district residency.
**Scholarships offered: *Merit:*** Academic scholarships; $2,000-$12,500 per year; renewable. ***Athletic:*** 4 full-time freshmen received athletic scholarships; average amount $13,950.
**Additional info:** Institutional need-based grant provided based on remaining need after being awarded all scholarships and Federal Student Aid. First time freshmen awarded 50% of remaining need and 45% for continuing students.

**FINANCIAL AID PROCEDURES**
**Forms required:** FAFSA.

**Dates and Deadlines:** Applicants notified on a rolling basis starting 2/1.

**CONTACT**
Nicole Ferguson, Director of Financial Aid
999 Tahoe Boulevard, Incline Village, NV 89451-4269
(775) 831-1314 ext. 7440

## Truckee Meadows Community College
Reno, Nevada
www.tmcc.edu                     Federal Code: 010363

**2-year public** community and technical college in large city.
**Enrollment:** 8,861 undergrads, 72% part-time. 758 full-time freshmen.
**Selectivity:** Open admission; but selective for some programs.

**BASIC COSTS (2015-2016)**
**Tuition and fees:** $2,805; out-of-state residents $9,450.
**Per-credit charge:** $88.

**FINANCIAL AID PICTURE**
**Students with need:** Work study available nights, weekends, and for part-time students.
**Students without need:** No-need awards available for academics, art, leadership, minority status, music/drama, state/district residency.
**Additional info:** Institutional grants to state residents, short-term emergency loans available. Work-study applications must reply within 10 days of notification.

**FINANCIAL AID PROCEDURES**
**Forms required:** FAFSA, institutional form.
**Dates and Deadlines:** Priority date 1/15; no closing date.
**Transfers:** Priority date 3/9; no deadline. Must provide academic transcript from previous institution.

**CONTACT**
Sharon Wurm, Director of Financial Aid, Scholarships and Student Employment
7000 Dandini Boulevard, Reno, NV 89512
(775) 673-7072

## University of Nevada: Las Vegas
Las Vegas, Nevada
www.unlv.edu                     Federal Code: 002569

**4-year public** university in very large city.
**Enrollment:** 23,329 undergrads, 25% part-time. 3,658 full-time freshmen.
**Selectivity:** Admits over 75% of applicants. GED not accepted.

**BASIC COSTS (2015-2016)**
**Tuition and fees:** $6,823; out-of-state residents $20,733.
**Per-credit charge:** $199.
**Room and board:** $10,730.

**FINANCIAL AID PICTURE (2015-2016)**
**Students with need:** Out of 3,194 full-time freshmen who applied for aid, 2,561 were judged to have need. Of these, 2,439 received aid, and 376 had their full need met. Average financial aid package met 72% of need; average scholarship/grant was $6,193; average loan was $3,179. For part-time students, average financial aid package was $9,220.
**Students without need:** 491 full-time freshmen who did not demonstrate need for aid received scholarships/grants; average award was $4,031. No-need awards available for academics, alumni affiliation, athletics, music/drama.
**Scholarships offered:** 64 full-time freshmen received athletic scholarships; average amount $20,832.

**Additional info:** Tuition reduction for state residents through consortium programs and for out-of-state students graduating from high schools in designated counties bordering Nevada, for military dependents residing in-state, and for dependents of children of alumni not residing in-state.

### FINANCIAL AID PROCEDURES
**Forms required:** FAFSA.

**Dates and Deadlines:** Priority date 2/1; no closing date. Applicants notified on a rolling basis starting 3/20; must reply within 6 week(s) of notification.

### CONTACT
Norm Bedford, Director of Financial Aid & Scholarships
4505 Maryland Parkway, Box 451021, Las Vegas, NV 89154-1021
(702) 895-3424

## University of Nevada: Reno
Reno, Nevada
www.unr.edu                                    Federal Code: 002568

**4-year public** university in small city.
**Enrollment:** 17,295 undergrads, 14% part-time. 3,851 full-time freshmen.
**Selectivity:** Admits over 75% of applicants. GED not accepted.

### BASIC COSTS (2015-2016)
**Tuition and fees:** $6,882; out-of-state residents $20,792.
**Per-credit charge:** $199.
**Room and board:** $9,861.

### FINANCIAL AID PICTURE (2014-2015)
**Students with need:** Out of 2,690 full-time freshmen who applied for aid, 1,892 were judged to have need. Of these, 1,892 received aid, and 220 had their full need met. Average financial aid package met 62% of need; average scholarship/grant was $5,490; average loan was $3,365. For part-time students, average financial aid package was $5,097.
**Students without need:** 1,028 full-time freshmen who did not demonstrate need for aid received scholarships/grants; average award was $2,821. No-need awards available for academics, alumni affiliation, art, athletics.
**Scholarships offered: Merit:** Presidential scholarship: $5,000 per year; 3.5 unweighted GPA and 1380 SAT (exclusive of writing)/31 ACT required; must be admitted by 2/1 of year prior to enrollment and meet Nevada residency requirements. Additional scholarships: $2,500-$5,000; based on combination of test scores and unweighted GPA. **Athletic:** 76 full-time freshmen received athletic scholarships; average amount $21,830.
**Additional info:** Reduced out-of-state tuition available for participants in WUE program.

### FINANCIAL AID PROCEDURES
**Forms required:** FAFSA.

**Dates and Deadlines:** Priority date 3/1; no closing date. Applicants notified on a rolling basis starting 4/1; must reply by 6/1.

**Transfers:** No deadline. Applicants notified on a rolling basis; must reply within 2 week(s) of notification. 2.0 transfer GPA required to be eligible for aid.

### CONTACT
Tim Wolfe, Director, Student Financial Services
Mail Stop 120, Reno, NV 89557
(775) 784-4666

## Western Nevada College
Carson City, Nevada
www.wnc.edu                                    Federal Code: 013896

**2-year public** community college in small city.
**Enrollment:** 3,327 undergrads, 59% part-time. 267 full-time freshmen.
**Selectivity:** Open admission; but selective for some programs.

### BASIC COSTS (2015-2016)
**Tuition and fees:** $2,805; out-of-state residents $9,450.
**Per-credit charge:** $88.

### FINANCIAL AID PICTURE (2014-2015)
**Students with need:** Out of 203 full-time freshmen who applied for aid, 185 were judged to have need. Of these, 185 received aid, and 1 had their full need met. Need-based aid available for part-time students.
**Students without need:** No-need awards available for academics, athletics, state/district residency.

### FINANCIAL AID PROCEDURES
**Forms required:** FAFSA.

**Dates and Deadlines:** Priority date 4/1; no closing date. Applicants notified on a rolling basis; must reply within 3 week(s) of notification.

**Transfers:** No deadline. Applicants notified on a rolling basis; must reply within 3 week(s) of notification. Loans received at other schools counted toward limit.

### CONTACT
JW Lazzari, Associate Director of Financial Assistance
2201 West College Parkway, Carson City, NV 89703-7399
(775) 445-3264

# New Hampshire

## Colby-Sawyer College
New London, New Hampshire
www.colby-sawyer.edu                           Federal Code: 002572

**4-year private** liberal arts college in small town.
**Enrollment:** 1,206 undergrads, 4% part-time. 268 full-time freshmen.
**Selectivity:** Admits 50 to 75% of applicants.

### BASIC COSTS (2016-2017)
**Tuition and fees:** $39,190.
**Room and board:** $13,260.

### FINANCIAL AID PICTURE (2015-2016)
**Students with need:** 70% of average financial aid package awarded as scholarships/grants, 30% awarded as loans/jobs. Work study available nights, weekends, and for part-time students.
**Students without need:** No-need awards available for academics, alumni affiliation, art, leadership, minority status, music/drama.

### FINANCIAL AID PROCEDURES
**Forms required:** FAFSA.

**Dates and Deadlines:** Priority date 2/15; closing date 3/1. Applicants notified on a rolling basis starting 2/1; must reply by 5/1.

**Transfers:** Priority date 3/1; closing date 4/15. Applicants notified on a rolling basis starting 12/15; must reply within 2 week(s) of notification.

### CONTACT
Beth Renzulli, Director of Financial Aid
541 Main Street, New London, NH 03257-7835
(603) 526-3717

## Daniel Webster College
Nashua, New Hampshire
www.dwc.edu                                    Federal Code: 004731

**4-year for-profit** business and engineering college in small city.
**Enrollment:** 636 undergrads, 5% part-time. 147 full-time freshmen.
**Selectivity:** Admits 50 to 75% of applicants.

## BASIC COSTS (2015-2016)

**Tuition and fees:** $15,630.
**Room and board:** $10,970.

## FINANCIAL AID PICTURE

**Students with need:** Need-based aid available for full-time and part-time students. Work study available nights, weekends, and for part-time students.
**Students without need:** No-need awards available for academics.

## FINANCIAL AID PROCEDURES

**Forms required:** FAFSA, institutional form.
**Dates and Deadlines:** Priority date 3/1; no closing date. Applicants notified on a rolling basis starting 3/15; must reply within 2 week(s) of notification.
**Transfers:** No deadline. Applicants notified on a rolling basis starting 3/15; must reply within 2 week(s) of notification.

## CONTACT

Darla Ammidown, Director of Financial Operations
20 University Drive, Nashua, NH 03063
(603) 577-6590

# Dartmouth College

Hanover, New Hampshire
www.dartmouth.edu

Federal Code: 002573
CSS Code: 3351

**4-year private** university and liberal arts college in large town.
**Enrollment:** 4,214 undergrads. 1,112 full-time freshmen.
**Selectivity:** Admits less than 50% of applicants.

## BASIC COSTS (2015-2016)

**Tuition and fees:** $49,506.
**Room and board:** $14,238.
**Additional info:** First-Year Students have additional room charges and fees of $390.

## FINANCIAL AID PICTURE (2015-2016)

**Students with need:** Out of 679 full-time freshmen who applied for aid, 553 were judged to have need. Of these, 553 received aid, and 553 had their full need met. Average financial aid package met 100% of need; average scholarship/grant was $46,917; average loan was $4,312. Need-based aid available for part-time students.
**Students without need:** This college awards aid only to students with need.

## FINANCIAL AID PROCEDURES

**Forms required:** FAFSA, CSS PROFILE.
**Dates and Deadlines:** Closing date 2/1. Applicants notified by 4/2; must reply by 5/1.
**Transfers:** Closing date 3/1. Applicants notified by 4/2; must reply by 5/1. Grant budget for transfer students is limited. Some admitted transfer students may not have their full needs met.

## CONTACT

Gordon Koff, Director of Financial Aid
6016 McNutt Hall, Hanover, NH 03755
(603) 646-2451

# Franklin Pierce University

Rindge, New Hampshire
www.franklinpierce.edu

Federal Code: 002575

**4-year private** university and liberal arts college in small town.
**Enrollment:** 1,657 undergrads, 12% part-time. 420 full-time freshmen.
**Selectivity:** Admits over 75% of applicants.

## BASIC COSTS (2015-2016)

**Tuition and fees:** $33,320.

---

**Room and board:** $12,546.

## FINANCIAL AID PICTURE (2015-2016)

**Students with need:** Out of 396 full-time freshmen who applied for aid, 361 were judged to have need. Of these, 361 received aid, and 67 had their full need met. Average financial aid package met 70% of need; average scholarship/grant was $20,147; average loan was $3,936. For part-time students, average financial aid package was $12,476.
**Students without need:** 86 full-time freshmen who did not demonstrate need for aid received scholarships/grants; average award was $13,934. No-need awards available for academics, art, athletics, leadership.
**Scholarships offered:** *Merit:* Trustee, Presidential, Provost, Deans, Transfer, Achieve, Success, Opportunity, Mascenic, Monadonock, International, Academic Ambition, Athletic, and Alumni scholarships range from $1,000 to $25,000. Marlin Fitzwater Mass Communication: $2,000; 6 awarded. Robert Alvin Performing Arts-Theater, Music, Dance; $2,000; 2 awarded in each category. Leadership Scholarship: $2,000; 10 awarded. *Athletic:* 29 full-time freshmen received athletic scholarships; average amount $14,359.

## FINANCIAL AID PROCEDURES

**Forms required:** FAFSA.
**Dates and Deadlines:** Priority date 3/1; no closing date. Applicants notified on a rolling basis starting 3/1.
**Transfers:** No deadline. Applicants notified on a rolling basis starting 3/1; must reply within 2 week(s) of notification.

## CONTACT

Ken Ferreira, Executive Director of Student Financial Services
40 University Drive, Rindge, NH 03461-0060
(603) 899-4180

# Granite State College

Concord, New Hampshire
www.granite.edu

Federal Code: 031013

**4-year public** liberal arts college in large town.
**Enrollment:** 1,812 undergrads, 44% part-time. 65 full-time freshmen.
**Selectivity:** Open admission; but selective for some programs.

## BASIC COSTS (2015-2016)

**Tuition and fees:** $8,940; out-of-state residents $9,900.
**Per-credit charge:** $293; out-of-state residents $325.

## FINANCIAL AID PICTURE

**Students with need:** Need-based aid available for full-time and part-time students. Work study available nights.
**Students without need:** This college awards aid only to students with need.

## FINANCIAL AID PROCEDURES

**Forms required:** FAFSA, institutional form.
**Dates and Deadlines:** Applicants notified on a rolling basis starting 4/15.
**Transfers:** No deadline. Applicants notified on a rolling basis starting 4/15.

## CONTACT

Mac Broderick, Director of Financial Aid
25 Hall Street, Concord, NH 03301-7317
(603) 228-3000 ext. 324

# Great Bay Community College

Portsmouth, New Hampshire
www.greatbay.edu

Federal Code: 002583

**2-year public** community and technical college in small town.
**Enrollment:** 1,887 undergrads.
**Selectivity:** Open admission; but selective for some programs.

**BASIC COSTS (2015-2016)**
**Tuition and fees:** $6,660; out-of-state residents $14,310.
**Per-credit charge:** $200; out-of-state residents $455.
**Additional info:** New England Regional tuition: $300 per credit hour; Graduation Fee $100.

**FINANCIAL AID PICTURE**
**Students with need:** Need-based aid available for full-time and part-time students. Work study available nights, weekends, and for part-time students.
**Students without need:** This college awards aid only to students with need.

**FINANCIAL AID PROCEDURES**
**Forms required:** FAFSA, institutional form.
**Dates and Deadlines:** Applicants notified on a rolling basis; must reply within 2 week(s) of notification.
**Transfers:** No deadline. Applicants notified on a rolling basis; must reply within 2 week(s) of notification.

**CONTACT**
Lauren Hughes, Director of Financial Aid
320 Corporate Drive, Portsmouth, NH 03801
(603) 772-1194

## Keene State College
Keene, New Hampshire
www.keene.edu
Federal Code: 002590

**4-year public** liberal arts college in small city.
**Enrollment:** 4,186 undergrads, 2% part-time. 1,266 full-time freshmen.
**Selectivity:** Admits over 75% of applicants.

**BASIC COSTS (2015-2016)**
**Tuition and fees:** $13,228; out-of-state residents $21,408.
**Per-credit charge:** $446; out-of-state residents $790.
**Room and board:** $9,712.

**FINANCIAL AID PICTURE (2014-2015)**
**Students with need:** Out of 1,150 full-time freshmen who applied for aid, 883 were judged to have need. Of these, 868 received aid, and 86 had their full need met. Average financial aid package met 62% of need; average scholarship/grant was $7,480; average loan was $3,567. For part-time students, average financial aid package was $5,628.
**Students without need:** 215 full-time freshmen who did not demonstrate need for aid received scholarships/grants; average award was $3,518. No-need awards available for academics, alumni affiliation, art, music/drama.

**FINANCIAL AID PROCEDURES**
**Forms required:** FAFSA.
**Dates and Deadlines:** Closing date 3/1. Applicants notified on a rolling basis; must reply within 4 week(s) of notification.
**Transfers:** Applicants notified on a rolling basis.

**CONTACT**
Patricia Blodgett, Director of Financial Aid
229 Main Street, Keene, NH 03435-2604
(603) 358-2280

## Lakes Region Community College
Laconia, New Hampshire
www.lrcc.edu
Federal Code: 007555

**2-year public** community and technical college in small city.
**Enrollment:** 894 undergrads.
**Selectivity:** Open admission; but selective for some programs.

**BASIC COSTS (2015-2016)**
**Tuition and fees:** $6,180; out-of-state residents $13,830.
**Per-credit charge:** $200; out-of-state residents $455.
**Additional info:** New England Regional tuition: $300 per credit hour.

**FINANCIAL AID PICTURE**
**Students with need:** Need-based aid available for full-time and part-time students.

**FINANCIAL AID PROCEDURES**
**Forms required:** FAFSA, institutional form.
**Dates and Deadlines:** Priority date 5/1; no closing date.

**CONTACT**
Kristen Purrington, Financial Aid Officer
379 Belmont Road, Laconia, NH 03246-9204
(603) 524-3207

## Manchester Community College
Manchester, New Hampshire
www.mccnh.edu
Federal Code: 002582

**2-year public** community and technical college in small city.
**Enrollment:** 3,075 undergrads.
**Selectivity:** Open admission; but selective for some programs.

**BASIC COSTS (2015-2016)**
**Tuition and fees:** $6,420; out-of-state residents $14,070.
**Per-credit charge:** $200; out-of-state residents $455.
**Additional info:** New England Regional tuition: $300 per credit hour.

**FINANCIAL AID PICTURE**
**Students with need:** Need-based aid available for full-time and part-time students. Work study available nights, weekends, and for part-time students.
**Students without need:** This college awards aid only to students with need.
**Scholarships offered:** NH high school valedictorians receive 100% tuition scholarship.

**FINANCIAL AID PROCEDURES**
**Forms required:** FAFSA, institutional form.
**Dates and Deadlines:** Priority date 5/1; no closing date. Applicants notified on a rolling basis starting 4/15; must reply within 2 week(s) of notification.

**CONTACT**
Stephanie Weldon, Financial Aid Officer
1066 Front Street, Manchester, NH 03102-8518
(603) 668-6706 ext. 352

## Mount Washington College
Manchester, New Hampshire
www.mountwashington.edu
Federal Code: 004729

**4-year for-profit** business and junior college in small city.
**Enrollment:** 1,511 undergrads.
**Selectivity:** Open admission; but selective for some programs.

**BASIC COSTS (2015-2016)**
**Additional info:** Degree program tuition: 8-week term tuition (per 3-credit course) $1,125; 8-week term tuition per credit $375. 20-week non-term tuition (textbooks included): full-time enrollment status (12-15 credit hours per payment period) $2,200.00, book fee $200; per 3 credit course (over 15 credit hours per payment period) $250, book fee $50. Enrollment fee: $10. Additional fees may apply.

**FINANCIAL AID PICTURE**
**Students with need:** Need-based aid available for full-time and part-time students. Work study available nights, weekends, and for part-time students.

**Students without need:** This college awards aid only to students with need.

**Additional info:** Two private loans available to assist students in paying their balance; Tree Loan, SLM Loan.

## FINANCIAL AID PROCEDURES
**Forms required:** FAFSA, institutional form.
**Dates and Deadlines:** Priority date 5/1; no closing date. Applicants notified on a rolling basis starting 3/1; must reply within 3 week(s) of notification.

## CONTACT
Shaman Quinn, Director of Financial Aid
3 Sundial Avenue, Manchester, NH 03103
(603) 668-6660 ext. 2210

## Nashua Community College
Nashua, New Hampshire
www.nashuacc.edu                    Federal Code: 009236

**2-year public** community and technical college in small city.
**Enrollment:** 1,697 undergrads, 64% part-time. 256 full-time freshmen.
**Selectivity:** Open admission; but selective for some programs.

### BASIC COSTS (2015-2016)
**Tuition and fees:** $6,480; out-of-state residents $14,130.
**Per-credit charge:** $200; out-of-state residents $455.
**Additional info:** New England Regional tuition: $300 per credit hour.

### FINANCIAL AID PICTURE (2014-2015)
**Students with need:** Out of 206 full-time freshmen who applied for aid, 174 were judged to have need. Of these, 158 received aid, and 5 had their full need met. Average financial aid package met 62% of need; average scholarship/grant was $4,698; average loan was $2,932. For part-time students, average financial aid package was $4,658.
**Students without need:** This college awards aid only to students with need.

### FINANCIAL AID PROCEDURES
**Forms required:** FAFSA.
**Dates and Deadlines:** Priority date 7/18; no closing date. Applicants notified on a rolling basis starting 3/1; must reply within 2 week(s) of notification.

### CONTACT
Anne Eule, Director of Financial Aid
505 Amherst Street, Nashua, NH 03063-1026
(603) 578-8903

## New England College
Henniker, New Hampshire
www.nec.edu                    Federal Code: 002579

**4-year private** liberal arts and teachers college in small town.
**Enrollment:** 1,805 undergrads, 2% part-time. 397 full-time freshmen.
**Selectivity:** Admits over 75% of applicants.

### BASIC COSTS (2016-2017)
**Tuition and fees:** $34,800.
**Per-credit charge:** $1,625.
**Room and board:** $13,500.
**Additional info:** Tuition/fee waivers available for adults.

### FINANCIAL AID PICTURE (2015-2016)
**Students with need:** Out of 340 full-time freshmen who applied for aid, 321 were judged to have need. Of these, 320 received aid, and 99 had their full need met. Average financial aid package met 79% of need; average scholarship/grant was $19,440; average loan was $13,151. For part-time students, average financial aid package was $17,008.

**Students without need:** 43 full-time freshmen who did not demonstrate need for aid received scholarships/grants; average award was $19,393. No-need awards available for academics, alumni affiliation, art, job skills, leadership, music/drama, state/district residency.
**Scholarships offered:** Russell Durgin veteran scholarship, up to $16,000. Any veteran is eligible regardless of time of service.
**Additional info:** Significant scholarship programs for veterans including non-Post 911 eligible veterans.

### FINANCIAL AID PROCEDURES
**Forms required:** FAFSA, institutional form.
**Dates and Deadlines:** Closing date 9/1. Applicants notified on a rolling basis starting 1/12; must reply within 4 week(s) of notification.
**Transfers:** No deadline. Applicants notified on a rolling basis starting 1/1; must reply within 4 week(s) of notification. May 1 deadline for state grant consideration.

### CONTACT
Kristen Blase, Director of Student Financial Services
15 Main Street, Henniker, NH 03242
(603) 428-2226

## New Hampshire Institute of Art
Manchester, New Hampshire
www.nhia.edu                    Federal Code: 031823

**4-year private** visual arts college in small city.
**Enrollment:** 383 undergrads, 8% part-time. 102 full-time freshmen.
**Selectivity:** Admits 50 to 75% of applicants.

### BASIC COSTS (2016-2017)
**Tuition and fees:** $25,790.
**Room and board:** $10,990.
**Additional info:** Tuition at time of enrollment locked for 4 years.

### FINANCIAL AID PICTURE (2015-2016)
**Students with need:** 58% of average financial aid package awarded as scholarships/grants, 42% awarded as loans/jobs. Need-based aid available for part-time students. Work study available nights.
**Students without need:** No-need awards available for academics, art.

### FINANCIAL AID PROCEDURES
**Forms required:** FAFSA.
**Dates and Deadlines:** Priority date 3/1; no closing date. Applicants notified on a rolling basis starting 3/15; must reply within 2 week(s) of notification.

### CONTACT
Elayne Peloquin, Director of Financial Aid
148 Concord Street, Manchester, NH 03104
(603) 836-2578

## NHTI-Concord's Community College
Concord, New Hampshire
www.nhti.edu                    Federal Code: 002581

**2-year public** community and technical college in large town.
**Enrollment:** 3,642 undergrads, 51% part-time. 781 full-time freshmen.
**Selectivity:** Open admission; but selective for some programs.

### BASIC COSTS (2015-2016)
**Tuition and fees:** $6,660; out-of-state residents $14,310.
**Per-credit charge:** $200; out-of-state residents $455.
**Room and board:** $8,754.
**Additional info:** New England Regional tuition: $300 per credit hour.

### FINANCIAL AID PICTURE (2014-2015)
**Students with need:** Out of 690 full-time freshmen who applied for aid, 583 were judged to have need. Of these, 549 received aid, and 24 had their

full need met. Average financial aid package met 58% of need; average scholarship/grant was $4,419; average loan was $3,016. For part-time students, average financial aid package was $5,127.

**Students without need:** This college awards aid only to students with need.

**Additional info:** 60% of students who apply receive some form of financial aid. State school; all financial aid need-based, primarily from federal sources. No scholarships awarded.

## FINANCIAL AID PROCEDURES

**Forms required:** FAFSA.

**Dates and Deadlines:** Priority date 5/1; no closing date. Applicants notified on a rolling basis starting 6/1; must reply within 2 week(s) of notification.

**Transfers:** No deadline. Applicants notified on a rolling basis.

## CONTACT

Sheri Gonthier, Financial Aid Director
31 College Drive, Concord, NH 03301
(603) 271-7136

# Northeast Catholic College
Warner, New Hampshire
www.northeastcatholic.edu          Federal Code: 022233

**4-year private** liberal arts college in small town, affiliated with Roman Catholic Church.

**Enrollment:** 89 undergrads, 1% part-time. 36 full-time freshmen.

**Selectivity:** Admits less than 50% of applicants.

## BASIC COSTS (2015-2016)

**Tuition and fees:** $21,200.

**Room and board:** $8,000.

## FINANCIAL AID PICTURE

**Students with need:** Need-based aid available for full-time and part-time students. Work study available nights, weekends, and for part-time students.

**Students without need:** This college awards aid only to students with need.

**Scholarships offered:** Presidential Scholarship: four year, full tuition scholarship (not including room and board costs); 1 awarded annually to incoming freshman. Dignitas Scholarship: amount varies; awarded to students who have demonstrated leadership or initiative in various ministry activities.

## FINANCIAL AID PROCEDURES

**Forms required:** institutional form.

**Dates and Deadlines:** Priority date 3/15; no closing date. Applicants notified on a rolling basis starting 3/15.

**Transfers:** No deadline. Applicants notified on a rolling basis; must reply within 4 week(s) of notification. Certain scholarships that are available to freshman are also available to new transfer students.

## CONTACT

Marie Lasher, Director of Financial Aid
511 Kearsarge Mountain Road, Warner, NH 03278
(603) 456-2656

# Plymouth State University
Plymouth, New Hampshire
www.plymouth.edu          Federal Code: 002591

**4-year public** university and teachers college in small town.

**Enrollment:** 4,042 undergrads, 5% part-time. 750 full-time freshmen.

**Selectivity:** Admits 50 to 75% of applicants.

## BASIC COSTS (2015-2016)

**Tuition and fees:** $13,128; out-of-state residents $21,208.

**Per-credit charge:** $446; out-of-state residents $783.

**Room and board:** $10,868.

## FINANCIAL AID PICTURE (2014-2015)

**Students with need:** Out of 697 full-time freshmen who applied for aid, 539 were judged to have need. Of these, 538 received aid, and 94 had their full need met. Average financial aid package met 56% of need; average scholarship/grant was $4,581; average loan was $3,429. For part-time students, average financial aid package was $5,961.

**Students without need:** 148 full-time freshmen who did not demonstrate need for aid received scholarships/grants; average award was $2,890. No-need awards available for academics, art, leadership, music/drama.

## FINANCIAL AID PROCEDURES

**Forms required:** FAFSA.

**Dates and Deadlines:** Priority date 3/1; no closing date. Applicants notified on a rolling basis starting 3/1; must reply by 5/1.

**Transfers:** Applicants notified on a rolling basis starting 3/1.

## CONTACT

Crystal Gaff, Director of Financial Aid
17 High Street MSC 52, Plymouth, NH 03264-1595
(603) 535-2338

# River Valley Community College
Claremont, New Hampshire
www.rivervalley.edu          Federal Code: 007560

**2-year public** community college in large town.

**Enrollment:** 719 undergrads.

**Selectivity:** Open admission; but selective for some programs.

## BASIC COSTS (2015-2016)

**Tuition and fees:** $6,150; out-of-state residents $13,800.

**Per-credit charge:** $200; out-of-state residents $455.

**Additional info:** New England Regional tuition: $300 per credit hour.

## FINANCIAL AID PICTURE

**Students with need:** Need-based aid available for full-time and part-time students.

**Students without need:** This college awards aid only to students with need.

## FINANCIAL AID PROCEDURES

**Forms required:** FAFSA.

**Dates and Deadlines:** Closing date 4/1. Applicants notified on a rolling basis; must reply within 2 week(s) of notification.

## CONTACT

Julia Dower, Director of Financial Aid
One College Drive, Claremont, NH 03743-9707
(603) 542-7744 ext. 5725

# Rivier University
Nashua, New Hampshire
www.rivier.edu          Federal Code: 002586

**4-year private** university and nursing college in small city, affiliated with Roman Catholic Church.

**Enrollment:** 1,344 undergrads, 42% part-time. 183 full-time freshmen.

**Selectivity:** Admits 50 to 75% of applicants.

## BASIC COSTS (2015-2016)

**Tuition and fees:** $29,400.

**Per-credit charge:** $960.

**Room and board:** $11,310.

**Additional info:** Tuition/fee waivers available for unemployed or children of unemployed.

## FINANCIAL AID PICTURE

**Students with need:** Need-based aid available for full-time and part-time students. Work study available nights, weekends, and for part-time students.
**Students without need:** No-need awards available for academics, alumni affiliation.

**Scholarships offered:** Dean's Scholarship: $6,000 for residents, $5,000 for commuters; minimum 1000 SAT (exclusive of Writing); 3.0 GPA; renewable with minimum 2.67 GPA. Presidential Scholarship: $7,000 for residents, $6,000 for commuters; minimum 1150 SAT (exclusive of Writing); 3.4 GPA; renewable with minimum 3.0 GPA. Catholic High School Grant: $4,000 for residents, $3,000 for commuters; for students graduating from Catholic high school; renewable with 2.5 GPA. Honors Scholarship: for honors program participants; $10,000 for residents, $2,000 for commuters. Alumni Scholarship: $2,000; for children of Rivier alumni; renewable with minimum 2.0 GPA. Trustee Scholarship: $8,000 for residents, $7,000 for commuters; minimum 1200 SAT (exclusive of Writing); 3.4 GPA; renewable with minimum 3.0 GPA. Founders Scholarship for National Merit Finalists: full tuition; renewable with minimum 3.0 GPA.

## FINANCIAL AID PROCEDURES

**Forms required:** FAFSA.
**Dates and Deadlines:** Priority date 3/1; no closing date. Applicants notified on a rolling basis starting 3/1; must reply by 5/1 or within 2 week(s) of notification.
**Transfers:** No deadline. Applicants notified on a rolling basis starting 3/1; must reply by 5/1 or within 2 week(s) of notification. Scholarship for transfer students with minimum 2.5 GPA and 12 transferable credits.

## CONTACT

Valerie Patnaude, Director of Financial Aid
420 South Main Street, Nashua, NH 03060-5086
(603) 897-8510

## Saint Anselm College

Manchester, New Hampshire — Federal Code: 002587
www.anselm.edu — CSS Code: 3748

**4-year private** nursing and liberal arts college in small city, affiliated with Roman Catholic Church.
**Enrollment:** 1,908 undergrads, 2% part-time. 528 full-time freshmen.
**Selectivity:** Admits 50 to 75% of applicants.

### BASIC COSTS (2015-2016)

**Tuition and fees:** $37,694.
**Room and board:** $13,334.
**Additional info:** Tuition/fee waivers available for minority students.

### FINANCIAL AID PICTURE (2015-2016)

**Students with need:** Out of 483 full-time freshmen who applied for aid, 389 were judged to have need. Of these, 389 received aid, and 116 had their full need met. Average financial aid package met 81% of need; average scholarship/grant was $22,396; average loan was $2,828. For part-time students, average financial aid package was $4,664.
**Students without need:** 124 full-time freshmen who did not demonstrate need for aid received scholarships/grants; average award was $13,354. No-need awards available for academics, alumni affiliation, athletics, leadership, music/drama, state/district residency.
**Scholarships offered:** *Merit:* Scholarships range from $7,000 to $20,000; based on grades, test results (of considered), and extracurricular experience. *Athletic:* 40 full-time freshmen received athletic scholarships; average amount $10,872.

### FINANCIAL AID PROCEDURES

**Forms required:** FAFSA, CSS PROFILE.

**Dates and Deadlines:** Priority date 3/15; closing date 3/15. Applicants notified on a rolling basis starting 3/1; must reply by 5/1 or within 2 week(s) of notification.
**Transfers:** Merit scholarships are awarded to qualified transfer students.

## CONTACT

Elizabeth Keuffel, Director of Financial Aid Systems and Compliance
100 Saint Anselm Drive, Manchester, NH 03102-1310
(603) 641-7110

## Southern New Hampshire University

Manchester, New Hampshire
www.snhu.edu — Federal Code: 002580

**4-year private** university and culinary school in small city.
**Enrollment:** 3,027 undergrads, 2% part-time. 788 full-time freshmen.
**Selectivity:** Admits over 75% of applicants.

### BASIC COSTS (2015-2016)

**Tuition and fees:** $30,386.
**Per-credit charge:** $1,250.
**Room and board:** $11,798.

### FINANCIAL AID PICTURE (2015-2016)

**Students with need:** Out of 707 full-time freshmen who applied for aid, 639 were judged to have need. Of these, 637 received aid, and 104 had their full need met. Average financial aid package met 70% of need; average scholarship/grant was $4,220; average loan was $3,247. For part-time students, average financial aid package was $16,496.
**Students without need:** 121 full-time freshmen who did not demonstrate need for aid received scholarships/grants; average award was $7,220. No-need awards available for academics, alumni affiliation, art, athletics, job skills, leadership, music/drama, state/district residency.
**Scholarships offered:** *Merit:* Scholarships up to $20,000 are available to students based primarily on high school GPA. *Athletic:* 9 full-time freshmen received athletic scholarships; average amount $9,971.

### FINANCIAL AID PROCEDURES

**Forms required:** FAFSA.
**Dates and Deadlines:** Priority date 3/15; closing date 6/30. Applicants notified on a rolling basis starting 3/15; must reply within 3 week(s) of notification.

### CONTACT

Benjamin Johnson, Associate VP of Student Financial Aid Services
2500 North River Road, Manchester, NH 03106-1045
(603) 668-2211

## Thomas More College of Liberal Arts

Merrimack, New Hampshire
www.thomasmorecollege.edu — Federal Code: 030431

**4-year private** liberal arts college in small city, affiliated with Roman Catholic Church.
**Enrollment:** 89 undergrads.

### BASIC COSTS (2015-2016)

**Tuition and fees:** $20,400.
**Per-credit charge:** $850.
**Room and board:** $9,500.

### FINANCIAL AID PICTURE

**Students with need:** Need-based aid available for full-time students. Work study available nights, weekends, and for part-time students.
**Students without need:** No-need awards available for academics.

**Scholarships offered:** Thomas More Scholarship: full or partial tuition (several awarded); based on superior academic achievement, exceptional promise or potential. Faith and Reason Essay Contest: up to $7,500 per year for 4 years; based on essay.

### FINANCIAL AID PROCEDURES
**Forms required:** FAFSA.
**Dates and Deadlines:** Priority date 5/1; no closing date. Applicants notified on a rolling basis starting 5/15; must reply within 2 week(s) of notification.
**Transfers:** No deadline. Applicants notified on a rolling basis; must reply within 2 week(s) of notification.

### CONTACT
Clint Hanson, Director of Financial Aid
Six Manchester Street, Merrimack, NH 03054-4818
(603) 880-8308 ext. 23

## University of New Hampshire
Durham, New Hampshire
www.unh.edu                          Federal Code: 002589

**4-year public** university in small town.
**Enrollment:** 12,788 undergrads, 2% part-time. 3,090 full-time freshmen.
**Selectivity:** Admits over 75% of applicants.

### BASIC COSTS (2015-2016)
**Tuition and fees:** $16,986; out-of-state residents $30,256.
**Per-credit charge:** $585; out-of-state residents $1,138.
**Room and board:** $10,618.
**Additional info:** Tuition rates are based on full-time registration (12-20 credits). Students who register for fewer than 12 credits are charged per credit hour. Students who register for more than 20 credit hours are charged per credit hour for each credit over 20. Tuition/fee waivers available for minority students.

### FINANCIAL AID PICTURE (2014-2015)
**Students with need:** Out of 2,764 full-time freshmen who applied for aid, 2,236 were judged to have need. Of these, 2,202 received aid, and 377 had their full need met. Average financial aid package met 78% of need; average scholarship/grant was $5,412; average loan was $2,651. For part-time students, average financial aid package was $13,753.
**Students without need:** 491 full-time freshmen who did not demonstrate need for aid received scholarships/grants; average award was $8,190. No-need awards available for academics, art, athletics, leadership, music/drama, ROTC.
**Scholarships offered:** *Merit:* Presidential Scholarship: half tuition. Various other awards recognizing outstanding high school achievement determined during freshmen candidate application review process; no additional application materials required. *Athletic:* 46 full-time freshmen received athletic scholarships; average amount $29,922.

### FINANCIAL AID PROCEDURES
**Forms required:** FAFSA.
**Dates and Deadlines:** Closing date 3/1. Applicants notified on a rolling basis starting 3/1; must reply by 5/1.
**Transfers:** Applicants notified on a rolling basis.

### CONTACT
Susan Allen, Director of Financial Aid
3 Garrison Avenue, Durham, NH 03824
(603) 862-3600

## University of New Hampshire at Manchester
Manchester, New Hampshire
www.manchester.unh.edu               Federal Code: 002589

**4-year public** university and liberal arts college in small city.
**Enrollment:** 719 undergrads.

### BASIC COSTS (2015-2016)
**Tuition and fees:** $14,955; out-of-state residents $28,225.
**Per-credit charge:** $572; out-of-state residents $1,125.
**Additional info:** New England Regional Student Program tuition is 175% of in-state tuition.

### FINANCIAL AID PICTURE
**Students with need:** Work study available nights, weekends, and for part-time students.
**Students without need:** No-need awards available for academics.

### FINANCIAL AID PROCEDURES
**Forms required:** FAFSA.
**Dates and Deadlines:** Closing date 3/1. Applicants notified by 4/1; must reply within 2 week(s) of notification.

### CONTACT
Sharon Eaton, Assistant Director of Financial Aid
88 Commercial Street, Manchester, NH 03101-1113
(603) 641-4189

## White Mountains Community College
Berlin, New Hampshire
www.wmcc.edu                         Federal Code: 005291

**2-year public** community college in large town.
**Enrollment:** 627 undergrads.
**Selectivity:** Open admission; but selective for some programs.

### BASIC COSTS (2015-2016)
**Tuition and fees:** $6,510; out-of-state residents $14,160.
**Per-credit charge:** $200; out-of-state residents $455.
**Additional info:** New England Regional tuition: $300 per credit hour.

### FINANCIAL AID PICTURE
**Students with need:** Need-based aid available for full-time and part-time students.
**Students without need:** This college awards aid only to students with need.

### FINANCIAL AID PROCEDURES
**Forms required:** FAFSA, institutional form.
**Dates and Deadlines:** Priority date 5/1; no closing date. Applicants notified on a rolling basis starting 5/1; must reply within 2 week(s) of notification.
**Transfers:** No deadline. Applicants notified on a rolling basis starting 5/1; must reply within 2 week(s) of notification.

### CONTACT
2020 Riverside Drive, Berlin, NH 03570

# New Jersey

## Atlantic Cape Community College
Mays Landing, New Jersey
www.atlantic.edu                     Federal Code: 002596

**2-year public** culinary school and community college in small town.
**Enrollment:** 3,675 full-time undergrads.

**Selectivity:** Open admission; but selective for some programs.

**BASIC COSTS (2015-2016)**

**Tuition and fees:** $4,266; out-of-district residents $5,946; out-of-state residents $7,536.

**Per-credit charge:** $116; out-of-district residents $172; out-of-state residents $225.

**Additional info:** Higher tuition for culinary arts program; Installment plan available. Tuition/fee waivers available for unemployed or children of unemployed.

**FINANCIAL AID PICTURE**

**Students with need:** Need-based aid available for full-time and part-time students.

**FINANCIAL AID PROCEDURES**

**Forms required:** FAFSA, institutional form.

**Dates and Deadlines:** Priority date 5/1; no closing date. Applicants notified on a rolling basis starting 5/1.

**CONTACT**

Linda Desantis, Director of Financial Aid and Veterans' Affairs

5100 Black Horse Pike, Mays Landing, NJ 08330-2699

(609) 343-5082

## Berkeley College

Woodland Park, New Jersey

www.berkeleycollege.edu          Federal Code: 007502

**4-year for-profit** business college in large town.

**Enrollment:** 3,806 undergrads, 16% part-time. 623 full-time freshmen.

**Selectivity:** Admits over 75% of applicants.

**BASIC COSTS (2015-2016)**

**Tuition and fees:** $24,300.

**Additional info:** Certificate tuition varies from $14,800-$27,950 including books, background check where appropriate, and cost of first certification/licensure exam; fees are $1,200.

**FINANCIAL AID PICTURE**

**Students with need:** Need-based aid available for full-time students.

**Students without need:** No-need awards available for academics, alumni affiliation.

**FINANCIAL AID PROCEDURES**

**Forms required:** FAFSA.

**CONTACT**

Howard Leslie, Vice President Financial Aid

44 Rifle Camp Road, Woodland Park, NJ 07424-0440

(973) 278-5400

## Bloomfield College

Bloomfield, New Jersey

www.bloomfield.edu          Federal Code: 002597

**4-year private** nursing and liberal arts college in large town, affiliated with Presbyterian Church (USA).

**Enrollment:** 1,937 undergrads, 10% part-time. 432 full-time freshmen.

**Selectivity:** Admits 50 to 75% of applicants.

**BASIC COSTS (2016-2017)**

**Tuition and fees:** $28,600.

**Per-credit charge:** $894.

**Room and board:** $11,500.

**FINANCIAL AID PICTURE (2015-2016)**

**Students with need:** Out of 432 full-time freshmen who applied for aid, 413 were judged to have need. Of these, 410 received aid, and 66 had their

full need met. Average financial aid package met 78% of need; average scholarship/grant was $18,952. For part-time students, average financial aid package was $10,079.

**Students without need:** 16 full-time freshmen who did not demonstrate need for aid received scholarships/grants; average award was $14,073. No-need awards available for academics, alumni affiliation, athletics, leadership.

**Scholarships offered:** *Merit:* Trustee Scholar Award: $8,000-full tuition; 3.6 GPA, 900 SAT required. Presidential Scholarship: $6,000-full tuition; 3.0 GPA and 900 SAT required. Community Service Scholarships: up to $5,000; for students with commitment to community service. *Athletic:* 28 full-time freshmen received athletic scholarships; average amount $12,895.

**FINANCIAL AID PROCEDURES**

**Forms required:** FAFSA.

**Dates and Deadlines:** Priority date 3/15; closing date 6/1. Applicants notified on a rolling basis starting 3/15; must reply within 2 week(s) of notification.

**Transfers:** Applicants notified on a rolling basis starting 3/15; must reply within 2 week(s) of notification. Transfer Scholarship: $5,000-full tuition; for transfer students from 2-year colleges with 3.0 GPA. Phi Theta Kappa Transfer Scholarships: up to full tuition; for day transfer students from 2-year colleges with 3.5 GPA with a completed AA/AS degree and are members of Phi Theta Kappa.

**CONTACT**

Breanne Simkin, Director of Financial Aid

One Park Place, Bloomfield, NJ 07003

(973) 748-9000 ext. 1212

## Brookdale Community College

Lincroft, New Jersey

www.brookdalecc.edu          Federal Code: 008404

**2-year public** community college in small city.

**Enrollment:** 12,077 undergrads.

**Selectivity:** Open admission; but selective for some programs.

**BASIC COSTS (2015-2016)**

**Tuition and fees:** $4,567; out-of-district residents $8,249; out-of-state residents $8,999.

**Per-credit charge:** $123; out-of-district residents $246; out-of-state residents $271.

**Additional info:** Tuition/fee waivers available for unemployed or children of unemployed.

**FINANCIAL AID PICTURE**

**Students with need:** Need-based aid available for full-time and part-time students.

**Students without need:** No-need awards available for academics, athletics.

**FINANCIAL AID PROCEDURES**

**Forms required:** FAFSA, institutional form.

**Dates and Deadlines:** Priority date 5/1; no closing date. Applicants notified on a rolling basis starting 5/1; must reply within 2 week(s) of notification.

**CONTACT**

Stephanie Fitzsimmons, Director of Financial Aid

765 Newman Springs Road, Lincroft, NJ 07738

(732) 224-2362

## Caldwell University

Caldwell, New Jersey

www.caldwell.edu          Federal Code: 002598

**4-year private** liberal arts college in large town, affiliated with Roman Catholic Church.

**Enrollment:** 1,595 undergrads, 14% part-time. 375 full-time freshmen.

**Selectivity:** Admits 50 to 75% of applicants.

## BASIC COSTS (2015-2016)
**Tuition and fees:** $31,200.
**Room and board:** $10,965.
**Additional info:** Tuition/fee waivers available for adults.

## FINANCIAL AID PICTURE (2014-2015)
**Students with need:** Out of 374 full-time freshmen who applied for aid, 374 were judged to have need. Of these, 374 received aid, and 46 had their full need met. Average financial aid package met 75% of need; average scholarship/grant was $22,757; average loan was $3,229. For part-time students, average financial aid package was $10,258.
**Students without need:** 53 full-time freshmen who did not demonstrate need for aid received scholarships/grants; average award was $16,832. No-need awards available for academics, alumni affiliation, art, athletics, leadership, music/drama, religious affiliation.
**Scholarships offered:** 29 full-time freshmen received athletic scholarships; average amount $5,576.

## FINANCIAL AID PROCEDURES
**Forms required:** FAFSA, state aid form, institutional form.
**Dates and Deadlines:** Priority date 4/1; no closing date. Applicants notified on a rolling basis starting 3/1; must reply within 4 week(s) of notification.
**Transfers:** No deadline. Applicants notified on a rolling basis; must reply within 4 week(s) of notification. Students who have filed for aid through the state previously must file FAFSA by 6/1 for succeeding year.

## CONTACT
Eileen Felske
120 Bloomfield Avenue, Caldwell, NJ 07006-6195
(973) 618-3221

# Camden County College
Blackwood, New Jersey
www.camdencc.edu                Federal Code: 006865

**2-year public** community college in large town.
**Enrollment:** 10,284 undergrads, 47% part-time. 1,597 full-time freshmen.
**Selectivity:** Open admission; but selective for some programs.

## BASIC COSTS (2016-2017)
**Tuition and fees:** $4,320; out-of-district residents $4,440; out-of-state residents $4,440.
**Per-credit charge:** $107; out-of-district residents $111; out-of-state residents $111.
**Additional info:** Tuition/fee waivers available for unemployed or children of unemployed.

## FINANCIAL AID PICTURE
**Students with need:** Need-based aid available for full-time and part-time students.
**Students without need:** No-need awards available for academics, state/district residency.

## FINANCIAL AID PROCEDURES
**Forms required:** FAFSA, institutional form.
**Dates and Deadlines:** Priority date 5/1; no closing date. Applicants notified on a rolling basis starting 7/1.
**Transfers:** No deadline.

## CONTACT
Felicia Bryant, Director of Financial Aid
Box 200, Blackwood, NJ 08012
(856) 227-7200

# Centenary College
Hackettstown, New Jersey
www.centenarycollege.edu          Federal Code: 002599

**4-year private** liberal arts college in large town, affiliated with United Methodist Church.
**Enrollment:** 1,548 undergrads, 5% part-time. 252 full-time freshmen.
**Selectivity:** Admits over 75% of applicants.

## BASIC COSTS (2015-2016)
**Tuition and fees:** $31,654.
**Per-credit charge:** $580.
**Room and board:** $10,730.

## FINANCIAL AID PICTURE (2014-2015)
**Students with need:** Out of 223 full-time freshmen who applied for aid, 201 were judged to have need. Of these, 201 received aid, and 39 had their full need met. Average financial aid package met 79% of need; average scholarship/grant was $22,920; average loan was $5,112. For part-time students, average financial aid package was $6,028.
**Students without need:** 32 full-time freshmen who did not demonstrate need for aid received scholarships/grants; average award was $14,017. No-need awards available for academics, religious affiliation.
**Scholarships offered:** Academic awards: based on 2.5 GPA, 800 SAT (exclusive of Writing) or 16 ACT. Leadership awards: based on demonstrated leadership ability and potential. Equine Award. Centenary Resident Grant. Out-of-State Centenary Grant. Skylands Centenary Grant. Centenary United Methodist Scholarship.

## FINANCIAL AID PROCEDURES
**Forms required:** FAFSA.
**Dates and Deadlines:** Priority date 2/15; closing date 9/1. Applicants notified on a rolling basis starting 3/1.
**Transfers:** Students from New Jersey colleges who have received tuition aid grants (TAG) must apply by state deadline. Students must submit financial aid transcripts from all previous institutions attended.

## CONTACT
Tonya Williams, Director of Financial Aid
400 Jefferson Street, Hackettstown, NJ 07840-9989

# The College of New Jersey
Ewing, New Jersey
www.tcnj.edu                     Federal Code: 002642

**4-year public** liberal arts college in large town.
**Enrollment:** 6,584 undergrads, 3% part-time. 1,413 full-time freshmen.
**Selectivity:** Admits less than 50% of applicants.

## BASIC COSTS (2015-2016)
**Tuition and fees:** $15,466; out-of-state residents $26,397.
**Per-credit charge:** $386; out-of-state residents $772.
**Room and board:** $12,498.
**Additional info:** Tuition/fee waivers available for unemployed or children of unemployed.

## FINANCIAL AID PICTURE (2014-2015)
**Students with need:** Out of 1,229 full-time freshmen who applied for aid, 788 were judged to have need. Of these, 719 received aid, and 63 had their full need met. Average financial aid package met 42% of need; average scholarship/grant was $14,316; average loan was $3,632. For part-time students, average financial aid package was $4,155.
**Students without need:** 158 full-time freshmen who did not demonstrate need for aid received scholarships/grants; average award was $4,550. No-need awards available for academics, art, music/drama.

**Additional info:** Merit scholarships available to New Jersey high school graduates based on academic distinction. Limited number of scholarships available to out-of-state students who demonstrate exceptional academic achievement in high school and on SAT. The EOF Promise Award meets the direct cost of attendance freshman and sophomore years, with merit scholarship awards available in junior and senior years.

## FINANCIAL AID PROCEDURES

**Forms required:** FAFSA.

**Dates and Deadlines:** Priority date 3/1; closing date 10/1. Applicants notified on a rolling basis starting 6/1; must reply within 2 week(s) of notification.

**Transfers:** No deadline. Applicants notified on a rolling basis; must reply within 2 week(s) of notification.

## CONTACT

Wil Casaine, Executive Director of Financial Aid
Office of Undergraduate Admissions PO Box 7718, Ewing, NJ 08628-0718
(609) 771-2211

# College of St. Elizabeth

Morristown, New Jersey
www.cse.edu                 Federal Code: 002600

**4-year private** liberal arts college for women in large town, affiliated with Roman Catholic Church.

**Enrollment:** 769 undergrads, 31% part-time. 141 full-time freshmen.

**Selectivity:** Admits 50 to 75% of applicants.

## BASIC COSTS (2015-2016)

**Tuition and fees:** $31,679.

**Per-credit charge:** $929.

**Room and board:** $12,744.

**Additional info:** Tuition/fee waivers available for adults.

## FINANCIAL AID PICTURE (2014-2015)

**Students with need:** Out of 134 full-time freshmen who applied for aid, 134 were judged to have need. Of these, 134 received aid, and 132 had their full need met. Average financial aid package met 61% of need; average scholarship/grant was $24,726; average loan was $3,476. For part-time students, average financial aid package was $4,915.

**Students without need:** 79 full-time freshmen who did not demonstrate need for aid received scholarships/grants; average award was $14,213. No-need awards available for academics, alumni affiliation, art, leadership, state/district residency.

**Scholarships offered:** Presidential Scholarship: full-tuition; for campus residents. Elizabethan Scholarship: $8,000-$10,000. Seton Scholarship: $3,000-$7,000. Awards guaranteed to eligible students who apply by 3/1 and enroll by 5/1. International scholarships: tuition, room and board; awarded annually for fall semester only to first year students enrolled in Women's College; based on academic record, SAT (if submitted) and TOEFL score.

## FINANCIAL AID PROCEDURES

**Forms required:** FAFSA.

**Dates and Deadlines:** Closing date 10/1. Applicants notified on a rolling basis starting 11/15; must reply by 5/1 or within 2 week(s) of notification.

**Transfers:** Priority date 4/15; closing date 8/20. Scholarships available for full-time students who enroll immediately following full-time enrollment at another college. Applicants must have completed 32 credits and have 3.0 GPA. Awards range from $3,500-half tuition. Minimum of 5 awarded annually. Preference given to applications received by 6/1. Limited number of partial scholarships awarded to international students.

## CONTACT

Jacqueline Weiskopff, Director of Financial Aid
2 Convent Road, Morristown, NJ 07960-6989
(973) 290-4445

# County College of Morris

Randolph, New Jersey
www.ccm.edu                 Federal Code: 007106

**2-year public** community college in large town.

**Enrollment:** 7,170 undergrads.

**Selectivity:** Open admission; but selective for some programs.

## BASIC COSTS (2015-2016)

**Tuition and fees:** $4,570; out-of-district residents $8,200; out-of-state residents $11,290.

**Per-credit charge:** $121; out-of-district residents $242; out-of-state residents $345.

**Additional info:** Tuition/fee waivers available for unemployed or children of unemployed.

## FINANCIAL AID PICTURE

**Students with need:** Need-based aid available for full-time and part-time students.

**Students without need:** No-need awards available for athletics.

## FINANCIAL AID PROCEDURES

**Forms required:** FAFSA.

**Dates and Deadlines:** Priority date 3/1; no closing date. Applicants notified on a rolling basis starting 5/1.

## CONTACT

Harvey Willis, Director, Financial Aid
214 Center Grove Road, Randolph, NJ 07869-2086
(973) 328-5230

# Cumberland County College

Vineland, New Jersey
www.cccnj.edu                 Federal Code: 002601

**2-year public** community college in small city.

**Enrollment:** 3,453 undergrads.

**Selectivity:** Open admission; but selective for some programs.

## BASIC COSTS (2015-2016)

**Tuition and fees:** $4,290; out-of-district residents $6,540; out-of-state residents $14,460.

**Per-credit charge:** $113; out-of-district residents $188; out-of-state residents $452.

**Additional info:** In-state, out-of-district students will be charged $123 per-credit-hour with appropriate chargeback documentation. Tuition/fee waivers available for unemployed or children of unemployed.

## FINANCIAL AID PICTURE

**Students with need:** Need-based aid available for full-time and part-time students.

**Students without need:** No-need awards available for academics.

## FINANCIAL AID PROCEDURES

**Forms required:** FAFSA.

**Dates and Deadlines:** Applicants notified on a rolling basis; must reply within 3 week(s) of notification.

## CONTACT

Maurice Thomas, Director, Financial Aid
PO Box 1500, Vineland, NJ 08362-9912
(856) 691-8600 ext. 1311

## DeVry University: North Brunswick
North Brunswick, New Jersey
www.devry.edu                    Federal Code: 009228

**4-year for-profit** university in small city.
**Enrollment:** 930 undergrads.

**BASIC COSTS (2015-2016)**
**Tuition and fees:** $17,132.
**Per-credit charge:** $609.

**FINANCIAL AID PICTURE**
**Students with need:** Need-based aid available for full-time and part-time students.
**Students without need:** This college awards aid only to students with need.

**FINANCIAL AID PROCEDURES**
**Forms required:** FAFSA.
**Dates and Deadlines:** Applicants notified on a rolling basis.

**CONTACT**
630 US Highway One, North Brunswick, NJ 08902-3362
(800) 333-3879

## Drew University
Madison, New Jersey
www.drew.edu                    Federal Code: 002603

**4-year private** university and liberal arts college in large town, affiliated with United Methodist Church.
**Enrollment:** 1,346 undergrads, 1% part-time. 302 full-time freshmen.
**Selectivity:** Admits 50 to 75% of applicants.

**BASIC COSTS (2015-2016)**
**Tuition and fees:** $46,384.
**Per-credit charge:** $1,898.
**Room and board:** $12,672.

**FINANCIAL AID PICTURE (2014-2015)**
**Students with need:** Out of 245 full-time freshmen who applied for aid, 220 were judged to have need. Of these, 220 received aid, and 35 had their full need met. Average financial aid package met 79% of need; average scholarship/grant was $32,459; average loan was $3,417.
**Students without need:** 75 full-time freshmen who did not demonstrate need for aid received scholarships/grants; average award was $20,621. No-need awards available for academics, art, leadership, minority status, music/drama.
**Scholarships offered:** The Baldwin Honors Scholarship: $25,000 per year; awarded to students who have earned approximately an A average while enrolled in their high school's most rigorous college preparatory program; students must have a minimum SAT score in the low to mid-1200s (Critical Reading + Mathematics) or a total ACT score of 27. The Presidential Scholarship: $20,000 per year; awarded to students with a high school GPA in the A- range in an honors curriculum; students must have an SAT score in the mid to high-1100s (Critical Reading + Mathematics) or a total ACT score of 26. Students intending to major or participate in the performing or fine arts may submit a digital recording of musical or theatrical performances or a digital portfolio of art work in place of standardized testing results. After successful completion of their first year, Baldwin and Presidential Scholars are eligible to receive an additional fellowship of up to $3,500 to support academically related initiatives including independent research, community service activities, internships, study abroad, writing, directing, or producing an original play. The Dean's Scholarship: $15,000 per year; awarded to students with a minimum high school GPA in the B+ range in an honors curriculum; awarded entirely on the basis of high school academic achievement so standardized test results are not required. Civic Engagement Scholarships:

$2,500 per year; awarded to students who complete a special application for the award and who have demonstrated a sustained commitment to community service and civic engagement throughout their high school years. After the successful completion of their first year, Civic Scholars are eligible to receive a fellowship of up to $5,000 for related initiatives.

**FINANCIAL AID PROCEDURES**
**Forms required:** FAFSA.
**Dates and Deadlines:** Closing date 2/15. Applicants notified by 3/25; must reply by 5/1.
**Transfers:** Closing date 4/1.

**CONTACT**
Colby McCarthy, Director of Financial Assistance
36 Madison Avenue, Madison, NJ 07940-4063
(973) 408-3112

## Eastern International College
Jersey City, New Jersey
www.eicollege.edu                    Federal Code: 031226

**2-year for-profit** health science and nursing college in very large city.
**Enrollment:** 433 undergrads, 26% part-time. 160 full-time freshmen.
**Selectivity:** Open admission.

**BASIC COSTS (2015-2016)**
**Additional info:** Associate degree programs annual tuition: Nursing $15,100, lab and supply fees $2,000; Dental Hygiene $17,100, lab and supply fees $3,000; Diagnostic Medical Sonography $15,100, lab and supply fees $400; Medical Assistant $9,500, lab and supply fees $400; Cardiovascular Technology $13,600, lab and supply fees $400. Bachelor degree annual tuition: Diagnostic Medical Sonography $15,100, lab and supply fees $600. Registration fee $100. Tuition at time of enrollment locked for 2 years.

**FINANCIAL AID PICTURE (2014-2015)**
**Students with need:** Out of 156 full-time freshmen who applied for aid, 119 were judged to have need. Of these, 119 received aid, and 108 had their full need met. Average financial aid package met 89% of need; average scholarship/grant was $17,811; average loan was $5,250. For part-time students, average financial aid package was $12,360.
**Students without need:** No-need awards available for academics.

**FINANCIAL AID PROCEDURES**
**Forms required:** FAFSA, state aid form.
**Dates and Deadlines:** Closing date 6/1. Applicants notified on a rolling basis; must reply within 2 week(s) of notification.
**Transfers:** No deadline. Applicants notified on a rolling basis; must reply within 2 week(s) of notification. Students transferring from another institution during the same award year in which aid was disbursed must ensure withdrawal and acknowledgment to receive no further funds from the transferring school.

**CONTACT**
Kinga Gizynska, Financial Aid Director
684 Newark Avenue, Jersey City, NJ 07306
(201) 216-9901

## Essex County College
Newark, New Jersey
www.essex.edu                    Federal Code: 007107

**2-year public** community college in large city.
**Enrollment:** 9,828 undergrads, 45% part-time. 1,771 full-time freshmen.
**Selectivity:** Open admission; but selective for some programs.

**BASIC COSTS (2015-2016)**
**Tuition and fees:** $4,680; out-of-district residents $8,175; out-of-state residents $8,175.
**Per-credit charge:** $117; out-of-district residents $233; out-of-state residents $233.
**Additional info:** Tuition/fee waivers available for unemployed or children of unemployed.

**FINANCIAL AID PICTURE (2015-2016)**
**Students with need:** For part-time students, average financial aid package was $1,889.

**FINANCIAL AID PROCEDURES**
**Forms required:** FAFSA, institutional form.
**Dates and Deadlines:** Priority date 6/30; no closing date. Applicants notified on a rolling basis starting 6/15; must reply within 3 week(s) of notification.

**CONTACT**
Mildred Cofer, Director of Financial Aid
303 University Avenue, Newark, NJ 07102
(973) 877-3000

## Felician University
Lodi, New Jersey
www.felician.edu                    Federal Code: 002610

**4-year private** liberal arts college in large town, affiliated with Roman Catholic Church.
**Enrollment:** 1,600 undergrads, 13% part-time. 270 full-time freshmen.
**Selectivity:** Admits over 75% of applicants.

**BASIC COSTS (2015-2016)**
**Tuition and fees:** $31,335.
**Per-credit charge:** $975.
**Room and board:** $11,900.
**Additional info:** Tuition/fee waivers available for adults.

**FINANCIAL AID PICTURE (2014-2015)**
**Students with need:** Out of 265 full-time freshmen who applied for aid, 265 were judged to have need. Of these, 265 received aid, and 18 had their full need met. Average financial aid package met 45% of need; average scholarship/grant was $14,534; average loan was $3,260. For part-time students, average financial aid package was $5,592.
**Students without need:** 10 full-time freshmen who did not demonstrate need for aid received scholarships/grants; average award was $12,718. No-need awards available for academics, athletics.
**Scholarships offered:** 33 full-time freshmen received athletic scholarships; average amount $13,872.

**FINANCIAL AID PROCEDURES**
**Forms required:** FAFSA, state aid form.
**Dates and Deadlines:** Priority date 2/15; no closing date. Applicants notified on a rolling basis starting 4/1; must reply within 2 week(s) of notification.

**CONTACT**
Cynthia Montalvo, Director of Financial Aid
262 South Main Street, Lodi, NJ 07644-2198
(201) 559-6000 ext. 6010

## Georgian Court University
Lakewood, New Jersey
www.georgian.edu                    Federal Code: 002608

**4-year private** university and liberal arts college in large town, affiliated with Roman Catholic Church.
**Enrollment:** 1,352 undergrads, 8% part-time. 149 full-time freshmen.
**Selectivity:** Admits over 75% of applicants.

**BASIC COSTS (2015-2016)**
**Tuition and fees:** $31,618.
**Per-credit charge:** $690.
**Room and board:** $10,808.

**FINANCIAL AID PICTURE (2015-2016)**
**Students with need:** Out of 147 full-time freshmen who applied for aid, 135 were judged to have need. Of these, 135 received aid, and 43 had their full need met. Average financial aid package met 79% of need; average scholarship/grant was $16,142; average loan was $5,936. For part-time students, average financial aid package was $10,492.
**Students without need:** 13 full-time freshmen who did not demonstrate need for aid received scholarships/grants; average award was $13,092. No-need awards available for academics, alumni affiliation, art, athletics, leadership, religious affiliation, state/district residency.
**Scholarships offered:** 3 full-time freshmen received athletic scholarships; average amount $15,667.

**FINANCIAL AID PROCEDURES**
**Forms required:** FAFSA.
**Dates and Deadlines:** Priority date 4/15; closing date 7/1. Applicants notified on a rolling basis; must reply within 2 week(s) of notification.
**Transfers:** Transfer students who have outstanding financial obligations to previous college or who are in default are not admitted before being cleared by previous college or following federal guidelines concerning defaults.

**CONTACT**
Randy Brown, Director of Financial Aid
900 Lakewood Avenue, Lakewood, NJ 08701-2697
(732) 987-2258

## Hudson County Community College
Jersey City, New Jersey
www.hccc.edu                    Federal Code: 012954

**2-year public** community college in small city.
**Enrollment:** 8,510 undergrads, 31% part-time. 2,580 full-time freshmen.
**Selectivity:** Open admission; but selective for some programs.

**BASIC COSTS (2015-2016)**
**Tuition and fees:** $5,083; out-of-district residents $8,743; out-of-state residents $12,403.
**Per-credit charge:** $122; out-of-district residents $244; out-of-state residents $366.

**FINANCIAL AID PICTURE (2014-2015)**
**Students with need:** Out of 2,580 full-time freshmen who applied for aid, 2,580 were judged to have need. Of these, 2,099 received aid, and 19 had their full need met. Average financial aid package met 36% of need; average scholarship/grant was $4,968; average loan was $2,745. For part-time students, average financial aid package was $2,583.
**Students without need:** This college awards aid only to students with need.

**FINANCIAL AID PROCEDURES**
**Forms required:** FAFSA.
**Dates and Deadlines:** Priority date 7/15; no closing date. Applicants notified on a rolling basis starting 6/1; must reply within 1 week(s) of notification.
**Transfers:** No deadline.

**CONTACT**
Pamela Littles, Associate Dean of Student Financial Assistance
70 Sip Avenue, 1st Floor, Jersey City, NJ 07306
(201) 360-4200

## Kean University
Union, New Jersey
www.kean.edu                           Federal Code: 002622

**4-year public** university and liberal arts college in small city.
**Enrollment:** 11,755 undergrads, 22% part-time. 1,490 full-time freshmen.
**Selectivity:** Admits 50 to 75% of applicants.

### BASIC COSTS (2015-2016)
**Tuition and fees:** $11,581; out-of-state residents $18,183.
**Per-credit charge:** $295; out-of-state residents $500.
**Room and board:** $12,565.
**Additional info:** Tuition/fee waivers available for unemployed or children of unemployed.

### FINANCIAL AID PICTURE (2015-2016)
**Students with need:** Out of 1,332 full-time freshmen who applied for aid, 1,165 were judged to have need. Of these, 1,096 received aid, and 6 had their full need met. Average financial aid package met 82% of need; average scholarship/grant was $8,555; average loan was $3,387. For part-time students, average financial aid package was $6,589.
**Students without need:** 28 full-time freshmen who did not demonstrate need for aid received scholarships/grants; average award was $4,688. No-need awards available for academics, art, leadership, music/drama.
**Scholarships offered:** Freshman merit scholarships: renewable each year with 3.0 GPA and full-time enrollment. William Livingston Scholarship: full in-state tuition and fees; 3.5 GPA and 1300 SAT/29 ACT required. Kean Scholarship: $4,000; 3.5 GPA and 1250 SAT/28 ACT required. Trustee Scholarship: $3,000; 3.0 GPA and 1200 SAT/26 ACT required. Presidential Scholarship; $2,500; 3.0 GPA and 1150 SAT/25 ACT required. Academic Merit Scholarship: $2,000; 3.0 GPA and 1100 SAT/24 ACT required. SAT scores exclusive of Writing; GPAs are unweighted.

### FINANCIAL AID PROCEDURES
**Forms required:** FAFSA.
**Dates and Deadlines:** Closing date 4/17. Applicants notified on a rolling basis starting 3/1; must reply by 5/1.
**Transfers:** No deadline. Applicants notified on a rolling basis starting 10/1; must reply by 5/1. Aid is Awarded to Transfer students based upon number of credits completed/awarded, at time of transfer. Transfer students can apply for Merit Scholarships offered by the University through the Foundation Office/Scholarship office.

### CONTACT
Sherrell Watson-Hall, Director Financial Aid
Office of Admissions - Kean Hall, Union, NJ 07083-0411
(908) 737-3190

## Mercer County Community College
Trenton, New Jersey
www.mccc.edu                           Federal Code: 002641

**2-year public** community college in small city.
**Enrollment:** 7,012 undergrads, 57% part-time. 1,128 full-time freshmen.
**Selectivity:** Open admission.

### BASIC COSTS (2015-2016)
**Tuition and fees:** $4,610; out-of-district residents $6,035; out-of-state residents $8,675.
**Per-credit charge:** $119; out-of-district residents $166; out-of-state residents $254.
**Additional info:** Tuition/fee waivers available for unemployed or children of unemployed.

### FINANCIAL AID PICTURE
**Students with need:** Need-based aid available for full-time and part-time students. Work study available nights.

**Students without need:** No-need awards available for academics, athletics, state/district residency.
**Scholarships offered:** MCCC Foundation Scholarship: $2,500; top 25% of high school class; 15 total awards. NJ STARS program: for top 20% of high school class.

### FINANCIAL AID PROCEDURES
**Forms required:** FAFSA.
**Dates and Deadlines:** Closing date 5/1. Applicants notified on a rolling basis.

### CONTACT
PO Box B, Trenton, NJ 08690-1099
(609) 570-3210

## Middlesex County College
Edison, New Jersey
www.middlesexcc.edu                    Federal Code: 002615

**2-year public** community college in small city.
**Enrollment:** 10,675 undergrads.
**Selectivity:** Open admission; but selective for some programs.

### BASIC COSTS (2015-2016)
**Tuition and fees:** $4,301; out-of-state residents $8,516.
**Per-credit charge:** $106; out-of-state residents $212.

### FINANCIAL AID PICTURE
**Students with need:** Need-based aid available for full-time and part-time students.

### FINANCIAL AID PROCEDURES
**Forms required:** FAFSA, institutional form.
**Dates and Deadlines:** Priority date 4/1; no closing date. Applicants notified on a rolling basis starting 5/4.

### CONTACT
Brian Clemmons, Financial Aid Director
2600 Woodbridge Avenue, Edison, NJ 08818-3050
(732) 906-3520 ext. 3520

## Monmouth University
West Long Branch, New Jersey
www.monmouth.edu                       Federal Code: 002616

**4-year private** university in small town.
**Enrollment:** 4,661 undergrads, 5% part-time. 1,128 full-time freshmen.
**Selectivity:** Admits over 75% of applicants.

### BASIC COSTS (2015-2016)
**Tuition and fees:** $33,728.
**Per-credit charge:** $956.
**Room and board:** $12,506.

### FINANCIAL AID PICTURE (2015-2016)
**Students with need:** Out of 1,034 full-time freshmen who applied for aid, 889 were judged to have need. Of these, 889 received aid, and 119 had their full need met. Average financial aid package met 66% of need; average scholarship/grant was $11,806; average loan was $3,474. For part-time students, average financial aid package was $9,718.
**Students without need:** 218 full-time freshmen who did not demonstrate need for aid received scholarships/grants; average award was $10,496. No-need awards available for academics, alumni affiliation, art, athletics, state/district residency.
**Scholarships offered:** *Merit:* Academic Excellence Awards: $2,000-$21,000; based on SAT and GPA; renewable annually as long as required GPA is maintained. *Athletic:* 78 full-time freshmen received athletic scholarships; average amount $23,919.

## FINANCIAL AID PROCEDURES
**Forms required:** FAFSA.
**Dates and Deadlines:** Priority date 2/15; no closing date. Applicants notified on a rolling basis starting 3/1; must reply within 2 week(s) of notification.
**Transfers:** No deadline. Applicants notified on a rolling basis; must reply within 2 week(s) of notification.

## CONTACT
Claire Alasio, Associate Vice President for Enrollment Management
400 Cedar Avenue, West Long Branch, NJ 07764-1898
(732) 571-3463

# Montclair State University
Montclair, New Jersey
www.montclair.edu                    Federal Code: 002617

**4-year public** university in large town.
**Enrollment:** 16,129 undergrads, 11% part-time. 2,889 full-time freshmen.
**Selectivity:** Admits 50 to 75% of applicants.

## BASIC COSTS (2015-2016)
**Tuition and fees:** $11,773; out-of-state residents $20,320.
**Per-credit charge:** $284; out-of-state residents $569.
**Room and board:** $13,884.
**Additional info:** Tuition/fee waivers available for unemployed or children of unemployed.

## FINANCIAL AID PICTURE (2014-2015)
**Students with need:** Out of 2,625 full-time freshmen who applied for aid, 2,174 were judged to have need. Of these, 1,950 received aid, and 22 had their full need met. For part-time students, average financial aid package was $5,704.
**Students without need:** 135 full-time freshmen who did not demonstrate need for aid received scholarships/grants; average award was $5,359. No-need awards available for academics, alumni affiliation, art.

## FINANCIAL AID PROCEDURES
**Forms required:** FAFSA.
**Dates and Deadlines:** Priority date 3/15; no closing date. Applicants notified on a rolling basis starting 4/1; must reply within 2 week(s) of notification.
**Transfers:** Applicants notified on a rolling basis starting 4/1. Students will be eligible for financial aid beginning fall semester of the academic year for which they are admitted.

## CONTACT
James Anderson, Director of Financial Aid
One Normal Avenue, Montclair, NJ 07043
(973) 655-4461

# New Jersey City University
Jersey City, New Jersey
www.njcu.edu                    Federal Code: 002613

**4-year public** university in small city.
**Enrollment:** 6,201 undergrads, 23% part-time. 624 full-time freshmen.
**Selectivity:** Admits over 75% of applicants.

## BASIC COSTS (2015-2016)
**Tuition and fees:** $11,179; out-of-state residents $20,008.
**Room and board:** $11,618.

## FINANCIAL AID PICTURE (2014-2015)
**Students with need:** Out of 609 full-time freshmen who applied for aid, 553 were judged to have need. Of these, 530 received aid. For part-time students, average financial aid package was $5,072.

**Students without need:** 21 full-time freshmen who did not demonstrate need for aid received scholarships/grants; average award was $6,792. No-need awards available for academics.

## FINANCIAL AID PROCEDURES
**Forms required:** FAFSA.
**Dates and Deadlines:** Priority date 4/15; no closing date. Applicants notified by 5/15.

## CONTACT
Frank Cuozzo, Director, Financial Aid
2039 Kennedy Boulevard, Jersey City, NJ 07305-1597
(201) 200-3173

# New Jersey Institute of Technology
Newark, New Jersey
www.njit.edu                    Federal Code: 002621

**4-year public** university in large city.
**Enrollment:** 7,049 undergrads, 13% part-time. 956 full-time freshmen.
**Selectivity:** Admits 50 to 75% of applicants.

## BASIC COSTS (2015-2016)
**Tuition and fees:** $16,108; out-of-state residents $30,326.
**Per-credit charge:** $511; out-of-state residents $1,182.
**Room and board:** $13,296.

## FINANCIAL AID PICTURE (2014-2015)
**Students with need:** Out of 880 full-time freshmen who applied for aid, 725 were judged to have need. Of these, 725 received aid, and 97 had their full need met. Average financial aid package met 61% of need; average scholarship/grant was $12,902; average loan was $3,801. For part-time students, average financial aid package was $6,240.
**Students without need:** 183 full-time freshmen who did not demonstrate need for aid received scholarships/grants; average award was $13,168. No-need awards available for academics, alumni affiliation, athletics, job skills, leadership, minority status, religious affiliation, ROTC, state/district residency.
**Scholarships offered:** 30 full-time freshmen received athletic scholarships; average amount $21,280.
**Additional info:** Extensive co-op program for all majors.

## FINANCIAL AID PROCEDURES
**Forms required:** FAFSA.
**Dates and Deadlines:** Priority date 3/15; no closing date. Applicants notified on a rolling basis starting 12/1; must reply by 5/1 or within 2 week(s) of notification.
**Transfers:** No deadline. Applicants notified on a rolling basis starting 1/1; must reply within 2 week(s) of notification.

## CONTACT
Ivon Nunez, Director of Financial Aid
University Heights, Newark, NJ 07102
(973) 596-3479

# Ocean County College
Toms River, New Jersey
www.ocean.edu                    Federal Code: 002624

**2-year public** community college in small city.
**Enrollment:** 7,535 undergrads, 40% part-time. 1,545 full-time freshmen.
**Selectivity:** Open admission; but selective for some programs.

## BASIC COSTS (2015-2016)
**Tuition and fees:** $4,255; out-of-district residents $5,035; out-of-state residents $7,735.

**Per-credit charge:** $109; out-of-district residents $135; out-of-state residents $225.

**Additional info:** Tuition/fee waivers available for unemployed or children of unemployed.

### FINANCIAL AID PICTURE (2014-2015)

**Students with need:** 56% of average financial aid package awarded as scholarships/grants, 44% awarded as loans/jobs. Need-based aid available for part-time students. Work study available nights, weekends, and for part-time students.

**Students without need:** No-need awards available for academics, state/district residency.

### FINANCIAL AID PROCEDURES

**Forms required:** FAFSA.

**Dates and Deadlines:** Priority date 5/31; closing date 10/1. Applicants notified on a rolling basis starting 7/15; must reply within 1 week(s) of notification.

### CONTACT

Eileen Buckle, Director of Financial Aid
College Drive, Toms River, NJ 08754-2001
(732) 255-0400

## Passaic County Community College

Paterson, New Jersey
www.pccc.edu      Federal Code: 009994

**2-year public** community college in small city.
**Enrollment:** 8,389 undergrads.
**Selectivity:** Open admission; but selective for some programs.

### BASIC COSTS (2015-2016)

**Tuition and fees:** $4,410; out-of-district residents $5,115; out-of-state residents $7,755.

**Per-credit charge:** $112; out-of-district residents $135; out-of-state residents $223.

**Additional info:** Tuition/fee waivers available for unemployed or children of unemployed.

### FINANCIAL AID PICTURE

**Students with need:** Need-based aid available for full-time and part-time students.

**Students without need:** No-need awards available for academics.

**Additional info:** Limited scholarship funds available for low income students eligible for federal or state aid.

### FINANCIAL AID PROCEDURES

**Forms required:** FAFSA.

**Dates and Deadlines:** Priority date 8/1; no closing date. Applicants notified on a rolling basis starting 8/1; must reply within 2 week(s) of notification.

**Transfers:** Priority date 5/15; closing date 6/30.

### CONTACT

Eddie Viera, Director of Financial Aid
One College Boulevard, Paterson, NJ 07505-1179
(973) 684-6100

## Pillar College

Newark, New Jersey
www.pillar.edu      Federal Code: 036663

**4-year private** Bible and liberal arts college in large city, affiliated with Christian Church.
**Enrollment:** 369 undergrads.

### BASIC COSTS (2015-2016)

**Tuition and fees:** $19,440.
**Per-credit charge:** $785.

### FINANCIAL AID PICTURE

**Students with need:** Need-based aid available for full-time and part-time students. Work study available nights.

**Students without need:** This college awards aid only to students with need.

### FINANCIAL AID PROCEDURES

**Forms required:** FAFSA, state aid form.

**Dates and Deadlines:** Applicants notified on a rolling basis starting 1/31.

### CONTACT

Joel Davis, AVP of Finanance
60 Park Place, Suite 701, Newark, NJ 07102
(973) 803-5000 ext. 1030

## Princeton University

Princeton, New Jersey
www.princeton.edu      Federal Code: 002627

**4-year private** university in large town.
**Enrollment:** 5,260 undergrads. 1,313 full-time freshmen.
**Selectivity:** Admits less than 50% of applicants.

### BASIC COSTS (2015-2016)

**Tuition and fees:** $43,450.
**Room and board:** $14,160.

### FINANCIAL AID PICTURE (2014-2015)

**Students with need:** Out of 882 full-time freshmen who applied for aid, 770 were judged to have need. Of these, 770 received aid, and 770 had their full need met. Average financial aid package met 100% of need; average scholarship/grant was $44,115.

**Students without need:** This college awards aid only to students with need.

**Additional info:** All aid need-based; all aid grant money (no loans); institution meets full demonstrated need. FAFSA due 4/15; financial aid application due 11/15 for early action applicants.

### FINANCIAL AID PROCEDURES

**Forms required:** FAFSA, institutional form.

**Dates and Deadlines:** Closing date 2/1. Applicants notified by 3/31; must reply by 5/1.

### CONTACT

Robin Moscato, Director of Financial Aid
Princeton University, Princeton, NJ 08542-0430
(609) 258-3330

## Ramapo College of New Jersey

Mahwah, New Jersey
www.ramapo.edu      Federal Code: 009344

**4-year public** liberal arts college in large town.
**Enrollment:** 5,425 undergrads, 9% part-time. 974 full-time freshmen.
**Selectivity:** Admits 50 to 75% of applicants.

### BASIC COSTS (2015-2016)

**Tuition and fees:** $13,698; out-of-state residents $22,563.
**Per-credit charge:** $277; out-of-state residents $554.
**Room and board:** $11,640.
**Additional info:** Tuition/fee waivers available for unemployed or children of unemployed.

## FINANCIAL AID PICTURE (2014-2015)

**Students with need:** Out of 827 full-time freshmen who applied for aid, 602 were judged to have need. Of these, 567 received aid, and 74 had their full need met. Average financial aid package met 48% of need; average scholarship/grant was $13,049; average loan was $3,301. For part-time students, average financial aid package was $1,536.

**Students without need:** 97 full-time freshmen who did not demonstrate need for aid received scholarships/grants; average award was $9,249. No-need awards available for academics, leadership, state/district residency.

### FINANCIAL AID PROCEDURES

**Forms required:** FAFSA, state aid form.

**Dates and Deadlines:** Priority date 3/1; no closing date. Applicants notified on a rolling basis starting 4/1; must reply by 5/1 or within 2 week(s) of notification.

**Transfers:** No deadline. Applicants notified on a rolling basis.

### CONTACT

Frederick O'Neill, Director of Financial Aid
505 Ramapo Valley Road, Mahwah, NJ 07430-1680
(201) 684-7549

## Raritan Valley Community College

Branchburg, New Jersey
www.raritanval.edu                    Federal Code: 007731

**2-year public** community college in large town.

**Enrollment:** 6,722 undergrads, 51% part-time. 1,097 full-time freshmen.

**Selectivity:** Open admission; but selective for some programs.

### BASIC COSTS (2015-2016)

**Tuition and fees:** $5,034; out-of-district residents $5,934; out-of-state residents $5,934.

**Per-credit charge:** $137; out-of-district residents $167; out-of-state residents $167.

**Additional info:** Tuition/fee waivers available for unemployed or children of unemployed.

### FINANCIAL AID PICTURE

**Students with need:** Need-based aid available for full-time and part-time students.

**Students without need:** No-need awards available for academics.

### FINANCIAL AID PROCEDURES

**Forms required:** FAFSA.

**Dates and Deadlines:** Applicants notified on a rolling basis starting 4/1.

### CONTACT

Leonard Mesonas, Director of Financial Aid
118 Lamington Road, Branchburg, NJ 08876-1265
(908) 526-1200 ext. 8273

## Rider University

Lawrenceville, New Jersey
www.rider.edu                    Federal Code: 002628

**4-year private** university in small town.

**Enrollment:** 4,039 undergrads, 9% part-time. 861 full-time freshmen.

**Selectivity:** Admits 50 to 75% of applicants.

### BASIC COSTS (2015-2016)

**Tuition and fees:** $38,360.

**Per-credit charge:** $1,110.

**Room and board:** $13,770.

## FINANCIAL AID PICTURE (2015-2016)

**Students with need:** Average financial aid package met 73% of need; average scholarship/grant was $24,203; average loan was $3,876. For part-time students, average financial aid package was $7,003.

**Students without need:** No-need awards available for academics, leadership.

### FINANCIAL AID PROCEDURES

**Forms required:** FAFSA.

**Dates and Deadlines:** Priority date 3/1; no closing date. Applicants notified on a rolling basis starting 3/1.

**Transfers:** No deadline.

### CONTACT

Director of Student Financial Services
2083 Lawrenceville Road, Lawrenceville, NJ 08648-3099
(609) 896-5360

## Rowan College at Burlington County

Pemberton, New Jersey
www.bcc.edu/rcbc                    Federal Code: 007730

**2-year public** community college in small town.

**Enrollment:** 8,014 undergrads, 48% part-time. 1,494 full-time freshmen.

**Selectivity:** Open admission; but selective for some programs.

### BASIC COSTS (2016-2017)

**Tuition and fees:** $4,065; out-of-district residents $4,545; out-of-state residents $6,495.

**Per-credit charge:** $100; out-of-district residents $116; out-of-state residents $181.

**Additional info:** Tuition/fee waivers available for unemployed or children of unemployed.

### FINANCIAL AID PICTURE (2014-2015)

**Students with need:** Need-based aid available for full-time and part-time students. Work study available nights, weekends, and for part-time students.

**Students without need:** This college awards aid only to students with need.

### FINANCIAL AID PROCEDURES

**Forms required:** FAFSA.

**Dates and Deadlines:** Applicants notified on a rolling basis.

### CONTACT

Jaclyn Angermeier, Chief Financial Officer
601 Pemberton Browns Mills Road, Pemberton, NJ 08068-1599
(609) 894-9311 ext. 1575

## Rowan College at Gloucester

Sewell, New Jersey
www.rcgc.edu                    Federal Code: 006901

**2-year public** community and liberal arts college in large town.

**Enrollment:** 6,128 undergrads.

**Selectivity:** Open admission; but selective for some programs.

### BASIC COSTS (2015-2016)

**Tuition and fees:** $4,125; out-of-district residents $4,815; out-of-state residents $8,415.

**Per-credit charge:** $97; out-of-district residents $120; out-of-state residents $240.

**Additional info:** Tuition/fee waivers available for unemployed or children of unemployed.

### FINANCIAL AID PICTURE

**Students with need:** Need-based aid available for full-time and part-time students. Work study available nights.

PART III: FINANCIAL AID COLLEGE BY COLLEGE

## FINANCIAL AID PROCEDURES
**Forms required:** FAFSA, institutional form.
**Dates and Deadlines:** Priority date 5/1; no closing date. Applicants notified on a rolling basis starting 3/20.

## CONTACT
Michael Chando, Executive Director, Admissions & Financial Aid
1400 Tanyard Road, Sewell, NJ 08080
(856) 415-2219

## Rowan University
Glassboro, New Jersey
www.rowan.edu                    Federal Code: 002609

**4-year public** university in large town.
**Enrollment:** 13,003 undergrads, 10% part-time. 1,913 full-time freshmen.
**Selectivity:** Admits 50 to 75% of applicants.

### BASIC COSTS (2016-2017)
**Tuition and fees:** $12,864; out-of-state residents $20,978.
**Per-credit charge:** $355; out-of-state residents $669.
**Room and board:** $11,627.

### FINANCIAL AID PICTURE (2014-2015)
**Students with need:** Out of 1,731 full-time freshmen who applied for aid, 1,252 were judged to have need. Of these, 1,193 received aid, and 138 had their full need met. Average financial aid package met 71% of need; average scholarship/grant was $9,121; average loan was $3,274. For part-time students, average financial aid package was $5,262.
**Students without need:** 298 full-time freshmen who did not demonstrate need for aid received scholarships/grants; average award was $6,699. No-need awards available for academics, art, music/drama.

### FINANCIAL AID PROCEDURES
**Forms required:** FAFSA.
**Dates and Deadlines:** Priority date 3/16; no closing date. Applicants notified on a rolling basis starting 3/16.
**Transfers:** No deadline. Applicants notified on a rolling basis starting 3/1; must reply within 3 week(s) of notification.

### CONTACT
Jeff Hand
Savitz Hall, 201 Mullica Hill Road, Glassboro, NJ 08028-1701
(856) 256-4250

## Rutgers, The State University of New Jersey: Camden Campus
Camden, New Jersey
www.camden.rutgers.edu           Federal Code: 002629

**4-year public** university in small city.
**Enrollment:** 4,835 undergrads, 19% part-time. 422 full-time freshmen.
**Selectivity:** Admits 50 to 75% of applicants.

### BASIC COSTS (2015-2016)
**Tuition and fees:** $14,000; out-of-state residents $28,890.
**Per-credit charge:** $361; out-of-state residents $848.
**Room and board:** $11,710.
**Additional info:** School of Business and School of Nursing tuition and fees are slightly higher. Tuition/fee waivers available for unemployed or children of unemployed.

### FINANCIAL AID PICTURE (2014-2015)
**Students with need:** Out of 377 full-time freshmen who applied for aid, 314 were judged to have need. Of these, 314 received aid, and 13 had their full need met. Average financial aid package met 61% of need; average

scholarship/grant was $11,513; average loan was $3,849. For part-time students, average financial aid package was $4,943.
**Students without need:** 14 full-time freshmen who did not demonstrate need for aid received scholarships/grants; average award was $15,720. No-need awards available for academics, alumni affiliation, art, athletics, leadership, music/drama, state/district residency.
**Scholarships offered:** Outstanding Scholarship Recruitment Program: $2,500-$7,500; for selected in-state resident applicants based on SAT and class rank; 2,500 awarded. Carr Scholarship: $10,000; for selected minority applicants; 150 awarded. Class of 1941 Scholarship: $1,941; descendant of 1941 alumni preferred; 1 awarded. National Merit Scholarship for National Merit finalists; $1,000-$2,000; 15 or more awarded. National Achievement Scholarship for National Achievement finalists: $1,000-$2,000; 2 awarded. Rockland County-Herman T. Hopper Scholarship: out-of-state tuition; for Rockland County, New York resident; 1 awarded. Academic Achievement Award: $1,000; for in-state and out-of-state minority students; 20 awarded. Alumni Federation Scholarship: $1,000; for children of Rutgers University alumni; 20 awarded. National Scholarship: $5,000; for out-of-state students; about 100 awarded university-wide.

### FINANCIAL AID PROCEDURES
**Forms required:** FAFSA.
**Dates and Deadlines:** Priority date 3/15; no closing date. Applicants notified on a rolling basis starting 3/1; must reply within 4 week(s) of notification.

### CONTACT
406 Penn Street, Camden, NJ 08102
(856) 225-6039

## Rutgers, The State University of New Jersey: New Brunswick/Piscataway Campus
Piscataway, New Jersey
www.newbrunswick.rutgers.edu     Federal Code: 002629

**4-year public** university in small city.
**Enrollment:** 35,102 undergrads, 5% part-time. 6,602 full-time freshmen.
**Selectivity:** Admits 50 to 75% of applicants.

### BASIC COSTS (2015-2016)
**Tuition and fees:** $14,131; out-of-state residents $29,521.
**Per-credit charge:** $361; out-of-state residents $863.
**Room and board:** $12,054.
**Additional info:** Tuition and Fees listed are for the School of Arts and Sciences. School of Engineering, School of Pharmacy, School of Environmental & Biological Sciences and School of Business tuition and fees are slightly higher. Tuition/fee waivers available for unemployed or children of unemployed.

### FINANCIAL AID PICTURE (2015-2016)
**Students with need:** Out of 4,368 full-time freshmen who applied for aid, 3,489 were judged to have need. Of these, 3,489 received aid, and 192 had their full need met. Average financial aid package met 56% of need; average scholarship/grant was $12,575; average loan was $4,036. For part-time students, average financial aid package was $4,467.
**Students without need:** 350 full-time freshmen who did not demonstrate need for aid received scholarships/grants; average award was $8,839. No-need awards available for academics, alumni affiliation, art, athletics, leadership, music/drama, state/district residency.
**Scholarships offered:** *Merit:* Outstanding Scholarship Recruitment Program: $2,500-$7,500; for selected in-state resident applicants based on SAT and class rank; 2,500 awarded. Carr Scholarship: $10,000; for selected minority applicants; 150 awarded. Class of 1941 Scholarship: $1,941; descendant of Class of 1941 alumni preferred; 1 awarded. National Merit Scholarship: $1,000-$2,000; for National Merit finalists; 15 or more awarded. National Achievement Scholarship: $1,000-$2,000; for National Achievement finalists;

2 awarded. Rockland County-Herman T. Hopper Scholarship: out-of-state tuition; for Rockland County, New York resident; 1 awarded. Academic Achievement Award: $1,000; 20 awarded; for minority students. Alumni Federation Scholarship: $1,000; for children of Rutgers University alumni; 20 awarded. National Scholarship: $5,000; for out-of-state students; about 100 awards university-wide. *Athletic:* 108 full-time freshmen received athletic scholarships; average amount $25,547.

### FINANCIAL AID PROCEDURES

**Forms required:** FAFSA.

**Dates and Deadlines:** Priority date 3/15; no closing date. Applicants notified on a rolling basis starting 3/1; must reply within 4 week(s) of notification.

### CONTACT

65 Davidson Road, Room 202, Piscataway, NJ 08854-8097

(848) 932-7057

## Rutgers, The State University of New Jersey: Newark Campus

Newark, New Jersey

www.newark.rutgers.edu          Federal Code: 002629

**4-year public** university in large city.

**Enrollment:** 7,208 undergrads, 14% part-time. 1,192 full-time freshmen.

**Selectivity:** Admits 50 to 75% of applicants.

### BASIC COSTS (2015-2016)

**Tuition and fees:** $13,597; out-of-state residents $28,987.

**Per-credit charge:** $361; out-of-state residents $863.

**Room and board:** $12,841.

**Additional info:** School of Business and School of Nursing tuition and fees are slightly higher. Tuition/fee waivers available for unemployed or children of unemployed.

### FINANCIAL AID PICTURE (2014-2015)

**Students with need:** Out of 797 full-time freshmen who applied for aid, 736 were judged to have need. Of these, 736 received aid, and 14 had their full need met. Average financial aid package met 62% of need; average scholarship/grant was $12,235; average loan was $4,262. For part-time students, average financial aid package was $5,112.

**Students without need:** 8 full-time freshmen who did not demonstrate need for aid received scholarships/grants; average award was $9,750. No-need awards available for academics, alumni affiliation, art, athletics, leadership, music/drama, state/district residency.

**Scholarships offered:** Outstanding Scholarship Recruitment Program: $2,500-$7,500; for selected in-state resident applicants; based on SAT and class rank; 2,500 awarded. Carr Scholarship: $10,000; for selected minority applicants; 150 awarded. Class of 1941 Scholarship: $1,941; descendant of Class of 1941 alumni preferred; 1 awarded. National Merit Scholarship: $1,000-$2,000; for National Merit finalists; 15 or more awarded. National Achievement Scholarship: $1,000-$2,000; for National Achievement finalists; 2 awarded. Rockland County-Herman T. Hopper Scholarship: out-of-state tuition; for Rockland County, New York resident; 1 awarded. Academic Achievement Award: $1,000; for in-and out-of-state minority students; 20 awarded. Alumni Federation Scholarship: $1,000; for children of Rutgers University alumni; 20 awarded. James Bryan Scholarship: $400; for selected in-state freshmen; 3 awarded. National Scholarship: $5,000; for out-of-state students; about 100 awards university-wide.

### FINANCIAL AID PROCEDURES

**Forms required:** FAFSA.

**Dates and Deadlines:** Priority date 3/15; no closing date. Applicants notified on á rolling basis starting 3/1; must reply within 2 week(s) of notification.

### CONTACT

249 University Avenue, Newark, NJ 07102-1896

(973) 353-5151

## Saint Peter's University

Jersey City, New Jersey

www.saintpeters.edu          Federal Code: 002638

**4-year private** university in small city, affiliated with Roman Catholic Church.

**Enrollment:** 2,424 undergrads, 9% part-time. 568 full-time freshmen.

**Selectivity:** Admits 50 to 75% of applicants.

### BASIC COSTS (2015-2016)

**Tuition and fees:** $34,198.

**Per-credit charge:** $1,020.

**Room and board:** $14,468.

### FINANCIAL AID PICTURE

**Students with need:** Need-based aid available for full-time students.

**Students without need:** No-need awards available for academics, athletics.

**Scholarships offered:** Academic Awards: full tuition; based on 1100 SAT (exclusive of Writing), 3.0 GPA, and top 20% of class; 50 awarded. Incentive Awards: $500-$4,000; for selected applicants with some qualities necessary for academic awards but who are otherwise ineligible. Residential Grants: $500-$2,500 toward housing; based on academics and extracurricular activities.

**Additional info:** Cooperative education internships available in all majors, with average salaries exceeding $5,200.

### FINANCIAL AID PROCEDURES

**Forms required:** FAFSA, state aid form.

**Dates and Deadlines:** Priority date 3/15; no closing date. Applicants notified on a rolling basis starting 2/15; must reply by 5/1 or within 2 week(s) of notification.

**Transfers:** Student and parents (if dependent students) must be New Jersey residents for at least 1 year prior to start date. Students must complete renewal application before 6/1.

### CONTACT

Jennifer Ragsdale, Director of Financial Aid

2641 Kennedy Boulevard, Jersey City, NJ 07306

(201) 761-6060

## Salem Community College

Carneys Point, New Jersey

www.salemcc.edu          Federal Code: 005461

**2-year public** community and junior college in small town.

**Enrollment:** 1,025 undergrads.

**Selectivity:** Open admission; but selective for some programs.

### BASIC COSTS (2015-2016)

**Tuition and fees:** $4,104; out-of-district residents $4,794; out-of-state residents $5,544.

**Per-credit charge:** $102; out-of-district residents $125; out-of-state residents $150.

**Additional info:** Special Program costs as required. Tuition/fee waivers available for unemployed or children of unemployed.

### FINANCIAL AID PICTURE

**Students with need:** Need-based aid available for full-time and part-time students.

**Students without need:** No-need awards available for academics, athletics, state/district residency.

### FINANCIAL AID PROCEDURES

**Forms required:** FAFSA, institutional form.

**Dates and Deadlines:** Priority date 6/1; no closing date. Applicants notified on a rolling basis starting 4/1; must reply within 2 week(s) of notification.

CONTACT

Ron Burkhardt, Director of Financial Aid

460 Hollywood Avenue, Carneys Point, NJ 08069-2799

(856) 351-2699

## Seton Hall University

South Orange, New Jersey

www.shu.edu                    Federal Code: 002632

**4-year private** university in large town, affiliated with Roman Catholic Church.

**Enrollment:** 5,818 undergrads.

**BASIC COSTS (2015-2016)**

**Tuition and fees:** $38,272.

**Per-credit charge:** $1,095.

**Room and board:** $14,154.

**FINANCIAL AID PICTURE**

**Students with need:** Need-based aid available for full-time and part-time students. Work study available nights, weekends, and for part-time students.

**Students without need:** No-need awards available for academics, alumni affiliation, athletics, leadership, music/drama, ROTC.

**FINANCIAL AID PROCEDURES**

**Forms required:** FAFSA.

CONTACT

Javonda Asante, Director of Financial Aid

400 South Orange Avenue, South Orange, NJ 07079-2680

(800) 222-7183

## Stevens Institute of Technology

Hoboken, New Jersey

www.stevens.edu                Federal Code: 002639

**4-year private** university and engineering college in small city.

**Enrollment:** 2,956 undergrads. 686 full-time freshmen.

**Selectivity:** Admits less than 50% of applicants.

**BASIC COSTS (2016-2017)**

**Tuition and fees:** $48,838.

**Room and board:** $13,500.

**FINANCIAL AID PICTURE (2014-2015)**

**Students with need:** 69% of average financial aid package awarded as scholarships/grants, 31% awarded as loans/jobs. Need-based aid available for part-time students. Work study available nights, weekends, and for part-time students.

**Students without need:** No-need awards available for academics, leadership, music/drama, ROTC.

**Scholarships offered:** Neupauer Scholarship: full tuition; for top candidates in freshman class. Edwin A. Stevens Scholarship: $3,000-$20,000; for top candidates in freshman class. Becton Dickinson Scholarship: full tuition; for top student pursuing engineering degree. DeBaun Performing Arts Scholarship: $1,000-$5,000.

**FINANCIAL AID PROCEDURES**

**Forms required:** FAFSA.

**Dates and Deadlines:** Priority date 2/15; no closing date. Applicants notified on a rolling basis starting 3/30; must reply by 5/1 or within 2 week(s) of notification.

**Transfers:** Transfer merit scholarships, Phi Theta Kappa awards.

CONTACT

Louis Mayer, CFO, VP for Finance and Treasurer

One Castle Point on Hudson, Hoboken, NJ 07030-5991

(201) 216-5215

## Stockton University

Galloway, New Jersey

www.stockton.edu               Federal Code: 009345

**4-year public** liberal arts college in large town.

**Enrollment:** 7,765 undergrads, 5% part-time. 1,151 full-time freshmen.

**Selectivity:** Admits 50 to 75% of applicants.

**BASIC COSTS (2015-2016)**

**Tuition and fees:** $12,820; out-of-state residents $19,472.

**Room and board:** $11,707.

**Additional info:** Tuition/fee waivers available for unemployed or children of unemployed.

**FINANCIAL AID PICTURE (2015-2016)**

**Students with need:** Out of 1,083 full-time freshmen who applied for aid, 845 were judged to have need. Of these, 831 received aid, and 293 had their full need met. Average financial aid package met 76% of need; average scholarship/grant was $9,681; average loan was $3,360. For part-time students, average financial aid package was $9,619.

**Students without need:** 131 full-time freshmen who did not demonstrate need for aid received scholarships/grants; average award was $6,967. No-need awards available for academics, art, leadership, minority status, music/drama, state/district residency.

**Scholarships offered:** Freshman Scholarship Program: $2,000-$18,000; based on class rank in top 15%, SAT.

**Additional info:** Institutional grants are provided to the neediest incoming students.

**FINANCIAL AID PROCEDURES**

**Forms required:** FAFSA, state aid form.

**Dates and Deadlines:** Priority date 3/1; no closing date. Applicants notified on a rolling basis starting 4/1; must reply within 2 week(s) of notification.

**Transfers:** Applicants notified on a rolling basis starting 4/1; must reply within 2 week(s) of notification.

CONTACT

Jeanne Lewis, Director of Financial Aid

101 Vera King Farris Drive, Galloway, NJ 08205

(609) 652-4201

## Sussex County Community College

Newton, New Jersey

www.sussex.edu                 Federal Code: 025688

**2-year public** community college in small town.

**Enrollment:** 2,482 undergrads.

**Selectivity:** Open admission; but selective for some programs.

**BASIC COSTS (2015-2016)**

**Tuition and fees:** $6,000; out-of-district residents $7,950; out-of-state residents $9,900.

**Additional info:** Tuition/fee waivers available for unemployed or children of unemployed.

**FINANCIAL AID PICTURE**

**Students with need:** Need-based aid available for full-time and part-time students. Work study available nights, weekends, and for part-time students.

**Students without need:** This college awards aid only to students with need.

**FINANCIAL AID PROCEDURES**

**Forms required:** FAFSA, state aid form.

**Dates and Deadlines:** Closing date 6/1. Applicants notified on a rolling basis starting 5/1; must reply within 2 week(s) of notification.

## CONTACT

Diane Pienta-Lett, Director, Financial Aid
One College Hill Road, Newton, NJ 07860
(973) 300-2225

## Thomas Edison State University

Trenton, New Jersey
www.tesu.edu                    Federal Code: 011648

**4-year public** university in small city.
**Enrollment:** 17,590 undergrads, 99% part-time.
**Selectivity:** Open admission; but selective for some programs.

### BASIC COSTS (2015-2016)

**Tuition and fees:** $6,266; out-of-state residents $9,167.
**Per-credit charge:** $183; out-of-state residents $247.
**Additional info:** Tuition provided represents the College's Comprehensive Tuition Plan, which enables students to take 36 credits over a 12 month period. The College offers several other tuition plans.

### FINANCIAL AID PICTURE (2014-2015)

**Students with need:** 21% of average financial aid package awarded as scholarships/grants, 79% awarded as loans/jobs. Need-based aid available for part-time students.
**Students without need:** This college awards aid only to students with need.
**Additional info:** Financial aid applications should be received two months before each new term begins.

### FINANCIAL AID PROCEDURES

**Forms required:** FAFSA, institutional form.
**Dates and Deadlines:** Applicants notified on a rolling basis starting 3/1; must reply within 4 week(s) of notification.
**Transfers:** No deadline. Applicants notified on a rolling basis; must reply within 4 week(s) of notification.

### CONTACT

James Owens, Director of Financial Aid
111 West State Street, Trenton, NJ 08608-1176
(609) 633-9658

## Union County College

Cranford, New Jersey
www.ucc.edu                    Federal Code: 002643

**2-year public** community college in large town.
**Enrollment:** 10,745 undergrads, 56% part-time. 1,460 full-time freshmen.
**Selectivity:** Open admission; but selective for some programs.

### BASIC COSTS (2015-2016)

**Tuition and fees:** $4,450; out-of-district residents $8,900; out-of-state residents $8,900.
**Per-credit charge:** $177; out-of-district residents $354; out-of-state residents $354.
**Additional info:** Tuition/fee waivers available for unemployed or children of unemployed.

### FINANCIAL AID PICTURE

**Students with need:** Need-based aid available for full-time and part-time students. Work study available nights, weekends, and for part-time students.
**Students without need:** This college awards aid only to students with need.

### FINANCIAL AID PROCEDURES

**Forms required:** FAFSA, institutional form.
**Dates and Deadlines:** Priority date 5/1; no closing date. Must reply within 2 week(s) of notification.

## CONTACT

Dayne Chance, Director of Financial Aid
1033 Springfield Avenue, Cranford, NJ 07016-1528
(908) 709-7137

## Warren County Community College

Washington, New Jersey
www.warren.edu                    Federal Code: 016857

**2-year public** community college in small town.
**Enrollment:** 1,257 undergrads, 49% part-time. 218 full-time freshmen.
**Selectivity:** Open admission; but selective for some programs.

### BASIC COSTS (2015-2016)

**Tuition and fees:** $4,410; out-of-district residents $4,710; out-of-state residents $5,310.
**Per-credit charge:** $127; out-of-district residents $137; out-of-state residents $157.
**Additional info:** Tuition/fee waivers available for unemployed or children of unemployed.

### FINANCIAL AID PICTURE

**Students with need:** Need-based aid available for full-time and part-time students. Work study available nights, weekends, and for part-time students.
**Students without need:** This college awards aid only to students with need.

### FINANCIAL AID PROCEDURES

**Forms required:** FAFSA, institutional form.
**Dates and Deadlines:** Closing date 7/1. Applicants notified on a rolling basis; must reply within 2 week(s) of notification.
**Transfers:** No deadline. Applicants notified on a rolling basis.

### CONTACT

Debra Wulff, Director of Financial Aid
475 Route 57 West, Washington, NJ 07882-4343
(908) 835-2456

## William Paterson University of New Jersey

Wayne, New Jersey
www.wpunj.edu                    Federal Code: 002625

**4-year public** university and liberal arts college in large town.
**Enrollment:** 9,272 undergrads, 17% part-time. 1,334 full-time freshmen.
**Selectivity:** Admits 50 to 75% of applicants.

### BASIC COSTS (2015-2016)

**Tuition and fees:** $12,365; out-of-state residents $20,125.
**Per-credit charge:** $289; out-of-state residents $545.
**Room and board:** $10,885.
**Additional info:** Tuition/fee waivers available for unemployed or children of unemployed.

### FINANCIAL AID PICTURE (2015-2016)

**Students with need:** Out of 1,267 full-time freshmen who applied for aid, 1,052 were judged to have need. Of these, 1,035 received aid, and 332 had their full need met. For part-time students, average financial aid package was $9,044.
**Students without need:** 96 full-time freshmen who did not demonstrate need for aid received scholarships/grants; average award was $6,210. No-need awards available for academics, art, music/drama.
**Scholarships offered:** Trustee Scholarships: $2,000-$8,000; for full time freshmen. Honors College Scholarship: $2,000; for full time freshmen enrolled in program. Talent Awards for Music and Art Students: up to $9,000; based on audition.

**FINANCIAL AID PROCEDURES**

**Forms required:** FAFSA.

**Dates and Deadlines:** Priority date 4/1; no closing date. Applicants notified by 4/15.

**Transfers:** Priority date 4/1; no deadline. Applicants notified on a rolling basis starting 4/1; must reply within 2 week(s) of notification.

**CONTACT**

Michael Corso, Director of Financial Aid

300 Pompton Road, Wayne, NJ 07470

(973) 720-3945

# New Mexico

## Brookline College: Albuquerque

Albuquerque, New Mexico

www.brooklinecollege.edu          Federal Code: 022188

**2-year for-profit** branch campus and career college in large city.

**Enrollment:** 357 undergrads.

**Selectivity:** Open admission.

**BASIC COSTS (2015-2016)**

**Additional info:** Diploma programs: $15,225;Associate degree programs:$30,000; Bachelor's degree programs:$49,467-$85,000. Fees vary by course and program. All fees are subject to change.

**FINANCIAL AID PICTURE**

**Students with need:** Need-based aid available for full-time students.

**Students without need:** This college awards aid only to students with need.

**FINANCIAL AID PROCEDURES**

**Forms required:** FAFSA, institutional form.

**CONTACT**

Genna Gillary, Corporate Manager of Financial Aid

4201 Central Avenue NW, Suite J, Albuquerque, NM 87105-1649

(505) 880-2877

## Central New Mexico Community College

Albuquerque, New Mexico

www.cnm.edu          Federal Code: 004742

**2-year public** community and technical college in very large city.

**Enrollment:** 24,171 undergrads, 67% part-time. 1,929 full-time freshmen.

**Selectivity:** Open admission.

**BASIC COSTS (2015-2016)**

**Tuition and fees:** $1,484; out-of-state residents $6,740.

**Per-credit charge:** $51; out-of-state residents $270.

**Additional info:** CNM is a 100% commuter campus. There is no on-campus room and board.

**FINANCIAL AID PICTURE (2014-2015)**

**Students with need:** Out of 1,711 full-time freshmen who applied for aid, 1,445 were judged to have need. Of these, 1,385 received aid. Need-based aid available for part-time students.

**Students without need:** 19 full-time freshmen who did not demonstrate need for aid received scholarships/grants; average award was $3,199.

**FINANCIAL AID PROCEDURES**

**Forms required:** FAFSA.

**Dates and Deadlines:** Priority date 5/1; no closing date. Applicants notified on a rolling basis starting 5/1.

**CONTACT**

Lee Carrillo, Director of Financial Aid

525 Buena Vista Drive, SE, Albuquerque, NM 87106

(505) 224-3090

## Clovis Community College

Clovis, New Mexico

www.clovis.edu          Federal Code: 004743

**2-year public** community and junior college in large town.

**Enrollment:** 1,850 undergrads, 68% part-time. 143 full-time freshmen.

**Selectivity:** Open admission; but selective for some programs.

**BASIC COSTS (2015-2016)**

**Tuition and fees:** $1,176; out-of-district residents $1,248; out-of-state residents $2,376.

**FINANCIAL AID PICTURE (2014-2015)**

**Students with need:** 86% of average financial aid package awarded as scholarships/grants, 14% awarded as loans/jobs. Need-based aid available for part-time students. Work study available nights, weekends, and for part-time students.

**Students without need:** No-need awards available for academics, state/district residency.

**Additional info:** Endowment of over $1,000,000 to assist nursing students.

**FINANCIAL AID PROCEDURES**

**Forms required:** FAFSA.

**Dates and Deadlines:** Priority date 9/1; no closing date. Applicants notified on a rolling basis starting 4/15.

**Transfers:** No deadline. Applicants notified on a rolling basis starting 4/15.

**CONTACT**

April Chavez, Director of Financial Aid

417 Schepps Boulevard, Clovis, NM 88101-8381

(575) 769-4060

## Dona Ana Community College of New Mexico State University

Las Cruces, New Mexico

www.dacc.nmsu.edu          Federal Code: 002657

**2-year public** branch campus and community college in small city.

**Enrollment:** 9,280 undergrads.

**Selectivity:** Open admission; but selective for some programs.

**BASIC COSTS (2015-2016)**

**Tuition and fees:** $1,632; out-of-district residents $1,968; out-of-state residents $5,184.

**Per-credit charge:** $68; out-of-district residents $82; out-of-state residents $216.

**Room and board:** $5,784.

**FINANCIAL AID PICTURE**

**Students with need:** Need-based aid available for full-time and part-time students.

**FINANCIAL AID PROCEDURES**

**Forms required:** FAFSA.

**Dates and Deadlines:** Priority date 3/1; no closing date. Applicants notified on a rolling basis starting 5/1.

**CONTACT**

Gladys Chairez, Financial Aid Director

MSC-3DA, Las Cruces, NM 88003-8001

(505) 527-7510

## Eastern New Mexico University
Portales, New Mexico
www.enmu.edu                          Federal Code: 002651

**4-year public** university in large town.
**Enrollment:** 3,627 undergrads.
**Selectivity:** Admits less than 50% of applicants.

**BASIC COSTS (2015-2016)**
**Tuition and fees:** $5,168; out-of-state residents $10,943.
**Per-credit charge:** $136; out-of-state residents $376.
**Room and board:** $6,718.
**Additional info:** Tuition at time of enrollment locked for 4 years.

**FINANCIAL AID PICTURE**
**Students with need:** Need-based aid available for full-time and part-time students. Work study available nights, weekends, and for part-time students.
**Students without need:** No-need awards available for academics, alumni affiliation, art, athletics, leadership, music/drama, state/district residency.
**Scholarships offered:** Admissions scholarships are available based on SAT or ACT scores.

**FINANCIAL AID PROCEDURES**
**Forms required:** FAFSA.
**Dates and Deadlines:** Applicants notified on a rolling basis starting 5/1.
**Transfers:** No deadline. Applicants notified on a rolling basis starting 4/1; must reply by 8/31. Child care grants and non-need-based college work study limited to New Mexico residents.

**CONTACT**
Brent Small, Director of Financial Aid
1500 South Avenue K, Portales, NM 88130
(575) 562-2194

## Eastern New Mexico University: Roswell
Roswell, New Mexico
www.roswell.enmu.edu                  Federal Code: 002651

**2-year public** branch campus and community college in large town.
**Enrollment:** 1,878 undergrads.
**Selectivity:** Open admission; but selective for some programs.

**BASIC COSTS (2015-2016)**
**Tuition and fees:** $1,752; out-of-district residents $1,860; out-of-state residents $4,356.
**Room and board:** $8,090.

**FINANCIAL AID PICTURE**
**Students with need:** Need-based aid available for full-time and part-time students. Work study available nights, weekends, and for part-time students.
**Students without need:** No-need awards available for academics.

**FINANCIAL AID PROCEDURES**
**Forms required:** FAFSA.
**Dates and Deadlines:** Priority date 4/1; no closing date. Applicants notified on a rolling basis starting 4/1; must reply within 3 week(s) of notification.

**CONTACT**
Analisa Bhakta, Director of Financial Aid
PO Box 6000, Roswell, NM 88202-6000
(575) 624-7152

## Institute of American Indian Arts
Santa Fe, New Mexico
www.iaia.edu                          Federal Code: 014152

**4-year public** visual arts and liberal arts college in small city.
**Enrollment:** 263 undergrads.

**BASIC COSTS (2015-2016)**
**Tuition and fees:** $4,440; out-of-state residents $4,440.
**Per-credit charge:** $175.83.
**Room and board:** $8,140.

**FINANCIAL AID PICTURE**
**Students with need:** Need-based aid available for full-time and part-time students.

**FINANCIAL AID PROCEDURES**
**Forms required:** FAFSA, institutional form.
**Dates and Deadlines:** Priority date 3/15; no closing date. Applicants notified on a rolling basis starting 5/1.

**CONTACT**
Lara Barela, Financial Aid Director
83 Avan Nu Po Road, Santa Fe, NM 87508-1300
(505) 424-5724

## Luna Community College
Las Vegas, New Mexico
www.luna.edu                          Federal Code: 009962

**2-year public** community and liberal arts college in large town.
**Enrollment:** 1,739 undergrads.
**Selectivity:** Open admission; but selective for some programs and for out-of-state students.

**BASIC COSTS (2015-2016)**
**Tuition and fees:** $886; out-of-district residents $1,198; out-of-state residents $2,230.
**Per-credit charge:** $35; out-of-district residents $48; out-of-state residents $91.

**FINANCIAL AID PICTURE**
**Students with need:** Work study available nights.
**Students without need:** No-need awards available for academics, athletics, state/district residency.

**CONTACT**
Michael Montoya, Financial Aid Director
366 Luna Drive, Las Vegas, NM 87701
(505) 454-2500 ext. 2002

## Mesalands Community College
Tucumcari, New Mexico
www.mesalands.edu                     Federal Code: 032063

**2-year public** community and technical college in small town.
**Enrollment:** 563 undergrads.
**Selectivity:** Open admission; but selective for some programs.

**BASIC COSTS (2015-2016)**
**Tuition and fees:** $2,115; out-of-state residents $3,225.
**Per-credit charge:** $50; out-of-state residents $91.

**FINANCIAL AID PICTURE (2014-2015)**
**Students with need:** 92% of average financial aid package awarded as scholarships/grants, 8% awarded as loans/jobs. Need-based aid available for part-time students. Work study available nights.
**Students without need:** No-need awards available for academics, athletics, leadership, minority status, state/district residency.

**FINANCIAL AID PROCEDURES**
**Forms required:** FAFSA.
**Dates and Deadlines:** Priority date 3/31; no closing date. Applicants notified on a rolling basis starting 4/1; must reply within 3 week(s) of notification.

## CONTACT

Jessica Elebario, Director of Financial Aid
911 South Tenth Street, Tucumcari, NM 88401
(575) 461-4413 ext. 136

---

# Navajo Technical University

Crownpoint, New Mexico
www.navajotech.edu                    Federal Code: 016119

**2-year public** college in rural community.
**Enrollment:** 1,383 undergrads. 242 full-time freshmen.
**Selectivity:** Open admission.

## BASIC COSTS (2015-2016)

**Tuition and fees:** $2,460; out-of-district residents $4,170.
**Per-credit charge:** $71.25; out-of-district residents $143.
**Room and board:** $6,270.
**Additional info:** Tuition at time of enrollment locked for 2 years; tuition/fee waivers available for minority students.

## FINANCIAL AID PICTURE (2014-2015)

**Students with need:** Out of 242 full-time freshmen who applied for aid, 220 were judged to have need. Of these, 220 received aid, and 120 had their full need met. Average financial aid package met 55% of need; average scholarship/grant was $6,502. For part-time students, average financial aid package was $5,767.
**Students without need:** No-need awards available for academics.
**Scholarships offered:** *Merit:* Boeing Scholarship: amount varies; number of recipients varies. Tom Davis Scholarship: $500 award; 10 recipients per semester. *Athletic:* 1 full-time freshmen received athletic scholarships; average amount $2,600.

## FINANCIAL AID PROCEDURES

**Forms required:** FAFSA, institutional form.
**Dates and Deadlines:** Priority date 6/30; no closing date. Applicants notified on a rolling basis starting 8/5; must reply by 11/30 or within 4 week(s) of notification.
**Transfers:** Priority date 7/31; no deadline. Applicants notified by 9/30; must reply within 4 week(s) of notification.

## CONTACT

Tyrrell Hardy, Financial Aid Officer
PO Box 849, Crownpoint, NM 87313
(505) 786-4309

---

# New Mexico Highlands University

Las Vegas, New Mexico
www.nmhu.edu                    Federal Code: 002653

**4-year public** university in large town.
**Enrollment:** 2,128 undergrads, 31% part-time. 275 full-time freshmen.
**Selectivity:** Open admission.

## BASIC COSTS (2016-2017)

**Tuition and fees:** $4,800; out-of-state residents $7,534.
**Per-credit charge:** $140; out-of-state residents $254.
**Room and board:** $7,164.

## FINANCIAL AID PICTURE (2014-2015)

**Students with need:** Out of 251 full-time freshmen who applied for aid, 214 were judged to have need. Of these, 210 received aid, and 21 had their full need met. For part-time students, average financial aid package was $1,816.
**Students without need:** 255 full-time freshmen who did not demonstrate need for aid received scholarships/grants; average award was $2,654. No-need awards available for academics, alumni affiliation, art, athletics, music/drama, state/district residency.

---

**Scholarships offered:** 31 full-time freshmen received athletic scholarships; average amount $1,020.
**Additional info:** Work study funds available on no-need basis to state residents.

## FINANCIAL AID PROCEDURES

**Forms required:** FAFSA.
**Dates and Deadlines:** Applicants notified on a rolling basis starting 3/15; must reply within 2 week(s) of notification.
**Transfers:** Closing date 6/30.

## CONTACT

Eileen Sedillo, Director of Financial Aid
Box 9000, Las Vegas, NM 87701
(505) 454-3318

---

# New Mexico Institute of Mining and Technology

Socorro, New Mexico
www.nmt.edu                    Federal Code: 002654

**4-year public** engineering and liberal arts college in small town.
**Enrollment:** 1,502 undergrads, 5% part-time. 338 full-time freshmen.
**Selectivity:** Admits less than 50% of applicants.

## BASIC COSTS (2015-2016)

**Tuition and fees:** $6,613; out-of-state residents $19,137.
**Per-credit charge:** $232; out-of-state residents $754.
**Room and board:** $7,586.

## FINANCIAL AID PICTURE (2015-2016)

**Students with need:** Out of 324 full-time freshmen who applied for aid, 180 were judged to have need. Of these, 178 received aid, and 36 had their full need met. Average financial aid package met 84% of need; average scholarship/grant was $4,582; average loan was $2,939. For part-time students, average financial aid package was $8,932.
**Students without need:** 139 full-time freshmen who did not demonstrate need for aid received scholarships/grants; average award was $6,215. No-need awards available for academics, alumni affiliation, minority status, state/district residency.
**Additional info:** Campus research projects offer student employment based on abilities, interest, and merit.

## FINANCIAL AID PROCEDURES

**Forms required:** FAFSA, institutional form.
**Dates and Deadlines:** Priority date 5/1; no closing date. Applicants notified on a rolling basis starting 5/1; must reply within 2 week(s) of notification.
**Transfers:** Priority date 3/1; no deadline. Applicants notified on a rolling basis starting 4/1; must reply within 2 week(s) of notification. Financial aid transcripts required from all colleges attended.

## CONTACT

Marliss Monette, Director of Financial Aid
801 Leroy Place, Socorro, NM 87801
(575) 835-5333

---

# New Mexico Junior College

Hobbs, New Mexico
www.nmjc.edu                    Federal Code: 002655

**2-year public** community and technical college in large town.
**Enrollment:** 2,949 undergrads.
**Selectivity:** Open admission; but selective for some programs.

## BASIC COSTS (2015-2016)

**Tuition and fees:** $1,248; out-of-district residents $1,704; out-of-state residents $1,896.

**Per-credit charge:** $35; out-of-district residents $54; out-of-state residents $62.

**Room and board:** $4,150.

## FINANCIAL AID PICTURE

**Students with need:** Need-based aid available for full-time and part-time students. Work study available nights, weekends, and for part-time students.

**Students without need:** No-need awards available for academics, art, athletics, leadership, music/drama.

## FINANCIAL AID PROCEDURES

**Forms required:** FAFSA.

**Dates and Deadlines:** Priority date 6/1; no closing date. Applicants notified on a rolling basis; must reply within 2 week(s) of notification.

## CONTACT

Kerrie Mitchell, Director of Financial Aid

5317 Lovington Highway, Hobbs, NM 88240

(575) 392-4510

## New Mexico Military Institute
Roswell, New Mexico
www.nmmi.edu                    Federal Code: 002656

**2-year public** junior and military college in small city.

**Enrollment:** 428 undergrads. 315 full-time freshmen.

## BASIC COSTS (2015-2016)

**Tuition and fees:** $7,454; out-of-state residents $12,725.

**Room and board:** $5,170.

## FINANCIAL AID PICTURE

**Students with need:** Need-based aid available for full-time students.

**Students without need:** No-need awards available for academics, alumni affiliation, athletics, leadership, minority status, music/drama, ROTC, state/district residency.

## FINANCIAL AID PROCEDURES

**Forms required:** FAFSA.

**Dates and Deadlines:** Priority date 2/1; no closing date. Applicants notified on a rolling basis starting 2/1; must reply within 3 week(s) of notification.

**Transfers:** No deadline. Applicants notified on a rolling basis; must reply within 3 week(s) of notification. New Mexico Scholars Program, New Mexico Lottery Success Scholarship programs available.

## CONTACT

Sonya Rodriguez, Director of Admissions & Financial Aid

101 West College Boulevard, Roswell, NM 88201-5173

(575) 624-8066

## New Mexico State University
Las Cruces, New Mexico
www.nmsu.edu                    Federal Code: 002657

**4-year public** university in small city.

**Enrollment:** 12,104 undergrads, 15% part-time. 1,848 full-time freshmen.

**Selectivity:** Admits 50 to 75% of applicants.

## BASIC COSTS (2015-2016)

**Tuition and fees:** $6,729; out-of-state residents $21,234.

**Room and board:** $7,572.

## FINANCIAL AID PICTURE (2014-2015)

**Students with need:** Out of 1,658 full-time freshmen who applied for aid, 1,347 were judged to have need. Of these, 1,346 received aid, and 153 had their full need met. Average financial aid package met 64% of need; average scholarship/grant was $7,053; average loan was $3,162. For part-time students, average financial aid package was $6,067.

**Students without need:** 363 full-time freshmen who did not demonstrate need for aid received scholarships/grants; average award was $3,134. No-need awards available for academics, alumni affiliation, art, athletics, leadership, minority status, music/drama, ROTC, state/district residency.

**Scholarships offered:** 38 full-time freshmen received athletic scholarships; average amount $9,307.

## FINANCIAL AID PROCEDURES

**Forms required:** FAFSA.

**Dates and Deadlines:** Priority date 1/1; closing date 3/1. Applicants notified on a rolling basis starting 4/1.

**Transfers:** No deadline. Applicants notified on a rolling basis starting 4/9; must reply within 4 week(s) of notification.

## CONTACT

Jerry Martinez, Director of Financial Aid

Box 30001, MSC 3A, Las Cruces, NM 88003-8001

(575) 646-4105

## New Mexico State University at Alamogordo
Alamogordo, New Mexico
www.nmsua.edu                    Federal Code: 002658

**2-year public** branch campus college in large town.

**Enrollment:** 1,849 undergrads, 48% part-time. 198 full-time freshmen.

**Selectivity:** Open admission; but selective for some programs.

## BASIC COSTS (2015-2016)

**Tuition and fees:** $2,064; out-of-district residents $2,424; out-of-state residents $5,376.

**Per-credit charge:** $78; out-of-district residents $93; out-of-state residents $216.

## FINANCIAL AID PICTURE

**Students with need:** Need-based aid available for full-time and part-time students. Work study available nights.

**Students without need:** No-need awards available for academics, state/district residency. .

## FINANCIAL AID PROCEDURES

**Forms required:** FAFSA, institutional form.

**Dates and Deadlines:** Priority date 3/1; no closing date.

## CONTACT

Vandeen McKenzie, Financial Aid Director

2400 North Scenic Drive, Alamogordo, NM 88310

(575) 439-3600

## New Mexico State University at Carlsbad
Carlsbad, New Mexico
www.cavern.nmsu.edu              Federal Code: 002657

**2-year public** branch campus and community college in large town.

**Enrollment:** 1,360 undergrads.

**Selectivity:** Open admission; but selective for some programs.

## BASIC COSTS (2015-2016)

**Tuition and fees:** $1,208; out-of-district residents $1,952; out-of-state residents $3,968.

**Per-credit charge:** $42; out-of-district residents $73.

## FINANCIAL AID PICTURE

**Students with need:** Need-based aid available for full-time and part-time students. Work study available nights.

**Students without need:** No-need awards available for academics, state/district residency.

**FINANCIAL AID PROCEDURES**

**Forms required:** FAFSA.

**Dates and Deadlines:** Priority date 3/1; no closing date. Applicants notified on a rolling basis starting 5/1; must reply within 4 week(s) of notification.

**CONTACT**

Diana Campos, Financial Aid Coordinator

1500 University Drive, Carlsbad, NM 88220

(575) 234-9226

## New Mexico State University at Grants

Grants, New Mexico

www.grants.nmsu.edu          Federal Code: 008854

**2-year public** branch campus and community college in small town.

**Enrollment:** 821 undergrads.

**Selectivity:** Open admission.

**BASIC COSTS (2015-2016)**

**Tuition and fees:** $1,896; out-of-district residents $2,112; out-of-state residents $3,936.

**FINANCIAL AID PICTURE**

**Students with need:** Need-based aid available for full-time and part-time students. Work study available nights, weekends, and for part-time students.

**FINANCIAL AID PROCEDURES**

**Forms required:** FAFSA, institutional form.

**Dates and Deadlines:** Priority date 3/5; no closing date. Applicants notified on a rolling basis starting 6/15; must reply by 8/28.

**CONTACT**

Beth Armstead, Vice President for Student Services

1500 North Third Street, Grants, NM 87020

(505) 287-6678

## Northern New Mexico College

Espanola, New Mexico

www.nnmc.edu          Federal Code: 005286

**4-year public** business and nursing college in small town.

**Enrollment:** 1,601 undergrads.

**Selectivity:** Open admission; but selective for some programs and for out-of-state students.

**BASIC COSTS (2015-2016)**

**Tuition and fees:** $2,183.

**FINANCIAL AID PICTURE**

**Students with need:** Need-based aid available for full-time students.

**Students without need:** This college awards aid only to students with need.

**FINANCIAL AID PROCEDURES**

**Forms required:** FAFSA.

**Dates and Deadlines:** Priority date 3/1; no closing date. Applicants notified on a rolling basis starting 6/1; must reply within 2 week(s) of notification.

**CONTACT**

Jacob Pacheco, Director of Financial Aid

921 Paseo de Onate, Espanola, NM 87532

(505) 747-2128 ext. 128

## St. John's College

Santa Fe, New Mexico

www.sjc.edu          Federal Code: 002093

**4-year private** liberal arts college in small city.

**Enrollment:** 324 undergrads, 2% part-time. 90 full-time freshmen.

**Selectivity:** Admits over 75% of applicants.

**BASIC COSTS (2015-2016)**

**Tuition and fees:** $49,269.

**Room and board:** $10,890.

**FINANCIAL AID PICTURE (2015-2016)**

**Students with need:** Out of 80 full-time freshmen who applied for aid, 76 were judged to have need. Of these, 76 received aid, and 70 had their full need met. Average financial aid package met 93% of need; average scholarship/grant was $31,415; average loan was $5,500. For part-time students, average financial aid package was $21,350.

**Students without need:** 27 full-time freshmen who did not demonstrate need for aid received scholarships/grants; average award was $12,200. No-need awards available for academics.

**Scholarships offered:** *Merit:* Merit awards: range from $18,000 to $23,000; awarded on the strength of the admission application. *Athletic:* 14 full-time freshmen received athletic scholarships; average amount $18,800.

**Additional info:** FAFSA is the only application used to apply for financial aid. Priority filing date is 2/15 for entering students and 3/1 for continuing students. CSS profile is optional for domestic students but required for international students.

**FINANCIAL AID PROCEDURES**

**Forms required:** FAFSA.

**Dates and Deadlines:** Priority date 2/15; no closing date. Applicants notified on a rolling basis starting 12/15; must reply by 5/1 or within 2 week(s) of notification.

**Transfers:** Applicants notified on a rolling basis starting 2/15; must reply by 5/1 or within 2 week(s) of notification.

**CONTACT**

Michael Rodriguez, Director of Financial Aid

1160 Camino Cruz Blanca, Santa Fe, NM 87505

(505) 984-6058

## San Juan College

Farmington, New Mexico

www.sanjuancollege.edu          Federal Code: 002660

**2-year public** community and technical college in large town.

**Enrollment:** 5,669 undergrads.

**Selectivity:** Open admission.

**BASIC COSTS (2015-2016)**

**Tuition and fees:** $1,750; out-of-state residents $4,990.

**Per-credit charge:** $46; out-of-state residents $146.

**FINANCIAL AID PICTURE**

**Students with need:** Need-based aid available for full-time and part-time students. Work study available nights, weekends, and for part-time students.

**Students without need:** No-need awards available for academics, state/district residency.

**FINANCIAL AID PROCEDURES**

**Forms required:** FAFSA, institutional form.

**Dates and Deadlines:** Applicants notified on a rolling basis starting 7/1; must reply within 2 week(s) of notification.

**CONTACT**

Mindi-Kim Schrum, Director for Financial Aid

4601 College Boulevard, Farmington, NM 87402-4699

(505) 566-3323

## Santa Fe Community College
Santa Fe, New Mexico
www.sfcc.edu                    Federal Code: 016065

**2-year public** community college in small city.
**Enrollment:** 4,437 undergrads.
**Selectivity:** Open admission; but selective for some programs.

**BASIC COSTS (2015-2016)**
**Tuition and fees:** $1,196; out-of-district residents $1,484; out-of-state residents $2,600.
**Per-credit charge:** $45; out-of-district residents $57; out-of-state residents $103.

**FINANCIAL AID PICTURE**
**Students with need:** Need-based aid available for full-time and part-time students. Work study available nights, weekends, and for part-time students.
**Students without need:** No-need awards available for academics, state/district residency.

**FINANCIAL AID PROCEDURES**
**Forms required:** FAFSA, institutional form.
**Dates and Deadlines:** Priority date 5/1; no closing date. Applicants notified on a rolling basis starting 6/1; must reply within 4 week(s) of notification.

**CONTACT**
Scott Whitaker, Financial Aid Director
6401 Richards Avenue, Santa Fe, NM 87508-4887
(505) 428-1268

## Santa Fe University of Art and Design
Santa Fe, New Mexico
www.santafeuniversity.edu        Federal Code: 002649

**4-year for-profit** visual arts and liberal arts college in small city.
**Enrollment:** 849 undergrads. 221 full-time freshmen.

**BASIC COSTS (2016-2017)**
**Tuition and fees:** $32,346.
**Room and board:** $9,546.

**FINANCIAL AID PICTURE (2015-2016)**
**Students with need:** Out of 190 full-time freshmen who applied for aid, 171 were judged to have need. Of these, 171 received aid, and 14 had their full need met. Average financial aid package met 59% of need; average scholarship/grant was $17,635; average loan was $3,319. For part-time students, average financial aid package was $6,037.
**Students without need:** 34 full-time freshmen who did not demonstrate need for aid received scholarships/grants; average award was $11,204. No-need awards available for academics, art, music/drama, state/district residency.

**FINANCIAL AID PROCEDURES**
**Forms required:** FAFSA.
**Dates and Deadlines:** Priority date 3/15; no closing date. Applicants notified on a rolling basis starting 3/1.
**Transfers:** No deadline. Applicants notified on a rolling basis starting 3/1. Financial Aid is not credited to student accounts until all financial aid transcripts received.

**CONTACT**
Celeste Franklin, Director of Financial Aid
1600 Saint Michael's Drive, Santa Fe, NM 87505-7634
(505) 473-6454

## Southwest University of Visual Arts
Albuquerque, New Mexico
www.suva.edu                    Federal Code: 024915

**4-year for-profit** visual arts college in very large city.
**Enrollment:** 209 undergrads.

**BASIC COSTS (2015-2016)**
**Tuition and fees:** $22,944.
**Additional info:** Estimated total costs for books and supplies for each program: $3,900-$4,750. Tuition at time of enrollment locked for 4 years.

**FINANCIAL AID PICTURE**
**Students with need:** Work study available nights, weekends, and for part-time students.
**Students without need:** No-need awards available for academics.
**Scholarships offered:** Board of Trustees Scholarship, Transfer Student Scholarship, Scholarship for Continuing Students.

**FINANCIAL AID PROCEDURES**
**Forms required:** FAFSA.
**Transfers:** No deadline. Applicants notified on a rolling basis.

**CONTACT**
Registrar, Office of Institutional Effectiveness
5000 Marble Avenue NE, Albuquerque, NM 87119
(520) 325-0123

## Southwestern Indian Polytechnic Institute
Albuquerque, New Mexico
www.sipi.edu                    Federal Code: 011185

**2-year public** community and technical college in large city.
**Enrollment:** 397 undergrads, 13% part-time. 245 full-time freshmen.
**Selectivity:** Open admission.

**BASIC COSTS (2016-2017)**
**Tuition and fees:** $730.
**Room and board:** $450.
**Additional info:** Tuition/fee waivers available for minority students.

**FINANCIAL AID PICTURE (2014-2015)**
**Students with need:** Out of 192 full-time freshmen who applied for aid, 192 were judged to have need. Of these, 192 received aid. Average financial aid package met 30% of need; average scholarship/grant was $1,292. Need-based aid available for part-time students.
**Students without need:** No-need awards available for academics, leadership, minority status.
**Additional info:** Students with valid membership in recognized Indian tribe attend tuition-free.

**FINANCIAL AID PROCEDURES**
**Forms required:** FAFSA, institutional form.
**Dates and Deadlines:** Closing date 3/1. Applicants notified on a rolling basis starting 9/30.
**Transfers:** Priority date 9/13; no deadline.

**CONTACT**
Joseph Carpio, Director Admissions & Financial aid
PO Box 10146, Albuquerque, NM 87184
(505) 346-2361

## University of New Mexico
Albuquerque, New Mexico
www.unm.edu                    Federal Code: 002663

**4-year public** university in very large city.
**Enrollment:** 19,886 undergrads, 20% part-time. 3,289 full-time freshmen.
**Selectivity:** Admits 50 to 75% of applicants.

### BASIC COSTS (2015-2016)
**Tuition and fees:** $6,664; out-of-state residents $21,304.
**Room and board:** $8,690.
**Additional info:** N/A.

### FINANCIAL AID PICTURE
**Students with need:** Need-based aid available for full-time and part-time students. Work study available nights, weekends, and for part-time students.
**Students without need:** No-need awards available for academics, alumni affiliation, art, athletics, job skills, leadership, minority status, music/drama, religious affiliation, ROTC, state/district residency.
**Scholarships offered:** Bridge to Success Scholarship and Success Grant: first semester only; requires New Mexico residency; full-time status in degree-granting program; acceptable GED test score and/or requisite high school GPA per sponsor. NM Legislature Lottery Scholarship: second and subsequent semesters; requires New Mexico residency; full-time status in degree-granting program; acceptable GED test score and/or requisite high school GPA; 15 or more credit hours with a 2.5 GPA in the first semester.

### FINANCIAL AID PROCEDURES
**Forms required:** FAFSA.
**Dates and Deadlines:** Priority date 3/1; no closing date. Applicants notified on a rolling basis starting 3/31.

### CONTACT
Brian Malone, Director of Student Financial Aid
Office of Admissions, Albuquerque, NM 87196-4895
(505) 277-8900

## University of the Southwest
Hobbs, New Mexico
www.usw.edu                    Federal Code: 013935

**4-year private** business, liberal arts and teachers college in large town, affiliated with nondenominational tradition.
**Enrollment:** 430 undergrads, 40% part-time. 111 full-time freshmen.
**Selectivity:** Open admission; but selective for some programs.

### BASIC COSTS (2015-2016)
**Tuition and fees:** $15,660.
**Per-credit charge:** $522.
**Room and board:** $7,303.

### FINANCIAL AID PICTURE
**Students with need:** Need-based aid available for full-time and part-time students. Work study available nights, weekends, and for part-time students.
**Students without need:** No-need awards available for academics, athletics, leadership.

### FINANCIAL AID PROCEDURES
**Forms required:** FAFSA.
**Dates and Deadlines:** Priority date 4/1; closing date 6/1. Applicants notified on a rolling basis starting 4/1; must reply within 2 week(s) of notification.
**Transfers:** Applicants notified on a rolling basis starting 4/1; must reply within 2 week(s) of notification.

### CONTACT
Dawney Kringle, Director of Financial Aid
6610 North Lovington Highway, #506, Hobbs, NM 88240
(575) 492-2114

## Western New Mexico University
Silver City, New Mexico
www.wnmu.edu                    Federal Code: 002664

**4-year public** university in large town.
**Enrollment:** 1,869 undergrads, 25% part-time. 324 full-time freshmen.
**Selectivity:** Open admission.

### BASIC COSTS (2015-2016)
**Tuition and fees:** $6,417; out-of-state residents $15,035.
**Room and board:** $7,010.

### FINANCIAL AID PICTURE (2014-2015)
**Students with need:** Out of 270 full-time freshmen who applied for aid, 269 were judged to have need. Of these, 269 received aid. Average financial aid package met 64% of need; average scholarship/grant was $4,753; average loan was $2,979. For part-time students, average financial aid package was $7,023.
**Students without need:** 14 full-time freshmen who did not demonstrate need for aid received scholarships/grants; average award was $4,667. No-need awards available for academics, art, athletics, music/drama.
**Scholarships offered:** 49 full-time freshmen received athletic scholarships; average amount $2,063.

### FINANCIAL AID PROCEDURES
**Forms required:** FAFSA, institutional form.
**Dates and Deadlines:** Priority date 3/1; no closing date. Applicants notified on a rolling basis starting 3/1; must reply within 2 week(s) of notification.

### CONTACT
Charles Kelly, Director of Financial Aid
Castorena 106, Silver City, NM 88062
(505) 538-6173

# New York

## Adelphi University
Garden City, New York
www.adelphi.edu                    Federal Code: 002666

**4-year private** university in large town.
**Enrollment:** 4,813 undergrads, 9% part-time. 854 full-time freshmen.
**Selectivity:** Admits 50 to 75% of applicants.

### BASIC COSTS (2015-2016)
**Tuition and fees:** $34,034.
**Per-credit charge:** $990.
**Room and board:** $13,510.

### FINANCIAL AID PICTURE (2015-2016)
**Students with need:** Out of 750 full-time freshmen who applied for aid, 636 were judged to have need. Of these, 614 received aid, and 6 had their full need met. Average financial aid package met 18% of need; average scholarship/grant was $7,417; average loan was $3,902. Need-based aid available for part-time students.
**Students without need:** 147 full-time freshmen who did not demonstrate need for aid received scholarships/grants; average award was $18,224. No-need awards available for academics, alumni affiliation, art, athletics, leadership, minority status, music/drama, religious affiliation.
**Scholarships offered:** *Merit:* Trustee Scholarships: for full-time freshmen with the most outstanding academic achievement and co-curricular activities, minimum 2020 score on SAT and rank in top 10% of high school class; 12 available. Presidential Scholarship: typically have minimum SAT of 1950 and rank in top 10% of high school class; $15,000-$16,000 depending upon the individual's academic profile; 25 available. Provost Scholarship: minimum SAT

of 1800 and rank in the top 15% of high school class or have minimum transfer GPA of 3.5; $12,000 to $14,500; 55 available. Dean's Scholarship: for full-time freshmen with very good academic performances. Generally minimum SAT scores 1580 to 1790 and rank in top 25% of high school class. *Athletic:* 18 full-time freshmen received athletic scholarships; average amount $19,999.

## FINANCIAL AID PROCEDURES

**Forms required:** FAFSA, state aid form.

**Dates and Deadlines:** Priority date 3/1; no closing date. Applicants notified on a rolling basis starting 3/1.

**Transfers:** No deadline. Applicants notified on a rolling basis.

## CONTACT

Sheryl Mihopulos, Assistant Vice President
One South Avenue, Levermore 110, Garden City, NY 11530-0701
(516) 877-3080

## Adirondack Community College
Queensbury, New York
www.sunyacc.edu                   Federal Code: 002860

**2-year public** community college in large town.
**Enrollment:** 3,300 undergrads.
**Selectivity:** Open admission; but selective for some programs.

### BASIC COSTS (2015-2016)
**Tuition and fees:** $4,419; out-of-state residents $8,403.
**Per-credit charge:** $166; out-of-state residents $332.
**Room and board:** $10,460.

### FINANCIAL AID PICTURE
**Students with need:** Need-based aid available for full-time and part-time students.
**Students without need:** No-need awards available for academics, state/district residency.
**Scholarships offered:** Academic Excellence Scholarship: $750 per semester for up to 4 semesters; for local high school graduates who are 1st or 2nd in class, GPA 3.5. Hill Scholarship: $500 per semester for 4 semesters; for Fort Edward High School graduate.

### FINANCIAL AID PROCEDURES
**Forms required:** FAFSA, state aid form, institutional form.
**Dates and Deadlines:** Priority date 4/15; no closing date. Applicants notified on a rolling basis starting 5/1.

### CONTACT
Maureen Reilly, Director of Financial Aid
640 Bay Road, Queensbury, NY 12804
(518) 743-2223

## Albany College of Pharmacy and Health Sciences
Albany, New York                   Federal Code: 002885
www.acphs.edu                      CSS Code: 2013

**4-year private** health science and pharmacy college in small city.
**Enrollment:** 1,003 undergrads, 1% part-time. 189 full-time freshmen.
**Selectivity:** Admits 50 to 75% of applicants.

### BASIC COSTS (2015-2016)
**Tuition and fees:** $31,081.
**Per-credit charge:** $1,010.
**Room and board:** $10,410.

### FINANCIAL AID PICTURE
**Students with need:** Need-based aid available for full-time and part-time students. Work study available nights, weekends, and for part-time students.
**Students without need:** No-need awards available for academics, alumni affiliation, athletics, state/district residency.

### FINANCIAL AID PROCEDURES
**Forms required:** FAFSA. CSS PROFILE priority date November 15.
**Dates and Deadlines:** Priority date 2/1; closing date 5/1. Applicants notified by 3/1; must reply within 2 week(s) of notification.
**Transfers:** Applicants notified by 4/1; must reply within 2 week(s) of notification.

### CONTACT
Kathleen Montague, Director of Financial Aid
106 New Scotland Avenue, Albany, NY 12208-3492
(518) 694-7256

## Alfred University
Alfred, New York
www.alfred.edu                     Federal Code: 002668

**4-year private** university in rural community.
**Enrollment:** 1,754 undergrads.
**Selectivity:** Admits 50 to 75% of applicants.

### BASIC COSTS (2015-2016)
**Tuition and fees:** $30,200.
**Per-credit charge:** $930.
**Room and board:** $11,960.
**Additional info:** Tuition figures provided are for the College of Liberal Arts & Sciences and Professional Studies. Tuition for the School of Art & Design and Biomaterials, Ceramic, Materials Science, and Glass Engineering is $23,664 for non-NYS residents and $17,200 for NYS residents. Tuition for Mechanical, Renewable, and Undecided Engineering is $23,664.

### FINANCIAL AID PICTURE
**Students with need:** Need-based aid available for full-time students. Work study available nights, weekends, and for part-time students.
**Students without need:** No-need awards available for academics, art, leadership, music/drama.

### FINANCIAL AID PROCEDURES
**Forms required:** FAFSA, state aid form, institutional form.
**Dates and Deadlines:** Closing date 3/15. Applicants notified on a rolling basis starting 2/15; must reply by 5/1 or within 2 week(s) of notification.
**Transfers:** No deadline. Applicants notified on a rolling basis starting 2/15; must reply by 5/1 or within 2 week(s) of notification.

### CONTACT
Earl Pierce, Director of Student Financial Aid
Alumni Hall, Alfred, NY 14802-1205
(607) 871-2159

## American Academy McAllister Institute of Funeral Service
New York, New York
www.funeraleducation.org           Federal Code: 010813

**2-year private** school of mortuary science in very large city.
**Enrollment:** 493 undergrads, 77% part-time. 29 full-time freshmen.
**Selectivity:** Admits over 75% of applicants.

### BASIC COSTS (2016-2017)
**Tuition and fees:** $14,410.
**Per-credit charge:** $475.

**FINANCIAL AID PICTURE**

**Students with need:** Need-based aid available for full-time students.

**Students without need:** This college awards aid only to students with need.

**Additional info:** Financial aid application due 30 days before start of semester.

**FINANCIAL AID PROCEDURES**

**Forms required:** FAFSA, state aid form.

**Dates and Deadlines:** Applicants notified on a rolling basis starting 7/1; must reply by 9/1 or within 3 week(s) of notification.

**Transfers:** Priority date 6/1.

**CONTACT**

Natalie Givan, Financial Aid Administrator

619 West 54th Street, 2nd Floor, New York, NY 10019-3602

(212) 757-1190

## American Academy of Dramatic Arts
New York, New York
www.aada.edu                    Federal Code: 007465

**2-year private** junior and performing arts college in very large city.

**Enrollment:** 290 undergrads.

**BASIC COSTS (2015-2016)**

**Tuition and fees:** $30,650.

**FINANCIAL AID PICTURE**

**Students with need:** Need-based aid available for full-time students.

**Students without need:** This college awards aid only to students with need.

**Scholarships offered:** Merit awards: $1,000-$6,000 for first-year students; Scholarships of $500-$4,000 available for second year; Scholarships of $500-$6,000 available for post-degree third year.

**Additional info:** Need-based incentive grants of $200-$2,000 for first-year students.

**FINANCIAL AID PROCEDURES**

**Forms required:** FAFSA, institutional form.

**Dates and Deadlines:** Applicants notified on a rolling basis.

**CONTACT**

Roberto Lopez, Financial Aid Director

120 Madison Avenue, New York, NY 10016

(212) 686-9244 ext. 342

## ASA College
Brooklyn, New York
www.asa.edu                     Federal Code: 030955

**2-year for-profit** technical and career college in very large city.

**Enrollment:** 4,551 undergrads, 6% part-time. 1,217 full-time freshmen.

**Selectivity:** Open admission.

**BASIC COSTS (2015-2016)**

**Tuition and fees:** $12,898.

**Per-credit charge:** $520.

**Room and board:** $9,200.

**FINANCIAL AID PICTURE (2014-2015)**

**Students with need:** 69% of average financial aid package awarded as scholarships/grants, 31% awarded as loans/jobs. Need-based aid available for part-time students. Work study available nights, weekends, and for part-time students.

**Students without need:** No-need awards available for academics, alumni affiliation, athletics, leadership, state/district residency.

**FINANCIAL AID PROCEDURES**

**Forms required:** FAFSA, state aid form.

**Dates and Deadlines:** Applicants notified on a rolling basis starting 7/13; must reply by 10/13.

**Transfers:** No deadline. Applicants notified on a rolling basis starting 7/13; must reply by 10/13.

**CONTACT**

Victoria Shtamler, Vice President of Student Financial Services

81 Willoughby Street, Brooklyn, NY 11201

(718) 522-9073 ext. 2037

## Bard College
Annandale-on-Hudson, New York    Federal Code: 002671
www.bard.edu                          CSS Code: 2037

**4-year private** liberal arts college in small town, affiliated with Episcopal Church.

**Enrollment:** 1,962 undergrads, 2% part-time. 447 full-time freshmen.

**Selectivity:** Admits less than 50% of applicants.

**BASIC COSTS (2016-2017)**

**Tuition and fees:** $51,614.

**Per-credit charge:** $1,585.

**Room and board:** $14,540.

**FINANCIAL AID PICTURE (2015-2016)**

**Students with need:** Out of 307 full-time freshmen who applied for aid, 285 were judged to have need. Of these, 285 received aid, and 85 had their full need met. Average financial aid package met 81% of need; average scholarship/grant was $38,766; average loan was $5,649. For part-time students, average financial aid package was $14,382.

**Students without need:** 3 full-time freshmen who did not demonstrate need for aid received scholarships/grants; average award was $16,000. No-need awards available for academics.

**Scholarships offered:** Distinguished Scientist Scholarship: full tuition; for students intending to major in math or sciences; 10-20 awarded annually.

**Additional info:** Excellence and Equal Cost Program for students who graduate in top 10 of public high school class lowers fees to levels equivalent to those at home state university or college.

**FINANCIAL AID PROCEDURES**

**Forms required:** FAFSA, CSS PROFILE, state aid form.

**Dates and Deadlines:** Closing date 2/15. Applicants notified by 4/1; must reply by 5/1.

**Transfers:** Applicants notified by 4/1; must reply by 5/1.

**CONTACT**

Denise Ackerman, Director of Financial Aid

30 Campus Road, Annandale-on-Hudson, NY 12504-5000

(845) 758-7526

## Barnard College
New York, New York               Federal Code: 002708
www.barnard.edu                       CSS Code: 2038

**4-year private** liberal arts college for women in very large city.

**Enrollment:** 2,536 undergrads, 1% part-time. 635 full-time freshmen.

**Selectivity:** Admits less than 50% of applicants.

**BASIC COSTS (2015-2016)**

**Tuition and fees:** $47,631.

**Per-credit charge:** $1,530.

**Room and board:** $15,110.

## FINANCIAL AID PICTURE (2015-2016)
**Students with need:** Out of 357 full-time freshmen who applied for aid, 287 were judged to have need. Of these, 287 received aid, and 281 had their full need met. Average financial aid package met 100% of need; average scholarship/grant was $44,840; average loan was $3,258.
**Students without need:** This college awards aid only to students with need.

## FINANCIAL AID PROCEDURES
**Forms required:** FAFSA, state aid form. CSS Profile required for returning students, except those who had a parent contribution less than $2,000 in the prior academic year. Returning international students also not required to complete the CSS Profile.
**Dates and Deadlines:** Closing date 2/15. Applicants notified by 3/31; must reply by 5/1.
**Transfers:** Closing date 4/16. Transfers admitted in the spring are not eligible for institutional grant aid.

## CONTACT
Nanette Dilauro, Director of Financial Aid
3009 Broadway, New York, NY 10027-6598
(212) 854-2154

## Berkeley College
White Plains, New York
www.berkeleycollege.edu          Federal Code: 007421

**4-year for-profit** branch campus and business college in small city.
**Enrollment:** 465 undergrads, 8% part-time. 100 full-time freshmen.

## BASIC COSTS (2015-2016)
**Tuition and fees:** $24,300.
**Per-credit charge:** $525.
**Room only:** $9,000.

## FINANCIAL AID PICTURE
**Students with need:** Need-based aid available for full-time students.
**Students without need:** No-need awards available for academics, alumni affiliation.

## FINANCIAL AID PROCEDURES
**Forms required:** FAFSA.
**Dates and Deadlines:** Applicants notified on a rolling basis starting 3/1; must reply within 6 week(s) of notification.

## CONTACT
Howard Leslie, VP, Financial Aid
99 Church Street, White Plains, NY 10601
(914) 694-1122

## Berkeley College of New York City
New York, New York
www.berkeleycollege.edu          Federal Code: 007502

**4-year for-profit** business college in very large city.
**Enrollment:** 3,935 undergrads, 12% part-time. 409 full-time freshmen.

## BASIC COSTS (2015-2016)
**Tuition and fees:** $24,300.
**Per-credit charge:** $525.

## FINANCIAL AID PICTURE
**Students with need:** Need-based aid available for full-time students.
**Students without need:** No-need awards available for academics, alumni affiliation.

## FINANCIAL AID PROCEDURES
**Forms required:** FAFSA.

**Dates and Deadlines:** Applicants notified on a rolling basis starting 3/1; must reply within 6 week(s) of notification.
**Transfers:** New York State TAP Grant eligibility may be affected.

## CONTACT
Howard Leslie, Vice President Financial Aid
3 East 43rd Street, New York, NY 10017
(212) 986-4343

## Boricua College
New York, New York
www.boricuacollege.edu          Federal Code: 013029

**4-year private** liberal arts college in very large city.
**Enrollment:** 1,019 undergrads.

## BASIC COSTS (2015-2016)
**Tuition and fees:** $10,100.

## FINANCIAL AID PICTURE
**Students with need:** Need-based aid available for full-time students.

## FINANCIAL AID PROCEDURES
**Forms required:** FAFSA, state aid form.
**Dates and Deadlines:** Priority date 4/30; no closing date. Applicants notified on a rolling basis; must reply within 3 week(s) of notification.

## CONTACT
Rosalia Cruz, Director of Financial Aid
3755 Broadway, New York, NY 10032
(212) 694-1000 ext. 611

## Briarcliffe College
Bethpage, New York
www.briarcliffe.edu          Federal Code: 020757

**4-year for-profit** business and career college in large town.
**Enrollment:** 1,719 undergrads.

## BASIC COSTS (2015-2016)
**Additional info:** Associate programs: $23,280-$37,440. Bachelor's programs: $21,930-$74,880.

## FINANCIAL AID PICTURE
**Students with need:** Need-based aid available for full-time and part-time students.
**Students without need:** No-need awards available for academics, alumni affiliation.

## FINANCIAL AID PROCEDURES
**Forms required:** FAFSA, state aid form, institutional form.
**Dates and Deadlines:** Applicants notified on a rolling basis.

## CONTACT
Cindy Roys, Director of Financial Aid
1055 Stewart Avenue, Bethpage, NY 11714
(516) 918-3600

## Broome Community College
Binghamton, New York
www.sunybroome.edu          Federal Code: 002862

**2-year public** community college in small city.
**Enrollment:** 5,539 undergrads.
**Selectivity:** Open admission; but selective for some programs.

**BASIC COSTS (2015-2016)**
**Tuition and fees:** $4,811; out-of-state residents $9,035.
**Per-credit charge:** $176; out-of-state residents $352.
**Room and board:** $10,362.

**FINANCIAL AID PICTURE**
**Students with need:** Need-based aid available for full-time and part-time students. Work study available nights.

**FINANCIAL AID PROCEDURES**
**Forms required:** FAFSA.
**Dates and Deadlines:** Priority date 3/1; no closing date. Applicants notified on a rolling basis starting 3/15; must reply within 2 week(s) of notification.

**CONTACT**
Laura Hodel, Director of Financial Aid
Box 1017, Binghamton, NY 13902
(607) 778-5028

## Bryant & Stratton College: Albany
Albany, New York
www.bryantstratton.edu          Federal Code: 004749

**2-year for-profit** business and career college in small city.
**Enrollment:** 481 undergrads.

**BASIC COSTS (2015-2016)**
**Tuition and fees:** $17,190.
**Per-credit charge:** $573.
**Additional info:** Tuition and fees may vary by program.

**FINANCIAL AID PICTURE**
**Students with need:** Need-based aid available for full-time and part-time students. Work study available nights, weekends, and for part-time students.
**Students without need:** This college awards aid only to students with need.

**FINANCIAL AID PROCEDURES**
**Forms required:** FAFSA, state aid form.
**Dates and Deadlines:** Closing date 9/17. Applicants notified on a rolling basis.

**CONTACT**
Jackie Rivers, FA Coordinator
1259 Central Avenue, Albany, NY 12205
(518) 437-1802

## Bryant & Stratton College: Syracuse
Syracuse, New York
www.bryantstratton.edu          Federal Code: 008276

**2-year for-profit** business and junior college in small city.
**Enrollment:** 503 undergrads.
**Selectivity:** Open admission.

**BASIC COSTS (2015-2016)**
**Tuition and fees:** $17,190.
**Per-credit charge:** $573.
**Room and board:** $8,880.

**FINANCIAL AID PICTURE**
**Students with need:** Work study available nights, weekends, and for part-time students.
**Students without need:** This college awards aid only to students with need.

**FINANCIAL AID PROCEDURES**
**Forms required:** FAFSA.

**Dates and Deadlines:** Closing date 9/17. Applicants notified on a rolling basis starting 10/1.
**Transfers:** Priority date 5/1.

**CONTACT**
Tami Eiklor, Financial Aid Supervisor
953 James Street, Syracuse, NY 13203
(315) 472-6603

## Bryant & Stratton College: Syracuse North
Liverpool, New York
www.bryantstratton.edu

**2-year for-profit** career college in small city.
**Enrollment:** 466 undergrads.

**BASIC COSTS (2015-2016)**
**Tuition and fees:** $17,190.
**Per-credit charge:** $573.
**Room and board:** $8,880.

**FINANCIAL AID PICTURE**
**Students with need:** Need-based aid available for full-time and part-time students. Work study available nights.
**Students without need:** This college awards aid only to students with need.

**FINANCIAL AID PROCEDURES**
**Forms required:** FAFSA, state aid form, institutional form.
**Dates and Deadlines:** Closing date 9/17.
**Transfers:** No deadline.

**CONTACT**
Stacey McConnell, Financial Services Manager
8687 Carling Road, Liverpool, NY 13090
(315) 652-6500

## Canisius College
Buffalo, New York
www.canisius.edu          Federal Code: 002681

**4-year private** liberal arts and teachers college in large city, affiliated with Roman Catholic Church.
**Enrollment:** 2,552 undergrads, 1% part-time. 605 full-time freshmen.
**Selectivity:** Admits over 75% of applicants.

**BASIC COSTS (2015-2016)**
**Tuition and fees:** $34,690.
**Per-credit charge:** $950.
**Room and board:** $12,766.
**Additional info:** Tuition/fee waivers available for minority students.

**FINANCIAL AID PICTURE (2015-2016)**
**Students with need:** Out of 561 full-time freshmen who applied for aid, 508 were judged to have need. Of these, 508 received aid, and 156 had their full need met. Average financial aid package met 84% of need; average scholarship/grant was $25,939; average loan was $3,922. Need-based aid available for part-time students.
**Students without need:** 90 full-time freshmen who did not demonstrate need for aid received scholarships/grants; average award was $17,975. No-need awards available for academics, alumni affiliation, art, athletics, job skills, minority status, music/drama, ROTC.
**Scholarships offered:** *Merit:* Trustee's Scholarship: $18,000. Dean's Scholarship: $13,000-$14,000. Benefactor's Scholarship: $10,000-$11,000. All based on high school average and SAT/ACT; renewable; open to U.S. and Canadian

residents. Transfer scholarships: $6,000-$12,000; based on 2.5 GPA. International students scholarships: up to $17,000; based on SAT (if taken) and TOEFL scores. Specialized scholarships: urban leadership, art, music, dance. **Athletic:** 25 full-time freshmen received athletic scholarships; average amount $23,016.

### FINANCIAL AID PROCEDURES

**Forms required:** FAFSA, state aid form.
**Dates and Deadlines:** Priority date 2/15; no closing date. Applicants notified on a rolling basis starting 3/1.

### CONTACT

Curtis Gaume, Director of Student Financial Aid
2001 Main Street, Buffalo, NY 14208-1098
(800) 541-6348

## Cayuga Community College

Auburn, New York
www.cayuga-cc.edu                    Federal Code: 002861

**2-year public** community college in large town.
**Enrollment:** 2,527 undergrads, 29% part-time. 522 full-time freshmen.
**Selectivity:** Open admission; but selective for some programs.

### BASIC COSTS (2015-2016)

**Tuition and fees:** $4,742; out-of-state residents $9,068.
**Per-credit charge:** $178; out-of-state residents $356.

### FINANCIAL AID PICTURE (2014-2015)

**Students with need:** 56% of average financial aid package awarded as scholarships/grants, 44% awarded as loans/jobs. Need-based aid available for part-time students. Work study available nights, weekends, and for part-time students.
**Students without need:** This college awards aid only to students with need.

### FINANCIAL AID PROCEDURES

**Forms required:** FAFSA, state aid form.
**Dates and Deadlines:** Priority date 5/1; no closing date. Applicants notified on a rolling basis starting 4/1.
**Transfers:** No deadline.

### CONTACT

Cathleen Patella, Director of Student Financial Aid and Compliance
197 Franklin Street, Auburn, NY 13021-3099
(315) 255-1743 ext. 2470

## Cazenovia College

Cazenovia, New York
www.cazenovia.edu                    Federal Code: 002685

**4-year private** liberal arts and career college in small town.
**Enrollment:** 1,050 undergrads, 10% part-time. 250 full-time freshmen.
**Selectivity:** Admits over 75% of applicants.

### BASIC COSTS (2015-2016)

**Tuition and fees:** $31,754.
**Room and board:** $12,826.

### FINANCIAL AID PICTURE

**Students with need:** Need-based aid available for full-time and part-time students. Work study available nights, weekends, and for part-time students.
**Students without need:** No-need awards available for academics, leadership.

### FINANCIAL AID PROCEDURES

**Forms required:** FAFSA, state aid form.

**Dates and Deadlines:** Priority date 3/1; no closing date. Applicants notified on a rolling basis starting 3/1; must reply by 5/1 or within 2 week(s) of notification.
**Transfers:** No deadline. Applicants notified on a rolling basis starting 11/1; must reply by 5/1 or within 2 week(s) of notification.

### CONTACT

Christine Mandel, Director of Financial Aid
3 Sullivan Street, Cazenovia, NY 13035
(315) 655-7887

## City University of New York: Baruch College

New York, New York
www.baruch.cuny.edu                  Federal Code: 007273

**4-year public** business and liberal arts college in very large city.
**Enrollment:** 14,896 undergrads, 25% part-time. 1,468 full-time freshmen.
**Selectivity:** Admits less than 50% of applicants.

### BASIC COSTS (2015-2016)

**Tuition and fees:** $6,861; out-of-state residents $17,331.
**Per-credit charge:** $275; out-of-state residents $560.
**Additional info:** Room / Housing Rates vary depending on room sizes among other factors, ranges from $12,152 to $12,990.

### FINANCIAL AID PICTURE

**Students with need:** Need-based aid available for full-time and part-time students.
**Students without need:** No-need awards available for academics, state/district residency.
**Scholarships offered:** Honors college scholarships based on SAT scores and high school GPA.

### FINANCIAL AID PROCEDURES

**Forms required:** FAFSA, state aid form.
**Dates and Deadlines:** Priority date 4/15; no closing date. Applicants notified on a rolling basis starting 4/15; must reply within 2 week(s) of notification.
**Transfers:** No deadline. Applicants notified on a rolling basis; must reply within 2 week(s) of notification.

### CONTACT

Elizabeth Riquez, Director of Financial Aid
One Bernard Baruch Way, Box H-0720, New York, NY 10010-5585
(646) 312-1360

## City University of New York: Borough of Manhattan Community College

New York, New York
www.bmcc.cuny.edu                    Federal Code: 002691

**2-year public** community college in very large city.
**Enrollment:** 26,560 undergrads, 32% part-time. 5,570 full-time freshmen.
**Selectivity:** Open admission; but selective for some programs.

### BASIC COSTS (2015-2016)

**Tuition and fees:** $5,169; out-of-state residents $9,969.
**Per-credit charge:** $210; out-of-state residents $320.
**Additional info:** Tuition/fee waivers available for unemployed or children of unemployed.

### FINANCIAL AID PICTURE (2014-2015)

**Students with need:** Out of 4,760 full-time freshmen who applied for aid, 4,760 were judged to have need. Of these, 4,668 received aid. Need-based aid available for part-time students.

**Students without need:** This college awards aid only to students with need.

### FINANCIAL AID PROCEDURES

**Forms required:** FAFSA, state aid form, institutional form.
**Dates and Deadlines:** Priority date 5/1; no closing date. Applicants notified on a rolling basis starting 4/15.
**Transfers:** No deadline. Applicants notified on a rolling basis starting 6/1; must reply within 2 week(s) of notification.

### CONTACT

Howard Entin, Director of Financial Aid
199 Chambers Street, New York, NY 10007
(212) 220-1430

## City University of New York: Bronx Community College

Bronx, New York
www.bcc.cuny.edu                    Federal Code: 002692

**2-year public** community college in very large city.
**Enrollment:** 11,434 undergrads.
**Selectivity:** Open admission.

### BASIC COSTS (2015-2016)

**Tuition and fees:** $5,205; out-of-state residents $10,005.
**Per-credit charge:** $210; out-of-state residents $320.

### FINANCIAL AID PICTURE

**Students with need:** Need-based aid available for full-time and part-time students. Work study available nights, weekends, and for part-time students.
**Students without need:** This college awards aid only to students with need.

### FINANCIAL AID PROCEDURES

**Forms required:** FAFSA.
**Dates and Deadlines:** Closing date 6/30. Applicants notified on a rolling basis starting 8/1.

### CONTACT

Sinu Jacob, Financial Aid Officer
2155 University Avenue, Bronx, NY 10453
(718) 289-5700

## City University of New York: Brooklyn College

Brooklyn, New York
www.brooklyn.cuny.edu              Federal Code: 002687

**4-year public** liberal arts college in very large city.
**Enrollment:** 13,172 undergrads, 23% part-time. 1,327 full-time freshmen.
**Selectivity:** Admits less than 50% of applicants.

### BASIC COSTS (2015-2016)

**Tuition and fees:** $6,838; out-of-state residents $17,308.
**Per-credit charge:** $275; out-of-state residents $560.
**Additional info:** Room/Housing Rates range from $12,418 to $17,520, depending on room sizes among other factors.

### FINANCIAL AID PICTURE (2015-2016)

**Students with need:** Out of 1,285 full-time freshmen who applied for aid, 1,200 were judged to have need. Of these, 1,060 received aid, and 785 had their full need met. Average financial aid package met 88% of need; average scholarship/grant was $3,400; average loan was $3,000. For part-time students, average financial aid package was $2,800.

**Students without need:** 42 full-time freshmen who did not demonstrate need for aid received scholarships/grants; average award was $1,500. No-need awards available for academics, art, leadership, music/drama, state/district residency.
**Scholarships offered:** Presidential Scholarship: 8 tuition payments totaling $16,000; 25 awarded. Freshman Scholarships: $1,000-$2,000 for the first year of study. Many scholarships are based on degree of study, academic merit, and community service. Scholarships are subject to financial availability.

### FINANCIAL AID PROCEDURES

**Forms required:** FAFSA.
**Dates and Deadlines:** Priority date 4/11; no closing date. Applicants notified on a rolling basis starting 5/11.
**Transfers:** Priority date 4/1; no deadline. Must reply within 6 week(s) of notification. Transfer-day orientation offered each semester. Students receive instruction on the rules and regulations of all programs with important deadlines. Students are urged to apply for federal, state and scholarship application as soon as possible. If any students do not qualify for grants and or scholarships, they are asked to consider students loan or to make a tuition plan with the bursar's office.

### CONTACT

Ahad Farhang, Director of Financial Aid
2900 Bedford Avenue, Brooklyn, NY 11210
(718) 951-5051

## City University of New York: City College

New York, New York
www.ccny.cuny.edu                   Federal Code: 002688

**4-year public** university and liberal arts college in very large city.
**Enrollment:** 13,294 undergrads, 27% part-time. 1,607 full-time freshmen.
**Selectivity:** Admits less than 50% of applicants.

### BASIC COSTS (2015-2016)

**Tuition and fees:** $6,740; out-of-state residents $17,210.
**Per-credit charge:** $275; out-of-state residents $560.
**Additional info:** Room/Housing Rates range from $12,370 to $18,086 depending on room sizes among other factors. Tuition/fee waivers available for minority students.

### FINANCIAL AID PICTURE (2015-2016)

**Students with need:** 73% of average financial aid package awarded as scholarships/grants, 27% awarded as loans/jobs. Need-based aid available for part-time students. Work study available nights, weekends, and for part-time students.
**Students without need:** No-need awards available for academics, alumni affiliation, art, leadership, music/drama, state/district residency.

### FINANCIAL AID PROCEDURES

**Forms required:** FAFSA, state aid form.
**Dates and Deadlines:** Priority date 3/15; no closing date. Applicants notified on a rolling basis starting 4/1.
**Transfers:** Priority date 3/31; no deadline. Applicants notified on a rolling basis starting 3/31.

### CONTACT

Arshaw Ramkaran, Director of Financial Aid
160 Convent Avenue, A100, New York, NY 10031
(212) 650-7000

## City University of New York: College of Staten Island

Staten Island, New York
www.csi.cuny.edu — Federal Code: 002698

**4-year public** liberal arts college in large city.
**Enrollment:** 12,298 undergrads, 21% part-time. 2,400 full-time freshmen.
**Selectivity:** Admits over 75% of applicants.

### BASIC COSTS (2015-2016)
**Tuition and fees:** $6,889; out-of-state residents $17,359.
**Per-credit charge:** $275; out-of-state residents $560.
**Additional info:** Room/Housing Rates range from $11,103 to $15,561 depending on room sizes among other factors.

### FINANCIAL AID PICTURE (2014-2015)
**Students with need:** Out of 2,036 full-time freshmen who applied for aid, 1,882 were judged to have need. Of these, 1,394 received aid, and 195 had their full need met. Average financial aid package met 69% of need; average scholarship/grant was $5,622; average loan was $3,598. For part-time students, average financial aid package was $3,855.
**Students without need:** No-need awards available for academics, alumni affiliation, art, leadership, minority status, music/drama, state/district residency.

### FINANCIAL AID PROCEDURES
**Forms required:** FAFSA, state aid form.
**Dates and Deadlines:** Priority date 3/30; no closing date. Applicants notified on a rolling basis starting 6/1.

### CONTACT
Philippe Marius, Director of Financial Aid
2800 Victory Boulevard 2A-103, Staten Island, NY 10314
(718) 982-2030

## City University of New York: CUNY Online

New York, New York
http://sps.cuny.edu/ — Federal Code: 004765

**4-year public** university in very large city.
**Enrollment:** 1,098 undergrads.
**Selectivity:** Open admission; but selective for some programs.

### FINANCIAL AID PICTURE
**Students with need:** Need-based aid available for full-time and part-time students.
**Students without need:** This college awards aid only to students with need.

### FINANCIAL AID PROCEDURES
**Dates and Deadlines:** Closing date 8/1.
**Transfers:** Closing date 4/15. Applicants notified on a rolling basis starting 6/1.

### CONTACT
Felix Huertas, Financial Aid and Student Support Specialist
119 West 31st Street, New York, NY 10001-3507
(646) 664-8720

## City University of New York: Guttman Community College

New York, New York
www.guttman.cuny.edu — Federal Code: 042101

**2-year public** community college in very large city.
**Enrollment:** 691 undergrads.

### BASIC COSTS (2015-2016)
**Tuition and fees:** $5,193; out-of-state residents $9,993.
**Per-credit charge:** $210; out-of-state residents $320.

### FINANCIAL AID PICTURE
**Students with need:** Need-based aid available for full-time and part-time students.

### FINANCIAL AID PROCEDURES
**Forms required:** FAFSA, state aid form.
**Dates and Deadlines:** Closing date 6/30. Applicants notified on a rolling basis starting 4/1.

### CONTACT
Vera Senese, Director of Financial Aid
50 West 40th Street, New York, NY 10018
(646) 313-8080

## City University of New York: Hostos Community College

Bronx, New York
www.hostos.cuny.edu — Federal Code: 008611

**2-year public** community college in very large city.
**Enrollment:** 6,427 undergrads.
**Selectivity:** Open admission; but selective for some programs.

### BASIC COSTS (2015-2016)
**Tuition and fees:** $5,206; out-of-state residents $10,006.
**Per-credit charge:** $210; out-of-state residents $320.

### FINANCIAL AID PICTURE
**Students with need:** Need-based aid available for full-time and part-time students.

### FINANCIAL AID PROCEDURES
**Forms required:** FAFSA.
**Dates and Deadlines:** Priority date 7/1; no closing date. Applicants notified on a rolling basis; must reply within 3 week(s) of notification.

### CONTACT
Joseph Alicea, Director of Financial Aid
500 Grand Concourse, Bronx, NY 10451
(718) 518-6555

## City University of New York: Hunter College

New York, New York
www.hunter.cuny.edu/main/ — Federal Code: 002689

**4-year public** liberal arts college in very large city.
**Enrollment:** 15,465 undergrads, 23% part-time. 2,168 full-time freshmen.
**Selectivity:** Admits less than 50% of applicants.

### BASIC COSTS (2015-2016)
**Tuition and fees:** $6,780; out-of-state residents $17,250.
**Per-credit charge:** $275; out-of-state residents $560.
**Additional info:** Room/Housing Rates range from $4,407 to $14,096 depending on room sizes among other factors.

### FINANCIAL AID PICTURE (2015-2016)
**Students with need:** Out of 1,776 full-time freshmen who applied for aid, 1,338 were judged to have need. Of these, 1,231 received aid, and 265 had their full need met. Average financial aid package met 73% of need; average scholarship/grant was $8,713; average loan was $4,177. For part-time students, average financial aid package was $5,243.

**Students without need:** 190 full-time freshmen who did not demonstrate need for aid received scholarships/grants; average award was $3,001. No-need awards available for academics.

## FINANCIAL AID PROCEDURES

**Forms required:** FAFSA, state aid form.
**Dates and Deadlines:** Priority date 5/1; no closing date. Applicants notified on a rolling basis starting 5/15.

## CONTACT

Aristalia Cortorreal Diaz, Director of Financial Aid
695 Park Avenue, New York, NY 10065
(212) 772-4820

## City University of New York: John Jay College of Criminal Justice
New York, New York
www.jjay.cuny.edu                          Federal Code: 002693

**4-year public** liberal arts college in very large city.
**Enrollment:** 12,545 undergrads, 19% part-time. 13,794 full-time freshmen.
**Selectivity:** Admits 50 to 75% of applicants.

## BASIC COSTS (2015-2016)

**Tuition and fees:** $6,810; out-of-state residents $17,280.
**Per-credit charge:** $275; out-of-state residents $560.
**Additional info:** Room/Housing Rates range from $14,550 to $22,100 depending on room sizes among other factors.

## FINANCIAL AID PICTURE (2014-2015)

**Students with need:** Out of 2,940 full-time freshmen who applied for aid, 2,703 were judged to have need. Of these, 2,489 received aid. Average financial aid package met 85% of need; average scholarship/grant was $2,889; average loan was $4,152. For part-time students, average financial aid package was $4,619.

## FINANCIAL AID PROCEDURES

**Forms required:** FAFSA, state aid form.
**Dates and Deadlines:** Priority date 4/30; no closing date. Applicants notified on a rolling basis starting 4/1; must reply within 2 week(s) of notification.
**Transfers:** Closing date 4/30.

## CONTACT

Sylvia Lopez-Crespo, Director of Financial Aid
524 West 59th Street, New York, NY 10019
(212) 237-8149

## City University of New York: Kingsborough Community College
Brooklyn, New York
www.kbcc.cuny.edu                          Federal Code: 002694

**2-year public** community college in very large city.
**Enrollment:** 12,847 undergrads.
**Selectivity:** Open admission.

## BASIC COSTS (2015-2016)

**Tuition and fees:** $5,201; out-of-state residents $10,001.
**Per-credit charge:** $210; out-of-state residents $320.

## FINANCIAL AID PICTURE

**Students with need:** Need-based aid available for full-time and part-time students.
**Students without need:** This college awards aid only to students with need.

## FINANCIAL AID PROCEDURES

**Forms required:** FAFSA.
**Dates and Deadlines:** Closing date 4/30. Applicants notified on a rolling basis; must reply within 2 week(s) of notification.

## CONTACT

Wayne Harewood, Director of Financial Aid
2001 Oriental Boulevard, Brooklyn, NY 11235
(718) 368-4644

## City University of New York: LaGuardia Community College
Long Island City, New York
www.lagcc.cuny.edu                          Federal Code: 010051

**2-year public** community college in very large city.
**Enrollment:** 16,062 undergrads, 35% part-time. 2,610 full-time freshmen.
**Selectivity:** Open admission.

## BASIC COSTS (2015-2016)

**Tuition and fees:** $5,217; out-of-state residents $10,017.
**Per-credit charge:** $210; out-of-state residents $320.
**Additional info:** Tuition/fee waivers available for adults, minority students, unemployed or children of unemployed.

## FINANCIAL AID PICTURE (2014-2015)

**Students with need:** Out of 2,364 full-time freshmen who applied for aid, 2,279 were judged to have need. Of these, 1,945 received aid, and 2 had their full need met. Average financial aid package met 32% of need; average scholarship/grant was $4,307; average loan was $1,415. For part-time students, average financial aid package was $1,828.
**Students without need:** This college awards aid only to students with need.

## FINANCIAL AID PROCEDURES

**Forms required:** FAFSA, state aid form, institutional form.
**Dates and Deadlines:** Closing date 4/15. Applicants notified on a rolling basis starting 3/1; must reply within 4 week(s) of notification.
**Transfers:** No deadline. Applicants notified on a rolling basis.

## CONTACT

Gail Baksh-Jarrett, Executive Director of Student Financial Services
31-10 Thomson Avenue, Long Island City, NY 11101
(718) 482-7218

## City University of New York: Lehman College
Bronx, New York
www.lehman.edu                          Federal Code: 007022

**4-year public** liberal arts college in very large city.
**Enrollment:** 9,874 undergrads, 37% part-time. 610 full-time freshmen.
**Selectivity:** Admits less than 50% of applicants.

## BASIC COSTS (2015-2016)

**Tuition and fees:** $6,759; out-of-state residents $17,229.
**Per-credit charge:** $275; out-of-state residents $560.
**Additional info:** Room/Housing Rates range from $9,432 to $11,142 depending on room sizes among other factors.

## FINANCIAL AID PICTURE (2014-2015)

**Students with need:** Need-based aid available for part-time students.
**Students without need:** This college awards aid only to students with need.

## FINANCIAL AID PROCEDURES

**Forms required:** FAFSA, state aid form.

**Dates and Deadlines:** Applicants notified on a rolling basis starting 3/1.
**Transfers:** No deadline. Applicants notified on a rolling basis starting 3/1.

**CONTACT**
David Martinez, Director of Financial Aid
250 Bedford Park Boulevard West, Bronx, NY 10468
(718) 960-8545

## City University of New York: Medgar Evers College
Brooklyn, New York
www.mec.cuny.edu — Federal Code: 010097

**4-year public** liberal arts college in very large city.
**Enrollment:** 6,257 undergrads, 30% part-time. 1,013 full-time freshmen.
**Selectivity:** Open admission; but selective for some programs.

**BASIC COSTS (2015-2016)**
**Tuition and fees:** $6,683; out-of-state residents $17,153.
**Per-credit charge:** $275; out-of-state residents $560.

**FINANCIAL AID PICTURE (2014-2015)**
**Students with need:** 84% of average financial aid package awarded as scholarships/grants, 16% awarded as loans/jobs. Need-based aid available for part-time students. Work study available weekends and for part-time students.
**Students without need:** No-need awards available for academics, leadership.

**FINANCIAL AID PROCEDURES**
**Forms required:** FAFSA, state aid form.
**Dates and Deadlines:** Priority date 1/2; closing date 6/1. Applicants notified on a rolling basis; must reply within 3 week(s) of notification.
**Transfers:** Priority date 3/1. Must reply within 2 week(s) of notification.

**CONTACT**
Conley James, Director of Financial Aid
1665 Bedford Avenue, Brooklyn, NY 11225-2201
(718) 270-6194

## City University of New York: New York City College of Technology
Brooklyn, New York
www.citytech.cuny.edu — Federal Code: 002696

**4-year public** technical college in very large city.
**Enrollment:** 16,297 undergrads, 34% part-time. 3,279 full-time freshmen.
**Selectivity:** Open admission; but selective for some programs.

**BASIC COSTS (2015-2016)**
**Tuition and fees:** $6,720; out-of-state residents $17,190.
**Per-credit charge:** $275; out-of-state residents $560.

**FINANCIAL AID PICTURE**
**Students with need:** Need-based aid available for full-time and part-time students.
**Students without need:** No-need awards available for state/district residency.
**Additional info:** Foreign students applying for aid must have resided in New York for at least 1 year.

**FINANCIAL AID PROCEDURES**
**Forms required:** FAFSA.
**Dates and Deadlines:** Priority date 3/31; no closing date.

**CONTACT**
Sandra Higgins, Director of Financial Aid
300 Jay Street Namm G17, Brooklyn, NY 11201
(718) 260-5700

## City University of New York: Queens College
Flushing, New York
www.qc.cuny.edu — Federal Code: 002690

**4-year public** liberal arts college in very large city.
**Enrollment:** 15,148 undergrads, 24% part-time. 1,514 full-time freshmen.
**Selectivity:** Admits less than 50% of applicants.

**BASIC COSTS (2015-2016)**
**Tuition and fees:** $6,777; out-of-state residents $17,247.
**Per-credit charge:** $275; out-of-state residents $560.
**Additional info:** Room/Housing Rates range from $11,330 to $16,900 depending on room sizes among other factors.

**FINANCIAL AID PICTURE (2015-2016)**
**Students with need:** Out of 1,150 full-time freshmen who applied for aid, 780 were judged to have need. Of these, 745 received aid, and 634 had their full need met. Average financial aid package met 95% of need; average scholarship/grant was $5,011; average loan was $4,870. For part-time students, average financial aid package was $2,500.
**Students without need:** 50 full-time freshmen who did not demonstrate need for aid received scholarships/grants; average award was $7,800. No-need awards available for academics, athletics, state/district residency.
**Scholarships offered:** 25 full-time freshmen received athletic scholarships; average amount $6,268.

**FINANCIAL AID PROCEDURES**
**Forms required:** FAFSA, state aid form, institutional form.
**Dates and Deadlines:** Priority date 2/15; no closing date. Applicants notified on a rolling basis starting 3/1; must reply within 3 week(s) of notification.
**Transfers:** Priority date 5/1; no deadline. Applicants notified on a rolling basis.

**CONTACT**
Clifford Couloute, Director of Financial Aid
6530 Kissena Boulevard, Jefferson 117, Flushing, NY 11367-1597
(718) 997-5123

## City University of New York: Queensborough Community College
Bayside, New York
www.qcc.cuny.edu — Federal Code: 002697

**2-year public** community college in very large city.
**Enrollment:** 13,692 undergrads, 32% part-time. 3,063 full-time freshmen.
**Selectivity:** Open admission.

**BASIC COSTS (2015-2016)**
**Tuition and fees:** $5,209; out-of-state residents $10,009.
**Per-credit charge:** $210; out-of-state residents $320.

**FINANCIAL AID PICTURE**
**Students with need:** Need-based aid available for full-time students.

**FINANCIAL AID PROCEDURES**
**Forms required:** FAFSA, institutional form.
**Dates and Deadlines:** Applicants notified on a rolling basis starting 7/15.

## CONTACT

Veronica Lukas, Director of Enrollment Management and Student Financial Services

222-05 56th Avenue, Bayside, NY 11364-1497

(718) 631-6267

## City University of New York: York College

Jamaica, New York

www.york.cuny.edu

Federal Code: 004759

**4-year public** liberal arts college in very large city.

**Enrollment:** 7,264 undergrads, 29% part-time. 995 full-time freshmen.

### BASIC COSTS (2015-2016)

**Tuition and fees:** $6,747; out-of-state residents $17,217.

**Per-credit charge:** $275; out-of-state residents $560.

### FINANCIAL AID PICTURE

**Students with need:** Need-based aid available for full-time and part-time students.

**Students without need:** No-need awards available for academics.

### FINANCIAL AID PROCEDURES

**Forms required:** FAFSA, state aid form.

**Dates and Deadlines:** Priority date 4/1; closing date 5/30. Applicants notified on a rolling basis starting 2/15; must reply within 4 week(s) of notification.

**Transfers:** No deadline. Applicants notified on a rolling basis starting 3/1.

### CONTACT

Beverly Brown, Director of Financial Aid

94-20 Guy R. Brewer Boulevard., Room 1B07, Jamaica, NY 11451

(718) 262-2230

## Clarkson University

Potsdam, New York

www.clarkson.edu

Federal Code: 002699

**4-year private** university in small town.

**Enrollment:** 3,153 undergrads. 792 full-time freshmen.

**Selectivity:** Admits 50 to 75% of applicants.

### BASIC COSTS (2016-2017)

**Tuition and fees:** $46,132.

**Per-credit charge:** $1,505.

**Room and board:** $14,260.

**Additional info:** Tuition/fee waivers available for minority students.

### FINANCIAL AID PICTURE (2015-2016)

**Students with need:** Out of 713 full-time freshmen who applied for aid, 637 were judged to have need. Of these, 636 received aid, and 128 had their full need met. Average financial aid package met 89% of need; average scholarship/grant was $31,060; average loan was $3,417. Need-based aid available for part-time students.

**Students without need:** 142 full-time freshmen who did not demonstrate need for aid received scholarships/grants; average award was $23,196. No-need awards available for academics, alumni affiliation, leadership, minority status, ROTC.

**Scholarships offered:** *Merit:* Scholarships ranging from $500 to $28,000 in value, including the Clarkson Scholarship, Clarkson Merit Scholarship, CU PLTW Scholarship, CU FIRST Robotics Scholarship, CU WACE National CO-OP, CU SAE Scholarship, Clarkson Adirondack Scholars Award, Spirit of Innovation, Holcroft Alumni Recognition Awards, Alumni Family Award, and the Alumni Legacy Award. Many require high school grades averaging 85 or higher. Some require a recommendation from a Clarkson alumnus. Most are

not limited by major or to a specific number of scholarships awarded. *Athletic:* 8 full-time freshmen received athletic scholarships; average amount $41,419.

### FINANCIAL AID PROCEDURES

**Forms required:** FAFSA, state aid form.

**Dates and Deadlines:** Priority date 2/15; closing date 3/1. Applicants notified on a rolling basis starting 3/14; must reply by 5/1 or within 2 week(s) of notification.

**Transfers:** Closing date 4/15. Applicants notified on a rolling basis starting 3/1. Transfer Leadership & Achievement scholarships, Phi Theta Kappa scholarships and Alpha Beta Gamma awards available in addition to state and federal programs.

### CONTACT

Kara Pitts, Director of New Student Financial Assistance

Holcroft House, Potsdam, NY 13699

(800) 527-6577

## Clinton Community College

Plattsburgh, New York

www.clinton.edu

Federal Code: 006787

**2-year public** community and career college in large town.

**Enrollment:** 937 undergrads, 3% part-time. 360 full-time freshmen.

**Selectivity:** Open admission; but selective for some programs and for out-of-state students.

### BASIC COSTS (2015-2016)

**Tuition and fees:** $5,122; out-of-state residents $10,122.

**Per-credit charge:** $175; out-of-state residents $383.

**Room and board:** $9,518.

### FINANCIAL AID PICTURE

**Students with need:** Need-based aid available for full-time and part-time students.

**Students without need:** This college awards aid only to students with need.

### FINANCIAL AID PROCEDURES

**Forms required:** FAFSA, state aid form.

**Dates and Deadlines:** Priority date 6/12; no closing date. Applicants notified on a rolling basis starting 4/12; must reply within 2 week(s) of notification.

### CONTACT

Mary LaPierre, Director of Financial Aid

136 Clinton Point Drive, Plattsburgh, NY 12901

(518) 562-4125

## Cochran School of Nursing

Yonkers, New York

www.cochranschoolofnursing.us

Federal Code: 006443

**2-year private** nursing college in small city.

**Enrollment:** 89 undergrads, 87% part-time.

### BASIC COSTS (2015-2016)

**Tuition and fees:** $11,132.

**Per-credit charge:** $563.

### FINANCIAL AID PICTURE (2015-2016)

**Students with need:** 25% of average financial aid package awarded as scholarships/grants, 75% awarded as loans/jobs. Need-based aid available for part-time students.

**Students without need:** This college awards aid only to students with need.

## FINANCIAL AID PROCEDURES
**Forms required:** FAFSA.
**Dates and Deadlines:** Closing date 4/30. Applicants notified on a rolling basis.
**Transfers:** No deadline.

## CONTACT
Maria Goncalves, Financial Aid Officer
967 North Broadway, Yonkers, NY 10701
(914) 964-4316

## Colgate University
Hamilton, New York
www.colgate.edu

Federal Code: 002701
CSS Code: 2086

**4-year private** university and liberal arts college in small town.
**Enrollment:** 2,834 undergrads. 773 full-time freshmen.
**Selectivity:** Admits less than 50% of applicants.

### BASIC COSTS (2015-2016)
**Tuition and fees:** $49,970.
**Room and board:** $12,570.

### FINANCIAL AID PICTURE (2015-2016)
**Students with need:** Out of 332 full-time freshmen who applied for aid, 290 were judged to have need. Of these, 290 received aid, and 290 had their full need met. Average financial aid package met 100% of need; average scholarship/grant was $45,417; average loan was $1,498.
**Students without need:** No-need awards available for athletics.
**Scholarships offered:** 80 full-time freshmen received athletic scholarships; average amount $36,500.

### FINANCIAL AID PROCEDURES
**Forms required:** CSS PROFILE.
**Dates and Deadlines:** Priority date 1/15; closing date 1/15. Applicants notified by 3/20; must reply by 5/1.
**Transfers:** Closing date 3/15. Applicants notified by 4/15; must reply by 5/15 or within 2 week(s) of notification. Financial aid for transfer students extremely limited.

### CONTACT
Marcelle Tyburski, Director of Financial Aid
13 Oak Drive, Hamilton, NY 13346-1383
(315) 228-7431

## College of Mount St. Vincent
Riverdale, New York
www.mountsaintvincent.edu

Federal Code: 002703

**4-year private** liberal arts college in very large city, affiliated with Roman Catholic Church.
**Enrollment:** 1,585 undergrads, 5% part-time. 321 full-time freshmen.
**Selectivity:** Admits over 75% of applicants.

### BASIC COSTS (2015-2016)
**Tuition and fees:** $35,130.
**Per-credit charge:** $940.
**Room and board:** $8,720.

### FINANCIAL AID PICTURE
**Students with need:** Need-based aid available for full-time students.
**Students without need:** No-need awards available for academics, alumni affiliation, leadership.

### FINANCIAL AID PROCEDURES
**Forms required:** FAFSA, state aid form.

**Dates and Deadlines:** Priority date 3/1; no closing date. Applicants notified on a rolling basis starting 3/1; must reply by 5/1 or within 3 week(s) of notification.
**Transfers:** Priority date 5/15. Applicants notified on a rolling basis starting 3/1; must reply by 5/1 or within 3 week(s) of notification.

## CONTACT
Monica Simotas, Director of Financial Aid
6301 Riverdale Avenue, Riverdale, NY 10471-1093
(718) 405-3289

## College of New Rochelle
New Rochelle, New York
www.cnr.edu

Federal Code: 002704

**4-year private** nursing and liberal arts college in small city, affiliated with Roman Catholic Church.
**Enrollment:** 570 undergrads, 11% part-time. 88 full-time freshmen.
**Selectivity:** Admits less than 50% of applicants.

### BASIC COSTS (2016-2017)
**Tuition and fees:** $34,648.
**Room and board:** $13,208.

### FINANCIAL AID PICTURE
**Students with need:** Need-based aid available for full-time and part-time students. Work study available nights, weekends, and for part-time students.
**Students without need:** No-need awards available for academics, art, leadership, music/drama.

### FINANCIAL AID PROCEDURES
**Forms required:** FAFSA, institutional form.
**Dates and Deadlines:** Priority date 2/1; no closing date. Applicants notified on a rolling basis starting 1/1; must reply within 2 week(s) of notification.
**Transfers:** No deadline. Applicants notified on a rolling basis.

### CONTACT
Ann Pelak, Director of Financial Aid
29 Castle Place, New Rochelle, NY 10805-2339
(914) 654-5225

## College of Saint Rose
Albany, New York
www.strose.edu

Federal Code: 002705

**4-year private** liberal arts college in small city.
**Enrollment:** 2,626 undergrads, 3% part-time. 534 full-time freshmen.
**Selectivity:** Admits over 75% of applicants.

### BASIC COSTS (2016-2017)
**Tuition and fees:** $30,692.
**Per-credit charge:** $986.
**Room and board:** $12,356.

### FINANCIAL AID PICTURE (2014-2015)
**Students with need:** Out of 511 full-time freshmen who applied for aid, 470 were judged to have need. Of these, 470 received aid, and 65 had their full need met. Average financial aid package met 79% of need; average scholarship/grant was $11,463; average loan was $3,725. For part-time students, average financial aid package was $5,539.
**Students without need:** 46 full-time freshmen who did not demonstrate need for aid received scholarships/grants; average award was $11,897. No-need awards available for academics, alumni affiliation, art, athletics, music/drama.
**Scholarships offered:** *Merit:* Academic, music, art, athletic awards based on talent. *Athletic:* 11 full-time freshmen received athletic scholarships; average amount $26,026.

**FINANCIAL AID PROCEDURES**

**Forms required:** FAFSA.

**Dates and Deadlines:** Priority date 2/1; closing date 4/1. Applicants notified on a rolling basis starting 3/1; must reply by 5/1 or within 2 week(s) of notification.

**Transfers:** Applicants notified on a rolling basis starting 2/1; must reply by 5/1 or within 2 week(s) of notification.

**CONTACT**

Steve Dwire, Director of Financial Aid
432 Western Avenue, Albany, NY 12203
(518) 458-5464

## College of Westchester

White Plains, New York
www.cw.edu                    Federal Code: 005208

**2-year for-profit** business and career college in small city.

**Enrollment:** 962 undergrads, 12% part-time. 204 full-time freshmen.

**Selectivity:** Admits over 75% of applicants.

**BASIC COSTS (2016-2017)**

**Tuition and fees:** $23,350.

**Additional info:** Tuition/fee waivers available for unemployed or children of unemployed.

**FINANCIAL AID PICTURE (2014-2015)**

**Students with need:** 65% of average financial aid package awarded as scholarships/grants, 35% awarded as loans/jobs. Need-based aid available for part-time students. Work study available nights, weekends, and for part-time students.

**Students without need:** No-need awards available for academics, alumni affiliation.

**FINANCIAL AID PROCEDURES**

**Forms required:** FAFSA, state aid form, institutional form.

**Dates and Deadlines:** Applicants notified on a rolling basis starting 2/7; must reply within 2 week(s) of notification.

**CONTACT**

Dianne Pepitone, Director, Student Financial Services
325 Central Avenue, White Plains, NY 10606
(914) 831-0473

## Columbia University

New York, New York           Federal Code: E00485
www.columbia.edu             CSS Code: 2116

**4-year private** university in very large city.

**Enrollment:** 6,102 undergrads. 1,398 full-time freshmen.

**Selectivity:** Admits less than 50% of applicants.

**BASIC COSTS (2015-2016)**

**Tuition and fees:** $53,000.

**Room and board:** $12,860.

**FINANCIAL AID PICTURE (2015-2016)**

**Students with need:** Out of 879 full-time freshmen who applied for aid, 730 were judged to have need. Of these, 730 received aid, and 730 had their full need met. Average financial aid package met 100% of need; average scholarship/grant was $48,172.

**Students without need:** This college awards aid only to students with need.

**Additional info:** Institution has eliminated student loans for those receiving Columbia need-based aid and replaced them with additional University grants, and significantly reduced the parent contribution for families making less than $100,000 per year.

**FINANCIAL AID PROCEDURES**

**Forms required:** FAFSA, CSS PROFILE.

**Dates and Deadlines:** Priority date 3/1; no closing date. Applicants notified by 4/1; must reply by 5/1 or within 2 week(s) of notification.

**Transfers:** Closing date 3/1. Applicants notified by 5/15.

**CONTACT**

Jessica Marinaccio, Dean of Undergraduate Admissions & Financial Aid
1130 Amsterdam Avenue, New York, NY 10027
(212) 854-3711

## Columbia University: School of General Studies

New York, New York
www.gs.columbia.edu          Federal Code: E00487

**4-year private** university and liberal arts college in very large city.

**Enrollment:** 2,005 undergrads, 23% part-time. 41 full-time freshmen.

**Selectivity:** Admits less than 50% of applicants.

**BASIC COSTS (2015-2016)**

**Tuition and fees:** $51,114.

**Per-credit charge:** $1,630.

**Room and board:** $10,356.

**FINANCIAL AID PICTURE (2014-2015)**

**Students with need:** Out of 34 full-time freshmen who applied for aid, 28 were judged to have need. Of these, 27 received aid. Average financial aid package met 34% of need; average scholarship/grant was $16,007; average loan was $7,760. For part-time students, average financial aid package was $21,178.

**Students without need:** 4 full-time freshmen who did not demonstrate need for aid received scholarships/grants; average award was $10,625. No-need awards available for academics.

**Scholarships offered:** All applicants should submit General Studies Application for Financial Aid.

**FINANCIAL AID PROCEDURES**

**Forms required:** FAFSA, institutional form.

**Dates and Deadlines:** Closing date 6/1. Applicants notified on a rolling basis; must reply within 3 week(s) of notification.

**Transfers:** Applicants notified on a rolling basis starting 4/1.

**CONTACT**

William Bailey, Director of Educational Financing
408 Lewisohn Hall, Mail Code 4101, New York, NY 10027
(212) 854-5410

## Columbia-Greene Community College

Hudson, New York
www.sunycgcc.edu             Federal Code: 006789

**2-year public** community college in small town.

**Enrollment:** 1,261 undergrads, 44% part-time. 263 full-time freshmen.

**BASIC COSTS (2015-2016)**

**Tuition and fees:** $4,552; out-of-state residents $8,752.

**Per-credit charge:** $175; out-of-state residents $350.

**FINANCIAL AID PICTURE**

**Students with need:** Need-based aid available for full-time and part-time students. Work study available nights, weekends, and for part-time students.

**FINANCIAL AID PROCEDURES**

**Forms required:** FAFSA, institutional form.

## CONTACT
Joel Phelps, Director of Financial Aid
4400 Route 23, Hudson, NY 12534
(518) 828-4181 ext. 3360

## Concordia College
Bronxville, New York
www.concordia-ny.edu          Federal Code: 002709

**4-year private** liberal arts college in small town, affiliated with Lutheran Church - Missouri Synod.
**Enrollment:** 886 undergrads.

### BASIC COSTS (2015-2016)
**Tuition and fees:** $29,700.
**Room and board:** $11,024.

### FINANCIAL AID PICTURE
**Students with need:** Need-based aid available for full-time and part-time students. Work study available nights, weekends, and for part-time students.
**Students without need:** No-need awards available for academics, athletics, leadership, music/drama, religious affiliation.
**Scholarships offered:** Fellows Scholarship: $15,000 a year; for 1800 SAT (exclusive of Writing) and 3.5/4.0 GPA. Merit Scholarships: $6,000-$9,000 for 80 average and above. Athletic, Faith Based, and Leadership Scholarships are also available.

### FINANCIAL AID PROCEDURES
**Forms required:** FAFSA, state aid form.
**Dates and Deadlines:** Priority date 4/1; no closing date. Applicants notified on a rolling basis starting 2/15; must reply by 5/1 or within 3 week(s) of notification.
**Transfers:** Priority date 6/1; no deadline. Applicants notified on a rolling basis starting 4/1; must reply by 8/1 or within 3 week(s) of notification.

### CONTACT
Kenneth Fick, Director of Financial Aid
171 White Plains Road, Bronxville, NY 10708-1923
(914) 337-9300 ext. 2146

## Cooper Union for the Advancement of Science and Art
New York, New York          Federal Code: 002710
www.cooper.edu          CSS Code: 2097

**4-year private** visual arts and engineering college in very large city.
**Enrollment:** 873 undergrads. 223 full-time freshmen.
**Selectivity:** Admits less than 50% of applicants.

### BASIC COSTS (2015-2016)
**Tuition and fees:** $42,650.
**Per-credit charge:** $1,200.
**Room only:** $11,560.
**Additional info:** All incoming undergraduate students receive at a minimum, a half-tuition scholarship. Cooper Union provides to those that demonstrate need, additional assistance to cover the remaining costs of attending, including tuition, room and board, books and supplies, personal expenses and transportation.

### FINANCIAL AID PICTURE (2014-2015)
**Students with need:** Out of 150 full-time freshmen who applied for aid, 135 were judged to have need. Of these, 135 received aid, and 135 had their full need met. Average financial aid package met 92% of need; average scholarship/grant was $20,143; average loan was $2,842. Need-based aid available for part-time students.

**Students without need:** 91 full-time freshmen who did not demonstrate need for aid received scholarships/grants; average award was $23,036. No-need awards available for academics.
**Scholarships offered:** All undergraduate students receive at a minimum, half-tuition merit scholarships currently worth about $20,000 annually. In addition, exceptional students offered smaller merit scholarships typically in the $2,000-4,000 range.
**Additional info:** All Pell eligible students receive a full tuition scholarship. All undergraduate students receive at a minimum half-tuition merit scholarships. Late financial aid applications processed on rolling basis.

### FINANCIAL AID PROCEDURES
**Forms required:** FAFSA, CSS PROFILE.
**Dates and Deadlines:** Priority date 3/1; closing date 5/1. Applicants notified on a rolling basis starting 12/20; must reply by 6/30 or within 2 week(s) of notification.
**Transfers:** Priority date 4/1. Applicants notified by 6/1; must reply by 6/30 or within 2 week(s) of notification.

### CONTACT
Charlie Xu, Director of Financial Aid
30 Cooper Square, Suite 300, New York, NY 10003-7183
(212) 353-4130

## Cornell University
Ithaca, New York          Federal Code: 002711
www.cornell.edu          CSS Code: 2098

**4-year private** university in large town.
**Enrollment:** 14,226 undergrads. 3,180 full-time freshmen.
**Selectivity:** Admits less than 50% of applicants.

### BASIC COSTS (2016-2017)
**Tuition and fees:** $50,953.
**Room and board:** $13,900.

### FINANCIAL AID PICTURE (2014-2015)
**Students with need:** Out of 1,718 full-time freshmen who applied for aid, 1,431 were judged to have need. Of these, 1,431 received aid, and 1,431 had their full need met. Average financial aid package met 100% of need; average scholarship/grant was $39,787; average loan was $4,031.
**Students without need:** This college awards aid only to students with need.

### FINANCIAL AID PROCEDURES
**Forms required:** FAFSA, CSS PROFILE.
**Dates and Deadlines:** Closing date 2/15. Applicants notified by 4/1; must reply by 5/1.
**Transfers:** Applicants notified on a rolling basis starting 5/1; must reply by 7/1. Submit Cornell aid application forms in addition to regular required forms.

### CONTACT
Susan Hitchcock, Director, Financial Aid and Student Employment
410 Thurston Avenue, Ithaca, NY 14850
(607) 255-5145

## Corning Community College
Corning, New York          Federal Code: 002863
www.corning-cc.edu          CSS Code: 2106

**2-year public** community college in large town.
**Enrollment:** 2,558 undergrads, 30% part-time. 665 full-time freshmen.
**Selectivity:** Open admission; but selective for some programs.

## BASIC COSTS (2015-2016)

**Tuition and fees:** $4,774; out-of-state residents $9,004.
**Per-credit charge:** $177; out-of-state residents $354.
**Room and board:** $9,000.

## FINANCIAL AID PICTURE (2014-2015)

**Students with need:** Need-based aid available for full-time and part-time students. Work study available weekends and for part-time students.
**Students without need:** This college awards aid only to students with need.

## FINANCIAL AID PROCEDURES

**Forms required:** FAFSA, CSS PROFILE, state aid form.
**Dates and Deadlines:** Applicants notified on a rolling basis starting 4/1; must reply within 4 week(s) of notification.

## CONTACT

Barbara Snow, Director of Financial Aid
One Academic Drive, Corning, NY 14830
(607) 962-9011

# Culinary Institute of America
Hyde Park, New York
www.ciachef.edu                    Federal Code: 007304

**4-year private** culinary school in large town.
**Enrollment:** 2,859 undergrads. 587 full-time freshmen.
**Selectivity:** Admits over 75% of applicants.

## BASIC COSTS (2015-2016)

**Tuition and fees:** $29,250.
**Room and board:** $9,880.

## FINANCIAL AID PICTURE (2015-2016)

**Students with need:** Out of 510 full-time freshmen who applied for aid, 467 were judged to have need. Of these, 467 received aid, and 188 had their full need met. Average financial aid package met 80% of need; average scholarship/grant was $11,277; average loan was $3,268. Need-based aid available for part-time students.
**Students without need:** 43 full-time freshmen who did not demonstrate need for aid received scholarships/grants; average award was $7,166. No-need awards available for academics, alumni affiliation, job skills, leadership.

## FINANCIAL AID PROCEDURES

**Forms required:** FAFSA, state aid form.
**Dates and Deadlines:** Applicants notified on a rolling basis starting 3/5; must reply within 2 week(s) of notification.

## CONTACT

Kathleen Gailor, Director of Financial Aid
1946 Campus Drive, Hyde Park, NY 12538-1499
(845) 451-1243

# Daemen College
Amherst, New York
www.daemen.edu                    Federal Code: 002808

**4-year private** liberal arts college in small city.
**Enrollment:** 1,968 undergrads, 15% part-time. 419 full-time freshmen.
**Selectivity:** Admits less than 50% of applicants.

## BASIC COSTS (2015-2016)

**Tuition and fees:** $25,995.
**Per-credit charge:** $850.
**Room and board:** $12,050.

## FINANCIAL AID PICTURE (2014-2015)

**Students with need:** Out of 377 full-time freshmen who applied for aid, 342 were judged to have need. Of these, 342 received aid, and 137 had their full need met. Average financial aid package met 83% of need; average scholarship/grant was $11,205; average loan was $3,942. For part-time students, average financial aid package was $20,181.
**Students without need:** 101 full-time freshmen who did not demonstrate need for aid received scholarships/grants; average award was $12,582. No-need awards available for academics, art, athletics, leadership.
**Scholarships offered:** *Merit:* President's Scholarship, Dean's Scholarship, Alumni Grant: $2,500-$10,000; renewable awards to freshmen and transfers; based on high school GPA and SAT scores. Trustee Scholarship: $17,000; 2 awards; and $14,000; 4 awards. Renewable visual arts scholarships: $5,000; 2 awards. *Athletic:* 4 full-time freshmen received athletic scholarships; average amount $19,773.

## FINANCIAL AID PROCEDURES

**Forms required:** FAFSA, state aid form.
**Dates and Deadlines:** Priority date 2/1; no closing date. Applicants notified on a rolling basis starting 2/1; must reply within 2 week(s) of notification.

## CONTACT

Jeffrey Pagano, Director of Financial Aid
4380 Main Street, Amherst, NY 14226-3592
(716) 839-8254

# Davis College
Johnson City, New York
www.davisny.edu                    Federal Code: 015291

**4-year private** Bible college in large town, affiliated with nondenominational tradition.
**Enrollment:** 231 undergrads.

## BASIC COSTS (2015-2016)

**Tuition and fees:** $12,390.
**Per-credit charge:** $450.
**Room and board:** $7,200.
**Additional info:** Tuition at time of enrollment locked for 4 years.

## FINANCIAL AID PICTURE

**Students with need:** Need-based aid available for full-time and part-time students. Work study available nights, weekends, and for part-time students.
**Students without need:** No-need awards available for academics, alumni affiliation.
**Scholarships offered:** Heart for Ministry Scholarship: based on personal essay and recommendations about a student's involvement in ministry or the community.

## FINANCIAL AID PROCEDURES

**Forms required:** FAFSA, state aid form, institutional form.
**Dates and Deadlines:** Applicants notified on a rolling basis.
**Transfers:** No deadline. Applicants notified on a rolling basis.

## CONTACT

Will Reichel, Director of Financial Aid
400 Riverside Drive, Johnson City, NY 13790
(607) 729-1581 ext. 331

# DeVry College of New York: Midtown Campus
New York, New York
www.devry.edu                    Federal Code: 003099

**4-year for-profit** business and technical college in very large city.
**Enrollment:** 936 undergrads.

## BASIC COSTS (2015-2016)
**Tuition and fees:** $17,132.
**Per-credit charge:** $609.
**Additional info:** Annual tuition: $10,810-$21,163; fees $50-$90.

## FINANCIAL AID PICTURE
**Students with need:** Need-based aid available for full-time and part-time students.
**Students without need:** This college awards aid only to students with need.

## CONTACT
180 Madison Avenue, Suite 900, New York, NY 10016

# Dominican College of Blauvelt
Orangeburg, New York
www.dc.edu
Federal Code: 002713

**4-year private** health science and liberal arts college in small town.
**Enrollment:** 1,552 undergrads, 13% part-time. 363 full-time freshmen.
**Selectivity:** Admits 50 to 75% of applicants.

## BASIC COSTS (2015-2016)
**Tuition and fees:** $26,450.
**Per-credit charge:** $776.
**Room and board:** $12,120.

## FINANCIAL AID PICTURE (2015-2016)
**Students with need:** Out of 363 full-time freshmen who applied for aid, 346 were judged to have need. Of these, 335 received aid, and 42 had their full need met. Average financial aid package met 70% of need; average scholarship/grant was $20,124; average loan was $4,122. For part-time students, average financial aid package was $7,245.
**Students without need:** 23 full-time freshmen who did not demonstrate need for aid received scholarships/grants; average award was $10,413. No-need awards available for academics, athletics.
**Scholarships offered:** *Merit:* All applicants considered for non-need based scholarships or grants based on high school GPA and SAT/ACT scores. *Athletic:* 23 full-time freshmen received athletic scholarships; average amount $6,870.
**Additional info:** Individual financial aid counseling available.

## FINANCIAL AID PROCEDURES
**Forms required:** FAFSA, state aid form.
**Dates and Deadlines:** Priority date 2/15; no closing date. Applicants notified on a rolling basis starting 2/1; must reply within 2 week(s) of notification.

## CONTACT
Stacy Salinas, Director of Financial Aid
470 Western Highway, Orangeburg, NY 10962-1210
(845) 848-7821

# Dowling College
Oakdale, New York
www.dowling.edu
Federal Code: 002667

**4-year private** business, liberal arts and teachers college in large town.
**Enrollment:** 1,152 undergrads, 15% part-time. 182 full-time freshmen.
**Selectivity:** Admits 50 to 75% of applicants.

## BASIC COSTS (2015-2016)
**Tuition and fees:** $29,100.
**Per-credit charge:** $1,215.
**Room and board:** $11,120.

## FINANCIAL AID PICTURE (2014-2015)
**Students with need:** Out of 157 full-time freshmen who applied for aid, 156 were judged to have need. Of these, 156 received aid, and 11 had their

full need met. Average financial aid package met 40% of need; average scholarship/grant was $11,512; average loan was $3,264. For part-time students, average financial aid package was $8,285.
**Students without need:** 107 full-time freshmen who did not demonstrate need for aid received scholarships/grants; average award was $9,232. No-need awards available for academics, alumni affiliation, athletics.
**Scholarships offered:** 35 full-time freshmen received athletic scholarships; average amount $8,708.

## FINANCIAL AID PROCEDURES
**Forms required:** FAFSA, state aid form.
**Dates and Deadlines:** Priority date 2/15; no closing date. Applicants notified on a rolling basis starting 3/15; must reply within 2 week(s) of notification.
**Transfers:** No deadline. Applicants notified on a rolling basis. Academic scholarships available for transfers with 60 credits or the equivalent of an associate degree.

## CONTACT
Carla Guevara, Director of Financial Aid
150 Idle Hour Boulevard, Oakdale, NY 11769-1999
(631) 244-3110

# Dutchess Community College
Poughkeepsie, New York
www.sunydutchess.edu
Federal Code: 002864

**2-year public** community college in large town.
**Enrollment:** 6,327 undergrads, 34% part-time. 1,713 full-time freshmen.
**Selectivity:** Open admission; but selective for some programs.

## BASIC COSTS (2015-2016)
**Tuition and fees:** $3,900; out-of-state residents $7,260.
**Per-credit charge:** $140; out-of-state residents $280.
**Room and board:** $9,750.

## FINANCIAL AID PICTURE (2014-2015)
**Students with need:** 73% of average financial aid package awarded as scholarships/grants, 27% awarded as loans/jobs. Need-based aid available for part-time students.
**Students without need:** No-need awards available for academics.
**Scholarships offered:** Dutchess County high school graduates in top 10% of their class; full tuition payment for 4 full-time consecutive semesters.

## FINANCIAL AID PROCEDURES
**Forms required:** FAFSA, state aid form.
**Dates and Deadlines:** Priority date 5/1; no closing date. Applicants notified on a rolling basis starting 5/15; must reply within 2 week(s) of notification.

## CONTACT
Susan Mead, Director of Financial Aid
53 Pendell Road, Poughkeepsie, NY 12601-1595
(845) 431-8030

# D'Youville College
Buffalo, New York
www.dyc.edu

**4-year private** health science and liberal arts college in large city.
**Enrollment:** 1,707 undergrads, 17% part-time. 232 full-time freshmen.
**Selectivity:** Admits 50 to 75% of applicants.

## BASIC COSTS (2015-2016)
**Tuition and fees:** $24,370.
**Per-credit charge:** $745.
**Room and board:** $11,180.

## FINANCIAL AID PICTURE (2015-2016)

**Students with need:** Out of 218 full-time freshmen who applied for aid, 196 were judged to have need. Of these, 196 received aid, and 41 had their full need met. Average financial aid package met 73% of need; average scholarship/grant was $15,650; average loan was $3,609. For part-time students, average financial aid package was $8,004.

**Students without need:** 43 full-time freshmen who did not demonstrate need for aid received scholarships/grants; average award was $9,459. No-need awards available for academics, leadership, religious affiliation, ROTC.

**Scholarships offered:** Presidential Honors Scholarship: for students with 1100 SAT (Math and Verbal) or 24 ACT Composite; covers 50% tuition and 25% of standard double room rate. Academic Initiative Scholarship: For students with 1000-1090 SAT (math & verbal scores only) or 21-23 ACT score and an 85 high school average. The award is for 25% of tuition and 50% of the standard double room rate in Marguerite Hall or 50% of the standard room rate in the apartments for full-time students. Achievement Scholarship: For students with 900-1090 SAT score or 19-23 ACT and an 80-84 high school average, demonstrated leadership and community service. The awards range from $1,000-$4,000. Transfer Achievement Scholarship: For students with a G.P.A. of 2.75-4.0 from previously attended institution(s). The award amounts range from $2,500-$5,000. All awards are renewable for the standard duration of the specific academic program and have GPA and other requirements.

## FINANCIAL AID PROCEDURES

**Forms required:** FAFSA, state aid form.

**Dates and Deadlines:** Priority date 3/1; no closing date. Applicants notified on a rolling basis starting 4/1; must reply within 2 week(s) of notification.

**Transfers:** Applicants notified on a rolling basis starting 4/1; must reply within 2 week(s) of notification. .

## CONTACT

Matthew Metz, Director of Financial Aid
320 Porter Avenue, Buffalo, NY 14201-1084

# Eastman School of Music of the University of Rochester

Rochester, New York          Federal Code: 008124
www.esm.rochester.edu          CSS Code: 2224

**4-year private** music and performing arts college in small city.

**Enrollment:** 565 undergrads. 131 full-time freshmen.

**Selectivity:** Admits less than 50% of applicants.

## BASIC COSTS (2015-2016)

**Tuition and fees:** $49,108.

**Per-credit charge:** $1,490.

**Room and board:** $14,294.

## FINANCIAL AID PICTURE

**Students with need:** Need-based aid available for full-time and part-time students.

**Students without need:** No-need awards available for academics, alumni affiliation, job skills, leadership, minority status, music/drama, state/district residency.

**Scholarships offered:** All merit scholarships awarded based on admission criteria and do not require separate application, audition, or interview.

## FINANCIAL AID PROCEDURES

**Forms required:** FAFSA, state aid form, institutional form. CSS Profile required for International students only.

**Dates and Deadlines:** Closing date 2/28. Applicants notified by 4/15; must reply by 5/1 or within 2 week(s) of notification.

**Transfers:** No deadline. Applicants notified by 4/15; must reply by 5/1 or within 2 week(s) of notification.

## CONTACT

Mary Ellen Nugent, Director of Financial Aid
26 Gibbs Street, Rochester, NY 14604-2599
(585) 274-1070

# Elmira Business Institute

Elmira, New York
www.ebi-college.com

**2-year for-profit** business, health science, technical and career college in large town.

**Enrollment:** 196 undergrads.

**Selectivity:** Open admission.

## FINANCIAL AID PICTURE

**Students with need:** Need-based aid available for full-time and part-time students.

**Students without need:** This college awards aid only to students with need.

## FINANCIAL AID PROCEDURES

**Forms required:** FAFSA, state aid form.

**Dates and Deadlines:** Priority date 5/1; no closing date. Applicants notified on a rolling basis starting 1/1; must reply within 1 week(s) of notification.

## CONTACT

Financial Aid Director
303 North Main Street, Elmira, NY 14901
(607) 733-7177

# Elmira Business Institute: Vestal

Vestal, New York
www.elmirabusinessinstitute.edu          Federal Code: 009044

**2-year for-profit** business, health science, technical and career college in small city.

**Enrollment:** 400 undergrads.

**Selectivity:** Open admission.

## FINANCIAL AID PICTURE

**Students with need:** Need-based aid available for full-time and part-time students.

**Students without need:** This college awards aid only to students with need.

## FINANCIAL AID PROCEDURES

**Forms required:** FAFSA, state aid form.

**Dates and Deadlines:** Applicants notified on a rolling basis starting 1/1; must reply within 1 week(s) of notification.

## CONTACT

Jeffrey Wood, Director of Finanical Services
4100 Vestal Road, Vestal, NY 13850
(607) 729-8915

# Elmira College

Elmira, New York
www.elmira.edu          Federal Code: 002718

**4-year private** liberal arts and teachers college in large town.

**Enrollment:** 1,252 undergrads, 10% part-time. 255 full-time freshmen.

**Selectivity:** Admits over 75% of applicants. GED not accepted.

## BASIC COSTS (2015-2016)

**Tuition and fees:** $39,950.

**Per-credit charge:** $1,094.
**Room and board:** $12,000.

## FINANCIAL AID PICTURE (2015-2016)
**Students with need:** Out of 236 full-time freshmen who applied for aid, 220 were judged to have need. Of these, 220 received aid, and 38 had their full need met. Average financial aid package met 76% of need; average scholarship/grant was $27,992; average loan was $3,481. Need-based aid available for part-time students.

**Students without need:** 35 full-time freshmen who did not demonstrate need for aid received scholarships/grants; average award was $21,855. No-need awards available for academics, leadership, ROTC, state/district residency.

**Scholarships offered:** Valedictorian and salutatorian awards: 30 anticipated awards; full-tuition; renewable for 3 years provided student maintains certain GPA. Additional scholarships: $26,000, $23,000, $21,000, $16,000 or $13,000; based on GPA, test scores, class rank, leadership; renewable for 3 additional years provided student maintains certain GPA.

**Additional info:** Sibling Scholarship program provides 50% discount on second immediate family member's room and board, regardless of need.

## FINANCIAL AID PROCEDURES
**Forms required:** FAFSA, state aid form.
**Dates and Deadlines:** Priority date 2/1; no closing date. Applicants notified on a rolling basis starting 2/1; must reply by 5/1 or within 2 week(s) of notification.
**Transfers:** No deadline. Applicants notified on a rolling basis starting 2/1; must reply by 5/1 or within 2 week(s) of notification. Award for enrolled U.S. citizens from outside New York State. New merit scholarship for transfer students.

## CONTACT
Kathleen Cohen, Dean of Financial Aid
One Park Place, Elmira, NY 14901
(607) 735-1728

## Erie Community College
Buffalo, New York
www.ecc.edu                    Federal Code: 010684

**2-year public** community college in large city.
**Enrollment:** 10,027 undergrads, 22% part-time. 2,374 full-time freshmen.
**Selectivity:** Open admission; but selective for some programs.

## BASIC COSTS (2015-2016)
**Tuition and fees:** $5,188; out-of-state residents $9,783.
**Per-credit charge:** $192; out-of-state residents $384.

## FINANCIAL AID PICTURE (2014-2015)
**Students with need:** 83% of average financial aid package awarded as scholarships/grants, 17% awarded as loans/jobs. Need-based aid available for part-time students. Work study available weekends and for part-time students.
**Students without need:** This college awards aid only to students with need.

## FINANCIAL AID PROCEDURES
**Forms required:** FAFSA, state aid form.
**Dates and Deadlines:** Priority date 5/1; no closing date. Applicants notified on a rolling basis starting 4/1; must reply within 2 week(s) of notification.

## CONTACT
Scott Weltjen, Director of Financial Aid
6205 Main Street, Williamsville, NY 14221-7095
(716) 851-1677

## Eugene Lang College The New School for Liberal Arts
New York, New York
www.newschool.edu              Federal Code: 002780

**4-year private** liberal arts college in very large city.
**Enrollment:** 1,506 undergrads, 5% part-time. 406 full-time freshmen.
**Selectivity:** Admits 50 to 75% of applicants.

## BASIC COSTS (2015-2016)
**Tuition and fees:** $43,006.
**Per-credit charge:** $1,430.
**Room and board:** $17,235.

## FINANCIAL AID PICTURE (2014-2015)
**Students with need:** Out of 259 full-time freshmen who applied for aid, 235 were judged to have need. Of these, 235 received aid, and 25 had their full need met. Average financial aid package met 71% of need; average scholarship/grant was $19,886; average loan was $5,605. For part-time students, average financial aid package was $13,963.

**Students without need:** 98 full-time freshmen who did not demonstrate need for aid received scholarships/grants; average award was $9,413. No-need awards available for academics, art, leadership, minority status, music/drama, state/district residency.

## FINANCIAL AID PROCEDURES
**Forms required:** FAFSA, state aid form.
**Dates and Deadlines:** Closing date 3/1. Applicants notified on a rolling basis starting 4/1; must reply within 4 week(s) of notification.
**Transfers:** Must reply within 4 week(s) of notification.

## CONTACT
Lisa Shaheen, Director of Student Financial Aid
79 Fifth Avenue, New York, NY 10003
(212) 229-8930

## Excelsior College
Albany, New York
www.excelsior.edu              Federal Code: 014251

**4-year private** virtual liberal arts college in small city.
**Enrollment:** 36,927 undergrads, 100% part-time.
**Selectivity:** Open admission; but selective for some programs.

## BASIC COSTS (2016-2017)
**Additional info:** Undergraduate per credit hour charge: $490. For students committed to taking at least 12 Excelsior College credits prior to graduation the enrollment fee is waived. An enrollment fee of up to $1,065 may be charged for evaluation of credits earned elsewhere. Students enrolled via a partnership (academic, corporate, military) qualify for different fees, tuition, credit requirements and rules based on the individual partnership agreement. Students taking 12 credits annually are not subject to $495 annual student services fee.

## FINANCIAL AID PICTURE (2014-2015)
**Students with need:** 32% of average financial aid package awarded as scholarships/grants, 68% awarded as loans/jobs.
**Students without need:** This college awards aid only to students with need.
**Scholarships offered:** Excelsior College has endowed scholarships for a number of student types and various programs.
**Additional info:** Excelsior College is Title IV eligible for its course-based degree programs; approved for all veterans' education benefit programs.

## FINANCIAL AID PROCEDURES
**Dates and Deadlines:** Applicants notified on a rolling basis; must reply within 2 week(s) of notification.

**CONTACT**

Thomas Dalton, Assistant Vice President for Enrollment Management, Financial Aid

7 Columbia Circle, Albany, NY 12203

(518) 464-8500

## Fashion Institute of Technology

New York, New York

www.fitnyc.edu                      Federal Code: 002866

**4-year public** visual arts and business college in very large city.

**Enrollment:** 8,229 undergrads, 11% part-time. 1,241 full-time freshmen.

**Selectivity:** Admits less than 50% of applicants.

**BASIC COSTS (2015-2016)**

**Tuition and fees:** $5,230; out-of-state residents $14,230.

**Per-credit charge:** $188; out-of-state residents $563.

**Room and board:** $13,291.

**FINANCIAL AID PICTURE (2014-2015)**

**Students with need:** 59% of average financial aid package awarded as scholarships/grants, 41% awarded as loans/jobs. Need-based aid available for part-time students. Work study available nights, weekends, and for part-time students.

**Students without need:** This college awards aid only to students with need.

**FINANCIAL AID PROCEDURES**

**Forms required:** FAFSA, state aid form.

**Dates and Deadlines:** Priority date 2/15; no closing date. Applicants notified on a rolling basis starting 4/15; must reply within 2 week(s) of notification.

**Transfers:** Applicants notified by 4/15; must reply within 2 week(s) of notification.

**CONTACT**

Mina Friedmann, Director of Financial Aid

227 West 27th Street, New York, NY 10001-5992

(212) 217-3560

## Finger Lakes Community College

Canandaigua, New York

www.flcc.edu                       Federal Code: 007532

**2-year public** community college in small town.

**Enrollment:** 3,906 undergrads, 25% part-time. 1,270 full-time freshmen.

**Selectivity:** Open admission; but selective for some programs.

**BASIC COSTS (2015-2016)**

**Tuition and fees:** $4,704; out-of-state residents $8,884.

**Per-credit charge:** $168; out-of-state residents $336.

**FINANCIAL AID PICTURE (2014-2015)**

**Students with need:** Out of 1,179 full-time freshmen who applied for aid, 1,001 were judged to have need. Of these, 929 received aid. Need-based aid available for part-time students.

**Students without need:** This college awards aid only to students with need.

**FINANCIAL AID PROCEDURES**

**Forms required:** FAFSA, state aid form.

**Dates and Deadlines:** Priority date 3/15; no closing date. Applicants notified on a rolling basis starting 4/1; must reply within 2 week(s) of notification.

**CONTACT**

Susan Romano, Director, Financial Aid

3325 Marvin Sands Drive, Canandaigua, NY 14424-8395

(585) 785-1275

## Five Towns College

Dix Hills, New York

www.ftc.edu                        Federal Code: 012561

**4-year for-profit** business and performing arts college in large town.

**Enrollment:** 630 undergrads, 3% part-time. 118 full-time freshmen.

**Selectivity:** Admits 50 to 75% of applicants.

**BASIC COSTS (2015-2016)**

**Tuition and fees:** $21,870.

**Per-credit charge:** $875.

**Room and board:** $12,270.

**FINANCIAL AID PICTURE (2014-2015)**

**Students with need:** Out of 104 full-time freshmen who applied for aid, 104 were judged to have need. Of these, 97 received aid, and 26 had their full need met. Average financial aid package met 68% of need; average scholarship/grant was $4,450; average loan was $3,344. For part-time students, average financial aid package was $8,195.

**Students without need:** 13 full-time freshmen who did not demonstrate need for aid received scholarships/grants; average award was $3,565. No-need awards available for academics, art, leadership, music/drama.

**FINANCIAL AID PROCEDURES**

**Forms required:** FAFSA, state aid form.

**Dates and Deadlines:** Priority date 4/30; no closing date. Applicants notified on a rolling basis starting 3/1; must reply within 4 week(s) of notification.

**Transfers:** No deadline. Applicants notified on a rolling basis starting 1/1; must reply within 4 week(s) of notification.

**CONTACT**

Jason LaBonte, Director of Financial Aid

305 North Service Road, Dix Hills, NY 11746-6055

(631) 656-2164

## Fordham University

Bronx, New York                    Federal Code: 002722

www.fordham.edu                         CSS Code: 2259

**4-year private** university in very large city, affiliated with Roman Catholic Church.

**Enrollment:** 8,701 undergrads, 5% part-time. 2,229 full-time freshmen.

**Selectivity:** Admits less than 50% of applicants.

**BASIC COSTS (2015-2016)**

**Tuition and fees:** $46,932.

**Room and board:** $16,350.

**FINANCIAL AID PICTURE (2014-2015)**

**Students with need:** Out of 1,959 full-time freshmen who applied for aid, 1,465 were judged to have need. Of these, 1,465 received aid, and 472 had their full need met. Average financial aid package met 82% of need; average scholarship/grant was $25,614; average loan was $5,337. For part-time students, average financial aid package was $14,118.

**Students without need:** 547 full-time freshmen who did not demonstrate need for aid received scholarships/grants; average award was $14,899. No-need awards available for academics, athletics, ROTC.

**Scholarships offered:** 37 full-time freshmen received athletic scholarships; average amount $32,806.

**FINANCIAL AID PROCEDURES**

**Forms required:** FAFSA, CSS PROFILE, state aid form.

**Dates and Deadlines:** Closing date 2/10. Applicants notified on a rolling basis starting 3/31; must reply by 5/1 or within 2 week(s) of notification.

**Transfers:** Priority date 2/10; closing date 5/1. Applicants notified on a rolling basis starting 5/1. Transfer students are only eligible for need based aid.

**CONTACT**
Angela Van Dekker, Assistant Vice President of Student Financial Services
Office of Undergraduate Admission, Fordham University, Bronx, NY 10458-9993
(718) 817-3800

## Fulton-Montgomery Community College
Johnstown, New York
www.fmcc.suny.edu                     Federal Code: 002867

**2-year public** community college in large town.
**Enrollment:** 1,961 undergrads.
**Selectivity:** Open admission; but selective for some programs.

**BASIC COSTS (2015-2016)**
**Tuition and fees:** $4,420; out-of-state residents $8,320.
**Per-credit charge:** $163; out-of-state residents $326.
**Room and board:** $11,000.

**FINANCIAL AID PICTURE**
**Students with need:** Need-based aid available for full-time and part-time students. Work study available nights, weekends, and for part-time students.
**Students without need:** No-need awards available for academics.

**FINANCIAL AID PROCEDURES**
**Forms required:** FAFSA, state aid form.
**Dates and Deadlines:** Priority date 6/1; no closing date. Applicants notified on a rolling basis starting 6/15; must reply within 2 week(s) of notification.

**CONTACT**
Rebecca Cozzocrea, Coordinator of Financial Aid
2805 State Highway 67, Johnstown, NY 12095
(518) 736-4651 ext. 8201

## Genesee Community College
Batavia, New York
www.genesee.edu                     Federal Code: 006782

**2-year public** community college in large town.
**Enrollment:** 3,715 undergrads, 28% part-time. 894 full-time freshmen.
**Selectivity:** Open admission; but selective for some programs.

**BASIC COSTS (2015-2016)**
**Tuition and fees:** $4,410; out-of-state residents $5,010.
**Room and board:** $8,475.

**FINANCIAL AID PICTURE (2014-2015)**
**Students with need:** Out of 733 full-time freshmen who applied for aid, 550 were judged to have need. Of these, 550 received aid, and 320 had their full need met. Average financial aid package met 80% of need; average scholarship/grant was $5,155; average loan was $3,750. For part-time students, average financial aid package was $3,200.
**Students without need:** 25 full-time freshmen who did not demonstrate need for aid received scholarships/grants; average award was $2,200. No-need awards available for academics, alumni affiliation, athletics, leadership, state/district residency.
**Scholarships offered:** 25 full-time freshmen received athletic scholarships; average amount $2,200.

**FINANCIAL AID PROCEDURES**
**Forms required:** FAFSA, state aid form.
**Dates and Deadlines:** Priority date 3/1; closing date 5/1. Applicants notified on a rolling basis starting 4/15; must reply within 2 week(s) of notification.
**Transfers:** No deadline.

**CONTACT**
Joseph Bailey, Director of Student Financial Services/Assistant Dean for Enrollment Services
One College Road, Batavia, NY 14020-9704
(585) 345-6900

## Globe Institute of Technology
New York, New York
www.globe.edu                     Federal Code: 025408

**4-year for-profit** university and business college in very large city.
**Enrollment:** 447 undergrads, 2% part-time. 139 full-time freshmen.
**Selectivity:** Open admission; but selective for some programs.

**BASIC COSTS (2015-2016)**
**Additional info:** Tuition/fee waivers available for adults, minority students, unemployed or children of unemployed.

**FINANCIAL AID PICTURE (2014-2015)**
**Students with need:** 73% of average financial aid package awarded as scholarships/grants, 27% awarded as loans/jobs. Need-based aid available for part-time students. Work study available nights, weekends, and for part-time students.
**Students without need:** No-need awards available for academics, athletics.

**FINANCIAL AID PROCEDURES**
**Forms required:** FAFSA, state aid form, institutional form.
**Dates and Deadlines:** Applicants notified on a rolling basis.
**Transfers:** No deadline. Applicants notified on a rolling basis.

**CONTACT**
Tatyana Nusenbaum, Director of Financial Aid
500 Seventh Avenue, 2nd Floor, New York, NY 10018
(212) 349-4330

## Hamilton College
Clinton, New York
www.hamilton.edu             Federal Code: 002728
                             CSS Code: 2286

**4-year private** liberal arts college in rural community.
**Enrollment:** 1,861 undergrads. 473 full-time freshmen.
**Selectivity:** Admits less than 50% of applicants.

**BASIC COSTS (2015-2016)**
**Tuition and fees:** $49,500.
**Room and board:** $12,570.

**FINANCIAL AID PICTURE (2015-2016)**
**Students with need:** Out of 267 full-time freshmen who applied for aid, 253 were judged to have need. Of these, 253 received aid, and 253 had their full need met. Average financial aid package met 100% of need; average scholarship/grant was $40,802; average loan was $3,226.
**Students without need:** This college awards aid only to students with need.

**FINANCIAL AID PROCEDURES**
**Forms required:** FAFSA, CSS PROFILE, state aid form, institutional form.
**Dates and Deadlines:** Closing date 2/15. Applicants notified by 4/1; must reply by 5/1.
**Transfers:** Closing date 4/15. Applicants notified by 5/10; must reply by 5/23.

**CONTACT**
Cameron Feist, Director of Financial Aid
198 College Hill Road, Clinton, NY 13323-1293
(315) 859-4413

## Hartwick College
Oneonta, New York
www.hartwick.edu                    Federal Code: 002729

**4-year private** liberal arts college in large town.
**Enrollment:** 1,383 undergrads, 2% part-time. 292 full-time freshmen.
**Selectivity:** Admits over 75% of applicants.

### BASIC COSTS (2016-2017)
**Tuition and fees:** $42,860.
**Per-credit charge:** $1,350.
**Room and board:** $11,510.

### FINANCIAL AID PICTURE (2015-2016)
**Students with need:** Out of 268 full-time freshmen who applied for aid, 254 were judged to have need. Of these, 254 received aid, and 53 had their full need met. Average financial aid package met 82% of need; average scholarship/grant was $27,415; average loan was $4,902. For part-time students, average financial aid package was $12,250.
**Students without need:** 38 full-time freshmen who did not demonstrate need for aid received scholarships/grants; average award was $22,929. No-need awards available for academics, alumni affiliation, art, athletics, music/drama.
**Scholarships offered:** 4 full-time freshmen received athletic scholarships; average amount $17,743.

### FINANCIAL AID PROCEDURES
**Forms required:** FAFSA.
**Dates and Deadlines:** Priority date 2/15; no closing date. Applicants notified on a rolling basis starting 1/15; must reply by 5/1 or within 2 week(s) of notification.
**Transfers:** Priority date 8/1; no deadline. Applicants notified on a rolling basis starting 3/15; must reply within 2 week(s) of notification.

### CONTACT
Melissa Allen, Director of Financial Aid
1 Hartwick Drive, Oneonta, NY 13820-4022
(607) 431-4130

## Helene Fuld College of Nursing
New York, New York
www.helenefuld.edu                    Federal Code: 015395

**2-year private** nursing and junior college in very large city.
**Enrollment:** 448 undergrads, 55% part-time.

### BASIC COSTS (2015-2016)
**Tuition and fees:** $19,099.
**Per-credit charge:** $341.

### FINANCIAL AID PICTURE
**Students with need:** Need-based aid available for full-time and part-time students.
**Students without need:** This college awards aid only to students with need.

### FINANCIAL AID PROCEDURES
**Forms required:** FAFSA, state aid form.
**Dates and Deadlines:** Closing date 6/30. Applicants notified on a rolling basis.

### CONTACT
Andrine Thomas, Financial Aid Counselor and Loan Coordinator
24 East 120th Street, New York, NY 10035
(212) 616-7253

## Herkimer County Community College
Herkimer, New York
www.herkimer.edu                    Federal Code: 004788

**2-year public** community college in small town.
**Enrollment:** 2,125 undergrads, 18% part-time. 749 full-time freshmen.
**Selectivity:** Open admission; but selective for some programs.

### BASIC COSTS (2015-2016)
**Tuition and fees:** $4,640; out-of-state residents $7,700.
**Per-credit charge:** $139; out-of-state residents $278.
**Room and board:** $9,550.
**Additional info:** Tuition/fee waivers available for unemployed or children of unemployed.

### FINANCIAL AID PICTURE
**Students with need:** Need-based aid available for full-time and part-time students. Work study available nights, weekends, and for part-time students.

### FINANCIAL AID PROCEDURES
**Forms required:** FAFSA, state aid form.
**Dates and Deadlines:** Closing date 4/1. Applicants notified on a rolling basis starting 4/1; must reply within 2 week(s) of notification.

### CONTACT
Susan Tripp, Director of Financial Aid
100 Reservoir Road, Herkimer, NY 13350-1598
(315) 866-0300 ext. 8282

## Hilbert College
Hamburg, New York
www.hilbert.edu                    Federal Code: 002735

**4-year private** liberal arts college in small city, affiliated with Roman Catholic Church.
**Enrollment:** 864 undergrads, 9% part-time. 151 full-time freshmen.
**Selectivity:** Admits over 75% of applicants.

### BASIC COSTS (2015-2016)
**Tuition and fees:** $20,700.
**Per-credit charge:** $505.
**Room and board:** $9,380.
**Additional info:** Tuition/fee waivers available for adults, minority students.

### FINANCIAL AID PICTURE (2015-2016)
**Students with need:** Out of 89 full-time freshmen who applied for aid, 80 were judged to have need. Of these, 80 received aid, and 9 had their full need met. Average financial aid package met 72% of need; average scholarship/grant was $14,081; average loan was $3,777. For part-time students, average financial aid package was $5,336.
**Students without need:** 10 full-time freshmen who did not demonstrate need for aid received scholarships/grants; average award was $6,925. No-need awards available for academics, alumni affiliation, leadership, minority status.

### FINANCIAL AID PROCEDURES
**Forms required:** FAFSA, state aid form.
**Dates and Deadlines:** Priority date 3/1; no closing date. Applicants notified on a rolling basis starting 3/1; must reply within 2 week(s) of notification.
**Transfers:** No deadline. Applicants notified on a rolling basis; must reply within 2 week(s) of notification.

### CONTACT
Beverly Chudy, Director of Student Financial Aid
5200 South Park Avenue, Hamburg, NY 14075-1597
(716) 649-7900

# Hobart and William Smith Colleges

Geneva, New York — Federal Code: 002731
www.hws.edu — CSS Code: 2294

**4-year private** liberal arts college in large town.
**Enrollment:** 2,257 undergrads. 555 full-time freshmen.
**Selectivity:** Admits 50 to 75% of applicants.

## BASIC COSTS (2015-2016)
**Tuition and fees:** $49,677.
**Room and board:** $12,583.

## FINANCIAL AID PICTURE (2014-2015)
**Students with need:** Out of 439 full-time freshmen who applied for aid, 354 were judged to have need. Of these, 354 received aid, and 238 had their full need met. Average financial aid package met 80% of need; average scholarship/grant was $29,520; average loan was $3,265. For part-time students, average financial aid package was $4,997.
**Students without need:** 194 full-time freshmen who did not demonstrate need for aid received scholarships/grants; average award was $13,481. No-need awards available for academics, alumni affiliation, art, leadership, music/drama, religious affiliation.
**Scholarships offered:** Cornelius and Muriel P. Wood Scholarship: full tuition for 4 years. Richard Hersh Scholarship: full tuition and fees for 4 years. Trustee and Blackwell Scholarships for Academic Excellence: $25,000 annually, for 4 years; based on GPA, test scores, class standing. Faculty Scholarships: $17,000. Presidential Leaders and Service Scholarships: $5,000-$15,000; based on academic excellence, leadership, service, personal qualities. Arts Scholarships: $3,000-$15,000; for special talent in studio art/architecture, creative writing, music, theater, and/or dance.

## FINANCIAL AID PROCEDURES
**Forms required:** FAFSA, CSS PROFILE, state aid form.
**Dates and Deadlines:** Priority date 2/1; closing date 2/1. Applicants notified by 4/1; must reply by 5/1 or within 2 week(s) of notification.
**Transfers:** No deadline. Applicants notified on a rolling basis; must reply within 2 week(s) of notification.

## CONTACT
Beth Nepa, Director of Financial Aid Services
629 South Main Street, Geneva, NY 14456
(315) 781-3315

# Hofstra University

Hempstead, New York
www.hofstra.edu — Federal Code: 002732

**4-year private** university in large city.
**Enrollment:** 6,716 undergrads, 5% part-time. 1,713 full-time freshmen.
**Selectivity:** Admits 50 to 75% of applicants.

## BASIC COSTS (2015-2016)
**Tuition and fees:** $40,460.
**Per-credit charge:** $1,325.
**Room and board:** $13,330.
**Additional info:** Tuition at time of enrollment locked for 4 years.

## FINANCIAL AID PICTURE (2014-2015)
**Students with need:** Out of 1,479 full-time freshmen who applied for aid, 1,244 were judged to have need. Of these, 1,244 received aid, and 287 had their full need met. Average financial aid package met 66% of need; average scholarship/grant was $19,719; average loan was $3,469. For part-time students, average financial aid package was $9,533.
**Students without need:** 353 full-time freshmen who did not demonstrate need for aid received scholarships/grants; average award was $17,815. No-need awards available for academics, alumni affiliation, art, athletics, leadership, minority status, music/drama, ROTC, state/district residency.

**Scholarships offered:** *Merit:* University Trustee Scholars Program: Full-tuition; number awarded varies but approximately 30 offered; candidates are selected based on the information supplied on their admission application. University Presidential Scholars Program: Partial tuition; number award varies. University Provosts Scholars Program: Partial tuition; number awarded varies; for students with high academic achievement and usually 30% of admitted students. University Dean's Scholars Program: Partial tuition; number awarded varies; for students with high academic achievement and usually 20% of admitted students. *Athletic:* 24 full-time freshmen received athletic scholarships; average amount $22,252.

## FINANCIAL AID PROCEDURES
**Forms required:** FAFSA, state aid form.
**Dates and Deadlines:** Priority date 2/15; no closing date. Applicants notified on a rolling basis starting 3/1; must reply by 5/1 or within 2 week(s) of notification.

## CONTACT
Sandra Mervius, Director of Financial Aid
Admissions Center, 100 Hofstra University, Hempstead, NY 11549-1450
(516) 463-8000

# Houghton College

Houghton, New York
www.houghton.edu — Federal Code: 002734

**4-year private** liberal arts college in rural community, affiliated with Wesleyan Church.
**Enrollment:** 1,009 undergrads, 2% part-time. 267 full-time freshmen.
**Selectivity:** Admits over 75% of applicants.

## BASIC COSTS (2015-2016)
**Tuition and fees:** $29,458.
**Per-credit charge:** $1,230.
**Room and board:** $8,498.
**Additional info:** Tuition/fee waivers available for minority students.

## FINANCIAL AID PICTURE (2015-2016)
**Students with need:** Out of 243 full-time freshmen who applied for aid, 227 were judged to have need. Of these, 226 received aid, and 62 had their full need met. Average financial aid package met 81% of need; average scholarship/grant was $12,334; average loan was $4,067. For part-time students, average financial aid package was $3,762.
**Students without need:** 30 full-time freshmen who did not demonstrate need for aid received scholarships/grants; average award was $17,178. No-need awards available for academics, alumni affiliation, art, minority status, music/drama, religious affiliation, ROTC, state/district residency.
**Scholarships offered:** Academic Scholarships: $4,000-$10,000. Heritage Scholarships: $12,000. Phi Theta Kappa: $4,000. Art Scholarships: $1,000-$5,000 (based on art portfolio). Music Scholarships: $1,000-$12,500 (based on audition). Excellence Scholarships: $1,000-$4,000. James S. Luckey Scholarship: full tuition.
**Additional info:** Loan Repayment Assistance Program (LRAP) to all new students. Offered through a partnership with the LRAP Foundation, this program covers up to 100% of all federal, private, and parent PLUS loans at no cost to the student or parent.

## FINANCIAL AID PROCEDURES
**Forms required:** FAFSA.
**Dates and Deadlines:** Priority date 3/1; no closing date. Applicants notified on a rolling basis starting 3/1.
**Transfers:** No deadline. Applicants notified on a rolling basis starting 3/15; must reply by 5/1 or within 4 week(s) of notification.

## CONTACT
Marianne Loper, Director of Student Financial Services
1 Willard Avenue/PO Box 128, Houghton, NY 14744-0128
(585) 567-9328

## Institute of Design and Construction
Brooklyn, New York
www.idc.edu                    Federal Code: 012107

**2-year private** junior and technical college in very large city.
**Enrollment:** 65 undergrads.
**Selectivity:** Open admission.

### BASIC COSTS (2015-2016)
**Tuition and fees:** $10,950.
**Per-credit charge:** $355.

### FINANCIAL AID PICTURE
**Students with need:** Need-based aid available for full-time and part-time students.
**Students without need:** This college awards aid only to students with need.

### FINANCIAL AID PROCEDURES
**Forms required:** FAFSA, state aid form, institutional form.
**Dates and Deadlines:** Applicants notified on a rolling basis starting 3/1; must reply within 4 week(s) of notification.
**Transfers:** Priority date 7/1; no deadline. Applicants notified on a rolling basis starting 7/1; must reply within 4 week(s) of notification.

### CONTACT
Giovanny Santana, Assistant Director of Financial Aid
141 Willoughby Street, Brooklyn, NY 11201-5380
(718) 855-3661 ext. 19

## Iona College
New Rochelle, New York
www.iona.edu                   Federal Code: 002737

**4-year private** business and liberal arts college in small city, affiliated with Roman Catholic Church.
**Enrollment:** 3,018 undergrads, 2% part-time. 838 full-time freshmen.
**Selectivity:** Admits over 75% of applicants.

### BASIC COSTS (2015-2016)
**Tuition and fees:** $35,324.
**Per-credit charge:** $1,100.
**Room and board:** $13,980.

### FINANCIAL AID PICTURE
**Students with need:** Need-based aid available for full-time and part-time students. Work study available nights.
**Students without need:** No-need awards available for academics, alumni affiliation, athletics.

### FINANCIAL AID PROCEDURES
**Forms required:** FAFSA, state aid form.
**Dates and Deadlines:** Priority date 4/15; no closing date. Applicants notified on a rolling basis starting 3/1; must reply by 5/1 or within 2 week(s) of notification.
**Transfers:** No deadline. Applicants notified on a rolling basis starting 3/1; must reply within 2 week(s) of notification.

### CONTACT
Mary Grant, Director of Financial Aid
715 North Avenue, New Rochelle, NY 10801-1890
(914) 633-2497

## Island Drafting and Technical Institute
Amityville, New York
www.idti.edu                   Federal Code: 007375

**2-year for-profit** technical and career college in large town.
**Enrollment:** 110 undergrads.
**Selectivity:** Open admission; but selective for some programs.

### BASIC COSTS (2015-2016)
**Tuition and fees:** $16,200.
**Per-credit charge:** $525.

### FINANCIAL AID PICTURE
**Students with need:** Need-based aid available for full-time students.
**Students without need:** This college awards aid only to students with need.

### FINANCIAL AID PROCEDURES
**Dates and Deadlines:** Applicants notified on a rolling basis.

### CONTACT
Daniel Greener, Financial Aid Office
128 Broadway, Amityville, NY 11701-2704
(631) 691-8733 ext. 115

## Ithaca College
Ithaca, New York              Federal Code: 002739
www.ithaca.edu                CSS Code: 2325

**4-year private** health science and liberal arts college in large town.
**Enrollment:** 6,278 undergrads, 1% part-time. 1,808 full-time freshmen.
**Selectivity:** Admits 50 to 75% of applicants.

### BASIC COSTS (2016-2017)
**Tuition and fees:** $41,776.
**Per-credit charge:** $1,393.
**Room and board:** $14,990.
**Additional info:** Tuition/fee waivers available for minority students.

### FINANCIAL AID PICTURE (2015-2016)
**Students with need:** Out of 1,561 full-time freshmen who applied for aid, 1,273 were judged to have need. Of these, 1,273 received aid, and 656 had their full need met. Average financial aid package met 90% of need; average scholarship/grant was $25,597; average loan was $5,528. For part-time students, average financial aid package was $20,727.
**Students without need:** 423 full-time freshmen who did not demonstrate need for aid received scholarships/grants; average award was $14,714. No-need awards available for academics, alumni affiliation, leadership, minority status, music/drama, ROTC.
**Scholarships offered:** President's Scholarship: $20,000; approximately top 10% of applicants. Dean's Scholarship: $13,000-$17,000; approximately top 11% to 35% of applicants. ALANA Scholarship: $2,000-$5,000; representatives of minority groups who show excellent academic achievement. Flora Brown Award: $10,000-$13,000. MLK Scholarship: $25,000 to full tuition; academic excellence; community service involvement; approximately 15. Ithaca Leadership Scholarship: $7,000; record of leadership and above average academic performance; approximately 120. Ithaca Premier Talent Scholarship: maximum $18,000 for music and theater majors; approximately 35. Park Scholar Achievement award: full cost of attendance; outstanding achievement in communications; approximately 20. Ithaca College Merit Scholarship, and Ithaca College National Merit Recognition Award: up to $2,000; for students who designate Ithaca their first-choice institution to National Merit Scholarship Corporation.

### FINANCIAL AID PROCEDURES
**Forms required:** FAFSA, CSS PROFILE.
**Dates and Deadlines:** Priority date 2/1; no closing date. Applicants notified on a rolling basis starting 2/15; must reply by 5/1.

**Transfers:** No deadline. Applicants notified on a rolling basis starting 2/15; must reply by 5/1. All institutional need-based and merit awards available for freshmen are also available for transfers.

**CONTACT**
Lisa Hoskey, Director, Student Financial Services
953 Danby Road, Ithaca, NY 14850-7002
(607) 274-3131

# Jamestown Business College
Jamestown, New York
www.jamestownbusinesscollege.edu
Federal Code: 008495

**2-year for-profit** business and junior college in large town.
**Enrollment:** 296 undergrads, 3% part-time. 95 full-time freshmen.
**Selectivity:** Admits over 75% of applicants.

**BASIC COSTS (2015-2016)**
**Tuition and fees:** $12,300.

**FINANCIAL AID PICTURE (2014-2015)**
**Students with need:** 79% of average financial aid package awarded as scholarships/grants, 21% awarded as loans/jobs. Need-based aid available for part-time students.
**Students without need:** No-need awards available for academics.

**FINANCIAL AID PROCEDURES**
**Forms required:** FAFSA, state aid form.
**Dates and Deadlines:** Applicants notified on a rolling basis starting 2/15.
**Transfers:** Priority date 3/1; no deadline. Applicants notified on a rolling basis starting 5/1.

**CONTACT**
Diane Sturzenbecker, Financial Aid Officer
7 Fairmount Avenue, Jamestown, NY 14701-0429
(716) 664-5100

# Jamestown Community College
Jamestown, New York
www.sunyjcc.edu
Federal Code: 002869

**2-year public** community college in large town.
**Enrollment:** 2,889 undergrads, 23% part-time. 866 full-time freshmen.
**Selectivity:** Open admission; but selective for some programs.

**BASIC COSTS (2015-2016)**
**Tuition and fees:** $5,152; out-of-state residents $9,622.
**Per-credit charge:** $188; out-of-state residents $377.
**Room and board:** $10,740.

**FINANCIAL AID PICTURE (2015-2016)**
**Students with need:** Out of 816 full-time freshmen who applied for aid, 680 were judged to have need. Of these, 679 received aid, and 18 had their full need met. Need-based aid available for part-time students.
**Students without need:** 37 full-time freshmen who did not demonstrate need for aid received scholarships/grants; average award was $4,287. No-need awards available for academics, alumni affiliation, art, athletics, music/drama, state/district residency.
**Scholarships offered:** 100% resident tuition scholarship (less federal and state grants) for students who apply for admissions by 3/1 and are in the top 20% of their high school graduating class with Regents diploma if residents of Chautauqua, Cattaraugus, or Allegany counties. Guaranteed in-state tuition rate for students in Warren, Potter, McKean, Forest, Elk and Cameron counties in Pennsylvania, in top 20% of graduating class with an academic diploma.

**FINANCIAL AID PROCEDURES**
**Forms required:** FAFSA, state aid form.
**Dates and Deadlines:** Priority date 3/1; no closing date. Applicants notified on a rolling basis starting 4/15.

**CONTACT**
Laurie Vorp, Executive Director of Student Finance and Records
525 Falconer Street, Jamestown, NY 14702-0020
(800) 388-8557

# Jefferson Community College
Watertown, New York
www.sunyjefferson.edu
Federal Code: 002870

**2-year public** community college in large town.
**Enrollment:** 3,009 undergrads, 29% part-time. 767 full-time freshmen.
**Selectivity:** Open admission; but selective for some programs.

**BASIC COSTS (2015-2016)**
**Tuition and fees:** $4,739; out-of-state residents $7,019.
**Per-credit charge:** $174; out-of-state residents $269.
**Room and board:** $10,050.

**FINANCIAL AID PICTURE**
**Students with need:** Need-based aid available for full-time and part-time students.
**Students without need:** This college awards aid only to students with need.

**FINANCIAL AID PROCEDURES**
**Forms required:** FAFSA, state aid form, institutional form.
**Dates and Deadlines:** Priority date 4/1; closing date 8/15. Applicants notified on a rolling basis starting 4/15; must reply within 2 week(s) of notification.
**Transfers:** No deadline.

**CONTACT**
James Ambrose, Director of Financial Aid
1220 Coffeen Street, Watertown, NY 13601
(315) 786-2355

# Jewish Theological Seminary of America
New York, New York
www.jtsa.edu/list

**4-year private** liberal arts college in very large city, affiliated with Jewish faith.
**Enrollment:** 158 undergrads. 41 full-time freshmen.
**Selectivity:** Admits 50 to 75% of applicants.

**BASIC COSTS (2015-2016)**
**Tuition and fees:** $20,340.
**Per-credit charge:** $1,080.
**Room only:** $11,720.
**Additional info:** Tuition/fee waivers available for adults.

**FINANCIAL AID PICTURE (2014-2015)**
**Students with need:** Out of 20 full-time freshmen who applied for aid, 16 were judged to have need. Of these, 16 received aid, and 7 had their full need met. Average financial aid package met 88% of need; average scholarship/grant was $34,537; average loan was $3,138. Need-based aid available for part-time students.
**Students without need:** 8 full-time freshmen who did not demonstrate need for aid received scholarships/grants; average award was $10,000. No-need awards available for academics, leadership.

**FINANCIAL AID PROCEDURES**
**Forms required:** FAFSA, institutional form.

**Dates and Deadlines:** Closing date 3/1. Applicants notified by 4/1; must reply within 2 week(s) of notification.

**CONTACT**
Linda Levine, Registrar/Director of Financial Aid
3080 Broadway, New York, NY 10025
(212) 678-8007

## Juilliard School
New York, New York
www.juilliard.edu

Federal Code: 002742
CSS Code: 2340

**4-year private** music and performing arts college in very large city.
**Enrollment:** 489 undergrads. 109 full-time freshmen.
**Selectivity:** Admits less than 50% of applicants.

**BASIC COSTS (2016-2017)**
**Tuition and fees:** $41,460.
**Room and board:** $15,380.

**FINANCIAL AID PICTURE (2015-2016)**
**Students with need:** 84% of average financial aid package awarded as scholarships/grants, 16% awarded as loans/jobs. Need-based aid available for part-time students. Work study available nights, weekends, and for part-time students.
**Students without need:** No-need awards available for music/drama.

**FINANCIAL AID PROCEDURES**
**Forms required:** FAFSA, CSS PROFILE, institutional form.
**Dates and Deadlines:** Closing date 3/1. Applicants notified by 4/1; must reply by 5/1.
**Transfers:** Applicants notified by 4/1; must reply by 5/1 or within 2 week(s) of notification.

**CONTACT**
Tina Gonzalez, Director of Financial Aid
60 Lincoln Center Plaza, New York, NY 10023-6588
(212) 799-5000 ext. 211

## Keuka College
Keuka Park, New York
www.keuka.edu

Federal Code: 002744

**4-year private** liberal arts college in rural community, affiliated with American Baptist Churches in the USA.
**Enrollment:** 1,717 undergrads, 22% part-time. 318 full-time freshmen.
**Selectivity:** Admits over 75% of applicants.

**BASIC COSTS (2016-2017)**
**Tuition and fees:** $29,506.
**Per-credit charge:** $952.
**Room and board:** $11,070.

**FINANCIAL AID PICTURE (2015-2016)**
**Students with need:** Out of 312 full-time freshmen who applied for aid, 293 were judged to have need. Of these, 293 received aid, and 26 had their full need met. For part-time students, average financial aid package was $7,401.
**Students without need:** 22 full-time freshmen who did not demonstrate need for aid received scholarships/grants; average award was $13,303. No-need awards available for academics, alumni affiliation, leadership, minority status.

**FINANCIAL AID PROCEDURES**
**Forms required:** FAFSA.

**Dates and Deadlines:** Priority date 3/15; no closing date. Applicants notified on a rolling basis starting 2/1; must reply by 5/1 or within 2 week(s) of notification.

**CONTACT**
Jen Bates, Executive Directror of Financial Aid
141 Central Avenue, Keuka Park, NY 14478-0098
(315) 279-5232

## The King's College
New York, New York
www.tkc.edu

Federal Code: 040953

**4-year private** liberal arts college in very large city, affiliated with nondenominational tradition.
**Enrollment:** 490 undergrads, 2% part-time. 143 full-time freshmen.
**Selectivity:** Admits less than 50% of applicants.

**BASIC COSTS (2015-2016)**
**Tuition and fees:** $33,270.
**Per-credit charge:** $1,370.
**Room only:** $13,000.

**FINANCIAL AID PICTURE (2014-2015)**
**Students with need:** Out of 127 full-time freshmen who applied for aid, 107 were judged to have need. Of these, 107 received aid, and 8 had their full need met. Average financial aid package met 60% of need; average scholarship/grant was $21,130; average loan was $2,579. For part-time students, average financial aid package was $10,887.
**Students without need:** 34 full-time freshmen who did not demonstrate need for aid received scholarships/grants; average award was $15,411. No-need awards available for academics, leadership.
**Scholarships offered:** Presidential Scholarships: unlimited number; based on composite SAT/ACT and high school GPA.

**FINANCIAL AID PROCEDURES**
**Forms required:** FAFSA.
**Dates and Deadlines:** Priority date 3/15; no closing date. Applicants notified on a rolling basis starting 2/15.

**CONTACT**
Anna Peters, Director of Financial Aid
56 Broadway, New York, NY 10004
(646) 237-8902

## Le Moyne College
Syracuse, New York
www.lemoyne.edu

Federal Code: 002748

**4-year private** liberal arts college in small city, affiliated with Roman Catholic Church.
**Enrollment:** 2,769 undergrads, 10% part-time. 678 full-time freshmen.
**Selectivity:** Admits 50 to 75% of applicants.

**BASIC COSTS (2016-2017)**
**Tuition and fees:** $33,030.
**Per-credit charge:** $672.
**Room and board:** $12,970.

**FINANCIAL AID PICTURE (2014-2015)**
**Students with need:** Out of 647 full-time freshmen who applied for aid, 570 were judged to have need. Of these, 570 received aid, and 154 had their full need met. Average financial aid package met 80% of need; average scholarship/grant was $20,903; average loan was $3,573. For part-time students, average financial aid package was $6,417.

**Students without need:** 59 full-time freshmen who did not demonstrate need for aid received scholarships/grants; average award was $7,098. No-need awards available for academics, alumni affiliation, athletics, leadership, minority status, ROTC.

**Scholarships offered: *Merit:*** Presidential Scholarship: $23,750 per year for 4 years; based on 95% GPA, 1300 SAT/29 ACT; must maintain 3.25 GPA. Dean Scholarship: $17,500 per year for 4 years; based on 92% GPA, 1200 SAT/27 ACT; must maintain 3.0 GPA. Ignatian Scholarship: $17,500 per year for 4 years; awarded to students from Jesuit high schools with superior academic records; must maintain 3.0 GPA. Leader Scholarship: $12,500 per year for 4 years; based on 85% GPA, 1050 SAT/22 ACT; must remain in good academic standing. Loyola Scholarship: $17,500 per year for 4 years; for multicultural students with demonstrated academic excellence; must maintain 3.0 GPA. Academic scholarships are based on review of the student's admission application. The annual strength of the applicant pool will dictate how many awards will be offered at each level. To be considered, students must file an admission application by February 1. ***Athletic:*** 58 full-time freshmen received athletic scholarships; average amount $9,585.

**Additional info:** Parent loan program at low interest, monthly payment plans and alternative loans for students.

## FINANCIAL AID PROCEDURES

**Forms required:** FAFSA, state aid form.

**Dates and Deadlines:** Priority date 2/15; no closing date. Applicants notified by 3/15; must reply by 5/1 or within 2 week(s) of notification.

**Transfers:** Priority date 5/1; no deadline. Applicants notified on a rolling basis starting 3/15; must reply by 5/1 or within 2 week(s) of notification.

## CONTACT

Sharon Halpin, Director of Financial Aid
1419 Salt Springs Road, Syracuse, NY 13214-1301
(315) 445-4400

## LIM College

New York, New York
www.limcollege.edu                     Federal Code: 007466

**4-year for-profit** business college in very large city.
**Enrollment:** 1,515 undergrads, 6% part-time. 285 full-time freshmen.
**Selectivity:** Admits over 75% of applicants.

### BASIC COSTS (2016-2017)
**Tuition and fees:** $25,725.
**Per-credit charge:** $805.
**Room and board:** $20,350.

### FINANCIAL AID PICTURE (2014-2015)
**Students with need:** Out of 269 full-time freshmen who applied for aid, 209 were judged to have need. Of these, 205 received aid, and 5 had their full need met. Average financial aid package met 34% of need; average scholarship/grant was $9,624; average loan was $3,288. For part-time students, average financial aid package was $4,913.

**Students without need:** 40 full-time freshmen who did not demonstrate need for aid received scholarships/grants; average award was $5,125. No-need awards available for academics, leadership, state/district residency.

**Scholarships offered:** LIM College Fashion Scholarship (Honors) Program: Awards of $6,000 and above are available to incoming freshmen with a minimum 90 average and a SAT score of 1100 or above on the Critical Reading and Math sections (24 on the ACT). Students will be evaluated on a first come, first served basis. Additional academic criteria will be considered prior to inviting students into the program.

### FINANCIAL AID PROCEDURES
**Forms required:** FAFSA, state aid form.
**Dates and Deadlines:** Priority date 3/1; closing date 11/15. Applicants notified on a rolling basis starting 2/25; must reply by 7/31 or within 2 week(s) of notification.

**Transfers:** No deadline. Applicants notified on a rolling basis starting 2/25.

## CONTACT

Christopher Barto, Dean of Student Financial Services
12 East 53rd Street, New York, NY 10022
(212) 752-1530

## LIU Brooklyn

Brooklyn, New York
http://liu.edu/brooklyn              Federal Code: 002751

**4-year private** university and liberal arts college in very large city.
**Enrollment:** 4,568 undergrads, 12% part-time. 808 full-time freshmen.
**Selectivity:** Admits over 75% of applicants.

### BASIC COSTS (2015-2016)
**Tuition and fees:** $35,546.
**Per-credit charge:** $1,051.
**Room and board:** $12,600.

### FINANCIAL AID PICTURE (2015-2016)
**Students with need:** Out of 704 full-time freshmen who applied for aid, 679 were judged to have need. Of these, 679 received aid, and 42 had their full need met. Average financial aid package met 55% of need; average scholarship/grant was $16,243; average loan was $3,682. For part-time students, average financial aid package was $6,646.

**Students without need:** 6 full-time freshmen who did not demonstrate need for aid received scholarships/grants; average award was $13,750. No-need awards available for academics, alumni affiliation, art, athletics, leadership, music/drama, ROTC.

**Scholarships offered:** 65 full-time freshmen received athletic scholarships; average amount $28,162.

### FINANCIAL AID PROCEDURES
**Forms required:** FAFSA.
**Dates and Deadlines:** Priority date 2/15; no closing date. Applicants notified on a rolling basis starting 2/1; must reply within 4 week(s) of notification.
**Transfers:** No deadline. Applicants notified on a rolling basis.

### CONTACT
Joseph Schaefer, Chief of Administration and Student Affairs
1 University Plaza, Brooklyn, NY 11201-8423
(718) 488-1037

## LIU Post

Brookville, New York
www.liu.edu/post                    Federal Code: 002751

**4-year private** university and liberal arts college in small town.
**Enrollment:** 3,443 undergrads, 11% part-time. 466 full-time freshmen.
**Selectivity:** Admits over 75% of applicants.

### BASIC COSTS (2015-2016)
**Tuition and fees:** $35,446.
**Per-credit charge:** $1,051.
**Room and board:** $13,138.

### FINANCIAL AID PICTURE (2014-2015)
**Students with need:** Out of 440 full-time freshmen who applied for aid, 371 were judged to have need. Of these, 371 received aid, and 61 had their full need met. Average financial aid package met 58% of need; average scholarship/grant was $10,335; average loan was $3,468. For part-time students, average financial aid package was $5,653.

**Students without need:** 24 full-time freshmen who did not demonstrate need for aid received scholarships/grants; average award was $16,344. No-need awards available for academics, alumni affiliation, art, athletics, leadership, music/drama, ROTC.

**Scholarships offered:** 79 full-time freshmen received athletic scholarships; average amount $13,850.

**FINANCIAL AID PROCEDURES**
**Forms required:** FAFSA, state aid form.
**Dates and Deadlines:** Priority date 2/15; closing date 2/15. Applicants notified on a rolling basis starting 2/1; must reply by 5/1 or within 2 week(s) of notification.
**Transfers:** No deadline. Applicants notified on a rolling basis.

**CONTACT**
Joseph Schaefer
720 Northern Boulevard, Brookville, NY 11548-1300
(516) 299-2553

## Long Island Business Institute
Flushing, New York
www.libi.edu                    Federal Code: 020937

**2-year for-profit** business and career college in very large city.
**Enrollment:** 1,104 undergrads, 15% part-time. 181 full-time freshmen.
**Selectivity:** Admits over 75% of applicants.

**BASIC COSTS (2016-2017)**
**Tuition and fees:** $14,769.

**FINANCIAL AID PICTURE (2015-2016)**
**Students with need:** For part-time students, average financial aid package was $2,150.
**Students without need:** No-need awards available for academics.

**FINANCIAL AID PROCEDURES**
**Forms required:** FAFSA, state aid form.
**Dates and Deadlines:** Closing date 5/1. Applicants notified by 1/1; must reply by 4/30.

**CONTACT**
Nazaret Kiregian, Director of Financial Aid
136-18 39th Avenue, 5th Floor, Flushing, NY 11354
(631) 499-7100 ext. 13

## Manhattan College
Riverdale, New York
www.manhattan.edu              Federal Code: 002758

**4-year private** engineering and liberal arts college in very large city, affiliated with Roman Catholic Church.
**Enrollment:** 3,576 undergrads, 5% part-time. 893 full-time freshmen.
**Selectivity:** Admits 50 to 75% of applicants.

**BASIC COSTS (2015-2016)**
**Tuition and fees:** $38,900.
**Room and board:** $14,430.

**FINANCIAL AID PICTURE (2014-2015)**
**Students with need:** Out of 839 full-time freshmen who applied for aid, 830 were judged to have need. Of these, 795 received aid, and 294 had their full need met. Average financial aid package met 80% of need; average scholarship/grant was $21,362. Need-based aid available for part-time students.
**Students without need:** This college awards aid only to students with need.
**Scholarships offered:** 27 full-time freshmen received athletic scholarships; average amount $23,496.

**FINANCIAL AID PROCEDURES**
**Forms required:** FAFSA.

**Dates and Deadlines:** Priority date 3/1; closing date 4/15. Applicants notified on a rolling basis starting 2/15; must reply by 5/1.
**Transfers:** Priority date 4/1; no deadline.

**CONTACT**
Denise Scalzo, Director of Student Financial Aid
4513 Manhattan College Parkway, Riverdale, NY 10471
(718) 862-7100

## Manhattan School of Music
New York, New York            Federal Code: 002759
www.msmnyc.edu                CSS Code: 2396

**4-year private** music college in very large city.
**Enrollment:** 410 undergrads.

**BASIC COSTS (2015-2016)**
**Tuition and fees:** $42,500.
**Per-credit charge:** $1,750.
**Room and board:** $12,260.

**FINANCIAL AID PICTURE**
**Students with need:** Need-based aid available for full-time and part-time students. Work study available nights, weekends, and for part-time students.
**Students without need:** No-need awards available for academics, alumni affiliation, leadership, music/drama.

**FINANCIAL AID PROCEDURES**
**Forms required:** FAFSA, institutional form. Returning International students are required to complete the CSS Profile on a yearly basis.
**Dates and Deadlines:** Closing date 3/1. Applicants notified by 4/1; must reply by 5/1 or within 2 week(s) of notification.
**Transfers:** Applicants notified by 4/1; must reply by 5/1 or within 2 week(s) of notification. CSS PROFILE required for transfer students.

**CONTACT**
Amy Anderson, Associate Dean for Enrollment Management
120 Claremont Avenue, New York, NY 10027-4698
(212) 749-2802 ext. 4463

## Manhattanville College
Purchase, New York
www.manhattanville.edu         Federal Code: 002760

**4-year private** liberal arts and teachers college in small town.
**Enrollment:** 1,744 undergrads. 451 full-time freshmen.
**Selectivity:** Admits 50 to 75% of applicants.

**BASIC COSTS (2015-2016)**
**Tuition and fees:** $36,220.
**Per-credit charge:** $810.
**Room and board:** $14,520.

**FINANCIAL AID PICTURE (2015-2016)**
**Students with need:** Out of 391 full-time freshmen who applied for aid, 355 were judged to have need. Of these, 355 received aid, and 57 had their full need met. Average financial aid package met 68% of need; average scholarship/grant was $5,889; average loan was $3,468. For part-time students, average financial aid package was $8,283.
**Students without need:** 178 full-time freshmen who did not demonstrate need for aid received scholarships/grants; average award was $18,298. No-need awards available for academics, alumni affiliation, art, music/drama.
**Additional info:** Upper level students may earn additional money and academic credit through internship program.

**FINANCIAL AID PROCEDURES**
**Forms required:** FAFSA, state aid form.

**Dates and Deadlines:** Closing date 3/1. Applicants notified on a rolling basis starting 2/15; must reply by 5/1 or within 2 week(s) of notification.
**Transfers:** No deadline.

### CONTACT

Robert Gilmore, Director of Financial Aid
2900 Purchase Street, Purchase, NY 10577
(914) 323-5357

## Mannes College The New School for Music
New York, New York
www.newschool.edu          Federal Code: 002780

**4-year private** music college in very large city.
**Enrollment:** 519 undergrads, 3% part-time. 129 full-time freshmen.
**Selectivity:** Admits 50 to 75% of applicants. GED not accepted.

### BASIC COSTS (2015-2016)
**Tuition and fees:** $43,006.
**Per-credit charge:** $1,430.
**Room and board:** $18,465.

### FINANCIAL AID PICTURE (2014-2015)
**Students with need:** Out of 94 full-time freshmen who applied for aid, 83 were judged to have need. Of these, 83 received aid, and 9 had their full need met. Average financial aid package met 63% of need; average scholarship/grant was $10,086; average loan was $5,594. For part-time students, average financial aid package was $4,961.
**Students without need:** 31 full-time freshmen who did not demonstrate need for aid received scholarships/grants; average award was $15,258. No-need awards available for academics, art, leadership, minority status, music/drama, state/district residency.

### FINANCIAL AID PROCEDURES
**Forms required:** FAFSA, state aid form.
**Dates and Deadlines:** Closing date 3/1. Applicants notified on a rolling basis starting 4/1; must reply within 4 week(s) of notification.

### CONTACT

Lisa Shaheen, Director of Student Financial Aid
79 Fifth Avenue, Floor 5, New York, NY 10003
(212) 229-8930

## Maria College
Albany, New York
www.mariacollege.edu          Federal Code: 002763

**2-year private** health science and liberal arts college in small city.
**Enrollment:** 770 undergrads, 62% part-time. 58 full-time freshmen.
**Selectivity:** Admits less than 50% of applicants.

### BASIC COSTS (2015-2016)
**Tuition and fees:** $13,570.
**Per-credit charge:** $555.

### FINANCIAL AID PICTURE (2014-2015)
**Students with need:** 48% of average financial aid package awarded as scholarships/grants, 52% awarded as loans/jobs. Need-based aid available for part-time students. Work study available nights, weekends, and for part-time students.
**Students without need:** This college awards aid only to students with need.

### FINANCIAL AID PROCEDURES
**Forms required:** FAFSA, state aid form.

**Dates and Deadlines:** Applicants notified on a rolling basis starting 3/1; must reply within 2 week(s) of notification.
**Transfers:** No deadline. Applicants notified on a rolling basis; must reply within 2 week(s) of notification.

### CONTACT

Donna Myers, Financial Aid
700 New Scotland Avenue, Albany, NY 12208
(518) 861-2586

## Marist College
Poughkeepsie, New York
www.marist.edu          Federal Code: 002765

**4-year private** liberal arts college in small city.
**Enrollment:** 5,205 undergrads, 6% part-time. 1,209 full-time freshmen.
**Selectivity:** Admits less than 50% of applicants.

### BASIC COSTS (2015-2016)
**Tuition and fees:** $32,750.
**Per-credit charge:** $634.
**Room and board:** $14,100.
**Additional info:** Tuition/fee waivers available for minority students.

### FINANCIAL AID PICTURE (2015-2016)
**Students with need:** Out of 983 full-time freshmen who applied for aid, 726 were judged to have need. Of these, 726 received aid, and 128 had their full need met. Average financial aid package met 66% of need; average scholarship/grant was $17,763; average loan was $3,917. For part-time students, average financial aid package was $6,981.
**Students without need:** 333 full-time freshmen who did not demonstrate need for aid received scholarships/grants; average award was $8,568. No-need awards available for academics, athletics, music/drama, ROTC, state/district residency.
**Scholarships offered:** *Merit:* Awards vary, as much as $12,000 per recipient. *Athletic:* 90 full-time freshmen received athletic scholarships; average amount $16,855.

### FINANCIAL AID PROCEDURES
**Forms required:** FAFSA. PROFILE required for early decision and early action applicants.
**Dates and Deadlines:** Priority date 2/15; closing date 5/1. Applicants notified on a rolling basis starting 4/1; must reply by 5/1 or within 2 week(s) of notification.
**Transfers:** No deadline. Applicants notified on a rolling basis. FAFSA should be filed as soon as possible after January 1.

### CONTACT

Joseph Weglarz, Executive Director, Student Financial Services
3399 North Road, Poughkeepsie, NY 12601-1387
(845) 575-3230

## Marymount Manhattan College
New York, New York
www.mmm.edu          Federal Code: 002769

**4-year private** liberal arts and performing arts college in very large city.
**Enrollment:** 1,875 undergrads, 9% part-time. 487 full-time freshmen.
**Selectivity:** Admits over 75% of applicants.

### BASIC COSTS (2015-2016)
**Tuition and fees:** $28,700.
**Per-credit charge:** $912.
**Room and board:** $15,500.
**Additional info:** Tuition/fee waivers available for adults.

## FINANCIAL AID PICTURE (2014-2015)

**Students with need:** Out of 409 full-time freshmen who applied for aid, 360 were judged to have need. Of these, 358 received aid, and 20 had their full need met. Average financial aid package met 50% of need; average scholarship/grant was $14,371; average loan was $3,307. For part-time students, average financial aid package was $7,589.

**Students without need:** 48 full-time freshmen who did not demonstrate need for aid received scholarships/grants; average award was $8,802. No-need awards available for academics, art, leadership, music/drama, state/district residency.

**Scholarships offered:** Prospective Freshmen are considered for academic scholarships based on an equal weighting of the SAT (critical reading and math) or ACT Composite score and the academic GPA at time of application. Presidential Scholarship: $12,000 per year. Dean's Scholarship: $10,000 per year. Trustees' Scholarship: $8,000 per year. Recognition Award: $6,000 per year. Talent scholarships: awarded to full-time, degree-seeking entering freshmen in any of the following majors: Acting (BFA), Art (BA), Dance (BA and BFA) and Theatre (BA). Awards range from $1,000 to $6,000 per academic year based on audition or portfolio review.

**Additional info:** Limited international scholarships for top applicants and diplomats.

## FINANCIAL AID PROCEDURES

**Forms required:** FAFSA, state aid form.

**Dates and Deadlines:** Priority date 3/15; no closing date. Applicants notified on a rolling basis starting 3/15; must reply by 5/1 or within 2 week(s) of notification.

**Transfers:** Must submit academic transcripts from previous institutions. Transfer Monitoring is performed in accordance with federal regulations for all transfer students to ensure that students do not exceed their annual federal aid limits.

## CONTACT

Maria DeInnocentiis, Asst Vice President - Financial & Registration Services
221 East 71st Street, New York, NY 10021-4597
(212) 517-0556

## Medaille College

Buffalo, New York
www.medaille.edu
Federal Code: 002777

**4-year private** liberal arts college in large city.
**Enrollment:** 2,160 undergrads.

### BASIC COSTS (2015-2016)

**Tuition and fees:** $26,252.
**Per-credit charge:** $925.
**Room and board:** $12,460.
**Additional info:** Tuition/fee waivers available for adults.

### FINANCIAL AID PICTURE

**Students with need:** Need-based aid available for full-time and part-time students. Work study available nights, weekends, and for part-time students.
**Students without need:** No-need awards available for academics, leadership.
**Scholarships offered:** Available from $1,000 to $10,500.

### FINANCIAL AID PROCEDURES

**Forms required:** FAFSA, state aid form.
**Dates and Deadlines:** Priority date 3/1; no closing date. Applicants notified on a rolling basis starting 3/1; must reply within 2 week(s) of notification.
**Transfers:** Applicants notified on a rolling basis starting 3/1.

### CONTACT

Catherine Buzanski, Director of Financial Aid
18 Agassiz Circle, Buffalo, NY 14214
(716) 880-2256

## Mercy College

Dobbs Ferry, New York
www.mercy.edu
Federal Code: 002772

**4-year private** liberal arts college in large town.
**Enrollment:** 6,410 undergrads, 18% part-time. 725 full-time freshmen.
**Selectivity:** Admits 50 to 75% of applicants.

### BASIC COSTS (2015-2016)

**Tuition and fees:** $18,076.
**Per-credit charge:** $735.
**Room and board:** $13,200.

### FINANCIAL AID PICTURE (2014-2015)

**Students with need:** Out of 701 full-time freshmen who applied for aid, 636 were judged to have need. Of these, 621 received aid, and 20 had their full need met. Average financial aid package met 54% of need; average scholarship/grant was $10,734; average loan was $3,204. For part-time students, average financial aid package was $5,255.

**Students without need:** 47 full-time freshmen who did not demonstrate need for aid received scholarships/grants; average award was $4,298. No-need awards available for academics, athletics.

**Scholarships offered:** 56 full-time freshmen received athletic scholarships; average amount $5,326.

### FINANCIAL AID PROCEDURES

**Forms required:** FAFSA, state aid form.

**Dates and Deadlines:** Priority date 2/15; no closing date. Applicants notified on a rolling basis starting 2/20; must reply by 5/1 or within 2 week(s) of notification.

**Transfers:** No deadline. Applicants notified on a rolling basis starting 4/1; must reply within 2 week(s) of notification.

### CONTACT

Margaret McGrail, Vice President for Student Services
555 Broadway, Dobbs Ferry, NY 10522
(888) 464-6737

## Metropolitan College of New York

New York, New York
www.metropolitan.edu
Federal Code: 009769

**4-year private** business and liberal arts college in very large city.
**Enrollment:** 779 undergrads, 12% part-time. 71 full-time freshmen.
**Selectivity:** Admits 50 to 75% of applicants.

### BASIC COSTS (2016-2017)

**Tuition and fees:** $18,730.
**Per-credit charge:** $747.

### FINANCIAL AID PICTURE (2015-2016)

**Students with need:** Out of 60 full-time freshmen who applied for aid, 59 were judged to have need. Of these, 59 received aid. Average financial aid package met 49% of need; average scholarship/grant was $11,211; average loan was $3,348. For part-time students, average financial aid package was $8,873.

**Students without need:** 7 full-time freshmen who did not demonstrate need for aid received scholarships/grants; average award was $2,677. No-need awards available for academics.

**Additional info:** Limited merit scholarships.

### FINANCIAL AID PROCEDURES

**Forms required:** FAFSA.

### CONTACT

Douane Campbell, Assistant Director of Financial Aid
431 Canal Street, New York, NY 10013-1919
(212) 343-1234 ext. 3500

## Mildred Elley: Albany

Albany, New York
www.mildred-elley.edu                    Federal Code: 022195

**2-year for-profit** junior and career college in small city.
**Enrollment:** 748 undergrads.
**Selectivity:** Open admission; but selective for some programs.

### BASIC COSTS (2015-2016)
**Additional info:** Tuition at time of enrollment locked for 2 years.

### FINANCIAL AID PICTURE
**Students with need:** Need-based aid available for full-time and part-time students. Work study available nights, weekends, and for part-time students.
**Students without need:** This college awards aid only to students with need.

### FINANCIAL AID PROCEDURES
**Forms required:** FAFSA, state aid form.
**Dates and Deadlines:** Applicants notified on a rolling basis starting 7/16; must reply within 2 week(s) of notification.
**Transfers:** No deadline. Applicants notified on a rolling basis starting 7/16; must reply within 2 week(s) of notification.

### CONTACT
Mary Ellen Duffy, Vice President of Financial Aid & Compliance
855 Central Avenue, Albany, NY 12206-1513
(518) 786-0855

## Mildred Elley: New York City

New York, New York
www.mildred-elley.edu                    Federal Code: 022195

**2-year for-profit** junior and career college in very large city.
**Enrollment:** 590 undergrads.
**Selectivity:** Open admission.

### BASIC COSTS (2015-2016)
**Additional info:** Tuition at time of enrollment locked for 2 years.

### FINANCIAL AID PICTURE
**Students with need:** Need-based aid available for full-time and part-time students. Work study available nights, weekends, and for part-time students.
**Students without need:** This college awards aid only to students with need.

### FINANCIAL AID PROCEDURES
**Forms required:** FAFSA, state aid form.
**Transfers:** No deadline. Applicants notified on a rolling basis.

### CONTACT
Mary Ellen Duffy, Director of Financial Aid
25 Broadway, 16th Floor, New York, NY 10004
(212) 380-9004 ext. 1626

## Mohawk Valley Community College

Utica, New York
www.mvcc.edu                             Federal Code: 002871

**2-year public** community college in small city.
**Enrollment:** 4,613 undergrads, 23% part-time. 1,197 full-time freshmen.
**Selectivity:** Open admission; but selective for some programs.

### BASIC COSTS (2015-2016)
**Tuition and fees:** $4,600; out-of-state residents $8,560.
**Per-credit charge:** $160; out-of-state residents $320.
**Room and board:** $10,090.

### FINANCIAL AID PICTURE (2015-2016)
**Students with need:** Out of 1,134 full-time freshmen who applied for aid, 629 were judged to have need. Of these, 629 received aid, and 541 had their full need met. Average financial aid package met 94% of need; average scholarship/grant was $6,517; average loan was $3,563. For part-time students, average financial aid package was $6,682.
**Additional info:** First year students must attend an orientation to receive Federal Work Study funds.

### FINANCIAL AID PROCEDURES
**Forms required:** FAFSA, state aid form.
**Dates and Deadlines:** Priority date 4/15; no closing date. Applicants notified on a rolling basis starting 3/1; must reply within 2 week(s) of notification.
**Transfers:** No deadline. Applicants notified on a rolling basis.

### CONTACT
Michael Pede, Director, Financial Aid
1101 Sherman Drive, Utica, NY 13501-5394
(315) 792-5415

## Molloy College

Rockville Centre, New York
www.molloy.edu                           Federal Code: 002775

**4-year private** liberal arts college in large town, affiliated with Roman Catholic Church.
**Enrollment:** 3,373 undergrads, 19% part-time. 490 full-time freshmen.
**Selectivity:** Admits over 75% of applicants.

### BASIC COSTS (2015-2016)
**Tuition and fees:** $28,030.
**Per-credit charge:** $890.
**Room and board:** $13,940.
**Additional info:** Tuition/fee waivers available for unemployed or children of unemployed.

### FINANCIAL AID PICTURE (2014-2015)
**Students with need:** Out of 465 full-time freshmen who applied for aid, 408 were judged to have need. Of these, 407 received aid, and 52 had their full need met. Average financial aid package met 60% of need; average scholarship/grant was $13,966; average loan was $3,242. For part-time students, average financial aid package was $6,022.
**Students without need:** 43 full-time freshmen who did not demonstrate need for aid received scholarships/grants; average award was $9,419. No-need awards available for academics, alumni affiliation, art, athletics, leadership, music/drama, religious affiliation.
**Scholarships offered:** *Merit:* Scholar's Program: full tuition for entering full-time freshmen; based on academic achievement and college aptitude test scores; minimum 95 percent high school average and either a minimum 1280 combined SAT score (Critical Reading, math) or a minimum 28 on the ACT; for renewal, must maintain at least a 3.5 cumulative index for a maximum of eight consecutive semesters taking a maximum of 16 credits each semester; recipients must also file required financial aid applications annually for renewal; application deadline: December 15. *Athletic:* 7 full-time freshmen received athletic scholarships; average amount $4,849.

### FINANCIAL AID PROCEDURES
**Forms required:** FAFSA, state aid form.
**Dates and Deadlines:** Priority date 4/15; closing date 5/1. Applicants notified on a rolling basis starting 2/1; must reply within 5 week(s) of notification.
**Transfers:** No deadline. All transfer applicants with a minimum of 30 credits and 3.0 GPA automatically considered for transfer scholarships ranging from $1,500-$3,000.

### CONTACT
Ana Lockward, Director of Financial Aid
PO Box 5002, Rockville Centre, NY 11571
(516) 323-4200

## Monroe College
Bronx, New York
www.monroecollege.edu
Federal Code: 004799

**4-year for-profit** business and health science college in very large city.
**Enrollment:** 6,178 undergrads, 23% part-time. 902 full-time freshmen.

**BASIC COSTS (2015-2016)**
**Tuition and fees:** $14,148.
**Per-credit charge:** $552.
**Room and board:** $8,810.

**FINANCIAL AID PICTURE**
**Students with need:** Need-based aid available for full-time and part-time students. Work study available nights, weekends, and for part-time students.
**Students without need:** This college awards aid only to students with need.

**FINANCIAL AID PROCEDURES**
**Forms required:** FAFSA.
**Dates and Deadlines:** Closing date 6/30. Applicants notified on a rolling basis starting 7/1.
**Transfers:** Applicants notified on a rolling basis.

**CONTACT**
Daniel Sharon, Financial Aid Director
2501 Jerome Avenue, Bronx, NY 10468
(718) 933-6700

## Monroe Community College
Rochester, New York
www.monroecc.edu
Federal Code: 002872

**2-year public** community college in large city.
**Enrollment:** 13,385 undergrads, 34% part-time. 2,892 full-time freshmen.
**Selectivity:** Open admission; but selective for some programs.

**BASIC COSTS (2015-2016)**
**Tuition and fees:** $4,043; out-of-state residents $7,843.
**Per-credit charge:** $159; out-of-state residents $318.
**Room only:** $6,170.

**FINANCIAL AID PICTURE**
**Students with need:** Need-based aid available for full-time and part-time students. Work study available nights, weekends, and for part-time students.
**Students without need:** This college awards aid only to students with need.

**FINANCIAL AID PROCEDURES**
**Forms required:** FAFSA, state aid form.
**Dates and Deadlines:** Priority date 3/30; no closing date. Applicants notified on a rolling basis starting 3/15; must reply within 2 week(s) of notification.
**Transfers:** No deadline. Applicants notified on a rolling basis starting 3/15; must reply within 2 week(s) of notification.

**CONTACT**
Jerome St. Croix, Director of Financial Aid
Office of Admissions-Monroe Community College, Rochester, NY 14692-8908
(585) 292-2050

## Mount Saint Mary College
Newburgh, New York
www.msmc.edu
Federal Code: 002778

**4-year private** liberal arts college in large town, affiliated with Roman Catholic Church.

**Enrollment:** 2,140 undergrads, 17% part-time. 422 full-time freshmen.
**Selectivity:** Admits over 75% of applicants.

**BASIC COSTS (2016-2017)**
**Tuition and fees:** $29,048.
**Per-credit charge:** $935.
**Room and board:** $14,104.
**Additional info:** Tuition/fee waivers available for adults.

**FINANCIAL AID PICTURE (2015-2016)**
**Students with need:** Out of 410 full-time freshmen who applied for aid, 360 were judged to have need. Of these, 360 received aid, and 62 had their full need met. Average financial aid package met 65% of need; average scholarship/grant was $16,426; average loan was $3,263. For part-time students, average financial aid package was $7,689.
**Students without need:** 59 full-time freshmen who did not demonstrate need for aid received scholarships/grants; average award was $11,907. No-need awards available for academics, alumni affiliation, leadership, ROTC, state/district residency.
**Scholarships offered:** Presidential Scholarship: approximately 65% of tuition in the year of enrollment; renewable for three years with minimum 3.0 GPA. Merit Awards: $3,000-$7,500; renewable each year with 2.5 GPA. Based on combined SAT/ACT test scores, GPA, and class rank.

**FINANCIAL AID PROCEDURES**
**Forms required:** FAFSA.
**Dates and Deadlines:** Priority date 2/15; closing date 3/1. Applicants notified on a rolling basis starting 3/1; must reply by 5/1.
**Transfers:** Applicants notified on a rolling basis starting 3/15; must reply by 5/1.

**CONTACT**
Barbara Winchell, Director of Financial Aid
330 Powell Avenue, Newburgh, NY 12550
(845) 569-3194

## Nassau Community College
Garden City, New York
www.ncc.edu
Federal Code: 002873

**2-year public** community college in large town.
**Enrollment:** 19,448 undergrads, 36% part-time. 3,813 full-time freshmen.
**Selectivity:** Open admission; but selective for some programs.

**BASIC COSTS (2015-2016)**
**Tuition and fees:** $4,888; out-of-state residents $9,422.
**Per-credit charge:** $189; out-of-state residents $378.

**FINANCIAL AID PICTURE**
**Students with need:** Need-based aid available for full-time and part-time students. Work study available nights, weekends, and for part-time students.
**Students without need:** No-need awards available for academics, minority status.

**FINANCIAL AID PROCEDURES**
**Forms required:** FAFSA, state aid form.
**Dates and Deadlines:** Priority date 6/7; no closing date. Applicants notified on a rolling basis; must reply within 1 week(s) of notification.

**CONTACT**
Patricia Noren, Director, Financial Aid Office
One Education Drive, Garden City, NY 11530
(516) 572-7259

## Nazareth College
Rochester, New York
www.naz.edu                   Federal Code: 002779

**4-year private** liberal arts college in large city.
**Enrollment:** 2,078 undergrads, 5% part-time. 519 full-time freshmen.
**Selectivity:** Admits over 75% of applicants.

**BASIC COSTS (2015-2016)**
**Tuition and fees:** $31,520.
**Per-credit charge:** $718.
**Room and board:** $12,918.
**Additional info:** Tuition/fee waivers available for minority students.

**FINANCIAL AID PICTURE (2015-2016)**
**Students with need:** Out of 497 full-time freshmen who applied for aid, 444 were judged to have need. Of these, 444 received aid, and 178 had their full need met. Average financial aid package met 84% of need; average scholarship/grant was $18,752; average loan was $3,598. For part-time students, average financial aid package was $12,356.
**Students without need:** 75 full-time freshmen who did not demonstrate need for aid received scholarships/grants; average award was $19,337. No-need awards available for academics, art, minority status, music/drama.

**FINANCIAL AID PROCEDURES**
**Forms required:** FAFSA, state aid form.
**Dates and Deadlines:** Closing date 2/15. Applicants notified on a rolling basis starting 2/1; must reply by 5/1.
**Transfers:** No deadline. Applicants notified on a rolling basis.

**CONTACT**
Janice Scheutzow, Director of Financial Aid
4245 East Avenue, Rochester, NY 14618-3790
(585) 389-2310

## New York Career Institute
New York, New York
www.nyci.edu                  Federal Code: 014576

**2-year for-profit** career college in very large city.
**Enrollment:** 420 undergrads.
**Selectivity:** Open admission.

**BASIC COSTS (2016-2017)**
**Tuition and fees:** $13,700.

**FINANCIAL AID PICTURE**
**Students with need:** Need-based aid available for full-time and part-time students. Work study available nights.
**Students without need:** This college awards aid only to students with need.

**FINANCIAL AID PROCEDURES**
**Dates and Deadlines:** Applicants notified on a rolling basis.

**CONTACT**
Brenda Soriano, Director of Student Financial Aid Services
11 Park Place, New York, NY 10007

## New York Institute of Technology
Old Westbury, New York
www.nyit.edu                  Federal Code: 002782

**4-year private** health science college in small town.
**Enrollment:** 3,950 undergrads, 12% part-time. 679 full-time freshmen.
**Selectivity:** Admits 50 to 75% of applicants.

**BASIC COSTS (2015-2016)**
**Tuition and fees:** $33,480.
**Per-credit charge:** $1,095.
**Room and board:** $13,090.
**Additional info:** Room and board cost is for a double at the Old Westbury campus.

**FINANCIAL AID PICTURE (2014-2015)**
**Students with need:** Out of 599 full-time freshmen who applied for aid, 529 were judged to have need. Of these, 527 received aid. For part-time students, average financial aid package was $9,234.
**Students without need:** 101 full-time freshmen who did not demonstrate need for aid received scholarships/grants; average award was $14,178. No-need awards available for academics, alumni affiliation, athletics.
**Scholarships offered:** 11 full-time freshmen received athletic scholarships; average amount $26,986.

**FINANCIAL AID PROCEDURES**
**Forms required:** FAFSA.
**Dates and Deadlines:** Priority date 3/1; no closing date. Applicants notified on a rolling basis starting 3/1; must reply within 4 week(s) of notification.

**CONTACT**
Rosemary Ferrucci, Associate Dean of Financial Aid
Box 8000, Old Westbury, NY 11568
(516) 686-3835

## New York School of Interior Design
New York, New York
www.nysid.edu                 Federal Code: 013606

**4-year private** visual arts college in very large city.
**Enrollment:** 335 undergrads, 62% part-time. 4 full-time freshmen.
**Selectivity:** Admits less than 50% of applicants.

**BASIC COSTS (2016-2017)**
**Tuition and fees:** $30,945.
**Per-credit charge:** $915.
**Room and board:** $21,000.

**FINANCIAL AID PICTURE (2015-2016)**
**Students with need:** Out of 4 full-time freshmen who applied for aid, 4 were judged to have need. Of these, 3 received aid. Average financial aid package met 5% of need; average scholarship/grant was $2,560; average loan was $3,500. For part-time students, average financial aid package was $4,916.
**Students without need:** No-need awards available for academics, art.

**FINANCIAL AID PROCEDURES**
**Forms required:** FAFSA, state aid form.
**Dates and Deadlines:** Priority date 8/1; no closing date. Applicants notified on a rolling basis starting 4/15; must reply within 2 week(s) of notification.
**Transfers:** Applicants notified on a rolling basis starting 4/15; must reply within 2 week(s) of notification.

**CONTACT**
Audrey Zahor, Financial Aid Coordinator
170 East 70th Street, New York, NY 10021-5110
(212) 472-1500 ext. 204

## New York University
New York, New York        Federal Code: 002785
www.nyu.edu               CSS Code: 2562

**4-year private** university in very large city.
**Enrollment:** 25,314 undergrads, 4% part-time. 5,886 full-time freshmen.

## BASIC COSTS (2015-2016)

**Tuition and fees:** $47,750.
**Per-credit charge:** $1,334.
**Room and board:** $17,580.
**Additional info:** Tuition at time of enrollment locked for 4 years.

## FINANCIAL AID PICTURE

**Students with need:** Need-based aid available for full-time and part-time students.

## FINANCIAL AID PROCEDURES

**Forms required:** FAFSA, CSS PROFILE.
**Dates and Deadlines:** Closing date 2/15. Applicants notified by 4/1; must reply by 5/1.
**Transfers:** Priority date 2/15. Applicants notified on a rolling basis; must reply within 3 week(s) of notification. Transfer students must apply for financial aid by November 1st if applicant is a Spring transfer. Spring transfer applicants begin receiving financial aid notification in mid-November. Transfer students must apply for financial aid by April 1st if applicant is a Summer or Fall transfer. Summer and Fall transfer applicants receive financial aid notification throughout the month of May. Fall transfer applicants for the College of Nursing Second Bachelor's Degree Program begin receiving financial aid notification in April.

## CONTACT

M J Knoll-Finn, Vice President for Enrollment Management
665 Broadway, 11th floor, New York, NY 10012-2339
(212) 998-4444

# Niagara County Community College
Sanborn, New York
www.niagaracc.suny.edu          Federal Code: 002874

**2-year public** community college in rural community.
**Enrollment:** 4,701 undergrads, 23% part-time. 1,220 full-time freshmen.
**Selectivity:** Open admission; but selective for some programs.

## BASIC COSTS (2015-2016)

**Tuition and fees:** $4,370; out-of-state residents $10,310.
**Per-credit charge:** $165; out-of-state residents $413.

## FINANCIAL AID PICTURE (2014-2015)

**Students with need:** 43% of average financial aid package awarded as scholarships/grants, 57% awarded as loans/jobs. Need-based aid available for part-time students. Work study available nights.
**Students without need:** This college awards aid only to students with need.
**Additional info:** Assistance offered with placing students in part-time employment through the Job Locator office. Students can charge books and food coupons.

## FINANCIAL AID PROCEDURES

**Forms required:** FAFSA, state aid form.
**Dates and Deadlines:** Priority date 4/1; no closing date. Applicants notified on a rolling basis starting 5/1; must reply within 2 week(s) of notification.
**Transfers:** Must file appropriate state and federal change forms at least 4 weeks before registration date.

## CONTACT

James Trimboli, Director of Financial Aid
3111 Saunders Settlement Road, Sanborn, NY 14132-9460
(716) 614-6266

# Niagara University
Niagara University, New York
www.niagara.edu          Federal Code: 002788

**4-year private** university in small city, affiliated with Roman Catholic Church.
**Enrollment:** 3,133 undergrads, 10% part-time. 643 full-time freshmen.
**Selectivity:** Admits 50 to 75% of applicants.

## BASIC COSTS (2016-2017)

**Tuition and fees:** $30,950.
**Per-credit charge:** $985.
**Room and board:** $12,700.
**Additional info:** Tuition at time of enrollment locked for 4 years.

## FINANCIAL AID PICTURE (2015-2016)

**Students with need:** Out of 589 full-time freshmen who applied for aid, 532 were judged to have need. Of these, 532 received aid, and 282 had their full need met. Average financial aid package met 84% of need; average scholarship/grant was $23,059; average loan was $4,568. For part-time students, average financial aid package was $9,442.
**Students without need:** 94 full-time freshmen who did not demonstrate need for aid received scholarships/grants; average award was $15,765. No-need awards available for academics, athletics, music/drama, ROTC.
**Scholarships offered:** *Merit:* Trustee Scholarship: $17,000-$22,000; minimum 95 average; 1150 SAT or 26 ACT; or 91 average; 1210 SAT or 27 ACT; unlimited. Presidential Scholarship: $16,000; 90 average; 1050 SAT or 23 ACT; or 85 average; 1120 SAT or 24 ACT; unlimited. Achievement Award: $14,000; mid to upper 80 average; 950-1050 SAT or 20-22 ACT; unlimited. Niagara University Grant: $9,000; mid 80 average; SAT above 950 or ACT above 20; unlimited. *Athletic:* 29 full-time freshmen received athletic scholarships; average amount $22,180.
**Additional info:** Opportunity program available for academically and economically disadvantaged students.

## FINANCIAL AID PROCEDURES

**Forms required:** FAFSA, state aid form.
**Dates and Deadlines:** Priority date 2/15; no closing date. Applicants notified on a rolling basis starting 3/1; must reply within 3 week(s) of notification.
**Transfers:** Must reply within 3 week(s) of notification. Academic scholarship available: $14,000 per year (3.75 GPA or higher); $13,000 per year (3.50 - 3.749 GPA); $12,000 per year (3.25-3.49 GPA); $11,000 per year (3.0 to 3.249 GPA); $9,000 per year (2.75-2.99 GPA); $8,000 per year (2.5 to 2.749 GPA).

## CONTACT

Katie Kocsis, Director of Financial Aid
Bailo Hall, Niagara University, NY 14109
(716) 286-8686

# North Country Community College
Saranac Lake, New York
www.nccc.edu          Federal Code: 007111

**2-year public** community college in small town.
**Enrollment:** 2,680 undergrads.
**Selectivity:** Open admission; but selective for some programs.

## BASIC COSTS (2015-2016)

**Tuition and fees:** $5,212; out-of-state residents $11,362.
**Per-credit charge:** $185; out-of-state residents $441.
**Room and board:** $9,480.
**Additional info:** Annual room rate based on single-occupancy bedroom within suite; no double-occupancy rooms available.

## FINANCIAL AID PICTURE

**Students with need:** Need-based aid available for full-time and part-time students. Work study available nights, weekends, and for part-time students.

**Students without need:** This college awards aid only to students with need.

**FINANCIAL AID PROCEDURES**
**Forms required:** FAFSA, state aid form:
**Dates and Deadlines:** Priority date 4/1; no closing date. Applicants notified on a rolling basis starting 4/1; must reply within 3 week(s) of notification.

**CONTACT**
Edwin Trathen, Vice President for Enrollment and Student Services
23 Santanoni Avenue, Saranac Lake, NY 12983
(518) 891-2915 ext. 229

## Nyack College
Nyack, New York
www.nyack.edu                    Federal Code: 002790

**4-year private** liberal arts and seminary college in large town, affiliated with Christian and Missionary Alliance.
**Enrollment:** 1,540 undergrads, 16% part-time. 240 full-time freshmen.
**Selectivity:** Admits over 75% of applicants.

**BASIC COSTS (2016-2017)**
**Tuition and fees:** $24,850.
**Per-credit charge:** $1,020.
**Room and board:** $9,200.

**FINANCIAL AID PICTURE (2014-2015)**
**Students with need:** Out of 217 full-time freshmen who applied for aid, 200 were judged to have need. Of these, 200 received aid, and 36 had their full need met. Average financial aid package met 61% of need; average scholarship/grant was $13,163; average loan was $2,946. For part-time students, average financial aid package was $3,798.
**Students without need:** 40 full-time freshmen who did not demonstrate need for aid received scholarships/grants; average award was $13,211. No-need awards available for academics, alumni affiliation, athletics, leadership, music/drama, religious affiliation, state/district residency.
**Scholarships offered:** 40 full-time freshmen received athletic scholarships; average amount $14,393.

**FINANCIAL AID PROCEDURES**
**Forms required:** FAFSA.
**Dates and Deadlines:** Priority date 3/31; no closing date. Applicants notified on a rolling basis starting 3/1; must reply within 4 week(s) of notification.

**CONTACT**
Dona Schepens, Assistant Treasurer
1 South Boulevard, Nyack, NY 10960-3698
(845) 675-4737

## Onondaga Community College
Syracuse, New York
www.sunyocc.edu                    Federal Code: 002875

**2-year public** community college in small city.
**Enrollment:** 8,009 undergrads, 28% part-time. 2,214 full-time freshmen.
**Selectivity:** Open admission; but selective for some programs.

**BASIC COSTS (2015-2016)**
**Tuition and fees:** $5,014; out-of-state residents $9,444.
**Per-credit charge:** $184; out-of-state residents $368.
**Room and board:** $8,900.

**FINANCIAL AID PICTURE (2014-2015)**
**Students with need:** Out of 2,045 full-time freshmen who applied for aid, 1,822 were judged to have need. Of these, 1,665 received aid, and 68 had their full need met. Average financial aid package met 56% of need; average

scholarship/grant was $5,814; average loan was $2,974. For part-time students, average financial aid package was $3,731.
**Students without need:** This college awards aid only to students with need.

**FINANCIAL AID PROCEDURES**
**Forms required:** FAFSA, state aid form.
**Dates and Deadlines:** Applicants notified on a rolling basis; must reply within 4 week(s) of notification.

**CONTACT**
Rebecca Rose, Director of Financial Aid
4585 West Seneca Turnpike, Syracuse, NY 13215-4585
(315) 498-2291

## Orange County Community College
Middletown, New York
www.sunyorange.edu                    Federal Code: 002876

**2-year public** community college in large town.
**Enrollment:** 5,353 undergrads, 41% part-time. 1,091 full-time freshmen.
**Selectivity:** Open admission; but selective for some programs.

**BASIC COSTS (2015-2016)**
**Tuition and fees:** $5,088; out-of-state residents $9,574.
**Per-credit charge:** $187; out-of-state residents $374.
**Additional info:** Tuition/fee waivers available for unemployed or children of unemployed.

**FINANCIAL AID PICTURE (2014-2015)**
**Students with need:** 57% of average financial aid package awarded as scholarships/grants, 43% awarded as loans/jobs. Need-based aid available for part-time students. Work study available nights.

**FINANCIAL AID PROCEDURES**
**Forms required:** FAFSA, state aid form, institutional form.
**Dates and Deadlines:** Priority date 4/15; closing date 7/1. Applicants notified on a rolling basis starting 4/1; must reply within 4 week(s) of notification.

**CONTACT**
John Ivankovic, Director of Financial Aid
115 South Street, Middletown, NY 10940-0115
(845) 341-4190

## Pace University
New York, New York
www.pace.edu                    Federal Code: 002791

**4-year private** university in very large city.
**Enrollment:** 5,811 undergrads, 9% part-time. 1,498 full-time freshmen.
**Selectivity:** Admits over 75% of applicants.

**BASIC COSTS (2015-2016)**
**Tuition and fees:** $41,281.
**Per-credit charge:** $1,140.
**Room and board:** $17,938.

**FINANCIAL AID PICTURE (2015-2016)**
**Students with need:** Out of 1,151 full-time freshmen who applied for aid, 1,043 were judged to have need. Of these, 1,041 received aid, and 124 had their full need met. Average financial aid package met 70% of need; average scholarship/grant was $26,608; average loan was $3,639. For part-time students, average financial aid package was $5,993.
**Students without need:** 346 full-time freshmen who did not demonstrate need for aid received scholarships/grants; average award was $19,556. No-need awards available for academics, alumni affiliation, athletics, music/drama.

**Scholarships offered:** 1 full-time freshmen received athletic scholarships; average amount $1,500.

**FINANCIAL AID PROCEDURES**

**Forms required:** FAFSA, state aid form.

**Dates and Deadlines:** Priority date 3/15; no closing date. Applicants notified on a rolling basis starting 3/1; must reply by 5/1 or within 2 week(s) of notification.

**Transfers:** Applicants notified on a rolling basis starting 3/1; must reply by 5/1 or within 2 week(s) of notification.

**CONTACT**

Mark Stephens, University Director, Financial Aid
1 Pace Plaza, New York, NY 10038-1598
(212) 346-1300

## Pace University: Pleasantville/Briarcliff

Pleasantville, New York
www.pace.edu                    Federal Code: 002791

**4-year private** university in small town.
**Enrollment:** 2,560 undergrads, 13% part-time. 554 full-time freshmen.
**Selectivity:** Admits over 75% of applicants.

**BASIC COSTS (2015-2016)**

**Tuition and fees:** $41,333.
**Per-credit charge:** $1,140.
**Room and board:** $15,010.

**FINANCIAL AID PICTURE (2015-2016)**

**Students with need:** Out of 516 full-time freshmen who applied for aid, 475 were judged to have need. Of these, 475 received aid, and 101 had their full need met. Average financial aid package met 82% of need; average scholarship/grant was $31,432; average loan was $3,612. For part-time students, average financial aid package was $5,773.

**Students without need:** 68 full-time freshmen who did not demonstrate need for aid received scholarships/grants; average award was $22,933. No-need awards available for academics, alumni affiliation, athletics, music/drama.

**Scholarships offered:** 9 full-time freshmen received athletic scholarships; average amount $10,879.

**FINANCIAL AID PROCEDURES**

**Forms required:** FAFSA, state aid form.

**Dates and Deadlines:** Priority date 3/15; no closing date. Applicants notified on a rolling basis starting 3/1; must reply by 5/1 or within 2 week(s) of notification.

**Transfers:** Applicants notified on a rolling basis starting 3/1; must reply by 5/1 or within 2 week(s) of notification.

**CONTACT**

Mark Stephens, Director of Financial Aid
861 Bedford Road, Pleasantville, NY 10570
(877) 672-1830

## Parsons The New School for Design

New York, New York
www.newschool.edu               Federal Code: 002780

**4-year private** visual arts college in very large city.
**Enrollment:** 4,185 undergrads, 11% part-time. 717 full-time freshmen.
**Selectivity:** Admits 50 to 75% of applicants.

**BASIC COSTS (2015-2016)**

**Tuition and fees:** $44,486.
**Per-credit charge:** $1,480.

**Room and board:** $17,235.

**FINANCIAL AID PICTURE (2014-2015)**

**Students with need:** Out of 314 full-time freshmen who applied for aid, 270 were judged to have need. Of these, 270 received aid, and 30 had their full need met. Average financial aid package met 70% of need; average scholarship/grant was $20,149; average loan was $5,575. For part-time students, average financial aid package was $5,690.

**Students without need:** 366 full-time freshmen who did not demonstrate need for aid received scholarships/grants; average award was $7,437. No-need awards available for academics, art, leadership, minority status, music/drama, state/district residency.

**FINANCIAL AID PROCEDURES**

**Forms required:** FAFSA, state aid form.

**Dates and Deadlines:** Closing date 3/1. Applicants notified on a rolling basis starting 4/1; must reply within 4 week(s) of notification.

**CONTACT**

Lisa Shaheen, Director of Student Financial Aid
79 Fifth Avenue, Floor 5, New York, NY 10003
(212) 229-8930

## Paul Smith's College

Paul Smiths, New York
www.paulsmiths.edu              Federal Code: 002795

**4-year private** culinary school and liberal arts college in rural community.
**Enrollment:** 877 undergrads.

**BASIC COSTS (2015-2016)**

**Tuition and fees:** $24,390.
**Room and board:** $11,680.

**FINANCIAL AID PICTURE**

**Students with need:** Need-based aid available for full-time students. Work study available nights, weekends, and for part-time students.

**Students without need:** No-need awards available for academics.

**Additional info:** Merit aid only for international students; no financial aid application required.

**FINANCIAL AID PROCEDURES**

**Forms required:** FAFSA.

**Dates and Deadlines:** Priority date 3/31; no closing date. Applicants notified on a rolling basis starting 3/5; must reply within 4 week(s) of notification.

**Transfers:** No deadline. Applicants notified by 2/5; must reply within 4 week(s) of notification.

**CONTACT**

Mary Ellen Chamberlain, Director of Financial Aid
PO Box 265, Routes 30 & 86, Paul Smiths, NY 12970-0265
(518) 327-6220

## Phillips Beth Israel School of Nursing

New York, New York
www.pbisn.edu                   Federal Code: 006438

**2-year private** nursing college in very large city.
**Enrollment:** 252 undergrads.

**BASIC COSTS (2015-2016)**

**Tuition and fees:** $24,120.
**Per-credit charge:** $500.

**FINANCIAL AID PICTURE**

**Students with need:** Need-based aid available for full-time and part-time students.

**Scholarships offered:** PVH Scholarship Program: full nursing course tuition; based on academic achievement. Karpas Scholarship Program: $3,000 a year awarded to senior students; based on academic achievement.

## FINANCIAL AID PROCEDURES

**Forms required:** FAFSA, state aid form, institutional form.
**Dates and Deadlines:** Closing date 6/30. Applicants notified by 8/1; must reply within 3 week(s) of notification.
**Transfers:** Priority date 6/1. Applicants notified by 8/1; must reply within 3 week(s) of notification.

## CONTACT

Thomas Zarkos, Financial Aid Director
776 Sixth Avenue, Fourth Floor, New York, NY 10001
(212) 614-6104

## Pratt Institute

Brooklyn, New York
www.pratt.edu          Federal Code: 002798

**4-year private** university and visual arts college in very large city.
**Enrollment:** 3,189 undergrads, 3% part-time. 703 full-time freshmen.
**Selectivity:** Admits 50 to 75% of applicants.

## BASIC COSTS (2016-2017)

**Tuition and fees:** $48,154.
**Per-credit charge:** $1,488.
**Room and board:** $12,026.

## FINANCIAL AID PICTURE

**Students with need:** Need-based aid available for full-time and part-time students.
**Students without need:** No-need awards available for academics.

## FINANCIAL AID PROCEDURES

**Forms required:** FAFSA, state aid form.
**Dates and Deadlines:** Closing date 3/1. Applicants notified on a rolling basis starting 4/15; must reply by 5/15.
**Transfers:** Must reply by 5/1 or within 2 week(s) of notification.

## CONTACT

Nedzad Goga, Director of Financial Aid
200 Willoughby Avenue, Brooklyn, NY 11205-3817
(718) 636-3519

## Rensselaer Polytechnic Institute

Troy, New York          Federal Code: 002803
www.rpi.edu          CSS Code: 2757

**4-year private** university in small city.
**Enrollment:** 5,781 undergrads. 1,379 full-time freshmen.
**Selectivity:** Admits less than 50% of applicants.

## BASIC COSTS (2015-2016)

**Tuition and fees:** $49,341.
**Per-credit charge:** $2,000.
**Room and board:** $14,095.
**Additional info:** Freshmen are required to have a laptop. Students may purchase a university-subsidized laptop costing approximately $1,650, or they may bring one with them but it must contain the software and capabilities required to complete the coursework.

## FINANCIAL AID PICTURE (2015-2016)

**Students with need:** Out of 1,065 full-time freshmen who applied for aid, 922 were judged to have need. Of these, 922 received aid, and 246 had their full need met. Average financial aid package met 87% of need; average scholarship/grant was $35,340; average loan was $4,695.

**Students without need:** 286 full-time freshmen who did not demonstrate need for aid received scholarships/grants; average award was $16,511. No-need awards available for academics, alumni affiliation, art, athletics, leadership, minority status, music/drama, ROTC.
**Scholarships offered:** *Merit:* Rensselaer Medals: $15,000; awarded by participating high schools for excellence in science and mathematics. *Athletic:* 12 full-time freshmen received athletic scholarships; average amount $60,564.

## FINANCIAL AID PROCEDURES

**Forms required:** FAFSA, CSS PROFILE.
**Dates and Deadlines:** Closing date 2/1. Applicants notified by 3/12.
**Transfers:** No deadline. Applicants notified on a rolling basis starting 3/31. Entering transfer students must complete two applications to apply for institutional and federal need-based aid: FAFSA and Transfer Financial Aid Application/Verification Worksheet (available upon acceptance). A number of special transfer scholarships available each year.

## CONTACT

Larry Chambers, Director of Financial Aid
110 Eighth Street, Troy, NY 12180-3590
(518) 276-6813

## Roberts Wesleyan College

Rochester, New York
www.roberts.edu          Federal Code: 002805

**4-year private** liberal arts college in large city, affiliated with Free Methodist Church of North America.
**Enrollment:** 1,282 undergrads.

## BASIC COSTS (2015-2016)

**Tuition and fees:** $29,036.
**Room and board:** $10,038.

## FINANCIAL AID PICTURE

**Students with need:** Need-based aid available for full-time and part-time students. Work study available nights, weekends, and for part-time students.
**Students without need:** No-need awards available for academics, alumni affiliation, art, athletics, music/drama, religious affiliation, ROTC.
**Additional info:** Dollars for Scholars offer matching grants of up to $750.

## FINANCIAL AID PROCEDURES

**Forms required:** FAFSA, state aid form.
**Dates and Deadlines:** Priority date 3/15; no closing date. Applicants notified on a rolling basis starting 2/28; must reply by 5/1 or within 2 week(s) of notification.
**Transfers:** No deadline. Applicants notified on a rolling basis starting 2/28; must reply within 3 week(s) of notification.

## CONTACT

Stephen Field, Director of Student Financial Services
2301 Westside Drive, Rochester, NY 14624-1997
(585) 594-6150

## Rochester Institute of Technology

Rochester, New York
www.rit.edu          Federal Code: 002806

**4-year private** university in large city.
**Enrollment:** 12,874 undergrads, 3% part-time. 2,903 full-time freshmen.
**Selectivity:** Admits 50 to 75% of applicants.

## BASIC COSTS (2015-2016)

**Tuition and fees:** $37,124.
**Per-credit charge:** $1,331.

**Room and board:** $11,918.

**Additional info:** Tuition/fee waivers available for unemployed or children of unemployed.

## FINANCIAL AID PICTURE (2015-2016)

**Students with need:** Out of 2,613 full-time freshmen who applied for aid, 2,247 were judged to have need. Of these, 2,247 received aid, and 1,798 had their full need met. Average financial aid package met 87% of need; average scholarship/grant was $22,000; average loan was $3,600. For part-time students, average financial aid package was $9,500.

**Students without need:** 550 full-time freshmen who did not demonstrate need for aid received scholarships/grants; average award was $12,000. No-need awards available for academics, art, leadership, ROTC.

**Scholarships offered:** Presidential Scholarships: $10,000-$16,000 per year; Qualifications: secondary school rank in the top 15% of high school class with 1330 or higher SAT combined score or ACT Composite of 29 or higher. Achievement Scholarships: $7,000-$10,000 per year; Qualifications A 1210 or higher SAT combined score or ACT Composite of 27 or higher and a B+ average in a strong college preparatory program.

**Additional info:** Most juniors and seniors participate in cooperative education program, earning an average $4,500-$6,500 per 3-month employment period through paid employment in jobs related to major.

## FINANCIAL AID PROCEDURES

**Forms required:** FAFSA, state aid form.

**Dates and Deadlines:** Priority date 3/1; no closing date. Applicants notified on a rolling basis starting 3/15; must reply by 5/1.

**Transfers:** Priority date 3/15. Applicants notified on a rolling basis starting 4/1; must reply by 5/1. Special merit scholarship programs available specifically for transfers with high GPA.

## CONTACT

Verna Hazen, Associate Vice President and Director of Financial Aid
60 Lomb Memorial Drive, Rochester, NY 14623-5604
(585) 475-2186

# Rockland Community College

Suffern, New York
www.sunyrockland.edu          Federal Code: 002877

**2-year public** community college in large town.
**Enrollment:** 6,040 undergrads.
**Selectivity:** Open admission.

## BASIC COSTS (2015-2016)

**Tuition and fees:** $4,654; out-of-state residents $8,953.
**Per-credit charge:** $180; out-of-state residents $360.

## FINANCIAL AID PICTURE

**Students with need:** Need-based aid available for full-time and part-time students. Work study available nights, weekends, and for part-time students.

**Scholarships offered:** Jack Watson Scholarship: minimum 3.5 high school GPA or 94 average in Regents; 5 awarded; $1,163 per semester; renewable for 2nd year. Alumni Scholarship: for children of alumni; 75 average; varying amounts.

## FINANCIAL AID PROCEDURES

**Forms required:** FAFSA, institutional form.

**Dates and Deadlines:** Priority date 5/31; no closing date. Applicants notified on a rolling basis starting 6/1.

## CONTACT

Debra Bouabidi, Director of Financial Aid
145 College Road, Suffern, NY 10901-3699
(845) 574-4282

# The Sage Colleges

Troy, New York
www.sage.edu          Federal Code: 002810

**4-year private** university in small city.
**Enrollment:** 1,618 undergrads, 12% part-time. 262 full-time freshmen.
**Selectivity:** Admits 50 to 75% of applicants.

## BASIC COSTS (2015-2016)

**Tuition and fees:** $28,400.
**Per-credit charge:** $900.
**Room and board:** $12,220.

## FINANCIAL AID PICTURE (2015-2016)

**Students with need:** Out of 257 full-time freshmen who applied for aid, 246 were judged to have need. Of these, 246 received aid. Need-based aid available for part-time students.

**Students without need:** 11 full-time freshmen who did not demonstrate need for aid received scholarships/grants; average award was $12,180. No-need awards available for academics, alumni affiliation, art, leadership, minority status, music/drama, state/district residency.

**Scholarships offered:** Multiple awards to qualified students: Presidential and Dean's scholarship, first-generation scholarship, valedictorian-salutatorian scholarship, student Sage scholarship, endowed scholarships for minority students and specific majors.

## FINANCIAL AID PROCEDURES

**Forms required:** FAFSA, state aid form.

**Dates and Deadlines:** Priority date 3/1; no closing date. Applicants notified on a rolling basis starting 3/1; must reply by 5/1 or within 2 week(s) of notification.

## CONTACT

Kelley Robinson, Director of Financial Aid
65 1st Street, Troy, NY 12180-4115
(518) 244-4525

# Saint Bonaventure University

St. Bonaventure, New York
www.sbu.edu          Federal Code: 002817

**4-year private** university in large town, affiliated with Roman Catholic Church.
**Enrollment:** 1,645 undergrads, 1% part-time. 438 full-time freshmen.
**Selectivity:** Admits 50 to 75% of applicants.

## BASIC COSTS (2015-2016)

**Tuition and fees:** $31,389.
**Per-credit charge:** $906.
**Room and board:** $11,728.
**Additional info:** Tuition/fee waivers available for minority students.

## FINANCIAL AID PICTURE (2014-2015)

**Students with need:** Out of 404 full-time freshmen who applied for aid, 364 were judged to have need. Of these, 364 received aid, and 73 had their full need met. Average financial aid package met 85% of need; average scholarship/grant was $20,524; average loan was $4,235. For part-time students, average financial aid package was $10,303.

**Students without need:** 67 full-time freshmen who did not demonstrate need for aid received scholarships/grants; average award was $13,931. No-need awards available for academics, athletics, minority status, music/drama, religious affiliation, ROTC, state/district residency.

**Scholarships offered:** *Merit:* Buckeye Award: $2,000; for first-time freshmen who graduate from a high school in Ohio (except students receiving athletic awards); renewable. Geographic Diversity Award: $2,000; given to all out-of-state students except those who graduate from high schools in Ohio, who will receive Buckeye Award. *Athletic:* 71 full-time freshmen received athletic scholarships; average amount $13,463.

**Additional info:** Families experiencing financial difficulties not adequately reflected by the FAFSA should contact the Office of Financial Assistance. Outside scholarships do not reduce other financial aid unless, when added to total aid, the new total exceeds need. If it exceeds need, then loans and work are reduced first.

### FINANCIAL AID PROCEDURES
**Forms required:** FAFSA, state aid form.
**Dates and Deadlines:** Priority date 2/15; no closing date. Applicants notified on a rolling basis starting 3/1; must reply by 5/1 or within 2 week(s) of notification.
**Transfers:** Priority date 3/1; no deadline. Applicants notified on a rolling basis starting 3/15; must reply by 5/1 or within 2 week(s) of notification.

### CONTACT
Troy Martin, Director of Financial Aid
Box D, St. Bonaventure, NY 14778
(716) 375-2400

## St. Elizabeth College of Nursing
Utica, New York
www.secon.edu                 Federal Code: 006461

**2-year private** nursing college in small city, affiliated with Roman Catholic Church.
**Enrollment:** 206 undergrads, 54% part-time. 9 full-time freshmen.
**Selectivity:** Admits 50 to 75% of applicants.

### BASIC COSTS (2015-2016)
**Tuition and fees:** $14,864.
**Per-credit charge:** $412.

### FINANCIAL AID PICTURE
**Students with need:** Need-based aid available for full-time and part-time students.

### FINANCIAL AID PROCEDURES
**Forms required:** FAFSA, state aid form.
**Dates and Deadlines:** Applicants notified on a rolling basis starting 1/1; must reply within 2 week(s) of notification.

### CONTACT
Sherry Wojnas, Director of Finance & Enrollment
2215 Genesee Street, Utica, NY 13501
(315) 801-8206

## St. Francis College
Brooklyn Heights, New York
www.sfc.edu                 Federal Code: 002820

**4-year private** liberal arts college in very large city, affiliated with Roman Catholic Church.
**Enrollment:** 2,578 undergrads, 7% part-time. 533 full-time freshmen.
**Selectivity:** Admits over 75% of applicants.

### BASIC COSTS (2015-2016)
**Tuition and fees:** $23,800.
**Per-credit charge:** $765.
**Room only:** $13,600.

### FINANCIAL AID PICTURE
**Students with need:** Need-based aid available for full-time and part-time students.
**Students without need:** No-need awards available for academics, athletics.

### FINANCIAL AID PROCEDURES
**Forms required:** FAFSA, state aid form.
**Dates and Deadlines:** Priority date 2/15; no closing date. Applicants notified on a rolling basis starting 3/15; must reply within 2 week(s) of notification.
**Transfers:** No deadline. Applicants notified on a rolling basis.

### CONTACT
Hellitz Lopez, Director of Student Financial Services
180 Remsen Street, Brooklyn Heights, NY 11201-9902
(718) 489-5255

## St. John Fisher College
Rochester, New York
www.sjfc.edu                 Federal Code: 002821

**4-year private** liberal arts college in large town, affiliated with Roman Catholic Church.
**Enrollment:** 2,791 undergrads, 6% part-time. 597 full-time freshmen.
**Selectivity:** Admits 50 to 75% of applicants. GED not accepted.

### BASIC COSTS (2016-2017)
**Tuition and fees:** $31,880.
**Per-credit charge:** $850.
**Room and board:** $11,740.

### FINANCIAL AID PICTURE (2014-2015)
**Students with need:** Out of 575 full-time freshmen who applied for aid, 504 were judged to have need. Of these, 504 received aid, and 186 had their full need met. Average financial aid package met 73% of need; average scholarship/grant was $18,180; average loan was $3,737.
**Students without need:** 93 full-time freshmen who did not demonstrate need for aid received scholarships/grants; average award was $11,360. No-need awards available for academics, leadership.
**Scholarships offered:** Scholarships range from $10,000 to $14,000. Honors and Science Scholars programs receive additional $3,000 annually. Fisher Service Scholars Program: one-half the total cost of education. First Generation Scholars Program: from $5,000 up to one-half of the total cost of education.

### FINANCIAL AID PROCEDURES
**Forms required:** FAFSA, state aid form.
**Dates and Deadlines:** Priority date 2/15; no closing date. Applicants notified on a rolling basis starting 3/15; must reply by 5/1 or within 3 week(s) of notification.
**Transfers:** No deadline. Applicants notified on a rolling basis starting 3/15; must reply within 3 week(s) of notification.

### CONTACT
Angela Monnat, Director of Financial Aid
3690 East Avenue, Rochester, NY 14618-3597
(585) 385-8042

## St. John's University
Queens, New York
www.stjohns.edu                 Federal Code: 002823

**4-year private** university in very large city, affiliated with Roman Catholic Church.
**Enrollment:** 11,248 undergrads, 2% part-time. 2,795 full-time freshmen.
**Selectivity:** Admits 50 to 75% of applicants.

### BASIC COSTS (2015-2016)
**Tuition and fees:** $38,680.
**Per-credit charge:** $1,262.
**Room and board:** $16,390.

**Additional info:** Tuition may vary by program and class year. Full-time freshman or transfer students are provided with a laptop for their entire St. John's career. Tuition at time of enrollment locked for 4 years.

### FINANCIAL AID PICTURE (2014-2015)

**Students with need:** Out of 2,534 full-time freshmen who applied for aid, 2,312 were judged to have need. Of these, 2,309 received aid, and 290 had their full need met. Average financial aid package met 86% of need; average scholarship/grant was $9,231; average loan was $3,658. For part-time students, average financial aid package was $17,237.

**Students without need:** 216 full-time freshmen who did not demonstrate need for aid received scholarships/grants; average award was $19,574. No-need awards available for academics, alumni affiliation, art, athletics, leadership, music/drama, religious affiliation, ROTC.

**Scholarships offered:** 52 full-time freshmen received athletic scholarships; average amount $30,013.

### FINANCIAL AID PROCEDURES

**Forms required:** FAFSA.

**Dates and Deadlines:** Priority date 2/1; no closing date. Applicants notified on a rolling basis starting 3/1; must reply within 2 week(s) of notification.

**Transfers:** No deadline. Applicants notified by 3/15; must reply by 5/1 or within 2 week(s) of notification. Scholarships available if 12 credits college study completed with a minimum GPA of 3.0.

### CONTACT

Jorge Rodriguez, Associate Vice President Student Financial Services
8000 Utopia Parkway, Queens, NY 11439
(718) 990-2000

## St. Joseph's College New York: Suffolk Campus

Patchogue, New York
www.sjcny.edu          Federal Code: 002825

**4-year private** liberal arts and teachers college in large town.
**Enrollment:** 2,846 undergrads, 16% part-time. 313 full-time freshmen.
**Selectivity:** Admits 50 to 75% of applicants.

### BASIC COSTS (2015-2016)

**Tuition and fees:** $24,130.
**Per-credit charge:** $760.

### FINANCIAL AID PICTURE (2014-2015)

**Students with need:** Out of 308 full-time freshmen who applied for aid, 242 were judged to have need. Of these, 240 received aid, and 95 had their full need met. Average financial aid package met 71% of need; average scholarship/grant was $12,518; average loan was $3,245. For part-time students, average financial aid package was $5,932.

**Students without need:** 63 full-time freshmen who did not demonstrate need for aid received scholarships/grants; average award was $10,206. No-need awards available for academics, alumni affiliation.

### FINANCIAL AID PROCEDURES

**Forms required:** FAFSA, state aid form.

**Dates and Deadlines:** Priority date 3/15; no closing date. Applicants notified on a rolling basis starting 3/30; must reply by 5/1 or within 2 week(s) of notification.

**Transfers:** No deadline. Applicants notified on a rolling basis starting 3/30; must reply by 5/1 or within 2 week(s) of notification.

### CONTACT

Amy Thompson, Director of Financial Aid
155 West Roe Boulevard, Patchogue, NY 11772-2325
(631) 687-2600

## St. Joseph's College of Nursing

Syracuse, New York
www.sjhcon.edu          Federal Code: 006467

**2-year private** nursing college in small city, affiliated with Roman Catholic Church.
**Enrollment:** 153 undergrads, 18% part-time. 1 full-time freshmen.

### BASIC COSTS (2016-2017)

**Tuition and fees:** $20,420.
**Per-credit charge:** $530.
**Room only:** $5,500.

### FINANCIAL AID PICTURE (2014-2015)

**Students with need:** 31% of average financial aid package awarded as scholarships/grants, 69% awarded as loans/jobs. Need-based aid available for part-time students.

**Students without need:** This college awards aid only to students with need.

### FINANCIAL AID PROCEDURES

**Forms required:** FAFSA, state aid form.

**Dates and Deadlines:** Priority date 3/1; no closing date. Applicants notified on a rolling basis starting 6/15.

### CONTACT

Jennifer Prutzman, Coordinator for Financial Aid
206 Prospect Avenue, Syracuse, NY 13203-1892
(315) 448-5040

## St. Joseph's College, New York

Brooklyn, New York
www.sjcny.edu          Federal Code: 002825

**4-year private** liberal arts and teachers college in very large city.
**Enrollment:** 967 undergrads, 22% part-time. 183 full-time freshmen.
**Selectivity:** Admits 50 to 75% of applicants.

### BASIC COSTS (2015-2016)

**Tuition and fees:** $24,120.
**Per-credit charge:** $760.

### FINANCIAL AID PICTURE (2014-2015)

**Students with need:** Out of 181 full-time freshmen who applied for aid, 153 were judged to have need. Of these, 152 received aid, and 20 had their full need met. Average financial aid package met 64% of need; average scholarship/grant was $15,341; average loan was $2,953. For part-time students, average financial aid package was $7,062.

**Students without need:** 28 full-time freshmen who did not demonstrate need for aid received scholarships/grants; average award was $9,941. No-need awards available for academics, alumni affiliation.

### FINANCIAL AID PROCEDURES

**Forms required:** FAFSA, state aid form.

**Dates and Deadlines:** Priority date 3/15; no closing date. Applicants notified on a rolling basis starting 3/30; must reply within 2 week(s) of notification.

**Transfers:** No deadline. Applicants notified on a rolling basis starting 3/30; must reply by 5/1 or within 2 week(s) of notification.

### CONTACT

Amy Thompson, Director of Financial Aid
245 Clinton Avenue, Brooklyn, NY 11205-3602
(718) 940-5700

## St. Lawrence University

Canton, New York
www.stlawu.edu                    Federal Code: 002829

**4-year private** liberal arts college in small town.
**Enrollment:** 2,404 undergrads. 680 full-time freshmen.
**Selectivity:** Admits less than 50% of applicants.

### BASIC COSTS (2016-2017)
**Tuition and fees:** $51,200.
**Room and board:** $13,190.

### FINANCIAL AID PICTURE (2015-2016)
**Students with need:** Out of 495 full-time freshmen who applied for aid, 429 were judged to have need. Of these, 429 received aid, and 119 had their full need met. Average financial aid package met 87% of need; average scholarship/grant was $37,312; average loan was $3,410.
**Students without need:** 235 full-time freshmen who did not demonstrate need for aid received scholarships/grants; average award was $19,320. No-need awards available for academics, alumni affiliation, athletics, leadership, minority status, ROTC, state/district residency.
**Scholarships offered:** *Merit:* Merit scholarships: $10,000 to $30,000 annually. Augsbury/North Country Scholarship: for students in some schools in northern New York and southern Ontario; nomination by counselor required. Community Service Scholarship: based on past and current service. Presidential Diversity Scholarship: for students of African American, Asian American, Hispanic American and Native American heritage and those who support multiculturalism. Sesquicentennial and University Scholarship: based on academic excellence, character and leadership. Vilas Scholarship: for students interested in business. Leadership Scholarship: based on evidence of leadership in schools and communities. *Athletic:* 8 full-time freshmen received athletic scholarships; average amount $44,275.

### FINANCIAL AID PROCEDURES
**Forms required:** FAFSA.
**Dates and Deadlines:** Priority date 2/1; closing date 2/1. Applicants notified by 3/30; must reply by 5/1 or within 2 week(s) of notification.
**Transfers:** Priority date 4/1; closing date 5/1. Applicants notified on a rolling basis starting 6/1; must reply within 2 week(s) of notification.

### CONTACT
Patricia Farmer, Director of Financial Aid
Payson Hall, Canton, NY 13617
(315) 229-5265

## St. Thomas Aquinas College

Sparkill, New York
www.stac.edu                      Federal Code: 002832

**4-year private** liberal arts college in large town.
**Enrollment:** 1,170 undergrads, 5% part-time. 272 full-time freshmen.
**Selectivity:** Admits over 75% of applicants.

### BASIC COSTS (2015-2016)
**Tuition and fees:** $28,740.
**Per-credit charge:** $900.
**Room and board:** $12,030.

### FINANCIAL AID PICTURE (2015-2016)
**Students with need:** Out of 250 full-time freshmen who applied for aid, 212 were judged to have need. Of these, 201 received aid, and 30 had their full need met. Average financial aid package met 34% of need; average scholarship/grant was $10,500; average loan was $3,300. For part-time students, average financial aid package was $9,000.
**Students without need:** 39 full-time freshmen who did not demonstrate need for aid received scholarships/grants; average award was $12,645. No-need awards available for academics, alumni affiliation, art, athletics, leadership, minority status, music/drama, religious affiliation.

**Scholarships offered:** 10 full-time freshmen received athletic scholarships; average amount $8,630.

### FINANCIAL AID PROCEDURES
**Forms required:** FAFSA.
**Dates and Deadlines:** Closing date 6/30. Applicants notified on a rolling basis starting 11/1; must reply within 4 week(s) of notification.
**Transfers:** Closing date 5/1. Applicants notified on a rolling basis; must reply within 4 week(s) of notification.

### CONTACT
Jean-Marie Mohr, Director of Financial Aid
125 Route 340, Sparkill, NY 10976-1050
(845) 398-4097

## Sarah Lawrence College

Bronxville, New York              Federal Code: 002813
www.sarahlawrence.edu             CSS Code: 2810

**4-year private** liberal arts college in small city.
**Enrollment:** 1,283 undergrads, 1% part-time. 353 full-time freshmen.
**Selectivity:** Admits 50 to 75% of applicants.

### BASIC COSTS (2015-2016)
**Tuition and fees:** $51,030.
**Per-credit charge:** $1,656.
**Room and board:** $14,700.

### FINANCIAL AID PICTURE (2015-2016)
**Students with need:** Out of 280 full-time freshmen who applied for aid, 234 were judged to have need. Of these, 233 received aid, and 43 had their full need met. Average financial aid package met 79% of need; average scholarship/grant was $37,713; average loan was $2,032. For part-time students, average financial aid package was $13,914.
**Students without need:** This college awards aid only to students with need.
**Scholarships offered:** Presidential and Dean Scholarships: available regardless of need to admitted students demonstrating substantial academic achievement, creativity and potential for leadership; available for up to four years of full-time study contingent on satisfactory academic progress.

### FINANCIAL AID PROCEDURES
**Forms required:** FAFSA, CSS PROFILE, state aid form.
**Dates and Deadlines:** Closing date 2/15. Applicants notified by 4/1; must reply by 5/1.
**Transfers:** Closing date 3/15. Applicants notified by 5/15. Spring Transfer student must submit financial aid forms by 11/1.

### CONTACT
Nicholas Salinas, Director of Financial Aid
1 Mead Way, Bronxville, NY 10708-5999
(914) 395-2570

## Schenectady County Community College

Schenectady, New York
www.sunysccc.edu                  Federal Code: 006785

**2-year public** community college in small city.
**Enrollment:** 3,293 undergrads, 34% part-time. 688 full-time freshmen.
**Selectivity:** Open admission; but selective for some programs.

### BASIC COSTS (2015-2016)
**Tuition and fees:** $3,934; out-of-state residents $7,462.
**Per-credit charge:** $147; out-of-state residents $294.

## FINANCIAL AID PICTURE (2014-2015)

**Students with need:** 58% of average financial aid package awarded as scholarships/grants, 42% awarded as loans/jobs. Need-based aid available for part-time students.

**Students without need:** This college awards aid only to students with need.

**Additional info:** Federal Work Study for full time students.

## FINANCIAL AID PROCEDURES

**Forms required:** FAFSA.

**Dates and Deadlines:** Priority date 5/1; no closing date. Applicants notified on a rolling basis starting 3/1; must reply by 8/31.

## CONTACT

Cynthia Decker, Director of Financial Aid
78 Washington Avenue, Schenectady, NY 12305
(518) 381-1352

## School of Visual Arts

New York, New York
www.sva.edu                          Federal Code: 007468

**4-year for-profit** visual arts college in very large city.

**Enrollment:** 3,581 undergrads, 4% part-time. 698 full-time freshmen.

**Selectivity:** Admits 50 to 75% of applicants.

## BASIC COSTS (2016-2017)

**Tuition and fees:** $36,500.

**Per-credit charge:** $1,270.

**Room only:** $15,400.

## FINANCIAL AID PICTURE (2015-2016)

**Students with need:** Out of 364 full-time freshmen who applied for aid, 335 were judged to have need. Of these, 318 received aid, and 8 had their full need met. Average financial aid package met 45% of need; average scholarship/grant was $14,447; average loan was $3,197. For part-time students, average financial aid package was $9,152.

**Students without need:** 54 full-time freshmen who did not demonstrate need for aid received scholarships/grants; average award was $11,562. No-need awards available for art.

**Scholarships offered:** SVA matching scholarship available to full- and part-time undergraduate and graduate students. SVA will match 25% of any outside scholarship, up to $2,500, that a student obtains.

## FINANCIAL AID PROCEDURES

**Forms required:** FAFSA, state aid form.

**Dates and Deadlines:** Priority date 2/1; closing date 3/1. Applicants notified on a rolling basis starting 2/15; must reply within 4 week(s) of notification.

**Transfers:** No deadline. Applicants notified on a rolling basis; must reply within 4 week(s) of notification.

## CONTACT

William Berrios, Director of Financial Aid
209 East 23rd Street, New York, NY 10010-3994
(212) 592-2030

## Siena College

Loudonville, New York
www.siena.edu                        Federal Code: 002816

**4-year private** liberal arts college in large town, affiliated with Roman Catholic Church.

**Enrollment:** 3,062 undergrads, 2% part-time. 709 full-time freshmen.

**Selectivity:** Admits 50 to 75% of applicants.

## BASIC COSTS (2016-2017)

**Tuition and fees:** $35,011.

**Per-credit charge:** $500.

**Room and board:** $14,105.

## FINANCIAL AID PICTURE (2014-2015)

**Students with need:** Out of 646 full-time freshmen who applied for aid, 564 were judged to have need. Of these, 564 received aid, and 185 had their full need met. Average financial aid package met 81% of need; average scholarship/grant was $23,060; average loan was $3,290. For part-time students, average financial aid package was $17,786.

**Students without need:** 127 full-time freshmen who did not demonstrate need for aid received scholarships/grants; average award was $13,408. No-need awards available for academics, athletics, leadership, minority status, ROTC, state/district residency.

**Scholarships offered:** 61 full-time freshmen received athletic scholarships; average amount $19,883.

## FINANCIAL AID PROCEDURES

**Forms required:** FAFSA, state aid form.

**Dates and Deadlines:** Priority date 2/15; closing date 5/1. Applicants notified by 4/1; must reply by 5/1.

**Transfers:** Priority date 3/1.

## CONTACT

Mary Lawyer, Associate Vice President for Enrollment Management
515 Loudon Road, Loudonville, NY 12211-1462
(518) 783-2427

## Skidmore College

Saratoga Springs, New York        Federal Code: 002814
www.skidmore.edu                       CSS Code: 2815

**4-year private** liberal arts college in large town.

**Enrollment:** 2,619 undergrads, 1% part-time. 686 full-time freshmen.

**Selectivity:** Admits less than 50% of applicants.

## BASIC COSTS (2015-2016)

**Tuition and fees:** $49,120.

**Per-credit charge:** $1,601.

**Room and board:** $13,072.

## FINANCIAL AID PICTURE (2015-2016)

**Students with need:** Out of 321 full-time freshmen who applied for aid, 220 were judged to have need. Of these, 220 received aid, and 220 had their full need met. Average financial aid package met 100% of need; average scholarship/grant was $42,000; average loan was $3,280. Need-based aid available for part-time students.

**Students without need:** 4 full-time freshmen who did not demonstrate need for aid received scholarships/grants; average award was $13,500. No-need awards available for music/drama.

**Scholarships offered:** Porter Presidential Scholarships in Science and Mathematics: $15,000 annually; based on outstanding ability and achievement in math, science, or computer science. Filene Undergraduate Music Scholarships: $12,000 annually; based on music ability.

## FINANCIAL AID PROCEDURES

**Forms required:** CSS PROFILE.

**Dates and Deadlines:** Closing date 2/1. Applicants notified by 4/1; must reply by 5/1.

**Transfers:** Priority date 4/1. Applicants notified on a rolling basis starting 4/15; must reply within 3 week(s) of notification. Some transfer students eligible for need-based grant assistance.

## CONTACT

Beth Post-Lundquist, Director of Financial Aid
815 North Broadway, Saratoga Springs, NY 12866
(518) 580-5750

## Suffolk County Community College

Selden, New York
www.sunysuffolk.edu                    Federal Code: 002878

**2-year public** community college in large town.
**Enrollment:** 26,600 undergrads.
**Selectivity:** Open admission; but selective for some programs.

### BASIC COSTS (2015-2016)
**Tuition and fees:** $5,280; out-of-state residents $9,850.
**Per-credit charge:** $191; out-of-state residents $392.

### FINANCIAL AID PICTURE
**Students with need:** Need-based aid available for full-time and part-time students. Work study available nights, weekends, and for part-time students.
**Students without need:** No-need awards available for academics, art, leadership, minority status, music/drama, state/district residency.

### FINANCIAL AID PROCEDURES
**Forms required:** FAFSA, state aid form.
**Dates and Deadlines:** Priority date 4/15; closing date 6/1. Applicants notified on a rolling basis starting 4/15; must reply within 2 week(s) of notification.
**Transfers:** No deadline. Applicants notified on a rolling basis starting 4/15.

### CONTACT
Nancy Dunnagan, Director of Financial Aid
533 College Road, Selden, NY 11784
(631) 451-4110

## Sullivan County Community College

Loch Sheldrake, New York
www.sunysullivan.edu                    Federal Code: 002879

**2-year public** community college in small town.
**Enrollment:** 1,079 undergrads, 27% part-time. 270 full-time freshmen.
**Selectivity:** Open admission; but selective for some programs.

### BASIC COSTS (2015-2016)
**Tuition and fees:** $5,500; out-of-state residents $10,174.
**Per-credit charge:** $195; out-of-state residents $312.
**Room and board:** $9,350.

### FINANCIAL AID PICTURE (2014-2015)
**Students with need:** 79% of average financial aid package awarded as scholarships/grants, 21% awarded as loans/jobs. Need-based aid available for part-time students.
**Additional info:** 60% of students hold part-time jobs locally.

### FINANCIAL AID PROCEDURES
**Forms required:** FAFSA.
**Dates and Deadlines:** Priority date 4/15; no closing date. Applicants notified on a rolling basis starting 5/15; must reply within 2 week(s) of notification.

### CONTACT
James Winderl, Director of Financial Aid
112 College Road, Loch Sheldrake, NY 12759-5151
(845) 434-5750 ext. 4231

## SUNY College at Brockport

Brockport, New York
www.brockport.edu                    Federal Code: 002841

**4-year public** liberal arts college in small town.
**Enrollment:** 6,993 undergrads, 9% part-time. 1,089 full-time freshmen.
**Selectivity:** Admits 50 to 75% of applicants.

### BASIC COSTS (2015-2016)
**Tuition and fees:** $7,898; out-of-state residents $17,748.
**Per-credit charge:** $270; out-of-state residents $680.
**Room and board:** $11,910.

### FINANCIAL AID PICTURE (2014-2015)
**Students with need:** Out of 923 full-time freshmen who applied for aid, 718 were judged to have need. Of these, 701 received aid, and 107 had their full need met. Average financial aid package met 75% of need; average scholarship/grant was $6,950; average loan was $4,896. For part-time students, average financial aid package was $5,289.
**Students without need:** 77 full-time freshmen who did not demonstrate need for aid received scholarships/grants; average award was $4,295. No-need awards available for academics, alumni affiliation, art, leadership, minority status, music/drama, ROTC.
**Scholarships offered:** Extraordinary Academic Scholarships: $2,250 to $6,470 per year; minimum qualifications include SAT scores of 1100 (24 ACT), rank in top 50% of class, 90 average or higher.

### FINANCIAL AID PROCEDURES
**Forms required:** FAFSA, state aid form.
**Dates and Deadlines:** Priority date 3/15; no closing date. Applicants notified on a rolling basis starting 3/1; must reply by 5/1.

### CONTACT
J Atkinson, Director of Enrollment Services/ Director of Financial Aid
350 New Campus Drive, Brockport, NY 14420-2915
(585) 395-2501

## SUNY College at Buffalo

Buffalo, New York
www.buffalostate.edu                    Federal Code: 002842

**4-year public** liberal arts and teachers college in large city.
**Enrollment:** 8,977 undergrads, 10% part-time. 1,835 full-time freshmen.
**Selectivity:** Admits 50 to 75% of applicants.

### BASIC COSTS (2015-2016)
**Tuition and fees:** $7,669; out-of-state residents $17,519.
**Room and board:** $12,332.
**Additional info:** Tuition/fee waivers available for minority students.

### FINANCIAL AID PICTURE
**Students with need:** Need-based aid available for full-time and part-time students.
**Students without need:** This college awards aid only to students with need.
**Scholarships offered:** Empire Minority Scholarships: $1,000 annually for 4 years. Honors Program: $2,000 for 2 years and $1,000 for remaining 2 years.

### FINANCIAL AID PROCEDURES
**Forms required:** FAFSA.
**Dates and Deadlines:** Priority date 3/1; closing date 5/1. Applicants notified on a rolling basis starting 5/1; must reply within 4 week(s) of notification.
**Transfers:** No deadline.

### CONTACT
Connie Cooke, Director of Financial Aid
1300 Elmwood Avenue, Moot Hall, Buffalo, NY 14222-1095
(716) 878-4902

## SUNY College at Cortland

Cortland, New York
www2.cortland.edu/home                    Federal Code: 002843

**4-year public** liberal arts and teachers college in large town.
**Enrollment:** 6,276 undergrads, 2% part-time. 945 full-time freshmen.

**Selectivity:** Admits 50 to 75% of applicants.

**BASIC COSTS (2015-2016)**
**Tuition and fees:** $8,050; out-of-state residents $17,900.
**Per-credit charge:** $270; out-of-state residents $680.
**Room and board:** $12,200.

**FINANCIAL AID PICTURE (2014-2015)**
**Students with need:** Out of 875 full-time freshmen who applied for aid, 634 were judged to have need. Of these, 602 received aid, and 62 had their full need met. Average financial aid package met 66% of need; average scholarship/grant was $5,062; average loan was $3,539. For part-time students, average financial aid package was $10,130.
**Students without need:** 25 full-time freshmen who did not demonstrate need for aid received scholarships/grants; average award was $4,175. No-need awards available for academics, art, leadership, minority status, music/drama, state/district residency.

**FINANCIAL AID PROCEDURES**
**Forms required:** FAFSA, state aid form.
**Dates and Deadlines:** Priority date 3/1; no closing date. Applicants notified on a rolling basis starting 3/15; must reply by 5/1 or within 4 week(s) of notification.

**CONTACT**
Karen Gallagher, Director of Financial Aid
PO Box 2000, Cortland, NY 13045-0900
(607) 753-4717

## SUNY College at Fredonia
Fredonia, New York
www.fredonia.edu                 Federal Code: 002844

**4-year public** liberal arts college in large town.
**Enrollment:** 4,557 undergrads, 2% part-time. 911 full-time freshmen.
**Selectivity:** Admits 50 to 75% of applicants.

**BASIC COSTS (2015-2016)**
**Tuition and fees:** $8,074; out-of-state residents $17,924.
**Per-credit charge:** $270; out-of-state residents $680.
**Room and board:** $12,500.

**FINANCIAL AID PICTURE (2015-2016)**
**Students with need:** Out of 853 full-time freshmen who applied for aid, 654 were judged to have need. Of these, 644 received aid, and 105 had their full need met. Average financial aid package met 62% of need; average scholarship/grant was $5,781; average loan was $5,472. For part-time students, average financial aid package was $5,208.
**Students without need:** 119 full-time freshmen who did not demonstrate need for aid received scholarships/grants; average award was $3,731. No-need awards available for academics, alumni affiliation, art, minority status, music/drama, state/district residency.
**Additional info:** More than 80% of students receive financial aid, and over $2 million in merit and need-based scholarships are available to academically qualified, new and returning students each year.

**FINANCIAL AID PROCEDURES**
**Forms required:** FAFSA, state aid form.
**Dates and Deadlines:** Applicants notified on a rolling basis starting 3/1; must reply by 5/1.
**Transfers:** Priority date 1/31; no deadline. Applicants notified on a rolling basis starting 10/15. Financial aid transcripts required from prior institutions attended.

**CONTACT**
Daniel Tramuta, Associate Vice President for Enrollment Services & Director of Financial Aid
280 Central Avenue, Fenner House, Fredonia, NY 14063-1136
(716) 673-3253

## SUNY College at Geneseo
Geneseo, New York
www.geneseo.edu                 Federal Code: 002845

**4-year public** liberal arts and teachers college in small town.
**Enrollment:** 5,548 undergrads, 2% part-time. 1,324 full-time freshmen.
**Selectivity:** Admits 50 to 75% of applicants.

**BASIC COSTS (2015-2016)**
**Tuition and fees:** $8,113; out-of-state residents $17,963.
**Per-credit charge:** $270; out-of-state residents $680.
**Room and board:** $11,980.

**FINANCIAL AID PICTURE (2015-2016)**
**Students with need:** Out of 1,139 full-time freshmen who applied for aid, 672 were judged to have need. Of these, 672 received aid, and 403 had their full need met. Average financial aid package met 60% of need; average scholarship/grant was $6,556; average loan was $4,018. Need-based aid available for part-time students.
**Students without need:** 92 full-time freshmen who did not demonstrate need for aid received scholarships/grants; average award was $1,850. No-need awards available for academics, art, leadership, minority status, music/drama, religious affiliation, state/district residency.

**FINANCIAL AID PROCEDURES**
**Forms required:** FAFSA, state aid form.
**Dates and Deadlines:** Closing date 2/15. Applicants notified on a rolling basis starting 3/15; must reply by 5/1.

**CONTACT**
Archie Cureton, Director of Financial Aid
1 College Circle, Geneseo, NY 14454-1401
(585) 245-5731

## SUNY College at New Paltz
New Paltz, New York
www.newpaltz.edu                 Federal Code: 002846

**4-year public** liberal arts college in large town.
**Enrollment:** 6,498 undergrads, 6% part-time. 1,069 full-time freshmen.
**Selectivity:** Admits less than 50% of applicants.

**BASIC COSTS (2015-2016)**
**Tuition and fees:** $7,760; out-of-state residents $17,610.
**Per-credit charge:** $270; out-of-state residents $680.
**Room and board:** $11,480.

**FINANCIAL AID PICTURE (2015-2016)**
**Students with need:** Out of 959 full-time freshmen who applied for aid, 655 were judged to have need. Of these, 646 received aid, and 55 had their full need met. Average financial aid package met 55% of need; average scholarship/grant was $5,194; average loan was $3,299. For part-time students, average financial aid package was $5,707.
**Students without need:** This college awards aid only to students with need.

**FINANCIAL AID PROCEDURES**
**Forms required:** FAFSA, state aid form.
**Dates and Deadlines:** Priority date 3/15; no closing date. Applicants notified on a rolling basis starting 4/1.
**Transfers:** No deadline. Applicants notified on a rolling basis starting 4/1; must reply within 4 week(s) of notification.

**CONTACT**
Maureen Lohan-Bremer, Director of Financial Aid
100 Hawk Drive, New Paltz, NY 12561-2443
(845) 257-3250

## SUNY College at Old Westbury

Old Westbury, New York
www.oldwestbury.edu                    Federal Code: 007109

**4-year public** business and liberal arts college in small city.
**Enrollment:** 3,998 undergrads, 13% part-time. 372 full-time freshmen.
**Selectivity:** Admits 50 to 75% of applicants.

### BASIC COSTS (2015-2016)

**Tuition and fees:** $7,643; out-of-state residents $17,493.
**Per-credit charge:** $270; out-of-state residents $680.
**Room and board:** $10,390.

### FINANCIAL AID PICTURE (2015-2016)

**Students with need:** Out of 368 full-time freshmen who applied for aid, 346 were judged to have need. Of these, 298 received aid, and 298 had their full need met. Average financial aid package met 55% of need; average scholarship/grant was $8,064; average loan was $3,519. For part-time students, average financial aid package was $5,204.
**Students without need:** No-need awards available for academics, alumni affiliation, state/district residency.

### FINANCIAL AID PROCEDURES

**Forms required:** FAFSA, state aid form, institutional form.
**Dates and Deadlines:** Closing date 4/1. Applicants notified on a rolling basis starting 4/15; must reply within 2 week(s) of notification.
**Transfers:** No deadline. Applicants notified on a rolling basis starting 4/15; must reply within 2 week(s) of notification. Financial aid transcript required.

### CONTACT

Mildred O'Keefe, Director of Financial Aid
Box 307, Old Westbury, NY 11568-0307
(516) 876-3222

## SUNY College at Oneonta

Oneonta, New York
www.oneonta.edu/home/default.asp
Federal Code: 002847

**4-year public** liberal arts college in large town.
**Enrollment:** 5,825 undergrads, 1% part-time. 1,130 full-time freshmen.
**Selectivity:** Admits less than 50% of applicants.

### BASIC COSTS (2015-2016)

**Tuition and fees:** $7,870; out-of-state residents $17,720.
**Room and board:** $11,842.

### FINANCIAL AID PICTURE

**Students with need:** Need-based aid available for full-time and part-time students. Work study available nights, weekends, and for part-time students.
**Students without need:** No-need awards available for academics, leadership, minority status, music/drama, state/district residency.
**Scholarships offered:** Presidential Scholarship: $5,870; awarded to students who have shown exceptional academic ability. Presidential Diversity Scholarship and Organization of Auxiliary Services Diversity Student Leadership Scholarship: $5,870; for students who will contribute to the diversity of the student body and who have shown exceptional academic ability and strong commitment to diversity through activities and leadership. Deans' Scholarship: $3,000; awarded based on academics. Oneonta Auxiliary Services Merit Scholarship: $2,000; awarded to applicants for academics, service, extracurricular activities. All scholarships are renewable.

### FINANCIAL AID PROCEDURES

**Forms required:** FAFSA.
**Dates and Deadlines:** Priority date 3/1; no closing date. Applicants notified on a rolling basis starting 3/1.
**Transfers:** No deadline. Applicants notified on a rolling basis starting 3/1.

### CONTACT

C Goodhue, Director of Student Financial Aid
Admissions Office, 116 Alumni Hall, Oneonta, NY 13820-4016
(607) 436-2532

## SUNY College at Oswego

Oswego, New York
www.oswego.edu                    Federal Code: 002848

**4-year public** university in large town.
**Enrollment:** 7,046 undergrads, 4% part-time. 1,481 full-time freshmen.
**Selectivity:** Admits 50 to 75% of applicants.

### BASIC COSTS (2015-2016)

**Tuition and fees:** $7,934; out-of-state residents $17,784.
**Per-credit charge:** $270; out-of-state residents $680.
**Room and board:** $12,990.

### FINANCIAL AID PICTURE (2015-2016)

**Students with need:** Out of 1,353 full-time freshmen who applied for aid, 1,026 were judged to have need. Of these, 1,018 received aid, and 61 had their full need met. Average financial aid package met 86% of need; average scholarship/grant was $8,121; average loan was $4,169. For part-time students, average financial aid package was $7,436.
**Students without need:** 340 full-time freshmen who did not demonstrate need for aid received scholarships/grants; average award was $1,925. No-need awards available for academics, state/district residency.
**Scholarships offered:** Annual scholarships: $500 to $4,400; based on class rank in top 15%. Additional residential scholarships for out-of-state students: $4,490 annually; requires on-campus housing.

### FINANCIAL AID PROCEDURES

**Forms required:** FAFSA, state aid form.
**Dates and Deadlines:** Priority date 2/15; no closing date. Applicants notified on a rolling basis starting 2/15; must reply by 5/1 or within 3 week(s) of notification.
**Transfers:** No deadline. Applicants notified on a rolling basis starting 3/1; must reply by 5/1 or within 21 week(s) of notification.

### CONTACT

Mark Humbert, Director of Financial Aid
229 Sheldon Hall, Oswego, NY 13126-3599
(315) 312-2248

## SUNY College at Plattsburgh

Plattsburgh, New York
www.plattsburgh.edu                    Federal Code: 002849

**4-year public** liberal arts and teachers college in large town.
**Enrollment:** 5,272 undergrads, 7% part-time. 1,035 full-time freshmen.
**Selectivity:** Admits less than 50% of applicants.

### BASIC COSTS (2015-2016)

**Tuition and fees:** $7,854; out-of-state residents $17,704.
**Per-credit charge:** $270; out-of-state residents $680.
**Room and board:** $11,270.

### FINANCIAL AID PICTURE (2014-2015)

**Students with need:** Out of 920 full-time freshmen who applied for aid, 670 were judged to have need. Of these, 648 received aid, and 139 had their full need met. Average financial aid package met 79% of need; average scholarship/grant was $7,906; average loan was $6,425. For part-time students, average financial aid package was $5,769.
**Students without need:** 198 full-time freshmen who did not demonstrate need for aid received scholarships/grants; average award was $3,434. No-need awards available for academics, alumni affiliation, art, leadership, minority status, music/drama, state/district residency.

**FINANCIAL AID PROCEDURES**

**Forms required:** FAFSA, state aid form.

**Dates and Deadlines:** Priority date 2/15; no closing date. Applicants notified on a rolling basis starting 3/1; must reply by 5/1.

**Transfers:** No deadline. Applicants notified on a rolling basis.

**CONTACT**

Todd Moravec, Director of Student Financial Services
Kehoe Administration Building, Plattsburgh, NY 12901
(518) 564-4076

## SUNY College at Potsdam

Potsdam, New York
www.potsdam.edu                    Federal Code: 002850

**4-year public** liberal arts and teachers college in large town.

**Enrollment:** 3,595 undergrads, 3% part-time. 848 full-time freshmen.

**Selectivity:** Admits 50 to 75% of applicants.

**BASIC COSTS (2015-2016)**

**Tuition and fees:** $7,908; out-of-state residents $17,758.

**Per-credit charge:** $270; out-of-state residents $680.

**Room and board:** $11,870.

**FINANCIAL AID PICTURE (2015-2016)**

**Students with need:** Out of 821 full-time freshmen who applied for aid, 680 were judged to have need. Of these, 676 received aid, and 324 had their full need met. Average financial aid package met 90% of need; average scholarship/grant was $10,710; average loan was $3,674. For part-time students, average financial aid package was $8,694.

**Students without need:** 85 full-time freshmen who did not demonstrate need for aid received scholarships/grants; average award was $3,249. No-need awards available for academics, art, leadership, music/drama.

**Scholarships offered:** Mt. Emmons Scholarship: covers balance of in-state tuition and mandatory fees after TAP awards; $500 book stipend; residence hall fee waiver and board; renewable with minimum 3.25 GPA; 5 awarded. Freshman Scholars Program: begins at $1,000 annually; minimum high school GPA of 88 (on a 100 scale) or minimum SAT score of 1100 (Critical Reading and Math) or minimum ACT score of 24; participation, leadership in extracurricular activities and community service; renewable for three years with a minimum 3.25 cumulative GPA.

**Additional info:** Apply early to access limited, need-based awards.

**FINANCIAL AID PROCEDURES**

**Forms required:** FAFSA, state aid form.

**Dates and Deadlines:** Priority date 3/1; closing date 5/1. Applicants notified on a rolling basis starting 2/1; must reply by 5/1 or within 4 week(s) of notification.

**Transfers:** Transfer Scholars Program for incoming transfer students based upon outstanding academic achievement as measured by previous college GPA. $1,000-$3,000 to students with minimum cumulative GPA of 3.25 and higher. Renewable for 1 year with cumulative 3.25 GPA.

**CONTACT**

Susan Godreau, Director of Financial Aid
44 Pierrepont Avenue, Potsdam, NY 13676
(315) 267-2162

## SUNY College at Purchase

Purchase, New York
www.purchase.edu                    Federal Code: 006791

**4-year public** university and liberal arts college in large town.

**Enrollment:** 3,923 undergrads, 6% part-time. 780 full-time freshmen.

**Selectivity:** Admits less than 50% of applicants.

**BASIC COSTS (2015-2016)**

**Tuition and fees:** $8,267; out-of-state residents $18,117.

**Per-credit charge:** $270; out-of-state residents $680.

**Room and board:** $12,576.

**FINANCIAL AID PICTURE (2015-2016)**

**Students with need:** Out of 686 full-time freshmen who applied for aid, 480 were judged to have need. Of these, 478 received aid, and 4 had their full need met. Average financial aid package met 44% of need; average scholarship/grant was $8,586; average loan was $3,387. For part-time students, average financial aid package was $8,748.

**Students without need:** 78 full-time freshmen who did not demonstrate need for aid received scholarships/grants; average award was $2,508. No-need awards available for academics, art, minority status, music/drama.

**Additional info:** All applicants automatically considered for scholarship upon review of applications, essays, auditions, and/or portfolio.

**FINANCIAL AID PROCEDURES**

**Forms required:** FAFSA, state aid form.

**Dates and Deadlines:** Priority date 2/1; no closing date. Applicants notified on a rolling basis starting 3/1; must reply within 2 week(s) of notification.

**Transfers:** Financial aid transcripts required from all previously attended institutions.

**CONTACT**

Corey York, Director of Financial Aid
735 Anderson Hill Road, Purchase, NY 10577-1400
(914) 251-6350

## SUNY College of Agriculture and Technology at Cobleskill

Cobleskill, New York
www.cobleskill.edu                    Federal Code: 002856

**2-year public** agricultural and technical college in small town.

**Enrollment:** 2,419 undergrads, 4% part-time. 797 full-time freshmen.

**Selectivity:** Admits over 75% of applicants.

**BASIC COSTS (2015-2016)**

**Tuition and fees:** $7,951; out-of-state residents $17,301.

**Per-credit charge:** $269.58; out-of-state residents $680.

**Room and board:** $12,606.

**FINANCIAL AID PICTURE (2014-2015)**

**Students with need:** Out of 675 full-time freshmen who applied for aid, 660 were judged to have need. Of these, 656 received aid, and 6 had their full need met. Average financial aid package met 44% of need; average scholarship/grant was $7,008; average loan was $3,437. For part-time students, average financial aid package was $6,109.

**Students without need:** 33 full-time freshmen who did not demonstrate need for aid received scholarships/grants; average award was $2,451. No-need awards available for academics, alumni affiliation, leadership.

**Additional info:** Application deadline for scholarships March 15. Separate application required, available through admissions office.

**FINANCIAL AID PROCEDURES**

**Forms required:** FAFSA, state aid form, institutional form.

**Dates and Deadlines:** Priority date 2/15; no closing date. Applicants notified on a rolling basis starting 3/1; must reply by 3/1.

**Transfers:** No deadline. Applicants notified on a rolling basis; must reply within 3 week(s) of notification.

**CONTACT**

Louise Biron, Director of Financial Aid
Knapp Hall, Cobleskill, NY 12043
(800) 295-8998

PART III: FINANCIAL AID COLLEGE BY COLLEGE

## SUNY College of Agriculture and Technology at Morrisville

Morrisville, New York
www.morrisville.edu                  Federal Code: 002859

**4-year public** agricultural and technical college in rural community.
**Enrollment:** 2,694 undergrads, 8% part-time. 772 full-time freshmen.
**Selectivity:** Admits 50 to 75% of applicants.

### BASIC COSTS (2015-2016)
**Tuition and fees:** $8,001; out-of-state residents $12,171.
**Per-credit charge:** $270; out-of-state residents $444.
**Room and board:** $13,488.
**Additional info:** Tuition/fee waivers available for unemployed or children of unemployed.

### FINANCIAL AID PICTURE (2014-2015)
**Students with need:** Out of 750 full-time freshmen who applied for aid, 685 were judged to have need. Of these, 684 received aid, and 6 had their full need met. Average financial aid package met 47% of need; average scholarship/grant was $7,133; average loan was $3,305. For part-time students, average financial aid package was $5,699.
**Students without need:** 86 full-time freshmen who did not demonstrate need for aid received scholarships/grants; average award was $1,804. No-need awards available for academics, alumni affiliation, leadership, minority status, state/district residency.
**Scholarships offered:** Mustang Merit Awards are offered upon acceptance and are assigned on a first-come, first served basis. Acceptance of any outstanding institutional scholarship offers are due no later than May 1. Failure to accept an offer by May 1 will result in forfeiture of the award, and balance is subject to reassignment. Foundation awards require a separate application due February 1.

### FINANCIAL AID PROCEDURES
**Forms required:** FAFSA, state aid form.
**Dates and Deadlines:** Priority date 2/1; no closing date. Applicants notified on a rolling basis starting 3/15; must reply by 5/1 or within 4 week(s) of notification.
**Transfers:** No deadline. Applicants notified on a rolling basis starting 3/15; must reply by 5/1 or within 4 week(s) of notification. Merit scholarships and preferential housing available to qualified transfer students.

### CONTACT
Dacia Banks, Director of Financial Aid
PO Box 901, Morrisville, NY 13408-0901

## SUNY College of Environmental Science and Forestry

Syracuse, New York
www.esf.edu                  Federal Code: 002851

**4-year public** university and liberal arts college in small city.
**Enrollment:** 1,753 undergrads, 2% part-time. 318 full-time freshmen.
**Selectivity:** Admits 50 to 75% of applicants.

### BASIC COSTS (2015-2016)
**Tuition and fees:** $7,717; out-of-state residents $17,567.
**Per-credit charge:** $270; out-of-state residents $680.
**Room and board:** $15,440.

### FINANCIAL AID PICTURE (2015-2016)
**Students with need:** Out of 295 full-time freshmen who applied for aid, 262 were judged to have need. Of these, 262 received aid, and 127 had their full need met. Average financial aid package met 82% of need; average scholarship/grant was $6,000; average loan was $4,100. For part-time students, average financial aid package was $4,191.

**Students without need:** 56 full-time freshmen who did not demonstrate need for aid received scholarships/grants; average award was $3,384. No-need awards available for academics, alumni affiliation, leadership, minority status, ROTC, state/district residency.
**Scholarships offered:** Merit scholarships: up to 50% of undergraduate tuition; based on high school grades, class rank, and SAT or ACT scores.

### FINANCIAL AID PROCEDURES
**Forms required:** FAFSA, state aid form.
**Dates and Deadlines:** Priority date 3/1; no closing date. Applicants notified on a rolling basis starting 3/15; must reply within 2 week(s) of notification.
**Transfers:** No deadline. Applicants notified on a rolling basis starting 3/15; must reply within 2 week(s) of notification.

### CONTACT
Mark Hill, Director of Financial Aid
Gateway Center, Syracuse, NY 13210
(315) 470-6670

## SUNY College of Technology at Alfred

Alfred, New York
www.alfredstate.edu                  Federal Code: 002854

**2-year public** liberal arts and technical college in rural community.
**Enrollment:** 3,669 undergrads, 8% part-time. 1,053 full-time freshmen.
**Selectivity:** Admits 50 to 75% of applicants.

### BASIC COSTS (2015-2016)
**Tuition and fees:** $8,057; out-of-state residents $11,327.
**Per-credit charge:** $270; out-of-state residents $406.
**Room and board:** $11,430.
**Additional info:** Tuition for Out-of-State Full-time Bachelor's degree-seeking students is $16,320; per credit hour is $680.

### FINANCIAL AID PICTURE (2015-2016)
**Students with need:** Out of 1,017 full-time freshmen who applied for aid, 890 were judged to have need. Of these, 877 received aid, and 97 had their full need met. Average financial aid package met 58% of need; average scholarship/grant was $8,007; average loan was $3,635. For part-time students, average financial aid package was $6,049.
**Students without need:** 55 full-time freshmen who did not demonstrate need for aid received scholarships/grants; average award was $3,531. No-need awards available for academics, alumni affiliation, job skills, music/drama, state/district residency.

### FINANCIAL AID PROCEDURES
**Forms required:** FAFSA, state aid form.
**Dates and Deadlines:** Applicants notified on a rolling basis starting 3/1; must reply within 4 week(s) of notification.
**Transfers:** No deadline. Applicants notified on a rolling basis starting 3/15; must reply within 4 week(s) of notification.

### CONTACT
Jane Gilliland, Senior Director Student Records and Financial Services
Huntington Administration Building, Alfred, NY 14802-1196
(607) 587-4253

## SUNY College of Technology at Canton

Canton, New York
www.canton.edu                  Federal Code: 002855

**2-year public** technical college in small town.
**Enrollment:** 3,040 undergrads, 13% part-time. 726 full-time freshmen.
**Selectivity:** Admits over 75% of applicants.

## BASIC COSTS (2015-2016)
**Tuition and fees:** $7,855; out-of-state residents $12,245.
**Per-credit charge:** $270; out-of-state residents $453.
**Room and board:** $11,800.

## FINANCIAL AID PICTURE (2014-2015)
**Students with need:** Out of 705 full-time freshmen who applied for aid, 625 were judged to have need. Of these, 617 received aid, and 105 had their full need met. Average financial aid package met 17% of need; average scholarship/grant was $8,060; average loan was $3,461. Need-based aid available for part-time students.
**Students without need:** 18 full-time freshmen who did not demonstrate need for aid received scholarships/grants; average award was $922. No-need awards available for academics, alumni affiliation, leadership, minority status, state/district residency.
**Additional info:** Students can apply after the priority deadline has passed, but not all types of aid will be available.

## FINANCIAL AID PROCEDURES
**Forms required:** FAFSA, state aid form.
**Dates and Deadlines:** Priority date 3/1; no closing date. Applicants notified on a rolling basis starting 2/15; must reply within 4 week(s) of notification.
**Transfers:** Financial aid transcripts required from all previously attended schools for mid-year transfers.

## CONTACT
Kerrie Cooper, Director of Financial Aid
34 Cornell Drive, Canton, NY 13617-1098
(315) 386-7616

# SUNY College of Technology at Delhi
Delhi, New York
www.delhi.edu                 Federal Code: 002857

2-year public liberal arts and technical college in rural community.
**Enrollment:** 3,392 undergrads, 25% part-time. 958 full-time freshmen.
**Selectivity:** Admits 50 to 75% of applicants.

## BASIC COSTS (2015-2016)
**Tuition and fees:** $8,075; out-of-state residents $12,445.
**Per-credit charge:** $270; out-of-state residents $452.
**Room and board:** $11,436.
**Additional info:** Out of State tuition listed is for Associate Programs only; the rate for Bachelor's Programs is: $16,320.

## FINANCIAL AID PICTURE (2014-2015)
**Students with need:** Out of 904 full-time freshmen who applied for aid, 801 were judged to have need. Of these, 793 received aid. For part-time students, average financial aid package was $5,147.

## FINANCIAL AID PROCEDURES
**Forms required:** FAFSA, state aid form.
**Dates and Deadlines:** Priority date 2/15; no closing date. Applicants notified on a rolling basis starting 3/1; must reply within 2 week(s) of notification.
**Transfers:** No deadline. Applicants notified on a rolling basis.

## CONTACT
Nancy Hughes, Financial Aid Director
2 Main Street, Delhi, NY 13753-1190
(607) 746-4000

# SUNY Downstate Medical Center
Brooklyn, New York
www.downstate.edu             Federal Code: 002839

Upper-division public health science and nursing college in very large city.
**Enrollment:** 348 undergrads.

## BASIC COSTS (2015-2016)
**Tuition and fees:** $7,074; out-of-state residents $16,924.
**Per-credit charge:** $270; out-of-state residents $680.
**Room only:** $4,550.

## FINANCIAL AID PICTURE
**Students with need:** Need-based aid available for full-time and part-time students.

## FINANCIAL AID PROCEDURES
**Forms required:** FAFSA.
**Dates and Deadlines:** Priority date 3/1; no closing date. Applicants notified on a rolling basis.

## CONTACT
James Newell, Director of Financial Aid
450 Clarkson Avenue, Box 60, Brooklyn, NY 11203-2098
(718) 270-2488

# SUNY Empire State College
Saratoga Springs, New York
www.esc.edu                   Federal Code: 010286

4-year public liberal arts college in large town.
**Enrollment:** 9,827 undergrads, 57% part-time. 156 full-time freshmen.
**Selectivity:** Admits over 75% of applicants.

## BASIC COSTS (2015-2016)
**Tuition and fees:** $6,985; out-of-state residents $16,835.
**Per-credit charge:** $270; out-of-state residents $680.

## FINANCIAL AID PICTURE
**Students with need:** Need-based aid available for full-time and part-time students.
**Students without need:** This college awards aid only to students with need.

## FINANCIAL AID PROCEDURES
**Forms required:** FAFSA, state aid form.
**Dates and Deadlines:** Priority date 4/1; no closing date. Applicants notified on a rolling basis; must reply within 3 week(s) of notification.
**Transfers:** No deadline. Applicants notified on a rolling basis.

## CONTACT
Kristina Delbridge, Director of Financial Aid
1 Union Avenue, Saratoga Springs, NY 12866
(518) 587-2100

# SUNY Farmingdale State College
Farmingdale, New York
www.farmingdale.edu           Federal Code: 002858

4-year public technical college in large town.
**Enrollment:** 7,977 undergrads, 22% part-time. 1,047 full-time freshmen.
**Selectivity:** Admits less than 50% of applicants.

## BASIC COSTS (2015-2016)
**Tuition and fees:** $7,808; out-of-state residents $17,658.
**Per-credit charge:** $270; out-of-state residents $680.
**Room and board:** $12,500.

## FINANCIAL AID PICTURE (2014-2015)
**Students with need:** Out of 869 full-time freshmen who applied for aid, 553 were judged to have need. Of these, 500 received aid, and 52 had their full need met. Average financial aid package met 62% of need; average scholarship/grant was $6,744; average loan was $3,645. For part-time students, average financial aid package was $4,525.

**Students without need:** 3 full-time freshmen who did not demonstrate need for aid received scholarships/grants; average award was $2,000. No-need awards available for academics, alumni affiliation, job skills, state/district residency.

## FINANCIAL AID PROCEDURES

**Forms required:** FAFSA.

**Dates and Deadlines:** Priority date 4/1; no closing date. Applicants notified on a rolling basis starting 3/1.

## CONTACT

Diane Kazanecki-Kempter, Director of Financial Aid

2350 Broadhollow Road, Farmingdale, NY 11735-1021

(631) 420-2578

# SUNY Maritime College

Throggs Neck, New York

www.sunymaritime.edu          Federal Code: 002853

**4-year public** technical and maritime college in very large city.

**Enrollment:** 1,667 undergrads, 3% part-time. 349 full-time freshmen.

**Selectivity:** Admits 50 to 75% of applicants.

## BASIC COSTS (2015-2016)

**Tuition and fees:** $7,809; out-of-state residents $17,659.

**Per-credit charge:** $270; out-of-state residents $680.

**Room and board:** $11,516.

## FINANCIAL AID PICTURE (2014-2015)

**Students with need:** Out of 198 full-time freshmen who applied for aid, 190 were judged to have need. Of these, 161 received aid, and 18 had their full need met. Average financial aid package met 43% of need; average scholarship/grant was $5,732; average loan was $3,255. For part-time students, average financial aid package was $4,601.

**Students without need:** 37 full-time freshmen who did not demonstrate need for aid received scholarships/grants; average award was $1,615. No-need awards available for academics, leadership, minority status, ROTC, state/district residency.

**Scholarships offered:** Freshmen New Student Scholarships: $2,500-$10,000 per year, for up to four years; the transfer scholarship award is $1,500 per year, for up to two years. Cadet Appointment Program Scholarship: four-year; full tuition scholarship for undergraduate studies for qualified New York State residents.

**Additional info:** The Strategic Sealift Officer Program is unique to the maritime schools. The program allows students earning unlimited licenses as Merchant Marine Deck or Engine Officers to be commissioned as an officer in the Navy Reserve upon graduation. Strategic Sealift Officers normally serve on inactive duty in the Individual Ready Reserve allowing them to work as civilians in the maritime industry. Qualified students may apply for the Student Incentive Payments funded by the U.S. Maritime Administration during their freshman year. SIP benefits amount to a maximum of $32,000; $4,000 per semester.

## FINANCIAL AID PROCEDURES

**Forms required:** FAFSA.

**Dates and Deadlines:** Priority date 3/15; closing date 7/15. Applicants notified on a rolling basis starting 3/15; must reply by 5/1.

**Transfers:** Must have minimum 2.0 cumulative GPA if degree has not yet been earned.

## CONTACT

Andrea Damar, Director of Financial Aid

6 Pennyfield Avenue, Throggs Neck, NY 10465

(718) 409-7268

# SUNY Polytechnic Institute

Utica, New York

www.sunypoly.edu          Federal Code: 011678

**4-year public** business and engineering college in small city.

**Enrollment:** 1,957 undergrads, 12% part-time. 347 full-time freshmen.

**Selectivity:** Admits 50 to 75% of applicants.

## BASIC COSTS (2015-2016)

**Tuition and fees:** $7,739; out-of-state residents $17,589.

**Per-credit charge:** $270; out-of-state residents $680.

**Room and board:** $11,714.

## FINANCIAL AID PICTURE (2015-2016)

**Students with need:** Out of 308 full-time freshmen who applied for aid, 235 were judged to have need. Of these, 235 received aid, and 235 had their full need met. Average financial aid package met 100% of need; average scholarship/grant was $8,242; average loan was $3,357. For part-time students, average financial aid package was $4,625.

**Students without need:** 84 full-time freshmen who did not demonstrate need for aid received scholarships/grants; average award was $4,879.

## FINANCIAL AID PROCEDURES

**Forms required:** FAFSA, state aid form.

**Dates and Deadlines:** Priority date 3/1; no closing date. Applicants notified on a rolling basis starting 3/15; must reply within 2 week(s) of notification.

**Transfers:** No deadline. Applicants notified on a rolling basis starting 3/15; must reply within 2 week(s) of notification.

## CONTACT

Melissa Rose, Director, Financial Aid

100 Seymour Road, Utica, NY 13502

(315) 792-7210

# SUNY University at Albany

Albany, New York

www.albany.edu          Federal Code: 002835

**4-year public** university in small city.

**Enrollment:** 12,698 undergrads, 4% part-time. 2,588 full-time freshmen.

**Selectivity:** Admits 50 to 75% of applicants.

## BASIC COSTS (2015-2016)

**Tuition and fees:** $8,996; out-of-state residents $22,116.

**Per-credit charge:** $270; out-of-state residents $816.

**Room and board:** $12,426.

## FINANCIAL AID PICTURE

**Students with need:** Need-based aid available for full-time and part-time students. Work study available nights, weekends, and for part-time students.

**Students without need:** No-need awards available for academics, athletics, state/district residency.

**Scholarships offered:** Presidential Scholarship: up to $4,000 per year for NY residents and $6,000 per year for out-of-state students; renewable; requires minimum 90 high school average and combined SAT Critical Reading and Math scores in the upper 1200s or higher.

## FINANCIAL AID PROCEDURES

**Forms required:** FAFSA.

**Dates and Deadlines:** Priority date 3/15; no closing date. Applicants notified on a rolling basis starting 3/20.

## CONTACT

Diane Corbett, Director of Financial Aid

Office of Undergraduate Admissions, University Hall, Albany, NY 12222

(518) 442-3202

## SUNY University at Binghamton
Binghamton, New York
www.binghamton.edu                    Federal Code: 002836

**4-year public** university in small city.
**Enrollment:** 13,465 undergrads, 3% part-time. 2,600 full-time freshmen.
**Selectivity:** Admits less than 50% of applicants.

### BASIC COSTS (2015-2016)
**Tuition and fees:** $9,053; out-of-state residents $22,173.
**Per-credit charge:** $270; out-of-state residents $816.
**Room and board:** $13,198.

### FINANCIAL AID PICTURE (2015-2016)
**Students with need:** Out of 2,129 full-time freshmen who applied for aid, 1,245 were judged to have need. Of these, 1,242 received aid, and 198 had their full need met. Average financial aid package met 66% of need; average scholarship/grant was $9,032; average loan was $3,695. For part-time students, average financial aid package was $7,434.
**Students without need:** 30 full-time freshmen who did not demonstrate need for aid received scholarships/grants; average award was $8,677. No-need awards available for academics, art, athletics, leadership, minority status, music/drama, state/district residency.
**Scholarships offered:** 84 full-time freshmen received athletic scholarships; average amount $11,727.
**Additional info:** Most institutional aid awarded on a first-come first-served basis while considering student's ability to pay (determined by use of the FAFSA application) and the student's academic achievement.

### FINANCIAL AID PROCEDURES
**Forms required:** FAFSA, state aid form.
**Dates and Deadlines:** Priority date 2/1; no closing date. Applicants notified on a rolling basis starting 3/4; must reply within 2 week(s) of notification.
**Transfers:** No deadline. Applicants notified on a rolling basis starting 3/7; must reply within 2 week(s) of notification. Awards based on self-reported grade level until an official transfer credit evaluation is completed.

### CONTACT
Dennis Chavez, Director, Financial Aid and Student Records
PO Box 6001, Binghamton, NY 13902-6001
(607) 777-2428

## SUNY University at Buffalo
Buffalo, New York
www.buffalo.edu                    Federal Code: 002837

**4-year public** university in large city.
**Enrollment:** 19,692 undergrads, 7% part-time. 3,498 full-time freshmen.
**Selectivity:** Admits 50 to 75% of applicants.

### BASIC COSTS (2015-2016)
**Tuition and fees:** $9,461; out-of-state residents $24,541.
**Per-credit charge:** $270; out-of-state residents $1,024.
**Room and board:** $13,061.
**Additional info:** Tuition/fee waivers available for adults, minority students.

### FINANCIAL AID PICTURE (2014-2015)
**Students with need:** Out of 2,756 full-time freshmen who applied for aid, 2,219 were judged to have need. Of these, 2,085 received aid. Average financial aid package met 64% of need; average scholarship/grant was $5,826; average loan was $3,525. For part-time students, average financial aid package was $5,727.
**Students without need:** 113 full-time freshmen who did not demonstrate need for aid received scholarships/grants; average award was $5,809. No-need awards available for academics, art, athletics, minority status, music/drama, state/district residency.

**Scholarships offered:** *Merit:* Presidential Scholarship: full cost of attendance; minimum 1470 SAT (Critical Reading and Math), or 33 ACT; unweighted high school average of 95 or better; 25 awards. Provost Scholarships: starts at $2,500; minimum high school average of 90; 1200 combined SAT (Critical Reading and Math) or ACT score of 27. Provost Scholarships for outstanding talent in the performing and creative arts: minimum unweighted high school average of 90; minimum 1230 combined SAT (Critical Reading and Math), or minimum 28 ACT. UB Buffalo Partnership Scholars Program: full tuition and fees for up to four consecutive years, a yearly book stipend of $600, and a laptop computer; for students from the Buffalo Public Schools who excel both academically and through civic service to their respective communities. *Athletic:* 60 full-time freshmen received athletic scholarships; average amount $14,963.

### FINANCIAL AID PROCEDURES
**Forms required:** FAFSA.
**Dates and Deadlines:** Priority date 3/1; no closing date. Applicants notified on a rolling basis starting 2/1; must reply by 5/1.

### CONTACT
John Gottardy, Director of Financial Aid
12 Capen Hall, Buffalo, NY 14260-1660
(716) 645-2450

## SUNY University at Stony Brook
Stony Brook, New York
www.stonybrook.edu                    Federal Code: 002838

**4-year public** university in large town.
**Enrollment:** 16,583 undergrads, 6% part-time. 2,852 full-time freshmen.
**Selectivity:** Admits less than 50% of applicants.

### BASIC COSTS (2015-2016)
**Tuition and fees:** $8,855; out-of-state residents $23,935.
**Per-credit charge:** $270; out-of-state residents $898.
**Room and board:** $12,032.

### FINANCIAL AID PICTURE (2014-2015)
**Students with need:** Out of 2,180 full-time freshmen who applied for aid, 1,535 were judged to have need. Of these, 1,520 received aid, and 294 had their full need met. Average financial aid package met 71% of need; average scholarship/grant was $9,316; average loan was $3,714. For part-time students, average financial aid package was $5,708.
**Students without need:** 442 full-time freshmen who did not demonstrate need for aid received scholarships/grants; average award was $4,106. No-need awards available for academics, alumni affiliation, art, athletics, job skills, leadership, music/drama.
**Scholarships offered:** 64 full-time freshmen received athletic scholarships; average amount $13,644.

### FINANCIAL AID PROCEDURES
**Forms required:** FAFSA, state aid form.
**Dates and Deadlines:** Priority date 3/1; no closing date. Applicants notified on a rolling basis starting 4/1; must reply by 5/1 or within 2 week(s) of notification.

### CONTACT
Jacqueline Pascariello, Director Financial Aid
118 Administration Building, Stony Brook, NY 11794-1901
(631) 632-6840

## SUNY Upstate Medical University
Syracuse, New York
www.upstate.edu                    Federal Code: 002840

**Upper-division public** health science and nursing college in small city.
**Enrollment:** 217 undergrads.

## BASIC COSTS (2015-2016)

**Tuition and fees:** $7,279; out-of-state residents $17,129.
**Per-credit charge:** $270; out-of-state residents $680.

## FINANCIAL AID PICTURE

**Students with need:** Need-based aid available for full-time and part-time students. Work study available nights, weekends, and for part-time students.
**Students without need:** This college awards aid only to students with need.

## FINANCIAL AID PROCEDURES

**Forms required:** FAFSA.
**Dates and Deadlines:** Priority date 3/1; no closing date. Applicants notified on a rolling basis starting 4/1; must reply within 2 week(s) of notification.
**Transfers:** Applicants notified on a rolling basis starting 4/15; must reply within 2 week(s) of notification.

## CONTACT

Mike Pede, Director of Financial Aid
766 Irving Avenue, Syracuse, NY 13210
(315) 464-4329

# Swedish Institute
New York, New York
www.swedishinstitute.edu          Federal Code: 021700

**2-year for-profit** health science college in very large city.
**Enrollment:** 700 undergrads.

## BASIC COSTS (2015-2016)

**Additional info:** Nursing: $568 per credit; 68 semester credits. Massage Therapy: $484 per credit; 64 semester credits. Advanced Personal Training: $493 per credit; 62 semester credits. Personal Training: $493 per credit; 37 semester credits. Clinical and Administrative Medical Assistant: $304 per credit; 90 quarter credits. Surgical Technologist: $368 per credit; 94.5 quarter credits. Medical Billing and Coding: $304 per credit; 48 quarter credits. One-time registration fee: $100. Program fees vary per term: ranges from $188 to $705.

## FINANCIAL AID PICTURE

**Students with need:** Need-based aid available for full-time and part-time students.
**Students without need:** This college awards aid only to students with need.

## FINANCIAL AID PROCEDURES

**Forms required:** FAFSA, institutional form.

## CONTACT

Alex Ormeno, Financial Aid Director
151 West 26th Street, New York, NY 10001
(212) 924-5900 ext. 223

# Syracuse University
Syracuse, New York          Federal Code: 002882
www.syr.edu          CSS Code: 2823

**4-year private** university in small city.
**Enrollment:** 14,620 undergrads, 3% part-time. 3,478 full-time freshmen.
**Selectivity:** Admits less than 50% of applicants.

## BASIC COSTS (2016-2017)

**Tuition and fees:** $45,022.
**Per-credit charge:** $1,891.
**Room and board:** $15,217.

## FINANCIAL AID PICTURE (2015-2016)

**Students with need:** Out of 2,363 full-time freshmen who applied for aid, 1,769 were judged to have need. Of these, 1,729 received aid, and 780 had their full need met. Average financial aid package met 96% of need; average scholarship/grant was $29,715; average loan was $4,600. Need-based aid available for part-time students.
**Students without need:** 498 full-time freshmen who did not demonstrate need for aid received scholarships/grants; average award was $11,540. No-need awards available for academics, art, athletics, music/drama, ROTC.
**Scholarships offered:** 78 full-time freshmen received athletic scholarships; average amount $54,080.

## FINANCIAL AID PROCEDURES

**Forms required:** FAFSA, CSS PROFILE.
**Dates and Deadlines:** Closing date 2/1. Applicants notified by 3/15; must reply by 5/1.
**Transfers:** Closing date 7/1. Applicants notified on a rolling basis starting 3/18; must reply by 5/1 or within 2 week(s) of notification.

## CONTACT

Ryan Williams, Associate Vice President Enrollment Management
900 South Crouse Avenue, Syracuse, NY 13244-5040
(315) 443-1513

# Technical Career Institutes
New York, New York
www.tcicollege.edu          Federal Code: 011031

**2-year for-profit** technical and career college in very large city.
**Enrollment:** 2,081 undergrads, 15% part-time. 342 full-time freshmen.
**Selectivity:** Open admission.

## BASIC COSTS (2015-2016)

**Tuition and fees:** $13,800.
**Per-credit charge:** $548.

## FINANCIAL AID PICTURE

**Students with need:** Need-based aid available for full-time and part-time students.
**Students without need:** No-need awards available for academics, alumni affiliation.

## FINANCIAL AID PROCEDURES

**Forms required:** FAFSA, institutional form.
**Dates and Deadlines:** Applicants notified on a rolling basis.

## CONTACT

Cynthia Fekaris, Vice President of Financial Aid
320 West 31st Street, New York, NY 10001
(212) 594-4000

# Tompkins Cortland Community College
Dryden, New York
www.TC3.edu          Federal Code: 006788

**2-year public** community college in small town.
**Enrollment:** 2,706 undergrads, 22% part-time. 773 full-time freshmen.
**Selectivity:** Open admission; but selective for some programs.

## BASIC COSTS (2015-2016)

**Tuition and fees:** $5,636; out-of-state residents $10,586.
**Per-credit charge:** $164; out-of-state residents $338.
**Room and board:** $10,980.

## FINANCIAL AID PICTURE

**Students with need:** Need-based aid available for full-time and part-time students. Work study available nights, weekends, and for part-time students.

**Students without need:** No-need awards available for academics.

## FINANCIAL AID PROCEDURES

**Forms required:** FAFSA, state aid form, institutional form.

**Dates and Deadlines:** Priority date 4/15; no closing date. Applicants notified on a rolling basis starting 3/15; must reply within 4 week(s) of notification.

## CONTACT

LaSonya Griggs, Director of Financial Aid
170 North Street, Dryden, NY 13053-0139
(607) 844-6580

## Touro College

New York, New York
www.touro.edu      Federal Code: 010142

**4-year private** liberal arts college in very large city.

**Enrollment:** 6,036 undergrads, 18% part-time. 522 full-time freshmen.

**Selectivity:** Admits less than 50% of applicants.

### BASIC COSTS (2016-2017)

**Tuition and fees:** $16,980.

**Per-credit charge:** $680.

**Room and board:** $11,970.

### FINANCIAL AID PICTURE (2015-2016)

**Students with need:** Average financial aid package met 40% of need; average scholarship/grant was $2,058; average loan was $1,799. For part-time students, average financial aid package was $1,807.

**Students without need:** No-need awards available for academics, alumni affiliation.

### FINANCIAL AID PROCEDURES

**Forms required:** FAFSA, state aid form, institutional form.

**Dates and Deadlines:** Priority date 5/15; closing date 8/15. Applicants notified on a rolling basis starting 5/1; must reply within 4 week(s) of notification.

### CONTACT

Carol Rosenbaum, Director of Financial Aid
27 West 23rd Street, New York, NY 10010
(212) 463-0400

## Trocaire College

Buffalo, New York
www.trocaire.edu      Federal Code: 002812

**2-year private** health science and career college in large city, affiliated with Roman Catholic Church.

**Enrollment:** 1,230 undergrads, 50% part-time. 110 full-time freshmen.

**Selectivity:** Open admission; but selective for some programs.

### BASIC COSTS (2015-2016)

**Tuition and fees:** $16,290.

**Per-credit charge:** $660.

### FINANCIAL AID PICTURE

**Students with need:** Need-based aid available for full-time and part-time students.

**Students without need:** No-need awards available for academics, alumni affiliation.

### FINANCIAL AID PROCEDURES

**Forms required:** FAFSA, state aid form.

**Dates and Deadlines:** Priority date 3/15; no closing date. Applicants notified on a rolling basis starting 3/1; must reply within 2 week(s) of notification.

## CONTACT

Janet McGrath, Director of Financial Aid
360 Choate Avenue, Buffalo, NY 14220
(716) 826-1200

## Ulster County Community College

Stone Ridge, New York
www.sunyulster.edu      Federal Code: 002880

**2-year public** community college in small town.

**Enrollment:** 1,907 undergrads, 32% part-time. 444 full-time freshmen.

**Selectivity:** Open admission; but selective for some programs.

### BASIC COSTS (2015-2016)

**Tuition and fees:** $5,010; out-of-state residents $9,240.

**Per-credit charge:** $159; out-of-state residents $318.

### FINANCIAL AID PICTURE (2014-2015)

**Students with need:** 68% of average financial aid package awarded as scholarships/grants, 32% awarded as loans/jobs. Need-based aid available for part-time students.

### FINANCIAL AID PROCEDURES

**Forms required:** FAFSA.

**Dates and Deadlines:** Priority date 6/1; no closing date. Applicants notified on a rolling basis starting 6/1; must reply within 2 week(s) of notification.

### CONTACT

Christopher Chang, Director of Financial Aid
Cottekill Road, Stone Ridge, NY 12484
(845) 687-5058

## Union College

Schenectady, New York      Federal Code: 002889
www.union.edu      CSS Code: 2920

**4-year private** engineering and liberal arts college in small city.

**Enrollment:** 2,206 undergrads. 568 full-time freshmen.

**Selectivity:** Admits less than 50% of applicants. GED not accepted.

### BASIC COSTS (2015-2016)

**Tuition and fees:** $50,013.

**Room and board:** $12,261.

### FINANCIAL AID PICTURE (2015-2016)

**Students with need:** Out of 347 full-time freshmen who applied for aid, 280 were judged to have need. Of these, 280 received aid, and 280 had their full need met. Average financial aid package met 100% of need; average scholarship/grant was $35,750; average loan was $3,570. Need-based aid available for part-time students.

**Students without need:** 194 full-time freshmen who did not demonstrate need for aid received scholarships/grants; average award was $9,500. No-need awards available for academics, ROTC.

### FINANCIAL AID PROCEDURES

**Forms required:** FAFSA, CSS PROFILE, state aid form.

**Dates and Deadlines:** Priority date 2/1; closing date 2/1. Applicants notified by 3/25; must reply by 5/1.

**Transfers:** No deadline. Applicants notified on a rolling basis; must reply within 2 week(s) of notification. Financial aid applicants must submit the CSS PROFILE form and FAFSA to their respective processing agencies at least two months prior to application deadline.

### CONTACT

Linda Parker, Director of Financial Aid
Grant Hall, 807 Union Street, Schenectady, NY 12308-3107
(518) 388-6123

## United States Merchant Marine Academy
Kings Point, New York
www.usmma.edu                    Federal Code: 002892

**4-year public** military and maritime college in large town.
**Enrollment:** 939 undergrads. 259 full-time freshmen.

### BASIC COSTS (2015-2016)
**Additional info:** All costs for tuition, board, books, and uniforms paid for by Federal Government. Students are required to purchase a compliant laptop computer, academic equipment (as needed), and pay for license fees, transportation costs, laundry and barber services. Students are not paid a monthly salary/stipend, unless they are at sea.

### FINANCIAL AID PICTURE (2014-2015)
**Students with need:** Out of 105 full-time freshmen who applied for aid, 63 were judged to have need. Of these, 63 received aid, and 63 had their full need met. Average financial aid package met 75% of need; average scholarship/grant was $4,285; average loan was $3,500.
**Students without need:** This college awards aid only to students with need.
**Scholarships offered:** Outside award scholarships welcomed and encouraged.
**Additional info:** Financial Aid awarded on a rolling basis; all students regarded as full time, undergraduates. The academy does not have institutional aid. Only Title IV FSA is awarded. Students will spend a cumulative period of one year at sea, where they will be paid a monthly salary of about $950.

### FINANCIAL AID PROCEDURES
**Forms required:** FAFSA, institutional form.
**Dates and Deadlines:** Applicants notified on a rolling basis starting 5/1; must reply within 8 week(s) of notification.
**Transfers:** No deadline. Applicants notified on a rolling basis. Transfer students regarded as freshmen, fall under freshmen aid criteria.

### CONTACT
Joseph Becker, Financial Aid Specialist
300 Steamboat Road, Admissions Center, Kings Point, NY 11024-1699
(516) 726-5638

## United States Military Academy
West Point, New York
www.westpoint.edu

**4-year public** military college in small town.
**Enrollment:** 4,348 undergrads. 1,236 full-time freshmen.
**Selectivity:** Admits less than 50% of applicants.

### BASIC COSTS (2016-2017)
**Additional info:** All Cadets are members of the United States Army and receive a full scholarship, room, board, and a monthly salary. However, an INITIAL DEPOSIT is required from all new incoming Cadets to cover the initial issue of uniforms, books, supplies, and equipment. Any Cadet who cannot meet the Initial Deposit will have their end of month pay reduced until their cadet account is in line.

### FINANCIAL AID PICTURE
**Additional info:** Scholarships can be accepted for a cadet to satisfy the requirement of the initial deposit. However, scholarships from any agency that states the scholarship is to be used for tuition and/or room and board will not be accepted since there is no charge for these items.

### CONTACT
646 Swift Road, West Point, NY 10996-1905

## University of Rochester
Rochester, New York          Federal Code: 002894
www.rochester.edu            CSS Code: 2928

**4-year private** university in large city.
**Enrollment:** 6,123 undergrads, 2% part-time. 1,406 full-time freshmen.
**Selectivity:** Admits less than 50% of applicants.

### BASIC COSTS (2016-2017)
**Tuition and fees:** $50,142.
**Per-credit charge:** $1,538.
**Room and board:** $14,890.

### FINANCIAL AID PICTURE (2014-2015)
**Students with need:** Out of 1,023 full-time freshmen who applied for aid, 794 were judged to have need. Of these, 792 received aid, and 722 had their full need met. Average financial aid package met 97% of need; average scholarship/grant was $40,556; average loan was $3,844. For part-time students, average financial aid package was $12,446.
**Students without need:** 432 full-time freshmen who did not demonstrate need for aid received scholarships/grants; average award was $13,179. No-need awards available for academics, alumni affiliation, art, leadership, music/drama, ROTC.
**Additional info:** Alternative loans and financing information available. Need-based aid available for eligible Mexican and Canadian citizens.

### FINANCIAL AID PROCEDURES
**Forms required:** FAFSA, CSS PROFILE, state aid form.
**Dates and Deadlines:** Closing date 2/15. Applicants notified by 4/1; must reply by 5/1.
**Transfers:** Priority date 2/15. Must reply by 8/1.

### CONTACT
Samantha Veeder, Associate Dean of College Enrollment/Director of Financial Aid
300 Wilson Boulevard, Rochester, NY 14627-0251
(585) 275-3226

## Utica College
Utica, New York
www.utica.edu                Federal Code: 002883

**4-year private** health science and liberal arts college in small city.
**Enrollment:** 3,041 undergrads, 21% part-time. 645 full-time freshmen.
**Selectivity:** Admits over 75% of applicants.

### BASIC COSTS (2016-2017)
**Tuition and fees:** $19,996.
**Room and board:** $10,434.

### FINANCIAL AID PICTURE (2015-2016)
**Students with need:** Out of 615 full-time freshmen who applied for aid, 572 were judged to have need. Of these, 572 received aid, and 68 had their full need met. Average financial aid package met 77% of need; average scholarship/grant was $6,136; average loan was $3,410. For part-time students, average financial aid package was $5,926.
**Students without need:** 66 full-time freshmen who did not demonstrate need for aid received scholarships/grants; average award was $20,978. No-need awards available for academics, alumni affiliation.

### FINANCIAL AID PROCEDURES
**Forms required:** FAFSA, state aid form.
**Dates and Deadlines:** Priority date 3/15; no closing date. Applicants notified on a rolling basis starting 3/1; must reply by 5/1.
**Transfers:** Applicants notified on a rolling basis.

**CONTACT**
Laura Bedford, Executive Director of Student Financial Services
1600 Burrstone Road, Utica, NY 13502-4892
(315) 792-3179

## Vassar College
Poughkeepsie, New York
www.vassar.edu
Federal Code: 002895
CSS Code: 2956

**4-year private** liberal arts college in small city.
**Enrollment:** 2,414 undergrads. 667 full-time freshmen.
**Selectivity:** Admits less than 50% of applicants.

**BASIC COSTS (2016-2017)**
**Tuition and fees:** $53,090.
**Room and board:** $12,400.

**FINANCIAL AID PICTURE (2015-2016)**
**Students with need:** Out of 505 full-time freshmen who applied for aid, 430 were judged to have need. Of these, 430 received aid, and 430 had their full need met. Average financial aid package met 100% of need; average scholarship/grant was $45,358; average loan was $2,493.
**Students without need:** This college awards aid only to students with need.
**Additional info:** No loans in the initial financial aid packages for students from families with total income used in need analysis of $60,000 or less.

**FINANCIAL AID PROCEDURES**
**Forms required:** FAFSA, CSS PROFILE.
**Dates and Deadlines:** Closing date 2/15. Applicants notified by 3/30; must reply by 5/1.
**Transfers:** Closing date 3/15. Applicants notified by 5/1; must reply within 4 week(s) of notification. Limited number of need-based award packages offered to transfers.

**CONTACT**
Jessica Bernier, Director of Financial Aid
Box 10, 124 Raymond Avenue, Poughkeepsie, NY 12604-0077
(845) 437-5320

## Vaughn College of Aeronautics and Technology
Flushing, New York
www.vaughn.edu
Federal Code: 002665

**4-year private** engineering college in very large city.
**Enrollment:** 1,525 undergrads, 20% part-time. 249 full-time freshmen.
**Selectivity:** Admits 50 to 75% of applicants.

**BASIC COSTS (2016-2017)**
**Tuition and fees:** $23,935.
**Per-credit charge:** $765.
**Room and board:** $13,575.

**FINANCIAL AID PICTURE (2015-2016)**
**Students with need:** Out of 230 full-time freshmen who applied for aid, 209 were judged to have need. Of these, 209 received aid, and 52 had their full need met. Average financial aid package met 92% of need; average scholarship/grant was $11,354; average loan was $2,851. For part-time students, average financial aid package was $6,133.
**Students without need:** 22 full-time freshmen who did not demonstrate need for aid received scholarships/grants; average award was $11,624. No-need awards available for academics, alumni affiliation.

**FINANCIAL AID PROCEDURES**
**Forms required:** FAFSA, state aid form.

**Dates and Deadlines:** Priority date 3/15; no closing date. Applicants notified on a rolling basis starting 4/15; must reply within 2 week(s) of notification.
**Transfers:** No deadline. Applicants notified on a rolling basis; must reply within 2 week(s) of notification.

**CONTACT**
Dorothy Martin, Director of Financial Aid
8601 23rd Avenue, Flushing, NY 11369
(718) 429-6600 ext. 100

## Villa Maria College of Buffalo
Buffalo, New York
www.villa.edu
Federal Code: 002896

**2-year private** visual arts and music college in large city, affiliated with Roman Catholic Church.
**Enrollment:** 541 undergrads, 23% part-time. 134 full-time freshmen.
**Selectivity:** Admits over 75% of applicants.

**BASIC COSTS (2015-2016)**
**Tuition and fees:** $19,910.
**Per-credit charge:** $645.
**Additional info:** Tuition/fee waivers available for unemployed or children of unemployed.

**FINANCIAL AID PICTURE (2014-2015)**
**Students with need:** 59% of average financial aid package awarded as scholarships/grants, 41% awarded as loans/jobs. Need-based aid available for part-time students.
**Students without need:** No-need awards available for academics, alumni affiliation, art, leadership.

**FINANCIAL AID PROCEDURES**
**Forms required:** FAFSA.
**Dates and Deadlines:** Applicants notified on a rolling basis starting 2/15; must reply within 2 week(s) of notification.
**Transfers:** No deadline. Applicants notified on a rolling basis starting 2/15; must reply within 2 week(s) of notification.

**CONTACT**
Aimee Murch, Director of Financial Aid and Veterans Affairs
240 Pine Ridge Road, Buffalo, NY 14225-3999
(716) 896-0700 ext. 1850

## Wagner College
Staten Island, New York
www.wagner.edu
Federal Code: 002899

**4-year private** liberal arts college in very large city, affiliated with Lutheran Church in America.
**Enrollment:** 1,741 undergrads, 2% part-time. 421 full-time freshmen.
**Selectivity:** Admits 50 to 75% of applicants.

**BASIC COSTS (2015-2016)**
**Tuition and fees:** $42,480.
**Room and board:** $13,000.
**Additional info:** Tuition/fee waivers available for unemployed or children of unemployed.

**FINANCIAL AID PICTURE (2015-2016)**
**Students with need:** Out of 348 full-time freshmen who applied for aid, 305 were judged to have need. Of these, 305 received aid, and 78 had their full need met. Average financial aid package met 78% of need; average scholarship/grant was $16,866; average loan was $2,197.
**Students without need:** 76 full-time freshmen who did not demonstrate need for aid received scholarships/grants; average award was $17,367. No-need awards available for academics, athletics, music/drama.

**Scholarships offered:** 21 full-time freshmen received athletic scholarships; average amount $31,850.

### FINANCIAL AID PROCEDURES
**Forms required:** FAFSA, state aid form.
**Dates and Deadlines:** Priority date 2/15; no closing date. Applicants notified on a rolling basis starting 3/1; must reply within 3 week(s) of notification.
**Transfers:** No deadline. Applicants notified on a rolling basis starting 3/1; must reply within 3 week(s) of notification.

### CONTACT
Theresa Weimer, Director of Financial Aid
One Campus Road, Staten Island, NY 10301
(718) 390-3183

## Webb Institute
Glen Cove, New York
www.webb.edu                    Federal Code: 002900

**4-year private** engineering college in large town.
**Enrollment:** 91 undergrads. 26 full-time freshmen.
**Selectivity:** Admits less than 50% of applicants. GED not accepted.

### BASIC COSTS (2016-2017)
**Tuition and fees:** $47,400.
**Room and board:** $14,400.
**Additional info:** All admitted students receive full-tuition scholarships.

### FINANCIAL AID PICTURE (2014-2015)
**Students with need:** Out of 11 full-time freshmen who applied for aid, 11 were judged to have need. Of these, 11 received aid. Average financial aid package met 80% of need; average scholarship/grant was $2,000; average loan was $3,340.
**Students without need:** This college awards aid only to students with need.
**Additional info:** Institutionally funded loans available.

### FINANCIAL AID PROCEDURES
**Forms required:** FAFSA, institutional form.
**Dates and Deadlines:** Closing date 7/1. Applicants notified on a rolling basis starting 6/1; must reply within 2 week(s) of notification.

### CONTACT
Lauri D'Ambra, Assistant Director of Financial Aid
298 Crescent Beach Road, Glen Cove, NY 11542-1398
(516) 671-8355 ext. 1107

## Wells College
Aurora, New York
www.wells.edu                   Federal Code: 002901

**4-year private** liberal arts college in rural community.
**Enrollment:** 572 undergrads, 2% part-time. 163 full-time freshmen.
**Selectivity:** Admits 50 to 75% of applicants.

### BASIC COSTS (2015-2016)
**Tuition and fees:** $37,500.
**Per-credit charge:** $1,250.
**Room and board:** $13,000.

### FINANCIAL AID PICTURE (2014-2015)
**Students with need:** Out of 161 full-time freshmen who applied for aid, 155 were judged to have need. Of these, 155 received aid, and 21 had their full need met. Average financial aid package met 83% of need; average scholarship/grant was $29,177; average loan was $3,768. For part-time students, average financial aid package was $955.

**Students without need:** 7 full-time freshmen who did not demonstrate need for aid received scholarships/grants; average award was $19,312. No-need awards available for academics, alumni affiliation, leadership.
**Scholarships offered:** Henry Wells Scholarship: guaranteed first-year internship or related experience and $3,000 stipend (unlocked in the Junior year), as well as internship or experiential learning program in student's upper-class years; tuition-based scholarship valued at up to $20,000 a year for four years. Thriving on Change Scholarship opportunity in the form of an essay competition from among incoming freshmen. Legacy Scholarships are available as well to qualifying individuals.

### FINANCIAL AID PROCEDURES
**Forms required:** FAFSA.
**Dates and Deadlines:** Priority date 2/15; no closing date. Applicants notified on a rolling basis starting 3/10; must reply by 5/1.
**Transfers:** Priority date 3/1; no deadline. Applicants notified on a rolling basis starting 3/1; must reply by 7/1.

### CONTACT
Laura Burns, Director of Financial Aid
170 Main Street, Aurora, NY 13026
(315) 364-3289

## Westchester Community College
Valhalla, New York
www.sunywcc.edu                 Federal Code: 002881

**2-year public** community college in large town.
**Enrollment:** 11,689 undergrads, 41% part-time. 2,023 full-time freshmen.
**Selectivity:** Open admission; but selective for some programs.

### BASIC COSTS (2015-2016)
**Tuition and fees:** $4,723; out-of-state residents $12,213.
**Per-credit charge:** $179; out-of-state residents $493.

### FINANCIAL AID PICTURE (2014-2015)
**Students with need:** Out of 1,617 full-time freshmen who applied for aid, 1,254 were judged to have need. Of these, 1,201 received aid. For part-time students, average financial aid package was $1,749.
**Students without need:** 13 full-time freshmen who did not demonstrate need for aid received scholarships/grants; average award was $939. No-need awards available for academics, leadership.

### FINANCIAL AID PROCEDURES
**Forms required:** FAFSA, state aid form.
**Dates and Deadlines:** Priority date 6/30; no closing date. Applicants notified on a rolling basis starting 4/1; must reply within 4 week(s) of notification.
**Transfers:** No deadline.

### CONTACT
Anita Cook, Director of Financial Aid
75 Grasslands Road, Valhalla, NY 10595
(914) 606-6773

## Yeshiva University
New York, New York
www.yu.edu                      Federal Code: 002903

**4-year private** university in very large city.
**Enrollment:** 2,744 undergrads, 2% part-time. 775 full-time freshmen.
**Selectivity:** Admits over 75% of applicants.

### BASIC COSTS (2015-2016)
**Tuition and fees:** $39,530.
**Per-credit charge:** $1,350.
**Room and board:** $11,250.

## FINANCIAL AID PICTURE (2015-2016)

**Students with need:** Out of 557 full-time freshmen who applied for aid, 438 were judged to have need. Of these, 431 received aid, and 134 had their full need met. Average financial aid package met 90% of need; average scholarship/grant was $12,700; average loan was $2,716. For part-time students, average financial aid package was $13,577.

**Students without need:** 195 full-time freshmen who did not demonstrate need for aid received scholarships/grants; average award was $9,506. No-need awards available for academics, state/district residency.

**Additional info:** Essays required of Distinguished Scholarship applicants.

## FINANCIAL AID PROCEDURES

**Forms required:** FAFSA.

**Dates and Deadlines:** Priority date 2/1; no closing date. Applicants notified on a rolling basis starting 3/15; must reply by 5/1.

## CONTACT

Robert Friedman, University Director of Student Finance
500 West 185th Street, New York, NY 10033
(212) 960-5399

## Yeshivat Mikdash Melech

Brooklyn, New York
www.mikdashmelech.net　　　　Federal Code: 014615

**5-year private** rabbinical college for men in very large city, affiliated with Jewish faith.

**Enrollment:** 17 undergrads.

**Selectivity:** Open admission; but selective for some programs.

## BASIC COSTS (2015-2016)

**Tuition and fees:** $8,100.

**Room and board:** $4,700.

**Additional info:** Tuition/fee waivers available for adults.

## FINANCIAL AID PICTURE

**Students with need:** Need-based aid available for full-time and part-time students. Work study available nights.

**Students without need:** No-need awards available for academics, leadership, religious affiliation.

## FINANCIAL AID PROCEDURES

**Forms required:** FAFSA, institutional form.

**Dates and Deadlines:** Applicants notified on a rolling basis starting 5/1.

**Transfers:** No deadline. Applicants notified on a rolling basis starting 5/1.

## CONTACT

Amram Sananes, Financial Aid Administrator
1326 Ocean Parkway, Brooklyn, NY 11230-9963
(718) 339-1090

# North Carolina

## Alamance Community College

Graham, North Carolina
www.alamancecc.edu　　　　Federal Code: 005463

**2-year public** community college in large town.

**Enrollment:** 4,042 undergrads, 38% part-time. 567 full-time freshmen.

**Selectivity:** Open admission; but selective for some programs.

## BASIC COSTS (2015-2016)

**Tuition and fees:** $2,190; out-of-state residents $7,950.

**Per-credit charge:** $72; out-of-state residents $264.

## FINANCIAL AID PICTURE (2014-2015)

**Students with need:** 94% of average financial aid package awarded as scholarships/grants, 6% awarded as loans/jobs. Need-based aid available for part-time students. Work study available nights.

**Students without need:** No-need awards available for academics, state/district residency.

## FINANCIAL AID PROCEDURES

**Forms required:** FAFSA.

**Dates and Deadlines:** Priority date 5/15; no closing date. Applicants notified on a rolling basis starting 3/15; must reply within 2 week(s) of notification.

**Transfers:** Supplemental educational opportunity grants limited.

## CONTACT

Sabrina Degain, Director of Financial Aid
Box 8000, Graham, NC 27253
(336) 506-4109

## Appalachian State University

Boone, North Carolina
www.appstate.edu　　　　Federal Code: 002906

**4-year public** university in large town.

**Enrollment:** 16,126 undergrads, 5% part-time. 3,030 full-time freshmen.

**Selectivity:** Admits 50 to 75% of applicants.

## BASIC COSTS (2015-2016)

**Tuition and fees:** $6,852; out-of-state residents $20,677.

**Room and board:** $7,845.

## FINANCIAL AID PICTURE (2014-2015)

**Students with need:** Out of 1,602 full-time freshmen who applied for aid, 1,570 were judged to have need. Of these, 1,465 received aid, and 321 had their full need met. Average financial aid package met 73% of need; average scholarship/grant was $8,203; average loan was $3,322. For part-time students, average financial aid package was $6,904.

**Students without need:** 81 full-time freshmen who did not demonstrate need for aid received scholarships/grants; average award was $3,788. No-need awards available for academics, alumni affiliation, art, athletics, job skills, leadership, minority status, music/drama, religious affiliation, ROTC, state/district residency.

**Scholarships offered: _Merit:_** Wilson Scholars Program: 4 awards available; full institutional cost with a summer stipend; based on academic, leadership, and community service. Chancellor's Scholarship: 10 awards available; full institutional cost; based on academic and leadership. Plemmons Leader Fellow Scholarship: 8-10 awards available; $1500 a year; based on academic and leadership. Diversity Scholarship: 12-15 awards available; $1000 a year; based on academic and leadership. **_Athletic:_** 47 full-time freshmen received athletic scholarships; average amount $10,251.

## FINANCIAL AID PROCEDURES

**Forms required:** FAFSA.

**Dates and Deadlines:** Priority date 3/1; no closing date. Applicants notified on a rolling basis starting 4/1; must reply within 3 week(s) of notification.

**Transfers:** No deadline. Applicants notified on a rolling basis starting 4/1; must reply within 3 week(s) of notification.

## CONTACT

Lori Townsend, Director of Financial Aid
ASU Box 32004, Boone, NC 28608
(828) 262-2190

## Barton College

Wilson, North Carolina
www.barton.edu　　　　Federal Code: 002908

**4-year private** liberal arts college in large town, affiliated with Christian Church (Disciples of Christ).

**Enrollment:** 975 undergrads, 7% part-time. 218 full-time freshmen.
**Selectivity:** Admits less than 50% of applicants.

**BASIC COSTS (2016-2017)**
**Tuition and fees:** $29,052.
**Per-credit charge:** $1,126.
**Room and board:** $9,634.
**Additional info:** Tuition/fee waivers available for adults.

**FINANCIAL AID PICTURE**
**Students with need:** Need-based aid available for full-time and part-time students. Work study available nights, weekends, and for part-time students.
**Students without need:** No-need awards available for academics, alumni affiliation, art, athletics, leadership, minority status, music/drama, religious affiliation, state/district residency.

**FINANCIAL AID PROCEDURES**
**Forms required:** FAFSA.
**Dates and Deadlines:** Priority date 4/1; no closing date. Applicants notified on a rolling basis starting 5/1; must reply within 2 week(s) of notification.
**Transfers:** No deadline. Applicants notified on a rolling basis; must reply within 2 week(s) of notification.

**CONTACT**
Bridget Ellis, Director of Financial Aid
Box 5000, Wilson, NC 27893-7000
(252) 399-6323

## Beaufort County Community College
Washington, North Carolina
www.beaufortccc.edu          Federal Code: 008558

**2-year public** community college in small town.
**Enrollment:** 1,385 undergrads.
**Selectivity:** Open admission; but selective for some programs.

**BASIC COSTS (2015-2016)**
**Tuition and fees:** $2,224; out-of-state residents $7,984.
**Per-credit charge:** $72; out-of-state residents $264.

**FINANCIAL AID PICTURE (2014-2015)**
**Students with need:** 99% of average financial aid package awarded as scholarships/grants, 1% awarded as loans/jobs. Need-based aid available for part-time students.
**Students without need:** No-need awards available for academics.

**FINANCIAL AID PROCEDURES**
**Forms required:** FAFSA, institutional form.
**Dates and Deadlines:** Closing date 8/1. Applicants notified on a rolling basis starting 5/1; must reply within 2 week(s) of notification.
**Transfers:** Priority date 6/16; no deadline.

**CONTACT**
Jo Woolard, Director of Student Financial Aid
Box 1069, Washington, NC 27889
(252) 940-6222

## Belmont Abbey College
Belmont, North Carolina
www.belmontabbeycollege.edu          Federal Code: 002910

**4-year private** liberal arts college in small town, affiliated with Roman Catholic Church.
**Enrollment:** 1,478 undergrads, 7% part-time. 311 full-time freshmen.
**Selectivity:** Admits 50 to 75% of applicants.

**BASIC COSTS (2015-2016)**
**Tuition and fees:** $18,500.

**Per-credit charge:** $617.
**Room and board:** $10,390.

**FINANCIAL AID PICTURE (2015-2016)**
**Students with need:** Out of 266 full-time freshmen who applied for aid, 208 were judged to have need. Of these, 208 received aid, and 25 had their full need met. Average financial aid package met 54% of need; average scholarship/grant was $9,410; average loan was $3,606. For part-time students, average financial aid package was $4,891.
**Students without need:** 112 full-time freshmen who did not demonstrate need for aid received scholarships/grants; average award was $4,594. No-need awards available for academics, athletics.
**Scholarships offered:** *Merit:* Many merit scholarships offered; ranging from $4,000 to $9,250; based solely on academic achievement. *Athletic:* 43 full-time freshmen received athletic scholarships; average amount $4,842.

**FINANCIAL AID PROCEDURES**
**Forms required:** FAFSA.
**Dates and Deadlines:** Priority date 4/1; no closing date. Applicants notified on a rolling basis starting 3/15; must reply within 2 week(s) of notification.
**Transfers:** Closing date 7/15. Applicants notified on a rolling basis starting 3/15; must reply within 2 week(s) of notification.

**CONTACT**
Anne Stevens, Director of Financial Aid
100 Belmont - Mt. Holly Road, Belmont, NC 28012-2795
(704) 461-6719

## Bennett College for Women
Greensboro, North Carolina
www.bennett.edu          Federal Code: 002911

**4-year private** liberal arts college for women in large city, affiliated with United Methodist Church.
**Enrollment:** 553 undergrads, 1% part-time. 164 full-time freshmen.

**BASIC COSTS (2015-2016)**
**Tuition and fees:** $17,130.
**Room and board:** $7,576.

**FINANCIAL AID PICTURE**
**Students with need:** Need-based aid available for full-time and part-time students.
**Students without need:** No-need awards available for academics, religious affiliation.

**FINANCIAL AID PROCEDURES**
**Forms required:** FAFSA, institutional form.
**Dates and Deadlines:** Closing date 4/15. Applicants notified by 7/15.

**CONTACT**
Shawn Guy, Director, Financial Aid
900 East Washington Street, Greensboro, NC 27401-3239
(336) 517-2209

## Bladen Community College
Dublin, North Carolina
www.bladencc.edu          Federal Code: 007987

**2-year public** community college in rural community.
**Enrollment:** 1,360 undergrads. 139 full-time freshmen.
**Selectivity:** Open admission; but selective for some programs.

**BASIC COSTS (2015-2016)**
**Tuition and fees:** $2,226; out-of-state residents $7,986.
**Per-credit charge:** $72; out-of-state residents $264.

## FINANCIAL AID PICTURE (2014-2015)

**Students with need:** Out of 127 full-time freshmen who applied for aid, 127 were judged to have need. Of these, 127 received aid, and 124 had their full need met. Average financial aid package met 58% of need; average scholarship/grant was $2,443. For part-time students, average financial aid package was $2,198.

**Students without need:** 2 full-time freshmen who did not demonstrate need for aid received scholarships/grants; average award was $875.

## FINANCIAL AID PROCEDURES

**Forms required:** FAFSA.

**Dates and Deadlines:** Priority date 6/1; closing date 7/1. Applicants notified on a rolling basis starting 8/1; must reply within 2 week(s) of notification.

## CONTACT

Samantha Benson, Financial Aid Director
Post Office Box 266, Dublin, NC 28332-0266
(910) 879-5562

## Blue Ridge Community College

Flat Rock, North Carolina
www.blueridge.edu                  Federal Code: 009684

**2-year public** community and technical college in large town.
**Enrollment:** 1,327 undergrads.
**Selectivity:** Open admission; but selective for some programs.

## BASIC COSTS (2015-2016)

**Tuition and fees:** $2,245; out-of-state residents $8,005.
**Per-credit charge:** $72; out-of-state residents $264.

## FINANCIAL AID PICTURE

**Students with need:** Need-based aid available for full-time and part-time students. Work study available nights.

**Students without need:** No-need awards available for academics, athletics, leadership, minority status, state/district residency.

## FINANCIAL AID PROCEDURES

**Forms required:** FAFSA, institutional form.

**Dates and Deadlines:** Priority date 6/30; no closing date. Applicants notified on a rolling basis starting 2/1; must reply within 4 week(s) of notification.

## CONTACT

Lisanne Masterson, Financial Aid Officer
180 West Campus Drive, Flat Rock, NC 28731-9624
(828) 694-1815

## Brevard College

Brevard, North Carolina
www.brevard.edu                    Federal Code: 002912

**4-year private** liberal arts college in small town, affiliated with United Methodist Church.
**Enrollment:** 720 undergrads.

## BASIC COSTS (2015-2016)

**Tuition and fees:** $26,980.
**Per-credit charge:** $525.
**Room and board:** $9,790.

## FINANCIAL AID PICTURE

**Students with need:** Need-based aid available for full-time and part-time students. Work study available nights, weekends, and for part-time students.

**Students without need:** No-need awards available for academics, art, athletics, leadership, music/drama, religious affiliation, state/district residency.

## FINANCIAL AID PROCEDURES

**Forms required:** FAFSA.

**Dates and Deadlines:** Priority date 2/1; no closing date. Applicants notified on a rolling basis starting 2/1; must reply by 5/1 or within 4 week(s) of notification.

**Transfers:** No deadline. Applicants notified on a rolling basis; must reply within 4 week(s) of notification. Phi Theta Kappa Scholarship.

## CONTACT

Caron Surrett, Director of Financial Aid
One Brevard College Drive, Brevard, NC 28712
(828) 884-8287

## Brunswick Community College

Bolivia, North Carolina
www.brunswickcc.edu                Federal Code: 015285

**2-year public** community college in small town.
**Enrollment:** 1,468 undergrads.
**Selectivity:** Open admission; but selective for some programs.

## BASIC COSTS (2015-2016)

**Tuition and fees:** $2,260; out-of-state residents $8,020.
**Per-credit charge:** $72; out-of-state residents $264.

## FINANCIAL AID PICTURE

**Students with need:** Need-based aid available for full-time and part-time students.

**Students without need:** No-need awards available for academics, state/district residency.

**Additional info:** Attendance required at financial aid orientation session for those receiving federal student aid.

## FINANCIAL AID PROCEDURES

**Forms required:** FAFSA, institutional form.

**Dates and Deadlines:** Priority date 6/1; closing date 6/15. Applicants notified on a rolling basis starting 3/1; must reply by 6/30 or within 2 week(s) of notification.

**Transfers:** Priority date 6/15; no deadline. Applicants notified on a rolling basis starting 3/1; must reply by 6/30 or within 2 week(s) of notification. Must submit all college transcripts. All transcripts must be evaluated prior to funds being applied to account.

## CONTACT

Tracy Somerlad, Director of Student Financial Resources
50 College Road NE, Bolivia, NC 28422
(910) 755-7322

## Cabarrus College of Health Sciences

Concord, North Carolina
www.cabarruscollege.edu            Federal Code: 015358

**4-year private** health science and nursing college in small city.
**Enrollment:** 423 undergrads, 63% part-time. 19 full-time freshmen.
**Selectivity:** Admits over 75% of applicants.

## BASIC COSTS (2015-2016)

**Tuition and fees:** $12,526.
**Per-credit charge:** $375.

## FINANCIAL AID PICTURE (2015-2016)

**Students with need:** 41% of average financial aid package awarded as scholarships/grants, 59% awarded as loans/jobs. Need-based aid available for part-time students.

**Students without need:** No-need awards available for academics, leadership, state/district residency.

**Scholarships offered:** New Cabarrus College Merit scholarship is offered to first time full time students who meet minimum GPA and Test scores. Information is available on our website and notice of scholarships level awards are sent by the Admissions department in the students acceptance letter.

### FINANCIAL AID PROCEDURES
**Forms required:** FAFSA, state aid form.
**Dates and Deadlines:** Closing date 4/15. Applicants notified on a rolling basis starting 6/30.

### CONTACT
Valerie Richard, Director of Financial Aid
401 Medical Park Drive, Concord, NC 28025-2405
(704) 403-2445

## Caldwell Community College and Technical Institute
Hudson, North Carolina
www.cccti.edu                    Federal Code: 004835

**2-year public** community and technical college in small town.
**Enrollment:** 3,940 undergrads.
**Selectivity:** Open admission; but selective for some programs.

### BASIC COSTS (2015-2016)
**Tuition and fees:** $2,236; out-of-state residents $7,996.
**Per-credit charge:** $72; out-of-state residents $264.

### FINANCIAL AID PICTURE
**Students with need:** Need-based aid available for full-time and part-time students.
**Students without need:** This college awards aid only to students with need.

### FINANCIAL AID PROCEDURES
**Forms required:** FAFSA.
**Dates and Deadlines:** Closing date 5/1. Applicants notified on a rolling basis starting 6/30.

### CONTACT
Shanna Kirby, Director of Financial Aid
2855 Hickory Boulevard, Hudson, NC 28638-2672
(828) 726-2713

## Campbell University
Buies Creek, North Carolina
www.campbell.edu                  Federal Code: 002913

**4-year private** university and liberal arts college in rural community, affiliated with Baptist faith.
**Enrollment:** 4,217 undergrads. 871 full-time freshmen.

### BASIC COSTS (2015-2016)
**Tuition and fees:** $28,635.
**Per-credit charge:** $575.
**Room and board:** $10,050.

### FINANCIAL AID PICTURE (2014-2015)
**Students with need:** Out of 808 full-time freshmen who applied for aid, 749 were judged to have need. Of these, 749 received aid, and 107 had their full need met. Average financial aid package met 82% of need; average scholarship/grant was $4,594; average loan was $2,935. For part-time students, average financial aid package was $18,339.
**Students without need:** 126 full-time freshmen who did not demonstrate need for aid received scholarships/grants; average award was $13,326. No-need awards available for academics, athletics, music/drama, religious affiliation, ROTC, state/district residency.

**Scholarships offered:** *Merit:* Presidential Scholarship: $13,000-$15,000. Campbell Scholarship: $7,000-$12,000. *Athletic:* 78 full-time freshmen received athletic scholarships; average amount $19,102.

### FINANCIAL AID PROCEDURES
**Forms required:** FAFSA.
**Dates and Deadlines:** Applicants notified on a rolling basis starting 2/1; must reply within 2 week(s) of notification.
**Transfers:** Priority date 3/12. Applicants notified on a rolling basis; must reply within 2 week(s) of notification.

### CONTACT
Michelle Day, Director of Financial Aid
PO Box 546, Buies Creek, NC 27506
(800) 334-4111 ext. 1310

## Cape Fear Community College
Wilmington, North Carolina
www.cfcc.edu                     Federal Code: 005320

**2-year public** community college in small city.
**Enrollment:** 8,067 undergrads, 52% part-time. 1,048 full-time freshmen.
**Selectivity:** Open admission; but selective for some programs.

### BASIC COSTS (2015-2016)
**Tuition and fees:** $2,498; out-of-state residents $8,258.
**Per-credit charge:** $76; out-of-state residents $268.

### FINANCIAL AID PICTURE (2015-2016)
**Students with need:** 59% of average financial aid package awarded as scholarships/grants, 41% awarded as loans/jobs. Need-based aid available for part-time students. Work study available nights.
**Students without need:** No-need awards available for academics, athletics, leadership.

### FINANCIAL AID PROCEDURES
**Forms required:** FAFSA.
**Dates and Deadlines:** Priority date 6/1; no closing date. Applicants notified on a rolling basis starting 4/1; must reply within 2 week(s) of notification.

### CONTACT
Rachel Cavenaugh, Interim Director of Financial Aid
411 North Front Street, Wilmington, NC 28401-3910
(910) 362-7055

## Carolina Christian College
Winston-Salem, North Carolina
www.carolina.edu

**4-year private** Bible college in large city, affiliated with nondenominational tradition.
**Enrollment:** 19 undergrads.
**Selectivity:** Open admission.

### FINANCIAL AID PICTURE
**Students with need:** Need-based aid available for full-time and part-time students.
**Students without need:** This college awards aid only to students with need.

### FINANCIAL AID PROCEDURES
**Forms required:** FAFSA.
**Dates and Deadlines:** Applicants notified on a rolling basis.
**Transfers:** No deadline. Applicants notified on a rolling basis.

**CONTACT**

Bryan Rhoden, Director of Financial Aid

PO Box 777, Winston-Salem, NC 27102

(336) 744-0900 ext. 202

## Carolinas College of Health Sciences

Charlotte, North Carolina

www.carolinascollege.edu          Federal Code: 031042

**2-year public** health science college in very large city.

**Enrollment:** 474 undergrads, 88% part-time. 2 full-time freshmen.

**Selectivity:** Open admission; but selective for some programs.

**BASIC COSTS (2015-2016)**

**Tuition and fees:** $9,630; out-of-state residents $9,630.

**Per-credit charge:** $323.

**FINANCIAL AID PICTURE (2014-2015)**

**Students with need:** Out of 2 full-time freshmen who applied for aid, 2 were judged to have need. Of these, 2 received aid, and 2 had their full need met. Average financial aid package met 75% of need; average scholarship/grant was $3,326; average loan was $5,443. Need-based aid available for part-time students.

**Students without need:** No-need awards available for academics.

**Additional info:** The College offers the Carolinas HealthCare System Educational Forgiveness Loan that allows students in a 2-year program to borrow up to $10,000 and up to $5,000 in a 1-year program. The loan may be forgiven if the student obtains an eligible full-time position after graduation.

**FINANCIAL AID PROCEDURES**

**Forms required:** FAFSA.

**Dates and Deadlines:** Priority date 5/1; no closing date. Applicants notified on a rolling basis starting 5/1.

**CONTACT**

Jill Powell, Financial Aid Coordinator

PO Box 32861, Charlotte, NC 28232-2861

(704) 355-8894

## Carteret Community College

Morehead City, North Carolina

www.carteret.edu          Federal Code: 008081

**2-year public** community and technical college in small town.

**Enrollment:** 1,382 undergrads.

**Selectivity:** Open admission; but selective for some programs.

**BASIC COSTS (2015-2016)**

**Tuition and fees:** $2,252; out-of-state residents $8,012.

**Per-credit charge:** $72; out-of-state residents $264.

**FINANCIAL AID PICTURE**

**Students with need:** Need-based aid available for full-time and part-time students.

**Students without need:** No-need awards available for academics, leadership, minority status, state/district residency.

**Additional info:** Institutional student loan program administered by college. Student may charge up to $600 for books, supplies and tuition per quarter. Repayment due by 11th week of semester.

**FINANCIAL AID PROCEDURES**

**Forms required:** FAFSA, institutional form.

**Dates and Deadlines:** Must reply within 2 week(s) of notification.

**CONTACT**

Brenda Long, Financial Aid Officer

3505 Arendell Street, Morehead City, NC 28557-2989

(252) 222-6297

## Catawba College

Salisbury, North Carolina

www.catawba.edu          Federal Code: 002914

**4-year private** liberal arts college in large town, affiliated with United Church of Christ.

**Enrollment:** 1,256 undergrads, 4% part-time. 344 full-time freshmen.

**Selectivity:** Admits less than 50% of applicants.

**BASIC COSTS (2016-2017)**

**Tuition and fees:** $29,333.

**Room and board:** $10,487.

**Additional info:** Tuition/fee waivers available for adults.

**FINANCIAL AID PICTURE (2014-2015)**

**Students with need:** Out of 324 full-time freshmen who applied for aid, 295 were judged to have need. Of these, 295 received aid, and 62 had their full need met. Average financial aid package met 75% of need; average scholarship/grant was $6,984; average loan was $4,090. For part-time students, average financial aid package was $5,887.

**Students without need:** 48 full-time freshmen who did not demonstrate need for aid received scholarships/grants; average award was $13,934. No-need awards available for academics, athletics, leadership, music/drama, religious affiliation, state/district residency.

**Scholarships offered:** 90 full-time freshmen received athletic scholarships; average amount $10,250.

**FINANCIAL AID PROCEDURES**

**Forms required:** FAFSA.

**Dates and Deadlines:** Priority date 3/15; no closing date. Applicants notified on a rolling basis starting 3/1; must reply within 2 week(s) of notification.

**CONTACT**

Dawn Snook, Director of Financial Aid

2300 West Innes Street, Salisbury, NC 28144-2488

(704) 637-4416

## Catawba Valley Community College

Hickory, North Carolina

www.cvcc.edu          Federal Code: 005318

**2-year public** community college in large town.

**Enrollment:** 4,165 undergrads.

**Selectivity:** Open admission; but selective for some programs.

**BASIC COSTS (2015-2016)**

**Tuition and fees:** $2,280; out-of-state residents $8,040.

**Per-credit charge:** $72; out-of-state residents $264.

**Additional info:** Tuition/fee waivers available for unemployed or children of unemployed.

**FINANCIAL AID PICTURE**

**Students with need:** Need-based aid available for full-time and part-time students. Work study available nights.

**Students without need:** No-need awards available for academics, leadership, music/drama.

**FINANCIAL AID PROCEDURES**

**Forms required:** FAFSA.

**Dates and Deadlines:** Closing date 3/15. Applicants notified on a rolling basis starting 5/15.

**CONTACT**

Debbie Barger, Director of Scholarships and Financial Aid

2550 Highway 70 SE, Hickory, NC 28602

(828) 327-7000 ext. 4214

## Central Carolina Community College
Sanford, North Carolina
www.cccc.edu                    Federal Code: 005449

**2-year public** community college in large town.
**Enrollment:** 3,656 undergrads, 48% part-time. 548 full-time freshmen.
**Selectivity:** Open admission; but selective for some programs.

### BASIC COSTS (2015-2016)
**Tuition and fees:** $2,268; out-of-state residents $8,028.
**Per-credit charge:** $72; out-of-state residents $264.

### FINANCIAL AID PICTURE (2014-2015)
**Students with need:** 100% of average financial aid package awarded as scholarships/grants, 0% awarded as loans/jobs. Need-based aid available for part-time students. Work study available nights.
**Students without need:** No-need awards available for academics, state/district residency.

### FINANCIAL AID PROCEDURES
**Forms required:** FAFSA.
**Dates and Deadlines:** Priority date 6/1; no closing date. Applicants notified on a rolling basis; must reply within 2 week(s) of notification.
**Transfers:** No deadline.

### CONTACT
Heather Willett, Dean Of Student Support Services
1105 Kelly Drive, Sanford, NC 27330
(919) 718-7229

## Central Piedmont Community College
Charlotte, North Carolina
www.cpcc.edu                    Federal Code: 002915

**2-year public** community college in very large city.
**Enrollment:** 18,092 undergrads, 63% part-time. 1,592 full-time freshmen.
**Selectivity:** Open admission; but selective for some programs.

### BASIC COSTS (2015-2016)
**Tuition and fees:** $2,326; out-of-state residents $8,086.
**Per-credit charge:** $72; out-of-state residents $264.

### FINANCIAL AID PICTURE (2014-2015)
**Students with need:** Need-based aid available for full-time and part-time students.
**Students without need:** No-need awards available for academics, minority status.

### FINANCIAL AID PROCEDURES
**Forms required:** FAFSA.
**Dates and Deadlines:** Priority date 4/1; closing date 6/1. Applicants notified on a rolling basis.

### CONTACT
Debbie Brooks, Director, Student Financial Aid
PO Box 35009, Charlotte, NC 28235-5009
(704) 330-6942

## Chowan University
Murfreesboro, North Carolina
www.chowan.edu                    Federal Code: 002916

**4-year private** university and liberal arts college in rural community, affiliated with Southern Baptist Convention.
**Enrollment:** 1,513 undergrads, 4% part-time. 552 full-time freshmen.
**Selectivity:** Admits 50 to 75% of applicants.

### BASIC COSTS (2015-2016)
**Tuition and fees:** $23,400.
**Per-credit charge:** $385.
**Room and board:** $8,680.

### FINANCIAL AID PICTURE (2015-2016)
**Students with need:** 71% of average financial aid package awarded as scholarships/grants, 29% awarded as loans/jobs. Need-based aid available for part-time students. Work study available nights, weekends, and for part-time students.
**Students without need:** No-need awards available for academics, athletics, leadership, music/drama, religious affiliation, state/district residency.

### FINANCIAL AID PROCEDURES
**Forms required:** FAFSA.
**Dates and Deadlines:** Priority date 3/1; no closing date. Applicants notified on a rolling basis starting 3/1; must reply within 2 week(s) of notification.

### CONTACT
Sharon Rose, Director of Financial Aid
One University Place, Murfreesboro, NC 27855-9901
(252) 398-1229

## Cleveland Community College
Shelby, North Carolina
www.clevelandcc.edu                    Federal Code: 008082

**2-year public** community college in large town.
**Enrollment:** 2,476 undergrads.
**Selectivity:** Open admission; but selective for some programs.

### BASIC COSTS (2015-2016)
**Tuition and fees:** $2,252; out-of-state residents $8,012.
**Per-credit charge:** $72; out-of-state residents $264.

### FINANCIAL AID PICTURE
**Students with need:** Need-based aid available for full-time and part-time students. Work study available nights.
**Students without need:** No-need awards available for academics.

### FINANCIAL AID PROCEDURES
**Forms required:** FAFSA.
**Dates and Deadlines:** Priority date 6/27; no closing date. Applicants notified on a rolling basis starting 3/15.

### CONTACT
Emily Hurdt, Financial Aid Coordinator
137 South Post Road, Shelby, NC 28152-6224
(704) 669-4204

## Coastal Carolina Community College
Jacksonville, North Carolina
www.coastalcarolina.edu                    Federal Code: 005316

**2-year public** community college in small city.
**Enrollment:** 3,930 undergrads, 47% part-time. 475 full-time freshmen.
**Selectivity:** Open admission; but selective for some programs.

### BASIC COSTS (2015-2016)
**Tuition and fees:** $2,190; out-of-state residents $7,950.
**Per-credit charge:** $72; out-of-state residents $264.

### FINANCIAL AID PICTURE
**Students with need:** Need-based aid available for full-time and part-time students. Work study available nights, weekends, and for part-time students.
**Students without need:** No-need awards available for academics, state/district residency.

## FINANCIAL AID PROCEDURES

**Forms required:** FAFSA, institutional form.

**Dates and Deadlines:** Priority date 5/15; no closing date. Applicants notified on a rolling basis starting 5/15; must reply within 2 week(s) of notification.

### CONTACT

Lyon Tammy, Director for Financial Aid Services

444 Western Boulevard, Jacksonville, NC 28546-6816

## College of the Albemarle

Elizabeth City, North Carolina

www.albemarle.edu          Federal Code: 002917

**2-year public** branch campus and community college in large town.

**Enrollment:** 1,473 undergrads, 55% part-time. 235 full-time freshmen.

**Selectivity:** Open admission; but selective for some programs.

### BASIC COSTS (2015-2016)

**Tuition and fees:** $2,287; out-of-state residents $8,047.

**Per-credit charge:** $72; out-of-state residents $264.

### FINANCIAL AID PICTURE

**Students with need:** Need-based aid available for full-time and part-time students.

**Students without need:** No-need awards available for academics, art, leadership, minority status, music/drama, state/district residency.

**Additional info:** Separate application must be submitted for COA Private Scholarships.

### FINANCIAL AID PROCEDURES

**Forms required:** FAFSA.

**Dates and Deadlines:** Priority date 3/15; closing date 6/1. Applicants notified on a rolling basis starting 5/1; must reply within 2 week(s) of notification.

### CONTACT

Angie Dawson, Director of Admissions and Financial Aid

1208 North Road Street, Elizabeth City, NC 27909

(252) 335-0821 ext. 2355

## Craven Community College

New Bern, North Carolina

www.cravencc.edu          Federal Code: 008086

**2-year public** community college in large town.

**Enrollment:** 2,840 undergrads.

**Selectivity:** Open admission; but selective for some programs.

### BASIC COSTS (2015-2016)

**Tuition and fees:** $2,326; out-of-state residents $8,086.

**Per-credit charge:** $72; out-of-state residents $264.

### FINANCIAL AID PICTURE

**Students with need:** Need-based aid available for full-time and part-time students.

### FINANCIAL AID PROCEDURES

**Forms required:** FAFSA.

**Dates and Deadlines:** Closing date 6/1. Applicants notified on a rolling basis.

### CONTACT

Kathy Banks, Director of Financial Aid

800 College Court, New Bern, NC 28562

(252) 638-7216

## Davidson College

Davidson, North Carolina          Federal Code: 002918

www.davidson.edu          CSS Code: 5150

**4-year private** liberal arts college in small town, affiliated with Presbyterian Church (USA).

**Enrollment:** 1,779 undergrads. 510 full-time freshmen.

**Selectivity:** Admits less than 50% of applicants. GED not accepted.

### BASIC COSTS (2015-2016)

**Tuition and fees:** $46,966.

**Room and board:** $13,153.

### FINANCIAL AID PICTURE (2015-2016)

**Students with need:** Out of 361 full-time freshmen who applied for aid, 265 were judged to have need. Of these, 265 received aid, and 265 had their full need met. Average financial aid package met 100% of need; average scholarship/grant was $37,846; average loan was $3,071. Need-based aid available for part-time students.

**Students without need:** 49 full-time freshmen who did not demonstrate need for aid received scholarships/grants; average award was $19,515. No-need awards available for academics, alumni affiliation, art, athletics, leadership, minority status, music/drama, ROTC.

**Scholarships offered:** *Merit:* Thompson S./Sarah S. Baker Scholarships: comprehensive fees; for first-time students with highest achievements; 3 awarded. John Montgomery Belk Scholarship: comprehensive fees; for Southeast applicants with highest achievements; 6 awarded. Amos Norris Scholarship: full cost; for first-time student athlete; 1 awarded. William Holt Terry Scholarships: full tuition; for first-year students with leadership skills and personal qualities; 2 awarded. John I. Smith Scholars Programs: full tuition; for first-year students with leadership, academic excellence, and commitment to community service; 2 awarded. *Athletic:* 37 full-time freshmen received athletic scholarships; average amount $15,995.

**Additional info:** The college has increased the money it provides for grants in financial aid packages and eliminated mandatory loans, allowing all students, regardless of socio-economic background, to graduate debt-free.

### FINANCIAL AID PROCEDURES

**Forms required:** FAFSA, CSS PROFILE.

**Dates and Deadlines:** Closing date 2/15. Applicants notified by 4/1; must reply by 5/1.

**Transfers:** Applicants notified by 5/15.

### CONTACT

David Gelinas, Director of Financial Aid

Box 7156, Davidson, NC 28035-7156

(704) 894-2232

## Davidson County Community College

Lexington, North Carolina

www.davidsonccc.edu          Federal Code: 002919

**2-year public** community college in large town.

**Enrollment:** 3,521 undergrads.

**Selectivity:** Open admission; but selective for some programs.

### BASIC COSTS (2015-2016)

**Tuition and fees:** $2,312; out-of-state residents $8,072.

**Per-credit charge:** $72; out-of-state residents $264.

### FINANCIAL AID PICTURE

**Students with need:** Need-based aid available for full-time and part-time students.

**Students without need:** No-need awards available for academics, leadership.

### FINANCIAL AID PROCEDURES

**Forms required:** FAFSA, institutional form.

**Dates and Deadlines:** Priority date 6/30; no closing date. Applicants notified on a rolling basis starting 7/31; must reply within 2 week(s) of notification.

**CONTACT**

Lori Blevins, Director, Admissions and Financial Aid

P O Box 1287, Lexington, NC 27293-1287

(336) 249-8186

## Duke University
Durham, North Carolina Federal Code: 002920
www.duke.edu CSS Code: 5156

**4-year private** university in large city.

**Enrollment:** 6,501 undergrads. 1,745 full-time freshmen.

**Selectivity:** Admits less than 50% of applicants. GED not accepted.

**BASIC COSTS (2016-2017)**

**Tuition and fees:** $51,265.

**Per-credit charge:** $1,489.

**Room and board:** $14,438.

**FINANCIAL AID PICTURE**

**Students with need:** Need-based aid available for full-time students.

**Students without need:** No-need awards available for academics, alumni affiliation, athletics, leadership, minority status, music/drama, religious affiliation, ROTC, state/district residency.

**FINANCIAL AID PROCEDURES**

**Forms required:** FAFSA, CSS PROFILE.

**Dates and Deadlines:** Closing date 3/15. Applicants notified by 4/1; must reply by 5/1.

**CONTACT**

Alison Rabil, Director of Financial Aid

2138 Campus Drive, Durham, NC 27708

(919) 684-6225

## Durham Technical Community College
Durham, North Carolina
www.durhamtech.edu Federal Code: 005448

**2-year public** community and technical college in small city.

**Enrollment:** 5,120 undergrads.

**Selectivity:** Open admission; but selective for some programs.

**BASIC COSTS (2015-2016)**

**Tuition and fees:** $2,252; out-of-state residents $8,012.

**Per-credit charge:** $72; out-of-state residents $264.

**FINANCIAL AID PICTURE (2015-2016)**

**Students with need:** 58% of average financial aid package awarded as scholarships/grants, 42% awarded as loans/jobs. Need-based aid available for part-time students. Work study available nights.

**Students without need:** No-need awards available for academics, minority status, state/district residency.

**Additional info:** Special funds available to single parents for tuition, fees, books, supplies and child care expenses.

**FINANCIAL AID PROCEDURES**

**Forms required:** FAFSA.

**Dates and Deadlines:** Applicants notified on a rolling basis starting 1/31; must reply within 3 week(s) of notification.

**CONTACT**

Everett Jeter, Director of Financial Aid

1637 Lawson Street, Durham, NC 27703

(919) 536-7209

## East Carolina University
Greenville, North Carolina
www.ecu.edu Federal Code: 002923

**4-year public** university in small city.

**Enrollment:** 21,697 undergrads, 11% part-time. 4,373 full-time freshmen.

**Selectivity:** Admits 50 to 75% of applicants.

**BASIC COSTS (2015-2016)**

**Tuition and fees:** $6,550; out-of-state residents $22,124.

**Room and board:** $9,319.

**FINANCIAL AID PICTURE (2015-2016)**

**Students with need:** Out of 3,614 full-time freshmen who applied for aid, 2,657 were judged to have need. Of these, 2,482 received aid, and 239 had their full need met. Average financial aid package met 61% of need; average scholarship/grant was $7,803; average loan was $5,635. For part-time students, average financial aid package was $7,749.

**Students without need:** 79 full-time freshmen who did not demonstrate need for aid received scholarships/grants; average award was $4,541. No-need awards available for academics, alumni affiliation, art, athletics, music/drama, ROTC.

**Scholarships offered:** 80 full-time freshmen received athletic scholarships; average amount $13,045.

**FINANCIAL AID PROCEDURES**

**Forms required:** FAFSA.

**Dates and Deadlines:** Priority date 3/1; no closing date. Applicants notified on a rolling basis starting 4/1; must reply within 3 week(s) of notification.

**CONTACT**

Julie Poorman, Director of Student Financial Aid

Office of Undergraduate Admissions, Greenville, NC 27858-4353

(252) 328-6610

## Edgecombe Community College
Tarboro, North Carolina
www.edgecombe.edu Federal Code: 008855

**2-year public** community college in large town.

**Enrollment:** 2,002 undergrads.

**Selectivity:** Open admission; but selective for some programs.

**BASIC COSTS (2015-2016)**

**Tuition and fees:** $2,253; out-of-state residents $8,053.

**Per-credit charge:** $75; out-of-state residents $265.

**FINANCIAL AID PICTURE**

**Students with need:** Need-based aid available for full-time and part-time students. Work study available nights, weekends, and for part-time students.

**Students without need:** This college awards aid only to students with need.

**FINANCIAL AID PROCEDURES**

**Forms required:** FAFSA, institutional form.

**Dates and Deadlines:** Applicants notified on a rolling basis starting 8/15; must reply within 3 week(s) of notification.

**Transfers:** No deadline.

**CONTACT**

Barbara Manning, Director of Financial Aid

2009 West Wilson Street, Tarboro, NC 27886

(252) 823-5166 ext. 250

## Elizabeth City State University

Elizabeth City, North Carolina
www.ecsu.edu                    Federal Code: 002926

**4-year public** liberal arts college in large town.
**Enrollment:** 2,276 undergrads.

**BASIC COSTS (2015-2016)**
**Tuition and fees:** $4,657; out-of-state residents $17,010.
**Room and board:** $7,844.

**FINANCIAL AID PICTURE**
**Students with need:** Need-based aid available for full-time students. Work study available nights, weekends, and for part-time students.
**Students without need:** No-need awards available for academics, athletics, minority status, ROTC, state/district residency.

**FINANCIAL AID PROCEDURES**
**Forms required:** FAFSA.
**Dates and Deadlines:** Priority date 3/15; closing date 6/1. Applicants notified on a rolling basis starting 6/1; must reply by 6/30 or within 3 week(s) of notification.
**Transfers:** Closing date 3/15. Applicants notified on a rolling basis starting 6/30; must reply within 3 week(s) of notification.

**CONTACT**
Kenneth Wilson, Associate Director of Financial Aid
1704 Weeksville Road, Campus Box 901, Elizabeth City, NC 27909
(252) 335-3283

## Elon University

Elon, North Carolina               Federal Code: 002927
www.elon.edu                          CSS Code: 5183

**4-year private** university and liberal arts college in large town.
**Enrollment:** 5,903 undergrads, 3% part-time. 1,509 full-time freshmen.
**Selectivity:** Admits 50 to 75% of applicants.

**BASIC COSTS (2015-2016)**
**Tuition and fees:** $32,172.
**Per-credit charge:** $1,012.
**Room and board:** $10,998.

**FINANCIAL AID PICTURE (2015-2016)**
**Students with need:** Out of 862 full-time freshmen who applied for aid, 486 were judged to have need. Of these, 485 received aid, and 73 had their full need met. Average financial aid package met 60% of need; average scholarship/grant was $13,546; average loan was $3,442. Need-based aid available for part-time students.
**Students without need:** 316 full-time freshmen who did not demonstrate need for aid received scholarships/grants; average award was $7,022. No-need awards available for academics, art, athletics, leadership, music/drama, religious affiliation.
**Scholarships offered:** *Merit:* Presidential Scholarships: up to $6,000 annually; based on academic credentials. Fellows Programs (Honors, Business, Communications, Elon College Fellows, Isabella Cannon Leadership, Teaching, International): $5,500-$13,500 annually; based on merit. Elon Teaching Fellows: $4,500 annually. Engineering Scholarships: $8,000 annually. Performing Arts Scholarships: $500-$6,000; talent-based. Music Scholarships: $500-$5,000; talent and need-based. Elon Engagement scholarships: up to $4,500. *Athletic:* 75 full-time freshmen received athletic scholarships; average amount $27,377.

**FINANCIAL AID PROCEDURES**
**Forms required:** FAFSA, CSS PROFILE, institutional form.
**Dates and Deadlines:** Priority date 2/15; no closing date. Applicants notified on a rolling basis starting 3/30.

**CONTACT**
Patrick Murphy, Director of Financial Planning
2700 Campus Box, Elon, NC 27244-2010
(336) 278-7640

## Fayetteville State University

Fayetteville, North Carolina
www.uncfsu.edu                    Federal Code: 002928

**4-year public** university in small city.
**Enrollment:** 5,087 undergrads, 24% part-time. 713 full-time freshmen.
**Selectivity:** Admits 50 to 75% of applicants.

**BASIC COSTS (2015-2016)**
**Tuition and fees:** $4,885; out-of-state residents $16,493.
**Room and board:** $7,130.

**FINANCIAL AID PICTURE (2014-2015)**
**Students with need:** Out of 686 full-time freshmen who applied for aid, 658 were judged to have need. Of these, 651 received aid, and 80 had their full need met. Average financial aid package met 78% of need; average scholarship/grant was $8,675; average loan was $3,420. For part-time students, average financial aid package was $7,044.
**Students without need:** No-need awards available for academics, alumni affiliation, athletics, music/drama, ROTC, state/district residency.

**FINANCIAL AID PROCEDURES**
**Forms required:** FAFSA.
**Dates and Deadlines:** Closing date 3/1. Applicants notified on a rolling basis starting 4/15; must reply within 2 week(s) of notification.

**CONTACT**
Kamesia Ewing, Director of Financial Aid
1200 Murchison Road, Fayetteville, NC 28301-4298
(910) 672-1325

## Fayetteville Technical Community College

Fayetteville, North Carolina
www.faytechcc.edu                 Federal Code: 007640

**2-year public** community and technical college in large city.
**Enrollment:** 9,645 undergrads, 54% part-time. 1,076 full-time freshmen.
**Selectivity:** Open admission; but selective for some programs.

**BASIC COSTS (2015-2016)**
**Tuition and fees:** $2,370; out-of-state residents $8,130.
**Per-credit charge:** $76; out-of-state residents $268.

**FINANCIAL AID PICTURE (2014-2015)**
**Students with need:** Out of 966 full-time freshmen who applied for aid, 807 were judged to have need. Of these, 780 received aid, and 780 had their full need met. Average financial aid package met 100% of need; average scholarship/grant was $1,352; average loan was $2,811. For part-time students, average financial aid package was $6,162.

**FINANCIAL AID PROCEDURES**
**Forms required:** FAFSA.
**Dates and Deadlines:** Applicants notified on a rolling basis starting 4/1.
**Transfers:** No deadline. Applicants notified on a rolling basis starting 4/1.

**CONTACT**
Tracie Hunter, Director of Financial Aid
2201 Hull Road, Fayetteville, NC 28303-0236
(910) 678-8448

## Forsyth Technical Community College
Winston-Salem, North Carolina
www.forsythtech.edu          Federal Code: 005317

**2-year public** community and technical college in small city.
**Enrollment:** 7,482 undergrads, 57% part-time. 8,396 full-time freshmen.
**Selectivity:** Open admission; but selective for some programs.

**BASIC COSTS (2015-2016)**
**Tuition and fees:** $2,326; out-of-state residents $8,086.
**Per-credit charge:** $72; out-of-state residents $264.

**FINANCIAL AID PICTURE (2014-2015)**
**Students with need:** Average financial aid package for all full-time undergraduates was $5,746; for part-time $3,086. 86% awarded as scholarships/grants, 14% awarded as loans/jobs. Work study available nights.
**Students without need:** No-need awards available for academics, alumni affiliation, leadership, state/district residency.
**Additional info:** Apply for aid as close to January 1 as possible for best consideration.

**FINANCIAL AID PROCEDURES**
**Forms required:** FAFSA.
**Dates and Deadlines:** Priority date 6/1; closing date 6/1. Applicants notified on a rolling basis starting 5/1.
**Transfers:** No deadline. Mid-year transfer students must submit a financial aid transcript from previous college in order for financial aid office to award any Federal Pell Grant funds to eligible students.

**CONTACT**
Ricky Hodges, Director of Student Financial Services
2100 Silas Creek Parkway, Winston-Salem, NC 27103

## Gardner-Webb University
Boiling Springs, North Carolina
www.gardner-webb.edu          Federal Code: 002929

**4-year private** university and liberal arts college in small town, affiliated with Southern Baptist Convention.
**Enrollment:** 2,617 undergrads. 460 full-time freshmen.

**BASIC COSTS (2015-2016)**
**Tuition and fees:** $28,280.
**Per-credit charge:** $447.
**Room and board:** $9,280.

**FINANCIAL AID PICTURE (2015-2016)**
**Students with need:** Out of 431 full-time freshmen who applied for aid, 389 were judged to have need. Of these, 389 received aid, and 86 had their full need met. Average financial aid package met 78% of need; average scholarship/grant was $7,715; average loan was $3,212. Need-based aid available for part-time students.
**Students without need:** 70 full-time freshmen who did not demonstrate need for aid received scholarships/grants; average award was $11,528. No-need awards available for academics, athletics, leadership, music/drama, religious affiliation, ROTC, state/district residency.
**Scholarships offered:** *Merit:* Presidential Fellow: full tuition, room and board for four years; 1 awarded. Academic Fellow: full tuition for four years; 4 awarded. Honors Scholarship $3000; 50 awarded. Selection based on academic accomplishments and interview. *Athletic:* 34 full-time freshmen received athletic scholarships; average amount $15,470.

**FINANCIAL AID PROCEDURES**
**Forms required:** FAFSA, state aid form.
**Dates and Deadlines:** Priority date 3/1; closing date 6/30. Applicants notified on a rolling basis starting 3/1; must reply within 2 week(s) of notification.
**Transfers:** No deadline. Applicants notified on a rolling basis starting 3/1; must reply within 2 week(s) of notification.

**CONTACT**
Summer Nance, Assistant Vice President for Financial Planning
PO Box 817, Boiling Springs, NC 28017
(704) 406-4243

## Gaston College
Dallas, North Carolina
www.gaston.edu          Federal Code: 002973

**2-year public** community college in small town.
**Enrollment:** 5,603 undergrads.
**Selectivity:** Open admission; but selective for some programs.

**BASIC COSTS (2015-2016)**
**Tuition and fees:** $2,577; out-of-state residents $8,722.

**FINANCIAL AID PICTURE**
**Students with need:** Need-based aid available for full-time students.
**Students without need:** No-need awards available for academics, state/district residency.
**Scholarships offered:** Academic Scholarship: over 30 available; $1,100; GPA of 3.0 or better. Careers Scholarship: 10 available; $1,100 each, must pursue career in specified engineering technologies or industrial technologies major and have GPA of 3.0 or better.
**Additional info:** Grants/scholarships available for women pursuing nontraditional roles.

**FINANCIAL AID PROCEDURES**
**Forms required:** FAFSA, institutional form.
**Dates and Deadlines:** Priority date 3/15; closing date 6/30. Applicants notified on a rolling basis.

**CONTACT**
Everett Jeter, Director of Financial Aid and Veterans Affairs
201 Highway 321 South, Dallas, NC 28034-1499
(704) 922-6227

## Greensboro College
Greensboro, North Carolina
www.greensboro.edu          Federal Code: 002930

**4-year private** liberal arts college in large city, affiliated with United Methodist Church.
**Enrollment:** 758 undergrads, 3% part-time. 227 full-time freshmen.
**Selectivity:** Admits over 75% of applicants.

**BASIC COSTS (2015-2016)**
**Tuition and fees:** $26,900.
**Room and board:** $10,100.

**FINANCIAL AID PICTURE (2015-2016)**
**Students with need:** 42% of average financial aid package awarded as scholarships/grants, 58% awarded as loans/jobs. Need-based aid available for part-time students. Work study available nights, weekends, and for part-time students.
**Students without need:** No-need awards available for academics, alumni affiliation, art, leadership, music/drama, religious affiliation, state/district residency.
**Scholarships offered:** Barrett Scholarships and Presidential Scholarships: full tuition; fees, room, and board; number of awards vary.

**FINANCIAL AID PROCEDURES**
**Forms required:** FAFSA, state aid form, institutional form.
**Dates and Deadlines:** Priority date 4/15; no closing date. Applicants notified on a rolling basis starting 2/1; must reply within 2 week(s) of notification.
**Transfers:** Closing date 4/15. Must reply within 4 week(s) of notification.

## CONTACT
Lindsay Latham, Director of Financial Aid
815 West Market Street, Greensboro, NC 27401-1875
(336) 272-7102 ext. 217

## Guilford College
Greensboro, North Carolina
www.guilford.edu                     Federal Code: 002931

**4-year private** liberal arts college in large city, affiliated with Society of Friends (Quaker).
**Enrollment:** 1,767 undergrads, 18% part-time. 351 full-time freshmen.
**Selectivity:** Admits 50 to 75% of applicants.

### BASIC COSTS (2015-2016)
**Tuition and fees:** $34,090.
**Per-credit charge:** $1,032.
**Room and board:** $9,560.

### FINANCIAL AID PICTURE (2014-2015)
**Students with need:** Out of 308 full-time freshmen who applied for aid, 256 were judged to have need. Of these, 256 received aid, and 37 had their full need met. Average financial aid package met 74% of need; average scholarship/grant was $7,204; average loan was $4,184. For part-time students, average financial aid package was $6,156.
**Students without need:** 95 full-time freshmen who did not demonstrate need for aid received scholarships/grants; average award was $14,848. No-need awards available for academics.
**Scholarships offered:** Honors Scholarship: $7,500 to full tuition. Presidential Scholarship: $5,000. Incentive grants: $3,000; based on participation or leadership in school or community activities. Quaker Leadership Scholarships: $3,000; candidates must be active members of the Religious Society of Friends.

### FINANCIAL AID PROCEDURES
**Forms required:** FAFSA.
**Dates and Deadlines:** Priority date 2/15; no closing date. Applicants notified on a rolling basis starting 3/1; must reply within 2 week(s) of notification.

### CONTACT
Brian De Young, Director of Student Financial Services
Admissions, New Garden Hall, Greensboro, NC 27410-4108
(336) 316-2354

## Guilford Technical Community College
Jamestown, North Carolina
www.gtcc.edu                     Federal Code: 004838

**2-year public** community and technical college in large city.
**Enrollment:** 11,292 undergrads, 54% part-time. 1,046 full-time freshmen.
**Selectivity:** Open admission; but selective for some programs.

### BASIC COSTS (2015-2016)
**Tuition and fees:** $2,251; out-of-state residents $8,011.
**Per-credit charge:** $72; out-of-state residents $264.

### FINANCIAL AID PICTURE
**Students with need:** Need-based aid available for full-time and part-time students.
**Students without need:** No-need awards available for academics, athletics, leadership, minority status, state/district residency.

### FINANCIAL AID PROCEDURES
**Forms required:** FAFSA.
**Dates and Deadlines:** Priority date 3/15; closing date 7/25. Applicants notified on a rolling basis starting 7/1; must reply within 2 week(s) of notification.

## CONTACT
Lisa Koretoff, Director of Financial Aid
PO Box 309, Jamestown, NC 27282
(336) 334-4822 ext. 50317

## Halifax Community College
Weldon, North Carolina
www.halifaxcc.edu                     Federal Code: 007986

**2-year public** community college in small town.
**Enrollment:** 1,154 undergrads. 198 full-time freshmen.
**Selectivity:** Open admission; but selective for some programs.

### BASIC COSTS (2015-2016)
**Tuition and fees:** $2,292; out-of-state residents $8,052.
**Per-credit charge:** $72; out-of-state residents $264.

### FINANCIAL AID PICTURE (2014-2015)
**Students with need:** Average financial aid package for all full-time undergraduates was $4,964; for part-time $4,770. 99% awarded as scholarships/grants, 1% awarded as loans/jobs. Work study available nights.
**Students without need:** No-need awards available for academics.

### FINANCIAL AID PROCEDURES
**Forms required:** FAFSA.
**Dates and Deadlines:** Priority date 6/1; no closing date. Applicants notified on a rolling basis starting 8/1; must reply within 2 week(s) of notification.
**Transfers:** No deadline. Applicants notified on a rolling basis; must reply within 2 week(s) of notification.

### CONTACT
Tara Keeter, Director, Financial Aid
100 College Drive, Drawer 809, Weldon, NC 27890
(252) 536-7223

## Haywood Community College
Clyde, North Carolina
www.haywood.edu                     Federal Code: 008083

**2-year public** community and technical college in rural community.
**Enrollment:** 1,614 undergrads.
**Selectivity:** Open admission; but selective for some programs.

### BASIC COSTS (2015-2016)
**Tuition and fees:** $2,263; out-of-state residents $8,023.
**Per-credit charge:** $72; out-of-state residents $264.

### FINANCIAL AID PICTURE
**Students with need:** Need-based aid available for full-time and part-time students.
**Students without need:** No-need awards available for academics.
**Additional info:** Complete FAFSA by priority filing date for consideration for institutional scholarships.

### FINANCIAL AID PROCEDURES
**Forms required:** FAFSA.
**Dates and Deadlines:** Priority date 6/1; no closing date. Applicants notified on a rolling basis starting 4/15; must reply within 2 week(s) of notification.

### CONTACT
Sayward Cabe, Director of Financial Aid
185 Freelander Drive, Clyde, NC 28721-9454
(828) 627-4506

## High Point University

High Point, North Carolina
www.highpoint.edu                    Federal Code: 002933

**4-year private** university and liberal arts college in small city, affiliated with United Methodist Church.
**Enrollment:** 4,362 undergrads, 1% part-time. 1,045 full-time freshmen.
**Selectivity:** Admits 50 to 75% of applicants.

### BASIC COSTS (2016-2017)
**Tuition and fees:** $33,405.
**Per-credit charge:** $927.
**Room and board:** $12,572.

### FINANCIAL AID PICTURE (2014-2015)
**Students with need:** Out of 972 full-time freshmen who applied for aid, 637 were judged to have need. Of these, 637 received aid, and 357 had their full need met. Average financial aid package met 56% of need; average scholarship/grant was $2,607; average loan was $3,500. For part-time students, average financial aid package was $3,107.
**Students without need:** 194 full-time freshmen who did not demonstrate need for aid received scholarships/grants; average award was $7,985. No-need awards available for academics, alumni affiliation, art, athletics, leadership, music/drama, religious affiliation, state/district residency.
**Scholarships offered:** *Merit:* Awarded annually to qualified freshmen: Presidential Fellowship: $9,000-$20,000. High Point Fellowship: $5,000-$9,000. High Point Scholarship: $2,000-$5,000. All scholarships based on merit. Application and interview required. *Athletic:* 71 full-time freshmen received athletic scholarships; average amount $16,603.

### FINANCIAL AID PROCEDURES
**Forms required:** FAFSA, state aid form.
**Dates and Deadlines:** Priority date 3/1; no closing date. Applicants notified on a rolling basis starting 4/1; must reply within 3 week(s) of notification.
**Transfers:** No deadline. Applicants notified on a rolling basis starting 5/1; must reply within 3 week(s) of notification.

### CONTACT
Ron Elmore, Director of Student Financial Services
One University Parkway, High Point, NC 27268-3598
(336) 841-9128

## Isothermal Community College

Spindale, North Carolina
www.isothermal.edu                    Federal Code: 002934

**2-year public** community college in small town.
**Enrollment:** 2,067 undergrads.
**Selectivity:** Open admission; but selective for some programs.

### BASIC COSTS (2015-2016)
**Tuition and fees:** $2,214; out-of-state residents $7,974.
**Per-credit charge:** $72; out-of-state residents $264.

### FINANCIAL AID PICTURE
**Students with need:** Need-based aid available for full-time and part-time students. Work study available nights.
**Students without need:** No-need awards available for academics, job skills, leadership, minority status, music/drama, state/district residency.

### FINANCIAL AID PROCEDURES
**Forms required:** FAFSA, institutional form.
**Dates and Deadlines:** Priority date 5/31; closing date 7/1. Applicants notified on a rolling basis starting 4/30; must reply within 4 week(s) of notification.

### CONTACT
Jeffery Boyle, Director of Financial Aid
PO Box 804, Spindale, NC 28160-0804
(828) 286-3636 ext. 468

## James Sprunt Community College

Kenansville, North Carolina
www.jamessprunt.edu                    Federal Code: 007687

**2-year public** community college in rural community.
**Enrollment:** 806 undergrads, 44% part-time. 137 full-time freshmen.
**Selectivity:** Open admission; but selective for some programs.

### BASIC COSTS (2015-2016)
**Tuition and fees:** $2,230; out-of-state residents $7,990.
**Per-credit charge:** $72; out-of-state residents $264.

### FINANCIAL AID PICTURE (2014-2015)
**Students with need:** Out of 130 full-time freshmen who applied for aid, 125 were judged to have need. Of these, 106 received aid. For part-time students, average financial aid package was $4,463.
**Students without need:** No-need awards available for academics, state/district residency.

### FINANCIAL AID PROCEDURES
**Forms required:** FAFSA, state aid form, institutional form.
**Dates and Deadlines:** Priority date 7/15; closing date 7/1. Applicants notified on a rolling basis starting 5/15; must reply within 2 week(s) of notification.

### CONTACT
Tracy Ward, Financial Aid Officer
PO Box 398, Kenansville, NC 28349-0398
(910) 296-2503

## Johnson and Wales University: Charlotte

Charlotte, North Carolina
www.jwu.edu

**4-year private** university in very large city.
**Enrollment:** 2,218 undergrads, 2% part-time. 700 full-time freshmen.
**Selectivity:** Admits 50 to 75% of applicants.

### BASIC COSTS (2015-2016)
**Tuition and fees:** $29,226.
**Room and board:** $12,732.

### FINANCIAL AID PICTURE (2015-2016)
**Students with need:** Out of 655 full-time freshmen who applied for aid, 601 were judged to have need. Of these, 601 received aid, and 77 had their full need met. Average financial aid package met 68% of need; average scholarship/grant was $9,159; average loan was $3,381. For part-time students, average financial aid package was $14,338.
**Students without need:** 53 full-time freshmen who did not demonstrate need for aid received scholarships/grants; average award was $9,679. No-need awards available for academics, alumni affiliation, leadership, state/district residency.

### FINANCIAL AID PROCEDURES
**Forms required:** FAFSA.
**Dates and Deadlines:** Applicants notified on a rolling basis starting 3/1.
**Transfers:** No deadline. Applicants notified on a rolling basis.

### CONTACT
Director of Financial Aid
801 West Trade Street, Charlotte, NC 28202
(800) 342-5598

## Johnson C. Smith University

Charlotte, North Carolina
www.jcsu.edu                    Federal Code: 002936

**4-year private** university and liberal arts college in very large city.
**Enrollment:** 1,371 undergrads, 4% part-time. 334 full-time freshmen.

**Selectivity:** Admits less than 50% of applicants.

### BASIC COSTS (2016-2017)
**Tuition and fees:** $18,236.
**Per-credit charge:** $418.
**Room and board:** $7,100.
**Additional info:** Tuition/fee waivers available for adults.

### FINANCIAL AID PICTURE (2015-2016)
**Students with need:** Out of 320 full-time freshmen who applied for aid, 306 were judged to have need. Of these, 304 received aid, and 14 had their full need met. Average financial aid package met 57% of need; average scholarship/grant was $13,414; average loan was $3,519. For part-time students, average financial aid package was $12,620.
**Students without need:** 14 full-time freshmen who did not demonstrate need for aid received scholarships/grants; average award was $12,757. No-need awards available for academics, athletics, music/drama, ROTC.
**Scholarships offered:** 8 full-time freshmen received athletic scholarships; average amount $6,362.

### FINANCIAL AID PROCEDURES
**Forms required:** FAFSA.
**Dates and Deadlines:** Priority date 3/1; no closing date. Applicants notified on a rolling basis starting 3/1; must reply within 2 week(s) of notification.
**Transfers:** No deadline. Applicants notified on a rolling basis starting 4/1; must reply within 2 week(s) of notification.

### CONTACT
Shelline Warren, Director of Financial Aid
100 Beatties Ford Road, Charlotte, NC 28216-5398
(704) 378-1035

## Johnston Community College
Smithfield, North Carolina
www.johnstoncc.edu                    Federal Code: 009336

**2-year public** community and technical college in large town.
**Enrollment:** 2,855 undergrads, 46% part-time. 415 full-time freshmen.
**Selectivity:** Open admission; but selective for some programs.

### BASIC COSTS (2015-2016)
**Tuition and fees:** $2,257; out-of-state residents $8,017.
**Per-credit charge:** $72; out-of-state residents $264.

### FINANCIAL AID PICTURE (2014-2015)
**Students with need:** 92% of average financial aid package awarded as scholarships/grants, 8% awarded as loans/jobs. Need-based aid available for part-time students.
**Students without need:** This college awards aid only to students with need.

### FINANCIAL AID PROCEDURES
**Forms required:** FAFSA.
**Dates and Deadlines:** Priority date 5/31; no closing date. Applicants notified on a rolling basis starting 6/1; must reply within 2 week(s) of notification.

### CONTACT
Betty Woodall, Financial Aid Director
PO Box 2350, Smithfield, NC 27577
(919) 209-2036

## Laurel University
High Point, North Carolina
www.laureluniversity.edu              Federal Code: 013819

**4-year private** university and Bible college in small city, affiliated with interdenominational tradition.

**Enrollment:** 125 undergrads.

### BASIC COSTS (2015-2016)
**Tuition and fees:** $13,030.
**Per-credit charge:** $410.
**Room only:** $3,000.

### FINANCIAL AID PICTURE
**Students with need:** Need-based aid available for full-time and part-time students. Work study available nights.
**Scholarships offered:** Early Acceptance; $100. Academic Honor; 10% of tuition.
**Additional info:** Early Acceptance Scholarships, Academic Honor Scholarships, Married Student Credit and Minister/Missionary Dependent Scholarship available.

### FINANCIAL AID PROCEDURES
**Forms required:** FAFSA.
**Dates and Deadlines:** Priority date 3/15; no closing date. Applicants notified on a rolling basis starting 6/1; must reply within 3 week(s) of notification.
**Transfers:** Closing date 3/15.

### CONTACT
Pamala Douglas, Director of Financial Aid
1215 Eastchester Drive, High Point, NC 27265-3115
(336) 887-3000 ext. 129

## Lees-McRae College
Banner Elk, North Carolina
www.lmc.edu                           Federal Code: 002923

**4-year private** liberal arts college in rural community, affiliated with Presbyterian Church (USA).
**Enrollment:** 1,032 undergrads. 197 full-time freshmen.
**Selectivity:** Admits 50 to 75% of applicants.

### BASIC COSTS (2015-2016)
**Tuition and fees:** $24,854.
**Per-credit charge:** $217.
**Room and board:** $9,782.

### FINANCIAL AID PICTURE (2015-2016)
**Students with need:** Out of 181 full-time freshmen who applied for aid, 166 were judged to have need. Of these, 166 received aid, and 3 had their full need met. Average financial aid package met 71% of need; average scholarship/grant was $9,993; average loan was $3,500. For part-time students, average financial aid package was $3,427.
**Students without need:** 23 full-time freshmen who did not demonstrate need for aid received scholarships/grants; average award was $7,783. No-need awards available for academics, athletics, leadership, music/drama, religious affiliation.
**Scholarships offered:** 57 full-time freshmen received athletic scholarships; average amount $7,794.

### FINANCIAL AID PROCEDURES
**Forms required:** FAFSA, state aid form.
**Dates and Deadlines:** Priority date 4/15; no closing date. Applicants notified on a rolling basis starting 3/1; must reply within 2 week(s) of notification.

### CONTACT
Cathy Shell, Director of Financial Aid
Box 128, Banner Elk, NC 28604
(828) 898-8740

## Lenoir Community College
Kinston, North Carolina
www.lenoircc.edu                    Federal Code: 002940

**2-year public** community college in large town.
**Enrollment:** 1,754 undergrads, 47% part-time. 247 full-time freshmen.
**Selectivity:** Open admission; but selective for some programs.

### BASIC COSTS (2015-2016)
**Tuition and fees:** $2,279; out-of-state residents $8,039.
**Per-credit charge:** $72; out-of-state residents $264.

### FINANCIAL AID PICTURE (2015-2016)
**Students with need:** 96% of average financial aid package awarded as scholarships/grants, 4% awarded as loans/jobs. Need-based aid available for part-time students. Work study available nights, weekends, and for part-time students.
**Students without need:** No-need awards available for academics, athletics, leadership, state/district residency.

### FINANCIAL AID PROCEDURES
**Forms required:** FAFSA.
**Dates and Deadlines:** Priority date 7/1; closing date 8/15. Applicants notified on a rolling basis starting 8/1; must reply within 2 week(s) of notification.

### CONTACT
J Gibbs, Director of Student Financial Aid
PO Box 188, Kinston, NC 28502-0188
(252) 527-6223 ext. 371

## Lenoir-Rhyne University
Hickory, North Carolina
www.lr.edu                    Federal Code: 002941

**4-year private** university and liberal arts college in large town, affiliated with Evangelical Lutheran Church in America.
**Enrollment:** 1,412 undergrads, 4% part-time. 341 full-time freshmen.
**Selectivity:** Admits over 75% of applicants.

### BASIC COSTS (2016-2017)
**Tuition and fees:** $33,730.
**Per-credit charge:** $1,395.
**Room and board:** $11,600.
**Additional info:** Tuition/fee waivers available for minority students.

### FINANCIAL AID PICTURE (2014-2015)
**Students with need:** Out of 327 full-time freshmen who applied for aid, 307 were judged to have need. Of these, 307 received aid, and 55 had their full need met. Average financial aid package met 73% of need; average scholarship/grant was $23,232; average loan was $2,939. For part-time students, average financial aid package was $7,714.
**Students without need:** 34 full-time freshmen who did not demonstrate need for aid received scholarships/grants; average award was $15,968. No-need awards available for academics, alumni affiliation, athletics, leadership, music/drama, religious affiliation.
**Scholarships offered:** 35 full-time freshmen received athletic scholarships; average amount $9,232.

### FINANCIAL AID PROCEDURES
**Forms required:** FAFSA.
**Dates and Deadlines:** Applicants notified on a rolling basis; must reply by 5/1 or within 3 week(s) of notification.

### CONTACT
Nick, Director of Financial Aid
LR Box 7227, Hickory, NC 28603
(800) 277-5721

## Livingstone College
Salisbury, North Carolina
www.livingstone.edu                    Federal Code: 002942

**4-year private** liberal arts college in large town, affiliated with African Methodist Episcopal Zion Church.
**Enrollment:** 1,262 undergrads.
**Selectivity:** Admits 50 to 75% of applicants.

### BASIC COSTS (2015-2016)
**Tuition and fees:** $17,246.
**Room and board:** $6,596.

### FINANCIAL AID PICTURE
**Students with need:** Need-based aid available for full-time and part-time students. Work study available nights, weekends, and for part-time students.
**Students without need:** No-need awards available for academics, alumni affiliation, athletics, leadership, music/drama, religious affiliation, ROTC, state/district residency.

### FINANCIAL AID PROCEDURES
**Forms required:** FAFSA, state aid form.
**Dates and Deadlines:** Priority date 3/15; closing date 6/30. Applicants notified by 5/1; must reply within 4 week(s) of notification.

### CONTACT
Stephanie McNeil, Director of Financial Aid
701 West Monroe Street, Salisbury, NC 28144-5213
(704) 216-6273

## Louisburg College
Louisburg, North Carolina
www.louisburg.edu                    Federal Code: 002943

**2-year private** junior college in small town, affiliated with United Methodist Church.
**Enrollment:** 704 undergrads. 351 full-time freshmen.
**Selectivity:** Admits over 75% of applicants.

### BASIC COSTS (2015-2016)
**Tuition and fees:** $17,346.
**Room and board:** $10,709.

### FINANCIAL AID PICTURE
**Students with need:** Need-based aid available for full-time students. Work study available nights, weekends, and for part-time students.
**Students without need:** No-need awards available for academics, art, athletics, leadership, minority status, music/drama, religious affiliation, state/district residency.
**Scholarships offered:** Academic Merit Scholarships: $2,000-$6,000. Leadership Scholarship: $1,000. Robbins Scholarship: $1,000.
**Additional info:** Job location and development program helps students obtain work in the community.

### FINANCIAL AID PROCEDURES
**Forms required:** FAFSA, state aid form.
**Dates and Deadlines:** Priority date 3/1; no closing date.

### CONTACT
Thomas Welch, Financial Services Director
501 North Main Street, Louisburg, NC 27549
(919) 497-3309

## Mars Hill University
Mars Hill, North Carolina
www.mhu.edu                          Federal Code: 002944

**4-year private** liberal arts college in small town, affiliated with Baptist faith.
**Enrollment:** 1,351 undergrads, 5% part-time. 403 full-time freshmen.
**Selectivity:** Admits 50 to 75% of applicants.

### BASIC COSTS (2015-2016)
**Tuition and fees:** $29,382.
**Per-credit charge:** $925.
**Room and board:** $8,234.

### FINANCIAL AID PICTURE (2015-2016)
**Students with need:** Out of 390 full-time freshmen who applied for aid, 372 were judged to have need. Of these, 372 received aid, and 58 had their full need met. Average financial aid package met 79% of need; average scholarship/grant was $9,498; average loan was $3,064. For part-time students, average financial aid package was $9,686.
**Students without need:** 42 full-time freshmen who did not demonstrate need for aid received scholarships/grants; average award was $7,765. No-need awards available for academics, athletics, state/district residency.
**Scholarships offered:** 22 full-time freshmen received athletic scholarships; average amount $9,431.

### FINANCIAL AID PROCEDURES
**Forms required:** FAFSA.
**Dates and Deadlines:** Priority date 3/15; no closing date. Applicants notified on a rolling basis starting 1/15; must reply within 2 week(s) of notification.
**Transfers:** No deadline. Applicants notified on a rolling basis; must reply within 2 week(s) of notification.

### CONTACT
Nichole Thomas, Director of Financial Aid
Mars Hill University Admissions Office, Mars Hill, NC 28754
(828) 689-1123

## Martin Community College
Williamston, North Carolina
www.martincc.edu                     Federal Code: 007988

**2-year public** community and technical college in small town.
**Enrollment:** 875 undergrads.
**Selectivity:** Open admission; but selective for some programs.

### BASIC COSTS (2015-2016)
**Tuition and fees:** $2,198; out-of-state residents $7,958.
**Per-credit charge:** $72; out-of-state residents $264.

### FINANCIAL AID PICTURE
**Students with need:** Need-based aid available for full-time and part-time students. Work study available nights.
**Students without need:** No-need awards available for academics.

### FINANCIAL AID PROCEDURES
**Forms required:** FAFSA.
**Dates and Deadlines:** Applicants notified on a rolling basis starting 5/1.

### CONTACT
Michelle Cobb, Director of Financial Aid
1161 Kehukee Park Road, Williamston, NC 27892-9988
(252) 789-0244

## Mayland Community College
Spruce Pine, North Carolina
www.mayland.edu                      Federal Code: 011197

**2-year public** community college in rural community.
**Enrollment:** 1,119 undergrads, 67% part-time. 84 full-time freshmen.
**Selectivity:** Open admission; but selective for some programs.

### BASIC COSTS (2015-2016)
**Tuition and fees:** $2,449; out-of-state residents $8,609.
**Per-credit charge:** $72; out-of-state residents $264.

### FINANCIAL AID PICTURE (2014-2015)
**Students with need:** 99% of average financial aid package awarded as scholarships/grants, 1% awarded as loans/jobs. Need-based aid available for part-time students.

### FINANCIAL AID PROCEDURES
**Forms required:** FAFSA, institutional form.
**Dates and Deadlines:** Priority date 3/15; closing date 6/30. Applicants notified on a rolling basis starting 6/15.

### CONTACT
Cassie Forbes, Director, Financial Aid
PO Box 547, Spruce Pine, NC 28777
(828) 766-1234

## McDowell Technical Community College
Marion, North Carolina
www.mcdowelltech.edu                 Federal Code: 008085

**2-year public** community and technical college in small town.
**Enrollment:** 1,323 undergrads.
**Selectivity:** Open admission; but selective for some programs.

### BASIC COSTS (2015-2016)
**Tuition and fees:** $2,213; out-of-state residents $7,973.
**Per-credit charge:** $72; out-of-state residents $264.

### FINANCIAL AID PICTURE
**Students with need:** Need-based aid available for full-time and part-time students. Work study available nights.
**Students without need:** This college awards aid only to students with need.

### FINANCIAL AID PROCEDURES
**Forms required:** FAFSA, institutional form.
**Dates and Deadlines:** Priority date 3/15; no closing date. Applicants notified on a rolling basis starting 7/1.

### CONTACT
Kim Ledbetter, Director of Financial Aid
54 College Drive, Marion, NC 28752
(828) 652-0602

## Meredith College
Raleigh, North Carolina
www.meredith.edu                     Federal Code: 002945

**4-year private** liberal arts college for women in large city.
**Enrollment:** 1,650 undergrads, 2% part-time. 439 full-time freshmen.
**Selectivity:** Admits 50 to 75% of applicants. GED not accepted.

### BASIC COSTS (2016-2017)
**Tuition and fees:** $34,907.
**Per-credit charge:** $864.
**Room and board:** $10,390.

## FINANCIAL AID PICTURE

**Students with need:** Need-based aid available for full-time and part-time students.

**Students without need:** No-need awards available for academics, art, leadership, minority status, music/drama, religious affiliation, state/district residency.

**Scholarships offered:** Presidential Scholarships: tuition plus a stipend for study abroad; based on superior academic ability and achievement; 3-5 awarded. Talent Scholarships: varying amounts; available for students planning to major in art, music, interior design and computer science/mathematics/pre-engineering; based on on-campus competition. Academic Merit Scholarships: ranging from $14,000-$18,000. Meredith Legacy Scholars: full, four-year scholarship.

## FINANCIAL AID PROCEDURES

**Forms required:** FAFSA.

**Dates and Deadlines:** Priority date 2/15; no closing date. Applicants notified on a rolling basis starting 3/15; must reply by 5/1 or within 2 week(s) of notification.

## CONTACT

Kevin Michaelsen, Director of Financial Assistance
3800 Hillsborough Street, Raleigh, NC 27607-5298
(919) 760-8565

## Methodist University
Fayetteville, North Carolina
www.methodist.edu                    Federal Code: 002946

**4-year private** liberal arts college in small city, affiliated with United Methodist Church.
**Enrollment:** 2,173 undergrads.

## BASIC COSTS (2015-2016)
**Tuition and fees:** $30,530.
**Per-credit charge:** $974.
**Room and board:** $11,344.

## FINANCIAL AID PICTURE

**Students with need:** Need-based aid available for full-time and part-time students. Work study available nights, weekends, and for part-time students.

**Students without need:** No-need awards available for academics, alumni affiliation, leadership, music/drama, religious affiliation.

**Scholarships offered:** Presidential Scholarship: $5,250-$17,000/yr; 3.1+ GPA, 1000+ SAT or 22+ ACT. Merit scholarship: $3,250-$4,250; residential freshmen; 2.9+ GPA, 900+ SAT or 19+ ACT; leadership. SAT scores exclusive of Writing.

## FINANCIAL AID PROCEDURES

**Forms required:** FAFSA, state aid form.

**Dates and Deadlines:** Priority date 8/1; no closing date. Applicants notified on a rolling basis starting 3/6; must reply within 2 week(s) of notification.

**Transfers:** No deadline. Applicants notified on a rolling basis; must reply within 2 week(s) of notification.

## CONTACT

Bonnie Adamson, Director of Financial Aid
5400 Ramsey Street, Fayetteville, NC 28311-1420
(910) 630-7192

## Mid-Atlantic Christian University
Elizabeth City, North Carolina
www.macuniversity.edu                    Federal Code: 014101

**4-year private** university and Bible college in large town, affiliated with Church of Christ.

**Enrollment:** 204 undergrads, 14% part-time. 55 full-time freshmen.
**Selectivity:** Admits less than 50% of applicants.

## BASIC COSTS (2015-2016)
**Tuition and fees:** $12,600.
**Per-credit charge:** $420.
**Room and board:** $8,200.

## FINANCIAL AID PICTURE

**Students with need:** Need-based aid available for full-time and part-time students. Work study available nights, weekends, and for part-time students.

**Students without need:** No-need awards available for academics, alumni affiliation, leadership, music/drama, religious affiliation.

**Scholarships offered:** Full tuition and half tuition available, based on demonstration of exceptional academic ability.

## FINANCIAL AID PROCEDURES

**Forms required:** FAFSA, institutional form.

**Dates and Deadlines:** Priority date 2/1; no closing date. Applicants notified on a rolling basis starting 5/1; must reply within 2 week(s) of notification.

**Transfers:** Priority date 3/1; no deadline. Applicants notified on a rolling basis starting 5/1; must reply within 2 week(s) of notification.

## CONTACT

Jenny Rowland, Financial Aid Administrator
715 North Poindexter Street, Elizabeth City, NC 27909
(252) 334-2020

## Miller-Motte College: Wilmington
Wilmington, North Carolina
www.miller-motte.edu                    Federal Code: E00896

**4-year for-profit** technical college in small city.
**Enrollment:** 3,463 undergrads.

## BASIC COSTS (2015-2016)
**Additional info:** Certificate programs: $9,660-$20,788, books and supplies $400-$3,900. Associate programs: $26,160-$29,136, books and supplies $4,550-$5,200. Bachelor's programs: $29,182-$31,048, books and supplies $3,900.

## FINANCIAL AID PICTURE

**Students with need:** Need-based aid available for full-time and part-time students. Work study available nights, weekends, and for part-time students.

**Students without need:** This college awards aid only to students with need.

## FINANCIAL AID PROCEDURES

**Forms required:** FAFSA, institutional form.

## CONTACT

Michele Carroll, Financial Services Manager
5000 Market Street, Wilmington, NC 28405
(910) 392-4660

## Mitchell Community College
Statesville, North Carolina
www.mitchellcc.edu                    Federal Code: 002947

**2-year public** community college in large town.
**Enrollment:** 2,672 undergrads.
**Selectivity:** Open admission; but selective for some programs.

## BASIC COSTS (2015-2016)
**Tuition and fees:** $2,228; out-of-state residents $7,988.
**Per-credit charge:** $72; out-of-state residents $264.

PART III: FINANCIAL AID COLLEGE BY COLLEGE

## FINANCIAL AID PICTURE
**Students with need:** Need-based aid available for full-time and part-time students.

## FINANCIAL AID PROCEDURES
**Forms required:** FAFSA, institutional form.
**Dates and Deadlines:** Applicants notified on a rolling basis starting 3/1; must reply within 2 week(s) of notification.
**Transfers:** Students are monitored through NSLDS's Transfer Monitoring List.

## CONTACT
Candace Cooper, Director of Financial Aid
500 West Broad Street, Statesville, NC 28677
(704) 878-3256

## Montgomery Community College
Troy, North Carolina
www.montgomery.edu                  Federal Code: 008087

**2-year public** community college in small town.
**Enrollment:** 809 undergrads.
**Selectivity:** Open admission; but selective for some programs.

### BASIC COSTS (2015-2016)
**Tuition and fees:** $2,277; out-of-state residents $8,037.
**Per-credit charge:** $72; out-of-state residents $264.

### FINANCIAL AID PICTURE
**Students with need:** Need-based aid available for full-time and part-time students. Work study available nights.
**Students without need:** No-need awards available for academics, minority status, state/district residency.

### FINANCIAL AID PROCEDURES
**Forms required:** FAFSA, institutional form.
**Dates and Deadlines:** Closing date 7/1. Applicants notified on a rolling basis starting 3/15; must reply by 7/1.
**Transfers:** Applicants notified on a rolling basis starting 3/15; must reply by 7/1.

### CONTACT
Doni Cody, Director of Financial Aid
1011 Page Street, Troy, NC 27371
(910) 576-6222 ext. 519

## Montreat College
Montreat, North Carolina
www.montreat.edu                  Federal Code: 002948

**4-year private** liberal arts college in small town, affiliated with Presbyterian Church Reformed and Independent.
**Enrollment:** 724 undergrads, 30% part-time. 111 full-time freshmen.
**Selectivity:** Admits 50 to 75% of applicants.

### BASIC COSTS (2015-2016)
**Tuition and fees:** $24,240.
**Room and board:** $8,266.

### FINANCIAL AID PICTURE (2014-2015)
**Students with need:** Out of 95 full-time freshmen who applied for aid, 85 were judged to have need. Of these, 85 received aid, and 19 had their full need met. Average financial aid package met 77% of need; average scholarship/grant was $17,229; average loan was $3,376. For part-time students, average financial aid package was $7,100.

**Students without need:** 23 full-time freshmen who did not demonstrate need for aid received scholarships/grants; average award was $11,849. No-need awards available for academics, alumni affiliation, art, athletics, leadership, minority status, music/drama, religious affiliation, state/district residency.
**Scholarships offered:** 24 full-time freshmen received athletic scholarships; average amount $4,030.

### FINANCIAL AID PROCEDURES
**Forms required:** FAFSA, state aid form.
**Dates and Deadlines:** Priority date 3/1; no closing date. Applicants notified on a rolling basis starting 3/1; must reply within 2 week(s) of notification.
**Transfers:** Priority date 4/1; no deadline. Applicants notified on a rolling basis starting 1/15; must reply within 2 week(s) of notification.

### CONTACT
Beth Pocock, Director of Financial Aid
P.O. Box 1267, Montreat, NC 28757
(800) 545-4656

## Nash Community College
Rocky Mount, North Carolina
www.nashcc.edu                  Federal Code: 008557

**2-year public** community and technical college in small city.
**Enrollment:** 1,939 undergrads, 46% part-time. 348 full-time freshmen.
**Selectivity:** Open admission; but selective for some programs.

### BASIC COSTS (2015-2016)
**Tuition and fees:** $2,776; out-of-state residents $8,966.
**Per-credit charge:** $72; out-of-state residents $264.

### FINANCIAL AID PICTURE
**Students with need:** Need-based aid available for full-time and part-time students. Work study available nights, weekends, and for part-time students.
**Students without need:** No-need awards available for academics.

### FINANCIAL AID PROCEDURES
**Forms required:** FAFSA, institutional form.
**Dates and Deadlines:** Priority date 6/30; no closing date. Applicants notified on a rolling basis starting 7/15.

### CONTACT
Tammy Lester, Financial Aid Officer
Box 7488, Rocky Mount, NC 27804-0488
(252) 451-8371

## North Carolina Agricultural and Technical State University
Greensboro, North Carolina
www.ncat.edu                  Federal Code: 002905

**4-year public** university in small city.
**Enrollment:** 9,036 undergrads.
**Selectivity:** Admits 50 to 75% of applicants.

### BASIC COSTS (2015-2016)
**Tuition and fees:** $5,972; out-of-state residents $18,732.
**Room and board:** $6,842.

### FINANCIAL AID PICTURE
**Students with need:** Need-based aid available for full-time and part-time students.
**Students without need:** No-need awards available for academics.

### FINANCIAL AID PROCEDURES
**Forms required:** FAFSA.

**Dates and Deadlines:** Priority date 3/1; no closing date. Applicants notified on a rolling basis starting 4/15; must reply within 2 week(s) of notification.

**CONTACT**
Sherri Avent, Director of Student Financial Aid
Webb Hall, Greensboro, NC 27411-0002
(336) 334-7973

## North Carolina Central University
Durham, North Carolina
www.nccu.edu                    Federal Code: 002950

**4-year public** university in small city.
**Enrollment:** 5,797 undergrads, 12% part-time. 1,101 full-time freshmen.
**Selectivity:** Admits 50 to 75% of applicants.

**BASIC COSTS (2015-2016)**
**Tuition and fees:** $5,755; out-of-state residents $17,793.
**Room and board:** $8,165.

**FINANCIAL AID PICTURE (2014-2015)**
**Students with need:** Out of 1,086 full-time freshmen who applied for aid, 1,030 were judged to have need. Of these, 1,025 received aid, and 50 had their full need met. Average financial aid package met 58% of need; average scholarship/grant was $8,138; average loan was $3,650. For part-time students, average financial aid package was $8,042.
**Students without need:** 4 full-time freshmen who did not demonstrate need for aid received scholarships/grants; average award was $6,372. No-need awards available for academics, alumni affiliation, art, athletics, leadership, music/drama, ROTC.
**Additional info:** Departmental grants based on need plus other available criteria.

**FINANCIAL AID PROCEDURES**
**Forms required:** FAFSA.
**Dates and Deadlines:** Closing date 3/1. Applicants notified by 3/1; must reply within 2 week(s) of notification.

**CONTACT**
Sharon Oliver, Director of Student Financial Aid
PO Box 19717, Durham, NC 27707
(919) 530-6180

## North Carolina State University
Raleigh, North Carolina
www.ncsu.edu                    Federal Code: 002972

**4-year public** university in large city.
**Enrollment:** 22,458 undergrads, 7% part-time. 4,209 full-time freshmen.
**Selectivity:** Admits 50 to 75% of applicants.

**BASIC COSTS (2015-2016)**
**Tuition and fees:** $8,581; out-of-state residents $24,932.
**Room and board:** $10,311.

**FINANCIAL AID PICTURE (2015-2016)**
**Students with need:** Out of 3,342 full-time freshmen who applied for aid, 2,010 were judged to have need. Of these, 1,972 received aid, and 473 had their full need met. Average financial aid package met 80% of need; average scholarship/grant was $10,186; average loan was $2,862. For part-time students, average financial aid package was $6,662.
**Students without need:** 193 full-time freshmen who did not demonstrate need for aid received scholarships/grants; average award was $6,876. No-need awards available for academics, alumni affiliation, athletics, leadership, ROTC, state/district residency.

**Scholarships offered:** *Merit:* Park Scholarships: 4 year scholarship that covers almost all expenses; approximately 50 awarded each year. Goodnight Scholarships: 4 year scholarship that covers more than 75% of all expenses; 50 awarded each year. Caldwell scholarships: awarded at end of freshmen year for 3 years covering most expenses. *Athletic:* 89 full-time freshmen received athletic scholarships; average amount $17,152.
**Additional info:** Freshman Merit Scholarships; students submitting complete admissions application by the November 1 Early Action deadline automatically considered, additional information may be required after initial review.

**FINANCIAL AID PROCEDURES**
**Forms required:** FAFSA.
**Dates and Deadlines:** Priority date 3/1; no closing date. Applicants notified on a rolling basis starting 4/1.

**CONTACT**
Krista Ringler Domnick, Director of Scholarships and Financial Aid
Campus Box 7103, Raleigh, NC 27695-7103
(919) 515-2421

## North Carolina Wesleyan College
Rocky Mount, North Carolina
www.ncwc.edu                    Federal Code: 002951

**4-year private** liberal arts college in small city, affiliated with United Methodist Church.
**Enrollment:** 2,119 undergrads, 19% part-time. 320 full-time freshmen.
**Selectivity:** Admits 50 to 75% of applicants.

**BASIC COSTS (2015-2016)**
**Tuition and fees:** $28,150.
**Per-credit charge:** $488.
**Room and board:** $9,524.

**FINANCIAL AID PICTURE**
**Students with need:** Need-based aid available for full-time and part-time students.
**Students without need:** No-need awards available for academics, religious affiliation.
**Additional info:** Scholarships based on GPA. Various scholarship and leadership awards available.

**FINANCIAL AID PROCEDURES**
**Forms required:** FAFSA.
**Dates and Deadlines:** Priority date 3/1; no closing date. Applicants notified on a rolling basis starting 1/1; must reply within 2 week(s) of notification.
**Transfers:** No deadline. Applicants notified on a rolling basis; must reply within 2 week(s) of notification.

**CONTACT**
Leah Hill, Director of Financial Aid
3400 North Wesleyan Boulevard, Rocky Mount, NC 27804
(252) 985-5295

## Pfeiffer University
Misenheimer, North Carolina
www.pfeiffer.edu                Federal Code: 002955

**4-year private** university and liberal arts college in rural community, affiliated with United Methodist Church.
**Enrollment:** 906 undergrads, 10% part-time. 213 full-time freshmen.
**Selectivity:** Admits less than 50% of applicants.

**BASIC COSTS (2015-2016)**
**Tuition and fees:** $27,125.

**Per-credit charge:** $598.
**Room and board:** $10,525.

## FINANCIAL AID PICTURE (2014-2015)
**Students with need:** Out of 166 full-time freshmen who applied for aid, 147 were judged to have need. Of these, 147 received aid, and 29 had their full need met. Average financial aid package met 77% of need; average scholarship/grant was $19,997; average loan was $4,089. For part-time students, average financial aid package was $7,952.
**Students without need:** 63 full-time freshmen who did not demonstrate need for aid received scholarships/grants; average award was $12,422. No-need awards available for academics, alumni affiliation, athletics, leadership, music/drama, religious affiliation, state/district residency.
**Scholarships offered: *Merit:*** Honor, Presidential, University, and Legacy Scholarships: $3,500 to full tuition per year. ***Athletic:*** 40 full-time freshmen received athletic scholarships; average amount $12,790.

## FINANCIAL AID PROCEDURES
**Forms required:** FAFSA, state aid form.
**Dates and Deadlines:** Priority date 4/15; no closing date. Applicants notified on a rolling basis starting 3/1; must reply within 2 week(s) of notification.
**Transfers:** Priority date 3/15.

## CONTACT
Amy Brown, Director of Financial Aid
PO Box 960, Misenheimer, NC 28109
(800) 336-2060

## Piedmont Community College
Roxboro, North Carolina
www.piedmontcc.edu          Federal Code: 009646

**2-year public** community college in small town.
**Enrollment:** 1,020 undergrads. 164 full-time freshmen.
**Selectivity:** Open admission; but selective for some programs.

### BASIC COSTS (2015-2016)
**Tuition and fees:** $2,232; out-of-state residents $7,992.
**Per-credit charge:** $72; out-of-state residents $264.

### FINANCIAL AID PICTURE (2014-2015)
**Students with need:** 99% of average financial aid package awarded as scholarships/grants, 1% awarded as loans/jobs. Need-based aid available for part-time students.

### FINANCIAL AID PROCEDURES
**Forms required:** FAFSA.
**Dates and Deadlines:** Priority date 4/1; no closing date. Applicants notified on a rolling basis starting 4/15; must reply within 2 week(s) of notification.

### CONTACT
Tasha Williams, Director of Financial Aid/Veterans Affairs
1715 College Drive, Roxboro, NC 27573-1197
(336) 599-1181 ext. 2159

## Piedmont International University
Winston-Salem, North Carolina
www.piedmontu.edu          Federal Code: 002956

**4-year private** university and seminary college in small city, affiliated with Baptist faith.
**Enrollment:** 351 undergrads, 42% part-time. 203 full-time freshmen.

### BASIC COSTS (2015-2016)
**Tuition and fees:** $9,580.
**Per-credit charge:** $295.
**Room and board:** $6,410.

**Additional info:** Tuition/fee waivers available for minority students.

## FINANCIAL AID PICTURE (2015-2016)
**Students with need:** Out of 19 full-time freshmen who applied for aid, 19 were judged to have need. Of these, 19 received aid, and 1 had their full need met. Average financial aid package met 68% of need; average scholarship/grant was $1,742; average loan was $1,732. For part-time students, average financial aid package was $2,472.
**Students without need:** 12 full-time freshmen who did not demonstrate need for aid received scholarships/grants; average award was $825. No-need awards available for academics, alumni affiliation, leadership, minority status, religious affiliation.

## FINANCIAL AID PROCEDURES
**Forms required:** FAFSA, institutional form.
**Dates and Deadlines:** Priority date 3/1; closing date 8/1. Applicants notified on a rolling basis starting 3/1; must reply within 2 week(s) of notification.
**Transfers:** Applicants notified on a rolling basis starting 3/1.

## CONTACT
Executive Vice President of Operations
420 South Boad Street, Winston-Salem, NC 27101-5133
(336) 714-7933

## Pitt Community College
Greenville, North Carolina
www.pittcc.edu          Federal Code: 004062

**2-year public** community and technical college in small city.
**Enrollment:** 8,521 undergrads.
**Selectivity:** Open admission; but selective for some programs.

### BASIC COSTS (2015-2016)
**Tuition and fees:** $2,234; out-of-state residents $7,994.
**Per-credit charge:** $72; out-of-state residents $264.

### FINANCIAL AID PICTURE
**Students with need:** Need-based aid available for full-time and part-time students. Work study available nights.
**Students without need:** No-need awards available for academics, athletics, ROTC.

### FINANCIAL AID PROCEDURES
**Forms required:** FAFSA.
**Dates and Deadlines:** Priority date 3/15; closing date 5/15. Applicants notified on a rolling basis starting 2/1.

### CONTACT
Tamara Glaspie, Financial Aid Director
PO Drawer 7007, Greenville, NC 27835-7007
(252) 483-7326

## Queens University of Charlotte
Charlotte, North Carolina
www.queens.edu          Federal Code: 002957

**4-year private** university in very large city, affiliated with Presbyterian Church (USA).
**Enrollment:** 1,551 undergrads, 13% part-time. 282 full-time freshmen.
**Selectivity:** Admits over 75% of applicants.

### BASIC COSTS (2015-2016)
**Tuition and fees:** $32,560.
**Per-credit charge:** $464.
**Room and board:** $11,390.

## FINANCIAL AID PICTURE (2015-2016)

**Students with need:** Out of 228 full-time freshmen who applied for aid, 173 were judged to have need. Of these, 173 received aid, and 45 had their full need met. Average financial aid package met 74% of need; average scholarship/grant was $8,183; average loan was $3,405. For part-time students, average financial aid package was $5,960.

**Students without need:** 103 full-time freshmen who did not demonstrate need for aid received scholarships/grants; average award was $12,738. No-need awards available for academics, art, athletics, leadership, minority status, music/drama, religious affiliation, state/district residency.

**Scholarships offered:** *Merit:* Presidential Scholarships: full tuition; based on special application/recommendations; deadline 12/13; up to 10 awarded. University Scholars (Trustee, Dean's & Alumni): range from $9,000-$15,000; based on admitted student's academic profile. *Athletic:* 44 full-time freshmen received athletic scholarships; average amount $12,023.

## FINANCIAL AID PROCEDURES

**Forms required:** FAFSA.

**Dates and Deadlines:** Applicants notified on a rolling basis starting 3/1; must reply by 5/1 or within 3 week(s) of notification.

**Transfers:** No deadline. Applicants notified on a rolling basis starting 3/15; must reply by 5/1 or within 3 week(s) of notification.

## CONTACT

Christy Majors, Assistant Vice President of Student Financial Services
1900 Selwyn Avenue, Charlotte, NC 28274-0001
(704) 337-2225

# Randolph Community College

Asheboro, North Carolina
www.randolph.edu                    Federal Code: 005447

**2-year public** community and technical college in large town.
**Enrollment:** 2,813 undergrads.
**Selectivity:** Open admission; but selective for some programs.

## BASIC COSTS (2015-2016)

**Tuition and fees:** $2,228; out-of-state residents $7,988.
**Per-credit charge:** $72; out-of-state residents $264.

## FINANCIAL AID PICTURE

**Students with need:** Need-based aid available for full-time and part-time students. Work study available nights.

**Students without need:** No-need awards available for academics, leadership, minority status, state/district residency.

## FINANCIAL AID PROCEDURES

**Forms required:** FAFSA.

**Dates and Deadlines:** Applicants notified on a rolling basis starting 3/1.

**Transfers:** No deadline. Applicants notified on a rolling basis starting 3/1.

## CONTACT

Chad Williams, Director of Student Support Services
629 Industrial Park Avenue, Asheboro, NC 27205
(336) 633-0200

# Richmond Community College

Hamlet, North Carolina
www.richmondcc.edu                  Federal Code: 005464

**2-year public** community college in small town.
**Enrollment:** 2,321 undergrads.
**Selectivity:** Open admission; but selective for some programs.

## BASIC COSTS (2015-2016)

**Tuition and fees:** $2,224; out-of-state residents $7,984.
**Per-credit charge:** $72; out-of-state residents $264.

## FINANCIAL AID PICTURE

**Students with need:** Need-based aid available for full-time and part-time students. Work study available nights.

**Students without need:** No-need awards available for academics, leadership.

## FINANCIAL AID PROCEDURES

**Forms required:** FAFSA, institutional form.

**Dates and Deadlines:** Closing date 7/25. Applicants notified on a rolling basis starting 7/8; must reply within 2 week(s) of notification.

## CONTACT

Bruce Blackmon, Director of Financial Aid
Box 1189, Hamlet, NC 28345
(910) 410-1726

# Roanoke-Chowan Community College

Ahoskie, North Carolina
www.roanokechowan.edu               Federal Code: 008613

**2-year public** community college in small town.
**Enrollment:** 903 undergrads. 59 full-time freshmen.
**Selectivity:** Open admission; but selective for some programs.

## BASIC COSTS (2015-2016)

**Tuition and fees:** $2,261; out-of-state residents $8,021.
**Per-credit charge:** $72; out-of-state residents $264.

## FINANCIAL AID PICTURE (2014-2015)

**Students with need:** Out of 56 full-time freshmen who applied for aid, 56 were judged to have need. Of these, 56 received aid, and 53 had their full need met. Average financial aid package met 95% of need; average scholarship/grant was $4,841; average loan was $1,364. Need-based aid available for part-time students.

**Students without need:** 3 full-time freshmen who did not demonstrate need for aid received scholarships/grants; average award was $926. No-need awards available for academics.

## FINANCIAL AID PROCEDURES

**Forms required:** FAFSA.

**Dates and Deadlines:** Priority date 3/15; no closing date. Applicants notified on a rolling basis starting 7/1.

## CONTACT

Crystal Harris, Financial Aid Director
109 Community College Road, Ahoskie, NC 27910-9522
(252) 862-1246

# Robeson Community College

Lumberton, North Carolina
www.robeson.edu                     Federal Code: 008612

**2-year public** community college in large town.
**Enrollment:** 1,867 undergrads.
**Selectivity:** Open admission; but selective for some programs.

## BASIC COSTS (2015-2016)

**Tuition and fees:** $2,285; out-of-state residents $8,045.
**Per-credit charge:** $72; out-of-state residents $264.

## FINANCIAL AID PICTURE

**Students with need:** Need-based aid available for full-time and part-time students.

## FINANCIAL AID PROCEDURES

**Forms required:** FAFSA.

**Dates and Deadlines:** Priority date 5/15; no closing date. Applicants notified on a rolling basis starting 7/31.

## CONTACT

Teresa Tubbs, Director of Financial Aid
PO Box 1420, Lumberton, NC 28359
(910) 272-3352

## Rockingham Community College

Wentworth, North Carolina
www.rockinghamcc.edu          Federal Code: 002958

**2-year public** community college in rural community.
**Enrollment:** 1,860 undergrads.
**Selectivity:** Open admission; but selective for some programs.

**BASIC COSTS (2015-2016)**
**Tuition and fees:** $2,256; out-of-state residents $8,016.
**Per-credit charge:** $72; out-of-state residents $264.

**FINANCIAL AID PICTURE**
**Students with need:** Need-based aid available for full-time and part-time students.
**Students without need:** No-need awards available for academics.

**FINANCIAL AID PROCEDURES**
**Forms required:** FAFSA, institutional form.
**Dates and Deadlines:** Priority date 3/15; no closing date. Must reply within 2 week(s) of notification.

## CONTACT

Evans Sarah, Director of Financial Aid
Box 38, Wentworth, NC 27375-0038
(336) 342-4261 ext. 2204

## Rowan-Cabarrus Community College

Salisbury, North Carolina
www.rccc.edu          Federal Code: 005754

**2-year public** community and technical college in large town.
**Enrollment:** 5,536 undergrads.
**Selectivity:** Open admission; but selective for some programs.

**BASIC COSTS (2015-2016)**
**Tuition and fees:** $2,289; out-of-state residents $8,049.
**Per-credit charge:** $72; out-of-state residents $264.

**FINANCIAL AID PICTURE**
**Students with need:** Need-based aid available for full-time and part-time students. Work study available nights.
**Students without need:** No-need awards available for academics, job skills, state/district residency.

**FINANCIAL AID PROCEDURES**
**Forms required:** FAFSA.
**Dates and Deadlines:** Priority date 3/15; no closing date. Applicants notified on a rolling basis starting 5/1; must reply within 3 week(s) of notification.
**Transfers:** No deadline.

## CONTACT

Lisa Ledbetter, Director, Financial Aid
Box 1595, Salisbury, NC 28145
(704) 637-0760 ext. 273

## St. Andrews University

Laurinburg, North Carolina
www.sa.edu          Federal Code: 002967

**4-year private** liberal arts college in large town, affiliated with Presbyterian Church (USA).

**Enrollment:** 601 undergrads, 7% part-time. 152 full-time freshmen.

**BASIC COSTS (2015-2016)**
**Tuition and fees:** $24,390.
**Per-credit charge:** $280.
**Room and board:** $10,194.

**FINANCIAL AID PICTURE**
**Students with need:** Need-based aid available for full-time students. Work study available nights, weekends, and for part-time students.
**Students without need:** No-need awards available for academics, alumni affiliation, art, athletics, job skills, leadership, music/drama, religious affiliation.

**FINANCIAL AID PROCEDURES**
**Dates and Deadlines:** Priority date 5/1; no closing date. Applicants notified on a rolling basis starting 3/1.
**Transfers:** No deadline. Applicants notified on a rolling basis starting 10/1; must reply within 2 week(s) of notification.

## CONTACT

Kimberly Driggers, Director of Student Financial Planning
1700 Dogwood Mile, Laurinburg, NC 28352
(910) 277-5560

## Saint Augustine's University

Raleigh, North Carolina
www.st-aug.edu          Federal Code: 002968

**4-year private** liberal arts college in large city, affiliated with Episcopal Church.
**Enrollment:** 810 undergrads, 1% part-time. 211 full-time freshmen.
**Selectivity:** Admits 50 to 75% of applicants.

**BASIC COSTS (2015-2016)**
**Tuition and fees:** $17,890.
**Per-credit charge:** $537.
**Room and board:** $7,692.

**FINANCIAL AID PICTURE (2015-2016)**
**Students with need:** Out of 138 full-time freshmen who applied for aid, 138 were judged to have need. Of these, 138 received aid, and 115 had their full need met. Average financial aid package met 65% of need; average scholarship/grant was $4,769; average loan was $6,160. For part-time students, average financial aid package was $6,794.
**Students without need:** No-need awards available for academics, art, athletics, leadership, minority status, music/drama, religious affiliation, ROTC, state/district residency.
**Scholarships offered: *Merit:*** Institutional Merit Scholarships based on high school record, evidence of leadership, and SAT score. ***Athletic:*** 1 full-time freshmen received athletic scholarships; average amount $6,500.

**FINANCIAL AID PROCEDURES**
**Forms required:** FAFSA, institutional form.
**Dates and Deadlines:** Priority date 3/15; no closing date. Applicants notified on a rolling basis starting 3/1; must reply within 2 week(s) of notification.
**Transfers:** Priority date 3/15; no deadline. Applicants notified on a rolling basis; must reply within 2 week(s) of notification.

## CONTACT

Nadine Ford, Director of Financial Aid
1315 Oakwood Avenue, Raleigh, NC 27610-2298
(919) 516-4131

## Salem College
Winston-Salem, North Carolina
www.salem.edu                    Federal Code: 002960

**4-year private** liberal arts college for women in small city, affiliated with Moravian Church in America.
**Enrollment:** 917 undergrads.

**BASIC COSTS (2015-2016)**
**Tuition and fees:** $25,930.
**Room and board:** $11,824.
**Additional info:** Tuition/fee waivers available for adults.

**FINANCIAL AID PICTURE**
**Students with need:** Need-based aid available for full-time and part-time students. Work study available nights, weekends, and for part-time students.
**Students without need:** No-need awards available for academics, alumni affiliation, leadership, minority status, music/drama, state/district residency.

**FINANCIAL AID PROCEDURES**
**Forms required:** FAFSA.
**Dates and Deadlines:** Priority date 3/1; no closing date. Applicants notified on a rolling basis starting 3/1; must reply by 5/1 or within 2 week(s) of notification.

**CONTACT**
Paul Coscia, Director of Financial Aid
601 South Church Street, Winston-Salem, NC 27108
(336) 721-2808

## Sampson Community College
Clinton, North Carolina
www.sampsoncc.edu                Federal Code: 007892

**2-year public** community and technical college in small town.
**Enrollment:** 1,539 undergrads.
**Selectivity:** Open admission; but selective for some programs.

**BASIC COSTS (2015-2016)**
**Tuition and fees:** $2,237; out-of-state residents $7,997.
**Per-credit charge:** $72; out-of-state residents $264.

**FINANCIAL AID PICTURE**
**Students with need:** Need-based aid available for full-time and part-time students.
**Students without need:** No-need awards available for academics, state/district residency.

**FINANCIAL AID PROCEDURES**
**Forms required:** FAFSA.
**Dates and Deadlines:** Priority date 5/1; no closing date. Applicants notified on a rolling basis starting 7/15; must reply within 2 week(s) of notification.

**CONTACT**
Judye Tart, Director of Financial Aid
PO Box 318, Clinton, NC 28329
(910) 592-8084 ext. 2024

## Sandhills Community College
Pinehurst, North Carolina
www.sandhills.edu                Federal Code: 002961

**2-year public** community college in large town.
**Enrollment:** 2,889 undergrads.
**Selectivity:** Open admission; but selective for some programs.

**BASIC COSTS (2015-2016)**
**Tuition and fees:** $2,326; out-of-state residents $8,086.
**Per-credit charge:** $72; out-of-state residents $264.

**FINANCIAL AID PICTURE (2015-2016)**
**Students with need:** 95% of average financial aid package awarded as scholarships/grants, 5% awarded as loans/jobs. Need-based aid available for part-time students.
**Students without need:** No-need awards available for academics, state/district residency.

**FINANCIAL AID PROCEDURES**
**Forms required:** FAFSA.
**Dates and Deadlines:** Closing date 7/14. Applicants notified on a rolling basis starting 5/1; must reply by 8/1 or within 4 week(s) of notification.

**CONTACT**
Lindsey Farmer, Director of Financial Aid
3395 Airport Road, Pinehurst, NC 28374
(910) 695-3743

## Shaw University
Raleigh, North Carolina
www.shawu.edu                    Federal Code: 002962

**4-year private** university and liberal arts college in large city, affiliated with Baptist faith.
**Enrollment:** 1,503 undergrads, 6% part-time. 399 full-time freshmen.
**Selectivity:** Admits 50 to 75% of applicants.

**BASIC COSTS (2015-2016)**
**Tuition and fees:** $14,840.
**Per-credit charge:** $492.
**Room and board:** $8,158.

**FINANCIAL AID PICTURE**
**Students with need:** Need-based aid available for full-time and part-time students. Work study available nights, weekends, and for part-time students.
**Students without need:** No-need awards available for academics, athletics, music/drama.
**Scholarships offered:** Presidential Scholarship: based on GPA and SAT.

**FINANCIAL AID PROCEDURES**
**Forms required:** FAFSA.
**Dates and Deadlines:** Priority date 3/1; closing date 6/30. Applicants notified on a rolling basis starting 3/15.

**CONTACT**
Ronald Dowdy, Vice President for Finance and Administration
118 East South Street, Raleigh, NC 27601
(919) 546-8240

## South College
Asheville, North Carolina
www.southcollegenc.edu           Federal Code: 010264

**2-year for-profit** health science and career college in small city.
**Enrollment:** 263 undergrads.
**Selectivity:** Open admission; but selective for some programs.

**BASIC COSTS (2015-2016)**
**Additional info:** Bachelor programs: Legal Studies $75,725, books and supplies $4,245. Radiological Sciences $75,725, books and supplies $5,243. Associate programs: Accounting $46,600, books and supplies $3,459. Business Administration $46,600, books and supplies $2,755. Criminal Justice $46,600, books and supplies $3,713. Medical Assisting $46,600, books and supplies $2,672. Nursing $50,300, books and supplies $3,485. Occupational

Therapy Assistant $49,800, books and supplies $3,473. Paralegal Studies $46,600, books and supplies $4,359. Physical Therapist Assistant $49,800, books and supplies $3,473. Radiologic Technology $4,800, books and supplies $4,821. Certificate programs: Medical Assisting $23,300, books and supplies $1,336. Surgical Technology $2,125, books and supplies $2,313.

**FINANCIAL AID PICTURE**

**Students with need:** Need-based aid available for full-time and part-time students.

**FINANCIAL AID PROCEDURES**

**Forms required:** FAFSA, institutional form.
**Dates and Deadlines:** Applicants notified on a rolling basis; must reply within 4 week(s) of notification.

**CONTACT**

Ronda Blackman, Financial Aid Director
140 Sweeten Creek Road, Asheville, NC 28803
(828) 398-2500

## South Piedmont Community College
Polkton, North Carolina
www.spcc.edu                    Federal Code: 007985

**2-year public** community college in small city.
**Enrollment:** 1,747 undergrads.
**Selectivity:** Open admission; but selective for some programs.

**BASIC COSTS (2015-2016)**
**Tuition and fees:** $2,305; out-of-state residents $8,065.

**FINANCIAL AID PICTURE**

**Students with need:** Need-based aid available for full-time and part-time students. Work study available nights.
**Additional info:** Small amount of non-federal scholarship aid available. FAFSA applications received before June 1 will receive first priority.

**FINANCIAL AID PROCEDURES**

**Forms required:** FAFSA.
**Dates and Deadlines:** Priority date 6/1; no closing date. Applicants notified on a rolling basis.

**CONTACT**

John Ratliff, Director of Financial Aid
PO Box 126, Polkton, NC 28135
(704) 272-5325

## Southeastern Community College
Whiteville, North Carolina
www.sccnc.edu                    Federal Code: 002964

**2-year public** community college in small town.
**Enrollment:** 1,044 undergrads, 42% part-time. 228 full-time freshmen.
**Selectivity:** Open admission; but selective for some programs.

**BASIC COSTS (2015-2016)**
**Tuition and fees:** $2,288; out-of-state residents $8,048.
**Per-credit charge:** $72; out-of-state residents $264.

**FINANCIAL AID PICTURE**

**Students with need:** Need-based aid available for full-time and part-time students.
**Students without need:** No-need awards available for academics, athletics, leadership, music/drama, state/district residency.

**FINANCIAL AID PROCEDURES**

**Forms required:** FAFSA.

**Dates and Deadlines:** Priority date 4/1; no closing date. Applicants notified on a rolling basis starting 6/1; must reply within 2 week(s) of notification.

**CONTACT**

Justin Cristello, Director of Financial Aid
4564 Chadbourn Highway, Whiteville, NC 28472-0151
(910) 642-7141 ext. 214

## Southwestern Community College
Sylva, North Carolina
www.southwesterncc.edu          Federal Code: 008466

**2-year public** community college in rural community.
**Enrollment:** 1,760 undergrads, 54% part-time. 202 full-time freshmen.
**Selectivity:** Open admission; but selective for some programs.

**BASIC COSTS (2015-2016)**
**Tuition and fees:** $2,251; out-of-state residents $8,011.
**Per-credit charge:** $72; out-of-state residents $264.

**FINANCIAL AID PICTURE**

**Students with need:** Need-based aid available for full-time and part-time students.

**FINANCIAL AID PROCEDURES**

**Forms required:** FAFSA.
**Dates and Deadlines:** Closing date 6/30. Applicants notified on a rolling basis starting 5/1; must reply within 2 week(s) of notification.

**CONTACT**

Melody Lawrence, Director of Financial Aid
447 College Drive, Sylva, NC 28779
(800) 447-4091 ext. 4224

## Stanly Community College
Albemarle, North Carolina
www.stanly.edu                  Federal Code: 011194

**2-year public** community college in large town.
**Enrollment:** 2,368 undergrads, 69% part-time. 266 full-time freshmen.
**Selectivity:** Open admission; but selective for some programs.

**BASIC COSTS (2015-2016)**
**Tuition and fees:** $2,326; out-of-state residents $8,086.
**Per-credit charge:** $72; out-of-state residents $264.

**FINANCIAL AID PICTURE (2014-2015)**

**Students with need:** Average financial aid package met 40% of need; average scholarship/grant was $4,892. Need-based aid available for part-time students.
**Students without need:** This college awards aid only to students with need.

**FINANCIAL AID PROCEDURES**

**Forms required:** FAFSA, institutional form.
**Dates and Deadlines:** Applicants notified on a rolling basis starting 6/1; must reply within 2 week(s) of notification.
**Transfers:** No deadline. Applicants notified on a rolling basis.

**CONTACT**

Petra Fields, Director of Financial Aid
141 College Drive, Albemarle, NC 28001
(704) 991-0231

## Surry Community College

Dobson, North Carolina
www.surry.edu                         Federal Code: 002970

**2-year public** community college in rural community.
**Enrollment:** 2,171 undergrads, 44% part-time. 379 full-time freshmen.
**Selectivity:** Open admission; but selective for some programs.

### BASIC COSTS (2015-2016)
**Tuition and fees:** $2,257; out-of-state residents $8,017.
**Per-credit charge:** $72; out-of-state residents $264.

### FINANCIAL AID PICTURE
**Students with need:** Need-based aid available for full-time and part-time students. Work study available nights.
**Students without need:** No-need awards available for academics.

### FINANCIAL AID PROCEDURES
**Forms required:** FAFSA, institutional form.
**Dates and Deadlines:** Closing date 5/1. Applicants notified on a rolling basis starting 6/1; must reply within 2 week(s) of notification.
**Transfers:** Priority date 6/1.

### CONTACT
Andrea Simpson, Director of Financial Aid
ATTN: Admissions Offfice 630 South Main Street, Dobson, NC 27017
(336) 386-3263

## Tri-County Community College

Murphy, North Carolina
www.tricountycc.edu                    Federal Code: 009430

**2-year public** community college in rural community.
**Enrollment:** 1,003 undergrads.
**Selectivity:** Open admission.

### BASIC COSTS (2015-2016)
**Tuition and fees:** $2,219; out-of-state residents $7,979.
**Per-credit charge:** $72; out-of-state residents $264.

### FINANCIAL AID PICTURE (2014-2015)
**Students with need:** 99% of average financial aid package awarded as scholarships/grants, 1% awarded as loans/jobs. Need-based aid available for part-time students.
**Students without need:** This college awards aid only to students with need.

### FINANCIAL AID PROCEDURES
**Forms required:** FAFSA.
**Dates and Deadlines:** Priority date 6/30; no closing date. Applicants notified on a rolling basis starting 6/1; must reply within 4 week(s) of notification.
**Transfers:** Must reply within 4 week(s) of notification.

### CONTACT
Diane Owl, Financial Aid Officer
21 Campus Circle, Murphy, NC 28906
(828) 837-6810

## University of Mount Olive

Mount Olive, North Carolina
www.mou.edu                            Federal Code: 002949

**4-year private** university in small town, affiliated with Free Will Baptists.
**Enrollment:** 3,152 undergrads, 56% part-time. 285 full-time freshmen.
**Selectivity:** Admits less than 50% of applicants.

### BASIC COSTS (2015-2016)
**Tuition and fees:** $18,400.
**Per-credit charge:** $420.
**Room and board:** $7,400.

### FINANCIAL AID PICTURE (2014-2015)
**Students with need:** Out of 259 full-time freshmen who applied for aid, 228 were judged to have need. Of these, 227 received aid, and 49 had their full need met. Average financial aid package met 72% of need; average scholarship/grant was $12,924; average loan was $3,288. For part-time students, average financial aid package was $6,850.
**Students without need:** 43 full-time freshmen who did not demonstrate need for aid received scholarships/grants; average award was $5,911. No-need awards available for academics, art, athletics, leadership, music/drama, religious affiliation.
**Scholarships offered:** 52 full-time freshmen received athletic scholarships; average amount $6,148.

### FINANCIAL AID PROCEDURES
**Forms required:** FAFSA, state aid form, institutional form.
**Dates and Deadlines:** Applicants notified on a rolling basis starting 3/1; must reply within 2 week(s) of notification.
**Transfers:** Special scholarship program available for transfers from North Carolina community colleges.

### CONTACT
Katrina Lee, Director of Financial Aid
634 Henderson Street, Mount Olive, NC 28365
(919) 658-7164

## University of North Carolina at Asheville

Asheville, North Carolina
www.unca.edu                           Federal Code: 002907

**4-year public** university and liberal arts college in small city.
**Enrollment:** 3,505 undergrads, 9% part-time. 628 full-time freshmen.
**Selectivity:** Admits over 75% of applicants. GED not accepted.

### BASIC COSTS (2015-2016)
**Tuition and fees:** $6,605; out-of-state residents $22,219.
**Room and board:** $8,332.

### FINANCIAL AID PICTURE (2014-2015)
**Students with need:** Out of 525 full-time freshmen who applied for aid, 344 were judged to have need. Of these, 341 received aid, and 68 had their full need met. Average financial aid package met 70% of need; average scholarship/grant was $5,995; average loan was $4,221. For part-time students, average financial aid package was $7,474.
**Students without need:** 47 full-time freshmen who did not demonstrate need for aid received scholarships/grants; average award was $2,207. No-need awards available for academics, alumni affiliation, art, athletics, job skills, leadership, music/drama, state/district residency.
**Scholarships offered:** *Merit:* University Laurels Program: a variety of scholarships, ranging from approximately $1,000 per year to full tuition, fees, room and board; to entering freshman who demonstrate high academic achievements. Leadership Scholarship: $1,000; renewable; solid academic record and leadership ability. *Athletic:* 17 full-time freshmen received athletic scholarships; average amount $11,061.

### FINANCIAL AID PROCEDURES
**Forms required:** FAFSA.
**Dates and Deadlines:** Priority date 3/1; no closing date. Applicants notified on a rolling basis starting 3/15.

### CONTACT
Elizabeth Bartlett, Associate Director of Financial Aid
CPO#1320, UNCA, Asheville, NC 28804-8502
(828) 251-6535

# University of North Carolina at Chapel Hill

Chapel Hill, North Carolina
www.unc.edu

Federal Code: 002974
CSS Code: 5816

**4-year public** university in small city.
**Enrollment:** 17,951 undergrads, 2% part-time. 3,976 full-time freshmen.
**Selectivity:** Admits less than 50% of applicants. GED not accepted.

## BASIC COSTS (2015-2016)
**Tuition and fees:** $8,591; out-of-state residents $33,673.
**Room and board:** $10,902.
**Additional info:** Fees may be higher for selected programs.

## FINANCIAL AID PICTURE (2014-2015)
**Students with need:** Out of 3,000 full-time freshmen who applied for aid, 1,789 were judged to have need. Of these, 1,789 received aid, and 1,555 had their full need met. Average financial aid package met 100% of need; average scholarship/grant was $16,972; average loan was $4,643. For part-time students, average financial aid package was $9,007.
**Students without need:** 102 full-time freshmen who did not demonstrate need for aid received scholarships/grants; average award was $9,501. No-need awards available for academics, alumni affiliation, art, athletics, leadership, music/drama, religious affiliation, state/district residency.
**Scholarships offered:** *Merit:* Morehead-Cain Scholarships: full tuition and expenses; based on academic merit, leadership, athletics, moral character; approximately 50 awarded. Robertson Scholarships: full tuition and expenses; based on academic merit, leadership, community service; 15-18 awarded. Carolina Scholars: $9,000 for in-state residents; cost of tuition, fees, room and board for non-NC residents; based on academic merit, leadership, residency specifications; 25-30 awarded with majority going to in-state residents. Pogue Scholarships: $9,000 for NC residents; cost of tuition, fees, room and board for non-NC residents; based on academic merit, leadership, involvement and interest in issues of diversity; up to 10 in-state and 3 out-of-state awarded. Colonel Robinson Scholarships: $9,000 for in-state residents; cost of tuition, fees, room and board for non-NC residents; based on academic merit; approximately 15 awarded to NC residents and 10 to non-NC residents. Old Well, College Fellows, and Founders Awards: $2,500-$6,000; based on academic merit, leadership, North Carolina residency; 15-20 awarded. *Athletic:* 77 full-time freshmen received athletic scholarships; average amount $28,267.
**Additional info:** 100% of all documented need met for both resident and non-resident undergraduates who qualify for need based aid, with a favorable mix of approximately 60% grants and scholarships and 40% loans and work study. A no-loans program available for qualifying low-income students (in-state or out-of-state) whose family's adjusted gross income does not exceed 200% of the federal poverty standard, indexed by family size.

## FINANCIAL AID PROCEDURES
**Forms required:** FAFSA, CSS PROFILE.
**Dates and Deadlines:** Priority date 3/1; no closing date. Applicants notified by 3/15; must reply by 5/1.

## CONTACT
Shirley Ort, Associate Provost and Director of Scholarships and Student Aid
Jackson Hall, Chapel Hill, NC 27599-2200
(919) 962-8396

# University of North Carolina at Charlotte

Charlotte, North Carolina
www.uncc.edu

Federal Code: 002975

**4-year public** university in very large city.
**Enrollment:** 22,686 undergrads, 13% part-time. 2,989 full-time freshmen.
**Selectivity:** Admits 50 to 75% of applicants.

## BASIC COSTS (2015-2016)
**Tuition and fees:** $6,531; out-of-state residents $19,702.
**Room and board:** $9,840.

## FINANCIAL AID PICTURE (2014-2015)
**Students with need:** Out of 2,511 full-time freshmen who applied for aid, 1,896 were judged to have need. Of these, 1,801 received aid, and 152 had their full need met. Average financial aid package met 63% of need; average scholarship/grant was $9,181; average loan was $3,697. For part-time students, average financial aid package was $7,277.
**Students without need:** 14 full-time freshmen who did not demonstrate need for aid received scholarships/grants; average award was $6,181. No-need awards available for academics, alumni affiliation, art, athletics, job skills, leadership, minority status, music/drama, religious affiliation, ROTC, state/district residency.
**Scholarships offered:** *Merit:* The Levine Scholars Program is a merit-based scholarship program, awarding 15 incoming freshmen students full tuition, room and board, and four summers of experiences to develop leadership skills, social awareness, and international perspective. Students must be nominated by their high school guidance counselor by October 15th of their senior year to be eligible for this scholars program. Students may join multiple honors programs and societies. *Athletic:* 8 full-time freshmen received athletic scholarships; average amount $6,115.

## FINANCIAL AID PROCEDURES
**Forms required:** FAFSA.
**Dates and Deadlines:** Priority date 3/1; no closing date. Applicants notified on a rolling basis starting 3/1; must reply within 3 week(s) of notification.
**Transfers:** Must reply within 2 week(s) of notification.

## CONTACT
Bruce Blackmon, Director of Student Financial Aid
Undergraduate Admissions- Cato Hall, Charlotte, NC 28223-0001
(704) 687-5504

# University of North Carolina at Greensboro

Greensboro, North Carolina
www.uncg.edu

Federal Code: 002976

**4-year public** university in large city.
**Enrollment:** 15,158 undergrads, 12% part-time. 2,757 full-time freshmen.
**Selectivity:** Admits 50 to 75% of applicants. GED not accepted.

## BASIC COSTS (2015-2016)
**Tuition and fees:** $6,733; out-of-state residents $21,595.
**Room and board:** $7,950.

## FINANCIAL AID PICTURE (2015-2016)
**Students with need:** Out of 2,483 full-time freshmen who applied for aid, 2,286 were judged to have need. Of these, 2,277 received aid, and 477 had their full need met. Average financial aid package met 57% of need; average scholarship/grant was $6,194; average loan was $3,376. For part-time students, average financial aid package was $6,492.
**Students without need:** 54 full-time freshmen who did not demonstrate need for aid received scholarships/grants; average award was $5,157. No-need awards available for academics, athletics, music/drama, religious affiliation, ROTC, state/district residency.
**Scholarships offered:** 34 full-time freshmen received athletic scholarships; average amount $15,191.

## FINANCIAL AID PROCEDURES
**Forms required:** FAFSA.
**Dates and Deadlines:** Priority date 3/1; no closing date. Applicants notified on a rolling basis starting 3/15; must reply within 3 week(s) of notification.

## CONTACT

Deborah Tollefson, Director of Financial Aid

PO Box 26170, Greensboro, NC 27402-6170

(336) 334-5702

## University of North Carolina at Pembroke

Pembroke, North Carolina

www.uncp.edu                                    Federal Code: 002954

**4-year public** university and liberal arts college in small town.

**Enrollment:** 5,508 undergrads, 18% part-time. 1,216 full-time freshmen.

**Selectivity:** Admits 50 to 75% of applicants.

### BASIC COSTS (2015-2016)

**Tuition and fees:** $5,534; out-of-state residents $15,982.

**Room and board:** $8,502.

### FINANCIAL AID PICTURE (2015-2016)

**Students with need:** Average financial aid package met 66% of need; average scholarship/grant was $7,144; average loan was $3,361. For part-time students, average financial aid package was $8,003.

**Students without need:** No-need awards available for academics, alumni affiliation, art, athletics, minority status, music/drama.

**Scholarships offered:** Academic Scholarships, Endowed Scholarship, University Incentive Scholarship, University Scholarships for Native Americans, Epsilon Sigma Alpha Scholarship.

### FINANCIAL AID PROCEDURES

**Forms required:** FAFSA.

**Dates and Deadlines:** Priority date 3/15; no closing date. Applicants notified on a rolling basis starting 4/15; must reply within 2 week(s) of notification.

**Transfers:** No deadline.

### CONTACT

Jenelle Handcox, Director of Financial Aid

Box 1510, Pembroke, NC 28372

(910) 521-6255

## University of North Carolina at Wilmington

Wilmington, North Carolina

www.uncw.edu                                    Federal Code: 002984

**4-year public** university in small city.

**Enrollment:** 12,982 undergrads, 11% part-time. 2,023 full-time freshmen.

**Selectivity:** Admits 50 to 75% of applicants.

### BASIC COSTS (2015-2016)

**Tuition and fees:** $6,690; out-of-state residents $20,556.

**Room and board:** $9,466.

### FINANCIAL AID PICTURE (2014-2015)

**Students with need:** Out of 1,759 full-time freshmen who applied for aid, 1,179 were judged to have need. Of these, 1,118 received aid, and 112 had their full need met. Average financial aid package met 62% of need; average scholarship/grant was $6,531; average loan was $3,461. For part-time students, average financial aid package was $6,543.

**Students without need:** 32 full-time freshmen who did not demonstrate need for aid received scholarships/grants; average award was $2,423. No-need awards available for academics, alumni affiliation, art, athletics, leadership, minority status, music/drama.

**Scholarships offered:** 51 full-time freshmen received athletic scholarships; average amount $7,712.

### FINANCIAL AID PROCEDURES

**Forms required:** FAFSA.

**Dates and Deadlines:** Priority date 3/1; no closing date. Applicants notified on a rolling basis starting 3/15; must reply within 3 week(s) of notification.

**Transfers:** No deadline. Applicants notified by 3/15; must reply within 3 week(s) of notification.

### CONTACT

Frederick Holding, Director of Financial Aid, Scholarships and Veterans Services

601 South College Road, Wilmington, NC 28403-5904

(910) 962-3177

## University of North Carolina School of the Arts

Winston-Salem, North Carolina

www.uncsa.edu/                                  Federal Code: 003981

**4-year public** visual arts and performing arts college in small city.

**Enrollment:** 850 undergrads, 1% part-time. 199 full-time freshmen.

**Selectivity:** Admits less than 50% of applicants.

### BASIC COSTS (2015-2016)

**Tuition and fees:** $8,917; out-of-state residents $24,337.

**Room and board:** $8,570.

### FINANCIAL AID PICTURE (2015-2016)

**Students with need:** Out of 163 full-time freshmen who applied for aid, 126 were judged to have need. Of these, 125 received aid, and 9 had their full need met. Average financial aid package met 56% of need; average scholarship/grant was $8,100; average loan was $3,693. For part-time students, average financial aid package was $9,199.

**Students without need:** 11 full-time freshmen who did not demonstrate need for aid received scholarships/grants; average award was $1,742. No-need awards available for academics, art, leadership, music/drama, state/district residency.

### FINANCIAL AID PROCEDURES

**Forms required:** FAFSA.

**Dates and Deadlines:** Priority date 3/1; no closing date. Applicants notified on a rolling basis starting 4/1; must reply within 2 week(s) of notification.

### CONTACT

Jane Kamiab, Director of Financial Aid

1533 South Main Street, Winston-Salem, NC 27127-2738

(336) 770-3297

## Vance-Granville Community College

Henderson, North Carolina

www.vgcc.edu                                    Federal Code: 009903

**2-year public** community college in large town.

**Enrollment:** 2,322 undergrads.

**Selectivity:** Open admission; but selective for some programs.

### BASIC COSTS (2015-2016)

**Tuition and fees:** $2,279; out-of-state residents $8,039.

**Per-credit charge:** $72; out-of-state residents $264.

### FINANCIAL AID PICTURE (2014-2015)

**Students with need:** 97% of average financial aid package awarded as scholarships/grants, 3% awarded as loans/jobs. Need-based aid available for part-time students.

**Students without need:** No-need awards available for academics, leadership, music/drama, state/district residency.

## FINANCIAL AID PROCEDURES

**Forms required:** FAFSA.

**Dates and Deadlines:** Priority date 3/15; no closing date. Applicants notified on a rolling basis starting 5/1; must reply within 2 week(s) of notification.

## CONTACT

Kali Brown, Director of Financial Aid

Box 917, Henderson, NC 27536

(252) 492-2061 ext. 3280

# Wake Forest University

Winston-Salem, North Carolina     Federal Code: 002978
www.wfu.edu                       CSS Code: 5885

**4-year private** university in small city.

**Enrollment:** 4,866 undergrads, 1% part-time. 1,284 full-time freshmen.

**Selectivity:** Admits less than 50% of applicants.

## BASIC COSTS (2016-2017)

**Tuition and fees:** $49,308.

**Per-credit charge:** $2,020.

**Room and board:** $14,748.

## FINANCIAL AID PICTURE (2015-2016)

**Students with need:** Out of 574 full-time freshmen who applied for aid, 441 were judged to have need. Of these, 441 received aid, and 441 had their full need met. Average financial aid package met 100% of need; average scholarship/grant was $42,212; average loan was $8,521. For part-time students, average financial aid package was $33,148.

**Students without need:** 20 full-time freshmen who did not demonstrate need for aid received scholarships/grants; average award was $29,718. No-need awards available for academics, alumni affiliation, art, athletics, leadership, music/drama, religious affiliation, ROTC, state/district residency.

**Scholarships offered:** *Merit:* Reynolds Scholarship: full tuition, room and board, books, fees for 4 years, also provides for summer study; 6 awarded. Joseph G. Gordon Scholarship: full tuition for 4 years; for underrepresented students with exceptional promise and leadership; 7 awarded. Carswell Scholarship: based on intellect and leadership; between 3/4 and full tuition for 4 years, including summer grant for travel and study projects; 10-12 awarded. Presidential Scholarship: for students gifted in areas such as writing, studio art, music theater, debate, leadership, dance, entrepreneurship, and community service; 20 awarded. Poteat Scholarship: $12,100; for North Carolina residents who are active members of a Baptist Church in North Carolina, must make an active contribution to church and society; 18 awarded. *Athletic:* 44 full-time freshmen received athletic scholarships; average amount $49,236.

**Additional info:** First-year students with an annual family income of less than $40,000 will have their student loans capped at $4,000 per year during their college years. Other financial aid to the students will come from grant and scholarship increases and work-study opportunities.

## FINANCIAL AID PROCEDURES

**Forms required:** FAFSA, CSS PROFILE, state aid form.

**Dates and Deadlines:** Priority date 2/15; closing date 3/1. Applicants notified on a rolling basis starting 4/1; must reply by 5/1 or within 4 week(s) of notification.

## CONTACT

William Wells, Director of Financial Aid

PO Box 7305, Winston-Salem, NC 27109-7305

(336) 758-5154

# Wake Technical Community College

Raleigh, North Carolina
www.waketech.edu                 Federal Code: 004844

**2-year public** community and technical college in large city.

**Enrollment:** 21,268 undergrads, 66% part-time. 1,958 full-time freshmen.

**Selectivity:** Open admission; but selective for some programs.

## BASIC COSTS (2015-2016)

**Tuition and fees:** $2,490; out-of-state residents $8,250.

**Per-credit charge:** $72; out-of-state residents $264.

## FINANCIAL AID PICTURE

**Students with need:** Need-based aid available for full-time and part-time students.

**Students without need:** No-need awards available for academics, job skills, leadership, ROTC, state/district residency.

## FINANCIAL AID PROCEDURES

**Forms required:** FAFSA, institutional form.

**Dates and Deadlines:** Priority date 3/15; no closing date. Applicants notified on a rolling basis starting 4/1; must reply within 2 week(s) of notification.

**Transfers:** Child care grant and NCCCS Grant and Loan Program available.

## CONTACT

Regina Huggins, Dean, Financial Aid

9101 Fayetteville Road, Raleigh, NC 27603

(919) 866-5410

# Warren Wilson College

Asheville, North Carolina
www.warren-wilson.edu            Federal Code: 002979

**4-year private** liberal arts college in small city.

**Enrollment:** 749 undergrads, 2% part-time. 234 full-time freshmen.

**Selectivity:** Admits over 75% of applicants.

## BASIC COSTS (2015-2016)

**Tuition and fees:** $32,560.

**Per-credit charge:** $1,334.

**Room and board:** $9,900.

**Additional info:** All resident students are required to work a total of 480 hours per year in the college's work program (15 hours per week, on average). For this, $3,480 earnings are credited toward tuition costs.

## FINANCIAL AID PICTURE (2014-2015)

**Students with need:** Out of 211 full-time freshmen who applied for aid, 191 were judged to have need. Of these, 191 received aid, and 59 had their full need met. Average financial aid package met 85% of need; average scholarship/grant was $6,161; average loan was $3,436. Need-based aid available for part-time students.

**Students without need:** 42 full-time freshmen who did not demonstrate need for aid received scholarships/grants; average award was $9,661. No-need awards available for academics, art, athletics, leadership, religious affiliation, state/district residency.

## FINANCIAL AID PROCEDURES

**Forms required:** FAFSA, state aid form.

**Dates and Deadlines:** Priority date 3/1; no closing date. Applicants notified on a rolling basis starting 3/1; must reply by 5/1 or within 3 week(s) of notification.

**Transfers:** No deadline. Applicants notified on a rolling basis starting 3/1; must reply within 3 week(s) of notification.

## CONTACT

Lori Lewis, Director of Financial Aid

PO Box 9000, Asheville, NC 28815-9000

(828) 771-2082

## Wayne Community College
Goldsboro, North Carolina
www.waynecc.edu                    Federal Code: 008216

**2-year public** community college in large town.
**Enrollment:** 2,773 undergrads.
**Selectivity:** Open admission; but selective for some programs.

### BASIC COSTS (2015-2016)
**Tuition and fees:** $2,252; out-of-state residents $8,012.
**Per-credit charge:** $72; out-of-state residents $264.

### FINANCIAL AID PICTURE
**Students with need:** Need-based aid available for full-time and part-time students.
**Students without need:** No-need awards available for academics.

### FINANCIAL AID PROCEDURES
**Forms required:** FAFSA.
**Dates and Deadlines:** Priority date 3/15; closing date 5/1. Applicants notified on a rolling basis starting 6/1; must reply within 2 week(s) of notification.
**Transfers:** Priority date 5/1; no deadline. Applicants notified on a rolling basis starting 4/1; must reply within 2 week(s) of notification.

### CONTACT
Brenda Mercer, Financial Aid Director
PO Box 8002, Goldsboro, NC 27533-8002
(919) 739-6735

## Western Carolina University
Cullowhee, North Carolina
www.wcu.edu                        Federal Code: 002981

**4-year public** university in small town.
**Enrollment:** 8,652 undergrads. 1,745 full-time freshmen.

### BASIC COSTS (2015-2016)
**Tuition and fees:** $6,903; out-of-state residents $17,296.
**Room and board:** $8,131.

### FINANCIAL AID PICTURE (2014-2015)
**Students with need:** Out of 1,588 full-time freshmen who applied for aid, 1,226 were judged to have need. Of these, 1,200 received aid, and 155 had their full need met. Average financial aid package met 64% of need; average scholarship/grant was $6,371; average loan was $5,403. For part-time students, average financial aid package was $6,135.
**Students without need:** 71 full-time freshmen who did not demonstrate need for aid received scholarships/grants; average award was $3,104. No-need awards available for academics, art, athletics, leadership, music/drama, state/district residency.
**Scholarships offered:** *Merit:* Institution awards merit-based scholarships each year to students that demonstrate excellent academic, athletic, artistic, professional, cultural and/or civic achievement. The number and amount of awards vary. *Athletic:* 20 full-time freshmen received athletic scholarships; average amount $8,375.

### FINANCIAL AID PROCEDURES
**Forms required:** FAFSA, institutional form.
**Dates and Deadlines:** Priority date 3/15; no closing date. Applicants notified on a rolling basis starting 4/1.

### CONTACT
Trina Orr, Director of Student Financial Aid
102 Camp Building, Cullowhee, NC 28723
(828) 227-7290

## Western Piedmont Community College
Morganton, North Carolina
www.wpcc.edu                       Federal Code: 002982

**2-year public** community and technical college in large town.
**Enrollment:** 2,153 undergrads.
**Selectivity:** Open admission; but selective for some programs.

### BASIC COSTS (2015-2016)
**Tuition and fees:** $2,259; out-of-state residents $8,019.
**Per-credit charge:** $72; out-of-state residents $264.

### FINANCIAL AID PICTURE
**Students with need:** Need-based aid available for full-time and part-time students.
**Students without need:** No-need awards available for academics.

### FINANCIAL AID PROCEDURES
**Forms required:** FAFSA.
**Dates and Deadlines:** Priority date 6/1; no closing date. Applicants notified on a rolling basis starting 6/15; must reply within 2 week(s) of notification.

### CONTACT
Dori Barron, Director of Financial Aid
1001 Burkemont Avenue, Morganton, NC 28655-4504
(828) 448-6042

## Wilkes Community College
Wilkesboro, North Carolina
www.wilkescc.edu                   Federal Code: 002983

**2-year public** community college in small town.
**Enrollment:** 2,999 undergrads. 2,718 full-time freshmen.
**Selectivity:** Open admission; but selective for some programs.

### BASIC COSTS (2015-2016)
**Tuition and fees:** $2,300; out-of-state residents $8,060.
**Per-credit charge:** $72; out-of-state residents $264.

### FINANCIAL AID PICTURE (2014-2015)
**Students with need:** Out of 1,900 full-time freshmen who applied for aid, 1,640 were judged to have need. Of these, 1,510 received aid, and 360 had their full need met. Average financial aid package met 45% of need; average scholarship/grant was $600; average loan was $1,250. Need-based aid available for part-time students.
**Students without need:** 60 full-time freshmen who did not demonstrate need for aid received scholarships/grants; average award was $300. No-need awards available for academics, art, job skills, leadership, minority status, music/drama, state/district residency.

### FINANCIAL AID PROCEDURES
**Forms required:** FAFSA.
**Dates and Deadlines:** Priority date 5/15; closing date 5/15. Applicants notified on a rolling basis starting 5/1; must reply by 8/1.
**Transfers:** No deadline. Must reply within 6 week(s) of notification.

### CONTACT
Vickie Call, Director of Financial Aid
1328 South Collegiate Drive, Wilkesboro, NC 28697-0120
(336) 838-6146

## William Peace University
Raleigh, North Carolina
www.peace.edu                      Federal Code: 002953

**4-year private** liberal arts college in large city, affiliated with Presbyterian Church (USA).

**Enrollment:** 1,038 undergrads, 15% part-time. 214 full-time freshmen.
**Selectivity:** Admits 50 to 75% of applicants.

**BASIC COSTS (2015-2016)**
**Tuition and fees:** $25,850.
**Per-credit charge:** $855.
**Room and board:** $9,900.

**FINANCIAL AID PICTURE (2015-2016)**
**Students with need:** Out of 199 full-time freshmen who applied for aid, 191 were judged to have need. Of these, 191 received aid, and 7 had their full need met. Average financial aid package met 61% of need; average scholarship/grant was $11,256; average loan was $4,284. For part-time students, average financial aid package was $12,342.
**Students without need:** 10 full-time freshmen who did not demonstrate need for aid received scholarships/grants; average award was $9,305. No-need awards available for academics, leadership, music/drama.

**FINANCIAL AID PROCEDURES**
**Forms required:** FAFSA.
**Dates and Deadlines:** Priority date 2/15; no closing date. Applicants notified on a rolling basis starting 2/15.
**Transfers:** Priority date 2/15; no deadline. Applicants notified on a rolling basis starting 2/3. Transfer merit scholarships available.

**CONTACT**
Angela Kirkley, Director of Financial Aid
15 East Peace Street, Raleigh, NC 27604-1194
(919) 508-2249

## Wilson Community College
Wilson, North Carolina
www.wilsoncc.edu
Federal Code: 004845

**2-year public** community college in large town.
**Enrollment:** 1,786 undergrads.
**Selectivity:** Open admission; but selective for some programs.

**BASIC COSTS (2015-2016)**
**Tuition and fees:** $2,727; out-of-state residents $8,055.

**FINANCIAL AID PICTURE**
**Students with need:** Need-based aid available for full-time and part-time students. Work study available nights.
**Students without need:** No-need awards available for academics.

**FINANCIAL AID PROCEDURES**
**Forms required:** FAFSA, institutional form.
**Dates and Deadlines:** Priority date 3/15; no closing date. Applicants notified on a rolling basis.
**Transfers:** No deadline. Applicants notified on a rolling basis.

**CONTACT**
Lisa Shearin, Director of Financial Aid and Veterans Affairs
Box 4305, Wilson, NC 27893-0305
(252) 246-1274

## Wingate University
Wingate, North Carolina
www.wingate.edu
Federal Code: 002985

**4-year private** university in small town.
**Enrollment:** 2,015 undergrads, 2% part-time. 642 full-time freshmen.
**Selectivity:** Admits 50 to 75% of applicants.

**BASIC COSTS (2016-2017)**
**Tuition and fees:** $29,170.
**Per-credit charge:** $915.

**Room and board:** $10,780.

**FINANCIAL AID PICTURE (2014-2015)**
**Students with need:** Out of 537 full-time freshmen who applied for aid, 485 were judged to have need. Of these, 444 received aid, and 89 had their full need met. Average financial aid package met 68% of need; average scholarship/grant was $20,657; average loan was $3,076. For part-time students, average financial aid package was $7,075.
**Students without need:** 123 full-time freshmen who did not demonstrate need for aid received scholarships/grants; average award was $12,782. No-need awards available for academics, alumni affiliation, art, athletics, music/drama, religious affiliation.
**Scholarships offered:** 67 full-time freshmen received athletic scholarships; average amount $9,571.
**Additional info:** Institutional aid may not be available after June 1.

**FINANCIAL AID PROCEDURES**
**Forms required:** FAFSA, state aid form.
**Dates and Deadlines:** Priority date 5/1; no closing date. Applicants notified on a rolling basis starting 3/15; must reply within 2 week(s) of notification.
**Transfers:** Priority date 3/1; no deadline. Applicants notified on a rolling basis; must reply within 2 week(s) of notification. Must submit financial aid transcripts from previous colleges attended.

**CONTACT**
Teresa Williams, Director of Financial Planning
220 N. Camden Drive, Wingate, NC 28174-0157
(704) 233-8209

## Winston-Salem State University
Winston-Salem, North Carolina
www.wssu.edu
Federal Code: 002986

**4-year public** university and health science college in small city.
**Enrollment:** 4,686 undergrads, 14% part-time. 865 full-time freshmen.
**Selectivity:** Admits 50 to 75% of applicants.

**BASIC COSTS (2015-2016)**
**Tuition and fees:** $5,707; out-of-state residents $15,523.
**Room and board:** $8,715.

**FINANCIAL AID PICTURE**
**Students with need:** Need-based aid available for full-time students.
**Students without need:** No-need awards available for academics, athletics, ROTC, state/district residency.

**FINANCIAL AID PROCEDURES**
**Forms required:** FAFSA.
**Dates and Deadlines:** Priority date 5/1; no closing date. Must reply within 2 week(s) of notification.
**Transfers:** Closing date 3/15. Applicants notified on a rolling basis.

**CONTACT**
Robert Muhammad, Director of Financial Aid
601 Martin Luther King Jr Drive, Winston-Salem, NC 27110
(336) 750-3280

# North Dakota

## Bismarck State College
Bismarck, North Dakota
www.bismarckstate.edu
Federal Code: 002988

**2-year public** community college in small city.
**Enrollment:** 3,175 undergrads, 29% part-time. 789 full-time freshmen.

**Selectivity:** Open admission; but selective for some programs.

**BASIC COSTS (2015-2016)**

**Tuition and fees:** $4,319; out-of-state residents $10,292.
**Per-credit charge:** $119; out-of-state residents $318.
**Room and board:** $6,578.
**Additional info:** Tuition/fee waivers available for minority students.

**FINANCIAL AID PICTURE**

**Students with need:** Need-based aid available for full-time and part-time students. Work study available nights, weekends, and for part-time students.
**Students without need:** This college awards aid only to students with need.

**FINANCIAL AID PROCEDURES**

**Forms required:** FAFSA.
**Dates and Deadlines:** Priority date 4/15; no closing date. Applicants notified on a rolling basis starting 5/1.
**Transfers:** Financial aid based on funds available.

**CONTACT**

Scott Lingen, Director of Financial Aid
PO Box 5587, Bismarck, ND 58506-5587
(701) 224-5494

## Cankdeska Cikana Community College

Fort Totten, North Dakota
www.littlehoop.edu                    Federal Code: 015793

**2-year public** community college in rural community.
**Enrollment:** 161 undergrads.
**Selectivity:** Open admission.

**BASIC COSTS (2015-2016)**

**Tuition and fees:** $3,300; out-of-state residents $3,300.
**Room and board:** $5,750.

**FINANCIAL AID PICTURE**

**Students with need:** Need-based aid available for full-time and part-time students.
**Students without need:** This college awards aid only to students with need.

**FINANCIAL AID PROCEDURES**

**Forms required:** FAFSA, institutional form.
**Dates and Deadlines:** Priority date 4/15; closing date 8/20. Applicants notified on a rolling basis.

**CONTACT**

Dixie Omen, Financial Aid Director
Box 269, Fort Totten, ND 58335
(701) 766-1374

## Dakota College at Bottineau

Bottineau, North Dakota
www.dakotacollege.edu                  Federal Code: 002995

**2-year public** nursing and junior college in small town.
**Enrollment:** 411 undergrads.
**Selectivity:** Open admission.

**BASIC COSTS (2015-2016)**

**Tuition and fees:** $4,181; out-of-state residents $5,872.
**Per-credit charge:** $141; out-of-state residents $211.
**Room and board:** $6,486.
**Additional info:** Full-time annual tuition for residents of South Dakota, Montana-$4,230; All Canadian Provinces $3,384. Tuition/fee waivers available for minority students.

**FINANCIAL AID PICTURE**

**Students with need:** Need-based aid available for full-time and part-time students. Work study available nights, weekends, and for part-time students.
**Students without need:** No-need awards available for academics, alumni affiliation, athletics, minority status, state/district residency.

**FINANCIAL AID PROCEDURES**

**Forms required:** FAFSA.
**Dates and Deadlines:** Priority date 4/15; no closing date. Applicants notified on a rolling basis starting 6/1; must reply within 2 week(s) of notification.

**CONTACT**

Valerie Heilman, Financial Aid Officer
105 Simrall Boulevard, Bottineau, ND 58318-1198
(701) 228-5437

## Dickinson State University

Dickinson, North Dakota
www.dickinsonstate.edu                 Federal Code: 002989

**4-year public** university in large town.
**Enrollment:** 1,134 undergrads, 22% part-time. 198 full-time freshmen.
**Selectivity:** Open admission; but selective for some programs.

**BASIC COSTS (2015-2016)**

**Tuition and fees:** $6,173; out-of-state residents $8,680.
**Per-credit charge:** $209; out-of-state residents $313.
**Room and board:** $6,480.
**Additional info:** Tuition/fee waivers available for minority students.

**FINANCIAL AID PICTURE (2015-2016)**

**Students with need:** Average financial aid package met 59% of need; average scholarship/grant was $6,125; average loan was $5,436. For part-time students, average financial aid package was $7,325.
**Students without need:** No-need awards available for academics, alumni affiliation, art, athletics, leadership, minority status, music/drama.

**FINANCIAL AID PROCEDURES**

**Forms required:** FAFSA.
**Dates and Deadlines:** Priority date 4/15; no closing date. Applicants notified on a rolling basis starting 5/15; must reply within 4 week(s) of notification.
**Transfers:** No deadline. Applicants notified on a rolling basis starting 5/15; must reply within 2 week(s) of notification.

**CONTACT**

Sandy Klein, Director of Financial Aid
291 Campus Drive, Dickinson, ND 58601-4896
(701) 483-2371

## Lake Region State College

Devils Lake, North Dakota
www.lrsc.edu                           Federal Code: 002991

**2-year public** community and technical college in small town.
**Enrollment:** 663 undergrads, 24% part-time. 195 full-time freshmen.
**Selectivity:** Open admission; but selective for some programs.

**BASIC COSTS (2015-2016)**

**Tuition and fees:** $4,138; out-of-state residents $4,138.
**Per-credit charge:** $136.
**Room and board:** $6,055.
**Additional info:** Tuition/fee waivers available for minority students.

**FINANCIAL AID PICTURE (2015-2016)**

**Students with need:** Out of 145 full-time freshmen who applied for aid, 112 were judged to have need. Of these, 110 received aid, and 51 had their full need met. Average financial aid package met 82% of need; average

scholarship/grant was $6,076; average loan was $4,704. For part-time students, average financial aid package was $9,765.

**Students without need:** 40 full-time freshmen who did not demonstrate need for aid received scholarships/grants; average award was $778. No-need awards available for academics, athletics, leadership, minority status, music/drama.

**Scholarships offered:** 19 full-time freshmen received athletic scholarships; average amount $2,191.

**FINANCIAL AID PROCEDURES**

**Forms required:** FAFSA.

**Dates and Deadlines:** Priority date 4/15; no closing date. Applicants notified on a rolling basis starting 5/15; must reply within 4 week(s) of notification.

**Transfers:** No deadline. Applicants notified on a rolling basis starting 5/15; must reply within 4 week(s) of notification.

**CONTACT**

Katie Nettell, Director of Financial Aid
1801 College Drive North, Devils Lake, ND 58301-1598
(701) 662-1516

# Mayville State University
Mayville, North Dakota
www.mayvillestate.edu                Federal Code: 002993

**4-year public** business and teachers college in small town.
**Enrollment:** 819 undergrads, 22% part-time. 136 full-time freshmen.
**Selectivity:** Open admission; but selective for some programs.

**BASIC COSTS (2015-2016)**
**Tuition and fees:** $6,380; out-of-state residents $8,845.
**Per-credit charge:** $205; out-of-state residents $308.
**Room and board:** $5,904.
**Additional info:** Full-time tuition for South Dakota, Montana, Kansas, Michigan, Missouri, Nebraska, Wisconsin, Indiana, Illinois, Manitoba, and Saskatchewan residents: $6163. All other states, except MN, and Canadian provinces: $7395. Tuition for Minnesota residents estimated at $5522. Tuition/fee waivers available for minority students.

**FINANCIAL AID PICTURE (2015-2016)**
**Students with need:** Out of 121 full-time freshmen who applied for aid, 87 were judged to have need. Of these, 87 received aid, and 19 had their full need met. Average financial aid package met 73% of need; average scholarship/grant was $5,666; average loan was $5,881. For part-time students, average financial aid package was $8,078.
**Students without need:** 26 full-time freshmen who did not demonstrate need for aid received scholarships/grants; average award was $2,126. No-need awards available for academics, athletics, leadership, minority status, music/drama, state/district residency.
**Scholarships offered:** 11 full-time freshmen received athletic scholarships; average amount $2,429.

**FINANCIAL AID PROCEDURES**
**Forms required:** FAFSA.
**Dates and Deadlines:** Priority date 2/15; no closing date. Applicants notified on a rolling basis starting 5/1; must reply within 2 week(s) of notification.
**Transfers:** No deadline. Applicants notified on a rolling basis starting 5/1; must reply within 2 week(s) of notification.

**CONTACT**
Shirley Hanson, Director of Financial Aid
330 Third Street, NE, Mayville, ND 58257-1299
(701) 788-4767

# Minot State University
Minot, North Dakota
www.minotstateu.edu            Federal Code: 002994

**4-year public** university and liberal arts college in large town.
**Enrollment:** 2,559 undergrads, 21% part-time. 316 full-time freshmen.
**Selectivity:** Admits 50 to 75% of applicants.

**BASIC COSTS (2015-2016)**
**Tuition and fees:** $6,391; out-of-state residents $6,391.
**Per-credit charge:** $266.
**Room and board:** $6,008.
**Additional info:** Tuition/fee waivers available for minority students.

**FINANCIAL AID PICTURE (2014-2015)**
**Students with need:** Out of 234 full-time freshmen who applied for aid, 131 were judged to have need. Of these, 130 received aid, and 40 had their full need met. Average financial aid package met 71% of need; average scholarship/grant was $5,255; average loan was $3,529. For part-time students, average financial aid package was $7,586.
**Students without need:** 67 full-time freshmen who did not demonstrate need for aid received scholarships/grants; average award was $992.6. No-need awards available for academics, alumni affiliation, art, athletics, minority status, music/drama, state/district residency.
**Scholarships offered:** 20 full-time freshmen received athletic scholarships; average amount $3,208.25.
**Additional info:** Scholarship application deadline is 2/15.

**FINANCIAL AID PROCEDURES**
**Forms required:** FAFSA.
**Dates and Deadlines:** Priority date 3/15; no closing date. Applicants notified on a rolling basis starting 5/1; must reply within 2 week(s) of notification.
**Transfers:** No deadline. Applicants notified by 5/1; must reply within 2 week(s) of notification.

**CONTACT**
Laurie Weber, Director of Financial Aid
500 University Avenue West, Minot, ND 58707-5002
(701) 858-3375

# North Dakota State College of Science
Wahpeton, North Dakota
www.ndscs.edu                Federal Code: 002996

**2-year public** junior and technical college in small town.
**Enrollment:** 2,095 undergrads, 20% part-time. 682 full-time freshmen.
**Selectivity:** Open admission; but selective for some programs.

**BASIC COSTS (2015-2016)**
**Tuition and fees:** $4,571; out-of-state residents $11,129.
**Per-credit charge:** $123; out-of-state residents $328.
**Room and board:** $6,448.
**Additional info:** Tuition/fee waivers available for minority students.

**FINANCIAL AID PICTURE (2014-2015)**
**Students with need:** Out of 625 full-time freshmen who applied for aid, 457 were judged to have need. Of these, 446 received aid, and 185 had their full need met. Average financial aid package met 69% of need; average scholarship/grant was $4,921; average loan was $5,386. For part-time students, average financial aid package was $7,847.
**Students without need:** 53 full-time freshmen who did not demonstrate need for aid received scholarships/grants; average award was $936. No-need awards available for academics, alumni affiliation, athletics, leadership, minority status, music/drama, state/district residency.
**Scholarships offered:** 2 full-time freshmen received athletic scholarships; average amount $3,763.

## FINANCIAL AID PROCEDURES

**Forms required:** FAFSA.

**Dates and Deadlines:** Priority date 4/15; closing date 4/15. Applicants notified on a rolling basis starting 6/1; must reply within 2 week(s) of notification.

**Transfers:** No deadline. Must reply within 2 week(s) of notification.

## CONTACT

Shelly Blome, Director of Financial Aid

800 North 6th Street, Wahpeton, ND 58076-0001

(701) 671-2207

# North Dakota State University

Fargo, North Dakota

www.ndsu.edu                    Federal Code: 002997

**4-year public** university in small city.

**Enrollment:** 11,609 undergrads, 9% part-time. 2,452 full-time freshmen.

**Selectivity:** Admits over 75% of applicants.

## BASIC COSTS (2015-2016)

**Tuition and fees:** $7,978; out-of-state residents $19,272.

**Per-credit charge:** $298; out-of-state residents $794.

**Room and board:** $7,502.

**Additional info:** Full-time annual tuition for residents of South Dakota, Montana, Manitoba, Saskatchewan: $10,144. Full-time annual tuition for residents of Minnesota: $7,574. Tuition/fee waivers available for minority students.

## FINANCIAL AID PICTURE (2014-2015)

**Students with need:** Out of 2,069 full-time freshmen who applied for aid, 1,311 were judged to have need. Of these, 1,272 received aid, and 510 had their full need met. Average financial aid package met 70% of need; average scholarship/grant was $5,124; average loan was $6,504. For part-time students, average financial aid package was $8,372.

**Students without need:** 198 full-time freshmen who did not demonstrate need for aid received scholarships/grants; average award was $1,953. No-need awards available for academics, alumni affiliation, art, athletics, leadership, minority status, music/drama, ROTC, state/district residency.

**Scholarships offered:** *Merit:* New Student Scholarships: vary in amount awarded; based on 25 ACT or 1200 SAT (exclusive of writing) and 3.5 GPA. *Athletic:* 47 full-time freshmen received athletic scholarships; average amount $8,861.

## FINANCIAL AID PROCEDURES

**Forms required:** FAFSA.

**Dates and Deadlines:** Closing date 3/15. Applicants notified on a rolling basis starting 4/20.

## CONTACT

Jeffrey Jacobs, Director of Student Financial Services

Dept. 2832, PO Box 6050, Fargo, ND 58108-6050

(701) 231-6200

# Rasmussen College: Bismarck

Bismarck, North Dakota

www.rasmussen.edu

**2-year for-profit** career college in small city.

**Enrollment:** 15 undergrads.

**Selectivity:** Open admission; but selective for some programs.

## BASIC COSTS (2016-2017)

**Tuition and fees:** $13,455.

**Per-credit charge:** $299.

## FINANCIAL AID PICTURE

**Students with need:** Need-based aid available for full-time and part-time students.

## FINANCIAL AID PROCEDURES

**Forms required:** FAFSA, institutional form.

**Dates and Deadlines:** Applicants notified on a rolling basis.

## CONTACT

Debora Murray, Director of Financial Services

1701 East Century Avenue, Bismarck, ND 58503

(701) 530-9600

# Rasmussen College: Fargo

Fargo, North Dakota

www.rasmussen.edu                    Federal Code: 004846

**4-year for-profit** career college in small city.

**Enrollment:** 395 undergrads.

**Selectivity:** Open admission; but selective for some programs.

## BASIC COSTS (2015-2016)

**Tuition and fees:** $13,455.

**Per-credit charge:** $299.

## FINANCIAL AID PICTURE

**Students with need:** Need-based aid available for full-time and part-time students.

## FINANCIAL AID PROCEDURES

**Forms required:** FAFSA, institutional form.

**Dates and Deadlines:** Applicants notified on a rolling basis.

## CONTACT

Debora Murray, Director of Financial Aid

4012 19th Avenue SW, Fargo, ND 58103

(701) 277-3889

# Sitting Bull College

Fort Yates, North Dakota

www.sittingbull.edu                    Federal Code: 014993

**2-year public** community college in small town.

**Enrollment:** 234 undergrads.

**Selectivity:** Open admission.

## BASIC COSTS (2015-2016)

**Tuition and fees:** $3,910; out-of-state residents $3,910.

## FINANCIAL AID PICTURE

**Students with need:** Need-based aid available for full-time and part-time students.

## FINANCIAL AID PROCEDURES

**Forms required:** FAFSA, institutional form.

**Dates and Deadlines:** Priority date 5/1; no closing date. Applicants notified on a rolling basis starting 7/15; must reply within 6 week(s) of notification.

**Transfers:** No deadline. Applicants notified on a rolling basis.

## CONTACT

Donna Seaboy, Financial Aid Director

9299 Hwy 24, Fort Yates, ND 58538

(701) 854-8013

# Trinity Bible College
Ellendale, North Dakota
www.trinitybiblecollege.edu          Federal Code: 012059

**4-year private** Bible college in rural community, affiliated with Assemblies of God.

**Enrollment:** 204 undergrads.

## BASIC COSTS (2016-2017)
**Tuition and fees:** $15,508.
**Room and board:** $5,746.

## FINANCIAL AID PICTURE
**Students with need:** Need-based aid available for full-time and part-time students. Work study available nights, weekends, and for part-time students.
**Students without need:** No-need awards available for academics, alumni affiliation, art, leadership, music/drama, religious affiliation.

## FINANCIAL AID PROCEDURES
**Forms required:** FAFSA.
**Dates and Deadlines:** Priority date 3/1; closing date 9/1. Applicants notified on a rolling basis starting 3/1; must reply within 3 week(s) of notification.

## CONTACT
Lorell Bradley, Financial Aid
50 6th Avenue South, Ellendale, ND 58436-7150
(701) 349-5416

# Turtle Mountain Community College
Belcourt, North Dakota
www.tm.edu          Federal Code: 009450

**2-year private** community college in rural community.
**Enrollment:** 550 undergrads. 123 full-time freshmen.
**Selectivity:** Open admission; but selective for some programs.

## BASIC COSTS (2015-2016)
**Tuition and fees:** $2,220.

## FINANCIAL AID PICTURE (2014-2015)
**Students with need:** Out of 123 full-time freshmen who applied for aid, 123 were judged to have need. Of these, 123 received aid, and 5 had their full need met. For part-time students, average financial aid package was $3,860.
**Students without need:** 35 full-time freshmen who did not demonstrate need for aid received scholarships/grants; average award was $1,000. No-need awards available for academics, athletics, job skills, leadership, minority status.
**Scholarships offered:** 4 full-time freshmen received athletic scholarships; average amount $818.

## FINANCIAL AID PROCEDURES
**Forms required:** FAFSA, institutional form.
**Dates and Deadlines:** Priority date 4/15; no closing date.

## CONTACT
Alexsis Marcellais, Financial Aid Director
PO Box 340, Belcourt, ND 58316

# United Tribes Technical College
Bismarck, North Dakota
www.uttc.edu          Federal Code: 014470

**2-year private** technical college in small city.
**Enrollment:** 394 undergrads.
**Selectivity:** Open admission; but selective for some programs.

## BASIC COSTS (2015-2016)
**Tuition and fees:** $3,650.
**Additional info:** Tuition/fee waivers available for adults, minority students.

## FINANCIAL AID PICTURE
**Students with need:** Need-based aid available for full-time and part-time students. Work study available nights, weekends, and for part-time students.

## FINANCIAL AID PROCEDURES
**Forms required:** FAFSA.
**Dates and Deadlines:** Priority date 5/29; closing date 6/30. Applicants notified on a rolling basis starting 5/29; must reply within 2 week(s) of notification.

## CONTACT
Kathlene Thurman, Financial Aid Director
3315 University Drive, Bismarck, ND 58504
(701) 255-3285 ext. 1211

# University of Jamestown
Jamestown, North Dakota
www.uj.edu          Federal Code: 002990

**4-year private** liberal arts college in large town, affiliated with Presbyterian Church (USA).
**Enrollment:** 860 undergrads, 2% part-time. 209 full-time freshmen.
**Selectivity:** Admits 50 to 75% of applicants.

## BASIC COSTS (2016-2017)
**Tuition and fees:** $20,510.
**Per-credit charge:** $435.
**Room and board:** $7,022.

## FINANCIAL AID PICTURE (2014-2015)
**Students with need:** Out of 178 full-time freshmen who applied for aid, 140 were judged to have need. Of these, 140 received aid, and 39 had their full need met. Average financial aid package met 78% of need; average scholarship/grant was $13,183; average loan was $3,297. For part-time students, average financial aid package was $6,790.
**Students without need:** 67 full-time freshmen who did not demonstrate need for aid received scholarships/grants; average award was $8,659. No-need awards available for academics, alumni affiliation, art, athletics, job skills, leadership, music/drama, religious affiliation.
**Scholarships offered:** *Merit:* Wilson Scholar: $14,000; minimum 3.6 GPA, and ACT25/SAT1150; 2 awarded. Distinguished Scholarship: $12,000; minimum 3.7 GPA and ACT25/SAT1180; 10 awarded. Presidential Scholarship: $10,000; minimum 3.7 GPA and ACT26/SAT1150. Honors Scholarship: $8,000; minimum 3.4 GPA and ACT23/SAT1070. Trustee Scholarship: $7,000; minimum 3.00 GPA and ACT21/SAT1000. Knight Award: $6,000; minimum 2.5 GPA and ACT19/SAT900. *Athletic:* 68 full-time freshmen received athletic scholarships; average amount $3,504.
**Additional info:** FAFSA must be received by April 15th for residents to be given first consideration for North Dakota state grants.

## FINANCIAL AID PROCEDURES
**Forms required:** FAFSA.
**Dates and Deadlines:** Priority date 3/15; no closing date. Applicants notified on a rolling basis starting 2/1; must reply within 2 week(s) of notification.
**Transfers:** No deadline. Applicants notified on a rolling basis starting 2/1; must reply within 2 week(s) of notification.

## CONTACT
Judy Hager, Director of Financial Aid
6081 College Lane, Jamestown, ND 58405
(701) 252-3467 ext. 5556

## University of Mary
Bismarck, North Dakota
www.umary.edu                    Federal Code: 002992

**4-year private** university in small city, affiliated with Roman Catholic Church.
**Enrollment:** 1,928 undergrads.

**BASIC COSTS (2015-2016)**
**Tuition and fees:** $16,490.
**Room and board:** $6,246.

**FINANCIAL AID PICTURE**
**Students with need:** Need-based aid available for full-time and part-time students. Work study available nights, weekends, and for part-time students.
**Students without need:** No-need awards available for academics, athletics, music/drama, religious affiliation, state/district residency.

**FINANCIAL AID PROCEDURES**
**Forms required:** FAFSA.
**Dates and Deadlines:** Priority date 3/1; no closing date. Applicants notified on a rolling basis starting 2/1; must reply within 2 week(s) of notification.
**Transfers:** No deadline. Applicants notified on a rolling basis starting 2/1; must reply within 2 week(s) of notification.

**CONTACT**
Janell Thomas, Director of Student Financial Aid
7500 University Drive, Bismarck, ND 58504-9652
(701) 355-8244

## University of North Dakota
Grand Forks, North Dakota
www.und.edu                    Federal Code: 003005

**4-year public** university in small city.
**Enrollment:** 10,809 undergrads, 16% part-time. 1,868 full-time freshmen.
**Selectivity:** Admits over 75% of applicants.

**BASIC COSTS (2015-2016)**
**Tuition and fees:** $7,965; out-of-state residents $18,899.
**Per-credit charge:** $273; out-of-state residents $728.
**Room and board:** $7,236.

**FINANCIAL AID PICTURE**
**Students with need:** Need-based aid available for full-time and part-time students.
**Scholarships offered:** Presidential Scholarship: $2,500-$3,000; based on 29 ACT/1290 SAT (exclusive of Writing) and 3.65 GPA; approximately 180 awarded. Community of Learner's Scholarship: $1,000 per year for 4 years; based on 24 ACT/1090 SAT (exclusive of Writing) and 3.0 GPA; approximately 600 awarded. Presidential Scholarship: $5,000 per year for 4 years; for National Merit Finalists listing UND as their first choice.

**FINANCIAL AID PROCEDURES**
**Forms required:** FAFSA.
**Dates and Deadlines:** Applicants notified on a rolling basis.

**CONTACT**
Janelle Kilgore, Director of Student Financial Aid
2901 University Avenue Stop 8264, Grand Forks, ND 58202-8264
(701) 777-3121

## Valley City State University
Valley City, North Dakota
www.vcsu.edu                    Federal Code: 003008

**4-year public** liberal arts and teachers college in small town.
**Enrollment:** 1,085 undergrads, 28% part-time. 173 full-time freshmen.

**Selectivity:** Admits over 75% of applicants.

**BASIC COSTS (2015-2016)**
**Tuition and fees:** $6,800; out-of-state residents $15,406.
**Per-credit charge:** $172; out-of-state residents $459.
**Room and board:** $6,000.
**Additional info:** Tuition/fee waivers available for minority students.

**FINANCIAL AID PICTURE (2015-2016)**
**Students with need:** 49% of average financial aid package awarded as scholarships/grants, 51% awarded as loans/jobs. Need-based aid available for part-time students. Work study available nights, weekends, and for part-time students.
**Students without need:** No-need awards available for academics, athletics, minority status, music/drama.
**Scholarships offered:** Presidents Scholarship: $2,500 per year for 4 years. Meredith Scholarship: $3,000 per year for 4 years; science or math students only. McCready Scholarship: tuition and books for 4 years.

**FINANCIAL AID PROCEDURES**
**Forms required:** FAFSA.
**Dates and Deadlines:** Priority date 3/15; no closing date. Applicants notified on a rolling basis starting 2/15; must reply within 4 week(s) of notification.

**CONTACT**
Betty Schumacher, Director of Financial Aid
101 College Street SW, Valley City, ND 58072-4098
(701) 845-7412

## Williston State College
Williston, North Dakota
www.willistonstate.edu                    Federal Code: 003007

**2-year public** community and junior college in large town.
**Enrollment:** 738 undergrads, 19% part-time. 281 full-time freshmen.
**Selectivity:** Open admission; but selective for some programs.

**BASIC COSTS (2015-2016)**
**Tuition and fees:** $5,233; out-of-state residents $5,233.
**Room and board:** $9,866.
**Additional info:** Tuition/fee waivers available for minority students.

**FINANCIAL AID PICTURE (2014-2015)**
**Students with need:** Need-based aid available for full-time and part-time students. Work study available nights, weekends, and for part-time students.
**Students without need:** No-need awards available for academics, athletics, music/drama.

**FINANCIAL AID PROCEDURES**
**Forms required:** FAFSA.
**Dates and Deadlines:** Priority date 3/15; no closing date. Applicants notified on a rolling basis starting 5/15.

**CONTACT**
Heather Fink, Financial Aid Director
1410 University Avenue, Williston, ND 58801
(701) 774-4248

# Ohio

## Antioch University Midwest
Yellow Springs, Ohio
www.antiochmidwest.edu                    Federal Code: E00553

**4-year private** university and branch campus college in small town.
**Enrollment:** 116 undergrads.

**BASIC COSTS (2015-2016)**
Tuition and fees: $16,210.

**FINANCIAL AID PICTURE**
**Students with need:** Need-based aid available for full-time and part-time students. Work study available nights, weekends, and for part-time students.

**FINANCIAL AID PROCEDURES**
**Forms required:** FAFSA, institutional form.
**Dates and Deadlines:** Applicants notified on a rolling basis starting 3/1; must reply within 2 week(s) of notification.
**Transfers:** No deadline. Applicants notified on a rolling basis starting 4/1; must reply within 2 week(s) of notification.

**CONTACT**
Kathy John, Director of Financial Aid
900 Dayton Street, Yellow Springs, OH 45387
(937) 769-1840

## Art Academy of Cincinnati
Cincinnati, Ohio
www.artacademy.edu                 Federal Code: 003011

**4-year private** visual arts college in large city.
**Enrollment:** 207 undergrads.

**BASIC COSTS (2015-2016)**
Tuition and fees: $27,758.
Per-credit charge: $1,121.
Room and board: $6,500.

**FINANCIAL AID PICTURE**
**Students with need:** Need-based aid available for full-time and part-time students.
**Students without need:** No-need awards available for academics, art.
**Scholarships offered:** Annual scholarships awarded to entering and transfer students and to continuing students based on portfolio competition.

**FINANCIAL AID PROCEDURES**
**Forms required:** FAFSA.
**Dates and Deadlines:** Priority date 4/1; no closing date. Applicants notified on a rolling basis starting 4/1.

**CONTACT**
Kris Olberding, Financial Aid Director
1212 Jackson Street, Cincinnati, OH 45202
(513) 562-8751

## Art Institute of Cincinnati
Cincinnati, Ohio
www.aic-arts.edu                   Federal Code: 014804

**2-year for-profit** visual arts college in large city.
**Enrollment:** 47 undergrads, 11% part-time. 8 full-time freshmen.
**Selectivity:** Admits over 75% of applicants.

**BASIC COSTS (2016-2017)**
Tuition and fees: $16,834.
**Additional info:** Tuition at time of enrollment locked for 2 years.

**FINANCIAL AID PICTURE (2014-2015)**
**Students with need:** Out of 7 full-time freshmen who applied for aid, 7 were judged to have need. Of these, 7 received aid. Average financial aid package met 90% of need; average scholarship/grant was $5,595. For part-time students, average financial aid package was $7,428.
**Students without need:** No-need awards available for academics, art.

**FINANCIAL AID PROCEDURES**
**Forms required:** FAFSA, institutional form.

**Dates and Deadlines:** Applicants notified on a rolling basis starting 9/1; must reply within 1 week(s) of notification.
**Transfers:** No deadline. Applicants notified on a rolling basis; must reply within 4 week(s) of notification.

**CONTACT**
Rita Schrand, Financial Aid Director
1171 East Kemper Road, Cincinnati, OH 45246
(513) 751-1206

## Ashland University
Ashland, Ohio
www.ashland.edu                    Federal Code: 003012

**4-year private** university and liberal arts college in large town, affiliated with Brethren Church.
**Enrollment:** 3,215 undergrads, 22% part-time. 587 full-time freshmen.
**Selectivity:** Admits over 75% of applicants.

**BASIC COSTS (2016-2017)**
Tuition and fees: $20,872.
Room and board: $9,602.
**Additional info:** Tuition/fee waivers available for minority students, unemployed or children of unemployed.

**FINANCIAL AID PICTURE (2015-2016)**
**Students with need:** Out of 546 full-time freshmen who applied for aid, 468 were judged to have need. Of these, 468 received aid. For part-time students, average financial aid package was $8,488.
**Students without need:** 87 full-time freshmen who did not demonstrate need for aid received scholarships/grants; average award was $7,306. No-need awards available for academics, alumni affiliation, art, athletics, job skills, leadership, minority status, music/drama, religious affiliation, state/district residency.
**Scholarships offered:** *Merit:* Four-year Freshmen merit awards: range from $26,000 to $46,000; based on high school GPA and highest ACT/SAT score received by March 1 of HS senior year. *Athletic:* 16 full-time freshmen received athletic scholarships; average amount $8,405.

**FINANCIAL AID PROCEDURES**
**Forms required:** FAFSA.
**Dates and Deadlines:** Priority date 3/15; no closing date. Applicants notified on a rolling basis starting 3/1.
**Transfers:** No deadline. Applicants notified on a rolling basis starting 3/15. Transfer scholarships based on college GPA: $7500 per year based on 3.75 GPA; $5500 per year based on 3.5 - 3.74 GPA; $4500 per year based on 3.25 - 3.49 GPA; $3500 per year based on 3.0 - 3.24 GPA.

**CONTACT**
Stephen Howell, Director of Financial Aid
401 College Avenue, Ashland, OH 44805-9981
(419) 289-5002

## Aultman College of Nursing and Health Sciences
Canton, Ohio
www.aultmancollege.edu             Federal Code: 006487

**2-year private** health science and nursing college in small city.
**Enrollment:** 362 undergrads, 82% part-time. 12 full-time freshmen.
**Selectivity:** Admits over 75% of applicants.

**BASIC COSTS (2016-2017)**
Tuition and fees: $15,915.
Per-credit charge: $523.

## FINANCIAL AID PICTURE (2014-2015)

**Students with need:** 31% of average financial aid package awarded as scholarships/grants, 69% awarded as loans/jobs. Need-based aid available for part-time students.

**Students without need:** This college awards aid only to students with need.

**Scholarships offered:** 1892 Scholarship: two $1,000 awards; for incoming fall or spring freshman based on 3.0 GPA, 25 ACT (or equivalent SAT score); one-page essay and 6 credit hours per semester required.

## FINANCIAL AID PROCEDURES

**Forms required:** FAFSA, institutional form.

**Dates and Deadlines:** Priority date 3/1; closing date 10/1. Applicants notified on a rolling basis starting 6/15; must reply within 2 week(s) of notification.

## CONTACT

Jennie Carlson, Financial Aid Administrator
2600 Sixth Street SW, Canton, OH 44710-1799
(330) 363-6479

## Baldwin Wallace University

Berea, Ohio
www.bw.edu                    Federal Code: 003014

**4-year private** university in large town, affiliated with United Methodist Church.

**Enrollment:** 3,310 undergrads, 8% part-time. 766 full-time freshmen.

**Selectivity:** Admits 50 to 75% of applicants.

## BASIC COSTS (2015-2016)

**Tuition and fees:** $29,908.

**Per-credit charge:** $929.

**Room and board:** $8,370.

**Additional info:** Tuition/fee waivers available for minority students.

## FINANCIAL AID PICTURE (2015-2016)

**Students with need:** Out of 707 full-time freshmen who applied for aid, 614 were judged to have need. Of these, 614 received aid, and 171 had their full need met. Average financial aid package met 86% of need; average scholarship/grant was $21,883; average loan was $4,083. For part-time students, average financial aid package was $10,034.

**Students without need:** 136 full-time freshmen who did not demonstrate need for aid received scholarships/grants; average award was $13,861. No-need awards available for academics, alumni affiliation, art, minority status, music/drama, religious affiliation, state/district residency.

**Scholarships offered:** Presidential Scholarship: $13,000; ACT 28 or SAT 1260 and above.

## FINANCIAL AID PROCEDURES

**Forms required:** FAFSA.

**Dates and Deadlines:** Priority date 8/15; no closing date. Applicants notified on a rolling basis starting 2/15.

## CONTACT

George Rolleston, Director of Financial Aid
275 Eastland Road, Berea, OH 44017-2088
(440) 826-2108

## Belmont College

St Clairsville, Ohio
www.belmontcollege.edu        Federal Code: 009941

**2-year public** community and technical college in small town.

**Enrollment:** 1,259 undergrads.

**Selectivity:** Open admission; but selective for some programs.

## BASIC COSTS (2015-2016)

**Tuition and fees:** $4,409; out-of-state residents $7,508.

**Per-credit charge:** $105; out-of-state residents $209.

**Additional info:** Tuition/fee waivers available for unemployed or children of unemployed.

## FINANCIAL AID PICTURE

**Students with need:** Need-based aid available for full-time and part-time students.

**Students without need:** No-need awards available for state/district residency.

## FINANCIAL AID PROCEDURES

**Forms required:** FAFSA.

**Dates and Deadlines:** Applicants notified on a rolling basis starting 6/1; must reply within 2 week(s) of notification.

## CONTACT

Jody Peeler, Associate Dean of Financial Aid
120 Fox Shannon Place, St. Clairsville, OH 43950
(740) 695-8510

## Bluffton University

Bluffton, Ohio
www.bluffton.edu              Federal Code: 003016

**4-year private** university and liberal arts college in small town, affiliated with Mennonite Church.

**Enrollment:** 833 undergrads, 11% part-time. 217 full-time freshmen.

**Selectivity:** Admits 50 to 75% of applicants.

## BASIC COSTS (2015-2016)

**Tuition and fees:** $30,168.

**Per-credit charge:** $1,238.

**Room and board:** $9,890.

## FINANCIAL AID PICTURE (2015-2016)

**Students with need:** Out of 205 full-time freshmen who applied for aid, 192 were judged to have need. Of these, 192 received aid, and 23 had their full need met. Average financial aid package met 75% of need; average scholarship/grant was $21,248; average loan was $4,363. For part-time students, average financial aid package was $8,741.

**Students without need:** 25 full-time freshmen who did not demonstrate need for aid received scholarships/grants; average award was $14,777. No-need awards available for academics, alumni affiliation, art, job skills, leadership, minority status, music/drama, religious affiliation, state/district residency.

**Additional info:** Tuition Equalization Program erases the difference between Bluffton's tuition and academic fees and that of the top state schools.

## FINANCIAL AID PROCEDURES

**Forms required:** FAFSA.

**Dates and Deadlines:** Priority date 5/1; closing date 10/1. Applicants notified on a rolling basis starting 3/1; must reply within 3 week(s) of notification.

## CONTACT

Christopher Fowler, Director of Financial Aid
1 University Drive, Bluffton, OH 45817-2104
(419) 358-3266

## Bowling Green State University

Bowling Green, Ohio
www.bgsu.edu                  Federal Code: 003018

**4-year public** university in large town.

**Enrollment:** 13,901 undergrads, 5% part-time. 3,020 full-time freshmen.

**Selectivity:** Admits over 75% of applicants.

## BASIC COSTS (2015-2016)

**Tuition and fees:** $10,726; out-of-state residents $18,262.
**Per-credit charge:** $379; out-of-state residents $693.
**Room and board:** $8,496.

## FINANCIAL AID PICTURE (2014-2015)

**Students with need:** Out of 2,747 full-time freshmen who applied for aid, 2,135 were judged to have need. Of these, 2,104 received aid, and 286 had their full need met. Average financial aid package met 78% of need; average scholarship/grant was $7,030; average loan was $3,509. For part-time students, average financial aid package was $9,646.

**Students without need:** 639 full-time freshmen who did not demonstrate need for aid received scholarships/grants; average award was $4,837. No-need awards available for academics, alumni affiliation, art, athletics, leadership, minority status, music/drama, ROTC, state/district residency.

**Scholarships offered:** 86 full-time freshmen received athletic scholarships; average amount $15,383.

## FINANCIAL AID PROCEDURES

**Forms required:** FAFSA.
**Dates and Deadlines:** Applicants notified on a rolling basis starting 4/15; must reply within 3 week(s) of notification.

## CONTACT

Tina Coulter, Director, Financial Aid
110 McFall Center, Bowling Green, OH 43403-0085
(419) 372-2651

# Bowling Green State University: Firelands College

Huron, Ohio
www.firelands.bgsu.edu          Federal Code: 003018

**2-year public** branch campus college in small town.
**Enrollment:** 1,464 undergrads, 35% part-time. 351 full-time freshmen.
**Selectivity:** Open admission.

## BASIC COSTS (2015-2016)

**Tuition and fees:** $4,946; out-of-state residents $12,254.
**Per-credit charge:** $196; out-of-state residents $501.

## FINANCIAL AID PICTURE

**Students with need:** Need-based aid available for full-time and part-time students.
**Students without need:** This college awards aid only to students with need.
**Scholarships offered:** Firelands Opportunities in College for Underrepresented Students Scholarship: full tuition; for historically underrepresented students in all Firelands majors; 4-6 awards annually.
**Additional info:** Scholarship application deadline May 1. Technology computer loan program available. Based on need, students may receive computer on semester by semester loan basis.

## FINANCIAL AID PROCEDURES

**Forms required:** FAFSA.
**Dates and Deadlines:** Priority date 3/1; no closing date. Applicants notified on a rolling basis starting 4/15; must reply within 2 week(s) of notification.

## CONTACT

Debralee Divers, Director of Enrollment Mgmt & Student Retention Services
One University Drive, Huron, OH 44839-9719
(419) 433-5560

# Brown Mackie College: Cincinnati

Cincinnati, Ohio
www.brownmackie.edu          Federal Code: 005127

**2-year for-profit** business and nursing college in large city.
**Enrollment:** 918 undergrads.
**Selectivity:** Open admission; but selective for some programs.

## BASIC COSTS (2015-2016)

**Tuition and fees:** $16,490.
**Per-credit charge:** $327.

## FINANCIAL AID PICTURE

**Students with need:** Need-based aid available for full-time and part-time students.
**Students without need:** This college awards aid only to students with need.

## FINANCIAL AID PROCEDURES

**Forms required:** FAFSA, state aid form, institutional form.
**Dates and Deadlines:** Priority date 3/15; no closing date. Applicants notified on a rolling basis.

## CONTACT

Charlene Howard, Director of Financial Aid
1011 Glendale-Milford Road, Cincinnati, OH 45215
(513) 771-2424

# Brown Mackie College: Findlay

Findlay, Ohio
www.brownmackie.edu          Federal Code: 026162

**2-year for-profit** business and junior college in small city.
**Enrollment:** 448 undergrads.
**Selectivity:** Open admission.

## BASIC COSTS (2015-2016)

**Tuition and fees:** $16,490.
**Per-credit charge:** $327.

## FINANCIAL AID PICTURE

**Students with need:** Need-based aid available for full-time and part-time students. Work study available nights, weekends, and for part-time students.
**Students without need:** No-need awards available for academics, state/district residency.

## FINANCIAL AID PROCEDURES

**Forms required:** FAFSA.
**Transfers:** No deadline.

## CONTACT

Brandy Lanagan, Director of Financial Aid
1700 Fostoria Avenue, Suite 100, Findlay, OH 45840
(419) 423-2211

# Brown Mackie College: North Canton

Canton, Ohio
www.brownmackie.edu          Federal Code: 030778

**2-year for-profit** career college in small city.
**Enrollment:** 471 undergrads.
**Selectivity:** Open admission.

## BASIC COSTS (2015-2016)

**Tuition and fees:** $16,490.
**Per-credit charge:** $327.

**FINANCIAL AID PICTURE**

**Students with need:** Work study available nights.

**FINANCIAL AID PROCEDURES**

**Forms required:** FAFSA.

**CONTACT**

Jessica Petitte, Director of Student Financial Services
4300 Munson Street Northwest, Canton, OH 44718-3674

## Bryant & Stratton College: Cleveland
Cleveland, Ohio
www.bryantstratton.edu          Federal Code: 022744

**2-year for-profit** technical and career college in very large city.
**Enrollment:** 291 undergrads.
**Selectivity:** Open admission; but selective for some programs.

**BASIC COSTS (2015-2016)**
**Tuition and fees:** $17,190.
**Per-credit charge:** $573.
**Additional info:** Tuition and fees may vary by program.

**FINANCIAL AID PICTURE**

**Students with need:** Need-based aid available for full-time and part-time students. Work study available nights.
**Students without need:** No-need awards available for academics.

**FINANCIAL AID PROCEDURES**

**Forms required:** FAFSA, institutional form.
**Dates and Deadlines:** Closing date 9/22. Applicants notified on a rolling basis starting 5/1; must reply within 2 week(s) of notification.
**Transfers:** No deadline. By state regulation, Ohio Institutional Grant can be awarded only 3 times a fiscal year.

**CONTACT**

DeAuntha Logan, Financial Aid Manager
3121 Euclid Avenue, Cleveland, OH 44115
(216) 771-1700

## Bryant & Stratton College: Eastlake
Eastlake, Ohio
www.bryantstratton.edu          Federal Code: 022744

**4-year for-profit** business college in small town.
**Enrollment:** 231 undergrads.
**Selectivity:** Open admission.

**BASIC COSTS (2015-2016)**
**Tuition and fees:** $17,190.
**Per-credit charge:** $573.
**Additional info:** Tuition and fees may vary by program.

**FINANCIAL AID PICTURE**

**Students with need:** Need-based aid available for full-time and part-time students.
**Students without need:** No-need awards available for academics.

**FINANCIAL AID PROCEDURES**

**Forms required:** FAFSA.
**Dates and Deadlines:** Applicants notified on a rolling basis.

**CONTACT**

Donna McCullough, Financial Aid Manager
35350 Curtis Boulevard, Eastlake, OH 44095
(440) 510-1112

## Bryant & Stratton College: Parma
Parma, Ohio
www.bryantstratton.edu          Federal Code: 015298

**4-year for-profit** nursing and junior college in small city.
**Enrollment:** 281 undergrads.
**Selectivity:** Open admission; but selective for some programs.

**BASIC COSTS (2015-2016)**
**Tuition and fees:** $17,190.
**Per-credit charge:** $573.

**FINANCIAL AID PICTURE**

**Students with need:** Need-based aid available for full-time and part-time students. Work study available nights.
**Students without need:** This college awards aid only to students with need.

**FINANCIAL AID PROCEDURES**

**Forms required:** FAFSA.
**Dates and Deadlines:** Closing date 9/22. Applicants notified on a rolling basis starting 6/1.
**Transfers:** Transfer form must be completed for state grant.

**CONTACT**

Laura Shannon, Financial Services Manager
12955 Snow Road, Parma, OH 44130-1013
(216) 265-3151 ext. 231

## Capital University
Columbus, Ohio
www.capital.edu          Federal Code: 003023

**4-year private** university in very large city, affiliated with Evangelical Lutheran Church in America.
**Enrollment:** 2,654 undergrads, 7% part-time. 710 full-time freshmen.
**Selectivity:** Admits 50 to 75% of applicants.

**BASIC COSTS (2015-2016)**
**Tuition and fees:** $32,830.
**Per-credit charge:** $1,088.
**Room and board:** $9,422.

**FINANCIAL AID PICTURE (2014-2015)**

**Students with need:** Out of 665 full-time freshmen who applied for aid, 601 were judged to have need. Of these, 601 received aid, and 180 had their full need met. Average financial aid package met 84% of need; average scholarship/grant was $23,151; average loan was $3,821. For part-time students, average financial aid package was $8,470.
**Students without need:** 108 full-time freshmen who did not demonstrate need for aid received scholarships/grants; average award was $19,966. No-need awards available for academics, alumni affiliation, art, leadership, minority status, music/drama, religious affiliation, state/district residency.
**Scholarships offered:** Scholarships and grants; $1,000 to full tuition.

**FINANCIAL AID PROCEDURES**

**Forms required:** FAFSA.
**Dates and Deadlines:** Priority date 3/1; no closing date. Applicants notified on a rolling basis starting 3/15; must reply by 5/1.
**Transfers:** Priority date 7/15.

**CONTACT**

Susan Kannenwischer, Director of Financial Aid
1 College and Main, Columbus, OH 43209-2394
(614) 236-6511

## Case Western Reserve University

Cleveland, Ohio                    Federal Code: E00077
www.case.edu                       CSS Code: 1105

**4-year private** university in very large city.
**Enrollment:** 5,039 undergrads, 1% part-time. 1,259 full-time freshmen.
**Selectivity:** Admits less than 50% of applicants.

**BASIC COSTS (2015-2016)**
**Tuition and fees:** $44,550.
**Per-credit charge:** $1,840.
**Room and board:** $13,850.

**FINANCIAL AID PICTURE (2015-2016)**
**Students with need:** Out of 857 full-time freshmen who applied for aid, 665 were judged to have need. Of these, 665 received aid, and 329 had their full need met. Average financial aid package met 87% of need; average scholarship/grant was $29,932; average loan was $4,357. For part-time students, average financial aid package was $19,203.
**Students without need:** 365 full-time freshmen who did not demonstrate need for aid received scholarships/grants; average award was $23,563. No-need awards available for academics, alumni affiliation, art, leadership, music/drama.

**FINANCIAL AID PROCEDURES**
**Forms required:** FAFSA, CSS PROFILE, institutional form.
**Dates and Deadlines:** Priority date 2/15; closing date 5/15. Applicants notified on a rolling basis starting 3/15; must reply by 5/1 or within 2 week(s) of notification.
**Transfers:** Priority date 2/15.

**CONTACT**
Venus Puliafico, Director of University Financial Aid
Wolstein Hall, Cleveland, OH 44106-7055
(216) 368-4530

## Cedarville University

Cedarville, Ohio
www.cedarville.edu                 Federal Code: 003025

**4-year private** university and liberal arts college in small town, affiliated with Baptist faith.
**Enrollment:** 3,061 undergrads, 2% part-time. 787 full-time freshmen.
**Selectivity:** Admits 50 to 75% of applicants.

**BASIC COSTS (2015-2016)**
**Tuition and fees:** $27,206.
**Per-credit charge:** $1,022.
**Room and board:** $6,542.

**FINANCIAL AID PICTURE (2014-2015)**
**Students with need:** Out of 694 full-time freshmen who applied for aid, 570 were judged to have need. Of these, 568 received aid, and 222 had their full need met. Average financial aid package met 28% of need; average scholarship/grant was $4,199; average loan was $4,560. For part-time students, average financial aid package was $6,077.
**Students without need:** 196 full-time freshmen who did not demonstrate need for aid received scholarships/grants; average award was $17,652. No-need awards available for academics, alumni affiliation, athletics, leadership, minority status, music/drama, ROTC, state/district residency.
**Scholarships offered:** 55 full-time freshmen received athletic scholarships; average amount $6,447.

**FINANCIAL AID PROCEDURES**
**Forms required:** FAFSA.
**Dates and Deadlines:** Priority date 3/1; no closing date. Applicants notified on a rolling basis starting 3/1; must reply within 3 week(s) of notification.
**Transfers:** No deadline. Applicants notified on a rolling basis starting 2/1.

**CONTACT**
Kim Jenerette, Executive Director of Financial Aid
251 North Main Street, Cedarville, OH 45314-0601
(937) 766-7866

## Central Ohio Technical College

Newark, Ohio
www.cotc.edu                       Federal Code: 011046

**2-year public** technical college in large town.
**Enrollment:** 2,721 undergrads, 66% part-time. 225 full-time freshmen.
**Selectivity:** Open admission; but selective for some programs.

**BASIC COSTS (2015-2016)**
**Tuition and fees:** $4,296; out-of-state residents $7,056.
**Per-credit charge:** $179; out-of-state residents $294.

**FINANCIAL AID PICTURE**
**Students with need:** Need-based aid available for full-time and part-time students. Work study available nights, weekends, and for part-time students.
**Students without need:** No-need awards available for academics, state/district residency.
**Scholarships offered:** Presidential Achievement Award: $1,800 annually; based on 3.0 GPA; 5 awarded. Minority Achievement Award: $850 annually; based on 2.5 GPA; 2 awarded.

**FINANCIAL AID PROCEDURES**
**Forms required:** FAFSA.
**Dates and Deadlines:** Priority date 2/15; no closing date. Applicants notified on a rolling basis starting 5/1; must reply within 3 week(s) of notification.

**CONTACT**
Faith Phillips, Director of Financial Aid
1179 University Drive, Newark, OH 43055
(740) 366-9435

## Central State University

Wilberforce, Ohio
www.centralstate.edu               Federal Code: 003026

**4-year public** university and liberal arts college in rural community.
**Enrollment:** 1,775 undergrads, 7% part-time. 510 full-time freshmen.
**Selectivity:** Admits less than 50% of applicants.

**BASIC COSTS (2015-2016)**
**Tuition and fees:** $6,246; out-of-state residents $13,928.
**Per-credit charge:** $267; out-of-state residents $612.
**Room and board:** $9,318.

**FINANCIAL AID PICTURE**
**Students with need:** Need-based aid available for full-time and part-time students. Work study available nights, weekends, and for part-time students.
**Students without need:** No-need awards available for academics, alumni affiliation, art, athletics, leadership, music/drama, religious affiliation, ROTC.

**FINANCIAL AID PROCEDURES**
**Forms required:** FAFSA, institutional form.
**Dates and Deadlines:** Priority date 2/15; no closing date. Applicants notified by 4/15; must reply by 5/1.
**Transfers:** No deadline.

**CONTACT**
Sonia Slomba, Director, Student Financial Aid Office
PO Box 1004, Wilberforce, OH 45384-1004
(937) 376-6519

## Chatfield College
Fayetteville, Ohio
www.chatfield.edu                  Federal Code: 010880

**2-year private** liberal arts college in rural community, affiliated with Roman Catholic Church.
**Enrollment:** 261 undergrads, 43% part-time. 42 full-time freshmen.
**Selectivity:** Open admission.

**BASIC COSTS (2015-2016)**
**Tuition and fees:** $9,645.
**Per-credit charge:** $386.

**FINANCIAL AID PICTURE**
**Students with need:** Need-based aid available for full-time and part-time students.
**Students without need:** No-need awards available for academics, leadership.
**Additional info:** Institutional grants/scholarships given primarily to first-year students to reduce debt load during initial year.

**FINANCIAL AID PROCEDURES**
**Forms required:** FAFSA, institutional form.
**Dates and Deadlines:** Priority date 5/1; closing date 8/3. Applicants notified on a rolling basis starting 4/1; must reply within 2 week(s) of notification.

**CONTACT**
Dawn Hundley
20918 State Route 251, St. Martin, OH 45118
(513) 875-3344

## Cincinnati Christian University
Cincinnati, Ohio
www.ccuniversity.edu               Federal Code: 003029

**4-year private** university in very large city, affiliated with Christian Church.
**Enrollment:** 569 undergrads, 13% part-time. 98 full-time freshmen.
**Selectivity:** Admits over 75% of applicants.

**BASIC COSTS (2015-2016)**
**Tuition and fees:** $15,966.
**Per-credit charge:** $570.
**Room and board:** $7,860.

**FINANCIAL AID PICTURE (2014-2015)**
**Students with need:** Out of 93 full-time freshmen who applied for aid, 82 were judged to have need. Of these, 82 received aid, and 7 had their full need met. Average financial aid package met 60% of need; average scholarship/grant was $9,295; average loan was $2,886. For part-time students, average financial aid package was $5,690.
**Students without need:** 12 full-time freshmen who did not demonstrate need for aid received scholarships/grants; average award was $4,696. No-need awards available for academics, athletics, leadership, minority status, music/drama, religious affiliation, state/district residency.
**Scholarships offered:** 8 full-time freshmen received athletic scholarships; average amount $9,163.

**FINANCIAL AID PROCEDURES**
**Forms required:** FAFSA.
**Dates and Deadlines:** Priority date 3/1; no closing date. Applicants notified on a rolling basis starting 4/1.
**Transfers:** No deadline.

**CONTACT**
Marcella Farmer, Financial Aid Director
2700 Glenway Avenue, Cincinnati, OH 45204-3200
(513) 244-8100 ext. 8450

## Cincinnati College of Mortuary Science
Cincinnati, Ohio
https://www.ccms.edu               Federal Code: 010906

**2-year private** school of mortuary science in very large city.
**Enrollment:** 100 undergrads.

**BASIC COSTS (2016-2017)**
**Tuition and fees:** $19,735.
**Per-credit charge:** $375.

**FINANCIAL AID PICTURE (2014-2015)**
**Students with need:** Need-based aid available for part-time students.
**Students without need:** This college awards aid only to students with need.

**FINANCIAL AID PROCEDURES**
**Forms required:** FAFSA.
**Transfers:** No deadline.

**CONTACT**
Leslie Boehm, Business Manager/Bursar
645 West North Bend Road, Cincinnati, OH 45224-1428
(513) 761-2020

## Cincinnati State Technical and Community College
Cincinnati, Ohio
www.cincinnatistate.edu            Federal Code: 010345

**2-year public** community and technical college in large city.
**Enrollment:** 7,983 undergrads, 65% part-time. 621 full-time freshmen.
**Selectivity:** Open admission; but selective for some programs.

**BASIC COSTS (2015-2016)**
**Tuition and fees:** $4,717; out-of-state residents $9,177.

**FINANCIAL AID PICTURE**
**Students with need:** Need-based aid available for full-time and part-time students. Work study available nights, weekends, and for part-time students.
**Students without need:** No-need awards available for academics, athletics, state/district residency.

**FINANCIAL AID PROCEDURES**
**Forms required:** FAFSA.
**Dates and Deadlines:** Priority date 2/15; no closing date. Applicants notified on a rolling basis starting 3/15; must reply within 4 week(s) of notification.

**CONTACT**
LaSaundra Craig, Director of Student Financial Aid/Scholarships
3520 Central Parkway, Cincinnati, OH 45223-2690
(513) 569-1530

## Clark State Community College
Springfield, Ohio
www.clarkstate.edu                 Federal Code: 004852

**2-year public** community college in small city.
**Enrollment:** 4,843 undergrads.
**Selectivity:** Open admission; but selective for some programs.

**BASIC COSTS (2015-2016)**
**Tuition and fees:** $4,180; out-of-state residents $7,820.
**Per-credit charge:** $121; out-of-state residents $243.

**FINANCIAL AID PICTURE**
**Students with need:** Work study available nights, weekends, and for part-time students.

PART III: FINANCIAL AID COLLEGE BY COLLEGE

**FINANCIAL AID PROCEDURES**

**Forms required:** FAFSA.

**Dates and Deadlines:** Priority date 6/15; no closing date. Applicants notified on a rolling basis.

**Transfers:** No deadline. Applicants notified on a rolling basis.

**CONTACT**

Kathy Klay, Director of Financial Aid

Box 570, Springfield, OH 45501-0570

(937) 328-6034

## Cleveland Institute of Art
Cleveland, Ohio
www.cia.edu                             Federal Code: 003982

**4-year private** visual arts college in large city.

**Enrollment:** 600 undergrads, 1% part-time. 168 full-time freshmen.

**Selectivity:** Admits 50 to 75% of applicants.

**BASIC COSTS (2015-2016)**

**Tuition and fees:** $38,487.

**Per-credit charge:** $1,500.

**Room and board:** $11,454.

**FINANCIAL AID PICTURE (2014-2015)**

**Students with need:** Out of 133 full-time freshmen who applied for aid, 128 were judged to have need. Of these, 128 received aid, and 11 had their full need met. Average financial aid package met 57% of need; average scholarship/grant was $21,357; average loan was $3,958. For part-time students, average financial aid package was $28,008.

**Students without need:** 22 full-time freshmen who did not demonstrate need for aid received scholarships/grants; average award was $12,409. No-need awards available for academics, art.

**FINANCIAL AID PROCEDURES**

**Forms required:** FAFSA.

**Dates and Deadlines:** Closing date 3/15. Applicants notified on a rolling basis starting 3/16; must reply within 2 week(s) of notification.

**Transfers:** Applicants notified on a rolling basis starting 4/1; must reply within 2 week(s) of notification.

**CONTACT**

Martin Carney, Director of Financial Aid

11610 Euclid Avenue, Cleveland, OH 44106-1710

(216) 421-7425

## Cleveland Institute of Music
Cleveland, Ohio
www.cim.edu                             Federal Code: 003031

**4-year private** music college in very large city.

**Enrollment:** 247 undergrads. 58 full-time freshmen.

**BASIC COSTS (2015-2016)**

**Tuition and fees:** $47,565.

**Per-credit charge:** $1,904.

**Room and board:** $13,890.

**FINANCIAL AID PICTURE (2014-2015)**

**Students with need:** Out of 49 full-time freshmen who applied for aid, 40 were judged to have need. Of these, 40 received aid, and 13 had their full need met. Average financial aid package met 78% of need; average scholarship/grant was $26,321; average loan was $3,653. Need-based aid available for part-time students.

**Students without need:** 18 full-time freshmen who did not demonstrate need for aid received scholarships/grants; average award was $18,444. No-need awards available for academics, music/drama.

**FINANCIAL AID PROCEDURES**

**Forms required:** FAFSA, institutional form.

**Dates and Deadlines:** Priority date 3/1; closing date 3/1. Applicants notified by 4/1; must reply by 5/1 or within 2 week(s) of notification.

**Transfers:** Priority date 3/1; closing date 3/1. Applicants notified by 4/1; must reply by 5/1 or within 2 week(s) of notification.

**CONTACT**

Kristie Gripp, Director of Financial Aid

11021 East Boulevard, Cleveland, OH 44106

(216) 795-3192

## Cleveland State University
Cleveland, Ohio
www.csuohio.edu                         Federal Code: 003032

**4-year public** university in large city.

**Enrollment:** 11,669 undergrads, 22% part-time. 1,847 full-time freshmen.

**Selectivity:** Admits over 75% of applicants.

**BASIC COSTS (2016-2017)**

**Tuition and fees:** $9,696; out-of-state residents $12,938.

**Per-credit charge:** $402; out-of-state residents $537.

**Room and board:** $12,500.

**FINANCIAL AID PICTURE (2015-2016)**

**Students with need:** 41% of average financial aid package awarded as scholarships/grants, 59% awarded as loans/jobs. Need-based aid available for part-time students. Work study available nights, weekends, and for part-time students.

**Students without need:** No-need awards available for academics, alumni affiliation, art, athletics, leadership, music/drama, ROTC.

**FINANCIAL AID PROCEDURES**

**Forms required:** FAFSA.

**Dates and Deadlines:** Priority date 2/15; no closing date. Applicants notified on a rolling basis starting 3/15; must reply within 4 week(s) of notification.

**CONTACT**

Rachel Schmidt, Director of Financial Aid

2121 Euclid Avenue, Cleveland, OH 44115-2214

(888) 278-6446

## College of Wooster
Wooster, Ohio                           Federal Code: 003037
www.wooster.edu                         CSS Code: 1134

**4-year private** liberal arts college in large town.

**Enrollment:** 2,026 undergrads. 566 full-time freshmen.

**Selectivity:** Admits 50 to 75% of applicants.

**BASIC COSTS (2015-2016)**

**Tuition and fees:** $44,950.

**Per-credit charge:** $1,386.

**Room and board:** $10,650.

**FINANCIAL AID PICTURE (2015-2016)**

**Students with need:** Out of 431 full-time freshmen who applied for aid, 356 were judged to have need. Of these, 356 received aid, and 213 had their full need met. Average financial aid package met 95% of need; average scholarship/grant was $29,714; average loan was $6,490. Need-based aid available for part-time students.

**Students without need:** 202 full-time freshmen who did not demonstrate need for aid received scholarships/grants; average award was $24,429. No-need awards available for academics, minority status, music/drama, religious affiliation.

## FINANCIAL AID PROCEDURES
**Forms required:** FAFSA, institutional form. Either CSS PROFILE or institution application for prospective students.
**Dates and Deadlines:** Priority date 2/15; no closing date. Applicants notified on a rolling basis starting 3/1; must reply by 5/1 or within 2 week(s) of notification.
**Transfers:** Priority date 4/1; no deadline. Applicants notified on a rolling basis.

## CONTACT
Joseph Winge, Director of Financial Aid
Gault Admissions Center, Wooster, OH 44691-2363
(330) 263-2317

## Columbus College of Art and Design
Columbus, Ohio
www.ccad.edu                    Federal Code: 003039

**4-year private** visual arts college in very large city.
**Enrollment:** 1,081 undergrads, 4% part-time. 236 full-time freshmen.
**Selectivity:** Admits less than 50% of applicants.

### BASIC COSTS (2015-2016)
**Tuition and fees:** $30,840.
**Per-credit charge:** $1,285.
**Room and board:** $8,390.

### FINANCIAL AID PICTURE (2015-2016)
**Students with need:** Average financial aid package met 59% of need; average scholarship/grant was $18,416; average loan was $5,999. For part-time students, average financial aid package was $10,122.
**Students without need:** No-need awards available for academics, art, ROTC, state/district residency.

### FINANCIAL AID PROCEDURES
**Forms required:** FAFSA.
**Dates and Deadlines:** Closing date 3/1. Applicants notified on a rolling basis starting 3/15; must reply within 2 week(s) of notification.
**Transfers:** Closing date 3/15. Applicants notified on a rolling basis.

### CONTACT
Anna Marie Schofield, Director of Financial Aid
60 Cleveland Avenue, Columbus, OH 43215-3875
(614) 222-3274

## Columbus State Community College
Columbus, Ohio
www.cscc.edu                    Federal Code: 006867

**2-year public** community and technical college in very large city.
**Enrollment:** 11,426 undergrads, 64% part-time. 1,048 full-time freshmen.
**Selectivity:** Open admission; but selective for some programs.

### BASIC COSTS (2015-2016)
**Tuition and fees:** $4,128; out-of-state residents $9,090.

### FINANCIAL AID PICTURE (2014-2015)
**Students with need:** Need-based aid available for part-time students.
**Students without need:** No-need awards available for academics, athletics, state/district residency.

### FINANCIAL AID PROCEDURES
**Forms required:** FAFSA.
**Dates and Deadlines:** Priority date 6/1; no closing date. Applicants notified on a rolling basis starting 4/1.

## CONTACT
David Metz, Director of Financial Aid
550 East Spring Street, Columbus, OH 43216-1609
(614) 287-2648

## Cuyahoga Community College
Cleveland, Ohio
www.tri-c.edu

**2-year public** community college in very large city.
**Enrollment:** 13,590 undergrads.
**Selectivity:** Open admission; but selective for some programs.

### BASIC COSTS (2015-2016)
**Tuition and fees:** $3,172; out-of-district residents $3,953; out-of-state residents $7,468.

### FINANCIAL AID PICTURE
**Students with need:** Need-based aid available for full-time and part-time students. Work study available nights, weekends, and for part-time students.
**Students without need:** No-need awards available for academics, art, athletics, leadership, minority status, music/drama.

### FINANCIAL AID PROCEDURES
**Forms required:** FAFSA, institutional form.
**Dates and Deadlines:** Applicants notified on a rolling basis starting 5/15.
**Transfers:** Priority date 5/13.

### CONTACT
Kimberly Nash-Yore
2900 Community College Avenue, Cleveland, OH 44115-2878

## Davis College
Toledo, Ohio
www.daviscollege.edu           Federal Code: 004855

**2-year for-profit** junior college in large city.
**Enrollment:** 190 undergrads, 74% part-time. 5 full-time freshmen.

### BASIC COSTS (2015-2016)
**Tuition and fees:** $16,800.
**Per-credit charge:** $350.

### FINANCIAL AID PICTURE
**Students with need:** Need-based aid available for full-time and part-time students. Work study available nights, weekends, and for part-time students.
**Students without need:** This college awards aid only to students with need.

### FINANCIAL AID PROCEDURES
**Forms required:** FAFSA.
**Dates and Deadlines:** Applicants notified on a rolling basis.
**Transfers:** No deadline. Applicants notified on a rolling basis. Student completes a clearance withdrawal letter that is completed from the previous school's financial aid office.

### CONTACT
Marilyn Bovia, Director of Financial Aid
4747 Monroe Street, Toledo, OH 43623
(419) 473-2700

## Daymar College: Chillicothe
Chillicothe, Ohio
www.daymarcollege.edu          Federal Code: 020568

**2-year for-profit** business college in large town.
**Enrollment:** 38 undergrads.

**Selectivity:** Open admission.

**BASIC COSTS (2015-2016)**

**Additional info:** Diploma programs: $17,000-$26,500. Associate programs: $33,000.

**FINANCIAL AID PICTURE**

**Students with need:** Need-based aid available for full-time and part-time students.

**Students without need:** This college awards aid only to students with need.

**Scholarships offered:** Ohio Legislative Scholarship: administered by the Ohio Council of Private Colleges and Schools, for Ohio-resident high school seniors nominated by their state representative who reviews applications; 2-year tuition for associate degree valued at $11,500.

**FINANCIAL AID PROCEDURES**

**Forms required:** FAFSA, institutional form.

**Transfers:** No deadline.

**CONTACT**

Connie Pruitt, Financial Aid Coordinator

1410 Industrial Drive, Chillicothe, OH 45601

(740) 774-2063

## Defiance College
Defiance, Ohio
www.defiance.edu                    Federal Code: 003041

**4-year private** liberal arts college in large town, affiliated with United Church of Christ.

**Enrollment:** 666 undergrads, 14% part-time. 183 full-time freshmen.

**Selectivity:** Admits 50 to 75% of applicants.

**BASIC COSTS (2015-2016)**

**Tuition and fees:** $31,082.

**Per-credit charge:** $485.

**Room and board:** $9,850.

**FINANCIAL AID PICTURE**

**Students with need:** Need-based aid available for full-time and part-time students. Work study available nights, weekends, and for part-time students.

**Students without need:** No-need awards available for academics, leadership, minority status, music/drama.

**Scholarships offered:** Presidential Scholar Program: $14,000 to full tuition; based on 3.5 GPA, 27 ACT/1210 SAT, and interview. Pilgrim Scholar Program: $13,000-$16,000; based on 3.2 GPA, 24 ACT/1090 SAT, and interview. Achievement Scholar Program: $12,000-$15,000; based on 2.8 GPA, 21 ACT/980 SAT, and interview. Defiance College Scholarship: $5,000-$10,000; based on 2.5-4.0 GPA and 18-36 ACT/850-1600 SAT.

**FINANCIAL AID PROCEDURES**

**Forms required:** FAFSA.

**Dates and Deadlines:** Priority date 4/1; no closing date. Applicants notified on a rolling basis starting 2/15; must reply by 5/1 or within 2 week(s) of notification.

**CONTACT**

Amy Francis, Director of Financial Aid

701 North Clinton Street, Defiance, OH 43512-1695

(419) 783-2458

## Denison University
Granville, Ohio
www.denison.edu                    Federal Code: 003042

**4-year private** liberal arts college in small town.

**Enrollment:** 2,255 undergrads. 632 full-time freshmen.

**Selectivity:** Admits less than 50% of applicants.

**BASIC COSTS (2015-2016)**

**Tuition and fees:** $47,290.

**Room and board:** $11,570.

**Additional info:** Tuition/fee waivers available for adults.

**FINANCIAL AID PICTURE (2015-2016)**

**Students with need:** Out of 435 full-time freshmen who applied for aid, 357 were judged to have need. Of these, 357 received aid, and 74 had their full need met. Average financial aid package met 90% of need; average scholarship/grant was $33,696; average loan was $3,464. Need-based aid available for part-time students.

**Students without need:** 263 full-time freshmen who did not demonstrate need for aid received scholarships/grants; average award was $22,140. No-need awards available for academics, alumni affiliation, art, leadership, minority status, music/drama, state/district residency.

**FINANCIAL AID PROCEDURES**

**Forms required:** FAFSA.

**Dates and Deadlines:** Priority date 3/15; no closing date. Applicants notified on a rolling basis starting 3/28.

**CONTACT**

Nancy Hoover, Director of Financial Aid and Student Employment

100 West College, Granville, OH 43023

(740) 587-6279

## DeVry University: Columbus
Columbus, Ohio
www.devry.edu                    Federal Code: 003099

**4-year for-profit** university in very large city.

**Enrollment:** 1,676 undergrads.

**BASIC COSTS (2015-2016)**

**Tuition and fees:** $17,132.

**Per-credit charge:** $609.

**FINANCIAL AID PICTURE**

**Students with need:** Need-based aid available for full-time and part-time students.

**Students without need:** This college awards aid only to students with need.

**FINANCIAL AID PROCEDURES**

**Forms required:** FAFSA.

**Dates and Deadlines:** Applicants notified on a rolling basis.

**CONTACT**

1350 Alum Creek Drive, Columbus, OH 43209-2705

(614) 253-7291

## Eastern Gateway Community College
Steubenville, Ohio
www.egcc.edu                    Federal Code: 007275

**2-year public** community college in large town.

**Enrollment:** 1,573 undergrads.

**Selectivity:** Open admission; but selective for some programs.

**BASIC COSTS (2015-2016)**

**Tuition and fees:** $3,460; out-of-district residents $3,640; out-of-state residents $4,480.

**Per-credit charge:** $111; out-of-district residents $117; out-of-state residents $145.

**Additional info:** Residents of 5 neighboring West Virginia counties eligible for in-state, out-of-district tuition rates.

## FINANCIAL AID PICTURE

**Students with need:** Need-based aid available for full-time and part-time students. Work study available nights, weekends, and for part-time students.
**Students without need:** This college awards aid only to students with need.
**Scholarships offered:** Horizon Grant: two-year tuition scholarship; awarded to all students graduating from a Jefferson County high school with 2.5 GPA; student must enroll full-time for fall semester immediately following high school graduation.

## FINANCIAL AID PROCEDURES

**Forms required:** FAFSA, institutional form.
**Dates and Deadlines:** Priority date 4/1; no closing date. Applicants notified on a rolling basis starting 6/15.

## CONTACT

Kelly Wilson, Director of Financial Aid
Eastern Gateway Community College- Jefferson County Campus,
Steubenville, OH 43952
(740) 264-5591 ext. 135

## Edison State Community College

Piqua, Ohio
www.edisonohio.edu                    Federal Code: 012750

**2-year public** community college in large town.
**Enrollment:** 1,773 undergrads, 68% part-time. 209 full-time freshmen.
**Selectivity:** Open admission; but selective for some programs.

## BASIC COSTS (2015-2016)

**Tuition and fees:** $4,234; out-of-state residents $7,843.
**Per-credit charge:** $120; out-of-state residents $241.

## FINANCIAL AID PICTURE (2014-2015)

**Students with need:** 98% of average financial aid package awarded as scholarships/grants, 2% awarded as loans/jobs. Need-based aid available for part-time students. Work study available nights, weekends, and for part-time students.
**Students without need:** No-need awards available for academics, alumni affiliation, art, athletics, job skills, leadership, minority status, state/district residency.

## FINANCIAL AID PROCEDURES

**Forms required:** FAFSA, institutional form.
**Dates and Deadlines:** Priority date 5/1; no closing date. Applicants notified on a rolling basis starting 5/15.

## CONTACT

Kathi Richards, Director of Student Financial Aid
1973 Edison Drive, Piqua, OH 45356-9253
(937) 778-7910

## ETI Technical College of Niles

Niles, Ohio
www.eticollege.edu                    Federal Code: 030790

**2-year for-profit** technical college in large town.
**Enrollment:** 37 undergrads. 2 full-time freshmen.
**Selectivity:** Open admission; but selective for some programs.

## BASIC COSTS (2015-2016)

**Tuition and fees:** $9,386.
**Per-credit charge:** $361.
**Additional info:** Tuition at time of enrollment locked for 2 years.

## FINANCIAL AID PICTURE (2015-2016)

**Students with need:** Out of 2 full-time freshmen who applied for aid, 2 were judged to have need. Of these, 2 received aid. Need-based aid available for part-time students.

## FINANCIAL AID PROCEDURES

**Forms required:** FAFSA.
**Dates and Deadlines:** Applicants notified on a rolling basis; must reply within 4 week(s) of notification.
**Transfers:** No deadline. Applicants notified on a rolling basis; must reply within 4 week(s) of notification.

## CONTACT

Kay Madigan, Financial Aid Director
2076 Youngstown Warren Road, Niles, OH 44446-4398
(330) 652-9919

## Fortis College: Centerville

Centerville, Ohio
www.fortis.edu                    Federal Code: 012267

**2-year for-profit** junior and technical college in large town.
**Enrollment:** 887 undergrads.
**Selectivity:** Open admission.

## BASIC COSTS (2015-2016)

**Additional info:** Bachelor: 20841; associate degree programs: $27,615-44,402; certificates: $16,670-21,902. Books and supplies range $450-3,100 depending on program level and course of study. All costs are subject to change.

## FINANCIAL AID PICTURE

**Students with need:** Need-based aid available for full-time and part-time students.
**Students without need:** This college awards aid only to students with need.

## FINANCIAL AID PROCEDURES

**Forms required:** FAFSA, institutional form.
**Dates and Deadlines:** Applicants notified on a rolling basis.

## CONTACT

Lynda Linsey, Director of Financial Aid
555 East Alex Bell Road, Centerville, OH 45459-9627

## Fortis College: Ravenna

Ravenna, Ohio
www.fortis.edu                    Federal Code: 016270

**2-year for-profit** business college in large town.
**Enrollment:** 269 undergrads.

## BASIC COSTS (2015-2016)

**Additional info:** Associate degree programs: $26,625-30,720; certificates: $14,147-21,621 depending on program level and course of study. All costs are subject to change.

## FINANCIAL AID PICTURE

**Students with need:** Need-based aid available for full-time and part-time students.
**Students without need:** This college awards aid only to students with need.

## FINANCIAL AID PROCEDURES

**Forms required:** FAFSA.
**Dates and Deadlines:** Applicants notified on a rolling basis.

**CONTACT**
Trudy Young, Financial Aid Director
653 Enterprise Parkway, Ravenna, OH 44266
(330) 297-7319

## Franciscan University of Steubenville
Steubenville, Ohio
www.franciscan.edu          Federal Code: 003036

**4-year private** university in large town, affiliated with Roman Catholic Church.
**Enrollment:** 2,036 undergrads, 2% part-time. 456 full-time freshmen.
**Selectivity:** Admits over 75% of applicants.

**BASIC COSTS (2015-2016)**
**Tuition and fees:** $24,780.
**Per-credit charge:** $810.
**Room and board:** $8,300.

**FINANCIAL AID PICTURE**
**Students with need:** Need-based aid available for full-time and part-time students. Work study available nights, weekends, and for part-time students.
**Students without need:** No-need awards available for academics, alumni affiliation, leadership, religious affiliation.

**FINANCIAL AID PROCEDURES**
**Forms required:** FAFSA.
**Dates and Deadlines:** Priority date 4/1; no closing date. Applicants notified on a rolling basis starting 2/15; must reply within 3 week(s) of notification.
**Transfers:** Closing date 8/1. Applicants notified on a rolling basis starting 2/15; must reply within 3 week(s) of notification.

**CONTACT**
John Herrmann, Director of Student Financial Services
1235 University Boulevard, Steubenville, OH 43952-1763
(740) 283-6226

## Franklin University
Columbus, Ohio
www.franklin.edu          Federal Code: 003046

**4-year private** university and business college in very large city.
**Enrollment:** 4,049 undergrads, 68% part-time. 11 full-time freshmen.
**Selectivity:** Open admission; but selective for some programs.

**BASIC COSTS (2015-2016)**
**Tuition and fees:** $14,545.
**Per-credit charge:** $484.

**FINANCIAL AID PICTURE**
**Students with need:** Need-based aid available for full-time and part-time students.
**Students without need:** No-need awards available for academics, leadership, minority status.

**FINANCIAL AID PROCEDURES**
**Forms required:** FAFSA.
**Dates and Deadlines:** Priority date 6/15; no closing date. Applicants notified on a rolling basis; must reply within 2 week(s) of notification.
**Transfers:** No deadline. Applicants notified on a rolling basis starting 3/15; must reply within 2 week(s) of notification. One scholarship specifically offered for transfer students: Transfer Scholarship.

**CONTACT**
Goldie Langley, Director of Financial Aid
201 South Grant Avenue, Columbus, OH 43215-5399
(614) 797-4700

## Gallipolis Career College
Gallipolis, Ohio
www.gallipoliscareercollege.com     Federal Code: 030079

**2-year for-profit** business and career college in small town.
**Enrollment:** 90 undergrads, 50% part-time. 4 full-time freshmen.
**Selectivity:** Open admission.

**BASIC COSTS (2016-2017)**
**Tuition and fees:** $7,620.

**FINANCIAL AID PICTURE (2014-2015)**
**Students with need:** 40% of average financial aid package awarded as scholarships/grants, 60% awarded as loans/jobs. Need-based aid available for part-time students.
**Students without need:** This college awards aid only to students with need.

**FINANCIAL AID PROCEDURES**
**Forms required:** FAFSA.

**CONTACT**
Jeanette Shirey, Financial Aid Administrator
1176 Jackson Pike, Suite 312, Gallipolis, OH 45631
(740) 446-4367

## God's Bible School and College
Cincinnati, Ohio
www.gbs.edu          Federal Code: 015691

**4-year private** Bible college in large city, affiliated with interdenominational tradition.
**Enrollment:** 304 undergrads.

**BASIC COSTS (2015-2016)**
**Tuition and fees:** $7,040.
**Per-credit charge:** $225.
**Room and board:** $4,050.

**FINANCIAL AID PICTURE**
**Students with need:** Need-based aid available for full-time and part-time students.
**Students without need:** No-need awards available for academics, leadership, music/drama, religious affiliation.
**Additional info:** Institutional work scholarships available.

**FINANCIAL AID PROCEDURES**
**Forms required:** FAFSA.
**Dates and Deadlines:** Priority date 4/30; no closing date. Applicants notified on a rolling basis.

**CONTACT**
Sharree Pouzar, Financial Aid Coordinator
1810 Young Street, Cincinnati, OH 45202-6838
(513) 721-7944 ext. 1161

## Heidelberg University
Tiffin, Ohio
www.heidelberg.edu          Federal Code: 003048

**4-year private** liberal arts college in large town, affiliated with United Church of Christ.
**Enrollment:** 1,026 undergrads, 2% part-time. 273 full-time freshmen.
**Selectivity:** Admits over 75% of applicants.

**BASIC COSTS (2015-2016)**
**Tuition and fees:** $28,500.

**Per-credit charge:** $720.
**Room and board:** $9,600.

## FINANCIAL AID PICTURE (2015-2016)
**Students with need:** Out of 266 full-time freshmen who applied for aid, 249 were judged to have need. Of these, 249 received aid, and 25 had their full need met. Average financial aid package met 79% of need; average scholarship/grant was $19,240; average loan was $4,000. Need-based aid available for part-time students.
**Students without need:** 22 full-time freshmen who did not demonstrate need for aid received scholarships/grants; average award was $13,464. No-need awards available for academics, alumni affiliation, music/drama, religious affiliation, state/district residency.

## FINANCIAL AID PROCEDURES
**Forms required:** FAFSA.
**Dates and Deadlines:** Priority date 3/1; no closing date. Applicants notified on a rolling basis starting 3/15; must reply by 5/1 or within 2 week(s) of notification.
**Transfers:** No deadline. Applicants notified on a rolling basis starting 3/1; must reply by 5/1 or within 2 week(s) of notification.

## CONTACT
Juli Weininger, Director of Financial Aid
310 East Market Street, Tiffin, OH 44883-2462
(419) 448-2293

## Hiram College
Hiram, Ohio      Federal Code: 003049
www.hiram.edu      CSS Code: 1297

**4-year private** liberal arts college in rural community, affiliated with Christian Church (Disciples of Christ).
**Enrollment:** 1,063 undergrads, 15% part-time. 160 full-time freshmen.
**Selectivity:** Admits 50 to 75% of applicants.

## BASIC COSTS (2015-2016)
**Tuition and fees:** $31,530.
**Room and board:** $10,190.

## FINANCIAL AID PICTURE
**Students with need:** Need-based aid available for full-time and part-time students. Work study available nights, weekends, and for part-time students.
**Students without need:** No-need awards available for academics, alumni affiliation, art, music/drama, religious affiliation.

## FINANCIAL AID PROCEDURES
**Forms required:** FAFSA. Not require for domestic applicants.
**Dates and Deadlines:** Priority date 2/15; no closing date. Applicants notified on a rolling basis starting 3/1; must reply by 5/1 or within 2 week(s) of notification.
**Transfers:** Transfer merit scholarships available. Phi Theta Kappa scholarships available.

## CONTACT
Andrea Caputo, Director of Student Financial Aid
P.O. Box 96, Hiram, OH 44234
(330) 569-5107

## Hocking College
Nelsonville, Ohio
www.hocking.edu      Federal Code: 007598

**2-year public** technical college in small town.
**Enrollment:** 3,130 undergrads.
**Selectivity:** Open admission; but selective for some programs.

## BASIC COSTS (2015-2016)
**Tuition and fees:** $4,390; out-of-state residents $8,780.
**Room and board:** $3,830.

## FINANCIAL AID PICTURE
**Students with need:** Need-based aid available for full-time and part-time students. Work study available nights, weekends, and for part-time students.
**Students without need:** No-need awards available for academics, minority status, state/district residency.

## FINANCIAL AID PROCEDURES
**Forms required:** FAFSA, institutional form.
**Dates and Deadlines:** Priority date 2/28; no closing date. Applicants notified on a rolling basis starting 4/15.
**Transfers:** No deadline. Applicants notified on a rolling basis. Non-entitlement aid awarded on first-come, first-served basis.

## CONTACT
Muriel Merchant, Director, Financial Aid
3301 Hocking Parkway, Nelsonville, OH 45764-9704
(740) 753-7080

## Hondros College
Westerville, Ohio
www.nursing.hondros.edu      Federal Code: 040743

**2-year for-profit** nursing college in very large city.
**Enrollment:** 1,520 undergrads.

## BASIC COSTS (2015-2016)
**Tuition and fees:** $17,825.

## FINANCIAL AID PICTURE
**Students with need:** Need-based aid available for full-time and part-time students.

## FINANCIAL AID PROCEDURES
**Forms required:** FAFSA.
**Transfers:** No deadline. Applicants notified on a rolling basis starting 2/1.

## CONTACT
Mary Cannon, Director of Financial Aid
4140 Executive Parkway, Westerville, OH 43081-3855
(614) 508-7200

## International College of Broadcasting
Dayton, Ohio
www.icb.edu      Federal Code: 013132

**2-year for-profit** technical college in small city.
**Enrollment:** 82 undergrads.
**Selectivity:** Open admission.

## BASIC COSTS (2015-2016)
**Tuition and fees:** $31,950.
**Per-credit charge:** $424.67.

## FINANCIAL AID PICTURE (2015-2016)
**Students with need:** Need-based aid available for full-time and part-time students.

## FINANCIAL AID PROCEDURES
**Forms required:** FAFSA.
**Dates and Deadlines:** Applicants notified on a rolling basis starting 11/1.

## CONTACT
Lizzie Miller, Financial Aid Director
6 South Smithville Road, Dayton, OH 45431
(937) 258-8251

## James A. Rhodes State College
Lima, Ohio
www.rhodesstate.edu                Federal Code: 010027

**2-year public** community and technical college in large town.
**Enrollment:** 3,416 undergrads.
**Selectivity:** Open admission; but selective for some programs.

### BASIC COSTS (2015-2016)
**Tuition and fees:** $4,806; out-of-state residents $9,611.
**Per-credit charge:** $160; out-of-state residents $320.

### FINANCIAL AID PICTURE
**Students with need:** Need-based aid available for full-time and part-time students. Work study available nights, weekends, and for part-time students.
**Students without need:** No-need awards available for academics.

### FINANCIAL AID PROCEDURES
**Forms required:** FAFSA.
**Dates and Deadlines:** Priority date 2/15; no closing date. Applicants notified on a rolling basis starting 5/1; must reply within 2 week(s) of notification.

### CONTACT
Cathy Kohli, Director of Financial Aid
4240 Campus Drive, PS 148, Lima, OH 45804-3597
(419) 995-8800

## John Carroll University
University Heights, Ohio
www.jcu.edu                Federal Code: 003050

**4-year private** university in large town, affiliated with Roman Catholic Church.
**Enrollment:** 2,994 undergrads.
**Selectivity:** Admits over 75% of applicants.

### BASIC COSTS (2016-2017)
**Tuition and fees:** $38,490.
**Per-credit charge:** $1,240.
**Room and board:** $11,250.

### FINANCIAL AID PICTURE (2014-2015)
**Students with need:** 76% of average financial aid package awarded as scholarships/grants, 24% awarded as loans/jobs. Need-based aid available for part-time students.
**Students without need:** No-need awards available for academics, alumni affiliation, leadership, minority status, ROTC, state/district residency.
**Additional info:** John Carroll grant combined with federal and state grant aid, and the Federal Stafford Loan program to meet the published flat, full-time tuition cost for Pell-eligible Ohio families.

### FINANCIAL AID PROCEDURES
**Forms required:** FAFSA.
**Dates and Deadlines:** Priority date 2/15; closing date 3/15. Applicants notified on a rolling basis starting 2/15; must reply by 5/1 or within 4 week(s) of notification.
**Transfers:** Priority date 5/1; closing date 8/1. Applicants notified on a rolling basis starting 4/1; must reply by 8/1 or within 3 week(s) of notification.

### CONTACT
Claudia Wenzel, Director of Financial Assistance
Office of Admission, University Heights, OH 44118-4581
(216) 397-4294

## Kaplan College: Dayton
Dayton, Ohio
www.dayton.kaplancollege.com                Federal Code: 020520

**2-year for-profit** technical college in very large city.
**Enrollment:** 317 undergrads.
**Selectivity:** Open admission; but selective for some programs.

### BASIC COSTS (2015-2016)
**Additional info:** Associate of Applied Science in Nursing: $41,095. Dental Assistant: $16,814. Electrical Technician: $20,944. Heating, Ventilation, and Air Conditioning/Refrigeration: $20,845. Intravenous (IV) Therapy: $609. Medical Assistant: $15,925. Pharmacy Technician: $15,954. Phlebotomy Technician: $970. Photographic Technology: $46,862. State Tested Nursing Assistant: $1,005.

### FINANCIAL AID PICTURE
**Students with need:** Need-based aid available for full-time and part-time students.

### FINANCIAL AID PROCEDURES
**Forms required:** FAFSA, institutional form.
**Dates and Deadlines:** Applicants notified on a rolling basis starting 3/1.

### CONTACT
Tiphany Pugh, Director of Operations
2800 East River Road, Dayton, OH 45439
(937) 294-6155

## Kent State University
Kent, Ohio
www.kent.edu                Federal Code: 003051

**4-year public** university in large town.
**Enrollment:** 22,779 undergrads, 11% part-time. 4,294 full-time freshmen.
**Selectivity:** Admits over 75% of applicants.

### BASIC COSTS (2015-2016)
**Tuition and fees:** $10,012; out-of-state residents $18,212.
**Per-credit charge:** $456; out-of-state residents $818.
**Room and board:** $10,334.

### FINANCIAL AID PICTURE (2015-2016)
**Students with need:** Out of 3,727 full-time freshmen who applied for aid, 2,940 were judged to have need. Of these, 2,925 received aid, and 258 had their full need met. Average financial aid package met 60% of need; average scholarship/grant was $5,813; average loan was $4,062. For part-time students, average financial aid package was $6,256.
**Students without need:** 936 full-time freshmen who did not demonstrate need for aid received scholarships/grants; average award was $5,398. No-need awards available for academics, alumni affiliation, art, athletics, leadership, minority status, music/drama, ROTC, state/district residency.
**Scholarships offered:** 46 full-time freshmen received athletic scholarships; average amount $18,159.
**Additional info:** Participant in US Department of Education's Quality Assurance Program and Experimental Sites Program.

### FINANCIAL AID PROCEDURES
**Forms required:** FAFSA.
**Dates and Deadlines:** Priority date 3/1; no closing date. Applicants notified by 3/15; must reply within 2 week(s) of notification.
**Transfers:** Applicants notified by 3/15; must reply within 2 week(s) of notification.

### CONTACT
Mark Evans, Director of Student Financial Aid
161 Schwartz Center, Kent, OH 44242-0001
(330) 672-2972

## Kent State University: Ashtabula

Ashtabula, Ohio
www.kent.edu/ashtabula          Federal Code: 003051

**2-year public** branch campus college in large town.
**Enrollment:** 2,095 undergrads, 46% part-time. 184 full-time freshmen.
**Selectivity:** Open admission; but selective for some programs.

### BASIC COSTS (2015-2016)
**Tuition and fees:** $5,664; out-of-state residents $13,864.
**Per-credit charge:** $258; out-of-state residents $620.

### FINANCIAL AID PICTURE (2015-2016)
**Students with need:** Out of 171 full-time freshmen who applied for aid, 147 were judged to have need. Of these, 144 received aid, and 1 had their full need met. Average financial aid package met 52% of need; average scholarship/grant was $4,773; average loan was $3,354. For part-time students, average financial aid package was $5,889.
**Students without need:** 1 full-time freshmen who did not demonstrate need for aid received scholarships/grants; average award was $1,000. No-need awards available for academics, alumni affiliation, art, athletics, leadership, minority status, music/drama, ROTC, state/district residency.

### FINANCIAL AID PROCEDURES
**Forms required:** FAFSA.
**Dates and Deadlines:** Priority date 3/1; no closing date. Applicants notified on a rolling basis starting 3/15; must reply within 2 week(s) of notification.

### CONTACT
Kristina Call, Financial Aid Coordinator
3300 Lake Road West, Ashtabula, OH 44004-2299
(440) 964-4591

## Kent State University: Geauga

Burton, Ohio
www.kent.edu/geauga          Federal Code: 003059

**2-year public** branch campus college in rural community.
**Enrollment:** 2,284 undergrads, 40% part-time. 277 full-time freshmen.
**Selectivity:** Open admission; but selective for some programs.

### BASIC COSTS (2015-2016)
**Tuition and fees:** $5,664; out-of-state residents $13,864.
**Per-credit charge:** $258; out-of-state residents $620.

### FINANCIAL AID PICTURE (2015-2016)
**Students with need:** Out of 202 full-time freshmen who applied for aid, 162 were judged to have need. Of these, 155 received aid, and 1 had their full need met. Average financial aid package met 52% of need; average scholarship/grant was $4,616; average loan was $3,298. For part-time students, average financial aid package was $6,090.
**Students without need:** 5 full-time freshmen who did not demonstrate need for aid received scholarships/grants; average award was $2,048. No-need awards available for academics, alumni affiliation, art, athletics, leadership, minority status, music/drama, ROTC, state/district residency.

### FINANCIAL AID PROCEDURES
**Forms required:** FAFSA.
**Dates and Deadlines:** Priority date 3/1; no closing date. Applicants notified by 3/15; must reply within 2 week(s) of notification.

### CONTACT
Donna Holcomb, Financial Aid Advisor
Office of Admissions, Burton, OH 44021
(440) 834-8846

## Kent State University: East Liverpool

East Liverpool, Ohio
www.kent.edu/columbiana          Federal Code: 003051

**2-year public** branch campus college in large town.
**Enrollment:** 1,168 undergrads, 42% part-time. 67 full-time freshmen.
**Selectivity:** Open admission; but selective for some programs.

### BASIC COSTS (2015-2016)
**Tuition and fees:** $5,664; out-of-state residents $13,864.
**Per-credit charge:** $258; out-of-state residents $620.

### FINANCIAL AID PICTURE (2015-2016)
**Students with need:** Out of 55 full-time freshmen who applied for aid, 48 were judged to have need. Of these, 48 received aid, and 1 had their full need met. Average financial aid package met 47% of need; average scholarship/grant was $4,992; average loan was $3,409. For part-time students, average financial aid package was $6,156.
**Students without need:** 6 full-time freshmen who did not demonstrate need for aid received scholarships/grants; average award was $750. No-need awards available for academics, alumni affiliation, art, athletics, leadership, minority status, music/drama, ROTC, state/district residency.

### FINANCIAL AID PROCEDURES
**Forms required:** FAFSA.
**Dates and Deadlines:** Priority date 3/1; no closing date. Applicants notified by 3/15; must reply within 2 week(s) of notification.

### CONTACT
Chris Winland, Administrative Assistant
400 East Fourth Street, East Liverpool, OH 43920
(330) 385-3805

## Kent State University: Salem

Salem, Ohio
www.kent.edu/columbiana          Federal Code: 003061

**2-year public** branch campus college in large town.
**Enrollment:** 1,565 undergrads, 28% part-time. 170 full-time freshmen.
**Selectivity:** Open admission; but selective for some programs.

### BASIC COSTS (2015-2016)
**Tuition and fees:** $5,664; out-of-state residents $13,664.
**Per-credit charge:** $258; out-of-state residents $620.

### FINANCIAL AID PICTURE (2015-2016)
**Students with need:** Out of 145 full-time freshmen who applied for aid, 135 were judged to have need. Of these, 133 received aid, and 1 had their full need met. Average financial aid package met 50% of need; average scholarship/grant was $4,853; average loan was $3,331. For part-time students, average financial aid package was $5,909.
**Students without need:** 11 full-time freshmen who did not demonstrate need for aid received scholarships/grants; average award was $1,133. No-need awards available for academics, alumni affiliation, art, athletics, leadership, minority status, music/drama, ROTC, state/district residency.

### FINANCIAL AID PROCEDURES
**Forms required:** FAFSA.
**Dates and Deadlines:** Priority date 3/1; no closing date. Applicants notified by 3/15; must reply within 2 week(s) of notification.
**Transfers:** Priority date 2/15.

### CONTACT
Angel Barcey, Administrative Clerk
2491 State Route 45 South, Salem, OH 44460

## Kent State University: Stark
Canton, Ohio
www.kent.edu/stark                    Federal Code: 003054

**2-year public** branch campus college in large town.
**Enrollment:** 4,332 undergrads, 30% part-time. 530 full-time freshmen.
**Selectivity:** Open admission; but selective for some programs.

### BASIC COSTS (2015-2016)
**Tuition and fees:** $5,664; out-of-state residents $13,864.
**Per-credit charge:** $258; out-of-state residents $620.

### FINANCIAL AID PICTURE (2015-2016)
**Students with need:** Out of 457 full-time freshmen who applied for aid,
375 were judged to have need. Of these, 368 received aid, and 14 had their
full need met. Average financial aid package met 57% of need; average
scholarship/grant was $4,456; average loan was $3,247. For part-time students, average financial aid package was $6,177.
**Students without need:** 55 full-time freshmen who did not demonstrate
need for aid received scholarships/grants; average award was $1,886. No-
need awards available for academics, alumni affiliation, art, athletics, leadership, minority status, music/drama, ROTC, state/district residency.

### FINANCIAL AID PROCEDURES
**Forms required:** FAFSA.
**Dates and Deadlines:** Priority date 3/1; no closing date. Applicants notified
by 3/15; must reply within 2 week(s) of notification.

### CONTACT
Mark Evans, Director Student Financial Aid
6000 Frank Avenue NW, Canton, OH 44720-7599
(330) 244-3251

## Kent State University: Trumbull
Warren, Ohio
www.kent.edu/trumbull                 Federal Code: 003051

**2-year public** branch campus college in small city.
**Enrollment:** 2,485 undergrads, 34% part-time. 234 full-time freshmen.
**Selectivity:** Open admission; but selective for some programs.

### BASIC COSTS (2015-2016)
**Tuition and fees:** $5,664; out-of-state residents $13,864.
**Per-credit charge:** $258; out-of-state residents $620.

### FINANCIAL AID PICTURE (2015-2016)
**Students with need:** Out of 210 full-time freshmen who applied for aid,
182 were judged to have need. Of these, 175 received aid, and 2 had their
full need met. Average financial aid package met 52% of need; average
scholarship/grant was $4,702; average loan was $3,351. For part-time students, average financial aid package was $6,276.
**Students without need:** 17 full-time freshmen who did not demonstrate
need for aid received scholarships/grants; average award was $985. No-need
awards available for academics, alumni affiliation, art, athletics, leadership,
minority status, music/drama, ROTC, state/district residency.

### FINANCIAL AID PROCEDURES
**Forms required:** FAFSA.
**Dates and Deadlines:** Priority date 3/1; no closing date. Applicants notified
by 3/15; must reply within 2 week(s) of notification.

### CONTACT
Sarah Helmick, Assistant Director Enrollment Management and Student
Services
4314 Mahoning Avenue, NW, Warren, OH 44483-1998
(330) 675-8970

## Kent State University: Tuscarawas
New Philadelphia, Ohio
www.kent.edu/tusc                     Federal Code: 003051

**2-year public** branch campus college in large town.
**Enrollment:** 1,861 undergrads, 34% part-time. 219 full-time freshmen.
**Selectivity:** Open admission; but selective for some programs and for out-
of-state students.

### BASIC COSTS (2015-2016)
**Tuition and fees:** $5,664; out-of-state residents $13,864.
**Per-credit charge:** $258; out-of-state residents $620.

### FINANCIAL AID PICTURE (2015-2016)
**Students with need:** Out of 170 full-time freshmen who applied for aid,
142 were judged to have need. Of these, 136 received aid. Average financial
aid package met 51% of need; average scholarship/grant was $4,242; aver-
age loan was $3,356. For part-time students, average financial aid package
was $5,881.
**Students without need:** 1 full-time freshmen who did not demonstrate
need for aid received scholarships/grants; average award was $4,000. No-
need awards available for academics, alumni affiliation, art, athletics, leadership, minority status, music/drama, ROTC, state/district residency.

### FINANCIAL AID PROCEDURES
**Forms required:** FAFSA.
**Dates and Deadlines:** Priority date 3/1; no closing date. Applicants notified
by 3/15; must reply within 2 week(s) of notification.
**Transfers:** Financial aid transcripts from all previous institutions required.

### CONTACT
Cheryl Walker
330 University Drive NE, New Philadelphia, OH 44663-9403
(330) 339-3391

## Kenyon College
Gambier, Ohio                         Federal Code: 003065
www.kenyon.edu                        CSS Code: 1370

**4-year private** liberal arts college in rural community, affiliated with
nondenominational tradition.
**Enrollment:** 1,698 undergrads. 493 full-time freshmen.
**Selectivity:** Admits less than 50% of applicants.

### BASIC COSTS (2015-2016)
**Tuition and fees:** $49,140.
**Room and board:** $11,890.

### FINANCIAL AID PICTURE (2015-2016)
**Students with need:** Out of 319 full-time freshmen who applied for aid,
224 were judged to have need. Of these, 224 received aid, and 143 had
their full need met. Average financial aid package met 100% of need; average scholarship/grant was $40,319; average loan was $2,602.
**Students without need:** 53 full-time freshmen who did not demonstrate
need for aid received scholarships/grants; average award was $19,153. No-
need awards available for academics, art, minority status, music/drama.
**Scholarships offered:** Honor Scholarships, Science Scholarships, Trustee
Opportunity Scholarships: averages around $16,000 a year; competitively
based on excellence in academic achievement, extracurricular leadership,
and community involvement. Distinguished Academic Scholarships: $2,000-
$10,000; based on academic accomplishment, standardized test results, and
extracurricular achievement. Scholarships for National Merit finalists available.
**Additional info:** Financial aid incentive guarantees a loan-free education for
25 students with the greatest need who bring the qualities of creativity, community service, and leadership.

## FINANCIAL AID PROCEDURES

**Forms required:** FAFSA, CSS PROFILE.
**Dates and Deadlines:** Closing date 2/15. Applicants notified by 4/1; must reply by 5/1.
**Transfers:** Closing date 4/15. Applicants notified by 5/15; must reply by 6/1.

## CONTACT

Craig Daugherty, Director of Financial Aid
Kenyon College Admissions Office, Ransom Hall, Gambier, OH 43022-9623
(740) 427-5430

## Kettering College

Kettering, Ohio
www.kc.edu                                    Federal Code: 007035

**4-year private** health science and nursing college in large city, affiliated with Seventh-day Adventists.
**Enrollment:** 626 undergrads, 48% part-time. 57 full-time freshmen.

### BASIC COSTS (2015-2016)

**Tuition and fees:** $13,680.
**Per-credit charge:** $456.
**Room only:** $3,800.

### FINANCIAL AID PICTURE

**Students with need:** Need-based aid available for full-time and part-time students.
**Students without need:** No-need awards available for academics.

### FINANCIAL AID PROCEDURES

**Forms required:** FAFSA, institutional form.
**Dates and Deadlines:** Priority date 3/31; no closing date. Applicants notified on a rolling basis starting 5/15; must reply within 3 week(s) of notification.

### CONTACT

Kim Snell, Director of Student Finance
3737 Southern Boulevard, Kettering, OH 45429-1299
(937) 296-7210

## Lake Erie College

Painesville, Ohio
www.lec.edu                                    Federal Code: 003066

**4-year private** liberal arts college in large town.
**Enrollment:** 804 undergrads.
**Selectivity:** Admits 50 to 75% of applicants.

### BASIC COSTS (2015-2016)

**Tuition and fees:** $29,162.
**Per-credit charge:** $736.
**Room and board:** $9,178.

### FINANCIAL AID PICTURE

**Students with need:** Need-based aid available for full-time and part-time students. Work study available nights, weekends, and for part-time students.
**Students without need:** No-need awards available for academics, art, athletics, leadership, music/drama, state/district residency.

### FINANCIAL AID PROCEDURES

**Forms required:** FAFSA.
**Dates and Deadlines:** Applicants notified on a rolling basis starting 2/15; must reply by 5/1 or within 4 week(s) of notification.
**Transfers:** No deadline.

### CONTACT

Tricia Pangonis, Director of Financial Aid
391 West Washington Street, Painesville, OH 44077-3389
(440) 375-7100

## Lakeland Community College

Kirtland, Ohio
www.lakelandcc.edu                             Federal Code: 006804

**2-year public** community and technical college in large town.
**Enrollment:** 5,726 undergrads.
**Selectivity:** Open admission; but selective for some programs.

### BASIC COSTS (2015-2016)

**Tuition and fees:** $3,287; out-of-district residents $4,136; out-of-state residents $9,176.
**Per-credit charge:** $98; out-of-district residents $126; out-of-state residents $294.

### FINANCIAL AID PICTURE

**Students with need:** Need-based aid available for full-time and part-time students. Work study available nights, weekends, and for part-time students.
**Students without need:** No-need awards available for academics, art, athletics, job skills, leadership, minority status, music/drama, state/district residency.
**Additional info:** Loans available for tuition and books.

### FINANCIAL AID PROCEDURES

**Forms required:** FAFSA, institutional form.
**Dates and Deadlines:** Closing date 3/1. Applicants notified on a rolling basis starting 5/1.
**Transfers:** Ohio Instructional Grant Transfer Form.

### CONTACT

Melissa Amspaugh, Director of Financial Aid
7700 Clocktower Drive, Kirtland, OH 44094-5198
(440) 525-7070

## Lincoln College of Technology: Dayton

Dayton, Ohio
www.swcollege.net                              Federal Code: 030161

**2-year for-profit** business college in small city.
**Enrollment:** 340 undergrads.
**Selectivity:** Open admission.

### BASIC COSTS (2015-2016)

**Additional info:** Certificate programs: $10,255. Diploma programs: $15,320 to $26,705. Associate programs: $30,515 to $33,048. Costs include total tuition, materials, tool fees, and registration fee.

### FINANCIAL AID PICTURE

**Students with need:** Need-based aid available for full-time and part-time students.
**Students without need:** This college awards aid only to students with need.

### FINANCIAL AID PROCEDURES

**Forms required:** FAFSA.

### CONTACT

Jill Matosky, Director of Financial Aid
111 West 1st Street, Dayton, OH 45402

## Lorain County Community College

Elyria, Ohio
www.lorainccc.edu                              Federal Code: 003068

**2-year public** community college in small city.
**Enrollment:** 8,907 undergrads, 65% part-time. 973 full-time freshmen.
**Selectivity:** Open admission.

## BASIC COSTS (2015-2016)

**Tuition and fees:** $3,077; out-of-district residents $3,679; out-of-state residents $7,302.

**Per-credit charge:** $118.34; out-of-district residents $141.39; out-of-state residents $280.84.

## FINANCIAL AID PICTURE (2014-2015)

**Students with need:** 67% of average financial aid package awarded as scholarships/grants, 33% awarded as loans/jobs. Need-based aid available for part-time students. Work study available nights, weekends, and for part-time students.

**Students without need:** No-need awards available for academics.

**Scholarships offered:** Presidential Scholarships and Trustee Scholarships available.

## FINANCIAL AID PROCEDURES

**Forms required:** FAFSA.

**Dates and Deadlines:** Priority date 8/15; no closing date. Applicants notified on a rolling basis starting 7/1; must reply within 3 week(s) of notification.

## CONTACT

Stephanie Sutton, Manager of Financial Aid
1005 Abbe Road North, Elyria, OH 44035-1691
(490) 366-4034

## Lourdes University
Sylvania, Ohio
www.lourdes.edu                    Federal Code: 003069

**4-year private** university in large town, affiliated with Roman Catholic Church.

**Enrollment:** 1,666 undergrads.

## BASIC COSTS (2015-2016)

**Tuition and fees:** $18,970.

**Per-credit charge:** $633.

**Room and board:** $9,800.

## FINANCIAL AID PICTURE

**Students with need:** Need-based aid available for full-time and part-time students. Work study available nights, weekends, and for part-time students.

**Students without need:** No-need awards available for academics, art, athletics, minority status, religious affiliation, ROTC, state/district residency.

## FINANCIAL AID PROCEDURES

**Forms required:** FAFSA.

**Dates and Deadlines:** Priority date 3/1; no closing date. Applicants notified on a rolling basis starting 3/1; must reply within 4 week(s) of notification.

**Transfers:** Must reply within 4 week(s) of notification.

## CONTACT

Deb LaJeunesse, Director of Financial Aid
6832 Convent Boulevard, Sylvania, OH 43560-2898
(419) 824-3732

## Malone University
Canton, Ohio
www.malone.edu                    Federal Code: 003072

**4-year private** university in small city, affiliated with Evangelical Friends Church-Eastern Region.

**Enrollment:** 1,293 undergrads, 10% part-time. 243 full-time freshmen.

**Selectivity:** Admits 50 to 75% of applicants.

## BASIC COSTS (2015-2016)

**Tuition and fees:** $27,440.

**Per-credit charge:** $470.

**Room and board:** $9,266.

## FINANCIAL AID PICTURE (2015-2016)

**Students with need:** Out of 239 full-time freshmen who applied for aid, 224 were judged to have need. Of these, 224 received aid, and 31 had their full need met. Average financial aid package met 80% of need; average scholarship/grant was $20,667; average loan was $4,434. For part-time students, average financial aid package was $7,441.

**Students without need:** 19 full-time freshmen who did not demonstrate need for aid received scholarships/grants; average award was $10,368. No-need awards available for academics, alumni affiliation, athletics, leadership, music/drama, religious affiliation.

**Scholarships offered:** 24 full-time freshmen received athletic scholarships; average amount $7,802.

**Additional info:** Prepayment discounts and employer deferred payments available for students in adult degree-completion programs. Employer deferred payment plan is available for traditional undergraduate students.

## FINANCIAL AID PROCEDURES

**Forms required:** FAFSA.

**Dates and Deadlines:** Priority date 3/1; closing date 7/31. Applicants notified on a rolling basis starting 3/1; must reply within 2 week(s) of notification.

**Transfers:** Applicants notified on a rolling basis starting 3/1; must reply within 2 week(s) of notification.

## CONTACT

Pamela Pustay, Director of Financial Aid
2600 Cleveland Avenue NW, Canton, OH 44709-3308
(330) 471-8100 ext. 8159

## Marietta College
Marietta, Ohio
www.marietta.edu                    Federal Code: 003073

**4-year private** liberal arts college in large town.

**Enrollment:** 1,215 undergrads, 3% part-time. 283 full-time freshmen.

**Selectivity:** Admits 50 to 75% of applicants.

## BASIC COSTS (2016-2017)

**Tuition and fees:** $35,330.

**Per-credit charge:** $1,140.

**Room and board:** $11,100.

## FINANCIAL AID PICTURE (2015-2016)

**Students with need:** Out of 243 full-time freshmen who applied for aid, 216 were judged to have need. Of these, 216 received aid, and 45 had their full need met. Average financial aid package met 79% of need; average scholarship/grant was $19,944; average loan was $3,759. Need-based aid available for part-time students.

**Students without need:** 30 full-time freshmen who did not demonstrate need for aid received scholarships/grants; average award was $17,378. No-need awards available for academics, alumni affiliation, art, music/drama.

**Additional info:** Auditions/portfolios for art, creative writing, music and theater required for competitive fine art scholarships.

## FINANCIAL AID PROCEDURES

**Forms required:** FAFSA.

**Dates and Deadlines:** Priority date 2/15; no closing date. Applicants notified on a rolling basis starting 3/15; must reply by 5/1 or within 2 week(s) of notification.

**Transfers:** Applicants notified on a rolling basis starting 4/1; must reply by 5/1 or within 2 week(s) of notification.

## CONTACT

Emily Schuck, Director of Student Financial Services
215 Fifth Street, Marietta, OH 45750-4005
(740) 376-4712

## Marion Technical College
Marion, Ohio
www.mtc.edu                    Federal Code: 010736

**2-year public** community and technical college in large town.
**Enrollment:** 1,681 undergrads, 70% part-time. 123 full-time freshmen.
**Selectivity:** Open admission; but selective for some programs.

### BASIC COSTS (2015-2016)
**Tuition and fees:** $4,782; out-of-state residents $6,702.
**Per-credit charge:** $170; out-of-state residents $220.

### FINANCIAL AID PICTURE (2014-2015)
**Students with need:** 59% of average financial aid package awarded as scholarships/grants, 41% awarded as loans/jobs. Need-based aid available for part-time students.
**Students without need:** This college awards aid only to students with need.
**Scholarships offered:** Foundation Scholarship; first year full tuition; for applicants in top 5% of class. President's Scholarship; $1,500; for applicants in top 50% of class. Tech Prep Scholarship; $1,200; for graduates of Tech Prep program. All scholarships require 2.5 GPA and successful completion of proficiency exams.

### FINANCIAL AID PROCEDURES
**Forms required:** FAFSA, institutional form.
**Dates and Deadlines:** Closing date 5/1. Applicants notified on a rolling basis.
**Transfers:** No deadline. Applicants notified on a rolling basis.

### CONTACT
Deb Langdon, Coordinator of Financial Aid
1467 Mt. Vernon Avenue, Marion, OH 43302-5694
(740) 389-4636 ext. 334

## Mercy College of Ohio
Toledo, Ohio
www.mercycollege.edu           Federal Code: 030970

**4-year private** health science and nursing college in large city, affiliated with Roman Catholic Church.
**Enrollment:** 1,239 undergrads, 63% part-time. 52 full-time freshmen.
**Selectivity:** Admits 50 to 75% of applicants.

### BASIC COSTS (2015-2016)
**Tuition and fees:** $12,530.
**Per-credit charge:** $381.

### FINANCIAL AID PICTURE (2014-2015)
**Students with need:** Need-based aid available for part-time students.
**Students without need:** 2 full-time freshmen who did not demonstrate need for aid received scholarships/grants; average award was $7,080. No-need awards available for academics, alumni affiliation, leadership, minority status.

### FINANCIAL AID PROCEDURES
**Forms required:** FAFSA.
**Dates and Deadlines:** Priority date 3/1; no closing date. Applicants notified on a rolling basis starting 3/1; must reply within 2 week(s) of notification.

### CONTACT
Julie Leslie, Financial Aid Director
2221 Madison Avenue, Toledo, OH 43604
(419) 251-1219

## Miami University: Hamilton
Hamilton, Ohio
www.ham.muohio.edu             Federal Code: 003077

**2-year public** branch campus college in small city.
**Enrollment:** 3,386 undergrads.
**Selectivity:** Open admission; but selective for some programs.

### BASIC COSTS (2015-2016)
**Tuition and fees:** $5,413; out-of-state residents $14,689.

### FINANCIAL AID PICTURE
**Students with need:** Need-based aid available for full-time and part-time students. Work study available nights, weekends, and for part-time students.
**Students without need:** No-need awards available for academics, athletics, leadership, minority status, state/district residency.
**Additional info:** Special gift funds for needy, multicultural students who enter with appropriate academic record. Separate application required for scholarships; closing date January 31.

### FINANCIAL AID PROCEDURES
**Forms required:** FAFSA.
**Dates and Deadlines:** Priority date 2/15; no closing date. Applicants notified on a rolling basis starting 4/1.
**Transfers:** Transfer students must complete one semester at Miami University to be considered for scholarships.

### CONTACT
Archie Nelson
1601 University Boulevard, Hamilton, OH 45011-3399
(513) 785-3123

## Miami University: Middletown
Middletown, Ohio
www.mid.muohio.edu             Federal Code: 003077

**2-year public** branch campus and community college in large town.
**Enrollment:** 2,034 undergrads.
**Selectivity:** Open admission; but selective for some programs.

### BASIC COSTS (2015-2016)
**Tuition and fees:** $5,413; out-of-state residents $14,689.
**Per-credit charge:** $216; out-of-state residents $602.

### FINANCIAL AID PICTURE
**Students with need:** Need-based aid available for full-time and part-time students.
**Students without need:** This college awards aid only to students with need.

### FINANCIAL AID PROCEDURES
**Forms required:** FAFSA.
**Dates and Deadlines:** Priority date 2/15; no closing date. Applicants notified on a rolling basis.
**Transfers:** Applicants must file by February 15 to be considered for campus-based aid or alumni scholarships.

### CONTACT
Archie Nelson, Director of Admissions and Financial Aid
4200 East University Boulevard, Middletown, OH 45042
(513) 727-3346

## Miami University: Oxford
Oxford, Ohio
www.MiamiOH.edu                Federal Code: 003077

**4-year public** university in large town.
**Enrollment:** 15,975 undergrads, 2% part-time. 3,641 full-time freshmen.

**Selectivity:** Admits 50 to 75% of applicants.

**BASIC COSTS (2015-2016)**
**Tuition and fees:** $14,287; out-of-state residents $30,987.
**Room and board:** $11,644.

**FINANCIAL AID PICTURE (2014-2015)**
**Students with need:** Out of 2,522 full-time freshmen who applied for aid, 1,421 were judged to have need. Of these, 1,388 received aid, and 314 had their full need met. Average financial aid package met 60% of need; average scholarship/grant was $10,176; average loan was $4,318. For part-time students, average financial aid package was $8,867.
**Students without need:** No-need awards available for academics, art, athletics, leadership, minority status, music/drama, ROTC, state/district residency.
**Additional info:** The Miami Access Initiative guarantees eligible students with scholarships and/or grants that meet or exceed the cost of tuition and academic fees. Academically competitive Ohio residents entering the Miami University Oxford campus as first-time, full-time freshmen in the fall semester and who have a total family income equal to or less than $35,000 will be considered.

**FINANCIAL AID PROCEDURES**
**Forms required:** FAFSA.
**Dates and Deadlines:** Priority date 2/15; no closing date. Applicants notified on a rolling basis starting 3/20; must reply by 5/1 or within 3 week(s) of notification.

**CONTACT**
Brent Shock, Director of Student Financial Assistance
301 South Campus Avenue, Oxford, OH 45056
(513) 529-8734

## Miami-Jacobs Career College: Columbus
Columbus, Ohio
www.miamijacobs.edu          Federal Code: 021521

**2-year for-profit** junior college in very large city.
**Enrollment:** 366 undergrads.

**BASIC COSTS (2015-2016)**
**Additional info:** Certificate programs: Dental Assisting $23,092, Massage Therapy $10,600, Medical Billing and Coding $23,495. Books and supplies $1,258-$3,600. Associate programs: Accounting $31,603, Business Administration $31,891, Criminal Justice $31,891, Electronic Health Records $31,699, Medical Assisting $31,891, Paralegal $31,891. Books and supplies $4,800.

**FINANCIAL AID PICTURE**
**Students with need:** Work study available nights.

**FINANCIAL AID PROCEDURES**
**Forms required:** FAFSA.

**CONTACT**
Lynn Mizanin, Director of Financial Aid
150 East Gay Street, 15th Floor, Columbus, OH 43215
(330) 867-4030

## Miami-Jacobs Career College: Dayton
Dayton, Ohio
www.miamijacobs.edu          Federal Code: 003076

**2-year for-profit** career college in small city.
**Enrollment:** 159 undergrads.

**BASIC COSTS (2015-2016)**
**Additional info:** Certificate programs: Massage Therapy $10,600, Medical Billing and Coding $23,495. Books and supplies $1,900-$3,600. Associate

programs: Business Administration $31,891, Criminal Justice $31,891, Electronic Health Records $31,699, Medical Assisting $31,891. Books and supplies $4,800.

**FINANCIAL AID PICTURE**
**Students with need:** Need-based aid available for full-time and part-time students.
**Students without need:** This college awards aid only to students with need.

**FINANCIAL AID PROCEDURES**
**Forms required:** FAFSA, institutional form.
**Dates and Deadlines:** Applicants notified on a rolling basis.

**CONTACT**
Marcia Byrd, Director of Financial Aid
110 North Patterson Boulevard, Dayton, OH 45402
(937) 461-5174

## Mount Carmel College of Nursing
Columbus, Ohio
www.mccn.edu          Federal Code: 030719

**4-year private** nursing college in very large city, affiliated with Roman Catholic Church.
**Enrollment:** 897 undergrads, 30% part-time. 88 full-time freshmen.
**Selectivity:** Admits over 75% of applicants.

**BASIC COSTS (2015-2016)**
**Tuition and fees:** $12,425.
**Per-credit charge:** $395.

**FINANCIAL AID PICTURE (2015-2016)**
**Students with need:** Out of 80 full-time freshmen who applied for aid, 65 were judged to have need. Of these, 59 received aid, and 1 had their full need met. Average financial aid package met 38% of need; average scholarship/grant was $6,036; average loan was $3,378. For part-time students, average financial aid package was $6,607.
**Students without need:** 14 full-time freshmen who did not demonstrate need for aid received scholarships/grants; average award was $2,325. No-need awards available for academics.

**FINANCIAL AID PROCEDURES**
**Forms required:** FAFSA.
**Dates and Deadlines:** Priority date 3/1; no closing date. Applicants notified on a rolling basis starting 5/31; must reply within 2 week(s) of notification.

**CONTACT**
Todd Everett, Financial Aid Director
127 South Davis Avenue, Columbus, OH 43222-1589
(614) 234-1842

## Mount St. Joseph University
Cincinnati, Ohio
www.msj.edu          Federal Code: 003033

**4-year private** liberal arts college in very large city, affiliated with Roman Catholic Church.
**Enrollment:** 1,405 undergrads, 22% part-time. 325 full-time freshmen.
**Selectivity:** Admits over 75% of applicants.

**BASIC COSTS (2015-2016)**
**Tuition and fees:** $27,500.
**Per-credit charge:** $500.
**Room and board:** $8,810.

## FINANCIAL AID PICTURE (2015-2016)

**Students with need:** Out of 316 full-time freshmen who applied for aid, 284 were judged to have need. Of these, 284 received aid, and 61 had their full need met. Average financial aid package met 83% of need; average scholarship/grant was $18,454; average loan was $3,915. For part-time students, average financial aid package was $8,260.

**Students without need:** 38 full-time freshmen who did not demonstrate need for aid received scholarships/grants; average award was $11,628. No-need awards available for academics, alumni affiliation, art, leadership, music/drama, ROTC, state/district residency.

**Scholarships offered:** Elizabeth Seton Scholarship: $13,000; 30-36 ACT 1330 SAT. Presidential Scholarship: $11,500; 26-36 ACT or 1170 SAT. Trustee Scholarship: $10,500; 24-25 ACT or 1090 SAT. Dean's Scholarship: $9,500; 22-23 ACT or 1020 SAT. Merit Award: $8,500; 20-21 ACT or 940 SAT.

## FINANCIAL AID PROCEDURES

**Forms required:** FAFSA.

**Dates and Deadlines:** Priority date 3/1; no closing date. Applicants notified on a rolling basis starting 1/31; must reply by 5/1 or within 4 week(s) of notification.

**Transfers:** Applicants notified on a rolling basis starting 2/15; must reply within 4 week(s) of notification. Transfer Scholarship; $5,000; 3.0 college GPA with at least 24 hours earned.

## CONTACT

Kathryn Kelly, Director of Student Administrative Services
5701 Delhi Road, Cincinnati, OH 45233-1670
(513) 244-4418

## Mount Vernon Nazarene University
Mount Vernon, Ohio
www.mvnu.edu                    Federal Code: 007085

**4-year private** university in large town, affiliated with Church of the Nazarene.

**Enrollment:** 1,697 undergrads, 15% part-time. 360 full-time freshmen.

**Selectivity:** Admits over 75% of applicants.

### BASIC COSTS (2016-2017)

**Tuition and fees:** $26,950.

**Per-credit charge:** $742.

**Room and board:** $7,550.

**Additional info:** Tuition/fee waivers available for minority students.

### FINANCIAL AID PICTURE (2015-2016)

**Students with need:** Out of 340 full-time freshmen who applied for aid, 303 were judged to have need. Of these, 297 received aid, and 113 had their full need met. Average financial aid package met 69% of need; average scholarship/grant was $20,801; average loan was $2,526. For part-time students, average financial aid package was $10,000.

**Students without need:** 57 full-time freshmen who did not demonstrate need for aid received scholarships/grants; average award was $14,522. No-need awards available for academics, art, athletics, minority status, music/drama, religious affiliation, state/district residency.

**Scholarships offered:** *Merit:* Academic scholarships: $4,000-$16,000; for first time students based on ACT/SAT and GPA. *Athletic:* 13 full-time freshmen received athletic scholarships; average amount $5,154.

**Additional info:** Transfer students are not awarded the same amount of academic scholarship.

### FINANCIAL AID PROCEDURES

**Forms required:** FAFSA.

**Dates and Deadlines:** Priority date 3/1; no closing date. Applicants notified on a rolling basis starting 3/4.

**Transfers:** No deadline. Applicants notified on a rolling basis starting 3/15; must reply within 2 week(s) of notification. Filing deadline for Ohio financial aid is October 1st.

## CONTACT

Jared Sponseller, Director of Student Financial Services
800 Martinsburg Road, Mount Vernon, OH 43050
(740) 392-6868 ext. 4520

## Muskingum University
New Concord, Ohio
www.muskingum.edu                    Federal Code: 003084

**4-year private** university and liberal arts college in small town, affiliated with Presbyterian Church (USA).

**Enrollment:** 1,580 undergrads, 12% part-time. 360 full-time freshmen.

**Selectivity:** Admits 50 to 75% of applicants.

### BASIC COSTS (2015-2016)

**Tuition and fees:** $26,082.

**Per-credit charge:** $550.

**Room and board:** $10,190.

**Additional info:** Tuition/fee waivers available for minority students.

### FINANCIAL AID PICTURE

**Students with need:** Need-based aid available for full-time and part-time students.

**Students without need:** No-need awards available for academics, alumni affiliation, art, leadership, minority status, music/drama, religious affiliation, state/district residency.

**Additional info:** Scholarship priority date February 1.

### FINANCIAL AID PROCEDURES

**Forms required:** FAFSA.

**Dates and Deadlines:** Priority date 3/1; no closing date. Applicants notified on a rolling basis starting 3/1; must reply by 5/1 or within 2 week(s) of notification.

**Transfers:** No deadline. Applicants notified on a rolling basis starting 3/1; must reply by 8/15 or within 2 week(s) of notification.

### CONTACT

Jeff Zellers, Vice President of Enrollment
163 Stormont Street, New Concord, OH 43762-1199
(740) 826-8139

## North Central State College
Mansfield, Ohio
www.ncstatecollege.edu                    Federal Code: 005313

**2-year public** community and technical college in small city.

**Enrollment:** 1,974 undergrads, 67% part-time. 261 full-time freshmen.

**Selectivity:** Open admission; but selective for some programs.

### BASIC COSTS (2015-2016)

**Tuition and fees:** $4,488; out-of-state residents $8,976.

**Per-credit charge:** $126; out-of-state residents $251.

### FINANCIAL AID PICTURE

**Students with need:** Need-based aid available for full-time and part-time students.

**Students without need:** This college awards aid only to students with need.

### FINANCIAL AID PROCEDURES

**Forms required:** FAFSA.

**Dates and Deadlines:** Priority date 4/1; no closing date. Applicants notified on a rolling basis starting 5/30; must reply within 1 week(s) of notification.

### CONTACT

James Phinney, Assistant Dean of Financial Aid
2441 Kenwood Circle, PO Box 698, Mansfield, OH 44901-0698
(419) 755-4899

## Northwest State Community College
Archbold, Ohio
www.northweststate.edu          Federal Code: 008677

**2-year public** community and technical college in small town.
**Enrollment:** 1,314 undergrads, 64% part-time. 143 full-time freshmen.
**Selectivity:** Open admission; but selective for some programs.

**BASIC COSTS (2015-2016)**
**Tuition and fees:** $4,780; out-of-state residents $9,310.
**Per-credit charge:** $157; out-of-state residents $308.

**FINANCIAL AID PICTURE (2014-2015)**
**Students with need:** 52% of average financial aid package awarded as scholarships/grants, 48% awarded as loans/jobs. Need-based aid available for part-time students.
**Students without need:** No-need awards available for academics.

**FINANCIAL AID PROCEDURES**
**Forms required:** FAFSA, institutional form.
**Dates and Deadlines:** Priority date 6/1; no closing date. Applicants notified on a rolling basis starting 4/1.
**Transfers:** No deadline. Applicants notified on a rolling basis starting 2/1.

**CONTACT**
Amber Yocom, Director of Financial Aid
22600 State Route 34, Archbold, OH 43502-9517
(419) 267-1333

## Notre Dame College
Cleveland, Ohio
www.notredamecollege.edu          Federal Code: 003085

**4-year private** nursing and liberal arts college in large town, affiliated with Roman Catholic Church.
**Enrollment:** 1,792 undergrads.

**BASIC COSTS (2015-2016)**
**Tuition and fees:** $27,520.
**Per-credit charge:** $535.
**Room and board:** $9,180.

**FINANCIAL AID PICTURE**
**Students with need:** Need-based aid available for full-time students.
**Students without need:** No-need awards available for academics, athletics, state/district residency.
**Scholarships offered:** Merit Scholarships; $2,500-$7,500; based on GPA and ACT or SAT scores. Presidential Scholarships; $3,000 awarded in addition to Merit Scholarships; based on 3.9 GPA and 27 ACT or 1210 SAT (exclusive of Writing).

**FINANCIAL AID PROCEDURES**
**Forms required:** FAFSA.
**Dates and Deadlines:** Closing date 5/1. Applicants notified on a rolling basis starting 1/1; must reply within 2 week(s) of notification.
**Transfers:** No deadline. Applicants notified on a rolling basis.

**CONTACT**
Mary McCrystal, Director of Student Financial Assistance
4545 College Road, Cleveland, OH 44121-4293
(216) 373-5263

## Oberlin College
Oberlin, Ohio          Federal Code: 003086
www.oberlin.edu          CSS Code: 1587

**4-year private** music nord liberal arts college in small town.
**Enrollment:** 2,912 undergrads, 1% part-time. 775 full-time freshmen.

**Selectivity:** Admits less than 50% of applicants. GED not accepted.

**BASIC COSTS (2015-2016)**
**Tuition and fees:** $50,594.
**Per-credit charge:** $2,040.
**Room and board:** $13,630.

**FINANCIAL AID PICTURE (2015-2016)**
**Students with need:** Out of 460 full-time freshmen who applied for aid, 388 were judged to have need. Of these, 388 received aid, and 388 had their full need met. Average financial aid package met 100% of need; average scholarship/grant was $33,033; average loan was $3,154. For part-time students, average financial aid package was $29,068.
**Students without need:** 280 full-time freshmen who did not demonstrate need for aid received scholarships/grants; average award was $13,425. No-need awards available for academics, music/drama.
**Scholarships offered:** Bonner Scholarship: based on community service. John Frederick Oberlin Scholarship: based on academic merit. Stern Scholarship: based on excellence in sciences. Stamps Leadership Scholarship: based on academic merit and leadership roles. Dean's Scholarship: available to Conservatory of Music students.

**FINANCIAL AID PROCEDURES**
**Forms required:** FAFSA, CSS PROFILE, institutional form.
**Dates and Deadlines:** Closing date 2/1. Applicants notified by 4/1; must reply by 5/1 or within 2 week(s) of notification.
**Transfers:** Closing date 3/1. Applicants notified by 5/15; must reply within 2 week(s) of notification. Limited scholarship funding available for transfer students.

**CONTACT**
Robert Reddy, Director of Financial Aid
Carnegie Building, 101 North Professor Street, Oberlin, OH 44074-1075
(440) 775-8142

## Ohio Business College: Sandusky
Sandusky, Ohio
www.ohiobusinesscollege.edu          Federal Code: 021585

**2-year for-profit** business college in small city.
**Enrollment:** 265 undergrads, 36% part-time. 26 full-time freshmen.
**Selectivity:** Open admission.

**BASIC COSTS (2015-2016)**
**Additional info:** Certificate programs: $3,255-$12,375, books and supplies $561-$3,240. Associate programs: $21,620-$25,380, books and supplies $5,820-$6,775.

**FINANCIAL AID PICTURE**
**Students with need:** Need-based aid available for full-time and part-time students.

**FINANCIAL AID PROCEDURES**
**Forms required:** FAFSA.

**CONTACT**
Gerilyn Wilson, Lead Financial Aid Administrator
5202 Timber Commons Drive, Sandusky, OH 44870
(419) 627-8345 ext. 14

## Ohio Business College: Sheffield
Sheffield Village, Ohio
www.ohiobusinesscollege.edu          Federal Code: 021585

**2-year for-profit** branch campus and business college in small city.
**Enrollment:** 410 undergrads.
**Selectivity:** Open admission.

**BASIC COSTS (2015-2016)**

**Additional info:** Certificate programs: $3,255-$12,375, books and supplies $561-$3,240. Associate programs: $21,620-$25,380, books and supplies $5,820-$6,775.

**FINANCIAL AID PICTURE**

**Students with need:** Need-based aid available for full-time and part-time students.

**FINANCIAL AID PROCEDURES**

**Forms required:** FAFSA.

**Dates and Deadlines:** Applicants notified on a rolling basis.

**CONTACT**

Becky Booher, Director of Financial Aid

5095 Waterford Drive, Sheffield Village, OH 44055

## Ohio Christian University
Circleville, Ohio
www.ohiochristian.edu            Federal Code: 003030

**4-year private** university and Bible college in large town, affiliated with Church of Christ.

**Enrollment:** 3,306 undergrads.

**Selectivity:** Admits 50 to 75% of applicants.

**BASIC COSTS (2015-2016)**

**Tuition and fees:** $18,165.

**Per-credit charge:** $800.

**Room and board:** $7,498.

**Additional info:** Tuition/fee waivers available for minority students.

**FINANCIAL AID PICTURE**

**Students with need:** Need-based aid available for full-time and part-time students.

**Students without need:** No-need awards available for academics, alumni affiliation, religious affiliation, state/district residency.

**Additional info:** Religious affiliation tuition discount.

**FINANCIAL AID PROCEDURES**

**Forms required:** FAFSA, institutional form.

**Dates and Deadlines:** Closing date 5/7. Applicants notified on a rolling basis starting 5/1; must reply within 2 week(s) of notification.

**Transfers:** Closing date 3/1. Applicants notified on a rolling basis; must reply within 2 week(s) of notification.

**CONTACT**

Wes Brothers, Director of Financial Aid

1476 Lancaster Pike, Circleville, OH 43113

(470) 477-7757

## Ohio Dominican University
Columbus, Ohio
www.ohiodominican.edu            Federal Code: 003035

**4-year private** university and liberal arts college in very large city, affiliated with Roman Catholic Church.

**Enrollment:** 1,213 undergrads, 8% part-time. 248 full-time freshmen.

**Selectivity:** Admits over 75% of applicants.

**BASIC COSTS (2015-2016)**

**Tuition and fees:** $30,270.

**Per-credit charge:** $600.

**Room and board:** $10,600.

**FINANCIAL AID PICTURE (2014-2015)**

**Students with need:** Need-based aid available for full-time and part-time students. Work study available nights, weekends, and for part-time students.

**Students without need:** No-need awards available for academics, athletics, state/district residency.

**FINANCIAL AID PROCEDURES**

**Forms required:** FAFSA.

**Dates and Deadlines:** Priority date 4/1; no closing date. Applicants notified on a rolling basis starting 3/1; must reply within 2 week(s) of notification.

**CONTACT**

Laura Meek, Director of Financial Aid

1216 Sunbury Road, Columbus, OH 43219

(614) 251-4778

## Ohio Northern University
Ada, Ohio
www.onu.edu            Federal Code: 003089

**4-year private** university in small town, affiliated with United Methodist Church.

**Enrollment:** 1,974 undergrads, 2% part-time. 585 full-time freshmen.

**Selectivity:** Admits 50 to 75% of applicants.

**BASIC COSTS (2016-2017)**

**Tuition and fees:** $29,820.

**Per-credit charge:** $1,180.

**Room and board:** $11,050.

**Additional info:** Tuition/fee waivers available for minority students.

**FINANCIAL AID PICTURE**

**Students with need:** Need-based aid available for full-time and part-time students. Work study available nights, weekends, and for part-time students.

**Students without need:** No-need awards available for academics, alumni affiliation, art, leadership, minority status, music/drama, ROTC, state/district residency.

**Scholarships offered:** Presidential Scholarships: $17,000 - $19,000 per year; Trustee Scholarships:$16,000 - $17,000 per year; Deans Scholarships: $14,000 - $15,000 per year; Faculty Scholarships: $9,000 - $10,000 per year.

**FINANCIAL AID PROCEDURES**

**Forms required:** FAFSA.

**CONTACT**

Melanie Weaver, Director of Financial Aid

525 South Main Street, Ada, OH 45810

(419) 772-2272

## Ohio State University Agricultural Technical Institute
Wooster, Ohio
www.ati.osu.edu            Federal Code: 003090

**2-year public** agricultural and branch campus college in large town.

**Enrollment:** 722 undergrads, 9% part-time. 330 full-time freshmen.

**Selectivity:** Open admission; but selective for out-of-state students.

**BASIC COSTS (2015-2016)**

**Tuition and fees:** $7,104; out-of-state residents $24,432.

**Room and board:** $8,130.

**FINANCIAL AID PICTURE (2015-2016)**

**Students with need:** Out of 300 full-time freshmen who applied for aid, 222 were judged to have need. Of these, 218 received aid, and 17 had their full need met. Average financial aid package met 51% of need; average scholarship/grant was $4,856; average loan was $3,912. For part-time students, average financial aid package was $7,194.

**Students without need:** This college awards aid only to students with need.

## FINANCIAL AID PROCEDURES

**Forms required:** FAFSA.

**Dates and Deadlines:** Priority date 2/15; no closing date. Applicants notified by 3/15; must reply by 5/1 or within 4 week(s) of notification.

**Transfers:** Priority date 2/1. Applicants notified by 4/1; must reply within 4 week(s) of notification.

## CONTACT

Barbara LaMoreaux, Coordinator, Financial Aid
1328 Dover Road, Wooster, OH 44691

# Ohio State University: Columbus Campus

Columbus, Ohio
www.osu.edu      Federal Code: 003090

**4-year public** university in very large city.

**Enrollment:** 44,131 undergrads, 7% part-time. 7,023 full-time freshmen.

**Selectivity:** Admits less than 50% of applicants.

## BASIC COSTS (2015-2016)

**Tuition and fees:** $10,037; out-of-state residents $27,365.

**Room and board:** $11,666.

## FINANCIAL AID PICTURE (2015-2016)

**Students with need:** Out of 5,632 full-time freshmen who applied for aid, 3,398 were judged to have need. Of these, 3,381 received aid, and 982 had their full need met. Average financial aid package met 74% of need; average scholarship/grant was $11,071; average loan was $3,601. For part-time students, average financial aid package was $9,004.

**Students without need:** 2,351 full-time freshmen who did not demonstrate need for aid received scholarships/grants; average award was $7,261. No-need awards available for academics, alumni affiliation, art, athletics, job skills, leadership, minority status, music/drama, ROTC, state/district residency.

**Scholarships offered:** 73 full-time freshmen received athletic scholarships; average amount $26,746.

## FINANCIAL AID PROCEDURES

**Forms required:** FAFSA.

**Dates and Deadlines:** Priority date 2/15; no closing date. Applicants notified by 3/31; must reply by 5/1 or within 4 week(s) of notification.

**Transfers:** Priority date 2/15. Applicants notified on a rolling basis starting 4/1; must reply within 4 week(s) of notification.

## CONTACT

Director of Student Financial Aid
Student Academic Services Building, 281 West Lane Avenue, Columbus, OH 43210
(614) 292-0300

# Ohio State University: Lima Campus

Lima, Ohio
www.lima.osu.edu      Federal Code: 003090

**4-year public** university and branch campus college in small city.

**Enrollment:** 928 undergrads, 13% part-time. 335 full-time freshmen.

**Selectivity:** Open admission; but selective for out-of-state students.

## BASIC COSTS (2015-2016)

**Tuition and fees:** $7,140; out-of-state residents $24,468.

## FINANCIAL AID PICTURE (2015-2016)

**Students with need:** Out of 314 full-time freshmen who applied for aid, 238 were judged to have need. Of these, 235 received aid, and 25 had their full need met. Average financial aid package met 55% of need; average scholarship/grant was $4,708; average loan was $3,534. For part-time students, average financial aid package was $6,810.

**Students without need:** 52 full-time freshmen who did not demonstrate need for aid received scholarships/grants; average award was $1,363. No-need awards available for academics, alumni affiliation, art, athletics, job skills, leadership, minority status, music/drama, ROTC, state/district residency.

## FINANCIAL AID PROCEDURES

**Forms required:** FAFSA.

**Dates and Deadlines:** Priority date 2/15; no closing date. Applicants notified by 3/15; must reply by 5/1 or within 4 week(s) of notification.

**Transfers:** Priority date 2/15. Applicants notified on a rolling basis starting 4/1; must reply within 4 week(s) of notification.

## CONTACT

4240 Campus Drive, Lima, OH 45804-3596
(614) 292-0300

# Ohio State University: Mansfield Campus

Mansfield, Ohio
www.mansfield.ohio-state.edu      Federal Code: 003090

**4-year public** university and branch campus college in large town.

**Enrollment:** 1,115 undergrads, 12% part-time. 514 full-time freshmen.

**Selectivity:** Open admission; but selective for out-of-state students.

## BASIC COSTS (2015-2016)

**Tuition and fees:** $7,140; out-of-state residents $24,468.

**Room only:** $5,970.

## FINANCIAL AID PICTURE (2015-2016)

**Students with need:** Out of 471 full-time freshmen who applied for aid, 394 were judged to have need. Of these, 390 received aid, and 27 had their full need met. Average financial aid package met 52% of need; average scholarship/grant was $5,049; average loan was $3,828. For part-time students, average financial aid package was $7,806.

**Students without need:** 53 full-time freshmen who did not demonstrate need for aid received scholarships/grants; average award was $1,761. No-need awards available for academics, alumni affiliation, art, athletics, job skills, leadership, minority status, music/drama, ROTC, state/district residency.

## FINANCIAL AID PROCEDURES

**Forms required:** FAFSA.

**Dates and Deadlines:** Priority date 2/15; no closing date. Applicants notified by 3/15; must reply by 5/1 or within 4 week(s) of notification.

**Transfers:** Applicants notified by 4/1; must reply within 4 week(s) of notification.

## CONTACT

Ken Sigler, Director of Admissions & Financial Aid
1760 University Drive, Mansfield, OH 44906
(419) 755-4011

# Ohio State University: Marion Campus

Marion, Ohio
www.osumarion.osu.edu      Federal Code: 003090

**4-year public** university and branch campus college in large town.

**Enrollment:** 1,016 undergrads, 16% part-time. 376 full-time freshmen.

**Selectivity:** Open admission; but selective for out-of-state students.

## BASIC COSTS (2015-2016)

**Tuition and fees:** $7,140; out-of-state residents $24,468.

## FINANCIAL AID PICTURE (2015-2016)

**Students with need:** Out of 345 full-time freshmen who applied for aid, 256 were judged to have need. Of these, 253 received aid, and 21 had their

full need met. Average financial aid package met 58% of need; average scholarship/grant was $5,050; average loan was $3,578. For part-time students, average financial aid package was $7,365.

**Students without need:** 72 full-time freshmen who did not demonstrate need for aid received scholarships/grants; average award was $2,160. No-need awards available for academics, alumni affiliation, art, athletics, job skills, leadership, minority status, music/drama, ROTC, state/district residency.

## FINANCIAL AID PROCEDURES

**Forms required:** FAFSA.

**Dates and Deadlines:** Priority date 2/15; no closing date. Applicants notified by 3/15; must reply by 5/1 or within 4 week(s) of notification.

**Transfers:** Priority date 2/15. Applicants notified by 4/1; must reply within 4 week(s) of notification.

## CONTACT

1465 Mount Vernon Avenue, Marion, OH 43302
(740) 389-6786 ext. 6273

## Ohio State University: Newark Campus
Newark, Ohio
www.newark.osu.edu          Federal Code: 003090

**4-year public** university and branch campus college in large town.
**Enrollment:** 2,362 undergrads, 14% part-time. 1,201 full-time freshmen.
**Selectivity:** Open admission; but selective for out-of-state students.

## BASIC COSTS (2015-2016)
**Tuition and fees:** $7,140; out-of-state residents $24,468.
**Room only:** $6,690.

## FINANCIAL AID PICTURE (2015-2016)
**Students with need:** Out of 1,056 full-time freshmen who applied for aid, 810 were judged to have need. Of these, 794 received aid, and 68 had their full need met. Average financial aid package met 52% of need; average scholarship/grant was $4,851; average loan was $3,640. For part-time students, average financial aid package was $7,150.

**Students without need:** 23 full-time freshmen who did not demonstrate need for aid received scholarships/grants; average award was $2,174. No-need awards available for academics, alumni affiliation, art, athletics, job skills, leadership, minority status, music/drama, ROTC, state/district residency.

## FINANCIAL AID PROCEDURES
**Forms required:** FAFSA.
**Dates and Deadlines:** Priority date 2/15; no closing date. Applicants notified by 3/15; must reply by 5/1 or within 4 week(s) of notification.
**Transfers:** Priority date 2/15. Applicants notified on a rolling basis starting 4/1; must reply within 4 week(s) of notification.

## CONTACT
1179 University Drive, Newark, OH 43055

## Ohio University
Athens, Ohio
www.ohio.edu          Federal Code: 003100

**4-year public** university in large town.
**Enrollment:** 20,652 undergrads, 16% part-time. 4,411 full-time freshmen.
**Selectivity:** Admits 50 to 75% of applicants.

## BASIC COSTS (2015-2016)
**Tuition and fees:** $11,548; out-of-state residents $20,512.
**Per-credit charge:** $547; out-of-state residents $989.
**Room and board:** $10,864.

## FINANCIAL AID PICTURE (2015-2016)
**Students with need:** Out of 3,672 full-time freshmen who applied for aid, 2,750 were judged to have need. Of these, 2,750 received aid, and 861 had their full need met. Average financial aid package met 51% of need; average scholarship/grant was $6,768; average loan was $2,801. For part-time students, average financial aid package was $5,361.

**Students without need:** 341 full-time freshmen who did not demonstrate need for aid received scholarships/grants; average award was $3,848. No-need awards available for academics, art, athletics, minority status, music/drama, religious affiliation, ROTC.

**Scholarships offered:** 23 full-time freshmen received athletic scholarships; average amount $23,468.

## FINANCIAL AID PROCEDURES
**Forms required:** FAFSA.
**Dates and Deadlines:** Closing date 3/15. Applicants notified on a rolling basis starting 4/1; must reply within 3 week(s) of notification.
**Transfers:** Priority date 5/15; no deadline. Applicants notified on a rolling basis starting 5/15.

## CONTACT
Valerie Miller, Director, Student Financial Aid and Scholarships
120 Chubb Hall, Athens, OH 45701-2979
(740) 593-4141

## Ohio University: Chillicothe Campus
Chillicothe, Ohio
www.chillicothe.ohiou.edu          Federal Code: 003102

**4-year public** branch campus college in large town.
**Enrollment:** 2,236 undergrads.
**Selectivity:** Open admission; but selective for some programs.

## BASIC COSTS (2015-2016)
**Tuition and fees:** $5,048; out-of-state residents $9,530.
**Per-credit charge:** $224; out-of-state residents $416.

## FINANCIAL AID PICTURE
**Students with need:** Need-based aid available for full-time and part-time students.

## FINANCIAL AID PROCEDURES
**Forms required:** FAFSA.
**Dates and Deadlines:** Applicants notified on a rolling basis.

## CONTACT
Ashlee Diggs, Coordinator of Student Activities
101 University Drive, Chillicothe, OH 45601
(740) 774-7228

## Ohio University: Eastern Campus
St. Clairsville, Ohio
www.eastern.ohiou.edu          Federal Code: 003101

**4-year public** branch campus college in small town.
**Enrollment:** 1,010 undergrads.
**Selectivity:** Open admission; but selective for some programs.

## BASIC COSTS (2015-2016)
**Tuition and fees:** $4,806; out-of-state residents $6,652.
**Per-credit charge:** $216; out-of-state residents $305.

## FINANCIAL AID PICTURE
**Students with need:** Need-based aid available for full-time and part-time students.
**Students without need:** No-need awards available for academics, alumni affiliation, minority status.

## FINANCIAL AID PROCEDURES

**Forms required:** FAFSA.

**Dates and Deadlines:** Priority date 3/15; no closing date.

**Transfers:** Priority date 3/1; closing date 5/1.

## CONTACT

Kevin Chenoweth, Student Services Manager

45425 National Road West, St. Clairsville, OH 43950-9724

(740) 695-1720 ext. 209

# Ohio University: Lancaster Campus

Lancaster, Ohio

www.lancaster.ohiou.edu        Federal Code: 003104

**4-year public** branch campus college in large town.

**Enrollment:** 2,596 undergrads.

**Selectivity:** Open admission; but selective for some programs.

## BASIC COSTS (2015-2016)

**Tuition and fees:** $4,994; out-of-state residents $9,530.

**Per-credit charge:** $224; out-of-state residents $416.

## FINANCIAL AID PICTURE

**Students with need:** Need-based aid available for full-time and part-time students.

**Additional info:** Scholarship application deadline April 1.

## FINANCIAL AID PROCEDURES

**Forms required:** FAFSA.

**Dates and Deadlines:** Priority date 2/15; no closing date. Applicants notified on a rolling basis; must reply within 2 week(s) of notification.

## CONTACT

Pat Fox, Coordinator of Financial Aid

1570 Granville Pike, Lancaster, OH 43130

(740) 654-6711 ext. 209

# Ohio University: Southern Campus at Ironton

Ironton, Ohio

www.southern.ohiou.edu        Federal Code: 003103

**4-year public** branch campus college in large town.

**Enrollment:** 2,072 undergrads.

**Selectivity:** Open admission.

## BASIC COSTS (2015-2016)

**Tuition and fees:** $4,806; out-of-state residents $6,652.

**Per-credit charge:** $216; out-of-state residents $305.

## FINANCIAL AID PICTURE

**Students with need:** Need-based aid available for full-time and part-time students.

**Students without need:** No-need awards available for academics, state/district residency.

## FINANCIAL AID PROCEDURES

**Forms required:** FAFSA.

**Dates and Deadlines:** Priority date 3/1; closing date 3/15. Applicants notified on a rolling basis starting 4/1.

## CONTACT

Jacki Adkins, Coordinator of Financial Aid and Scholarships

1804 Liberty Avenue, Ironton, OH 45638

(740) 533-4600

# Ohio University: Zanesville Campus

Zanesville, Ohio

www.ohio.edu/zanesville        Federal Code: 003108

**4-year public** branch campus college in large town.

**Enrollment:** 1,992 undergrads.

**Selectivity:** Open admission; but selective for some programs.

## BASIC COSTS (2015-2016)

**Tuition and fees:** $4,994; out-of-state residents $9,530.

**Per-credit charge:** $224; out-of-state residents $416.

## FINANCIAL AID PICTURE

**Students with need:** Need-based aid available for full-time and part-time students.

**Students without need:** No-need awards available for academics, minority status.

## FINANCIAL AID PROCEDURES

**Forms required:** FAFSA.

**Dates and Deadlines:** Priority date 3/15; no closing date. Applicants notified on a rolling basis starting 4/15; must reply within 2 week(s) of notification.

## CONTACT

Vicki DeLucas, Financial Aid Coordinator

1425 Newark Road, Zanesville, OH 43701

(740) 588-1439

# Ohio Valley College of Technology

East Liverpool, Ohio

www.ovct.edu        Federal Code: 016261

**2-year for-profit** junior and technical college in large town.

**Enrollment:** 146 undergrads.

## BASIC COSTS (2015-2016)

**Tuition and fees:** $27,360.

## FINANCIAL AID PICTURE

**Students with need:** Need-based aid available for full-time and part-time students.

**Students without need:** This college awards aid only to students with need.

## FINANCIAL AID PROCEDURES

**Forms required:** FAFSA.

**Dates and Deadlines:** Applicants notified on a rolling basis; must reply within 6 week(s) of notification.

## CONTACT

Rebecca Steckman, Regional Financial Aid Director

15258 State Route 170, East Liverpool, OH 43920-9585

(330) 385-1070

# Ohio Wesleyan University

Delaware, Ohio

www.owu.edu        Federal Code: 003109

**4-year private** liberal arts college in large town, affiliated with United Methodist Church.

**Enrollment:** 1,668 undergrads, 1% part-time. 484 full-time freshmen.

**Selectivity:** Admits 50 to 75% of applicants.

## BASIC COSTS (2015-2016)

**Tuition and fees:** $43,230.

**Room and board:** $11,540.

**FINANCIAL AID PICTURE (2014-2015)**

**Students with need:** Out of 404 full-time freshmen who applied for aid, 344 were judged to have need. Of these, 344 received aid, and 80 had their full need met. Average financial aid package met 79% of need; average scholarship/grant was $28,970; average loan was $3,558.

**Students without need:** 134 full-time freshmen who did not demonstrate need for aid received scholarships/grants; average award was $21,788. No-need awards available for academics, alumni affiliation, art, minority status, music/drama, religious affiliation, state/district residency.

**FINANCIAL AID PROCEDURES**

**Forms required:** FAFSA.

**Dates and Deadlines:** Priority date 2/15; no closing date. Applicants notified on a rolling basis starting 2/15; must reply by 5/1 or within 2 week(s) of notification.

**Transfers:** Priority date 2/15; no deadline. Applicants notified on a rolling basis starting 2/15; must reply by 5/1 or within 2 week(s) of notification.

**CONTACT**

Kevin Paskvan, Director of Financial Aid

61 South Sandusky Street, Delaware, OH 43015-2398

(740) 368-3050

## Otterbein University
Westerville, Ohio
www.otterbein.edu                    Federal Code: 003110

**4-year private** university and liberal arts college in large town, affiliated with United Methodist Church.

**Enrollment:** 2,343 undergrads, 9% part-time. 559 full-time freshmen.

**Selectivity:** Admits 50 to 75% of applicants.

**BASIC COSTS (2016-2017)**

**Tuition and fees:** $31,624.

**Room and board:** $10,006.

**Additional info:** Tuition/fee waivers available for adults, minority students.

**FINANCIAL AID PICTURE (2014-2015)**

**Students with need:** 65% of average financial aid package awarded as scholarships/grants, 35% awarded as loans/jobs. Work study available nights, weekends, and for part-time students.

**Students without need:** No-need awards available for academics, alumni affiliation, art, leadership, minority status, music/drama, state/district residency.

**FINANCIAL AID PROCEDURES**

**Forms required:** FAFSA.

**Dates and Deadlines:** Priority date 2/15; no closing date. Applicants notified on a rolling basis starting 2/15.

**Transfers:** Transfer students must complete appropriate state grant transfer paperwork.

**CONTACT**

Thomas Yarnell, Director of Financial Aid

One Otterbein College, Westerville, OH 43081

(614) 823-1502

## Owens Community College
Toledo, Ohio
www.owens.edu                    Federal Code: 005753

**2-year public** community college in large city.

**Enrollment:** 8,218 undergrads, 60% part-time. 859 full-time freshmen.

**Selectivity:** Open admission; but selective for some programs.

**BASIC COSTS (2015-2016)**

**Tuition and fees:** $4,414; out-of-state residents $8,698.

**Per-credit charge:** $153; out-of-state residents $306.

**FINANCIAL AID PICTURE (2015-2016)**

**Students with need:** 38% of average financial aid package awarded as scholarships/grants, 62% awarded as loans/jobs. Need-based aid available for part-time students. Work study available nights, weekends, and for part-time students.

**Students without need:** No-need awards available for academics, athletics, job skills, state/district residency.

**Additional info:** Other types of financial aid available: federal family education loan program, private foundation loan (SCHELL).

**FINANCIAL AID PROCEDURES**

**Forms required:** FAFSA.

**Dates and Deadlines:** Priority date 3/31; no closing date.

**CONTACT**

Andrea Morrow, Director, Financial Aid

30335 Oregon Road, Toledo, OH 43699-1947

(567) 661-7343

## Pontifical College Josephinum
Columbus, Ohio
www.pcj.edu                    Federal Code: 003113

**4-year private** liberal arts and seminary college for men in very large city, affiliated with Roman Catholic Church.

**Enrollment:** 110 undergrads.

**BASIC COSTS (2015-2016)**

**Tuition and fees:** $21,038.

**Room and board:** $9,300.

**FINANCIAL AID PICTURE**

**Students with need:** Need-based aid available for full-time and part-time students. Work study available nights, weekends, and for part-time students.

**Students without need:** This college awards aid only to students with need.

**FINANCIAL AID PROCEDURES**

**Forms required:** FAFSA, institutional form.

**Dates and Deadlines:** Priority date 9/2; no closing date. Applicants notified on a rolling basis starting 8/15; must reply within 2 week(s) of notification.

**CONTACT**

Marky Leichtnam, Director of Financial Aid

7625 North High Street, Columbus, OH 43235-1499

(614) 985-2212

## PowerSport Institute
North Randall, Ohio
www.psi-now.com

**2-year for-profit** technical college in very large city.

**Enrollment:** 75 undergrads.

**Selectivity:** Open admission.

**BASIC COSTS (2016-2017)**

**Tuition and fees:** $27,000.

**FINANCIAL AID PICTURE (2015-2016)**

**Students with need:** Average financial aid package met 100% of need; average scholarship/grant was $2,205.

**Students without need:** No-need awards available for academics.

**FINANCIAL AID PROCEDURES**

**Forms required:** FAFSA, institutional form.

**Dates and Deadlines:** Applicants notified on a rolling basis starting 1/15.

**Transfers:** No deadline.

**CONTACT**
Robin Coleman, Director of Financial Aid
21210 Emery Road, North Randall, OH 44128
(216) 881-1700 ext. 122

## Rosedale Bible College
Irwin, Ohio
www.rosedale.edu                    Federal Code: 034253

**2-year private** Bible and junior college in rural community, affiliated with Mennonite Church.
**Enrollment:** 56 undergrads.
**Selectivity:** Open admission.

**BASIC COSTS (2015-2016)**
**Tuition and fees:** $8,311.
**Per-credit charge:** $266.
**Room and board:** $5,650.

**FINANCIAL AID PICTURE**
**Students with need:** Need-based aid available for full-time and part-time students.
**Students without need:** No-need awards available for academics, leadership, religious affiliation.

**FINANCIAL AID PROCEDURES**
**Forms required:** FAFSA, institutional form.
**Dates and Deadlines:** Applicants notified on a rolling basis.
**Transfers:** Priority date 5/1. Applicants notified on a rolling basis.

**CONTACT**
Darnell Brenneman
2270 Rosedale Road, Irwin, OH 43029
(740) 857-1311 ext. 237

## School of Advertising Art
Kettering, Ohio
www.saa.edu                    Federal Code: 017160

**2-year for-profit** graphic design art college. in small city.
**Enrollment:** 173 undergrads.

**BASIC COSTS (2016-2017)**
**Tuition and fees:** $31,311.
**Additional info:** Tuition/fee waivers available for minority students.

**FINANCIAL AID PICTURE**
**Students with need:** Need-based aid available for full-time students.
**Students without need:** No-need awards available for academics, art, leadership, minority status.

**FINANCIAL AID PROCEDURES**
**Forms required:** FAFSA.
**Dates and Deadlines:** Priority date 7/1; no closing date. Applicants notified on a rolling basis starting 4/1; must reply by 7/1 or within 1 week(s) of notification.
**Transfers:** No deadline. Applicants notified on a rolling basis starting 4/1; must reply by 7/1 or within 1 week(s) of notification.

**CONTACT**
Tracy Gardner, Financial Aid Director
1725 East David Road, Kettering, OH 45440-1612
(937) 294-0592 ext. 106

## Shawnee State University
Portsmouth, Ohio
www.shawnee.edu                    Federal Code: 009942

**4-year public** university in large town.
**Enrollment:** 3,461 undergrads, 13% part-time. 883 full-time freshmen.
**Selectivity:** Open admission; but selective for some programs.

**BASIC COSTS (2015-2016)**
**Tuition and fees:** $7,364; out-of-state residents $12,761.
**Per-credit charge:** $260; out-of-state residents $485.
**Room and board:** $9,766.

**FINANCIAL AID PICTURE**
**Students with need:** Need-based aid available for full-time and part-time students.
**Additional info:** ACT recommended for scholarship applicants.

**FINANCIAL AID PROCEDURES**
**Forms required:** FAFSA.
**Dates and Deadlines:** Priority date 2/16; no closing date. Applicants notified on a rolling basis starting 3/15; must reply within 4 week(s) of notification.

**CONTACT**
Nicole Neal, Director Financial Aid
940 Second Street, Portsmouth, OH 45662
(740) 351-4243

## Sinclair Community College
Dayton, Ohio
www.sinclair.edu                    Federal Code: 003119

**2-year public** community college in small city.
**Enrollment:** 16,275 undergrads, 64% part-time. 2,022 full-time freshmen.
**Selectivity:** Open admission; but selective for some programs.

**BASIC COSTS (2015-2016)**
**Tuition and fees:** $2,971; out-of-district residents $4,388; out-of-state residents $8,472.
**Per-credit charge:** $99; out-of-district residents $146; out-of-state residents $282.

**FINANCIAL AID PICTURE**
**Students with need:** Need-based aid available for full-time and part-time students. Work study available nights, weekends, and for part-time students.
**Students without need:** No-need awards available for academics, alumni affiliation, art, athletics, leadership, minority status, music/drama, state/district residency.

**FINANCIAL AID PROCEDURES**
**Forms required:** FAFSA.
**Dates and Deadlines:** Priority date 5/1; no closing date. Applicants notified on a rolling basis starting 4/1.
**Transfers:** No deadline. Applicants notified on a rolling basis starting 4/1.

**CONTACT**
Matthew Moore, Director, Offfice of Financial Aid and Scholarships
444 West Third Street, Dayton, OH 45402-1460
(937) 512-3000

## Southern State Community College
Hillsboro, Ohio
www.sscc.edu                    Federal Code: 012870

**2-year public** community college in small town.
**Enrollment:** 2,218 undergrads.

**Selectivity:** Open admission; but selective for some programs.

## BASIC COSTS (2015-2016)
**Tuition and fees:** $4,364; out-of-state residents $7,938.
**Per-credit charge:** $162; out-of-state residents $306.

## FINANCIAL AID PICTURE
**Students with need:** Need-based aid available for full-time and part-time students. Work study available nights.
**Students without need:** No-need awards available for academics, art, athletics, music/drama.

## FINANCIAL AID PROCEDURES
**Forms required:** FAFSA, institutional form.
**Dates and Deadlines:** Priority date 7/1; closing date 9/1. Applicants notified by 4/15; must reply within 2 week(s) of notification.
**Transfers:** No deadline.

## CONTACT
Linda Myers, Financial Aid Director
100 Hobart Drive, Hillsboro, OH 45133
(937) 393-3431 ext. 2610

# Stark State College
North Canton, Ohio
www.starkstate.edu                Federal Code: 011141

**2-year public** community college in small city.
**Enrollment:** 8,959 undergrads, 64% part-time. 891 full-time freshmen.
**Selectivity:** Open admission; but selective for some programs.

## BASIC COSTS (2015-2016)
**Tuition and fees:** $4,608; out-of-state residents $7,338.
**Per-credit charge:** $117; out-of-state residents $208.

## FINANCIAL AID PICTURE (2014-2015)
**Students with need:** 41% of average financial aid package awarded as scholarships/grants, 59% awarded as loans/jobs. Need-based aid available for part-time students. Work study available nights, weekends, and for part-time students.
**Students without need:** This college awards aid only to students with need.

## FINANCIAL AID PROCEDURES
**Forms required:** FAFSA, institutional form.
**Dates and Deadlines:** Priority date 5/1; no closing date. Applicants notified on a rolling basis starting 4/1; must reply within 4 week(s) of notification.

## CONTACT
Amy Welty, Executive Director for Financial Aid, Registration and Enrollment Operations
6200 Frank Avenue NW, North Canton, OH 44720
(330) 494-6170 ext. 4369

# Stautzenberger College
Maumee, Ohio
www.sctoday.edu                Federal Code: 004866

**2-year for-profit** technical and career college in large town.
**Enrollment:** 708 undergrads.
**Selectivity:** Open admission; but selective for some programs.

## BASIC COSTS (2015-2016)
**Tuition and fees:** $5,850; out-of-state residents $10,350.

## FINANCIAL AID PICTURE
**Students with need:** Need-based aid available for full-time and part-time students.

**Students without need:** This college awards aid only to students with need.

## FINANCIAL AID PROCEDURES
**Forms required:** FAFSA.
**Dates and Deadlines:** Applicants notified on a rolling basis.

## CONTACT
Mari Huffman, Financial Aid Director
1796 Indian Wood Circle, Maumee, OH 43537-4007
(419) 866-0261

# Stautzenberger College: Brecksville
Brecksville, Ohio
www.sctoday.edu                Federal Code: 004866

**2-year for-profit** career college in large town.
**Enrollment:** 335 undergrads.
**Selectivity:** Open admission.

## BASIC COSTS (2015-2016)
**Tuition and fees:** $11,070.

## FINANCIAL AID PICTURE
**Students with need:** Need-based aid available for full-time and part-time students.
**Students without need:** This college awards aid only to students with need.

## FINANCIAL AID PROCEDURES
**Forms required:** FAFSA.
**Dates and Deadlines:** Applicants notified on a rolling basis.
**Transfers:** No deadline. Applicants notified on a rolling basis.

## CONTACT
Mari Huffman, Director of Financial Aid
8001 Katherine Boulevard, Brecksville, OH 44141

# Terra State Community College
Fremont, Ohio
www.terra.edu                Federal Code: 008278

**2-year public** community and technical college in large town.
**Enrollment:** 2,901 undergrads.
**Selectivity:** Open admission.

## BASIC COSTS (2015-2016)
**Tuition and fees:** $4,284; out-of-state residents $8,568.
**Per-credit charge:** $133; out-of-state residents $217.

## FINANCIAL AID PICTURE
**Students with need:** Need-based aid available for full-time and part-time students.
**Students without need:** No-need awards available for academics.

## FINANCIAL AID PROCEDURES
**Forms required:** FAFSA, institutional form.
**Dates and Deadlines:** Priority date 5/1; no closing date. Applicants notified on a rolling basis starting 5/15.

## CONTACT
Christina Bratton, Director of Financial Aid
2830 Napoleon Road, Fremont, OH 43420-9600
(419) 559-2387

## Tiffin University
Tiffin, Ohio
www.tiffin.edu                    Federal Code: 003121

**4-year private** university and liberal arts college in large town.
**Enrollment:** 2,309 undergrads, 22% part-time. 475 full-time freshmen.
**Selectivity:** Admits over 75% of applicants.

### BASIC COSTS (2015-2016)
**Tuition and fees:** $22,165.
**Per-credit charge:** $738.
**Room and board:** $10,196.

### FINANCIAL AID PICTURE (2015-2016)
**Students with need:** Average financial aid package met 67% of need; average scholarship/grant was $14,690. For part-time students, average financial aid package was $6,788.
**Students without need:** No-need awards available for academics, art, athletics, leadership, music/drama, state/district residency.

### FINANCIAL AID PROCEDURES
**Forms required:** FAFSA.
**Dates and Deadlines:** Applicants notified on a rolling basis starting 2/1; must reply within 2 week(s) of notification.
**Transfers:** No deadline.

### CONTACT
Cindy Little, Director of Financial Aid
155 Miami Street, Tiffin, OH 44883
(800) 968-6446 ext. 3415

## Trumbull Business College
Warren, Ohio
www.trumbull.edu                  Federal Code: 013585

**2-year for-profit** business college in large town.
**Enrollment:** 158 undergrads.
**Selectivity:** Open admission.

### BASIC COSTS (2015-2016)
**Tuition and fees:** $11,340.
**Per-credit charge:** $252.

### FINANCIAL AID PICTURE
**Students with need:** Need-based aid available for full-time and part-time students.

### FINANCIAL AID PROCEDURES
**Forms required:** FAFSA.

### CONTACT
Florence Henning, Financial Assistance Director
3200 Ridge Road, Warren, OH 44484
(330) 369-3200 ext. 12

## Union Institute & University
Cincinnati, Ohio
www.myunion.edu                   Federal Code: 010923

**4-year private** university in very large city.
**Enrollment:** 1,027 undergrads, 46% part-time. 6 full-time freshmen.

### BASIC COSTS (2015-2016)
**Tuition and fees:** $15,144.
**Per-credit charge:** $500.

### FINANCIAL AID PICTURE
**Students with need:** Need-based aid available for full-time and part-time students.
**Students without need:** No-need awards available for academics, state/district residency.

### FINANCIAL AID PROCEDURES
**Forms required:** FAFSA.
**Dates and Deadlines:** Must reply within 4 week(s) of notification.
**Transfers:** No deadline. Applicants notified on a rolling basis.

### CONTACT
Jean Pohlman, Director, Financial Aid
440 East McMillan Street, Cincinnati, OH 45206
(800) 861-6400 ext. 1115

## University of Akron
Akron, Ohio
www.uakron.edu                    Federal Code: 003123

**4-year public** university in small city.
**Enrollment:** 17,176 undergrads, 15% part-time. 3,652 full-time freshmen.
**Selectivity:** Admits over 75% of applicants.

### BASIC COSTS (2015-2016)
**Tuition and fees:** $10,509; out-of-state residents $19,040.
**Per-credit charge:** $359; out-of-state residents $715.
**Room and board:** $11,322.

### FINANCIAL AID PICTURE (2014-2015)
**Students with need:** Out of 3,476 full-time freshmen who applied for aid, 2,796 were judged to have need. Of these, 2,796 received aid, and 314 had their full need met. Average financial aid package met 53% of need; average scholarship/grant was $4,915; average loan was $3,255. For part-time students, average financial aid package was $3,453.
**Students without need:** 540 full-time freshmen who did not demonstrate need for aid received scholarships/grants; average award was $4,596. No-need awards available for academics, art, athletics, leadership, music/drama, ROTC, state/district residency.
**Scholarships offered:** *Merit:* Scholarships for Excellence: $6,000 per year; based on 3.8 GPA, 30 ACT, 1320 SAT (exclusive of Writing); deadline February 1. Presidential Scholarships: $3,000 per year; based on 3.8 GPA, 27 ACT, 1200 SAT. Honors Scholarships: $1,500-$3,000 per year; based on top 10% of class, 3.5 GPA; deadline December 31. Jim and Vanita Oelschlager Leadership Award: $1,000-$17,000 per year; based on leadership and service. Academic Scholarship: $500-$1,500 per year; based on upper 30% of high school class, 21 ACT, 3.0 GPA. Akron Advantage Award: non-resident surcharge reduction of 60% or 100%; for students who meet academic criteria from 49 states outside of Ohio plus U.S. territories. *Athletic:* 6 full-time freshmen received athletic scholarships; average amount $4,473.

### FINANCIAL AID PROCEDURES
**Forms required:** FAFSA, institutional form.
**Dates and Deadlines:** Priority date 3/1; no closing date. Applicants notified on a rolling basis starting 3/15; must reply within 2 week(s) of notification.
**Transfers:** Priority date 3/1; no deadline. Applicants notified on a rolling basis starting 6/15; must reply within 2 week(s) of notification.

### CONTACT
Jennifer Harpham, Executive Director, Student Financial Aid
Simmons Hall, Akron, OH 44325-2001
(330) 972-7032

## University of Akron: Wayne College
Orrville, Ohio
www.wayne.uakron.edu    Federal Code: 003123

**2-year public** branch campus and junior college in small town.
**Enrollment:** 2,604 undergrads.
**Selectivity:** Open admission.

**BASIC COSTS (2015-2016)**
**Tuition and fees:** $6,116; out-of-state residents $13,542.
**Per-credit charge:** $248; out-of-state residents $526.

**FINANCIAL AID PICTURE**
**Students with need:** Need-based aid available for full-time and part-time students. Work study available nights, weekends, and for part-time students.
**Students without need:** No-need awards available for academics, art, athletics, leadership, minority status, music/drama, state/district residency.
**Additional info:** All financial aid processed through University of Akron.

**FINANCIAL AID PROCEDURES**
**Forms required:** FAFSA, institutional form.
**Dates and Deadlines:** Closing date 3/15. Applicants notified on a rolling basis starting 4/15.

**CONTACT**
Theresa Rabbitts, Financial Aid Counselor
1901 Smucker Road, Orrville, OH 44667-9758
(330) 684-8900

## University of Cincinnati
Cincinnati, Ohio
www.uc.edu    Federal Code: 003125

**4-year public** university in large city.
**Enrollment:** 24,111 undergrads, 13% part-time. 4,394 full-time freshmen.
**Selectivity:** Admits over 75% of applicants.

**BASIC COSTS (2015-2016)**
**Tuition and fees:** $11,000; out-of-state residents $26,334.
**Per-credit charge:** $389; out-of-state residents $1,028.
**Room and board:** $10,750.

**FINANCIAL AID PICTURE (2015-2016)**
**Students with need:** Out of 3,706 full-time freshmen who applied for aid, 2,694 were judged to have need. Of these, 2,546 received aid, and 216 had their full need met. Average financial aid package met 48% of need; average scholarship/grant was $6,894; average loan was $3,718. For part-time students, average financial aid package was $7,234.
**Students without need:** 780 full-time freshmen who did not demonstrate need for aid received scholarships/grants; average award was $5,504. No-need awards available for academics, alumni affiliation, art, athletics, leadership, minority status, music/drama, ROTC, state/district residency.
**Scholarships offered:** 35 full-time freshmen received athletic scholarships; average amount $14,128.

**FINANCIAL AID PROCEDURES**
**Forms required:** FAFSA.
**Dates and Deadlines:** Applicants notified on a rolling basis starting 3/15; must reply within 2 week(s) of notification.

**CONTACT**
Randy Ulses, Director of Financial Aid
PO Box 210091, Cincinnati, OH 45221-0091
(513) 556-1000

## University of Cincinnati: Blue Ash College
Cincinnati, Ohio
www.rwc.uc.edu    Federal Code: 003125

**2-year public** branch campus college in large city.
**Enrollment:** 4,790 undergrads.
**Selectivity:** Open admission; but selective for some programs.

**BASIC COSTS (2015-2016)**
**Tuition and fees:** $6,024; out-of-state residents $14,808.
**Per-credit charge:** $251; out-of-state residents $617.

**FINANCIAL AID PICTURE**
**Students with need:** Need-based aid available for full-time and part-time students.
**Students without need:** This college awards aid only to students with need.
**Scholarships offered:** Dean's scholarships: $1,500; based on 2.5 GPA, tech prep program participation, 2-page essay; 10 available. Cincinnatus Scholarship Competition: $1,500 to full tuition, room, board and books; must have 26 ACT or be in top 5% of high school class to qualify.
**Additional info:** All financial aid applications and awards administered through main campus.

**FINANCIAL AID PROCEDURES**
**Forms required:** FAFSA.
**Dates and Deadlines:** Priority date 3/15; no closing date. Applicants notified on a rolling basis starting 3/15; must reply within 2 week(s) of notification.

**CONTACT**
Chris Powers, Director of Enrollment Management
9555 Plainfield Road, Cincinnati, OH 45236-1096
(513) 745-5740

## University of Cincinnati: Clermont College
Batavia, Ohio
www.ucclermont.edu    Federal Code: 003125

**2-year public** branch campus college in small town.
**Enrollment:** 2,590 undergrads, 36% part-time. 512 full-time freshmen.
**Selectivity:** Open admission; but selective for some programs.

**BASIC COSTS (2015-2016)**
**Tuition and fees:** $5,316; out-of-state residents $12,550.
**Per-credit charge:** $222; out-of-state residents $523.

**FINANCIAL AID PICTURE**
**Students with need:** Need-based aid available for full-time and part-time students. Work study available nights, weekends, and for part-time students.
**Students without need:** No-need awards available for academics, leadership, minority status, state/district residency.
**Additional info:** All financial aid applications and awards administered through Uptown campus except in-house loans and scholarships.

**FINANCIAL AID PROCEDURES**
**Forms required:** FAFSA.
**Dates and Deadlines:** Applicants notified on a rolling basis.
**Transfers:** No deadline. Applicants notified on a rolling basis starting 5/1.

**CONTACT**
Wanda Poling, University Services Associate I
4200 Clermont College Drive, Batavia, OH 45103
(513) 732-5202

## University of Dayton
Dayton, Ohio
www.udayton.edu                    Federal Code: 003127

**4-year private** university in small city, affiliated with Roman Catholic Church.
**Enrollment:** 8,556 undergrads, 4% part-time. 2,138 full-time freshmen.
**Selectivity:** Admits 50 to 75% of applicants.

**BASIC COSTS (2015-2016)**
**Tuition and fees:** $39,090.
**Room and board:** $12,190.
**Additional info:** Tuition/fee waivers available for adults, minority students.

**FINANCIAL AID PICTURE (2014-2015)**
**Students with need:** Out of 1,880 full-time freshmen who applied for aid, 1,359 were judged to have need. Of these, 1,359 received aid, and 265 had their full need met. Average financial aid package met 76% of need; average scholarship/grant was $23,014; average loan was $3,387. For part-time students, average financial aid package was $12,533.
**Students without need:** 650 full-time freshmen who did not demonstrate need for aid received scholarships/grants; average award was $13,664. No-need awards available for academics, alumni affiliation, art, athletics, job skills, leadership, minority status, music/drama, religious affiliation, ROTC, state/district residency.
**Scholarships offered: Merit:** Merit Scholarships: $1,000 to full tuition; based on GPA, ACT/SAT, service and leadership. Visual arts awards: amounts vary; based on student portfolios. Chaminade Scholarships: $2,500; for students accepted to Chaminade Scholars Program. National Merit Scholarships: $1,000 to $2,000; available to all students who are selected by the National Merit Scholarship Corporation and select UD as their first choice. Army ROTC awards: supplements U.S. Army ROTC awards with scholarship incentives. **Athletic:** 39 full-time freshmen received athletic scholarships; average amount $25,068.
**Additional info:** Guaranteed net-tuition for up to eight semesters of study. Students who visit campus and file the FAFSA prior to March 1st of their senior year in high school are eligible to receive up to $1,000 per year toward their textbooks.

**FINANCIAL AID PROCEDURES**
**Forms required:** FAFSA.
**Dates and Deadlines:** Priority date 3/1; no closing date. Applicants notified on a rolling basis starting 3/15; must reply within 2 week(s) of notification.
**Transfers:** Priority date 6/1; no deadline. Applicants notified on a rolling basis starting 3/15; must reply within 2 week(s) of notification. Students must submit FAFSA prior to October 1 each year for consideration for state funds.

**CONTACT**
Kathy McEuen Harmon, Dean of Admission and Financial Aid
300 College Park, Dayton, OH 45469-1310
(800) 837-7433

## University of Findlay
Findlay, Ohio
www.findlay.edu                    Federal Code: 003045

**4-year private** university and health science college in small city, affiliated with Church of God.
**Enrollment:** 2,882 undergrads, 7% part-time. 714 full-time freshmen.
**Selectivity:** Admits over 75% of applicants.

**BASIC COSTS (2015-2016)**
**Tuition and fees:** $31,508.
**Per-credit charge:** $678.
**Room and board:** $9,442.

**FINANCIAL AID PICTURE (2014-2015)**
**Students with need:** Out of 672 full-time freshmen who applied for aid, 538 were judged to have need. Of these, 538 received aid, and 107 had

their full need met. Average financial aid package met 82% of need; average scholarship/grant was $20,654; average loan was $3,248.
**Students without need:** 176 full-time freshmen who did not demonstrate need for aid received scholarships/grants; average award was $17,874. No-need awards available for academics, alumni affiliation, athletics, music/drama, state/district residency.
**Scholarships offered: Merit:** Full tuition available to select valedictorian/salutatorians. Automatic academic awards available based on GPA, test scores. **Athletic:** 80 full-time freshmen received athletic scholarships; average amount $11,021.

**FINANCIAL AID PROCEDURES**
**Forms required:** FAFSA.
**Dates and Deadlines:** Priority date 8/1; closing date 9/1. Applicants notified on a rolling basis starting 3/1; must reply within 2 week(s) of notification.
**Transfers:** No deadline.

**CONTACT**
Edward Recker, Director of Financial Aid
1000 North Main Street, Findlay, OH 45840-3653
(419) 434-4791

## University of Mount Union
Alliance, Ohio
www.mountunion.edu                 Federal Code: 003083

**4-year private** university in large town, affiliated with United Methodist Church.
**Enrollment:** 2,061 undergrads, 1% part-time. 682 full-time freshmen.
**Selectivity:** Admits over 75% of applicants.

**BASIC COSTS (2015-2016)**
**Tuition and fees:** $28,550.
**Room and board:** $9,540.
**Additional info:** Tuition/fee waivers available for minority students.

**FINANCIAL AID PICTURE (2014-2015)**
**Students with need:** Out of 626 full-time freshmen who applied for aid, 551 were judged to have need. Of these, 551 received aid, and 67 had their full need met. Average financial aid package met 78% of need; average scholarship/grant was $17,016; average loan was $5,827. For part-time students, average financial aid package was $15,452.
**Students without need:** 104 full-time freshmen who did not demonstrate need for aid received scholarships/grants; average award was $11,658. No-need awards available for academics, alumni affiliation, art, job skills, leadership, minority status, music/drama, religious affiliation, ROTC, state/district residency.

**FINANCIAL AID PROCEDURES**
**Forms required:** FAFSA.
**Dates and Deadlines:** Applicants notified on a rolling basis starting 3/15; must reply within 4 week(s) of notification.
**Transfers:** No deadline. Applicants notified on a rolling basis; must reply within 4 week(s) of notification.

**CONTACT**
Emily Mattison, Director of Student Financial Services
1972 Clark Avenue, Alliance, OH 44601-3993
(330) 823-2674

## University of Northwestern Ohio
Lima, Ohio
www.unoh.edu                       Federal Code: 004861

**2-year private** business and technical college in large town.
**Enrollment:** 3,628 full-time undergrads.

**BASIC COSTS (2015-2016)**

**Additional info:** College of Applied Technologies: $11,800; College of Business, Health Professions, and Occupational Professions: $12,300. Books, supplies, fees range depending on program level and course of study. All costs are subject to change. Tuition/fee waivers available for minority students.

**FINANCIAL AID PICTURE**

**Students with need:** Need-based aid available for full-time and part-time students. Work study available nights.

**Students without need:** No-need awards available for academics, job skills, minority status.

**FINANCIAL AID PROCEDURES**

**Forms required:** FAFSA.

**Dates and Deadlines:** Priority date 4/1; no closing date. Applicants notified on a rolling basis starting 4/30; must reply within 2 week(s) of notification.

**Transfers:** No deadline. Applicants notified on a rolling basis.

**CONTACT**

Wendell Schick, Director of Financial Aid
1441 North Cable Road, Lima, OH 45805
(419) 227-3141

## University of Rio Grande
Rio Grande, Ohio
www.rio.edu
Federal Code: 003116

**4-year private** community and liberal arts college in rural community.
**Enrollment:** 1,165 undergrads, 21% part-time. 264 full-time freshmen.
**Selectivity:** Open admission; but selective for some programs.

**BASIC COSTS (2015-2016)**

**Tuition and fees:** $23,860.
**Per-credit charge:** $970.
**Room and board:** $9,920.

**FINANCIAL AID PICTURE (2015-2016)**

**Students with need:** Out of 253 full-time freshmen who applied for aid, 253 were judged to have need. Of these, 238 received aid, and 170 had their full need met. Average financial aid package met 81% of need; average scholarship/grant was $3,248; average loan was $268. For part-time students, average financial aid package was $5,210.

**Students without need:** No-need awards available for academics, alumni affiliation, athletics, leadership, music/drama, state/district residency.

**Scholarships offered:** 208 full-time freshmen received athletic scholarships; average amount $3,303.

**FINANCIAL AID PROCEDURES**

**Forms required:** FAFSA.

**CONTACT**

Meghann Fraley, Financial Aid Director
218 North College Avenue, Rio Grande, OH 45674
(740) 245-7218

## University of Toledo
Toledo, Ohio
www.utoledo.edu
Federal Code: 003131

**4-year public** university in large city.
**Enrollment:** 14,990 undergrads, 16% part-time. 3,317 full-time freshmen.
**Selectivity:** Open admission; but selective for some programs and for out-of-state students.

**BASIC COSTS (2015-2016)**

**Tuition and fees:** $9,560; out-of-state residents $18,898.

**Per-credit charge:** $385; out-of-state residents $774.
**Room and board:** $11,494.

**FINANCIAL AID PICTURE (2015-2016)**

**Students with need:** Out of 3,004 full-time freshmen who applied for aid, 2,385 were judged to have need. Of these, 2,377 received aid, and 381 had their full need met. Average financial aid package met 63% of need; average scholarship/grant was $9,708; average loan was $3,498. For part-time students, average financial aid package was $7,406.

**Students without need:** 809 full-time freshmen who did not demonstrate need for aid received scholarships/grants; average award was $6,380. No-need awards available for academics, alumni affiliation, art, athletics, leadership, music/drama, ROTC, state/district residency.

**Scholarships offered:** 37 full-time freshmen received athletic scholarships; average amount $22,673.

**Additional info:** March priority date for federal aid. Students encouraged to apply as early as December for priority consideration for institutional aid.

**FINANCIAL AID PROCEDURES**

**Forms required:** FAFSA.

**Dates and Deadlines:** Priority date 3/1; no closing date. Applicants notified on a rolling basis starting 3/1; must reply within 8 week(s) of notification.

**Transfers:** Priority date 3/1.

**CONTACT**

Stephen Schissler, AVP Financial Aid & EnrollServ
2801 West Bancroft Street, Toledo, OH 43606-3390
(419) 530-8700

## Urbana University
Urbana, Ohio
www.urbana.edu
Federal Code: 003133

**4-year private** university in large town.
**Enrollment:** 787 undergrads.

**BASIC COSTS (2015-2016)**

**Tuition and fees:** $22,012.
**Per-credit charge:** $450.
**Room and board:** $8,938.

**FINANCIAL AID PICTURE**

**Students with need:** Need-based aid available for full-time and part-time students. Work study available nights, weekends, and for part-time students.

**Students without need:** No-need awards available for academics, alumni affiliation, athletics, music/drama.

**FINANCIAL AID PROCEDURES**

**Forms required:** FAFSA.

**Dates and Deadlines:** Priority date 4/1; closing date 8/15. Applicants notified on a rolling basis starting 3/1; must reply within 4 week(s) of notification.

**Transfers:** No deadline. Applicants notified on a rolling basis starting 3/1; must reply within 4 week(s) of notification.

**CONTACT**

Samuel Selvage, Director of Financial Aid
579 College Way, Urbana, OH 43078
(937) 772-9251

## Ursuline College
Pepper Pike, Ohio
www.ursuline.edu
Federal Code: 003134

**4-year private** liberal arts college for women in small town, affiliated with Roman Catholic Church.
**Enrollment:** 641 undergrads, 31% part-time. 114 full-time freshmen.

**Selectivity:** Admits over 75% of applicants.

**BASIC COSTS (2015-2016)**
**Tuition and fees:** $28,580.
**Per-credit charge:** $941.
**Room and board:** $9,490.

**FINANCIAL AID PICTURE (2015-2016)**
**Students with need:** Out of 111 full-time freshmen who applied for aid, 103 were judged to have need. Of these, 103 received aid, and 22 had their full need met. Average financial aid package met 84% of need; average scholarship/grant was $22,271; average loan was $4,407. For part-time students, average financial aid package was $8,530.
**Students without need:** 10 full-time freshmen who did not demonstrate need for aid received scholarships/grants; average award was $8,650. No-need awards available for academics, alumni affiliation, art, athletics, minority status.
**Scholarships offered:** *Merit:* Ursuline Scholarship: $5,000 to $7,500. Ursuline Award: $1,500 to $4,500. Presidential Scholarship: $11,000. Dean's Scholarship: $9,500. Unlimited number available for each; all renewable. *Athletic:* 19 full-time freshmen received athletic scholarships; average amount $11,688.

**FINANCIAL AID PROCEDURES**
**Forms required:** FAFSA.
**Dates and Deadlines:** Priority date 2/15; no closing date. Applicants notified on a rolling basis starting 2/15; must reply within 3 week(s) of notification.
**Transfers:** No deadline. Applicants notified on a rolling basis; must reply within 4 week(s) of notification.

**CONTACT**
Mary Lynn Perri, Director of Financial Aid
2550 Lander Road, Pepper Pike, OH 44124-4398
(440) 684-6114

## Virginia Marti College of Art and Design
Lakewood, Ohio
www.vmcad.edu                    Federal Code: 012896

**2-year for-profit** visual arts and business college in large city.
**Enrollment:** 160 undergrads.

**BASIC COSTS (2015-2016)**
**Additional info:** Bachelor degree programs: range from $21,060 -$21,450; Associates programs: $9,600. Books, supplies, fees range depending on program level and course of study. All costs are subject to change.

**FINANCIAL AID PICTURE**
**Students with need:** Need-based aid available for full-time students.
**Students without need:** This college awards aid only to students with need.

**FINANCIAL AID PROCEDURES**
**Forms required:** FAFSA.
**Dates and Deadlines:** Applicants notified on a rolling basis.

**CONTACT**
Martha Snodgrass, Financial Aid Officer
11724 Detroit Avenue, Lakewood, OH 44107

## Walsh University
North Canton, Ohio
www.walsh.edu                    Federal Code: 003135

**4-year private** university and liberal arts college in small city, affiliated with Roman Catholic Church.
**Enrollment:** 2,157 undergrads, 13% part-time. 439 full-time freshmen.

**Selectivity:** Admits over 75% of applicants.

**BASIC COSTS (2015-2016)**
**Tuition and fees:** $27,710.
**Per-credit charge:** $875.
**Room and board:** $9,920.

**FINANCIAL AID PICTURE (2015-2016)**
**Students with need:** Out of 406 full-time freshmen who applied for aid, 382 were judged to have need. Of these, 382 received aid, and 110 had their full need met. Average financial aid package met 66% of need; average scholarship/grant was $4,505; average loan was $3,472. For part-time students, average financial aid package was $6,612.
**Students without need:** 57 full-time freshmen who did not demonstrate need for aid received scholarships/grants; average award was $11,964. No-need awards available for academics, alumni affiliation, athletics, music/drama, religious affiliation, state/district residency.
**Scholarships offered:** 80 full-time freshmen received athletic scholarships; average amount $6,823.

**FINANCIAL AID PROCEDURES**
**Forms required:** FAFSA.
**Dates and Deadlines:** Priority date 5/1; no closing date. Applicants notified on a rolling basis starting 2/15.
**Transfers:** No deadline. Applicants notified on a rolling basis starting 3/15.

**CONTACT**
Holly Van Gilder, Financial Aid Director
2020 East Maple Street, North Canton, OH 44720-3396
(330) 490-7146

## Washington State Community College
Marietta, Ohio
www.wscc.edu                    Federal Code: 010453

**2-year public** community college in large town.
**Enrollment:** 1,136 undergrads.
**Selectivity:** Open admission; but selective for some programs.

**BASIC COSTS (2015-2016)**
**Tuition and fees:** $4,410; out-of-state residents $8,580.
**Per-credit charge:** $139; out-of-state residents $278.

**FINANCIAL AID PICTURE (2014-2015)**
**Students with need:** 40% of average financial aid package awarded as scholarships/grants, 60% awarded as loans/jobs.

**FINANCIAL AID PROCEDURES**
**Forms required:** FAFSA, institutional form.
**Dates and Deadlines:** Applicants notified on a rolling basis starting 5/15; must reply within 2 week(s) of notification.

**CONTACT**
Shannon Venezia, Director of Financial Aid
710 Colegate Drive, Marietta, OH 45750
(740) 568-1908

## Wilberforce University
Wilberforce, Ohio                Federal Code: 003141
www.wilberforce.edu              CSS Code: 1906

**4-year private** university and liberal arts college in rural community, affiliated with African Methodist Episcopal Church.
**Enrollment:** 594 undergrads. 195 full-time freshmen.
**Selectivity:** Admits less than 50% of applicants.

**BASIC COSTS (2015-2016)**
**Tuition and fees:** $13,250.

**Per-credit charge:** $501.

**Room and board:** $6,456.

**Additional info:** Tuition/fee waivers available for minority students.

**FINANCIAL AID PICTURE (2015-2016)**

**Students with need:** Out of 195 full-time freshmen who applied for aid, 193 were judged to have need. Of these, 193 received aid, and 13 had their full need met. Average financial aid package met 79% of need; average scholarship/grant was $13,282; average loan was $2,784. For part-time students, average financial aid package was $9,708.

**Students without need:** 1 full-time freshmen who did not demonstrate need for aid received scholarships/grants; average award was $3,000. No-need awards available for academics, alumni affiliation.

**Scholarships offered:** We encouraged prospective students to fill out their FAFSA as early as possible.

**FINANCIAL AID PROCEDURES**

**Forms required:** FAFSA, CSS PROFILE, institutional form.

**Dates and Deadlines:** Priority date 3/15; closing date 6/30. Applicants notified on a rolling basis starting 3/15; must reply within 2 week(s) of notification.

**CONTACT**

Terry Jeffries, VP - Enrollment Mgt, Financial Aid

1055 North Bickett Road, Wilberforce, OH 45384-1001

(937) 708-5727

## Wilmington College

Wilmington, Ohio

www.wilmington.edu                 Federal Code: 003142

**4-year private** agricultural and liberal arts college in large town, affiliated with Society of Friends (Quaker).

**Enrollment:** 1,200 undergrads.

**BASIC COSTS (2015-2016)**

**Tuition and fees:** $24,500.

**Room and board:** $9,500.

**FINANCIAL AID PICTURE**

**Students with need:** Need-based aid available for full-time and part-time students.

**Students without need:** No-need awards available for academics, alumni affiliation, religious affiliation, state/district residency.

**FINANCIAL AID PROCEDURES**

**Forms required:** FAFSA.

**Dates and Deadlines:** Priority date 3/31; closing date 6/1. Applicants notified on a rolling basis starting 3/1; must reply by 5/1 or within 2 week(s) of notification.

**CONTACT**

Cheryl Louallen, Director of Financial Aid

Box 1325 Pyle Center, Wilmington, OH 45177

(937) 382-6661 ext. 249

## Wittenberg University

Springfield, Ohio

www.wittenberg.edu                 Federal Code: 003143

**4-year private** liberal arts college in small city, affiliated with Evangelical Lutheran Church in America.

**Enrollment:** 1,706 undergrads. 493 full-time freshmen.

**Selectivity:** Admits over 75% of applicants.

**BASIC COSTS (2016-2017)**

**Tuition and fees:** $38,090.

**Per-credit charge:** $1,241.

**Room and board:** $10,126.

**Additional info:** Tuition/fee waivers available for adults.

**FINANCIAL AID PICTURE (2015-2016)**

**Students with need:** Out of 466 full-time freshmen who applied for aid, 411 were judged to have need. Of these, 411 received aid, and 185 had their full need met. Average financial aid package met 67% of need; average scholarship/grant was $27,177; average loan was $5,212. For part-time students, average financial aid package was $5,401.

**Students without need:** 82 full-time freshmen who did not demonstrate need for aid received scholarships/grants; average award was $19,984. No-need awards available for academics, alumni affiliation, art, minority status, music/drama, religious affiliation, state/district residency.

**Scholarships offered:** University Scholar Award: half tuition; renewable; based on academic achievement and other qualities. Broadwell Chinn Scholarship: half tuition; renewable; based on minority status, academic achievement, and other qualities.

**Additional info:** Auditions required of applicants for music, theater, and dance scholarships. Portfolio required of applicants for art scholarships.

**FINANCIAL AID PROCEDURES**

**Forms required:** FAFSA.

**Dates and Deadlines:** Priority date 3/1; no closing date. Applicants notified on a rolling basis starting 3/1; must reply by 5/1 or within 2 week(s) of notification.

**Transfers:** Priority date 5/15; no deadline. Applicants notified on a rolling basis starting 3/15; must reply by 5/15 or within 2 week(s) of notification. No special restrictions for transfer students. Transfer students receive free books.

**CONTACT**

Jonathan Green, Executive Director of Financial Aid

Ward Street and North Wittenberg, Springfield, OH 45501-0720

(937) 327-7321

## Wright State University

Dayton, Ohio

www.wright.edu                 Federal Code: 003078

**4-year public** university in small city.

**Enrollment:** 12,040 undergrads, 18% part-time. 2,244 full-time freshmen.

**Selectivity:** Admits over 75% of applicants.

**BASIC COSTS (2015-2016)**

**Tuition and fees:** $8,730; out-of-state residents $17,098.

**Per-credit charge:** $394; out-of-state residents $779.

**Room and board:** $9,304.

**FINANCIAL AID PICTURE (2015-2016)**

**Students with need:** 38% of average financial aid package awarded as scholarships/grants, 62% awarded as loans/jobs. Need-based aid available for part-time students. Work study available nights, weekends, and for part-time students.

**Students without need:** No-need awards available for academics, alumni affiliation, art, athletics, leadership, minority status, music/drama, ROTC, state/district residency.

**FINANCIAL AID PROCEDURES**

**Forms required:** FAFSA.

**Dates and Deadlines:** Priority date 3/1; no closing date. Applicants notified on a rolling basis starting 3/15.

**CONTACT**

Amy Barnhart, Assistant Vice President of Enrollment Management and Director of Financial Aid

3640 Colonel Glenn Highway, 108 SU, Dayton, OH 45435

(937) 775-4000

## Wright State University: Lake Campus
Celina, Ohio
http://lake.wright.edu/　　　　　Federal Code: 003078

**2-year public** branch campus college in large town.
**Enrollment:** 992 undergrads, 18% part-time. 249 full-time freshmen.
**Selectivity:** Open admission; but selective for some programs.

**BASIC COSTS (2015-2016)**
**Tuition and fees:** $5,842; out-of-state residents $14,022.
**Per-credit charge:** $265; out-of-state residents $650.

**FINANCIAL AID PICTURE**
**Students with need:** Need-based aid available for full-time and part-time students. Work study available nights, weekends, and for part-time students.
**Students without need:** No-need awards available for academics, alumni affiliation, art, athletics, leadership, minority status, music/drama, ROTC, state/district residency.

**FINANCIAL AID PROCEDURES**
**Forms required:** FAFSA.
**Dates and Deadlines:** Priority date 3/1; no closing date. Applicants notified on a rolling basis starting 3/15.

**CONTACT**
Amy Barnhart, Assistant Vice President of Enrollment Management and Director of Financial Aid
7600 Lake Campus Drive, State Route 703, Celina, OH 45822-2952
(937) 775-4000

## Xavier University
Cincinnati, Ohio
www.xavier.edu　　　　　Federal Code: 003144

**4-year private** university in large city, affiliated with Roman Catholic Church.
**Enrollment:** 4,461 undergrads, 5% part-time. 1,149 full-time freshmen.
**Selectivity:** Admits 50 to 75% of applicants.

**BASIC COSTS (2015-2016)**
**Tuition and fees:** $35,080.
**Per-credit charge:** $654.
**Room and board:** $11,380.

**FINANCIAL AID PICTURE (2014-2015)**
**Students with need:** For part-time students, average financial aid package was $7,642.
**Students without need:** No-need awards available for academics, alumni affiliation, art, athletics, leadership, music/drama, religious affiliation.
**Scholarships offered:** Saint Francis Xavier Scholarship: full tuition; based on leadership, talent and highest academic achievement; competitive; 10 awarded. Community Engaged Fellowship: $22,000; competitive; 10 awarded. Chancellor Scholarship: $21,000; based on leadership, talent, and highest academic achievement; number of awards varies. Trustee Scholarship: $20,000; based on academic achievement; number of awards varies. Presidential Scholarship: $19,000; based on academic achievement; number of awards varies. Deans Award: $18,000; based on academic achievement; number of awards varies. Miguel Pro Scholarship: amount varies; awarded annually to students committed to promoting diversity and demonstrate leadership; number varies. Francis X. Weninger Scholarship: amount varies; awarded annually to students who promote diversity in our society and who demonstrate leadership; number varies.

**FINANCIAL AID PROCEDURES**
**Forms required:** FAFSA.
**Dates and Deadlines:** Priority date 2/15; no closing date. Applicants notified on a rolling basis starting 3/1; must reply by 5/1.
**Transfers:** No deadline. Applicants notified on a rolling basis starting 3/1.

**CONTACT**
Aaron Meis, Dean of Undergraduate Admission & Financial Aid
3800 Victory Parkway, Cincinnati, OH 45207-5311
(513) 745-3142

## Youngstown State University
Youngstown, Ohio
www.ysu.edu　　　　　Federal Code: 003145

**4-year public** university in small city.
**Enrollment:** 10,255 undergrads, 17% part-time. 1,661 full-time freshmen.
**Selectivity:** Admits 50 to 75% of applicants.

**BASIC COSTS (2015-2016)**
**Tuition and fees:** $8,327; out-of-state residents $14,327.
**Per-credit charge:** $270; out-of-district residents $280; out-of-state residents $520.
**Room and board:** $8,990.

**FINANCIAL AID PICTURE (2014-2015)**
**Students with need:** Out of 1,513 full-time freshmen who applied for aid, 1,298 were judged to have need. Of these, 1,297 received aid, and 144 had their full need met. Average financial aid package met 33% of need; average scholarship/grant was $5,050; average loan was $3,013. For part-time students, average financial aid package was $7,105.
**Students without need:** 216 full-time freshmen who did not demonstrate need for aid received scholarships/grants; average award was $3,233. No-need awards available for academics, alumni affiliation, athletics, ROTC, state/district residency.
**Scholarships offered:** 101 full-time freshmen received athletic scholarships; average amount $10,502.

**FINANCIAL AID PROCEDURES**
**Forms required:** FAFSA, institutional form.
**Dates and Deadlines:** Priority date 2/15; no closing date. Applicants notified on a rolling basis starting 4/1; must reply within 2 week(s) of notification.

**CONTACT**
Elaine Ruse, Director of Financial Aid and Scholarships
One University Plaza, Youngstown, OH 44555-0001
(330) 941-3505

## Zane State College
Zanesville, Ohio
www.zanestate.edu　　　　　Federal Code: 008133

**2-year public** community and technical college in large town.
**Enrollment:** 2,607 undergrads.
**Selectivity:** Open admission; but selective for some programs.

**BASIC COSTS (2015-2016)**
**Tuition and fees:** $4,560; out-of-state residents $9,120.
**Per-credit charge:** $152; out-of-state residents $304.

**FINANCIAL AID PICTURE**
**Students with need:** Need-based aid available for full-time and part-time students.

**FINANCIAL AID PROCEDURES**
**Forms required:** FAFSA.
**Dates and Deadlines:** Priority date 5/1; closing date 6/30. Must reply by 9/1.

**CONTACT**
Amanda Reisinger, Financial Aid Director
1555 Newark Road, Zanesville, OH 43701-2626
(740) 454-2501 ext. 1275

# Oklahoma

## Bacone College

Muskogee, Oklahoma
www.bacone.edu                    Federal Code: 003147

**4-year private** liberal arts college in large town, affiliated with American Baptist Churches in the USA.
**Enrollment:** 968 undergrads.

**BASIC COSTS (2015-2016)**
**Tuition and fees:** $14,500.
**Room and board:** $10,000.

**FINANCIAL AID PICTURE**
**Students with need:** Need-based aid available for full-time and part-time students. Work study available nights, weekends, and for part-time students.
**Students without need:** This college awards aid only to students with need.

**FINANCIAL AID PROCEDURES**
**Forms required:** FAFSA.
**Dates and Deadlines:** Priority date 3/31; no closing date. Applicants notified on a rolling basis starting 4/1; must reply within 2 week(s) of notification.
**Transfers:** No deadline. Applicants notified on a rolling basis.

**CONTACT**
Misty Oleson, Director of Financial Aid
2299 Old Bacone Road, Muskogee, OK 74403
(918) 781-7340

## Cameron University

Lawton, Oklahoma
www.cameron.edu                   Federal Code: 003150

**4-year public** university in small city.
**Enrollment:** 4,361 undergrads, 27% part-time. 720 full-time freshmen.
**Selectivity:** Admits over 75% of applicants.

**BASIC COSTS (2015-2016)**
**Tuition and fees:** $5,580; out-of-state residents $14,190.
**Per-credit charge:** $132; out-of-state residents $419.
**Room and board:** $4,888.

**FINANCIAL AID PICTURE (2014-2015)**
**Students with need:** Out of 595 full-time freshmen who applied for aid, 486 were judged to have need. Of these, 467 received aid, and 75 had their full need met. Average financial aid package met 56% of need; average scholarship/grant was $6,005; average loan was $2,895. For part-time students, average financial aid package was $8,914.
**Students without need:** 32 full-time freshmen who did not demonstrate need for aid received scholarships/grants; average award was $1,727. No-need awards available for academics, alumni affiliation, art, athletics, leadership, minority status, music/drama, ROTC, state/district residency.
**Scholarships offered:** 27 full-time freshmen received athletic scholarships; average amount $4,178.

**FINANCIAL AID PROCEDURES**
**Dates and Deadlines:** Priority date 4/1; no closing date. Applicants notified on a rolling basis starting 4/1; must reply within 2 week(s) of notification.
**Transfers:** Priority date 6/1; no deadline. Applicants notified on a rolling basis starting 6/1. Academic transcripts required.

**CONTACT**
Director of Financial Assistance
2800 West Gore Boulevard, Lawton, OK 73505-6377
(580) 581-2293

## Carl Albert State College

Poteau, Oklahoma
www.carlalbert.edu                Federal Code: 003176

**2-year public** community and junior college in large town.
**Enrollment:** 2,856 undergrads.
**Selectivity:** Open admission; but selective for some programs.

**BASIC COSTS (2015-2016)**
**Tuition and fees:** $3,151; out-of-state residents $6,519.
**Per-credit charge:** $73; out-of-state residents $185.
**Room and board:** $4,222.
**Additional info:** Tuition/fee waivers available for minority students.

**FINANCIAL AID PICTURE**
**Students with need:** Need-based aid available for full-time and part-time students. Work study available nights.
**Students without need:** This college awards aid only to students with need.

**FINANCIAL AID PROCEDURES**
**Forms required:** FAFSA, institutional form.
**Dates and Deadlines:** Applicants notified on a rolling basis.

**CONTACT**
Robin Benson, Director of Financial Aid
1507 South McKenna, Poteau, OK 74953-5208
(918) 647-1343

## Connors State College

Warner, Oklahoma
www.connorsstate.edu              Federal Code: 003153

**2-year public** community and junior college in rural community.
**Enrollment:** 2,600 undergrads.
**Selectivity:** Open admission; but selective for some programs.

**BASIC COSTS (2015-2016)**
**Tuition and fees:** $3,798; out-of-state residents $8,500.
**Per-credit charge:** $84; out-of-state residents $241.
**Room and board:** $5,690.

**FINANCIAL AID PICTURE**
**Students with need:** Need-based aid available for full-time and part-time students.
**Students without need:** No-need awards available for academics, alumni affiliation, athletics, leadership, state/district residency.

**FINANCIAL AID PROCEDURES**
**Forms required:** FAFSA, institutional form.
**Dates and Deadlines:** Closing date 3/1. Applicants notified on a rolling basis starting 4/1; must reply within 2 week(s) of notification.

**CONTACT**
Jennifer Watkins, Director of Financial Aid
RR 1, Box 1000, Warner, OK 74469-9700
(918) 463-6220 ext. 6220

## East Central University

Ada, Oklahoma
www.ecok.edu                      Federal Code: 003154

**4-year public** university in large town.
**Enrollment:** 3,637 undergrads.

**BASIC COSTS (2015-2016)**
**Tuition and fees:** $5,824; out-of-state residents $14,132.

**Per-credit charge:** $150; out-of-state residents $427.
**Room and board:** $5,350.

## FINANCIAL AID PICTURE

**Students with need:** Need-based aid available for full-time and part-time students. Work study available nights, weekends, and for part-time students.
**Students without need:** No-need awards available for academics, athletics.

## FINANCIAL AID PROCEDURES

**Forms required:** FAFSA.
**Dates and Deadlines:** Closing date 3/1. Applicants notified on a rolling basis starting 4/15; must reply within 2 week(s) of notification.

## CONTACT

Becky Isaacs, Director of Financial Aid
PMBJ8, 1100 East 14th Street, Ada, OK 74820
(580) 559-5243

# Eastern Oklahoma State College

Wilburton, Oklahoma
www.eosc.edu                    Federal Code: 003155

**2-year public** community college in rural community.
**Enrollment:** 1,317 undergrads, 32% part-time. 947 full-time freshmen.
**Selectivity:** Open admission; but selective for some programs.

## BASIC COSTS (2015-2016)

**Tuition and fees:** $3,947; out-of-state residents $7,564.
**Per-credit charge:** $95.44; out-of-state residents $216.
**Room and board:** $5,370.
**Additional info:** Tuition/fee waivers available for adults.

## FINANCIAL AID PICTURE (2014-2015)

**Students with need:** Out of 899 full-time freshmen who applied for aid, 660 were judged to have need. Of these, 642 received aid, and 436 had their full need met. Average financial aid package met 55% of need; average scholarship/grant was $2,124; average loan was $3,290. For part-time students, average financial aid package was $3,510.
**Students without need:** This college awards aid only to students with need.
**Scholarships offered:** 63 full-time freshmen received athletic scholarships; average amount $2,093.

## FINANCIAL AID PROCEDURES

**Forms required:** FAFSA, institutional form.
**Dates and Deadlines:** Priority date 3/1; closing date 6/30. Applicants notified on a rolling basis starting 5/1; must reply within 2 week(s) of notification.
**Transfers:** Priority date 3/1; no deadline. Applicants notified on a rolling basis starting 5/1; must reply within 2 week(s) of notification.

## CONTACT

Mimi Kelley, Director of Financial Aid
1301 West Main Street, Wilburton, OK 74578-4999
(918) 465-1771

# Langston University

Langston, Oklahoma
www.langston.edu                Federal Code: 003157

**4-year public** university and liberal arts college in rural community.
**Enrollment:** 2,159 undergrads, 2% part-time. 692 full-time freshmen.
**Selectivity:** Admits 50 to 75% of applicants.

## BASIC COSTS (2015-2016)

**Tuition and fees:** $5,043; out-of-state residents $12,372.
**Per-credit charge:** $116; out-of-state residents $360.
**Room and board:** $8,982.

**Additional info:** Tuition at time of enrollment locked for 4 years.

## FINANCIAL AID PICTURE (2015-2016)

**Students with need:** Out of 608 full-time freshmen who applied for aid, 560 were judged to have need. Of these, 560 received aid. Average financial aid package met 60% of need; average scholarship/grant was $13,413; average loan was $11,550. For part-time students, average financial aid package was $1,310.
**Students without need:** This college awards aid only to students with need.

## FINANCIAL AID PROCEDURES

**Forms required:** FAFSA, state aid form.
**Dates and Deadlines:** Priority date 3/1; closing date 5/1. Applicants notified on a rolling basis starting 7/15; must reply within 2 week(s) of notification.

## CONTACT

Shelia McGill, Financial Aid Director
Box 728, Langston, OK 73050
(405) 466-3282

# Mid-America Christian University

Oklahoma City, Oklahoma
www.macu.edu                    Federal Code: 006942

**4-year private** university and liberal arts college in very large city, affiliated with Church of God.
**Enrollment:** 2,688 undergrads.
**Selectivity:** Open admission.

## BASIC COSTS (2015-2016)

**Tuition and fees:** $16,798.
**Room and board:** $7,380.

## FINANCIAL AID PICTURE

**Students with need:** Need-based aid available for full-time and part-time students.
**Students without need:** No-need awards available for academics, athletics, leadership, minority status, music/drama, religious affiliation.

## FINANCIAL AID PROCEDURES

**Forms required:** FAFSA.
**Dates and Deadlines:** Priority date 5/1; no closing date. Applicants notified on a rolling basis starting 5/1.

## CONTACT

Christina Padilla, Director of Student Financial Services
3500 SW 119th Street, Oklahoma City, OK 73170
(405) 692-3182

# Northeastern Oklahoma Agricultural and Mechanical College

Miami, Oklahoma
www.neo.edu                     Federal Code: 316000

**2-year public** community and junior college in large town.
**Enrollment:** 2,029 undergrads.
**Selectivity:** Open admission.

## BASIC COSTS (2015-2016)

**Tuition and fees:** $3,833; out-of-state residents $9,173.
**Per-credit charge:** $78; out-of-state residents $256.
**Room and board:** $5,768.

## FINANCIAL AID PICTURE

**Students with need:** Need-based aid available for full-time and part-time students. Work study available nights, weekends, and for part-time students.

**Students without need:** No-need awards available for academics, athletics, leadership, music/drama, state/district residency.

## FINANCIAL AID PROCEDURES

**Forms required:** FAFSA.

**Dates and Deadlines:** Priority date 4/1; no closing date. Applicants notified on a rolling basis starting 4/1; must reply by 8/30 or within 2 week(s) of notification.

**Transfers:** No deadline. Applicants notified on a rolling basis starting 4/1; must reply within 2 week(s) of notification.

## CONTACT

David Fisher, Director of Financial Aid
200 I Street Northeast, Miami, OK 74354-6497
(918) 540-6235

# Northeastern State University
Tahlequah, Oklahoma
www.nsuok.edu                     Federal Code: 003161

**4-year public** university in large town.

**Enrollment:** 7,036 undergrads, 29% part-time. 795 full-time freshmen.

**Selectivity:** Admits over 75% of applicants.

## BASIC COSTS (2015-2016)

**Tuition and fees:** $5,547; out-of-state residents $12,897.

**Per-credit charge:** $148; out-of-state residents $393.

**Room and board:** $6,490.

**Additional info:** Tuition/fee waivers available for adults, minority students.

## FINANCIAL AID PICTURE (2015-2016)

**Students with need:** Out of 735 full-time freshmen who applied for aid, 497 were judged to have need. Of these, 497 received aid, and 427 had their full need met. Average financial aid package met 98% of need; average scholarship/grant was $7,507; average loan was $4,993. For part-time students, average financial aid package was $11,285.

**Students without need:** 58 full-time freshmen who did not demonstrate need for aid received scholarships/grants; average award was $3,179. No-need awards available for academics, alumni affiliation, art, athletics, leadership, minority status, music/drama, religious affiliation, ROTC, state/district residency.

**Scholarships offered:** *Merit:* Academic scholarships: up to $10,092 a year for 4 years. Baccalaureate scholarships: up to $11,092. Collegiate scholarships: up to $4,150. Freshmen scholarships: up to $2,350. Green and White scholarships: up to $3,050. Honors scholarship: up to $9,092. Leadership scholarships: up to $9,101. Community Service scholarship: up to $8,092. University scholarships: up to $3,900. Valedictorians scholarship: up to $3,300. *Athletic:* 34 full-time freshmen received athletic scholarships; average amount $4,167.

**Additional info:** Off-campus job location and development program introduced to assist students with finding off-campus employers to earn money for college expenses.

## FINANCIAL AID PROCEDURES

**Forms required:** FAFSA.

**Dates and Deadlines:** Priority date 3/1; no closing date. Applicants notified on a rolling basis starting 3/1.

**Transfers:** Priority date 12/15; no deadline. State grant deadline is April 15.

## CONTACT

Teri Cochran, Director of Student Financial Services
600 North Grand Avenue, Tahlequah, OK 74464-2399
(918) 444-3456

# Northern Oklahoma College
Tonkawa, Oklahoma
www.noc.edu                      Federal Code: 003162

**2-year public** community college in small town.

**Enrollment:** 5,023 undergrads.

**Selectivity:** Open admission; but selective for out-of-state students.

## BASIC COSTS (2015-2016)

**Tuition and fees:** $3,249; out-of-state residents $8,409.

**Per-credit charge:** $78; out-of-state residents $250.

**Room and board:** $5,770.

**Additional info:** Tuition/fee waivers available for adults, minority students, unemployed or children of unemployed.

## FINANCIAL AID PICTURE

**Students with need:** Need-based aid available for full-time and part-time students.

**Students without need:** No-need awards available for academics, art, athletics, music/drama.

## FINANCIAL AID PROCEDURES

**Forms required:** FAFSA, institutional form.

**Dates and Deadlines:** Priority date 6/1; no closing date. Applicants notified on a rolling basis starting 4/1.

## CONTACT

Linda Brown, Director of Financial Aid
Box 310, Tonkawa, OK 74653-0310
(580) 628-6240

# Northwestern Oklahoma State University
Alva, Oklahoma
www.nwosu.edu                    Federal Code: 003163

**4-year public** university and teachers college in small town.

**Enrollment:** 1,799 undergrads.

**Selectivity:** Admits 50 to 75% of applicants.

## BASIC COSTS (2015-2016)

**Tuition and fees:** $5,821; out-of-state residents $12,271.

**Per-credit charge:** $172; out-of-state residents $387.

**Room and board:** $4,530.

## FINANCIAL AID PICTURE

**Students with need:** Need-based aid available for full-time and part-time students. Work study available nights, weekends, and for part-time students.

**Students without need:** No-need awards available for academics, alumni affiliation, art, athletics, leadership, music/drama.

## FINANCIAL AID PROCEDURES

**Forms required:** FAFSA.

**Dates and Deadlines:** Applicants notified on a rolling basis starting 5/1; must reply by 8/15.

## CONTACT

Rita Castleberry, Director of Financial Aid
709 Oklahoma Boulevard, Alva, OK 73717-2799
(580) 327-8542

# Oklahoma Baptist University
Shawnee, Oklahoma
www.okbu.edu                     Federal Code: 003164

**4-year private** university and liberal arts college in large town, affiliated with Southern Baptist Convention.

**Enrollment:** 1,847 undergrads, 4% part-time. 483 full-time freshmen.
**Selectivity:** Admits over 75% of applicants.

## BASIC COSTS (2016-2017)
**Tuition and fees:** $25,310.
**Room and board:** $7,010.
**Additional info:** Tuition/fee waivers available for minority students.

## FINANCIAL AID PICTURE (2014-2015)
**Students with need:** Out of 429 full-time freshmen who applied for aid, 378 were judged to have need. Of these, 378 received aid, and 125 had their full need met. Average financial aid package met 81% of need; average scholarship/grant was $8,557; average loan was $3,145. For part-time students, average financial aid package was $12,946.
**Students without need:** 103 full-time freshmen who did not demonstrate need for aid received scholarships/grants; average award was $8,973. No-need awards available for academics, art, athletics, leadership, minority status, music/drama, religious affiliation, ROTC.
**Scholarships offered:** 107 full-time freshmen received athletic scholarships; average amount $9,469.

## FINANCIAL AID PROCEDURES
**Forms required:** FAFSA.
**Dates and Deadlines:** Priority date 3/1; no closing date. Applicants notified on a rolling basis starting 2/1; must reply within 2 week(s) of notification.
**Transfers:** No deadline. Applicants notified on a rolling basis starting 2/1. Transfers receive 1 semester of financial aid on probationary basis. During probation semester, must meet SAP requirements in order to receive financial aid in subsequent semesters.

## CONTACT
Jonna Raney, Director of Student Financial Services
500 West University, Shawnee, OK 74804
(405) 585-5120

# Oklahoma Christian University
Oklahoma City, Oklahoma
www.oc.edu                          Federal Code: 003165

**4-year private** university in very large city, affiliated with Church of Christ.
**Enrollment:** 1,956 undergrads, 3% part-time. 452 full-time freshmen.
**Selectivity:** Admits 50 to 75% of applicants.

## BASIC COSTS (2015-2016)
**Tuition and fees:** $19,890.
**Per-credit charge:** $828.
**Room and board:** $7,030.

## FINANCIAL AID PICTURE (2014-2015)
**Students with need:** Out of 376 full-time freshmen who applied for aid, 305 were judged to have need. Of these, 302 received aid, and 137 had their full need met. Average financial aid package met 70% of need; average scholarship/grant was $3,261; average loan was $2,306. For part-time students, average financial aid package was $11,838.
**Students without need:** 139 full-time freshmen who did not demonstrate need for aid received scholarships/grants; average award was $6,279. No-need awards available for academics, art, athletics, music/drama, religious affiliation, ROTC.
**Scholarships offered:** 41 full-time freshmen received athletic scholarships; average amount $5,351.

## FINANCIAL AID PROCEDURES
**Forms required:** FAFSA.
**Dates and Deadlines:** Priority date 4/1; closing date 8/31. Applicants notified on a rolling basis starting 1/15; must reply within 4 week(s) of notification.
**Transfers:** Applicants notified on a rolling basis starting 3/1; must reply within 4 week(s) of notification. Will award based on unofficial transcript. Must have all official transcripts before awards will be disbursed.

## CONTACT
Clint LaRue, Director, Student Financial Services
Box 11000, Oklahoma City, OK 73136-1100
(405) 425-5190

# Oklahoma City Community College
Oklahoma City, Oklahoma
www.occc.edu                          Federal Code: 010391

**2-year public** community and technical college in very large city.
**Enrollment:** 13,000 undergrads.
**Selectivity:** Open admission; but selective for some programs.

## BASIC COSTS (2015-2016)
**Tuition and fees:** $3,391; out-of-state residents $8,425.
**Per-credit charge:** $88; out-of-state residents $255.
**Additional info:** Tuition/fee waivers available for adults.

## FINANCIAL AID PICTURE
**Students with need:** Need-based aid available for full-time and part-time students. Work study available nights, weekends, and for part-time students.
**Students without need:** No-need awards available for academics, alumni affiliation, art, leadership, music/drama, state/district residency.

## FINANCIAL AID PROCEDURES
**Forms required:** FAFSA.
**Dates and Deadlines:** Priority date 4/15; no closing date. Applicants notified on a rolling basis starting 2/15.
**Transfers:** Applicants notified on a rolling basis. Those with previous degrees or over 90 credit hours attempted must appeal for eligibility for federally funded financial assistance.

## CONTACT
Sonya Gore, Director of Financial Aid
7777 South May Avenue, Oklahoma City, OK 73159
(405) 682-7525

# Oklahoma City University
Oklahoma City, Oklahoma
www.okcu.edu                          Federal Code: 003166

**4-year private** university and liberal arts college in very large city, affiliated with United Methodist Church.
**Enrollment:** 1,783 undergrads, 9% part-time. 400 full-time freshmen.
**Selectivity:** Admits 50 to 75% of applicants.

## BASIC COSTS (2015-2016)
**Tuition and fees:** $30,726.
**Per-credit charge:** $925.
**Room and board:** $9,682.
**Additional info:** Tuition/fee waivers available for adults.

## FINANCIAL AID PICTURE (2015-2016)
**Students with need:** Average financial aid package met 65% of need; average scholarship/grant was $17,717; average loan was $3,381. For part-time students, average financial aid package was $8,019.
**Students without need:** No-need awards available for academics, alumni affiliation, art, athletics, leadership, music/drama, religious affiliation, ROTC, state/district residency.

## FINANCIAL AID PROCEDURES
**Forms required:** FAFSA.
**Dates and Deadlines:** Priority date 3/1; no closing date. Applicants notified on a rolling basis starting 3/1; must reply within 2 week(s) of notification.
**Transfers:** Applicants notified on a rolling basis; must reply within 2 week(s) of notification. Financial aid transcripts required from all previously attended institutions whether or not financial aid was received.

## CONTACT

Denise Flis, Senior Director, Student Financial Services
2501 North Blackwelder Avenue, Oklahoma City, OK 73106-1493
(405) 208-5211

## Oklahoma Panhandle State University
Goodwell, Oklahoma
www.opsu.edu                    Federal Code: 003174

**4-year public** university and liberal arts college in rural community.
**Enrollment:** 1,261 undergrads.

### BASIC COSTS (2015-2016)
**Tuition and fees:** $7,421; out-of-state residents $12,980.
**Per-credit charge:** $146; out-of-state residents $331.
**Room and board:** $4,708.
**Additional info:** Tuition at time of enrollment locked for 4 years.

### FINANCIAL AID PICTURE (2014-2015)
**Students with need:** 97% of average financial aid package awarded as scholarships/grants, 3% awarded as loans/jobs. Need-based aid available for part-time students.
**Students without need:** This college awards aid only to students with need.

### FINANCIAL AID PROCEDURES
**Forms required:** FAFSA, institutional form.
**Dates and Deadlines:** Priority date 3/15; no closing date.
**Transfers:** No deadline. Applicants notified on a rolling basis.

### CONTACT
Lori Ferguson, Director of Financial Aid
OPSU Admissions, Goodwell, OK 73939-0430
(580) 349-1566

## Oklahoma State University
Stillwater, Oklahoma
go.okstate.edu                  Federal Code: 003170

**4-year public** university in large town.
**Enrollment:** 20,752 undergrads, 12% part-time. 3,865 full-time freshmen.
**Selectivity:** Admits over 75% of applicants.

### BASIC COSTS (2015-2016)
**Tuition and fees:** $7,778; out-of-state residents $20,978.
**Per-credit charge:** $154; out-of-state residents $594.
**Room and board:** $7,450.

### FINANCIAL AID PICTURE (2014-2015)
**Students with need:** Out of 3,104 full-time freshmen who applied for aid, 2,153 were judged to have need. Of these, 2,089 received aid, and 338 had their full need met. Average financial aid package met 78% of need; average scholarship/grant was $7,337; average loan was $3,255. For part-time students, average financial aid package was $9,687.
**Students without need:** 1,102 full-time freshmen who did not demonstrate need for aid received scholarships/grants; average award was $6,348. No-need awards available for academics, alumni affiliation, art, athletics, leadership, minority status, music/drama, ROTC, state/district residency.
**Scholarships offered:** 63 full-time freshmen received athletic scholarships; average amount $12,522.
**Additional info:** In-state students who file the FAFSA and who have financial need may receive additional funding through the Academic Opportunity Scholarship program.

### FINANCIAL AID PROCEDURES
**Forms required:** FAFSA.

**Dates and Deadlines:** Priority date 2/1; no closing date. Applicants notified on a rolling basis starting 4/1; must reply by 5/1 or within 2 week(s) of notification.

### CONTACT
Chad Blew, Director of Scholarships & Financial Aid
219 Student Union, Stillwater, OK 74078
(405) 744-6604

## Oklahoma State University Institute of Technology: Okmulgee
Okmulgee, Oklahoma
www.osuit.edu                   Federal Code: 003172

**2-year public** branch campus and technical college in large town.
**Enrollment:** 2,167 undergrads, 22% part-time. 480 full-time freshmen.
**Selectivity:** Open admission; but selective for some programs.

### BASIC COSTS (2015-2016)
**Tuition and fees:** $4,860; out-of-state residents $10,470.
**Per-credit charge:** $124; out-of-state residents $311.
**Room and board:** $6,008.

### FINANCIAL AID PICTURE (2015-2016)
**Students with need:** Average financial aid package met 75% of need; average scholarship/grant was $7,145; average loan was $3,100. For part-time students, average financial aid package was $500.
**Students without need:** No-need awards available for academics, alumni affiliation, job skills, leadership, minority status, state/district residency.
**Additional info:** OSUIT Foundation Scholarship application due March 1.

### FINANCIAL AID PROCEDURES
**Forms required:** FAFSA.
**Dates and Deadlines:** Priority date 3/1; no closing date. Must reply within 4 week(s) of notification.
**Transfers:** Priority date 3/1. Applicants notified by 6/1; must reply within 4 week(s) of notification. Requirement of financial aid transcript from any institution(s) attended during transferring academic year.

### CONTACT
Diana Sanders, Financial Aid Director
1801 East Fourth Street, Okmulgee, OK 74447-3901
(918) 293-5290

## Oklahoma State University: Oklahoma City
Oklahoma City, Oklahoma
www.osuokc.edu/home             Federal Code: 009647

**2-year public** branch campus and technical college in very large city.
**Enrollment:** 5,537 undergrads, 66% part-time. 456 full-time freshmen.
**Selectivity:** Open admission; but selective for some programs.

### BASIC COSTS (2015-2016)
**Tuition and fees:** $3,634; out-of-state residents $9,922.
**Per-credit charge:** $95; out-of-state residents $305.
**Additional info:** Tuition/fee waivers available for adults, minority students.

### FINANCIAL AID PICTURE
**Students with need:** Need-based aid available for full-time and part-time students. Work study available nights, weekends, and for part-time students.
**Students without need:** This college awards aid only to students with need.

### FINANCIAL AID PROCEDURES
**Forms required:** FAFSA.

**Dates and Deadlines:** Priority date 7/19; no closing date. Applicants notified on a rolling basis starting 8/1; must reply within 2 week(s) of notification.
**Transfers:** Applicants notified on a rolling basis.

**CONTACT**
Bessie Carter, Director of Financial Aid & Scholarships
900 North Portland Avenue, Oklahoma City, OK 73107-6195
(405) 945-8646

## Oklahoma Wesleyan University
Bartlesville, Oklahoma
www.okwu.edu                           Federal Code: 003151

**4-year private** university and liberal arts college in large town, affiliated with Wesleyan Church.
**Enrollment:** 1,157 undergrads, 48% part-time. 193 full-time freshmen.
**Selectivity:** Admits 50 to 75% of applicants.

**BASIC COSTS (2015-2016)**
**Tuition and fees:** $24,108.
**Room and board:** $7,862.

**FINANCIAL AID PICTURE (2015-2016)**
**Students with need:** Out of 184 full-time freshmen who applied for aid, 162 were judged to have need. Of these, 162 received aid, and 20 had their full need met. Average financial aid package met 59% of need; average scholarship/grant was $11,588; average loan was $3,159. For part-time students, average financial aid package was $6,502.
**Students without need:** 29 full-time freshmen who did not demonstrate need for aid received scholarships/grants; average award was $6,343. No-need awards available for academics, alumni affiliation, athletics, leadership, music/drama, religious affiliation, state/district residency.
**Scholarships offered:** 36 full-time freshmen received athletic scholarships; average amount $5,572.

**FINANCIAL AID PROCEDURES**
**Forms required:** FAFSA, institutional form.
**Dates and Deadlines:** Priority date 3/1; no closing date. Applicants notified on a rolling basis starting 3/1; must reply by 5/1 or within 2 week(s) of notification.
**Transfers:** Closing date 8/1. Applicants notified on a rolling basis; must reply within 2 week(s) of notification.

**CONTACT**
Kandi Molder, Director of Student Financial Services
2201 Silver Lake Road, Bartlesville, OK 74006
(918) 335-6282

## Oral Roberts University
Tulsa, Oklahoma
www.oru.edu                            Federal Code: 003985

**4-year private** university and liberal arts college in large city, affiliated with nondenominational tradition.
**Enrollment:** 2,805 undergrads, 10% part-time. 430 full-time freshmen.
**Selectivity:** Admits less than 50% of applicants.

**BASIC COSTS (2015-2016)**
**Tuition and fees:** $24,792.
**Per-credit charge:** $998.
**Room and board:** $10,348.

**FINANCIAL AID PICTURE (2015-2016)**
**Students with need:** Average financial aid package met 91% of need; average scholarship/grant was $17,314; average loan was $7,077. For part-time students, average financial aid package was $5,163.

**Students without need:** No-need awards available for academics, alumni affiliation, art, athletics, leadership, music/drama.

**FINANCIAL AID PROCEDURES**
**Forms required:** FAFSA.
**Dates and Deadlines:** Priority date 3/15; closing date 4/19. Applicants notified on a rolling basis starting 3/15; must reply by 5/1.
**Transfers:** Priority date 3/30. Applicants notified on a rolling basis starting 4/1. Transfer applicants eligible for some scholarships.

**CONTACT**
William Womack, Director of Financial Aid
7777 South Lewis Avenue, Tulsa, OK 74171
(918) 495-6510

## Platt College: Oklahoma City Central
Oklahoma City, Oklahoma
www.plattcolleges.edu                  Federal Code: 023068

**2-year for-profit** branch campus and career college in small city.
**Enrollment:** 200 undergrads.
**Selectivity:** Open admission; but selective for some programs.

**BASIC COSTS (2015-2016)**
**Additional info:** Certificate programs: Dental Assistant $15,420; Medical Assistant $15,420. Associate programs: Practical Nursing $28,200; Nursing $36,020; Culinary Arts (Morning) $31,720. Bachelor's programs: Nursing $46,120; Hospitality and Restaurant Management $46,020.

**FINANCIAL AID PICTURE**
**Students with need:** Need-based aid available for full-time students.

**FINANCIAL AID PROCEDURES**
**Forms required:** FAFSA.

**CONTACT**
Amy Hocker, Financial Aid Director
309 South Ann Arbor, Oklahoma City, OK 73128
(405) 946-7799

## Platt College: Tulsa
Tulsa, Oklahoma
www.plattcolleges.edu                  Federal Code: 016312

**2-year for-profit** culinary school and health science college in large city.
**Enrollment:** 360 undergrads.
**Selectivity:** Open admission; but selective for some programs.

**BASIC COSTS (2015-2016)**
**Additional info:** Certificate programs: Dental Assistant $15,420; Medical Assistant $15,420; Pharmacy Technician $12,500; Pastry Arts (Morning) $22,520. Associate programs: Practical Nursing $28,200; Nursing $36,020; Culinary Arts (Morning) $31,720. Bachelor's programs: Nursing $46,120; Hospitality and Restaurant Management $46,020.

**FINANCIAL AID PICTURE**
**Students with need:** Need-based aid available for full-time and part-time students.
**Students without need:** This college awards aid only to students with need.

**FINANCIAL AID PROCEDURES**
**Forms required:** FAFSA.

**CONTACT**
Linda Bates, Director of Compliance-Financial Services
3801 South Sheridan, Tulsa, OK 74145-1132
(918) 663-9000

## Redlands Community College
El Reno, Oklahoma
www.redlandscc.edu                    Federal Code: 003156

**2-year public** community college in large town.
**Enrollment:** 2,500 undergrads.
**Selectivity:** Open admission; but selective for some programs.

**BASIC COSTS (2015-2016)**
**Tuition and fees:** $3,882; out-of-state residents $6,026.
**Per-credit charge:** $129; out-of-state residents $201.
**Room and board:** $7,468.
**Additional info:** Tuition/fee waivers available for adults.

**FINANCIAL AID PICTURE**
**Students with need:** Need-based aid available for full-time and part-time students. Work study available nights, weekends, and for part-time students.
**Students without need:** No-need awards available for academics, athletics, leadership.

**FINANCIAL AID PROCEDURES**
**Forms required:** FAFSA.
**Dates and Deadlines:** Priority date 8/1; no closing date. Applicants notified on a rolling basis starting 6/1; must reply within 6 week(s) of notification.
**Transfers:** No deadline. Applicants notified on a rolling basis; must reply within 6 week(s) of notification.

**CONTACT**
Karen Jeffers, Director of Financial Aid
1300 South Country Club Road, El Reno, OK 73036
(866) 415-6367 ext. 1442

## Rogers State University
Claremore, Oklahoma
www.rsu.edu                           Federal Code: 003168

**4-year public** university in large town.
**Enrollment:** 4,029 undergrads, 39% part-time. 657 full-time freshmen.
**Selectivity:** Admits over 75% of applicants.

**BASIC COSTS (2015-2016)**
**Tuition and fees:** $6,309; out-of-state residents $13,599.
**Per-credit charge:** $122; out-of-state residents $365.
**Room and board:** $7,705.

**FINANCIAL AID PICTURE (2015-2016)**
**Students with need:** Average financial aid package met 48% of need; average scholarship/grant was $6,437; average loan was $3,358. For part-time students, average financial aid package was $6,553.
**Students without need:** No-need awards available for academics, alumni affiliation, art, athletics, leadership, music/drama, state/district residency.

**FINANCIAL AID PROCEDURES**
**Forms required:** FAFSA.
**Dates and Deadlines:** Priority date 6/15; no closing date. Applicants notified on a rolling basis starting 4/1; must reply within 1 week(s) of notification.
**Transfers:** No deadline. Applicants notified on a rolling basis starting 4/1; must reply within 3 week(s) of notification.

**CONTACT**
Kelly Hicks, Director, Financial Aid
1701 West Will Rogers Boulevard, Claremore, OK 74017-3252
(918) 343-7553

## Rose State College
Midwest City, Oklahoma
www.rose.edu                          Federal Code: 009185

**2-year public** community college in small city.
**Enrollment:** 5,998 undergrads, 55% part-time. 923 full-time freshmen.
**Selectivity:** Open admission; but selective for some programs.

**BASIC COSTS (2015-2016)**
**Tuition and fees:** $3,375; out-of-state residents $9,752.
**Per-credit charge:** $92; out-of-state residents $304.
**Room only:** $6,000.

**FINANCIAL AID PICTURE (2014-2015)**
**Students with need:** 59% of average financial aid package awarded as scholarships/grants, 41% awarded as loans/jobs. Need-based aid available for part-time students. Work study available nights, weekends, and for part-time students.
**Students without need:** No-need awards available for academics, athletics, leadership.
**Additional info:** Ticket to Rose grant available to students from Midwest City/Choctaw high schools to cover unmet need in tuition/fees.

**FINANCIAL AID PROCEDURES**
**Forms required:** FAFSA.
**Dates and Deadlines:** Priority date 6/1; no closing date. Applicants notified on a rolling basis starting 3/1; must reply within 4 week(s) of notification.

**CONTACT**
Steven Daffer, Director of Financial Aid
6420 SE 15th Street, Midwest City, OK 73110-2799
(405) 733-7424

## St. Gregory's University
Shawnee, Oklahoma
www.stgregorys.edu                    Federal Code: 003183

**4-year private** university and liberal arts college in large town, affiliated with Roman Catholic Church.
**Enrollment:** 580 undergrads, 18% part-time. 86 full-time freshmen.
**Selectivity:** Admits 50 to 75% of applicants.

**BASIC COSTS (2015-2016)**
**Tuition and fees:** $24,480.
**Additional info:** Tuition/fee waivers available for adults.

**FINANCIAL AID PICTURE (2014-2015)**
**Students with need:** 90% of average financial aid package awarded as scholarships/grants, 10% awarded as loans/jobs. Need-based aid available for part-time students. Work study available nights, weekends, and for part-time students.
**Students without need:** No-need awards available for academics, alumni affiliation, art, athletics, job skills, leadership, music/drama, religious affiliation.
**Scholarships offered:** Leadership Scholarship; $500-$2,000. Academic Scholarship; $500-$5,100. Need-based scholarship; $500-$1,500.

**FINANCIAL AID PROCEDURES**
**Forms required:** FAFSA, institutional form.
**Dates and Deadlines:** Priority date 4/1; no closing date. Applicants notified on a rolling basis starting 2/15; must reply within 3 week(s) of notification.
**Transfers:** No deadline. Applicants notified on a rolling basis.

**CONTACT**
Marcia Cheers, Director of Financial Aid
1900 West MacArthur Drive, Shawnee, OK 74804
(405) 878-5412

# Seminole State College

Seminole, Oklahoma
www.sscok.edu                    Federal Code: 003178

**2-year public** community and junior college in small town.
**Enrollment:** 1,399 undergrads, 36% part-time. 335 full-time freshmen.
**Selectivity:** Open admission; but selective for some programs.

## BASIC COSTS (2015-2016)
**Tuition and fees:** $3,809; out-of-state residents $8,969.
**Per-credit charge:** $83; out-of-state residents $255.
**Room and board:** $7,070.

## FINANCIAL AID PICTURE
**Students with need:** Need-based aid available for full-time and part-time students.
**Students without need:** No-need awards available for academics, art, athletics, leadership, music/drama, state/district residency.

## FINANCIAL AID PROCEDURES
**Forms required:** FAFSA, institutional form.
**Dates and Deadlines:** Priority date 3/1; no closing date. Applicants notified on a rolling basis starting 3/1; must reply within 4 week(s) of notification.

## CONTACT
Melanie Rinehart, Director of Financial Assistance
PO Box 351, Seminole, OK 74818-0351
(405) 382-9247

# Southeastern Oklahoma State University

Durant, Oklahoma
www.se.edu                       Federal Code: 003179

**4-year public** liberal arts and teachers college in large town.
**Enrollment:** 3,209 undergrads, 24% part-time. 430 full-time freshmen.
**Selectivity:** Admits 50 to 75% of applicants.

## BASIC COSTS (2015-2016)
**Tuition and fees:** $6,075; out-of-state residents $14,713.
**Per-credit charge:** $184; out-of-state residents $472.
**Room and board:** $6,030.
**Additional info:** Tuition/fee waivers available for minority students.

## FINANCIAL AID PICTURE (2014-2015)
**Students with need:** Out of 418 full-time freshmen who applied for aid, 343 were judged to have need. Of these, 338 received aid, and 33 had their full need met. Average financial aid package met 50% of need; average scholarship/grant was $1,879; average loan was $1,393. For part-time students, average financial aid package was $5,953.
**Students without need:** 7 full-time freshmen who did not demonstrate need for aid received scholarships/grants; average award was $439. No-need awards available for academics, alumni affiliation, art, athletics, leadership, minority status, music/drama, state/district residency.
**Scholarships offered:** 54 full-time freshmen received athletic scholarships; average amount $2,789.

## FINANCIAL AID PROCEDURES
**Forms required:** FAFSA, institutional form.
**Dates and Deadlines:** Priority date 3/1; no closing date. Applicants notified on a rolling basis starting 4/1.

## CONTACT
Tony Lehrling, Director of Student Financial Aid
1405 North Fourth Avenue, PMB 4225, Durant, OK 74701-0607
(580) 745-2186

# Southern Nazarene University

Bethany, Oklahoma
www.snu.edu                      Federal Code: 003149

**4-year private** university and liberal arts college in large town, affiliated with Church of the Nazarene.
**Enrollment:** 1,639 undergrads, 3% part-time. 283 full-time freshmen.
**Selectivity:** Admits less than 50% of applicants.

## BASIC COSTS (2016-2017)
**Tuition and fees:** $24,468.
**Per-credit charge:** $790.
**Room and board:** $8,330.

## FINANCIAL AID PICTURE (2014-2015)
**Students with need:** 83% of average financial aid package awarded as scholarships/grants, 17% awarded as loans/jobs.
**Students without need:** No-need awards available for academics, athletics, ROTC, state/district residency.

## FINANCIAL AID PROCEDURES
**Forms required:** FAFSA, institutional form.
**Dates and Deadlines:** Priority date 3/1; no closing date. Applicants notified on a rolling basis starting 5/1; must reply within 2 week(s) of notification.

## CONTACT
Diana Lee, Director of Financial Assistance
6729 NW 39th Expressway, Bethany, OK 73008
(405) 491-6310

# Southwestern Christian University

Bethany, Oklahoma
www.swcu.edu                     Federal Code: 003180

**4-year private** university and liberal arts college in large town, affiliated with Pentecostal Holiness Church.
**Enrollment:** 713 undergrads. 126 full-time freshmen.

## BASIC COSTS (2015-2016)
**Tuition and fees:** $15,630.
**Per-credit charge:** $465.
**Room and board:** $6,200.

## FINANCIAL AID PICTURE (2014-2015)
**Students with need:** Average financial aid package met 82% of need; average scholarship/grant was $7,208; average loan was $3,321. For part-time students, average financial aid package was $17,392.
**Students without need:** 52 full-time freshmen who did not demonstrate need for aid received scholarships/grants; average award was $4,242. No-need awards available for academics, alumni affiliation, music/drama, religious affiliation, ROTC.
**Scholarships offered:** 50 full-time freshmen received athletic scholarships; average amount $5,652.

## FINANCIAL AID PROCEDURES
**Forms required:** FAFSA, institutional form.
**Dates and Deadlines:** Priority date 3/1; no closing date. Applicants notified on a rolling basis starting 4/1; must reply within 2 week(s) of notification.

## CONTACT
Kellye Johnson, Director of Financial Aid
Box 340, Bethany, OK 73008
(405) 789-7661 ext. 3456

## Southwestern Oklahoma State University

Weatherford, Oklahoma
www.swosu.edu                    Federal Code: 003181

**4-year public** university in large town.
**Enrollment:** 4,348 undergrads.

### BASIC COSTS (2015-2016)

**Tuition and fees:** $5,820; out-of-state residents $12,270.
**Per-credit charge:** $158; out-of-state residents $373.
**Room and board:** $5,220.

### FINANCIAL AID PICTURE

**Students with need:** Need-based aid available for full-time and part-time students.
**Students without need:** No-need awards available for academics, alumni affiliation, art, athletics, leadership, music/drama, state/district residency.

### FINANCIAL AID PROCEDURES

**Forms required:** FAFSA, institutional form.
**Dates and Deadlines:** Closing date 3/1. Applicants notified by 3/15.

### CONTACT

Jerome Wichert, Director of Student Financial Services
100 Campus Drive, Weatherford, OK 73096
(508) 774-3786

## Spartan College of Aeronautics and Technology

Tulsa, Oklahoma
www.spartan.edu

**4-year for-profit** technical college in large city.
**Enrollment:** 849 undergrads.

### BASIC COSTS (2015-2016)

**Tuition and fees:** $16,150.
**Additional info:** Annual cost shown is for Aviation Maintenance Technology program. Full program costs vary by program ranging from $20,060 to $73,209. Tuition at time of enrollment locked for 4 years.

### FINANCIAL AID PICTURE

**Students with need:** Need-based aid available for full-time and part-time students. Work study available nights, weekends, and for part-time students.

### FINANCIAL AID PROCEDURES

**Forms required:** FAFSA, institutional form.
**Dates and Deadlines:** Applicants notified on a rolling basis starting 2/1; must reply within 2 week(s) of notification.
**Transfers:** No deadline. Applicants notified on a rolling basis starting 2/1; must reply within 2 week(s) of notification.

### CONTACT

Christina Foster, Financial Aid Director
8820 East Pine Street, Tulsa, OK 74158-2833
(918) 836-6886

## Tulsa Community College

Tulsa, Oklahoma
www.tulsacc.edu                    Federal Code: 009763

**2-year public** community college in large city.
**Enrollment:** 14,069 undergrads, 61% part-time. 2,194 full-time freshmen.
**Selectivity:** Open admission; but selective for some programs.

### BASIC COSTS (2015-2016)

**Tuition and fees:** $3,623; out-of-state residents $9,803.

**Per-credit charge:** $91; out-of-state residents $297.
**Additional info:** Tuition/fee waivers available for minority students.

### FINANCIAL AID PICTURE (2015-2016)

**Students with need:** Average financial aid package met 70% of need; average scholarship/grant was $2,828; average loan was $1,576. For part-time students, average financial aid package was $9,297.
**Students without need:** No-need awards available for academics, art, job skills, leadership, minority status, state/district residency.

### FINANCIAL AID PROCEDURES

**Forms required:** FAFSA.
**Dates and Deadlines:** Priority date 6/1; no closing date. Applicants notified on a rolling basis starting 2/1.

### CONTACT

Karen Jeffers, Director of Financial Aid
6111 East Skelly Drive, Tulsa, OK 74135-6198
(918) 595-7155

## Tulsa Welding School

Tulsa, Oklahoma
www.weldingschool.com              Federal Code: 015733

**2-year for-profit** technical college in very large city.
**Enrollment:** 1,783 undergrads.
**Selectivity:** Open admission.

### BASIC COSTS (2015-2016)

**Additional info:** Program tuition varies from $14,300 to $38,957.

### FINANCIAL AID PICTURE (2014-2015)

**Students with need:** 42% of average financial aid package awarded as scholarships/grants, 58% awarded as loans/jobs.
**Students without need:** This college awards aid only to students with need.

### FINANCIAL AID PROCEDURES

**Forms required:** FAFSA.

### CONTACT

Teresa Franklin, Regional Financial Aid Director
2545 East 11th Street, Tulsa, OK 74104-3909
(918) 587-6789

## University of Central Oklahoma

Edmond, Oklahoma
www.uco.edu                        Federal Code: 003152

**4-year public** university in small city.
**Enrollment:** 14,788 undergrads, 29% part-time. 2,298 full-time freshmen.
**Selectivity:** Admits 50 to 75% of applicants.

### BASIC COSTS (2015-2016)

**Tuition and fees:** $6,096; out-of-state residents $14,972.
**Per-credit charge:** $172; out-of-state residents $468.
**Room and board:** $7,470.
**Additional info:** Tuition at time of enrollment locked for 4 years.

### FINANCIAL AID PICTURE (2014-2015)

**Students with need:** Average financial aid package met 62% of need; average scholarship/grant was $6,867; average loan was $3,125. For part-time students, average financial aid package was $5,301.
**Students without need:** No-need awards available for academics, alumni affiliation, art, athletics, leadership, minority status, music/drama, ROTC, state/district residency.

**FINANCIAL AID PROCEDURES**

**Forms required:** FAFSA, institutional form.

**Dates and Deadlines:** Priority date 5/31; no closing date. Applicants notified on a rolling basis.

**Transfers:** No deadline. Applicants notified on a rolling basis starting 5/1.

**CONTACT**

Susan Prater, Director of Student Financial Services

100 North University Drive, Edmond, OK 73034-0151

(405) 974-2727

## University of Oklahoma

Norman, Oklahoma

www.ou.edu                                              Federal Code: 003184

**4-year public** university in small city.

**Enrollment:** 21,525 undergrads, 13% part-time. 3,861 full-time freshmen.

**Selectivity:** Admits over 75% of applicants.

**BASIC COSTS (2015-2016)**

**Tuition and fees:** $10,090; out-of-state residents $23,476.

**Per-credit charge:** $143; out-of-state residents $589.

**Room and board:** $9,368.

**Additional info:** Tuition at time of enrollment locked for 4 years; tuition/fee waivers available for adults, minority students.

**FINANCIAL AID PICTURE (2014-2015)**

**Students with need:** Out of 2,809 full-time freshmen who applied for aid, 1,831 were judged to have need. Of these, 1,788 received aid, and 1,352 had their full need met. Average financial aid package met 76% of need; average scholarship/grant was $6,662; average loan was $3,597. For part-time students, average financial aid package was $8,943.

**Students without need:** 639 full-time freshmen who did not demonstrate need for aid received scholarships/grants; average award was $3,254. No-need awards available for academics, alumni affiliation, art, athletics, leadership, music/drama, ROTC.

**Scholarships offered:** 65 full-time freshmen received athletic scholarships; average amount $21,342.

**FINANCIAL AID PROCEDURES**

**Forms required:** FAFSA.

**Dates and Deadlines:** Priority date 3/1; no closing date. Applicants notified on a rolling basis starting 3/15.

**Transfers:** No deadline. Applicants notified on a rolling basis starting 4/1; must reply within 6 week(s) of notification.

**CONTACT**

Caryn Pacheco, Director of Financial Aid

1000 Asp Avenue, Room 127, Norman, OK 73019-4076

(405) 325-5505

## University of Science and Arts of Oklahoma

Chickasha, Oklahoma

www.usao.edu                                            Federal Code: 003167

**4-year public** university and liberal arts college in large town.

**Enrollment:** 845 undergrads.

**BASIC COSTS (2015-2016)**

**Tuition and fees:** $6,570; out-of-state residents $16,020.

**Per-credit charge:** $180; out-of-state residents $495.

**Room and board:** $5,800.

**Additional info:** Tuition at time of enrollment locked for 4 years.

**FINANCIAL AID PICTURE**

**Students with need:** Need-based aid available for full-time and part-time students. Work study available nights, weekends, and for part-time students.

**Students without need:** No-need awards available for academics, art, athletics, leadership, music/drama, state/district residency.

**FINANCIAL AID PROCEDURES**

**Forms required:** FAFSA.

**Dates and Deadlines:** Priority date 3/1; no closing date. Applicants notified on a rolling basis starting 3/1.

**Transfers:** No deadline. Applicants notified on a rolling basis starting 3/1; must reply within 4 week(s) of notification.

**CONTACT**

Laura Coponiti, Director of Financial Aid

1727 West Alabama, Chickasha, OK 73018-5322

(405) 574-1240

## University of Tulsa

Tulsa, Oklahoma

www.utulsa.edu                                          Federal Code: 003185

**4-year private** university in large city, affiliated with Presbyterian Church (USA).

**Enrollment:** 3,452 undergrads, 3% part-time. 710 full-time freshmen.

**Selectivity:** Admits less than 50% of applicants.

**BASIC COSTS (2016-2017)**

**Tuition and fees:** $41,024.

**Per-credit charge:** $1,453.

**Room and board:** $11,116.

**FINANCIAL AID PICTURE (2015-2016)**

**Students with need:** Out of 520 full-time freshmen who applied for aid, 391 were judged to have need. Of these, 390 received aid, and 216 had their full need met. Average financial aid package met 86% of need; average scholarship/grant was $6,508; average loan was $4,263. For part-time students, average financial aid package was $13,566.

**Students without need:** 251 full-time freshmen who did not demonstrate need for aid received scholarships/grants; average award was $19,540. No-need awards available for academics, alumni affiliation, art, athletics, leadership, minority status, music/drama, religious affiliation, ROTC.

**Scholarships offered:** 68 full-time freshmen received athletic scholarships; average amount $35,746.

**FINANCIAL AID PROCEDURES**

**Forms required:** FAFSA.

**Dates and Deadlines:** Priority date 3/1; no closing date. Applicants notified on a rolling basis starting 3/1; must reply by 5/1 or within 2 week(s) of notification.

**Transfers:** Priority date 5/1; no deadline. Applicants notified on a rolling basis starting 3/1; must reply by 5/1 or within 2 week(s) of notification.

**CONTACT**

Vicki Hendrickson, Director of Student Financial Services

Office of Admission, Tulsa, OK 74104-3189

(918) 631-2526

## Vatterott College: Oklahoma City

Oklahoma City, Oklahoma

www.vatterott.edu                                       Federal Code: 020693

**2-year for-profit** technical and career college in very large city.

**Enrollment:** 280 undergrads.

**Selectivity:** Open admission.

## BASIC COSTS (2015-2016)

**Additional info:** Diploma programs: (40 weeks) $18,884; (60 weeks) $28,034-$28,480. Associate programs: (70 weeks) $30,559-$37,450; (90 weeks) $39,114-$41,822. Costs include fees, books and supplies.

## FINANCIAL AID PICTURE

**Students with need:** Need-based aid available for full-time students.
**Students without need:** This college awards aid only to students with need.

## FINANCIAL AID PROCEDURES

**Forms required:** FAFSA.

## CONTACT

Janice Stepp, Director of Financial Aid
5537 Northwest Expressway, Oklahoma City, OK 73132
(405) 945-0088

---

## Western Oklahoma State College
Altus, Oklahoma
www.wosc.edu                        Federal Code: 003146

**2-year public** community college in large town.
**Enrollment:** 1,178 undergrads.
**Selectivity:** Open admission; but selective for some programs.

## BASIC COSTS (2015-2016)

**Tuition and fees:** $3,299; out-of-state residents $7,654.
**Per-credit charge:** $71; out-of-state residents $216.
**Room and board:** $4,250.

## FINANCIAL AID PICTURE (2014-2015)

**Students with need:** Need-based aid available for part-time students. Work study available nights, weekends, and for part-time students.
**Students without need:** No-need awards available for academics, alumni affiliation, art, athletics, leadership, music/drama, state/district residency.

## FINANCIAL AID PROCEDURES

**Forms required:** FAFSA, institutional form.
**Dates and Deadlines:** Closing date 3/1. Applicants notified on a rolling basis; must reply within 3 week(s) of notification.

## CONTACT

Myrna Cross, Director of Financial Aid/Veterans' Affairs
2801 North Main Street, Altus, OK 73521
(580) 477-7709

# Oregon

## Art Institute of Portland
Portland, Oregon
http://new.artinstitutes.edu/portland
                                     Federal Code: 007819

**4-year for-profit** visual arts and liberal arts college in large city.
**Enrollment:** 1,111 undergrads.

## BASIC COSTS (2015-2016)

**Tuition and fees:** $21,695.
**Per-credit charge:** $481.
**Room only:** $6,570.

## FINANCIAL AID PICTURE

**Students with need:** Need-based aid available for full-time and part-time students. Work study available nights, weekends, and for part-time students.

**Students without need:** No-need awards available for art.
**Additional info:** Applicants encouraged to apply early for financial aid. Scholarship deadlines range from January 1 to March 1.

## FINANCIAL AID PROCEDURES

**Forms required:** FAFSA.
**Dates and Deadlines:** Priority date 3/1; no closing date. Applicants notified on a rolling basis starting 1/1; must reply within 5 week(s) of notification.
**Transfers:** No deadline. Applicants notified on a rolling basis starting 1/1.

## CONTACT

Lauren Patterson, Director of Student Financial Services
1122 Northwest Davis Street, Portland, OR 97209-2911
(503) 382-4784

---

## Blue Mountain Community College
Pendleton, Oregon
www.bluecc.edu                        Federal Code: 003186

**2-year public** community college in large town.
**Enrollment:** 591 undergrads.
**Selectivity:** Open admission; but selective for some programs.

## BASIC COSTS (2015-2016)

**Tuition and fees:** $4,756; out-of-state residents $13,216.
**Per-credit charge:** $94; out-of-state residents $282.
**Additional info:** Students in limited entry programs such as dental and nursing and some academic programs such as agriculture, diesel, music and art pay additional program and/or course fees. Washington state, Idaho, Nevada, California and Montana residents all pay in-state rates.

## FINANCIAL AID PICTURE

**Students with need:** Need-based aid available for full-time and part-time students. Work study available nights, weekends, and for part-time students.
**Students without need:** No-need awards available for athletics, music/drama.

## FINANCIAL AID PROCEDURES

**Forms required:** FAFSA.
**Dates and Deadlines:** Priority date 3/30; no closing date. Applicants notified on a rolling basis starting 4/1; must reply within 2 week(s) of notification.

## CONTACT

Yadira Gonzalez, Director of Student Financial Assistance
2411 NW Carden Avenue, Pendleton, OR 97801
(541) 278-5790

---

## Central Oregon Community College
Bend, Oregon
www.cocc.edu                        Federal Code: 003188

**2-year public** community college in small city.
**Enrollment:** 5,321 undergrads, 54% part-time. 439 full-time freshmen.
**Selectivity:** Open admission; but selective for some programs.

## BASIC COSTS (2015-2016)

**Tuition and fees:** $4,444; out-of-district residents $5,749; out-of-state residents $11,419.
**Per-credit charge:** $91; out-of-district residents $120; out-of-state residents $246.
**Room and board:** $10,550.

## FINANCIAL AID PICTURE (2015-2016)

**Students with need:** Out of 320 full-time freshmen who applied for aid, 273 were judged to have need. Of these, 272 received aid, and 29 had their full need met. Average financial aid package met 70% of need; average

scholarship/grant was $5,978; average loan was $3,205. For part-time students, average financial aid package was $10,237.

**Students without need:** 4 full-time freshmen who did not demonstrate need for aid received scholarships/grants; average award was $3,000. No-need awards available for academics, leadership, state/district residency.

**Additional info:** Institution-sponsored short-term loans. Extensive part-time student employment.

### FINANCIAL AID PROCEDURES
**Forms required:** FAFSA.
**Dates and Deadlines:** Applicants notified on a rolling basis starting 4/1; must reply within 4 week(s) of notification.

### CONTACT
Kevin Multop, Director of Financial Aid
2600 Northwest College Way, Bend, OR 97703
(541) 383-7260

## Chemeketa Community College
Salem, Oregon
www.chemeketa.edu          Federal Code: 003218

**2-year public** community and junior college in small city.
**Enrollment:** 9,563 undergrads. 1,006 full-time freshmen.
**Selectivity:** Open admission; but selective for some programs.

### BASIC COSTS (2015-2016)
**Tuition and fees:** $4,230; out-of-state residents $11,520.
**Per-credit charge:** $80; out-of-state residents $242.

### FINANCIAL AID PICTURE (2014-2015)
**Students with need:** Out of 989 full-time freshmen who applied for aid, 907 were judged to have need. Of these, 866 received aid, and 6 had their full need met. Average financial aid package met 44% of need; average scholarship/grant was $4,056; average loan was $4,560. For part-time students, average financial aid package was $4,789.
**Students without need:** This college awards aid only to students with need.
**Scholarships offered:** 14 full-time freshmen received athletic scholarships; average amount $3,529.

### FINANCIAL AID PROCEDURES
**Forms required:** FAFSA.
**Dates and Deadlines:** Priority date 4/1; no closing date. Applicants notified on a rolling basis starting 6/30; must reply within 2 week(s) of notification.
**Transfers:** Priority date 6/30; no deadline. Applicants notified on a rolling basis; must reply within 4 week(s) of notification.

### CONTACT
Kathy Campbell, Financial Aid Director
Admissions Office, Salem, OR 97309-7070
(503) 399-5018

## Clackamas Community College
Oregon City, Oregon
www.clackamas.edu          Federal Code: 004878

**2-year public** community college in large town.
**Enrollment:** 6,100 undergrads, 57% part-time. 701 full-time freshmen.
**Selectivity:** Open admission; but selective for some programs.

### BASIC COSTS (2016-2017)
**Tuition and fees:** $4,623; out-of-state residents $11,559.
**Per-credit charge:** $87; out-of-state residents $249.

### FINANCIAL AID PICTURE
**Students with need:** Need-based aid available for full-time and part-time students. Work study available nights, weekends, and for part-time students.

**Students without need:** No-need awards available for academics, art, athletics, leadership, music/drama.
**Additional info:** Institutional tuition rebate guarantee. Frozen tuition rates for new fall students who graduate within 3 years. Any tuition increase levied by college during those 3 years will be refunded to student upon graduation.

### FINANCIAL AID PROCEDURES
**Forms required:** FAFSA, institutional form.
**Dates and Deadlines:** Applicants notified on a rolling basis starting 3/15; must reply within 3 week(s) of notification.
**Transfers:** No deadline. Applicants notified on a rolling basis starting 3/15; must reply within 3 week(s) of notification.

### CONTACT
Chippi Bello, Financial Aid Director
19600 Molalla Avenue, Oregon City, OR 97045
(503) 594-6100

## Clatsop Community College
Astoria, Oregon
www.clatsopcc.edu          Federal Code: 003189

**2-year public** community and maritime college in large town.
**Enrollment:** 619 undergrads.
**Selectivity:** Open admission; but selective for some programs.

### BASIC COSTS (2015-2016)
**Tuition and fees:** $4,995; out-of-state residents $9,450.
**Per-credit charge:** $99; out-of-state residents $198.

### FINANCIAL AID PICTURE
**Students with need:** Need-based aid available for full-time and part-time students.
**Students without need:** No-need awards available for academics, art, leadership, minority status, state/district residency.

### FINANCIAL AID PROCEDURES
**Forms required:** FAFSA, institutional form.
**Dates and Deadlines:** Priority date 5/1; no closing date. Applicants notified on a rolling basis starting 2/1.
**Transfers:** No deadline. Applicants notified on a rolling basis starting 2/1. Students who apply after July 1 may only be eligible for Pell Grants and loans depending on availability of funds. Reply deadline 1 week before start of classes.

### CONTACT
Lloyd Mueller, Director of Financial Aid
1651 Lexington, Astoria, OR 97103
(503) 338-2412

## Concordia University
Portland, Oregon
www.cu-portland.edu          Federal Code: 003191

**4-year private** liberal arts and teachers college in very large city, affiliated with Lutheran Church - Missouri Synod.
**Enrollment:** 1,168 undergrads, 13% part-time. 198 full-time freshmen.
**Selectivity:** Admits 50 to 75% of applicants.

### BASIC COSTS (2015-2016)
**Tuition and fees:** $28,420.
**Per-credit charge:** $885.
**Room and board:** $8,810.
**Additional info:** Tuition/fee waivers available for adults.

### FINANCIAL AID PICTURE (2014-2015)
**Students with need:** Out of 187 full-time freshmen who applied for aid, 149 were judged to have need. Of these, 149 received aid, and 33 had their

full need met. For part-time students, average financial aid package was $10,652.

**Students without need:** 46 full-time freshmen who did not demonstrate need for aid received scholarships/grants; average award was $7,935. No-need awards available for academics, athletics, leadership, music/drama, religious affiliation.

**Scholarships offered: *Merit:*** President's Scholarship; $13,500; Scholar's Scholarship $12,500; Regent's Scholarship $11,000; Provost's Scholarship $10,000; Dean's Award $8,000; University Award; $7,000; Cavalier's Award; $6,000; Faculty Award $3,500. Merit awarded based on academic index including HS GPA and ACT/SAT test scores. Honors Scholarship 50% tuition discount, acceptance to Honors Program. ***Athletic:*** 46 full-time freshmen received athletic scholarships; average amount $8,152.

**FINANCIAL AID PROCEDURES**

**Forms required:** FAFSA.

**Dates and Deadlines:** Applicants notified on a rolling basis starting 3/1.

**Transfers:** No deadline. Applicants notified on a rolling basis starting 3/1.

**CONTACT**

Robert Clarke, Financial Aid Director
2811 Northeast Holman Street, Portland, OR 97211-6099
(503) 280-8514

# Corban University
Salem, Oregon
www.corban.edu          Federal Code: 001339

**4-year private** liberal arts college in small city, affiliated with Baptist faith.
**Enrollment:** 985 undergrads, 5% part-time. 253 full-time freshmen.
**Selectivity:** Admits less than 50% of applicants.

**BASIC COSTS (2015-2016)**
**Tuition and fees:** $29,640.
**Per-credit charge:** $1,208.
**Room and board:** $9,240.

**FINANCIAL AID PICTURE (2014-2015)**
**Students with need:** Out of 235 full-time freshmen who applied for aid, 217 were judged to have need. Of these, 217 received aid, and 32 had their full need met. Average financial aid package met 67% of need; average scholarship/grant was $17,989; average loan was $3,872. For part-time students, average financial aid package was $9,262.
**Students without need:** 25 full-time freshmen who did not demonstrate need for aid received scholarships/grants; average award was $8,374. No-need awards available for academics, alumni affiliation, athletics, leadership, music/drama, ROTC.
**Scholarships offered:** 25 full-time freshmen received athletic scholarships; average amount $12,116.
**Additional info:** The Corban Promise is a policy to retire student debt. After graduation, students who work at least 30 hours a week with incomes below $37,000 will qualify for assistance which increases proportionately as income decreases. Incomes below $20,000 will be eligible for 100% reimbursement.

**FINANCIAL AID PROCEDURES**
**Forms required:** FAFSA.
**Dates and Deadlines:** Priority date 2/1; no closing date. Applicants notified on a rolling basis starting 2/20.

**CONTACT**
Ellen Zarfas, Director of Financial Aid
5000 Deer Park Drive SE, Salem, OR 97317-9392
(503) 375-7006

# Eastern Oregon University
La Grande, Oregon
www.eou.edu          Federal Code: 003193

**4-year public** university and liberal arts college in large town.
**Enrollment:** 2,765 undergrads, 37% part-time. 282 full-time freshmen.
**Selectivity:** Admits over 75% of applicants.

**BASIC COSTS (2015-2016)**
**Tuition and fees:** $7,756.5; out-of-state residents $17,994.
**Room and board:** $9,642.

**FINANCIAL AID PICTURE (2014-2015)**
**Students with need:** Out of 267 full-time freshmen who applied for aid, 230 were judged to have need. Of these, 229 received aid, and 40 had their full need met. Average financial aid package met 57% of need; average scholarship/grant was $6,609; average loan was $3,033. For part-time students, average financial aid package was $6,766.
**Students without need:** 26 full-time freshmen who did not demonstrate need for aid received scholarships/grants; average award was $1,759. No-need awards available for academics, art, leadership, minority status, music/drama, state/district residency.
**Scholarships offered: *Merit:*** University Scholars Scholarships; full-tuition; based on personal essay, recommendations, GPA, activities and awards. ***Athletic:*** 51 full-time freshmen received athletic scholarships; average amount $3,213.

**FINANCIAL AID PROCEDURES**
**Forms required:** FAFSA.
**Dates and Deadlines:** Priority date 1/1; no closing date. Applicants notified on a rolling basis starting 4/1; must reply within 4 week(s) of notification.
**Transfers:** No deadline. Applicants notified on a rolling basis.

**CONTACT**
Sandy Henry, Director of Financial Aid
One University Boulevard, La Grande, OR 97850
(541) 962-3550

# George Fox University
Newberg, Oregon
www.georgefox.edu          Federal Code: 003194

**4-year private** university and seminary college in large town, affiliated with Society of Friends (Quaker).
**Enrollment:** 2,558 undergrads, 8% part-time. 633 full-time freshmen.
**Selectivity:** Admits over 75% of applicants.

**BASIC COSTS (2016-2017)**
**Tuition and fees:** $33,730.
**Room and board:** $10,528.
**Additional info:** Tuition/fee waivers available for minority students.

**FINANCIAL AID PICTURE**
**Students with need:** Need-based aid available for full-time and part-time students. Work study available nights, weekends, and for part-time students.
**Students without need:** No-need awards available for academics, alumni affiliation, art, job skills, leadership, minority status, music/drama, religious affiliation.
**Scholarships offered:** Academic merit awards; $2,500-$15,000 per year; based on GPA, SAT/ACT and rigor of high school curriculum; renewable based on academic performance.
**Additional info:** Audition required for music and drama scholarships.

**FINANCIAL AID PROCEDURES**
**Forms required:** FAFSA, state aid form.
**Dates and Deadlines:** Priority date 2/1; no closing date. Applicants notified on a rolling basis starting 3/1; must reply within 6 week(s) of notification.
**Transfers:** Priority date 3/1.

**CONTACT**
James Oshiro, Director of Financial Aid
414 North Meridian Street #6089, Newberg, OR 97132-2697
(503) 554-2290

## Klamath Community College
Klamath Falls, Oregon
www.klamathcc.edu                    Federal Code: 034283

**2-year public** community college in small city.
**Enrollment:** 1,227 undergrads, 58% part-time. 83 full-time freshmen.
**Selectivity:** Open admission.

**BASIC COSTS (2015-2016)**
**Tuition and fees:** $4,606; out-of-state residents $7,823.
**Per-credit charge:** $90; out-of-state residents $161.

**FINANCIAL AID PICTURE**
**Students with need:** Need-based aid available for full-time and part-time students. Work study available nights.

**FINANCIAL AID PROCEDURES**
**Forms required:** FAFSA.
**Transfers:** No deadline. Applicants notified on a rolling basis.

**CONTACT**
Robin Sundseth, Financial Aid Director
7390 South 6th Street, Klamath Falls, OR 97603
(541) 882-3521

## Lane Community College
Eugene, Oregon
www.lanecc.edu                    Federal Code: 003196

**2-year public** community college in small city.
**Enrollment:** 8,370 undergrads, 54% part-time. 555 full-time freshmen.
**Selectivity:** Open admission; but selective for some programs.

**BASIC COSTS (2015-2016)**
**Tuition and fees:** $4,869; out-of-state residents $11,214.
**Per-credit charge:** $98; out-of-state residents $239.

**FINANCIAL AID PICTURE**
**Students with need:** Need-based aid available for full-time and part-time students. Work study available nights, weekends, and for part-time students.
**Students without need:** No-need awards available for art, athletics, minority status, music/drama.

**FINANCIAL AID PROCEDURES**
**Forms required:** FAFSA.
**Dates and Deadlines:** Closing date 2/15. Applicants notified on a rolling basis starting 6/1; must reply within 2 week(s) of notification.

**CONTACT**
Greg Holmes, Chief Financial Officer
4000 East 30th Avenue, Eugene, OR 97405
(541) 463-3100

## Lewis & Clark College
Portland, Oregon                    Federal Code: 003197
www.lclark.edu                      CSS Code: 4384

**4-year private** liberal arts college in very large city.
**Enrollment:** 2,085 undergrads. 654 full-time freshmen.
**Selectivity:** Admits 50 to 75% of applicants.

**BASIC COSTS (2016-2017)**
**Tuition and fees:** $46,894.
**Per-credit charge:** $2,327.
**Room and board:** $11,540.

**FINANCIAL AID PICTURE (2015-2016)**
**Students with need:** Out of 515 full-time freshmen who applied for aid, 390 were judged to have need. Of these, 389 received aid, and 107 had their full need met. Average financial aid package met 90% of need; average scholarship/grant was $29,808; average loan was $6,568. For part-time students, average financial aid package was $31,229.
**Students without need:** 213 full-time freshmen who did not demonstrate need for aid received scholarships/grants; average award was $15,836. No-need awards available for academics, leadership, music/drama.

**FINANCIAL AID PROCEDURES**
**Forms required:** FAFSA, CSS PROFILE.
**Dates and Deadlines:** Priority date 2/15; no closing date. Applicants notified on a rolling basis starting 3/15; must reply by 7/1 or within 2 week(s) of notification.
**Transfers:** The number of semesters a transfer student may receive institutionally-funded aid is prorated based on the number of transfer credits accepted. Students are notified of the number of semesters of institutional aid they are eligible to receive once the Registrar has completed their final transcript evaluation.

**CONTACT**
Anastacia Dillon, Director of Financial Aid
0615 SW Palatine Hill Road, Portland, OR 97219-7899
(503) 768-7090

## Linfield College
McMinnville, Oregon
www.linfield.edu                    Federal Code: 003198

**4-year private** nursing and liberal arts college in large town, affiliated with American Baptist Churches in the USA.
**Enrollment:** 1,663 undergrads, 2% part-time. 474 full-time freshmen.
**Selectivity:** Admits over 75% of applicants.

**BASIC COSTS (2015-2016)**
**Tuition and fees:** $38,654.
**Per-credit charge:** $1,192.
**Room and board:** $11,410.
**Additional info:** The room and board costs in 2015-2016 reflect board costs for entering first year students who will be required to attend January term.

**FINANCIAL AID PICTURE (2015-2016)**
**Students with need:** Out of 440 full-time freshmen who applied for aid, 380 were judged to have need. Of these, 380 received aid, and 98 had their full need met. Average financial aid package met 81% of need; average scholarship/grant was $28,864; average loan was $3,633. For part-time students, average financial aid package was $13,319.
**Students without need:** 88 full-time freshmen who did not demonstrate need for aid received scholarships/grants; average award was $18,627. No-need awards available for academics, leadership, minority status, music/drama.
**Scholarships offered:** National Merit Award: half to full-tuition for National Merit Finalists who list Linfield as first choice. Other scholarships based on academic record include Trustee Scholarships, Presidential Scholarships, Frances R. Linfield Scholarships, Faculty Scholarships, and Achievement Awards. The Academic Competitive Scholarships are sponsored by departments; separate application required. The Music department offers scholarships available by audition for majors, minors and non-majors. Leadership and Service Scholarship are based on high levels of leadership, initiative, and service to others through student government, school activities, community organizations, and religious or social service agencies.

## FINANCIAL AID PROCEDURES

**Forms required:** FAFSA.

**Dates and Deadlines:** Priority date 2/1; no closing date. Applicants notified on a rolling basis starting 4/1; must reply by 5/1 or within 2 week(s) of notification.

**Transfers:** Priority date 2/15. Applicants notified by 5/15; must reply by 6/15. Scholarships available for transfer students include Transfer Scholarships for students who have attended 2- or 4-year accredited colleges full-time and have 3.00 GPA. Honor Society Scholarships for members of Phi Theta Kappa or Alpha Gamma Sigma are available. Chemeketa Scholars at Linfield is a scholarship program for participants in the Chemeketa Scholars program at Chemeketa Community College (Oregon).

## CONTACT

Director of Financial Aid
900 Southeast Baker Street, McMinnville, OR 97128-6894
(503) 883-2225

## Linn-Benton Community College
Albany, Oregon
www.linnbenton.edu          Federal Code: 006938

**2-year public** community college in small city.

**Enrollment:** 5,635 undergrads, 52% part-time. 628 full-time freshmen.

**Selectivity:** Open admission; but selective for some programs.

### BASIC COSTS (2015-2016)

**Tuition and fees:** $4,694; out-of-state residents $9,977.

**Per-credit charge:** $96.61; out-of-state residents $225.43.

**Additional info:** Tuition/fee waivers available for unemployed or children of unemployed.

### FINANCIAL AID PICTURE (2014-2015)

**Students with need:** Out of 490 full-time freshmen who applied for aid, 430 were judged to have need. Of these, 412 received aid, and 21 had their full need met. Average financial aid package met 57% of need; average scholarship/grant was $4,943; average loan was $2,755. For part-time students, average financial aid package was $6,796.

**Students without need:** 38 full-time freshmen who did not demonstrate need for aid received scholarships/grants; average award was $1,948. No-need awards available for academics, alumni affiliation, art, athletics, leadership, music/drama.

**Scholarships offered:** 10 full-time freshmen received athletic scholarships; average amount $2,908.

### FINANCIAL AID PROCEDURES

**Forms required:** FAFSA.

**Dates and Deadlines:** Applicants notified on a rolling basis starting 3/30; must reply within 4 week(s) of notification.

### CONTACT

Elaine Robinson, Director, Financial Aid & Veteran's Affairs
6500 Pacific Blvd SW, Albany, OR 97321
(541) 917-4850

## Marylhurst University
Marylhurst, Oregon
www.marylhurst.edu          Federal Code: 003199

**4-year private** university and liberal arts college in large town, affiliated with Roman Catholic Church.

**Enrollment:** 503 undergrads, 71% part-time. 4 full-time freshmen.

**Selectivity:** Admits over 75% of applicants.

### BASIC COSTS (2015-2016)

**Tuition and fees:** $20,835.

**Per-credit charge:** $463.

### FINANCIAL AID PICTURE (2015-2016)

**Students with need:** Out of 4 full-time freshmen who applied for aid, 4 were judged to have need. Of these, 4 received aid. Average financial aid package met 63% of need; average scholarship/grant was $9,359; average loan was $3,791. For part-time students, average financial aid package was $10,250.

**Students without need:** No-need awards available for academics.

### FINANCIAL AID PROCEDURES

**Forms required:** FAFSA, institutional form.

**Dates and Deadlines:** Priority date 3/1; no closing date. Applicants notified on a rolling basis starting 5/1.

**Transfers:** No deadline. Applicants notified on a rolling basis starting 5/1.

### CONTACT

Tracy Reisinger, Director of Financial Aid
PO Box 261, Marylhurst, OR 97036-0261
(503) 699-6253

## Mt. Hood Community College
Gresham, Oregon
www.mhcc.edu          Federal Code: 003204

**2-year public** community college in small city.

**Enrollment:** 7,597 undergrads.

**Selectivity:** Open admission; but selective for some programs.

### BASIC COSTS (2015-2016)

**Tuition and fees:** $4,669; out-of-state residents $9,776.

**Per-credit charge:** $96; out-of-state residents $209.

### FINANCIAL AID PICTURE

**Students with need:** Need-based aid available for full-time and part-time students.

**Students without need:** No-need awards available for academics.

### FINANCIAL AID PROCEDURES

**Forms required:** FAFSA, institutional form.

**Dates and Deadlines:** Closing date 4/1. Applicants notified on a rolling basis starting 4/1; must reply within 2 week(s) of notification.

### CONTACT

Christi Hart, Financial Aid Director
26000 SE Stark Street, Gresham, OR 97030
(503) 491-7379

## Multnomah University
Portland, Oregon
www.multnomah.edu          Federal Code: 003206

**4-year private** university and seminary college in very large city, affiliated with interdenominational tradition.

**Enrollment:** 405 undergrads, 17% part-time. 88 full-time freshmen.

**Selectivity:** Admits 50 to 75% of applicants.

### BASIC COSTS (2016-2017)

**Tuition and fees:** $23,680.

**Per-credit charge:** $730.

**Room and board:** $7,820.

### FINANCIAL AID PICTURE (2014-2015)

**Students with need:** Out of 87 full-time freshmen who applied for aid, 73 were judged to have need. Of these, 65 received aid. Average financial aid package met 43% of need; average scholarship/grant was $10,847; average loan was $3,312. For part-time students, average financial aid package was $5,634.

**Students without need:** 9 full-time freshmen who did not demonstrate need for aid received scholarships/grants; average award was $6,333. No-need awards available for academics, alumni affiliation, athletics.

**FINANCIAL AID PROCEDURES**
**Forms required:** FAFSA.
**Dates and Deadlines:** Priority date 4/1; closing date 8/1. Applicants notified on a rolling basis starting 3/1; must reply within 2 week(s) of notification.
**Transfers:** Must reply within 2 week(s) of notification.

**CONTACT**
Mary McGlothlan, Director of Financial Aid
8435 Northeast Glisan Street, Portland, OR 97220
(503) 251-5336

## New Hope Christian College
Eugene, Oregon
www.newhope.edu — Federal Code: 015167

**4-year private** Bible college in small city, affiliated with nondenominational tradition.
**Enrollment:** 137 undergrads.

**BASIC COSTS (2015-2016)**
**Tuition and fees:** $17,530.
**Per-credit charge:** $550.
**Room and board:** $6,100.

**FINANCIAL AID PICTURE**
**Students with need:** Need-based aid available for full-time and part-time students. Work study available nights, weekends, and for part-time students.
**Students without need:** No-need awards available for academics, art, athletics, job skills, leadership, music/drama, religious affiliation, state/district residency.
**Scholarships offered:** Honors award; $300; 3.7 GPA required.
**Additional info:** Some early acceptance awards possible for those admitted by May 15. Distance awards to those coming from over 1,000 miles away. Some awards for husbands and wives enrolled at same time.

**FINANCIAL AID PROCEDURES**
**Forms required:** FAFSA, institutional form.
**Dates and Deadlines:** Priority date 4/1; closing date 8/1. Applicants notified on a rolling basis starting 2/1; must reply within 4 week(s) of notification.
**Transfers:** No deadline.

**CONTACT**
Casey Craigie, Director of Financial Aid
2155 Bailey Hill Road, Eugene, OR 97405
(800) 322-2638

## Northwest Christian University
Eugene, Oregon
www.nwcu.edu — Federal Code: 003208

**4-year private** university in small city, affiliated with Christian Church (Disciples of Christ).
**Enrollment:** 528 undergrads, 20% part-time. 83 full-time freshmen.
**Selectivity:** Admits 50 to 75% of applicants.

**BASIC COSTS (2015-2016)**
**Tuition and fees:** $27,490.
**Per-credit charge:** $908.
**Room and board:** $8,600.

**FINANCIAL AID PICTURE (2015-2016)**
**Students with need:** Out of 78 full-time freshmen who applied for aid, 65 were judged to have need. Of these, 65 received aid, and 12 had their full

need met. Average financial aid package met 77% of need; average scholarship/grant was $19,767; average loan was $2,808. For part-time students, average financial aid package was $6,971.
**Students without need:** 18 full-time freshmen who did not demonstrate need for aid received scholarships/grants; average award was $9,302. No-need awards available for academics, alumni affiliation, athletics, leadership, music/drama, religious affiliation.
**Scholarships offered:** *Merit:* Academic Scholarships; $4,000-$13,000; 2.80-4.00 unweighted GPA; not limited. Leadership Awards; $500-$1,000; school, community, church leadership roles; not limited. *Athletic:* 17 full-time freshmen received athletic scholarships; average amount $5,611.

**FINANCIAL AID PROCEDURES**
**Forms required:** FAFSA.
**Dates and Deadlines:** Priority date 3/1; no closing date. Applicants notified on a rolling basis starting 3/1; must reply within 2 week(s) of notification.
**Transfers:** No deadline. Applicants notified on a rolling basis starting 3/1; must reply within 2 week(s) of notification.

**CONTACT**
Jocelyn Hubbs, Director of Financial Aid
828 East 11th Avenue, Eugene, OR 97401-3745
(541) 684-7218

## Oregon College of Art & Craft
Portland, Oregon
www.ocac.edu — Federal Code: 030073

**4-year private** visual arts college in very large city.
**Enrollment:** 111 undergrads.

**BASIC COSTS (2015-2016)**
**Tuition and fees:** $28,730.

**FINANCIAL AID PICTURE**
**Students with need:** Need-based aid available for full-time and part-time students. Work study available weekends and for part-time students.
**Students without need:** No-need awards available for academics, art.

**FINANCIAL AID PROCEDURES**
**Forms required:** FAFSA.
**Dates and Deadlines:** Priority date 3/1; no closing date. Applicants notified on a rolling basis starting 3/1.

**CONTACT**
Linda Anderson, Financial Aid Director
8245 SW Barnes Road, Portland, OR 97225-6349
(971) 255-4224

## Oregon Health & Science University
Portland, Oregon
www.ohsu.edu — Federal Code: 004883

**3-year public** university and health science college in very large city.
**Enrollment:** 827 undergrads, 75% part-time.

**BASIC COSTS (2015-2016)**
**Tuition and fees:** $21,345; out-of-state residents $34,620.
**Per-credit charge:** $354; out-of-state residents $649.
**Additional info:** Tuition shown is for new 2015-2016 undergraduate nursing program; costs for other programs vary. The Required Fees amount includes student health insurance since it is required for all students.

**FINANCIAL AID PICTURE (2015-2016)**
**Students with need:** Average financial aid package for all full-time undergraduates was $13,880; for part-time $9,542. 21% awarded as scholarships/

grants, 79% awarded as loans/jobs. Work study available nights, weekends, and for part-time students.

**FINANCIAL AID PROCEDURES**
**Transfers:** Priority date 3/1; no deadline. Applicants notified on a rolling basis starting 5/1; must reply within 4 week(s) of notification.

**CONTACT**
Rachel Durbin, Director of Financial Aid
3181 SW Sam Jackson Park Road, Portland, OR 97239-3098
(503) 494-7800

## Oregon Institute of Technology
Klamath Falls, Oregon
www.oit.edu                Federal Code: 003211

**4-year public** career college in small city.
**Enrollment:** 3,446 undergrads.

**BASIC COSTS (2015-2016)**
**Tuition and fees:** $8,839; out-of-state residents $24,826.
**Room and board:** $8,530.
**Additional info:** Tuition/fee waivers available for minority students.

**FINANCIAL AID PICTURE**
**Students with need:** Need-based aid available for full-time and part-time students. Work study available weekends and for part-time students.
**Students without need:** No-need awards available for academics, athletics, leadership.

**FINANCIAL AID PROCEDURES**
**Forms required:** FAFSA.
**Dates and Deadlines:** Priority date 2/1; no closing date. Applicants notified on a rolling basis starting 4/1.
**Transfers:** Closing date 2/1.

**CONTACT**
Tracey Lehman, Director of Financial Aid
3201 Campus Drive, Klamath Falls, OR 97601
(541) 885-1280

## Oregon State University
Corvallis, Oregon
www.oregonstate.edu                Federal Code: 003210

**4-year public** university in small city.
**Enrollment:** 23,656 undergrads, 24% part-time. 3,453 full-time freshmen.
**Selectivity:** Admits over 75% of applicants.

**BASIC COSTS (2015-2016)**
**Tuition and fees:** $10,107; out-of-state residents $28,767.
**Per-credit charge:** $183; out-of-state residents $582.
**Room and board:** $12,156.

**FINANCIAL AID PICTURE (2014-2015)**
**Students with need:** Out of 2,950 full-time freshmen who applied for aid, 2,038 were judged to have need. Of these, 2,018 received aid, and 203 had their full need met. Average financial aid package met 67% of need; average scholarship/grant was $7,265; average loan was $3,749. For part-time students, average financial aid package was $11,199.
**Students without need:** 582 full-time freshmen who did not demonstrate need for aid received scholarships/grants; average award was $4,338. No-need awards available for academics, alumni affiliation, athletics, job skills, leadership, minority status, ROTC, state/district residency.
**Scholarships offered:** 71 full-time freshmen received athletic scholarships; average amount $29,349.

**FINANCIAL AID PROCEDURES**
**Forms required:** FAFSA.
**Dates and Deadlines:** Priority date 2/28; no closing date. Applicants notified on a rolling basis starting 4/1; must reply within 4 week(s) of notification.

**CONTACT**
Doug Severs, Director of Financial Aid & Scholarships
104 Kerr Administration Building, Corvallis, OR 97331-2130
(541) 731-2241

## Pacific Northwest College of Art
Portland, Oregon
www.pnca.edu                Federal Code: 003207

**4-year private** visual arts college in very large city.
**Enrollment:** 399 undergrads, 8% part-time. 70 full-time freshmen.
**Selectivity:** Admits over 75% of applicants.

**BASIC COSTS (2015-2016)**
**Tuition and fees:** $33,120.
**Per-credit charge:** $1,313.
**Room only:** $8,772.

**FINANCIAL AID PICTURE**
**Students with need:** Need-based aid available for full-time and part-time students. Work study available nights, weekends, and for part-time students.
**Students without need:** No-need awards available for academics, art.
**Scholarships offered:** Leta Kennedy Student Scholarships; $10,000; based on artistic merit. Dorothy Lemelson Scholarship; cost of attendance; based on artistic and academic merit; renewable up to 4 years; 1 awarded. Other renewable scholarships available.

**FINANCIAL AID PROCEDURES**
**Forms required:** FAFSA.
**Dates and Deadlines:** Priority date 3/1; no closing date. Applicants notified on a rolling basis starting 4/1; must reply by 5/1 or within 4 week(s) of notification.
**Transfers:** No deadline. Applicants notified on a rolling basis starting 4/1; must reply by 5/1 or within 4 week(s) of notification.

**CONTACT**
Heidi Locke, Director of Financial Aid
511 NW Broadway, Portland, OR 97209
(503) 821-8972

## Pacific University
Forest Grove, Oregon
www.pacificu.edu                Federal Code: 003212

**4-year private** university in large town, affiliated with United Church of Christ.
**Enrollment:** 1,884 undergrads, 1% part-time. 478 full-time freshmen.
**Selectivity:** Admits over 75% of applicants.

**BASIC COSTS (2016-2017)**
**Tuition and fees:** $41,054.
**Per-credit charge:** $1,672.
**Room and board:** $11,822.

**FINANCIAL AID PICTURE (2015-2016)**
**Students with need:** Out of 447 full-time freshmen who applied for aid, 393 were judged to have need. Of these, 393 received aid, and 72 had their full need met. Average financial aid package met 77% of need; average scholarship/grant was $11,440; average loan was $4,341. For part-time students, average financial aid package was $13,163.

**Students without need:** 81 full-time freshmen who did not demonstrate need for aid received scholarships/grants; average award was $19,599. No-need awards available for academics, alumni affiliation, art, music/drama.
**Scholarships offered:** Founder's Scholarship; $15,000. Honors Scholarship; $12,000. Presidential Scholarship; $10,000. Trustee Scholarship; $8,500. University Scholarship; $7,500. Pacific Opportunity Award; $5,000. Pacesetters Scholarship; $1,000-$3,000. Music and Forensics Talent Awards; $1,000-$3,000. Number of awards vary.

### FINANCIAL AID PROCEDURES
**Forms required:** FAFSA.
**Dates and Deadlines:** Priority date 3/1; no closing date. Applicants notified on a rolling basis starting 3/15.

### CONTACT
Michael Johnson, Director of Financial Aid
2043 College Way, Forest Grove, OR 97116-1797
(503) 352-2222

## Pioneer Pacific College
Wilsonville, Oregon
www.pioneerpacific.edu          Federal Code: 016520

**2-year for-profit** career college in large town.
**Enrollment:** 1,195 undergrads.
**Selectivity:** Open admission; but selective for some programs.

### FINANCIAL AID PICTURE
**Students with need:** Need-based aid available for full-time and part-time students.
**Students without need:** This college awards aid only to students with need.
**Scholarships offered:** High school scholarship program and community scholarship program available.

### FINANCIAL AID PROCEDURES
**Forms required:** FAFSA.
**Dates and Deadlines:** Applicants notified on a rolling basis starting 2/27.

### CONTACT
Mark Johnson, Executive Director of Financial Aid
27501 Southwest Parkway Avenue, Wilsonville, OR 97070
(503) 654-8000

## Portland Community College
Portland, Oregon
www.pcc.edu          Federal Code: 003213

**2-year public** community college in very large city.
**Enrollment:** 27,946 undergrads.
**Selectivity:** Open admission; but selective for some programs.

### BASIC COSTS (2015-2016)
**Tuition and fees:** $4,690; out-of-state residents $10,450.
**Per-credit charge:** $96; out-of-state residents $224.

### FINANCIAL AID PICTURE
**Students with need:** Need-based aid available for full-time and part-time students. Work study available nights, weekends, and for part-time students.
**Students without need:** This college awards aid only to students with need.

### FINANCIAL AID PROCEDURES
**Forms required:** FAFSA.
**Dates and Deadlines:** Priority date 3/1; no closing date. Applicants notified on a rolling basis starting 6/1; must reply within 3 week(s) of notification.

### CONTACT
Bert Logan, Director of Financial Aid
12000 SW 49th Avenue, Portland, OR 97219-7132
(503) 722-4934

## Portland State University
Portland, Oregon
www.pdx.edu          Federal Code: 003216

**4-year public** university in very large city.
**Enrollment:** 19,674 undergrads, 28% part-time. 1,599 full-time freshmen.
**Selectivity:** Admits over 75% of applicants.

### BASIC COSTS (2015-2016)
**Tuition and fees:** $8,124; out-of-state residents $24,009.
**Per-credit charge:** $152; out-of-state residents $505.
**Room and board:** $10,260.

### FINANCIAL AID PICTURE
**Students with need:** Need-based aid available for full-time and part-time students. Work study available nights, weekends, and for part-time students.
**Students without need:** No-need awards available for academics, alumni affiliation, art, athletics, leadership, minority status, music/drama, state/district residency.

### FINANCIAL AID PROCEDURES
**Forms required:** FAFSA.
**Dates and Deadlines:** Priority date 2/28; no closing date. Applicants notified on a rolling basis starting 3/15.
**Transfers:** No deadline. Applicants notified on a rolling basis.

### CONTACT
G Johnson, Director of Financial Aid and Scholarships
PO Box 751-ADM, Portland, OR 97207-0751
(800) 547-8887

## Reed College
Portland, Oregon          Federal Code: 003217
www.reed.edu          CSS Code: 4654

**4-year private** liberal arts college in very large city.
**Enrollment:** 1,396 undergrads, 1% part-time. 420 full-time freshmen.
**Selectivity:** Admits less than 50% of applicants.

### BASIC COSTS (2016-2017)
**Tuition and fees:** $52,150.
**Room and board:** $13,150.

### FINANCIAL AID PICTURE
**Students with need:** Need-based aid available for full-time students. Work study available nights, weekends, and for part-time students.
**Students without need:** This college awards aid only to students with need.
**Additional info:** College meets demonstrated need of continuing students who have attended Reed minimum of 2 semesters, who file financial aid applications on time, and who maintain satisfactory academic progress. Institutional aid consideration is for total of 8 semesters.

### FINANCIAL AID PROCEDURES
**Forms required:** FAFSA, CSS PROFILE.
**Dates and Deadlines:** Closing date 2/1. Applicants notified by 4/1; must reply by 5/1.
**Transfers:** Closing date 3/1. Applicants notified by 5/15; must reply by 6/1 or within 2 week(s) of notification.

PART III: FINANCIAL AID COLLEGE BY COLLEGE

## CONTACT

Milyon Trulove, Vice President of Admission and Financial Aid
3203 SE Woodstock Boulevard, Portland, OR 97202-8199
(800) 547-4750

## Rogue Community College

Grants Pass, Oregon
www.roguecc.edu                Federal Code: 010071

**2-year public** community college in large town.
**Enrollment:** 4,216 undergrads, 59% part-time. 344 full-time freshmen.
**Selectivity:** Open admission; but selective for some programs.

**BASIC COSTS (2015-2016)**
**Tuition and fees:** $4,905; out-of-state residents $5,850.
**Per-credit charge:** $95; out-of-state residents $116.
**Additional info:** Tuition/fee waivers available for unemployed or children of unemployed.

**FINANCIAL AID PICTURE (2014-2015)**
**Students with need:** Out of 304 full-time freshmen who applied for aid, 268 were judged to have need. Of these, 268 received aid, and 3 had their full need met. Average financial aid package met 65% of need; average scholarship/grant was $4,736; average loan was $2,881. For part-time students, average financial aid package was $8,180.
**Students without need:** 11 full-time freshmen who did not demonstrate need for aid received scholarships/grants; average award was $1,240. No-need awards available for academics.

**FINANCIAL AID PROCEDURES**
**Forms required:** FAFSA, institutional form.
**Dates and Deadlines:** Priority date 5/1; no closing date. Applicants notified on a rolling basis; must reply within 2 week(s) of notification.

## CONTACT

Anna Manley, Director of Financial Aid
3345 Redwood Highway, Grants Pass, OR 97527
(541) 956-7501 ext. 1

## Southern Oregon University

Ashland, Oregon
www.sou.edu                Federal Code: 003219

**4-year public** university and liberal arts college in large town.
**Enrollment:** 4,203 undergrads, 16% part-time. 795 full-time freshmen.
**Selectivity:** Admits over 75% of applicants.

**BASIC COSTS (2015-2016)**
**Tuition and fees:** $8,145; out-of-state residents $22,365.
**Per-credit charge:** $147; out-of-state residents $463.
**Room and board:** $12,105.
**Additional info:** Tuition/fee waivers available for minority students.

**FINANCIAL AID PICTURE (2015-2016)**
**Students with need:** 47% of average financial aid package awarded as scholarships/grants, 53% awarded as loans/jobs. Need-based aid available for part-time students. Work study available nights, weekends, and for part-time students.
**Students without need:** No-need awards available for academics, athletics.

**FINANCIAL AID PROCEDURES**
**Forms required:** FAFSA.
**Dates and Deadlines:** Priority date 3/1; no closing date. Applicants notified on a rolling basis starting 3/2; must reply within 4 week(s) of notification.

## CONTACT

Peggy Mezger, Director of Financial Aid
1250 Siskiyou Boulevard, Ashland, OR 97520-5032
(541) 552-6600

## Southwestern Oregon Community College

Coos Bay, Oregon
www.socc.edu                Federal Code: 003220

**2-year public** culinary school and community college in large town.
**Enrollment:** 2,306 undergrads.
**Selectivity:** Open admission; but selective for some programs.

**BASIC COSTS (2015-2016)**
**Tuition and fees:** $5,595; out-of-state residents $5,595.
**Room and board:** $7,400.
**Additional info:** Tuition/fee waivers available for adults, unemployed or children of unemployed.

**FINANCIAL AID PICTURE**
**Students with need:** Need-based aid available for full-time and part-time students.
**Students without need:** No-need awards available for art, athletics, leadership, music/drama.

**FINANCIAL AID PROCEDURES**
**Forms required:** FAFSA.
**Dates and Deadlines:** Closing date 3/1. Applicants notified on a rolling basis starting 5/1; must reply within 3 week(s) of notification.

## CONTACT

Avena Singh, Director of Financial Aid
1988 Newmark Avenue, Coos Bay, OR 97420-2956
(541) 888-7337

## Treasure Valley Community College

Ontario, Oregon
www.tvcc.cc                Federal Code: 003221

**2-year public** community college in large town.
**Enrollment:** 1,838 undergrads, 48% part-time. 320 full-time freshmen.
**Selectivity:** Open admission; but selective for some programs.

**BASIC COSTS (2016-2017)**
**Tuition and fees:** $5,310; out-of-state residents $5,760.
**Room and board:** $7,069.

**FINANCIAL AID PICTURE (2015-2016)**
**Students with need:** Out of 304 full-time freshmen who applied for aid, 290 were judged to have need. Of these, 287 received aid, and 10 had their full need met. Average financial aid package met 43% of need; average scholarship/grant was $5,556; average loan was $3,058. For part-time students, average financial aid package was $7,826.
**Students without need:** 4 full-time freshmen who did not demonstrate need for aid received scholarships/grants; average award was $837. No-need awards available for academics, athletics, leadership, music/drama.
**Scholarships offered:** 42 full-time freshmen received athletic scholarships; average amount $2,216.

**FINANCIAL AID PROCEDURES**
**Forms required:** FAFSA.
**Dates and Deadlines:** Applicants notified on a rolling basis starting 5/1.
**Transfers:** No deadline. Applicants notified on a rolling basis.

## CONTACT

Michelle McKay, Associate Vice President of Student Services
650 College Boulevard, Ontario, OR 97914-3423
(541) 881-5599

## Umpqua Community College

Roseburg, Oregon
www.umpqua.edu                    Federal Code: 003222

**2-year public** community college in large town.
**Enrollment:** 1,146 undergrads, 63% part-time. 182 full-time freshmen.
**Selectivity:** Open admission; but selective for some programs.

### BASIC COSTS (2015-2016)

**Tuition and fees:** $5,325; out-of-state residents $10,545.
**Per-credit charge:** $105; out-of-state residents $221.

### FINANCIAL AID PICTURE (2014-2015)

**Students with need:** Out of 182 full-time freshmen who applied for aid, 74 were judged to have need. Of these, 68 received aid, and 37 had their full need met. Average financial aid package met 84% of need; average scholarship/grant was $6,148. For part-time students, average financial aid package was $2,320.
**Students without need:** No-need awards available for academics, athletics.

### FINANCIAL AID PROCEDURES

**Forms required:** FAFSA, institutional form.
**Dates and Deadlines:** Priority date 3/10; no closing date. Applicants notified on a rolling basis starting 2/9; must reply within 2 week(s) of notification.

### CONTACT

Michelle Bergmann, Director of Financial Aid
1140 Umpqua College Road, Roseburg, OR 97470-0226
(541) 440-4602

## University of Oregon

Eugene, Oregon
www.uoregon.edu                    Federal Code: 003223

**4-year public** university in small city.
**Enrollment:** 20,220 undergrads, 8% part-time. 4,047 full-time freshmen.
**Selectivity:** Admits 50 to 75% of applicants.

### BASIC COSTS (2015-2016)

**Tuition and fees:** $10,289; out-of-state residents $32,024.
**Per-credit charge:** $189; out-of-state residents $672.
**Room and board:** $11,785.

### FINANCIAL AID PICTURE

**Students with need:** Need-based aid available for full-time and part-time students. Work study available nights, weekends, and for part-time students.
**Students without need:** No-need awards available for academics, athletics, leadership, minority status, music/drama, ROTC, state/district residency.
**Scholarships offered:** Stamps Leadership Scholarship: tuition, room, and board for 4 years of undergraduate study and up to $12,000 in enrichment funds over 4 years to pursue study abroad, unpaid internships, or other experiences; total over four years approximately $110,000; awarded competitively to outstanding incoming freshmen from Oregon; 5 per year awarded. Summit Scholarships: awards Oregon top scholars $5,000 per year for 4 years; out-of-state top scholars receive $8,000 per year for 4 years. Apex Scholarship: Oregon residents $3,000 per year for 4 years; out-of-state students receive $4,000 per year for 4 years.

### FINANCIAL AID PROCEDURES

**Forms required:** FAFSA.
**Dates and Deadlines:** Priority date 3/1; no closing date. Applicants notified on a rolling basis starting 4/15; must reply within 4 week(s) of notification.

## CONTACT

Jim Brooks, Asst VP/Director Financial Aid
1217 University of Oregon, Eugene, OR 97403-1217
(541) 346-3221

## University of Portland

Portland, Oregon
www.up.edu                    Federal Code: 003224

**4-year private** university in large city, affiliated with Roman Catholic Church.
**Enrollment:** 3,741 undergrads, 1% part-time. 941 full-time freshmen.
**Selectivity:** Admits 50 to 75% of applicants.

### BASIC COSTS (2015-2016)

**Tuition and fees:** $40,250.
**Per-credit charge:** $1,255.
**Room and board:** $11,902.

### FINANCIAL AID PICTURE (2015-2016)

**Students with need:** Out of 794 full-time freshmen who applied for aid, 626 were judged to have need. Of these, 624 received aid, and 61 had their full need met. Average financial aid package met 69% of need; average scholarship/grant was $23,025; average loan was $3,636. For part-time students, average financial aid package was $16,552.
**Students without need:** 293 full-time freshmen who did not demonstrate need for aid received scholarships/grants; average award was $17,079. No-need awards available for academics, athletics, leadership, minority status, music/drama, ROTC.
**Scholarships offered:** *Merit:* President's Scholarship; up to $10,000; based on academic excellence, school and community involvement, and other factors. Holy Cross Scholarship; up to $6,000; based on academic excellence, school and community involvement, and other factors. Arthur A. Schulte Scholarship; up to $6,000. *Athletic:* 31 full-time freshmen received athletic scholarships; average amount $23,189.

### FINANCIAL AID PROCEDURES

**Forms required:** FAFSA.
**Dates and Deadlines:** Priority date 3/1; no closing date. Applicants notified on a rolling basis starting 3/1; must reply by 5/1.
**Transfers:** No deadline. Applicants notified on a rolling basis; must reply within 4 week(s) of notification.

### CONTACT

Janet Turner, Director of Financial Aid
5000 North Willamette Boulevard, Portland, OR 97203-5798
(503) 943-7311

## Warner Pacific College

Portland, Oregon
www.warnerpacific.edu                    Federal Code: 003225

**4-year private** liberal arts college in very large city, affiliated with Church of God.
**Enrollment:** 519 undergrads, 6% part-time. 90 full-time freshmen.
**Selectivity:** Admits 50 to 75% of applicants.

### BASIC COSTS (2016-2017)

**Tuition and fees:** $22,710.
**Room and board:** $8,900.

### FINANCIAL AID PICTURE (2015-2016)

**Students with need:** Out of 84 full-time freshmen who applied for aid, 75 were judged to have need. Of these, 75 received aid, and 12 had their full need met. Average financial aid package met 59% of need; average scholarship/grant was $6,461; average loan was $3,607. For part-time students, average financial aid package was $14,807.

**Students without need:** 15 full-time freshmen who did not demonstrate need for aid received scholarships/grants; average award was $9,333. No-need awards available for academics, alumni affiliation, athletics, leadership, music/drama, religious affiliation.

**Scholarships offered:** 5 full-time freshmen received athletic scholarships; average amount $2,880.

## FINANCIAL AID PROCEDURES

**Forms required:** FAFSA.

**Dates and Deadlines:** Priority date 3/1; no closing date. Applicants notified on a rolling basis starting 3/1; must reply within 2 week(s) of notification.

**Transfers:** Applicants notified on a rolling basis starting 3/1; must reply within 2 week(s) of notification. Highest Academic Scholarships not available to transfer students. Phi Theta Kappa award available to transfers only.

## CONTACT

Cindy Pollard, Director of Student Financial Services and Financial Aid
2219 SE 68th Avenue, Portland, OR 97215-4026
(503) 517-1091

## Western Oregon University
Monmouth, Oregon
www.wou.edu                      Federal Code: 003209

**4-year public** liberal arts and teachers college in small town.
**Enrollment:** 4,788 undergrads, 15% part-time. 638 full-time freshmen.
**Selectivity:** Admits over 75% of applicants.

### BASIC COSTS (2015-2016)
**Tuition and fees:** $8,433; out-of-state residents $22,728.
**Per-credit charge:** $151; out-of-state residents $469.
**Room and board:** $9,672.
**Additional info:** Full participant in the Western Undergraduate Exchange (WUE) WUE Tuition is $10,215. Resident students can also select a Tuition Promise base tuition rate that is not subject to annual adjustments for 4 years. Tuition at time of enrollment locked for 4 years; tuition/fee waivers available for minority students.

### FINANCIAL AID PICTURE (2014-2015)
**Students with need:** Out of 616 full-time freshmen who applied for aid, 520 were judged to have need. Of these, 520 received aid, and 52 had their full need met. Average financial aid package met 56% of need; average scholarship/grant was $7,589; average loan was $3,071. For part-time students, average financial aid package was $6,866.
**Students without need:** 35 full-time freshmen who did not demonstrate need for aid received scholarships/grants; average award was $1,061. No-need awards available for academics, alumni affiliation, art, athletics, leadership, minority status, music/drama.
**Scholarships offered:** 12 full-time freshmen received athletic scholarships; average amount $2,597.

### FINANCIAL AID PROCEDURES
**Forms required:** FAFSA.
**Dates and Deadlines:** Priority date 2/1; no closing date. Applicants notified on a rolling basis starting 3/25; must reply within 3 week(s) of notification.

### CONTACT
Kella Helyer, Director of Financial Aid
345 North Monmouth Avenue, Monmouth, OR 97361
(503) 838-8475

## Willamette University
Salem, Oregon
www.willamette.edu              Federal Code: 003227

**4-year private** university and liberal arts college in small city, affiliated with United Methodist Church.

**Enrollment:** 1,938 undergrads; 1% part-time. 521 full-time freshmen.
**Selectivity:** Admits over 75% of applicants.

### BASIC COSTS (2015-2016)
**Tuition and fees:** $45,616.
**Room and board:** $11,200.

### FINANCIAL AID PICTURE (2015-2016)
**Students with need:** Out of 456 full-time freshmen who applied for aid, 363 were judged to have need. Of these, 363 received aid, and 113 had their full need met. Average financial aid package met 84% of need; average scholarship/grant was $29,199; average loan was $3,742. For part-time students, average financial aid package was $16,624.
**Students without need:** 152 full-time freshmen who did not demonstrate need for aid received scholarships/grants; average award was $19,925. No-need awards available for academics, alumni affiliation, leadership, minority status, music/drama, religious affiliation.
**Scholarships offered:** Academic merit awards; $5,000-$15,000; based on superior academic achievement and promise. Music, forensics, theater scholarships; average $3,000-$5,000; based on talent. Mark O. Hatfield Scholarship; full tuition; based on excellent academic record and demonstrated commitment to service leadership.

### FINANCIAL AID PROCEDURES
**Forms required:** FAFSA.
**Dates and Deadlines:** Priority date 2/1; no closing date. Applicants notified on a rolling basis starting 4/1; must reply by 5/1 or within 2 week(s) of notification.
**Transfers:** Applicants notified on a rolling basis starting 4/1; must reply by 5/1 or within 2 week(s) of notification.

### CONTACT
Patricia Hoban, Director of Financial Aid
900 State Street, Salem, OR 97301-3922
(503) 370-6273

# Pennsylvania

## Albright College
Reading, Pennsylvania
www.albright.edu                Federal Code: 003229

**4-year private** liberal arts college in small city, affiliated with United Methodist Church.
**Enrollment:** 2,228 undergrads. 493 full-time freshmen.
**Selectivity:** Admits less than 50% of applicants.

### BASIC COSTS (2015-2016)
**Tuition and fees:** $39,850.
**Per-credit charge:** $1,217.
**Room and board:** $10,770.
**Additional info:** Tuition/fee waivers available for minority students.

### FINANCIAL AID PICTURE (2015-2016)
**Students with need:** Out of 473 full-time freshmen who applied for aid, 445 were judged to have need. Of these, 445 received aid, and 41 had their full need met. Average financial aid package met 82% of need; average scholarship/grant was $30,490; average loan was $4,782. For part-time students, average financial aid package was $7,652.
**Students without need:** 122 full-time freshmen who did not demonstrate need for aid received scholarships/grants; average award was $16,344. No-need awards available for academics, art, music/drama, religious affiliation, state/district residency.

**Scholarships offered:** Academic scholarships range from $5,000 to full tuition per year. All scholarships and awards are renewable, typically contingent upon achieving a specified grade point average and/or service commitment.
**Additional info:** If student's financial aid and admission application is complete by 3/1, college will meet 100% of the family's institutionally determined need.

### FINANCIAL AID PROCEDURES
**Forms required:** FAFSA. The CSS Profile can be optionally completed in the fall prior to the start of student's college experience for early awarding.
**Dates and Deadlines:** Priority date 3/1; no closing date. Applicants notified on a rolling basis starting 11/20; must reply by 5/1 or within 2 week(s) of notification.
**Transfers:** Priority date 6/1; no deadline. Applicants notified on a rolling basis starting 2/15; must reply within 2 week(s) of notification.

### CONTACT
Chris Hanlon, Director of Financial Aid
North 13th and Bern Streets, Reading, PA 19612-5234
(800) 252-1856

## Allegheny College
Meadville, Pennsylvania
www.allegheny.edu                    Federal Code: 003230

**4-year private** liberal arts college in large town, affiliated with United Methodist Church.
**Enrollment:** 1,896 undergrads, 1% part-time. 489 full-time freshmen.
**Selectivity:** Admits 50 to 75% of applicants.

### BASIC COSTS (2016-2017)
**Tuition and fees:** $44,250.
**Per-credit charge:** $1,823.
**Room and board:** $11,170.

### FINANCIAL AID PICTURE (2015-2016)
**Students with need:** Out of 423 full-time freshmen who applied for aid, 375 were judged to have need. Of these, 375 received aid, and 157 had their full need met. Average financial aid package met 92% of need; average scholarship/grant was $32,544; average loan was $4,033. For part-time students, average financial aid package was $12,226.
**Students without need:** 107 full-time freshmen who did not demonstrate need for aid received scholarships/grants; average award was $19,878. No-need awards available for academics, leadership, minority status, state/district residency.
**Scholarships offered:** Trustee Scholarships: up to $22,500 per year available for entering freshman and $20,000 for entering transfer students.
**Additional info:** Non need-based financial aid also determined by extra-curricular and co-curricular involvement and special achievement or activities. Daytime work-study programs available.

### FINANCIAL AID PROCEDURES
**Forms required:** FAFSA.
**Dates and Deadlines:** Priority date 2/15; no closing date. Applicants notified on a rolling basis starting 3/1; must reply by 5/1 or within 4 week(s) of notification.
**Transfers:** Priority date 6/1; no deadline. Applicants notified on a rolling basis; must reply within 3 week(s) of notification.

### CONTACT
Jonathan Boleratz, Director of Financial Aid
Box 5, 520 North Main Street, Meadville, PA 16335
(800) 835-7780

## Alvernia University
Reading, Pennsylvania
www.alvernia.edu                    Federal Code: 003233

**4-year private** university and liberal arts college in small city, affiliated with Roman Catholic Church.
**Enrollment:** 2,177 undergrads, 19% part-time. 401 full-time freshmen.
**Selectivity:** Admits 50 to 75% of applicants.

### BASIC COSTS (2016-2017)
**Tuition and fees:** $32,270.
**Per-credit charge:** $870.
**Room and board:** $11,430.
**Additional info:** Tuition/fee waivers available for minority students.

### FINANCIAL AID PICTURE (2015-2016)
**Students with need:** Out of 387 full-time freshmen who applied for aid, 341 were judged to have need. Of these, 340 received aid, and 52 had their full need met. Average financial aid package met 70% of need; average scholarship/grant was $18,979; average loan was $3,206. For part-time students, average financial aid package was $6,506.
**Students without need:** 58 full-time freshmen who did not demonstrate need for aid received scholarships/grants; average award was $15,108. No-need awards available for academics, ROTC.
**Scholarships offered:** Presidential Scholarship: $14,000; minimum 1130 SAT (or 25 ACT) and minimum 3.5 GPA. Trustee's Scholarship: $12,000; minimum 1050 SAT (or 23 ACT) and minimum 3.2 GPA. Veronica Founder's Scholarship: $10,000; minimum 980 SAT (or 21 ACT) and 3.0 GPA.

### FINANCIAL AID PROCEDURES
**Forms required:** FAFSA, state aid form.
**Dates and Deadlines:** Priority date 5/1; no closing date. Applicants notified on a rolling basis starting 3/1; must reply by 5/1.
**Transfers:** Priority date 5/8; no deadline. Applicants notified on a rolling basis starting 2/20; must reply within 2 week(s) of notification.

### CONTACT
Christine Saadi, Associate Director of Financial Aid
400 St. Bernardine Street, Reading, PA 19607-1799
(610) 796-8356

## Antonelli Institute of Art and Photography
Erdenheim, Pennsylvania
www.antonelli.edu                    Federal Code: 007430

**2-year for-profit** visual arts and junior college in large town.
**Enrollment:** 189 undergrads.

### BASIC COSTS (2015-2016)
**Tuition and fees:** $20,920.
**Additional info:** Tuition quoted is for the photography degree program; annual tuition for the graphic design degree program is $18,820. Estimated kit and supply costs vary depending on degree program. All costs are subject to change.

### FINANCIAL AID PICTURE
**Students with need:** Need-based aid available for full-time and part-time students. Work study available nights.
**Students without need:** This college awards aid only to students with need.

### FINANCIAL AID PROCEDURES
**Forms required:** FAFSA.
**Dates and Deadlines:** Applicants notified on a rolling basis; must reply within 2 week(s) of notification.
**Transfers:** Priority date 3/15; closing date 8/1. Applicants notified on a rolling basis.

## CONTACT
Eugene Awot, Director of Financial Aid
300 Montgomery Avenue, Erdenheim, PA 19038-8242
(215) 836-2222

## Arcadia University
Glenside, Pennsylvania
www.arcadia.edu                    Federal Code: 003235

**4-year private** university in large town, affiliated with Presbyterian Church
(USA).
**Enrollment:** 2,501 undergrads, 5% part-time. 598 full-time freshmen.

### BASIC COSTS (2015-2016)
**Tuition and fees:** $39,560.
**Per-credit charge:** $640.
**Room and board:** $13,200.

### FINANCIAL AID PICTURE
**Students with need:** Need-based aid available for full-time and part-time students. Work study available nights, weekends, and for part-time students.
**Students without need:** No-need awards available for academics, alumni
affiliation, art, leadership, music/drama.
**Scholarships offered:** Distinguished Scholarships: $15,000-$20,500; for full-
time students based on grades, test scores, coursework taken, high school
rank and involvement. Arcadia University Achievement Awards: $1,000-
$14,500; for full-time students who have demonstrated outstanding leader-
ship, exceptional community and/or volunteer service or special talents. President's Scholarship: full tuition; based on academic excellence, outstanding
leadership, and community and volunteer service. Writing Achievement
Awards: offered to those who score among the highest in the applicant pool
annually on SAT or ACT writing sections.
**Additional info:** Automatic $1,000 renewable FAFSA Early Filer Grant for
new incoming full-time undergraduates who file FAFSA by March 1, listing
Arcadia as a recipient school on the form, and have a completed admissions
application on file by March 1.

### FINANCIAL AID PROCEDURES
**Forms required:** FAFSA, institutional form.
**Dates and Deadlines:** Priority date 3/1; no closing date. Applicants notified
on a rolling basis starting 2/1; must reply by 5/1.
**Transfers:** No deadline. Applicants notified on a rolling basis starting 2/1.

### CONTACT
Holly Kirkpatrick, Director of Enrollment Management and Director of
Financial Aid
450 South Easton Road, Glenside, PA 19038-3295
(215) 572-2980

## Art Institute of Philadelphia
Philadelphia, Pennsylvania
www.artinstitutes.edu/Philadelphia   Federal Code: 008350

**4-year for-profit** visual arts college in very large city.
**Enrollment:** 1,953 undergrads.

### BASIC COSTS (2015-2016)
**Tuition and fees:** $22,375.
**Room only:** $8,673.
**Additional info:** Additional fees may be apply. All costs are subject to
change.

### FINANCIAL AID PICTURE
**Students with need:** Need-based aid available for full-time and part-time students. Work study available nights, weekends, and for part-time students.

**Additional info:** Institute-sponsored scholarships available. May 1st application deadline for Pennsylvania State Grant.

### FINANCIAL AID PROCEDURES
**Forms required:** FAFSA, institutional form.
**Dates and Deadlines:** Applicants notified on a rolling basis starting 3/1;
must reply within 2 week(s) of notification.
**Transfers:** No deadline. Transfer students applying for financial aid must
meet standards for satisfactory academic progress as defined by State Grant
Program.

### CONTACT
Fatisha Strickland, Director of Student Financial Services
1622 Chestnut Street, Philadelphia, PA 19103-5198
(215) 567-7080 ext. 6392

## Art Institute of Pittsburgh
Pittsburgh, Pennsylvania
www.artinstitutes.edu/pittsburgh    Federal Code: 007470

**4-year for-profit** culinary school and visual arts college in large city.
**Enrollment:** 900 undergrads.

### BASIC COSTS (2016-2017)
**Tuition and fees:** $23,476.
**Room only:** $7,956.

### FINANCIAL AID PICTURE
**Students with need:** Need-based aid available for full-time and part-time students.

### FINANCIAL AID PROCEDURES
**Forms required:** FAFSA, institutional form.
**Dates and Deadlines:** Applicants notified on a rolling basis starting 4/15.

### CONTACT
Lara Hemwall, Director Student Financial Services
420 Boulevard of the Allies, Pittsburgh, PA 15219-1328
(412) 291-6200

## Berks Technical Institute
Wyomissing, Pennsylvania
www.berks.edu                      Federal Code: 017149

**2-year for-profit** business and technical college in small city.
**Enrollment:** 1,140 undergrads.

### BASIC COSTS (2015-2016)
**Additional info:** Tuition varies by program; total program tuition and fees
range from $27,849 to $32,455. Massage Therapy diploma program,
$10,600. Books and supplies vary depending on program and level. All costs
are subject to change.

### FINANCIAL AID PICTURE
**Students with need:** Need-based aid available for full-time and part-time students.
**Students without need:** This college awards aid only to students with
need.

### FINANCIAL AID PROCEDURES
**Forms required:** FAFSA, state aid form.
**Dates and Deadlines:** Applicants notified on a rolling basis; must reply
within 2 week(s) of notification.
**Transfers:** Deadline for first-time financial aid applicants is August 1. Dead-
line for renewal applicants is May 1.

**CONTACT**
Valerie Wessner, Senior Financial Aid Director
2205 Ridgewood Road, Wyomissing, PA 19610
(610) 372-1722

## Bidwell Training Center
Pittsburgh, Pennsylvania
www.bidwell-training.org　　　Federal Code: 031015

**1-year private** business and health science college in large city.
**Enrollment:** 150 undergrads.

**BASIC COSTS (2015-2016)**
**Tuition and fees:** $14,000.
**Additional info:** Cost quoted is for the chemical laboratory technician program. Tuition for other programs varies by program. All costs are subject to change.

**FINANCIAL AID PICTURE**
**Students with need:** Need-based aid available for full-time students.
**Students without need:** This college awards aid only to students with need.

**FINANCIAL AID PROCEDURES**
**Forms required:** FAFSA.
**Dates and Deadlines:** Applicants notified on a rolling basis.

**CONTACT**
Ken Huselton, Senior Director of Operations
1815 Metropolitan Street, Pittsburgh, PA 15233
(412) 323-4000

## Bloomsburg University of Pennsylvania
Bloomsburg, Pennsylvania
www.bloomu.edu　　　Federal Code: 003315

**4-year public** university in large town.
**Enrollment:** 8,931 undergrads, 6% part-time. 2,102 full-time freshmen.
**Selectivity:** Admits over 75% of applicants.

**BASIC COSTS (2015-2016)**
**Tuition and fees:** $9,326; out-of-state residents $19,916.
**Room and board:** $8,480.
**Additional info:** Tuition/fee waivers available for minority students.

**FINANCIAL AID PICTURE (2015-2016)**
**Students with need:** Out of 1,979 full-time freshmen who applied for aid, 1,375 were judged to have need. Of these, 1,339 received aid, and 131 had their full need met. Average financial aid package met 50% of need; average scholarship/grant was $6,053; average loan was $3,196. For part-time students, average financial aid package was $6,228.
**Students without need:** 63 full-time freshmen who did not demonstrate need for aid received scholarships/grants; average award was $2,639. No-need awards available for academics, art, athletics, job skills, leadership, minority status, music/drama, ROTC, state/district residency.
**Scholarships offered:** 47 full-time freshmen received athletic scholarships; average amount $2,740.

**FINANCIAL AID PROCEDURES**
**Forms required:** FAFSA.
**Dates and Deadlines:** Priority date 3/15; no closing date. Applicants notified on a rolling basis starting 4/1.
**Transfers:** Evaluation of transfer credits must be completed before financial aid can be finalized.

**CONTACT**
Amanda Kishbaugh, Interim Director of Financial Aid
104 Student Service Center, Bloomsburg, PA 17815
(570) 389-4297

## Bradford School: Pittsburgh
Pittsburgh, Pennsylvania
www.bradfordpittsburgh.edu　　　Federal Code: 009721

**2-year for-profit** junior college in very large city.
**Enrollment:** 439 full-time undergrads.

**BASIC COSTS (2015-2016)**
**Tuition and fees:** $15,340.
**Room and board:** $6,960.
**Additional info:** Estimated cost of books and supplies range from $1,180 to $1,800 depending on degree program. All costs are subject to change.

**FINANCIAL AID PICTURE**
**Students with need:** Need-based aid available for full-time students.

**FINANCIAL AID PROCEDURES**
**Forms required:** FAFSA.

**CONTACT**
Director of Financial Aid
125 West Station Square Drive, Pittsburgh, PA 15219
(412) 391-6710

## Bryn Athyn College
Bryn Athyn, Pennsylvania
www.brynathyn.edu　　　Federal Code: 003228

**4-year private** liberal arts college in small town, affiliated with Christian Church.
**Enrollment:** 273 undergrads, 3% part-time. 89 full-time freshmen.
**Selectivity:** Admits over 75% of applicants.

**BASIC COSTS (2015-2016)**
**Tuition and fees:** $19,353.
**Room and board:** $11,202.

**FINANCIAL AID PICTURE (2015-2016)**
**Students with need:** Out of 77 full-time freshmen who applied for aid, 69 were judged to have need. Of these, 69 received aid, and 9 had their full need met. Average financial aid package met 68% of need; average scholarship/grant was $11,288; average loan was $3,414. For part-time students, average financial aid package was $8,359.
**Students without need:** 14 full-time freshmen who did not demonstrate need for aid received scholarships/grants; average award was $6,795. No-need awards available for academics, religious affiliation.

**FINANCIAL AID PROCEDURES**
**Forms required:** FAFSA, state aid form.
**Dates and Deadlines:** Priority date 2/15; no closing date. Applicants notified on a rolling basis starting 3/15; must reply within 3 week(s) of notification.
**Transfers:** No deadline. Applicants notified on a rolling basis starting 7/1; must reply within 6 week(s) of notification.

**CONTACT**
Eiben Carole, Financial Aid Director
PO Box 462, Bryn Athyn, PA 19009-0462
(267) 502-2493

## Bryn Mawr College

Bryn Mawr, Pennsylvania
www.brynmawr.edu

Federal Code: 003237
CSS Code: 2049

**4-year private** liberal arts college for women in very large city.
**Enrollment:** 1,341 undergrads, 1% part-time. 385 full-time freshmen.
**Selectivity:** Admits less than 50% of applicants.

### BASIC COSTS (2015-2016)

**Tuition and fees:** $47,140.
**Room and board:** $14,850.

### FINANCIAL AID PICTURE (2015-2016)

**Students with need:** Out of 244 full-time freshmen who applied for aid, 198 were judged to have need. Of these, 198 received aid, and 198 had their full need met. Average financial aid package met 100% of need; average scholarship/grant was $38,885; average loan was $4,291. For part-time students, average financial aid package was $31,094.
**Students without need:** This college awards aid only to students with need.

### FINANCIAL AID PROCEDURES

**Forms required:** FAFSA, CSS PROFILE.
**Dates and Deadlines:** Priority date 2/5; closing date 3/1. Applicants notified by 3/23; must reply by 5/1.
**Transfers:** Closing date 3/15. Must reply by 5/1.

### CONTACT

Ethel Desmarais, Director of Financial Aid
101 North Merion Avenue, Bryn Mawr, PA 19010-2899
(610) 526-5245

## Bucknell University

Lewisburg, Pennsylvania
www.bucknell.edu

Federal Code: 003238
CSS Code: 2050

**4-year private** university in small town.
**Enrollment:** 3,522 undergrads. 938 full-time freshmen.
**Selectivity:** Admits less than 50% of applicants.

### BASIC COSTS (2016-2017)

**Tuition and fees:** $51,960.
**Per-credit charge:** $1,418.
**Room and board:** $12,656.

### FINANCIAL AID PICTURE (2015-2016)

**Students with need:** Out of 528 full-time freshmen who applied for aid, 417 were judged to have need. Of these, 417 received aid, and 379 had their full need met. Average financial aid package met 91% of need; average scholarship/grant was $27,400; average loan was $3,500.
**Students without need:** 80 full-time freshmen who did not demonstrate need for aid received scholarships/grants; average award was $13,007. No-need awards available for academics, art, athletics, leadership, music/drama, ROTC.
**Scholarships offered:** *Merit:* Scholarships available to a limited number of students who have demonstrated exceptional achievements in academics, art and performing arts, music, and athletics. *Athletic:* 36 full-time freshmen received athletic scholarships; average amount $33,689.

### FINANCIAL AID PROCEDURES

**Forms required:** FAFSA, CSS PROFILE.
**Dates and Deadlines:** Closing date 1/15. Applicants notified by 4/1; must reply by 5/1.
**Transfers:** Closing date 3/15. Applicants notified by 5/1; must reply by 6/1. Aid restricted to 2-year college graduates.

### CONTACT

Andrea Stauffer, Director of Financial Aid
Office of Admissions, Bucknell University, Lewisburg, PA 17837-9988
(570) 577-1331

## Bucks County Community College

Newtown, Pennsylvania
www.bucks.edu

Federal Code: 003239

**2-year public** community college in large town.
**Enrollment:** 8,532 undergrads, 65% part-time. 1,127 full-time freshmen.
**Selectivity:** Open admission; but selective for some programs.

### BASIC COSTS (2015-2016)

**Tuition and fees:** $5,210; out-of-district residents $9,260; out-of-state residents $13,310.
**Per-credit charge:** $135; out-of-district residents $270; out-of-state residents $405.

### FINANCIAL AID PICTURE

**Students with need:** Need-based aid available for full-time and part-time students. Work study available nights, weekends, and for part-time students.
**Students without need:** No-need awards available for academics, art, music/drama.
**Additional info:** Files are processed in order of receipt and completion date.

### FINANCIAL AID PROCEDURES

**Forms required:** FAFSA.
**Dates and Deadlines:** Closing date 5/1. Applicants notified on a rolling basis starting 6/1; must reply within 2 week(s) of notification.
**Transfers:** Applicants notified on a rolling basis starting 6/1; must reply within 2 week(s) of notification.

### CONTACT

Donna Wilkoski, Director of Financial Aid
275 Swamp Road, Newtown, PA 18940
(215) 968-8200

## Butler County Community College

Butler, Pennsylvania
www.bc3.edu

Federal Code: 003240

**2-year public** community college in small city.
**Enrollment:** 3,686 undergrads.
**Selectivity:** Open admission; but selective for some programs.

### BASIC COSTS (2015-2016)

**Tuition and fees:** $4,230; out-of-district residents $7,230; out-of-state residents $10,230.

### FINANCIAL AID PICTURE

**Students with need:** Need-based aid available for full-time and part-time students.
**Students without need:** No-need awards available for academics, state/district residency.

### FINANCIAL AID PROCEDURES

**Forms required:** FAFSA.
**Dates and Deadlines:** Priority date 4/15; no closing date. Applicants notified on a rolling basis starting 5/1; must reply within 2 week(s) of notification.

### CONTACT

Julianne Louttit, Director of Financial Aid
PO Box 1203, Butler, PA 16003-1203
(724) 287-8711 ext. 8329

## Cabrini College
Radnor, Pennsylvania
www.cabrini.edu                    Federal Code: 003241

**4-year private** liberal arts college in large town, affiliated with Roman Catholic Church.
**Enrollment:** 1,377 undergrads, 5% part-time. 394 full-time freshmen.
**Selectivity:** Admits 50 to 75% of applicants.

### BASIC COSTS (2016-2017)
**Tuition and fees:** $30,588.
**Per-credit charge:** $540.
**Room and board:** $12,026.

### FINANCIAL AID PICTURE (2014-2015)
**Students with need:** Out of 284 full-time freshmen who applied for aid, 253 were judged to have need. Of these, 253 received aid, and 50 had their full need met. For part-time students, average financial aid package was $10,625.
**Students without need:** 39 full-time freshmen who did not demonstrate need for aid received scholarships/grants; average award was $9,562. No-need awards available for academics, alumni affiliation, religious affiliation, ROTC, state/district residency.

### FINANCIAL AID PROCEDURES
**Forms required:** FAFSA.
**Dates and Deadlines:** Priority date 2/15; no closing date. Applicants notified on a rolling basis starting 3/1; must reply by 5/1.
**Transfers:** Achievement scholarships available.

### CONTACT
Betsy Gingerich, Director of Financial Aid
610 King of Prussia Road, Radnor, PA 19087-3698
(610) 902-8420

## Cairn University
Langhorne, Pennsylvania
www.cairn.edu                      Federal Code: 003351

**4-year private** university and Bible college in small town, affiliated with Christian Church.
**Enrollment:** 772 undergrads, 6% part-time. 159 full-time freshmen.
**Selectivity:** Admits over 75% of applicants.

### BASIC COSTS (2015-2016)
**Tuition and fees:** $23,920.
**Room and board:** $9,350.

### FINANCIAL AID PICTURE (2015-2016)
**Students with need:** Out of 148 full-time freshmen who applied for aid, 130 were judged to have need. Of these, 130 received aid, and 5 had their full need met. Average financial aid package met 77% of need; average scholarship/grant was $17,771; average loan was $3,860. For part-time students, average financial aid package was $4,935.
**Students without need:** 29 full-time freshmen who did not demonstrate need for aid received scholarships/grants; average award was $10,467. No-need awards available for academics, leadership, music/drama.
**Scholarships offered:** Cairn U Merit Scholarship based on high school GPA and SAT scores.

### FINANCIAL AID PROCEDURES
**Forms required:** FAFSA.
**Dates and Deadlines:** Priority date 3/1; no closing date. Applicants notified on a rolling basis starting 2/1; must reply within 2 week(s) of notification.
**Transfers:** Priority date 3/1; no deadline. Applicants notified on a rolling basis.

### CONTACT
Stephen Cassel, Director of Financial Aid
200 Manor Avenue, Langhorne, PA 19047-2990
(215) 702-4246

## California University of Pennsylvania
California, Pennsylvania
www.calu.edu                       Federal Code: 003316

**4-year public** university in small town.
**Enrollment:** 5,715 undergrads, 13% part-time. 1,015 full-time freshmen.
**Selectivity:** Admits over 75% of applicants.

### BASIC COSTS (2015-2016)
**Tuition and fees:** $9,936; out-of-state residents $13,466.
**Room and board:** $10,238.
**Additional info:** Tuition/fee waivers available for adults, minority students.

### FINANCIAL AID PICTURE (2014-2015)
**Students with need:** Out of 953 full-time freshmen who applied for aid, 809 were judged to have need. Of these, 809 received aid, and 49 had their full need met. Average financial aid package met 52% of need; average scholarship/grant was $6,678; average loan was $3,340. For part-time students, average financial aid package was $6,454.
**Students without need:** 36 full-time freshmen who did not demonstrate need for aid received scholarships/grants; average award was $3,421. No-need awards available for academics, athletics, leadership, minority status, music/drama, state/district residency.
**Scholarships offered:** 18 full-time freshmen received athletic scholarships; average amount $9,926.

### FINANCIAL AID PROCEDURES
**Forms required:** FAFSA.
**Dates and Deadlines:** Priority date 3/1; no closing date. Applicants notified on a rolling basis starting 4/1; must reply within 2 week(s) of notification.

### CONTACT
Jill Fernandes, Director of Financial Aid
250 University Avenue, California, PA 15419-1394
(724) 938-4415

## Cambria-Rowe Business College
Johnstown, Pennsylvania
www.crbc.net

**2-year for-profit** business and career college in small city.
**Enrollment:** 136 undergrads, 1% part-time. 33 full-time freshmen.
**Selectivity:** Open admission.

### BASIC COSTS (2015-2016)
**Tuition and fees:** $14,830.
**Per-credit charge:** $260.

### FINANCIAL AID PICTURE
**Students with need:** Need-based aid available for full-time and part-time students.
**Students without need:** No-need awards available for academics, leadership.
**Scholarships offered:** Presidential Grant (3 awarded) 50% tuition; FBLA Scholarship (2 awarded) $3,000.

### FINANCIAL AID PROCEDURES
**Forms required:** FAFSA, state aid form.
**Dates and Deadlines:** Applicants notified on a rolling basis.
**Transfers:** Closing date 5/1.

**CONTACT**
Linda Wess, Director of Financial Aid Services
221 Central Avenue, Johnstown, PA 15902

## Cambria-Rowe Business College: Indiana
Indiana, Pennsylvania
www.crbc.net                    Federal Code: 004889

**2-year for-profit** business and career college in small town.
**Enrollment:** 105 undergrads.

**BASIC COSTS (2015-2016)**
**Tuition and fees:** $14,830.
**Per-credit charge:** $260.

**FINANCIAL AID PICTURE**
**Students with need:** Need-based aid available for full-time and part-time students.
**Students without need:** No-need awards available for academics, leadership.

**FINANCIAL AID PROCEDURES**
**Forms required:** FAFSA, state aid form.
**Dates and Deadlines:** Applicants notified on a rolling basis.
**Transfers:** Closing date 5/1.

**CONTACT**
Linda Wess, Director of Financial Aid Services
422 South 13th Street, Indiana, PA 15701
(814) 536-5168

## Career Training Academy
New Kensington, Pennsylvania
www.careerta.edu                Federal Code: 026095

**2-year for-profit** career college in small town.
**Enrollment:** 171 undergrads.
**Selectivity:** Open admission; but selective for some programs.

**BASIC COSTS (2015-2016)**
**Additional info:** Tuition and fees for entire programs (diploma or associate degree) range from $10,200 to $23,053; programs vary from 6 to 18 months in duration. Additional expenses include books and supplies, which range from $1,183 to $3,952 depending upon program of study.

**FINANCIAL AID PICTURE**
**Students with need:** Need-based aid available for full-time students.
**Students without need:** This college awards aid only to students with need.
**Additional info:** Work study available after class day.

**FINANCIAL AID PROCEDURES**
**Forms required:** FAFSA, institutional form.

**CONTACT**
Amber Tate, Director of Financial Aid
950 Fifth Avenue, New Kensington, PA 15068

## Career Training Academy: Monroeville
Monroeville, Pennsylvania
www.careerta.edu                Federal Code: 026095

**2-year for-profit** branch campus college in small city.
**Enrollment:** 115 undergrads.
**Selectivity:** Open admission; but selective for some programs.

**BASIC COSTS (2015-2016)**
**Additional info:** Tuition and fees for entire programs (diploma or associate degree) range from $10,200 to $23,053; programs vary from 6 to 18 months in duration. Additional expenses include books and supplies, which range from $1,183 to $3,952 depending upon program of study.

**FINANCIAL AID PICTURE**
**Students with need:** Need-based aid available for full-time and part-time students.
**Students without need:** This college awards aid only to students with need.

**FINANCIAL AID PROCEDURES**
**Forms required:** FAFSA, state aid form, institutional form.

**CONTACT**
Amber Tate, Director of Financial Aid
4314 Old William Penn Highway #103, Monroeville, PA 15146
(724) 337-1000

## Carlow University
Pittsburgh, Pennsylvania
www.carlow.edu                  Federal Code: 003303

**4-year private** university in large city, affiliated with Roman Catholic Church.
**Enrollment:** 1,377 undergrads, 25% part-time. 219 full-time freshmen.
**Selectivity:** Admits over 75% of applicants.

**BASIC COSTS (2015-2016)**
**Tuition and fees:** $26,832.
**Per-credit charge:** $846.
**Room and board:** $10,572.
**Additional info:** Part-time traditionally-aged undergraduates pay $846 per-credit-hour. Both full-time and part-time non-traditionally-aged undergraduates pay $642 per-credit-hour. RN-to-BSN students pay $495 per-credit-hour.

**FINANCIAL AID PICTURE**
**Students with need:** Need-based aid available for full-time and part-time students. Work study available nights, weekends, and for part-time students.

**FINANCIAL AID PROCEDURES**
**Forms required:** FAFSA, state aid form.
**Dates and Deadlines:** Priority date 5/1; no closing date. Applicants notified on a rolling basis starting 2/15; must reply within 4 week(s) of notification.
**Transfers:** No deadline. Applicants notified on a rolling basis; must reply within 4 week(s) of notification.

**CONTACT**
Natalie Wilson, Director of Financial Aid
3333 Fifth Avenue, Pittsburgh, PA 15213-3165
(412) 578-6058

## Carnegie Mellon University
Pittsburgh, Pennsylvania          Federal Code: 003242
www.cmu.edu                       CSS Code: 2074

**4-year private** university in large city.
**Enrollment:** 6,362 undergrads, 2% part-time. 1,575 full-time freshmen.
**Selectivity:** Admits less than 50% of applicants.

**BASIC COSTS (2015-2016)**
**Tuition and fees:** $50,665.
**Room and board:** $12,830.

**FINANCIAL AID PICTURE (2015-2016)**
**Students with need:** Out of 1,010 full-time freshmen who applied for aid, 737 were judged to have need. Of these, 729 received aid, and 215 had their full need met. Average financial aid package met 84% of need; average

scholarship/grant was $31,926; average loan was $4,055. For part-time students, average financial aid package was $23,642.

**Students without need:** 77 full-time freshmen who did not demonstrate need for aid received scholarships/grants; average award was $13,140. No-need awards available for academics, art, leadership, minority status, music/drama, state/district residency.

**Additional info:** Early need analysis offered; merit awards available. Financial aid applicants will receive financial aid notification shortly after notification of admission or a spot on the waiting list.

### FINANCIAL AID PROCEDURES

**Forms required:** FAFSA, state aid form, institutional form. Required for institutional financial aid programs only. Not required if applying only for federal financial aid.

**Dates and Deadlines:** Priority date 2/15; closing date 4/15. Applicants notified by 4/15; must reply by 5/1.

**Transfers:** Students applying for spring transfer must file FAFSA by 11/1 and are notified of award 12/15 or soon after. College of Fine Arts applicants applying for fall transfer must file FAFSA by 2/15 and are notified of award by 4/15. All other applicants for fall transfer must submit FAFSA by 5/1 and are notified of award during the month of June.

### CONTACT

Judith Schneider, Interim Director of Student Financial Aid
5000 Forbes Avenue, Pittsburgh, PA 15213-3890
(412) 268-8186

## Cedar Crest College
Allentown, Pennsylvania
www.cedarcrest.edu                Federal Code: 003243

**4-year private** liberal arts college for women in small city.
**Enrollment:** 1,360 undergrads, 43% part-time. 179 full-time freshmen.
**Selectivity:** Admits 50 to 75% of applicants.

### BASIC COSTS (2015-2016)
**Tuition and fees:** $35,400.
**Room and board:** $10,765.

### FINANCIAL AID PICTURE (2015-2016)
**Students with need:** Out of 174 full-time freshmen who applied for aid, 164 were judged to have need. Of these, 164 received aid, and 11 had their full need met. Average financial aid package met 78% of need; average scholarship/grant was $27,930; average loan was $3,364. For part-time students, average financial aid package was $8,335.

**Students without need:** 13 full-time freshmen who did not demonstrate need for aid received scholarships/grants; average award was $18,680. No-need awards available for academics, alumni affiliation, art, music/drama.

**Scholarships offered:** Presidential Scholarship; up to half tuition; for freshmen with SAT scores over 1150 and in top 10% of class; renewable for four years with GPA of 3.0. 1867 Award; one-third of tuition; renewable for four years with GPA of 3.0; for freshmen with SAT of 1100 and in top 25% of class. Girl Scout Gold Awards; $1,000 per year; for recipients of the Girl Scout Gold Award. Art, Dance, and Performing Arts Scholarships; $1,500 per year; based on portfolio review, audition, and commitment to the creative process. Governor's School of Excellence Award; $1,000 per year; for graduates of Governor's Schools of Excellence. Hugh O'Brian Youth (HOBY) Awards; $1,000 per year; for freshmen who are HOBY alumnae. SAT scores exclusive of Writing portion.

### FINANCIAL AID PROCEDURES
**Forms required:** FAFSA.
**Dates and Deadlines:** Priority date 5/1; no closing date. Applicants notified on a rolling basis starting 9/15; must reply within 2 week(s) of notification.
**Transfers:** Must reply by 5/15. Certain academic scholarships are available for transfers only, such as the Phi Theta Kappa Scholarship, Lifelong Learning Transfer Scholarship and Traditional Transfer Scholarship.

### CONTACT

Valerie Kreiser, Director of Student Financial Services
100 College Drive, Allentown, PA 18104-6196
(610) 606-4653

## Central Penn College
Summerdale, Pennsylvania
www.centralpenn.edu             Federal Code: 004890

**4-year for-profit** technical and career college in rural community.
**Enrollment:** 1,286 undergrads, 44% part-time. 101 full-time freshmen.

### BASIC COSTS (2015-2016)
**Tuition and fees:** $22,868.
**Per-credit charge:** $453.
**Room and board:** $8,736.

### FINANCIAL AID PICTURE
**Students with need:** Need-based aid available for full-time and part-time students.

**Students without need:** No-need awards available for academics, alumni affiliation, job skills, leadership, minority status, state/district residency.

### FINANCIAL AID PROCEDURES
**Forms required:** FAFSA, state aid form, institutional form.
**Dates and Deadlines:** Priority date 3/15; no closing date. Applicants notified on a rolling basis starting 2/1; must reply within 2 week(s) of notification.

### CONTACT

Kathy Shepard, Financial Aid Director
College Hill and Valley Roads, Summerdale, PA 17093-0309
(717) 728-2261

## Chatham University
Pittsburgh, Pennsylvania
www.chatham.edu                Federal Code: 003244

**4-year private** university and liberal arts college in large city.
**Enrollment:** 695 undergrads, 12% part-time. 210 full-time freshmen.
**Selectivity:** Admits over 75% of applicants.

### BASIC COSTS (2015-2016)
**Tuition and fees:** $34,440.
**Per-credit charge:** $805.
**Room and board:** $10,720.

### FINANCIAL AID PICTURE (2015-2016)
**Students with need:** Out of 197 full-time freshmen who applied for aid, 163 were judged to have need. Of these, 163 received aid, and 37 had their full need met. Average financial aid package met 82% of need; average scholarship/grant was $9,487; average loan was $3,572. For part-time students, average financial aid package was $5,667.

**Students without need:** 34 full-time freshmen who did not demonstrate need for aid received scholarships/grants; average award was $15,432. No-need awards available for academics, alumni affiliation, art, music/drama.

**Scholarships offered:** Presidential Scholarship: up to annual tuition. Trustee Scholarship: $16,000. Dean Scholarship: $14,000. Founders' Scholarship: $12,000. Chatham Scholarship: $10,000. All based on academic excellence and renewable annually based on GPA of 2.8 or higher. The Presidential requires a 3.00 or higher for renewal.

### FINANCIAL AID PROCEDURES
**Forms required:** FAFSA.
**Dates and Deadlines:** Priority date 3/1; no closing date. Applicants notified on a rolling basis starting 3/1; must reply within 3 week(s) of notification.
**Transfers:** Special scholarships are available for transfer students.

**CONTACT**
Jennifer Burns, Director of Financial Aid
Woodland Road, Pittsburgh, PA 15232
(412) 365-2781

## Chestnut Hill College
Philadelphia, Pennsylvania
www.chc.edu                          Federal Code: 003245

**4-year private** liberal arts college in very large city, affiliated with Roman
Catholic Church.
**Enrollment:** 1,383 undergrads.
**Selectivity:** Admits over 75% of applicants.

**BASIC COSTS (2015-2016)**
**Tuition and fees:** $33,120.
**Per-credit charge:** $705.
**Room and board:** $10,200.

**FINANCIAL AID PICTURE (2015-2016)**
**Students with need:** Average financial aid package met 73% of need; average scholarship/grant was $23,712; average loan was $3,557. For part-time
students, average financial aid package was $8,112.
**Students without need:** No-need awards available for academics, art, athletics.
**Scholarships offered:** Full-tuition and partial-tuition awards based on academics.

**FINANCIAL AID PROCEDURES**
**Forms required:** FAFSA.
**Dates and Deadlines:** Priority date 2/15; no closing date. Applicants notified
on a rolling basis starting 2/16.
**Transfers:** Priority date 4/15; no deadline. Applicants notified on a rolling
basis starting 2/15.

**CONTACT**
Dawn Snook, Director of Financial Aid
9601 Germantown Avenue, Philadelphia, PA 19118-2693
(215) 248-7182

## Cheyney University of Pennsylvania
Cheyney, Pennsylvania
www.cheyney.edu                      Federal Code: 003317

**4-year public** university in small town.
**Enrollment:** 686 undergrads, 10% part-time. 100 full-time freshmen.
**Selectivity:** Admits less than 50% of applicants.

**BASIC COSTS (2015-2016)**
**Tuition and fees:** $9,344; out-of-state residents $13,934.
**Room and board:** $10,748.
**Additional info:** Tuition/fee waivers available for minority students.

**FINANCIAL AID PICTURE**
**Students with need:** Need-based aid available for full-time and part-time stu-
dents.
**Students without need:** No-need awards available for academics, athletics.

**FINANCIAL AID PROCEDURES**
**Forms required:** FAFSA.
**Dates and Deadlines:** Priority date 3/15; no closing date. Applicants notified
on a rolling basis starting 4/1; must reply within 2 week(s) of notification.

**CONTACT**
1837 University Circle, Cheyney, PA 19319-0019
(610) 399-2302

## Clarion University of Pennsylvania
Clarion, Pennsylvania
www.clarion.edu                      Federal Code: 003318

**4-year public** business and teachers college in small town.
**Enrollment:** 4,401 undergrads.

**BASIC COSTS (2015-2016)**
**Tuition and fees:** $10,190; out-of-state residents $13,720.
**Room and board:** $9,792.

**FINANCIAL AID PICTURE**
**Students with need:** Need-based aid available for full-time and part-time students.
**Students without need:** No-need awards available for academics, alumni
affiliation, art, athletics, job skills, leadership, minority status, music/drama,
state/district residency.

**FINANCIAL AID PROCEDURES**
**Forms required:** FAFSA, state aid form.
**Dates and Deadlines:** Priority date 5/1; no closing date. Applicants notified
on a rolling basis starting 3/30.

**CONTACT**
Ragan Griffin, Financial Aid Officer
840 Wood Street, Clarion, PA 16214
(814) 226-2315

## Commonwealth Technical Institute
Johnstown, Pennsylvania
www.hgac.org

**2-year private** technical college in small city.
**Enrollment:** 177 undergrads.
**Selectivity:** Open admission.

**BASIC COSTS (2015-2016)**
**Tuition and fees:** $11,152.
**Room and board:** $11,152.

**FINANCIAL AID PICTURE**
**Students with need:** Need-based aid available for full-time and part-time students. Work study available nights, weekends, and for part-time students.
**Students without need:** This college awards aid only to students with
need.

**FINANCIAL AID PROCEDURES**
**Forms required:** FAFSA.
**Dates and Deadlines:** Applicants notified on a rolling basis.
**Transfers:** No deadline. Applicants notified on a rolling basis.

**CONTACT**
Christopher Zakraysek, Financial Aid Director
727 Goucher Street, Johnstown, PA 15905-3902
(800) 762-4211

## Community College of Allegheny County
Pittsburgh, Pennsylvania
www.ccac.edu

**2-year public** community college in very large city.
**Enrollment:** 15,335 undergrads, 64% part-time. 1,888 full-time freshmen.
**Selectivity:** Open admission.

**BASIC COSTS (2015-2016)**
**Tuition and fees:** $4,064; out-of-district residents $7,206; out-of-state residents $10,349.

**Per-credit charge:** $105; out-of-district residents $210; out-of-state residents $314.

## FINANCIAL AID PICTURE

**Students with need:** Work study available nights, weekends, and for part-time students.

**Students without need:** No-need awards available for academics, minority status.

## FINANCIAL AID PROCEDURES

**Forms required:** FAFSA.

**Dates and Deadlines:** Applicants notified on a rolling basis starting 6/1.

## CONTACT

Jamie Hightower-Poindexter, Director of Financial Aid

808 Ridge Avenue, Pittsburgh, PA 15212

(412) 323-2323

## Community College of Beaver County

Monaca, Pennsylvania

www.ccbc.edu                    Federal Code: 006807

**2-year public** community college in small town.

**Enrollment:** 2,255 undergrads.

**Selectivity:** Open admission; but selective for some programs.

## BASIC COSTS (2015-2016)

**Tuition and fees:** $5,460; out-of-district residents $10,320; out-of-state residents $15,180.

**Per-credit charge:** $142; out-of-district residents $284; out-of-state residents $426.

## FINANCIAL AID PICTURE

**Students with need:** Need-based aid available for full-time and part-time students. Work study available nights, weekends, and for part-time students.

**Students without need:** No-need awards available for academics, athletics, state/district residency.

**Scholarships offered:** Academic Excellence Scholarship; full tuition.

## FINANCIAL AID PROCEDURES

**Forms required:** FAFSA, state aid form, institutional form.

**Dates and Deadlines:** Priority date 5/1; closing date 7/1. Applicants notified on a rolling basis starting 8/5; must reply within 2 week(s) of notification.

**Transfers:** Priority date 5/6.

## CONTACT

Janet Davidson, Director of Financial Aid

One Campus Drive, Monaca, PA 15061-2588

(724) 480-3501

## Community College of Philadelphia

Philadelphia, Pennsylvania

www.ccp.edu                    Federal Code: 003249

**2-year public** community college in very large city.

**Enrollment:** 17,948 undergrads, 71% part-time. 1,616 full-time freshmen.

**Selectivity:** Open admission; but selective for some programs.

## BASIC COSTS (2015-2016)

**Tuition and fees:** $5,550; out-of-district residents $10,140; out-of-state residents $14,730.

**Additional info:** In-state, out-of-district students pay an additional $10 nonresident capital fee per credit; out-of-state students pay an additional $20 nonresident capital fee per credit. Tuition/fee waivers available for unemployed or children of unemployed.

## FINANCIAL AID PICTURE (2014-2015)

**Students with need:** Need-based aid available for full-time and part-time students. Work study available nights, weekends, and for part-time students.

**Students without need:** This college awards aid only to students with need.

## FINANCIAL AID PROCEDURES

**Forms required:** FAFSA, institutional form.

**Dates and Deadlines:** Closing date 5/1. Applicants notified on a rolling basis.

**Transfers:** No deadline.

## CONTACT

Gim Lim, Director of Financial Aid

1700 Spring Garden Street, Philadelphia, PA 19130-3991

(215) 751-8270

## Consolidated School of Business: Lancaster

Lancaster, Pennsylvania

www.csb.edu                    Federal Code: 030299

**2-year for-profit** career college in small city.

**Enrollment:** 99 undergrads.

**Selectivity:** Open admission.

## BASIC COSTS (2015-2016)

**Additional info:** Associate degree programs: $28,200-$28,500; certificates: $14,600. Books and supplies range $1,450-$3,100 depending on program level and course of study. All costs are subject to change. Tuition at time of enrollment locked for 2 years; tuition/fee waivers available for unemployed or children of unemployed.

## FINANCIAL AID PICTURE

**Students with need:** Need-based aid available for full-time and part-time students.

**Students without need:** No-need awards available for academics, leadership.

## FINANCIAL AID PROCEDURES

**Forms required:** FAFSA, state aid form.

**Dates and Deadlines:** Applicants notified on a rolling basis.

## CONTACT

Gail Dougherty, Director of Financial Aid

2124 Ambassador Circle, Lancaster, PA 17603

(717) 394-6211

## Consolidated School of Business: York

York, Pennsylvania

www.csb.edu                    Federal Code: 022896

**2-year for-profit** career college in small city.

**Enrollment:** 107 undergrads.

**Selectivity:** Open admission.

## BASIC COSTS (2015-2016)

**Additional info:** Associate degree programs: $28,200-$28,500; certificates: $14,600. Books and supplies range $1,450-$3,100 depending on program level and course of study. All costs are subject to change. Tuition at time of enrollment locked for 2 years; tuition/fee waivers available for unemployed or children of unemployed.

## FINANCIAL AID PICTURE

**Students with need:** Need-based aid available for full-time and part-time students.

**Students without need:** No-need awards available for academics.

## FINANCIAL AID PROCEDURES

**Forms required:** FAFSA, state aid form.

**Dates and Deadlines:** Applicants notified on a rolling basis.

## CONTACT

Gail Dougherty, Director of Financial Aid

York City Business and Industry Park, York, PA 17404

(717) 764-9550

# Dean Institute of Technology

Pittsburgh, Pennsylvania

www.deantech.edu                Federal Code: 009186

**2-year for-profit** technical college in large city.

**Enrollment:** 166 undergrads.

**Selectivity:** Open admission.

## BASIC COSTS (2015-2016)

**Additional info:** Tuition varies by program and level. Associate's degrees: $22,700; Diplomas: $9,950-$10,500; Certificates: $3,000-$5,250. All costs are subject to change.

## FINANCIAL AID PICTURE

**Students with need:** Need-based aid available for full-time and part-time students.

## FINANCIAL AID PROCEDURES

**Forms required:** FAFSA.

**Dates and Deadlines:** Closing date 8/1. Applicants notified on a rolling basis; must reply within 8 week(s) of notification.

## CONTACT

Nancy Grom, Director of Financial Aid

1501 West Liberty Avenue, Pittsburgh, PA 15226

(412) 531-4433 ext. 121

# Delaware County Community College

Media, Pennsylvania

www.dccc.edu

**2-year public** community college in large town.

**Enrollment:** 11,742 undergrads. 1,397 full-time freshmen.

**Selectivity:** Open admission; but selective for some programs.

## BASIC COSTS (2015-2016)

**Tuition and fees:** $4,950; out-of-district residents $9,900; out-of-state residents $14,850.

**Per-credit charge:** $110; out-of-district residents $220; out-of-state residents $330.

## FINANCIAL AID PICTURE (2014-2015)

**Students with need:** Out of 838 full-time freshmen who applied for aid, 629 were judged to have need. Of these, 629 received aid, and 352 had their full need met. Average financial aid package met 90% of need; average scholarship/grant was $3,048; average loan was $3,500. For part-time students, average financial aid package was $4,724.

**Students without need:** No-need awards available for academics, job skills.

**Additional info:** DCCC provides federal, college-funded and international work study.

## FINANCIAL AID PROCEDURES

**Forms required:** FAFSA, state aid form.

**Dates and Deadlines:** Closing date 7/1. Applicants notified on a rolling basis.

**Transfers:** No deadline. Applicants notified on a rolling basis.

## CONTACT

Raymond Toole, Director, Financial Aid

901 South Media Line Road, Media, PA 19063

(610) 359-5330

# Delaware Valley University

Doylestown, Pennsylvania

www.delval.edu                Federal Code: 003252

**4-year private** university in large town.

**Enrollment:** 1,879 undergrads, 6% part-time. 471 full-time freshmen.

**Selectivity:** Admits 50 to 75% of applicants.

## BASIC COSTS (2015-2016)

**Tuition and fees:** $35,256.

**Per-credit charge:** $916.

**Room and board:** $12,618.

**Additional info:** Tuition/fee waivers available for adults.

## FINANCIAL AID PICTURE (2015-2016)

**Students with need:** Out of 438 full-time freshmen who applied for aid, 406 were judged to have need. Of these, 406 received aid, and 56 had their full need met. Average financial aid package met 68% of need; average scholarship/grant was $21,898; average loan was $3,720. For part-time students, average financial aid package was $7,133.

**Students without need:** 62 full-time freshmen who did not demonstrate need for aid received scholarships/grants; average award was $16,800. No-need awards available for academics, alumni affiliation, leadership, music/drama, state/district residency.

## FINANCIAL AID PROCEDURES

**Forms required:** FAFSA, state aid form.

**Dates and Deadlines:** Priority date 4/15; no closing date. Applicants notified on a rolling basis starting 3/31; must reply by 5/1 or within 2 week(s) of notification.

**Transfers:** No deadline. Applicants notified on a rolling basis; must reply by 4/1.

## CONTACT

Joan Hock, Director of Financial Aid

700 East Butler Avenue, Doylestown, PA 18901-2697

(215) 489-2272

# DeSales University

Center Valley, Pennsylvania

www.desales.edu                Federal Code: 003986

**4-year private** university in large town, affiliated with Roman Catholic Church.

**Enrollment:** 2,291 undergrads, 24% part-time. 427 full-time freshmen.

**Selectivity:** Admits over 75% of applicants.

## BASIC COSTS (2015-2016)

**Tuition and fees:** $33,350.

**Per-credit charge:** $1,335.

**Room and board:** $12,050.

## FINANCIAL AID PICTURE (2015-2016)

**Students with need:** Out of 407 full-time freshmen who applied for aid, 348 were judged to have need. Of these, 348 received aid, and 95 had their full need met. Average financial aid package met 77% of need; average scholarship/grant was $20,533; average loan was $3,518. For part-time students, average financial aid package was $6,919.

**Students without need:** 75 full-time freshmen who did not demonstrate need for aid received scholarships/grants; average award was $16,807. No-need awards available for academics, alumni affiliation, art, leadership, music/drama, religious affiliation, ROTC.

**Scholarships offered:** Presidential Scholarships; $18,000 to full tuition; top 5% of class and 1300 SAT. Trustee Scholarships; $6,000 to $10,000; top 15% of class, minimum 1200 SAT. DeSales Scholarships; $4,000; top 25% of class, minimum 1100 SAT. SAT scores exclusive of Writing.

## FINANCIAL AID PROCEDURES
**Forms required:** FAFSA.
**Dates and Deadlines:** Priority date 2/1; closing date 5/1. Applicants notified on a rolling basis starting 2/15; must reply by 5/1 or within 2 week(s) of notification.
**Transfers:** No deadline. Applicants notified on a rolling basis. Merit scholarships automatically awarded for transfer students with a qualifying GPA. Award amounts are based on factors such as GPA, courses completed, and credits accumulated. Three levels of transfer scholarships: $3,500, $5,000, and $8,000 per year.

## CONTACT
Joyce Farmer, Director of Financial Aid
2755 Station Avenue, Center Valley, PA 18034-9568
(610) 282-1100 ext. 1287

# DeVry University: Fort Washington
Fort Washington, Pennsylvania
www.devry.edu

**4-year for-profit** university in large town.
**Enrollment:** 436 undergrads.

## BASIC COSTS (2015-2016)
**Tuition and fees:** $13,380.
**Per-credit charge:** $475.

## FINANCIAL AID PICTURE
**Students with need:** Need-based aid available for full-time and part-time students.
**Students without need:** This college awards aid only to students with need.

## FINANCIAL AID PROCEDURES
**Forms required:** FAFSA.
**Dates and Deadlines:** Applicants notified on a rolling basis.

## CONTACT
1140 Virginia Drive, Fort Washington, PA 19034-3204
(215) 591-5724

# Dickinson College
Carlisle, Pennsylvania          Federal Code: 003253
www.dickinson.edu               CSS Code: 2186

**4-year private** liberal arts college in large town.
**Enrollment:** 2,381 undergrads. 731 full-time freshmen.
**Selectivity:** Admits less than 50% of applicants.

## BASIC COSTS (2015-2016)
**Tuition and fees:** $49,489.
**Per-credit charge:** $1,533.
**Room and board:** $12,362.

## FINANCIAL AID PICTURE (2015-2016)
**Students with need:** Out of 451 full-time freshmen who applied for aid, 396 were judged to have need. Of these, 396 received aid, and 349 had their full need met. Average financial aid package met 99% of need; average scholarship/grant was $36,639; average loan was $4,237. For part-time students, average financial aid package was $22,302.

**Students without need:** 137 full-time freshmen who did not demonstrate need for aid received scholarships/grants; average award was $10,648. No-need awards available for academics, leadership, ROTC.
**Scholarships offered:** John Dickinson and Benjamin Rush Scholarships; awarded to most academically competitive students. Additional Engage the World Fellowship for selected John Dickinson Scholarship winners. John Montgomery Scholarship; awarded to first-year students who possess strong credentials, talent in the arts, or competency in 2 foreign languages in addition to English. Scholars must also demonstrate strong leadership in high school and community.

## FINANCIAL AID PROCEDURES
**Forms required:** FAFSA, CSS PROFILE, state aid form.
**Dates and Deadlines:** Priority date 11/15; closing date 2/1. Applicants notified by 3/20; must reply by 5/1 or within 2 week(s) of notification.
**Transfers:** Closing date 4/1. Applicants notified by 5/15; must reply within 2 week(s) of notification.

## CONTACT
Richard Heckman, Director of Financial Aid
PO Box 1773, Carlisle, PA 17013-2896
(717) 245-1308

# Douglas Education Center
Monessen, Pennsylvania
www.dec.edu                     Federal Code: 013957

**2-year for-profit** visual arts and business college in small town.
**Enrollment:** 267 undergrads.
**Selectivity:** Open admission.

## BASIC COSTS (2015-2016)
**Additional info:** Tuition and fees vary depending on program. Examples of Associate's degree programs: Medical Assistant Program, $20,800; The Factory Digital Film-making Program, $33,500. Certificate programs: Cosmetology Program, $15,850; Esthetician and Nail Technologist Program, $4,675. Costs listed included tuition and fees; books, supplies, and additional costs vary by program. All costs are subject to change.

## FINANCIAL AID PICTURE
**Students with need:** Need-based aid available for full-time and part-time students.
**Students without need:** This college awards aid only to students with need.

## FINANCIAL AID PROCEDURES
**Forms required:** FAFSA.
**Dates and Deadlines:** Applicants notified on a rolling basis.

## CONTACT
Amanda Phillips, Director of Financial Aid
130 Seventh Street, Monessen, PA 15062
(724) 684-3684

# Drexel University
Philadelphia, Pennsylvania      Federal Code: 003256
www.drexel.edu                  CSS Code: 2194

**5-year private** university in very large city.
**Enrollment:** 16,050 undergrads, 12% part-time. 2,720 full-time freshmen.
**Selectivity:** Admits 50 to 75% of applicants.

## BASIC COSTS (2016-2017)
**Tuition and fees:** $51,065.
**Per-credit charge:** $1,094.
**Room and board:** $14,367.

## FINANCIAL AID PICTURE (2015-2016)

**Students with need:** Out of 2,282 full-time freshmen who applied for aid, 1,964 were judged to have need. Of these, 1,963 received aid, and 610 had their full need met. Average financial aid package met 81% of need; average scholarship/grant was $32,838; average loan was $8,769. For part-time students, average financial aid package was $18,160.

**Students without need:** 697 full-time freshmen who did not demonstrate need for aid received scholarships/grants; average award was $12,812. No-need awards available for academics, art, athletics, music/drama, ROTC, state/district residency.

**Scholarships offered:** 35 full-time freshmen received athletic scholarships; average amount $33,379.

## FINANCIAL AID PROCEDURES

**Forms required:** FAFSA, CSS PROFILE.

**Dates and Deadlines:** Closing date 1/28.

**Transfers:** Scholarships available in amounts up to $8,000. 3.2 GPA and 30 credit hours at time of application required for eligibility.

## CONTACT

Christopher Ferguson, Vice President & Dean of Admissions
3141 Chestnut Street, Philadelphia, PA 19104-2876
(215) 895-2537

## DuBois Business College
DuBois, Pennsylvania
www.dbcollege.edu          Federal Code: 004893

**2-year for-profit** business and technical college in large town.

**Enrollment:** 90 undergrads.

**Selectivity:** Open admission.

## BASIC COSTS (2015-2016)

**Additional info:** Diploma programs 9-12 months: $11,280-$15,040, lab fee $600-$800, books and supplies $3,368-$6,237. Associate programs 18-21 months: $22,560-$26,320, lab fee $1,200-$1,400, books and supplies $4,582-$7,882.

## FINANCIAL AID PICTURE

**Students with need:** Need-based aid available for full-time students.

## FINANCIAL AID PROCEDURES

**Forms required:** FAFSA.

**Dates and Deadlines:** Closing date 8/1. Applicants notified on a rolling basis.

## CONTACT

Karen Alderton, Financial Aid Director
One Beaver Drive, DuBois, PA 15801
(814) 371-6920

## Duquesne University
Pittsburgh, Pennsylvania
www.duq.edu          Federal Code: 003258

**4-year private** university in large city, affiliated with Roman Catholic Church.

**Enrollment:** 5,943 undergrads, 4% part-time. 1,332 full-time freshmen.

**Selectivity:** Admits over 75% of applicants.

## BASIC COSTS (2015-2016)

**Tuition and fees:** $33,778.

**Per-credit charge:** $1,119.

**Room and board:** $11,418.

## FINANCIAL AID PICTURE (2014-2015)

**Students with need:** Out of 1,165 full-time freshmen who applied for aid, 964 were judged to have need. Of these, 964 received aid, and 187 had

their full need met. Average financial aid package met 76% of need; average scholarship/grant was $18,586; average loan was $4,111. For part-time students, average financial aid package was $8,069.

**Students without need:** 346 full-time freshmen who did not demonstrate need for aid received scholarships/grants; average award was $12,909. No-need awards available for academics, alumni affiliation, athletics, music/drama, ROTC.

**Scholarships offered:** *Merit:* Competitive scholarships available for academically and/or artistically talented students. *Athletic:* 71 full-time freshmen received athletic scholarships; average amount $18,094.

## FINANCIAL AID PROCEDURES

**Forms required:** FAFSA, institutional form.

**Dates and Deadlines:** Closing date 5/1. Applicants notified on a rolling basis starting 3/1; must reply by 5/1 or within 3 week(s) of notification.

**Transfers:** No deadline. Must reply within 3 week(s) of notification.

## CONTACT

Richard Esposito, Director of Financial Aid
600 Forbes Avenue, Administration Building, Pittsburgh, PA 15282-0201
(412) 396-6607

## East Stroudsburg University of Pennsylvania
East Stroudsburg, Pennsylvania
www.esu.edu          Federal Code: 003320

**4-year public** university in large town.

**Enrollment:** 6,100 undergrads, 8% part-time. 1,269 full-time freshmen.

**Selectivity:** Open admission; but selective for some programs.

## BASIC COSTS (2015-2016)

**Tuition and fees:** $9,684; out-of-state residents $20,274.

**Room and board:** $8,126.

**Additional info:** Out-of-State tuition is $10,590 for domestic out-of-state students with high school GPA of at least 3.2 out of 4.0 and a combined Math and Critical Reading score on the SAT of at least 1,100 or a score of at least 24 on the ACT. Out-of-State tuition is $12,356 for transferring students with a minimum of 30 transferable credits and a GPA of 3.2 from higher education institutions attended.

## FINANCIAL AID PICTURE (2014-2015)

**Students with need:** Out of 1,204 full-time freshmen who applied for aid, 980 were judged to have need. Of these, 927 received aid, and 442 had their full need met. Average financial aid package met 45% of need; average scholarship/grant was $5,149; average loan was $3,239. For part-time students, average financial aid package was $4,782.

**Students without need:** 15 full-time freshmen who did not demonstrate need for aid received scholarships/grants; average award was $2,048. No-need awards available for academics, alumni affiliation, art, athletics, job skills, leadership, minority status, music/drama, state/district residency.

**Scholarships offered:** 23 full-time freshmen received athletic scholarships; average amount $2,547.

## FINANCIAL AID PROCEDURES

**Forms required:** FAFSA.

**Dates and Deadlines:** Priority date 2/14; no closing date. Applicants notified on a rolling basis starting 3/15; must reply by 5/1.

**Transfers:** Applicants notified by 4/1; must reply by 5/1.

## CONTACT

Kizzy Morris, Director of Enrollment Services and Registrar
200 Prospect Street, East Stroudsburg, PA 18301-2999
(570) 422-2800

## Eastern University
St. Davids, Pennsylvania
www.eastern.edu                    Federal Code: 003259

**4-year private** university in small town, affiliated with American Baptist Churches in the USA.
**Enrollment:** 2,163 undergrads, 14% part-time. 410 full-time freshmen.
**Selectivity:** Admits 50 to 75% of applicants.

**BASIC COSTS (2016-2017)**
**Tuition and fees:** $31,020.
**Per-credit charge:** $675.
**Room and board:** $10,674.

**FINANCIAL AID PICTURE (2014-2015)**
**Students with need:** Out of 285 full-time freshmen who applied for aid, 252 were judged to have need. Of these, 252 received aid, and 70 had their full need met. Average financial aid package met 76% of need; average scholarship/grant was $6,572; average loan was $3,771. For part-time students, average financial aid package was $9,591.
**Students without need:** 32 full-time freshmen who did not demonstrate need for aid received scholarships/grants; average award was $13,143. No-need awards available for academics, alumni affiliation, leadership, music/drama.
**Scholarships offered:** Academic scholarships ranging from $5,000-$14,000 per year.

**FINANCIAL AID PROCEDURES**
**Forms required:** FAFSA.
**Dates and Deadlines:** Applicants notified on a rolling basis starting 4/1.
**Transfers:** No deadline. Applicants notified on a rolling basis starting 3/15. Financial aid transcripts from previous institutions required.

**CONTACT**
Christal Jennings, Director of Financial Aid
1300 Eagle Road, St. Davids, PA 19087-3696
(610) 341-5842

## Edinboro University of Pennsylvania
Edinboro, Pennsylvania
www.edinboro.edu                   Federal Code: 003321

**4-year public** university in small town.
**Enrollment:** 5,142 undergrads, 8% part-time. 1,212 full-time freshmen.
**Selectivity:** Admits over 75% of applicants.

**BASIC COSTS (2015-2016)**
**Tuition and fees:** $9,506; out-of-state residents $9,860.
**Room and board:** $10,166.

**FINANCIAL AID PICTURE (2014-2015)**
**Students with need:** Out of 1,168 full-time freshmen who applied for aid, 1,030 were judged to have need. Of these, 1,016 received aid. Average financial aid package met 47% of need; average scholarship/grant was $4,711; average loan was $3,098. For part-time students, average financial aid package was $5,150.
**Students without need:** No-need awards available for academics, alumni affiliation, art, athletics, leadership, minority status, music/drama, ROTC, state/district residency.

**FINANCIAL AID PROCEDURES**
**Forms required:** FAFSA, state aid form.
**Dates and Deadlines:** Priority date 3/15; no closing date. Applicants notified on a rolling basis starting 2/15; must reply by 8/1.

**CONTACT**
200 East Normal Street, Edinboro, PA 16444
(888) 611-2680

## Elizabethtown College
Elizabethtown, Pennsylvania
www.etown.edu                      Federal Code: 003262

**4-year private** liberal arts college in large town, affiliated with Brethren Church.
**Enrollment:** 1,762 undergrads, 1% part-time. 504 full-time freshmen.
**Selectivity:** Admits 50 to 75% of applicants.

**BASIC COSTS (2015-2016)**
**Tuition and fees:** $41,710.
**Room and board:** $10,140.

**FINANCIAL AID PICTURE (2015-2016)**
**Students with need:** Out of 493 full-time freshmen who applied for aid, 441 were judged to have need. Of these, 441 received aid, and 98 had their full need met. Average financial aid package met 82% of need; average scholarship/grant was $27,128; average loan was $3,806. For part-time students, average financial aid package was $5,817.
**Students without need:** 88 full-time freshmen who did not demonstrate need for aid received scholarships/grants; average award was $22,040. No-need awards available for academics, alumni affiliation, art, music/drama, religious affiliation.
**Scholarships offered:** Presidential Scholarship: up to $25,000 annually; top percentages of class and minimum 1300 SAT score. Provost Scholarship: up to $22,500 annually; top 10% of class with minimum 1150 SAT; unlimited number awarded. Dean's Scholarship: up to $20,000 annually; for students with very strong academic achievement who do not qualify for other merit awards; unlimited number awarded. Music scholarships: up to $4,000; based on audition. Stamps Scholarship: full tuition, $4,000 enrichment fund and personal mentor.

**FINANCIAL AID PROCEDURES**
**Forms required:** FAFSA.
**Dates and Deadlines:** Priority date 3/15; no closing date. Applicants notified on a rolling basis starting 3/1; must reply by 5/1 or within 2 week(s) of notification.
**Transfers:** No deadline. Applicants notified on a rolling basis; must reply within 2 week(s) of notification.

**CONTACT**
Melodie Jackson, Director of Financial Aid
One Alpha Drive, Elizabethtown, PA 17022-2298
(717) 361-1302

## Franklin & Marshall College
Lancaster, Pennsylvania              Federal Code: 003265
www.fandm.edu                        CSS Code: 2261

**4-year private** liberal arts college in small city.
**Enrollment:** 2,219 undergrads. 592 full-time freshmen.
**Selectivity:** Admits less than 50% of applicants.

**BASIC COSTS (2015-2016)**
**Tuition and fees:** $50,400.
**Room and board:** $12,770.

**FINANCIAL AID PICTURE (2015-2016)**
**Students with need:** Out of 373 full-time freshmen who applied for aid, 298 were judged to have need. Of these, 298 received aid, and 298 had their full need met. Average financial aid package met 100% of need; average scholarship/grant was $43,342; average loan was $2,868.
**Students without need:** This college awards aid only to students with need.

**FINANCIAL AID PROCEDURES**
**Forms required:** FAFSA, CSS PROFILE.

**Dates and Deadlines:** Priority date 2/15; closing date 2/15. Applicants notified by 4/1; must reply by 5/1.

**Transfers:** Closing date 5/1. Applicants notified by 6/15.

**CONTACT**
Clarke Paine, Director of Student Aid
PO Box 3003, Lancaster, PA 17604-3003
(717) 291-3991

## Gannon University
Erie, Pennsylvania
www.gannon.edu                    Federal Code: 003266

**4-year private** university in small city, affiliated with Roman Catholic Church.
**Enrollment:** 2,661 undergrads, 5% part-time. 613 full-time freshmen.
**Selectivity:** Admits over 75% of applicants.

### BASIC COSTS (2015-2016)
**Tuition and fees:** $29,258.
**Per-credit charge:** $690.
**Room and board:** $11,710.
**Additional info:** $25 fee per-credit hour for part-time students. Tuition/fee waivers available for adults, unemployed or children of unemployed.

### FINANCIAL AID PICTURE (2015-2016)
**Students with need:** Out of 546 full-time freshmen who applied for aid, 496 were judged to have need. Of these, 496 received aid, and 122 had their full need met. Average financial aid package met 76% of need; average scholarship/grant was $21,000; average loan was $3,388. For part-time students, average financial aid package was $6,154.
**Students without need:** 89 full-time freshmen who did not demonstrate need for aid received scholarships/grants; average award was $15,144. No-need awards available for academics, athletics, leadership, music/drama, religious affiliation, ROTC.
**Scholarships offered:** *Merit:* Academic Awards: $1,000 to full tuition; based on high school rank, GPA, and test scores. Diocesan Scholarship: $1,000 Parish Grant; for students that belong to a parish within the Diocese of Erie. Diocesan High School Grant: $1,500; for students who attended a Catholic high school within the Diocese of Erie. Catholic High School Grant: $1,000; for any student who attended a Catholic high school outside of the Diocese of Erie. Athletic scholarships: $1,000 to full tuition, room and board. *Athletic:* 21 full-time freshmen received athletic scholarships; average amount $9,970.

### FINANCIAL AID PROCEDURES
**Forms required:** FAFSA.
**Dates and Deadlines:** Priority date 3/15; no closing date. Applicants notified on a rolling basis starting 11/1.
**Transfers:** Priority date 3/15; no deadline. Applicants notified on a rolling basis starting 11/1.

**CONTACT**
Sharon Krahe, Director of Financial Aid
109 University Square, Erie, PA 16541-0001
(814) 871-7337

## Geneva College
Beaver Falls, Pennsylvania
www.geneva.edu                    Federal Code: 003267

**4-year private** liberal arts college in large town, affiliated with Reformed Presbyterian Church of North America.
**Enrollment:** 1,458 undergrads. 374 full-time freshmen.
**Selectivity:** Admits 50 to 75% of applicants.

### BASIC COSTS (2015-2016)
**Tuition and fees:** $25,450.

**Per-credit charge:** $860.
**Room and board:** $9,630.
**Additional info:** Some lab and practicum courses require additional fees. Tuition/fee waivers available for minority students, unemployed or children of unemployed.

### FINANCIAL AID PICTURE (2014-2015)
**Students with need:** Out of 300 full-time freshmen who applied for aid, 267 were judged to have need. Of these, 266 received aid, and 46 had their full need met. Average financial aid package met 77% of need; average scholarship/grant was $16,855; average loan was $3,473. For part-time students, average financial aid package was $6,462.
**Students without need:** 45 full-time freshmen who did not demonstrate need for aid received scholarships/grants; average award was $10,802. No-need awards available for academics, alumni affiliation, music/drama, religious affiliation.
**Scholarships offered:** Academic scholarships, scholarships for National Merit finalists and semifinalists, grants for members of controlling church and other denominations identified by the college.

### FINANCIAL AID PROCEDURES
**Forms required:** FAFSA.
**Dates and Deadlines:** Priority date 3/15; no closing date. Applicants notified on a rolling basis starting 3/1; must reply by 5/1 or within 4 week(s) of notification.
**Transfers:** No deadline. Applicants notified on a rolling basis starting 3/1; must reply within 4 week(s) of notification.

**CONTACT**
Steven Bell, Director of Financial Aid
3200 College Avenue, Beaver Falls, PA 15010
(724) 847-6530

## Gettysburg College
Gettysburg, Pennsylvania            Federal Code: 003268
www.gettysburg.edu                  CSS Code: 2275

**4-year private** liberal arts college in large town, affiliated with Evangelical Lutheran Church in America.
**Enrollment:** 2,441 undergrads. 699 full-time freshmen.
**Selectivity:** Admits less than 50% of applicants.

### BASIC COSTS (2015-2016)
**Tuition and fees:** $49,140.
**Room and board:** $11,730.

### FINANCIAL AID PICTURE (2015-2016)
**Students with need:** Out of 449 full-time freshmen who applied for aid, 379 were judged to have need. Of these, 372 received aid, and 334 had their full need met. Average financial aid package met 90% of need; average scholarship/grant was $33,314; average loan was $5,223.
**Students without need:** 123 full-time freshmen who did not demonstrate need for aid received scholarships/grants; average award was $11,821. No-need awards available for academics, music/drama.
**Scholarships offered:** Lincoln, Presidential, David Wills, and 1832 Founders Scholarships based on high school GPA, class rank and standardized test scores. The number awarded varies. Wagnild Scholarship and Sunderman Scholarships for music talent; audition required.

### FINANCIAL AID PROCEDURES
**Forms required:** FAFSA, CSS PROFILE.
**Dates and Deadlines:** Closing date 2/1. Applicants notified by 3/18; must reply by 5/1.
**Transfers:** Priority date 4/15. Must reply within 2 week(s) of notification.

**CONTACT**
Christina Gormley, Director of Financial Aid
300 North Washington Street, Gettysburg, PA 17325-1400
(717) 337-6611

## Grove City College
Grove City, Pennsylvania
www.gcc.edu                    Federal Code: G03269

**4-year private** liberal arts college in small town, affiliated with nondenominational tradition.
**Enrollment:** 2,409 undergrads, 1% part-time. 547 full-time freshmen.
**Selectivity:** Admits over 75% of applicants.

### BASIC COSTS (2015-2016)
**Tuition and fees:** $16,154.
**Per-credit charge:** $524.
**Room and board:** $8,802.

### FINANCIAL AID PICTURE (2015-2016)
**Students with need:** Out of 346 full-time freshmen who applied for aid, 259 were judged to have need. Of these, 258 received aid, and 36 had their full need met. Average financial aid package met 56% of need; average scholarship/grant was $7,594. For part-time students, average financial aid package was $3,028.
**Students without need:** 59 full-time freshmen who did not demonstrate need for aid received scholarships/grants; average award was $3,739. No-need awards available for academics, leadership, music/drama.
**Scholarships offered:** Trustee Scholarships; $8,000 to full standard tuition, room, and board awards; issued to a select group of accepted students who meet academic requirements; 24 awarded. Presidential Scholarships; $1,000; awarded to all valedictorians in class of 30 or more and all salutatorians in class of 100 or more. National Merit Scholarships; $2,000; awarded to all National Merit Finalists. Engineering Scholarships; $2,500; 4 awarded. Leadership Scholarships; $2,500; 4 awarded.
**Additional info:** Institutional aid applications required for institutional need-based scholarships. Federal monies are not accepted (Pell Grant, Stafford Loan, Parent Plus Loan, GI Bill, or any other government scholarship or loan program).

### FINANCIAL AID PROCEDURES
**Forms required:** institutional form.
**Dates and Deadlines:** Closing date 4/15. Applicants notified on a rolling basis starting 3/15; must reply by 5/1.
**Transfers:** Closing date 8/15. Applicants notified on a rolling basis; must reply within 3 week(s) of notification.

### CONTACT
Thomas Ball, Director of Financial Aid
100 Campus Drive, Grove City, PA 16127-2104
(724) 458-3300

## Gwynedd Mercy University
Gwynedd Valley, Pennsylvania
www.gmercyu.edu                Federal Code: 003270

**4-year private** nursing and liberal arts college in large town, affiliated with Roman Catholic Church.
**Enrollment:** 1,935 undergrads, 7% part-time. 235 full-time freshmen.
**Selectivity:** Admits over 75% of applicants.

### BASIC COSTS (2016-2017)
**Tuition and fees:** $34,380.
**Per-credit charge:** $700.
**Room and board:** $11,300.
**Additional info:** Cost reported is annual tuition for allied health and nursing programs; tuition for other programs, $31,780.

### FINANCIAL AID PICTURE (2015-2016)
**Students with need:** Out of 228 full-time freshmen who applied for aid, 217 were judged to have need. Of these, 217 received aid, and 37 had their full need met. Average financial aid package met 73% of need; average

scholarship/grant was $20,419; average loan was $3,245. For part-time students, average financial aid package was $9,043.
**Students without need:** 17 full-time freshmen who did not demonstrate need for aid received scholarships/grants; average award was $14,852. No-need awards available for academics, alumni affiliation, leadership, minority status, religious affiliation, state/district residency.
**Scholarships offered:** Presidential scholarship; $10,000; must have 1200 SAT and be in top 30% of class, essay required; 2/15 deadline. Connelly Scholarship; $6,000-$7,000; must have 1100 SAT and be in top 50% of class. Mother Mary Bernard Scholarship; $4,500-$5,000; must have 1000 SAT, be in top 50% of class, and have documented leadership experience. Yearly scholarship for Catholic school graduates; $2,000 (tuition incentive grant). All SAT scores exclusive of Writing.

### FINANCIAL AID PROCEDURES
**Forms required:** FAFSA, institutional form.
**Dates and Deadlines:** Priority date 3/15; closing date 5/1. Applicants notified on a rolling basis starting 2/15; must reply by 5/1 or within 2 week(s) of notification.

### CONTACT
Elizabeth Howard, Director of Student Financial Aid
1325 Sumneytown Pike, Gwynedd Valley, PA 19437-0901
(215) 646-7300 ext. 21483

## Harcum College
Bryn Mawr, Pennsylvania
www.harcum.edu                 Federal Code: 003272

**2-year private** junior college in large town.
**Enrollment:** 1,663 undergrads.

### BASIC COSTS (2015-2016)
**Tuition and fees:** $22,060.
**Per-credit charge:** $695.
**Room and board:** $9,100.

### FINANCIAL AID PICTURE
**Students with need:** Need-based aid available for full-time and part-time students. Work study available nights.
**Students without need:** No-need awards available for academics, alumni affiliation, athletics, leadership.
**Scholarships offered:** Scholarships available based on academic achievement.

### FINANCIAL AID PROCEDURES
**Forms required:** FAFSA.
**Dates and Deadlines:** Priority date 4/15; closing date 5/1. Applicants notified on a rolling basis starting 3/1; must reply within 3 week(s) of notification.

### CONTACT
Melissa Walsh, Director of Financial Aid
750 Montgomery Avenue, Bryn Mawr, PA 19010-3476
(610) 526-6098

## Harrisburg Area Community College
Harrisburg, Pennsylvania
www.hacc.edu                   Federal Code: 003273

**2-year public** community college in small city.
**Enrollment:** 14,830 undergrads, 69% part-time. 1,314 full-time freshmen.
**Selectivity:** Open admission; but selective for some programs.

### BASIC COSTS (2015-2016)
**Tuition and fees:** $6,165; out-of-district residents $7,500; out-of-state residents $8,790.

**Per-credit charge:** $163; out-of-district residents $207; out-of-state residents $250.

**Additional info:** Required fees are $1,140 for sponsored In-State, $1,290 for Non-Sponsored In-State, and $1,440 for Out-Of-State.

**FINANCIAL AID PICTURE (2015-2016)**

**Students with need:** 99% of average financial aid package awarded as scholarships/grants, 1% awarded as loans/jobs. Need-based aid available for part-time students.

**Students without need:** No-need awards available for academics, art, leadership, music/drama, religious affiliation, state/district residency.

**Additional info:** Federal work study community service positions available.

**FINANCIAL AID PROCEDURES**

**Forms required:** FAFSA, state aid form, institutional form.

**Dates and Deadlines:** Priority date 4/15; no closing date. Applicants notified on a rolling basis starting 4/30.

**Transfers:** PHEAA state grants require separate academic progress review by financial aid staff.

**CONTACT**

James Carideo, Director of Financial Aid

One HACC Drive, Cooper 206, Harrisburg, PA 17110-2999

(717) 780-2330

## Harrisburg University of Science and Technology

Harrisburg, Pennsylvania

www.harrisburgu.edu                Federal Code: 039483

**4-year private** university in small city.

**Enrollment:** 278 undergrads.

**BASIC COSTS (2015-2016)**

**Tuition and fees:** $23,900.

**Per-credit charge:** $1,000.

**FINANCIAL AID PICTURE**

**Students with need:** Need-based aid available for full-time and part-time students. Work study available nights.

**Students without need:** No-need awards available for academics, leadership, state/district residency.

**Scholarships offered:** Various scholarships; $1,000-$18,000, depending on specific criteria.

**FINANCIAL AID PROCEDURES**

**Forms required:** FAFSA.

**Dates and Deadlines:** Applicants notified on a rolling basis; must reply within 2 week(s) of notification.

**Transfers:** Priority date 5/1; no deadline. Applicants notified on a rolling basis; must reply within 4 week(s) of notification.

**CONTACT**

Vincent Frank, Director of Financial Aid

326 Market Street, Harrisburg, PA 17101-2208

(717) 901-5115

## Haverford College

Haverford, Pennsylvania              Federal Code: 003274

www.haverford.edu                    CSS Code: 2289

**4-year private** liberal arts college in large town.

**Enrollment:** 1,229 undergrads. 346 full-time freshmen.

**Selectivity:** Admits less than 50% of applicants.

**BASIC COSTS (2015-2016)**

**Tuition and fees:** $49,098.

**Room and board:** $14,888.

**FINANCIAL AID PICTURE (2015-2016)**

**Students with need:** Out of 183 full-time freshmen who applied for aid, 176 were judged to have need. Of these, 176 received aid, and 176 had their full need met. Average financial aid package met 100% of need; average scholarship/grant was $47,009; average loan was $813.

**Students without need:** This college awards aid only to students with need.

**FINANCIAL AID PROCEDURES**

**Forms required:** FAFSA, CSS PROFILE.

**Dates and Deadlines:** Closing date 2/1. Applicants notified by 4/1; must reply by 5/1.

**Transfers:** Closing date 3/1.

**CONTACT**

Michael Colahan, Director of Financial Aid

370 Lancaster Avenue, Haverford, PA 19041-1392

(610) 896-1350

## Holy Family University

Philadelphia, Pennsylvania

www.holyfamily.edu                  Federal Code: 003275

**4-year private** university in very large city, affiliated with Roman Catholic Church.

**Enrollment:** 1,825 undergrads, 22% part-time. 341 full-time freshmen.

**Selectivity:** Admits 50 to 75% of applicants.

**BASIC COSTS (2015-2016)**

**Tuition and fees:** $29,168.

**Per-credit charge:** $603.

**Room and board:** $13,576.

**FINANCIAL AID PICTURE (2015-2016)**

**Students with need:** Out of 329 full-time freshmen who applied for aid, 303 were judged to have need. Of these, 303 received aid, and 54 had their full need met. Average financial aid package met 83% of need; average scholarship/grant was $19,706; average loan was $1,550. For part-time students, average financial aid package was $7,361.

**Students without need:** 38 full-time freshmen who did not demonstrate need for aid received scholarships/grants; average award was $15,592. No-need awards available for academics, athletics, leadership.

**Scholarships offered:** 34 full-time freshmen received athletic scholarships; average amount $6,015.

**FINANCIAL AID PROCEDURES**

**Forms required:** FAFSA.

**Dates and Deadlines:** Priority date 3/1; closing date 4/1. Applicants notified on a rolling basis starting 3/15; must reply within 4 week(s) of notification.

**Transfers:** Priority date 3/1; closing date 4/1. Applicants notified on a rolling basis starting 3/15.

**CONTACT**

Janice Hetrick, Director of Financial Aid

9801 Frankford Avenue, Philadelphia, PA 19114-2009

(267) 341-3233

## Hussian College, School of Art

Philadelphia, Pennsylvania

www.hussianart.edu                  Federal Code: 007469

**2-year for-profit** visual arts college in very large city.

**Enrollment:** 79 undergrads.

**BASIC COSTS (2015-2016)**
**Tuition and fees:** $18,050.

**FINANCIAL AID PICTURE**
**Students with need:** Need-based aid available for full-time students.

**FINANCIAL AID PROCEDURES**
**Forms required:** FAFSA, state aid form, institutional form.
**Dates and Deadlines:** Applicants notified on a rolling basis starting 2/15; must reply within 3 week(s) of notification.
**Transfers:** Priority date 3/15; no deadline. Applicants notified on a rolling basis starting 4/1. August 1 deadline for PHEAA State Grant consideration.

**CONTACT**
Susan Cohen, Financial Aid Director
The Bourse, Suite 300, Philadelphia, PA 19106
(215) 574-9600 ext. 206

## Immaculata University
Immaculata, Pennsylvania
www.immaculata.edu                    Federal Code: 003276

**4-year private** university and liberal arts college in large town, affiliated with Roman Catholic Church.
**Enrollment:** 1,694 undergrads, 40% part-time. 188 full-time freshmen.
**Selectivity:** Admits over 75% of applicants.

**BASIC COSTS (2016-2017)**
**Tuition and fees:** $35,210.
**Per-credit charge:** $530.
**Room and board:** $12,500.

**FINANCIAL AID PICTURE**
**Students with need:** Need-based aid available for full-time and part-time students. Work study available nights, weekends, and for part-time students.
**Students without need:** No-need awards available for academics, alumni affiliation, art, job skills, leadership, minority status, music/drama, religious affiliation, state/district residency.

**FINANCIAL AID PROCEDURES**
**Forms required:** FAFSA.
**Dates and Deadlines:** Priority date 2/15; closing date 4/15. Applicants notified on a rolling basis starting 2/1; must reply within 2 week(s) of notification.
**Transfers:** No deadline. Applicants notified on a rolling basis starting 1/1; must reply within 2 week(s) of notification.

**CONTACT**
Robert Forest, Director of Financial Aid
1145 King Road, Immaculata, PA 19345
(610) 647-4400 ext. 3026

## Indiana University of Pennsylvania
Indiana, Pennsylvania
www.iup.edu                           Federal Code: 003277

**4-year public** university in large town.
**Enrollment:** 11,237 undergrads, 5% part-time. 2,718 full-time freshmen.
**Selectivity:** Admits over 75% of applicants.

**BASIC COSTS (2015-2016)**
**Tuition and fees:** $9,936; out-of-state residents $20,526.
**Room and board:** $11,880.
**Additional info:** Out-of-state tuition is $9,884 for students in the Southwestern University of Finance and Economics (China) partnership. Tuition is

$12,002 for first-time freshmen admitted to main campus from Indiana, Maryland, Michigan, New Jersey, New York, Ohio, Virginia, and West Virginia or for first-time freshmen with a high school GPA of at least 3.0 out of 4.0.

**FINANCIAL AID PICTURE (2014-2015)**
**Students with need:** Out of 2,544 full-time freshmen who applied for aid, 2,067 were judged to have need. Of these, 2,032 received aid, and 189 had their full need met. Average financial aid package met 62% of need; average scholarship/grant was $6,645; average loan was $3,755. For part-time students, average financial aid package was $9,002.
**Students without need:** 85 full-time freshmen who did not demonstrate need for aid received scholarships/grants; average award was $1,856. No-need awards available for academics, alumni affiliation, art, athletics, job skills, leadership, music/drama, ROTC, state/district residency.
**Scholarships offered:** 87 full-time freshmen received athletic scholarships; average amount $5,257.

**FINANCIAL AID PROCEDURES**
**Forms required:** FAFSA.
**Dates and Deadlines:** Priority date 4/15; no closing date. Applicants notified on a rolling basis starting 3/14.
**Transfers:** Must reply within 2 week(s) of notification.

**CONTACT**
Tiffany Eicher, Interim Director of Financial Aid
120 Sutton Hall, 1011 South Drive, Indiana, PA 15705-1088
(724) 357-2218

## JNA Institute of Culinary Arts
Philadelphia, Pennsylvania
www.culinaryarts.edu                  Federal Code: 031033

**2-year for-profit** technical college in very large city.
**Enrollment:** 59 undergrads.
**Selectivity:** Open admission.

**BASIC COSTS (2015-2016)**
**Tuition and fees:** $12,725.
**Additional info:** Tuition listed is for the Food Service Diploma Program. Culinary Arts/Restaurant Management Associate Program is $25,300 with a $75 registration fee. All costs are subject to change.

**FINANCIAL AID PICTURE**
**Students with need:** Need-based aid available for full-time students.

**FINANCIAL AID PROCEDURES**
**Forms required:** FAFSA.

**CONTACT**
Joseph Digironimo, Financial Aid Director
1212 South Broad Street, Philadelphia, PA 19146
(215) 468-8800

## Johnson College
Scranton, Pennsylvania
www.johnson.edu                       Federal Code: 014734

**2-year private** technical college in small city.
**Enrollment:** 430 undergrads, 10% part-time. 155 full-time freshmen.

**BASIC COSTS (2015-2016)**
**Tuition and fees:** $17,684.
**Per-credit charge:** $510.
**Room and board:** $5,010.
**Additional info:** Required fees for Radiologic & Physical Therapist Assistant are $1950, Carpentry & HVAC fees are $1500, welding fees are $2050.

Other expenses include book, tools and supplies and are estimated at $2000 per semester.

## FINANCIAL AID PICTURE (2014-2015)

**Students with need:** Out of 149 full-time freshmen who applied for aid, 142 were judged to have need. Of these, 136 received aid, and 3 had their full need met. Average financial aid package met 41% of need; average scholarship/grant was $6,782; average loan was $2,967. For part-time students, average financial aid package was $5,881.

**Students without need:** 3 full-time freshmen who did not demonstrate need for aid received scholarships/grants; average award was $693. No-need awards available for academics.

## FINANCIAL AID PROCEDURES

**Forms required:** FAFSA.

**Dates and Deadlines:** Priority date 4/28; no closing date. Applicants notified on a rolling basis starting 3/15; must reply within 2 week(s) of notification.

**Transfers:** Priority date 5/1; no deadline. Applicants notified on a rolling basis starting 3/1; must reply within 2 week(s) of notification.

## CONTACT

Robin Walker, Director of Financial Aid
3427 North Main Avenue, Scranton, PA 18508
(570) 702-8915

# Juniata College
Huntingdon, Pennsylvania
www.juniata.edu                 Federal Code: 003279

**4-year private** liberal arts college in small town.
**Enrollment:** 1,470 undergrads. 359 full-time freshmen.
**Selectivity:** Admits over 75% of applicants.

## BASIC COSTS (2015-2016)
**Tuition and fees:** $40,600.
**Per-credit charge:** $1,610.
**Room and board:** $11,140.

## FINANCIAL AID PICTURE (2014-2015)

**Students with need:** Out of 309 full-time freshmen who applied for aid, 278 were judged to have need. Of these, 276 received aid, and 69 had their full need met. Average financial aid package met 83% of need; average scholarship/grant was $26,702; average loan was $4,688. Need-based aid available for part-time students.

**Students without need:** 79 full-time freshmen who did not demonstrate need for aid received scholarships/grants; average award was $20,588. No-need awards available for academics, alumni affiliation, art, minority status, music/drama.

**Scholarships offered:** Friendship Scholarship: $2,000; awarded to international student. Ray Day Scholarship: up to $8,000; for a minority student. Eagles Abroad Scholarship: international experience plus $3,000; based on commitment to international experience in France, Germany, Mexico, Spain, or Russia. James Quinter Scholarships: $25,000. Calvert Ellis Scholarships: $16,000-$24,000.

## FINANCIAL AID PROCEDURES

**Forms required:** FAFSA.

**Dates and Deadlines:** Closing date 2/15. Applicants notified on a rolling basis starting 3/1; must reply by 5/1.

**Transfers:** Applicants notified on a rolling basis starting 3/1; must reply by 5/1.

## CONTACT

Shane Himes, Director of Student Financial Planning
1700 Moore Street, Huntingdon, PA 16652-2196
(814) 641-3142

# Kaplan Career Institute: Broomall
Broomall, Pennsylvania
www.kaplancareerinstitute.com     Federal Code: 007781

**2-year for-profit** career college in large town.
**Enrollment:** 560 undergrads.
**Selectivity:** Open admission.

## BASIC COSTS (2015-2016)
**Additional info:** Associate degree program: Medical assisting $29,615. Diploma programs range from $15,464 to $18,965. Fees, books and supplies included. All fees subject to change.

## FINANCIAL AID PICTURE

**Students with need:** Need-based aid available for full-time and part-time students.

## FINANCIAL AID PROCEDURES

**Forms required:** FAFSA.

**Dates and Deadlines:** Applicants notified on a rolling basis.

## CONTACT

Sheena McGinley, Director of Financial Aid
1991 Sproul Road, Suite 42, Broomall, PA 19008

# Kaplan Career Institute: Harrisburg
Harrisburg, Pennsylvania
www.kaplancareerinstitute.com     Federal Code: 004910

**2-year for-profit** health science and technical college in small city.
**Enrollment:** 217 undergrads.
**Selectivity:** Open admission; but selective for some programs.

## BASIC COSTS (2015-2016)
**Additional info:** Associate degree programs: Computer networking technology $36,089; criminal justice $28,985. Diploma programs: Medical assistant $15,365; medical billing and coding $15,315. Fees, books and supplies included. All costs are subject to change.

## FINANCIAL AID PICTURE

**Students with need:** Need-based aid available for full-time and part-time students. Work study available nights.

## FINANCIAL AID PROCEDURES

**Forms required:** FAFSA, institutional form.

## CONTACT

Sarah Brooker, Financial Aid Director
5650 Derry Street, Harrisburg, PA 17111-4112

# Kaplan Career Institute: Pittsburgh
Pittsburgh, Pennsylvania
www.kaplancareerinstitute.com     Federal Code: 007436

**2-year for-profit** business and health science college in large city.
**Enrollment:** 444 undergrads.

## BASIC COSTS (2015-2016)
**Additional info:** Accounting Management: $31,809. Business Administration/Management: $31,837. Computer Numerical Control Machinist: $9,500. Criminal Justice: $31,775. Electrical Technician: $18,064. Federal, State and Local Payroll Tax Workshop: $510. Heating, Ventilation, Air Conditioning and Refrigeration: $17,104. Medical Assistant: $16,471. Medical Assisting: $31,789. Medical Billing and Coding: $13,536. Medical Office Assistant: $13,536. Occupational Therapy Assistant: $34,904. Practical Nursing: $29,806.

**FINANCIAL AID PICTURE**

**Students with need:** Need-based aid available for full-time and part-time students. Work study available nights.

**Students without need:** This college awards aid only to students with need.

**FINANCIAL AID PROCEDURES**

**Forms required:** FAFSA, state aid form, institutional form.

**Dates and Deadlines:** Closing date 4/30. Applicants notified on a rolling basis.

**CONTACT**

Chrissy Kapusniak, Director of Financial Aid

933 Penn Avenue, Pittsburgh, PA 15222

(412) 261-2647 ext. 265

## Keystone College

La Plume, Pennsylvania

www.keystone.edu     Federal Code: 003280

**4-year private** business and liberal arts college in rural community.

**Enrollment:** 1,360 undergrads.

**Selectivity:** Admits over 75% of applicants.

**BASIC COSTS (2015-2016)**

**Tuition and fees:** $24,700.

**Room and board:** $10,050.

**FINANCIAL AID PICTURE**

**Students with need:** Need-based aid available for full-time and part-time students. Work study available nights, weekends, and for part-time students.

**Students without need:** No-need awards available for academics, alumni affiliation, art.

**Scholarships offered:** Academic Excellence Scholarship: one-half up to full tuition; for full-time, first-time students in the top 5% of their class with SAT scores of 1100 or above (exclusive of Writing). Presidential Scholarship: up to $9,500 each year; based on class rank and SAT/ACT scores. Trustee Scholarship: up to $8,500 each year; based on class rank and SAT/ACT scores. Promise Award: up to $6,500 each year; for students demonstrating non-athletic leadership skills.

**FINANCIAL AID PROCEDURES**

**Forms required:** FAFSA, state aid form.

**Dates and Deadlines:** Priority date 4/1; closing date 5/1. Applicants notified on a rolling basis starting 2/1; must reply within 3 week(s) of notification.

**Transfers:** Must reply within 2 week(s) of notification.

**CONTACT**

Delaina Jayne, Director of Financial Assistance and Planning

One College Green, La Plume, PA 18440-1099

(570) 945-8134

## Keystone Technical Institute

Harrisburg, Pennsylvania

www.kti.edu     Federal Code: 022342

**2-year for-profit** culinary school and technical college in small city.

**Enrollment:** 341 undergrads.

**Selectivity:** Open admission.

**BASIC COSTS (2015-2016)**

**Additional info:** Tuition and fees vary by program. Associate's degrees: $23,141-$31,843; Certificate's: $2,941-$28,326. Books and supplies vary depending on program level and course of study. All costs are subject to change.

**FINANCIAL AID PICTURE**

**Students with need:** Need-based aid available for full-time and part-time students. Work study available nights.

**Students without need:** This college awards aid only to students with need.

**Scholarships offered:** Half-tuition scholarships; 13 available to degree-seeking students.

**FINANCIAL AID PROCEDURES**

**Forms required:** FAFSA, state aid form.

**Dates and Deadlines:** Closing date 8/1. Applicants notified on a rolling basis.

**Transfers:** State grant deadline for first-time recipients August 1. Renewal application deadline May 1.

**CONTACT**

Tracy Stewart, Financial Aid Coordinator

2301 Academy Drive, Harrisburg, PA 17112-1012

(717) 545-4747

## King's College

Wilkes-Barre, Pennsylvania

www.kings.edu     Federal Code: 003282

**4-year private** business and liberal arts college in small city, affiliated with Roman Catholic Church.

**Enrollment:** 1,859 undergrads, 3% part-time. 517 full-time freshmen.

**Selectivity:** Admits 50 to 75% of applicants.

**BASIC COSTS (2015-2016)**

**Tuition and fees:** $33,090.

**Per-credit charge:** $530.

**Room and board:** $11,958.

**FINANCIAL AID PICTURE (2015-2016)**

**Students with need:** Out of 498 full-time freshmen who applied for aid, 434 were judged to have need. Of these, 434 received aid, and 61 had their full need met. Average financial aid package met 71% of need; average scholarship/grant was $19,092; average loan was $3,471. For part-time students, average financial aid package was $4,967.

**Students without need:** 70 full-time freshmen who did not demonstrate need for aid received scholarships/grants; average award was $15,098. No-need awards available for academics, leadership, ROTC.

**Additional info:** Any minority student with financial need may receive some aid in the form of a diversity scholarship.

**FINANCIAL AID PROCEDURES**

**Forms required:** FAFSA.

**Dates and Deadlines:** Priority date 2/15; no closing date. Applicants notified on a rolling basis starting 3/1; must reply within 2 week(s) of notification.

**Transfers:** Priority date 2/1; no deadline. Applicants notified on a rolling basis; must reply by 5/1 or within 2 week(s) of notification.

**CONTACT**

Donna Cerza, Director of Financial Aid

133 North River Street, Wilkes-Barre, PA 18711

(570) 208-5868

## Kutztown University of Pennsylvania

Kutztown, Pennsylvania

www.kutztown.edu     Federal Code: 003322

**4-year public** university in small town.

**Enrollment:** 8,249 undergrads, 5% part-time. 1,778 full-time freshmen.

**Selectivity:** Admits over 75% of applicants.

## BASIC COSTS (2015-2016)

**Tuition and fees:** $9,145; out-of-state residents $19,735.

**Room and board:** $9,070.

**Additional info:** Out-of-State tuition is $10,590 for domestic out-of-state students with a high school GPA of at least 3.25 out of 4.0 and a combined Math and Critical Reading score on the SAT of at least 1,100. Tuition is $14,120 for domestic out-of-state students with a high school GPA of at least 3.0 out of 4.0 and a combined Math and Critical Reading score on the SAT of at least 1,000.

## FINANCIAL AID PICTURE (2014-2015)

**Students with need:** Out of 1,654 full-time freshmen who applied for aid, 1,324 were judged to have need. Of these, 1,288 received aid, and 70 had their full need met. Average financial aid package met 44% of need; average scholarship/grant was $5,889; average loan was $3,575. For part-time students, average financial aid package was $5,726.

**Students without need:** 156 full-time freshmen who did not demonstrate need for aid received scholarships/grants; average award was $711. No-need awards available for academics, art, athletics, leadership, minority status, music/drama.

**Scholarships offered:** 89 full-time freshmen received athletic scholarships; average amount $2,099.

## FINANCIAL AID PROCEDURES

**Forms required:** FAFSA.

**Dates and Deadlines:** Priority date 3/1; no closing date. Applicants notified on a rolling basis starting 3/30; must reply by 5/1 or within 4 week(s) of notification.

## CONTACT

Bernard McCree, Director of Financial Aid

Admissions Office, Kutztown, PA 19530-0730

(610) 683-4077

# La Roche College

Pittsburgh, Pennsylvania

www.laroche.edu     Federal Code: 003987

**4-year private** liberal arts college in large city, affiliated with Roman Catholic Church.

**Enrollment:** 1,359 undergrads, 14% part-time. 291 full-time freshmen.

**Selectivity:** Admits over 75% of applicants.

## BASIC COSTS (2015-2016)

**Tuition and fees:** $26,250.

**Per-credit charge:** $645.

**Room and board:** $10,630.

## FINANCIAL AID PICTURE (2015-2016)

**Students with need:** Out of 179 full-time freshmen who applied for aid, 168 were judged to have need. Of these, 168 received aid, and 62 had their full need met. Average financial aid package met 86% of need; average scholarship/grant was $9,275; average loan was $3,945. For part-time students, average financial aid package was $7,960.

**Students without need:** 11 full-time freshmen who did not demonstrate need for aid received scholarships/grants; average award was $18,870. No-need awards available for academics.

## FINANCIAL AID PROCEDURES

**Forms required:** FAFSA.

**Dates and Deadlines:** Priority date 5/1; no closing date. Applicants notified on a rolling basis starting 2/15; must reply within 2 week(s) of notification.

## CONTACT

Sharon Platt, Director of Financial Aid

9000 Babcock Boulevard, Pittsburgh, PA 15237

(412) 536-1125

# La Salle University

Philadelphia, Pennsylvania

www.lasalle.edu     Federal Code: 003287

**4-year private** university and liberal arts college in very large city, affiliated with Roman Catholic Church.

**Enrollment:** 3,801 undergrads, 12% part-time. 921 full-time freshmen.

**Selectivity:** Admits 50 to 75% of applicants.

## BASIC COSTS (2015-2016)

**Tuition and fees:** $41,100.

**Room and board:** $14,490.

## FINANCIAL AID PICTURE (2014-2015)

**Students with need:** Out of 863 full-time freshmen who applied for aid, 811 were judged to have need. Of these, 809 received aid, and 102 had their full need met. Average financial aid package met 74% of need; average scholarship/grant was $24,997; average loan was $3,576. For part-time students, average financial aid package was $7,500.

**Students without need:** 99 full-time freshmen who did not demonstrate need for aid received scholarships/grants; average award was $18,723. No-need awards available for academics, athletics, ROTC.

**Scholarships offered:** *Merit:* Christian Brothers Scholarship; full tuition; based on academics and extracurricular leadership. Community Service Scholarship; half tuition; based on involvement in community service and academics. *Athletic:* 40 full-time freshmen received athletic scholarships; average amount $17,393.

## FINANCIAL AID PROCEDURES

**Forms required:** FAFSA.

**Dates and Deadlines:** Priority date 2/15; no closing date. Applicants notified on a rolling basis starting 3/15; must reply by 5/1 or within 2 week(s) of notification.

**Transfers:** Applicants notified on a rolling basis starting 3/15; must reply by 5/1 or within 2 week(s) of notification.

## CONTACT

Joseph Alaimo, Financial Aid Director

1900 West Olney Avenue, Philadelphia, PA 19141-1199

(215) 951-1070

# Lackawanna College

Scranton, Pennsylvania

www.lackawanna.edu     Federal Code: 003283

**2-year private** junior college in small city.

**Enrollment:** 1,420 undergrads. 1,340 full-time freshmen.

**Selectivity:** Open admission.

## BASIC COSTS (2015-2016)

**Tuition and fees:** $14,210.

**Per-credit charge:** $465.

**Room and board:** $8,300.

## FINANCIAL AID PICTURE (2014-2015)

**Students with need:** Out of 1,337 full-time freshmen who applied for aid, 1,206 were judged to have need. Of these, 388 received aid, and 13 had their full need met. Average financial aid package met 14% of need; average scholarship/grant was $7,123; average loan was $3,060. For part-time students, average financial aid package was $5,677.

**Students without need:** 2 full-time freshmen who did not demonstrate need for aid received scholarships/grants; average award was $2,500. No-need awards available for academics, athletics.

**Scholarships offered:** 8 full-time freshmen received athletic scholarships; average amount $3,729.

## FINANCIAL AID PROCEDURES

**Forms required:** FAFSA, state aid form, institutional form.

**Dates and Deadlines:** Priority date 5/1; no closing date. Applicants notified on a rolling basis starting 5/1.

**Transfers:** No deadline. Applicants notified on a rolling basis starting 5/1; must reply by 5/1.

**CONTACT**
Matthew Peters, Director of Financial Aid
501 Vine Street, Scranton, PA 18509
(570) 961-7859

## Lafayette College

Easton, Pennsylvania
www.lafayette.edu

Federal Code: 003284
CSS Code: 2361

**4-year private** engineering and liberal arts college in large town.
**Enrollment:** 2,505 undergrads, 1% part-time. 672 full-time freshmen.
**Selectivity:** Admits less than 50% of applicants.

**BASIC COSTS (2015-2016)**
**Tuition and fees:** $47,010.
**Room and board:** $13,920.

**FINANCIAL AID PICTURE (2015-2016)**
**Students with need:** Out of 389 full-time freshmen who applied for aid, 204 were judged to have need. Of these, 204 received aid, and 204 had their full need met. Average financial aid package met 100% of need; average scholarship/grant was $39,316; average loan was $4,438. For part-time students, average financial aid package was $2,750.
**Students without need:** 44 full-time freshmen who did not demonstrate need for aid received scholarships/grants; average award was $26,145. No-need awards available for academics, athletics, leadership, ROTC.
**Scholarships offered: _Merit:_** Marquis Scholarships; $24,000 per year; based on academic merit, awarded to about 50 entering students. Marquis Fellowships; $40,000 per year, based on academic merit and day-long interview process, awarded to about 10 entering students. Both programs carry a $4,000 one-time stipend to be used for a study abroad program. Creative and Performing Arts Fellowships; based on application; $7,500 toward a studio or performing arts project to be used during four years at Lafayette. _**Athletic:**_ 62 full-time freshmen received athletic scholarships; average amount $35,438.
**Additional info:** Parent loans, up to $7,500 annually, available with college absorbing interest while student is enrolled. Family has 8 years after graduation to repay. Not limited to those demonstrating need.

**FINANCIAL AID PROCEDURES**
**Forms required:** FAFSA, CSS PROFILE.
**Dates and Deadlines:** Priority date 1/15; closing date 3/1. Applicants notified by 4/1; must reply by 5/1.
**Transfers:** Closing date 4/1. Applicants notified on a rolling basis starting 5/1; must reply within 2 week(s) of notification.

**CONTACT**
Ashley Bianchi, Director of Student Financial Aid
118 Markle Hall, Easton, PA 18042
(610) 330-5055

## Lancaster Bible College

Lancaster, Pennsylvania
www.lbc.edu

Federal Code: 003285

**4-year private** Bible college in small city, affiliated with nondenominational tradition.
**Enrollment:** 1,254 undergrads.

**BASIC COSTS (2015-2016)**
**Tuition and fees:** $19,980.

**Per-credit charge:** $670.
**Room and board:** $8,350.

**FINANCIAL AID PICTURE (2015-2016)**
**Students with need:** 65% of average financial aid package awarded as scholarships/grants, 35% awarded as loans/jobs. Need-based aid available for part-time students. Work study available nights, weekends, and for part-time students.
**Students without need:** No-need awards available for academics, alumni affiliation, leadership, music/drama.

**FINANCIAL AID PROCEDURES**
**Forms required:** FAFSA, state aid form.
**Dates and Deadlines:** Priority date 5/1; no closing date. Applicants notified on a rolling basis starting 3/1; must reply within 3 week(s) of notification.

**CONTACT**
Karen Fox, Director of Financial Aid
901 Eden Road, Lancaster, PA 17601-5036
(717) 560-8254

## Laurel Business Institute

Uniontown, Pennsylvania
www.laurel.edu

Federal Code: 017118

**2-year for-profit** technical and career college in large town.
**Enrollment:** 233 undergrads.

**BASIC COSTS (2015-2016)**
**Tuition and fees:** $9,694.
**Per-credit charge:** $295.
**Additional info:** Annual tuition varies by program and ranges from $4,397 to $6,274 per term; per-credit-hour charges range from $295 to $350.

**FINANCIAL AID PICTURE**
**Students with need:** Need-based aid available for full-time and part-time students.
**Students without need:** This college awards aid only to students with need.
**Scholarships offered:** One full tuition, several half tuition (including GED scholarships); based on high school transcripts or GED scores, letters of reference, and personal interview.

**FINANCIAL AID PROCEDURES**
**Forms required:** FAFSA, institutional form.
**Dates and Deadlines:** Applicants notified on a rolling basis; must reply within 4 week(s) of notification.
**Transfers:** No deadline. Must reply within 4 week(s) of notification.

**CONTACT**
Stephanie Migyanko, Director of Financial Aid
11 East Penn Street, Uniontown, PA 15401
(724) 439-4900

## Lebanon Valley College

Annville, Pennsylvania
www.lvc.edu

Federal Code: 003288

**4-year private** liberal arts college in small town, affiliated with United Methodist Church.
**Enrollment:** 1,651 undergrads, 3% part-time. 455 full-time freshmen.
**Selectivity:** Admits 50 to 75% of applicants.

**BASIC COSTS (2015-2016)**
**Tuition and fees:** $39,030.
**Per-credit charge:** $595.
**Room and board:** $10,510.

**Additional info:** Tuition/fee waivers available for minority students.

## FINANCIAL AID PICTURE (2015-2016)

**Students with need:** Out of 444 full-time freshmen who applied for aid, 420 were judged to have need. Of these, 420 received aid, and 92 had their full need met. Average financial aid package met 83% of need; average scholarship/grant was $25,445; average loan was $3,984. For part-time students, average financial aid package was $6,082.

**Students without need:** 61 full-time freshmen who did not demonstrate need for aid received scholarships/grants; average award was $15,022. No-need awards available for academics, alumni affiliation, music/drama.

**Scholarships offered:** Board of Trustees Scholarship; $22,000 per year. Presidential Scholarship; $20,000 per year. Dean's Scholarship; $18,000 per year. Alfred Tennyson Sumner Scholarship; $16,000 per year. Mary C. Weiss Scholarship; $14,000 per year. Institution awards merit-based scholarship based on strength and rigor of course work, grade-point average (GPA), class rank (if applicable), and SAT or ACT test scores (optional). Students applying for admission will be automatically evaluated for scholarships. Scholarships are awarded for up to a maximum of eight semesters as long as satisfactory academic progress is made. International and transfer students are also considered for merit scholarships. Strength of courses and grades earned in transferable courses are factors in determining scholarships for transfer students with more than 16 credits. High school credentials will also be factored for those with fewer than 16 credits.

## FINANCIAL AID PROCEDURES

**Forms required:** FAFSA.

**Dates and Deadlines:** Priority date 3/1; no closing date. Applicants notified on a rolling basis starting 3/1; must reply by 5/1 or within 2 week(s) of notification.

**Transfers:** No deadline. Applicants notified on a rolling basis starting 3/1; must reply by 5/1 or within 2 week(s) of notification. Students transferring 15 or fewer credits are considered for scholarships on the same basis as high school seniors. Students transferring 16 or more credits are considered for scholarships based on their college academic performance.

## CONTACT

Kendra Feigert, Director of Financial Aid
101 North College Avenue, Annville, PA 17003-1400
(717) 867-6181

## Lehigh Carbon Community College

Schnecksville, Pennsylvania
www.lccc.edu                          Federal Code: 006810

**2-year public** community college in small town.
**Enrollment:** 5,801 undergrads, 56% part-time. 994 full-time freshmen.
**Selectivity:** Open admission; but selective for some programs.

## BASIC COSTS (2015-2016)

**Tuition and fees:** $3,800; out-of-district residents $7,070; out-of-state residents $10,340.
**Per-credit charge:** $100; out-of-district residents $209; out-of-state residents $318.
**Additional info:** Tuition/fee waivers available for unemployed or children of unemployed.

## FINANCIAL AID PICTURE (2014-2015)

**Students with need:** Out of 874 full-time freshmen who applied for aid, 618 were judged to have need. Of these, 618 received aid, and 618 had their full need met. Average financial aid package met 100% of need; average scholarship/grant was $4,342; average loan was $2,898. For part-time students, average financial aid package was $3,824.

**Students without need:** 14 full-time freshmen who did not demonstrate need for aid received scholarships/grants; average award was $3,134. No-need awards available for academics, job skills.

## FINANCIAL AID PROCEDURES

**Forms required:** FAFSA.

**Dates and Deadlines:** Priority date 5/1; no closing date. Applicants notified on a rolling basis starting 1/1; must reply within 2 week(s) of notification.

**Transfers:** No deadline. Applicants notified on a rolling basis.

## CONTACT

Marian Snyder, Director of Financial Aid
4525 Education Park Drive, Schnecksville, PA 18078-2502
(610) 799-1133

## Lehigh University

Bethlehem, Pennsylvania                 Federal Code: 003289
www.lehigh.edu                          CSS Code: 2365

**4-year private** university in small city.
**Enrollment:** 5,054 undergrads, 1% part-time. 1,261 full-time freshmen.
**Selectivity:** Admits less than 50% of applicants.

## BASIC COSTS (2015-2016)

**Tuition and fees:** $46,230.
**Per-credit charge:** $1,915.
**Room and board:** $12,280.

## FINANCIAL AID PICTURE (2015-2016)

**Students with need:** Out of 770 full-time freshmen who applied for aid, 502 were judged to have need. Of these, 502 received aid, and 256 had their full need met. Average financial aid package met 95% of need; average scholarship/grant was $34,998; average loan was $3,996. For part-time students, average financial aid package was $17,782.

**Students without need:** 49 full-time freshmen who did not demonstrate need for aid received scholarships/grants; average award was $13,129. No-need awards available for academics, art, athletics, leadership, music/drama, ROTC.

**Scholarships offered:** *Merit:* Dean's Scholarships; $10,000; for academic excellence and leadership skills. Baker Scholarship; $3,000; for excellence in music or theater and superior academic record. Choral Arts Scholarships; $2,500; for singing talent. Performing Arts Scholarship; $3,000; for those who display exceptional theatrical talent (including performance, design, technical, and playwriting). Snyder Family Marching 97 Scholarships; $1,000-$2,500; for those who demonstrate musical talent and leadership and who fully participate in the marching band. Athletic Awards/Scholarships. *Athletic:* 65 full-time freshmen received athletic scholarships; average amount $37,245.

**Additional info:** Loans eliminated in financial aid packages for students eligible for financial aid and whose calculated total family income is less than $50,000. Loans limited to $3,000 in financial aid packages for students eligible for financial aid and who have a calculated total family income between $50,000 and $75,000.

## FINANCIAL AID PROCEDURES

**Forms required:** FAFSA, CSS PROFILE.

**Dates and Deadlines:** Closing date 2/15. Applicants notified by 3/30; must reply by 5/1 or within 3 week(s) of notification.

**Transfers:** Closing date 3/1. Applicants notified by 5/15; must reply within 3 week(s) of notification.

## CONTACT

Jennifer Mertz, Director of Financial Aid
27 Memorial Drive West, Bethlehem, PA 18015
(610) 758-3181

## Lincoln University
Lincoln University, Pennsylvania
www.lincoln.edu                     Federal Code: 003290

4-year public university and liberal arts college in small town.
**Enrollment:** 1,628 undergrads, 5% part-time. 453 full-time freshmen.
**Selectivity:** Admits over 75% of applicants.

### BASIC COSTS (2015-2016)
**Tuition and fees:** $10,289; out-of-state residents $15,081.
**Per-credit charge:** $309; out-of-state residents $509.
**Room and board:** $8,904.
**Additional info:** Tuition at time of enrollment locked for 4 years.

### FINANCIAL AID PICTURE
**Students with need:** Need-based aid available for full-time and part-time students. Work study available nights, weekends, and for part-time students.
**Students without need:** No-need awards available for academics, alumni affiliation, leadership, music/drama.

### FINANCIAL AID PROCEDURES
**Forms required:** FAFSA.
**Dates and Deadlines:** Closing date 5/1. Applicants notified on a rolling basis starting 4/1; must reply within 3 week(s) of notification.

### CONTACT
Kim Anderson, Director of Financial Aid
1570 Baltimore Pike, Lincoln University, PA 19352-0999
(800) 561-2606

## Lock Haven University of Pennsylvania
Lock Haven, Pennsylvania
www.lhup.edu                        Federal Code: 003323

4-year public university and liberal arts college in small town.
**Enrollment:** 4,158 undergrads, 7% part-time. 874 full-time freshmen.
**Selectivity:** Admits over 75% of applicants.

### BASIC COSTS (2015-2016)
**Tuition and fees:** $9,665; out-of-state residents $18,255.
**Room and board:** $9,344.
**Additional info:** Out-of-State tuition is $14,120 for domestic out-of-state students with a high school GPA of at least 3.25 out of 4.0.

### FINANCIAL AID PICTURE (2015-2016)
**Students with need:** Out of 834 full-time freshmen who applied for aid, 711 were judged to have need. Of these, 692 received aid, and 247 had their full need met. Average financial aid package met 85% of need; average scholarship/grant was $7,519; average loan was $3,225. For part-time students, average financial aid package was $6,187.
**Students without need:** 15 full-time freshmen who did not demonstrate need for aid received scholarships/grants; average award was $2,049. No-need awards available for academics, art, athletics, leadership, minority status, music/drama, ROTC, state/district residency.
**Scholarships offered:** 55 full-time freshmen received athletic scholarships; average amount $2,197.

### FINANCIAL AID PROCEDURES
**Forms required:** FAFSA, state aid form.
**Dates and Deadlines:** Closing date 3/15. Applicants notified on a rolling basis starting 3/15; must reply within 2 week(s) of notification.
**Transfers:** Priority date 3/15. Applicants notified on a rolling basis starting 3/15; must reply within 2 week(s) of notification.

### CONTACT
Robert Fryer, Director Financial Aid
LHU Office of Admissions, Lock Haven, PA 17745
(570) 484-2424

## Luzerne County Community College
Nanticoke, Pennsylvania
www.luzerne.edu                     Federal Code: 006811

2-year public community college in large town.
**Enrollment:** 5,227 undergrads, 50% part-time. 931 full-time freshmen.
**Selectivity:** Open admission; but selective for some programs.

### BASIC COSTS (2015-2016)
**Tuition and fees:** $4,770; out-of-district residents $8,370; out-of-state residents $11,970.
**Per-credit charge:** $120; out-of-district residents $240; out-of-state residents $360.

### FINANCIAL AID PICTURE
**Students with need:** Need-based aid available for full-time and part-time students.

### FINANCIAL AID PROCEDURES
**Forms required:** FAFSA, state aid form, institutional form.
**Dates and Deadlines:** Priority date 4/15; no closing date. Applicants notified on a rolling basis starting 7/1.

### CONTACT
Mark Carpentier, Director of Financial Aid
1333 South Prospect Street, Nanticoke, PA 18634-3899
(570) 740-0389

## Lycoming College
Williamsport, Pennsylvania
www.lycoming.edu                    Federal Code: 003293

4-year private liberal arts college in small city, affiliated with United Methodist Church.
**Enrollment:** 1,260 undergrads. 347 full-time freshmen.
**Selectivity:** Admits 50 to 75% of applicants.

### BASIC COSTS (2015-2016)
**Tuition and fees:** $35,900.
**Per-credit charge:** $1,100.
**Room and board:** $10,884.
**Additional info:** Tuition/fee waivers available for minority students.

### FINANCIAL AID PICTURE (2015-2016)
**Students with need:** Out of 318 full-time freshmen who applied for aid, 301 were judged to have need. Of these, 301 received aid, and 50 had their full need met. Average financial aid package met 84% of need; average scholarship/grant was $29,434; average loan was $3,816. Need-based aid available for part-time students.
**Students without need:** 44 full-time freshmen who did not demonstrate need for aid received scholarships/grants; average award was $23,781. No-need awards available for academics, art, minority status, music/drama, ROTC.

### FINANCIAL AID PROCEDURES
**Forms required:** FAFSA.
**Dates and Deadlines:** Priority date 5/1; no closing date. Applicants notified on a rolling basis starting 3/1; must reply by 5/1.
**Transfers:** No deadline.

### CONTACT
James Lakis, Director of Financial Aid
700 College Place, Williamsport, PA 17701
(570) 321-4026

# Manor College
Jenkintown, Pennsylvania
www.manor.edu — Federal Code: 003294

**2-year private** junior college in small town, affiliated with Ukrainian Catholic Church.
**Enrollment:** 678 undergrads, 37% part-time. 141 full-time freshmen.
**Selectivity:** Admits 50 to 75% of applicants.

## BASIC COSTS (2015-2016)
**Tuition and fees:** $16,550.
**Room and board:** $7,500.
**Additional info:** Full-time tuition for Dental Hygiene, Expanded Dental Functions Assisting, and Veterinary Technology is $16,700. Part-time tuition for these programs is $699 per credit. Tuition/fee waivers available for minority students, unemployed or children of unemployed.

## FINANCIAL AID PICTURE (2015-2016)
**Students with need:** Out of 133 full-time freshmen who applied for aid, 130 were judged to have need. Of these, 126 received aid, and 3 had their full need met. Average financial aid package met 65% of need; average scholarship/grant was $17,315; average loan was $6,355. For part-time students, average financial aid package was $9,973.
**Students without need:** This college awards aid only to students with need.
**Scholarships offered:** Basilian Scholarship; for every freshman with A or B high school average and minimum 900 SAT (exclusive of Writing).

## FINANCIAL AID PROCEDURES
**Forms required:** FAFSA, state aid form, institutional form.
**Dates and Deadlines:** Priority date 3/1; no closing date. Applicants notified on a rolling basis; must reply within 1 week(s) of notification.
**Transfers:** No deadline. Applicants notified on a rolling basis starting 12/1; must reply within 2 week(s) of notification.

## CONTACT
Chris Hartman, Director of Financial Aid
700 Fox Chase Road, Jenkintown, PA 19046-3319
(215) 884-6051

# Mansfield University of Pennsylvania
Mansfield, Pennsylvania
www.mansfield.edu — Federal Code: 003324

**4-year public** university in small town.
**Enrollment:** 2,194 undergrads, 7% part-time. 573 full-time freshmen.
**Selectivity:** Admits over 75% of applicants.

## BASIC COSTS (2015-2016)
**Tuition and fees:** $9,806; out-of-state residents $20,396.
**Room and board:** $11,912.
**Additional info:** Out-of-State tuition is $11,650 for all out-of-state students from New York and New Jersey.

## FINANCIAL AID PICTURE (2014-2015)
**Students with need:** Out of 557 full-time freshmen who applied for aid, 485 were judged to have need. Of these, 485 received aid, and 32 had their full need met. Average financial aid package met 93% of need; average scholarship/grant was $2,721; average loan was $2,286. For part-time students, average financial aid package was $5,004.
**Students without need:** 14 full-time freshmen who did not demonstrate need for aid received scholarships/grants; average award was $1,123. No-need awards available for academics, alumni affiliation, art, athletics, job skills, leadership, minority status, music/drama, religious affiliation, ROTC, state/district residency.
**Scholarships offered:** 4 full-time freshmen received athletic scholarships; average amount $1,489.

## FINANCIAL AID PROCEDURES
**Forms required:** FAFSA, state aid form.
**Dates and Deadlines:** Priority date 2/15; closing date 6/30. Applicants notified on a rolling basis starting 2/17; must reply within 4 week(s) of notification.

## CONTACT
Charles Scheetz, Director of Financial Aid
71 Academy Street, Mansfield, PA 16933
(570) 662-4129

# Marywood University
Scranton, Pennsylvania
www.marywood.edu — Federal Code: 003296

**4-year private** university in small city, affiliated with Roman Catholic Church.
**Enrollment:** 1,817 undergrads, 5% part-time. 369 full-time freshmen.
**Selectivity:** Admits 50 to 75% of applicants.

## BASIC COSTS (2015-2016)
**Tuition and fees:** $32,692.
**Per-credit charge:** $630.
**Room and board:** $13,900.

## FINANCIAL AID PICTURE (2015-2016)
**Students with need:** Out of 346 full-time freshmen who applied for aid, 309 were judged to have need. Of these, 307 received aid, and 72 had their full need met. Average financial aid package met 83% of need; average scholarship/grant was $22,362; average loan was $3,637. For part-time students, average financial aid package was $9,174.
**Students without need:** 48 full-time freshmen who did not demonstrate need for aid received scholarships/grants; average award was $17,043. No-need awards available for academics, alumni affiliation, art, leadership, music/drama, ROTC.

## FINANCIAL AID PROCEDURES
**Forms required:** FAFSA, state aid form.
**Dates and Deadlines:** Priority date 2/15; no closing date. Applicants notified on a rolling basis starting 3/15; must reply by 5/1 or within 3 week(s) of notification.
**Transfers:** No deadline. Applicants notified on a rolling basis starting 3/1; must reply by 5/1 or within 3 week(s) of notification.

## CONTACT
Barbara Schmitt, Director of Financial Aid
2300 Adams Avenue, Scranton, PA 18509-1598
(570) 348-6225

# Mercyhurst University
Erie, Pennsylvania
www.mercyhurst.edu — Federal Code: 003297

**4-year private** university and liberal arts college in small city, affiliated with Roman Catholic Church.
**Enrollment:** 2,457 undergrads.
**Selectivity:** Admits over 75% of applicants.

## BASIC COSTS (2015-2016)
**Tuition and fees:** $33,314.
**Per-credit charge:** $1,044.
**Room and board:** $11,232.
**Additional info:** Tuition/fee waivers available for adults, minority students, unemployed or children of unemployed.

## FINANCIAL AID PICTURE
**Students with need:** Need-based aid available for full-time and part-time students. Work study available nights, weekends, and for part-time students.

**Students without need:** No-need awards available for academics, alumni affiliation, art, athletics, leadership, minority status, music/drama, religious affiliation, ROTC.

### FINANCIAL AID PROCEDURES

**Forms required:** FAFSA.

**Dates and Deadlines:** Priority date 3/1; no closing date. Applicants notified on a rolling basis starting 2/15; must reply by 5/1 or within 2 week(s) of notification.

**Transfers:** No deadline. Applicants notified on a rolling basis; must reply within 2 week(s) of notification.

### CONTACT

Carrie Newman, Director of Student Financial Services
501 East 38th Street, Erie, PA 16546-0001
(814) 824-2288

## Messiah College
Mechanicsburg, Pennsylvania
www.messiah.edu                    Federal Code: 003298

**4-year private** liberal arts college in small town, affiliated with interdenominational tradition.

**Enrollment:** 2,723 undergrads, 2% part-time. 689 full-time freshmen.

**Selectivity:** Admits over 75% of applicants.

### BASIC COSTS (2015-2016)

**Tuition and fees:** $32,240.

**Per-credit charge:** $1,310.

**Room and board:** $9,630.

**Additional info:** Tuition/fee waivers available for adults, minority students.

### FINANCIAL AID PICTURE (2015-2016)

**Students with need:** Out of 603 full-time freshmen who applied for aid, 524 were judged to have need. Of these, 524 received aid, and 97 had their full need met. Average financial aid package met 73% of need; average scholarship/grant was $18,943; average loan was $3,769. For part-time students, average financial aid package was $6,466.

**Students without need:** 163 full-time freshmen who did not demonstrate need for aid received scholarships/grants; average award was $15,295. No-need awards available for academics, art, leadership, music/drama, religious affiliation.

### FINANCIAL AID PROCEDURES

**Forms required:** FAFSA.

**Dates and Deadlines:** Priority date 4/1; no closing date. Applicants notified on a rolling basis starting 3/15; must reply by 5/1 or within 4 week(s) of notification.

### CONTACT

Greg Gearhart, Director of Financial Aid
One College Avenue, Suite 3005, Mechanicsburg, PA 17055
(717) 691-6007

## Metropolitan Career Center Computer Technology Institute
Philadelphia, Pennsylvania
www.cti-careers.org                    Federal Code: 031091

**2-year private** technical and career college in very large city.

**Enrollment:** 34 undergrads.

### BASIC COSTS (2015-2016)

**Tuition and fees:** $12,147.

**Per-credit charge:** $387.

**Additional info:** Full program cost is $23,994; does not include all fees and supplies.

### FINANCIAL AID PICTURE

**Students with need:** Need-based aid available for full-time and part-time students. Work study available nights.

**Students without need:** This college awards aid only to students with need.

### FINANCIAL AID PROCEDURES

**Forms required:** FAFSA, state aid form.

**Dates and Deadlines:** Applicants notified on a rolling basis starting 1/1; must reply within 2 week(s) of notification.

**Transfers:** No deadline. Applicants notified on a rolling basis starting 1/1; must reply within 2 week(s) of notification. Because we offer transfer enrollment on a rolling basis, aid is process based on need and remaining eligibility of financial aid at any given start date.

### CONTACT

Timothy Donohue, Controller
100 South Broad Street, Suite 830, Philadelphia, PA 19110
(215) 568-7937

## Millersville University of Pennsylvania
Millersville, Pennsylvania
www.millersville.edu                    Federal Code: 003325

**4-year public** university and liberal arts college in small town.

**Enrollment:** 6,981 undergrads, 12% part-time. 1,341 full-time freshmen.

**Selectivity:** Admits 50 to 75% of applicants.

### BASIC COSTS (2015-2016)

**Tuition and fees:** $10,918; out-of-state residents $20,108.

**Room and board:** $12,188.

**Additional info:** There is a out-of-state tuition reduction program; depending on academic major and qualifications, some students may qualify for a reduced tuition rate of $12,356 or $14,120 for STEM majors.

### FINANCIAL AID PICTURE (2014-2015)

**Students with need:** Out of 1,249 full-time freshmen who applied for aid, 949 were judged to have need. Of these, 914 received aid, and 63 had their full need met. Average financial aid package met 60% of need; average scholarship/grant was $5,483; average loan was $3,295. For part-time students, average financial aid package was $5,883.

**Students without need:** 32 full-time freshmen who did not demonstrate need for aid received scholarships/grants; average award was $3,246. No-need awards available for academics, athletics, minority status.

**Scholarships offered:** 32 full-time freshmen received athletic scholarships; average amount $2,068.

### FINANCIAL AID PROCEDURES

**Forms required:** FAFSA.

**Dates and Deadlines:** Priority date 3/15; no closing date. Applicants notified on a rolling basis starting 3/19; must reply within 2 week(s) of notification.

### CONTACT

Dwight Horsey, Director of Financial Aid and Assistant Vice President for Enrollment Management
PO Box 1002, Millersville, PA 17551-0302
(717) 871-5100

## Misericordia University
Dallas, Pennsylvania
www.misericordia.edu                    Federal Code: 003247

**4-year private** health science and liberal arts college in large town, affiliated with Roman Catholic Church.

**Enrollment:** 2,298 undergrads, 22% part-time. 434 full-time freshmen.
**Selectivity:** Admits 50 to 75% of applicants.

**BASIC COSTS (2016-2017)**
**Tuition and fees:** $30,740.
**Per-credit charge:** $575.
**Room and board:** $13,150.
**Additional info:** Tuition/fee waivers available for adults, minority students.

**FINANCIAL AID PICTURE (2015-2016)**
**Students with need:** Out of 425 full-time freshmen who applied for aid, 366 were judged to have need. Of these, 366 received aid, and 94 had their full need met. Average financial aid package met 82% of need; average scholarship/grant was $17,497; average loan was $7,102. For part-time students, average financial aid package was $5,851.
**Students without need:** 58 full-time freshmen who did not demonstrate need for aid received scholarships/grants; average award was $13,517. No-need awards available for academics, alumni affiliation, leadership, minority status, state/district residency.
**Scholarships offered:** McAuley Award; $1,000-$5,000 per year; based on out-of-classroom activities. Academic Scholarship; $2,000-$15,000 per year; based on academic abilities.

**FINANCIAL AID PROCEDURES**
**Forms required:** FAFSA.
**Dates and Deadlines:** Priority date 3/1; closing date 5/1. Applicants notified on a rolling basis starting 3/15.
**Transfers:** No deadline. Applicants notified on a rolling basis starting 3/15.

**CONTACT**
Jane Dessoye, Executive Director of Enrollment Management
301 Lake Street, Dallas, PA 18612-1098
(570) 674-6280

## Montgomery County Community College
Blue Bell, Pennsylvania
www.mc3.edu                    Federal Code: 004452

**2-year public** community college in large town.
**Enrollment:** 10,482 undergrads, 64% part-time. 1,474 full-time freshmen.
**Selectivity:** Open admission; but selective for some programs.

**BASIC COSTS (2015-2016)**
**Tuition and fees:** $4,920; out-of-district residents $9,240; out-of-state residents $13,560.
**Per-credit charge:** $134; out-of-district residents $268; out-of-state residents $402.
**Additional info:** Additional fees for Culinary Courses may apply.

**FINANCIAL AID PICTURE (2014-2015)**
**Students with need:** Out of 1,002 full-time freshmen who applied for aid, 856 were judged to have need. Of these, 760 received aid, and 56 had their full need met. Average financial aid package met 21% of need; average scholarship/grant was $2,915; average loan was $1,621. For part-time students, average financial aid package was $2,825.
**Students without need:** 123 full-time freshmen who did not demonstrate need for aid received scholarships/grants; average award was $2,690. No-need awards available for academics.

**FINANCIAL AID PROCEDURES**
**Forms required:** FAFSA.
**Dates and Deadlines:** Priority date 5/1; no closing date. Applicants notified on a rolling basis starting 2/1.
**Transfers:** No deadline.

**CONTACT**
Tracey Richards, Director of Financial Aid
340 DeKalb Pike, Blue Bell, PA 19422
(215) 641-6566

## Moore College of Art and Design
Philadelphia, Pennsylvania
www.moore.edu                    Federal Code: 003300

**4-year private** visual arts college for women in very large city.
**Enrollment:** 406 undergrads, 3% part-time. 96 full-time freshmen.
**Selectivity:** Admits 50 to 75% of applicants.

**BASIC COSTS (2015-2016)**
**Tuition and fees:** $37,098.
**Room and board:** $13,836.

**FINANCIAL AID PICTURE**
**Students with need:** Need-based aid available for full-time and part-time students.
**Students without need:** No-need awards available for academics, art, leadership.

**FINANCIAL AID PROCEDURES**
**Forms required:** FAFSA.
**Dates and Deadlines:** Priority date 3/1; closing date 5/1. Applicants notified on a rolling basis starting 2/15; must reply within 2 week(s) of notification.
**Transfers:** Priority date 5/1; no deadline.

**CONTACT**
Devon Weaver, Director of Financial Aid
The Parkway at 20th Street, Philadelphia, PA 19103-1179
(215) 568-4515

## Moravian College
Bethlehem, Pennsylvania
www.moravian.edu                    Federal Code: 003301

**4-year private** liberal arts and seminary college in small city, affiliated with Moravian Church in America.
**Enrollment:** 1,765 undergrads, 5% part-time. 523 full-time freshmen.
**Selectivity:** Admits 50 to 75% of applicants.

**BASIC COSTS (2015-2016)**
**Tuition and fees:** $38,832.
**Per-credit charge:** $1,035.
**Room and board:** $11,636.

**FINANCIAL AID PICTURE (2015-2016)**
**Students with need:** Average financial aid package met 77% of need; average scholarship/grant was $25,311; average loan was $3,957. For part-time students, average financial aid package was $8,479.
**Students without need:** No-need awards available for academics, alumni affiliation, art, leadership, music/drama, religious affiliation, ROTC, state/district residency.
**Scholarships offered:** $2,000 to entering freshmen graduating from a Lehigh County or Northampton County High School; $2,000 residential grant for entering freshmen who reside on campus.

**FINANCIAL AID PROCEDURES**
**Forms required:** FAFSA, institutional form.
**Dates and Deadlines:** Priority date 3/1; no closing date. Applicants notified on a rolling basis starting 2/25; must reply by 5/1.

**CONTACT**
Dennis Levy, Director of Financial Aid Services
1200 Main Street, Bethlehem, PA 18018
(610) 861-1330

## Mount Aloysius College

Cresson, Pennsylvania
www.mtaloy.edu
Federal Code: 003302

**4-year private** liberal arts college in small town, affiliated with Roman Catholic Church.
**Enrollment:** 1,472 undergrads, 21% part-time. 364 full-time freshmen.
**Selectivity:** Open admission; but selective for some programs.

### BASIC COSTS (2015-2016)

**Tuition and fees:** $21,360.
**Per-credit charge:** $720.
**Room and board:** $9,552.
**Additional info:** Tuition/fee waivers available for unemployed or children of unemployed.

### FINANCIAL AID PICTURE (2015-2016)

**Students with need:** Out of 364 full-time freshmen who applied for aid, 296 were judged to have need. Of these, 296 received aid. Average financial aid package met 35% of need; average scholarship/grant was $6,400; average loan was $3,500. For part-time students, average financial aid package was $5,800.
**Students without need:** 68 full-time freshmen who did not demonstrate need for aid received scholarships/grants; average award was $5,200. No-need awards available for academics, art, leadership, music/drama, religious affiliation.

### FINANCIAL AID PROCEDURES

**Forms required:** FAFSA.
**Dates and Deadlines:** Priority date 4/1; no closing date. Applicants notified on a rolling basis starting 3/15; must reply within 2 week(s) of notification.
**Transfers:** No deadline.

### CONTACT

Stacy Schenk, Director of Financial Aid
7373 Admiral Peary Highway, Cresson, PA 16630
(814) 886-6357

## Muhlenberg College

Allentown, Pennsylvania
Federal Code: 003304
www.muhlenberg.edu
CSS Code: 2424

**4-year private** liberal arts college in small city, affiliated with Evangelical Lutheran Church in America.
**Enrollment:** 2,302 undergrads, 2% part-time. 582 full-time freshmen.
**Selectivity:** Admits less than 50% of applicants.

### BASIC COSTS (2015-2016)

**Tuition and fees:** $46,160.
**Per-credit charge:** $1,341.25.
**Room and board:** $10,770.

### FINANCIAL AID PICTURE (2015-2016)

**Students with need:** Out of 372 full-time freshmen who applied for aid, 273 were judged to have need. Of these, 273 received aid, and 85 had their full need met. Average financial aid package met 93% of need; average scholarship/grant was $32,445; average loan was $3,852. For part-time students, average financial aid package was $6,970.
**Students without need:** 244 full-time freshmen who did not demonstrate need for aid received scholarships/grants; average award was $12,981. No-need awards available for academics, art, leadership, music/drama, ROTC.

### FINANCIAL AID PROCEDURES

**Forms required:** FAFSA, CSS PROFILE, institutional form.
**Dates and Deadlines:** Closing date 2/15. Applicants notified by 4/1; must reply by 5/1.

**Transfers:** Closing date 4/15. Applicants notified by 6/1; must reply by 7/1. Transfers awarded aid on a funds-available basis after returning students and freshmen have been served.

### CONTACT

Gregory Mitton, Director of Financial Aid
2400 Chew Street, Allentown, PA 18104
(484) 664-3175

## Neumann University

Aston, Pennsylvania
www.neumann.edu
Federal Code: 003988

**4-year private** university in large town, affiliated with Roman Catholic Church.
**Enrollment:** 2,358 undergrads, 24% part-time. 415 full-time freshmen.
**Selectivity:** Admits over 75% of applicants.

### BASIC COSTS (2015-2016)

**Tuition and fees:** $26,918.
**Per-credit charge:** $589.
**Room and board:** $11,754.

### FINANCIAL AID PICTURE (2014-2015)

**Students with need:** Out of 401 full-time freshmen who applied for aid, 377 were judged to have need. Of these, 377 received aid. Average financial aid package met 70% of need; average scholarship/grant was $6,738; average loan was $3,500.
**Students without need:** This college awards aid only to students with need.

### FINANCIAL AID PROCEDURES

**Forms required:** FAFSA.
**Dates and Deadlines:** Applicants notified on a rolling basis; must reply within 2 week(s) of notification.
**Transfers:** No deadline. Applicants notified on a rolling basis; must reply within 2 week(s) of notification.

### CONTACT

Andrea Del Vacchio, Director of Financial Assistance
Office of Admissions, Aston, PA 19014-1298
(610) 558-5521

## New Castle School of Trades

New Castle, Pennsylvania
www.ncstrades.edu
Federal Code: 007780

**2-year for-profit** technical college in large town.
**Enrollment:** 825 undergrads.

### BASIC COSTS (2015-2016)

**Additional info:** Tuition varies by program; $5,970 to $19,650. Books and tool expenses also vary by program. All costs are subject to change.

### FINANCIAL AID PICTURE

**Students with need:** Need-based aid available for full-time and part-time students.

### CONTACT

Trudy Sotter, Financial Aid
4117 Pulaski Road, New Castle, PA 16101
(724) 964-8811

# Northampton Community College

Bethlehem, Pennsylvania
www.northampton.edu                Federal Code: 007191

**2-year public** community college in small city.
**Enrollment:** 9,727 undergrads, 53% part-time. 1,499 full-time freshmen.
**Selectivity:** Open admission; but selective for some programs.

## BASIC COSTS (2015-2016)
**Tuition and fees:** $3,990; out-of-district residents $8,700; out-of-state residents $12,840.
**Per-credit charge:** $94; out-of-district residents $188; out-of-state residents $282.
**Room and board:** $8,092.
**Additional info:** Tuition/fee waivers available for unemployed or children of unemployed.

## FINANCIAL AID PICTURE (2015-2016)
**Students with need:** 73% of average financial aid package awarded as scholarships/grants, 27% awarded as loans/jobs. Need-based aid available for part-time students. Work study available nights, weekends, and for part-time students.
**Students without need:** No-need awards available for academics, alumni affiliation, art, leadership, minority status, music/drama, state/district residency.

## FINANCIAL AID PROCEDURES
**Forms required:** FAFSA, state aid form.
**Dates and Deadlines:** Priority date 3/31; no closing date. Applicants notified on a rolling basis starting 4/1.

## CONTACT
Cindy King, Director of Financial Aid
3835 Green Pond Road, Bethlehem, PA 18020-7599
(610) 861-5510

# Orleans Technical Institute

Philadelphia, Pennsylvania
www.orleanstech.edu                Federal Code: 021830

**2-year private** technical and career college in very large city.
**Enrollment:** 548 undergrads.

## BASIC COSTS (2015-2016)
**Additional info:** Tuition and required fees vary by program and range from $12,990 to $13,791. Books and supplies range from $526 to $1,415. All costs are subject to change.

## FINANCIAL AID PICTURE
**Students with need:** Need-based aid available for full-time and part-time students. Work study available nights, weekends, and for part-time students.
**Students without need:** No-need awards available for academics.

## FINANCIAL AID PROCEDURES
**Forms required:** FAFSA, institutional form.
**Dates and Deadlines:** Applicants notified on a rolling basis.

## CONTACT
Latanya Byrd, Director of Student Financial Services
2770 Red Lion Road, Philadelphia, PA 19114
(215) 728-4736 ext. 4736

# Peirce College

Philadelphia, Pennsylvania
www.peirce.edu                Federal Code: 003309

**4-year private** business and technical college in very large city.
**Enrollment:** 1,622 undergrads, 81% part-time. 32 full-time freshmen.

**Selectivity:** Open admission; but selective for some programs.

## BASIC COSTS (2016-2017)
**Tuition and fees:** $17,940.
**Per-credit charge:** $578.

## FINANCIAL AID PICTURE (2014-2015)
**Students with need:** Out of 32 full-time freshmen who applied for aid, 30 were judged to have need. Of these, 30 received aid. Average financial aid package met 51% of need; average scholarship/grant was $6,128; average loan was $2,798. For part-time students, average financial aid package was $6,073.
**Students without need:** 1 full-time freshmen who did not demonstrate need for aid received scholarships/grants; average award was $12,150. No-need awards available for academics, alumni affiliation, leadership, state/district residency.
**Additional info:** Tuition discounts available for US students serving in US military and in protect-and-serve fields.

## FINANCIAL AID PROCEDURES
**Forms required:** FAFSA.
**Dates and Deadlines:** Priority date 5/1; no closing date. Applicants notified on a rolling basis starting 5/1.
**Transfers:** No deadline. Applicants notified on a rolling basis.

## CONTACT
Kristina Fripps, Director, Student Financial Aid
1420 Pine Street, Philadelphia, PA 19102-4699
(888) 467-3472 ext. 9370

# Penn State Abington

Abington, Pennsylvania
www.abington.psu.edu                Federal Code: 003329

**4-year public** branch campus college in small city.
**Enrollment:** 3,490 undergrads, 12% part-time. 893 full-time freshmen.
**Selectivity:** Admits over 75% of applicants.

## BASIC COSTS (2015-2016)
**Tuition and fees:** $13,954; out-of-state residents $21,266.
**Per-credit charge:** $535; out-of-state residents $847.

## FINANCIAL AID PICTURE (2014-2015)
**Students with need:** Out of 747 full-time freshmen who applied for aid, 614 were judged to have need. Of these, 596 received aid, and 18 had their full need met. Average financial aid package met 57% of need; average scholarship/grant was $7,747; average loan was $3,320. For part-time students, average financial aid package was $5,729.
**Students without need:** 62 full-time freshmen who did not demonstrate need for aid received scholarships/grants; average award was $4,406. No-need awards available for academics, alumni affiliation, ROTC.

## FINANCIAL AID PROCEDURES
**Forms required:** FAFSA.
**Dates and Deadlines:** Priority date 2/15; no closing date. Applicants notified on a rolling basis.
**Transfers:** No deadline. Applicants notified on a rolling basis. Schools required to obtain student aid information through National Student Loan Data System (NSLDS).

## CONTACT
Anna Griswold, Assistant Vice President for Undergraduate Education & Executive Director for Student Aid
1600 Woodland Road, Abington, PA 19001
(814) 865-6301

## Penn State Altoona
Altoona, Pennsylvania
www.altoona.psu.edu          Federal Code: 003329

**4-year public** branch campus college in small city.
**Enrollment:** 3,772 undergrads, 3% part-time. 1,482 full-time freshmen.
**Selectivity:** Admits over 75% of applicants.

### BASIC COSTS (2015-2016)
**Tuition and fees:** $14,610; out-of-state residents $22,344.
**Per-credit charge:** $569; out-of-state residents $891.
**Room and board:** $10,920.

### FINANCIAL AID PICTURE (2014-2015)
**Students with need:** Out of 1,239 full-time freshmen who applied for aid, 982 were judged to have need. Of these, 939 received aid, and 53 had their full need met. Average financial aid package met 56% of need; average scholarship/grant was $6,573; average loan was $3,469. For part-time students, average financial aid package was $7,420.
**Students without need:** 147 full-time freshmen who did not demonstrate need for aid received scholarships/grants; average award was $3,526. No-need awards available for academics, alumni affiliation, ROTC.

### FINANCIAL AID PROCEDURES
**Forms required:** FAFSA.
**Dates and Deadlines:** Priority date 2/15; no closing date. Applicants notified on a rolling basis.
**Transfers:** No deadline. Applicants notified on a rolling basis. Schools required to obtain student aid information through National Student Loan Data System (NSLDS).

### CONTACT
Anna Griswold, Assistant Vice President for Undergraduate Education & Executive Director for Student Aid
3000 Ivyside Park, Altoona, PA 16801
(814) 865-6301

## Penn State Beaver
Monaca, Pennsylvania
www.br.psu.edu          Federal Code: 003329

**4-year public** branch campus college in small town.
**Enrollment:** 639 undergrads, 5% part-time. 216 full-time freshmen.
**Selectivity:** Admits over 75% of applicants.

### BASIC COSTS (2015-2016)
**Tuition and fees:** $13,660; out-of-state residents $20,346.
**Per-credit charge:** $524; out-of-state residents $809.
**Room and board:** $10,920.

### FINANCIAL AID PICTURE (2014-2015)
**Students with need:** Out of 198 full-time freshmen who applied for aid, 168 were judged to have need. Of these, 167 received aid, and 6 had their full need met. Average financial aid package met 67% of need; average scholarship/grant was $7,478; average loan was $3,475. For part-time students, average financial aid package was $6,493.
**Students without need:** 23 full-time freshmen who did not demonstrate need for aid received scholarships/grants; average award was $2,655. No-need awards available for academics, alumni affiliation, ROTC.

### FINANCIAL AID PROCEDURES
**Forms required:** FAFSA.
**Dates and Deadlines:** Priority date 2/15; no closing date. Applicants notified on a rolling basis.
**Transfers:** No deadline. Applicants notified on a rolling basis. Schools required to obtain student aid information through National Student Loan Data System (NSLDS).

### CONTACT
Anna Griswold, Assistant Vice President for Undergraduate Education & Executive Director for Student Aid
100 University Drive, Monaca, PA 15061
(814) 865-6301

## Penn State Berks
Reading, Pennsylvania
www.bk.psu.edu          Federal Code: 003329

**4-year public** branch campus college in small city.
**Enrollment:** 2,778 undergrads, 7% part-time. 846 full-time freshmen.
**Selectivity:** Admits over 75% of applicants.

### BASIC COSTS (2015-2016)
**Tuition and fees:** $14,610; out-of-state residents $22,344.
**Per-credit charge:** $569; out-of-state residents $891.
**Room and board:** $11,950.

### FINANCIAL AID PICTURE (2014-2015)
**Students with need:** Out of 745 full-time freshmen who applied for aid, 612 were judged to have need. Of these, 594 received aid, and 25 had their full need met. Average financial aid package met 59% of need; average scholarship/grant was $6,835; average loan was $3,503. For part-time students, average financial aid package was $6,272.
**Students without need:** 41 full-time freshmen who did not demonstrate need for aid received scholarships/grants; average award was $2,710. No-need awards available for academics, alumni affiliation, ROTC.

### FINANCIAL AID PROCEDURES
**Forms required:** FAFSA.
**Dates and Deadlines:** Priority date 2/15; no closing date. Applicants notified on a rolling basis.
**Transfers:** No deadline. Applicants notified on a rolling basis. Schools required to obtain student aid information through National Student Loan Data System (NSLDS).

### CONTACT
Anna Griswold, Assistant Vice President for Undergraduate Education & Executive Director for Student Aid
Tulpehocken Road, Reading, PA 19610
(814) 865-6301

## Penn State Brandywine
Media, Pennsylvania
www.brandywine.psu.edu          Federal Code: 006922

**4-year public** branch campus college in small town.
**Enrollment:** 1,291 undergrads, 9% part-time. 382 full-time freshmen.
**Selectivity:** Admits over 75% of applicants.

### BASIC COSTS (2015-2016)
**Tuition and fees:** $13,964; out-of-state residents $21,158.
**Per-credit charge:** $535; out-of-state residents $842.

### FINANCIAL AID PICTURE (2014-2015)
**Students with need:** Out of 335 full-time freshmen who applied for aid, 255 were judged to have need. Of these, 249 received aid, and 9 had their full need met. Average financial aid package met 61% of need; average scholarship/grant was $6,811; average loan was $3,398. For part-time students, average financial aid package was $6,869.
**Students without need:** 52 full-time freshmen who did not demonstrate need for aid received scholarships/grants; average award was $3,840. No-need awards available for academics, alumni affiliation, ROTC.

### FINANCIAL AID PROCEDURES
**Forms required:** FAFSA.

**Dates and Deadlines:** Priority date 2/15; no closing date. Applicants notified on a rolling basis.

**Transfers:** No deadline. Applicants notified on a rolling basis. Schools required to obtain student aid information through National Student Loan Data System (NSLDS).

**CONTACT**

Anna Griswold, Assistant Vice President for Undergraduate Education & Executive Director for Student Aid

25 Yearsley Mill Road, Media, PA 19063

(814) 865-6301

## Penn State DuBois

DuBois, Pennsylvania

http://dubois.psu.edu                    Federal Code: 003335

**4-year public** branch campus college in small town.

**Enrollment:** 512 undergrads, 7% part-time. 150 full-time freshmen.

**Selectivity:** Admits over 75% of applicants.

**BASIC COSTS (2015-2016)**

**Tuition and fees:** $13,546; out-of-state residents $20,232.

**Per-credit charge:** $524; out-of-state residents $809.

**FINANCIAL AID PICTURE (2014-2015)**

**Students with need:** Out of 141 full-time freshmen who applied for aid, 125 were judged to have need. Of these, 124 received aid, and 4 had their full need met. Average financial aid package met 63% of need; average scholarship/grant was $6,813; average loan was $3,220. For part-time students, average financial aid package was $8,116.

**Students without need:** 10 full-time freshmen who did not demonstrate need for aid received scholarships/grants; average award was $1,793. No-need awards available for academics, alumni affiliation, ROTC.

**FINANCIAL AID PROCEDURES**

**Forms required:** FAFSA.

**Dates and Deadlines:** Priority date 2/15; no closing date. Applicants notified on a rolling basis.

**Transfers:** No deadline. Applicants notified on a rolling basis. Schools required to obtain student aid information through National Student Loan Data System (NSLDS).

**CONTACT**

Anna Griswold, Assistant Vice President for Undergraduate Education & Executive Director for Student Aid

1 College Place, DuBois, PA 15801

(814) 865-6301

## Penn State Erie, The Behrend College

Erie, Pennsylvania

http://psbehrend.psu.edu                    Federal Code: 003329

**4-year public** branch campus college in small city.

**Enrollment:** 4,092 undergrads, 4% part-time. 1,178 full-time freshmen.

**Selectivity:** Admits over 75% of applicants.

**BASIC COSTS (2015-2016)**

**Tuition and fees:** $14,610; out-of-state residents $22,344.

**Per-credit charge:** $569; out-of-state residents $891.

**Room and board:** $10,920.

**FINANCIAL AID PICTURE (2014-2015)**

**Students with need:** Out of 924 full-time freshmen who applied for aid, 747 were judged to have need. Of these, 731 received aid, and 29 had their full need met. Average financial aid package met 58% of need; average

scholarship/grant was $6,901; average loan was $3,512. For part-time students, average financial aid package was $6,342.

**Students without need:** 83 full-time freshmen who did not demonstrate need for aid received scholarships/grants; average award was $2,736. No-need awards available for academics, alumni affiliation, ROTC.

**FINANCIAL AID PROCEDURES**

**Forms required:** FAFSA.

**Dates and Deadlines:** Priority date 2/15; no closing date. Applicants notified on a rolling basis.

**Transfers:** No deadline. Applicants notified on a rolling basis. Schools required to obtain student aid information through National Student Loan Data System (NSLDS).

**CONTACT**

Anna Griswold, Assistant Vice President for Undergraduate Education & Executive Director for Student Aid

Metzgar Admissions & Alumni Center, Erie, PA 16563

(814) 865-6301

## Penn State Fayette, The Eberly Campus

Lemont Furnace, Pennsylvania

www.fe.psu.edu                    Federal Code: 003329

**4-year public** branch campus college in large town.

**Enrollment:** 671 undergrads, 13% part-time. 194 full-time freshmen.

**Selectivity:** Admits over 75% of applicants.

**BASIC COSTS (2015-2016)**

**Tuition and fees:** $13,608; out-of-state residents $20,294.

**Per-credit charge:** $524; out-of-state residents $809.

**FINANCIAL AID PICTURE (2014-2015)**

**Students with need:** Out of 181 full-time freshmen who applied for aid, 149 were judged to have need. Of these, 147 received aid, and 9 had their full need met. Average financial aid package met 63% of need; average scholarship/grant was $6,230; average loan was $3,331. For part-time students, average financial aid package was $7,592.

**Students without need:** 29 full-time freshmen who did not demonstrate need for aid received scholarships/grants; average award was $2,500. No-need awards available for academics, alumni affiliation, ROTC.

**FINANCIAL AID PROCEDURES**

**Forms required:** FAFSA.

**Dates and Deadlines:** Priority date 2/15; no closing date. Applicants notified on a rolling basis.

**Transfers:** No deadline. Applicants notified on a rolling basis. Schools required to obtain student aid information through National Student Loan Data System (NSLDS).

**CONTACT**

Anna Griswold, Assistant Vice President for Undergraduate Education & Executive Director for Student Aid

110 Eberly Building, Lemont Furnace, PA 15456

(814) 865-6301

## Penn State Greater Allegheny

McKeesport, Pennsylvania

http://ga.psu.edu                    Federal Code: 003329

**4-year public** branch campus college in large town.

**Enrollment:** 532 undergrads, 9% part-time. 182 full-time freshmen.

**Selectivity:** Admits over 75% of applicants.

**BASIC COSTS (2015-2016)**

**Tuition and fees:** $13,660; out-of-state residents $20,346.

**Per-credit charge:** $524; out-of-state residents $809.
**Room and board:** $10,920.

## FINANCIAL AID PICTURE (2014-2015)
**Students with need:** Out of 168 full-time freshmen who applied for aid, 150 were judged to have need. Of these, 150 received aid, and 11 had their full need met. Average financial aid package met 68% of need; average scholarship/grant was $7,609; average loan was $3,459. For part-time students, average financial aid package was $7,341.
**Students without need:** 10 full-time freshmen who did not demonstrate need for aid received scholarships/grants; average award was $5,100. No-need awards available for academics, alumni affiliation, ROTC.

## FINANCIAL AID PROCEDURES
**Forms required:** FAFSA.
**Dates and Deadlines:** Priority date 2/15; no closing date. Applicants notified on a rolling basis.
**Transfers:** No deadline. Applicants notified on a rolling basis. Schools required to obtain student aid information through National Student Loan Data System (NSLDS).

## CONTACT
Anna Griswold, Assistant Vice President for Undergraduate Education & Executive Director for Student Aid
123 Frable Building, McKeesport, PA 15132
(814) 865-6301

# Penn State Harrisburg
Middletown, Pennsylvania
www.hbg.psu.edu                          Federal Code: 003329

**4-year public** branch campus college in small town.
**Enrollment:** 3,740 undergrads, 9% part-time. 792 full-time freshmen.
**Selectivity:** Admits over 75% of applicants.

## BASIC COSTS (2015-2016)
**Tuition and fees:** $14,610; out-of-state residents $22,344.
**Per-credit charge:** $569; out-of-state residents $891.
**Room and board:** $12,450.

## FINANCIAL AID PICTURE (2014-2015)
**Students with need:** Out of 575 full-time freshmen who applied for aid, 464 were judged to have need. Of these, 449 received aid, and 24 had their full need met. Average financial aid package met 55% of need; average scholarship/grant was $7,218; average loan was $3,530. For part-time students, average financial aid package was $6,868.
**Students without need:** 107 full-time freshmen who did not demonstrate need for aid received scholarships/grants; average award was $1,869. No-need awards available for academics, alumni affiliation, ROTC.

## FINANCIAL AID PROCEDURES
**Forms required:** FAFSA.
**Dates and Deadlines:** Priority date 2/15; no closing date. Applicants notified on a rolling basis.
**Transfers:** No deadline. Applicants notified on a rolling basis. Schools required to obtain student aid information through National Student Loan Data System (NSLDS).

## CONTACT
Anna Griswold, Assistant Vice President for Undergraduate Education & Executive Director for Student Aid
Swatara Building, Middletown, PA 17057
(814) 865-6301

# Penn State Hazleton
Hazleton, Pennsylvania
http://hazleton.psu.edu/                 Federal Code: 003338

**4-year public** branch campus college in large town.
**Enrollment:** 753 undergrads, 4% part-time. 304 full-time freshmen.
**Selectivity:** Admits over 75% of applicants.

## BASIC COSTS (2015-2016)
**Tuition and fees:** $13,902; out-of-state residents $21,096.
**Per-credit charge:** $535; out-of-state residents $842.
**Room and board:** $10,920.

## FINANCIAL AID PICTURE (2014-2015)
**Students with need:** Out of 278 full-time freshmen who applied for aid, 253 were judged to have need. Of these, 250 received aid, and 8 had their full need met. Average financial aid package met 60% of need; average scholarship/grant was $7,557; average loan was $3,344. For part-time students, average financial aid package was $7,412.
**Students without need:** 30 full-time freshmen who did not demonstrate need for aid received scholarships/grants; average award was $3,331. No-need awards available for academics, alumni affiliation, ROTC.

## FINANCIAL AID PROCEDURES
**Forms required:** FAFSA.
**Dates and Deadlines:** Priority date 2/15; no closing date. Applicants notified on a rolling basis.
**Transfers:** No deadline. Applicants notified on a rolling basis. Schools required to obtain student aid information through National Student Loan Data System (NSLDS).

## CONTACT
Anna Griswold, Assistant Vice President for Undergraduate Education & Executive Director for Student Aid
110 Schiavo Hall, University Park, PA 18202
(814) 865-6301

# Penn State Lehigh Valley
Center Valley, Pennsylvania
www.lv.psu.edu                           Federal Code: 003329

**4-year public** branch campus college in rural community.
**Enrollment:** 773 undergrads, 11% part-time. 212 full-time freshmen.
**Selectivity:** Admits over 75% of applicants.

## BASIC COSTS (2015-2016)
**Tuition and fees:** $13,964; out-of-state residents $21,158.
**Per-credit charge:** $535; out-of-state residents $842.

## FINANCIAL AID PICTURE (2014-2015)
**Students with need:** Out of 191 full-time freshmen who applied for aid, 144 were judged to have need. Of these, 137 received aid, and 6 had their full need met. Average financial aid package met 57% of need; average scholarship/grant was $7,495; average loan was $3,389. For part-time students, average financial aid package was $7,419.
**Students without need:** 31 full-time freshmen who did not demonstrate need for aid received scholarships/grants; average award was $2,386. No-need awards available for academics, alumni affiliation, ROTC.

## FINANCIAL AID PROCEDURES
**Forms required:** FAFSA.
**Dates and Deadlines:** Priority date 2/15; no closing date. Applicants notified on a rolling basis.
**Transfers:** No deadline. Applicants notified on a rolling basis. Schools required to obtain student aid information through National Student Loan Data System (NSLDS).

**CONTACT**
Anna Griswold, Assistant Vice President for Undergraduate Education & Executive Director for Student Aid
2809 Saucon Valley Road, Center Vally, PA 18034
(814) 865-6301

## Penn State Mont Alto
Mont Alto, Pennsylvania
www.ma.psu.edu                          Federal Code: 003329

**4-year public** branch campus college in rural community.
**Enrollment:** 809 undergrads, 19% part-time. 267 full-time freshmen.
**Selectivity:** Admits over 75% of applicants.

**BASIC COSTS (2015-2016)**
**Tuition and fees:** $13,670; out-of-state residents $20,356.
**Per-credit charge:** $524; out-of-state residents $809.
**Room and board:** $10,920.

**FINANCIAL AID PICTURE (2014-2015)**
**Students with need:** Out of 257 full-time freshmen who applied for aid, 221 were judged to have need. Of these, 219 received aid, and 12 had their full need met. Average financial aid package met 62% of need; average scholarship/grant was $6,387; average loan was $3,578. For part-time students, average financial aid package was $6,927.
**Students without need:** 17 full-time freshmen who did not demonstrate need for aid received scholarships/grants; average award was $3,275. No-need awards available for academics, alumni affiliation, ROTC.

**FINANCIAL AID PROCEDURES**
**Forms required:** FAFSA.
**Dates and Deadlines:** Priority date 2/15; no closing date. Applicants notified on a rolling basis starting 3/1.
**Transfers:** No deadline. Applicants notified on a rolling basis. Schools required to obtain student aid information through National Student Loan Data System (NSLDS).

**CONTACT**
Anna Griswold, Assistant Vice President for Undergraduate Education & Executive Director for Student Aid
1 Campus Drive, Mont Alto, PA 17237
(814) 865-6301

## Penn State New Kensington
New Kensington, Pennsylvania
www.nk.psu.edu                          Federal Code: 003329

**4-year public** branch campus college in large town.
**Enrollment:** 598 undergrads, 17% part-time. 185 full-time freshmen.
**Selectivity:** Admits over 75% of applicants.

**BASIC COSTS (2015-2016)**
**Tuition and fees:** $13,608; out-of-state residents $20,294.
**Per-credit charge:** $524; out-of-state residents $809.

**FINANCIAL AID PICTURE (2014-2015)**
**Students with need:** Out of 169 full-time freshmen who applied for aid, 131 were judged to have need. Of these, 131 received aid, and 22 had their full need met. Average financial aid package met 67% of need; average scholarship/grant was $5,710; average loan was $3,188. For part-time students, average financial aid package was $6,462.
**Students without need:** 30 full-time freshmen who did not demonstrate need for aid received scholarships/grants; average award was $3,524. No-need awards available for academics, alumni affiliation, ROTC.

**FINANCIAL AID PROCEDURES**
**Forms required:** FAFSA.

**Dates and Deadlines:** Priority date 2/15; no closing date. Applicants notified on a rolling basis.
**Transfers:** No deadline. Applicants notified on a rolling basis. Schools required to obtain student aid information through National Student Loan Data System (NSLDS).

**CONTACT**
Anna Griswold, Assistant Vice President for Undergraduate Education & Executive Director for Student Aid
3550 Seventh Street Road, New Kensington, PA 15068
(814) 865-6301

## Penn State Schuylkill
Schuylkill Haven, Pennsylvania
www.sl.psu.edu                          Federal Code: 003329

**4-year public** branch campus college in small town.
**Enrollment:** 720 undergrads, 16% part-time. 247 full-time freshmen.
**Selectivity:** Admits 50 to 75% of applicants.

**BASIC COSTS (2015-2016)**
**Tuition and fees:** $13,902; out-of-state residents $21,096.
**Per-credit charge:** $535; out-of-state residents $842.
**Room and board:** $8,060.

**FINANCIAL AID PICTURE (2014-2015)**
**Students with need:** Out of 233 full-time freshmen who applied for aid, 210 were judged to have need. Of these, 208 received aid, and 13 had their full need met. Average financial aid package met 63% of need; average scholarship/grant was $6,779; average loan was $3,339. For part-time students, average financial aid package was $6,638.
**Students without need:** 25 full-time freshmen who did not demonstrate need for aid received scholarships/grants; average award was $2,942. No-need awards available for academics, alumni affiliation, ROTC.

**FINANCIAL AID PROCEDURES**
**Forms required:** FAFSA.
**Dates and Deadlines:** Priority date 2/15; no closing date. Applicants notified on a rolling basis.
**Transfers:** No deadline. Applicants notified on a rolling basis. Schools required to obtain student aid information through National Student Loan Data System (NSLDS).

**CONTACT**
Anna Griswold, Assistant Vice President for Undergraduate Education & Executive Director for Student Aid
102 Administration Building, Schuylkill Haven, PA 17972
(814) 865-6301

## Penn State Shenango
Sharon, Pennsylvania
www.shenango.psu.edu                    Federal Code: 003329

**4-year public** branch campus college in large town.
**Enrollment:** 436 undergrads, 38% part-time. 74 full-time freshmen.
**Selectivity:** Admits 50 to 75% of applicants.

**BASIC COSTS (2015-2016)**
**Tuition and fees:** $13,354; out-of-state residents $19,910.
**Per-credit charge:** $504; out-of-state residents $793.

**FINANCIAL AID PICTURE (2014-2015)**
**Students with need:** Out of 73 full-time freshmen who applied for aid, 64 were judged to have need. Of these, 64 received aid, and 4 had their full need met. Average financial aid package met 62% of need; average scholarship/grant was $7,526; average loan was $3,333. For part-time students, average financial aid package was $8,218.

**Students without need:** 7 full-time freshmen who did not demonstrate need for aid received scholarships/grants; average award was $2,090. No-need awards available for academics, alumni affiliation, ROTC.

### FINANCIAL AID PROCEDURES

**Forms required:** FAFSA.

**Dates and Deadlines:** Priority date 2/15; no closing date. Applicants notified on a rolling basis.

**Transfers:** No deadline. Applicants notified on a rolling basis. Schools required to obtain student aid information through National Student Loan Data System (NSLDS).

### CONTACT

Anna Griswold, Assistant Vice President for Undergraduate Education & Executive Director for Student Aid
147 Shenango Avenue, Sharon, PA 16146
(814) 865-6301

## Penn State University Park

University Park, Pennsylvania
www.psu.edu                    Federal Code: 003329

**4-year public** university in large town.

**Enrollment:** 40,179 undergrads, 2% part-time. 8,166 full-time freshmen.

**Selectivity:** Admits 50 to 75% of applicants.

### BASIC COSTS (2015-2016)

**Tuition and fees:** $17,514; out-of-state residents $31,346.

**Per-credit charge:** $691; out-of-state residents $1,267.

**Room and board:** $10,920.

### FINANCIAL AID PICTURE (2014-2015)

**Students with need:** Out of 5,891 full-time freshmen who applied for aid, 3,819 were judged to have need. Of these, 3,516 received aid, and 302 had their full need met. Average financial aid package met 58% of need; average scholarship/grant was $7,052; average loan was $3,540. For part-time students, average financial aid package was $7,728.

**Students without need:** 652 full-time freshmen who did not demonstrate need for aid received scholarships/grants; average award was $4,540. No-need awards available for academics, alumni affiliation, athletics, ROTC.

**Scholarships offered:** 142 full-time freshmen received athletic scholarships; average amount $23,866.

### FINANCIAL AID PROCEDURES

**Forms required:** FAFSA.

**Dates and Deadlines:** Priority date 2/15; no closing date. Applicants notified on a rolling basis.

**Transfers:** No deadline. Applicants notified on a rolling basis. Schools required to obtain student aid information through National Student Loan Data System (NSLDS).

### CONTACT

Anna Griswold, Assistant Vice President for Undergraduate Education & Executive Director for Student Aid
201 Shields Building, University Park, PA 16802
(814) 865-6301

## Penn State Wilkes-Barre

Lehman, Pennsylvania
www.wb.psu.edu                    Federal Code: 003329

**4-year public** branch campus college in small city.

**Enrollment:** 460 undergrads, 6% part-time. 137 full-time freshmen.

**Selectivity:** Admits over 75% of applicants.

### BASIC COSTS (2015-2016)

**Tuition and fees:** $13,598; out-of-state residents $20,284.

**Per-credit charge:** $524; out-of-state residents $809.

### FINANCIAL AID PICTURE (2014-2015)

**Students with need:** Out of 130 full-time freshmen who applied for aid, 100 were judged to have need. Of these, 98 received aid, and 10 had their full need met. Average financial aid package met 64% of need; average scholarship/grant was $6,485; average loan was $3,241. For part-time students, average financial aid package was $4,712.

**Students without need:** 11 full-time freshmen who did not demonstrate need for aid received scholarships/grants; average award was $2,148. No-need awards available for academics, alumni affiliation, ROTC.

### FINANCIAL AID PROCEDURES

**Forms required:** FAFSA.

**Dates and Deadlines:** Priority date 2/15; no closing date. Applicants notified on a rolling basis.

**Transfers:** No deadline. Applicants notified on a rolling basis. Schools required to obtain student aid information through National Student Loan Data System (NSLDS).

### CONTACT

Anna Griswold, Assistant Vice President for Undergraduate Education & Executive Director for Student Aid
Hayfield House 101, Lehman, PA 18627
(814) 865-6301

## Penn State Worthington Scranton

Dunmore, Pennsylvania
www.sn.psu.edu                    Federal Code: 003344

**4-year public** branch campus college in large town.

**Enrollment:** 967 undergrads, 12% part-time. 263 full-time freshmen.

**Selectivity:** Admits over 75% of applicants.

### BASIC COSTS (2015-2016)

**Tuition and fees:** $13,902; out-of-state residents $21,096.

**Per-credit charge:** $535; out-of-state residents $842.

### FINANCIAL AID PICTURE (2014-2015)

**Students with need:** Out of 251 full-time freshmen who applied for aid, 209 were judged to have need. Of these, 199 received aid, and 9 had their full need met. Average financial aid package met 61% of need; average scholarship/grant was $6,816; average loan was $3,390. For part-time students, average financial aid package was $6,039.

**Students without need:** 20 full-time freshmen who did not demonstrate need for aid received scholarships/grants; average award was $3,773. No-need awards available for academics, alumni affiliation, ROTC.

### FINANCIAL AID PROCEDURES

**Forms required:** FAFSA.

**Dates and Deadlines:** Priority date 2/15; no closing date. Applicants notified on a rolling basis.

**Transfers:** No deadline. Applicants notified on a rolling basis. Schools required to obtain student aid information through National Student Loan Data System (NSLDS).

### CONTACT

Anna Griswold, Assistant Vice President for Undergraduate Education & Executive Director for Student Aid
Dawson Building, Room 5, 120 Ridge View Drive, Dunmore, PA 18512
(814) 865-6301

## Penn State York
York, Pennsylvania
www.yk.psu.edu                    Federal Code: 003329

**4-year public** branch campus college in large town.
**Enrollment:** 935 undergrads, 14% part-time. 298 full-time freshmen.
**Selectivity:** Admits over 75% of applicants.

### BASIC COSTS (2015-2016)
**Tuition and fees:** $13,964; out-of-state residents $21,158.
**Per-credit charge:** $535; out-of-state residents $842.

### FINANCIAL AID PICTURE (2014-2015)
**Students with need:** Out of 221 full-time freshmen who applied for aid, 179 were judged to have need. Of these, 177 received aid, and 4 had their full need met. Average financial aid package met 62% of need; average scholarship/grant was $6,499; average loan was $3,349. For part-time students, average financial aid package was $5,816.
**Students without need:** 45 full-time freshmen who did not demonstrate need for aid received scholarships/grants; average award was $2,758. No-need awards available for academics, alumni affiliation, ROTC.

### FINANCIAL AID PROCEDURES
**Forms required:** FAFSA.
**Dates and Deadlines:** Priority date 2/15; no closing date. Applicants notified on a rolling basis.
**Transfers:** No deadline. Applicants notified on a rolling basis. Schools required to obtain student aid information through National Student Loan Data System (NSLDS).

### CONTACT
Anna Griswold, Assistant Vice President for Undergraduate Education & Executive Director for Student Aid
Room 139, Main Classroom Building, 1031 Edgecomb Avenue, York, PA 17403
(814) 865-6301

## Pennsylvania Academy of the Fine Arts
Philadelphia, Pennsylvania
www.pafa.edu                    Federal Code: 014653

**4-year private** visual arts college in very large city.
**Enrollment:** 195 undergrads, 2% part-time. 37 full-time freshmen.

### BASIC COSTS (2016-2017)
**Tuition and fees:** $36,058.
**Per-credit charge:** $1,154.

### FINANCIAL AID PICTURE
**Students with need:** Need-based aid available for full-time and part-time students.
**Students without need:** No-need awards available for academics, alumni affiliation, art.

### FINANCIAL AID PROCEDURES
**Forms required:** FAFSA.
**Dates and Deadlines:** Closing date 3/1. Applicants notified on a rolling basis; must reply by 5/1 or within 14 week(s) of notification.
**Transfers:** Applicants notified on a rolling basis starting 1/31; must reply by 5/1 or within 4 week(s) of notification.

### CONTACT
Dana Moore, Director of Financial Aid
128 North Broad Street, Philadelphia, PA 19102
(215) 972-2019

## Pennsylvania College of Art and Design
Lancaster, Pennsylvania
www.pcad.edu                    Federal Code: 016021

**4-year private** visual arts college in small city.
**Enrollment:** 220 undergrads, 5% part-time. 59 full-time freshmen.
**Selectivity:** Admits less than 50% of applicants.

### BASIC COSTS (2015-2016)
**Tuition and fees:** $22,800.
**Per-credit charge:** $888.
**Additional info:** Additional fees for required laptop, camera, software purchase: $3,400.

### FINANCIAL AID PICTURE (2014-2015)
**Students with need:** Out of 57 full-time freshmen who applied for aid, 53 were judged to have need. Of these, 53 received aid, and 2 had their full need met. Need-based aid available for part-time students.
**Students without need:** 4 full-time freshmen who did not demonstrate need for aid received scholarships/grants; average award was $1,932. No-need awards available for academics, art.

### FINANCIAL AID PROCEDURES
**Forms required:** FAFSA, state aid form.
**Dates and Deadlines:** Priority date 3/1; no closing date. Applicants notified on a rolling basis starting 4/15.

### CONTACT
David Hershey, Director of Financial Aid
PO Box 59, Lancaster, PA 17608-0059

## Pennsylvania College of Technology
Williamsport, Pennsylvania
www.pct.edu                    Federal Code: 003395

**4-year public** technical college in large town.
**Enrollment:** 5,416 undergrads, 15% part-time. 1,145 full-time freshmen.
**Selectivity:** Open admission; but selective for some programs.

### BASIC COSTS (2015-2016)
**Tuition and fees:** $15,810; out-of-state residents $22,470.
**Room and board:** $11,108.

### FINANCIAL AID PICTURE (2014-2015)
**Students with need:** 38% of average financial aid package awarded as scholarships/grants, 62% awarded as loans/jobs. Need-based aid available for part-time students. Work study available nights, weekends, and for part-time students.
**Students without need:** No-need awards available for academics, alumni affiliation, leadership, ROTC.

### FINANCIAL AID PROCEDURES
**Forms required:** FAFSA, institutional form.
**Dates and Deadlines:** Priority date 4/15; no closing date. Applicants notified on a rolling basis starting 6/1; must reply by 7/1 or within 4 week(s) of notification.
**Transfers:** No deadline. Applicants notified on a rolling basis.

### CONTACT
Dennis Correll, Associate Dean for Financial Aid and Admissions
One College Avenue, Williamsport, PA 17701-5799
(570) 327-4766

# Pennsylvania Highlands Community College

Johnstown, Pennsylvania
www.pennhighlands.edu                Federal Code: 031804

**2-year public** community college in large town.
**Enrollment:** 1,295 undergrads, 36% part-time. 222 full-time freshmen.
**Selectivity:** Open admission.

## BASIC COSTS (2015-2016)
**Tuition and fees:** $5,670; out-of-district residents $7,710; out-of-state residents $10,650.
**Per-credit charge:** $127; out-of-district residents $195; out-of-state residents $293.
**Additional info:** Lab/Material Fees for specific courses depending on consumable supplies and materials required: $10-$950.

## FINANCIAL AID PICTURE (2015-2016)
**Students with need:** 52% of average financial aid package awarded as scholarships/grants, 48% awarded as loans/jobs. Need-based aid available for part-time students. Work study available nights.
**Students without need:** No-need awards available for academics, state/district residency.

## FINANCIAL AID PROCEDURES
**Forms required:** FAFSA.
**Dates and Deadlines:** Closing date 4/1. Applicants notified on a rolling basis; must reply by 8/1.

## CONTACT
Brenda Coughenour, Director of Financial Aid
101 Community College Way, Johnstown, PA 15904
(814) 262-6454

# Pennsylvania Institute of Technology

Media, Pennsylvania
www.pit.edu                Federal Code: 010998

**2-year private** junior and technical college in small town.
**Enrollment:** 595 undergrads, 49% part-time. 166 full-time freshmen.
**Selectivity:** Open admission; but selective for some programs.

## BASIC COSTS (2015-2016)
**Tuition and fees:** $13,200.
**Additional info:** Tuition varies by program. School of Professional Programs certificates tuition is $15,450; Practical nursing program tuition is $21,500.

## FINANCIAL AID PICTURE
**Students with need:** Need-based aid available for full-time and part-time students.
**Students without need:** No-need awards available for academics, leadership.
**Scholarships offered:** Presidential Scholarship: half tuition; for current high school graduates; SAT scores required.
**Additional info:** Application deadline of May 1 for PHEAA and Philadelphia State Grant aid.

## FINANCIAL AID PROCEDURES
**Forms required:** FAFSA, state aid form, institutional form.
**Dates and Deadlines:** Applicants notified on a rolling basis starting 7/1.
**Transfers:** No deadline. Applicants notified on a rolling basis starting 7/1.

## CONTACT
Laura Blomgren, Director of Financial Aid
800 Manchester Avenue, Media, PA 19063-4098
(610) 892-1536

# Philadelphia University

Philadelphia, Pennsylvania
www.PhilaU.edu                Federal Code: 003354

**4-year private** university in very large city.
**Enrollment:** 2,788 undergrads, 12% part-time. 507 full-time freshmen.
**Selectivity:** Admits 50 to 75% of applicants.

## BASIC COSTS (2015-2016)
**Tuition and fees:** $36,520.
**Per-credit charge:** $605.
**Room and board:** $12,140.

## FINANCIAL AID PICTURE (2015-2016)
**Students with need:** Out of 474 full-time freshmen who applied for aid, 411 were judged to have need. Of these, 411 received aid, and 92 had their full need met. Average financial aid package met 79% of need; average scholarship/grant was $27,568; average loan was $3,741. Need-based aid available for part-time students.
**Students without need:** 85 full-time freshmen who did not demonstrate need for aid received scholarships/grants; average award was $12,760. No-need awards available for academics, athletics.
**Scholarships offered:** 8 full-time freshmen received athletic scholarships; average amount $9,750.

## FINANCIAL AID PROCEDURES
**Forms required:** FAFSA.
**Dates and Deadlines:** Priority date 3/1; closing date 4/15. Applicants notified on a rolling basis starting 3/1; must reply by 5/1.

## CONTACT
Lisa Cooper, Director of Financial Aid
4201 Henry Avenue, Philadelphia, PA 19144
(215) 951-2940

# Pittsburgh Institute of Aeronautics

Pittsburgh, Pennsylvania
www.pia.edu                Federal Code: 005310

**2-year private** technical college in large city.
**Enrollment:** 176 undergrads. 49 full-time freshmen.
**Selectivity:** Open admission.

## BASIC COSTS (2015-2016)
**Tuition and fees:** $15,600.

## FINANCIAL AID PICTURE
**Students with need:** Need-based aid available for full-time students.

## FINANCIAL AID PROCEDURES
**Forms required:** FAFSA.
**Dates and Deadlines:** Priority date 5/1; no closing date. Applicants notified on a rolling basis.
**Transfers:** No deadline. Applicants notified on a rolling basis.

## CONTACT
Jonathan Vukmanic, Director of Financial Aid
PO Box 10897, Pittsburgh, PA 15236-0897
(412) 346-2100

# Pittsburgh Institute of Mortuary Science

Pittsburgh, Pennsylvania
www.pims.edu                Federal Code: 010814

**2-year private** technical college in large city.
**Enrollment:** 248 undergrads.

**BASIC COSTS (2015-2016)**
**Tuition and fees:** $14,125.
**Per-credit charge:** $290.

**FINANCIAL AID PICTURE**
**Students with need:** Need-based aid available for full-time and part-time students.

**FINANCIAL AID PROCEDURES**
**Forms required:** FAFSA.
**Dates and Deadlines:** Applicants notified on a rolling basis.
**Transfers:** No deadline. Applicants notified on a rolling basis.

**CONTACT**
Karen Rocco, Financial Aid Officer
5808 Baum Boulevard, Pittsburgh, PA 15206-3706
(412) 362-8500

## Point Park University
Pittsburgh, Pennsylvania
www.pointpark.edu                    Federal Code: 003357

**4-year private** university in large city.
**Enrollment:** 3,140 undergrads. 558 full-time freshmen.
**Selectivity:** Admits 50 to 75% of applicants.

**BASIC COSTS (2015-2016)**
**Tuition and fees:** $28,250.
**Per-credit charge:** $766.
**Room and board:** $10,620.
**Additional info:** Students in Conservatory of Performing Arts pay full-time tuition of $34,400 per year ($976 per-credit hour). Required fees, room and board are the same for COPA and non-COPA students.

**FINANCIAL AID PICTURE (2015-2016)**
**Students with need:** Out of 558 full-time freshmen who applied for aid, 500 were judged to have need. Of these, 500 received aid, and 94 had their full need met. Average financial aid package met 75% of need; average scholarship/grant was $19,551; average loan was $4,603. For part-time students, average financial aid package was $8,125.
**Students without need:** 57 full-time freshmen who did not demonstrate need for aid received scholarships/grants; average award was $13,160. No-need awards available for academics, athletics, music/drama.
**Scholarships offered:** 16 full-time freshmen received athletic scholarships; average amount $7,527.

**FINANCIAL AID PROCEDURES**
**Forms required:** FAFSA.
**Dates and Deadlines:** Priority date 3/15; closing date 12/1. Applicants notified by 2/15; must reply within 2 week(s) of notification.
**Transfers:** No deadline. Applicants notified on a rolling basis starting 2/15. Merit aid is awarded on GPA only.

**CONTACT**
Sheila Nelson-Hensley, Director of Financial Aid
201 Wood Street, Pittsburgh, PA 15222-1984
(412) 392-3930

## Restaurant School at Walnut Hill College
Philadelphia, Pennsylvania
www.walnuthillcollege.edu            Federal Code: 015499

**4-year for-profit** culinary school and business college in very large city.
**Enrollment:** 380 undergrads.

**BASIC COSTS (2015-2016)**
**Tuition and fees:** $23,850.

**Additional info:** Cost of books and supplies vary. All costs are subject to change.

**FINANCIAL AID PICTURE**
**Students with need:** Need-based aid available for full-time students.
**Students without need:** No-need awards available for leadership.

**FINANCIAL AID PROCEDURES**
**Forms required:** FAFSA, state aid form, institutional form.

**CONTACT**
Caitlin Snedeker, Director of Financial Aid
4207 Walnut Street, Philadelphia, PA 19104
(267) 295-2311

## Robert Morris University
Moon Township, Pennsylvania
www.rmu.edu                          Federal Code: 001746

**4-year private** university in large town.
**Enrollment:** 4,485 undergrads, 12% part-time. 865 full-time freshmen.
**Selectivity:** Admits over 75% of applicants.

**BASIC COSTS (2015-2016)**
**Tuition and fees:** $27,194.
**Per-credit charge:** $845.
**Room and board:** $12,130.

**FINANCIAL AID PICTURE (2015-2016)**
**Students with need:** Out of 779 full-time freshmen who applied for aid, 688 were judged to have need. Of these, 688 received aid, and 84 had their full need met. Average financial aid package met 74% of need; average scholarship/grant was $17,356; average loan was $4,880. For part-time students, average financial aid package was $6,086.
**Students without need:** 144 full-time freshmen who did not demonstrate need for aid received scholarships/grants; average award was $12,563. No-need awards available for academics, athletics, ROTC.
**Scholarships offered:** 36 full-time freshmen received athletic scholarships; average amount $21,376.

**FINANCIAL AID PROCEDURES**
**Forms required:** FAFSA.
**Dates and Deadlines:** Applicants notified on a rolling basis starting 2/15.

**CONTACT**
Stephanie Hendershot, Director of Financial Aid
6001 University Boulevard, Moon Township, PA 15108-1189
(412) 397-6250

## Rosedale Technical Institute
Pittsburgh, Pennsylvania
www.rosedaletech.org                 Federal Code: 012050

**2-year private** technical and career college in large city.
**Enrollment:** 330 full-time undergrads.
**Selectivity:** Open admission; but selective for some programs.

**BASIC COSTS (2015-2016)**
**Tuition and fees:** $14,530.

**FINANCIAL AID PICTURE**
**Students with need:** Need-based aid available for full-time students.

**FINANCIAL AID PROCEDURES**
**Forms required:** FAFSA.
**Dates and Deadlines:** Closing date 8/1.

**CONTACT**
Anna Bartolini, Director of Financial Aid
215 Beecham Drive, Pittsburgh, PA 15205-9791
(412) 521-6200

## Rosemont College
Rosemont, Pennsylvania
www.rosemont.edu                    Federal Code: 003360

**4-year private** liberal arts college in small town, affiliated with Roman Catholic Church.
**Enrollment:** 529 undergrads, 14% part-time. 135 full-time freshmen.
**Selectivity:** Admits 50 to 75% of applicants.

**BASIC COSTS (2016-2017)**
**Tuition and fees:** $19,480.
**Per-credit charge:** $1,200.
**Room and board:** $11,500.
**Additional info:** Tuition/fee waivers available for adults.

**FINANCIAL AID PICTURE**
**Students with need:** Need-based aid available for full-time and part-time students. Work study available nights, weekends, and for part-time students.
**Students without need:** No-need awards available for academics, alumni affiliation, athletics, leadership.
**Scholarships offered:** Sister Maria Stella Kelly Art Scholarship; merit award based on artistic excellence for students intending to major in Studio Art. Cornelian Scholarship; full tuition scholarship awarded annually to two outstanding graduates of Catholic high schools.

**FINANCIAL AID PROCEDURES**
**Forms required:** FAFSA.
**Dates and Deadlines:** Priority date 2/15; no closing date. Applicants notified on a rolling basis starting 3/5; must reply within 4 week(s) of notification.
**Transfers:** No deadline. Applicants notified on a rolling basis starting 3/1.

**CONTACT**
Deborah Cawley, Director of Enrollment Services and Financial Aid Compliance
1400 Montgomery Avenue, Rosemont, PA 19010-1699
(610) 527-0200 ext. 2214

## St. Charles Borromeo Seminary - Overbrook
Wynnewood, Pennsylvania
www.scs.edu                        Federal Code: 016229

**4-year private** seminary college for men in large town, affiliated with Roman Catholic Church.
**Enrollment:** 55 undergrads.

**BASIC COSTS (2015-2016)**
**Tuition and fees:** $20,050.
**Room and board:** $12,925.

**FINANCIAL AID PICTURE**
**Students with need:** Need-based aid available for full-time students.
**Students without need:** No-need awards available for religious affiliation.

**FINANCIAL AID PROCEDURES**
**Forms required:** FAFSA, institutional form.
**Dates and Deadlines:** Closing date 4/15. Applicants notified on a rolling basis starting 6/1; must reply by 6/1 or within 4 week(s) of notification.

**CONTACT**
Nora Downey, Financial Aid Coordinator
100 East Wynnewood Road, Wynnewood, PA 19096
(610) 785-6582

## St. Francis University
Loretto, Pennsylvania
www.francis.edu                    Federal Code: 003366

**4-year private** university and liberal arts college in rural community, affiliated with Roman Catholic Church.
**Enrollment:** 1,703 undergrads, 6% part-time. 413 full-time freshmen.
**Selectivity:** Admits 50 to 75% of applicants.

**BASIC COSTS (2015-2016)**
**Tuition and fees:** $32,128.
**Per-credit charge:** $971.
**Room and board:** $11,082.
**Additional info:** Tuition/fee waivers available for adults.

**FINANCIAL AID PICTURE**
**Students with need:** Need-based aid available for full-time and part-time students. Work study available nights, weekends, and for part-time students.
**Students without need:** No-need awards available for academics, alumni affiliation, athletics, music/drama, religious affiliation.
**Scholarships offered:** Red Flash Co-Curricular Award: $1,000-$6,000; 2.5 GPA minimum. Assisi Scholarship: $3,000-$7,000; 3.2 GPA,1020 SAT, 22 ACT minimum. Presidential Scholarship: $7,500-$10,000; 3.5 GPA, 1100 SAT, 24 ACT minimum. Founders Award: $10,500-$16,000; 3.7 GPA, 1250 SAT, 28 ACT minimum. Franciscan Scholarship: $2,000 over four years awarded to graduates of a Catholic high school.

**FINANCIAL AID PROCEDURES**
**Forms required:** FAFSA.
**Dates and Deadlines:** Priority date 5/1; no closing date. Applicants notified on a rolling basis starting 3/1.
**Transfers:** No deadline. Applicants notified on a rolling basis. Associate degree transfer scholarship based on academic achievement. Returning adult student scholarships available to qualifying transfers after one semester.

**CONTACT**
Jamie Kosh, Director of Financial Aid
Box 600, Loretto, PA 15940

## Saint Joseph's University
Philadelphia, Pennsylvania
www.sju.edu                        Federal Code: 003367

**4-year private** university in very large city, affiliated with Roman Catholic Church.
**Enrollment:** 5,250 undergrads, 12% part-time. 1,179 full-time freshmen.
**Selectivity:** Admits over 75% of applicants.

**BASIC COSTS (2015-2016)**
**Tuition and fees:** $42,180.
**Room and board:** $14,928.
**Additional info:** Traditional undergraduate day students taking additional credits over 5 courses pay an additional per-credit-hour fee of $1,349. Part-time, adult undergraduate evening division per-credit-hour fee is $557 (non-traditional, adult continuing education). Business and Psychology majors are required to have a laptop but are not required to purchase from the University.

**FINANCIAL AID PICTURE (2015-2016)**
**Students with need:** Out of 987 full-time freshmen who applied for aid, 778 were judged to have need. Of these, 778 received aid, and 165 had their full need met. Average financial aid package met 76% of need; average scholarship/grant was $22,874; average loan was $3,281. Need-based aid available for part-time students.
**Students without need:** 305 full-time freshmen who did not demonstrate need for aid received scholarships/grants; average award was $13,234. No-need awards available for academics, alumni affiliation, art, athletics, minority status, music/drama, ROTC.

**Scholarships offered:** 44 full-time freshmen received athletic scholarships; average amount $23,709.

## FINANCIAL AID PROCEDURES

**Forms required:** FAFSA.

**Dates and Deadlines:** Priority date 2/15; no closing date. Applicants notified on a rolling basis starting 3/31; must reply by 5/1.

**Transfers:** Financial aid for transfer students subject to availability of funds.

## CONTACT

Eileen Tucker, Director of Financial Aid

5600 City Avenue, Philadelphia, PA 19131

## St. Vincent College

Latrobe, Pennsylvania

www.stvincent.edu                    Federal Code: 003368

**4-year private** liberal arts college in large town, affiliated with Roman Catholic Church.

**Enrollment:** 1,596 undergrads, 1% part-time. 445 full-time freshmen.

**Selectivity:** Admits 50 to 75% of applicants.

## BASIC COSTS (2015-2016)

**Tuition and fees:** $32,770.

**Per-credit charge:** $986.

**Room and board:** $10,793.

## FINANCIAL AID PICTURE (2015-2016)

**Students with need:** Out of 408 full-time freshmen who applied for aid, 355 were judged to have need. Of these, 355 received aid, and 91 had their full need met. Average financial aid package met 84% of need; average scholarship/grant was $6,153; average loan was $3,341. For part-time students, average financial aid package was $3,396.

**Students without need:** 87 full-time freshmen who did not demonstrate need for aid received scholarships/grants; average award was $1,877. No-need awards available for academics, alumni affiliation, art, leadership, minority status, music/drama, religious affiliation, state/district residency.

**Scholarships offered:** Academic Merit Scholarship: $5,000 to $14,000, based on high school GPA, class rank, and SAT scores. Leadership Merit Grant: $500 to $3,000, based on extracurricular activities and recommendations. Competitive scholarships from $4,000 to full tuition.

## FINANCIAL AID PROCEDURES

**Forms required:** FAFSA.

**Dates and Deadlines:** Priority date 5/1; no closing date. Applicants notified on a rolling basis starting 10/1; must reply within 4 week(s) of notification.

**Transfers:** Applicants notified on a rolling basis starting 3/1; must reply within 2 week(s) of notification.

## CONTACT

Mary Gazal, Director of Financial Aid

300 Fraser Purchase Road, Latrobe, PA 15650-2690

(800) 782-5549

## Seton Hill University

Greensburg, Pennsylvania

www.setonhill.edu                    Federal Code: 003362

**4-year private** university and liberal arts college in large town, affiliated with Roman Catholic Church.

**Enrollment:** 1,564 undergrads, 5% part-time. 330 full-time freshmen.

**Selectivity:** Admits over 75% of applicants.

## BASIC COSTS (2015-2016)

**Tuition and fees:** $32,420.

**Per-credit charge:** $832.

**Room and board:** $10,868.

**Additional info:** Tuition/fee waivers available for adults.

## FINANCIAL AID PICTURE (2014-2015)

**Students with need:** Out of 307 full-time freshmen who applied for aid, 283 were judged to have need. Of these, 283 received aid, and 58 had their full need met. Average financial aid package met 76% of need; average scholarship/grant was $20,017; average loan was $5,858. For part-time students, average financial aid package was $10,802.

**Students without need:** 47 full-time freshmen who did not demonstrate need for aid received scholarships/grants; average award was $12,916. No-need awards available for academics, alumni affiliation, art, athletics, music/drama.

**Scholarships offered:** *Merit:* Presidential and Seton Scholarships; up to full tuition per academic year; given to top students. *Athletic:* 48 full-time freshmen received athletic scholarships; average amount $11,792.

## FINANCIAL AID PROCEDURES

**Forms required:** FAFSA, state aid form, institutional form.

**Dates and Deadlines:** Priority date 5/1; no closing date. Applicants notified on a rolling basis starting 11/30.

**Transfers:** Priority date 8/1; closing date 8/15. Applicants notified on a rolling basis starting 1/1; must reply within 2 week(s) of notification. Scholarship available for full-time transfer students with 3.5 GPA.

## CONTACT

Tracey Snyder de Baez, Director of Financial Aid

1 Seton Hill Drive, Greensburg, PA 15601 .

(724) 838-4293

## Shippensburg University of Pennsylvania

Shippensburg, Pennsylvania

www.ship.edu                    Federal Code: 003326

**4-year public** university in small town.

**Enrollment:** 5,963 undergrads, 5% part-time. 1,385 full-time freshmen.

**Selectivity:** Admits over 75% of applicants.

## BASIC COSTS (2015-2016)

**Tuition and fees:** $10,052; out-of-state residents $18,878.

**Room and board:** $11,428.

**Additional info:** $10,590 for Dual Admit (out-of-state) students and $12,356 for STEM (Science, Technology, Engineering, or Math) and High Achieving (1200 SAT or top 10% of their class) out-of-state students.

## FINANCIAL AID PICTURE (2015-2016)

**Students with need:** Out of 1,285 full-time freshmen who applied for aid, 1,005 were judged to have need. Of these, 993 received aid, and 71 had their full need met. Average financial aid package met 49% of need; average scholarship/grant was $6,302; average loan was $3,466. For part-time students, average financial aid package was $5,758.

**Students without need:** 97 full-time freshmen who did not demonstrate need for aid received scholarships/grants; average award was $3,379. No-need awards available for academics, athletics.

**Scholarships offered:** 80 full-time freshmen received athletic scholarships; average amount $2,643.

## FINANCIAL AID PROCEDURES

**Forms required:** FAFSA.

**Dates and Deadlines:** Priority date 3/15; no closing date. Applicants notified on a rolling basis; must reply within 2 week(s) of notification.

**Transfers:** No deadline. Applicants notified on a rolling basis; must reply within 2 week(s) of notification.

## CONTACT

Trina Snyder, Interim Director of Financial Aid

1871 Old Main Drive, Shippensburg, PA 17257-2299

(717) 477-1131

## Slippery Rock University of Pennsylvania
Slippery Rock, Pennsylvania
www.sru.edu                     Federal Code: 003327

**4-year public** university in small town.
**Enrollment:** 7,471 undergrads, 6% part-time. 1,523 full-time freshmen.
**Selectivity:** Admits 50 to 75% of applicants.

### BASIC COSTS (2015-2016)
**Tuition and fees:** $9,645; out-of-state residents $13,175.
**Room and board:** $10,022.
**Additional info:** Out-of-State tuition is $10,590 for freshmen or transfer students with a high school GPA of at least 3.0 out of 4.0, or returning students with a GPA of at least 2.5.

### FINANCIAL AID PICTURE (2015-2016)
**Students with need:** Out of 1,443 full-time freshmen who applied for aid, 1,104 were judged to have need. Of these, 1,092 received aid, and 143 had their full need met. Average financial aid package met 56% of need; average scholarship/grant was $5,971; average loan was $3,559. For part-time students, average financial aid package was $5,359.
**Students without need:** 152 full-time freshmen who did not demonstrate need for aid received scholarships/grants; average award was $2,881. No-need awards available for academics, alumni affiliation, art, athletics, job skills, leadership, minority status, music/drama, ROTC, state/district residency.
**Scholarships offered:** 57 full-time freshmen received athletic scholarships; average amount $3,405.
**Additional info:** May 1 closing date for Pennsylvania state grants.

### FINANCIAL AID PROCEDURES
**Forms required:** FAFSA.
**Dates and Deadlines:** Priority date 5/1; no closing date. Applicants notified on a rolling basis starting 3/15.

### CONTACT
Alyssa Dobson, Director of Financial Aid
1 Morrow Way, Slippery Rock, PA 16057-1383
(724) 738-2044

## South Hills School of Business & Technology
State College, Pennsylvania
www.southhills.edu              Federal Code: 013263

**2-year for-profit** business and technical college in large town.
**Enrollment:** 630 undergrads.
**Selectivity:** Open admission; but selective for some programs.

### BASIC COSTS (2015-2016)
**Additional info:** Tuition varies by program. Associate's programs: $33,042-$54,846. Books and supplies also vary by program. All costs are subject to change.

### FINANCIAL AID PICTURE
**Students with need:** Need-based aid available for full-time and part-time students.
**Students without need:** This college awards aid only to students with need.

### FINANCIAL AID PROCEDURES
**Forms required:** FAFSA.
**Dates and Deadlines:** Closing date 6/30. Applicants notified on a rolling basis starting 7/5.
**Transfers:** No deadline. Must reply by 6/14.

### CONTACT
Anne Falk, Financial Aid Director
480 Waupelani Drive, State College, PA 16801-4516
(814) 234-7755

## Summit University
Clarks Summit, Pennsylvania
https://www.summitu.edu         Federal Code: 002670

**4-year private** university and Bible college in small city, affiliated with Baptist faith.
**Enrollment:** 553 undergrads.

### BASIC COSTS (2015-2016)
**Tuition and fees:** $23,140.
**Per-credit charge:** $650.
**Room and board:** $5,800.

### FINANCIAL AID PICTURE
**Students with need:** Need-based aid available for full-time and part-time students. Work study available nights, weekends, and for part-time students.
**Students without need:** No-need awards available for academics, leadership, music/drama, religious affiliation.

### FINANCIAL AID PROCEDURES
**Forms required:** FAFSA, institutional form.
**Dates and Deadlines:** Closing date 5/1. Applicants notified on a rolling basis starting 4/1.

### CONTACT
Steve Brown, Director of Student Financial Services
538 Venard Road, Clarks Summit, PA 18411-1297
(570) 585-9215

## Susquehanna University
Selinsgrove, Pennsylvania       Federal Code: 003369
www.susqu.edu                   CSS Code: 2820

**4-year private** university and liberal arts college in small town, affiliated with Evangelical Lutheran Church in America.
**Enrollment:** 2,126 undergrads, 1% part-time. 666 full-time freshmen.
**Selectivity:** Admits over 75% of applicants.

### BASIC COSTS (2016-2017)
**Tuition and fees:** $44,340.
**Per-credit charge:** $1,375.
**Room and board:** $11,620.

### FINANCIAL AID PICTURE (2015-2016)
**Students with need:** Out of 603 full-time freshmen who applied for aid, 537 were judged to have need. Of these, 537 received aid, and 113 had their full need met. Average financial aid package met 85% of need; average scholarship/grant was $30,505; average loan was $2,862. For part-time students, average financial aid package was $12,200.
**Students without need:** 125 full-time freshmen who did not demonstrate need for aid received scholarships/grants; average award was $22,701. No-need awards available for academics, alumni affiliation, leadership, minority status, music/drama, ROTC.
**Scholarships offered:** Academic scholarships; $1,000 to $16,000; renewable annually; based on outstanding academic achievement, personal accomplishment, and/or musical talent. Alumni scholarships; $2,500; for 5 new legacy students with best academic records. Annual scholarships; $2,500; to dependent children of ordained Lutheran clergy. Founder Scholarships; Full tuition; renewable annually; based on outstanding academic achievement and personal accomplishment. University Assistantships; beginning at $5,000

annually, includes professional work experience with a faculty or staff mentor.

**Additional info:** Graduated pay scale for federal work-study program. $1,000 Visit Grant awarded to enrolling students who make an official campus visit between March 1 of sophomore year and March 1 of senior year of high school.

## FINANCIAL AID PROCEDURES
**Forms required:** FAFSA, CSS PROFILE.
**Dates and Deadlines:** Priority date 3/1; closing date 5/1. Applicants notified on a rolling basis starting 3/15; must reply by 5/1.
**Transfers:** Priority date 5/1; closing date 7/1. Applicants notified on a rolling basis. Transfer students eligible for financial aid and scholarship consideration.

## CONTACT
Erin Wolfe, Director of Financial Aid
514 University Avenue, Selinsgrove, PA 17870-1164
(570) 372-4450

## Swarthmore College
Swarthmore, Pennsylvania     Federal Code: 003370
www.swarthmore.edu     CSS Code: 2821

**4-year private** liberal arts college in small town.
**Enrollment:** 1,566 undergrads. 407 full-time freshmen.
**Selectivity:** Admits less than 50% of applicants.

### BASIC COSTS (2016-2017)
**Tuition and fees:** $47,442.
**Room and board:** $13,958.

### FINANCIAL AID PICTURE (2015-2016)
**Students with need:** Out of 274 full-time freshmen who applied for aid, 237 were judged to have need. Of these, 237 received aid, and 237 had their full need met. Average financial aid package met 100% of need; average scholarship/grant was $46,053.
**Students without need:** 1 full-time freshmen who did not demonstrate need for aid received scholarships/grants. No-need awards available for academics, leadership, state/district residency.
**Additional info:** All aid is loan-free and packaged to meet full demonstrated need. Financial aid program includes work-study opportunities.

### FINANCIAL AID PROCEDURES
**Forms required:** FAFSA, CSS PROFILE, state aid form.
**Dates and Deadlines:** Closing date 2/15. Applicants notified by 4/1; must reply by 5/1.
**Transfers:** Closing date 4/1. Applicants notified by 5/15. No aid consideration for foreign national transfer applicants.

### CONTACT
Varo Duffins, Director of Financial Aid
500 College Avenue, Swarthmore, PA 19081
(610) 328-8358

## Talmudical Yeshiva of Philadelphia
Philadelphia, Pennsylvania     Federal Code: 012523

**4-year private** rabbinical college for men in very large city, affiliated with Jewish faith.
**Enrollment:** 115 undergrads. 36 full-time freshmen.
**Selectivity:** Admits over 75% of applicants.

### BASIC COSTS (2015-2016)
**Tuition and fees:** $8,750.
**Room and board:** $7,100.

### FINANCIAL AID PICTURE
**Students with need:** Need-based aid available for full-time students.
**Students without need:** This college awards aid only to students with need.

### FINANCIAL AID PROCEDURES
**Forms required:** FAFSA, institutional form.
**Dates and Deadlines:** Priority date 8/1; closing date 5/1. Applicants notified on a rolling basis starting 3/15; must reply within 2 week(s) of notification.

### CONTACT
Chaya Hoberman, Financial Aid Officer
6063 Drexel Road, Philadelphia, PA 19131
(215) 477-1000

## Temple University
Philadelphia, Pennsylvania
www.temple.edu     Federal Code: 003371

**4-year public** university in very large city.
**Enrollment:** 27,983 undergrads, 10% part-time. 4,472 full-time freshmen.
**Selectivity:** Admits 50 to 75% of applicants.

### BASIC COSTS (2016-2017)
**Tuition and fees:** $15,688; out-of-state residents $25,994.
**Per-credit charge:** $573; out-of-state residents $899.
**Room and board:** $11,146.

### FINANCIAL AID PICTURE (2014-2015)
**Students with need:** Out of 3,940 full-time freshmen who applied for aid, 3,196 were judged to have need. Of these, 3,180 received aid, and 932 had their full need met. Average financial aid package met 70% of need; average scholarship/grant was $7,029; average loan was $3,596. For part-time students, average financial aid package was $10,658.
**Students without need:** 687 full-time freshmen who did not demonstrate need for aid received scholarships/grants; average award was $8,264. No-need awards available for academics, art, athletics, music/drama, ROTC.
**Scholarships offered:** 68 full-time freshmen received athletic scholarships; average amount $28,642.

### FINANCIAL AID PROCEDURES
**Forms required:** FAFSA.
**Dates and Deadlines:** Closing date 3/1. Applicants notified on a rolling basis starting 2/15; must reply by 5/1 or within 3 week(s) of notification.
**Transfers:** Priority date 3/1; no deadline. Must reply within 2 week(s) of notification.

### CONTACT
Craig Fennell, Director, Student Financial Services
103 Conwell Hall, Philadelphia, PA 19122-6096
(215) 204-2244

## Thiel College
Greenville, Pennsylvania
www.thiel.edu     Federal Code: 003376

**4-year private** liberal arts college in small town, affiliated with Evangelical Lutheran Church in America.
**Enrollment:** 903 undergrads. 274 full-time freshmen.
**Selectivity:** Admits 50 to 75% of applicants.

### BASIC COSTS (2015-2016)
**Tuition and fees:** $28,868.
**Per-credit charge:** $880.
**Room and board:** $11,336.
**Additional info:** Required fees include technology fee of $950, student services fee of $630, and health & wellness fee of $250.

### FINANCIAL AID PICTURE (2014-2015)

**Students with need:** Out of 270 full-time freshmen who applied for aid, 253 were judged to have need. Of these, 253 received aid, and 19 had their full need met. Average financial aid package met 69% of need; average scholarship/grant was $19,115; average loan was $3,851. For part-time students, average financial aid package was $15,726.

**Students without need:** 18 full-time freshmen who did not demonstrate need for aid received scholarships/grants; average award was $13,485. No-need awards available for academics, alumni affiliation, leadership, music/drama, religious affiliation.

### FINANCIAL AID PROCEDURES

**Forms required:** FAFSA, state aid form.

**Dates and Deadlines:** Priority date 3/15; no closing date. Applicants notified on a rolling basis starting 2/15; must reply within 2 week(s) of notification.

**Transfers:** Priority date 6/1; no deadline. Applicants notified on a rolling basis starting 2/15; must reply within 2 week(s) of notification.

### CONTACT

Cynthia Farrell, Executive Director of Student Financial Services
75 College Avenue, Greenville, PA 16125-2181
(724) 589-2250

## Thomas Jefferson University

Philadelphia, Pennsylvania
www.jefferson.edu                    Federal Code: 012393

**4-year private** university and health science college in very large city.
**Enrollment:** 789 undergrads.

### BASIC COSTS (2015-2016)

**Additional info:** Costs vary according to program. Examples of full-time (academic year) tuition rates for bachelor's degree programs in radiologic sciences: $30,223; bachelor's degree program in occupational therapy: $31,027. All full-time students pay an annual technology fee; $500, and a library fee; $350. Academic fees vary by program. On-campus room and board ranges from $708-$2335 per month depending on the facility.

### FINANCIAL AID PICTURE

**Students with need:** Need-based aid available for full-time and part-time students. Work study available nights, weekends, and for part-time students.

**Students without need:** No-need awards available for academics, leadership, state/district residency.

**Scholarships offered:** Range of merit-based scholarships available for selected applicants.

**Additional info:** Applicants must use the IRS DRT process on the FAFSA.

### FINANCIAL AID PROCEDURES

**Forms required:** FAFSA, institutional form.

**Dates and Deadlines:** Closing date 4/1. Applicants notified on a rolling basis starting 4/1; must reply within 2 week(s) of notification.

**Transfers:** Applicants notified on a rolling basis starting 11/15; must reply within 2 week(s) of notification.

### CONTACT

Susan McFadden, University Director of Financial Aid
130 South Ninth Street, Edison Building, Suite 100, Philadelphia, PA 19107
(215) 955-2867

## Triangle Tech: Bethlehem

Bethlehem, Pennsylvania
www.triangle-tech.edu                Federal Code: 014895

**2-year for-profit** branch campus and technical college in small city.
**Enrollment:** 120 undergrads. 51 full-time freshmen.
**Selectivity:** Open admission.

### BASIC COSTS (2016-2017)

**Tuition and fees:** $16,779.
**Additional info:** Fees will vary depending on program.

### FINANCIAL AID PICTURE (2014-2015)

**Students with need:** Out of 49 full-time freshmen who applied for aid, 48 were judged to have need. Of these, 48 received aid. Average financial aid package met 72% of need; average scholarship/grant was $3,852; average loan was $2,686. Need-based aid available for part-time students.

**Students without need:** No-need awards available for academics.

### FINANCIAL AID PROCEDURES

**Forms required:** FAFSA.

**Dates and Deadlines:** Applicants notified on a rolling basis.

### CONTACT

Catherine Waxter, Director of Financial Aid
3184 Airport Road, Bethlehem, PA 18017
(610) 266-2910

## Triangle Tech: DuBois

Falls Creek, Pennsylvania
www.triangle-tech.edu                Federal Code: 021744

**2-year for-profit** technical college in large town.
**Enrollment:** 133 undergrads. 65 full-time freshmen.
**Selectivity:** Open admission.

### BASIC COSTS (2015-2016)

**Tuition and fees:** $16,542.
**Additional info:** Fees will vary depending on program.

### FINANCIAL AID PICTURE (2014-2015)

**Students with need:** Out of 65 full-time freshmen who applied for aid, 61 were judged to have need. Of these, 61 received aid, and 19 had their full need met. Average financial aid package met 31% of need; average scholarship/grant was $6,607; average loan was $3,333. Need-based aid available for part-time students.

**Students without need:** This college awards aid only to students with need.

### FINANCIAL AID PROCEDURES

**Forms required:** FAFSA, state aid form, institutional form.

**Dates and Deadlines:** Applicants notified on a rolling basis.

### CONTACT

Catherine Waxter, Corporate Director of Financial Aid
225 Tannery Row Road, Falls Creek, PA 15840-3333
(724) 832-1050

## Triangle Tech: Erie

Erie, Pennsylvania
www.triangle-tech.edu                Federal Code: 014417

**2-year for-profit** technical and career college in small city.
**Enrollment:** 30 undergrads. 27 full-time freshmen.
**Selectivity:** Open admission.

### BASIC COSTS (2015-2016)

**Tuition and fees:** $16,409.
**Additional info:** Fees will vary depending on program.

### FINANCIAL AID PICTURE (2014-2015)

**Students with need:** Out of 26 full-time freshmen who applied for aid, 25 were judged to have need. Of these, 25 received aid, and 21 had their full need met. Average financial aid package met 84% of need; average scholarship/grant was $5,370; average loan was $2,811. Need-based aid available for part-time students.

**Students without need:** This college awards aid only to students with need.

**FINANCIAL AID PROCEDURES**

**Forms required:** FAFSA.

**Dates and Deadlines:** Applicants notified on a rolling basis.

**CONTACT**

Cathy Waxter, Corporate Director of Financial Aid

2000 Liberty Street, Erie, PA 16502-2594

(724) 832-1050

## Triangle Tech: Greensburg
Greensburg, Pennsylvania
www.triangle-tech.edu          Federal Code: 014895

**2-year for-profit** technical college in large town.

**Enrollment:** 163 undergrads. 85 full-time freshmen.

**Selectivity:** Open admission.

**BASIC COSTS (2015-2016)**

**Tuition and fees:** $16,530.

**Additional info:** Fees will vary depending on program.

**FINANCIAL AID PICTURE (2014-2015)**

**Students with need:** Out of 82 full-time freshmen who applied for aid, 82 were judged to have need. Of these, 82 received aid, and 34 had their full need met. Average financial aid package met 41% of need; average scholarship/grant was $6,355; average loan was $2,873. Need-based aid available for part-time students.

**Students without need:** 4 full-time freshmen who did not demonstrate need for aid received scholarships/grants; average award was $4,054.

**FINANCIAL AID PROCEDURES**

**Forms required:** FAFSA, institutional form.

**Dates and Deadlines:** Applicants notified on a rolling basis starting 1/1.

**Transfers:** No deadline.

**CONTACT**

Catherine Waxter, Director of Financial Aid

222 East Pittsburgh Street, Suite A, Greensburg, PA 15601-3304

(724) 832-1050

## Triangle Tech: Pittsburgh
Pittsburgh, Pennsylvania
www.triangle-tech.edu          Federal Code: 007839

**2-year for-profit** technical college in large city.

**Enrollment:** 169 undergrads. 89 full-time freshmen.

**Selectivity:** Open admission; but selective for some programs.

**BASIC COSTS (2016-2017)**

**Tuition and fees:** $16,586.

**Additional info:** Fees will vary depending on program.

**FINANCIAL AID PICTURE (2014-2015)**

**Students with need:** Out of 89 full-time freshmen who applied for aid, 89 were judged to have need. Of these, 89 received aid, and 13 had their full need met. Average financial aid package met 15% of need; average scholarship/grant was $5,637; average loan was $2,809. Need-based aid available for part-time students.

**Students without need:** 3 full-time freshmen who did not demonstrate need for aid received scholarships/grants; average award was $4,054. No-need awards available for academics, state/district residency.

**FINANCIAL AID PROCEDURES**

**Forms required:** FAFSA, institutional form.

**Dates and Deadlines:** Applicants notified on a rolling basis.

**Transfers:** No deadline.

**CONTACT**

Cathy Waxter, Corporate Director of Financial Aid

1940 Perrysville Avenue, Pittsburgh, PA 15214-3897

(412) 359-1000

## Triangle Tech: Sunbury
Sunbury, Pennsylvania
www.triangle-tech.edu

**2-year for-profit** technical college in large town.

**Enrollment:** 111 undergrads. 62 full-time freshmen.

**Selectivity:** Open admission.

**BASIC COSTS (2016-2017)**

**Tuition and fees:** $16,692.

**Additional info:** Fees will vary by program.

**FINANCIAL AID PICTURE (2014-2015)**

**Students with need:** Out of 62 full-time freshmen who applied for aid, 62 were judged to have need. Of these, 58 received aid, and 56 had their full need met. Average financial aid package met 97% of need; average scholarship/grant was $6,564; average loan was $3,155. Need-based aid available for part-time students.

**Students without need:** 3 full-time freshmen who did not demonstrate need for aid received scholarships/grants; average award was $4,054.

**FINANCIAL AID PROCEDURES**

**Forms required:** FAFSA, state aid form, institutional form.

**Dates and Deadlines:** Applicants notified on a rolling basis.

**Transfers:** No deadline.

**CONTACT**

Cathy Waxter, Director of Financial Aid

191 Performance Road, Sunbury, PA 17801

## University of Pennsylvania
Philadelphia, Pennsylvania          Federal Code: 003378
www.upenn.edu          CSS Code: 2926

**4-year private** university in very large city.

**Enrollment:** 9,726 undergrads, 3% part-time. 2,350 full-time freshmen.

**Selectivity:** Admits less than 50% of applicants.

**BASIC COSTS (2015-2016)**

**Tuition and fees:** $49,536.

**Per-credit charge:** $1,399.

**Room and board:** $13,990.

**FINANCIAL AID PICTURE (2014-2015)**

**Students with need:** Out of 1,318 full-time freshmen who applied for aid, 1,066 were judged to have need. Of these, 1,066 received aid, and 1,066 had their full need met. Average financial aid package met 100% of need; average scholarship/grant was $42,150; average loan was $83. Need-based aid available for part-time students.

**Students without need:** This college awards aid only to students with need.

**Additional info:** All loans have been eliminated from need-based aid packages.

**FINANCIAL AID PROCEDURES**

**Forms required:** FAFSA, CSS PROFILE, institutional form.

**Dates and Deadlines:** Priority date 2/15; no closing date. Applicants notified on a rolling basis starting 4/1; must reply by 5/1.

**Transfers:** Priority date 3/15. Applicants notified on a rolling basis starting 5/15; must reply within 4 week(s) of notification.

**CONTACT**

1 College Hall, Philadelphia, PA 19104-6376

(215) 898-1988

## University of Pittsburgh

Pittsburgh, Pennsylvania

www.pitt.edu                     Federal Code: 008815

**4-year public** university in large city.

**Enrollment:** 18,655 undergrads, 5% part-time. 3,845 full-time freshmen.

**Selectivity:** Admits 50 to 75% of applicants. GED not accepted.

**BASIC COSTS (2015-2016)**

**Tuition and fees:** $18,192; out-of-state residents $28,958.

**Per-credit charge:** $720; out-of-state residents $1,169.

**Room and board:** $10,900.

**FINANCIAL AID PICTURE (2014-2015)**

**Students with need:** Out of 3,180 full-time freshmen who applied for aid, 2,160 were judged to have need. Of these, 2,089 received aid, and 326 had their full need met. Average financial aid package met 61% of need; average scholarship/grant was $9,239; average loan was $4,747. For part-time students, average financial aid package was $6,970.

**Students without need:** 235 full-time freshmen who did not demonstrate need for aid received scholarships/grants; average award was $10,312. No-need awards available for academics, athletics, minority status.

**Scholarships offered:** *Merit:* Academic Scholarships; $1,000 to full tuition, room and board; renewable up to 4 years with 3.0 GPA. *Athletic:* 102 full-time freshmen received athletic scholarships; average amount $13,130.

**FINANCIAL AID PROCEDURES**

**Forms required:** FAFSA.

**Dates and Deadlines:** Priority date 3/1; no closing date. Applicants notified on a rolling basis starting 3/15.

**Transfers:** Priority date 5/1; no deadline. Applicants notified on a rolling basis. Transfer students not eligible for freshman scholarships.

**CONTACT**

Marc Harding, Chief Enrollment Officer

4227 Fifth Avenue, 1st Floor, Alumni Hall, Pittsburgh, PA 15260

(412) 624-7488

## University of Pittsburgh at Bradford

Bradford, Pennsylvania

www.upb.pitt.edu                Federal Code: 003380

**4-year public** university in large town.

**Enrollment:** 1,435 undergrads, 6% part-time. 391 full-time freshmen.

**Selectivity:** Admits 50 to 75% of applicants.

**BASIC COSTS (2015-2016)**

**Tuition and fees:** $13,372; out-of-state residents $24,188.

**Per-credit charge:** $518; out-of-district residents $969.

**Room and board:** $8,592.

**FINANCIAL AID PICTURE (2014-2015)**

**Students with need:** Out of 365 full-time freshmen who applied for aid, 326 were judged to have need. Of these, 324 received aid, and 63 had their full need met. Average financial aid package met 75% of need; average scholarship/grant was $9,669; average loan was $5,616. For part-time students, average financial aid package was $10,630.

**Students without need:** 33 full-time freshmen who did not demonstrate need for aid received scholarships/grants; average award was $5,540. No-need awards available for academics, alumni affiliation, ROTC, state/district residency.

**Scholarships offered:** Panther Scholarship; for full-time on-campus residents or students who commute from Cameron, Elk, Forest, McKean, Potter, or Warren counties. Valedictorian/Salutatorian Scholarship; for Pennsylvania students. International Student Scholarship; for international students who plan to enroll full-time and reside on campus.

**FINANCIAL AID PROCEDURES**

**Forms required:** FAFSA.

**Dates and Deadlines:** Priority date 3/1; no closing date. Applicants notified on a rolling basis starting 4/1; must reply within 2 week(s) of notification.

**Transfers:** No deadline. Applicants notified on a rolling basis starting 4/1; must reply within 2 week(s) of notification. Transfers must meet academic policy guidelines.

**CONTACT**

Melissa Ibanez, Director of Financial Aid

300 Campus Drive, Bradford, PA 16701

(814) 362-7550

## University of Pittsburgh at Greensburg

Greensburg, Pennsylvania

www.greensburg.pitt.edu           Federal Code: 003381

**4-year public** branch campus and liberal arts college in large town.

**Enrollment:** 1,559 undergrads, 6% part-time. 423 full-time freshmen.

**Selectivity:** Admits 50 to 75% of applicants.

**BASIC COSTS (2015-2016)**

**Tuition and fees:** $13,382; out-of-state residents $24,198.

**Per-credit charge:** $518; out-of-state residents $969.

**Room and board:** $9,750.

**FINANCIAL AID PICTURE (2014-2015)**

**Students with need:** Out of 380 full-time freshmen who applied for aid, 314 were judged to have need. Of these, 309 received aid, and 65 had their full need met. Average financial aid package met 72% of need; average scholarship/grant was $8,355; average loan was $5,535. For part-time students, average financial aid package was $8,244.

**Students without need:** 40 full-time freshmen who did not demonstrate need for aid received scholarships/grants; average award was $4,319. No-need awards available for academics, leadership, minority status, state/district residency.

**FINANCIAL AID PROCEDURES**

**Forms required:** FAFSA, state aid form.

**Dates and Deadlines:** Priority date 2/15; no closing date. Applicants notified on a rolling basis starting 3/15; must reply within 3 week(s) of notification.

**Transfers:** No deadline.

**CONTACT**

Brandi Darr, Director of Financial Aid

150 Finoli Drive, Greensburg, PA 15601

(724) 836-9881

## University of Pittsburgh at Johnstown

Johnstown, Pennsylvania

www.upj.pitt.edu                Federal Code: 008815

**4-year public** engineering and liberal arts college in small city.

**Enrollment:** 2,814 undergrads, 3% part-time. 799 full-time freshmen.

**Selectivity:** Admits over 75% of applicants.

**BASIC COSTS (2015-2016)**

**Tuition and fees:** $13,374; out-of-state residents $24,190.

**Per-credit charge:** $518; out-of-state residents $969.

**Room and board:** $9,200.

## FINANCIAL AID PICTURE (2014-2015)

**Students with need:** Out of 729 full-time freshmen who applied for aid, 605 were judged to have need. Of these, 598 received aid, and 85 had their full need met. Average financial aid package met 64% of need; average scholarship/grant was $6,890; average loan was $3,433. For part-time students, average financial aid package was $4,331.

**Students without need:** 62 full-time freshmen who did not demonstrate need for aid received scholarships/grants; average award was $4,135. No-need awards available for academics, alumni affiliation, athletics, leadership, ROTC, state/district residency.

**Scholarships offered:** *Merit:* Achievement, Presidential, and Leadership Scholarships; $2,500 to full tuition yearly; based on high school GPA and SAT/ACT scores. *Athletic:* 25 full-time freshmen received athletic scholarships; average amount $3,951.

## FINANCIAL AID PROCEDURES

**Forms required:** FAFSA, state aid form.

**Dates and Deadlines:** Priority date 4/1; no closing date. Applicants notified on a rolling basis starting 3/1; must reply within 2 week(s) of notification.

## CONTACT

Jeanine Lawn, Director of Financial Aid
450 Schoolhouse Road, 157 Blackington Hall, Johnstown, PA 15904-1200
(800) 881-5544

# University of Pittsburgh at Titusville
Titusville, Pennsylvania
www.upt.pitt.edu
Federal Code: 008815

**2-year public** branch campus and liberal arts college in small town.
**Enrollment:** 342 undergrads, 15% part-time. 153 full-time freshmen.
**Selectivity:** Admits over 75% of applicants.

## BASIC COSTS (2015-2016)

**Tuition and fees:** $11,584; out-of-state residents $21,146.
**Per-credit charge:** $448; out-of-state residents $846.
**Room and board:** $10,224.

## FINANCIAL AID PICTURE (2014-2015)

**Students with need:** Out of 150 full-time freshmen who applied for aid, 141 were judged to have need. Of these, 141 received aid, and 20 had their full need met. Average financial aid package met 68% of need; average scholarship/grant was $8,018; average loan was $6,153. For part-time students, average financial aid package was $10,410.

**Students without need:** 7 full-time freshmen who did not demonstrate need for aid received scholarships/grants; average award was $2,786. No-need awards available for academics, state/district residency.

**Scholarships offered:** Rees scholarships; $2,000; awarded to top 5 students with science as a major; renewable with 3.0 GPA and continued science major. Presidential scholarships; $2,500; based on high school academic record; 10 awarded.

## FINANCIAL AID PROCEDURES

**Forms required:** FAFSA.

**Dates and Deadlines:** Priority date 3/1; no closing date. Applicants notified on a rolling basis starting 3/1; must reply within 2 week(s) of notification.

**Transfers:** No deadline. Applicants notified on a rolling basis starting 4/1; must reply within 2 week(s) of notification. Pennsylvania residents must apply by 5/1 for PHEAA. Transfer students must have completed 24 credits to renew. Information retrieved from NSLDS is utilized to determine transfer student eligibility for financial aid.

## CONTACT

Melissa Ibanez, Director of Financial Aid
UPT Admissions Office, Titusville, PA 16354-0287
(814) 827-4495

# University of Scranton
Scranton, Pennsylvania
www.scranton.edu
Federal Code: 003384

**4-year private** university and liberal arts college in small city, affiliated with Roman Catholic Church.
**Enrollment:** 3,793 undergrads, 3% part-time. 909 full-time freshmen.
**Selectivity:** Admits 50 to 75% of applicants.

## BASIC COSTS (2015-2016)

**Tuition and fees:** $41,044.
**Per-credit charge:** $1,044.
**Room and board:** $13,918.

## FINANCIAL AID PICTURE

**Students with need:** Need-based aid available for full-time and part-time students. Work study available nights, weekends, and for part-time students.
**Students without need:** No-need awards available for academics, ROTC.

## FINANCIAL AID PROCEDURES

**Forms required:** FAFSA.

**Dates and Deadlines:** Priority date 2/15; no closing date. Applicants notified on a rolling basis starting 3/15; must reply by 5/1 or within 2 week(s) of notification.

**Transfers:** Institutional grants available based on financial need.

## CONTACT

William Burke, Director of Financial Aid
800 Linden Street, Scranton, PA 18510-4699
(570) 941-7700

# University of the Arts
Philadelphia, Pennsylvania
www.uarts.edu
Federal Code: 003350

**4-year private** visual arts and performing arts college in very large city.
**Enrollment:** 1,675 undergrads, 2% part-time. 404 full-time freshmen.
**Selectivity:** Admits 50 to 75% of applicants.

## BASIC COSTS (2015-2016)

**Tuition and fees:** $39,908.
**Per-credit charge:** $1,663.
**Room and board:** $14,552.

## FINANCIAL AID PICTURE (2015-2016)

**Students with need:** Out of 372 full-time freshmen who applied for aid, 334 were judged to have need. Of these, 334 received aid, and 66 had their full need met. Average financial aid package met 68% of need; average scholarship/grant was $24,604; average loan was $3,466. For part-time students, average financial aid package was $16,195.

**Students without need:** 74 full-time freshmen who did not demonstrate need for aid received scholarships/grants; average award was $15,129. No-need awards available for academics, art, music/drama.

**Scholarships offered:** Merit awards; available to students who demonstrate exceptional talent and academic abilities.

## FINANCIAL AID PROCEDURES

**Forms required:** FAFSA, state aid form.

**Dates and Deadlines:** Priority date 3/1; no closing date. Applicants notified on a rolling basis starting 2/15; must reply by 5/1 or within 2 week(s) of notification.

**Transfers:** Undergraduate transfers not eligible for federal, state, or university aid if 4-year degree previously conferred.

## CONTACT

Michael Light, Director, Student Financial Services
320 South Broad Street, Philadelphia, PA 19102
(215) 717-6170

## University of the Sciences
Philadelphia, Pennsylvania
www.usciences.edu                                    Federal Code: 003353

**4-year private** health science and pharmacy college in very large city.
**Enrollment:** 2,238 undergrads, 1% part-time. 360 full-time freshmen.
**Selectivity:** Admits 50 to 75% of applicants.

### BASIC COSTS (2015-2016)
**Tuition and fees:** $37,466.
**Per-credit charge:** $1,485.
**Room and board:** $14,646.

### FINANCIAL AID PICTURE (2014-2015)
**Students with need:** Out of 341 full-time freshmen who applied for aid,
305 were judged to have need. Of these, 305 received aid, and 128 had
their full need met. Average financial aid package met 42% of need; average
scholarship/grant was $10,174; average loan was $3,617. For part-time students, average financial aid package was $3,124.
**Students without need:** 19 full-time freshmen who did not demonstrate
need for aid received scholarships/grants; average award was $15,702. No-
need awards available for academics, athletics.
**Scholarships offered:** *Merit:* Freshman students are considered for merit
scholarships upon time of application. Scholarship notification will be provided with admission decision. No additional essays or applications are
required for merit scholarship consideration. *Athletic:* 4 full-time freshmen
received athletic scholarships; average amount $12,084.

### FINANCIAL AID PROCEDURES
**Forms required:** FAFSA.
**Dates and Deadlines:** Priority date 3/15; no closing date. Applicants notified
on a rolling basis starting 2/15; must reply by 5/1 or within 2 week(s) of notification.

### CONTACT
Paula Lehrberger, Director of Financial Aid
600 South 43rd Street, Philadelphia, PA 19104-4495
(215) 596-8894

## University of Valley Forge
Phoenixville, Pennsylvania
www.valleyforge.edu                                  Federal Code: 003306

**4-year private** university and liberal arts college in large town, affiliated with
Assemblies of God.
**Enrollment:** 770 undergrads, 21% part-time. 125 full-time freshmen.
**Selectivity:** Admits over 75% of applicants.

### BASIC COSTS (2015-2016)
**Tuition and fees:** $20,424.
**Room and board:** $8,116.
**Additional info:** Cost of $700 for mandatory laptop is included in the
required fees.

### FINANCIAL AID PICTURE (2015-2016)
**Students with need:** Average financial aid package met 51% of need; average scholarship/grant was $10,025; average loan was $3,447. For part-time
students, average financial aid package was $7,638.
**Students without need:** No-need awards available for academics, leadership, music/drama, religious affiliation, state/district residency.
**Scholarships offered:** Trustee's Scholarship, President's Elite Scholarship,
President's Plus Scholarship, Dean's Scholarship, Professor's Scholarship;
ranging from full tuition (minimum 3.5 GPA, 1300 SAT or 29 ACT, and upper
10% class rank) to $1,000 (minimum 3.3 GPA and 1030 SAT or 22 ACT);
application required for awards; renewable with specified GPA requirement;.

### FINANCIAL AID PROCEDURES
**Forms required:** FAFSA.

**Dates and Deadlines:** Priority date 5/1; no closing date. Applicants notified
on a rolling basis starting 3/1.
**Transfers:** No deadline. Applicants notified on a rolling basis starting 3/15;
must reply within 3 week(s) of notification.

### CONTACT
Linda Stein, Director of Financial Aid
1401 Charlestown Road, Phoenixville, PA 19460-2373
(610) 917-1475

## Ursinus College
Collegeville, Pennsylvania                           Federal Code: 003385
www.ursinus.edu                                      CSS Code: 2931

**4-year private** liberal arts college in small town.
**Enrollment:** 1,629 undergrads. 429 full-time freshmen.
**Selectivity:** Admits over 75% of applicants.

### BASIC COSTS (2015-2016)
**Tuition and fees:** $47,700.
**Per-credit charge:** $1,484.
**Room and board:** $11,900.

### FINANCIAL AID PICTURE (2015-2016)
**Students with need:** Out of 388 full-time freshmen who applied for aid,
333 were judged to have need. Of these, 333 received aid, and 70 had their
full need met. Average financial aid package met 88% of need; average
scholarship/grant was $33,250; average loan was $3,370.
**Students without need:** 95 full-time freshmen who did not demonstrate
need for aid received scholarships/grants; average award was $22,328. No-
need awards available for academics, alumni affiliation, leadership, minority
status, music/drama, state/district residency.

### FINANCIAL AID PROCEDURES
**Forms required:** FAFSA, CSS PROFILE.
**Dates and Deadlines:** Closing date 2/15. Applicants notified by 3/15; must
reply by 5/1 or within 2 week(s) of notification.
**Transfers:** Closing date 8/1.

### CONTACT
Suzanne Sparrow, Director of Scholarships and Financial Aid
PO Box 1000, Collegeville, PA 19426-1000
(610) 409-3600

## Valley Forge Military College
Wayne, Pennsylvania
www.vfmac.edu                                        Federal Code: 003386

**2-year private** junior and military college in small city.
**Enrollment:** 347 undergrads. 177 full-time freshmen.
**Selectivity:** Admits less than 50% of applicants.

### BASIC COSTS (2015-2016)
**Tuition and fees:** $29,975.
**Room and board:** $14,700.

### FINANCIAL AID PICTURE (2014-2015)
**Students with need:** Out of 147 full-time freshmen who applied for aid,
147 were judged to have need. Of these, 122 received aid, and 32 had their
full need met. Average financial aid package met 72% of need; average
scholarship/grant was $22,000.
**Students without need:** This college awards aid only to students with
need.
**Scholarships offered:** 73 full-time freshmen received athletic scholarships;
average amount $6,000.

**Additional info:** Students enrolled in advanced military science program can receive up to $5,000 from the Army. In addition, competitively awarded ROTC scholarships pay average of another $14,100 per school year for direct educational expenses.

**FINANCIAL AID PROCEDURES**
**Forms required:** FAFSA.
**Dates and Deadlines:** Priority date 5/1; closing date 5/1. Applicants notified on a rolling basis starting 5/15; must reply by 5/1 or within 2 week(s) of notification.
**Transfers:** No deadline. Applicants notified on a rolling basis; must reply by 5/1 or within 2 week(s) of notification. Must submit transcripts from all previously attended colleges, even if aid was not received.

**CONTACT**
Michelle Molina, Financial Aid Director
1001 Eagle Road, Wayne, PA 19087
(610) 989-1300 ext. 1306

## Vet Tech Institute
Pittsburgh, Pennsylvania
www.vettechinstitute.edu          Federal Code: 008568

**2-year for-profit** health science and technical college in large city.
**Enrollment:** 385 undergrads.

**BASIC COSTS (2015-2016)**
**Tuition and fees:** $14,680.

**FINANCIAL AID PICTURE**
**Students with need:** Work study available nights.
**Students without need:** No-need awards available for academics.
**Scholarships offered:** $1,000 scholarships; 5 offered to commuters. $2,000 scholarships; 2 offered to students not living at home. Awarded based on results of examination given at school in November and March.

**FINANCIAL AID PROCEDURES**
**Forms required:** FAFSA, state aid form.
**Dates and Deadlines:** Applicants notified on a rolling basis.

**CONTACT**
Donna Durr, Financial Aid Director
125 Seventh Street, Pittsburgh, PA 15222-3400
(800) 570-0693

## Villanova University
Villanova, Pennsylvania          Federal Code: 003388
www.villanova.edu                CSS Code: 2959

**4-year private** university in large town, affiliated with Roman Catholic Church.
**Enrollment:** 7,002 undergrads, 6% part-time. 1,700 full-time freshmen.
**Selectivity:** Admits less than 50% of applicants.

**BASIC COSTS (2016-2017)**
**Tuition and fees:** $47,766.
**Per-credit charge:** $1,960.
**Room and board:** $12,720.

**FINANCIAL AID PICTURE (2015-2016)**
**Students with need:** Out of 1,160 full-time freshmen who applied for aid, 868 were judged to have need. Of these, 849 received aid, and 173 had their full need met. Average financial aid package met 80% of need; average scholarship/grant was $31,640; average loan was $3,835. For part-time students, average financial aid package was $6,697.

**Students without need:** 88 full-time freshmen who did not demonstrate need for aid received scholarships/grants; average award was $11,120. No-need awards available for academics, alumni affiliation, athletics, leadership, minority status, religious affiliation, ROTC.
**Scholarships offered:** 51 full-time freshmen received athletic scholarships; average amount $41,937.

**FINANCIAL AID PROCEDURES**
**Forms required:** FAFSA, CSS PROFILE.
**Dates and Deadlines:** Closing date 2/7. Applicants notified by 4/1; must reply by 5/1 or within 2 week(s) of notification.
**Transfers:** Closing date 7/15. Applicants notified on a rolling basis starting 5/1; must reply within 2 week(s) of notification.

**CONTACT**
Bonnie Lee Behm, Director of Financial Assistance
Austin Hall, 800 Lancaster Avenue, Villanova, PA 19085-1672
(610) 519-4010

## Washington & Jefferson College
Washington, Pennsylvania
www.washjeff.edu          Federal Code: 003389

**4-year private** liberal arts college in large town.
**Enrollment:** 1,307 undergrads. 389 full-time freshmen.
**Selectivity:** Admits less than 50% of applicants.

**BASIC COSTS (2015-2016)**
**Tuition and fees:** $43,226.
**Per-credit charge:** $1,075.
**Room and board:** $11,406.

**FINANCIAL AID PICTURE (2015-2016)**
**Students with need:** Out of 351 full-time freshmen who applied for aid, 314 were judged to have need. Of these, 314 received aid, and 50 had their full need met. Average financial aid package met 78% of need; average scholarship/grant was $14,582; average loan was $3,496. Need-based aid available for part-time students.
**Students without need:** 74 full-time freshmen who did not demonstrate need for aid received scholarships/grants; average award was $19,679. No-need awards available for academics, alumni affiliation, leadership.
**Scholarships offered:** Presidential Scholarship and Scholars Award: based on distinguished academic performance. Joseph Hardy Sr. Scholarship: for students in entrepreneurial studies program. Dean's Award: based on academic performance in high school, distinguished achievement outside the classroom, and good citizenship. Challenge Grant: for students who show academic promise. Alumni Scholarship: for students whose father and/or mother are alumni. Greb Endowed Student International Travel Award Fund and the Swick International Programs Endowed Fund which provide assistance to students who wish to study abroad. The Magellan Project: for students who want to pursue interesting summer projects domestically or abroad.
**Additional info:** Give It Forward Together is a special fund for students whose economic situations change dramatically while they are enrolled at W&J.

**FINANCIAL AID PROCEDURES**
**Forms required:** FAFSA.
**Dates and Deadlines:** Priority date 2/15; no closing date. Applicants notified on a rolling basis starting 3/1; must reply by 5/1.
**Transfers:** Must reply within 2 week(s) of notification. Students should complete the FAFSA as soon as possible. Financial aid awards will be made when FAFSA has been received and the student has been accepted for admission. For students selected for verification, these awards are estimated until the required tax documentation has been received and reviewed.

**CONTACT**
Michelle Anderson, Director of Financial Aid
60 South Lincoln Street, Washington, PA 15301
(724) 223-6019

## Waynesburg University
Waynesburg, Pennsylvania
www.waynesburg.edu                Federal Code: 003391

**4-year private** liberal arts college in small town, affiliated with Presbyterian Church (USA).
**Enrollment:** 1,422 undergrads, 7% part-time. 356 full-time freshmen.
**Selectivity:** Admits over 75% of applicants.

### BASIC COSTS (2015-2016)
**Tuition and fees:** $22,030.
**Per-credit charge:** $900.
**Room and board:** $9,170.

### FINANCIAL AID PICTURE (2015-2016)
**Students with need:** Average financial aid package met 81% of need; average scholarship/grant was $14,533; average loan was $3,997. For part-time students, average financial aid package was $6,081.
**Students without need:** No-need awards available for academics, alumni affiliation, job skills, state/district residency.
**Scholarships offered:** A.B. Miller Scholarship: $15,000. Presidential Honor Scholarship: $12,000. Honor Scholarship: $10,000.

### FINANCIAL AID PROCEDURES
**Forms required:** FAFSA, state aid form.
**Dates and Deadlines:** Applicants notified on a rolling basis starting 2/15; must reply within 2 week(s) of notification.
**Transfers:** No deadline. Applicants notified on a rolling basis; must reply within 2 week(s) of notification.

### CONTACT
Matthew Stokan, Director of Financial Aid
51 West College Street, Waynesburg, PA 15370-1222
(724) 852-6312

## West Chester University of Pennsylvania
West Chester, Pennsylvania
www.wcupa.edu                Federal Code: 003328

**4-year public** university in large town.
**Enrollment:** 13,956 undergrads, 9% part-time. 2,344 full-time freshmen.
**Selectivity:** Admits 50 to 75% of applicants.

### BASIC COSTS (2015-2016)
**Tuition and fees:** $9,462; out-of-state residents $20,052.
**Room and board:** $12,780.
**Additional info:** Required fees listed are for in-state students; out-of-state students are charged $2,630.

### FINANCIAL AID PICTURE (2014-2015)
**Students with need:** Out of 2,119 full-time freshmen who applied for aid, 1,530 were judged to have need. Of these, 1,530 received aid, and 88 had their full need met. Average financial aid package met 40% of need; average scholarship/grant was $5,574; average loan was $3,450. For part-time students, average financial aid package was $5,872.
**Students without need:** 44 full-time freshmen who did not demonstrate need for aid received scholarships/grants; average award was $4,271. No-need awards available for academics, art, athletics, leadership, music/drama.
**Scholarships offered:** 21 full-time freshmen received athletic scholarships; average amount $2,298.

**FINANCIAL AID PROCEDURES**
**Forms required:** FAFSA.
**Dates and Deadlines:** Priority date 3/1; no closing date. Applicants notified on a rolling basis starting 4/1; must reply within 4 week(s) of notification.
**Transfers:** Must reply within 4 week(s) of notification.

**CONTACT**
Dana Parker, Director of Financial Aid
Emil H. Messikomer Hall, West Chester, PA 19383
(610) 436-2627

## Westminster College
New Wilmington, Pennsylvania
www.westminster.edu                Federal Code: 003392

**4-year private** liberal arts college in small town, affiliated with Presbyterian Church (USA).
**Enrollment:** 1,103 undergrads, 2% part-time. 288 full-time freshmen.
**Selectivity:** Admits over 75% of applicants.

### BASIC COSTS (2015-2016)
**Tuition and fees:** $34,105.
**Per-credit charge:** $1,055.
**Room and board:** $10,370.
**Additional info:** Tuition/fee waivers available for adults.

### FINANCIAL AID PICTURE (2014-2015)
**Students with need:** Out of 273 full-time freshmen who applied for aid, 255 were judged to have need. Of these, 255 received aid, and 48 had their full need met. Average financial aid package met 81% of need; average scholarship/grant was $24,300; average loan was $3,736. For part-time students, average financial aid package was $7,974.
**Students without need:** 30 full-time freshmen who did not demonstrate need for aid received scholarships/grants; average award was $19,379. No-need awards available for academics, alumni affiliation, leadership, minority status, music/drama, religious affiliation, state/district residency.

### FINANCIAL AID PROCEDURES
**Forms required:** FAFSA, institutional form.
**Dates and Deadlines:** Priority date 5/1; no closing date. Applicants notified on a rolling basis starting 3/1; must reply by 5/1 or within 3 week(s) of notification.

### CONTACT
Cheryl Gerber, Director of Financial Aid
Remick Hall, Westminster College, New Wilmington, PA 16172-0001
(724) 946-7102

## Westmoreland County Community College
Youngwood, Pennsylvania
www.wccc.edu                Federal Code: 010176

**2-year public** community college in small town.
**Enrollment:** 4,694 undergrads, 47% part-time. 887 full-time freshmen.
**Selectivity:** Open admission; but selective for some programs.

### BASIC COSTS (2016-2017)
**Tuition and fees:** $5,070; out-of-district residents $8,730; out-of-state residents $12,390.
**Per-credit charge:** $122; out-of-district residents $244; out-of-state residents $366.

### FINANCIAL AID PICTURE
**Students with need:** Need-based aid available for full-time and part-time students. Work study available nights.

**Students without need:** No-need awards available for academics.

## FINANCIAL AID PROCEDURES
**Forms required:** FAFSA, institutional form.
**Dates and Deadlines:** Applicants notified on a rolling basis starting 5/1.

## CONTACT
Sheila Nelson-Hensley, Director of Financial Aid
145 Pavilion Lane, Youngwood, PA 15697
(724) 925-4063

## Widener University
Chester, Pennsylvania
www.widener.edu                    Federal Code: 003313

**4-year private** university in large town.
**Enrollment:** 3,293 undergrads, 11% part-time. 846 full-time freshmen.
**Selectivity:** Admits 50 to 75% of applicants.

### BASIC COSTS (2015-2016)
**Tuition and fees:** $41,224.
**Per-credit charge:** $1,346.
**Room and board:** $13,092.

### FINANCIAL AID PICTURE (2015-2016)
**Students with need:** Out of 829 full-time freshmen who applied for aid, 731 were judged to have need. Of these, 730 received aid, and 161 had their full need met. Average financial aid package met 79% of need; average scholarship/grant was $29,270; average loan was $3,670. For part-time students, average financial aid package was $8,010.
**Students without need:** 98 full-time freshmen who did not demonstrate need for aid received scholarships/grants; average award was $23,740. No-need awards available for academics, leadership, music/drama, ROTC.
**Scholarships offered:** Academic Scholarships; $4,000 to full tuition; based on SAT and GPA; renewable. Music, leadership, and community service scholarships; based on performance evaluations.

### FINANCIAL AID PROCEDURES
**Forms required:** FAFSA.
**Dates and Deadlines:** Priority date 2/15; no closing date. Applicants notified on a rolling basis starting 3/15; must reply within 4 week(s) of notification.
**Transfers:** Transfer scholarships; $2,500 to $10,000; based on GPA and minimum of 24 transferable credits.

### CONTACT
Thomas Malloy, Executive Director of Enrollment Services
One University Place, Chester, PA 19013
(610) 499-4174

## Wilkes University
Wilkes-Barre, Pennsylvania
www.wilkes.edu                    Federal Code: 003394

**4-year private** university in small city.
**Enrollment:** 2,358 undergrads, 5% part-time. 581 full-time freshmen.
**Selectivity:** Admits over 75% of applicants.

### BASIC COSTS (2015-2016)
**Tuition and fees:** $32,356.
**Per-credit charge:** $855.
**Room and board:** $13,266.

### FINANCIAL AID PICTURE (2015-2016)
**Students with need:** Out of 551 full-time freshmen who applied for aid, 505 were judged to have need. Of these, 505 received aid, and 51 had their full need met. Average financial aid package met 76% of need; average

scholarship/grant was $22,578; average loan was $4,045. For part-time students, average financial aid package was $13,812.
**Students without need:** 40 full-time freshmen who did not demonstrate need for aid received scholarships/grants; average award was $14,624. No-need awards available for academics, leadership, minority status, music/drama.

### FINANCIAL AID PROCEDURES
**Forms required:** FAFSA.
**Dates and Deadlines:** Priority date 3/1; no closing date. Applicants notified on a rolling basis starting 3/1.

### CONTACT
Melanie Wade, Vice President of Enrollment Services
84 West South Street, Wilkes-Barre, PA 18766
(570) 408-2000

## Williamson College of the Trades
Media, Pennsylvania
www.williamson.edu

**2-year private** technical college for men in large town, affiliated with nondenominational tradition.
**Enrollment:** 265 undergrads. 100 full-time freshmen.

### BASIC COSTS (2015-2016)
**Additional info:** Required fees for personal clothing and tools for the freshman year average $1,330.

### FINANCIAL AID PICTURE (2014-2015)
**Students with need:** Out of 100 full-time freshmen who applied for aid, 100 were judged to have need. Of these, 100 received aid, and 100 had their full need met. Average financial aid package met 100% of need; average scholarship/grant was $27,000.
**Students without need:** This college awards aid only to students with need.
**Additional info:** Each enrolled student receives a full scholarship covering tuition, room and board, and textbooks for the three-year program.

### FINANCIAL AID PROCEDURES
**Dates and Deadlines:** Closing date 2/22. Applicants notified by 5/1; must reply by 5/15.

### CONTACT
Jay Merillat, Dean of Enrollments
106 S. New Middletown Rd., Media, PA 19063
(610) 566-1776 ext. 235

## Wilson College
Chambersburg, Pennsylvania
www.wilson.edu                    Federal Code: 003396

**4-year private** liberal arts college in large town, affiliated with Presbyterian Church (USA).
**Enrollment:** 689 undergrads.

### BASIC COSTS (2015-2016)
**Tuition and fees:** $24,392.
**Room and board:** $10,912.

### FINANCIAL AID PICTURE
**Students with need:** Need-based aid available for full-time and part-time students.
**Students without need:** No-need awards available for academics, alumni affiliation, leadership, religious affiliation, state/district residency.

**Scholarships offered:** Presidential Merit Scholarship; $12,000 cumulative GPA 3.75 or higher; Dean's Merit Scholarship; $9,000, 3.40 to 3.74 cumulative GPA; Leadership Merit Scholarship; $3,000 to $6,000, 3.0-3.39 cumulative GPA. Scholarships for full-time students who are members of Presbyterian Church, USA. Curran Scholarships; awarded to incoming students with significant community service.

**FINANCIAL AID PROCEDURES**

**Forms required:** FAFSA, state aid form, institutional form.
**Dates and Deadlines:** Priority date 4/30; no closing date. Applicants notified on a rolling basis starting 2/15.
**Transfers:** Priority date 4/30; no deadline. Applicants notified on a rolling basis starting 2/15; must reply by 5/1 or within 3 week(s) of notification. Tuition scholarships available to transfer articulation students who hold associate degrees from Harrisburg Area Community College, Hagerstown Community College, Central Penn College, Luzerne County Community College, Lehigh Carbon Community College, Harcum College, Cottey College, Frederick Community College, Howard Community College; transfer merit scholarships for students with 3.0 GPA from 25% to 50% tuition, Phi Theta Kappa scholarship.

**CONTACT**

Linda Brittain, Dean of Financial Aid
1015 Philadelphia Avenue, Chambersburg, PA 17201-1285
(717) 262-2016

## York College of Pennsylvania
York, Pennsylvania
www.ycp.edu                                   Federal Code: 003399

**4-year private** liberal arts college in small city.
**Enrollment:** 4,421 undergrads, 8% part-time. 898 full-time freshmen.
**Selectivity:** Admits less than 50% of applicants.

**BASIC COSTS (2015-2016)**
**Tuition and fees:** $18,240.
**Per-credit charge:** $510.
**Room and board:** $10,160.

**FINANCIAL AID PICTURE (2015-2016)**
**Students with need:** Out of 824 full-time freshmen who applied for aid, 642 were judged to have need. Of these, 642 received aid, and 175 had their full need met. Average financial aid package met 70% of need; average scholarship/grant was $5,219; average loan was $6,231. For part-time students, average financial aid package was $7,882.
**Students without need:** 246 full-time freshmen who did not demonstrate need for aid received scholarships/grants; average award was $5,681. No-need awards available for academics, alumni affiliation, minority status, music/drama.
**Scholarships offered:** All accepted freshman applicants considered for merit scholarships, including Presidential and Dean's Scholarships, based on academic criteria GPA, rank, test scores. Scholarship awards reduce tuition to approximately $7,000-$11,500 annually for many students, not including additional eligibility for need-based financial aid.

**FINANCIAL AID PROCEDURES**
**Forms required:** FAFSA.
**Dates and Deadlines:** Applicants notified on a rolling basis starting 3/1; must reply within 4 week(s) of notification.
**Transfers:** No deadline. Applicants notified on a rolling basis starting 3/1; must reply within 4 week(s) of notification. Transfer Merit Scholarship: $2,000; $1,000 per semester for entering transfer students with minimum 3.3 GPA.

**CONTACT**
Calvin Williams, Director of Financial Aid
441 Country Club Road, York, PA 17403-3651
(717) 849-1682

## YTI Career Institute: Lancaster
Lancaster, Pennsylvania
www.yti.edu

**2-year for-profit** technical and career college in small city.
**Enrollment:** 421 undergrads. 145 full-time freshmen.
**Selectivity:** Open admission; but selective for some programs.

**BASIC COSTS (2015-2016)**
**Additional info:** Diploma program costs range from $3,000 to $20,100; associate degree programs range from $26,270 to $35,900. Books and supplies range from $450 to $4,500, depending on program. Tuition at time of enrollment locked for 2 years.

**FINANCIAL AID PICTURE**
**Students with need:** Need-based aid available for full-time and part-time students.
**Students without need:** This college awards aid only to students with need.

**FINANCIAL AID PROCEDURES**
**Forms required:** FAFSA.
**Dates and Deadlines:** Applicants notified on a rolling basis; must reply within 4 week(s) of notification.
**Transfers:** No deadline. Applicants notified on a rolling basis; must reply within 4 week(s) of notification.

**CONTACT**
Tracey Cole, Director of Financial Aid
3050 Hempland Road, Lancaster, PA 17601
(717) 757-1100

# Puerto Rico

## American University of Puerto Rico
Bayamon, Puerto Rico
www.aupr.edu                                  Federal Code: 011941

**4-year private** university and business college in large city.
**Enrollment:** 1,650 undergrads, 17% part-time. 213 full-time freshmen.

**BASIC COSTS (2016-2017)**
**Tuition and fees:** $7,036.
**Additional info:** Tuition/fee waivers available for minority students.

**FINANCIAL AID PICTURE (2014-2015)**
**Students with need:** 85% of average financial aid package awarded as scholarships/grants, 15% awarded as loans/jobs. Need-based aid available for part-time students.
**Students without need:** This college awards aid only to students with need.

**FINANCIAL AID PROCEDURES**
**Forms required:** FAFSA, institutional form.
**Dates and Deadlines:** Priority date 4/30; closing date 5/31. Applicants notified by 6/1; must reply within 2 week(s) of notification.

**CONTACT**
Raquel Torres, Director of Bursar's Office
PO Box 2037, Bayamon, PR 00960-2037
(787) 620-2040 ext. 2031

## Atlantic University College

Guaynabo, Puerto Rico
www.atlanticu.edu                    Federal Code: 016871

**4-year private** liberal arts college in small city.
**Enrollment:** 1,429 undergrads.
**Selectivity:** Open admission.

### FINANCIAL AID PICTURE

**Students with need:** Need-based aid available for full-time and part-time students. Work study available nights.
**Students without need:** This college awards aid only to students with need.

### FINANCIAL AID PROCEDURES

**Forms required:** FAFSA, institutional form.
**Dates and Deadlines:** Closing date 6/30. Applicants notified on a rolling basis starting 4/1; must reply within 2 week(s) of notification.
**Transfers:** Priority date 1/7; closing date 6/7.

### CONTACT

Janice Rivera, Director of Financial Aid
PO Box 3918, Guaynabo, PR 00970
(787) 789-4251

## Bayamon Central University

Bayamon, Puerto Rico
www.ucb.edu.pr                    Federal Code: 010015

**4-year private** university in small city, affiliated with Roman Catholic Church.
**Enrollment:** 438 undergrads, 43% part-time. 177 full-time freshmen.
**Selectivity:** Admits 50 to 75% of applicants.

### BASIC COSTS (2015-2016)

**Additional info:** Tuition/fee waivers available for unemployed or children of unemployed.

### FINANCIAL AID PICTURE

**Students with need:** Need-based aid available for full-time and part-time students. Work study available nights.
**Students without need:** This college awards aid only to students with need.

### FINANCIAL AID PROCEDURES

**Forms required:** FAFSA, institutional form.
**Dates and Deadlines:** Priority date 5/31; closing date 7/2. Applicants notified on a rolling basis starting 5/31; must reply within 6 week(s) of notification.
**Transfers:** No deadline. Applicants notified on a rolling basis starting 4/30.

### CONTACT

Edna Ortiz, Director of Financial Aid Office
PO Box 1725, Bayamon, PR 00960-1725
(787) 786-3030 ext. 2116

## Caribbean University

Bayamon, Puerto Rico
www.caribbean.edu                    Federal Code: 012525

**4-year private** university in small city.
**Enrollment:** 3,448 undergrads, 26% part-time. 413 full-time freshmen.
**Selectivity:** Open admission; but selective for some programs.

### BASIC COSTS (2016-2017)

**Tuition and fees:** $6,180.
**Per-credit charge:** $180.

### FINANCIAL AID PICTURE

**Students with need:** Need-based aid available for full-time and part-time students. Work study available nights, weekends, and for part-time students.
**Students without need:** This college awards aid only to students with need.

### FINANCIAL AID PROCEDURES

**Forms required:** FAFSA.
**Dates and Deadlines:** Priority date 5/30; no closing date. Applicants notified on a rolling basis starting 7/30; must reply within 2 week(s) of notification.
**Transfers:** Closing date 5/30. Applicants notified on a rolling basis.

### CONTACT

Hector Gracia, Financial Aid Director
PO Box 493, Bayamon, PR 00960-0493
(787) 780-0070 ext. 1125

## Columbia Central University: Caguas

Caguas, Puerto Rico
www.columbiacentral.edu                    Federal Code: 013517

**4-year for-profit** university and branch campus college in large city.
**Enrollment:** 1,535 undergrads.
**Selectivity:** Open admission; but selective for some programs.

### BASIC COSTS (2015-2016)

**Tuition and fees:** $6,290.
**Additional info:** Additional fees may apply.

### FINANCIAL AID PICTURE

**Students with need:** Need-based aid available for full-time and part-time students.
**Students without need:** This college awards aid only to students with need.

### FINANCIAL AID PROCEDURES

**Forms required:** FAFSA, state aid form, institutional form.

### CONTACT

Gloria Mirabal, Financial Aid Director
PO Box 8517, Caguas, PR 00726-8517
(787) 743-4041 ext. 223

## Columbia Central University: Yauco

Yauco, Puerto Rico
www.columbiacentral.edu                    Federal Code: 008902

**2-year for-profit** business and health science college in large town.
**Enrollment:** 626 undergrads, 50% part-time. 73 full-time freshmen.
**Selectivity:** Open admission; but selective for some programs.

### BASIC COSTS (2015-2016)

**Tuition and fees:** $6,290.
**Additional info:** Additional fees may apply.

### FINANCIAL AID PICTURE (2014-2015)

**Students with need:** Out of 71 full-time freshmen who applied for aid, 71 were judged to have need. Of these, 71 received aid. For part-time students, average financial aid package was $4,657.
**Students without need:** This college awards aid only to students with need.

### FINANCIAL AID PROCEDURES

**Forms required:** FAFSA, institutional form.

### CONTACT

Gloria Mirabal, Director of Financial Aid
PO Box 3062, Yauco, PR 00698-3062
(787) 856-0845 ext. 112

## Conservatory of Music of Puerto Rico
San Juan, Puerto Rico
www.cmpr.edu    Federal Code: 010819

**4-year public** music college in large city.
**Enrollment:** 411 undergrads, 32% part-time. 34 full-time freshmen.
**Selectivity:** Admits 50 to 75% of applicants.

### BASIC COSTS (2015-2016)
**Additional info:** Tuition at time of enrollment locked for 4 years.

### FINANCIAL AID PICTURE (2015-2016)
**Students with need:** Average financial aid package met 33% of need; average scholarship/grant was $5,301; average loan was $3,811. For part-time students, average financial aid package was $33.
**Students without need:** This college awards aid only to students with need.

### FINANCIAL AID PROCEDURES
**Forms required:** FAFSA.
**Dates and Deadlines:** Priority date 12/15; no closing date. Applicants notified on a rolling basis starting 4/30.
**Transfers:** No deadline. Applicants notified on a rolling basis.

### CONTACT
Luis Diaz, Financial Aid Administrator
951 Ave. Ponce de Leon, San Juan, PR 00907-3373
(787) 751-0160 ext. 231

## EDIC College
Caguas, Puerto Rico
www.ediccollege.com    Federal Code: 030219

**2-year for-profit** health science and technical college in large city.
**Enrollment:** 880 full-time undergrads.
**Selectivity:** Open admission; but selective for some programs.

### BASIC COSTS (2015-2016)
**Tuition and fees:** $6,625.
**Per-credit charge:** $275.

### FINANCIAL AID PICTURE
**Students with need:** Need-based aid available for full-time and part-time students. Work study available nights.
**Students without need:** This college awards aid only to students with need.

### FINANCIAL AID PROCEDURES
**Forms required:** FAFSA, state aid form, institutional form.
**Dates and Deadlines:** Applicants notified on a rolling basis.
**Transfers:** No deadline. Applicants notified on a rolling basis.

### CONTACT
Julio Melendez, Financial Aid Director
Box 9120, Caguas, PR 00726-9120
(787) 744-8519

## EDP University of Puerto Rico: Hato Rey
San Juan, Puerto Rico
www.edpuniversity.edu    Federal Code: 021651

**4-year for-profit** university in very large city.
**Enrollment:** 1,603 undergrads. 93 full-time freshmen.
**Selectivity:** Admits over 75% of applicants.

### BASIC COSTS (2015-2016)
**Additional info:** General courses: $156 per-credit. Health courses: $160 per credit. Certificate Degree: $186 per credit. Additional fees may apply. Tuition at time of enrollment locked for 4 years.

### FINANCIAL AID PICTURE (2014-2015)
**Students with need:** Out of 91 full-time freshmen who applied for aid, 83 were judged to have need. Of these, 83 received aid. Average financial aid package met 89% of need; average scholarship/grant was $5,366; average loan was $3,328. For part-time students, average financial aid package was $5,531.
**Students without need:** This college awards aid only to students with need.

### FINANCIAL AID PROCEDURES
**Forms required:** FAFSA.
**Dates and Deadlines:** Applicants notified on a rolling basis.
**Transfers:** No deadline. Applicants notified on a rolling basis.

### CONTACT
Yaitzaenid Gonzalez Melendez, Fincial Aid Administrator
PO Box 192303, Hato Rey, PR 00919-2303
(787) 765-3560 ext. 278

## EDP University of Puerto Rico: San Sebastian
San Sebastian, Puerto Rico
www.edpuniverstiy.edu    Federal Code: 021651

**4-year for-profit** university in small city.
**Enrollment:** 1,112 undergrads, 31% part-time. 163 full-time freshmen.
**Selectivity:** Admits over 75% of applicants.

### BASIC COSTS (2015-2016)
**Additional info:** General courses: $156 per-credit. Health courses: $160 per credit. Certificate Degree: $186 per credit. Additional fees may apply. Tuition at time of enrollment locked for 4 years.

### FINANCIAL AID PICTURE (2014-2015)
**Students with need:** Out of 160 full-time freshmen who applied for aid, 154 were judged to have need. Of these, 154 received aid. Average financial aid package met 96% of need; average scholarship/grant was $5,260; average loan was $3,013. For part-time students, average financial aid package was $4,925.
**Students without need:** This college awards aid only to students with need.

### FINANCIAL AID PROCEDURES
**Forms required:** FAFSA.
**Dates and Deadlines:** Closing date 6/30. Applicants notified on a rolling basis.
**Transfers:** No deadline. Applicants notified on a rolling basis.

### CONTACT
Yaitzanid Gonzalez, Financial Aid Adininstartor
PO Box 1674, San Sebastian, PR 00685
(787) 896-2252

## Escuela de Artes Plasticas de Puerto Rico
San Juan, Puerto Rico
www.eap.edu    Federal Code: 017345

**4-year public** visual arts college in large city.
**Enrollment:** 573 undergrads, 27% part-time. 91 full-time freshmen.
**Selectivity:** Admits over 75% of applicants.

## FINANCIAL AID PICTURE

**Students with need:** Need-based aid available for full-time and part-time students.

**Students without need:** This college awards aid only to students with need.

## FINANCIAL AID PROCEDURES

**Forms required:** FAFSA.

**Dates and Deadlines:** Priority date 4/11; closing date 5/18. Applicants notified by 7/11.

## CONTACT

Alfred Diaz, Financial Aid Officer
PO Box 9021112, San Juan, PR 00902-1112

## Huertas College

Caguas, Puerto Rico
www.huertas.edu                    Federal Code: 014105

**2-year for-profit** junior and technical college in large city.
**Enrollment:** 1,280 undergrads, 12% part-time. 242 full-time freshmen.
**Selectivity:** Open admission.

## BASIC COSTS (2015-2016)

**Tuition and fees:** $6,550.
**Per-credit charge:** $218.

## FINANCIAL AID PICTURE (2015-2016)

**Students with need:** Out of 225 full-time freshmen who applied for aid, 225 were judged to have need. Of these, 225 received aid, and 225 had their full need met. Need-based aid available for part-time students.
**Students without need:** This college awards aid only to students with need.

## FINANCIAL AID PROCEDURES

**Forms required:** FAFSA, institutional form.
**Dates and Deadlines:** Applicants notified on a rolling basis.

## CONTACT

Wanda Ortiz, Financial Aid Director
PO Box 8429, Caguas, PR 00726
(787) 746-1400

## Humacao Community College

Humacao, Puerto Rico
www.hccpr.edu                     Federal Code: 014952

**2-year private** business and community college in small city.
**Enrollment:** 506 undergrads, 20% part-time. 114 full-time freshmen.
**Selectivity:** Open admission.

## BASIC COSTS (2016-2017)

**Tuition and fees:** $5,382.

## FINANCIAL AID PICTURE (2014-2015)

**Students with need:** Out of 114 full-time freshmen who applied for aid, 114 were judged to have need. Of these, 114 received aid. Average financial aid package met 100% of need; average scholarship/grant was $5,765. Need-based aid available for part-time students.
**Students without need:** This college awards aid only to students with need.

## FINANCIAL AID PROCEDURES

**Forms required:** FAFSA, state aid form, institutional form.
**Dates and Deadlines:** Priority date 1/1; closing date 6/30. Applicants notified on a rolling basis starting 3/4; must reply within 2 week(s) of notification.
**Transfers:** No deadline.

## CONTACT

Cheryle Perez, Financial Aid Director
PO Box 9139, Humacao, PR 00792-9139
(787) 852-1430 ext. 234

## ICPR Junior College

San Juan, Puerto Rico
www.icprjc.edu                    Federal Code: 011940

**2-year for-profit** business, junior and career college in large city.
**Enrollment:** 2,554 undergrads.
**Selectivity:** Open admission.

## BASIC COSTS (2015-2016)

**Additional info:** Tuition for Nursing Program, Medical Sonography, Culinary Arts, and Pharmacy is $6,809. Tuition for other programs is $6,450.

## FINANCIAL AID PICTURE (2015-2016)

**Students with need:** 75% of average financial aid package awarded as scholarships/grants, 25% awarded as loans/jobs. Need-based aid available for part-time students. Work study available nights.
**Students without need:** No-need awards available for academics, state/district residency.

## FINANCIAL AID PROCEDURES

**Forms required:** FAFSA, institutional form.
**Dates and Deadlines:** Closing date 6/14. Applicants notified on a rolling basis starting 11/15.
**Transfers:** No deadline.

## CONTACT

Palmira Arroyo, Financial Aid Director
PO Box 190304, San Juan, PR 00919-0304
(787) 753-6335 ext. 4201

## Inter American University of Puerto Rico: Aguadilla Campus

Aguadilla, Puerto Rico
www.aguadilla.inter.edu             Federal Code: 003939

**4-year private** university and liberal arts college in small city.
**Enrollment:** 4,198 undergrads, 12% part-time. 841 full-time freshmen.
**Selectivity:** Admits 50 to 75% of applicants.

## BASIC COSTS (2015-2016)

**Additional info:** Tuition at time of enrollment locked for 4 years.

## FINANCIAL AID PICTURE (2015-2016)

**Students with need:** 77% of average financial aid package awarded as scholarships/grants, 23% awarded as loans/jobs. Need-based aid available for part-time students. Work study available nights, weekends, and for part-time students.
**Students without need:** No-need awards available for academics.

## FINANCIAL AID PROCEDURES

**Forms required:** FAFSA.
**Dates and Deadlines:** Closing date 4/30. Applicants notified by 6/16; must reply by 8/8.
**Transfers:** No deadline.

## CONTACT

Gloria Cortes, Director of Financial Aid
Box 20000, Aguadilla, PR 00605
(787) 891-0925 ext. 2747

## Inter American University of Puerto Rico: Arecibo Campus

Arecibo, Puerto Rico
www.arecibo.inter.edu                     Federal Code: 005026

**4-year private** liberal arts college in small city.
**Enrollment:** 4,303 undergrads.

### FINANCIAL AID PICTURE
**Students with need:** Need-based aid available for full-time and part-time students. Work study available nights, weekends, and for part-time students.
**Students without need:** No-need awards available for academics, athletics.

### FINANCIAL AID PROCEDURES
**Forms required:** FAFSA, institutional form.
**Dates and Deadlines:** Closing date 5/15. Applicants notified on a rolling basis.

### CONTACT
Ramon de Jesus, Director of Financial Aid
PO Box 4050, Arecibo, PR 00614-4050
(787) 878-5475 ext. 2275

## Inter American University of Puerto Rico: Barranquitas Campus

Barranquitas, Puerto Rico
www.br.inter.edu                     Federal Code: 005027

**4-year private** university and branch campus college in large town.
**Enrollment:** 2,073 undergrads.

### BASIC COSTS (2015-2016)
**Additional info:** Tuition/fee waivers available for adults, minority students.

### FINANCIAL AID PICTURE
**Students with need:** Need-based aid available for full-time and part-time students.
**Students without need:** This college awards aid only to students with need.

### FINANCIAL AID PROCEDURES
**Forms required:** FAFSA.
**Dates and Deadlines:** Closing date 4/30. Applicants notified on a rolling basis; must reply within 2 week(s) of notification.

### CONTACT
Eduardo Fontanez, Financial Aid Director
PO Box 517, Barranquitas, PR 00794
(787) 857-3600 ext. 2050

## Inter American University of Puerto Rico: Bayamon Campus

Bayamon, Puerto Rico
www.bayamon.inter.edu                     Federal Code: 003938

**4-year private** university and engineering college in small city.
**Enrollment:** 4,481 undergrads, 12% part-time. 950 full-time freshmen.
**Selectivity:** Admits 50 to 75% of applicants.

### BASIC COSTS (2016-2017)
**Tuition and fees:** $6,090.
**Per-credit charge:** $180.

### FINANCIAL AID PICTURE (2015-2016)
**Students with need:** Average financial aid package met 5% of need; average scholarship/grant was $701; average loan was $96. For part-time students, average financial aid package was $164.

**Students without need:** This college awards aid only to students with need.

### FINANCIAL AID PROCEDURES
**Forms required:** FAFSA.
**Dates and Deadlines:** Priority date 6/30; no closing date. Applicants notified on a rolling basis starting 5/10.

### CONTACT
Hector Vargas, Director of Student Services
500 Dr. John Will Harris Road, Bayamon, PR 00957
(787) 279-1912 ext. 2025

## Inter American University of Puerto Rico: Fajardo Campus

Fajardo, Puerto Rico
www.fajardo.inter.edu                     Federal Code: 010763

**4-year private** university and branch campus college in large town.
**Enrollment:** 2,226 undergrads, 15% part-time. 471 full-time freshmen.

### BASIC COSTS (2015-2016)
**Tuition and fees:** $5,876.
**Per-credit charge:** $178.

### FINANCIAL AID PICTURE (2014-2015)
**Students with need:** 78% of average financial aid package awarded as scholarships/grants, 22% awarded as loans/jobs. Need-based aid available for part-time students. Work study available nights, weekends, and for part-time students.
**Students without need:** This college awards aid only to students with need.

### FINANCIAL AID PROCEDURES
**Forms required:** FAFSA.
**Dates and Deadlines:** Closing date 4/30. Applicants notified by 2/1; must reply within 2 week(s) of notification.
**Transfers:** Priority date 1/1; closing date 4/9. Applicants notified on a rolling basis starting 1/15; must reply within 2 week(s) of notification.

### CONTACT
Lydia Santiago, Dean of Administration
Call Box 70003, Fajardo, PR 00738-7003
(787) 863-2390 ext. 2309

## Inter American University of Puerto Rico: Guayama Campus

Guayama, Puerto Rico
www.guayama.inter.edu                     Federal Code: 010764

**4-year private** university in large town.
**Enrollment:** 1,898 undergrads, 15% part-time. 256 full-time freshmen.
**Selectivity:** Admits less than 50% of applicants.

### BASIC COSTS (2015-2016)
**Tuition and fees:** $6,072.

### FINANCIAL AID PICTURE
**Students with need:** Need-based aid available for full-time and part-time students. Work study available nights, weekends, and for part-time students.
**Students without need:** This college awards aid only to students with need.

### FINANCIAL AID PROCEDURES
**Forms required:** FAFSA, institutional form.
**Dates and Deadlines:** Closing date 4/29. Applicants notified by 6/15; must reply by 7/30.

**Transfers:** No deadline.

**CONTACT**

Jose Vechini-Rodriguez, Director of Financial Aid

PO Box 10004, Guayama, PR 00785

(787) 864-2222 ext. 2206

## Inter American University of Puerto Rico: Metropolitan Campus

San Juan, Puerto Rico

www.metro.inter.edu/index.asp        Federal Code: 003940

**4-year private** branch campus college in large city.

**Enrollment:** 6,339 undergrads, 17% part-time. 671 full-time freshmen.

**Selectivity:** Admits less than 50% of applicants.

### FINANCIAL AID PICTURE (2015-2016)

**Students with need:** Average financial aid package met 4% of need; average scholarship/grant was $594; average loan was $150. For part-time students, average financial aid package was $602.

### FINANCIAL AID PROCEDURES

**Forms required:** FAFSA.

**Dates and Deadlines:** Closing date 4/30. Applicants notified on a rolling basis.

### CONTACT

Lillian Concepcion, Director of Financial Aid

Box 191293, San Juan, PR 00919-1293

(787) 250-1912 ext. 2185

## Inter American University of Puerto Rico: Ponce Campus

Mercedita, Puerto Rico

ponce.inter.edu        Federal Code: 005029

**4-year private** university in large town.

**Enrollment:** 5,011 undergrads, 13% part-time. 925 full-time freshmen.

**Selectivity:** Admits 50 to 75% of applicants.

### BASIC COSTS (2015-2016)

**Tuition and fees:** $6,030.

**Per-credit charge:** $178.

### FINANCIAL AID PICTURE (2015-2016)

**Students with need:** Average financial aid package met 2% of need; average scholarship/grant was $262; average loan was $224. For part-time students, average financial aid package was $465.

**Students without need:** This college awards aid only to students with need.

**Scholarships offered:** Scholarship program for first-time freshmen with a high school academic index of 3.0 or higher.

### FINANCIAL AID PROCEDURES

**Forms required:** FAFSA.

### CONTACT

Miriam Martinez, Acting Director of Financial Aid

104 Turpo Industrial Park, Mercedita, PR 00715-1602

(787) 284-1912 ext. 2018

## Inter American University of Puerto Rico: San German Campus

San German, Puerto Rico

www.sg.inter.edu        Federal Code: 00714

**4-year private** university in large town.

**Enrollment:** 4,243 undergrads, 10% part-time. 1,034 full-time freshmen.

**Selectivity:** Admits 50 to 75% of applicants.

### BASIC COSTS (2015-2016)

**Tuition and fees:** $6,030.

**Per-credit charge:** $178.

**Room and board:** $2,700.

### FINANCIAL AID PICTURE (2014-2015)

**Students with need:** Out of 1,011 full-time freshmen who applied for aid, 996 were judged to have need. Of these, 627 received aid, and 2 had their full need met. Average financial aid package met 3% of need; average scholarship/grant was $201; average loan was $245. For part-time students, average financial aid package was $174.

**Students without need:** No-need awards available for academics, athletics.

**Scholarships offered:** 25 full-time freshmen received athletic scholarships; average amount $812.

### FINANCIAL AID PROCEDURES

**Forms required:** FAFSA, institutional form.

**Dates and Deadlines:** Closing date 5/14. Applicants notified on a rolling basis; must reply by 8/1.

### CONTACT

Maria Lugo, Director of Financial Aid

Box 5100, San German, PR 00683-9801

(787) 264-1912 ext. 7250

## National University College: Arecibo

Arecibo, Puerto Rico

www.nuc.edu        Federal Code: 015953

**3-year for-profit** career college in small city.

**Enrollment:** 1,450 undergrads, 34% part-time. 199 full-time freshmen.

### BASIC COSTS (2015-2016)

**Additional info:** Tuition per-credit-hour charge $170. Registration fee $25 per term. Administrative service and technological resources fee $100 per term. Additional fees may apply.

### FINANCIAL AID PICTURE

**Students with need:** Need-based aid available for full-time and part-time students. Work study available nights, weekends, and for part-time students.

### FINANCIAL AID PROCEDURES

**Forms required:** FAFSA.

**Dates and Deadlines:** Priority date 12/31; closing date 4/30. Applicants notified on a rolling basis starting 5/2; must reply by 5/15 or within 2 week(s) of notification.

**Transfers:** No deadline.

### CONTACT

Evelyn Quinones, Director of Financial Aid

PO Box 4035, MSC 452, Arecibo, PR 00614

(787) 879-5044 ext. 5220

## National University College: Bayamon

Bayamon, Puerto Rico

www.nuc.edu        Federal Code: 015953

**3-year for-profit** career college in large town.

**Enrollment:** 3,305 undergrads, 40% part-time. 885 full-time freshmen.

## BASIC COSTS (2015-2016)

**Additional info:** Tuition per-credit-hour charge $170. Registration fee $25 per term. Administrative service and technological resources fee $100 per term. Additional fees may apply.

## FINANCIAL AID PICTURE

**Students with need:** Need-based aid available for full-time and part-time students. Work study available nights, weekends, and for part-time students.
**Students without need:** This college awards aid only to students with need.

## FINANCIAL AID PROCEDURES

**Forms required:** FAFSA.
**Dates and Deadlines:** Priority date 12/31; closing date 4/30. Applicants notified on a rolling basis starting 5/2; must reply by 5/15 or within 2 week(s) of notification.
**Transfers:** No deadline.

## CONTACT

Ivelisse Rios, Director of Financial Aid
PO Box 2036, Bayamon, PR 00960
(787) 780-5134 ext. 4020

## National University College: Ponce

Coto Laurel, Puerto Rico
www.nuc.edu

**3-year for-profit** career college in large city.
**Enrollment:** 1,229 undergrads, 23% part-time. 218 full-time freshmen.

## BASIC COSTS (2015-2016)

**Additional info:** Tuition per-credit-hour charge $170. Registration fee $25 per term. Administrative service and technological resources fee $100 per term. Additional fees may apply.

## FINANCIAL AID PICTURE

**Students with need:** Need-based aid available for full-time and part-time students. Work study available nights, weekends, and for part-time students.
**Students without need:** This college awards aid only to students with need.

## FINANCIAL AID PROCEDURES

**Forms required:** FAFSA.
**Dates and Deadlines:** Priority date 12/31; closing date 4/30. Applicants notified on a rolling basis starting 5/2; must reply by 5/15 or within 2 week(s) of notification.
**Transfers:** No deadline.

## CONTACT

Tereangeli Toledo, Director of Financial Aid
PO Box 801243, Coto Laurel, PR 00780-1243

## National University College: Rio Grande

Rio Grande, Puerto Rico
www.nuc.edu                          Federal Code: E01213

**3-year for-profit** career college in small town.
**Enrollment:** 1,816 undergrads, 41% part-time. 195 full-time freshmen.

## BASIC COSTS (2015-2016)

**Additional info:** Tuition per-credit-hour charge $170. Registration fee $25 per term. Administrative service and technological resources fee $100 per term. Additional fees may apply.

## FINANCIAL AID PICTURE

**Students with need:** Need-based aid available for full-time and part-time students. Work study available nights, weekends, and for part-time students.

**Students without need:** This college awards aid only to students with need.

## FINANCIAL AID PROCEDURES

**Forms required:** FAFSA.
**Dates and Deadlines:** Priority date 12/31; closing date 4/30. Must reply by 5/15 or within 2 week(s) of notification.
**Transfers:** No deadline.

## CONTACT

Nelson Diaz, Director of Financial Aid
PO Box 3064, Rio Grande, PR 00745
(787) 809-5110 ext. 6314

## Pontifical Catholic University of Puerto Rico

Ponce, Puerto Rico
www.pucpr.edu                          Federal Code: 003936

**4-year private** university in small city, affiliated with Roman Catholic Church.
**Enrollment:** 5,427 undergrads.

## BASIC COSTS (2015-2016)

**Tuition and fees:** $6,270.
**Per-credit charge:** $190.
**Room only:** $1,300.

## FINANCIAL AID PICTURE

**Students with need:** Need-based aid available for full-time and part-time students. Work study available nights, weekends, and for part-time students.
**Students without need:** No-need awards available for academics, athletics, music/drama.

## FINANCIAL AID PROCEDURES

**Forms required:** FAFSA.
**Dates and Deadlines:** Closing date 5/15. Applicants notified by 6/15; must reply within 4 week(s) of notification.
**Transfers:** Priority date 5/11. Applicants notified by 6/15; must reply within 4 week(s) of notification. Distribution of awards based on availability of funds when application received.

## CONTACT

Maria Nolasco, Director of Financial Aid
2250 Las Americas Avenue, Suite 284, Ponce, PR 00717-9777
(787) 651-2041

## Theological University of the Caribbean

Saint Just, Puerto Rico
www.utcpr.edu

**4-year private** Bible and seminary college in small city, affiliated with Church of God.
**Enrollment:** 242 undergrads, 40% part-time. 6 full-time freshmen.
**Selectivity:** Admits over 75% of applicants.

## BASIC COSTS (2016-2017)

**Tuition and fees:** $4,448.
**Per-credit charge:** $130.
**Room and board:** $2,400.

## FINANCIAL AID PICTURE (2015-2016)

**Students with need:** Out of 6 full-time freshmen who applied for aid, 6 were judged to have need. Of these, 6 received aid. Average financial aid package met 60% of need. Need-based aid available for part-time students.
**Students without need:** This college awards aid only to students with need.

## FINANCIAL AID PROCEDURES
**Forms required:** FAFSA.

## CONTACT
Frankie Negron, Administration Dean
PO Box 901, Saint Just, PR 00978-0901
(787) 761-0640 ext. 265

## Turabo University
Gurabo, Puerto Rico
www.ut.suagm.edu
Federal Code: 011719

**4-year private** university and engineering college in small city.
**Enrollment:** 14,696 undergrads, 27% part-time. 2,224 full-time freshmen.
**Selectivity:** Admits 50 to 75% of applicants.

### FINANCIAL AID PICTURE (2014-2015)
**Students with need:** Need-based aid available for full-time and part-time students.
**Students without need:** This college awards aid only to students with need.

### FINANCIAL AID PROCEDURES
**Forms required:** FAFSA.
**Dates and Deadlines:** Priority date 5/30; no closing date.

### CONTACT
Carmen Rivera-Lopez, Admissions and Financial Aid Director
PO Box 3030, Gurabo, PR 00778
(787) 743-7979 ext. 4350

## Universal Technology College of Puerto Rico
Aguadilla, Puerto Rico
www.unitecpr.edu
Federal Code: 030297

**2-year private** health science and career college in small city.
**Enrollment:** 1,260 undergrads.
**Selectivity:** Open admission.

### FINANCIAL AID PICTURE
**Students with need:** Need-based aid available for full-time and part-time students. Work study available nights, weekends, and for part-time students.
**Students without need:** This college awards aid only to students with need.

### FINANCIAL AID PROCEDURES
**Forms required:** FAFSA, state aid form, institutional form.
**Dates and Deadlines:** Priority date 4/30; closing date 6/30. Applicants notified on a rolling basis starting 2/1; must reply by 6/30.
**Transfers:** No deadline.

### CONTACT
Samuel Hernandez, Financial Aid Administrator
Apartado 1955, Victoria Station, Aguadilla, PR 00605
(787) 882-2065 ext. 313

## Universidad Adventista de las Antillas
Mayaguez, Puerto Rico
www.uaa.edu
Federal Code: 005019

**4-year private** university and liberal arts college in small city, affiliated with Seventh-day Adventists.
**Enrollment:** 1,304 undergrads, 6% part-time. 219 full-time freshmen.

---

**Selectivity:** Open admission; but selective for some programs.

### BASIC COSTS (2015-2016)
**Tuition and fees:** $6,850.
**Per-credit charge:** $175.
**Room and board:** $5,200.

### FINANCIAL AID PICTURE (2014-2015)
**Students with need:** Out of 219 full-time freshmen who applied for aid, 205 were judged to have need. Of these, 205 received aid. Need-based aid available for part-time students.
**Students without need:** 14 full-time freshmen who did not demonstrate need for aid received scholarships/grants; average award was $2,500.

### FINANCIAL AID PROCEDURES
**Forms required:** FAFSA, institutional form.
**Dates and Deadlines:** Applicants notified on a rolling basis starting 8/15; must reply within 3 week(s) of notification.
**Transfers:** No deadline. Applicants notified on a rolling basis.

### CONTACT
Awilda Matos, Director of Financial Aid
PO Box 118, Mayaguez, PR 00681-0118
(787) 834-9595 ext. 2200

## Universidad del Este
Carolina, Puerto Rico
www.suagm.edu/une
Federal Code: 011718

**4-year private** university in small city.
**Enrollment:** 11,825 undergrads, 28% part-time. 1,842 full-time freshmen.
**Selectivity:** Open admission; but selective for some programs.

### FINANCIAL AID PICTURE
**Students with need:** Need-based aid available for full-time and part-time students. Work study available nights, weekends, and for part-time students.
**Students without need:** This college awards aid only to students with need.

### FINANCIAL AID PROCEDURES
**Forms required:** FAFSA, state aid form, institutional form.
**Dates and Deadlines:** Priority date 5/30; no closing date.

### CONTACT
Norberto Pag|fan, Financial Aid Director
PO Box 2010, Carolina, PR 00984-2010
(787) 257-7373 ext. 3304

## Universidad Metropolitana
San Juan, Puerto Rico
www.suagm.edu/umet
Federal Code: 025875

**4-year private** university and liberal arts college in large city.
**Enrollment:** 11,589 undergrads, 22% part-time. 2,050 full-time freshmen.
**Selectivity:** Admits 50 to 75% of applicants.

### FINANCIAL AID PICTURE
**Students with need:** Need-based aid available for full-time and part-time students. Work study available nights.
**Students without need:** This college awards aid only to students with need.

### FINANCIAL AID PROCEDURES
**Forms required:** FAFSA.
**Dates and Deadlines:** Priority date 5/30; no closing date.

## CONTACT

Julio Rodriguez, Financial Aid Director

Apartado 21150, San Juan, PR 00928

(787) 766-1717 ext. 6587

## Universidad Pentecostal Mizpa

San Juan, Puerto Rico

www.mizpa.edu                    Federal Code: 035313

**4-year private** university and Bible college in very large city, affiliated with Pentecostal Holiness Church.

**Enrollment:** 290 undergrads, 50% part-time. 10 full-time freshmen.

### BASIC COSTS (2016-2017)

**Tuition and fees:** $5,150.

**Per-credit charge:** $155.

**Room and board:** $3,760.

### FINANCIAL AID PICTURE (2015-2016)

**Students with need:** 96% of average financial aid package awarded as scholarships/grants, 4% awarded as loans/jobs. Need-based aid available for part-time students.

**Students without need:** This college awards aid only to students with need.

### FINANCIAL AID PROCEDURES

**Forms required:** FAFSA.

### CONTACT

Ismael Soto, Administrative Dean

RR 16 Box 4800, San Juan, PR 00926

(787) 720-4476 ext. 233

## Universidad Politecnica de Puerto Rico

Hato Rey, Puerto Rico

www.pupr.edu                     Federal Code: 014255

**5-year private** university and engineering college in large city.

**Enrollment:** 3,475 undergrads, 54% part-time. 323 full-time freshmen.

**Selectivity:** Admits over 75% of applicants.

### BASIC COSTS (2016-2017)

**Tuition and fees:** $8,040.

**Per-credit charge:** $200.

### FINANCIAL AID PICTURE (2015-2016)

**Students with need:** Average financial aid package met 49% of need; average scholarship/grant was $4,486; average loan was $2,068. For part-time students, average financial aid package was $11,390.

**Students without need:** No-need awards available for academics, music/drama.

### FINANCIAL AID PROCEDURES

**Forms required:** FAFSA.

**Dates and Deadlines:** Priority date 5/15; closing date 6/30. Applicants notified by 7/15.

### CONTACT

Sergio Villoldo, Director of Financial Aid

PO Box 192017, San Juan, PR 00919-2017

(787) 622-8000 ext. 249

## University College of San Juan

San Juan, Puerto Rico

www.cunisanjuan.edu              Federal Code: 010567

**4-year public** university and community college in large city.

**Enrollment:** 1,429 undergrads, 13% part-time. 244 full-time freshmen.

**Selectivity:** Admits 50 to 75% of applicants.

### FINANCIAL AID PICTURE (2014-2015)

**Students with need:** Out of 215 full-time freshmen who applied for aid, 215 were judged to have need. Of these, 215 received aid, and 215 had their full need met. Average financial aid package met 100% of need; average scholarship/grant was $4,690. For part-time students, average financial aid package was $2,175.

**Students without need:** This college awards aid only to students with need.

### FINANCIAL AID PROCEDURES

**Forms required:** FAFSA, state aid form, institutional form.

**Dates and Deadlines:** Applicants notified on a rolling basis starting 8/1.

**Transfers:** Financial aid transcripts.

### CONTACT

Kennia Santos, Director of Financial Aid

180 Jose R. Oliver Avenue, San Juan, PR 00918

(787) 480-2400 ext. 2425

## University of Puerto Rico: Aguadilla

Aguadilla, Puerto Rico

www.uprag.edu                    Federal Code: 012123

**4-year public** liberal arts and technical college in small city.

**Enrollment:** 2,573 undergrads, 7% part-time. 771 full-time freshmen.

**Selectivity:** Admits less than 50% of applicants.

### BASIC COSTS (2015-2016)

**Tuition and fees:** $2,014.

### FINANCIAL AID PICTURE (2015-2016)

**Students with need:** 98% of average financial aid package awarded as scholarships/grants, 2% awarded as loans/jobs. Need-based aid available for part-time students.

**Students without need:** This college awards aid only to students with need.

### FINANCIAL AID PROCEDURES

**Forms required:** FAFSA, institutional form.

**Dates and Deadlines:** Closing date 5/6. Applicants notified on a rolling basis starting 4/1; must reply within 1 week(s) of notification.

**Transfers:** No deadline.

### CONTACT

Yanira Matos, Financial Aid Director

Box 6150, Aguadilla, PR 00604-6150

(787) 890-0109

## University of Puerto Rico: Arecibo

Arecibo, Puerto Rico

www.upra.edu                     Federal Code: 007228

**4-year public** university and liberal arts college in small city.

**Enrollment:** 3,881 undergrads, 6% part-time. 944 full-time freshmen.

**Selectivity:** Admits over 75% of applicants.

### BASIC COSTS (2015-2016)

**Tuition and fees:** $2,014.

## FINANCIAL AID PICTURE (2014-2015)

**Students with need:** 92% of average financial aid package awarded as scholarships/grants, 8% awarded as loans/jobs. Need-based aid available for part-time students. Work study available nights, weekends, and for part-time students.

**Students without need:** This college awards aid only to students with need.

## FINANCIAL AID PROCEDURES

**Forms required:** FAFSA, institutional form.

**Dates and Deadlines:** Priority date 5/4; closing date 6/30. Applicants notified on a rolling basis starting 1/1; must reply within 4 week(s) of notification.

**Transfers:** Closing date 5/30. Must reply within 4 week(s) of notification.

## CONTACT

Daliana Fresse, Financial Aid Officer
PO Box 4010, Arecibo, PR 00614-4010
(787) 815-0000 ext. 4501

## University of Puerto Rico: Carolina Regional College

Carolina, Puerto Rico
www.uprc.edu                    Federal Code: 003942

**4-year public** university in small city.

**Enrollment:** 3,678 undergrads, 18% part-time. 918 full-time freshmen.

**Selectivity:** Admits less than 50% of applicants.

## BASIC COSTS (2015-2016)

**Tuition and fees:** $2,691.

## FINANCIAL AID PICTURE (2014-2015)

**Students with need:** 92% of average financial aid package awarded as scholarships/grants, 8% awarded as loans/jobs. Need-based aid available for part-time students.

**Students without need:** This college awards aid only to students with need.

## FINANCIAL AID PROCEDURES

**Forms required:** FAFSA, state aid form, institutional form.

**Dates and Deadlines:** Closing date 4/30. Applicants notified on a rolling basis starting 6/10.

## CONTACT

Rafael Ruiz, Financial Aid Director
PO Box 4800, Carolina, PR 00984-4800
(787) 769-0188

## University of Puerto Rico: Cayey University College

Cayey, Puerto Rico
www.cayey.upr.edu                    Federal Code: 007206

**4-year public** university and liberal arts college in large town.

**Enrollment:** 3,737 undergrads.

## BASIC COSTS (2015-2016)

**Tuition and fees:** $2,014.

**Additional info:** Tuition at time of enrollment locked for 4 years.

## FINANCIAL AID PICTURE

**Students with need:** Need-based aid available for full-time and part-time students. Work study available weekends and for part-time students.

**Students without need:** This college awards aid only to students with need.

## FINANCIAL AID PROCEDURES

**Forms required:** FAFSA.

**Dates and Deadlines:** Closing date 6/30. Applicants notified by 7/30.

**Transfers:** Priority date 1/30; closing date 2/28.

## CONTACT

Sonia Placeres, Director of Financial Aid
Oficina de Admisiones UPR- Cayey, Cayey, PR 00737-2230
(787) 738-2161 ext. 2061

## University of Puerto Rico: Humacao

Humacao, Puerto Rico
www.uprh.edu                    Federal Code: 003942

**4-year public** university and liberal arts college in small city.

**Enrollment:** 3,732 undergrads, 6% part-time. 983 full-time freshmen.

**Selectivity:** Admits less than 50% of applicants.

## BASIC COSTS (2015-2016)

**Tuition and fees:** $2,014.

## FINANCIAL AID PICTURE

**Students with need:** Need-based aid available for full-time and part-time students.

**Students without need:** No-need awards available for academics, athletics, music/drama.

## FINANCIAL AID PROCEDURES

**Forms required:** FAFSA.

**Dates and Deadlines:** Priority date 3/1; closing date 6/30. Applicants notified on a rolling basis starting 4/30; must reply by 7/31.

## CONTACT

Brunilda Lopez, Director of Financial Aid
Call Box 860, Humacao, PR 00792
(787) 850-9342

## University of Puerto Rico: Mayaguez

Mayaguez, Puerto Rico
www.uprm.edu                    Federal Code: 003944

**5-year public** university, agricultural and engineering college in small city.

**Enrollment:** 11,518 undergrads, 6% part-time. 2,135 full-time freshmen.

**Selectivity:** Admits over 75% of applicants.

## BASIC COSTS (2015-2016)

**Tuition and fees:** $2,014.

**Per-credit charge:** $55; out-of-state residents $114.

## FINANCIAL AID PICTURE (2014-2015)

**Students with need:** Out of 1,826 full-time freshmen who applied for aid, 1,688 were judged to have need. Of these, 1,482 received aid, and 2 had their full need met. Average financial aid package met 44% of need; average scholarship/grant was $5,577; average loan was $3,382. For part-time students, average financial aid package was $3,348.

**Students without need:** This college awards aid only to students with need.

**Scholarships offered:** 18 full-time freshmen received athletic scholarships; average amount $1,195.

## FINANCIAL AID PROCEDURES

**Forms required:** FAFSA, institutional form.

**Dates and Deadlines:** Priority date 1/30; closing date 6/30. Applicants notified on a rolling basis starting 6/30.

**Transfers:** Must reply by 6/30. Deadline according to admission date.

**CONTACT**
Nannette Hérnandez, Director of Financial Aid
Admissions Office, Mayaguez, PR 00681-9000
(787) 265-1920

## University of Puerto Rico: Medical Sciences
San Juan, Puerto Rico
www.rcm.upr.edu                         Federal Code: 003945

**4-year public** university in large city.
**Enrollment:** 489 undergrads.

**BASIC COSTS (2015-2016)**
**Tuition and fees:** $2,196.
**Per-credit charge:** $55; out-of-state residents $120.

**FINANCIAL AID PICTURE**
**Students with need:** Need-based aid available for full-time and part-time students. Work study available nights, weekends, and for part-time students.
**Students without need:** This college awards aid only to students with need.

**FINANCIAL AID PROCEDURES**
**Forms required:** FAFSA, institutional form.
**Dates and Deadlines:** Priority date 4/30; closing date 6/15. Applicants notified on a rolling basis starting 8/1; must reply within 2 week(s) of notification.

**CONTACT**
Rafael Solis, Director of Financial Aid
PO Box 365067, San Juan, PR 00936-5067
(787) 758-2525 ext. 3205

## University of Puerto Rico: Ponce
Ponce, Puerto Rico
www.uprp.edu                           Federal Code: 009652

**4-year public** university and branch campus college in small city.
**Enrollment:** 3,543 undergrads, 7% part-time. 927 full-time freshmen.
**Selectivity:** Admits 50 to 75% of applicants.

**BASIC COSTS (2015-2016)**
**Tuition and fees:** $2,019.
**Additional info:** Tuition at time of enrollment locked for 4 years.

**FINANCIAL AID PICTURE (2015-2016)**
**Students with need:** 94% of average financial aid package awarded as scholarships/grants, 6% awarded as loans/jobs.
**Students without need:** This college awards aid only to students with need.

**FINANCIAL AID PROCEDURES**
**Forms required:** FAFSA, institutional form.
**Dates and Deadlines:** Closing date 5/30.

**CONTACT**
Arturo Almodovar, Director
Box 7186, Ponce, PR 00732
(787) 844-8181 ext. 2555

## University of Puerto Rico: Rio Piedras
San Juan, Puerto Rico
www.uprrp.edu                          Federal Code: 007108

**4-year public** university in very large city.
**Enrollment:** 13,002 undergrads, 11% part-time. 2,727 full-time freshmen.

**Selectivity:** Admits less than 50% of applicants.

**BASIC COSTS (2015-2016)**
**Tuition and fees:** $2,014.
**Room and board:** $8,280.

**FINANCIAL AID PICTURE (2014-2015)**
**Students with need:** 96% of average financial aid package awarded as scholarships/grants, 4% awarded as loans/jobs. Need-based aid available for part-time students.
**Students without need:** This college awards aid only to students with need.
**Additional info:** Tuition waived for honor students, athletes, members of chorus, and others with special talents.

**FINANCIAL AID PROCEDURES**
**Forms required:** FAFSA.
**Dates and Deadlines:** Closing date 4/1.

**CONTACT**
Samarie Cunningham, Director of Financial Aid
Box 21907, San Juan, PR 00931-1907

## University of Puerto Rico: Utuado
Utuado, Puerto Rico
uprutuado.edu                          Federal Code: 010922

**4-year public** agricultural college in large town.
**Enrollment:** 1,405 undergrads, 4% part-time. 564 full-time freshmen.
**Selectivity:** Admits less than 50% of applicants.

**BASIC COSTS (2015-2016)**
**Tuition and fees:** $2,019.
**Per-credit charge:** $55; out-of-state residents $114.

**FINANCIAL AID PICTURE (2014-2015)**
**Students with need:** 85% of average financial aid package awarded as scholarships/grants, 15% awarded as loans/jobs. Need-based aid available for part-time students. Work study available nights.
**Students without need:** This college awards aid only to students with need.

**FINANCIAL AID PROCEDURES**
**Forms required:** FAFSA.
**Dates and Deadlines:** Priority date 5/31; no closing date. Applicants notified on a rolling basis starting 9/30; must reply within 4 week(s) of notification.
**Transfers:** Priority date 5/30; closing date 6/15. Closing date for Pell Grant applicants March 31.

**CONTACT**
Edymariel Cortes, Financial Aid Director
PO Box 2500, Utuado, PR 00641
(787) 894-2828 ext. 2601

## University of the Sacred Heart
San Juan, Puerto Rico
www.sagrado.edu                        Federal Code: 003937

**4-year private** university and liberal arts college in large city, affiliated with Roman Catholic Church.
**Enrollment:** 4,420 undergrads.

**BASIC COSTS (2015-2016)**
**Tuition and fees:** $6,950.
**Per-credit charge:** $195.
**Room only:** $3,100.

**FINANCIAL AID PICTURE**

**Students with need:** Need-based aid available for full-time and part-time students.

**Students without need:** No-need awards available for academics, athletics.

**FINANCIAL AID PROCEDURES**

**Forms required:** FAFSA, institutional form.

**Dates and Deadlines:** Priority date 4/30; closing date 5/30. Applicants notified on a rolling basis starting 6/15; must reply by 8/30.

**Transfers:** No deadline.

**CONTACT**

June Adrade, Director of Financial Aid

Universidad del Sagrado Corazon Oficina de Nuevo Ingreso, San Juan, PR 00914-0383

# Rhode Island

## Brown University

Providence, Rhode Island

www.brown.edu

Federal Code: 003401

CSS Code: 3094

**4-year private** university and liberal arts college in small city.

**Enrollment:** 6,320 undergrads. 1,613 full-time freshmen.

**Selectivity:** Admits less than 50% of applicants.

**BASIC COSTS (2016-2017)**

**Tuition and fees:** $51,366.

**Room and board:** $13,200.

**FINANCIAL AID PICTURE (2015-2016)**

**Students with need:** Out of 826 full-time freshmen who applied for aid, 721 were judged to have need. Of these, 721 received aid, and 721 had their full need met. Average financial aid package met 100% of need; average scholarship/grant was $42,109; average loan was $4,841. For part-time students, average financial aid package was $31,404.

**Students without need:** This college awards aid only to students with need.

**FINANCIAL AID PROCEDURES**

**Forms required:** FAFSA, CSS PROFILE.

**Dates and Deadlines:** Closing date 2/1. Applicants notified by 4/1; must reply by 5/1.

**Transfers:** Financial aid for transfer applicants is limited. Transfer admissions are not need-blind. If awarded financial aid, your demonstrated need will be met. In order for an applicant to be considered for available funds, each candidate for financial aid must check "yes" to the Financial Aid question on Form 1 of the admission application and complete the appropriate application forms by the requisite deadlines.

**CONTACT**

James Tilton, Director of Financial Aid

Box 1876, Providence, RI 02912

(401) 863-2721

## Bryant University

Smithfield, Rhode Island

www.bryant.edu

Federal Code: 003402

**4-year private** business and liberal arts college in large town.

**Enrollment:** 3,430 undergrads, 2% part-time. 908 full-time freshmen.

**Selectivity:** Admits 50 to 75% of applicants.

**BASIC COSTS (2016-2017)**

**Tuition and fees:** $40,962.

**Per-credit charge:** $1,005.

**Room and board:** $14,975.

**FINANCIAL AID PICTURE (2015-2016)**

**Students with need:** Out of 692 full-time freshmen who applied for aid, 597 were judged to have need. Of these, 595 received aid, and 141 had their full need met. Average financial aid package met 48% of need; average scholarship/grant was $8,993; average loan was $3,813. For part-time students, average financial aid package was $10,405.

**Students without need:** 226 full-time freshmen who did not demonstrate need for aid received scholarships/grants; average award was $15,392. No-need awards available for academics, athletics, minority status, ROTC.

**Scholarships offered:** 36 full-time freshmen received athletic scholarships; average amount $23,416.

**FINANCIAL AID PROCEDURES**

**Forms required:** FAFSA.

**Dates and Deadlines:** Priority date 2/15; closing date 2/15. Applicants notified by 3/24; must reply by 5/1.

**Transfers:** Closing date 4/1.

**CONTACT**

John Canning, Director of Financial Aid

1150 Douglas Pike, Smithfield, RI 02917-1291

(401) 232-6020

## Community College of Rhode Island

Warwick, Rhode Island

www.ccri.edu

Federal Code: 004916

**2-year public** community college in small city.

**Enrollment:** 15,255 undergrads, 69% part-time. 1,557 full-time freshmen.

**Selectivity:** Open admission; but selective for some programs.

**BASIC COSTS (2015-2016)**

**Tuition and fees:** $4,266; out-of-state residents $11,496.

**Per-credit charge:** $180; out-of-state residents $534.

**Additional info:** Tuition/fee waivers available for unemployed or children of unemployed.

**FINANCIAL AID PICTURE**

**Students with need:** Need-based aid available for full-time and part-time students. Work study available nights, weekends, and for part-time students.

**Students without need:** No-need awards available for athletics.

**FINANCIAL AID PROCEDURES**

**Forms required:** FAFSA, institutional form.

**Dates and Deadlines:** Priority date 3/1; closing date 7/1. Applicants notified on a rolling basis starting 5/1; must reply within 2 week(s) of notification.

**CONTACT**

Joel Friedman, Director of Financial Aid

400 East Avenue, Warwick, RI 02886-1807

(401) 825-2003

## Johnson & Wales University: Providence

Providence, Rhode Island

http://admissions.jwu.edu/

Federal Code: 003404

**4-year private** university in small city.

**Enrollment:** 8,718 undergrads, 7% part-time. 2,040 full-time freshmen.

**Selectivity:** Admits over 75% of applicants.

**BASIC COSTS (2015-2016)**

**Tuition and fees:** $29,226.

**Room and board:** $12,186.

### FINANCIAL AID PICTURE (2015-2016)

**Students with need:** Out of 1,944 full-time freshmen who applied for aid, 1,579 were judged to have need. Of these, 1,577 received aid, and 247 had their full need met. Average financial aid package met 70% of need; average scholarship/grant was $6,048; average loan was $3,395. For part-time students, average financial aid package was $12,225.

**Students without need:** 315 full-time freshmen who did not demonstrate need for aid received scholarships/grants; average award was $9,619. No-need awards available for academics, alumni affiliation, leadership, state/district residency.

### FINANCIAL AID PROCEDURES

**Forms required:** FAFSA.

**Dates and Deadlines:** Applicants notified on a rolling basis starting 3/1; must reply within 2 week(s) of notification.

**Transfers:** Transfer scholarships available.

### CONTACT

Lynn Robinson, Director of Financial Aid
8 Abbott Park Place, Providence, RI 02903
(800) 342-5598 ext. 4648

## New England Institute of Technology

East Greenwich, Rhode Island
www.neit.edu                              Federal Code: 007845

**4-year private** health science and technical college in small city.
**Enrollment:** 2,813 undergrads, 16% part-time. 417 full-time freshmen.
**Selectivity:** Open admission; but selective for some programs.

### BASIC COSTS (2016-2017)

**Tuition and fees:** $24,651.
**Per-credit charge:** $465.
**Additional info:** Tuition at time of enrollment locked for 4 years.

### FINANCIAL AID PICTURE (2014-2015)

**Students with need:** 33% of average financial aid package awarded as scholarships/grants, 67% awarded as loans/jobs. Need-based aid available for part-time students. Work study available nights, weekends, and for part-time students.

**Students without need:** No-need awards available for academics.

### FINANCIAL AID PROCEDURES

**Forms required:** FAFSA.

**Transfers:** No deadline.

### CONTACT

Anna Kelly, Director of Financial Aid
One New England Tech Boulevard, East Greenwich, RI 02818
(401) 739-5000 ext. 3354

## Providence College

Providence, Rhode Island                  Federal Code: 003406
www.providence.edu                        CSS Code: 3693

**4-year private** liberal arts college in small city, affiliated with Roman Catholic Church.
**Enrollment:** 4,119 undergrads, 5% part-time. 1,033 full-time freshmen.
**Selectivity:** Admits 50 to 75% of applicants. GED not accepted.

### BASIC COSTS (2015-2016)

**Tuition and fees:** $45,400.
**Per-credit charge:** $1,590.
**Room and board:** $13,390.
**Additional info:** Tuition/fee waivers available for minority students.

### FINANCIAL AID PICTURE (2015-2016)

**Students with need:** Out of 732 full-time freshmen who applied for aid, 495 were judged to have need. Of these, 495 received aid, and 138 had their full need met. Average financial aid package met 84% of need; average scholarship/grant was $26,300; average loan was $4,855. For part-time students, average financial aid package was $6,004.

**Students without need:** 158 full-time freshmen who did not demonstrate need for aid received scholarships/grants; average award was $20,388. No-need awards available for academics, athletics, leadership, minority status, music/drama, ROTC.

**Scholarships offered:** 64 full-time freshmen received athletic scholarships; average amount $35,581.

### FINANCIAL AID PROCEDURES

**Forms required:** FAFSA, CSS PROFILE.

**Dates and Deadlines:** Priority date 2/1; closing date 2/1. Applicants notified by 3/16; must reply by 5/1.

**Transfers:** Priority date 4/15; closing date 4/15. Applicants notified on a rolling basis starting 4/15; must reply within 2 week(s) of notification.

### CONTACT

Sandra Oliveira, Director of Financial Aid
Harkins Hall 103, 1 Cunningham Square, Providence, RI 02918-0001
(401) 865-2286

## Rhode Island College

Providence, Rhode Island
www.ric.edu                               Federal Code: 003407

**4-year public** liberal arts and teachers college in small city.
**Enrollment:** 7,216 undergrads, 23% part-time. 1,087 full-time freshmen.
**Selectivity:** Admits 50 to 75% of applicants.

### BASIC COSTS (2015-2016)

**Tuition and fees:** $8,197; out-of-state residents $19,858.
**Per-credit charge:** $280; out-of-state residents $690.
**Room and board:** $10,718.
**Additional info:** Connecticut and Massachusetts students whose permanent address is within a 50-mile radius of the College pay the in-state tuition rate plus 50%. Tuition/fee waivers available for unemployed or children of unemployed.

### FINANCIAL AID PICTURE (2015-2016)

**Students with need:** Out of 1,023 full-time freshmen who applied for aid, 805 were judged to have need. Of these, 762 received aid, and 106 had their full need met. Average financial aid package met 69% of need; average scholarship/grant was $7,702; average loan was $3,486. For part-time students, average financial aid package was $5,946.

**Students without need:** 42 full-time freshmen who did not demonstrate need for aid received scholarships/grants; average award was $2,655. No-need awards available for academics, alumni affiliation, art, music/drama.

**Scholarships offered:** Presidential Scholarships: $2,000 per year; for entering freshmen in the top 30% of class; minimum combined SAT score of 1100 (exclusive of Writing); must apply for admission by December 15; approximately 100 awards.

### FINANCIAL AID PROCEDURES

**Forms required:** FAFSA, institutional form.

**Dates and Deadlines:** Priority date 3/1; no closing date. Applicants notified on a rolling basis starting 3/15; must reply by 5/1 or within 3 week(s) of notification.

**Transfers:** Priority date 5/15. Applicants notified on a rolling basis starting 3/15; must reply by 5/1 or within 3 week(s) of notification.

### CONTACT

Kenneth Ferus, Director of Financial Aid
600 Mount Pleasant Avenue, Providence, RI 02908
(401) 456-8033

## Rhode Island School of Design

Providence, Rhode Island                    Federal Code: 003409
www.risd.edu                                          CSS Code: 3726

**4-year private** visual arts college in small city.
**Enrollment:** 2,014 undergrads. 464 full-time freshmen.
**Selectivity:** Admits less than 50% of applicants.

### BASIC COSTS (2015-2016)
**Tuition and fees:** $45,840.
**Room and board:** $12,600.

### FINANCIAL AID PICTURE (2015-2016)
**Students with need:** Out of 284 full-time freshmen who applied for aid, 208 were judged to have need. Of these, 208 received aid. Average financial aid package met 67% of need; average scholarship/grant was $24,005; average loan was $3,500.
**Students without need:** No-need awards available for academics, art.

### FINANCIAL AID PROCEDURES
**Forms required:** FAFSA, CSS PROFILE.
**Dates and Deadlines:** Closing date 2/15. Applicants notified by 4/1; must reply by 5/1.
**Transfers:** Closing date 3/15. Applicants notified by 4/25; must reply by 5/22. Transfer students with previous undergraduate degree not eligible for scholarship aid.

### CONTACT
Anthony Gallonio, Director of Financial Aid
2 College Street, Providence, RI 02903-2784
(401) 454-6661

## Roger Williams University

Bristol, Rhode Island                        Federal Code: 003410
www.rwu.edu                                          CSS Code: 3729

**4-year private** university in large town.
**Enrollment:** 4,481 undergrads, 12% part-time. 1,023 full-time freshmen.
**Selectivity:** Admits over 75% of applicants.

### BASIC COSTS (2015-2016)
**Tuition and fees:** $31,800.
**Per-credit charge:** $1,249.
**Room and board:** $15,172.
**Additional info:** Tuition at time of enrollment locked for 4 years.

### FINANCIAL AID PICTURE (2015-2016)
**Students with need:** Out of 922 full-time freshmen who applied for aid, 714 were judged to have need. Of these, 704 received aid, and 51 had their full need met. Average financial aid package met 86% of need; average scholarship/grant was $14,634; average loan was $3,500. For part-time students, average financial aid package was $7,144.
**Students without need:** 150 full-time freshmen who did not demonstrate need for aid received scholarships/grants; average award was $12,171. No-need awards available for academics, leadership.

### FINANCIAL AID PROCEDURES
**Forms required:** FAFSA. New students must complete CSS PROFILE by January 1.
**Dates and Deadlines:** Priority date 1/1; closing date 2/1. Applicants notified on a rolling basis starting 3/15; must reply by 5/1 or within 2 week(s) of notification.
**Transfers:** Must reply by 5/1.

### CONTACT
Tracy DaCosta, Assistant Vice President of Enrollment Management
1 Old Ferry Road, Bristol, RI 02809-2921
(401) 254-3100

## Salve Regina University

Newport, Rhode Island
www.salve.edu                                Federal Code: 003411

**4-year private** university and liberal arts college in large town, affiliated with Roman Catholic Church.
**Enrollment:** 2,123 undergrads, 6% part-time. 557 full-time freshmen.
**Selectivity:** Admits 50 to 75% of applicants.

### BASIC COSTS (2015-2016)
**Tuition and fees:** $36,740.
**Per-credit charge:** $1,206.
**Room and board:** $13,250.

### FINANCIAL AID PICTURE (2015-2016)
**Students with need:** Out of 514 full-time freshmen who applied for aid, 440 were judged to have need. Of these, 440 received aid, and 53 had their full need met. Average financial aid package met 74% of need; average scholarship/grant was $23,958; average loan was $3,920. For part-time students, average financial aid package was $4,146.
**Students without need:** 278 full-time freshmen who did not demonstrate need for aid received scholarships/grants; average award was $13,540. No-need awards available for academics, alumni affiliation, art, ROTC.

### FINANCIAL AID PROCEDURES
**Forms required:** FAFSA.
**Dates and Deadlines:** Priority date 3/1; no closing date. Applicants notified on a rolling basis starting 1/3; must reply by 5/1 or within 2 week(s) of notification.
**Transfers:** No deadline. Applicants notified on a rolling basis starting 3/1; must reply by 5/1 or within 2 week(s) of notification. Must provide financial aid transcripts from previous institutions attended.

### CONTACT
Anne McDermott, Director of Financial Aid
100 Ochre Point Avenue, Newport, RI 02840-4192
(401) 341-2901

## University of Rhode Island

Kingston, Rhode Island
www.uri.edu                                  Federal Code: 003414

**4-year public** university in small town.
**Enrollment:** 13,342 undergrads, 8% part-time. 2,987 full-time freshmen.
**Selectivity:** Admits 50 to 75% of applicants.

### BASIC COSTS (2015-2016)
**Tuition and fees:** $12,862; out-of-state residents $28,852.
**Per-credit charge:** $474; out-of-state residents $1,124.
**Room and board:** $11,956.
**Additional info:** Tuition/fee waivers available for unemployed or children of unemployed.

### FINANCIAL AID PICTURE (2015-2016)
**Students with need:** Out of 2,362 full-time freshmen who applied for aid, 1,888 were judged to have need. Of these, 1,753 received aid, and 66 had their full need met. Average financial aid package met 64% of need; average scholarship/grant was $10,254; average loan was $5,855. For part-time students, average financial aid package was $9,473.
**Students without need:** 270 full-time freshmen who did not demonstrate need for aid received scholarships/grants; average award was $6,632. No-need awards available for academics, alumni affiliation, art, athletics, music/drama, ROTC.
**Scholarships offered:** *Merit:* Centennial and University Merit Scholarships of varying amounts are awarded by our Admission Office at the time of admission. Criteria are posted on the Admission web site. *Athletic:* 11 full-time freshmen received athletic scholarships; average amount $8,551.

**FINANCIAL AID PROCEDURES**

**Forms required:** FAFSA.

**Dates and Deadlines:** Priority date 3/1; no closing date. Applicants notified on a rolling basis starting 3/15; must reply by 5/1.

**Transfers:** No deadline. Applicants notified on a rolling basis starting 4/1; must reply within 2 week(s) of notification.

**CONTACT**

Bonnie Saccucci, Senior Associate Director of Enrollment Services

Newman Hall, Kingston, RI 02881-1322

(401) 874-9500

# South Carolina

## Aiken Technical College
Aiken, South Carolina
www.atc.edu
Federal Code: 010056

**2-year public** community and technical college in small city.

**Enrollment:** 2,259 undergrads.

**Selectivity:** Open admission; but selective for some programs.

**BASIC COSTS (2015-2016)**

**Tuition and fees:** $5,246; out-of-district residents $5,696; out-of-state residents $8,020.

**Per-credit charge:** $164; out-of-district residents $179; out-of-state residents $254.

**FINANCIAL AID PICTURE**

**Students with need:** Need-based aid available for full-time and part-time students. Work study available nights, weekends, and for part-time students.

**Students without need:** No-need awards available for academics, leadership, minority status, state/district residency.

**Scholarships offered:** Vernon Ford Scholarships; $1,000 annually; based on 3.0 GPA; 8 awarded. Presidential Scholarship; $10,000 annually; 10 awarded.

**FINANCIAL AID PROCEDURES**

**Forms required:** FAFSA.

**Dates and Deadlines:** Priority date 6/1; closing date 7/1. Applicants notified on a rolling basis starting 4/1; must reply within 2 week(s) of notification.

**Transfers:** Priority date 6/1. Applicants notified on a rolling basis; must reply within 2 week(s) of notification.

**CONTACT**

Sue Sims, Director of Financial Aid

PO Drawer 696, Aiken, SC 29802

(803) 593-9954 ext. 1261

## Allen University
Columbia, South Carolina
www.allenuniversity.edu
Federal Code: 003417

**4-year private** university and liberal arts college in large city, affiliated with African Methodist Episcopal Church.

**Enrollment:** 670 undergrads.

**BASIC COSTS (2015-2016)**

**Tuition and fees:** $12,640.

**Per-credit charge:** $450.

**Room and board:** $6,660.

**FINANCIAL AID PICTURE**

**Students with need:** Need-based aid available for full-time and part-time students.

**Students without need:** No-need awards available for academics, athletics, music/drama, ROTC.

**FINANCIAL AID PROCEDURES**

**Forms required:** FAFSA.

**Dates and Deadlines:** Priority date 4/15; closing date 7/20. Applicants notified on a rolling basis starting 4/1; must reply within 2 week(s) of notification.

**Transfers:** No deadline.

**CONTACT**

Shelline Warren, Financial Aid Director

1530 Harden Street, Columbia, SC 29204

(803) 376-5930

## Anderson University
Anderson, South Carolina
www.andersonuniversity.edu
Federal Code: 003418

**4-year private** university in large town, affiliated with Southern Baptist Convention.

**Enrollment:** 2,632 undergrads, 9% part-time. 664 full-time freshmen.

**Selectivity:** Admits 50 to 75% of applicants.

**BASIC COSTS (2015-2016)**

**Tuition and fees:** $24,860.

**Per-credit charge:** $560.

**Room and board:** $8,860.

**Additional info:** Tuition/fee waivers available for adults.

**FINANCIAL AID PICTURE (2014-2015)**

**Students with need:** Out of 632 full-time freshmen who applied for aid, 511 were judged to have need. Of these, 511 received aid, and 158 had their full need met. Average financial aid package met 77% of need; average scholarship/grant was $17,539; average loan was $3,939. For part-time students, average financial aid package was $5,992.

**Students without need:** 153 full-time freshmen who did not demonstrate need for aid received scholarships/grants; average award was $11,383. No-need awards available for academics, art, athletics, leadership, minority status, music/drama, religious affiliation, state/district residency.

**Scholarships offered:** 45 full-time freshmen received athletic scholarships; average amount $3,151.

**FINANCIAL AID PROCEDURES**

**Forms required:** FAFSA, state aid form.

**Dates and Deadlines:** Priority date 3/1; closing date 6/30. Applicants notified on a rolling basis starting 3/15; must reply by 5/1 or within 2 week(s) of notification.

**Transfers:** No deadline. Applicants notified on a rolling basis. Transfers are awarded based on college GPA on a different merit scale than Firs-time-freshmen.

**CONTACT**

Allison Sullivan, Director of Financial Aid & Planning

316 Boulevard, Anderson, SC 29621-4002

(864) 231-2070

## Benedict College
Columbia, South Carolina
www.benedict.edu
Federal Code: 003420

**4-year private** liberal arts college in large city, affiliated with American Baptist Churches in the USA.

**Enrollment:** 2,464 undergrads.

**Selectivity:** Admits over 75% of applicants.

## BASIC COSTS (2015-2016)
**Tuition and fees:** $18,286.
**Per-credit charge:** $548.
**Room and board:** $8,104.

## FINANCIAL AID PICTURE
**Students with need:** Need-based aid available for full-time and part-time students.

## FINANCIAL AID PROCEDURES
**Forms required:** FAFSA.
**Dates and Deadlines:** Priority date 4/15; no closing date. Applicants notified on a rolling basis starting 4/15.

## CONTACT
Sul Black, Director of Financial Aid
1600 Harden Street, Columbia, SC 29204
(803) 253-5105

# Bob Jones University
Greenville, South Carolina
www.bju.edu          Federal Code: 003421

**4-year private** Bible, liberal arts and seminary college in small city, affiliated with nondenominational tradition.
**Enrollment:** 2,467 undergrads, 2% part-time. 608 full-time freshmen.
**Selectivity:** Admits over 75% of applicants.

## BASIC COSTS (2015-2016)
**Tuition and fees:** $14,900.
**Per-credit charge:** $680.
**Room and board:** $6,280.

## FINANCIAL AID PICTURE (2014-2015)
**Students with need:** Out of 530 full-time freshmen who applied for aid, 442 were judged to have need. Of these, 442 received aid, and 131 had their full need met. Average financial aid package met 50% of need; average scholarship/grant was $12,105; average loan was $12,054. Need-based aid available for part-time students.
**Students without need:** 57 full-time freshmen who did not demonstrate need for aid received scholarships/grants; average award was $4,731. No-need awards available for academics, alumni affiliation, state/district residency.

## FINANCIAL AID PROCEDURES
**Forms required:** FAFSA.
**Dates and Deadlines:** Priority date 3/1; closing date 7/1. Applicants notified on a rolling basis.
**Transfers:** Applicants notified on a rolling basis.

## CONTACT
Susan Young, Director of Financial Aid
1700 Wade Hampton Boulevard, Greenville, SC 29614
(864) 242-5100 ext. 3040

# Central Carolina Technical College
Sumter, South Carolina
www.cctech.edu          Federal Code: 003995

**2-year public** community and technical college in large town.
**Enrollment:** 4,300 undergrads.
**Selectivity:** Open admission; but selective for some programs.

## BASIC COSTS (2015-2016)
**Tuition and fees:** $4,950; out-of-district residents $5,790; out-of-state residents $8,460.

**Per-credit charge:** $165; out-of-district residents $193; out-of-state residents $282.

## FINANCIAL AID PICTURE
**Students with need:** Need-based aid available for full-time and part-time students. Work study available nights.

## FINANCIAL AID PROCEDURES
**Forms required:** FAFSA.
**Dates and Deadlines:** Applicants notified on a rolling basis starting 4/11; must reply within 2 week(s) of notification.

## CONTACT
Sarah Dowd, Director of Financial Aid
506 North Guignard Drive, Sumter, SC 29150-2499
(803) 778-7831

# Charleston Southern University
Charleston, South Carolina
www.csuniv.edu          Federal Code: 003419

**4-year private** university and liberal arts college in large city, affiliated with Southern Baptist Convention.
**Enrollment:** 3,112 undergrads.
**Selectivity:** Admits 50 to 75% of applicants.

## BASIC COSTS (2015-2016)
**Tuition and fees:** $23,400.
**Per-credit charge:** $470.
**Room and board:** $9,270.

## FINANCIAL AID PICTURE
**Students with need:** Need-based aid available for full-time and part-time students. Work study available nights, weekends, and for part-time students.
**Students without need:** No-need awards available for academics, athletics, religious affiliation, ROTC.

## FINANCIAL AID PROCEDURES
**Forms required:** FAFSA, state aid form.
**Dates and Deadlines:** Priority date 4/15; no closing date. Applicants notified on a rolling basis starting 3/1; must reply within 2 week(s) of notification.

## CONTACT
Jenna Parish, Director of Financial Aid
9200 University Boulevard, Charleston, SC 29406
(843) 863-7050

# The Citadel
Charleston, South Carolina
www.citadel.edu          Federal Code: 003423

**4-year public** military college in large city.
**Enrollment:** 2,616 undergrads, 6% part-time. 602 full-time freshmen.
**Selectivity:** Admits over 75% of applicants.

## BASIC COSTS (2015-2016)
**Tuition and fees:** $13,024; out-of-state residents $33,440.
**Per-credit charge:** $442; out-of-state residents $820.
**Room and board:** $6,381.

## FINANCIAL AID PICTURE (2015-2016)
**Students with need:** Out of 499 full-time freshmen who applied for aid, 373 were judged to have need. Of these, 361 received aid, and 74 had their full need met. Average financial aid package met 53% of need; average scholarship/grant was $14,525; average loan was $3,440. For part-time students, average financial aid package was $6,518.

**Students without need:** 134 full-time freshmen who did not demonstrate need for aid received scholarships/grants; average award was $8,100. No-need awards available for academics, alumni affiliation, athletics, leadership, minority status, music/drama, religious affiliation, ROTC, state/district residency.

**Scholarships offered:** 62 full-time freshmen received athletic scholarships; average amount $23,904.

**FINANCIAL AID PROCEDURES**

**Forms required:** FAFSA.

**Dates and Deadlines:** Priority date 3/1; no closing date. Applicants notified on a rolling basis starting 4/1; must reply within 2 week(s) of notification.

**Transfers:** No deadline. Applicants notified on a rolling basis starting 4/1; must reply within 2 week(s) of notification.

**CONTACT**

Henry Fuller, Director of Financial Aid
171 Moultrie Street, Charleston, SC 29409
(843) 953-5187

## Claflin University
Orangeburg, South Carolina
www.claflin.edu                    Federal Code: 003424

**4-year private** liberal arts college in large town, affiliated with United Methodist Church.

**Enrollment:** 1,809 full-time undergrads.

**BASIC COSTS (2015-2016)**

**Tuition and fees:** $15,520.

**Room and board:** $8,674.

**FINANCIAL AID PICTURE**

**Students with need:** Need-based aid available for full-time and part-time students. Work study available nights.

**FINANCIAL AID PROCEDURES**

**Forms required:** FAFSA.

**Dates and Deadlines:** Closing date 4/15. Applicants notified on a rolling basis starting 5/3; must reply within 2 week(s) of notification.

**Transfers:** No deadline. Applicants notified on a rolling basis.

**CONTACT**

Terria Williams, Director of Financial Aid
400 Magnolia Street, Orangeburg, SC 29115
(803) 535-5334

## Clemson University
Clemson, South Carolina
www.clemson.edu                    Federal Code: 003425

**4-year public** university and engineering college in large town.

**Enrollment:** 17,740 undergrads, 3% part-time. 3,448 full-time freshmen.

**Selectivity:** Admits 50 to 75% of applicants.

**BASIC COSTS (2015-2016)**

**Tuition and fees:** $13,882; out-of-state residents $32,800.

**Per-credit charge:** $601; out-of-state residents $1,423.

**Room and board:** $8,718.

**FINANCIAL AID PICTURE (2015-2016)**

**Students with need:** Out of 2,765 full-time freshmen who applied for aid, 1,750 were judged to have need. Of these, 1,710 received aid, and 372 had their full need met. Average financial aid package met 61% of need; average scholarship/grant was $10,776; average loan was $3,485. For part-time students, average financial aid package was $5,547.

**Students without need:** 923 full-time freshmen who did not demonstrate need for aid received scholarships/grants; average award was $6,926. No-need awards available for academics, alumni affiliation, art, athletics, leadership, minority status, music/drama, ROTC, state/district residency.

**Scholarships offered:** 89 full-time freshmen received athletic scholarships; average amount $24,196.

**FINANCIAL AID PROCEDURES**

**Forms required:** FAFSA.

**Dates and Deadlines:** Priority date 3/1; no closing date. Applicants notified by 4/1.

**Transfers:** Priority date 4/1. Applicants notified on a rolling basis starting 6/1; must reply within 3 week(s) of notification. Transfer students must earn 12 semester hours before being considered for institutional scholarship.

**CONTACT**

Chuck Knepfle, Director of Student Financial Aid
105 Sikes Hall, Clemson, SC 29634-5124
(864) 656-2280

## Clinton College
Rock Hill, South Carolina
www.clintoncollege.edu/

**2-year private** junior and liberal arts college in small city.

**Enrollment:** 184 undergrads.

**Selectivity:** Open admission.

**BASIC COSTS (2015-2016)**

**Tuition and fees:** $6,751.

**Per-credit charge:** $400.

**Room and board:** $9,551.

**Additional info:** Off-campus residents pay $400 less in fees.

**FINANCIAL AID PICTURE**

**Students with need:** Need-based aid available for full-time and part-time students.

**Students without need:** This college awards aid only to students with need.

**FINANCIAL AID PROCEDURES**

**Forms required:** FAFSA.

**Transfers:** No deadline.

**CONTACT**

Sadie Jumper, Coordinator of Financial Aid
1029 Crawford Road, Rock Hill, SC 29730

## Coastal Carolina University
Conway, South Carolina
www.coastal.edu                    Federal Code: 003451

**4-year public** university in large town.

**Enrollment:** 9,289 undergrads, 6% part-time. 2,374 full-time freshmen.

**Selectivity:** Admits 50 to 75% of applicants.

**BASIC COSTS (2015-2016)**

**Tuition and fees:** $10,530; out-of-state residents $24,320.

**Per-credit charge:** $442; out-of-state residents $1,010.

**Room and board:** $8,690.

**FINANCIAL AID PICTURE (2014-2015)**

**Students with need:** Out of 2,171 full-time freshmen who applied for aid, 1,785 were judged to have need. Of these, 1,754 received aid, and 103 had their full need met. Average financial aid package met 44% of need; average scholarship/grant was $4,784; average loan was $8,453. For part-time students, average financial aid package was $4,844.

**Students without need:** 417 full-time freshmen who did not demonstrate need for aid received scholarships/grants; average award was $12,749. No-need awards available for academics, art, athletics, leadership, ROTC.
**Scholarships offered:** 77 full-time freshmen received athletic scholarships; average amount $9,409.

### FINANCIAL AID PROCEDURES
**Forms required:** FAFSA.
**Dates and Deadlines:** Priority date 3/1; no closing date. Applicants notified on a rolling basis starting 3/1; must reply by 5/15.
**Transfers:** No deadline. Applicants notified on a rolling basis starting 3/1; must reply within 4 week(s) of notification.

### CONTACT
Wendy Watts, Director of Financial Aid and Scholarships
PO Box 261954, Conway, SC 29528-6054
(843) 349-2313

## Coker College
Hartsville, South Carolina
www.coker.edu                    Federal Code: 003427

**4-year private** liberal arts college in large town.
**Enrollment:** 1,091 undergrads, 12% part-time. 221 full-time freshmen.
**Selectivity:** Admits less than 50% of applicants.

### BASIC COSTS (2015-2016)
**Tuition and fees:** $26,568.
**Room and board:** $8,242.
**Additional info:** Tuition/fee waivers available for adults.

### FINANCIAL AID PICTURE (2014-2015)
**Students with need:** Need-based aid available for full-time and part-time students. Work study available nights, weekends, and for part-time students.
**Students without need:** No-need awards available for academics, alumni affiliation, art, athletics, leadership, music/drama.
**Scholarships offered:** Scholarships for Excellence; up to $17,000 per year; awarded to students showing potential for continued high performance and leadership.
**Additional info:** Endowed scholarship program for qualified applicants. June 1 deadline for filing South Carolina Tuition Grant forms.

### FINANCIAL AID PROCEDURES
**Forms required:** FAFSA.
**Dates and Deadlines:** Priority date 4/1; closing date 6/1. Applicants notified on a rolling basis starting 3/1; must reply by 5/1 or within 3 week(s) of notification.
**Transfers:** No deadline.

### CONTACT
Betty Williams, Director of Financial Aid
300 East College Avenue, Hartsville, SC 29550
(843) 383-8055

## College of Charleston
Charleston, South Carolina
www.cofc.edu                    Federal Code: 003428

**4-year public** liberal arts college in large city.
**Enrollment:** 10,033 undergrads, 5% part-time. 2,161 full-time freshmen.
**Selectivity:** Admits over 75% of applicants.

### BASIC COSTS (2015-2016)
**Tuition and fees:** $11,220; out-of-state residents $28,764.
**Per-credit charge:** $454; out-of-state residents $1,185.
**Room and board:** $11,629.

**Additional info:** Room costs are the weighted average of a tiered dorm pricing system. Room costs range from $5,866 to $10,070 per academic year with the majority of available rooms at $8,758.

### FINANCIAL AID PICTURE (2014-2015)
**Students with need:** Out of 1,567 full-time freshmen who applied for aid, 1,068 were judged to have need. Of these, 1,024 received aid, and 236 had their full need met. Average financial aid package met 58% of need; average scholarship/grant was $3,317; average loan was $2,968. For part-time students, average financial aid package was $8,752.
**Students without need:** 544 full-time freshmen who did not demonstrate need for aid received scholarships/grants; average award was $10,240. No-need awards available for academics, alumni affiliation, art, athletics, music/drama.
**Scholarships offered:** 27 full-time freshmen received athletic scholarships; average amount $19,438.

### FINANCIAL AID PROCEDURES
**Forms required:** FAFSA.
**Dates and Deadlines:** Priority date 3/1; no closing date. Applicants notified on a rolling basis starting 4/1; must reply within 8 week(s) of notification.

### CONTACT
Donald Griggs, Director of Financial Assistance and Veterans Affairs
Admissions, Charleston, SC 29424-0001
(843) 953-5540

## Columbia College
Columbia, South Carolina
www.columbiasc.edu               Federal Code: 003430

**4-year private** liberal arts college for women in large city, affiliated with United Methodist Church.
**Enrollment:** 1,552 undergrads, 36% part-time. 178 full-time freshmen.
**Selectivity:** Admits over 75% of applicants.

### BASIC COSTS (2015-2016)
**Tuition and fees:** $28,100.
**Per-credit charge:** $725.
**Room and board:** $7,400.

### FINANCIAL AID PICTURE (2015-2016)
**Students with need:** Average financial aid package met 79% of need; average scholarship/grant was $23,134; average loan was $2,862. For part-time students, average financial aid package was $6,650.
**Students without need:** No-need awards available for academics, alumni affiliation, art, athletics, leadership, music/drama.
**Scholarships offered:** Founders Scholarship; up to full tuition. Presidential Scholarships; up to $14,000. Trustees Scholarships; up to $12,000. Momentum Scholarships; up to full tuition.

### FINANCIAL AID PROCEDURES
**Forms required:** FAFSA.
**Dates and Deadlines:** Priority date 4/1; no closing date. Applicants notified on a rolling basis starting 3/15; must reply within 4 week(s) of notification.
**Transfers:** Priority date 4/15; closing date 8/1. Applicants notified on a rolling basis starting 3/15; must reply within 4 week(s) of notification. Must meet institutional standards of satisfactory academic progress.

### CONTACT
Donna Quick, Director of Financial Aid
1301 Columbia College Drive, Columbia, SC 29203
(803) 786-3612

# Columbia International University
Columbia, South Carolina
www.ciu.edu                          Federal Code: 003429

**4-year private** university and Bible college in small city, affiliated with interdenominational tradition.
**Enrollment:** 535 undergrads, 8% part-time. 138 full-time freshmen.
**Selectivity:** Admits less than 50% of applicants.

## BASIC COSTS (2016-2017)
**Tuition and fees:** $21,450.
**Per-credit charge:** $850.
**Room and board:** $7,760.

## FINANCIAL AID PICTURE (2014-2015)
**Students with need:** Out of 92 full-time freshmen who applied for aid, 81 were judged to have need. Of these, 81 received aid, and 8 had their full need met. Average financial aid package met 66% of need; average scholarship/grant was $14,525; average loan was $3,325. For part-time students, average financial aid package was $5,936.
**Students without need:** 57 full-time freshmen who did not demonstrate need for aid received scholarships/grants; average award was $2,696. No-need awards available for academics, alumni affiliation, athletics, leadership, minority status, music/drama, state/district residency.
**Scholarships offered: *Merit:*** Merit Scholarships; $1,000-$7,000. ***Athletic:*** 3 full-time freshmen received athletic scholarships; average amount $5,833.
**Additional info:** Spouse scholarship program.

## FINANCIAL AID PROCEDURES
**Forms required:** FAFSA, state aid form, institutional form.
**Dates and Deadlines:** Priority date 4/15; no closing date. Applicants notified on a rolling basis starting 3/1; must reply within 2 week(s) of notification.
**Transfers:** No deadline. Applicants notified on a rolling basis starting 3/15; must reply within 2 week(s) of notification. FAFSA must be processed by June 30 for state need-based aid. State aid requires 1-year residency prior to award in most cases. Non-need-based state aid requires graduation from state high school.

## CONTACT
Patty Hix, Director of Financial Aid
PO Box 3122, Columbia, SC 29230-3122
(803) 807-5036

# Converse College
Spartanburg, South Carolina
www.converse.edu                     Federal Code: 003431

**4-year private** university and liberal arts college for women in large town.
**Enrollment:** 796 undergrads, 6% part-time. 212 full-time freshmen.
**Selectivity:** Admits 50 to 75% of applicants.

## BASIC COSTS (2015-2016)
**Tuition and fees:** $16,850.
**Per-credit charge:** $875.
**Room and board:** $9,995.

## FINANCIAL AID PICTURE (2015-2016)
**Students with need:** Average financial aid package met 65% of need; average scholarship/grant was $12,531; average loan was $3,701. Need-based aid available for part-time students.
**Students without need:** No-need awards available for academics, art, athletics, music/drama, ROTC, state/district residency.

## FINANCIAL AID PROCEDURES
**Forms required:** FAFSA.
**Dates and Deadlines:** Priority date 3/1; no closing date. Applicants notified on a rolling basis starting 3/1; must reply by 5/1 or within 2 week(s) of notification.

**Transfers:** No deadline. Applicants notified on a rolling basis starting 3/1; must reply by 5/1 or within 2 week(s) of notification.

## CONTACT
James Kellam, Director of Financial Planning
580 East Main Street, Spartanburg, SC 29302-0006
(864) 596-9019

# Denmark Technical College
Denmark, South Carolina
www.denmarktech.edu                  Federal Code: 005363

**2-year public** technical college in small town.
**Enrollment:** 988 undergrads.
**Selectivity:** Open admission.

## BASIC COSTS (2015-2016)
**Tuition and fees:** $3,486; out-of-state residents $6,756.
**Room and board:** $3,858.

## FINANCIAL AID PICTURE
**Students with need:** Need-based aid available for full-time and part-time students.

## FINANCIAL AID PROCEDURES
**Forms required:** FAFSA.
**Dates and Deadlines:** Applicants notified on a rolling basis starting 6/1; must reply within 2 week(s) of notification.

## CONTACT
Laura Fogel, Director of Financial Aid
1126 Solomon Blatt Boulevard, Denmark, SC 29042
(803) 793-5161

# Erskine College
Due West, South Carolina
www.erskine.edu                      Federal Code: 003432

**4-year private** liberal arts and seminary college in rural community, affiliated with Associate Reformed Presbyterian Church.
**Enrollment:** 619 undergrads.

## BASIC COSTS (2015-2016)
**Tuition and fees:** $33,315.
**Per-credit charge:** $1,150.
**Room and board:** $10,500.

## FINANCIAL AID PICTURE
**Students with need:** Need-based aid available for full-time and part-time students. Work study available nights, weekends, and for part-time students.
**Students without need:** No-need awards available for academics, alumni affiliation, athletics, leadership, minority status, music/drama, religious affiliation, state/district residency.
**Additional info:** Filing deadline 5/1 for institutional form, 6/30 for state form.

## FINANCIAL AID PROCEDURES
**Forms required:** FAFSA, state aid form, institutional form.
**Dates and Deadlines:** Priority date 4/1; no closing date. Applicants notified on a rolling basis starting 12/15; must reply within 2 week(s) of notification.
**Transfers:** Closing date 5/1. South Carolina residents must have earned 24 hours in previous year to receive tuition grant and 30 hours plus 3.0 GPA to receive the Life Scholarship.

## CONTACT
Michelle Lodato, Director of Financial Aid
PO Box 338, Due West, SC 29639-0338
(864) 379-8832

## Florence-Darlington Technical College

Florence, South Carolina
www.fdtc.edu                    Federal Code: 003990

**2-year public** community and technical college in small city.
**Enrollment:** 6,214 undergrads.
**Selectivity:** Open admission; but selective for some programs.

### BASIC COSTS (2015-2016)
**Tuition and fees:** $5,060; out-of-district residents $5,390; out-of-state residents $7,670.
**Per-credit charge:** $163; out-of-district residents $174; out-of-state residents $250.

### FINANCIAL AID PICTURE
**Students with need:** Need-based aid available for full-time and part-time students.
**Students without need:** No-need awards available for academics.

### FINANCIAL AID PROCEDURES
**Forms required:** FAFSA.
**Dates and Deadlines:** Priority date 5/1; no closing date. Applicants notified on a rolling basis starting 7/1; must reply within 2 week(s) of notification.
**Transfers:** Priority date 4/1; no deadline.

### CONTACT
Tony Otto, Director of Financial Assistance
PO Box 100548, Florence, SC 29501-0548
(843) 661-8085

## Forrest Junior College

Anderson, South Carolina
www.forrestcollege.edu            Federal Code: 004924

**2-year for-profit** business college in large town.
**Enrollment:** 86 undergrads. 16 full-time freshmen.
**Selectivity:** Open admission; but selective for some programs.

### BASIC COSTS (2016-2017)
**Tuition and fees:** $9,195.
**Per-credit charge:** $245.

### FINANCIAL AID PICTURE (2014-2015)
**Students with need:** Out of 16 full-time freshmen who applied for aid, 16 were judged to have need. Of these, 16 received aid, and 15 had their full need met. Average financial aid package met 90% of need; average loan was $3,500. Need-based aid available for part-time students.
**Students without need:** This college awards aid only to students with need.

### FINANCIAL AID PROCEDURES
**Forms required:** FAFSA.
**Dates and Deadlines:** Applicants notified on a rolling basis starting 4/30; must reply by 5/31 or within 4 week(s) of notification.
**Transfers:** No deadline. Applicants notified on a rolling basis; must reply within 3 week(s) of notification.

### CONTACT
Kathy Montgomery, Finance Coordinator
601 East River Street, Anderson, SC 29624
(864) 225-7653 ext. 2209

## Francis Marion University

Florence, South Carolina
www.fmarion.edu                  Federal Code: 009226

**4-year public** university and liberal arts college in small city.
**Enrollment:** 3,258 undergrads, 5% part-time. 737 full-time freshmen.

**Selectivity:** Admits 50 to 75% of applicants.

### BASIC COSTS (2015-2016)
**Tuition and fees:** $10,100; out-of-state residents $19,668.
**Per-credit charge:** $478; out-of-state residents $956.
**Room and board:** $7,472.

### FINANCIAL AID PICTURE (2015-2016)
**Students with need:** Out of 645 full-time freshmen who applied for aid, 581 were judged to have need. Of these, 580 received aid, and 60 had their full need met. Average financial aid package met 70% of need; average scholarship/grant was $8,998; average loan was $3,382. For part-time students, average financial aid package was $7,070.
**Students without need:** 4 full-time freshmen who did not demonstrate need for aid received scholarships/grants; average award was $3,825. No-need awards available for academics, alumni affiliation, art, athletics, leadership, minority status, music/drama, religious affiliation, ROTC, state/district residency.
**Scholarships offered:** 20 full-time freshmen received athletic scholarships; average amount $5,266.

### FINANCIAL AID PROCEDURES
**Forms required:** FAFSA.
**Dates and Deadlines:** Priority date 3/1; no closing date. Applicants notified on a rolling basis starting 1/30.
**Transfers:** Priority date 3/1; no deadline. Applicants notified on a rolling basis starting 1/30. Institutional scholarships available after one semester completed in residence.

### CONTACT
Kim Ellisor, Director of Financial Assistance
PO Box 100547, Florence, SC 29502-0547
(843) 661-1190

## Furman University

Greenville, South Carolina        Federal Code: 003434
www.furman.edu                    CSS Code: 5222

**4-year private** liberal arts college in small city.
**Enrollment:** 2,713 undergrads, 4% part-time. 669 full-time freshmen.
**Selectivity:** Admits 50 to 75% of applicants.

### BASIC COSTS (2015-2016)
**Tuition and fees:** $46,012.
**Per-credit charge:** $1,426.
**Room and board:** $11,522.

### FINANCIAL AID PICTURE (2015-2016)
**Students with need:** Out of 438 full-time freshmen who applied for aid, 352 were judged to have need. Of these, 352 received aid, and 93 had their full need met. Average financial aid package met 79% of need; average scholarship/grant was $32,120; average loan was $5,038. Need-based aid available for part-time students.
**Students without need:** 246 full-time freshmen who did not demonstrate need for aid received scholarships/grants; average award was $18,939. No-need awards available for academics, alumni affiliation, art, athletics, leadership, music/drama, religious affiliation, ROTC, state/district residency.
**Scholarships offered:** 61 full-time freshmen received athletic scholarships; average amount $38,662.
**Additional info:** 5-point comprehensive education financing plan includes financial aid packaging, money management counseling, debt management counseling, outside scholarship coordination, summer job-match program.

### FINANCIAL AID PROCEDURES
**Forms required:** FAFSA, CSS PROFILE, state aid form, institutional form.
**Dates and Deadlines:** Closing date 1/15. Applicants notified by 4/1; must reply by 5/1 or within 2 week(s) of notification.

**Transfers:** Closing date 6/1. For South Carolina Tuition Grant, must have earned 24 credits in previous year. For Life Scholarship, must have 3.0 cumulative GPA and 30 credits earned.

### CONTACT
Forrest Stuart, Associate Vice President for Financial Aid
3300 Poinsett Highway, Greenville, SC 29613
(864) 294-2204

## Greenville Technical College
Greenville, South Carolina
www.gvltec.edu                          Federal Code: 003991

**2-year public** community and technical college in large city.
**Enrollment:** 10,929 undergrads, 56% part-time. 1,548 full-time freshmen.
**Selectivity:** Open admission; but selective for some programs.

### BASIC COSTS (2015-2016)
**Tuition and fees:** $5,220; out-of-district residents $5,670; out-of-state residents $10,500.

### FINANCIAL AID PICTURE (2014-2015)
**Students with need:** 53% of average financial aid package awarded as scholarships/grants, 47% awarded as loans/jobs. Need-based aid available for part-time students. Work study available nights, weekends, and for part-time students.
**Students without need:** No-need awards available for academics, state/district residency.

### FINANCIAL AID PROCEDURES
**Forms required:** FAFSA.
**Dates and Deadlines:** Priority date 5/1; no closing date. Applicants notified on a rolling basis starting 5/1; must reply within 2 week(s) of notification.
**Transfers:** Priority date 10/1; no deadline. Applicants notified on a rolling basis starting 11/15; must reply within 2 week(s) of notification.

### CONTACT
Jeff Dennis, Financial Aid Director
PO Box 5616, Greenville, SC 29606-5616
(864) 250-8000

## Horry-Georgetown Technical College
Conway, South Carolina
www.hgtc.edu                            Federal Code: 004925

**2-year public** community and technical college in large town.
**Enrollment:** 6,354 undergrads, 53% part-time. 695 full-time freshmen.
**Selectivity:** Open admission; but selective for some programs.

### BASIC COSTS (2015-2016)
**Tuition and fees:** $3,960; out-of-district residents $4,902; out-of-state residents $6,918.
**Per-credit charge:** $154; out-of-district residents $193; out-of-state residents $278.

### FINANCIAL AID PICTURE (2014-2015)
**Students with need:** 61% of average financial aid package awarded as scholarships/grants, 39% awarded as loans/jobs. Need-based aid available for part-time students.
**Students without need:** No-need awards available for academics, state/district residency.
**Additional info:** Participates in South Carolina lottery tuition assistance program. Full-time technical college students who are state residents receive assistance for tuition not covered by federal or need-based grants.

### FINANCIAL AID PROCEDURES
**Forms required:** FAFSA.

**Dates and Deadlines:** Priority date 4/1; closing date 6/30. Applicants notified on a rolling basis starting 4/1.

### CONTACT
Susan Thompson, Director of Financial Aid and Veterans Affairs
PO Box 261966, Conway, SC 29528-6066
(843) 349-5251

## Lander University
Greenwood, South Carolina
www.lander.edu                          Federal Code: 003435

**4-year public** liberal arts and teachers college in large town.
**Enrollment:** 2,670 undergrads. 543 full-time freshmen.

### BASIC COSTS (2015-2016)
**Tuition and fees:** $10,752; out-of-state residents $20,370.
**Per-credit charge:** $448; out-of-state residents $849.
**Room and board:** $8,246.

### FINANCIAL AID PICTURE (2014-2015)
**Students with need:** Out of 497 full-time freshmen who applied for aid, 426 were judged to have need. Of these, 426 received aid, and 78 had their full need met. Average financial aid package met 70% of need; average scholarship/grant was $9,144; average loan was $3,198. For part-time students, average financial aid package was $6,367.
**Students without need:** 62 full-time freshmen who did not demonstrate need for aid received scholarships/grants; average award was $5,180. No-need awards available for academics, alumni affiliation, art, athletics, job skills, leadership, minority status, music/drama, religious affiliation, ROTC, state/district residency.
**Scholarships offered:** 16 full-time freshmen received athletic scholarships; average amount $8,416.

### FINANCIAL AID PROCEDURES
**Forms required:** FAFSA.
**Dates and Deadlines:** Priority date 11/1; closing date 8/1. Applicants notified on a rolling basis starting 12/15.

### CONTACT
Fred Hardin, Director of Financial Aid
Stanley Avenue, Greenwood, SC 29649-2099
(864) 388-8340

## Limestone College
Gaffney, South Carolina
www.limestone.edu                       Federal Code: 003436

**4-year private** liberal arts college in large town, affiliated with nondenominational tradition.
**Enrollment:** 1,227 undergrads. 427 full-time freshmen.
**Selectivity:** Admits 50 to 75% of applicants.

### BASIC COSTS (2016-2017)
**Tuition and fees:** $23,900.
**Per-credit charge:** $996.
**Room and board:** $8,550.

### FINANCIAL AID PICTURE (2015-2016)
**Students with need:** Out of 386 full-time freshmen who applied for aid, 355 were judged to have need. Of these, 354 received aid, and 39 had their full need met. Average financial aid package met 62% of need; average scholarship/grant was $16,185; average loan was $3,292. For part-time students, average financial aid package was $9,025.

**Students without need:** 65 full-time freshmen who did not demonstrate need for aid received scholarships/grants; average award was $6,783. No-need awards available for academics, art, athletics, job skills, leadership, music/drama, religious affiliation, ROTC, state/district residency.
**Scholarships offered: _Merit:_** Presidential Scholarship: full tuition; 1300 SAT, 3.5 GPA. Academic Dean Scholarships: partial tuition; 3.0 GPA. Founders Scholarships: partial tuition. McMillan Scholarships: 3.0 GPA or above. R.S. Campbell Scholarship: SAT above 1100; GPA 3.25 or above; 1 available. Leadership Scholarship: partial tuition. Drada Hoover Scholarship: SAT 1200 or higher exclusive of Writing; GPA 3.5, top 10% of graduating class. Founders scholarship for students with a 2.0 or higher. **_Athletic:_** 48 full-time freshmen received athletic scholarships; average amount $13,234.

## FINANCIAL AID PROCEDURES
**Forms required:** FAFSA.
**Dates and Deadlines:** Priority date 2/1; no closing date. Applicants notified on a rolling basis starting 1/15; must reply within 3 week(s) of notification.
**Transfers:** Priority date 5/1; no deadline. Applicants notified on a rolling basis; must reply within 3 week(s) of notification.

## CONTACT
Bobby Greer, Director of Financial Aid
1115 College Drive, Gaffney, SC 29340-3799
(800) 795-7151 ext. 8231

# Medical University of South Carolina
Charleston, South Carolina
www.musc.edu                    Federal Code: 003438

**Upper-division public** university in small city.
**Enrollment:** 205 undergrads.

## FINANCIAL AID PICTURE
**Students with need:** Need-based aid available for full-time and part-time students.

## FINANCIAL AID PROCEDURES
**Forms required:** FAFSA.
**Dates and Deadlines:** Priority date 10/3; closing date 3/4. Applicants notified on a rolling basis starting 4/30.

## CONTACT
Cecile Kamath, Director, Student Financial Aid
41 Bee Street, Charleston, SC 29425-2030
(843) 792-2536

# Midlands Technical College
Columbia, South Carolina
www.midlandstech.edu            Federal Code: 003993

**2-year public** community and technical college in large city.
**Enrollment:** 10,946 undergrads.
**Selectivity:** Open admission; but selective for some programs.

## BASIC COSTS (2015-2016)
**Tuition and fees:** $4,930; out-of-district residents $6,100; out-of-state residents $14,350.
**Additional info:** General education courses require additional $27 per-credit-hour fee, technical courses require additional $12 per-credit-hour fee.

## FINANCIAL AID PICTURE
**Students with need:** Need-based aid available for full-time and part-time students.
**Students without need:** This college awards aid only to students with need.

## FINANCIAL AID PROCEDURES
**Forms required:** FAFSA.
**Dates and Deadlines:** Priority date 4/15; no closing date. Applicants notified on a rolling basis; must reply within 2 week(s) of notification.

## CONTACT
Angela Williams, Director of Student Financial Services
PO Box 2408, Columbia, SC 29202
(803) 738-7792

# Morris College
Sumter, South Carolina
www.morris.edu                  Federal Code: 003439

**4-year private** liberal arts college in large town, affiliated with Baptist faith.
**Enrollment:** 774 undergrads, 2% part-time. 213 full-time freshmen.
**Selectivity:** Admits over 75% of applicants.

## BASIC COSTS (2015-2016)
**Tuition and fees:** $11,454.
**Per-credit charge:** $471.
**Room and board:** $5,216.

## FINANCIAL AID PICTURE (2015-2016)
**Students with need:** Average financial aid package met 67% of need; average scholarship/grant was $7,455; average loan was $5,446. For part-time students, average financial aid package was $7,642.
**Students without need:** No-need awards available for academics, athletics, music/drama, state/district residency.
**Scholarships offered:** Presidential Scholarship; $750-$2,500; rank in the first quarter of graduating class; larger awards available to salutatorians ($2,000) and valedictorians ($2,500); awards renewable up to 4 years if student maintains B average and excellent citizenship record. Luns C. Richardson Endowed Scholarship; $4,500; for full-time students with 3.5 college prep GPA, exceptional letters of recommendation from at least 2 classroom teachers and one guidance counselor, principal, or assistant principal.

## FINANCIAL AID PROCEDURES
**Forms required:** FAFSA, institutional form.
**Dates and Deadlines:** Priority date 3/31; closing date 3/31. Applicants notified on a rolling basis starting 4/1; must reply within 2 week(s) of notification.
**Transfers:** Must reply within 2 week(s) of notification.

## CONTACT
Sandra Gibson, Financial Aid Officer
100 West College Street, Sumter, SC 29150-3599
(803) 934-3238

# Newberry College
Newberry, South Carolina
www.newberry.edu                Federal Code: 003440

**4-year private** liberal arts college in large town, affiliated with Evangelical Lutheran Church in America.
**Enrollment:** 1,048 undergrads, 2% part-time. 277 full-time freshmen.
**Selectivity:** Admits 50 to 75% of applicants.

## BASIC COSTS (2015-2016)
**Tuition and fees:** $25,000.
**Per-credit charge:** $735.
**Room and board:** $9,550.
**Additional info:** Tuition at time of enrollment locked for 4 years.

## FINANCIAL AID PICTURE (2014-2015)
**Students with need:** Out of 264 full-time freshmen who applied for aid, 245 were judged to have need. Of these, 245 received aid, and 23 had their

full need met. Average financial aid package met 69% of need; average scholarship/grant was $20,370; average loan was $3,488. For part-time students, average financial aid package was $3,804.

**Students without need:** 31 full-time freshmen who did not demonstrate need for aid received scholarships/grants; average award was $11,656. No-need awards available for academics, alumni affiliation, athletics, music/drama, ROTC.

**Scholarships offered:** 22 full-time freshmen received athletic scholarships; average amount $11,777.

### FINANCIAL AID PROCEDURES
**Forms required:** FAFSA.

**Dates and Deadlines:** Priority date 3/15; no closing date. Applicants notified on a rolling basis starting 3/15; must reply by 8/20.

**Transfers:** No deadline. Applicants notified on a rolling basis.

### CONTACT
Danielle Bell, Director of Financial Aid
2100 College Street, Newberry, SC 29108
(803) 321-5127

## North Greenville University
Tigerville, South Carolina
www.ngu.edu                    Federal Code: 003441

**4-year private** university and liberal arts college in rural community, affiliated with Southern Baptist Convention.

**Enrollment:** 2,289 undergrads, 3% part-time. 528 full-time freshmen.

**Selectivity:** Admits 50 to 75% of applicants.

### BASIC COSTS (2015-2016)
**Tuition and fees:** $16,290.

**Per-credit charge:** $390.

**Room and board:** $9,640.

### FINANCIAL AID PICTURE
**Students with need:** Need-based aid available for full-time and part-time students.

**Students without need:** No-need awards available for academics, athletics, leadership, music/drama, religious affiliation, state/district residency.

### FINANCIAL AID PROCEDURES
**Forms required:** FAFSA.

**Dates and Deadlines:** Priority date 6/1; closing date 6/30. Applicants notified on a rolling basis starting 8/1; must reply within 2 week(s) of notification.

**Transfers:** No deadline.

### CONTACT
Mike Jordan, Director of Financial Aid
PO Box 1892, Tigerville, SC 29688-1892
(864) 977-7050

## Orangeburg-Calhoun Technical College
Orangeburg, South Carolina
www.octech.edu                    Federal Code: 006815

**2-year public** community and technical college in large town.

**Enrollment:** 2,399 undergrads.

**Selectivity:** Open admission; but selective for some programs.

### BASIC COSTS (2015-2016)
**Tuition and fees:** $4,970; out-of-district residents $5,930; out-of-state residents $7,706.

**Per-credit charge:** $160; out-of-district residents $200; out-of-state residents $274.

### FINANCIAL AID PICTURE
**Students with need:** Need-based aid available for full-time and part-time students.

**Students without need:** This college awards aid only to students with need.

**Scholarships offered:** College Foundation Scholarship; full academic tuition; for high school valedictorians and salutatorians.

### FINANCIAL AID PROCEDURES
**Forms required:** FAFSA, institutional form.

**Dates and Deadlines:** Priority date 6/4; no closing date. Applicants notified on a rolling basis starting 5/1; must reply within 2 week(s) of notification.

**Transfers:** Priority date 6/1. Financial aid transcripts required of mid-year transfers prior to disbursement of aid.

### CONTACT
Bobbie Felder, Director of Institutional Research
3250 St. Matthews Road, Orangeburg, SC 29118-8222
(803) 535-1368

## Piedmont Technical College
Greenwood, South Carolina
www.ptc.edu                    Federal Code: 003992

**2-year public** community and technical college in small city.

**Enrollment:** 4,369 undergrads, 59% part-time. 601 full-time freshmen.

**Selectivity:** Open admission; but selective for some programs.

### BASIC COSTS (2015-2016)
**Tuition and fees:** $4,955; out-of-district residents $5,645; out-of-state residents $7,145.

**Per-credit charge:** $159; out-of-district residents $182; out-of-state residents $232.

### FINANCIAL AID PICTURE (2014-2015)
**Students with need:** 99% of average financial aid package awarded as scholarships/grants, 1% awarded as loans/jobs. Need-based aid available for part-time students. Work study available nights.

**Students without need:** This college awards aid only to students with need.

### FINANCIAL AID PROCEDURES
**Forms required:** FAFSA.

**Dates and Deadlines:** Priority date 5/1; no closing date. Applicants notified on a rolling basis starting 6/1; must reply within 2 week(s) of notification.

### CONTACT
Missy Perry, Director of Financial Aid
620 North Emerald Road, Greenwood, SC 29646
(864) 941-8365

## Presbyterian College
Clinton, South Carolina
www.presby.edu                    Federal Code: 003445

**4-year private** pharmacy and liberal arts college in small town, affiliated with Presbyterian Church (USA).

**Enrollment:** 963 undergrads, 1% part-time. 262 full-time freshmen.

**Selectivity:** Admits 50 to 75% of applicants.

### BASIC COSTS (2015-2016)
**Tuition and fees:** $36,130.

**Per-credit charge:** $1,384.

**Room and board:** $9,750.

### FINANCIAL AID PICTURE (2015-2016)
**Students with need:** Out of 257 full-time freshmen who applied for aid, 214 were judged to have need. Of these, 214 received aid. Average financial

aid package met 28% of need; average scholarship/grant was $28,790; average loan was $3,660. For part-time students, average financial aid package was $2,377.

**Students without need:** 48 full-time freshmen who did not demonstrate need for aid received scholarships/grants; average award was $16,100. No-need awards available for academics, alumni affiliation, art, athletics, job skills, leadership, minority status, music/drama, religious affiliation, ROTC, state/district residency.

**Scholarships offered:** *Merit:* Academic and leadership scholarships: applications by December 5; number and amounts awarded vary; music awards based on audition. *Athletic:* 19 full-time freshmen received athletic scholarships; average amount $20,825.

### FINANCIAL AID PROCEDURES

**Forms required:** FAFSA.

**Dates and Deadlines:** Priority date 3/15; closing date 6/30. Applicants notified on a rolling basis starting 3/15; must reply by 7/1.

**Transfers:** No deadline. Applicants notified on a rolling basis starting 5/1; must reply within 1 week(s) of notification.

### CONTACT

Linda McAnnally, Director of Financial Aid
503 South Broad Street, Clinton, SC 29325-2865
(864) 833-8290

## South Carolina State University
Orangeburg, South Carolina
www.scsu.edu                    Federal Code: 003446

**4-year public** university in large town.
**Enrollment:** 2,410 undergrads, 8% part-time. 490 full-time freshmen.
**Selectivity:** Admits over 75% of applicants.

### BASIC COSTS (2015-2016)
**Tuition and fees:** $10,088; out-of-state residents $19,856.
**Per-credit charge:** $420; out-of-state residents $827.
**Room and board:** $9,402.

### FINANCIAL AID PICTURE (2014-2015)
**Students with need:** 60% of average financial aid package awarded as scholarships/grants, 40% awarded as loans/jobs. Need-based aid available for part-time students.
**Students without need:** No-need awards available for academics, alumni affiliation, athletics.

### FINANCIAL AID PROCEDURES
**Forms required:** FAFSA, state aid form, institutional form.
**Dates and Deadlines:** Closing date 5/1. Applicants notified on a rolling basis starting 5/15; must reply by 7/1 or within 4 week(s) of notification.
**Transfers:** Must reply by 7/1 or within 2 week(s) of notification. Must provide documentation on amount of state aid received, and which semesters it was received, prior to transfer.

### CONTACT
CC Jackson, Director of Financial Aid
300 College Street NE, Orangeburg, SC 29117
(803) 536-8221

## Southern Wesleyan University
Central, South Carolina
www.swu.edu                    Federal Code: 003422

**4-year private** university and liberal arts college in small town, affiliated with Wesleyan Church.
**Enrollment:** 1,400 undergrads.

### BASIC COSTS (2015-2016)
**Tuition and fees:** $23,470.
**Per-credit charge:** $930.
**Room and board:** $8,020.

### FINANCIAL AID PICTURE
**Students with need:** Need-based aid available for full-time students. Work study available nights, weekends, and for part-time students.
**Students without need:** No-need awards available for academics, athletics, music/drama.

### FINANCIAL AID PROCEDURES
**Forms required:** FAFSA, institutional form.
**Dates and Deadlines:** Priority date 3/31; closing date 6/30. Applicants notified on a rolling basis starting 2/1; must reply within 2 week(s) of notification.
**Transfers:** Priority date 4/1. Applicants notified on a rolling basis starting 2/1; must reply within 2 week(s) of notification.

### CONTACT
Kim Jenerette, Financial Aid Director
PO Box 1020, Central, SC 29630-1020
(800) 289-1292

## Spartanburg Community College
Spartanburg, South Carolina
www.sccsc.edu                    Federal Code: 003994

**2-year public** community and technical college in small city.
**Enrollment:** 4,163 undergrads, 47% part-time. 689 full-time freshmen.
**Selectivity:** Open admission; but selective for some programs.

### BASIC COSTS (2015-2016)
**Tuition and fees:** $4,092; out-of-district residents $5,110; out-of-state residents $8,372.
**Per-credit charge:** $171; out-of-district residents $213; out-of-state residents $349.

### FINANCIAL AID PICTURE
**Students with need:** Need-based aid available for full-time and part-time students.
**Students without need:** No-need awards available for academics.
**Additional info:** Participates in South Carolina lottery tuition assistance program. Full-time technical college students who are state residents receive assistance for tuition not covered by federal or need-based grants.

### FINANCIAL AID PROCEDURES
**Forms required:** FAFSA.
**Dates and Deadlines:** Priority date 2/28; closing date 5/1. Applicants notified on a rolling basis starting 5/1.
**Transfers:** No deadline. Applicants notified on a rolling basis starting 8/15.

### CONTACT
Jeff Boyle, Director of Financial Aid
Box 4386, Spartanburg, SC 29305-4386
(864) 592-4810

## Spartanburg Methodist College
Spartanburg, South Carolina
www.smcsc.edu                    Federal Code: 003447

**2-year private** junior and liberal arts college in small city, affiliated with United Methodist Church.
**Enrollment:** 769 undergrads, 1% part-time. 440 full-time freshmen.
**Selectivity:** Admits 50 to 75% of applicants.

**BASIC COSTS (2016-2017)**

**Tuition and fees:** $17,500.

**Room and board:** $9,100.

**Additional info:** Tuition/fee waivers available for adults, unemployed or children of unemployed.

**FINANCIAL AID PICTURE**

**Students with need:** Need-based aid available for full-time and part-time students. Work study available weekends and for part-time students.

**Students without need:** No-need awards available for academics, athletics, religious affiliation.

**Scholarships offered:** Milliken Scholars; $4,100. Camak Scholars; $3,500. Trustee Scholars; $3,000. Presidential Scholars; $2,400.

**FINANCIAL AID PROCEDURES**

**Forms required:** FAFSA, state aid form.

**Dates and Deadlines:** Priority date 6/30; closing date 8/22. Applicants notified on a rolling basis starting 3/1; must reply within 2 week(s) of notification.

**Transfers:** No deadline. Applicants notified on a rolling basis starting 3/1; must reply within 2 week(s) of notification. To be eligible for financial aid, full time students must pass the equivalent of 12 hours.

**CONTACT**

Kendra Strange, Director of Financial Aid

1000 Powell Mill Road, Spartanburg, SC 29301-5899

(864) 587-4298

## Technical College of the Lowcountry
Beaufort, South Carolina
www.tcl.edu                    Federal Code: 009910

**2-year public** community and technical college in small city.

**Enrollment:** 2,332 undergrads.

**Selectivity:** Open admission; but selective for some programs.

**BASIC COSTS (2015-2016)**

**Tuition and fees:** $5,200; out-of-district residents $5,950; out-of-state residents $11,320.

**Per-credit charge:** $166; out-of-district residents $191; out-of-state residents $370.

**FINANCIAL AID PICTURE**

**Students with need:** Need-based aid available for full-time and part-time students.

**Students without need:** This college awards aid only to students with need.

**Additional info:** State lottery aid may be available to South Carolina residents who take 6 credit hours or more.

**FINANCIAL AID PROCEDURES**

**Forms required:** FAFSA.

**CONTACT**

Cleo Martin, Director of Financial Aid

921 South Ribaut Road, Beaufort, SC 29901-1288

(843) 525-8337

## Tri-County Technical College
Pendleton, South Carolina
www.tctc.edu                    Federal Code: 004926

**2-year public** community and technical college in small town.

**Enrollment:** 5,322 undergrads.

**Selectivity:** Open admission; but selective for some programs.

**BASIC COSTS (2015-2016)**

**Tuition and fees:** $4,959; out-of-district residents $6,459; out-of-state residents $11,019.

**Per-credit charge:** $165; out-of-district residents $215; out-of-state residents $367.

**FINANCIAL AID PICTURE**

**Students with need:** Need-based aid available for full-time and part-time students. Work study available nights.

**Students without need:** No-need awards available for academics, state/district residency.

**Scholarships offered:** General and departmental scholarships; amounts vary; some have special qualification criteria, such as student's career field or place of residency; more than 125 awarded.

**Additional info:** Deadline for application to institutional scholarships 4/2.

**FINANCIAL AID PROCEDURES**

**Forms required:** FAFSA.

**Dates and Deadlines:** Priority date 4/1; closing date 7/30. Applicants notified on a rolling basis starting 6/15; must reply within 2 week(s) of notification.

**Transfers:** No deadline. Applicants notified on a rolling basis starting 6/1.

**CONTACT**

Sarah Dowd, Director of Financial Aid

PO Box 587, Pendleton, SC 29670

(864) 646-1650

## Trident Technical College
Charleston, South Carolina
www.tridenttech.edu              Federal Code: 004920

**2-year public** community and technical college in large city.

**Enrollment:** 12,892 undergrads.

**Selectivity:** Open admission; but selective for some programs.

**BASIC COSTS (2015-2016)**

**Tuition and fees:** $4,070; out-of-district residents $4,512; out-of-state residents $7,676.

**Per-credit charge:** $168; out-of-district residents $187; out-of-state residents $319.

**FINANCIAL AID PICTURE**

**Students with need:** Need-based aid available for full-time and part-time students. Work study available nights, weekends, and for part-time students.

**Students without need:** No-need awards available for academics, alumni affiliation, state/district residency.

**FINANCIAL AID PROCEDURES**

**Forms required:** FAFSA.

**Dates and Deadlines:** Applicants notified on a rolling basis; must reply within 6 week(s) of notification.

**Transfers:** No deadline. Applicants notified on a rolling basis; must reply within 6 week(s) of notification.

**CONTACT**

Ellen Green, Director of Financial Aid/Veterans Assistance

PO Box 118067, AM-M, Charleston, SC 29423-8067

(843) 574-6147

## University of South Carolina: Aiken
Aiken, South Carolina
http://web.usca.edu/             Federal Code: 003449

**4-year public** university and liberal arts college in large town.

**Enrollment:** 3,082 undergrads, 16% part-time. 595 full-time freshmen.

**Selectivity:** Admits 50 to 75% of applicants.

## BASIC COSTS (2015-2016)
**Tuition and fees:** $9,878; out-of-state residents $19,472.
**Per-credit charge:** $400; out-of-state residents $799.
**Room and board:** $7,290.

## FINANCIAL AID PICTURE (2014-2015)
**Students with need:** Out of 593 full-time freshmen who applied for aid, 432 were judged to have need. Of these, 428 received aid, and 95 had their full need met. Average financial aid package met 67% of need; average scholarship/grant was $6,686; average loan was $3,114. For part-time students, average financial aid package was $7,712.
**Students without need:** 26 full-time freshmen who did not demonstrate need for aid received scholarships/grants; average award was $2,782. No-need awards available for academics, alumni affiliation, art, athletics, leadership, minority status, music/drama, state/district residency.
**Scholarships offered:** 26 full-time freshmen received athletic scholarships; average amount $3,693.
**Additional info:** Students must be enrolled at least half time and be able to present documentation which verifies eligibility to work in the U.S.

## FINANCIAL AID PROCEDURES
**Forms required:** FAFSA.
**Dates and Deadlines:** Priority date 3/15; no closing date. Applicants notified on a rolling basis starting 4/20; must reply within 2 week(s) of notification.
**Transfers:** Financial aid transcripts from previous institutions required.

## CONTACT
Linda Aubrey-Higgins, Director of Financial Aid
471 University Parkway, Aiken, SC 29801-6399
(803) 641-3476

# University of South Carolina: Beaufort
Bluffton, South Carolina
www.uscb.edu                    Federal Code: 003450

**4-year public** university and liberal arts college in large town.
**Enrollment:** 1,966 undergrads, 13% part-time. 506 full-time freshmen.
**Selectivity:** Admits 50 to 75% of applicants.

## BASIC COSTS (2015-2016)
**Tuition and fees:** $9,848; out-of-state residents $19,982.
**Per-credit charge:** $394; out-of-state residents $817.
**Room and board:** $8,297.
**Additional info:** Active duty military pay reduced tuition. Some courses require additional fees.

## FINANCIAL AID PICTURE
**Students with need:** Need-based aid available for full-time and part-time students. Work study available nights, weekends, and for part-time students.
**Students without need:** No-need awards available for academics, art, athletics, leadership, religious affiliation, state/district residency.

## FINANCIAL AID PROCEDURES
**Forms required:** FAFSA.
**Dates and Deadlines:** Priority date 3/1; no closing date. Applicants notified on a rolling basis starting 5/1; must reply within 2 week(s) of notification.
**Transfers:** No deadline. Applicants notified on a rolling basis starting 5/1.

## CONTACT
Patricia Greene, Director and VA Coordinator of Financial Aid
One University Boulevard, Bluffton, SC 29909
(843) 521-3104

# University of South Carolina: Columbia
Columbia, South Carolina
www.sc.edu                    Federal Code: 003448

**4-year public** university in small city.
**Enrollment:** 24,899 undergrads.
**Selectivity:** Admits 50 to 75% of applicants.

## BASIC COSTS (2015-2016)
**Tuition and fees:** $11,482; out-of-state residents $30,298.
**Per-credit charge:** $461; out-of-state residents $1,246.
**Room and board:** $9,872.
**Additional info:** Health professions including public health, nursing and social work require additional fees.

## FINANCIAL AID PICTURE
**Students with need:** Need-based aid available for full-time and part-time students. Work study available nights, weekends, and for part-time students.
**Students without need:** No-need awards available for academics, alumni affiliation, art, athletics, job skills, leadership, minority status, music/drama, religious affiliation, ROTC, state/district residency.

## FINANCIAL AID PROCEDURES
**Forms required:** FAFSA.
**Dates and Deadlines:** Priority date 4/1; no closing date. Applicants notified on a rolling basis starting 4/1.
**Transfers:** Applicants notified on a rolling basis starting 4/1.

## CONTACT
Edgar Miller, Director of Financial Aid and Scholarships
Office of Undergraduate Admissions, Columbia, SC 29208
(803) 777-8134

# University of South Carolina: Salkehatchie
Allendale, South Carolina
uscsalkehatchie.sc.edu                    Federal Code: 003454

**2-year public** branch campus college in rural community.
**Enrollment:** 730 full-time undergrads.

## BASIC COSTS (2015-2016)
**Tuition and fees:** $6,878; out-of-state residents $9,980.
**Per-credit charge:** $270; out-of-state residents $400.

## FINANCIAL AID PICTURE
**Students with need:** Need-based aid available for full-time and part-time students. Work study available nights, weekends, and for part-time students.
**Students without need:** No-need awards available for academics.

## FINANCIAL AID PROCEDURES
**Forms required:** FAFSA.
**Dates and Deadlines:** Priority date 4/30; no closing date. Applicants notified on a rolling basis starting 6/1.

## CONTACT
Julie Hadwin, Director of Financial Aid
PO Box 617, Allendale, SC 29810
(803) 584-3446

# University of South Carolina: Sumter
Sumter, South Carolina
www.uscsumter.edu                    Federal Code: 003426

**2-year public** branch campus college in small city.
**Enrollment:** 650 undergrads.

**BASIC COSTS (2015-2016)**

**Tuition and fees:** $6,886; out-of-state residents $16,606.
**Per-credit charge:** $262; out-of-state residents $656.

**FINANCIAL AID PICTURE**

**Students with need:** Need-based aid available for full-time and part-time students. Work study available nights, weekends, and for part-time students.
**Students without need:** This college awards aid only to students with need.

**FINANCIAL AID PROCEDURES**

**Forms required:** FAFSA.
**Dates and Deadlines:** Priority date 4/15; no closing date. Applicants notified on a rolling basis starting 4/16; must reply within 2 week(s) of notification.

**CONTACT**

200 Miller Road, Sumter, SC 29150-2498
(803) 938-3766

# University of South Carolina: Union

Union, South Carolina
uscunion.sc.edu                    Federal Code: 004927

**2-year public** branch campus and liberal arts college in small town.
**Enrollment:** 430 full-time undergrads.

**BASIC COSTS (2015-2016)**

**Tuition and fees:** $6,886; out-of-state residents $16,606.
**Per-credit charge:** $262; out-of-state residents $656.

**FINANCIAL AID PICTURE**

**Students with need:** Work study available nights, weekends, and for part-time students.
**Students without need:** This college awards aid only to students with need.

**FINANCIAL AID PROCEDURES**

**Forms required:** FAFSA.
**Dates and Deadlines:** Priority date 4/15; no closing date. Applicants notified on a rolling basis starting 7/15; must reply within 2 week(s) of notification.

**CONTACT**

Bobby Holcombe, Financial Aid Director
PO Drawer 729, Union, SC 29379
(864) 429-8728

# University of South Carolina: Upstate

Spartanburg, South Carolina
www.uscupstate.edu                 Federal Code: 006951

**4-year public** university in small city.
**Enrollment:** 5,153 undergrads.

**BASIC COSTS (2015-2016)**

**Tuition and fees:** $10,818; out-of-state residents $21,468.
**Per-credit charge:** $432; out-of-state residents $876.
**Room and board:** $7,848.

**FINANCIAL AID PICTURE**

**Students with need:** Need-based aid available for full-time and part-time students. Work study available nights, weekends, and for part-time students.
**Students without need:** No-need awards available for academics, athletics, minority status, ROTC, state/district residency.
**Additional info:** Out-of-state students who are recipients of financial aid may qualify for out-of-state fee waiver. Educational benefits available to veterans and children of deceased/disabled veterans.

**FINANCIAL AID PROCEDURES**

**Forms required:** FAFSA, institutional form.

**Dates and Deadlines:** Priority date 3/1; closing date 7/15. Applicants notified on a rolling basis starting 5/17; must reply within 2 week(s) of notification.
**Transfers:** Students eligible for financial assistance for total of 5 years or 10 full-time semesters at all post-secondary institutions attended for the bachelor's degree, and 5 full-time semesters of enrollment for associate's degree in nursing.

**CONTACT**

Bonnie Carson, Director of Financial Aid
800 University Way, Spartanburg, SC 29303
(864) 503-5974

# Voorhees College

Denmark, South Carolina
www.voorhees.edu                   Federal Code: 003455

**4-year private** liberal arts college in small town, affiliated with Episcopal Church.
**Enrollment:** 434 undergrads, 3% part-time. 104 full-time freshmen.
**Selectivity:** Admits over 75% of applicants.

**BASIC COSTS (2015-2016)**

**Tuition and fees:** $12,630.
**Per-credit charge:** $484.
**Room and board:** $7,346.

**FINANCIAL AID PICTURE (2014-2015)**

**Students with need:** Need-based aid available for full-time and part-time students. Work study available nights, weekends, and for part-time students.

**FINANCIAL AID PROCEDURES**

**Forms required:** FAFSA, institutional form.
**Dates and Deadlines:** Priority date 4/15; no closing date. Applicants notified on a rolling basis starting 3/1; must reply within 2 week(s) of notification.

**CONTACT**

Augusta Kitchen, Director of Student Financial Aid
213 Wiggins Road, Denmark, SC 29042
(803) 780-1159

# Williamsburg Technical College

Kingstree, South Carolina
www.wiltech.edu                    Federal Code: 009322

**2-year public** community and technical college in small town.
**Enrollment:** 686 undergrads, 71% part-time. 44 full-time freshmen.
**Selectivity:** Open admission.

**BASIC COSTS (2015-2016)**

**Tuition and fees:** $4,008; out-of-district residents $4,128; out-of-state residents $7,608.

**FINANCIAL AID PICTURE (2014-2015)**

**Students with need:** Need-based aid available for part-time students. Work study available nights.
**Students without need:** No-need awards available for academics, leadership, minority status, state/district residency.
**Additional info:** Tuition waivers for children of war veterans.

**FINANCIAL AID PROCEDURES**

**Forms required:** FAFSA.
**Dates and Deadlines:** Applicants notified on a rolling basis starting 7/1; must reply within 4 week(s) of notification.

**CONTACT**

601 Martin Luther King Avenue, Kingstree, SC 29556-4197
(843) 355-4166

## Winthrop University

Rock Hill, South Carolina
www.winthrop.edu                    Federal Code: 003456

**4-year public** university in small city.
**Enrollment:** 4,786 undergrads, 5% part-time. 1,018 full-time freshmen.
**Selectivity:** Admits 50 to 75% of applicants.

### BASIC COSTS (2015-2016)

**Tuition and fees:** $14,456; out-of-state residents $27,704.
**Per-credit charge:** $590; out-of-state residents $1,142.
**Room and board:** $8,320.

### FINANCIAL AID PICTURE (2014-2015)

**Students with need:** Out of 947 full-time freshmen who applied for aid, 822 were judged to have need. Of these, 821 received aid, and 150 had their full need met. Average financial aid package met 63% of need; average scholarship/grant was $9,441; average loan was $3,382. For part-time students, average financial aid package was $4,259.
**Students without need:** 97 full-time freshmen who did not demonstrate need for aid received scholarships/grants; average award was $6,161. No-need awards available for academics, art, athletics, leadership, music/drama.
**Scholarships offered:** *Merit:* Academic scholarships; $1,500-full tuition and board; awarded to approximately one-third of entering freshman class each year. *Athletic:* 22 full-time freshmen received athletic scholarships; average amount $6,886.

### FINANCIAL AID PROCEDURES

**Forms required:** FAFSA.
**Dates and Deadlines:** Priority date 3/15; no closing date. Applicants notified on a rolling basis starting 4/1; must reply within 2 week(s) of notification.
**Transfers:** Transfer students are not eligible for academic scholarship their first year.

### CONTACT

Michelle Hare, Director, Office of Financial Aid
701 Oakland Avenue, Rock Hill, SC 29733
(803) 323-2189

## Wofford College

Spartanburg, South Carolina
www.wofford.edu                     Federal Code: 003457

**4-year private** liberal arts college in small city, affiliated with United Methodist Church.
**Enrollment:** 1,596 undergrads, 2% part-time. 442 full-time freshmen.
**Selectivity:** Admits 50 to 75% of applicants.

### BASIC COSTS (2015-2016)

**Tuition and fees:** $38,705.
**Room and board:** $11,180.

### FINANCIAL AID PICTURE (2015-2016)

**Students with need:** Out of 373 full-time freshmen who applied for aid, 282 were judged to have need. Of these, 281 received aid, and 124 had their full need met. Average financial aid package met 90% of need; average scholarship/grant was $29,962; average loan was $3,371. For part-time students, average financial aid package was $20,828.
**Students without need:** 104 full-time freshmen who did not demonstrate need for aid received scholarships/grants; average award was $15,172. No-need awards available for academics, art, athletics, job skills, leadership, minority status, music/drama, religious affiliation, ROTC, state/district residency.
**Scholarships offered:** 54 full-time freshmen received athletic scholarships; average amount $22,591.

### FINANCIAL AID PROCEDURES

**Forms required:** FAFSA.

**Dates and Deadlines:** Priority date 3/1; no closing date. Applicants notified on a rolling basis starting 3/15.

### CONTACT

Carolyn Sparks, Director of Financial Aid
429 North Church Street, Spartanburg, SC 29303-3663
(864) 597-4160

## York Technical College

Rock Hill, South Carolina
www.yorktech.edu                    Federal Code: 003996

**2-year public** community and technical college in large town.
**Enrollment:** 4,416 undergrads.
**Selectivity:** Open admission; but selective for some programs.

### BASIC COSTS (2015-2016)

**Tuition and fees:** $5,020; out-of-district residents $5,470; out-of-state residents $11,350.
**Per-credit charge:** $161; out-of-district residents $176; out-of-state residents $372.

### FINANCIAL AID PICTURE

**Students with need:** Need-based aid available for full-time and part-time students. Work study available nights.
**Students without need:** No-need awards available for academics, leadership, state/district residency.

### FINANCIAL AID PROCEDURES

**Forms required:** FAFSA.
**Dates and Deadlines:** Priority date 6/1; no closing date. Applicants notified on a rolling basis starting 4/1; must reply within 2 week(s) of notification.
**Transfers:** No deadline. Applicants notified on a rolling basis starting 4/1; must reply within 2 week(s) of notification.

### CONTACT

Angela Fowler, Director of Financial Aid
452 South Anderson Road, Rock Hill, SC 29730
(803) 327-8005

# South Dakota

## Augustana University

Sioux Falls, South Dakota
www.augie.edu                       Federal Code: 003458

**4-year private** university in small city, affiliated with Evangelical Lutheran Church in America.
**Enrollment:** 1,563 undergrads, 4% part-time. 367 full-time freshmen.
**Selectivity:** Admits 50 to 75% of applicants.

### BASIC COSTS (2015-2016)

**Tuition and fees:** $29,730.
**Per-credit charge:** $450.
**Room and board:** $7,404.
**Additional info:** Tuition/fee waivers available for minority students.

### FINANCIAL AID PICTURE (2015-2016)

**Students with need:** Out of 290 full-time freshmen who applied for aid, 246 were judged to have need. Of these, 246 received aid, and 54 had their full need met. Average financial aid package met 100% of need; average scholarship/grant was $22,705; average loan was $4,806. For part-time students, average financial aid package was $9,437.

**Students without need:** 118 full-time freshmen who did not demonstrate need for aid received scholarships/grants; average award was $16,119. No-need awards available for academics, alumni affiliation, art, athletics, leadership, minority status, music/drama, religious affiliation, ROTC, state/district residency.

**Scholarships offered: *Merit:*** Distinguished Scholars Scholarships: Trustees and Presidential Scholarships for students with a 27 ACT or above and 3.5 GPA and above. ProMusica scholarships, ProDramatis scholarships, ProArtis Scholarships; Fryxell Scholarships for journalism/English majors. ***Athletic:*** 44 full-time freshmen received athletic scholarships; average amount $11,132.

### FINANCIAL AID PROCEDURES
**Forms required:** FAFSA.
**Dates and Deadlines:** Priority date 3/1; no closing date. Applicants notified on a rolling basis starting 4/1; must reply within 4 week(s) of notification.
**Transfers:** No deadline. Applicants notified on a rolling basis starting 4/1; must reply within 4 week(s) of notification.

### CONTACT
Tresse Evenson, Director of Financial Aid
2001 South Summit Avenue, Sioux Falls, SD 57197-9990
(605) 274-5216

## Black Hills State University
Spearfish, South Dakota
www.bhsu.edu                          Federal Code: 003459

**4-year public** university in large town.
**Enrollment:** 2,858 undergrads.

### BASIC COSTS (2015-2016)
**Tuition and fees:** $8,004; out-of-state residents $10,092.
**Per-credit charge:** $139; out-of-state residents $209.
**Room and board:** $6,458.

### FINANCIAL AID PICTURE
**Students with need:** Need-based aid available for full-time and part-time students.
**Students without need:** This college awards aid only to students with need.

### FINANCIAL AID PROCEDURES
**Forms required:** FAFSA.
**Dates and Deadlines:** Closing date 2/15. Applicants notified on a rolling basis starting 5/15; must reply within 3 week(s) of notification.

### CONTACT
Deb Henriksen, Director of Financial Aid
1200 University Street, Spearfish, SD 57799
(605) 642-6581

## Dakota State University
Madison, South Dakota
www.dsu.edu                           Federal Code: 003463

**4-year public** university in small town.
**Enrollment:** 1,896 undergrads, 34% part-time. 269 full-time freshmen.
**Selectivity:** Admits over 75% of applicants.

### BASIC COSTS (2015-2016)
**Tuition and fees:** $8,754; out-of-state residents $10,842.
**Per-credit charge:** $139; out-of-state residents $209.
**Room and board:** $6,060.

### FINANCIAL AID PICTURE (2014-2015)
**Students with need:** Out of 247 full-time freshmen who applied for aid, 197 were judged to have need. Of these, 195 received aid, and 18 had their

full need met. Average financial aid package met 79% of need; average scholarship/grant was $4,377; average loan was $3,427. For part-time students, average financial aid package was $5,810.
**Students without need:** 39 full-time freshmen who did not demonstrate need for aid received scholarships/grants; average award was $4,679. No-need awards available for academics, alumni affiliation, art, athletics, leadership, minority status, music/drama, state/district residency.
**Scholarships offered:** 35 full-time freshmen received athletic scholarships; average amount $2,450.
**Additional info:** Application deadline for grants and scholarships 3/1. No deadline for loan and job applications.

### FINANCIAL AID PROCEDURES
**Forms required:** FAFSA.
**Dates and Deadlines:** Priority date 3/1; no closing date. Applicants notified on a rolling basis starting 4/1; must reply within 2 week(s) of notification.
**Transfers:** Priority date 4/1; no deadline. Applicants notified on a rolling basis starting 4/1; must reply within 2 week(s) of notification.

### CONTACT
Denise Grayson, Financial Aid Director
820 North Washington Avenue, Madison, SD 57042
(605) 256-5152

## Dakota Wesleyan University
Mitchell, South Dakota
www.dwu.edu                           Federal Code: 003461

**4-year private** university and liberal arts college in large town, affiliated with United Methodist Church.
**Enrollment:** 795 undergrads.

### BASIC COSTS (2015-2016)
**Tuition and fees:** $24,800.
**Room and board:** $6,800.

### FINANCIAL AID PICTURE
**Students with need:** Need-based aid available for full-time and part-time students. Work study available nights, weekends, and for part-time students.
**Students without need:** No-need awards available for academics, alumni affiliation, art, athletics, leadership, minority status, music/drama, religious affiliation.

### FINANCIAL AID PROCEDURES
**Forms required:** FAFSA.
**Dates and Deadlines:** Priority date 4/1; no closing date. Applicants notified on a rolling basis starting 3/1; must reply within 2 week(s) of notification.
**Transfers:** No deadline. Applicants notified on a rolling basis starting 3/1; must reply within 2 week(s) of notification.

### CONTACT
Kristy O'Kief, Director of Financial Aid
1200 West University Avenue, Mitchell, SD 57301-4398
(605) 995-2667

## Globe University: Sioux Falls
Sioux Falls, South Dakota
www.globeuniversity.edu               Federal Code: 004642

**2-year for-profit** career college in small city.
**Enrollment:** 138 undergrads.
**Selectivity:** Open admission.

### BASIC COSTS (2015-2016)
**Tuition and fees:** $18,702.
**Per-credit charge:** $390.

## FINANCIAL AID PICTURE

**Students with need:** Need-based aid available for full-time and part-time students.

## FINANCIAL AID PROCEDURES

**Forms required:** FAFSA, institutional form.

**Dates and Deadlines:** Applicants notified on a rolling basis starting 7/1; must reply within 2 week(s) of notification.

## CONTACT

Elizabeth Augustine, Financial Aid Manager
5101 South Broadband Lane, Sioux Falls, SD 57108
(605) 977-0705

# Kilian Community College

Sioux Falls, South Dakota
www.kilian.edu                    Federal Code: 015000

**2-year private** community college in small city.
**Enrollment:** 145 undergrads, 90% part-time. 3 full-time freshmen.
**Selectivity:** Open admission.

## BASIC COSTS (2015-2016)

**Tuition and fees:** $10,650.
**Per-credit charge:** $355.

## FINANCIAL AID PICTURE

**Students with need:** Need-based aid available for full-time and part-time students. Work study available nights.
**Students without need:** No-need awards available for academics, leadership.

## FINANCIAL AID PROCEDURES

**Forms required:** FAFSA, institutional form.
**Dates and Deadlines:** Applicants notified on a rolling basis starting 7/1; must reply within 2 week(s) of notification.
**Transfers:** No deadline. Applicants notified on a rolling basis starting 7/1; must reply within 2 week(s) of notification.

## CONTACT

Mary Klockman, Director of Financial Aid
300 East 6th Street, Sioux Falls, SD 57103-7020
(605) 221-3105

# Lake Area Technical Institute

Watertown, South Dakota
www.lakeareatech.edu               Federal Code: 005309

**2-year public** technical college in large town.
**Enrollment:** 1,691 undergrads, 9% part-time. 465 full-time freshmen.
**Selectivity:** Open admission; but selective for some programs.

## BASIC COSTS (2015-2016)

**Tuition and fees:** $6,089; out-of-state residents $6,089.
**Per-credit charge:** $109.

## FINANCIAL AID PICTURE (2014-2015)

**Students with need:** Out of 463 full-time freshmen who applied for aid, 380 were judged to have need. Of these, 378 received aid, and 29 had their full need met. Average financial aid package met 54% of need; average scholarship/grant was $4,383; average loan was $4,024. For part-time students, average financial aid package was $5,357.
**Students without need:** This college awards aid only to students with need.

## FINANCIAL AID PROCEDURES

**Forms required:** FAFSA.

**Dates and Deadlines:** Priority date 4/1; no closing date. Applicants notified on a rolling basis starting 5/1.
**Transfers:** No deadline. Applicants notified on a rolling basis.

## CONTACT

Marlene Seeklander, Financial Aid Director
PO Box 730, Watertown, SD 57201
(605) 882-5284

# Mitchell Technical Institute

Mitchell, South Dakota
www.mitchelltech.edu              Federal Code: 008284

**2-year public** technical college in large town.
**Enrollment:** 1,096 undergrads, 23% part-time. 347 full-time freshmen.
**Selectivity:** Admits 50 to 75% of applicants.

## BASIC COSTS (2015-2016)

**Tuition and fees:** $5,880; out-of-state residents $5,880.
**Per-credit charge:** $109.

## FINANCIAL AID PICTURE (2015-2016)

**Students with need:** Average financial aid package met 52% of need; average scholarship/grant was $4,463; average loan was $2,965. For part-time students, average financial aid package was $4,952.
**Students without need:** No-need awards available for academics, alumni affiliation, job skills.
**Scholarships offered:** Star Student program; $1,000 the first semester (and up to $3,000 total); to students with 24 ACT and 3.0 GPA.

## FINANCIAL AID PROCEDURES

**Forms required:** FAFSA.
**Dates and Deadlines:** Applicants notified on a rolling basis; must reply within 3 week(s) of notification.
**Transfers:** No deadline. Applicants notified on a rolling basis.

## CONTACT

Morgan Huber, Financial Aid Coordinator
1800 E Spruce Street, Mitchell, SD 57301
(605) 995-3052

# Mount Marty College

Yankton, South Dakota
www.mtmc.edu                      Federal Code: 003465

**4-year private** liberal arts college in large town, affiliated with Roman Catholic Church.
**Enrollment:** 590 undergrads, 17% part-time. 101 full-time freshmen.
**Selectivity:** Admits 50 to 75% of applicants.

## BASIC COSTS (2015-2016)

**Tuition and fees:** $24,306.
**Room and board:** $7,326.

## FINANCIAL AID PICTURE (2015-2016)

**Students with need:** Out of 96 full-time freshmen who applied for aid, 82 were judged to have need. Of these, 82 received aid, and 34 had their full need met. Average financial aid package met 88% of need; average scholarship/grant was $16,975; average loan was $5,115. For part-time students, average financial aid package was $12,388.
**Students without need:** 13 full-time freshmen who did not demonstrate need for aid received scholarships/grants; average award was $10,540. No-need awards available for academics, athletics, leadership, music/drama, religious affiliation.
**Scholarships offered:** 6 full-time freshmen received athletic scholarships; average amount $4,000.

**Additional info:** Prestige scholarships application deadline 2/1.

**FINANCIAL AID PROCEDURES**

**Forms required:** FAFSA, institutional form.

**Dates and Deadlines:** Priority date 3/1; no closing date. Applicants notified on a rolling basis starting 3/15; must reply within 2 week(s) of notification.

**Transfers:** No deadline. Applicants notified on a rolling basis; must reply within 2 week(s) of notification.

**CONTACT**

Kenneth Kocer, Director of Financial Assistance

1105 West Eighth Street, Yankton, SD 57078

(605) 668-1589

## National American University: Rapid City

Rapid City, South Dakota

www.national.edu                    Federal Code: 004057

**4-year for-profit** business and technical college in small city.

**Enrollment:** 1,479 undergrads.

**Selectivity:** Open admission; but selective for some programs.

**BASIC COSTS (2015-2016)**

**Tuition and fees:** $15,750.

**Per-credit charge:** $330.

**Additional info:** Additional fees may apply.

**FINANCIAL AID PICTURE**

**Students with need:** Need-based aid available for full-time and part-time students. Work study available nights, weekends, and for part-time students.

**Students without need:** This college awards aid only to students with need.

**Scholarships offered:** Reduced tuition to military students and military dependents with a valid military ID card.

**FINANCIAL AID PROCEDURES**

**Forms required:** FAFSA, institutional form.

**Dates and Deadlines:** Applicants notified on a rolling basis; must reply within 4 week(s) of notification.

**CONTACT**

Cheryl Bullinger, Director of Financial Aid

5301 S. Hwy 16, Rapid City, SD 57701

## Northern State University

Aberdeen, South Dakota

www.northern.edu                    Federal Code: 003466

**4-year public** university and liberal arts college in large town.

**Enrollment:** 1,693 undergrads.

**BASIC COSTS (2015-2016)**

**Tuition and fees:** $7,977; out-of-state residents $10,065.

**Per-credit charge:** $139; out-of-state residents $209.

**Room and board:** $7,088.

**FINANCIAL AID PICTURE**

**Students with need:** Need-based aid available for full-time and part-time students. Work study available nights, weekends, and for part-time students.

**Students without need:** No-need awards available for academics, art, athletics, leadership, minority status, music/drama.

**Scholarships offered:** WolfPACT Scholarship; $5,000-$12,000; based on ACT.

**FINANCIAL AID PROCEDURES**

**Forms required:** FAFSA.

**Dates and Deadlines:** Priority date 3/1; no closing date. Applicants notified on a rolling basis starting 4/15; must reply within 2 week(s) of notification.

**Transfers:** Applicants notified by 4/15; must reply within 2 week(s) of notification. Financial aid transcript(s) required from all schools previously attended.

**CONTACT**

Sharon Kienow, Director of Student Financial Assistance

1200 South Jay Street, Aberdeen, SD 57401-7198

(605) 626-2640

## Presentation College

Aberdeen, South Dakota

www.presentation.edu                    Federal Code: 003467

**4-year private** business and health science college in large town, affiliated with Roman Catholic Church.

**Enrollment:** 750 undergrads.

**BASIC COSTS (2015-2016)**

**Tuition and fees:** $17,990.

**Room and board:** $8,690.

**FINANCIAL AID PICTURE**

**Students with need:** Need-based aid available for full-time and part-time students. Work study available nights, weekends, and for part-time students.

**FINANCIAL AID PROCEDURES**

**Forms required:** FAFSA.

**Dates and Deadlines:** Priority date 4/1; no closing date. Applicants notified on a rolling basis starting 5/1; must reply within 2 week(s) of notification.

**CONTACT**

Janel Wagner, Financial Aid Director

1500 North Main Street, Aberdeen, SD 57401

(605) 229-8429

## Sinte Gleska University

Mission, South Dakota

www.sintegleska.edu                    Federal Code: 014303

**4-year public** university and liberal arts college in rural community.

**Enrollment:** 690 undergrads.

**Selectivity:** Open admission.

**BASIC COSTS (2015-2016)**

**Tuition and fees:** $3,640.

**Per-credit charge:** $110.

**FINANCIAL AID PICTURE**

**Students with need:** Need-based aid available for full-time and part-time students.

**FINANCIAL AID PROCEDURES**

**Forms required:** FAFSA.

**CONTACT**

William Hay, Director of Financial Aid

Box 105, Mission, SD 57555

## Sisseton Wahpeton College

Sisseton, South Dakota

www.swc.tc                    Federal Code: 016080

**2-year public** technical college in large town.

**Enrollment:** 127 undergrads, 35% part-time. 24 full-time freshmen.

**Selectivity:** Open admission.

## BASIC COSTS (2015-2016)
**Tuition and fees:** $3,940.
**Per-credit charge:** $115.
**Additional info:** Non-ISC funded students pay $125 per-credit-hour.

## FINANCIAL AID PICTURE
**Students with need:** Need-based aid available for full-time and part-time students.

## FINANCIAL AID PROCEDURES
**Forms required:** FAFSA.
**Dates and Deadlines:** Priority date 12/15; no closing date. Applicants notified on a rolling basis.

## CONTACT
Sylvan Flute, Financial Aid Director
BIA 700, Box 689, Sisseton, SD 57262-0689
(605) 698-3966 ext. 1183

# South Dakota School of Mines and Technology
Rapid City, South Dakota
www.sdsmt.edu                    Federal Code: 003470

**4-year public** university in small city.
**Enrollment:** 2,359 undergrads, 13% part-time. 593 full-time freshmen.
**Selectivity:** Admits over 75% of applicants.

## BASIC COSTS (2015-2016)
**Tuition and fees:** $8,763; out-of-state residents $11,823.
**Per-credit charge:** $151; out-of-state residents $346.
**Room and board:** $7,300.

## FINANCIAL AID PICTURE (2014-2015)
**Students with need:** Out of 570 full-time freshmen who applied for aid, 340 were judged to have need. Of these, 340 received aid, and 120 had their full need met. Average financial aid package met 76% of need; average scholarship/grant was $4,526; average loan was $3,612. For part-time students, average financial aid package was $10,868.
**Students without need:** 161 full-time freshmen who did not demonstrate need for aid received scholarships/grants; average award was $2,673. No-need awards available for academics, athletics, leadership, minority status, ROTC.
**Scholarships offered:** Presidential Scholarship; $1,000-$4,000; 5 awarded. Surbeck Scholars; $7,000; 2 awarded. All based on ACT/SAT, GPA, and class rank. Number of awards may vary from year to year depending on availability of funding.
**Additional info:** Closing date for scholarship applications 2/1.

## FINANCIAL AID PROCEDURES
**Forms required:** FAFSA.
**Dates and Deadlines:** Applicants notified on a rolling basis starting 4/15; must reply within 3 week(s) of notification.
**Transfers:** Must reply by 5/1 or within 6 week(s) of notification.

## CONTACT
David Martin, Director of Financial Aid
501 East St. Joseph Street, Rapid City, SD 57701
(605) 394-2274

# South Dakota State University
Brookings, South Dakota
www.sdstate.edu                    Federal Code: 003471

**4-year public** university in large town.
**Enrollment:** 9,835 undergrads, 13% part-time. 2,116 full-time freshmen.

**Selectivity:** Admits over 75% of applicants.

## BASIC COSTS (2015-2016)
**Tuition and fees:** $8,172; out-of-state residents $10,343.
**Per-credit charge:** $145; out-of-state residents $217.
**Room and board:** $7,462.

## FINANCIAL AID PICTURE (2014-2015)
**Students with need:** Out of 1,806 full-time freshmen who applied for aid, 1,366 were judged to have need. Of these, 1,360 received aid, and 148 had their full need met. Average financial aid package met 44% of need; average scholarship/grant was $3,585; average loan was $3,493. Need-based aid available for part-time students.
**Students without need:** 418 full-time freshmen who did not demonstrate need for aid received scholarships/grants; average award was $1,791. No-need awards available for academics, alumni affiliation, art, athletics, leadership, minority status, music/drama, state/district residency.
**Scholarships offered:** 92 full-time freshmen received athletic scholarships; average amount $9,187.

## FINANCIAL AID PROCEDURES
**Forms required:** FAFSA.
**Dates and Deadlines:** Priority date 3/10; no closing date. Applicants notified on a rolling basis starting 4/1; must reply within 3 week(s) of notification.
**Transfers:** No deadline. Applicants notified on a rolling basis starting 4/1; must reply within 3 week(s) of notification.

## CONTACT
Carolyn Halgerson, Director of Financial Aid
Box 2201 SAD 200, Brookings, SD 57007-0649
(605) 688-4695

# Southeast Technical Institute
Sioux Falls, South Dakota
www.southeasttech.edu                    Federal Code: 008285

**2-year public** technical college in small city.
**Enrollment:** 1,899 undergrads, 32% part-time. 367 full-time freshmen.
**Selectivity:** Open admission; but selective for some programs.

## BASIC COSTS (2015-2016)
**Tuition and fees:** $6,600; out-of-state residents $6,600.
**Per-credit charge:** $109.

## FINANCIAL AID PICTURE (2014-2015)
**Students with need:** 27% of average financial aid package awarded as scholarships/grants, 73% awarded as loans/jobs. Need-based aid available for part-time students.
**Students without need:** This college awards aid only to students with need.

## FINANCIAL AID PROCEDURES
**Forms required:** FAFSA.
**Dates and Deadlines:** Priority date 5/1; no closing date. Applicants notified on a rolling basis starting 5/1; must reply within 3 week(s) of notification.

## CONTACT
Lynette Grabowska, Financial Aid Officer
2320 North Career Avenue, Sioux Falls, SD 57107
(605) 367-7867

# University of Sioux Falls
Sioux Falls, South Dakota
www.usiouxfalls.edu                    Federal Code: 003469

**4-year private** university and liberal arts college in small city, affiliated with American Baptist Churches in the USA.

**Enrollment:** 951 undergrads.

**BASIC COSTS (2015-2016)**
**Tuition and fees:** $26,240.
**Room and board:** $6,900.
**Additional info:** Tuition/fee waivers available for adults.

**FINANCIAL AID PICTURE**
**Students with need:** Need-based aid available for full-time and part-time students. Work study available nights, weekends, and for part-time students.
**Students without need:** No-need awards available for academics, art, athletics, music/drama.

**FINANCIAL AID PROCEDURES**
**Forms required:** FAFSA.
**Dates and Deadlines:** Priority date 3/1; no closing date. Applicants notified on a rolling basis starting 3/1; must reply within 2 week(s) of notification.
**Transfers:** Applicants notified on a rolling basis; must reply within 2 week(s) of notification.

**CONTACT**
Karrie Morgan, Director of Financial Aid
1101 West 22nd Street, Sioux Falls, SD 57105-1699
(605) 331-6623

## University of South Dakota
Vermillion, South Dakota
www.usd.edu                    Federal Code: 003474

**4-year public** university in large town.
**Enrollment:** 6,331 undergrads.

**BASIC COSTS (2015-2016)**
**Tuition and fees:** $8,457; out-of-state residents $11,337.
**Per-credit charge:** $145; out-of-state residents $217.05.
**Room and board:** $7,605.

**FINANCIAL AID PICTURE**
**Students with need:** Need-based aid available for full-time students.
**Students without need:** No-need awards available for academics, art, athletics, leadership, minority status, music/drama, ROTC.

**FINANCIAL AID PROCEDURES**
**Forms required:** FAFSA.
**Dates and Deadlines:** Priority date 3/15; no closing date. Applicants notified on a rolling basis starting 5/5.
**Transfers:** Priority date 5/1.

**CONTACT**
Julie Pier, Director of Student Financial Aid
414 East Clark Street, Vermillion, SD 57069-2390
(605) 677-5446

## Western Dakota Technical Institute
Rapid City, South Dakota
www.wdt.edu                    Federal Code: 010170

**2-year public** technical college in small city.
**Enrollment:** 810 undergrads.
**Selectivity:** Open admission; but selective for some programs.

**BASIC COSTS (2015-2016)**
**Tuition and fees:** $5,850; out-of-state residents $5,850.
**Per-credit charge:** $109.

**FINANCIAL AID PICTURE**
**Students with need:** Need-based aid available for full-time and part-time students. Work study available nights, weekends, and for part-time students.

**FINANCIAL AID PROCEDURES**
**Forms required:** FAFSA.
**Dates and Deadlines:** Priority date 4/20; no closing date. Applicants notified on a rolling basis starting 4/30; must reply within 2 week(s) of notification.

**CONTACT**
Starla Russell, Manager of Financial Aid
800 Mickelson Drive, Rapid City, SD 57703
(605) 718-2416

# Tennessee

## American Baptist College
Nashville, Tennessee
www.abcnash.edu                    Federal Code: 010460

**4-year private** Bible and liberal arts college in large city, affiliated with Baptist faith.
**Enrollment:** 160 undergrads.

**BASIC COSTS (2015-2016)**
**Tuition and fees:** $11,894.
**Room only:** $6,240.

**FINANCIAL AID PICTURE**
**Students with need:** Need-based aid available for full-time students.

**FINANCIAL AID PROCEDURES**
**Forms required:** FAFSA.
**Dates and Deadlines:** Priority date 5/1; no closing date. Applicants notified on a rolling basis; must reply within 2 week(s) of notification.
**Transfers:** Priority date 1/15; closing date 5/1. Applicants notified on a rolling basis starting 6/1; must reply by 7/1.

**CONTACT**
1800 Baptist World Center Drive, Nashville, TN 37207
(615) 687-6896 ext. 2227

## Aquinas College
Nashville, Tennessee
www.aquinascollege.edu                    Federal Code: 003477

**4-year private** liberal arts college in very large city, affiliated with Roman Catholic Church.
**Enrollment:** 335 undergrads.

**BASIC COSTS (2015-2016)**
**Tuition and fees:** $20,550.
**Room and board:** $8,900.

**FINANCIAL AID PICTURE**
**Students with need:** Need-based aid available for full-time and part-time students. Work study available nights, weekends, and for part-time students.
**Students without need:** No-need awards available for academics, alumni affiliation, leadership, religious affiliation.

**FINANCIAL AID PROCEDURES**
**Forms required:** FAFSA.
**Dates and Deadlines:** Priority date 2/15; no closing date. Applicants notified on a rolling basis starting 2/15; must reply within 2 week(s) of notification.
**Transfers:** No deadline. Applicants notified on a rolling basis; must reply within 2 week(s) of notification. Transfer students may receive a scholarship based on GPA.

**CONTACT**

Cynthia Piana, Senior Associate Director of Financial Aid

4210 Harding Pike, Nashville, TN 37205-2086

(615) 297-7545 ext. 442

## Austin Peay State University

Clarksville, Tennessee

www.apsu.edu                    Federal Code: 003478

**4-year public** university and liberal arts college in small city.

**Enrollment:** 8,915 undergrads, 24% part-time. 1,184 full-time freshmen.

**Selectivity:** Admits over 75% of applicants.

**BASIC COSTS (2015-2016)**

**Tuition and fees:** $7,801; out-of-state residents $23,371.

**Per-credit charge:** $252; out-of-state residents $870.

**Room and board:** $9,550.

**FINANCIAL AID PICTURE (2014-2015)**

**Students with need:** Out of 1,142 full-time freshmen who applied for aid, 959 were judged to have need. Of these, 949 received aid. For part-time students, average financial aid package was $7,876.

**Students without need:** 164 full-time freshmen who did not demonstrate need for aid received scholarships/grants; average award was $5,279. No-need awards available for academics, art, athletics, leadership, music/drama, ROTC, state/district residency.

**Scholarships offered:** 19 full-time freshmen received athletic scholarships; average amount $7,513.

**FINANCIAL AID PROCEDURES**

**Forms required:** FAFSA.

**Dates and Deadlines:** Priority date 2/3; no closing date. Applicants notified on a rolling basis starting 4/7.

**CONTACT**

Donna Price, Director of Financial Aid

PO Box 4548, Clarksville, TN 37044-4548

(931) 221-7907

## Belmont University

Nashville, Tennessee

www.belmont.edu                  Federal Code: 003479

**4-year private** university in very large city, affiliated with Christian Church.

**Enrollment:** 5,933 undergrads, 5% part-time. 1,392 full-time freshmen.

**Selectivity:** Admits over 75% of applicants.

**BASIC COSTS (2015-2016)**

**Tuition and fees:** $30,000.

**Per-credit charge:** $1,090.

**Room and board:** $10,970.

**FINANCIAL AID PICTURE (2014-2015)**

**Students with need:** Out of 1,138 full-time freshmen who applied for aid, 802 were judged to have need. Of these, 802 received aid, and 92 had their full need met. Average financial aid package met 59% of need; average scholarship/grant was $15,453; average loan was $3,584. For part-time students, average financial aid package was $6,702.

**Students without need:** 402 full-time freshmen who did not demonstrate need for aid received scholarships/grants; average award was $6,800. No-need awards available for academics, art, athletics, leadership, music/drama, religious affiliation, state/district residency.

**Scholarships offered:** 25 full-time freshmen received athletic scholarships; average amount $17,396.

**FINANCIAL AID PROCEDURES**

**Forms required:** FAFSA.

**Dates and Deadlines:** Priority date 3/1; no closing date. Applicants notified on a rolling basis starting 3/15; must reply by 5/1 or within 2 week(s) of notification.

**Transfers:** Applicants notified on a rolling basis starting 3/1; must reply by 5/1 or within 2 week(s) of notification. Scholarships available.

**CONTACT**

Patricia Smedley, Director of Student Financial Services

1900 Belmont Boulevard, Nashville, TN 37212-3757

(615) 460-6403

## Bethel University

McKenzie, Tennessee

www.bethelu.edu                  Federal Code: 003480

**4-year private** university and liberal arts college in small town, affiliated with Cumberland Presbyterian Church.

**Enrollment:** 5,236 undergrads.

**Selectivity:** Admits over 75% of applicants.

**BASIC COSTS (2015-2016)**

**Tuition and fees:** $15,714.

**Per-credit charge:** $440.

**Room and board:** $8,782.

**FINANCIAL AID PICTURE (2014-2015)**

**Students with need:** Need-based aid available for part-time students. Work study available nights, weekends, and for part-time students.

**Students without need:** No-need awards available for academics, athletics, music/drama, religious affiliation, state/district residency.

**FINANCIAL AID PROCEDURES**

**Forms required:** FAFSA, institutional form.

**Dates and Deadlines:** Priority date 3/3; closing date 6/30. Applicants notified on a rolling basis starting 1/1; must reply within 2 week(s) of notification.

**Transfers:** No deadline. Financial aid transcripts from previously attended institutions required.

**CONTACT**

Janie Burns, University Director of Financial Aid

325 Cherry Avenue, McKenzie, TN 38201

(731) 352-6418

## Bryan College: Dayton

Dayton, Tennessee

www.bryan.edu                    Federal Code: 003536

**4-year private** liberal arts college in small town, affiliated with interdenominational tradition.

**Enrollment:** 999 undergrads, 19% part-time. 156 full-time freshmen.

**Selectivity:** Admits less than 50% of applicants.

**BASIC COSTS (2015-2016)**

**Tuition and fees:** $23,300.

**Room and board:** $6,690.

**Additional info:** Tuition/fee waivers available for adults, minority students, unemployed or children of unemployed.

**FINANCIAL AID PICTURE (2015-2016)**

**Students with need:** Out of 144 full-time freshmen who applied for aid, 113 were judged to have need. Of these, 113 received aid, and 75 had their full need met. Average financial aid package met 50% of need; average scholarship/grant was $15,050; average loan was $3,300. For part-time students, average financial aid package was $22,100.

**Students without need:** No-need awards available for academics, alumni affiliation, art, athletics, job skills, leadership, music/drama.

## FINANCIAL AID PROCEDURES
**Forms required:** FAFSA.
**Dates and Deadlines:** Priority date 1/31; no closing date. Applicants notified on a rolling basis starting 1/1; must reply within 2 week(s) of notification.

## CONTACT
David Haggard, Director of Financial Aid
721 Bryan Drive, Dayton, TN 37321-7000
(423) 775-7339

## Carson-Newman University
Jefferson City, Tennessee
www.cn.edu                            Federal Code: 003481

**4-year private** liberal arts college in small town, affiliated with Southern Baptist Convention.
**Enrollment:** 1,698 undergrads, 2% part-time. 491 full-time freshmen.
**Selectivity:** Admits 50 to 75% of applicants.

### BASIC COSTS (2015-2016)
**Tuition and fees:** $25,360.
**Per-credit charge:** $1,010.
**Room and board:** $7,640.
**Additional info:** Tuition/fee waivers available for adults, minority students.

### FINANCIAL AID PICTURE (2014-2015)
**Students with need:** Out of 420 full-time freshmen who applied for aid, 420 were judged to have need. Of these, 420 received aid, and 92 had their full need met. Average financial aid package met 81% of need; average scholarship/grant was $19,124; average loan was $2,713. For part-time students, average financial aid package was $7,538.
**Students without need:** 43 full-time freshmen who did not demonstrate need for aid received scholarships/grants; average award was $10,886. No-need awards available for academics, art, athletics, leadership, music/drama, religious affiliation, ROTC, state/district residency.
**Scholarships offered:** 24 full-time freshmen received athletic scholarships; average amount $12,637.

### FINANCIAL AID PROCEDURES
**Forms required:** FAFSA.
**Dates and Deadlines:** Priority date 2/1; no closing date. Applicants notified on a rolling basis starting 2/1; must reply by 5/1.

### CONTACT
Danette Seale, Director of Financial Aid
1646 Russell Avenue, Jefferson City, TN 37760
(865) 471-3247

## Chattanooga State Community College
Chattanooga, Tennessee
www.chattanoogastate.edu          Federal Code: 003998

**2-year public** community and technical college in small city.
**Enrollment:** 9,374 undergrads.
**Selectivity:** Open admission; but selective for some programs.

### BASIC COSTS (2015-2016)
**Tuition and fees:** $4,153; out-of-state residents $16,123.

### FINANCIAL AID PICTURE
**Students with need:** Need-based aid available for full-time and part-time students. Work study available nights, weekends, and for part-time students.
**Students without need:** No-need awards available for state/district residency.

### FINANCIAL AID PROCEDURES
**Forms required:** FAFSA.

**Dates and Deadlines:** Priority date 6/1; no closing date. Applicants notified on a rolling basis starting 4/1; must reply within 2 week(s) of notification.

## CONTACT
Julae Grosz, Director of Financial Aid
4501 Amnicola Highway, Chattanooga, TN 37406
(423) 697-4402

## Christian Brothers University
Memphis, Tennessee
www.cbu.edu                          Federal Code: 003482

**4-year private** university in very large city, affiliated with Roman Catholic Church.
**Enrollment:** 1,408 undergrads, 8% part-time. 354 full-time freshmen.
**Selectivity:** Admits less than 50% of applicants.

### BASIC COSTS (2015-2016)
**Tuition and fees:** $30,186.
**Per-credit charge:** $1,025.
**Room and board:** $6,920.
**Additional info:** Tuition/fee waivers available for adults.

### FINANCIAL AID PICTURE (2014-2015)
**Students with need:** Out of 354 full-time freshmen who applied for aid, 285 were judged to have need. Of these, 283 received aid, and 70 had their full need met. Average financial aid package met 82% of need; average scholarship/grant was $21,450; average loan was $3,024. For part-time students, average financial aid package was $6,028.
**Students without need:** 69 full-time freshmen who did not demonstrate need for aid received scholarships/grants; average award was $17,055. No-need awards available for academics, alumni affiliation, athletics, music/drama, state/district residency.
**Scholarships offered:** 15 full-time freshmen received athletic scholarships; average amount $8,648.
**Additional info:** ROTC scholarships available to qualified applicants.

### FINANCIAL AID PROCEDURES
**Forms required:** FAFSA.
**Dates and Deadlines:** Priority date 2/15; no closing date. Applicants notified on a rolling basis starting 3/1; must reply within 2 week(s) of notification.
**Transfers:** No deadline. Applicants notified on a rolling basis starting 3/1; must reply within 2 week(s) of notification.

### CONTACT
John Lewis, Director of Financial Aid
650 East Parkway South, Memphis, TN 38104-5519
(901) 321-3305

## Cleveland State Community College
Cleveland, Tennessee
www.clevelandstatecc.edu          Federal Code: 003999

**2-year public** community college in small city.
**Enrollment:** 2,387 undergrads, 34% part-time. 777 full-time freshmen.
**Selectivity:** Open admission; but selective for some programs.

### BASIC COSTS (2015-2016)
**Tuition and fees:** $4,127; out-of-state residents $15,917.
**Per-credit charge:** $152; out-of-state residents $627.

### FINANCIAL AID PICTURE (2015-2016)
**Students with need:** Out of 532 full-time freshmen who applied for aid, 361 were judged to have need. Of these, 361 received aid, and 59 had their full need met. Average financial aid package met 63% of need; average

scholarship/grant was $2,498; average loan was $1,479. For part-time students, average financial aid package was $3,329.

**Students without need:** 171 full-time freshmen who did not demonstrate need for aid received scholarships/grants; average award was $1,970. No-need awards available for athletics, minority status.

**Scholarships offered:** 12 full-time freshmen received athletic scholarships; average amount $683.

### FINANCIAL AID PROCEDURES

**Forms required:** FAFSA, institutional form.

**Dates and Deadlines:** Priority date 5/15; no closing date. Applicants notified on a rolling basis starting 7/1; must reply within 2 week(s) of notification.

**Transfers:** Closing date 7/27.

### CONTACT

Jamie Hamby, Director of Financial Aid
3535 Adkisson Drive, Cleveland, TN 37320-3570
(423) 472-7141 ext. 215

## Columbia State Community College
Columbia, Tennessee
www.columbiastate.edu          Federal Code: 003483

**2-year public** community college in large town.
**Enrollment:** 4,271 undergrads.
**Selectivity:** Open admission; but selective for some programs.

### BASIC COSTS (2015-2016)
**Tuition and fees:** $4,099; out-of-state residents $16,069.

### FINANCIAL AID PICTURE (2014-2015)
**Students with need:** 75% of average financial aid package awarded as scholarships/grants, 25% awarded as loans/jobs. Need-based aid available for part-time students.

**Students without need:** No-need awards available for academics, athletics, state/district residency.

### FINANCIAL AID PROCEDURES
**Forms required:** FAFSA, institutional form.
**Dates and Deadlines:** Priority date 3/15; closing date 7/31. Applicants notified on a rolling basis starting 5/15; must reply within 2 week(s) of notification.

### CONTACT
Cherry Johnson, Director of Financial Aid
1665 Hampshire Pike, Columbia, TN 38401
(931) 540-8267

## Cumberland University
Lebanon, Tennessee
www.cumberland.edu          Federal Code: 003485

**4-year private** university and liberal arts college in large town.
**Enrollment:** 1,142 undergrads.

### BASIC COSTS (2015-2016)
**Tuition and fees:** $21,210.
**Per-credit charge:** $840.
**Room and board:** $8,000.

### FINANCIAL AID PICTURE
**Students with need:** Need-based aid available for full-time and part-time students.
**Students without need:** No-need awards available for academics, art, athletics, music/drama.

### FINANCIAL AID PROCEDURES
**Forms required:** FAFSA, institutional form.

**Dates and Deadlines:** Priority date 2/1; no closing date. Applicants notified on a rolling basis starting 5/1; must reply within 2 week(s) of notification.
**Transfers:** Priority date 2/15. Applicants notified on a rolling basis starting 5/1.

### CONTACT
Beatrice LaChance, Executive Director of Enrollment Services
1 Cumberland Square, Lebanon, TN 37087
(615) 444-2562 ext. 1249

## Daymar Institute: Nashville
Nashville, Tennessee
www.daymarinstitute.edu          Federal Code: 004934

**2-year for-profit** career college in very large city.
**Enrollment:** 410 undergrads.
**Selectivity:** Open admission; but selective for some programs.

### BASIC COSTS (2015-2016)
**Additional info:** Diploma programs: $22,000-$26,500. Associate programs: $33,000.

### FINANCIAL AID PICTURE
**Students with need:** Need-based aid available for full-time and part-time students. Work study available nights.
**Students without need:** This college awards aid only to students with need.
**Additional info:** Financial aid form for in-state applicants must be filed before 5/1.

### FINANCIAL AID PROCEDURES
**Forms required:** FAFSA.
**Dates and Deadlines:** Applicants notified on a rolling basis.
**Transfers:** Students must notify Tennessee Student Assistance Corporation of institutional change before appropriate deadlines.

### CONTACT
Janie Rager, Director of Financial Services
340 & 283 Plus Park at Pavilion Boulevard, Nashville, TN 37217
(615) 361-7555

## Dyersburg State Community College
Dyersburg, Tennessee
www.dscc.edu          Federal Code: 006835

**2-year public** community college in large town.
**Enrollment:** 1,930 undergrads, 37% part-time. 531 full-time freshmen.
**Selectivity:** Open admission; but selective for some programs.

### BASIC COSTS (2015-2016)
**Tuition and fees:** $4,127; out-of-state residents $16,097.
**Per-credit charge:** $152; out-of-state residents $627.

### FINANCIAL AID PICTURE (2014-2015)
**Students with need:** 76% of average financial aid package awarded as scholarships/grants, 24% awarded as loans/jobs. Need-based aid available for part-time students.
**Students without need:** No-need awards available for academics, alumni affiliation, athletics, job skills, leadership, minority status, music/drama, state/district residency.

### FINANCIAL AID PROCEDURES
**Forms required:** FAFSA.
**Dates and Deadlines:** Priority date 3/1; no closing date. Applicants notified on a rolling basis starting 3/1; must reply within 2 week(s) of notification.
**Transfers:** Priority date 3/1.

**CONTACT**
Sandra Rockett, Director of Financial Aid
1510 Lake Road, Dyersburg, TN 38024
(731) 286-3238

## East Tennessee State University
Johnson City, Tennessee
www.etsu.edu              Federal Code: 003487

**4-year public** university in small city.
**Enrollment:** 10,960 undergrads, 14% part-time. 1,976 full-time freshmen.
**Selectivity:** Admits over 75% of applicants.

**BASIC COSTS (2015-2016)**
**Tuition and fees:** $8,477; out-of-state residents $26,147.
**Per-credit charge:** $271; out-of-state residents $972.
**Room and board:** $9,280.

**FINANCIAL AID PICTURE**
**Students with need:** Need-based aid available for full-time and part-time students. Work study available nights, weekends, and for part-time students.
**Students without need:** No-need awards available for academics, alumni affiliation, art, athletics, leadership, minority status, music/drama, religious affiliation, ROTC, state/district residency.
**Additional info:** Housing costs payable by installment.

**FINANCIAL AID PROCEDURES**
**Forms required:** FAFSA.
**Dates and Deadlines:** Priority date 4/15; no closing date. Applicants notified on a rolling basis starting 4/15; must reply within 3 week(s) of notification.

**CONTACT**
Margaret Miller, Director of Financial Aid
ETSU Box 70731, Johnson City, TN 37614
(423) 439-4300

## Fisk University
Nashville, Tennessee
www.fisk.edu              Federal Code: 003490

**4-year private** liberal arts college in very large city.
**Enrollment:** 805 undergrads.
**Selectivity:** Admits over 75% of applicants.

**BASIC COSTS (2015-2016)**
**Tuition and fees:** $21,480.
**Room and board:** $10,276.

**FINANCIAL AID PICTURE**
**Students with need:** Need-based aid available for full-time and part-time students.
**Students without need:** This college awards aid only to students with need.

**FINANCIAL AID PROCEDURES**
**Forms required:** FAFSA.
**Dates and Deadlines:** Priority date 3/1; closing date 7/1. Applicants notified on a rolling basis starting 4/1; must reply within 2 week(s) of notification.

**CONTACT**
Mary Chambliss, Director of Financial Aid
1000 Seventeenth Avenue North, Nashville, TN 37208-3051
(615) 329-8585

## Freed-Hardeman University
Henderson, Tennessee
www.fhu.edu              Federal Code: 003492

**4-year private** university and liberal arts college in small town, affiliated with Church of Christ.
**Enrollment:** 1,260 undergrads, 3% part-time. 422 full-time freshmen.
**Selectivity:** Admits over 75% of applicants.

**BASIC COSTS (2015-2016)**
**Tuition and fees:** $21,500.
**Per-credit charge:** $700.
**Room and board:** $7,580.
**Additional info:** There are NO additional fees, such as parking, lab, freshmen orientation, or graduation fees. Tuition/fee waivers available for minority students.

**FINANCIAL AID PICTURE**
**Students with need:** Need-based aid available for full-time and part-time students. Work study available nights, weekends, and for part-time students.
**Students without need:** No-need awards available for academics, art, athletics, leadership, minority status, music/drama.

**FINANCIAL AID PROCEDURES**
**Forms required:** FAFSA, institutional form.
**Dates and Deadlines:** Priority date 2/1; no closing date. Applicants notified on a rolling basis starting 3/10; must reply within 4 week(s) of notification.

**CONTACT**
Summer Judd, Director of Financial Aid
158 East Main Street, Henderson, TN 38340
(731) 989-6662

## Jackson State Community College
Jackson, Tennessee
www.jscc.edu              Federal Code: 004937

**2-year public** community college in small city.
**Enrollment:** 3,243 undergrads.
**Selectivity:** Open admission; but selective for some programs.

**BASIC COSTS (2015-2016)**
**Tuition and fees:** $4,398; out-of-state residents $16,368.
**Per-credit charge:** $152; out-of-state residents $475.
**Additional info:** Tuition/fee waivers available for adults, minority students.

**FINANCIAL AID PICTURE**
**Students with need:** Need-based aid available for full-time and part-time students.
**Students without need:** No-need awards available for academics, art, athletics, job skills, leadership, minority status, music/drama.

**FINANCIAL AID PROCEDURES**
**Forms required:** FAFSA, institutional form.
**Dates and Deadlines:** Priority date 3/15; no closing date. Applicants notified on a rolling basis starting 5/15; must reply within 2 week(s) of notification.

**CONTACT**
Dewana Latimer, Director of Financial Aid
2046 North Parkway, Jackson, TN 38301-3797
(731) 425-2605

## John A. Gupton College
Nashville, Tennessee
www.guptoncollege.edu              Federal Code: 008859

**2-year private** school of mortuary science in large city.
**Enrollment:** 119 undergrads.

**Selectivity:** Open admission; but selective for some programs.

## BASIC COSTS (2016-2017)
**Tuition and fees:** $10,040.
**Per-credit charge:** $310.
**Room only:** $3,600.

## FINANCIAL AID PICTURE
**Students with need:** Need-based aid available for full-time and part-time students.
**Students without need:** This college awards aid only to students with need.

## FINANCIAL AID PROCEDURES
**Forms required:** FAFSA.
**Dates and Deadlines:** Applicants notified on a rolling basis; must reply within 2 week(s) of notification.
**Transfers:** No deadline. Applicants notified on a rolling basis starting 1/1; must reply within 2 week(s) of notification.

## CONTACT
Joanna Hayes Dickens, Director of Financial Aid
1616 Church Street, Nashville, TN 37203-2920
(615) 327-3927

## Johnson University
Knoxville, Tennessee
www.johnsonu.edu                    Federal Code: 003495

**4-year private** university and Bible college in large city, affiliated with Christian Church.
**Enrollment:** 1,099 undergrads.

## BASIC COSTS (2015-2016)
**Tuition and fees:** $12,650.
**Room and board:** $5,750.
**Additional info:** Tuition/fee waivers available for minority students.

## FINANCIAL AID PICTURE
**Students with need:** Need-based aid available for full-time and part-time students. Work study available nights, weekends, and for part-time students.
**Students without need:** No-need awards available for academics, leadership, minority status, music/drama, religious affiliation, state/district residency.

## FINANCIAL AID PROCEDURES
**Forms required:** FAFSA, institutional form.
**Dates and Deadlines:** Closing date 3/1. Applicants notified on a rolling basis starting 4/30; must reply by 8/25 or within 2 week(s) of notification.
**Transfers:** No deadline.

## CONTACT
Larry Rector, Financial Aid Director
7900 Johnson Drive, Knoxville, TN 37998-0001
(865) 251-2303

## King University
Bristol, Tennessee
www.king.edu                    Federal Code: 003496

**4-year private** nursing and liberal arts college in large town, affiliated with Presbyterian Church (USA).
**Enrollment:** 2,118 undergrads.

## BASIC COSTS (2015-2016)
**Tuition and fees:** $26,480.
**Room and board:** $8,180.

## FINANCIAL AID PICTURE
**Students with need:** Need-based aid available for full-time and part-time students. Work study available nights, weekends, and for part-time students.
**Students without need:** No-need awards available for academics, art, athletics, job skills, music/drama, state/district residency.

## FINANCIAL AID PROCEDURES
**Forms required:** FAFSA.
**Dates and Deadlines:** Priority date 3/1; no closing date. Applicants notified on a rolling basis starting 3/1; must reply within 2 week(s) of notification.

## CONTACT
Chrystal Jefferson, Financial Aid Director
1350 King College Road, Bristol, TN 37620-2699
(423) 652-4725

## Lane College
Jackson, Tennessee
www.lanecollege.edu                    Federal Code: 003499

**4-year private** liberal arts college in small city, affiliated with Christian Methodist Episcopal Church.
**Enrollment:** 1,376 undergrads, 2% part-time. 444 full-time freshmen.
**Selectivity:** Admits 50 to 75% of applicants.

## BASIC COSTS (2015-2016)
**Tuition and fees:** $9,930.
**Per-credit charge:** $375.
**Room and board:** $6,620.

## FINANCIAL AID PICTURE (2015-2016)
**Students with need:** Out of 444 full-time freshmen who applied for aid, 444 were judged to have need. Of these, 437 received aid. Average financial aid package met 50% of need; average scholarship/grant was $7,996; average loan was $3,448. For part-time students, average financial aid package was $10,019.
**Students without need:** 2 full-time freshmen who did not demonstrate need for aid received scholarships/grants; average award was $5,500. No-need awards available for academics, athletics, religious affiliation.
**Scholarships offered:** 12 full-time freshmen received athletic scholarships; average amount $5,684.

## FINANCIAL AID PROCEDURES
**Forms required:** FAFSA.
**Dates and Deadlines:** Priority date 3/1; no closing date. Applicants notified on a rolling basis starting 3/31; must reply within 2 week(s) of notification.
**Transfers:** No deadline. Applicants notified on a rolling basis; must reply within 2 week(s) of notification.

## CONTACT
Tony Calhoun, Director of Financial Aid
545 Lane Avenue, Jackson, TN 38301-4598
(731) 426-7537

## Lee University
Cleveland, Tennessee
www.leeuniversity.edu                    Federal Code: 003500

**4-year private** university and liberal arts college in large town, affiliated with Church of God.
**Enrollment:** 4,151 undergrads, 9% part-time. 826 full-time freshmen.
**Selectivity:** Open admission; but selective for some programs.

## BASIC COSTS (2015-2016)
**Tuition and fees:** $15,000.
**Per-credit charge:** $600.
**Room and board:** $7,045.

**FINANCIAL AID PICTURE (2015-2016)**

**Students with need:** Out of 757 full-time freshmen who applied for aid, 597 were judged to have need. Of these, 596 received aid, and 145 had their full need met. Average financial aid package met 63% of need; average scholarship/grant was $11,325; average loan was $3,201. For part-time students, average financial aid package was $6,709.

**Students without need:** 153 full-time freshmen who did not demonstrate need for aid received scholarships/grants; average award was $8,888. No-need awards available for academics, alumni affiliation, athletics, leadership, minority status, music/drama, religious affiliation, state/district residency.

**Scholarships offered:** 35 full-time freshmen received athletic scholarships; average amount $8,816.

**FINANCIAL AID PROCEDURES**

**Forms required:** FAFSA.

**Dates and Deadlines:** Priority date 3/15; no closing date. Applicants notified on a rolling basis starting 2/1.

**CONTACT**

Marian Dill, Director of Student Financial Aid
1120 North Ocoee Street, Cleveland, TN 37320-3450
(423) 614-8304

## LeMoyne-Owen College
Memphis, Tennessee
www.loc.edu                              Federal Code: 003501

**4-year private** liberal arts college in very large city, affiliated with Baptist faith.

**Enrollment:** 945 undergrads.

**BASIC COSTS (2015-2016)**

**Tuition and fees:** $10,680.

**Per-credit charge:** $436.

**Room and board:** $5,910.

**FINANCIAL AID PICTURE**

**Students with need:** Need-based aid available for full-time and part-time students.

**Students without need:** No-need awards available for academics, athletics, music/drama.

**FINANCIAL AID PROCEDURES**

**Forms required:** FAFSA.

**Dates and Deadlines:** Priority date 4/15; no closing date. Applicants notified on a rolling basis starting 4/1.

**Transfers:** No deadline. Applicants notified on a rolling basis starting 4/1.

**CONTACT**

Phyllis Torry, Financial Aid Director
807 Walker Avenue, Memphis, TN 38126
(901) 435-1550

## Lincoln College of Technology: Nashville
Nashville, Tennessee
www.nadcedu.com                          Federal Code: 007440

**1-year for-profit** technical college in large city.

**Enrollment:** 1,782 undergrads.

**BASIC COSTS (2015-2016)**

**Additional info:** Certificate programs: $14,754. Diploma programs: $29,867 to $36,344. Associate programs: $35,817. Costs include total tuition, materials, tool fees, and registration fee.

**FINANCIAL AID PICTURE**

**Students with need:** Need-based aid available for full-time students. Work study available nights, weekends, and for part-time students.

**Students without need:** This college awards aid only to students with need.

**FINANCIAL AID PROCEDURES**

**Forms required:** FAFSA, state aid form.

**Dates and Deadlines:** Applicants notified on a rolling basis.

**CONTACT**

Chris Biddle, Director of Financial Aid
1524 Gallatin Road, Nashville, TN 37206
(615) 650-8202

## Lincoln Memorial University
Harrogate, Tennessee
www.lmunet.edu                           Federal Code: 003502

**4-year private** university and liberal arts college in small town.

**Enrollment:** 1,617 undergrads.

**BASIC COSTS (2015-2016)**

**Tuition and fees:** $20,546.

**Per-credit charge:** $834.

**Room and board:** $7,300.

**FINANCIAL AID PICTURE**

**Students with need:** Need-based aid available for full-time and part-time students.

**Students without need:** No-need awards available for academics, alumni affiliation, athletics, music/drama, ROTC.

**FINANCIAL AID PROCEDURES**

**Forms required:** FAFSA.

**Dates and Deadlines:** Priority date 2/15; no closing date. Applicants notified on a rolling basis starting 3/15; must reply within 3 week(s) of notification.

**CONTACT**

Bryan Erslan, Director of Financial Aid
6965 Cumberland Gap Parkway, Harrogate, TN 37752-1901
(423) 869-6336

## Lipscomb University
Nashville, Tennessee
www.lipscomb.edu                         Federal Code: 003486

**4-year private** university and liberal arts college in very large city, affiliated with Church of Christ.

**Enrollment:** 3,024 undergrads, 10% part-time. 662 full-time freshmen.

**Selectivity:** Admits 50 to 75% of applicants.

**BASIC COSTS (2015-2016)**

**Tuition and fees:** $28,624.

**Per-credit charge:** $1,110.

**Room and board:** $11,032.

**FINANCIAL AID PICTURE (2015-2016)**

**Students with need:** Out of 662 full-time freshmen who applied for aid, 430 were judged to have need. Of these, 430 received aid, and 108 had their full need met. Average financial aid package met 62% of need; average scholarship/grant was $3,599; average loan was $3,514. For part-time students, average financial aid package was $8,526.

**Students without need:** 231 full-time freshmen who did not demonstrate need for aid received scholarships/grants; average award was $12,709. No-need awards available for academics, art, athletics, leadership, minority status, music/drama, religious affiliation, state/district residency.

**Scholarships offered:** 22 full-time freshmen received athletic scholarships; average amount $16,013.

**FINANCIAL AID PROCEDURES**
**Forms required:** FAFSA.
**Dates and Deadlines:** Priority date 3/31; no closing date. Applicants notified on a rolling basis starting 3/1.

**CONTACT**
Karita Waters, Director of Financial Aid
One University Park Drive, Nashville, TN 37204-3951
(615) 966-1791

## Martin Methodist College
Pulaski, Tennessee
www.martinmethodist.edu                Federal Code: 003504

**4-year private** liberal arts college in small town, affiliated with United Methodist Church.
**Enrollment:** 1,050 undergrads.

**BASIC COSTS (2015-2016)**
**Tuition and fees:** $23,100.
**Room and board:** $8,400.

**FINANCIAL AID PICTURE**
**Students with need:** Need-based aid available for full-time and part-time students. Work study available nights, weekends, and for part-time students.
**Students without need:** No-need awards available for academics, art, athletics, leadership, music/drama, religious affiliation, state/district residency.
**Scholarships offered:** Two full academic scholarships per year awarded through interview and essay competition.

**FINANCIAL AID PROCEDURES**
**Forms required:** FAFSA, institutional form.
**Dates and Deadlines:** Applicants notified on a rolling basis starting 3/1; must reply within 2 week(s) of notification.
**Transfers:** Closing date 9/13.

**CONTACT**
Emma Hlubb, Director of Financial Aid
433 West Madison, Pulaski, TN 38478-2799
(931) 363-9804

## Maryville College
Maryville, Tennessee
www.maryvillecollege.edu                Federal Code: 003505

**4-year private** liberal arts college in large town, affiliated with Presbyterian Church (USA).
**Enrollment:** 1,170 undergrads, 1% part-time. 338 full-time freshmen.
**Selectivity:** Admits 50 to 75% of applicants.

**BASIC COSTS (2015-2016)**
**Tuition and fees:** $32,866.
**Per-credit charge:** $825.
**Room and board:** $10,442.

**FINANCIAL AID PICTURE (2015-2016)**
**Students with need:** Out of 338 full-time freshmen who applied for aid, 296 were judged to have need. Of these, 296 received aid, and 78 had their full need met. Average financial aid package met 90% of need; average scholarship/grant was $28,621; average loan was $3,492. For part-time students, average financial aid package was $16,258.
**Students without need:** 42 full-time freshmen who did not demonstrate need for aid received scholarships/grants; average award was $24,281. No-need awards available for academics, alumni affiliation, art, leadership, minority status, music/drama, religious affiliation, state/district residency.

**FINANCIAL AID PROCEDURES**
**Forms required:** FAFSA.
**Dates and Deadlines:** Priority date 2/1; no closing date. Applicants notified on a rolling basis starting 3/12; must reply by 5/1 or within 4 week(s) of notification.

**CONTACT**
Alayne Bowman, Asst. Director of Financial Aid
502 East Lamar Alexander Parkway, Maryville, TN 37804-5907
(865) 981-8100

## Memphis College of Art
Memphis, Tennessee
www.mca.edu                Federal Code: 003507

**4-year private** visual arts college in very large city.
**Enrollment:** 357 undergrads, 15% part-time. 80 full-time freshmen.
**Selectivity:** Admits less than 50% of applicants.

**BASIC COSTS (2015-2016)**
**Tuition and fees:** $30,250.
**Room and board:** $8,550.
**Additional info:** Room and board are estimated amounts.

**FINANCIAL AID PICTURE**
**Students with need:** Need-based aid available for full-time and part-time students. Work study available nights.
**Students without need:** No-need awards available for academics, art.
**Additional info:** Students considered for institutional resources through admissions application process.

**FINANCIAL AID PROCEDURES**
**Forms required:** FAFSA.
**Dates and Deadlines:** Priority date 2/15; no closing date. Applicants notified on a rolling basis starting 3/15; must reply within 3 week(s) of notification.
**Transfers:** Applicants notified on a rolling basis; must reply within 3 week(s) of notification. Grants of $1,000 awarded to students who attended accredited junior or community college earning at least 60 credit hours.

**CONTACT**
Aaron White, Director of Financial Aid
1930 Poplar Avenue, Memphis, TN 38104-2764
(901) 272-5138

## Middle Tennessee State University
Murfreesboro, Tennessee
www.mtsu.edu                Federal Code: 003510

**4-year public** university in small city.
**Enrollment:** 19,446 undergrads, 17% part-time. 2,758 full-time freshmen.
**Selectivity:** Admits 50 to 75% of applicants.

**BASIC COSTS (2015-2016)**
**Tuition and fees:** $8,404; out-of-state residents $25,972.
**Per-credit charge:** $268; out-of-state residents $965.
**Room and board:** $8,550.

**FINANCIAL AID PICTURE (2014-2015)**
**Students with need:** Average financial aid package met 69% of need; average scholarship/grant was $6,285; average loan was $3,282. For part-time students, average financial aid package was $5,037.
**Students without need:** No-need awards available for academics, leadership.
**Additional info:** Deadline for scholarships 2/15.

**FINANCIAL AID PROCEDURES**
**Forms required:** FAFSA.

**Dates and Deadlines:** Priority date 3/1; no closing date. Applicants notified on a rolling basis starting 4/15; must reply within 2 week(s) of notification.

**CONTACT**
David Hutton, Director of Student Financial Aid
1301 East Main Street, Murfreesboro, TN 37132
(615) 898-2830

## Miller-Motte Technical College: Clarksville

Clarksville, Tennessee
www.miller-motte.edu          Federal Code: 026142

**2-year for-profit** business and health science college in small city.
**Enrollment:** 404 undergrads.
**Selectivity:** Open admission; but selective for some programs.

**BASIC COSTS (2015-2016)**
**Additional info:** Certificate programs: $10,200-$20,788, books and supplies $400-$3,000. Associate programs: $25,080-$33,180, books and supplies $3,600-$4,800.

**FINANCIAL AID PICTURE**
**Students with need:** Need-based aid available for full-time and part-time students. Work study available nights, weekends, and for part-time students.
**Students without need:** This college awards aid only to students with need.

**FINANCIAL AID PROCEDURES**
**Forms required:** FAFSA, institutional form.
**Dates and Deadlines:** Applicants notified on a rolling basis.
**Transfers:** No deadline.

**CONTACT**
Debbie Stratman, Financial Aid Director
1820 Business Park Drive, Clarksville, TN 37040
(931) 553-0071

## Milligan College

Milligan College, Tennessee
www.milligan.edu          Federal Code: 003511

**4-year private** liberal arts college in small city, affiliated with Christian Church.
**Enrollment:** 832 undergrads, 6% part-time. 187 full-time freshmen.
**Selectivity:** Admits 50 to 75% of applicants.

**BASIC COSTS (2015-2016)**
**Tuition and fees:** $29,830.
**Room and board:** $6,500.

**FINANCIAL AID PICTURE (2015-2016)**
**Students with need:** Average financial aid package met 83% of need; average scholarship/grant was $20,659; average loan was $4,063. For part-time students, average financial aid package was $10,187.
**Students without need:** No-need awards available for academics, art, athletics, leadership, minority status, music/drama.

**FINANCIAL AID PROCEDURES**
**Forms required:** FAFSA.
**Dates and Deadlines:** Closing date 3/1. Applicants notified on a rolling basis starting 3/15; must reply within 2 week(s) of notification.

**CONTACT**
Diane Keasling, Coordinator of Financial Aid
Box 210, Milligan College, TN 37682
(800) 447-4880

## Motlow State Community College

Lynchburg, Tennessee
www.mscc.edu          Federal Code: 006836

**2-year public** community college in rural community.
**Enrollment:** 5,065 undergrads, 47% part-time. 1,636 full-time freshmen.
**Selectivity:** Open admission; but selective for some programs.

**BASIC COSTS (2015-2016)**
**Tuition and fees:** $4,129; out-of-state residents $16,099.

**FINANCIAL AID PICTURE**
**Students with need:** Need-based aid available for full-time and part-time students.
**Students without need:** No-need awards available for academics, alumni affiliation, art, athletics, leadership, music/drama.

**FINANCIAL AID PROCEDURES**
**Forms required:** FAFSA, institutional form.
**Dates and Deadlines:** Closing date 2/15. Applicants notified on a rolling basis starting 3/15.
**Transfers:** No deadline. Applicants notified on a rolling basis starting 3/15.

**CONTACT**
Joe Myers, Director of Financial Aid and Scholarships
Box 8500, Lynchburg, TN 37352-8500
(931) 393-1553

## Nashville State Community College

Nashville, Tennessee
www.nscc.edu          Federal Code: 007534

**2-year public** community and technical college in very large city.
**Enrollment:** 7,979 undergrads, 48% part-time. 1,769 full-time freshmen.
**Selectivity:** Open admission; but selective for some programs.

**BASIC COSTS (2015-2016)**
**Tuition and fees:** $4,053; out-of-state residents $16,023.
**Per-credit charge:** $152; out-of-state residents $627.

**FINANCIAL AID PICTURE (2014-2015)**
**Students with need:** Need-based aid available for part-time students. Work study available nights, weekends, and for part-time students.
**Students without need:** No-need awards available for academics, minority status.

**FINANCIAL AID PROCEDURES**
**Forms required:** FAFSA.
**Dates and Deadlines:** Priority date 3/1; closing date 7/1. Applicants notified on a rolling basis starting 6/1; must reply within 2 week(s) of notification.

**CONTACT**
Josh Moran, Director of Financial Aid
120 White Bridge Road, Nashville, TN 37209-4515
(615) 353-3250

## National College: Bristol

Bristol, Tennessee
www.national-college.edu          Federal Code: 003726

**2-year for-profit** business college in large town.
**Enrollment:** 92 undergrads.
**Selectivity:** Open admission.

**BASIC COSTS (2016-2017)**
**Tuition and fees:** $14,460.
**Per-credit charge:** $317.

**FINANCIAL AID PICTURE**

**Students with need:** Need-based aid available for full-time and part-time students.

**Students without need:** This college awards aid only to students with need.

**FINANCIAL AID PROCEDURES**

**Forms required:** FAFSA.

**Dates and Deadlines:** Applicants notified on a rolling basis starting 9/1.

**CONTACT**

Pam Cotton, Director of Financial Aid Compliance and Auditing
1328 Highway 11W, Bristol, TN 37620

## National College: Nashville

Nashville, Tennessee
www.ncbt.edu                     Federal Code: 003726

**2-year for-profit** business and technical college in large city.
**Enrollment:** 102 undergrads.
**Selectivity:** Open admission.

**BASIC COSTS (2016-2017)**

**Tuition and fees:** $14,460.
**Per-credit charge:** $317.

**FINANCIAL AID PICTURE**

**Students with need:** Need-based aid available for full-time and part-time students.

**Students without need:** This college awards aid only to students with need.

**FINANCIAL AID PROCEDURES**

**Forms required:** FAFSA.

**CONTACT**

Pam Cotton, Director of Financial Aid Compliance and Auditing
1638 Bell Road, Nashville, TN 37211
(615) 333-3344

## Northeast State Community College

Blountville, Tennessee
www.NortheastState.edu           Federal Code: 005378

**2-year public** community and technical college in small city.
**Enrollment:** 6,084 undergrads.
**Selectivity:** Open admission; but selective for some programs.

**BASIC COSTS (2015-2016)**

**Tuition and fees:** $4,115; out-of-state residents $16,085.

**FINANCIAL AID PICTURE**

**Students with need:** Need-based aid available for full-time and part-time students. Work study available nights.

**Students without need:** No-need awards available for academics, alumni affiliation, art, job skills, leadership, minority status, music/drama, religious affiliation.

**FINANCIAL AID PROCEDURES**

**Forms required:** FAFSA.

**Dates and Deadlines:** Priority date 3/31; no closing date. Applicants notified on a rolling basis starting 3/1; must reply within 3 week(s) of notification.

**CONTACT**

Cruzita Lucero, Director of Financial Aid
Box 246, Blountville, TN 37617-0246
(423) 323-0252

## Nossi College of Art

Nashville, Tennessee
www.nossi.edu                    Federal Code: 017347

**2-year for-profit** visual arts and technical college in large town.
**Enrollment:** 268 undergrads. 62 full-time freshmen.

**BASIC COSTS (2016-2017)**

**Tuition and fees:** $17,700.

**FINANCIAL AID PICTURE**

**Students with need:** Need-based aid available for full-time and part-time students.

**CONTACT**

Mary Kidd, Financial Aid Director
590 Cheron Road, Nashville, TN 37115
(615) 514-2787

## O'More College of Design

Franklin, Tennessee
www.omorecollege.edu             Federal Code: 014663

**4-year private** visual arts college in large town.
**Enrollment:** 176 undergrads, 16% part-time. 24 full-time freshmen.

**BASIC COSTS (2015-2016)**

**Tuition and fees:** $27,360.
**Per-credit charge:** $1,112.

**FINANCIAL AID PICTURE**

**Students with need:** Need-based aid available for full-time and part-time students. Work study available nights, weekends, and for part-time students.

**Students without need:** This college awards aid only to students with need.

**FINANCIAL AID PROCEDURES**

**Forms required:** FAFSA.

**Dates and Deadlines:** Closing date 4/7.

**Transfers:** Priority date 4/7; no deadline. Applicants notified by 6/10.

**CONTACT**

Jerry Masterson, Financial Aid Director
423 South Margin Street, Franklin, TN 37064-0908
(615) 794-4254 ext. 238

## Pellissippi State Community College

Knoxville, Tennessee
www.pstcc.edu                    Federal Code: 012693

**2-year public** community and technical college in small city.
**Enrollment:** 10,325 undergrads.
**Selectivity:** Open admission.

**BASIC COSTS (2015-2016)**

**Tuition and fees:** $4,168; out-of-state residents $15,728.

**FINANCIAL AID PICTURE**

**Students with need:** Need-based aid available for full-time and part-time students. Work study available nights, weekends, and for part-time students.

**Students without need:** No-need awards available for academics, art, minority status, music/drama.

**FINANCIAL AID PROCEDURES**

**Forms required:** FAFSA.

**Dates and Deadlines:** Priority date 5/1; no closing date. Applicants notified on a rolling basis starting 7/15; must reply within 2 week(s) of notification.

## CONTACT

Richard Smelser, Director of Financial Aid
Box 22990, Knoxville, TN 37933-0990
(423) 694-6565

# Remington College: Memphis
Memphis, Tennessee
www.memphis.remingtoncollege.edu

**2-year private** business and technical college in very large city.
**Enrollment:** 1,361 undergrads.

## BASIC COSTS (2015-2016)

**Additional info:** Diploma programs: ventilation and air conditioning $20,995; medical assisting $19,990; medical billing and coding $15,995; pharmacy technician $19,990. Associate programs: business administration $33,900; business office management $33,900; computer and network administration $33,900; criminal justice $33,900; electronics and computer technology $33,900. Bahelor's program: criminal justice $24,700.

## FINANCIAL AID PICTURE

**Students with need:** Need-based aid available for full-time and part-time students.
**Students without need:** This college awards aid only to students with need.

## FINANCIAL AID PROCEDURES

**Forms required:** FAFSA, institutional form.
**Dates and Deadlines:** Applicants notified on a rolling basis; must reply within 2 week(s) of notification.

## CONTACT

James Dunn, National Director of Financial Aid
2710 Nonconnah Boulevard, Memphis, TN 38132

# Rhodes College
Memphis, Tennessee            Federal Code: 003519
www.rhodes.edu                    CSS Code: 1730

**4-year private** liberal arts college in very large city, affiliated with Presbyterian Church (USA).
**Enrollment:** 2,031 undergrads. 562 full-time freshmen.
**Selectivity:** Admits less than 50% of applicants.

## BASIC COSTS (2016-2017)

**Tuition and fees:** $43,224.
**Per-credit charge:** $1,800.
**Room and board:** $10,746.

## FINANCIAL AID PICTURE (2015-2016)

**Students with need:** Out of 478 full-time freshmen who applied for aid, 293 were judged to have need. Of these, 293 received aid, and 185 had their full need met. Average financial aid package met 93% of need; average scholarship/grant was $26,954; average loan was $2,887.
**Students without need:** 227 full-time freshmen who did not demonstrate need for aid received scholarships/grants; average award was $21,164. No-need awards available for academics, art, minority status, music/drama, religious affiliation.
**Additional info:** Auditions required for theater and music achievement awards and art achievement awards. Interviews recommended for merit scholarships. Notification of admissions decision for Bellingrath Scholarship applicants by 3/15; must reply by 5/1.

## FINANCIAL AID PROCEDURES

**Forms required:** FAFSA, CSS PROFILE.
**Dates and Deadlines:** Priority date 3/1; closing date 3/1. Must reply by 5/1.

## CONTACT

Michael Morgan, Director of Financial Aid
2000 North Parkway, Memphis, TN 38112
(901) 843-3810

# Roane State Community College
Harriman, Tennessee
www.roanestate.edu            Federal Code: 009914

**2-year public** community and junior college in small town.
**Enrollment:** 4,421 undergrads.
**Selectivity:** Open admission; but selective for some programs.

## BASIC COSTS (2015-2016)

**Tuition and fees:** $4,131; out-of-state residents $16,101.
**Per-credit charge:** $152; out-of-state residents $627.

## FINANCIAL AID PICTURE

**Students with need:** Need-based aid available for full-time and part-time students. Work study available nights, weekends, and for part-time students.
**Students without need:** No-need awards available for academics, art, athletics, leadership, music/drama, state/district residency.

## FINANCIAL AID PROCEDURES

**Forms required:** FAFSA, institutional form.
**Dates and Deadlines:** Priority date 4/1; no closing date. Applicants notified on a rolling basis starting 5/1.

## CONTACT

Robin Townson, Director, Financial Aid
276 Patton Lane, Harriman, TN 37748
(865) 882-4545

# Sewanee: The University of the South
Sewanee, Tennessee            Federal Code: 003534
www.sewanee.edu                   CSS Code: 1842

**4-year private** university and liberal arts college in small town, affiliated with Episcopal Church.
**Enrollment:** 1,689 undergrads. 469 full-time freshmen.
**Selectivity:** Admits less than 50% of applicants. GED not accepted.

## BASIC COSTS (2015-2016)

**Tuition and fees:** $38,700.
**Per-credit charge:** $1,350.
**Room and board:** $11,050.
**Additional info:** Tuition at time of enrollment locked for 4 years.

## FINANCIAL AID PICTURE (2015-2016)

**Students with need:** Out of 323 full-time freshmen who applied for aid, 235 were judged to have need. Of these, 235 received aid, and 70 had their full need met. Average financial aid package met 91% of need; average scholarship/grant was $24,549; average loan was $3,791.
**Students without need:** 151 full-time freshmen who did not demonstrate need for aid received scholarships/grants; average award was $11,704. No-need awards available for academics, art, religious affiliation, state/district residency.
**Scholarships offered:** Benedict Scholarship; full tuition, fees, room and board annually; 2 awarded. Wilkins Scholarship; $15,000 annually; $60,000 total; number awarded determined annually. Quintard Award; $12,000 annually; $48,000 total; number awarded determined annually. Fairbanks Award; $10,000 annually; $40,000 total; number awarded determined annually. Otey Award; $5,000 annually; $20,000 total; number awarded determined annually. Georgia4 Scholarship; $4,000 annually; $16,000 total; all students admitted from Georgia.

## FINANCIAL AID PROCEDURES

**Forms required:** FAFSA, CSS PROFILE.

**Dates and Deadlines:** Priority date 2/1; closing date 2/1. Applicants notified on a rolling basis starting 3/1; must reply by 5/1 or within 2 week(s) of notification.

## CONTACT

Beth Cragar, Associate Dean of Admission for Financial Aid
Office of Admission, Sewanee, TN 37383-1000
(931) 598-1312

# South College

Knoxville, Tennessee
www.southcollegetn.edu          Federal Code: 004938

**4-year for-profit** career college in small city.

**Enrollment:** 1,139 undergrads.

## BASIC COSTS (2015-2016)

**Tuition and fees:** $20,475.

## FINANCIAL AID PICTURE

**Students with need:** Need-based aid available for full-time and part-time students.

**Students without need:** This college awards aid only to students with need.

## FINANCIAL AID PROCEDURES

**Forms required:** FAFSA, institutional form.

**Dates and Deadlines:** Applicants notified on a rolling basis.

**Transfers:** Priority date 2/1; no deadline. Applicants notified on a rolling basis starting 6/1; must reply within 4 week(s) of notification.

## CONTACT

Larry Broadwater, Financial Aid Director
3904 Lonas Drive, Knoxville, TN 37909
(865) 251-1800

# Southern Adventist University

Collegedale, Tennessee
www.southern.edu          Federal Code: 003518

**4-year private** university and liberal arts college in small town, affiliated with Seventh-day Adventists.

**Enrollment:** 2,697 undergrads, 17% part-time. 535 full-time freshmen.

**Selectivity:** Admits 50 to 75% of applicants.

## BASIC COSTS (2015-2016)

**Tuition and fees:** $20,650.

**Per-credit charge:** $840.

**Room and board:** $5,980.

## FINANCIAL AID PICTURE (2014-2015)

**Students with need:** Average financial aid package met 70% of need; average scholarship/grant was $11,093; average loan was $3,905. For part-time students, average financial aid package was $6,584.

**Students without need:** No-need awards available for academics, alumni affiliation, art, athletics, leadership, music/drama.

**Scholarships offered:** Freshman scholarships; based on GPA, ACT/SAT, leadership positions held.

## FINANCIAL AID PROCEDURES

**Forms required:** FAFSA.

**Dates and Deadlines:** Priority date 3/1; no closing date. Applicants notified on a rolling basis starting 2/15; must reply within 2 week(s) of notification.

**Transfers:** No deadline. Applicants notified on a rolling basis.

## CONTACT

Paula Walter, Associate Vice President for Enrollment Services
PO Box 370, Collegedale, TN 37315-0370
(423) 236-2835

# Southwest Tennessee Community College

Memphis, Tennessee
www.southwest.tn.edu          Federal Code: 010439

**2-year public** community college in very large city.

**Enrollment:** 8,402 undergrads.

**Selectivity:** Open admission; but selective for some programs.

## BASIC COSTS (2015-2016)

**Tuition and fees:** $3,963; out-of-state residents $15,363.

**Per-credit charge:** $152; out-of-state residents $627.

**Additional info:** Tuition/fee waivers available for minority students.

## FINANCIAL AID PICTURE

**Students with need:** Need-based aid available for full-time and part-time students. Work study available nights, weekends, and for part-time students.

**Students without need:** No-need awards available for academics, athletics, minority status, music/drama, state/district residency.

**Additional info:** State grants available to eligible students who apply by 4/1.

## FINANCIAL AID PROCEDURES

**Forms required:** FAFSA.

**Dates and Deadlines:** Closing date 3/15. Applicants notified on a rolling basis starting 6/1; must reply within 4 week(s) of notification.

**Transfers:** Priority date 4/15; closing date 6/30.

## CONTACT

Lechelle Davenport, Director Financial Aid
PO Box 780, Memphis, TN 38101-0780
(901) 333-5957

# Tennessee State University

Nashville, Tennessee
www.tnstate.edu          Federal Code: 003522

**4-year public** university in very large city.

**Enrollment:** 7,176 undergrads, 17% part-time. 1,389 full-time freshmen.

**Selectivity:** Admits 50 to 75% of applicants.

## BASIC COSTS (2015-2016)

**Tuition and fees:** $7,417; out-of-state residents $20,773.

**Per-credit charge:** $253; out-of-state residents $783.

**Room and board:** $7,130.

**Additional info:** Tuition/fee waivers available for minority students.

## FINANCIAL AID PICTURE (2015-2016)

**Students with need:** Out of 1,318 full-time freshmen who applied for aid, 1,249 were judged to have need. Of these, 1,215 received aid, and 18 had their full need met. Average financial aid package met 29% of need; average scholarship/grant was $3,186; average loan was $1,947. For part-time students, average financial aid package was $2,869.

**Students without need:** 36 full-time freshmen who did not demonstrate need for aid received scholarships/grants; average award was $6,478. No-need awards available for academics.

**Scholarships offered:** 1 full-time freshmen received athletic scholarships; average amount $11,635.

## FINANCIAL AID PROCEDURES

**Forms required:** FAFSA.

**Dates and Deadlines:** Priority date 4/1; no closing date. Applicants notified on a rolling basis starting 4/15; must reply within 3 week(s) of notification.

**CONTACT**
Cynthia Brooks, Vice President of Finance/Accounting
3500 John A. Merritt Boulevard, Nashville, TN 37209-1561
(615) 963-5701

## Tennessee Technological University
Cookeville, Tennessee
www.tntech.edu                    Federal Code: 003523

**4-year public** university in large town.
**Enrollment:** 9,475 undergrads, 9% part-time. 1,577 full-time freshmen.

**BASIC COSTS (2015-2016)**
**Tuition and fees:** $8,353; out-of-state residents $24,559.
**Per-credit charge:** $285; out-of-state residents $928.
**Room and board:** $9,418.
**Additional info:** Tuition/fee waivers available for minority students.

**FINANCIAL AID PICTURE**
**Students with need:** Need-based aid available for full-time and part-time students. Work study available nights, weekends, and for part-time students.
**Students without need:** No-need awards available for academics, alumni affiliation, art, athletics, leadership, minority status, music/drama, ROTC, state/district residency.
**Scholarships offered:** Presidential Scholarship; $4,000 renewable annually. Awarded to National Merit Finalists.
**Additional info:** Tuition and/or fee waivers available for children of Tennessee public school teachers.

**FINANCIAL AID PROCEDURES**
**Forms required:** FAFSA.
**Dates and Deadlines:** Priority date 3/15; no closing date. Applicants notified on a rolling basis starting 3/15; must reply within 2 week(s) of notification.
**Transfers:** No deadline. Applicants notified on a rolling basis starting 6/1; must reply within 2 week(s) of notification.

**CONTACT**
Lester McKenzie, Director of Student Financial Aid
Office of Admissions, Cookeville, TN 38505-0001
(931) 372-3073

## Tennessee Wesleyan College
Athens, Tennessee
www.twcnet.edu                    Federal Code: 003525

**4-year private** liberal arts and teachers college in large town, affiliated with United Methodist Church.
**Enrollment:** 1,014 undergrads, 6% part-time. 459 full-time freshmen.
**Selectivity:** Admits 50 to 75% of applicants.

**BASIC COSTS (2015-2016)**
**Tuition and fees:** $22,900.
**Per-credit charge:** $570.
**Room and board:** $7,310.
**Additional info:** Tuition/fee waivers available for minority students.

**FINANCIAL AID PICTURE (2014-2015)**
**Students with need:** Out of 238 full-time freshmen who applied for aid, 215 were judged to have need. Of these, 204 received aid, and 40 had their full need met. Average financial aid package met 67% of need; average scholarship/grant was $17,001; average loan was $2,995. For part-time students, average financial aid package was $7,232.

**Students without need:** 16 full-time freshmen who did not demonstrate need for aid received scholarships/grants; average award was $10,166. No-need awards available for academics, alumni affiliation, athletics, minority status, music/drama, religious affiliation.
**Scholarships offered:** 20 full-time freshmen received athletic scholarships; average amount $12,585.

**FINANCIAL AID PROCEDURES**
**Forms required:** FAFSA, institutional form.
**Dates and Deadlines:** Priority date 2/15; no closing date. Applicants notified on a rolling basis starting 2/15; must reply within 2 week(s) of notification.

**CONTACT**
Lacey Weese, Director of Financial Aid
204 East College Street, Athens, TN 37303
(423) 746-5215

## Trevecca Nazarene University
Nashville, Tennessee
www.trevecca.edu                    Federal Code: 003526

**4-year private** university and liberal arts college in very large city, affiliated with Church of the Nazarene.
**Enrollment:** 1,762 undergrads, 29% part-time. 354 full-time freshmen.
**Selectivity:** Admits 50 to 75% of applicants.

**BASIC COSTS (2015-2016)**
**Tuition and fees:** $23,748.
**Room and board:** $8,300.

**FINANCIAL AID PICTURE (2014-2015)**
**Students with need:** 44% of average financial aid package awarded as scholarships/grants, 56% awarded as loans/jobs.
**Students without need:** No-need awards available for academics, alumni affiliation, athletics, leadership, minority status, music/drama, religious affiliation.

**FINANCIAL AID PROCEDURES**
**Dates and Deadlines:** Priority date 3/1; no closing date. Applicants notified on a rolling basis starting 3/1.

**CONTACT**
Eddie White, Director of Financial Aid
333 Murfreesboro Road, Nashville, TN 37210
(615) 248-1242

## Tusculum College
Greeneville, Tennessee
www.tusculum.edu                    Federal Code: 003527

**4-year private** liberal arts college in large town, affiliated with Presbyterian Church (USA).
**Enrollment:** 1,619 undergrads, 7% part-time. 283 full-time freshmen.
**Selectivity:** Admits 50 to 75% of applicants.

**BASIC COSTS (2016-2017)**
**Tuition and fees:** $23,125.
**Per-credit charge:** $718.
**Room and board:** $8,500.

**FINANCIAL AID PICTURE (2015-2016)**
**Students with need:** Out of 274 full-time freshmen who applied for aid, 262 were judged to have need. Of these, 258 received aid, and 38 had their full need met. Average financial aid package met 71% of need; average scholarship/grant was $9,691; average loan was $3,416. For part-time students, average financial aid package was $6,608.

**Students without need:** 12 full-time freshmen who did not demonstrate need for aid received scholarships/grants; average award was $8,608. No-need awards available for academics, athletics, leadership, religious affiliation, state/district residency.
**Scholarships offered:** 6 full-time freshmen received athletic scholarships; average amount $8,250.

## FINANCIAL AID PROCEDURES
**Forms required:** FAFSA.
**Dates and Deadlines:** Closing date 2/15. Applicants notified on a rolling basis starting 3/15; must reply within 3 week(s) of notification.

## CONTACT
Karen Sartain, Director of Financial Aid
60 Shiloh Road, Greeneville, TN 37743
(423) 636-7376

# Union University
Jackson, Tennessee
www.uu.edu                          Federal Code: 003528

**4-year private** university and liberal arts college in small city, affiliated with Southern Baptist Convention.
**Enrollment:** 2,567 undergrads. 340 full-time freshmen.

## BASIC COSTS (2015-2016)
**Tuition and fees:** $29,190.
**Per-credit charge:** $940.
**Room and board:** $9,090.
**Additional info:** Tuition/fee waivers available for minority students.

## FINANCIAL AID PICTURE (2015-2016)
**Students with need:** Out of 309 full-time freshmen who applied for aid, 269 were judged to have need. Of these, 269 received aid, and 48 had their full need met. Average financial aid package met 65% of need; average scholarship/grant was $6,244; average loan was $3,418. For part-time students, average financial aid package was $7,103.
**Students without need:** 69 full-time freshmen who did not demonstrate need for aid received scholarships/grants; average award was $14,039. No-need awards available for academics, alumni affiliation, art, athletics, job skills, leadership, minority status, music/drama, religious affiliation, state/district residency.
**Scholarships offered:** *Merit:* Www.uu.edu. *Athletic:* 14 full-time freshmen received athletic scholarships; average amount $19,195.
**Additional info:** Www.uu.edu.

## FINANCIAL AID PROCEDURES
**Forms required:** FAFSA, institutional form.
**Dates and Deadlines:** Priority date 2/1; closing date 2/1. Applicants notified on a rolling basis starting 3/1; must reply by 5/1 or within 2 week(s) of notification.
**Transfers:** Priority date 2/1; closing date 2/1. Applicants notified on a rolling basis starting 3/1; must reply by 5/1 or within 2 week(s) of notification.

## CONTACT
John Windham, Director of Student Financial Planning
1050 Union University Drive, Jackson, TN 38305-3697
(731) 661-5015

# University of Memphis
Memphis, Tennessee
www.memphis.edu                     Federal Code: 003509

**4-year public** university in very large city.
**Enrollment:** 15,548 undergrads, 23% part-time. 2,049 full-time freshmen.
**Selectivity:** Admits over 75% of applicants.

## BASIC COSTS (2015-2016)
**Tuition and fees:** $9,269; out-of-state residents $20,981.
**Per-credit charge:** $305; out-of-state residents $793.
**Room and board:** $9,061.
**Additional info:** Reduced out of state tuition rate possible for students who graduated from a high school within 250-mile radius of University of Memphis. Tuition/fee waivers available for adults, minority students.

## FINANCIAL AID PICTURE (2015-2016)
**Students with need:** Out of 1,902 full-time freshmen who applied for aid, 1,494 were judged to have need. Of these, 1,293 received aid, and 374 had their full need met. Average financial aid package met 82% of need; average scholarship/grant was $6,820; average loan was $3,283. For part-time students, average financial aid package was $5,824.
**Students without need:** 391 full-time freshmen who did not demonstrate need for aid received scholarships/grants; average award was $7,679. No-need awards available for academics, alumni affiliation, art, athletics, leadership, music/drama, ROTC, state/district residency.
**Scholarships offered:** *Merit:* Cecil C. Humphreys Presidential Scholarship: $7,500; minimum 30 ACT/1330 SAT (CR+M), 3.5 or higher cumulative high school grade point average. Provost Scholarship: $5,500; minimum 28 ACT/1250 SAT (CR+M), 3.25 or higher cumulative high school grade point average. Valedictorian Scholarship: $4,500; recipient must attend a Tennessee accredited or state approved high school from the following Mississippi counties: DeSoto, Marshall, Tate, Tunica, or Crittenden County in Arkansas. Students must also rank number one in the class and meet the admission requirements. Dean's Scholarship: $3,000; minimum 25 ACT/1130 SAT (CR+M), 3.00 or higher cumulative high school grade point average. Emerging Leaders Scholarship: $5,500; requires a separate application; minimum 21 ACT/980 SAT (CR+M) 3.00 or higher cumulative high school grade point average. *Athletic:* 77 full-time freshmen received athletic scholarships; average amount $15,128.

## FINANCIAL AID PROCEDURES
**Dates and Deadlines:** Priority date 3/1; closing date 5/1. Applicants notified on a rolling basis starting 3/15; must reply by 8/1.

## CONTACT
Richard Ritzman, Director of Student Financial Aid
101 Wilder Tower, Memphis, TN 38152
(901) 678-4825

# University of Tennessee: Chattanooga
Chattanooga, Tennessee
www.utc.edu                         Federal Code: 003529

**4-year public** university in small city.
**Enrollment:** 9,977 undergrads, 12% part-time. 1,853 full-time freshmen.
**Selectivity:** Admits over 75% of applicants.

## BASIC COSTS (2015-2016)
**Tuition and fees:** $8,356; out-of-state residents $24,474.
**Per-credit charge:** $276; out-of-state residents $948.
**Room and board:** $8,388.

## FINANCIAL AID PICTURE (2015-2016)
**Students with need:** Out of 1,751 full-time freshmen who applied for aid, 1,127 were judged to have need. Of these, 1,112 received aid, and 200 had their full need met. Average financial aid package met 68% of need; average scholarship/grant was $8,140; average loan was $3,324. For part-time students, average financial aid package was $9,044.
**Students without need:** 232 full-time freshmen who did not demonstrate need for aid received scholarships/grants; average award was $3,068. No-need awards available for academics, alumni affiliation, art, athletics, leadership, music/drama, ROTC, state/district residency.
**Scholarships offered:** 23 full-time freshmen received athletic scholarships; average amount $15,206.

**FINANCIAL AID PROCEDURES**
**Forms required:** FAFSA.
**Dates and Deadlines:** Priority date 5/1; no closing date. Applicants notified on a rolling basis starting 3/1; must reply within 4 week(s) of notification.
**Transfers:** Applicants notified on a rolling basis starting 3/1; must reply within 6 week(s) of notification.

**CONTACT**
Jennifer Buckles, Director of Financial Aid
615 McCallie Avenue, Chattanooga, TN 37403
(423) 425-4677

## University of Tennessee: Knoxville
Knoxville, Tennessee
www.utk.edu                                Federal Code: 003530

**4-year public** university in large city.
**Enrollment:** 21,661 undergrads, 6% part-time. 4,700 full-time freshmen.
**Selectivity:** Admits over 75% of applicants.

**BASIC COSTS (2015-2016)**
**Tuition and fees:** $12,436; out-of-state residents $30,626.
**Per-credit charge:** $359; out-of-state residents $1,110.
**Room and board:** $9,926.
**Additional info:** Out-of-state students pay additional required fees of $230.

**FINANCIAL AID PICTURE (2015-2016)**
**Students with need:** Out of 4,429 full-time freshmen who applied for aid, 2,804 were judged to have need. Of these, 2,804 received aid, and 702 had their full need met. Average financial aid package met 62% of need; average scholarship/grant was $11,049; average loan was $5,234. For part-time students, average financial aid package was $12,105.
**Students without need:** This college awards aid only to students with need.
**Scholarships offered:** 97 full-time freshmen received athletic scholarships; average amount $27,648.
**Additional info:** Application priority date for scholarships 2/1.

**FINANCIAL AID PROCEDURES**
**Forms required:** FAFSA.
**Dates and Deadlines:** Priority date 2/15; no closing date. Applicants notified on a rolling basis starting 3/15; must reply within 3 week(s) of notification.
**Transfers:** Priority date 4/1; no deadline. Applicants notified on a rolling basis starting 4/15; must reply within 3 week(s) of notification.

**CONTACT**
Jeff Gerkin, Director of Financial Aid
320 Student Services Building, Circle Park, Knoxville, TN 37996-0230
(865) 974-3131

## University of Tennessee: Martin
Martin, Tennessee
www.utm.edu                                Federal Code: 003531

**4-year public** university in small town.
**Enrollment:** 5,988 undergrads, 10% part-time. 1,010 full-time freshmen.
**Selectivity:** Admits 50 to 75% of applicants.

**BASIC COSTS (2015-2016)**
**Tuition and fees:** $8,326; out-of-state residents $22,270.
**Per-credit charge:** $288; out-of-state residents $869.
**Room and board:** $5,896.

**FINANCIAL AID PICTURE (2015-2016)**
**Students with need:** Out of 981 full-time freshmen who applied for aid, 739 were judged to have need. Of these, 730 received aid, and 157 had their full need met. Average financial aid package met 79% of need; average

scholarship/grant was $6,735; average loan was $3,314. For part-time students, average financial aid package was $11,490.
**Students without need:** This college awards aid only to students with need.
**Scholarships offered:** 110 full-time freshmen received athletic scholarships; average amount $10,384.

**FINANCIAL AID PROCEDURES**
**Forms required:** FAFSA.
**Dates and Deadlines:** Priority date 2/15; no closing date. Applicants notified by 3/15; must reply within 2 week(s) of notification.

**CONTACT**
Amy Mistric, Coordinator III
201 Administration Building, Martin, TN 38238
(731) 881-7040

## Vanderbilt University
Nashville, Tennessee               Federal Code: 003535
www.vanderbilt.edu                      CSS Code: 1871

**4-year private** university in very large city.
**Enrollment:** 6,857 undergrads, 1% part-time. 1,607 full-time freshmen.
**Selectivity:** Admits less than 50% of applicants.

**BASIC COSTS (2015-2016)**
**Tuition and fees:** $44,712.
**Room and board:** $14,670.

**FINANCIAL AID PICTURE (2015-2016)**
**Students with need:** Out of 1,027 full-time freshmen who applied for aid, 854 were judged to have need. Of these, 839 received aid, and 839 had their full need met. Average financial aid package met 100% of need; average scholarship/grant was $41,718; average loan was $2,781.
**Students without need:** 147 full-time freshmen who did not demonstrate need for aid received scholarships/grants; average award was $18,787. No-need awards available for academics, athletics, leadership, music/drama, ROTC, state/district residency.
**Scholarships offered:** *Merit:* Scholarship programs; full-tuition plus summer stipends for study abroad, research or service projects; approximately 250 awarded. *Athletic:* 58 full-time freshmen received athletic scholarships; average amount $44,501.
**Additional info:** Financial aid packages awarded to incoming and returning undergraduate students are need-based loan-free.

**FINANCIAL AID PROCEDURES**
**Forms required:** FAFSA, CSS PROFILE.
**Dates and Deadlines:** Priority date 2/1; no closing date. Applicants notified by 4/1; must reply by 5/1.
**Transfers:** Priority date 2/15. Must reply within 2 week(s) of notification.

**CONTACT**
Brent Tener, Director of Student Financial Aid
2305 West End Avenue, Nashville, TN 37203-1727
(615) 322-3591

## Volunteer State Community College
Gallatin, Tennessee
www.volstate.edu                           Federal Code: 009912

**2-year public** community and junior college in large town.
**Enrollment:** 6,536 undergrads, 36% part-time. 1,110 full-time freshmen.
**Selectivity:** Open admission; but selective for some programs.

**BASIC COSTS (2015-2016)**
**Tuition and fees:** $3,925; out-of-state residents $15,325.

**Additional info:** Tuition/fee waivers available for adults, minority students.

**FINANCIAL AID PICTURE (2014-2015)**

**Students with need:** Out of 1,054 full-time freshmen who applied for aid, 785 were judged to have need. Of these, 785 received aid, and 70 had their full need met. Average financial aid package met 57% of need; average scholarship/grant was $4,553; average loan was $2,550. For part-time students, average financial aid package was $3,968.

**Students without need:** 20 full-time freshmen who did not demonstrate need for aid received scholarships/grants; average award was $1,609. No-need awards available for academics, art, athletics, leadership, minority status, music/drama, state/district residency.

**Scholarships offered:** 2 full-time freshmen received athletic scholarships; average amount $1,144.

**FINANCIAL AID PROCEDURES**

**Forms required:** FAFSA, institutional form.

**Dates and Deadlines:** Priority date 4/15; no closing date. Applicants notified on a rolling basis; must reply within 2 week(s) of notification.

**Transfers:** No deadline. Applicants notified on a rolling basis; must reply within 2 week(s) of notification.

**CONTACT**

Sue Pedigo, Director of Financial Aid

1480 Nashville Pike, Gallatin, TN 37066-3188

(615) 452-8600 ext. 3456

## Walters State Community College

Morristown, Tennessee

www.ws.edu  Federal Code: 008863

**2-year public** culinary school and community college in small city.

**Enrollment:** 4,553 undergrads, 30% part-time. 943 full-time freshmen.

**Selectivity:** Open admission; but selective for some programs.

**BASIC COSTS (2015-2016)**

**Tuition and fees:** $4,116; out-of-state residents $16,086.

**Additional info:** Tuition/fee waivers available for minority students.

**FINANCIAL AID PICTURE (2014-2015)**

**Students with need:** Out of 937 full-time freshmen who applied for aid, 755 were judged to have need. Of these, 753 received aid, and 75 had their full need met. Average financial aid package met 58% of need; average scholarship/grant was $4,713. For part-time students, average financial aid package was $3,823.

**Students without need:** 178 full-time freshmen who did not demonstrate need for aid received scholarships/grants; average award was $3,661. No-need awards available for academics, athletics, minority status, music/drama, state/district residency.

**Scholarships offered:** 11 full-time freshmen received athletic scholarships; average amount $446.

**FINANCIAL AID PROCEDURES**

**Forms required:** FAFSA.

**Dates and Deadlines:** Priority date 6/30; no closing date. Applicants notified by 5/10.

**Transfers:** No deadline. Applicants notified on a rolling basis.

**CONTACT**

Terri Stansberry, Director of Financial Aid

500 South Davy Crockett Parkway, Morristown, TN 37813-6899

(423) 585-6811

## Watkins College of Art, Design & Film

Nashville, Tennessee

www.watkins.edu

**4-year private** visual arts college in very large city.

**Enrollment:** 305 undergrads.

**Selectivity:** Admits less than 50% of applicants.

**BASIC COSTS (2015-2016)**

**Tuition and fees:** $23,100.

**Per-credit charge:** $715.

**Room only:** $6,380.

**FINANCIAL AID PICTURE**

**Students with need:** Need-based aid available for full-time and part-time students. Work study available nights, weekends, and for part-time students.

**Students without need:** No-need awards available for academics, art, minority status.

**FINANCIAL AID PROCEDURES**

**Forms required:** FAFSA, institutional form.

**Dates and Deadlines:** Priority date 4/1; closing date 8/1. Applicants notified on a rolling basis starting 5/1; must reply within 2 week(s) of notification.

**CONTACT**

Regina Gilbert, Director of Financial Aid

2298 Rosa L. Parks Boulevard, Nashville, TN 37228

(615) 277-7420

## Welch College

Nashville, Tennessee

www.welch.edu  Federal Code: 030018

**4-year private** Bible and teachers college in very large city, affiliated with Free Will Baptists.

**Enrollment:** 243 undergrads, 9% part-time. 46 full-time freshmen.

**Selectivity:** Open admission.

**BASIC COSTS (2015-2016)**

**Tuition and fees:** $17,398.

**Room and board:** $7,048.

**FINANCIAL AID PICTURE (2014-2015)**

**Students with need:** Out of 46 full-time freshmen who applied for aid, 45 were judged to have need. Of these, 45 received aid. Average financial aid package met 41% of need; average scholarship/grant was $5,944; average loan was $3,500. For part-time students, average financial aid package was $10,232.

**Students without need:** 2 full-time freshmen who did not demonstrate need for aid received scholarships/grants; average award was $4,750. No-need awards available for academics, alumni affiliation, art, music/drama.

**Scholarships offered:** Presidential Honors Scholarship: $1,000 per semester, renewable for 8 semesters; high school GPA 3.5+, and ACT 29+, must maintain college GPA 3.25; awarded to four students yearly.

**FINANCIAL AID PROCEDURES**

**Forms required:** FAFSA, institutional form.

**Dates and Deadlines:** Priority date 4/15; no closing date. Applicants notified on a rolling basis starting 3/15; must reply within 2 week(s) of notification.

**Transfers:** No deadline.

**CONTACT**

Angie Edgmon, Financial Aid Coordinator

3606 West End Avenue, Nashville, TN 37205-2403

(615) 844-5214

PART III: FINANCIAL AID COLLEGE BY COLLEGE

## Williamson College

Franklin, Tennessee
www.williamsoncc.edu
Federal Code: 035315

**4-year private** liberal arts college in small city, affiliated with interdenominational tradition.
**Enrollment:** 69 undergrads.
**Selectivity:** Open admission; but selective for some programs.

### BASIC COSTS (2015-2016)
**Tuition and fees:** $11,550.
**Per-credit charge:** $375.

### FINANCIAL AID PICTURE
**Students with need:** Need-based aid available for full-time and part-time students.
**Students without need:** No-need awards available for academics, state/district residency.
**Scholarships offered:** Williamson is offering a new College Bound Scholarship for incoming freshman who are Tennessee residents, ACT/SAT scores of 21/980, who maintain full-time enrollment with a 3.0GPA. Click here, http://www.williamsoncc.edu/scholarships/, for more information on our scholarship program.

### FINANCIAL AID PROCEDURES
**Forms required:** FAFSA.
**Dates and Deadlines:** Priority date 5/1; no closing date. Applicants notified on a rolling basis starting 5/1; must reply within 2 week(s) of notification.
**Transfers:** No deadline. Applicants notified on a rolling basis starting 5/1; must reply within 2 week(s) of notification.

### CONTACT
Laura Flowers, Director of Financial Aid
274 Mallory Station Road, Franklin, TN 37067
(615) 550-3170

# Texas

## Abilene Christian University

Abilene, Texas
www.acu.edu
Federal Code: 003537

**4-year private** university in small city, affiliated with Church of Christ.
**Enrollment:** 3,695 undergrads, 3% part-time. 974 full-time freshmen.
**Selectivity:** Admits less than 50% of applicants.

### BASIC COSTS (2015-2016)
**Tuition and fees:** $30,830.
**Per-credit charge:** $1,280.
**Room and board:** $9,310.

### FINANCIAL AID PICTURE (2014-2015)
**Students with need:** Out of 847 full-time freshmen who applied for aid, 700 were judged to have need. Of these, 700 received aid, and 189 had their full need met. Average financial aid package met 73% of need; average scholarship/grant was $20,695; average loan was $3,577. For part-time students, average financial aid package was $19,978.
**Students without need:** 283 full-time freshmen who did not demonstrate need for aid received scholarships/grants; average award was $11,758. No-need awards available for academics, art, athletics, leadership, minority status, music/drama, religious affiliation, state/district residency.
**Scholarships offered:** *Merit:* Presidential Scholarship: half or full tuition; based on interview, ACT or SAT scores. Academic Scholarship: $3,000-$14,000; based on ACT/SAT, class rank, and performance in high school

courses. Transfer Scholarship: $4,000-$8,000; based on GPA. *Athletic:* 72 full-time freshmen received athletic scholarships; average amount $20,171.
**Additional info:** Early estimate service available.

### FINANCIAL AID PROCEDURES
**Forms required:** FAFSA.
**Dates and Deadlines:** Priority date 3/1; no closing date. Applicants notified on a rolling basis starting 4/1.

### CONTACT
Student Financial Services
ACU Box 29000, Abilene, TX 79699
(325) 674-6850

## Alvin Community College

Alvin, Texas
www.alvincollege.edu
Federal Code: 003539

**2-year public** community and liberal arts college in large town.
**Enrollment:** 5,116 undergrads.
**Selectivity:** Open admission; but selective for some programs.

### BASIC COSTS (2015-2016)
**Tuition and fees:** $1,814; out-of-district residents $3,164; out-of-state residents $4,664.
**Per-credit charge:** $45; out-of-district residents $90; out-of-state residents $140.

### FINANCIAL AID PICTURE (2014-2015)
**Students with need:** 94% of average financial aid package awarded as scholarships/grants, 6% awarded as loans/jobs. Need-based aid available for part-time students. Work study available nights, weekends, and for part-time students.
**Students without need:** This college awards aid only to students with need.

### FINANCIAL AID PROCEDURES
**Forms required:** FAFSA.
**Dates and Deadlines:** Applicants notified on a rolling basis; must reply within 2 week(s) of notification.

### CONTACT
Dora Sims, Director of Student Financial Aid and Placement
3110 Mustang Road, Alvin, TX 77511-4898
(281) 756-3524

## Angelina College

Lufkin, Texas
www.angelina.edu
Federal Code: 006661

**2-year public** community college in large town.
**Enrollment:** 5,236 undergrads, 74% part-time. 491 full-time freshmen.
**Selectivity:** Open admission; but selective for some programs.

### BASIC COSTS (2015-2016)
**Tuition and fees:** $2,220; out-of-district residents $3,480; out-of-state residents $4,860.
**Per-credit charge:** $62; out-of-district residents $104; out-of-state residents $150.
**Room and board:** $5,600.

### FINANCIAL AID PICTURE
**Students with need:** Need-based aid available for full-time and part-time students. Work study available nights.
**Students without need:** No-need awards available for academics, art, athletics, job skills, leadership, music/drama, state/district residency.

**Scholarships offered:** Angelina Challenge Award: $750 per semester; available to graduating seniors from the six Angelina County high schools; students must receive less than $1,000 in other need-based aid.

## FINANCIAL AID PROCEDURES
**Forms required:** FAFSA.
**Dates and Deadlines:** Priority date 7/15; no closing date. Applicants notified on a rolling basis starting 3/15.
**Transfers:** No deadline. Applicants notified on a rolling basis starting 4/1. Transfer students must provide the financial aid office with an official transcript from all colleges previously attended. All transfer credit will be used to calculate maximum time frame for Title IV funds and for completion pace.

## CONTACT
Susan Jones, Director of Financial Aid
PO Box 1768, Lufkin, TX 75902-1768
(936) 633-5291

## Angelo State University
San Angelo, Texas
www.angelo.edu                     Federal Code: 003541

**4-year public** university in small city.
**Enrollment:** 5,403 undergrads, 12% part-time. 1,281 full-time freshmen.
**Selectivity:** Admits over 75% of applicants.

### BASIC COSTS (2015-2016)
**Tuition and fees:** $7,864; out-of-state residents $19,564.
**Per-credit charge:** $162; out-of-state residents $552.
**Room and board:** $7,702.
**Additional info:** Angelo State University also offers a guaranteed tuition program that locks in tuition price for four years.

### FINANCIAL AID PICTURE (2014-2015)
**Students with need:** Out of 1,125 full-time freshmen who applied for aid, 855 were judged to have need. Of these, 854 received aid, and 163 had their full need met. Average financial aid package met 83% of need; average scholarship/grant was $3,598; average loan was $3,203. For part-time students, average financial aid package was $8,854.
**Students without need:** 251 full-time freshmen who did not demonstrate need for aid received scholarships/grants; average award was $3,828. No-need awards available for academics, art, athletics, leadership, music/drama, ROTC, state/district residency.
**Scholarships offered:** 78 full-time freshmen received athletic scholarships; average amount $5,191.

### FINANCIAL AID PROCEDURES
**Forms required:** FAFSA.
**Dates and Deadlines:** Priority date 4/1; no closing date. Applicants notified on a rolling basis starting 4/1; must reply within 4 week(s) of notification.
**Transfers:** Applicants notified on a rolling basis starting 4/1; must reply within 4 week(s) of notification.

### CONTACT
William Bloom, Financial Aid Director
ASU Station #11014, San Angelo, TX 76909-1014
(325) 942-2246

## Arlington Baptist College
Arlington, Texas
www.arlingtonbaptistcollege.edu     Federal Code: 014305

**4-year private** Bible and teachers college in very large city, affiliated with Baptist faith.
**Enrollment:** 212 undergrads, 15% part-time. 43 full-time freshmen.
**Selectivity:** Open admission.

### BASIC COSTS (2015-2016)
**Tuition and fees:** $11,010.
**Per-credit charge:** $335.
**Room and board:** $5,800.

### FINANCIAL AID PICTURE (2014-2015)
**Students with need:** Out of 40 full-time freshmen who applied for aid, 38 were judged to have need. Of these, 38 received aid. Need-based aid available for part-time students.
**Students without need:** This college awards aid only to students with need.
**Scholarships offered:** 8 full-time freshmen received athletic scholarships; average amount $2,000.

### FINANCIAL AID PROCEDURES
**Forms required:** FAFSA, institutional form.
**Dates and Deadlines:** Closing date 8/15. Applicants notified on a rolling basis starting 12/1; must reply by 8/15.
**Transfers:** Priority date 4/16; closing date 6/16. Applicants notified by 12/1; must reply by 8/5.

### CONTACT
David Ingram, Business Manager
3001 West Division Street, Arlington, TX 76012
(817) 461-8741 ext. 114

## Art Institute of Dallas
Dallas, Texas
www.aid.edu                     Federal Code: 017360

**4-year for-profit** visual arts college in very large city.
**Enrollment:** 1,155 undergrads.
**Selectivity:** Open admission; but selective for some programs.

### FINANCIAL AID PICTURE
**Students with need:** Need-based aid available for full-time students.

### FINANCIAL AID PROCEDURES
**Forms required:** FAFSA.
**Dates and Deadlines:** Applicants notified on a rolling basis.

### CONTACT
Jeff Clark, Financial Aid Director
Two North Park, 8080 Park Lane, Dallas, TX 75231
(214) 692-8080

## Austin College
Sherman, Texas
www.austincollege.edu            Federal Code: 003543

**4-year private** liberal arts and teachers college in small city, affiliated with Presbyterian Church (USA).
**Enrollment:** 1,250 undergrads, 1% part-time. 355 full-time freshmen.
**Selectivity:** Admits 50 to 75% of applicants.

### BASIC COSTS (2015-2016)
**Tuition and fees:** $36,230.
**Room and board:** $11,793.

### FINANCIAL AID PICTURE (2015-2016)
**Students with need:** Out of 306 full-time freshmen who applied for aid, 257 were judged to have need. Of these, 257 received aid, and 166 had their full need met. Average financial aid package met 95% of need; average scholarship/grant was $28,997; average loan was $5,531. For part-time students, average financial aid package was $7,258.

**Students without need:** 86 full-time freshmen who did not demonstrate need for aid received scholarships/grants; average award was $21,169. No-need awards available for academics, alumni affiliation, art, leadership, music/drama, religious affiliation.

## FINANCIAL AID PROCEDURES

**Forms required:** FAFSA.

**Dates and Deadlines:** Priority date 4/1; no closing date. Applicants notified on a rolling basis starting 2/15; must reply by 5/1.

**Transfers:** Applicants notified on a rolling basis starting 3/1; must reply by 5/1.

## CONTACT

Laurie Coulter, Executive Director of Financial Aid

900 North Grand Avenue, Suite 6N, Sherman, TX 75090-4400

(903) 813-2900

## Austin Community College

Austin, Texas

www.austincc.edu                    Federal Code: 012015

**2-year public** community college in very large city.

**Enrollment:** 41,574 undergrads. 2,225 full-time freshmen.

**Selectivity:** Open admission; but selective for some programs.

## BASIC COSTS (2015-2016)

**Tuition and fees:** $2,550; out-of-district residents $9,210; out-of-state residents $11,340.

**Per-credit charge:** $67; out-of-district residents $289; out-of-state residents $360.

**Additional info:** In-district and Out-of-district students pay the same tuition, but there is an additional Out-of-district fee that is charged to Out-of-district students.

## FINANCIAL AID PICTURE (2014-2015)

**Students with need:** Out of 1,323 full-time freshmen who applied for aid, 1,012 were judged to have need. Of these, 855 received aid. Need-based aid available for part-time students.

## FINANCIAL AID PROCEDURES

**Forms required:** FAFSA.

**Dates and Deadlines:** Priority date 4/1; closing date 6/1. Applicants notified on a rolling basis starting 3/30; must reply within 2 week(s) of notification.

## CONTACT

Terry Bazan, Director, Financial Assistance

PO Box 15306, Austin, TX 78761-5306

(512) 223-7550

## Austin Graduate School of Theology

Austin, Texas

www.austingrad.edu                    Federal Code: 017322

**Upper-division private** Bible and seminary college in very large city, affiliated with Church of Christ.

**Enrollment:** 20 undergrads.

## BASIC COSTS (2015-2016)

**Tuition and fees:** $10,850.

**Per-credit charge:** $350.

## FINANCIAL AID PICTURE

**Students with need:** Need-based aid available for full-time and part-time students. Work study available nights.

**Students without need:** No-need awards available for academics, leadership.

**Additional info:** Generous scholarships for students taking at least 12 hours. Federal work study program available. Institutional work study program (need-based) available.

## FINANCIAL AID PROCEDURES

**Forms required:** FAFSA, institutional form.

**Dates and Deadlines:** Priority date 7/1; closing date 8/1.

**Transfers:** No deadline.

## CONTACT

Dave Arthur, Vice President

7640 Guadalupe Street, Austin, TX 78752-1333

(512) 476-2772

## Baptist Missionary Association Theological Seminary

Jacksonville, Texas

www.bmats.edu                    Federal Code: 016525

**4-year private** Bible and seminary college in large town, affiliated with Baptist faith.

**Enrollment:** 63 undergrads. 871 full-time freshmen.

**Selectivity:** Open admission; but selective for some programs.

## BASIC COSTS (2015-2016)

**Tuition and fees:** $5,550.

**Per-credit charge:** $180.

**Additional info:** $100 distance learning fee added per course.

## FINANCIAL AID PICTURE (2014-2015)

**Students with need:** Out of 790 full-time freshmen who applied for aid, 577 were judged to have need. Of these, 550 received aid, and 37 had their full need met. Average financial aid package met 58% of need; average scholarship/grant was $6,233; average loan was $5,766. For part-time students, average financial aid package was $6,107.

**Students without need:** 46 full-time freshmen who did not demonstrate need for aid received scholarships/grants; average award was $4,700. No-need awards available for academics, state/district residency.

## FINANCIAL AID PROCEDURES

**Forms required:** FAFSA.

**Dates and Deadlines:** Priority date 3/1; no closing date. Applicants notified on a rolling basis starting 3/1; must reply by 3/1.

## CONTACT

Philip Attebery, Dean/Registrar

1530 East Pine Street, Jacksonville, TX 75766

(903) 586-2501

## Baylor University

Waco, Texas

www.baylor.edu                    Federal Code: 003545

**4-year private** university in small city, affiliated with Baptist faith.

**Enrollment:** 14,139 undergrads, 2% part-time. 3,393 full-time freshmen.

**Selectivity:** Admits less than 50% of applicants.

## BASIC COSTS (2016-2017)

**Tuition and fees:** $42,096.

**Per-credit charge:** $1,583.

**Room and board:** $11,654.

## FINANCIAL AID PICTURE (2015-2016)

**Students with need:** Out of 2,559 full-time freshmen who applied for aid, 1,939 were judged to have need. Of these, 1,939 received aid, and 328 had their full need met. Average financial aid package met 70% of need; average

scholarship/grant was $22,926; average loan was $2,602. For part-time students, average financial aid package was $13,177.

**Students without need:** 1,345 full-time freshmen who did not demonstrate need for aid received scholarships/grants; average award was $14,165. No-need awards available for academics, art, athletics, job skills, leadership, music/drama, religious affiliation, ROTC.

**Scholarships offered:** *Merit:* Regent's Scholarship; full tuition; limited to National Merit finalists who list Baylor as first choice; unlimited number. President's Scholarship; Provost's Scholarship; Dean's Scholarship also available. *Athletic:* 81 full-time freshmen received athletic scholarships; average amount $35,450.

**FINANCIAL AID PROCEDURES**

**Forms required:** FAFSA. CSS PROFILE accepted but not required for international applicants.

**Dates and Deadlines:** Applicants notified on a rolling basis starting 3/1; must reply by 5/1 or within 2 week(s) of notification.

**Transfers:** No deadline. Applicants notified on a rolling basis starting 3/1; must reply by 5/1 or within 2 week(s) of notification.

**CONTACT**

Lyn Kinyon, Assistant Vice President
One Bear Place #97056, Waco, TX 76798-7056
(800) 229-5678

## Blinn College

Brenham, Texas
www.blinn.edu                    Federal Code: 003549

**2-year public** community college in large town.
**Enrollment:** 18,021 undergrads, 43% part-time. 5,398 full-time freshmen.
**Selectivity:** Open admission; but selective for some programs.

**BASIC COSTS (2015-2016)**

**Tuition and fees:** $2,820; out-of-district residents $4,890; out-of-state residents $7,380.
**Per-credit charge:** $48; out-of-district residents $117; out-of-state residents $200.
**Room and board:** $6,100.

**FINANCIAL AID PICTURE**

**Students with need:** Need-based aid available for full-time and part-time students.

**FINANCIAL AID PROCEDURES**

**Forms required:** FAFSA, institutional form.
**Dates and Deadlines:** Priority date 6/1; no closing date. Applicants notified on a rolling basis starting 7/1.
**Transfers:** Applicants notified on a rolling basis starting 5/15.

**CONTACT**

Brent Williford, Dean of Financial Aid and Veteran Services
902 College Avenue, Brenham, TX 77833
(979) 830-4149

## Brazosport College

Lake Jackson, Texas
www.brazosport.edu                Federal Code: 007287

**2-year public** community college in large town.
**Enrollment:** 4,173 undergrads, 81% part-time. 232 full-time freshmen.
**Selectivity:** Open admission; but selective for some programs.

**BASIC COSTS (2015-2016)**

**Tuition and fees:** $2,505; out-of-district residents $3,525; out-of-state residents $5,145.

**Per-credit charge:** $62; out-of-district residents $96; out-of-state residents $150.

**FINANCIAL AID PICTURE**

**Students with need:** Need-based aid available for full-time and part-time students.
**Students without need:** No-need awards available for academics, art, job skills, leadership, music/drama, state/district residency.

**FINANCIAL AID PROCEDURES**

**Forms required:** FAFSA, institutional form.
**Dates and Deadlines:** Priority date 7/1; no closing date. Applicants notified on a rolling basis starting 5/1.

**CONTACT**

Kay Wright, Director of Financial Aid
500 College Drive, Lake Jackson, TX 77566
(979) 230-3377

## Cedar Valley College

Lancaster, Texas
www.cedarvalleycollege.edu         Federal Code: 014035

**2-year public** community college in large town.
**Enrollment:** 4,954 undergrads. 399 full-time freshmen.
**Selectivity:** Open admission.

**BASIC COSTS (2015-2016)**

**Tuition and fees:** $1,770; out-of-district residents $3,330; out-of-state residents $5,220.
**Per-credit charge:** $59; out-of-district residents $111; out-of-state residents $174.

**FINANCIAL AID PICTURE (2014-2015)**

**Students with need:** Out of 399 full-time freshmen who applied for aid, 273 were judged to have need. Of these, 273 received aid.

**FINANCIAL AID PROCEDURES**

**Forms required:** FAFSA.
**Dates and Deadlines:** Priority date 5/1; no closing date. Applicants notified on a rolling basis.

**CONTACT**

Cathy Adams, Director of Financial Aid
3030 North Dallas Avenue, Lancaster, TX 75134
(972) 587-2599

## Central Texas College

Killeen, Texas
www.ctcd.edu                      Federal Code: 004003

**2-year public** community college in small city.
**Enrollment:** 11,442 undergrads, 80% part-time. 569 full-time freshmen.
**Selectivity:** Open admission; but selective for some programs.

**BASIC COSTS (2015-2016)**

**Tuition and fees:** $2,280; out-of-district residents $2,940; out-of-state residents $6,420.
**Per-credit charge:** $76; out-of-district residents $98; out-of-state residents $214.
**Room and board:** $4,800.

**FINANCIAL AID PICTURE**

**Students with need:** Need-based aid available for full-time and part-time students. Work study available nights, weekends, and for part-time students.
**Students without need:** This college awards aid only to students with need.

## FINANCIAL AID PROCEDURES

**Forms required:** FAFSA, institutional form.

**Dates and Deadlines:** Closing date 6/1. Applicants notified on a rolling basis starting 3/1; must reply within 4 week(s) of notification.

### CONTACT

Annabelle Smith, Associate Dean, Financial Aid and Veteran Services

Central Texas College, Killeen, TX 76540-1800

(254) 526-1508

## Cisco College

Cisco, Texas

www.cisco.edu                    Federal Code: 003553

**2-year public** community college in small town.

**Enrollment:** 3,480 undergrads.

**Selectivity:** Open admission.

### BASIC COSTS (2016-2017)

**Tuition and fees:** $2,790; out-of-district residents $3,540; out-of-state residents $4,620.

**Per-credit charge:** $93; out-of-district residents $118; out-of-state residents $154.

**Room and board:** $4,152.

### FINANCIAL AID PICTURE (2014-2015)

**Students with need:** 59% of average financial aid package awarded as scholarships/grants, 41% awarded as loans/jobs.

**Students without need:** No-need awards available for athletics, music/drama.

**Additional info:** Financial aid application deadline July 1 for Fall semester, November 1 for Spring semester.

### FINANCIAL AID PROCEDURES

**Forms required:** FAFSA.

**Dates and Deadlines:** Closing date 7/1. Applicants notified on a rolling basis starting 8/15.

**Transfers:** Transfer students must submit school code change on the FAFSA to have Student Aid Report sent to Cisco College. Students selected for verification must complete the verification process with college before financial aid can be awarded even if they have award letter from previous institution. Eligibility for financial assistance will be determined once the Student Aid Report is received.

### CONTACT

Linda Sellers, Director of Financial Aid

101 College Heights, Cisco, TX 76437

(254) 442-5151

## Clarendon College

Clarendon, Texas

www.clarendoncollege.edu         Federal Code: 003554

**2-year public** community college in rural community.

**Enrollment:** 1,350 undergrads.

**Selectivity:** Open admission; but selective for some programs.

### BASIC COSTS (2015-2016)

**Tuition and fees:** $3,030; out-of-district residents $3,720; out-of-state residents $4,650.

**Room and board:** $4,176.

### FINANCIAL AID PICTURE

**Students with need:** Need-based aid available for full-time and part-time students. Work study available nights, weekends, and for part-time students.

**Students without need:** No-need awards available for academics, art, athletics, leadership, music/drama, state/district residency.

**Scholarships offered:** Named and endowed scholarships available based on academic achievement, need, and/or other requirements as stipulated by the scholarship donor.

### FINANCIAL AID PROCEDURES

**Forms required:** FAFSA, institutional form.

**Dates and Deadlines:** Priority date 8/1; no closing date. Applicants notified on a rolling basis starting 5/15; must reply by 8/15 or within 2 week(s) of notification.

**Transfers:** No deadline. Applicants notified on a rolling basis starting 11/15; must reply within 4 week(s) of notification.

### CONTACT

Susan Russell, Associate Dean of Financial Aid

PO Box 968, Clarendon, TX 79226

(806) 874-3571 ext. 112

## Coastal Bend College

Beeville, Texas

www.coastalbend.edu              Federal Code: 003546

**2-year public** community college in large town.

**Enrollment:** 2,382 undergrads.

**Selectivity:** Open admission; but selective for some programs.

### BASIC COSTS (2015-2016)

**Tuition and fees:** $2,646; out-of-district residents $4,506; out-of-state residents $4,956.

**Per-credit charge:** $70; out-of-district residents $132; out-of-state residents $147.

**Room and board:** $5,200.

### FINANCIAL AID PICTURE

**Students with need:** Need-based aid available for full-time and part-time students.

**Students without need:** No-need awards available for academics, leadership.

### FINANCIAL AID PROCEDURES

**Forms required:** FAFSA, institutional form.

**Dates and Deadlines:** Priority date 4/1; no closing date. Applicants notified on a rolling basis starting 5/1; must reply within 2 week(s) of notification.

**Transfers:** No deadline. Applicants notified on a rolling basis.

### CONTACT

Nora Morales, Director of Financial Aid

3800 Charco Road, Beeville, TX 78102

(361) 354-2238

## College of the Mainland

Texas City, Texas

www.com.edu                      Federal Code: 007096

**2-year public** community and technical college in large town.

**Enrollment:** 4,013 undergrads, 78% part-time. 161 full-time freshmen.

**Selectivity:** Open admission; but selective for some programs.

### BASIC COSTS (2015-2016)

**Tuition and fees:** $1,773; out-of-district residents $2,973; out-of-state residents $3,873.

### FINANCIAL AID PICTURE (2014-2015)

**Students with need:** Out of 107 full-time freshmen who applied for aid, 90 were judged to have need. Of these, 82 received aid, and 8 had their full need met. Average financial aid package met 64% of need; average scholarship/grant was $5,265; average loan was $3,562. For part-time students, average financial aid package was $4,518.

**Students without need:** This college awards aid only to students with need.

### FINANCIAL AID PROCEDURES

**Forms required:** FAFSA.

**Dates and Deadlines:** Priority date 6/1; no closing date. Applicants notified on a rolling basis starting 5/1; must reply within 4 week(s) of notification.

### CONTACT

Carl Gordon, Director, Student Financial Services
1200 Amburn Road, Texas City, TX 77591
(409) 933-8274

## Collin County Community College District

McKinney, Texas
www.collin.edu                    Federal Code: 016792

**2-year public** community college in large city.
**Enrollment:** 24,185 undergrads, 61% part-time. 3,047 full-time freshmen.
**Selectivity:** Open admission; but selective for some programs.

### BASIC COSTS (2016-2017)

**Tuition and fees:** $1,434; out-of-district residents $2,344; out-of-state residents $4,144.
**Per-credit charge:** $39; out-of-district residents $78; out-of-state residents $138.

### FINANCIAL AID PICTURE (2014-2015)

**Students with need:** 68% of average financial aid package awarded as scholarships/grants, 32% awarded as loans/jobs. Need-based aid available for part-time students. Work study available nights, weekends, and for part-time students.

**Students without need:** No-need awards available for academics, art, athletics, job skills, leadership, minority status, music/drama, state/district residency.

### FINANCIAL AID PROCEDURES

**Forms required:** FAFSA, institutional form.

**Dates and Deadlines:** Priority date 6/1; no closing date. Applicants notified on a rolling basis starting 5/1; must reply within 2 week(s) of notification.

**Transfers:** Applicants must have cumulative GPA of 2.0 and less than 90 transferable credit hours.

### CONTACT

Alan Pixley, Director, Financial Aid & Veterans Affairs
2800 East Spring Creek Parkway, Plano, TX 75074
(972) 881-5760

## Commonwealth Institute of Funeral Service

Houston, Texas
www.commonwealthinst.org           Federal Code: 003556

**2-year private** school of mortuary science in very large city.
**Enrollment:** 226 undergrads.

### FINANCIAL AID PICTURE

**Students with need:** Need-based aid available for full-time and part-time students.

**Students without need:** This college awards aid only to students with need.

**Scholarships offered:** Scholarship awards: $250-$500 based on funds available; recipients selected on academic achievement, leadership and professional promise, as well as any stipulations by the donor, by a committee of Commonwealth Institute graduate employers, alumni, and benefactors.

### FINANCIAL AID PROCEDURES

**Forms required:** FAFSA.

**Dates and Deadlines:** Priority date 8/31; no closing date. Applicants notified on a rolling basis starting 7/12.

### CONTACT

Jessika Jenkins, Director of Financial Aid
415 Barren Springs Drive, Houston, TX 77090-5913
(281) 873-0262

## Concordia University Texas

Austin, Texas
www.concordia.edu                  Federal Code: 003557

**4-year private** university and liberal arts college in very large city, affiliated with Lutheran Church - Missouri Synod.
**Enrollment:** 1,525 undergrads. 235 full-time freshmen.

### BASIC COSTS (2015-2016)

**Tuition and fees:** $28,160.
**Per-credit charge:** $905.
**Room and board:** $9,284.
**Additional info:** Tuition/fee waivers available for adults.

### FINANCIAL AID PICTURE (2014-2015)

**Students with need:** Out of 215 full-time freshmen who applied for aid, 181 were judged to have need. Of these, 179 received aid, and 45 had their full need met. Average financial aid package met 77% of need; average scholarship/grant was $17,243; average loan was $7,179. For part-time students, average financial aid package was $8,755.

**Students without need:** 46 full-time freshmen who did not demonstrate need for aid received scholarships/grants; average award was $13,738. No-need awards available for academics, leadership, music/drama, religious affiliation.

### FINANCIAL AID PROCEDURES

**Forms required:** FAFSA.

**Dates and Deadlines:** Priority date 5/1; no closing date. Applicants notified on a rolling basis starting 2/15; must reply within 3 week(s) of notification.

**Transfers:** Priority date 5/1; no deadline. Applicants notified on a rolling basis starting 2/15; must reply within 3 week(s) of notification. Academic transcripts from all previously attended trade/technical schools and colleges/universities required.

### CONTACT

Russell Jeffrey, Director, Financial Services
11400 Concordia University Drive, Austin, TX 78726
(512) 313-4681

## Criswell College

Dallas, Texas
www.criswell.edu

**4-year private** Bible and seminary college in very large city, affiliated with Southern Baptist Convention.
**Enrollment:** 262 undergrads.

### BASIC COSTS (2015-2016)

**Tuition and fees:** $10,120.
**Per-credit charge:** $315.

### FINANCIAL AID PICTURE

**Students with need:** Work study available nights.

### FINANCIAL AID PROCEDURES

**Forms required:** FAFSA, institutional form.

**Dates and Deadlines:** Closing date 4/15. Applicants notified on a rolling basis.

**CONTACT**

Ta Lisa Pollard, Director of Financial Aid

4010 Gaston Avenue, Dallas, TX 75246-1537

(214) 828-1393

## Dallas Baptist University
Dallas, Texas
www.dbu.edu                                    Federal Code: 003560

**4-year private** university in very large city, affiliated with Baptist faith.

**Enrollment:** 3,220 undergrads, 26% part-time. 496 full-time freshmen.

**Selectivity:** Admits less than 50% of applicants.

**BASIC COSTS (2016-2017)**

**Tuition and fees:** $26,180.

**Per-credit charge:** $846.

**Room and board:** $7,533.

**FINANCIAL AID PICTURE (2015-2016)**

**Students with need:** Out of 429 full-time freshmen who applied for aid, 307 were judged to have need. Of these, 303 received aid, and 122 had their full need met. Average financial aid package met 63% of need; average scholarship/grant was $4,032; average loan was $3,377. For part-time students, average financial aid package was $6,949.

**Students without need:** 120 full-time freshmen who did not demonstrate need for aid received scholarships/grants; average award was $9,203. No-need awards available for academics, athletics, job skills, leadership, music/drama, religious affiliation.

**Scholarships offered:** 29 full-time freshmen received athletic scholarships; average amount $16,647.

**FINANCIAL AID PROCEDURES**

**Forms required:** FAFSA, institutional form.

**Dates and Deadlines:** Applicants notified on a rolling basis starting 2/1.

**Transfers:** No deadline. Applicants notified on a rolling basis.

**CONTACT**

Lee Ferguson, Director of Financial Aid

3000 Mountain Creek Parkway, Dallas, TX 75211-9299

(214) 333-5363

## Dallas Christian College
Dallas, Texas
www.dallas.edu                                 Federal Code: 006941

**4-year private** Bible college in very large city, affiliated with nondenominational tradition.

**Enrollment:** 315 undergrads, 23% part-time. 59 full-time freshmen.

**BASIC COSTS (2015-2016)**

**Tuition and fees:** $15,500.

**Per-credit charge:** $488.

**Room and board:** $7,920.

**FINANCIAL AID PICTURE**

**Students with need:** Need-based aid available for full-time and part-time students.

**Students without need:** This college awards aid only to students with need.

**FINANCIAL AID PROCEDURES**

**Forms required:** FAFSA, institutional form.

**Dates and Deadlines:** Priority date 5/15; no closing date. Applicants notified on a rolling basis; must reply within 2 week(s) of notification.

**Transfers:** Priority date 5/1; no deadline. Applicants notified on a rolling basis; must reply within 2 week(s) of notification.

**CONTACT**

Dana Mingo, Financial Aid Director

2700 Christian Parkway, Dallas, TX 75234-7299

(972) 241-3371 ext. 143

## Del Mar College
Corpus Christi, Texas
www.delmar.edu                                 Federal Code: 003563

**2-year public** community college in large city.

**Enrollment:** 10,159 undergrads, 74% part-time. 458 full-time freshmen.

**Selectivity:** Open admission; but selective for some programs.

**BASIC COSTS (2015-2016)**

**Tuition and fees:** $2,914; out-of-district residents $4,414; out-of-state residents $5,524.

**Per-credit charge:** $56; out-of-district residents $106; out-of-state residents $143.

**FINANCIAL AID PICTURE**

**Students with need:** Need-based aid available for full-time and part-time students. Work study available nights, weekends, and for part-time students.

**FINANCIAL AID PROCEDURES**

**Forms required:** FAFSA, institutional form.

**Dates and Deadlines:** Priority date 5/1; no closing date. Applicants notified on a rolling basis starting 7/1; must reply within 2 week(s) of notification.

**CONTACT**

Nancy Briseno, Director of Financial Aid Services

101 Baldwin Boulevard, Corpus Christi, TX 78404-3897

(361) 698-1293

## DeVry University: Irving
Dallas, Texas
www.devry.edu                                  Federal Code: 010139

**4-year for-profit** university in small city.

**Enrollment:** 578 undergrads.

**BASIC COSTS (2015-2016)**

**Tuition and fees:** $17,132.

**Per-credit charge:** $609.

**FINANCIAL AID PICTURE**

**Students with need:** Need-based aid available for full-time and part-time students.

**Students without need:** This college awards aid only to students with need.

**CONTACT**

Nga Phan, Director, Financial Aid

4800 Regent Boulevard, Suite 200, Dallas, TX 75063-2439

(972) 929-9740

## East Texas Baptist University
Marshall, Texas
www.etbu.edu                                   Federal Code: 003564

**4-year private** university and liberal arts college in large town, affiliated with Baptist faith.

**Enrollment:** 1,139 undergrads, 4% part-time. 363 full-time freshmen.

**Selectivity:** Admits 50 to 75% of applicants.

## BASIC COSTS (2015-2016)
**Tuition and fees:** $24,218.
**Per-credit charge:** $775.
**Room and board:** $8,629.

## FINANCIAL AID PICTURE (2014-2015)
**Students with need:** Out of 346 full-time freshmen who applied for aid, 323 were judged to have need. Of these, 323 received aid, and 53 had their full need met. Average financial aid package met 31% of need; average scholarship/grant was $6,312; average loan was $3,091. For part-time students, average financial aid package was $5,320.
**Students without need:** 40 full-time freshmen who did not demonstrate need for aid received scholarships/grants; average award was $9,979. No-need awards available for academics, alumni affiliation, leadership, religious affiliation, state/district residency.

## FINANCIAL AID PROCEDURES
**Forms required:** FAFSA, institutional form.
**Dates and Deadlines:** Priority date 6/1; no closing date. Applicants notified on a rolling basis starting 1/1.
**Transfers:** Applicants notified on a rolling basis starting 1/1.

## CONTACT
Tommy Young, Director of Financial Aid
One Tiger Drive, Marshall, TX 75670-1498
(903) 923-2138

# Eastfield College
Mesquite, Texas
www.efc.dcccd.edu          Federal Code: 008510

**2-year public** community and liberal arts college in small city.
**Enrollment:** 10,890 undergrads, 73% part-time. 714 full-time freshmen.
**Selectivity:** Open admission.

## BASIC COSTS (2015-2016)
**Tuition and fees:** $1,770; out-of-district residents $3,330; out-of-state residents $5,220.
**Per-credit charge:** $59; out-of-district residents $111; out-of-state residents $174.

## FINANCIAL AID PICTURE
**Students with need:** Need-based aid available for full-time and part-time students. Work study available nights, weekends, and for part-time students.
**Scholarships offered:** Lecroy Scholars Program; $600 per semester; based on demonstrated church, community, or academic leadership and 3.0 GPA; requires enrollment in at least 12 credit hours; 5-10 awarded. Erin Tierney Kramp Encouragement Program; $600 per semester; based on demonstrated courage in the face of adversity, moral character, leadership, and high academic standards; requires enrollment in 8 hours for awarding semester, and maintenance of high academic standards; 2 awarded.

## FINANCIAL AID PROCEDURES
**Forms required:** FAFSA, institutional form.
**Dates and Deadlines:** Priority date 5/1; no closing date. Applicants notified on a rolling basis starting 4/15.

## CONTACT
Dana Mingo, Dean of Financial Aid
3737 Motley Drive, Mesquite, TX 75150
(972) 860-8385

# El Centro College
Dallas, Texas
www.elcentrocollege.edu          Federal Code: 004453

**2-year public** community college in very large city.
**Enrollment:** 8,212 undergrads, 85% part-time. 246 full-time freshmen.
**Selectivity:** Open admission; but selective for some programs.

## BASIC COSTS (2015-2016)
**Tuition and fees:** $1,770; out-of-district residents $3,330; out-of-state residents $5,220.
**Per-credit charge:** $59; out-of-district residents $111; out-of-state residents $200.
**Additional info:** Tuition/fee waivers available for minority students, unemployed or children of unemployed.

## FINANCIAL AID PICTURE
**Students with need:** Need-based aid available for full-time and part-time students.
**Additional info:** Interview required for financial aid applicants.

## FINANCIAL AID PROCEDURES
**Forms required:** FAFSA.
**Dates and Deadlines:** Priority date 5/1; no closing date. Applicants notified on a rolling basis; must reply within 2 week(s) of notification.
**Transfers:** Financial aid transcript may be required from previous institutions attended.

## CONTACT
Pamela Lucas, Director
801 Main Street, Dallas, TX 75202
(214) 860-2099

# El Paso Community College
El Paso, Texas
www.epcc.edu          Federal Code: 010387

**2-year public** community college in very large city.
**Enrollment:** 27,488 undergrads.
**Selectivity:** Open admission; but selective for some programs.

## BASIC COSTS (2015-2016)
**Tuition and fees:** $2,970; out-of-state residents $5,040.
**Per-credit charge:** $84; out-of-state residents $153.
**Additional info:** Out of state student per credit hour rate is $200 for 1st credit hour, $306 for 2 credit hours, $459 for 3 credit hours. Each additional credit hour is $153.

## FINANCIAL AID PICTURE
**Students with need:** Work study available nights, weekends, and for part-time students.
**Students without need:** No-need awards available for academics, athletics.

## FINANCIAL AID PROCEDURES
**Forms required:** FAFSA, institutional form.
**Dates and Deadlines:** Priority date 5/1; no closing date. Applicants notified on a rolling basis starting 7/1; must reply within 2 week(s) of notification.

## CONTACT
Linda Gonzalez-Hensgen, Director of Student Financial Services
Box 20500, El Paso, TX 79998
(915) 831-2566

## Frank Phillips College

Borger, Texas
www.fpctx.edu                                 Federal Code: 003568

**2-year public** community and junior college in large town.
**Enrollment:** 569 undergrads.
**Selectivity:** Open admission.

### BASIC COSTS (2015-2016)

**Tuition and fees:** $2,755; out-of-district residents $3,445; out-of-state residents $3,743.
**Room and board:** $4,670.

### FINANCIAL AID PICTURE

**Students with need:** Need-based aid available for full-time and part-time students. Work study available nights, weekends, and for part-time students.
**Students without need:** No-need awards available for academics, athletics, music/drama, state/district residency.
**Additional info:** Some Texas fire department and police department personnel, active duty military personnel, children of military missing in action may qualify for reduced or waived tuition. Out-of-state tuition waived for students living in Oklahoma counties adjacent to Texas.

### FINANCIAL AID PROCEDURES

**Forms required:** FAFSA, institutional form.
**Dates and Deadlines:** Closing date 7/1. Applicants notified on a rolling basis; must reply within 2 week(s) of notification.
**Transfers:** No deadline. Applicants notified on a rolling basis.

### CONTACT

Beverly Fields, Director of Financial Services
Box 5118, Borger, TX 79008-5118
(806) 457-4200 ext. 796

## Galveston College

Galveston, Texas
www.gc.edu                                    Federal Code: 004972

**2-year public** community college in small city.
**Enrollment:** 1,751 undergrads, 72% part-time. 113 full-time freshmen.
**Selectivity:** Open admission; but selective for some programs.

### BASIC COSTS (2015-2016)

**Tuition and fees:** $1,900; out-of-district residents $2,260; out-of-state residents $4,150.
**Per-credit charge:** $37; out-of-district residents $49; out-of-state residents $112.

### FINANCIAL AID PICTURE

**Students with need:** Need-based aid available for full-time and part-time students.
**Students without need:** This college awards aid only to students with need.

### FINANCIAL AID PROCEDURES

**Forms required:** FAFSA.
**Dates and Deadlines:** Priority date 6/7; no closing date. Applicants notified on a rolling basis starting 6/1.

### CONTACT

Ron Crumedy, V.P. of Student Services/Director of Finanical Aid
4015 Avenue Q, Galveston, TX 77550-7447
(409) 944-1235

## Grayson College

Denison, Texas
www.grayson.edu                               Federal Code: 003570

**2-year public** community and technical college in large town.
**Enrollment:** 4,500 undergrads. 767 full-time freshmen.
**Selectivity:** Open admission; but selective for some programs.

### BASIC COSTS (2015-2016)

**Tuition and fees:** $2,310; out-of-district residents $3,450; out-of-state residents $4,830.
**Per-credit charge:** $49; out-of-district residents $87; out-of-state residents $133.
**Room and board:** $5,340.
**Additional info:** Tuition at time of enrollment locked for 2 years.

### FINANCIAL AID PICTURE (2014-2015)

**Students with need:** Out of 714 full-time freshmen who applied for aid, 666 were judged to have need. Of these, 666 received aid, and 1 had their full need met. For part-time students, average financial aid package was $4,405.
**Students without need:** 52 full-time freshmen who did not demonstrate need for aid received scholarships/grants; average award was $1,572. No-need awards available for academics, alumni affiliation, art, athletics, job skills, leadership, minority status, music/drama, state/district residency.
**Scholarships offered:** 33 full-time freshmen received athletic scholarships; average amount $5,761.
**Additional info:** Short term loans available.

### FINANCIAL AID PROCEDURES

**Forms required:** FAFSA.
**Dates and Deadlines:** Priority date 6/1; no closing date. Applicants notified on a rolling basis; must reply within 5 week(s) of notification.
**Transfers:** No deadline. Applicants notified on a rolling basis; must reply within 5 week(s) of notification.

### CONTACT

Donna King, Director of Financial Aid
6101 Grayson Drive, Denison, TX 75020
(903) 463-8642

## Hallmark University

San Antonio, Texas
www.hallmarkuniversity.edu                    Federal Code: 010509

**2-year private** business and health science college in very large city.
**Enrollment:** 582 undergrads. 124 full-time freshmen.
**Selectivity:** Admits over 75% of applicants.

### BASIC COSTS (2016-2017)

**Additional info:** Tuition and fees vary by program.

### FINANCIAL AID PICTURE (2015-2016)

**Students with need:** 25% of average financial aid package awarded as scholarships/grants, 75% awarded as loans/jobs.

### FINANCIAL AID PROCEDURES

**Forms required:** FAFSA, institutional form.
**Dates and Deadlines:** Applicants notified on a rolling basis.
**Transfers:** No deadline. Applicants notified on a rolling basis.

### CONTACT

Grace Calixto, Director of Financial Planning
Hallmark University, San Antonio, TX 78230-1736
(210) 690-9000 ext. 211

## Hardin-Simmons University
Abilene, Texas
www.hsutx.edu                    Federal Code: 003571

**4-year private** university in small city, affiliated with Baptist faith.
**Enrollment:** 1,599 undergrads, 8% part-time. 413 full-time freshmen.
**Selectivity:** Admits 50 to 75% of applicants.

**BASIC COSTS (2016-2017)**
**Tuition and fees:** $25,830.
**Room and board:** $8,138.
**Additional info:** Tuition at time of enrollment locked for 4 years.

**FINANCIAL AID PICTURE (2015-2016)**
**Students with need:** Out of 412 full-time freshmen who applied for aid, 325 were judged to have need. Of these, 325 received aid, and 114 had their full need met. Average financial aid package met 90% of need; average scholarship/grant was $8,245; average loan was $3,080. For part-time students, average financial aid package was $10,899.
**Students without need:** 87 full-time freshmen who did not demonstrate need for aid received scholarships/grants; average award was $14,537. No-need awards available for academics, alumni affiliation, art, leadership, minority status, music/drama, religious affiliation.

**FINANCIAL AID PROCEDURES**
**Forms required:** FAFSA.
**Dates and Deadlines:** Priority date 3/1; no closing date. Applicants notified on a rolling basis starting 3/1; must reply by 6/1.
**Transfers:** No deadline. Applicants notified on a rolling basis starting 2/1.

**CONTACT**
Bridget Moore, Director of Financial Aid & Scholarships
PO Box 16050, Abilene, TX 79698-0001
(325) 670-1206

## Hill College
Hillsboro, Texas
www.hillcollege.edu              Federal Code: 003573

**2-year public** community college in small town.
**Enrollment:** 4,098 undergrads.
**Selectivity:** Open admission; but selective for some programs.

**BASIC COSTS (2015-2016)**
**Tuition and fees:** $2,370; out-of-district residents $3,120; out-of-state residents $3,520.
**Room and board:** $3,650.
**Additional info:** Cost 1516: t&f confirmed via website - http://www.hillcollege.edu/Admissions_and_Aid/FinAid/fees.html. et 9/9.

**FINANCIAL AID PICTURE**
**Students with need:** Need-based aid available for full-time and part-time students.
**Students without need:** No-need awards available for academics, athletics, music/drama.

**FINANCIAL AID PROCEDURES**
**Forms required:** FAFSA, institutional form.
**Dates and Deadlines:** Closing date 7/31. Applicants notified on a rolling basis.

**CONTACT**
Susan Russell, Director of Student Financial Aid
112 Lamar Drive, Hillsboro, TX 76645
(254) 659-7600

## Houston Baptist University
Houston, Texas
www.hbu.edu                      Federal Code: 003576

**4-year private** university and liberal arts college in very large city, affiliated with Baptist faith.
**Enrollment:** 2,240 undergrads, 6% part-time. 544 full-time freshmen.
**Selectivity:** Admits less than 50% of applicants.

**BASIC COSTS (2015-2016)**
**Tuition and fees:** $29,800.
**Room and board:** $7,715.

**FINANCIAL AID PICTURE (2015-2016)**
**Students with need:** Out of 472 full-time freshmen who applied for aid, 430 were judged to have need. Of these, 426 received aid, and 57 had their full need met. Average financial aid package met 71% of need; average scholarship/grant was $19,007; average loan was $4,109. For part-time students, average financial aid package was $14,197.
**Students without need:** 114 full-time freshmen who did not demonstrate need for aid received scholarships/grants; average award was $12,159. No-need awards available for academics, alumni affiliation, art, athletics, music/drama.
**Scholarships offered:** *Merit:* Endowed Academic Scholarship; full or three-quarters tuition for four years; limited number available. Founders Academic Scholarship; $15,000 per year, renewable; minimum 1170 SAT or 26 ACT required for freshmen. Presidential Academic Scholarship; $14,000 per year, renewable; minimum 1140 SAT or 25 ACT required for freshmen. Legacy Grant; $13,000 per year, renewable; minimum 1010 SAT or 22 ACT required for freshmen. All SAT scores are exclusive of Writing. Ministerial Dependents Grant; $2,000 per year; for dependent children of ordained/licensed Southern Baptist ministers and missionaries. Grants-In-Aid; awards vary; for students who contribute special abilities or services to the University; awarded in music, art, athletics and nursing. Church Matching Award; awards vary. *Athletic:* 53 full-time freshmen received athletic scholarships; average amount $25,480.

**FINANCIAL AID PROCEDURES**
**Forms required:** FAFSA.
**Dates and Deadlines:** Applicants notified on a rolling basis starting 3/15; must reply within 4 week(s) of notification.

**CONTACT**
Jene Gabbard, Senior Director of Financial Aid and Scholarships
7502 Fondren Road, Houston, TX 77074-3298
(281) 649-3471

## Houston Community College System
Houston, Texas
www.hccs.edu                     Federal Code: 010422

**2-year public** community college in very large city.
**Enrollment:** 56,359 undergrads, 70% part-time. 3,544 full-time freshmen.
**Selectivity:** Open admission; but selective for some programs.

**BASIC COSTS (2016-2017)**
**Tuition and fees:** $2,031; out-of-district residents $4,191; out-of-state residents $4,686.
**Additional info:** All required fees are included in the tuition figures.

**FINANCIAL AID PICTURE (2015-2016)**
**Students with need:** Out of 2,361 full-time freshmen who applied for aid, 2,046 were judged to have need. Of these, 2,046 received aid, and 1,956 had their full need met. Average financial aid package met 78% of need; average loan was $2,600. Need-based aid available for part-time students.
**Students without need:** No-need awards available for academics, state/district residency.

**Additional info:** Although financial aid applications can be submitted at any time during the academic year, FAFSA's received after priority filing date of April 15 will be considered for funding only after all on-time filers have been awarded and then only if funds are available.

**FINANCIAL AID PROCEDURES**

**Forms required:** FAFSA.

**Dates and Deadlines:** Priority date 4/15; closing date 6/30. Applicants notified on a rolling basis starting 3/15.

**CONTACT**

Joellen Soucier, Executive Director of Financial Aid
PO Box 667517, MC 1136, Houston, TX 77266-7517
(713) 718-2000 ext. OPT2

## Howard College

Big Spring, Texas
www.howardcollege.edu                    Federal Code: 003574

**2-year public** community college in large town.

**Enrollment:** 4,360 undergrads, 78% part-time. 320 full-time freshmen.

**Selectivity:** Open admission; but selective for some programs.

**BASIC COSTS (2015-2016)**

**Tuition and fees:** $2,542; out-of-district residents $3,772; out-of-state residents $5,402.

**Per-credit charge:** $67; out-of-district residents $106; out-of-state residents $159.

**Room and board:** $4,530.

**FINANCIAL AID PICTURE**

**Students with need:** Need-based aid available for full-time and part-time students.

**Students without need:** No-need awards available for academics, art, athletics, leadership, music/drama.

**FINANCIAL AID PROCEDURES**

**Forms required:** FAFSA, institutional form.

**Dates and Deadlines:** Priority date 4/1; no closing date. Applicants notified on a rolling basis starting 7/15; must reply within 2 week(s) of notification.

**CONTACT**

Candice Draper, Director of Financial Aid
1001 Birdwell Lane, Big Spring, TX 79720
(432) 264-5083

## Howard Payne University

Brownwood, Texas
www.hputx.edu                    Federal Code: 003575

**4-year private** university and liberal arts college in large town, affiliated with Baptist faith.

**Enrollment:** 951 undergrads. 300 full-time freshmen.

**Selectivity:** Admits over 75% of applicants.

**BASIC COSTS (2015-2016)**

**Tuition and fees:** $25,600.

**Per-credit charge:** $760.

**Room and board:** $7,489.

**FINANCIAL AID PICTURE (2014-2015)**

**Students with need:** Out of 288 full-time freshmen who applied for aid, 270 were judged to have need. Of these, 269 received aid, and 64 had their full need met. Average financial aid package met 78% of need; average scholarship/grant was $17,215; average loan was $3,412. For part-time students, average financial aid package was $6,539.

**Students without need:** 28 full-time freshmen who did not demonstrate need for aid received scholarships/grants; average award was $13,487. No-need awards available for academics, alumni affiliation, art, leadership, music/drama, religious affiliation, state/district residency.

**Scholarships offered:** Merit-based scholarship available to all approved home school applicants, $5,000 annually ($20,000 over 4 years).

**FINANCIAL AID PROCEDURES**

**Forms required:** FAFSA, institutional form.

**Dates and Deadlines:** Applicants notified on a rolling basis starting 2/15; must reply within 2 week(s) of notification.

**CONTACT**

Glenda Huff, Director of Student Financial Aid
1000 Fisk Street, Brownwood, TX 76801-2794
(325) 649-8015

## Huston-Tillotson University

Austin, Texas
www.htu.edu                    Federal Code: 003577

**4-year private** business and liberal arts college in very large city, affiliated with United Methodist Church.

**Enrollment:** 968 undergrads, 5% part-time. 203 full-time freshmen.

**Selectivity:** Admits less than 50% of applicants.

**BASIC COSTS (2015-2016)**

**Tuition and fees:** $14,346.

**Room and board:** $7,568.

**FINANCIAL AID PICTURE (2014-2015)**

**Students with need:** For part-time students, average financial aid package was $7,062.

**Students without need:** No-need awards available for academics, athletics, leadership, minority status, music/drama, religious affiliation, state/district residency.

**FINANCIAL AID PROCEDURES**

**Forms required:** FAFSA, institutional form.

**Dates and Deadlines:** Priority date 3/15; no closing date. Applicants notified on a rolling basis starting 4/8; must reply within 2 week(s) of notification.

**Transfers:** No deadline.

**CONTACT**

Melanie Johnson, Assistant Director of Financial Aid
900 Chicon Street, Austin, TX 78702-2795
(512) 505-3031

## Jacksonville College

Jacksonville, Texas
www.jacksonville-college.edu                    Federal Code: 003579

**2-year private** junior and liberal arts college in large town, affiliated with Baptist faith.

**Enrollment:** 304 undergrads.

**Selectivity:** Open admission.

**BASIC COSTS (2015-2016)**

**Tuition and fees:** $7,700.

**Per-credit charge:** $210.

**Room and board:** $6,000.

**FINANCIAL AID PICTURE (2015-2016)**

**Students with need:** 93% of average financial aid package awarded as scholarships/grants, 7% awarded as loans/jobs. Need-based aid available for part-time students.

**Students without need:** No-need awards available for academics, athletics, leadership, music/drama, religious affiliation, state/district residency.

**FINANCIAL AID PROCEDURES**

**Forms required:** FAFSA, state aid form, institutional form.

**Dates and Deadlines:** Priority date 8/1; no closing date. Applicants notified on a rolling basis.

**Transfers:** No deadline. Applicants notified on a rolling basis.

**CONTACT**

Paul Galyean, Financial Aid Officer

105 B.J. Albritton Drive, Jacksonville, TX 75766-4759

(903) 586-2518 ext. 7135

## Jarvis Christian College

Hawkins, Texas

www.jarvis.edu                    Federal Code: 003637

**4-year private** liberal arts college in rural community, affiliated with Christian Church (Disciples of Christ).

**Enrollment:** 863 undergrads, 2% part-time. 186 full-time freshmen.

**Selectivity:** Open admission; but selective for some programs.

**BASIC COSTS (2015-2016)**

**Tuition and fees:** $11,369.

**Per-credit charge:** $420.

**Room and board:** $8,183.

**FINANCIAL AID PICTURE (2014-2015)**

**Students with need:** Out of 181 full-time freshmen who applied for aid, 181 were judged to have need. Of these, 175 received aid, and 174 had their full need met. Average financial aid package met 96% of need; average scholarship/grant was $9,387; average loan was $9,923. For part-time students, average financial aid package was $9,121.

**Students without need:** No-need awards available for academics, athletics, religious affiliation.

**Scholarships offered:** 43 full-time freshmen received athletic scholarships; average amount $8,925.

**Additional info:** High school transcript required for scholarship consideration.

**FINANCIAL AID PROCEDURES**

**Forms required:** FAFSA, state aid form.

**Dates and Deadlines:** Applicants notified on a rolling basis starting 5/1; must reply by 5/30 or within 2 week(s) of notification.

**Transfers:** Priority date 4/15; no deadline. Applicants notified on a rolling basis starting 7/1; must reply within 2 week(s) of notification.

**CONTACT**

Rosamond Gholson, Interim Director of Financial Aid

PO Box 1470, Hawkins, TX 75765-1470

(903) 730-4890 ext. 2410

## Kilgore College

Kilgore, Texas

www.kilgore.edu                    Federal Code: 003580

**2-year public** community college in large town.

**Enrollment:** 5,630 undergrads, 60% part-time. 677 full-time freshmen.

**Selectivity:** Open admission; but selective for some programs.

**BASIC COSTS (2015-2016)**

**Tuition and fees:** $1,830; out-of-district residents $3,900; out-of-state residents $5,400.

**Per-credit charge:** $32; out-of-district residents $101; out-of-state residents $151.

**Room and board:** $4,640.

**Additional info:** Tuition/fee waivers available for unemployed or children of unemployed.

**FINANCIAL AID PICTURE**

**Students with need:** Need-based aid available for full-time and part-time students.

**Students without need:** No-need awards available for academics, alumni affiliation, art, athletics, job skills, leadership, music/drama, state/district residency.

**Scholarships offered:** Presidential Scholarships: tuition, fees and books for 4 semesters; ACT 25 or top 10% of senior class; 20 available; renewable at 2.5 GPA.

**Additional info:** State of Texas grants and loans available for honor graduates with unmet needs and for non-traditional students.

**FINANCIAL AID PROCEDURES**

**Forms required:** FAFSA, state aid form, institutional form.

**Dates and Deadlines:** Priority date 6/1; closing date 7/1. Applicants notified on a rolling basis starting 3/1; must reply within 2 week(s) of notification.

**Transfers:** No deadline. Transfer students must submit financial aid transcript from previous school plus all appropriate internal aid forms and show proof of high school graduation or GED.

**CONTACT**

Annette Morgan, Director of Financial Aid

1100 Broadway, Kilgore, TX 75662-3299

(903) 983-8183

## The King's University

Southlake, Texas

www.tku.edu                    Federal Code: 035163

**4-year private** Bible and seminary college in very large city, affiliated with nondenominational tradition.

**Enrollment:** 473 undergrads.

**BASIC COSTS (2015-2016)**

**Tuition and fees:** $12,690.

**Per-credit charge:** $398.

**Additional info:** Tuition/fee waivers available for adults.

**FINANCIAL AID PICTURE**

**Students with need:** Need-based aid available for full-time and part-time students. Work study available nights, weekends, and for part-time students.

**Additional info:** Specific scholarships may require specific essays.

**FINANCIAL AID PROCEDURES**

**Forms required:** FAFSA.

**Dates and Deadlines:** Applicants notified on a rolling basis; must reply within 4 week(s) of notification.

**CONTACT**

Jackie Wadleigh, Director of Financial Aid

2121 E Southlake Blvd, Southlake, TX 76092

(817) 552-7341

## Lamar State College at Orange

Orange, Texas

www.lsco.edu                    Federal Code: 016748

**2-year public** junior and liberal arts college in small city.

**Enrollment:** 1,841 undergrads.

**Selectivity:** Open admission; but selective for some programs.

**BASIC COSTS (2015-2016)**

**Tuition and fees:** $4,807; out-of-state residents $16,507.

**Per-credit charge:** $125; out-of-state residents $515.

### FINANCIAL AID PICTURE

**Students with need:** Need-based aid available for full-time and part-time students.

**Students without need:** This college awards aid only to students with need.

### FINANCIAL AID PROCEDURES

**Forms required:** FAFSA, institutional form.

**Dates and Deadlines:** Priority date 4/1; no closing date. Applicants notified on a rolling basis starting 5/15; must reply within 2 week(s) of notification.

### CONTACT

Kerry Olson, Director of Financial Aid
410 Front Street, Orange, TX 77630
(409) 882-3317

## Lamar State College at Port Arthur

Port Arthur, Texas
www.lamarpa.edu                    Federal Code: 016666

**2-year public** community and technical college in small city.

**Enrollment:** 1,802 undergrads.

**Selectivity:** Open admission.

### BASIC COSTS (2015-2016)

**Tuition and fees:** $5,553; out-of-state residents $16,393.

**Per-credit charge:** $128; out-of-state residents $518.

### FINANCIAL AID PICTURE

**Students with need:** Need-based aid available for full-time and part-time students. Work study available nights.

**Students without need:** This college awards aid only to students with need.

### FINANCIAL AID PROCEDURES

**Forms required:** FAFSA, institutional form.

**Dates and Deadlines:** Priority date 4/1; no closing date. Applicants notified on a rolling basis starting 4/15; must reply within 2 week(s) of notification.

### CONTACT

Connie Riley, Director of Financial Aid
Box 310, Port Arthur, TX 77641-0310
(409) 984-6203

## Lamar University

Beaumont, Texas
www.lamar.edu                    Federal Code: 003581

**4-year public** university in small city.

**Enrollment:** 9,009 undergrads, 30% part-time. 1,306 full-time freshmen.

**Selectivity:** Admits over 75% of applicants.

### BASIC COSTS (2016-2017)

**Tuition and fees:** $9,362; out-of-state residents $21,062.

**Per-credit charge:** $230; out-of-state residents $620.

**Room and board:** $7,870.

### FINANCIAL AID PICTURE (2014-2015)

**Students with need:** Out of 1,098 full-time freshmen who applied for aid, 858 were judged to have need. Of these, 843 received aid, and 105 had their full need met. Average financial aid package met 50% of need; average scholarship/grant was $6,750; average loan was $2,758. For part-time students, average financial aid package was $4,633.

**Students without need:** This college awards aid only to students with need.

### FINANCIAL AID PROCEDURES

**Forms required:** FAFSA, institutional form.

**Dates and Deadlines:** Priority date 4/1; no closing date. Applicants notified on a rolling basis starting 4/1; must reply within 2 week(s) of notification.

### CONTACT

Jill Rowley, Director of Financial Aid
Box 10009, Beaumont, TX 77710
(409) 880-8450

## Lee College

Baytown, Texas
www.lee.edu                    Federal Code: 003583

**2-year public** community college in small city.

**Enrollment:** 6,817 undergrads.

**Selectivity:** Open admission; but selective for some programs.

### BASIC COSTS (2015-2016)

**Tuition and fees:** $2,058; out-of-district residents $2,958; out-of-state residents $4,368.

**Per-credit charge:** $50; out-of-district residents $80; out-of-state residents $127.

### FINANCIAL AID PICTURE

**Students with need:** Need-based aid available for full-time and part-time students.

**Students without need:** No-need awards available for academics, art, athletics, job skills, leadership, music/drama.

### FINANCIAL AID PROCEDURES

**Forms required:** FAFSA.

**Dates and Deadlines:** Priority date 4/1; no closing date. Applicants notified on a rolling basis starting 6/1.

**Transfers:** Priority date 4/15; no deadline. Applicants notified on a rolling basis.

### CONTACT

Sharon Steele, Financial Aid Officer
Box 818, Baytown, TX 77522-0818
(281) 425-6388

## LeTourneau University

Longview, Texas
www.letu.edu                    Federal Code: 003584

**4-year private** university in small city, affiliated with nondenominational tradition.

**Enrollment:** 1,933 undergrads, 36% part-time. 273 full-time freshmen.

**Selectivity:** Admits less than 50% of applicants.

### BASIC COSTS (2016-2017)

**Tuition and fees:** $28,480.

**Room and board:** $9,770.

### FINANCIAL AID PICTURE (2015-2016)

**Students with need:** Out of 247 full-time freshmen who applied for aid, 211 were judged to have need. Of these, 211 received aid, and 16 had their full need met. Average financial aid package met 78% of need; average scholarship/grant was $18,937; average loan was $4,214. For part-time students, average financial aid package was $8,269.

**Students without need:** 43 full-time freshmen who did not demonstrate need for aid received scholarships/grants; average award was $11,516. No-need awards available for academics, leadership, minority status, religious affiliation, state/district residency.

## FINANCIAL AID PROCEDURES
**Forms required:** FAFSA.
**Dates and Deadlines:** Priority date 2/15; no closing date. Applicants notified on a rolling basis starting 3/15; must reply within 2 week(s) of notification.

## CONTACT
PO Box 7001, Longview, TX 75607-7001
(903) 233-4350

## Lone Star College System
The Woodlands, Texas
www.lonestar.edu                Federal Code: 011145

**2-year public** community college in very large city.
**Enrollment:** 83,932 undergrads, 71% part-time. 2,635 full-time freshmen.
**Selectivity:** Open admission; but selective for some programs.

## BASIC COSTS (2016-2017)
**Tuition and fees:** $1,864; out-of-district residents $3,964; out-of-state residents $4,414.
**Per-credit charge:** $42; out-of-district residents $112; out-of-state residents $127.

## FINANCIAL AID PICTURE (2014-2015)
**Students with need:** Out of 1,484 full-time freshmen who applied for aid, 1,266 were judged to have need. Of these, 922 received aid, and 13 had their full need met. Average financial aid package met 42% of need; average scholarship/grant was $2,245; average loan was $1,353. For part-time students, average financial aid package was $2,033.
**Students without need:** 27 full-time freshmen who did not demonstrate need for aid received scholarships/grants; average award was $761. No-need awards available for academics.

## FINANCIAL AID PROCEDURES
**Forms required:** FAFSA.
**Dates and Deadlines:** Priority date 5/10; no closing date. Applicants notified on a rolling basis starting 4/1.

## CONTACT
Donna King, AVC - Student Success/Financial Aid
5000 Research Forest Drive, The Woodlands, TX 77381-4356
(281) 290-2700

## Lubbock Christian University
Lubbock, Texas
www.lcu.edu                Federal Code: 003586

**4-year private** university and liberal arts college in small city, affiliated with Church of Christ.
**Enrollment:** 1,496 undergrads, 15% part-time. 250 full-time freshmen.
**Selectivity:** Admits over 75% of applicants.

## BASIC COSTS (2015-2016)
**Tuition and fees:** $20,360.
**Per-credit charge:** $652.
**Room and board:** $6,070.

## FINANCIAL AID PICTURE (2014-2015)
**Students with need:** Out of 176 full-time freshmen who applied for aid, 143 were judged to have need. Of these, 143 received aid, and 13 had their full need met. Average financial aid package met 69% of need; average scholarship/grant was $10,419; average loan was $4,216. For part-time students, average financial aid package was $7,405.
**Students without need:** 39 full-time freshmen who did not demonstrate need for aid received scholarships/grants; average award was $4,542. No-need awards available for academics, athletics, leadership, music/drama, religious affiliation.

**Scholarships offered:** 21 full-time freshmen received athletic scholarships; average amount $11,304.

## FINANCIAL AID PROCEDURES
**Forms required:** FAFSA, institutional form.
**Dates and Deadlines:** Priority date 6/1; no closing date. Applicants notified on a rolling basis starting 3/1.
**Transfers:** No deadline. Applicants notified on a rolling basis starting 3/1.

## CONTACT
Amy Hardesty, Director, Financial Assistance
5601 19th Street, Lubbock, TX 79407-2099
(806) 720-7176

## McLennan Community College
Waco, Texas
www.mclennan.edu                Federal Code: 003590

**2-year public** community and junior college in small city.
**Enrollment:** 8,305 undergrads, 58% part-time. 889 full-time freshmen.
**Selectivity:** Open admission; but selective for some programs.

## BASIC COSTS (2015-2016)
**Tuition and fees:** $3,450; out-of-district residents $3,990; out-of-state residents $5,700.
**Per-credit charge:** $106; out-of-district residents $124; out-of-state residents $181.

## FINANCIAL AID PICTURE
**Students with need:** Need-based aid available for full-time and part-time students.
**Students without need:** No-need awards available for athletics.
**Scholarships offered:** Academic scholarship: awarded to individuals selected for Tartan scholar's program.

## FINANCIAL AID PROCEDURES
**Forms required:** FAFSA.
**Dates and Deadlines:** Closing date 6/1. Applicants notified on a rolling basis starting 5/1.

## CONTACT
James Kubacak, Director of Financial Aid
1400 College Drive, Waco, TX 76708
(254) 299-8698

## McMurry University
Abilene, Texas
www.mcm.edu                Federal Code: 003591

**4-year private** university and liberal arts college in small city, affiliated with United Methodist Church.
**Enrollment:** 1,002 undergrads, 9% part-time. 207 full-time freshmen.
**Selectivity:** Admits 50 to 75% of applicants.

## BASIC COSTS (2015-2016)
**Tuition and fees:** $25,588.
**Per-credit charge:** $799.
**Room and board:** $8,162.
**Additional info:** Students pay a block tuition rate for 12 or more hours per semester for fall and spring semesters. Required fees (other than the $175 freshmen orientation fee) are included in tuition cost. The use of a tablet PC and school-related software is also included in tuition cost.

## FINANCIAL AID PICTURE (2014-2015)
**Students with need:** Out of 145 full-time freshmen who applied for aid, 141 were judged to have need. Of these, 141 received aid, and 10 had their full need met. Average financial aid package met 71% of need; average

scholarship/grant was $16,862; average loan was $4,318. For part-time students, average financial aid package was $7,970.

**Students without need:** 9 full-time freshmen who did not demonstrate need for aid received scholarships/grants; average award was $10,450. No-need awards available for academics, art, athletics, job skills, leadership, music/drama, religious affiliation.

**FINANCIAL AID PROCEDURES**
**Forms required:** FAFSA, state aid form, institutional form.
**Dates and Deadlines:** Priority date 3/15; no closing date. Applicants notified on a rolling basis starting 2/15; must reply within 3 week(s) of notification.
**Transfers:** No deadline. Applicants notified on a rolling basis starting 2/15; must reply by 6/30.

**CONTACT**
Lori Herrick, Director of Financial Aid
South 14th and Sayles Boulevard, Abilene, TX 79697-0001
(325) 793-4713

## Midland College
Midland, Texas
www.midland.edu                 Federal Code: 009797

**2-year public** community college in small city.
**Enrollment:** 5,430 undergrads.
**Selectivity:** Open admission; but selective for some programs.

**BASIC COSTS (2015-2016)**
**Tuition and fees:** $2,460; out-of-district residents $3,960; out-of-state residents $5,160.
**Per-credit charge:** $154; out-of-district residents $204; out-of-state residents $392.
**Room and board:** $4,700.

**FINANCIAL AID PICTURE**
**Students with need:** Need-based aid available for full-time and part-time students.
**Students without need:** No-need awards available for academics, athletics, minority status, music/drama, state/district residency.
**Scholarships offered:** Legacy Scholarship: varying amounts; renewable; available for full-time or part-time study to graduates of Midland County High Schools.

**FINANCIAL AID PROCEDURES**
**Forms required:** FAFSA.
**Dates and Deadlines:** Priority date 4/2; closing date 6/1. Applicants notified on a rolling basis starting 5/15; must reply within 2 week(s) of notification.
**Transfers:** No deadline.

**CONTACT**
Yolanda Ramos, Director of Financial Aid
3600 North Garfield, Midland, TX 79705
(432) 685-5511

## Midwestern State University
Wichita Falls, Texas
www.mwsu.edu                 Federal Code: 003592

**4-year public** university and liberal arts college in small city.
**Enrollment:** 5,277 undergrads, 23% part-time. 794 full-time freshmen.
**Selectivity:** Admits over 75% of applicants.

**BASIC COSTS (2015-2016)**
**Tuition and fees:** $8,005; out-of-state residents $9,955.
**Per-credit charge:** $171; out-of-state residents $236.
**Room and board:** $7,070.

**Additional info:** Tuition at time of enrollment locked for 4 years.

**FINANCIAL AID PICTURE (2015-2016)**
**Students with need:** Out of 741 full-time freshmen who applied for aid, 539 were judged to have need. Of these, 536 received aid, and 293 had their full need met. Average financial aid package met 70% of need; average scholarship/grant was $8,369; average loan was $5,177. For part-time students, average financial aid package was $5,810.
**Students without need:** 152 full-time freshmen who did not demonstrate need for aid received scholarships/grants; average award was $2,033. No-need awards available for academics, alumni affiliation, art, athletics, leadership, music/drama.
**Scholarships offered:** 22 full-time freshmen received athletic scholarships; average amount $6,632.

**FINANCIAL AID PROCEDURES**
**Forms required:** FAFSA, institutional form.
**Dates and Deadlines:** Priority date 3/1; no closing date. Applicants notified on a rolling basis starting 4/15; must reply within 4 week(s) of notification.
**Transfers:** No deadline. Applicants notified on a rolling basis starting 4/15; must reply within 4 week(s) of notification.

**CONTACT**
Kathy Pennartz, Director of Financial Aid
3410 Taft Boulevard, Wichita Falls, TX 76308-2099
(940) 397-4119

## Mountain View College
Dallas, Texas
www.mvc.dcccd.edu                 Federal Code: 008503

**2-year public** community college in very large city.
**Enrollment:** 7,300 undergrads, 76% part-time. 626 full-time freshmen.
**Selectivity:** Open admission; but selective for some programs.

**BASIC COSTS (2015-2016)**
**Tuition and fees:** $1,770; out-of-district residents $3,330; out-of-state residents $5,220.
**Per-credit charge:** $59; out-of-district residents $111; out-of-state residents $200.
**Additional info:** Tuition/fee waivers available for adults.

**FINANCIAL AID PICTURE**
**Students with need:** Need-based aid available for full-time and part-time students. Work study available nights, weekends, and for part-time students.

**FINANCIAL AID PROCEDURES**
**Forms required:** FAFSA, institutional form.
**Dates and Deadlines:** Priority date 5/1; no closing date. Applicants notified on a rolling basis starting 6/1.

**CONTACT**
Pam Shuttlesworth, Director of Financial Aid
Attn: Admissions, Dallas, TX 75211-6599
(214) 860-8688

## Navarro College
Corsicana, Texas
www.navarrocollege.edu                 Federal Code: 003593

**2-year public** community and junior college in large town.
**Enrollment:** 9,478 undergrads, 62% part-time. 1,201 full-time freshmen.
**Selectivity:** Open admission; but selective for some programs.

**BASIC COSTS (2016-2017)**
**Tuition and fees:** $2,188; out-of-district residents $3,388; out-of-state residents $4,888.

**Room and board:** $5,504.

**FINANCIAL AID PICTURE (2014-2015)**
**Students with need:** 66% of average financial aid package awarded as scholarships/grants, 34% awarded as loans/jobs.

**FINANCIAL AID PROCEDURES**
**Forms required:** FAFSA.
**Dates and Deadlines:** Priority date 6/1; no closing date. Applicants notified on a rolling basis starting 7/1; must reply within 2 week(s) of notification.

**CONTACT**
KrIstal Nicholson, Director of Financial Aid
3200 West Seventh Avenue, Corsicana, TX 75110
(903) 875-7362

## North Central Texas College
Gainesville, Texas
www.nctc.edu                 Federal Code: 003558

**2-year public** community college in large city.
**Enrollment:** 9,427 undergrads, 68% part-time. 1,068 full-time freshmen.
**Selectivity:** Open admission; but selective for some programs.

**BASIC COSTS (2015-2016)**
**Tuition and fees:** $2,280; out-of-district residents $3,540; out-of-state residents $6,000.
**Per-credit charge:** $50; out-of-district residents $92; out-of-state residents $174.
**Room and board:** $3,888.

**FINANCIAL AID PICTURE**
**Students with need:** Need-based aid available for full-time and part-time students. Work study available nights.
**Students without need:** This college awards aid only to students with need.

**FINANCIAL AID PROCEDURES**
**Forms required:** FAFSA.
**Dates and Deadlines:** Priority date 5/1; closing date 6/1. Applicants notified on a rolling basis starting 6/1; must reply within 4 week(s) of notification.

**CONTACT**
Ashley Tatum, Director of Financial Aid
1525 West California Street, Gainesville, TX 76240
(940) 668-4242

## North Lake College
Irving, Texas
www.northlakecollege.edu       Federal Code: 014036

**2-year public** community and liberal arts college in large city.
**Enrollment:** 7,793 undergrads.
**Selectivity:** Open admission.

**BASIC COSTS (2015-2016)**
**Tuition and fees:** $1,770; out-of-district residents $3,330; out-of-state residents $5,220.
**Per-credit charge:** $59; out-of-district residents $111; out-of-state residents $200.

**FINANCIAL AID PICTURE**
**Students with need:** Need-based aid available for full-time and part-time students. Work study available nights, weekends, and for part-time students.
**Students without need:** No-need awards available for academics, minority status, state/district residency.

**FINANCIAL AID PROCEDURES**
**Forms required:** FAFSA, state aid form.
**Dates and Deadlines:** Priority date 3/1; closing date 5/1. Applicants notified on a rolling basis starting 7/1.
**Transfers:** Priority date 2/1. Applicants notified on a rolling basis starting 8/1.

**CONTACT**
Paul Felix, Director of Financial Aid
5001 North MacArthur Boulevard, Irving, TX 75038-3899
(972) 273-3321

## Northeast Texas Community College
Mount Pleasant, Texas
www.ntcc.edu                 Federal Code: 016396

**2-year public** community college in large town.
**Enrollment:** 3,037 undergrads.
**Selectivity:** Open admission; but selective for some programs.

**BASIC COSTS (2015-2016)**
**Tuition and fees:** $2,506; out-of-district residents $4,276; out-of-state residents $5,696.
**Room and board:** $5,800.

**FINANCIAL AID PICTURE**
**Students with need:** Need-based aid available for full-time and part-time students.

**FINANCIAL AID PROCEDURES**
**Forms required:** FAFSA, institutional form.
**Dates and Deadlines:** Priority date 6/1; no closing date. Applicants notified on a rolling basis starting 6/1.

**CONTACT**
Kim Lawrence, Dean of Enrollment Management & Director of Financial Aid
2886 FM 1735, Mount Pleasant, TX 75455
(903) 434-8142

## Northwest Vista College
San Antonio, Texas
www.alamo.edu/nvc            Federal Code: 033723

**2-year public** community college in very large city.
**Enrollment:** 13,505 undergrads, 69% part-time. 1,222 full-time freshmen.
**Selectivity:** Open admission.

**BASIC COSTS (2015-2016)**
**Tuition and fees:** $2,088; out-of-district residents $5,550; out-of-state residents $10,740.

**FINANCIAL AID PICTURE**
**Students with need:** Need-based aid available for full-time and part-time students. Work study available nights, weekends, and for part-time students.
**Students without need:** No-need awards available for academics, leadership.

**FINANCIAL AID PROCEDURES**
**Forms required:** FAFSA.
**Dates and Deadlines:** Priority date 4/1; no closing date. Applicants notified on a rolling basis starting 5/15; must reply within 2 week(s) of notification.

**CONTACT**
Rosalinda Encina, Associate Director of Student Financial Services
3535 North Ellison Drive, San Antonio, TX 78251-4217
(210) 486-4600

## Northwood University: Texas

Cedar Hill, Texas

www.northwood.edu

Federal Code: 013040

**4-year private** university and business college in large town.

**Enrollment:** 208 undergrads.

### BASIC COSTS (2015-2016)

**Tuition and fees:** $24,170.

**Per-credit charge:** $883.

**Room and board:** $9,590.

### FINANCIAL AID PICTURE

**Students with need:** Need-based aid available for full-time and part-time students. Work study available nights, weekends, and for part-time students.

**Students without need:** No-need awards available for academics, athletics, leadership.

**Scholarships offered:** Academic Scholarships: $4,000-$10,000; based on test scores and GPA; unlimited number awarded.

### FINANCIAL AID PROCEDURES

**Forms required:** FAFSA.

**Dates and Deadlines:** Priority date 3/1; no closing date. Applicants notified on a rolling basis starting 3/1.

**Transfers:** No deadline. Applicants notified on a rolling basis.

### CONTACT

Mark Martin, Director of Financial Aid

1114 West FM 1382, Cedar Hill, TX 75104-1204

(989) 837-4997

## Odessa College

Odessa, Texas

www.odessa.edu

Federal Code: 003596

**2-year public** community college in small city.

**Enrollment:** 5,569 undergrads, 68% part-time. 484 full-time freshmen.

**Selectivity:** Open admission; but selective for some programs.

### BASIC COSTS (2015-2016)

**Tuition and fees:** $2,580; out-of-district residents $3,900; out-of-state residents $5,160.

**Room and board:** $5,200.

### FINANCIAL AID PICTURE (2015-2016)

**Students with need:** Need-based aid available for full-time and part-time students. Work study available nights.

**Students without need:** No-need awards available for academics, athletics, music/drama.

### FINANCIAL AID PROCEDURES

**Forms required:** FAFSA.

**Dates and Deadlines:** Priority date 5/1; no closing date. Applicants notified on a rolling basis starting 6/1.

### CONTACT

Dee Nesmith, Director of Student Financial Aid

201 West University, Odessa, TX 79764-7127

(432) 335-6429

## Our Lady of the Lake University of San Antonio

San Antonio, Texas

www.ollusa.edu

Federal Code: 003598

**4-year private** university in very large city, affiliated with Roman Catholic Church.

**Enrollment:** 1,498 undergrads, 11% part-time. 357 full-time freshmen.

**Selectivity:** Admits 50 to 75% of applicants.

### BASIC COSTS (2015-2016)

**Tuition and fees:** $26,148.

**Per-credit charge:** $811.

**Room and board:** $7,556.

### FINANCIAL AID PICTURE (2014-2015)

**Students with need:** Out of 347 full-time freshmen who applied for aid, 324 were judged to have need. Of these, 324 received aid, and 114 had their full need met. Average financial aid package met 89% of need; average scholarship/grant was $9,545; average loan was $3,516. For part-time students, average financial aid package was $9,931.

**Students without need:** 29 full-time freshmen who did not demonstrate need for aid received scholarships/grants; average award was $9,646. No-need awards available for academics, alumni affiliation, art, athletics, music/drama, religious affiliation.

**Scholarships offered:** *Merit:* General academic scholarship; $1,205 awarded yearly, renewable. Art/fine arts and music; 4 awarded yearly, renewable. Children of faculty/staff; 60 awarded yearly, renewable. All based on GPA scores and high school record. *Athletic:* 8 full-time freshmen received athletic scholarships; average amount $12,180.

### FINANCIAL AID PROCEDURES

**Forms required:** FAFSA, institutional form.

**Dates and Deadlines:** Priority date 5/1; no closing date. Applicants notified on a rolling basis starting 3/1; must reply within 2 week(s) of notification.

### CONTACT

Esmeralda Flores, Director of Financial Aid

411 Southwest 24th Street, San Antonio, TX 78207-4689

(210) 434-6711 ext. 3958

## Palo Alto College

San Antonio, Texas

www.alamo.edu/pac

Federal Code: 016615

**2-year public** community college in very large city.

**Enrollment:** 8,671 undergrads.

**Selectivity:** Open admission.

### BASIC COSTS (2015-2016)

**Tuition and fees:** $2,088; out-of-district residents $5,550; out-of-state residents $10,740.

### FINANCIAL AID PICTURE (2014-2015)

**Students with need:** 82% of average financial aid package awarded as scholarships/grants, 18% awarded as loans/jobs. Need-based aid available for part-time students.

**Students without need:** This college awards aid only to students with need.

**Scholarships offered:** Alamo Community College District Scholarship: $1,000; 50 awarded.

### FINANCIAL AID PROCEDURES

**Forms required:** FAFSA, state aid form.

**Dates and Deadlines:** Priority date 4/1; closing date 5/1. Applicants notified on a rolling basis starting 5/31.

### CONTACT

Shirley Leija, Director of Financial Aid

1400 West Villaret Boulevard, San Antonio, TX 78224-2499

(210) 486-3600

## Panola College

Carthage, Texas
www.panola.edu                          Federal Code: 003600

**2-year public** community and junior college in small town.
**Enrollment:** 2,674 undergrads, 50% part-time. 383 full-time freshmen.
**Selectivity:** Open admission; but selective for some programs.

### BASIC COSTS (2015-2016)

**Tuition and fees:** $2,190; out-of-district residents $2,910; out-of-state residents $3,375.
**Per-credit charge:** $60; out-of-state residents $200.
**Room and board:** $4,600.

### FINANCIAL AID PICTURE (2014-2015)

**Students with need:** Need-based aid available for part-time students.
**Students without need:** No-need awards available for academics, alumni affiliation, art, athletics, leadership, music/drama.
**Scholarships offered:** Several departmental and organization-sponsored scholarships, Presidential scholarship, Dean's scholarship.

### FINANCIAL AID PROCEDURES

**Forms required:** FAFSA, institutional form.
**Dates and Deadlines:** Priority date 6/1; no closing date. Applicants notified on a rolling basis starting 6/1.
**Transfers:** No deadline. Applicants notified on a rolling basis.

### CONTACT

Denise Welch, Director of Financial Aid
1109 West Panola Street, Carthage, TX 75633
(903) 693-2039

## Paris Junior College

Paris, Texas
www.parisjc.edu                         Federal Code: 003601

**2-year public** community and junior college in large town.
**Enrollment:** 4,998 undergrads.
**Selectivity:** Open admission; but selective for some programs.

### BASIC COSTS (2015-2016)

**Tuition and fees:** $1,890; out-of-district residents $2,970; out-of-state residents $4,380.
**Per-credit charge:** $50; out-of-district residents $86; out-of-state residents $133.
**Room and board:** $5,442.

### FINANCIAL AID PICTURE (2014-2015)

**Students with need:** 99% of average financial aid package awarded as scholarships/grants, 1% awarded as loans/jobs. Need-based aid available for part-time students.
**Students without need:** No-need awards available for athletics, music/drama.

### FINANCIAL AID PROCEDURES

**Forms required:** FAFSA.
**Dates and Deadlines:** Applicants notified on a rolling basis starting 6/1.

### CONTACT

Linda Slawson, Director of Financial Aid
2400 Clarksville Street, Paris, TX 75460
(903) 782-0429

## Paul Quinn College

Dallas, Texas
www.pqc.edu                             Federal Code: 003602

**4-year private** liberal arts college in very large city, affiliated with African Methodist Episcopal Church.
**Enrollment:** 420 undergrads.

### BASIC COSTS (2015-2016)

**Tuition and fees:** $8,275.
**Per-credit charge:** $240.63.
**Room and board:** $6,000.

### FINANCIAL AID PICTURE

**Students with need:** Need-based aid available for full-time and part-time students.
**Students without need:** This college awards aid only to students with need.
**Scholarships offered:** Presidential Scholarship: 100% tuition, fees, room and board; top 15% of class; minimum 3.5 GPA (3.7 for transfer students); at least 23 on the ACT or 1590 on the SAT; essay; renewable. Paul Quinn Scholarship: 50% of tuition, room and board; top 25% of class; minimum 3.25 GPA (3.5 for transfer students); at least 20 on the ACT or 1410 on the SAT; essay; renewable.

### FINANCIAL AID PROCEDURES

**Forms required:** FAFSA, institutional form.
**Dates and Deadlines:** Priority date 7/1; no closing date. Applicants notified on a rolling basis starting 7/15; must reply within 2 week(s) of notification.

### CONTACT

3837 Simpson Stuart Road, Dallas, TX 75241
(214) 379-5497

## Prairie View A&M University

Prairie View, Texas
www.pvamu.edu                           Federal Code: 003630

**4-year public** university in small town.
**Enrollment:** 6,923 undergrads, 9% part-time. 1,589 full-time freshmen.
**Selectivity:** Admits over 75% of applicants.

### BASIC COSTS (2015-2016)

**Tuition and fees:** $9,745; out-of-state residents $22,272.
**Per-credit charge:** $228.33; out-of-state residents $645.88.
**Room and board:** $7,849.
**Additional info:** Tuition at time of enrollment locked for 4 years.

### FINANCIAL AID PICTURE (2014-2015)

**Students with need:** Out of 1,475 full-time freshmen who applied for aid, 1,199 were judged to have need. Of these, 992 received aid, and 9 had their full need met. Average financial aid package met 87% of need; average scholarship/grant was $4,120; average loan was $3,875. For part-time students, average financial aid package was $13,394.
**Students without need:** 36 full-time freshmen who did not demonstrate need for aid received scholarships/grants; average award was $2,510. No-need awards available for academics, athletics, ROTC.
**Scholarships offered:** 8 full-time freshmen received athletic scholarships; average amount $10,051.

### FINANCIAL AID PROCEDURES

**Forms required:** FAFSA.
**Dates and Deadlines:** Closing date 3/15. Applicants notified by 6/1; must reply by 8/1.
**Transfers:** Applicants notified by 6/1; must reply by 8/1. Minimum 2.0 GPA from all colleges attended required to be considered for financial aid.

## CONTACT

Ralph Perri, Director of Financial Aid and Scholarships
PO Box 519, MS 1009, Prairie View, TX 77446
(936) 261-1000

## Ranger College

Ranger, Texas
www.rangercollege.edu
Federal Code: 003603

**2-year public** junior college in rural community.
**Enrollment:** 1,856 undergrads.
**Selectivity:** Open admission; but selective for some programs.

### FINANCIAL AID PICTURE (2014-2015)

**Students with need:** 71% of average financial aid package awarded as scholarships/grants, 29% awarded as loans/jobs. Need-based aid available for part-time students.
**Students without need:** This college awards aid only to students with need.

### FINANCIAL AID PROCEDURES

**Forms required:** FAFSA.
**Dates and Deadlines:** Priority date 7/28; no closing date. Applicants notified on a rolling basis; must reply within 2 week(s) of notification.
**Transfers:** No deadline. Applicants notified on a rolling basis; must reply within 2 week(s) of notification.

### CONTACT

Don Hilton, Financial Aid Director
1100 College Circle, Ranger, TX 76470
(254) 647-3234 ext. 117

## Remington College: Westchase Campus

Houston, Texas
http://houston.remingtoncollege.edu
Federal Code: E00672

**2-year private** technical college in very large city.
**Enrollment:** 609 undergrads.
**Selectivity:** Open admission.

### BASIC COSTS (2015-2016)

**Additional info:** Cost of diploma programs in Medical Assisting, Medical Billing and Coding, Pharmacy Technician: $15,995; Electronic Technology, $20,995; Cosmetology, $21,700; Medical Assisting (with or without X-Ray Tech), $19,990; Associate degree programs in Business Office Management, Criminal Justice, $33,900. Includes books, equipment, lab fees, and uniforms (if necessary).

### FINANCIAL AID PICTURE

**Students with need:** Need-based aid available for full-time and part-time students. Work study available nights.
**Students without need:** No-need awards available for state/district residency.

### FINANCIAL AID PROCEDURES

**Forms required:** FAFSA, institutional form.
**Dates and Deadlines:** Applicants notified on a rolling basis.

### CONTACT

James Dunn, National Director of Financial Aid
3110 Hayes Road, Suite 380, Houston, TX 77082

## Rice University

Houston, Texas
www.rice.edu
Federal Code: 003604
CSS Code: 6609

**4-year private** university in very large city.
**Enrollment:** 3,879 undergrads, 1% part-time. 968 full-time freshmen.
**Selectivity:** Admits less than 50% of applicants.

### BASIC COSTS (2015-2016)

**Tuition and fees:** $42,253.
**Room and board:** $13,650.

### FINANCIAL AID PICTURE (2015-2016)

**Students with need:** Out of 745 full-time freshmen who applied for aid, 380 were judged to have need. Of these, 377 received aid, and 376 had their full need met. Average financial aid package met 100% of need; average scholarship/grant was $36,568; average loan was $2,675. Need-based aid available for part-time students.
**Students without need:** 83 full-time freshmen who did not demonstrate need for aid received scholarships/grants; average award was $24,208. No-need awards available for academics, art, athletics, leadership, minority status, music/drama, ROTC, state/district residency.
**Scholarships offered:** 58 full-time freshmen received athletic scholarships; average amount $43,705.

### FINANCIAL AID PROCEDURES

**Forms required:** FAFSA, CSS PROFILE.
**Dates and Deadlines:** Closing date 3/1. Applicants notified by 4/1; must reply by 5/1.
**Transfers:** Priority date 4/1.

### CONTACT

Anne Walker, Director of Student Financial Services
6100 Main Street, Houston, TX 77251-1892
(713) 348-4958

## Richland College

Dallas, Texas
www.rlc.dcccd.edu
Federal Code: 008504

**2-year public** community college in very large city.
**Enrollment:** 12,762 undergrads.
**Selectivity:** Open admission.

### BASIC COSTS (2015-2016)

**Tuition and fees:** $1,770; out-of-district residents $3,330; out-of-state residents $5,220.
**Per-credit charge:** $59; out-of-district residents $111; out-of-state residents $200.

### FINANCIAL AID PICTURE

**Students with need:** Need-based aid available for full-time and part-time students. Work study available nights.
**Students without need:** No-need awards available for art, leadership, music/drama.

### FINANCIAL AID PROCEDURES

**Forms required:** FAFSA.
**Dates and Deadlines:** Priority date 5/11; no closing date. Applicants notified on a rolling basis starting 6/1; must reply within 2 week(s) of notification.

### CONTACT

Sylvia Holmes, Director of Financial Aid
12800 Abrams Road, Dallas, TX 75243-2199
(972) 238-6188

## St. Edward's University
Austin, Texas
www.stedwards.edu                     Federal Code: 003621

**4-year private** university and liberal arts college in very large city, affiliated with Roman Catholic Church.
**Enrollment:** 4,020 undergrads, 12% part-time. 873 full-time freshmen.
**Selectivity:** Admits over 75% of applicants.

### BASIC COSTS (2016-2017)
**Tuition and fees:** $40,828.
**Per-credit charge:** $1,348.
**Room and board:** $12,172.

### FINANCIAL AID PICTURE (2015-2016)
**Students with need:** Out of 716 full-time freshmen who applied for aid, 613 were judged to have need. Of these, 606 received aid, and 66 had their full need met. Average financial aid package met 75% of need; average scholarship/grant was $20,893; average loan was $3,486. For part-time students, average financial aid package was $11,612.
**Students without need:** 68 full-time freshmen who did not demonstrate need for aid received scholarships/grants; average award was $18,294. No-need awards available for academics, athletics, music/drama, state/district residency.
**Scholarships offered: *Merit:*** President's Excellence Scholarship: $20,000 per year; minimum 1300 SAT; top 15% of class. Academic Scholar Award: $7,000-$20,000 per year; minimum 1100 SAT; top 25% of class. All SAT scores exclusive of Writing section. ***Athletic:*** 53 full-time freshmen received athletic scholarships; average amount $20,483.

### FINANCIAL AID PROCEDURES
**Forms required:** FAFSA.
**Dates and Deadlines:** Priority date 2/1; no closing date. Applicants notified on a rolling basis starting 2/1; must reply by 5/1 or within 2 week(s) of notification.
**Transfers:** No deadline. Applicants notified on a rolling basis starting 2/1; must reply within 2 week(s) of notification.

### CONTACT
Doris Constantine, Associate VP and Director of Student Financial Services
3001 South Congress Avenue, Austin, TX 78704-6489
(512) 448-8523

## St. Mary's University
San Antonio, Texas
www.stmarytx.edu                      Federal Code: 003623

**4-year private** university and liberal arts college in very large city, affiliated with Roman Catholic Church.
**Enrollment:** 2,305 undergrads, 5% part-time. 469 full-time freshmen.
**Selectivity:** Admits 50 to 75% of applicants.

### BASIC COSTS (2016-2017)
**Tuition and fees:** $28,200.
**Per-credit charge:** $855.
**Room and board:** $9,300.

### FINANCIAL AID PICTURE (2014-2015)
**Students with need:** Out of 399 full-time freshmen who applied for aid, 368 were judged to have need. Of these, 368 received aid, and 31 had their full need met. Average financial aid package met 73% of need; average scholarship/grant was $19,362; average loan was $4,116. For part-time students, average financial aid package was $8,655.
**Students without need:** 89 full-time freshmen who did not demonstrate need for aid received scholarships/grants; average award was $17,813. No-need awards available for academics, alumni affiliation, athletics, music/drama, religious affiliation, ROTC, state/district residency.

**Scholarships offered:** 25 full-time freshmen received athletic scholarships; average amount $14,251.

### FINANCIAL AID PROCEDURES
**Dates and Deadlines:** Priority date 3/31; no closing date. Applicants notified on a rolling basis starting 3/1; must reply by 5/1 or within 2 week(s) of notification.

### CONTACT
David Krause, Director of Financial Assistance
One Camino Santa Maria, San Antonio, TX 78228-8504
(210) 436-3141

## St. Philip's College
San Antonio, Texas
www.alamo.edu/spc                     Federal Code: 003608

**2-year public** community college in very large city.
**Enrollment:** 10,739 undergrads.
**Selectivity:** Open admission; but selective for some programs.

### BASIC COSTS (2015-2016)
**Tuition and fees:** $2,088; out-of-district residents $5,550; out-of-state residents $10,740.

### FINANCIAL AID PICTURE (2014-2015)
**Students with need:** 74% of average financial aid package awarded as scholarships/grants, 26% awarded as loans/jobs. Need-based aid available for part-time students. Work study available nights, weekends, and for part-time students.
**Students without need:** This college awards aid only to students with need.

### FINANCIAL AID PROCEDURES
**Forms required:** FAFSA.

### CONTACT
Harold Whitis, District Director of Student Financial Services
1801 Martin Luther King Drive, San Antonio, TX 78203
(210) 486-2600

## Sam Houston State University
Huntsville, Texas
www.shsu.edu                          Federal Code: 003606

**4-year public** university in large town.
**Enrollment:** 17,401 undergrads, 19% part-time. 2,310 full-time freshmen.
**Selectivity:** Admits 50 to 75% of applicants.

### BASIC COSTS (2015-2016)
**Tuition and fees:** $9,337; out-of-state residents $21,037.
**Per-credit charge:** $216; out-of-state residents $606.
**Room and board:** $8,676.

### FINANCIAL AID PICTURE (2014-2015)
**Students with need:** Out of 2,017 full-time freshmen who applied for aid, 1,575 were judged to have need. Of these, 1,574 received aid, and 234 had their full need met. Average financial aid package met 63% of need; average scholarship/grant was $9,054; average loan was $3,000. For part-time students, average financial aid package was $7,749.
**Students without need:** 203 full-time freshmen who did not demonstrate need for aid received scholarships/grants; average award was $2,545. No-need awards available for academics, alumni affiliation, art, athletics, leadership, music/drama, religious affiliation, ROTC, state/district residency.
**Scholarships offered:** 46 full-time freshmen received athletic scholarships; average amount $10,899.

## FINANCIAL AID PROCEDURES
**Forms required:** FAFSA.
**Dates and Deadlines:** Priority date 3/15; no closing date. Applicants notified on a rolling basis starting 4/1; must reply within 4 week(s) of notification.
**Transfers:** No deadline. Applicants notified on a rolling basis starting 3/15; must reply within 4 week(s) of notification.

## CONTACT
Lydia Hall, Director of Financial Aid
Box 2418, Huntsville, TX 77341-2418
(936) 294-1774

# San Antonio College
San Antonio, Texas
www.alamo.edu/sac            Federal Code: 009163

**2-year public** community college in very large city.
**Enrollment:** 19,523 undergrads.
**Selectivity:** Open admission; but selective for some programs.

## BASIC COSTS (2015-2016)
**Tuition and fees:** $2,088; out-of-district residents $5,550; out-of-state residents $10,740.

## FINANCIAL AID PICTURE
**Students with need:** Need-based aid available for full-time and part-time students. Work study available nights, weekends, and for part-time students.
**Students without need:** This college awards aid only to students with need.
**Additional info:** Leveraging Educational Assistance Partnership, public student incentive grant, towards excellence access and success grants (Texas and Texas II grants) available.

## FINANCIAL AID PROCEDURES
**Forms required:** FAFSA.
**Dates and Deadlines:** Priority date 3/1; closing date 5/1.

## CONTACT
Rose Carreon-Munoz, Associate Director of Student Financial Services
1300 San Pedro Avenue, San Antonio, TX 78212-4299
(210) 486-0600

# San Jacinto College
Pasadena, Texas
www.sanjac.edu

**2-year public** community and technical college in very large city.
**Enrollment:** 23,870 undergrads, 75% part-time. 2,414 full-time freshmen.
**Selectivity:** Open admission; but selective for some programs.

## BASIC COSTS (2015-2016)
**Tuition and fees:** $1,690; out-of-district residents $2,950; out-of-state residents $4,750.
**Per-credit charge:** $47; out-of-district residents $89; out-of-state residents $149.

## FINANCIAL AID PICTURE (2014-2015)
**Students with need:** Out of 1,617 full-time freshmen who applied for aid, 1,426 were judged to have need. Of these, 1,017 received aid, and 1 had their full need met. Average financial aid package met 26% of need; average scholarship/grant was $5,003; average loan was $3,328. For part-time students, average financial aid package was $3,461.
**Students without need:** This college awards aid only to students with need.

## FINANCIAL AID PROCEDURES
**Forms required:** FAFSA.

**Dates and Deadlines:** Priority date 6/30; no closing date. Applicants notified on a rolling basis starting 5/1; must reply within 4 week(s) of notification.
**Transfers:** Priority date 10/31. Applicants notified on a rolling basis starting 4/1; must reply within 4 week(s) of notification. All transfer students must have all transcripts evaluated by the Enrollment Service office.

## CONTACT
Robert Merino, Director of Financial Aid
8060 Spencer Highway, Pasadena, TX 77505-5999
(281) 998-6150

# Schreiner University
Kerrville, Texas
www.schreiner.edu            Federal Code: 003610

**4-year private** liberal arts college in large town, affiliated with Presbyterian Church (USA).
**Enrollment:** 1,126 undergrads, 7% part-time. 277 full-time freshmen.
**Selectivity:** Admits over 75% of applicants.

## BASIC COSTS (2015-2016)
**Tuition and fees:** $25,086.
**Per-credit charge:** $999.
**Room and board:** $9,540.

## FINANCIAL AID PICTURE (2014-2015)
**Students with need:** Out of 277 full-time freshmen who applied for aid, 230 were judged to have need. Of these, 230 received aid, and 38 had their full need met. Average financial aid package met 70% of need; average scholarship/grant was $15,429; average loan was $3,061. For part-time students, average financial aid package was $14,068.
**Students without need:** 47 full-time freshmen who did not demonstrate need for aid received scholarships/grants; average award was $9,977. No-need awards available for academics, art, leadership, music/drama, religious affiliation.
**Scholarships offered:** Awards for students with exceptional academic achievement and leadership abilities; partial and full tuition; 3.5 GPA and 1100 SAT (exclusive of Writing) or 24 ACT.

## FINANCIAL AID PROCEDURES
**Forms required:** FAFSA.
**Dates and Deadlines:** Priority date 5/1; no closing date. Applicants notified on a rolling basis starting 2/15; must reply within 2 week(s) of notification.
**Transfers:** No deadline.

## CONTACT
Toni Bryant, Associate Dean of Admissions & Financial Aid
2100 Memorial Boulevard, Kerrville, TX 78028-5697
(830) 896-5411

# South Plains College
Levelland, Texas
www.southplainscollege.edu            Federal Code: 003611

**2-year public** community and junior college in large town.
**Enrollment:** 7,863 undergrads, 41% part-time. 1,764 full-time freshmen.
**Selectivity:** Open admission; but selective for some programs.

## BASIC COSTS (2016-2017)
**Tuition and fees:** $3,784; out-of-district residents $4,720; out-of-state residents $5,104.
**Per-credit charge:** $29; out-of-district residents $68; out-of-state residents $84.
**Room and board:** $3,900.

## FINANCIAL AID PICTURE (2014-2015)

**Students with need:** 76% of average financial aid package awarded as scholarships/grants, 24% awarded as loans/jobs. Need-based aid available for part-time students.

**Students without need:** No-need awards available for academics, art, athletics, leadership, music/drama, state/district residency.

## FINANCIAL AID PROCEDURES

**Forms required:** FAFSA.

**Dates and Deadlines:** Priority date 6/1; no closing date. Applicants notified on a rolling basis starting 6/30; must reply within 2 week(s) of notification.

## CONTACT

Suzan Nazworth, Director of Financial Aid
1401 South College Avenue, Levelland, TX 79336
(806) 894-9611

# South Texas College

McAllen, Texas
www.southtexascollege.edu          Federal Code: 031034

**2-year public** community and technical college in very large city.
**Enrollment:** 31,143 undergrads.
**Selectivity:** Open admission; but selective for some programs.

## BASIC COSTS (2015-2016)

**Tuition and fees:** $3,480; out-of-district residents $3,753; out-of-state residents $4,470.

## FINANCIAL AID PICTURE

**Students with need:** Need-based aid available for full-time and part-time students.

**Students without need:** No-need awards available for academics.

## FINANCIAL AID PROCEDURES

**Forms required:** FAFSA.

**Dates and Deadlines:** Priority date 3/15; no closing date. Applicants notified on a rolling basis starting 4/15.

**Transfers:** No deadline. Applicants notified by 5/15; must reply within 4 week(s) of notification.

## CONTACT

Miguel Galvan, Director of Financial Aid
3201 West Pecan Boulevard, McAllen, TX 78502
(956) 872-8375

# Southern Methodist University

Dallas, Texas          Federal Code: 003613
www.smu.edu          CSS Code: 6660

**4-year private** university in very large city, affiliated with United Methodist Church.
**Enrollment:** 6,348 undergrads, 3% part-time. 1,374 full-time freshmen.
**Selectivity:** Admits less than 50% of applicants. GED not accepted.

## BASIC COSTS (2015-2016)

**Tuition and fees:** $48,190.
**Per-credit charge:** $1,787.
**Room and board:** $15,575.

## FINANCIAL AID PICTURE (2015-2016)

**Students with need:** Out of 669 full-time freshmen who applied for aid, 438 were judged to have need. Of these, 435 received aid, and 168 had their full need met. Average financial aid package met 88% of need; average scholarship/grant was $20,909; average loan was $3,358. For part-time students, average financial aid package was $19,614.

**Students without need:** 548 full-time freshmen who did not demonstrate need for aid received scholarships/grants; average award was $21,192. No-need awards available for academics, alumni affiliation, art, athletics, leadership, music/drama.

**Scholarships offered:** 69 full-time freshmen received athletic scholarships; average amount $50,753.

## FINANCIAL AID PROCEDURES

**Forms required:** FAFSA, CSS PROFILE.

**Dates and Deadlines:** Priority date 2/15; no closing date. Applicants notified on a rolling basis starting 4/1; must reply within 3 week(s) of notification.

**Transfers:** Priority date 4/1. Merit scholarships available for community college and senior institution honor transfers. Students entering without scholarship aid will receive need-based aid up to cost of tuition.

## CONTACT

Marc Peterson, Executive Director of Enrollment Services
PO Box 750181, Dallas, TX 75275-0181
(214) 768-2068

# Southwest Texas Junior College

Uvalde, Texas
www.swtjc.edu          Federal Code: 003614

**2-year public** community and junior college in large town.
**Enrollment:** 5,608 undergrads, 66% part-time.
**Selectivity:** Open admission.

## BASIC COSTS (2015-2016)

**Tuition and fees:** $2,617; out-of-district residents $4,207; out-of-state residents $5,107.
**Per-credit charge:** $57; out-of-district residents $110; out-of-state residents $140.
**Room and board:** $3,600.

## FINANCIAL AID PICTURE

**Students with need:** Need-based aid available for full-time and part-time students.

## FINANCIAL AID PROCEDURES

**Forms required:** FAFSA.

**Dates and Deadlines:** Priority date 6/15; no closing date. Applicants notified on a rolling basis starting 5/1; must reply within 2 week(s) of notification.

**Transfers:** Financial aid application deadline for specific scholarships 4/1; priority deadline for grants 5/1.

## CONTACT

Yvette Hernandez, Director of Financial Aid
2401 Garner Field Road, Uvalde, TX 78801
(830) 591-7368

# Southwestern Adventist University

Keene, Texas
www.swau.edu          Federal Code: 003619

**4-year private** university and liberal arts college in small town, affiliated with Seventh-day Adventists.
**Enrollment:** 724 undergrads, 9% part-time. 147 full-time freshmen.
**Selectivity:** Admits less than 50% of applicants.

## BASIC COSTS (2015-2016)

**Tuition and fees:** $19,916.
**Per-credit charge:** $804.
**Room and board:** $7,400.

## FINANCIAL AID PICTURE (2014-2015)

**Students with need:** Out of 147 full-time freshmen who applied for aid, 137 were judged to have need. Of these, 136 received aid, and 15 had their

full need met. Average financial aid package met 63% of need; average scholarship/grant was $11,624; average loan was $2,976. For part-time students, average financial aid package was $11,049.

**Students without need:** 21 full-time freshmen who did not demonstrate need for aid received scholarships/grants; average award was $9,550. No-need awards available for academics, leadership, music/drama.

## FINANCIAL AID PROCEDURES

**Forms required:** FAFSA, institutional form.

**Dates and Deadlines:** Priority date 3/15; no closing date. Applicants notified on a rolling basis starting 3/15.

**Transfers:** No deadline. Applicants notified on a rolling basis.

## CONTACT

Patricia Norwood, Assistant Vice President for Financial Administration, Student Finance
Box 567, Keene, TX 76059
(817) 202-6262

## Southwestern Assemblies of God University

Waxahachie, Texas
www.sagu.edu              Federal Code: 003616

**4-year private** university and Bible college in large town, affiliated with Assemblies of God.

**Enrollment:** 1,639 undergrads, 13% part-time. 270 full-time freshmen.

### BASIC COSTS (2015-2016)

**Tuition and fees:** $20,530.
**Per-credit charge:** $655.
**Room and board:** $6,660.

### FINANCIAL AID PICTURE

**Students with need:** Need-based aid available for full-time and part-time students.

### FINANCIAL AID PROCEDURES

**Forms required:** FAFSA.

**Dates and Deadlines:** Priority date 3/1; no closing date. Applicants notified on a rolling basis starting 6/1; must reply within 2 week(s) of notification.

### CONTACT

Jeff Francis, Senior Director of Financial Aid
1200 Sycamore Street, Waxahachie, TX 75165
(972) 825-4730

## Southwestern Baptist Theological Seminary

Fort Worth, Texas
www.swbts.edu

**4-year private** Bible and seminary college in very large city, affiliated with Christian Church.

**Enrollment:** 580 undergrads.

### BASIC COSTS (2016-2017)

**Tuition and fees:** $14,640.
**Per-credit charge:** $470.
**Room only:** $1,890.

### FINANCIAL AID PICTURE (2015-2016)

**Students with need:** Need-based aid available for full-time and part-time students.

### CONTACT

Adam Mallette, Director of Student Services
PO Box 22000, Fort Worth, TX 76122
(817) 923-1921 ext. 3080

## Southwestern Christian College

Terrell, Texas
www.swcc.edu              Federal Code: 003618

**4-year private** Bible and liberal arts college in large town, affiliated with Church of Christ.

**Enrollment:** 149 undergrads, 10% part-time. 55 full-time freshmen.

**Selectivity:** Open admission.

### BASIC COSTS (2015-2016)

**Tuition and fees:** $8,042.
**Per-credit charge:** $295.
**Room and board:** $5,334.

### FINANCIAL AID PICTURE

**Students with need:** Need-based aid available for full-time and part-time students.

**Students without need:** No-need awards available for academics, athletics, music/drama.

### FINANCIAL AID PROCEDURES

**Forms required:** FAFSA.

**Dates and Deadlines:** Closing date 6/1. Applicants notified on a rolling basis starting 7/15; must reply within 2 week(s) of notification.

### CONTACT

Tonya Dean, Director of Financial Aid
Box 10, Terrell, TX 75160
(972) 524-3341 ext. 124

## Southwestern University

Georgetown, Texas
www.southwestern.edu      Federal Code: 003620

**4-year private** liberal arts and performing arts college in large town, affiliated with United Methodist Church.

**Enrollment:** 1,514 undergrads, 1% part-time. 359 full-time freshmen.

**Selectivity:** Admits less than 50% of applicants.

### BASIC COSTS (2015-2016)

**Tuition and fees:** $37,560.
**Per-credit charge:** $1,565.
**Room and board:** $11,498.

### FINANCIAL AID PICTURE (2015-2016)

**Students with need:** Out of 316 full-time freshmen who applied for aid, 245 were judged to have need. Of these, 245 received aid, and 68 had their full need met. Average financial aid package met 92% of need; average scholarship/grant was $30,100; average loan was $4,106. For part-time students, average financial aid package was $15,165.

**Students without need:** 114 full-time freshmen who did not demonstrate need for aid received scholarships/grants; average award was $20,581. No-need awards available for academics, alumni affiliation, art, leadership, minority status, music/drama, religious affiliation.

**Scholarships offered:** Academic Merit Scholarships; $2,000 to $22,000 per year. Brown Scholarships; full tuition, average room and average board. National Merit Finalist Awards; $2,000 per year. Fine Arts Scholarships; $3,500 to $10,000 per year; for students majoring in art, music or theater; based on talent, auditions or portfolio review. Music Performance Awards; up to $2,500; based on talent and awarded to non-fine arts majors who wish to participate in university ensemble. Dixon Scholarship; $5,000 per year or full tuition; awarded to high-achieving African-American, Hispanic, and Native American students. Beneficiary Grants; $6,000 per year; awarded to dependents of United Methodist clergy. Preministerial Scholarships; $3,000 per year; to students interested in full-time ministry careers.

### FINANCIAL AID PROCEDURES

**Forms required:** FAFSA.

**Dates and Deadlines:** Priority date 3/1; no closing date. Applicants notified on a rolling basis starting 3/1; must reply by 5/1 or within 2 week(s) of notification.

**Transfers:** Applicants notified on a rolling basis starting 3/1; must reply by 5/1 or within 2 week(s) of notification.

### CONTACT

James Gaeta, Director of Financial Aid
PO Box 770, Georgetown, TX 78627-0770
(512) 863-1259

## Stephen F. Austin State University
Nacogdoches, Texas
www.sfasu.edu                    Federal Code: 003624

**4-year public** university in large town.
**Enrollment:** 10,562 undergrads, 11% part-time. 2,005 full-time freshmen.
**Selectivity:** Admits 50 to 75% of applicants.

### BASIC COSTS (2015-2016)
**Tuition and fees:** $9,342; out-of-state residents $21,042.
**Per-credit charge:** $235; out-of-state residents $625.
**Room and board:** $8,868.

### FINANCIAL AID PICTURE (2014-2015)
**Students with need:** Out of 1,732 full-time freshmen who applied for aid, 1,361 were judged to have need. Of these, 1,361 received aid, and 128 had their full need met. Average financial aid package met 56% of need; average scholarship/grant was $9,101; average loan was $3,626. For part-time students, average financial aid package was $8,833.
**Students without need:** 179 full-time freshmen who did not demonstrate need for aid received scholarships/grants; average award was $3,420. No-need awards available for academics, alumni affiliation, art, leadership, music/drama, state/district residency.
**Scholarships offered:** *Merit:* Academic Excellence Scholarship Program; $3,000 per year; rank in top 10% of high school class or top quartile class with 1100 SAT (exclusive of Writing) or 24 ACT; renewable with 3.5 GPA. Dugas Honors Scholarship; $2,500 per semester; active member of School of Honors. University Scholars Program; $2,000 per semester; minimum 1220 SAT, 27 ACT, 3.0 GPA maintenance; up to 11 awarded. Student Foundation Association Leadership Scholarship; amounts vary; demonstrated leadership capabilities and academic achievement throughout high school career; 1 awarded. *Athletic:* 44 full-time freshmen received athletic scholarships; average amount $7,664.
**Additional info:** For students who qualify, Purple Promise tuition guarantee program covers the remaining balance of any tuition and mandatory fees not covered by other gift aid, for 15 hours per regular semester for up to 4 years.

### FINANCIAL AID PROCEDURES
**Forms required:** FAFSA.
**Dates and Deadlines:** Priority date 4/1; no closing date. Applicants notified on a rolling basis starting 4/1.

### CONTACT
H. Rachele Garrett, Director of Financial Aid
Box 13051, SFA Station, Nacogdoches, TX 75962-3051
(936) 468-2403

## Sul Ross State University
Alpine, Texas
www.sulross.edu                  Federal Code: 003625

**4-year public** university in small town.
**Enrollment:** 1,354 undergrads, 20% part-time. 332 full-time freshmen.
**Selectivity:** Admits over 75% of applicants.

### BASIC COSTS (2015-2016)
**Tuition and fees:** $7,211; out-of-state residents $18,911.
**Room and board:** $7,810.

### FINANCIAL AID PICTURE (2014-2015)
**Students with need:** For part-time students, average financial aid package was $6,460.
**Students without need:** No-need awards available for academics, alumni affiliation, art, leadership, music/drama, state/district residency.

### FINANCIAL AID PROCEDURES
**Forms required:** FAFSA.
**Dates and Deadlines:** Priority date 3/1; no closing date. Applicants notified by 3/3.

### CONTACT
Michael Corbett, Director
PO Box C-2, Alpine, TX 79832
(432) 837-8050

## Tarleton State University
Stephenville, Texas
www.tarleton.edu                 Federal Code: 003631

**4-year public** university in large town.
**Enrollment:** 10,749 undergrads, 23% part-time. 2,073 full-time freshmen.
**Selectivity:** Admits 50 to 75% of applicants.

### BASIC COSTS (2015-2016)
**Tuition and fees:** $7,705; out-of-state residents $19,714.
**Per-credit charge:** $154; out-of-state residents $554.25.
**Room and board:** $8,832.

### FINANCIAL AID PICTURE (2014-2015)
**Students with need:** Out of 1,774 full-time freshmen who applied for aid, 1,340 were judged to have need. Of these, 1,322 received aid, and 90 had their full need met. Average financial aid package met 58% of need; average scholarship/grant was $7,284; average loan was $3,089. For part-time students, average financial aid package was $6,527.
**Students without need:** No-need awards available for academics, alumni affiliation, athletics, leadership, music/drama, ROTC.
**Additional info:** Tuition guarantee program covers tuition and fees for qualified freshman.

### FINANCIAL AID PROCEDURES
**Forms required:** FAFSA.
**Dates and Deadlines:** Priority date 3/15; no closing date. Applicants notified on a rolling basis starting 5/1; must reply within 2 week(s) of notification.
**Transfers:** No deadline.

### CONTACT
Kathy Purvis, Executive Director, Student Financial Aid
Box T-0030, Stephenville, TX 76402
(254) 968-9070

PART III: FINANCIAL AID COLLEGE BY COLLEGE

## Tarrant County College
Fort Worth, Texas
www.tccd.edu                    Federal Code: 003626

**2-year public** community college in very large city.
**Enrollment:** 52,613 undergrads.
**Selectivity:** Open admission; but selective for some programs.

**BASIC COSTS (2016-2017)**
**Tuition and fees:** $1,770; out-of-district residents $3,180; out-of-state residents $7,650.
**Per-credit charge:** $59; out-of-district residents $106; out-of-state residents $255.

**FINANCIAL AID PICTURE (2014-2015)**
**Students with need:** 71% of average financial aid package awarded as scholarships/grants, 29% awarded as loans/jobs. Need-based aid available for part-time students.
**Students without need:** No-need awards available for academics.

**FINANCIAL AID PROCEDURES**
**Forms required:** FAFSA, institutional form.
**Dates and Deadlines:** Priority date 5/1; no closing date. Applicants notified on a rolling basis starting 5/1; must reply within 2 week(s) of notification.
**Transfers:** No deadline. Applicants notified on a rolling basis.

**CONTACT**
Samantha Stalnaker, District Director of Financial Aid
300 Trinity Campus Circle, Fort Worth, TX 76102-1964
(817) 515-4243

## Temple College
Temple, Texas
www.templejc.edu                Federal Code: 003627

**2-year public** community college in small city.
**Enrollment:** 4,874 undergrads.
**Selectivity:** Open admission; but selective for some programs.

**BASIC COSTS (2015-2016)**
**Tuition and fees:** $2,670; out-of-district residents $4,770; out-of-state residents $7,170.
**Per-credit charge:** $89; out-of-district residents $159; out-of-state residents $239.

**FINANCIAL AID PICTURE**
**Students with need:** Need-based aid available for full-time and part-time students. Work study available nights.
**Students without need:** This college awards aid only to students with need.

**FINANCIAL AID PROCEDURES**
**Forms required:** FAFSA.
**Dates and Deadlines:** Priority date 6/1; no closing date. Applicants notified on a rolling basis starting 5/1; must reply within 4 week(s) of notification.
**Transfers:** No deadline. Applicants notified on a rolling basis starting 5/1; must reply within 4 week(s) of notification.

**CONTACT**
Patricia Goodman, Director of Financial Aid
2600 South First Street, Temple, TX 76504-7435
(254) 298-8321

## Texarkana College
Texarkana, Texas
www.texarkanacollege.edu        Federal Code: 003628

**2-year public** community college in small city.
**Enrollment:** 1,386 full-time undergrads.
**Selectivity:** Open admission.

**BASIC COSTS (2015-2016)**
**Tuition and fees:** $2,420; out-of-district residents $3,890; out-of-state residents $5,300.
**Per-credit charge:** $48; out-of-district residents $97; out-of-state residents $144.

**FINANCIAL AID PICTURE (2014-2015)**
**Students with need:** 70% of average financial aid package awarded as scholarships/grants, 30% awarded as loans/jobs. Need-based aid available for part-time students. Work study available nights.
**Students without need:** No-need awards available for academics, art, music/drama.
**Scholarships offered:** The Presidential Scholarship will be awarded in the full amount of tuition and fees. This Scholarship is intended for the completion of an Associate degree and will be awarded for two years or until the completion of 60 credit hours. If you are a current-year graduate and have a cumulative, unweighted GPA of 3.25 and are ranked in the top 15% of your class or in the top 10 graduates of your class, you are guaranteed acceptance for this scholarship. If you have a 3.25 GPA but do not meet the other criteria, you may still apply; please write a paragraph with 300 words or less describing your academic and career goals and attach to your application. Priority will be given to students who meet the application deadline of April 1. All recipients must be TSI met in all areas.

**FINANCIAL AID PROCEDURES**
**Forms required:** FAFSA, institutional form.
**Dates and Deadlines:** Priority date 7/24; no closing date. Applicants notified on a rolling basis starting 3/1.
**Transfers:** Closing date 5/1. Applicants notified on a rolling basis.

**CONTACT**
Susan Johnston, Director of Financial Aid
2500 North Robison Road, Texarkana, TX 75599
(903) 823-3163

## Texas A&M International University
Laredo, Texas
www.tamiu.edu                   Federal Code: 009651

**4-year public** university in small city.
**Enrollment:** 6,349 undergrads, 28% part-time. 879 full-time freshmen.
**Selectivity:** Admits less than 50% of applicants.

**BASIC COSTS (2015-2016)**
**Tuition and fees:** $7,990; out-of-state residents $19,894.
**Room and board:** $8,259.

**FINANCIAL AID PICTURE**
**Students with need:** Need-based aid available for full-time and part-time students. Work study available nights, weekends, and for part-time students.
**Students without need:** No-need awards available for academics, art, athletics, leadership, music/drama.

**FINANCIAL AID PROCEDURES**
**Forms required:** FAFSA, institutional form.
**Dates and Deadlines:** Priority date 3/15; no closing date. Applicants notified on a rolling basis starting 4/15; must reply within 2 week(s) of notification.
**Transfers:** No deadline. Applicants notified on a rolling basis starting 11/30; must reply within 2 week(s) of notification.

**CONTACT**
Laura Elizondo, Director of Financial Aid
5201 University Boulevard, Laredo, TX 78041-1900
(956) 326-2225

## Texas A&M University
College Station, Texas
www.tamu.edu                    Federal Code: 003632

**4-year public** university in small city.
**Enrollment:** 48,708 undergrads, 11% part-time. 9,489 full-time freshmen.
**Selectivity:** Admits 50 to 75% of applicants.

**BASIC COSTS (2015-2016)**
**Tuition and fees:** $9,428; out-of-state residents $28,021.
**Per-credit charge:** $227; out-of-state residents $847.
**Room and board:** $10,338.

**FINANCIAL AID PICTURE (2014-2015)**
**Students with need:** Out of 7,375 full-time freshmen who applied for aid, 4,582 were judged to have need. Of these, 4,463 received aid, and 1,716 had their full need met. Average financial aid package met 73% of need; average scholarship/grant was $11,610; average loan was $5,900. For part-time students, average financial aid package was $10,219.
**Students without need:** 1,024 full-time freshmen who did not demonstrate need for aid received scholarships/grants; average award was $3,824. No-need awards available for academics, alumni affiliation, art, athletics, job skills, leadership, music/drama, religious affiliation, ROTC, state/district residency.
**Scholarships offered:** *Merit:* Texas residents; Regents scholarship, additional $5,000 annually for 4 years, first-generation students incomes <$40,000. Aggie Assurance, minimum scholarships, grants for Pell students, incomes <$30,000; incomes <$60,000 gift aid for tuition only. Students must maintain a 2.5 GPA. *Athletic:* 9 full-time freshmen received athletic scholarships; average amount $7,008.
**Additional info:** Short-term loans available.

**FINANCIAL AID PROCEDURES**
**Forms required:** FAFSA.
**Dates and Deadlines:** Priority date 3/15; no closing date. Applicants notified on a rolling basis starting 4/1.

**CONTACT**
Delisa Falks, Executive Director, Scholarships and Financial Aid
750 Agronomy Road, Suite 1601, College Station, TX 77843-0200
(979) 845-3236

## Texas A&M University-Baylor College of Dentistry
Dallas, Texas
www.bcd.tamhsc.edu              Federal Code: 004948

**Upper-division public** health science college in very large city.
**Enrollment:** 59 undergrads.

**FINANCIAL AID PICTURE**
**Students with need:** Need-based aid available for full-time and part-time students.
**Students without need:** No-need awards available for academics.

**FINANCIAL AID PROCEDURES**
**Forms required:** FAFSA, institutional form.
**Dates and Deadlines:** Priority date 3/15; no closing date. Applicants notified on a rolling basis starting 6/1; must reply within 2 week(s) of notification.

**CONTACT**
Kay Egbert, Director of Student Aid
PO Box 660677, Dallas, TX 75266-0677

## Texas A&M University-Commerce
Commerce, Texas
www.tamuc.edu                   Federal Code: 003565

**4-year public** university in small town.
**Enrollment:** 7,642 undergrads, 29% part-time. 960 full-time freshmen.
**Selectivity:** Admits less than 50% of applicants.

**BASIC COSTS (2016-2017)**
**Tuition and fees:** $7,432; out-of-state residents $19,132.
**Per-credit charge:** $160; out-of-state residents $550.
**Room and board:** $8,326.

**FINANCIAL AID PICTURE (2014-2015)**
**Students with need:** Out of 894 full-time freshmen who applied for aid, 755 were judged to have need. Of these, 742 received aid, and 78 had their full need met. Average financial aid package met 72% of need; average scholarship/grant was $10,903; average loan was $3,459. For part-time students, average financial aid package was $6,303.
**Students without need:** 67 full-time freshmen who did not demonstrate need for aid received scholarships/grants; average award was $2,145. No-need awards available for academics, alumni affiliation, art, athletics, job skills, leadership, music/drama, ROTC, state/district residency.
**Scholarships offered:** 23 full-time freshmen received athletic scholarships; average amount $4,393.
**Additional info:** Work-study also available for full-time students.

**FINANCIAL AID PROCEDURES**
**Forms required:** FAFSA.
**Dates and Deadlines:** Priority date 4/1; no closing date. Applicants notified on a rolling basis starting 5/1; must reply within 4 week(s) of notification.

**CONTACT**
Maria Ramos, Director of Financial Aid and Scholarships
Box 3011, Commerce, TX 75429-3011
(903) 886-5091

## Texas A&M University-Corpus Christi
Corpus Christi, Texas
www.tamucc.edu                  Federal Code: 011161

**4-year public** university in large city.
**Enrollment:** 9,801 undergrads, 25% part-time. 2,145 full-time freshmen.
**Selectivity:** Admits over 75% of applicants.

**BASIC COSTS (2015-2016)**
**Tuition and fees:** $8,620; out-of-state residents $20,208.
**Per-credit charge:** $174.27; out-of-state residents $560.24.
**Room and board:** $9,874.

**FINANCIAL AID PICTURE (2015-2016)**
**Students with need:** Out of 1,785 full-time freshmen who applied for aid, 1,363 were judged to have need. Of these, 1,315 received aid, and 41 had their full need met. Average financial aid package met 52% of need; average scholarship/grant was $6,812; average loan was $3,375. For part-time students, average financial aid package was $7,056.
**Students without need:** 163 full-time freshmen who did not demonstrate need for aid received scholarships/grants; average award was $2,332. No-need awards available for academics, art, athletics, leadership, music/drama, ROTC.
**Scholarships offered:** 55 full-time freshmen received athletic scholarships; average amount $10,136.

## FINANCIAL AID PROCEDURES

**Forms required:** FAFSA.

**Dates and Deadlines:** Priority date 3/31; closing date 6/30. Applicants notified on a rolling basis starting 4/1; must reply within 2 week(s) of notification.

**Transfers:** No deadline. Applicants notified on a rolling basis starting 4/1; must reply within 2 week(s) of notification.

## CONTACT

Jeannie Gage, Director, Financial Assistance

6300 Ocean Drive, Unit 5774, Corpus Christi, TX 78412-5774

(361) 825-2338

## Texas A&M University-Galveston

Galveston, Texas

www.tamug.edu                    Federal Code: 003632

**4-year public** university and maritime college in small city.

**Enrollment:** 2,168 undergrads.

### BASIC COSTS (2015-2016)

**Tuition and fees:** $9,988; out-of-state residents $22,260.

**Per-credit charge:** $257; out-of-state residents $666.

**Room and board:** $10,026.

### FINANCIAL AID PICTURE

**Students with need:** Need-based aid available for full-time and part-time students. Work study available nights, weekends, and for part-time students.

**Students without need:** No-need awards available for academics, state/district residency.

### FINANCIAL AID PROCEDURES

**Forms required:** FAFSA.

**Dates and Deadlines:** Priority date 4/1; no closing date. Applicants notified on a rolling basis starting 3/15; must reply within 3 week(s) of notification.

### CONTACT

Cheryl Grefenstette-Moon, Executive Director of Enrollment Services

PO Box 1675, Galveston, TX 77553-1675

(409) 740-4500

## Texas A&M University-Kingsville

Kingsville, Texas

www.tamuk.edu                    Federal Code: 003639

**4-year public** university in large town.

**Enrollment:** 5,630 undergrads, 10% part-time. 1,125 full-time freshmen.

**Selectivity:** Admits over 75% of applicants.

### BASIC COSTS (2015-2016)

**Tuition and fees:** $7,700; out-of-state residents $20,190.

**Room and board:** $7,344.

**Additional info:** Tuition at time of enrollment locked for 4 years.

### FINANCIAL AID PICTURE (2014-2015)

**Students with need:** Out of 1,019 full-time freshmen who applied for aid, 900 were judged to have need. Of these, 886 received aid, and 131 had their full need met. Average financial aid package met 71% of need; average scholarship/grant was $1,922; average loan was $2,261. For part-time students, average financial aid package was $9,020.

**Students without need:** 5 full-time freshmen who did not demonstrate need for aid received scholarships/grants; average award was $1,900. No-need awards available for academics, athletics, leadership, minority status, state/district residency.

**Scholarships offered:** 31 full-time freshmen received athletic scholarships; average amount $5,643.

## FINANCIAL AID PROCEDURES

**Forms required:** FAFSA.

**Dates and Deadlines:** Priority date 3/15; no closing date. Applicants notified on a rolling basis starting 4/15; must reply within 12 week(s) of notification.

## CONTACT

Darylann Thomas, Executive Director of Financial Aid

MSC 128, Kingsville, TX 78363-8202

(361) 593-3911

## Texas A&M University-Texarkana

Texarkana, Texas

www.tamut.edu                    Federal Code: 031703

**Upper-division public** university in small city.

**Enrollment:** 1,415 undergrads, 34% part-time. 151 full-time freshmen.

### BASIC COSTS (2015-2016)

**Tuition and fees:** $7,036; out-of-state residents $19,568.

**Room and board:** $7,872.

### FINANCIAL AID PICTURE (2014-2015)

**Students with need:** Out of 136 full-time freshmen who applied for aid, 107 were judged to have need. Of these, 107 received aid, and 17 had their full need met. Average financial aid package met 88% of need; average scholarship/grant was $11,547; average loan was $2,684. For part-time students, average financial aid package was $7,520.

**Students without need:** 41 full-time freshmen who did not demonstrate need for aid received scholarships/grants; average award was $3,203. No-need awards available for academics, alumni affiliation, art, athletics, job skills, leadership, music/drama, state/district residency.

**Scholarships offered:** 9 full-time freshmen received athletic scholarships; average amount $911.

### FINANCIAL AID PROCEDURES

**Forms required:** FAFSA.

**Dates and Deadlines:** Priority date 3/15; closing date 9/30. Applicants notified on a rolling basis; must reply within 4 week(s) of notification.

**Transfers:** Priority date 3/15; closing date 9/30. Applicants notified on a rolling basis; must reply within 10 week(s) of notification. Transfer students must have completed minimum of 54 semester hours of transferable college credit to apply for financial aid and notified applicants must reply within 45 days from date of award letter. Exceptions made on individual basis. April 1 financial aid deadline for scholarships.

### CONTACT

Michael Fuller, Director of Financial Aid

7101 University Avenue, Texarkana, TX 75503

(903) 233-3066

## Texas Christian University

Fort Worth, Texas                Federal Code: 003636

www.tcu.edu                      CSS Code: 6820

**4-year private** university in very large city, affiliated with Christian Church (Disciples of Christ).

**Enrollment:** 8,851 undergrads, 3% part-time. 2,070 full-time freshmen.

**Selectivity:** Admits less than 50% of applicants. GED not accepted.

### BASIC COSTS (2016-2017)

**Tuition and fees:** $42,670.

**Room and board:** $12,000.

**Additional info:** Tuition/fee waivers available for adults, minority students.

### FINANCIAL AID PICTURE (2015-2016)

**Students with need:** Out of 1,299 full-time freshmen who applied for aid, 866 were judged to have need. Of these, 860 received aid, and 319 had

their full need met. Average financial aid package met 70% of need; average scholarship/grant was $25,971; average loan was $2,734. For part-time students, average financial aid package was $14,162.

**Students without need:** 592 full-time freshmen who did not demonstrate need for aid received scholarships/grants; average award was $16,037. No-need awards available for academics, alumni affiliation, art, minority status, music/drama, religious affiliation, ROTC, state/district residency.

**Scholarships offered:** 92 full-time freshmen received athletic scholarships; average amount $23,414.

**FINANCIAL AID PROCEDURES**
**Forms required:** FAFSA, CSS PROFILE.
**Dates and Deadlines:** Priority date 5/1; closing date 5/1. Applicants notified on a rolling basis starting 3/15; must reply by 5/1.
**Transfers:** Priority date 6/1. Applicants notified on a rolling basis starting 6/15. Transfer students must submit both the FAFSA and the CSS PROFILE to receive financial aid.

**CONTACT**
Michael Scott, Director of Scholarships and Student Financial Aid
TCU Box 297013, Fort Worth, TX 76129
(817) 257-7858

## Texas College
Tyler, Texas
www.texascollege.edu          Federal Code: 003638

**4-year private** liberal arts college in small city, affiliated with Christian Methodist Episcopal Church.
**Enrollment:** 813 undergrads.
**Selectivity:** Open admission.

**BASIC COSTS (2015-2016)**
**Tuition and fees:** $10,008.
**Room and board:** $8,000.

**FINANCIAL AID PICTURE**
**Students with need:** Need-based aid available for full-time and part-time students.
**Students without need:** No-need awards available for academics, athletics, leadership, music/drama.

**FINANCIAL AID PROCEDURES**
**Forms required:** FAFSA, institutional form.
**Dates and Deadlines:** Priority date 6/1; no closing date. Applicants notified on a rolling basis starting 4/15.

**CONTACT**
Angela Marshall, Director of Financial Aid
2404 North Grand Avenue, Tyler, TX 75712-4500
(903) 593-8311 ext. 2208

## Texas Lutheran University
Seguin, Texas
www.tlu.edu          Federal Code: 003641

**4-year private** university and liberal arts college in large town, affiliated with Evangelical Lutheran Church in America.
**Enrollment:** 1,319 undergrads, 3% part-time. 395 full-time freshmen.
**Selectivity:** Admits 50 to 75% of applicants.

**BASIC COSTS (2015-2016)**
**Tuition and fees:** $27,900.
**Per-credit charge:** $915.
**Room and board:** $9,390.

**FINANCIAL AID PICTURE (2015-2016)**
**Students with need:** 74% of average financial aid package awarded as scholarships/grants, 26% awarded as loans/jobs. Need-based aid available for part-time students. Work study available nights, weekends, and for part-time students.
**Students without need:** No-need awards available for academics, alumni affiliation, leadership, music/drama, religious affiliation.
**Scholarships offered:** National Merit Finalist Scholarship; full tuition. Pacesetter Award for College Excellence; up to $18,000 a year. Locus Aduro Award in Dramatic Media; up to $18,000 a year. Da capo Award in Music; up to $18,000 a year. TLU CHOICE Scholarship; difference between cost at TLU and University of Texas-Austin or Texas AM-College Station. Presidential Scholarship; up to $11,000 a year. Academic Excellence Award; up to $9,000 a year.

**FINANCIAL AID PROCEDURES**
**Forms required:** FAFSA.
**Dates and Deadlines:** Priority date 4/1; no closing date. Applicants notified on a rolling basis starting 3/1; must reply within 4 week(s) of notification.
**Transfers:** No deadline. Applicants notified on a rolling basis starting 3/1; must reply within 6 week(s) of notification.

**CONTACT**
Bonnie Trevino, Director Financial Aid
1000 West Court Street, Seguin, TX 78155-5999
(830) 372-8075

## Texas Southern University
Houston, Texas
www.tsu.edu          Federal Code: 003642

**4-year public** university in very large city.
**Enrollment:** 6,696 undergrads, 12% part-time. 1,391 full-time freshmen.
**Selectivity:** Admits 50 to 75% of applicants.

**BASIC COSTS (2015-2016)**
**Tuition and fees:** $8,726; out-of-state residents $20,426.
**Room and board:** $10,566.
**Additional info:** Tuition/fee waivers available for minority students.

**FINANCIAL AID PICTURE**
**Students with need:** Need-based aid available for full-time and part-time students. Work study available nights, weekends, and for part-time students.
**Students without need:** This college awards aid only to students with need.

**FINANCIAL AID PROCEDURES**
**Forms required:** FAFSA.
**Dates and Deadlines:** Priority date 5/15; no closing date. Applicants notified on a rolling basis starting 6/1.
**Transfers:** Priority date 4/1; closing date 8/30.

**CONTACT**
Linda Ballard, Director of Financial Aid
3100 Cleburne Street, Houston, TX 77004
(713) 313-7071

## Texas State Technical College
Waco, Texas
www.tstc.edu          Federal Code: 003634

**2-year public** technical college in small city.
**Enrollment:** 8,160 undergrads, 54% part-time. 1,044 full-time freshmen.
**Selectivity:** Open admission.

**BASIC COSTS (2015-2016)**
**Tuition and fees:** $4,434; out-of-state residents $9,660.

**Room and board:** $5,370.

**FINANCIAL AID PICTURE (2015-2016)**

**Students with need:** 68% of average financial aid package awarded as scholarships/grants, 32% awarded as loans/jobs. Need-based aid available for part-time students.

**Students without need:** This college awards aid only to students with need.

**FINANCIAL AID PROCEDURES**

**Forms required:** FAFSA.

**Dates and Deadlines:** Priority date 6/1; no closing date. Applicants notified on a rolling basis starting 5/15.

**Transfers:** No deadline. Applicants notified on a rolling basis.

**CONTACT**

Jackie Adler, Director, Financial Aid

3801 Campus Drive, Waco, TX 76705

(254) 867-4814

## Texas State Technical College: Harlingen

Harlingen, Texas

www.tstc.edu/                 Federal Code: 009225

**2-year public** technical college in small city.

**Enrollment:** 3,022 undergrads, 62% part-time. 271 full-time freshmen.

**Selectivity:** Open admission; but selective for some programs.

**BASIC COSTS (2015-2016)**

**Tuition and fees:** $4,434; out-of-state residents $9,660.

**Room and board:** $4,270.

**FINANCIAL AID PICTURE (2015-2016)**

**Students with need:** 86% of average financial aid package awarded as scholarships/grants, 14% awarded as loans/jobs. Need-based aid available for part-time students.

**FINANCIAL AID PROCEDURES**

**Forms required:** FAFSA, institutional form.

**Dates and Deadlines:** Priority date 3/1; no closing date. Applicants notified on a rolling basis.

**CONTACT**

Fred Pena, Director of Financial Aid

1902 North Loop 499, Harlingen, TX 78550-3697

(956) 364-4337

## Texas State Technical College: West Texas

Sweetwater, Texas

www.westtexas.tstc.edu          Federal Code: 009932

**2-year public** technical college in large town.

**Enrollment:** 897 undergrads.

**Selectivity:** Open admission; but selective for some programs.

**BASIC COSTS (2015-2016)**

**Tuition and fees:** $4,434; out-of-state residents $9,660.

**Room and board:** $5,280.

**FINANCIAL AID PICTURE**

**Students with need:** Need-based aid available for full-time and part-time students. Work study available nights, weekends, and for part-time students.

**Students without need:** No-need awards available for academics, leadership.

**FINANCIAL AID PROCEDURES**

**Forms required:** FAFSA, institutional form.

**Dates and Deadlines:** Priority date 5/1; closing date 7/1. Applicants notified on a rolling basis starting 7/1.

**Transfers:** No deadline. Applicants notified on a rolling basis starting 7/1; must reply by 8/20.

**CONTACT**

Gail Johnson, Director of Financial Aid

300 Homer K Taylor Drive, Sweetwater, TX 79556

(325) 235-7419

## Texas State University

San Marcos, Texas

www.txstate.edu                 Federal Code: 003615

**4-year public** university in large town.

**Enrollment:** 33,480 undergrads, 18% part-time. 5,476 full-time freshmen.

**Selectivity:** Admits 50 to 75% of applicants.

**BASIC COSTS (2015-2016)**

**Tuition and fees:** $9,944; out-of-state residents $21,644.

**Per-credit charge:** $251; out-of-state residents $641.

**Room and board:** $7,840.

**Additional info:** Tuition at time of enrollment locked for 4 years.

**FINANCIAL AID PICTURE (2015-2016)**

**Students with need:** Out of 5,476 full-time freshmen who applied for aid, 3,503 were judged to have need. Of these, 3,342 received aid, and 371 had their full need met. Average financial aid package met 85% of need; average scholarship/grant was $8,779; average loan was $4,983. For part-time students, average financial aid package was $7,881.

**Students without need:** 476 full-time freshmen who did not demonstrate need for aid received scholarships/grants; average award was $3,125. No-need awards available for academics, art, athletics, leadership, minority status, music/drama, ROTC, state/district residency.

**Scholarships offered:** *Merit:* Terry Foundation Scholarship; $12,500; 16 awarded. McCoy Scholarship of Excellence; $8,000; number awarded varies. McCoy Scholarship of Distinction; $5,000; number varies. University Scholars; $3,000; 8 awarded. Lone Star Scholarship; $2,500; 10 awarded. *Athletic:* 27 full-time freshmen received athletic scholarships; average amount $9,233.

**Additional info:** Federal and state work study programs are available for those that qualify. Employment time varies by hiring departments.

**FINANCIAL AID PROCEDURES**

**Forms required:** FAFSA.

**Dates and Deadlines:** Priority date 4/1; no closing date. Applicants notified on a rolling basis starting 5/1; must reply within 3 week(s) of notification.

**CONTACT**

Christopher Murr, Director of Financial Aid & Scholarship Office

429 North Guadalupe Street, San Marcos, TX 78666-5709

(512) 245-2315

## Texas Tech University

Lubbock, Texas

www.ttu.edu                     Federal Code: 003644

**4-year public** university in small city.

**Enrollment:** 28,868 undergrads, 10% part-time. 5,519 full-time freshmen.

**Selectivity:** Admits 50 to 75% of applicants.

**BASIC COSTS (2015-2016)**

**Tuition and fees:** $9,567; out-of-state residents $21,267.

**Per-credit charge:** $220; out-of-state residents $610.

**Room and board:** $8,405.

## FINANCIAL AID PICTURE (2014-2015)

**Students with need:** Out of 3,610 full-time freshmen who applied for aid, 2,651 were judged to have need. Of these, 2,651 received aid, and 421 had their full need met. Average financial aid package met 73% of need; average scholarship/grant was $8,247; average loan was $5,002. For part-time students, average financial aid package was $10,216.

**Students without need:** 726 full-time freshmen who did not demonstrate need for aid received scholarships/grants; average award was $3,665. No-need awards available for academics, art, athletics, job skills, leadership, music/drama, ROTC.

**Scholarships offered:** *Merit:* Presidential Scholarships: National Merit Finalist, approximately $25,000 per year; $6,000 per year, top 10% of high school graduating class and SAT 1400 or ACT 32; $4,000 per year, top 10% of high school class and SAT 1300 or ACT 29; $3,500 per year, top 10% of high school class and SAT 1250 or ACT 28; $3,000 per year, top 10% of high school class and SAT 1200 or ACT 27; $5,000 per year, top 11%-25% of high school class and SAT 1500 or ACT 34; $4,000 per year, top 11%-25% of high school class and SAT 1400 or ACT 32; $3,500 per year, top 11%-25% of high school class and SAT 1300 or ACT 29; $3,000 per year, top 11%-25% of high school class and SAT 1200 or ACT 27. All are renewable for up to 4 years. *Athletic:* 33 full-time freshmen received athletic scholarships; average amount $14,359.

**Additional info:** Red Raider Guarantee program provides free tuition and mandatory fees for up to 15 credit hours per semester to new entering freshman who are Texas residents, enrolled full-time with family adjusted gross incomes that do not exceed $40,000. Eligible students who complete and submit the Free Application for Federal Student Aid (FAFSA) by required deadline are guaranteed to receive funds based on available state and federal allocations. Applications received after the deadline will be awarded based on available funding. Students may qualify for the program for up to eight (8) semesters of full-time enrollment.

## FINANCIAL AID PROCEDURES

**Forms required:** FAFSA.

**Dates and Deadlines:** Priority date 3/15; no closing date. Applicants notified on a rolling basis; must reply within 2 week(s) of notification.

## CONTACT

Becky Wilson, Director of Financial Aid
Box 45005, Lubbock, TX 79409-5005
(806) 742-3681

# Texas Tech University Health Sciences Center
Lubbock, Texas
www.ttuhsc.edu  Federal Code: 010674

**Upper-division public** university in small city.
**Enrollment:** 1,221 undergrads.

## BASIC COSTS (2015-2016)
**Tuition and fees:** $9,312; out-of-state residents $21,012.
**Room and board:** $9,964.
**Additional info:** Figures shown are for traditional BSN in the School of Nursing.

## FINANCIAL AID PICTURE
**Students with need:** Need-based aid available for full-time and part-time students.
**Students without need:** No-need awards available for academics.

## FINANCIAL AID PROCEDURES
**Transfers:** No deadline. Applicants notified on a rolling basis.

## CONTACT
Marcus Wilson, Director, Financial Aid
3601 Fourth Street, Lubbock, TX 79430

# Texas Wesleyan University
Fort Worth, Texas
www.txwes.edu  Federal Code: 003645

**4-year private** university in very large city, affiliated with United Methodist Church.
**Enrollment:** 1,780 undergrads, 13% part-time. 310 full-time freshmen.
**Selectivity:** Admits less than 50% of applicants.

## BASIC COSTS (2015-2016)
**Tuition and fees:** $24,454.
**Per-credit charge:** $735.
**Room and board:** $8,651.

## FINANCIAL AID PICTURE (2014-2015)
**Students with need:** Out of 190 full-time freshmen who applied for aid, 172 were judged to have need. Of these, 170 received aid, and 35 had their full need met. Average financial aid package met 79% of need; average scholarship/grant was $19,605; average loan was $3,026. For part-time students, average financial aid package was $10,658.
**Students without need:** This college awards aid only to students with need.
**Scholarships offered:** 7 full-time freshmen received athletic scholarships; average amount $10,670.

## FINANCIAL AID PROCEDURES
**Forms required:** FAFSA.
**Dates and Deadlines:** Priority date 3/1; no closing date. Applicants notified on a rolling basis.

## CONTACT
Laurie Rosenkrantz, Financial Aid Director
1201 Wesleyan Street, Fort Worth, TX 76105-1536
(817) 531-4420

# Texas Woman's University
Denton, Texas
www.twu.edu  Federal Code: 003646

**4-year public** university in small city.
**Enrollment:** 8,803 undergrads, 25% part-time. 1,133 full-time freshmen.
**Selectivity:** Admits 50 to 75% of applicants.

## BASIC COSTS (2015-2016)
**Tuition and fees:** $8,522; out-of-state residents $20,222.
**Per-credit charge:** $198.32; out-of-state residents $588.32.
**Room and board:** $7,443.

## FINANCIAL AID PICTURE
**Students with need:** Need-based aid available for full-time and part-time students. Work study available nights, weekends, and for part-time students.
**Students without need:** No-need awards available for academics, art, athletics, music/drama, ROTC.
**Scholarships offered:** Chancellor's Endowed Scholarship; full tuition and fees, room and board; based on high school valedictorian status, extracurricular activities, SAT score; 2 awarded. Presidential Scholarship; full tuition and fees; awarded to valedictorian or salutatorian. Honors Scholarship; $1,500 annually up to 4 years; based on admission to honors program and SAT score. New Freshman Scholarship; $1,500 annually up to 4 years; based on SAT/ACT score, class rank and GPA. Transfer Student Scholarship; $1,500 annually up to 4 years; based on GPA, must have completed at least 12 credit hours. New Student Scholarship; $1,800 annually up to 4 years; based on high school rank, ACT/SAT score; 150 awarded.

## FINANCIAL AID PROCEDURES
**Forms required:** FAFSA.
**Dates and Deadlines:** Priority date 4/1; no closing date.

**CONTACT**
Governor Jackson, Director of Financial Aid
Box 425589, Denton, TX 76204-5589
(940) 898-3064

## Trinity University
San Antonio, Texas                          Federal Code: 003647
www.trinity.edu                                  CSS Code: 6831

**4-year private** university in very large city, affiliated with Presbyterian Church (USA).
**Enrollment:** 2,253 undergrads, 3% part-time. 602 full-time freshmen.
**Selectivity:** Admits less than 50% of applicants.

**BASIC COSTS (2016-2017)**
**Tuition and fees:** $39,560.
**Per-credit charge:** $1,624.
**Room and board:** $12,754.

**FINANCIAL AID PICTURE (2015-2016)**
**Students with need:** Out of 421 full-time freshmen who applied for aid, 269 were judged to have need. Of these, 269 received aid, and 222 had their full need met. Average financial aid package met 98% of need; average scholarship/grant was $29,089; average loan was $4,468. For part-time students, average financial aid package was $1,990.
**Students without need:** 312 full-time freshmen who did not demonstrate need for aid received scholarships/grants; average award was $19,066. No-need awards available for academics, art, leadership, music/drama.

**FINANCIAL AID PROCEDURES**
**Forms required:** FAFSA, CSS PROFILE.
**Dates and Deadlines:** Priority date 2/15; no closing date. Applicants notified by 3/15; must reply by 5/1.
**Transfers:** Priority date 5/1; no deadline.

**CONTACT**
Glendi Gaddis, Director of Financial Aid
One Trinity Place, San Antonio, TX 78212-7200
(210) 999-8315

## Trinity Valley Community College
Athens, Texas
www.tvcc.edu                                  Federal Code: 003572

**2-year public** community college in large town.
**Enrollment:** 6,254 undergrads, 69% part-time. 466 full-time freshmen.
**Selectivity:** Open admission; but selective for some programs.

**BASIC COSTS (2015-2016)**
**Tuition and fees:** $2,340; out-of-district residents $4,110; out-of-state residents $4,680.
**Per-credit charge:** $34; out-of-district residents $93; out-of-state residents $112.
**Room and board:** $5,580.
**Additional info:** Tuition/fee waivers available for adults.

**FINANCIAL AID PICTURE**
**Students with need:** Need-based aid available for full-time and part-time students. Work study available nights, weekends, and for part-time students.
**Students without need:** No-need awards available for academics, athletics.

**FINANCIAL AID PROCEDURES**
**Forms required:** FAFSA, institutional form.
**Dates and Deadlines:** Closing date 7/1. Applicants notified on a rolling basis starting 7/1; must reply within 2 week(s) of notification.
**Transfers:** Students on suspension at previous institution ineligible to receive aid.

**CONTACT**
Jennifer Evilsizer
100 Cardinal Drive, Athens, TX 75751
(903) 675-6233

## Tyler Junior College
Tyler, Texas
www.tjc.edu                                  Federal Code: 003648

**2-year public** community and junior college in small city.
**Enrollment:** 10,887 undergrads, 45% part-time. 2,466 full-time freshmen.
**Selectivity:** Open admission; but selective for some programs.

**BASIC COSTS (2015-2016)**
**Tuition and fees:** $2,352; out-of-district residents $3,762; out-of-state residents $4,362.
**Per-credit charge:** $30; out-of-district residents $77; out-of-state residents $97.
**Room and board:** $7,022.

**FINANCIAL AID PICTURE (2014-2015)**
**Students with need:** Out of 2,089 full-time freshmen who applied for aid, 1,612 were judged to have need. Of these, 1,597 received aid, and 45 had their full need met. Average financial aid package met 57% of need; average scholarship/grant was $4,042; average loan was $2,003. For part-time students, average financial aid package was $5,068.
**Students without need:** 134 full-time freshmen who did not demonstrate need for aid received scholarships/grants; average award was $3,715. No-need awards available for academics, alumni affiliation, art, athletics, music/drama.
**Scholarships offered:** 131 full-time freshmen received athletic scholarships; average amount $7,994.

**FINANCIAL AID PROCEDURES**
**Forms required:** FAFSA, institutional form.
**Dates and Deadlines:** Priority date 4/1; closing date 6/1. Applicants notified on a rolling basis starting 4/1; must reply within 2 week(s) of notification.
**Transfers:** Financial aid transcript required if student enrolled same year elsewhere.

**CONTACT**
Devon Wiggins, Director of Student Financial Aid and Scholarship
Box 9020, Tyler, TX 75711-9020
(903) 510-2385

## University of Dallas
Irving, Texas
www.udallas.edu                              Federal Code: 003651

**4-year private** university and liberal arts college in small city, affiliated with Roman Catholic Church.
**Enrollment:** 1,336 undergrads, 2% part-time. 393 full-time freshmen.
**Selectivity:** Admits over 75% of applicants.

**BASIC COSTS (2016-2017)**
**Tuition and fees:** $37,230.
**Room and board:** $11,540.

**FINANCIAL AID PICTURE (2015-2016)**
**Students with need:** Out of 316 full-time freshmen who applied for aid, 268 were judged to have need. Of these, 268 received aid, and 57 had their full need met. Average financial aid package met 83% of need; average scholarship/grant was $28,287; average loan was $4,386. For part-time students, average financial aid package was $11,256.

**Students without need:** 117 full-time freshmen who did not demonstrate need for aid received scholarships/grants; average award was $21,813. No-need awards available for academics, alumni affiliation, art, minority status, music/drama, religious affiliation, ROTC, state/district residency.

**FINANCIAL AID PROCEDURES**

**Forms required:** FAFSA.

**Dates and Deadlines:** Priority date 3/1; closing date 8/1. Applicants notified on a rolling basis starting 3/1; must reply by 5/1 or within 4 week(s) of notification.

**Transfers:** No deadline. Applicants notified on a rolling basis starting 3/1; must reply by 5/1 or within 4 week(s) of notification.

**CONTACT**

Taryn Anderson, Director of Financial Aid
1845 East Northgate Drive, Irving, TX 75062-4736
(972) 721-5266

## University of Houston

Houston, Texas
www.uh.edu                          Federal Code: 003652

**4-year public** university in very large city.

**Enrollment:** 33,404 undergrads, 27% part-time. 4,010 full-time freshmen.

**Selectivity:** Admits 50 to 75% of applicants.

**BASIC COSTS (2015-2016)**

**Tuition and fees:** $10,664; out-of-state residents $25,364.

**Per-credit charge:** $305; out-of-state residents $795.

**FINANCIAL AID PICTURE (2015-2016)**

**Students with need:** Out of 3,093 full-time freshmen who applied for aid, 2,484 were judged to have need. Of these, 2,412 received aid, and 459 had their full need met. Average financial aid package met 66% of need; average scholarship/grant was $9,671; average loan was $5,270. For part-time students, average financial aid package was $9,226.

**Students without need:** 417 full-time freshmen who did not demonstrate need for aid received scholarships/grants; average award was $4,676. No-need awards available for academics, alumni affiliation, art, athletics, job skills, leadership, music/drama, ROTC, state/district residency.

**Scholarships offered:** 36 full-time freshmen received athletic scholarships; average amount $8,298.

**Additional info:** The Cougar Promise guarantees free tuition and mandatory fees to new in-state freshmen with family incomes at or below $45,000. Qualifying students will have tuition and fees guaranteed for up to four years as long as students continue to meet eligibility criteria and maintain at least a 2.5 GPA. Covers tuition and fees during the fall and spring semesters only. Eligibility is determined when a student fills out the FAFSA. Those who miss the April 1 deadline will be awarded based on the availability of funds.

**FINANCIAL AID PROCEDURES**

**Forms required:** FAFSA.

**Dates and Deadlines:** Priority date 4/1; no closing date. Applicants notified on a rolling basis starting 5/1.

**Transfers:** Applicants notified on a rolling basis starting 4/1; must reply by 7/1.

**CONTACT**

Scott Moore, Interim Executive Director
Office of Admission, Houston, TX 77004
(713) 743-1010

## University of Houston-Clear Lake

Houston, Texas
www.uhcl.edu                         Federal Code: 011711

**4-year public** university in very large city.

**Enrollment:** 5,403 undergrads, 51% part-time. 174 full-time freshmen.

**Selectivity:** Admits 50 to 75% of applicants.

**BASIC COSTS (2015-2016)**

**Tuition and fees:** $6,639; out-of-state residents $21,099.

**Per-credit charge:** $200; out-of-state residents $682.

**FINANCIAL AID PICTURE (2014-2015)**

**Students with need:** Out of 152 full-time freshmen who applied for aid, 122 were judged to have need. Of these, 105 received aid, and 19 had their full need met. Average financial aid package met 65% of need; average scholarship/grant was $10,871; average loan was $2,744. For part-time students, average financial aid package was $5,700.

**Students without need:** 36 full-time freshmen who did not demonstrate need for aid received scholarships/grants; average award was $5,861. No-need awards available for academics, art, leadership, state/district residency.

**Scholarships offered:** Non-need, merit based scholarships will be available to entering freshmen.

**Additional info:** UHCL offers the automatic transfer scholarship to any first-time transfer student if their transfer GPA is 2.75 or above upon receiving all transcripts. No application necessary for the scholarship.

**FINANCIAL AID PROCEDURES**

**Forms required:** FAFSA.

**Dates and Deadlines:** Priority date 3/15; no closing date. Applicants notified on a rolling basis starting 5/1; must reply within 2 week(s) of notification.

**Transfers:** No deadline. Applicants notified on a rolling basis starting 5/15; must reply within 4 week(s) of notification.

**CONTACT**

Billy Satterfield, Executive Director of Student Financial Aid/Registrar
2700 Bay Area Boulevard, Houston, TX 77058-1098
(281) 283-2480

## University of Houston-Downtown

Houston, Texas
www.uhd.edu                          Federal Code: 003612

**4-year public** university in very large city.

**Enrollment:** 13,101 undergrads, 49% part-time. 914 full-time freshmen.

**Selectivity:** Admits over 75% of applicants.

**BASIC COSTS (2015-2016)**

**Tuition and fees:** $6,938; out-of-state residents $18,638.

**Per-credit charge:** $193; out-of-state residents $583.

**Additional info:** College of Business tuition rates are an additional $2 per credit hour. College of Science and Technology tuition rates are an additional $3 per credit hour.

**FINANCIAL AID PICTURE (2014-2015)**

**Students with need:** Out of 813 full-time freshmen who applied for aid, 731 were judged to have need. Of these, 654 received aid, and 8 had their full need met. Average financial aid package met 62% of need; average scholarship/grant was $8,903; average loan was $4,560. For part-time students, average financial aid package was $8,257.

**FINANCIAL AID PROCEDURES**

**Forms required:** FAFSA.

**Dates and Deadlines:** Priority date 4/1; no closing date. Applicants notified on a rolling basis starting 2/1; must reply within 4 week(s) of notification.

**Transfers:** No deadline. Applicants notified on a rolling basis starting 4/15; must reply within 4 week(s) of notification.

**CONTACT**

LaTasha Goudeau, Director of Scholarships and Financial Aid
One Main Street, Suite S350, Houston, TX 77002
(713) 221-8041

## University of Houston-Victoria
Victoria, Texas
www.uhv.edu                         Federal Code: 013231

**4-year public** university in small city.
**Enrollment:** 2,991 undergrads.

### BASIC COSTS (2015-2016)
**Tuition and fees:** $7,086; out-of-state residents $18,786.
**Per-credit charge:** $183; out-of-state residents $573.
**Room and board:** $7,664.

### FINANCIAL AID PICTURE
**Students with need:** Need-based aid available for full-time and part-time students. Work study available weekends and for part-time students.
**Students without need:** No-need awards available for academics, athletics, leadership, state/district residency.
**Additional info:** Short-term loans available at registration.

### FINANCIAL AID PROCEDURES
**Forms required:** FAFSA, institutional form.
**Dates and Deadlines:** Priority date 3/15; no closing date. Applicants notified on a rolling basis starting 3/30; must reply within 3 week(s) of notification.
**Transfers:** No deadline. Applicants notified on a rolling basis; must reply within 3 week(s) of notification.

### CONTACT
Carolyn Mallory, Financial Aid Director
3007 North Ben Wilson, Victoria, TX 77901-4450
(361) 570-4131

## University of Mary Hardin-Baylor
Belton, Texas
www.umhb.edu                        Federal Code: 003588

**4-year private** university in large town, affiliated with Baptist faith.
**Enrollment:** 3,173 undergrads, 8% part-time. 725 full-time freshmen.
**Selectivity:** Admits over 75% of applicants.

### BASIC COSTS (2016-2017)
**Tuition and fees:** $26,650.
**Per-credit charge:** $810.
**Room and board:** $7,300.
**Additional info:** Tuition/fee waivers available for minority students.

### FINANCIAL AID PICTURE (2015-2016)
**Students with need:** Out of 603 full-time freshmen who applied for aid, 526 were judged to have need. Of these, 526 received aid, and 43 had their full need met. Average financial aid package met 63% of need; average scholarship/grant was $15,392; average loan was $3,240. For part-time students, average financial aid package was $9,058.
**Students without need:** 90 full-time freshmen who did not demonstrate need for aid received scholarships/grants; average award was $7,411. No-need awards available for academics, alumni affiliation, art, leadership, music/drama, religious affiliation.

### FINANCIAL AID PROCEDURES
**Forms required:** FAFSA.
**Dates and Deadlines:** Priority date 2/15; no closing date. Applicants notified on a rolling basis starting 2/15; must reply within 2 week(s) of notification.
**Transfers:** No deadline. Applicants notified on a rolling basis starting 11/1; must reply within 2 week(s) of notification.

### CONTACT
Ron Brown, Director of Financial Aid
900 College Street, Belton, TX 76513
(254) 295-4517

## University of North Texas
Denton, Texas
www.unt.edu                         Federal Code: 003594

**4-year public** university in small city.
**Enrollment:** 30,503 undergrads, 18% part-time. 4,361 full-time freshmen.
**Selectivity:** Admits 50 to 75% of applicants.

### BASIC COSTS (2015-2016)
**Tuition and fees:** $10,091; out-of-state residents $21,791.
**Per-credit charge:** $253; out-of-state residents $643.
**Room and board:** $8,199.

### FINANCIAL AID PICTURE (2015-2016)
**Students with need:** Out of 3,752 full-time freshmen who applied for aid, 2,852 were judged to have need. Of these, 2,754 received aid, and 365 had their full need met. Average financial aid package met 69% of need; average scholarship/grant was $10,846; average loan was $3,134. For part-time students, average financial aid package was $7,109.
**Students without need:** 568 full-time freshmen who did not demonstrate need for aid received scholarships/grants; average award was $9,789.
**Scholarships offered:** 25 full-time freshmen received athletic scholarships; average amount $12,391.

### FINANCIAL AID PROCEDURES
**Forms required:** FAFSA.
**Dates and Deadlines:** Priority date 3/15; no closing date. Applicants notified on a rolling basis starting 4/1.

### CONTACT
Zelma DeLeon, Director of Financial Aid
1401 West Prairie Suite 309, Denton, TX 76203-5017
(940) 565-2302

## University of St. Thomas
Houston, Texas
www.stthom.edu                      Federal Code: 003654

**4-year private** university and liberal arts college in very large city, affiliated with Roman Catholic Church.
**Enrollment:** 1,729 undergrads, 22% part-time. 237 full-time freshmen.
**Selectivity:** Admits over 75% of applicants.

### BASIC COSTS (2016-2017)
**Tuition and fees:** $30,310.
**Per-credit charge:** $999.
**Room and board:** $8,500.

### FINANCIAL AID PICTURE (2015-2016)
**Students with need:** Out of 191 full-time freshmen who applied for aid, 166 were judged to have need. Of these, 161 received aid, and 25 had their full need met. Average financial aid package met 75% of need; average scholarship/grant was $22,566; average loan was $3,281. For part-time students, average financial aid package was $10,684.
**Students without need:** 67 full-time freshmen who did not demonstrate need for aid received scholarships/grants; average award was $11,024. No-need awards available for academics, athletics, music/drama, religious affiliation, ROTC.
**Scholarships offered:** 9 full-time freshmen received athletic scholarships; average amount $5,647.

### FINANCIAL AID PROCEDURES
**Forms required:** FAFSA.
**Dates and Deadlines:** Priority date 4/15; no closing date. Applicants notified on a rolling basis starting 2/15; must reply within 2 week(s) of notification.

## CONTACT

Lynda McKendree, Dean of Scholarships and Financial Aid

3800 Montrose Boulevard, Houston, TX 77006-4626

(713) 942-3465

# University of Texas at Arlington

Arlington, Texas

www.uta.edu                    Federal Code: 003656

**4-year public** university in large city.

**Enrollment:** 30,358 undergrads.

## BASIC COSTS (2015-2016)

**Tuition and fees:** $8,878; out-of-state residents $21,114.

**Room and board:** $8,398.

## FINANCIAL AID PICTURE

**Students with need:** Need-based aid available for full-time and part-time students. Work study available nights, weekends, and for part-time students.

**Students without need:** No-need awards available for academics, art, athletics, leadership, music/drama, ROTC.

**Scholarships offered:** Academic Scholarships: $1,000-$4,000 per year; renewable; based on minimum SAT 1050 (exclusive of Writing) or ACT 22, top 25% of high school class.

**Additional info:** Free tuition to eligible students whose household income is $65,000 or less through the Maverick Promise program.

## FINANCIAL AID PROCEDURES

**Forms required:** FAFSA.

**Dates and Deadlines:** Priority date 4/15; no closing date. Applicants notified on a rolling basis starting 4/1; must reply within 3 week(s) of notification.

**Transfers:** Must reply within 3 week(s) of notification. To receive Texas grant or Texas B on Time loan, student must have either received Texas grant or completed associates degree at prior school.

## CONTACT

Karen Krause, Director of Financial Aid

UTA Box 19088, Arlington, TX 76019

(817) 272-3561

# University of Texas at Austin

Austin, Texas

www.utexas.edu                Federal Code: 003658

**4-year public** university in very large city.

**Enrollment:** 39,057 undergrads, 7% part-time. 7,743 full-time freshmen.

**Selectivity:** Admits less than 50% of applicants.

## BASIC COSTS (2015-2016)

**Tuition and fees:** $9,830; out-of-state residents $34,836.

**Room and board:** $11,456.

## FINANCIAL AID PICTURE (2015-2016)

**Students with need:** Out of 5,879 full-time freshmen who applied for aid, 3,314 were judged to have need. Of these, 3,308 received aid, and 778 had their full need met. Average financial aid package met 68% of need; average scholarship/grant was $9,229; average loan was $3,306. Need-based aid available for part-time students.

**Students without need:** 48 full-time freshmen who did not demonstrate need for aid received scholarships/grants; average award was $5,995. No-need awards available for academics, art, athletics, leadership, music/drama, ROTC, state/district residency.

## FINANCIAL AID PROCEDURES

**Forms required:** FAFSA, institutional form.

**Dates and Deadlines:** Priority date 3/15; no closing date. Applicants notified on a rolling basis starting 3/15; must reply by 5/1 or within 3 week(s) of notification.

**Transfers:** Limited number of scholarship funds available for transfer students.

## CONTACT

Diane Sprague, Director of Financial Aid

PO Box 8058, Austin, TX 78713-8058

(512) 475-6282

# University of Texas at Brownsville

Brownsville, Texas

www.utb.edu                    Federal Code: 030646

**4-year public** university in small city.

**Enrollment:** 6,798 undergrads.

## FINANCIAL AID PICTURE

**Students with need:** Need-based aid available for full-time and part-time students. Work study available nights.

**Students without need:** No-need awards available for academics, alumni affiliation, art, athletics, minority status, music/drama, state/district residency.

## FINANCIAL AID PROCEDURES

**Forms required:** FAFSA.

**Dates and Deadlines:** Priority date 3/1; closing date 8/15. Must reply by 7/1 or within 12 week(s) of notification.

**Transfers:** Priority date 4/1; closing date 7/25.

## CONTACT

Arnold Trejo, Director of Financial Aid

One West University Blvd., Brownsville, TX 78520

(956) 882-8277

# University of Texas at Dallas

Richardson, Texas

www.utdallas.edu              Federal Code: 009741

**4-year public** university in very large city.

**Enrollment:** 15,283 undergrads, 18% part-time. 2,480 full-time freshmen.

**Selectivity:** Admits 50 to 75% of applicants.

## BASIC COSTS (2015-2016)

**Tuition and fees:** $11,806; out-of-state residents $31,328.

**Per-credit charge:** $393.53; out-of-state residents $1,044.27.

**Room and board:** $9,944.

**Additional info:** Tuition at time of enrollment locked for 4 years.

## FINANCIAL AID PICTURE (2014-2015)

**Students with need:** Out of 1,794 full-time freshmen who applied for aid, 1,329 were judged to have need. Of these, 1,298 received aid, and 397 had their full need met. Average financial aid package met 76% of need; average scholarship/grant was $11,085; average loan was $3,318. For part-time students, average financial aid package was $7,362.

**Students without need:** 638 full-time freshmen who did not demonstrate need for aid received scholarships/grants; average award was $13,459. No-need awards available for academics.

**Scholarships offered:** Eugene McDermott Scholars Program Awards; full tuition and fees plus domestic and international travel costs for enhancement of scholar's education; based on being in top 10% of high school class, high scores on entrance exams, evidence of leadership abilities; 20 awarded. Academic Excellence Scholarships; based on SAT/ACT, class rank, high school GPA, AP/Honors work; Achievement level is $3,000/year, Distinction covers tuition/mandatory fees, Honors covers tuition/mandatory fees plus $3,000 stipend.

**FINANCIAL AID PROCEDURES**

**Forms required:** FAFSA.

**Dates and Deadlines:** Priority date 3/31; closing date 4/12. Applicants notified on a rolling basis starting 3/1; must reply within 2 week(s) of notification.

**Transfers:** Priority date 4/1. Applicants notified on a rolling basis; must reply within 2 week(s) of notification.

**CONTACT**

Beth Tolan, Director of Financial Aid

Admission and Enrollment Services, Richardson, TX 75080-3021

(972) 883-2941

## University of Texas at El Paso

El Paso, Texas

www.utep.edu                    Federal Code: 003661

**4-year public** university in very large city.

**Enrollment:** 20,004 undergrads. 2,908 full-time freshmen.

**BASIC COSTS (2015-2016)**

**Tuition and fees:** $7,059; out-of-state residents $18,169.

**Per-credit charge:** $186.86; out-of-state residents $555.54.

**Room only:** $4,806.

**FINANCIAL AID PICTURE (2014-2015)**

**Students with need:** Out of 2,757 full-time freshmen who applied for aid, 2,328 were judged to have need. Of these, 2,266 received aid, and 263 had their full need met. Average financial aid package met 68% of need; average scholarship/grant was $9,916; average loan was $4,265. For part-time students, average financial aid package was $9,523.

**Students without need:** 168 full-time freshmen who did not demonstrate need for aid received scholarships/grants; average award was $2,988. No-need awards available for academics, alumni affiliation, art, athletics, job skills, leadership, minority status, music/drama, religious affiliation, ROTC, state/district residency.

**Scholarships offered:** 28 full-time freshmen received athletic scholarships; average amount $11,200.

**Additional info:** Emergency loans available.

**FINANCIAL AID PROCEDURES**

**Forms required:** FAFSA, institutional form.

**Dates and Deadlines:** Priority date 3/15; no closing date. Must reply within 2 week(s) of notification.

**Transfers:** No deadline. Must reply within 2 week(s) of notification.

**CONTACT**

Ron Williams, Director of Financial Aid

500 West University Avenue, El Paso, TX 79968

(915) 747-5204

## University of Texas at San Antonio

San Antonio, Texas

www.utsa.edu                    Federal Code: 010115

**4-year public** university in very large city.

**Enrollment:** 23,921 undergrads, 16% part-time. 4,948 full-time freshmen.

**Selectivity:** Admits over 75% of applicants.

**BASIC COSTS (2015-2016)**

**Tuition and fees:** $8,737; out-of-state residents $20,890.

**Per-credit charge:** $199.41; out-of-state residents $605.

**Room and board:** $7,564.

**FINANCIAL AID PICTURE (2014-2015)**

**Students with need:** Out of 4,245 full-time freshmen who applied for aid, 3,410 were judged to have need. Of these, 3,283 received aid, and 203 had

their full need met. Average financial aid package met 61% of need; average scholarship/grant was $8,071; average loan was $3,266. For part-time students, average financial aid package was $5,283.

**Students without need:** 288 full-time freshmen who did not demonstrate need for aid received scholarships/grants; average award was $2,755. No-need awards available for academics, alumni affiliation, art, athletics, job skills, leadership, music/drama, ROTC, state/district residency.

**Scholarships offered:** 60 full-time freshmen received athletic scholarships; average amount $13,161.

**FINANCIAL AID PROCEDURES**

**Forms required:** FAFSA.

**Dates and Deadlines:** Priority date 3/15; no closing date. Applicants notified on a rolling basis starting 4/1.

**Transfers:** No deadline. Applicants notified on a rolling basis starting 4/1; must reply within 4 week(s) of notification.

**CONTACT**

Lisa Blazer, Assistant Vice President of Financial Aid

One UTSA Circle, San Antonio, TX 78249-0617

(210) 458-7828

## University of Texas at Tyler

Tyler, Texas

www.uttyler.edu                    Federal Code: 011163

**4-year public** university in small city.

**Enrollment:** 6,059 undergrads, 25% part-time. 767 full-time freshmen.

**Selectivity:** Admits 50 to 75% of applicants.

**BASIC COSTS (2015-2016)**

**Tuition and fees:** $7,312; out-of-state residents $19,236.

**Per-credit charge:** $50; out-of-state residents $440.

**Room and board:** $7,775.

**FINANCIAL AID PICTURE**

**Students with need:** Need-based aid available for full-time and part-time students.

**Students without need:** No-need awards available for academics, art, music/drama.

**Additional info:** Apply early for all programs.

**FINANCIAL AID PROCEDURES**

**Forms required:** FAFSA, state aid form.

**Dates and Deadlines:** Priority date 4/1; no closing date. Applicants notified on a rolling basis starting 4/15; must reply within 2 week(s) of notification.

**CONTACT**

Marquita Hackett, Director of Student Financial Aid

3900 University Boulevard, Tyler, TX 75799

(903) 566-7180

## University of Texas Health Science Center at Houston

Houston, Texas

www.uth.tmc.edu                    Federal Code: 013956

**Upper-division public** university and health science college in very large city.

**Enrollment:** 657 undergrads, 18% part-time.

**FINANCIAL AID PICTURE**

**Students with need:** Need-based aid available for full-time and part-time students.

**Students without need:** This college awards aid only to students with need.

## FINANCIAL AID PROCEDURES

**Forms required:** FAFSA, institutional form.

**Dates and Deadlines:** Applicants notified on a rolling basis starting 6/1.

## CONTACT

Araceli Alvarez, Director of Student Financial Aid

Box 20036, Houston, TX 77225

(713) 500-3860

# University of Texas Medical Branch at Galveston

Galveston, Texas

www.utmb.edu                    Federal Code: 013976

**Upper-division public** health science and nursing college in large town.

**Enrollment:** 745 undergrads, 17% part-time.

## FINANCIAL AID PICTURE

**Students with need:** Need-based aid available for full-time and part-time students. Work study available nights, weekends, and for part-time students.

**Students without need:** No-need awards available for academics, minority status, state/district residency.

## FINANCIAL AID PROCEDURES

**Forms required:** FAFSA.

**Dates and Deadlines:** Applicants notified on a rolling basis; must reply within 4 week(s) of notification.

## CONTACT

Carol Cromie, Assistant Director of Enrollment Services for Financial Aid

301 University Boulevard, Galveston, TX 77555-1305

(409) 772-1215

# University of Texas of the Permian Basin

Odessa, Texas

www.utpb.edu                    Federal Code: 009930

**4-year public** university in small city.

**Enrollment:** 3,436 undergrads, 40% part-time. 391 full-time freshmen.

**Selectivity:** Admits over 75% of applicants.

## BASIC COSTS (2015-2016)

**Tuition and fees:** $6,458; out-of-district residents $7,508; out-of-state residents $7,508.

**Per-credit charge:** $168; out-of-district residents $202.88; out-of-state residents $202.88.

**Room and board:** $8,904.

## FINANCIAL AID PICTURE (2014-2015)

**Students with need:** Out of 330 full-time freshmen who applied for aid, 254 were judged to have need. Of these, 254 received aid, and 215 had their full need met. Average financial aid package met 75% of need; average scholarship/grant was $8,360; average loan was $2,713. For part-time students, average financial aid package was $3,010.

**Students without need:** 106 full-time freshmen who did not demonstrate need for aid received scholarships/grants; average award was $4,530. No-need awards available for academics, art, athletics, leadership, music/drama, state/district residency.

**Scholarships offered:** 19 full-time freshmen received athletic scholarships; average amount $4,420.

## FINANCIAL AID PROCEDURES

**Forms required:** FAFSA.

**Dates and Deadlines:** Priority date 7/15; no closing date. Applicants notified on a rolling basis starting 3/15.

## CONTACT

Charles Kerestly, Director of Financial Aid

4901 East University, Odessa, TX 79762

(432) 552-2620

# University Of Texas Rio Grande Valley

Edinburg, Texas

www.utrgv.edu

**4-year public** university in small city.

**Enrollment:** 24,677 undergrads, 29% part-time. 3,943 full-time freshmen.

**Selectivity:** Admits over 75% of applicants.

## FINANCIAL AID PICTURE (2015-2016)

**Students with need:** Out of 3,574 full-time freshmen who applied for aid, 3,366 were judged to have need. Of these, 3,366 received aid, and 111 had their full need met. Average financial aid package met 68% of need; average scholarship/grant was $10,191; average loan was $3,252. For part-time students, average financial aid package was $6,037.

**Students without need:** 116 full-time freshmen who did not demonstrate need for aid received scholarships/grants; average award was $3,542. No-need awards available for academics, alumni affiliation, art, athletics, leadership, music/drama.

**Scholarships offered:** 35 full-time freshmen received athletic scholarships; average amount $9,197.

## FINANCIAL AID PROCEDURES

**Forms required:** FAFSA.

**Dates and Deadlines:** Priority date 3/15; no closing date. Applicants notified on a rolling basis.

## CONTACT

1201 West University Drive, Edinburg, TX 78539

# University of Texas-Pan American

Edinburg, Texas

www.utpa.edu                    Federal Code: 003599

**4-year public** university in small city.

**Enrollment:** 17,994 undergrads.

## BASIC COSTS (2015-2016)

**Tuition and fees:** $7,292; out-of-state residents $18,992.

**Per-credit charge:** $194; out-of-state residents $584.

**Room and board:** $6,592.

## FINANCIAL AID PICTURE

**Students with need:** Need-based aid available for full-time and part-time students.

**Students without need:** No-need awards available for academics, alumni affiliation, art, athletics, ROTC.

## FINANCIAL AID PROCEDURES

**Forms required:** FAFSA.

**Dates and Deadlines:** Priority date 3/15; no closing date. Applicants notified on a rolling basis starting 3/15.

**Transfers:** No deadline. Applicants notified on a rolling basis.

## CONTACT

Elaine Rivera, Executive Director of Student Financial Services

1201 West University Drive, Edinburg, TX 78539-2999

(956) 665-2501

# University of the Incarnate Word

San Antonio, Texas

www.uiw.edu                                  Federal Code: 003578

**4-year private** university in very large city, affiliated with Roman Catholic Church.

**Enrollment:** 6,249 undergrads, 32% part-time. 913 full-time freshmen.

**Selectivity:** Admits over 75% of applicants.

## BASIC COSTS (2015-2016)

**Tuition and fees:** $27,798.

**Per-credit charge:** $850.

**Room and board:** $11,364.

## FINANCIAL AID PICTURE (2014-2015)

**Students with need:** Out of 803 full-time freshmen who applied for aid, 734 were judged to have need. Of these, 733 received aid, and 78 had their full need met. Average financial aid package met 63% of need; average scholarship/grant was $17,375; average loan was $3,544. For part-time students, average financial aid package was $6,425.

**Students without need:** 157 full-time freshmen who did not demonstrate need for aid received scholarships/grants; average award was $9,053. No-need awards available for academics, alumni affiliation, art, athletics, leadership, minority status, music/drama, religious affiliation, ROTC.

**Scholarships offered:** 37 full-time freshmen received athletic scholarships; average amount $22,891.

**Additional info:** Students encouraged to pursue outside scholarship programs.

## FINANCIAL AID PROCEDURES

**Forms required:** FAFSA.

**Dates and Deadlines:** Priority date 4/1; no closing date. Applicants notified on a rolling basis starting 2/15; must reply within 2 week(s) of notification.

**Transfers:** No deadline. Applicants notified on a rolling basis starting 2/15.

## CONTACT

Amy Carcanagues, Director of Financial Assistance

4301 Broadway, San Antonio, TX 78209-6397

(210) 829-6008

# Vernon College

Vernon, Texas

www.vernoncollege.edu                        Federal Code: 010060

**2-year public** community and junior college in large town.

**Enrollment:** 2,367 undergrads.

**Selectivity:** Open admission; but selective for some programs.

## BASIC COSTS (2015-2016)

**Tuition and fees:** $2,640; out-of-district residents $4,050; out-of-state residents $6,000.

**Per-credit charge:** $48; out-of-district residents $95; out-of-state residents $200.

**Room and board:** $3,912.

## FINANCIAL AID PICTURE (2015-2016)

**Students with need:** 65% of average financial aid package awarded as scholarships/grants, 35% awarded as loans/jobs. Need-based aid available for part-time students. Work study available nights, weekends, and for part-time students.

**Students without need:** This college awards aid only to students with need.

## FINANCIAL AID PROCEDURES

**Forms required:** FAFSA.

**Dates and Deadlines:** Priority date 7/1; no closing date. Applicants notified on a rolling basis starting 4/1.

**Transfers:** No deadline. Applicants notified on a rolling basis.

## CONTACT

Melissa Elliott, Director of Financial Aid

4400 College Drive, Vernon, TX 76384-4092

(940) 552-6291

# Vet Tech Institute of Houston

Houston, Texas

www.bradfordschools.com

**2-year for-profit** technical college in very large city.

**Enrollment:** 260 undergrads.

## BASIC COSTS (2015-2016)

**Additional info:** Cost for full-time students entering Fall 2015, $6,780 per semester; Spring 2016, $6,780 per semester. Books and supplies vary from semester to semester, ranging from $100 to $1,500.

## FINANCIAL AID PICTURE

**Students with need:** Need-based aid available for full-time students.

## CONTACT

4669 Southwest Freeway, Houston, TX 77027

# Victoria College

Victoria, Texas

www.victoriacollege.edu                       Federal Code: 003662

**2-year public** community college in small city.

**Enrollment:** 3,410 undergrads, 67% part-time. 362 full-time freshmen.

**Selectivity:** Open admission; but selective for some programs.

## BASIC COSTS (2015-2016)

**Tuition and fees:** $2,640; out-of-district residents $4,050; out-of-state residents $4,650.

**Per-credit charge:** $46; out-of-district residents $93; out-of-state residents $200.

## FINANCIAL AID PICTURE (2014-2015)

**Students with need:** 69% of average financial aid package awarded as scholarships/grants, 31% awarded as loans/jobs.

**Students without need:** No-need awards available for academics, art, minority status, music/drama.

## FINANCIAL AID PROCEDURES

**Forms required:** FAFSA, institutional form.

**Dates and Deadlines:** Priority date 4/15; no closing date. Applicants notified on a rolling basis.

## CONTACT

Kim Obsta, Director of Financial Aid

2200 East Red River, Victoria, TX 77901

(361) 572-6415

# Wade College

Dallas, Texas

www.wadecollege.edu                           Federal Code: 010130

**2-year for-profit** business and career college in very large city.

**Enrollment:** 250 undergrads.

**Selectivity:** Open admission; but selective for some programs.

## BASIC COSTS (2015-2016)

**Tuition and fees:** $15,575.

**Per-credit charge:** $515.

**Additional info:** Books/Supplies $0 (all inclusive tuition/books/fees). Tuition shown for the Associate of Arts degree in Merchandising and Design. Bachelor of Arts per credit-hour charge of $585. Tuition at time of enrollment locked for 2 years.

**FINANCIAL AID PICTURE**
**Students with need:** Need-based aid available for full-time and part-time students.
**Students without need:** This college awards aid only to students with need.

**FINANCIAL AID PROCEDURES**
**Forms required:** FAFSA.
**Dates and Deadlines:** Applicants notified on a rolling basis; must reply within 4 week(s) of notification.

**CONTACT**
Lisa Hoover, Director of Financial Services
1950 North Stemmons Freeway, Suite 4080, Dallas, TX 75207
(214) 637-3530

## Wayland Baptist University
Plainview, Texas
www.wbu.edu                  Federal Code: 003663

**4-year private** university and liberal arts college in large town, affiliated with Southern Baptist Convention.
**Enrollment:** 3,583 undergrads, 71% part-time. 267 full-time freshmen.
**Selectivity:** Admits over 75% of applicants.

**BASIC COSTS (2015-2016)**
**Tuition and fees:** $16,830.
**Per-credit charge:** $525.
**Room and board:** $5,952.

**FINANCIAL AID PICTURE (2015-2016)**
**Students with need:** Out of 228 full-time freshmen who applied for aid, 207 were judged to have need. Of these, 188 received aid, and 13 had their full need met. Average financial aid package met 56% of need; average scholarship/grant was $10,962; average loan was $3,487. For part-time students, average financial aid package was $6,874.
**Students without need:** 26 full-time freshmen who did not demonstrate need for aid received scholarships/grants; average award was $5,500. No-need awards available for academics, art, athletics, leadership, music/drama, religious affiliation, state/district residency.
**Scholarships offered:** 28 full-time freshmen received athletic scholarships; average amount $7,988.

**FINANCIAL AID PROCEDURES**
**Forms required:** FAFSA, institutional form.
**Dates and Deadlines:** Applicants notified on a rolling basis starting 2/1; must reply within 2 week(s) of notification.
**Transfers:** No deadline. Applicants notified on a rolling basis.

**CONTACT**
Karen LaQuey, Director of Financial Aid
1900 West Seventh Street, CMB #1294, Plainview, TX 79072
(806) 291-3520

## Weatherford College
Weatherford, Texas
www.wc.edu                  Federal Code: 003664

**2-year public** community college in large town.
**Enrollment:** 5,316 undergrads.
**Selectivity:** Open admission; but selective for some programs.

**BASIC COSTS (2015-2016)**
**Tuition and fees:** $2,400; out-of-district residents $3,720; out-of-state residents $5,280.
**Room and board:** $7,430.

**FINANCIAL AID PICTURE**
**Students with need:** Work study available nights, weekends, and for part-time students.
**Students without need:** This college awards aid only to students with need.

**FINANCIAL AID PROCEDURES**
**Forms required:** FAFSA.
**Dates and Deadlines:** Priority date 7/3; no closing date. Applicants notified on a rolling basis; must reply within 2 week(s) of notification.

**CONTACT**
Donnie Purvis, Director, Financial Aid
225 College Park Drive, Weatherford, TX 76086
(817) 598-6295

## West Coast University: Dallas
Dallas, Texas
www.westcoastuniversity.edu          Federal Code: 036983

**4-year for-profit** branch campus and nursing college in very large city.
**Enrollment:** 428 undergrads.
**Selectivity:** Open admission; but selective for some programs.

**FINANCIAL AID PICTURE**
**Students with need:** Need-based aid available for full-time and part-time students. Work study available nights, weekends, and for part-time students.
**Students without need:** No-need awards available for academics.

**FINANCIAL AID PROCEDURES**
**Forms required:** FAFSA, institutional form.
**Dates and Deadlines:** Closing date 6/30. Applicants notified on a rolling basis.

**CONTACT**
Monita Saunders, Director of Financial Aid
8435 North Stemmons Freeway, Dallas, TX 75247
(214) 453-4533

## West Texas A&M University
Canyon, Texas
www.wtamu.edu                Federal Code: 003665

**4-year public** university in large town.
**Enrollment:** 7,253 undergrads, 22% part-time. 1,354 full-time freshmen.
**Selectivity:** Admits 50 to 75% of applicants.

**BASIC COSTS (2016-2017)**
**Tuition and fees:** $7,936; out-of-state residents $8,959.

**FINANCIAL AID PICTURE (2014-2015)**
**Students with need:** Out of 1,101 full-time freshmen who applied for aid, 906 were judged to have need. Of these, 906 received aid, and 70 had their full need met. Average financial aid package met 61% of need; average scholarship/grant was $6,584; average loan was $3,209. For part-time students, average financial aid package was $5,181.
**Students without need:** 121 full-time freshmen who did not demonstrate need for aid received scholarships/grants; average award was $1,669. No-need awards available for academics, art, athletics, leadership, music/drama.
**Scholarships offered:** 97 full-time freshmen received athletic scholarships; average amount $6,853.
**Additional info:** Scholarship deadline February 1.

**FINANCIAL AID PROCEDURES**
**Forms required:** FAFSA.
**Dates and Deadlines:** Priority date 4/15; no closing date. Applicants notified on a rolling basis starting 3/1; must reply within 2 week(s) of notification.
**Transfers:** No deadline. Applicants notified on a rolling basis; must reply within 2 week(s) of notification. Must provide financial aid transcripts through last semester of attendance. All academic transcripts must be on file.

**CONTACT**
Marian Giesecke, Director of Financial Aid
WTAMU Box 60907, Canyon, TX 79016-0001
(806) 651-2055

## Western Technical College
El Paso, Texas
www.westerntech.edu                    Federal Code: 014535

**2-year for-profit** technical college in very large city.
**Enrollment:** 773 undergrads.
**Selectivity:** Open admission; but selective for some programs.

**BASIC COSTS (2015-2016)**
**Tuition and fees:** $13,989.
**Room and board:** $10,185.

**FINANCIAL AID PICTURE (2014-2015)**
**Students with need:** 40% of average financial aid package awarded as scholarships/grants, 60% awarded as loans/jobs. Need-based aid available for part-time students.
**Students without need:** This college awards aid only to students with need.

**FINANCIAL AID PROCEDURES**
**Forms required:** FAFSA.
**Dates and Deadlines:** Applicants notified on a rolling basis.

**CONTACT**
Danielle Picchi, Financial Aid Director
9624 Plaza Circle, El Paso, TX 79927
(915) 532-3737 ext. 8105

## Western Technical College: Diana Drive
El Paso, Texas
www.westerntech.edu                    Federal Code: 014535

**2-year for-profit** branch campus and technical college in very large city.
**Enrollment:** 482 undergrads.
**Selectivity:** Open admission; but selective for some programs.

**FINANCIAL AID PICTURE (2014-2015)**
**Students with need:** 42% of average financial aid package awarded as scholarships/grants, 58% awarded as loans/jobs.

**CONTACT**
Danielle Picchi, Director of Financial Aid
9451 Diana Drive, El Paso, TX 79924
(915) 532-3737 ext. 8105

## Western Texas College
Snyder, Texas
www.wtc.edu                    Federal Code: 009549

**2-year public** community and junior college in large town.
**Enrollment:** 1,491 undergrads.
**Selectivity:** Open admission; but selective for some programs.

**BASIC COSTS (2015-2016)**
**Tuition and fees:** $2,460; out-of-district residents $3,510; out-of-state residents $4,620.
**Room and board:** $5,100.

**FINANCIAL AID PICTURE (2014-2015)**
**Students with need:** 82% of average financial aid package awarded as scholarships/grants, 18% awarded as loans/jobs. Need-based aid available for part-time students. Work study available nights, weekends, and for part-time students.
**Students without need:** No-need awards available for academics, art, athletics, leadership, music/drama, state/district residency.

**FINANCIAL AID PROCEDURES**
**Forms required:** FAFSA, state aid form, institutional form.
**Dates and Deadlines:** Priority date 5/1; no closing date. Applicants notified on a rolling basis starting 5/1; must reply within 2 week(s) of notification.
**Transfers:** No deadline. Applicants notified on a rolling basis.

**CONTACT**
Greg Torres, Director of Student Financial Aid
6200 College Avenue, Snyder, TX 79549
(866) 270-6184

## Wharton County Junior College
Wharton, Texas
www.wcjc.edu                    Federal Code: 003668

**2-year public** community and junior college in small town.
**Enrollment:** 7,416 undergrads, 61% part-time. 1,195 full-time freshmen.
**Selectivity:** Open admission; but selective for some programs.

**BASIC COSTS (2015-2016)**
**Tuition and fees:** $2,640; out-of-state residents $5,130.
**Per-credit charge:** $32; out-of-state residents $64.
**Room and board:** $4,100.

**FINANCIAL AID PICTURE (2014-2015)**
**Students with need:** 68% of average financial aid package awarded as scholarships/grants, 32% awarded as loans/jobs. Need-based aid available for part-time students.
**Students without need:** No-need awards available for academics, athletics, music/drama.

**FINANCIAL AID PROCEDURES**
**Forms required:** FAFSA, institutional form.
**Dates and Deadlines:** Closing date 6/1. Applicants notified on a rolling basis starting 3/1; must reply within 8 week(s) of notification.

**CONTACT**
Richard Hyde, Director of Financial Aid
911 Boling Highway, Wharton, TX 77488-0080
(979) 532-4560 ext. 6345

## Wiley College
Marshall, Texas
www.wileyc.edu                    Federal Code: 003669

**4-year private** liberal arts college in large town, affiliated with United Methodist Church.
**Enrollment:** 1,172 undergrads, 6% part-time. 239 full-time freshmen.
**Selectivity:** Open admission; but selective for some programs.

**BASIC COSTS (2016-2017)**
**Tuition and fees:** $11,828.
**Per-credit charge:** $318.
**Room and board:** $7,052.

### FINANCIAL AID PICTURE (2014-2015)

**Students with need:** Out of 204 full-time freshmen who applied for aid, 198 were judged to have need. Of these, 194 received aid, and 14 had their full need met. Average financial aid package met 57% of need; average scholarship/grant was $8,970; average loan was $3,090. Need-based aid available for part-time students.

**Students without need:** 36 full-time freshmen who did not demonstrate need for aid received scholarships/grants; average award was $14,554.

**Scholarships offered:** 4 full-time freshmen received athletic scholarships; average amount $107,887.

### FINANCIAL AID PROCEDURES

**Forms required:** FAFSA, institutional form.

**Dates and Deadlines:** Priority date 4/15; closing date 4/15. Applicants notified on a rolling basis.

### CONTACT

Cecelia Jones, Director of Financial Aid
711 Wiley Avenue, Marshall, TX 75670
(903) 927-3217

# Utah

## Brigham Young University

Provo, Utah
www.byu.edu                    Federal Code: 003670

**4-year private** university in small city, affiliated with Church of Jesus Christ of Latter-day Saints.

**Enrollment:** 30,221 undergrads, 10% part-time. 4,015 full-time freshmen.

**Selectivity:** GED not accepted.

### BASIC COSTS (2015-2016)

**Tuition and fees:** $5,150.

**Room and board:** $7,330.

### FINANCIAL AID PICTURE (2014-2015)

**Students with need:** Out of 1,993 full-time freshmen who applied for aid, 1,268 were judged to have need. Of these, 1,152 received aid, and 18 had their full need met. Average financial aid package met 30% of need; average scholarship/grant was $4,908; average loan was $3,241. For part-time students, average financial aid package was $4,459.

**Students without need:** 1,516 full-time freshmen who did not demonstrate need for aid received scholarships/grants; average award was $3,910. No-need awards available for academics, art, athletics, leadership, minority status, music/drama, religious affiliation, ROTC, state/district residency.

**Scholarships offered:** 109 full-time freshmen received athletic scholarships; average amount $6,590.

**Additional info:** Students notified of scholarships on or about 4/20.

### FINANCIAL AID PROCEDURES

**Forms required:** FAFSA.

**Dates and Deadlines:** Priority date 4/15; no closing date. Applicants notified on a rolling basis starting 4/1.

**Transfers:** Must provide financial aid transcript.

### CONTACT

Julie Saville, Institutional Assessment and Analysis
A-153 ASB, Provo, UT 84602
(801) 422-4104

## Broadview Entertainment Arts University

Salt Lake City, Utah
www.broadviewuniversity.edu        Federal Code: 011166

**2-year for-profit** university and visual arts college in small city.

**Enrollment:** 151 undergrads.

**Selectivity:** Open admission.

### BASIC COSTS (2015-2016)

**Tuition and fees:** $18,027.

**Per-credit charge:** $375.

**Additional info:** Per-credit-hour charge for 1-11 hours, $435; for 12-16 hours, $375. Course fees: $100 to $650 per course.

### FINANCIAL AID PICTURE

**Students with need:** Need-based aid available for full-time and part-time students.

### FINANCIAL AID PROCEDURES

**Forms required:** FAFSA, institutional form.

**Dates and Deadlines:** Applicants notified on a rolling basis starting 7/1; must reply within 2 week(s) of notification.

### CONTACT

Julie Wilbur, Director of Financial Aid
240 East Morris Avenue, Salt Lake City, UT 84115
(801) 300-4300

## Broadview University: Layton

Layton, Utah
www.broadviewuniversity.edu        Federal Code: 011166

**2-year for-profit** university and career college in small city.

**Enrollment:** 163 undergrads.

**Selectivity:** Open admission.

### BASIC COSTS (2015-2016)

**Tuition and fees:** $18,027.

**Per-credit charge:** $375.

**Additional info:** Per-credit-hour charge for 1-11 hours, $435; for 12-16 hours, $375. Course fees: $100 to $650 per course.

### FINANCIAL AID PICTURE

**Students with need:** Need-based aid available for full-time and part-time students.

### FINANCIAL AID PROCEDURES

**Forms required:** FAFSA, institutional form.

**Dates and Deadlines:** Applicants notified on a rolling basis starting 7/1; must reply within 2 week(s) of notification.

### CONTACT

Lina Okazaki, Financial Aid Manager
869 West Hill Field Road, Layton, UT 84041
(801) 660-6000

## Broadview University: Orem

Orem, Utah
www.broadviewuniversity.edu        Federal Code: 011166

**4-year for-profit** university and career college in small city.

**Enrollment:** 124 undergrads.

**Selectivity:** Open admission.

### BASIC COSTS (2015-2016)

**Tuition and fees:** $18,027.

**Per-credit charge:** $375.

**Additional info:** Per-credit-hour charge for 1-11 hours, $435; for 12-16 hours, $375. Course fees: $100 to $650 per course.

### FINANCIAL AID PICTURE

**Students with need:** Need-based aid available for full-time and part-time students.

### FINANCIAL AID PROCEDURES

**Forms required:** FAFSA, institutional form.

**Dates and Deadlines:** Applicants notified on a rolling basis starting 7/1; must reply within 2 week(s) of notification.

### CONTACT

Julie Wilbur, Financial Aid Manager
898 North 1200 West, Orem, UT 84057
(801) 822-5800

## Broadview University: West Jordan

West Jordan, Utah
www.broadviewuniversity.edu        Federal Code: 011166

**2-year for-profit** technical and career college in small city.
**Enrollment:** 237 undergrads.
**Selectivity:** Open admission; but selective for some programs.

### BASIC COSTS (2015-2016)

**Tuition and fees:** $18,027.
**Per-credit charge:** $375.
**Additional info:** Per-credit-hour charge for 1-11 hours, $435; for 12-16 hours, $375. Course fees: $100 to $650 per course.

### FINANCIAL AID PICTURE

**Students with need:** Need-based aid available for full-time and part-time students.

### FINANCIAL AID PROCEDURES

**Forms required:** FAFSA, institutional form.

**Dates and Deadlines:** Applicants notified on a rolling basis starting 7/1; must reply within 2 week(s) of notification.

### CONTACT

Kristi Snow, Financial Aid Manager
1902 West 7800 South, West Jordan, UT 84088
(801) 304-4224

## Dixie State University

St George, Utah
www.dixie.edu        Federal Code: 003671

**4-year public** university in small city.
**Enrollment:** 7,208 undergrads, 27% part-time. 1,440 full-time freshmen.
**Selectivity:** Open admission; but selective for some programs.

### BASIC COSTS (2015-2016)

**Tuition and fees:** $4,620; out-of-state residents $13,206.
**Per-credit charge:** $158; out-of-state residents $505.
**Room and board:** $6,098.

### FINANCIAL AID PICTURE (2015-2016)

**Students with need:** Out of 1,009 full-time freshmen who applied for aid, 862 were judged to have need. Of these, 862 received aid, and 488 had their full need met. Average financial aid package met 38% of need; average scholarship/grant was $6,195; average loan was $3,408. For part-time students, average financial aid package was $8,208.

**Students without need:** 3 full-time freshmen who did not demonstrate need for aid received scholarships/grants; average award was $933. No-need

awards available for academics, alumni affiliation, art, athletics, job skills, leadership, minority status, music/drama, state/district residency.

**Scholarships offered:** 51 full-time freshmen received athletic scholarships; average amount $4,825.

### FINANCIAL AID PROCEDURES

**Forms required:** FAFSA.

**Dates and Deadlines:** Priority date 5/1; closing date 6/30. Applicants notified on a rolling basis starting 3/1.

**Transfers:** Applicants notified on a rolling basis starting 3/1.

### CONTACT

JD Robertson, Director of Financial Aid
225 South 700 East, St. George, UT 84770-3876
(435) 652-7575

## Independence University

Murray, Utah
www.independence.edu        Federal Code: 014683

**4-year for-profit** business and health science college in very large city.
**Enrollment:** 1,280 undergrads.
**Selectivity:** Open admission.

### BASIC COSTS (2015-2016)

**Additional info:** Diploma programs: $15,042-$19,447. Associate programs: $34,390-$51,188. Bachelor's programs: $55,800-$81,719. Additional $4,000 fee for Workshop courses and any pre-requisites.

### FINANCIAL AID PICTURE

**Students with need:** Need-based aid available for full-time students.
**Students without need:** This college awards aid only to students with need.
**Additional info:** Financial aid available for resident students only, not correspondence students.

### FINANCIAL AID PROCEDURES

**Forms required:** FAFSA.

**Dates and Deadlines:** Closing date 7/23. Applicants notified on a rolling basis.

**Transfers:** No deadline. Applicants notified on a rolling basis.

### CONTACT

Lana Moon, Director of Finance
4021 South 700 East, Suite 400, Murray, UT 84107

## LDS Business College

Salt Lake City, Utah
www.ldsbc.edu        Federal Code: 003672

**2-year private** business and career college in large city, affiliated with Church of Jesus Christ of Latter-day Saints.
**Enrollment:** 2,168 undergrads.
**Selectivity:** Open admission; but selective for some programs.

### BASIC COSTS (2015-2016)

**Tuition and fees:** $3,160.
**Room and board:** $5,582.

### FINANCIAL AID PICTURE

**Students with need:** Need-based aid available for full-time and part-time students.
**Students without need:** No-need awards available for academics, leadership.
**Scholarships offered:** Service scholarships; half-tuition for one semester; for Church of Jesus Christ of Latter-day Saints missionaries who have returned from mission within past year.

## FINANCIAL AID PROCEDURES

**Forms required:** FAFSA.

**Dates and Deadlines:** Priority date 7/1; no closing date. Applicants notified on a rolling basis starting 3/1; must reply by 7/1 or within 3 week(s) of notification.

**Transfers:** No deadline. Applicants notified on a rolling basis starting 1/1.

## CONTACT

Melanie Conover, Manager of Student Financial Services

95 North 300 West, Salt Lake City, UT 84101-3500

(801) 524-8111

## Neumont University

Salt Lake City, Utah

www.neumont.edu                    Federal Code: 009948

**4-year for-profit** engineering and technical college in very large city.

**Enrollment:** 429 undergrads. 136 full-time freshmen.

**Selectivity:** Admits over 75% of applicants.

### BASIC COSTS (2016-2017)

**Tuition and fees:** $24,450.

**Per-credit charge:** $495.

**Room only:** $5,670.

### FINANCIAL AID PICTURE (2014-2015)

**Students with need:** Out of 75 full-time freshmen who applied for aid, 75 were judged to have need. Of these, 75 received aid. Average financial aid package met 14% of need; average scholarship/grant was $2,719. Need-based aid available for part-time students.

**Students without need:** 61 full-time freshmen who did not demonstrate need for aid received scholarships/grants; average award was $1,347. No-need awards available for academics, job skills, leadership, state/district residency.

### FINANCIAL AID PROCEDURES

**Forms required:** FAFSA, institutional form.

**Dates and Deadlines:** Closing date 8/1. Applicants notified on a rolling basis.

**Transfers:** No deadline. Applicants notified on a rolling basis starting 8/1.

### CONTACT

Nate Blanchard, Director of Financial Aid

143 South Main Street, Salt Lake City, UT 84111

(801) 302-2870

## Salt Lake Community College

Salt Lake City, Utah

www.slcc.edu                    Federal Code: 005220

**2-year public** community and technical college in very large city.

**Enrollment:** 22,326 undergrads. 67% part-time. 1,415 full-time freshmen.

**Selectivity:** Open admission; but selective for some programs.

### BASIC COSTS (2015-2016)

**Tuition and fees:** $3,568; out-of-state residents $11,336.

**Additional info:** Tuition/fee waivers available for adults, minority students.

### FINANCIAL AID PICTURE

**Students with need:** Need-based aid available for full-time and part-time students. Work study available nights, weekends, and for part-time students.

**Students without need:** No-need awards available for academics, alumni affiliation, art, athletics, leadership, minority status, music/drama.

### FINANCIAL AID PROCEDURES

**Forms required:** FAFSA, institutional form.

**Dates and Deadlines:** Priority date 5/1; no closing date. Applicants notified on a rolling basis starting 5/1; must reply within 4 week(s) of notification.

### CONTACT

Cristi Millard, Director of Financial Aid

4600 South Redwood Road, Salt Lake City, UT 84130-0808

(801) 957-4410

## Snow College

Ephraim, Utah

www.snow.edu                    Federal Code: 003679

**2-year public** junior college in small town.

**Enrollment:** 4,605 undergrads.

**Selectivity:** Open admission.

### BASIC COSTS (2015-2016)

**Tuition and fees:** $3,484; out-of-state residents $11,676.

**Per-credit charge:** $137; out-of-state residents $497.

**Room only:** $1,750.

**Additional info:** Tuition/fee waivers available for unemployed or children of unemployed.

### FINANCIAL AID PICTURE

**Students with need:** Need-based aid available for full-time students.

**Students without need:** No-need awards available for academics, alumni affiliation, athletics, leadership, music/drama, state/district residency.

### FINANCIAL AID PROCEDURES

**Forms required:** FAFSA, institutional form.

**Dates and Deadlines:** Priority date 3/1; closing date 6/1. Applicants notified on a rolling basis starting 8/1; must reply within 1 week(s) of notification.

**Transfers:** Priority date 3/15; closing date 6/15. Applicants notified on a rolling basis. F.A.T. required for mid-year transfers.

### CONTACT

Jack Dalene, Director of Financial Aid

150 East College Avenue, Ephraim, UT 84627

(435) 283-7132

## Southern Utah University

Cedar City, Utah

www.suu.edu                    Federal Code: 003678

**4-year public** university in large town.

**Enrollment:** 5,977 undergrads, 10% part-time. 1,168 full-time freshmen.

**Selectivity:** Admits 50 to 75% of applicants.

### BASIC COSTS (2015-2016)

**Tuition and fees:** $6,300; out-of-state residents $19,132.

**Room and board:** $6,957.

### FINANCIAL AID PICTURE (2014-2015)

**Students with need:** Out of 889 full-time freshmen who applied for aid, 730 were judged to have need. Of these, 728 received aid, and 72 had their full need met. Average financial aid package met 61% of need; average scholarship/grant was $4,310; average loan was $3,111. For part-time students, average financial aid package was $5,111.

**Students without need:** 326 full-time freshmen who did not demonstrate need for aid received scholarships/grants; average award was $5,822. No-need awards available for academics, alumni affiliation, art, athletics, job skills, leadership, minority status, music/drama, ROTC, state/district residency.

**Scholarships offered:** 57 full-time freshmen received athletic scholarships; average amount $8,744.

## FINANCIAL AID PROCEDURES
**Forms required:** FAFSA.
**Dates and Deadlines:** Priority date 12/1; no closing date. Applicants notified on a rolling basis starting 11/1; must reply by 5/1.

## CONTACT
Jan Carey-McDonald, Director of Financial Aid and Scholarships
351 West University Boulevard, Cedar City, UT 84720
(435) 586-7735

# University of Utah
Salt Lake City, Utah
www.utah.edu                    Federal Code: 003675

**4-year public** university in very large city.
**Enrollment:** 22,761 undergrads, 26% part-time. 3,086 full-time freshmen.
**Selectivity:** Admits over 75% of applicants.

## BASIC COSTS (2015-2016)
**Tuition and fees:** $8,197; out-of-state residents $26,022.
**Room and board:** $9,000.

## FINANCIAL AID PICTURE (2015-2016)
**Students with need:** Out of 2,057 full-time freshmen who applied for aid, 1,456 were judged to have need. Of these, 1,442 received aid, and 222 had their full need met. Average financial aid package met 66% of need; average scholarship/grant was $7,988; average loan was $3,286. For part-time students, average financial aid package was $16,055.
**Students without need:** 1,478 full-time freshmen who did not demonstrate need for aid received scholarships/grants; average award was $6,691. No-need awards available for academics, alumni affiliation, art, athletics, leadership, minority status, music/drama, ROTC, state/district residency.
**Scholarships offered:** 66 full-time freshmen received athletic scholarships; average amount $24,699.

## FINANCIAL AID PROCEDURES
**Forms required:** FAFSA.
**Dates and Deadlines:** Priority date 3/15; no closing date. Applicants notified on a rolling basis starting 4/1; must reply within 6 week(s) of notification.
**Transfers:** No deadline. Applicants notified on a rolling basis starting 4/15; must reply within 6 week(s) of notification.

## CONTACT
John Curl, Director of Financial Aid and Scholarship
201 South 1460 East, Room 250 S, Salt Lake City, UT 84112-9057
(801) 581-6211

# Utah State University
Logan, Utah
www.usu.edu                    Federal Code: 003677

**4-year public** university in small city.
**Enrollment:** 22,265 undergrads, 24% part-time. 4,292 full-time freshmen.

## BASIC COSTS (2015-2016)
**Tuition and fees:** $6,663; out-of-state residents $19,133.
**Room and board:** $5,790.

## FINANCIAL AID PICTURE (2015-2016)
**Students with need:** Out of 2,658 full-time freshmen who applied for aid, 2,094 were judged to have need. Of these, 2,036 received aid, and 305 had their full need met. Average financial aid package met 61% of need; average scholarship/grant was $4,399; average loan was $3,319. For part-time students, average financial aid package was $5,611.

**Students without need:** 339 full-time freshmen who did not demonstrate need for aid received scholarships/grants; average award was $7,276. No-need awards available for academics, alumni affiliation, art, athletics, leadership, minority status, music/drama, religious affiliation, ROTC, state/district residency.
**Scholarships offered:** 68 full-time freshmen received athletic scholarships; average amount $16,295.

## FINANCIAL AID PROCEDURES
**Forms required:** FAFSA.
**Dates and Deadlines:** Applicants notified on a rolling basis starting 4/1; must reply within 4 week(s) of notification.
**Transfers:** No deadline. Applicants notified on a rolling basis starting 4/1; must reply within 4 week(s) of notification.

## CONTACT
Patti Kohler, Director of Financial Aid
0160 Old Main Hill, Logan, UT 84322-0160
(435) 797-0173

# Utah Valley University
Orem, Utah
www.uvu.edu                    Federal Code: 004027

**4-year public** university and technical college in small city.
**Enrollment:** 25,751 undergrads, 36% part-time. 3,165 full-time freshmen.
**Selectivity:** Open admission.

## BASIC COSTS (2015-2016)
**Tuition and fees:** $5,386; out-of-state residents $15,202.

## FINANCIAL AID PICTURE (2015-2016)
**Students with need:** Out of 1,874 full-time freshmen who applied for aid, 1,453 were judged to have need. Of these, 1,392 received aid, and 201 had their full need met. Average financial aid package met 68% of need; average scholarship/grant was $4,701; average loan was $2,315. For part-time students, average financial aid package was $5,949.
**Students without need:** 54 full-time freshmen who did not demonstrate need for aid received scholarships/grants; average award was $1,746. No-need awards available for academics, alumni affiliation, art, athletics, ROTC.
**Scholarships offered:** 28 full-time freshmen received athletic scholarships; average amount $4,115.

## FINANCIAL AID PROCEDURES
**Forms required:** FAFSA.
**Dates and Deadlines:** Applicants notified on a rolling basis.
**Transfers:** No deadline.

## CONTACT
Trish Howard, Director of Financial Aid and Scholarship
800 West University Parkway, Orem, UT 84058-5999
(801) 863-8442

# Weber State University
Ogden, Utah
https://www.weber.edu                    Federal Code: 003680

**4-year public** university in small city.
**Enrollment:** 17,795 undergrads, 39% part-time. 2,168 full-time freshmen.
**Selectivity:** Open admission; but selective for some programs.

## BASIC COSTS (2015-2016)
**Tuition and fees:** $5,339; out-of-state residents $14,252.
**Room and board:** $4,596.

## FINANCIAL AID PICTURE
**Students with need:** Need-based aid available for full-time and part-time students. Work study available nights, weekends, and for part-time students.

**Students without need:** This college awards aid only to students with need.

**Additional info:** Dream Weber program provides free tuition and general student fees to students whose annual household income is $40,000 or less.

### FINANCIAL AID PROCEDURES

**Forms required:** FAFSA, institutional form.

**Dates and Deadlines:** Priority date 3/1; no closing date. Applicants notified on a rolling basis starting 3/15; must reply within 2 week(s) of notification.

### CONTACT

Jed Spencer, Director of Financial Aid

1137 University Circle, Ogden, UT 84408-1137

(801) 626-7569

## Western Governors University

Salt Lake City, Utah

www.wgu.edu                     Federal Code: 033394

**4-year private** virtual university in very large city.

**Enrollment:** 61,027 undergrads. 149 full-time freshmen.

**Selectivity:** Open admission; but selective for some programs.

### BASIC COSTS (2015-2016)

**Tuition and fees:** $6,070.

### FINANCIAL AID PICTURE (2014-2015)

**Students with need:** Out of 123 full-time freshmen who applied for aid, 87 were judged to have need. Of these, 87 received aid, and 26 had their full need met. Average financial aid package met 100% of need; average scholarship/grant was $4,483; average loan was $1,436.

**Students without need:** This college awards aid only to students with need.

### FINANCIAL AID PROCEDURES

**Forms required:** FAFSA.

**Dates and Deadlines:** Applicants notified on a rolling basis.

**Transfers:** No deadline. Applicants notified on a rolling basis.

### CONTACT

Robert Collins, VP for Financial Aid

4001 South 700 East, Salt Lake City, UT 84107

(877) 435-7948 ext. 3104

## Westminster College

Salt Lake City, Utah

www.westminstercollege.edu       Federal Code: 003681

**4-year private** liberal arts college in very large city.

**Enrollment:** 2,135 undergrads, 5% part-time. 464 full-time freshmen.

**Selectivity:** Admits over 75% of applicants.

### BASIC COSTS (2016-2017)

**Tuition and fees:** $32,104.

**Per-credit charge:** $1,316.

**Room and board:** $8,974.

### FINANCIAL AID PICTURE (2015-2016)

**Students with need:** Out of 385 full-time freshmen who applied for aid, 310 were judged to have need. Of these, 310 received aid, and 77 had their full need met. Average financial aid package met 81% of need; average scholarship/grant was $21,011; average loan was $3,018. For part-time students, average financial aid package was $9,910.

**Students without need:** 127 full-time freshmen who did not demonstrate need for aid received scholarships/grants; average award was $14,131. No-need awards available for academics, alumni affiliation, art, athletics, leadership, minority status, music/drama, ROTC.

**Scholarships offered:** 17 full-time freshmen received athletic scholarships; average amount $4,015.

### FINANCIAL AID PROCEDURES

**Forms required:** FAFSA.

**Dates and Deadlines:** Priority date 4/15; no closing date. Applicants notified on a rolling basis starting 3/1; must reply within 3 week(s) of notification.

**Transfers:** No deadline. Applicants notified on a rolling basis starting 3/1; must reply within 3 week(s) of notification. Full-time transfer students with 3.0 GPA eligible for work study, loans, scholarships and grants. Merit scholarships based on cumulative transfer GPA range from $7,000-$12,000 per year.

### CONTACT

Jenny Ryan, Director of Financial Aid

1840 South 1300 East, Salt Lake City, UT 84105

(801) 832-2500

# Vermont

## Bennington College

Bennington, Vermont                Federal Code: 003682

www.bennington.edu                     CSS Code: 3080

**4-year private** liberal arts college in large town.

**Enrollment:** 683 undergrads. 192 full-time freshmen.

**Selectivity:** Admits 50 to 75% of applicants.

### BASIC COSTS (2015-2016)

**Tuition and fees:** $48,220.

**Room and board:** $14,200.

### FINANCIAL AID PICTURE (2014-2015)

**Students with need:** Out of 155 full-time freshmen who applied for aid, 155 were judged to have need. Of these, 155 received aid, and 5 had their full need met. Average financial aid package met 77% of need; average scholarship/grant was $25,079; average loan was $3,116. Need-based aid available for part-time students.

**Students without need:** 32 full-time freshmen who did not demonstrate need for aid received scholarships/grants; average award was $14,283. No-need awards available for academics, alumni affiliation, art, leadership, minority status, music/drama.

**Additional info:** All applicants for undergraduate admission considered for scholarships based on quality of overall application.

### FINANCIAL AID PROCEDURES

**Forms required:** FAFSA, institutional form. CSS PROFILE required of early decision applicants only.

**Dates and Deadlines:** Priority date 1/15; closing date 2/15. Applicants notified by 3/26; must reply by 5/1.

**Transfers:** Priority date 3/15; closing date 8/1. Applicants notified on a rolling basis starting 5/1; must reply by 6/1 or within 2 week(s) of notification.

### CONTACT

Heather Clifford, Director of Financial Aid

One College Drive, Bennington, VT 05201-6003

(802) 440-4325

## Burlington College

Burlington, Vermont

www.burlington.edu                  Federal Code: 012183

**4-year private** liberal arts college in small city.

**Enrollment:** 177 undergrads.

**BASIC COSTS (2015-2016)**
**Tuition and fees:** $23,656.
**Per-credit charge:** $981.01.
**Room only:** $7,200.
**Additional info:** Tuition at time of enrollment locked for 4 years.

**FINANCIAL AID PICTURE**
**Students with need:** Need-based aid available for full-time and part-time students. Work study available nights, weekends, and for part-time students.
**Students without need:** No-need awards available for academics, leadership.

**FINANCIAL AID PROCEDURES**
**Forms required:** FAFSA.
**Dates and Deadlines:** Applicants notified on a rolling basis starting 2/15.
**Transfers:** No deadline. Applicants notified on a rolling basis starting 2/15.

**CONTACT**
Joanna Morse, Director of Financial Aid
351 North Avenue, Burlington, VT 05401
(802) 862-9616 ext. 337

## Castleton State College
Castleton, Vermont
www.castleton.edu                  Federal Code: 003683

**4-year public** liberal arts college in small town.
**Enrollment:** 1,890 undergrads, 9% part-time. 367 full-time freshmen.

**BASIC COSTS (2015-2016)**
**Tuition and fees:** $11,282; out-of-state residents $26,690.
**Per-credit charge:** $427; out-of-state residents $1,069.
**Room and board:** $9,696.
**Additional info:** Nursing students pay $13,320 in-state, $28,728 out-of-state. Qualified international students and New England Board of Higher Education rate for students from other New England states: 150% of Vermont resident tuition [$15,408]. International rate for qualified nursing students $20,016. International students pay a $100 international fee per semester.

**FINANCIAL AID PICTURE**
**Students with need:** Need-based aid available for full-time and part-time students.
**Students without need:** No-need awards available for academics, alumni affiliation, music/drama, state/district residency.

**FINANCIAL AID PROCEDURES**
**Forms required:** FAFSA.
**Dates and Deadlines:** Priority date 4/1; no closing date. Applicants notified by 2/21; must reply within 2 week(s) of notification.

**CONTACT**
Kathy O'Meara, Financial Aid Director
Seminary Street, Castleton, VT 05735
(802) 468-1286

## Champlain College
Burlington, Vermont
www.champlain.edu                  Federal Code: 003684

**4-year private** liberal arts and career college in small city.
**Enrollment:** 3,249 undergrads, 27% part-time. 553 full-time freshmen.
**Selectivity:** Admits 50 to 75% of applicants.

**BASIC COSTS (2015-2016)**
**Tuition and fees:** $37,536.
**Per-credit charge:** $1,560.
**Room and board:** $14,050.

**FINANCIAL AID PICTURE (2015-2016)**
**Students with need:** Out of 473 full-time freshmen who applied for aid, 405 were judged to have need. Of these, 404 received aid, and 70 had their full need met. Average financial aid package met 70% of need; average scholarship/grant was $19,068; average loan was $3,969. For part-time students, average financial aid package was $6,136.
**Students without need:** 125 full-time freshmen who did not demonstrate need for aid received scholarships/grants; average award was $8,737. No-need awards available for academics, leadership, minority status.

**FINANCIAL AID PROCEDURES**
**Forms required:** FAFSA.
**Dates and Deadlines:** Priority date 2/15; no closing date. Applicants notified on a rolling basis starting 3/1; must reply by 5/1 or within 2 week(s) of notification.
**Transfers:** No deadline. Applicants notified on a rolling basis starting 3/1; must reply within 2 week(s) of notification.

**CONTACT**
Kristi Jovell, Director of Financial Aid
PO Box 670, Burlington, VT 05402-0670
(802) 860-2777

## College of St. Joseph in Vermont
Rutland, Vermont
www.csj.edu                  Federal Code: 003685

**4-year private** liberal arts and teachers college in large town, affiliated with Roman Catholic Church.
**Enrollment:** 230 undergrads.

**BASIC COSTS (2015-2016)**
**Tuition and fees:** $21,900.
**Per-credit charge:** $285.
**Room and board:** $10,500.

**FINANCIAL AID PICTURE**
**Students with need:** Need-based aid available for full-time and part-time students. Work study available nights, weekends, and for part-time students.
**Students without need:** No-need awards available for academics, alumni affiliation.

**FINANCIAL AID PROCEDURES**
**Forms required:** FAFSA, institutional form.
**Dates and Deadlines:** Priority date 3/1; no closing date. Applicants notified on a rolling basis starting 3/1.
**Transfers:** No deadline. Applicants notified on a rolling basis starting 3/1.

**CONTACT**
Julie Rosmus, Financial Aid Director
71 Clement Road, Rutland, VT 05701-3899
(802) 773-5900 ext. 3262

## Community College of Vermont
Montpelier, Vermont
www.ccv.edu                  Federal Code: 011167

**2-year public** community and liberal arts college in small town.
**Enrollment:** 3,883 undergrads.
**Selectivity:** Open admission.

**BASIC COSTS (2015-2016)**
**Tuition and fees:** $7,530; out-of-state residents $14,910.
**Per-credit charge:** $246; out-of-state residents $492.
**Additional info:** New England Board of Higher Education rate for students from other New England states: 150% of Vermont resident tuition. Available

to degree candidates in academic areas not offered by educational institutions in their home states.

## FINANCIAL AID PICTURE

**Students with need:** Need-based aid available for full-time and part-time students. Work study available nights, weekends, and for part-time students.
**Students without need:** This college awards aid only to students with need.

## FINANCIAL AID PROCEDURES

**Forms required:** FAFSA, state aid form, institutional form.
**Dates and Deadlines:** Applicants notified on a rolling basis starting 9/1; must reply within 3 week(s) of notification.

## CONTACT

Pam Chisholm, Associate Dean of Enrollment
PO Box 489, Montpelier, VT 05601
(802) 828-2800

## Goddard College

Plainfield, Vermont
www.goddard.edu                    Federal Code: 003686

**4-year private** liberal arts college in rural community.
**Enrollment:** 181 undergrads, 4% part-time. 5 full-time freshmen.

### BASIC COSTS (2015-2016)
**Tuition and fees:** $15,476.
**Room and board:** $1,564.

### FINANCIAL AID PICTURE (2014-2015)
**Students with need:** Out of 4 full-time freshmen who applied for aid, 4 were judged to have need. Of these, 3 received aid. Average financial aid package met 30% of need; average scholarship/grant was $11,630; average loan was $4,216. For part-time students, average financial aid package was $9,295.
**Students without need:** 1 full-time freshmen who did not demonstrate need for aid received scholarships/grants; average award was $1,000. No-need awards available for academics, art, job skills, leadership, music/drama, state/district residency.

### FINANCIAL AID PROCEDURES
**Forms required:** FAFSA.
**Dates and Deadlines:** Applicants notified on a rolling basis starting 4/15; must reply within 4 week(s) of notification.
**Transfers:** No deadline. Applicants notified on a rolling basis starting 4/15; must reply within 4 week(s) of notification.

### CONTACT
Beverly Jene, Director of Financial Aid
123 Pitkin Road, Plainfield, VT 05667
(800) 468-4888

## Green Mountain College

Poultney, Vermont
www.greenmtn.edu                    Federal Code: 003687

**4-year private** liberal arts college in small town, affiliated with United Methodist Church.
**Enrollment:** 582 undergrads, 3% part-time. 132 full-time freshmen.
**Selectivity:** Admits 50 to 75% of applicants.

### BASIC COSTS (2015-2016)
**Tuition and fees:** $35,340.
**Per-credit charge:** $1,130.
**Room and board:** $11,492.

### FINANCIAL AID PICTURE (2015-2016)
**Students with need:** Out of 118 full-time freshmen who applied for aid, 111 were judged to have need. Of these, 111 received aid, and 23 had their full need met. Average financial aid package met 83% of need; average scholarship/grant was $29,878; average loan was $3,480. For part-time students, average financial aid package was $14,964.
**Students without need:** 24 full-time freshmen who did not demonstrate need for aid received scholarships/grants; average award was $18,816. No-need awards available for academics, alumni affiliation, religious affiliation, state/district residency.
**Additional info:** Service/recognition awards available to all students, determined by admission application and supplemental documentation. VT resident grant matching UVM tuition, to help meet on average 90% of a student's demonstrated need.

### FINANCIAL AID PROCEDURES
**Forms required:** FAFSA.
**Dates and Deadlines:** Priority date 3/1; no closing date. Applicants notified on a rolling basis starting 11/1; must reply by 5/1 or within 3 week(s) of notification.
**Transfers:** No deadline. Applicants notified on a rolling basis; must reply by 5/1 or within 3 week(s) of notification.

### CONTACT
Wendy Ellis, Director of Student Financial Services
One Brennan Circle, Poultney, VT 05764
(802) 287-8210

## Johnson State College

Johnson, Vermont
www.jsc.edu                    Federal Code: 003688

**4-year public** liberal arts college in small town.
**Enrollment:** 1,320 undergrads, 28% part-time. 195 full-time freshmen.

### BASIC COSTS (2015-2016)
**Tuition and fees:** $11,018; out-of-state residents $23,714.
**Per-credit charge:** $416; out-of-state residents $945.
**Room and board:** $9,696.
**Additional info:** New England Board of Higher Education rate for students from other New England states: 150% of Vermont resident tuition. Available to degree candidates in academic areas not offered by educational institutions in their home states.

### FINANCIAL AID PICTURE (2015-2016)
**Students with need:** Need-based aid available for full-time and part-time students.
**Students without need:** No-need awards available for academics, alumni affiliation, art, leadership, music/drama, state/district residency.

### FINANCIAL AID PROCEDURES
**Forms required:** FAFSA, state aid form.
**Dates and Deadlines:** Priority date 3/1; no closing date. Applicants notified on a rolling basis starting 2/15; must reply within 3 week(s) of notification.
**Transfers:** No deadline. Applicants notified on a rolling basis starting 2/15; must reply within 3 week(s) of notification. Financial aid transcripts from previously attended colleges required.

### CONTACT
Lisa Cummings, Director of Financial Aid
337 College Hill, Johnson, VT 05656
(800) 635-1207

PART III: FINANCIAL AID COLLEGE BY COLLEGE

## Landmark College
Putney, Vermont
www.landmark.edu                    Federal Code: 017157

**2-year private** liberal arts college in small town.
**Enrollment:** 452 undergrads.

**BASIC COSTS (2015-2016)**
**Tuition and fees:** $52,792.
**Room and board:** $10,710.
**Additional info:** Required fees include laptop computer, protective sleeve, warranty, and Office software. Students who already own a Tablet/PC with Windows 8 can apply for an exception.

**FINANCIAL AID PICTURE**
**Students with need:** Need-based aid available for full-time and part-time students. Work study available nights, weekends, and for part-time students.
**Students without need:** No-need awards available for academics, art, leadership, minority status, music/drama.
**Additional info:** Students encouraged to apply to state departments of vocational rehabilitation for additional financial assistance.

**FINANCIAL AID PROCEDURES**
**Forms required:** FAFSA.
**Dates and Deadlines:** Priority date 2/15; no closing date. Applicants notified on a rolling basis starting 3/15; must reply within 2 week(s) of notification.
**Transfers:** Applicants notified on a rolling basis; must reply within 2 week(s) of notification.

**CONTACT**
Jennifer Desmarais, Director of Financial Aid
19 River Road South, Putney, VT 05346
(802) 387-6718

## Lyndon State College
Lyndonville, Vermont
www.lyndonstate.edu                  Federal Code: 003689

**4-year public** liberal arts and teachers college in small town.
**Enrollment:** 1,447 undergrads.

**BASIC COSTS (2015-2016)**
**Tuition and fees:** $11,018; out-of-state residents $22,418.
**Per-credit charge:** $416; out-of-state residents $891.
**Room and board:** $9,696.
**Additional info:** New England Board of Higher Education rate for students from other New England states: 150% of Vermont resident tuition. Available to degree candidates in academic areas not offered by educational institutions in their home states. Tuition/fee waivers available for unemployed or children of unemployed.

**FINANCIAL AID PICTURE**
**Students with need:** Need-based aid available for full-time and part-time students. Work study available nights, weekends, and for part-time students.
**Students without need:** No-need awards available for academics, leadership.

**FINANCIAL AID PROCEDURES**
**Forms required:** FAFSA.
**Dates and Deadlines:** Priority date 2/1; no closing date. Applicants notified on a rolling basis starting 4/1; must reply within 2 week(s) of notification.

**CONTACT**
Tanya Bradley, Director of Financial Aid
1001 College Road, Lyndonville, VT 05851
(802) 626-6218

## Marlboro College
Marlboro, Vermont
www.marlboro.edu                     Federal Code: 003690

**4-year private** liberal arts college in rural community.
**Enrollment:** 182 undergrads, 2% part-time. 35 full-time freshmen.

**BASIC COSTS (2015-2016)**
**Tuition and fees:** $39,250.
**Per-credit charge:** $1,280.
**Room and board:** $10,590.

**FINANCIAL AID PICTURE (2015-2016)**
**Students with need:** Out of 34 full-time freshmen who applied for aid, 31 were judged to have need. Of these, 31 received aid. Average financial aid package met 78% of need; average scholarship/grant was $29,231; average loan was $3,451. Need-based aid available for part-time students.
**Students without need:** 3 full-time freshmen who did not demonstrate need for aid received scholarships/grants; average award was $13,000. No-need awards available for academics, leadership.

**FINANCIAL AID PROCEDURES**
**Forms required:** FAFSA.
**Dates and Deadlines:** Closing date 3/1. Applicants notified on a rolling basis starting 3/1; must reply within 2 week(s) of notification.

**CONTACT**
Cathy Fuller, Associate Director of Financial Aid
PO Box A, Marlboro, VT 05344-0300
(802) 258-9237

## Middlebury College
Middlebury, Vermont                  Federal Code: 003691
www.middlebury.edu                         CSS Code: 3526

**4-year private** liberal arts college in small town.
**Enrollment:** 2,516 undergrads, 1% part-time. 589 full-time freshmen.
**Selectivity:** Admits less than 50% of applicants.

**BASIC COSTS (2015-2016)**
**Tuition and fees:** $47,828.
**Room and board:** $13,628.

**FINANCIAL AID PICTURE (2015-2016)**
**Students with need:** Out of 339 full-time freshmen who applied for aid, 287 were judged to have need. Of these, 287 received aid, and 287 had their full need met. Average financial aid package met 100% of need; average scholarship/grant was $42,741; average loan was $3,766. Need-based aid available for part-time students.
**Students without need:** This college awards aid only to students with need.
**Additional info:** Need-blind admissions policy; meets full demonstrated financial need of students who qualify for admission, to extent resources permit.

**FINANCIAL AID PROCEDURES**
**Forms required:** FAFSA, CSS PROFILE, institutional form.
**Dates and Deadlines:** Priority date 11/15; closing date 2/1. Applicants notified by 4/1; must reply by 5/1.
**Transfers:** Closing date 3/1. Applicants notified by 4/10; must reply by 5/1.

**CONTACT**
Kim Downs-Burns, Associate VP for SFS, Student Financial Services
The Emma Willard House, Middlebury, VT 05753-6002
(802) 443-5158

## New England Culinary Institute

Montpelier, Vermont
www.neci.edu                    Federal Code: 015904

**2-year for-profit** culinary school in small town.
**Enrollment:** 462 undergrads.

### BASIC COSTS (2015-2016)
**Tuition and fees:** $31,390.
**Room and board:** $8,000.

### FINANCIAL AID PICTURE
**Students with need:** Need-based aid available for full-time students. Work study available nights, weekends, and for part-time students.
**Students without need:** No-need awards available for academics, alumni affiliation, job skills, leadership.

### FINANCIAL AID PROCEDURES
**Forms required:** FAFSA, state aid form.
**Dates and Deadlines:** Applicants notified on a rolling basis.
**Transfers:** No deadline. Applicants notified on a rolling basis; must reply within 4 week(s) of notification.

### CONTACT
Marianne Werner, Associate Director of Financial Aid
56 College Street, Montpelier, VT 05602
(802) 225-3242

## Norwich University

Northfield, Vermont
www.norwich.edu                 Federal Code: 003692

**4-year private** university and military college in small town.
**Enrollment:** 2,806 undergrads, 19% part-time. 674 full-time freshmen.
**Selectivity:** Admits 50 to 75% of applicants.

### BASIC COSTS (2016-2017)
**Tuition and fees:** $37,354.
**Per-credit charge:** $1,036.
**Room and board:** $12,920.

### FINANCIAL AID PICTURE (2015-2016)
**Students with need:** Average financial aid package met 79% of need; average scholarship/grant was $27,184; average loan was $4,849. For part-time students, average financial aid package was $6,107.
**Students without need:** No-need awards available for academics, ROTC, state/district residency.
**Additional info:** Winners of ROTC scholarships receive full room and board; must maintain 2.75 GPA. Renewable up to 4 years.

### FINANCIAL AID PROCEDURES
**Forms required:** FAFSA.
**Dates and Deadlines:** Priority date 3/1; no closing date. Applicants notified on a rolling basis starting 2/15; must reply by 8/1.

### CONTACT
Martin Daniels, Director of Financial Aid
158 Harmon Drive, Northfield, VT 05663
(802) 485-2015

## Saint Michael's College

Colchester, Vermont
www.smcvt.edu                   Federal Code: 003694

**4-year private** liberal arts college in small city, affiliated with Roman Catholic Church.

**Enrollment:** 1,941 undergrads, 1% part-time. 464 full-time freshmen.
**Selectivity:** Admits over 75% of applicants.

### BASIC COSTS (2015-2016)
**Tuition and fees:** $40,750.
**Per-credit charge:** $1,300.
**Room and board:** $10,975.

### FINANCIAL AID PICTURE (2015-2016)
**Students with need:** Out of 378 full-time freshmen who applied for aid, 297 were judged to have need. Of these, 297 received aid, and 115 had their full need met. Average financial aid package met 81% of need; average scholarship/grant was $22,338; average loan was $5,070. Need-based aid available for part-time students.
**Students without need:** 160 full-time freshmen who did not demonstrate need for aid received scholarships/grants; average award was $17,140. No-need awards available for academics, art, athletics, music/drama, ROTC.
**Scholarships offered:** 6 full-time freshmen received athletic scholarships; average amount $51,800.

### FINANCIAL AID PROCEDURES
**Forms required:** FAFSA, state aid form.
**Dates and Deadlines:** Priority date 2/1; no closing date. Applicants notified on a rolling basis starting 3/21; must reply by 5/1 or within 2 week(s) of notification.
**Transfers:** Must reply within 2 week(s) of notification.

### CONTACT
Daniel Couture, Director of Student Financial Services
One Winooski Park, Colchester, VT 05439
(802) 654-3244

## Southern Vermont College

Bennington, Vermont
www.svc.edu                     Federal Code: 003693

**4-year private** liberal arts college in large town.
**Enrollment:** 431 undergrads, 3% part-time. 90 full-time freshmen.
**Selectivity:** Admits 50 to 75% of applicants.

### BASIC COSTS (2015-2016)
**Tuition and fees:** $23,260.
**Room and board:** $10,700.

### FINANCIAL AID PICTURE (2014-2015)
**Students with need:** Out of 85 full-time freshmen who applied for aid, 85 were judged to have need. Of these, 85 received aid. Average financial aid package met 47% of need; average loan was $4,500. Need-based aid available for part-time students.
**Students without need:** 5 full-time freshmen who did not demonstrate need for aid received scholarships/grants; average award was $9,000. No-need awards available for academics, leadership.
**Scholarships offered:** Merit scholarships; based on GPA and SAT/ACT.

### FINANCIAL AID PROCEDURES
**Forms required:** FAFSA.
**Dates and Deadlines:** Priority date 3/1; no closing date. Applicants notified on a rolling basis starting 3/1; must reply by 5/1 or within 2 week(s) of notification.
**Transfers:** No deadline. Applicants notified on a rolling basis starting 3/15; must reply by 5/1. No limitations on aid for transfer students.

### CONTACT
Jennifer Macksey, Chief Financial and Administrative Officer
982 Mansion Drive, Bennington, VT 05201-6002
(802) 447-6336

## Sterling College

Craftsbury Common, Vermont
www.sterlingcollege.edu          Federal Code: 014991

**4-year private** liberal arts college in rural community.
**Enrollment:** 119 undergrads. 20 full-time freshmen.
**Selectivity:** Admits 50 to 75% of applicants.

### BASIC COSTS (2016-2017)
**Tuition and fees:** $36,577.
**Room and board:** $4,780.

### FINANCIAL AID PICTURE
**Students with need:** Need-based aid available for full-time and part-time students. Work study available nights, weekends, and for part-time students.
**Students without need:** No-need awards available for academics, leadership, state/district residency.
**Scholarships offered:** Gladys Brooks: up to $6,000; academic merit, resident of Northeast Kingdom of Vermont, leadership. Presidential Scholarship: up to $5,000; significant academic merit and achievement. Achievement Scholarships: up to $5,000; significant life achievement. Vermont Scholarship: up to $2,000; for Vermont residents. Service Scholarship: up to $5,000; significant service. Bounder Scholarship: $500; applicants who live west of the Mississippi or in the Deep South. SCA Award: $1,000; alumni of Student Conservation Association. Transfer Award: $1,000. Vermont Youth Conservation Corps Award: $1,000; awarded to alumni of VYCC. Work-Learning-Service Credit: $800/semester.

### FINANCIAL AID PROCEDURES
**Forms required:** FAFSA, state aid form, institutional form.
**Dates and Deadlines:** Priority date 3/15; no closing date. Applicants notified on a rolling basis starting 2/1; must reply by 5/1 or within 3 week(s) of notification.
**Transfers:** Applicants notified on a rolling basis starting 2/1; must reply within 3 week(s) of notification.

### CONTACT
Tim Patterson, Director of Admission and Financial Aid
PO Box 72, Craftsbury Common, VT 05827-0072
(800) 648-3591 ext. 3

## University of Vermont

Burlington, Vermont
www.uvm.edu          Federal Code: 003696

**4-year public** university in large town.
**Enrollment:** 10,081 undergrads, 4% part-time. 2,283 full-time freshmen.
**Selectivity:** Admits 50 to 75% of applicants.

### BASIC COSTS (2015-2016)
**Tuition and fees:** $16,738; out-of-state residents $39,130.
**Per-credit charge:** $611; out-of-state residents $1,544.
**Room and board:** $11,180.

### FINANCIAL AID PICTURE (2014-2015)
**Students with need:** Out of 1,777 full-time freshmen who applied for aid, 1,347 were judged to have need. Of these, 1,347 received aid, and 228 had their full need met. Average financial aid package met 70% of need; average scholarship/grant was $16,660; average loan was $3,655. For part-time students, average financial aid package was $13,346.
**Students without need:** 765 full-time freshmen who did not demonstrate need for aid received scholarships/grants; average award was $11,096. No-need awards available for academics, alumni affiliation, athletics, leadership, minority status, music/drama, ROTC, state/district residency.
**Scholarships offered:** 50 full-time freshmen received athletic scholarships; average amount $25,978.

### FINANCIAL AID PROCEDURES
**Forms required:** FAFSA.
**Dates and Deadlines:** Priority date 2/10; no closing date. Applicants notified on a rolling basis starting 3/31; must reply within 4 week(s) of notification.
**Transfers:** Priority date 3/1; no deadline. Applicants notified on a rolling basis starting 3/15; must reply within 4 week(s) of notification. Merit scholarships are now available to transfer students.

### CONTACT
Marie Johnson, Director Student Financial Services
194 South Prospect Street, Burlington, VT 05401-3596
(802) 656-5700

## Vermont Technical College

Randolph Center, Vermont
www.vtc.edu          Federal Code: 003698

**4-year public** nursing and technical college in small town.
**Enrollment:** 1,372 undergrads, 22% part-time. 507 full-time freshmen.
**Selectivity:** Admits 50 to 75% of applicants.

### BASIC COSTS (2015-2016)
**Tuition and fees:** $13,490; out-of-state residents $24,866.
**Per-credit charge:** $519; out-of-state residents $993.
**Room and board:** $9,696.

### FINANCIAL AID PICTURE (2014-2015)
**Students with need:** Out of 440 full-time freshmen who applied for aid, 402 were judged to have need. Of these, 398 received aid, and 17 had their full need met. Average financial aid package met 44% of need; average scholarship/grant was $6,028; average loan was $3,528. For part-time students, average financial aid package was $7,602.
**Students without need:** 6 full-time freshmen who did not demonstrate need for aid received scholarships/grants; average award was $6,952. No-need awards available for academics.

### FINANCIAL AID PROCEDURES
**Forms required:** FAFSA.
**Dates and Deadlines:** Priority date 3/1; no closing date. Applicants notified on a rolling basis starting 1/31; must reply within 2 week(s) of notification.

### CONTACT
Cathy McCullough, Director of Financial Aid
PO Box 500, Randolph Center, VT 05061-0500
(800) 965-8790

# Virginia

## American National University: Charlottesville

Charlottesville, Virginia
www.an.edu          Federal Code: 003726

**2-year for-profit** business college in small city.
**Enrollment:** 115 undergrads.
**Selectivity:** Open admission.

### BASIC COSTS (2016-2017)
**Tuition and fees:** $14,460.
**Per-credit charge:** $317.

### FINANCIAL AID PICTURE
**Students with need:** Need-based aid available for full-time and part-time students.

**Students without need:** This college awards aid only to students with need.

**FINANCIAL AID PROCEDURES**
**Forms required:** FAFSA.
**Dates and Deadlines:** Applicants notified on a rolling basis.

**CONTACT**
Pam Cotton, Director of Financial Aid Compliance and Auditing
3926 Seminole Trail, Charlottesville, VA 22903
(540) 986-1800

## American National University: Danville
Danville, Virginia
www.an.edu                     Federal Code: 003726

**2-year for-profit** branch campus and business college in small city.
**Enrollment:** 123 undergrads.
**Selectivity:** Open admission.

**BASIC COSTS (2016-2017)**
**Tuition and fees:** $14,460.
**Per-credit charge:** $317.

**FINANCIAL AID PICTURE**
**Students with need:** Need-based aid available for full-time and part-time students.
**Students without need:** This college awards aid only to students with need.

**FINANCIAL AID PROCEDURES**
**Forms required:** FAFSA.
**Dates and Deadlines:** Applicants notified on a rolling basis starting 9/1.

**CONTACT**
Pam Cotton, Director of Financial Aid Compliance and Auditing
336 Old Riverside Drive, Danville, VA 24541
(540) 986-1800

## American National University: Harrisonburg
Harrisonburg, Virginia
www.an.edu                     Federal Code: 003726

**2-year for-profit** business college in large town.
**Enrollment:** 95 undergrads.
**Selectivity:** Open admission; but selective for some programs.

**BASIC COSTS (2016-2017)**
**Tuition and fees:** $14,460.
**Per-credit charge:** $317.

**FINANCIAL AID PICTURE**
**Students with need:** Need-based aid available for full-time and part-time students.
**Students without need:** This college awards aid only to students with need.

**FINANCIAL AID PROCEDURES**
**Forms required:** FAFSA.
**Dates and Deadlines:** Applicants notified on a rolling basis starting 9/1.

**CONTACT**
Pam Cotton, Director of Financial Aid Compliance and Auditing
1515 Country Club Road, Harrisonburg, VA 22802
(540) 986-1800

## American National University: Lynchburg
Lynchburg, Virginia
www.an.edu                     Federal Code: 010489

**2-year for-profit** business college in small city.
**Enrollment:** 118 undergrads.
**Selectivity:** Open admission.

**BASIC COSTS (2016-2017)**
**Tuition and fees:** $14,460.
**Per-credit charge:** $317.

**FINANCIAL AID PICTURE**
**Students with need:** Need-based aid available for full-time and part-time students.
**Students without need:** This college awards aid only to students with need.

**FINANCIAL AID PROCEDURES**
**Forms required:** FAFSA.
**Dates and Deadlines:** Applicants notified on a rolling basis starting 9/1.

**CONTACT**
Pam Cotton, Director of Financial Aid Compliance and Auditing
104 Candlewood Court, Lynchburg, VA 24502
(540) 986-1000

## American National University: Martinsville
Martinsville, Virginia
www.an.edu                     Federal Code: 003726

**2-year for-profit** business and junior college in small city.
**Enrollment:** 91 undergrads.
**Selectivity:** Open admission.

**BASIC COSTS (2016-2017)**
**Tuition and fees:** $14,460.
**Per-credit charge:** $317.

**FINANCIAL AID PICTURE**
**Students with need:** Need-based aid available for full-time and part-time students.
**Students without need:** This college awards aid only to students with need.

**FINANCIAL AID PROCEDURES**
**Forms required:** FAFSA.
**Dates and Deadlines:** Applicants notified on a rolling basis.

**CONTACT**
Pam Cotton, Director of Financial Aid Compliance and Auditing
905 North Memorial Boulevard, Martinsville, VA 24112
(540) 986-1800

## American National University: Salem
Roanoke, Virginia
www.an.edu                     Federal Code: 003726

**4-year for-profit** business college in large city.
**Enrollment:** 145 undergrads.
**Selectivity:** Open admission.

**BASIC COSTS (2016-2017)**
**Tuition and fees:** $14,460.

**Per-credit charge:** $317.

## FINANCIAL AID PICTURE

**Students with need:** Need-based aid available for full-time and part-time students.

**Students without need:** This college awards aid only to students with need.

## FINANCIAL AID PROCEDURES

**Forms required:** FAFSA.

**Dates and Deadlines:** Applicants notified on a rolling basis.

## CONTACT

Pam Cotton, Director of Financial Aid Compliance and Auditing
1813 East Main Street, Salem, VA 24153
(540) 986-1800

## Art Institute of Washington

Arlington, Virginia
www.aiw.artinstitutes.edu          Federal Code: 009270

**4-year for-profit** culinary school and visual arts college in small city.
**Enrollment:** 878 undergrads.

## BASIC COSTS (2015-2016)

**Tuition and fees:** $21,970.
**Per-credit charge:** $486.
**Room only:** $10,398.

## FINANCIAL AID PICTURE

**Students with need:** Need-based aid available for part-time students.

## FINANCIAL AID PROCEDURES

**Forms required:** FAFSA, institutional form.

## CONTACT

Sam Miller, Director of Student Financial Services
1820 North Fort Myer Drive, Arlington, VA 22209-1802
(703) 358-9550

## Averett University

Danville, Virginia
www.averett.edu          Federal Code: 003702

**4-year private** university and liberal arts college in large town, affiliated with Baptist faith.
**Enrollment:** 873 undergrads, 2% part-time. 266 full-time freshmen.
**Selectivity:** Admits 50 to 75% of applicants.

## BASIC COSTS (2015-2016)

**Tuition and fees:** $30,900.
**Per-credit charge:** $1,290.
**Room and board:** $8,700.

## FINANCIAL AID PICTURE (2015-2016)

**Students with need:** Out of 244 full-time freshmen who applied for aid, 225 were judged to have need. Of these, 225 received aid, and 23 had their full need met. Average financial aid package met 68% of need; average scholarship/grant was $18,693; average loan was $3,745. For part-time students, average financial aid package was $7,383.

**Students without need:** 41 full-time freshmen who did not demonstrate need for aid received scholarships/grants; average award was $12,766. No-need awards available for academics, alumni affiliation, art, job skills, leadership, minority status, music/drama, religious affiliation, state/district residency.

**Scholarships offered:** Founders Scholarship; $9,000; awarded to students for their quality academic preparation; renewable. Horizon Scholarship;

$4,000; based on academic performance; renewable. Phi Theta Kappa Scholarship; $1,000; awarded to community college students who are members of Phi Theta Kappa; must be enrolled in a traditional program; renewable with 3.0 GPA. Ministerial Tuition Discount; $400 (resident students), $200 (commuters); for full-time students who are children of ministers or students preparing for church-related vocations; renewable. Presidential scholarship; $14,000. Deans Scholarship; $12,000.

## FINANCIAL AID PROCEDURES

**Forms required:** FAFSA, state aid form.

**Dates and Deadlines:** Applicants notified on a rolling basis starting 2/15; must reply within 2 week(s) of notification.

**Transfers:** No deadline. Applicants notified on a rolling basis starting 2/15; must reply within 2 week(s) of notification.

## CONTACT

Carl Bradsher, Director of Student Financial Services
Office of Admissions, Danville, VA 24541
(434) 791-5890

## Blue Ridge Community College

Weyers Cave, Virginia
www.brcc.edu          Federal Code: 006819

**2-year public** community college in large town.
**Enrollment:** 4,388 undergrads.
**Selectivity:** Open admission; but selective for some programs.

## BASIC COSTS (2015-2016)

**Tuition and fees:** $5,019; out-of-state residents $10,317.
**Per-credit charge:** $138; out-of-state residents $315.
**Additional info:** Out-of-state students pay an additional $540 capital outlay fee.

## FINANCIAL AID PICTURE

**Students with need:** Need-based aid available for full-time and part-time students.

**Students without need:** No-need awards available for academics, job skills, leadership, minority status.

## FINANCIAL AID PROCEDURES

**Forms required:** FAFSA, institutional form.

**Dates and Deadlines:** Priority date 5/1; no closing date. Applicants notified on a rolling basis starting 5/30; must reply within 2 week(s) of notification.

## CONTACT

Robert Clemmer, Financial Aid Director
Box 80, Weyers Cave, VA 24486-9989
(540) 234-9261 ext. 2223

## Bluefield College

Bluefield, Virginia
www.bluefield.edu          Federal Code: 003703

**4-year private** liberal arts and teachers college in small town, affiliated with Baptist faith.
**Enrollment:** 914 undergrads, 15% part-time. 150 full-time freshmen.
**Selectivity:** Admits over 75% of applicants.

## BASIC COSTS (2015-2016)

**Tuition and fees:** $23,295.
**Per-credit charge:** $971.
**Room and board:** $8,185.

## FINANCIAL AID PICTURE (2014-2015)

**Students with need:** Out of 137 full-time freshmen who applied for aid, 124 were judged to have need. Of these, 124 received aid, and 18 had their

full need met. Average financial aid package met 64% of need; average scholarship/grant was $14,671; average loan was $3,700. For part-time students, average financial aid package was $4,806.

**Students without need:** 26 full-time freshmen who did not demonstrate need for aid received scholarships/grants; average award was $5,636. No-need awards available for academics, art, athletics, music/drama.

**Scholarships offered:** 26 full-time freshmen received athletic scholarships; average amount $8,470.

### FINANCIAL AID PROCEDURES
**Forms required:** FAFSA, state aid form.
**Dates and Deadlines:** Priority date 6/1; no closing date. Applicants notified on a rolling basis starting 3/1; must reply within 3 week(s) of notification.
**Transfers:** No deadline. Applicants notified on a rolling basis starting 3/1; must reply within 3 week(s) of notification. Transfer students are not eligible to participate in academic essay competition in which students compete for full-tuition and half-tuition scholarships.

### CONTACT
Carly Kestner, Director of Financial Aid
3000 College Avenue, Bluefield, VA 24605
(276) 326-4215

## Bridgewater College
Bridgewater, Virginia
www.bridgewater.edu Federal Code: 003704

**4-year private** liberal arts college in small town, affiliated with Church of the Brethren.
**Enrollment:** 1,823 undergrads. 542 full-time freshmen.
**Selectivity:** Admits less than 50% of applicants.

### BASIC COSTS (2016-2017)
**Tuition and fees:** $32,590.
**Room and board:** $11,920.

### FINANCIAL AID PICTURE (2015-2016)
**Students with need:** Out of 520 full-time freshmen who applied for aid, 469 were judged to have need. Of these, 469 received aid, and 124 had their full need met. Average financial aid package met 86% of need; average scholarship/grant was $26,134; average loan was $4,283. Need-based aid available for part-time students.
**Students without need:** 75 full-time freshmen who did not demonstrate need for aid received scholarships/grants; average award was $19,786. No-need awards available for academics, minority status, music/drama, religious affiliation, state/district residency.
**Scholarships offered:** Renewable academic scholarships are provided to freshmen based on high school grade point average and other criteria from the applicant's record.

### FINANCIAL AID PROCEDURES
**Forms required:** FAFSA, state aid form.
**Dates and Deadlines:** Priority date 3/1; no closing date. Applicants notified on a rolling basis starting 3/15; must reply by 5/1 or within 2 week(s) of notification.
**Transfers:** No deadline. Applicants notified on a rolling basis starting 3/15; must reply by 5/1 or within 2 week(s) of notification.

### CONTACT
Scott Morrison, Director of Financial Aid
402 East College Street, Bridgewater, VA 22812-1599
(540) 828-5377

## Bryant & Stratton College: Richmond
Richmond, Virginia
www.bryantstratton.edu Federal Code: 010061

**2-year for-profit** career college in small city.
**Enrollment:** 626 undergrads.
**Selectivity:** Open admission; but selective for some programs.

### BASIC COSTS (2015-2016)
**Tuition and fees:** $17,190.
**Per-credit charge:** $573.
**Additional info:** Tuition and fees may vary by program.

### FINANCIAL AID PICTURE
**Students with need:** Need-based aid available for full-time and part-time students. Work study available nights.
**Students without need:** This college awards aid only to students with need.

### FINANCIAL AID PROCEDURES
**Forms required:** FAFSA.
**Dates and Deadlines:** Closing date 9/17.
**Transfers:** No deadline.

### CONTACT
Eddie Webster, Financial Aid Manager
8141 Hull Street Road, Richmond, VA 23235
(804) 745-2444

## Bryant & Stratton College: Virginia Beach
Virginia Beach, Virginia
www.bryantstratton.edu Federal Code: 002678

**2-year for-profit** business and junior college in large city.
**Enrollment:** 585 undergrads.
**Selectivity:** Open admission; but selective for some programs.

### BASIC COSTS (2015-2016)
**Tuition and fees:** $17,190.
**Per-credit charge:** $573.
**Additional info:** Tuition and fees may vary by program.

### FINANCIAL AID PICTURE
**Students with need:** Need-based aid available for full-time and part-time students. Work study available nights.

### FINANCIAL AID PROCEDURES
**Forms required:** FAFSA.
**Dates and Deadlines:** Closing date 9/17. Applicants notified on a rolling basis.

### CONTACT
Bethann Verbal, Director of Financial Aid
301 Centre Pointe Drive, Virginia Beach, VA 23462-4417
(757) 499-7900

## Central Virginia Community College
Lynchburg, Virginia
www.cvcc.vccs.edu Federal Code: 004988

**2-year public** community college in small city.
**Enrollment:** 2,737 undergrads.
**Selectivity:** Open admission; but selective for some programs.

### BASIC COSTS (2015-2016)
**Tuition and fees:** $4,470; out-of-state residents $9,768.

**Per-credit charge:** $134; out-of-state residents $311.

**Additional info:** Out-of-state students pay an additional $540 capital outlay fee.

## FINANCIAL AID PICTURE

**Students with need:** Need-based aid available for full-time students.

**Students without need:** No-need awards available for academics, alumni affiliation.

**Additional info:** Payment plan available.

## FINANCIAL AID PROCEDURES

**Forms required:** FAFSA.

**Dates and Deadlines:** Priority date 3/15; no closing date. Applicants notified on a rolling basis starting 5/1; must reply within 2 week(s) of notification.

## CONTACT

Michael Farris, Dean of Enrollment Management

3506 Wards Road, Lynchburg, VA 24502-2498

(434) 832-7814

## Christendom College

Front Royal, Virginia

www.christendom.edu

**4-year private** liberal arts college in large town, affiliated with Roman Catholic Church.

**Enrollment:** 469 undergrads.

**Selectivity:** Admits over 75% of applicants.

## BASIC COSTS (2015-2016)

**Tuition and fees:** $24,780.

**Room and board:** $8,980.

## FINANCIAL AID PICTURE (2015-2016)

**Students with need:** Out of 109 full-time freshmen who applied for aid, 89 were judged to have need. Of these, 89 received aid. Average financial aid package met 85% of need; average scholarship/grant was $18,049; average loan was $7,460.

**Students without need:** 44 full-time freshmen who did not demonstrate need for aid received scholarships/grants; average award was $13,861. No-need awards available for academics, alumni affiliation.

**Scholarships offered:** Padre Pio Full-Tuition Scholarship.

**Additional info:** Institution does not accept direct federal aid, nor does it participate in indirect programs of federal aid.

## FINANCIAL AID PROCEDURES

**Forms required:** institutional form.

**Dates and Deadlines:** Priority date 4/1; closing date 6/1. Applicants notified on a rolling basis starting 2/1; must reply within 4 week(s) of notification.

## CONTACT

Alisa Polk, Financial Aid Officer

134 Christendom Drive, Front Royal, VA 22630

(800) 877-5456

## Christopher Newport University

Newport News, Virginia

www.cnu.edu                    Federal Code: 003706

**4-year public** university and liberal arts college in small city.

**Enrollment:** 5,040 undergrads, 2% part-time. 1,224 full-time freshmen.

**Selectivity:** Admits 50 to 75% of applicants. GED not accepted.

## BASIC COSTS (2015-2016)

**Tuition and fees:** $12,526; out-of-state residents $23,428.

**Per-credit charge:** $317; out-of-state residents $772.

**Room and board:** $10,614.

**Additional info:** Out-of-state students pay annual $396 capital fee.

## FINANCIAL AID PICTURE (2015-2016)

**Students with need:** Out of 989 full-time freshmen who applied for aid, 590 were judged to have need. Of these, 563 received aid, and 36 had their full need met. Average financial aid package met 68% of need; average scholarship/grant was $6,535; average loan was $3,387. For part-time students, average financial aid package was $5,237.

**Students without need:** 179 full-time freshmen who did not demonstrate need for aid received scholarships/grants; average award was $1,760. No-need awards available for academics, alumni affiliation, art, leadership, music/drama, state/district residency.

## FINANCIAL AID PROCEDURES

**Forms required:** FAFSA.

**Dates and Deadlines:** Priority date 3/1; no closing date. Applicants notified on a rolling basis starting 3/1; must reply by 5/1.

**Transfers:** No deadline. Applicants notified on a rolling basis starting 3/1; must reply within 3 week(s) of notification.

## CONTACT

Lisa Raines, Vice Provost Enrollment Services and Student Success

1 Avenue of the Arts, Newport News, VA 23606-3072

(757) 594-7170

## College of William and Mary

Williamsburg, Virginia          Federal Code: 003705

www.wm.edu                     CSS Code: 5115

**4-year public** university in large town.

**Enrollment:** 6,260 undergrads, 1% part-time. 1,517 full-time freshmen.

**Selectivity:** Admits less than 50% of applicants.

## BASIC COSTS (2015-2016)

**Tuition and fees:** $19,372; out-of-state residents $40,516.

**Per-credit charge:** $370; out-of-state residents $1,120.

**Room and board:** $10,978.

## FINANCIAL AID PICTURE

**Students with need:** Need-based aid available for full-time and part-time students.

**Students without need:** No-need awards available for academics, art, athletics, music/drama, ROTC.

## FINANCIAL AID PROCEDURES

**Forms required:** FAFSA, CSS PROFILE.

**Dates and Deadlines:** Priority date 3/1; no closing date. Applicants notified on a rolling basis starting 3/15; must reply by 5/1.

**Transfers:** Priority date 3/1. Applicants notified by 3/15.

## CONTACT

Edward Irish, Director of Student Financial Aid

PO Box 8795, Williamsburg, VA 23187-8795

(757) 221-2420

## Dabney S. Lancaster Community College

Clifton Forge, Virginia

www.dslcc.edu                  Federal Code: 004996

**2-year public** community and technical college in small town.

**Enrollment:** 667 undergrads.

**Selectivity:** Open admission; but selective for some programs.

## BASIC COSTS (2015-2016)

**Tuition and fees:** $4,365; out-of-state residents $9,663.

**Per-credit charge:** $134; out-of-state residents $311.

## FINANCIAL AID PICTURE

**Students with need:** Need-based aid available for full-time and part-time students. Work study available nights.

**Students without need:** This college awards aid only to students with need.

## FINANCIAL AID PROCEDURES

**Forms required:** FAFSA.

**Dates and Deadlines:** Priority date 3/1; closing date 6/30. Applicants notified on a rolling basis starting 4/15; must reply within 2 week(s) of notification.

## CONTACT

Joy Broyles, Coordinator of Financial Aid and Veterans Affairs
1000 Dabney Drive, Clifton Forge, VA 24422
(540) 863-2861

# Danville Community College

Danville, Virginia
www.dcc.vccs.edu          Federal Code: 003758

**2-year public** community college in small city.

**Enrollment:** 1,972 undergrads.

**Selectivity:** Open admission; but selective for some programs.

## BASIC COSTS (2015-2016)

**Tuition and fees:** $4,350; out-of-state residents $9,648.

**Per-credit charge:** $134; out-of-state residents $311.

**Additional info:** Out-of-state students pay an additional $540 capital outlay fee.

## FINANCIAL AID PICTURE

**Students with need:** Need-based aid available for full-time and part-time students.

**Students without need:** This college awards aid only to students with need.

**Scholarships offered:** Educational Foundation Scholarship: $250 to $1,500; based on separate application; deadline mid-March prior to award year.

## FINANCIAL AID PROCEDURES

**Forms required:** FAFSA.

**Dates and Deadlines:** Priority date 6/1; no closing date. Applicants notified on a rolling basis starting 5/1; must reply within 2 week(s) of notification.

**Transfers:** Limited aid available to transfer students admitted in spring semester.

## CONTACT

Mary Gore, Assistant Coordinator of Financial Aid
1008 South Main Street, Danville, VA 24541
(434) 797-8439

# DeVry University: Arlington

Arlington, Virginia
www.devry.edu

**4-year for-profit** university in very large city.

**Enrollment:** 424 undergrads.

## BASIC COSTS (2015-2016)

**Tuition and fees:** $17,132.

**Per-credit charge:** $609.

## FINANCIAL AID PICTURE

**Students with need:** Need-based aid available for full-time and part-time students.

**Students without need:** This college awards aid only to students with need.

## FINANCIAL AID PROCEDURES

**Forms required:** FAFSA.

**Dates and Deadlines:** Applicants notified on a rolling basis.

## CONTACT

Director of Student Finance
2450 Crystal Drive, Arlington, VA 22202
(703) 414-4000

# Eastern Mennonite University

Harrisonburg, Virginia
www.emu.edu          Federal Code: 003708

**4-year private** university and liberal arts college in small city, affiliated with Mennonite Church.

**Enrollment:** 1,214 undergrads, 10% part-time. 254 full-time freshmen.

**Selectivity:** Admits 50 to 75% of applicants.

## BASIC COSTS (2015-2016)

**Tuition and fees:** $32,300.

**Per-credit charge:** $1,300.

**Room and board:** $10,250.

## FINANCIAL AID PICTURE

**Students with need:** Need-based aid available for full-time and part-time students. Work study available nights, weekends, and for part-time students.

**Students without need:** No-need awards available for academics, alumni affiliation, art, leadership, religious affiliation, state/district residency.

**Scholarships offered:** President's Scholarship; minimum 3.9 GPA. Academic Achievement Scholarship; minimum 3.2 GPA. University Grant; minimum 2.5 GPA. 920 SAT (exclusive of Writing) or 20 ACT required for all scholarships. Amounts based on GPA and test scores; no limit on number of awards. Full-tuition scholarships available for 2 honors program applicants with highest test scores and GPA; half tuition scholarships available for next 10 candidates.

## FINANCIAL AID PROCEDURES

**Forms required:** FAFSA, state aid form.

**Dates and Deadlines:** Priority date 3/1; no closing date. Applicants notified on a rolling basis starting 3/1; must reply within 4 week(s) of notification.

**Transfers:** No deadline. Applicants notified on a rolling basis starting 3/1; must reply within 4 week(s) of notification.

## CONTACT

Michele Hensley, Director of Financial Assistance
1200 Park Road, Harrisonburg, VA 22802-2462
(540) 432-4137

# Eastern Shore Community College

Melfa, Virginia
www.es.vccs.edu          Federal Code: 003748

**2-year public** community college in rural community.

**Enrollment:** 503 undergrads.

**Selectivity:** Open admission; but selective for some programs.

## BASIC COSTS (2015-2016)

**Tuition and fees:** $4,395; out-of-state residents $9,693.

**Per-credit charge:** $134; out-of-state residents $311.

**Additional info:** Out-of-state students pay an additional $18 per credit hour for a Capital Fee.

## FINANCIAL AID PICTURE

**Students with need:** Need-based aid available for full-time and part-time students.

**Students without need:** This college awards aid only to students with need.

**Additional info:** ESCC is a member of the Servicemembers Opportunity Colleges program.

### FINANCIAL AID PROCEDURES

**Forms required:** FAFSA.

**Dates and Deadlines:** Priority date 5/1; no closing date. Applicants notified on a rolling basis starting 6/1; must reply within 2 week(s) of notification.

### CONTACT

Carole Read, Financial Aid Officer
29300 Lankford Highway, Melfa, VA 23410-9755
(757) 789-1733

## ECPI University

Virginia Beach, Virginia
www.ecpi.edu                    Federal Code: 010198

**4-year for-profit** university and health science college in very large city.
**Enrollment:** 10,242 undergrads.

### BASIC COSTS (2015-2016)

**Tuition and fees:** $15,420.

### FINANCIAL AID PICTURE

**Students with need:** Need-based aid available for full-time and part-time students. Work study available nights.
**Students without need:** No-need awards available for academics.

### FINANCIAL AID PROCEDURES

**Forms required:** FAFSA.

**Dates and Deadlines:** Applicants notified on a rolling basis.

**Transfers:** No deadline. Applicants notified on a rolling basis.

### CONTACT

Kathi Turner, Director of Financial Aid
5555 Greenwich Road, Suite 300, Virginia Beach, VA 23462-6542
(757) 671-7171 ext. 55351

## Emory & Henry College

Emory, Virginia
www.ehc.edu                     Federal Code: 003709

**4-year private** liberal arts college in rural community, affiliated with United Methodist Church.
**Enrollment:** 1,010 undergrads, 1% part-time. 303 full-time freshmen.
**Selectivity:** Admits over 75% of applicants.

### BASIC COSTS (2015-2016)

**Tuition and fees:** $30,900.
**Room and board:** $10,510.

### FINANCIAL AID PICTURE (2015-2016)

**Students with need:** Out of 289 full-time freshmen who applied for aid, 265 were judged to have need. Of these, 265 received aid, and 87 had their full need met. Average financial aid package met 91% of need; average scholarship/grant was $25,667; average loan was $3,262. For part-time students, average financial aid package was $3,505.
**Students without need:** 15 full-time freshmen who did not demonstrate need for aid received scholarships/grants; average award was $18,520. No-need awards available for academics, alumni affiliation, art, music/drama, state/district residency.
**Additional info:** Virginia residents eligible for additional in-state tuition grants.

### FINANCIAL AID PROCEDURES

**Forms required:** FAFSA.

**Dates and Deadlines:** Priority date 4/1; no closing date. Applicants notified on a rolling basis starting 2/1; must reply within 3 week(s) of notification.

**Transfers:** Closing date 5/15. Applicants notified on a rolling basis starting 2/15; must reply by 6/15 or within 4 week(s) of notification. Financial aid based on academic credits accepted for transfer.

### CONTACT

Scarlett Blevins, Director of Financial Aid and Student Services
PO Box 10, Emory, VA 24327
(276) 944-6115

## Ferrum College

Ferrum, Virginia
www.ferrum.edu                  Federal Code: 003711

**4-year private** liberal arts college in rural community, affiliated with United Methodist Church.
**Enrollment:** 1,451 undergrads.

### BASIC COSTS (2015-2016)

**Tuition and fees:** $30,835.
**Per-credit charge:** $615.
**Room and board:** $10,320.

### FINANCIAL AID PICTURE

**Students with need:** Need-based aid available for full-time and part-time students.
**Students without need:** No-need awards available for academics, leadership, religious affiliation, state/district residency.

### FINANCIAL AID PROCEDURES

**Forms required:** FAFSA, state aid form.

**Dates and Deadlines:** Applicants notified on a rolling basis.

### CONTACT

Heather Hollandsworth, Director of Financial Aid
Spilman-Daniel House, 40 Stratton Lane, Ferrum, VA 24088
(540) 365-4282

## George Mason University

Fairfax, Virginia
www2.gmu.edu                    Federal Code: 003749

**4-year public** university in large town.
**Enrollment:** 22,304 undergrads, 18% part-time. 3,046 full-time freshmen.
**Selectivity:** Admits 50 to 75% of applicants.

### BASIC COSTS (2015-2016)

**Tuition and fees:** $10,952; out-of-state residents $31,598.
**Per-credit charge:** $332; out-of-state residents $1,193.
**Room and board:** $10,510.

### FINANCIAL AID PICTURE (2014-2015)

**Students with need:** Out of 2,480 full-time freshmen who applied for aid, 1,755 were judged to have need. Of these, 1,667 received aid, and 95 had their full need met. Average financial aid package met 64% of need; average scholarship/grant was $6,540; average loan was $3,415. For part-time students, average financial aid package was $7,086.
**Students without need:** 279 full-time freshmen who did not demonstrate need for aid received scholarships/grants; average award was $4,351. No-need awards available for academics, athletics, minority status, music/drama, ROTC.
**Scholarships offered:** 66 full-time freshmen received athletic scholarships; average amount $19,739.

### FINANCIAL AID PROCEDURES

**Forms required:** FAFSA.

**Dates and Deadlines:** Closing date 3/1. Applicants notified on a rolling basis starting 4/1; must reply within 3 week(s) of notification.

**CONTACT**

Sandra Tarbox, Director, Student Financial Aid

4400 University Drive, MSN 3A4, Fairfax, VA 22030-4444

(703) 993-2353

## Germanna Community College

Locust Grove, Virginia

www.germanna.edu                    Federal Code: 008660

**2-year public** community college in rural community.

**Enrollment:** 7,379 undergrads.

**Selectivity:** Open admission; but selective for some programs.

**BASIC COSTS (2015-2016)**

**Tuition and fees:** $4,575; out-of-state residents $9,873.

**Per-credit charge:** $135; out-of-state residents $312.

**Additional info:** Out-of-state students pay an additional $540 capital outlay fee.

**FINANCIAL AID PICTURE**

**Students with need:** Need-based aid available for full-time and part-time students.

**Students without need:** No-need awards available for academics.

**FINANCIAL AID PROCEDURES**

**Forms required:** FAFSA.

**Dates and Deadlines:** Priority date 4/1; no closing date. Applicants notified on a rolling basis starting 5/15; must reply within 2 week(s) of notification.

**CONTACT**

Michael Farris, Financial Aid Coordinator

2130 Germanna Highway, Locust Grove, VA 22508-2102

(540) 423-9124

## Hampden-Sydney College

Hampden-Sydney, Virginia

www.hsc.edu                    Federal Code: 003713

**4-year private** liberal arts college for men in small town, affiliated with Presbyterian Church (USA).

**Enrollment:** 1,087 undergrads. 305 full-time freshmen.

**Selectivity:** Admits 50 to 75% of applicants.

**BASIC COSTS (2015-2016)**

**Tuition and fees:** $41,310.

**Room and board:** $13,060.

**FINANCIAL AID PICTURE (2015-2016)**

**Students with need:** Out of 251 full-time freshmen who applied for aid, 200 were judged to have need. Of these, 200 received aid, and 39 had their full need met. Average financial aid package met 77% of need; average scholarship/grant was $28,626; average loan was $3,810. For part-time students, average financial aid package was $1,550.

**Students without need:** 105 full-time freshmen who did not demonstrate need for aid received scholarships/grants; average award was $19,993. No-need awards available for academics, leadership, minority status, music/drama, ROTC, state/district residency.

**Scholarships offered:** Allan Scholarship: $30,000 annually. Venable Scholarship: $25,000 annually. Patrick Henry Scholarship: $20,000 annually. Achievement Awards: range from $5,000-$15,000 annually.

**FINANCIAL AID PROCEDURES**

**Forms required:** FAFSA, state aid form.

**Dates and Deadlines:** Priority date 3/1; closing date 5/1. Applicants notified by 3/15; must reply by 5/1 or within 2 week(s) of notification.

**Transfers:** Priority date 7/1; no deadline. Applicants notified on a rolling basis starting 3/1; must reply within 2 week(s) of notification.

**CONTACT**

Zita Barree, Director of Financial Aid

PO Box 667, Hampden-Sydney, VA 23943

(434) 223-6119

## Hampton University

Hampton, Virginia

www.hamptonu.edu                    Federal Code: 003714

**4-year private** university in small city.

**Enrollment:** 3,419 undergrads, 5% part-time. 750 full-time freshmen.

**Selectivity:** Admits 50 to 75% of applicants.

**BASIC COSTS (2016-2017)**

**Tuition and fees:** $23,992.

**Per-credit charge:** $548.

**Room and board:** $10,684.

**FINANCIAL AID PICTURE (2014-2015)**

**Students with need:** Out of 632 full-time freshmen who applied for aid, 507 were judged to have need. Of these, 484 received aid, and 189 had their full need met. Average financial aid package met 39% of need; average scholarship/grant was $5,138; average loan was $5,396. For part-time students, average financial aid package was $3,926.

**Students without need:** 27 full-time freshmen who did not demonstrate need for aid received scholarships/grants; average award was $3,309. No-need awards available for academics, athletics, job skills, leadership, music/drama, ROTC.

**Scholarships offered:** 55 full-time freshmen received athletic scholarships; average amount $12,185.

**FINANCIAL AID PROCEDURES**

**Forms required:** FAFSA.

**Dates and Deadlines:** Priority date 2/15; closing date 4/15. Applicants notified on a rolling basis starting 3/1; must reply within 2 week(s) of notification.

**CONTACT**

Martin Miles, Financial Aid Director

Office of Admission, Hampton, VA 23668

(800) 624-3341

## Hollins University

Roanoke, Virginia

www.hollins.edu                    Federal Code: 003715

**4-year private** university and liberal arts college for women in small city.

**Enrollment:** 630 undergrads, 2% part-time. 196 full-time freshmen.

**Selectivity:** Admits 50 to 75% of applicants.

**BASIC COSTS (2015-2016)**

**Tuition and fees:** $35,635.

**Per-credit charge:** $1,094.

**Room and board:** $12,300.

**FINANCIAL AID PICTURE (2015-2016)**

**Students with need:** Out of 182 full-time freshmen who applied for aid, 164 were judged to have need. Of these, 164 received aid, and 36 had their full need met. Average financial aid package met 84% of need; average scholarship/grant was $30,113; average loan was $3,725. For part-time students, average financial aid package was $13,452.

**Students without need:** 32 full-time freshmen who did not demonstrate need for aid received scholarships/grants; average award was $25,759. No-need awards available for academics, alumni affiliation, art, leadership, music/drama, state/district residency.

**Scholarships offered:** Batten Scholar: full tuition; academic merit. Hollins Scholar Awards: $15,000-$17,000; academic merit. Hollins Recognition Awards: $7,500-$14,000; academic merit. Leadership Awards: $1,000-$5,000; organizational involvement. Creative Talent Awards: $1,000-$5,000; distinguished achievement in art, photography/film, creative writing, music, dance or theater. Science & Math Award: $1,000-$5,000. Half off tuition for 2 years for incoming transfer students with at least a 2.75 college GPA.

**FINANCIAL AID PROCEDURES**

**Forms required:** FAFSA, state aid form.

**Dates and Deadlines:** Priority date 2/15; no closing date. Applicants notified on a rolling basis starting 3/1; must reply by 5/1.

**Transfers:** Priority date 7/1; closing date 7/15.

**CONTACT**

Mary Jean Sullivan, Director of Scholarships and Financial Assistance

PO Box 9707, Roanoke, VA 24020-1707

(540) 362-6332

## J. Sargeant Reynolds Community College

Richmond, Virginia

www.reynolds.edu                    Federal Code: 003759

**2-year public** community college in very large city.

**Enrollment:** 9,152 undergrads, 67% part-time. 943 full-time freshmen.

**Selectivity:** Open admission; but selective for some programs.

**BASIC COSTS (2015-2016)**

**Tuition and fees:** $4,653; out-of-state residents $9,951.

**Per-credit charge:** $138; out-of-state residents $313.

**Additional info:** Out-of-state students pay an additional $540 capital outlay fee.

**FINANCIAL AID PICTURE (2014-2015)**

**Students with need:** Out of 545 full-time freshmen who applied for aid, 541 were judged to have need. Of these, 541 received aid. Need-based aid available for part-time students.

**Students without need:** No-need awards available for academics.

**FINANCIAL AID PROCEDURES**

**Forms required:** FAFSA.

**Dates and Deadlines:** Closing date 4/15. Applicants notified on a rolling basis starting 7/15; must reply within 2 week(s) of notification.

**CONTACT**

Kiesha Pope, Director of Financial Aid

PO Box 85622, Richmond, VA 23285-5622

(804) 523-5137

## James Madison University

Harrisonburg, Virginia

www.jmu.edu                    Federal Code: 003721

**4-year public** university in large town.

**Enrollment:** 19,019 undergrads, 4% part-time. 4,324 full-time freshmen.

**Selectivity:** Admits 50 to 75% of applicants.

**BASIC COSTS (2015-2016)**

**Tuition and fees:** $10,018; out-of-state residents $25,142.

**Per-credit charge:** $190; out-of-state residents $676.

**Room and board:** $9,396.

**FINANCIAL AID PICTURE (2015-2016)**

**Students with need:** Out of 3,685 full-time freshmen who applied for aid, 1,952 were judged to have need. Of these, 1,713 received aid, and 1,532 had their full need met. Average financial aid package met 40% of need;

average scholarship/grant was $7,861; average loan was $3,474. For part-time students, average financial aid package was $6,914.

**Students without need:** 94 full-time freshmen who did not demonstrate need for aid received scholarships/grants; average award was $4,235. No-need awards available for academics, alumni affiliation, art, athletics, leadership, minority status, music/drama, state/district residency.

**Scholarships offered:** 79 full-time freshmen received athletic scholarships; average amount $21,210.

**FINANCIAL AID PROCEDURES**

**Forms required:** FAFSA.

**Dates and Deadlines:** Priority date 3/1; no closing date. Applicants notified on a rolling basis starting 4/1; must reply within 4 week(s) of notification.

**Transfers:** Applicants notified on a rolling basis starting 4/1; must reply within 4 week(s) of notification.

**CONTACT**

Lisa Tumer, Director of Financial Aid and Scholarships

Sonner Hall, MSC 0101, Harrisonburg, VA 22807

(540) 568-7820

## Jefferson College of Health Sciences

Roanoke, Virginia

www.jchs.edu                    Federal Code: 009893

**4-year private** health science and nursing college in small city.

**Enrollment:** 787 undergrads, 17% part-time. 108 full-time freshmen.

**BASIC COSTS (2015-2016)**

**Tuition and fees:** $24,400.

**Per-credit charge:** $695.

**Room only:** $5,870.

**FINANCIAL AID PICTURE**

**Students with need:** Need-based aid available for full-time and part-time students.

**Students without need:** No-need awards available for academics.

**FINANCIAL AID PROCEDURES**

**Forms required:** FAFSA, institutional form.

**Dates and Deadlines:** Applicants notified on a rolling basis; must reply within 2 week(s) of notification.

**CONTACT**

Deborah Johnson, Financial Aid Officer

101 Elm Avenue, SE, Roanoke, VA 24013-2222

(540) 985-8483

## John Tyler Community College

Chester, Virginia

www.jtcc.edu                    Federal Code: 004004

**2-year public** community college in small city.

**Enrollment:** 6,220 undergrads, 61% part-time. 825 full-time freshmen.

**Selectivity:** Open admission; but selective for some programs.

**BASIC COSTS (2015-2016)**

**Tuition and fees:** $4,345; out-of-state residents $9,643.

**Per-credit charge:** $134; out-of-state residents $311.

**Additional info:** Out-of-state students pay an additional $540 capital outlay fee.

**FINANCIAL AID PICTURE**

**Students with need:** Need-based aid available for full-time and part-time students. Work study available nights, weekends, and for part-time students.

**Students without need:** No-need awards available for academics, state/district residency.

**FINANCIAL AID PROCEDURES**
**Forms required:** FAFSA.
**Dates and Deadlines:** Priority date 4/1; no closing date. Applicants notified on a rolling basis starting 5/30.

**CONTACT**
Tony Jones, Director of Financial Aid
13101 Jefferson Davis Highway, Chester, VA 23831-5316
(855) 874-6684

## Liberty University
Lynchburg, Virginia
www.liberty.edu                Federal Code: 010392

**4-year private** university in small city, affiliated with Christian Church.
**Enrollment:** 12,999 undergrads, 3% part-time. 2,941 full-time freshmen.
**Selectivity:** Admits less than 50% of applicants.

**BASIC COSTS (2016-2017)**
**Tuition and fees:** $23,020.
**Per-credit charge:** $917.
**Room and board:** $9,306.

**FINANCIAL AID PICTURE (2015-2016)**
**Students with need:** Out of 2,750 full-time freshmen who applied for aid, 2,484 were judged to have need. Of these, 2,484 received aid, and 54 had their full need met. Average financial aid package met 28% of need; average scholarship/grant was $11,807; average loan was $3,434. For part-time students, average financial aid package was $6,411.
**Students without need:** 262 full-time freshmen who did not demonstrate need for aid received scholarships/grants; average award was $8,241. No-need awards available for academics, alumni affiliation, athletics, leadership, music/drama, religious affiliation, ROTC, state/district residency.
**Scholarships offered:** *Merit:* Liberty Academic Achievement Scholarship: up to $6,000; additional $3,500 could be applied if student is also accepted into the Honors Program; based on high school grades and standardized test scores. *Athletic:* 11 full-time freshmen received athletic scholarships; average amount $9,844.

**FINANCIAL AID PROCEDURES**
**Forms required:** FAFSA, state aid form.
**Dates and Deadlines:** Priority date 1/15; no closing date. Applicants notified on a rolling basis starting 3/15; must reply within 3 week(s) of notification.
**Transfers:** Applicants notified on a rolling basis starting 3/15; must reply within 3 week(s) of notification.

**CONTACT**
Robert Ritz, Vice President of Student Financial Aid
1971 University Boulevard, Lynchburg, VA 24515
(434) 582-2270

## Longwood University
Farmville, Virginia
www.longwood.edu                Federal Code: 003719

**4-year public** university in small town.
**Enrollment:** 4,399 undergrads, 6% part-time. 1,077 full-time freshmen.
**Selectivity:** Admits over 75% of applicants.

**BASIC COSTS (2015-2016)**
**Tuition and fees:** $11,910; out-of-state residents $26,070.
**Per-credit charge:** $239; out-of-state residents $688.
**Room and board:** $10,272.

**FINANCIAL AID PICTURE (2014-2015)**
**Students with need:** Out of 861 full-time freshmen who applied for aid, 613 were judged to have need. Of these, 574 received aid, and 192 had

their full need met. Average financial aid package met 80% of need; average scholarship/grant was $7,443; average loan was $4,407. For part-time students, average financial aid package was $11,590.
**Students without need:** 50 full-time freshmen who did not demonstrate need for aid received scholarships/grants; average award was $4,452. No-need awards available for academics, alumni affiliation, art, athletics, leadership, music/drama, ROTC, state/district residency.
**Scholarships offered:** 26 full-time freshmen received athletic scholarships; average amount $14,990.

**FINANCIAL AID PROCEDURES**
**Forms required:** FAFSA.
**Dates and Deadlines:** Priority date 3/1; no closing date. Applicants notified on a rolling basis starting 4/1; must reply within 4 week(s) of notification.
**Transfers:** Closing date 3/1. Applicants notified by 4/1; must reply by 5/1.

**CONTACT**
Melissa Shepherd, Director of Financial Aid
201 High Street, Farmville, VA 23909-1898
(434) 395-2077

## Lord Fairfax Community College
Middletown, Virginia
www.lfcc.edu                Federal Code: 008659

**2-year public** community college in small town.
**Enrollment:** 4,262 undergrads.
**Selectivity:** Open admission; but selective for some programs.

**BASIC COSTS (2015-2016)**
**Tuition and fees:** $4,424; out-of-state residents $9,722.
**Per-credit charge:** $135; out-of-state residents $312.
**Additional info:** Out-of-state students pay an additional $540 capital outlay fee.

**FINANCIAL AID PICTURE**
**Students with need:** Need-based aid available for full-time and part-time students.
**Students without need:** This college awards aid only to students with need.

**FINANCIAL AID PROCEDURES**
**Forms required:** FAFSA.
**Dates and Deadlines:** Priority date 5/1; no closing date. Applicants notified on a rolling basis starting 6/1.

**CONTACT**
Aaron Whitacre, Director of Financial Aid
173 Skirmisher Lane, Middletown, VA 22645
(540) 868-7274

## Lynchburg College
Lynchburg, Virginia
www.lynchburg.edu                Federal Code: 003720

**4-year private** liberal arts college in small city, affiliated with Christian Church (Disciples of Christ).
**Enrollment:** 2,064 undergrads, 4% part-time. 527 full-time freshmen.
**Selectivity:** Admits 50 to 75% of applicants.

**BASIC COSTS (2016-2017)**
**Tuition and fees:** $36,620.
**Per-credit charge:** $490.
**Room and board:** $10,120.
**Additional info:** Tuition/fee waivers available for adults.

## FINANCIAL AID PICTURE (2015-2016)

**Students with need:** Out of 476 full-time freshmen who applied for aid, 423 were judged to have need. Of these, 423 received aid, and 109 had their full need met. Average financial aid package met 78% of need; average scholarship/grant was $23,854; average loan was $2,239. For part-time students, average financial aid package was $6,075.

**Students without need:** 98 full-time freshmen who did not demonstrate need for aid received scholarships/grants; average award was $17,842. No-need awards available for academics, art, leadership, music/drama, state/district residency.

## FINANCIAL AID PROCEDURES

**Forms required:** FAFSA.

**Dates and Deadlines:** Priority date 3/1; no closing date. Applicants notified on a rolling basis starting 3/5; must reply within 2 week(s) of notification.

**Transfers:** Priority date 7/1; no deadline. Applicants notified on a rolling basis starting 3/5; must reply within 2 week(s) of notification.

## CONTACT

Timothy Saulnier, Director of Financial Aid
1501 Lakeside Drive, Lynchburg, VA 24501-3199
(434) 544-8228

---

# Mary Baldwin College
Staunton, Virginia
www.mbc.edu                    Federal Code: 003723

**4-year private** liberal arts college for women in large town, affiliated with Presbyterian Church (USA).
**Enrollment:** 1,265 undergrads.
**Selectivity:** Admits over 75% of applicants.

## BASIC COSTS (2015-2016)
**Tuition and fees:** $30,331.
**Per-credit charge:** $450.
**Room and board:** $9,000.

## FINANCIAL AID PICTURE
**Students with need:** Need-based aid available for full-time and part-time students.
**Students without need:** No-need awards available for academics, leadership, state/district residency.

## FINANCIAL AID PROCEDURES
**Forms required:** FAFSA, state aid form.
**Dates and Deadlines:** Priority date 3/1; no closing date. Applicants notified on a rolling basis starting 2/27; must reply by 5/1 or within 2 week(s) of notification.
**Transfers:** No deadline. Applicants notified on a rolling basis starting 2/1; must reply by 5/1.

## CONTACT
Robin Dietrich, Financial Aid Director
Office of Admissions, Staunton, VA 24401
(540) 887-7022

---

# Marymount University
Arlington, Virginia
www.marymount.edu              Federal Code: 003724

**4-year private** university in small city, affiliated with Roman Catholic Church.
**Enrollment:** 2,305 undergrads, 9% part-time. 388 full-time freshmen.
**Selectivity:** Admits over 75% of applicants.

## BASIC COSTS (2015-2016)
**Tuition and fees:** $28,310.
**Per-credit charge:** $910.

---

**Room and board:** $12,220.

## FINANCIAL AID PICTURE
**Students with need:** Need-based aid available for full-time and part-time students.
**Students without need:** No-need awards available for academics, alumni affiliation, leadership, music/drama, ROTC, state/district residency.
**Scholarships offered:** Freshman Scholarship: guaranteed for full-time freshman with 3.3 GPA and 1050 SAT (exclusive of Writing); renewable for 4 years for students who maintain academic eligibility.

## FINANCIAL AID PROCEDURES
**Forms required:** FAFSA.
**Dates and Deadlines:** Priority date 3/1; no closing date. Applicants notified by 3/15; must reply within 2 week(s) of notification.
**Transfers:** No deadline. Applicants notified on a rolling basis starting 3/15; must reply within 2 week(s) of notification. Academic scholarships available; apply by 5/1.

## CONTACT
Debbie Raines, Director of Financial Aid
2807 North Glebe Road, Arlington, VA 22207-4224
(703) 284-1530

---

# Miller-Motte Technical College: Lynchburg
Lynchburg, Virginia
www.miller-motte.edu          Federal Code: 004992

**2-year for-profit** technical college in small city.
**Enrollment:** 409 undergrads.
**Selectivity:** Open admission.

## BASIC COSTS (2015-2016)
**Additional info:** Management: $25,563; books and supplies $3,200. Medical Assisting: $27,963; books and supplies $3,200. Surgical Technology: $27,232; books and supplies $2,400. Criminal Justice: $25,563; books and supplies $3,200. Healthcare Technology: $27,963; books and supplies $3,200. Electronic Health Records: $27,963; books and supplies $3,200. Network Administration and Security: $27,483; books and supplies $3,200. Massage Therapy: $10,600; books and supplies $1,900. Figures are for total program cost.

## FINANCIAL AID PICTURE
**Students with need:** Need-based aid available for full-time and part-time students. Work study available nights.
**Students without need:** This college awards aid only to students with need.

## FINANCIAL AID PROCEDURES
**Forms required:** FAFSA.
**Dates and Deadlines:** Applicants notified on a rolling basis.

## CONTACT
Kim Hodges, Director of Financial Aid
1011 Creekside Lane, Lynchburg, VA 24502
(434) 239-5222

---

# Mountain Empire Community College
Big Stone Gap, Virginia
www.mecc.edu                  Federal Code: 009629

**2-year public** community college in small town.
**Enrollment:** 2,924 undergrads.
**Selectivity:** Open admission; but selective for some programs.

## BASIC COSTS (2015-2016)
**Tuition and fees:** $4,365; out-of-state residents $9,663.
**Per-credit charge:** $134; out-of-state residents $311.
**Additional info:** Out-of-state students pay an additional $540 capital outlay fee.

## FINANCIAL AID PICTURE
**Students with need:** Need-based aid available for full-time and part-time students.
**Students without need:** No-need awards available for academics, state/district residency.
**Scholarships offered:** Presidential Honor Scholarship; full tuition; for valedictorian or salutatorian. Dean's Academic Honor Award; $500-$1,000; for top 10 in graduating class.
**Additional info:** The college does not participate in loan programs. All financial aid is in form of grants, scholarships, or work study.

## FINANCIAL AID PROCEDURES
**Forms required:** FAFSA.
**Dates and Deadlines:** Priority date 5/1; no closing date. Applicants notified on a rolling basis starting 1/1.

## CONTACT
Kristy Hall, Director of Enrollment Services
3441 Mountain Empire Road, Big Stone Gap, VA 24219
(276) 523-2400

# New River Community College
Dublin, Virginia
www.nr.edu
Federal Code: 005223

**2-year public** community college in rural community.
**Enrollment:** 4,200 undergrads.
**Selectivity:** Open admission.

## BASIC COSTS (2015-2016)
**Tuition and fees:** $4,352; out-of-state residents $9,650.
**Per-credit charge:** $134; out-of-state residents $311.

## FINANCIAL AID PICTURE
**Students with need:** Need-based aid available for full-time and part-time students.

## FINANCIAL AID PROCEDURES
**Forms required:** FAFSA, institutional form.
**Dates and Deadlines:** Closing date 4/15. Applicants notified on a rolling basis.

## CONTACT
Lori Nunn, Director of Financial Aid
5251 College Dr, Dublin, VA 24084
(540) 674-3615

# Norfolk State University
Norfolk, Virginia
www.nsu.edu
Federal Code: 003765

**4-year public** university in small city.
**Enrollment:** 5,284 undergrads, 17% part-time. 557 full-time freshmen.

## BASIC COSTS (2015-2016)
**Tuition and fees:** $8,366; out-of-state residents $20,884.
**Per-credit charge:** $325; out-of-state residents $718.
**Room and board:** $8,668.

## FINANCIAL AID PICTURE
**Students with need:** Need-based aid available for full-time and part-time students.

**Students without need:** No-need awards available for academics, alumni affiliation, athletics, leadership, music/drama, ROTC, state/district residency.

## FINANCIAL AID PROCEDURES
**Forms required:** FAFSA.
**Dates and Deadlines:** Priority date 5/31; no closing date. Applicants notified on a rolling basis starting 4/1; must reply within 2 week(s) of notification.

## CONTACT
Kevin Burns, Director of Student Financial Services
700 Park Avenue, Norfolk, VA 23504
(757) 823-8381

# Old Dominion University
Norfolk, Virginia
www.odu.edu
Federal Code: 003728

**4-year public** university in large city.
**Enrollment:** 19,870 undergrads, 23% part-time. 2,931 full-time freshmen.
**Selectivity:** Admits over 75% of applicants.

## BASIC COSTS (2015-2016)
**Tuition and fees:** $9,768; out-of-state residents $26,508.
**Per-credit charge:** $316; out-of-state residents $874.
**Room and board:** $10,404.

## FINANCIAL AID PICTURE (2015-2016)
**Students with need:** Out of 2,624 full-time freshmen who applied for aid, 2,086 were judged to have need. Of these, 2,012 received aid, and 390 had their full need met. Average financial aid package met 49% of need; average scholarship/grant was $7,330; average loan was $3,512. For part-time students, average financial aid package was $6,493.
**Students without need:** 319 full-time freshmen who did not demonstrate need for aid received scholarships/grants; average award was $5,182. No-need awards available for academics, alumni affiliation, art, athletics, leadership, music/drama, ROTC, state/district residency.
**Scholarships offered:** 74 full-time freshmen received athletic scholarships; average amount $20,031.

## FINANCIAL AID PROCEDURES
**Forms required:** FAFSA.
**Dates and Deadlines:** Priority date 2/15; closing date 3/15. Applicants notified on a rolling basis starting 3/15; must reply within 2 week(s) of notification.
**Transfers:** Applicants notified on a rolling basis starting 3/1; must reply within 2 week(s) of notification.

## CONTACT
Vera Riddick, Director of Financial Aid
108 Rollins Hall, Norfolk, VA 23529
(757) 683-3683

# Patrick Henry College
Purcellville, Virginia
www.phc.edu
Federal Code: 039513
CSS Code: 2804

**4-year private** liberal arts college in small town, affiliated with nondenominational tradition.
**Enrollment:** 294 undergrads, 5% part-time. 89 full-time freshmen.
**Selectivity:** Admits over 75% of applicants.

## BASIC COSTS (2015-2016)
**Tuition and fees:** $27,922.
**Per-credit charge:** $1,163.
**Room and board:** $10,727.

**FINANCIAL AID PICTURE (2014-2015)**
**Students with need:** Out of 58 full-time freshmen who applied for aid, 38 were judged to have need. Of these, 38 received aid. Average financial aid package met 35% of need; average scholarship/grant was $5,200; average loan was $11,600. For part-time students, average financial aid package was $11,580.
**Students without need:** 47 full-time freshmen who did not demonstrate need for aid received scholarships/grants; average award was $10,600. No-need awards available for academics, leadership, music/drama.

**FINANCIAL AID PROCEDURES**
**Forms required:** CSS PROFILE.
**Dates and Deadlines:** Priority date 3/15; closing date 6/15. Applicants notified on a rolling basis starting 3/1; must reply within 4 week(s) of notification.

**CONTACT**
William Kellaris, Director of Financial Aid
10 Patrick Henry Circle, Purcellville, VA 20132-3197
(540) 441-8140

## Patrick Henry Community College
Martinsville, Virginia
www.ph.vccs.edu          Federal Code: 003751

**2-year public** community college in large town.
**Enrollment:** 2,200 undergrads.
**Selectivity:** Open admission.

**BASIC COSTS (2015-2016)**
**Tuition and fees:** $4,360; out-of-state residents $9,658.
**Per-credit charge:** $134; out-of-state residents $311.
**Additional info:** Out-of-state students pay an additional $540 capital outlay fee.

**FINANCIAL AID PICTURE**
**Students with need:** Need-based aid available for full-time and part-time students.

**FINANCIAL AID PROCEDURES**
**Forms required:** FAFSA.
**Dates and Deadlines:** Priority date 6/1; no closing date. Applicants notified on a rolling basis starting 6/15.

**CONTACT**
Cindy Keller, Financial Aid
645 Patriot Avenue, Martinsville, VA 24112
(276) 656-0317

## Paul D. Camp Community College
Franklin, Virginia
www.pdc.edu          Federal Code: 009159

**2-year public** community college in small town.
**Enrollment:** 789 undergrads.
**Selectivity:** Open admission; but selective for some programs.

**BASIC COSTS (2015-2016)**
**Tuition and fees:** $4,340; out-of-state residents $10,178.
**Per-credit charge:** $134; out-of-state residents $329.

**FINANCIAL AID PICTURE (2014-2015)**
**Students with need:** Need-based aid available for part-time students. Work study available nights, weekends, and for part-time students.
**Students without need:** This college awards aid only to students with need.

**FINANCIAL AID PROCEDURES**
**Forms required:** FAFSA.
**Dates and Deadlines:** Priority date 5/15; no closing date. Applicants notified on a rolling basis starting 8/1; must reply within 2 week(s) of notification.

**CONTACT**
Teresa Harrison, Financial Aid Coordinator
100 North College Drive, Franklin, VA 23851-0737
(757) 569-6715

## Piedmont Virginia Community College
Charlottesville, Virginia
www.pvcc.edu          Federal Code: 009928

**2-year public** community college in large town.
**Enrollment:** 3,502 undergrads.
**Selectivity:** Open admission; but selective for some programs.

**BASIC COSTS (2015-2016)**
**Tuition and fees:** $4,445; out-of-state residents $9,743.
**Per-credit charge:** $135; out-of-state residents $312.
**Additional info:** Out-of-state students pay an additional $540 capital outlay fee.

**FINANCIAL AID PICTURE**
**Students with need:** Need-based aid available for full-time and part-time students. Work study available nights, weekends, and for part-time students.
**Students without need:** No-need awards available for academics.

**FINANCIAL AID PROCEDURES**
**Forms required:** FAFSA.
**Dates and Deadlines:** Applicants notified on a rolling basis starting 4/1.
**Transfers:** Must meet Satisfactory Academic Progress standards.

**CONTACT**
Carol Larson, Director of Financial Aid
501 College Drive, Charlottesville, VA 22902-7589
(434) 961-6545

## Radford University
Radford, Virginia
www.radford.edu          Federal Code: 003732

**4-year public** university in large town.
**Enrollment:** 8,839 undergrads, 4% part-time. 1,960 full-time freshmen.
**Selectivity:** Admits over 75% of applicants.

**BASIC COSTS (2015-2016)**
**Tuition and fees:** $9,809; out-of-state residents $21,647.
**Per-credit charge:** $283; out-of-state residents $773.
**Room and board:** $8,677.
**Additional info:** Room rate reflects weighted average room rate. Board rate reflects 19 meal plan.

**FINANCIAL AID PICTURE (2015-2016)**
**Students with need:** Out of 1,678 full-time freshmen who applied for aid, 1,219 were judged to have need. Of these, 1,151 received aid, and 275 had their full need met. Average financial aid package met 74% of need; average scholarship/grant was $7,750; average loan was $3,344. For part-time students, average financial aid package was $6,511.
**Students without need:** 67 full-time freshmen who did not demonstrate need for aid received scholarships/grants; average award was $5,500. No-need awards available for academics, alumni affiliation, art, athletics, leadership, music/drama, ROTC, state/district residency.
**Scholarships offered:** *Merit:* Presidential Scholarship: $500 to $16,000; 3.5 GPA or higher; 1180 SAT combined critical reading and math sections or 26 ACT composite; 134 awarded. Academic Excellence Scholarship: $1,000 to

$5,000; 3.5 GPA or higher; 1100 SAT combined on critical reading and math sections or 24 ACT composite; 145 awarded. *Athletic:* 29 full-time freshmen received athletic scholarships; average amount $9,596.

**Additional info:** Student's need and grades considered. Top consideration given to those with greatest need and who apply by deadline.

### FINANCIAL AID PROCEDURES

**Forms required:** FAFSA.

**Dates and Deadlines:** Priority date 2/15; no closing date. Applicants notified on a rolling basis starting 4/15; must reply within 2 week(s) of notification.

### CONTACT

Barbara Porter, Director of Financial Aid
PO Box 6903, Radford, VA 24142
(540) 831-5408

## Randolph College

Lynchburg, Virginia
www.randolphcollege.edu          Federal Code: 003734

**4-year private** liberal arts college in small city, affiliated with United Methodist Church.

**Enrollment:** 665 undergrads, 1% part-time. 184 full-time freshmen.

**Selectivity:** Admits over 75% of applicants.

### BASIC COSTS (2015-2016)

**Tuition and fees:** $35,410.

**Per-credit charge:** $1,450.

**Room and board:** $12,106.

**Additional info:** Tuition/fee waivers available for adults.

### FINANCIAL AID PICTURE (2015-2016)

**Students with need:** Out of 155 full-time freshmen who applied for aid, 144 were judged to have need. Of these, 144 received aid, and 36 had their full need met. Average financial aid package met 76% of need; average scholarship/grant was $25,373; average loan was $3,707. For part-time students, average financial aid package was $16,242.

**Students without need:** 59 full-time freshmen who did not demonstrate need for aid received scholarships/grants; average award was $22,134. No-need awards available for academics, alumni affiliation, art, music/drama, religious affiliation, state/district residency.

**Scholarships offered:** Gottwald Scholarship: full tuition plus travel stipend; based on academic profile; approximately 3 awarded in each class. Presidential Scholars: $17,500; renewable annually; based on academic profile.

### FINANCIAL AID PROCEDURES

**Forms required:** FAFSA.

**Dates and Deadlines:** Priority date 4/1; no closing date. Applicants notified on a rolling basis; must reply by 5/1 or within 2 week(s) of notification.

**Transfers:** Applicants notified on a rolling basis starting 3/1; must reply by 5/1 or within 2 week(s) of notification.

### CONTACT

Debi Woodall-Stevens, Director of Student Financial Services
2500 Rivermont Avenue, Lynchburg, VA 24503-1555
(434) 947-8128

## Randolph-Macon College

Ashland, Virginia
www.rmc.edu          Federal Code: 003733

**4-year private** liberal arts college in small town, affiliated with United Methodist Church.

**Enrollment:** 1,405 undergrads, 2% part-time. 404 full-time freshmen.

**Selectivity:** Admits 50 to 75% of applicants.

### BASIC COSTS (2016-2017)

**Tuition and fees:** $38,730.

**Room and board:** $11,180.

### FINANCIAL AID PICTURE (2015-2016)

**Students with need:** Out of 381 full-time freshmen who applied for aid, 307 were judged to have need. Of these, 307 received aid, and 98 had their full need met. Average financial aid package met 83% of need; average scholarship/grant was $24,571; average loan was $5,015. For part-time students, average financial aid package was $11,774.

**Students without need:** 97 full-time freshmen who did not demonstrate need for aid received scholarships/grants; average award was $18,471. No-need awards available for academics, alumni affiliation, minority status, religious affiliation, ROTC, state/district residency.

**Scholarships offered:** Presidential Scholarships: $14,500 up to full-tuition; based solely on the student's academic record and extra-curricular activities; renewable for up to four years. All applicants for admissions considered for academic awards.

### FINANCIAL AID PROCEDURES

**Forms required:** FAFSA, state aid form.

**Dates and Deadlines:** Priority date 2/15; closing date 3/1. Applicants notified on a rolling basis starting 3/1; must reply by 5/1 or within 2 week(s) of notification.

**Transfers:** Applicants notified by 3/1; must reply by 5/1 or within 2 week(s) of notification.

### CONTACT

Mary Neal, Director of Financial Aid
PO Box 5005, Ashland, VA 23005-5505
(804) 752-7529

## Rappahannock Community College

Glenns, Virginia
www.rappahannock.edu          Federal Code: 009160

**2-year public** community college in rural community.

**Enrollment:** 1,791 undergrads.

**Selectivity:** Open admission; but selective for some programs.

### BASIC COSTS (2015-2016)

**Tuition and fees:** $4,460; out-of-state residents $9,758.

**Per-credit charge:** $134; out-of-state residents $311.

**Additional info:** Out-of-state students pay an additional $540 capital outlay fee.

### FINANCIAL AID PICTURE

**Students with need:** Need-based aid available for full-time and part-time students.

### FINANCIAL AID PROCEDURES

**Forms required:** FAFSA, institutional form.

**Dates and Deadlines:** Priority date 4/15; no closing date. Applicants notified on a rolling basis starting 6/30.

**Transfers:** No deadline. Applicants notified on a rolling basis.

### CONTACT

Sherika Charity, Director of Financial Aid
12745 College Drive, Glenns, VA 23149-2616
(804) 758-6737

## Regent University

Virginia Beach, Virginia
www.regent.edu          Federal Code: 030913

**4-year private** university in large city, affiliated with interdenominational tradition.

**Enrollment:** 2,867 undergrads, 38% part-time. 301 full-time freshmen.
**Selectivity:** Admits over 75% of applicants.

## BASIC COSTS (2015-2016)
**Tuition and fees:** $16,700.
**Per-credit charge:** $530.
**Room and board:** $8,480.

## FINANCIAL AID PICTURE (2015-2016)
**Students with need:** Out of 267 full-time freshmen who applied for aid, 233 were judged to have need. Of these, 232 received aid, and 42 had their full need met. Average financial aid package met 53% of need; average scholarship/grant was $9,395; average loan was $3,424. For part-time students, average financial aid package was $6,820.
**Students without need:** 59 full-time freshmen who did not demonstrate need for aid received scholarships/grants; average award was $7,293. No-need awards available for academics, alumni affiliation, leadership, ROTC.

## FINANCIAL AID PROCEDURES
**Forms required:** FAFSA, state aid form, institutional form.
**Dates and Deadlines:** Priority date 3/15; no closing date. Applicants notified on a rolling basis; must reply within 2 week(s) of notification.
**Transfers:** Priority date 7/1; no deadline. Applicants notified on a rolling basis starting 3/15; must reply within 2 week(s) of notification. Must be able to determine number of transfer credits before full award package is offered. Student should submit all academic transcripts in a timely manner to ensure transfer articulation occurs in a timely manner.

## CONTACT
Dotti Davidson, Director of Financial Aid
1000 Regent University Drive, Virginia Beach, VA 23464-9800
(757) 352-4125

## Richard Bland College
Petersburg, Virginia
www.rbc.edu                          Federal Code: 003707

**2-year public** junior and liberal arts college in small city.
**Enrollment:** 1,528 undergrads: 924 full-time freshmen.

## BASIC COSTS (2015-2016)
**Tuition and fees:** $5,493; out-of-state residents $15,236.
**Per-credit charge:** $245; out-of-state residents $652.
**Room and board:** $10,572.

## FINANCIAL AID PICTURE
**Students with need:** Need-based aid available for full-time and part-time students.
**Students without need:** No-need awards available for academics.
**Scholarships offered:** Presidential Scholarships: average $1,000; for full-time first-time Virginia residents; based on minimum 3.5 GPA.

## FINANCIAL AID PROCEDURES
**Forms required:** FAFSA.
**Dates and Deadlines:** Priority date 3/1; no closing date. Must reply by 5/1 or within 2 week(s) of notification.
**Transfers:** No deadline. Applicants notified on a rolling basis; must reply within 2 week(s) of notification.

## CONTACT
Emily Martin, Director of Financial Aid
8311 Halifax Road, Petersburg, VA 23805
(804) 862-6223

## Roanoke College
Salem, Virginia
www.roanoke.edu                      Federal Code: 003736

**4-year private** liberal arts college in large town, affiliated with Evangelical Lutheran Church in America.
**Enrollment:** 1,961 undergrads, 2% part-time. 507 full-time freshmen.
**Selectivity:** Admits 50 to 75% of applicants.

## BASIC COSTS (2016-2017)
**Tuition and fees:** $41,304.
**Per-credit charge:** $475.
**Room and board:** $12,810.
**Additional info:** Freshmen commuter students pay a lower total of required fees: $1334. Tuition/fee waivers available for adults.

## FINANCIAL AID PICTURE (2015-2016)
**Students with need:** Out of 454 full-time freshmen who applied for aid, 387 were judged to have need. Of these, 387 received aid, and 97 had their full need met. Average financial aid package met 81% of need; average scholarship/grant was $27,462; average loan was $4,270. For part-time students, average financial aid package was $13,725.
**Students without need:** 115 full-time freshmen who did not demonstrate need for aid received scholarships/grants; average award was $17,224. No-need awards available for academics, art, minority status, music/drama, religious affiliation.
**Scholarships offered:** William Beard Scholarship: up to 2 awarded; full tuition; room and board for four years. David Bittle Scholarship: up to 6 awarded; full tuition for four years. A.M. Bowman Scholarships: up to 50 awarded; $7,000 annually; added to previously awarded college scholarships. Christopher Baughman Scholarship: up to 60 awarded; $4,500 per year; added to previously awarded college scholarships. Julius Dreher Scholarship: up to 75 awarded; $1,500 per year; added to previously awarded college scholarships. John Morehead Scholarship: $1,000 per year; added to previously awarded college scholarships.

## FINANCIAL AID PROCEDURES
**Forms required:** FAFSA, state aid form.
**Dates and Deadlines:** Priority date 3/1; no closing date. Applicants notified on a rolling basis; must reply within 2 week(s) of notification.
**Transfers:** No deadline. Applicants notified on a rolling basis starting 10/15; must reply within 2 week(s) of notification.

## CONTACT
Thomas Blair, Director of Financial Aid
221 College Lane, Salem, VA 24153-3794
(540) 375-2235

## Shenandoah University
Winchester, Virginia
www.su.edu                           Federal Code: 003737

**4-year private** university in large town, affiliated with United Methodist Church.
**Enrollment:** 1,991 undergrads, 3% part-time. 446 full-time freshmen.
**Selectivity:** Admits over 75% of applicants.

## BASIC COSTS (2016-2017)
**Tuition and fees:** $31,322.
**Per-credit charge:** $877.
**Room and board:** $9,990.

## FINANCIAL AID PICTURE (2015-2016)
**Students with need:** Out of 398 full-time freshmen who applied for aid, 343 were judged to have need. Of these, 343 received aid. Average financial aid package met 32% of need; average scholarship/grant was $5,150; average loan was $2,841. For part-time students, average financial aid package was $18,986.

**Students without need:** 101 full-time freshmen who did not demonstrate need for aid received scholarships/grants; average award was $11,074. No-need awards available for academics, music/drama, religious affiliation.

## FINANCIAL AID PROCEDURES
**Forms required:** FAFSA, state aid form.
**Dates and Deadlines:** Applicants notified on a rolling basis starting 3/15; must reply within 4 week(s) of notification.
**Transfers:** No deadline. Applicants notified on a rolling basis starting 3/15; must reply within 4 week(s) of notification.

## CONTACT
Nancy Bragg, Director of Financial Aid
Office of Admissions, Winchester, VA 22601-5195
(540) 665-4538

# Southern Virginia University
Buena Vista, Virginia
www.svu.edu                Federal Code: 003738

**4-year private** liberal arts college in small town, affiliated with Church of Jesus Christ of Latter-day Saints.
**Enrollment:** 703 undergrads.

## BASIC COSTS (2015-2016)
**Tuition and fees:** $14,900.
**Per-credit charge:** $665.
**Room and board:** $7,600.

## FINANCIAL AID PICTURE
**Students with need:** Need-based aid available for full-time students.
**Students without need:** No-need awards available for academics, art, athletics, leadership, music/drama, ROTC.

## FINANCIAL AID PROCEDURES
**Forms required:** FAFSA, state aid form.
**Dates and Deadlines:** Priority date 5/1; no closing date. Applicants notified on a rolling basis starting 2/15.
**Transfers:** No deadline. Applicants notified on a rolling basis starting 3/1.

## CONTACT
John Brandt, Director of Financial Aid
One University Hill Drive, Buena Vista, VA 24416-3097
(540) 261-4351

# Southside Virginia Community College
Alberta, Virginia
www.southside.edu          Federal Code: 008661

**2-year public** community college in rural community.
**Enrollment:** 2,509 undergrads, 55% part-time. 161 full-time freshmen.
**Selectivity:** Open admission; but selective for some programs.

## BASIC COSTS (2015-2016)
**Tuition and fees:** $4,350; out-of-state residents $9,648.
**Per-credit charge:** $134; out-of-state residents $311.

## FINANCIAL AID PICTURE
**Students with need:** Need-based aid available for full-time and part-time students. Work study available nights.
**Students without need:** No-need awards available for academics.
**Scholarships offered:** Academic Merit Award: $1,500; for high school graduates within college's service area with 3.0 GPA who do not receive at least $1,500 in need-based aid.

## FINANCIAL AID PROCEDURES
**Forms required:** FAFSA.

**Dates and Deadlines:** Priority date 6/1; closing date 8/1. Applicants notified on a rolling basis starting 6/15.
**Transfers:** State aid limited to in-state residents.

## CONTACT
Sally Tharrington, Director of Financial Aid
109 Campus Drive, Alberta, VA 23821
(434) 736-2091

# Southwest Virginia Community College
Richlands, Virginia
www.sw.edu                 Federal Code: 007260

**2-year public** community college in small town.
**Enrollment:** 1,838 undergrads.
**Selectivity:** Open admission; but selective for some programs.

## BASIC COSTS (2015-2016)
**Tuition and fees:** $4,335; out-of-state residents $9,633.
**Per-credit charge:** $134; out-of-state residents $310.
**Additional info:** Out-of-state students pay an additional $540 capital outlay fee.

## FINANCIAL AID PICTURE (2014-2015)
**Students with need:** Need-based aid available for full-time and part-time students.
**Students without need:** This college awards aid only to students with need.

## FINANCIAL AID PROCEDURES
**Forms required:** FAFSA, institutional form.
**Dates and Deadlines:** Priority date 5/30; no closing date. Applicants notified on a rolling basis starting 7/1.

## CONTACT
Virginia Stevens, Administrative and Office Specialist III, Financial Aid
PO Box SVCC, Richlands, VA 24641-1101
(276) 964-7290

# Stratford University: Falls Church
Falls Church, Virginia
www.stratford.edu          Federal Code: 017053

**4-year for-profit** health science and career college in large city.
**Enrollment:** 625 undergrads.
**Selectivity:** Open admission.

## BASIC COSTS (2015-2016)
**Tuition and fees:** $16,750.
**Additional info:** NSG course tuition is $410 per credit.

## FINANCIAL AID PICTURE (2015-2016)
**Students with need:** Need-based aid available for part-time students. Work study available nights, weekends, and for part-time students.
**Students without need:** This college awards aid only to students with need.

## FINANCIAL AID PROCEDURES
**Forms required:** FAFSA.
**Dates and Deadlines:** Applicants notified on a rolling basis starting 1/1.
**Transfers:** No deadline. Applicants notified on a rolling basis starting 1/1.

## CONTACT
Michael Hargrave, Corporate Financial Aid Director
7777 Leesburg Pike Suite 1LN, Falls Church, VA 22043

---

## Stratford University: Woodbridge
Woodbridge, Virginia
www.stratford.edu                    Federal Code: 017053

**4-year for-profit** university and branch campus college in large town.
**Enrollment:** 450 undergrads.
**Selectivity:** Open admission.

**BASIC COSTS (2015-2016)**
**Tuition and fees:** $11,100.
**Per-credit charge:** $370.
**Additional info:** Classes with lab components or additional instructional materials will require extra fees. Books are included in tuition.

**FINANCIAL AID PICTURE (2014-2015)**
**Students with need:** 43% of average financial aid package awarded as scholarships/grants, 57% awarded as loans/jobs.

**FINANCIAL AID PROCEDURES**
**Forms required:** FAFSA.

**CONTACT**
John Dovi, Chief Financial Officer
14349 Gideon Drive, Woodbridge, VA 22192
(703) 897-1982

## Sweet Briar College
Sweet Briar, Virginia
www.sbc.edu                    Federal Code: 003742

**4-year private** liberal arts college for women in rural community.
**Enrollment:** 236 undergrads, 2% part-time. 154 full-time freshmen.
**Selectivity:** Admits over 75% of applicants.

**BASIC COSTS (2016-2017)**
**Tuition and fees:** $36,425.
**Per-credit charge:** $1,050.
**Room and board:** $12,635.
**Additional info:** Tuition/fee waivers available for adults.

**FINANCIAL AID PICTURE (2014-2015)**
**Students with need:** Out of 145 full-time freshmen who applied for aid, 127 were judged to have need. Of these, 127 received aid, and 16 had their full need met. Average financial aid package met 73% of need; average scholarship/grant was $25,651; average loan was $5,631. Need-based aid available for part-time students.
**Students without need:** 26 full-time freshmen who did not demonstrate need for aid received scholarships/grants; average award was $17,630. No-need awards available for academics, art, leadership, music/drama, state/district residency.
**Scholarships offered:** Founders and Prothro Scholarships; up to $15,000. Commonwealth Scholarships; up to $13,000. Betty Bean Black Scholarships; up to $12,000. Sweet Briar Scholarships; up to $9,000; for students with special talents in specific area. All awards based on academic qualifications; renewable annually with specified GPA.

**FINANCIAL AID PROCEDURES**
**Forms required:** FAFSA.
**Dates and Deadlines:** Priority date 2/15; no closing date. Applicants notified on a rolling basis starting 3/1; must reply by 5/1.
**Transfers:** Closing date 7/15.

**CONTACT**
Bobbi Carpenter, Director of Financial Aid
PO Box 1052, Sweet Briar, VA 24595-1502

## Thomas Nelson Community College
Hampton, Virginia
www.tncc.edu                    Federal Code: 006871

**2-year public** community college in small city.
**Enrollment:** 7,970 undergrads.
**Selectivity:** Open admission; but selective for some programs.

**BASIC COSTS (2015-2016)**
**Tuition and fees:** $4,416; out-of-state residents $9,714.
**Per-credit charge:** $136; out-of-state residents $313.
**Additional info:** Out-of-state students pay an additional $540 capital outlay fee.

**FINANCIAL AID PICTURE**
**Students with need:** Need-based aid available for full-time and part-time students. Work study available nights.

**FINANCIAL AID PROCEDURES**
**Forms required:** FAFSA, institutional form.
**Dates and Deadlines:** Priority date 5/1; no closing date. Applicants notified on a rolling basis starting 6/1; must reply within 2 week(s) of notification.
**Transfers:** No deadline. Applicants notified on a rolling basis; must reply within 2 week(s) of notification.

**CONTACT**
Kathryn Anderson, Director of Financial Aid, Veterans Affairs, and Scholarships
PO Box 9407, Hampton, VA 23670
(757) 825-2848

## Tidewater Community College
Norfolk, Virginia
www.tcc.edu                    Federal Code: 003712

**2-year public** community college in large city.
**Enrollment:** 24,631 undergrads.
**Selectivity:** Open admission; but selective for some programs.

**BASIC COSTS (2015-2016)**
**Tuition and fees:** $5,171; out-of-state residents $10,469.
**Per-credit charge:** $136; out-of-state residents $313.
**Additional info:** Out-of-state students pay an additional $540 capital outlay fee.

**FINANCIAL AID PICTURE**
**Students with need:** Need-based aid available for full-time and part-time students.

**FINANCIAL AID PROCEDURES**
**Forms required:** FAFSA.
**Dates and Deadlines:** Priority date 4/1; no closing date. Applicants notified on a rolling basis starting 4/1.

**CONTACT**
300 Granby Street, Norfolk, VA 23510
(757) 822-1360

## University of Mary Washington
Fredericksburg, Virginia
www.umw.edu                    Federal Code: 003746

**4-year public** university in small city.
**Enrollment:** 4,262 undergrads, 11% part-time. 840 full-time freshmen.
**Selectivity:** Admits over 75% of applicants.

## BASIC COSTS (2015-2016)

**Tuition and fees:** $10,974; out-of-state residents $24,814.
**Per-credit charge:** $395; out-of-state residents $983.
**Room and board:** $10,202.

## FINANCIAL AID PICTURE (2014-2015)

**Students with need:** Out of 665 full-time freshmen who applied for aid, 367 were judged to have need. Of these, 349 received aid, and 52 had their full need met. Average financial aid package met 50% of need; average scholarship/grant was $2,851; average loan was $3,502. For part-time students, average financial aid package was $5,499.

**Students without need:** 253 full-time freshmen who did not demonstrate need for aid received scholarships/grants; average award was $2,390. No-need awards available for academics, alumni affiliation, art, leadership, music/drama, state/district residency.

**Scholarships offered:** Scholarships awarded annually equal to tuition, fees, room and board given to select incoming freshmen with exceptional academic records (Washington scholarships to Virginia residents, Alvey scholarship when available to non-resident). In addition, merit awards up to $4,000 in-state and $8,000 out-of state based on high school GPA and SAT/ACT scores.

## FINANCIAL AID PROCEDURES

**Forms required:** FAFSA.
**Dates and Deadlines:** Priority date 3/15; closing date 6/1. Applicants notified on a rolling basis starting 3/15; must reply by 5/1 or within 2 week(s) of notification.
**Transfers:** Applicants notified on a rolling basis starting 3/15; must reply by 5/1 or within 2 week(s) of notification.

## CONTACT

Heidi Hunter-Goldsworthy, Director of Financial Aid
1301 College Avenue, Fredericksburg, VA 22401-5300
(540) 654-2468

# University of Richmond

Richmond, Virginia      Federal Code: 003744
www.richmond.edu      CSS Code: 5569

**4-year private** university and liberal arts college in small city.
**Enrollment:** 2,889 undergrads, 1% part-time. 806 full-time freshmen.
**Selectivity:** Admits less than 50% of applicants.

## BASIC COSTS (2016-2017)

**Tuition and fees:** $49,420.
**Per-credit charge:** $2,471.
**Room and board:** $11,460.

## FINANCIAL AID PICTURE (2015-2016)

**Students with need:** Out of 487 full-time freshmen who applied for aid, 342 were judged to have need. Of these, 342 received aid, and 294 had their full need met. Average financial aid package met 100% of need; average scholarship/grant was $39,666; average loan was $3,065. For part-time students, average financial aid package was $42,619.

**Students without need:** 58 full-time freshmen who did not demonstrate need for aid received scholarships/grants; average award was $41,154. No-need awards available for academics, art, athletics, leadership, music/drama, ROTC.

**Scholarships offered:** *Merit:* Richmond Scholars: full-tuition; up to 45 awarded to entering freshmen. Presidential Scholarships: one-third tuition. *Athletic:* 59 full-time freshmen received athletic scholarships; average amount $30,915.

## FINANCIAL AID PROCEDURES

**Forms required:** FAFSA, CSS PROFILE.
**Dates and Deadlines:** Closing date 2/15. Applicants notified by 4/1; must reply within 4 week(s) of notification.

**Transfers:** Applicants notified by 4/15; must reply within 4 week(s) of notification.

## CONTACT

Cynthia Deffenbaugh, Director of Financial Aid
Brunet Hall: 28 Westhampton Way, Richmond, VA 23173
(804) 289-8438

# University of the Potomac

Herndon, Virginia
www.potomac.edu      Federal Code: 032183

**4-year for-profit** business college in large town.
**Enrollment:** 15 undergrads.
**Selectivity:** Open admission.

## BASIC COSTS (2015-2016)

**Additional info:** Bachelor degree programs: $541; Associate degree programs: $541; certificates: $250. Books and supplies range depending on program level and course of study. All costs are subject to change.

## FINANCIAL AID PICTURE

**Students with need:** Need-based aid available for full-time and part-time students.

## FINANCIAL AID PROCEDURES

**Forms required:** FAFSA, institutional form.
**Dates and Deadlines:** Applicants notified on a rolling basis.

## CONTACT

David Rivers, Director of Financial Aid
2070 Chain Bridge Road, Vienna, VA 20170
(602) 734-4372

# University of Virginia

Charlottesville, Virginia      Federal Code: 003745
www.virginia.edu      CSS Code: 5820

**4-year public** university in small city.
**Enrollment:** 15,690 undergrads, 3% part-time. 3,672 full-time freshmen.
**Selectivity:** Admits less than 50% of applicants.

## BASIC COSTS (2015-2016)

**Tuition and fees:** $14,468; out-of-state residents $43,082.
**Per-credit charge:** $363; out-of-state residents $1,350.
**Room and board:** $10,400.
**Additional info:** All Commerce students both in-state and out-of-state pay an additional $5,000 Tuition Differential in 2014-15 and beyond. 1st-year Engineering students both in-state and out-of-state pay an additional $4,000 Tuition Differential in 2015-16. 2nd and 3rd year Engineering students both in-state and out-of-state pay an additional $2,000 Tuition Differential in 2015-16. 3rd and 4th year Batten school students both in-state and out-of-state pay an additional $2,500 Tuition Differential in 2015-16.

## FINANCIAL AID PICTURE (2015-2016)

**Students with need:** Out of 2,638 full-time freshmen who applied for aid, 1,275 were judged to have need. Of these, 1,275 received aid, and 1,275 had their full need met. Average financial aid package met 100% of need; average scholarship/grant was $19,470; average loan was $5,208. For part-time students, average financial aid package was $12,397.

**Students without need:** 87 full-time freshmen who did not demonstrate need for aid received scholarships/grants; average award was $7,100. No-need awards available for academics, athletics, leadership, minority status, music/drama, state/district residency.

**Scholarships offered:** 112 full-time freshmen received athletic scholarships; average amount $26,119.

**FINANCIAL AID PROCEDURES**
**Forms required:** FAFSA, CSS PROFILE.
**Dates and Deadlines:** Priority date 3/1; no closing date. Must reply by 5/1.

**CONTACT**
Scott Miller, Director of Financial Aid
Box 400160, Charlottesville, VA 22904-4160
(434) 982-6000

## University of Virginia's College at Wise
Wise, Virginia
www.uvawise.edu                    Federal Code: 003747

**4-year public** liberal arts college in small town.
**Enrollment:** 1,396 undergrads, 5% part-time. 286 full-time freshmen.
**Selectivity:** Admits over 75% of applicants.

**BASIC COSTS (2015-2016)**
**Tuition and fees:** $9,355; out-of-state residents $24,957.
**Per-credit charge:** $216; out-of-state residents $874.
**Room and board:** $10,256.

**FINANCIAL AID PICTURE (2014-2015)**
**Students with need:** Out of 275 full-time freshmen who applied for aid, 232 were judged to have need. Of these, 232 received aid, and 47 had their full need met. Average financial aid package met 75% of need; average scholarship/grant was $8,889; average loan was $2,907. For part-time students, average financial aid package was $7,560.
**Students without need:** 25 full-time freshmen who did not demonstrate need for aid received scholarships/grants; average award was $4,856. No-need awards available for academics, alumni affiliation, art, athletics, job skills, leadership, music/drama, religious affiliation, state/district residency.
**Scholarships offered:** 24 full-time freshmen received athletic scholarships; average amount $5,165.

**FINANCIAL AID PROCEDURES**
**Forms required:** FAFSA.
**Dates and Deadlines:** Closing date 4/1. Applicants notified on a rolling basis starting 2/16; must reply within 4 week(s) of notification.
**Transfers:** Applicants notified on a rolling basis.

**CONTACT**
Rebecca Huffman, Director of Financial Aid
1 College Avenue, Wise, VA 24293-4412
(276) 328-0139

## Virginia Baptist College
Fredericksburg, Virginia
www.vbc.edu                        Federal Code: 038626

**4-year private** Bible college in large city, affiliated with Baptist faith.
**Enrollment:** 72 undergrads, 40% part-time. 7 full-time freshmen.
**Selectivity:** Open admission.

**BASIC COSTS (2015-2016)**
**Tuition and fees:** $5,540.
**Per-credit charge:** $210.
**Room only:** $3,200.

**FINANCIAL AID PICTURE (2015-2016)**
**Students with need:** Out of 5 full-time freshmen who applied for aid, 5 were judged to have need. Of these, 5 received aid, and 5 had their full need met. Average financial aid package met 100% of need; average scholarship/grant was $3,663. For part-time students, average financial aid package was $3,125.
**Students without need:** 1 full-time freshmen who did not demonstrate need for aid received scholarships/grants; average award was $500. No-need

awards available for academics, alumni affiliation, leadership, religious affiliation.

**FINANCIAL AID PROCEDURES**
**Forms required:** FAFSA, institutional form.
**Dates and Deadlines:** Applicants notified on a rolling basis.
**Transfers:** No deadline. Applicants notified on a rolling basis.

**CONTACT**
Sherry Davis, Business Manager
4105 Plank Road, Fredericksburg, VA 22407
(540) 785-5440 ext. 308

## Virginia Commonwealth University
Richmond, Virginia
www.vcu.edu                        Federal Code: 003735

**4-year public** university in small city.
**Enrollment:** 22,516 undergrads, 11% part-time. 3,565 full-time freshmen.
**Selectivity:** Admits 50 to 75% of applicants.

**BASIC COSTS (2015-2016)**
**Tuition and fees:** $12,772; out-of-state residents $30,838.
**Per-credit charge:** $365; out-of-state residents $988.
**Room and board:** $9,586.

**FINANCIAL AID PICTURE (2014-2015)**
**Students with need:** Out of 3,111 full-time freshmen who applied for aid, 2,459 were judged to have need. Of these, 2,220 received aid, and 812 had their full need met. Average financial aid package met 52% of need; average scholarship/grant was $7,771; average loan was $3,351. For part-time students, average financial aid package was $5,593.
**Students without need:** 333 full-time freshmen who did not demonstrate need for aid received scholarships/grants; average award was $8,588. No-need awards available for academics, alumni affiliation, art, athletics, leadership, music/drama.
**Scholarships offered:** 31 full-time freshmen received athletic scholarships; average amount $19,542.

**FINANCIAL AID PROCEDURES**
**Forms required:** FAFSA.
**Dates and Deadlines:** Priority date 3/1; no closing date. Applicants notified on a rolling basis starting 4/1; must reply within 2 week(s) of notification.
**Transfers:** Applicants notified by 4/1.

**CONTACT**
Marc Vernon, Executive Director of Financial Aid
Box 842526, Richmond, VA 23284-2526
(804) 828-6669

## Virginia Military Institute
Lexington, Virginia
www.vmi.edu                        Federal Code: 003753

**4-year public** liberal arts and military college in small town.
**Enrollment:** 1,717 undergrads. 434 full-time freshmen.
**Selectivity:** Admits 50 to 75% of applicants. GED not accepted.

**BASIC COSTS (2015-2016)**
**Tuition and fees:** $16,536; out-of-state residents $39,550.
**Room and board:** $8,666.

**FINANCIAL AID PICTURE (2014-2015)**
**Students with need:** Out of 372 full-time freshmen who applied for aid, 265 were judged to have need. Of these, 260 received aid, and 130 had their full need met. Average financial aid package met 85% of need; average scholarship/grant was $15,054; average loan was $3,672.

**Students without need:** 49 full-time freshmen who did not demonstrate need for aid received scholarships/grants; average award was $3,823. No-need awards available for academics, alumni affiliation, athletics, leadership, music/drama, ROTC, state/district residency.

**Scholarships offered:** *Merit:* Institute Scholarship: up to $25,000; 10-12 awarded; based on superior academic performance, demonstrated character and leadership, extracurricular activities, 3.7 GPA, 1250 SAT (exclusive of Writing) or 27 ACT, rank in top 5% of class. *Athletic:* 30 full-time freshmen received athletic scholarships; average amount $14,875.

### FINANCIAL AID PROCEDURES

**Forms required:** FAFSA, institutional form.

**Dates and Deadlines:** Priority date 3/1; closing date 3/1. Applicants notified on a rolling basis starting 4/1; must reply by 5/1.

### CONTACT

Timothy Golden, Director of Financial Aid
VMI Office of Admissions, Lexington, VA 24450-9967
(540) 464-7208

## Virginia Polytechnic Institute and State University
Blacksburg, Virginia
www.vt.edu                    Federal Code: 003754

**4-year public** university in large town.

**Enrollment:** 25,327 undergrads, 2% part-time. 5,474 full-time freshmen.

**Selectivity:** Admits 50 to 75% of applicants.

### BASIC COSTS (2015-2016)

**Tuition and fees:** $12,485; out-of-state residents $28,525.

**Per-credit charge:** $437; out-of-state residents $1,105.

**Room and board:** $8,266.

**Additional info:** Out-of-state students pay an additional $604 for Capital & Equipment Fee (o-o-s student fees $2593). Tuition/fee waivers available for unemployed or children of unemployed.

### FINANCIAL AID PICTURE (2014-2015)

**Students with need:** Out of 4,232 full-time freshmen who applied for aid, 2,418 were judged to have need. Of these, 2,121 received aid, and 395 had their full need met. Average financial aid package met 64% of need; average scholarship/grant was $7,469; average loan was $4,078. Need-based aid available for part-time students.

**Students without need:** 575 full-time freshmen who did not demonstrate need for aid received scholarships/grants; average award was $3,482. No-need awards available for academics, art, athletics, leadership, minority status, music/drama, ROTC, state/district residency.

**Scholarships offered:** 93 full-time freshmen received athletic scholarships; average amount $25,420.

### FINANCIAL AID PROCEDURES

**Forms required:** FAFSA.

**Dates and Deadlines:** Closing date 3/1. Applicants notified by 4/1; must reply by 5/1 or within 4 week(s) of notification.

**Transfers:** Applicants notified by 4/1. Based on family EFC per FAFSA and available resources. Significant academic scholarships for graduates of Virginia Community College System.

### CONTACT

Beth Armstrong, Director of Financial Aid
925 Prices Fork Road, Blacksburg, VA 24061-0202
(540) 231-5179

## Virginia State University
Petersburg, Virginia
www.vsu.edu                    Federal Code: 003764

**4-year public** university in large town.

**Enrollment:** 4,176 undergrads, 5% part-time. 906 full-time freshmen.

**Selectivity:** Admits over 75% of applicants.

### BASIC COSTS (2015-2016)

**Tuition and fees:** $8,226; out-of-state residents $17,760.

**Per-credit charge:** $358; out-of-state residents $793.

**Room and board:** $10,252.

### FINANCIAL AID PICTURE (2014-2015)

**Students with need:** Out of 833 full-time freshmen who applied for aid, 833 were judged to have need. Of these, 833 received aid, and 284 had their full need met. Average financial aid package met 60% of need; average scholarship/grant was $5,940; average loan was $3,500. Need-based aid available for part-time students. .

**Students without need:** 190 full-time freshmen who did not demonstrate need for aid received scholarships/grants; average award was $500. No-need awards available for academics, alumni affiliation, art, athletics, job skills, leadership, minority status, music/drama, religious affiliation, ROTC.

**Scholarships offered:** *Merit:* Presidential Scholarships: $7,000; based on 3.2 GPA; 1100 SAT/24 ACT. Provost's Scholarships: $3,500; based on 3.0 GPA; 1000 SAT/21 ACT. Fine and Performing Arts Scholarships: $1,500; based on outstanding talent in music or fine arts; audition or portfolio may be required; recommendation required. Math, Science, and Technology Scholarships: $1,500; based on 3.0 GPA; above average ability in math, science, or technology; recommendation and essay required. *Athletic:* 20 full-time freshmen received athletic scholarships; average amount $500.

**Additional info:** Strongly recommend that students apply for scholarship assistance through federal, state, local and private agencies.

### FINANCIAL AID PROCEDURES

**Forms required:** FAFSA, institutional form.

**Dates and Deadlines:** Priority date 3/31; closing date 5/1. Applicants notified on a rolling basis starting 3/1; must reply within 2 week(s) of notification.

**Transfers:** Priority date 3/1.

### CONTACT

Myra Phillips, Director, Financial Aid
1 Hayden Drive, Petersburg, VA 23806
(804) 524-5990

## Virginia Union University
Richmond, Virginia
www.vuu.edu                    Federal Code: 003766

**4-year private** university and liberal arts college in small city, affiliated with Baptist faith.

**Enrollment:** 1,441 undergrads, 2% part-time. 449 full-time freshmen.

**Selectivity:** Admits less than 50% of applicants.

### BASIC COSTS (2015-2016)

**Tuition and fees:** $15,746.

**Per-credit charge:** $447.

**Room and board:** $8,074.

### FINANCIAL AID PICTURE (2015-2016)

**Students with need:** Out of 447 full-time freshmen who applied for aid, 430 were judged to have need. Of these, 430 received aid, and 31 had their full need met. Average financial aid package met 51% of need; average scholarship/grant was $10,168; average loan was $3,219. For part-time students, average financial aid package was $8,012.

**Students without need:** 11 full-time freshmen who did not demonstrate need for aid received scholarships/grants; average award was $8,271. No-need awards available for academics, athletics, ROTC, state/district residency.

**Scholarships offered:** 3 full-time freshmen received athletic scholarships; average amount $9,546.

## FINANCIAL AID PROCEDURES

**Forms required:** FAFSA.

**Dates and Deadlines:** Priority date 4/27; no closing date. Applicants notified on a rolling basis starting 5/1; must reply within 2 week(s) of notification.

**Transfers:** No deadline. Student must submit financial aid transcript from all prior schools attended before receiving aid.

## CONTACT

Antoinette House, Director of Financial Aid
1500 North Lombardy Street, Richmond, VA 23220
(804) 257-5882

## Virginia Wesleyan College

Norfolk, Virginia
www.vwc.edu                          Federal Code: 003767

**4-year private** liberal arts college in large city, affiliated with United Methodist Church.

**Enrollment:** 1,410 undergrads, 6% part-time. 406 full-time freshmen.

**Selectivity:** Admits over 75% of applicants.

### BASIC COSTS (2015-2016)

**Tuition and fees:** $34,428.

**Per-credit charge:** $1,408.

**Room and board:** $8,680.

**Additional info:** Tuition/fee waivers available for adults.

### FINANCIAL AID PICTURE (2014-2015)

**Students with need:** Out of 406 full-time freshmen who applied for aid, 368 were judged to have need. Of these, 368 received aid, and 67 had their full need met. Average financial aid package met 71% of need; average scholarship/grant was $21,369; average loan was $6,356. For part-time students, average financial aid package was $7,083.

**Students without need:** 38 full-time freshmen who did not demonstrate need for aid received scholarships/grants; average award was $16,023. No-need awards available for academics, alumni affiliation, leadership, religious affiliation, ROTC, state/district residency.

### FINANCIAL AID PROCEDURES

**Forms required:** FAFSA, state aid form.

**Dates and Deadlines:** Priority date 3/1; no closing date. Applicants notified on a rolling basis starting 2/15; must reply by 5/1 or within 2 week(s) of notification.

**Transfers:** No deadline. Applicants notified on a rolling basis starting 2/15; must reply by 5/1 or within 2 week(s) of notification. 4-semester maximum of special aid available for students who graduated with 3.0 GPA and earned an associate degree from local community college. Must enroll full time and maintain 2.5 GPA minimum.

### CONTACT

Teresa Rhyne, Director of Financial Aid
1584 Wesleyan Drive, Norfolk, VA 23502-5599
(757) 455-3345

## Virginia Western Community College

Roanoke, Virginia
www.virginiawestern.edu          Federal Code: 003760

**2-year public** community college in small city.

**Enrollment:** 5,264 undergrads, 54% part-time. 974 full-time freshmen.

**Selectivity:** Open admission; but selective for some programs.

### BASIC COSTS (2015-2016)

**Tuition and fees:** $4,713; out-of-state residents $10,551.

**Per-credit charge:** $136; out-of-state residents $313.

**Additional info:** Out-of-state students pay an additional $540 capital outlay fee.

### FINANCIAL AID PICTURE

**Students with need:** Need-based aid available for full-time and part-time students.

**Students without need:** No-need awards available for academics, state/district residency.

**Scholarships offered:** CCAP scholarships; for qualifying graduates of local high schools.

### FINANCIAL AID PROCEDURES

**Forms required:** FAFSA.

**Dates and Deadlines:** Applicants notified on a rolling basis starting 4/1.

**Transfers:** No deadline. Applicants notified on a rolling basis.

### CONTACT

Chad Sartini, Financial Aid Officer
3094 Colonial Avenue, Roanoke, VA 24013
(855) 874-6690

## Washington and Lee University

Lexington, Virginia                  Federal Code: 003768
www.wlu.edu                          CSS Code: 5887

**4-year private** university and liberal arts college in small town.

**Enrollment:** 1,844 undergrads. 454 full-time freshmen.

**Selectivity:** Admits less than 50% of applicants.

### BASIC COSTS (2016-2017)

**Tuition and fees:** $48,267.

**Per-credit charge:** $1,689.

**Room and board:** $11,380.

### FINANCIAL AID PICTURE (2015-2016)

**Students with need:** Out of 233 full-time freshmen who applied for aid, 201 were judged to have need. Of these, 201 received aid, and 201 had their full need met. Average financial aid package met 100% of need; average scholarship/grant was $40,857; average loan was $816. Need-based aid available for part-time students.

**Students without need:** 17 full-time freshmen who did not demonstrate need for aid received scholarships/grants; average award was $41,148. No-need awards available for academics.

**Additional info:** W&L Promise guarantees free tuition to any undergraduate student with family income below $75,000. All students meeting the relevant Early Decision I, Early Decision II, or Regular Decision need-based financial aid deadline will receive aid package that covers their family's institutionally determined need. Loan assistance offered only to offset any additional educational expenses.

### FINANCIAL AID PROCEDURES

**Forms required:** FAFSA, CSS PROFILE.

**Dates and Deadlines:** Priority date 2/15; closing date 2/15. Applicants notified by 4/1; must reply by 5/1.

**Transfers:** Transfer students awarded institutional funds only after commitments to enrolled students are met. Notification usually in late summer.

### CONTACT

Jim Kaster, Director of Student Financial Aid
204 West Washington Street, Lexington, VA 24450-2116
(540) 458-8720

## Wytheville Community College
Wytheville, Virginia
www.wcc.vccs.edu    Federal Code: 003761

**2-year public** community college in small town.
**Enrollment:** 1,733 undergrads.
**Selectivity:** Open admission; but selective for some programs.

**BASIC COSTS (2015-2016)**
**Tuition and fees:** $4,380; out-of-state residents $9,678.
**Per-credit charge:** $134; out-of-state residents $311.
**Additional info:** Out-of-state students pay an additional $540 capital outlay fee.

**FINANCIAL AID PICTURE**
**Students with need:** Need-based aid available for full-time and part-time students.
**Students without need:** This college awards aid only to students with need.

**FINANCIAL AID PROCEDURES**
**Forms required:** FAFSA, institutional form.
**Dates and Deadlines:** Priority date 4/1; no closing date. Applicants notified on a rolling basis starting 5/1; must reply within 4 week(s) of notification.

**CONTACT**
Mary Gallagher, Financial Aid Coordinator
1000 East Main Street, Wytheville, VA 24382
(540) 223-4703

# Washington

## Antioch University Seattle
Seattle, Washington
www.antiochseattle.edu    Federal Code: 003010

**Upper-division private** university and liberal arts college in very large city.
**Enrollment:** 230 undergrads.
**Selectivity:** Open admission; but selective for some programs.

**BASIC COSTS (2015-2016)**
**Tuition and fees:** $27,435.
**Per-credit charge:** $600.

**FINANCIAL AID PICTURE**
**Students with need:** Need-based aid available for full-time and part-time students. Work study available nights, weekends, and for part-time students.

**FINANCIAL AID PROCEDURES**
**Forms required:** FAFSA, state aid form.
**Dates and Deadlines:** Priority date 4/15; no closing date. Applicants notified on a rolling basis starting 3/15; must reply within 2 week(s) of notification.
**Transfers:** Applicants notified on a rolling basis starting 3/15; must reply within 2 week(s) of notification.

**CONTACT**
Betsy Raleigh, Vice President for Finance and Administration
2326 Sixth Avenue, Seattle, WA 98121-1814
(206) 268-4010

## Art Institute of Seattle
Seattle, Washington
www.ais.edu    Federal Code: 016210

**4-year for-profit** culinary school and visual arts college in very large city.
**Enrollment:** 1,703 undergrads.

**Selectivity:** Open admission; but selective for some programs.

**BASIC COSTS (2015-2016)**
**Additional info:** Diploma programs range from $20,520-$22,669; Associates programs: $44,110-$46,264; Bachelors programs: $87,450-$89,914. Books, supplies, fees range depending on program level and course of study. All costs are subject to change.

**FINANCIAL AID PICTURE**
**Students with need:** Need-based aid available for full-time and part-time students. Work study available nights, weekends, and for part-time students.
**Students without need:** No-need awards available for academics, art.

**FINANCIAL AID PROCEDURES**
**Forms required:** FAFSA, state aid form.
**Dates and Deadlines:** Applicants notified on a rolling basis.

**CONTACT**
Angela Hedwall, Director of Student Financial Services
2323 Elliott Avenue, Seattle, WA 98121-1622
(206) 448-2501

## Bastyr University
Kenmore, Washington
www.bastyr.edu    Federal Code: 016059

**Upper-division private** university and health science college in small city.
**Enrollment:** 287 undergrads, 24% part-time.

**BASIC COSTS (2015-2016)**
**Tuition and fees:** $24,273.
**Room and board:** $15,550.

**FINANCIAL AID PICTURE (2014-2015)**
**Students with need:** Average financial aid package for all full-time undergraduates was $18,194; for part-time $14,865. 31% awarded as scholarships/grants, 69% awarded as loans/jobs. Work study available nights, weekends, and for part-time students.
**Students without need:** No-need awards available for academics, alumni affiliation, job skills, leadership.

**FINANCIAL AID PROCEDURES**
**Forms required:** FAFSA, institutional form.
**Dates and Deadlines:** Priority date 4/15; no closing date. Applicants notified on a rolling basis starting 2/1; must reply within 2 week(s) of notification.
**Transfers:** No deadline. Applicants notified on a rolling basis; must reply within 3 week(s) of notification.

**CONTACT**
Danette Wells, Director of Financial Aid
14500 Juanita Drive, NE, Kenmore, WA 98028
(425) 602-3080

## Bates Technical College
Tacoma, Washington
www.bates.ctc.edu    Federal Code: 012259

**2-year public** technical college in small city.
**Enrollment:** 995 undergrads.
**Selectivity:** Open admission; but selective for some programs.

**BASIC COSTS (2015-2016)**
**Tuition and fees:** $4,703; out-of-state residents $10,106.
**Per-credit charge:** $84; out-of-state residents $204.

**FINANCIAL AID PICTURE**
**Students with need:** Need-based aid available for full-time and part-time students. Work study available nights.

**Students without need:** This college awards aid only to students with need.

### FINANCIAL AID PROCEDURES

**Forms required:** FAFSA, institutional form.
**Dates and Deadlines:** Applicants notified on a rolling basis starting 9/7.
**Transfers:** No deadline. Applicants notified on a rolling basis.

### CONTACT

Susan Neese, Financial Aid Officer
1101 South Yakima Avenue, Tacoma, WA 98405
(253) 680-7025

## Bellevue College
Bellevue, Washington
www.bellevuecollege.edu                    Federal Code: 003769

**2-year public** community college in small city.
**Enrollment:** 13,469 undergrads.
**Selectivity:** Open admission; but selective for some programs.

### BASIC COSTS (2015-2016)

**Tuition and fees:** $4,077; out-of-state residents $9,480.
**Per-credit charge:** $85; out-of-state residents $206.

### FINANCIAL AID PICTURE

**Students with need:** Need-based aid available for full-time and part-time students. Work study available nights, weekends, and for part-time students.
**Students without need:** No-need awards available for academics, athletics.

### FINANCIAL AID PROCEDURES

**Forms required:** FAFSA, institutional form.
**Dates and Deadlines:** Priority date 4/16; no closing date. Applicants notified on a rolling basis starting 8/1.

### CONTACT

Sherri Ballantyne, Assistant Dean, Financial Aid
3000 Landerholm Circle SE, Bellevue, WA 98007-6484
(425) 564-2227

## Bellingham Technical College
Bellingham, Washington
www.btc.edu                                Federal Code: 016227

**2-year public** technical college in small city.
**Enrollment:** 2,112 undergrads.
**Selectivity:** Open admission; but selective for some programs.

### BASIC COSTS (2015-2016)

**Tuition and fees:** $3,775; out-of-state residents $9,178.
**Per-credit charge:** $81; out-of-state residents $201.

### FINANCIAL AID PICTURE (2014-2015)

**Students with need:** 60% of average financial aid package awarded as scholarships/grants, 40% awarded as loans/jobs. Need-based aid available for part-time students.
**Students without need:** This college awards aid only to students with need.

### FINANCIAL AID PROCEDURES

**Forms required:** FAFSA, institutional form.
**Dates and Deadlines:** Priority date 3/1; no closing date. Applicants notified on a rolling basis starting 7/1; must reply within 2 week(s) of notification.

### CONTACT

Crystal Bagby, Director of Financial Aid
3028 Lindbergh Avenue, Bellingham, WA 98225-1599
(360) 752-8351

## Big Bend Community College
Moses Lake, Washington
www.bigbend.edu                            Federal Code: 003770

**2-year public** community college in large town.
**Enrollment:** 1,614 undergrads, 23% part-time. 332 full-time freshmen.
**Selectivity:** Open admission; but selective for some programs.

### BASIC COSTS (2015-2016)

**Tuition and fees:** $4,071; out-of-state residents $9,474.
**Per-credit charge:** $85; out-of-state residents $206.
**Additional info:** Room charge is $2,790 for single and $3,330 for double occupancy. Tuition/fee waivers available for unemployed or children of unemployed.

### FINANCIAL AID PICTURE (2014-2015)

**Students with need:** 71% of average financial aid package awarded as scholarships/grants, 29% awarded as loans/jobs. Need-based aid available for part-time students. Work study available nights, weekends, and for part-time students.
**Students without need:** This college awards aid only to students with need.

### FINANCIAL AID PROCEDURES

**Forms required:** FAFSA, institutional form.
**Dates and Deadlines:** Priority date 4/15; no closing date. Applicants notified on a rolling basis starting 5/15; must reply within 2 week(s) of notification.

### CONTACT

Jeremy Iverson, Director of Financial Aid
7662 Chanute Street NE, Moses Lake, WA 98837-3299
(509) 793-2034

## Cascadia College
Bothell, Washington
www.cascadia.edu                           Federal Code: 034835

**2-year public** community college in large town.
**Enrollment:** 2,327 undergrads, 43% part-time. 369 full-time freshmen.
**Selectivity:** Open admission.

### BASIC COSTS (2015-2016)

**Tuition and fees:** $3,947; out-of-state residents $9,350.
**Per-credit charge:** $83; out-of-state residents $203.

### FINANCIAL AID PICTURE

**Students with need:** Work study available nights, weekends, and for part-time students.

### FINANCIAL AID PROCEDURES

**Forms required:** FAFSA, institutional form.
**Dates and Deadlines:** Priority date 4/15; no closing date.

### CONTACT

Deann Holliday, Director of Student Financial Services
18345 Campus Way, NE, Bothell, WA 98011
(425) 352-8324

## Central Washington University
Ellensburg, Washington
www.cwu.edu                                Federal Code: 003771

**4-year public** university in large town.
**Enrollment:** 10,102 undergrads, 11% part-time. 1,340 full-time freshmen.
**Selectivity:** Admits over 75% of applicants.

## BASIC COSTS (2015-2016)
**Tuition and fees:** $8,688; out-of-state residents $21,501.
**Room and board:** $9,780.

## FINANCIAL AID PICTURE (2014-2015)
**Students with need:** Out of 1,163 full-time freshmen who applied for aid, 855 were judged to have need. Of these, 855 received aid, and 311 had their full need met. Average financial aid package met 84% of need; average scholarship/grant was $8,869; average loan was $3,812. For part-time students, average financial aid package was $7,187.
**Students without need:** 2 full-time freshmen who did not demonstrate need for aid received scholarships/grants; average award was $1,250. No-need awards available for academics, alumni affiliation, art, athletics, job skills, leadership, minority status, music/drama, religious affiliation, ROTC, state/district residency.
**Scholarships offered:** Merit Tuition Awards are offered to incoming students. Eligibility is based on a prospective student's admissions application.

## FINANCIAL AID PROCEDURES
**Forms required:** FAFSA.
**Dates and Deadlines:** Priority date 3/1; closing date 5/1. Applicants notified on a rolling basis starting 5/15; must reply within 4 week(s) of notification.
**Transfers:** Equal Opportunity Grant available for junior-level transfers from selected Washington counties. May receive up to $2,500/year for three years. Phi Theta Kappa Transfer Honors Program: $1200.

## CONTACT
Adrian Naranjo, Director of Financial Aid
400 East University Way, Ellensburg, WA 98926-7463
(509) 963-1611

## Centralia College
Centralia, Washington
www.centralia.edu                           Federal Code: 003772

**2-year public** community college in large town.
**Enrollment:** 2,097 undergrads.
**Selectivity:** Open admission; but selective for some programs.

## BASIC COSTS (2015-2016)
**Tuition and fees:** $4,211; out-of-state residents $9,204.
**Per-credit charge:** $85; out-of-state residents $196.
**Additional info:** Tuition/fee waivers available for unemployed or children of unemployed.

## FINANCIAL AID PICTURE
**Students with need:** Need-based aid available for full-time and part-time students.
**Students without need:** No-need awards available for academics, alumni affiliation, art, athletics, leadership, minority status, music/drama.

## FINANCIAL AID PROCEDURES
**Forms required:** FAFSA, institutional form.
**Dates and Deadlines:** Priority date 5/1; closing date 9/1. Applicants notified on a rolling basis starting 7/10; must reply within 2 week(s) of notification.

## CONTACT
Tracy Smothers, Director of Financial Aid
600 Centralia College Boulevard, Centralia, WA 98531
(360) 736-9391 ext. 234

## City University of Seattle
Seattle, Washington
www.cityu.edu                               Federal Code: 013022

**4-year private** university in very large city.
**Enrollment:** 905 undergrads.

**Selectivity:** Open admission; but selective for some programs.
## BASIC COSTS (2015-2016)
**Tuition and fees:** $16,020.
**Per-credit charge:** $356.

## FINANCIAL AID PICTURE (2014-2015)
**Students with need:** Need-based aid available for full-time and part-time students.
**Students without need:** No-need awards available for academics, alumni affiliation, leadership, minority status, state/district residency.
**Additional info:** All degree programs approved for veteran's administration education benefits.

## FINANCIAL AID PROCEDURES
**Forms required:** FAFSA.
**Dates and Deadlines:** Applicants notified on a rolling basis starting 5/1.

## CONTACT
Darcy Keller, Director of Financial Aid
521 Wall Street, Seattle, WA 98121
(800) 426-5596

## Clark College
Vancouver, Washington
www.clark.edu                               Federal Code: 003773

**2-year public** community college in small city.
**Enrollment:** 8,234 undergrads, 48% part-time. 827 full-time freshmen.
**Selectivity:** Open admission; but selective for some programs.

## BASIC COSTS (2015-2016)
**Tuition and fees:** $3,930; out-of-state residents $9,333.
**Per-credit charge:** $82; out-of-state residents $203.
**Additional info:** Tuition/fee waivers available for unemployed or children of unemployed.

## FINANCIAL AID PICTURE (2014-2015)
**Students with need:** 77% of average financial aid package awarded as scholarships/grants, 23% awarded as loans/jobs. Need-based aid available for part-time students. Work study available nights, weekends, and for part-time students.
**Students without need:** No-need awards available for academics, alumni affiliation, art, athletics, leadership, minority status, music/drama, state/district residency.
**Scholarships offered:** Clark College Foundation Scholarships: $500 to full tuition; recipients selected from those completing Clark's Foundation Standard Scholarship application form.

## FINANCIAL AID PROCEDURES
**Forms required:** FAFSA.
**Dates and Deadlines:** Priority date 5/18; no closing date. Applicants notified on a rolling basis starting 6/1; must reply within 2 week(s) of notification.

## CONTACT
Karen Driscoll, Director of Financial Aid
Welcome Center, MS PUB002, Vancouver, WA 98663
(360) 992-2153

## Clover Park Technical College
Lakewood, Washington
www.cptc.edu                                Federal Code: 015984

**2-year public** technical college in small city.
**Enrollment:** 4,509 undergrads.
**Selectivity:** Open admission; but selective for some programs.

## BASIC COSTS (2015-2016)

**Tuition and fees:** $3,886; out-of-state residents $9,289.
**Per-credit charge:** $82; out-of-state residents $202.

## FINANCIAL AID PICTURE

**Students with need:** Need-based aid available for full-time and part-time students. Work study available nights, weekends, and for part-time students.
**Students without need:** This college awards aid only to students with need.

## FINANCIAL AID PROCEDURES

**Forms required:** FAFSA, institutional form.
**Dates and Deadlines:** Closing date 4/12. Applicants notified on a rolling basis starting 5/1.

## CONTACT

Wendy Joseph, Financial Aid Director
4500 Steilacoom Boulevard, SW, Lakewood, WA 98499-4098
(253) 589-5660

# Columbia Basin College
Pasco, Washington
www.columbiabasin.edu          Federal Code: 003774

**2-year public** community college in small city.
**Enrollment:** 1,595 undergrads.
**Selectivity:** Open admission; but selective for some programs.

## BASIC COSTS (2015-2016)

**Tuition and fees:** $4,241; out-of-state residents $9,644.
**Per-credit charge:** $82; out-of-state residents $202.
**Additional info:** Tuition/fee waivers available for unemployed or children of unemployed.

## FINANCIAL AID PICTURE

**Students with need:** Need-based aid available for full-time and part-time students. Work study available nights, weekends, and for part-time students.
**Students without need:** No-need awards available for academics, athletics, state/district residency.

## FINANCIAL AID PROCEDURES

**Forms required:** FAFSA, institutional form.
**Dates and Deadlines:** Closing date 4/15. Applicants notified on a rolling basis starting 6/15; must reply within 2 week(s) of notification.

## CONTACT

Ceci Ratliff, Director of Student Financial Services
2600 North 20th Avenue, Pasco, WA 99301
(509) 542-4715

# Cornish College of the Arts
Seattle, Washington
www.cornish.edu          Federal Code: 012315

**4-year private** visual arts and performing arts college in very large city.
**Enrollment:** 720 undergrads, 1% part-time. 143 full-time freshmen.
**Selectivity:** Admits 50 to 75% of applicants.

## BASIC COSTS (2015-2016)

**Tuition and fees:** $37,240.
**Per-credit charge:** $1,535.
**Room and board:** $10,680.

## FINANCIAL AID PICTURE (2014-2015)

**Students with need:** Out of 123 full-time freshmen who applied for aid, 116 were judged to have need. Of these, 116 received aid, and 8 had their full need met. Average financial aid package met 54% of need; average

scholarship/grant was $17,190; average loan was $3,171. For part-time students, average financial aid package was $19,546.
**Students without need:** 27 full-time freshmen who did not demonstrate need for aid received scholarships/grants; average award was $7,566. No-need awards available for academics, art, music/drama.

## FINANCIAL AID PROCEDURES

**Forms required:** FAFSA.
**Dates and Deadlines:** Priority date 2/15; no closing date. Applicants notified on a rolling basis starting 3/15; must reply by 5/1 or within 2 week(s) of notification.
**Transfers:** No deadline. Applicants notified on a rolling basis; must reply by 2/15.

## CONTACT

Monique Theriault, Director for Financial Aid
1000 Lenora Street, Seattle, WA 98121
(206) 726-5014

# DeVry University: Federal Way
Federal Way, Washington
www.devry.edu

**4-year for-profit** university in large city.
**Enrollment:** 311 undergrads.

## BASIC COSTS (2015-2016)

**Tuition and fees:** $18,959.
**Per-credit charge:** $609.
**Additional info:** Annual tuition: $10,810-$21,163; fees $50-$90.

## FINANCIAL AID PICTURE

**Students with need:** Need-based aid available for full-time and part-time students.
**Students without need:** This college awards aid only to students with need.

## FINANCIAL AID PROCEDURES

**Forms required:** FAFSA.
**Dates and Deadlines:** Applicants notified on a rolling basis.

## CONTACT

3600 South 344th Way, Federal Way, WA 98001-9558
(253) 943-3060

# DigiPen Institute of Technology
Redmond, Washington
www.digipen.edu          Federal Code: 037243

**4-year for-profit** visual arts and engineering college in large town.
**Enrollment:** 978 full-time undergrads. 154 full-time freshmen.
**Selectivity:** Admits less than 50% of applicants.

## BASIC COSTS (2016-2017)

**Tuition and fees:** $28,100.
**Per-credit charge:** $930.
**Additional info:** Flat-rate fee structure; students typically take 18-20 credits each semester which equates to 36-40 credits per year. Tuition for this credit amount is $28,800 and $31,600 for nonresident aliens.

## FINANCIAL AID PICTURE (2014-2015)

**Students with need:** Out of 116 full-time freshmen who applied for aid, 94 were judged to have need. Of these, 94 received aid, and 44 had their full need met. Average financial aid package met 79% of need; average scholarship/grant was $8,097; average loan was $3,361. For part-time students, average financial aid package was $5,968.

**Students without need:** No-need awards available for academics, art, leadership.

**Scholarships offered:** First Scholarship: $5,000; based on essay and academic record; 2 awarded. Art scholarship: up to $10,000; for incoming student who demonstrates considerable artistic talent; 2 awarded. Limited number of scholarships up to $10,000, offered to incoming students who have demonstrated academic achievements and are likely to make a positive impact in the DigiPen community and their chosen field.

**Additional info:** Federal Work Study available. Many aid programs are on a first-come, first-served basis.

### FINANCIAL AID PROCEDURES

**Forms required:** FAFSA.

**Dates and Deadlines:** Priority date 2/1; closing date 4/15. Applicants notified on a rolling basis starting 2/15; must reply within 2 week(s) of notification.

**Transfers:** No deadline. Must reply within 2 week(s) of notification. Transfer students should meet with a financial aid administrator as soon as they are accepted. Must submit prior financial aid history to determine eligibility.

### CONTACT

Trinity Huttner, Director of Financial Aid
9931 Willows Road NE, Redmond, WA 98052
(425) 629-5002

## Eastern Washington University

Cheney, Washington
www.ewu.edu                           Federal Code: 003775

**4-year public** university in large town.
**Enrollment:** 10,761 undergrads, 9% part-time. 1,662 full-time freshmen.
**Selectivity:** Admits over 75% of applicants.

### BASIC COSTS (2015-2016)

**Tuition and fees:** $7,866; out-of-state residents $22,272.
**Per-credit charge:** $214; out-of-state residents $657.
**Room and board:** $10,263.

### FINANCIAL AID PICTURE (2014-2015)

**Students with need:** Out of 1,450 full-time freshmen who applied for aid, 1,112 were judged to have need. Of these, 1,077 received aid, and 317 had their full need met. Average financial aid package met 57% of need; average scholarship/grant was $8,521; average loan was $3,068. For part-time students, average financial aid package was $9,649.

**Students without need:** 167 full-time freshmen who did not demonstrate need for aid received scholarships/grants; average award was $2,855. No-need awards available for academics, alumni affiliation, art, athletics, job skills, music/drama, state/district residency.

**Scholarships offered:** *Merit:* Killin Scholarship: full tuition; three awards; for academic excellence; must have 3.7 GPA and 1100 SAT score (exclusive of Writing). Honors Scholarship: $4,000; 38 awards; for academic excellence. Presidential Scholarship: $3,000; 75 awards; based on GPA, SAT, early admission. *Athletic:* 47 full-time freshmen received athletic scholarships; average amount $12,278.

**Additional info:** The High Demand Scholarship program helps low income students pursue "high demand" careers.

### FINANCIAL AID PROCEDURES

**Forms required:** FAFSA.

**Dates and Deadlines:** Priority date 2/15; no closing date. Applicants notified on a rolling basis starting 4/1; must reply within 4 week(s) of notification.

**Transfers:** No deadline. Applicants notified on a rolling basis.

### CONTACT

Bruce DeFrates, Director of Financial Aid
304 Sutton Hall, Cheney, WA 99004
(509) 359-2314

## Edmonds Community College

Lynnwood, Washington
www.edcc.edu                          Federal Code: 005001

**2-year public** community college in small city.
**Enrollment:** 9,540 undergrads.
**Selectivity:** Open admission; but selective for some programs.

### BASIC COSTS (2015-2016)

**Tuition and fees:** $4,308; out-of-state residents $9,711.
**Per-credit charge:** $85; out-of-state residents $206.
**Additional info:** Room fee ranges $2,085-$3,375 depending on unit.

### FINANCIAL AID PICTURE

**Students with need:** Need-based aid available for full-time and part-time students. Work study available nights.

**Students without need:** No-need awards available for athletics.

### FINANCIAL AID PROCEDURES

**Forms required:** FAFSA, institutional form.

**Dates and Deadlines:** Priority date 5/1; no closing date. Applicants notified on a rolling basis starting 6/1; must reply within 4 week(s) of notification.

### CONTACT

Rae-Ellen Reas, Senior Associate Dean of Enrollment and Financial Services
20000 68th Avenue West, Lynnwood, WA 98036-5912
(425) 640-1457

## Everett Community College

Everett, Washington
www.everettcc.edu                     Federal Code: 003776

**2-year public** community college in small city.
**Enrollment:** 6,990 undergrads.
**Selectivity:** Open admission; but selective for some programs.

### BASIC COSTS (2015-2016)

**Tuition and fees:** $4,101; out-of-state residents $9,504.
**Per-credit charge:** $85; out-of-state residents $206.
**Additional info:** Room ranges $5,100-$6,495 depending on unit.

### FINANCIAL AID PICTURE

**Students with need:** Need-based aid available for full-time and part-time students. Work study available nights, weekends, and for part-time students.

**Students without need:** No-need awards available for academics, alumni affiliation, art, athletics, job skills, leadership, minority status, music/drama, state/district residency.

### FINANCIAL AID PROCEDURES

**Forms required:** FAFSA, institutional form.

**Dates and Deadlines:** Priority date 5/5; no closing date. Applicants notified on a rolling basis starting 4/15; must reply within 4 week(s) of notification.

**Transfers:** No deadline. Applicants notified on a rolling basis starting 6/15; must reply within 4 week(s) of notification.

### CONTACT

Andrea Wilson, Director of Student Financial Services
2000 Tower Street, Everett, WA 98201-1352
(425) 388-9280

## Evergreen State College

Olympia, Washington
www.evergreen.edu                     Federal Code: 008155

**4-year public** liberal arts college in small city.
**Enrollment:** 3,821 undergrads, 6% part-time. 527 full-time freshmen.

**Selectivity:** Admits over 75% of applicants.

## BASIC COSTS (2015-2016)
**Tuition and fees:** $8,380; out-of-state residents $22,795.
**Per-credit charge:** $250; out-of-state residents $731.
**Room and board:** $9,492.

## FINANCIAL AID PICTURE (2014-2015)
**Students with need:** Out of 425 full-time freshmen who applied for aid, 341 were judged to have need. Of these, 324 received aid, and 32 had their full need met. Average financial aid package met 56% of need; average scholarship/grant was $8,832; average loan was $3,362. For part-time students, average financial aid package was $7,094.
**Students without need:** 6 full-time freshmen who did not demonstrate need for aid received scholarships/grants; average award was $6,435. No-need awards available for academics, art, athletics, leadership, state/district residency.
**Scholarships offered:** 3 full-time freshmen received athletic scholarships; average amount $3,055.
**Additional info:** Application packets for all scholarships and tuition awards EXCEPT the Merit Award (due by May 2) must be received by February 1. To meet the financial aid priority deadline, the Federal Processor must process the official results of the FAFSA by March 1. FAFSA applications that are rejected or incomplete cannot be considered for priority awarding.

## FINANCIAL AID PROCEDURES
**Forms required:** FAFSA.
**Dates and Deadlines:** Priority date 3/1; no closing date. Applicants notified on a rolling basis starting 4/1; must reply within 6 week(s) of notification.

## CONTACT
Tracy Hall, Director of Financial Aid
2700 Evergreen Parkway NW, Olympia, WA 98505
(360) 867-6205

# Gonzaga University
Spokane, Washington
www.gonzaga.edu                    Federal Code: 003778

**4-year private** university and liberal arts college in large city, affiliated with Roman Catholic Church.
**Enrollment:** 4,960 undergrads, 1% part-time. 1,048 full-time freshmen.
**Selectivity:** Admits 50 to 75% of applicants. GED not accepted.

## BASIC COSTS (2015-2016)
**Tuition and fees:** $37,990.
**Per-credit charge:** $1,055.
**Room and board:** $10,440.
**Additional info:** Tuition/fee waivers available for adults.

## FINANCIAL AID PICTURE (2014-2015)
**Students with need:** Out of 877 full-time freshmen who applied for aid, 638 were judged to have need. Of these, 638 received aid, and 167 had their full need met. Average financial aid package met 79% of need; average scholarship/grant was $20,411; average loan was $4,714. For part-time students, average financial aid package was $23,733.
**Students without need:** 379 full-time freshmen who did not demonstrate need for aid received scholarships/grants; average award was $12,659. No-need awards available for academics, alumni affiliation, athletics, leadership, minority status, music/drama, ROTC.
**Scholarships offered:** *Merit:* All freshmen are considered for Academic Merit Scholarships: awards range from $3,000 to $10,000. *Athletic:* 44 full-time freshmen received athletic scholarships; average amount $20,797.

## FINANCIAL AID PROCEDURES
**Forms required:** FAFSA.
**Dates and Deadlines:** Priority date 2/1; closing date 6/30. Applicants notified on a rolling basis starting 3/1; must reply by 5/1.

**Transfers:** No deadline. Applicants notified on a rolling basis; must reply by 4/15 or within 3 week(s) of notification.

## CONTACT
Jim White, Director of Financial Aid
502 East Boone Avenue, Spokane, WA 99258-0001
(509) 313-5816

# Grays Harbor College
Aberdeen, Washington
www.ghc.edu                    Federal Code: 003779

**2-year public** community college in large town.
**Enrollment:** 1,970 undergrads.
**Selectivity:** Open admission; but selective for some programs.

## BASIC COSTS (2015-2016)
**Tuition and fees:** $4,041; out-of-state residents $9,444.
**Per-credit charge:** $85; out-of-state residents $206.
**Additional info:** Tuition/fee waivers available for adults, unemployed or children of unemployed.

## FINANCIAL AID PICTURE
**Students with need:** Need-based aid available for full-time and part-time students. Work study available nights.
**Students without need:** No-need awards available for academics, art, athletics, music/drama.

## FINANCIAL AID PROCEDURES
**Forms required:** FAFSA, institutional form.
**Dates and Deadlines:** Closing date 5/1. Applicants notified on a rolling basis starting 5/15.

## CONTACT
Stacey Savino, Assistant Dean of Financial Aid
1620 Edward P Smith Drive, Aberdeen, WA 98520
(360) 538-4081

# Green River Community College
Auburn, Washington
www.greenriver.edu                    Federal Code: 003780

**2-year public** community college in large town.
**Enrollment:** 5,463 undergrads.
**Selectivity:** Open admission; but selective for some programs.

## BASIC COSTS (2015-2016)
**Tuition and fees:** $4,341; out-of-state residents $9,744.
**Per-credit charge:** $85; out-of-state residents $206.

## FINANCIAL AID PICTURE
**Students with need:** Need-based aid available for full-time and part-time students.
**Students without need:** This college awards aid only to students with need.

## FINANCIAL AID PROCEDURES
**Forms required:** FAFSA, institutional form.
**Dates and Deadlines:** Closing date 4/15. Applicants notified on a rolling basis starting 6/30; must reply within 2 week(s) of notification.

## CONTACT
Mary Edington, Director of Financial Aid
12401 SE 320th Street, Auburn, WA 98092
(253) 833-9111 ext. 2440

## Heritage University
Toppenish, Washington
www.heritage.edu                Federal Code: 003777

**4-year private** liberal arts and teachers college in small town, affiliated with interdenominational tradition.
**Enrollment:** 819 undergrads, 10% part-time. 103 full-time freshmen.
**Selectivity:** Open admission.

### BASIC COSTS (2015-2016)
**Tuition and fees:** $19,242.
**Per-credit charge:** $793.

### FINANCIAL AID PICTURE
**Students with need:** Need-based aid available for full-time and part-time students. Work study available nights, weekends, and for part-time students.
**Students without need:** No-need awards available for academics, leadership, minority status.
**Additional info:** Undergraduates eligible for and receiving Federal Pell Grant and/or State Need Grant can receive institutional grant aid necessary to reduce their gap with tuition to no more than their eligibility for subsidized Stafford loans.

### FINANCIAL AID PROCEDURES
**Forms required:** FAFSA, institutional form.
**Dates and Deadlines:** Priority date 2/10; no closing date. Applicants notified on a rolling basis starting 3/1; must reply within 2 week(s) of notification.
**Transfers:** No deadline. Applicants notified on a rolling basis starting 3/1; must reply within 2 week(s) of notification. A request to the State is made to continue awarding State Need Grant funds to transfer students if they were receiving these funds at their previous institution.

### CONTACT
Oscar Verduzco, Director of Financial Aid
3240 Fort Road, Toppenish, WA 98948-9599
(509) 865-8502

## Highline College
Des Moines, Washington
www.highline.edu                Federal Code: 003781

**2-year public** community college in small city.
**Enrollment:** 6,489 undergrads.
**Selectivity:** Open admission; but selective for some programs.

### BASIC COSTS (2015-2016)
**Tuition and fees:** $4,034; out-of-state residents $9,437.
**Per-credit charge:** $85; out-of-state residents $206.

### FINANCIAL AID PICTURE
**Students with need:** Need-based aid available for full-time and part-time students.

### FINANCIAL AID PROCEDURES
**Forms required:** FAFSA.
**Dates and Deadlines:** Priority date 6/1; no closing date. Applicants notified on a rolling basis starting 6/1.

### CONTACT
Lorraine Odom, Director of Financial Aid
2400 South 240th Street, Des Moines, WA 98198-9800
(206) 878-3710

## Lake Washington Institute of Technology
Kirkland, Washington
www.lwtech.edu                Federal Code: 005373

**2-year public** technical college in large town.
**Enrollment:** 1,651 undergrads, 35% part-time. 239 full-time freshmen.
**Selectivity:** Open admission; but selective for some programs.

### BASIC COSTS (2015-2016)
**Tuition and fees:** $4,461; out-of-state residents $9,864.
**Per-credit charge:** $85; out-of-state residents $206.

### FINANCIAL AID PICTURE
**Students with need:** Need-based aid available for full-time and part-time students.

### FINANCIAL AID PROCEDURES
**Forms required:** FAFSA, institutional form.
**Dates and Deadlines:** Closing date 3/15. Applicants notified on a rolling basis starting 5/1.

### CONTACT
Bill Chaney, Director of Financial Aid
West Building, W201, Kirkland, WA 98034
(425) 739-8119

## Lower Columbia College
Longview, Washington
www.lowercolumbia.edu                Federal Code: 003782

**2-year public** community college in small city.
**Enrollment:** 1,411 undergrads, 40% part-time. 255 full-time freshmen.
**Selectivity:** Open admission; but selective for some programs.

### BASIC COSTS (2015-2016)
**Tuition and fees:** $4,212; out-of-state residents $9,615.
**Per-credit charge:** $85; out-of-state residents $205.
**Additional info:** Tuition/fee waivers available for adults, unemployed or children of unemployed.

### FINANCIAL AID PICTURE
**Students with need:** Need-based aid available for full-time and part-time students.

### FINANCIAL AID PROCEDURES
**Forms required:** FAFSA, institutional form.
**Dates and Deadlines:** Priority date 5/26; no closing date. Applicants notified on a rolling basis starting 4/8; must reply within 2 week(s) of notification.
**Transfers:** State-need grant awards transfer with students if previously awarded at another WA institution; SEOG usually not available to transfer students. Student employment, loans, Pell Grant available.

### CONTACT
Marisa Geier, Director of Financial Aid
1600 Maple Street, Longview, WA 98632-0310
(360) 442-2390

## North Seattle College
Seattle, Washington
www.northseattle.edu                Federal Code: 009704

**2-year public** community college in very large city.
**Enrollment:** 2,356 undergrads, 55% part-time. 318 full-time freshmen.
**Selectivity:** Open admission.

### BASIC COSTS (2015-2016)
**Tuition and fees:** $4,019; out-of-state residents $9,422.

**Per-credit charge:** $85; out-of-state residents $206.
**Additional info:** Tuition/fee waivers available for adults, unemployed or children of unemployed.

### FINANCIAL AID PICTURE (2014-2015)

**Students with need:** 87% of average financial aid package awarded as scholarships/grants, 13% awarded as loans/jobs. Need-based aid available for part-time students. Work study available weekends and for part-time students.

### FINANCIAL AID PROCEDURES

**Forms required:** FAFSA.
**Dates and Deadlines:** Priority date 3/15; closing date 6/30. Applicants notified on a rolling basis starting 6/1; must reply by 9/15.
**Transfers:** Applicants notified on a rolling basis starting 6/1; must reply by 9/15.

### CONTACT

Brianne Sanchez, Director of Financial Aid and Veterans Services
9600 College Way North, Seattle, WA 98103-3599
(206) 934-4706

## Northwest College of Art & Design

Poulsbo, Washington
www.ncad.edu                          Federal Code: 026021

**4-year for-profit** visual arts college in small town.
**Enrollment:** 99 undergrads.

### BASIC COSTS (2015-2016)

**Tuition and fees:** $19,050.
**Per-credit charge:** $800.

### FINANCIAL AID PICTURE

**Students with need:** Need-based aid available for full-time and part-time students.
**Students without need:** No-need awards available for academics, art, state/district residency.

### FINANCIAL AID PROCEDURES

**Forms required:** FAFSA.
**Dates and Deadlines:** Priority date 3/1; closing date 6/1. Applicants notified on a rolling basis.

### CONTACT

Mac Fox, Financial Aid Officer/Title IX Coordinator
16301 Creative Drive NE, Poulsbo, WA 98370-8651
(360) 697-8133

## Northwest Indian College

Bellingham, Washington
www.nwic.edu                          Federal Code: 021800

**2-year public** tribal college in small town.
**Enrollment:** 616 undergrads.
**Selectivity:** Open admission.

### BASIC COSTS (2015-2016)

**Tuition and fees:** $4,455; out-of-state residents $11,079.
**Per-credit charge:** $105; out-of-state residents $289.
**Room and board:** $4,950.
**Additional info:** Tuition/fee waivers available for minority students.

### FINANCIAL AID PICTURE

**Students with need:** Need-based aid available for full-time and part-time students.
**Students without need:** No-need awards available for academics.

### FINANCIAL AID PROCEDURES

**Forms required:** FAFSA, institutional form.
**Dates and Deadlines:** Applicants notified on a rolling basis.
**Transfers:** No deadline. Applicants notified on a rolling basis.

### CONTACT

Raymond Burns, Director of Admissions and Financial Aid
2522 Kwina Road, Bellingham, WA 98226-9217
(360) 676-2772 ext. 4206

## Northwest School of Wooden Boatbuilding

Port Hadlock, Washington
www.nwswb.edu

**1-year private** technical and maritime college in small town.
**Enrollment:** 62 undergrads.
**Selectivity:** Open admission; but selective for some programs.

### BASIC COSTS (2016-2017)

**Tuition and fees:** $14,650.
**Per-credit charge:** $225.
**Additional info:** Tuition information is for 9-month diploma program. 12-month degree program: $19,400.

### FINANCIAL AID PICTURE

**Students with need:** Need-based aid available for full-time students.
**Students without need:** This college awards aid only to students with need.

### FINANCIAL AID PROCEDURES

**Forms required:** FAFSA, institutional form.

### CONTACT

Katie Whalen, Financial Aid Director
42 North Water Street, Port Hadlock, WA 98339

## Northwest University

Kirkland, Washington
www.northwestu.edu                    Federal Code: 003783

**4-year private** university and liberal arts college in small city, affiliated with Assemblies of God.
**Enrollment:** 1,619 undergrads, 22% part-time. 900 full-time freshmen.
**Selectivity:** Admits over 75% of applicants.

### BASIC COSTS (2015-2016)

**Tuition and fees:** $28,086.
**Room and board:** $7,790.

### FINANCIAL AID PICTURE (2014-2015)

**Students with need:** Out of 851 full-time freshmen who applied for aid, 529 were judged to have need. Of these, 479 received aid, and 236 had their full need met. Average financial aid package met 70% of need; average scholarship/grant was $8,691; average loan was $3,297. For part-time students, average financial aid package was $6,066.
**Students without need:** 57 full-time freshmen who did not demonstrate need for aid received scholarships/grants; average award was $6,878. No-need awards available for academics, art, athletics, leadership, music/drama, religious affiliation.
**Scholarships offered:** 12 full-time freshmen received athletic scholarships; average amount $9,594.

### FINANCIAL AID PROCEDURES

**Forms required:** FAFSA, institutional form.
**Dates and Deadlines:** Priority date 2/15; closing date 8/1. Applicants notified on a rolling basis starting 3/3; must reply within 4 week(s) of notification.

**Transfers:** No deadline. Applicants notified on a rolling basis starting 3/30; must reply within 4 week(s) of notification.

## CONTACT

Roger Wilson, Director of Financial Aid
5520 108th Avenue, NE, Kirkland, WA 98083-0579
(425) 889-5210

## Olympic College

Bremerton, Washington
www.olympic.edu                    Federal Code: 003784

**2-year public** community and liberal arts college in large town.
**Enrollment:** 7,881 undergrads.
**Selectivity:** Open admission; but selective for some programs.

### BASIC COSTS (2015-2016)

**Tuition and fees:** $4,521; out-of-state residents $9,924.
**Per-credit charge:** $85; out-of-state residents $206.
**Room only:** $4,500.

### FINANCIAL AID PICTURE

**Students with need:** Need-based aid available for full-time and part-time students. Work study available nights.
**Students without need:** No-need awards available for academics, state/district residency.
**Additional info:** Waivers available for select groups including Fallen Veterans, Children of Deceased or Disabled Law Enforcement Officers, and others.

### FINANCIAL AID PROCEDURES

**Forms required:** FAFSA, institutional form.
**Dates and Deadlines:** Priority date 3/1; no closing date. Applicants notified on a rolling basis starting 6/1; must reply within 2 week(s) of notification.
**Transfers:** No deadline. Applicants notified on a rolling basis starting 1/2.

### CONTACT

Heidi Townsend, Director Student Financial Services
1600 Chester Avenue, Bremerton, WA 98337-1699
(360) 475-7160

## Pacific Lutheran University

Tacoma, Washington
www.plu.edu                         Federal Code: 003785

**4-year private** university in small city, affiliated with Evangelical Lutheran Church in America.
**Enrollment:** 2,809 undergrads, 2% part-time. 642 full-time freshmen.
**Selectivity:** Admits over 75% of applicants.

### BASIC COSTS (2015-2016)

**Tuition and fees:** $37,950.
**Per-credit charge:** $1,175.
**Room and board:** $10,330.

### FINANCIAL AID PICTURE (2015-2016)

**Students with need:** Out of 583 full-time freshmen who applied for aid, 511 were judged to have need. Of these, 509 received aid, and 146 had their full need met. Average financial aid package met 89% of need; average scholarship/grant was $26,137; average loan was $6,776. For part-time students, average financial aid package was $16,284.
**Students without need:** 117 full-time freshmen who did not demonstrate need for aid received scholarships/grants; average award was $19,945. No-need awards available for academics, alumni affiliation, art, leadership, music/drama, religious affiliation, ROTC.

### FINANCIAL AID PROCEDURES

**Forms required:** FAFSA.
**Dates and Deadlines:** Priority date 1/15; no closing date. Applicants notified on a rolling basis starting 3/1; must reply by 5/1 or within 3 week(s) of notification.
**Transfers:** Applicants notified on a rolling basis; must reply by 5/1. Reply by 05/01 but are able to make accommodations if this is not possible.

### CONTACT

Kay Soltis, Director of Financial Aid
12180 Park Ave South, Tacoma, WA 98447-0003
(253) 535-7134

## Peninsula College

Port Angeles, Washington
www.pencol.edu                      Federal Code: 003786

**2-year public** community college in large town.
**Enrollment:** 1,386 undergrads.
**Selectivity:** Open admission; but selective for some programs.

### BASIC COSTS (2015-2016)

**Tuition and fees:** $4,344; out-of-state residents $9,747.
**Per-credit charge:** $85; out-of-state residents $206.
**Additional info:** Tuition/fee waivers available for unemployed or children of unemployed.

### FINANCIAL AID PICTURE

**Students with need:** Need-based aid available for full-time and part-time students.
**Students without need:** No-need awards available for academics, athletics, job skills.

### FINANCIAL AID PROCEDURES

**Forms required:** FAFSA, institutional form.
**Dates and Deadlines:** Closing date 4/1. Applicants notified on a rolling basis starting 6/1; must reply within 2 week(s) of notification.

### CONTACT

Krista Francis, Director of Financial Aid
1502 East Lauridsen Boulevard, Port Angeles, WA 98362
(360) 417-6390

## Pierce College

Lakewood, Washington
www.pierce.ctc.edu                  Federal Code: 005000

**2-year public** community college in small city.
**Enrollment:** 6,805 undergrads.
**Selectivity:** Open admission; but selective for some programs.

### BASIC COSTS (2015-2016)

**Tuition and fees:** $4,187; out-of-state residents $9,590.
**Per-credit charge:** $85; out-of-state residents $206.
**Additional info:** Tuition/fee waivers available for unemployed or children of unemployed.

### FINANCIAL AID PICTURE

**Students with need:** Need-based aid available for full-time and part-time students.
**Students without need:** No-need awards available for academics, athletics, music/drama.

### FINANCIAL AID PROCEDURES

**Forms required:** FAFSA, institutional form.
**Dates and Deadlines:** Closing date 5/1. Applicants notified on a rolling basis starting 4/15.

## CONTACT

Mary Richards, Assistant Financial Aid Director

9401 Farwest Drive SW, Lakewood, WA 98498-1999

(253) 964-6544

## Renton Technical College

Renton, Washington

www.RTC.edu                                    Federal Code: 014001

**2-year public** technical college in large town.

**Enrollment:** 3,359 undergrads.

**Selectivity:** Open admission; but selective for some programs.

### BASIC COSTS (2015-2016)

**Tuition and fees:** $4,161; out-of-state residents $9,564.

**Per-credit charge:** $85; out-of-state residents $206.

### FINANCIAL AID PICTURE

**Students with need:** Need-based aid available for full-time and part-time students.

**Students without need:** This college awards aid only to students with need.

### FINANCIAL AID PROCEDURES

**Forms required:** FAFSA, institutional form.

**Dates and Deadlines:** Priority date 5/1; closing date 7/1. Applicants notified on a rolling basis.

### CONTACT

Debbie Solomon, Director of Financial Aid

3000 NE Fourth Street, Renton, WA 98056-4195

(425) 235-5841

## Saint Martin's University

Lacey, Washington

www.stmartin.edu                              Federal Code: 003794

**4-year private** university in large town, affiliated with Roman Catholic Church.

**Enrollment:** 1,177 undergrads, 16% part-time. 103 full-time freshmen.

**Selectivity:** Admits over 75% of applicants.

### BASIC COSTS (2015-2016)

**Tuition and fees:** $33,194.

**Per-credit charge:** $1,095.

**Room and board:** $10,340.

**Additional info:** Students in Accounting, Business, Computer Science, Engineering, and Nursing classes pay additional $60 per semester credit hour fee.

### FINANCIAL AID PICTURE (2014-2015)

**Students with need:** Out of 99 full-time freshmen who applied for aid, 91 were judged to have need. Of these, 90 received aid, and 28 had their full need met. Average financial aid package met 82% of need; average scholarship/grant was $23,250; average loan was $2,823. For part-time students, average financial aid package was $9,995.

**Students without need:** 12 full-time freshmen who did not demonstrate need for aid received scholarships/grants; average award was $13,393. No-need awards available for academics, alumni affiliation, art, athletics, leadership, minority status, music/drama, religious affiliation, ROTC, state/district residency.

**Scholarships offered:** 16 full-time freshmen received athletic scholarships; average amount $9,962.

### FINANCIAL AID PROCEDURES

**Forms required:** FAFSA.

**Dates and Deadlines:** Priority date 3/1; no closing date. Applicants notified on a rolling basis starting 2/15; must reply within 3 week(s) of notification.

### CONTACT

Michael Grosso, Director, Office of Financial Aid

5000 Abbey Way SE, Lacey, WA 98503-7500

(360) 438-4397

## Seattle Central College

Seattle, Washington

www.seattlecentral.edu                        Federal Code: 003787

**2-year public** community and technical college in very large city.

**Enrollment:** 8,154 undergrads.

**Selectivity:** Open admission; but selective for some programs.

### BASIC COSTS (2015-2016)

**Tuition and fees:** $3,712; out-of-state residents $9,115.

**Per-credit charge:** $78; out-of-state residents $198.

**Additional info:** Tuition/fee waivers available for unemployed or children of unemployed.

### FINANCIAL AID PICTURE

**Students with need:** Need-based aid available for full-time and part-time students. Work study available nights, weekends, and for part-time students.

**Students without need:** This college awards aid only to students with need.

**Additional info:** Currently enrolled international students can apply for institutional scholarship in second year of study.

### FINANCIAL AID PROCEDURES

**Forms required:** FAFSA, institutional form.

**Dates and Deadlines:** Closing date 7/27. Applicants notified on a rolling basis; must reply within 2 week(s) of notification.

### CONTACT

Noel McBride, Assistant Dean, Financial Student Services

1701 Broadway, Seattle, WA 98122

(206) 587-3844

## Seattle Pacific University

Seattle, Washington

www.spu.edu                                   Federal Code: 003788

**4-year private** university in very large city, affiliated with Free Methodist Church of North America.

**Enrollment:** 3,187 undergrads, 3% part-time. 687 full-time freshmen.

**Selectivity:** Admits over 75% of applicants.

### BASIC COSTS (2015-2016)

**Tuition and fees:** $37,086.

**Per-credit charge:** $1,019.

**Room and board:** $10,353.

### FINANCIAL AID PICTURE (2015-2016)

**Students with need:** Out of 611 full-time freshmen who applied for aid, 519 were judged to have need. Of these, 518 received aid, and 39 had their full need met. Average financial aid package met 81% of need; average scholarship/grant was $27,581; average loan was $3,773. For part-time students, average financial aid package was $24,350.

**Students without need:** 149 full-time freshmen who did not demonstrate need for aid received scholarships/grants; average award was $22,805. No-need awards available for academics, alumni affiliation, art, athletics, leadership, minority status, music/drama, religious affiliation, ROTC.

**Scholarships offered:** 8 full-time freshmen received athletic scholarships; average amount $19,765.

**FINANCIAL AID PROCEDURES**
**Forms required:** FAFSA.
**Dates and Deadlines:** Priority date 2/1; no closing date. Applicants notified on a rolling basis starting 3/15; must reply by 5/1 or within 3 week(s) of notification.
**Transfers:** No deadline. Applicants notified on a rolling basis starting 3/13; must reply by 5/1 or within 4 week(s) of notification.

**CONTACT**
Jordan Grant, Director of Financial Aid
3307 Third Avenue West, Suite 115, Seattle, WA 98119-1997
(206) 281-2061

## Seattle University
Seattle, Washington
www.seattleu.edu                Federal Code: 003790

**4-year private** university in very large city, affiliated with Roman Catholic Church.
**Enrollment:** 4,670 undergrads, 5% part-time. 996 full-time freshmen.
**Selectivity:** Admits 50 to 75% of applicants.

**BASIC COSTS (2015-2016)**
**Tuition and fees:** $39,690.
**Per-credit charge:** $866.
**Room and board:** $11,121.

**FINANCIAL AID PICTURE (2015-2016)**
**Students with need:** Out of 846 full-time freshmen who applied for aid, 665 were judged to have need. Of these, 665 received aid, and 81 had their full need met. Average financial aid package met 69% of need; average scholarship/grant was $22,736; average loan was $3,521. For part-time students, average financial aid package was $20,303.
**Students without need:** 91 full-time freshmen who did not demonstrate need for aid received scholarships/grants; average award was $14,655. No-need awards available for academics, alumni affiliation, athletics, leadership, minority status, music/drama, ROTC, state/district residency.
**Scholarships offered:** 45 full-time freshmen received athletic scholarships; average amount $25,251.

**FINANCIAL AID PROCEDURES**
**Forms required:** FAFSA.
**Dates and Deadlines:** Priority date 2/1; no closing date. Applicants notified on a rolling basis; must reply by 5/1 or within 2 week(s) of notification.

**CONTACT**
Jeff Scofield, Director of Student Financial Services
901 12th Avenue, Seattle, WA 98122-4340
(206) 296-2000

## Shoreline Community College
Shoreline, Washington
www.shoreline.edu                Federal Code: 003791

**2-year public** community college in small city.
**Enrollment:** 2,990 undergrads.
**Selectivity:** Open admission; but selective for some programs.

**BASIC COSTS (2015-2016)**
**Tuition and fees:** $4,208; out-of-state residents $9,611.
**Per-credit charge:** $84; out-of-state residents $205.

**FINANCIAL AID PICTURE**
**Students with need:** Work study available nights, weekends, and for part-time students.
**Additional info:** Tuition and/or fee waiver for students with need on space-available basis.

**FINANCIAL AID PROCEDURES**
**Forms required:** FAFSA, institutional form.
**Dates and Deadlines:** Closing date 3/31. Applicants notified on a rolling basis starting 8/1; must reply within 3 week(s) of notification.

**CONTACT**
Ted Haase, Director of Financial Services
16101 Greenwood Avenue North, Seattle, WA 98133
(206) 546-4762

## Skagit Valley College
Mount Vernon, Washington
www.skagit.edu                Federal Code: 003792

**2-year public** community college in large town.
**Enrollment:** 5,977 undergrads.
**Selectivity:** Open admission; but selective for some programs.

**BASIC COSTS (2015-2016)**
**Tuition and fees:** $4,448; out-of-state residents $9,851.
**Per-credit charge:** $85; out-of-state residents $205.
**Additional info:** Tuition/fee waivers available for unemployed or children of unemployed.

**FINANCIAL AID PICTURE**
**Students with need:** Need-based aid available for full-time and part-time students. Work study available nights, weekends, and for part-time students.
**Students without need:** This college awards aid only to students with need.

**FINANCIAL AID PROCEDURES**
**Forms required:** FAFSA, institutional form.
**Dates and Deadlines:** Priority date 5/1; no closing date. Applicants notified on a rolling basis starting 7/1; must reply within 2 week(s) of notification.

**CONTACT**
Crystal Allison, Associate Dean for Financial Aid
2405 East College Way, Mount Vernon, WA 98273
(360) 416-7666

## South Puget Sound Community College
Olympia, Washington
www.spscc.ctc.edu                Federal Code: 005372

**2-year public** community and junior college in small city.
**Enrollment:** 3,585 undergrads.
**Selectivity:** Open admission; but selective for some programs.

**BASIC COSTS (2015-2016)**
**Tuition and fees:** $4,068; out-of-state residents $9,471.
**Per-credit charge:** $85; out-of-state residents $206.

**FINANCIAL AID PICTURE**
**Students with need:** Need-based aid available for full-time and part-time students.
**Students without need:** No-need awards available for academics, athletics.

**FINANCIAL AID PROCEDURES**
**Forms required:** FAFSA, institutional form.
**Dates and Deadlines:** Priority date 5/1; closing date 6/27. Applicants notified on a rolling basis starting 7/10; must reply within 2 week(s) of notification.

**CONTACT**
2011 Mottman Road, SW, Olympia, WA 98512-6218
(360) 596-5232

## South Seattle College

Seattle, Washington
www.southseattle.edu                    Federal Code: 009706

**2-year public** community college in very large city.
**Enrollment:** 3,592 undergrads.
**Selectivity:** Open admission; but selective for some programs.

**BASIC COSTS (2015-2016)**
**Tuition and fees:** $3,901; out-of-state residents $9,304.
**Per-credit charge:** $87; out-of-state residents $207.
**Additional info:** Tuition/fee waivers available for unemployed or children of unemployed.

**FINANCIAL AID PICTURE (2014-2015)**
**Students with need:** Average financial aid package for all full-time undergraduates was $5,392. 92% awarded as scholarships/grants, 8% awarded as loans/jobs. Need-based aid available for part-time students.
**Students without need:** No-need awards available for academics, state/district residency.

**FINANCIAL AID PROCEDURES**
**Forms required:** FAFSA, institutional form.
**Dates and Deadlines:** Priority date 3/15; closing date 5/9. Applicants notified on a rolling basis starting 7/1.

**CONTACT**
Maria Rebecchi, Financial Aid Manager
6000 16th Avenue, SW, Seattle, WA 98106-1499
(206) 934-5317

## Spokane Falls Community College

Spokane, Washington
www.spokanefalls.edu                    Federal Code: 009544

**2-year public** community college in small city.
**Enrollment:** 8,530 undergrads.
**Selectivity:** Open admission; but selective for some programs.

**BASIC COSTS (2015-2016)**
**Tuition and fees:** $4,535; out-of-state residents $9,938.
**Per-credit charge:** $85; out-of-state residents $206.
**Additional info:** Tuition/fee waivers available for unemployed or children of unemployed.

**FINANCIAL AID PICTURE**
**Students with need:** Need-based aid available for full-time and part-time students.
**Students without need:** This college awards aid only to students with need.

**FINANCIAL AID PROCEDURES**
**Forms required:** FAFSA, institutional form.
**Dates and Deadlines:** Priority date 5/13; no closing date. Applicants notified on a rolling basis starting 5/15; must reply within 2 week(s) of notification.

**CONTACT**
Jille Shankar, Associate Dean of Financial Aid and Student Employment
3410 West Fort George Wright Drive, Spokane, WA 99224
(509) 533-3550

## Tacoma Community College

Tacoma, Washington
www.tacomacc.edu                    Federal Code: 003796

**2-year public** community college in small city.
**Enrollment:** 7,384 undergrads.

**Selectivity:** Open admission; but selective for some programs.

**BASIC COSTS (2015-2016)**
**Tuition and fees:** $4,251; out-of-state residents $9,654.
**Per-credit charge:** $85; out-of-state residents $206.
**Additional info:** Tuition/fee waivers available for unemployed or children of unemployed.

**FINANCIAL AID PICTURE**
**Students with need:** Need-based aid available for full-time and part-time students. Work study available nights, weekends, and for part-time students.
**Students without need:** This college awards aid only to students with need.

**FINANCIAL AID PROCEDURES**
**Forms required:** FAFSA, institutional form.
**Dates and Deadlines:** Priority date 3/26; no closing date. Applicants notified on a rolling basis starting 7/20; must reply within 4 week(s) of notification.

**CONTACT**
Kim Matison, Director, Financial Aid Services
6501 South 19th Street, Tacoma, WA 98466-9971
(253) 566-5080

## Trinity Lutheran College

Everett, Washington
www.tlc.edu                    Federal Code: 013525

**4-year private** liberal arts college in small city, affiliated with Lutheran Church.
**Enrollment:** 195 undergrads.

**BASIC COSTS (2015-2016)**
**Tuition and fees:** $29,650.
**Per-credit charge:** $1,208.
**Room only:** $5,800.

**FINANCIAL AID PICTURE**
**Students with need:** Need-based aid available for full-time and part-time students. Work study available nights, weekends, and for part-time students.
**Students without need:** No-need awards available for academics, alumni affiliation, art, athletics, leadership, music/drama, religious affiliation.

**FINANCIAL AID PROCEDURES**
**Forms required:** FAFSA, institutional form.
**Dates and Deadlines:** Closing date 3/1. Applicants notified on a rolling basis starting 3/15; must reply within 2 week(s) of notification.
**Transfers:** No deadline. Applicants notified on a rolling basis starting 3/15; must reply within 2 week(s) of notification.

**CONTACT**
Andrea Paull, Interim Dean of Admissions & Financial Aid
2802 Wetmore Avenue, Everett, WA 98201
(425) 249-4800

## University of Puget Sound

Tacoma, Washington
www.pugetsound.edu                    Federal Code: 003797

**4-year private** university and liberal arts college in small city.
**Enrollment:** 2,476 undergrads, 1% part-time. 652 full-time freshmen.
**Selectivity:** Admits over 75% of applicants.

**BASIC COSTS (2015-2016)**
**Tuition and fees:** $44,976.
**Per-credit charge:** $1,411.
**Room and board:** $11,480.

## FINANCIAL AID PICTURE (2015-2016)

**Students with need:** Out of 490 full-time freshmen who applied for aid, 354 were judged to have need. Of these, 354 received aid, and 65 had their full need met. Average financial aid package met 76% of need; average scholarship/grant was $24,324; average loan was $5,018. Need-based aid available for part-time students.

**Students without need:** 294 full-time freshmen who did not demonstrate need for aid received scholarships/grants; average award was $15,014. No-need awards available for academics, alumni affiliation, art, leadership, music/drama, religious affiliation.

**Scholarships offered:** Alumni, Faculty, Dean's, President's, Trustee Scholarships: all incoming freshman considered; $15,000-$19,000; based on the student's overall admission application, including academic performance in high school and standardized test scores; no separate scholarship application required.

## FINANCIAL AID PROCEDURES

**Forms required:** FAFSA. Students applying for Early Decision must complete the CSS PROFILE for notification of need-based financial aid eligibility.

**Dates and Deadlines:** Priority date 2/1; no closing date. Applicants notified by 3/15; must reply by 5/1 or within 2 week(s) of notification.

**Transfers:** Priority date 3/1; no deadline. Applicants notified on a rolling basis starting 3/15.

## CONTACT

Maggie Mittuch, Associate Vice President of Student Financial Services
1500 North Warner Street, Tacoma, WA 98416-1062
(253) 879-3214

## University of Washington
Seattle, Washington
www.washington.edu                 Federal Code: 003798

**4-year public** university in very large city.
**Enrollment:** 30,022 undergrads, 6% part-time. 6,716 full-time freshmen.
**Selectivity:** Admits 50 to 75% of applicants.

## BASIC COSTS (2015-2016)

**Tuition and fees:** $11,839; out-of-state residents $34,143.
**Per-credit charge:** $359; out-of-state residents $1,102.
**Room and board:** $11,310.

## FINANCIAL AID PICTURE (2015-2016)

**Students with need:** Out of 4,573 full-time freshmen who applied for aid, 2,755 were judged to have need. Of these, 2,572 received aid, and 1,100 had their full need met. Average financial aid package met 82% of need; average scholarship/grant was $15,000; average loan was $5,500. For part-time students, average financial aid package was $12,000.

**Students without need:** 330 full-time freshmen who did not demonstrate need for aid received scholarships/grants; average award was $6,400. No-need awards available for academics, alumni affiliation, art, athletics, leadership, music/drama, ROTC, state/district residency.

**Scholarships offered:** 50 full-time freshmen received athletic scholarships; average amount $10,500.

**Additional info:** Tuition not due until third week of term.

## FINANCIAL AID PROCEDURES

**Forms required:** FAFSA.

**Dates and Deadlines:** Priority date 2/28; no closing date. Applicants notified on a rolling basis starting 4/1; must reply by 5/1 or within 3 week(s) of notification.

**Transfers:** Closing date 2/28.

## CONTACT

Kay Lewis, Director of Student Financial Aid
1410 Northeast Campus Parkway, Box 355852, Seattle, WA 98195-5852
(206) 543-6101

## University of Washington Bothell
Bothell, Washington
www.uwb.edu                 Federal Code: 003798

**4-year public** branch campus college in large town.
**Enrollment:** 4,660 undergrads, 13% part-time. 674 full-time freshmen.
**Selectivity:** Admits over 75% of applicants.

## BASIC COSTS (2015-2016)

**Tuition and fees:** $11,758; out-of-state residents $34,062.
**Per-credit charge:** $376; out-of-state residents $1,119.
**Room and board:** $10,833.

## FINANCIAL AID PICTURE (2015-2016)

**Students with need:** Out of 397 full-time freshmen who applied for aid, 342 were judged to have need. Of these, 321 received aid, and 100 had their full need met. Average financial aid package met 82% of need; average scholarship/grant was $15,000; average loan was $5,500. For part-time students, average financial aid package was $12,000.

**Students without need:** 25 full-time freshmen who did not demonstrate need for aid received scholarships/grants; average award was $5,100. No-need awards available for academics, alumni affiliation, art, athletics, leadership, music/drama, ROTC, state/district residency.

## FINANCIAL AID PROCEDURES

**Forms required:** FAFSA.

**Dates and Deadlines:** Priority date 2/28; no closing date. Applicants notified on a rolling basis starting 4/1; must reply by 5/1 or within 3 week(s) of notification.

## CONTACT

Danette Iyall, Assistant Director, Financial Aid
Box 358500, Enrollment Management, Bothell, WA 98011
(425) 352-5240

## University of Washington Tacoma
Tacoma, Washington
www.tacoma.uw.edu                 Federal Code: 003798

**4-year public** university in small city.
**Enrollment:** 3,884 undergrads, 11% part-time. 447 full-time freshmen.
**Selectivity:** Admits over 75% of applicants.

## BASIC COSTS (2015-2016)

**Tuition and fees:** $11,905; out-of-state residents $34,209.
**Per-credit charge:** $359; out-of-state residents $1,102.
**Room and board:** $10,833.

## FINANCIAL AID PICTURE (2015-2016)

**Students with need:** Out of 397 full-time freshmen who applied for aid, 342 were judged to have need. Of these, 321 received aid, and 100 had their full need met. Average financial aid package met 82% of need; average scholarship/grant was $15,000; average loan was $5,500. For part-time students, average financial aid package was $12,000.

**Students without need:** 25 full-time freshmen who did not demonstrate need for aid received scholarships/grants; average award was $5,100. No-need awards available for academics, alumni affiliation, art, athletics, leadership, music/drama, ROTC, state/district residency.

## FINANCIAL AID PROCEDURES

**Forms required:** FAFSA.

**Dates and Deadlines:** Priority date 2/28; no closing date. Applicants notified by 4/1; must reply by 5/1.

**Transfers:** Applicants notified on a rolling basis starting 11/15.

## CONTACT

Kimberly Fee, Director for Financial Aid and Scholarships
Campus Box 358430, Tacoma, WA 98402-3100
(253) 692-4374

## Walla Walla Community College
Walla Walla, Washington
www.wwcc.edu                    Federal Code: 005006

**2-year public** community and technical college in large town.
**Enrollment:** 6,572 undergrads.
**Selectivity:** Open admission; but selective for some programs.

### BASIC COSTS (2015-2016)
**Tuition and fees:** $4,203; out-of-state residents $9,606.
**Per-credit charge:** $85; out-of-state residents $206.
**Additional info:** Tuition/fee waivers available for unemployed or children of unemployed.

### FINANCIAL AID PICTURE
**Students with need:** Need-based aid available for full-time and part-time students. Work study available nights.
**Students without need:** No-need awards available for academics, athletics, leadership, music/drama.

### FINANCIAL AID PROCEDURES
**Forms required:** FAFSA, institutional form.
**Dates and Deadlines:** Priority date 3/1; no closing date. Applicants notified on a rolling basis starting 6/1; must reply within 2 week(s) of notification.

### CONTACT
Danielle Hodgen, Director of Financial Aid
500 Tausick Way, Walla Walla, WA 99362-9972
(509) 527-4301

## Walla Walla University
College Place, Washington
www.wallawalla.edu              Federal Code: 003799

**4-year private** university and liberal arts college in large town, affiliated with Seventh-day Adventists.
**Enrollment:** 1,622 undergrads, 4% part-time. 346 full-time freshmen.
**Selectivity:** Open admission; but selective for some programs.

### BASIC COSTS (2016-2017)
**Tuition and fees:** $26,982.
**Room and board:** $6,990.

### FINANCIAL AID PICTURE (2014-2015)
**Students with need:** Out of 274 full-time freshmen who applied for aid, 234 were judged to have need. Of these, 234 received aid, and 76 had their full need met. Average financial aid package met 93% of need; average scholarship/grant was $5,433; average loan was $3,127. For part-time students, average financial aid package was $18,067.
**Students without need:** 108 full-time freshmen who did not demonstrate need for aid received scholarships/grants; average award was $9,932. No-need awards available for academics, leadership, music/drama, state/district residency.

### FINANCIAL AID PROCEDURES
**Forms required:** FAFSA, institutional form.
**Dates and Deadlines:** Priority date 4/30; no closing date. Applicants notified on a rolling basis starting 2/15.

### CONTACT
Cassie Ragenovich, Director of Student Financial Services
204 South College Avenue, College Place, WA 99324-3000
(509) 527-2815

## Washington State University
Pullman, Washington
www.wsu.edu                     Federal Code: 003800

**4-year public** university in large town.
**Enrollment:** 24,100 undergrads, 12% part-time. 4,357 full-time freshmen.
**Selectivity:** Admits over 75% of applicants.

### BASIC COSTS (2015-2016)
**Tuition and fees:** $10,916; out-of-state residents $24,516.
**Per-credit charge:** $546; out-of-state residents $1,226.
**Room and board:** $11,356.
**Additional info:** Note that fees vary by campus.

### FINANCIAL AID PICTURE (2014-2015)
**Students with need:** Out of 3,699 full-time freshmen who applied for aid, 2,823 were judged to have need. Of these, 2,659 received aid, and 398 had their full need met. Average financial aid package met 63% of need; average scholarship/grant was $11,772; average loan was $3,516. For part-time students, average financial aid package was $7,801.
**Students without need:** 724 full-time freshmen who did not demonstrate need for aid received scholarships/grants; average award was $3,752. No-need awards available for academics, alumni affiliation, art, athletics, job skills, leadership, minority status, music/drama, religious affiliation, ROTC, state/district residency.
**Scholarships offered:** *Merit:* Regents Scholars Program: Distinguished Regents Scholars receive tuition and fees; Regents Scholars receive $4,000 per year; renewable; based on high school GPA, standardized test scores, community, civic, and co-curricular involvement; educator or tribal council recommendations; residency; 10 Distinguished Regents Scholar awards, number of Regents Scholar awards varies. University Achievement Award: $2,000 to $4,000; granted to Washington high school students who meet GPA and SAT/ACT requirements and apply for freshman admission to Pullman campus by January 31 priority date; renewable for one year. Cougar Academic Award: $4,000 or $9,000 per year; renewable for three years; out-of-state students; based on high school grades, standardized test scores. Lighty Leadership Award: full tuition for out-of-state students; based on academic achievement and community involvement; preference to applicants from Northern California; number varies. National Merit Scholarships: full tuition for up to four years for National Merit semifinalists who list Washington State University as their first choice and enroll fall semester after high school graduation; number varies. *Athletic:* 69 full-time freshmen received athletic scholarships; average amount $28,783.

### FINANCIAL AID PROCEDURES
**Forms required:** FAFSA.
**Dates and Deadlines:** Closing date 1/31. Applicants notified on a rolling basis starting 4/15; must reply within 2 week(s) of notification.
**Transfers:** No deadline. Applicants notified on a rolling basis starting 4/15. Transfer Achievement Award offered to entering transfer students who have already earned their associate degree and are transferring to the Pullman campus. Must be residents of Washington, have a minimum grade point average of 3.0, and demonstrate financial need through the FAFSA. Award is valued at $2,500 and renewable for a second year.

### CONTACT
Brian Dixon, Director of Financial Aid and Scholarships
370 Lighty Student Services Bldg, Pullman, WA 99164-1067
(509) 335-9711

## Wenatchee Valley College
Wenatchee, Washington
www.wvc.edu                     Federal Code: 003801

**2-year public** community college in large town.
**Enrollment:** 2,465 undergrads.

**Selectivity:** Open admission; but selective for some programs.

## BASIC COSTS (2015-2016)
**Tuition and fees:** $3,951; out-of-state residents $9,354.
**Per-credit charge:** $85; out-of-state residents $206.
**Room only:** $3,975.
**Additional info:** Tuition/fee waivers available for adults, unemployed or children of unemployed.

## FINANCIAL AID PICTURE
**Students with need:** Need-based aid available for full-time and part-time students.
**Students without need:** No-need awards available for academics, athletics.

## FINANCIAL AID PROCEDURES
**Forms required:** FAFSA.
**Dates and Deadlines:** Closing date 3/1. Applicants notified by 7/2; must reply within 3 week(s) of notification.
**Transfers:** Priority date 3/1. Applicants notified on a rolling basis.

## CONTACT
Kevin Berg, Financial Aid Director
1300 Fifth Street, Wenatchee, WA 98801-1799
(509) 682-6845

# Western Washington University
Bellingham, Washington
www.wwu.edu                    Federal Code: 003802

**4-year public** university in small city.
**Enrollment:** 14,336 undergrads, 8% part-time. 2,783 full-time freshmen.
**Selectivity:** Admits over 75% of applicants.

## BASIC COSTS (2015-2016)
**Tuition and fees:** $8,611; out-of-state residents $20,963.
**Room and board:** $10,342.
**Additional info:** Tuition/fee waivers available for adults, minority students.

## FINANCIAL AID PICTURE (2015-2016)
**Students with need:** Out of 2,298 full-time freshmen who applied for aid, 1,522 were judged to have need. Of these, 1,484 received aid, and 333 had their full need met. Average financial aid package met 87% of need; average scholarship/grant was $9,297; average loan was $3,804. For part-time students, average financial aid package was $11,710.
**Students without need:** 73 full-time freshmen who did not demonstrate need for aid received scholarships/grants; average award was $2,141. No-need awards available for academics, alumni affiliation, art, athletics, job skills, leadership, minority status, music/drama, state/district residency.
**Scholarships offered:** 21 full-time freshmen received athletic scholarships; average amount $6,054.
**Additional info:** Short-term student loans ranging from $100 to $1,000 available on a quarterly basis.

## FINANCIAL AID PROCEDURES
**Forms required:** FAFSA.
**Dates and Deadlines:** Priority date 2/15; no closing date. Applicants notified on a rolling basis starting 3/20; must reply by 5/11 or within 3 week(s) of notification.
**Transfers:** No deadline. Applicants notified on a rolling basis starting 3/20; must reply within 3 week(s) of notification. Some state aid not available for out-of-state transfer students.

## CONTACT
Jim DeWilde, Associate Director of Financial Aid
516 High Street, Bellingham, WA 98225-9009
(360) 650-3470

# Whatcom Community College
Bellingham, Washington
www.whatcom.ctc.edu            Federal Code: 010364

**2-year public** community college in small city.
**Enrollment:** 4,020 full-time undergrads.
**Selectivity:** Open admission; but selective for some programs.

## BASIC COSTS (2015-2016)
**Tuition and fees:** $4,400; out-of-state residents $9,803.
**Per-credit charge:** $85; out-of-state residents $206.

## FINANCIAL AID PICTURE
**Students with need:** Need-based aid available for full-time and part-time students. Work study available nights.
**Students without need:** No-need awards available for academics, athletics, state/district residency.

## FINANCIAL AID PROCEDURES
**Forms required:** FAFSA, institutional form.
**Dates and Deadlines:** Closing date 4/1. Applicants notified on a rolling basis starting 7/1; must reply within 3 week(s) of notification.

## CONTACT
David Klaffke, Director of Financial Aid
237 West Kellogg Road, Bellingham, WA 98226
(360) 383-3010

# Whitman College
Walla Walla, Washington         Federal Code: 003803
www.whitman.edu                 CSS Code: 4951

**4-year private** liberal arts college in large town.
**Enrollment:** 1,444 undergrads, 1% part-time. 364 full-time freshmen.
**Selectivity:** Admits less than 50% of applicants.

## BASIC COSTS (2015-2016)
**Tuition and fees:** $46,138.
**Per-credit charge:** $1,907.
**Room and board:** $11,564.

## FINANCIAL AID PICTURE (2015-2016)
**Students with need:** Out of 237 full-time freshmen who applied for aid, 183 were judged to have need. Of these, 183 received aid, and 89 had their full need met. Average financial aid package met 96% of need; average scholarship/grant was $33,224; average loan was $4,453. For part-time students, average financial aid package was $37,135.
**Students without need:** 90 full-time freshmen who did not demonstrate need for aid received scholarships/grants; average award was $9,751. No-need awards available for academics, art, minority status, music/drama.

## FINANCIAL AID PROCEDURES
**Forms required:** FAFSA, CSS PROFILE.
**Dates and Deadlines:** Priority date 11/15; closing date 2/1. Applicants notified by 4/1; must reply by 5/1.
**Transfers:** Closing date 3/1. Applicants notified by 4/22; must reply by 5/15.

## CONTACT
Tony Cabasco, Dean of Admission and Financial Aid
345 Boyer Avenue, Walla Walla, WA 99362-2046
(509) 527-5178

# Whitworth University
Spokane, Washington
www.whitworth.edu              Federal Code: 003804

**4-year private** university and liberal arts college in large city, affiliated with Presbyterian Church (USA).

**Enrollment:** 2,320 undergrads, 1% part-time. 583 full-time freshmen.
**Selectivity:** Admits 50 to 75% of applicants.

### BASIC COSTS (2015-2016)
**Tuition and fees:** $39,096.
**Per-credit charge:** $1,590.
**Room and board:** $10,714.
**Additional info:** Tuition/fee waivers available for minority students.

### FINANCIAL AID PICTURE (2015-2016)
**Students with need:** Out of 513 full-time freshmen who applied for aid, 443 were judged to have need. Of these, 441 received aid, and 72 had their full need met. Average financial aid package met 81% of need; average scholarship/grant was $26,608; average loan was $4,249. For part-time students, average financial aid package was $20,642.
**Students without need:** 133 full-time freshmen who did not demonstrate need for aid received scholarships/grants; average award was $18,616. No-need awards available for academics, alumni affiliation, art, minority status, music/drama, ROTC.
**Scholarships offered:** Mind & Heart Scholarship: $22,000 per year for four years; 3.75 GPA and 2020 SAT/30 ACT. Presidential Scholarship: $20,000 per year for four years; 4.0 GPA regardless of test scores or 3.75 GPA and 1870 SAT/28 ACT. Trustee Scholarship: $18,000 per year for four years; 3.9 GPA regardless of test scores or 3.6 GPA and 1800 SAT/27 ACT. Whitworth Scholarship: $16,000 per year for four years; 3.5 GPA regardless of test scores or 1720 SAT/25 ACT. Founder's Scholarship: $14,000 per year for four years; 3.4-3.49 GPA regardless of test scores or 1650 SAT/24 ACT.

### FINANCIAL AID PROCEDURES
**Forms required:** FAFSA.
**Dates and Deadlines:** Priority date 3/1; no closing date. Applicants notified on a rolling basis starting 3/15.
**Transfers:** Priority date 4/1; no deadline. Applicants notified on a rolling basis starting 3/15.

### CONTACT
Traci Stensland, Director of Financial Aid
300 West Hawthorne Road, Spokane, WA 99251-0002
(509) 777-3215

## Yakima Valley Community College
Yakima, Washington
www.yvcc.edu                          Federal Code: 003805

**2-year public** community college in small city.
**Enrollment:** 4,105 undergrads.
**Selectivity:** Open admission; but selective for some programs.

### BASIC COSTS (2015-2016)
**Tuition and fees:** $4,319; out-of-state residents $9,722.
**Per-credit charge:** $85; out-of-state residents $206.
**Additional info:** Tuition/fee waivers available for unemployed or children of unemployed.

### FINANCIAL AID PICTURE
**Students with need:** Need-based aid available for full-time and part-time students. Work study available nights, weekends, and for part-time students.
**Students without need:** No-need awards available for athletics.

### FINANCIAL AID PROCEDURES
**Forms required:** FAFSA.
**Dates and Deadlines:** Closing date 4/15. Applicants notified on a rolling basis starting 8/1; must reply within 2 week(s) of notification.
**Transfers:** Priority date 4/15; no deadline. Applicants notified on a rolling basis starting 8/1; must reply within 2 week(s) of notification.

### CONTACT
Janet Cantelon, Director, Office of Student Financial Aid
PO Box 22520, Yakima, WA 98907-2520
(509) 574-6855

# West Virginia

## Alderson-Broaddus University
Philippi, West Virginia
www.ab.edu                           Federal Code: 003806

**4-year private** liberal arts college in small town, affiliated with American Baptist Churches in the USA.
**Enrollment:** 1,066 undergrads, 2% part-time. 333 full-time freshmen.
**Selectivity:** Admits 50 to 75% of applicants.

### BASIC COSTS (2015-2016)
**Tuition and fees:** $24,140.
**Per-credit charge:** $798.
**Room and board:** $7,606.

### FINANCIAL AID PICTURE (2015-2016)
**Students with need:** Out of 317 full-time freshmen who applied for aid, 289 were judged to have need. Of these, 289 received aid, and 79 had their full need met. Average financial aid package met 91% of need; average scholarship/grant was $18,841; average loan was $3,526. For part-time students, average financial aid package was $7,553.
**Students without need:** 33 full-time freshmen who did not demonstrate need for aid received scholarships/grants; average award was $10,727. No-need awards available for academics, athletics, music/drama, state/district residency.
**Scholarships offered:** *Merit:* IMPACT Scholarship: $15,000; 25 ACT or 1150 SAT and 3.5 GPA required for consideration; 5 awards. *Athletic:* 16 full-time freshmen received athletic scholarships; average amount $14,943.

### FINANCIAL AID PROCEDURES
**Forms required:** FAFSA, state aid form.
**Dates and Deadlines:** Priority date 3/1; no closing date. Applicants notified on a rolling basis starting 3/1; must reply within 2 week(s) of notification.

### CONTACT
Amy King, Director of Financial Aid
101 College Hill Drive, Philippi, WV 26416
(304) 457-6354

## American National University: Princeton
Princeton, West Virginia
www.an.edu                           Federal Code: 003726

**2-year for-profit** business college in small city.
**Enrollment:** 104 undergrads.
**Selectivity:** Open admission.

### BASIC COSTS (2016-2017)
**Tuition and fees:** $14,460.
**Per-credit charge:** $317.

### FINANCIAL AID PICTURE
**Students with need:** Need-based aid available for full-time and part-time students.
**Students without need:** This college awards aid only to students with need.

### FINANCIAL AID PROCEDURES
**Forms required:** FAFSA.
**Dates and Deadlines:** Applicants notified on a rolling basis starting 9/1.

### CONTACT
Pam Cotton, Director of Financial Aid Compliance and Auditing
421 Hilltop Drive, Princeton, WV 24739

## American Public University System
Charles Town, West Virginia
www.apus.edu                    Federal Code: 038193

**4-year for-profit** virtual university in small town.
**Enrollment:** 40,833 undergrads, 91% part-time. 309 full-time freshmen.
**Selectivity:** Open admission.

### BASIC COSTS (2015-2016)
**Tuition and fees:** $8,100.
**Per-credit charge:** $270.
**Additional info:** Required technology fee of $50 per course.

### FINANCIAL AID PICTURE (2014-2015)
**Students with need:** Out of 286 full-time freshmen who applied for aid, 285 were judged to have need. Of these, 284 received aid. Average financial aid package met 53% of need; average scholarship/grant was $2,502; average loan was $1,732. For part-time students, average financial aid package was $2,615.
**Additional info:** Students should complete a Federal Student Aid Intent Form and register for classes at least 37 days prior to start to allow sufficient time for financial aid process.

### FINANCIAL AID PROCEDURES
**Forms required:** FAFSA, institutional form.
**Dates and Deadlines:** Applicants notified on a rolling basis starting 3/1.
**Transfers:** Must reply within 2 week(s) of notification. Students should ensure that financial aid is processed and confirmed at least 10-14 days prior to beginning a semester.

### CONTACT
Keith Wellings, Vice President, Financial Aid and Compliance
111 West Congress Street, Charles Town, WV 25414
(877) 777-9081

## Appalachian Bible College
Mount Hope, West Virginia
https://abc.edu                    Federal Code: 007544

**4-year private** Bible college in large town, affiliated with nondenominational tradition.
**Enrollment:** 173 undergrads, 3% part-time. 34 full-time freshmen.

### BASIC COSTS (2015-2016)
**Tuition and fees:** $13,590.
**Per-credit charge:** $355.
**Room and board:** $7,350.

### FINANCIAL AID PICTURE
**Students with need:** Need-based aid available for full-time and part-time students.
**Students without need:** No-need awards available for leadership.
**Scholarships offered:** Christian Workers' Children Scholarship: $4,000 per year; maintain 2.75 GPA for renewal. Church Matching Scholarship: Totals up to $5,000 per year; based on church endorsement. Scholastic Achievement Scholarship: $1,000 per year; based on 24 ACT or 1650 SAT.

### FINANCIAL AID PROCEDURES
**Forms required:** FAFSA, state aid form, institutional form.
**Dates and Deadlines:** Priority date 6/15; closing date 9/15. Applicants notified on a rolling basis starting 1/15.
**Transfers:** Applicants notified on a rolling basis starting 1/15.

### CONTACT
Deana Steinke, Director of Financial Aid
Director of Admissions, Mount Hope, WV 25880
(304) 877-6428 ext. 321

## Bethany College
Bethany, West Virginia
www.bethanywv.edu                    Federal Code: 003808

**4-year private** liberal arts college in rural community, affiliated with Christian Church (Disciples of Christ).
**Enrollment:** 700 undergrads, 1% part-time. 208 full-time freshmen.
**Selectivity:** Admits 50 to 75% of applicants.

### BASIC COSTS (2015-2016)
**Tuition and fees:** $26,500.
**Per-credit charge:** $1,065.
**Room and board:** $9,800.

### FINANCIAL AID PICTURE (2015-2016)
**Students with need:** Out of 208 full-time freshmen who applied for aid, 191 were judged to have need. Of these, 191 received aid, and 34 had their full need met. Average financial aid package met 81% of need; average scholarship/grant was $9,532; average loan was $4,753. For part-time students, average financial aid package was $16,841.
**Students without need:** No-need awards available for academics, alumni affiliation, leadership, music/drama, religious affiliation, state/district residency.
**Additional info:** Scholarships available for travel program.

### FINANCIAL AID PROCEDURES
**Forms required:** FAFSA.
**Dates and Deadlines:** Priority date 3/1; no closing date. Applicants notified on a rolling basis starting 2/15; must reply within 2 week(s) of notification.
**Transfers:** No deadline.

### CONTACT
Jason McClain, Director of Financial Aid
Office of Enrollment, Bethany, WV 26032-0428
(304) 829-7611

## Blue Ridge Community and Technical College
Martinsburg, West Virginia
www.blueridgectc.edu                    Federal Code: 039573

**2-year public** community and technical college in small city.
**Enrollment:** 2,016 undergrads, 47% part-time. 265 full-time freshmen.
**Selectivity:** Open admission.

### BASIC COSTS (2015-2016)
**Tuition and fees:** $3,696; out-of-state residents $6,456.
**Per-credit charge:** $144; out-of-state residents $278.

### FINANCIAL AID PICTURE
**Students with need:** Need-based aid available for full-time and part-time students.

### FINANCIAL AID PROCEDURES
**Forms required:** FAFSA.
**Dates and Deadlines:** Applicants notified on a rolling basis; must reply within 2 week(s) of notification.

### CONTACT
Director of Financial Aid
13650 Apple Harvest Drive, Martinsburg, WV 25403
(304) 260-4380 ext. 2105

## Bluefield State College
Bluefield, West Virginia
www.bluefieldstate.edu                  Federal Code: 003809

**4-year public** liberal arts and technical college in large town.
**Enrollment:** 1,486 undergrads, 18% part-time. 267 full-time freshmen.
**Selectivity:** Admits over 75% of applicants.

**BASIC COSTS (2015-2016)**
**Tuition and fees:** $6,120; out-of-state residents $11,280.
**Per-credit charge:** $254; out-of-state residents $468.
**Additional info:** Tuition for students residing in bordering counties is $8,700.

**FINANCIAL AID PICTURE (2015-2016)**
**Students with need:** Out of 255 full-time freshmen who applied for aid, 223 were judged to have need. Of these, 223 received aid, and 20 had their full need met. Average financial aid package met 59% of need; average scholarship/grant was $3,507; average loan was $3,424. For part-time students, average financial aid package was $2,891.
**Students without need:** 19 full-time freshmen who did not demonstrate need for aid received scholarships/grants; average award was $1,311. No-need awards available for academics, athletics.
**Scholarships offered:** 8 full-time freshmen received athletic scholarships; average amount $1,463.

**FINANCIAL AID PROCEDURES**
**Forms required:** FAFSA, institutional form.
**Dates and Deadlines:** Priority date 3/1; no closing date. Applicants notified on a rolling basis starting 6/1.
**Transfers:** No deadline.

**CONTACT**
Tom Ilse, Director of Financial Aid
219 Rock Street, Bluefield, WV 24701
(304) 327-4020

## Concord University
Athens, West Virginia
www.concord.edu                  Federal Code: 003810

**4-year public** university and liberal arts college in small town.
**Enrollment:** 2,250 undergrads.

**BASIC COSTS (2015-2016)**
**Tuition and fees:** $6,744; out-of-state residents $14,824.
**Per-credit charge:** $281; out-of-state residents $618.
**Room and board:** $8,668.

**FINANCIAL AID PICTURE (2015-2016)**
**Students with need:** Average financial aid package met 90% of need; average scholarship/grant was $4,781; average loan was $2,596. For part-time students, average financial aid package was $6,211.
**Students without need:** No-need awards available for academics, alumni affiliation, leadership.
**Additional info:** March 1 priority deadline for state forms. April 15 priority deadline for FAFSA.

**FINANCIAL AID PROCEDURES**
**Forms required:** FAFSA.
**Dates and Deadlines:** Priority date 3/1; no closing date. Applicants notified on a rolling basis starting 5/1; must reply within 2 week(s) of notification.

**CONTACT**
Debra Turner, Director of Financial Aid
PO Box 1000, Athens, WV 24712-1000
(304) 384-6069

## Davis and Elkins College
Elkins, West Virginia
www.dewv.edu                  Federal Code: 003811

**4-year private** liberal arts college in small town, affiliated with Presbyterian Church (USA).
**Enrollment:** 874 undergrads.

**BASIC COSTS (2015-2016)**
**Tuition and fees:** $27,842.
**Room and board:** $9,250.

**FINANCIAL AID PICTURE**
**Students with need:** Need-based aid available for full-time and part-time students. Work study available nights, weekends, and for part-time students.
**Students without need:** No-need awards available for academics, alumni affiliation, art, athletics, leadership, music/drama, religious affiliation, state/district residency.
**Scholarships offered:** Highlands Scholarship Program: $14,000 for residential students; $11,000 for commuter students; for freshmen students from surrounding seven counties with at least 2.5 GPA.

**FINANCIAL AID PROCEDURES**
**Forms required:** FAFSA.
**Dates and Deadlines:** Priority date 3/1; closing date 8/1. Applicants notified on a rolling basis; must reply by 8/30.
**Transfers:** Applicants notified on a rolling basis; must reply by 8/30.

**CONTACT**
Matthew Summers, Director of Financial Planning
100 Campus Drive, Elkins, WV 26241-3996
(304) 637-1990

## Eastern West Virginia Community and Technical College
Moorefield, West Virginia
www.easternwv.edu

**2-year public** community and technical college in rural community.
**Enrollment:** 526 undergrads.
**Selectivity:** Open admission.

**FINANCIAL AID PICTURE**
**Students with need:** Need-based aid available for full-time and part-time students.

**FINANCIAL AID PROCEDURES**
**Forms required:** FAFSA, institutional form.
**Dates and Deadlines:** Priority date 6/1; no closing date. Applicants notified on a rolling basis; must reply within 2 week(s) of notification.

**CONTACT**
Amanda Sites, Director of Financial Aid
316 Eastern Drive, Moorefield, WV 26836
(304) 434-8000

## Fairmont State University
Fairmont, West Virginia
www.fairmontstate.edu                  Federal Code: 003812

**4-year public** university in large town.
**Enrollment:** 3,707 undergrads, 13% part-time. 680 full-time freshmen.
**Selectivity:** Admits 50 to 75% of applicants.

**BASIC COSTS (2015-2016)**
**Tuition and fees:** $6,620; out-of-state residents $13,970.

**Per-credit charge:** $268; out-of-state residents $574.
**Room and board:** $8,766.
**Additional info:** Tuition/fee waivers available for adults, minority students.

**FINANCIAL AID PICTURE (2014-2015)**
**Students with need:** Out of 661 full-time freshmen who applied for aid, 510 were judged to have need. Of these, 499 received aid, and 52 had their full need met. Average financial aid package met 72% of need; average scholarship/grant was $6,596; average loan was $3,015. For part-time students, average financial aid package was $4,792.
**Students without need:** This college awards aid only to students with need.
**Scholarships offered:** 17 full-time freshmen received athletic scholarships; average amount $5,315.

**FINANCIAL AID PROCEDURES**
**Forms required:** FAFSA.
**Dates and Deadlines:** Closing date 3/1. Applicants notified on a rolling basis starting 4/1; must reply within 2 week(s) of notification.
**Transfers:** Academic transcripts required.

**CONTACT**
Patricia Weimer, Director of Financial Aid and Scholarships
Office of Admissions, Fairmont, WV 26554-2470
(304) 367-4213

## Glenville State College
Glenville, West Virginia
www.glenville.edu                    Federal Code: 003813

**4-year public** liberal arts and teachers college in small town.
**Enrollment:** 1,243 undergrads, 16% part-time. 287 full-time freshmen.
**Selectivity:** Admits 50 to 75% of applicants.

**BASIC COSTS (2015-2016)**
**Tuition and fees:** $7,032; out-of-state residents $15,888.
**Per-credit charge:** $293; out-of-state residents $662.
**Additional info:** Tuition for students in residing in border counties is $11,472.

**FINANCIAL AID PICTURE**
**Students with need:** Need-based aid available for full-time and part-time students. Work study available nights, weekends, and for part-time students.
**Students without need:** No-need awards available for academics, athletics, music/drama, state/district residency.

**FINANCIAL AID PROCEDURES**
**Forms required:** FAFSA.
**Dates and Deadlines:** Priority date 2/1; no closing date. Applicants notified on a rolling basis starting 3/1; must reply within 3 week(s) of notification.

**CONTACT**
Karen Lay, Director of Financial Aid
200 High Street, Glenville, WV 26351-1292
(304) 462-4103

## Marshall University
Huntington, West Virginia
www.marshall.edu                    Federal Code: 003815

**4-year public** university in small city.
**Enrollment:** 8,780 undergrads, 10% part-time. 1,900 full-time freshmen.
**Selectivity:** Admits over 75% of applicants.

**BASIC COSTS (2015-2016)**
**Tuition and fees:** $6,814; out-of-state residents $15,602.
**Per-credit charge:** $238.75; out-of-state residents $605.

**Room and board:** $9,832.

**FINANCIAL AID PICTURE (2015-2016)**
**Students with need:** Out of 1,831 full-time freshmen who applied for aid, 1,383 were judged to have need. Of these, 1,371 received aid, and 428 had their full need met. Average financial aid package met 49% of need; average scholarship/grant was $6,685; average loan was $5,416. For part-time students, average financial aid package was $5,099.
**Students without need:** 323 full-time freshmen who did not demonstrate need for aid received scholarships/grants; average award was $2,419. No-need awards available for academics, alumni affiliation, art, athletics, minority status, music/drama, ROTC, state/district residency.
**Scholarships offered:** *Merit:* Michael Perry Scholarship: $500 based on 3.2 GPA and 20 ACT; $750 based on 3.5 GPA and 23 ACT, or 3.2 GPA and 25 ACT; one-year only. Presidential Scholarship: $1,250; 3.5 GPA and 25 ACT; renewable with 3.5 GPA. John Marshall Scholarship: tuition waiver plus $1,250 stipend; 3.5 GPA and 30 ACT; renewable yearly with 3.5 GPA. Yeager scholarship: full tuition and fees; full room and board; book allowance; stipend; personal computer for use during program; $4,000 toward study abroad; 28 ACT/1260 SAT (exclusive of Writing). *Athletic:* 91 full-time freshmen received athletic scholarships; average amount $11,365.

**FINANCIAL AID PROCEDURES**
**Forms required:** FAFSA, state aid form.
**Dates and Deadlines:** Priority date 3/1; no closing date. Applicants notified on a rolling basis starting 4/1.
**Transfers:** Priority date 1/1.

**CONTACT**
Kathy Bialk, Director of Financial Aid
One John Marshall Drive, Huntington, WV 25755
(304) 696-3162

## Mountain State College
Parkersburg, West Virginia
www.msc.edu                    Federal Code: 005008

**2-year for-profit** junior and career college in large town.
**Enrollment:** 189 undergrads.
**Selectivity:** Open admission.

**FINANCIAL AID PICTURE**
**Students with need:** Work study available nights, weekends, and for part-time students.

**FINANCIAL AID PROCEDURES**
**Forms required:** FAFSA.
**Dates and Deadlines:** Applicants notified on a rolling basis.

**CONTACT**
Faye Wagoner, Director of Student Financial Services
1508 Spring Street, Parkersburg, WV 26101-3993
(304) 485-5487

## Ohio Valley University
Vienna, West Virginia
www.ovu.edu                    Federal Code: 003819

**4-year private** university and liberal arts college in small city, affiliated with Church of Christ.
**Enrollment:** 411 undergrads, 5% part-time. 101 full-time freshmen.
**Selectivity:** Admits less than 50% of applicants.

**BASIC COSTS (2015-2016)**
**Tuition and fees:** $19,840.
**Per-credit charge:** $530.

**Room and board:** $7,220.

## FINANCIAL AID PICTURE (2014-2015)

**Students with need:** Out of 93 full-time freshmen who applied for aid, 88 were judged to have need. Of these, 86 received aid, and 19 had their full need met. Average financial aid package met 70% of need; average scholarship/grant was $11,523; average loan was $3,320. Need-based aid available for part-time students.

**Students without need:** 8 full-time freshmen who did not demonstrate need for aid received scholarships/grants; average award was $4,718. No-need awards available for academics, athletics, leadership, music/drama, state/district residency.

**Scholarships offered:** 13 full-time freshmen received athletic scholarships; average amount $8,073.

## FINANCIAL AID PROCEDURES

**Forms required:** FAFSA.

**Dates and Deadlines:** Priority date 2/15; no closing date. Applicants notified on a rolling basis starting 3/1; must reply within 4 week(s) of notification.

**Transfers:** No deadline. Applicants notified on a rolling basis starting 3/15; must reply within 4 week(s) of notification.

## CONTACT

Dennis Cox, Director of Student Financial Services
One Campus View Drive, Vienna, WV 26105
(304) 865-6081

## Potomac State College of West Virginia University

Keyser, West Virginia
www.potomacstatecollege.edu          Federal Code: 003829

**2-year public** branch campus and junior college in small town.

**Enrollment:** 1,224 undergrads, 6% part-time. 581 full-time freshmen.

**Selectivity:** Open admission; but selective for out-of-state students.

## BASIC COSTS (2015-2016)

**Tuition and fees:** $3,864; out-of-state residents $10,080.

**Room and board:** $8,476.

**Additional info:** Tuition for students residing in border counties is $6,240.

## FINANCIAL AID PICTURE

**Students with need:** Need-based aid available for full-time and part-time students.

**Students without need:** No-need awards available for academics, athletics.

## FINANCIAL AID PROCEDURES

**Forms required:** FAFSA.

**Dates and Deadlines:** Priority date 3/1; no closing date. Applicants notified on a rolling basis starting 3/15; must reply within 2 week(s) of notification.

**Transfers:** Applicants notified on a rolling basis starting 3/1; must reply within 3 week(s) of notification.

## CONTACT

Harlan Shreve, Chief Business Officer
75 Arnold Street, Keyser, WV 26726
(304) 788-6820

## Salem International University

Salem, West Virginia
www.salemu.edu          Federal Code: 003820

**4-year for-profit** university and liberal arts college in rural community.

**Enrollment:** 402 undergrads.

## BASIC COSTS (2015-2016)

**Additional info:** Certificate programs: $20,925-$25,740, room and board $7,000. Associate programs: $35,400-$47,190, room and board $14,000. Bachelor's programs: $35,400-$70,800, room and board $14,000-$28,000.

## FINANCIAL AID PICTURE

**Students with need:** Need-based aid available for full-time and part-time students. Work study available nights, weekends, and for part-time students.

**Students without need:** No-need awards available for academics.

**Scholarships offered:** Scholarships; extensive amount awarded; based on high school GPA, standardized test scores. Breed-related awards; for students in equine career and industry management program. Awards for GED diploma recipients; based on academic excellence.

## FINANCIAL AID PROCEDURES

**Forms required:** FAFSA.

**Dates and Deadlines:** Priority date 4/15; no closing date. Applicants notified on a rolling basis starting 2/15; must reply within 4 week(s) of notification.

**Transfers:** Priority date 3/1; closing date 4/15. Applicants notified on a rolling basis starting 3/1.

## CONTACT

Marty Mehringer, Vice President for Financial Aid and Compliance
223 West Main Street, Salem, WV 26426

## Shepherd University

Shepherdstown, West Virginia
www.shepherd.edu          Federal Code: 003822

**4-year public** university in small town.

**Enrollment:** 3,320 undergrads, 12% part-time. 631 full-time freshmen.

**Selectivity:** Admits over 75% of applicants.

## BASIC COSTS (2015-2016)

**Tuition and fees:** $6,830; out-of-state residents $16,628.

**Per-credit charge:** $278; out-of-state residents $687.

**Room and board:** $9,682.

**Additional info:** Tuition/fee waivers available for minority students.

## FINANCIAL AID PICTURE (2015-2016)

**Students with need:** Out of 616 full-time freshmen who applied for aid, 430 were judged to have need. Of these, 421 received aid, and 133 had their full need met. Average financial aid package met 78% of need; average scholarship/grant was $5,559; average loan was $3,299. For part-time students, average financial aid package was $10,746.

**Students without need:** 159 full-time freshmen who did not demonstrate need for aid received scholarships/grants; average award was $10,721. No-need awards available for academics, art, athletics, job skills, leadership, minority status, music/drama, state/district residency.

**Scholarships offered:** 70 full-time freshmen received athletic scholarships; average amount $6,074.

## FINANCIAL AID PROCEDURES

**Forms required:** FAFSA, state aid form.

**Dates and Deadlines:** Priority date 3/1; no closing date. Applicants notified on a rolling basis starting 3/15; must reply within 3 week(s) of notification.

**Transfers:** No deadline. Applicants notified on a rolling basis starting 11/1; must reply within 3 week(s) of notification.

## CONTACT

Joyce Cabral, Director of Financial Aid
PO Box 5000, Shepherdstown, WV 25443-5000
(304) 876-5470

## Southern West Virginia Community and Technical College

Mount Gay, West Virginia
www.southernwv.edu                    Federal Code: 003816

**2-year public** community and technical college in small town.
**Enrollment:** 2,002 undergrads.
**Selectivity:** Open admission; but selective for some programs.

**BASIC COSTS (2015-2016)**
**Tuition and fees:** $3,582; out-of-state residents $5,298.
**Per-credit charge:** $133; out-of-state residents $202.

**FINANCIAL AID PICTURE**
**Students with need:** Need-based aid available for full-time and part-time students.

**FINANCIAL AID PROCEDURES**
**Forms required:** FAFSA.
**Dates and Deadlines:** Applicants notified on a rolling basis.

**CONTACT**
August Kafer, Financial Aid Director
PO Box 2900, Mount Gay, WV 25637
(304) 896-7382

## University of Charleston

Charleston, West Virginia
www.ucwv.edu                          Federal Code: 003818

**4-year private** university in small city.
**Enrollment:** 1,706 undergrads, 24% part-time. 316 full-time freshmen.
**Selectivity:** Admits 50 to 75% of applicants.

**BASIC COSTS (2015-2016)**
**Tuition and fees:** $27,100.
**Room and board:** $9,100.

**FINANCIAL AID PICTURE**
**Students with need:** Need-based aid available for full-time and part-time students. Work study available nights, weekends, and for part-time students.
**Students without need:** No-need awards available for academics, alumni affiliation, art, athletics, leadership, music/drama, ROTC.
**Additional info:** All university tuition discounts (scholarships) based on family or student need and talent. Higher need awards given to middle and lower income students.

**FINANCIAL AID PROCEDURES**
**Forms required:** FAFSA, state aid form, institutional form.
**Dates and Deadlines:** Priority date 3/1; closing date 8/15. Applicants notified on a rolling basis starting 3/1; must reply by 5/1 or within 4 week(s) of notification.
**Transfers:** Applicants notified on a rolling basis starting 4/1; must reply by 5/1 or within 4 week(s) of notification.

**CONTACT**
Nina Morton, Director of Financial Aid
2300 MacCorkle Avenue, SE, Charleston, WV 25304
(304) 357-4947

## Valley College

Martinsburg, West Virginia
www.valley.edu                        Federal Code: G26094

**2-year for-profit** career college in large town.
**Enrollment:** 140 undergrads.

**Selectivity:** Open admission.

**FINANCIAL AID PICTURE**
**Students with need:** Need-based aid available for full-time and part-time students.

**FINANCIAL AID PROCEDURES**
**Forms required:** FAFSA, institutional form.
**Dates and Deadlines:** Applicants notified on a rolling basis.
**Transfers:** No deadline. Applicants notified on a rolling basis.

**CONTACT**
Kellie Thayer, Director of Financial Aid
287 Aikens Center, Martinsburg, WV 25404
(304) 263-0979

## West Liberty University

West Liberty, West Virginia
www.westliberty.edu                   Federal Code: 003823

**4-year public** university in rural community.
**Enrollment:** 2,013 undergrads, 8% part-time. 403 full-time freshmen.
**Selectivity:** Admits 50 to 75% of applicants.

**BASIC COSTS (2015-2016)**
**Tuition and fees:** $6,702; out-of-state residents $14,112.
**Per-credit charge:** $273; out-of-state residents $581.75.
**Room and board:** $8,810.

**FINANCIAL AID PICTURE**
**Students with need:** Need-based aid available for full-time and part-time students. Work study available nights, weekends, and for part-time students.
**Students without need:** No-need awards available for academics, alumni affiliation, art, athletics, music/drama, state/district residency.
**Additional info:** Non-need based student employment available at food service, college union, bookstore, and tutoring office. Resident assistant and campus security jobs also available.

**FINANCIAL AID PROCEDURES**
**Forms required:** FAFSA.
**Dates and Deadlines:** Priority date 3/1; no closing date. Applicants notified on a rolling basis starting 3/1; must reply within 2 week(s) of notification.
**Transfers:** Financial aid transcript required from all previous colleges attended regardless of whether aid was received.

**CONTACT**
Katie Cooper, Director of Financial Aid
208 University Drive, West Liberty, WV 26074
(304) 336-8016

## West Virginia Junior College

Morgantown, West Virginia
www.wvjc.edu                          Federal Code: 005007

**2-year for-profit** junior college in large town.
**Enrollment:** 291 undergrads.
**Selectivity:** Open admission.

**BASIC COSTS (2015-2016)**
**Additional info:** Associate programs: $25,250, books and supplies $420.

**FINANCIAL AID PICTURE**
**Students with need:** Need-based aid available for full-time and part-time students.

**FINANCIAL AID PROCEDURES**
**Forms required:** FAFSA.
**Dates and Deadlines:** Applicants notified on a rolling basis.

**CONTACT**
Patricia Callen, Executive Director
148 Willey Street, Morgantown, WV 26505

## West Virginia Junior College: Bridgeport
Bridgeport, West Virginia
www.wvjc.edu                       Federal Code: 010573

**2-year for-profit** health science and junior college in large town.
**Enrollment:** 188 undergrads.
**Selectivity:** Open admission; but selective for some programs.

**BASIC COSTS (2015-2016)**
**Additional info:** Diploma programs: $16,850-$20,282, books and supplies
$280. Associate programs: $25,250, books and supplies $420.

**FINANCIAL AID PICTURE**
**Students with need:** Need-based aid available for full-time and part-time students.

**FINANCIAL AID PROCEDURES**
**Forms required:** FAFSA, state aid form.

**CONTACT**
Frances Jenkins, Financial Aid Director
176 Thompson Drive, Bridgeport, WV 26330
(304) 842-4007 ext. 105

## West Virginia Junior College: Charleston
Charleston, West Virginia
www.wvjc.edu                       Federal Code: 010573

**2-year for-profit** junior and career college in small city.
**Enrollment:** 213 undergrads.
**Selectivity:** Open admission.

**BASIC COSTS (2015-2016)**
**Additional info:** Diploma programs: $16,850-$20,282, books and supplies
$280. Associate programs: $25,250, books and supplies $420.

**FINANCIAL AID PICTURE**
**Students with need:** Need-based aid available for full-time and part-time students.

**FINANCIAL AID PROCEDURES**
**Forms required:** FAFSA.
**Dates and Deadlines:** Applicants notified on a rolling basis.

**CONTACT**
Katherine Barnes, Financial Aid Director
1000 Virginia Street East, Charleston, WV 25301

## West Virginia Northern Community College
Wheeling, West Virginia
www.wvncc.edu                      Federal Code: 010920

**2-year public** community and technical college in large town.
**Enrollment:** 1,429 undergrads, 43% part-time. 285 full-time freshmen.
**Selectivity:** Open admission; but selective for some programs.

**BASIC COSTS (2015-2016)**
**Tuition and fees:** $3,275; out-of-state residents $9,875.
**Additional info:** Tuition/fee waivers available for adults.

**FINANCIAL AID PICTURE (2014-2015)**
**Students with need:** 75% of average financial aid package awarded as
scholarships/grants, 25% awarded as loans/jobs. Need-based aid available
for part-time students.

**FINANCIAL AID PROCEDURES**
**Forms required:** FAFSA, institutional form.
**Dates and Deadlines:** Priority date 3/15; no closing date. Applicants notified
on a rolling basis starting 3/10.

**CONTACT**
Janet Fike, Vice President of Student Services/Director of Financial Aid
1704 Market Street, Wheeling, WV 26003
(304) 214-8844

## West Virginia State University
Institute, West Virginia
www.wvstateu.edu                   Federal Code: 003826

**4-year public** liberal arts and teachers college in small town.
**Enrollment:** 2,033 undergrads, 11% part-time. 356 full-time freshmen.
**Selectivity:** Admits over 75% of applicants.

**BASIC COSTS (2015-2016)**
**Tuition and fees:** $6,662; out-of-state residents $15,572.
**Per-credit charge:** $273; out-of-state residents $644.
**Room and board:** $10,806.
**Additional info:** Tuition for students residing in bordering counties is
$12,156.

**FINANCIAL AID PICTURE**
**Students with need:** Need-based aid available for full-time and part-time students. Work study available nights, weekends, and for part-time students.
**Students without need:** No-need awards available for academics, athletics,
ROTC, state/district residency.

**FINANCIAL AID PROCEDURES**
**Dates and Deadlines:** Applicants notified on a rolling basis.
**Transfers:** Closing date 6/30. Applicants notified on a rolling basis starting
3/1; must reply within 2 week(s) of notification.

**CONTACT**
JoAnn Ross, Director of Financial Aid
124 Ferrell Hall, Institute, WV 25112-1000
(304) 204-4369

## West Virginia University
Morgantown, West Virginia
www.wvu.edu                        Federal Code: 003827

**4-year public** university in small city.
**Enrollment:** 21,580 undergrads, 5% part-time. 4,948 full-time freshmen.
**Selectivity:** Admits over 75% of applicants.

**BASIC COSTS (2015-2016)**
**Tuition and fees:** $7,632; out-of-district residents $7,632; out-of-state residents $21,432.
**Room and board:** $9,872.

**FINANCIAL AID PICTURE (2014-2015)**
**Students with need:** Out of 4,305 full-time freshmen who applied for aid,
2,939 were judged to have need. Of these, 2,883 received aid, and 617 had
their full need met. Average financial aid package met 72% of need; average
scholarship/grant was $4,814; average loan was $2,826. For part-time students, average financial aid package was $4,969.

PART III: FINANCIAL AID COLLEGE BY COLLEGE

**Students without need:** 910 full-time freshmen who did not demonstrate need for aid received scholarships/grants; average award was $2,382. No-need awards available for academics, alumni affiliation, art, athletics, job skills, leadership, minority status, music/drama, religious affiliation, ROTC, state/district residency.
**Scholarships offered:** 64 full-time freshmen received athletic scholarships; average amount $20,863.

**FINANCIAL AID PROCEDURES**
**Forms required:** FAFSA, state aid form.
**Dates and Deadlines:** Closing date 3/1. Applicants notified on a rolling basis starting 3/15; must reply within 2 week(s) of notification.
**Transfers:** Applicants notified on a rolling basis starting 4/1; must reply within 4 week(s) of notification. Transfer scholarship available to those students who apply by 7/1 and transfer minimum of 15 hours with 3.0 GPA.

**CONTACT**
Sandra Oerly-Bennett, Executive Director of Financial Aid
Office of Admissions, Morgantown, WV 26506-6009
(800) 344-9881

## West Virginia University at Parkersburg
Parkersburg, West Virginia
www.wvup.edu          Federal Code: 003828

**2-year public** community college in large town.
**Enrollment:** 3,800 undergrads.
**Selectivity:** Open admission; but selective for some programs.

**BASIC COSTS (2015-2016)**
**Tuition and fees:** $3,660; out-of-state residents $13,020.

**FINANCIAL AID PICTURE**
**Students with need:** Need-based aid available for full-time and part-time students. Work study available nights, weekends, and for part-time students.
**Students without need:** No-need awards available for academics, leadership, state/district residency.

**FINANCIAL AID PROCEDURES**
**Forms required:** FAFSA.
**Dates and Deadlines:** Priority date 3/1; no closing date. Applicants notified on a rolling basis; must reply within 2 week(s) of notification.

**CONTACT**
August Kafer, Director of Financial Aid
300 Campus Drive, Parkersburg, WV 26104-8647
(304) 424-8210

## West Virginia University Institute of Technology
Montgomery, West Virginia
www.wvutech.edu          Federal Code: 003825

**4-year public** engineering and liberal arts college in small town.
**Enrollment:** 1,116 undergrads, 12% part-time. 299 full-time freshmen.
**Selectivity:** Admits 50 to 75% of applicants.

**BASIC COSTS (2015-2016)**
**Tuition and fees:** $7,632; out-of-state residents $21,432.
**Per-credit charge:** $318; out-of-state residents $893.
**Room and board:** $9,872.

**FINANCIAL AID PICTURE (2014-2015)**
**Students with need:** Out of 258 full-time freshmen who applied for aid, 204 were judged to have need. Of these, 204 received aid, and 61 had their

full need met. Average financial aid package met 7% of need; average scholarship/grant was $5,394; average loan was $2,532. For part-time students, average financial aid package was $4,588.
**Students without need:** 19 full-time freshmen who did not demonstrate need for aid received scholarships/grants; average award was $1,992. No-need awards available for academics, alumni affiliation, art, athletics, job skills, leadership, minority status, music/drama, ROTC, state/district residency.
**Scholarships offered:** *Merit:* Academic scholarships; students meeting academic criteria will receive scholarship/tuition waiver offer; renewable each year upon meeting the stated requirements. *Athletic:* 5 full-time freshmen received athletic scholarships; average amount $1,350.

**FINANCIAL AID PROCEDURES**
**Forms required:** FAFSA.
**Dates and Deadlines:** Closing date 3/1. Applicants notified on a rolling basis starting 3/15; must reply within 2 week(s) of notification.
**Transfers:** No deadline. Applicants notified on a rolling basis starting 3/21; must reply within 4 week(s) of notification.

**CONTACT**
Michael White, Director of Financial Aid Services
405 Fayette Pike, Montgomery, WV 25136-2436
(304) 442-3140

## West Virginia Wesleyan College
Buckhannon, West Virginia
www.wvwc.edu          Federal Code: 003830

**4-year private** liberal arts college in small town, affiliated with United Methodist Church.
**Enrollment:** 1,371 undergrads, 1% part-time. 392 full-time freshmen.
**Selectivity:** Admits over 75% of applicants.

**BASIC COSTS (2015-2016)**
**Tuition and fees:** $28,992.
**Room and board:** $8,066.

**FINANCIAL AID PICTURE (2015-2016)**
**Students with need:** 77% of average financial aid package awarded as scholarships/grants, 23% awarded as loans/jobs. Need-based aid available for part-time students. Work study available nights, weekends, and for part-time students.
**Students without need:** No-need awards available for academics, alumni affiliation, art, athletics, leadership, music/drama, religious affiliation.

**FINANCIAL AID PROCEDURES**
**Forms required:** FAFSA.
**Dates and Deadlines:** Priority date 2/15; no closing date. Applicants notified on a rolling basis starting 3/1; must reply within 4 week(s) of notification.
**Transfers:** No deadline. Applicants notified on a rolling basis starting 3/15; must reply within 4 week(s) of notification. Financial aid transcripts required from all institutions previously attended.

**CONTACT**
Susan George, Director of Financial Aid
59 College Avenue, Buckhannon, WV 26201-2998
(304) 473-8080

## Wheeling Jesuit University
Wheeling, West Virginia
www.wju.edu          Federal Code: 003831

**4-year private** university and liberal arts college in small city, affiliated with Roman Catholic Church.
**Enrollment:** 1,131 undergrads.

## BASIC COSTS (2015-2016)
**Tuition and fees:** $28,030.
**Room and board:** $7,070.

## FINANCIAL AID PICTURE (2015-2016)
**Students with need:** Average financial aid package met 93% of need; average scholarship/grant was $9,997; average loan was $4,457. For part-time students, average financial aid package was $3,146.
**Students without need:** No-need awards available for academics, alumni affiliation, athletics, music/drama, religious affiliation.

## FINANCIAL AID PROCEDURES
**Forms required:** FAFSA.
**Dates and Deadlines:** Priority date 3/1; closing date 8/1. Applicants notified on a rolling basis starting 3/10; must reply within 2 week(s) of notification.
**Transfers:** No deadline. Applicants notified on a rolling basis starting 3/10; must reply within 2 week(s) of notification. Academic scholarships available to qualified transfer students.

## CONTACT
Christie Tomczyk, Director of Financial Aid
316 Washington Avenue, Wheeling, WV 26003-6295
(304) 243-2304

# Wisconsin

## Alverno College
Milwaukee, Wisconsin
www.alverno.edu                    Federal Code: 003832

**4-year private** liberal arts college for women in very large city, affiliated with Roman Catholic Church.
**Enrollment:** 1,528 undergrads, 23% part-time. 225 full-time freshmen.
**Selectivity:** Admits 50 to 75% of applicants.

## BASIC COSTS (2015-2016)
**Tuition and fees:** $25,660.
**Per-credit charge:** $1,041.
**Room and board:** $7,634.

## FINANCIAL AID PICTURE (2015-2016)
**Students with need:** Out of 214 full-time freshmen who applied for aid, 203 were judged to have need. Of these, 203 received aid. For part-time students, average financial aid package was $14,766.
**Students without need:** 16 full-time freshmen who did not demonstrate need for aid received scholarships/grants; average award was $11,625. No-need awards available for academics, alumni affiliation.
**Scholarships offered:** Four-year academic scholarships: range from $20,000 to $66,000. Clare Scholarships: $12,000 for four years or $48,000. Must be from a high school that is part of the Archdiocese of Milwaukee, GPA of 2.8 or higher, replaces four-year academic scholarship.

## FINANCIAL AID PROCEDURES
**Forms required:** FAFSA.
**Dates and Deadlines:** Priority date 3/1; no closing date. Applicants notified on a rolling basis starting 3/1; must reply within 2 week(s) of notification.
**Transfers:** No deadline. Applicants notified on a rolling basis; must reply within 2 week(s) of notification. Transfer students are eligible for academic scholarships.

## CONTACT
Amy Christen, Director of Financial Aid
3400 South 43rd Street, Milwaukee, WI 53234-3922
(414) 382-6046

## Bellin College
Green Bay, Wisconsin
www.bellincollege.edu              Federal Code: 006639

**4-year private** Nursing + Health Sciences in small city.
**Enrollment:** 315 undergrads, 36% part-time. 27 full-time freshmen.
**Selectivity:** Admits over 75% of applicants.

## BASIC COSTS (2016-2017)
**Tuition and fees:** $21,140.
**Per-credit charge:** $998.

## FINANCIAL AID PICTURE (2014-2015)
**Students with need:** Average financial aid package for all full-time undergraduates was $20,892; for part-time $17,452. 36% awarded as scholarships/grants, 64% awarded as loans/jobs. Work study available nights, weekends, and for part-time students.
**Students without need:** No-need awards available for academics.
**Scholarships offered:** Academic Scholarship: $10,000-40,000 renewable conditionally. Spread over length of enrollment; based on high school GPA, ACT scores or transfer GPA.
**Additional info:** Freshmen and sophomores receive aid through University of Wisconsin-Green Bay. Juniors and seniors receive aid through Bellin College. All aid stats reflect only those enrolled students receiving aid through Bellin College. Bellin College does not award federal and state aid to first-time full time freshman. Those students receive aid through UWGB.

## FINANCIAL AID PROCEDURES
**Forms required:** FAFSA.
**Dates and Deadlines:** Priority date 3/1; no closing date. Applicants notified on a rolling basis starting 4/1; must reply within 2 week(s) of notification.
**Transfers:** Priority date 3/1; no deadline. Applicants notified on a rolling basis starting 4/1; must reply within 2 week(s) of notification.

## CONTACT
Lena Goodman, Director of Financial Aid
3201 Eaton Road, Green Bay, WI 54311
(920) 433-6638

## Beloit College
Beloit, Wisconsin
www.beloit.edu                     Federal Code: 003835

**4-year private** liberal arts college in large town.
**Enrollment:** 1,271 undergrads. 392 full-time freshmen.
**Selectivity:** Admits 50 to 75% of applicants.

## BASIC COSTS (2015-2016)
**Tuition and fees:** $45,050.
**Per-credit charge:** $1,394.
**Room and board:** $7,890.

## FINANCIAL AID PICTURE (2015-2016)
**Students with need:** Out of 316 full-time freshmen who applied for aid, 274 were judged to have need. Of these, 274 received aid, and 85 had their full need met. Average financial aid package met 95% of need; average scholarship/grant was $31,060; average loan was $5,354.
**Students without need:** 112 full-time freshmen who did not demonstrate need for aid received scholarships/grants; average award was $23,659. No-need awards available for academics, leadership, minority status, music/drama.
**Scholarships offered:** Presidential Scholarships: $18,000-$25,000 per year; Eaton Scholarships: $10,000-$18,000 per year; The American Field Service/Rotary Overseas/Youth for Understanding/U.S Citizens Living Overseas: $5,000 per year; The Charles Winter Wood Scholarship for underrepresented students: Up to $40,000 per year; The Founders Scholarship for National Merit Finalists: $5,000 per year; Music scholarships: $5,000 per year.

**FINANCIAL AID PROCEDURES**

**Forms required:** FAFSA. PROFILE required for early decision/early action applicants only.

**Dates and Deadlines:** Priority date 3/1; closing date 3/1. Applicants notified on a rolling basis starting 3/1; must reply by 5/1.

**Transfers:** No deadline. Applicants notified on a rolling basis starting 4/1; must reply by 5/1 or within 2 week(s) of notification.

**CONTACT**

Jon Urish, Director of Student Financial Services

700 College Street, Beloit, WI 53511-5595

(608) 363-2663

## Blackhawk Technical College

Janesville, Wisconsin

www.blackhawk.edu                Federal Code: 005390

**2-year public** technical college in small city.

**Enrollment:** 2,249 undergrads, 58% part-time. 208 full-time freshmen.

**Selectivity:** Open admission; but selective for some programs.

**BASIC COSTS (2015-2016)**

**Tuition and fees:** $4,045; out-of-state residents $5,971.

**Per-credit charge:** $128; out-of-state residents $193.

**Additional info:** Material fees vary by program: Minimum $4.50 per course. $10 per credit for online courses.

**FINANCIAL AID PICTURE (2014-2015)**

**Students with need:** 54% of average financial aid package awarded as scholarships/grants, 46% awarded as loans/jobs. Need-based aid available for part-time students. Work study available nights.

**FINANCIAL AID PROCEDURES**

**Forms required:** FAFSA.

**Dates and Deadlines:** Closing date 4/30. Applicants notified on a rolling basis starting 3/15.

**CONTACT**

Deena Wettstein, Director of Financial Aid

PO Box 5009, Janesville, WI 53547-5009

(608) 757-7664

## Bryant & Stratton College: Milwaukee

Milwaukee, Wisconsin

www.bryantstratton.edu            Federal Code: 005009

**2-year for-profit** business and junior college in very large city.

**Enrollment:** 1,266 undergrads.

**BASIC COSTS (2015-2016)**

**Tuition and fees:** $17,190.

**Per-credit charge:** $573.

**Additional info:** Tuition and fees may vary by program.

**FINANCIAL AID PICTURE**

**Students with need:** Work study available nights.

**Students without need:** This college awards aid only to students with need.

**FINANCIAL AID PROCEDURES**

**Forms required:** FAFSA.

**Dates and Deadlines:** Closing date 9/22. Applicants notified on a rolling basis; must reply within 2 week(s) of notification.

**CONTACT**

Robert Hoffman, Financial Aid Manager

310 West Wisconsin Avenue, Suite 500, Milwaukee, WI 53203

(414) 276-5200

## Cardinal Stritch University

Milwaukee, Wisconsin

www.stritch.edu                  Federal Code: 003837

**4-year private** university in very large city, affiliated with Roman Catholic Church.

**Enrollment:** 1,971 undergrads, 11% part-time. 159 full-time freshmen.

**Selectivity:** Admits over 75% of applicants.

**BASIC COSTS (2015-2016)**

**Tuition and fees:** $27,540.

**Per-credit charge:** $840.

**Room and board:** $7,700.

**FINANCIAL AID PICTURE (2015-2016)**

**Students with need:** Out of 130 full-time freshmen who applied for aid, 117 were judged to have need. Of these, 117 received aid, and 17 had their full need met. Average financial aid package met 83% of need; average scholarship/grant was $22,011; average loan was $3,328. For part-time students, average financial aid package was $7,018.

**Students without need:** 42 full-time freshmen who did not demonstrate need for aid received scholarships/grants; average award was $19,575. No-need awards available for academics, alumni affiliation, art, athletics, music/drama, religious affiliation.

**Scholarships offered:** 18 full-time freshmen received athletic scholarships; average amount $5,463.

**FINANCIAL AID PROCEDURES**

**Forms required:** FAFSA.

**Dates and Deadlines:** Priority date 3/15; no closing date. Applicants notified on a rolling basis starting 2/19; must reply within 2 week(s) of notification.

**CONTACT**

Mark Quistorf, Director of Financial Aid

6801 North Yates Road, Box 516, Milwaukee, WI 53217-7516

(414) 410-4048

## Carroll University

Waukesha, Wisconsin

www.carrollu.edu                 Federal Code: 003838

**4-year private** university and liberal arts college in small city, affiliated with Presbyterian Church (USA).

**Enrollment:** 3,021 undergrads.

**BASIC COSTS (2015-2016)**

**Tuition and fees:** $29,535.

**Per-credit charge:** $370.

**Room and board:** $9,032.

**FINANCIAL AID PICTURE**

**Students with need:** Need-based aid available for full-time and part-time students. Work study available nights, weekends, and for part-time students.

**Students without need:** No-need awards available for academics, alumni affiliation, art, leadership, music/drama, ROTC.

**FINANCIAL AID PROCEDURES**

**Forms required:** FAFSA.

**Dates and Deadlines:** Applicants notified on a rolling basis starting 2/15; must reply by 5/1 or within 2 week(s) of notification.

**Transfers:** No deadline. Applicants notified on a rolling basis starting 2/15.

**CONTACT**

Dawn Scott, Director of Student Financial Services

100 North East Avenue, Waukesha, WI 53186-9988

(262) 524-7296

## Carthage College

Kenosha, Wisconsin
www.carthage.edu                    Federal Code: 003839

**4-year private** liberal arts college in small city, affiliated with Evangelical Lutheran Church in America.
**Enrollment:** 2,863 undergrads, 8% part-time. 751 full-time freshmen.
**Selectivity:** Admits 50 to 75% of applicants.

### BASIC COSTS (2015-2016)
**Tuition and fees:** $38,375.
**Room and board:** $10,460.
**Additional info:** Tuition/fee waivers available for minority students.

### FINANCIAL AID PICTURE
**Students with need:** Need-based aid available for full-time and part-time students.
**Students without need:** No-need awards available for academics, alumni affiliation, art, leadership, minority status, music/drama, religious affiliation.
**Scholarships offered:** Presidential Scholarship Program: range from 75% tuition to full tuition; room and board; renewable; separate scholarship application; 35 awarded. Business Scholarship: three awarded; range from $27,000/year to full tuition; renewable; requires separate scholarship application; restricted to accounting, finance, management and marketing majors. Multicultural Scholarship: four awarded; full tuition; renewable; requires separate scholarship application. Math/Science Scholarship: three awarded; range from $27,000/year to full tuition; renewable; requires separate scholarship application; restricted to math and natural science majors. Modern Language Scholarship: eight awarded; $27,000/year; renewable; requires separate scholarship application; restricted to Chinese, French, German and Japanese majors. Fine Arts Scholarships: $500-$10,000/year; renewable; requires separate audition/portfolio; open to majors and non majors in music and theater and majors in studio art or graphic design. Tarble Scholarships: number awarded variable; up to $25,000 year; renewable; requires separate scholarship application; restricted to California residents.

### FINANCIAL AID PROCEDURES
**Forms required:** FAFSA.
**Dates and Deadlines:** Priority date 2/15; no closing date. Applicants notified on a rolling basis starting 3/1.
**Transfers:** Priority date 2/15; no deadline. Applicants notified on a rolling basis starting 3/1.

### CONTACT
Vatistas Vatistas, Director of Financial Aid
2001 Alford Park Drive, Kenosha, WI 53140-1994
(262) 551-6001

## Chippewa Valley Technical College

Eau Claire, Wisconsin
www.cvtc.edu                        Federal Code: 005304

**2-year public** technical college in small city.
**Enrollment:** 4,197 undergrads, 53% part-time. 538 full-time freshmen.
**Selectivity:** Open admission; but selective for some programs.

### BASIC COSTS (2015-2016)
**Tuition and fees:** $4,102; out-of-state residents $6,028.
**Per-credit charge:** $128; out-of-state residents $193.

### FINANCIAL AID PICTURE (2014-2015)
**Students with need:** Need-based aid available for full-time and part-time students. Work study available nights, weekends, and for part-time students.

### FINANCIAL AID PROCEDURES
**Forms required:** FAFSA.
**Dates and Deadlines:** Priority date 3/15; no closing date. Applicants notified on a rolling basis starting 4/30; must reply within 2 week(s) of notification.

### CONTACT
Barbara Cloutier, Financial Aid Manager
620 West Clairemont Avenue, Eau Claire, WI 54701-6162
(715) 833-6252

## College of Menominee Nation

Keshena, Wisconsin
www.menominee.edu                   Federal Code: 031251

**2-year private** community college in rural community.
**Enrollment:** 661 undergrads.
**Selectivity:** Open admission; but selective for some programs.

### BASIC COSTS (2015-2016)
**Tuition and fees:** $7,600.
**Room and board:** $6,800.

### FINANCIAL AID PICTURE
**Students with need:** Need-based aid available for full-time and part-time students. Work study available nights.
**Students without need:** This college awards aid only to students with need.

### FINANCIAL AID PROCEDURES
**Forms required:** FAFSA.
**Dates and Deadlines:** Priority date 4/15; no closing date. Applicants notified on a rolling basis.
**Transfers:** No deadline. Applicants notified on a rolling basis.

### CONTACT
Nicole Fish, Financial Aid Director
N 172 State Highway 47/55, Keshena, WI 54135-1179
(715) 799-5600 ext. 3039

## Columbia College of Nursing

Glendale, Wisconsin
www.ccon.edu                        Federal Code: 041594

**4-year private** nursing college in very large city.
**Enrollment:** 150 undergrads, 13% part-time.

### BASIC COSTS (2015-2016)
**Tuition and fees:** $27,330.
**Per-credit charge:** $795.

### FINANCIAL AID PICTURE (2015-2016)
**Students with need:** Average financial aid package for all full-time undergraduates was $11,039; for part-time $10,586. 34% awarded as scholarships/grants, 66% awarded as loans/jobs.
**Students without need:** No-need awards available for academics.

### FINANCIAL AID PROCEDURES
**Forms required:** FAFSA. CCON is an upper division school and all students are junior or senior level students and 100% of student body transfers in.
**Dates and Deadlines:** Priority date 4/15; no closing date. Applicants notified on a rolling basis starting 4/15; must reply by 6/1.
**Transfers:** No deadline. Applicants notified on a rolling basis starting 3/1; must reply by 6/1.

### CONTACT
Wendy Hilvo, Financial Aid Director
4425 North Port Washington Road, Glendale, WI 53212-1099
(414) 326-2337

## Concordia University Wisconsin
Mequon, Wisconsin
www.cuw.edu                    Federal Code: 003842

**4-year private** university and liberal arts college in large town, affiliated with Lutheran Church - Missouri Synod.
**Enrollment:** 4,057 undergrads, 26% part-time. 619 full-time freshmen.
**Selectivity:** Admits 50 to 75% of applicants.

### BASIC COSTS (2015-2016)
**Tuition and fees:** $26,900.
**Room and board:** $9,980.

### FINANCIAL AID PICTURE (2015-2016)
**Students with need:** Out of 589 full-time freshmen who applied for aid, 505 were judged to have need. Of these, 505 received aid, and 160 had their full need met. Average financial aid package met 80% of need; average scholarship/grant was $15,624; average loan was $7,191. For part-time students, average financial aid package was $6,083.
**Students without need:** 108 full-time freshmen who did not demonstrate need for aid received scholarships/grants; average award was $12,354. No-need awards available for academics, art, minority status, music/drama.

### FINANCIAL AID PROCEDURES
**Forms required:** FAFSA.
**Dates and Deadlines:** Priority date 3/15; closing date 4/15. Applicants notified on a rolling basis starting 2/15; must reply within 3 week(s) of notification.

### CONTACT
Steve Taylor, Director of Financial Aid
12800 North Lake Shore Drive, Mequon, WI 53097
(262) 243-4392

## Edgewood College
Madison, Wisconsin
www.edgewood.edu               Federal Code: 003848

**4-year private** liberal arts college in small city, affiliated with Roman Catholic Church.
**Enrollment:** 1,758 undergrads, 12% part-time. 301 full-time freshmen.
**Selectivity:** Admits over 75% of applicants.

### BASIC COSTS (2015-2016)
**Tuition and fees:** $26,550.
**Per-credit charge:** $835.
**Room and board:** $9,400.

### FINANCIAL AID PICTURE (2014-2015)
**Students with need:** Out of 276 full-time freshmen who applied for aid, 239 were judged to have need. Of these, 239 received aid, and 29 had their full need met. Average financial aid package met 78% of need; average scholarship/grant was $16,868; average loan was $4,421. For part-time students, average financial aid package was $7,287.
**Students without need:** 56 full-time freshmen who did not demonstrate need for aid received scholarships/grants; average award was $7,140. No-need awards available for academics, alumni affiliation, art, leadership, music/drama, religious affiliation.
**Scholarships offered:** Alumni Award: $500-$1,500. Bonner Leaders Award: $1,000-$2,000. Capital City Award: $500-$2,000. College Access Award: $500-$2,000. Community Scholars Award: full tuition. Cor Ad Cor Award: $500-$3,000. Friends of Northern Wisconsin Award: $500-$3,000. Forward Wisconsin Award: $500-$3,000. Mazzuchelli Award: $500-$2,000. Predolin Scholarship: $4,000-$6,000. Talent Scholarships: $1000-$3,000. Voyager Scholarship: $500-$4,000. Aspiring Writer Scholarship: $1,000-$3,000. Fine Arts Scholarship in Art: $1,000-$3,000. Fine Arts Scholarship in Music:

$1,000-$3,000. Fine Arts Scholarship in Theatre: $1,000-$3,000. World Languages Scholarship: $1,000-$3,000.

### FINANCIAL AID PROCEDURES
**Forms required:** FAFSA.
**Dates and Deadlines:** Priority date 3/1; no closing date. Applicants notified on a rolling basis starting 3/15; must reply by 5/1.
**Transfers:** Priority date 3/1; no deadline. Applicants notified on a rolling basis starting 3/15; must reply by 5/1 or within 2 week(s) of notification. Transfer Partnership Award (Half Tuition for the Academic Year) available.

### CONTACT
Kari Gribble, Director of Edgewood Central and Financial Aid
1000 Edgewood College Drive, Madison, WI 53711-1997
(608) 663-4300

## Fox Valley Technical College
Appleton, Wisconsin
www.fvtc.edu                   Federal Code: 009744

**2-year public** technical college in small city.
**Enrollment:** 6,621 undergrads, 63% part-time. 409 full-time freshmen.
**Selectivity:** Open admission; but selective for some programs.

### BASIC COSTS (2015-2016)
**Tuition and fees:** $4,373; out-of-state residents $6,299.
**Per-credit charge:** $128; out-of-state residents $193.

### FINANCIAL AID PICTURE (2014-2015)
**Students with need:** 44% of average financial aid package awarded as scholarships/grants, 56% awarded as loans/jobs. Need-based aid available for part-time students. Work study available weekends and for part-time students.
**Students without need:** This college awards aid only to students with need.

### FINANCIAL AID PROCEDURES
**Forms required:** FAFSA.
**Dates and Deadlines:** Priority date 4/15; no closing date. Applicants notified on a rolling basis.

### CONTACT
Stacy Doran, Director Student Financial Services
1825 North Bluemound Drive, Appleton, WI 54912-2277
(920) 735-5650

## Gateway Technical College
Kenosha, Wisconsin
www.gtc.edu                    Federal Code: 005389

**2-year public** technical college in small city.
**Enrollment:** 6,291 undergrads.
**Selectivity:** Open admission; but selective for some programs.

### BASIC COSTS (2015-2016)
**Tuition and fees:** $4,176; out-of-state residents $6,102.
**Per-credit charge:** $128; out-of-state residents $193.

### FINANCIAL AID PICTURE
**Students with need:** Need-based aid available for full-time and part-time students.
**Students without need:** No-need awards available for state/district residency.

### FINANCIAL AID PROCEDURES
**Forms required:** FAFSA, institutional form.
**Dates and Deadlines:** Priority date 7/1; no closing date. Applicants notified on a rolling basis starting 5/1; must reply within 2 week(s) of notification.

**CONTACT**
Justin Kehring, Director of Student Financial Aid
400 County Road H, Elkhorn, WI 53121
(262) 564-3072

## Globe University: Appleton
Grand Chute, Wisconsin
www.globeuniversity.edu　　　　Federal Code: 004642

**2-year for-profit** career college in small city.
**Enrollment:** 203 undergrads.
**Selectivity:** Open admission.

**BASIC COSTS (2015-2016)**
**Tuition and fees:** $18,702.

**FINANCIAL AID PICTURE**
**Students with need:** Need-based aid available for full-time and part-time students.

**FINANCIAL AID PROCEDURES**
**Forms required:** FAFSA, institutional form.
**Dates and Deadlines:** Applicants notified on a rolling basis starting 7/1; must reply within 2 week(s) of notification.

**CONTACT**
Jonathan Allen, Financial Aid Manager
5045 West Grande Market Drive, Grand Chute, WI 54913
(920) 364-1100

## Globe University: Eau Claire
Eau Claire, Wisconsin
www.globeuniversity.edu　　　　Federal Code: 004642

**2-year for-profit** career college in small city.
**Enrollment:** 153 undergrads.
**Selectivity:** Open admission.

**BASIC COSTS (2015-2016)**
**Tuition and fees:** $18,702.

**FINANCIAL AID PICTURE**
**Students with need:** Need-based aid available for full-time and part-time students.

**FINANCIAL AID PROCEDURES**
**Forms required:** FAFSA, institutional form.
**Dates and Deadlines:** Applicants notified on a rolling basis starting 7/1; must reply within 2 week(s) of notification.

**CONTACT**
Kenton Davis, Financial Aid Manager
4955 Bullis Farm Road, Eau Claire, WI 54701
(715) 855-6600

## Globe University: Green Bay
Green Bay, Wisconsin
www.globeuniversity.edu　　　　Federal Code: 004642

**4-year for-profit** university and career college in small city.
**Enrollment:** 185 undergrads.
**Selectivity:** Open admission.

**BASIC COSTS (2015-2016)**
**Tuition and fees:** $18,702.

**FINANCIAL AID PICTURE**
**Students with need:** Need-based aid available for full-time and part-time students.

**FINANCIAL AID PROCEDURES**
**Forms required:** FAFSA, institutional form.
**Dates and Deadlines:** Applicants notified on a rolling basis starting 7/1; must reply within 2 week(s) of notification.

**CONTACT**
Kristin Thyrion, Financial Aid Manager
2620 Development Drive, Green Bay, WI 54311
(920) 264-1600

## Globe University: La Crosse
Onalaska, Wisconsin
www.globeuniversity.edu　　　　Federal Code: 004642

**2-year for-profit** career college in large town.
**Enrollment:** 178 undergrads.
**Selectivity:** Open admission.

**BASIC COSTS (2015-2016)**
**Tuition and fees:** $18,702.

**FINANCIAL AID PICTURE**
**Students with need:** Need-based aid available for full-time and part-time students.

**FINANCIAL AID PROCEDURES**
**Forms required:** FAFSA, institutional form.
**Dates and Deadlines:** Applicants notified on a rolling basis starting 7/1; must reply within 2 week(s) of notification.

**CONTACT**
Michael Waters, Financial Aid Manager
2651 Midwest Drive, Onalaska, WI 54650
(608) 779-8600

## Globe University: Madison East
Madison, Wisconsin
www.globeuniversity.edu　　　　Federal Code: 004642

**2-year for-profit** career college in small city.
**Enrollment:** 217 undergrads.
**Selectivity:** Open admission.

**BASIC COSTS (2015-2016)**
**Tuition and fees:** $18,702.

**FINANCIAL AID PICTURE**
**Students with need:** Need-based aid available for full-time and part-time students.

**FINANCIAL AID PROCEDURES**
**Forms required:** FAFSA, institutional form.
**Dates and Deadlines:** Applicants notified on a rolling basis starting 7/1; must reply within 2 week(s) of notification.

**CONTACT**
Bill Vache, Director of Financial Aid
4901 Eastpark Boulevard, Madison, WI 53718
(608) 216-9400

## Globe University: Middleton
Middleton, Wisconsin
www.globeuniversity.edu        Federal Code: 004642

**2-year for-profit** career college in large town.
**Enrollment:** 182 undergrads.
**Selectivity:** Open admission.

**BASIC COSTS (2015-2016)**
**Tuition and fees:** $18,702; out-of-state residents $26,352.

**FINANCIAL AID PICTURE**
**Students with need:** Need-based aid available for full-time and part-time students.

**FINANCIAL AID PROCEDURES**
**Forms required:** FAFSA, institutional form.
**Dates and Deadlines:** Applicants notified on a rolling basis starting 7/1; must reply within 2 week(s) of notification.

**CONTACT**
Brittanie Dempsey, Financial Aid Manager
1345 Deming Way, Middleton, WI 53562
(608) 830-6900

## Globe University: Wausau
Rothschild, Wisconsin
www.globeuniversity.edu        Federal Code: 004642

**2-year for-profit** career college in small town.
**Enrollment:** 122 undergrads.
**Selectivity:** Open admission.

**BASIC COSTS (2015-2016)**
**Tuition and fees:** $18,702.

**FINANCIAL AID PICTURE**
**Students with need:** Need-based aid available for full-time and part-time students.

**FINANCIAL AID PROCEDURES**
**Forms required:** FAFSA, institutional form.
**Dates and Deadlines:** Applicants notified on a rolling basis starting 7/1; must reply within 2 week(s) of notification.

**CONTACT**
Cheng Heu, Financial Aid Manager
1480 Country Road XX, Rothschild, WI 54474
(715) 301-1300

## Herzing University: Madison
Madison, Wisconsin
www.herzing.edu/madison        Federal Code: 009621

**3-year for-profit** business and career college in small city.
**Enrollment:** 2,369 undergrads.
**Selectivity:** Open admission; but selective for some programs.

**BASIC COSTS (2015-2016)**
**Additional info:** Certificate programs: $13,670 to $26,820. Associate programs: $26,180 to $53,640. Bachelor's programs: $61,515 to $88,065.

**FINANCIAL AID PICTURE**
**Students with need:** Need-based aid available for full-time and part-time students.

**FINANCIAL AID PROCEDURES**
**Forms required:** FAFSA, institutional form.

**Dates and Deadlines:** Applicants notified on a rolling basis.

**CONTACT**
Beverly Faga, Director of Financial Services
5218 East Terrace Drive, Madison, WI 53718
(608) 249-6611

## Lac Courte Oreilles Ojibwa Community College
Hayward, Wisconsin
www.lco.edu        Federal Code: 017199

**2-year public** community college in small town.
**Enrollment:** 309 undergrads, 51% part-time. 25 full-time freshmen.
**Selectivity:** Open admission.

**BASIC COSTS (2015-2016)**
**Tuition and fees:** $5,700.
**Per-credit charge:** $190.

**FINANCIAL AID PICTURE**
**Students with need:** Need-based aid available for full-time students.

**FINANCIAL AID PROCEDURES**
**Forms required:** FAFSA.
**Dates and Deadlines:** Applicants notified on a rolling basis.

**CONTACT**
Jason Parolin, Financial Aid Director
13466 West Trepania Road, Hayward, WI 54843

## Lakeland College
Sheboygan, Wisconsin
www.lakeland.edu        Federal Code: 003854

**4-year private** liberal arts college in small city, affiliated with United Church of Christ.
**Enrollment:** 2,196 undergrads, 58% part-time. 241 full-time freshmen.

**BASIC COSTS (2015-2016)**
**Tuition and fees:** $25,050.
**Room and board:** $8,620.
**Additional info:** There are flight fees on a per courses basis for the Aviation Minor.

**FINANCIAL AID PICTURE**
**Students with need:** Need-based aid available for full-time and part-time students. Work study available nights, weekends, and for part-time students.
**Students without need:** No-need awards available for academics, alumni affiliation, art, religious affiliation.
**Scholarships offered:** Trustees' Scholarship: $11,000; minimum GPA of 3.5 and minimum ACT of 24. Presidential Scholarship: $8,000; 3.25-3.49 GPA and 21 or greater ACT. Dean's Scholarship: $7,000; 3.0-3.24 GPA and 21 or greater ACT. Faculty Scholarship: $6,000; 2.75-2.99 GPA and 19 or greater ACT.

**FINANCIAL AID PROCEDURES**
**Forms required:** FAFSA, institutional form.
**Dates and Deadlines:** Priority date 3/15; no closing date. Applicants notified on a rolling basis starting 2/15; must reply within 2 week(s) of notification.

**CONTACT**
Patty Taylor, Director of Financial Aid
Box 359, Sheboygan, WI 53082-0359
(920) 565-1032

## Lakeshore Technical College
Cleveland, Wisconsin
www.gotoltc.edu                    Federal Code: 009194

**2-year public** technical college in rural community.
**Enrollment:** 2,138 undergrads.
**Selectivity:** Open admission; but selective for some programs.

### BASIC COSTS (2015-2016)
**Tuition and fees:** $4,064; out-of-state residents $5,990.
**Per-credit charge:** $128; out-of-state residents $193.

### FINANCIAL AID PICTURE (2014-2015)
**Students with need:** 64% of average financial aid package awarded as scholarships/grants, 36% awarded as loans/jobs. Need-based aid available for part-time students. Work study available nights.
**Students without need:** This college awards aid only to students with need.

### FINANCIAL AID PROCEDURES
**Forms required:** FAFSA, institutional form.
**Dates and Deadlines:** Priority date 6/1; no closing date. Applicants notified on a rolling basis starting 6/1; must reply within 3 week(s) of notification.

### CONTACT
Jessica Hemenway, Financial Aid Manager
1290 North Avenue, Cleveland, WI 53015-9761
(920) 693-1118

## Lawrence University
Appleton, Wisconsin              Federal Code: 003856
www.lawrence.edu                      CSS Code: 1398

**4-year private** music and liberal arts college in small city.
**Enrollment:** 1,527 undergrads, 2% part-time. 394 full-time freshmen.
**Selectivity:** Admits 50 to 75% of applicants.

### BASIC COSTS (2015-2016)
**Tuition and fees:** $43,740.
**Room and board:** $9,210.

### FINANCIAL AID PICTURE (2015-2016)
**Students with need:** Out of 311 full-time freshmen who applied for aid, 234 were judged to have need. Of these, 234 received aid, and 107 had their full need met. Average financial aid package met 97% of need; average scholarship/grant was $31,540; average loan was $4,771. For part-time students, average financial aid package was $28,468.
**Students without need:** 157 full-time freshmen who did not demonstrate need for aid received scholarships/grants; average award was $22,551. No-need awards available for academics, alumni affiliation, leadership, minority status, music/drama.
**Scholarships offered:** Scholarships range from $5,000 to $23,000 per year.

### FINANCIAL AID PROCEDURES
**Forms required:** FAFSA. CSS PROFILE required for applicants seeking institutionally-funded need-based aid.
**Dates and Deadlines:** Priority date 3/1; no closing date. Applicants notified on a rolling basis starting 3/1; must reply by 5/1 or within 2 week(s) of notification.
**Transfers:** Priority date 4/1. Applicants notified on a rolling basis starting 5/23.

### CONTACT
Ken Anselment, Dean of Admissions and Financial Aid
711 East Boldt Way SPC 29, Appleton, WI 54911-5699
(920) 832-6583

## Maranatha Baptist University
Watertown, Wisconsin
www.mbu.edu                        Federal Code: 016394

**4-year private** Bible and liberal arts college in large town, affiliated with Baptist faith.
**Enrollment:** 730 undergrads, 14% part-time. 157 full-time freshmen.
**Selectivity:** Admits 50 to 75% of applicants.

### BASIC COSTS (2015-2016)
**Tuition and fees:** $13,940.
**Room and board:** $6,550.

### FINANCIAL AID PICTURE (2014-2015)
**Students with need:** Out of 150 full-time freshmen who applied for aid, 132 were judged to have need. Of these, 132 received aid, and 10 had their full need met. Average financial aid package met 55% of need; average scholarship/grant was $7,389; average loan was $3,266. For part-time students, average financial aid package was $5,919.
**Students without need:** 19 full-time freshmen who did not demonstrate need for aid received scholarships/grants; average award was $3,461. No-need awards available for academics, alumni affiliation.

### FINANCIAL AID PROCEDURES
**Forms required:** FAFSA.
**Dates and Deadlines:** Priority date 3/1; no closing date. Applicants notified on a rolling basis starting 2/1; must reply within 2 week(s) of notification.
**Transfers:** Financial aid transcript or equivalent required.

### CONTACT
Randy Hibbs, Financial Aid Director
745 West Main Street, Watertown, WI 53094
(920) 206-2318

## Marian University
Fond du Lac, Wisconsin
www.marianuniversity.edu           Federal Code: 003861

**4-year private** university and liberal arts college in large town, affiliated with Roman Catholic Church.
**Enrollment:** 1,538 undergrads, 16% part-time. 250 full-time freshmen.
**Selectivity:** Admits over 75% of applicants.

### BASIC COSTS (2015-2016)
**Tuition and fees:** $27,310.
**Per-credit charge:** $430.
**Room and board:** $6,750.

### FINANCIAL AID PICTURE (2014-2015)
**Students with need:** Out of 249 full-time freshmen who applied for aid, 233 were judged to have need. Of these, 233 received aid, and 27 had their full need met. Average financial aid package met 55% of need; average scholarship/grant was $7,647; average loan was $6,720. For part-time students, average financial aid package was $4,500.
**Students without need:** 16 full-time freshmen who did not demonstrate need for aid received scholarships/grants; average award was $10,455. No-need awards available for academics, state/district residency.
**Scholarships offered:** Academic Achievement Award: $7,500; based on 3.5 GPA, 25 ACT, top 15% of class; 7 awarded. Presidential Scholarship: $5,000; based on 3.1 GPA, top 20% of class. Naber Leadership Scholarship: $3,000; based on 2.5 GPA, top 50% of class.

### FINANCIAL AID PROCEDURES
**Forms required:** FAFSA, institutional form.
**Dates and Deadlines:** Priority date 3/1; no closing date. Applicants notified on a rolling basis starting 3/1; must reply within 4 week(s) of notification.
**Transfers:** No deadline. Applicants notified on a rolling basis; must reply within 4 week(s) of notification.

## CONTACT
Pam Warren, Associate Director of Financial Aid
45 South National Avenue, Fond du Lac, WI 54935-4699
(920) 923-7614

---

## Marquette University
Milwaukee, Wisconsin
www.marquette.edu          Federal Code: 003863

**4-year private** university in very large city, affiliated with Roman Catholic Church.
**Enrollment:** 8,143 undergrads, 2% part-time. 1,872 full-time freshmen.
**Selectivity:** Admits 50 to 75% of applicants.

### BASIC COSTS (2015-2016)
**Tuition and fees:** $37,170.
**Per-credit charge:** $995.
**Room and board:** $11,220.

### FINANCIAL AID PICTURE (2015-2016)
**Students with need:** Out of 1,520 full-time freshmen who applied for aid, 1,162 were judged to have need. Of these, 1,162 received aid, and 292 had their full need met. Average financial aid package met 77% of need; average scholarship/grant was $21,049; average loan was $3,655. For part-time students, average financial aid package was $7,260.
**Students without need:** 678 full-time freshmen who did not demonstrate need for aid received scholarships/grants; average award was $11,540. No-need awards available for academics, athletics, leadership, music/drama, ROTC.
**Scholarships offered:** 40 full-time freshmen received athletic scholarships; average amount $26,022.

### FINANCIAL AID PROCEDURES
**Forms required:** FAFSA.
**Dates and Deadlines:** Priority date 2/1; no closing date. Applicants notified on a rolling basis starting 3/5; must reply by 5/1 or within 3 week(s) of notification.
**Transfers:** No deadline. Applicants notified on a rolling basis starting 3/15; must reply by 5/1 or within 3 week(s) of notification. Transfer scholarships available.

### CONTACT
Susan Teerink, Director of Student Financial Aid
PO Box 1881, Milwaukee, WI 53201-1881
(414) 288-0200

---

## Mid-State Technical College
Wisconsin Rapids, Wisconsin
www.mstc.edu          Federal Code: 005380

**2-year public** technical college in large town.
**Enrollment:** 3,100 undergrads.
**Selectivity:** Open admission; but selective for some programs.

### BASIC COSTS (2015-2016)
**Tuition and fees:** $4,044; out-of-state residents $5,970.
**Per-credit charge:** $128; out-of-state residents $193.

### FINANCIAL AID PICTURE
**Students with need:** Need-based aid available for full-time and part-time students. Work study available nights, weekends, and for part-time students.
**Students without need:** No-need awards available for academics, leadership.

### FINANCIAL AID PROCEDURES
**Forms required:** FAFSA.

**Dates and Deadlines:** Priority date 4/15; no closing date. Applicants notified on a rolling basis starting 5/30; must reply within 2 week(s) of notification.
**Transfers:** No deadline.

### CONTACT
Mary Jo Green, Financial Aid Supervisor
500 32nd Street North, Wisconsin Rapids, WI 54494
(715) 422-5501

---

## Milwaukee Area Technical College
Milwaukee, Wisconsin
www.matc.edu          Federal Code: 003866

**2-year public** junior and technical college in very large city.
**Enrollment:** 14,574 undergrads, 71% part-time. 623 full-time freshmen.
**Selectivity:** Open admission; but selective for some programs.

### BASIC COSTS (2015-2016)
**Tuition and fees:** $4,794; out-of-state residents $6,720.
**Per-credit charge:** $145; out-of-state residents $209.
**Additional info:** Tuition/fee waivers available for minority students.

### FINANCIAL AID PICTURE (2014-2015)
**Students with need:** 52% of average financial aid package awarded as scholarships/grants, 48% awarded as loans/jobs. Need-based aid available for part-time students.
**Students without need:** No-need awards available for academics.

### FINANCIAL AID PROCEDURES
**Forms required:** FAFSA.
**Dates and Deadlines:** Priority date 3/15; no closing date. Applicants notified on a rolling basis starting 4/15.
**Transfers:** No deadline. Applicants notified on a rolling basis starting 4/15.

### CONTACT
Camille Nicolai, Director of Financial Aid
700 West State Street, Milwaukee, WI 53233-1443
(414) 297-8875

---

## Milwaukee Institute of Art & Design
Milwaukee, Wisconsin
www.miad.edu          Federal Code: 014203

**4-year private** visual arts college in very large city.
**Enrollment:** 621 undergrads, 3% part-time. 143 full-time freshmen.
**Selectivity:** Admits 50 to 75% of applicants.

### BASIC COSTS (2015-2016)
**Tuition and fees:** $33,560.
**Per-credit charge:** $1,073.
**Room and board:** $9,050.

### FINANCIAL AID PICTURE (2014-2015)
**Students with need:** Out of 137 full-time freshmen who applied for aid, 125 were judged to have need. Of these, 125 received aid, and 16 had their full need met. Average financial aid package met 65% of need; average scholarship/grant was $19,094; average loan was $4,691. For part-time students, average financial aid package was $13,896.
**Students without need:** 18 full-time freshmen who did not demonstrate need for aid received scholarships/grants; average award was $12,569. No-need awards available for academics, art.

### FINANCIAL AID PROCEDURES
**Forms required:** FAFSA.
**Dates and Deadlines:** Priority date 2/15; no closing date. Applicants notified on a rolling basis starting 3/1; must reply by 5/1 or within 4 week(s) of notification.

**Transfers:** No deadline. Applicants notified on a rolling basis starting 4/1; must reply by 5/1 or within 2 week(s) of notification.

**CONTACT**
Carol Masse, Executive Director of Financial Aid
273 East Erie Street, Milwaukee, WI 53202
(414) 847-3270

## Milwaukee School of Engineering
Milwaukee, Wisconsin
www.msoe.edu                              Federal Code: 003868

**4-year private** university in very large city.
**Enrollment:** 2,712 undergrads, 6% part-time. 558 full-time freshmen.
**Selectivity:** Admits 50 to 75% of applicants.

**BASIC COSTS (2016-2017)**
**Tuition and fees:** $37,980.
**Per-credit charge:** $630.
**Room and board:** $8,835.
**Additional info:** Tuition/fee waivers available for minority students.

**FINANCIAL AID PICTURE (2014-2015)**
**Students with need:** Out of 524 full-time freshmen who applied for aid, 452 were judged to have need. Of these, 452 received aid, and 86 had their full need met. Average financial aid package met 83% of need; average scholarship/grant was $24,676; average loan was $3,552. For part-time students, average financial aid package was $7,800.
**Students without need:** 115 full-time freshmen who did not demonstrate need for aid received scholarships/grants; average award was $14,749. No-need awards available for academics, ROTC.
**Scholarships offered:** Presidential Scholarship: full tuition; awarded to students with high academic standing; 8 awarded.

**FINANCIAL AID PROCEDURES**
**Forms required:** FAFSA.
**Dates and Deadlines:** Priority date 3/15; no closing date. Applicants notified on a rolling basis starting 3/1; must reply within 2 week(s) of notification.
**Transfers:** Applicants notified on a rolling basis.

**CONTACT**
Steven Midthun, Director, Financial Aid
1025 North Broadway, Milwaukee, WI 53202-3109
(414) 277-7223

## Moraine Park Technical College
Fond du Lac, Wisconsin
www.morainepark.edu                       Federal Code: 005303

**2-year public** technical college in large town.
**Enrollment:** 3,143 undergrads.
**Selectivity:** Open admission; but selective for some programs.

**BASIC COSTS (2015-2016)**
**Tuition and fees:** $4,252; out-of-state residents $6,178.
**Per-credit charge:** $128; out-of-state residents $193.

**FINANCIAL AID PICTURE**
**Students with need:** Need-based aid available for full-time and part-time students. Work study available nights.
**Students without need:** No-need awards available for academics, job skills, leadership, minority status, state/district residency.

**FINANCIAL AID PROCEDURES**
**Forms required:** FAFSA, institutional form.
**Dates and Deadlines:** Priority date 5/1; no closing date. Applicants notified on a rolling basis starting 5/15; must reply within 2 week(s) of notification.

**Transfers:** Priority date 4/15; no deadline. Applicants notified on a rolling basis starting 5/15.

**CONTACT**
Julie Waldvogel, Financial Aid Associate
235 North National Avenue, Fond du Lac, WI 54935-1940

## Mount Mary University
Milwaukee, Wisconsin
www.mtmary.edu                            Federal Code: 003869

**4-year private** university and liberal arts college for women in very large city, affiliated with Roman Catholic Church.
**Enrollment:** 804 undergrads, 11% part-time. 147 full-time freshmen.
**Selectivity:** Admits 50 to 75% of applicants.

**BASIC COSTS (2015-2016)**
**Tuition and fees:** $26,760.
**Per-credit charge:** $795.
**Room and board:** $7,890.

**FINANCIAL AID PICTURE (2014-2015)**
**Students with need:** Average financial aid package met 77% of need; average scholarship/grant was $21,603; average loan was $3,292. For part-time students, average financial aid package was $6,748.
**Students without need:** No-need awards available for academics, alumni affiliation, art, leadership, music/drama.

**FINANCIAL AID PROCEDURES**
**Forms required:** FAFSA.
**Dates and Deadlines:** Priority date 3/1; no closing date. Applicants notified on a rolling basis starting 3/1; must reply within 2 week(s) of notification.
**Transfers:** Must reply within 2 week(s) of notification.

**CONTACT**
Debra Duff, Director of Financial Aid
2900 North Menomonee River Parkway, Milwaukee, WI 53222-4597
(414) 930-3044

## Nicolet Area Technical College
Rhinelander, Wisconsin
www.nicoletcollege.edu                    Federal Code: 008919

**2-year public** community and technical college in small town.
**Enrollment:** 1,139 undergrads.
**Selectivity:** Open admission; but selective for some programs.

**BASIC COSTS (2015-2016)**
**Tuition and fees:** $4,046; out-of-state residents $5,972.
**Per-credit charge:** $128; out-of-state residents $193.

**FINANCIAL AID PICTURE (2014-2015)**
**Students with need:** 71% of average financial aid package awarded as scholarships/grants, 29% awarded as loans/jobs. Need-based aid available for part-time students.

**FINANCIAL AID PROCEDURES**
**Forms required:** FAFSA.
**Dates and Deadlines:** Priority date 4/15; no closing date. Applicants notified on a rolling basis starting 6/1; must reply within 2 week(s) of notification.
**Transfers:** No deadline. Applicants notified on a rolling basis; must reply within 2 week(s) of notification.

**CONTACT**
Jill Price, Director of Financial Aid
Box 518, Rhinelander, WI 54501
(715) 365-4423

# Northcentral Technical College

Wausau, Wisconsin
www.ntc.edu                                   Federal Code: 005387

**2-year public** community and technical college in small city.
**Enrollment:** 3,710 undergrads, 61% part-time. 322 full-time freshmen.
**Selectivity:** Open admission; but selective for some programs.

## BASIC COSTS (2015-2016)
**Tuition and fees:** $4,308; out-of-state residents $6,234.
**Per-credit charge:** $128; out-of-state residents $193.

## FINANCIAL AID PICTURE (2015-2016)
**Students with need:** 59% of average financial aid package awarded as scholarships/grants, 41% awarded as loans/jobs. Need-based aid available for part-time students. Work study available nights.

## FINANCIAL AID PROCEDURES
**Forms required:** FAFSA.
**Dates and Deadlines:** Applicants notified on a rolling basis.
**Transfers:** No deadline.

## CONTACT
Jeff Cichon, Director of Financial Aid
1000 West Campus Drive, Wausau, WI 54401
(715) 675-3331 ext. 5862

# Northeast Wisconsin Technical College

Green Bay, Wisconsin
www.nwtc.edu                                  Federal Code: 005301

**2-year public** community and technical college in small city.
**Enrollment:** 8,526 undergrads.
**Selectivity:** Open admission; but selective for some programs.

## BASIC COSTS (2015-2016)
**Tuition and fees:** $4,274; out-of-state residents $6,200.
**Per-credit charge:** $128; out-of-state residents $192.

## FINANCIAL AID PICTURE
**Students with need:** Need-based aid available for full-time and part-time students. Work study available nights, weekends, and for part-time students.

## FINANCIAL AID PROCEDURES
**Forms required:** FAFSA.
**Dates and Deadlines:** Priority date 4/15; no closing date. Applicants notified on a rolling basis starting 6/1; must reply within 2 week(s) of notification.
**Transfers:** No deadline. Applicants notified on a rolling basis starting 6/1; must reply within 2 week(s) of notification.

## CONTACT
Emily Ysebaert, Financial Aid Director
2740 West Mason Street, Green Bay, WI 54307-9042
(920) 498-5444

# Northland College

Ashland, Wisconsin
www.northland.edu                             Federal Code: 003875

**4-year private** liberal arts college in small town, affiliated with United Church of Christ.
**Enrollment:** 518 undergrads, 1% part-time. 128 full-time freshmen.
**Selectivity:** Admits 50 to 75% of applicants.

## BASIC COSTS (2015-2016)
**Tuition and fees:** $32,754.
**Per-credit charge:** $600.

**Room and board:** $8,349.
**Additional info:** Tuition at time of enrollment locked for 4 years; tuition/fee waivers available for unemployed or children of unemployed.

## FINANCIAL AID PICTURE (2015-2016)
**Students with need:** Out of 122 full-time freshmen who applied for aid, 108 were judged to have need. Of these, 108 received aid, and 26 had their full need met. Average financial aid package met 87% of need; average scholarship/grant was $24,770; average loan was $4,407. For part-time students, average financial aid package was $15,133.
**Students without need:** 17 full-time freshmen who did not demonstrate need for aid received scholarships/grants; average award was $19,430. No-need awards available for academics, alumni affiliation, art, job skills, leadership, minority status, music/drama, religious affiliation, state/district residency.

## FINANCIAL AID PROCEDURES
**Forms required:** FAFSA.
**Dates and Deadlines:** Priority date 3/15; no closing date. Applicants notified on a rolling basis starting 3/1; must reply by 5/1 or within 4 week(s) of notification.
**Transfers:** No deadline.

## CONTACT
Heather Shelly, Director of Financial Aid
1411 Ellis Avenue, Ashland, WI 54806-3999
(715) 682-1255

# Rasmussen College: Appleton

Appleton, Wisconsin
www.rasmussen.edu

**4-year for-profit** branch campus and career college in small city.
**Enrollment:** 374 undergrads.
**Selectivity:** Open admission; but selective for some programs.

## BASIC COSTS (2016-2017)
**Tuition and fees:** $13,455.
**Per-credit charge:** $299.

## FINANCIAL AID PICTURE
**Students with need:** Need-based aid available for full-time and part-time students.

## FINANCIAL AID PROCEDURES
**Forms required:** FAFSA, institutional form.
**Dates and Deadlines:** Applicants notified on a rolling basis.

## CONTACT
Debora Murray, Director of Financial Aid
3500 East Destination Drive, Appleton, WI 54915

# Rasmussen College: Green Bay

Green Bay, Wisconsin
www.rasmussen.edu

**2-year for-profit** career college in small city.
**Enrollment:** 441 undergrads.
**Selectivity:** Open admission; but selective for some programs.

## BASIC COSTS (2016-2017)
**Tuition and fees:** $13,455.
**Per-credit charge:** $299.

## FINANCIAL AID PICTURE
**Students with need:** Need-based aid available for full-time and part-time students.

## FINANCIAL AID PROCEDURES
**Forms required:** FAFSA, institutional form.
**Dates and Deadlines:** Applicants notified on a rolling basis.

## CONTACT
Debora Murray, Financial Aid Director
904 South Taylor Street, Suite 100, Green Bay, WI 54303-2349

# Rasmussen College: Wausau
Wausau, Wisconsin
www.rasmussen.edu

**2-year for-profit** career college in large town.
**Enrollment:** 346 undergrads.
**Selectivity:** Open admission; but selective for some programs.

## BASIC COSTS (2016-2017)
**Tuition and fees:** $13,455.
**Per-credit charge:** $299.

## FINANCIAL AID PICTURE
**Students with need:** Need-based aid available for full-time and part-time students.

## FINANCIAL AID PROCEDURES
**Forms required:** FAFSA, institutional form.
**Dates and Deadlines:** Applicants notified on a rolling basis.

## CONTACT
Debora Murray, Director of Financial Aid
1101 Westwood Drive, Wausau, WI 54401

# Ripon College
Ripon, Wisconsin
www.ripon.edu          Federal Code: 003884

**4-year private** liberal arts college in small town.
**Enrollment:** 781 undergrads. 216 full-time freshmen.
**Selectivity:** Admits 50 to 75% of applicants.

## BASIC COSTS (2016-2017)
**Tuition and fees:** $38,325.
**Per-credit charge:** $1,200.
**Room and board:** $8,177.

## FINANCIAL AID PICTURE (2015-2016)
**Students with need:** Out of 208 full-time freshmen who applied for aid, 188 were judged to have need. Of these, 188 received aid, and 49 had their full need met. Average financial aid package met 87% of need; average scholarship/grant was $27,230; average loan was $4,325. Need-based aid available for part-time students.
**Students without need:** 27 full-time freshmen who did not demonstrate need for aid received scholarships/grants; average award was $18,808. No-need awards available for academics, alumni affiliation, art, leadership, minority status, music/drama, religious affiliation, ROTC, state/district residency.
**Scholarships offered:** Pickard Scholarship Competition: $22,000-$30,000 per year; based on 3.8 GPA, 28 ACT/1260 SAT; invitation only. Knop Scholars Program: full-tuition; for natural science or math major; based on 3.8 GPA, top 5% of class, interview; invitation only; one awarded. Rolling Academic Scholarships: $14,000 to $18,000 per year; consideration given to students who have academic and/or leadership achievements in their schools and communities. Army ROTC Scholarships: up to $5,000 per year. Diversity Scholarships: $20,000. Communication Consortium Scholarships: $20,000; interview required. Art Scholarships: $20,000 maximum award; portfolio required. Theater Scholarships: up to $20,000; interview required. Music Scholarships: $20,000; audition required. Evans Achievement Awards: $10,000 per year; not available to academic scholarship recipients. Boy/Girl

State Scholarships: up to $16,000. Legacy Awards: $8,000. United Church of Christ Scholarships: $8,000; application required. Alumni Award; $8,000: recommendation letter from alumnus required.

## FINANCIAL AID PROCEDURES
**Forms required:** FAFSA.
**Dates and Deadlines:** Priority date 3/1; closing date 6/15. Applicants notified on a rolling basis starting 3/1; must reply within 2 week(s) of notification.
**Transfers:** Priority date 3/1; no deadline. Applicants notified on a rolling basis starting 3/1; must reply within 2 week(s) of notification.

## CONTACT
David Woodward, Director of Financial Aid
300 West Seward Street, Ripon, WI 54971-0248
(920) 748-8301

# St. Norbert College
De Pere, Wisconsin
www.snc.edu          Federal Code: 003892

**4-year private** liberal arts college in large town, affiliated with Roman Catholic Church.
**Enrollment:** 2,052 undergrads, 1% part-time. 536 full-time freshmen.
**Selectivity:** Admits over 75% of applicants.

## BASIC COSTS (2015-2016)
**Tuition and fees:** $34,237.
**Per-credit charge:** $1,051.
**Room and board:** $8,794.

## FINANCIAL AID PICTURE (2014-2015)
**Students with need:** Out of 490 full-time freshmen who applied for aid, 428 were judged to have need. Of these, 428 received aid, and 99 had their full need met. Average financial aid package met 84% of need; average scholarship/grant was $20,551; average loan was $3,701. For part-time students, average financial aid package was $8,476.
**Students without need:** 101 full-time freshmen who did not demonstrate need for aid received scholarships/grants; average award was $11,240. No-need awards available for academics, art, leadership, minority status, music/drama, ROTC, state/district residency.

## FINANCIAL AID PROCEDURES
**Forms required:** FAFSA.
**Dates and Deadlines:** Priority date 3/1; no closing date. Applicants notified by 3/15; must reply within 2 week(s) of notification.

## CONTACT
Jessica Rafeld, Director of Financial Aid
100 Grant Street, De Pere, WI 54115-2099
(888) 786-6721

# Silver Lake College of the Holy Family
Manitowoc, Wisconsin
www.sl.edu          Federal Code: 003850

**4-year private** liberal arts college in large town, affiliated with Roman Catholic Church.
**Enrollment:** 296 undergrads.

## BASIC COSTS (2015-2016)
**Tuition and fees:** $14,650.
**Room and board:** $12,760.

## FINANCIAL AID PICTURE
**Students with need:** Need-based aid available for full-time and part-time students. Work study available nights, weekends, and for part-time students.

**Students without need:** No-need awards available for academics, art, athletics, leadership, music/drama, state/district residency.

## FINANCIAL AID PROCEDURES

**Forms required:** FAFSA.

**Dates and Deadlines:** Priority date 5/1; no closing date. Applicants notified on a rolling basis starting 3/15.

**Transfers:** No deadline. Applicants notified on a rolling basis starting 3/15. Transfer Merit Scholarships and Phi Theta Kappa Scholarships available, as well as other institutional scholarship and grant assistance.

## CONTACT

Corey Givens-Novak, Director of Student Financial Aid

2406 South Alverno Road, Manitowoc, WI 54220-9319

(920) 686-6175

## Southwest Wisconsin Technical College

Fennimore, Wisconsin

www.swtc.edu                    Federal Code: 007699

**2-year public** technical college in rural community.

**Enrollment:** 1,356 undergrads.

**Selectivity:** Open admission; but selective for some programs.

### BASIC COSTS (2015-2016)

**Tuition and fees:** $4,114; out-of-state residents $6,040.

**Per-credit charge:** $128; out-of-state residents $193.

### FINANCIAL AID PICTURE

**Students with need:** Work study available nights.

### FINANCIAL AID PROCEDURES

**Forms required:** FAFSA, institutional form.

**Dates and Deadlines:** Priority date 4/15; no closing date. Applicants notified on a rolling basis starting 5/15; must reply within 4 week(s) of notification.

### CONTACT

Joy Kite, Director of Financial Aid

1800 Bronson Boulevard, Fennimore, WI 53809

(608) 822-2319

## University of Wisconsin-Baraboo/Sauk County

Baraboo, Wisconsin

www.baraboo.uwc.edu              Federal Code: 003897

**2-year public** branch campus and liberal arts college in large town.

**Enrollment:** 600 undergrads.

### BASIC COSTS (2015-2016)

**Tuition and fees:** $5,178; out-of-state residents $12,162.

**Per-credit charge:** $198; out-of-state residents $489.

### FINANCIAL AID PICTURE

**Students with need:** Need-based aid available for full-time and part-time students. Work study available nights.

**Students without need:** This college awards aid only to students with need.

**Scholarships offered:** Campus scholarships: $250 to full tuition.

### FINANCIAL AID PROCEDURES

**Forms required:** FAFSA, institutional form.

**Dates and Deadlines:** Priority date 4/15; no closing date. Applicants notified on a rolling basis starting 4/15; must reply within 3 week(s) of notification.

**Transfers:** Must reply within 3 week(s) of notification.

## CONTACT

Marilyn Krump, Director of Student Financial Aid

1006 Connie Road, Baraboo, WI 53913-1098

(608) 263-7727

## University of Wisconsin-Barron County

Rice Lake, Wisconsin

www.barron.uwc.edu              Federal Code: 003897

**2-year public** branch campus and junior college in small town.

**Enrollment:** 422 undergrads.

### BASIC COSTS (2015-2016)

**Tuition and fees:** $5,184; out-of-state residents $12,168.

**Per-credit charge:** $198; out-of-state residents $489.

### FINANCIAL AID PICTURE

**Students with need:** Need-based aid available for full-time and part-time students.

### FINANCIAL AID PROCEDURES

**Forms required:** FAFSA.

**Dates and Deadlines:** Priority date 4/15; no closing date. Applicants notified on a rolling basis starting 6/1.

### CONTACT

William Trippett, Director of Student Financial Aid

1800 College Drive, Rice Lake, WI 54868

## University of Wisconsin-Eau Claire

Eau Claire, Wisconsin

www.uwec.edu                    Federal Code: 003917

**4-year public** university in small city.

**Enrollment:** 9,697 undergrads, 6% part-time. 2,007 full-time freshmen.

**Selectivity:** Admits over 75% of applicants.

### BASIC COSTS (2015-2016)

**Tuition and fees:** $8,822; out-of-state residents $16,395.

**Per-credit charge:** $307; out-of-state residents $622.

**Room and board:** $7,322.

**Additional info:** Fees include mandatory textbook rental fees.

### FINANCIAL AID PICTURE (2014-2015)

**Students with need:** Out of 1,732 full-time freshmen who applied for aid, 1,107 were judged to have need. Of these, 1,094 received aid, and 240 had their full need met. Average financial aid package met 87% of need; average scholarship/grant was $5,932; average loan was $3,994. For part-time students, average financial aid package was $6,588.

**Students without need:** 110 full-time freshmen who did not demonstrate need for aid received scholarships/grants; average award was $1,761. No-need awards available for academics, art, leadership, minority status, music/drama, state/district residency.

**Scholarships offered:** Wisconsin Academic Excellence Scholars: $2,250; Mark of Excellence Award: $2,000 various; Diversity Scholar: up to $6,000; Diversity Achievement: up to $2000; Blugold Fellowship: $1,500 scholarship and $1,200 research stipend; Freshman Honor Scholarship: $1,000; Centennial Scholarship: $5,000.

### FINANCIAL AID PROCEDURES

**Forms required:** FAFSA.

**Dates and Deadlines:** Priority date 4/15; no closing date. Applicants notified on a rolling basis starting 4/15.

### CONTACT

Kathleen Sahlhoff, Director of Financial Aid

111 Schofield Hall, Eau Claire, WI 54701

(715) 836-3373

# University of Wisconsin-Fond du Lac

Fond du Lac, Wisconsin
www.fdl.uwc.edu                    Federal Code: 003897

**2-year public** liberal arts college in large town.
**Enrollment:** 626 undergrads.

## BASIC COSTS (2015-2016)
**Tuition and fees:** $5,209; out-of-state residents $12,193.
**Per-credit charge:** $198; out-of-state residents $489.

## FINANCIAL AID PICTURE
**Students with need:** Need-based aid available for full-time and part-time students.
**Students without need:** No-need awards available for academics, leadership, music/drama.

## FINANCIAL AID PROCEDURES
**Forms required:** FAFSA.
**Dates and Deadlines:** Priority date 4/15; no closing date. Applicants notified on a rolling basis starting 6/1; must reply within 2 week(s) of notification.

## CONTACT
William Trippett, Director of Student Financial Aid
400 University Drive, Fond du Lac, WI 54935-2950
(608) 262-5928

# University of Wisconsin-Fox Valley

Menasha, Wisconsin
www.uwfox.uwc.edu                    Federal Code: 011459

**2-year public** liberal arts college in small city.
**Enrollment:** 1,549 undergrads.
**Selectivity:** Admits over 75% of applicants.

## BASIC COSTS (2015-2016)
**Tuition and fees:** $5,294; out-of-state residents $12,278.

## FINANCIAL AID PICTURE
**Students with need:** Need-based aid available for full-time and part-time students. Work study available nights, weekends, and for part-time students.
**Students without need:** No-need awards available for academics, leadership.

## FINANCIAL AID PROCEDURES
**Forms required:** FAFSA.
**Dates and Deadlines:** Priority date 4/15; no closing date. Applicants notified on a rolling basis starting 6/1; must reply within 3 week(s) of notification.

## CONTACT
William Trippett, Director of Student Financial Aid
1478 Midway Road, Menasha, WI 54952-2850
(608) 262-5928

# University of Wisconsin-Green Bay

Green Bay, Wisconsin
www.uwgb.edu                    Federal Code: 003899

**4-year public** university and liberal arts college in small city.
**Enrollment:** 5,487 undergrads, 28% part-time. 760 full-time freshmen.
**Selectivity:** Admits over 75% of applicants.

## BASIC COSTS (2015-2016)
**Tuition and fees:** $7,824; out-of-state residents $15,397.
**Per-credit charge:** $262; out-of-state residents $578.
**Room and board:** $7,270.

## FINANCIAL AID PICTURE (2015-2016)
**Students with need:** Out of 702 full-time freshmen who applied for aid, 471 were judged to have need. Of these, 456 received aid, and 106 had their full need met. Average financial aid package met 70% of need; average scholarship/grant was $6,244; average loan was $3,161. For part-time students, average financial aid package was $6,556.
**Students without need:** 45 full-time freshmen who did not demonstrate need for aid received scholarships/grants; average award was $1,379. No-need awards available for academics, art, athletics, leadership, minority status, music/drama.
**Scholarships offered:** 33 full-time freshmen received athletic scholarships; average amount $10,046.
**Additional info:** Auditions required for music and theater scholarships. Tuition is waived for eligible Wisconsin veterans and their family members under the Wisconsin GI Bill. Veterans from outside of Wisconsin are charged the in-state tuition rate regardless of residency. Waivers for children of Wisconsin police/firemen who were slain in the line of duty.

## FINANCIAL AID PROCEDURES
**Forms required:** FAFSA.
**Dates and Deadlines:** Priority date 4/1; no closing date. Applicants notified on a rolling basis starting 1/1; must reply within 3 week(s) of notification.
**Transfers:** Must reply within 3 week(s) of notification.

## CONTACT
James Rohan, Director of Financial Aid and Student Employment
2420 Nicolet Drive, Green Bay, WI 54311-7001
(920) 465-2075

# University of Wisconsin-La Crosse

La Crosse, Wisconsin
www.uwlax.edu                    Federal Code: 003919

**4-year public** university in small city.
**Enrollment:** 9,424 undergrads, 4% part-time. 1,985 full-time freshmen.
**Selectivity:** Admits over 75% of applicants.

## BASIC COSTS (2015-2016)
**Tuition and fees:** $8,832; out-of-state residents $16,783.
**Per-credit charge:** $316; out-of-state residents $647.
**Room and board:** $5,850.

## FINANCIAL AID PICTURE (2014-2015)
**Students with need:** Out of 1,710 full-time freshmen who applied for aid, 1,035 were judged to have need. Of these, 1,026 received aid, and 198 had their full need met. Average financial aid package met 68% of need; average scholarship/grant was $5,493; average loan was $3,375. For part-time students, average financial aid package was $6,107.
**Students without need:** 140 full-time freshmen who did not demonstrate need for aid received scholarships/grants; average award was $2,192. No-need awards available for academics, alumni affiliation, art, leadership, minority status, music/drama.

## FINANCIAL AID PROCEDURES
**Forms required:** FAFSA.
**Dates and Deadlines:** Priority date 3/15; no closing date. Applicants notified on a rolling basis starting 4/1.

## CONTACT
Louise Janke, Director of Financial Aid
1725 State Street, Cleary Center, La Crosse, WI 54601
(608) 785-8604

# University of Wisconsin-Madison

Madison, Wisconsin
www.wisc.edu                Federal Code: 003895

**4-year public** university in small city.
**Enrollment:** 29,580 undergrads, 5% part-time. 6,259 full-time freshmen.
**Selectivity:** Admits less than 50% of applicants.

**BASIC COSTS (2015-2016)**
**Tuition and fees:** $10,415; out-of-state residents $29,665.
**Per-credit charge:** $386; out-of-state residents $1,188.
**Room and board:** $8,804.
**Additional info:** Wisconsin has a tuition reciprocity agreement with Minnesota. Minnesota students pay $12,240 plus required fees ($1142).

**FINANCIAL AID PICTURE (2015-2016)**
**Students with need:** 56% of average financial aid package awarded as scholarships/grants, 44% awarded as loans/jobs. Need-based aid available for part-time students.
**Students without need:** No-need awards available for academics, alumni affiliation, art, athletics, job skills, leadership, minority status, music/drama, ROTC, state/district residency.

**FINANCIAL AID PROCEDURES**
**Forms required:** FAFSA.
**Dates and Deadlines:** Applicants notified on a rolling basis starting 4/1; must reply within 3 week(s) of notification.

**CONTACT**
Terry Ruzicka, Interim Director of Student Financial Aid
702 West Johnson Street, Suite 1101, Madison, WI 53715-1007
(608) 262-3060

# University of Wisconsin-Manitowoc

Manitowoc, Wisconsin
www.manitowoc.uwc.edu        Federal Code: 003897

**2-year public** branch campus and liberal arts college in large town.
**Enrollment:** 508 undergrads.

**BASIC COSTS (2015-2016)**
**Tuition and fees:** $5,108; out-of-state residents $12,092.
**Per-credit charge:** $198; out-of-state residents $489.

**FINANCIAL AID PICTURE**
**Students with need:** Need-based aid available for full-time and part-time students. Work study available nights.
**Students without need:** This college awards aid only to students with need.

**FINANCIAL AID PROCEDURES**
**Forms required:** FAFSA.
**Dates and Deadlines:** Priority date 3/1; no closing date. Applicants notified on a rolling basis starting 5/1; must reply within 2 week(s) of notification.
**Transfers:** Priority date 5/1; no deadline.

**CONTACT**
Bill Trippett, Director of Student Financial Aid
705 Viebahn Street, Manitowoc, WI 54220-6699
(920) 683-4707

# University of Wisconsin-Marathon County

Wausau, Wisconsin
www.uwmc.uwc.edu            Federal Code: 003903

**2-year public** liberal arts college in small city.
**Enrollment:** 1,138 undergrads.

**BASIC COSTS (2015-2016)**
**Tuition and fees:** $5,132; out-of-state residents $12,116.
**Per-credit charge:** $198; out-of-district residents $489.
**Room and board:** $4,924.

**FINANCIAL AID PICTURE**
**Students with need:** Need-based aid available for full-time and part-time students. Work study available nights.
**Students without need:** This college awards aid only to students with need.

**FINANCIAL AID PROCEDURES**
**Forms required:** FAFSA, institutional form.
**Dates and Deadlines:** Priority date 4/15; no closing date. Applicants notified on a rolling basis starting 6/1; must reply within 3 week(s) of notification.

**CONTACT**
Bill Trippett, Director of Student Financial Aid
518 South Seventh Avenue, Wausau, WI 54401-5396
(715) 261-6235

# University of Wisconsin-Marinette

Marinette, Wisconsin
www.marinette.uwc.edu        Federal Code: 003897

**2-year public** branch campus and liberal arts college in large town.
**Enrollment:** 350 undergrads.

**BASIC COSTS (2015-2016)**
**Tuition and fees:** $5,105; out-of-state residents $12,089.
**Per-credit charge:** $198; out-of-state residents $489.

**FINANCIAL AID PICTURE**
**Students with need:** Need-based aid available for full-time and part-time students. Work study available nights.
**Students without need:** This college awards aid only to students with need.

**FINANCIAL AID PROCEDURES**
**Forms required:** FAFSA.
**Dates and Deadlines:** Priority date 4/15; no closing date. Applicants notified on a rolling basis.

**CONTACT**
Bill Trippett, Director of Student Financial Aid
750 West Bay Shore Street, Marinette, WI 54143
(715) 735-4301

# University of Wisconsin-Marshfield/ Wood County

Marshfield, Wisconsin
www.marshfield.uwc.edu        Federal Code: 003897

**2-year public** branch campus college in small city.
**Enrollment:** 650 undergrads.

**BASIC COSTS (2015-2016)**
**Tuition and fees:** $5,288; out-of-state residents $12,272.
**Per-credit charge:** $198; out-of-state residents $489.
**Room only:** $4,800.

**FINANCIAL AID PICTURE**
**Students with need:** Need-based aid available for full-time and part-time students. Work study available nights, weekends, and for part-time students.
**Students without need:** No-need awards available for academics.
**Scholarships offered:** Special Entering Scholarships: $1,000; based on academic excellence; 2 awarded. Ken and Ardyce Helting Scholarship: $1,000;

priority given to physically challenged or learning disabled; 1 awarded. Vale-dictorian, Salutatorian and National Merit Finalist and Semi-Finalists: $1,000; ACT of 25 or better. Greenhouse Scholarship: priority to students in Environmental Studies; 1 awarded. Patrice Ptacek Memorial Scholarship: 2 letters of recommendation; 1 awarded. Woman of the Future Scholarship: $1,000; must be full-time female freshman entering sophomore year, well-defined career goals other than nursing; 1 awarded.

### FINANCIAL AID PROCEDURES

**Forms required:** FAFSA.

**Dates and Deadlines:** Closing date 4/15. Applicants notified on a rolling basis starting 4/1.

**Transfers:** Priority date 4/15; no deadline. Applicants notified on a rolling basis starting 4/1.

### CONTACT

William Trippett, Director of Student Financial Aid
2000 West Fifth Street, Marshfield, WI 54449
(715) 389-6500

## University of Wisconsin-Milwaukee

Milwaukee, Wisconsin
www.uwm.edu                          Federal Code: 003896

**4-year public** university in very large city.

**Enrollment:** 20,886 undergrads. 3,215 full-time freshmen.

**Selectivity:** Admits 50 to 75% of applicants.

### BASIC COSTS (2015-2016)

**Tuition and fees:** $9,429; out-of-state residents $19,602.

**Room and board:** $10,030.

### FINANCIAL AID PICTURE (2014-2015)

**Students with need:** Out of 2,944 full-time freshmen who applied for aid, 2,417 were judged to have need. Of these, 2,351 received aid, and 655 had their full need met. Average financial aid package met 39% of need; average scholarship/grant was $6,340; average loan was $3,508. For part-time students, average financial aid package was $6,489.

**Students without need:** 31 full-time freshmen who did not demonstrate need for aid received scholarships/grants; average award was $1,836. No-need awards available for academics, art, athletics, leadership, music/drama.

**Scholarships offered:** 18 full-time freshmen received athletic scholarships; average amount $5,539.

### FINANCIAL AID PROCEDURES

**Forms required:** FAFSA.

**Dates and Deadlines:** Priority date 3/1; no closing date. Applicants notified on a rolling basis starting 3/15.

**Transfers:** Priority date 3/1; no deadline. Applicants notified on a rolling basis.

### CONTACT

Seth Zlotocha, Interim Director of Financial Aid
P.O. Box 413, Milwaukee, WI 53201
(414) 229-6300

## University of Wisconsin-Oshkosh

Oshkosh, Wisconsin
www.uwosh.edu                        Federal Code: 003920

**4-year public** university in small city.

**Enrollment:** 9,935 undergrads, 14% part-time. 1,553 full-time freshmen.

**Selectivity:** Admits 50 to 75% of applicants.

### FINANCIAL AID PICTURE

**Students with need:** Need-based aid available for full-time and part-time students.

**Students without need:** No-need awards available for academics, art, job skills, leadership, minority status, music/drama, ROTC, state/district residency.

### FINANCIAL AID PROCEDURES

**Forms required:** FAFSA.

**Dates and Deadlines:** Priority date 3/15; no closing date. Applicants notified on a rolling basis starting 4/15; must reply within 2 week(s) of notification.

**Transfers:** Must send financial aid transcript to university.

### CONTACT

Kim Donat, Director of Financial Aid
800 Algoma Boulevard, Oshkosh, WI 54901-8602
(920) 424-3377

## University of Wisconsin-Parkside

Kenosha, Wisconsin
www.uwp.edu                          Federal Code: 005015

**4-year public** university in small city.

**Enrollment:** 4,168 undergrads, 22% part-time. 577 full-time freshmen.

**Selectivity:** Admits over 75% of applicants.

### BASIC COSTS (2015-2016)

**Tuition and fees:** $7,481; out-of-state residents $15,470.

**Per-credit charge:** $262; out-of-state residents $595.

**Room and board:** $7,712.

**Additional info:** Minnesota reciprocity tuition: $293.15 per-credit-hour. Midwest Student Exchange Program tuition: $393.65 per-credit-hour.

### FINANCIAL AID PICTURE (2014-2015)

**Students with need:** Out of 470 full-time freshmen who applied for aid, 363 were judged to have need. Of these, 363 received aid, and 56 had their full need met. Average financial aid package met 66% of need; average scholarship/grant was $6,574; average loan was $3,471. For part-time students, average financial aid package was $6,147.

**Students without need:** 42 full-time freshmen who did not demonstrate need for aid received scholarships/grants; average award was $4,276. No-need awards available for academics, art, athletics, leadership, music/drama, state/district residency.

**Scholarships offered:** 41 full-time freshmen received athletic scholarships; average amount $7,481.

### FINANCIAL AID PROCEDURES

**Forms required:** FAFSA.

**Dates and Deadlines:** Priority date 3/15; no closing date. Applicants notified on a rolling basis starting 4/1; must reply within 2 week(s) of notification.

### CONTACT

Kristina Klemens, Interim Director of Financial Aid
PO Box 2000, Kenosha, WI 53141-2000
(262) 595-2574

## University of Wisconsin-Platteville

Platteville, Wisconsin
www.uwplatt.edu                      Federal Code: 003921

**4-year public** university in large town.

**Enrollment:** 7,785 undergrads, 9% part-time. 1,579 full-time freshmen.

**Selectivity:** Admits over 75% of applicants.

### BASIC COSTS (2015-2016)

**Tuition and fees:** $7,488; out-of-state residents $15,339.

**Room and board:** $7,160.

### FINANCIAL AID PICTURE (2015-2016)

**Students with need:** Out of 1,364 full-time freshmen who applied for aid, 1,203 were judged to have need. Of these, 1,203 received aid, and 290 had

their full need met. Average financial aid package met 64% of need; average scholarship/grant was $4,093; average loan was $2,830. For part-time students, average financial aid package was $3,276.

**Students without need:** This college awards aid only to students with need.

### FINANCIAL AID PROCEDURES

**Forms required:** FAFSA.

**Dates and Deadlines:** Priority date 3/15; no closing date. Applicants notified on a rolling basis starting 6/1; must reply within 2 week(s) of notification.

### CONTACT

Shelia Trotter, Assoicate Director of Financial Aid
One University Plaza, Platteville, WI 53818
(608) 342-1836

## University of Wisconsin-Richland

Richland Center, Wisconsin
www.richland.uwc.edu                    Federal Code: 003897

**2-year public** liberal arts college in small town.
**Enrollment:** 320 undergrads.
**Selectivity:** Open admission; but selective for some programs.

### BASIC COSTS (2015-2016)

**Tuition and fees:** $5,330; out-of-state residents $12,314.
**Per-credit charge:** $198; out-of-state residents $489.

### FINANCIAL AID PICTURE

**Students with need:** Need-based aid available for full-time and part-time students. Work study available nights, weekends, and for part-time students.
**Students without need:** This college awards aid only to students with need.

### FINANCIAL AID PROCEDURES

**Forms required:** FAFSA.

**Dates and Deadlines:** Priority date 4/1; no closing date. Applicants notified on a rolling basis starting 5/15; must reply within 3 week(s) of notification.

### CONTACT

William Trippett, Director of Student Financial Aid
1200 Highway 14 West, Richland Center, WI 53581
(608) 647-6186 ext. 3

## University of Wisconsin-River Falls

River Falls, Wisconsin
www.uwrf.edu                    Federal Code: 003923

**4-year public** university and liberal arts college in large town.
**Enrollment:** 5,278 undergrads, 9% part-time. 863 full-time freshmen.
**Selectivity:** Admits over 75% of applicants.

### BASIC COSTS (2015-2016)

**Tuition and fees:** $7,937; out-of-state residents $15,510.
**Room and board:** $6,475.

### FINANCIAL AID PICTURE (2014-2015)

**Students with need:** Out of 792 full-time freshmen who applied for aid, 565 were judged to have need. Of these, 521 received aid, and 15 had their full need met. Average financial aid package met 52% of need; average scholarship/grant was $4,608; average loan was $3,953. For part-time students, average financial aid package was $5,799.
**Students without need:** This college awards aid only to students with need.

### FINANCIAL AID PROCEDURES

**Forms required:** FAFSA.

**Dates and Deadlines:** Priority date 3/15; no closing date. Applicants notified on a rolling basis starting 4/15.
**Transfers:** No deadline. Applicants notified on a rolling basis starting 4/1.

### CONTACT

Robert Bode, Director of Financial Aid
410 South 3rd Street, River Falls, WI 54022-5001
(715) 425-3141

## University of Wisconsin-Rock County

Janesville, Wisconsin
www.rock.uwc.edu                    Federal Code: 003897

**2-year public** branch campus and liberal arts college in small city.
**Enrollment:** 1,220 undergrads.

### BASIC COSTS (2015-2016)

**Tuition and fees:** $5,118; out-of-state residents $12,102.
**Per-credit charge:** $198; out-of-state residents $489.

### FINANCIAL AID PICTURE

**Students with need:** Need-based aid available for full-time and part-time students. Work study available nights, weekends, and for part-time students.
**Students without need:** This college awards aid only to students with need.

### FINANCIAL AID PROCEDURES

**Forms required:** FAFSA, institutional form.

**Dates and Deadlines:** Closing date 3/15. Applicants notified on a rolling basis starting 6/1; must reply within 3 week(s) of notification.

### CONTACT

William Trippet, Director of Student Financial Aid
2909 Kellogg Avenue, Janesville, WI 53546-5699
(608) 758-6565 ext. 200

## University of Wisconsin-Sheboygan

Sheboygan, Wisconsin
www.sheboygan.uwc.edu                    Federal Code: 003897

**2-year public** community and liberal arts college in small city.
**Enrollment:** 769 undergrads.
**Selectivity:** Open admission.

### BASIC COSTS (2015-2016)

**Tuition and fees:** $5,136; out-of-state residents $12,120.

### FINANCIAL AID PICTURE

**Students with need:** Need-based aid available for full-time and part-time students.
**Students without need:** No-need awards available for academics, art, leadership, music/drama.

### FINANCIAL AID PROCEDURES

**Forms required:** FAFSA, institutional form.

**Dates and Deadlines:** Priority date 4/15; no closing date. Applicants notified on a rolling basis starting 6/1; must reply within 2 week(s) of notification.
**Transfers:** No deadline. Applicants notified on a rolling basis.

### CONTACT

Mary Balde, Student Financial Aid Officer
One University Drive, Sheboygan, WI 53081
(920) 459-6633

## University of Wisconsin-Stevens Point

Stevens Point, Wisconsin
www.uwsp.edu
Federal Code: 003924

**4-year public** university in large town.
**Enrollment:** 8,684 undergrads. 1,617 full-time freshmen.

### BASIC COSTS (2015-2016)
**Tuition and fees:** $7,491; out-of-state residents $15,758.
**Per-credit charge:** $262.43; out-of-state residents $606.87.
**Room and board:** $7,012.

### FINANCIAL AID PICTURE (2014-2015)
**Students with need:** Out of 1,461 full-time freshmen who applied for aid, 932 were judged to have need. Of these, 932 received aid, and 104 had their full need met. Average financial aid package met 65% of need; average scholarship/grant was $5,371; average loan was $4,253. For part-time students, average financial aid package was $6,942.
**Students without need:** 85 full-time freshmen who did not demonstrate need for aid received scholarships/grants; average award was $1,454. No-need awards available for academics, alumni affiliation, art, music/drama, ROTC.
**Additional info:** Tuition discounts offered to qualified residents from other states. Tuition waiver for state veterans.

### FINANCIAL AID PROCEDURES
**Forms required:** FAFSA.
**Dates and Deadlines:** Priority date 3/15; closing date 5/1. Applicants notified on a rolling basis starting 3/1; must reply within 4 week(s) of notification.
**Transfers:** No deadline.

### CONTACT
Paul Watson, Director of Financial Aid
Student Services Center, Stevens Point, WI 54481
(715) 346-4771

## University of Wisconsin-Stout

Menomonie, Wisconsin
www.uwstout.edu
Federal Code: 003915

**4-year public** university in large town.
**Enrollment:** 8,194 undergrads, 17% part-time. 1,520 full-time freshmen.
**Selectivity:** Admits over 75% of applicants.

### BASIC COSTS (2015-2016)
**Tuition and fees:** $9,203; out-of-state residents $16,949.
**Per-credit charge:** $234; out-of-state residents $492.
**Room and board:** $6,504.
**Additional info:** Laptop is included with payment of fees.

### FINANCIAL AID PICTURE (2015-2016)
**Students with need:** Out of 1,326 full-time freshmen who applied for aid, 916 were judged to have need. Of these, 886 received aid, and 126 had their full need met. Average financial aid package met 80% of need; average scholarship/grant was $5,795; average loan was $3,748. For part-time students, average financial aid package was $8,489.
**Students without need:** 57 full-time freshmen who did not demonstrate need for aid received scholarships/grants; average award was $2,561. No-need awards available for academics.
**Scholarships offered:** Wisconsin Academic Excellence Scholarship: $2,250; selected by high school. National Merit Finalist Scholarship: $2,000; automatically awarded to NMSQT finalist. National Merit Semifinalist Scholarship: $1,000; automatically awarded to NMSQT semifinalist. Chancellor's Academic Honor Scholarship: $1,000; automatically awarded to top 5% of high school class with ACT of 25 who enroll by July 15.

### FINANCIAL AID PROCEDURES
**Forms required:** FAFSA.

**Dates and Deadlines:** Priority date 3/15; no closing date. Applicants notified on a rolling basis starting 3/21; must reply within 4 week(s) of notification.

### CONTACT
Beth Boisen, Director of Financial Aid
1 Clocktower Plaza, Menomonie, WI 54751
(715) 232-1363

## University of Wisconsin-Superior

Superior, Wisconsin
www.uwsuper.edu
Federal Code: 003925

**4-year public** university and liberal arts college in small city.
**Enrollment:** 2,254 undergrads, 17% part-time. 357 full-time freshmen.
**Selectivity:** Admits 50 to 75% of applicants.

### BASIC COSTS (2015-2016)
**Tuition and fees:** $8,036; out-of-state residents $15,609.
**Per-credit charge:** $272; out-of-state residents $588.
**Room and board:** $6,410.

### FINANCIAL AID PICTURE (2015-2016)
**Students with need:** Out of 267 full-time freshmen who applied for aid, 201 were judged to have need. Of these, 193 received aid, and 36 had their full need met. Average financial aid package met 82% of need; average scholarship/grant was $5,225; average loan was $3,592. For part-time students, average financial aid package was $8,975.
**Students without need:** 21 full-time freshmen who did not demonstrate need for aid received scholarships/grants; average award was $1,543. No-need awards available for academics, alumni affiliation, art, leadership, minority status, music/drama, state/district residency.
**Additional info:** Non resident Tuition Waiver (NTW) available to non-resident students on limited basis.

### FINANCIAL AID PROCEDURES
**Forms required:** FAFSA.
**Dates and Deadlines:** Priority date 3/15; no closing date. Applicants notified on a rolling basis starting 4/1; must reply by 5/1 or within 4 week(s) of notification.
**Transfers:** No deadline. Applicants notified on a rolling basis starting 3/15; must reply by 5/1 or within 4 week(s) of notification.

### CONTACT
Donna Dahlvang, Director of Financial Aid
Belknap and Catlin, Superior, WI 54880
(715) 394-8200

## University of Wisconsin-Washington County

West Bend, Wisconsin
www.washington.uwc.edu
Federal Code: 003897

**2-year public** branch campus and liberal arts college in large town.
**Enrollment:** 810 undergrads.

### BASIC COSTS (2015-2016)
**Tuition and fees:** $5,094; out-of-state residents $12,078.
**Per-credit charge:** $198; out-of-state residents $489.

### FINANCIAL AID PICTURE
**Students with need:** Need-based aid available for full-time and part-time students. Work study available weekends and for part-time students.
**Students without need:** No-need awards available for academics.

### FINANCIAL AID PROCEDURES
**Forms required:** FAFSA.

**Dates and Deadlines:** Priority date 4/15; no closing date. Applicants notified on a rolling basis starting 4/30; must reply within 3 week(s) of notification. **Transfers:** No deadline.

### CONTACT
Maria Graciano, Director of Student Financial Aid
400 University Drive, West Bend, WI 53095
(262) 335-5207

## University of Wisconsin-Waukesha
Waukesha, Wisconsin
www.waukesha.uwc.edu                    Federal Code: 003897

**2-year public** branch campus and junior college in small city.
**Enrollment:** 1,929 undergrads.

### BASIC COSTS (2015-2016)
**Tuition and fees:** $5,102; out-of-state residents $12,086.
**Per-credit charge:** $198; out-of-state residents $489.

### FINANCIAL AID PICTURE
**Students with need:** Need-based aid available for full-time and part-time students. Work study available nights, weekends, and for part-time students.
**Students without need:** No-need awards available for academics, alumni affiliation, art, leadership, minority status, music/drama, state/district residency.
**Scholarships offered:** University of Wisconsin-Waukesha Scholarship Program: numerous scholarships; amounts vary.

### FINANCIAL AID PROCEDURES
**Forms required:** FAFSA.
**Dates and Deadlines:** Priority date 4/1; no closing date. Applicants notified on a rolling basis starting 4/1; must reply within 3 week(s) of notification.

### CONTACT
Bill Trippett, Director of Student Financial Aid
1500 North University Drive, Waukesha, WI 53188
(262) 521-5210

## University of Wisconsin-Whitewater
Whitewater, Wisconsin
www.uww.edu                    Federal Code: 003926

**4-year public** university in large town.
**Enrollment:** 10,584 undergrads, 7% part-time. 2,179 full-time freshmen.
**Selectivity:** Admits 50 to 75% of applicants.

### BASIC COSTS (2015-2016)
**Tuition and fees:** $7,600; out-of-state residents $15,173.
**Per-credit charge:** $262; out-of-state residents $316.
**Room and board:** $6,144.

### FINANCIAL AID PICTURE (2015-2016)
**Students with need:** Average financial aid package met 58% of need; average scholarship/grant was $5,320; average loan was $3,397. Need-based aid available for part-time students.
**Students without need:** No-need awards available for academics, art, leadership, minority status, music/drama, state/district residency.

### FINANCIAL AID PROCEDURES
**Forms required:** FAFSA.
**Dates and Deadlines:** Priority date 3/1; no closing date. Applicants notified on a rolling basis starting 4/1; must reply within 3 week(s) of notification.
**Transfers:** No deadline. Applicants notified on a rolling basis starting 4/1; must reply within 3 week(s) of notification.

### CONTACT
Carol Miller, Director of Financial Aid
800 West Main Street, Whitewater, WI 53190-1790
(262) 472-1130

## Viterbo University
La Crosse, Wisconsin
www.viterbo.edu                    Federal Code: 003911

**4-year private** university in small city, affiliated with Roman Catholic Church.
**Enrollment:** 1,983 undergrads.

### BASIC COSTS (2015-2016)
**Tuition and fees:** $25,050.
**Room and board:** $8,260.
**Additional info:** Tuition/fee waivers available for minority students.

### FINANCIAL AID PICTURE
**Students with need:** Need-based aid available for full-time and part-time students. Work study available nights, weekends, and for part-time students.
**Students without need:** No-need awards available for academics, alumni affiliation, art, athletics, leadership, minority status, music/drama, ROTC.
**Scholarships offered:** Fine arts scholarships: up to $10,000 per year; for incoming full-time freshmen and transfer students talented in areas of art, music or theater. Dr. Scholl Scholarship: full, 4-year tuition; must enroll full-time and maintain 3.5 GPA, 1 awarded. Viterbo University Scholarship: $1,000-$8,000 per year; based on academic history; incoming freshmen and transfers automatically considered; renewable.

### FINANCIAL AID PROCEDURES
**Forms required:** FAFSA, institutional form.
**Dates and Deadlines:** Priority date 3/15; no closing date. Applicants notified on a rolling basis starting 4/1; must reply within 3 week(s) of notification.

### CONTACT
Terry Norman, Director of Financial Aid
900 Viterbo Drive, La Crosse, WI 54601-8804
(608) 796-3900

## Waukesha County Technical College
Pewaukee, Wisconsin
www.wctc.edu                    Federal Code: 005294

**2-year public** technical college in large town.
**Enrollment:** 4,889 undergrads, 68% part-time. 274 full-time freshmen.
**Selectivity:** Open admission; but selective for some programs.

### BASIC COSTS (2015-2016)
**Tuition and fees:** $4,083; out-of-state residents $6,009.
**Per-credit charge:** $128; out-of-state residents $193.
**Additional info:** Materials fees vary by program; minimum $5 per course. $10 per credit fee for online courses.

### FINANCIAL AID PICTURE (2014-2015)
**Students with need:** 34% of average financial aid package awarded as scholarships/grants, 66% awarded as loans/jobs. Work study available nights.
**Students without need:** No-need awards available for academics.

### FINANCIAL AID PROCEDURES
**Forms required:** FAFSA.
**Dates and Deadlines:** Priority date 4/1; no closing date. Applicants notified on a rolling basis starting 4/30.

### CONTACT
Tim Jacobson, Financial Aid Manager
Office of Admissions, C-019, Pewaukee, WI 53072
(262) 691-5436

## Western Technical College

La Crosse, Wisconsin
www.westerntc.edu                    Federal Code: 003840

**2-year public** community and technical college in small city.
**Enrollment:** 4,525 undergrads.
**Selectivity:** Open admission; but selective for some programs.

### BASIC COSTS (2015-2016)
**Tuition and fees:** $4,164; out-of-state residents $6,090.
**Per-credit charge:** $126; out-of-state residents $189.
**Additional info:** Tuition/fee waivers available for unemployed or children of unemployed.

### FINANCIAL AID PICTURE
**Students with need:** Need-based aid available for full-time and part-time students. Work study available nights, weekends, and for part-time students.

### FINANCIAL AID PROCEDURES
**Forms required:** FAFSA, institutional form.
**Dates and Deadlines:** Priority date 3/1; no closing date. Applicants notified on a rolling basis starting 4/1.

### CONTACT
Jerolyn Grandall, Student Financial Services Manager
400 Seventh St N, La Crosse, WI 54601
(608) 785-9302

## Wisconsin Indianhead Technical College

Shell Lake, Wisconsin
www.witc.edu                    Federal Code: 011824

**2-year public** technical college in small town.
**Enrollment:** 2,558 undergrads, 56% part-time. 290 full-time freshmen.
**Selectivity:** Open admission; but selective for some programs.

### BASIC COSTS (2015-2016)
**Tuition and fees:** $4,655; out-of-state residents $6,575.
**Per-credit charge:** $126; out-of-state residents $189.

### FINANCIAL AID PICTURE (2014-2015)
**Students with need:** 55% of average financial aid package awarded as scholarships/grants, 45% awarded as loans/jobs. Need-based aid available for part-time students. Work study available nights, weekends, and for part-time students.
**Students without need:** This college awards aid only to students with need.

### FINANCIAL AID PROCEDURES
**Forms required:** FAFSA.
**Dates and Deadlines:** Priority date 4/15; no closing date. Applicants notified on a rolling basis starting 4/15; must reply by 9/1 or within 4 week(s) of notification.

### CONTACT
Terry Klein, Director of Financial Aid
505 Pine Ridge Drive, Shell Lake, WI 54871
(715) 468-2815 ext. 2243

## Wisconsin Lutheran College

Milwaukee, Wisconsin
www.wlc.edu                    Federal Code: 014658

**4-year private** liberal arts college in very large city, affiliated with Wisconsin Evangelical Lutheran Synod.
**Enrollment:** 1,060 undergrads.

### BASIC COSTS (2015-2016)
**Tuition and fees:** $27,040.
**Per-credit charge:** $720.
**Room and board:** $9,250.

### FINANCIAL AID PICTURE
**Students with need:** Need-based aid available for full-time and part-time students.
**Students without need:** No-need awards available for academics, art, leadership, music/drama, ROTC.

### FINANCIAL AID PROCEDURES
**Forms required:** FAFSA, institutional form.
**Dates and Deadlines:** Priority date 3/1; no closing date. Applicants notified on a rolling basis starting 3/15; must reply within 2 week(s) of notification.
**Transfers:** No deadline. Applicants notified on a rolling basis; must reply within 2 week(s) of notification. Transfer scholarship and transfer grant available for qualifying students.

### CONTACT
Linda Loeffel, Financial Aid Director
8800 West Bluemound Road, Milwaukee, WI 53226-4699
(414) 443-8856

# Wyoming

## Casper College

Casper, Wyoming
www.caspercollege.edu                    Federal Code: 003928

**2-year public** community college in small city.
**Enrollment:** 2,429 undergrads, 31% part-time. 597 full-time freshmen.
**Selectivity:** Open admission; but selective for some programs and for out-of-state students.

### BASIC COSTS (2015-2016)
**Tuition and fees:** $2,640; out-of-state residents $6,624.
**Per-credit charge:** $83; out-of-state residents $249.
**Room and board:** $6,294.
**Additional info:** Western Undergraduate Exchange (WUE) students qualify for reduced rates.

### FINANCIAL AID PICTURE
**Students with need:** Need-based aid available for full-time and part-time students. Work study available nights, weekends, and for part-time students.
**Students without need:** No-need awards available for academics, art, athletics, leadership, music/drama, state/district residency.

### FINANCIAL AID PROCEDURES
**Forms required:** FAFSA.
**Dates and Deadlines:** Priority date 3/15; no closing date. Applicants notified on a rolling basis starting 4/1.
**Transfers:** No deadline. Applicants notified on a rolling basis starting 4/1.

### CONTACT
Darry Voigt, Executive Director Enrollment Services
125 College Drive, Casper, WY 82601
(307) 268-2510

## Central Wyoming College

Riverton, Wyoming
www.cwc.edu                    Federal Code: 005018

**2-year public** community college in large town.
**Enrollment:** 1,045 undergrads, 43% part-time. 222 full-time freshmen.

**Selectivity:** Open admission; but selective for some programs.

## BASIC COSTS (2015-2016)
**Tuition and fees:** $2,892; out-of-state residents $6,876.
**Per-credit charge:** $83; out-of-state residents $249.
**Room and board:** $5,130.
**Additional info:** Western Undergraduate Exchange (WUE) students qualify for reduced rates.

## FINANCIAL AID PICTURE (2015-2016)
**Students with need:** Out of 144 full-time freshmen who applied for aid, 105 were judged to have need. Of these, 105 received aid. Need-based aid available for part-time students.
**Students without need:** No-need awards available for academics, alumni affiliation, art, athletics, leadership, minority status, music/drama, state/district residency.
**Scholarships offered:** Honors Scholarships: in-state tuition and general fees plus $300 book stipend; for graduating high school seniors with 3.5 GPA or 25 ACT. Seniors Scholarships: in-state tuition; for graduating high school seniors with 3.0-3.49 GPA or 22 ACT. Full academic scholarships: in-state tuition, general fees, room and board, books and supplies; for Wyoming National Merit finalists.

## FINANCIAL AID PROCEDURES
**Forms required:** FAFSA, institutional form.
**Dates and Deadlines:** Priority date 4/15; no closing date. Applicants notified on a rolling basis starting 5/1; must reply within 2 week(s) of notification.

## CONTACT
Scott McFarland, Director of Financial Aid
2660 Peck Avenue, Riverton, WY 82501
(307) 855-2150

# Eastern Wyoming College
Torrington, Wyoming
www.ewc.wy.edu                    Federal Code: 003929

**2-year public** community college in small town.
**Enrollment:** 611 undergrads, 34% part-time. 179 full-time freshmen.
**Selectivity:** Open admission.

## BASIC COSTS (2015-2016)
**Tuition and fees:** $2,712; out-of-state residents $6,696.
**Room and board:** $6,136.
**Additional info:** Western Undergraduate Exchange (WUE) students qualify for reduced rates.

## FINANCIAL AID PICTURE
**Students with need:** Need-based aid available for full-time and part-time students. Work study available nights, weekends, and for part-time students.
**Students without need:** No-need awards available for academics, alumni affiliation, art, athletics, leadership, music/drama.
**Additional info:** Installment payment plan on room and board contracts offered.

## FINANCIAL AID PROCEDURES
**Forms required:** FAFSA, institutional form.
**Dates and Deadlines:** Priority date 3/15; no closing date. Applicants notified on a rolling basis starting 1/1.

## CONTACT
Susan Stephenson, Financial Aid Director
3200 West C Street, Torrington, WY 82240
(800) 658-3195 ext. 8325

# Laramie County Community College
Cheyenne, Wyoming
www.lccc.wy.edu                    Federal Code: 009259

**2-year public** community college in small city.
**Enrollment:** 3,021 undergrads, 41% part-time. 326 full-time freshmen.
**Selectivity:** Open admission; but selective for some programs.

## BASIC COSTS (2015-2016)
**Tuition and fees:** $3,144; out-of-state residents $7,128.
**Room and board:** $7,200.
**Additional info:** Western Undergraduate Exchange (WUE) students qualify for reduced tuition and fees $4,128.

## FINANCIAL AID PICTURE (2014-2015)
**Students with need:** Out of 266 full-time freshmen who applied for aid, 200 were judged to have need. Of these, 193 received aid, and 34 had their full need met. Average financial aid package met 71% of need; average scholarship/grant was $1,694; average loan was $2,796. For part-time students, average financial aid package was $4,096.
**Students without need:** 133 full-time freshmen who did not demonstrate need for aid received scholarships/grants; average award was $1,195. No-need awards available for academics, alumni affiliation, art, athletics, job skills, leadership, minority status, music/drama, religious affiliation, state/district residency.
**Scholarships offered:** 42 full-time freshmen received athletic scholarships; average amount $7,173.

## FINANCIAL AID PROCEDURES
**Forms required:** FAFSA, institutional form.
**Dates and Deadlines:** Priority date 4/1; no closing date. Applicants notified on a rolling basis starting 4/1; must reply within 2 week(s) of notification.
**Transfers:** No deadline. Applicants notified on a rolling basis starting 4/1; must reply within 2 week(s) of notification.

## CONTACT
Jennifer Almli, Director of Financial Aid
1400 East College Drive, Cheyenne, WY 82007-3299
(307) 778-1281

# Northwest College
Powell, Wyoming
www.nwc.edu                    Federal Code: 003931

**2-year public** community and junior college in small town.
**Enrollment:** 1,425 undergrads, 35% part-time. 304 full-time freshmen.
**Selectivity:** Open admission; but selective for some programs and for out-of-state students.

## BASIC COSTS (2015-2016)
**Tuition and fees:** $2,779; out-of-state residents $6,763.
**Per-credit charge:** $83; out-of-state residents $249.
**Room and board:** $5,198.
**Additional info:** The WUE (Western Undergraduate Exchange) program provides discounted tuition rates for residents of the following states: AK, AZ, CA, CNMI, CO, HI, ID, MT, NV, NM, ND, OR, SD, UT, & WA. Nebraska residents also qualify for this reduced rate.

## FINANCIAL AID PICTURE
**Students with need:** Need-based aid available for full-time and part-time students. Work study available nights, weekends, and for part-time students.
**Students without need:** No-need awards available for academics, alumni affiliation, art, athletics, leadership, music/drama, state/district residency.

## FINANCIAL AID PROCEDURES
**Forms required:** FAFSA, institutional form.
**Dates and Deadlines:** Priority date 3/1; no closing date. Applicants notified on a rolling basis; must reply within 2 week(s) of notification.

CONTACT

Shaman Quinn, Financial Aid and Scholarships Director

Orendorff Building, Powell, WY 82435-1898

(307) 754-6158

## Sheridan College
Sheridan, Wyoming
www.sheridan.edu                 Federal Code: 003930

**2-year public** community college in large town.

**Enrollment:** 1,941 undergrads, 35% part-time. 498 full-time freshmen.

**Selectivity:** Open admission; but selective for some programs.

**BASIC COSTS (2015-2016)**

**Tuition and fees:** $2,952; out-of-state residents $6,936.

**Per-credit charge:** $83; out-of-state residents $249.

**Room and board:** $6,170.

**Additional info:** Western Undergraduate Exchange (WUE) students qualify for reduced rates.

**FINANCIAL AID PICTURE**

**Students with need:** Need-based aid available for full-time and part-time students. Work study available nights, weekends, and for part-time students.

**Students without need:** No-need awards available for academics, art, athletics, leadership, music/drama, state/district residency.

**Scholarships offered:** Academic scholarships; in-state tuition and fees; based on 25 ACT/1120 SAT (exclusive of Writing); renewable.

**FINANCIAL AID PROCEDURES**

**Forms required:** FAFSA, institutional form.

**Dates and Deadlines:** Priority date 3/1; no closing date. Applicants notified on a rolling basis; must reply within 3 week(s) of notification.

CONTACT

Kristen Gast, Director of Financial Aid

PO Box 1500, Sheridan, WY 82801-1500

(307) 674-6446 ext. 2100

## University of Wyoming
Laramie, Wyoming
www.uwyo.edu                     Federal Code: 003932

**4-year public** university in large town.

**Enrollment:** 9,842 undergrads, 15% part-time. 1,554 full-time freshmen.

**Selectivity:** Admits over 75% of applicants.

**BASIC COSTS (2015-2016)**

**Tuition and fees:** $4,891; out-of-state residents $15,631.

**Per-credit charge:** $119; out-of-state residents $477.

**Room and board:** $10,037.

**FINANCIAL AID PICTURE (2014-2015)**

**Students with need:** Out of 1,207 full-time freshmen who applied for aid, 761 were judged to have need. Of these, 753 received aid, and 176 had their full need met. Average financial aid package met 65% of need; average scholarship/grant was $5,255; average loan was $3,163. For part-time students, average financial aid package was $5,506.

**Students without need:** 441 full-time freshmen who did not demonstrate need for aid received scholarships/grants; average award was $4,169. No-need awards available for academics, alumni affiliation, art, athletics, leadership, minority status, music/drama, ROTC, state/district residency.

**Scholarships offered:** *Merit:* Western Heritage Scholarship: number awarded and packages vary. President's High School Honor Scholarship: covers undergraduate fees and tuition; number awarded varies. *Athletic:* 34 full-time freshmen received athletic scholarships; average amount $1,792.

**FINANCIAL AID PROCEDURES**

**Forms required:** FAFSA.

**Dates and Deadlines:** Priority date 3/1; no closing date. Applicants notified on a rolling basis starting 4/3; must reply within 3 week(s) of notification.

CONTACT

Kathy Bobbitt, Director of Student Financial Aid

Dept 3435, Laramie, WY 82071

(307) 766-2116

## Western Wyoming Community College
Rock Springs, Wyoming
www.westernwyoming.edu           Federal Code: 003933

**2-year public** community college in large town.

**Enrollment:** 1,797 undergrads, 39% part-time. 175 full-time freshmen.

**Selectivity:** Open admission; but selective for some programs.

**BASIC COSTS (2015-2016)**

**Tuition and fees:** $2,400; out-of-state residents $6,384.

**Per-credit charge:** $101; out-of-state residents $267.

**Room and board:** $4,472.

**Additional info:** Western Undergraduate Exchange (WUE) students qualify for reduced rates.

**FINANCIAL AID PICTURE (2014-2015)**

**Students with need:** 54% of average financial aid package awarded as scholarships/grants, 46% awarded as loans/jobs. Need-based aid available for part-time students.

**Students without need:** No-need awards available for academics, art, athletics, music/drama, state/district residency.

**FINANCIAL AID PROCEDURES**

**Forms required:** FAFSA.

**Dates and Deadlines:** Priority date 4/1; no closing date. Applicants notified on a rolling basis starting 2/15; must reply within 2 week(s) of notification.

CONTACT

Nicole Castillon, Financial Aid Officer

Box 428, Rock Springs, WY 82902-0428

(307) 382-1643

# Part IV

Scholarship Lists

# Academic scholarships

## Alabama
Alabama State University
Amridge University
Athens State University
Bevill State Community College
Birmingham-Southern College
Bishop State Community College
Calhoun Community College
Central Alabama Community College
Chattahoochee Valley Community College
Enterprise State Community College
Faulkner State Community College
Faulkner University
Gadsden State Community College
George C. Wallace Community College at
  Dothan
George C. Wallace State Community College
  at Selma
Huntingdon College
Jacksonville State University
Jefferson Davis Community College
Jefferson State Community College
Judson College
Lurleen B. Wallace Community College
Northeast Alabama Community College
Northwest-Shoals Community College
Oakwood University
Samford University
Selma University
Shelton State Community College
Snead State Community College
Southeastern Bible College
Spring Hill College
Stillman College
Talladega College
Troy University
Tuskegee University
University of Alabama
University of Alabama
  Birmingham
  Huntsville
University of Mobile
University of Montevallo
University of North Alabama
University of South Alabama
University of West Alabama
Wallace State Community College at
  Hanceville

## Alaska
Alaska Bible College
Alaska Pacific University
University of Alaska
  Anchorage
  Fairbanks
  Southeast

## Arizona
Arizona Christian University
Arizona State University
Arizona Western College
DeVry University
  Phoenix
Dine College
Eastern Arizona College
Grand Canyon University
Mesa Community College
Northern Arizona University
Northland Pioneer College
Pima Community College
Prescott College
Scottsdale Community College
South Mountain Community College
Southwest University of Visual Arts

Tohono O'odham Community College
University of Advancing Technology
University of Arizona
Yavapai College

## Arkansas
Arkansas Northeastern College
Arkansas State University
Arkansas State University
  Beebe
  Mid-South
  Mountain Home
Arkansas Tech University
Black River Technical College
Central Baptist College
College of the Ouachitas
Crowley's Ridge College
Ecclesia College
Harding University
Henderson State University
Hendrix College
John Brown University
Lyon College
National Park College
North Arkansas College
Northwest Arkansas Community College
Ouachita Baptist University
Philander Smith College
Phillips Community College of the University
  of Arkansas
Rich Mountain Community College
Southeast Arkansas College
Southern Arkansas University
Southern Arkansas University Tech
University of Arkansas
  Community College at Batesville
  Community College at Hope
  Community College at Morrilton
  for Medical Sciences
  Fort Smith
  Little Rock
  Monticello
  Pine Bluff
University of Central Arkansas
University of the Ozarks
Williams Baptist College

## California
Academy of Art University
Alliant International University
American Academy of Dramatic Arts: West
Art Institute of California
  Los Angeles
  Orange County
Azusa Pacific University
Bethesda University of California
Biola University
Brandman University
California Baptist University
California College of the Arts
California Institute of Integral Studies
California Institute of the Arts
California Lutheran University
California Maritime Academy
California Polytechnic State University: San
  Luis Obispo
California State Polytechnic University:
  Pomona
California State University
  Bakersfield
  Channel Islands
  Chico
  Dominguez Hills
  East Bay
  Fresno

  Fullerton
  Long Beach
  Monterey Bay
  Northridge
  San Marcos
  Stanislaus
Chaffey College
Chapman University
Charles Drew University of Medicine and
  Science
Claremont McKenna College
Cogswell Polytechnical College
College of the Canyons
College of the Desert
Columbia College
Concordia University Irvine
Deep Springs College
DeVry University
  Pomona
Dominican University of California
East Los Angeles College
El Camino College
Empire College
Fashion Institute of Design and Merchandising
  Los Angeles
  San Diego
  San Francisco
Fresno Pacific University
Glendale Community College
Golden Gate University
Golden West College
Harvey Mudd College
Holy Names University
Hope International University
Humboldt State University
Humphreys College
Imperial Valley College
John F. Kennedy University
John Paul the Great Catholic University
La Sierra University
Life Pacific College
Loyola Marymount University
The Master's College
Mendocino College
Menlo College
Merced College
Mills College
Mount Saint Mary's University
Mount San Jacinto College
Napa Valley College
Notre Dame de Namur University
Occidental College
Otis College of Art and Design
Pacific States University
Pacific Union College
Pepperdine University
Pitzer College
Point Loma Nazarene University
Providence Christian College
Riverside City College
St. Mary's College of California
Samuel Merritt University
San Diego Christian College
San Diego State University
San Francisco Art Institute
San Francisco State University
San Joaquin Delta College
San Jose State University
Santa Clara University
Santa Rosa Junior College
Scripps College
Simpson University
Soka University of America
Sonoma State University
Southern California Institute of Architecture
SUM Bible College & Theological Seminary
Taft College
University of California
  Berkeley
  Davis
  Los Angeles
  Merced
  Riverside

  San Diego
  Santa Barbara
  Santa Cruz
University of La Verne
University of Redlands
University of San Diego
University of San Francisco
University of Southern California
University of the Pacific
University of the West
Vanguard University of Southern California
West Coast University
  Los Angeles
West Coast University: Ontario
West Coast University: Orange County
Westmont College
Whittier College
William Jessup University
Woodbury University
Yuba College

## Colorado
Adams State University
Arapahoe Community College
Colorado Christian University
Colorado College
Colorado Heights University
Colorado Mesa University
Colorado Northwestern Community College
Colorado School of Mines
Colorado State University
Colorado State University
  Pueblo
Colorado Technical University
Community College of Aurora
Community College of Denver
DeVry University
  Westminster
Fort Lewis College
Front Range Community College
Johnson & Wales University
  Denver
Lamar Community College
Naropa University
Nazarene Bible College
Northeastern Junior College
Otero Junior College
Pueblo Community College
Red Rocks Community College
Regis University
Rocky Mountain College of Art & Design
Trinidad State Junior College
University of Colorado
  Boulder
  Colorado Springs
  Denver
University of Denver
University of Northern Colorado
Western State Colorado University
Westwood College
  Denver North

## Connecticut
Albertus Magnus College
Central Connecticut State University
Fairfield University
Goodwin College
Housatonic Community College
Lincoln College of New England
Lyme Academy College of Fine Arts
Mitchell College
Norwalk Community College
Quinnipiac University
Sacred Heart University
St. Vincent's College
Southern Connecticut State University
Trinity College
Tunxis Community College
University of Bridgeport
University of Connecticut
University of Hartford
University of New Haven

University of Saint Joseph
Western Connecticut State University

### Delaware

Delaware College of Art and Design
Delaware State University
Delaware Technical Community College
    Jack F. Owens Campus
    Stanton/Wilmington Campus
    Terry Campus
Goldey-Beacom College
University of Delaware
Wesley College
Wilmington University

### District of Columbia

American University
Catholic University of America
George Washington University
Howard University
Trinity Washington University

### Florida

Art Institute of Fort Lauderdale
Ave Maria University
Baptist College of Florida
Barry University
Beacon College
Bethune-Cookman University
Broward College
Brown Mackie College
    Miami
Carlos Albizu University
Chipola College
College of Central Florida
Daytona State College
DeVry University
    Miramar
    Orlando
Eastern Florida State College
Eckerd College
Flagler College
Florida Agricultural and Mechanical University
Florida Atlantic University
Florida College
Florida Gateway College
Florida Gulf Coast University
Florida Institute of Technology
Florida International University
Florida Keys Community College
Florida National University
Florida Southern College
Florida SouthWestern State College
Florida State College at Jacksonville
Florida State University
Gulf Coast State College
Hillsborough Community College
Hobe Sound Bible College
Hodges University
Indian River State College
International Academy of Design and
    Technology: Tampa
Jacksonville University
Johnson & Wales University
    North Miami
Johnson University: Florida
Jones College
Jose Maria Vargas University
Keiser University
Lake-Sumter State College
Lynn University
Miami Dade College
New College of Florida
North Florida Community College
Northwest Florida State College
Nova Southeastern University
Palm Beach Atlantic University
Palm Beach State College
Pasco-Hernando State College
Pensacola State College
Polk State College
Ringling College of Art and Design
Rollins College

Saint Leo University
St. Petersburg College
Saint Thomas University
Santa Fe College
Schiller International University
Seminole State College of Florida
South Florida State College
Southeastern University
State College of Florida, Manatee-Sarasota
Stetson University
Tallahassee Community College
Trinity Baptist College
Trinity College of Florida
University of Central Florida
University of Florida
University of Miami
University of North Florida
University of South Florida
University of South Florida
    Sarasota-Manatee
University of Tampa
University of West Florida
Warner University
Webber International University

### Georgia

Abraham Baldwin Agricultural College
Agnes Scott College
Albany State University
Albany Technical College
Andrew College
Armstrong State University
Art Institute of Atlanta
Athens Technical College
Augusta University
Berry College
Brenau University
Brewton-Parker College
Central Georgia Technical College
Clark Atlanta University
Clayton State University
College of Coastal Georgia
Columbus State University
Covenant College
Dalton State College
Darton College
DeVry University
    Decatur
East Georgia State College
Emmanuel College
Emory University
Fort Valley State University
Georgia College and State University
Georgia Gwinnett College
Georgia Highlands College
Georgia Institute of Technology
Georgia Perimeter College
Georgia Piedmont Technical College
Georgia Southern University
Georgia Southwestern State University
Georgia State University
Gordon State College
Herzing University
    Atlanta
Kennesaw State University
LaGrange College
Life University
Luther Rice University
Mercer University
Middle Georgia State College
Morehouse College
Oglethorpe University
Oxford College of Emory University
Paine College
Piedmont College
Point University
Reinhardt University
Savannah College of Art and Design
Savannah State University
Savannah Technical College
Shorter University
South Georgia State College
Spelman College

Thomas University
Toccoa Falls College
Truett-McConnell College
University of Georgia
University of North Georgia
University of West Georgia
Valdosta State University
Wesleyan College
Wiregrass Georgia Technical College
Young Harris College

### Hawaii

Brigham Young University-Hawaii
Chaminade University of Honolulu
Hawaii Pacific University
Hawaii Tokai International College
University of Hawaii
    Hilo
    Honolulu Community College
    Kapiolani Community College
    Manoa
    West Oahu
    Windward Community College

### Idaho

Boise Bible College
Boise State University
Brigham Young University-Idaho
College of Idaho
College of Western Idaho
Eastern Idaho Technical College
Idaho State University
Lewis-Clark State College
New Saint Andrews College
North Idaho College
Northwest Nazarene University
University of Idaho

### Illinois

Augustana College
Aurora University
Benedictine University
Benedictine University at Springfield
Black Hawk College
Blackburn College
Blessing-Rieman College of Nursing
Bradley University
Carl Sandburg College
Chicago State University
College of DuPage
College of Lake County
Columbia College Chicago
Concordia University Chicago
Danville Area Community College
DePaul University
DeVry University
    Chicago
    Online
Dominican University
East-West University
Eastern Illinois University
Elgin Community College
Elmhurst College
Eureka College
Governors State University
Greenville College
Harper College
Heartland Community College
Highland Community College
Illinois Central College
Illinois College
Illinois Eastern Community Colleges
    Frontier Community College
    Lincoln Trail College
    Olney Central College
    Wabash Valley College
Illinois Institute of Art
    Schaumburg
Illinois Institute of Technology
Illinois State University
Illinois Valley Community College
Illinois Wesleyan University

International Academy of Design and
    Technology
    Chicago
Joliet Junior College
Judson University
Kaskaskia College
Kendall College
Kishwaukee College
Knox College
Lake Forest College
Lake Land College
Lewis University
Lincoln Christian University
Lincoln College
Lincoln Land Community College
Loyola University Chicago
MacCormac College
MacMurray College
McHenry County College
McKendree University
Midstate College
Millikin University
Monmouth College
Moody Bible Institute
Moraine Valley Community College
Morrison Institute of Technology
National-Louis University
North Central College
North Park University
Northeastern Illinois University
Northern Illinois University
Northwestern College
Oakton Community College
Olivet Nazarene University
Parkland College
Principia College
Quincy University
Resurrection University
Richland Community College
Robert Morris University: Chicago
Rockford University
Roosevelt University
Rush University
Saint Anthony College of Nursing
St. Francis Medical Center College of Nursing
Saint Xavier University
Sauk Valley Community College
School of the Art Institute of Chicago
Shawnee Community College
Shimer College
South Suburban College of Cook County
Southeastern Illinois College
Southern Illinois University Carbondale
Southern Illinois University Edwardsville
Southwestern Illinois College
Spoon River College
Trinity Christian College
Trinity College of Nursing & Health Sciences
Trinity International University
Triton College
University of Chicago
University of Illinois
    Chicago
    Springfield
    Urbana-Champaign
University of St. Francis
VanderCook College of Music
Waubonsee Community College
Western Illinois University
Wheaton College

### Indiana

Ancilla College
Anderson University
Ball State University
Bethel College
Butler University
Calumet College of St. Joseph
DePauw University
Earlham College
Franklin College
Goshen College
Grace College

Hanover College
Holy Cross College
Huntington University
Indiana State University
Indiana University
  Bloomington
  East
  Kokomo
  Northwest
  Purdue University Fort Wayne
  Purdue University Indianapolis
  South Bend
  Southeast
Indiana Wesleyan University
Manchester University
Marian University
Oakland City University
Purdue University
Purdue University
  Calumet
  North Central
Rose-Hulman Institute of Technology
Saint Joseph's College
St. Mary-of-the-Woods College
Saint Mary's College
Taylor University
Trine University
University of Evansville
University of Indianapolis
University of Notre Dame
University of Saint Francis
University of Southern Indiana
Valparaiso University
Vincennes University
Wabash College

**Iowa**
Allen College
Briar Cliff University
Buena Vista University
Central College
Clarke University
Coe College
Cornell College
Des Moines Area Community College
Dordt College
Drake University
Ellsworth Community College
Emmaus Bible College
Faith Baptist Bible College and Theological
  Seminary
Graceland University
Grand View University
Grinnell College
Hawkeye Community College
Iowa Central Community College
Iowa State University
Iowa Wesleyan College
Kaplan University
  Cedar Falls
  Cedar Rapids
  Davenport
  Mason City
Loras College
Luther College
Mercy College of Health Sciences
Morningside College
Mount Mercy University
North Iowa Area Community College
Northeast Iowa Community College
Northwestern College
St. Ambrose University
St. Luke's College
Simpson College
Southeastern Community College
Southwestern Community College
University of Dubuque
University of Iowa
University of Northern Iowa
Upper Iowa University
Vatterott College
  Des Moines
Waldorf University

Wartburg College
Western Iowa Tech Community College
William Penn University

**Kansas**
Allen County Community College
Baker University
Barclay College
Barton County Community College
Benedictine College
Bethany College
Bethel College
Butler Community College
Central Christian College of Kansas
Coffeyville Community College
Colby Community College
Cowley County Community College
Dodge City Community College
Donnelly College
Emporia State University
Fort Hays State University
Friends University
Garden City Community College
Hesston College
Highland Community College
Hutchinson Community College
Independence Community College
Johnson County Community College
Kansas City Kansas Community College
Kansas State University
Kansas Wesleyan University
Labette Community College
Manhattan Area Technical College
Manhattan Christian College
McPherson College
MidAmerica Nazarene University
Neosho County Community College
Newman University
North Central Kansas Technical College
Ottawa University
Pittsburg State University
Pratt Community College
Seward County Community College
Southwestern College
Sterling College
Tabor College
University of Kansas
University of Kansas Medical Center
University of St. Mary
Washburn University
Wichita Area Technical College
Wichita State University

**Kentucky**
Alice Lloyd College
Asbury University
Ashland Community and Technical College
Beckfield College
Bellarmine University
Big Sandy Community and Technical College
Bluegrass Community and Technical College
Brescia University
Campbellsville University
Centre College
Clear Creek Baptist Bible College
Daymar College
  Bowling Green
  Owensboro
Eastern Kentucky University
Georgetown College
Hopkinsville Community College
Jefferson Community and Technical College
Kentucky Christian University
Kentucky Mountain Bible College
Kentucky State University
Kentucky Wesleyan College
Maysville Community and Technical College
Midway College
Morehead State University
Murray State University
National College
  Danville
  Florence

  Lexington
  Louisville
  Pikeville
  Richmond
Northern Kentucky University
Owensboro Community and Technical College
St. Catharine College
Somerset Community College
Southeast Kentucky Community and Technical
  College
Spalding University
Spencerian College
Spencerian College: Lexington
Sullivan College of Technology and Design
Thomas More College
Transylvania University
Union College
University of Kentucky
University of Louisville
University of the Cumberlands
Western Kentucky University

**Louisiana**
Baton Rouge Community College
Bossier Parish Community College
Centenary College of Louisiana
Delgado Community College
Dillard University
Grambling State University
Louisiana College
Louisiana State University
  Alexandria
  Health Sciences Center
  Shreveport
Louisiana State University and Agricultural and
  Mechanical College
Louisiana Tech University
Loyola University New Orleans
McNeese State University
Nicholls State University
Northwestern State University
Remington College
  Baton Rouge
St. Joseph Seminary College
South Louisiana Community College
Southeastern Louisiana University
Southern University and Agricultural and
  Mechanical College
Tulane University
University of Holy Cross
University of Louisiana at Monroe
University of New Orleans
Xavier University of Louisiana

**Maine**
Bowdoin College
College of the Atlantic
Eastern Maine Community College
Husson University
Maine College of Art
Maine Maritime Academy
Saint Joseph's College of Maine
Thomas College
Unity College
University of Maine
University of Maine
  Augusta
  Farmington
  Fort Kent
  Machias
  Presque Isle
University of New England
University of Southern Maine
Washington County Community College
York County Community College

**Maryland**
Allegany College of Maryland
Bowie State University
Capitol Technology University
Carroll Community College
Cecil College
Chesapeake College

College of Southern Maryland
Community College of Baltimore County
Coppin State University
Frederick Community College
Frostburg State University
Garrett College
Goucher College
Hood College
Johns Hopkins University
Johns Hopkins University: Peabody
  Conservatory of Music
Loyola University Maryland
Maryland Institute College of Art
McDaniel College
Montgomery College
Mount St. Mary's University
Notre Dame of Maryland University
Prince George's Community College
St. John's College
St. Mary's College of Maryland
Salisbury University
Stevenson University
Towson University
University of Maryland
  Baltimore County
  College Park
  Eastern Shore
  University College
Washington Adventist University
Washington College
Wor-Wic Community College

**Massachusetts**
American International College
Anna Maria College
Assumption College
Babson College
Bard College at Simon's Rock
Bay Path University
Bay State College
Becker College
Benjamin Franklin Institute of Technology
Bentley University
Berklee College of Music
Berkshire Community College
Boston Architectural College
Boston Baptist College
Boston College
Boston University
Brandeis University
Bridgewater State University
Bristol Community College
Bunker Hill Community College
Cape Cod Community College
Clark University
College of the Holy Cross
Curry College
Dean College
Eastern Nazarene College
Elms College
Emerson College
Emmanuel College
Endicott College
Fisher College
Fitchburg State University
Framingham State University
Franklin W. Olin College of Engineering
Gordon College
Hampshire College
Hellenic College/Holy Cross
Holyoke Community College
Laboure College
Lasell College
Lesley University
Massachusetts College of Art and Design
Massachusetts College of Liberal Arts
Massachusetts Maritime Academy
MCPHS University
Merrimack College
Montserrat College of Art
Mount Holyoke College
Mount Wachusett Community College
New England Conservatory of Music

Newbury College
Nichols College
North Shore Community College
Northeastern University
Northern Essex Community College
Northpoint Bible College
Pine Manor College
Quinsigamond Community College
Regis College
Salem State University
School of the Museum of Fine Arts
Simmons College
Smith College
Springfield College
Stonehill College
Suffolk University
Tufts University
University of Massachusetts
    Amherst
    Boston
    Dartmouth
    Lowell
Wentworth Institute of Technology
Western New England University
Westfield State University
Wheaton College
Wheelock College
Worcester Polytechnic Institute
Worcester State University

## Michigan
Adrian College
Albion College
Alma College
Alpena Community College
Andrews University
Aquinas College
Baker College
    Auburn Hills
    Cadillac
    Clinton Township
    Flint
    Jackson
    Muskegon
    Owosso
    Port Huron
Bay College
Calvin College
Central Michigan University
Cleary University
College for Creative Studies
Concordia University
Cornerstone University
Davenport University
Delta College
Eastern Michigan University
Ferris State University
Finlandia University
Glen Oaks Community College
Gogebic Community College
Grace Bible College
Grand Rapids Community College
Grand Valley State University
Great Lakes Christian College
Henry Ford Community College
Hillsdale College
Hope College
Jackson College
Kalamazoo College
Kalamazoo Valley Community College
Kellogg Community College
Kettering University
Kirtland Community College
Kuyper College
Lake Superior State University
Lansing Community College
Lawrence Technological University
Macomb Community College
Madonna College
Marygrove College
Michigan State University
Michigan Technological University
Mid Michigan Community College

Monroe County Community College
Montcalm Community College
Mott Community College
Northern Michigan University
Northwestern Michigan College
Northwood University
    Michigan
Oakland Community College
Oakland University
Olivet College
Robert B. Miller College
Rochester College
Sacred Heart Major Seminary
Saginaw Valley State University
Schoolcraft College
Southwestern Michigan College
Spring Arbor University
University of Detroit Mercy
University of Michigan
University of Michigan
    Dearborn
    Flint
Walsh College of Accountancy and Business
    Administration
Washtenaw Community College
Wayne State University
Western Michigan University

## Minnesota
Art Institutes International Minnesota
Augsburg College
Bemidji State University
Bethany Lutheran College
Bethel University
Brown College
    Mendota Heights
Carleton College
College of St. Benedict
College of St. Scholastica
Concordia College: Moorhead
Concordia University St. Paul
Crossroads College
Crown College
Dakota County Technical College
Fond du Lac Tribal and Community College
Gustavus Adolphus College
Hamline University
Itasca Community College
Lake Superior College
Le Cordon Bleu College of Culinary Arts
    Minneapolis-St. Paul
Macalester College
Martin Luther College
McNally Smith College of Music
Metropolitan State University
Minneapolis College of Art and Design
Minnesota State College - Southeast Technical
Minnesota State Community and Technical
    College
Minnesota State University
    Mankato
    Moorhead
National American University
    Bloomington
Normandale Community College
North Central University
North Hennepin Community College
Northland Community & Technical College
Northwest Technical College
Northwestern Health Sciences University
Oak Hills Christian College
Pine Technical & Community College
Rainy River Community College
St. Catherine University
Saint Cloud State University
St. Cloud Technical and Community College
St. John's University
St. Mary's University of Minnesota
St. Olaf College
Southwest Minnesota State University
University of Minnesota
    Crookston
    Duluth

    Morris
    Rochester
    Twin Cities
University of Northwestern - St. Paul
University of St. Thomas
Winona State University

## Mississippi
Alcorn State University
Belhaven University
Blue Mountain College
Coahoma Community College
Copiah-Lincoln Community College
Delta State University
East Central Community College
East Mississippi Community College
Hinds Community College
Holmes Community College
Itawamba Community College
Jackson State University
Jones County Junior College
Meridian Community College
Millsaps College
Mississippi College
Mississippi Delta Community College
Mississippi Gulf Coast Community College
Mississippi State University
Mississippi University for Women
Mississippi Valley State University
Northeast Mississippi Community College
Pearl River Community College
Rust College
Tougaloo College
University of Mississippi
University of Mississippi Medical Center
University of Southern Mississippi
William Carey University

## Missouri
Avila University
Calvary Bible College and Theological
    Seminary
Central Methodist University
Chamberlain College of Nursing
    St. Louis
College of the Ozarks
Columbia College
Conception Seminary College
Cottey College
Crowder College
Culver-Stockton College
DeVry University
    Kansas City
Drury University
East Central College
Fontbonne University
Goldfarb School of Nursing at Barnes-Jewish
    College
Hannibal-LaGrange University
Harris-Stowe State University
Jefferson College
Kansas City Art Institute
Lincoln University
Lindenwood University
Maryville University of Saint Louis
Metropolitan Community College - Kansas City
Mineral Area College
Missouri Baptist University
Missouri Southern State University
Missouri State University
Missouri State University: West Plains
Missouri Tech
Missouri University of Science and Technology
Missouri Valley College
Missouri Western State University
Moberly Area Community College
North Central Missouri College
Northwest Missouri State University
Ozark Christian College
Park University
Research College of Nursing
Rockhurst University
St. Charles Community College

St. Louis Community College
Saint Louis University
Southeast Missouri State University
Southwest Baptist University
State Fair Community College
State Technical College of Missouri
Stephens College
Three Rivers Community College
Truman State University
University of Central Missouri
University of Missouri
    Columbia
    Kansas City
    St. Louis
Washington University in St. Louis
Webster University
Westminster College
William Jewell College
William Woods University

## Montana
Blackfeet Community College
Carroll College
Chief Dull Knife College
Dawson Community College
Flathead Valley Community College
Fort Peck Community College
Little Big Horn College
Miles Community College
Montana State University
Montana State University
    Billings
    Great Falls College
    Northern
Montana Tech of the University of Montana
Rocky Mountain College
University of Great Falls
University of Montana
University of Montana: Western

## Nebraska
Bellevue University
BryanLGH College of Health Sciences
Central Community College
Chadron State College
Clarkson College
College of Saint Mary
Concordia University
Creative Center
Creighton University
Doane College
Grace University
Hastings College
Metropolitan Community College
Mid-Plains Community College
Midland University
Nebraska Christian College
Nebraska College of Technical Agriculture
Nebraska Methodist College of Nursing and
    Allied Health
Nebraska Wesleyan University
Northeast Community College
Peru State College
Southeast Community College
Union College
University of Nebraska
    Kearney
    Lincoln
    Omaha
Wayne State College
Western Nebraska Community College
York College

## Nevada
Art Institute of Las Vegas
Roseman University of Health Sciences
Sierra Nevada College
Truckee Meadows Community College
University of Nevada
    Las Vegas
    Reno
Western Nevada College

**New Hampshire**
Colby-Sawyer College
Daniel Webster College
Franklin Pierce University
Keene State College
Mount Washington College
New England College
New Hampshire Institute of Art
Plymouth State University
Rivier University
Saint Anselm College
Southern New Hampshire University
Thomas More College of Liberal Arts
University of New Hampshire
University of New Hampshire at Manchester

**New Jersey**
Berkeley College
Bloomfield College
Brookdale Community College
Caldwell University
Camden County College
Centenary College
The College of New Jersey
College of St. Elizabeth
Cumberland County College
DeVry University
    North Brunswick
Drew University
Eastern International College
Felician University
Georgian Court University
Kean University
Mercer County Community College
Monmouth University
Montclair State University
New Jersey City University
New Jersey Institute of Technology
Ocean County College
Passaic County Community College
Pillar College
Ramapo College of New Jersey
Raritan Valley Community College
Rider University
Rowan College at Burlington County
Rowan University
Rutgers, The State University of New Jersey
    Camden Campus
    New Brunswick/Piscataway Campus
    Newark Campus
Saint Peter's University
Salem Community College
Seton Hall University
Stevens Institute of Technology
Stockton University
Sussex County Community College
Union County College
Warren County Community College
William Paterson University of New Jersey

**New Mexico**
Clovis Community College
Eastern New Mexico University
Eastern New Mexico University: Roswell
Luna Community College
Mesalands Community College
Navajo Technical University
New Mexico Highlands University
New Mexico Institute of Mining and
    Technology
New Mexico Junior College
New Mexico Military Institute
New Mexico State University
New Mexico State University
    Alamogordo
    Carlsbad
Northern New Mexico College
St. John's College
San Juan College
Santa Fe Community College
Santa Fe University of Art and Design
Southwest University of Visual Arts
Southwestern Indian Polytechnic Institute

University of New Mexico
University of the Southwest
Western New Mexico University

**New York**
Adelphi University
Adirondack Community College
Albany College of Pharmacy and Health
    Sciences
Alfred University
ASA College
Bard College
Berkeley College
Berkeley College of New York City
Briarcliffe College
Bryant & Stratton College
    Albany
    Syracuse
Canisius College
Cayuga Community College
Cazenovia College
City University of New York
    Baruch College
    Brooklyn College
    City College
    College of Staten Island
    Hunter College
    Medgar Evers College
    Queens College
    York College
Clarkson University
College of Mount St. Vincent
College of New Rochelle
College of Saint Rose
College of Westchester
Columbia University
    School of General Studies
Concordia College
Cooper Union for the Advancement of Science
    and Art
Corning Community College
Culinary Institute of America
Daemen College
Davis College
Dominican College of Blauvelt
Dowling College
Dutchess Community College
D'Youville College
Eastman School of Music of the University of
    Rochester
Elmira Business Institute
Elmira Business Institute: Vestal
Elmira College
Eugene Lang College The New School for
    Liberal Arts
Finger Lakes Community College
Five Towns College
Fordham University
Fulton-Montgomery Community College
Genesee Community College
Globe Institute of Technology
Hartwick College
Hilbert College
Hobart and William Smith Colleges
Hofstra University
Houghton College
Iona College
Ithaca College
Jamestown Business College
Jamestown Community College
Jefferson Community College
Jewish Theological Seminary of America
Keuka College
The King's College
Le Moyne College
LIM College
Long Island Business Institute
Long Island University
    LIU Brooklyn
    LIU Post
Manhattan College
Manhattan School of Music
Manhattanville College

Mannes College The New School for Music
Marist College
Marymount Manhattan College
Medaille College
Mercy College
Metropolitan College of New York
Mildred Elley
    Albany
    New York City
Molloy College
Monroe College
Monroe Community College
Mount Saint Mary College
Nassau Community College
Nazareth College
New York Institute of Technology
New York School of Interior Design
Niagara County Community College
Niagara University
Nyack College
Onondaga Community College
Pace University
Pace University: Pleasantville/Briarcliff
Parsons The New School for Design
Paul Smith's College
Pratt Institute
Rensselaer Polytechnic Institute
Roberts Wesleyan College
Rochester Institute of Technology
The Sage Colleges
Saint Bonaventure University
St. Francis College
St. John Fisher College
St. John's University
St. Joseph's College New York: Suffolk
    Campus
St. Joseph's College, New York
St. Lawrence University
St. Thomas Aquinas College
Sarah Lawrence College
Schenectady County Community College
Siena College
Suffolk County Community College
SUNY
    College at Brockport
    College at Buffalo
    College at Cortland
    College at Fredonia
    College at Geneseo
    College at New Paltz
    College at Old Westbury
    College at Oneonta
    College at Oswego
    College at Plattsburgh
    College at Potsdam
    College at Purchase
    College of Agriculture and Technology at
        Cobleskill
    College of Agriculture and Technology at
        Morrisville
    College of Environmental Science and
        Forestry
    College of Technology at Alfred
    College of Technology at Canton
    Farmingdale State College
    Maritime College
    University at Albany
    University at Binghamton
    University at Buffalo
    University at Stony Brook
Syracuse University
Technical Career Institutes
Tompkins Cortland Community College
Touro College
Trocaire College
Union College
University of Rochester
Utica College
Vaughn College of Aeronautics and Technology
Villa Maria College of Buffalo
Wagner College
Webb Institute
Wells College

Westchester Community College
Yeshiva University
Yeshivat Mikdash Melech

**North Carolina**
Alamance Community College
Appalachian State University
Asheville-Buncombe Technical Community
    College
Barton College
Beaufort County Community College
Belmont Abbey College
Bennett College for Women
Blue Ridge Community College
Brevard College
Brunswick Community College
Cabarrus College of Health Sciences
Campbell University
Cape Fear Community College
Carolinas College of Health Sciences
Carteret Community College
Catawba College
Catawba Valley Community College
Central Carolina Community College
Central Piedmont Community College
Chowan University
Cleveland Community College
Coastal Carolina Community College
College of the Albemarle
Davidson College
Davidson County Community College
Duke University
Durham Technical Community College
East Carolina University
Elizabeth City State University
Elon University
Fayetteville State University
Forsyth Technical Community College
Gardner-Webb University
Gaston College
Greensboro College
Guilford College
Guilford Technical Community College
Halifax Community College
Haywood Community College
High Point University
Isothermal Community College
James Sprunt Community College
Johnson and Wales University
    Charlotte
Johnson C. Smith University
Johnston Community College
Lees-McRae College
Lenoir Community College
Lenoir-Rhyne University
Livingstone College
Louisburg College
Mars Hill University
Martin Community College
McDowell Technical Community College
Meredith College
Methodist University
Mid-Atlantic Christian University
Montgomery Community College
Montreat College
Nash Community College
North Carolina Agricultural and Technical State
    University
North Carolina Central University
North Carolina State University
North Carolina Wesleyan College
Pfeiffer University
Piedmont International University
Pitt Community College
Queens University of Charlotte
Randolph Community College
Richmond Community College
Roanoke-Chowan Community College
Rockingham Community College
Rowan-Cabarrus Community College
St. Andrews University
Saint Augustine's University
Salem College

Sampson Community College
Sandhills Community College
Shaw University
Southeastern Community College
Stanly Community College
Surry Community College
University of Mount Olive
University of North Carolina
   Asheville
   Chapel Hill
   Charlotte
   Greensboro
   Pembroke
   School of the Arts
   Wilmington
Vance-Granville Community College
Wake Forest University
Wake Technical Community College
Warren Wilson College
Wayne Community College
Western Carolina University
Western Piedmont Community College
Wilkes Community College
William Peace University
Wilson Community College
Wingate University
Winston-Salem State University

## North Dakota
Bismarck State College
Dakota College at Bottineau
Dickinson State University
Lake Region State College
Mayville State University
Minot State University
North Dakota State College of Science
North Dakota State University
Trinity Bible College
Turtle Mountain Community College
University of Jamestown
University of Mary
Valley City State University
Williston State College

## Ohio
Art Academy of Cincinnati
Art Institute of Cincinnati
Ashland University
Aultman College of Nursing and Health
   Sciences
Baldwin Wallace University
Bluffton University
Bowling Green State University
Bowling Green State University: Firelands
   College
Brown Mackie College
   Findlay
Bryant & Stratton College
   Cleveland
   Eastlake
   Parma
Capital University
Case Western Reserve University
Cedarville University
Central Ohio Technical College
Central State University
Chatfield College
Cincinnati Christian University
Cincinnati State Technical and Community
   College
Cleveland Institute of Art
Cleveland Institute of Music
Cleveland State University
College of Wooster
Columbus College of Art and Design
Columbus State Community College
Cuyahoga Community College
Defiance College
Denison University
DeVry University
   Columbus
Eastern Gateway Community College
Edison State Community College

Franciscan University of Steubenville
Franklin University
God's Bible School and College
Heidelberg University
Hiram College
Hocking College
James A. Rhodes State College
John Carroll University
Kent State University
Kent State University
   Ashtabula
   East Liverpool
   Geauga
   Salem
   Stark
   Trumbull
   Tuscarawas
Kenyon College
Kettering College
Lake Erie College
Lakeland Community College
Lorain County Community College
Lourdes University
Malone University
Marietta College
Marion Technical College
Mercy College of Ohio
Miami University
   Hamilton
   Oxford
Mount Carmel College of Nursing
Mount St. Joseph University
Mount Vernon Nazarene University
Muskingum University
Northwest State Community College
Notre Dame College
Oberlin College
Ohio Christian University
Ohio Dominican University
Ohio Northern University
Ohio State University
   Agricultural Technical Institute
   Columbus Campus
   Lima Campus
   Mansfield Campus
   Marion Campus
   Newark Campus
Ohio University
Ohio University
   Eastern Campus
   Southern Campus at Ironton
   Zanesville Campus
Ohio Wesleyan University
Otterbein University
Owens Community College
Pontifical College Josephinum
PowerSport Institute
Rosedale Bible College
School of Advertising Art
Sinclair Community College
Southern State Community College
Stark State College
Terra State Community College
Tiffin University
Union Institute & University
University of Akron
University of Akron: Wayne College
University of Cincinnati
University of Cincinnati
   Blue Ash College
   Clermont College
University of Dayton
University of Findlay
University of Mount Union
University of Northwestern Ohio
University of Rio Grande
University of Toledo
Urbana University
Ursuline College
Walsh University
Wilberforce University
Wilmington College
Wittenberg University

Wright State University
Wright State University: Lake Campus
Xavier University
Youngstown State University

## Oklahoma
Cameron University
Carl Albert State College
Connors State College
East Central University
Eastern Oklahoma State College
Langston University
Mid-America Christian University
Northeastern Oklahoma Agricultural and
   Mechanical College
Northeastern State University
Northern Oklahoma College
Northwestern Oklahoma State University
Oklahoma Baptist University
Oklahoma Christian University
Oklahoma City Community College
Oklahoma City University
Oklahoma Panhandle State University
Oklahoma State University
Oklahoma State University
   Institute of Technology: Okmulgee
   Oklahoma City
Oklahoma Wesleyan University
Oral Roberts University
Redlands Community College
Rogers State University
Rose State College
St. Gregory's University
Seminole State College
Southeastern Oklahoma State University
Southern Nazarene University
Southwestern Christian University
Southwestern Oklahoma State University
Tulsa Community College
University of Central Oklahoma
University of Oklahoma
University of Science and Arts of Oklahoma
University of Tulsa
Western Oklahoma State College

## Oregon
Central Oregon Community College
Chemeketa Community College
Clackamas Community College
Clatsop Community College
Concordia University
Corban University
Eastern Oregon University
George Fox University
Lewis & Clark College
Linfield College
Linn-Benton Community College
Marylhurst University
Mt. Hood Community College
Multnomah University
New Hope Christian College
Northwest Christian University
Oregon College of Art & Craft
Oregon Institute of Technology
Oregon State University
Pacific Northwest College of Art
Pacific University
Portland State University
Rogue Community College
Southern Oregon University
Treasure Valley Community College
Umpqua Community College
University of Oregon
University of Portland
Warner Pacific College
Western Oregon University
Willamette University

## Pennsylvania
Albright College
Allegheny College
Alvernia University
Arcadia University

Berks Technical Institute
Bloomsburg University of Pennsylvania
Bryn Athyn College
Bryn Mawr College
Bucknell University
Bucks County Community College
Butler County Community College
Cabrini College
Cairn University
California University of Pennsylvania
Cambria-Rowe Business College
Cambria-Rowe Business College: Indiana
Carnegie Mellon University
Cedar Crest College
Central Penn College
Chatham University
Chestnut Hill College
Cheyney University of Pennsylvania
Clarion University of Pennsylvania
Community College of Allegheny County
Community College of Beaver County
Consolidated School of Business
   Lancaster
   York
Delaware County Community College
Delaware Valley University
DeSales University
DeVry University
   Fort Washington
Dickinson College
Drexel University
Duquesne University
East Stroudsburg University of Pennsylvania
Eastern University
Edinboro University
   Pennsylvania
Elizabethtown College
Gannon University
Geneva College
Gettysburg College
Grove City College
Gwynedd Mercy University
Harcum College
Harrisburg Area Community College
Harrisburg University of Science and
   Technology
Holy Family University
Immaculata University
Indiana University of Pennsylvania
Johnson College
Juniata College
Keystone College
King's College
Kutztown University of Pennsylvania
La Roche College
La Salle University
Lackawanna College
Lafayette College
Lancaster Bible College
Laurel Technical Institute
Lebanon Valley College
Lehigh Carbon Community College
Lehigh University
Lincoln University
Lock Haven University of Pennsylvania
Lycoming College
Manor College
Mansfield University of Pennsylvania
Marywood University
Mercyhurst University
Messiah College
Millersville University of Pennsylvania
Misericordia University
Montgomery County Community College
Moore College of Art and Design
Moravian College
Mount Aloysius College
Muhlenberg College
Neumann University
Northampton Community College
Orleans Technical Institute
Peirce College
Penn State

Abington
Altoona
Beaver
Berks
Brandywine
DuBois
Erie, The Behrend College
Fayette, The Eberly Campus
Greater Allegheny
Harrisburg
Hazleton
Lehigh Valley
Mont Alto
New Kensington
Schuylkill
Shenango
University Park
Wilkes-Barre
Worthington Scranton
York
Pennsylvania Academy of the Fine Arts
Pennsylvania College of Art and Design
Pennsylvania College of Health Sciences
Pennsylvania College of Technology
Pennsylvania Highlands Community College
Pennsylvania Institute of Technology
Philadelphia University
Point Park University
Robert Morris University
Rosemont College
St. Francis University
Saint Joseph's University
St. Vincent College
Seton Hill University
Shippensburg University of Pennsylvania
Slippery Rock University of Pennsylvania
Summit University
Susquehanna University
Swarthmore College
Temple University
Thiel College
Thomas Jefferson University
Triangle Tech
    Bethlehem
    DuBois
    Pittsburgh
University of Pittsburgh
University of Pittsburgh
    Bradford
    Greensburg
    Johnstown
    Titusville
University of Scranton
University of the Arts
University of the Sciences
University of Valley Forge
Ursinus College
Valley Forge Military College
Vet Tech Institute
Villanova University
Washington & Jefferson College
Waynesburg University
West Chester University of Pennsylvania
Westminster College
Westmoreland County Community College
Widener University
Wilkes University
Wilson College
York College of Pennsylvania
YTI Career Institute
    Lancaster

## Puerto Rico
ICPR Junior College
Inter American University of Puerto Rico
    Aguadilla Campus
    Arecibo Campus
    Bayamon Campus
    Ponce Campus
    San German Campus
Pontifical Catholic University of Puerto Rico
Turabo University
Universidad del Este

Universidad Metropolitana
Universidad Pentecostal Mizpa
Universidad Politecnica de Puerto Rico
University of Puerto Rico
    Bayamon University College
    Cayey University College
    Humacao
    Mayaguez
    Utuado
University of the Sacred Heart

## Rhode Island
Bryant University
Johnson & Wales University
    Providence
New England Institute of Technology
Providence College
Rhode Island College
Rhode Island School of Design
Roger Williams University
Salve Regina University
University of Rhode Island

## South Carolina
Aiken Technical College
Allen University
Anderson University
Bob Jones University
Charleston Southern University
The Citadel
Clemson University
Coastal Carolina University
Coker College
College of Charleston
Columbia College
Columbia International University
Converse College
Erskine College
Florence-Darlington Technical College
Francis Marion University
Furman University
Greenville Technical College
Horry-Georgetown Technical College
Lander University
Limestone College
Morris College
Newberry College
North Greenville University
Piedmont Technical College
Presbyterian College
South Carolina State University
Southern Wesleyan University
Spartanburg Community College
Spartanburg Methodist College
Tri-County Technical College
Trident Technical College
University of South Carolina
    Aiken
    Beaufort
    Columbia
    Salkehatchie
    Sumter
    Union
    Upstate
Williamsburg Technical College
Winthrop University
Wofford College
York Technical College

## South Dakota
Augusta University
    Augustana University
Black Hills State University
Dakota State University
Dakota Wesleyan University
Kilian Community College
Mitchell Technical Institute
Mount Marty College
Northern State University
South Dakota School of Mines and Technology
South Dakota State University
Southeast Technical Institute

University of Sioux Falls
University of South Dakota

## Tennessee
Aquinas College
Austin Peay State University
Belmont University
Bethel University
Bryan College
    Dayton
Carson-Newman University
Christian Brothers University
Columbia State Community College
Cumberland University
Dyersburg State Community College
East Tennessee State University
Fisk University
Freed-Hardeman University
Jackson State Community College
Johnson University
King University
Lane College
Lee University
LeMoyne-Owen College
Lincoln Memorial University
Lipscomb University
Martin Methodist College
Maryville College
Memphis College of Art
Middle Tennessee State University
Milligan College
Motlow State Community College
Nashville State Community College
National College
    Bristol
    Nashville
Northeast State Community College
O'More College of Design
Pellissippi State Community College
Rhodes College
Roane State Community College
Sewanee: The University of the South
Southern Adventist University
Southwest Tennessee Community College
Tennessee State University
Tennessee Technological University
Tennessee Wesleyan College
Trevecca Nazarene University
Tusculum College
Union University
University of Memphis
University of Tennessee
    Chattanooga
    Knoxville
    Martin
Vanderbilt University
Volunteer State Community College
Walters State Community College
Watkins College of Art, Design & Film
Welch College
Williamson College

## Texas
Abilene Christian University
Alvin Community College
Amarillo College
Angelina College
Angelo State University
Arlington Baptist College
Austin College
Austin Graduate School of Theology
Baptist Missionary Association Theological
    Seminary
Baylor University
Brazosport College
Brookhaven College
Central Texas College
Clarendon College
Coastal Bend College
College of the Mainland
Collin County Community College District
Commonwealth Institute of Funeral Service
Concordia University Texas

Dallas Baptist University
East Texas Baptist University
El Paso Community College
Frank Phillips College
Galveston College
Grayson College
Hardin-Simmons University
Hill College
Houston Baptist University
Houston Community College System
Howard College
Howard Payne University
Huston-Tillotson University
Jacksonville College
Jarvis Christian College
Kilgore College
Lamar University
Lee College
LeTourneau University
Lone Star College System
Lubbock Christian University
McMurry University
Midland College
Midwestern State University
North Central Texas College
North Lake College
Northwest Vista College
Northwood University
    Texas
Odessa College
Our Lady of the Lake University of San
    Antonio
Palo Alto College
Panola College
Paul Quinn College
Prairie View A&M University
Ranger College
Rice University
St. Edward's University
St. Mary's University
Sam Houston State University
San Jacinto College
Schreiner University
South Plains College
South Texas College
Southern Methodist University
Southwestern Adventist University
Southwestern Christian College
Southwestern University
Stephen F. Austin State University
Sul Ross State University
Tarleton State University
Tarrant County College
Texarkana College
Texas A&M International University
Texas A&M University
Texas A&M University
    Baylor College of Dentistry
    Commerce
    Corpus Christi
    Galveston
    Kingsville
    Texarkana
Texas Christian University
Texas College
Texas Lutheran University
Texas Southern University
Texas State Technical College
Texas State Technical College
    West Texas
Texas State University
Texas Tech University
Texas Tech University Health Sciences Center
Texas Wesleyan University
Texas Woman's University
Trinity University
Trinity Valley Community College
Tyler Junior College
University of Dallas
University of Houston
University of Houston
    Clear Lake
    Victoria

University of Mary Hardin-Baylor
University of St. Thomas
University of Texas
  Arlington
  Austin
  Brownsville
  Dallas
  El Paso
  Medical Branch at Galveston
  Pan American
  the Permian Basin
  San Antonio
  Tyler
University Of Texas Rio Grande Valley
University of the Incarnate Word
Vernon College
Victoria College
Wayland Baptist University
West Coast University: Dallas
West Texas A&M University
Western Texas College
Wharton County Junior College

### Utah
Brigham Young University
Dixie State University
LDS Business College
Neumont University
Salt Lake Community College
Snow College
Southern Utah University
University of Utah
Utah State University
Utah Valley University
Weber State University
Western Governors University
Westminster College

### Vermont
Bennington College
Burlington College
Castleton State College
Champlain College
College of St. Joseph in Vermont
Goddard College
Green Mountain College
Johnson State College
Landmark College
Lyndon State College
Marlboro College
New England Culinary Institute
Norwich University
Saint Michael's College
Southern Vermont College
Sterling College
University of Vermont
Vermont Technical College

### Virginia
American National University
  Charlottesville
  Danville
  Harrisonburg
  Lynchburg
  Martinsville
Averett University
Blue Ridge Community College
Bluefield College
Bridgewater College
Bryant & Stratton College
  Richmond
Central Virginia Community College
Christendom College
Christopher Newport University
College of William and Mary
DeVry University
  Arlington
Eastern Mennonite University
ECPI University
Emory & Henry College
Ferrum College
George Mason University
Germanna Community College

Hampden-Sydney College
Hampton University
Hollins University
J. Sargeant Reynolds Community College
James Madison University
Jefferson College of Health Sciences
John Tyler Community College
Liberty University
Longwood University
Lynchburg College
Mary Baldwin College
Marymount University
Mountain Empire Community College
Norfolk State University
Northern Virginia Community College
Old Dominion University
Patrick Henry College
Paul D. Camp Community College
Piedmont Virginia Community College
Radford University
Randolph College
Randolph-Macon College
Regent University
Richard Bland College
Roanoke College
Shenandoah University
Southern Virginia University
Southside Virginia Community College
Southwest Virginia Community College
Stratford University: Falls Church
Sweet Briar College
University of Mary Washington
University of Richmond
University of Virginia
University of Virginia's College at Wise
Virginia Baptist College
Virginia Commonwealth University
Virginia Military Institute
Virginia Polytechnic Institute and State
  University
Virginia State University
Virginia Union University
Virginia Wesleyan College
Virginia Western Community College
Washington and Lee University
Wytheville Community College

### Washington
Art Institute of Seattle
Bastyr University
Bellevue College
Big Bend Community College
Central Washington University
Centralia College
City University of Seattle
Clark College
Clover Park Technical College
Columbia Basin College
Cornish College of the Arts
DeVry University
  Federal Way
DigiPen Institute of Technology
Eastern Washington University
Everett Community College
Evergreen State College
Gonzaga University
Grays Harbor College
Heritage University
Northwest College of Art & Design
Northwest Indian College
Northwest University
Olympic College
Pacific Lutheran University
Peninsula College
Pierce College
Saint Martin's University
Seattle Pacific University
Seattle University
Skagit Valley College
South Puget Sound Community College
South Seattle College
Tacoma Community College
Trinity Lutheran College

University of Puget Sound
University of Washington
University of Washington Bothell
University of Washington Tacoma
Walla Walla Community College
Walla Walla University
Washington State University
Wenatchee Valley College
Western Washington University
Whatcom Community College
Whitman College
Whitworth University

### West Virginia
Alderson-Broaddus University
American National University
  Princeton
Bethany College
Bluefield State College
Concord University
Davis and Elkins College
Fairmont State University
Glenville State College
Marshall University
Ohio Valley University
Potomac State College of West Virginia
  University
Salem International University
Shepherd University
University of Charleston
West Liberty University
West Virginia State University
West Virginia University
West Virginia University at Parkersburg
West Virginia University Institute of
  Technology
West Virginia Wesleyan College
Wheeling Jesuit University

### Wisconsin
Alverno College
Bellin College
Beloit College
Cardinal Stritch University
Carroll University
Carthage College
College of Menominee Nation
Columbia College of Nursing
Concordia University Wisconsin
Edgewood College
Lakeland College
Lakeshore Technical College
Lawrence University
Maranathan Baptist University
  Maranatha Baptist University
Marian University
Marquette University
Mid-State Technical College
Milwaukee Area Technical College
Milwaukee Institute of Art & Design
Milwaukee School of Engineering
Moraine Park Technical College
Mount Mary University
Northland College
Ripon College
St. Norbert College
Silver Lake College of the Holy Family
University of Wisconsin
  Baraboo/Sauk County
  Eau Claire
  Fond du Lac
  Fox Valley
  Green Bay
  La Crosse
  Madison
  Marshfield/Wood County
  Milwaukee
  Oshkosh
  Parkside
  Richland
  River Falls
  Rock County
  Sheboygan

  Stevens Point
  Stout
  Superior
  Washington County
  Waukesha
  Whitewater
Viterbo University
Waukesha County Technical College
Wisconsin Lutheran College

### Wyoming
Casper College
Central Wyoming College
Eastern Wyoming College
Laramie County Community College
Northwest College
Sheridan College
University of Wyoming
Western Wyoming Community College

# Art scholarships

**Alabama**
Alabama State University
Athens State University
Birmingham-Southern College
Chattahoochee Valley Community College
Enterprise State Community College
Faulkner State Community College
Gadsden State Community College
Jacksonville State University
Jefferson State Community College
Judson College
Lurleen B. Wallace Community College
Northeast Alabama Community College
Northwest-Shoals Community College
Samford University
Selma University
Shelton State Community College
Snead State Community College
Southern Union State Community College
Spring Hill College
Talladega College
Troy University
University of Alabama
University of Alabama
 Birmingham
 Huntsville
University of Montevallo
University of North Alabama
University of South Alabama
University of West Alabama

**Alaska**
Alaska Pacific University
University of Alaska
 Anchorage
 Fairbanks

**Arizona**
Arizona State University
Arizona Western College
Eastern Arizona College
Grand Canyon University
Northern Arizona University
Northland Pioneer College
Pima Community College
University of Advancing Technology
University of Arizona

**Arkansas**
Arkansas Northeastern College
Arkansas State University
Harding University
Henderson State University
Hendrix College
John Brown University
Lyon College
Ouachita Baptist University
Southern Arkansas University
University of Arkansas
 Little Rock
 Pine Bluff
University of Central Arkansas
University of the Ozarks
Williams Baptist College

**California**
Academy of Art University
Art Institute of California
 Orange County
Biola University
California Baptist University
California College of the Arts
California Institute of Integral Studies
California Institute of the Arts
California Lutheran University
California Polytechnic State University: San
 Luis Obispo
California State University
 Bakersfield

Chico
Dominguez Hills
Fresno
Fullerton
Long Beach
Stanislaus
Chapman University
College of the Canyons
College of the Desert
Columbia College
 Hollywood
El Camino College
Irvine Valley College
La Sierra University
Laguna College of Art and Design
Loyola Marymount University
Marymount California University
The Master's College
Notre Dame de Namur University
Otis College of Art and Design
Pacific Union College
Pepperdine University
Point Loma Nazarene University
Riverside City College
San Diego State University
San Francisco Art Institute
San Jose State University
Santa Rosa Junior College
Sonoma State University
University of California
 Los Angeles
 Riverside
 San Diego
 Santa Cruz
University of La Verne
University of Redlands
University of Southern California
Westmont College
Whittier College
William Jessup University

**Colorado**
Adams State University
Arapahoe Community College
Colorado Mesa University
Colorado State University
Colorado State University
 Pueblo
Fort Lewis College
Naropa University
Northeastern Junior College
Pueblo Community College
Rocky Mountain College of Art & Design
University of Colorado
 Boulder
 Denver
University of Denver
Western State Colorado University

**Connecticut**
Fairfield University
Lyme Academy College of Fine Arts
Mitchell College
Sacred Heart University
University of Bridgeport
University of Connecticut
University of Hartford
University of New Haven
Western Connecticut State University

**Delaware**
Delaware College of Art and Design
Delaware State University
University of Delaware

**District of Columbia**
George Washington University
Howard University

**Florida**
Barry University
Chipola College
Digital Media Arts College
Eckerd College
Flagler College
Florida Agricultural and Mechanical University
Florida International University
Florida Keys Community College
Florida Southern College
Florida SouthWestern State College
Florida State College at Jacksonville
Florida State University
Hillsborough Community College
Jacksonville University
Lake-Sumter State College
Miami Dade College
North Florida Community College
Nova Southeastern University
Palm Beach Atlantic University
Ringling College of Art and Design
Rollins College
St. Petersburg College
Santa Fe College
Seminole State College of Florida
State College of Florida, Manatee-Sarasota
Stetson University
Tallahassee Community College
University of Florida
University of South Florida
University of South Florida
 Sarasota-Manatee
University of Tampa
University of West Florida
Warner University

**Georgia**
Andrew College
Armstrong State University
Art Institute of Atlanta
Augusta University
Berry College
Brenau University
Clark Atlanta University
Columbus State University
Covenant College
Darton College
Emmanuel College
Emory University
Georgia College and State University
Georgia Highlands College
Georgia Perimeter College
Georgia Southern University
Georgia Southwestern State University
Georgia State University
Kennesaw State University
LaGrange College
Mercer University
Middle Georgia State College
Morehouse College
Oglethorpe University
Piedmont College
Reinhardt University
Savannah College of Art and Design
Shorter University
University of North Georgia
University of West Georgia
Valdosta State University
Wesleyan College
Young Harris College

**Hawaii**
Brigham Young University-Hawaii
University of Hawaii
 Hilo
 Manoa

**Idaho**
Boise State University
Brigham Young University-Idaho
Idaho State University
Lewis-Clark State College

North Idaho College
University of Idaho

**Illinois**
American Academy of Art
Augustana College
Aurora University
Benedictine University at Springfield
Black Hawk College
Bradley University
Carl Sandburg College
College of DuPage
College of Lake County
Columbia College Chicago
Danville Area Community College
DePaul University
Dominican University
Eastern Illinois University
Elgin Community College
Elmhurst College
Eureka College
Greenville College
Harper College
Illinois College
Illinois Institute of Art
 Schaumburg
Illinois State University
Illinois Valley Community College
Illinois Wesleyan University
Judson University
Knox College
Lake Forest College
Lewis University
Lincoln College
Loyola University Chicago
McKendree University
Millikin University
Monmouth College
North Central College
North Park University
Northeastern Illinois University
Northern Illinois University
Oakton Community College
Olivet Nazarene University
Parkland College
Quincy University
Richland Community College
Robert Morris University: Chicago
Roosevelt University
School of the Art Institute of Chicago
Shawnee Community College
South Suburban College of Cook County
Southeastern Illinois College
Southern Illinois University Carbondale
Southern Illinois University Edwardsville
Southwestern Illinois College
Spoon River College
Trinity Christian College
University of Illinois
 Chicago
 Springfield
 Urbana-Champaign
University of St. Francis
Waubonsee Community College
Western Illinois University
Wheaton College

**Indiana**
Anderson University
Bethel College
Calumet College of St. Joseph
Franklin College
Goshen College
Grace College
Hanover College
Huntington University
Indiana State University
Indiana University
 Bloomington
 Purdue University Fort Wayne
 Southeast
Indiana Wesleyan University
Marian University

St. Mary-of-the-Woods College
Saint Mary's College
Taylor University
University of Evansville
University of Indianapolis
University of Saint Francis
University of Southern Indiana
Valparaiso University
Vincennes University
Wabash College

**Iowa**
Briar Cliff University
Buena Vista University
Central College
Clarke University
Coe College
Cornell College
Dordt College
Drake University
Ellsworth Community College
Graceland University
Grand View University
Iowa Central Community College
Iowa State University
Iowa Wesleyan College
Kirkwood Community College
Loras College
Luther College
Morningside College
Mount Mercy University
North Iowa Area Community College
Northwestern College
St. Ambrose University
Simpson College
Southeastern Community College
University of Iowa
University of Northern Iowa
Western Iowa Tech Community College

**Kansas**
Allen County Community College
Baker University
Benedictine College
Bethany College
Bethel College
Butler Community College
Coffeyville Community College
Cowley County Community College
Emporia State University
Fort Hays State University
Friends University
Garden City Community College
Hesston College
Highland Community College
Hutchinson Community College
Independence Community College
Kansas City Kansas Community College
Kansas State University
Kansas Wesleyan University
McPherson College
Neosho County Community College
Newman University
Pittsburg State University
Pratt Community College
Sterling College
Tabor College
University of Kansas
University of St. Mary
Washburn University
Wichita State University

**Kentucky**
Asbury University
Bellarmine University
Brescia University
Campbellsville University
Centre College
Eastern Kentucky University
Georgetown College
Jefferson Community and Technical College
Kentucky State University
Kentucky Wesleyan College

Midway College
Morehead State University
Murray State University
Northern Kentucky University
Owensboro Community and Technical College
Spalding University
Sullivan College of Technology and Design
Thomas More College
Transylvania University
University of Kentucky
University of Louisville
Western Kentucky University

**Louisiana**
Centenary College of Louisiana
Dillard University
Grambling State University
Louisiana College
Louisiana Tech University
Loyola University New Orleans
McNeese State University
Northwestern State University
University of Louisiana at Monroe
Xavier University of Louisiana

**Maine**
Maine College of Art
University of Maine
York County Community College

**Maryland**
Bowie State University
Carroll Community College
Chesapeake College
Goucher College
Maryland Institute College of Art
Montgomery College
Mount St. Mary's University
Notre Dame of Maryland University
Salisbury University
Stevenson University
Towson University
University of Maryland
    Baltimore County
    College Park
    Eastern Shore
Washington College

**Massachusetts**
Boston Architectural College
Boston University
Bristol Community College
Cape Cod Community College
Dean College
Endicott College
Gordon College
Hampshire College
Holyoke Community College
Lesley University
Massachusetts College of Art and Design
Massachusetts College of Liberal Arts
Montserrat College of Art
Mount Wachusett Community College
School of the Museum of Fine Arts
Springfield College
University of Massachusetts
    Amherst
    Lowell

**Michigan**
Adrian College
Albion College
Alma College
Alpena Community College
Aquinas College
Calvin College
Central Michigan University
College for Creative Studies
Concordia University
Eastern Michigan University
Ferris State University
Glen Oaks Community College
Gogebic Community College
Grand Valley State University

Hillsdale College
Hope College
Jackson College
Kalamazoo College
Kellogg Community College
Madonna University
Marygrove College
Michigan State University
Mid Michigan Community College
Monroe County Community College
Mott Community College
Northern Michigan University
Northwestern Michigan College
Oakland University
Olivet College
Saginaw Valley State University
Southwestern Michigan College
Spring Arbor University
University of Michigan
University of Michigan
    Dearborn
    Flint
Wayne State University
Western Michigan University

**Minnesota**
Augsburg College
Bemidji State University
Bethany Lutheran College
Bethel University
College of St. Benedict
Concordia College: Moorhead
Concordia University St. Paul
Gustavus Adolphus College
Hamline University
Minneapolis College of Art and Design
Minnesota State Community and Technical
    College
Minnesota State University
    Mankato
    Moorhead
Normandale Community College
North Hennepin Community College
Saint Cloud State University
St. John's University
St. Mary's University of Minnesota
St. Olaf College
Southwest Minnesota State University
University of Minnesota
    Duluth
    Twin Cities
Winona State University

**Mississippi**
Belhaven University
Blue Mountain College
Copiah-Lincoln Community College
Delta State University
East Central Community College
East Mississippi Community College
Hinds Community College
Itawamba Community College
Meridian Community College
Millsaps College
Mississippi College
Mississippi State University
Tougaloo College
University of Mississippi
University of Southern Mississippi
William Carey University

**Missouri**
Avila University
College of the Ozarks
Columbia College
Cottey College
Crowder College
Culver-Stockton College
Drury University
East Central College
Fontbonne University
Hannibal-LaGrange University
Harris-Stowe State University

Jefferson College
Kansas City Art Institute
Lincoln University
Lindenwood University
Maryville University of Saint Louis
Mineral Area College
Missouri Southern State University
Missouri State University
Missouri Western State University
Moberly Area Community College
Northwest Missouri State University
Park University
St. Charles Community College
St. Louis Community College
Saint Louis University
Southeast Missouri State University
Southwest Baptist University
State Fair Community College
Truman State University
University of Central Missouri
University of Missouri
    Columbia
    Kansas City
    St. Louis
Washington University in St. Louis
Webster University
William Woods University

**Montana**
Carroll College
Dawson Community College
Montana State University
Montana State University
    Billings
University of Great Falls
University of Montana: Western

**Nebraska**
Central Community College
Chadron State College
Concordia University
Creative Center
Creighton University
Doane College
Hastings College
Mid-Plains Community College
Midland University
Nebraska Wesleyan University
Peru State College
University of Nebraska
    Kearney
    Lincoln
    Omaha
Wayne State College
Western Nebraska Community College

**Nevada**
Sierra Nevada College
Truckee Meadows Community College
University of Nevada
    Reno

**New Hampshire**
Colby-Sawyer College
Franklin Pierce University
Keene State College
New England College
New Hampshire Institute of Art
Plymouth State University
Southern New Hampshire University
University of New Hampshire

**New Jersey**
Caldwell University
The College of New Jersey
College of St. Elizabeth
Drew University
Georgian Court University
Kean University
Monmouth University
Montclair State University
Rowan University
Rutgers, The State University of New Jersey
    Camden Campus

New Brunswick/Piscataway Campus
Newark Campus
Stockton University
Union County College
William Paterson University of New Jersey

### New Mexico
Eastern New Mexico University
New Mexico Highlands University
New Mexico Junior College
New Mexico State University
Santa Fe University of Art and Design
University of New Mexico
Western New Mexico University

### New York
Adelphi University
Alfred University
Canisius College
City University of New York
   Brooklyn College
   City College
   College of Staten Island
College of New Rochelle
College of Saint Rose
Daemen College
Eugene Lang College The New School for
   Liberal Arts
Five Towns College
Hartwick College
Hobart and William Smith Colleges
Hofstra University
Houghton College
Jamestown Community College
Long Island University
   LIU Brooklyn
   LIU Post
Manhattanville College
Mannes College The New School for Music
Marymount Manhattan College
Molloy College
Nazareth College
New York School of Interior Design
Parsons The New School for Design
Rensselaer Polytechnic Institute
Roberts Wesleyan College
Rochester Institute of Technology
The Sage Colleges
St. John's University
St. Thomas Aquinas College
School of Visual Arts
Suffolk County Community College
SUNY
   College at Brockport
   College at Cortland
   College at Fredonia
   College at Geneseo
   College at New Paltz
   College at Plattsburgh
   College at Potsdam
   College at Purchase
   University at Binghamton
   University at Buffalo
   University at Stony Brook
Syracuse University
University of Rochester
Villa Maria College of Buffalo

### North Carolina
Appalachian State University
Barton College
Brevard College
College of the Albemarle
Davidson College
East Carolina University
Elon University
Greensboro College
High Point University
Louisburg College
Meredith College
Montreat College
North Carolina Central University
Queens University of Charlotte

St. Andrews University
Saint Augustine's University
University of Mount Olive
University of North Carolina
   Asheville
   Chapel Hill
   Charlotte
   Pembroke
   School of the Arts
   Wilmington
Wake Forest University
Warren Wilson College
Western Carolina University
Wilkes Community College
Wingate University

### North Dakota
Bismarck State College
Dickinson State University
Minot State University
North Dakota State University
Trinity Bible College
University of Jamestown

### Ohio
Art Academy of Cincinnati
Art Institute of Cincinnati
Ashland University
Baldwin Wallace University
Bluffton University
Bowling Green State University
Bowling Green State University: Firelands
   College
Capital University
Case Western Reserve University
Central State University
Cleveland Institute of Art
Cleveland State University
Columbus College of Art and Design
Cuyahoga Community College
Denison University
Edison State Community College
Hiram College
Kent State University
Kent State University
   Ashtabula
   East Liverpool
   Geauga
   Salem
   Stark
   Trumbull
   Tuscarawas
Kenyon College
Lake Erie College
Lakeland Community College
Lourdes University
Marietta College
Miami University
   Oxford
Mount St. Joseph University
Mount Vernon Nazarene University
Muskingum University
Ohio Northern University
Ohio State University
   Agricultural Technical Institute
   Columbus Campus
   Lima Campus
   Mansfield Campus
   Marion Campus
   Newark Campus
Ohio University
Ohio Wesleyan University
Otterbein University
Pontifical College Josephinum
School of Advertising Art
Sinclair Community College
Southern State Community College
Tiffin University
University of Akron
University of Akron: Wayne College
University of Cincinnati
University of Dayton
University of Mount Union

University of Toledo
Ursuline College
Wittenberg University
Wright State University
Wright State University: Lake Campus
Xavier University

### Oklahoma
Cameron University
Carl Albert State College
Northeastern State University
Northern Oklahoma College
Northwestern Oklahoma State University
Oklahoma Baptist University
Oklahoma Christian University
Oklahoma City Community College
Oklahoma City University
Oklahoma Panhandle State University
Oklahoma State University
Oral Roberts University
Rogers State University
St. Gregory's University
Seminole State College
Southeastern Oklahoma State University
Southwestern Oklahoma State University
Tulsa Community College
University of Central Oklahoma
University of Oklahoma
University of Science and Arts of Oklahoma
University of Tulsa
Western Oklahoma State College

### Oregon
Art Institute of Portland
Clackamas Community College
Clatsop Community College
Eastern Oregon University
George Fox University
Lane Community College
Linn-Benton Community College
New Hope Christian College
Oregon College of Art & Craft
Pacific Northwest College of Art
Pacific University
Portland State University
Southwestern Oregon Community College
Western Oregon University

### Pennsylvania
Albright College
Arcadia University
Berks Technical Institute
Bloomsburg University of Pennsylvania
Bucknell University
Bucks County Community College
Carnegie Mellon University
Cedar Crest College
Chatham University
Chestnut Hill College
Clarion University of Pennsylvania
DeSales University
Drexel University
East Stroudsburg University of Pennsylvania
Edinboro University
   Pennsylvania
Elizabethtown College
Harrisburg Area Community College
Immaculata University
Indiana University of Pennsylvania
Juniata College
Keystone College
Kutztown University of Pennsylvania
Lehigh University
Lock Haven University of Pennsylvania
Lycoming College
Mansfield University of Pennsylvania
Marywood University
Mercyhurst University
Messiah College
Moore College of Art and Design
Moravian College
Mount Aloysius College
Muhlenberg College

Northampton Community College
Pennsylvania Academy of the Fine Arts
Pennsylvania College of Art and Design
Saint Joseph's University
St. Vincent College
Seton Hill University
Slippery Rock University of Pennsylvania
Temple University
University of the Arts
West Chester University of Pennsylvania

### Puerto Rico
Colegio de Cinematografía, Artes y Televisión
Humacao Community College
University of Puerto Rico
   Mayaguez

### Rhode Island
Rhode Island College
Rhode Island School of Design
Salve Regina University
University of Rhode Island

### South Carolina
Anderson University
Clemson University
Coastal Carolina University
Coker College
College of Charleston
Columbia College
Converse College
Francis Marion University
Furman University
Lander University
Limestone College
Presbyterian College
University of South Carolina
   Aiken
   Beaufort
   Columbia
Winthrop University
Wofford College

### South Dakota
Augusta University
   Augustana University
Dakota State University
Dakota Wesleyan University
Northern State University
South Dakota State University
University of Sioux Falls
University of South Dakota

### Tennessee
Austin Peay State University
Belmont University
Bryan College
   Dayton
Carson-Newman University
Cumberland University
East Tennessee State University
Freed-Hardeman University
Jackson State Community College
King University
Lipscomb University
Martin Methodist College
Maryville College
Memphis College of Art
Milligan College
Motlow State Community College
Northeast State Community College
O'More College of Design
Pellissippi State Community College
Rhodes College
Roane State Community College
Sewanee: The University of the South
Southern Adventist University
Tennessee Technological University
Union University
University of Memphis
University of Tennessee
   Chattanooga
   Knoxville
   Martin

Volunteer State Community College
Watkins College of Art, Design & Film
Welch College

## Texas
Abilene Christian University
Angelina College
Angelo State University
Austin College
Baylor University
Brazosport College
Clarendon College
College of the Mainland
Collin County Community College District
Galveston College
Grayson College
Hardin-Simmons University
Houston Baptist University
Howard College
Howard Payne University
Kilgore College
Lee College
McMurry University
Midwestern State University
Our Lady of the Lake University of San
    Antonio
Panola College
Rice University
Richland College
Sam Houston State University
San Jacinto College
Schreiner University
South Plains College
Southern Methodist University
Southwestern University
Stephen F. Austin State University
Sul Ross State University
Temple College
Texarkana College
Texas A&M International University
Texas A&M University
Texas A&M University
    Commerce
    Corpus Christi
    Texarkana
Texas Christian University
Texas State University
Texas Tech University
Texas Wesleyan University
Texas Woman's University
Trinity University
Tyler Junior College
University of Dallas
University of Houston
University of Houston
    Clear Lake
University of Mary Hardin-Baylor
University of Texas
    Arlington
    Austin
    Brownsville
    El Paso
    Pan American
    the Permian Basin
    San Antonio
    Tyler
University Of Texas Rio Grande Valley
University of the Incarnate Word
Victoria College
Wayland Baptist University
West Texas A&M University
Western Texas College

## Utah
Brigham Young University
Dixie State University
Salt Lake Community College
Southern Utah University
University of Utah
Utah State University
Utah Valley University
Weber State University
Westminster College

## Vermont
Bennington College
Goddard College
Johnson State College
Landmark College
Saint Michael's College

## Virginia
Averett University
Bluefield College
Christopher Newport University
College of William and Mary
Eastern Mennonite University
Emory & Henry College
Hollins University
James Madison University
Longwood University
Lynchburg College
Old Dominion University
Radford University
Randolph College
Roanoke College
Southern Virginia University
Sweet Briar College
University of Mary Washington
University of Richmond
University of Virginia's College at Wise
Virginia Commonwealth University
Virginia Polytechnic Institute and State
    University
Virginia State University

## Washington
Art Institute of Seattle
Big Bend Community College
Central Washington University
Centralia College
Clark College
Cornish College of the Arts
DigiPen Institute of Technology
Eastern Washington University
Everett Community College
Evergreen State College
Grays Harbor College
Northwest College of Art & Design
Northwest University
Pacific Lutheran University
Saint Martin's University
Seattle Pacific University
Trinity Lutheran College
University of Puget Sound
University of Washington
University of Washington Bothell
University of Washington Tacoma
Washington State University
Western Washington University
Whitman College
Whitworth University

## West Virginia
Davis and Elkins College
Fairmont State University
Marshall University
Shepherd University
University of Charleston
West Liberty University
West Virginia University
West Virginia University Institute of
    Technology
West Virginia Wesleyan College

## Wisconsin
Cardinal Stritch University
Carroll University
Carthage College
Concordia University Wisconsin
Edgewood College
Lakeland College
Milwaukee Institute of Art & Design
Mount Mary University
Northland College
Ripon College
St. Norbert College

Silver Lake College of the Holy Family
University of Wisconsin
    Baraboo/Sauk County
    Eau Claire
    Green Bay
    La Crosse
    Madison
    Manitowoc
    Milwaukee
    Oshkosh
    Parkside
    Richland
    River Falls
    Sheboygan
    Stevens Point
    Superior
    Waukesha
    Whitewater
Viterbo University
Wisconsin Lutheran College

## Wyoming
Casper College
Central Wyoming College
Eastern Wyoming College
Laramie County Community College
Northwest College
Sheridan College
University of Wyoming
Western Wyoming Community College

# Athletic scholarships

## Archery

**Arizona**
Dine College M,W

**California**
College of the Redwoods M

**Georgia**
Emmanuel College M,W

**Kentucky**
Midway College W
University of the Cumberlands M,W

## Badminton

**California**
Fresno City College M,W

**New Jersey**
New Jersey Institute of Technology M

## Baseball

**Alabama**
Alabama Agricultural and Mechanical
    University M
Alabama Southern Community College M
Alabama State University M
Auburn University M
Auburn University at Montgomery M
Central Alabama Community College M
Chattahoochee Valley Community College M
Concordia College M
Enterprise State Community College M
Faulkner State Community College M
George C. Wallace Community College at
    Dothan M
George C. Wallace State Community College
    at Selma M
Jacksonville State University M
Jefferson Davis Community College M
Lawson State Community College M
Lurleen B. Wallace Community College M
Marion Military Institute M
Miles College M
Samford University M
Selma University M
Shelton State Community College M
Snead State Community College M
Southern Union State Community College M
Spring Hill College M
Troy University M
Tuskegee University M
University of Alabama M
University of Alabama
    Birmingham M
    Huntsville M
University of Mobile M
University of Montevallo M
University of North Alabama M
University of South Alabama M
University of West Alabama M
Wallace State Community College at
    Hanceville M

**Arizona**
Arizona Christian University M
Arizona State University M

Arizona Western College M
Central Arizona College M
Chandler-Gilbert Community College M
Cochise College M
Eastern Arizona College M
GateWay Community College M
Grand Canyon University M
Mesa Community College M
Paradise Valley Community College M
Pima Community College M
Scottsdale Community College M
South Mountain Community College M
University of Arizona M
Yavapai College M

**Arkansas**
Arkansas State University M
Arkansas Tech University M
Crowley's Ridge College M
Ecclesia College M
Harding University M
Henderson State University M
Lyon College M
North Arkansas College M
Ouachita Baptist University M
Southern Arkansas University M
University of Arkansas M
University of Arkansas
    Fort Smith M
    Little Rock M
    Pine Bluff M
University of Central Arkansas M
Williams Baptist College M

**California**
Academy of Art University M
Azusa Pacific University M
Biola University M
California Baptist University M
California Polytechnic State University: San
    Luis Obispo M
California State Polytechnic University:
    Pomona M
California State University
    Chico M
    Dominguez Hills M
    Fresno M
    Fullerton M
    Long Beach M
    Los Angeles M
    Monterey Bay M
    Northridge M
    Sacramento M
    San Bernardino M
    Stanislaus M
Concordia University Irvine M
Fresno City College M
Fresno Pacific University M
Grossmont College M
Holy Names University M
Hope International University M
La Sierra University M
Loyola Marymount University M
The Master's College M
Menlo College M
Pepperdine University M
Point Loma Nazarene University M
St. Mary's College of California M
San Diego Christian College M
San Diego State University M
San Jose State University M
Santa Clara University M
Simpson University M
Sonoma State University M
Stanford University M

University of California
    Berkeley M
    Davis M
    Irvine M
    Los Angeles M
    Riverside M
    Santa Barbara M
University of San Diego M
University of San Francisco M
University of Southern California M
University of the Pacific M
Vanguard University of Southern California M
Westmont College M
William Jessup University M
Yuba College M

**Colorado**
Colorado Christian University M
Colorado Mesa University M
Colorado Northwestern Community College M
Colorado School of Mines M
Colorado State University
    Pueblo M
Lamar Community College M
Metropolitan State University of Denver M
Northeastern Junior College M
Otero Junior College M
Regis University M
Trinidad State Junior College M
University of Colorado
    Colorado Springs M
University of Northern Colorado M

**Connecticut**
Central Connecticut State University M
Fairfield University M
Post University M
Quinnipiac University M
Sacred Heart University M
Southern Connecticut State University M
University of Bridgeport M
University of Connecticut M
University of Hartford M
University of New Haven M

**Delaware**
Delaware State University M
Delaware Technical Community College
    Jack F. Owens Campus M
University of Delaware M
Wilmington University M

**District of Columbia**
George Washington University M
Georgetown University M

**Florida**
Ave Maria University M
Barry University M
Bethune-Cookman University M
Chipola College M
College of Central Florida M
Daytona State College M
Eastern Florida State College M
Eckerd College M
Edward Waters College M
Embry-Riddle Aeronautical University M
Flagler College M
Florida Atlantic University M
Florida Gulf Coast University M
Florida Institute of Technology M
Florida Memorial University M
Florida Southern College M
Florida State College at Jacksonville M
Florida State University M
Gulf Coast State College M
Hillsborough Community College M
Indian River State College M
Jacksonville University M
Lake-Sumter State College M
Lynn University M
Miami Dade College M
North Florida Community College M
Northwest Florida State College M

Nova Southeastern University M
Palm Beach Atlantic University M
Palm Beach State College M
Pasco-Hernando State College M
Pensacola State College M
Polk State College M
Rollins College M
Saint Johns River State College M
Saint Leo University M
St. Petersburg College M
Saint Thomas University M
Santa Fe College M
South Florida State College M
Southeastern University M
State College of Florida, Manatee-Sarasota M
Stetson University M
Tallahassee Community College M
University of Central Florida M
University of Florida M
University of Miami M
University of North Florida M
University of South Florida M
University of Tampa M
University of West Florida M
Warner University M
Webber International University M

**Georgia**
Abraham Baldwin Agricultural College M
Albany State University M
Andrew College M
Armstrong State University M
Augusta University M
Brewton-Parker College M
Clark Atlanta University M
Columbus State University M
Darton College M
East Georgia State College M
Emmanuel College M
Georgia College and State University M
Georgia Gwinnett College M
Georgia Highlands College M,W
Georgia Institute of Technology M
Georgia Perimeter College M
Georgia Southern University M
Georgia Southwestern State University M
Georgia State University M
Gordon State College M
Kennesaw State University M
Mercer University M
Middle Georgia State College M
Morehouse College M
Paine College M
Point University M
Reinhardt University M
Savannah State University M
Shorter University M
Thomas University M
Truett-McConnell College M
University of Georgia M
University of North Georgia M
University of West Georgia M
Valdosta State University M
Young Harris College M

**Hawaii**
Hawaii Pacific University M
University of Hawaii
    Manoa M

**Idaho**
College of Idaho M
College of Southern Idaho M
Lewis-Clark State College M
Northwest Nazarene University M

**Illinois**
Benedictine University at Springfield M
Black Hawk College M
Bradley University M
Carl Sandburg College M
Chicago State University M
College of Lake County M
Danville Area Community College M

Eastern Illinois University M
Elgin Community College M
Highland Community College M
Illinois Central College M
Illinois Eastern Community Colleges
    Lincoln Trail College M
    Olney Central College M
    Wabash Valley College M
Illinois Institute of Technology M
Illinois State University M
John A. Logan College M
John Wood Community College M
Judson University M
Kankakee Community College M
Kaskaskia College M
Kishwaukee College M
Lake Land College M
Lewis and Clark Community College M
Lewis University M
Lincoln Christian University M
Lincoln College M
Lincoln Land Community College M
McHenry County College M
McKendree University M
Moraine Valley Community College M
Morton College M
Northern Illinois University M
Northwestern University M
Olivet Nazarene University M
Parkland College M
Quincy University M
Rend Lake College M
Robert Morris University: Chicago M
Saint Xavier University M
Sauk Valley Community College M
South Suburban College of Cook County M
Southeastern Illinois College M
Southern Illinois University Carbondale M
Southern Illinois University Edwardsville M
Southwestern Illinois College M
Spoon River College M
Trinity Christian College M
Trinity International University M
University of Illinois
    Chicago M
    Springfield M
    Urbana-Champaign M
University of St. Francis M
Western Illinois University M

**Indiana**
Ancilla College M
Ball State University M
Bethel College M
Butler University M
Calumet College of St. Joseph M
Goshen College M
Grace College M
Holy Cross College M
Huntington University M
Indiana Institute of Technology M
Indiana State University M
Indiana University
    Bloomington M
    Purdue University Fort Wayne M
    Southeast M
Indiana Wesleyan University M
Marian University M
Oakland City University M
Purdue University M
Purdue University
    Calumet M
    North Central M
Saint Joseph's College M
Taylor University M
University of Evansville M
University of Indianapolis M
University of Notre Dame M
University of Saint Francis M
University of Southern Indiana M
Valparaiso University M
Vincennes University M

**Iowa**
Briar Cliff University M
Clarke University M
Des Moines Area Community College M
Dordt College M
Ellsworth Community College M
Graceland University M
Grand View University M
Iowa Central Community College M
Iowa Lakes Community College M
Iowa Western Community College M
Kirkwood Community College M
Morningside College M
Mount Mercy University M
Muscatine Community College M
North Iowa Area Community College M
Northwestern College M
St. Ambrose University M
Southeastern Community College M
Southwestern Community College M
University of Iowa M
Upper Iowa University M
Waldorf University M
William Penn University M

**Kansas**
Allen County Community College M
Baker University M
Barton County Community College M
Benedictine College M
Bethany College M
Brown Mackie College
    Salina M
Butler Community College M
Central Christian College of Kansas M
Cloud County Community College M
Coffeyville Community College M
Colby Community College M
Cowley County Community College M
Dodge City Community College M
Emporia State University M
Fort Scott Community College M
Friends University M
Garden City Community College M
Hesston College M
Highland Community College M
Hutchinson Community College M
Independence Community College M
Johnson County Community College M
Kansas City Kansas Community College M
Kansas State University M
Kansas Wesleyan University M
Labette Community College M
McPherson College M
MidAmerica Nazarene University M
Neosho County Community College M
Newman University M
Ottawa University M
Pittsburg State University M
Pratt Community College M
Seward County Community College M
Sterling College M
Tabor College M
University of Kansas M
University of St. Mary M
Washburn University M
Wichita State University M

**Kentucky**
Alice Lloyd College M
Asbury University M
Bellarmine University M
Brescia University M
Campbellsville University M
Eastern Kentucky University M
Georgetown College M
Kentucky State University M
Kentucky Wesleyan College M
Lindsey Wilson College M
Morehead State University M
Murray State University M
Northern Kentucky University M
St. Catharine College M

Union College M
University of Kentucky M
University of Louisville M
University of Pikeville M
University of the Cumberlands M
Western Kentucky University M

**Louisiana**
Bossier Parish Community College M
Delgado Community College M
Grambling State University M
Louisiana State University
    Eunice M
    Shreveport M
Louisiana State University and Agricultural and
    Mechanical College M
Louisiana Tech University M
Loyola University New Orleans M
McNeese State University M
Nicholls State University M
Northwestern State University M
Southeastern Louisiana University M
Southern University and Agricultural and
    Mechanical College M
Tulane University M
University of Louisiana at Lafayette M
University of Louisiana at Monroe M
University of New Orleans M

**Maine**
University of Maine M

**Maryland**
Anne Arundel Community College M
Chesapeake College M
College of Southern Maryland M
Community College of Baltimore County M
Coppin State University M
Garrett College M
Hagerstown Community College M
Harford Community College M
Mount St. Mary's University M
Towson University M
University of Maryland
    Baltimore County M
    College Park M
    Eastern Shore M

**Massachusetts**
American International College M
Boston College M
Merrimack College M
Northeastern University M
Stonehill College M
University of Massachusetts
    Amherst M
    Lowell M

**Michigan**
Aquinas College M
Central Michigan University M
Cleary University M
Concordia University M
Davenport University M
Eastern Michigan University M
Glen Oaks Community College M
Hillsdale College M
Kalamazoo Valley Community College M
Kellogg Community College M
Lake Michigan College M
Lansing Community College M
Macomb Community College M
Madonna University M
Marygrove College M
Michigan State University M
Mott Community College M
Muskegon Community College M
Northwood University
    Michigan M
Oakland University M
Rochester College M
Saginaw Valley State University M
St. Clair County Community College M
Siena Heights University M

Spring Arbor University M
University of Michigan M
Wayne State University M
Western Michigan University M

**Minnesota**
Concordia University St. Paul M
Minnesota State University
    Mankato M
Saint Cloud State University M
Southwest Minnesota State University M
University of Minnesota
    Crookston M
    Duluth M
    Twin Cities M
Winona State University M

**Mississippi**
Alcorn State University M
Belhaven University M
Blue Mountain College M
Copiah-Lincoln Community College M
Delta State University M
East Central Community College M
East Mississippi Community College M
Hinds Community College M
Holmes Community College M
Itawamba Community College M
Jackson State University M
Jones County Junior College M
Meridian Community College M
Mississippi Gulf Coast Community College M
Mississippi State University M
Mississippi Valley State University M
Northwest Mississippi Community College M
Southwest Mississippi Community College M
University of Mississippi M
University of Southern Mississippi M
William Carey University M

**Missouri**
Avila University M
Central Methodist University M
College of the Ozarks M
Crowder College M
Culver-Stockton College M
Drury University M
Evangel University M
Hannibal-LaGrange University M
Harris-Stowe State University M
Jefferson College M
Lincoln University M
Lindenwood University M
Maryville University of Saint Louis M
Metropolitan Community College - Kansas City
    M
Mineral Area College M
Missouri Baptist University M
Missouri Southern State University M
Missouri State University M
Missouri University of Science and Technology
    M
Missouri Valley College M
Missouri Western State University M
North Central Missouri College M
Northwest Missouri State University M
Park University M
Research College of Nursing M
Rockhurst University M
St. Louis Community College M
Saint Louis University M
Southeast Missouri State University M
Southwest Baptist University M
Three Rivers Community College M
Truman State University M
University of Central Missouri M
University of Missouri
    Columbia M
    St. Louis M
William Jewell College M
William Woods University M

## Montana
Miles Community College M
Montana State University
　　Billings M

## Nebraska
Bellevue University M
Concordia University M
Creighton University M
Doane College M
Grace University M
Hastings College M
Mid-Plains Community College M
Midland University M
Peru State College M
University of Nebraska
　　Kearney M
　　Lincoln M
　　Omaha M
Wayne State College M
Western Nebraska Community College M
York College M

## Nevada
University of Nevada
　　Las Vegas M
　　Reno M

## New Hampshire
Franklin Pierce University M
Mount Washington College M
Southern New Hampshire University M

## New Jersey
Bloomfield College M
Brookdale Community College M
Caldwell University M
County College of Morris M
Fairleigh Dickinson University
　　Metropolitan Campus M
Mercer County Community College M
Monmouth University M
New Jersey Institute of Technology M
Raritan Valley Community College M
Rider University M
Rowan College at Burlington County M
Rutgers, The State University of New Jersey
　　New Brunswick/Piscataway Campus M
Saint Peter's University M
Salem Community College M
Seton Hall University M
Sussex County Community College M

## New Mexico
Eastern New Mexico University M
New Mexico Highlands University M
New Mexico Junior College M
New Mexico Military Institute M
New Mexico State University M
University of New Mexico M
University of the Southwest M

## New York
Adelphi University M
ASA College M
Canisius College M
City University of New York
　　Queens College M
College of Saint Rose M
Concordia College M
Dominican College of Blauvelt M
Dowling College M
Fordham University M
Globe Institute of Technology M
Hofstra University M
Iona College M
Le Moyne College M
Long Island University
　　LIU Brooklyn M
　　LIU Post M
Manhattan College M
Marist College M
Mercy College M
Molloy College M

Monroe College M
Monroe Community College M
New York Institute of Technology M
Niagara University M
Nyack College M
Orange County Community College M
Pace University M
Pace University: Pleasantville/Briarcliff M
Saint Bonaventure University M
St. John's University M
St. Thomas Aquinas College M
Siena College M
SUNY
　　University at Albany M
　　University at Binghamton M
　　University at Buffalo M
　　University at Stony Brook M
Wagner College M

## North Carolina
Appalachian State University M
Barton College M
Belmont Abbey College M
Brevard College M
Campbell University M
Catawba College M
Chowan University M
Davidson College M
Duke University M
East Carolina University M
Elizabeth City State University M
Elon University M
Gardner-Webb University M
Guilford Technical Community College M
High Point University M
Lenoir Community College M
Lenoir-Rhyne University M
Louisburg College M
Mars Hill University M
Montreat College M
North Carolina Agricultural and Technical State
　　University M
North Carolina State University M
Pitt Community College M
Saint Augustine's University M
Southeastern Community College M
University of Mount Olive M
University of North Carolina
　　Asheville M
　　Chapel Hill M
　　Charlotte M
　　Greensboro M
　　Wilmington M
Wake Forest University M
Western Carolina University M
Wingate University M

## North Dakota
Bismarck State College M
Dakota College at Bottineau M
Dickinson State University M
Lake Region State College M
Mayville State University M
Minot State University M
North Dakota State University M
University of Jamestown M
University of Mary M
University of North Dakota M
Valley City State University M
Williston State College M

## Ohio
Ashland University M
Bowling Green State University M
Cedarville University M
Clark State Community College M
Kent State University M
Lake Erie College M
Lakeland Community College M
Lourdes University M
Malone University M
Miami University
　　Oxford M

Mount Vernon Nazarene University M
Notre Dame College M
Ohio Dominican University M
Ohio State University
　　Columbus Campus M
Ohio University M
Owens Community College M
Shawnee State University M
Sinclair Community College M
Tiffin University M
University of Cincinnati M
University of Dayton M
University of Findlay M
University of Rio Grande M
University of Toledo M
Urbana University M
Walsh University M
Wright State University M
Xavier University M
Youngstown State University M

## Oklahoma
Bacone College M
Cameron University M
Carl Albert State College M
Connors State College M
East Central University M
Eastern Oklahoma State College M
Mid-America Christian University M
Northeastern Oklahoma Agricultural and
　　Mechanical College M
Northeastern State University M
Northern Oklahoma College M
Northwestern Oklahoma State University M
Oklahoma Baptist University M
Oklahoma Christian University M
Oklahoma City University M
Oklahoma Panhandle State University M
Oklahoma State University M
Oklahoma Wesleyan University M
Oral Roberts University M
Redlands Community College M
Rogers State University M
Rose State College M
St. Gregory's University M
Seminole State College M
Southeastern Oklahoma State University M
Southern Nazarene University M
Southwestern Oklahoma State University M
University of Central Oklahoma M
University of Oklahoma M
University of Science and Arts of Oklahoma M
Western Oklahoma State College M

## Oregon
Blue Mountain Community College M
Chemeketa Community College M
Clackamas Community College M
Concordia University M
Corban University M
Lane Community College M
Linn-Benton Community College M
Mt. Hood Community College M
Oregon Institute of Technology M
Oregon State University M
Portland State University M
Southwestern Oregon Community College M
Treasure Valley Community College M
University of Oregon M
University of Portland M
Western Oregon University M

## Pennsylvania
Bloomsburg University of Pennsylvania M
California University of Pennsylvania M
Chestnut Hill College M
Clarion University of Pennsylvania M
East Stroudsburg University of Pennsylvania M
Gannon University M
Indiana University of Pennsylvania M
Kutztown University of Pennsylvania M
La Salle University M
Lackawanna College M

Lock Haven University of Pennsylvania M
Mansfield University of Pennsylvania M
Mercyhurst University M
Millersville University of Pennsylvania M
Penn State
　　University Park M
Philadelphia University M
Point Park University M
Saint Joseph's University M
Seton Hill University M
Shippensburg University of Pennsylvania M
Slippery Rock University of Pennsylvania M
University of Pittsburgh M
University of the Sciences M
Villanova University M
West Chester University of Pennsylvania M

## Puerto Rico
Inter American University of Puerto Rico
　　Aguadilla Campus M
　　Bayamon Campus M
　　Metropolitan Campus M
　　Ponce Campus M
　　San German Campus M
Turabo University M
Universidad del Este M
Universidad Metropolitana M
University of Puerto Rico
　　Arecibo M
　　Carolina Regional College M
　　Humacao M
　　Mayaguez M
　　Utuado M

## Rhode Island
Bryant University M
Community College of Rhode Island M
University of Rhode Island M

## South Carolina
Anderson University M
Charleston Southern University M
The Citadel M
Claflin University M
Clemson University M
Coastal Carolina University M
Coker College M
College of Charleston M
Erskine College M
Francis Marion University M
Furman University M
Lander University M
Limestone College M
Morris College M
Newberry College M
North Greenville University M
Presbyterian College M
Southern Wesleyan University M
Spartanburg Methodist College M
University of South Carolina
　　Aiken M
　　Columbia M
　　Sumter M
　　Upstate M
Voorhees College M
Winthrop University M
Wofford College M

## South Dakota
Augusta University
　　Augustana University M
Dakota State University M
Dakota Wesleyan University M
Mount Marty College M
Northern State University M
University of Sioux Falls M

## Tennessee
Austin Peay State University M
Belmont University M
Bethel University M
Bryan College
　　Dayton M
Carson-Newman University M

Chattanooga State Community College M
Christian Brothers University M
Cleveland State Community College M
Columbia State Community College M
Cumberland University M
Dyersburg State Community College M
East Tennessee State University M
Freed-Hardeman University M
Hiwassee College M
Jackson State Community College M
King University M
Lee University M
LeMoyne-Owen College M
Lincoln Memorial University M
Lipscomb University M
Martin Methodist College M
Middle Tennessee State University M
Milligan College M
Motlow State Community College M
Roane State Community College M
Southwest Tennessee Community College M
Tennessee Technological University M
Tennessee Wesleyan College M
Trevecca Nazarene University M
Tusculum College M
Union University M
University of Memphis M
University of Tennessee
    Knoxville M
    Martin M
Vanderbilt University M
Walters State Community College M

**Texas**
Abilene Christian University M
Alvin Community College M
Angelina College M
Angelo State University M
Baylor University M
Blinn College M
Brookhaven College M
Clarendon College M
Dallas Baptist University M
El Paso Community College M
Frank Phillips College M
Galveston College M
Grayson College M
Hill College M
Houston Baptist University M
Howard College M
Jarvis Christian College M
Lamar University M
Laredo Community College M
Lubbock Christian University M
McLennan Community College M
Midland College M
North Central Texas College M
Northeast Texas Community College M
Odessa College M
Panola College M
Paris Junior College M
Prairie View A&M University M
Ranger College M
Rice University M
St. Edward's University M
St. Mary's University M
Sam Houston State University M
San Jacinto College M
Southwestern Assemblies of God University M
Stephen F. Austin State University M
Tarleton State University M
Texas A&M University M
Texas A&M University
    Corpus Christi M
Texas Christian University M
Texas Southern University M
Texas State University M
Texas Tech University M
Texas Wesleyan University M
University of Houston M
University of Texas
    Arlington M
    Austin M

Pan American M
    of the Permian Basin M
    San Antonio M
University of the Incarnate Word M
Vernon College M
Wayland Baptist University M
Weatherford College M
West Texas A&M University M
Western Texas College M
Wharton County Junior College M
Wiley College M

**Utah**
Brigham Young University M
Dixie State University M
Salt Lake Community College M
University of Utah M
Utah Valley University M

**Virginia**
Bluefield College M
College of William and Mary M
George Mason University M
James Madison University M
Liberty University M
Longwood University M
Norfolk State University M
Old Dominion University M
Radford University M
University of Richmond M
University of Virginia M
University of Virginia's College at Wise M
Virginia Commonwealth University M
Virginia Military Institute M
Virginia Polytechnic Institute and State
    University M
Virginia State University M

**Washington**
Big Bend Community College M
Central Washington University M
Centralia College M
Columbia Basin College M
Edmonds Community College M
Everett Community College M
Gonzaga University M
Grays Harbor College M
Green River Community College M
Lower Columbia College M
Olympic College M
Pierce College M
Saint Martin's University M
Shoreline Community College M
Skagit Valley College M
Spokane Community College M
Tacoma Community College M
University of Washington M
Walla Walla Community College M
Washington State University M
Yakima Valley Community College M

**West Virginia**
Alderson-Broaddus University M
Bluefield State College M
Concord University M
Davis and Elkins College M
Fairmont State University M
Marshall University M
Ohio Valley University M
Potomac State College of West Virginia
    University M
Salem International University M
Shepherd University M
University of Charleston M
West Liberty University M
West Virginia State University M
West Virginia University M
West Virginia University Institute of
    Technology M
West Virginia Wesleyan College M
Wheeling Jesuit University M

**Wisconsin**
University of Wisconsin
    Milwaukee M
    Parkside M
Viterbo University M

# Basketball

**Alabama**
Alabama Agricultural and Mechanical
    University M,W
Alabama Southern Community College M,W
Alabama State University M,W
Auburn University M,W
Auburn University at Montgomery M,W
Chattahoochee Valley Community College M,W
Concordia College M,W
Enterprise State Community College M,W
Faulkner State Community College M,W
Faulkner University M,W
Gadsden State Community College M,W
George C. Wallace State Community College
    at Selma M,W
Jacksonville State University M,W
Jefferson Davis Community College M
Judson College W
Lawson State Community College M,W
Lurleen B. Wallace Community College M,W
Marion Military Institute M
Miles College M,W
Samford University M,W
Shelton State Community College M,W
Snead State Community College M,W
Southern Union State Community College M,W
Spring Hill College M,W
Troy University M,W
Tuskegee University M,W
University of Alabama M,W
University of Alabama
    Birmingham M,W
    Huntsville M,W
University of Mobile M,W
University of Montevallo M,W
University of North Alabama M,W
University of South Alabama M,W
University of West Alabama M,W
Wallace State Community College at
    Hanceville M,W

**Alaska**
University of Alaska
    Anchorage M,W
    Fairbanks M,W

**Arizona**
Arizona Christian University M,W
Arizona State University M,W
Arizona Western College M,W
Central Arizona College M,W
Chandler-Gilbert Community College M,W
Cochise College M,W
Eastern Arizona College M,W
Embry-Riddle Aeronautical University
    Prescott Campus M
Grand Canyon University M,W
Mesa Community College M,W
Northern Arizona University M,W
Pima Community College M,W
Scottsdale Community College M,W
South Mountain Community College M,W
University of Arizona M,W
Yavapai College M,W

**Arkansas**
Arkansas State University M,W
Arkansas Tech University M,W
Crowley's Ridge College M,W
Ecclesia College M,W
Harding University M,W
Henderson State University M,W
John Brown University M,W

Lyon College M,W
North Arkansas College M,W
Ouachita Baptist University M,W
Philander Smith College M,W
Southern Arkansas University M,W
University of Arkansas M,W
University of Arkansas
    Fort Smith M,W
    Little Rock M,W
    Monticello M,W
    Pine Bluff M,W
University of Central Arkansas M,W
Williams Baptist College M,W

**California**
Academy of Art University M,W
Azusa Pacific University M,W
Biola University M,W
California Baptist University M,W
California Polytechnic State University: San
    Luis Obispo M,W
California State Polytechnic University:
    Pomona M,W
California State University
    Bakersfield M
    Chico M,W
    Dominguez Hills M,W
    Fresno M,W
    Fullerton M,W
    Long Beach M,W
    Los Angeles M,W
    Monterey Bay M,W
    Northridge M,W
    Sacramento M,W
    San Bernardino M,W
    Stanislaus M,W
Concordia University Irvine M,W
Dominican University of California M,W
Fresno City College M,W
Fresno Pacific University M,W
Grossmont College M,W
Holy Names University M,W
Hope International University M,W
Humboldt State University M,W
La Sierra University M,W
Loyola Marymount University M,W
The Master's College M,W
Menlo College M,W
Notre Dame de Namur University M,W
Pepperdine University M,W
Point Loma Nazarene University M,W
St. Mary's College of California M,W
San Diego Christian College M,W
San Diego State University M,W
San Jose State University M,W
Santa Clara University M,W
Simpson University M,W
Sonoma State University M,W
Stanford University M,W
University of California
    Berkeley M,W
    Davis M,W
    Irvine M,W
    Los Angeles M,W
    Merced M,W
    Riverside M,W
    Santa Barbara M,W
University of San Diego M,W
University of San Francisco M,W
University of Southern California M,W
University of the Pacific M,W
Vanguard University of Southern California
    M,W
Westmont College M,W
William Jessup University M,W
Yuba College M,W

**Colorado**
Adams State University M,W
Colorado Christian University M,W
Colorado Mesa University M,W
Colorado Northwestern Community College
    M,W

Colorado School of Mines M,W
Colorado State University M,W
Colorado State University
 Pueblo M,W
Fort Lewis College M,W
Lamar Community College M,W
Metropolitan State University of Denver M,W
Northeastern Junior College M,W
Otero Junior College M,W
Regis University M,W
Trinidad State Junior College M,W
University of Colorado
 Boulder M,W
 Colorado Springs M,W
University of Denver M,W
University of Northern Colorado M,W
Western State Colorado University M,W

### Connecticut
Central Connecticut State University M,W
Fairfield University M,W
Post University M,W
Quinnipiac University M,W
Sacred Heart University M,W
Southern Connecticut State University M,W
University of Bridgeport M,W
University of Connecticut M,W
University of Hartford M,W
University of New Haven M,W

### Delaware
Delaware State University M,W
Delaware Technical Community College
 Stanton/Wilmington Campus M,W
Goldey-Beacom College M,W
University of Delaware M,W
Wilmington University M,W

### District of Columbia
American University M,W
George Washington University M,W
Georgetown University M,W
Howard University M,W
University of the District of Columbia M,W

### Florida
Ave Maria University M,W
Barry University M,W
Bethune-Cookman University M,W
Chipola College M,W
College of Central Florida M,W
Daytona State College M,W
Eastern Florida State College M,W
Eckerd College M,W
Edward Waters College M,W
Embry-Riddle Aeronautical University M,W
Flagler College M,W
Florida Agricultural and Mechanical University
 M
Florida Atlantic University M,W
Florida College M
Florida Gulf Coast University M,W
Florida Institute of Technology M,W
Florida Memorial University M,W
Florida Southern College M,W
Florida State College at Jacksonville M,W
Florida State University M,W
Gulf Coast State College M,W
Hillsborough Community College M,W
Indian River State College M,W
Jacksonville University M,W
Lynn University M,W
Miami Dade College M,W
North Florida Community College W
Northwest Florida State College M,W
Nova Southeastern University M,W
Palm Beach Atlantic University M,W
Palm Beach State College M,W
Pasco-Hernando State College M
Pensacola State College M,W
Polk State College M
Rollins College M,W
Saint Leo University M,W
St. Petersburg College M,W

Santa Fe College M,W
Southeastern University M,W
State College of Florida, Manatee-Sarasota M
Stetson University M,W
Tallahassee Community College M,W
University of Central Florida M,W
University of Florida M,W
University of Miami M,W
University of North Florida M,W
University of South Florida M,W
University of Tampa M,W
University of West Florida M,W
Warner University M,W
Webber International University M,W

### Georgia
Albany State University M,W
Andrew College W
Armstrong State University M,W
Augusta University M,W
Brenau University W
Brewton-Parker College M,W
Clark Atlanta University M,W
Clayton State University M,W
College of Coastal Georgia M,W
Columbus State University M,W
Darton College W
East Georgia State College M,W
Emmanuel College M,W
Fort Valley State University M,W
Georgia College and State University M,W
Georgia Highlands College M,W
Georgia Institute of Technology M,W
Georgia Perimeter College M,W
Georgia Southern University M,W
Georgia Southwestern State University M,W
Georgia State University M,W
Gordon State College M
Kennesaw State University M,W
Life University M
Mercer University M,W
Middle Georgia State College M,W
Morehouse College M
Paine College M,W
Point University M,W
Reinhardt University M,W
Savannah State University M,W
Shorter University M,W
Truett-McConnell College M,W
University of Georgia M,W
University of North Georgia M,W
University of West Georgia M,W
Valdosta State University M,W
Young Harris College M,W

### Hawaii
Brigham Young University-Hawaii M,W
Chaminade University of Honolulu M,W
Hawaii Pacific University M,W
University of Hawaii
 Hilo M
 Manoa M,W

### Idaho
Boise State University M,W
College of Idaho M,W
College of Southern Idaho M,W
Idaho State University M,W
Lewis-Clark State College M,W
North Idaho College M,W
Northwest Nazarene University M,W
University of Idaho M,W

### Illinois
Benedictine University at Springfield M,W
Black Hawk College M,W
Bradley University M,W
Carl Sandburg College M,W
Chicago State University M,W
College of Lake County M,W
Danville Area Community College M,W
DePaul University M,W
Eastern Illinois University M,W
Elgin Community College M,W

Governors State University M,W
Highland Community College M,W
Illinois Central College M,W
Illinois Eastern Community Colleges
 Lincoln Trail College M,W
 Olney Central College M,W
 Wabash Valley College M,W
Illinois State University M,W
John A. Logan College M,W
John Wood Community College M,W
Judson University M,W
Kankakee Community College M,W
Kaskaskia College M,W
Kishwaukee College M,W
Lake Land College M,W
Lewis and Clark Community College M,W
Lewis University M,W
Lincoln Christian University M,W
Lincoln College M,W
Lincoln Land Community College M,W
Loyola University Chicago M,W
McHenry County College M,W
McKendree University M,W
Moraine Valley Community College M,W
Morton College M,W
Northern Illinois University M,W
Northwestern University M,W
Olivet Nazarene University M,W
Parkland College M,W
Quincy University M,W
Rend Lake College M,W
Robert Morris University: Chicago M,W
Saint Xavier University M
Sauk Valley Community College M,W
Shawnee Community College M,W
South Suburban College of Cook County M,W
Southeastern Illinois College M,W
Southern Illinois University Carbondale M,W
Southern Illinois University Edwardsville M,W
Southwestern Illinois College M,W
Trinity Christian College M,W
Trinity International University M,W
University of Illinois
 Chicago M,W
 Springfield M,W
 Urbana-Champaign M,W
University of St. Francis M,W
Waubonsee Community College M,W
Western Illinois University M,W

### Indiana
Ancilla College M,W
Ball State University M,W
Bethel College M,W
Butler University M,W
Calumet College of St. Joseph M,W
Goshen College M,W
Grace College M,W
Holy Cross College M,W
Huntington University M,W
Indiana Institute of Technology M,W
Indiana State University M,W
Indiana University
 Bloomington M,W
 Northwest M,W
 Purdue University Fort Wayne M,W
 Purdue University Indianapolis M,W
 South Bend M,W
 Southeast M,W
Indiana Wesleyan University M,W
Marian University M,W
Oakland City University M,W
Purdue University M,W
Purdue University
 Calumet M,W
 North Central M
Saint Joseph's College M,W
St. Mary-of-the-Woods College W
Taylor University M,W
University of Evansville M,W
University of Indianapolis M,W
University of Notre Dame M,W
University of Saint Francis M,W

University of Southern Indiana M,W
Valparaiso University M,W
Vincennes University M,W

### Iowa
Briar Cliff University M,W
Clarke University M,W
Des Moines Area Community College M,W
Dordt College M,W
Drake University M,W
Ellsworth Community College M,W
Graceland University M,W
Grand View University M,W
Iowa Central Community College M,W
Iowa Lakes Community College M,W
Iowa State University M,W
Iowa Western Community College M,W
Kirkwood Community College M,W
Marshalltown Community College M,W
Morningside College M,W
Mount Mercy University M,W
North Iowa Area Community College M,W
Northwestern College M,W
St. Ambrose University M,W
Southeastern Community College M,W
Southwestern Community College M,W
University of Iowa M,W
University of Northern Iowa M,W
Upper Iowa University M,W
Waldorf University M,W
William Penn University M,W

### Kansas
Allen County Community College M,W
Baker University M,W
Barton County Community College M,W
Benedictine College M,W
Bethany College M,W
Bethel College M,W
Brown Mackie College
 Salina M,W
Butler Community College M,W
Central Christian College of Kansas M,W
Cloud County Community College M,W
Coffeyville Community College M,W
Colby Community College M,W
Cowley County Community College M,W
Dodge City Community College M,W
Emporia State University M,W
Fort Hays State University M,W
Fort Scott Community College M,W
Friends University M,W
Garden City Community College M,W
Hesston College M,W
Highland Community College M,W
Hutchinson Community College M,W
Independence Community College M,W
Johnson County Community College M,W
Kansas City Kansas Community College M,W
Kansas State University M,W
Kansas Wesleyan University M,W
Labette Community College M,W
McPherson College M,W
MidAmerica Nazarene University M,W
Neosho County Community College M,W
Newman University M,W
Northwest Kansas Technical College M,W
Ottawa University M,W
Pittsburg State University M,W
Pratt Community College M,W
Seward County Community College M,W
Southwestern College M,W
Sterling College M,W
Tabor College M,W
University of Kansas M,W
University of St. Mary M,W
Washburn University M,W
Wichita State University M,W

### Kentucky
Alice Lloyd College M,W
Asbury University M,W
Bellarmine University M,W

Brescia University M,W
Campbellsville University M,W
Eastern Kentucky University M,W
Georgetown College M,W
Kentucky State University M,W
Kentucky Wesleyan College M,W
Lindsey Wilson College M,W
Midway College W
Morehead State University M,W
Murray State University M,W
Northern Kentucky University M,W
St. Catharine College M,W
Union College M,W
University of Kentucky M,W
University of Louisville M,W
University of Pikeville M,W
University of the Cumberlands M,W
Western Kentucky University M,W

**Louisiana**
Bossier Parish Community College M,W
Dillard University M,W
Grambling State University M,W
Louisiana State University
    Eunice W
    Shreveport M,W
Louisiana State University and Agricultural and
    Mechanical College M,W
Louisiana Tech University M,W
Loyola University New Orleans M,W
McNeese State University M,W
Nicholls State University M,W
Northwestern State University M,W
Southeastern Louisiana University M,W
Southern University
    New Orleans M,W
Southern University and Agricultural and
    Mechanical College M,W
Tulane University M,W
University of Louisiana at Lafayette M,W
University of Louisiana at Monroe M,W
University of New Orleans M,W
Xavier University of Louisiana M,W

**Maine**
University of Maine M,W
University of Maine
    Augusta M,W

**Maryland**
Allegany College of Maryland M,W
Anne Arundel Community College M,W
Bowie State University M,W
Chesapeake College M,W
College of Southern Maryland M,W
Community College of Baltimore County M,W
Coppin State University M,W
Garrett College M,W
Hagerstown Community College M,W
Harford Community College M,W
Howard Community College M,W
Loyola University Maryland M,W
Morgan State University M,W
Mount St. Mary's University M,W
Towson University M,W
University of Maryland
    Baltimore County M,W
    College Park M,W
    Eastern Shore M,W
Washington Adventist University M,W

**Massachusetts**
American International College M,W
Assumption College M,W
Bentley University M,W
Boston College M,W
Boston University M,W
College of the Holy Cross M,W
Merrimack College M,W
Northeastern University M,W
Roxbury Community College M
Stonehill College M,W

University of Massachusetts
    Amherst M,W
    Lowell M,W

**Michigan**
Alpena Community College M,W
Aquinas College M,W
Central Michigan University M,W
Concordia University M,W
Cornerstone University M,W
Davenport University M,W
Delta College M,W
Eastern Michigan University M,W
Ferris State University M,W
Glen Oaks Community College M,W
Gogebic Community College M,W
Grand Valley State University M,W
Hillsdale College M,W
Kalamazoo Valley Community College M,W
Kellogg Community College M,W
Lake Michigan College M,W
Lake Superior State University M,W
Lansing Community College M,W
Lawrence Technological University M,W
Macomb Community College M,W
Madonna University M,W
Marygrove College M,W
Michigan State University M,W
Michigan Technological University M,W
Mott Community College M,W
Muskegon Community College M,W
Northern Michigan University M,W
Northwood University
    Michigan M,W
Oakland Community College M,W
Oakland University M,W
Rochester College M,W
Saginaw Valley State University M,W
St. Clair County Community College M,W
Siena Heights University M,W
Spring Arbor University M,W
University of Detroit Mercy M,W
University of Michigan M,W
University of Michigan
    Dearborn M,W
Wayne State University M,W
Western Michigan University M,W

**Minnesota**
Bemidji State University M,W
Concordia University St. Paul M,W
Minnesota State University
    Mankato M,W
    Moorhead M,W
Saint Cloud State University M,W
Southwest Minnesota State University M,W
University of Minnesota
    Crookston M,W
    Duluth M,W
    Twin Cities M,W
Winona State University M,W

**Mississippi**
Alcorn State University M,W
Belhaven University M,W
Blue Mountain College M,W
Coahoma Community College M,W
Copiah-Lincoln Community College M,W
Delta State University M,W
East Central Community College M,W
East Mississippi Community College M,W
Hinds Community College M,W
Holmes Community College M,W
Itawamba Community College M,W
Jackson State University M,W
Jones County Junior College M,W
Meridian Community College M,W
Mississippi Gulf Coast Community College
    M,W
Mississippi State University M,W
Mississippi Valley State University M,W
Northwest Mississippi Community College
    M,W

Southwest Mississippi Community College
    M,W
Tougaloo College M,W
University of Mississippi M,W
University of Southern Mississippi M,W
William Carey University M,W

**Missouri**
Avila University M,W
Central Methodist University M,W
College of the Ozarks M,W
Columbia College M,W
Cottey College W
Crowder College W
Culver-Stockton College M,W
Drury University M,W
Evangel University M,W
Hannibal-LaGrange University M,W
Harris-Stowe State University M,W
Jefferson College W
Lincoln University M,W
Lindenwood University M,W
Maryville University of Saint Louis M,W
Metropolitan Community College - Kansas City
    M,W
Mineral Area College M,W
Missouri Baptist University M,W
Missouri Southern State University M,W
Missouri State University M,W
Missouri State University: West Plains M
Missouri University of Science and Technology
    M,W
Missouri Valley College M,W
Missouri Western State University M,W
Moberly Area Community College M,W
North Central Missouri College M,W
Northwest Missouri State University M,W
Park University M,W
Research College of Nursing M,W
Rockhurst University M,W
St. Louis Community College M,W
Saint Louis University M,W
Southeast Missouri State University M,W
Southwest Baptist University M,W
State Fair Community College M,W
Stephens College W
Three Rivers Community College M,W
Truman State University M,W
University of Central Missouri M,W
University of Missouri
    Columbia M,W
    Kansas City M,W
    St. Louis M,W
William Jewell College M,W
William Woods University M,W

**Montana**
Carroll College M,W
Dawson Community College M,W
Miles Community College M,W
Montana State University M,W
Montana State University
    Billings M,W
    Northern M,W
Montana Tech of the University of Montana
    M,W
Rocky Mountain College M,W
University of Great Falls M,W
University of Montana M,W
University of Montana: Western M,W

**Nebraska**
Bellevue University M
Central Community College M
Chadron State College M,W
College of Saint Mary W
Concordia University M,W
Creighton University M,W
Doane College M,W
Grace University M,W
Hastings College M,W
Mid-Plains Community College M,W
Midland University M,W

Northeast Community College M,W
Peru State College M,W
University of Nebraska
    Kearney M,W
    Lincoln M,W
    Omaha M,W
Wayne State College M,W
Western Nebraska Community College M,W
York College M,W

**Nevada**
University of Nevada
    Las Vegas M,W
    Reno M,W

**New Hampshire**
Franklin Pierce University M,W
Mount Washington College M,W
Saint Anselm College M,W
Southern New Hampshire University M,W
University of New Hampshire M,W

**New Jersey**
Bloomfield College M,W
Brookdale Community College M,W
Caldwell University M,W
County College of Morris M,W
Essex County College M,W
Fairleigh Dickinson University
    Metropolitan Campus M,W
Felician University M,W
Georgian Court University M,W
Mercer County Community College M,W
Monmouth University M,W
New Jersey Institute of Technology M,W
Raritan Valley Community College M,W
Rider University M,W
Rowan College at Burlington County M,W
Rutgers, The State University of New Jersey
    New Brunswick/Piscataway Campus
    M,W
Saint Peter's University M,W
Salem Community College M,W
Seton Hall University M,W
Union County College W

**New Mexico**
Eastern New Mexico University M,W
New Mexico Highlands University M,W
New Mexico Junior College M,W
New Mexico Military Institute M
New Mexico State University M,W
University of New Mexico M,W
University of the Southwest M,W
Western New Mexico University M,W

**New York**
Adelphi University M,W
ASA College M,W
Canisius College M,W
City University of New York
    Queens College M,W
Colgate University M,W
College of Saint Rose M,W
Concordia College M,W
Daemen College M,W
Dominican College of Blauvelt M,W
Dowling College M,W
Fordham University M,W
Genesee Community College M,W
Globe Institute of Technology M,W
Hofstra University M,W
Iona College M,W
Le Moyne College M,W
Long Island University
    LIU Brooklyn M,W
    LIU Post M,W
Manhattan College M,W
Marist College M,W
Mercy College M,W
Molloy College M,W
Monroe College M
Monroe Community College M
New York Institute of Technology M,W

Niagara County Community College M,W
Niagara University M,W
Nyack College M,W
Orange County Community College M,W
Pace University M,W
Pace University: Pleasantville/Briarcliff M,W
Roberts Wesleyan College M,W
Saint Bonaventure University M,W
St. Francis College M,W
St. John's University M,W
St. Thomas Aquinas College M,W
Siena College M,W
SUNY
 University at Albany M,W
 University at Binghamton M,W
 University at Buffalo M,W
 University at Stony Brook M,W
Syracuse University M,W
Wagner College M,W

**North Carolina**
Appalachian State University M,W
Barton College M,W
Belmont Abbey College M,W
Brevard College M,W
Campbell University M,W
Catawba College M,W
Chowan University M,W
Davidson College M,W
Duke University M,W
East Carolina University M,W
Elizabeth City State University M,W
Elon University M,W
Fayetteville State University M,W
Gardner-Webb University M,W
Guilford Technical Community College M,W
High Point University M,W
Johnson C. Smith University M,W
Lees-McRae College M,W
Lenoir Community College M,W
Lenoir-Rhyne University M,W
Livingstone College M,W
Louisburg College M,W
Mars Hill University M,W
Montreat College M,W
North Carolina Agricultural and Technical State
 University M,W
North Carolina Central University M,W
North Carolina State University M,W
Queens University of Charlotte M,W
St. Andrews University M,W
Saint Augustine's University M,W
Shaw University M,W
University of Mount Olive M,W
University of North Carolina
 Asheville M,W
 Chapel Hill M,W
 Charlotte M,W
 Greensboro M,W
 Wilmington M,W
Wake Forest University M,W
Western Carolina University M,W
Wingate University M,W
Winston-Salem State University M,W

**North Dakota**
Bismarck State College M,W
Dakota College at Bottineau M,W
Dickinson State University M,W
Lake Region State College M,W
Mayville State University M,W
Minot State University M,W
North Dakota State College of Science M,W
North Dakota State University M,W
University of Jamestown M,W
University of Mary M,W
University of North Dakota M,W
Valley City State University M,W
Williston State College M,W

**Ohio**
Ashland University M,W
Bowling Green State University M,W

Cedarville University M,W
Central State University M,W
Cincinnati State Technical and Community
 College M,W
Clark State Community College M,W
Cleveland State University M,W
Columbus State Community College M,W
Edison State Community College M,W
Kent State University M,W
Lake Erie College M,W
Lakeland Community College M,W
Lourdes University M,W
Malone University M,W
Miami University
 Oxford M,W
Mount Vernon Nazarene University M,W
Notre Dame College M,W
Ohio Dominican University M,W
Ohio State University
 Columbus Campus M,W
Ohio University M,W
Owens Community College M,W
Shawnee State University M,W
Sinclair Community College M,W
Southern State Community College M,W
Tiffin University M,W
University of Akron M,W
University of Cincinnati M,W
University of Dayton M,W
University of Findlay M,W
University of Rio Grande M,W
University of Toledo M,W
Urbana University M,W
Ursuline College W
Walsh University M,W
Wright State University M,W
Xavier University M,W
Youngstown State University M,W

**Oklahoma**
Bacone College M,W
Cameron University M,W
Carl Albert State College M,W
Connors State College M,W
East Central University M,W
Eastern Oklahoma State College M,W
Langston University M,W
Mid-America Christian University M,W
Northeastern Oklahoma Agricultural and
 Mechanical College M,W
Northeastern State University M,W
Northern Oklahoma College M,W
Northwestern Oklahoma State University M,W
Oklahoma Baptist University M,W
Oklahoma Christian University M,W
Oklahoma City University M,W
Oklahoma Panhandle State University M,W
Oklahoma State University M,W
Oklahoma Wesleyan University M,W
Oral Roberts University M,W
Redlands Community College M,W
Rogers State University M,W
St. Gregory's University M,W
Seminole State College M,W
Southeastern Oklahoma State University M,W
Southern Nazarene University M,W
Southwestern Oklahoma State University M,W
University of Central Oklahoma M,W
University of Oklahoma M,W
University of Science and Arts of Oklahoma
 M,W
University of Tulsa M,W
Western Oklahoma State College M,W

**Oregon**
Blue Mountain Community College M,W
Chemeketa Community College M,W
Clackamas Community College M,W
Concordia University M,W
Corban University M,W
Eastern Oregon University M,W
Lane Community College M,W
Linn-Benton Community College M,W

Mt. Hood Community College M,W
Multnomah University M,W
Northwest Christian University M,W
Oregon Institute of Technology M,W
Oregon State University M,W
Portland Community College M,W
Portland State University M,W
Southern Oregon University M,W
Southwestern Oregon Community College
 M,W
Treasure Valley Community College M,W
University of Oregon M,W
University of Portland M,W
Warner Pacific College M,W
Western Oregon University M,W

**Pennsylvania**
Bloomsburg University of Pennsylvania M,W
Bucknell University M,W
California University of Pennsylvania M,W
Carlow University M,W
Chestnut Hill College M,W
Cheyney University of Pennsylvania M,W
Clarion University of Pennsylvania M,W
Drexel University M,W
Duquesne University M,W
East Stroudsburg University of Pennsylvania
 M,W
Edinboro University
 of Pennsylvania M,W
Gannon University M,W
Harcum College M,W
Holy Family University M,W
Indiana University of Pennsylvania M,W
Kutztown University of Pennsylvania M,W
La Salle University M,W
Lackawanna College M,W
Lafayette College M,W
Lehigh University M,W
Lock Haven University of Pennsylvania M,W
Mansfield University of Pennsylvania M,W
Mercyhurst University M,W
Millersville University of Pennsylvania M,W
Penn State
 University Park M,W
Philadelphia University M,W
Point Park University M,W
Robert Morris University M,W
St. Francis University M,W
Saint Joseph's University M,W
Seton Hill University M,W
Shippensburg University of Pennsylvania M,W
Slippery Rock University of Pennsylvania M,W
Temple University M,W
University of Pittsburgh M,W
University of Pittsburgh
 Johnstown M,W
 Titusville M,W
University of the Sciences M,W
Valley Forge Military College M,W
Villanova University M,W
West Chester University of Pennsylvania M,W

**Puerto Rico**
Bayamon Central University M,W
Inter American University of Puerto Rico
 Aguadilla Campus M,W
 Arecibo Campus M
 Bayamon Campus M,W
 Fajardo Campus M
 Guayama Campus M,W
 Metropolitan Campus M,W
 Ponce Campus M,W
 San German Campus M,W
Turabo University M,W
Universidad del Este M,W
Universidad Metropolitana M,W
Universidad Politecnica de Puerto Rico M
University of Puerto Rico
 Arecibo M,W
 Bayamon University College M,W
 Carolina Regional College M,W
 Cayey University College M,W

Humacao M,W
Mayaguez M,W
Ponce M,W
Utuado M,W
University of the Sacred Heart M

**Rhode Island**
Bryant University M,W
Community College of Rhode Island M,W
Providence College M,W
University of Rhode Island M,W

**South Carolina**
Allen University M,W
Anderson University M,W
Charleston Southern University M,W
The Citadel M
Claflin University M,W
Clemson University M,W
Coastal Carolina University M,W
Coker College M,W
College of Charleston M,W
Columbia College W
Columbia International University M,W
Converse College W
Erskine College M,W
Francis Marion University M,W
Furman University M,W
Lander University M,W
Limestone College M,W
Morris College M,W
Newberry College M,W
North Greenville University M,W
Presbyterian College M,W
South Carolina State University M,W
Southern Wesleyan University M,W
Spartanburg Methodist College M,W
University of South Carolina
 Aiken M,W
 Columbia M,W
 Upstate M,W
Voorhees College M,W
Winthrop University M,W
Wofford College M,W

**South Dakota**
Augusta University
 Augustana University M,W
Black Hills State University M,W
Dakota State University M,W
Dakota Wesleyan University M,W
Mount Marty College M,W
Northern State University M,W
South Dakota School of Mines and Technology
 M,W
South Dakota State University M,W
University of Sioux Falls M,W
University of South Dakota M,W

**Tennessee**
Austin Peay State University M,W
Belmont University M,W
Bethel University M,W
Bryan College
 Dayton M,W
Carson-Newman University M,W
Chattanooga State Community College M,W
Christian Brothers University M,W
Cleveland State Community College M,W
Columbia State Community College M,W
Cumberland University M,W
Dyersburg State Community College M,W
East Tennessee State University M,W
Freed-Hardeman University M,W
Hiwassee College M,W
Jackson State Community College M,W
King University M,W
Lane College M,W
Lee University M,W
LeMoyne-Owen College M,W
Lincoln Memorial University M,W
Lipscomb University M,W
Martin Methodist College M,W
Middle Tennessee State University M,W

Milligan College M,W
Motlow State Community College M,W
Roane State Community College M,W
Southwest Tennessee Community College M,W
Tennessee State University M,W
Tennessee Technological University M,W
Tennessee Wesleyan College M,W
Trevecca Nazarene University M,W
Tusculum College M,W
Union University M,W
University of Memphis M,W
University of Tennessee
    Chattanooga M,W
    Knoxville M,W
    Martin M,W
Vanderbilt University M,W
Volunteer State Community College M,W
Walters State Community College M,W

**Texas**
Abilene Christian University M,W
Angelina College M,W
Angelo State University M,W
Baylor University M,W
Blinn College M,W
Brookhaven College M
Clarendon College M,W
Collin County Community College District M,W
Dallas Baptist University M
Frank Phillips College M,W
Hill College M,W
Houston Baptist University M,W
Howard College M,W
Jacksonville College M,W
Jarvis Christian College M,W
Kilgore College M,W
Lamar University M,W
Lee College M
Lubbock Christian University M,W
McLennan Community College M,W
Midland College M,W
Midwestern State University M,W
Odessa College M,W
Panola College M,W
Paris Junior College M,W
Prairie View A&M University M,W
Ranger College M,W
Rice University M,W
St. Edward's University M,W
St. Mary's University M,W
Sam Houston State University M,W
San Jacinto College M,W
South Plains College M,W
Southern Methodist University M,W
Southwestern Assemblies of God University M,W
Stephen F. Austin State University M,W
Tarleton State University M,W
Temple College M,W
Texas A&M University M,W
Texas A&M University
    Commerce M,W
    Corpus Christi M,W
Texas Christian University M,W
Texas Southern University M,W
Texas State University M,W
Texas Tech University M,W
Texas Wesleyan University M,W
Texas Woman's University W
Trinity Valley Community College M,W
Tyler Junior College M,W
University of Houston M,W
University of North Texas M,W
University of St. Thomas M,W
University of Texas
    Arlington M,W
    Austin M,W
    Pan American M,W
    of the Permian Basin M,W
    San Antonio M,W
University of the Incarnate Word M,W
Wayland Baptist University M,W

Weatherford College M,W
West Texas A&M University M,W
Western Texas College M,W
Wiley College M,W

**Utah**
Brigham Young University M,W
Dixie State University M,W
Salt Lake Community College M,W
Snow College M,W
Southern Utah University M,W
University of Utah M,W
Utah State University M,W
Utah Valley University M,W
Weber State University M,W
Westminster College M,W

**Vermont**
Saint Michael's College M,W
University of Vermont M,W

**Virginia**
Bluefield College M,W
College of William and Mary M,W
George Mason University M,W
Hampton University M,W
James Madison University M,W
Liberty University M,W
Longwood University M,W
Norfolk State University M,W
Old Dominion University M,W
Radford University M,W
University of Richmond M,W
University of Virginia M,W
University of Virginia's College at Wise M,W
Virginia Commonwealth University M,W
Virginia Military Institute M
Virginia Polytechnic Institute and State University M,W
Virginia State University M,W
Virginia Union University M,W

**Washington**
Big Bend Community College M,W
Central Washington University M,W
Centralia College M,W
Clark College M,W
Columbia Basin College M,W
Eastern Washington University M,W
Edmonds Community College M,W
Everett Community College M,W
Evergreen State College M,W
Gonzaga University M,W
Grays Harbor College M,W
Green River Community College M,W
Highline College M,W
Lower Columbia College M,W
Northwest Indian College M,W
Northwest University M,W
Olympic College M,W
Peninsula College M,W
Pierce College M,W
Saint Martin's University M,W
Seattle Pacific University M,W
Seattle University M,W
Shoreline Community College M,W
Skagit Valley College M,W
Spokane Community College M,W
Tacoma Community College M,W
University of Washington M,W
Walla Walla Community College M,W
Washington State University M,W
Western Washington University M,W
Whatcom Community College M,W
Yakima Valley Community College M,W

**West Virginia**
Alderson-Broaddus University M,W
Bluefield State College M,W
Concord University M,W
Davis and Elkins College M,W
Fairmont State University M,W
Glenville State College M,W
Marshall University M,W

Ohio Valley University M,W
Potomac State College of West Virginia University M,W
Salem International University M,W
Shepherd University M,W
University of Charleston M,W
West Liberty University M,W
West Virginia State University M,W
West Virginia University M,W
West Virginia University Institute of Technology M,W
West Virginia Wesleyan College M,W
Wheeling Jesuit University M,W

**Wisconsin**
Cardinal Stritch University M,W
Marquette University M,W
Silver Lake College of the Holy Family M,W
University of Wisconsin
    Green Bay M,W
    Madison M,W
    Milwaukee M,W
    Parkside M,W
Viterbo University M,W

**Wyoming**
Casper College M,W
Central Wyoming College M,W
Eastern Wyoming College M,W
Laramie County Community College M
Northwest College M,W
Sheridan College M,W
University of Wyoming M,W
Western Wyoming Community College M,W

# Bowling

**Alabama**
Spring Hill College M,W

**Arizona**
Arizona Christian University M,W

**Arkansas**
Arkansas State University W
University of Arkansas
    Pine Bluff W

**Connecticut**
Post University W
Sacred Heart University W

**Delaware**
Delaware State University W

**District of Columbia**
Howard University W

**Florida**
Bethune-Cookman University W
Webber International University M,W

**Georgia**
Emmanuel College M,W
Life University M,W

**Illinois**
Judson University M,W
McKendree University M,W
Robert Morris University: Chicago M,W
University of St. Francis M,W

**Indiana**
Ancilla College M,W
Calumet College of St. Joseph M,W
Huntington University M,W
Indiana Institute of Technology M,W
Marian University M,W
Valparaiso University W
Vincennes University M,W

**Iowa**
Clarke University M,W
Graceland University M,W
Grand View University M,W
Iowa Central Community College M,W
St. Ambrose University M,W
Waldorf University M,W

**Kansas**
Baker University W
Kansas Wesleyan University M,W
Newman University M,W
Wichita State University M,W

**Kentucky**
Campbellsville University M,W
St. Catharine College M,W
University of Pikeville M,W
University of the Cumberlands M,W

**Louisiana**
Southern University and Agricultural and Mechanical College W

**Maryland**
Bowie State University W
Coppin State University W
Morgan State University W
University of Maryland
    Eastern Shore W

**Michigan**
Aquinas College M
Cleary University M,W
Concordia University M,W
Davenport University M,W
Kirtland Community College M,W
Lawrence Technological University M,W
Saginaw Valley State University M
Schoolcraft College M,W

**Mississippi**
Jackson State University W
Mississippi Valley State University M,W

**Missouri**
Culver-Stockton College M,W
Lincoln University W
Missouri Baptist University M,W

**Nebraska**
Hastings College M,W
Midland University M,W
University of Nebraska
    Lincoln W

**New Jersey**
Caldwell University W
Fairleigh Dickinson University
    Metropolitan Campus W
Monmouth University W

**New York**
Adelphi University W
Daemen College W
Long Island University
    LIU Brooklyn W
Molloy College W

**North Carolina**
Blue Ridge Community College M
Chowan University W
Elizabeth City State University W
Johnson C. Smith University W
Livingstone College M,W
North Carolina Central University W
Saint Augustine's University W
Shaw University W

**Ohio**
Notre Dame College M,W
Urbana University M,W
Ursuline College W

**Pennsylvania**
Chestnut Hill College W
Cheyney University of Pennsylvania W
Duquesne University W
Kutztown University of Pennsylvania W

**Tennessee**
Bethel University M,W
Martin Methodist College M,W

**Texas**
Jarvis Christian College M,W
Prairie View A&M University W
Sam Houston State University W
Stephen F. Austin State University W
Texas Southern University W

**Virginia**
Norfolk State University W

**Wisconsin**
Viterbo University M,W

# Cheerleading

**Alabama**
Alabama Southern Community College M,W
Auburn University at Montgomery M,W
Faulkner State Community College M,W
Shelton State Community College M,W
Southern Union State Community College M,W
Troy University M,W
Tuskegee University M,W
University of Alabama M,W
University of Alabama
    Huntsville M,W
University of Mobile W
University of North Alabama M,W
University of South Alabama M,W
University of West Alabama M,W
Wallace State Community College at
    Hanceville M,W

**Arizona**
Arizona Christian University W
Arizona Western College M,W

**Arkansas**
Arkansas Tech University M,W
John Brown University M,W
Lyon College M,W
North Arkansas College W
University of Arkansas
    Fort Smith M,W
    Little Rock W
    Monticello M,W
University of Central Arkansas M,W
Williams Baptist College M,W

**California**
California Baptist University W
Concordia University Irvine M,W
Hope International University M,W
San Jose State University M,W

**Delaware**
Delaware State University M,W
University of Delaware M,W

**Florida**
University of Central Florida M,W
University of Florida M,W
Warner University M,W
Webber International University M,W

**Georgia**
Brenau University W
Brewton-Parker College M,W
Columbus State University M,W
Emmanuel College M,W
Gordon State College W
Point University W

Reinhardt University M,W
Young Harris College M,W

**Hawaii**
Hawaii Pacific University M,W
University of Hawaii
    Manoa M,W

**Idaho**
Boise State University M,W
North Idaho College M,W

**Illinois**
Benedictine University at Springfield M,W
Judson University M,W
Kaskaskia College M,W
Lewis University W
McKendree University M,W
Northwestern University M,W
Olivet Nazarene University M,W
Robert Morris University: Chicago M,W
University of St. Francis M,W

**Indiana**
Ancilla College M,W
Bethel College M,W
Grace College M,W
Indiana Institute of Technology M,W
Indiana Wesleyan University M,W
Marian University M,W
Oakland City University W
University of Saint Francis W

**Iowa**
Briar Cliff University W
Graceland University M,W
Grand View University W
Iowa Western Community College M,W
Kirkwood Community College W
Northwestern College M,W
St. Ambrose University M,W
Waldorf University M,W
William Penn University M,W

**Kansas**
Allen County Community College M,W
Baker University M,W
Barton County Community College M,W
Benedictine College M,W
Bethany College M,W
Central Christian College of Kansas M,W
Cloud County Community College M,W
Coffeyville Community College M,W
Colby Community College M,W
Cowley County Community College M,W
Dodge City Community College M,W
Emporia State University M,W
Fort Scott Community College W
Friends University M,W
Garden City Community College M,W
Highland Community College M,W
Hutchinson Community College M,W
Independence Community College M,W
Kansas Wesleyan University M,W
Labette Community College M,W
McPherson College M,W
MidAmerica Nazarene University M,W
Neosho County Community College M,W
Newman University M,W
Ottawa University M,W
Pratt Community College M,W
Seward County Community College M,W
Southwestern College M,W
Tabor College M,W
University of St. Mary M,W
Washburn University M,W
Wichita State University M,W

**Kentucky**
Bellarmine University M,W
Campbellsville University M,W
Georgetown College W
Kentucky State University W
Northern Kentucky University M,W

St. Catharine College M,W
Union College M,W
University of Pikeville M,W
University of the Cumberlands M,W

**Louisiana**
Bossier Parish Community College M,W
Loyola University New Orleans M,W
McNeese State University M,W
University of Louisiana at Lafayette M,W
University of Louisiana at Monroe M,W

**Maryland**
Morgan State University W

**Massachusetts**
American International College M,W

**Michigan**
Concordia University M,W
Cornerstone University M,W
Davenport University W
Northwood University
    Michigan M,W
Siena Heights University M,W
University of Detroit Mercy W
University of Michigan M,W
Wayne State University M,W

**Mississippi**
Copiah-Lincoln Community College M,W
East Central Community College M,W
East Mississippi Community College M,W
Hinds Community College M,W
Itawamba Community College M,W
Mississippi Gulf Coast Community College
    M,W
Northwest Mississippi Community College W
Southwest Mississippi Community College
    M,W
University of Mississippi M,W
William Carey University M,W

**Missouri**
Avila University W
Central Methodist University W
Culver-Stockton College M,W
Drury University W
Evangel University M,W
Hannibal-LaGrange University M,W
Harris-Stowe State University M,W
Lincoln University W
Maryville University of Saint Louis M,W
Missouri Baptist University M,W
Missouri Valley College M,W
Moberly Area Community College M,W
Northwest Missouri State University M,W
Southeast Missouri State University M,W
University of Missouri
    Kansas City M,W
William Jewell College M,W
William Woods University W

**Montana**
Rocky Mountain College M,W

**Nebraska**
Concordia University W
Doane College W
Hastings College W
Midland University M,W
Peru State College W
York College M,W

**Nevada**
University of Nevada
    Las Vegas M,W
    Reno M,W

**New Mexico**
New Mexico Junior College M,W

**New York**
ASA College W
Hofstra University M,W
Nyack College M,W

**North Carolina**
Brevard College M,W
Elon University M,W
Gardner-Webb University M,W
Lenoir-Rhyne University M,W
Mars Hill University M,W
Methodist University M,W
Queens University of Charlotte M,W
University of North Carolina
    Wilmington M,W

**Ohio**
Ashland University W
Kent State University M,W
Lourdes University M,W
Notre Dame College W
Tiffin University M,W
University of Rio Grande M,W
Urbana University M,W
Wright State University M,W

**Oklahoma**
Bacone College M,W
Cameron University M,W
Carl Albert State College W
Connors State College M,W
Eastern Oklahoma State College M,W
Langston University M,W
Mid-America Christian University M,W
Northeastern Oklahoma Agricultural and
    Mechanical College M,W
Northern Oklahoma College M,W
Northwestern Oklahoma State University M,W
Oklahoma Christian University M,W
Oklahoma City University M,W
Oklahoma Panhandle State University M,W
Oklahoma State University M,W
Oral Roberts University M,W
Rogers State University M,W
St. Gregory's University M,W
Southeastern Oklahoma State University M,W
Southern Nazarene University M,W
Southwestern Oklahoma State University M,W
University of Oklahoma M,W
University of Science and Arts of Oklahoma
    M,W
University of Tulsa M,W
Western Oklahoma State College M,W

**Oregon**
Southwestern Oregon Community College
    M,W

**Pennsylvania**
Gannon University W
Lackawanna College M,W
Millersville University of Pennsylvania M,W
St. Francis University M,W
Seton Hill University M,W

**Puerto Rico**
Inter American University of Puerto Rico
    Aguadilla Campus M,W
University of Puerto Rico
    Carolina Regional College M,W
    Cayey University College M,W
    Humacao M,W

**South Carolina**
Anderson University W
Clemson University M,W
Limestone College M,W
Morris College M,W
Newberry College M,W
North Greenville University M,W
Presbyterian College M,W
Spartanburg Methodist College M,W
University of South Carolina
    Columbia M,W

**South Dakota**
Dakota Wesleyan University M,W
University of Sioux Falls M,W

**Tennessee**
Bethel University M,W
Bryan College
 Dayton M,W
Cumberland University M,W
Dyersburg State Community College M,W
Freed-Hardeman University W
Hiwassee College M,W
King University M,W
Lee University M,W
Martin Methodist College W
Tennessee Technological University M,W
Tennessee Wesleyan College M,W
Tusculum College W
University of Memphis M,W
University of Tennessee
 Martin W

**Texas**
Angelina College M,W
Baylor University W
Clarendon College M,W
East Texas Baptist University M,W
Houston Baptist University M,W
Howard College M,W
Jacksonville College M,W
Paris Junior College M,W
Ranger College M,W
Sam Houston State University M,W
San Jacinto College M,W
South Plains College M,W
Southern Methodist University M,W
Southwestern Assemblies of God University W
Tarleton State University M,W
Temple College M,W
Texas Southern University M,W
Texas Wesleyan University M,W
Tyler Junior College M,W
University of Texas
 Pan American M,W
 of the Permian Basin M,W
Wayland Baptist University M,W

**Utah**
Brigham Young University M,W
Snow College M,W
Southern Utah University M,W
Weber State University M,W

**Virginia**
Liberty University M,W
Old Dominion University M,W

**Washington**
University of Washington M,W

**West Virginia**
Alderson-Broaddus University M,W
University of Charleston M,W

**Wyoming**
University of Wyoming M,W
Western Wyoming Community College M,W

## Cricket

**California**
College of the Redwoods M

## Cross-country

**Alabama**
Alabama Agricultural and Mechanical
 University M,W
Alabama State University M,W
Auburn University M,W
Auburn University at Montgomery M,W
Jacksonville State University M,W
Miles College M,W

Samford University M,W
Spring Hill College M,W
Troy University M,W
University of Alabama M,W
University of Alabama
 Birmingham W
 Huntsville M,W
University of Mobile M,W
University of North Alabama M,W
University of South Alabama M,W
University of West Alabama M,W

**Alaska**
University of Alaska
 Anchorage M,W
 Fairbanks M,W

**Arizona**
Arizona Christian University M,W
Arizona State University M,W
Central Arizona College M,W
Dine College M,W
Embry-Riddle Aeronautical University
 Prescott Campus M,W
GateWay Community College M,W
Grand Canyon University M,W
Mesa Community College M,W
Northern Arizona University M,W
Paradise Valley Community College M,W
Pima Community College M,W
University of Arizona M,W
Yavapai College W

**Arkansas**
Arkansas State University M,W
Arkansas Tech University W
Ecclesia College M,W
Harding University M,W
Henderson State University W
John Brown University M,W
Lyon College M,W
Ouachita Baptist University W
Southern Arkansas University M,W
University of Arkansas M,W
University of Arkansas
 Fort Smith M,W
 Little Rock M,W
 Monticello W
 Pine Bluff M,W
University of Central Arkansas M,W

**California**
Academy of Art University M,W
Azusa Pacific University M,W
Biola University M,W
California Baptist University M,W
California Polytechnic State University: San
 Luis Obispo M,W
California State Polytechnic University:
 Pomona M,W
California State University
 Chico M,W
 Dominguez Hills W
 Fresno M,W
 Fullerton M,W
 Long Beach M,W
 Los Angeles M,W
 Monterey Bay M,W
 Northridge M,W
 Sacramento M,W
 Stanislaus M,W
Concordia University Irvine M,W
Fresno City College M,W
Fresno Pacific University M,W
Holy Names University M,W
Hope International University M,W
Humboldt State University M,W
Loyola Marymount University M,W
The Master's College M,W
Menlo College M,W
Notre Dame de Namur University M,W
Pepperdine University M,W
Point Loma Nazarene University W
St. Mary's College of California M,W

San Diego Christian College M,W
San Diego State University W
San Jose State University M,W
Santa Clara University M,W
Santiago Canyon College M,W
Simpson University M,W
Soka University of America M,W
Stanford University M,W
University of California
 Berkeley M,W
 Davis M,W
 Irvine M,W
 Los Angeles M,W
 Merced M,W
 Riverside M,W
 Santa Barbara M,W
University of San Diego M,W
University of San Francisco M,W
University of Southern California W
University of the Pacific W
Vanguard University of Southern California
 M,W
Westmont College M,W
William Jessup University M,W

**Colorado**
Adams State University M,W
Colorado Christian University M,W
Colorado Mesa University M,W
Colorado School of Mines M,W
Colorado State University M,W
Colorado State University
 Pueblo M,W
Fort Lewis College M,W
Regis University M,W
University of Colorado
 Boulder M,W
 Colorado Springs M,W
University of Northern Colorado W
Western State Colorado University M,W

**Connecticut**
Central Connecticut State University M,W
Fairfield University M,W
Post University M,W
Quinnipiac University M,W
Sacred Heart University M,W
Southern Connecticut State University M,W
University of Bridgeport M,W
University of Connecticut M,W
University of Hartford M,W
University of New Haven M,W

**Delaware**
Delaware State University M,W
Goldey-Beacom College M,W
Wilmington University M,W

**District of Columbia**
American University M,W
George Washington University M,W
Georgetown University M,W
Howard University M,W

**Florida**
Ave Maria University M,W
Bethune-Cookman University M,W
Chipola College W
Embry-Riddle Aeronautical University M,W
Flagler College M,W
Florida Atlantic University M,W
Florida Institute of Technology M,W
Florida Southern College M,W
Florida State University M,W
Jacksonville University W
Lynn University W
Nova Southeastern University M,W
Palm Beach Atlantic University W
Pasco-Hernando State College W
Saint Leo University M,W
Saint Thomas University M,W
South Florida State College W
Southeastern University M,W
Stetson University M,W

University of Central Florida W
University of Florida M,W
University of Miami M,W
University of North Florida M,W
University of Tampa M,W
University of West Florida M,W
Warner University M,W
Webber International University M,W

**Georgia**
Albany State University M,W
Augusta University M,W
Brenau University W
Brewton-Parker College M,W
Clark Atlanta University M,W
Clayton State University M,W
Columbus State University M,W
Darton College M,W
Emmanuel College M,W
Georgia College and State University M,W
Georgia Institute of Technology M,W
Georgia Southern University W
Georgia Southwestern State University W
Georgia State University M,W
Gordon State College M,W
Kennesaw State University M,W
Life University M,W
Mercer University M,W
Morehouse College M
Paine College M,W
Point University M,W
Reinhardt University M,W
Savannah College of Art and Design M,W
Savannah State University M,W
Shorter University M,W
Truett-McConnell College M,W
University of Georgia M,W
University of West Georgia M,W
Valdosta State University M,W
Young Harris College M,W

**Hawaii**
Brigham Young University-Hawaii M,W
Chaminade University of Honolulu M,W
Hawaii Pacific University M,W
University of Hawaii
 Hilo M,W
 Manoa W

**Idaho**
Boise State University M,W
College of Idaho M,W
Idaho State University M,W
Lewis-Clark State College M,W
Northwest Nazarene University M,W
University of Idaho M,W

**Illinois**
Benedictine University at Springfield M,W
Bradley University M,W
Chicago State University M,W
College of Lake County M,W
Danville Area Community College M,W
DePaul University M,W
Eastern Illinois University M,W
Illinois Central College M,W
Illinois Institute of Technology M,W
Illinois State University M,W
Judson University M,W
Kaskaskia College M,W
Lewis University M,W
Lincoln College M,W
Loyola University Chicago M,W
McKendree University M,W
Moraine Valley Community College M,W
Morton College M,W
Northern Illinois University W
Northwestern University W
Olivet Nazarene University M,W
Quincy University M,W
Robert Morris University: Chicago M,W
Saint Xavier University M,W
Sauk Valley Community College M,W
Southern Illinois University Carbondale M,W

Southern Illinois University Edwardsville M,W
Spoon River College M,W
Trinity Christian College M,W
University of Illinois
    Chicago M,W
    Springfield M,W
    Urbana-Champaign M,W
University of St. Francis M,W
Waubonsee Community College M,W
Western Illinois University M,W

**Indiana**
Ancilla College M,W
Ball State University W
Bethel College M,W
Butler University M,W
Calumet College of St. Joseph M,W
Goshen College M,W
Grace College M,W
Huntington University M,W
Indiana Institute of Technology M,W
Indiana State University M,W
Indiana University
    Bloomington M,W
    Purdue University Fort Wayne M,W
    Purdue University Indianapolis M,W
Indiana Wesleyan University M,W
Marian University M,W
Oakland City University M,W
Purdue University M,W
Purdue University
    Calumet M,W
Saint Joseph's College M,W
St. Mary-of-the-Woods College W
Taylor University M,W
University of Evansville M,W
University of Indianapolis M,W
University of Notre Dame M,W
University of Saint Francis M,W
University of Southern Indiana M,W
Valparaiso University M,W
Vincennes University M,W

**Iowa**
Briar Cliff University M,W
Clarke University M,W
Dordt College M,W
Drake University M,W
Ellsworth Community College M,W
Graceland University M,W
Grand View University M,W
Iowa Central Community College M,W
Iowa State University M,W
Iowa Western Community College M,W
Morningside College M,W
Mount Mercy University M,W
North Iowa Area Community College M,W
Northwestern College M,W
St. Ambrose University M,W
Scott Community College M,W
University of Iowa M,W
University of Northern Iowa M,W
Upper Iowa University M
Waldorf University M,W
William Penn University M,W

**Kansas**
Allen County Community College M,W
Baker University M,W
Barton County Community College M,W
Benedictine College M,W
Bethany College M,W
Bethel College M,W
Butler Community College M,W
Central Christian College of Kansas M,W
Cloud County Community College M,W
Coffeyville Community College M,W
Colby Community College M,W
Cowley County Community College M,W
Dodge City Community College M,W
Emporia State University M,W
Fort Hays State University M,W
Friends University M,W

Garden City Community College M,W
Hesston College M,W
Highland Community College M,W
Hutchinson Community College M,W
Johnson County Community College M,W
Kansas City Kansas Community College M,W
Kansas State University M,W
Kansas Wesleyan University M,W
McPherson College M,W
Neosho County Community College M,W
Newman University M,W
Northwest Kansas Technical College M,W
Ottawa University M,W
Pittsburg State University M,W
Pratt Community College M,W
Southwestern College M,W
Sterling College M,W
Tabor College M,W
University of Kansas M,W
University of St. Mary M,W
Wichita State University M,W

**Kentucky**
Asbury University M,W
Bellarmine University M,W
Brescia University M,W
Campbellsville University M,W
Eastern Kentucky University M,W
Georgetown College M,W
Kentucky State University M,W
Kentucky Wesleyan College M,W
Lindsey Wilson College M,W
Midway College W
Morehead State University M,W
Murray State University W
Northern Kentucky University M,W
St. Catharine College M,W
Union College M,W
University of Kentucky M,W
University of Louisville M,W
University of Pikeville M,W
University of the Cumberlands M,W
Western Kentucky University M,W

**Louisiana**
Dillard University M,W
Grambling State University M,W
Louisiana State University and Agricultural and
    Mechanical College M,W
Louisiana Tech University M,W
Loyola University New Orleans M,W
McNeese State University M,W
Nicholls State University M,W
Northwestern State University M,W
Southeastern Louisiana University M,W
Southern University
    New Orleans M,W
Southern University and Agricultural and
    Mechanical College M,W
Tulane University M,W
University of Louisiana at Lafayette M,W
University of Louisiana at Monroe M,W
University of New Orleans M,W
Xavier University of Louisiana M,W

**Maine**
University of Maine M,W

**Maryland**
Bowie State University M,W
Community College of Baltimore County W
Coppin State University M,W
Hagerstown Community College M,W
Harford Community College M,W
Loyola University Maryland M,W
Morgan State University M,W
Mount St. Mary's University M,W
Towson University W
University of Maryland
    Baltimore County M,W
    College Park W
    Eastern Shore M,W
Washington Adventist University M,W

**Massachusetts**
American International College M,W
Boston College M,W
Boston University M,W
College of the Holy Cross W
Merrimack College W
Northeastern University M,W
Stonehill College M,W
University of Massachusetts
    Amherst M,W
    Lowell M,W

**Michigan**
Aquinas College M,W
Central Michigan University M,W
Cleary University M,W
Concordia University M,W
Cornerstone University M,W
Davenport University M,W
Eastern Michigan University M,W
Ferris State University M,W
Gogebic Community College M,W
Grand Valley State University M,W
Hillsdale College M,W
Kirtland Community College M,W
Lake Superior State University M,W
Lansing Community College M,W
Lawrence Technological University M,W
Macomb Community College M,W
Madonna University M,W
Marygrove College M,W
Michigan State University M,W
Michigan Technological University M,W
Mott Community College M,W
Muskegon Community College M,W
Northern Michigan University W
Northwood University
    Michigan M,W
Oakland Community College M,W
Oakland University M,W
Saginaw Valley State University M,W
Siena Heights University M,W
Spring Arbor University M,W
University of Detroit Mercy M,W
University of Michigan M,W
Wayne State University M,W
Western Michigan University W

**Minnesota**
Concordia University St. Paul M,W
Minnesota State University
    Mankato M,W
    Moorhead M,W
Saint Cloud State University M,W
University of Minnesota
    Duluth M,W
    Twin Cities M,W
Winona State University M,W

**Mississippi**
Alcorn State University M,W
Belhaven University M,W
Blue Mountain College M,W
Delta State University W
Jackson State University M,W
Mississippi State University M,W
Mississippi Valley State University M,W
Tougaloo College M,W
University of Mississippi M,W
University of Southern Mississippi M,W

**Missouri**
Avila University M,W
Central Methodist University M,W
Columbia College M,W
Culver-Stockton College M,W
Drury University M,W
Evangel University M,W
Hannibal-LaGrange University M,W
Lincoln University W
Lindenwood University M,W
Maryville University of Saint Louis M,W

Metropolitan Community College - Kansas City
    W
Missouri Baptist University M,W
Missouri Southern State University M,W
Missouri State University M,W
Missouri University of Science and Technology
    M,W
Missouri Valley College M,W
Northwest Missouri State University M,W
Park University M,W
Saint Louis University M,W
Southeast Missouri State University M,W
Southwest Baptist University M,W
Stephens College W
Truman State University M,W
University of Central Missouri M,W
University of Missouri
    Columbia M,W
    Kansas City M,W
William Jewell College M,W
William Woods University M,W

**Montana**
Carroll College M,W
Flathead Valley Community College M,W
Montana State University M,W
Montana State University
    Billings M,W
Rocky Mountain College M,W
University of Great Falls M,W
University of Montana M,W

**Nebraska**
College of Saint Mary W
Concordia University M,W
Creighton University M,W
Doane College M,W
Hastings College M,W
Midland University M,W
Peru State College W
University of Nebraska
    Kearney M,W
    Lincoln M,W
Wayne State College M,W
York College M,W

**Nevada**
University of Nevada
    Las Vegas W
    Reno W

**New Hampshire**
Franklin Pierce University M,W
Saint Anselm College M,W
Southern New Hampshire University M,W
University of New Hampshire M,W

**New Jersey**
Bloomfield College M,W
Caldwell University M,W
Fairleigh Dickinson University
    Metropolitan Campus M,W
Felician University M,W
Georgian Court University M,W
Monmouth University M,W
Rider University M,W
Rutgers, The State University of New Jersey
    New Brunswick/Piscataway Campus
    M,W
Saint Peter's University M,W
Seton Hall University M,W

**New Mexico**
Eastern New Mexico University M,W
Navajo Technical University M,W
New Mexico Highlands University M,W
New Mexico Junior College M,W
New Mexico State University M,W
University of New Mexico M,W
University of the Southwest M,W

**New York**
Adelphi University M,W
Canisius College M,W

City University of New York
    Queens College M,W
College of Saint Rose W
Concordia College M,W
Daemen College M,W
Dominican College of Blauvelt M,W
Dowling College M,W
Fordham University M,W
Hofstra University M,W
Iona College M,W
Le Moyne College M,W
Long Island University
    LIU Brooklyn W
    LIU Post M,W
Manhattan College M,W
Marist College M,W
Molloy College M,W
New York Institute of Technology M,W
Niagara University M,W
Nyack College M,W
Pace University M,W
Pace University: Pleasantville/Briarcliff M,W
Roberts Wesleyan College M,W
St. Francis College M,W
St. John's University W
St. Thomas Aquinas College M,W
Siena College M,W
SUNY
    University at Albany M,W
    University at Binghamton M,W
    University at Buffalo M,W
    University at Stony Brook M,W
Syracuse University M,W
Wagner College M,W

### North Carolina

Appalachian State University M,W
Barton College M,W
Belmont Abbey College M,W
Brevard College M,W
Campbell University M,W
Catawba College M,W
Chowan University M,W
Davidson College M,W
East Carolina University M,W
Elon University M,W
Fayetteville State University M,W
Gardner-Webb University M,W
High Point University M,W
Johnson C. Smith University M,W
Lees-McRae College M,W
Lenoir-Rhyne University M,W
Livingstone College M,W
Mars Hill University M,W
Montreat College M,W
North Carolina Agricultural and Technical State
    University M,W
North Carolina Central University M,W
North Carolina State University M,W
Queens University of Charlotte M,W
St. Andrews University M,W
Saint Augustine's University M,W
Shaw University M,W
University of Mount Olive M,W
University of North Carolina
    Asheville M,W
    Chapel Hill M,W
    Charlotte M,W
    Greensboro M,W
    Wilmington M,W
Wake Forest University M,W
Western Carolina University M,W
Wingate University M,W
Winston-Salem State University M,W

### North Dakota

Dickinson State University M,W
Minot State University M,W
North Dakota State University M,W
University of Jamestown M,W
University of Mary M,W
University of North Dakota M,W
Valley City State University M,W

### Ohio

Ashland University M,W
Bowling Green State University M,W
Cedarville University M,W
Central State University M,W
Cleveland State University W
Kent State University M,W
Lake Erie College M,W
Lourdes University M,W
Malone University M,W
Miami University
    Oxford M,W
Mount Vernon Nazarene University M,W
Notre Dame College M,W
Ohio Dominican University M,W
Ohio State University
    Columbus Campus M,W
Ohio University M,W
Shawnee State University M,W
Tiffin University M,W
University of Akron M,W
University of Cincinnati M,W
University of Dayton M,W
University of Findlay M,W
University of Rio Grande M,W
University of Toledo M,W
Urbana University M,W
Ursuline College W
Walsh University M,W
Wright State University M,W
Xavier University M,W
Youngstown State University M,W

### Oklahoma

Cameron University M
East Central University M,W
Langston University M,W
Northwestern Oklahoma State University M,W
Oklahoma Baptist University M,W
Oklahoma Christian University M,W
Oklahoma City University M,W
Oklahoma Panhandle State University M,W
Oklahoma State University M,W
Oklahoma Wesleyan University M,W
Oral Roberts University M,W
Rogers State University M,W
St. Gregory's University M,W
Southeastern Oklahoma State University W
Southern Nazarene University M,W
Southwestern Oklahoma State University W
University of Central Oklahoma W
University of Oklahoma M,W
University of Science and Arts of Oklahoma
    M,W
University of Tulsa M,W

### Oregon

Clackamas Community College M,W
Concordia University M,W
Corban University M,W
Eastern Oregon University M,W
Lane Community College M,W
Mt. Hood Community College M,W
Multnomah University M,W
Northwest Christian University M,W
Oregon Institute of Technology M,W
Portland State University M,W
Southern Oregon University M,W
Southwestern Oregon Community College
    M,W
Treasure Valley Community College M,W
University of Oregon M,W
University of Portland M,W
Warner Pacific College M,W
Western Oregon University M,W

### Pennsylvania

Bloomsburg University of Pennsylvania M,W
Bucknell University W
California University of Pennsylvania M,W
Carlow University M,W
Chestnut Hill College M,W
Cheyney University of Pennsylvania M,W

Clarion University of Pennsylvania M,W
Duquesne University M,W
East Stroudsburg University of Pennsylvania
    M,W
Edinboro University
    of Pennsylvania M,W
Gannon University M,W
Holy Family University M,W
Indiana University of Pennsylvania M,W
Kutztown University of Pennsylvania M,W
La Salle University M,W
Lackawanna College M,W
Lehigh University M,W
Lock Haven University of Pennsylvania M,W
Mansfield University of Pennsylvania W
Mercyhurst University M,W
Millersville University of Pennsylvania W
Penn State
    University Park M,W
Philadelphia University M,W
Point Park University M,W
St. Francis University M,W
Saint Joseph's University M,W
Seton Hill University M,W
Shippensburg University of Pennsylvania M,W
Slippery Rock University of Pennsylvania M,W
Temple University M,W
University of Pittsburgh M,W
University of the Sciences M,W
Valley Forge Military College M,W
Villanova University M,W
West Chester University of Pennsylvania M,W

### Puerto Rico

Bayamon Central University M,W
Inter American University of Puerto Rico
    Aguadilla Campus M,W
    Bayamon Campus M,W
    Guayama Campus M,W
    Ponce Campus M,W
    San German Campus M,W
Turabo University M,W
Universidad del Este M,W
Universidad Metropolitana M,W
University of Puerto Rico
    Arecibo W
    Cayey University College M,W
    Humacao M,W
    Mayaguez M,W
    Ponce M,W
    Utuado M,W
University of the Sacred Heart M,W

### Rhode Island

Bryant University M,W
Providence College M,W
University of Rhode Island M,W

### South Carolina

Anderson University M,W
Charleston Southern University M,W
The Citadel M,W
Claflin University M,W
Clemson University M,W
Coastal Carolina University M,W
Coker College M,W
College of Charleston M,W
Columbia College W
Columbia International University M,W
Converse College W
Erskine College M,W
Francis Marion University M,W
Furman University M,W
Limestone College M,W
Morris College M,W
Newberry College M,W
North Greenville University M,W
Presbyterian College M,W
South Carolina State University M,W
Southern Wesleyan University M,W
Spartanburg Methodist College M,W
University of South Carolina
    Aiken W

Columbia W
Upstate M,W
Voorhees College M,W
Winthrop University M,W
Wofford College M,W

### South Dakota

Augusta University
    Augustana University M,W
Black Hills State University M,W
Dakota State University M,W
Dakota Wesleyan University M,W
Mount Marty College M,W
Northern State University M,W
South Dakota School of Mines and Technology
    M,W
South Dakota State University M,W
University of Sioux Falls M,W
University of South Dakota M,W

### Tennessee

Austin Peay State University M,W
Belmont University M,W
Bethel University M,W
Bryan College
    Dayton M,W
Carson-Newman University M,W
Christian Brothers University M,W
Cumberland University M,W
East Tennessee State University M,W
Hiwassee College M,W
King University M,W
Lee University M,W
LeMoyne-Owen College M
Lincoln Memorial University M,W
Lipscomb University M,W
Middle Tennessee State University M,W
Milligan College M,W
Tennessee Technological University M,W
Tennessee Wesleyan College M,W
Trevecca Nazarene University M,W
Tusculum College M,W
Union University M,W
University of Memphis M,W
University of Tennessee
    Chattanooga M,W
    Martin M,W
Vanderbilt University M,W

### Texas

Abilene Christian University M,W
Angelo State University M,W
Baylor University M,W
Clarendon College M,W
Dallas Baptist University W
Houston Baptist University M,W
Lamar University M,W
Lubbock Christian University M,W
Midwestern State University W
Odessa College M,W
Prairie View A&M University M,W
Rice University M,W
St. Edward's University M,W
Sam Houston State University M,W
South Plains College M,W
Southern Methodist University W
Southwestern Assemblies of God University
    M,W
Stephen F. Austin State University M,W
Tarleton State University M,W
Texas A&M University
    Commerce M,W
Texas Christian University M,W
Texas Southern University M,W
Texas State University M,W
Texas Tech University M,W
Texas Wesleyan University M,W
University of Houston ·M,W
University of North Texas M,W
University of Texas
    Austin M,W
    Pan American M,W
    of the Permian Basin M,W

San Antonio M,W
University of the Incarnate Word M,W
Wayland Baptist University M,W
West Texas A&M University M,W
Western Texas College M,W

**Utah**
Brigham Young University M,W
Dixie State University M,W
Southern Utah University M,W
University of Utah W
Utah State University M,W
Utah Valley University M,W
Westminster College M,W

**Vermont**
University of Vermont M,W

**Virginia**
Bluefield College M,W
College of William and Mary M,W
George Mason University M,W
Hampton University M,W
James Madison University W
Liberty University M,W
Longwood University M,W
Norfolk State University M,W
Radford University M,W
University of Richmond W
University of Virginia M,W
University of Virginia's College at Wise M,W
Virginia Commonwealth University M,W
Virginia Military Institute M,W
Virginia Polytechnic Institute and State
  University M,W
Virginia State University M,W
Virginia Union University M,W

**Washington**
Central Washington University M,W
Clark College M,W
Eastern Washington University M,W
Everett Community College M,W
Gonzaga University M,W
Highline College M,W
Northwest University M,W
Saint Martin's University M,W
Seattle Pacific University M,W
Seattle University M,W
Spokane Community College M,W
Trinity Lutheran College M,W
University of Washington M,W
Washington State University M,W
Western Washington University M,W

**West Virginia**
Alderson-Broaddus University M,W
Bluefield State College M,W
Concord University M,W
Davis and Elkins College M,W
Fairmont State University M,W
Glenville State College M,W
Marshall University M,W
Ohio Valley University M,W
Potomac State College of West Virginia
  University M,W
University of Charleston M,W
West Liberty University M,W
West Virginia State University W
West Virginia University W
West Virginia Wesleyan College M,W
Wheeling Jesuit University M,W

**Wisconsin**
Cardinal Stritch University M,W
Marquette University M,W
Silver Lake College of the Holy Family M,W
University of Wisconsin
  Green Bay M,W
  Madison M,W
  Milwaukee M,W
  Parkside M,W
Viterbo University M,W

**Wyoming**
Central Wyoming College M
Sheridan College M,W
University of Wyoming M,W

# Diving

**Alabama**
Auburn University M,W
University of Alabama M,W

**Arizona**
Arizona State University M,W
Northern Arizona University W
University of Arizona M,W

**Arkansas**
Ouachita Baptist University M,W
University of Arkansas W

**California**
California Baptist University M,W
California State University
  Fresno W
  Northridge M,W
College of the Redwoods M
San Diego State University W
Soka University of America M,W
Stanford University M,W
University of California
  Berkeley M,W
  Davis W
  Los Angeles M,W
University of San Diego W
University of Southern California M,W

**Colorado**
Colorado State University W
Colorado State University
  Pueblo W
University of Denver M,W

**Connecticut**
Central Connecticut State University W
Fairfield University M,W
University of Connecticut M,W

**District of Columbia**
George Washington University M,W
Georgetown University M,W
Howard University M,W

**Florida**
Florida State University M,W
Indian River State College M,W
Nova Southeastern University M,W
University of Florida M,W
University of Miami M,W

**Georgia**
Georgia Institute of Technology M,W
Georgia Southern University W
University of Georgia M,W

**Hawaii**
University of Hawaii
  Manoa M,W

**Idaho**
University of Idaho W

**Illinois**
Illinois Institute of Technology M,W
Illinois State University W
Lincoln College M,W
McKendree University M,W
Northwestern University M,W
Southern Illinois University Carbondale M,W
University of Illinois
  Chicago M,W
  Urbana-Champaign W
Western Illinois University M,W

**Indiana**
Ball State University M,W
Indiana State University W
Indiana University
  Bloomington M,W
  Purdue University Indianapolis M,W
Purdue University M,W
University of Evansville M,W
University of Notre Dame M,W
Valparaiso University M,W

**Iowa**
University of Iowa M,W

**Kentucky**
Asbury University M,W
University of Kentucky M,W
University of Louisville M,W

**Louisiana**
Louisiana State University and Agricultural and
  Mechanical College M,W

**Maine**
University of Maine W

**Maryland**
Loyola University Maryland M,W
Towson University M,W

**Massachusetts**
Boston College M,W
Boston University M,W
Northeastern University W
University of Massachusetts
  Amherst M,W

**Michigan**
Eastern Michigan University M,W
Grand Valley State University M,W
Michigan State University M,W
Northern Michigan University W
Oakland University M,W
University of Michigan M,W
Wayne State University M,W

**Minnesota**
Minnesota State University
  Mankato M,W
  Moorhead W
Saint Cloud State University M,W
University of Minnesota
  Twin Cities M,W

**Mississippi**
Delta State University M,W

**Missouri**
Drury University M,W
Lindenwood University M,W
Maryville University of Saint Louis W
Saint Louis University M,W
University of Missouri
  Columbia M,W

**Nebraska**
University of Nebraska
  Kearney W

**Nevada**
University of Nevada
  Las Vegas M,W
  Reno W

**New Hampshire**
University of New Hampshire W

**New Jersey**
Rider University M,W
Rutgers, The State University of New Jersey
  New Brunswick/Piscataway Campus
  M,W
Saint Peter's University M,W

**New Mexico**
University of New Mexico W

**New York**
College of Saint Rose M,W
Fordham University M,W
Iona College M,W
Le Moyne College M,W
Marist College M,W
Niagara University M,W
Pace University M,W
Pace University: Pleasantville/Briarcliff M
Saint Bonaventure University M,W
St. Francis College M,W
Siena College W
SUNY
  University at Binghamton M,W
  University at Buffalo M,W
  University at Stony Brook W

**North Carolina**
Davidson College M,W
East Carolina University M,W
University of North Carolina
  Chapel Hill M,W
  Wilmington M,W

**North Dakota**
University of North Dakota M,W

**Ohio**
Ashland University M,W
Cleveland State University M,W
Malone University M,W
Miami University
  Oxford M,W
Notre Dame College M,W
Ohio University W
University of Akron W
University of Cincinnati M,W
University of Findlay M,W
University of Toledo W
Wright State University M,W

**Oklahoma**
Oklahoma Baptist University M,W

**Pennsylvania**
Clarion University of Pennsylvania M,W
Drexel University M,W
La Salle University M,W
Lehigh University M,W
Penn State
  University Park M,W
St. Francis University W
University of Pittsburgh M,W
Villanova University W
West Chester University of Pennsylvania M,W

**Rhode Island**
Bryant University M,W
University of Rhode Island W

**South Carolina**
Clemson University M,W
University of South Carolina
  Columbia M,W

**South Dakota**
South Dakota State University M,W
University of South Dakota M,W

**Texas**
Southern Methodist University M,W
Texas A&M University M,W
Texas Christian University M,W
University of Houston W
University of North Texas W
University of Texas
  Austin M,W

**Utah**
Brigham Young University M,W
University of Utah M,W

**Vermont**
University of Vermont W

**Virginia**
George Mason University M,W
James Madison University W
Liberty University W
Old Dominion University M,W
University of Richmond W
University of Virginia M,W
Virginia Military Institute M
Virginia Polytechnic Institute and State
    University M,W

**West Virginia**
West Virginia University M,W

**Wisconsin**
University of Wisconsin
    Green Bay M,W
    Milwaukee M,W

**Wyoming**
University of Wyoming M,W

# Equestrian

**California**
California State University
    Fresno W

**Delaware**
Delaware State University W

**Georgia**
Savannah College of Art and Design M,W
University of Georgia W

**Idaho**
College of Southern Idaho M,W

**Indiana**
St. Mary-of-the-Woods College W

**Kentucky**
Midway College W

**Minnesota**
University of Minnesota
    Crookston W

**Montana**
University of Montana: Western M,W

**Nebraska**
Nebraska College of Technical Agriculture
    M,W

**North Carolina**
St. Andrews University M,W

**Ohio**
Tiffin University M,W

**Oklahoma**
Northeastern Oklahoma Agricultural and
    Mechanical College M,W
Oklahoma Panhandle State University M,W
Oklahoma State University W

**Pennsylvania**
Seton Hill University W

**South Carolina**
University of South Carolina
    Columbia W

**South Dakota**
South Dakota State University W

**Tennessee**
University of Tennessee
    Martin W

**Texas**
Baylor University W
Southern Methodist University W
Texas A&M University W
Texas Christian University W
West Texas A&M University W

**Wyoming**
Laramie County Community College M,W

# Fencing

**California**
Stanford University M,W

**Illinois**
Northwestern University W

**Indiana**
University of Notre Dame M,W

**Michigan**
University of Detroit Mercy M,W
Wayne State University M,W

**New Jersey**
Fairleigh Dickinson University
    Metropolitan Campus W
New Jersey Institute of Technology M,W
Rutgers, The State University of New Jersey
    New Brunswick/Piscataway Campus
    M,W

**New York**
City University of New York
    Queens College W
Long Island University
    LIU Post W
St. John's University M,W

**North Carolina**
University of North Carolina
    Chapel Hill M,W

**Ohio**
Cleveland State University M,W
Ohio State University
    Columbus Campus M,W

**Pennsylvania**
Bucknell University M,W
Penn State
    University Park M,W
Temple University W

# Field Hockey

**California**
Stanford University W
University of California
    Berkeley W
    Davis W
University of the Pacific W

**Connecticut**
Fairfield University W
Quinnipiac University W
Sacred Heart University W
Southern Connecticut State University W
University of Connecticut W

**Delaware**
University of Delaware W

**District of Columbia**
American University W
Georgetown University W

**Illinois**
Northwestern University W

**Indiana**
Ball State University W

**Iowa**
University of Iowa W

**Kentucky**
Bellarmine University W
University of Louisville W

**Maine**
University of Maine W

**Maryland**
Towson University W
University of Maryland
    College Park W

**Massachusetts**
American International College W
Boston College W
Boston University W
College of the Holy Cross W
Merrimack College W
Northeastern University W
Stonehill College W
University of Massachusetts
    Lowell W

**Michigan**
Central Michigan University W
Michigan State University W
University of Michigan W

**Missouri**
Lindenwood University W
Missouri State University W
Saint Louis University W

**New Hampshire**
Franklin Pierce University W
Saint Anselm College W
University of New Hampshire W

**New Jersey**
Monmouth University W
Rider University W
Rutgers, The State University of New Jersey
    New Brunswick/Piscataway Campus W

**New York**
Adelphi University W
Colgate University W
Dowling College W
Hofstra University W
Long Island University
    LIU Brooklyn W
    LIU Post W
Mercy College W
Pace University W
Pace University: Pleasantville/Briarcliff W
Siena College W
SUNY
    University at Albany W
Syracuse University W

**North Carolina**
Appalachian State University W
Davidson College W
Duke University W
University of North Carolina
    Chapel Hill W
Wake Forest University W

**Ohio**
Kent State University W
Miami University
    Oxford W
Ohio State University
    Columbus Campus W
Ohio University W

**Pennsylvania**
Bloomsburg University of Pennsylvania W
Bucknell University W
Drexel University W
East Stroudsburg University of Pennsylvania W
Indiana University of Pennsylvania W
Kutztown University of Pennsylvania W
La Salle University W
Lafayette College W
Lehigh University W
Lock Haven University of Pennsylvania W
Mansfield University of Pennsylvania W
Mercyhurst University W
Millersville University of Pennsylvania W
Penn State
    University Park W
Robert Morris University W
St. Francis University W
Saint Joseph's University W
Seton Hill University W
Shippensburg University of Pennsylvania W
Slippery Rock University of Pennsylvania W
Temple University W
Villanova University W
West Chester University of Pennsylvania W

**Rhode Island**
Bryant University W
Providence College W

**South Carolina**
Limestone College W
Newberry College W

**Vermont**
University of Vermont W

**Virginia**
College of William and Mary W
James Madison University W
Liberty University W
Longwood University W
Old Dominion University W
University of Richmond W
University of Virginia W
Virginia Commonwealth University W

# Football (non-tackle)

**Alabama**
Faulkner University M

**Illinois**
Olivet Nazarene University M

# Football (tackle)

**Alabama**
Alabama Agricultural and Mechanical
    University M
Alabama State University M
Auburn University M
Jacksonville State University M
Miles College M
Samford University M
Troy University M
Tuskegee University M
University of Alabama M
University of Alabama
    Birmingham M
University of North Alabama M
University of West Alabama M

**Arizona**
Arizona Christian University M
Arizona State University M
Arizona Western College M

Eastern Arizona College M
Mesa Community College M
Northern Arizona University M
Pima Community College M
Scottsdale Community College M
University of Arizona M

**Arkansas**
Arkansas State University M
Arkansas Tech University M
Harding University M
Henderson State University M
Ouachita Baptist University M
Southern Arkansas University M
University of Arkansas M
University of Arkansas
 Monticello M
 Pine Bluff M
University of Central Arkansas M

**California**
Azusa Pacific University M
California Polytechnic State University: San
 Luis Obispo M
California State University
 Fresno M
 Sacramento M
Fresno City College M
Grossmont College M
Humboldt State University M
San Diego State University M
San Jose State University M
Stanford University M
University of California
 Berkeley M
 Davis M
 Los Angeles M
University of Southern California M
Yuba College M

**Colorado**
Adams State University M
Colorado Mesa University M
Colorado School of Mines M
Colorado State University M
Colorado State University
 Pueblo M
Fort Lewis College M
University of Colorado
 Boulder M
University of Northern Colorado M
Western State Colorado University M

**Connecticut**
Central Connecticut State University M
Sacred Heart University M
Southern Connecticut State University M
University of Connecticut M
University of New Haven M

**Delaware**
Delaware State University M
University of Delaware M

**District of Columbia**
Georgetown University M
Howard University M

**Florida**
Ave Maria University M
Bethune-Cookman University M
Florida Agricultural and Mechanical University
 M
Florida Atlantic University M
Florida State University M
Southeastern University M
University of Central Florida M
University of Florida M
University of Miami M
University of South Florida M
Webber International University M

**Georgia**
Albany State University M
Clark Atlanta University M

Fort Valley State University M
Georgia Institute of Technology M
Georgia Military College M
Georgia Southern University M
Georgia State University M
Kennesaw State University M
Mercer University M
Morehouse College M
Point University M
Reinhardt University M
Savannah State University M
Shorter University M
University of Georgia M
University of West Georgia M
Valdosta State University M

**Hawaii**
University of Hawaii
 Manoa M

**Idaho**
Boise State University M
Idaho State University M
University of Idaho M

**Illinois**
Eastern Illinois University M
Illinois State University M
McKendree University M
Northwestern University M
Olivet Nazarene University M
Quincy University M
Robert Morris University: Chicago M
Saint Xavier University M
Southern Illinois University Carbondale M
Trinity International University M
University of Illinois
 Urbana-Champaign M
University of St. Francis M
Western Illinois University M

**Indiana**
Ball State University M
Indiana State University M
Indiana University
 Bloomington M
Marian University M
Purdue University M
Saint Joseph's College M
Taylor University M
University of Indianapolis M
University of Notre Dame M
University of Saint Francis M

**Iowa**
Briar Cliff University M
Dordt College M
Ellsworth Community College M
Graceland University M
Grand View University M
Iowa Central Community College M
Iowa State University M
Iowa Western Community College M
Morningside College M
Northwestern College M
St. Ambrose University M
University of Iowa M
University of Northern Iowa M
Upper Iowa University M
Waldorf University M
William Penn University M

**Kansas**
Baker University M
Benedictine College M
Bethany College M
Bethel College M
Butler Community College M
Coffeyville Community College M
Dodge City Community College M
Emporia State University M
Fort Hays State University M
Fort Scott Community College M
Friends University M

Garden City Community College M
Highland Community College M
Hutchinson Community College M
Independence Community College M
Kansas State University M
Kansas Wesleyan University M
McPherson College M
MidAmerica Nazarene University M
Ottawa University M
Pittsburg State University M
Southwestern College M
Sterling College M
Tabor College M
University of Kansas M
University of St. Mary M
Washburn University M

**Kentucky**
Campbellsville University M
Eastern Kentucky University M
Georgetown College M
Kentucky Christian University M
Kentucky State University M
Kentucky Wesleyan College M
Lindsey Wilson College M
Murray State University M
Union College M
University of Kentucky M
University of Louisville M
University of Pikeville M
University of the Cumberlands M
Western Kentucky University M

**Louisiana**
Grambling State University M
Louisiana State University and Agricultural and
 Mechanical College M
Louisiana Tech University M
McNeese State University M
Nicholls State University M
Northwestern State University M
Southeastern Louisiana University M
Southern University and Agricultural and
 Mechanical College M
Tulane University M
University of Louisiana at Lafayette M
University of Louisiana at Monroe M

**Maine**
University of Maine M

**Maryland**
Bowie State University M
Morgan State University M
Towson University M
University of Maryland
 College Park M

**Massachusetts**
American International College M
Boston College M
College of the Holy Cross M
Merrimack College M
Stonehill College M
University of Massachusetts
 Amherst M

**Michigan**
Central Michigan University M
Concordia University M
Eastern Michigan University M
Ferris State University M
Grand Valley State University M
Hillsdale College M
Michigan State University M
Michigan Technological University M
Northern Michigan University M
Northwood University
 Michigan M
Saginaw Valley State University M
Siena Heights University M
University of Michigan M
Wayne State University M
Western Michigan University M

**Minnesota**
Bemidji State University M
Concordia University St. Paul M
Minnesota State University
 Mankato M
 Moorhead M
Saint Cloud State University M
Southwest Minnesota State University M
University of Minnesota
 Crookston M
 Duluth M
 Twin Cities M
Winona State University M

**Mississippi**
Alcorn State University M
Belhaven University M
Coahoma Community College M
Copiah-Lincoln Community College M
Delta State University M
East Central Community College M
East Mississippi Community College M
Hinds Community College M
Holmes Community College M
Itawamba Community College M
Jackson State University M
Jones County Junior College M
Mississippi Gulf Coast Community College M
Mississippi State University M
Mississippi Valley State University M
Northwest Mississippi Community College M
Southwest Mississippi Community College M
University of Mississippi M
University of Southern Mississippi M

**Missouri**
Avila University M
Central Methodist University M
Culver-Stockton College M
Evangel University M
Lincoln University M
Lindenwood University M
Missouri Baptist University M
Missouri Southern State University M
Missouri State University M
Missouri University of Science and Technology
 M
Missouri Valley College M
Missouri Western State University M
Northwest Missouri State University M
Southeast Missouri State University M
Southwest Baptist University M
Truman State University M
University of Central Missouri M
University of Missouri
 Columbia M
William Jewell College M

**Montana**
Carroll College M
Montana State University M
Montana State University
 Northern M
Montana Tech of the University of Montana M
Rocky Mountain College M
University of Montana M
University of Montana: Western M

**Nebraska**
Chadron State College M
Concordia University M
Doane College M
Hastings College M
Midland University M
Peru State College M
University of Nebraska
 Kearney M
 Lincoln M
Wayne State College M

**Nevada**
University of Nevada
 Las Vegas M
 Reno M

## New Hampshire
Saint Anselm College M
University of New Hampshire M

## New Jersey
Monmouth University M
Rutgers, The State University of New Jersey
    New Brunswick/Piscataway Campus M

## New Mexico
Eastern New Mexico University M
New Mexico Highlands University M
New Mexico Military Institute M
New Mexico State University M
University of New Mexico M
Western New Mexico University M

## New York
ASA College M
Fordham University M
Long Island University
    LIU Post M
Pace University M
Pace University: Pleasantville/Briarcliff M
SUNY
    University at Albany M
    University at Buffalo M
    University at Stony Brook M
Syracuse University M
Wagner College M

## North Carolina
Appalachian State University M
Brevard College M
Catawba College M
Chowan University M
Duke University M
East Carolina University M
Elizabeth City State University M
Elon University M
Fayetteville State University M
Gardner-Webb University M
Johnson C. Smith University M
Lenoir-Rhyne University M
Livingstone College M
Mars Hill University M
North Carolina Agricultural and Technical State
    University M
North Carolina Central University M
North Carolina State University M
Saint Augustine's University M
Shaw University M
University of North Carolina
    Chapel Hill M
    Charlotte M
Wake Forest University M
Western Carolina University M
Wingate University M
Winston-Salem State University M

## North Dakota
Dickinson State University M
Mayville State University M
Minot State University M
North Dakota State College of Science M
North Dakota State University M
University of Jamestown M
University of Mary M
University of North Dakota M
Valley City State University M

## Ohio
Ashland University M
Bowling Green State University M
Kent State University M
Lake Erie College M
Malone University M
Miami University
    Oxford M
Notre Dame College M
Ohio Dominican University M
Ohio State University
    Columbus Campus M
Ohio University M

Tiffin University M
University of Akron M
University of Cincinnati M
University of Findlay M
University of Toledo M
Urbana University M
Walsh University M
Youngstown State University M

## Oklahoma
Bacone College M
East Central University M
Langston University M
Northeastern Oklahoma Agricultural and
    Mechanical College M
Northeastern State University M
Northwestern Oklahoma State University M
Oklahoma Baptist University M
Oklahoma Panhandle State University M
Oklahoma State University M
Southeastern Oklahoma State University M
Southern Nazarene University M
Southwestern Oklahoma State University M
University of Central Oklahoma M
University of Oklahoma M
University of Tulsa M

## Oregon
Eastern Oregon University M
Oregon State University M
Portland State University M
Southern Oregon University M
University of Oregon M
Western Oregon University M

## Pennsylvania
Bloomsburg University of Pennsylvania M
Bucknell University M
California University of Pennsylvania M
Chestnut Hill College M
Cheyney University of Pennsylvania M
Clarion University of Pennsylvania M
Duquesne University M
East Stroudsburg University of Pennsylvania M
Edinboro University
    of Pennsylvania M
Gannon University M
Indiana University of Pennsylvania M
Kutztown University of Pennsylvania M
Lackawanna College M
Lehigh University M
Lock Haven University of Pennsylvania M
Mansfield University of Pennsylvania M
Mercyhurst University M
Millersville University of Pennsylvania M
Penn State
    University Park M
Robert Morris University M
St. Francis University M
Seton Hill University M
Shippensburg University of Pennsylvania M
Slippery Rock University of Pennsylvania M
Temple University M
University of Pittsburgh M
Valley Forge Military College M
Villanova University M
West Chester University of Pennsylvania M

## Rhode Island
Bryant University M
University of Rhode Island M

## South Carolina
Charleston Southern University M
The Citadel M
Clemson University M
Coastal Carolina University M
Furman University M
Limestone College M
Newberry College M
North Greenville University M
Presbyterian College M
South Carolina State University M

University of South Carolina
    Columbia M
Wofford College M

## South Dakota
Augusta University
    Augustana University M
Black Hills State University M
Dakota State University M
Dakota Wesleyan University M
Northern State University M
South Dakota School of Mines and Technology
    M
South Dakota State University M
University of Sioux Falls M
University of South Dakota M

## Tennessee
Austin Peay State University M
Bethel University M
Carson-Newman University M
Cumberland University M
Lane College M
Middle Tennessee State University M
Tennessee State University M
Tennessee Technological University M
Tusculum College M
University of Memphis M
University of Tennessee
    Chattanooga M
    Knoxville M
    Martin M
Vanderbilt University M

## Texas
Abilene Christian University M
Angelo State University M
Baylor University M
Blinn College M
Houston Baptist University M
Kilgore College M
Midwestern State University M
Prairie View A&M University M
Rice University M
Sam Houston State University M
Southern Methodist University M
Southwestern Assemblies of God University M
Stephen F. Austin State University M
Tarleton State University M
Texas A&M University M
Texas A&M University
    Commerce M
Texas Christian University M
Texas Southern University M
Texas State University M
Texas Tech University M
Trinity Valley Community College M
Tyler Junior College M
University of Houston M
University of North Texas M
University of Texas
    Austin M
    San Antonio M
Wayland Baptist University M
West Texas A&M University M

## Utah
Brigham Young University M
Dixie State University M
Snow College M
Southern Utah University M
University of Utah M
Utah State University M
Weber State University M

## Virginia
Bluefield College M
College of William and Mary M
Hampton University M
James Madison University M
Liberty University M
Norfolk State University M
Old Dominion University M
University of Richmond M

University of Virginia M
University of Virginia's College at Wise M
Virginia Military Institute M
Virginia Polytechnic Institute and State
    University M
Virginia State University M
Virginia Union University M

## Washington
Central Washington University M
Eastern Washington University M
University of Washington M
Washington State University M

## West Virginia
Alderson-Broaddus University M
Concord University M
Fairmont State University M
Glenville State College M
Marshall University M
Shepherd University M
University of Charleston M
West Liberty University M
West Virginia State University M
West Virginia University M
West Virginia Wesleyan College M

## Wisconsin
University of Wisconsin
    Madison M

## Wyoming
University of Wyoming M

# Golf

## Alabama
Alabama State University M,W
Auburn University M,W
Central Alabama Community College M
Faulkner State Community College M,W
Faulkner University M,W
Jacksonville State University M,W
Samford University M,W
Spring Hill College M,W
Troy University M,W
University of Alabama M,W
University of Alabama
    Birmingham M,W
University of Mobile M,W
University of Montevallo M,W
University of North Alabama M,W
University of South Alabama M,W
University of West Alabama M,W
Wallace State Community College at
    Hanceville M,W

## Arizona
Arizona Christian University M,W
Arizona State University M,W
Chandler-Gilbert Community College M,W
Eastern Arizona College M
Embry-Riddle Aeronautical University
    Prescott Campus M,W
GateWay Community College M,W
Grand Canyon University M,W
Mesa Community College M,W
Northern Arizona University W
Paradise Valley Community College M,W
Pima Community College M,W
Scottsdale Community College M
University of Arizona M,W

## Arkansas
Arkansas State University M,W
Arkansas Tech University M,W
Ecclesia College M,W
Harding University M,W
Henderson State University M,W
John Brown University M,W
Lyon College M,W
University of Arkansas M,W

University of Arkansas
　　Fort Smith M,W
　　Little Rock M,W
　　Monticello M,W
　　Pine Bluff M,W
University of Central Arkansas M,W

**California**
Academy of Art University M,W
Biola University M,W
California Baptist University M,W
California Polytechnic State University: San
　　Luis Obispo M,W
California State University
　　Bakersfield M
　　Chico M,W
　　Dominguez Hills M
　　Fresno M,W
　　Fullerton M,W
　　Long Beach M,W
　　Monterey Bay M,W
　　Northridge M
　　Sacramento M,W
　　San Bernardino M
　　Stanislaus M
Dominican University of California M,W
Fresno City College M,W
Holy Names University M,W
Hope International University M,W
Loyola Marymount University M
The Master's College M
Menlo College M,W
Notre Dame de Namur University M
Pepperdine University M,W
Point Loma Nazarene University W
St. Mary's College of California M
San Diego State University M,W
San Jose State University M,W
Santa Clara University M,W
Santiago Canyon College M,W
Simpson University M,W
Sonoma State University M
Stanford University M,W
University of California
　　Berkeley M,W
　　Davis M,W
　　Irvine M,W
　　Los Angeles M,W
　　Riverside M
　　Santa Barbara M
University of San Diego M
University of San Francisco M,W
University of Southern California M,W
University of the Pacific M
William Jessup University M

**Colorado**
Adams State University M,W
Colorado Christian University M,W
Colorado Mesa University M,W
Colorado State University M,W
Colorado State University
　　Pueblo M,W
Fort Lewis College M
Lamar Community College M
Northeastern Junior College M,W
Otero Junior College M,W
Regis University M,W
University of Colorado
　　Boulder M,W
　　Colorado Springs M,W
University of Denver M,W
University of Northern Colorado M,W

**Connecticut**
Central Connecticut State University M,W
Fairfield University M,W
Post University M,W
Quinnipiac University W
Sacred Heart University M,W
University of Connecticut M
University of Hartford M,W

**Delaware**
Goldey-Beacom College M
Wilmington University M

**District of Columbia**
George Washington University M
Georgetown University M,W

**Florida**
Ave Maria University M,W
Barry University M,W
Bethune-Cookman University M,W
Daytona State College W
Eastern Florida State College M
Eckerd College M,W
Embry-Riddle Aeronautical University M,W
Flagler College M,W
Florida Atlantic University M,W
Florida Gulf Coast University M,W
Florida Institute of Technology M,W
Florida Southern College M,W
Florida State University M,W
Jacksonville University M,W
Lynn University M,W
Nova Southeastern University M,W
Palm Beach Atlantic University M,W
Rollins College M,W
Saint Leo University M,W
Saint Thomas University M
Southeastern University M
Stetson University M,W
University of Central Florida M,W
University of Florida M,W
University of Miami W
University of North Florida M,W
University of South Florida M,W
University of Tampa M,W
University of West Florida M,W
Warner University M,W
Webber International University M,W

**Georgia**
Abraham Baldwin Agricultural College M
Andrew College M
Armstrong State University M
Augusta University M,W
Brenau University W
Brewton-Parker College M
Clayton State University M
College of Coastal Georgia M,W
Columbus State University M,W
Darton College M
Emmanuel College M,W
Georgia College and State University M
Georgia Institute of Technology M
Georgia Southern University M
Georgia Southwestern State University M
Georgia State University M,W
Kennesaw State University M,W
Mercer University M,W
Paine College M
Point University M,W
Reinhardt University M
Savannah College of Art and Design M,W
Shorter University M,W
Thomas University M,W
Truett-McConnell College M,W
University of Georgia M,W
University of North Georgia M,W
University of West Georgia M,W
Valdosta State University M
Young Harris College M,W

**Hawaii**
Chaminade University of Honolulu M
Hawaii Pacific University M
University of Hawaii
　　Hilo M
　　Manoa M,W

**Idaho**
Boise State University M,W
College of Idaho M,W
Idaho State University W

Lewis-Clark State College M,W
Northwest Nazarene University M
University of Idaho M,W

**Illinois**
Benedictine University at Springfield M,W
Black Hawk College M
Bradley University M,W
Chicago State University M,W
College of Lake County M,W
DePaul University M
Eastern Illinois University M,W
Elgin Community College M
Highland Community College M
Illinois Central College M
Illinois Eastern Community Colleges
　　Frontier Community College M,W
Illinois State University M,W
John A. Logan College M,W
Judson University M,W
Kaskaskia College M,W
Kishwaukee College M,W
Lewis and Clark Community College M
Lewis University M,W
Lincoln College M,W
Loyola University Chicago M,W
McKendree University M,W
Moraine Valley Community College M
Northern Illinois University M,W
Northwestern University M,W
Olivet Nazarene University M
Parkland College M
Quincy University M,W
Rend Lake College M,W
Robert Morris University: Chicago M,W
Sauk Valley Community College M
Southern Illinois University Carbondale M,W
Southern Illinois University Edwardsville M,W
University of Illinois
　　Springfield M,W
　　Urbana-Champaign M,W
University of St. Francis M,W
Waubonsee Community College M
Western Illinois University M,W

**Indiana**
Ancilla College M,W
Ball State University M,W
Bethel College M,W
Butler University M,W
Calumet College of St. Joseph M,W
Grace College M,W
Holy Cross College M,W
Huntington University M,W
Indiana Institute of Technology M,W
Indiana State University W
Indiana University
　　Bloomington M,W
　　Purdue University Fort Wayne M,W
　　Purdue University Indianapolis M,W
Indiana Wesleyan University M,W
Marian University M,W
Oakland City University M,W
Purdue University M,W
Purdue University
　　Calumet M
　　North Central M
Saint Joseph's College M,W
St. Mary-of-the-Woods College W
Taylor University M
University of Evansville M,W
University of Indianapolis M,W
University of Notre Dame M,W
University of Saint Francis M,W
University of Southern Indiana M,W
Valparaiso University M,W
Vincennes University M

**Iowa**
Briar Cliff University M,W
Clarke University M,W
Dordt College M,W
Drake University M,W

Ellsworth Community College M,W
Graceland University M,W
Grand View University M,W
Iowa Central Community College M,W
Iowa Lakes Community College M,W
Iowa State University M,W
Iowa Western Community College M,W
Kirkwood Community College M
Marshalltown Community College M,W
Morningside College M,W
Mount Mercy University M,W
North Iowa Area Community College M,W
Northwestern College M,W
St. Ambrose University M,W
Southeastern Community College M,W
Southwestern Community College M
University of Iowa M,W
University of Northern Iowa M,W
Upper Iowa University M,W
Waldorf University M,W
William Penn University M,W

**Kansas**
Allen County Community College M
Baker University M,W
Barton County Community College M,W
Bethany College M,W
Bethel College M,W
Central Christian College of Kansas M,W
Coffeyville Community College M,W
Colby Community College M,W
Dodge City Community College M,W
Friends University M
Garden City Community College M
Hutchinson Community College M
Johnson County Community College M
Kansas City Kansas Community College M
Kansas State University M,W
Kansas Wesleyan University M,W
Newman University M,W
Northwest Kansas Technical College M,W
Ottawa University M
Pittsburg State University M
Southwestern College M,W
Sterling College M,W
University of Kansas M,W
Washburn University M
Wichita State University M,W

**Kentucky**
Asbury University M,W
Bellarmine University M,W
Brescia University M,W
Campbellsville University M,W
Eastern Kentucky University M,W
Georgetown College M,W
Kentucky State University M
Kentucky Wesleyan College M,W
Lindsey Wilson College M,W
Midway College W
Morehead State University M
Murray State University M,W
Northern Kentucky University M,W
St. Catharine College M,W
Union College M,W
University of Kentucky M,W
University of Louisville M,W
University of Pikeville M,W
University of the Cumberlands M,W
Western Kentucky University M,W

**Louisiana**
Grambling State University M
Louisiana State University and Agricultural and
　　Mechanical College M,W
Louisiana Tech University M
Loyola University New Orleans M,W
McNeese State University M,W
Nicholls State University M
Southeastern Louisiana University M
Southern University and Agricultural and
　　Mechanical College M
University of Louisiana at Lafayette M

University of Louisiana at Monroe M
University of New Orleans M

**Maryland**
College of Southern Maryland M,W
Coppin State University W
Harford Community College M
Loyola University Maryland M
Towson University M,W
University of Maryland
College Park M,W

**Massachusetts**
American International College M
Boston College M,W
Merrimack College W
University of Massachusetts
Lowell M

**Michigan**
Aquinas College M,W
Cleary University M,W
Concordia University M,W
Cornerstone University M,W
Davenport University M,W
Eastern Michigan University M,W
Ferris State University M,W
Grand Valley State University M,W
Hillsdale College M
Kirtland Community College M,W
Lake Superior State University M,W
Lawrence Technological University M,W
Madonna University M,W
Marygrove College M,W
Michigan State University M,W
Mott Community College M
Muskegon Community College M
Northern Michigan University M
Northwood University
Michigan M,W
Oakland Community College M
Oakland University M,W
Saginaw Valley State University M
Siena Heights University M,W
Spring Arbor University M,W
University of Detroit Mercy M,W
University of Michigan M,W
Wayne State University M,W
Western Michigan University W

**Minnesota**
Concordia University St. Paul M,W
Minnesota State University
Mankato M,W
Moorhead W
Saint Cloud State University M,W
Southwest Minnesota State University W
University of Minnesota
Crookston M,W
Twin Cities M,W
Winona State University M,W

**Mississippi**
Alcorn State University M,W
Belhaven University M,W
Blue Mountain College M,W
Copiah-Lincoln Community College M
Delta State University M
East Central Community College M
East Mississippi Community College M,W
Hinds Community College M
Itawamba Community College M
Jackson State University M,W
Meridian Community College M
Mississippi Gulf Coast Community College M
Mississippi State University M,W
Mississippi Valley State University M,W
Northwest Mississippi Community College M
University of Mississippi M,W
University of Southern Mississippi M,W
William Carey University M,W

**Missouri**
Avila University M,W
Central Methodist University M

Columbia College M,W
Culver-Stockton College M,W
Drury University M,W
Evangel University M,W
Hannibal-LaGrange University M,W
Lincoln University M,W
Lindenwood University M,W
Maryville University of Saint Louis M,W
Missouri Baptist University M,W
Missouri Southern State University M
Missouri State University M,W
Missouri Valley College M,W
Missouri Western State University M
Northwest Missouri State University W
Park University W
Research College of Nursing M,W
Southwest Baptist University M
Stephens College W
Truman State University W
University of Central Missouri M
University of Missouri
Columbia M,W
Kansas City M,W
St. Louis M,W
William Jewell College M,W
William Woods University M,W

**Montana**
Carroll College M,W
Miles Community College M,W
Montana State University W
Montana State University
Billings M,W
Northern W
Montana Tech of the University of Montana M,W
Rocky Mountain College M,W
University of Great Falls M,W
University of Montana W

**Nebraska**
Bellevue University M,W
Chadron State College W
College of Saint Mary W
Concordia University M,W
Creighton University M,W
Doane College M,W
Hastings College M,W
Mid-Plains Community College M
Midland University M,W
Peru State College W
University of Nebraska
Kearney M,W
Lincoln M,W
Omaha M,W
York College M,W

**Nevada**
University of Nevada
Las Vegas M,W
Reno M,W

**New Hampshire**
Franklin Pierce University M
Saint Anselm College M

**New Jersey**
Brookdale Community College M
Fairleigh Dickinson University
Metropolitan Campus M,W
Monmouth University M,W
Rider University M
Rowan College at Burlington County M,W
Rutgers, The State University of New Jersey
New Brunswick/Piscataway Campus M,W
Saint Peter's University M
Salem Community College M
Seton Hall University M,W

**New Mexico**
New Mexico Junior College M
New Mexico Military Institute M
New Mexico State University M,W

University of New Mexico M,W
University of the Southwest M,W
Western New Mexico University M,W

**New York**
Adelphi University M,W
Canisius College M
College of Saint Rose W
Concordia College M
Daemen College M
Dominican College of Blauvelt M
Dowling College M
Hofstra University M,W
Iona College M
Le Moyne College M,W
Long Island University
LIU Brooklyn M,W
Manhattan College M
Niagara University M,W
Nyack College M
Pace University: Pleasantville/Briarcliff W
Roberts Wesleyan College M
Saint Bonaventure University M
St. John's University M,W
Siena College M,W
SUNY
University at Albany W
University at Binghamton M
Wagner College M,W

**North Carolina**
Appalachian State University M,W
Barton College M
Belmont Abbey College M,W
Brevard College M
Campbell University M,W
Catawba College M,W
Chowan University M
Davidson College M
Duke University M,W
East Carolina University M,W
Elizabeth City State University M
Elon University M,W
Fayetteville State University M
Gardner-Webb University M,W
High Point University M,W
Johnson C. Smith University M
Johnston Community College M
Lenoir-Rhyne University M,W
Mars Hill University M
Montreat College M,W
North Carolina Central University M,W
North Carolina State University M,W
Pitt Community College M
Queens University of Charlotte M,W
St. Andrews University M
Saint Augustine's University M
University of Mount Olive M
University of North Carolina
Chapel Hill M,W
Charlotte M
Greensboro M,W
Wilmington M,W
Wake Forest University M,W
Western Carolina University M,W
Wingate University M,W

**North Dakota**
Dickinson State University M,W
Minot State University W
North Dakota State University W
University of Jamestown M,W
University of Mary W
University of North Dakota M,W
Valley City State University M,W

**Ohio**
Ashland University M,W
Bowling Green State University M,W
Cedarville University M
Central State University M,W
Cleveland State University M,W
Columbus State Community College M,W
Kent State University M,W

Lake Erie College M,W
Lakeland Community College M
Lourdes University M,W
Malone University M,W
Miami University
Oxford M
Mount Vernon Nazarene University M,W
Notre Dame College M,W
Ohio Dominican University M,W
Ohio State University
Columbus Campus M,W
Ohio University M,W
Owens Community College M
Shawnee State University M
Tiffin University M,W
University of Akron M
University of Cincinnati M,W
University of Dayton M
University of Findlay M,W
University of Toledo M,W
Urbana University M,W
Ursuline College W
Walsh University M,W
Wright State University M
Xavier University M,W
Youngstown State University M,W

**Oklahoma**
Bacone College M,W
Cameron University M,W
East Central University M,W
Mid-America Christian University M
Northeastern State University M,W
Northwestern Oklahoma State University M,W
Oklahoma Baptist University M,W
Oklahoma Christian University M
Oklahoma City University M,W
Oklahoma Panhandle State University M,W
Oklahoma State University M,W
Oklahoma Wesleyan University M,W
Oral Roberts University M,W
Redlands Community College W
Rogers State University M,W
St. Gregory's University W
Seminole State College M,W
Southeastern Oklahoma State University M
Southern Nazarene University M,W
Southwestern Oklahoma State University M,W
University of Central Oklahoma M,W
University of Oklahoma M,W
University of Tulsa M,W

**Oregon**
Concordia University M,W
Corban University M,W
Multnomah University M,W
Northwest Christian University M,W
Oregon State University M,W
Portland State University W
Southwestern Oregon Community College M,W
University of Oregon M,W
Warner Pacific College M,W

**Pennsylvania**
California University of Pennsylvania M,W
Carlow University M,W
Chestnut Hill College M,W
Clarion University of Pennsylvania M
Drexel University M
Gannon University M,W
Indiana University of Pennsylvania M
Kutztown University of Pennsylvania W
La Salle University M,W
Lackawanna College M
Lehigh University M,W
Mercyhurst University M,W
Millersville University of Pennsylvania M,W
Penn State
University Park M,W
Philadelphia University M
St. Francis University M,W
Saint Joseph's University M

Seton Hill University W
Temple University M
University of the Sciences M,W
West Chester University of Pennsylvania M,W

**Rhode Island**
Bryant University M
University of Rhode Island M

**South Carolina**
Anderson University M,W
Charleston Southern University M,W
The Citadel W
Clemson University M
Coastal Carolina University M,W
Coker College M,W
College of Charleston M,W
Columbia College W
Converse College W
Erskine College M,W
Francis Marion University M
Furman University M,W
Lander University M,W
Limestone College M,W
Newberry College M,W
North Greenville University M,W
Presbyterian College M,W
Southern Wesleyan University M
Spartanburg Methodist College M,W
University of South Carolina
    Aiken M
    Columbia M,W
Winthrop University M,W
Wofford College M,W

**South Dakota**
Augusta University
    Augustana University M,W
Dakota Wesleyan University M,W
Mount Marty College M,W
South Dakota School of Mines and Technology
    M,W
South Dakota State University M,W
University of Sioux Falls M,W

**Tennessee**
Austin Peay State University M,W
Belmont University M,W
Bethel University M,W
Bryan College
    Dayton M,W
Carson-Newman University M
Christian Brothers University M,W
Cumberland University M,W
East Tennessee State University M,W
Hiwassee College M,W
King University M,W
Lee University M,W
LeMoyne-Owen College M,W
Lincoln Memorial University M,W
Lipscomb University M,W
Martin Methodist College M,W
Middle Tennessee State University M,W
Milligan College M
Tennessee Technological University M,W
Tennessee Wesleyan College M,W
Trevecca Nazarene University M,W
Tusculum College M,W
Union University M,W
University of Memphis M,W
University of Tennessee
    Chattanooga M,W
    Knoxville M,W
    Martin M
Vanderbilt University M,W
Walters State Community College M,W

**Texas**
Abilene Christian University M
Baylor University M,W
Dallas Baptist University W
Houston Baptist University M,W
Jacksonville College M,W
Jarvis Christian College M

Lamar University M,W
Lubbock Christian University M,W
McLennan Community College M
Midland College M
Midwestern State University M,W
Odessa College M
Paris Junior College M
Prairie View A&M University M,W
Ranger College M,W
Rice University M
St. Edward's University M,W
St. Mary's University M,W
Sam Houston State University M,W
Southern Methodist University M,W
Stephen F. Austin State University M,W
Tarleton State University W
Texas A&M University M,W
Texas A&M University
    Commerce M
    Corpus Christi W
Texas Christian University M,W
Texas Southern University M,W
Texas State University M,W
Texas Tech University M,W
Texas Wesleyan University M,W
Tyler Junior College M,W
University of Houston M,W
University of North Texas M,W
University of St. Thomas M,W
University of Texas
    Austin M,W
    Brownsville M,W
    Pan American M,W
    San Antonio M,W
University of the Incarnate Word M,W
Wayland Baptist University M,W
West Texas A&M University M,W
Western Texas College M,W

**Utah**
Brigham Young University M,W
Dixie State University M,W
Southern Utah University M,W
University of Utah M
Utah State University M
Utah Valley University M,W
Weber State University M,W
Westminster College M,W

**Virginia**
Bluefield College M
College of William and Mary M,W
George Mason University M
Hampton University M,W
James Madison University M,W
Liberty University M
Longwood University M,W
Old Dominion University M,W
Radford University M,W
University of Richmond M,W
University of Virginia M,W
Virginia Commonwealth University M
Virginia Polytechnic Institute and State
    University M,W
Virginia State University M,W
Virginia Union University M,W

**Washington**
Centralia College W
Columbia Basin College M,W
Eastern Washington University W
Edmonds Community College M,W
Gonzaga University M,W
Grays Harbor College M,W
Green River Community College M
Olympic College M,W
Saint Martin's University M,W
Seattle University M,W
Skagit Valley College M,W
Spokane Community College M,W
Trinity Lutheran College M,W
University of Washington M,W
Walla Walla Community College M,W

Washington State University M,W
Western Washington University M,W

**West Virginia**
Alderson-Broaddus University M,W
Bluefield State College M
Concord University M
Davis and Elkins College M
Fairmont State University M,W
Glenville State College M,W
Marshall University M,W
Ohio Valley University M,W
Salem International University M,W
Shepherd University M
University of Charleston M
West Liberty University M,W
West Virginia State University M
West Virginia University Institute of
    Technology M
West Virginia Wesleyan College M,W
Wheeling Jesuit University M,W

**Wisconsin**
Cardinal Stritch University M,W
Silver Lake College of the Holy Family M,W
University of Wisconsin
    Green Bay M,W
    Madison M,W
    Parkside M
Viterbo University M,W

**Wyoming**
Central Wyoming College M,W
Eastern Wyoming College M
University of Wyoming M,W

# Gymnastics

**Alabama**
Auburn University W
University of Alabama W

**Alaska**
University of Alaska
    Anchorage W

**Arizona**
Arizona State University W
University of Arizona W

**Arkansas**
University of Arkansas W

**California**
California State University
    Sacramento W
San Jose State University W
Stanford University M,W
University of California
    Berkeley M,W
    Davis W
    Los Angeles W
    Santa Barbara W

**Colorado**
University of Denver W

**Connecticut**
Southern Connecticut State University W
University of Bridgeport W

**District of Columbia**
George Washington University W

**Florida**
University of Florida W

**Georgia**
University of Georgia W

**Idaho**
Boise State University W

**Illinois**
Illinois State University W
Northern Illinois University W

University of Illinois
    Chicago M,W
    Urbana-Champaign M,W

**Indiana**
Ball State University W

**Iowa**
Iowa State University W
University of Iowa M,W

**Kansas**
Fort Hays State University M

**Kentucky**
University of Kentucky W

**Louisiana**
Louisiana State University and Agricultural and
    Mechanical College W

**Maryland**
Towson University W
University of Maryland
    College Park W
Washington Adventist University M,W

**Michigan**
Central Michigan University W
Eastern Michigan University W
Michigan State University W
University of Michigan M,W
Western Michigan University W

**Minnesota**
University of Minnesota
    Twin Cities M,W

**Missouri**
Lindenwood University W
Southeast Missouri State University W
University of Missouri
    Columbia W

**Nebraska**
University of Nebraska
    Lincoln M,W

**New Hampshire**
University of New Hampshire W

**New Jersey**
Rutgers, The State University of New Jersey
    New Brunswick/Piscataway Campus W

**North Carolina**
North Carolina State University W
University of North Carolina
    Chapel Hill W

**Ohio**
Bowling Green State University W
Kent State University W
Ohio State University
    Columbus Campus M,W

**Oklahoma**
University of Oklahoma M,W

**Oregon**
Oregon State University W

**Pennsylvania**
Penn State
    University Park M,W
Temple University W
University of Pittsburgh W
West Chester University of Pennsylvania W

**Tennessee**
Southern Adventist University M,W

**Texas**
Texas Woman's University W

**Utah**
Brigham Young University W
Southern Utah University W

University of Utah W
Utah State University W

**Virginia**
College of William and Mary M,W

**Washington**
Seattle Pacific University W
University of Washington W

**West Virginia**
Alderson-Broaddus University W
West Virginia University W

# Ice hockey

**Alabama**
University of Alabama
Huntsville M

**Alaska**
University of Alaska
Anchorage M
Fairbanks M

**Arizona**
Arizona State University M

**Colorado**
Colorado College M
University of Denver M

**Connecticut**
Quinnipiac University M,W
Sacred Heart University M,W
University of Connecticut M,W

**Georgia**
Life University M

**Indiana**
University of Notre Dame M

**Maine**
University of Maine M,W

**Massachusetts**
American International College M
Bentley University M
Boston College M,W
Boston University M,W
College of the Holy Cross M
Merrimack College M,W
Northeastern University M,W
University of Massachusetts
Amherst M
Lowell M

**Michigan**
Davenport University M
Ferris State University M
Lake Superior State University M
Michigan State University M
Michigan Technological University M
Northern Michigan University M
University of Michigan M
Western Michigan University M

**Minnesota**
Bemidji State University M,W
Minnesota State University
Mankato M,W
Saint Cloud State University M,W
University of Minnesota
Duluth M,W
Twin Cities M,W

**Missouri**
Lindenwood University W

**Nebraska**
Midland University M,W
University of Nebraska
Omaha M

**New Hampshire**
Franklin Pierce University M,W
University of New Hampshire M,W

**New York**
Canisius College M
Clarkson University M,W
Colgate University M,W
Monroe Community College M
Niagara University M
Rensselaer Polytechnic Institute M,W
St. Lawrence University M,W
Syracuse University W

**North Dakota**
Dakota College at Bottineau M
University of North Dakota M,W
Williston State College M

**Ohio**
Bowling Green State University M
Miami University
Oxford M
Ohio State University
Columbus Campus M,W

**Pennsylvania**
Mercyhurst University M,W
Penn State
University Park M,W
Robert Morris University M,W

**Rhode Island**
Providence College M,W

**Vermont**
University of Vermont M,W

**Wisconsin**
University of Wisconsin
Madison M,W

# Judo

**Puerto Rico**
Inter American University of Puerto Rico
Aguadilla Campus M,W
Ponce Campus M,W
Turabo University W
Universidad Metropolitana M,W
University of Puerto Rico
Arecibo M,W
Humacao M,W
Utuado M

# Lacrosse

**Arizona**
Arizona State University W

**California**
California State University
Fresno W
Concordia University Irvine M,W
Dominican University of California M
Notre Dame de Namur University M
St. Mary's College of California W
San Diego State University W
Stanford University W
University of California
Davis W

**Colorado**
Adams State University M,W
Colorado Mesa University M,W
Colorado State University
Pueblo M,W
Fort Lewis College W
Regis University W

University of Colorado
Boulder W
Colorado Springs W
University of Denver M,W

**Connecticut**
Central Connecticut State University W
Fairfield University M,W
Post University M,W
Quinnipiac University M,W
Sacred Heart University M,W
Southern Connecticut State University W
University of Bridgeport M,W
University of Connecticut W
University of Hartford M
University of New Haven W

**Delaware**
Delaware Technical Community College
Terry Campus M
University of Delaware M,W
Wilmington University W

**District of Columbia**
American University W
Georgetown University M,W
Howard University W

**Florida**
Florida Institute of Technology M
Florida Southern College M,W
Jacksonville University M,W
Lynn University M
Saint Leo University M,W
Stetson University W
University of Florida W
University of Tampa M

**Georgia**
Emmanuel College M,W
Kennesaw State University W
Mercer University M,W
Point University M,W
Savannah College of Art and Design M,W
Shorter University M,W
Truett-McConnell College W
Young Harris College M,W

**Illinois**
Judson University M
McKendree University W
Northwestern University W
Robert Morris University: Chicago M,W

**Indiana**
Ancilla College M,W
Bethel College W
Indiana Institute of Technology M,W
University of Notre Dame M,W

**Iowa**
Clarke University M,W
St. Ambrose University M

**Kansas**
University of St. Mary M,W

**Kentucky**
Asbury University M,W
Bellarmine University M
Georgetown College W
University of Louisville W
University of Pikeville W
University of the Cumberlands M,W

**Maryland**
Anne Arundel Community College M,W
Community College of Baltimore County M,W
Harford Community College M,W
Howard Community College M,W
Johns Hopkins University M,W
Loyola University Maryland M,W
Mount St. Mary's University M,W
Towson University M,W

University of Maryland
College Park M,W

**Massachusetts**
American International College M,W
Boston College W
Boston University W
College of the Holy Cross M,W
Merrimack College M,W
Stonehill College W
University of Massachusetts
Amherst M,W
Lowell M,W

**Michigan**
Cleary University M,W
Davenport University M
Lawrence Technological University M,W
Siena Heights University M,W
University of Detroit Mercy M,W
University of Michigan M,W

**Minnesota**
Concordia University St. Paul W
University of Minnesota
Duluth M,W

**Missouri**
Lindenwood University M,W
Missouri Baptist University M,W
Missouri Valley College M,W

**Nebraska**
Midland University W

**Nevada**
Sierra Nevada College M,W

**New Hampshire**
Franklin Pierce University M,W
Saint Anselm College M,W
Southern New Hampshire University M,W
University of New Hampshire W

**New Jersey**
Caldwell University W
Georgian Court University M,W
Monmouth University M,W
Rutgers, The State University of New Jersey
New Brunswick/Piscataway Campus
M,W
Union County College M

**New York**
Adelphi University M,W
Canisius College M,W
City University of New York
Queens College W
Colgate University M,W
College of Saint Rose M
Dominican College of Blauvelt M,W
Dowling College M,W
Hofstra University M,W
Iona College W
Le Moyne College M,W
Long Island University
LIU Brooklyn W
LIU Post M,W
Manhattan College M,W
Marist College M,W
Mercy College M,W
Molloy College M,W
Monroe Community College M
New York Institute of Technology M
Niagara University W
Nyack College W
Pace University M,W
Pace University: Pleasantville/Briarcliff M,W
Roberts Wesleyan College M,W
St. John's University M
Siena College M,W
SUNY
University at Albany M,W
University at Binghamton M,W
University at Stony Brook M,W

Syracuse University M,W
Wagner College M,W

**North Carolina**
Belmont Abbey College M,W
Brevard College M,W
Campbell University W
Catawba College M,W
Chowan University M,W
Davidson College W
Duke University M
Elon University W
High Point University M,W
Laurel University M
Lees-McRae College M,W
Lenoir-Rhyne University M,W
Mars Hill University M
Queens University of Charlotte M,W
St. Andrews University M
University of North Carolina
    Chapel Hill M,W
Wingate University M,W

**Ohio**
Lake Erie College M,W
Lourdes University M,W
Notre Dame College W
Ohio State University
    Columbus Campus M,W
Tiffin University W
University of Cincinnati W
University of Findlay W
Urbana University W
Ursuline College W
Walsh University M,W

**Oklahoma**
Oklahoma Baptist University W

**Oregon**
University of Oregon W

**Pennsylvania**
Bloomsburg University of Pennsylvania W
Bucknell University M,W
Chestnut Hill College M,W
Drexel University M,W
Duquesne University W
Gannon University W
Holy Family University W
Indiana University of Pennsylvania W
Kutztown University of Pennsylvania W
La Salle University W
Lehigh University M,W
Lock Haven University of Pennsylvania W
Mercyhurst University M,W
Millersville University of Pennsylvania W
Penn State
    University Park M,W
Philadelphia University W
Robert Morris University M,W
St. Francis University W
Saint Joseph's University M,W
Seton Hill University M,W
Shippensburg University of Pennsylvania W
Slippery Rock University of Pennsylvania W
Temple University W
West Chester University of Pennsylvania W

**Rhode Island**
Bryant University M,W
Providence College M

**South Carolina**
Coastal Carolina University W
Coker College M,W
Columbia College W
Converse College W
Erskine College W
Furman University M,W
Limestone College W
Newberry College W
North Greenville University M,W
Presbyterian College W

**Tennessee**
Tennessee Wesleyan College M,W
Tusculum College M,W
Vanderbilt University W

**Utah**
Westminster College M,W

**Vermont**
University of Vermont M,W

**Virginia**
College of William and Mary W
George Mason University W
James Madison University W
Liberty University W
Longwood University W
Old Dominion University W
Radford University W
University of Richmond M,W
University of Virginia M,W
Virginia Commonwealth University W
Virginia Military Institute M
Virginia Polytechnic Institute and State
    University W

**West Virginia**
Alderson-Broaddus University M,W
Potomac State College of West Virginia
    University M,W
Shepherd University W
West Virginia Wesleyan College W
Wheeling Jesuit University M,W

**Wisconsin**
Marquette University M,W

## Rifle

**Alabama**
Jacksonville State University M,W

**Alaska**
University of Alaska
    Fairbanks M,W

**Georgia**
Columbus State University M,W
Emmanuel College M,W
Georgia Southern University W
University of North Georgia M,W

**Iowa**
Iowa Central Community College M,W

**Kentucky**
Morehead State University M,W
Murray State University M,W
University of Kentucky M,W

**Mississippi**
University of Mississippi W

**Nebraska**
Concordia University M,W
Midland University M,W
University of Nebraska
    Lincoln W

**Nevada**
University of Nevada
    Reno M,W

**Ohio**
Ohio State University
    Columbus Campus M
University of Akron W

**Pennsylvania**
University of the Sciences M,W

**South Carolina**
The Citadel M,W

**Tennessee**
Bethel University M,W
University of Memphis M,W
University of Tennessee
    Martin M,W

**Texas**
Texas Christian University W

**Virginia**
Virginia Military Institute M,W

**West Virginia**
West Virginia University M,W

## Rodeo

**Alabama**
Troy University M,W
University of West Alabama M,W

**Arizona**
Central Arizona College M,W
Cochise College M,W
Dine College M,W

**Arkansas**
Southern Arkansas University M,W
University of Arkansas
    Monticello M,W

**Colorado**
Colorado Northwestern Community College
    M,W
Northeastern Junior College M,W
Otero Junior College M,W

**Idaho**
Boise State University M,W
College of Southern Idaho M,W

**Iowa**
Iowa Central Community College M,W

**Kansas**
Coffeyville Community College M,W
Colby Community College M
Dodge City Community College M,W
Fort Hays State University M
Fort Scott Community College M,W
Garden City Community College M,W
Northwest Kansas Technical College M,W
Pratt Community College M,W

**Louisiana**
McNeese State University M,W

**Mississippi**
East Mississippi Community College M,W

**Missouri**
Missouri Valley College M,W
Northwest Missouri State University M,W

**Montana**
Dawson Community College M,W
Miles Community College M,W
Montana State University M,W
Montana State University
    Northern M,W
University of Montana: Western M,W

**Nebraska**
Chadron State College M,W
Mid-Plains Community College M,W
Nebraska College of Technical Agriculture
    M,W

**New Mexico**
Eastern New Mexico University M,W
Navajo Technical University M,W
New Mexico Junior College M,W

**North Dakota**
Dickinson State University M

**Oklahoma**
Bacone College M,W
Connors State College M,W
Northeastern Oklahoma Agricultural and
    Mechanical College M,W
Northwestern Oklahoma State University M,W
Oklahoma Panhandle State University M,W
Southeastern Oklahoma State University M,W
Southwestern Oklahoma State University M,W
Western Oklahoma State College M,W

**Oregon**
Blue Mountain Community College M,W
Eastern Oregon University M,W
Treasure Valley Community College M,W

**Tennessee**
University of Tennessee
    Martin M,W

**Texas**
Clarendon College M,W
Hill College M,W
Howard College M,W
North Central Texas College M
Northeast Texas Community College M,W
Odessa College M,W
Panola College M,W
Ranger College M,W
Sam Houston State University M,W
South Plains College M,W
Tarleton State University M,W
University of Texas
    Pan American W
Vernon College M,W
Weatherford College M,W
Western Texas College M,W
Wharton County Junior College M,W

**Washington**
Central Washington University M,W
Walla Walla Community College M,W

**Wyoming**
Casper College M,W
Central Wyoming College M,W
Eastern Wyoming College M,W
Laramie County Community College M,W
Northwest College M,W
Sheridan College M,W
University of Wyoming M,W

## Rowing (crew)

**Alabama**
University of Alabama W

**California**
California State University
    Sacramento W
Humboldt State University W
Loyola Marymount University W
St. Mary's College of California W
San Diego State University W
Stanford University M,W
University of California
    Berkeley M,W
    Los Angeles M,W
University of San Diego W
University of Southern California W

**Connecticut**
Fairfield University M,W
University of Connecticut W

**Delaware**
University of Delaware W

**District of Columbia**
George Washington University M,W
Georgetown University M,W

**Florida**
Ave Maria University W
Barry University W
Florida Institute of Technology M,W
Jacksonville University M,W
Nova Southeastern University W
Stetson University W
University of Central Florida W
University of Miami W
University of Tampa W

**Indiana**
Indiana University
    Bloomington W
University of Notre Dame W

**Iowa**
University of Iowa W

**Kansas**
Kansas State University W
University of Kansas W

**Kentucky**
University of Louisville W

**Massachusetts**
Boston College W
Boston University M,W
College of the Holy Cross W
Merrimack College W
Northeastern University M,W
University of Massachusetts
    Amherst W

**Michigan**
Eastern Michigan University W
Michigan State University W
University of Michigan W

**Nebraska**
Creighton University W

**New Jersey**
Rutgers, The State University of New Jersey
    New Brunswick/Piscataway Campus
    M,W

**New York**
Fordham University W
Manhattan College W
Marist College W
SUNY
    University at Buffalo W
Syracuse University M,W

**North Carolina**
Duke University W
University of North Carolina
    Chapel Hill W

**Oklahoma**
Oklahoma City University M,W
University of Central Oklahoma W
University of Oklahoma W
University of Tulsa W

**Pennsylvania**
Drexel University M,W
Duquesne University W
La Salle University M,W
Lehigh University W
Mercyhurst University M,W
Philadelphia University M,W
Robert Morris University W
Saint Joseph's University M,W
Temple University M,W

**Rhode Island**
University of Rhode Island W

**South Carolina**
Clemson University W

**Tennessee**
University of Tennessee
    Knoxville W

**Texas**
Southern Methodist University W
University of Texas
    Austin W

**Virginia**
George Mason University W
Old Dominion University W
University of Virginia W

**Washington**
Gonzaga University W
Seattle Pacific University W
University of Washington M,W
Washington State University W
Western Washington University M,W

**West Virginia**
University of Charleston W
West Virginia University W

**Wisconsin**
University of Wisconsin
    Madison M,W

# Rugby

**California**
University of California
    Berkeley M

**Connecticut**
Quinnipiac University W

**Georgia**
Life University M,W

**Indiana**
Bethel College M

**Massachusetts**
American International College M,W

**Michigan**
Davenport University M,W

**Pennsylvania**
West Chester University of Pennsylvania W

**Washington**
Central Washington University M,W

# Skiing

**Alaska**
University of Alaska
    Anchorage M,W
    Fairbanks M,W

**Colorado**
Colorado Mountain College M,W
University of Colorado
    Boulder M,W
University of Denver M,W
Western State Colorado University M,W

**Idaho**
College of Idaho M,W

**Michigan**
Michigan Technological University M,W
Northern Michigan University M,W

**Minnesota**
Saint Cloud State University W
University of Minnesota
    Twin Cities M,W

**Montana**
Montana State University W
Rocky Mountain College M,W

**Nevada**
Sierra Nevada College M,W

**New Hampshire**
Saint Anselm College M,W
University of New Hampshire M,W

**New Mexico**
University of New Mexico M,W

**Tennessee**
Carson-Newman University M,W

**Utah**
University of Utah M,W
Westminster College M,W

**Vermont**
University of Vermont M,W

**Wisconsin**
University of Wisconsin
    Green Bay M,W

# Skin diving

**Florida**
Flagler College M,W

# Soccer

**Alabama**
Auburn University W
Auburn University at Montgomery M,W
Judson College W
Samford University W
Spring Hill College M,W
Troy University W
University of Alabama W
University of Alabama
    Birmingham M,W
    Huntsville M,W
University of Mobile M,W
University of Montevallo M,W
University of North Alabama W
University of South Alabama W
University of West Alabama M,W

**Arizona**
Arizona Christian University M,W
Arizona State University W
Arizona Western College M,W
Chandler-Gilbert Community College M,W
Cochise College W
Embry-Riddle Aeronautical University
    Prescott Campus M,W
GateWay Community College M
Grand Canyon University M,W
Mesa Community College M,W
Northern Arizona University W
Paradise Valley Community College M,W
Pima Community College M,W
Scottsdale Community College M,W
South Mountain Community College M
University of Arizona W
Yavapai College M

**Arkansas**
Arkansas State University W
Ecclesia College M,W
Harding University M,W

John Brown University M,W
Lyon College M,W
Ouachita Baptist University M,W
University of Arkansas W
University of Arkansas
    Little Rock M,W
    Pine Bluff W
University of Central Arkansas M,W
Williams Baptist College M

**California**
Academy of Art University M,W
Azusa Pacific University M,W
Bethesda University of California M
Biola University M,W
California Baptist University M,W
California Polytechnic State University: San
    Luis Obispo M,W
California State Polytechnic University:
    Pomona M,W
California State University
    Bakersfield M,W
    Chico M,W
    Dominguez Hills M,W
    Fresno W
    Fullerton M,W
    Los Angeles M,W
    Monterey Bay M,W
    Northridge M
    Sacramento M,W
    San Bernardino M,W
    Stanislaus M,W
Concordia University Irvine M,W
Dominican University of California M,W
Fresno City College M,W
Fresno Pacific University M,W
Grossmont College W
Holy Names University M,W
Hope International University M,W
Humboldt State University M,W
Loyola Marymount University M,W
The Master's College M,W
Menlo College M,W
Notre Dame de Namur University M,W
Pepperdine University W
Point Loma Nazarene University M,W
St. Mary's College of California M,W
San Diego Christian College M,W
San Diego State University M,W
San Jose State University M,W
Santa Clara University M,W
Santiago Canyon College M,W
Simpson University M,W
Soka University of America M,W
Sonoma State University M,W
Stanford University M,W
University of California
    Berkeley M,W
    Davis M,W
    Irvine M,W
    Los Angeles M,W
    Merced M,W
    Riverside M,W
    Santa Barbara M,W
University of San Diego M,W
University of San Francisco M,W
University of Southern California W
University of the Pacific W
Vanguard University of Southern California
    M,W
Westmont College M,W
William Jessup University M,W
Yuba College M,W

**Colorado**
Adams State University M,W
Colorado Christian University M,W
Colorado College W
Colorado Mesa University M,W
Colorado School of Mines M,W
Colorado State University W
Colorado State University
    Pueblo M,W

Fort Lewis College M,W
Metropolitan State University of Denver M,W
Northeastern Junior College M,W
Otero Junior College M,W
Regis University M,W
Trinidad State Junior College M,W
University of Colorado
 Boulder W
 Colorado Springs M,W
University of Denver M,W
University of Northern Colorado W

**Connecticut**
Central Connecticut State University M,W
Fairfield University M,W
Post University M,W
Quinnipiac University M,W
Sacred Heart University M,W
Southern Connecticut State University M,W
University of Bridgeport M,W
University of Connecticut M,W
University of Hartford M,W
University of New Haven M,W

**Delaware**
Delaware State University W
Delaware Technical Community College
 Stanton/Wilmington Campus M
 Terry Campus M
Goldey-Beacom College M,W
University of Delaware M,W
Wilmington University M,W

**District of Columbia**
American University M,W
George Washington University M,W
Georgetown University M,W
Howard University M,W

**Florida**
Ave Maria University M,W
Barry University M,W
Eastern Florida State College M,W
Eckerd College M,W
Embry-Riddle Aeronautical University M,W
Flagler College M,W
Florida Atlantic University M,W
Florida College M,W
Florida Institute of Technology M,W
Florida Southern College M,W
Florida State University W
Jacksonville University M,W
Lynn University M,W
Nova Southeastern University M,W
Palm Beach Atlantic University M,W
Polk State College W
Rollins College M,W
Saint Leo University M,W
Saint Thomas University M,W
Southeastern University M,W
Stetson University M,W
University of Central Florida M,W
University of Florida W
University of Miami W
University of North Florida M,W
University of South Florida M,W
University of Tampa M,W
University of West Florida M,W
Warner University M,W
Webber International University M,W

**Georgia**
Abraham Baldwin Agricultural College W
Andrew College M,W
Brenau University W
Brewton-Parker College M,W
Clayton State University M,W
Columbus State University W
Darton College M,W
Emmanuel College M,W
Georgia College and State University M,W
Georgia Gwinnett College M,W
Georgia Military College M,W
Georgia Perimeter College M,W

Georgia Southern University M,W
Georgia Southwestern State University M,W
Georgia State University M,W
Gordon State College W
Kennesaw State University W
Mercer University M,W
Middle Georgia State College M,W
Point University M,W
Reinhardt University M,W
Savannah College of Art and Design M,W
Shorter University M,W
Thomas University M,W
Truett-McConnell College M,W
University of Georgia W
University of North Georgia M,W
University of West Georgia W
Valdosta State University W
Young Harris College M,W

**Hawaii**
Brigham Young University-Hawaii M,W
Chaminade University of Honolulu M,W
Hawaii Pacific University M,W
University of Hawaii
 Manoa W

**Idaho**
Boise State University W
College of Idaho M,W
Idaho State University W
Northwest Nazarene University W
University of Idaho W

**Illinois**
Benedictine University at Springfield M,W
Bradley University M
Chicago State University W
College of Lake County M,W
DePaul University M,W
Eastern Illinois University M,W
Elgin Community College M,W
Illinois Central College M,W
Illinois Institute of Technology M,W
Illinois State University W
Judson University M,W
Kankakee Community College M
Kaskaskia College M,W
Kishwaukee College M
Lewis and Clark Community College M,W
Lewis University M,W
Lincoln Christian University M,W
Lincoln College M,W
Lincoln Land Community College M
Loyola University Chicago M,W
McHenry County College M
McKendree University M,W
Moraine Valley Community College M,W
Morton College M
Northern Illinois University M,W
Northwestern University M,W
Olivet Nazarene University M,W
Parkland College M,W
Quincy University M,W
Robert Morris University: Chicago M,W
Saint Xavier University M,W
South Suburban College of Cook County M
Southern Illinois University Edwardsville M,W
Southwestern Illinois College M
Trinity Christian College M,W
Trinity International University M,W
University of Illinois
 Chicago M
 Springfield M,W
 Urbana-Champaign W
University of St. Francis M,W
Waubonsee Community College M,W
Western Illinois University M,W

**Indiana**
Ancilla College M,W
Ball State University W
Bethel College M,W
Butler University M,W
Calumet College of St. Joseph M,W

Goshen College M,W
Grace College M,W
Holy Cross College M,W
Huntington University M,W
Indiana Institute of Technology M,W
Indiana State University W
Indiana University
 Bloomington M,W
 Purdue University Fort Wayne M,W
 Purdue University Indianapolis M,W
Indiana Wesleyan University M,W
Marian University M,W
Oakland City University M,W
Purdue University W
Purdue University
 Calumet M,W
Saint Joseph's College M,W
St. Mary-of-the-Woods College W
Taylor University M,W
University of Evansville M,W
University of Indianapolis M,W
University of Notre Dame M,W
University of Saint Francis M,W
University of Southern Indiana M,W
Valparaiso University M,W

**Iowa**
Briar Cliff University M,W
Clarke University M,W
Dordt College M,W
Drake University M,W
Graceland University M,W
Grand View University M,W
Iowa Central Community College M,W
Iowa State University W
Iowa Western Community College M,W
Kirkwood Community College M
Morningside College M,W
Mount Mercy University M,W
North Iowa Area Community College M
Northwestern College M,W
St. Ambrose University M,W
Scott Community College M,W
University of Iowa W
University of Northern Iowa W
Upper Iowa University M,W
Waldorf University M,W
William Penn University M,W

**Kansas**
Allen County Community College M,W
Baker University M,W
Barton County Community College M,W
Benedictine College M,W
Bethany College M,W
Bethel College M,W
Butler Community College W
Central Christian College of Kansas M,W
Cloud County Community College M,W
Coffeyville Community College M,W
Dodge City Community College M,W
Emporia State University W
Friends University M,W
Garden City Community College M,W
Hesston College M,W
Hutchinson Community College W
Johnson County Community College M
Kansas City Kansas Community College M
Kansas State University W
Kansas Wesleyan University M,W
MidAmerica Nazarene University M,W
Neosho County Community College M,W
Newman University M,W
Northwest Kansas Technical College M,W
Ottawa University M,W
Southwestern College M,W
Sterling College M,W
Tabor College M,W
University of Kansas W
University of St. Mary M,W
Washburn University W

**Kentucky**
Asbury University M,W
Bellarmine University M,W
Brescia University M,W
Campbellsville University M,W
Georgetown College M,W
Kentucky Wesleyan College M,W
Lindsey Wilson College M,W
Midway College W
Morehead State University W
Murray State University W
Northern Kentucky University M,W
St. Catharine College M,W
Union College M,W
University of Kentucky M,W
University of Louisville M,W
University of Pikeville M,W
University of the Cumberlands M,W

**Louisiana**
Louisiana State University and Agricultural and
 Mechanical College W
McNeese State University W
Nicholls State University W
Northwestern State University W
Southeastern Louisiana University W
Southern University and Agricultural and
 Mechanical College W
University of Louisiana at Lafayette W
University of Louisiana at Monroe W

**Maine**
University of Maine M,W
University of Maine
 Augusta M,W

**Maryland**
Anne Arundel Community College W
Chesapeake College W
College of Southern Maryland M,W
Community College of Baltimore County M,W
Hagerstown Community College M,W
Harford Community College M,W
Loyola University Maryland M,W
Mount St. Mary's University W
Towson University W
University of Maryland
 College Park M,W
Washington Adventist University M,W

**Massachusetts**
American International College M,W
Boston College M,W
Boston University M,W
College of the Holy Cross M,W
Merrimack College M,W
Northeastern University M,W
Stonehill College M,W
University of Massachusetts
 Amherst M,W
 Lowell M,W

**Michigan**
Aquinas College M,W
Central Michigan University W
Cleary University M,W
Concordia University M,W
Cornerstone University M,W
Davenport University M,W
Delta College W
Eastern Michigan University W
Ferris State University W
Grand Valley State University W
Lake Michigan College M,W
Lawrence Technological University M,W
Madonna University M,W
Marygrove College M,W
Michigan State University M,W
Michigan Technological University W
Northern Michigan University W
Northwood University
 Michigan M,W
Oakland University M,W
Rochester College M,W

Saginaw Valley State University M,W
Schoolcraft College M,W
Siena Heights University M,W
Spring Arbor University M,W
University of Detroit Mercy M,W
University of Michigan M,W
Western Michigan University M,W

**Minnesota**
Bemidji State University W
Concordia University St. Paul W
Minnesota State University
    Mankato W
    Moorhead W
Saint Cloud State University W
Southwest Minnesota State University W
University of Minnesota
    Crookston W
    Duluth W
    Twin Cities W
Winona State University W

**Mississippi**
Alcorn State University W
Belhaven University M,W
Delta State University M,W
East Central Community College M,W
Hinds Community College M,W
Holmes Community College M
Jackson State University W
Jones County Junior College M,W
Meridian Community College M,W
Mississippi Gulf Coast Community College M,W
Mississippi State University W
Northwest Mississippi Community College M,W
Southwest Mississippi Community College M,W
University of Mississippi W
University of Southern Mississippi W
William Carey University M,W

**Missouri**
Avila University M,W
Central Methodist University M,W
Columbia College M,W
Culver-Stockton College M,W
Drury University M,W
East Central College M
Hannibal-LaGrange University M,W
Harris-Stowe State University M,W
Jefferson College M
Lindenwood University M,W
Maryville University of Saint Louis M,W
Metropolitan Community College - Kansas City M,W
Missouri Baptist University M,W
Missouri Southern State University M,W
Missouri State University M,W
Missouri University of Science and Technology M,W
Missouri Valley College M,W
Northwest Missouri State University W
Park University M,W
Research College of Nursing M,W
Rockhurst University M,W
St. Louis Community College M
Saint Louis University M,W
Southeast Missouri State University W
Southwest Baptist University M,W
Stephens College W
Truman State University M,W
University of Central Missouri W
University of Missouri
    Columbia W
    Kansas City M,W
    St. Louis M,W
William Jewell College M,W
William Woods University M,W

**Montana**
Carroll College M,W
Montana State University
    Billings M,W

Rocky Mountain College M,W
University of Great Falls W
University of Montana W

**Nebraska**
Bellevue University M,W
College of Saint Mary W
Concordia University M,W
Creighton University M,W
Doane College M,W
Grace University M,W
Hastings College M,W
Midland University M,W
University of Nebraska
    Lincoln W
    Omaha M,W
Wayne State College W
Western Nebraska Community College M,W
York College M,W

**Nevada**
University of Nevada
    Las Vegas M,W
    Reno W

**New Hampshire**
Franklin Pierce University M,W
Mount Washington College M,W
Saint Anselm College M,W
Southern New Hampshire University M,W
University of New Hampshire M,W

**New Jersey**
Bloomfield College M,W
Caldwell University M,W
County College of Morris W
Essex County College M
Fairleigh Dickinson University
    Metropolitan Campus M,W
Felician University M,W
Georgian Court University M,W
Mercer County Community College M,W
Monmouth University M,W
New Jersey Institute of Technology M,W
Rider University M,W
Rowan College at Burlington County M,W
Rutgers, The State University of New Jersey
    New Brunswick/Piscataway Campus M,W
Saint Peter's University M,W
Salem Community College W
Seton Hall University M,W
Sussex County Community College W

**New Mexico**
Eastern New Mexico University M,W
New Mexico Highlands University W
New Mexico State University W
University of New Mexico M,W
University of the Southwest M,W

**New York**
Adelphi University M,W
ASA College M
Bryant & Stratton College
    Syracuse M,W
Canisius College M,W
City University of New York
    Queens College M,W
Colgate University M,W
College of Saint Rose M,W
Concordia College M,W
Daemen College M,W
Dominican College of Blauvelt M,W
Dowling College M,W
Fordham University M,W
Globe Institute of Technology M
Hartwick College M
Hofstra University M,W
Iona College M,W
Le Moyne College M,W
Long Island University
    LIU Brooklyn M,W
    LIU Post M,W

Manhattan College M,W
Marist College M,W
Mercy College M,W
Molloy College M,W
Monroe Community College M,W
New York Institute of Technology M,W
Niagara University M,W
Nyack College M,W
Pace University W
Pace University: Pleasantville/Briarcliff W
Roberts Wesleyan College M,W
Saint Bonaventure University M,W
St. Francis College M
St. John's University M,W
St. Thomas Aquinas College M,W
Siena College M,W
SUNY
    University at Albany M,W
    University at Binghamton M,W
    University at Buffalo M,W
    University at Stony Brook M,W
Syracuse University M,W
Wagner College W

**North Carolina**
Appalachian State University M,W
Barton College M,W
Belmont Abbey College M,W
Brevard College M,W
Campbell University M,W
Catawba College M,W
Chowan University M,W
Davidson College M,W
Duke University M,W
East Carolina University W
Elon University M,W
Gardner-Webb University M,W
High Point University M,W
Laurel University M,W
Lees-McRae College M,W
Lenoir-Rhyne University M,W
Louisburg College M,W
Mars Hill University M,W
Montreat College M,W
North Carolina State University M,W
Queens University of Charlotte M,W
St. Andrews University M,W
University of Mount Olive M,W
University of North Carolina
    Asheville M,W
    Chapel Hill M,W
    Charlotte M,W
    Greensboro M,W
    Pembroke W
    Wilmington M,W
Wake Forest University M,W
Western Carolina University W
Wingate University M,W

**North Dakota**
North Dakota State University W
University of Jamestown M,W
University of Mary M,W
University of North Dakota W

**Ohio**
Ashland University M,W
Bowling Green State University M,W
Bryant & Stratton College
    Eastlake M
Cedarville University M,W
Cincinnati State Technical and Community College M,W
Cleveland State University M,W
Kent State University W
Lake Erie College M,W
Lakeland Community College M
Malone University M,W
Miami University
    Oxford M,W
Mount Vernon Nazarene University M,W
Notre Dame College M,W
Ohio Dominican University M,W

Ohio State University
    Columbus Campus M,W
Ohio University W
Owens Community College M,W
Shawnee State University M,W
Southern State Community College M
Tiffin University M,W
University of Akron M,W
University of Cincinnati M,W
University of Dayton M,W
University of Findlay M,W
University of Rio Grande M,W
University of Toledo W
Urbana University W
Ursuline College W
Walsh University M,W
Wright State University M,W
Xavier University M,W
Youngstown State University W

**Oklahoma**
Bacone College M,W
East Central University W
Eastern Oklahoma State College M,W
Mid-America Christian University M,W
Northeastern Oklahoma Agricultural and Mechanical College M,W
Northeastern State University M,W
Northern Oklahoma College M,W
Northwestern Oklahoma State University W
Oklahoma Baptist University M,W
Oklahoma Christian University M,W
Oklahoma City University M,W
Oklahoma State University W
Oklahoma Wesleyan University M,W
Oral Roberts University M,W
Rogers State University M,W
Rose State College M,W
St. Gregory's University M,W
Southern Nazarene University M,W
Southwestern Oklahoma State University M,W
University of Central Oklahoma W
University of Oklahoma W
University of Science and Arts of Oklahoma M,W
University of Tulsa M,W

**Oregon**
Concordia University M,W
Corban University M,W
Eastern Oregon University M,W
Lane Community College M,W
Multnomah University M
Northwest Christian University M,W
Oregon Institute of Technology W
Oregon State University M,W
Portland State University W
Southern Oregon University W
Southwestern Oregon Community College M,W
Treasure Valley Community College M,W
University of Oregon W
University of Portland M,W
Warner Pacific College M,W
Western Oregon University W

**Pennsylvania**
Bloomsburg University of Pennsylvania M,W
Bucknell University M,W
California University of Pennsylvania M,W
Carlow University W
Chestnut Hill College M,W
Clarion University of Pennsylvania W
Drexel University M,W
Duquesne University M,W
East Stroudsburg University of Pennsylvania M,W
Edinboro University
    of Pennsylvania W
Gannon University M,W
Harcum College M,W
Holy Family University M,W
Indiana University of Pennsylvania W

Kutztown University of Pennsylvania W
La Salle University M,W
Lackawanna College W
Lafayette College M
Lehigh University M,W
Lock Haven University of Pennsylvania M,W
Mercyhurst University M,W
Millersville University of Pennsylvania M,W
Penn State
University Park M,W
Philadelphia University M,W
Point Park University M,W
Robert Morris University M,W
St. Francis University M,W
Saint Joseph's University M,W
Seton Hill University M,W
Shippensburg University of Pennsylvania M,W
Slippery Rock University of Pennsylvania M,W
Temple University M,W
University of Pittsburgh M,W
Valley Forge Military College M,W
Villanova University M,W
West Chester University of Pennsylvania M,W

**Puerto Rico**
Inter American University of Puerto Rico
Aguadilla Campus M,W
Bayamon Campus M
Guayama Campus M
Ponce Campus M,W
San German Campus M
Turabo University M
Universidad Metropolitana M,W
University of Puerto Rico
Arecibo M,W
Carolina Regional College M
Cayey University College M,W
Mayaguez M
Utuado M,W

**Rhode Island**
Bryant University M,W
Community College of Rhode Island M,W
Providence College M,W
University of Rhode Island M,W

**South Carolina**
Anderson University M,W
Charleston Southern University M,W
The Citadel W
Clemson University M,W
Coastal Carolina University M,W
Coker College M,W
College of Charleston M,W
Columbia College W
Columbia International University M
Converse College W
Erskine College M,W
Francis Marion University M,W
Furman University M,W
Lander University M,W
Limestone College M,W
Newberry College M,W
North Greenville University M,W
Presbyterian College M,W
South Carolina State University W
Southern Wesleyan University M,W
Spartanburg Methodist College M,W
University of South Carolina
Aiken M,W
Columbia M,W
Upstate M,W
Winthrop University M
Wofford College M,W

**South Dakota**
Augusta University
Augustana University W
Dakota Wesleyan University M,W
Mount Marty College M,W
Northern State University W
South Dakota State University W
University of Sioux Falls W
University of South Dakota W

**Tennessee**
Austin Peay State University W
Belmont University M,W
Bethel University M,W
Bryan College
Dayton M,W
Carson-Newman University M,W
Christian Brothers University M,W
Cumberland University M,W
East Tennessee State University M,W
Freed-Hardeman University M,W
Hiwassee College M,W
King University M,W
Lee University M,W
Lincoln Memorial University M,W
Lipscomb University M,W
Martin Methodist College M,W
Middle Tennessee State University W
Milligan College M,W
Tennessee Technological University W
Tennessee Wesleyan College M,W
Trevecca Nazarene University M,W
Tusculum College M,W
Union University M,W
University of Memphis M,W
University of Tennessee
Chattanooga W
Knoxville W
Martin W
Vanderbilt University W

**Texas**
Abilene Christian University W
Angelo State University W
Baylor University W
Brookhaven College W
Dallas Baptist University W
Hill College W
Houston Baptist University M,W
Jacksonville College M,W
Jarvis Christian College M,W
Lubbock Christian University M,W
Midwestern State University M,W
Northeast Texas Community College M,W
Paris Junior College M,W
Prairie View A&M University W
Ranger College M,W
Rice University W
St. Edward's University M,W
St. Mary's University M,W
Sam Houston State University W
San Jacinto College M
Southern Methodist University M,W
Southwestern Assemblies of God University M,W
Stephen F. Austin State University W
Texas A&M University W
Texas A&M University
Commerce W
Corpus Christi W
Texas Christian University W
Texas Southern University W
Texas State University W
Texas Tech University W
Texas Wesleyan University M,W
Texas Woman's University W
Tyler Junior College M
University of Houston W
University of North Texas W
University of St. Thomas M
University of Texas
Austin W
Brownsville M,W
of the Permian Basin M,W
San Antonio W
University of the Incarnate Word M,W
Wayland Baptist University M,W
West Texas A&M University M,W
Western Texas College M,W

**Utah**
Brigham Young University W
Dixie State University M,W

Southern Utah University W
University of Utah W
Utah State University W
Utah Valley University W
Weber State University W
Westminster College M,W

**Vermont**
University of Vermont M,W

**Virginia**
Bluefield College M,W
College of William and Mary M,W
George Mason University M,W
James Madison University M,W
Liberty University M,W
Longwood University M,W
Old Dominion University M,W
Radford University M,W
University of Richmond W
University of Virginia M,W
Virginia Commonwealth University M,W
Virginia Military Institute M,W
Virginia Polytechnic Institute and State University M,W

**Washington**
Central Washington University W
Clark College M,W
Columbia Basin College M,W
Eastern Washington University W
Edmonds Community College M,W
Everett Community College M,W
Evergreen State College M,W
Gonzaga University M,W
Green River Community College M
Highline College M,W
Lower Columbia College W
Northwest University M,W
Peninsula College M,W
Pierce College M
Saint Martin's University M,W
Seattle Pacific University M,W
Seattle University M,W
Shoreline Community College M,W
Skagit Valley College M,W
Spokane Community College W
Tacoma Community College M,W
Trinity Lutheran College M,W
University of Washington M,W
Walla Walla Community College M,W
Washington State University W
Western Washington University M,W
Whatcom Community College M,W
Yakima Valley Community College W

**West Virginia**
Alderson-Broaddus University M,W
Concord University W
Davis and Elkins College M,W
Marshall University M,W
Ohio Valley University M,W
Salem International University M,W
Shepherd University M,W
University of Charleston M,W
West Virginia University M,W
West Virginia Wesleyan College M,W
Wheeling Jesuit University M,W

**Wisconsin**
Cardinal Stritch University M,W
Marquette University M,W
Silver Lake College of the Holy Family M,W
University of Wisconsin
Green Bay M,W
Madison M,W
Milwaukee M,W
Parkside M,W
Viterbo University M,W

**Wyoming**
Central Wyoming College M,W
Laramie County Community College M,W
Northwest College M,W

Sheridan College M,W
University of Wyoming W
Western Wyoming Community College M,W

## Softball

**Alabama**
Alabama Southern Community College W
Alabama State University W
Auburn University W
Central Alabama Community College W
Chattahoochee Valley Community College W
Concordia College W
Enterprise State Community College W
Faulkner State Community College W
Faulkner University W
Gadsden State Community College W
George C. Wallace Community College at Dothan W
George C. Wallace State Community College at Selma W
Jacksonville State University W
Jefferson Davis Community College W
Judson College W
Lurleen B. Wallace Community College W
Marion Military Institute W
Miles College W
Samford University W
Shelton State Community College W
Snead State Community College W
Southern Union State Community College W
Spring Hill College W
Troy University W
Tuskegee University W
University of Alabama W
University of Alabama
Birmingham W
Huntsville W
University of Mobile W
University of Montevallo W
University of North Alabama W
University of West Alabama W
Wallace State Community College at Hanceville W

**Arizona**
Arizona Christian University W
Arizona State University W
Arizona Western College W
Central Arizona College W
Chandler-Gilbert Community College W
Eastern Arizona College W
Embry-Riddle Aeronautical University
Prescott Campus W
GateWay Community College W
Grand Canyon University W
Mesa Community College W
Paradise Valley Community College W
Pima Community College W
Scottsdale Community College W
South Mountain Community College W
University of Arizona W

**Arkansas**
Arkansas Tech University W
Crowley's Ridge College W
Ecclesia College W
Henderson State University W
Lyon College W
North Arkansas College W
Ouachita Baptist University W
Southern Arkansas University W
University of Arkansas W
University of Arkansas
Monticello W
Pine Bluff W
University of Central Arkansas W
Williams Baptist College W

**California**
Academy of Art University W
Azusa Pacific University W

Biola University W
California Baptist University W
California Polytechnic State University: San
    Luis Obispo W
California State University
    Bakersfield W
    Chico W
    Dominguez Hills W
    Fresno W
    Fullerton W
    Long Beach W
    Monterey Bay W
    Northridge W
    Sacramento W
    San Bernardino W
    Stanislaus W
Concordia University Irvine W
Dominican University of California W
Fresno City College W
Grossmont College W
Holy Names University W
Hope International University W
Humboldt State University W
La Sierra University W
Loyola Marymount University W
Menlo College W
Notre Dame de Namur University W
St. Mary's College of California W
San Diego Christian College W
San Diego State University W
San Jose State University W
Santa Clara University W
Sonoma State University W
Stanford University W
University of California
    Berkeley W
    Davis W
    Los Angeles W
    Riverside W
    Santa Barbara W
University of San Diego W
University of the Pacific W
Vanguard University of Southern California W
William Jessup University W
Yuba College W

## Colorado
Adams State University W
Colorado Mesa University W
Colorado Northwestern Community College W
Colorado School of Mines W
Colorado State University W
Colorado State University
    Pueblo W
Fort Lewis College W
Lamar Community College W
Northeastern Junior College W
Otero Junior College W
Regis University W
Trinidad State Junior College W
University of Colorado
    Colorado Springs W
University of Northern Colorado W

## Connecticut
Central Connecticut State University W
Fairfield University W
Post University W
Quinnipiac University W
Sacred Heart University W
Southern Connecticut State University W
University of Bridgeport W
University of Connecticut W
University of New Haven W

## Delaware
Delaware State University W
Delaware Technical Community College
    Jack F. Owens Campus W
    Stanton/Wilmington Campus W
    Terry Campus W
Goldey-Beacom College W

University of Delaware W
Wilmington University W

## District of Columbia
Georgetown University W

## Florida
Ave Maria University W
Barry University W
Bethune-Cookman University W
Chipola College W
College of Central Florida W
Daytona State College W
Eastern Florida State College W
Eckerd College W
Edward Waters College W
Embry-Riddle Aeronautical University W
Flagler College W
Florida Atlantic University W
Florida Gulf Coast University W
Florida Institute of Technology W
Florida Southern College W
Florida State College at Jacksonville W
Florida State University W
Gulf Coast State College W
Hillsborough Community College W
Indian River State College W
Jacksonville University W
Lake-Sumter State College W
Lynn University W
Miami Dade College W
North Florida Community College W
Northwest Florida State College W
Nova Southeastern University W
Palm Beach Atlantic University W
Palm Beach State College W
Pasco-Hernando State College W
Pensacola State College W
Polk State College W
Rollins College W
Saint Johns River State College W
Saint Leo University W
St. Petersburg College W
Saint Thomas University W
Santa Fe College W
South Florida State College W
Southeastern University W
State College of Florida, Manatee-Sarasota W
Stetson University W
Tallahassee Community College W
University of Central Florida W
University of Florida W
University of North Florida W
University of Tampa W
University of West Florida W
Warner University W
Webber International University W

## Georgia
Abraham Baldwin Agricultural College W
Albany State University W
Andrew College W
Armstrong State University W
Augusta University W
Brenau University W
Brewton-Parker College W
Clark Atlanta University W
College of Coastal Georgia W
Columbus State University W
Darton College W
East Georgia State College W
Emmanuel College W
Georgia College and State University W
Georgia Gwinnett College W
Georgia Highlands College M,W
Georgia Institute of Technology W
Georgia Military College W
Georgia Perimeter College W
Georgia Southern University W
Georgia Southwestern State University W
Georgia State University W
Gordon State College W
Kennesaw State University W

Mercer University W
Middle Georgia State College W
Paine College W
Point University W
Reinhardt University W
Shorter University W
South Georgia State College W
Thomas University W
Truett-McConnell College W
University of Georgia W
University of North Georgia W
University of West Georgia W
Valdosta State University W
Young Harris College W

## Hawaii
Brigham Young University-Hawaii W
Chaminade University of Honolulu W
Hawaii Pacific University W
University of Hawaii
    Hilo W
    Manoa W

## Idaho
Boise State University W
College of Idaho W
College of Southern Idaho M,W
Idaho State University W
North Idaho College W
Northwest Nazarene University W

## Illinois
Benedictine University at Springfield W
Black Hawk College W
Bradley University W
Carl Sandburg College W
College of Lake County W
Danville Area Community College W
DePaul University W
Eastern Illinois University W
Elgin Community College W
Highland Community College W
Illinois Central College W
Illinois Eastern Community Colleges
    Lincoln Trail College W
    Olney Central College W
    Wabash Valley College W
Illinois State University W
John A. Logan College W
John Wood Community College W
Judson University W
Kankakee Community College W
Kaskaskia College W
Kishwaukee College W
Lake Land College W
Lewis University W
Lincoln College W
Lincoln Land Community College W
Loyola University Chicago W
McHenry County College W
McKendree University W
Moraine Valley Community College W
Morton College W
Northern Illinois University W
Northwestern University W
Olivet Nazarene University W
Parkland College W
Quincy University W
Rend Lake College W
Robert Morris University: Chicago W
Saint Xavier University W
Sauk Valley Community College W
Shawnee Community College W
South Suburban College of Cook County W
Southeastern Illinois College W
Southern Illinois University Carbondale W
Southern Illinois University Edwardsville W
Southwestern Illinois College W
Spoon River College W
Trinity Christian College W
Trinity International University W
University of Illinois
    Chicago W

    Springfield W
    Urbana-Champaign W
University of St. Francis W
Waubonsee Community College W
Western Illinois University W

## Indiana
Ancilla College W
Ball State University W
Bethel College W
Butler University W
Calumet College of St. Joseph W
Goshen College W
Grace College W
Huntington University W
Indiana Institute of Technology W
Indiana State University W
Indiana University
    Bloomington W
    Purdue University Fort Wayne W
    Purdue University Indianapolis W
Indiana Wesleyan University W
Marian University W
Oakland City University W
Purdue University W
Purdue University
    Calumet W
    North Central W
Saint Joseph's College W
St. Mary-of-the-Woods College W
Taylor University W
University of Evansville W
University of Indianapolis W
University of Notre Dame W
University of Saint Francis W
University of Southern Indiana W
Valparaiso University W

## Iowa
Briar Cliff University W
Clarke University W
Dordt College W
Drake University W
Ellsworth Community College W
Graceland University W
Grand View University W
Iowa Central Community College W
Iowa Lakes Community College W
Iowa State University W
Iowa Western Community College W
Kirkwood Community College W
Marshalltown Community College W
Morningside College W
Mount Mercy University W
Muscatine Community College W
North Iowa Area Community College W
Northwestern College W
St. Ambrose University W
Southeastern Community College W
Southwestern Community College W
University of Iowa W
University of Northern Iowa W
Upper Iowa University W
Waldorf University W
William Penn University W

## Kansas
Allen County Community College W
Baker University W
Barton County Community College W
Benedictine College W
Bethany College W
Brown Mackie College
    Salina W
Butler Community College W
Central Christian College of Kansas W
Cloud County Community College W
Coffeyville Community College W
Colby Community College W
Cowley County Community College W
Dodge City Community College W
Emporia State University W
Fort Hays State University W

Fort Scott Community College W
Friends University W
Garden City Community College W
Hesston College W
Highland Community College W
Hutchinson Community College W
Independence Community College W
Johnson County Community College W
Kansas City Kansas Community College W
Kansas Wesleyan University W
Labette Community College W
McPherson College W
MidAmerica Nazarene University W
Neosho County Community College W
Newman University W
Ottawa University W
Pittsburg State University W
Pratt Community College W
Seward County Community College W
Southwestern College W
Sterling College W
Tabor College W
University of Kansas W
University of St. Mary W
Washburn University W
Wichita State University W

**Kentucky**
Asbury University W
Bellarmine University W
Brescia University W
Campbellsville University W
Eastern Kentucky University W
Georgetown College W
Kentucky State University W
Kentucky Wesleyan College W
Lindsey Wilson College W
Midway College W
Morehead State University W
Murray State University W
Northern Kentucky University W
St. Catharine College W
Union College W
University of Kentucky W
University of Louisville M
University of Pikeville W
University of the Cumberlands W
Western Kentucky University W

**Louisiana**
Bossier Parish Community College W
Louisiana State University
    Eunice W
Louisiana State University and Agricultural and
    Mechanical College W
Louisiana Tech University W
McNeese State University W
Nicholls State University W
Northwestern State University W
Southeastern Louisiana University W
Southern University and Agricultural and
    Mechanical College W
University of Louisiana at Lafayette W
University of Louisiana at Monroe W

**Maine**
University of Maine W

**Maryland**
Bowie State University W
Chesapeake College W
College of Southern Maryland W
Community College of Baltimore County W
Coppin State University W
Garrett College W
Hagerstown Community College W
Harford Community College W
Morgan State University W
Mount St. Mary's University W
Towson University W
University of Maryland
    College Park W
    Eastern Shore W

**Massachusetts**
American International College W
Boston College W
Boston University W
College of the Holy Cross W
Merrimack College W
Stonehill College W
University of Massachusetts
    Amherst W
    Lowell W

**Michigan**
Alpena Community College W
Aquinas College W
Central Michigan University W
Cleary University W
Concordia University W
Cornerstone University W
Davenport University W
Delta College W
Eastern Michigan University W
Ferris State University W
Glen Oaks Community College W
Grand Valley State University W
Henry Ford Community College W
Hillsdale College W
Kalamazoo Valley Community College W
Kellogg Community College W
Lake Michigan College W
Lake Superior State University W
Lansing Community College W
Madonna University W
Michigan State University W
Mott Community College W
Muskegon Community College W
Northwood University
    Michigan W
Oakland Community College W
Oakland University W
Rochester College W
Saginaw Valley State University W
St. Clair County Community College W
Siena Heights University W
Spring Arbor University W
University of Detroit Mercy W
University of Michigan W
University of Michigan
    Dearborn W
Wayne State University W
Western Michigan University W

**Minnesota**
Bemidji State University W
Concordia University St. Paul W
Minnesota State University
    Mankato W
    Moorhead W
Saint Cloud State University W
Southwest Minnesota State University W
University of Minnesota
    Crookston W
    Duluth W
    Twin Cities W
Winona State University W

**Mississippi**
Alcorn State University W
Belhaven University W
Blue Mountain College W
Copiah-Lincoln Community College W
Delta State University W
East Central Community College W
East Mississippi Community College W
Hinds Community College W
Holmes Community College W
Itawamba Community College W
Jackson State University W
Jones County Junior College W
Meridian Community College W
Mississippi Gulf Coast Community College W
Mississippi State University W
Mississippi Valley State University W
Northwest Mississippi Community College W

Southwest Mississippi Community College W
University of Mississippi W
University of Southern Mississippi W
William Carey University W

**Missouri**
Avila University W
Central Methodist University W
Columbia College W
Cottey College W
Culver-Stockton College W
Drury University W
East Central College W
Evangel University W
Hannibal-LaGrange University W
Harris-Stowe State University W
Jefferson College W
Lincoln University W
Lindenwood University W
Maryville University of Saint Louis W
Metropolitan Community College - Kansas City
    W
Missouri Baptist University W
Missouri Southern State University W
Missouri State University W
Missouri University of Science and Technology
    W
Missouri Valley College W
Missouri Western State University W
North Central Missouri College W
Northwest Missouri State University W
Park University W
Research College of Nursing W
Rockhurst University W
St. Louis Community College W
Saint Louis University W
Southeast Missouri State University W
Southwest Baptist University W
Stephens College W
Three Rivers Community College W
Truman State University W
University of Central Missouri W
University of Missouri
    Columbia W
    Kansas City W
    St. Louis W
William Jewell College W
William Woods University W

**Montana**
Carroll College W
Montana State University
    Billings W
University of Great Falls W
University of Montana W

**Nebraska**
Bellevue University W
College of Saint Mary W
Concordia University W
Creighton University W
Doane College W
Grace University W
Hastings College W
Mid-Plains Community College W
Midland University W
Peru State College W
University of Nebraska
    Kearney W
    Lincoln W
    Omaha W
Wayne State College W
Western Nebraska Community College W
York College W

**Nevada**
University of Nevada
    Las Vegas W
    Reno W

**New Hampshire**
Franklin Pierce University W
Mount Washington College W

Saint Anselm College W
Southern New Hampshire University M,W

**New Jersey**
Bloomfield College W
Brookdale Community College W
Caldwell University W
County College of Morris W
Fairleigh Dickinson University
    Metropolitan Campus W
Felician University W
Georgian Court University W
Mercer County Community College W
Monmouth University W
Raritan Valley Community College W
Rider University W
Rowan College at Burlington County W
Rutgers, The State University of New Jersey
    New Brunswick/Piscataway Campus W
Saint Peter's University W
Salem Community College W
Seton Hall University W

**New Mexico**
Eastern New Mexico University W
New Mexico Highlands University W
New Mexico State University W
University of New Mexico W
University of the Southwest W
Western New Mexico University W

**New York**
Adelphi University W
Canisius College W
City University of New York
    Queens College W
Colgate University W
College of Saint Rose W
Concordia College W
Dominican College of Blauvelt W
Dowling College W
Fordham University W
Hofstra University W
Iona College W
Le Moyne College W
Long Island University
    LIU Brooklyn W
    LIU Post W
Manhattan College W
Marist College W
Mercy College W
Molloy College W
New York Institute of Technology W
Niagara University W
Nyack College W
Orange County Community College W
Pace University: Pleasantville/Briarcliff W
Saint Bonaventure University W
St. John's University W
St. Thomas Aquinas College W
Siena College W
SUNY
    University at Albany W
    University at Binghamton W
    University at Buffalo W
    University at Stony Brook W
Syracuse University W
Wagner College W

**North Carolina**
Appalachian State University W
Barton College W
Belmont Abbey College W
Brevard College W
Campbell University W
Catawba College W
Chowan University W
East Carolina University W
Elizabeth City State University W
Elon University W
Fayetteville State University W
Gardner-Webb University W
Johnson C. Smith University W
Lees-McRae College W

Lenoir-Rhyne University W
Louisburg College W
Mars Hill University W
Montreat College W
North Carolina Central University W
North Carolina State University W
Pitt Community College W
Queens University of Charlotte W
St. Andrews University W
Saint Augustine's University W
Shaw University W
University of Mount Olive W
University of North Carolina
    Chapel Hill W
    Charlotte W
    Greensboro W
    Wilmington W
Western Carolina University W
Wingate University W
Winston-Salem State University W

**North Dakota**
Dakota College at Bottineau W
Dickinson State University W
Lake Region State College W
Mayville State University W
Minot State University W
North Dakota State University W
University of Jamestown W
University of Mary W
University of North Dakota W
Valley City State University W
Williston State College W

**Ohio**
Ashland University W
Bowling Green State University W
Cedarville University W
Cleveland State University W
Kent State University W
Lake Erie College W
Lakeland Community College W
Lourdes University W
Malone University W
Miami University
    Oxford W
Mount Vernon Nazarene University W
Notre Dame College W
Ohio Dominican University W
Ohio University W
Owens Community College W
Shawnee State University W
Sinclair Community College W
Southern State Community College W
Tiffin University W
University of Akron W
University of Dayton W
University of Findlay W
University of Rio Grande W
University of Toledo W
Urbana University W
Ursuline College W
Walsh University W
Wright State University W
Youngstown State University W

**Oklahoma**
Bacone College W
Cameron University W
Carl Albert State College W
Connors State College W
East Central University W
Eastern Oklahoma State College W
Mid-America Christian University W
Northeastern Oklahoma Agricultural and
    Mechanical College W
Northeastern State University W
Northern Oklahoma College W
Northwestern Oklahoma State University W
Oklahoma Baptist University W
Oklahoma Christian University W
Oklahoma City University W
Oklahoma Panhandle State University M,W

Oklahoma State University W
Oklahoma Wesleyan University W
Rogers State University W
Rose State College W
St. Gregory's University W
Seminole State College W
Southeastern Oklahoma State University W
Southern Nazarene University W
Southwestern Oklahoma State University W
University of Central Oklahoma W
University of Oklahoma W
University of Science and Arts of Oklahoma W
University of Tulsa W
Western Oklahoma State College W

**Oregon**
Blue Mountain Community College W
Clackamas Community College W
Concordia University W
Corban University W
Eastern Oregon University W
Mt. Hood Community College W
Northwest Christian University W
Oregon Institute of Technology W
Oregon State University W
Portland State University W
Southern Oregon University W
Southwestern Oregon Community College W
Treasure Valley Community College W
University of Oregon W

**Pennsylvania**
Bloomsburg University of Pennsylvania W
Bucknell University W
California University of Pennsylvania W
Carlow University W
Chestnut Hill College W
Clarion University of Pennsylvania W
Drexel University W
East Stroudsburg University of Pennsylvania W
Edinboro University
    of Pennsylvania W
Gannon University W
Holy Family University W
Indiana University of Pennsylvania W
Kutztown University of Pennsylvania W
La Salle University W
Lackawanna College W
Lehigh University W
Lock Haven University of Pennsylvania W
Mansfield University of Pennsylvania W
Mercyhurst University W
Millersville University of Pennsylvania W
Penn State
    University Park W
Philadelphia University W
Point Park University W
Robert Morris University W
St. Francis University W
Saint Joseph's University W
Seton Hill University W
Shippensburg University of Pennsylvania W
Slippery Rock University of Pennsylvania W
University of Pittsburgh W
University of the Sciences W
Villanova University W
West Chester University of Pennsylvania W

**Puerto Rico**
Inter American University of Puerto Rico
    Aguadilla Campus M,W
    Bayamon Campus M,W
    Guayama Campus M,W
    Ponce Campus M,W
Universidad del Este W
Universidad Metropolitana W
University of Puerto Rico
    Arecibo W
    Carolina Regional College W
    Cayey University College W
    Humacao W
    Mayaguez W

    Ponce M,W
    Utuado M

**Rhode Island**
Bryant University W
Community College of Rhode Island W
Providence College W
University of Rhode Island W

**South Carolina**
Anderson University W
Charleston Southern University W
Claflin University W
Coastal Carolina University W
Coker College W
College of Charleston W
Columbia College W
Erskine College W
Francis Marion University W
Furman University W
Lander University W
Limestone College W
Morris College W
Newberry College W
North Greenville University W
Presbyterian College W
South Carolina State University W
Southern Wesleyan University W
Spartanburg Methodist College W
University of South Carolina
    Aiken W
    Columbia W
    Upstate W
Voorhees College W
Winthrop University W

**South Dakota**
Augusta University
    Augustana University W
Dakota State University W
Dakota Wesleyan University W
Mount Marty College W
Northern State University W
South Dakota State University M,W
University of Sioux Falls W
University of South Dakota W

**Tennessee**
Austin Peay State University W
Belmont University W
Bethel University W
Bryan College
    Dayton W
Carson-Newman University W
Christian Brothers University W
Cleveland State Community College W
Columbia State Community College W
Cumberland University W
Dyersburg State Community College W
East Tennessee State University W
Freed-Hardeman University W
Hiwassee College W
Jackson State Community College W
King University W
Lee University W
LeMoyne-Owen College W
Lincoln Memorial University W
Lipscomb University W
Martin Methodist College W
Middle Tennessee State University W
Milligan College W
Motlow State Community College W
Roane State Community College W
Southwest Tennessee Community College W
Tennessee Technological University W
Tennessee Wesleyan College W
Trevecca Nazarene University W
Tusculum College W
Union University W
University of Tennessee
    Chattanooga W
    Knoxville W
    Martin W
Walters State Community College W

**Texas**
Abilene Christian University W
Alvin Community College W
Angelina College W
Angelo State University W
Baylor University W
Blinn College M
Clarendon College W
Frank Phillips College W
Galveston College W
Grayson College W
Hill College W
Houston Baptist University W
Howard College W
Kilgore College W
Lubbock Christian University W
McLennan Community College W
Midland College W
Midwestern State University W
Northeast Texas Community College W
Odessa College W
Paris Junior College W
Prairie View A&M University W
Ranger College W
St. Edward's University W
St. Mary's University W
Sam Houston State University W
San Jacinto College W
Southwestern Assemblies of God University W
Stephen F. Austin State University W
Tarleton State University W
Temple College W
Texas A&M University W
Texas Southern University W
Texas State University W
Texas Tech University W
Texas Wesleyan University W
Texas Woman's University W
University of Houston W
University of North Texas W
University of Texas
    Arlington W
    Austin W
    of the Permian Basin W
    San Antonio W
University of the Incarnate Word W
Vernon College W
Weatherford College W
Western Texas College W
Wiley College W

**Utah**
Brigham Young University W
Dixie State University W
Salt Lake Community College W
Snow College W
Southern Utah University W
University of Utah W
Utah State University W
Utah Valley University W
Weber State University W

**Virginia**
Bluefield College W
George Mason University W
Hampton University W
James Madison University W
Liberty University W
Longwood University W
Norfolk State University W
Radford University W
University of Virginia W
University of Virginia's College at Wise W
Virginia Polytechnic Institute and State
    University W
Virginia State University W
Virginia Union University W

**Washington**
Big Bend Community College W
Central Washington University W
Centralia College W
Columbia Basin College W

Edmonds Community College W
Everett Community College W
Grays Harbor College W
Green River Community College W
Highline College W
Lower Columbia College W
Northwest University W
Olympic College W
Pierce College W
Saint Martin's University W
Seattle University W
Shoreline Community College W
Skagit Valley College W
Spokane Community College W
University of Washington W
Walla Walla Community College W
Western Washington University W
Yakima Valley Community College W

**West Virginia**
Alderson-Broaddus University W
Bluefield State College W
Concord University W
Davis and Elkins College W
Fairmont State University W
Glenville State College W
Marshall University W
Ohio Valley University W
Potomac State College of West Virginia
   University W
Salem International University W
Shepherd University W
University of Charleston W
West Liberty University W
West Virginia State University W
West Virginia University Institute of
   Technology W
West Virginia Wesleyan College W
Wheeling Jesuit University W

**Wisconsin**
Cardinal Stritch University W
University of Wisconsin
      Green Bay W
      Madison W
      Parkside W
Viterbo University W

# Squash

**Pennsylvania**
Drexel University M,W

# Swimming

**Alabama**
Auburn University M,W
University of Alabama M,W

**Alaska**
University of Alaska
      Fairbanks W

**Arizona**
Arizona State University M,W
Grand Canyon University M,W
Northern Arizona University W
University of Arizona M,W

**Arkansas**
Henderson State University M,W
Ouachita Baptist University M,W
University of Arkansas W
University of Arkansas
      Little Rock M,W

**California**
Biola University M,W
California Baptist University M,W

California Polytechnic State University: San
   Luis Obispo M,W
California State University
      Bakersfield M,W
      Fresno W
      Northridge M,W
      San Bernardino M,W
Concordia University Irvine M,W
Fresno Pacific University M,W
Grossmont College M,W
Loyola Marymount University W
Pepperdine University W
San Diego State University W
San Jose State University W
Soka University of America M,W
Stanford University M,W
University of California
      Berkeley M,W
      Davis W
      Los Angeles M,W
      Santa Barbara M,W
University of San Diego W
University of Southern California M,W
University of the Pacific M,W
Vanguard University of Southern California
   M,W

**Colorado**
Adams State University W
Colorado Mesa University M,W
Colorado State University W
Colorado State University
      Pueblo W
University of Denver M,W
University of Northern Colorado W

**Connecticut**
Central Connecticut State University W
Fairfield University M,W
Sacred Heart University W
Southern Connecticut State University M,W
University of Bridgeport M,W
University of Connecticut M,W

**Delaware**
University of Delaware W

**District of Columbia**
George Washington University M,W
Georgetown University M,W
Howard University M,W

**Florida**
Florida Atlantic University M,W
Florida Institute of Technology M,W
Florida Southern College M,W
Florida State University M,W
Indian River State College M,W
Lynn University W
Nova Southeastern University M,W
Saint Leo University M,W
University of Florida M,W
University of Miami W
University of North Florida W
University of Tampa M,W

**Georgia**
Brenau University W
Darton College M,W
Emmanuel College M,W
Georgia Institute of Technology M,W
Georgia Southern University W
Life University M,W
Point University M,W
Savannah College of Art and Design M,W
University of Georgia M,W

**Hawaii**
University of Hawaii
      Manoa M,W

**Idaho**
Boise State University W
College of Idaho M,W
University of Idaho W

**Illinois**
Eastern Illinois University M,W
Illinois Institute of Technology M,W
Illinois State University W
Lewis University M,W
Lincoln College M,W
McKendree University M,W
Northwestern University M,W
Olivet Nazarene University M,W
Quincy University W
Southern Illinois University Carbondale M,W
University of Illinois
      Chicago M,W
      Urbana-Champaign W
Western Illinois University M,W

**Indiana**
Ball State University M,W
Indiana State University W
Indiana University
      Bloomington M,W
      Purdue University Indianapolis M,W
Purdue University M,W
University of Evansville M,W
University of Indianapolis M,W
University of Notre Dame M,W
Valparaiso University M,W

**Iowa**
Iowa Central Community College M,W
Iowa State University W
Morningside College M,W
University of Iowa M,W
University of Northern Iowa W

**Kansas**
Tabor College M,W
University of Kansas W

**Kentucky**
Asbury University M,W
Bellarmine University M,W
Campbellsville University M,W
Lindsey Wilson College M,W
St. Catharine College M
University of Kentucky M,W
University of Louisville M,W
University of the Cumberlands M,W

**Louisiana**
Louisiana State University and Agricultural and
      Mechanical College M,W
Tulane University W
University of Louisiana at Monroe M,W

**Maine**
University of Maine W

**Maryland**
Loyola University Maryland M,W
Mount St. Mary's University W
Towson University M,W

**Massachusetts**
Boston College M,W
Boston University M,W
College of the Holy Cross W
Merrimack College W
Northeastern University W
University of Massachusetts
      Amherst M,W

**Michigan**
Eastern Michigan University M,W
Grand Valley State University M,W
Hillsdale College W
Michigan State University M,W
Northern Michigan University W
Oakland University M,W
University of Michigan M,W
Wayne State University M,W

**Minnesota**
Minnesota State University
      Mankato M,W

Saint Cloud State University M,W
University of Minnesota
      Twin Cities M,W

**Mississippi**
Delta State University M,W

**Missouri**
Drury University M,W
Lindenwood University M,W
Maryville University of Saint Louis W
Missouri State University M,W
Missouri University of Science and Technology
   M
Saint Louis University M,W
Truman State University W
University of Missouri
      Columbia M,W
William Jewell College M,W

**Nebraska**
College of Saint Mary W
University of Nebraska
      Kearney W
      Lincoln W
      Omaha W

**Nevada**
University of Nevada
      Las Vegas M,W
      Reno W

**New Hampshire**
Franklin Pierce University W
University of New Hampshire W

**New Jersey**
Monmouth University M,W
New Jersey Institute of Technology M,W
Rider University M,W
Rutgers, The State University of New Jersey
      New Brunswick/Piscataway Campus
      M,W
Saint Peter's University M,W
Seton Hall University M,W

**New Mexico**
New Mexico State University W
University of New Mexico W

**New York**
Adelphi University M,W
Canisius College M,W
City University of New York
      Queens College M,W
College of Saint Rose M,W
Fordham University M,W
Iona College M,W
Le Moyne College M,W
Long Island University
      LIU Brooklyn M,W
      LIU Post W
Manhattan College M,W
Marist College M,W
Monroe Community College M,W
Niagara University M,W
Pace University M,W
Pace University: Pleasantville/Briarcliff M,W
Saint Bonaventure University M,W
St. Francis College M,W
Siena College W
SUNY
      University at Binghamton M,W
      University at Buffalo M,W
Wagner College W

**North Carolina**
Campbell University W
Catawba College M,W
Chowan University W
Davidson College M,W
East Carolina University M,W
Gardner-Webb University M,W
Lenoir-Rhyne University M,W
Mars Hill University M,W

North Carolina Agricultural and Technical State
    University W
North Carolina State University M,W
Queens University of Charlotte M,W
University of North Carolina
    Chapel Hill M,W
    Wilmington M,W
Wingate University M,W

**North Dakota**
University of North Dakota M,W

**Ohio**
Ashland University M,W
Bowling Green State University W
Cleveland State University M,W
Lake Erie College M,W
Malone University M,W
Miami University
    Oxford M,W
Notre Dame College M,W
Ohio State University
    Columbus Campus M,W
Ohio University W
University of Akron W
University of Cincinnati M,W
University of Findlay M,W
University of Toledo W
Urbana University M,W
Ursuline College W
Wright State University M,W
Xavier University M,W
Youngstown State University W

**Oklahoma**
Oklahoma Baptist University M,W

**Oregon**
Oregon State University W

**Pennsylvania**
Bloomsburg University of Pennsylvania M,W
Bucknell University M,W
California University of Pennsylvania W
Clarion University of Pennsylvania M,W
Drexel University M,W
Duquesne University W
East Stroudsburg University of Pennsylvania W
Edinboro University
    of Pennsylvania W
Gannon University M,W
Indiana University of Pennsylvania W
Kutztown University of Pennsylvania W
La Salle University M,W
Lehigh University M,W
Lock Haven University of Pennsylvania W
Mansfield University of Pennsylvania W
Millersville University of Pennsylvania W
Penn State
    University Park M,W
St. Francis University W
Shippensburg University of Pennsylvania M,W
University of Pittsburgh M,W
Villanova University W
West Chester University of Pennsylvania M,W

**Puerto Rico**
Bayamon Central University M,W
Inter American University of Puerto Rico
    Aguadilla Campus M,W
    Bayamon Campus M,W
    Ponce Campus M,W
Turabo University M,W
University of Puerto Rico
    Cayey University College M
    Humacao M,W
    Mayaguez M,W
University of the Sacred Heart M,W

**Rhode Island**
Bryant University M,W
University of Rhode Island W

**South Carolina**
Columbia College W
Converse College W

Limestone College M,W
University of South Carolina
    Columbia M,W

**South Dakota**
Northern State University W
South Dakota State University M,W
University of South Dakota M,W

**Tennessee**
King University M,W
University of Tennessee
    Knoxville M,W
Vanderbilt University W

**Texas**
Rice University W
Southern Methodist University M,W
Texas A&M University M,W
Texas Christian University M,W
University of Houston W
University of North Texas W
University of Texas
    Austin M,W
    of the Permian Basin M,W
University of the Incarnate Word M,W
Wayland Baptist University M,W

**Utah**
Brigham Young University M,W
University of Utah M,W

**Vermont**
University of Vermont W

**Virginia**
George Mason University M,W
James Madison University W
Liberty University W
University of Richmond W
University of Virginia M,W
Virginia Military Institute M
Virginia Polytechnic Institute and State
    University M,W

**Washington**
Seattle University M,W
Trinity Lutheran College M,W
Washington State University W

**West Virginia**
Alderson-Broaddus University M,W
Davis and Elkins College M,W
Fairmont State University M,W
Marshall University W
West Virginia University M,W
West Virginia Wesleyan College M,W
Wheeling Jesuit University M,W

**Wisconsin**
University of Wisconsin
    Green Bay M,W
    Madison M,W
    Milwaukee M,W

**Wyoming**
University of Wyoming M,W

## Synchronized swimming

**Alabama**
University of Alabama
    Birmingham W

**California**
Stanford University W

**New York**
Canisius College W

**Texas**
University of the Incarnate Word W

## Table tennis

**Arizona**
South Mountain Community College M,W

**Florida**
Flagler College M,W

**Puerto Rico**
Inter American University of Puerto Rico
    Aguadilla Campus M,W
    Bayamon Campus M,W
    Metropolitan Campus M,W
    Ponce Campus M,W
Universidad Metropolitana M,W
Universidad Politecnica de Puerto Rico M,W
University of Puerto Rico
    Arecibo M,W
    Cayey University College M,W
    Mayaguez M,W
    Ponce M,W
    Utuado M,W

**Texas**
Texas Wesleyan University M,W

## Tennis

**Alabama**
Alabama Agricultural and Mechanical
    University M,W
Alabama State University M,W
Auburn University M,W
Auburn University at Montgomery M,W
Central Alabama Community College W
Faulkner State Community College M,W
Gadsden State Community College M
Jacksonville State University M,W
Judson College W
Marion Military Institute M,W
Samford University M,W
Snead State Community College W
Spring Hill College M,W
Troy University M,W
Tuskegee University M,W
University of Alabama M,W
University of Alabama
    Birmingham M,W
    Huntsville M,W
University of Mobile M,W
University of Montevallo W
University of North Alabama M,W
University of South Alabama M,W
University of West Alabama M,W

**Arizona**
Arizona Christian University M,W
Arizona State University W
Eastern Arizona College W
GateWay Community College M,W
Grand Canyon University M,W
Northern Arizona University M,W
Paradise Valley Community College M,W
Pima Community College M,W
South Mountain Community College M,W
University of Arizona M,W

**Arkansas**
Arkansas State University W
Arkansas Tech University W

Harding University M,W
Henderson State University W
John Brown University M,W
Ouachita Baptist University M,W
Southern Arkansas University W
University of Arkansas M,W
University of Arkansas
    Fort Smith W
    Little Rock M,W
    Pine Bluff M,W
University of Central Arkansas W

**California**
Academy of Art University W
Azusa Pacific University M
Biola University M,W
California Polytechnic State University: San
    Luis Obispo M,W
California State University
    Bakersfield W
    Fresno M,W
    Fullerton W
    Long Beach W
    Los Angeles M,W
    Northridge W
    Sacramento M,W
Concordia University Irvine M,W
Dominican University of California W
Fresno City College M,W
Fresno Pacific University M,W
Grossmont College M,W
Holy Names University M,W
Hope International University M,W
Loyola Marymount University M,W
Notre Dame de Namur University W
Pepperdine University M,W
Point Loma Nazarene University M,W
St. Mary's College of California M,W
San Diego Christian College M,W
San Diego State University M,W
San Jose State University W
Santa Clara University M,W
Sonoma State University M,W
Stanford University M,W
University of California
    Berkeley M,W
    Davis M,W
    Irvine M,W
    Los Angeles M,W
    Santa Barbara M,W
University of San Diego M,W
University of San Francisco M,W
University of Southern California M,W
University of the Pacific M,W
Westmont College M,W

**Colorado**
Colorado Christian University M,W
Colorado Mesa University M,W
Colorado State University W
Colorado State University
    Pueblo M,W
Metropolitan State University of Denver M,W
University of Colorado
    Boulder W
University of Denver M,W
University of Northern Colorado M,W

**Connecticut**
Fairfield University M,W
Post University M,W
Quinnipiac University M,W
Sacred Heart University M,W
University of Connecticut M,W
University of Hartford M,W
University of New Haven W

**Delaware**
Delaware State University W
Goldey-Beacom College W

**District of Columbia**
George Washington University M,W
Georgetown University M,W
Howard University M,W

## Florida
Ave Maria University M,W
Barry University M,W
Bethune-Cookman University M,W
Eastern Florida State College W
Eckerd College M,W
Embry-Riddle Aeronautical University M,W
Flagler College M,W
Florida Atlantic University M,W
Florida Gulf Coast University M,W
Florida Institute of Technology M,W
Florida Southern College M,W
Florida State College at Jacksonville W
Florida State University M,W
Hillsborough Community College W
Lynn University M,W
Palm Beach Atlantic University M,W
Rollins College M,W
Saint Leo University M,W
Saint Thomas University M,W
Southeastern University M,W
Stetson University M,W
University of Central Florida M,W
University of Florida M,W
University of Miami M,W
University of North Florida M,W
University of South Florida M,W
University of Tampa W
University of West Florida M,W
Warner University M,W
Webber International University M,W

## Georgia
Abraham Baldwin Agricultural College M,W
Albany State University W
Armstrong State University M,W
Augusta University W
Brenau University W
Clark Atlanta University W
Clayton State University W
College of Coastal Georgia M,W
Columbus State University M,W
Emmanuel College M,W
Fort Valley State University M,W
Georgia College and State University M,W
Georgia Gwinnett College M,W
Georgia Institute of Technology M,W
Georgia Perimeter College M,W
Georgia Southern University M,W
Georgia Southwestern State University M,W
Georgia State University M,W
Kennesaw State University M,W
Mercer University M,W
Morehouse College M
Point University M,W
Reinhardt University M,W
Savannah College of Art and Design M,W
Savannah State University W
Shorter University M,W
South Georgia State College W
University of Georgia M,W
University of North Georgia M,W
University of West Georgia W
Valdosta State University M,W
Young Harris College M,W

## Hawaii
Brigham Young University-Hawaii M,W
Chaminade University of Honolulu W
Hawaii Pacific University M,W
University of Hawaii
    Hilo M,W
    Manoa M,W

## Idaho
Boise State University M,W
College of Idaho W
Idaho State University M,W
Lewis-Clark State College M,W
University of Idaho M,W

## Illinois
Bradley University W
Chicago State University M,W

College of Lake County M,W
DePaul University M,W
Eastern Illinois University M,W
Elgin Community College M,W
Illinois State University M,W
Judson University M,W
Kaskaskia College M,W
Lewis and Clark Community College M,W
Lewis University M,W
McHenry County College M,W
McKendree University M,W
Moraine Valley Community College M,W
Northern Illinois University M,W
Northwestern University M,W
Olivet Nazarene University M,W
Quincy University M,W
Rend Lake College W
Robert Morris University: Chicago W
Sauk Valley Community College M,W
Southern Illinois University Carbondale M,W
Southern Illinois University Edwardsville M,W
University of Illinois
    Chicago M,W
    Springfield M,W
    Urbana-Champaign M,W
University of St. Francis M,W
Waubonsee Community College M,W
Western Illinois University M,W

## Indiana
Ancilla College M,W
Ball State University M,W
Bethel College M,W
Butler University M,W
Calumet College of St. Joseph M,W
Goshen College M,W
Grace College M,W
Huntington University M,W
Indiana Institute of Technology M,W
Indiana University
    Bloomington M,W
    Purdue University Fort Wayne M,W
    Purdue University Indianapolis M,W
Indiana Wesleyan University M,W
Marian University M,W
Oakland City University M,W
Purdue University M,W
Purdue University
    Calumet M,W
Saint Joseph's College M,W
Taylor University M,W
University of Evansville W
University of Indianapolis M,W
University of Notre Dame M,W
University of Saint Francis M,W
University of Southern Indiana M,W
Valparaiso University M,W

## Iowa
Briar Cliff University M,W
Drake University M,W
Graceland University M,W
Grand View University M,W
Iowa Central Community College M,W
Iowa State University W
Morningside College M,W
Northwestern College W
St. Ambrose University M,W
University of Iowa M,W
University of Northern Iowa W
Upper Iowa University W

## Kansas
Baker University M,W
Barton County Community College M,W
Bethany College M,W
Bethel College M,W
Central Christian College of Kansas M,W
Cowley County Community College M,W
Emporia State University M,W
Fort Hays State University W
Friends University M,W
Hesston College M,W

Johnson County Community College M,W
Kansas State University W
Kansas Wesleyan University M,W
Labette Community College W
McPherson College M,W
Newman University M,W
Seward County Community College M,W
Southwestern College M,W
Tabor College M,W
University of Kansas W
Washburn University M,W
Wichita State University M,W

## Kentucky
Asbury University M,W
Bellarmine University M,W
Brescia University M,W
Campbellsville University M,W
Eastern Kentucky University M,W
Georgetown College M,W
Kentucky Wesleyan College W
Lindsey Wilson College M,W
Midway College W
Morehead State University M,W
Murray State University M,W
Northern Kentucky University M,W
St. Catharine College M
Union College M,W
University of Kentucky M,W
University of Louisville M,W
University of Pikeville M,W
University of the Cumberlands M,W
Western Kentucky University M,W

## Louisiana
Dillard University M,W
Grambling State University M,W
Louisiana State University
    Shreveport W
Louisiana State University and Agricultural and
    Mechanical College M,W
Louisiana Tech University M,W
Loyola University New Orleans M,W
McNeese State University W
Nicholls State University M,W
Northwestern State University W
Southeastern Louisiana University W
Southern University and Agricultural and
    Mechanical College W
Tulane University M,W
University of Louisiana at Lafayette M,W
University of New Orleans M,W
Xavier University of Louisiana M,W

## Maryland
College of Southern Maryland M,W
Coppin State University M,W
Harford Community College M,W
Loyola University Maryland M,W
Morgan State University M,W
Mount St. Mary's University M,W
Towson University W
University of Maryland
    College Park W
    Eastern Shore M,W

## Massachusetts
American International College M,W
Boston College M,W
Boston University W
Merrimack College M,W
Stonehill College M,W
University of Massachusetts
    Amherst W

## Michigan
Aquinas College M,W
Cleary University M,W
Davenport University M,W
Eastern Michigan University W
Ferris State University M,W
Grand Valley State University M,W
Hillsdale College M,W
Lake Superior State University M,W

Lawrence Technological University M,W
Michigan State University M,W
Michigan Technological University M,W
Northwood University
    Michigan M,W
Oakland Community College W
Oakland University W
Saginaw Valley State University W
Spring Arbor University M,W
University of Detroit Mercy M,W
University of Michigan M,W
Wayne State University M,W
Western Michigan University M,W

## Minnesota
Bemidji State University W
Minnesota State University
    Mankato W
    Moorhead W
Saint Cloud State University M,W
Southwest Minnesota State University W
University of Minnesota
    Crookston W
    Duluth W
    Twin Cities M,W
Winona State University W

## Mississippi
Alcorn State University M,W
Belhaven University M,W
Copiah-Lincoln Community College M,W
Delta State University M,W
East Central Community College M
Hinds Community College M,W
Holmes Community College M,W
Jackson State University M,W
Jones County Junior College M,W
Meridian Community College M,W
Mississippi Gulf Coast Community College
    M,W
Mississippi State University M,W
Mississippi Valley State University M,W
Northwest Mississippi Community College
    M,W
Tougaloo College M,W
University of Mississippi M,W
University of Southern Mississippi M,W

## Missouri
Drury University M,W
Evangel University M,W
Lincoln University W
Lindenwood University M,W
Maryville University of Saint Louis W
Missouri Baptist University M,W
Missouri Valley College M,W
Missouri Western State University W
Northwest Missouri State University M,W
Research College of Nursing M,W
Rockhurst University M,W
Saint Louis University M,W
Southeast Missouri State University W
Southwest Baptist University M,W
Stephens College W
University of Missouri
    Columbia W
    Kansas City M,W
    St. Louis M,W
William Jewell College M,W
William Woods University M,W

## Montana
Montana State University M,W
Montana State University
    Billings M,W
University of Montana M,W

## Nebraska
College of Saint Mary W
Concordia University M,W
Creighton University M,W
Hastings College M,W
Midland University M,W
University of Nebraska

Kearney M,W
Lincoln M,W
Omaha M,W

**Nevada**
University of Nevada
Las Vegas M,W
Reno M,W

**New Hampshire**
Franklin Pierce University M,W
Saint Anselm College M,W
Southern New Hampshire University M,W

**New Jersey**
Bloomfield College M
Caldwell University M,W
Fairleigh Dickinson University
Metropolitan Campus M,W
Georgian Court University W
Monmouth University M,W
New Jersey Institute of Technology M,W
Rider University M,W
Rutgers, The State University of New Jersey
New Brunswick/Piscataway Campus
M,W
Saint Peter's University M,W
Seton Hall University W

**New Mexico**
New Mexico Military Institute M
New Mexico State University M,W
University of New Mexico M,W
University of the Southwest M,W
Western New Mexico University M,W

**New York**
Adelphi University M,W
ASA College M,W
City University of New York
Queens College M,W
College of Saint Rose W
Concordia College M,W
Daemen College M,W
Fordham University W
Hofstra University M,W
Le Moyne College M,W
Long Island University
LIU Brooklyn W
LIU Post W
Marist College M,W
Molloy College W
New York Institute of Technology M,W
Niagara University M,W
Roberts Wesleyan College M,W
Saint Bonaventure University M,W
St. Francis College M,W
St. John's University M,W
Siena College M,W
SUNY
University at Albany W
University at Binghamton M,W
University at Buffalo M,W
University at Stony Brook M,W
Syracuse University W
Wagner College M,W

**North Carolina**
Appalachian State University M,W
Barton College M,W
Belmont Abbey College M,W
Brevard College M,W
Campbell University M,W
Catawba College M,W
Chowan University M,W
Davidson College M,W
Duke University M,W
East Carolina University M,W
Elizabeth City State University W
Elon University M,W
Fayetteville State University W
Gardner-Webb University M,W
Johnson C. Smith University M,W
Lees-McRae College M,W

Lenoir-Rhyne University M,W
Mars Hill University M,W
North Carolina Agricultural and Technical State
University W
North Carolina Central University M,W
North Carolina State University M,W
Queens University of Charlotte M,W
St. Andrews University W
Saint Augustine's University M,W
Shaw University M,W
University of Mount Olive M,W
University of North Carolina
Asheville M,W
Chapel Hill M,W
Charlotte M,W
Greensboro M,W
Wilmington M,W
Wake Forest University M,W
Western Carolina University W
Wingate University M,W
Winston-Salem State University M,W

**North Dakota**
University of Mary W
University of North Dakota W

**Ohio**
Ashland University W
Bowling Green State University W
Cedarville University M,W
Central State University M,W
Cleveland State University M,W
Miami University
Oxford W
Ohio Dominican University M,W
Ohio State University
Columbus Campus M,W
Shawnee State University W
Tiffin University M,W
University of Akron W
University of Cincinnati W
University of Dayton M,W
University of Findlay M,W
University of Toledo M,W
Ursuline College W
Walsh University M,W
Wright State University M,W
Xavier University M,W
Youngstown State University M,W

**Oklahoma**
Bacone College M,W
Cameron University M,W
East Central University M,W
Northeastern State University W
Oklahoma Baptist University M,W
Oklahoma State University M,W
Oklahoma Wesleyan University M,W
Oral Roberts University M,W
Seminole State College M,W
Southeastern Oklahoma State University M,W
Southern Nazarene University M,W
University of Central Oklahoma W
University of Oklahoma M,W
University of Tulsa M,W

**Oregon**
Portland State University W
Southern Oregon University W
Treasure Valley Community College M,W
University of Oregon M,W
University of Portland M,W

**Pennsylvania**
Bloomsburg University of Pennsylvania M,W
California University of Pennsylvania W
Carlow University W
Chestnut Hill College M,W
Clarion University of Pennsylvania W
Drexel University M,W
Duquesne University W
East Stroudsburg University of Pennsylvania W
Edinboro University
of Pennsylvania M,W

Holy Family University W
Indiana University of Pennsylvania W
Kutztown University of Pennsylvania M,W
La Salle University M,W
Lehigh University M,W
Mercyhurst University M,W
Millersville University of Pennsylvania M,W
Penn State
University Park M,W
Philadelphia University M,W
St. Francis University M,W
Saint Joseph's University M,W
Seton Hill University W
Shippensburg University of Pennsylvania W
Slippery Rock University of Pennsylvania W
Temple University M,W
University of Pittsburgh W
University of the Sciences M,W
West Chester University of Pennsylvania M,W

**Puerto Rico**
Inter American University of Puerto Rico
Aguadilla Campus M,W
Bayamon Campus M,W
Ponce Campus M,W
San German Campus M,W
Turabo University M,W
Universidad Metropolitana M,W
Universidad Politecnica de Puerto Rico M,W
University of Puerto Rico
Bayamon University College M,W
Carolina Regional College M,W
Cayey University College M,W
Mayaguez M,W
Ponce M,W
University of the Sacred Heart M

**Rhode Island**
Bryant University M,W
University of Rhode Island W

**South Carolina**
Anderson University M,W
Charleston Southern University M,W
The Citadel M
Clemson University M,W
Coastal Carolina University M,W
Coker College M,W
College of Charleston M,W
Columbia College W
Converse College W
Erskine College M,W
Francis Marion University M,W
Furman University M,W
Lander University M,W
Limestone College M,W
Newberry College M,W
North Greenville University M,W
Presbyterian College M,W
South Carolina State University M,W
Spartanburg Methodist College M,W
University of South Carolina
Aiken M,W
Columbia M,W
Upstate M,W
Winthrop University M,W
Wofford College M,W

**South Dakota**
Augusta University
Augustana University M,W
Mount Marty College W
South Dakota State University M,W
University of Sioux Falls W

**Tennessee**
Austin Peay State University M,W
Belmont University M,W
Bethel University M,W
Carson-Newman University M,W
Christian Brothers University M,W
Cumberland University M,W
East Tennessee State University M,W
King University M,W

Lee University M,W
LeMoyne-Owen College M,W
Lincoln Memorial University M,W
Lipscomb University M,W
Martin Methodist College M,W
Middle Tennessee State University M,W
Milligan College M,W
Tennessee Technological University M
Tennessee Wesleyan College M,W
Tusculum College M,W
Union University M,W
University of Memphis M,W
University of Tennessee
Chattanooga M,W
Knoxville M,W
Martin W
Vanderbilt University M,W

**Texas**
Abilene Christian University M,W
Baylor University M,W
Collin County Community College District M,W
Dallas Baptist University W
Jacksonville College M,W
Lamar University M,W
Laredo Community College M,W
Midwestern State University M,W
North Central Texas College W
Prairie View A&M University M,W
Rice University M,W
St. Edward's University M,W
St. Mary's University M,W
Sam Houston State University W
Southern Methodist University M,W
Stephen F. Austin State University W
Tarleton State University M,W
Temple College M,W
Texas A&M University M,W
Texas A&M University
Corpus Christi M,W
Texas Christian University M,W
Texas Southern University M,W
Texas State University W
Texas Tech University M,W
Texas Wesleyan University W
Tyler Junior College M,W
University of Houston W
University of North Texas W
University of Texas
Arlington M,W
Austin M,W
Pan American M,W
of the Permian Basin M,W
San Antonio M,W
University of the Incarnate Word M,W

**Utah**
Brigham Young University M,W
Dixie State University W
Southern Utah University M,W
University of Utah M,W
Utah State University M,W
Weber State University M,W

**Virginia**
Bluefield College M,W
College of William and Mary M,W
George Mason University M,W
Hampton University M,W
James Madison University M,W
Liberty University M,W
Longwood University M,W
Norfolk State University M,W
Old Dominion University M,W
Radford University M,W
University of Richmond M,W
University of Virginia M,W
University of Virginia's College at Wise M,W
Virginia Commonwealth University M,W
Virginia Military Institute M
Virginia Polytechnic Institute and State
University M,W

Virginia State University M,W
Virginia Union University M,W

**Washington**
Eastern Washington University M,W
Gonzaga University M,W
Green River Community College M,W
Seattle University M,W
Shoreline Community College M,W
Skagit Valley College M,W
Spokane Community College M,W
Trinity Lutheran College M,W
University of Washington M,W
Washington State University W

**West Virginia**
Alderson-Broaddus University W
Bluefield State College M,W
Concord University M,W
Davis and Elkins College M,W
Fairmont State University M,W
Marshall University W
Salem International University M
Shepherd University M,W
University of Charleston M,W
West Liberty University M,W
West Virginia State University M,W
West Virginia University W
West Virginia Wesleyan College M,W

**Wisconsin**
Cardinal Stritch University M,W
Marquette University M,W
University of Wisconsin
    Green Bay M,W
    Madison M,W
    Milwaukee W

**Wyoming**
University of Wyoming W

## Track and field

**Alabama**
Alabama Agricultural and Mechanical
    University M,W
Alabama State University M,W
Auburn University M,W
Miles College M,W
Samford University M,W
Spring Hill College M,W
Troy University M,W
Tuskegee University M,W
University of Alabama M,W
University of Alabama
    Birmingham W
    Huntsville M,W
University of Mobile M,W
University of South Alabama M,W
University of West Alabama M,W

**Arizona**
Arizona Christian University M,W
Arizona State University M,W
Central Arizona College M,W
Grand Canyon University M,W
Mesa Community College M,W
Northern Arizona University M,W
Paradise Valley Community College M,W
Pima Community College M,W
University of Arizona M,W

**Arkansas**
Arkansas State University M,W
Harding University M,W
Southern Arkansas University M,W
University of Arkansas M,W
University of Arkansas
    Little Rock M,W
    Pine Bluff M,W
University of Central Arkansas M,W

**California**
Academy of Art University M,W
Azusa Pacific University M,W
Biola University M,W
California Baptist University M,W
California Polytechnic State University: San
    Luis Obispo M,W
California State Polytechnic University:
    Pomona M,W
California State University
    Bakersfield M,W
    Chico M,W
    Dominguez Hills W
    Fresno M,W
    Fullerton M,W
    Long Beach M,W
    Los Angeles M,W
    Northridge M,W
    Sacramento M,W
    Stanislaus M,W
Concordia University Irvine M,W
Fresno City College M,W
Fresno Pacific University M,W
Hope International University M,W
Humboldt State University M,W
The Master's College M,W
Menlo College M,W
Pepperdine University M,W
Point Loma Nazarene University W
St. Mary's College of California M,W
San Diego State University M,W
San Jose State University W
Santa Clara University M,W
Santiago Canyon College M,W
Soka University of America M,W
Sonoma State University W
Stanford University M,W
University of California
    Berkeley M,W
    Davis M,W
    Irvine M,W
    Los Angeles M,W
    Santa Barbara M,W
University of San Diego W
University of San Francisco M,W
University of Southern California M,W
Vanguard University of Southern California
    M,W
Westmont College M,W
William Jessup University M,W
Yuba College M,W

**Colorado**
Adams State University M,W
Colorado Mesa University M,W
Colorado School of Mines M,W
Colorado State University M,W
Colorado State University
    Pueblo M,W
University of Colorado
    Boulder M,W
    Colorado Springs M,W
University of Northern Colorado M,W
Western State Colorado University M,W

**Connecticut**
Central Connecticut State University M,W
Post University M,W
Quinnipiac University W
Sacred Heart University M,W
Southern Connecticut State University M,W
University of Connecticut M,W
University of New Haven M,W

**Delaware**
Delaware State University M,W
University of Delaware W

**District of Columbia**
American University M,W
Georgetown University M,W
Howard University M,W

**Florida**
Bethune-Cookman University M,W
Edward Waters College M
Embry-Riddle Aeronautical University M,W
Flagler College M,W
Florida Agricultural and Mechanical University
    M,W
Florida Atlantic University W
Florida Institute of Technology M,W
Florida Memorial University M
Florida State University M,W
Jacksonville University W
Nova Southeastern University M,W
University of Central Florida W
University of Florida M,W
University of Miami M,W
University of North Florida M,W
University of South Florida M,W
University of West Florida M,W
Warner University M,W
Webber International University M,W

**Georgia**
Albany State University M,W
Brenau University W
Clark Atlanta University M,W
Columbus State University M,W
Emmanuel College M,W
Fort Valley State University M,W
Georgia Institute of Technology M,W
Georgia Southern University W
Georgia State University W
Kennesaw State University M,W
Mercer University W
Morehouse College M
Paine College M,W
Savannah State University M,W
Shorter University M,W
University of Georgia M,W
University of West Georgia W

**Hawaii**
University of Hawaii
    Manoa W

**Idaho**
Boise State University M,W
College of Idaho M,W
Idaho State University M,W
Lewis-Clark State College M,W
Northwest Nazarene University M,W
University of Idaho M,W

**Illinois**
Bradley University M,W
Chicago State University M,W
DePaul University M,W
Eastern Illinois University M,W
Illinois State University M,W
Judson University M,W
Lewis University M,W
Lincoln College M,W
Loyola University Chicago M,W
McKendree University M,W
Northern Illinois University W
Olivet Nazarene University M,W
Robert Morris University: Chicago M,W
Southern Illinois University Carbondale M,W
Southern Illinois University Edwardsville M,W
Trinity Christian College M,W
University of Illinois
    Chicago M,W
    Springfield W
    Urbana-Champaign M,W
University of St. Francis M,W
Western Illinois University M,W

**Indiana**
Ancilla College M,W
Ball State University W
Bethel College M,W
Butler University M,W
Goshen College M,W
Grace College M,W

Huntington University M,W
Indiana Institute of Technology M,W
Indiana State University M,W
Indiana University
    Bloomington M,W
    Purdue University Fort Wayne W
Indiana Wesleyan University M,W
Marian University M,W
Purdue University M,W
Saint Joseph's College M,W
Taylor University M,W
University of Indianapolis M,W
University of Notre Dame M,W
University of Saint Francis M,W
Valparaiso University M,W
Vincennes University M,W

**Iowa**
Briar Cliff University M,W
Clarke University M,W
Dordt College M,W
Drake University M,W
Graceland University M,W
Iowa Central Community College M,W
Iowa State University M,W
Iowa Western Community College M,W
Morningside College M,W
Mount Mercy University M,W
North Iowa Area Community College M,W
Northwestern College M,W
St. Ambrose University M,W
University of Iowa M,W
University of Northern Iowa M,W
Waldorf University M,W
William Penn University M,W

**Kansas**
Allen County Community College M,W
Baker University M,W
Barton County Community College M,W
Benedictine College M,W
Bethany College M,W
Bethel College M,W
Butler Community College M,W
Cloud County Community College M,W
Coffeyville Community College M,W
Colby Community College M,W
Cowley County Community College M,W
Dodge City Community College M,W
Emporia State University M,W
Fort Hays State University M,W
Friends University M,W
Garden City Community College M,W
Highland Community College M,W
Hutchinson Community College M,W
Johnson County Community College M,W
Kansas City Kansas Community College M,W
Kansas State University M,W
Kansas Wesleyan University M,W
McPherson College M,W
Neosho County Community College M,W
Northwest Kansas Technical College M,W
Ottawa University M,W
Pittsburg State University M,W
Pratt Community College M,W
Southwestern College M,W
Sterling College M,W
Tabor College M,W
University of Kansas M,W
University of St. Mary M,W
Wichita State University M,W

**Kentucky**
Bellarmine University M,W
Brescia University M,W
Campbellsville University M,W
Eastern Kentucky University M,W
Georgetown College M,W
Kentucky State University M,W
Lindsey Wilson College M,W
Midway College W
Morehead State University M,W
Murray State University W

Northern Kentucky University M,W
St. Catharine College M,W
University of Kentucky M,W
University of Louisville M,W
University of Pikeville M,W
University of the Cumberlands M,W
Western Kentucky University M,W

### Louisiana
Dillard University M,W
Grambling State University M,W
Louisiana State University and Agricultural and
   Mechanical College M,W
Louisiana Tech University M,W
McNeese State University M,W
Nicholls State University W
Northwestern State University M,W
Southeastern Louisiana University M,W
Southern University and Agricultural and
   Mechanical College M,W
Tulane University M,W
University of Louisiana at Lafayette M,W
University of Louisiana at Monroe M,W
University of New Orleans M,W

### Maine
University of Maine M,W

### Maryland
Bowie State University M,W
Community College of Baltimore County W
Coppin State University M,W
Hagerstown Community College M,W
Morgan State University M,W
Mount St. Mary's University M,W
Towson University W
University of Maryland
   College Park M,W
   Eastern Shore M,W
Washington Adventist University M,W

### Massachusetts
American International College M,W
Boston College M,W
Boston University M,W
College of the Holy Cross W
Merrimack College M,W
Northeastern University M,W
Stonehill College M,W
University of Massachusetts
   Amherst M,W
   Lowell M,W

### Michigan
Aquinas College M,W
Central Michigan University M,W
Concordia University M,W
Cornerstone University M,W
Davenport University M,W
Eastern Michigan University M,W
Ferris State University M,W
Grand Valley State University M,W
Hillsdale College M,W
Lake Superior State University M,W
Macomb Community College M,W
Marygrove College M,W
Michigan State University M,W
Michigan Technological University M,W
Northern Michigan University W
Northwood University
   Michigan M,W
Saginaw Valley State University M,W
Siena Heights University M,W
University of Detroit Mercy M,W
University of Michigan M,W
Western Michigan University W

### Minnesota
Bemidji State University M,W
Concordia University St. Paul M,W
Minnesota State University
   Mankato M,W
   Moorhead M,W
Saint Cloud State University M,W

University of Minnesota
   Duluth M,W
   Twin Cities M,W
Winona State University W

### Mississippi
Alcorn State University M,W
Hinds Community College M,W
Holmes Community College M
Jackson State University M,W
Mississippi State University M,W
Mississippi Valley State University M,W
University of Mississippi M,W
University of Southern Mississippi M,W

### Missouri
Central Methodist University M,W
Culver-Stockton College M,W
Drury University M,W
Evangel University M,W
Hannibal-LaGrange University M,W
Lincoln University M,W
Lindenwood University M,W
Maryville University of Saint Louis M,W
Missouri Baptist University M,W
Missouri Southern State University M,W
Missouri State University M,W
Missouri University of Science and Technology
   M,W
Missouri Valley College M,W
Northwest Missouri State University M,W
Park University M,W
Saint Louis University M,W
Southeast Missouri State University M,W
Southwest Baptist University M,W
Truman State University M,W
University of Central Missouri M,W
University of Missouri
   Columbia M,W
   Kansas City M,W
William Jewell College M,W
William Woods University M,W

### Montana
Montana State University M,W
Montana State University
   Billings M,W
Rocky Mountain College M,W
University of Montana M,W

### Nebraska
Chadron State College M,W
Concordia University M,W
Doane College M,W
Hastings College M,W
Midland University M,W
University of Nebraska
   Kearney M,W
   Lincoln M,W
   Omaha W
Wayne State College M,W
York College M,W

### Nevada
University of Nevada
   Las Vegas W
   Reno W

### New Hampshire
Franklin Pierce University M,W
University of New Hampshire M,W

### New Jersey
Caldwell University M,W
Essex County College M,W
Fairleigh Dickinson University
   Metropolitan Campus M,W
Felician University M,W
Georgian Court University M,W
Monmouth University M,W
Rider University M,W
Rutgers, The State University of New Jersey
   New Brunswick/Piscataway Campus
   M,W
Saint Peter's University M,W

### New Mexico
Eastern New Mexico University M,W
New Mexico Highlands University W
New Mexico Military Institute M
New Mexico State University W
University of New Mexico M,W
University of the Southwest M,W

### New York
Adelphi University M,W
City University of New York
   Queens College M,W
College of Saint Rose M,W
Daemen College M,W
Dominican College of Blauvelt M,W
Fordham University M,W
Iona College M,W
Le Moyne College M,W
Long Island University
   LIU Brooklyn M,W
   LIU Post M,W
Manhattan College M,W
Marist College M,W
Molloy College M,W
Niagara University W
Roberts Wesleyan College M,W
St. Francis College M,W
St. John's University W
St. Thomas Aquinas College M,W
SUNY
   University at Albany M,W
   University at Binghamton M,W
   University at Buffalo M,W
   University at Stony Brook M,W
Syracuse University M,W
Wagner College M,W

### North Carolina
Appalachian State University M,W
Barton College M,W
Belmont Abbey College M,W
Brevard College M,W
Campbell University M,W
Davidson College M,W
East Carolina University M,W
Elon University W
Fayetteville State University W
Gardner-Webb University M,W
High Point University M,W
Johnson C. Smith University M,W
Lees-McRae College M,W
Lenoir-Rhyne University M,W
Livingstone College M,W
Mars Hill University M,W
Montreat College M,W
North Carolina Agricultural and Technical State
   University M,W
North Carolina Central University M,W
North Carolina State University M,W
Queens University of Charlotte M,W
Saint Augustine's University M,W
Shaw University M,W
University of Mount Olive M,W
University of North Carolina
   Asheville M,W
   Chapel Hill M,W
   Charlotte M,W
   Wilmington M,W
Wake Forest University M,W
Western Carolina University M,W
Winston-Salem State University M,W

### North Dakota
Dickinson State University M,W
Minot State University M,W
North Dakota State University M,W
University of Jamestown M,W
University of Mary M,W
University of North Dakota M,W
Valley City State University M,W

### Ohio
Ashland University M,W
Bowling Green State University W

Cedarville University M,W
Central State University M,W
Kent State University M,W
Lake Erie College M,W
Malone University M,W
Miami University
   Oxford M,W
Mount Vernon Nazarene University M,W
Notre Dame College M,W
Ohio Dominican University M,W
Ohio State University
   Columbus Campus M,W
Ohio University W
Tiffin University M,W
University of Akron M,W
University of Cincinnati M,W
University of Dayton W
University of Findlay M,W
University of Rio Grande M,W
University of Toledo W
Ursuline College W
Walsh University M,W
Wright State University W
Xavier University M,W
Youngstown State University M,W

### Oklahoma
Bacone College M,W
Langston University M,W
Oklahoma Baptist University M,W
Oklahoma Christian University M,W
Oklahoma City University M,W
Oklahoma State University M,W
Oklahoma Wesleyan University M,W
Oral Roberts University M,W
Rogers State University M,W
St. Gregory's University M,W
Southern Nazarene University M,W
University of Central Oklahoma W
University of Oklahoma M,W
University of Tulsa M,W

### Oregon
Clackamas Community College M,W
Concordia University M,W
Corban University M,W
Eastern Oregon University M,W
Lane Community College M,W
Mt. Hood Community College M,W
Northwest Christian University M,W
Oregon Institute of Technology M,W
Portland State University M,W
Southern Oregon University M,W
Southwestern Oregon Community College
   M,W
Treasure Valley Community College M,W
University of Oregon M,W
University of Portland M,W
Warner Pacific College M,W
Western Oregon University M,W

### Pennsylvania
Bloomsburg University of Pennsylvania M,W
Bucknell University W
California University of Pennsylvania M,W
Chestnut Hill College M,W
Cheyney University of Pennsylvania M,W
Clarion University of Pennsylvania M,W
Duquesne University M,W
East Stroudsburg University of Pennsylvania
   M,W
Edinboro University
   of Pennsylvania M,W
Harcum College M,W
Holy Family University M,W
Indiana University of Pennsylvania M,W
Kutztown University of Pennsylvania M,W
La Salle University M,W .
Lehigh University M,W
Lock Haven University of Pennsylvania M,W
Millersville University of Pennsylvania W
Penn State
   University Park M,W

Robert Morris University W
St. Francis University M,W
Saint Joseph's University M,W
Seton Hill University M,W
Shippensburg University of Pennsylvania M,W
Slippery Rock University of Pennsylvania M,W
Temple University W
University of Pittsburgh M,W
Villanova University M,W
West Chester University of Pennsylvania M,W

**Puerto Rico**
Bayamon Central University M,W
Inter American University of Puerto Rico
    Aguadilla Campus M,W
    Bayamon Campus M,W
    Fajardo Campus M,W
    Guayama Campus M,W
    Metropolitan Campus M,W
    Ponce Campus M,W
    San German Campus M,W
Turabo University M,W
Universidad del Este M,W
Universidad Metropolitana M,W
Universidad Politecnica de Puerto Rico M,W
University of Puerto Rico
    Arecibo M,W
    Bayamon University College M,W
    Carolina Regional College M,W
    Humacao M,W
    Mayaguez M,W
    Ponce M,W
    Utuado M,W
University of the Sacred Heart M,W

**Rhode Island**
Bryant University M,W
Providence College M,W
University of Rhode Island M,W

**South Carolina**
Anderson University M,W
Charleston Southern University M,W
The Citadel M,W
Claflin University M,W
Clemson University M,W
Coastal Carolina University M,W
Converse College W
Furman University M,W
Limestone College M,W
Morris College M,W
North Greenville University M,W
South Carolina State University M,W
University of South Carolina
    Columbia M,W
    Upstate M,W
Voorhees College M,W
Winthrop University M,W
Wofford College M,W

**South Dakota**
Augusta University
    Augustana University M,W
Black Hills State University M,W
Dakota State University M,W
Dakota Wesleyan University M,W
Mount Marty College M,W
Northern State University M,W
South Dakota School of Mines and Technology
    M,W
South Dakota State University M,W
University of Sioux Falls M,W
University of South Dakota M,W

**Tennessee**
Austin Peay State University W
Belmont University M,W
Bethel University M,W
Bryan College
    Dayton M,W
Christian Brothers University M,W
East Tennessee State University M,W
King University M,W
Lipscomb University M,W

Middle Tennessee State University M,W
Milligan College M,W
Tennessee Technological University W
Trevecca Nazarene University M,W
University of Memphis M,W
University of Tennessee
    Chattanooga M,W
    Knoxville M,W
Vanderbilt University W

**Texas**
Abilene Christian University M,W
Angelo State University M,W
Baylor University M,W
Dallas Baptist University W
Houston Baptist University M,W
Jarvis Christian College M,W
Lamar University M,W
Prairie View A&M University M,W
Rice University M,W
Sam Houston State University M,W
South Plains College M,W
Stephen F. Austin State University M,W
Tarleton State University M,W
Texas A&M University M,W
Texas A&M University
    Commerce M,W
    Corpus Christi M,W
Texas Christian University M,W
Texas Southern University M,W
Texas State University M,W
Texas Tech University M,W
Texas Wesleyan University M,W
University of Houston M,W
University of North Texas M,W
University of Texas
    Austin M,W
    Pan American M,W
    San Antonio M,W
University of the Incarnate Word M,W
Wayland Baptist University M,W
Western Texas College M,W
Wiley College M,W

**Utah**
Brigham Young University M,W
Southern Utah University M,W
University of Utah W
Utah State University M,W
Utah Valley University M,W
Weber State University M,W
Westminster College M,W

**Vermont**
University of Vermont M,W

**Virginia**
College of William and Mary M,W
George Mason University M,W
Hampton University M,W
James Madison University W
Liberty University M,W
Norfolk State University M,W
Radford University W
University of Richmond W
University of Virginia M,W
Virginia Commonwealth University M,W
Virginia Military Institute M,W
Virginia Polytechnic Institute and State
    University M,W
Virginia State University M,W
Virginia Union University M,W

**Washington**
Central Washington University M,W
Clark College M,W
Eastern Washington University M,W
Evergreen State College M,W
Highline College M,W
Northwest University M,W
Saint Martin's University M,W
Seattle Pacific University M,W
Seattle University M,W
Spokane Community College M,W

Trinity Lutheran College M,W
University of Washington M,W
Washington State University M,W
Western Washington University M,W

**West Virginia**
Alderson-Broaddus University M,W
Glenville State College M,W
Marshall University W
University of Charleston W
West Liberty University M,W
West Virginia University W
West Virginia Wesleyan College M,W
Wheeling Jesuit University M,W

**Wisconsin**
Cardinal Stritch University M,W
Marquette University M,W
University of Wisconsin
    Madison M,W
    Milwaukee M,W
    Parkside M,W

**Wyoming**
University of Wyoming M,W

## Triathlon

**Alabama**
University of West Alabama W

**New York**
Daemen College W

## Volleyball

**Alabama**
Alabama Agricultural and Mechanical
    University W
Alabama State University W
Auburn University W
Faulkner State Community College M,W
Faulkner University W
Gadsden State Community College W
Jacksonville State University W
Jefferson Davis Community College W
Judson College W
Lawson State Community College W
Miles College M,W
Samford University W
Southern Union State Community College W
Spring Hill College W
Troy University W
Tuskegee University W
University of Alabama W
University of Alabama
    Birmingham W
    Huntsville W
University of Mobile W
University of Montevallo W
University of North Alabama W
University of South Alabama W
University of West Alabama W
Wallace State Community College at
    Hanceville W

**Alaska**
University of Alaska
    Anchorage W
    Fairbanks W

**Arizona**
Arizona Christian University W
Arizona State University W
Arizona Western College W
Chandler-Gilbert Community College W
Eastern Arizona College W
Embry-Riddle Aeronautical University
    Prescott Campus W

Grand Canyon University M,W
Northern Arizona University W
Pima Community College W
Scottsdale Community College W
University of Arizona W
Yavapai College W

**Arkansas**
Arkansas State University W
Arkansas Tech University W
Crowley's Ridge College W
Harding University W
Henderson State University W
John Brown University W
Lyon College W
Ouachita Baptist University W
Philander Smith College W
Southern Arkansas University W
University of Arkansas W
University of Arkansas
    Fort Smith W
    Little Rock W
    Pine Bluff W
University of Central Arkansas W
Williams Baptist College W

**California**
Academy of Art University W
Azusa Pacific University W
Biola University W
California Baptist University M,W
California Polytechnic State University: San
    Luis Obispo W
California State Polytechnic University:
    Pomona W
California State University
    Bakersfield W
    Chico W
    Dominguez Hills W
    Fresno W
    Fullerton W
    Long Beach M,W
    Los Angeles W
    Monterey Bay W
    Northridge M,W
    Sacramento W
    San Bernardino W
    Stanislaus W
Concordia University Irvine M,W
Dominican University of California W
Fresno City College W
Fresno Pacific University W
Grossmont College M,W
Holy Names University M,W
Hope International University M,W
Humboldt State University W
Loyola Marymount University W
The Master's College W
Menlo College W
Notre Dame de Namur University W
Pepperdine University M,W
Point Loma Nazarene University W
St. Mary's College of California W
San Diego Christian College W
San Diego State University W
San Jose State University W
Santa Clara University W
Simpson University W
Sonoma State University W
Stanford University W
University of California
    Berkeley W
    Davis W
    Irvine M,W
    Los Angeles W
    Merced M,W
    Riverside W
    Santa Barbara M,W
University of San Diego W
University of San Francisco W
University of Southern California M,W
University of the Pacific M,W
Vanguard University of Southern California W

Westmont College W
William Jessup University W
Yuba College W

## Colorado
Adams State University W
Colorado Christian University W
Colorado Mesa University W
Colorado Northwestern Community College W
Colorado School of Mines W
Colorado State University W
Colorado State University
    Pueblo W
Fort Lewis College W
Lamar Community College W
Metropolitan State University of Denver W
Northeastern Junior College W
Otero Junior College W
Regis University W
Trinidad State Junior College W
University of Colorado
    Boulder W
    Colorado Springs W
University of Denver W
University of Northern Colorado W
Western State Colorado University W

## Connecticut
Central Connecticut State University W
Fairfield University W
Post University W
Quinnipiac University W
Sacred Heart University M,W
Southern Connecticut State University W
University of Bridgeport W
University of Connecticut W
University of Hartford W
University of New Haven W

## Delaware
Delaware State University W
Goldey-Beacom College W
University of Delaware W
Wilmington University W

## District of Columbia
American University W
George Washington University W
Georgetown University W
Howard University W

## Florida
Ave Maria University W
Barry University M,W
Bethune-Cookman University W
College of Central Florida W
Daytona State College W
Eastern Florida State College W
Eckerd College W
Embry-Riddle Aeronautical University W
Flagler College W
Florida Agricultural and Mechanical University
    W
Florida Atlantic University W
Florida College W
Florida Gulf Coast University W
Florida Institute of Technology W
Florida Memorial University W
Florida Southern College W
Florida State College at Jacksonville W
Florida State University W
Gulf Coast State College W
Hillsborough Community College W
Indian River State College W
Jacksonville University W
Lake-Sumter State College W
Lynn University W
Miami Dade College W
Nova Southeastern University W
Palm Beach Atlantic University W
Palm Beach State College W
Pasco-Hernando State College W
Pensacola State College W
Polk State College W

Rollins College W
Saint Johns River State College W
Saint Leo University W
St. Petersburg College W
Saint Thomas University W
South Florida State College W
Southeastern University W
State College of Florida, Manatee-Sarasota W
Stetson University W
University of Central Florida W
University of Florida W
University of Miami W
University of North Florida W
University of South Florida M,W
University of Tampa W
University of West Florida W
Warner University M,W
Webber International University W

## Georgia
Abraham Baldwin Agricultural College W
Albany State University W
Andrew College W
Armstrong State University W
Augusta University W
Brenau University W
Brewton-Parker College W
Clark Atlanta University W
College of Coastal Georgia W
Emmanuel College M,W
Fort Valley State University W
Georgia Institute of Technology W
Georgia Southern University W
Georgia State University W
Kennesaw State University W
Life University M
Mercer University W
Paine College W
Point University W
Savannah State University W
Shorter University W
Truett-McConnell College W
University of Georgia W
University of West Georgia W
Valdosta State University W

## Hawaii
Brigham Young University-Hawaii W
Chaminade University of Honolulu W
Hawaii Pacific University W
University of Hawaii
    Hilo W
    Manoa M,W

## Idaho
Boise State University W
College of Idaho W
College of Southern Idaho W
Idaho State University W
Lewis-Clark State College W
North Idaho College W
Northwest Nazarene University W
University of Idaho W

## Illinois
Benedictine University at Springfield W
Black Hawk College W
Bradley University W
Carl Sandburg College W
Chicago State University W
College of Lake County W
DePaul University W
Eastern Illinois University W
Elgin Community College W
Highland Community College W
Illinois Central College W
Illinois Institute of Technology W
Illinois State University W
John A. Logan College W
Judson University W
Kankakee Community College W
Kaskaskia College W
Kishwaukee College W
Lake Land College W

Lewis and Clark Community College W
Lewis University M,W
Lincoln Christian University W
Lincoln College W
Loyola University Chicago M,W
McHenry County College W
McKendree University M,W
Moraine Valley Community College W
Morton College W
Northern Illinois University W
Northwestern University W
Olivet Nazarene University W
Parkland College W
Quincy University M,W
Rend Lake College W
Robert Morris University: Chicago M,W
Saint Xavier University W
Sauk Valley Community College W
Shawnee Community College W
South Suburban College of Cook County W
Southern Illinois University Carbondale W
Southern Illinois University Edwardsville W
Southwestern Illinois College W
Trinity Christian College W
Trinity International University W
University of Illinois
    Chicago W
    Springfield W
    Urbana-Champaign W
University of St. Francis W
Waubonsee Community College W
Western Illinois University W

## Indiana
Ancilla College W
Ball State University M,W
Bethel College W
Butler University W
Calumet College of St. Joseph M,W
Goshen College W
Grace College W
Huntington University W
Indiana Institute of Technology W
Indiana State University W
Indiana University
    Bloomington W
    Purdue University Fort Wayne M,W
    Purdue University Indianapolis W
    Southeast W
Indiana Wesleyan University W
Marian University W
Oakland City University W
Purdue University W
Purdue University
    Calumet W
    North Central W
Saint Joseph's College W
Taylor University W
University of Evansville W
University of Indianapolis W
University of Notre Dame W
University of Saint Francis W
University of Southern Indiana W
Valparaiso University W
Vincennes University W

## Iowa
Briar Cliff University W
Clarke University M,W
Des Moines Area Community College W
Dordt College W
Drake University W
Ellsworth Community College W
Graceland University M,W
Grand View University M,W
Iowa Central Community College W
Iowa Lakes Community College W
Iowa State University W
Iowa Western Community College W
Kirkwood Community College W
Morningside College W
Mount Mercy University W
North Iowa Area Community College W

Northwestern College W
St. Ambrose University M,W
Southeastern Community College W
Southwestern Community College W
University of Iowa W
University of Northern Iowa W
Upper Iowa University W
Waldorf University W
William Penn University W

## Kansas
Allen County Community College W
Baker University W
Barton County Community College W
Benedictine College W
Bethany College W
Bethel College W
Butler Community College W
Central Christian College of Kansas W
Cloud County Community College W
Coffeyville Community College W
Colby Community College W
Cowley County Community College W
Dodge City Community College W
Emporia State University W
Fort Hays State University W
Fort Scott Community College W
Friends University W
Garden City Community College W
Hesston College W
Highland Community College W
Hutchinson Community College W
Independence Community College W
Johnson County Community College W
Kansas City Kansas Community College W
Kansas State University W
Kansas Wesleyan University W
Labette Community College W
McPherson College W
MidAmerica Nazarene University W
Neosho County Community College W
Newman University W
Ottawa University W
Pittsburg State University W
Pratt Community College W
Seward County Community College W
Southwestern College W
Sterling College W
Tabor College W
University of Kansas W
University of St. Mary W
Washburn University W
Wichita State University W

## Kentucky
Asbury University W
Bellarmine University W
Brescia University W
Campbellsville University W
Eastern Kentucky University W
Georgetown College W
Kentucky State University W
Kentucky Wesleyan College W
Lindsey Wilson College W
Midway College W
Morehead State University W
Murray State University W
Northern Kentucky University W
St. Catharine College W
Union College W
University of Kentucky W
University of Louisville W
University of Pikeville W
University of the Cumberlands W
Western Kentucky University W

## Louisiana
Dillard University W
Louisiana State University and Agricultural and
    Mechanical College W
Louisiana Tech University W
Loyola University New Orleans W
McNeese State University W

Nicholls State University W
Northwestern State University W
Southeastern Louisiana University W
Southern University and Agricultural and
　Mechanical College W
Tulane University W
University of Louisiana at Lafayette W
University of Louisiana at Monroe W
University of New Orleans W
Xavier University of Louisiana W

## Maine
University of Maine W

## Maryland
Bowie State University W
Chesapeake College W
College of Southern Maryland W
Community College of Baltimore County W
Coppin State University W
Garrett College W
Hagerstown Community College W
Harford Community College W
Loyola University Maryland W
Morgan State University W
Towson University W
University of Maryland
　College Park W
　Eastern Shore W

## Massachusetts
American International College W
Boston College W
College of the Holy Cross W
Merrimack College W
Northeastern University W
Stonehill College W
University of Massachusetts
　Lowell W

## Michigan
Alpena Community College W
Aquinas College W
Central Michigan University W
Concordia University W
Cornerstone University W
Davenport University W
Eastern Michigan University W
Ferris State University W
Gogebic Community College M,W
Grand Valley State University W
Hillsdale College W
Kalamazoo Valley Community College W
Kellogg Community College W
Lake Michigan College W
Lake Superior State University W
Lansing Community College W
Lawrence Technological University W
Macomb Community College W
Madonna University W
Marygrove College W
Michigan State University W
Michigan Technological University W
Mott Community College W
Muskegon Community College W
Northern Michigan University W
Northwood University
　Michigan W
Oakland Community College W
Oakland University W
Rochester College W
Saginaw Valley State University W
St. Clair County Community College W
Schoolcraft College W
Siena Heights University M,W
Spring Arbor University W
University of Michigan W
University of Michigan
　Dearborn W
Wayne State University W
Western Michigan University W

## Minnesota
Bemidji State University W
Concordia University St. Paul W

Minnesota State University
　Mankato W
　Moorhead W
Saint Cloud State University W
Southwest Minnesota State University W
University of Minnesota
　Crookston W
　Duluth W
　Twin Cities W
Winona State University W

## Mississippi
Alcorn State University W
Belhaven University W
Jackson State University W
Mississippi State University W
Mississippi Valley State University W
University of Mississippi W
University of Southern Mississippi W

## Missouri
Avila University W
Central Methodist University W
College of the Ozarks W
Columbia College W
Cottey College W
Culver-Stockton College M,W
Drury University W
East Central College W
Evangel University W
Hannibal-LaGrange University M,W
Harris-Stowe State University W
Jefferson College W
Lindenwood University M,W
Maryville University of Saint Louis W
Metropolitan Community College - Kansas City
　W
Mineral Area College W
Missouri Baptist University M,W
Missouri Southern State University W
Missouri State University W
Missouri State University: West Plains W
Missouri Valley College M,W
Missouri Western State University W
Northwest Missouri State University W
Park University M,W
Research College of Nursing W
Rockhurst University W
Saint Louis University W
Southeast Missouri State University W
Southwest Baptist University W
Stephens College W
Truman State University W
University of Central Missouri W
University of Missouri
　Columbia W
　Kansas City W
　St. Louis W
William Jewell College W
William Woods University W

## Montana
Carroll College W
Montana State University W
Montana State University
　Billings W
　Northern W
Montana Tech of the University of Montana W
Rocky Mountain College W
University of Great Falls W
University of Montana W
University of Montana: Western W

## Nebraska
Bellevue University W
Central Community College W
Chadron State College W
College of Saint Mary W
Concordia University W
Creighton University W
Doane College W
Grace University W
Hastings College W
Mid-Plains Community College W

Midland University W
Peru State College W
University of Nebraska
　Kearney W
　Lincoln W
　Omaha W
Wayne State College W
Western Nebraska Community College W
York College W

## Nevada
University of Nevada
　Las Vegas W
　Reno W

## New Hampshire
Franklin Pierce University W
Mount Washington College M,W
Saint Anselm College W
University of New Hampshire W

## New Jersey
Bloomfield College W
Caldwell University W
County College of Morris W
Fairleigh Dickinson University
　Metropolitan Campus W
Georgian Court University W
New Jersey Institute of Technology M,W
Rider University W
Rutgers, The State University of New Jersey
　New Brunswick/Piscataway Campus W
　Newark Campus M
Saint Peter's University W
Seton Hall University W

## New Mexico
Eastern New Mexico University W
New Mexico Highlands University W
New Mexico State University W
University of New Mexico W
University of the Southwest W
Western New Mexico University W

## New York
Adelphi University W
Canisius College W
City University of New York
　Queens College W
Colgate University W
College of Saint Rose W
Concordia College W
Daemen College W
Dominican College of Blauvelt W
Dowling College W
Fordham University W
Globe Institute of Technology W
Hofstra University W
Iona College W
Le Moyne College W
Long Island University
　LIU Brooklyn W
　LIU Post W
Manhattan College W
Marist College W
Mercy College W
Molloy College W
New York Institute of Technology W
Niagara University W
Nyack College W
Pace University W
Pace University: Pleasantville/Briarcliff W
Roberts Wesleyan College W
St. Francis College W
St. John's University W
Siena College W
SUNY
　University at Albany W
　University at Binghamton W
　University at Buffalo W
　University at Stony Brook M,W
Syracuse University W

## North Carolina
Appalachian State University W
Barton College M,W
Belmont Abbey College M,W
Brevard College W
Campbell University W
Catawba College W
Chowan University W
Davidson College W
Duke University W
East Carolina University M,W
Elizabeth City State University W
Elon University W
Fayetteville State University W
Gardner-Webb University W
Guilford Technical Community College W
High Point University W
Johnson C. Smith University W
Laurel University W
Lees-McRae College M,W
Lenoir Community College W
Lenoir-Rhyne University W
Livingstone College W
Louisburg College W
Mars Hill University W
Montreat College W
North Carolina Agricultural and Technical State
　University W
North Carolina Central University W
North Carolina State University W
Pitt Community College W
Queens University of Charlotte W
St. Andrews University W
Saint Augustine's University W
Shaw University W
Southeastern Community College W
University of Mount Olive W
University of North Carolina
　Asheville W
　Chapel Hill W
　Charlotte W
　Greensboro W
　Wilmington W
Wake Forest University W
Western Carolina University W
Wingate University W
Winston-Salem State University W

## North Dakota
Bismarck State College W
Dakota College at Bottineau W
Dickinson State University W
Lake Region State College W
Mayville State University W
Minot State University W
North Dakota State College of Science W
North Dakota State University W
University of Jamestown W
University of Mary W
University of North Dakota W
Valley City State University W
Williston State College W

## Ohio
Ashland University W
Bowling Green State University W
Cedarville University W
Central State University W
Clark State Community College W
Cleveland State University W
Columbus State Community College W
Kent State University W
Lake Erie College W
Lakeland Community College W
Lourdes University M,W
Malone University W
Miami University
　Oxford W
Mount Vernon Nazarene University W
Notre Dame College W
Ohio Dominican University W
Ohio State University
　Columbus Campus M,W

Ohio University W
Owens Community College W
Shawnee State University W
Sinclair Community College W
Southern State Community College W
Tiffin University W
University of Akron W
University of Cincinnati W
University of Dayton W
University of Findlay W
University of Rio Grande W
University of Toledo W
Urbana University W
Ursuline College W
Walsh University W
Wright State University W
Xavier University W
Youngstown State University W

**Oklahoma**
Bacone College W
Cameron University W
East Central University W
Langston University W
Mid-America Christian University W
Northeastern Oklahoma Agricultural and
    Mechanical College W
Northwestern Oklahoma State University M,W
Oklahoma Baptist University W
Oklahoma City University W
Oklahoma Panhandle State University W
Oklahoma Wesleyan University W
Oral Roberts University W
Redlands Community College W
St. Gregory's University W
Seminole State College W
Southeastern Oklahoma State University W
Southern Nazarene University W
University of Central Oklahoma W
University of Oklahoma W
University of Tulsa W

**Oregon**
Blue Mountain Community College W
Chemeketa Community College W
Clackamas Community College W
Concordia University W
Corban University W
Eastern Oregon University W
Linn-Benton Community College W
Mt. Hood Community College W
Multnomah University W
Northwest Christian University W
Oregon Institute of Technology W
Oregon State University W
Portland State University W
Southern Oregon University W
Southwestern Oregon Community College W
Treasure Valley Community College W
University of Oregon W
University of Portland W
Warner Pacific College W
Western Oregon University W

**Pennsylvania**
Bucknell University W
California University of Pennsylvania W
Carlow University W
Chestnut Hill College W
Cheyney University of Pennsylvania W
Duquesne University W
East Stroudsburg University of Pennsylvania W
Edinboro University
    of Pennsylvania W
Gannon University W
Harcum College W
Holy Family University W
Indiana University of Pennsylvania W
Kutztown University of Pennsylvania W
La Salle University W
Lackawanna College W
Lehigh University W
Lock Haven University of Pennsylvania W

Mercyhurst University W
Millersville University of Pennsylvania W
Penn State
    Lehigh Valley M
    University Park M,W
Philadelphia University W
Point Park University W
Robert Morris University W
St. Francis University M,W
Seton Hill University W
Shippensburg University of Pennsylvania W
Slippery Rock University of Pennsylvania W
Temple University W
University of Pittsburgh W
University of the Sciences W
Villanova University W
West Chester University of Pennsylvania W

**Puerto Rico**
Bayamon Central University M,W
Inter American University of Puerto Rico
    Aguadilla Campus M,W
    Bayamon Campus M,W
    Metropolitan Campus M,W
    Ponce Campus M,W
    San German Campus M,W
Turabo University M,W
Universidad del Este M,W
Universidad Metropolitana M,W
Universidad Politecnica de Puerto Rico M,W
University of Puerto Rico
    Arecibo M,W
    Bayamon University College M,W
    Carolina Regional College M,W
    Cayey University College M,W
    Humacao M,W
    Mayaguez M,W
    Ponce M,W
    Utuado M,W
University of the Sacred Heart M,W

**Rhode Island**
Bryant University W
Community College of Rhode Island W
University of Rhode Island W

**South Carolina**
Anderson University W
Charleston Southern University W
The Citadel W
Claflin University W
Clemson University W
Coastal Carolina University W
Coker College M,W
College of Charleston W
Columbia College W
Converse College W
Erskine College W
Francis Marion University W
Furman University W
Lander University W
Limestone College M,W
Morris College W
Newberry College W
North Greenville University M,W
Presbyterian College W
South Carolina State University W
Southern Wesleyan University W
Spartanburg Methodist College W
University of South Carolina
    Aiken W
    Columbia W
    Upstate W
Winthrop University W
Wofford College W

**South Dakota**
Augusta University
    Augustana University W
Black Hills State University W
Dakota State University W
Dakota Wesleyan University W
Mount Marty College W
Northern State University W

South Dakota School of Mines and Technology
    W
South Dakota State University W
University of Sioux Falls W

**Tennessee**
Austin Peay State University W
Belmont University W
Bethel University W
Bryan College
    Dayton W
Carson-Newman University W
Christian Brothers University W
Cumberland University W
East Tennessee State University W
Freed-Hardeman University W
Hiwassee College W
King University M,W
Lane College W
Lee University W
LeMoyne-Owen College W
Lincoln Memorial University W
Lipscomb University W
Martin Methodist College W
Middle Tennessee State University W
Milligan College W
Tennessee Technological University W
Tennessee Wesleyan College W
Trevecca Nazarene University W
Tusculum College W
Union University W
University of Memphis W
University of Tennessee
    Chattanooga W
    Knoxville W
    Martin W

**Texas**
Abilene Christian University W
Angelo State University W
Baylor University W
Blinn College W
Brookhaven College W
Clarendon College W
Dallas Baptist University W
Frank Phillips College W
Hill College W
Houston Baptist University W
Jarvis Christian College M,W
Lamar University W
Laredo Community College W
Lee College W
Lubbock Christian University W
Midland College W
Midwestern State University W
North Central Texas College W
Panola College W
Paris Junior College W
Prairie View A&M University M,W
Ranger College W
Rice University W
St. Edward's University W
St. Mary's University W
Sam Houston State University W
San Jacinto College W
Southern Methodist University W
Southwestern Assemblies of God University W
Stephen F. Austin State University W
Tarleton State University W
Temple College W
Texas A&M University W
Texas A&M University
    Commerce W
    Corpus Christi W
Texas Christian University W
Texas Southern University W
Texas State University W
Texas Tech University W
Texas Wesleyan University W
Texas Woman's University W
Tyler Junior College W
University of Houston W
University of North Texas W

University of St. Thomas W
University of Texas
    Arlington W
    Austin W
    Brownsville W
    Pan American W
    of the Permian Basin W
    San Antonio W
University of the Incarnate Word W
Vernon College W
Wayland Baptist University W
West Texas A&M University W
Western Texas College W
Wharton County Junior College W
Wiley College W

**Utah**
Brigham Young University M,W
Dixie State University W
Salt Lake Community College W
Snow College W
Southern Utah University W
University of Utah W
Utah State University W
Utah Valley University W
Weber State University W
Westminster College W

**Virginia**
Bluefield College M,W
College of William and Mary W
George Mason University M,W
Hampton University W
James Madison University W
Liberty University W
Norfolk State University W
Radford University W
University of Virginia W
University of Virginia's College at Wise W
Virginia Commonwealth University W
Virginia Polytechnic Institute and State
    University W
Virginia State University W
Virginia Union University W

**Washington**
Big Bend Community College W
Central Washington University W
Centralia College W
Clark College W
Columbia Basin College W
Eastern Washington University W
Edmonds Community College W
Everett Community College W
Evergreen State College W
Gonzaga University W
Grays Harbor College W
Green River Community College W
Highline College W
Lower Columbia College W
Northwest University W
Olympic College W
Pierce College W
Saint Martin's University W
Seattle University W
Shoreline Community College W
Skagit Valley College W
Spokane Community College W
Tacoma Community College W
University of Washington W
Walla Walla Community College W
Washington State University W
Western Washington University W
Whatcom Community College W
Yakima Valley Community College W

**West Virginia**
Alderson-Broaddus University M,W
Bluefield State College W
Concord University W
Davis and Elkins College W
Fairmont State University W
Glenville State College W
Marshall University W

Ohio Valley University W
Salem International University W
Shepherd University W
University of Charleston W
West Liberty University W
West Virginia State University W
West Virginia University W
West Virginia University Institute of
    Technology W
West Virginia Wesleyan College W
Wheeling Jesuit University W

**Wisconsin**
Cardinal Stritch University M,W
Marquette University W
Silver Lake College of the Holy Family W
University of Wisconsin
    Green Bay W
    Madison W
    Milwaukee M,W
    Parkside W
Viterbo University W

**Wyoming**
Casper College W
Central Wyoming College W
Eastern Wyoming College W
Laramie County Community College W
Northwest College W
Sheridan College W
University of Wyoming W
Western Wyoming Community College W

# Water polo

**Arizona**
Arizona State University W

**California**
California Baptist University M,W
California State University
    Bakersfield W
    Long Beach M,W
    Monterey Bay W
Concordia University Irvine M,W
Fresno Pacific University M,W
Grossmont College M,W
Loyola Marymount University M,W
Pepperdine University M
San Diego State University W
San Jose State University M,W
Santa Clara University M,W
Sonoma State University W
Stanford University M,W
University of California
    Berkeley M,W
    Davis M,W
    Irvine M,W
University of Southern California M,W
University of the Pacific M,W

**District of Columbia**
George Washington University M

**Florida**
Florida Atlantic University W.

**Hawaii**
University of Hawaii
    Manoa W

**Illinois**
McKendree University M,W

**Indiana**
Indiana University
    Bloomington W

**Michigan**
University of Michigan W

**New York**
City University of New York
    Queens College M

Fordham University M
Hartwick College W
Iona College M,W
Marist College W
St. Francis College M,W
Siena College W
Wagner College W

**Pennsylvania**
Gannon University M,W
La Salle University M,W
Mercyhurst University M,W

**Puerto Rico**
University of Puerto Rico
    Mayaguez M

**Virginia**
Virginia Military Institute M,W

# Weight lifting

**New York**
United States Merchant Marine Academy
    M,W

**Puerto Rico**
Inter American University of Puerto Rico
    Aguadilla Campus M,W
    Ponce Campus M,W
    San German Campus M,W
Turabo University M,W
Universidad del Este M
Universidad Metropolitana M,W
University of Puerto Rico
    Arecibo M,W
    Carolina Regional College M,W
    Cayey University College M,W
    Humacao M,W
    Utuado M,W

# Wrestling

**Arizona**
Arizona State University M
Embry-Riddle Aeronautical University
    Prescott Campus M
Grand Canyon University M

**Arkansas**
Ouachita Baptist University M

**California**
California Baptist University M
California Polytechnic State University: San
    Luis Obispo M
California State University
    Bakersfield M
Fresno City College M
Menlo College M,W
Stanford University M
University of California
    Los Angeles M,W

**Colorado**
Adams State University M
Colorado Mesa University M
Colorado School of Mines M
Colorado State University
    Pueblo M
Otero Junior College M
University of Northern Colorado M
Western State Colorado University M

**Connecticut**
Sacred Heart University M

**District of Columbia**
American University M

**Georgia**
Brewton-Parker College M
Darton College M
Emmanuel College M,W
Life University M,W
Shorter University M
Truett-McConnell College M

**Idaho**
Boise State University M
North Idaho College M

**Illinois**
City Colleges of Chicago
    Wilbur Wright College M,W
Lincoln College M
McKendree University M,W
Northern Illinois University M
Northwestern University M
Southern Illinois University Edwardsville M
University of Illinois
    Urbana-Champaign M

**Indiana**
Ancilla College M
Calumet College of St. Joseph M
Indiana Institute of Technology M
Indiana University
    Bloomington M
Purdue University M
University of Indianapolis M

**Iowa**
Briar Cliff University M
Ellsworth Community College M
Graceland University M
Grand View University M
Iowa Central Community College M
Iowa State University M
Iowa Western Community College M
North Iowa Area Community College M
Northwestern College M
University of Iowa M
University of Northern Iowa M
Upper Iowa University M
Waldorf University M,W
William Penn University M

**Kansas**
Baker University M
Benedictine College M
Bethany College M
Colby Community College M
Fort Hays State University M
Kansas Wesleyan University M
Labette Community College M
Neosho County Community College M
Newman University M
Northwest Kansas Technical College M,W
Pratt Community College M

**Kentucky**
Campbellsville University M,W
Lindsey Wilson College M
St. Catharine College M
University of the Cumberlands M,W

**Maryland**
University of Maryland
    College Park M

**Massachusetts**
American International College M

**Michigan**
Central Michigan University M
Davenport University M
Eastern Michigan University M
Michigan State University M

Muskegon Community College M
University of Michigan M

**Minnesota**
Minnesota State University
    Mankato M
    Moorhead M
Saint Cloud State University M
Southwest Minnesota State University M
University of Minnesota
    Twin Cities M

**Missouri**
Hannibal-LaGrange University M
Lindenwood University M
Maryville University of Saint Louis M
Missouri Baptist University M,W
Missouri Valley College M,W
University of Central Missouri M
University of Missouri
    Columbia M

**Montana**
Montana State University
    Northern M
University of Great Falls M

**Nebraska**
Chadron State College M
Concordia University M
Hastings College M
Midland University M,W
University of Nebraska
    Kearney M
    Lincoln M
York College M

**New Jersey**
Rider University M
Rutgers, The State University of New Jersey
    New Brunswick/Piscataway Campus M

**New York**
Hofstra University M
Long Island University
    LIU Post M
Niagara County Community College M
SUNY
    University at Binghamton M
    University at Buffalo M

**North Carolina**
Appalachian State University M
Belmont Abbey College M
Campbell University M
Davidson College M
Duke University M
Gardner-Webb University M
North Carolina State University M
University of North Carolina
    Chapel Hill M

**North Dakota**
Dickinson State University M
North Dakota State University M
University of Jamestown M,W
University of Mary M

**Ohio**
Ashland University M
Cleveland State University M
Kent State University M
Lake Erie College M
Notre Dame College M
Ohio State University
    Columbus Campus M
Ohio University M
Tiffin University M
University of Findlay M

**Oklahoma**
Bacone College M
Northeastern Oklahoma Agricultural and
    Mechanical College M
Oklahoma City University M,W

Oklahoma State University M
University of Central Oklahoma M
University of Oklahoma M

### Oregon
Clackamas Community College M
Oregon State University M
Southern Oregon University M
Southwestern Oregon Community College M

### Pennsylvania
Bloomsburg University of Pennsylvania M
Bucknell University M
Clarion University of Pennsylvania M
Drexel University M
East Stroudsburg University of Pennsylvania M
Edinboro University
    of Pennsylvania M
Gannon University M
Kutztown University of Pennsylvania M
Lehigh University M
Lock Haven University of Pennsylvania M
Mercyhurst University M
Millersville University of Pennsylvania M
Penn State
    University Park M
Seton Hill University M
Shippensburg University of Pennsylvania M
University of Pittsburgh M
University of Pittsburgh
    Johnstown M

### Puerto Rico
Inter American University of Puerto Rico
    Aguadilla Campus M
    Bayamon Campus M
    Ponce Campus M,W
University of Puerto Rico
    Arecibo M
    Bayamon University College M
    Humacao M
    Mayaguez M
    Utuado M
University of the Sacred Heart M

### South Carolina
Anderson University M
The Citadel M
Coker College M
Limestone College M
Newberry College M
Spartanburg Methodist College M

### South Dakota
Augusta University
    Augustana University M
Dakota Wesleyan University M
Northern State University M
South Dakota State University M

### Tennessee
Carson-Newman University M
Cumberland University M
King University M,W
University of Tennessee
    Chattanooga M

### Texas
Wayland Baptist University M,W

### Utah
Utah Valley University M

### Virginia
George Mason University M
Old Dominion University M
University of Virginia M
Virginia Military Institute M
Virginia Polytechnic Institute and State
    University M

### Washington
Highline College M

### West Virginia
Alderson-Broaddus University M
West Liberty University M
West Virginia University M

### Wisconsin
University of Wisconsin
    Madison M
    Parkside M

### Wyoming
Northwest College M
University of Wyoming M
Western Wyoming Community College M

# Music/drama scholarships

## Alabama
Alabama State University
Bevill State Community College
Birmingham-Southern College
Central Alabama Community College
Chattahoochee Valley Community College
Enterprise State Community College
Faulkner State Community College
Faulkner University
Gadsden State Community College
Huntingdon College
Jacksonville State University
Jefferson State Community College
Judson College
Lurleen B. Wallace Community College
Northeast Alabama Community College
Northwest-Shoals Community College
Samford University
Selma University
Shelton State Community College
Snead State Community College
Talladega College
Troy University
University of Alabama
University of Alabama
    Birmingham
    Huntsville
University of Mobile
University of Montevallo
University of North Alabama
University of South Alabama
University of West Alabama
Wallace State Community College at
    Hanceville

## Alaska
Alaska Pacific University
University of Alaska
    Anchorage
    Fairbanks
    Southeast

## Arizona
Arizona Christian University
Arizona State University
Arizona Western College
Eastern Arizona College
Grand Canyon University
Northern Arizona University
Northland Pioneer College
Pima Community College
South Mountain Community College
University of Arizona

## Arkansas
Arkansas Northeastern College
Arkansas State University
Arkansas State University
    Beebe
Arkansas Tech University
Black River Technical College
Central Baptist College
Crowley's Ridge College
Ecclesia College
Harding University
Henderson State University
Hendrix College
John Brown University
Lyon College
National Park College
Northwest Arkansas Community College
Ouachita Baptist University
Philander Smith College
Phillips Community College of the University
    of Arkansas

Southern Arkansas University
University of Arkansas
    Fort Smith
    Little Rock
    Monticello
    Pine Bluff
University of Central Arkansas
University of the Ozarks
Williams Baptist College

## California
American Jewish University
Azusa Pacific University
Bethesda University of California
Biola University
California Baptist University
California Institute of Integral Studies
California Institute of the Arts
California Lutheran University
California Polytechnic State University: San
    Luis Obispo
California State University
    Bakersfield
    Chico
    Dominguez Hills
    East Bay
    Fresno
    Fullerton
    Long Beach
    Stanislaus
Chapman University
College of the Canyons
College of the Desert
Concordia University Irvine
Dominican University of California
El Camino College
Fresno Pacific University
Holy Names University
Hope International University
Irvine Valley College
La Sierra University
Loyola Marymount University
Marymount California University
The Master's College
Mendocino College
Mills College
Mount Saint Mary's University
Mount San Jacinto College
Notre Dame de Namur University
Occidental College
Pacific Union College
Pepperdine University
Point Loma Nazarene University
Providence Christian College
Riverside City College
St. Mary's College of California
San Diego Christian College
San Diego State University
San Francisco Conservatory of Music
San Jose State University
Santa Clara University
Santa Rosa Junior College
Shasta Bible College and Graduate School
Simpson University
Sonoma State University
University of California
    Riverside
    San Diego
    Santa Cruz
University of La Verne
University of Redlands
University of San Diego
University of Southern California
University of the Pacific

Vanguard University of Southern California
Westmont College
Whittier College
William Jessup University
Yuba College

## Colorado
Adams State University
Arapahoe Community College
Colorado Christian University
Colorado Mesa University
Colorado School of Mines
Colorado State University
Colorado State University
    Pueblo
Community College of Aurora
Fort Lewis College
Naropa University
Northeastern Junior College
Pueblo Community College
Regis University
University of Colorado
    Boulder
    Denver
University of Denver
University of Northern Colorado
Western State Colorado University

## Connecticut
Fairfield University
Sacred Heart University
University of Bridgeport
University of Connecticut
University of Hartford
Western Connecticut State University

## Delaware
University of Delaware

## District of Columbia
American University
Catholic University of America
George Washington University
Howard University

## Florida
Ave Maria University
Baptist College of Florida
Barry University
Bethune-Cookman University
Chipola College
College of Central Florida
Daytona State College
Eckerd College
Flagler College
Florida Agricultural and Mechanical University
Florida Atlantic University
Florida College
Florida Gateway College
Florida Gulf Coast University
Florida Institute of Technology
Florida International University
Florida Southern College
Florida SouthWestern State College
Florida State College at Jacksonville
Florida State University
Gulf Coast State College
Hillsborough Community College
Indian River State College
Jacksonville University
Johnson University: Florida
Lynn University
Miami Dade College
North Florida Community College
Nova Southeastern University
Palm Beach Atlantic University
Pensacola State College
Rollins College
St. Petersburg College
Santa Fe College
Seminole State College of Florida
South Florida State College
Southeastern University
State College of Florida, Manatee-Sarasota

Stetson University
Tallahassee Community College
University of Florida
University of Miami
University of North Florida
University of South Florida
University of South Florida
    Sarasota-Manatee
University of Tampa
University of West Florida
Warner University

## Georgia
Agnes Scott College
Albany State University
Andrew College
Armstrong State University
Augusta University
Berry College
Brenau University
Clark Atlanta University
Clayton State University
Columbus State University
Covenant College
Darton College
Emmanuel College
Emory University
Fort Valley State University
Georgia College and State University
Georgia Institute of Technology
Georgia Perimeter College
Georgia Southern University
Georgia Southwestern State University
Georgia State University
Gordon State College
Kennesaw State University
LaGrange College
Mercer University
Middle Georgia State College
Morehouse College
Oglethorpe University
Paine College
Piedmont College
Reinhardt University
Savannah College of Art and Design
Savannah State University
Shorter University
Spelman College
Truett-McConnell College
University of North Georgia
University of West Georgia
Valdosta State University
Wesleyan College
Young Harris College

## Hawaii
Brigham Young University-Hawaii
Hawaii Pacific University
University of Hawaii
    Hilo
    Manoa

## Idaho
Boise Bible College
Boise State University
Brigham Young University-Idaho
Idaho State University
Lewis-Clark State College
North Idaho College
Northwest Nazarene University
University of Idaho

## Illinois
Augustana College
Aurora University
Benedictine University
Black Hawk College
Bradley University
Carl Sandburg College
College of DuPage
College of Lake County
Columbia College Chicago
Concordia University Chicago
Danville Area Community College

DePaul University
Eastern Illinois University
Elgin Community College
Elmhurst College
Eureka College
Harper College
Illinois Central College
Illinois College
Illinois State University
Illinois Valley Community College
Illinois Wesleyan University
Judson University
Kishwaukee College
Knox College
Lake Forest College
Lewis University
Lincoln College
Loyola University Chicago
McHenry County College
McKendree University
Millikin University
Monmouth College
Moody Bible Institute
North Central College
North Park University
Northeastern Illinois University
Northern Illinois University
Northwestern University
Oakton Community College
Olivet Nazarene University
Parkland College
Quincy University
Richland Community College
Robert Morris University: Chicago
Rockford University
Saint Xavier University
Shawnee Community College
South Suburban College of Cook County
Southeastern Illinois College
Southern Illinois University Carbondale
Southern Illinois University Edwardsville
Southwestern Illinois College
Spoon River College
Trinity Christian College
Trinity International University
University of Illinois
    Springfield
    Urbana-Champaign
University of St. Francis
VanderCook College of Music
Waubonsee Community College
Western Illinois University
Wheaton College

**Indiana**
Anderson University
Ball State University
Bethel College
Butler University
Calumet College of St. Joseph
DePauw University
Franklin College
Goshen College
Grace College
Hanover College
Huntington University
Indiana State University
Indiana University
    Bloomington
    Purdue University Fort Wayne
    Southeast
Indiana Wesleyan University
Manchester University
Marian University
Purdue University
Saint Joseph's College
St. Mary-of-the-Woods College
Saint Mary's College
Taylor University
Trine University
University of Evansville
University of Indianapolis
University of Saint Francis

University of Southern Indiana
Valparaiso University
Vincennes University
Wabash College

**Iowa**
Briar Cliff University
Buena Vista University
Central College
Clarke University
Coe College
Cornell College
Dordt College
Drake University
Ellsworth Community College
Emmaus Bible College
Faith Baptist Bible College and Theological
    Seminary
Graceland University
Grand View University
Iowa Central Community College
Iowa State University
Iowa Wesleyan College
Iowa Western Community College
Kirkwood Community College
Luther College
Morningside College
Mount Mercy University
Northwestern College
St. Ambrose University
Simpson College
Southwestern Community College
University of Dubuque
University of Iowa
University of Northern Iowa
Waldorf University
Wartburg College
Western Iowa Tech Community College
William Penn University

**Kansas**
Allen County Community College
Baker University
Barclay College
Benedictine College
Bethany College
Bethel College
Butler Community College
Central Christian College of Kansas
Coffeyville Community College
Colby Community College
Cowley County Community College
Dodge City Community College
Emporia State University
Fort Hays State University
Friends University
Garden City Community College
Hesston College
Highland Community College
Hutchinson Community College
Independence Community College
Kansas City Kansas Community College
Kansas State University
Kansas Wesleyan University
Manhattan Christian College
McPherson College
MidAmerica Nazarene University
Neosho County Community College
Newman University
Ottawa University
Pittsburg State University
Pratt Community College
Southwestern College
Sterling College
Tabor College
University of Kansas
University of St. Mary
Washburn University

**Kentucky**
Asbury University
Ashland Community and Technical College
Bellarmine University

Brescia University
Campbellsville University
Centre College
Eastern Kentucky University
Georgetown College
Kentucky Christian University
Kentucky Mountain Bible College
Kentucky State University
Kentucky Wesleyan College
Morehead State University
Murray State University
Northern Kentucky University
Owensboro Community and Technical College
Thomas More College
Transylvania University
Union College
University of Kentucky
University of Louisville
University of the Cumberlands
Western Kentucky University

**Louisiana**
Bossier Parish Community College
Centenary College of Louisiana
Delgado Community College
Dillard University
Grambling State University
Louisiana College
Louisiana State University and Agricultural and
    Mechanical College
Louisiana Tech University
Loyola University New Orleans
McNeese State University
Nicholls State University
Northwestern State University
Southeastern Louisiana University
Tulane University
University of Louisiana at Monroe
University of New Orleans
Xavier University of Louisiana

**Maine**
University of Maine
University of Maine
    Augusta
    Farmington
University of Southern Maine

**Maryland**
Bowie State University
Goucher College
Hood College
Johns Hopkins University: Peabody
    Conservatory of Music
Montgomery College
Notre Dame of Maryland University
Salisbury University
Towson University
University of Maryland
    Baltimore County
    College Park
    Eastern Shore
Washington College

**Massachusetts**
Anna Maria College
Assumption College
Berklee College of Music
Boston Conservatory
Boston University
Bristol Community College
Cape Cod Community College
College of the Holy Cross
Dean College
Emerson College
Endicott College
Gordon College
Hampshire College
Holyoke Community College
Massachusetts College of Liberal Arts
Merrimack College
Mount Wachusett Community College
New England Conservatory of Music
North Shore Community College

Northpoint Bible College
Springfield College
University of Massachusetts
    Amherst
    Lowell
Western New England University

**Michigan**
Adrian College
Albion College
Alma College
Alpena Community College
Andrews University
Aquinas College
Calvin College
Central Michigan University
Concordia University
Cornerstone University
Eastern Michigan University
Ferris State University
Gogebic Community College
Grace Bible College
Grand Valley State University
Great Lakes Christian College
Hillsdale College
Hope College
Kalamazoo College
Kellogg Community College
Kuyper College
Macomb Community College
Madonna University
Marygrove College
Michigan State University
Monroe County Community College
Mott Community College
Northern Michigan University
Northwestern Michigan College
Oakland University
Olivet College
Rochester College
Saginaw Valley State University
Schoolcraft College
Southwestern Michigan College
Spring Arbor University
University of Michigan
University of Michigan
    Dearborn
    Flint
Wayne State University
Western Michigan University

**Minnesota**
Augsburg College
Bemidji State University
Bethany Lutheran College
Bethel University
College of St. Benedict
College of St. Scholastica
Concordia College: Moorhead
Concordia University St. Paul
Crossroads College
Crown College
Gustavus Adolphus College
Hamline University
Martin Luther College
McNally Smith College of Music
Minnesota State Community and Technical
    College
Minnesota State University
    Mankato
    Moorhead
Normandale Community College
North Central University
Saint Cloud State University
St. John's University
St. Mary's University of Minnesota
St. Olaf College
Southwest Minnesota State University
University of Minnesota
    Crookston
    Duluth
    Twin Cities
University of Northwestern - St. Paul

University of St. Thomas
Winona State University

## Mississippi
Belhaven University
Blue Mountain College
Copiah-Lincoln Community College
Delta State University
East Central Community College
East Mississippi Community College
Hinds Community College
Itawamba Community College
Jackson State University
Meridian Community College
Millsaps College
Mississippi College
Mississippi Gulf Coast Community College
Mississippi State University
Mississippi University for Women
Northeast Mississippi Community College
Pearl River Community College
Rust College
Tougaloo College
University of Mississippi
University of Southern Mississippi
William Carey University

## Missouri
Avila University
Calvary Bible College and Theological
    Seminary
Central Methodist University
College of the Ozarks
Columbia College
Cottey College
Crowder College
Culver-Stockton College
Drury University
East Central College
Fontbonne University
Hannibal-LaGrange University
Harris-Stowe State University
Jefferson College
Lincoln University
Lindenwood University
Maryville University of Saint Louis
Mineral Area College
Missouri Baptist University
Missouri Southern State University
Missouri State University
Missouri University of Science and Technology
Missouri Western State University
Moberly Area Community College
Northwest Missouri State University
Park University
Rockhurst University
St. Charles Community College
St. Louis Community College
Saint Louis University
Southeast Missouri State University
Southwest Baptist University
State Fair Community College
Stephens College
Truman State University
University of Central Missouri
University of Missouri
    Columbia
    Kansas City
    St. Louis
Webster University
Westminster College
William Jewell College
William Woods University

## Montana
Carroll College
Dawson Community College
Montana State University
Montana State University
    Billings
Montana Tech of the University of Montana
University of Great Falls
University of Montana

## Nebraska
Central Community College
Chadron State College
College of Saint Mary
Concordia University
Creighton University
Doane College
Grace University
Hastings College
Mid-Plains Community College
Midland University
Nebraska Wesleyan University
Northeast Community College
Peru State College
University of Nebraska
    Kearney
    Lincoln
    Omaha
Wayne State College
Western Nebraska Community College
York College

## Nevada
Truckee Meadows Community College
University of Nevada
    Las Vegas

## New Hampshire
Colby-Sawyer College
Keene State College
New England College
Plymouth State University
Saint Anselm College
Southern New Hampshire University
University of New Hampshire

## New Jersey
Caldwell University
The College of New Jersey
Drew University
Kean University
Rowan University
Rutgers, The State University of New Jersey
    Camden Campus
    New Brunswick/Piscataway Campus
    Newark Campus
Seton Hall University
Stevens Institute of Technology
Stockton University
William Paterson University of New Jersey

## New Mexico
Eastern New Mexico University
New Mexico Highlands University
New Mexico Junior College
New Mexico Military Institute
New Mexico State University
Santa Fe University of Art and Design
University of New Mexico
Western New Mexico University

## New York
Adelphi University
Alfred University
Canisius College
City University of New York
    Brooklyn College
    City College
    College of Staten Island
College of New Rochelle
College of Saint Rose
Concordia College
Corning Community College
Eastman School of Music of the University of
    Rochester
Eugene Lang College The New School for
    Liberal Arts
Five Towns College
Hartwick College
Hobart and William Smith Colleges
Hofstra University
Houghton College
Ithaca College
Jamestown Community College

Juilliard School
Long Island University
    LIU Brooklyn
    LIU Post
Manhattan School of Music
Manhattanville College
Mannes College The New School for Music
Marist College
Marymount Manhattan College
Molloy College
Monroe Community College
Nazareth College
Niagara University
Nyack College
Pace University
Pace University: Pleasantville/Briarcliff
Parsons The New School for Design
Rensselaer Polytechnic Institute
Roberts Wesleyan College
The Sage Colleges
Saint Bonaventure University
St. John's University
St. Thomas Aquinas College
Skidmore College
Suffolk County Community College
SUNY
    College at Brockport
    College at Cortland
    College at Fredonia
    College at Geneseo
    College at New Paltz
    College at Oneonta
    College at Plattsburgh
    College at Potsdam
    College at Purchase
    College of Technology at Alfred
    University at Binghamton
    University at Buffalo
    University at Stony Brook
Syracuse University
University of Rochester
Wagner College

## North Carolina
Appalachian State University
Barton College
Brevard College
Campbell University
Catawba College
Catawba Valley Community College
Chowan University
College of the Albemarle
Davidson College
Duke University
East Carolina University
Elon University
Fayetteville State University
Gardner-Webb University
Greensboro College
High Point University
Isothermal Community College
Johnson C. Smith University
Lees-McRae College
Lenoir-Rhyne University
Livingstone College
Louisburg College
Meredith College
Methodist University
Mid-Atlantic Christian University
Montreat College
North Carolina Central University
Pfeiffer University
Queens University of Charlotte
St. Andrews University
Saint Augustine's University
Salem College
Shaw University
Southeastern Community College
University of Mount Olive
University of North Carolina
    Asheville
    Chapel Hill
    Charlotte

Greensboro
Pembroke
School of the Arts
Wilmington
Vance-Granville Community College
Wake Forest University
Western Carolina University
Wilkes Community College
William Peace University
Wingate University

## North Dakota
Bismarck State College
Dickinson State University
Lake Region State College
Mayville State University
Minot State University
North Dakota State College of Science
North Dakota State University
Trinity Bible College
University of Jamestown
University of Mary
Valley City State University
Williston State College

## Ohio
Ashland University
Baldwin Wallace University
Bluffton University
Bowling Green State University
Bowling Green State University: Firelands
    College
Capital University
Case Western Reserve University
Cedarville University
Central State University
Cincinnati Christian University
Cleveland Institute of Music
Cleveland State University
College of Wooster
Cuyahoga Community College
Defiance College
Denison University
God's Bible School and College
Heidelberg University
Hiram College
Kent State University
Kent State University
    Ashtabula
    East Liverpool
    Geauga
    Salem
    Stark
    Trumbull
    Tuscarawas
Kenyon College
Lake Erie College
Lakeland Community College
Malone University
Marietta College
Miami University
    Oxford
Mount St. Joseph University
Mount Vernon Nazarene University
Muskingum University
Oberlin College
Ohio Northern University
Ohio State University
    Agricultural Technical Institute
    Columbus Campus
    Lima Campus
    Mansfield Campus
    Marion Campus
    Newark Campus
Ohio University
Ohio Wesleyan University
Otterbein University
Pontifical College Josephinum
Sinclair Community College
Southern State Community College
Tiffin University
University of Akron
University of Akron: Wayne College

University of Cincinnati
University of Dayton
University of Findlay
University of Mount Union
University of Rio Grande
University of Toledo
Urbana University
Walsh University
Wittenberg University
Wright State University
Wright State University: Lake Campus
Xavier University

## Oklahoma
Cameron University
Carl Albert State College
Eastern Oklahoma State College
Langston University
Mid-America Christian University
Northeastern Oklahoma Agricultural and
    Mechanical College
Northeastern State University
Northern Oklahoma College
Northwestern Oklahoma State University
Oklahoma Baptist University
Oklahoma Christian University
Oklahoma City Community College
Oklahoma City University
Oklahoma Panhandle State University
Oklahoma State University
Oklahoma Wesleyan University
Oral Roberts University
Rogers State University
St. Gregory's University
Seminole State College
Southeastern Oklahoma State University
Southwestern Christian University
Southwestern Oklahoma State University
University of Central Oklahoma
University of Oklahoma
University of Science and Arts of Oklahoma
University of Tulsa
Western Oklahoma State College

## Oregon
Blue Mountain Community College
Clackamas Community College
Concordia University
Corban University
Eastern Oregon University
George Fox University
Lane Community College
Lewis & Clark College
Linfield College
Linn-Benton Community College
New Hope Christian College
Northwest Christian University
Pacific University
Portland State University
Southwestern Oregon Community College
Treasure Valley Community College
University of Oregon
University of Portland
Warner Pacific College
Western Oregon University
Willamette University

## Pennsylvania
Albright College
Arcadia University
Berks Technical Institute
Bloomsburg University of Pennsylvania
Bucknell University
Bucks County Community College
Cairn University
California University of Pennsylvania
Carnegie Mellon University
Cedar Crest College
Chatham University
Clarion University of Pennsylvania
Delaware Valley University
DeSales University
Drexel University

Duquesne University
East Stroudsburg University of Pennsylvania
Eastern University
Edinboro University
    Pennsylvania
Elizabethtown College
Gannon University
Geneva College
Gettysburg College
Grove City College
Harrisburg Area Community College
Immaculata University
Indiana University of Pennsylvania
Juniata College
Kutztown University of Pennsylvania
Lancaster Bible College
Lebanon Valley College
Lehigh University
Lincoln University
Lock Haven University of Pennsylvania
Lycoming College
Mansfield University of Pennsylvania
Marywood University
Mercyhurst University
Messiah College
Moravian College
Mount Aloysius College
Muhlenberg College
Northampton Community College
Point Park University
St. Francis University
Saint Joseph's University
St. Vincent College
Seton Hill University
Slippery Rock University of Pennsylvania
Summit University
Susquehanna University
Temple University
Thiel College
University of the Arts
University of Valley Forge
Ursinus College
Valley Forge Military College
West Chester University of Pennsylvania
Westminster College
Widener University
Wilkes University
York College of Pennsylvania

## Puerto Rico
Colegio de Cinematografía, Artes y Televisión
Humacao Community College
Inter American University of Puerto Rico
    Ponce Campus
Pontifical Catholic University of Puerto Rico
Universidad Politecnica de Puerto Rico
University of Puerto Rico
    Aguadilla
    Humacao
    Mayaguez

## Rhode Island
Providence College
Rhode Island College
University of Rhode Island

## South Carolina
Allen University
Anderson University
The Citadel
Clemson University
Coker College
College of Charleston
Columbia College
Columbia International University
Converse College
Erskine College
Francis Marion University
Furman University
Lander University
Limestone College
Morris College
Newberry College

North Greenville University
Presbyterian College
Southern Wesleyan University
University of South Carolina
    Aiken
    Columbia
Winthrop University
Wofford College

## South Dakota
Augusta University
    Augustana University
Dakota State University
Dakota Wesleyan University
Mount Marty College
Northern State University
South Dakota State University
University of Sioux Falls
University of South Dakota

## Tennessee
Austin Peay State University
Belmont University
Bethel University
Bryan College
    Dayton
Carson-Newman University
Christian Brothers University
Cumberland University
Dyersburg State Community College
East Tennessee State University
Fisk University
Freed-Hardeman University
Jackson State Community College
Johnson University
King University
Lee University
LeMoyne-Owen College
Lincoln Memorial University
Lipscomb University
Martin Methodist College
Maryville College
Milligan College
Motlow State Community College
Northeast State Community College
Pellissippi State Community College
Rhodes College
Roane State Community College
Southern Adventist University
Southwest Tennessee Community College
Tennessee Technological University
Tennessee Wesleyan College
Trevecca Nazarene University
Union University
University of Memphis
University of Tennessee
    Chattanooga
    Knoxville
    Martin
Vanderbilt University
Volunteer State Community College
Walters State Community College
Welch College

## Texas
Abilene Christian University
Angelina College
Angelo State University
Austin College
Baylor University
Brazosport College
Brookhaven College
Cisco College
Clarendon College
College of the Mainland
Collin County Community College District
Concordia University Texas
Dallas Baptist University
Frank Phillips College
Galveston College
Grayson College
Hardin-Simmons University
Hill College

Houston Baptist University
Howard College
Howard Payne University
Huston-Tillotson University
Jacksonville College
Kilgore College
Lee College
Lubbock Christian University
McMurry University
Midland College
Midwestern State University
Odessa College
Our Lady of the Lake University of San
    Antonio
Panola College
Paris Junior College
Ranger College
Rice University
Richland College
St. Edward's University
St. Mary's University
Sam Houston State University
San Jacinto College
Schreiner University
South Plains College
Southern Methodist University
Southwestern Adventist University
Southwestern Christian College
Southwestern University
Stephen F. Austin State University
Sul Ross State University
Tarleton State University
Temple College
Texarkana College
Texas A&M International University
Texas A&M University
Texas A&M University
    Commerce
    Corpus Christi
    Texarkana
Texas Christian University
Texas College
Texas Lutheran University
Texas State University
Texas Tech University
Texas Wesleyan University
Texas Woman's University
Trinity University
Tyler Junior College
University of Dallas
University of Houston
University of Mary Hardin-Baylor
University of St. Thomas
University of Texas
    Arlington
    Austin
    Brownsville
    El Paso
    the Permian Basin
    San Antonio
    Tyler
University Of Texas Rio Grande Valley
University of the Incarnate Word
Vernon College
Victoria College
Wayland Baptist University
West Texas A&M University
Western Texas College
Wharton County Junior College

## Utah
Brigham Young University
Dixie State University
Salt Lake Community College
Snow College
Southern Utah University
University of Utah
Utah State University
Weber State University
Westminster College

## Vermont
Bennington College
Castleton State College

Goddard College
Johnson State College
Landmark College
Saint Michael's College
University of Vermont

## Virginia
Averett University
Bluefield College
Bridgewater College
Christopher Newport University
College of William and Mary
Emory & Henry College
George Mason University
Hampden-Sydney College
Hampton University
Hollins University
James Madison University
Liberty University
Longwood University
Lynchburg College
Marymount University
Norfolk State University
Old Dominion University
Patrick Henry College
Radford University
Randolph College
Roanoke College
Shenandoah University
Southern Virginia University
Sweet Briar College
University of Mary Washington
University of Richmond
University of Virginia
University of Virginia's College at Wise
Virginia Commonwealth University
Virginia Military Institute
Virginia Polytechnic Institute and State
    University
Virginia State University

## Washington
Big Bend Community College
Central Washington University
Centralia College
Clark College
Cornish College of the Arts
Eastern Washington University
Everett Community College
Gonzaga University
Grays Harbor College
Northwest University
Pacific Lutheran University
Pierce College
Saint Martin's University
Seattle Pacific University
Seattle University
Trinity Lutheran College
University of Puget Sound
University of Washington
University of Washington Bothell
University of Washington Tacoma
Walla Walla Community College
Walla Walla University
Washington State University
Western Washington University
Whitman College
Whitworth University

## West Virginia
Alderson-Broaddus University
Bethany College
Davis and Elkins College
Fairmont State University
Glenville State College
Marshall University
Ohio Valley University
Shepherd University
University of Charleston
West Liberty University
West Virginia University
West Virginia University Institute of
    Technology

West Virginia Wesleyan College
Wheeling Jesuit University

## Wisconsin
Beloit College
Cardinal Stritch University
Carroll University
Carthage College
Concordia University Wisconsin
Edgewood College
Lawrence University
Marquette University
Mount Mary University
Northland College
Ripon College
St. Norbert College
Silver Lake College of the Holy Family
University of Wisconsin
    Baraboo/Sauk County
    Eau Claire
    Fond du Lac
    Green Bay
    La Crosse
    Madison
    Manitowoc
    Milwaukee
    Oshkosh
    Parkside
    Richland
    River Falls
    Rock County
    Sheboygan
    Stevens Point
    Superior
    Waukesha
    Whitewater
Viterbo University
Wisconsin Lutheran College

## Wyoming
Casper College
Central Wyoming College
Eastern Wyoming College
Laramie County Community College
Northwest College
Sheridan College
University of Wyoming
Western Wyoming Community College

# ROTC scholarships

## Air Force ROTC

### Alabama
Alabama State University
Auburn University
Auburn University at Montgomery
Birmingham-Southern College
Bishop State Community College
Faulkner University
Huntingdon College
Jefferson State Community College
Marion Military Institute
Miles College
Samford University
Shelton State Community College
Spring Hill College
Stillman College
Troy University
Tuskegee University
University of Alabama
University of Alabama
 Birmingham
University of Mobile
University of Montevallo
University of South Alabama
University of West Alabama

### Alaska
Alaska Pacific University
University of Alaska
 Anchorage

### Arizona
Arizona Christian University
Arizona State University
Coconino County Community College
DeVry University
 Phoenix
Embry-Riddle Aeronautical University
 Prescott Campus
Estrella Mountain Community College
GateWay Community College
Mesa Community College
Northern Arizona University
Phoenix College
Pima Community College
University of Arizona
Yavapai College

### Arkansas
John Brown University
Northwest Arkansas Community College
University of Arkansas
University of Arkansas
 Fort Smith

### California
Azusa Pacific University
Biola University
California Baptist University
California Institute of Technology
California Lutheran University
California Maritime Academy
California State University
 Dominguez Hills
 Fresno
 Los Angeles
 Northridge
 Sacramento
 San Bernardino
 San Marcos
Canada College
Chabot College
Chapman University

Claremont McKenna College
College of the Sequoias
Cuyamaca College
De Anza College
Dominican University of California
Foothill College
Fresno City College
Harvey Mudd College
Holy Names University
Irvine Valley College
Los Angeles Mission College
Loyola Marymount University
The Master's College
Menlo College
Mission College
Mount San Antonio College
National University
Notre Dame de Namur University
Occidental College
Ohlone College
Pepperdine University
Pitzer College
Point Loma Nazarene University
Pomona College
Riverside City College
Sacramento City College
St. Mary's College of California
Samuel Merritt University
San Diego Christian College
San Diego City College
San Diego State University
San Francisco State University
San Jose State University
Santa Clara University
Scripps College
Solano Community College
Sonoma State University
Stanford University
University of California
 Berkeley
 Davis
 Irvine
 Los Angeles
 Riverside
 Santa Barbara
 Santa Cruz
University of Redlands
University of San Diego
University of San Francisco
University of Southern California
University of the Pacific
Vanguard University of Southern California
West Coast University: Orange County
West Valley College
Westmont College
William Jessup University

### Colorado
Arapahoe Community College
Colorado Christian University
Colorado School of Mines
Colorado State University
Metropolitan State University of Denver
Red Rocks Community College
Regis University
University of Colorado
 Boulder
 Denver
University of Denver
University of Northern Colorado

### Connecticut
Capital Community College
Central Connecticut State University
Eastern Connecticut State University

Fairfield University
Quinnipiac University
Sacred Heart University
Southern Connecticut State University
Tunxis Community College
University of Connecticut
University of Hartford
University of New Haven
Wesleyan University
Western Connecticut State University
Yale University

### Delaware
Delaware State University
University of Delaware
Wilmington University

### District of Columbia
American University
Catholic University of America
George Washington University
Georgetown University
Howard University
Trinity Washington University
University of the District of Columbia

### Florida
Barry University
Bethune-Cookman University
Broward College
Daytona State College
Eastern Florida State College
Eckerd College
Embry-Riddle Aeronautical University
Florida Agricultural and Mechanical University
Florida Atlantic University
Florida College
Florida International University
Florida Southern College
Florida State University
Lynn University
Miami Dade College
Saint Leo University
Santa Fe College
Tallahassee Community College
University of Central Florida
University of Florida
University of Miami
University of South Florida
University of Tampa
University of West Florida
Valencia College

### Georgia
Agnes Scott College
Clayton State University
Emory University
Georgia Institute of Technology
Georgia State University
Kennesaw State University
Morehouse College
Oglethorpe University
Oxford College of Emory University
Spelman College
University of Georgia
University of West Georgia
Valdosta State University

### Hawaii
Brigham Young University-Hawaii
Chaminade University of Honolulu
Hawaii Pacific University
University of Hawaii
 Honolulu Community College
 Manoa
 West Oahu

### Idaho
Lewis-Clark State College
University of Idaho

### Illinois
Elmhurst College
Illinois Institute of Technology

John A. Logan College
Lewis University
Lincoln Land Community College
Loyola University Chicago
McKendree University
North Central College
North Park University
Northeastern Illinois University
Northwestern University
Parkland College
Saint Xavier University
Shawnee Community College
Shimer College
Southern Illinois University Carbondale
Southern Illinois University Edwardsville
Southwestern Illinois College
University of Chicago
University of Illinois
 Chicago
 Urbana-Champaign
Wheaton College

### Indiana
Bethel College
Butler University
DePauw University
Holy Cross College
Indiana State University
Indiana University
 Bloomington
 Purdue University Indianapolis
 South Bend
 Southeast
Purdue University
Rose-Hulman Institute of Technology
St. Mary-of-the-Woods College
Saint Mary's College
Trine University
University of Notre Dame
Valparaiso University
Vincennes University

### Iowa
Coe College
Drake University
Grand View University
Hawkeye Community College
Iowa State University
Iowa Western Community College
University of Iowa

### Kansas
Baker University
Kansas State University
Manhattan Christian College
MidAmerica Nazarene University
University of Kansas
University of St. Mary
Washburn University

### Kentucky
Asbury University
Bellarmine University
Centre College
Georgetown College
Kentucky State University
Midway College
Northern Kentucky University
Spalding University
Thomas More College
Transylvania University
University of Kentucky
University of Louisville
Western Kentucky University

### Louisiana
Dillard University
Grambling State University
Louisiana State University and Agricultural and
 Mechanical College
Louisiana Tech University
Loyola University New Orleans
Our Lady of the Lake College

Southern University
New Orleans
Southern University and Agricultural and
Mechanical College
Tulane University
University of Holy Cross
University of New Orleans
Xavier University of Louisiana

**Maine**
University of Maine
Augusta
University of Southern Maine

**Maryland**
Anne Arundel Community College
Bowie State University
Goucher College
Johns Hopkins University
Loyola University Maryland
Prince George's Community College
Salisbury University
Stevenson University
Towson University
University of Maryland
Baltimore County
College Park

**Massachusetts**
American International College
Amherst College
Anna Maria College
Assumption College
Bay Path University
Becker College
Bentley University
Boston College
Boston University
Brandeis University
Bridgewater State University
Clark University
College of the Holy Cross
Eastern Nazarene College
Elms College
Emmanuel College
Harvard College
Holyoke Community College
Massachusetts Institute of Technology
MCPHS University
Merrimack College
Middlesex Community College
Mount Holyoke College
Nichols College
Northeastern University
Pine Manor College
Quinsigamond Community College
Salem State University
Smith College
Springfield College
Tufts University
University of Massachusetts
Amherst
Boston
Lowell
Wellesley College
Wentworth Institute of Technology
Western New England University
Westfield State University
Williams College
Worcester Polytechnic Institute
Worcester State University

**Michigan**
Central Michigan University
Concordia University
Eastern Michigan University
Finlandia University
Lansing Community College
Lawrence Technological University
Michigan State University
Michigan Technological University
Oakland University
Olivet College
Spring Arbor University

University of Michigan
University of Michigan
Dearborn
Wayne State University

**Minnesota**
Anoka-Ramsey Community College
Augsburg College
Bethel University
Century College
College of St. Scholastica
Concordia College: Moorhead
Concordia University St. Paul
Hamline University
Inver Hills Community College
Macalester College
Minnesota State University
Moorhead
North Central University
North Hennepin Community College
St. Catherine University
University of Minnesota
Crookston
Duluth
Twin Cities
University of Northwestern - St. Paul
University of St. Thomas

**Mississippi**
Belhaven University
East Mississippi Community College
Jackson State University
Millsaps College
Mississippi College
Mississippi State University
Mississippi University for Women
Northwest Mississippi Community College
University of Mississippi
University of Southern Mississippi
William Carey University

**Missouri**
Central Methodist University
Columbia College
Fontbonne University
Harris-Stowe State University
Lincoln University
Lindenwood University
Missouri University of Science and Technology
Saint Louis University
Southeast Missouri State University
Stephens College
University of Central Missouri
University of Missouri
Columbia
St. Louis
Washington University in St. Louis
Webster University
Westminster College

**Montana**
Montana State University

**Nebraska**
Bellevue University
Clarkson College
College of Saint Mary
Concordia University
Creighton University
Doane College
Grace University
Nebraska Methodist College of Nursing and
Allied Health
Nebraska Wesleyan University
University of Nebraska
Lincoln
Medical Center
Omaha
York College

**Nevada**
Nevada State College
University of Nevada
Las Vegas

**New Hampshire**
Colby-Sawyer College
Daniel Webster College
Franklin Pierce University
Granite State College
Keene State College
New England College
Plymouth State University
Rivier University
University of New Hampshire

**New Jersey**
Brookdale Community College
The College of New Jersey
Fairleigh Dickinson University
College at Florham
Metropolitan Campus
Felician University
Kean University
Monmouth University
New Jersey City University
New Jersey Institute of Technology
Princeton University
Ramapo College of New Jersey
Raritan Valley Community College
Rutgers, The State University of New Jersey
Camden Campus
New Brunswick/Piscataway Campus
Newark Campus
Saint Peter's University
Stevens Institute of Technology
Union County College
William Paterson University of New Jersey

**New Mexico**
Central New Mexico Community College
Dona Ana Community College of New Mexico
State University
National American University
Albuquerque
New Mexico State University
New Mexico State University
Alamogordo
University of New Mexico

**New York**
Adelphi University
Barnard College
Cazenovia College
City University of New York
Queens College
Clarkson University
College of Mount St. Vincent
College of Saint Rose
Columbia University
Columbia University
School of General Studies
Cornell University
Dowling College
Elmira College
Fordham University
Hamilton College
Hobart and William Smith Colleges
Hudson Valley Community College
Iona College
Ithaca College
Le Moyne College
Manhattan College
Maria College
Mercy College
Mesivta Torah Vodaath Seminary
Mohawk Valley Community College
Monroe Community College
Nazareth College
New York Institute of Technology
New York University
Onondaga Community College
Pace University
Rensselaer Polytechnic Institute
Roberts Wesleyan College
Rochester Institute of Technology
The Sage Colleges
St. Francis College

St. John Fisher College
St. Lawrence University
St. Thomas Aquinas College
Schenectady County Community College
Siena College
Skidmore College
SUNY
College at Brockport
College at Cortland
College at Geneseo
College at Old Westbury
College at Oswego
College at Potsdam
College of Agriculture and Technology at
Morrisville
College of Environmental Science and
Forestry
College of Technology at Canton
Farmingdale State College
University at Albany
University at Binghamton
University at Stony Brook
SUNY Polytechnic Institute
Syracuse University
Union College
United States Merchant Marine Academy
University of Rochester
Utica College
Vaughn College of Aeronautics and Technology

**North Carolina**
Belmont Abbey College
Bennett College for Women
Catawba College
Catawba Valley Community College
Davidson College
Duke University
East Carolina University
Elon University
Fayetteville State University
Gardner-Webb University
Greensboro College
High Point University
Meredith College
Methodist University
North Carolina Agricultural and Technical State
University
North Carolina Central University
North Carolina State University
Randolph Community College
University of Mount Olive
University of North Carolina
Chapel Hill
Charlotte
Greensboro
Pembroke
William Peace University
Wingate University

**North Dakota**
Mayville State University
North Dakota State University
University of North Dakota

**Ohio**
Ashland University
Baldwin Wallace University
Bowling Green State University
Capital University
Case Western Reserve University
Cedarville University
Central State University
Cleveland Institute of Art
Cleveland State University
Columbus State Community College
Cuyahoga Community College
Franciscan University of Steubenville
Heidelberg University
Hiram College
Hocking College
John Carroll University
Kent State University
Kent State University

East Liverpool
Salem
Stark
Trumbull
Tuscarawas
Lourdes University
Miami University
Hamilton
Middletown
Oxford
Mount Carmel College of Nursing
Mount St. Joseph University
Ohio Christian University
Ohio Northern University
Ohio State University
Agricultural Technical Institute
Columbus Campus
Lima Campus
Mansfield Campus
Marion Campus
Newark Campus
Ohio University
Ohio University
Lancaster Campus
Ohio Wesleyan University
Otterbein University
Sinclair Community College
Tiffin University
University of Akron
University of Akron: Wayne College
University of Cincinnati
University of Cincinnati
Blue Ash College
University of Dayton
University of Findlay
University of Mount Union
University of Toledo
Wilberforce University
Wittenberg University
Wright State University
Xavier University
Youngstown State University

**Oklahoma**
Langston University
Northeastern Oklahoma Agricultural and
Mechanical College
Oklahoma Baptist University
Oklahoma Christian University
Oklahoma City University
Oklahoma State University
Oral Roberts University
Rose State College
St. Gregory's University
Southern Nazarene University
University of Oklahoma
University of Tulsa

**Oregon**
Concordia University
Corban University
George Fox University
Linfield College
Linn-Benton Community College
Oregon State University
Pacific University
Portland State University
University of Oregon
University of Portland
Warner Pacific College
Western Oregon University
Willamette University

**Pennsylvania**
Bloomsburg University of Pennsylvania
Bryn Athyn College
Bryn Mawr College
Cabrini College
Cairn University
Carlow University
Carnegie Mellon University
Chatham University
Drexel University

Duquesne University
East Stroudsburg University of Pennsylvania
Eastern University
Keystone College
King's College
La Roche College
La Salle University
Lincoln University
Marywood University
Misericordia University
Neumann University
Penn State
Abington
Altoona
Brandywine
Hazleton
New Kensington
University Park
Wilkes-Barre
Worthington Scranton
Point Park University
Robert Morris University
Rosemont College
Saint Joseph's University
St. Vincent College
Swarthmore College
Temple University
Thomas Jefferson University
University of Pennsylvania
University of Pittsburgh
University of Pittsburgh
Greensburg
University of Scranton
University of the Sciences
Valley Forge Military College
Villanova University
Washington & Jefferson College
West Chester University of Pennsylvania
Widener University
Wilkes University

**Puerto Rico**
Bayamon Central University
Inter American University of Puerto Rico
Aguadilla Campus
Bayamon Campus
Fajardo Campus
Metropolitan Campus
San German Campus
Pontifical Catholic University of Puerto Rico
Turabo University
Universidad Metropolitana
Universidad Politecnica de Puerto Rico
University of Puerto Rico
Mayaguez
Rio Piedras

**Rhode Island**
Brown University

**South Carolina**
Anderson University
Benedict College
Charleston Southern University
The Citadel
Claflin University
Clemson University
College of Charleston
Southern Wesleyan University
Tri-County Technical College
University of South Carolina
Columbia
Salkehatchie
Winthrop University

**South Dakota**
Augusta University
Augustana University
Dakota State University
South Dakota State University
University of Sioux Falls

**Tennessee**
Austin Peay State University
Belmont University

Christian Brothers University
LeMoyne-Owen College
Lipscomb University
Middle Tennessee State University
Rhodes College
Southwest Tennessee Community College
Tennessee State University
Tennessee Technological University
Tennessee Wesleyan College
University of Memphis
University of Tennessee
Knoxville
Vanderbilt University
Welch College

**Texas**
Alvin Community College
Angelo State University
Austin Community College
Baylor University
College of the Mainland
Collin County Community College District
Concordia University Texas
Dallas Baptist University
Houston Baptist University
Houston Community College System
Huston-Tillotson University
Lamar University
Lone Star College System
Lubbock Christian University
McLennan Community College
Midwestern State University
North Central Texas College
Prairie View A&M University
Rice University
St. Edward's University
St. Mary's University
San Antonio College
San Jacinto College
Southern Methodist University
Tarrant County College
Texas A&M University
Texas A&M University
Commerce
Texas Christian University
Texas Lutheran University
Texas State University
Texas Tech University
Texas Wesleyan University
Texas Woman's University
Trinity University
University of Dallas
University of Houston
University of Houston
Downtown
Victoria
University of Mary Hardin-Baylor
University of North Texas
University of St. Thomas
University of Texas
Arlington
Austin
Dallas
San Antonio
University of the Incarnate Word
Wayland Baptist University
Weatherford College

**Utah**
Brigham Young University
LDS Business College
Salt Lake Community College
University of Utah
Utah State University
Utah Valley University
Weber State University
Westminster College

**Vermont**
Lyndon State College
Norwich University
Saint Michael's College

**Virginia**
George Mason University
James Madison University
Liberty University
Mary Baldwin College
Piedmont Virginia Community College
University of Virginia
Virginia Military Institute
Virginia Polytechnic Institute and State
University

**Washington**
Central Washington University
Clark College
Highline College
Saint Martin's University
Seattle Pacific University
Seattle University
South Puget Sound Community College
Spokane Community College
University of Washington
University of Washington Bothell
University of Washington Tacoma
Washington State University

**West Virginia**
Fairmont State University
Shepherd University
West Virginia University

**Wisconsin**
Alverno College
Carroll University
Carthage College
Edgewood College
Maranathan Baptist University
Maranatha Baptist University
Marquette University
Milwaukee School of Engineering
University of Wisconsin
Madison
Milwaukee
Stout
Superior
Whitewater
Wisconsin Lutheran College

**Wyoming**
Laramie County Community College
University of Wyoming

## Army ROTC

**Alabama**
Alabama Agricultural and Mechanical
University
Alabama State University
Auburn University
Auburn University at Montgomery
Birmingham-Southern College
Bishop State Community College
Faulkner University
Gadsden State Community College
Huntingdon College
Jacksonville State University
Jefferson State Community College
Judson College
Marion Military Institute
Miles College
Samford University
Shelton State Community College
Southern Union State Community College
Spring Hill College
Stillman College
Talladega College
Troy University
Tuskegee University
University of Alabama
University of Alabama
Birmingham
Huntsville

University of Mobile
University of Montevallo
University of North Alabama
University of South Alabama

**Alaska**
University of Alaska
    Anchorage
    Fairbanks

**Arizona**
Arizona State University
Coconino County Community College
Embry-Riddle Aeronautical University
    Prescott Campus
GateWay Community College
Grand Canyon University
Mesa Community College
Northern Arizona University
Paradise Valley Community College
Phoenix College
Pima Community College
Southwest University of Visual Arts
University of Arizona
Yavapai College

**Arkansas**
Arkansas State University
Arkansas State University
    Beebe
Arkansas Tech University
Central Baptist College
College of the Ouachitas
Henderson State University
Hendrix College
John Brown University
Northwest Arkansas Community College
Ouachita Baptist University
University of Arkansas
University of Arkansas
    Fort Smith
    Little Rock
    Monticello
    Pine Bluff
University of Central Arkansas
Williams Baptist College

**California**
Azusa Pacific University
Biola University
California Baptist University
California Institute of Technology
California Lutheran University
California Polytechnic State University: San
    Luis Obispo
California State Polytechnic University:
    Pomona
California State University
    Dominguez Hills
    Fresno
    Fullerton
    Long Beach
    Los Angeles
    Northridge
    Sacramento
    San Bernardino
    San Marcos
Canada College
Chabot College
Chapman University
City College of San Francisco
Claremont McKenna College
De Anza College
Diablo Valley College
Foothill College
Fresno City College
Harvey Mudd College
Holy Names University
Hope International University
Los Angeles Mission College
Loyola Marymount University
The Master's College
Mills College
National University

Occidental College
Pepperdine University
Pitzer College
Point Loma Nazarene University
Pomona College
Riverside City College
Sacramento City College
St. Mary's College of California
Samuel Merritt University
San Diego Christian College
San Diego City College
San Diego State University
San Francisco State University
San Jose State University
Santa Clara University
Scripps College
Sonoma State University
Stanford University
University of California
    Berkeley
    Davis
    Irvine
    Los Angeles
    Riverside
    Santa Barbara
    Santa Cruz
University of La Verne
University of Redlands
University of San Diego
University of San Francisco
University of Southern California
Vanguard University of Southern California
West Valley College
Westmont College
Whittier College

**Colorado**
Arapahoe Community College
Colorado Christian University
Colorado College
Colorado School of Mines
Colorado State University
Colorado State University
    Pueblo
Colorado Technical University
Community College of Denver
Johnson & Wales University
    Denver
Metropolitan State University of Denver
Red Rocks Community College
Regis University
University of Colorado
    Boulder
    Colorado Springs
    Denver
University of Denver
University of Northern Colorado

**Connecticut**
Capital Community College
Central Connecticut State University
Eastern Connecticut State University
Fairfield University
Quinnipiac University
Southern Connecticut State University
Trinity College
Tunxis Community College
University of Bridgeport
University of Connecticut
University of Hartford
University of New Haven
Western Connecticut State University
Yale University

**Delaware**
Delaware State University
University of Delaware
Wesley College
Wilmington University

**District of Columbia**
American University
Catholic University of America
George Washington University

Georgetown University
Howard University
Trinity Washington University
University of the District of Columbia

**Florida**
Barry University
Bethune-Cookman University
Broward College
Daytona State College
Eastern Florida State College
Eckerd College
Embry-Riddle Aeronautical University
Florida Agricultural and Mechanical University
Florida Atlantic University
Florida College
Florida Institute of Technology
Florida International University
Florida Memorial University
Florida Southern College
Florida State College at Jacksonville
Florida State University
Hillsborough Community College
Jacksonville University
Miami Dade College
Northwest Florida State College
Palm Beach Atlantic University
Pasco-Hernando State College
Pensacola State College
Polk State College
Saint Leo University
Santa Fe College
Seminole State College of Florida
Southeastern University
Stetson University
Tallahassee Community College
University of Central Florida
University of Florida
University of Miami
University of North Florida
University of South Florida
University of South Florida
    Saint Petersburg
University of Tampa
University of West Florida
Valencia College

**Georgia**
Agnes Scott College
Albany State University
Armstrong State University
Augusta University
Clark Atlanta University
Clayton State University
Columbus State University
Covenant College
East Georgia State College
Emory University
Fort Valley State University
Georgia College and State University
Georgia Gwinnett College
Georgia Institute of Technology
Georgia Military College
Georgia Southern University
Georgia State University
Kennesaw State University
Mercer University
Middle Georgia State College
Morehouse College
Oglethorpe University
Oxford College of Emory University
Paine College
Savannah State University
Spelman College
University of Georgia
University of North Georgia
Wesleyan College

**Hawaii**
Brigham Young University-Hawaii
Chaminade University of Honolulu
Hawaii Pacific University
University of Hawaii

Hilo
Honolulu Community College
Manoa
West Oahu
Windward Community College

**Idaho**
Boise State University
Brigham Young University-Idaho
College of Idaho
Idaho State University
Lewis-Clark State College
North Idaho College
Northwest Nazarene University
University of Idaho

**Illinois**
Aurora University
Benedictine University
Bradley University
Carl Sandburg College
Chicago State University
DePaul University
Eastern Illinois University
Elmhurst College
Illinois Institute of Technology
Illinois State University
Illinois Wesleyan University
John A. Logan College
Judson University
Kankakee Community College
Kaskaskia College
Kishwaukee College
Lewis and Clark Community College
Lewis University
Lincoln Land Community College
Loyola University Chicago
McKendree University
Monmouth College
North Central College
North Park University
Northeastern Illinois University
Northern Illinois University
Northwestern University
Olivet Nazarene University
Parkland College
Robert Morris University: Chicago
Shawnee Community College
Shimer College
Southern Illinois University Carbondale
Southern Illinois University Edwardsville
Southwestern Illinois College
Spoon River College
University of Chicago
University of Illinois
    Chicago
    Urbana-Champaign
University of St. Francis
Waubonsee Community College
Western Illinois University
Wheaton College

**Indiana**
Ball State University
Bethel College
Butler University
DePauw University
Franklin College
Holy Cross College
Indiana Institute of Technology
Indiana State University
Indiana University
    Bloomington
    Kokomo
    Northwest
    Purdue University Fort Wayne
    Purdue University Indianapolis
    South Bend
    Southeast
Indiana Wesleyan University
Marian University
Purdue University

Purdue University
    Calumet
Rose-Hulman Institute of Technology
St. Mary-of-the-Woods College
Saint Mary's College
University of Evansville
University of Indianapolis
University of Notre Dame
University of Southern Indiana
Valparaiso University
Vincennes University

### Iowa
Allen College
Briar Cliff University
Buena Vista University
Clarke University
Coe College
Drake University
Grand View University
Hawkeye Community College
Iowa State University
Iowa Western Community College
Loras College
Morningside College
University of Dubuque
University of Iowa
University of Northern Iowa

### Kansas
Baker University
Benedictine College
Haskell Indian Nations University
Kansas State University
Manhattan Christian College
MidAmerica Nazarene University
Pittsburg State University
University of Kansas
University of St. Mary
Washburn University

### Kentucky
Asbury University
Bellarmine University
Campbellsville University
Centre College
Eastern Kentucky University
Elizabethtown Community and Technical
    College
Georgetown College
Jefferson Community and Technical College
Kentucky State University
Kentucky Wesleyan College
Midway College
Morehead State University
Murray State University
Northern Kentucky University
Owensboro Community and Technical College
Spalding University
Thomas More College
Transylvania University
University of Kentucky
University of Louisville
Western Kentucky University

### Louisiana
Dillard University
Grambling State University
Louisiana College
Louisiana State University
    Alexandria
    Shreveport
Louisiana State University and Agricultural and
    Mechanical College
Louisiana Tech University
Loyola University New Orleans
Northwestern State University
Our Lady of the Lake College
Southeastern Louisiana University
Southern University
    New Orleans
Southern University and Agricultural and
    Mechanical College
Tulane University

University of Holy Cross
University of Louisiana at Lafayette
University of Louisiana at Monroe
University of New Orleans
Xavier University of Louisiana

### Maine
Colby College
Eastern Maine Community College
Husson University
Maine Maritime Academy
Saint Joseph's College of Maine
University of Maine
University of Maine
    Augusta
University of New England
University of Southern Maine

### Maryland
Allegany College of Maryland
Anne Arundel Community College
Bowie State University
Capitol Technology University
Coppin State University
Goucher College
Hood College
Johns Hopkins University
Loyola University Maryland
Maryland Institute College of Art
McDaniel College
Morgan State University
Mount St. Mary's University
Notre Dame of Maryland University
Prince George's Community College
Salisbury University
Stevenson University
Towson University
University of Baltimore
University of Maryland
    Baltimore County
    College Park

### Massachusetts
American International College
Amherst College
Assumption College
Babson College
Bay Path University
Becker College
Bentley University
Boston College
Boston University
Brandeis University
Bridgewater State University
Clark University
College of the Holy Cross
Curry College
Eastern Nazarene College
Elms College
Emmanuel College
Endicott College
Fisher College
Fitchburg State University
Gordon College
Hampshire College
Harvard College
Holyoke Community College
Massachusetts Institute of Technology
Massachusetts Maritime Academy
MCPHS University
Middlesex Community College
Mount Holyoke College
Mount Wachusett Community College
Nichols College
Northeastern University
Pine Manor College
Quinsigamond Community College
Regis College
Roxbury Community College
Salem State University
Simmons College
Smith College
Springfield College

Stonehill College
Suffolk University
Tufts University
University of Massachusetts
    Amherst
    Boston
    Dartmouth
    Lowell
Wellesley College
Wentworth Institute of Technology
Western New England University
Westfield State University
Wheaton College
Worcester Polytechnic Institute
Worcester State University

### Michigan
Adrian College
Alma College
Aquinas College
Baker College
    Jackson
Calvin College
Central Michigan University
Concordia University
Cornerstone University
Davenport University
Eastern Michigan University
Ferris State University
Finlandia University
Grace Bible College
Hope College
Kalamazoo College
Kuyper College
Lansing Community College
Madonna University
Michigan State University
Michigan Technological University
Northern Michigan University
Olivet College
Spring Arbor University
University of Michigan
University of Michigan
    Dearborn
    Flint
Washtenaw Community College
Wayne State University
Western Michigan University

### Minnesota
Anoka-Ramsey Community College
Augsburg College
Bethany Lutheran College
Bethel University
College of St. Benedict
Concordia College: Moorhead
Concordia University St. Paul
Crown College
Gustavus Adolphus College
Hamline University
Inver Hills Community College
Macalester College
Minnesota State University
    Mankato
    Moorhead
North Central University
North Hennepin Community College
St. Catherine University
Saint Cloud State University
St. John's University
St. Mary's University of Minnesota
University of Minnesota
    Twin Cities
University of Northwestern - St. Paul
University of St. Thomas
Winona State University

### Mississippi
Alcorn State University
Belhaven University
Delta State University
East Mississippi Community College
Hinds Community College

Jackson State University
Jones County Junior College
Millsaps College
Mississippi College
Mississippi State University
Mississippi University for Women
Mississippi Valley State University
Northeast Mississippi Community College
Tougaloo College
University of Mississippi
University of Southern Mississippi
William Carey University

### Missouri
Avila University
Calvary Bible College and Theological
    Seminary
Central Methodist University
College of the Ozarks
Columbia College
Drury University
Evangel University
Fontbonne University
Harris-Stowe State University
Lincoln University
Lindenwood University
Maryville University of Saint Louis
Metropolitan Community College - Kansas City
Missouri Baptist University
Missouri Southern State University
Missouri State University
Missouri University of Science and Technology
Missouri Valley College
Missouri Western State University
Northwest Missouri State University
Park University
Research College of Nursing
Rockhurst University
Saint Louis University
Southwest Baptist University
State Fair Community College
Stephens College
Truman State University
University of Central Missouri
University of Missouri
    Columbia
    Kansas City
    St. Louis
Washington University in St. Louis
Webster University
Wentworth Military Junior College
Westminster College
William Jewell College
William Woods University

### Montana
Carroll College
Montana State University
Montana State University
    Billings
Rocky Mountain College
University of Montana

### Nebraska
Bellevue University
BryanLGH College of Health Sciences
Chadron State College
Clarkson College
College of Saint Mary
Concordia University
Creighton University
Doane College
Nebraska Wesleyan University
University of Nebraska
    Kearney
    Lincoln
    Medical Center
    Omaha
Wayne State College
York College

### Nevada
College of Southern Nevada
Truckee Meadows Community College

University of Nevada
Las Vegas
Reno

**New Hampshire**
Colby-Sawyer College
Daniel Webster College
Dartmouth College
Franklin Pierce University
Granite State College
Keene State College
New England College
Plymouth State University
Rivier University
Saint Anselm College
Southern New Hampshire University
University of New Hampshire

**New Jersey**
Berkeley College
Bloomfield College
Brookdale Community College
Caldwell University
The College of New Jersey
Fairleigh Dickinson University
College at Florham
Metropolitan Campus
Felician University
Kean University
Middlesex County College
Monmouth University
New Jersey City University
New Jersey Institute of Technology
Princeton University
Ramapo College of New Jersey
Raritan Valley Community College
Rider University
Rowan University
Rutgers, The State University of New Jersey
Camden Campus
New Brunswick/Piscataway Campus
Newark Campus
Saint Peter's University
Seton Hall University
Stevens Institute of Technology

**New Mexico**
Central New Mexico Community College
Dona Ana Community College of New Mexico
State University
New Mexico Military Institute
New Mexico State University
Southwest University of Visual Arts
University of New Mexico

**New York**
Adelphi University
Alfred University
Barnard College
Canisius College
Cazenovia College
City University of New York
Baruch College
City College
Lehman College
Queens College
York College
Clarkson University
Colgate University
College of Mount St. Vincent
College of New Rochelle
College of Saint Rose
Columbia University
Columbia University
School of General Studies
Cooper Union for the Advancement of Science
and Art
Cornell University
Daemen College
Dowling College
D'Youville College
Elmira College
Erie Community College
Fordham University

Genesee Community College
Hamilton College
Herkimer County Community College
Hilbert College
Hobart and William Smith Colleges
Hofstra University
Houghton College
Hudson Valley Community College
Iona College
Ithaca College
The King's College
Le Moyne College
Long Island University
LIU Brooklyn
LIU Post
Manhattan College
Manhattanville College
Maria College
Marist College
Medaille College
Mercy College
Mohawk Valley Community College
Molloy College
Monroe College
Monroe Community College
Mount Saint Mary College
Nazareth College
New York Institute of Technology
New York University
Niagara County Community College
Niagara University
Onondaga Community College
Pace University
Pratt Institute
Rensselaer Polytechnic Institute
Roberts Wesleyan College
Rochester Institute of Technology
The Sage Colleges
Saint Bonaventure University
St. Francis College
St. John Fisher College
St. John's University
St. Lawrence University
Siena College
Skidmore College
SUNY
College at Brockport
College at Buffalo
College at Cortland
College at Fredonia
College at Geneseo
College at Old Westbury
College at Oswego
College at Plattsburgh
College at Potsdam
College of Agriculture and Technology at
Morrisville
College of Environmental Science and
Forestry
College of Technology at Alfred
College of Technology at Canton
Farmingdale State College
Maritime College
University at Albany
University at Binghamton
University at Buffalo
University at Stony Brook
Upstate Medical University
SUNY Polytechnic Institute
Syracuse University
Talmudical Seminary Oholei Torah
Union College
United States Merchant Marine Academy
University of Rochester
Utica College
Vaughn College of Aeronautics and Technology
Wagner College

**North Carolina**
Appalachian State University
Belmont Abbey College
Bennett College for Women
Campbell University

Catawba College
Davidson College
Duke University
East Carolina University
Elizabeth City State University
Elon University
Fayetteville State University
Gardner-Webb University
Greensboro College
High Point University
Johnson and Wales University
Charlotte
Livingstone College
Meredith College
Methodist University
Mid-Atlantic Christian University
North Carolina Agricultural and Technical State
University
North Carolina Central University
North Carolina State University
North Carolina Wesleyan College
Pfeiffer University
Pitt Community College
Saint Augustine's University
Salem College
Shaw University
University of North Carolina
Chapel Hill
Charlotte
Greensboro
Pembroke
Wake Forest University
Wake Technical Community College
William Peace University
Wingate University
Winston-Salem State University

**North Dakota**
Mayville State University
North Dakota State University
University of North Dakota

**Ohio**
Ashland University
Baldwin Wallace University
Bowling Green State University
Capital University
Case Western Reserve University
Cedarville University
Central State University
Cincinnati State Technical and Community
College
Cleveland Institute of Art
Cleveland State University
Columbus State Community College
Denison University
DeVry University
Columbus
Franciscan University of Steubenville
Franklin University
Heidelberg University
Hiram College
Hocking College
John Carroll University
Kent State University
Kent State University
East Liverpool
Salem
Stark
Trumbull
Tuscarawas
Lourdes University
Miami University
Oxford
Mount Carmel College of Nursing
Mount St. Joseph University
Notre Dame College
Ohio Dominican University
Ohio Northern University
Ohio State University
Agricultural Technical Institute
Columbus Campus
Lima Campus

Mansfield Campus
Marion Campus
Newark Campus
Ohio University
Ohio University
Lancaster Campus
Ohio Wesleyan University
Otterbein University
Sinclair Community College
Tiffin University
University of Akron
University of Akron: Wayne College
University of Cincinnati
University of Cincinnati
Blue Ash College
Clermont College
University of Dayton
University of Findlay
University of Mount Union
University of Northwestern Ohio
University of Toledo
Urbana University
Ursuline College
Wilberforce University
Wittenberg University
Wright State University
Xavier University
Youngstown State University

**Oklahoma**
Cameron University
Langston University
Northeastern State University
Oklahoma Christian University
Oklahoma City University
Oklahoma State University
Southern Nazarene University
University of Central Oklahoma
University of Oklahoma

**Oregon**
Central Oregon Community College
Corban University
Eastern Oregon University
Lewis & Clark College
Linn-Benton Community College
Oregon State University
Pacific University
Portland State University
Southern Oregon University
University of Oregon
University of Portland
Western Oregon University
Willamette University

**Pennsylvania**
Albright College
Alvernia University
Arcadia University
Bloomsburg University of Pennsylvania
Bryn Athyn College
Bucknell University
Cabrini College
California University of Pennsylvania
Carlow University
Carnegie Mellon University
Chatham University
Cheyney University of Pennsylvania
Clarion University of Pennsylvania
Community College of Philadelphia
DeSales University
Dickinson College
Drexel University
Duquesne University
East Stroudsburg University of Pennsylvania
Eastern University
Edinboro University
Pennsylvania
Gannon University
Geneva College
Gettysburg College
Harrisburg Area Community College
Holy Family University

Immaculata University
Indiana University of Pennsylvania
Keystone College
King's College
Kutztown University of Pennsylvania
La Roche College
La Salle University
Lackawanna College
Lafayette College
Lehigh Carbon Community College
Lehigh University
Lincoln University
Lock Haven University of Pennsylvania
Lycoming College
Mansfield University of Pennsylvania
Marywood University
Mercyhurst University
Millersville University of Pennsylvania
Misericordia University
Moravian College
Muhlenberg College
Neumann University
Penn State
   Abington
   Altoona
   Berks
   Brandywine
   Erie, The Behrend College
   Harrisburg
   Lehigh Valley
   Mont Alto
   University Park
   Wilkes-Barre
   Worthington Scranton
Pennsylvania College of Technology
Point Park University
Robert Morris University
Rosemont College
St. Francis University
Saint Joseph's University
St. Vincent College
Seton Hill University
Shippensburg University of Pennsylvania
Slippery Rock University of Pennsylvania
Summit University
Susquehanna University
Swarthmore College
Temple University
University of Pennsylvania
University of Pittsburgh
University of Pittsburgh
   Bradford
   Greensburg
   Johnstown
University of Scranton
University of the Sciences
Valley Forge Military College
Villanova University
Washington & Jefferson College
Waynesburg University
West Chester University of Pennsylvania
Westminster College
Widener University
Wilkes University
Wilson College

## Puerto Rico
American University of Puerto Rico
Bayamon Central University
Caribbean University
EDP University of Puerto Rico: Hato Rey
Inter American University of Puerto Rico
   Aguadilla Campus
   Arecibo Campus
   Bayamon Campus
   Guayama Campus
   Metropolitan Campus
   San German Campus
Pontifical Catholic University of Puerto Rico
Turabo University
Universidad del Este
Universidad Metropolitana
Universidad Politecnica de Puerto Rico

University of Puerto Rico
   Aguadilla
   Arecibo
   Bayamon University College
   Cayey University College
   Mayaguez
   Ponce
   Rio Piedras
   Utuado

## Rhode Island
Brown University
Bryant University
Community College of Rhode Island
Johnson & Wales University
   Providence
Providence College
Rhode Island College
Rhode Island School of Design
Roger Williams University
Salve Regina University
University of Rhode Island

## South Carolina
Allen University
Benedict College
Charleston Southern University
The Citadel
Claflin University
Clemson University
Coastal Carolina University
Columbia College
Converse College
Francis Marion University
Furman University
Greenville Technical College
Lander University
Limestone College
Morris College
Newberry College
North Greenville University
Orangeburg-Calhoun Technical College
Presbyterian College
South Carolina State University
Southern Wesleyan University
Spartanburg Methodist College
Tri-County Technical College
University of South Carolina
   Columbia
   Lancaster
   Salkehatchie
   Sumter
   Upstate
Voorhees College
Winthrop University
Wofford College

## South Dakota
Augusta University
   Augustana University
Black Hills State University
Dakota State University
Dakota Wesleyan University
Mount Marty College
National American University
   Rapid City
South Dakota School of Mines and Technology
South Dakota State University
University of South Dakota

## Tennessee
Austin Peay State University
Belmont University
Carson-Newman University
Christian Brothers University
Cumberland University
East Tennessee State University
Fisk University
Jackson State Community College
Lane College
LeMoyne-Owen College
Lincoln Memorial University
Lipscomb University
Middle Tennessee State University

Pellissippi State Community College
Rhodes College
Southwest Tennessee Community College
Tennessee Technological University
Tennessee Wesleyan College
Trevecca Nazarene University
Union University
University of Memphis
University of Tennessee
   Chattanooga
   Knoxville
   Martin
Vanderbilt University
Walters State Community College
Welch College

## Texas
Angelina College
Austin Community College
Baylor University
Central Texas College
Concordia University Texas
Dallas Baptist University
Del Mar College
El Centro College
El Paso Community College
Houston Baptist University
Houston Community College System
Huston-Tillotson University
Laredo Community College
Lone Star College System
Lubbock Christian University
Northwest Vista College
Our Lady of the Lake University of San
   Antonio
Palo Alto College
Prairie View A&M University
Rice University
St. Edward's University
St. Mary's University
St. Philip's College
Sam Houston State University
San Antonio College
San Jacinto College
Southern Methodist University
Southwestern Assemblies of God University
Stephen F. Austin State University
Tarleton State University
Tarrant County College
Texas A&M International University
Texas A&M University
Texas A&M University
   Corpus Christi
   Kingsville
Texas Christian University
Texas Lutheran University
Texas Southern University
Texas State University
Texas Tech University
Texas Wesleyan University
Texas Woman's University
Trinity University
University of Dallas
University of Houston
University of Houston
   Downtown
University of Mary Hardin-Baylor
University of North Texas
University of St. Thomas
University of Texas
   Arlington
   Austin
   Brownsville
   Dallas
   Pan American
   San Antonio
University Of Texas Rio Grande Valley
University of the Incarnate Word
Wayland Baptist University

## Utah
Brigham Young University
Dixie State University

LDS Business College
Salt Lake Community College
Southern Utah University
University of Utah
Utah State University
Utah Valley University
Weber State University
Westminster College

## Vermont
Castleton State College
Champlain College
Johnson State College
Lyndon State College
Middlebury College
Norwich University
Saint Michael's College
University of Vermont
Vermont Technical College

## Virginia
Christopher Newport University
College of William and Mary
George Mason University
Hampden-Sydney College
Hampton University
James Madison University
John Tyler Community College
Liberty University
Longwood University
Mary Baldwin College
Marymount University
Norfolk State University
Old Dominion University
Piedmont Virginia Community College
Radford University
Randolph-Macon College
Regent University
Richard Bland College
Southern Virginia University
Southside Virginia Community College
Tidewater Community College
University of Mary Washington
University of Richmond
University of Virginia
University of Virginia's College at Wise
Virginia Commonwealth University
Virginia Military Institute
Virginia Polytechnic Institute and State
   University
Virginia State University
Virginia Union University
Virginia Wesleyan College
Washington and Lee University

## Washington
Central Washington University
Clark College
DeVry University
   Federal Way
Eastern Washington University
Gonzaga University
Highline College
Northwest University
Pacific Lutheran University
Pierce College
Saint Martin's University
Seattle Pacific University
Seattle University
Spokane Community College
Spokane Falls Community College
University of Puget Sound
University of Washington
University of Washington Bothell
University of Washington Tacoma
Walla Walla University
Washington State University
Whitworth University

## West Virginia
Fairmont State University
Glenville State College
Marshall University
West Virginia State University

West Virginia University
West Virginia University Institute of
Technology

### Wisconsin
Alverno College
Bellin College
Carroll University
Edgewood College
Maranathan Baptist University
    Maranatha Baptist University
Marian University
Marquette University
Milwaukee School of Engineering
Ripon College
St. Norbert College
University of Wisconsin
    Eau Claire
    Green Bay
    La Crosse
    Madison
    Milwaukee
    Oshkosh
    Parkside
    Platteville
    River Falls
    Stevens Point
    Stout
    Whitewater
Viterbo University

### Wyoming
Laramie County Community College
University of Wyoming

# Naval ROTC

### Alabama
Auburn University
Stillman College
Tuskegee University

### Arizona
Arizona State University
GateWay Community College
Mesa Community College
Pima Community College
University of Arizona

### California
California Maritime Academy
California State University
    San Marcos
Contra Costa College
Diablo Valley College
Foothill College
Loyola Marymount University
Mission College
National University
Point Loma Nazarene University
Riverside City College
Sacramento City College
Samuel Merritt University
San Diego State University
Sonoma State University
Stanford University
University of California
    Berkeley
    Davis
    Los Angeles
    Santa Cruz
University of Redlands
University of San Diego
University of Southern California

### Colorado
Regis University
University of Colorado
    Boulder

### Connecticut
Capital Community College
Tunxis Community College
Yale University

### District of Columbia
Catholic University of America
George Washington University
Georgetown University
University of the District of Columbia

### Florida
Embry-Riddle Aeronautical University
Florida Agricultural and Mechanical University
Florida State College at Jacksonville
Florida State University
Jacksonville University
Pasco-Hernando State College
Tallahassee Community College
University of Florida
University of North Florida
University of South Florida
University of Tampa

### Georgia
Armstrong State University
Clark Atlanta University
Clayton State University
Emory University
Georgia Institute of Technology
Georgia State University
Morehouse College
Oglethorpe University
Oxford College of Emory University
Savannah State University
Spelman College

### Hawaii
Brigham Young University-Hawaii

### Idaho
Lewis-Clark State College
University of Idaho

### Illinois
Illinois Institute of Technology
Lincoln Land Community College
Loyola University Chicago
Northwestern University
Parkland College
Shawnee Community College
Shimer College
University of Illinois
    Chicago
    Urbana-Champaign

### Indiana
Indiana University
    South Bend
Purdue University
Saint Mary's College
University of Notre Dame

### Iowa
Hawkeye Community College
Iowa State University

### Kansas
University of Kansas
Washburn University

### Louisiana
Dillard University
Louisiana State University and Agricultural and
    Mechanical College
Loyola University New Orleans
Southern University
    New Orleans
Southern University and Agricultural and
    Mechanical College
Tulane University
University of Holy Cross
University of New Orleans
Xavier University of Louisiana

### Maine
Husson University
Maine Maritime Academy
University of Maine
University of Maine
    Augusta

### Maryland
University of Maryland
    Baltimore County
    College Park

### Massachusetts
Boston College
Boston University
College of the Holy Cross
Harvard College
Massachusetts Institute of Technology
Massachusetts Maritime Academy
MCPHS University
Northeastern University
Tufts University
University of Massachusetts
    Boston
Worcester Polytechnic Institute
Worcester State University

### Michigan
Eastern Michigan University
Finlandia University
University of Michigan
University of Michigan
    Dearborn

### Minnesota
Anoka-Ramsey Community College
Augsburg College
Macalester College
North Hennepin Community College
University of Minnesota
    Twin Cities
University of St. Thomas

### Mississippi
Tougaloo College
University of Mississippi

### Missouri
Columbia College
Lincoln University
Stephens College
University of Missouri
    Columbia

### Nebraska
BryanLGH College of Health Sciences
Nebraska Wesleyan University
University of Nebraska
    Lincoln
York College

### New Hampshire
Daniel Webster College
Rivier University

### New Jersey
Princeton University
Rutgers, The State University of New Jersey
    New Brunswick/Piscataway Campus
    Newark Campus

### New Mexico
Central New Mexico Community College
National American University
    Albuquerque
University of New Mexico

### New York
Barnard College
College of New Rochelle
College of Saint Rose
Columbia University
Columbia University
    School of General Studies
Cornell University

Eastman School of Music of the University of
    Rochester
Fordham University
Maria College
Mesivta Torah Vodaath Seminary
Molloy College
Monroe Community College
Rensselaer Polytechnic Institute
Rochester Institute of Technology
The Sage Colleges
St. John Fisher College
SUNY
    College at Brockport
    Farmingdale State College
    Maritime College
Talmudical Seminary Oholei Torah
Union College
United States Merchant Marine Academy
University of Rochester

### North Carolina
Duke University
North Carolina State University
University of North Carolina
    Chapel Hill

### Ohio
Cleveland Institute of Art
Cuyahoga Community College
Miami University
    Hamilton
    Middletown
    Oxford
Mount Carmel College of Nursing
Ohio State University
    Agricultural Technical Institute
    Columbus Campus
    Lima Campus
    Mansfield Campus
    Marion Campus
    Newark Campus
Ohio University
    Lancaster Campus
University of Cincinnati
    Blue Ash College

### Oklahoma
University of Oklahoma

### Oregon
Linn-Benton Community College
Oregon State University
Western Oregon University

### Pennsylvania
Carlow University
Carnegie Mellon University
Chatham University
Drexel University
Duquesne University
Penn State
    University Park
Robert Morris University
Saint Joseph's University
Swarthmore College
Temple University
Thomas Jefferson University
University of Pennsylvania
University of Pittsburgh
Villanova University
Widener University

### Puerto Rico
Inter American University of Puerto Rico
    Bayamon Campus
    Ponce Campus
Universidad Metropolitana

### Rhode Island
Brown University

### South Carolina
Allen University
The Citadel

University of South Carolina
  Columbia
  Salkehatchie

**Tennessee**
Belmont University
Christian Brothers University
Fisk University
Tennessee Wesleyan College
University of Memphis
Vanderbilt University

**Texas**
Houston Baptist University
Huston-Tillotson University
Prairie View A&M University
Rice University
Texas A&M University
Texas A&M University
  Galveston
University of Houston
University of Texas
  Arlington
  Austin

**Utah**
University of Utah
Weber State University
Westminster College

**Vermont**
Norwich University

**Virginia**
Hampton University
Mary Baldwin College
Norfolk State University
Old Dominion University
Regent University
Tidewater Community College
University of Virginia
Virginia Military Institute
Virginia Polytechnic Institute and State
  University

**Washington**
Seattle Pacific University
Seattle University
Spokane Community College
University of Washington
University of Washington Bothell
University of Washington Tacoma
Washington State University

**Wisconsin**
Edgewood College
Marquette University
Milwaukee School of Engineering
University of Wisconsin
  Madison
  Milwaukee

# Glossary

**Accelerated program.** A college program of study completed in less time than is usually required, most often by attending classes in summer or by taking extra courses during the regular academic terms.

**Accreditation.** A process that ensures that a college meets acceptable standards in its programs, facilities, and services. Only colleges that are accredited by an agency recognized by the U.S. Department of Education may distribute federal financial aid to their students. Every college described in this book is accredited by such an agency.

**ACT.** A college admission examination given at test centers on specified dates. Please visit the organization's website for further information.

**Advanced placement.** Admission or assignment of a first-year college student to an advanced course in a certain subject on the basis of evidence that he or she has successfuly completed the equivalent of the college's course in that subject.

**Advanced Placement Program (AP).** An academic program of the College Board that provides high school students with the opportunity to study and learn at the college level. AP offers courses in 38 subjects, each culminating in a rigorous exam. High schools offer the courses and administer the exams to interested students. Most colleges and universities accept qualifying AP Exam scores for credit, advanced placement or both.

**Agricultural college.** A college or university that primarily trains students in the agricultural sciences and agribusiness operations.

**American Opportunity Tax Credit.** A federal income tax credit of as much as $2,500 per year, available for the first four years of college for each eligible student in a family. The amount of the credit is determined by income eligibility guidelines. See also *Lifetime Learning Tax Credit.*

**AmeriCorps.** A national network of community service programs for which people volunteer and from which they earn an education award that can used to pay for college or pay back student loans.

**Articulation agreement.** A formal agreement between two colleges to facilitate the successful transfer of students from one college to the other without duplication of course work.

**Associate degree.** A degree granted by a college or university upon completion of a two-year, full-time program of study or its part-time equivalent. In general, the associate of arts (A.A.) or associate of science (A.S.) program is similar to the first two years of a four-year college curriculum. The associate in applied science (A.A.S.) is awarded by many colleges on completion of technological or vocational programs of study.

**Award letter.** A means of notifying admitted students of the financial aid being offered by the college or university. The award letter provides information on the types and amounts of aid offered, as well as the students' responsibilities, and the conditions governing the awards. Usually the award letter gives students the opportunity to accept or decline the aid offered, and a deadline by which to respond.

**Bachelor's degree.** A degree received upon completion of a four- or five-year full-time program of study (or its part-time equivalent) at a college or university. The bachelor of arts (B.A.), bachelor of science (B.S.) and bachelor of fine arts (B.F.A.) are the most common such degrees. College policies vary as to the types of degrees awarded in each major.

**Bible college.** An undergraduate institution whose program, in addition to a general education in the liberal arts, includes a significant element of Bible study. Most Bible colleges seek to prepare their students for vocational or lay Christian ministry.

**Branch campus.** A part of a college, university or community college that is geographically separate from the main campus, has its own faculty and administration, and may have separate admissions requirements and degree programs.

**Bursar.** The college official responsible for handling billing and payments for tuition, fees, housing, etc.

**Business college.** A college that primarily prepares students to work in an office or entrepreneurial setting. The curriculum may focus on management, clerical positions, or both.

**Campus.** The physical location of a college or university. Includes classroom buildings, libraries, research facilities, dormitories, dining halls and administration buildings.

**Campus-based programs.** Federal financial aid programs that are administered directly by the college's financial aid office, which awards these funds to students using federal guidelines. Includes the Federal Supplemental Educational Opportunity Grant Program, Federal Perkins Loan Program and the Federal Work-Study Program.

**Candidates' reply date.** The date by which admitted students must accept or decline an offer of admission and (if any) the college's offer of financial aid. Most colleges and universities follow the College Board-sponsored Candidates' Reply Date Agreement (CRDA), under which they agree to not require a decision from applicants for admission in the fall semester before May 1. The purpose of this agreement is to give applicants time to hear from all the colleges to which they have applied before having to make a commitment to any of them.

**Career college.** Usually a for-profit two-year college that trains students for specific occupations. Also known as a vocational/technical school.

**CB code.** A four-digit College Board code number that students use to designate colleges or scholarship programs to receive their SAT score reports.

**Certificate.** An award for completing a particular program or course of study, sometimes given by two-year colleges or vocational or technical schools.

**CLEP®.** See *College-Level Examination Program*.

**College.** The generic term for an institution of higher education. Also a term used to designate divisions within a university.

**College-Level Examination Program (CLEP).** A program in which students receive college credit by earning a qualifying score in any of 33 examinations in business, composition and literature, world languages, history and social sciences, and science and mathematics. Sponsored by the College Board, exams are administered at over 1,800 test centers. Over 2,900 colleges and universities grant credit for passing a CLEP exam.

**Community/junior college.** A college offering two-year programs leading to an associate degree. Community colleges are public institutions, while junior colleges are privately operated on a not-for-profit basis. Most two-year colleges offer both vocational programs (also called "career" or "terminal" programs), as well as the first two years of a four-year program ("academic" or "transfer" programs). Students in the vocational program usually go directly into a career after graduation, while students in the academic program usually intend to transfer to a four-year institution or an upper-division college.

**Comprehensive fee.** If the college combines tuition, fees, room, and board expenses, that single figure is called a comprehensive fee.

**Consortium.** A group of colleges and universities that share a common geographic location. Consortiums of colleges in the same local area often allow students at one institution to take classes at neighboring consortium colleges and use facilities such as libraries at the member colleges. Larger consortiums, at the state or regional level, may offer in-state tuition to out-of-state students.

**Cooperative education (co-op).** A program in which students alternate class attendance and employment in business, industry, or government. Co-op students are typically paid for their work and may receive academic credit for their participation in the program. Under a cooperative plan, five years are normally required for completion of a bachelor's degree, but graduates have the advantage of about a year's practical work experience in addition to their studies.

**Core curriculum.** A group of courses, usually in the liberal arts, designated by a college as one of the requirements for a degree. Some colleges have both core-curriculum requirements and general-education requirements.

**Cost of attendance.** A number of expenses, among them tuition and fees (including loan fees), books and supplies, and the student's living expenses while attending school. The cost of attendance is estimated by the school, within guidelines established by federal regulation. The cost of attendance is compared with the student's expected family contribution to determine the student's need for financial aid.

**Coverdell Education Savings Account (ESA).** A federal income-tax provision (formerly referred to as the Education IRA) that enables taxpayers to establish a college savings plan. A maximum of $2,000 may be contributed annually to the account, which earns interest and/or dividends on a tax-free basis.

**Credit/placement by examination.** Academic credit or placement out of introductory courses granted by a college to entering students who have demonstrated proficiency in college-level studies through examinations such as those administered by the College Board's AP and CLEP programs.

**Credit Hour.** The standard unit of measurement for a college course. Each credit hour requires one classroom hour per week. Most college courses are offered in one to five credit-hour increments. For financial aid purposes, students taking at least 12 credit hours of classes in a semester are considered to be attending the college full-time, and students taking at least six credit hours are considered half-time.

**CSS code.** A four-digit College Board number that students use to designate colleges or scholarship programs to receive their CSS/Financial Aid PROFILE information. If a college requires financial aid applicants to submit the PROFILE, its CSS code will appear in its description in Part III of this book. A complete list of all CSS codes can also be viewed on the PROFILE website.

**CSS/Financial Aid PROFILE.** A Web-based application service offered by the College Board and used by some colleges, universities, and private scholarship programs to award their private financial aid funds. Students complete the application online. The College Board processes and reports the application data to institutions. The PROFILE is not a federal form and may not be used to apply for federal student aid.

**Culinary school.** A vocational college that primarily prepares students to work as chefs or caterers.

**Deferred admission.** Postponing enrollment, usually for one year, after being accepted for admission by a college.

**Degree.** An award given by a college or university certifying that a student has completed a course of study. *See* bachelor's degree, associate degree, graduate degree. *See also* Certificate.

**Dependent student.** For federal financial aid purposes, such students are either under the age of 24, attend an undergraduate program, are not married, do not have children of their own, are not orphans or wards of the court, or veterans of the active-duty armed services. The term is used to define eligibility for certain financial aid programs, regardless of whether or not the student lives with a parent, receives financial support from a parent, or is claimed on a parent's tax return. If a student is defined as dependent, parental financial information must be supplied on the Free Application for Federal Student Aid (FAFSA) and on institutional aid applications.

**Direct Loan Program.** See *Federal Direct Loan Program.*

**District.** See *In-district tuition.*

**Dual enrollment.** The practice in which a student enrolls in college courses while still in high school, earning both high school and college credit for his or her work.

**Early Action.** A nonbinding early decision program in which a student can receive an admission decision from one or more colleges and universities earlier than the standard response date but is not required to accept the admission offer or to make a deposit before May 1. Compare to *Early Decision*, which is a binding program.

**Early action single choice.** An early action program in which the student may only apply early action to one college or university.

**Early Decision.** A binding program where students can receive an admission decision from one college or university before applications are due for regular admission. Participating students commit to enroll at the college if admitted and offered a satisfactory financial aid package.

**Elective.** A course, not required for one's chosen major or the college's core curriculum, that is selected to fulfill credit hours required for graduation.

**Employer tuition assistance.** Money that employers offer to employees or their dependents for use in paying education costs. Tuition assistance is considered an outside resource when colleges award financial aid.

**Engineering college/institute/school.** An institution of higher education that primarily prepares students for careers as licensed professional engineers or engineering technologists.

**Expected family contribution (EFC).** The total amount students and their families are expected to pay toward college costs from their income and assets for one academic year. The amount is derived from a need analysis of the family's overall financial circumstances. The *federal methodology* is used to determine a student's eligibility for federal and state student aid. Colleges and private aid programs may use a different methodology to determine eligibility for nonfederal financial aid. Frequently, these private institutions use the *institutional methodology*.

**FAFSA.** See *Free Application for Federal Student Aid*.

**FAFSA on the Web.** An electronic option for completing the Free Application for Federal Student Aid (www.fafsa.ed.gov).

**Family Educational Rights and Privacy Act (FERPA).** A federal law that protects the privacy of student education records. The law applies to all schools that receive funds under an applicable program of the U.S. Department of Education. FERPA gives parents certain rights with respect to their children's education records. These rights transfer to the student when he or she reaches the age of 18 or attends a school beyond the high school level.

**Federal code number.** A six-digit number that identifies a specific college to which students want their FAFSA information submitted. Each college's federal code appears in its profile in Part III of this book. Formerly known as the Title IV code.

**Federal Direct Loan Program.** A program whereby participating schools administer federal loans that students and parents borrow directly from the U.S. Department of Education. Direct loans include the subsidized and unsubsidized Federal Stafford Loan, PLUS Loan, and Loan Consolidation programs.

**Federal methodology (FM).** A need-analysis formula used by colleges and universities to determine students' financial need for the purpose of awarding federal financial aid. Most colleges also use this methodology to determine need for the purpose of awarding their own institutional funds, but some colleges use the *institutional methodology* for that. The federal methodology uses information submitted by students on the FAFSA to assess their ability to pay for college and calculate their expected family contribution.

**Federal Parents' Loan for Undergraduate Students (PLUS).** A *federal direct loan program* that permits parents of undergraduate students to borrow up to the full cost of education, less any other financial aid the student may have received.

**Federal Pell Grant Program.** A federally sponsored and administered program that provides need-based grants to undergraduate students. Congress annually sets the dollar range. Eligibility for Pell Grants is based on a student's expected family contribution, the total cost of attendance at the college, and whether the student is attending the college full time or part time.

**Federal Perkins Loan Program.** A federally funded campus-based program that provides low-interest student loans. The maximum amount of loan funds available to an individual for undergraduate study is $27,500. Repayment need not begin until completion of the student's education, and it may be deferred for limited periods of service in the military, Peace Corps or approved comparable organizations. The total debt may be forgiven by the federal government if the recipient enters a career of service as a public health nurse, law enforcement officer, public school teacher or social worker.

**Federal Stafford Loan.** A *federal direct loan program* that allows students to borrow money for educational expenses. Subsidized Stafford loans are offered by colleges based on need. The federal government pays the interest on subsidized loans while the borrower is in college, and repayment does not begin until completion of the student's education. Unsubsidized Stafford loans are non-need based; anyone may apply for one regardless of their ability to pay for college. The interest on unsubsidized loans begins accumulating immediately. For both programs, the amounts that may be borrowed depend on the student's year in school.

**Federal student aid.** A number of programs sponsored by the federal government that award students loans, grants or work-study jobs for the purpose of meeting their financial need. To receive any federal student aid, a student must demonstrate financial need by filing the Free Application for Federal Student Aid and meet certain other eligibility requirements.

**Federal Supplemental Educational Opportunity Grant Program (SEOG).** A federal campus-based program that provides need-based grants of up to $4,000 a year for undergraduate study. Each college is given a certain total amount of SEOG money each year to distribute among their financial aid applicants and determines the amount to which the student is entitled.

**Federal Work-Study Program.** A campus-based financial aid program that allows students to meet some of their financial need by working on- or off-campus while attending school. The wages earned are used to help pay the student's educational costs for the academic year. Job opportunities vary from campus to campus. The time commitment for a work-study job is usually between 10 and 15 hours each week.

**Fee waiver.** The waiver that significantly reduces the amount a student must pay for an application for admission, application for institutional financial aid, standardized tests or other college-related expenses. Fee waivers are most commonly awarded to low-income students, but are sometimes also awarded to students who are senior citizens or in the military. See also *Tuition and fee waiver*.

**Financial aid.** Money awarded to students to help them pay for college. Financial aid comes in the form of gifts (scholarships and grants) and self-help aid (loans and work-study opportunities). Most aid is awarded on the basis of financial need, but some awards are non-need based. Both need-based and non-need-based aid may or may not be offered on the additional basis of merit.

**Financial aid application form.** A form that collects information on the student, his or her income and assets, and (for dependent students) his or her parents' income and assets.

**Financial aid award letter.** See *Award letter*.

**Financial aid package.** The total financial aid offered to a student by a college, including all loans, grants, scholarships and work-study opportunities.

**Financial Aid PROFILE.** See *CSS/Financial Aid PROFILE*.

**Financial need.** The difference between the total cost of attending a college and a student's expected family contribution (EFC). Financial aid grants, loans and work-study will be offered by each college to fill all or a portion of the student's need.

**529 Plan.** See *Section 529 Plan*.

**Fixed interest rate.** An interest rate on a loan that is fixed for the lifetime of the loan. Compare to *Variable interest rate*.

**For-profit college/university.** A higher-education institution not supported by taxes and operated as a for-profit business, either as a publicly traded corporation or as a privately held company. Sometimes referred to as a "proprietary" college.

**Free Application for Federal Student Aid (FAFSA).** A form completed by all applicants for federal student aid. The FAFSA is available on the Web at www.fafsa.ed.gov. In many states, completion of the FAFSA is also sufficient to establish eligibility for state-sponsored aid programs. There is no charge for completing the FAFSA, and you can file it anytime after October 1 of the year before the year for which you are seeking aid (e.g., after October 1, 2016, for the academic year 2017–18).

**FSA ID.** A username and password combination that serves as a student's or parent's identifier to allow access to personal information in various U.S. Department of Education systems and acts as a digital signature on the FAFSA.

**Full need.** A student's entire financial need at a college. A college that offers a financial aid package covering the complete difference between the cost of attendance and the expected family contribution is "meeting full need." See also *Gapping*.

**Full-time status.** Enrollment at a college or university for 12 or more credit hours per semester. Students must be enrolled full time to qualify for the maximum award available to them from federal grant programs.

**Gapping.** A practice by which a college does not meet the full financial need of an admitted student, leaving a gap that must be filled by the student's own financial resources, in addition to the student's expected family contribution.

**General education requirements.** Courses that give undergraduates a background in all major academic disciplines: natural sciences, social sciences, mathematics, literature, language and fine arts. Most colleges have general education requirements that students complete in their first and second years, giving students a chance to sample a wide range of courses before selecting a major. Some colleges refer to general education courses as the core curriculum; at others, a few courses within the general education requirements are core courses that all students must take.

**Gift aid.** Financial aid in the form of scholarships or grants that do not have to be repaid.

**Grade point average (GPA) or ratio.** A system used by many schools for evaluating the overall scholastic performance of students. Grade points are determined by first multiplying the number of hours given for a course by the numerical value of the grade and then dividing the sum of all grade points by the total number of hours carried. The most common system of numerical values for grades is A = 4, B = 3, C = 2, D = 1, and E or F = 0. Also called quality point average or ratio.

**Graduate degree.** A degree pursued after a student has earned a bachelor's degree. The master's degree, which requires one to three years of study, is usually the degree earned after the bachelor's. The doctoral degree requires further study. Professional degrees are also graduate degrees.

**Grant.** A financial aid award given to a student that does not have to be paid back. The terms "grant" and "scholarship" are often used interchangeably to refer to gift aid, but grants tend to be awarded solely on the basis of financial need, while scholarships may require the student to demonstrate merit.

**Half-time status.** Enrollment at a college or university for at least 6 credit hours per semester, but fewer than the 12 credit hours required to qualify as full time. Students must be enrolled at least half time to qualify for federal student aid loan programs.

**Health sciences college.** An institution of higher education that primarily prepares students to enter work in a clinic, hospital or private medical practice. For a complete description of health-related fields of study, see the *College Board Book of Majors*.

**Independent student.** For financial aid purposes, a student who is either age 24 or older, married, a veteran, an orphan, or has legal dependents. Independent students do not need to provide parental information to be considered for federal financial aid programs. However, private institutions may require independent students to provide parental information on their institutional forms in order to be considered for nonfederal sources of funding.

**In-district tuition.** The tuition charged by a community college or state university to residents of the district from which it draws tax support. Districts are usually individual counties or cities, but sometimes are larger.

**Individual Retirement Account (IRA).** A retirement account that earns tax-free income. Money withdrawn for college expenses is not charged the penalty that normally would be incurred for withdrawing IRA money before age 59½, but is taxed as regular income.

**In-state tuition.** The tuition that a public institution charges residents of its state. Some community colleges and state universities charge this rate to students who are not residents of their district, but who are residents of their state.

**Institutional form.** A financial aid application form custom-made by a particular college or university. Some institutional forms are designed to collect additional information on a family's finances beyond what is collected on the FAFSA, and are required of all financial aid applicants. Others serve specific purposes and are only required from certain students, for example early decision applicants or student athletes.

**Institutional Methodology (IM).** A need-analysis formula used by some colleges and universities to determine students' financial need and award their own institutional funds. Compared to the *federal methodology*, the IM takes into account a broader and deeper picture of family assets to determine a student's expected family contribution. Most colleges that use the IM collect this additional information through the CSS/Financial Aid PROFILE form, but some collect it using their own customized institutional forms.

**International Baccalaureate (IB).** A high school curriculum offered by some schools in the United States and other countries. Some colleges award credit for completion of this curriculum. Please visit the organization's website for further information.

**Internship.** Any short-term, supervised work, usually related to a student's major, for which academic credit is earned. The work can be full time or part time, on or off campus, paid or unpaid. Some majors require the student to complete an internship.

**IRS Data Retrieval Tool.** Accessible from FAFSA on the Web, this tool allows you or your parents to access the IRS tax return information needed to complete the FAFSA and to transfer the data directly onto your FAFSA online. For many colleges, the IRS Data Retrieval process is the preferred means of completing your FAFSA.

**Junior college.** See *Community/junior college.*

**Liberal arts.** The study of the humanities (literature, the arts and philosophy), history, foreign languages, social sciences, mathematics and natural sciences. Liberal arts study guides students in developing general knowledge and reasoning ability rather than specific skills.

**Liberal arts college.** A college that emphasizes the liberal arts in its core curriculum and academic offerings and does not offer vocation or professional programs.

**Lifetime Learning Tax Credit.** A federal income tax credit of as much as $2,000 per household annually; available to eligible taxpayers based on "out-of-pocket" tuition and fee expenditures, according to income eligibility guidelines. See also *American Opportunity Tax Credit.*

**Major.** The subject area in which students concentrate during their undergraduate study. At most colleges, students take one-third to one-half of their courses in the major; the rest of their course work is devoted to core requirements and electives.

**Maritime college/institute/academy.** An institution of higher education that prepares students to operate commercial shipping or fishing vessels. Upon graduation, students of most maritime academies are commissioned as officers in the United States Merchant Marine, and simultaneously commissioned as officers in the U.S. Navy Reserve.

**Master Promissory Note (MPN).** A special type of promissory note used to obtain a Federal Stafford loan. The MPN is designated for use as both a single-year and a multi-year note (for four-year and graduate/professional schools). Borrowers can sign a MPN once, the time they first borrow, and then receive additional loans during the same year or in subsequent years without signing an additional note.

**Merit aid.** Financial aid awarded on the basis of academic qualifications, artistic or athletic talent, leadership qualities, or similar qualities. Most merit aid comes in the form of scholarships. Merit aid may be non-need based, or the merit criteria may be in addition to a requirement that the student demonstrate financial need.

**Military college/institute/academy.** An institution of higher education that prepares students (who are called "cadets" while enrolled) to become active-duty officers in the armed services. The curriculum usually combines a study of the liberal arts, military science and engineering. Cadets usually participate in military training assignments during the summer term in addition to attending the college in the fall and spring semesters.

**Minor.** Course work that is not as extensive as that in a major but gives students some specialized knowledge of a second field.

**NCAA.** The National Collegiate Athletic Association. The largest collegiate athletic association, it oversees the most athletic scholarship money. The NCAA governs league play in 23 championship sports.

**Need analysis.** The process of analyzing the student's household and financial information to calculate an EFC and financial need. See also *Federal Methodology, Institutional Methodology.*

**Need-analysis form.** See *Financial aid application form.*

**Need-based aid.** Financial aid (scholarships, grants, loans or work-study opportunities) given to students who have demonstrated financial need, calculated by subtracting the student's expected family contribution from a college's total cost of attendance. The largest source of need-based aid is the federal government, but colleges, states and private foundations also award need-based aid to eligible students.

**Need-blind admission.** The policy of determining whether a student should be admitted to a college without regard to his or her financial need.

**Non-need-based aid.** Financial aid awarded without regard to the student's demonstrated ability to pay for college. Unsubsidized loans and scholarships awarded solely on the basis of merit are both non-need based. Some financial aid sponsors also offer non-need-based grants tied not to merit, but to other qualities, such as state of residence or participation in ROTC.

**Nursing college.** An institution of higher education that primarily prepares students to become registered nurses (RNs) or licensed practical nurses (LPNs).

**Open admission.** The college admissions policy of admitting high school graduates and other adults generally without regard to conventional academic qualifications, such as high school subjects, high school grades and admission test scores. Virtually all applicants with high school diplomas or their equivalent are accepted, although some programs of study may have additional requirements.

**Origination fee.** A fee charged to a borrower to cover the costs of processing a loan. The origination fee is usually a percentage of the total amount being borrowed. The origination fee for any loan will be disclosed in the promissory note for that loan.

**Out-of-state tuition.** The tuition a public college or university charges residents of other states.

**Parents' contribution.** The amount a student's parents are expected to pay toward college costs from their income and assets. It is derived from need analysis of the parents' overall financial situation. The parents' contribution and the student's contribution together constitute the total expected family contribution (EFC).

**Parents' Loan for Undergraduate Students.** See *Federal Parents' Loan for Undergraduate Students.*

**Part-time status.** Enrollment at a college or university for 11 or fewer credit hours per semester.

**Pell Grant.** See *Federal Pell Grant Program.*

**Perkins Loan.** See *Federal Perkins Loan Program.*

**PLUS loan.** See *Federal Parents' Loan for Undergraduate Students.*

**Prepaid tuition plan.** See *Section 529 Plans.*

**Portfolio.** A collection of a student's work that demonstrates skills and accomplishments. Portfolios may be physical or electronic. There are academic portfolios that include student written papers and projects, and also portfolios that include created objects — art, photography, fashion illustrations, and more. Some scholarship programs request a portfolio.

**Priority date.** The date by which applications for financial aid must be received to be given the strongest possible consideration. The college will consider the financial need of applicants who make the priority date before any other applicants. Qualified applicants who do not make the priority date are considered on a first-come, first-served basis, and are only offered financial aid if (and to the extent to which) the college still has sufficient money left over after all the offers it has made. Can also refer to the priority date for admission applications, where, again, the college will make offers to the priority applicants first, and then consider subsequent applicants on a first-come, first-served basis, making offers only if there is still room in the incoming class.

**Private college/university.** An educational institution of higher education not supported by public taxes and operated on a not-for-profit basis. May be independent or affiliated with a religious denomination.

**PROFILE.** See *CSS/Financial Aid PROFILE.*

**Promissory note.** A binding legal document that a borrower signs to get a loan. By signing this note, a borrower promises to repay the loan, with interest, in specified installments. The promissory note also includes any information about origination fees, grace periods, deferment or cancellation provisions, and the borrower's rights and responsibilities with respect to that loan.

**Proprietary college/university.** See *For-profit college/university.*

**PSAT/NMSQT® (Preliminary SAT/National Merit Scholarship Qualifying Test).** A comprehensive program that helps schools put students on the path to college. The PSAT/NMSQT is administered by high schools to sophomores and juniors each year in October and serves as the qualifying test for scholarships awarded by the National Merit Scholarship Corporation.

**Public college/university.** An institution of higher education supported by public taxes.

**Quarter.** An academic calendar period of about 12 weeks. Four quarters make up an academic year, but at colleges using the quarter system, students make normal academic progress by attending three quarters each year. In some colleges, students can accelerate their progress by attending all four quarters in one or more years.

**Reciprocity agreement:** An agreement between neighboring states that allows residents to attend a public college in either state at the *in-state tuition* rate.

**Regular admission.** At colleges with early action or early decision plans, "regular" admission is the round of admission conducted in January or February, after the early admission rounds.

**Renewal FAFSA.** A simplified reapplication form for federal student aid. The Renewal FAFSA allows continuing students to update the prior year's FAFSA, rather than completing the entire FAFSA for each award year.

**Reserve Officers Training Corps (ROTC).** Programs conducted by certain colleges in cooperation with the United States Air Force, Army and Navy reserves. Participating students may receive a merit scholarship while they are in college, and will enter the reserves of their service branch as an officer upon graduation. Naval ROTC includes the Marine Corps. (The Coast Guard and Merchant Marine do not sponsor ROTC programs.) Local recruiting offices of the services themselves can supply detailed information about these programs, as can participating colleges.

**Residency requirements.** The minimum number of terms that a student must spend taking courses on campus (as opposed to independent study, transfer credits from other colleges or credit-by-examination) to be eligible for graduation. Can also refer to the minimum amount of time a student is required to have lived in-state in order to qualify for the in-state tuition rate at a public college or university.

**Rolling admission.** An admission procedure by which the college considers each student's application as soon as all the required credentials, such as school record and test scores, have been received. The college usually notifies an applicant of its decision without delay. At many colleges, rolling admission allows for early notification and works much like nonbinding early action programs.

**Room and board.** The cost of housing and meals for students who reside on campus and/or dine in college-operated meal halls.

**Safety school.** A college you'd like to attend that's also sure to accept you. Usually a public college in your state that is not selective in its admission criteria or practices open admissions.

**SAR.** See *Student Aid Report*.

**SAT.** A college admission exam that tests reading, writing and language, and mathematics skills. It is given on specified dates throughout the year at test centers in the United States and other countries. The SAT is used by most colleges and sponsors of financial aid programs.

**Satisfactory academic progress.** Standards set by a college or university to determine whether a student is meeting sufficient academic standards. The student must achieve these standards to continue to receive financial aid.

**SAT Subject Tests.** Admission tests in specific subjects given at test centers in the United States and other countries on specified dates throughout the year. The tests are used by colleges for help in both evaluating applicants for admission and determining course placement, and exemption of enrolled first-year students.

**Scholarship.** A type of financial aid that doesn't have to be repaid. Grants are often based on financial need. Scholarships may be based on need, on need combined with merit, or solely on the basis of merit or some other qualification, such as minority status.

**School.** In this book, used generically to refer interchangeably to colleges, universities and other institutions of higher education. At some universities, a "school" is a subdivision of the university — for example, the administrative unit that offers nursing courses may be called the "college of nursing" at one institution, and the "school of nursing" at another.

**Section 529 Plans.** State-sponsored college savings programs commonly referred to as "529 Plans" after the section of the Internal Revenue Code that provides the plan's tax breaks. There are two kinds: Section 529 college savings plans and Section 529 prepaid tuition plans.

**Section 529 Prepaid Tuition Plan.** State-sponsored plans through which parents can pay in advance for tuition at public institutions in their state of residence.

**Self-help aid.** Student financial aid, such as loans and work-study jobs, that requires repayment or employment.

**Semester.** A period of about 16 weeks. Colleges on a semester system offer two semesters of instruction a year; there may also be an additional summer session.

**SEOG.** See *Federal Supplemental Educational Opportunity Grant.*

**Simplified needs test.** In Federal Methodology need analysis, the simplified needs test excludes assets from the Expected Family Contribution calculation for low- to moderate-income families who file simplified tax returns (1040A, 1040EZ).

**Stafford Loan.** See *Federal Stafford Loan Program.*

**Student Aid Report (SAR).** A report produced by the U.S. Department of Education and sent to students in response to their having filed the Free Application for Federal Student Aid (FAFSA). The SAR contains information the student provided on the FAFSA as well as the federally calculated expected family contribution.

**Student expense budget.** A calculation of the annual cost of attending college that is used to determine your financial need. Student expense budgets usually include tuition and fees, books and supplies, room and board, personal expenses, and transportation. Sometimes additional expenses are included for students with special education needs, students who have a disability, or students who are married or have children.

**Student's contribution.** The amount you are expected to pay toward college costs from your income and assets. The amount is derived from a need analysis of your resources. Your contribution and your parents' contribution together compose the total expected family contribution.

**Study abroad.** Any arrangement by which a student completes part of the college program — typically the junior year but sometimes only a semester or a summer — by studying in another country. A college may operate a campus abroad, or it may have a cooperative agreement with some other U.S. college or an institution of the other country.

**Subsidized loan.** A loan awarded to a student on the basis of financial need. The federal government or the state awarding the loan pays the borrower's interest while they are in college at least half-time, thereby subsidizing the loan.

**Supplemental Educational Opportunity Grant.** See *Federal Supplemental Educational Opportunity Grant.*

**Taxable income.** Income earned from wages, salaries and tips, as well as from interest income, dividends, alimony, estates or trust income, business or farm profits, and rental or property income. Some scholarship awards must be reported as taxable income.

**Teacher Education Assistance for College and Higher Education (TEACH) Grant.** A federal grant program that provides up to $4,000 per year to students who intend to teach in a public or private elementary or secondary school serving students from low-income families. Recipients must teach in such a school for at least four academic years within eight years of completing the program of study for which they received the grant.

**Teacher's college.** A college that specializes in preparing students to teach in elementary or secondary schools. Most teacher's colleges offer a curriculum that combines a study of the liberal arts with the study of pedagogy.

**Technical college/school.** A college that offers a wide variety of vocational programs to students.

**Terminal program.** An education program designed to prepare students for immediate employment. These programs usually can be completed in fewer than four years beyond high school and are available in most community colleges and trade schools.

**Title IV code.** See *Federal code number.*

**Transcript.** A copy of a student's official academic record listing all courses taken and grades received.

**Transfer program.** An academic program in a community or junior college primarily for students who plan to continue their studies in a four-year college or university.

**Transfer student.** A student who has attended another college for any period, which may be defined by various colleges as any time from a single term up to three years. A transfer student may receive credit for all or some of the courses successfully completed before the transfer.

**Trimester.** An academic calendar period of about 15 weeks. Three trimesters make up one year. Students normally progress by attending two of the trimesters each year and in some colleges can accelerate their progress by attending all three trimesters in one or more years.

**Tuition.** The price of instruction at a college. Tuition may be charged per term or per credit hour.

**Tuition and fee waiver.** Some colleges reduce the tuition and/or fees for some categories of students, such as adults, senior citizens or children of alumni.

**Two-year college.** A college that offers only two years of undergraduate study. See *Community/junior college*; see also *Upper-division college*.

**Undergraduate.** A student in the freshman, sophomore, junior or senior year of study, as opposed to a graduate student who has earned an undergraduate degree and is pursuing a master's, doctoral or professional degree.

**University.** An institution of higher education that is divided into several colleges, schools or institutes.

**Unmet need.** The difference between a specific student's total available resources and the total cost for the student's attendance at a specific institution.

**Unsubsidized loan.** An education loan that is non-need based and therefore not subsidized by the federal government; the borrower is responsible for accrued interest throughout the life of the loan.

**Upper-division college.** A college that offers only the junior and senior years of study. Students must complete their freshman and sophomore years at other institutions before entering the upper-division institution to earn their bachelor's degree.

**Variable interest rate.** An interest rate that changes on an annual basis to better reflect market rates.

**Virtual college/university.** A degree-granting, accredited institution wherein all courses are delivered by distance learning, with no physical campus.

**Work-study.** An arrangement by which a student combines employment and college study. The employment may be an integral part of the academic program (as in cooperative education and internships) or simply a means of paying for college (as in the need-based *Federal Work-Study Program*).

# Alphabetical Index of Colleges

# Applying to College?

## Remove the anxiety with these helpful guides.

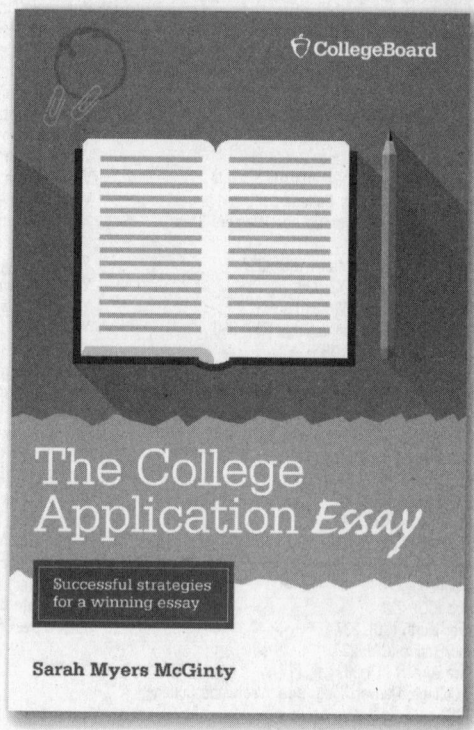

**Campus Visits & College Interviews, 3rd Edition**

By Zola Dincin Schneider & Norman G. Schneider

184 pages, paperback
ISBN: 978-0-87447-988-1

Price: $14.99

**The College Application Essay, 6th Edition**

By Sarah Myers McGinty

160 pages, paperback
ISBN: 978-1-4573-0428-6

Price: $15.99

◉ CollegeBoard

# More College Planning Resources
## from the College Board

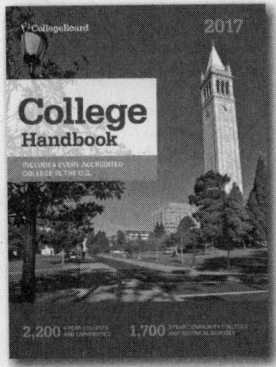

### College Handbook 2017

The only guide listing all accredited universities, two-year and four-year colleges, and technical schools in the United States — more than 3,900 in total.

2,400 pages, paperback
ISBN: 978-1-4573-0773-7
**$31.99**

### The Official SAT Study Guide™: for the Redesigned SAT

The SAT changed in March 2016, and there's only one guide with official practice tests from the test maker. Includes four redesigned SATs, sets of practice questions, official answer explanations, and a comprehensive review of everything on the test.

650 pages, trade paper
ISBN: 978-1-4573-0430-9
**$24.99**

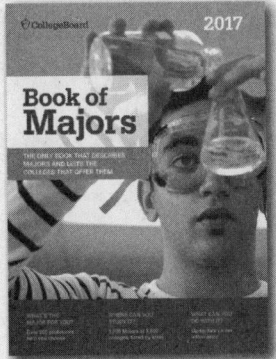

### Book of Majors 2017

Explore in-depth descriptions of 200 majors, and see where over 1,100 majors are offered at colleges nationwide.

1,350 pages, paperback
ISBN: 978-1-4573-0774-4
**$28.99**

### Get It Together for College, 3rd Edition

Take advantage of expert tips that help students stay on top of the college admission process.

226 pages, paperback
ISBN: 978-1-4573-0429-3
**$15.99**

## PAYING FOR COLLEGE

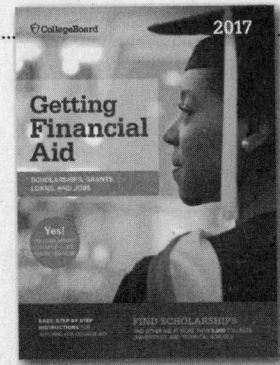

### Getting Financial Aid 2017

A must-have book in today's economy, this is the perfect resource for families managing the high cost of college. This easy step-by-step guide shows why, when, and how to apply for financial aid.

1,050 pages, paperback
ISBN: 978-1-4573-0775-1
**$23.99**

### Scholarship Handbook 2017

The most complete and comprehensive guide to help families tap into the more than 1.7 million scholarships, internships, and loans available to students each year.

624 pages, paperback
ISBN: 978-1-4573-0776-8
**$31.99**

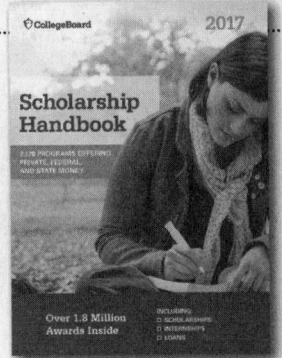

Available wherever books are sold. Distributed by Macmillan.

 **CollegeBoard**

00245-014b

# Official SAT Practice

## CollegeBoard + KHANACADEMY

Start practicing now with Official SAT Practice on Khan Academy.

## Benefit from:

Personalized instruction tailored to your strengths and weaknesses.

Practice questions approved by the test maker, and official SAT practice tests.

SAT

Engaging lessons that build familiarity with the SAT format, question styles, and testing experience.

## Get started at
## satpractice.org